2003

JANUARY

M	T	W	T	F	S	S
		1	2	3	4	5
6	7	8	9	10	11	12
13	14	15	16	17	18	19
20	21	22	23	24	25	26
27	28	29	30	31		

FEBRUARY

M	T	W	T	F		
3	4	5	6	7		
10	11	12	13	14		
17	18	19	20	21	22	23
24	25	26	27	28		

					15	16
17	18	19	20	21	22	23
24	25	26	27	28	29	30

APRIL

M	T	W	T	F	S	S
	1	2	3	4	5	6
7	8	9	10	11	12	13
14	15	16	17	18	19	20
21	22	23	24	25	26	27
28	29	30				

MAY

M	T	W	T	F	S	S
			1	2	3	4
5	6	7	8	9	10	11
12	13	14	15	16	17	18
19	20	21	22	23	24	25
26	27	28	29	30	31	

JUNE

M	T	W	T	F	S	S
30						1
2	3	4	5	6	7	8
9	10	11	12	13	14	15
16	17	18	19	20	21	22
23	24	25	26	27	28	29

JULY

M	T	W	T	F	S	S
	1	2	3	4	5	6
7	8	9	10	11	12	13
14	15	16	17	18	19	20
21	22	23	24	25	26	27
28	29	30	31			

AUGUST

M	T	W	T	F	S	S
				1	2	3
4	5	6	7	8	9	10
11	12	13	14	15	16	17
18	19	20	21	22	23	24
25	26	27	28	29	30	31

SEPTEMBER

M	T	W	T	F	S	S
1	2	3	4	5	6	7
8	9	10	11	12	13	14
15	16	17	18	19	20	21
22	23	24	25	26	27	28
29	30					

OCTOBER

M	T	W	T	F	S	S
		1	2	3	4	5
6	7	8	9	10	11	12
13	14	15	16	17	18	19
20	21	22	23	24	25	26
27	28	29	30	31		

NOVEMBER

M	T	W	T	F	S	S
					1	2
3	4	5	6	7	8	9
10	11	12	13	14	15	16
17	18	19	20	21	22	23
24	25	26	27	28	29	30

DECEMBER

M	T	W	T	F	S	S
1	2	3	4	5	6	7
8	9	10	11	12	13	14
15	16	17	18	19	20	21
22	23	24	25	26	27	28
29	30	31				

2004

JANUARY

M	T	W	T	F	S	S
			1	2	3	4
5	6	7	8	9	10	11
12	13	14	15	16	17	18
19	20	21	22	23	24	25
26	27	28	29	30	31	

FEBRUARY

M	T	W	T	F	S	S
						1
2	3	4	5	6	7	8
9	10	11	12	13	14	15
16	17	18	19	20	21	22
23	24	25	26	27	28	29

MARCH

M	T	W	T	F	S	S
1	2	3	4	5	6	7
8	9	10	11	12	13	14
15	16	17	18	19	20	21
22	23	24	25	26	27	28
29	30	31				

APRIL

M	T	W	T	F	S	S
			1	2	3	4
5	6	7	8	9	10	11
12	13	14	15	16	17	18
19	20	21	22	23	24	25
26	27	28	29	30		

MAY

M	T	W	T	F	S	S
31					1	2
3	4	5	6	7	8	9
10	11	12	13	14	15	16
17	18	19	20	21	22	23
24	25	26	27	28	29	30

JUNE

M	T	W	T	F	S	S
	1	2	3	4	5	6
7	8	9	10	11	12	13
14	15	16	17	18	19	20
21	22	23	24	25	26	27
28	29	30				

JULY

M	T	W	T	F	S	S
			1	2	3	4
5	6	7	8	9	10	11
12	13	14	15	16	17	18
19	20	21	22	23	24	25
26	27	28	29	30	31	

AUGUST

M	T	W	T	F	S	S
30	31					1
2	3	4	5	6	7	8
9	10	11	12	13	14	15
16	17	18	19	20	21	22
23	24	25	26	27	28	29

SEPTEMBER

M	T	W	T	F	S	S
		1	2	3	4	5
6	7	8	9	10	11	12
13	14	15	16	17	18	19
20	21	22	23	24	25	26
27	28	29	30			

OCTOBER

M	T	W	T	F	S	S
				1	2	3
4	5	6	7	8	9	10
11	12	13	14	15	16	17
18	19	20	21	22	23	24
25	26	27	28	29	30	31

NOVEMBER

M	T	W	T	F	S	S
1	2	3	4	5	6	7
8	9	10	11	12	13	14
15	16	17	18	19	20	21
22	23	24	25	26	27	28
29	30					

DECEMBER

M	T	W	T	F	S	S
		1	2	3	4	5
6	7	8	9	10	11	12
13	14	15	16	17	18	19
20	21	22	23	24	25	26
27	28	29	30	31		

Court Hearings: in public (open court), in private, or confidential

Type of proceedings	*Court:* C-confidential O-open P-private	*References (figures refer to endnotes)*
Adoption Act 1976	C	
Child Abduction and Custody Act 1985	C	
Child Support Act 1991 – appeals	C/P	1
Committal for breach of a court order or undertaking	O	
Children Act 1989	C	
Domestic Proceedings and Magistrates' Courts Act 1978 (1) Finance (2) Personal protection	 C P	 2
Family Law Act 1996, Pt IV	P	2
Family Law Act 1986, Pt III (eg parentage declarations)	O	FPR 1991, rr 3.16(12) and 2.28(1)
Inheritance (Provision for Family and Dependants) Act 1975	C	
Civil Procedure Act 1997: search orders; freezing injunctions (s 7(1))	P/C	3 P: if no disclosure ordered C: if application in civil proceedings (CPR 1998, Pt 25) and involves eg personal financial matters (CPR 1998, r 39.2(3)(*c*))
Married Women's Property Act 1882	C	
Matrimonial Causes Act 1973 (1) Divorce (2) Children (s 41) (3) Ancillary relief (except s 37(2)(*a*)) (4) Restraint of disposal (s 37(2)(*a*))	 O C C P	 FPR 1991, r 2.28(1) 3
Matrimonial and Family Proceedings Act 1984, Pt III	C	
Protection from Harassment Act 1997	O	C: if welfare of children involved (CPR 1998, r 39.2(3)(*d*))
Supreme Court Act 1981 s 37 (inherent jurisdiction): (1) *Shipman* order (2) *Mareva* (and CPA 1997, s 7(1)(*a*))	 P P	 3 3
Trusts of Land and Appointment of Trustees Act 1996, s 14	O	C: if involving personal financial matters or the welfare of children (eg alongside CA 1989, s 15) (CPR 1998, r 39.2(3)(*c*), (*d*))
Wardship and inherent jurisdiction	C	

1 As proceedings relating to a child these may be confidential; but since they are essentially inter parties, they may be conducted in private.

2 Save where children are involved, when they will normally be confidential (see *Clibbery v Allan*).

3 Though listed as private, these proceedings may attract the same restrictions as to openness of court as the proceedings to which they are interlocutory.

THE FAMILY COURT PRACTICE 2003

THE FAMILY COURT PRACTICE 2003

Family Law

Family Law is a publishing imprint of

Jordan Publishing Limited
21 St Thomas Street
Bristol BS1 6JS

British Library Cataloguing-in-Publication Data
A catalogue record for this book is available from the British Library.

ISSN 1350–1860

ISBN 0 85308 864 0

The publishers are grateful to the Secretariat of the Principal Registry of the Family Division for providing updated texts of a number of practice directions issued by the Division which are set out in Part IV of the work.

The kind permission of the President of the Family Division to reproduce certain materials from the *Children Act Advisory Committee Annual Report 1992/93*, *1993/94* and *1994/95* and the *Handbook of Best Practice in Children Act cases* is also gratefully acknowledged.

This volume is produced in-house by Jordans using composition software developed by TSO Content Solutions Limited, Epsom, Surrey.

SENIOR LEGAL EDITOR: Gregory Woodgate LLB, LLM, Barrister

SYSTEMS PRODUCTION EDITOR: Paul Tomlin BA

COMMISSIONING EDITOR: Martin West LLB, Solicitor

PUBLISHER: Richard Hudson MA, Barrister

The Tables and Index are researched and compiled by Josephine Joyce.

Printed in Great Britain by William Clowes Ltd, Beccles, Suffolk, England

EDITOR-IN-CHIEF
The Hon Mrs Justice Bracewell

GENERAL EDITOR
District Judge Anthony Cleary
Birmingham County Court

CONSULTING EDITOR
The Hon Mrs Justice Black

CONTRIBUTORS
District Judge Gordon Ashton
Preston County Court

David Brewer BA, Barrister
Clerk to the Justices, Wiltshire

Jane Bridge LLB (Hons)
Barrister

David Burrows BA
Solicitor Advocate

Alastair Haig-Haddow BA
Barrister

Louise Hallam MA, LLB (Hons)
Barrister

David Hershman QC

District Judge Robert Hill
Kingston upon Hull County Court
Visiting Professor of Law, Leeds Metropolitan University

Andrew McFarlane QC

Her Honour Judge Nasreen Pearce

Maggie Silver BA, Solicitor
Principal Legal Adviser (Family),
North & East Surrey Magistrates' Court

District Judge William Vincent
Worcester County Court

Preface

When first published in 1993, *The Family Court Practice* was new and innovative, designed to meet the need for a definitive work of reference covering the entire range of family proceedings at every level of court. It was hoped then that it might stand alongside *The Supreme Court Practice* and *The County Court Practice* as the comprehensive and authoritative guide for practitioners.

Over the ensuing years the hope has become reality and as civil procedure has changed so *The Family Court Practice* has been updated annually to reflect developments in law and procedure. The work is now universally accepted as a standard book of reference for judges and practitioners throughout the jurisdiction.

Congratulations are due to the team of contributors who have achieved so much in just a few years.

The Hon Mrs Justice Bracewell
Family Division February 2001

Contents

PART I: Procedural Guides

For an alphabetical list see **Notes to Procedural Guides** at p 5

APPLICATIONS FOR RELIEF OTHER THAN DIVORCE

APPLICATIONS FOR RELIEF BY WAY OF DIVORCE, JUDICIAL SEPARATION OR NULLITY

MISCELLANEOUS

PART II: Statutes

PART III: Statutory Instruments

PART IV: Practice Directions

PART V: CPR Practice Directions

PART VI: European Regulations

Introduction

This Edition takes us into our second decade. One small sentence, behind which lies an exciting array of historical endeavour – from the publisher's initial faith in the editorial team's ability to design the work from scratch, to the recruitment of a team of authors who, both past and present (including several who have remained in place throughout the decade) have proved to be masters of their fields. A number have taken silk, and we have lost one to the High Court bench, but all have produced narratives of enduring quality and authority, such that the work has now found a place on most, if not all, Family benches throughout the jurisdiction, and in the offices of Family practitioners, both solicitors and the Bar, in numbers which increase year-on-year. In flattering imitation, the innovative design of the Procedural Guides has been copied by other practice works, while our stated policy of ensuring that the work remains in one volume continues to be welcomed by both advocates and the judiciary.

His Honour Judge Nigel Fricker has retired – practitioners who recognised his authority in the field of emergency remedies may not be aware of his substantial contribution, both as consulting editor and author, to the genesis and endurance of this work. His name leaves the spine of the book, but his influence and contribution endure.

So far, so good. Now for the bad news. While Family law may not exactly be in a mess, there is trouble around and about. Recent Introductions have commented unfavourably on the unhappy contrast between the current state of the Family Proceedings Rules 1991 and their more fluent cousins, the Civil Procedure Rules 1998 and supplementary Practice Directions.

The progress towards convergence in this last year might be likened to the administration of sticking-plaster. Enforcement has been addressed, but only in part. The gaggle of Practice Directions, Notes, Circulars and Protocols remain unattended to, cluttering Part IV of this work rather like a bewildered crowd of ticket-holders clustered around the turnstiles, seeking entry to a match played many seasons before. A protocol has been introduced for the instruction of joint experts (but does not quite mirror the CPR counterpart), and a protocol for the management of Children Act proceedings is under consideration.

Parliament lurches between domestic issues – those concerning, at least in the public gaze, hunting with dogs – and foreign policy, where it argues within itself, apparently with increasing impotence, about war in the Middle East. While just off-stage, to the concern of practitioners and, if they only understood the implications, the amazement of the public, the legislature is seriously addressing the legal recognition of same-sex relationships by creating legally binding civil partnerships, accompanied by property and inheritance rights. Hopefully, it might just dawn on Parliament that legislation of this nature would have enormous repercussions on the Matrimonial Causes Act 1973, Inheritance legislation, and indeed on marriage itself.

The Audit Commission, in late 2002, poured scorn on the culture of "targets", many if not all of which, said the Commission, had been ill thought-out and were presented with inadequate consideration being given to either definition or justification. Most, if not all, were simply unsustainable or pointless. This finding does not sit comfortably with the expressed justification for, and the Prime Minister's introduction to, the amending Adoption legislation.

A significant number of contact disputes in private law continue their bitter procession to the Court of Appeal, the tip of an iceberg of anger and rancour that in calmer and more responsible moments the parents might find shameful. Last year this Introduction commended the report of Mr Justice Wall's committee. More recently, an interdisciplinary conference revisited the issue. In general terms, it is recognised that education leading to an early awareness of the effect of these disputes on both children and adults is beneficial. In some US States for example, opposing parents are obliged to view a video, a resource which should bear careful scrutiny in this country. It is acknowledged that this is a funding issue, but this form of intervention is not a new idea, having been trailed as an introduction to the ill-fated Family Law Act 1996. That received the support of the Government of the day, but the response of this Government, of providing funds for a clutch of Contact Centres might be seen as too little, and given the stage of the dispute, too late.

And too little is all that can be said of Graduated Fees. The Bar is being driven from the practice of Family law or is obliged, at the least, to turn away publicly funded cases. This form of cost-cutting is mean and destructive.

Little, if any, attention seems to be paid to the continuing crisis in CAFCASS. Local managers are struggling with staff reductions and increasing demand. In public law, tens of unallocated appointments in each local authority area mean that children's interests are not receiving the attention they demand, while private family disputes, in which the judge requires investigation by, and the input of, a Children and Family Reporter, are themselves increasingly delayed by a similar inability to allocate. CAFCASS Legal is under such strain that an increasing number of cases are turned away, and the Service will, sometime in 2003, have to present a revised Practice Note to the President of the Family Division to explain how representation of children can be arranged, and funded. Needless to say, this disarray affects the more intractable and serious children cases.

CAFCASS is not alone. The agencies which bickered among themselves, to the concern of this Introduction in 2002, do not appear to have experienced an increase in their resourcing, in terms of money or manpower. Thus, at the mournful table around which, last year, sat the shades of Maria Caldwell and Victoria Climbié, looking accusingly on the failures of social services and other statutory agencies to protect them, this year another chair is drawn up, occupied by Ainlee Walker. How many more chairs are to be occupied at this ghastly banquet?

But subscribers may be forgiven for eschewing the increasingly depressing view of Family legislation and funding which has been mirrored within this Introduction over recent editions. Surely, they will say, the fact that the Child Support Agency's computer system is (after more than a year's delay) at last on-line, and has now enabled a new and simplified regime to be engaged, is good news? Subscribers will judge for themselves.

This year, the publishers have included amendments to the Family Proceedings Rules 1991 (which were not laid before Parliament until February), the Child Support Act regime, which came into force on 3 March, and further Adoption Rules (affecting inter-country adoption) which will come into force later in the year. Otherwise, save where narratives have taken account of subsequent developments, the law is stated as at 1 January 2003.

Anthony Cleary
Birmingham

March 2003

Table of Statutes

References are to page numbers. **Bold** references indicate where material is set out in full.

Table of Statutory Instruments

References are to page numbers. **Bold** references indicate where material is set out in full.

A chronological list of statutory instruments referred to in this work appears at the end of the alpahabetical list below.

Chronological list of statutory instruments

1922 Maintenance Orders (Facilities for Enforcement) Rules 1922, SR & O 1922/1355
1950 Maintenance Orders Act 1950 (Summary Jurisdiction) Rules 1950, SI 1950/2035
1952 Magistrates' Courts Rules 1952, SI 1952/2190
1959 Magistrates' Courts (Maintenance Orders Act 1958) Rules 1959, SI 1959/3
1965 Rules of the Supreme Court 1965, SI 1965/1776
1967 Rules of the Supreme Court (Amendment No 1) 1967, SI 1967/829
1968 Rules of the Supreme Court (Amendment No 1) 1968, SI 1968/1244
Secretary of State for Social Services Order 1968, SI 1968/1699
Magistrates' Courts Rules 1968, SI 1968/1920
1969 Rules of the Supreme Court (Amendment) 1969, SI 1969/1105
1970 Rules of the Supreme Court (Amendment) 1970, SI 1970/671
Rules of the Supreme Court (Amendment No 2) 1970, SI 1970/944
Rules of the Supreme Court (Amendment No 3) 1970, SI 1970/1208
1971 Magistrates' Courts (Attachment of Earnings) Rules 1971, SI 1971/809
Rules of the Supreme Court (Amendment No 4) 1971, SI 1971/1269
Blood Tests (Evidence of Paternity) Regulations 1971, SI 1971/1861
Rules of the Supreme Court (Amendment No 5) 1971, SI 1971/1955
1973 Adoption (Designation of Overseas Adoptions) Order 1973, SI 1973/19
Rules of the Supreme Court (Amendment) 1973, SI 1973/1384
Northern Ireland (Modification of Enactments – No 1) Order 1973, SI 1973/2163
1974 Reciprocal Enforcement of Maintenance Orders (Designation of Reciprocating Countries) Order 1974, SI 1974/556
Magistrates' Courts (Reciprocal Enforcement of Maintenance Orders) Rules 1974, SI 1974/668
Magistrates' Courts (Guardianship of Minors) Rules 1974, SI 1974/706
Rules of the Supreme Court (Amendment No 3) 1974, SI 1974/1360
1975 Magistrates' Courts (Reciprocal Enforcement of Maintenance Orders) (Republic of Ireland) Rules 1975, SI 1975/286
Recovery Abroad of Maintenance (Convention Countries) Order 1975, SI 1975/423
Magistrates' Courts (Recovery Abroad of Maintenance) Rules 1975, SI 1975/488
Forms of Adoption Entry Regulations 1975, SI 1975/1959
Reciprocal Enforcement of Maintenance Orders (Designation of Reciprocating Countries) Order 1975, SI 1975/2187
Magistrates' Courts (Reciprocal Enforcement of Maintenance Orders) (Amendment) Rules 1975, SI 1975/2236
1976 Rules of the Supreme Court (Amendment) 1976, SI 1976/337
Adoption (County Court) Rules 1976, SI 1976/1644
Adoption (High Court) Rules 1976, SI 1976/1645
Magistrates' Courts (Adoption) Rules 1976, SI 1976/1768
1977 Matrimonial Causes Rules 1977, SI 1977/334
Rules of the Supreme Court (Amendment No 2) 1977, SI 1977/960
Rules of the Supreme Court (Amendment No 3) 1977, SI 1977/1955
Supplementary Benefits etc (Consequential Provisions) (Northern Ireland) Order 1977, SI 1977/2158
1978 Convention Adoption Rules 1978, SI 1978/417
Rules of the Supreme Court (Amendment No 3) 1978, SI 1978/579
Convention Adoption (Miscellaneous Provisions) Order 1978, SI 1978/1432

1979 Reciprocal Enforcement of Maintenance Orders (Designation of Reciprocating Countries) Order 1979, SI 1979/115
Magistrates' Courts (Reciprocal Enforcement of Maintenance Orders) (Amendment) Rules 1979, SI 1979/170
Rules of the Supreme Court (Amendment No 2) 1979, SI 1979/402
Rules of the Supreme Court (Amendment No 4) 1979, SI 1979/1542
Magistrates' Courts (Recovery Abroad of Maintenance) (Amendment) Rules 1979, SI 1979/1561
Rules of the Supreme Court (Writ and Appearance) 1979, SI 1979/1716
1980 Magistrates' Courts (Reciprocal Enforcement of Maintenance Orders) (Hague Convention Countries) Rules 1980, SI 1980/108
Maintenance Orders (Northern Ireland Consequential Amendments) Order 1980, SI 1980/564
Rules of the Supreme Court (Amendment) 1980, SI 1980/629
Rules of the Supreme Court (Amendment No 2) 1980, SI 1980/1010
Magistrates' Courts (Recovery Abroad of Maintenance) (Amendment) Rules 1980, SI 1980/1584
Magistrates' Courts (Guardianship of Minors) (Amendment) Rules 1980, SI 1980/1585
Magistrates' Courts (Maintenance Orders Act 1950) (Amendment) Rules 1980, SI 1980/1895
Magistrates' Courts (Maintenance Orders Act 1958) (Amendment) Rules 1980, SI 1980/1896
1981 County Court Rules (Northern Ireland), SI 1981/225
Magistrates' Courts Rules 1981, SI 1981/552
Magistrates' Courts (Forms) Rules 1981, SI 1981/553
Magistrates' Courts (Northern Ireland) Order 1981, SI 1981/1675
County Court Rules 1981, SI 1981/1687
Rules of the Supreme Court (Amendment No 2) 1981, SI 1981/1734
1982 County Court Rules 1981 (Amendment) Rules 1982, SI 1982/436
County Court (Forms) Rules 1982, SI 1982/586
Rules of the Supreme Court (Amendment No 2) 1982, SI 1982/1111
County Court Rules 1981 (Amendment No 2) Rules 1982, SI 1982/1140
County Court Rules 1981 (Amendment No 3) Rules 1982, SI 1982/1794
1983 Magistrates' Courts (Amendment) Rules 1983, SI 1983/523
Civil Courts Order 1983, SI 1983/713
Reciprocal Enforcement of Maintenance Orders (Designation of Reciprocating Countries) Order 1983, SI 1983/1125
Magistrates' Courts (Reciprocal Enforcement of Maintenance Orders) (Amendment) Rules 1983, SI 1983/1148
Rules of the Supreme Court (Amendment No 2) 1983, SI 1983/1181
County Court (Amendment No 2) Rules 1983, SI 1983/1716
Adoption Agency Regulations 1983, SI 1983/1964
1984 Adoption Rules 1984, SI 1984/265
Criminal Penalties etc (Increase) Order 1984, SI 1984/447
Magistrates' Courts (Adoption) Rules 1984, SI 1984/611
County Court (Amendment No 2) Rules 1984, SI 1984/878
Rules of the Supreme Court (Amendment) 1984, SI 1984/1051
1985 Rules of the Supreme Court (Amendment) 1985, SI 1985/69
County Court (Amendment) Rules 1985, SI 1985/566
County Court (Amendment) (No 2) Rules 1985, SI 1985/1269
1986 Rules of the Supreme Court (Amendment) 1986, SI 1986/632
County Court (Amendment) Rules 1986, SI 1986/636
Hong Kong (British Nationality) Order 1986, SI 1986/948
Magistrates' Courts (Child Abduction and Custody) Rules 1986, SI 1986/1141
Child Abduction and Custody (Parties to Conventions) Order 1986, SI 1986/1159
Insolvency Rules 1986, SI 1986/1925
Magistrates' Courts (Civil Jurisdiction and Judgments Act 1982) Rules 1986, SI 1986/1962
Administration of Insolvent Estates of Deceased Persons Order 1986, SI 1986/1999

1987 Rules of the Supreme Court (Amendment) 1987, SI 1987/1423
Data Protection (Subject Access) Fees Regulations 1987, SI 1987/1507
Income Support (General) Regulations 1987, SI 1987/1967
Non-Contentious Probate Rules 1987, SI 1987/2024
1988 Rules of the Supreme Court (Northern Ireland) 1988, SI 1988/71
Magistrates' Courts (Family Law Act 1986) Rules (Northern Ireland) 1988, SI 1988/113
County Court (Amendment) Rules 1988, SI 1988/278
Rules of the Supreme Court (Amendment) 1988, SI 1988/298
Magistrates' Courts (Family Law Act 1986) Rules 1988, SI 1988/329
Magistrates' Courts (Increase of Lump Sums) Order 1988, SI 1988/1069
Rules of the Supreme Court (Amendment No 2) 1988, SI 1988/1340
Magistrates' Courts (Criminal Justice Act 1988) (Miscellaneous Amendments) Regulations 1988, SI 1988/2132
1989 County Court (Amendment) Rules 1989, SI 1989/236
Civil Legal Aid (General) Regulations 1989, SI 1989/339
Magistrates' Courts (Family Law Reform Act 1987) (Miscellaneous Amendments) Rules 1989, SI 1989/384
Blood Tests (Evidence of Paternity) (Amendment) Regulations 1989, SI 1989/776
Rules of the Supreme Court (Amendment No 3) 1989, SI 1989/1307
Civil Jurisdiction and Judgments Act 1982 (Amendment) Order 1989, SI 1989/1346
County Court (Amendment No 3) Rules 1989, SI 1989/1838
County Court (Amendment No 4) Rules 1989, SI 1989/2426
Rules of the Supreme Court (Amendment No 4) 1989, SI 1989/2427
1990 Blood Tests (Evidence of Paternity) (Amendment) Regulations 1990, SI 1990/359
Magistrates' Courts (Civilian Fine Enforcement Officers) Rules 1990, SI 1990/1190
Magistrates' Courts (Civilian Fine Enforcement Officers) (No 2) Rules 1990, SI 1990/2260
Civil Jurisdiction and Judgments Act 1982 (Amendment) Order 1990, SI 1990/2591
1991 Attachment of Earnings (Employer's Deduction) Order 1991, SI 1991/356
County Court (Amendment) Rules 1991, SI 1991/525
High Court and County Courts Jurisdiction Order 1991, SI 1991/724
Blood Tests (Evidence of Paternity) (Amendment) (No 2) Regulations 1991, SI 1991/839
Contact with Children Regulations 1991, SI 1991/891
Adopted Persons (Contact Register) (Fees) Rules 1991, SI 1991/952
Children (Admissibility of Hearsay Evidence) Order 1991, SI 1991/1115
County Court (Amendment No 2) Rules 1991, SI 1991/1126
County Courts (Interest on Judgment Debts) Order 1991, SI 1991/1184
High Court (Distribution of Business) Order 1991, SI 1991/1210
County Court Remedies Regulations 1991, SI 1991/1222
Family Proceedings Rules 1991, SI 1991/1247
County Court (Amendment No 3) Rules 1991, SI 1991/1328
Rules of the Supreme Court (Amendment No 2) 1991, SI 1991/1329
Family Proceedings Courts (Children Act 1989) Rules 1991, SI 1991/1395
Family Proceedings Courts (Constitution) Rules 1991, SI 1991/1405
Emergency Protection Order (Transfer of Responsibilities) Regulations 1991, SI 1991/1414
Family Proceedings Courts (Constitution) (Metropolitan Areas) Rules 1991, SI 1991/1426
Parental Responsibility Agreement Regulations 1991, SI 1991/1478
Children (Secure Accommodation) Regulations 1991, SI 1991/1505
Children (Allocation of Proceedings) Order 1991, SI 1991/1677
Family Law Act 1986 (Dependent Territories) Order 1991, SI 1991/1723
Children (Allocation of Proceedings) (Appeals) Order 1991, SI 1991/1801
Family Proceedings (Costs) Rules 1991, SI 1991/1832

County Court Appeals Order 1991, SI 1991/1877
Adoption (Amendment) Rules 1991, SI 1991/1880
County Court (Amendment No 4) Rules 1991, SI 1991/1882
Adopted Persons (Birth Records) Regulations 1991, SI 1991/1981
Family Proceedings Courts (Matrimonial Proceedings etc) Rules 1991, SI 1991/1991
Children (Secure Accommodation) (No 2) Regulations 1991, SI 1991/2034
Legal Aid in Family Proceedings (Remuneration) Regulations 1991, SI 1991/2038
Magistrates' Courts (Costs Against Legal Representatives in Civil Proceedings) Rules 1991, SI 1991/2096
Legal Aid in Family Proceedings (Remuneration) (Amendment) Regulations 1991, SI 1991/2112
Family Proceedings (Amendment) Rules 1991, SI 1991/2113
Rules of the Supreme Court (Amendment No 4) 1991, SI 1991/2671
1992 Family Proceedings (Amendment) Rules 1992, SI 1992/456
Magistrates' Courts (Maintenance Enforcement Act 1991) (Miscellaneous Amendments) Rules 1992, SI 1992/457
Legal Aid in Family Proceedings (Remuneration) (Amendment) Regulations 1992, SI 1992/596
Rules of the Supreme Court (Amendment) 1992, SI 1992/638
Transfer of Functions (Magistrates' Courts and Family Law) Order 1992, SI 1992/709
Magistrates' Courts (Miscellaneous Amendments) Rules 1992, SI 1992/729
County Court (Amendment) Rules 1992, SI 1992/793
Transfer of Functions (Science) Order 1992, SI 1992/1296
Child Support (Information, Evidence and Disclosure) Regulations 1992, SI 1992/1812
Rules of the Supreme Court (Amendment No 2) 1992, SI 1992/1907
Child Support (Collection and Enforcement) Regulations 1992, SI 1992/1989
Family Proceedings (Amendment No 2) Rules 1992, SI 1992/2067
Family Proceedings Courts (Miscellaneous Amendments) Rules 1992, SI 1992/2068
Children (Secure Accommodation) Amendment Regulations 1992, SI 1992/2117
Child Support Commissioners (Procedure) Regulations 1992, SI 1992/2640
Child Support (Collection and Enforcement of Other Forms of Maintenance) Regulations 1992, SI 1992/2643
Child Support (Maintenance Arrangements and Jurisdiction) Regulations 1992, SI 1992/2645
1993 Family Proceedings (Amendment) Rules 1993, SI 1993/295
Judgment Debts (Rate of Interest) Order 1993, SI 1993/564
Recovery of Maintenance (United States of America) Order 1993, SI 1993/591
Reciprocal Enforcement of Maintenance Orders (Hague Convention Countries) Order 1993, SI 1993/593
Reciprocal Enforcement of Maintenance Orders (Republic of Ireland) Order 1993, SI 1993/594
Magistrates' Courts (Reciprocal Enforcement of Maintenance Orders) (Miscellaneous Amendments) Rules 1993, SI 1993/617
Child Maintenance (Written Agreements) Order 1993, SI 1993/620
Children (Admissibility of Hearsay Evidence) Order 1993, SI 1993/621
High Court (Distribution of Business) Order 1993, SI 1993/622
Maintenance Orders (Backdating) Order 1993, SI 1993/623
Children (Allocation of Proceedings) (Amendment) Order 1993, SI 1993/624
Family Proceedings Courts (Child Support Act 1991) Rules 1993, SI 1993/627
County Court (Amendment) Rules 1993, SI 1993/711
Child Support (Miscellaneous Amendments) Regulations 1993, SI 1993/913
Legal Aid in Family Proceedings (Remuneration) (Amendment) Regulations 1993, SI 1993/1117
Magistrates' Courts (Miscellaneous Amendments) Rules 1993, SI 1993/1183

Family Law (Northern Ireland) Order 1993, SI 1993/1576
Family Law (Northern Ireland Consequential Amendments) Order 1993, SI 1993/1577
Magistrates' Courts Fees (Amendment) Order 1993, SI 1993/1889
Education Act 1993 (Commencement No 1 and Transitional Provisions) Order 1993, SI 1993/1975
Rules of the Supreme Court (Amendment) 1993, SI 1993/2133
County Court (Amendment No 2) Rules 1993, SI 1993/2150
Child Abduction and Custody (Parties to Conventions) Order 1993, SI 1993/3144
County Court (Amendment No 4) Rules 1993, SI 1993/3273
1994 Legal Aid in Civil Proceedings (Remuneration) Regulations 1994, SI 1994/228
Legal Aid in Family Proceedings (Remuneration) (Amendment) Regulations 1994, SI 1994/230
Enrolment of Deeds (Change of Name) Regulations 1994, SI 1994/604
Child Support Act 1991 (Consequential Amendments) Order 1994, SI 1994/731
Commissioners for Oaths (Prescribed Bodies) Regulations 1994, SI 1994/1380
Human Fertilisation and Embryology Act 1990 (Commencement No 5) Order 1994, SI 1994/1776
Reciprocal Enforcement of Maintenance Orders (Hague Convention Countries) (Variation) Order 1994, SI 1994/1902
Rules of the Supreme Court (Amendment) 1994, SI 1994/1975
Children (Allocation of Proceedings) (Amendment) Order 1994, SI 1994/2164
Family Proceedings (Amendment) (No 2) Rules 1994, SI 1994/2165
Family Proceedings Courts (Children Act 1989) (Amendment) Rules 1994, SI 1994/2166
County Court (Amendment No 3) Rules 1994, SI 1994/2403
Parental Orders (Human Fertilisation and Embryology) Regulations 1994, SI 1994/2767
Child Abduction and Custody Act 1985 (Isle of Man) Order 1994, SI 1994/2799
Family Law Act 1986 (Dependent Territories) (Amendment) Order 1994, SI 1994/2800
Family Proceedings (Amendment) (No 3) Rules 1994, SI 1994/2890
Children (Allocation of Proceedings) (Amendment) (No 2) Order 1994, SI 1994/3138
Family Proceedings (Amendment) (No 4) Rules 1994, SI 1994/3155
Family Proceedings Courts (Children Act 1989) (Amendment) (No 2) Rules 1994, SI 1994/3156
Parental Responsibility Agreement (Amendment) Regulations 1994, SI 1994/3157
Magistrates' Courts Fees (Amendment) Order 1994, SI 1994/3250
1995 Child Support (Miscellaneous Amendments) Regulations 1995, SI 1995/123
County Court Remedies (Amendment) Regulations 1995, SI 1995/206
Children (Northern Ireland) Order 1995, SI 1995/755
Children (Northern Ireland Consequential Amendments) Order 1995, SI 1995/756
County Court (Amendment) Rules 1995, SI 1995/969
Child Support and Income Support (Amendment) Regulations 1995, SI 1995/1045
Children (Secure Accommodation) Amendment Regulations 1995, SI 1995/1398
Children (Allocation of Proceedings) (Amendment) Order 1995, SI 1995/1649
Commissioners for Oaths (Prescribed Bodies) Regulations 1995, SI 1995/1676
Reciprocal Enforcement of Maintenance Orders (United States of America) Order 1995, SI 1995/2709
Magistrates' Courts (Reciprocal Enforcement of Maintenance Orders) (United States of America) Rules 1995, SI 1995/2802
County Court (Amendment No 3) Rules 1995, SI 1995/2838
Transfer of Functions (Science) Order 1995, SI 1995/2985
Child Support (Miscellaneous Amendments) (No 2) Regulations 1995, SI 1995/3261
1996 Transfer of Functions (Registration and Statistics) Order 1996, SI 1996/273
Legal Aid in Civil Proceedings (Remuneration) (Amendment) Regulations 1996, SI 1996/645

Legal Aid in Family Proceedings (Remuneration) (Amendment) Regulations 1996, SI 1996/650
Local Government Changes for England (Magistrates' Courts) Regulations 1996, SI 1996/674
Magistrates' Courts (Wales) (Consequences of Local Government Changes) Order 1996, SI 1996/675
Children Act 1989 (Amendment) (Children's Services Planning) Order 1996, SI 1996/785
Family Proceedings (Amendment) Rules 1996, SI 1996/816
Legal Aid in Family Proceedings (Remuneration) (Amendment) (No 2) Regulations 1996, SI 1996/1555
Family Proceedings (Amendment) (No 2) Rules 1996, SI 1996/1674
Pensions Act 1995 (Commencement) (No 5) Order 1996, SI 1996/1675
Recovery Abroad of Maintenance (Convention Countries) Order 1996, SI 1996/1925
County Court (Amendment) Rules 1996, SI 1996/2181
County Court (Amendment No 2) Rules 1996, SI 1996/2810
Rules of the Supreme Court (Amendment) 1996, SI 1996/2892
Attachment of Debts (Expenses) Order 1996, SI 1996/3098
County Court (Amendment No 3) Rules 1996, SI 1996/3218

1997 Housing Act 1996 (Consequential Amendments) Order 1997, SI 1997/74
Magistrates' Courts (Amendment) Rules 1997, SI 1997/706
Family Proceedings (Amendment No 2) Rules 1997, SI 1997/1056
County Court (Amendment) Rules 1997, SI 1997/1837
Family Law Act 1996 (Commencement No. 2) Order 1997, SI 1997/1892
Family Proceedings (Amendment No 3) Rules 1997, SI 1997/1893
Family Proceedings Courts (Matrimonial Proceedings etc) (Amendment) Rules 1997, SI 1997/1894
Family Proceedings Courts (Children Act 1989) (Amendment) Rules 1997, SI 1997/1895
Family Law Act 1996 (Part IV) (Allocation of Proceedings) Order 1997, SI 1997/1896
Children (Allocation of Proceedings) (Amendment) Order 1997, SI 1997/1897
Family Law Act 1996 (Modifications of Enactments) Order 1997, SI 1997/1898
Legal Aid in Family Proceedings (Remuneration) (Amendment) Regulations 1997, SI 1997/2394
Child Abduction and Custody (Cayman Islands) Order 1997, SI 1997/2574

1998 Rules of the Supreme Court (Amendment) 1998, SI 1998/1898
Children (Allocation of Proceedings) (Amendment) Order 1998, SI 1998/2166
Family Law Act 1996 (Commencement) (No 3) Order 1998, SI 1998/2572
Reserve Forces Act 1996 (Consequential Provisions etc) Regulations, SI 1998/3086
Civil Procedure Rules 1998, SI 1998/3132

1999 Children (Allocation of Proceedings) (Amendment) Order 1999, SI 1999/524
Supreme Court Fees Order 1999, SI 1999/687
Non-Contentious Probate Fees Order 1999, SI 1999/688
County Court Fees Order 1999, SI 1999/689
Family Proceedings Fees Order 1999, SI 1999/690
Civil Procedure (Amendment) Rules 1999, SI 1999/1008
Family Proceedings (Miscellaneous Amendments) Rules 1999, SI 1999/1012
Reciprocal Enforcement of Maintenance Orders (Hague Convention Countries) (Variation) Order 1999, SI 1999/1318
Adoption (Amendment) Rules 1999, SI 1999/1477
Magistrates' Courts (Reciprocal Enforcement of Maintenance Orders) (Hague Convention Countries) Rules 1999, SI 1999/2002
Family Proceedings Fees (Amendment) Order 1999, SI 1999/2549
Magistrates' Courts (Miscellaneous Amendments) Rules 1999, SI 1999/2765
Justices' Clerks Rules 1999, SI 1999/2784
Legal Aid in Civil Proceedings (Remuneration) (Amendment) Regulations 1999, SI 1999/3098
Family Proceedings (Amendment No 2) Rules 1999, SI 1999/3491

2000 Health Act 1999 (Supplementary, Consequential etc Provisions) Order 2000, SI 2000/90
Child Support (Maintenance Calculation Procedure) Regulations 2000, SI 2000/157
Civil Procedure (Amendment) Rules 2000, SI 2000/221
Community Legal Service (Costs) Regulations 2000, SI 2000/441
Community Legal Service (Financial) Regulations 2000, SI 2000/516
Family Proceedings Fees (Amendment) Order 2000, SI 2000/640
Conditional Fee Agreements Regulations 2000, SI 2000/692
Access to Justice (Membership Organisation) Regulations 2000, SI 2000/693
Health Act 1999 (Supplementary, Consequential etc Provisions) (No 2) Order 2000, SI 2000/694
Community Legal Service (Cost Protection) Regulations 2000, SI 2000/824
Family Proceedings Fees (Amendment No 2) Order 2000, SI 2000/938
Civil Procedure (Amendment No 2) Rules 2000, SI 2000/940
Pensions on Divorce etc (Provision of Information) Regulations 2000, SI 2000/1048
Pensions on Divorce (Charging) Regulations, SI 2000/1049
Access to Justice Act 1999 (Destination of Appeals) Order 2000, SI 2000/1071
Divorce etc (Pensions) Regulations 2000, SI 2000/1123
Family Proceedings (Amendment) Rules 2000, SI 2000/1247
Civil Procedure (Amendment No 3) Rules 2000, SI 2000/1317
Family Proceedings Fees (Amendment No 3) Order 2000, SI 2000/1545
Civil Jurisdiction and Judgments Act 1982 (Amendment) Order 2000, SI 2000/1824
Maintenance Orders (Facilities for Enforcement) (Amendment) Rules 2000, SI 2000/1875
Civil Procedure (Amendment No 4) Rules 2000, SI 2000/2092
Family Proceedings (Amendment) Rules 2000, SI 2000/2267
Children (Allocation of Proceedings) (Amendment) Order 2000, SI 2000/2670
Pension Sharing (Consequential and Miscellaneous Amendments) Regulations 2000), SI 2000/2691
Sharing of State Scheme Rights (Provision of Information and Valuations) Regulations 2000, SI 2000/2693
Sharing of State Scheme Rights (Provision of Information and Valuation) (No 2) Regulations 2000, SI 2000/2914
Magistrates' Courts (Amendment) Rules 2000, SI 2000/3361

2001 Child Support (Information, Evidence and Disclosure and Maintenance Arrangements and Jurisdiction) (Amendment) Regulations 2000, SI 2001/161
Child Support (Collection and Enforcement and Miscellaneous Amendments) Regulations 2000, SI 2001/162
Magistrates' Courts (Amendment) Rules 2001, SI 2001/167
Civil Procedure (Amendment) Rules 2001, SI 2001/256
European Communities (Matrimonial Jurisdiction and Judgments) Regulations 2001, SI 2001/310
Reciprocal Enforcement of Maintenance Orders (Variation) Order 2001, SI 2001/410
Magistrates' Courts (Amendment No 2) Rules 2001, SI 2001/610
Magistrates' Courts (Transfer of Justices' Clerks' Functions) (Miscellaneous Amendments) Rules 2001, SI 2001/615
Access to Justice Act 1999 (Transfer of Justices' Clerks' Functions) Order 2001, SI 2001/618
European Communities (Matrimonial Jurisdiction and Judgments) (Northern Ireland) Regulations 2001, SI 2001/660
Children (Allocation of Proceedings) (Amendment) Order 2001, SI 2001/775
Family Proceedings Courts (Family Law Act 1986) Rules 2001, SI 2001/778
Family Proceedings Courts (Children Act 1989) (Amendment) Rules 2001, SI 2001/818
Adoption (Amendment) Rules 2001, SI 2001/819
Magistrates' Courts (Adoption) (Amendment) Rules 2001, SI 2001/820
Family Proceedings (Amendment) Rules 2001, SI 2001/821
Community Legal Service (Costs) (Amendment) Regulations 2001, SI 2001/822

Community Legal Service (Cost Protection) (Amendment) Regulations 2001, SI 2001/823
Legal Aid in Family Proceedings (Remuneration) (Amendment) Regulations 2001, SI 2001/830
Community Legal Service (Funding) (Counsel in Family Proceedings) Order 2001, SI 2001/1077
Adoption of Children from Overseas Regulations 2001, SI 2001/1251
Legal Aid in Family Proceedings (Remuneration) (Amendment) (No 2) Regulations 2001, SI 2001/1255
Civil Procedure (Amendment No 2) Rules 2001, SI 2001/1388
Children (Allocation of Proceedings) (Amendment) (No 2) Order 2001, SI 2001/1656
Civil Procedure (Amendment No 3) Rules 2001, SI 2001/1769
Local Authorities (Executive and Alternative Arrangements) (Modification of Enactments and Other Provisions) (England) Order 2001, SI 2001/2237
Legal Aid in Family Proceedings (Remuneration) (Amendment) (No 3) Regulations 2001, SI 2001/2417
Reciprocal Enforcement of Maintenance Orders (Hague Convention Countries) (Variation) Order 2001, SI 2001/2567
Reciprocal Enforcement of Maintenance Orders (Designation of Reciprocating Countries) Order 2001, SI 2001/3501
Financial Services and Markets Act 2000 (Consequential Amendments and Repeals) Order 2001, SI 2001/3649
Community Legal Service (Cost Protection) (Amendment No 2) Regulations 2001, SI 2001/3812
Child Abduction and Custody (Parties to Conventions) (Amendment) Order 2001, SI 2001/3923
Civil Jurisdiction and Judgments Order 2001, SI 2001/3929
Civil Procedure (Amendment No 5) Rules 2001, SI 2001/4015

2002 Magistrates' Courts (Civil Jurisdiction and Judgments Act 1982) (Amendment) Rules 2002, SI 2002/194
Civil Procedure (Modification of Enactments) Order 2002, SI 2002/439
Children Act (Miscellaneous Amendments) (England) Regulations 2002, SI 2002/546
Legal Aid in Family Proceedings (Remuneration) (Amendment) Regulations 2002, SI 2002/710
Reciprocal Enforcement of Maintenance Orders (Designation of Reciprocating Countries) Order 2002, SI 2002/788
Magistrates' Courts (Reciprocal Enforcement of Maintenance Orders) (Amendment) Rules 2002, SI 2002/1734
Child Support Appeals (Jurisdiction of Courts) Order 2002, SI 2002/1915
Civil Procedure (Amendment) Rules 2002, SI 2002/2058
National Health Service Reform and Health Care Professions Act 2002 (Supplementary, Consequential etc Provisions) Regulations 2002, SI 2002/2469
Reciprocal Enforcement of Maintenance Orders (Hague Convention Countries) (Variation) Order 2002, SI 2002/2838
Recovery Abroad of Maintenance (Convention Countries) Order 2002, SI 2002/2839
Children and Family Court Advisory and Support Service (Miscellaneous Amendments) Order 2002, SI 2002/3220

2003 Intercountry Adoption (Hague Convention) Regulations 2003, SI 2003/118
Adoption (Amendment) Rules 2003, SI 2003/183
Family Proceedings (Amendment) Rules 2003, SI 2003/184

Table of Cases

References are to page numbers.

Table of Practice Directions

References are to page numbers. **Bold** references indicate where material is set out in full.

Table of CPR PDs

References are to page numbers. **Bold** references indicate where material is set out in full.

Abbreviations

AA 1976	Adoption Act 1976
AEA 1971	Attachment of Earnings Act 1971
AJA 1876	Appellate Jurisdiction Act 1876
AJA 1920/1960/1969/1970	Administration of Justice Act 1920/1960/1969/1970
AJA 1999	Access to Justice Act 1999
AJ(A)A 1934	Administration of Justice (Appeals) Act 1934
AR 1984	Adoption Rules 1984
CA 1989	Children Act 1989
CACA 1985	Child Abduction and Custody Act 1985
C(AHE)O 1992	Children (Admissibility of Hearsay Evidence) Order 1992
C(AP)(A)O 1991	Children (Allocation of Proceedings) Appeals Order 1991
C(AP)O 1991	Children (Allocation of Proceedings) Order 1991
CCA 1981	Contempt of Court Act 1981
CCA 1984	County Courts Act 1984
CCAO 1991	County Court Appeals Order 1991
CCFO 1999	County Court Fees Order 1999
CC(F)R 1982	County Court (Forms) Rules 1982
CC(IJD)O 1991	County Courts (Interest on Judgment Debts) Order 1991
CCR	County Court Rules 1981
CCRR 1991	County Court Remedies Regulations 1991
CJCSA 2000	Criminal Justice and Court Services Act 2000
CJJA 1982/1991	Civil Jurisdiction and Judgments Act 1982/1991
CLA(G)R 1989	Civil Legal Aid (General) Regulations 1989
CLSA 1990	Courts and Legal Services Act 1990
CLS(C)R 2000	Community Legal Service (Costs) Regulations 2000
CLS(CP)R 2000	Community Legal Service (Cost Protection) Regulations 2000
CLS(F)R 2000	Community Legal Service (Financial) Regulations 2000
COA 1979	Charging Orders Act 1979
CPR 1998	Civil Procedure Rules 1998
CPR 1998, Sch 1, RSC	Rules taken from the Rules of the Supreme Court 1965 and set out (as amended) in Schedule 1 to CPR
CPR 1998, Sch 2, CCR	Rules taken from the County Court Rules 1981 and set out (as amended) in Schedule 2 to CPR
CSA 1991/1995	Child Support Act 1991/1995
C(SA)R 1991	Children (Secure Accommodation) Regulations 1991
C(SA)(No 2)R 1991	Children (Secure Accommodation) (No 2) Regulations 1991
CS(CE)R 1992	Child Support (Collection and Enforcement) Regulations 1992
CS(CEOFM)R 1992	Child Support (Collection and Enforcement of Other Forms of Maintenance) Regulations 1992
CS(IED)R 1992	Child Support (Information, Evidence and Disclosure) Regulations 1992
CS(MAP)R 1992	Child Support (Maintenance Assessment Procedure) Regulations 1992
CS(MASC)R 1992	Child Support (Maintenance Assessments and Special Cases) Regulations 1992
CSR	Court of Session Rules
DA 1869	Debtors Act 1869
DAP(RP)A 1968	Domestic and Appellate Proceedings (Restriction of Publicity) Act 1968
DMPA 1973	Domicile and Matrimonial Proceedings Act 1973
DPMCA 1978	Domestic Proceedings and Magistrates' Courts Act 1978

D(P)R 2000	Divorce etc (Pensions) Regulations 2000
FJ(RE)A 1933	Foreign Judgments (Reciprocal Enforcement) Act 1933
FLA 1986/1996	Family Law Act 1986/1996
FLA 1986(DT)O 1991	Family Law Act 1986 (Dependent Territories) Order 1991
FLA(Pt IV)(AP)O 1997	Family Law Act 1996 (Part IV) (Allocation of Proceedings) Order 1997
FLRA 1969/1987	Family Law Reform Act 1969/1987
FP(AJ)D 1999	Family Proceedings (Allocation to Judiciary) Directions 1999
FPC(CA 1989)R 1991	Family Proceedings Courts (Children Act 1989) Rules 1991
FPC(CSA 1991)R 1993	Family Proceedings Courts (Child Support Act 1991) Rules 1993
FPC(MP etc)R 1991	Family Proceedings Courts (Matrimonial Proceedings etc) Rules 1991
FPFO 1999	Family Proceedings Fees Order 1999
FPR 1991	Family Proceedings Rules 1991
GALRO(P)R 1991	Guardians Ad Litem and Reporting Officers (Panels) Regulations 1991
HCCCJO 1991	High Court and County Courts Jurisdiction Order 1991
HFEA 1990	Human Fertilisation and Embryology Act 1990
HLPD	House of Lords Practice Directions and Standing Orders Applicable to Civil Appeals
IA 1978	Interpretation Act 1978
I(PFD)A 1975	Inheritance (Provision for Family and Dependants) Act 1975
JA 1838	Judgments Act 1838
JCR 1999	Justices' Clerks Rules 1999
LAA 1988	Legal Aid Act 1988
LAAR 1989	Legal Advice and Assistance Regulations 1989
LACP(R)R 1994	Legal Aid in Civil Proceedings (Remuneration) Regulations 1994
LAFP(R)R 1991	Legal Aid in Family Proceedings (Remuneration) Regulations 1991
LR(MP)A 1970	Law Reform (Miscellaneous Provisions) Act 1970
MA 1949	Marriage Act 1949
MCA 1973	Matrimonial Causes Act 1973
MCA 1980	Magistrates' Courts Act 1980
MC(AE)R 1971	Magistrates' Courts (Attachment of Earnings) Rules 1971
MC(A)R 1984	Magistrates' Courts (Adoption) Rules 1984
MC(CJJA 1982)R 1986	Magistrates' Courts (Civil Jurisdiction and Judgments Act 1982) Rules 1986
MCF(A)O 1992	Magistrates' Courts Fees (Amendment) Order 1992
MC(GM)R 1974	Magistrates' Courts (Guardianship of Minors) Rules 1974
MC(MOA 1958)R 1959	Magistrates' Courts (Maintenance Orders Act 1958) Rules 1959
MD(PM)A 1958	Matrimonial Causes (Property and Maintenance) Act 1958
MCR 1981	Magistrates' Courts Rules 1981
MC(RAM)R 1975	Magistrates' Courts (Recovery Abroad of Maintenance) Rules 1975
MC(REMO)(HCC)R 1980	Magistrates' Courts (Reciprocal Enforcement of Maintenance Orders) (Hague Convention Countries) Rules 1980
MC(REMO)R 1974	Magistrates' Courts (Reciprocal Enforcement of Maintenance Orders) Rules 1974
MC(REMO)(RI)R 1975	Magistrates' Courts (Reciprocal Enforcement of Maintenance Orders) (Republic of Ireland) Rules 1975
MC(REMO)(USA)R 1995	Magistrates' Courts (Reciprocal Enforcement of Maintenance Orders) (United States of America) Rules 1995

MEA 1991	Maintenance Enforcement Act 1991
MFPA 1984	Matrimonial and Family Proceedings Act 1984
MOA 1950/1958	Maintenance Orders Act 1950/1958
MOA 1950(SJ)R 1950	Maintenance Orders Act 1950 (Summary Jurisdiction) Rules 1950
MO(FE)A 1920	Maintenance Orders (Facilities for Enforcement) Act 1920
MO(FE)R 1922	Maintenance Orders (Facilities for Enforcement) Rules 1922
MO(RE)A 1972	Maintenance Orders (Reciprocal Enforcement) Act 1972
MPPA 1970	Matrimonial Proceedings and Property Act 1970
MWPA 1882/1964	Married Women's Property Act 1882/1964
PD	Practice Direction, Registrar's Direction, Secretary's Circular etc
PD [number]	Practice Direction which supplements Part [number] of CPR 1998
PD(PI)R 2000	Pensions on Divorce etc (Provision of Information) Regulations 2000
PHA 1997	Protection from Harassment Act 1997
PO(HFE)R 1994	Parental Orders (Human Fertilisation and Embryology) Regulations 1994
RAM(CC)O 1975	Recovery Abroad of Maintenance (Convention Countries) Order 1975
REMO(HCC)O 1993	Reciprocal Enforcement of Maintenance Orders (Hague Convention Countries) Order 1993
REMO(RI)O 1993	Reciprocal Enforcement of Maintenance Orders (Republic of Ireland) Order 1993
REMO(USA)O 1995	Reciprocal Enforcement of Maintenance Orders (United States of America) Order 1995
RM(USA)O 1979	Recovery of Maintenance (United States of America) Order 1979
RRCOSC 1988	Act of Sederunt (Rules for the Registration of Custody Orders of the Sheriff Court) 1988
RSC	Rules of the Supreme Court 1965
SCA 1981	Supreme Court Act 1981
SCFO 1999	Supreme Court Fees Order 1999
SJ(P)A 1881	Summary Jurisdiction (Process) Act 1881
SSAA 1992	Social Security Administration Act 1992
WRPA 1999	Welfare Reform and Pensions Act 1999

PART I

Procedural Guides

PART I: Procedural Guides

Contents

APPLICATIONS FOR RELIEF OTHER THAN DIVORCE

APPLICATIONS FOR RELIEF BY WAY OF DIVORCE, JUDICIAL SEPARATION OR NULLITY

ENFORCEMENT OF ORDERS

Notes to Procedural Guides

(1) Index

PART I

(2) Civil Procedure Rules 1998

The Civil Procedure Rules 1998 came into operation on 26 April 1999. They do not apply to "family proceedings" as defined by Matrimonial and Family Proceedings Act 1984, s 32 (with the exception of costs issues arising in all such proceedings and expert evidence in ancillary relief proceedings) but are applicable to other forms of family process. Thus, there are four principal rules regimes applicable to the proceedings covered by this volume:

(i) Family Proceedings Rules 1991;

(ii) Rules of the Supreme Court 1965 and County Court Rules 1981 ("old style") which will continue to govern "family proceedings" for as long as CPR 1998 do not apply directly to such proceedings within the meaning of MFPA 1984, s 32;

(iii) Rules of the Supreme Court 1965 and County Court Rules 1981 ("new style" – ie as modified to bring them into line with CPR 1998 and set out in Schs 1 and 2 thereto);

(iv) Civil Procedure Rules 1998 which govern applications under the Inheritance (Provision for Family and Dependants) Act 1975, Protection from Harassment Act 1997, Trusts of Land and Appointment of Trustees Act 1996, s 14, judicial review proceedings and appeals to the Court of Appeal.

NB For a detailed examination of the procedural regime applicable to any individual form of family process see Table set out in the annotations under FPR 1991, r 1.3.

(3) Fees

Information concerning fees payable is included, where appropriate, in the following Guides. However, **no** fee is payable:

(*a*) in family proceedings in the High Court and county courts where the applicant:

- (i) is receiving advice and assistance under Legal Aid Act 1988, Pts II/III; or
- (ii) is receiving Legal Help as defined in, and provided in accordance with, the Funding Code in connection with the matter to which the proceedings relate; or
- (iii) is acting in person and is receiving income support, working families' tax credit, disabled person's tax credit or income-based jobseeker's allowance; or
- (iv) is a child or, if over 18, seeks financial relief under Children Act 1989, Sch 1, para 2 (Family Proceedings Fees Order 1999, art 4);

(*b*) in proceedings in the magistrates' courts where the applicant is receiving services funded by the Legal Services Commission as part of the Community Legal Service or is in receipt of income support, working families' tax credit or income-based jobseeker's allowance, or for enforcement of an order made in the magistrates' court (Magistrates' Courts Act 1980, Sch 6, Pt I, Note 1); or

(*c*) in any other proceedings where it appears to the Lord Chancellor that payment of fees would cause exceptional hardship (Family Proceedings Fees Order 1999, art 5; Supreme Court Fees Order 1999, art 6; County Court Fees Order 1999, art 6).

1: Contribution Order

Legal background

Where a local authority is looking after a child, it has to consider whether it should recover contributions towards that child's maintenance from either of his parents (where he is under 16) or from the child himself (where he is 16 or over) (CA 1989, Sch 2, para 21). If the local authority decides that it is reasonable to recover a contribution, it will first serve a contribution notice on the proposed contributor specifying the weekly sum he should contribute and the arrangements for payment (CA 1989, Sch 2, para 22). An agreement may then be reached between the authority and the contributor, but if no agreement is reached within one month from the service of the contribution notice, or if the contributor subsequently serves a notice withdrawing his agreement, the authority may apply to the court for a contribution order (CA 1989, Sch 2, para 23). The court may make an order requiring the contributor to contribute a weekly sum towards the child's maintenance. In fixing the sum, the court must have regard to the contributor's means and must not specify a sum greater than that specified in the local authority's contribution notice. A contribution order may be varied or revoked by the court (CA 1989, Sch 2, para 23(8)). Alternatively, a subsequent contribution agreement between the local authority and the contributor in accordance with para 23(6) will have the effect of discharging the order.

Procedure

Who may apply	Local authority looking after child	CA 1989, Sch 2, para 23
Which court	Magistrates' court	C(AP)O 1991, art 3(1)
	Proceedings can be transferred sideways but not upwards	C(AP)O 1991, arts 6, 7(2)
Which proceedings	Freestanding application	
Variation or discharge of order by which court	Court by which original order made	C(AP)O 1991, art 4(1)
Application	*Initial application* On Form C1, with sufficient copies for each respondent	
	Copy of contribution notice	
	Copy of any contributor's notice under CA 1989, Sch 2, para 22(8) withdrawing agreement	FPC(CA 1989)R 1991, rr 4(1), 30(1)
	Fee payable: £30	MCA 1980, Sch 6, Pt I
	Variation/revocation application On Form C1, with sufficient copies for each respondent	
	Copy of contribution order	FPC(CA 1989)R 1991, rr 4(1), 30(3)
	Fee payable: £20	MCA 1980, Sch 6, Pt I
Respondents	*Initial application* Contributor	
	Variation/revocation application Where local authority is applicant, contributor	

	Where contributor is applicant, local authority	FPC(CA 1989)R 1991, r 7, Sch 2
Additional persons to whom notice in Form C6A is to be given	Local authority providing accommodation for child	
	Person caring for child at commencement of proceedings	
	Person providing a s 51 refuge for child	FPC(CA 1989)R 1991, r 4, Sch 2
Service	Copy of application, together with Form C6, to be served on respondents at least 14 days before date of hearing or directions appointment	FPC(CA 1989)R 1991, r 4(1)
	Form C6A to be served on additional persons at same time as application etc served on respondents	FPC(CA 1989)R 1991, r 4(3)
	At or before first directions appointment or hearing, applicant must file statement in Form C9 to prove that requirements for service have been complied with	FPC(CA 1989)R 1991, r 7
Ex parte	May not be available	FPC(CA 1989)R 1991, r 4(4)
Joinder or removal of parties	By court order, of its own motion or on written request	FPC(CA 1989)R 1991, r 7
Answer to application	No provision either forbidding or permitting an answer	
Directions	As to the powers of the justices' clerk or the court, see —	FPC(CA 1989)R 1991, r 14
Children's guardian	Not "specified proceedings"	CA 1989, s 41(6); FPC (CA 1989)R 1991, r 2(2)
Who has power to make the order	A magistrates' court; however, justices' clerk or single justice has no such power	JCR 1999; CA 1989, s 93(2)(i), Sch 2, para 23(2); FPC(CA 1989)R 1991, r 2(5)
Order	Form C21	FPC(CA 1989)R 1991, r 21(7)
Appeals	See Guide 70	CA 1989, s 94, Sch 2, para 23(11)

2: Financial Relief for a Child in the High Court or County Court under Children Act 1989, Sch 1

Legal background

Subject to the provisions of the Child Support Act 1991 (see **Interface with Child Support Act 1991** under MCA 1973, s 23 and **Outline of new bases for child support calculation** under CSA 1991, s 4), which leave the court with a limited role in ordering maintenance or variation of maintenance agreements in respect of children, CA 1989, Sch 1 provides three forms of financial relief for a child: first, CA 1989, Sch 1, para 1 enables a maintenance order, settlement and transfer of property order to be made in favour of a child against either or both of its parents; secondly, para 2 enables a periodical payments order and lump sum order to be made in favour of a child who has reached 18 where (i) the child's parents are not living with each other, (ii) there was not in force a periodical payments order for the child immediately before he reached 16, and (iii) he is undergoing education or training or there are special circumstances (orders under both paras 1 and 2 may be varied or extended under para 6); and, thirdly, by CA 1989, Sch 1, paras 10 and 11, the court may vary a maintenance agreement containing financial arrangements for the child either during the lifetime of the parent or after the death of one of them. For the reasons set out under CA 1989, s 15, if a child's parents are married, the greater procedural powers that are available make it more advantageous for an application for financial relief against a parent by a child to be brought under Matrimonial Causes Act 1973, ss 23, 24 and 27 and for an alteration of a maintenance agreement to be brought under MCA 1973, ss 35 and 36; however, where the parents are not married, there is no jurisdiction apart from CA 1989, Sch 1.

CA 1989, Sch 1 (except where financial relief is also sought by or on behalf of an adult, in which case the application should proceed as an application for ancillary relief) is governed by FPR 1991, Part IV; FPR 1991, r 4.1(2)(*d*) refers. The High Court and county courts have equal jurisdiction.

Procedure

Who may apply	*Application for child under 18* Parent or guardian of child or holder of residence order	CA 1989, Sch 1, para 1(1)
	The order will be made either on the application of the above or without an application on the making, varying or discharging of a residence order	CA 1989, Sch 1, para 1(6)
	Application by child over 18 The child who is over 18 and:	
	who is or will be undergoing education or training or where there are special circumstances	CA 1989, Sch 1, para 2(1)(*a*), (*b*)
	who has not had in force a periodical payments order immediately before he was 16	CA 1989, Sch 1, para 2(3), (6)
	whose parents are not living together	CA 1989, Sch 1, para 2(4)

	Variation application Any of the persons set out above, with, additionally on an application under CA 1989, Sch 1, para 1, the child himself if he has reached 16	CA 1989, Sch 1, para 6(4)
	Application to alter maintenance agreement Either party to the agreement or a personal representative	CA 1989, Sch 1, paras 10(2), 11(1)
Application	To the High Court or county court on Forms C1 and C10, with statement of means on Form C10A. The applicant must lodge one set of the above forms for the court and sufficient copies to serve on each of the respondents; the court will provide Forms C6 (notice to parties), C6A (notice to non-parties), where appropriate, and C7 (acknowledgement), the first two of which will have been endorsed by the court with the date, and the applicant must serve these documents on each of the respondents in accordance with FPR 1991, r 4.8; at the first appointment, the applicant must file at court Form C9 (statement of service)	FPR 1991, r 4.4(1), (1A), (2), (3), (6)
Fee payable	£80	FPFO 1999, fee 2.2
Respondents	Any parent who is not an applicant and any person whom the applicant believes to be interested in or affected by the proceedings. All respondents must receive at least 14 days' notice prior to the hearing or directions appointment	FPR 1991, App 3
Respondent's answer	Respondent must file Form C9 within 14 days of service	FPR 1991, r 4.9(1)
Directions/Interim orders	The court (which will usually be the district judge) may make an interim order for periodical payments	CA 1989, Sch 1, para 9
	The court can fix a timetable for service of documents and filing of written statements, including the filing by the respondent of a statement of means in Form C10A	FPR 1991, rr 4.14(2), 4.17
	Court can join or discharge parties and give such directions as it thinks fit	FPR 1991, r 4.7; CA 1989, Sch 1, para 9(1)(*b*)
Order	*Application for child under 18* Periodical payments Secured periodical payments Lump sum	

	Settlement of property or transfer of property	
	Application by child over 18 Periodical payments	
	Lump sum	
	Application to alter maintenance agreement Varying or revoking any financial arrangements contained in the maintenance agreement, including inserting provision for periodical payments or for security for increasing or decreasing the level of periodical payments	
	All applications, once made, can only be withdrawn with leave	FPR 1991, r 4.5
Appeals	See Guides 72–75	

3: Financial Relief for a Child in a Magistrates' Court under Children Act 1989, Sch 1

Legal background

CA 1989, Sch 1 provides three forms of financial relief for a child in a magistrates' court: first, CA 1989, Sch 1, para 1 enables a periodical payments order or lump sum order to be made in favour of a child against either or both of its parents; secondly, para 2 enables a periodical payments order and lump sum order to be made in favour of a child who has reached 18 where (i) the child's parents are not living with each other, (ii) there was not in force a periodical payments order for the child immediately before he reached 16, and (iii) he is undergoing education or training or there are special circumstances; and, thirdly, a limited power to vary maintenance agreements under para 10. Orders under paras 1 and 2 may be varied or extended under para 6.

CA 1989, Sch 1 is governed by the Family Proceedings Courts (Children Act 1989) Rules 1991. There is a concurrent jurisdiction with the High Court and county courts for the making of these orders, but the High Court and county courts have additional powers under CA 1989, Sch 1 to make secured periodical payments orders, orders for the settlement or transfer of property and wider powers to vary the terms of maintenance agreements (see Guide 2).

Where the parties are married to each other, application for financial provision for a child may also be made under the Domestic Proceedings and Magistrates' Courts Act 1978. The magistrates' jurisdiction to make orders for financial relief in respect of a child under CA 1989, Sch 1 or DPMCA 1978 is limited by the provisions of the Child Support Act 1991 (see **Interface with Child Support Act 1991** under MCA 1973, s 23 and **Outline of new bases for child support calculation** under CSA 1991, s 4). A claim for child maintenance against a step-parent is unaffected by CSA 1991.

Procedure

Who may apply	*Application for child under 18* Parent or guardian of child or holder of residence order	CA 1989, Sch 1, para 1(1)

	The order may be made either on the application of the above or without an application on the making, varying or discharging of a residence order	CA 1989, Sch 1, para 1(6)
	Where the child is a ward of court, the court may exercise any of its powers under Sch 1, even if no application has been made	CA 1989, Sch 1, para 1(7)
	Application by child over 18 The child who is over 18 and:	
	who is or will be undergoing education or training or where there are special circumstances	CA 1989, Sch 1, para 2(1)(*a*), (*b*)
	who has not had in force a periodical payments order immediately before he was 16	CA 1989, Sch 1, para 2(3), (6)
	whose parents are not living together	CA 1989, Sch 1, para 2(4)
	Variation application Any of the persons set out above, with, additionally on an application under CA 1989, Sch 1, para 1, the child himself if he has reached 16	CA 1989, Sch 1, para 6(4)
	Application to alter maintenance agreement Either party to the agreement	CA 1989, Sch 1, para 10(2)
Application	To any magistrates' court, except in the case of an application under CA 1989, Sch 1, para 10 where the application must be made to a magistrates' court acting for the commission area in which at least one of the parties to the agreement resides	CA 1989, Sch 1, para 10(6)
	The application must be made on Forms C1 and C10, with statement of means on Form C10A	
	The applicant must file with the justices' clerk one set of the above forms for the court and sufficient copies to serve on each of the respondents; once the hearing date has been filled in, the applicant must serve the documents on each of the respondents	FPC(CA 1989)R 1991, r 4(1)
	At or before the first directions appointment or hearing, the applicant must file a statement in Form C9 that service has been effected of a copy of the application on each respondent and notice of the proceedings under r 4(3)	FPC(CA 1989)R 1991, r 8(7)
	Fee payable: £30	MCA 1980, Sch 6, Pt I

Respondents	Any parent who is not an applicant and any person whom the applicant believes to be interested in or affected by the proceedings. All respondents must receive at least 14 days' notice of any hearing or directions appointment	FPC(CA 1989)R 1991, Sch 2
Respondent's acknowledgement	Respondent must file Form C7 within 14 days of service	FPC(CA 1989)R 1991, r 9
Directions/Interim orders	The court may make an interim order for periodical payments	CA 1989, Sch 1, para 9
	The court or justices' clerk can give directions for the conduct of proceedings	FPC(CA 1989)R 1991, r 14
	The court can, on written request, order that a person be joined as a party or cease to be a party	FPC(CA 1989)R 1991, r 7
Order	*Application for financial relief* Periodical payments	CA 1989, Sch 1, paras 1–4
	Lump sum	CA 1989, Sch 1, para 5
	Application to alter maintenance agreement Where the agreement contains provision for periodical payments by either of the parties, an order varying or terminating those payments	CA 1989, Sch 1, para 10(6)
	All applications, once made, can only be withdrawn with leave	FPC(CA 1989)R 1991, r 5
	Reasons and findings of fact for the court's decision must be recorded and stated	FPC(CA 1989)R 1991, r 21(5), (6); *S v S* [1993]1 FLR 606
Appeals	See Guide 70	

4: Declaration of Proprietary Rights under Married Women's Property Act 1882, s 17

General note

The Family Proceedings (Amendment No 2) Rules 1999 have amended FPR 1991, rr 2.52–2.77 in respect of claims for ancillary relief started on or after 5 June 2000. The amended version of the rules is printed in this edition. A claim under the Married Women's Property Act 1882 is not a claim for ancillary relief. Family Proceedings (Amendment No 2) Rules 1999, r 20 provides that the unamended version of those rules applies to a claim under MWPA 1882. The unamended version, whose broad thrust is not substantially different from the current version of the rules, is contained in earlier editions of *The Family Court Practice*. Throughout this Guide the references are to the unamended rules.

Legal background

Both the High Court and county courts have equal jurisdiction on an application by a husband or wife, fiancé or fiancée to declare and enforce their proprietary rights in respect of any property which they possess or control at the time of the application or, as extended by s 7 of the Matrimonial Causes (Property and Maintenance) Act 1958, that they formerly possessed or controlled. The use of Married Women's Property Act 1882, s 17 has been strongly disapproved when Matrimonial Causes Act 1973, ss 23 and 24 are available but it is useful in two circumstances: (i) where a declaration of beneficial ownership is needed if there are doubts about the solvency of one of the parties; (ii) as suggested in *Wicks v Wicks* [1998] 1 FLR 470 where an order for sale is required prior to the ancillary relief hearing.

Wicks v Wicks suggested that if an order for possession of the assets was also required the application under MWPA 1882 should be linked with an application under Family Law Act 1996, Pt IV (an alternative is to proceed under Guide 5).

Procedure

Who may apply	Either spouse or fiancé(e), provided application made within 3 years of decree absolute or termination of engagement	MPPA 1970, s 39; LR(MP)A 1970, s 2(2)
Application and supporting affidavit and court	*If made in existing ancillary relief proceedings* By Form M11 in those ancillary relief proceedings	FPR 1991, r 3.6(2)
	Form M11 should state whether title is registered and give particulars of mortgage	FPR 1991, r 3.6(4)
	Supporting affidavit should set out full details of case	FPR 1991, r 3.6(1)
	If no ancillary relief proceedings By originating summons in High Court and originating application in county court in Form M23	FPR 1991, r 3.6(1)
	High Court applicant can choose his registry	FPR 1991, r 3.6(1)(*a*)
	County court applicant must choose the divorce county court in which any suit for divorce etc is proceeding or is intended to be commenced or the court for the district in which either the applicant or respondent resides	FPR 1991, r 3.6(3)
	application must identify whether land is registered or unregistered and give particulars of mortgage	FPR 1991, r 3.6(4)
	supporting affidavit should set out full details of case	FPR 1991, r 3.6(1)
	If commenced in principal registry If divorce etc proceedings commenced or about to be commenced in principal registry and treated as if in county court, applicant has option of issuing proceedings in principal registry as if in county court	FPR 1991, r 3.7

	Otherwise, issue in principal registry as High Court proceedings.	
Fee payable	£120	FPFO 1999, fee 1.1
Respondent	Other spouse or fiancé(e) Any mortgagee should be served and may apply to intervene	FPR 1991, r 3.6(6)
Respondent's affidavit	Respondent must file affidavit within 28 days of service of application; power exists to debar from defending	FPR 1991, r 3.6(7), (8)
Request for information	By letter, followed by application for an order for information and documents	FPR 1991, rr 2.63, 3.6(10)
Directions, injunctions or interim orders	District judge may: grant injunctions ancillary to claim, make interim orders and conduct final hearing, subject to power to refer application to judge give directions order the discovery and production of any documents or require further affidavits from the parties, order the attendance of anyone and take oral evidence	FPR 1991, rr 2.62(4), 2.64(2), 2.65, 3.6(9) FPR 1991, r 2.62(5) FPR 1991, rr 2.62(4), 3.6(10)
Documents	Schedule and chronology of events Succinct affidavits Paginated indexed bundles of documents with Civil Evidence Act notice; see under —	MCA 1973, s 25; *PD of 31 January 1995*
Order	Declare and enforce proprietary rights of both parties including: ordering sale and ordering payment of lump sum equal to value of assessed interest	MC(PM)A 1958, s 7(7) *Bothe v Amos* [1976] Fam 46
Appeals	See Guides 72–75	

5: Order under Trusts of Land and Appointment of Trustees Act 1996, s 14

Legal background

Trusts of Land and Appointment of Trustees Act 1996, s 14 entitles a trustee or a beneficiary of the proceeds of sale of land to apply for any order relating to the exercise by the trustees of any of their functions (including the power of exclusion and the power of sale), or declaring the nature and extent of a person's interest in a trust of land. This section is, therefore, considerably wider than the repealed Law of Property Act 1925, s 30 (which entitled one joint owner of a property to apply for its sale, independent of any divorce proceedings), and enables the court to make a long-term exclusion order. The 1996 Act is in force from 1 January 1997 and, by virtue of s 1(1)(*a*), applies to trusts of land created before that date. The court does not have jurisdiction under the Matrimonial Causes Act 1973 to order a sale pending a final ancillary relief hearing (*Wicks v Wicks* [1998] 1 FLR 470). TLATA 1996, s 14 gives the court jurisdiction to order a sale with vacant possession pending a final ancillary relief order but, unless a case of urgency for an immediate sale can be made out, if divorce proceedings are pending or are likely to be filed shortly, the application is at risk of being consolidated with those proceedings (*Williams v Williams* [1976] Ch 278). By virtue of the High Court and County Courts Jurisdiction Order 1991 (as amended), the county court's jurisdiction is unlimited. Section 14 of the 1996 Act is to be read together with ss 13 and 15. An application under TLATA 1996 is governed by CPR 1998, Pt 8. See also *Practice Direction (Alternative Procedure for Claims)* (PD 8), set out in Part V of this work and *Practice Direction (How to Make Claims in the Schedule Rules and Other Claims)* (PD 8B), set out in Section 2 of the *Civil Court Service* (Jordan Publishing Ltd).

Procedure

Who may apply	A trustee, a joint legal or beneficial owner, or a judgment creditor holding a charging order	*Midland Bank v Pike* [1988] 2 All ER 434
Which court	If in the High Court, the Chancery Division or, if a family case, the Family Division	*Williams v Williams* [1976] Ch 278
	If in the county court, the court for the district in which the defendant lives or carries on business or the property is situated; but if divorce proceedings are pending in another court, apply at time of issuing application for matter to be transferred to that court under CPR 1998, r 30.2	PD 8B, para B.6
Application	Claim Form N208 complying with CPR 1998, r 8.2, with written evidence in support of claim verified by statement of truth	CPR 1998, rr 8.2, 8.5
Fee payable	county court: £120 High Court: £120	CCFO 1999, fee 1.3 SCFO 1999, fee 1.2
Defendant	Any other owner or person with an interest in the property should be served.	
Defendant's response	Whilst there is no requirement for filing a defence, the defendant must within 14 days file an acknowledgment of service in Form N210 complying with CPR 1998, r 8.3, with written evidence opposing the claim verified by statement of truth	CPR 1998, rr 8.3–8.5

Directions	Either immediately the Claim Form is issued or when the time for filing the acknowledgment of service has expired the court will fix a hearing date or give directions and/or fix a directions appointment on its own motion or on application	PD 8, para 4.1
	The claim is treated as allocated to the multi-track	CPR 1998, r 8.9(c)
	Directions given in pursuance of the overriding objective to actively case manage will include:	
	(i) whether the case should proceed as a Part 7 claim	CPR 1998, r 8.1(3)
	(ii) allowing a party to take part in absence of acknowledgment of service	CPR 1998, r 8.4
	(iii) giving judgment if no real prospect of success in making or defending claim	
	(iv) fixing timetable for final hearing	CPR 1998, r 3.4, Pt 24
Order	Grant of, or refusal to grant, order for sale, either unconditionally or on terms, eg applicant to provide smaller house for respondent, or respondent to pay occupation rent, or judgment debtor to pay debt by instalments; order excluding one party, and declaration as to interest in the trust	*Chapman v Chapman* (1962) 4 CL 441; *Dennis v McDonald* [1982] 2 WLR 275
Appeals	See Guides 72–75	

6: Financial Provision Order under Matrimonial Causes Act 1973, s 27

General note

The Family Proceedings (Amendment No 2) Rules 1999 have amended FPR 1991, rr 2.52–2.77 in respect of claims for ancillary relief started on or after 5 June 2000. The amended version of the rules is printed in this edition. A claim for failure to provide reasonable maintenance is not a claim for ancillary relief. Family Proceedings (Amendment No 2) Rules 1999, r 20 provides that the unamended version of those rules applies to a claim for failure to provide reasonable maintenance. The unamended version, whose broad thrust is not substantially different from the current version of the rules, is contained in earlier editions of *The Family Court Practice*. Throughout this Guide the references are to the unamended rules.

Legal background

Subject to the effect of the Child Support Act 1991 (see **Interface with Child Support Act 1991** under MCA 1973, s 23 and **Outline of new bases for child support calculation** under CSA 1991, s 4), Matrimonial Causes Act 1973, s 27 enables a spouse to apply to the High Court or a county court for periodical payments, secured periodical payments and a lump sum (but not a transfer of property) for him or herself and/or the children without the necessity of filing a petition for divorce, judicial separation or nullity. Once failure to provide reasonable maintenance is proved, the application is determined on the same principles as if such a petition had been filed, except that there is no presumption that the marriage has broken down. The jurisdictional requirement as to domicile or habitual residence is the same as for a petition, except that under MCA 1973, s 27 the applicant can establish jurisdiction on the additional ground that the respondent is resident in England and Wales at the date of the application.

The procedural steps suggested below are set out on the basis that the application is made in the county court. While the definition of "court" incorporated into MCA 1973, s 27 by s 52(1) includes the High Court, FPR 1991, r 3.1(2) envisages the application being made in the county court. It is suggested, therefore, that the application is launched in the county court and, if it is wished that it proceed in the High Court, the applicant should apply to transfer to the High Court when applying for directions.

Procedure

Who may apply	Either spouse	MCA 1973, s 27(1), (2)
Application	Originating application on Form M19 to divorce county court of applicant's choice	FPR 1991, r 3.1(1), (2)
Fee payable	£120	FPFO 1999, fee 1.1
Lead affidavit	The affidavit should contain: formal particulars of the marriage, the court's jurisdiction, children and previous proceedings disclosure of means facts relied on	FPR 1991, r 3.1(3)(*a*); App 2, paras 1(*a*), (*c*), (*d*), (*f*), (*i*)
Respondent	The other spouse	FPR 1991, r 3.1(4)
	If there is an allegation of adultery or improper association with a named person, the court may direct service on that person	FPR 1991, rr 2.60, 3.1(7)
Respondent's affidavit in answer	Unless there is a challenge to jurisdiction, affidavit of means and stating case within 28 days of service of originating application on him	FPR 1991, r 3.1(5)–(8)
Applicant's affidavit in reply	Within 14 days of receipt of respondent's affidavit; otherwise, no further affidavit possible without leave	FPR 1991, r 3.1(9)
Request for information	By letter, followed by application for an order for information and documents	FPR 1991, rr 2.63, 3.1(10)
Consent application	File proposed consent order and statement of information	FPR 1991, rr 2.61, 3.1(10)
Directions	Dual purpose: explore possibility of a settlement; prepare case for final hearing	

	Order to provide information or documents	FPR 1991, r 2.63
	Further affidavits, attendance of witnesses or leave to call any expert evidence	FPR 1991, r 2.62(4), (5)
	Production of documents	FPR 1991, r 2.62(7)–(9)
	Transfer or setting down	FPR 1991, r 10.10
Interim orders	Unfettered power to make interim orders for periodical payments, but not interim lump sum	MCA 1973, ss 27(5), 31; *Wicks v Wicks* [1998] 1 FLR 470, CA
Documents for final hearing	Schedule Succinct affidavits of the minimum number possible Paginated and indexed bundle of documents including estimate of costs prefaced with Civil Evidence Act notice; see under —	MCA 1973, s 25; *PD of 31 January 1995*
Order	Periodical payments and/or secured periodical payments for spouse and/or children	MCA 1973, s 27(6)(*a*), (*b*), (*d*), (*e*)
	Lump sum for spouse and/or children; for wording of roll-over of statutory charge, see —	MCA 1973, s 27(6)(*c*), (*f*); *PD of 19 August 1991*
	No power to award interest on lump sum before it is paid (no MCA 1973, s 23(6) equivalent) but interest as judgment debt after time for payment has expired	CC(IJD)O 1991
Appeals	See Guides 72–75	

7: Variation of a Maintenance Agreement

General note

The Family Proceedings (Amendment No 2) Rules 1999 have amended FPR 1991, rr 2.52–2.77 in respect of claims for ancillary relief started on or after 5 June 2000. The amended version of the rules is printed in this edition. A claim to vary a maintenance agreement is not a claim for ancillary relief. Family Proceedings (Amendment No 2) Rules 1999, r 20 provides that the unamended version of those rules applies to a claim to vary a maintenance agreement. The unamended version, whose broad thrust is not substantially different from the current version of the rules, is contained in earlier editions of *The Family Court Practice*. Throughout this Guide the references are to the unamended rules.

Legal background

The court's power to vary a maintenance agreement during the lives of the parties (Matrimonial Causes Act 1973, s 35) or on the death of one of the parties (MCA 1973, s 36) is exercised by the High Court or a county court, subject to the minor exception that a magistrates' court can vary a maintenance agreement if it includes no provision for periodical payments or the application is to vary or terminate those payments. FPR 1991, r 3.2 provides that a maintenance agreement to be altered during joint lives may be made in the divorce county court only. The procedural steps suggested below for altering such an agreement are set out on the basis that the application is lodged in the county court. A transfer to the High Court can be sought at directions. FPR 1991, r 3.3 provides that an application to vary a maintenance agreement after the death of one party may be made in either the High Court or a county court. As noted to MCA 1973, s 36, the county court's jurisdiction is now unlimited.

Child Support Act 1991, s 9 limits the court's power, in respect of child maintenance, to vary a maintenance agreement made after 5 April 1993 to the categories summarised at **Interface with Child Support Act 1991** under MCA 1973, s 23.

Procedure

Who may apply	*Lifetime application* Either spouse	MCA 1973, s 35(1)
	Application after death of one party The personal representatives of the deceased or the surviving spouse	MCA 1973, s 36(1)
	If application is made more than 6 months after the grant of probate, leave is required	MCA 1973, s 36(2)
Application and supporting documents	*Lifetime application* Originating application on Form M21	FPR 1991, r 3.2(1)
	Supporting affidavit exhibiting copy of the agreement and verifying Form M21	FPR 1991, r 3.2(3)
	Application is made to the divorce county court of the applicant's choice	FPR 1991, r 3.2(2)
	Application after death of one party Originating summons if in High Court or originating application if in county court on Form M22	FPR 1991, r 3.2(1)
	Supporting affidavit exhibiting agreement and official copy of the grant of probate and the will, disclosing means, stating facts relied on and providing formal details	FPR 1991, r 3.3(2)
	If in the county court, file in the court for the district in which the deceased resided	CCR Ord 48, r 3(1)
Fee payable	£120	FPFO 1999, fee 1.1
Respondents	The other spouse or his personal representatives	FPR 1991, r 3.4(1)–(3)
	Any other party whom the district judge directs should be served	FPR 1991, r 2.60
Respondent's affidavit	*Lifetime application* Affidavit disclosing means and stating case within 28 days of service of application	FPR 1991, r 3.2(5)

	Application after death of one party Affidavit by personal representative within 28 days of service of application giving full particulars of the value of the deceased's estate and the persons beneficially interested	FPR 1991, r 3.4(4)(*a*), (*b*), (*c*)
Request for information	Request by letter followed by application for an order for information and documents	FPR 1991, rr 2.63, 3.5
Directions	Dual purpose: explore possibility of a settlement; prepare case for final hearing	
	Order to provide information or documents	FPR 1991, r 2.63
	Further affidavits, discovery and production of documents by parties and orders for attendance of witnesses, including witnesses who are not parties	FPR 1991, r 2.62(4), (5)
	Transfer to High Court or between courts	FPR 1991, r 10.10; CCR Ord 48, r 9
Documents for final hearing	Schedule and chronology of events	
	Succinct affidavits of the minimum number possible	
	Paginated and indexed bundle of documents, including valuations and estimate of costs prefaced with Civil Evidence Act notice; see under —	MCA 1973, s 25; *PD of 31 January 1995*
Order	Vary or revoke financial arrangements contained in agreement, or insert financial arrangements into agreement for benefit of spouse or child	MCA 1973, ss 34(2), 35(2), 36(1)
	Statutory charge can be rolled over on MCA 1973, s 35 but not s 36 application	CLA(G)R 1989, reg 94(*d*)(i)
	For wording of roll-over, see —	*PD of 19 August 1991*
Appeals	See Guides 72–75	

8: Claim for Financial Provision under the Inheritance (Provision for Family and Dependants) Act 1975

Legal background

A claim may be made against the estate of a deceased person by certain members of the deceased's family and dependants categorised in the Inheritance (Provision for Family and Dependants) Act 1975, s 1 (as amended by the Law Reform (Succession)

Act 1995) for financial provision out of the net estate of the deceased, on the ground that the disposition of the deceased's estate effected by his will and/or under the laws of intestacy is not such as to make reasonable financial provision for the applicant. Special provisions are set out in I(PFD)A 1975, s 14 in respect of cases where a party to the marriage dies within 12 months of the decree of divorce, nullity or judicial separation and an application for financial provision has not been made or determined. Section 2 sets out the court's powers to make orders and s 3 details the matters which the court must take into account. Unless the court gives permission extending the time limit, the application must be made within six months of the date on which representation is first granted (s 4).

The procedure for both the High Court and county court is governed by CPR 1998, Pt 57. See also *Practice Direction (Probate)* (PD 57) and *Practice Direction (Alternative Procedure for Claims)* (PD 8), set out in Part V of this work; and *Practice Direction (How to Make Claims in the Schedule Rules and Other Claims)* (PD 8B), set out in Section 2 of the *Civil Court Service* (Jordan Publishing Ltd).

Procedure

Who may apply	The spouse of the deceased The former spouse of the deceased who has not remarried A cohabitant of the deceased A child of the deceased Any person who was treated as a child of the family Any other person who immediately before the death of the deceased was being maintained by him	I(PFD)A 1975, s 1
Which court	High Court (Chancery or Family Division) or county court	CPR 1998, r 57.15; I(PFD)A 1975, s 22
	District judges (including District judges of the Principal Registry of the Family Division) have jurisdiction to hear such applications	*PD of 22 April 1999*
Application	*High Court/county court* By Part 8 claim form which should be entitled "In the estate of ... deceased" and "In the matter of I(PFD)A 1975"	CPR 1998, rr 57.16, 8.2; PD 8B
Time limit	The claim must be issued within 6 months of the date on which representation is taken out (unless extended by the court). Application to extend the time limit must be included in the claim form	I(PFD)A 1975, s 4
Documents	The applicant must file with the claim form a witness statement/affidavit in support exhibiting an official copy of the grant of representation and of every testamentary document admitted to proof	CPR 1998, rr 57.16(3), 8.5(1), (2)

Defendants	Personal representatives	
	Beneficiaries	
	Other persons affected by the claim	
	Any other person directed by the court to be added	CPR 1998, r 19.7
Service	Acknowledgement of service must be filed within 21 days after service of the claim form and served on the claimant and other parties if served within the jurisdiction	CPR 1998, rr 57.16(4), 8.3(1), 10.3(1)
	otherwise, in accordance with CPR 1998, r 10.3(2) and Sch 1, RSC Ord 11, r 1A	CPR 1998, r 10.3(2)
Statement/Affidavit in answer	Must be filed by the personal representatives within 21 days after service of the claim form (it should include the matters set out in PD 57, para 16)	CPR 1998, r 57.16(4), (5); PD 57, para 16
	May be filed by other defendants within 21 days after service of the claim form	CPR 1998, r 57.16(4)
Service of answer	Every defendant who files any written evidence within 21 days in answer must serve a copy on the claimant and every other defendant who is not represented by the same solicitor	CPR 1998, r 57.16(4)
Reply	A claimant may serve a statement in reply on all other parties within 14 days of service of the defendant's evidence on him	CPR 1998, r 8.5(5), (6)
Directions	At the same time as issuing the claim form a directions hearing may be requested	PD 8, para 4.1
	The court will in any event give directions after the defendant has filed the acknowledgement of service or after the time for filing it has expired	PD 8, para 4.2
Fee payable	High Court: £120	SCFO 1999, fee 1.2
	county court: £120	CCFO 1999, fee 1.3
Order	Periodical payments	I(PFD)A 1975, s 2(1)(*a*)
	Lump sum	I(PFD)A 1975, s 2(1)(*b*)
	Transfer of property	I(PFD)A 1975, s 2(1)(*c*)
	Settlement of property	I(PFD)A 1975, s 2(1)(*d*)
	Acquisition, transfer and settlement of property	I(PFD)A 1975, s 2(1)(*e*)
	Variation of antenuptial and post-nuptial settlement	I(PFD)A 1975, s 2(1)(*f*)

	Variation or discharge of secured periodical payments	I(PFD)A 1975, s 16
	Variation or revocation of maintenance agreements	I(PFD)A 1975, s 17
	Order relating to disposition intended to defeat a claim under the Act	I(PFD)A 1975, ss 10, 11
	Treatment of deceased's former beneficial interest in joint property as part of his estate and not passing by survivorship	I(PFD)A 1975, s 9
Appeals	See Guides 72, 73, 75	

9: Financial Provision in the Magistrates' Court

Legal background

Three separate forms of application for financial provision may be made under the Domestic Proceedings and Magistrates' Courts Act 1978: an application under DPMCA 1978, s 2 based on the grounds in s 1 (failure to provide reasonable maintenance for the applicant or for any child of the family, behaviour or desertion); an application under DPMCA 1978, s 6 based on agreed financial provision; or an application under DPMCA 1978, s 7 based on the level of maintenance paid in the three months preceding the date of the application while the parties have been living apart by agreement.

There is provision for the "conversion" of an application under DPMCA 1978, s 2 to an application under s 6, and for the "conversion" of an application under s 7 to an application under s 2.

Financial provision may be made for either party to the marriage and for any child of the family (as defined in DPMCA 1978, s 88). The court is required to have regard to the matters contained in DPMCA 1978, s 3 in assessing the amount of any order.

A lump sum order is available under DPMCA 1978, s 2(1)(*b*) for the benefit of a spouse and under s 2(1)(*d*) for the benefit of a child of the family. The amount of any lump sum order under s 2 is limited to £1,000. Lump sum orders are also available under DPMCA 1978, s 6(2)(*b*) to a spouse and s 6(2)(*d*) for a child of the family. There is no limit to the amount of a lump sum order under s 6.

The term of a periodical payments order to a spouse is governed by DPMCA 1978, s 4; the term of an order to or for a child of the family is governed by DPMCA 1978, s 5. Financial provision for children is also available under CA 1989, Sch 1.

Periodical payments and lump sum orders payable by instalments may be ordered to be paid under Magistrates' Courts Act 1980, s 59 either directly between the parties, through the justices' chief executive, by standing order or by an attachment of earnings order.

This must now be read subject to Child Support Act 1991, s 8(1), (3), which deprives the court of any power which it would otherwise have to make, vary or revive any maintenance order in relation to the child and non-resident parent concerned in any case where the Child Support Agency would have jurisdiction to make a maintenance calculation with respect to a qualifying child and non-resident parent of his. Any such application must now be made to the Secretary of State and not to the courts.

Procedure

Who may apply	Either party to a marriage	DPMCA 1978, ss 1, 6(1), 7(1)

Which court	A magistrates' court with jurisdiction for the commission area in which the applicant or respondent ordinarily resides	DPMCA 1978, s 30; MCA 1980, s 52
Application	*Under DPMCA 1978, s 2* On Form 1 (MAT 1) *Under DPMCA 1978, s 6* On Form 2 (MAT 2) *Under DPMCA 1978, s 7* On Form 3 (MAT 3)	FPC(MP etc)R 1991, r 3(1)(*a*), Sch 1
	Sufficient copies must be filed for one to be served on the respondent.	
	An oral application may be made when an application under DPMCA 1978, s 2 is converted to an application under s 6	FPC(MP etc)R 1991, r 3(3)
	Fee payable: £30	MCA 1980, Sch 6, Pt I
Respondent	The other party to the marriage	
Service	At least 21 days before the date fixed for the hearing, by personal service or first-class post if the respondent is not acting by solicitor; otherwise, on the solicitor by first-class post, document exchange or fax, or as directed by the justices' clerk or the court	FPC(MP etc)R 1991, rr 3(1)(*b*), 4
	At or before the first directions appointment or the first hearing, the applicant must serve a statement of service.	
Answer to application	Must be filed and served by respondent within 14 days of service of the application	FPC(MP etc)R 1991, r 5
Directions	May be given by the justices' clerk or court on own motion (after notice of intention given), on a party's written request filed and served, or on written request by consent or (in an urgent case) orally without notice	FPC(MP etc)R 1991, rr 6, 8
	Directions for the conduct of the proceedings may include the timetable for the proceedings, variation of the time within which or by which an act is required to be done, the service of documents, the submission of evidence and attendance at a directions appointment or hearing.	
Order	Form 9 (MAT 9)	FPC(MP etc)R 1991, r 12(7)(*a*)

Additional or alternative orders	Interim order	DPMCA 1978, s 19
	Financial provision for child	CA 1989, Sch 1
	Costs	FPC(MP etc)R 1991, r 13
	Adjournment for reconciliation and report	DPMCA 1978, s 26
Variation, revival and revocation	Application may be made by either party, or by a child who has attained the age of 16 on Form 4 (MAT 4)	DPMCA 1978, ss 20, 20A, 20ZA, 20(12); FPC(MP etc)R 1991, r 3(1)(*a*)
	Jurisdiction may exist even where a party resides outside England and Wales	FPC(MP etc)R 1991, r 22(1)
	Notice	FPC(MP etc)R 1991, r 22(2), (4), (5)
	The order may only be increased if the payer appears or a statement of service is filed	FPC(MP etc)R 1991, r 22(4)
Appeals	See Guide 71	

10: "Non-molestation" and/or Occupation Order in Pending Family Proceedings, or under Family Law Act 1996, Part IV

Legal background

Where no family proceedings are pending, a free-standing application under FLA 1996, Pt IV can be issued in a divorce county court (so designated under Matrimonial and Family Proceedings Act 1984, s 33), a family hearing centre or care centre (see Children (Allocation of Proceedings) Order 1991, Schs 1 and 2 respectively) or the Principal Registry of the Family Division (Family Law Act 1996 (Part IV) (Allocation of Proceedings) Order 1997, art 16). Alternatively, subject to FLA 1996, s 59 and Sch 7, para 1, proceedings under Pt IV may be commenced in a family proceedings court.

An application by an applicant under the age of 18, or for leave under s 43 (applications by children under 16) must be made in the High Court.

Where "family proceedings" (see FLA 1996, s 63) are pending in a county court or family proceedings court, an application under FLA 1996, Pt IV may be made in those proceedings.

Personal protection in the form of a "non-molestation order" is available to "associated persons", a term widely defined in s 62(3). "Molestation" is not defined in the Act. It includes violence and threats of violence but is not confined to such acts (see s 42).

"Occupation orders" are available under ss 33, 35, 36, 37 and 38. Each section is self-contained, setting out who may apply and the court's powers. In practice, most applications will be under s 33. If an application is made under the wrong section, the court can make an order under another section (s 39). The court can include ancillary provisions (s 40).

A power of arrest may be attached to a non-molestation order or an occupation order. In certain circumstances, the court has a duty to attach a power of arrest (s 47(2)). Attaching a power of arrest is now the rule rather than the exception (see s 47).

Where injunctive relief from tortious molestation (including harassment within the meaning of the Protection from Harassment Act 1997) is sought, see Guide 11. For example, a person who is not an "associated person" within FLA 1996, Pt IV may need to sue in tort.

Procedure

What is a "non-molestation" order?	An order prohibiting the respondent from molesting another person who is associated with the respondent and/or relevant child	FLA 1996, s 42(1)
Who may apply for a "non-molestation" order?	An associated person; a person is associated with another person if:	FLA 1996, s 62(3)
	they are or have been married	
	they are cohabitants or former cohabitants	
	they live or have lived in the same household, otherwise than merely by reason of one of them being the other's employee, tenant, lodger or boarder	
	they are relatives (as defined)	FLA 1996, s 63(1)
	they have agreed to marry one another (whether or not that agreement has been terminated)	
	in relation to a child both persons are parents or have or have had parental responsibility for the child	FLA 1996, s 62(4)
	they are parties to the same family proceedings	FLA 1996, s 63(1), (2)
Who may apply for an "occupation order" under s 33?	An applicant who is entitled to occupy a dwelling-house by virtue of a beneficial estate or interest or contract or by virtue of any enactment giving him the right to remain in occupation or who has matrimonial home rights. The respondent is an "associated person"	FLA 1996, s 30
	The dwelling-house must be, have been, or have been intended to be, the home of the applicant and respondent	FLA 1996, s 33
Who may apply for an "occupation order" under s 35?	An applicant former spouse who is not entitled to occupy; the respondent is entitled to occupy; the dwelling-house was or was intended to be their matrimonial home	FLA 1996, s 35
Who may apply for an "occupation order" under s 36?	An applicant cohabitant or former cohabitant who is not entitled to occupy; the respondent is entitled to occupy; the dwelling-house is, was, or was intended to be the home where they live together as husband and wife	FLA 1996, s 36

Who may apply for an "occupation order" under s 37?	An applicant spouse or former spouse where neither applicant nor respondent spouse or former spouse is entitled to occupy; the dwelling-house must be or have been the matrimonial home	FLA 1996, s 37
Who may apply for an "occupation order" under s 38?	An applicant cohabitant or former cohabitant where neither applicant nor respondent cohabitant or former cohabitant is entitled to occupy. The dwelling-house must be or have been the home in which they live together as husband and wife	FLA 1996, s 38
How is the application made?	In all cases, on Form FL401 supported by a "sworn statement" (which must state the grounds). A draft of the order sought should also be provided	FPR 1991, r 3.8; FPC(MP etc)R 1991, r 3A; CCR Ord 13, r 6
Which court?	County court which is a divorce county court, family hearing centre or care centre. Lambeth, Shoreditch and Woolwich county courts also have jurisdiction. The Principal Registry is treated as a county court	FLA(Pt IV)(AP)O 1997
	Family proceedings court (subject to FLA 1996, s 59)	FLA(Pt IV)(AP)O 1997, art 4
	High Court, if the applicant is under 18 or seeks leave under s 43	FLA(Pt IV)(AP)O 1997, art 4(2)
Fee payable	£40	FPFO 1999, fee 1.3
Transfer of proceedings	Court may transfer proceedings to a more convenient court	FPR 1991, rr 3.8(9), 10.10; FPC(MP etc)R 1991, r 3A(8); Form FL417
Ex parte applications	In any case where it considers it is "just and convenient" to do so the court can make a non-molestation order or an occupation order on an ex parte basis. The court must have regard to "all the circumstances", including the criteria in s 45(2)	FLA 1996, s 45(1), (2)
	The sworn statement must state the reasons why notice was not given	FPR 1991, r 3.8(5); FPC(MP etc)R 1991, r 3A(4)
	If an ex parte order is made there must be a "full hearing" as soon as just and convenient	FLA 1996, s 45(3)
Service of ex parte order	Respondent must be personally served with: a copy of the order made (Form FL404)	

	a copy of the application in Form FL401 a copy of the sworn statement in support of the application notice of the date of the full hearing in Form FL402.	FPR 1991, r 3.9(2); FPC(MP etc)R 1991, r 12A(2)
Application on notice	Notice in Form FL402, together with a copy of the application in Form FL401 and the sworn statement in support must be served on the respondent personally not less than 2 days before the application is to be heard	FPR 1991, r 3.8(6); FPC(MP etc)R 1991, r 3A(5)
	Before the application is served, the court can abridge time for service	FPR 1991, r 3.8(7); FPC(MP etc)R 1991, r 3A(6)
	If the application is for an occupation order under ss 33, 35 or 36 a copy of the application and notice in Form FL416 must be served by first class post on the mortgagee or landlord	FPR 1991, r 3.8(11); FPC(MP etc)R 1991, r 3A(10)
Proof of service	After service, the applicant must file a statement in Form FL415	FPR 1991, r 3.8(15); FPC(MP etc)R 1991, r 3A(11)
Response	Respondent may, but is not required to, serve a sworn statement in reply and/or make a cross-application	CCR Ord 13, r 6(4A)
Hearing	An application for a non-molestation order or an occupation order is dealt with in chambers unless the court otherwise directs	FPR 1991, r 3.9(1)
	The application in the county court is heard by a district judge or Circuit judge	FP(AJ)D 1999 (as amended by FP(AJ)(A)D 2002)
	The applicant must submit a draft of the order sought. It should be drafted in Form FL404 and based on the specimen clauses 1–41 as appropriate	FPR 1991, r 3.9(6)(*b*); CCR Ord 13, r 6(6)
	The court keeps a record of the hearing in Form FL405	FPR 1991, r 3.9(6)(*a*); FPC(MP etc)R 1991, r 12A(1)(*a*)
Orders available	*Non-molestation order* An order may forbid molestation in general or particular acts of molestation or both	FLA 1996, s 42(6)
	See also specimen clauses 38–41 in Form FL404, set out in —	FPR 1991, App 1; FPC(MP etc)R 1991, Sch 1

	Occupation order under s 33 An order may:	
	enforce the applicant's entitlement to remain in occupation as against the respondent	
	require the respondent to permit the applicant to enter and remain in the dwelling-house or part of the dwelling-house	
	regulate the occupation of the dwelling-house by either or both of the parties	
	if the respondent is entitled [to occupy], prohibit, suspend or restrict the exercise by him of his right to occupy the dwelling-house	
	if the respondent has matrimonial home rights in relation to the dwelling-house and the applicant is the other spouse, restrict or terminate those rights	
	require the respondent to leave the dwelling-house or part of the dwelling-house	
	exclude the respondent from a defined area in which the dwelling-house is included	
	See specimen clauses 1–12 in Form FL404, set out in —	FPR 1991, App 1
	For additional provisions, see s 40; and specimen clauses 24–31 in Form FL404, set out in —	FPR 1991, App 1
	Occupation orders under ss 35, 36 Mandatory provisions are set out in ss 35(3), (4), 36(3), (4), and discretionary provisions in ss 35(5), 36(6)	
	See specimen clauses 13–19 in Form FL404, set out in —	FPR 1991, App 1
	For additional provisions, see s 40; and specimen clauses 24–31 in Form FL404, set out in —	FPR 1991, App 1
	Occupation orders under ss 37, 38 See ss 37(3), 38(3); and specimen clauses 20–23 in Form FL404, set out in —	FPR 1991, App 1
Duration of non-molestation orders	For a specified period or until further order	FLA 1996, s 42(7)
	Application for extension of the order is made in Form FL403	FPR 1991, r 3.9(8)
Duration of occupation orders	*Applicant with estate or interest etc or with matrimonial home rights* for a specified period	

	until the occurrence of a specified event	
	or until further order	FLA 1996, s 33(10)
	Application for extension of the order is made in Form FL403	FPR 1991, r 3.9(8)
	Spouse or former spouse not entitled to an interest for a maximum of 6 months, but can be renewed any number of times	FLA 1996, ss 35(10), 37(5)
	Application for extension of the order is made in Form FL403	FPR 1991, r 3.9(8)
	Cohabitant or former cohabitant not entitled to an interest for a maximum of 6 months, but can be renewed only once	FLA 1996, ss 36(10), 38(6)
	Application for extension of the order is made in Form FL403	FPR 1991, r 3.9(8)
Penal notice	A penal notice must be endorsed on an order before it can be enforced by committal	CCR Ord 29, r 1(3)
	A penal notice is therefore mandatory if the order includes a non-molestation order, and discretionary if it does not; see Notice A in Form FL404, set out in —	FPR 1991, App 1; FPC(MP etc)R 1991, Sch 1
Power of arrest	The court "*shall* attach a power of arrest to one or more provisions of the order unless satisfied that ... the applicant ... will be adequately protected without [it]" if the respondent has used or threatened violence	FLA 1996, s 47(2)
	If the order is made ex parte, the court *may* attach a power of arrest if "the respondent has used or threatened violence ..." and "there is a risk of significant harm ... if the power of arrest is not attached ..."	FLA 1996, s 47(3)
Undertakings	The court may accept an undertaking. The court "shall not accept an undertaking ... in any case where ... a power of arrest would be attached to the order"	FLA 1996, s 46(1), (3)
	The court must deliver a copy of the undertaking to the party giving the undertaking	CCR Ord 29, r 1A
Service of injunction	Personal service of an order is required	FPR 1991, r 3.9(4); FPC(MP etc)R 1991, r 12A(2)
	The applicant's solicitor should endeavour to effect service as soon as possible	

	An injunction directing an act to be done cannot be enforced unless it is served before the time within which the act is to be done has expired; an injunction cannot be enforced unless the respondent knows about it	RSC Ord 45, r 7(2); FPC(MP etc)R 1991, r 20(6), (11), (12); CCR Ord 29, r 1(2)
	Form FL406 (containing only those provisions of the order to which a power of arrest has been attached) must be delivered to the officer in charge of any police station for the applicant's address or such other police station as the court may specify. The form must be served together with a statement showing that the respondent has been served with the order or otherwise informed of its terms	FPR 1991, r 3.9A(1); FPC(MP etc)R 1991, r 20(1)(*b*)
	A copy of an occupation order made under s 33, 35 or 36 must be served by the applicant by first class post on the mortgagee or landlord	FPC(MP etc)R 1991, r 12A(4)

11: Personal Protection Injunction based in Torts

Legal background

The High Court and county courts have jurisdiction to grant an injunction for personal protection by forbidding harassment under the Protection from Harassment Act 1997 or any conduct which amounts to a recognised form of tort (*Patel v Patel* [1988] 2 FLR 179; *Khorasandjian v Bush* [1993] 2 FLR 66). Such proceedings are not "family proceedings", and remedies under FLA 1996, Pt IV, such as occupation orders and powers of arrest, are not available; however a warrant of arrest can be granted in respect of a breach (PHA 1997, s 3(3), (5)). In *Burris v Azadani* [1996] 1 FLR 266, the Court of Appeal held that, where it is necessary to make the injunction effective for the protection of the applicant, an "exclusion zone" can be ordered forbidding the defendant to go within a specified area around the applicant's home. On this basis, it would appear that an exclusion zone could also be provided around the applicant's place of work.

For precedents and an outline of the law and practice, see *Emergency Remedies in the Family Courts* (Family Law, 2000).

Injunctions forbidding molestation and regulating occupation of the family home under Family Law Act 1996, Part IV

Where the victim and the perpetrator of harassment or molestation are "associated persons" within FLA 1996, s 62(3), the remedies under that Act are more comprehensive, particularly if occupation of the family home is an issue. See Guide 10.

Free-standing injunction by application in a county court under Protection from Harassment Act 1997

An injunction can be granted in a county court (as in the High Court) without a claim for damages or other relief, by virtue of County Courts Act 1984, s 38. Such an injunction is "free-standing", like an injunction under FLA 1996. However, whereas an injunction under FLA 1996 is applied for by way of an application in Form FL401 under FPR 1991, r 3.8, an application for a free-standing injunction under PHA 1997 is governed by the CPR

PART I

1998 and is begun by a civil Claim Form N1 together with N16A injunction application (county court) or Application Notice Form N244 (High Court).

Under the CPR, proceedings are commenced by "claim form" (see Pt 7). Particulars of claim must be included in the claim form or in a separate document served with, or within 14 days after service of, the claim form. Particulars of claim must include "a concise statement of the facts on which the claimant relies" (r 16.4(1)) and they must be verified by a "statement of truth" (see rr 2.3 and 22.1). Interim remedies are also governed by Pt 25: see in particular *Practice Direction – Interim Injunctions* (PD 25) which supplements Pt 25. Best practice for making a free-standing application is to file N1 incorporating short particulars of claim, which can, but need not, include a claim for damages, together with an application in Form N16A (county court) or Application Notice in Form N244 (High Court), provided that the evidence setting out the relevant facts is given in Form N16A or N244, or in witness statement(s), verified by a statement of truth.

Procedure

Who may apply	Victim of tort committed or threatened	*Khorasandjian v Bush* [1993] 2 FLR 66
	An injunction based in tort can be granted only when a tortious act has been or is likely to be committed	*Khorasandjian v Bush* (above); *Patel v Patel* [1988] 2 FLR 179 at 180H; PHA 1997, s 3(1)
	Application for an interim injunction may be made by the defendant to the claim	CPR 1998, rr 25.1(1)(*a*), 25.2(1)
Which court	High Court or the county court for the district where the claimant or defendant resides	PHA 1997, s 3(3); CPR 1998, Sch 1, RSC Ord 94, r 16(6)
Application	Claim Form N1 (including the specified details and a statement of truth) must be issued, unless the court allows the application to be made before proceedings are started because the matter is urgent or there are good reasons for not giving notice	CPR 1998, rr 2.3(1), 7.2(1), 16.2(1), 16.3(2), 22.1(1)(*a*), 25.2(1), (2), 25.3(1); PD 25, para 4.4
	An urgent application for an injunction should be made as an interim application in pending proceedings (begun by Form N1), by application notice in Form N16A (county court) or Form N244 (High Court)	CPR 1998, Pt 23; PD 23; CPR 1998, r 25.1(1)(*a*); PD 25, para 2.1
	Particulars of claim including the specified details should be included in the Claim Form N1 if practicable, and this should be done where a free-standing injunction is sought	CPR 1998, r 16.4(1); PD 16, para 3.1
	Otherwise, particulars of claim including a statement of truth may be served separately	CPR 1998, rr 2.3(1), 22.1(1)(*a*); PD 16, para 3.2

	The forms for the defendant to respond must be served with the particulars of claim, whether those are included in Form N1 or served subsequently	CPR 1998, r 7.8(1)
	Damages can be claimed, but need not be, as a free-standing injunction can be sought in a county court as well as the High Court	PHA 1997, s 3; CCA 1984, s 38
	An application for an interim injunction must be supported by evidence, ie a witness statement, unless the court orders otherwise	CPR 1998, r 25.3(2)
	Where the claimant is relying on the evidence of a medical practitioner, eg of personal injury, the report must be served with the particulars of claim	PD 16, para 4.3
Fee	£120 (non-money claim) payable on issue of application in Form N16A or N244 together with Claim Form N1	CCFO 1999, fee 1.3
Oral application without documents	The court can dispense with the requirement for an application notice and in cases of extreme urgency can grant an interim injunction by telephone. However, the court should be expected to require an undertaking to file evidence, verified by a statement of truth, notice of application and, if not yet done, issue a claim form	CPR 1998, r 23.3(2)(*b*); PD 25, paras 4.2, 4.5, 5.1(2)
	Such an undertaking must be strictly complied with	*Re S (A Child) (Family Division: Without Notice Orders)* [2001] 1 All ER 362
Application begun without notice	An interim injunction can be granted without notice of the application having been given, where the matter is urgent and the court considers that there are good reasons for not giving notice	CPR 1998, rr 25.2(1), (2), 25.3(1)
	However, in an urgent case informal notice, ie short notice, of application for a personal protection injunction is better practice than no notice, unless the circumstances require secrecy	PD 23, para 4.2
	If a claim form has already been served, the applicant should take steps to tell the respondent that the application is being made without full notice unless secrecy is essential	PD 25, para 4.3

	The reasons for not giving notice must be stated in the evidence in support	CPR 1998, r 25.3(3); PD 25, para 3.4
	The court will give directions as to commencement of the claim unless the applicant undertakes to issue a claim form immediately	PD 25, para 4.4(1)
	If the application is made before the application notice has been issued, the notice and evidence in support and fee must be filed on the same or next working day (or as ordered by the court), as should the claim form and fee, if not already issued	PD 25, paras 4.4(3), 5.1(4), (5)
	The respondent against whom an interim injunction is granted may apply to have it set aside or varied, but must apply within 7 days after it is served or at the return date provided in the order	CPR 1998, r 23.10(1), (2); PD 25, para 5.1(3)
Evidence	Applications for interim injunctions must be supported by evidence, ie set out in a document verified by a statement of truth, which may be in a witness statement or the statement of case or the application itself	CPR 1998, r 25.3(2); PD 25, para 3.2
	The evidence must set out the facts on which the applicant relies for the claim including all material facts of which the court should be made aware	PD 25, para 3.3
	The statement of case and any witness statement must be verified by a statement of truth	CPR 1998, r 22.1(1)
Service of notice	The application and evidence in support must be served as soon as practicable after it is filed and at least 3 working days before the hearing to give valid notice, unless the court shortens the time	CPR 1998, rr 2.8, 3.1(2)(*a*), 23.7(1)(*a*); PD 25, para 2.2
	Informal notice (ie less than 3 days) is better than no notice	*G v G* [1990] 1 FLR 395
	Where proceedings have commenced, informal notice should be given unless secrecy is essential	PD 25, para 4.3(3)
Response	Note that the defendant to claim must respond by filing a defence or an acknowledgment of service or an admission, or else default judgment may be entered	CPR 1998, rr 7.8, 9.2, 12.3

	Respondent to application for injunction may:	
	(i) elect not to oppose	CPR 1998, r 23.11(1)
	(ii) oppose in whole or in part by filing and serving evidence	
	(iii) make his own application in like form	
Hearing	CPR 1998 do not require the hearing of an interim application to be conducted in open court in public	CPR 1998, rr 23.8, 25.1, 25.2, 39.2(1)
	The applicant should submit a draft of the injunction in typescript (in Form N16 in a county court) and on disk (in a format compatible with the word processing format used by the court) if he has not filed one already	CPR 1998, r 23.7(3)(*b*); PD 25, paras 2.4, 4.3
Orders available	Order may forbid any tort already committed or threatened, provided it is sufficiently established by evidence verified by a statement of truth and/or oral evidence	*Khorasandjian v Bush* (above)
	Where necessary for the protection of the applicant, an exclusion zone can be provided around her home, or, apparently, her place of work	*Burris v Azadani* [1996] 1 FLR 266
	Power of arrest is not available in support of an injunction in civil proceedings forbidding torts (though a warrant of arrest can be granted after the event)	PHA 1997, s 3(3), (4)
Order made without notice: duration and review	If an injunction is granted at a hearing of which the respondent has not been given notice:	
	a return date must (unless the court orders otherwise) be given for a hearing at which the respondent can be present	PD 25, para 5.1(3)
	the respondent is in any event entitled within 7 days of service on him to apply to have the order set aside	CPR 1998, r 23.10; Form N16
	Where an injunction is granted without notice having been given, it is good practice for the court to order that it runs to a date later than the return date, so that there is no hiatus until an injunction granted on notice can be served.	

Undertakings	An enforceable undertaking can be accepted by the court	CPR 1998, Sch 2, CCR Ord 29, r 1A; *Hussain v Hussain* [1986] 2 FLR 271
Form of injunction order or undertaking: penal notice and clear instructions	To be enforceable, when served an injunction order must have prominently displayed on the front a warning notice of the consequences of disobedience	CPR 1998, Sch 1, RSC Ord 45, r 7(4); CPR 1998, Sch 2, CCR Ord 29, r 1(3); Form N16A
	Any order for an injunction must set out clearly what the respondent must do or not do (in a county court the injunction should be issued in Form N138)	PD 25, para 5.2
	An undertaking given to a county court must be recorded in Form N117. If, exceptionally, the court is asked to accept an undertaking in the absence of the giver, he will need to have signed an adapted Form N117.	
Service of injunction or delivery of form of undertaking	Before an injunction can be enforced it must have been personally served on the respondent, before any alleged breach, unless the court has dispensed with service or he was present when the order was made or he has been notified of the terms of the order	CPR 1998, Sch 1, RSC Ord 45, r 7(2), (6), (7); CPR 1998, Sch 2, CCR Ord 29, r 1(2), (6), (7)
	An undertaking becomes enforceable when and because it is given to the court; however, unless a record of it is given to the person who gave it, difficulties can arise on enforcement proceedings, and in county courts a copy is required to be delivered to the giver by the court or, failing that, served by the applicant	CPR 1998, Sch 2, CCR Ord 29, r 1A(*a*); *Hussain v Hussain* [1986] 2 FLR 271
Duration of interim injunction made on notice	An interim injunction granted on notice can be ordered to last until a fixed date or trial or further order	PD 25, para 5.2
	If the claim is stayed other than by agreement between the parties, an interim injunction shall be set aside unless the court orders that it should continue to have effect	CPR 1998, r 25.10
Warrant for arrest	Application for a warrant of arrest in respect of disobedience of an injunction prohibiting harassment should be made in the High Court if the order was made there or, if the order was made in a county court, the application may be made in any county court	PHA 1997, s 3(4), (5)

	The formal requirements upon making application for a warrant are provided by rules; see Guide 38 for practice	CPR 1998, Sch 1, RSC Ord 94, r 16

12: Transfer of a Tenancy under Family Law Act 1996, Part IV

General note

The Family Proceedings (Amendment No 2) Rules 1999 have amended FPR 1991, rr 2.52–2.77 in respect of claims for ancillary relief started on or after 5 June 2000. The amended version of the rules is printed in this edition. A claim to transfer a tenancy under Family Law Act 1996, Pt IV is not a claim for ancillary relief. Family Proceedings (Amendment No 2) Rules 1999, r 20 provides that the unamended version of those rules applies to a claim to transfer a tenancy under FLA 1996, Pt IV. The unamended version, whose broad thrust is not substantially different from the current version of the rules, is contained in earlier editions of *The Family Court Practice*. Throughout this Guide the references are to the unamended rules.

Legal background

Since the coming into force of FLA 1996, Pt IV on 1 October 1997, the court is empowered to transfer tenancies, both contractual and statutory, between cohabitants who no longer live together as husband and wife, as well as between spouses and former spouses. As set out in FLA 1996, Sch 7, para 10, the person to whom the tenancy is transferred can be ordered to pay compensation to the other party. The power to transfer the tenancy to a former spouse arises on decree nisi; the order becomes effective on decree absolute; and there is a prohibition on applying if that former spouse has remarried. If there is a decree of judicial separation, the power to transfer arises after the decree is pronounced. A tenancy in the other spouse's name, or in joint names, can be destroyed by the unilateral surrender or giving of notice to quit by one tenant without consultation with the other (*Hammersmith and Fulham London Borough Council v Monk* [1992] 1 AC 478, [1992] 1 FLR 465). A party should ask for an undertaking that the tenancy will not be surrendered and then serve that undertaking on the landlord. If the undertaking is not given the applicant should apply for an injunction and serve the order on the landlord (*Bater v Greenwich London Borough Council* [1999] 2 FLR 993). Matrimonial Causes Act 1973, s 37(2)(*a*) does not apply to FLA 1996, Pt IV but FPR 1991, r 3.8 expressly incorporates r 3.6(9) empowering an injunction to be granted.

Procedure

Who may apply	Either spouse, but a decree of judicial separation must be granted before the order is made	FLA 1996, Sch 7, para 2(2)
	Either former spouse, but a decree nisi must be granted before the order is made and the applicant must not have remarried; if application is for the transfer of a statutory tenancy or contractual tenancy containing a prohibition on assignment, it must be made before decree absolute	FLA 1996, Sch 7, para 13

	A cohabitant who is no longer living with the other cohabitant as husband and wife	FLA 1996, Sch 7, para 3
Application	By originating summons in High Court or originating application in county court in Form M23 supported by affidavit	FPR 1991, r 3.8(12)
Fee payable	£40	FPFO 1999, fee 1.3
Which court	If judicial separation, divorce or nullity proceedings are pending, in that court	FLA 1996, Sch 7, para 2(2)
	Otherwise, if in the county court, in the district where applicant or respondent lives; if in the High Court, the applicant has the choice	FPR 1991, r 3.6(3)
Respondent	The other spouse or cohabitant	
	Service must be effected on the landlord, who is entitled to be heard	FPR 1991, r 3.8(12)
	After serving application, applicant should file Form FL415	FPR 1991, r 3.8(15)
Interlocutory injunction	Initial application made ex parte to district judge	FPR 1991, rr 3.6(9), 3.8(14)
	By summons if in High Court, or notice of application in accordance with CCR Ord 13, r 1 if in county court, with supporting affidavit to restrain surrender/notice to quit being given by other party to tenancy in his sole name/joint tenancy pending hearing	
Respondent's affidavit	Filed 14 days after time for acknowledgement of service, setting out grounds in opposition; respondent may be debarred from defending	FPR 1991, rr 3.6(7), (8), 3.8(14)
Request for information	Request by letter, followed by application for an order for information and documents	FPR 1991, rr 2.63, 3.8(13)
Directions	The application may be heard by the district judge (in chambers). Power to make interim orders and give directions for discovery of documents and calling of witnesses	FPR 1991, rr 2.62(4)–(6), 3.6(7)–(9), 3.8(13), (14)
Documents	Schedule and chronology of events	
	Succinct affidavits	
	Paginated indexed bundles of document; see under —	MCA 1973, s 25; *PD of 31 January 1995*
Order	Transfer of tenancy or statutory tenancy	FLA 1996, Sch 7, paras 7–9

	Payment by the spouse or cohabitant to whom the tenancy is transferred, to the other; deferment of payment or payment by instalments if transferee's financial hardship greater than transferor's	FLA 1996, Sch 7, para 10
	Order that both liable to discharge obligations prior to date of transfer and indemnity	FLA 1996, Sch 7, para 11
Appeals	See Guides 72–75	

13: Parental Order under Human Fertilisation and Embryology Act 1990, s 30

Legal background

An application under s 30 of the 1990 Act for a parental order may be made only by a married couple, both of whom must be aged 18 or over, in respect of a child who is genetically the child of the husband or the wife or both, but who was carried by a surrogate. The child must be living with the applicants, who must be domiciled in the United Kingdom, the Channel Islands or the Isle of Man. The provisions of the Act, and the regulations and rules made thereunder, simplify the existing provisions of the Adoption Act 1976, as amended. The application must be made within 6 months of the birth of the child, or within 6 months after 1 November 1994 (when the section came into force).

The procedure to be followed in the High Court and county courts is prescribed by the Family Proceedings (Amendment) (No 2) Rules 1994, which amend the Family Proceedings Rules 1991 so as to incorporate the new provisions. The Family Proceedings Courts (Children Act 1989) (Amendment) Rules 1994 amend the Family Proceedings Courts (Children Act 1989) Rules 1991 to incorporate the new provisions which prescribe the procedure to be followed in family proceedings courts. The Parental Orders (Human Fertilisation and Embryology) Regulations 1994 provide for certain provisions of the Adoption Act 1976 (in particular, ss 27(1), 29(2)) to apply with appropriate modification to applications under s 30 of the 1990 Act. Both sets of rules provide for the procedure to be followed in connection with these and other interlocutory applications.

Procedure

Who may apply	Husband and wife	HFEA 1990, s 30; FPR 1991, r 4A.2; FPC(CA 1989)R 1991, r 21C
Which court	Family proceedings court, unless there are proceedings pending or in progress which concern the child, in which case application should be made to the court where the proceedings are pending	C(AP)O 1991, art 3
	In certain circumstances, proceedings may be transferred sideways, upwards or downwards	C(AP)O 1991, arts 6–13
Which proceedings	Freestanding application	HFEA 1990, s 30

Application	On Form C51, with sufficient copies for each respondent	FPR 1991, r 4.4; FPC(CA 1989)R 1991, r 21C
Respondents	Birth parents, ie birth mother (woman who carried the child) and birth father (father of the child as defined by s 28 of the Act), except where the applicants seek to dispense with their agreement	FPR 1991, r 4A.1, App 3; FPC(CA 1989)R 1991, r 21C, Sch 2
	the child	
	any other person with parental responsibility for the child at the date of the application	FPR 1991, r 4A.3; FPC(CA 1989)R 1991, r 21C
Additional persons to whom notice is to be given	Any local authority or voluntary organisation that has at any time provided accommodation for the child	FPR 1991, r 4A.3, App 3; FPC(CA 1989)R 1991, r 21C
Service	Copy of the application, and notice of application endorsed with hearing/ directions appointment date, to be served on respondents at least 14 days before that date	FPR 1991, r 4.4(1), App 3; FPC(CA 1989)R 1991, Sch 2
	Written notice of proceedings and of date and place of hearing/directions appointment to be given at least 14 days before that date	FPR 1991, r 4.4(3); FPC(CA 1989)R 1991, r 4(3)
Acknowledgement	Each respondent must file and serve acknowledgement on all other parties in Form C52	FPR 1991, r 4A.4; FPC(CA 1989)R 1991, r 21D
Parental consent	Evidence of consent to be given in writing (the parental agreement form C(PA)M given by some courts for use by the birth parents wishing to give their consent is inappropriate and has now been discontinued)	AA 1976, s 61; PO(HFE)R 1994, Sch 1, para 5
Parental order reporter	Court must consider appointment of parental order reporter as soon as practicable	CA 1989, s 41(1); FPR 1991, r 4A.5; FPC(CA 1989)R 1991, r 21E
Directions	As to the powers of the justices' clerk or the court, see —	FPR 1991, r 4.14; FPC(CA 1989)R 1991, r 14
Attendance	Personal attendance by the applicants is required	FPR 1991, r 4A.6; FPC(CA 1989)R 1991, r 21F
Order	Parental order in Form C53	HFEA 1990, s 30; FPR 1991, App 1; FPC(CA 1989)R 1991, Sch 1
Additional orders made on notice	Leave to remove the child from his home	AA 1976, s 27(1); PO(HFE)R 1994

	Return of the child taken in breach	AA 1976, s 29(1)
	Preventing removal of a child from the applicant's home	AA 1976, s 29(2); FPR 1991, r 4A.10; FPC(CA 1989)R 1991, r 21J
	Issue of a search warrant	AA 1976, s 29(4)
Who has power to make the order	High Court judge, Circuit judge nominated for public or private family law proceedings	
	A district judge in relation to interlocutory matters, where the order is to be returnable to the Circuit judge and is the first order of its type in the proceedings whilst pending in the county court or magistrates' court	FP(AJ)D 1999, Sch, para (*m*) (as substituted by FP(AJ)(A)D 2002)

14: Declaration as to Marital Status

Legal background

Family Law Act 1986, s 55 allows the court to make a declaration that a marriage: (*a*) was valid at its inception; (*b*) subsisted on a particular date; or (*c*) did not subsist on a particular date. If the truth of the proposition sought to be declared is established, the court is obliged to make the declaration, unless to do so would manifestly be contrary to public policy (FLA 1986, s 58(1)). If made, a declaration binds the world and not just the parties (FLA 1986, s 58(2)).

Subject to specific provision, FPR 1991 apply to proceedings for a declaration as they apply to matrimonial causes (FPR 1991, r 3.16(12)).

Procedure

Who may apply	A party to the marriage in question and any other person who has a sufficient interest	FLA 1986, s 55(1), (3); see also under FPR 1991, r 3.12
Which court	High Court or county court	FLA 1986, ss 55(1), 63; see also under FPR 1991, r 3.12
Pre-application requirement	Papers must be served on Attorney General at least 1 month before petition is filed	FPR 1991, r 3.16(4)
Application	By petition containing, unless otherwise directed, the details required by FPR 1991, r 3.12(1)–(2), App 2, para 4 and, where relevant, r 3.16(2)	FPR 1991, rr 2.2(1), 3.12(1), (2), 3.16(2), (12)
	Fee payable: £150	FPFO 1999, fee 1.2
Documents to accompany petition	Any marriage certificate or divorce/annulment/legal separation decree where relevant (and with an authenticated English translation where relevant)	FPR 1991, r 3.12(3), (4)

	Affidavit verifying petition and identifying those affected	FPR 1991, r 3.16(1)
Respondents	The parties (or other party) to the marriage in question	FPR 1991, r 3.12(5)
Other parties	The Attorney General has the right to intervene in accordance with —	FLA 1986, s 59(2); FPR 1991, r 3.16(7), (9), (10)
	For joinder of other parties, see —	FPR 1991, r 3.16(6), (8)
Service	In accordance with FPR 1991, rr 2.9 (generally), 9.3 (service on person under disability), 10.6 (service out of England and Wales)	FPR 1991, r 3.16(12)
Answer to petition	28 days after service of petition	FPR 1991, rr 2.12(1), 3.16(12), 10.8(2)(*a*)
Other interlocutory procedures	As in matrimonial proceedings	FPR 1991, rr 2.13–2.25, 3.16(12)
Hearing	As in matrimonial proceedings	FPR 1991, rr 2.32–2.42, 3.16(12)
Order	A declaration that the marriage:	
	was valid at its inception	
	subsisted on a particular date	
	did not subsist on a particular date	FLA 1986, s 55
Form	M29	FPR 1991, r 3.16(11)
Appeals	See Guide 75	

15: Decree of Divorce, Judicial Separation or Nullity on Undefended Cause

Legal background

A marriage may be dissolved on the ground that it has broken down irretrievably (Matrimonial Causes Act 1973, s 1(1)). To prove that the marriage has broken down irretrievably, the petitioner must prove one or more of five facts set out in MCA 1973, s 1(2). If satisfied on the fact(s), the court grants a decree of divorce (MCA 1973, s 1(4)), which in the first instance is a decree nisi. This cannot be made absolute for six weeks (MCA 1973, s 1(5), as varied by Matrimonial Causes (Decree Absolute) General Order 1972).

A marriage may be annulled on the ground that it is void as set out in MCA 1973, s 11, or that it is voidable as set out in MCA 1973, s 12. Any decree is a decree nisi which cannot be made absolute for six weeks (MCA 1973, s 15 which applies s 1(5) to nullity causes).

Parties to a marriage may be judicially separated on the ground that one or more of the facts set out in MCA 1973, s 1(2) is proved (MCA 1973, s 17(1)). The procedure is that a decree of judicial separation is granted, ie that is to say, there is no decree nisi and a subsequent decree absolute. A party to the marriage may rely on a decree of judicial separation as proof of the fact(s) on which the decree was granted in subsequent divorce proceedings (MCA 1973, s 4(2)).

Procedure

Who may apply	Either party to the marriage	MCA 1973, s 1(1)
Which court	Principal Registry of the Family Division or any divorce county court	FPR 1991, r 2.6(1)
Application	By petition, containing information required by FPR 1991, App 2	FPR 1991, rr 2.2(1), 2.3
	The petition must be accompanied by:	
	copies for service on all other parties	FPR 1991, r 2.6(5)
	statement of arrangements for the children	FPR 1991, rr 2.2(2), 2.6(5)
	marriage certificate	FPR 1991, r 2.6(2)
	reconciliation statement (if solicitor acting)	MCA 1973, s 6(1); FPR 1991, r 2.6(3)
	public funding certificate (if any) and notice thereof	Funding Code, Procedures, paras C16.2 and C16.3
	court fee or "fee exempt" form	FPFO 1999, art 4
	Fee payable: £150	FPFO 1999, fee 1.2
Parties	As respondent, other party to the marriage	
	As co-respondent, anyone with whom respondent is alleged to have committed adultery, save as in FPR 1991, r 2.7(1), (2), (5), or, if the court so directs, anyone with whom petitioner alleges respondent had an improper association	MCA 1973, s 49(1); FPR 1991, r 2.7(1), (3)
	As party cited, person named as co-respondent above in any answer	FPR 1991, r 2.16(1)
	As intervener, anyone applying to and satisfying the court that it is in his interest to be joined	MCA 1973, s 49(5)
Service	Personally or by post on respondent and co-respondent (and party cited, if applicable)	FPR 1991, r 2.9(1), (4)
	Documents for service:	
	petition	
	statement of arrangements (respondent only)	FPR 1991, r 2.6(6)
	notice of proceedings	
	acknowledgement of service (Form M6)	FPR 1991, r 2.6(6)
	notice of public funding (if any)	Funding Code, Procedures, paras C16.2 and C16.3
	Alternatively, service may be:	

	deemed	FPR 1991, r 2.9(6)
	effected by court bailiff	FPR 1991, r 2.9(4)
	substituted, including by advertisement	FPR 1991, r 2.9(9)
	dispensed with by the court	FPR 1991, r 2.9(11)
Acknowledgement of service	A party served may:	
	acknowledge service on Form M6 stating no intention to defend	
	indicate an intention to defend in Form M6 (notice of intention to defend)	FPR 1991, r 10.8(1)
	Notice of intention to defend must be given within 8 days of service	FPR 1991, r 10.8(2)(*a*)
	A party need not indicate an intention to defend only to be heard on issues as to:	
	children	FPR 1991, r 2.40
	financial relief	FPR 1991, r 2.52
	costs	FPR 1991, r 2.37(1)
Amendment and supplemental petitions	Filed as of right before answer filed; thereafter, filing only with leave	FPR 1991, r 2.11(1)
	Fee payable: £50	FPFO 1999, fee 1.4
	No further pleading can be filed or amended after directions for trial have been given	FPR 1991, r 2.14
Directions for trial	Directions may be:	
	in the special procedure list or	FPR 1991, r 2.24(3)
	for cause to be heard in open court	FPR 1991, r 2.24(2), (5)
	Application for directions is made to the district judge	FPR 1991, r 2.24(1)
	Place of trial is specified in the directions	FPR 1991, rr 2.25, 2.32(2)–(6)
	Special arrangements exist for medical reports in certain nullity proceedings	FPR 1991, rr 2.22, 2.23
Trial	Hearing is by judge alone in open court; however, evidence as to capacity in nullity cases is given in camera	FPR 1991, rr 2.28(1), 2.32(1); MCA 1973, s 48(2)
	Oral evidence only, save as in defended suits (see Evidence in Guide 16)	FPR 1991, r 2.32(1)
Special procedure	In the case of petitions for divorce or judicial separation:	
	where undefended or	

	where under MCA 1973, s 1(2)(*d*) the respondent has indicated his consent or	
	unless otherwise directed on filing request for directions, petitioner also files affidavit in Form M7(*a*), (*b*), (*c*), (*d*) or (*e*)	
	on filing of affidavit in Form M7, district judge gives directions for trial by entering cause in special procedure list	FPR 1991, r 2.24(3)(*a*)
	On causes in special procedure list, district judge considers:	
	evidence in support of prayer for decree	
	arrangements for children	
	costs	
	If satisfied on consideration of evidence filed by petitioner, district judge certifies entitlement to a decree	FPR 1991, r 2.36(1)(*a*)
	If not satisfied, district judge offers opportunity to file further evidence or removes cause from special procedure list	FPR 1991, r 2.36(1)(*b*)
	If entitlement to a decree certified, court fixes date for pronouncement of decree in open court	FPR 1991, r 2.24(2)
Children	If no contested children application is pending, district judge considers evidence filed concerning the children (if any) and:	MCA 1973, s 41(1); FPR 1991, rr 2.39(1), 2.40(1)
	certifies that there are no relevant children	FPR 1991, r 2.39(2)(*a*)
	certifies that there are relevant children but court need not exercise statutory powers concerning them	FPR 1991, r 2.39(2)(*b*)
	gives directions for the provision of further information	FPR 1991, r 2.39(3)
Decree	In cases of divorce or nullity, the decree is initially a "decree nisi"	MCA 1973, ss 1(5), 15
	Subject to MCA 1973, ss 10(2) and 41(1), application for the decree nisi to be made absolute can be made:	
	by the petitioner after 6 weeks	MCA 1973, s 1(5); FPR 1991, r 2.49
	Fee payable: £30	FPFO 1999, fee 4.1
	by the respondent on application on notice 3 months thereafter	MCA 1973, s 9(2); FPR 1991, r 2.50(2)
	Fee payable: £60	FPFO 1999, fee 4.3

	However, if application is made more than 12 months after decree, the district judge will require an explanation	FPR 1991, r 2.49, proviso
Costs	Any party may be heard on costs even though:	
	no answer filed	FPR 1991, r 2.37(1)
	no acknowledgement of service returned to court indicating a wish to be heard on costs	FPR 1991, r 2.37(2)
	If costs claimed in petition, district judge under special procedure may:	
	certify if satisfied as to entitlement	FPR 1991, r 2.36(3)(*a*)
	if not satisfied, order party objecting to pay to attend court to pursue objection	FPR 1991, r 2.36(3)(*b*)
	Court hearing decree nisi deals with application for costs: principles for award of costs	CPR 1998, r 44.3
Appeals	To a judge, where no error of the court is alleged, within 6 weeks	FPR 1991, r 2.42(1), (4)
	Otherwise, see Guides 72, 75	

15A: Staying Grant of Decree Absolute under Matrimonial Causes Act 1973, s 10A

Legal background

Matrimonial Causes Act 1973, s 10A provides that, where a couple were married in accordance with "the usages of the Jews" or other religious usages which prescribe final dissolution, the grant of a decree absolute can be stayed. No decree absolute will be granted until the court is satisfied by a declaration of both parties that the marriage is also dissolved in accordance with "those [Jewish or other] usages". FPR 1991, rr 2.45A and 2.45B provide the regulatory framework for an application under s 10A.

Procedure

Who may apply	Either party to the marriage; though in Jewish marriages it is more likely to be the wife (whether respondent or petitioner)	MCA 1973, s 10A(2)
Time for application	After decree nisi, but before grant of decree absolute	MCA 1973, s 10A(1)
	NB: Because of the time-frame from grant of decree nisi, prompt application is essential	

Application	On notice with affidavit in support setting out grounds of application	FPR 1991, r 2.45A(2), (3) (by reference to r 2.42(3))
Fee on application	£60	
Effect of order	Stay on grant of decree absolute until parties jointly declare that they have co-operated in arranging dissolution of their marriage in accordance with their religious usages	
Stay lifted	Upon filing declaration containing:	MCA 1973, s 10A(4)
	signature of both parties	FPR 1991, r 2.45B(1)(*a*)
	particulars of MCA 1973 proceedings	FPR 1991, r 2.45B(1)(*b*)
	confirmation that necessary religious steps have been taken to dissolve the marriage	FPR 1991, r 2.45B(1)(*c*)
	Declaration should be accompanied by a certificate of dissolution from relevant religious authority (unless otherwise directed)	FPR 1991, r 2.45B(1)(*d*)

16: Decree of Divorce, Judicial Separation or Nullity on Defended Cause

Legal background

See Guide 15.

Which rules of court
Defended causes, as family proceedings, are still dealt with under the "old" procedural regime (ie RSC 1965 and CCR 1981).

Procedure

Answer to petition	Any respondent or co-respondent who:	
	wishes to defend the petition or to dispute any of the facts in it	FPR 1991, r 2.12(1)(*a*)
	wishes to cross-pray (respondent only)	FPR 1991, r 2.12(1)(*b*)
	wishes to oppose the grant of a decree under MCA 1973, s 5(1) (respondent to a petition under MCA 1973, s 1(2)(*e*) only)	FPR 1991, r 2.12(1)(*c*)
	must file an answer containing information set out in FPR 1991	FPR 1991, r 2.15(1)–(4)

	A party cited may similarly file an answer	FPR 1991, rr 2.12, 2.16(2)
	Must be filed within 29 days (21 days plus time for filing notice of intention to defend (8 days))	FPR 1991, rr 2.12(1), 10.8(2)
	Fee payable: £100	FPFO 1999, fee 1.5
Reply	Petitioner may file reply to the answer	FPR 1991, r 2.13(1)
	Must be filed within 14 days from receipt of answer	FPR 1991, r 2.13(1)
Documents	The answer or reply must be accompanied by:	
	copies for service on other parties	FPR 1991, r 2.17
	public funding certificate (if any) and notice thereof	Funding Code, Procedures, paras C16.2 and C16.3
Service	Court serves petition, with Forms M5 and M6 attached	FPR 1991, r 2.17
	Personally or by post on respondent and co-respondent (and party cited, if applicable)	FPR 1991, r 2.9(1), (4)
	Documents for service:	
	petition	
	statement of arrangements (respondent only)	FPR 1991, r 2.6(6)
	notice of proceedings (Form M5)	
	acknowledgement of service (Form M6)	FPR 1991, r 2.6(6)
	notice of public funding	Funding Code, Procedures, paras C16.2 and C16.3
	Alternatively, service may be:	
	deemed	FPR 1991, r 2.9(6)
	effected by court bailiff	FPR 1991, r 2.9(4)
	substituted, including by advertisement	FPR 1991, r 2.9(9)
	dispensed with by the court	FPR 1991, r 2.9(11)
Particulars	Party on whom pleading is served may "within a reasonable time" seek further particulars:	
	by request to the party serving the pleading	
	or (failing a response) by application to the court	FPR 1991, r 2.19(1)
	Fee payable: £60	FPFO 1999, fee 4.3
Discovery of documents	Duty of discovery exists in defended causes, whether in the High Court or county court	RSC Ord 24, r 1(1); FPR 1991, r 2.20(1)

	Must be by list:	
	by mutual exchange or	RSC Ord 24, r 2(1)
	by court order on court's own motion or on a party's application to the district judge	RSC Ord 24, r 3(1)
	Must be 14 days after close of pleadings (ie, in matrimonial causes, 14 days from service of the answer)	RSC Ord 24, r 2(1); FPR 1991, r 2.20(2)
	Service is effected on other parties (ie not filed at court)	RSC Ord 24, r 2(1); FPR 1991, r 2.20(3)
	Time for inspection of documents in list must be given on service	RSC Ord 24, r 9
Interrogatories	Discovery by interrogatories is available in defended causes, whether in the High Court or county court	RSC Ord 26, r 1(1); FPR 1991, r 2.21(1), (3)
	Service is effected by any party on another; interrogatories must at the same time be filed at court	RSC Ord 26, r 1(1); FPR 1991, r 2.21(2)
	Time for service is not specified; time for reply must be stated in interrogatories, and may not in any event be less than 28 days	RSC Ord 26, r 2(1)(*a*)
	If replies are not given or are inadequate, application may be made to the court for an order for replies	RSC Ord 26, rr 1(2), 4(1), 5(2)
	Fee payable: £60	FPFO 1999, fee 4.3
Evidence	Evidence on deposition may be ordered on application to the district judge; appropriate rules in RSC and CCR apply	FPR 1991, r 2.29
	In the High Court, a subpoena is issued on filing a praecipe	FPR 1991, r 2.30; RSC Ord 38, r 14(5)
	In the county court, a witness summons is issued on filing a request	CCR Ord 20, r 12
	Issue is as of right for open court hearings; leave is required for chambers hearings (only on directions in county court)	CCR Ord 20, r 12(8); RSC Ord 32, r 7(1)
	At the trial, evidence is oral and given in open court, except:	FPR 1991, r 2.28(1)
	judge has discretion to refuse to admit evidence	FPR 1991, r 2.28(2)
	party may apply for evidence to be given on affidavit	RSC Ord 38, r 2; FPR 1991, r 2.28(3)(*a*)
	party may apply for evidence to be given by other means, eg documents, video link etc	RSC Ord 26, r 3; FPR 1991, r 2.28(3)(*b*)

	Application may be to a district judge (if before trial) or to the judge at the trial or where he is seised of the case	FPR 1991, r 2.28(4), (5)
Request for directions for trial	Party intending to request directions gives notice to other parties containing:	
	his desired place of trial	
	number of witnesses to be called on his behalf	
	their addresses	FPR 1991, r 2.25(3)
	Fee payable: £30	FPFO 1999, fee 4.2
	Notice must be given 8 days before making request	
	If the party to whom notice is given does not consent to the place of trial, he applies to district judge for trial at another place; if he does consent, he sends a statement confirming receipt of notice and giving details of witnesses as above	FPR 1991, r 2.25(4)
	Application or statement must be made 8 days after receipt of notice.	
	Party giving notice files:	
	request for directions stating place of trial desired, details of witnesses and addresses where he and they reside, (if applicable) that no statement in response to the notice received and time estimate for trial	FPR 1991, r 2.25(5)
	any statement in response (under FPR 1991, r 2.25(4))	
	new time estimate, if original appears inaccurate	FPR 1991, r 2.25(6)
Directions for trial	If satisfied as to the matters set out in FPR 1991, r 2.24(1), the district judge may give directions for trial, generally following an appointment before him	FPR 1991, r 2.24(1), (2), (4)
	Directions must cover:	
	future course of the cause	
	any ancillary relief applications	
	evidence concerning arrangements for the children	FPR 1991, r 2.24(4), (6)
	determination of place of trial, having regard to the factors in FPR 1991, r 2.25(7)	FPR 1991, r 2.25(1)
	filing of a schedule of allegations and counter-allegations of unreasonable behaviour	FPR 1991, r 2.26(1)

	After giving directions, the district judge considers the arrangements for the children	FPR 1991, rr 2.24(4), 2.39(1)
Children	If no contested children application is pending, district judge considers evidence filed concerning the children (if any) and:	MCA 1973, s 41(1); FPR 1991, rr 2.39(1), 2.40(1)
	certifies that there are no relevant children	FPR 1991, r 2.39(2)(*a*)
	certifies that there are relevant children but court need not exercise statutory powers concerning them	FPR 1991, r 2.39(2)(*b*)
	gives directions for the provision of further information	FPR 1991, r 2.39(3)
Trial	A preliminary issue may be ordered to be tried separately; application for such a trial is made on notice to the district judge	FPR 1991, r 2.33
	Place of trial is fixed on directions and in accordance with FPR 1991, r 2.32; may be varied on application on notice of any party; court of trial is generally the county court, but in cases of complexity etc there may be a transfer to the High Court	FPR 1991, rr 2.25(1), (8), 2.32(2)–(4), 10.10, 10.11; *PD of 5 June 1992*
	Setting down for trial Court fixes date, place and time of trial	FPR 1991, r 2.32(5)
	Mode of trial Trial is by judge alone hearing oral evidence in open court, subject to:	FPR 1991, r 2.32(1)
	hearing in camera applied for (rarely ordered)	*Scott v Scott* (1913) FLR Rep 657, HL
	evidence being adduced by other means (eg evidence on deposition, by affidavit, from documents etc)	FPR 1991, rr 2.28, 2.29
	evidence of marriage outside England and Wales	FPR 1991, r 10.14
Decree	If satisfied on the evidence that a fact under MCA 1973, s 1(2) is proved, the court grants a decree unless:	MCA 1973, s 1(4)
	it is satisfied that the marriage has not broken down irretrievably	MCA 1973, s 1(4)
	an application is made under MCA 1973, s 5	MCA 1973, s 5(2)(*b*)
	In cases of divorce or nullity, the decree is initially a "decree nisi"	MCA 1973, ss 1(5), 15
	Subject to MCA 1973, ss 10(2) and 41(1), application for the decree nisi to be made absolute can be made:	

	by the petitioner after 6 weeks	MCA 1973, s 1(5); FPR 1991, r 2.49
	Fee payable: £30	FPFO 1999, fee 4.1
	by the respondent on application on notice 3 months thereafter	MCA 1973, s 9(2); FPR 1991, r 2.50(2)
	Fee payable: £60	FPFO 1999, fee 4.3
	However, if application is made more than 12 months after decree, the district judge will require an explanation	FPR 1991, r 2.49, proviso
Costs	In the discretion of the court	CPR 1998, r 44.3; see also *Gojkovic v Gojkovic (No 2)* [1991] 2 FLR 233
Appeals	To a judge, where no error of the court is alleged, within 6 weeks	FPR 1991, r 2.42(1), (4)
	Otherwise, see Guides 72, 75	

17: Maintenance Pending Suit, Financial Provision and Property Adjustment Orders, including Pension Sharing and Attachment Orders and Applications under Matrimonial Causes Act 1973, s 10(2) for Consideration of the Respondent's Financial Position

General note

(i) For applications made by filing a notice of application before 5 June 2000 see *The Family Court Practice 1999* at Guide 17 (s 10(2) applications), Guide 18 (ss 22–24 applications) or, if the claim is proceeding in a pilot scheme area, Guide 19.

(ii) For applications started by filing Form A or Form B between 5 June 2000 and 30 November 2000 see Guide 17 in *The Family Court Practice 2000*.

(iii) This Guide covers applications under MCA 1973, s 10(2) and applications for maintenance pending suit, financial provision and property adjustment orders (including pension sharing and adjustment) where the Form A or B was filed after 1 December 2000. Pension sharing is available where the petition was also filed after 1 December 2000.

Legal background

The Family Proceedings Rules, as amended in 1999, provide a new procedural code governing applications under MCA 1973, s 10(2) for the court to consider the financial position of the respondent and all applications for ancillary relief (maintenance pending suit, financial provision and property adjustment, including pension earmarking, now known as attachment, variation applications under MCA 1973, s 31 and avoidance of disposition applications under MCA 1973, s 37) where the application was made by filing Form A or B on or after 5 June 2000. These rules incorporate the Overriding Objective introduced by CPR 1998 and rules for expert evidence and costs but do *not* apply to pre-5 June 2000 proceedings unless the court specifically directs (Family Proceedings

(Amendment No 2) Rules 1999, r 1(3)(*a*)). Pension sharing is available where the petition has been filed on or after 1 December 2000. Consequently, FPR 1991, r 2.70 (the rule formerly covering pension attachment and now covering both pension attachment and sharing) has been redrawn. The new rule applies only where the Form A has been filed on or after 1 December 2000 (Family Proceedings (Amendment) Rules 2000, r 2(1)).

Matrimonial Causes Act 1973, s 10(2) enables the court to consider the financial position of a respondent to a petition based on 5 years' separation or 2 years' separation with consent before allowing the decree to be made absolute. MCA 1973, ss 22 (maintenance pending suit), 23 (periodical payments and lump sum for a party to the marriage and the children, including pension attachment – formerly called earmarking – under ss 23B and 23C) and 24 (property adjustment including pension sharing under ss 24B and C) enable the court in a suit for divorce, judicial separation or nullity to make wide-ranging orders allocating the income and capital of both parties between themselves and in respect of any children. Additionally, where the petition has been filed after 1 December 2000 in divorce and nullity only a pension sharing order can be made under s 24B. A pension sharing and attachment order cannot be made for a party to the marriage before court against the same pension arrangement. A *Brooks v Brooks* variation of a pension fund is only possible if the application has been made before 1 December 2000 (Welfare Reform and Pensions Act 1999, s 85(4)).

The court's limited powers to order child maintenance are summarised at **Interface with Child Support Act 1991** under MCA 1973, s 23 and **Outline of new bases for child support calculation** under CSA 1991, s 4.

The court's power to impose a clean break does not apply to judicial separation (MCA 1973, s 25A). The court has power to order the sale of property (MCA 1973, s 24A), and will exercise its discretion in accordance with MCA 1973, ss 25 and 25A.

If a party remarries before making an application for a financial provision or property adjustment order, that party is barred by MCA 1973, s 28(3) from making the application for himself or herself (although an application for children is unaffected by the s 28(3) bar). Remarriage after an application is made but before it is heard is not a bar to jurisdiction, although a periodical payments or secured periodical payments order ends on the remarriage of the payee.

Procedure

Who may apply	***Claim for spouse*** ***MCA 1973, s 10(2)*** The respondent to a petition under MCA 1973, s 1(2)(*d*) or (*e*) in the court of the decree proceedings at any time after the petition is filed but before the decree is made absolute	MCA 1973, s 10(2); *PD of 7 November 1973*
	MCA 1973, ss 22–24 Either spouse provided not remarried at time that the application is made	
	Claim for children Parent or guardian	
	Person who is applying for, is entitled to apply for or who has been granted a residence order	
	Local authority to whose care the child has been committed	
	Official Solicitor	
	Child, if given leave to intervene	FPR 1991, r 2.54
Application	***MCA 1973, s 10(2)*** Form B	FPR 1991, r 2.45

	MCA 1973, ss 22–24	
	Form A stating, if claim is to land, registration and mortgage details and interest of any third party and if claim for pension attachment or pension sharing details of requested order	FPR 1991, rr 2.59(2), 2.61A
	If claim omitted from petition or answer claiming relief, leave is needed to make claim. If application for leave made before decree nisi apply on notice to other party with supporting sworn statement for leave to amend the petition/answer to incorporate the claim	*PD of 5 March 1957*
	If made after decree nisi has been pronounced, make application for leave on Form A and support application with sworn statement	FPR 1991, r 2.53(2)
Fee payable	Where order agreed: £30	FPFO 1999, fee 4.1
	Otherwise: £80	FPFO 1999, fee 4.4
Who is to be served and by whom	The court serves other spouse (within 4 days of filing of notice) inserting on Form A date of first appointment within 12–16 weeks	FPR 1991, r 2.61A
	The applicant serves:	
	(*a*) any mortgagee of property subject to a property adjustment claim	FPR 1991, r 2.59(4)
	(*b*) any party having an interest in a property subject to a property adjustment claim	FPR 1991, r 2.59(3)
	(*c*) if application is for an order for a variation of settlement, including for a variation of a pension fund, the trustees of the settlement and the settlor	FPR 1991, r 2.59(3)
	(*d*) if application is for attachment or pension sharing, the person responsible for the pension arrangement (the pension provider)	FPR 1991, r 2.70(6), (7)
	(*e*) if court so directs, any person who is both named and charged with an allegation of adultery or of improper association in any document	FPR 1991, r 2.60(1)
	(*f*) any other person that the district judge may direct	FPR 1991, r 2.59(3)
Filing and exchange of Form E	Five weeks prior to first appointment simultaneous exchange of sworn statements annexing (only):	FPR 1991, r 2.61B(1)–(5)

	(i) any valuation of matrimonial home or other property in last 6 months and recent mortgage statement (ii) bank and building society statements for last year (iii) surrender values of life policies (iv) if interest in a company, last 2 years' accounts and any document relied on to support valuation of company (v) Cash equivalent transfer value and other information of pension arrangement or shareable state scheme rights as set out in Divorce etc (Provision of Information) Regulations 2000, regs 2, 3 and Sharing of State Scheme Rights (Provision of Information and Valuation) Regulations 2000, reg 2	FPR 1991, r 2.61B(3)(*c*)
	(vi) last 3 pay slips and latest P60 (vii) accounts for last 2 years if self-employed (NB There is a restriction on requesting or giving disclosure)	FPR 1991, r 2.61B(6)
	Party with pension rights within 1 week of receiving notification of the date of the first appointment must, unless he already has a CETV less than 1 year old, request from his pension provider the information set out in (v) above and serve it on the other party within 7 days of receiving it	FPR 1991, r 2.70(2)–(5)
Interim applications	*Applications for maintenance pending suit or interim periodical payments* Made at any stage by notice of application on 14 days notice to other party. If application made before Form E filed, support with draft order and short sworn statement disclosing means Unless Form E filed respondent must, at least 1 week before the hearing, file and serve short sworn statement disclosing means	FPR 1991, r 2.69F(1)–(5)
	(NB: No power to make interim lump sum, property adjustment order or order for sale. For order for sale pending ancillary relief hearing see Guide 5)	MCA 1973, ss 23(1)(*c*), 24; *Wicks v Wicks* [1998] 1 FLR 470
	Application for any other interim order Made at any stage with or without notice.	FPR 1991, r 2.69F(6)–(8)

	For applications to restrain future dealings under MCA 1973, s 37(2)(*a*) see Guide 19.	
Action to be taken at least 14 days before first appointment	Both parties file and serve: (i) Concise statement of issues (ii) Chronology (iii) Questionnaire for further information and documents (iv) Form G (whether or not party can proceed to FDR at first appointment) and (applicant only) confirmation of service of mortgagee, third party owners and pension provider	FPR 1991, r 2.61B(7)
The first appointment	Both parties must attend personally and estimates of costs incurred to date in Form H (and if application for summary assessment of costs or costs on account, costs estimate of the hearing) must be produced	FPR 1991, rr 2.61D(5), 2.61F
	Active case management by the district judge pursuant to the overriding objective will include:	
	(i) answering questionnaires and disclosure of documents	FPR 1991, r 2.61D(2)(*a*)
	(ii) valuation of assets and expert evidence	FPR 1991, rr 2.61C, 2.61D(2)(*b*)
	(iii) other evidence (subject to the court exercising its right to control the evidence at the conclusion of the FDR)	FPR 1991, r 2.61D(2)(*b*)
	(iv) if pension sharing or attachment, whether the pension provider has been served, has had 21 days to object and, if he is objecting, arrangements for his objection to be heard	FPR 1991, r 2.70(6)–(12)
	Whether CETV etc details have been provided	FPR 1991, r 2.70(3)
	Whether there should be expert evidence by an actuary or independent financial adviser	
	(v) fixing the next stage of the case (usually an FDR)	FPR 1991, r 2.61D(2)(*c*)
	(NB No entitlement to further disclosure except in accordance with directions given or with permission)	FPR 1991, r 2.61D(3)

Action after first appointment	Implementation of directions: Seven days before the FDR appointment, the applicant gives notice to the court of all open, without prejudice and *Calderbank* offers	FPR 1991, r 2.61E(3), (4)
	Immediately before FDR up-to-date costs estimate (and if summary assessment of order for costs of the hearing is sought, costs estimate of the hearing)	FPR 1991, r 2.61F
FDR appointment	Both parties attend personally and use best endeavours to reach agreement	FPR 1991, r 2.61E(6), (9)
	No privilege attaches to any prior offer. All FDR discussions are completely privileged. If no agreement is reached the district judge will play no further part in the case. At conclusion of the FDR, parties filing privileged documents request their return	*President's Direction of 25 May 2000;* FPR 1991, r 2.61E(1)–(6)
	District judge can adjourn, make a consent order, fix a final hearing and will give any case management directions which were not made at the first appointment	FPR 1991, r 2.61E(8)
Action between FDR appointment and final hearing	Implementation of directions: Statement of open proposals filed and served at court, by the applicant 14 days before the final hearing, and by the respondent 7 days before	FPR 1991, r 2.69E
Documents for final hearing	Paginated and indexed bundle of documents	*President's Direction of 10 March 2000*
	Costs estimate	FPR 1991, r 2.61F
Order	Maintenance pending suit	MCA 1973, s 22
	Periodical payments and/or secured periodical payments for spouse and/or children (by standing order or by direct debit)	MCA 1973, s 23(1)(*a*), (*b*), (*d*), (*e*)
	Lump sum for spouse and/or children; for wording of roll-over of statutory charge, see —	MCA 1973, s 23(1)(*c*), (*f*); *PD of 19 August 1991*
	Interest on lump sum before and after payment due	MCA 1973, s 23(6); JA 1838
	Property adjustment order; for wording of roll-over of statutory charge, see —	MCA 1973, s 24; *PD of 19 August 1991*

	Order for sale of property, with a direction that vacant possession be given	MCA 1973, s 24A; FPR 1991, r 2.64(3)
	If there is to be a complete, clean break (divorce or nullity only), a direction preventing an application to extend the term of the periodical payments order or to apply again	MCA 1973, ss 28(1A), 25A(3)
	A pension sharing order is for a percentage of the cash equivalent transfer value valued at a date specified by the court	MCA 1973, s 21A; PD(PI)R 2000, reg 3; D(P)R 2000, reg 3
	A pension sharing order cannot take effect until 7 days after the time for appealing has expired	D(P)R 2000, reg 9
	A pension attachment order is for a percentage of the benefit and if the benefit is for a lump sum the pension member can be required to commute but he cannot be ordered to commute on any date	MCA 1973, s 25B(5), (7)
	A pension sharing or attachment order must contain an annex in a prescribed form (a copy of which is obtainable from the court office) setting out its salient points	FPR 1991, r 2.70(14), (15)
	Costs including payment on account and interest	CPR 1998, r 44.3; FPR 1991, r 2.69B
Service and implementation of pension orders	Within 7 days of making the order or decree absolute, whichever is the later, the court serves order for pension sharing or attachment on pension provider together with copy of the decree	FPR 1991, r 2.70(16), (17)
	Parties serve on the pension provider formal information including, in the case of a pension attachment order, bank account details of the applicant	PD(PI)R 2000, reg 5
	4 month period that the pension provider has to implement the order then starts. Within 3 weeks of receiving pension sharing order pension provider gives notice of charges	PD(PI)R 2000, reg 7
Pension provider's obligations	Percentage debited from member's share and transferred to applicant by way of pension credit either in internal or external transfer. Pension provider then gives notice of completion of this process	PD(PI)R 2000, reg 8
Appeals	See Guides 72–75	

18: Variation Order

General note

This Guide applies to variation applications started by Form A on or after 5 June 2000. For variation applications made before that date see Guide 20 in *The Family Court Practice 1999* or, if the court is in a pilot scheme area, Guide 19.

Legal background

The orders that can be varied under Matrimonial Causes Act 1973, s 31 include those for maintenance pending suit, periodical payments, lump sum by instalments and deferred pension attachment lump sums and in extremely limited circumstances, namely where the order has both not taken effect and the decree has not been made absolute, a pension sharing order. The court's powers under MCA 1973, s 31(1) are extensive and include, in the absence of a MCA 1973, s 28(1A) direction, the power to extend the term of a fixed-term order. If an application is being made to discharge the order in its entirety, because for example a capital sum is offered, a direction under MCA 1973, s 25A(3) and Inheritance (Provision for Family and Dependants) Act 1975 dismissal should also be sought.

The court's power to vary a child maintenance order which was made before 5 April 1993 is undoubted (see Child Support Act 1991 ss 4(10), 8(3A)). *V v V (Child Maintenance)* [2001] 2 FLR 799 has established that the court can vary a child maintenance order made after April 1993. See **Interface with Child Support Act 1991** under MCA 1973, s 23.

The court is able to capitalise periodical payments at the request of the payee by making a lump sum or property adjustment order (in respect of petitions whenever issued) or a pension sharing order (in respect of petitions issued after 1 December 2000). See **Further capital order now possible on application of either party for clean break on variation application** under MCA 1973, s 31.

A variation application to extend the term of a periodical payments order should be made *prior* to the expiration of the term but can be heard after the order has expired (*Jones v Jones* [2000] 2 FLR 307).

Procedure

Who may apply	Payer or payee	
Application	By Form A (which is served by the court on the respondent and gives notice of the first appointment in 12–16 weeks time). Form A should: identify the order to be varied state the order the applicant seeks if a clean break is proposed, request MCA 1973, s 25A(3) direction, I(PFD)A 1975 dismissal and (if the clean break is to be deferred) MCA 1973, s 28(1A) prohibition on extension if there are arrears, request remission	FP(A No 2)R 1999, r 1(2); FPR 1991, rr 1.2(1), 2.61A

	if it is sought to recover from the payee monies which she was no longer entitled to in view of changed circumstances under MCA 1973, s 33, state the amount requested to be paid back	
Fee payable	Where order agreed: £30	FPFO 1999, fee 4.1
	Otherwise: £80	FPFO 1999, fee 4.4
Filing and exchange of Form E	Five weeks prior to the first appointment simultaneous exchange of sworn statements annexing (only):	FPR 1991, r 2.61B(1)–(5)
	(i) any valuation of matrimonial home or other property in last 6 months and recent mortgage statement	
	(ii) bank and building society statements for last year	
	(iii) surrender values of life policies	
	(iv) if interest in a company, last 2 years' accounts and any document relied on to support valuation of company	
	(v) pension scheme valuation or letter of request	
	(vi) last 3 pay slips and latest P60	
	(vii) accounts for last 2 years if self-employed	
	Restriction on requesting or giving disclosure	FPR 1991, r 2.61B(6)
	NB as a variation application is an application for ancillary relief a person with pension rights is required within 7 days of receiving notification of the first appointment to obtain an updated CETV and serve it on the other party	FPR 1991, r 2.70(1)–(5)
Interim applications	*Application for interim variation order*	
	Made at any stage by notice of application on 14 days notice to other party. If application made before Form E filed, support with draft order and short sworn statement disclosing means	
	Unless Form E filed respondent must, at least 1 week before the hearing, file and serve short sworn statement disclosing means	FPR 1991, r 2.69F(1)–(5)
	Application for any other interim order	
	Made at any stage with or without notice	FPR 1991, r 2.69F(6)–(8)

	For applications to restrain future dealings under MCA 1973, s 37(2)(*a*) see Guide 19.	
Action to be taken at least 14 days before first appointment	Both parties file and serve: (i) Concise statement of issues (ii) Chronology (iii) Questionnaire for further information and documents (iv) Form G (whether or not party can proceed to FDR at first appointment) and (applicant only) confirmation of service of mortgagee, third party owners and pension trustees	FPR 1991, r 2.61B(7)
The first appointment	Both parties must attend personally and estimates of costs incurred to date (and if application for summary assessment of costs or costs on account, costs estimate of the hearing) must be produced	FPR 1991, rr 2.61D(5), 2.61F
	Active case management by the district judge pursuant to the overriding objective will include:	
	(i) answering questionnaires and disclosure of documents	FPR 1991, r 2.61D(2)(*a*)
	(ii) valuation of assets and expert evidence	FPR 1991, rr 2.61C, 2.61D(2)(*b*)
	(iii) other evidence (subject to the court exercising its right to control the evidence at the conclusion of the FDR)	FPR 1991, r 2.61D(2)(*b*)
	(iv) fixing the next stage of the case (usually an FDR)	FPR 1991, r 2.61D(2)(*c*)
	(NB No entitlement to further disclosure except in accordance with directions given or with permission)	FPR 1991, r 2.61D(3)
Action after first appointment	Implementation of directions:	
	Seven days before the FDR appointment, the applicant gives notice to the court of all open, without prejudice and *Calderbank* offers	FPR 1991, r 2.61E(3), (4)
	Immediately before FDR up-to-date costs estimate (and if summary assessment of order for costs of the hearing is sought, costs estimate of the hearing)	FPR 1991, r 2.61F

FDR appointment	Both parties attend personally and use best endeavours to reach agreement	FPR 1991, r 2.61E(6), (9)
	No privilege attaches to any prior offer. All FDR discussions are completely privileged. If no agreement is reached the district judge will play no further part in the case. At conclusion of the FDR, parties filing privileged documents request their return	FPR 1991, r 2.61E(1)–(6)
	District judge can adjourn, make a consent order, fix a final hearing and will give any case management directions which were not made at the first appointment	FPR 1991, r 2.61E(8)
Action between FDR appointment and final hearing	Implementation of directions:	
	Statement of open proposals filed and served at court, by the applicant 14 days before the final hearing, and by the respondent 7 days before	FPR 1991, r 2.69E
Documents for final hearing	Paginated and indexed bundle of documents	
	Costs estimate	FPR 1991, r 2.61F
Order	Discharge, with MCA 1973, ss 25A(3), 28(1A) and I(PFD)A 1975 dismissal directions and direction for lump sum property adjustment or pension sharing	MCA 1973, s 31(1), (7A)–(7G)
	Vary, suspend or revive order or extend term	MCA 1973, s 31(1)
	Remit arrears	MCA 1973, s 31(2A)
	Order payee to repay to payer the monies already paid	MCA 1973, s 33
	Costs including payment on account	CPR 1998, r 44.3; FPR 1991, r 2.69B
Appeals	See Guides 72–75	

19: Restraining Future Disposals or Dealings with Property

Legal background

There are two separate jurisdictional frameworks enabling the court to grant injunctions to protect a claim for financial relief. The first which is specific to matrimonial financial proceedings is MCA 1973, s 37(2)(*a*) which enables an applicant to a claim for maintenance pending suit, a financial provision, property adjustment or pension sharing order, a variation of maintenance or for relief due to the other party's wilful neglect to maintain, to apply to the court if it is thought that the other party is about to deal with his assets in such a way as to defeat the claim, for the court to restrain those anticipated dealings. The injunction can be made in either the High or county court. Procedure is governed by FPR 1991, r 2.68.

The second is the general framework which applies to all civil claims. It has two separate bases, namely (i) the court's inherent jurisdiction to freeze assets where the balance of convenience favours such a course (*Roche v Roche* (1981) Fam Law 243; *Shipman v Shipman* [1991] 1 FLR 250); (ii) under Supreme Court Act 1981, s 37(1) as fortified by Civil Procedure Act 1997, s 7 (set out in the annotations thereunder). Under these Acts the court can make injunctions including freezing injunctions (formerly called *Mareva* injunctions) against assets either in England and Wales or worldwide and make search orders (formerly called *Anton Piller* orders) whereby a home or business premises is searched under the auspices of a supervising solicitor. Search orders (which may only be made in exceptional circumstances in family cases – *A v A* [1997] Fam Law 301) must be made in the High Court but all other orders can, if appropriate, be made in the county as well as the High Court (County Court Remedies Regulations 1991, reg 3(3)). Procedure for a matrimonial applicant for injunctions applicable to all civil claims is still governed by the original RSC and CCR (except to the small extent that the CPR 1998 have been imported into them eg expert evidence and costs: see annotation **Civil Procedure Rules 1998** under FPR 1991, r 1.3). Nevertheless, in the three years since the CPR have been in force the practice of granting civil injunctions has moved on. It is suggested that good practice dictates that procedure for the matrimonial applicant should follow general civil procedure as closely as possible.

An injunction may be applied for on notice or (if the applicant shows good grounds for no notice) without notice. The applicant for an injunction without notice is under a strict obligation to give full disclosure of facts which militate against an order being made (*Re W (Ex Parte Orders)* [2000] 2 FLR 927) and, if not, is at risk of being denied an order at the with notice hearing. Further, the absent respondent is entitled to copies of the material read by the judge and a note of what took place at the without notice hearing.

To prevent a tenant surrendering a tenancy (which cannot be subsequently set aside by an avoidance of disposition order) where an undertaking not to so surrender has not been given, a party should apply for an injunction to restrain the surrender, serving any injunction on the landlord (*Bater v Greenwich London Borough Council* [1999] 2 FLR 993).

Procedure

Who may apply	An applicant who has a validly constituted application for financial relief (ie for an order under MCA 1973, s 22, 23, 24, 24B, 27, 31 or 35)	MCA 1973, s 37(1), (2)
	An application for an order under MCA 1973, s 22, 23, 24 or 24B is, if the applicant is the petitioner or a respondent who has filed an answer claiming relief, contained in the petition or answer	FPR 1991, r 2.53(1)
	Otherwise, the application is made on Form A	FPR 1991, rr 2.53(3), 2.54(1)
	Injunctions under SCA 1981/CPA 1997/inherent jurisdiction may be granted if undertaking to file claim	RSC Ord 29, r 1(3); CCR Ord 13, r 6(4); *PD 25 – Interim Injunctions*, para 5.1(2), (5)
Application and supporting documents	(i) Application Notice setting out what order and briefly why	CPR 1998, r 23.6

	(ii) Draft order (plus disk) (if civil injunction, in format of annex to CPR *PD 25 – Interim Injunctions*)	
	(iii) Affidavit containing supporting evidence including reason if application without notice	CPR 1998, r 25.3; *PD 25 – Interim Injunctions*, para 3.1
Fee payable	on notice: £60	FPFO 1999, fee 4.3
	without notice: £30	FPFO 1999, fee 4.1
Arrangements for hearing	*Injunction under MCA 1973, s 37(2)(a)* Usually heard by district judge, but can be heard by judge	FPR 1991, r 2.68(1), (2)
	Injunctions under inherent jurisdiction, SCA 1981 and CPA 1997 Under the CPR, search orders and freezing injunctions can only be made by High Court judges and any other judge duly authorised	*PD 25 – Interim Injunctions*, para 1.1
	Only the High Court can make a search order but the county court may make any injunction including a freezing injunction	CCRR 1991, regs 2(*a*), 3(1), (3)(*a*)
	Under RSC and CCR any injunction (including a freezing injunction) can be heard by either a circuit or district judge. At the time of listing it is wise to write for confirmation that the district judge will accept jurisdiction	RSC Ord 32, r 11(1)(*d*); CCR Ord 1, r 6, Ord 13, r 6(2)
Without Notice Hearings	Applicant must give full disclosure of facts adverse to his case, undertaking to serve order, application notice and supporting evidence (and if no claim yet filed, to do so)	CPR 1998, r 23.9(2); *PD 25 – Interim Injunctions*, para 5.1; *Re W* [2000] 2 FLR 927
	Order must state right of respondent to set aside or vary and give date for with notice hearing	CPR 1998, r 23.9(3); *PD 25 – Interim Injunctions*, para 5.1
Who is to be served	Other spouse on two days clear notice (CPR: three clear days)	CCR Ord 13, r 1(2); RSC Ord 32, r 3; CPR 1998, r 23.7(1)
	Power to abridge/extend time	CCR Ord 13, r 4; RSC Ord 3, r 5; CPR 1998, r 3.1(2)(*a*)
Order	Subject to the fact that the order must set out clearly and in plain English what the respondent must do and not do, whatever order is necessary to protect the claim, including a freezing injunction or an order for surrender of passport and restraining the respondent from leaving the jurisdiction	*Bayer AG v Winter* [1986] 1 WLR 497

	Although not normally required, applicant may be required to give an undertaking as to damages, particularly if order may impact on third party rights	*Re W (Ex parte Orders)* [2000] 2 FLR 927
Appeals	See Guides 72–75	

20: Avoidance of Disposition Order

General note

This Guide applies to applications for an avoidance of disposition order started by filing Form A on or after 5 June 2000. For applications started before that date see Guide 22 in *The Family Court Practice 1999* or, if the court is in a pilot scheme area, Guide 19.

Legal background

If an applicant for an order under Matrimonial Causes Act 1973, s 37(2)(*b*) or (*c*) is seeking to set aside a transaction that has already taken place, the third party involved has to show under MCA 1973, s 37(4), first, that the transaction was made for valuable consideration, secondly, that he acted in good faith and, thirdly, that he had no notice of any intention on the other spouse's part to defeat the claim for financial relief. Unlike an application under MCA 1973, s 37(2)(*a*) to restrain anticipated dealings, applications under s 37(2)(*b*) and (*c*) are for an avoidance of disposition order and consequently are within the definition of "ancillary relief". Thus, the new code of rules for ancillary relief claims provided for by the Family Proceedings (Amendment No 2) Rules 1999 applies.

The applicant will often allege that the person to whom the disposal was made acted in bad faith. Accordingly, there may be good reason to believe that the third party will himself try to dispose of the asset before the hearing to set aside the transaction, and so careful consideration must be given to apply to prevent that course of action occurring. Under MCA 1973, s 37(2)(*a*), the court's power to restrain anticipated dealings extends only to dealings by a party to the marriage. An application should therefore be made under the court's inherent jurisdiction and under Supreme Court Act 1981, s 37; Civil Procedure Act 1997, s 7 (as extended to the county court by County Courts Act 1984, s 38), that application being initially made without notice at the time that the application for the avoidance of disposition order is filed so as to restrain the third party from disposing of the property. That application should be linked to any MCA 1973, s 37(2)(*a*) application to restrain future dealings by the other spouse. Procedure for both applications is set out in Guide 19.

Procedure

Who may apply	A party with a validly constituted notice of application for financial relief (ie for an order under MCA 1973, s 22, 23, 24 – including a pension sharing order, 27, 31 or 35) which is either contained in the petition or answer or alternatively contained in Form A	MCA 1973, s 37(1), (2); FPR 1991, rr 2.53(3), 2.54(1)
Application	Form A which, if it relates to land, should identify the land's title and give details of any mortgage or any third party interest therein	FPR 1991, rr 2.59(2), 2.61A

	The notice must also clearly identify the transaction that it is sought to set aside, and the name and address of the person in whose favour the disposition has been made.	
Fee payable	£30	FPFO 1999, fee 4.1
Injunctive relief	If it is suspected that the respondent may make a further disposition or that the person in whose favour the disposition was made may himself dispose of the property, at the time of issuing Form A the applicant should apply with supporting sworn statement, initially without notice, for: an MCA 1973, s 37(2)(*a*) injunction against the respondent and/or an order that the person in whose favour the disposition has been made should be made a party to the proceedings and for an injunction under the court's inherent jurisdiction, SCA 1981, and CPA 1997, restraining any disposition by him of that property Additionally, an application for an interim order may be made at any time with or without notice	FPR 1991, r 2.69F(6)
Who is to be served and by whom	The court serves other spouse (within 4 days of filing of notice) inserting on Form A date of first appointment within 12–16 weeks	FPR 1991, r 2.61A
	The applicant serves the person in whose favour the disposition has been made and any other person (such as a joint owner) that the district judge directs	FPR 1991, r 2.59(3)
Filing and exchange of Form E	Five weeks prior to the first appointment simultaneous exchange of sworn statements in Form E annexing only those documents set out in r 2.61B which are relevant on an avoidance of disposition claim	FPR 1991, r 2.61B(1)–(5)

Action to be taken at least 14 days before first appointment	Both parties file and serve: (i) Concise statement of issues (ii) Chronology (iii) Questionnaire for further information and documents (iv) Form G (whether or not party can proceed to FDR at first appointment)	FPR 1991, r 2.61B(7)
	and (applicant only) confirmation of service on the person in whose favour the disposition has been made	FPR 1991, r 2.61B
The first appointment	Both parties must attend personally and estimates of costs incurred to date (and if application for summary assessment of costs or costs on account, costs estimate of the hearing) must be produced	FPR 1991, rr 2.61D(5), 2.61F
	Active case management by the district judge pursuant to the overriding objective will include:	
	(i) answering questionnaires and disclosure of documents	FPR 1991, r 2.61D(2)(*a*)
	(ii) valuation of assets and expert evidence	FPR 1991, rr 2.61C, 2.61D(2)(*b*)
	(iii) other evidence (subject to the court exercising its right to control the evidence at the conclusion of the FDR)	FPR 1991, r 2.61D(2)(*b*)
	(iv) fixing the next stage of the case (usually an FDR)	FPR 1991, r 2.61D(2)(*c*)
	(NB No entitlement to further disclosure except in accordance with directions given or with permission)	FPR 1991, r 2.61D(3)
Action after first appointment	Implementation of directions:	
	Seven days before the FDR appointment, the applicant gives notice to the court of all open, without prejudice and *Calderbank* offers	FPR 1991, r 2.61E(3), (4)
	Immediately before FDR up-to-date costs estimate (and if summary assessment of order for costs of the hearing is sought, costs estimate of the hearing)	FPR 1991, r 2.61F
FDR appointment	Both parties attend personally and use best endeavours to reach agreement	FPR 1991, r 2.61E(6), (9)

	No privilege attaches to any prior offer. All FDR discussions are completely privileged. If no agreement is reached the district judge will play no further part in the case. At conclusion of the FDR, parties filing privileged documents request their return	FPR 1991, r 2.61E(1)–(6)
	District judge can adjourn, make a consent order, fix a final hearing and will give any case management directions which were not made at the first appointment	FPR 1991, r 2.61E(8)
	The application should if possible be heard at the same time as any related application for financial relief	FPR 1991, r 2.62(2)
Action between FDR appointment and final hearing	Implementation of directions:	
	Statement of open proposals filed and served at court, by the applicant 14 days before the final hearing, and by the respondent 7 days before	FPR 1991, r 2.69E
Documents for final hearing	Paginated and indexed bundle of documents	
	Costs estimate	FPR 1991, r 2.61F
Order	On setting aside the disposition, the court can give consequential directions including requiring the making of payment or for the disposal of any property	MCA 1973, s 37(3)
Appeals	See Guides 72–75	

21: Financial Relief after Overseas Proceedings

General note

The Family Proceedings (Amendment No 2) Rules 1999 have amended FPR 1991, rr 2.52–2.77 in respect of claims for ancillary relief started on or after 5 June 2000. The amended version of the rules is printed in this edition. A claim for financial relief after overseas proceedings is not a claim for ancillary relief. Family Proceedings (Amendment No 2) Rules 1999, r 20 provides that the unamended version of those rules applies to a claim for financial relief after overseas proceedings. The unamended version, whose broad thrust is not substantially different from the current version of the rules, is contained in earlier editions of *The Family Court Practice*. Throughout this Guide the references are to the unamended rules.

Legal background

Matrimonial and Family Proceedings Act 1984, ss 12 to 27 allow a party to a marriage which has been ended by overseas proceedings (whether judicial or, for instance, by talaq) which are recognised in England and Wales to apply for financial relief in, broadly speaking, the same way as if the marriage had been ended here. The court can make financial provision, property adjustment orders, including pension sharing, orders for sale and orders for the transfer of a tenancy. An application for financial relief after an overseas divorce must first have leave. Jurisdiction to hear an application for leave depends on domicile, habitual residence for one year or the existence of a matrimonial home within the jurisdiction (if the sole ground for establishing jurisdiction is a matrimonial home, the court can only make capital orders in respect of that property and cannot make income or other capital orders for the applicant and the children). If the applicant is unable to apply for leave because one year's habitual residence has not yet been established, the applicant can still apply under MFPA 1984, s 24 to restrain the respondent from disposing of assets. Additionally, once leave to apply is granted, the applicant can restrain anticipated dealings and set aside past dealings whose intention was to defeat the claim for financial relief.

Remarriage bars an application in the same way as Matrimonial Causes Act 1973, s 28(3); MFPA 1984, s 12(2) refers.

The court's limited powers to order child maintenance are summarised at **Interface with Child Support Act 1991** under MCA 1973, s 23 and **Outline of new bases for child support calculation** under CSA 1991, s 4.

Procedure

Who may apply for leave	A party whose marriage has been ended by overseas proceedings (judicial or otherwise) recognised in England and Wales and who can establish domicile, one year's habitual residence or the existence of a matrimonial home within the jurisdiction	MFPA 1984, ss 12, 15
Application for leave	Ex parte by originating summons in Form M25 out of the principal registry to the judge (not district judge) supported by affidavit setting out:	
	formal details required by FPR 1991, r 3.17(2)	
	grounds for jurisdiction required by MFPA 1984, s 15	
	all facts relied on, including the considerations for exercise of discretion under MFPA 1984, s 16(2)	FPR 1991, r 3.17
	Fee payable: £30	FPFO 1999, fee 4.1
Order	Grant or refusal of leave, with or without conditions	MFPA 1984, s 13
Form of application	Once leave has been granted, by originating summons on Form M26 out of the principal registry, with affidavit disclosing means and stating case. Form M26 can include claims on behalf of applicant and children for:	
	financial provision, property adjustment and sale orders	MCA 1973, ss 23–24A; MFPA 1984, s 17
	interim order for maintenance for applicant and/or children	MFPA 1984, s 14; FPR 1991, r 3.18(4)

	avoidance of transaction order (ie restraining future dispositions and setting aside past dispositions)	MFPA 1984, s 23; FPR 1991, r 3.18(4)
	transfer of a contractual or statutory tenancy	MFPA 1984, s 22; FPR 1991, r 3.18(7)
	The summons must identify whether the land is registered and, if so, title number, whether there is any mortgagee, other joint owner, landlord and, in an avoidance and transaction application, the person to whom the asset has been transferred	FPR 1991, rr 2.59, 3.18(3), (6), (7)
	Fee payable: £60	FPFO 1999, fee 4.3
Respondent	The other party to the marriage	
	The mortgagee, the party to whom property has been transferred, the landlord and any other third party having an interest in the disputed asset must also be served	
Injunction	If respondent is about to deal with property to defeat claim, apply to judge (not district judge) by summons in High Court or notice of application in accordance with CCR Ord 13, r 1 if in county court supported by affidavit, initially ex parte, for injunction to restrain future dealing	MFPA 1984, s 23(2)(*a*); FPR 1991, r 3.18(8)
Respondent's affidavit	The respondent has 31 days to return his acknowledgement of service and thereafter a further 28 days to file and serve his affidavit in answer	FPR 1991, r 3.18(5)
Request for information	Request by letter followed by application for an order for information and documents	FPR 1991, rr 2.63, 3.18(3)
Directions	The district judge may give directions, including ordering the parties to give discovery and produce documents and ordering any person (including a non-party) to attend to give evidence	FPR 1991, rr 2.62(5), 3.18(3)
Interim order	The judge must hear all other applications, including an order for interim maintenance	MFPA 1984, s 14
Consent orders	Two copies of the draft of the proposed order, one signed by the respondent to the application signifying his agreement and statement of information in Form M1	FPR 1991, rr 2.61, 3.18(3)

Orders	Periodical payments, secured periodical payments and lump sum for the applicant and the children, but no power to award interest on lump sum	MFPA 1984, ss 17, 21
	Property adjustment order for the spouse and/or children and an order for sale	MFPA 1984, ss 17, 21
	Transfer of a statutory or contractual tenancy	MFPA 1984, s 22
	Setting aside a disposition made with the intention of defeating a claim for financial relief	MFPA 1984, s 23
	If only fact establishing jurisdiction is existence of matrimonial home in England and Wales, the court can only make orders in relation to that asset and cannot make any income order for applicant or children	MFPA 1984, s 20
Appeals	See Guides 72–75	

22: Restraining Anticipated Dealings Pending an Application for Financial Relief after Overseas Proceedings

Legal background

Matrimonial and Family Proceedings Act 1984, s 24 enables the court to restrain anticipated dealings with property where the sole potential ground on which the applicant is able to claim jurisdiction for financial relief after overseas proceedings is one year's habitual residence, and that year has not yet been completed.

Procedure

Who may apply	A party to a marriage that has been ended overseas by means of judicial or other proceedings recognised in England and Wales who intends to apply for financial relief as soon as he or she has been habitually resident for one year	MFPA 1984, ss 12(1), 24(1)(*a*), (*b*)
Application and supporting affidavit	By originating summons on Form M27 out of the principal registry, supported by affidavit setting out all supporting facts	MFPA 1984, s 24(3)
	Consider applying ex parte initially	FPR 1991, r 3.19(1), (4)
	Application heard by judge (not district judge).	

Fee payable	£30 (ex parte application) £60 (application on notice)	FPFO 1999, fee 4.1 FPFO 1999, fee 4.3
Respondent	The other party to the marriage	
Service	Form M27, supporting affidavit, notice of any ex parte injunction, notice of proceedings and Form M28 must be served on the respondent; acknowledgement of service must be returned within 31 days	FPR 1991, r 3.19(2)
Respondent's affidavit	Respondent must file his affidavit in answer within 28 days after the 31 days allowed for acknowledgement of service	FPR 1991, r 3.19(3)
Order	Injunction restraining any disposition, transfer out of the jurisdiction or other dealing with any property	MFPA 1984, s 24(1)
Appeals	See Guides 74, 75	

23: Enforcement of an Order for Financial Provision in a Magistrates' Court

Legal background

The authority and procedure for the enforcement of magistrates' court maintenance orders are contained in Maintenance Orders Act 1958, Magistrates' Courts (Maintenance Orders Act 1958) Rules 1959, Magistrates' Courts Act 1980 and Magistrates' Courts Rules 1981.

The orders under the following provisions are enforceable as magistrates' court maintenance orders: Maintenance Orders (Facilities for Enforcement) Act 1920; National Assistance Act 1948, s 43; Maintenance Orders Act 1950, Pt II; Affiliation Proceedings Act 1957; Maintenance Orders Act 1958; Matrimonial Proceedings (Magistrates' Courts) Act 1960; Guardianship of Minors Act 1971; Maintenance Orders (Reciprocal Enforcement) Act 1972; Guardianship Act 1973; Supplementary Benefits Act 1976, s 18; Domestic Proceedings and Magistrates' Courts Act 1978, Pt I; Child Care Act 1980; Social Security Act 1986, s 24; Children Act 1989, Sch 1.

Procedure

Notification of arrears	The justices' chief executive must, unless it appears to him unnecessary or inexpedient to do so, give written notice where, in the case of payments required to be made monthly or less frequently, the arrears amount to twice the sum payable periodically or, in any other case, to four times the sum payable periodically	MCR 1981, r 40

Who may apply	The person entitled to payment including, where payment is made through the court, the justices' chief executive	
Which court	The court which made the order (or the court where the order is registered) or, where it would be more convenient, the court acting for the area where the complainant or defendant resides. Venue to be decided by the person to whom the complaint is made, ie a justice of the peace or, if the complaint is not on oath, a justices' clerk	MCR 1981, r 59
Application	By way of complaint	MCA 1980, s 93; MCR 1981, r 4(1)
Fee payable	None	
Process	A summons may be issued or, if the complaint is in writing and on oath, a warrant with or without bail may be issued	MCR 1981, rr 59, 96, 98
Service	Service of a summons may be effected by personal service or, provided that it is proved that the summons came to the defendant's knowledge, by leaving it with some person at his last known or usual place of residence or (except in the case of HM Forces personnel) by post at his last known or usual place of residence	MCR 1981, r 99
Non-appearance	If the defendant fails to appear, the court may, if satisfied as to reasonable service, proceed in his absence or, if the complaint is substantiated on oath and the defendant has not already given evidence in the proceedings, issue a warrant If the complainant fails to appear, the court may dismiss the complaint or, if evidence has been received on a previous occasion, proceed in the absence of the complainant If neither party appears, the court may dismiss the complaint	MCA 1980, ss 55–57
Procedure at the hearing	The general procedure on the hearing of a complaint applies	MCA 1980, s 53
Orders available	Adjournment	MCA 1980, s 54
	Distress warrant (immediate or postponed)	MCA 1980, ss 76(1), 77; MCR 1981, r 54

	Warrant of commitment to prison (immediate or postponed), maximum period of committal being 6 weeks	MCA 1980, ss 76(1), (2), (3), 77, Sch 4; MC(MOA 1958)R 1959, r 23
	For payment after imprisonment imposed, see —	MCA 1980, ss 79, 80(2); MCR 1981, rr 55, 64
	While a person is in custody under a warrant of commitment for arrears, further arrears under the order may not accrue, unless the court otherwise directs	MCA 1980, s 94
Alternative orders	The court may also order direct payments between the parties, payments through the justices' chief executive, payments by standing order or payments under an attachment of earnings order	MCA 1980, ss 59, 95
	The court may remit all or part of the arrears, but it must, unless it considers it to be unnecessary or impracticable, give prior notice to the person in whose favour the order was made or, if a child, to the person with whom the child has its home	MCA 1980, s 95; MCR 1981, r 44
Appeals	See Guide 71	

24: Enforcement of an Order other than for the Payment of Money in a Magistrates' Court

Legal background

An order for anything other than the payment of money or to abstain from doing anything may be enforced under Magistrates' Courts Act 1980, s 63(3), either by order on complaint or on the court's own motion. Where the court acts on its own motion, the relevant provisions of MCA 1980 have been amended by Contempt of Court Act 1981, s 17 and Sch 3.

Caution should be exercised when dealing with the person with whom a child has his residence for breach of a contact order. A variation of the contact order, if acceptable to both parents, will be preferable to punishment for breach of the order (*T v T* (1984) *The Times*, 19 July). See also *Re H (A Minor) (Contact: Enforcement)* [1996] 1 FLR 614.

Section 63(3), as amended, is intended to be used only in the event of deliberate and wilful disobedience of an order of the court.

The proceedings attract the full protection of ECHR Article 6 and, in particular, the minimum rights in Article 6.3.

Procedure

Availability	The court may act of its own motion or by order on complaint	CCA 1981, s 17(1)

	Where the breach is of an order made under FLA 1996, s 42, enforcement proceedings are commenced by the exercise of a power of arrest attached to the order or by the issue of a warrant on an application substantiated on oath	FLA 1996, s 47
Which court	A magistrates' court has jurisdiction to hear a complaint if the complaint relates to anything done or left undone within the commission area	MCA 1980, s 52
	Where enforcement proceedings have been commenced by the exercise of a power of arrest attached to an order made under FLA 1996, s 42, the constable is required to bring the arrested person before any magistrates' court	FLA 1996, ss 47(7), 63
	Where enforcement proceedings are to be commenced by application for a warrant of arrest under FLA 1996, s 47(8), application may be made to any magistrates' court	FLA 1996, ss 47(8), 63
	There is power to transfer proceedings to another court once they have been commenced	FLA(Pt IV)(AP)O 1997
Forms	Where enforcement proceedings have been commenced by way of complaint, no form is prescribed, but a summons should be issued which cites the disobedience of the order and requires the defendant to appear to show cause why an order requiring him to pay money or be committed to prison should not be made; clear details of the breach, including date, time and place must be given	*P v W (Access Order: Breach)* [1984] Fam 32
	Where proceedings are commenced by way of an application under FLA 1996, s 47(8), any warrant issued must be in Form FL408	FPC(MP etc)R 1991, r 20
	Fee payable for complaint or application: £3.50	MCA 1980, Sch 6, Pt I
	Fee payable for summons and copy: £3.50	MCA 1980, Sch 6, Pt I
	Fee payable for warrant and copy: £6.50	MCA 1980, Sch 6, Pt I

Service	If a summons has been issued, personal service is required; however, the summons may be left with some person at the defendant's last known or usual place of abode or be sent by post, provided that it is proved that the summons came to the defendant's knowledge	
	The complainant is responsible for service	
	Proof of service by certificate is permissible	MCR 1981, rr 67, 99
Orders available	Where the order to be enforced was made in family proceedings, an order that the enforcement proceedings be treated as family proceedings	MCA 1980, s 65(2)
	An order to pay £50 for every day during which he is in default or a sum not exceeding £5,000	
	Committal to prison for a period not exceeding two months or until he has remedied his default	MCA 1980, s 63(3)
	A hospital or guardianship order	FLA 1996, ss 50, 51
Imprisonment	Occupation/non-molestation orders under FLA 1996, Pt IV and exclusion orders under CA 1989, ss 38A, 44A are enforceable by way of suspended committal	FLA 1996, s 50
	Consecutive committal orders are not available	*Head v Head* [1982] 1 WLR 1186
	No procedure is prescribed for formally accepting that the default has been remedied and for ordering the defaulter's release from prison. A certificate of the justice of the peace who ordered committal, addressed to the governor of the prison, would appear to be appropriate	
Appeals	See Guide 71	

25: Reciprocal Enforcement

Legal background

The provisions for enforcing in other countries judgments and orders (including maintenance orders) made in England and Wales, and vice versa, and for making in England and Wales claims for maintenance against persons resident in other countries, and vice versa, are complex. The Table and Procedural Guides which follow constitute an outline of the relevant procedures and their availability. However, reference should always be made to the text of the rules, statutes and, where appropriate, international conventions from which the remedies derive. Moreover, no attempt is made to provide a comprehensive account of the particular requirements of individual countries. Before expense is undertaken in attempting to pursue a remedy abroad, enquiry should be made of a local lawyer as to any requirements of a particular territory and, indeed, as to the likelihood of the remedy being effective, for example because of stringent exchange control regulation. For enforcement abroad of residence (custody) and contact (access) orders and recovery of children abducted abroad, see Guides 64, 65 and 65A.

How to use the Table

Identify from the list below the activity to be undertaken. The number (1 to 6) associated with it is the number of a vertical column in the Table. Locate the territory concerned on the left-hand side of the Table and note the letter reference(s) given (A to N) in the chosen column beside it. Find the letter reference(s) in the Procedural Guides (25A to 25N) which follow the Table. Each Guide deals with the English (and Welsh) aspect of "outward" enforcement (ie an applicant in England pursuing a remedy abroad) and, so far as appropriate, "inward" enforcement (ie a foreign applicant pursuing the equivalent remedy in England).

The presence of more than one letter reference indicates that alternative remedies may be available to the applicant. The absence of any indicates that no appropriate remedy has been discovered by the authors. However, the information has had to be gathered from a wide range of sources and international arrangements are constantly changing. It is always worth checking the up-to-date position: in the case of maintenance orders, assistance can usually be obtained from the Reciprocal Enforcement of Maintenance Orders Section, Family Policy Division 1, Lord Chancellor's Department, Southside, 105 Victoria Street, London SW1E 6QT, telephone 020 7210 1260 or 1239.

In the Table, lower case letters in parentheses refer to notes given at the foot of the Table.

The cases to which the Table refers

1 A maintenance order having been made in England or Wales, the payee seeks to enforce it abroad, and vice versa
2 Application in England and Wales for a provisional maintenance order against a respondent abroad, and vice versa
3 Applicant in England or Wales makes a maintenance claim for transmission abroad for determination there against a respondent there, and vice versa
4 Application to vary, discharge or revoke an order which has been registered or made under Case 1, 2 or 3
5 A money judgment having been given in England or Wales, the creditor seeks to enforce it abroad, and vice versa
6 A judgment or order including a non-monetary provision having been given or made in England or Wales, the person entitled to the benefit of that provision seeks to enforce it abroad, and vice versa

Table

CASE	1	2	3	4	5	6
Scotland and Northern Ireland	C			D	N	N
Akrotiri (Sovereign Base Area)					J	
Algeria			H	I		
Anguilla	E	F		G	J	
Antigua and Barbuda	A	B			J	
Antilles (n)						
Aruba (n)						
Australia	E(h)	F(h)	H	G(h),I	K	

Austria	L		H	I	M	M
Bahamas	A	B			J	
Barbados	E	F	H	G,I	J	
Belgium	L		H	I	M	M
Belize	A	B			J	
Bermuda	E	F		G	J	
Bosnia and Herzegovina			H	I		
Botswana	A	B			J	
Brazil			H	I		
British Indian Ocean Territory					J	
British Virgin Islands	A	B				
Brunei Darussalam	E(l)	F(l)		G(l)		
Burkina Faso			H	I		
Canada:						
Federal Court					K	
Alberta	E(ab)	F(abc)		G(ab)		
British Columbia	E	F		G	K	
Manitoba	E	F		G	K	
New Brunswick	E(abc)	F(abc)		G(abc)	K	
Newfoundland and Labrador	E	F		G	K	
Northwest Territories	E(abc)	F(abc)		G(abc)		
Nunavut	E(abc)	F(abc)		G(abc)		
Nova Scotia	E(ab)	F(ab)		G(ab)	K	
Ontario	E(b)	F(b)		G(b)	K	
Prince Edward Island	A	B			K	
Saskatchewan	E(b)	F(bc)		G(b)	K	
Yukon	A	B			K	
Cape Verde Islands			H	I		
Cayman Islands	A	B			J	
Central African Republic			H	I		
Chile			H	I		
Christmas Island	A	B			J	
Cocos (Keeling) Islands	A	B			J	
Comoro Archipelago			H	I		
Croatia			H	I		
Cyprus	A	B	H	I	J	
Czech Republic, The	E(h)	F(h)	H	G(h),I		
Denmark	E(h),L	F(h)	H	G(h),I	M	M
Dhekelia (Sovereign Base Area)					J	
Dominica	A	B			J	
Ecuador			H	I		
Estonia	E(h)	F(h)		G(h)		

Falkland Islands	E	F		G	J	
Fiji	E	F		G	J	
Finland	E(h),L	F(h)	H	G(h),I	M	M
France (f)	E(h),L	F(h)	H	G(h),I	M	M
French Guiana (f)			H	I		
French Polynesia			H	I		
Gambia	A	B			J	
Germany	E(h),L	F(h)	H	G(h),I	M	M
Ghana	E(bc)	F(bc)		G(bc)	J	
Gibraltar	E,L	F		G	M	M
Greece	L		H	I	M	M
Grenada	A	B			J	
Guadeloupe (f)			H	I		
Guatemala			H	I		
Guernsey	A	B			K	
Guyana	A	B			J	
Haiti			H	I		
Holy See *see* Vatican						
Hong Kong	E	F		G	J	
Hungary			H	I		
Iceland	L				M	M
India	E(abc)	F(abc)		G(abc)	J(z)	
Ireland, Republic of	E(i),L	F(i)	H	G(i)	M	M
Isle of Man	E	F		G	K(d)	
Israel			H	I	K	
Italy	E(h),L	F(h)	H	G(h),I	M	M
Jamaica	A	B			J	
Jersey	A	B			K(e)	
Kenya	E(bc)	F(bc)		G(bc)	J	
Kiribati	A	B			J	
Lesotho	A	B			J	
Luxembourg	E(h),L	F(h)	H	G(h),I	M	M
Macedonia (former Yugoslav republic)			H	I		
Malawi	A	B			J	
Malaysia	A	B			J	
Malta and Gozo	E	F		G	J	
Martinique (f)			H	I		
Mauritius	A	B			J	
Mexico			H	I		
Monaco			H	I		
Montserrat	A	B			J	
Morocco			H	I		

Nauru	E	F		G		
Netherlands (n)	E(h),L	F(h)	H	G(h),I	M	M
New Caledonia and Dependencies			H	I		
New Zealand	E	F	H	G,I	J	
Niger			H	I		
Nigeria	A	B			J	
Norfolk Island	E(a)	F(a)	H	G(a),I	J	
Norway	E(h),L	F(h)	H	G(h),I	M	M
Pakistan			H	I	K	
Papua New Guinea	E	F(c)		G	J	
Philippines			H	I		
Poland	E(h)	F(h)	H	G(h),I		
Polynesia, French *see* French Polynesia						
Portugal	E(h),L	F(h)	H	G(h),I	M	M
Réunion (f)			H	I		
Romania			H	I		
St Kitts and Nevis	A	B			J	
St Helena	E	F		G	J	
St Lucia	A	B			J	
St Pierre et Miquelon			H	I		
St Vincent and the Grenadines	A	B			J	
Seychelles	A	B			J	
Sierra Leone	A	B			J	
Singapore	E	F		G	J	
Slovakia	E(h)	F(h)	H	G(h),I		
Slovenia			H	I		
Solomon Islands	A	B			J	
South Africa	E(bc)	F(bc)		G(bc)		
Spain	E(h),L	F(h)	H	G(h),I	M	M
Sri Lanka	A	B	H	I	J	
Surinam			H	I	K	
Swaziland	A	B			J	
Sweden	E(h),L	F(h)	H	G(h),I	M	M
Switzerland	E(h),L	F(h)	H	G(h),I	M	M
Tanzania (except Zanzibar)	E(abc)	F(abc)		G(abc)	J	
Tonga					K	
Trinidad and Tobago	A	B			J	
Tunisia			H	I		
Turkey	E(h)	F(h)	H	G(h),I		
Turks and Caicos Islands	E(abc)	F(abc)		G(abc)	J	
Tuvalu	A	B			J	

Uganda	A	B			J
United States of America	E(x)		H(u)	G(x), I(u)	
Uruguay			H	I	
Vatican			H	I	
Virgin Islands (UK) *see* British Virgin Islands					
Yugoslavia			H	I	
Zambia	A	B			J
Zanzibar	A	B			J
Zimbabwe	E(bc)	F(bc)		G(bc)	J

Notes

(a) Other than orders obtained by or in favour of a public authority
(b) Other than orders for the payment of birth and funeral expenses of child
(c) Other than affiliation orders
(d) County court judgments and orders must have first been transferred to the High Court
(e) High Court judgments and orders only
(f) For some purposes, France includes the overseas departments of Guadeloupe, Guiana, Martinique and Réunion
(h) MO(RE)A 1972, Pt I applies to the Hague Convention countries as modified by SI 1993/593 and SI 1999/1318
(i) MO(RE)A 1972, Pt I applies to the Republic of Ireland as modified by SI 1993/594
(l) Other than lump sum orders
(n) For most purposes, the Netherlands include the Netherlands Antilles and Aruba
(u) MO(RE)A 1972, Pt II applies, as modified by SI 1993/591, to the following states: Colorado, Georgia, Hawaii, Idaho, Illinois, Michigan, New Hampshire, New Mexico, Ohio, Rhode Island, Tennessee
(x) MO(RE)A 1972, Pt I applies to some States in the United States of America as modified by REMO(USA)O 1995, together with MC(REMO)(HCC)R 1980 as modified by MC(REMO)(USA)R 1995. The States concerned are: Alaska, Arizona, Arkansas, California, Connecticut, Delaware, Florida, Indiana, Iowa, Kansas, Kentucky, Louisiana, Maine, Maryland, Massachusetts, Minnesota, Missouri, Montana, Nebraska, Nevada, New Jersey, New York, North Carolina, North Dakota, Oklahoma, Oregon, Pennsylvania, South Dakota, Texas, Utah, Vermont, Virginia, Washington, West Virginia, Wisconsin, Wyoming. With the exception of West Virginia, Pt II of the Act formerly applied to all of these States. Existing maintenance claims in all of these States (except West Virginia) and claims where no maintenance order is existing continue to operate under MO(RE)A 1972, Pt II
(z) The territories named in SI 1958/425.

25A: Maintenance Order having been Made in England or Wales, Payee Seeks to Enforce it Abroad, and Vice Versa

OUTWARD

Registration abroad of maintenance order made in England or Wales

Who may apply	The payee under a maintenance order made in England or Wales where the payer resides in a Commonwealth country which is not designated as a reciprocating country under MO(RE)A 1972, Pt I	MO(FE)A 1920, s 2
Which court	*High Court order* The principal registry or the district registry if the cause is proceeding there	FPR 1991, r 7.17(4)
	County court order Although MO(FE)A 1920 refers to "a court in England" (Wales is included for the purposes of the Act), the rule under which application is made refers only to a maintenance order made in the High Court. If possible, it is prudent to seek to transfer to the High Court before the order is made; otherwise (ie if the maintenance order has already been made in the county court), the proceedings should be transferred to the High Court under MFPA 1984, s 39 as a preliminary step.	
	Magistrates' court order The magistrates' court which made the order	MO(FE)A 1920, s 2
Documents required	*High Court (or transferred county court) order* A certified copy of the maintenance order An affidavit stating the reason for believing that the payer is residing in the territory in question So far as known, his address and occupation Any other information required by the law of that territory for the purpose of enforcement of the order	

	It is therefore necessary to enquire in advance as to the particular requirements of the territory and to disclose the result in the affidavit	FPR 1991, r 7.17(2)
	In the case of Canada, if the payer's address is unknown the court can cause enquiries to be made	*PD of 10 February 1976*
	Magistrates' court order A certified copy of the order Information sufficient to ascertain the whereabouts of the payer (including his last known address) Information sufficient to identify the payer (including where possible a photograph) A certificate of marriage A certificate of the birth of the child (where maintenance is payable in respect of a child) The name and address of the justices' chief executive	MO(FE)A 1920, ss 2, 8
Fee payable	High Court and county court: £30 Magistrates' court: none prescribed	FPFO 1999, fee 4.1
What happens next	If satisfied, the court sends the documents to the Lord Chancellor for transmission to the governor of that part of Her Majesty's dominions	MO(FE)A 1920, s 2
Variation or discharge	MO(FE)A 1920 contains no provisions affecting the court's power to vary or discharge a maintenance order, but enforcement will be subject to any equivalent powers which the corresponding legislation in the country of registration may accord to its courts	
Appeals	See Guides 71, 73	

INWARD

Registration in England of maintenance order made abroad

Who may apply	The Lord Chancellor, on receipt of a maintenance order made in a Commonwealth country which is not designated as a reciprocating country under MO(RE)A 1972, Pt I	MO(FE)A 1920, s 1

Which court	If the maintenance order was made by a court of superior jurisdiction, the Principal Registry of the Family Division; otherwise, the magistrates' court where the defendant resides	FPR 1991, r 7.17(1); MO(FE)A 1920, s 1; MO(FE)R 1922, r 1
Fee payable	High Court or magistrates' court: none	
What happens next	The senior district judge or justices' chief executive as the case may be enters the order in the register. In the magistrates' court, unless it is satisfied that it is undesirable to do so, the court will order payment to be made through an officer of the court or such other person as the court may specify. The order has full retrospective effect from the date specified in the order. Registration is an administrative act and the defendant cannot appeal against registration of the order	MO(FE)A 1920, s 1
Enforcement	*High Court* The order is enforceable as a High Court maintenance order and all proceedings may be taken on it as if it had been made by the High Court (including further registration in the magistrates' court)	MO(FE)A 1920, s 1(1)
	Magistrates' court The order is enforceable as a magistrates' court maintenance order. Monies collected are to be sent to the court which made the order or to such other person or authority as that court or the Lord Chancellor may from time to time direct. Monies collected for the following countries are to be sent to the courts direct: Newfoundland, Prince Edward Island, Yukon, Cocos (Keeling) Islands, Christmas Island (Indian Ocean), Guernsey and Jersey. If the court is in a colony not possessing responsible government or in a British Protectorate, the monies are to be paid to the Crown Agents for Overseas Governments and Administrations, 4 Millbank, London SW1	MO(FE)R 1922, r 6

	Enforcement proceedings are subject to the modifications of MCA 1980, ss 76 and 93, as specified in MOA 1950, s 18	MO(FE)A 1920, s 6

25B: Application in England and Wales for a Provisional Maintenance Order against a Respondent Abroad, and Vice Versa

OUTWARD

Confirmation abroad of provisional maintenance order made in England and Wales

Who may apply	An applicant for maintenance against a person who lives in one of the countries to which the Act is extended by Order in Council; there is no power under the Act to make a provisional affiliation order	MO(FE)A 1920, ss 3, 10
Which court	The magistrates' court acting for the area in which the applicant resides	*Collister v Collister* [1972] 1 All ER 334
What happens next	The court must hear an application for a maintenance order as if the respondent had received reasonable notice of the date of the hearing and the respondent had failed to appear; if satisfied of the justice of the application, the court must make a provisional maintenance order The evidence of any witnesses must be taken down as a deposition	MO(FE)A 1920, s 3(1), (2)
Documents required	Where a provisional maintenance order is made, the court must send to the Lord Chancellor, for transmission to the appropriate authority of the relevant country, the following documents: the depositions a certified copy of the order a statement of possible grounds of opposition (see Home Office Circular 469, 726/4) information for facilitating the identification of the person and ascertaining his whereabouts a photograph, where available	

	a marriage certificate the birth certificate(s) of any child(ren) for whom maintenance has been ordered, where appropriate. There is provision for the taking of further evidence and for the rescission of the provisional order on the remittal of the case to the original court by the foreign court	MO(FE)A 1920, s 3(3), (4); MO(FE)R 1922, r 7
Fee payable	None prescribed	

INWARD

Confirmation in England and Wales of provisional maintenance order made abroad

Application	The application for confirmation is sent by the Lord Chancellor to the appropriate court on receipt of the relevant documents from the foreign court	MO(FE)A 1920, s 4
Which court	The documents are to be sent to the justices' chief executive acting for the area within which the respondent is alleged to be living	MO(FE)R 1922, r 1
Documents required	The following documents should be sent to the justices' chief executive: the depositions a certified copy of the order a statement of possible grounds of opposition (see Home Office Circular 469, 726/4) information for facilitating the identification of the person and ascertaining his whereabouts a photograph, where available a marriage certificate the birth certificate(s) of any child(ren) for whom maintenance has been ordered, where appropriate a requisition for the notice to be served	MO(FE)A 1920, s 4(1)
Fee payable	None	
What happens next	A notice should be issued and served	MO(FE)R 1922, Sch 2, para 3

	At the hearing, it is open to the respondent only to oppose the confirmation of the order on any grounds on which he might have opposed the making of the original order If the respondent does not appear, it is open to the court to confirm the order with or without modifications If the respondent appears and the court is satisfied that it is necessary to obtain further evidence, it may adjourn the proceedings and/or remit the case to the court which made the original order	MO(FE)A 1920, s 4(2)–(5)
Enforcement	The order is enforceable as a magistrates' court maintenance order Monies collected are to be sent to the court which made the order or to such other person or authority as that court or the Lord Chancellor may from time to time direct Monies collected for the following countries are to be sent to the courts direct: Newfoundland, Prince Edward Island, Yukon, Cocos (Keeling) Islands, Christmas Island (Indian Ocean), Guernsey and Jersey If the court is in a colony not possessing responsible government or in a British Protectorate, the monies are to be paid to the Crown Agents for Overseas Governments and Administrations, 4 Millbank, London SW1	MO(FE)R 1922, r 6
	Enforcement proceedings are subject to the modifications of MCA 1980, ss 76 and 93, as specified in MOA 1950, s 18	MO(FE)A 1920, s 6

25C: Maintenance Order having been Made in England or Wales, Payee Seeks to Enforce it in Scotland or Northern Ireland, and Vice Versa

OUTWARD

Registration in Scotland or Northern Ireland of maintenance order made in England or Wales

Who may apply	The person entitled to payments under the order or on that person's behalf	MOA 1950(SJ)R 1950, r 2
Which court	The appropriate court is the court which made the order or to which the proceedings have since been transferred	MOA 1950, s 17(1)
Application	*High Court or county court* The applicant files in the court or registry in which the cause or matter is proceeding a certified copy of the order, an affidavit and a copy of the affidavit. The affidavit must state: the address and occupation of the payer the date the order was served on him or the reason why service has not been effected the reason why it is convenient that the order should be enforceable in Scotland or Northern Ireland the amount of any arrears that the order is not already registered	FPR 1991, r 7.19(1)
	Magistrates' court Applicant to make an oral or written application for the registration of the order Unless the applicant appears in person, a statutory declaration must be lodged containing the following information: the address of the person liable to make payments under the order the reason why it is convenient that the order should be enforced in Scotland or Northern Ireland unless a certificate of arrears is lodged, the amount of any arrears due under the order	

	a statement that the order is not already registered under Part II of the Act	MOA 1950, s 17; MOA 1950(SJ)R 1950, r 2
Fee payable	High Court and county court: £30 Magistrates' court: none	FPFO 1999, fee 9.1 MCA 1980, Sch 6, Pt I, Note 1(*b*)
What happens next	*High Court or county court* If the district judge is satisfied, the court sends the certified copy order and the affidavit to (in the case of a High Court order) the Court of Session or the Supreme Court of Northern Ireland or (in the case of a county court order) the Sheriff Court or the court of summary jurisdiction in whose area the payer resides, and the order is registered in that court	MOA 1950, s 17; FPR 1991, r 7.19(2), (6)
	Magistrates' court If the justice is satisfied that the payer resides in Scotland or Northern Ireland and that it is convenient that the order should be enforced there, he requires the clerk to send to the sheriff-clerk (in Scotland) or the clerk of the court in Northern Ireland: a certified copy of the order the certificate of arrears (in Form 3 of MOA 1950(SJ)R 1950) or statutory declaration (if any) if no statutory declaration has been lodged, written notice of the address of the person liable to make payments under the order. The court to which the documents are to be sent is the sheriff court or the court of summary jurisdiction having jurisdiction in the place where the person liable to make payments resides. The addresses of sheriff-clerks can be obtained from Home Office Circular No 241/1950. The addresses of courts of summary jurisdiction in Northern Ireland can be obtained from the Lord Chancellor's Department. The justices' chief executive of the original court must enter a memorandum of the proceedings in the register and, on receipt of notice of registration, must enter particulars in the register	MOA 1950, s 17; MOA 1950(SJ)R 1950, r 2(3), (4)

Transfer of registration	Once an order has been registered in the High Court in Northern Ireland or in a court of summary jurisdiction there, either party may apply to the court which made the order for its registration in a court of summary jurisdiction or the High Court in Northern Ireland instead	CJJA 1982, s 36
Enforcement	The order is enforceable as if it had been made in the court in which the order is registered. In Northern Ireland, enforcement is undertaken by the court. In Scotland, proceedings for enforcement must be taken in the payee's own name and legal representation is advisable	MOA 1950, ss 18, 20(3)
Appeals	See Guides 71–73	

INWARD

Registration in England and Wales of maintenance order made in Scotland or Northern Ireland

Application	Application for registration is made by the original court sending prescribed documents to the court in England	MOA 1950, s 17(1)(*b*), (*c*); MOA 1950(SJ)R 1950, r 7
Which court	If the order was made by the Court of Session or the Supreme Court of Northern Ireland, it is transmitted to the principal registry for registration; otherwise, the court of registration is the court of summary jurisdiction acting for the place in England in which the defendant appears to be	MOA 1950, s 17(3)(*b*); FPR 1991, r 7.20(1); MOA 1950(SJ)R 1950, r 7
Fee payable	High Court: none prescribed Magistrates' court: none prescribed	
What happens next	On receipt of the certified copy of the maintenance order, the proper officer of the principal registry or the justices' chief executive must cause the order to be registered in that court and gives written notice of the registration of the order to the original court	MOA 1950, s 17(4); FPR 1991, r 7.20(1); MOA 1950(SJ)R 1950, r 7
Enforcement	The order may be enforced in all respects as if it had been made by the court in which it is registered and as if that court had had jurisdiction to make it.	

	A Scottish order which carries interest will continue to do so if registered in the High Court, but not if registered in a magistrates' court.	
	The senior district judge of the principal registry may, on written application, order that an order registered there may be enforced in a district registry	FPR 1991, r 7.20(6)
	The order is enforceable as a magistrates' court maintenance order subject to the amendment of MCA 1980, ss 76 and 93 (means of payments orders); see Guide 23	MOA 1950, s 18(1), (1A), (2), (2ZA), (2ZB)
Payment of money	On registration in the magistrates' court, the court orders payments to be made through the collecting officer of the court or through the collecting officer of some other court of summary jurisdiction.	
	An alternative means of payment order may be made on enforcement of the order (see Guide 33).	

25D: Variation or Discharge of Registered Maintenance Orders and Cancellation of Registration (Scotland and Northern Ireland)

Variation or discharge	*Maintenance order made by or registered in the High Court* The court which made the order retains the exclusive jurisdiction to vary or discharge it. However, in the case of a Scottish order registered in the High Court, the payer on application may adduce in the High Court evidence for the purpose of variation or discharge proceedings in the original court. The application is made by lodging in the principal registry a request for an appointment before a district judge. Notice of the appointment is given by post to both parties	FPR 1991, r 7.20(3); MOA 1950, s 21
	Any other case Application to vary the rate of payments must be made to the court in which the order is registered; however, application to vary it in any other respect or to discharge it must be made to the court which made it	

	Either party may, on application to the other court, adduce his evidence there for transmission to the court hearing the variation or discharge application	MOA 1950, s 22
	If the order is varied, notice of the variation is to be given to the prescribed officer of the court which made the order and any court in which the order is registered. The notice must consist of a certified copy of the order of variation	MOA 1950, s 23; MOA 1950(SJ)R 1950, r 10
Fee payable	High Court and county court: £60	FPFO 1999, fee 4.3
	Magistrates' court: none	MCA 1980, Sch 6, Pt I
Cancellation	The payee may apply to the court where the order is registered to cancel the registration, in the High Court ex parte by affidavit to the district judge and in the magistrates' court by lodging a written application stating the date of registration together with a copy of the order with the justices' chief executive of the court. The order will then be cancelled unless a variation application is pending. The court of registration gives notice of the cancellation to the original court	FPR 1991, r 7.20(5); MOA 1950, s 24; MOA 1950(SJ)R 1950, rr 11, 12, 12A
	The payer may apply to the original court if he has ceased to reside in the jurisdiction of the court where the order is registered; if satisfied, the court sends notice to the court of registration which cancels the registration	MOA 1950, s 24(2)
Fee payable	High Court and county court: £60	FPFO 1999, fee 4.3
	Magistrates' court: none	

25E: Maintenance Order having been Made in England or Wales, Payee Seeks to Enforce it Abroad, and Vice Versa

OUTWARD

Registration abroad of maintenance order made in England

Who may apply	The payee under the order	MO(RE)A 1972, s 2(1)

Which court	*High Court or county court* The court or registry in which the order was made *Magistrates' court* Application is to be made to the justices' chief executive of the magistrates' court which made the order	MO(RE)A 1972, s 2(1); MC(REMO)R 1974, r 3
Application	*High Court or county court* The following must be filed: an affidavit stating the reasons for believing that the payer resides in the country in question, and the current arrears, the date to which they are calculated and the date the next payment falls due a certified copy of the maintenance order a statement giving all known information as to the payer's whereabouts all known information to help identify the payer (including employer, occupation and date and place of issue of passport) if possible, a photograph of the payer	FPR 1991, r 7.31
	In the cases of Australia, Canada, New Zealand and South Africa, if the payer's address is unknown the court can cause enquiries to be made	*PD of 10 February 1976*
	Magistrates' court The application must: specify the date on which the order was made contain such particulars as are known to the applicant of the whereabouts of the payer and the nature and location of his assets specify any matters likely to assist in the identification of the payer where possible, be accompanied by a recent photograph of the payer. The court, if satisfied that the payer is residing in a reciprocating country, will send the relevant documents to the Lord Chancellor with a view to their being transmitted to the responsible authority in the reciprocating country	MO(RE)A 1972, s 2

	If the applicant relies on the alternative ground (added into MO(RE)A 1972 by CJJA 1982, Sch 11, Pt III, paras 8, 9(*a*)) that the payer has assets in the foreign country, the affidavit or application should also give reasons for believing that fact and set out the nature and location of the assets.	
Fee payable	High Court or county court: £30 Magistrates' court: none	FPFO 1999, fee 9.2 MCA 1980, Sch 6, Pt I, Note 1(*b*)
Applicability to Ireland	MO(RE)A 1972, Pt I applies to the Republic of Ireland as modified by SI 1993/594. In addition to the basic requirements, the applicant files a statement that the payer appeared in the proceedings or a document (or certified copy) establishing that notice of the proceedings was served on him, a document establishing that notice of the order was sent to him and a certified copy of any legal aid certificate held by the payee for those proceedings	MO(RE)A 1972, s 2, as modified; FPR 1991, r 7.37(2)
	The procedure for registration on the basis of assets in the foreign country is not available in the Republic of Ireland. A remedy may, however, exist under CJJA 1982 and reference should be made to Guide 25L.	
Applicability to Hague Convention countries	MO(RE)A 1972, Pt I applies to Hague Convention countries as modified by SI 1993/593 and SI 1999/1318. In addition to the basic requirements, the affidavit or application must state whether the time for appealing against the order has expired and whether an appeal is pending. The applicant files in addition a statement as to whether the payer appeared in the proceedings and, if not, a document (or certified copy) establishing that notice of the proceedings including notice of the substance of the claim was served on him, a document which establishes that notice of the order was sent to him and a statement whether the payee had legal aid for those proceedings or the instant application with a certified copy of any such legal aid certificate	MO(RE)A 1972, s 2; FPR 1991 r 7.38(3), (4)

	The procedure for registration on the basis of assets in the foreign country is not available in Hague Convention countries. A remedy may, however, exist in the case of the EU and, soon, for EFTA countries under CJJA 1982; reference should be made to Guide 25L.	
Applicability to United States of America	MO(RE)A 1972, Pt I, as modified by SI 1995/2709, applies to most States in the United States of America. The application follows the procedure for Hague Convention countries, except that the information required from the applicant is to be in the form of a sworn statement	MC(REMO)(USA)R 1995, r 3(*b*)
Restrictions	In the case of territories indicated (a), (b) or (c) in the Table, the facility does not exist to enforce respectively (a) orders obtained by or in favour of a public authority, (b) orders for the payment of birth or funeral expenses of a child, or (c) affiliation orders	
What happens next	If satisfied, the court sends the relevant documents to the Lord Chancellor with a view to their being transmitted to the responsible authority in the reciprocating country, provided the Lord Chancellor is satisfied that there is sufficient information. He has a discretion to transmit them or not. The relevant documents are: a certified copy of the maintenance order (or, for the USA, three certified copies) a certificate signed by the proper officer certifying that the order is enforceable in the United Kingdom a certificate of arrears so signed a statement giving such information as the officer possesses as to the whereabouts of the payer and the nature and location of his assets in that country a statement giving such information as the officer possesses for facilitating the identification of the payer where available, a photograph of the payer.	
Appeals	See Guides 71–73	

INWARD

Registration in England of maintenance order made abroad

Who may apply	Where the Lord Chancellor receives a certified copy of a maintenance order made by a court in a reciprocating country and it appears that the payer is residing or has assets in the United Kingdom, he must send it to the prescribed officer of the appropriate court	MO(RE)A 1972, s 6(2)
Which court	The appropriate court is the magistrates' court where the payer resides or where the payer has assets. If the justices' chief executive receives a certified order and, after taking such steps as he considers appropriate, is satisfied that the payer is not residing and has no assets within the jurisdiction of the court, he will return the order to the Lord Chancellor with a statement giving such information as he possesses as to the whereabouts of the payer and the nature and location of his assets	MO(RE)A 1972, s 6(4)
Fee payable	None prescribed	
What happens next	Unless the justices' chief executive returns the order to the Lord Chancellor under MO(RE)A 1972, s 6(4), he registers the order by means of a signed entry in his register and specifies the section of the Act under which the order is registered	MO(RE)A 1972, s 6(3); MC(REMO)R 1974, r 8(1), (3)
Enforcement	The order is enforceable as a magistrates' court maintenance order. For the purposes of enforcement of the order, MCA 1980, ss 76 and 93 are modified in accordance with MO(RE)A 1972, ss 8(4A) and (4B) (see also Guide 23) The justices' chief executive is under a duty, in any case where the order is in arrears to an amount equal to four weekly payments, to take enforcement proceedings in his own name. The justices' chief executive is also under a duty to take reasonable steps to notify the payee of the steps available for the enforcement of the order	MO(RE)A 1972, s 8; MC(REMO)R 1974, rr 9, 9A

Applicability to Ireland	The provisions outlined above apply equally to orders made in the Republic of Ireland and registered in the United Kingdom under the Act, except for the modifications made by REMO(RI)O 1993. The main differences are that:	
	under s 6, the order will not be registered if such registration is contrary to public policy, if the payer did not appear and was not duly served with the summons, or if the order is irreconcilable with a judgment given in the United Kingdom in proceedings between the same parties	MO(RE)A 1972, s 6(5), as modified
	on registration, notice must be given on the form specified in MC(REMO)(RI)R 1975, Sch, Pt I and notice must also be given to the payer	MO(RE)A 1972, s 6(6), as modified
	a right of appeal against registration is provided	MO(RE)A 1972, s 6(7)–(9), as modified
	a right of appeal against refusal to register is provided	MO(RE)A 1972, s 6(10), (11), as modified; MC(REMO)(RI)R 1975, r 9
	written authority to enforce the order is required	MC(REMO)(RI)R 1975, r 10
	partial registration and enforcement of the order is authorised	MO(RE)A 1972, s 8(2A), (2B)
	the order is expressed to be enforceable as an affiliation order	MO(RE)A 1972, s 8(4), as modified
Applicability to Hague Convention countries	The provisions outlined above apply equally to orders made in a Hague Convention country, except for the modifications made by REMO(HCC)O 1993 and REMO(HCC)(V)O 1999. The main differences are that:	
	registration may be refused if there was an error of jurisdiction in the court which made the order, if registration is manifestly contrary to public policy, if the order was obtained by fraud in connection with a matter of procedure, if there are similar proceedings pending between the same parties in the United Kingdom and those proceedings were the first to be instituted or if the order is incompatible with a similar order between the parties in the United Kingdom or in another country and the latter order fulfils the conditions necessary for registration	

	the justices' chief executive will refuse to register the order if the payer did not appear in the proceedings in which the order was made and there was a defect of service	
	an appeals procedure is prescribed and forms are prescribed for the purposes of giving notices under the modified Act and for the purposes of any appeal	MO(RE)A 1972, s 6, as modified by REMO(HCC)O 1993, REMO(HCC)(V)O 1999 and MC(REMO)(HCC)R 1980
Applicability to United States of America	The provisions outlined above apply equally to orders from the States specified in REMO(USA)O 1995	MO(RE)A 1972, s 6, as modified by REMO(USA)O 1995 and MC(REMO)(USA)R 1995, r 3(*b*)
Payment of money	The sum to be paid, if expressed in a foreign currency, is calculated on the basis of the rate of exchange prevailing at the date of registration of the order or the date of last variation. A written certificate of a bank officer in the United Kingdom is evidence of the rate of exchange prevailing at that time	
	Payments under the order are to be made to the justices' chief executive of the registering court. The justices' chief executive is required to send the payments to the court which made the order or to such other person or authority as the Secretary of State may direct	
	If the court which made the order is in one of the countries listed in MC(REMO)R 1974, Sch 2, any such sums must be sent to the Crown Agents for Overseas Governments and Administrations for transmission to the person to whom they are due	MO(RE)A 1972, s 16; MC(REMO)R 1974, r 9

25F: Application in England and Wales for a Provisional Maintenance Order against a Respondent Abroad, and Vice Versa

OUTWARD

Confirmation abroad of provisional maintenance order made in England and Wales

Who may apply	Any person entitled to make an application for a maintenance order	
Which court	A magistrates' court has jurisdiction as if the respondent resided in England and Wales and as if notice of hearing had been duly served on him	MO(RE)A 1972, s 3(1)
Fee payable	None prescribed	
What happens next	The court hears the application and may make a provisional maintenance order For procedure, see — If a provisional maintenance order is made, the justices' chief executive sends the following documents to the Lord Chancellor for transmission to the responsible authority in the reciprocating country: a certified copy of the maintenance order a document authenticated in accordance with MC(REMO)R 1974, r 5, setting out or summarising the evidence given in the proceedings a certificate signed by the justices' clerk of possible grounds of opposition a statement giving such information as was available to the court as to the whereabouts of the payer a statement giving such information as the justices' clerk possesses for facilitating the identification of the payer where available, a photograph of the payer.	 MC(REMO)R 1974, Sch A1

Applicability to Ireland	A separate procedure exists for making maintenance orders in England and Wales against persons resident in the Republic of Ireland	
	An applicant for a maintenance order who is habitually resident in England and Wales may make application for an order	MO(RE)A 1972, s 3(1), as modified by REMO(RI)O 1993
	The application is made to the magistrates' court which would have jurisdiction to make a maintenance order if the respondent were residing in England and Wales and a notice of hearing had been duly served on him	
	On hearing the application, the court may make a provisional maintenance order	MO(RE)A 1972, s 3(1), (2), as modified
	For procedure, see —	MC(REMO)(RI)R 1975, Sch A1
	On the making of a provisional order, the following documents must be sent to the Lord Chancellor for transmission to the responsible authority in Ireland:	
	a certified copy of the maintenance order	
	a document setting out or summarising the evidence given in the proceedings authenticated by a certificate signed by one of the justices before whom the evidence was given that the document is the original or a true copy	
	a certificate signed by the justices' clerk of the possible grounds of opposition	
	a notice addressed to the payer stating that a provisional order has been made, that it has no effect unless or until confirmed with or without alteration by the court making the order and that, in considering whether or not to confirm the provisional order, the court will take into account any representations made or any evidence adduced by or on behalf of the payer within 3 weeks from the date of service of the notice	
	a statement giving such information as the justices' clerk possesses as to the whereabouts of the payer	

	a statement giving such information as the officer possesses for facilitating the identification of the payer	
	where available, a photograph of the payer	MO(RE)A 1972, s 3(5), as modified
	The court is obliged to take into account any representations made or evidence adduced by or on behalf of the respondent, and a copy of any representations or evidence must be served by the justices' chief executive on the applicant before the hearing	
	The applicant must be notified in writing of any date fixed for the hearing of the representations or evidence in the document	
	The court may not confirm, with or without alteration, the order earlier than 3 weeks after the date of service of the notice mentioned above	
	The court will not confirm the order unless the first 4 documents above have been served on the payer in accordance with the law of Ireland	MO(RE)A 1972, s 3(6), (6A), (6B), as modified
	Where a maintenance order has been made, the justices' chief executive sends to the payer by registered post notice of the confirmation of the order and to the Lord Chancellor the following documents for transmission to the responsible authority in the Republic of Ireland:	
	a certified copy of the order	
	a certificate signed by the justices' chief executive certifying that the order is enforceable in the United Kingdom	
	if the payer did not appear in the proceedings in which the order was confirmed, the original or a certified copy of a document that establishes that the first 4 documents referred to above have been served on the payer	
	a document that establishes that notice of the confirmation of the order was sent to the respondent	
	if the payee received legal aid in the proceedings, a written statement to that effect	MO(RE)A 1972, s 3(6C), as modified

Applicability to Hague Convention countries	A separate procedure exists for making maintenance orders against payers resident in a Hague Convention country	MO(RE)A 1972, s 3, as modified by REMO(HCC)O 1993 and REMO(HCC)(V)O 1999
	An applicant who is habitually resident in England and Wales may make application for a maintenance order	MO(RE)A 1972, s 3(1), as modified
	The application is made to the court which would have jurisdiction to make a maintenance order if the respondent were residing in England and Wales and a notice of hearing had been duly served on him	
	On hearing an application, the court may make a maintenance order	MO(RE)A 1972, s 3(1), (3), as modified
	For procedure, see —	MC(REMO)(HCC)R 1980, Sch 1A
	On the making of an application the following documents must be sent to the Lord Chancellor for transmission to the appropriate authority in the Hague Convention country:	
	notice of the institution of the proceedings, including notice of the substance of the application	
	a statement signed by the justices' chief executive giving such information as he possesses as to the whereabouts of the respondent	
	a statement giving such information as the officer possesses for facilitating the identification of the respondent	
	where available, a photograph of the respondent	
	The notice mentioned above must be served in accordance with the laws of the Hague Convention country or in such other manner as the Lord Chancellor may authorise at least 6 weeks before the hearing at which any order is made	MO(RE)A 1972, s 3(5), (6C), as modified
	The court is obliged to take into account any representations made or evidence adduced by or on behalf of the respondent, and a copy of any representations or evidence must be served by the justices' clerk on the applicant before the hearing	MO(RE)A 1972, s 3(6), (6A), as modified

	The justices' chief executive must give the respondent notice in writing of the date fixed for the hearing	MO(RE)A 1972, s 3(6B), as modified
	Where a maintenance order has been made, the justices' chief executive must send the following documents to the Lord Chancellor for transmission to the appropriate authority in the Hague Convention country with a view to recognition and enforcement of the order:	
	a certified copy of the order	
	a certificate signed by the justices' chief executive certifying that the order is enforceable and that it is no longer subject to the ordinary forms of review	
	a written statement signed by the justices' chief executive as to whether the respondent appeared and, if not, the original or a certified copy of a document that establishes that the notice of the institution of the proceedings and substance of the application was duly served	
	a document that establishes that notice of the order was sent to the respondent	
	a written statement signed by the justices' chief executive as to whether or not the applicant received legal aid in the proceedings	MO(RE)A 1972, s 3(6D), as modified

INWARD

Confirmation in England and Wales of maintenance order made abroad

Who may apply	Where the Lord Chancellor receives a certified copy of a provisional order from a reciprocating country and it appears that the payer under the order is residing in the United Kingdom, he must send the relevant documents to the justices' chief executive of the appropriate court	MO(RE)A 1972, s 7(2)
Which court	The appropriate court is the court having jurisdiction where the payer resides or where the payer has assets	MO(RE)A 1972, s 21

Documents required	The Lord Chancellor must send to the justices' chief executive a certified copy of the order, a duly authenticated document setting out or summarising the evidence and a statement of possible grounds of opposition	MO(RE)A 1972, s 7(2)
Fee payable	None prescribed	
What happens next	A notice must be issued and served in accordance with MC(REMO)R 1974, Sch A1, para 3. The court then proceeds as if an application for a maintenance order had been made against the payer If the payer establishes any defence he might have raised in the proceedings in which the order was made, the court will refuse to confirm the order. In any other case, the court confirms the order either with or without such alteration as the court thinks reasonable If the court confirms the order, the justices' chief executive registers the order. At the same time as confirming the order, the court will make an order as to the method of payment (payment to a chief executive of a court, payment by standing order to a clerk of a court or payment under an attachment of earnings order) If the court refuses to confirm the order, the justices' chief executive must return the documents to the Lord Chancellor. If the summons cannot be served, the justices' chief executive returns the documents to the Lord Chancellor, together with a statement giving such information as he possesses as to the whereabouts of the payer.	
Applicability to Ireland	A separate procedure exists for the confirmation in England and Wales of maintenance orders made in the Republic of Ireland The main differences are that the order may not be registered if: such registration is contrary to public policy the payer did not appear and was not duly served with the summons	MO(RE)A 1972, s 6, as modified by REMO(RI)O 1993

	the order is irreconcilable with a judgment given in the United Kingdom in proceedings between the same parties	MO(RE)A 1972, s 6(5), as modified
	On registration, notice must be given in the form specified in MC(REMO)(RI)R 1975, Sch, Pt I and notice must also be given to the payer	MO(RE)A 1972, s 6(6), as modified
	A right of appeal against registration is provided	MO(RE)A 1972, s 6(7)–(9), as modified
	A right of appeal against refusal to register is provided	MO(RE)A 1972, s 6(10), (11), as modified; MC(REMO)(RI)R 1975, r 9
	Written authority to enforce the order is required	MC(REMO)(RI)R 1975, r 10
	Partial registration and enforcement of the order is authorised	MO(RE)A 1972, s 8(2A), (2B)
	The order is expressed to be enforceable as an affiliation order	MO(RE)A 1972, s 8(4), as modified
Applicability to Hague Convention countries	A separate procedure exists for the registration in a United Kingdom court of an order made in a Hague Convention country	MO(RE)A 1972, s 6, as modified by REMO(HCC)O 1993, REMO(HCC)(V)O 1999 and MC(REMO)(HCC)R 1980
	The following differences are of importance:	
	registration may be refused if there was an error of jurisdiction in the court which made the order, if registration is manifestly contrary to public policy, if the order was obtained by fraud in connection with a matter of procedure, if there are similar proceedings pending between the same parties in the United Kingdom and those proceedings were the first to be instituted or if the order is incompatible with a similar order between the parties in the United Kingdom or in another country and the latter order fulfils the conditions necessary for registration	
	the justices' chief executive will refuse to register the order if the payer did not appear in the proceedings in which the order was made and there was a defect in service	

	an appeals procedure is prescribed and forms are prescribed for the purposes of giving notices under the modified Act and for the purposes of any appeal partial registration and enforcement, on request, is permissible	MO(RE)A 1972, s 6, as modified
Enforcement	The order is enforceable as a magistrates' court maintenance order. For the purposes of enforcement of the order, MCA 1980, ss 76 and 93 are modified in accordance with MO(RE)A 1972, s 8(4A), (4B) The justices' chief executive is under a duty, in any case where the order is in arrears to an amount equal to four weekly payments, to take enforcement proceedings in his own name. The justices' chief executive is also under a duty to take reasonable steps to notify the payee of the steps available for the enforcement of the order	MO(RE)A 1972, s 8; MC(REMO)R 1974, rr 9, 9A
Payment of money	The sum to be paid, if expressed in a foreign currency, is calculated on the basis of the rate of exchange prevailing at the date of registration of the order or the date of last variation. A written certificate of a bank officer in the United Kingdom is evidence of the rate of exchange prevailing at that time Payments under the order are to be made to the justices' chief executive of the registering court. The justices' chief executive is required to send the payments to the court which made the order or to such other person or authority as the Lord Chancellor may direct If the court which made the order is in one of the countries listed in MC(REMO)R 1974, Sch 2, any such sums must be sent to the Crown Agents for Overseas Governments and Administrations for transmission to the person to whom they are due	MO(RE)A 1972, s 16; MC(REMO)R 1974, r 9

25G: Application to Vary, Discharge or Revoke an Order Registered under the Maintenance Orders (Reciprocal Enforcement) Act 1972, Pt I

Legal background

Where a maintenance order has been registered abroad under MO(RE)A 1972 for enforcement, the power to vary the order under the provision ordinarily applicable (eg MCA 1973, s 3(1)) is modified by MO(RE)A 1972, s 5.

Procedure

General position	In addition to its usual powers, the court may vary such a maintenance order by a provisional order. If the court proposes to increase the payments, the order varying *must* be a provisional order, unless both the payer and payee appear or the applicant appears and the process has been duly served on the other party	MO(RE)A 1972, s 5(3)
	For procedure, see —	MC(REMO)R 1974, Sch A1
	If the order is a provisional order, the court sends a certified copy of it and a note or a summary of the evidence taken, authenticated in accordance with the rules, to the foreign court for confirmation	MO(RE)A 1972, s 5(4); FPR 1991, r 7.32; MC(REMO)R 1974, r 6
	The court in the reciprocating country may, under powers given to it by its own laws, transmit to the original court in England and Wales which made the order a provisional order varying or revoking it, together with an authenticated note or summary of the evidence which it heard. The court must then proceed as if the application to vary or revoke had been made to it and may confirm or refuse to confirm the order. If it confirms a variation order, it may do so with or without alteration	MO(RE)A 1972, s 5(5), (6)
	The order, whether provisional or not, must state the date from which it takes effect; in the case of a provisional order, it does so in the form in which it is confirmed (ie subject to any alteration made by the confirming court)	MO(RE)A 1972, s 5(7)
	There is no right of appeal against the making of a provisional order	MO(RE)A 1972, s 12(1)

Fee payable	None prescribed	
Applicability to Ireland	The provisional order procedure does not apply. When a maintenance order has been registered under MO(RE)A 1972, s 2 in the Republic of Ireland for enforcement and the payee applies for its variation or discharge, certified copies of the application and of the affidavit, or in the magistrates' court the evidence, in support are sent by the court to the Lord Chancellor for transmission to the responsible body in Ireland for service on the payer. The court must allow 3 weeks from the date of service and must take into account any representations made and evidence adduced by the payer before varying or revoking the order	MO(RE)A 1972, s 5, as substituted by REMO(RI)O 1993
	For procedure, see —	MC(REMO)(RI)R 1975, Sch A1
	The order is immediately effective and a certified copy of it and details of the service of the application are sent to the Irish court by which the order is being enforced	MO(RE)A 1972, s 5(4)–(6), as substituted
Applicability to Hague Convention countries	Article 12 of the Hague Convention states: "There shall be no review by the authority of the State addressed of the merits of the decision" and the Permanent Bureau in the Hague has confirmed that the intention of Art 12 is to prevent receiving countries from varying orders except for the method of payment	REMO(HCC)(V)O 1999
	Any request by a payer living in the UK for variation of an order made by a Hague Convention country and registered in the UK should be sent to the Reciprocal Enforcement of Maintenance Orders (REMO) Section at Lord Chancellor's Department, Selborne House, 54–60 Victoria Street, London SW1E 6QW for onward transmission to the overseas authority	

Applicability to United States of America	The provisional order procedure does not apply. When a maintenance order has been registered under MO(RE)A 1972 for enforcement and the payee applies for variation or revocation, the justices' chief executive sends to the Lord Chancellor notice of the institution of proceedings, including notice of the substance of the application, with a view to its being transmitted to the appropriate authority in the specified State for service on the payer and also sends to the payer notice in writing of the date fixed for the hearing by post to his last known or usual place of abode	MO(RE)A 1972, s 5(4), as modified by REMO(USA)O 1995
	The order may not be varied or revoked unless the notice is served by the appropriate authority, and any representations and evidence adduced by the payer must be served on the payee before the hearing and taken into account by the court	MO(RE)A 1972, s 5(5), as modified by REMO(USA)O 1995
	Where the application is made by the payer, the justices' chief executive is required to arrange for the service of notice of institution of the proceedings, including notice of the substance of the application, on the payee	MO(RE)A 1972, s 5(6), as modified by REMO(USA)O 1995
	Where the order is varied or revoked, the justices' chief executive must send to the Lord Chancellor three certified copies of the order and a written statement signed by the justices' clerk as to whether both parties appeared in the proceedings and, if only the applicant appeared, the original or certified copy of the document establishing proof of service of the notice of the proceedings upon the other party. The Lord Chancellor will send these documents to the appropriate authority in the specified State for registration and enforcement	MO(RE)A 1972, s 5(7), as modified by REMO(USA)O 1995
	The variation or revocation takes effect as from the date of the order but, in the case of revocation, arrears continue to be enforceable	MO(RE)A 1972, s 5(8), (9), as modified by REMO(USA)O 1995

25H: Applicant in England or Wales Makes Maintenance Claim for Transmission Abroad for Determination There against Respondent, and Vice Versa

OUTWARD

Application by person in England or Wales for recovery etc of maintenance in a convention country

General position	A person in the United Kingdom who claims to be entitled to recover, in a convention country, maintenance from another person is required to make an application to the Lord Chancellor The application must be made through the justices' chief executive acting for the area in which the applicant resides and the chief executive is under a duty to assist the applicant complete the relevant forms. No forms are prescribed, but a set of forms are recommended in Home Office Circular 54/1975 The Lord Chancellor is under a duty to forward the application to the appropriate authority in the convention country unless he is satisfied that the application is not made in good faith or that it does not comply with the requirements of the law applied in that country. If the Lord Chancellor requires further information, he can request the justices' chief executive to obtain the information from the court, and the court is under a duty to furnish the information	MO(RE)A 1972, s 26
Fee payable	None prescribed	

Applicability to United States of America	For the states specified in RM(USA)O 1993, there is an additional requirement for a certificate signed by a justice to the effect that the application sets out facts from which it may be determined that the respondent owes a duty to maintain the applicant and any other person named in the application, and that a court in the specified state may "obtain jurisdiction of the respondent" or his property must be registered in the court by the justices' chief executive	MO(RE)A 1972, s 26(3A)

INWARD

Pursuit in England of a claim for maintenance made in a convention country

General position	Where the Lord Chancellor receives an application from the appropriate authority in a convention country for the recovery of maintenance, he sends the claim to the chief executive of the magistrates' court for the area in which the respondent is residing. The claim is to be treated as an application for an appropriate order made at a time when the application was received by the Lord Chancellor	MO(RE)A 1972, ss 27A, 27B
	If a notice of hearing cannot be served, the justices' chief executive of the court is required to return the application and documents to the Lord Chancellor, together with such information he may have as to the whereabouts of the respondent or, if the justices' chief executive is satisfied that the respondent is residing in the area of another magistrates' court, he may send the documents to the justices' chief executive of that court and notify the Lord Chancellor accordingly	MO(RE)A 1972, s 27B(3), (4)
	For procedure, see —	MC(RAM)R 1975, Sch 2
	If the court makes an order, the clerk must register the order and, at the time of making the order, the court orders payments to be made to the justices' chief executive of a magistrates' court or to a justices' chief executive by standing order or by an attachment of earnings order	

	The justices' chief executive must also notify the Lord Chancellor that the order has been registered	MO(RE)A 1972, s 27C; MC(RAM)R 1975, r 6
	Where the application is for an order under DPMCA 1978, s 2, the provisions of the 1978 Act are modified by MO(RE)A 1972, ss 28 and 28A. The order is, unless for the time being registered in the High Court, enforceable as a magistrates' court maintenance order as defined in MCA 1980, s 150(1). The power of the court to make orders for the method of payment under MCA 1980, ss 76 and 93 is modified	MO(RE)A 1972, s 33; see also MC(RAM)R 1975, r 7
	There is power to transfer the order to another magistrates' court if the payer moves to the jurisdiction of that court	MO(RE)A 1972, s 32
	Payments received by the justices' chief executive under the order must be sent to the Lord Chancellor by post	MC(RAM)R 1975, r 7
Fee payable	None prescribed	

25I: Variation and Revocation of Orders Registered under the Maintenance Orders (Reciprocal Enforcement) Act 1972, Pt II

General position	Jurisdiction to vary or revoke an order registered under MO(RE)A 1972, Pt II may only be exercised by the registering court and, where the registering court revokes an order, it must cancel the registration	MO(RE)A 1972, s 34(1), (2)
	Application is made through the appropriate authority in the convention country and transmitted to the Lord Chancellor, who then sends it together with any accompanying documents (which may include evidence taken in the convention country and which is admissible under MO(RE)A 1972, s 36) to the justices' chief executive of the registering court	MO(RE)A 1972, s 34(3)
	For procedure, see —	MC(RAM)R 1975, Sch 2

	On the variation of a registered order, if the court is satisfied that payment has not been made in accordance with the order, the court may also order that payments are made to the justices' chief executive of that court or of any other magistrates' court, either directly or by standing order, or the court may order payment by attachment of earnings	MO(RE)A 1972, s 34A
	The application is treated as if an application for variation had been made, and the court must proceed as if the applicant were before the court	MO(RE)A 1972, s 35(3)
	Where the respondent does not appear, if the court is satisfied that the respondent is residing outside England and Wales and that notice of the proceedings has been given in the prescribed form, the court may nevertheless proceed	MO(RE)A 1972, s 35(3); MC(RAM)R 1975, r 8, Sch 2
	Where the court makes or refuses to make an order, any person has the same right of appeal as they would have if the registered order had been made by that court	MO(RE)A 1972, s 34(4)
Fee payable	None prescribed	

25J: Money Judgment or Order having been Made in England or Wales, Payee Seeks to Enforce it in a Commonwealth Country, and Vice Versa

Legal background

The reader is reminded that this Guide deals only with "family proceedings". Procedural changes made by the Civil Procedure Rules 1998 do not (yet) apply to such proceedings (see further annotations under FPR 1991, r 1.3). For a description of the steps to be taken in proceedings which are not "family proceedings" and which are governed by CPR 1998, see the *Civil Court Service* (Jordan Publishing Ltd).

OUTWARD

Enforcement in certain Commonwealth countries of a High Court judgment or order for payment of a sum of money

Who may apply	The judgment creditor under a judgment or order given or made by the High Court	AJA 1920, ss 10(1), 12(1)

Which court	The principal registry or district registry in which the cause is proceeding	
Documents required	An affidavit which must: give particulars of the judgment or order show that the creditor wishes to enforce in a specified Commonwealth territory to which the Act extends state the name, trade or business and usual last known place of residence of both the creditor and the debtor, so far as known	RSC Ord 71, r 13(1), (2)
Fee payable	£30	FPFO 1999, fee 14.5
What happens next	The court issues to the creditor a certified copy of the judgment or order, ie an office copy bearing an appropriate certificate signed by the district judge. The creditor must transmit the copy to the territory in question and secure enforcement in accordance with its procedures	
Limitations	The Commonwealth country's relevant provisions may contain conditions similar to those which apply to judgments and orders sought to be registered for enforcement in England and Wales (see INWARD section below)	
Note	A county court judgment or order transferred to the High Court under FPR 1991, r 7.3 may also be enforced by this method, provided that the Commonwealth country's court interprets its relevant provisions as accommodating that situation	

INWARD

Enforcement in England and Wales of a money judgment or order of a superior court in certain Commonwealth countries

Who may apply	A judgment creditor under a judgment or order obtained in a superior court in the Commonwealth country	AJA 1920, ss 9(1), 12(1)

Which court	The High Court; RSC seem to assume that the application will be made to the Queen's Bench Division but, if the judgment or order was made in proceedings which in England and Wales would have been family proceedings, the application may be more appropriately made to the Principal Registry of the Family Division	
Application	In the first instance, ex parte by affidavit. However, the court may direct that an originating summons (RSC App A, Form 10) be issued	RSC Ord 71, r 2
Documents required	An affidavit: exhibiting the judgment or order or an authenticated copy and (if it is not in English) a translation certified by a notary public or verified by affidavit stating the name, trade or business and usual or last known address of the debtor and creditor, so far as known confirming the creditor's entitlement to enforce the judgment or order, the amount outstanding under it and that it does not contravene AJA 1920, s 9(2) (see Limitations below) verifying that Protection of Trading Interests Act 1980, s 5 does not apply	RSC Ord 71, r 3
Fee payable	£120	FPFO 1999, fee 1.1
What happens next	Security may be required for the costs of registration and of any application by the debtor to set the registration aside. The order must state a period (during which execution cannot be issued) when the debtor may apply to set the registration aside, and that period may be extended from time to time	RSC Ord 71, rr 4, 5
Service	Notice (as well as the order, if made on summons) must be served on the debtor giving details of the judgment or order and the order for registration, giving the creditor's or his solicitor's name and address for service and telling the debtor of his right to apply to set the registration aside and the time within which the application must be made	RSC Ord 71, r 7

Setting aside	An application by the debtor to set aside the registration is made by summons supported by affidavit. The court may order an issue to be tried. The registration may be set aside if the court finds that the judgment or order contravenes AJA 1920, s 9(2) (see Limitations below), that it is not just or convenient that it be enforced in England and Wales or that there is some other sufficient reason to set aside the registration	RSC Ord 71, r 9
	Fee payable: £60	FPFO 1999, fee 4.3
Enforcement	Execution cannot be issued until the time specified in the order for registration (as extended) has expired and any application to set aside has been disposed of. An affidavit of service of the notice on the debtor must be filed	RSC Ord 71, r 10
Limitations	The application must generally be made within 12 months of the date of the judgment or order, although the court has power to allow a later application	AJA 1920, s 9(1)
	A judgment or order cannot be registered for enforcement in England and Wales under this provision if:	
	the original court acted without jurisdiction	
	the debtor did not live or carry on business within that court's jurisdiction and did not appear or submit to the court's jurisdiction	
	the debtor (being the defendant) was not duly served with the court's process and did not appear	
	the judgment or order was obtained by fraud	
	the debtor satisfies the court that an appeal is pending or that he is entitled to, and intends to, appeal	
	the action would not have been entertained by the High Court for some public policy or similar reason	AJA 1920, s 9(2)
Appeals	See Guides 73, 75	

25K: Enforcement Abroad of an English or Welsh Judgment or Order for Payment of a Sum of Money, and Vice Versa

Legal background

The reader is reminded that this Guide deals only with "family proceedings". Procedural changes made by the Civil Procedure Rules 1998 do not (yet) apply to such proceedings (see further annotations under FPR 1991, r 1.3). For a description of the steps to be taken in proceedings which are not "family proceedings" and which are governed by CPR 1998, see the *Civil Court Service* (Jordan Publishing Ltd).

OUTWARD

Enforcement abroad of a judgment or order for payment of a sum of money

Who may apply	The judgment creditor under a judgment or order for payment or a sum of money given or made by a court in England or Wales in civil proceedings or, if for compensation or damages to an injured party, in criminal proceedings, but not taxes etc or a fine or other penalty	FJ(RE)A 1933, ss 10(2), 11(1)
Which court	The court which made the order and, if the High Court, the principal registry or district registry in which the cause is proceeding	
Documents required	*High Court* An affidavit which must:	
	give particulars of the proceedings in which the judgment or order was obtained	
	have annexed a copy of the petition or other originating process, evidence of service on the respondent, copies of any pleadings and a statement of the grounds on which the judgment or order was based	
	state whether the respondent did or did not object to the jurisdiction and, if so, on what grounds	
	show that the judgment or order is not subject to any stay of execution	
	state that the time for appealing has expired or give the date when it will expire, and state whether notice of appeal has been given	
	state the rate at which the judgment or order carries interest	RSC Ord 71, r 13(1), (3)

	County court (NB See Limitations below) An affidavit sworn by the creditor's solicitor (or by himself if he is acting in person) which must: give particulars of the proceedings in which the judgment or order was obtained have annexed evidence of service on the respondent of the petition or other originating process (unless it was served by the court), copies of any pleadings and a statement of the grounds on which the judgment or order was based state whether the respondent did or did not object to the jurisdiction and, if so, on what grounds show that the judgment or order is not subject to any stay of execution state that the time for appealing or applying for a rehearing has expired or give the date when it will expire, and state whether notice of appeal has been given or application for a rehearing has been made state whether interest is recoverable on the judgment or order or part of it and, if so, the rate and period in respect of which it is recoverable	CCR Ord 35, r 2
	Magistrates' court No rules exist under which application may be made in respect of a magistrates' court order	
Fee payable	High Court: £30	FPFO 1999, fee 14.5
	County court: £30	FPFO 1999, fee 4.1
What happens next	In the High Court or the county court, the creditor receives from the court a sealed copy of the judgment or order appropriately certified by the district judge and a sealed certificate signed by him setting out, in essence, the information required to be given in the affidavit and any other particulars which it may be necessary to give to the foreign court The creditor must then apply to the relevant court or authority in the foreign state in accordance with its law and procedures for enforcement of the judgment there	

Limitations	If the judgment or order was given or made by a court other than the High Court, its enforceability in a particular country depends on the terms of the individual arrangements made with that country. Reference to the Statutory Instrument enabling that country's judgments to be enforced here will give an indication, as the reciprocal arrangements will be equivalent. Further enquiry may be made of the Magistrates' Courts Division of the Lord Chancellor's Department, Selborne House, 54–60 Victoria Street, London SW1E 6QW (Tel: 020 7210 8500) The foreign country's relevant provisions may impose conditions similar to those which the Act applies in the case of foreign judgments sought to be enforced in the UK (see INWARD section below).	

INWARD

Enforcement in England and Wales of a foreign judgment or order for payment of a sum of money

Who may apply	The judgment creditor under the judgment or order	FJ(RE)A 1933, s 2(1)
Which court	The High Court only; RSC seem to assume that the application will be made to the Queen's Bench Division but, if the judgment or order was made in proceedings which in England and Wales would have been family proceedings, the application may be more appropriately made to the Principal Registry of the Family Division	
Application	In the first instance, ex parte by affidavit. If not content that the application be made ex parte, the court may direct the issue of an originating summons in Form 10	RSC Ord 71, r 2
Documents required	An affidavit: exhibiting the judgment or order or an authenticated copy and (if it is not in English) a translation certified by a notary public or verified by affidavit	

	stating the name, trade or business and usual or last known address of the debtor and creditor, so far as known confirming the creditor's entitlement to enforce the judgment or order, the amount outstanding under it, that it can be enforced by execution in the original country and that any registration is not liable to be set aside under FJ(RE)A 1933, s 4 (see Setting aside below) specifying the interest (if any) then due on it under the law of the original country verifying that the Protection of Trading Interests Act 1980, s 5 does not apply If there are several provisions in the judgment, it must be made clear which ones are to be registered The Order in Council applying FJ(RE)A 1933 to the country may also require further evidence to be given as to the enforceability of the judgment or the accrual of interest	RSC Ord 71, r 3
Fee payable	£120	FPFO 1999, fee 1.1
What happens next	Security may be required for the costs of registration and of any application by the debtor to set the registration aside. The order must state a period (during which execution cannot be issued) when the debtor may apply to set the registration aside, and that period may be extended from time to time	RSC Ord 71, rr 4, 5
Service	Notice (as well as the order, if made on summons) must be served on the debtor giving details of the judgment or order and the order for registration, giving the creditor's or his solicitor's name and address for service and telling the debtor of his right to apply to set the registration aside and the time within which the application must be made	RSC Ord 71, r 7
Setting aside	An application by the debtor to set aside the registration is made by summons supported by affidavit. The court may order an issue to be tried The registration *must* be set aside if the court finds that:	

	the Act does not apply to the judgment, or was contravened in effecting the registration	
	the original court acted without jurisdiction	
	the debtor (being the defendant) had insufficient notice to enable him to defend and did not appear	
	the judgment was obtained by fraud	
	enforcement would be contrary to public policy or	
	the benefit of the judgment is not vested in the applicant	
	The registration *may* be set aside if, before the judgment, another court of competent jurisdiction had already decided the issue; it may also be set aside if there is an appeal pending against the judgment or if the debtor is entitled to and intends to appeal	FJ(RE)A 1933, s 4; RSC Ord 71, r 9
	Fee payable: £60	FPFO 1999, fee 4.3
Enforcement	Execution cannot be issued until the time specified in the order for registration (as extended) has expired and any application to set aside has been disposed of. An affidavit of service of the notice on the debtor must be filed	RSC Ord 71, r 10
Limitations	FJ(RE)A 1933 applies only to the judgments and orders of the courts identified in the Statutory Instruments applying it to the particular country. (Statutory Instruments made before the Act was amended, with effect from 1 January 1987, by CJJA 1982 applied the Act only to superior courts.) A judgment or order cannot be registered if it could not be enforced by execution in the original country, if it is fully paid (though if partly paid it can be registered as to the balance), or if it was given or made more than 6 years before the application for registration	FJ(RE)A 1933, ss 1(1)(*c*), 2(1)
	Enforcement more than six years after the judgment is registered will not be allowed except in a special case, notwithstanding that a longer limitation period applies in the country where the judgment was given	*Anne-Margaret Duer v Peter Nigel Frazer* [2001] 1 WLR 919, [2001] 1 All ER 249, QBD (Evans-Lombe J)
Appeals	See Guides 73, 75	

25L: Enforcement in a European Union or EFTA Country of a Maintenance Order Made in England and Wales, and Vice Versa

OUTWARD

Enforcement in a European Union or EFTA country of a maintenance order

General position	In the cases of the High Court and county court, the procedure is identical to that in respect of other judgments and orders (see Guide 25M). If the order has been registered in the magistrates' court, a certificate as to the payments made and arrears accrued under it while it has been registered may be obtained from the justices' chief executive. Accordingly, the following description deals only with the position in the magistrates' court	MC(CJJA 1982)R 1986, r 12(5)
Who may apply	Any interested party	CJJA 1982, s 12
Which court	The court which made the order	MC(CJJA 1982)R 1986, r 12(1)
Application	Made in writing to the justices' chief executive. The application is for a copy of the order and a certificate as to it and the proceedings in which it was made. The application must give: the names of the parties to the proceedings in which the order was made the date or approximate date and the nature of those proceedings the Contracting State in which the application for recognition or enforcement was or is to be made the postal address of the applicant	MC(CJJA 1982)R 1986, r 12(1), (2)
What happens next	The justices' chief executive sends to the applicant a copy of the order with a certificate certifying that it is a true copy and giving particulars of the proceedings in which it was made. The applicant must then deliver these documents to the appropriate authority in the State in question	MC(CJJA 1982)R 1986, r 12(3), (4)

Alternative procedures	The procedures afforded by MO(RE)A 1972 (see Guides 25E and 25H) continue to be available in respect of the countries where they are indicated in the Table	
Recent EU members	The more recent members of the European Union may not yet have put in place the facilities for enforcement under this provision	

INWARD

Enforcement in England and Wales of a maintenance order made in a European Union or EFTA country

Who may apply	Any interested party	CJJA 1982, Sch 1, Art 31
Which court	The appropriate court is the magistrates' court. Jurisdiction is based on domicile, or, if the payer is not domiciled in England or Wales, the place of enforcement. Accordingly, the justices' chief executive may make enquiry as to the payer's residence and location of his assets If the payer resides within the jurisdiction of his court the justices' chief executive must register the order; otherwise, he may: refuse to register the order, returning the documents to the Lord Chancellor with such information as he has concerning the payer's whereabouts and the nature and location of his assets or if the payer has assets which could be reached through further registration in the High Court, register the order in his court If the justices' chief executive is of the opinion that the order (or part of it) might appropriately be registered in the High Court, he must tell the applicant of his opinion and that such further registration is possible	CJJA 1982, Sch 1, Art 32; MC(CJJA 1982)R 1986, r 4
Application	The application (including the documents supplied by the foreign court) is lodged with the Lord Chancellor for transmission to the appropriate court. Authenticated copy orders are deemed to be true copies, and other documents required to be produced are admissible in evidence	CJJA 1982, s 11, Sch 1, Art 32

What happens next	If the justices' chief executive refuses the application, he notifies the applicant. If he registers the order, he notifies the Lord Chancellor, the applicant and the payer	MC(CJJA 1982)R 1986, r 4
Enforcement	On registration, the order is enforceable as if it had been made by the magistrates' court, except that payments must be made only to the justices' chief executive and sent by him to the original court (or to such other person or authority as that court or the Lord Chancellor may direct); the justices' chief executive may, or, if at least 4 weeks' arrears accrue, must (unless it appears unreasonable to do so), take steps in his own name to enforce the order whether or not the payee so requests The justices' chief executive is also under a duty to take reasonable steps to notify the payee of the methods of enforcement available	CJJA 1982, s 5(5); MC(CJJA 1982)R 1986, r 6
Recent EU members	The more recent members of the European Union may not yet have put in place the facilities for enforcement under this provision.	

25M: Enforcement in a European Union or EFTA Country of a Judgment or Order (other than a Maintenance Order) Made in England or Wales, and Vice Versa

Legal background

The Brussels Convention under which these arrangements are made does not extend to "rights in property arising out of a matrimonial relationship" (Article 1). Lump sum and transfer of property orders which are of this character will not be enforceable under the Convention, but those which make provision akin to maintenance will be (*Van den Boogard v Laumen* [1997] 2 FLR 399, ECJ).

The reader is reminded that this Guide deals only with "family proceedings". Procedural changes made by the Civil Procedure Rules 1998 do not (yet) apply to such proceedings (see further annotations under FPR 1991, r 1.3). For a description of the steps to be taken in proceedings which are not "family proceedings" and which are governed by CPR 1998, see the *Civil Court Service* (Jordan Publishing Ltd).

OUTWARD

Enforcement in a European Union or EFTA country of any High Court or county court judgment or order

Who may apply	Any interested party	CJJA 1982, s 12
Which court	The court which made the order. In the case of the High Court, the application will in practice be dealt with by the Principal Registry of the Family Division, notwithstanding the apparent requirement of RSC Ord 71, r 26 that it be made to the Queen's Bench Division.	
Application	Made by filing an affidavit which must: give particulars of the proceedings in which the judgment was obtained have annexed to it: (i) in the High Court only, a copy of the originating process and evidence of service thereof (unless it was served by the court) (ii) copies of the pleadings (if any) (iii) a statement of the grounds on which the judgment was based (iv) if appropriate, a copy of any legal aid certificate or "green form" in force for the proceedings state whether the defendant did or did not object to the jurisdiction and, if so, on what grounds show that the judgment has been served and that it is not subject to any stay of execution state: (i) that the time for appealing (or, in the county court, applying for a rehearing) has expired or the date on which that time will expire (ii) whether notice of appeal has been given (or an application for a rehearing has been made) state: (i) whether the judgment provides for payment of a sum or sums of money (ii) whether interest is recoverable on the judgment or part of it and if so the rate of interest, the date from which it is recoverable and the date it ceases to accrue (Note: no more than 6 years' interest may be recovered (*Lowsley and another v Forbes* [1998] 3 All ER 897, HL)) Form PF 163 may be used.	RSC Ord 71, r 36; CCR Ord 35, r 3

Fee payable	High Court: £30 County court: £30	FPFO 1999, fee 14.5 FPFO 1999, fee 4.1
What happens next	If the district judge is satisfied, the court issues a certified copy of the judgment and a certificate in Form 110 prescribed by RSC, adapted as necessary and signed by the district judge The applicant must apply to the relevant court or authority in the foreign State in accordance with its law and procedures for enforcement of the judgment there	RSC Ord 71, r 36; CCR Ord 35, r 3 CJJA 1991, Sch 1, Arts 31–35
Recent EU members	The more recent members of the European Union may not yet have put in place the facilities for enforcement under this provision	
Appeals	See Guides 72, 73	

INWARD

Enforcement in England and Wales of a judgment or order (other than a maintenance order) made in a European Union or EFTA country

Who may apply	Any interested party	CJJA 1982, Sch 1, Art 31
Which court	High Court. The application will in practice be dealt with by the Principal Registry of the Family Division, notwithstanding the apparent requirement of RSC Ord 71, r 26 that it be made to the Queen's Bench Division.	CJJA 1982, s 4(1)
Application	Ex parte by affidavit which must: exhibit: (i) the judgment or order or an authenticated copy, with documents to show that it is enforceable in the original country and has been served (ii) if a default judgment, evidence of service of the document instituting proceedings or equivalent (iii) evidence of any legal aid held by the creditor in the original country (iv) an authenticated translation of any document not in English	

	state: (i) whether the judgment or order provides for payment of money (ii) whether interest is payable on all or part of it under the law of the original country and, if so, the rate and the dates from and to which it is payable (Note: no more than 6 years' interest will be enforceable in any event (*Lowsley and another v Forbes* [1998] 3 All ER 897, HL)) give an address for service in England or Wales for the applicant and state the debtor's usual or last known address or place of business show how the applicant is the person entitled under the judgment or order and how much is owing under it Form PF 159 may be used.	RSC Ord 71, rr 27, 28
Fee payable	£120	FPFO 1999, fee 1.1
Order	Drawn up by the applicant, stating the period for appeal against it and that the judgment or order will not be enforced by execution until that period has expired Form PF 160 may be used.	RSC Ord 71, rr 27, 28
Service	Notice of the registration of the judgment or order must be served on the debtor, stating full particulars of the judgment or order registered and of the order for registration, the name and address for service of the applicant, the right of the debtor to appeal against the registration and the time for such an appeal (1 month from service, which may be extended in the case of a debtor not domiciled in a convention country on application made within 2 months after service) Form PF 161 may be used.	RSC Ord 71, rr 32, 33
Appeal by debtor	The debtor has a right of appeal but, since the court is not permitted to review the foreign judgment, the appeal may extend only to the grounds on which registration could have been refused, ie that the judgment is one which would not be recognised here for the reasons set out in CJJA 1982, Sch 1, Arts 27, 28. The appeal is by summons to a judge Form PF 162 may be used. Fee payable: £80	CJJA 1982, Sch 1, Art 36; RSC Ord 71, r 33(1) FPFO 1999, fee 5.1

Appeal by creditor	Appeal by creditor from district judge's refusal to register, see —	Guide 73
Enforcement	Execution may not be issued, nor may the judgment or order be otherwise enforced, until the time for appeal (including any extension) has expired and any appeal has been disposed of. This does not prevent an application, for example, to prevent the disposal of assets	CJJA 1982, Sch 1, Art 39; RSC Ord 71, r 34
Limitation	Enforcement more than six years after the judgment is registered will not be allowed except in a special case, notwithstanding that a longer limitation period applies in the country where the judgment was given	*Anne-Margaret Duer v Peter Nigel Frazer* [2001] 1 WLR 919, [2001] 1 All ER 249, QBD (Evans-Lombe J)
Recent EU members	The more recent members of the European Union may not yet have put in place the facilities for enforcement under this provision.	

25N: Enforcement in Scotland or Northern Ireland of a Judgment or Order (other than a Maintenance Order) of an English or Welsh Court other than a Magistrates' Court, and Vice Versa

Legal background

The reader is reminded that this Guide deals only with "family proceedings". Procedural changes made by the Civil Procedure Rules 1998 do not (yet) apply to such proceedings (see further annotations under FPR 1991, r 1.3). For a description of the steps to be taken in proceedings which are not "family proceedings" and which are governed by CPR 1998, see the *Civil Court Service* (Jordan Publishing Ltd).

OUTWARD

Enforcement in Scotland or Northern Ireland of an existing High Court or county court judgment or order (other than a maintenance order)

Who may apply	Any interested party	CJJA 1982, Sch 6, para 2(1), Sch 7, para 2(1)

Which court	The principal registry, district registry or county court in which the judgment or order was given or made	
Documents required	*Monetary provisions of a judgment or order* A certificate in Form 111 prescribed by RSC (adapted as necessary) and an affidavit. In the High Court the affidavit must be made by the party entitled to enforce the judgment. In the county court it must be made by his solicitor unless he is acting in person. It must:	
	give particulars of the judgment, stating the sum or aggregate of the sums (including costs) payable and unsatisfied under its money provisions, the rate of interest, if any, payable on it, the date or time from which interest began to accrue and, in the county court, the rate of payment (if any) specified	
	verify that the time for appealing against the judgment (or, in the county court, for applying for a rehearing) has expired or that any appeal (or rehearing) has been disposed of and that enforcement of the judgment is not stayed or suspended	
	give the usual or last known addresses of the creditor and the debtor	RSC Ord 71, r 37(3); CCR Ord 35, r 5
	High Court Form PF 164 may be used, adapted as necessary for the county court.	
	Non-monetary provisions of a judgment or order An affidavit which, in the High Court, must be made by person entitled to enforce the judgment or order and, in the county court, must be made by his solicitor unless he is acting in person. It must:	
	give particulars of the judgment	
	verify that the time for appealing against the judgment (or, in the county court, for applying for a rehearing) has expired or that any appeal (or rehearing) has been disposed of and that enforcement of the judgment is not stayed or suspended	
	give the usual or last known addresses of the creditor and the debtor	RSC Ord 71, r 38(5), (6); CCR Ord 35, r 6(1), (2)

	High Court Form PF 165 may be used, adapted as necessary for the county court.	
Fee payable	High Court: £30 County court: £30	FPFO 1999, fee 14.5 FPFO 1999, fee 4.1
What happens next	*Monetary provisions* The certificate is completed by the proper officer and issued to the creditor, who uses it to found the appropriate steps in Scotland or Northern Ireland *Non-monetary provisions* The court provides a certified copy of the judgment and a certificate annexed to it in Form 112 prescribed by RSC adapted as necessary. The applicant uses these documents to found the appropriate application in Scotland or Northern Ireland	CJJA 1982, Sch 6 CJJA 1982, Sch 7
Appeals	Not applicable	

INWARD

Enforcement in England and Wales of a judgment or order (other than a maintenance order) of a Scottish or Northern Irish court other than a magistrates' court

Who may apply	Any interested party	CJJA 1982, Sch 6, para 2(1), Sch 7, para 2(1)
Which court	High Court. The application will in practice be dealt with by the Principal Registry of the Family Division, notwithstanding the apparent assumption in RSC Ord 71, rr 37(1), 38(1) that it be made to the Queen's Bench Division.	
Application	*Monetary provisions* No application as such is made. *Non-monetary provisions* Ex parte in the first instance, but the court may direct the issue of an originating summons in Form 10	RSC Ord 71, r 38(1)
Documents required	*Monetary provisions* A certificate of the judgment or order issued within the preceding 6 months by the Scottish or Northern Irish court, together with a copy certified by the applicant's solicitor to be a true copy	RSC Ord 71, r 37(1)

	Non-monetary provisions A certified copy of the judgment or order and the prescribed form of certificate issued within the previous 6 months by the Scottish or Northern Irish court	CJJA 1982, Sch 7, para 5(3); RSC Ord 71, r 38(2)
Fee payable	£120	FPFO 1999, fee 1.1
What happens next	*Monetary provisions* The certified copy is sealed by the court and returned as evidence of the registration of the judgment or order, which may then be enforced as a judgment or order of the High Court	CJJA 1982, Sch 6, paras 5, 6; RSC Ord 71, r 37(2)
	Non-monetary provisions The judgment or order must not be registered if compliance would breach the law in England and Wales; otherwise, the court must order it to be registered. If the order is granted, the applicant must draw it up. The order must state the period within which an appeal may be made against the order for registration and that execution will not be issued on the judgment or order until that period has expired. This is taken to refer to the respondent's right to apply to set aside the registration. No period is in fact specified in the Act or Rules, but it seems likely that the court would apply by analogy the 1-month period applicable under RSC Ord 71, r 33 in the case of an order made in a convention country	CJJA 1982, Sch 7, para 5(4), (5); RSC Ord 71, rr 30, 38(3)
Service	*Monetary provisions* There is no requirement for notice of the registration to be served. *Non-monetary provisions* Notice of the registration must be served on the person against whom the order was made, giving full particulars of the judgment or order registered and the order for registration, the name of the applicant and his address for service within England and Wales. It must state the right of that person to appeal against the registration and the period within which the appeal must be made. This provision is taken to refer to the right of the person against whom the order was made to apply to set aside the registration. The order is then enforceable as if made by the High Court	CJJA 1982, Sch 7, para 6; RSC Ord 71, rr 32, 38(3)

	Form PF 161, in an adapted form, may be used.	
Costs and interest	*Monetary provisions* The costs of obtaining and registering the certificate are added to the judgment debt. Interest continues to accrue at the rate stated in the certificate, including interest from the date of registration on the added costs. No other interest is recoverable	CJJA 1982, Sch 6, paras 7, 8
	Non-monetary provisions The costs of obtaining the copy order and certificate and of registration are recoverable as if the original order included an order for their payment, but interest is recoverable on those costs as if, on registration, the High Court had ordered their payment	CJJA 1982, Sch 7, para 7
Stay and setting aside	If satisfied that the debtor is entitled to and intends to appeal against or apply to have set aside the judgment or order, the court may stay enforcement on such terms as it thinks fit and for such period as appears to be sufficient. On the application of any interested party, the court *must* set aside the registration if satisfied that registration was contrary to the provisions of the relevant Schedule, and it *may* set the registration aside if the issue in the original proceedings had previously been decided by another court of competent jurisdiction	CJJA 1982, Sch 6, paras 9, 10, Sch 7, paras 8, 9
	Any application to set aside the registration must be made by summons, supported by an affidavit. The court may order an issue to be tried	RSC Ord 71, rr 9(1), (2), 38(4)
	Fee payable: £60	FPFO 1999, fee 4.3
Appeals	Appeal against master's refusal, see —	Guide 73
	Appeal from application to set aside, see —	Guide 75

26: Registration in a Magistrates' Court of a Maintenance Order Made in the High Court or a County Court

Legal background

The person entitled to receive payment under a maintenance order made by the High Court or a county court may apply to that court for its registration in a magistrates' court and, provided that it remains registered, it is treated as a magistrates' court order for the purpose of enforcement and (broadly) variation.

Procedure

Availability	Only "maintenance orders" may be registered, but this expression includes lump sum orders. Although an application may be made and granted while enforcement process is outstanding in the original court, the registration will not be effected until that process has been completed	MOA 1958, s 1(1)
	The grant of the application will become void if the enforcement process is not completed within 14 days	MOA 1958, s 2(2); FPR 1991, r 7.23(2)
	A nominal order for a spouse only will not be registered, and a maintenance pending suit or interim order will only be registered in special circumstances	*PD of 10 March 1980*
Application	Two copies of the application form and a certified copy of the order are lodged in the court which made the order (or the court to which the cause has since been transferred). Since the application does not of itself constitute enforcement, no affidavit is needed and leave is not required	
	If the application is granted, the order is registered in the magistrates' court for the place where the payer resides	FPR 1991, r 7.23(1)
	The magistrates' court has no discretion to decline registration	MOA 1958, s 2(5)
Fee payable	£30	FPFO 1999, fee 9.1
Effect	Any attachment of earnings order ceases to have effect	AEA 1971, s 11(1)(*a*)
	Unless a means of payment order under MEA 1991 is in force, future payments must be ordered to be paid through the magistrates' clerk	MOA 1958, s 2(6ZA)(*b*)

	Where the payee is receiving income support, this enables the payee to divert the payments to the Benefits Agency, enabling her (or him) to receive full benefit regardless of any irregularity in payment	*PD of 22 May 1975*
	The order is enforceable only as if it were an order made by the magistrates' court	MOA 1958, s 3
	Variation proceedings must be in the magistrates' court, unless there is an application to vary some provision (eg extension of the term of the order) other than merely the rate of payment or the payer is outside England and Wales; in either of those cases, the application is to the original court. In any event, the magistrates' court may remit a variation application made to it to the original court for hearing	MOA 1958, s 4
Cancellation	The person entitled to receive payment may simply give notice to the magistrates' court. The original court may give such a notice, but only where it varies or discharges the maintenance order.	
	The notice has the effect of cancelling the registration as soon as any outstanding enforcement process or variation application has been concluded	MOA 1958, s 5
	Fee payable: none prescribed	
Form	Application on FPR 1991, Form M33	
Appeals	See Guides 72, 73	

27: Attachment of Earnings Order (High Court or County Court)

Legal background

Where the debtor is in employment, the court may order his employer to deduct periodic amounts from his earnings and remit them to the court against the amount(s) due under the order to be enforced. The position varies according to whether the attachment of earnings order is to secure (*a*) a qualifying periodical maintenance order (including some lump sum orders), (*b*) some other maintenance order (including a lump sum order) or (*c*) an order which is not a maintenance order.

The reader is reminded that this Guide deals only with "family proceedings". Procedural changes made by the Civil Procedure Rules 1998 do not (yet) apply to such proceedings (see further annotations under FPR 1991, r 1.3). For a description of the steps to be taken in proceedings which are not "family proceedings" and which are governed by CPR 1998, see the relevant Guide in the *Civil Court Service* (Jordan Publishing Ltd).

Procedure

Availability	Leave is required if it is sought to enforce arrears more than 12 months old under a financial provision or similar order	MCA 1973, s 32
	The application for leave is made to the district judge on notice to the debtor and may be issued with (and made returnable with) the attachment of earnings application itself	FPR 1991, r 10.9
	The court has a discretion whether to make the attachment of earnings order or not. If the circumstances would require the creditor to obtain leave before issuing execution against goods, similar considerations apply as on an application for such leave.	
	Qualifying periodical maintenance order The person to whom the payments are to be made, the person (if different) who applied for the maintenance order or the debtor may apply at any time; otherwise, the court may make an order of its own motion on making the maintenance order or in the course of any proceedings relating to it	MEA 1991, s 1(1), (3)
	Other maintenance order The person to whom the payments are to be made may apply at any time	AEA 1971, s 3
	The debtor may apply on the making or variation of the maintenance order	CCR Ord 27, r 17(4)
	Other order The person to whom the payments are to be made may apply if the debtor has defaulted under the order, but only if the amount due under the order is (or was when it was made) at least £50	AEA 1971, ss 1(2)(*b*), 3(3); CCR Ord 27, r 7(9)

Application	*Qualifying periodical maintenance order* No change was made to the rules of court when MEA 1991 came into force on 1 April 1992. A free-standing application by the creditor need not rely on the Act, and the applicant should follow the procedure provided for other maintenance orders. If the application is to be made on the hearing of another matter, or is to be made by the debtor, adequate notice must be given to the other party	
	High Court No rules currently exist. The county court procedure should be adapted (or the application may be made to the county court)	CCR Ord 25, r 11
	The High Court has power to make an attachment of earnings order only to secure a High Court maintenance order, unless the proceedings in the principal registry are treated as pending in a divorce county court	AEA 1971, s 1(1); FPR 1991, r 7.1(4)
	County court The application is filed in the court which made the order	CCR Ord 27, r 17(2)
	The creditor must file an affidavit showing how the amount due and any interest claimed are calculated, together with a further copy of the interest calculation	FPR 1991, r 7.1(1); CCR Ord 25, r 5A
	If the application is to enforce a maintenance order, a return date is given before the district judge, which the applicant should attend	
Fee payable	High Court: £60	FPFO 1999, fee 4.3
	County court: £50 for each person against whom the order is sought (NB it appears that no fee is payable if the order is made of the court's own motion)	FPFO 1999, fee 12.7
Debtor's address	It is for the creditor to provide the address of the debtor. In case of difficulty, assistance may sometimes be obtained from certain Government departments	*PD of 13 February 1989*
Powers of the court	The court has wide powers to require the debtor to provide the information needed to deal with the application	AEA 1971, s 14

	Provision is also made for where a debtor fails to attend or provide information	AEA 1971, s 23; CCR Ord 27, r 8
Order	The debtor's employer must make periodic deductions from his pay and remit them to the court, which passes them on to the creditor. Where the payee is receiving income support, this enables the payee to divert the payments to the Benefits Agency enabling her (or him) to receive full benefit, regardless of any irregularity in payment	*PD of 22 May 1975*
Forms	Request for order N337 will need adaptation for a maintenance order case. The court prepares Notice to the debtor in form N55 (debt) or N55(1) (maintenance)	
Appeals	See Guides 72, 73 NB Appeal from a district judge's committal order under AEA 1971, s 23 also lies direct to the Court of Appeal but this route will rarely be appropriate	AJA 1960, s 13; *King v Read & Slack* (unreported) 18 November 1996, CA

28: Charging Order

Legal background

The court may impose a charge on the debtor's interest in land, securities or a fund in court. The effect of this remedy is to provide security for the debt, rather than enforce it but, having made a charging order, the court may appoint a receiver of the income generated by the property charged (see Guide 36) and/or may order its sale.

The reader is reminded that this Guide deals only with "family proceedings". Procedural changes made by the Civil Procedure Rules 1998 do not (yet) apply to such proceedings (see further annotations under FPR 1991, r 1.3). For a description of the steps to be taken in proceedings which are not "family proceedings" and which are governed by CPR 1998, Pt 73 (which came into force on 25 March 2002, replacing RSC Ord 50 and CCR Ord 31), see the relevant Guide in the *Civil Court Service* (Jordan Publishing Ltd) and also Vincent, *Enforcement of Judgments – The New Rules* (A Special Bulletin, Jordan Publishing Ltd, 2002).

Procedure

Availability	Leave is required if it is sought to enforce arrears more than 12 months old under a financial provision or similar order	MCA 1973, s 32
	The application for leave is made to the district judge on notice to the debtor	FPR 1991, r 10.9

	Otherwise, the creditor may apply at any time. However, the court has a discretion whether to make the charging order or not; if the circumstances would require the creditor to obtain leave before issuing execution against goods, similar considerations apply as on an application for such leave; only in exceptional circumstances will an order be made if the debtor is not in default.	
	In addition, an order will not be made if the debt is the subject of a county court instalment order which is up to date when the application is made	*Mercantile Credit Co Ltd v Ellis* (1987) *The Times*, 1 April
	An instalment order made subsequently will not prevent a charging order being confirmed	*Ropaigealach v Allied Irish Bank plc* [2001] EWCA Civ 1790, CA
Which court	*High Court order* In the case of a maintenance or lump sum order or an order for over £5,000, the application may be made to the High Court (in the principal registry or the district registry in which the cause or matter is proceeding)	COA 1979, s 1(2)(*b*), (*c*)
	In any case, the application may be made to the county court in whose district the debtor resides or carries on business (or, if none, the county court in whose district the creditor resides or carries on business)	CCR Ord 31, r 1(1)(*c*)
	County court order The application must be made to the county court which made the order, or to the county court to which the cause or matter has since been transferred	CCR Ord 31, r 1(1)(*b*)
Application	The application is made by filing an affidavit giving the name and address of the debtor and all known creditors and details of the asset sought to be charged and setting out how the amount due and any interest claimed are calculated, together (in the county court) with a further copy of the interest calculation. Any other person interested (eg the debtor's spouse or a co-owner) should be identified	RSC Ord 50, r 1(3); CCR Ord 31, r 1(2), Ord 25, r 5A; FPR 1991, r 7.1(1)
	If satisfied, the district judge makes the order temporarily and a return date is given.	
Fee payable	High Court: £50 for each person against whom the order is sought	FPFO 1999, fee 14.3

	County court: £50 for each person against whom the order is sought	FPFO 1999, fee 12.4
Debtor's address	It is for the creditor to provide the address of the debtor. In case of difficulty, assistance may sometimes be obtained from certain Government departments	*PD of 13 February 1989*
Service	The creditor serves the order and copy affidavit on (i) the debtor, (ii) the other creditors (High Court, if so directed; county court, unless otherwise directed), and (iii) any other person directed by the court, by first-class post. An affidavit of service should be filed	RSC Ord 50, r 2; CCR Ord 31, r 1(6), (9)
Order	Initially made in temporary form ("order nisi"). On the hearing, it is either confirmed (made "absolute") or discharged	
Registration	A charging order affecting an interest in land can and should be protected by registration at HM Land Registry or HM Land Charges Registry as appropriate when it is first made as an order nisi; if it is discharged on the hearing, the registration must be removed by the creditor	
Order for sale	The judgment creditor holding a charging order may apply for an order for sale of the property charged	
	If the debt secured does not exceed £30,000, the application may be made to the county court; in any case, the application may be made to the Chancery Division of the High Court	CCA 1984, s 23(*c*); CCR Ord 31, r 4; RSC Ord 50, r 9A
	Such a free-standing application will not be "family proceedings" and will be governed by CPR 1998 and in particular Pt 8 and r 73.10 of those rules and the Practice Directions supplementing them.	
	If the interest charged is merely a beneficial interest under a trust (eg if the property is in the joint names of the debtor and another), the creditor may apply (see Guide 5) for an order for sale of the trust property; in this case, the county court has jurisdiction irrespective of the amount of the debt or the value of the property	TLATA 1996, s 14; HCCCJO 1991, art 2(1)(*a*)

	The court will have regard to the relative values of the debt and the property charged, and will be reluctant to make an order where either is small.	
Appeals	See Guides 72, 73	

29: Writ or Warrant of Delivery

Legal background

In the High Court, a writ of delivery is issued to the sheriff and, in the county court, a delivery warrant is issued to the bailiff, requiring him physically to take the goods from the person against whom the order was made. If the order provides the alternative of payment of the value of the goods, the writ or warrant will require the sheriff or bailiff to levy execution for the value if the goods cannot be uplifted, unless the court has ordered otherwise.

The reader is reminded that this Guide deals only with "family proceedings". Procedural changes made by the Civil Procedure Rules 1998 do not (yet) apply to such proceedings (see further annotations under FPR 1991, r 1.3). For a description of the steps to be taken in proceedings which are not "family proceedings" and which are governed by CPR 1998, see the relevant Guide in the *Civil Court Service* (Jordan Publishing Ltd).

Procedure

Availability	Leave is required to issue the writ or warrant if more than 6 years have elapsed since the order, if there has been a change of parties or (High Court only) if the order was conditional; otherwise, the person in whose favour the order is made may issue the writ or warrant as soon as it is made or, if it allows a time for compliance, as soon as that time has expired	RSC Ord 46, r 2; CCR Ord 26, r 5
	The court has a general power to stay execution of an order on the ground of matters which have occurred since it was made	CCA 1984, ss 38, 76; RSC Ord 45, r 11
Issue	*High Court* The applicant files a praecipe together with the form of writ for sealing, and then serves the sealed writ on the under-sheriff in whose area the goods are situated	RSC Ord 46, r 6
	County court The applicant files a form of request for the issue of the warrant	CCR Ord 26, rr 1, 16
Fee payable	*High Court* £20 (NB a further fee is payable to the sheriff)	FPFO 1999, fee 14.1

	County court £80 No further court fee is payable if the writ or warrant is issued also to recover money.	FPFO 1999, fee 12.6
Form	*High Court* Praecipe in Form PF90; writ in Form 64 or 65 *County court* Request in Form N324	
Appeals	See Guides 72, 73	

30: Execution against Goods

Legal background

In the High Court, a writ of fieri facias is issued to the sheriff and, in the county court, a warrant of execution is issued to the bailiff, requiring him to seize and sell the debtor's goods to produce the amount due under the order. The court may stay or suspend the execution if there are special circumstances or if the debtor is unable to pay.

The reader is reminded that this Guide deals only with "family proceedings". Procedural changes made by the Civil Procedure Rules 1998 do not (yet) apply to such proceedings (see further annotations under FPR 1991, r 1.3). For a description of the steps to be taken in proceedings which are not "family proceedings" and which are governed by CPR 1998, see the relevant Guide in the *Civil Court Service* (Jordan Publishing Ltd).

Procedure

Availability	Leave is required if it is sought to enforce arrears more than 12 months old under a financial provision or similar order or where a variation application is pending	MCA 1973, s 32; FPR 1991, r 7.1(2)
	The application for leave is made to a district judge on notice to the debtor	FPR 1991, r 10.9
	Leave is also required to issue the writ or warrant if more than 6 years have elapsed since the order, if there has been a change of parties, if the order was conditional (High Court only), in certain circumstances if the order was against the estate of a deceased person or if a receiver or sequestrator has been appointed. In these cases the application may be made either ex parte or on notice according to circumstance.	

	Otherwise, the person in whose favour the order is made may issue the writ or warrant as soon as it is made or, if it allows a time for compliance, then as soon as that time has expired	RSC Ord 46, r 2; CCR Ord 26, r 5
	In the county court, if the debt is the subject of an instalment order, the warrant may not be issued so long as the payments are up to date	CCA 1984, s 86
	If the payments are in arrears, a warrant can be issued for all or part of the debt then unpaid	CCR Ord 26, r 1(2)
	The court has a general power to stay execution of an order on the ground of matters which have occurred since it was made. The county court has a similar power in the case of monetary orders on the ground of inability to pay, whenever arising	CCA 1984, ss 38, 71(2), 76; RSC Ord 45, r 11
	A county court order other than for periodical payments or arrears thereof may be transferred to the High Court and enforced as a High Court order. The application is made to the county court ex parte by affidavit, stating the amount which remains due under the order. The transfer has immediate effect	FPR 1991, r 7.3
Issue	*High Court* The applicant files an affidavit showing the amount due and how it is calculated and a praecipe together with the form of writ for sealing; he then serves the sealed writ on the under-sheriff in whose area the debtor has goods	RSC Ord 46, r 6; FPR 1991, r 7.1(1)
	County court The applicant files an affidavit showing how the amount due and any interest claimed are calculated, together with a further copy of the interest calculation and a form of request for the issue of the warrant	CCR Ord 25, r 5A, Ord 26, r 1; FPR 1991, r 7.1(1)
Fee payable	*High Court* £20 (NB a further fee is payable to the sheriff)	FPFO 1999, fee 14.1
	County court £25 (debt up to £125)	FPFO 1999, fee 12.1(*a*)
	£45 (debt over £125)	FPFO 1999, fee 12.1(*b*)
Debtor's address	It is for the creditor to provide the address of the debtor. In case of difficulty, assistance may sometimes be obtained from certain Government departments	*PD of 13 February 1989*

Form	*High Court* Praecipe in Form PF86; Writ in Form Nos 53 to 63 *County court* Request in Form N323	
Appeals	Application for leave or for stay, see —	Guides 72, 73

31: Garnishee Order

Legal background

The court may order a person (the garnishee) who owes money to the debtor to pay it instead to the creditor in reduction of a judgment debt. The debt attached is usually, but is not limited to, a balance in the debtor's bank or building society account.

The reader is reminded that this Guide deals only with "family proceedings". Procedural changes made by the Civil Procedure Rules 1998 do not (yet) apply to such proceedings (see further annotations under FPR 1991, r 1.3). For a description of the steps to be taken in proceedings which are not "family proceedings" and which are governed by CPR 1998, Pt 72 (which came into force on 25 March 2002, replacing RSC Ord 49 and CCR Ord 30), see the relevant Guide in the *Civil Court Service* (Jordan Publishing Ltd) and also Vincent, *Enforcement of Judgments – The New Rules* (A Special Bulletin, Jordan Publishing Ltd, 2002).

Procedure

Availability	The garnishee must be within England and Wales, and the amount due to the applicant must exceed £50	RSC Ord 49, r 1(1); CCR Ord 30, r 1(1)
	Leave is required if it is sought to enforce arrears more than 12 months old under a financial provision or similar order	MCA 1973, s 32
	The application for leave is made to the district judge on notice to the debtor	FPR 1991, r 10.9
	The court has a discretion whether to make a garnishee order or not; if the circumstances would require the creditor to obtain leave before issuing execution against goods, similar considerations apply as on an application for such leave	

Application	Made by filing in the court in which the cause or matter is proceeding an affidavit giving the name and address of the debtor, identifying the order and saying how much is due and how it and any interest claimed are calculated, giving details of the garnishee and the debt due from him to the debtor, identifying (if the garnishee is a bank or building society etc) the branch in question and (county court only) showing the arrears under any instalment order and attaching a copy of any interest calculation.	
	If satisfied, the district judge makes a temporary order which binds the debt in the hands of the garnishee and a return date is given	RSC Ord 49, r 2; CCR Ord 25, r 5A, Ord 30, r 2; FPR 1991, r 7.1(1)
Fee payable	High Court: £50 for each person against whom the order is sought	FPFO 1999, fee 14.3
	County court: £50 for each person against whom the order is sought	FPFO 1999, fee 12.4
Debtor's address	It is for the creditor to provide the address of the debtor. In case of difficulty, assistance may sometimes be obtained from certain Government departments	*PD of 13 February 1989*
Service	The order is served on the garnishee in the same manner as a fixed date summons (ie usually by the court by post) in the county court, and personally in the High Court, at least 15 days before the hearing and by posting to the debtor at least 7 days later but 7 days before the hearing	RSC Ord 49, r 3; CCR Ord 30, r 3
Order	If the garnishee disputes his liability to the debtor, the district judge may determine the issue summarily or give directions for trial. If the order is made absolute (the remedy is in any event discretionary), it requires the garnishee to make payment direct to the creditor	RSC Ord 49, r 5; CCR Ord 30, rr 8, 9
Form	Affidavit in Form PF100 (High Court) or Form N349 (county court)	
Appeals	See Guides 72, 73	

32: Committal by way of Judgment Summons

Legal background

The court may imprison for up to 6 weeks a person who has been ordered to pay maintenance (including a lump sum), who has or has had the means to pay it and who neglects or refuses or has neglected or refused to do so.

FPR 1991 have been amended with effect from 24 February 2003 to require the creditor to file and serve in advance his evidence to prove the debtor's means and neglect or refusal. Other procedural changes have also been made to reflect the view of judgment summons proceedings expressed in *Mubarak v Mubarak* [2001] 1 FLR 698, CA that they are penal in character.

Procedure

Availability	The remedy is only available in the case of a maintenance order (including a lump sum order)	AJA 1970, s 11, Sch 8
	Leave is required if it is sought to enforce arrears more than 12 months old under a financial provision or similar order. The application for leave may be combined with the summons, the prescribed forms including such an application for use if required	MCA 1973, s 32
	Leave of the judge is required before the summons is issued if the debtor is in default under a committal order made on an earlier judgment summons	FPR 1991, r 7.4(4)
	A committal order will not be made unless refusal or neglect to pay, notwithstanding the means to pay, is proved	DA 1869, s 5
Which court	The High Court may hear a judgment summons to enforce a High Court maintenance order; the county court may hear a judgment summons to enforce a High Court or a county court maintenance order	FPR 1991, r 7.4(2)
Application	A request is filed, together with an affidavit as to the amount due, either in the principal registry or in the district registry (if a High Court order) or the divorce county court which is most convenient, having regard to the debtor's residence or place of business. If this is not the court which made the order, the affidavit should exhibit a copy of the order	FPR 1991, rr 7.1(1), 7.4(2), (3)
	All of the evidence intended to be relied on at the hearing must be filed at the same time	FPR 1991, r 7.4(3A)

	If interest is claimed, the affidavit should set out the calculation and (in the county court) a copy of the calculation should be filed	CCR Ord 25, r 5A
Fee payable	High Court: £80 County court: £80	FPFO 1999, fee 14.4 FPFO 1999, fee 12.5
Service	The judgment summons is issued by the court and must be served personally 14 days before the hearing; travelling expenses must be paid or tendered	FPR 1991, r 7.4(5)
	The written evidence upon which the creditor intends to rely must be served with the judgment summons	FPR 1991, r 7.4(5)
	It is for the creditor to provide the address of the debtor. In case of difficulty, assistance may sometimes be obtained from certain Government departments	*PD of 13 February 1989*
Evidence	The evidence adduced by the creditor must prove beyond reasonable doubt that the debtor has or has had the means to pay and that he has neglected or refused or is neglecting or refusing to pay	FPR 1991, r 7.4(7B)(*c*)
Debtor's attendance	If the debtor fails to attend, the court may order him to attend an adjourned hearing and, if he disobeys, commit him for up to 14 days	CCA 1984, s 110; CCR Ord 28, r 4
	However, as the proceedings are penal in character, the debtor cannot be compelled to give evidence	FPR 1991, r 7.4(7C)
	If the judge is satisfied that the judgment summons and evidence have been duly served, he may be prepared to proceed in the debtor's absence.	
Order	If satisfied of his neglect or refusal to pay, the judge may commit the debtor to prison for up to 6 weeks, but may and usually will suspend the order on condition that he makes payment (by instalments or otherwise)	DA 1869, s 5; FPR 1991, r 7.4(10)
	Alternatively, the judge may make a new order for payment	FPR 1991, r 7.4(9)
Form	Request in Form M16	
Appeals	See Guide 75	

33: Means of Payment Order

Legal background

The court may order the debtor to make the required payments by standing order or by direct debit, and to open an account for the purpose.

Procedure

Availability	The order to be enforced must be a "qualifying periodical maintenance order", ie one made when the debtor was ordinarily resident in England and Wales; it includes a lump sum order if the sum is payable by instalments	MEA 1991, s 1(2), (10)
	Any interested party may apply. If the order is sought to enforce arrears more than 12 months old, leave must be obtained (but may be requested in the same application)	MCA 1973, s 32
	An order may be made when the maintenance order is made or at any time thereafter, on application or (in the course of any proceedings concerning the maintenance order) of the court's own motion; similarly, the court may revoke, suspend, revive or vary such an order	MEA 1991, s 1(1), (3), (7)
	An order to open an account cannot be made until the debtor has been given an opportunity to do so voluntarily	MEA 1991, s 1(6)
Application	In the course of proceedings concerning the maintenance order, the court will generally consider an oral invitation to exercise its powers, but it must (if practicable) give every interested party the opportunity to make representations; if a party is absent, this may necessitate an adjournment so that notice can be given	MEA 1991, s 1(8)
	Otherwise, the application is to the district judge on notice and, if some other application is pending, may conveniently be made so as to be returnable on the same occasion	FPR 1991, r 10.9
	The creditor must file an affidavit showing how the amount due and any interest claimed are calculated, together with (in the county court) a copy of the interest calculation	CCR Ord 25, r 5A; FPR 1991, r 7.1(1)

Fee payable	£60 (NB it appears that no fee is payable if the order is made of the court's own motion)	FPFO 1999, fee 4.3
Debtor's address	It is for the creditor to provide the address of the debtor. In case of difficulty, assistance may sometimes be obtained from certain Government departments	*PD of 13 February 1989*
Appeals	See Guides 72, 73, 75	

34: Oral Examination of the Debtor

Legal background

The court may order the debtor to attend and be cross-examined as to his means to pay the amount ordered or otherwise to comply with the order if it is not for payment of money. This procedure, while not itself an enforcement measure, is a valuable aid to enforcement.

The reader is reminded that this Guide deals only with "family proceedings". Procedural changes made by the Civil Procedure Rules 1998 do not (yet) apply to such proceedings (see further annotations under FPR 1991, r 1.3). For a description of the steps to be taken in proceedings which are not "family proceedings" and which are governed by CPR 1998, Pt 71 (which came into force on 25 March 2002, replacing RSC Ord 48 and CCR Ord 25, r 3), see the relevant Guide in the *Civil Court Service* (Jordan Publishing Ltd) and also Vincent, *Enforcement of Judgments – The New Rules* (A Special Bulletin, Jordan Publishing Ltd, 2002).

Procedure

Availability	The person who obtained the order may apply for an order for oral examination at any time thereafter, but the application may be refused as oppressive if the debtor has not had the opportunity to comply; the application must be made to the High Court if the order was made by the High Court	RSC Ord 48, r 1; CCR Ord 25, r 3(1)
	If the order was made by a divorce county court, the application must be made to the divorce county court nearest to the debtor's residence or place of business	FPR 1991, r 7.1(5)(*a*)
Application	The application is made ex parte in the High Court, by affidavit, and in the county court is supported by an affidavit verifying the amount due and how it is arrived at	
	The grounds of application should be given	RSC Ord 48, r 1; FPR 1991, r 7.1(5)(*b*)
	If interest is claimed, the calculation should be set out and (in the county court) a copy filed	CCR Ord 25, r 5A

	If the court is not the one which made the order, a copy of the order must be exhibited.	
Fee payable	High Court: £40 County court: £40	FPFO 1999, fee 14 FPFO 1999, fee 12.3
Order	If the order is made, it requires the debtor to attend at a court office on a specified appointment and to submit to cross-examination. The High Court may order the examination to take place at a district registry or a county court.	
Service	In the High Court, the order must be served personally, and the debtor's expenses paid or tendered or a solicitor's undertaking given	RSC Ord 48, r 1
	In the county court, the order is initially served as if a default summons (ie usually by post) but, if the debtor fails to attend, a further order is made which is served personally; conduct money must be paid if the debtor so requests	CCR Ord 25, r 3
	It is for the creditor to provide the address of the debtor. In case of difficulty, assistance may sometimes be obtained from certain Government departments	*PD of 13 February 1989*
Examination	Conducted by the district judge or a senior member of the court staff. The creditor or his solicitor should attend to cross-examine the debtor. If not, the officer may be prepared to put standard questions to the debtor, but this is rarely appropriate in family proceedings	
Failure to attend	In the High Court, this constitutes contempt and is punishable by committal.	
	In the county court, this is dealt with by a further order to attend, disobedience of which is punishable by committal	CCR Ord 25, r 3(4), (5)
Appeals	See Guides 72, 73	

35: Writ or Warrant of Possession of Land

Legal background

In the High Court, a writ of possession is issued to the sheriff and, in the county court, a possession warrant is issued to the bailiff, requiring him physically to take possession of the land (and buildings) and give it to the person in whose favour the order was made.

The reader is reminded that this Guide deals only with "family proceedings". Procedural changes made by the Civil Procedure Rules 1998 do not (yet) apply to such proceedings (see further annotations under FPR 1991, r 1.3). For a description of the steps to be taken in proceedings which are not "family proceedings" and which are governed by CPR 1998, see the relevant Guide in the *Civil Court Service* (Jordan Publishing Ltd).

Procedure

Availability	In the High Court, leave is generally required	RSC Ord 45, r 3(2), Ord 46, r 2
	In the county court, leave is required if more than 6 years have elapsed since the order or if there has been a change of parties	CCR Ord 26, r 5
	Otherwise, the person in whose favour the order is made may issue the writ or warrant as soon as it is made or, if it allows a time for compliance, as soon as that time has expired.	
	The court has a general power to stay execution of an order on the ground of matters which have occurred since it was made	CCA 1984, ss 38, 76; RSC Ord 45, r 11
Application for leave	In the High Court, the application for leave is made by summons to the district judge if the possession order was conditional, if 6 years have elapsed since it was made or if the person against whom it is to be enforced has changed; otherwise, ex parte by affidavit, which must give details of any occupiers other than the defendant and of any tenancies held by them	RSC Ord 46, r 4; *PD of 19 January 1972*
	In the county court, the application is made ex parte by affidavit, although the district judge may require notice to be given	CCR Ord 25, r 3
Issue	*High Court* The applicant files a praecipe together with the form of writ for sealing, and then serves the sealed writ on the under-sheriff in whose area the land is situated	RSC Ord 46, r 6
	County court The applicant files a form of request for the issue of the warrant	CCR Ord 26, r 1
Fee payable	*High Court* £20 (NB a further fee is payable to the sheriff)	FPFO 1999, fee 14.1
	County court £80	FPFO 1999, fee 12.6

	No further court fee is payable if the writ or warrant is issued also to recover money.	
Forms	*High Court* Praecipe in Form PF88 or 89; writ in Form No 66 *County court* Request in Form N325	
Appeals	Application for leave or for stay, see —	Guides 72, 73

36: Appointment of a Receiver by way of Equitable Execution

Legal background

Where the debtor has assets which cannot be reached by other enforcement methods, the court may appoint a receiver to take them and apply them (or the income from them) to the payment of the amount due under the order.

The reader is reminded that this Guide deals only with "family proceedings". Procedural changes made by the Civil Procedure Rules 1998 do not (yet) apply to such proceedings (see further annotations under FPR 1991, r 1.3). For a description of the steps to be taken in proceedings which are not "family proceedings" and which are governed by CPR 1998, see the relevant Guide in the *Civil Court Service* (Jordan Publishing Ltd).

Procedure

Availability	A county court has all the necessary powers of the High Court in this regard, and also has express powers to appoint a receiver of interests in land. The powers of either court are entirely discretionary	CCA 1984, ss 38, 107
	If the order is sought to enforce arrears more than 12 months old, leave must be obtained (but may be requested in the same application)	MCA 1973, s 32
Application	In the High Court, the application is made by summons to the district judge	RSC Ord 30, r 1, Ord 51, r 2
	In the county court, the application is made on notice to the district judge	FPR 1991, r 10.9
	In either case, the application must be supported by an affidavit verifying the amount due and showing how it is arrived at	FPR 1991, r 7.1(1)

	If interest is claimed, the calculation should be set out in the affidavit and (in the county court) a copy of it filed	CCR Ord 25, r 5A
Fee payable	High Court: £50 for each person against whom the order is sought	FPFO 1999, fee 14.3
	County court: £50 for each person against whom the order is sought	FPFO 1999, fee 12.4
Appeals	See Guides 72, 73	

37: Writ of Sequestration

Legal background

In the High Court, the person in whose favour an order has been made may issue a writ of sequestration requiring the sequestrators named to take possession of all the assets of the person against whom it was made if he has not complied with it. The remedy is appropriate in circumstances where committal for contempt might be imposed, save that the restrictions on the court's power to commit for non-compliance with an order to pay money do not apply to sequestration. The county court also may exercise this remedy, but it is usually considered more appropriate to transfer a county court order to the High Court and make the application there.

The reader is reminded that this Guide deals only with "family proceedings". Procedural changes made by the Civil Procedure Rules 1998 do not (yet) apply to such proceedings (see further annotations under FPR 1991, r 1.3). For a description of the steps to be taken in proceedings which are not "family proceedings" and which are governed by CPR 1998, see the relevant Guide in the *Civil Court Service* (Jordan Publishing Ltd).

Procedure

Availability	Leave is always required and is generally only granted in the largest cases, in view of the considerable expense involved	RSC Ord 45, r 5(1)(i)
Application	In the High Court, by motion to a judge; it must be supported by an affidavit	RSC Ord 46, r 5
	No rules exist in the county court; in the event that an application for leave is to be made there, the High Court procedure should be followed as nearly as may be	CCA 1984, s 76
Fee payable	£60	FPFO 1999, fee 4.3
Service	The notice of motion and a copy of the affidavit must usually be served personally	RSC Ord 46, r 5

Subsequent procedure	If leave is granted, the applicant files a praecipe, presents the form of writ for sealing and serves the writ on the sequestrators named in it	RSC Ord 46, r 6
Form	No form is prescribed for the notice of motion or affidavit; writ of sequestration in Form No 67	
Appeals	See Guide 75	

38: Committal and Arrest for Disobedience of an Injunctive Order or Breach of an Undertaking in the High Court, County Court or Magistrates' Court

Legal background

An injunctive order (including a non-molestation order or occupation order under FLA 1996, Pt IV; a CA 1989, s 8 order to which a penal notice has been attached; and an order under PHA 1997) directing a person to do an act at or within a specified time, or to abstain from doing an act, or an undertaking to like effect which incorporates a penal warning notice, may be enforced by committal proceedings initiated by the person entitled to the benefit of the direction or undertaking. Orders and undertakings for payment of money in general cannot be enforced by committal for contempt (*Nwogbe v Nwogbe* [2000] 2 FLR 744) and should not have a penal notice incorporated or attached. Some money orders may be enforceable by judgment summons under the Debtors Acts 1869 and 1878 (see Guide 32). Personal service of an injunctive order is required by CPR 1998, Sch 1, RSC Ord 45, r 7, CPR 1998, Sch 2, CCR Ord 29, r 1(2) and Family Proceedings Courts (Matrimonial Proceedings etc) Rules 1991, r 20(7). The court can dispense with service or provide for some other form of service, but an injunction cannot be enforced unless it can be proved that the person to whom it was directed knew about the order and, where an act is directed to be done, the order must have been served before the time set for the act to be done. "Any procedural defect in the commencement or conduct by the applicant of a committal application may be waived by the court if satisfied that no injustice has been caused to the respondent by the defect" (*Practice Direction (Committal Applications)*, para 10; *Nicholls v Nicholls* [1997] 1 FLR 649).

Which rules of court

Applications for committal in respect of injunctive orders are interlocutory in nature (*Savings and Investment Bank v Gasco Investments (Netherlands) BV (No 2)* [1988] Ch 422, [1988] 2 WLR 1212). Consequently, if the injunctive order was made in family proceedings an application for committal is made in family proceedings and RSC Ord 52 and CCR Ord 29, unrevised, apply. If the injunctive order was made in non-family civil proceedings, the same rules apply but in their new placement in CPR 1998, Schs 1 and 2. As there is no material difference in the substance of practice, only changes in some of the language (eg claim form and application notice), the text of these rules will be found in the Schedules to the CPR 1998. *Practice Direction (Judgments and Orders)* (PD 40B), paras 8.1 and 9, *Practice Direction (Committal Applications)* and *President's Direction of 16 March 2001 (Committal Applications and Proceedings in which a Committal Order may be Made)* apply.

Committal proceedings begun by notice to show good reason

The standard procedure for beginning proceedings for committal for enforcement of an injunction or an undertaking is by way of notice to show good reason why an order for committal should not be made, begun by summons (High Court, Family Division), application notice or Part 8 claim form (High Court, Queen's Bench and Chancery Divisions), Form N78 (county court) or FL 418 (magistrates' court). This is the appropriate way to start proceedings based on more than one alleged disobedience or breach or where there is no immediate urgency.

Committal proceedings begun by arrest under a power of arrest

The power to arrest, for breach of a non-molestation or occupation order granted under FLA 1996, s 47(3), provides the police with authority to intervene and stop a breach while it is happening or where they have reason to believe that such a breach has occurred. A power of arrest can also be exercised after the disobedience has ended and after an arrest for a criminal offence (*Wheeldon v Wheeldon* [1998] 1 FLR 463). Where there has been serious violence the police are more likely to arrest under their criminal powers of arrest. Where the police use the civil power of arrest the arrested person must be brought before the court within 24 hours (FLA 1996, s 47(7)).

There is no power to attach a power of arrest to an injunction against torts under the Protection from Harassment Act 1997 or common law.

Committal proceedings begun by arrest under a warrant of arrest

FLA 1996, s 47(8), (9) extended to the High Court and county courts a power previously available only in family proceedings courts. This power is available where no power of arrest was attached to the breached direction (s 47(8)). The court can issue a warrant for the arrest of a person where the court has reasonable grounds, substantiated on oath (s 47(9)), to believe that he has failed to comply with a non-molestation or occupation order made under FLA 1996, Pt IV.

Protection from Harassment Act 1997, s 3(3)–(5) provides the High Court and county courts with the power to issue a warrant of arrest where the court has reasonable grounds, substantiated on oath (s 3(5)), to believe that the respondent has failed to comply with an injunction which forbids harassment.

Remand following arrest

Once an arrested respondent is before the court, the court can immediately deal with the breach for which he has been arrested or adjourn (whether or not upon enlarged injunctive provisions). If adjourning, the court has power to remand. The power to remand is given to the High Court and county courts by FLA 1996, s 47(11) and Sch 5, and exists in a magistrates' court by virtue of Magistrates' Courts Act 1980, ss 128 and 129. The remand can be in custody or on bail. Under FLA 1996, s 48, the power to remand can be exercised to enable a medical report to be made on the respondent.

There is no power to remand under Protection from Harassment Act 1997.

Conduct of committal proceedings when the respondent is before the court, whether on notice or following an arrest

Whether the respondent or defendant appears on notice in answer to a notice to show good reason, or following an arrest, the procedure to be followed for the determination of whether the respondent has disobeyed an order or breached an undertaking, and the disposal powers of the court, are the same. However, an arrest is executed upon the basis of the breach(es) which led to the arrest, and earlier breaches should not be dealt with unless the court considers it just to dispense with service of a notice to show good reason. This is the import of FPR 1991, r 3.9A(4), FPC(MP etc)R 1991, r 20(4)(*a*), and (in respect of harassment under PHA 1997) CPR 1998, Sch 1, RSC Ord 94, r 16(5)(*a*). Arrest is an alternative procedure for bringing an alleged contemnor before the court, without a notice to show good reason having been issued and served. Once the court commences determination of whether a breach is proved, the hearing procedure leading to a finding of contempt and disposal is the same.

Penalties

The court can order imprisonment (immediate or suspended) and/or a fine, or adjourn consideration of penalty for a fixed period. Other disposals or remedies for enforcement may be more appropriate. The common disposal orders are set out in county court Form N79 and family proceedings court Form FL419.

Procedure

Preliminary matters	An injunctive order must be served personally on the person to whom it is directed, unless there has been an order for substituted service or dispensing with service	CPR 1998, Sch 1, RSC Ord 45, r 7(2); CPR 1998, Sch 2, CCR Ord 29, r 1(2); FPC(MP etc)R 1991, r 20(6)
	However, pending service, if the respondent disobeys an injunctive order which requires him to abstain from doing an act, the court can impose a penalty if it is satisfied that he knew about the terms of the order	CPR 1998, Sch 1, RSC Ord 45, r 7(6); CPR 1998, Sch 2, CCR Ord 29, r 1(2)(*a*); FPC(MP etc)R 1991, r 20(11)
	Proof of service of the order is required. In the High Court and county courts this is usually by affidavit. In magistrates' courts, by Form FL415	
	A mandatory injunctive order directing a person to do an act cannot be enforced unless it was served before the time at or by which the act was directed to be done	CPR 1998, Sch 1, RSC Ord 45, r 7(2); CPR 1998, Sch 2, CCR Ord 29, r 1(2)(*b*); FPC(MP etc)R 1991, r 20(6)(*b*)
	An undertaking becomes enforceable on being given to and accepted by the court; however the court can require the giver to sign a statement to the effect that he understands the terms of his undertaking and the consequences of failure to comply with it	*Hussain v Hussain* [1986] 2 FLR 271; PD 40B, para 9.3
	A copy of the undertaking in Form N117 in a county court, D787 in the Principal Registry or FL422 in a family proceedings court, is required to be delivered to the giver of the undertaking, but the giver is bound even if he does not receive a copy	CPR 1998, Sch 2, CCR Ord 29, r 1A; FPC(MP etc)R 1991, r 20(14)
Who may apply for committal or enforcement?	Person in whose favour the injunctive order was granted or the undertaking was given	CPR 1998, Sch 1, RSC Ord 45, r 5; Ord 52, r 4; CPR 1998, Sch 2, CCR Ord 29, r 1(4); FPC(MP etc)R 1991, r 20(8)
Which court?	The court which granted the injunctive order or undertaking	*PD (Committal)*, paras 1.2, 1.3
	The powers of county courts to deal with disobedience or breach are the same as the High Court	CCA 1981; CCA 1984, s 38
	Magistrates' courts statutory powers to deal with disobedience or breach are limited to imposing immediate or suspended committal, fine or adjourning consideration of penalty	MCA 1980, s 63(3); FLA 1996, s 50(1); FPC(MP etc)R, 1991 r 20(16), (18)

Application by summons (FD), application notice (QBD and non-family proceedings in a county court) or notice to show good reason (family proceedings in a county court)	In the Family Division of the High Court, by summons supported by an affidavit. In the Queen's Bench Division, by an application notice supported by affidavit	FPR 1991, r 7.2(1); CPR 1998, Sch 1, RSC Ord 52, r 4; *PD (Committal)*, paras 2, 3; N244
	In a county court, by application notice or request for notice, supported by affidavit, for issue of notice in Form N78. A draft Form N78 is usually accepted as the application, though a Part 8 claim form is required in PHA 1997 proceedings	CC(F)R 1982; CPR 1998, Sch 2, CCR Ord 29, r 1(4), (4A); *PD (Committal)*, paras 2.2, 2.5, 3.1
	In a magistrates' court, by request, supported by statement declaring the facts recited are true, for issue of notice in Form FL 418. The request is usually a draft Form N418	FPC(MP etc)R 1991, r 20(8), (9)(*c*)
	In every case, the summons or notice must "identify, separately and numerically, each alleged act of contempt"	*PD (Committal)*, para 2.5(2)
	The affidavit or statement in support should narrate the facts relied on, but the list must be given in the summons, application notice, Part 8 claim form or notice to show good reason	CPR 1998, Sch 2, CCR Ord 29, r 1(4A); FPC(MP etc)R 1991, r 20(9)(*b*); *Harmsworth v Harmsworth* [1988] 1 FLR 349 at 354D–355B
	Fee payable on application in family proceedings in High Court or county court: £60	FPFO 1999, fee 4.3
	No fee payable in magistrates' court.	
Application for warrant of arrest under FLA 1996, s 47(8)	Application is made, without notice to the respondent, in Form FL408, to "the relevant judicial authority", ie the convenient court in whichever tier of court the injunctive order was granted	FLA 1996, ss 47(8), 63(1); FPR 1991, r 3.9A(3); FPC(MP etc)R 1991, r 20(3)
	The application must be substantiated on oath and the court must have reasonable grounds for believing that the respondent has failed to comply with an order, or part of an order to which no power of arrest had been attached	FLA 1996, s 47(9)
	The warrant is executed in the High Court by the Tipstaff, in the county court by the bailiffs (or, in each case, by the police on request), and in the magistrates' court by the police	Form FL408
	In the magistrates' court the justices' clerk is responsible for delivering the warrant to the police	FPC(MP etc)R 1991, r 20(3)

Application for warrant of arrest under PHA 1997, s 3(3)	Application is made, without notice to the respondent, to the convenient court in whichever tier of court the injunctive order was granted	PHA 1997, s 3(4)
	The application must be substantiated on oath and the court must have reasonable grounds for believing that the respondent has done something which is prohibited by the injunction	PHA 1997, s 3(5); CPR 1998, Sch 1, RSC Ord 94, r 16(4)
Production in court following arrest under FLA 1996, s 47	A person arrested under a power of arrest must be brought before the relevant judicial authority within 24 hours not including Sunday, Christmas Day or Good Friday	FLA 1996, s 47(7)
	Neither FLA 1996 nor the rules prescribe how soon a person arrested under a warrant of arrest must be brought before the court	FLA 1996, s 47(8)–(10)
Procedures open to court under FLA 1996, ss 47, 48 when arrested person produced in court	The court may hear the facts upon which the arrest was based, and decide penalty or	FLA 1996, s 47(7)(*b*), (10)
	adjourn for not more than 14 days, in which case the respondent must be given not less than 2 days' notice of the adjourned hearing, or	FPR 1991, r 3.9A(4); FPC(MP etc)R 1991, r 20(4)
	remand in custody for a period not exceeding 8 days or	FLA 1996, s 47(11), Sch 5 para 2(5)
	remand on bail on conditions and/or recognisances	FLA 1996, s 47(11), (12), Sch 5 para 2(5)
	where the court has reason to suspect mental illness or severe mental impairment, the court may remand, to enable a medical examination and report, for not more than 3 weeks if in custody or 4 weeks if on bail	FLA 1996, s 48
Powers of court under PHA 1997, s 3(5) when arrested person produced in court	The court may hear the facts upon which the arrest was based, and decide penalty, or adjourn for not more than 14 days, in which case the defendant must be given not less than 2 days' notice of the adjourned hearing	CPR 1998, Sch 1, RSC Ord 94, r 16(5)
Hearing without notice to the respondent	In exceptional circumstances, the court may, without notice having been given to the respondent, deal with an application begun by notice to show good reason, by dispensing with service of the summons or notice	CPR 1998, Sch 1, RSC Ord 52, r 4(3); CPR 1998, Sch 2, CCR Ord 29, r 1(7); FPC(MP etc)R 1991, r 20(12)

	It is not appropriate for a court to proceed without notice where arrest under a power or warrant can be achieved under FLA 1996, s 47, or under PHA 1997, s 3(5). However, where a power or warrant of arrest is not available, proceeding without notice may exceptionally be appropriate. When the court takes this exceptional step and imposes imprisonment, the court should fix a date and time for the contemnor to be brought before the court	CPR 1998, Sch 2, CCR Ord 29, r 1(8)
Service of summons or Form N78	Personal service of the summons or Form N78, and affidavit in support, is required at least 2 working days before the hearing	CPR 1998, Sch 1, RSC Ord 52, r 4(2); CPR 1998, Sch 2, CCR Ord 29, r 1(4), (4A); FPC(MP etc)R 1991, r 3A(5), 20(8), (9)
	In civil proceedings under CPR 1998 a period of 14 clear days after service is required unless the court directs otherwise	*PD (Committal)*, para 4.2
	However, this does not apply in family proceedings where, instead, the court will allow the respondent "adequate time" to prepare his defence	*PD of 16 March 2001*, para 1.1
	By way of exception, where the committal order was made in family proceedings, the court can:	
	order substituted service (not available in magistrates' courts)	RSC Ord 65, r 4(2); CCR Ord 7, r 8
	abridge time-limit for service	RSC Ord 8, r 2(2); CCR Ord 13, r 4(1); FPC(MP etc)R 1991, r 3A(6); *PD (Committal)*, para 4.2
	in exceptional cases, dispense with service	see Hearing without notice to the respondent (above)
Service of notice of adjourned hearing	Where a hearing is adjourned, personal service of notice of the adjourned hearing is required, unless the respondent was present in court and was told when and where the adjourned hearing would resume and/or was remanded under FLA 1996, s 47(7), (10), Sch 5 or MCA 1980, ss 128, 129	*Chiltern DC v Keane* [1985] 1 WLR 619 at 622H–623C
Case management	The court can make directions at any time as to service of evidence and conduct of the proceedings, or strike out an inappropriate application	*PD (Committal)*, paras 4.3, 5

The hearing	Which judge? District judges as well as High Court and circuit judges have power to hear committal proceedings under FLA 1996, Pt IV	FLA 1996, ss 58, 63(1)
	However district judges do not have power to hear committal proceedings under PHA 1997	PHA 1997, s 3(3), (4) only gives power to issue a warrant; *PD (Committal)*, para 11
	Normally held in open court, unless it relates to the welfare of a child or to a person suffering from mental disorder. A finding of contempt in private must be announced in public	CPR 1998, Sch 1, RSC Ord 52, r 6(1); *PD (Committal)*, para 9
	The court can proceed if the respondent, having been duly served, fails to attend	*Payne v Payne* [1979] CAT 209
	The court cannot grant legal aid to a person who answers to an application for committal, but may invite a solicitor to represent him by providing "Help at Court"	AJA 1999, Pt I
	Note that the power of the court to *grant* legal representation in contempt cases applies only to a contempt in the face of the court	AJA 1999, s 12(2), Sch 3
	Procedure is akin to criminal trial; see *Emergency Remedies in the Family Courts* E [15.158]. The criminal standard of proof ("beyond reasonable doubt" applies)	*Dean v Dean* [1987] 1 FLR 517
	An application notice can be amended with the permission of the court but not otherwise	*PD (Committal)*, para 2.6(3)
	An alleged contemnor cannot be directed or compelled to give information	*PD (Committal)*, paras 6, 7; *Comet Products UK Ltd v Hawkex Plastics Ltd* [1971] 2 QB 67, [1971] 2 WLR 361
	A deliberate act or failure to act (actus reus) with knowledge of the terms of the order (mens rea) must be proved	*DG of Fair Trading v Smiths Concrete* [1992] QB 213
Powers of court	The disposal must be proportionate to the seriousness of the contempt, reflect the court's disapproval and be designed to secure compliance in future. The court should briefly explain its reasons for the choice of disposal	*Hale v Tanner* [2000] 2 FLR 879
	Committal to prison is appropriate only where no reasonable alternative exists	*Hale v Tanner* (above)

	Imprisonment is restricted to total of 2 years in the High Court or a county court, 2 months in a magistrates' court, and must be for a fixed term	CCA 1981, s 14; MCA 1980, s 63(3)
	Sentence can be suspended or adjourned on terms	FLA 1996, s 50(1); CPR 1998, Sch 1, RSC Ord 52, r 7(1); FPC(MP etc)R 1991, r 20(16), (18); *George v George* [1986] 2 FLR 347
	Person under the age of 21 can be detained under CJA 1982, s 9(1)	*R v Selby Justices ex parte Frame* [1991] 2 WLR 965
	Person under the age of 18 cannot be committed to any form of detention	*R v Selby Justices* (above)
	Mental Health Act powers are available	CCA 1981, s 14; MHA 1983, ss 35, 37, 38
	Fine can be imposed	*Hale v Tanner* [2000] 2 FLR 879
	A fresh injunction can be granted	*Coats v Chadwick* [1894] 1 Ch 347
	A power of arrest can be attached, if available, to the injunctive order	*Ansah v Ansah* (1976) FLR Rep 9
	Sequestration, damages and other means of enforcement are available in the High Court and county court, see Fricker and Bean, *Enforcement of Injunctions and Undertakings* (Family Law, 1991), Ch 5	CPR 1998, Sch 1, RSC Ord 45, rr 5(1), 8; *Rose v Laskington* [1990] QB 562
Form of order	The order must specify "exact details" of each contempt found proved and specify the disposal ordered	*Nguyen v Phung* [1984] FLR 773 at 778C; *Re C (A Minor) (Contempt)* [1986] 1 FLR 578 at 585A
	Where sentence is suspended or adjourned, the period of suspension or adjournment and the precise terms for activation must be specified	*Pidduck v Molloy* [1992] 2 FLR 202; CPR 1998, Sch 1, RSC Ord 52, r 7(1)
	In the High Court, the order is issued in Form A85 and warrant in Form PF303. In a county court, Form N79 and warrant in Form N80. In a magistrates' court, Form FL419 and warrant in Form FL420	
Service of order	Where immediate imprisonment or detention is imposed, the court serves the order	CPR 1998, Sch 2, CCR Ord 29, r 1(5); *Clarke v Clarke* [1990] 2 FLR 115
	Where sentence is suspended, the applicant must serve the order, unless the court directs otherwise	CPR 1998, Sch 1, RSC Ord 52, r 7(2); FPC(MP etc)R 1991, r 20(17)

Review by Official Solicitor	The court sends a copy of every committal order and relevant details to the Official Solicitor, who reviews the case and may apply or appeal of his own motion or at the contemnor's request	*Lord Chancellor's Direction of 29 May 1963; Secretary's Circular of 28 September 1981*
Discharge of contemnor	A contemnor is entitled to apply to purge his contempt and be discharged from prison	CPR 1998, Sch 1, RSC Ord 52, r 8(1); CPR 1998, Sch 2, CCR Ord 29, r 3(1)
	In the High Court, if the committal order was made in family proceedings, the application is made by notice of motion which must be served at least 2 working days before the hearing	RSC Ord 8, r 2(2)
	If the committal was made in civil proceedings, the application notice must be served as soon as practicable after it is filed and at least 3 days before the hearing	CPR 1998, r 23.7(1)
	In a county court or a magistrates' court, one working day suffices	CPR 1998, Sch 2, CCR Ord 29, r 3(1); FPC(MP etc)R 1991, r 20(15)
	The contemnor should be in court	*PD of 25 July 1983*
	On an application to purge, the court can say "yes", "no" or "not yet"	*Harris v Harris* [2001] EWCA Civ 1645, [2002] 1 FLR 248
Appeals	See Guide 75	

39: Consent to Marriage of a Minor

Legal background

Marriage Act 1949, s 3(1) sets out a general rule that those under the age of 18, who are not widows or widowers, may not marry under a superintendent registrar's certificate or a common licence without the consent of the persons mentioned in MA 1949, s 3(1A) (usually the parents but with variations according to circumstances, eg where a residence order is in force or the child has a guardian). MA 1949, s 3(1)(*b*) allows the court, on application, to give consent instead of any person whose consent is required and who refuses that consent.

Procedure

Who may apply	The person who needs the consent to marry	
Which court	High Court	
	county court for the district in which any applicant or respondent resides or	

	magistrates' court in a commission area in which any applicant or respondent resides	MA 1949, s 3(1)(*b*), (5)
Application	By originating summons in the High Court	RSC Ord 5, r 3
	By originating application in a county court	CCR Ord 3, r 4
	Fee payable in High Court or county court: £120	FPFO 1999, fee 1.1
	Orally or in writing in a magistrates' court	MC(GM)R 1974, r 5(1)
	Fee payable in magistrates' court: £3.50	MCA 1980, Sch 6, Pt I
	A next friend is unnecessary	FPR 1991, r 3.20(3)
Respondents	Those refusing consent in the case of an application under s 3(1)(*b*)	MC(GM)R 1974, r 5(2)
	None in the case of an application under s 3(1)(*a*)	FPR 1991, r 3.20(4)
Service	Effected 7 days before the hearing (unless otherwise ordered) in a county court or the High Court	FPR 1991, rr 3.20(5), 10.2, 10.3
	By the justices' clerk on receiving the application in a magistrates' court	MC(GM)R 1974, r 5(2)
Remaining stages of proceedings	As on originating summons, generally in the High Court	RSC generally
	As on originating application, generally in a county court	CCR generally
	MCA 1980, Pt II and MCR 1981, r 14 govern the hearing	MC(GM)R 1974, r 5(4); IA 1978, s 17(2)(*a*)
	In the High Court and county courts, a district judge may hear the proceedings in chambers	FPR 1991, r 3.20(1), (2)

40: Declaration of Parentage and Parentage Appeals under the Child Support Act 1991

Legal background

Child Support Act 1991, s 27(1) enables the Secretary of State for Social Security or a person with care to apply to the court where there is a question under the Act as to a child's parentage which has not already been resolved by another court. Where a question arises as to the child's parentage on a calculation of child support maintenance, any appeal on this point goes to a court rather than to a child support appeal tribunal (CSA 1991, s 20 and Child Support Appeals (Jurisdiction of Courts) Order 2002, art 4).

Procedure

Who may apply	Person with care, or Secretary of State	CSA 1991, s 27(1); FLA 1986, s 55A
Which court	Magistrates' court Proceedings may be transferred	C(AP)O 1991, art 3(1)(*s*), (*t*) C(AP)O 1991, arts 6–13
Application	No form prescribed by FPC(CA 1989)R 1991, r 4(1)(*a*); thus, apply in writing, giving relevant details	FPC(MP etc)R 1991, r 4(1), as applied by FPC(CSA 1991)R 1993, r 4(1)
Fee payable	£30	MCA 1980, Sch 6, Pt I
Respondents	*Section 20 appeal* Secretary of State *Section 27 application* Alleged parent	FPC(CSA 1991)R 1993, r 4(2) FPC(CSA 1991)R 1993, r 4(3)
Time for service	None prescribed, but it seems reasonable to assume 21 days as for applications under CA 1989, s 8 or Sch 1	FPC(MP etc)R 1991, r 4(1)(*b*), (3), Sch 2, col (ii), as applied
Transfer	If transferred, case proceeds as if by originating summons/application, and all existing directions stand	FPR 1991, r 3.21
Answer to application	No form is prescribed, but a written answer must be filed, indicating intention to defend or not to defend, within 14 days from service of application	FPC(MP etc)R 1991, r 5, as applied
Directions	The issue of whether to give directions must be considered by the justices' clerk or the court	FPR 1991, r 3.21(2); FPC(MP etc)R 1991, r 6(1), as applied
Scientific tests	May be made on application by either party to the proceedings or by court of its own motion	FLRA 1969, s 20
Power to make the order	*Family proceedings court* Magistrates *High Court or county court* On s 20 appeal, judge only; on s 27 application, judge or district judge	FPC(MP etc)R 1991, r 12, as applied FPR 1991, r 3.21(4)
Costs	In the discretion of the court; but see —	FLRA 1969, s 20(6); CSA 1991, s 27A(1)
CLS funding	Available for s 20 appeals and s 27 applications in all courts	AJA 1999, s 6, Sch 2, para 2(1), (3)(*g*)
Appeals	*Family proceedings court* To the High Court	RSC Ord 55; see Guide 70

	High Court or county court From district judge to judge	FPR 1991, r 8.1, RSC Ord 58; see Guides 71, 72
	From judge to Court of Appeal	CPR 1998, Pt 52; see Guide 75

41: Declaration of Legitimacy or Legitimation

Legal background

Family Law Act 1986, s 56(1)(*b*), (2) (substituted by Family Law Reform Act 1987) allows any court to make a declaration that the applicant (*a*) is the legitimate child of his parents, (*b*) has become a legitimated person or (*c*) has not become a legitimated person; (*b*) and (*c*) can be sought as alternatives under FLA 1986, s 56(2). If the truth of the proposition sought to be declared is established, the court is obliged to make the declaration, unless to do so would manifestly be contrary to public policy (FLA 1986, s 58(1)). If made, a declaration binds the world, not just the parties (FLA 1986, s 58(2)).

Subject to specific provision, FPR 1991 apply to proceedings for a declaration as they apply to matrimonial causes (FPR 1991, r 3.16(12)).

Procedure

Who may apply	Any person (in effect, the person whose status is in question)	FLA 1986, s 56(1), (2); see also under FPR 1991, r 3.14
Which court	High Court or a county court	FLA 1986, ss 56(1), (2), 63; see also under FPR 1991, r 3.14
Pre-application requirement	Papers must be served on Attorney General at least 1 month before petition is filed	FPR 1991, r 3.16(4)
Application	By petition containing, unless otherwise directed, the details required by FPR 1991, r 3.14(1), App 2, para 4, and, where relevant, r 3.16(2)	FPR 1991, rr 2.2(1), 3.14(1), 3.16(2), (12)
	Fee payable: £150	FPFO 1999, fee 1.2
Documents to accompany petition	A copy of the petitioner's birth certificate (unless otherwise directed)	FPR 1991, r 3.14(2)
	Affidavit verifying petition and identifying those affected	FPR 1991, r 3.16(1)
Respondents	The petitioner's parents (if alive)	FPR 1991, r 3.14(3)
Other parties	The Attorney General has the right to intervene in accordance with —	FLA 1986, s 59(2); FPR 1991, r 3.16(7), (9), (10)
	For joinder of other parties, see —	FPR 1991, r 3.16(6), (8)

Service	In accordance with FPR 1991, rr 2.9 (generally), 9.3 (service on person under disability), 10.6 (service out of England and Wales)	FPR 1991, r 3.16(12)
Answer to petition	28 days after service of petition	FPR 1991, rr 2.12(1), 3.16(12), 10.8(2)(*a*)
Other interlocutory procedures	As in matrimonial proceedings	FPR 1991, rr 3.16(12), 2.13–2.25
Hearing	As in matrimonial proceedings	FPR 1991, rr 2.32–2.42, 3.16(12)
Order	A declaration that the applicant: is the legitimate child of his parents has become a legitimated person has not become a legitimated person	FLA 1986, s 56(1)(*b*), (2)
Form	M31	FPR 1991, r 3.16(11)
Appeals	See Guide 75	

42: Declaration of Parentage under the Family Law Act 1986

Legal background

Family Law Act 1986, s 55A (which was introduced by Child Support, Pensions and Social Security Act 2000, s 83 and replaces FLA 1986, s 56(1)(*a*)) allows any court to make a declaration that a person named in the application is or was the parent of another person so named. If the truth of the proposition sought to be declared is established, the court is obliged to make the declaration, unless to do so would manifestly be contrary to public policy (FLA 1986, s 58(1)). If made, a declaration binds the world and not just the parties (FLA 1986, s 58(2)). When a declaration of parentage is made, the court notifies the Registrar General of the declaration. Under Births and Deaths Registration Act 1953, s 14A, the Registrar General has a discretion to authorise the re-registration of the birth on the basis of the declaration. An alternative procedure is available under BDRA 1953, s 10A (as amended by Children Act 1975, s 93(2)), which provides for the re-registration of the birth of an illegitimate child in the Register of Births by entering the name of the father either at the joint request of the parents or at the request of the mother on the production of Statutory Declarations, parental responsibility agreement or parental responsibility order.

It should be noted that, subject to specific provision, FPR 1991 apply to proceedings for a declaration as they apply to matrimonial causes (FPR 1991, r 3.16(12)).

Procedure

Who may apply	A parent, the child or any other person with sufficient personal interest	FLA 1986, s 55A – see also under FPR 1991, r 3.13

Which court	High Court, a county court or a magistrates' court	FLA 1986, s 55A – see also under FPR 1991, r 3.13
Application	By petition containing, unless otherwise directed, the details required by FPR 1991, r 3.13(1), App 2, para 4, and, where relevant, r 3.16(2)	FPR 1991, rr 2.2(1), 3.13(1), 3.16(2), (12)
	Fee payable: £150	FPFO 1999, fee 1.2
Documents to accompany petition	A copy of the birth certificate of the person whose parentage is in issue (unless otherwise directed)	FPR 1991, r 3.13(2)
	Affidavit verifying petition and identifying those affected	FPR 1991, r 3.16(1)
Respondents	The person whose parentage is in issue and anybody who is alleged to be the mother or father of that person (excluding the petitioner)	FPR 1991, r 3.13(3)
Other parties	The Attorney General has the right to intervene in accordance with —	FLA 1986, s 59(2); FPR 1991, r 3.16(7), (9), (10)
	For joinder of other parties, see —	FPR 1991, r 3.16(6), (8)
Service	In accordance with FPR 1991, rr 2.9 (generally), 9.3 (service on person under disability), 10.6 (service out of England and Wales)	FPR 1991, r 3.16(12)
Answer to petition	28 days after service of petition	FPR 1991, rr 2.12(1), 3.16(12), 10.8(2)(*a*)
Other interlocutory procedures	As in matrimonial proceedings	FPR 1991, rr 2.13–2.25, 3.16(12)
Hearing	As in matrimonial proceedings	FPR 1991, rr 2.32–2.42, 3.16(12)
Order	A declaration that a person named in the application is or was the parent of another person so named	FLA 1986, s 55A
Form	M30 (High Court/county court)	FPR 1991, r 3.16(11)
	FL424 (magistrates' court)	FPC(MP etc)R 1991, r 3B(13)
Appeals	See Guide 75	

43: Child Assessment Order

Legal background

Under CA 1989, s 43, the court may make a child assessment order authorising a medical, psychiatric or other assessment on the application of a local authority, or of the NSPCC or any other person authorised by the secretary of state to bring care proceedings provided it is satisfied (*a*) that the applicant has reasonable cause to suspect that the child is suffering or is likely to suffer significant harm, (*b*) that an assessment of the child's health or development or of the way in which he has been treated is required to enable the applicant to determine whether or not the child is suffering or likely to suffer significant harm and (*c*) that it is unlikely that such an assessment will be made (or be satisfactory) in the absence of an order.

The order must specify the date on which the assessment is to begin and must be for a period not exceeding seven days. If necessary, it can include a direction that the child lives away from home for a specified period for the purposes of the assessment and regulate contact with him while he is away. If the child is of sufficient understanding to make an informed decision, he may override the court's order by refusing to submit to the assessment.

If the court is satisfied that there are grounds for an emergency protection order and that it ought to make such an order rather than the child assessment order sought, it must not make a child assessment order and may make an emergency protection order instead.

Procedure

Who may apply	Local authority or authorised person (ie officer of NSPCC or anyone authorised by Secretary of State)	CA 1989, ss 31(9), 43(1), (13)
Which court	Magistrates' court, unless pending proceedings or application arises out of a s 37 investigation by local authority, in which case apply to court where proceedings pending/court which required investigation	C(AP)O 1991, art 3
	Proceedings may be transferable sideways, upwards or downwards	C(AP)O 1991, arts 6–13
Which proceedings	Freestanding application	CA 1989, s 43(1)
Application	On Form C1 and Supplement C16, with copies for each respondent	FPR 1991, r 4.4(1); FPC(CA 1989)R 1991, r 4(1)
	Fee in High Court or county court: £80	FPFO 1999, fee 2.8(*a*)
	Fee in magistrates' court: £50	MCA 1980, Sch 6, Pt I
Respondents	Every person whom applicant believes has parental responsibility Every person whom applicant believes had parental responsibility prior to care order The child	FPR 1991, r 4.7, App 3; FPC(CA 1989)R 1991, r 7, Sch 2

Additional persons to whom notice in Form C6A is to be given	Local authority providing accommodation for child Persons caring for child at commencement of proceedings and every person whom applicant believes is caring for child Person providing a s 51 refuge for child Every person whom applicant believes is a parent Every person in whose favour a contact order is in force Every person allowed to have contact by a s 34 order	FPR 1991, r 4.4, App 3; FPC(CA 1989)R 1991, r 4, Sch 2 – note also the slight difference in terminology in CA 1989, s 43(11)
Service	Copy of application, together with Form C6, to be served on respondents at least 7 days before date of hearing or directions appointment	FPR 1991, rr 4.4(1), 4.8; FPC(CA 1989)R 1991, rr 4(1), 8
	Form C6A to be served on additional persons at same time as application etc served on respondents	FPR 1991, r 4.4(3); FPC(CA 1989)R 1991, r 4(3)
	At or before first directions appointment or hearing, applicant must file statement in Form C9 to prove that requirements for service have been complied with	FPR 1991, r 4.7; FPC (CA 1989)R 1991, r 7
Ex parte	May not be available	FPR 1991, r 4.4(4); FPC (CA 1989)R 1991, r 4(4)
Joinder or removal of parties	By court order, of its own motion or on written request	FPR 1991, r 4.7; FPC(CA 1989)R 1991, r 7
Answer to application	Under FPR 1991, respondent may file an answer; serve on other parties	FPR 1991, r 4.9(3), (4)
	Under FPC(CA 1989)R 1991, no provision either forbidding or permitting an answer	
Directions	As to the powers of the justices' clerk or the court, see —	FPR 1991, r 4.14; FPC(CA 1989)R 1991, r 14
Children's guardian	Must normally be appointed	CA 1989, s 41(1)
Special requirements	Bar on application for further order within 6 months from disposal of first application unless leave given	CA 1989, s 91(15)

Who has power to make the order	High Court or nominated county court judge, any district judge of the principal registry or nominated district judge outside the principal registry	FP(AJ)D 1999, Sch, para (*j*) (as substituted by FP(AJ)(A)D 2002)
	A magistrates' court; however, justices' clerk or single justice has no such power	JCR 1999; CA 1989, s 93(2)(*i*); FPC(CA 1989)R 1991, r 2(5)
Order	Form C39	FPR 1991, r 4.21(5), App 1; FPC(CA 1989)R 1991, r 21(7), Sch 1
Additional or alternative orders	Emergency protection order	CA 1989, s 43(3), (4)
	No order	CA 1989, s 1(5)
Appeals	See Guides 70, 72–75	

44: Variation or Discharge of a Child Assessment Order

Legal background

CA 1989, s 43(12) (as given effect by FPR 1991 and FPC(CA 1989)R 1991) enables an application to be made for the variation or discharge of a child assessment order. The rules state that such an application can be made "in any circumstances" (FPR 1991, r 4.2(3); FPC(CA 1989)R 1991, r 2(3)).

Procedure

Who may apply	Local authority or authorised person on whose application the order was originally made A parent Any person with parental responsibility Any other person caring for child Any person in whose favour a contact order is in force Any person who is allowed to have contact by a s 34 order The child	CA 1989, s 43(12); FPR 1991, r 4.2(3); FPC(CA 1989)R 1991, r 2(3)
Which court	The court which made the original order	C(AP)O 1991, art 4(1)
	Proceedings may be transferable sideways, upwards or downwards	C(AP)O 1991, arts 6–13
Which proceedings	Freestanding application	CA 1989, s 43(11); FPR 1991, r 4.2(3); FPC(CA 1989)R 1991, r 2(3)

Application	On Form C1, with copies for each respondent	FPR 1991, r 4.4(1); FPC(CA 1989)R 1991, r 4(1)
	Fee in High Court or county court: £80	FPFO 1999, fee 2.9(*a*)
	Fee in magistrates' court: £20	MCA 1980, Sch 6, Pt I
Respondents	Every person whom applicant believes has parental responsibility	
	Every person whom applicant believes had parental responsibility prior to care order	
	The child	
	The parties to the original proceedings	FPR 1991, r 4.7, App 3; FPC(CA 1989)R 1991, r 7, Sch 2
Additional persons to whom notice in Form C6A is to be given	Those persons referred to in CA 1989, s 43(11)(*a*)–(*e*) who were not party to application for original order	FPR 1991, r 4.4, App 3; FPC(CA 1989)R 1991, r 4, Sch 2
Service	Copy of application, together with Form C6, to be served on respondents at least 2 days before date of hearing or directions appointment	FPR 1991, rr 4.4(1), 4.8; FPC(CA 1989)R 1991, rr 4(1), 8
	Form C6A to be served on additional persons at same time as application etc served on respondents	FPR 1991, r 4.4(3); FPC(CA 1989)R 1991, r 4(3)
	At or before first directions appointment or hearing, applicant must file statement in Form C9 to prove that requirements for service have been complied with	FPR 1991, r 4.7; FPC (CA 1989)R 1991, r 7
Ex parte	May not be available	FPR 1991, r 4.4(1); FPC (CA 1989)R 1991, r 4(4)
Joinder or removal of parties	By court order, of its own motion or on written request	FPR 1991, r 4.7; FPC(CA 1989)R 1991, r 7
Answer to application	Under FPR 1991, respondent may file an answer; serve on other parties	FPR 1991, r 4.9(3), (4)
	Under FPC(CA 1989)R 1991, no provision either forbidding or permitting an answer	
Directions	As to the powers of the justices' clerk or the court, see —	FPR 1991, r 4.14; FPC(CA 1989)R 1991, r 14
Children's guardian	Must normally be appointed	CA 1989, s 41(1)

Who has power to make the order	High Court or nominated county court judge, any district judge of the principal registry or nominated district judge outside the principal registry	FP(AJ)D 1999, Sch, para (*j*) (as substituted by FP(AJ)(A)D 2002)
	A magistrates' court; however, justices' clerk or single justice has no such power	JCR 1999; CA 1989, s 93(2)(*i*); FPC(CA 1989)R 1991, r 2(5)
Order	Form C21	
Additional or alternative orders	As for initial application	
Appeals	See Guides 70, 72–75	

45: Emergency Protection Order

Legal background

An emergency protection order (EPO) may be sought under CA 1989, s 44, in order to ensure the short-term safety of a child where it appears that the child may be at risk. It can authorise the applicant to remove a child from where he is (eg from his home) to a safe place or to keep him in a safe place (eg a hospital). The maximum duration of an order is generally eight days in the first instance but there can be one extension for a maximum of seven days (see CA 1989, s 45). The grounds for making an order differ according to the status of the applicant. All applicants may rely on the ground that there is reasonable cause to believe that the child is likely to suffer significant harm if he is not removed to accommodation provided by or on behalf of the applicant, or does not remain where he is.

Where the applicant is a local authority which is making enquiries under CA 1989, s 47(1)(*b*), about a child in its area, it can obtain an order on the alternative ground that the enquiries are being frustrated by access to the child being unreasonably refused to a person authorised to seek access to the child and that it has reasonable cause to believe that access to the child is urgently required. Where the applicant is an authorised person, an order can be made on the ground that the applicant is making enquiries into the welfare of a child whom he has reasonable cause to suspect is suffering or is likely to suffer significant harm, that the enquiries are being frustrated by access being unreasonably refused to a person authorised to seek access and that the applicant has reasonable cause to believe that access to the child is urgently required.

Various directions may be given at the same time as an EPO is made (for example, as to medical, psychiatric or other assessment of the child and as to contact with him) and, under CA 1989, s 48, supplementary provisions can also be included in the order requiring another person to disclose information as to the child's whereabouts, authorising the applicant to enter specified premises to search for the child or for another child and authorising a constable to assist in the execution of the EPO.

Section 44A enables the court to include an exclusion requirement in an EPO and to attach a power of arrest to that provision. The purpose of an exclusion requirement is to safeguard a child by removing from the scene (whether from the child's home or from part of it or from the area in which it is situated) a person who poses a threat to the child.

There is no appeal against the grant of or refusal to grant an EPO, but, if an order is made, an application to discharge it may be possible.

Procedure

Who may apply	Any person including a local authority or an authorised person such as the NSPCC or a designated police officer	CA 1989, ss 44(1), 46(7)
Which court	Magistrates' court, unless pending proceedings or application arises out of a CA 1989, s 37 investigation by local authority, in which case application is to the court where proceedings are pending or the court which required investigation	C(AP)O 1991, art 3
	Proceedings commenced in the magistrates' court can be transferred sideways but not upwards	C(AP)O 1991, arts 6, 7(2)
	Proceedings commenced in the county court or High Court can be transferred between county courts, and between High Court and county court but not down to magistrates' court	C(AP)O 1991, arts 10–13
Which proceedings	Freestanding application	CA 1989, ss 44(1), 46(7)
	EPO can be made on application for child assessment order	CA 1989, s 43(3), (4)
Application	On Form C1 and Supplement C11, with copies for each respondent; see below for ex parte applications	FPR 1991, r 4.4(1); FPC(CA 1989)R 1991, r 4(1)
	Fee in High Court or county court: £80	FPFO 1999, fee 2.9(*b*)
	No fee in magistrates' court	MCA 1980, Sch 6, Pt I
Respondents	Every person whom applicant believes has parental responsibility Every person whom applicant believes had parental responsibility prior to care order The child	FPR 1991, r 4.7, App 3; FPC(CA 1989)R 1991, r 7, Sch 2
Additional persons to whom notice in Form C6A is to be given	Local authority providing accommodation for child Persons caring for child at commencement of proceedings Person providing a CA 1989, s 51 refuge for child Every person whom applicant believes is a parent	FPR 1991, r 4.4, App 3; FPC(CA 1989)R 1991, r 4, Sch 2
Service	Copy of application, together with Form C6, to be served on respondents at least 1 day before date of hearing or directions appointment	FPR 1991, rr 4.4(1), 4.8; FPC(CA 1989)R 1991, rr 4(1), 8

	Form C6A to be served on additional persons at same time as application etc served on respondents	FPR 1991, r 4.4(3); FPC(CA 1989)R 1991, r 4(3)
	At or before first directions appointment or hearing, applicant must file statement in Form C9 to prove that requirements for service have been complied with	FPR 1991, r 4.7; FPC (CA 1989)R 1991, r 7
Ex parte	Permitted (leave of justices' clerk required in magistrates' court)	
	High Court or county court Where application made by telephone, file Form C1 and Supplement C11 within 24 hours after application	
	Where made otherwise, file at time application made	
	Magistrates' court File Form C1 and Supplement C11 when emergency protection order application made or as directed by justices' clerk	
	Any court Serve copy of application on each respondent (see above) within 48 hours after making of order	FPR 1991, r 4.4(4); FPC(CA 1989)R 1991, r 4(4)
Joinder or removal of parties	By court order, of its own motion or on written request	FPR 1991, r 4.7; FPC(CA 1989)R 1991, r 7
Answer to application	Under FPR 1991, respondent may file an answer; serve on other parties	FPR 1991, r 4.9(3), (4)
	Under FPC(CA 1989)R 1991, no provision either forbidding or permitting an answer	
Directions	As to the powers of the justices' clerk or the court, see —	FPR 1991, r 4.14; FPC(CA 1989)R 1991, r 14
Children's guardian	Must normally be appointed	CA 1989, s 41(1)
Who has power to make the order	High Court or nominated county court judge, any district judge of the principal registry or nominated district judge outside the principal registry	FP(AJ)D 1999, Sch, para (*j*) (as substituted by FP(AJ)(A)D 2002)
	A magistrates' court	
	A single justice may grant an EPO ex parte	CA 1989, s 93(2)(*i*); FPC(CA 1989)R 1991, r 2(5)
	A justices' clerk has no such power	JCR 1999

Order	On Form C23 (naming child wherever reasonably practicable or describing him as clearly as possible)	FPR 1991, r 4.21(5), App 1; FPC(CA 1989)R 1991, r 21(7), Sch 1; CA 1989, s 44(14)
	If ex parte, applicant to serve copy within 48 hours after making of order on: each party any person with actual care of child or who had actual care immediately before order local authority in whose area child lives or is found	FPR 1991, r 4.21(7); FPC(CA 1989)1991, r 21(8)
Additional or alternative orders	No order	CA 1989, s 1(5)
Procedure for exclusion requirements	Applicant for EPO prepares separate statement of evidence in support re: exclusion requirement	
	Applicant serves statement and copy of order containing exclusion requirement (and of any power of arrest attached) personally on relevant person (ie person who is excluded) and informs relevant person of right to apply to vary/discharge exclusion requirement	CA 1989, s 44A; FPR 1991, r 4.24A(2); FPC(CA 1989)1991, r 25A(2)
	If power of arrest attached, once relevant person served with order/informed of terms, copy of order shall be delivered to police together with statement showing relevant person served/informed of terms	FPR 1991, r 4.24A(3); FPC(CA 1989)1991, r 25A(3)
	Unless relevant person given notice and attended hearing, if power of arrest attached to exclusion order, court must announce in open court at earliest opportunity the name of person and fact that such order made	*President's Direction of 17 December 1997 (Children Act 1989: Exclusion Requirement)*
	Consent of person who is assuming care of child is required	CA 1989, s 44A(2); FPR 1991, r 4.24; FPC(CA 1989)1991, r 25
Appeals	None possible	CA 1989, s 45(10)

46: Discharge of an Emergency Protection Order

Legal background

With two exceptions, CA 1989, s 45(8) enables an application to be made for the discharge of an emergency protection order (EPO). An application for discharge cannot be heard before the expiry of 72 hours from the making of the original order, although there is nothing to prevent the application being filed sooner. The exceptional cases in which no discharge application is possible are (*a*) where the person who wishes to apply for the discharge was given due notice of the hearing at which the original order was made and was present at the hearing, and (*b*) where the period of the EPO has been extended (CA 1989, s 45(11)).

Section 45(8A), (8B) deals with applications to vary or discharge an EPO insofar as it imposes an exclusion requirement, or to vary or discharge the attendant power of arrest.

Procedure

Who may apply	The child A parent Any person with parental responsibility Any person with whom the child was living immediately before the emergency protection order was made	CA 1989, s 45(8)
Which court	The court which made the original order	C(AP)O 1991, art 4(1)
	Proceedings commenced in the magistrates' court can be transferred sideways but not upwards	C(AP)O 1991, arts 6, 7(2)
	Proceedings commenced in the county court or High Court can be transferred between county courts, and between High Court and county court but not down to magistrates' court	C(AP)O 1991, arts 10–13
Which proceedings	Freestanding application	CA 1989, s 45(8)
Application	On Form C2, with copies for each respondent	FPR 1991, r 4.4(1); FPC(CA 1989)R 1991, r 4(1)
Fee payable	High Court and county court: £80	FPFO 1999, fee 2.9(*b*)
	Magistrates' courts: in principle, £20	MCA 1980, Sch 6, Pt I
Respondents	Every person whom applicant believes has parental responsibility Every person whom applicant believes had parental responsibility prior to care order	

	The child The parties to the original proceedings	FPR 1991, r 4.7; FPC(CA 1989)R 1991, r 7
Additional persons to whom notice in Form C6A is to be given	Local authority providing accommodation for child Persons caring for child at commencement of proceedings Person providing a CA 1989, s 51 refuge for child	FPR 1991, r 4.4, App 3; FPC(CA 1989)R 1991, r 4, Sch 2
Service	Copy of application, together with Form C6, to be served on respondents at least 1 day before date of hearing or directions appointment	FPR 1991, rr 4.4(1), 4.8; FPC(CA 1989)R 1991, rr 4(1), 8
	Form C6A to be served on additional persons at same time as application etc served on respondents	FPR 1991, r 4.4(3); FPC(CA 1989)R 1991, r 4(3)
	At or before first directions appointment or hearing, applicant must file statement in Form C9 to prove that requirements for service have been complied with	FPR 1991, r 4.7; FPC(CA 1989)R 1991, r 7
Ex parte	May not be available	FPR 1991, r 4.4(4); FPC (CA 1989)R 1991, r 4(4)
Joinder or removal of parties	By court order, of its own motion or on written request	FPR 1991, r 4.7; FPC(CA 1989)R 1991, r 7
Answer to application	Under FPR 1991, respondent may file an answer; serve on other parties	FPR 1991, r 4.9(3), (4)
	Under FPC(CA 1989)R 1991, no provision either forbidding or permitting an answer	
Directions	As to the powers of the justices' clerk or the court, see —	FPR 1991, r 4.14; FPC(CA 1989)R 1991, r 14
Children's guardian	Must normally be appointed	CA 1989, s 41(1)
Special requirements	No application allowed where applicant had proper notice of original application and was present at the hearing or where EPO has already been extended	CA 1989, s 45(11)
	Application must not be heard until at least 72 hours have elapsed from making of original EPO	CA 1989, s 45(9)

Who has power to make the order	High Court or nominated county court judge, any district judge of the principal registry or nominated district judge outside the principal registry	FP(AJ)D 1999, Sch, para (*j*) (as substituted by FP(AJ)(A)D 2002)
	A magistrates' court; however, justices' clerk or single justice has no such power	JCR 1999; CA 1989, s 93(2)(*i*); FPC(CA 1989)R 1991, r 2(5)
Order	Form C24	FPR 1991, r 4.21(5), App 1; FPC(CA 1989)R 1991, r 21(7), Sch 1
Procedure for variation/discharge of exclusion requirements and attendant power of arrest	Application for variation/discharge re: exclusion requirement or re: power of arrest by person to whom it applies, Form C2 suggested	CA 1989, s 45(8A), (8B)
	Applicant serves parties to the proceedings with application for variation/discharge	FPR 1991, r 4.24A(5); FPC(CA 1989)R 1991, r 25A(5)
	Consider giving notice to person caring for child	FPR 1991, App 3; FPC(CA 1989)R 1991, Sch 2
	For steps to be taken on variation/discharge affecting exclusion requirement/power of arrest, see—	FPR 1991, r 4.24A(4), (6); FPC(CA 1989)R 1991, r 25A(4), (6)
Appeals	None possible	CA 1989, s 45(10)

47: Extension of an Emergency Protection Order, Warrant under CA 1989, s 48(9) or Variation of Directions as to Contact or Assessment under CA 1989, s 44(9)(b)

Legal background

An emergency protection order (EPO) can be extended once for a period not exceeding 7 days if the court has reasonable cause to believe that the child concerned is likely to suffer significant harm if the order is not extended (CA 1989, s 45(4)–(6)). Where a person is attempting to exercise powers under an EPO and has been prevented from doing so by being refused entry to the premises concerned or access to the child concerned or is likely to be so prevented, the court may issue a warrant authorising a constable to give assistance, using reasonable force if necessary (CA 1989, s 48(9)).

When making an EPO or at any time whilst such an order is in force, the court may give directions under CA 1989, s 44(6) with respect to contact with the child concerned and as to medical or psychiatric examination or other assessment of him. Application may be made at any time under CA 1989, s 44(9) for such directions to be varied.

Procedure

Who may apply	*Extension of EPO* Any person who has parental responsibility as a result of an EPO and is entitled to apply for a care order	CA 1989, s 45(4)
	CA 1989, s 48(9) warrant Any person	CA 1989, s 48(9)
	CA 1989, s 44(9)(b) variation Parties to original application	
	Children's guardian	
	Local authority in whose area child is ordinarily resident Anyone named in the directions	CA 1989, s 44(9); FPR 1991, r 4.2(4); FPC(CA 1989)R 1991, r 2(4)
Which court	The court which made the original order	C(AP)O 1991, art 4(1); CA 1989, s 48
	Proceedings commenced in the magistrates' court can be transferred sideways but not upwards	C(AP)O 1991, arts 6, 7(2)
	Proceedings commenced in the county court or High Court can be transferred between county courts, and between High Court and county court but not down to magistrates' court	C(AP)O 1991, arts 10–13
Which proceedings	Freestanding application	CA 1989, ss 44(9), 45(4), 48(9)
Application	*Extension of EPO* On Form C2, with copies for each respondent	FPR 1991, r 4.4(1); FPC(CA 1989)R 1991, r 4(1)
	High Court and county court: £80	FPFO 1999, fee 2.9(*b*)
	Magistrates' court: in principle, £20	MCA 1980, Sch 6, Pt I
	CA 1989, s 48(9) warrant On Form C1 and Supplement C12 (naming child wherever reasonably practicable or describing him as clearly as possible), with copies for each respondent	CA 1989, s 48(13); FPR 1991, r 4.4(1); FPC(CA 1989)R 1991, r 4(1)
	High Court and county court: £80	FPFO 1999, fee 2.9(*b*)
	No fee in magistrates' court	MCA 1980, Sch 6, Pt I
	CA 1989, s 44(9)(b) variation On Form C2, with copies for each respondent	FPR 1991, r 4.4(1); FPC(CA 1989)R 1991, r 4(1)
	High Court and county court: £80	FPFO 1999, fee 2.9(*b*)
	Magistrates' court: in principle, £20	MCA 1980, Sch 6, Pt I
Respondents	*In all cases* Every person whom applicant believes has parental responsibility	

	Every person whom applicant believes had parental responsibility prior to care order The child AND *Extension of EPO or CA 1989, s 44(9)(b) variation* The parties to the original EPO proceedings *CA 1989, s 44(9)(b) variation* Any person who was caring for child prior to making of the order Any person whose contact with child is affected by the direction which is to be varied	FPR 1991, r 4.7, App 3; FPC(CA 1989)R 1991, r 7, Sch 2
Additional persons to whom notice is to be given	*In all cases* Local authority providing accommodation for child Persons caring for child at commencement of proceedings Person providing a CA 1989, s 51 refuge for child AND *CA 1989, s 44(9)(b) variation* Local authority in whose area child is living Any person whom applicant believes is affected by the direction which is to be varied	FPR 1991, r 4.4, App 3; FPC(CA 1989)R 1991, r 4, Sch 2
Service	Copy of application, together with Form C6, to be served on respondents at least 1 day before date of hearing or directions appointment	FPR 1991, rr 4.4(1), 4.8; FPC(CA 1989)R 1991, rr 4(1), 8
	Form C6A to be served on additional persons at same time as application etc served on respondents	FPR 1991, r 4.4(3); FPC(CA 1989)R 1991, r 4(3)
	At or before first directions appointment or hearing, applicant must file statement in Form C9 to prove that requirements for service have been complied with	FPR 1991, r 4.7; FPC (CA 1989)R 1991, r 7
Ex parte	*Extension of EPO or CA 1989, s 44(9)(b) variation* May not be available *CA 1989, s 48(9) warrant* In High Court or county court, Form C1 and Supplement C12 is filed within 24 hours after application where made by telephone; otherwise, filed at time when application made	

	In magistrates' court, application must be made with leave of justices' clerk; Form C1 and Supplement C12 is filed when application made or as directed by justices' clerk	FPR 1991, r 4.4(4); FPC(CA 1989)R 1991, r 4(4)
Joinder or removal of parties	By court order, of its own motion or on written request	FPR 1991, r 4.7; FPC(CA 1989)R 1991, r7
Answer to application	Under FPR 1991, respondent may file an answer; serve on other parties	FPR 1991, r 4.9(3), (4)
	Under FPC(CA 1989)R 1991, no provision either forbidding or permitting an answer	
Directions	As to the powers of the justices' clerk or the court, see —	FPR 1991, r 4.14, FPC(CA 1989)R 1991, r 14
Children's guardian	Must normally be appointed	CA 1989, s 41(1)
Who has power to make the order	High Court or nominated county court judge, any district judge of the principal registry or nominated district judge outside the principal registry	FP(AJ)D 1999, Sch, para (*j*) (as substituted by FP(AJ)(A)D 2002)
	A magistrates' court	
	A single justice may grant an ex parte warrant under CA 1989, s 48(9) and variation under s 44(9)(*b*), but may not extend an EPO	CA 1989, s 93(2)(*i*); FPC(CA 1989)R 1991, r 2(5)
	A justices' clerk has no such power	JCR 1999
Order	*Extension of EPO* Form C24	
	CA 1989, s 48(9) warrant Form C25 (naming child wherever reasonably practicable or describing him as clearly as possible). If ex parte, applicant must serve copy, within 48 hours of making of order, on each party, on any person with actual care of child or who had actual care immediately before order and on the local authority in whose area the child lives or is found	CA 1989, s 48(13); FPR 1991, r 4.21(5), (7), App 1; FPC(CA 1989)R 1991, r 21(7), (8), Sch 1
	CA 1989, s 44(9)(b) variation Form C24	FPR 1991, r 4.21(5), App 1; FPC(CA 1989)R 1991, r 21(7), Sch 1
Appeals	*Extension of EPO or CA 1989, s 44(9)(b) variation* None permitted	

	CA 1989, s 48(9) warrant See Guides 70, 72–75	CA 1989, s 45(10)

48: Recovery Order

Legal background

Where it appears to the court that there is reason to believe that a child who is in care or is the subject of an emergency protection order or is in police protection, is missing or has been unlawfully taken or kept away or has run away or is staying away from the person who has care of him under the care order etc, it may make a recovery order under CA 1989, s 50. The order has the following effects: (*a*) it operates as a direction to any person who is in a position to do so to produce the child to any authorised person on request; (*b*) it authorises any authorised person to remove the child; (*c*) it requires any person who has information as to the child's whereabouts to disclose that information, if asked to do so, to a constable or an officer of the court; and (*d*) it authorises a constable to enter any premises specified in the order and search for the child, using reasonable force if necessary. A recovery order is open-ended, remaining in force until it is discharged or until the child is recovered.

Procedure

Who may apply	Any person with parental responsibility for child by virtue of care order or emergency protection order Where child is in police protection, designated officer	CA 1989, s 50(4)
Which court	Magistrates' court, unless pending proceedings in which case apply to court where proceedings pending Proceedings may be transferable sideways, upwards or downwards, depending on circumstances	C(AP)O 1991, art 3 C(AP)O 1991, arts 6–13
Which proceedings	Freestanding application	CA 1989, s 50(4)
Application	On Form C1 and Supplement C18, with sufficient copies for each respondent; see below for ex parte applications High Court and county court: £80 No fee payable in magistrates' court	FPR 1991, r 4.4(1); FPC(CA 1989)R 1991, r 4(1) FPFO 1999, fee 2.10 MCA 1980, Sch 6, Pt I
Respondents	Every person whom applicant believes has parental responsibility Every person whom applicant believes had parental responsibility prior to care order The child	

	Person whom applicant alleges to have effected, or to have been or to be responsible for, taking or keeping of child	FPR 1991, r 4.7, App 3; FPC(CA 1989)R 1991, r 7, Sch 2
Additional persons to whom notice is to be given	Local authority providing accommodation for child Persons caring for child at commencement of proceedings	
	Person providing a CA 1989, s 51 refuge for child	FPR 1991, r 4.4, App 3; FPC(CA 1989)R 1991, r 4, Sch 2
Service	Copy of application, together with Form C6, to be served on respondents at least 1 day before date of hearing or directions appointment	FPR 1991, rr 4.4(1), 4.8; FPC(CA 1989)R 1991, rr 4(1), 8
	Form C6A to be served on additional persons at same time as application etc served on respondents	FPR 1991, r 4.4(3); FPC(CA 1989)R 1991, r 4(3)
	At or before first directions appointment or hearing, applicant must file statement in Form C9 to prove that requirements for service have been complied with	FPR 1991, r 4.7; FPC (CA 1989)R 1991, r 7
Ex parte	Permitted (leave of justices' clerk required in magistrates' court) *High court or county court* Where application is made by telephone, file Form C1 and Supplement C18 within 24 hours after application Where made otherwise, file at time application made *Magistrates' court* File Form C1 and Supplement C18 when application made or as directed by justices' clerk	FPR 1991, r 4.4(4); FPC(CA 1989)R 1991, r 4(4)
Joinder or removal of parties	By court order, of its own motion or on written request	FPR 1991, r 4.7; FPC(CA 1989)R 1991, r 7
Answer to application	Under FPR 1991, respondent may file answer; serve on other parties Under FPC(CA 1989)R 1991, no provision either forbidding or permitting an answer	FPR 1991, r 4.9(3), (4)
Directions	As to the powers of the justices' clerk or the court, see —	FPR 1991, r 4.14, FPC(CA 1989)R 1991, r 14
Children's guardian	Must normally be appointed	CA 1989, s 41(1)

Who has power to make the order	High Court or nominated county court judge, any district judge of the principal registry or nominated district judge outside the principal registry	FP(AJ)D 1999, Sch, para (*j*) (as substituted by FP(AJ)(A)D 2002)
	A magistrates' court A single justice may grant an ex parte order	CA 1989, s 93(2)(*i*); FPC(CA 1989)R 1991, r 2(5)
	A justices' clerk has no such power	JCR 1999
Order	Form C29 (naming child and any person with parental responsibility by virtue of care order or emergency protection order or designated officer where child in police protection)	FPR 1991, r 4.21(5), App 1; FPC(CA 1989)R 1991, r 21(7), Sch 1; CA 1989, s 50(5)
	If ex parte, applicant to serve copy within 48 hours after making of order on: every party any person with actual care of child or who had actual care immediately before order local authority in whose area child lives or is found	FPR 1991, r 4.21(7); FPC(CA 1989)R 1991, r 21(8)
Appeals	See Guides 70, 72–75	

49: Parental Responsibility Order

Legal background

Parental responsibility comprises all the rights, duties, powers, responsibilities and authority which, by law, a parent has in relation to a child and his property, or which a guardian of a child's estate has in relation to his property (CA 1989, s 3).

A child's mother always has parental responsibility for the child; however, if she was not married to the child's father at the time of the birth, the father will only acquire parental responsibility by marrying the mother, by making a formal parental responsibility agreement with her (using Form C(PRA)) or by obtaining an order from the court (CA 1989, s 4, to be read in conjunction with Family Law Reform Act 1987, s 1(2)). The court must make such an order where it makes a residence order in favour of the father (CA 1989, s 12(1)); otherwise, it is in the court's discretion whether to grant a specific application under CA 1989, s 4.

The court may subsequently revoke such an order and also a parental responsibility agreement (which may not be revoked merely by agreement).

Procedure

Who may apply	Father without parental responsibility	CA 1989, s 4(1)(*a*)

Which court	Any court (subject to certain exceptions)	CA 1989, ss 10(1), 92(7); C(AP)O 1991, arts 4, 14, 19; FPR 1991, r 2.40(1)
	Proceedings can be transferred sideways, upwards or downwards, using order in Form C49	C(AP)O 1991, arts 5, 6, 8, 10, 12, 13, 15, 19
Which proceedings	Freestanding application	CA 1989, s 4(1)
	Court must make order on making residence order in favour of father without parental responsibility even if no specific application is made	CA 1989, s 12(1)
Application	On Form C1, with sufficient copies for each respondent	FPR 1991, r 4.4(1)(*a*), App 1; FPC(CA 1989)R 1991, r 4(1)(*a*), Sch 1
	Fee payable: £80	FPFO 1999, fee 2.1(*a*)
Respondents	Notice to be served in Form C6 on every person with parental responsibility and on every person with parental responsibility before care order	FPR 1991, r 4.7, App 3; FPC(CA 1989)R 1991, r 7, Sch 2
Additional persons to be served with notice of the proceedings	Notice to be served in Form C6A on local authority, if providing accommodation, and on person caring for child or providing refuge	FPR 1991, r 4.4, App 3; FPC(CA 1989)R 1991, r 4, Sch 2
Service	Applicant must serve a copy of the application, together with Form C6 (endorsed with date fixed for hearing), on each respondent at least 14 days before the hearing; notice of the proceedings must be served in Form C6A (endorsed with date fixed for hearing) on other persons to be served at least 14 days before the hearing	FPR 1991, r 4.4, App 3; FPC(CA 1989)R 1991, r 4, Sch 2
	At or before first directions appointment or hearing, applicant must file statement in Form C9 to prove that requirements for service have been complied with	FPR 1991, r 4.8(7); FPC(CA 1989)R 1991, r 8(7)
Answer to application	Respondent to an application in the High Court or a county court (but not a family proceedings court) may file a written answer and serve it on the other parties to the proceedings not less than 2 days before the hearing	FPR 1991, r 4.9(3), (4)
Joinder or removal of parties	By court order, of its own motion or on written request on Form C2	FPR 1991, r 4.7; FPC(CA 1989)R 1991, r 7

Directions	As to applications for directions, see —	FPR 1991, r 4.14(2), (3), (4); FPC(CA 1989)R 1991, r 14(2), (5), (6)
	NB A written request for directions must be made on Form C2	
	As to the directions which may be given (eg timetable for the proceedings, submission of evidence or transfer of proceedings to another court), see —	FPR 1991, r 4.14(2); FPC(CA 1989)R 1991, r 14(2)
	As to timing of proceedings, see —	FPR 1991, r 4.15; FPC(CA 1989)R 1991, r 15
	As to attendance at the directions hearing, see —	FPR 1991, r 4.16; FPC(CA 1989)R 1991, r 16
Order	Conferring parental responsibility on the father, in Form C45	CA 1989, ss 4(1)(*a*), 12(1); FPR 1991, r 4.21(5), App 1; FPC(CA 1989)R 1991, r 21(7)(*a*), Sch 1
Appeals	See Guides 70, 72, 73, 75	

50: Discharge of a Parental Responsibility Order or a Parental Responsibility Agreement

Legal background

For parental responsibility orders, see Guide 49.

Procedure

Who may apply	Any person with parental responsibility; the child (with leave)	CA 1989, s 4(3)
Which court	Any court (subject to certain exceptions)	CA 1989, ss 10(1), 92(7); C(AP)O 1991, arts 4, 14; FPR 1991, r 2.40(1)
	A district judge of the principal registry can hear any application under CA 1989, s 4(3)	FP(AJ)D 1999, Sch, para (*f*) (as substituted by FP(AJ)(A)D 2002)
	Proceedings can be transferred sideways, upwards or downwards, using order in Form C49	C(AP)O 1991, arts 5, 6, 8, 10, 12, 13, 15, 19
Which proceedings	Freestanding application	CA 1989, s 4(3)
Application	On Form C1, with sufficient copies for each respondent	FPR 1991, r 4.4; FPC(CA 1989)R 1991, r 4

	Fee payable: £80	FPFO 1999, fee 2.1(*a*)
	Child should obtain the necessary leave, using Form C2	FPR 1991, r 4.3; FPC(CA 1989)R 1991, r 3
Respondents	Notice to be served in Form C6 on every person with parental responsibility; every person with parental responsibility before care order and on other parties to original proceedings (where the appointment had been by the court)	FPR 1991, r 4.7, App 3; FPC(CA 1989)R 1991, r 7, Sch 2
Additional persons to be served with notice of the proceedings	Notice to be served in Form C6A on local authority, if providing accommodation, and on person caring for child or providing refuge	FPR 1991, r 4.4, App 3; FPC(CA 1989)R 1991, r 4, Sch 2
Service	Applicant must serve a copy of the application, together with Form C6 (endorsed with date fixed for hearing), on each respondent at least 14 days before the hearing; notice of the proceedings must be served in Form C6A (endorsed with date fixed for hearing) on other persons to be served at least 14 days before the hearing	FPR 1991, r 4.4, App 3; FPC(CA 1989)R 1991, r 4, Sch 2
	At or before first directions appointment or hearing, applicant must file statement in Form C9 to prove that requirements for service have been complied with	FPR 1991, r 4.8(7); FPC(CA 1989)R 1991, r 8(7)
Answer to application	Respondent may file a written answer and serve it on the other parties to the proceedings not less than 2 days before the hearing (but no answers in magistrates' courts)	FPR 1991, r 4.9(3), (4)
Joinder or removal of parties	By court order, of its own motion or on written request on Form C2	FPR 1991, r 4.7; FPC(CA 1989)R 1991, r 7
Directions	As to applications for directions, see —	FPR 1991, r 4.14(2), (3), (4); FPC(CA 1989)R 1991, r 14(2), (5), (6)
	NB A written request for directions must be made on Form C2	
	As to the directions which may be given (eg as to timetable for the proceedings, submission of evidence or transfer of proceedings to another court), see —	FPR 1991, r 4.14(2); FPC(CA 1989)R 1991, r 14(2)
	As to timing of proceedings, see —	FPR 1991, r 4.15; FPC(CA 1989)R 1991, r 15

	As to attendance at the directions hearing, see —	FPR 1991, r 4.16; FPC(CA 1989)R 1991, r 16
Order	Form C45, for termination of parental responsibility order or parental responsibility agreement	FPR 1991, r 4.21(5); FPC(CA 1989)R 1991, r 21(7)
Appeals	See Guides 70, 72, 73, 75	

51: Appointment or Removal of a Guardian

Legal background

A guardian usually stands in the shoes of a parent when a child no longer has a parent with parental responsibility living (although one may also be appointed where a parent who had the benefit of a residence order dies regardless of whether the non-resident parent survives).

Under CA 1989, s 5, a guardian may be appointed in writing by a parent with parental responsibility, the appointment to take effect when he dies (if he has a residence order) or when the last surviving parent with parental responsibility dies. In default (or in addition), the court has a concurrent right of appointment. The court may also terminate (under CA 1989, s 6(7)) the appointment of a guardian, whether he had been appointed by the court or a parent.

Procedure

Who may apply	*Appointment* Any person (the proposed guardian)	CA 1989, s 5(1)
	Removal Any person with parental responsibility or, with leave, the child	CA 1989, s 6(7)
Which court	Any court (subject to certain exceptions)	CA 1989, ss 10(1), 92(7); C(AP)O 1991, arts 4, 14, 19; FPR 1991, r 2.40(1)
	A district judge nominated for private or public family law proceedings can hear any application under CA 1989, s 5(1) or 6(7); a district judge or deputy district judge can hear interlocutory matters or unopposed hearings	FP(AJ)D 1999, Sch, para (*f*) (as substituted by FP(AJ)(A)D 2002)
	Proceedings can be transferred sideways, upwards or downwards, using order in Form C49	C(AP)O 1991, arts 5, 6, 8, 10, 12, 13, 15, 19
Which proceedings	Freestanding application; own motion order in any family proceedings	CA 1989, ss 5(1), (2), 6(7)
Application	*Appointment* On Form C1	

	Fee payable: £80	FPFO 1999, fee 2.1(*a*)
	Removal On Form C1, with sufficient copies for each respondent	FPR 1991, r 4.4, App 3; FPC(CA 1989)R 1991, r 4, Sch 1
	Fee payable: £80	FPFO 1999, fee 2.1(*b*)
Respondents	Notice to be served in Form C6 on every person with parental responsibility, every person with parental responsibility before a care order, and (on application to discharge court-appointed guardian) parties to the original proceedings	FPR 1991, r 4.7, App 3; FPC(CA 1989)R 1991, r 7, Sch 2
Additional persons to whom notice in Form C6A is to be given	Local authority, if providing accommodation	
	Person caring for child or providing refuge	
	If application is for appointment, father without parental responsibility	FPR 1991, r 4.4, App 3; FPC(CA 1989)R 1991, r 4, Sch 2
Service	Applicant must serve a copy of the application, together with Form C6 (endorsed with date fixed for hearing), on each respondent at least 14 days before the hearing; notice of the proceedings must be served in Form C6A (endorsed with date fixed for hearing) on other persons to be served at least 14 days before the hearing	FPR 1991, r 4.4, App 3; FPC(CA 1989)R 1991, r 4, Sch 2
	At or before first directions appointment or hearing, applicant must file statement in Form C9 to prove that requirements for service have been complied with	FPR 1991, r 4.8(7); FPC (CA 1989)R 1991, r 8(7)
Joinder of parties	By court order, of its own motion or on written request on Form C2	FPR 1991, r 4.7; FPC(CA 1989)R 1991, r 7
Answer to application	Respondent may file a written answer and serve it on the other parties to the proceedings not less than 2 days before the hearing (but no answers in magistrates' courts)	FPR 1991, r 4.9(3), (4)
Directions	As to applications for directions, see —	FPR 1991, r 4.14(2), (3), (4); FPC(CA 1989)R 1991, r 14(2), (5), (6)
	NB A written request for directions must be made on Form C2	
	As to the directions which may be given (eg as to timetable for the proceedings, submission of evidence or transfer of proceedings to another court), see —	FPR 1991, r 4.14(2); FPC(CA 1989)R 1991, r 14(2)

	As to timing of proceedings, see —	FPR 1991, r 4.15; FPC(CA 1989)R 1991, r 15
	As to attendance at the directions hearing, see —	FPR 1991, r 4.16; FPC(CA 1989)R 1991, r 16
Order	On Form C46, appointing a guardian, in which case the appointee assumes parental responsibility until the appointment is brought to an end by the court	CA 1989, ss 5(1), (6), 6(7); FPR 1991, r 4.21(5), App 1; FPC(CA 1989)R 1991, r 21(7)(*a*), Sch 1
	On Form C46, bringing to an end the appointment of a guardian under CA 1989, s 5 (whether made by the court or not)	CA 1989, s 6(7); FPR 1991, r 4.21(5), App 1; FPC(CA 1989)R 1991, r 21(7)(*a*), Sch 1
Appeals	See Guides 70, 72–74	

52: Residence or Contact Order (or Discharge or Variation of the Same)

Legal background

A residence order is available under CA 1989, s 8 and settles the arrangements as to the person with whom a child is to live (CA 1989, s 8(1)). Such an order automatically confers parental responsibility on any person in whose favour it is made for as long as the order is in force (CA 1989, s 12(2)).

A contact order is also available under CA 1989, s 8 and requires the person with whom a child lives, or is to live, to allow the child to visit or stay with the person named in the order, or for that person and the child otherwise to have contact with each other (CA 1989, s 8(1)).

An order for "no contact" does fall within the definition of "contact order" in CA 1989, s 8(1) (*Nottinghamshire County Council v P* [1993] 2 FLR 134 at 143G, per Sir Stephen Brown P).

Procedure

Who may apply	Parent or guardian	
	Residence order holder	
	Either party to marriage	
	Person with whom child has lived for 3 of the last 5 years and within the preceding 3 months	
	Person with consent of those with parental responsibility	
	Application to discharge or vary may be made by previous applicant or person named in order (in case of contact order only)	

	Any person with leave, except a local authority; special requirements apply to some foster-parents	CA 1989, ss 9(2)–(4), 10
Fee payable	Application to discharge or vary: £80	FPFO 1999, fee 2.1(*a*)
	Application for leave: £80	FPFO 1999, fee 2.1(*a*)
Which court	Any court (subject to certain exceptions)	CA 1989, ss 10(1), 92(7); C(AP)O 1991, arts 4, 14, 19–20; FPR 1991, r 2.40(1)
	A district judge of the principal registry or a district judge nominated for private or public law proceedings can hear any application for a s 8 order. A district judge in a county court, in an application for a s 8 order, can hear interlocutory matters, unopposed trials and some opposed trials in limited circumstances. A deputy district judge can hear interlocutory matters and unopposed hearings	FP(AJ)D 1999, Sch, para (*g*) (as substituted by FP(AJ)(A)D 2002)
	Proceedings can be transferred sideways, upwards or downwards, using order in Form C49	C(AP)O 1991, arts 5, 6, 8, 10, 12, 13, 16
Which proceedings	Freestanding application	CA 1989, s 10(2)
	Application made in family proceedings	CA 1989, s 10(1)(*a*)
	On court's own motion in family proceedings	CA 1989, s 10(1)(*b*)
	If matrimonial proceedings are pending, any application must be made in those proceedings	FPR 1991, r 2.40(1)
Application	On Form C1, with sufficient copies for each respondent	FPR 1991, r 4.4, App 1; FPC(CA 1989)R 1991, r 4, Sch 1
	Fee payable: £80	FPFO 1999, fee 2.1(*a*)
Respondents	Notice to be served in Form C6 on every person with parental responsibility, every person with parental responsibility prior to care order, and (on application to discharge or vary) parties to proceedings where order was made	FPR 1991, r 4.7, App 3; FPC(CA 1989)R 1991, r 7, Sch 2
Additional persons to whom notice in Form C6A is to be given	Local authority, if providing accommodation for child	
	Person caring for child or providing refuge	

	Person named in a court order (unless not relevant) Party to pending proceedings Person with whom the child has lived for 3 years	FPR 1991, r 4.4, App 3; FPC(CA 1989)R 1991, r 4, Sch 2
Service	Applicant must serve a copy of the application, together with Form C6 (endorsed with date fixed for hearing), on each respondent at least 14 days before the hearing, unless emergency (see Ex parte procedure below)	
	Notice of the proceedings must be served in Form C6A (endorsed with date fixed for hearing) on other persons to be served	FPR 1991, r 4.4, App 3; FPC(CA 1989)R 1991, r 4, Sch 2
	At or before first directions appointment or hearing, applicant must file statement in Form C9 to prove that requirements for service have been complied with	FPR 1991, r 4.8(7); FPC(CA 1989)R 1991, r 8(7)
Power to abridge time-limits	In appropriate cases, court has power to abridge time-limits set by rules	FPR 1991, r 4.14(2)(*b*); FPC(CA 1989)R 1991, r 14(2)(*b*)
	Court has power to abridge time for service	FPR 1991, r 4.8(8), FPC(CA 1989)R 1991, r 8(8)
Ex parte procedure	If ex parte order obtained by telephone, file application within 24 hours; otherwise, file at time application is made (NB ex parte residence orders will be made only in exceptional circumstances)	*Re G* [1993] 1 FLR 910; *Re P* [1993] 1 FLR 915
	If an order is made, it must be served on respondents within 48 hours	FPR 1991, r 4.4(4); FPC(CA 1989)R 1991, r 4(4)
Joinder or removal of parties	By court order, of its own motion or on written request on Form C2	FPR 1991, r 4.7; FPC(CA 1989)R 1991, r 7
Acknowledgement of application	Respondent must file acknowledgement of application in Form C7 and serve it on the parties within 14 days of service of the application	FPR 1991, r 4.1(2)(*d*); FPC(CA 1989)R 1991, r 9
Answer to application	Respondent to an application in the High Court or a county court (but not a family proceedings court) may file a written answer and serve it on the other parties to the proceedings not less than 2 days before the hearing	FPR 1991, r 4.9(3), (4)

Withdrawal of application	Permitted only with leave; application may be made orally if parties and welfare officer present; otherwise, by written request on Form C2 giving reasons, served on parties	
	If by consent, court may grant request without a hearing; otherwise, hearing on 7 days' notice	FPR 1991, r 4.5; FPC(CA 1989)R 1991, r 5
Directions	Court may give directions of own motion or on written (or oral, if urgent) request, subject to certain procedural requirements	FPR 1991, r 4.14(2), (3), (4); FPC(CA 1989)R 1991, r 14(2), (5), (6)
	NB A written request for directions must be made on Form C2	
	As to the directions which may be given (eg as to timetable for the proceedings, submission of evidence or transfer of proceedings to another court), see —	FPR 1991, r 4.14(2); FPC(CA 1989)R 1991, r 14(2)
	As to timing of proceedings, see —	FPR 1991, r 4.15; FPC(CA 1989)R 1991, r 15
	As to attendance at the directions hearing, see —	FPR 1991, r 4.16; FPC(CA 1989)R 1991, r 16
Order	On Form C43, making, discharging or varying a residence order or contact order (including an order for "no contact"); order may contain directions and conditions	CA 1989, ss 8, 11(7); FPR 1991, r 4.21(5), App 1; FPC(CA 1989)R 1991, r 21(7), (9), Sch 1
	Penal notice may be attached on specific application (High Court or county court only)	FPR 1991, r 4.21A
Additional or alternative orders	Parental responsibility order (Form C45)	CA 1989, s 4(1)(*a*)
	Appointment of guardian (Form C46)	CA 1989, s 5(2)
	Family assistance order (in exceptional circumstances and only with the consent of persons named) (Form C42)	CA 1989, s 16
	Financial provision order (Form C21)	CA 1989, Sch 1, para 1
	Supervision order (Form C35)	CA 1989, ss 31(1)(*b*), 35, 38
	Education supervision order (provided the application is made by a local education authority) (Form C37)	CA 1989, s 36(1)
Restrictions on court's powers	A contact order may not be made in respect of a child in care	CA 1989, s 9(1)

Appeals	See Guides 70, 72, 73, 75	

53: Specific Issue Order or Prohibited Steps Order (or Discharge or Variation of the Same)

Legal background

A specific issue order is defined by CA 1989, s 8(1) as an order giving directions for the purpose of determining a specific question which has arisen, or which may arise, in connection with any aspect of parental responsibility for a child. In effect it is used to settle ad hoc disputes where those who share parental responsibility cannot agree over the issue in question.

A prohibited steps order is also defined by CA 1989, s 8(1), and means an order specifying that no step which could be taken by a parent in meeting his or her parental responsibility for a child, and which is of a kind specified in the order, can be taken by any person without the consent of the court. This is a negative version of a specific issue order.

Procedure

Who may apply	Parent or guardian	
	Residence order holder	
	Application to discharge or vary may be made by previous applicant	
	Any person with leave	CA 1989, s 10
Which court	Any court (subject to certain exceptions)	CA 1989, ss 10(1), 92(7); FPR 1991, r 2.40(1); C(AP)O 1991, arts 4, 14, 19, 20
	A district judge of the principal registry or a district judge nominated for private or public law proceedings can hear any application for a s 8 order. A district judge in a county court, in an application for a s 8 order, can hear interlocutory matters, unopposed trials and some opposed trials in limited circumstances. A deputy district judge can hear interlocutory matters and unopposed hearings	FP(AJ)D 1999, Sch, para (*g*) (as substituted by FP(AJ)(A)D 2002)
	Proceedings can be transferred sideways, upwards or downwards, using order in Form C49	C(AP)O 1991, arts 4, 6, 8, 10, 12, 13, 16
Which proceedings	Freestanding application	CA 1989, s 10(2)
	Application made in family proceedings	CA 1989, s 10(1)(*a*)
	On court's own motion in family proceedings	CA 1989, s 10(1)(*b*)

	If matrimonial proceedings are pending, any application must be made in those proceedings	FPR 1991, r 2.40(1)
Application	On Form C1, with sufficient copies for service on each respondent	FPR 1991, r 4.4, App 1; FPC(CA 1989)R 1991, r 4, Sch 1
	Fee payable on application: £80	FPFO 1999, fee 2.1(*a*)
	Fee payable on application to discharge or vary order: £80	FPFO 1999, fee 2.1(*a*)
Respondents	Notice to be served in Form C6 on every person with parental responsibility, every person with parental responsibility prior to care order, and (on application to discharge or vary) parties to proceedings where order was made	FPR 1991, r 4.7, App 3; FPC(CA 1989)R 1991, r 7, Sch 2
Additional persons to whom notice in Form C6A is to be given	Local authority, if providing accommodation for child Person caring for child or providing refuge Person named in a court order (unless not relevant) Party to pending proceedings Person with whom the child has lived for 3 years	FPR 1991, r 4.4, App 3; FPC(CA 1989)R 1991, r 4, Sch 2
Service	At least 14 days, unless emergency (see Ex parte procedure below)	
	Applicant must serve copy of application, together with Form C6 (endorsed with date fixed for hearing) on each respondent Notice of the proceedings must be served in Form C6A (endorsed with date fixed for hearing) on other persons to be served	FPR 1991, r 4.4, App 3; FPC(CA 1989)R 1991, r 4, Sch 2
	At or before first directions appointment or hearing, applicant must file statement in Form C9 to prove that requirements for service have been complied with	FPR 1991, r 4.8(7); FPC (CA 1989)R 1991, r 8(7)
Power to abridge time-limits	In appropriate cases, court has power to abridge time-limits set by rules	FPR 1991, r 4.14(2)(*b*); FPC(CA 1989)R 1991, r 14(2)(*b*)
	Court has power to abridge time for service	FPR 1991, r 4.8(8); FPC(CA 1989)R 1991, r 8(8)

Ex parte procedure	If ex parte order obtained by telephone, file application within 24 hours; otherwise, file at time application is made	
	If an order is made, it must be served on respondents within 48 hours	FPR 1991, r 4.4(4); FPC(CA 1989)R 1991, r 4(4)
Joinder or removal of parties	By court order, of its own motion or on written request on Form C2	FPR 1991, r 4.7; FPC(CA 1989)R 1991, r 7
Acknowledgement of application	Respondent must file acknowledgement of application in Form C7 and serve it on the parties within 14 days of service of the application	FPR 1991, r 4.9(1); FPC(CA 1989)R 1991, r 9
Answer to application	Respondent to an application in the High Court or a county court (but not a family proceedings court) may file a written answer and serve it on the other parties to the proceedings not less than 2 days before the hearing	FPR 1991, r 4.9(3), (4)
Directions	As to applications for directions, see —	FPR 1991, r 4.14(2), (3), (4); FPC(CA 1989)R 1991, r 14(2), (5), (6)
	NB A written request for directions must be made on Form C2	
	As to the directions which may be given (eg as to timetable for the proceedings, submission of evidence or transfer of proceedings to another court), see —	FPR 1991, r 4.14(2); FPC(CA 1989)R 1991, r 14(2)
	As to timing of proceedings, see —	FPR 1991, r 4.15; FPC(CA 1989)R 1991, r 15
	As to attendance at the directions hearing, see —	FPR 1991, r 4.16; FPC(CA 1989)R 1991, r 16
Order	On Form C43, making, discharging or varying a specific issue order or prohibited steps order; order may contain directions and conditions	CA 1989, ss 8, 11(7); FPR 1991, r 4.21(5), App 1; FPC(CA 1989)R 1991, r 21(7)(*a*), Sch 1
	Penal notice may be attached on specific application	FPR 1991, r 4.21A
Appeals	See Guides 70, 72, 73, 75	

54: Private Law Proceedings for the Disclosure of Information as to the Whereabouts of a Child

Legal background

Family Law Act 1986, s 33, provides a power for any court, in any proceedings in relation to a child within Part I of that Act brought in that court, to order "any person" to disclose information to the court as to the whereabouts of the child if his whereabouts are not sufficiently known. In the High Court, this adds nothing to the court's inherent powers, but a county court or family proceedings court can proceed in this way only under s 33. The order directs that the information be given to the court, not to a party (*Chief Constable of West Yorkshire Police v S* [1998] 2 FLR 973).

Application ex parte or on notice?
Where it is likely that the person who has the child may remove the child to frustrate the proceedings or order, an application may be made ex parte; where the risk of the child being removed is negligible, it will usually be appropriate to apply on notice.

Procedure

Pre-condition	Missing child who is subject of proceedings or order within FLA 1986, Part I	FLA 1986, s 33
	"Part I order" includes proceedings for or in relation to a CA 1989, s 8 order, or previous custody order, and similar orders made in Scotland, Northern Ireland and specified dependent territories; it does not include an order in proceedings for adoption or under CA 1989, Pt IV or V (public law); for more details of meaning of "Part I order", see under —	FLA 1986, s 25
	Where application is made in relation to an order made in Scotland, Northern Ireland or a specified dependent territory, the order must have been registered in the High Court, and proceedings for enforcement must have been begun in that court	FLA 1986 ss 25(3), 27(1), 29(1), 32(1)
	For recovery order in public law proceedings under CA 1989, see —	CA 1989, s 50
Who may apply	Any party with a legitimate interest in CA 1989, s 8 proceedings	
	A person who has registered an order made elsewhere in the UK or a specified dependent territory, being a person on whom rights are conferred by the order	FLA 1986, s 27(1)

Who may be directed to provide information	Any person can be so directed; see also Duty of person to whom order is directed, below	FLA 1986, s 33(1)
	Where a mother has taken a child to stay at a women's refuge, the police should not be directed to disclose the address	*Chief Constable of West Yorkshire Police v S* [1998] 2 FLR 973
Which court	Where made in pending proceedings or in relation to a subsisting s 8 order, the application should be made in the same court	FLA 1986, s 33(1)
	Where made in relation to an order registered in the High Court, the application must be made in the High Court	FLA 1986, ss 25(3), 29(1), 32(1)
Form of application	On Form C4, which should be supported by evidence. Where the application is made in proceedings in the High Court or a county court under, or in relation to an order under, CA 1989, s 8 (or previous custody order), or is made in a family proceedings court, a statement which complies with FPR 1991, r 4.17(1)(*a*)/FPC(CA 1989)R 1991, r 17(1)(*a*) should be ready for use at the hearing	FPR 1991, rr 4.4(1A), 6.17(2); FPC(CA 1989)R 1991, rr 4(1A), 31A(2)
	Where the application is made in the High Court otherwise than in relation to proceedings under CA 1989, s 8 (or previous custody order), an affidavit should be made in support.	
Fee payable	High Court or county court: £60	FPFO 1999, fee 4.3
	Magistrates' court: £20	MCA 1980, Sch 6, Pt I
Ex parte practice	Application may be made ex parte; in an emergency, it may be made by telephone, in which case Form C4 must be (i) filed within 24 hours and (ii) served within 48 hours after the making of the order	FPR 1991, r 6.17(4); FPC(CA 1989)R 1991, r 31A(4)
	In a family proceedings court, an application ex parte by telephone is impractical, as there is no provision for the application to be heard by a single justice	FPC(CA 1989)R 1991, rr 2(5), 31A
Service of application where made on notice	2 days' notice in a county court, or reasonable or adequate notice in a family proceedings court (NB FPR 1991 and FPC(CA 1989)R 1991 and the Appendix/Schedule thereto do not specify the period of notice required for an application made in pending proceedings)	CCR Ord 13, r 1(2); MCA 1980, s 55(3), (4)

Inter partes response by respondent	The respondent should appear, and may prepare a statement which complies with FPR 1991, r 4.17(1)(*a*)/FPC(CA 1989)R 1991, r 17(1)(*a*), or affidavit, as appropriate.	
Hearing	Judge or district judge in chambers, in High Court or county court; magistrates in family proceedings court	FP(AJ)D 1999, Sch, para (*n*) (as substituted by FP(AJ)(A)D 2002); FPR 1991, r 4.16(7) (in relation to s 8 proceedings); FPC(CA 1989)R 1991, rr 2(5), 31A
	Leave needed to rely on statement of evidence in pending s 8 proceedings	FPR 1991, r 4.17(1), (3); FPC(CA 1989)R 1991, r 17(1), (3)
	Applicant should submit draft order, including formulation of the way in which the order should require information to be provided to the court; see —	Form C30
Form of order	C30 (note that C30 incorporates a penal notice)	FPR 1991, r 6.17(2); FPC(CA 1989)R 1991, r 31A(2)
Service of order	Personal service is advisable if penal enforcement may be needed	CCR Ord 29, r 1A; MCA 1980, s 63(3)
Duty of person to whom order is directed	Person to whom order is directed must, forthwith after service, disclose to the court, in the way specified in the order, "all the information" he has about the whereabouts of the child; the court will decide what to do with the information	FLA 1986, s 33(1); see also *Re B* [1993] 1 FLR 191
	Refusal to comply cannot be excused on the basis that giving the information may tend to incriminate the giver (NB the statement or admission cannot be used in criminal proceedings other than for perjury)	FLA 1986, s 33(2)
	Legal professional privilege is no answer to the order; see under —	FLA 1986, s 33

55: Private Law Proceedings for an Order Authorising the Taking Charge of, and Delivery of, a Child

Legal background

Under Family Law Act 1986, s 34 any court may authorise "an officer of the court or a constable to take charge of [a] child and deliver him to" a person entitled, under an order within Part I of that Act, to have the child given up to him. The authority under a s 34 order includes the power to "enter and search any premises where ... the child may be found, and to use such force as may be necessary". In the High Court, this power adds nothing to its inherent powers, but a county court or a family proceedings court can proceed in this way only under s 34. The powers under s 34 become available to the court only after "the child has not been given up in accordance with the order" which entitles a person to have the child given up to him: thus, unlike the inherent power of the High Court, this power cannot be used if there has been no disobedience of a previous order.

Suitability of order under s 34
An order which authorises the use of force to take charge of a child should not be granted, nor should the powers under a s 34 order be exercised, unless this is in the interests of the welfare of the child. Use of this power is more likely to be appropriate for achieving transfer of residence than for achieving contact.

Ex parte or on notice?
Where it is likely that the party who has the child may remove the child to frustrate the order, an application ex parte is appropriate. Where the risk is negligible, it will usually be appropriate to apply on notice.

Exercise of the power under a s 34 order
Only "an officer of the court or a constable" can exercise the power under a s 34 order. County court bailiffs are not trained for this work and do not undertake it. The police cannot be compelled to act: *R v Chief Constable of Cheshire* [1990] 1 FLR 70. Although a solicitor is an officer of the Supreme Court (Solicitors Act 1974, s 50), he is not an officer of either a county court (County Courts Act 1984, s 147) or a family proceedings court.

An order under s 34 authorises taking charge of the child, but it is not directive. Anyone seeking to exercise the authority should exercise discretion, having regard to the welfare of the child.

Procedure

Pre-condition	Failure to comply with an order (within FLA 1986, Part I) to give up a child	FLA 1986, s 34
	"Part I order" includes a CA 1989, s 8 order, or previous custody order, and similar orders made in Scotland and Northern Ireland; it does not include an order in proceedings for adoption or under CA 1989, Pt IV or V (public law); for more details of meaning of "Part I order", see under—	FLA 1986, s 25

	In a county court, a specific order to give up the child must have been ignored	FLA 1986, s 34; CCR Ord 29, r 1(1)
	In a family proceedings court, failure to comply with a residence order which has been served is sufficient	CA 1989, s 14(1), (2)
	The order to give up the child may be in the form of a condition or direction under CA 1989, s 11(7) attached to a s 8 order, and may be attached when the s 8 order is first made, or later.	
	Where the order was made elsewhere in the UK or in a specified dependent territory, it must have been registered in the High Court, and proceedings for enforcement must have been begun in that court	FLA 1986, ss 25(3), 27(1), 29(1), 32(1)
	For recovery order in public law proceedings under CA 1989, see —	CA 1989, s 50
Who may apply	Any party with a legitimate interest in s 8 proceedings	FLA 1986, s 34
	A person who has registered an order made elsewhere in the UK or a specified dependent territory, being a person on whom rights have been conferred by the order	FLA 1986, s 27(1)
Which court	In respect of an order made in England and Wales, the court which made the order not complied with	FLA 1986, s 34(1)
	Where made in relation to an order registered in the High Court, the application must be made in the High Court	FLA 1986, ss 25(3), 29(1), 32(1)
Form of application	On Form C3, which should be supported by evidence. Where the application is made in proceedings in the High Court or a county court in relation to an order under CA 1989, s 8 (or previous custody order), or is made in a family proceedings court, a statement which complies with FPR 1991, r 4.17(1)(*a*)/FPC(CA 1989)R 1991, r 17(1)(*a*) should be ready for use at the hearing	FPR 1991, rr 4.4(1A), 6.17(3); FPC(CA 1989)R 1991, rr 4(1A), 31A(3)
	Where the application is made in the High Court or otherwise than in relation to proceedings under CA 1989, s 8 (or previous custody order), an affidavit should be made in support.	

Fee payable	High Court or county court: £60 Magistrates' court: £20	FPFO 1999, fee 4.3 MCA 1980, Sch 6, Pt I
Ex parte practice	Application may be made ex parte; in an emergency, it may be made by telephone, in which case Form C3 must be (i) filed within 24 hours and (ii) served within 48 hours after the making of the order	FPR 1991, r 6.17(4); FPC(CA 1989)R 1991, r 31A(4)
	In a family proceedings court, an application ex parte by telephone is impractical, as there is no provision for the application to be heard by a single justice	FPC(CA 1989)R 1991, rr 2(5), 31A
Service of application where made on notice	2 days' notice in a county court, or reasonable or adequate notice in a family proceedings court (NB FPR 1991 and FPC(CA 1989)R 1991 and the Appendix/Schedule thereto do not specify the period of notice required for an application made in pending proceedings)	CCR Ord 13, r 1(2); MCA 1980, s 55(3), (4)
	Personal service is advisable so that the court may be satisfied that the respondent is aware of the hearing.	
Inter partes response by respondent	The respondent should appear, and may prepare a statement which complies with FPR 1991, r 4.17(1)(*a*)/FPC(CA 1989)R 1991, r 17(1)(*a*), or affidavit, as appropriate.	
Hearing	Judge or district judge in chambers, in High Court or a county court; magistrates in family proceedings court	FP(AJ)D 1999, Sch, para (*n*) (as substituted by FP(AJ)(A)D 2002); FPR 1991, r 4.16(7) (for s 8 proceedings); FPC(CA 1989)R 1991, rr 2(5), 31A
	Leave needed to rely on statement of evidence in pending s 8 proceedings	FPR 1991, r 4.17(1), (3); FPC(CA 1989)R 1991, r 17(1), (3)
	Applicant should submit draft order	Form C31
Form of order	C31	FPR 1991, r 6.17(3); FPC(CA 1989)R 1991, r 31A(3)
"Unless" order	C31 may be adapted to state that, unless the respondent hands over the child at a specified time and place, the power may be exercised thereafter. This allows the respondent to save face by delivering the child.	

56: Care or Supervision Order

Legal background

By virtue of CA 1989, s 31, the court may only make an order placing a child in the care of a local authority or putting him under the supervision of a local authority or a probation officer if it is satisfied about the threshold criteria, ie that the child is suffering or is likely to suffer significant harm and that the harm or likelihood of harm is attributable to the care given to him (or likely to be given to him if an order were not made) falling below a reasonable standard or his being beyond parental control. Once the court has found the threshold criteria proved, it must go on to decide whether or not to make an order and, if so, which sort of order would be appropriate. In so doing, it must take into account the CA 1989, s 1(1) welfare principle and the checklist of factors set out in CA 1989, s 1(3), as well as bearing in mind the general principle that delay is likely to prejudice the welfare of the child (CA 1989, s 1(2)). It must not make an order unless it considers that to do so would be better for the child than to make no order at all (CA 1989, s 1(5)).

While a care order is in force, the designated local authority has a duty to receive the child into its care and to keep him in its care for the duration of the order (see CA 1989, s 33(1)). Subject to certain restrictions set out in CA 1989, s 33, the local authority has parental responsibility for the child and has the power to decide what role his parents or guardian may play in the child's life. The order can be discharged or a supervision order substituted on an application under CA 1989, s 39, or it may be discharged by the making of a residence order in respect of the child (CA 1989, s 91(1)).

A supervision order lasts for one year in the first instance (though it can subsequently be extended so as to run for a period of up to three years from the date on which it was originally made) and imposes a general duty on the supervisor to advise, assist and befriend the child (see CA 1989, s 35 and Sch 3, Pts I and II which set out the provisions as to supervision orders in more detail). The supervisor must take such steps as are reasonably necessary to give effect to the order and, where the order is not wholly complied with or where he considers that it may not be necessary any more, he must consider whether he should apply to the court for it to be varied or discharged. The order can be discharged or varied on an application under CA 1989, s 39. A subsequent care order also discharges a supervision order (CA 1989, s 91(3)).

Where the main care or supervision proceedings are adjourned or the court gives a direction to the local authority under CA 1989, s 37(1) to investigate the child's circumstances, CA 1989, s 38(1) permits the making of an interim care or supervision order, provided that the court is satisfied that there are reasonable grounds for believing that the grounds for a full order exist (CA 1989, s 38(2)). There are stringent restrictions on the duration of interim orders (see CA 1989, s 38(4)). Directions with regard to the medical or psychiatric examination or other assessment of the child can be given either at the time of making an interim care or supervision order or at any time while it is in force (CA 1989, s 38(6)–(8)) and can be varied on application. Section 38A enables the court to include an exclusion requirement in an interim care order and to attach a power of arrest to that provision. The purpose of an exclusion requirement is to safeguard a child by removing from the scene (whether from the child's home or from part of it or from the area in which it is situated) a person who poses a threat to the child. Application can be made to vary or discharge the exclusion requirement and attendant power of arrest (CA 1989, s 39).

Procedure

Who may apply	Any local authority or authorised person (ie officer of NSPCC or anyone authorised by the Secretary of State)	CA 1989, s 31(1), (9)

Which court	Magistrates' court unless pending proceedings or application arises out of a CA 1989, s 37 investigation by local authority, in which case apply to court where proceedings pending or court which requires investigation	C(AP)O 1991, art 3
	Proceedings may be transferable sideways, upwards or downwards, depending on circumstances	C(AP)O 1991, arts 6–13
Which proceedings	Freestanding application or application in other family proceedings	CA 1989, s 31(4)
	Court may make supervision order on application for care order or vice versa, but otherwise has no power to make full care or supervision order of its own motion	CA 1989, s 31(1), (5)
Application	On Form C1 and Supplement C13, with copies for each respondent	FPR 1991, r 4.4(1); FPC(CA 1989)R 1991, r 4(1)
	Cases commenced in or transferred to the Family Division at the Royal Courts of Justice will be allocated to a High Court judge and special procedures apply	*President's Direction of 22 March 2002*
	Fee in High Court or county court (upon commencement of s 31 application): £80	FPFO 1999, fee 2.4(*a*)
	plus additional fee of £30 on an application for an interim care or supervision order where an application for a care or supervision order has already been made and at least one interim care order/interim supervision order has been made in the proceedings	FPFO 1999, fee 2.13(*a*)
	Fee in magistrates' court: £50	MCA 1980, Sch 6, Pt I
Respondents	Every person whom applicant believes has parental responsibility The child	FPR 1991, r 4.7, App 3; FPC(CA 1989)R 1991, r 7, Sch 2
Additional persons to whom notice in Form C6A is to be given	Local authority providing accommodation for child	
	Persons caring for child at commencement of proceedings	
	Person providing a CA 1989, s 51 refuge for child	
	Every person whom applicant believes is a party to pending relevant proceedings re same child	
	Every person whom applicant believes is a parent without parental responsibility for child	FPR 1991, r 4.4, App 3; FPC(CA 1989)R 1991, r 7, Sch 2

Service	Copy of application, together with Form C6, to be served on respondents at least 3 days before date of hearing or directions appointment	FPR 1991, rr 4.4(1), 4.8; FPC(CA 1989)R 1991, rr 4(1), 8
	Form C6A to be served on additional persons at same time as application etc served on respondents	FPR 1991, r 4.4(3); FPC(CA 1989)R 1991, r 4(3)
	At or before first directions appointment or hearing, applicant must file statement in Form C9 to prove that requirements for service have been complied with	FPR 1991, r 4.7; FPC (CA 1989)R 1991, r 7
Ex parte	May not be available (but see below as to interim orders)	FPR 1991, r 4.4(4); FPC (CA 1989)R 1991, r 4(4)
Joinder or removal of parties	By court order, of its own motion or on written request	FPR 1991, r 4.7; FPC(CA 1989)R 1991, r 7
Answer to application	Under FPR 1991, respondent may file answer; serve on other parties	FPR 1991, r 4.9(3), (4)
	Under FPC(CA 1989)R 1991, no provision either forbidding or permitting an answer	
Directions	As to the powers of the justices' clerk or the court, see —	FPR 1991, r 4.14; FPC(CA 1989)R 1991, r 14
Children's guardian	Must normally be appointed	CA 1989, s 41(1)
Interim orders	Unless leave given, interim application must be in writing on notice (can be included on Form C1)	FPR 1991, r 4.14(7); FPC(CA 1989)R 1991, r 14(9)
	With leave, interim order can be sought without formal written application or notice	
Who has power to make the order	High Court judge, nominated county court judge or any district judge of the principal registry	FP(AJ)D 1999, Sch, paras (*h*), (*i*) (as substituted by FP(AJ)(A)D 2002)
	A nominated district judge outside the principal registry (in relation to s 31 applications – interlocutory matters and unopposed trials only)	FP(AJ)D 1999, Sch, para (*h*) (as substituted by FP(AJ)(A)D 2002)
	A magistrates' court	
	A justices' clerk or single justice has limited power to make interim orders by consent, but no power to make full care or supervision orders	JCR 1999; CA 1989, s 93(2)(*i*); FPC(CA 1989)R 1991, rr 2(5)(*b*), 28
Order	*Interim care order* Form C33	

	Care order Form C32 *Supervision order (interim or full)* Form C35	FPR 1991, r 4.21(5), App 1; FPC(CA 1989)R 1991, r 21(7), Sch 1
Additional or alternative orders available without prior application	Interim care/supervision order with or without directions as to assessment	CA 1989, s 38(1), (6)
	Care order/supervision order	CA 1989, s 31(1), (5)
	Residence order (but not in favour of local authority and not with a care order)	CA 1989, ss 9(2), 10(1), 91(1)
	Prohibited steps order (but subject to s 9(5) and not with a care order)	CA 1989, ss 9(1), 10(1)
	Specific issue order (but subject to s 9(5) and not with a care order)	CA 1989, ss 9(1), 10(1)
	Section 8 contact order (but not in favour of local authority and not with a care order)	CA 1989, ss 9(1), (2), 10(1)
	Section 34 contact order (in conjunction with care order)	CA 1989, s 34(5)
	Family assistance order	CA 1989, s 16(1)
	Order appointing children's guardian	CA 1989, s 5(2)
	Order terminating appointment of guardian	CA 1989, s 6(7)(*c*)
	Order for financial relief (in certain limited circumstances only)	CA 1989, s 15, Sch 1
	No order	CA 1989, s 1(5)
	There is no reason why other orders (eg a parental responsibility order under s 4) should not be sought at the same time as a care or supervision order in an appropriate case, but a prior application would need to be made in accordance with the rules (FPR 1991 and FPC(CA 1989)R 1991).	
Procedure for exclusion requirements	Applicant for interim care order prepares separate statement of evidence in support re: exclusion requirement	
	Applicant serves statement and copy of order containing exclusion requirement (and of any power of arrest attached) personally on relevant person (ie person who is excluded) and informs relevant person of right to apply to vary/discharge exclusion requirement	CA 1989, s 38A; FPR 1991, r 4.24A(2); FPC(CA 1989)1991, r 25A(2)

	If power of arrest attached, once relevant person served with order/informed of terms, copy of order must be delivered to police together with statement showing relevant person served/informed of terms	FPR 1991, r 4.24A(3); FPC(CA 1989)1991, r 25A(3)
	Unless relevant person given notice and attended hearing, if power of arrest attached to exclusion order, court must announce in open court at earliest opportunity the name of person and fact that such order made	*President's Direction of 17 December 1997 (Children Act 1989: Exclusion Requirement)*
	Consent of person who is assuming care of child is required	CA 1989, s 38A(2); FPR 1991, r 4.24; FPC(CA 1989)1991, r 25
Variation/discharge of exclusion requirement and attendant power of arrest	Application for variation/discharge re: exclusion requirement or re: power of arrest by person to whom it applies, Form C2 suggested	CA 1989, s 39(3A), (3B)
	Applicant serves parties to the proceedings with application for variation/discharge	FPR 1991, r 4.24A(5); FPC(CA 1989)R 1991, r 25A(5)
	Consider giving notice to person caring for child	FPR 1991, App 3; FPC(CA 1989)R 1991, Sch 2
	For steps to be taken on variation/discharge affecting exclusion requirement/power of arrest, see—	FPR 1991, r 4.24A(4), (6); FPC(CA 1989)R 1991, r 25A(4), (6)
Appeals	See Guides 70, 72–75	

57: Discharge etc of a Care or Supervision Order, Substitution of a Supervision Order for a Care Order or Variation or Extension of a Supervision Order

Legal background

Under CA 1989, s 39, application may be made for the discharge of a care or supervision order or the variation of a supervision order. CA 1989, s 39(4) also empowers the court, on application, to substitute a supervision order for a care order, regardless of whether the threshold provisions set out in CA 1989, s 31(2) are satisfied at the time. In considering all s 39 applications, the court must apply the principle that the child's welfare is paramount (CA 1989, s 1(1)) and have regard to the checklist of factors in CA 1989, s 1(3) as well as to its duty not to make an order unless to do so would be more beneficial for the child than not to do so (CA 1989, s 1(5)).

Since the making of a residence order in relation to a child who is the subject of a care order discharges the care order (CA 1989, s 9(1)), an application for a residence order can, in an appropriate case, be an alternative to an application under s 39(1) for discharge.

An application to extend the length of a supervision order should be made by the supervisor under CA 1989, Sch 3, para 6(3) rather than in reliance on the more general power in s 39(2) to vary a supervision order.

Procedure

Who may apply	The child Any person with parental responsibility for the child *Discharge of care order* Local authority designated in order *Discharge of supervision order* Supervisor and, where application is to vary a requirement affecting a person with whom child is living, that person	CA 1989, s 39(1)–(3)
	Extension of supervision order Supervisor only	CA 1989, Sch 3, para 6(3)
Which court	The court which made the original order	C(AP)O 1991, art 4(1)
	Proceedings may be transferable sideways, upwards or downwards, depending on circumstances	C(AP)O 1991, arts 6–13
Which proceedings	Freestanding application	
Application	On Form C1, with sufficient copies for each respondent	FPR 1991, r 4.4(1); FPC(CA 1989)R 1991, r 4(1)
	Fee in High Court or county court: £80	FPFO 1999, fee 2.4(*b*)
	Fee in magistrates' court: £20	MCA 1980, Sch 6, Pt I
Respondents	Every person whom applicant believes has parental responsibility Every person whom applicant believes had parental responsibility prior to care order The child The parties to the original proceedings The supervisor (supervision order only)	FPR 1991, r 4.7, App 3; FPC(CA 1989)R 1991, r 7, Sch 2
Additional persons to whom notice in Form C6A is to be given	Local authority providing accommodation for child Persons caring for child at commencement of proceedings Person providing a CA 1989, s 51 refuge for child	FPR 1991 r 4.4, App 3; FPC(CA 1989)R 1991, r 4, Sch 2

Service	Copy of application, together with Form C6, to be served on respondent at least 7 days before date of hearing or directions appointment	FPR 1991, rr 4.4(1), 4.8; FPC(CA 1989)R 1991, rr 4(1), 8
	Form C6A to be served on additional persons at same time as application etc served on respondents	FPR 1991, r 4.4(3); FPC(CA 1989)R 1991, r 4(3)
	At or before first directions appointment or hearing, applicant must file statement in Form C9 to prove that requirements for service have been complied with	FPR 1991, r 4.7; FPC (CA 1989)R 1991, r 7
Ex parte	May not be available	FPR 1991, r 4.4(4); FPC(CA 1989)R 1991, r 4(4)
Joinder or removal of parties	By court order, of its own motion or on written request	FPR 1991, r 4.7; FPC(CA 1989)R 1991, r 7
Answer to application	Under FPR 1991, respondent may file answer; serve on other parties	FPR 1991, r 4.9(3), (4)
	Under FPC(CA 1989)R 1991, no provision either forbidding or permitting an answer	
Directions	As to the powers of the justices' clerk or the court, see—	FPR 1991, r 4.14; FPC(CA 1989)R 1991, r 14
Children's guardian	Must normally be appointed	CA 1989, s 41(1)
Special requirements	Following application for discharge of care order, supervision order, education supervision order, or for substitution of supervision order for care order or for child assessment order, bar on further application within 6 months from disposal of application, unless leave given	CA 1989, s 91(15)
Who has power to make the order	High Court judge, nominated Circuit judge or any district judge of the principal registry	FP(AJ)D 1999, Sch, paras (*h*), (*j*) (as substituted by FP(AJ)(A)D 2002)
	A nominated district judge outside the principal registry (in relation to variation applications under CA 1989, s 39(3), all stages of application; in relation to other s 39 applications, interlocutory matters and unopposed trials only)	FP(AJ)D 1999, Sch, paras (*h*), (*j*) (as substituted by FP(AJ)(A)D 2002)
	A magistrates' court; however, justices' clerk or single justice has no such power	JCR 1999; CA 1989, s 93(2)(*i*); FPC(CA 1989)R 1991, r 2(5)

Order	*Discharge of care order* Form C32 *Other applications* Form C36	FPR 1991, r 4.21(5), App 1; FPC(CA 1989)R 1991, r 21(7), Sch 1
Additional or alternative orders available on applications under CA 1989, s 39 without prior application	Section 8 order (residence, prohibited steps, specific issue or contact), but subject to certain restrictions	CA 1989, ss 9(1), (2), 10(1), 91(1)
	Section 34 contact order (if care order is to continue)	CA 1989, s 34(5)
	Family assistance order	CA 1989, s 16(1)
	Order appointing children's guardian	CA 1989, s 5(2)
	Order terminating appointment of guardian	CA 1989, s 6(7)(*c*)
	Order for financial relief (in certain limited circumstances only)	CA 1989, s 15, Sch 1
	No order	CA 1989, s 1(5)
	There is no reason why other orders (eg a parental responsibility order under s 4) should not be sought in an appropriate case at the same time as an application for discharge or variation is made, but a prior application would need to be made in accordance with the rules (FPR 1991 and FPC(CA 1989)R 1991).	
Appeals	See Guides 70, 72–75	

58: Regulating Contact with Children in Care

Legal background

The local authority has a duty to allow reasonable contact between a child in care and the child's parents, guardian, any person who had a residence order immediately before the care order was made and any person who had care of the child immediately before the care order by virtue of an order made under the High Court's inherent jurisdiction (CA 1989, s 34(1)). As a matter of urgency, the local authority may withhold contact for a period of up to seven days if it is satisfied that it is necessary to do so to safeguard or promote the child's welfare (CA 1989, s 34(6)). If this is not sufficient to cover the situation, an order authorising the local authority to refuse contact to a named person can be obtained from the court under CA 1989, s 34(4) and is not limited in time.

The court also has a general power to make such an order (with or without conditions, CA 1989, s 34(7)) as it considers appropriate with respect to the contact that is to be allowed between the child and a named person (CA 1989, s 34(2), (3)), and this can be used to define contact where there is dissatisfaction with the level of contact the local authority has decided upon, to resolve a dispute with the local authority as to whether contact needs to be supervised etc. CA 1989, s 8 contact orders cannot co-exist with a care order and the position is therefore regulated exclusively by CA 1989, s 34. If a CA 1989, s 8 contact order existed prior to the making of the care order, the care order will automatically discharge it (CA 1989, s 91(2)), and no s 8 contact order can be made in relation to a child in care (CA 1989, s 9(1)).

Procedure

Who may apply	Local authority Child AND (unless application is for refusal of contact) Parent Children's guardian Person who had residence order immediately prior to care order Person who had care of child immediately prior to care order by virtue of High Court order under inherent jurisdiction Any other person with leave	CA 1989, s 34(2)–(4)
Which court	Magistrates' court unless pending proceedings, in which case apply to court where proceedings pending	C(AP)O 1991, art 3
	Proceedings may be transferable sideways, upwards or downwards, depending on circumstances	C(AP)O 1991, arts 6–13
Which proceedings	Freestanding application	CA 1989, s 34(2)–(4)
	When making care order or in any family proceedings in connection with child in care, even though no application has been made	CA 1989, s 34(5)
Application	*Contact* Form C1 and Supplement C15, with sufficient copies for each respondent *Refusal of contact* Form C1 and Supplement C14, with sufficient copies for each respondent	FPR 1991, r 4.4(1); FPC(CA 1989)R 1991, r 4(1)
	Fee in High Court or county court: £80	FPFO 1999, fee 2.5(*a*)
	Fee in magistrates' court: £20	MCA 1980, Sch 6, Pt I
Respondents	Every person whom applicant believes has parental responsibility Every person whom applicant believes had parental responsibility prior to care order The child The person whose contact with the child is the subject of the application	FPR 1991, r 4.7, App 3; FPC(CA 1989)R 1991, r 7, Sch 2

Additional persons to whom notice in Form C6A is to be given	Local authority providing accommodation for child Persons caring for child at commencement of proceedings Person providing a s 51 refuge for child	FPR 1991, r 4.4, App 3; FPC(CA 1989)R 1991, r 4, Sch 2
Service	Copy of application, together with Form C6, to be served on respondents at least 3 days before date of hearing or directions appointment	FPR 1991, rr 4.4(1), 4.8; FPC(CA 1989)R 1991, rr 4(1), 8
	Form C6A to be served on additional persons at same time as application etc served on respondents	FPR 1991, r 4.4(3); FPC(CA 1989)R 1991, r 4(3)
	At or before first directions appointment or hearing, applicant must file statement in Form C9 to prove that requirements for service have been complied with	FPR 1991, r 4.7; FPC (CA 1989)R 1991, r 7
Ex parte	May not be available	FPR 1991, r 4.4(4); FPC (CA 1989)R 1991, r 4(4)
Joinder or removal of parties	By court order, of its own motion or on written request	FPR 1991, r 4.7; FPC(CA 1989)R 1991, r 7
Answer to application	Under FPR 1991, respondent may file answer; serve on other parties	FPR 1991, r 4.9(3), (4)
	Under FPC(CA 1989)R 1991, no provision either forbidding or permitting an answer	
Directions	As to the powers of the justices' clerk or the court, see —	FPR 1991, r 4.14; FPC(CA 1989)R 1991, r 14
Children's guardian	Must normally be appointed	CA 1989, s 41(1)
Special requirements	Bar on further application within 6 months from refusal of application unless leave given	CA 1989, s 91(17)
Who has power to make the order	High Court judge, nominated county court judge or any district judge of the principal registry	FP(AJ)D 1999, Sch, para (*h*) (as substituted by FP(AJ)(A)D 2002)
	A nominated district judge outside the principal registry, in relation to interlocutory matters, unopposed trials and opposed hearings where the application is for a contact order and the principle of contact is unopposed	FP(AJ)D 1999, Sch, para (*h*) (as substituted by FP(AJ)(A)D 2002)
	A magistrates' court	

	A justices' clerk or single justice has no such power, although a single justice may grant leave to make the application	JCR 1999; FPC(CA 1989)R 1991, r 2(5)(*c*)
Order	Form C34	FPR 1991, r 4.21(5), App 1; FPC(CA 1989)R 1991, r 21(7), Sch 1
Additional or alternative orders	Residence order in favour of someone other than local authority (but subject to CA 1989, s 9 restrictions, and note that effect would be to discharge care order)	CA 1989, ss 9(1), (2), 10(1), 91(1)
	No order	CA 1989, s 1(5)
	Other orders which are theoretically possible but very unlikely to be appropriate:	
	family assistance order	CA 1989, s 16(1)
	order appointing children's guardian/terminating appointment	CA 1989, ss 5(2), 6(7)(*c*)
Appeals	See Guides 70, 72–75	

59: Discharge or Variation of an Order Regulating Contact with Children in Care

Legal background

An order under CA 1989, s 34 may be varied or discharged by the court on an application under CA 1989, s 34(9); alternatively, the local authority and the person entitled to contact can agree a variation in accordance with the Contact with Children Regulations 1991, SI 1991/891.

Procedure

Who may apply	Local authority	
	The child	
	The person named in the order	CA 1989, s 34(9)
Which court	The court which made the original order	C(AP)O 1991, art 4(1)
	Proceedings may be transferable sideways, upwards or downwards, depending on circumstances	C(AP)O 1991, arts 6–13
Which proceedings	Freestanding application	CA 1989, s 34(9)
	In any family proceedings in connection with child in care, even though no application has been made	CA 1989, s 34(5)

Application	On Form C1, with copies for each respondent	FPR 1991, r 4.4(1); FPC(CA 1989)R 1991, r 4(1)
	Fee in High Court or county court: £80	FPFO 1999, fee 2.5(*a*)
	Fee in magistrates' court: £20	MCA 1980, Sch 6, Pt I
Respondents	As for initial application, *plus* the parties to the original proceedings	FPR 1991, r 4.7, App 3; FPC(CA 1989)R 1991, r 7, Sch 2
Additional persons to whom notice in Form C6A is to be given	Local authority providing accommodation for child Persons caring for child at commencement of proceedings Person providing a s 51 refuge for child	FPR 1991 r 4.4, App 3; FPC(CA 1989)R 1991, r 4, Sch 2
Service	Copy of application, together with Form C6, to be served on respondents at least 3 days before date of hearing or directions appointment	FPR 1991, rr 4.4(1), 4.8; FPC(CA 1989)R 1991, rr 4(1), 8
	Form C6A to be served on additional persons at same time as application etc served on respondents	FPR 1991, r 4.4(3); FPC(CA 1989)R 1991, r 4(3)
	At or before first directions appointment or hearing, applicant must file statement in Form C9 to prove that requirements for service have been complied with	FPR 1991, r 4.7; FPC (CA 1989)R 1991, r 7
Ex parte	May not be available	FPR 1991, r 4.4(4); FPC(CA 1989)R 1991, r 4(4)
Joinder or removal of parties	By court order, of its own motion or on written request	FPR 1991, r 4.7; FPC(CA 1989)R 1991, r 7
Answer to application	Under FPR 1991, respondent may file answer; serve on other parties	FPR 1991, r 4.9(3), (4)
	Under FPC(CA 1989)R 1991, no provision either forbidding or permitting an answer	
Directions	As to the powers of the justices' clerk or the court, see —	FPR 1991, r 4.14; FPC(CA 1989)R 1991, r 14
Children's guardian	Must normally be appointed	CA 1989, s 41(1)
Special requirements	Bar on further application within 6 months from refusal of application unless leave given	CA 1989, s 91(17)

Who has power to make the order	High Court judge, nominated county court judge or any district judge of the principal registry	FP(AJ)D 1999, Sch, para (*h*) (as substituted by FP(AJ)(A)D 2002)
	A nominated district judge outside the principal registry, in relation to interlocutory matters, unopposed trials and opposed hearings where the application is for a contact order and the principle of contact is unopposed	FP(AJ)D 1999, Sch, para (*h*) (as substituted by FP(AJ)(A)D 2002)
	A magistrates' court; however, justices' clerk or single justice has no such power	JCR 1999; CA 1989, s 93(2)(*i*); FPC(CA 1989)R 1991, r 2(5)
Order	Form C21	
Additional or alternative orders	Residence order in favour of someone other than local authority (but subject to CA 1989, s 9 restrictions, and note that effect would be to discharge care order)	CA 1989, ss 9(1), (2), 10(1), 91(1)
	No order	CA 1989, s 1(5)
	Other orders which are theoretically possible but very unlikely to be appropriate:	
	family assistance order	CA 1989, s 16(1)
	order appointing children's guardian/terminating appointment	CA 1989, ss 5(2), 6(7)(*c*)
Appeals	See Guides 70, 72–75	

60: Secure Accommodation Order

Legal background

Restricting the liberty of a child is a serious step and is therefore strictly regulated by CA 1989, s 25 and by the Children (Secure Accommodation) Regulations 1991 and the Children (Secure Accommodation) (No 2) Regulations 1991. With certain exceptions, a child may not be placed or kept in secure accommodation unless either he has a history of absconding and is likely to abscond if kept in any other type of accommodation and, if he absconds, to suffer significant harm or he is likely to injure himself or others if kept in any other type of accommodation. Where either of these criteria is satisfied, a child may be kept in secure accommodation for a maximum of 72 hours without court authority but, if there is a need to detain him for longer, an application must be made to the court. If the court is satisfied that the relevant criteria are met, it will make an order authorising the child to be kept in secure accommodation for a specified maximum period of time (up to three months for a first application and up to six months on any further application).

Procedure

Who may apply	Where local authority looking after child, only the local authority	C(SA)R 1991, reg 8

	Where health authority, National Health Service trust or local education authority providing accommodation for child, only the health authority etc, unless local authority looking after child	C(SA)(No 2)R 1991, reg 2(1)
	Where child provided with accommodation in residential care home, nursing home or mental nursing home, only the person providing such accommodation, unless local authority looking after child	C(SA)(No 2)R 1991, reg 2(2)
Which court	Magistrates' court, unless pending proceedings, in which case apply to court where proceedings pending	C(AP)O 1991, art 3(1), (3)
	Proceedings may be transferable sideways, upwards or downwards, depending on circumstances	C(AP)O 1991, arts 6–13
Which proceedings	Freestanding application	
Which court for variation, extension or discharge of order	Court by which original order made	C(AP)O 1991, art 4(1)
Application	On Form C1 and Supplement C20, with sufficient copies for each respondent	FPR 1991, r 4.4(1); FPC(CA 1989)R 1991, r 4(1)
	Fee payable in High Court or county court: £80	FPFO 1999, fee 2.3(*a*)
	Fee payable in magistrates' court: None	MCA 1980, Sch 6, Pt I
Respondents	Every person whom applicant believes has parental responsibility Every person whom applicant believes had parental responsibility prior to care order The child Where application is to vary etc, parties to original proceedings	FPR 1991, r 4.7, App 3; FPC(CA 1989)R 1991, r 7, Sch 2
Additional persons to whom notice in Form C6A is to be given	Local authority providing accommodation for child Person caring for child at commencement of proceedings Person providing a CA 1989, s 51 refuge for child	FPR 1991, r 4.4, App 3; FPC(CA 1989)R 1991, r 4, Sch 2
Additional persons to be notified of intention to apply	Where application relates to child already kept in secure accommodation in a community home: child's independent visitor, if appointed	

	any other person whom local authority considers should be informed	C(SA)R 1991, reg 14
Service	Copy of application, together with Form C6, to be served on respondent at least 1 day before date of hearing or directions appointment	FPR 1991, rr 4.4(1), 4.8; FPC(CA 1989)R 1991, rr 4(1), 8
	Form C6A to be served on additional persons at same time as application etc served on respondents	FPR 1991, r 4.4(3); FPC(CA 1989)R 1991, r 4(3)
	At or before first directions appointment or hearing, applicant must file statement in Form C9 to prove that requirements for service have been complied with	FPR 1991, r 4.7; FPC (CA 1989)R 1991, r 7
Ex parte	May not be available	FPR 1991, r 4.4(4); FPC(CA 1989)R 1991, r 4(4)
Joinder or removal of parties	By court order, of its own motion or on written request	FPR 1991, r 4.7; FPC(CA 1989)R 1991, r 7
Answer to application	Under FPR 1991, respondent may file answer; serve on other parties	FPR 1991, r 4.9(3), (4)
	Under FPC(CA 1989)R 1991, no provision either forbidding or permitting an answer	
Directions	As to the powers of the justices' clerk or the court, see —	FPR 1991, r 4.14; FPC(CA 1989)R 1991, r 14
Children's guardian	Must normally be appointed	CA 1989, s 41(1)
Special requirements	Order may not be made unless child is legally represented or has been told of the right to apply for CLS funding and given opportunity to do so and has refused or failed to apply	CA 1989, s 25(6)
Who has power to make the order	High Court judge, nominated county court judge or any district judge of the principal registry	FP(AJ)D 1999, Sch, para (*h*) (as substituted by FP(AJ)(A)D 2002)
	A district judge nominated for public family law proceedings, in relation to interlocutory matters, or unopposed hearings	FP(AJ)D 1999, Sch, para (*h*) (as substituted by FP(AJ)(A)D 2002)
	A magistrates' court; however, justices' clerk or single justice has no such power	JCR 1999; CA 1989, s 93(2)(*i*); FPC(CA 1989)R 1991, r 2(5)
Order	Form C26	FPR 1991, r 4.21(5), App 1; FPC(CA 1989)R 1991, r 21(7), Sch 1

Additional or alternative orders	No order	CA 1989, s 1(5)
	Wide range of alternative orders may be available, eg s 8 orders, since CA 1989, s 25 proceedings in magistrates' courts are "family proceedings" by virtue of s 92(2)	*Oxfordshire County Council v R* [1992] 1 FLR 648
Appeals	See Guides 70, 72–75	

61: Education Supervision Order

Legal background

If the court is satisfied that a child of compulsory school age is not being properly educated it can make an education supervision order (ESO) putting him under the supervision of a designated local education authority (CA 1989, s 36). In making a decision whether or not to grant an ESO, the court must take into account the CA 1989, s 1(1) welfare principle and the checklist of factors set out in CA 1989, s 1(3), as well as bearing in mind the general principle that delay is likely to prejudice the welfare of the child (CA 1989, s 1(2)). It must not make an order unless it considers that to do so would be better for the child than to make no order at all (CA 1989, s 1(5)). An ESO cannot be made in respect of a child who is in the care of a local authority (CA 1989, s 36(6)), but there is no bar on the co-existence of an ESO and a supervision order, in which case the supervision order will take precedence (CA 1989, Sch 3, para 14).

Detailed provisions as to the effect and duration etc of an ESO can be found in CA 1989, Sch 3, Pt III. In the first instance the order lasts for one year but can be extended subsequently. It imposes a general duty on the supervisor to advise, assist, befriend and give directions to the child and his parents to ensure that he is properly educated. A parent who persistently fails to comply with a direction given under an ESO can be guilty of an offence under CA 1989, Sch 3, para 18. Where the child persistently fails to comply with any directions given under an ESO, the local education authority must notify the appropriate local authority who then has to investigate the child's circumstances and may see fit to apply for a care order (CA 1989, Sch 3, para 19).

Procedure

Who may apply	Any local education authority	CA 1989, s 36(1)
Which court	Magistrates' court, unless pending proceedings or application arises out of a s 37 investigation by local authority, in which case apply to court where proceedings pending or court which required investigation	C(AP)O 1991, art 3
	Proceedings may be transferable sideways, upwards or downwards, depending on circumstances	C(AP)O 1991, arts 6–13
Which proceedings	Freestanding application	CA 1989, s 36(1)
Application	On Form C1 and Supplement C17, with sufficient copies for each respondent	FPR 1991, r 4.4(1); FPC(CA 1989)R 1991, r 4(1)
	Fee in High Court or county court: £80	FPFO 1999, fee 2.7(*a*)

	Fee in magistrates' court: £50	MCA 1980, Sch 6, Pt I
Respondents	Every person whom applicant believes has parental responsibility The child	FPR 1991, r 4.7, App 3; FPC(CA 1989)R 1991, r 7, Sch 2
Additional persons to whom notice in Form C6A is to be given	Local authority providing accommodation for child Persons caring for child at commencement of proceedings Person providing a CA 1989, s 51 refuge for child	FPR 1991, r 4.4, App 3; FPC(CA 1989)R 1991, r 4, Sch 2
Service	Copy of application, together with Form C6, to be served on respondents at least 7 days before date of hearing or directions appointment	FPR 1991, rr 4.4(1), 4.8; FPC(CA 1989)R 1991, rr 4(1), 8
	Form C6A to be served on additional persons at same time as application etc served on respondents	FPR 1991, r 4.4(3); FPC(CA 1989)R 1991, r 4(3)
	At or before first directions appointment or hearing, applicant must file statement in Form C9 to prove that requirements for service have been complied with	FPR 1991, r 4.7; FPC (CA 1989)R 1991, r 7
Ex parte	May not be available	FPR 1991, r 4.4(4); FPC(CA 1989)R 1991, r 4(4)
Joinder or removal of parties	By court order, of its own motion or on written request	FPR 1991, r 4.7; FPC(CA 1989)R 1991, r 7
Answer to application	Under FPR 1991, respondent may file answer; serve on other parties at least 2 days before date fixed for hearing of application Under FPC(CA 1989)R 1991, no provision either forbidding or permitting an answer	FPR 1991, r 4.9(3), (4)
Directions	As to the powers of the justices' clerk or the court, see —	FPR 1991, r 4.14; FPC(CA 1989)R 1991, r 14
Children's guardian	Not "specified proceedings"	CA 1989, s 41(1)
Special requirements	Local education authority must consult local authority social services committee before applying	CA 1989, s 36(8)
Who has power to make the order	High Court judge, nominated county court judge, any district judge of the principal registry or nominated district judge outside the principal registry	FP(AJ)D 1999, Sch, para (*j*) (as substituted by FP(AJ)(A)D 2002)

	A magistrates' court; however, justices' clerk or single justice has no such power	JCR 1999; CA 1989, s 93(2)(*i*); FPC(CA 1989)R 1991, r 2(5)
Order	Form C37	FPR 1991, r 4.21(5), App 1; FPC(CA 1989)R 1991, r 21(7)
Additional or alternative orders	Direction requiring local authority to investigate with a view to care or supervision order	CA 1989, s 37(1)
	CA 1989, s 8 order (but subject to restrictions in CA 1989, s 9)	CA 1989, s 10(1)
	Family assistance order	CA 1989, s 16(1)
	Order appointing children's guardian or terminating appointment	CA 1989, ss 5(2), 6(7)(*c*)
	No order	CA 1989, s 1(5)
Appeals	See Guides 70, 72–75	

62: Extension of an Education Supervision Order

Legal background

An education supervision order (ESO) may be extended by the court (CA 1989, Sch 3, para 15(2)). Application must be made during the currency of the order (para 15(2)) but may not be made earlier than three months before the date on which the order is due to expire (para 15(3)). There can be more than one extension, each extension being for not more than three years (para 15(4), (5)).

Procedure

Who may apply	Local education authority in whose favour order was made	CA 1989, Sch 3, para 15(2)
Which court	The court which made the original order	C(AP)O 1991, art 4
	Proceedings may be transferable sideways, upwards or downwards, depending on circumstances	C(AP)O 1991, arts 6–13
Which proceedings	Freestanding application	CA 1989, Sch 3, para 15(2)
Application	On Form C1 and Supplement C17A	FPR 1991, r 4.4(1); FPC(CA 1989)R 1991, r 4(1)
	Fee in High Court or county court: £80	FPFO 1999, fee 2.7(*b*)
	Fee in magistrates' court: £20	MCA 1980, Sch 6, Pt I

Respondents	Every person whom applicant believes has parental responsibility The child The parties to the original application	FPR 1991, r 4.7, App 3; FPC(CA 1989)R 1991, r 7, Sch 2
Additional persons to whom notice in Form C6A is to be given	Local authority providing accommodation for child Persons caring for child at commencement of proceedings Person providing a s 51 refuge for child	FPR 1991, r 4.4, App 3; FPC(CA 1989)R 1991, r 4, Sch 2
Service	Copy of application, together with Form C6, to be served on respondents at least 7 days before date of hearing or directions appointment	FPR 1991, rr 4.4(1), 4.8; FPC(CA 1989)R 1991, rr 4(1), 8
	Form C6A to be served on additional persons at same time as application etc served on respondents	FPR 1991, r 4.4(3); FPC(CA 1989)R 1991, r 4(3)
	At or before first directions appointment or hearing, applicant must file statement in Form C9 to prove that requirements for service have been complied with	FPR 1991, r 4.7; FPC (CA 1989)R 1991, r 7
Ex parte	May not be available	FPR 1991, r 4.4(4); FPC(CA 1989)R 1991, r 4(4)
Joinder or removal of parties	By court order, of its own motion or on written request	FPR 1991, r 4.7; FPC(CA 1989)R 1991, r 7
Answer to application	Under FPR 1991, respondent may file answer; serve on other parties at least 2 days before date fixed for hearing of application	FPR 1991, r 4.9(3), (4)
	Under FPC(CA 1989)R 1991, no provision either forbidding or permitting an answer	
Directions	As to the powers of the justices' clerk or the court, see —	FPR 1991, r 4.14; FPC(CA 1989)R 1991, r 14
Children's guardian	Not "specified proceedings"	CA 1989, s 41(1)
Special requirements	No application earlier than 3 months before expiry date of order	CA 1989, Sch 3, para 15(3)
Who has power to make the order	High Court judge, nominated county court judge, any district judge of the principal registry or nominated district judge outside the principal registry	FP(AJ)D 1999, Sch, para (*j*) (as substituted by FP(AJ)(A)D 2002)

	A magistrates' court; however, justices' clerk or single justice has no such power	JCR 1999; CA 1989, s 93(2)(*i*); FPC(CA 1989)R 1991, r 2(5)
Order	Form C38	FPR 1991, r 4.21(5), App 1; FPC(CA 1989)R 1991, r 21(7), Sch 1
Additional or alternative orders	Direction requiring local authority to investigate with a view to care or supervision order	CA 1989, s 37(1)
	CA 1989, s 8 order (but subject to restrictions in CA 1989, s 9)	CA 1989, s 10(1)
	Family assistance order	CA 1989, s 16(1)
	Order appointing children's guardian or terminating appointment	CA 1989, ss 5(2), 6(7)(*c*)
	No order	CA 1989, s 1(5)
Appeals	See Guides 70, 72–75	

63: Discharge of an Education Supervision Order

Legal background

An education supervision order (ESO) may be discharged by the court on an application under CA 1989, Sch 3, para 17. On discharging an ESO, the court may direct the local authority within whose area the child lives, or will live, to investigate the child's circumstances (CA 1989, Sch 3, para 17(2)).

Procedure

Who may apply	The child	
	A parent	
	The local education authority concerned	CA 1989, Sch 3, para 17(1)
Which court	The court which made the original order	C(AP)O 1991, art 4
	Proceedings may be transferable sideways, upwards or downwards, depending on circumstances	C(AP)O 1991, arts 6–13
Which proceedings	Freestanding application	CA 1989, Sch 3, para 17(1)
Application	On Form C1, with copies for each respondent	FPR 1991, r 4.4(1); FPC(CA 1989)R 1991, r 4(1)
	Fee in High Court or county court: £80	FPFO 1999, fee 2.7(*b*)
	Fee in magistrates' court: £20	MCA 1980, Sch 6, Pt I

Respondents	Every person whom applicant believes has parental responsibility The child The local education authority concerned The parties to the original proceedings	FPR 1991, r 4.7, App 3; FPC(CA 1989)R 1991, r 7, Sch 2
Additional persons in Form C6A to whom notice is to be given	Local authority providing accommodation for child Persons caring for child at commencement of proceedings Person providing a CA 1989, s 51 refuge for child	FPR 1991, r 4.4, App 3; FPC(CA 1989)R 1991, r 4, Sch 2
Service	Copy of application, together with Form C6, to be served on respondents at least 7 days before date of hearing or directions appointment	FPR 1991, rr 4.4(1), 4.8; FPC(CA 1989)R 1991, rr 4(1), 8
	Form C6A to be served on additional persons at same time as application etc served on respondents	FPR 1991, r 4.4(3); FPC(CA 1989)R 1991, r 4(3)
	At or before first directions appointment or hearing, applicant must file statement in Form C9 to prove that requirements for service have been complied with	FPR 1991, r 4.7; FPC (CA 1989)R 1991, r 7
Ex parte	May not be available	FPR 1991, r 4.4(4); FPC(CA 1989)R 1991, r 4(4)
Joinder or removal of parties	By court order, of its own motion or on written request	FPR 1991, r 4.7; FPC(CA 1989)R 1991, r 7
Answer to application	Under FPR 1991, respondent may file answer; serve on other parties at least 2 days before date fixed for hearing of application	FPR 1991, r 4.9(3), (4)
	Under FPC(CA 1989)R 1991, no provision either forbidding or permitting an answer	
Directions	As to the powers of the justices' clerk or the court, see —	FPR 1991, r 4.14; FPC(CA 1989)R 1991, r 14
Children's guardian	Not "specified proceedings"	CA 1989, s 41(1)
Who has power to make the order	High Court judge, nominated county court judge, any district judge of the principal registry or nominated district judge outside the principal registry	FP(AJ)D 1999, Sch, para (*j*) (as substituted by FP(AJ)(A)D 2002)

	A magistrates' court; however, justices' clerk or single justice has no such power	JCR 1999; CA 1989, s 93(2)(*i*); FPC(CA 1989)R 1991, r 2(5)
Order	Form C38	FPR 1991, r 4.21(5), App 1; FPC(CA 1989)R 1991, r 21(7), Sch 1
Additional or alternative orders	Direction requiring local authority to investigate with a view to care or supervision order	CA 1989, s 37(1)
	CA 1989, s 8 order (but subject to restrictions in CA 1989, s 9)	CA 1989, s 10(1)
	Family assistance order	CA 1989, s 16(1)
	Order appointing children's guardian or terminating appointment	CA 1989, ss 5(2), 6(7)(*c*)
	No order	CA 1989, s 1(5)
Appeals	See Guides 70, 72–75	

64: Application in Respect of an Abducted Child under the Hague Convention 1980 or European Convention 1980

Legal background

The Child Abduction and Custody Act 1985 ratifies the Hague Convention of 25 October 1980 and the European Convention of 20 May 1980. Applications under the Hague Convention are made: (*a*) to secure the prompt return of children wrongfully removed to or retained in any Contracting State; or (*b*) to ensure that rights of custody and of access under the law of the Contracting State are effectively respected in the other Contracting State.

Applications under the European Convention are made for: (*a*) recognition and enforcement of a custody order, including enforcement by means of returning the child to the person in whose favour the custody order was made; (*b*) recognition of a custody or contact order; or (*c*) recognition and enforcement of a contact order.

Procedure

Who may apply	*Hague Convention* Any person, institution or body who claims that a child has been removed or retained in breach of custody or access rights	CACA 1985, Sch 1, Art 3
	European Convention Any person who has a court order giving them rights of custody and contact	CACA 1985, Sch 2, Arts 1, 8
Which court	High Court	CACA 1985, s 4
Conditions to be met	*Hague Convention* The child must be under 16	CACA 1985, Sch 1, Art 4

	The child must have been habitually resident in a Contracting State immediately before his removal or breach of contact rights	
	The child must have been taken or retained after the date on which the Convention came into force between the two countries	
	European Convention The child must be under 16	CACA 1985, Sch 2, Art 1
	At the time of removal the applicant must have a custody or contact order made in his favour	CACA 1985, Sch 2, Art 4
	The child must have been removed in breach of those custody or contact rights to another Contracting State	CACA 1985, Sch 1, Art 3
	If, at the time of removal, there is no custody order in force, the Convention may apply to an order made after the removal if it also contains a declaration that the removal was wrongful	CACA 1985, Sch 2, Art 12
Application procedure in England and Wales	By originating summons in RSC, App A, Form 10 and must contain the required information	FPR 1991, rr 6.2–6.4
Documents	*Hague Convention* Authenticated copy of any relevant decision or agreement	
	Certificate or affidavit concerning the relevant law of the Contracting State	CACA 1985, Sch 1, Art 8
	Any other relevant document	
	European Convention Document of authorisation	
	Copy court order	
	Evidence of service	
	Document establishing that the order is enforceable in the Contracting State	
	Statement indicating the whereabouts of the child	CACA 1985, Sch 2, Art 14
Defendants	The abductor	
	The harbourer	
	The parent or guardian within the UK	
	Any person in whose favour a custody order has been made	
	Any other person who has an interest in the welfare of the child	FPR 1991, r 6.5

Service	The acknowledgement of service must be filed within 7 days of service of the originating summons unless extended by the court	FPR 1991, r 6.6
Affidavit in answer	Must be filed within 7 days of service of the originating summons	FPR 1991, r 6.7(2)
Affidavit in reply	Must be filed within 7 days of service of the affidavit in answer	FPR 1991, r 6.7(3)
Orders	All the orders under the inherent jurisdiction, including:	
	collection and location orders in the prescribed form – see *Emergency Remedies in the Family Courts* (Issue 12)	
	disclosure of whereabouts	CACA 1985, s 24A
	attendance order	
	surrender of passport	
	port alert	
	flight information	
	publicity	
	injunction prohibiting further removal and removal from UK	
	injunction freezing assets	
	any other direction	
	contact order	CACA 1985, s 5
Appeals	See Guide 75	

65: Application for Registration of an Order under the Family Law Act 1986 in Respect of an Abducted Child

Legal background

Application for the registration of a Part I order may be made by any person in whose favour rights have been conferred by the order, in another part of the United Kingdom under Family Law Act 1986, s 27, or in the Isle of Man under a corresponding provision. If the order was made in the family proceedings court, the procedure laid down in the Magistrates' Courts (Family Law Act 1986) Rules 1988 should be followed. In the case of an order made in the High Court in England and Wales and Northern Ireland, the Court of Session in Scotland and the High Court of Justice of the Isle of Man the following procedure applies.

Procedure

Who may apply	Any person on whom rights are conferred by a Part I order	FLA 1986, s 27

Which court	(*a*) Application in respect of High Court orders must be made to the court which made the order, that is:	FLA 1986, s 27
	(i) High Court in England and Wales and Northern Ireland	FPR 1991, r 7.7(1)
	(ii) The Court of Session in Scotland	FLA 1986(DT)O 1991
	(iii) High Court of Justice of the Isle of Man	FLA 1986(DT)O 1991; FPR 1991, rr 6.11, 7.7(1)
	(*b*) Applications in respect of an order made in the county court must be made to the county court which made the order	FLA 1986, s 27; FPR 1991, r 7.8(2)
Which Department	In respect of High Court orders the application should be made as follows:	
	in the principal registry, to the family proceedings clerk	
	in the district registry, to the court manager	FPR 1991, r 1.2(1)
	in Northern Ireland, to the master (care and protection) of the High Court	FPR 1991, r 7.7(1)
	in Scotland, to the deputy principal clerk of session or the sheriff clerk, as the case may be	CSR 260R; RRCOSC 1988, r 3(1)
	in the Isle of Man, the corresponding officer of the High Court of Justice of the Isle of Man	FPR 1991, r 7.7(1)
	In respect of an order made by the county court, to the court manager	
Application	Request in writing signed by or on behalf of the applicant	FPR 1991, r 7.8; Ord 90 (NI); CSR 260R (Scotland)
Documents	Copy of the letter of application Affidavit by the applicant Copy of the affidavit Certified copy of the order Certified copy of any order which has varied the original order	FPR 1991, r 7.8(1); Ord 90 (NI); CSR 260R; RRCOSC 1988, r 3(2)

65A: Application to Enforce a Registered Order in Respect of an Abducted Child under the Family Law Act 1986

Procedure

Which court	As under Guide 65, the court at which the order is registered	FLA 1986, s 27
Application	If proceeding in the High Court, in England and Wales, by originating summons in RSC, App A, Form 10.	
	In the county court, by originating application supported by affidavit	
	In Scotland, by petition	CSR 260V
Defendant	The abductor	
Service	No specific rules, but the court will give directions	FLA 1986, s 27; FPR 1991, r 7.12
	In Scotland, usually 21 days unless the court otherwise directs	CSR 260V(4)
Orders	All the orders under the inherent jurisdiction, including:	
	collection and location orders (formerly known as find and return and search and locate orders)	For prescribed forms see *Emergency Remedies in the Family Courts* (Issue 12)
	disclosure of whereabouts	CACA 1985, s 24A
	attendance order	
	surrender of passport	
	port alert	
	flight information	
	publicity	
	injunction prohibiting further removal and removal from UK	
	injunction freezing assets	
	any other direction	
	contact order	CACA 1985, s 5

66: Wardship, and Other Applications, under the Inherent Jurisdiction of the High Court

Legal background

The inherent jurisdiction of the High Court is generally unrestricted and unlimited, except insofar as restrictions have been imposed by statutes or by judicial decisions of the court itself. The most significant statutory restriction on the court's jurisdiction is that imposed by CA 1989, s 100 in the use of its inherent jurisdiction by local authorities. The court's inherent jurisdiction is not restricted to wardship, as wardship is just one of the ways in which the court exercises its inherent jurisdiction in relation to children; in such cases (save for the restrictions imposed) the court has powers to make such orders as are deemed necessary for the protection of the child. There may, however, be circumstances where the court is asked to exercise its inherent jurisdiction to protect the interest of a child, even though the child has not been warded, eg where the court is asked to give directions on medical treatment to be given to, or withdrawn from, a child.

Procedure

Who may apply	Local authority (subject to the restrictions imposed by CA 1989, s 100 and only with leave)	
	Any person with a genuine interest in the person who is the subject of the proceedings	FPR 1991, r 5.1(6)
	The ward (wardship only)	FPR 1991, r 9.2A; see also *Re CT (A Minor)* [1993] 2 FLR 278
Which court	Family Division of the High Court (principal registry or district registry)	SCA 1981, Sch 1
	Proceedings may be transferred to an appropriate county court	MFPA 1984, s 38(2)
Application	*Wardship* By originating summons in Form 8, as adapted (Form FD 582)	FPR 1991, r 5.1
	Other applications By originating summons, other than an ex parte summons, in RSC App A, Form 8	RSC Ord 7, r 2(2)
	If ex parte, by originating summons in RSC App A, Form 11	RSC Ord 7, r 2(2)
Service	Unless the court otherwise directs, the acknowledgement of service must be filed with 14 days of service, if served within the jurisdiction	RSC Ord 12, r 5(*a*)
	If served outside the jurisdiction, the court should give directions, unless the provisions of RSC Ord 11, r 1(3) apply	RSC Ord 10, r 2(2); Ord 11, r 4(4); Ord 12, r 5(*b*)
Documents	*Wardship* Affidavit in support	FPR 1991, r 5.1

	Certified copy of birth certificate or copy of entry in the Adopted Children Register	FPR 1991, r 5.1(5)(*a*)
	Other applications On inter partes application:	
	plaintiff's evidence must be filed before the expiration of 14 days after the defendant has acknowledged service	RSC Ord 28, r 1A(1)
	On ex parte application:	
	applicant must file his evidence not less than 4 clear days before the hearing	RSC Ord 28, r 1A(2)
	By reason of the urgency of such applications, the court generally accepts the evidence when the application is made.	
Defendant	Usually the parent or guardian of the child	
	Any other person who has an interest in or relation to the child	
	The ward, with leave (wardship only)	FPR 1991, rr 5.1(3), (6), 9.2(1), (2), (7); *L v L* [1994] 1 FLR 156
Affidavit in answer	*Wardship* No specific provisions in FPR 1991, and so the provisions of RSC Ord 28, r 1A(4) apply, unless the court directs otherwise	
	The court will generally give directions and set a timetable on the first appointment (see Directions below)	
	Other applications Defendant must file his evidence within 28 days of service of the plaintiff's evidence, unless the court directs otherwise	RSC Ord 28, rr 1A(4), 2(2)
Directions	*Wardship* A request for the first appointment must be made within 21 days of the issue of the originating summons	SCA 1981, s 41(2); FPR 1991, r 5.3(1)
	Other applications The registry, on issuing the summons, should fix a date for directions before a judge of the Family Division on the first available date after 8 weeks	RSC Ord 28, r 2(1)
	In the case of an ex parte application, the time for the directions appointment will usually be abridged on the applicant's application	RSC Ord 28, r 2(2)

	On the hearing for directions, if the case appears complex and uncertain in its outcome, the judge may give further directions, including directions for trial	*Re C* [1990] 2 FLR 527
Orders	Any order, directions or declaration sought and consequential orders which may be necessary	
	Where appropriate, any of the following orders:	
	collection and location orders in the prescribed form – see *Emergency Remedies in the Family Courts* (Issue 12)	
	disclosure of whereabouts	CACA 1985, s 24A
	attendance order	
	surrender of passport	
	port alert	
	flight information	
	publicity	
	injunction prohibiting further removal and removal from UK	
	injunction freezing assets	
	any other direction	
	contact order	CACA 1985, s 5
	Where appropriate, any order under CA 1989, s 8	
Appeals	See Guide 75	

67: Declaration Freeing a Child for Adoption

Legal background

Under Adoption Act 1976, s 18, on an application by an adoption agency, an authorised court can make an order declaring a child to be free for adoption. On the making of the order, parental responsibility for the child is given to the applicant adoption agency, and parental responsibility held by any person prior to the making of the order is extinguished (AA 1976, s 18(5)). Any previous care order ceases to have effect. The requirements regarding the parent's agreement in respect of any subsequent adoption application are satisfied and, subject to a successful application to revoke the freeing order (under AA 1976, s 20 or the inherent jurisdiction), the parent has no rights or role in relation to any such adoption application. A freeing order may be made to facilitate the prospect of an adoption in a foreign jurisdiction (*Re S (Freeing for Adoption)* [2002] EWCA Civ 798, [2002] 2 FLR 681).

Proceedings under AA 1976 are "family proceedings" under CA 1989, s 8 and FLA 1996, Pt IV; therefore the court may make orders under CA 1989, Pt II or non-molestation orders within adoption proceedings. The *President's Guidelines of 1 October 2001 (Adoption Proceedings: A New Approach)* (set out in Part IV of this work) give detailed procedural guidance.

Procedure

Who may apply	An adoption agency	AA 1976, s 18(1)
Which court	If child is in England and Wales when application made:	
	High Court (Principal Registry of the Family Division)	
	adoption centre county court family proceedings court	AA 1976, s 62(2); C(AP)O 1991
	If child is not in Great Britain when application made:	
	High Court only	AA 1976, s 62(3)
	Proceedings can be transferred sideways, upwards or downwards	C(AP)O 1991
Application	Originating summons or originating application in Form 1	AR 1984, r 4, Form 1; MC(A)R 1984, r 4, Form 1
	Can only be made if one of the child's parents or guardians consents to the making of the application *or* the child is in local authority care and the local authority are applying to dispense with parents' consent	AA 1976, s 18(2), (2A)
	Fee payable in High Court or county court: £120	FPFO 1999, fee 3.1
	Fee payable in family proceedings court: £30	MCA 1980, Sch 6, Pt I
Respondents	Each parent (with parental responsibility) or guardian of the child	
	Any local authority or voluntary organisation which has parental responsibility for, or is looking after or caring for, the child	
	Any person liable to maintain child	
	The child (in the High Court)	
	Court may add any other person or body (including child in county court) as a respondent	AR 1984, r 4(2), (3); MC(A)R 1984, r 4(2), (3)
Documents	The applicant must file:	
	3 copies of originating process	
	3 copies of Sch 2 report	
	birth certificate or certificate of previous adoption	
	any document re evidence of parental consent	
	if application to dispense with consent, 3 copies of statement of facts	AR 1984, r 4, Form 1; MC(A)R 1984, r 4, Form 1

Parental consent	Court must be satisfied in the case of each parent or guardian of the child that *either* he freely, with full understanding, agrees generally and unconditionally to the making of an adoption order *or* that his consent should be dispensed with under AA 1976, s 16(2)	AA 1976, s 18(1)
	Consent may not be dispensed with unless child placed for adoption or likely to be placed	AA 1976, s 18(3)
	Consent of mother is ineffective if given within 6 weeks of birth	AA 1976, s 18(4)
Natural father	If child's father does not have parental responsibility, the court must be satisfied that he has no intention of applying for a parental responsibility order or a residence order *or*, if he did, the application would be likely to be refused	AA 1976, s 18(7)
Reporting officer	Appointed if parent appears willing to consent to adoption	AR 1984, r 5; MC(A)R 1984, r 5
Children's guardian	Appointed if parent appears unwilling to consent to adoption or if special circumstances and welfare require it	AR 1984, r 6; MC(A)R 1984, r 6
Hearing	Notice to be served on all parties, the reporting officer and the children's guardian	AR 1984, r 9(1); MC(A)R 1984, r 9(1)
	Proceedings under AA 1976 are "family proceedings"	CA 1989, s 8(4); FLA 1996, s 63(2)
	At least 4 weeks before final hearing the court must consider documents and give directions	AR 1984, r 9(3)
	The court should decide first whether adoption is in the child's best interests and second whether consent should be dispensed with	*Re D (A Minor) (Adoption: Freeing Order)* [1991] 1 FLR 48
	Where a court hears an application to free for adoption together with an application for a care order, the application for the care order is the primary application	*Re D (Simultaneous Applications for Care Order and Freeing Order)* [1999] 2 FLR 49
	Before making a freeing order, the court must be satisfied that each parent or guardian has been given an opportunity to declare that they prefer not to be involved in future questions of the child's welfare	AA 1976, s 18(6)
	No order can be made without the attendance of the child (unless there are special circumstances) and of an authorised officer of the applicant	AR 1984, r 10(4), (5); MC(A)R 1984, r 10(4), (5)

Order	The order declares that the child is free for adoption	AR 1984, Form 12; MC(A)R 1984, Form 10
Revocation of a freeing order	Where parent has not declared that he wishes no further part in child's future, he may, in limited circumstances, apply to revoke the freeing order	AA 1976, s 20
	The application must be made in the original freeing proceedings	AR 1984, r 12(1); MC(A)R 1984, r 12(1), Form 4
	If AA 1976, s 20 does not apply, the court may revoke the order under the inherent jurisdiction	*Re C (Adoption: Freeing Order)* [1999] 1 FLR 348
Appeals	See Guides 71, 74, 75	

68: Adoption Order

Legal background

An adoption order is an order giving parental responsibility for a child to the adopters made on their application to an authorised court (Adoption Act 1976, s 12(1)). At the same time, the making of an adoption order operates to extinguish permanently the parental responsibility which any person had for the child immediately before the making of the order (AA 1976, s 12(2)). An adoption order is irrevocable, save in the very restricted circumstances of AA 1976, s 52 (revocation on subsequent legitimation). The adopted child is deemed to be the adopter's legitimate child, as if he had been born to the adopter(s) in marriage (AA 1976, s 39). Adoption is therefore the legal process by which a child becomes a permanent and full member of a new family.

Proceedings under AA 1976 are "family proceedings" under CA 1989, s 8 and FLA 1996, Pt IV; therefore the court may make orders under CA 1989, Pt II or non-molestation orders within adoption proceedings. The *President's Guidelines of 1 October 2001 (Adoption Proceedings: A New Approach)* (set out in Part IV of this work) give detailed procedural guidance.

Procedure

Who may apply	*Married applicants* Each applicant must be over 21 (save for the child's parent who must be over 18)	AA 1976, s 14
	At least one of the applicants must be domiciled in the UK, Channel Islands or the Isle of Man (unless it is a Convention case)	AA 1976, s 14(2)
	The applicants must be married to each other	AA 1976, s 14(1)
	Sole applicant Must be over 21	AA 1976, s 15(1)
	Must be unmarried or satisfy court that spouse cannot be found, or is separated, or mentally/physically incapable of applying	AA 1976, s 15(1)

	Must be domiciled in the UK, Channel Islands or the Isle of Man (unless it is a Convention case)	AA 1976, s 15(2)
Who may be adopted	Adoption order may be made only in respect of a child (a person under the age of 18) who has never been married	AA 1976, ss 12(1), (5), 72(1)
	Child must be at least 19 weeks old	AA 1976, s 13(1)
	Child must live with adopters for preceding 13 weeks (in the case of a parent, step-parent or relative applicant, or adoption agency/High Court placement), or for 12 months (all other cases)	AA 1976, s 13(1), (2)
	Proper notice of intention to apply to adopt must have been given to local authority	AA 1976, s 22
	The court must not be denied jurisdiction by AA 1976, s 24	AA 1976, s 24
	The child must be either in England and Wales or outside Great Britain when the application is made	AA 1976, s 62
Which court	If child is in England and Wales when application made:	
	High Court (Principal Registry of the Family Division)	
	adoption centre county court	AA 1976, s 62(2); C(AP)O 1991
	family proceedings court	
	If child is not in Great Britain when application made:	
	High Court only	AA 1976, s 62(3)
	Proceedings can be transferred sideways, upwards or downwards	C(AP)O 1991
Application	Originating summons or originating application in Form 6	AR 1984, r 15, Form 6; MC(A)R 1984, r 15, Form 6
	If the applicant wishes his identity to be kept confidential, he may apply for a serial number to be issued	AR 1984, r 14; MC(A)R 1984, r 14
	Fee payable in High Court or county court: £120	FPFO 1999, fee 3.1
	Fee payable in magistrates' court: £30	MCA 1980, Sch 6, Pt I
Respondents	Each parent (with parental responsibility) or guardian of the child (unless the child is free for adoption)	
	Any adoption agency that has parental responsibility under a freeing order	

	Any adoption agency involved in the adoption arrangements	
	Any local authority to whom notice has been given under AA 1976, s 22	
	Any local authority or voluntary organisation which has parental responsibility for, or is looking after or caring for, the child	
	Any person liable to maintain the child	
	The spouse of a married sole applicant	
	The child (in the High Court)	
	Court can join any other person or body (including child in county court) as a respondent	AR 1984, r 15(2), (3); MC(A)R 1984, r 15(2), (3)
Documents	The applicant must file:	
	3 copies of originating process	
	birth certificate or certificate of previous adoption	
	any document re evidence of parental consent	
	copy of any freeing order	
	if application to dispense with consent, 3 copies of statement of facts	
	marriage certificate of married applicants	
	medical report on each applicant and the child (not required in agency cases)	AR 1984, r 15(4), Form 6; MC(A)R 1984, r 15(4), Form 6
	The relevant adoption agency (not the applicant) must file a Sch 2 report	AR 1984, r 22; MC(A)R 1984, r 22
Parental consent	Unless the child is free for adoption, court must be satisfied in the case of each parent or guardian of the child that *either* he freely, with full understanding, agrees generally and unconditionally to the making of an adoption order *or* that his consent should be dispensed with under AA 1976, s 16(2)	AA 1976, s 16(1)
	Consent of mother is ineffective if given within 6 weeks of birth	AA 1976, s 16(4)
Reporting officer	Appointed if parent appears willing to consent to adoption	AR 1984, r 17; MC(A)R 1984, r 17
Children's guardian	Appointed if parent appears unwilling to consent to adoption or if special circumstances and welfare require it	AR 1984, r 18; MC(A)R 1984, r 18

Hearing	Notice to be served on all parties, the reporting officer and the children's guardian	AR 1984, r 21(1); MC(A)R 1984, r 21(1)
	Proceedings under AA 1976 are "family proceedings"	CA 1989, s 8(4); FLA 1996, s 63(2)
	At least 4 weeks before final hearing the court must consider documents and give directions	AR 1984, r 21(5)
	No order can be made without the attendance of the child (unless there are special circumstances)	AR 1984, r 23(4), (5); MC(A)R 1984, r 23(4), (5)
Order	An adoption order gives parental responsibility to the adopters and extinguishes any previous parental responsibility and any earlier court orders. The child is treated as if he was born to the adopter(s) in marriage	AA 1976, ss 12, 39; AR 1984, Form 15; MC(A)R 1984, Form 13
	An adoption order may contain such terms and conditions as the court thinks fit	AA 1976, s 12(6)
Appeals	See Guides 71, 74, 75	

69: Application for Judicial Review

Legal background

Judicial review is the process whereby the High Court exercises its supervisory jurisdiction to review the legality and validity of the actions and decisions of persons or bodies exercising administrative powers, whether of a legislative, executive, judicial or adjudicatory character. The jurisdiction is over the proceedings and decisions of inferior courts (such as magistrates' courts and county courts), tribunals and other bodies performing public acts and duties. It is not a system of appeal. The procedure must be used where the claimant is seeking a mandatory order (formerly known as an order of mandamus), a prohibiting order (formerly known as an order of prohibition) or a quashing order (formerly known as an order of certiorari). The procedure for an application for judicial review is prescribed by CPR 1998, Pt 54 and accompanying Practice Direction (PD54) and Supreme Court Act 1981, ss 29 to 31 (and County Courts Act 1984, ss 83 and 84). Judicial review claims are dealt with in the Administrative Court (see further annotation under CPR 1998, r 54.1).

Procedure

Who may apply	Any person with sufficient interest in the matter subject to the proposed review	SCA 1981, s 31(3)
Application for permission	Made by filing a claim form (N461) promptly, and in any event within 3 months of the decision, in the Administrative Court in London (or Wales where there is a devolution issue or an issue concerning the National Assembly)	CPR 1998, r 54.5

The claim form must include or be accompanied by	(i) a detailed statement of the claimant's grounds for bringing the claim for judicial review (ii) a statement of facts relied on (iii) any application to extend the time limit for filing the claim form (iv) any application for directions (v) a time estimate for the hearing	PD54, para 5.6
Additional documents to accompany the claim form	(i) written evidence in support of the claim (verified by a statement of truth) (ii) a copy of the order complained of (iii) where the decision complained of relates to a decision of a court or tribunal, an approved copy of the reasons for the decision (iv) copies of any documents on which the claimant proposes to rely (v) copies of any statutory material (vi) a list of essential documents for advance reading by the court (with page references to passages); and if necessary, reasons why the documents cannot be filed and details of any person considered to be an interested party	PD54, paras 5.7, 5.10
Human Rights Act 1998	Where the applicant seeks to raise any issue under the Human Rights Act 1998, or seeks a remedy under that Act, the claim form must: (*a*) state that there is a claim in respect of a HRA issue; and (*b*) give details of the alleged convention right infringed (*c*) specify the relief sought (*d*) state if the relief sought includes a declaration of incompatibility or damages in respect of a judicial act (*e*) where there is a claim for a declaration of incompatibility, provide details of the legislative provision (*f*) where the claim relates to unlawfulness by another court or tribunal, give details of the finding (*g*) where the claim relates to a judicial act, give details of the act complained of and the court or tribunal concerned	PD 16, para 15.1

Acknowledgment of service	Must be filed within 21 days of service of the claim form	CPR 1998, r 54.8(2)(*a*)
	and served within 7 days of filing	CPR 1998, r 54.8(2)(*b*)
Determination of permission application	Usually determined without a hearing	PD54, para 8.4
	Reasons being provided (on form JRJ)	PD54, para 9.1
	If refused without a hearing (or granted on terms), a request for reconsideration (at an oral hearing) must be filed within 7 days of the reasons given for refusal	CPR 1998, r 54.12
	If refused after a hearing, an application or permission may be made to the Court of Appeal within 7 days of the refusal	CPR 1998, r 52.15
	Fee payable: £30 (to HM Paymaster General)	
Application	The application must proceed on the claim form (see above) used to seek leave.	
	Where the claimant seeks to rely on additional grounds he must give notice no later than 7 days before the hearing	PD54, para 11.1
	Fee payable: £120	
Defendants	Where the claim relates to proceedings in a court or tribunal all parties to those proceedings must be named in the claim form as an interested party	PD54, para 5.1
	The claimant must serve all the parties within 7 days of the issue of the claim form	CPR 1998, r 54.7; PD54, para 6.1
	The claimant must lodge a certificate of service in the Administrative Court within 7 days of service	
Additional persons to be served	The claim form must be served by the claimant upon any person the claimant considers to be an interested party within 7 days of the date of issue	CPR 1998, r 54.7
	Any person may apply for permission to file evidence or make representations at the hearing	CPR 1998, r 54.17
Response	A defendant or any other person served with the claim form who wishes to contest or support the claim must:	

	(*a*) file an acknowledgment of service (form N462) within 21 days setting out a summary of the grounds for contesting the claim and the name and address of any person claiming to be an interested party; (*b*) serve the acknowedgment of service on the claimant and interested persons within 7 days of filing (the court will do this if requested)	CPR 1998, r 54.8
	(*c*) file and serve detailed grounds and any written evidence within 35 days after service of the order giving permission	CPR 1998, r 54.14
Case Management Directions	Directions may be given as to service or evidence	CPR 1998, r 54.10
	Where a claim is under the Human Rights Act 1998 a direction may be made for giving notice to the Crown or joining the Crown as a party	CPR 1998, r 19.4A
	Case management directions may be sought	CPR 1998, Pt 23
Interim remedy	A range of interim orders may be sought (including an interim injunction or declaration)	CPR 1998, Pt 25
Documents	The claimant must file two copies of a paginated and indexed bundle which must include the documents of the other parties	PD54, para 5.9
	The claimant should also provide a paginated indexed bundle of statutory material	PD54, para 5.9
	Skeleton argument must be filed by the claimant not less than 21 working days before the hearing (or the warned date for hearing) and by the defendant or any other person wishing to make representations not less than 14 days before the hearing	PD54, para 15.1
	The skeleton argument must contain:	PD54, para 15.3
	(*a*) a time estimate; (*b*) a list of issues; (*c*) a list of legal points with justification for citing more than one authority on any proposition of law	*PD of 9 April 2001*
	(*d*) a chronology; (*e*) a list of essential reading (where only part of a page needs to be read, that part should be marked (not highlighted)) and;	

	(*f*) a list of persons referred to	
Hearing	When an application is ready to be heard it will be entered in the Administrative Court Warned List and all involved will be notified. The case will usually be heard by a single judge in open court but may be heard by two or more judges sitting as the Divisional Court	
Order	The court may:	
	make a mandatory order, a prohibiting order or a quashing order	CPR 1998, rr 54.2, 54.3
	grant an injunction or declaration	SCA 1981, s 30
	award damages	SCA 1981, s 31(4)
Appeals	To the Court of Appeal – Permission to appeal is required either from the Administrative Court or from the Court of Appeal within 14 days of the decision	CPR 1998, Pt 52

70: Appeal from a Family Proceedings Court under the Children Act 1989

Legal background

An appeal from a family proceedings court in relation to a decision made in proceedings under CA 1989 is to the High Court in accordance with the provisions of CA 1989, s 94. The only exception is where the court has refused an application to transfer care proceedings in accordance with the Children (Allocation of Proceedings) Order 1991, in which case a further application is made to a district judge of the appropriate care centre and not to the High Court.

Subject to certain exceptions, an appeal may be made by any party to the proceedings against any order, or the refusal to make an order. There is no requirement that permission to appeal be obtained first and, therefore, an appeal may be made as of right. The restrictions on an appeal relate to certain types of order: there is no appeal against the decision of the court to decline jurisdiction (CA 1989, s 94(2)); to make or refuse to make an emergency protection order (CA 1989, s 45(10)); or against an interim periodical payments order (CA 1989, s 94(3)). Special provisions apply to orders for the transfer of proceedings (see C(AP)O 1991).

Procedure

Who may appeal	Any party to the hearing against an order or refusal to make an order	CA 1989, s 94
	any person interested, aggrieved or prejudicially affected	*Re M (Prohibited Steps: Application for Leave)* [1993] 1 FLR 275
	except where the order was an interim periodical payments order	CA 1989, s 94(3)

Which court	High Court (ie High Court judge of the Family Division in open court)	CA 1989, s 94; FPR 1991, r 4.22(8); *PD of 31 January 1992*
	Where the decision is a refusal to transfer care proceedings to a county court, further application may be made to the district judge of the care centre listed in C(AP)O 1991, Sch 2	C(AP)O 1991, art 9
Procedure on appeal	By notice of appeal to be filed and served within 14 days of the determination, unless the appeal is under CA 1989, s 38(1), in which case within 7 days or, with leave of the court, within such other time as is directed	FPR 1991, r 4.22(3)
	The appeal must be made to:	
	the principal registry (where the family proceedings court is in the London Commission Area); or	
	the district registry which is in the same place as, or is nearest to, the care centre for the family proceedings court	FPR 1991, r 4.22(2A)
	Fee payable: £80	
Respondents	The parties to the proceedings and any children's guardian	FPR 1991, r 4.22(2)
Answer	A respondent's notice may be filed and served within 14 days of receipt of the notice of appeal, unless the appeal is under s 38(1) where no respondent's notice may be filed	FPR 1991, r 4.22(5), (6)
Documents	The appellant must file and serve a paginated and indexed bundle with a summary of the hearing, a statement of issues, a chronology and skeleton arguments. The bundle should contain:	*PD of 10 March 2000*
	a certified copy of the application and order	
	a copy of the notes of evidence	
	a copy of the reasons for the decision	
	This should be done as soon as practicable after filing and serving the notice of appeal	FPR 1991, r 4.22(2)
	The reports and witness statements filed for the original hearing must also be filed and served	*Re U(T) (A Minor)* [1993] 2 FCR 565

	The notes of evidence or reasons should state the parties who were represented and the statements which were before the court	*Leicestershire CC v G* [1994] 2 FLR 329
	Citation of judgments must comply with PD	*PD of 9 April 2001*
Directions	Applications to: amend the grounds of appeal dismiss the appeal by consent or withdraw the appeal may be made to the district judge	FPR 1991, r 4.22(7)
Listing	The appellant, and other parties, must notify the court of the time estimate for the hearing of the appeal	*PD of 22 November 1993*
Order	The order on appeal is treated as an order of the family proceedings court	CA 1989, s 94(9)
Powers of the court	The High Court may:	
	make such orders as may be necessary to give effect to the determination of the appeal	CA 1989, s 94(4)
	make such incidental or consequential orders as appear just	CA 1989, s 94(5)
Appeals	To the Court of Appeal (with permission); or	SCA 1981, s 16; CPR 1998, r 52.13
	to the House of Lords, if a certificate has been issued by the judge under AJA 1969, s 12	AJA 1969, s 12; HLPD, Dirs 1.4, 6

71: Appeal from a Magistrates' Court or Family Proceedings Court not under the Children Act 1989

Legal background

An appeal from any decision of the magistrates' court lies to the High Court (Supreme Court Act 1981, s 28(3)). The procedure for appeals relating to proceedings under CA 1989 is considered separately and is governed by CA 1989, s 94 and FPR 1991, r 4.22. Appeals other than under CA 1989 are governed by FPR 1991, r 8.2 (for appeals under the Domestic Proceedings and Magistrates' Courts Act 1978), r 8.3 (for appeals under Administration of Justice Act 1960, s 13) and under RSC Ord 55 (for all other proceedings).

Where there is no specific provision under FPR 1991, rr 8.1, 8.2, for those particular appeals it seems RSC Ord 55 will apply. In order to determine the appropriate procedure, a proposed appellant must consider first whether the proceedings which are to be the subject of the appeal are proceedings to which CA 1989 applies (for which, see FPR 1991, r 4.1(2)). If not, then consider whether FPR 1991, rr 8.1 and 8.2 apply (subject in any event to RSC Ord 55). Otherwise, the procedure is governed by RSC Ord 55. An appeal by way of notice of motion (Ord 55) is appropriate in respect of orders made under the now repealed Guardianship of Minors Act 1971.

Which rules of court

As an appeal to the High Court in "family proceedings" (as defined by MFPA 1984, s 32) does not fall within the definition of "civil proceedings" under CPR 1998, r 2.1 and the "old" RSC have not been repealed (The Civil Procedure (Amendment) Rules 2000 repealed only those parts of RSC which were incorporated in CPR 1998, Sch 1), it is assumed that they will continue to apply, unamended, to family proceedings. For a detailed examination of the procedural regime applicable to such an appeal see the annotations under FPR 1991, r 1.3 and, in particular, the Table contained therein.

Procedure

Who may appeal	Any party to the hearing	
Which court	High Court	RSC Ord 55, r 1(1)
	Where the decision of the High Court is final, a divisional court; otherwise, by a single judge	RSC Ord 55, r 2
	On appeal under DPMCA 1978 or AJA 1960, s 13, a divisional court of the Family Division of the High Court	FPR 1991, rr 8.2(1), 8.3
Procedure on appeal	By notice of motion which must be served and lodged within 28 days of decision	RSC Ord 55, r 4(2)
	On appeal under DPMCA 1978, notice of motion must be served and lodged within 6 weeks of the decision	FPR 1991, r 8.2(1)
	On appeal under AJA 1960, s 13, no more than 4 clear days between decision and hearing; notice must be served not less than 1 day before hearing	RSC Ord 109, r 2(4), (5)
	On appeal under FLA 1996, s 61, within 14 days of the decision by notice of appeal	FPR 1991, r 8.1A(1)(*a*)
	A supplementary notice may be served not less than 7 days before the hearing, which must be lodged within 2 days of service	RSC Ord 55, r 6
	Fee payable: £50	
Respondents	The parties to the original hearing directly affected by the appeal	RSC Ord 55, r 4(1)(*a*)
Additional persons to be served	The clerk to the justices	RSC Ord 55, r 4; FPR 1991, r 8.1A(2) for appeals under FLA 1996, Pt IV
Service	In accordance with RSC Ord 65, r 5	FPR 1991, r 8.2(3)

Documents	For appeals under FPR 1991, rr 8.2 and 8.3, the appellant must lodge 3 copies of:	
	the summons and order appealed against	
	the clerk's notes of evidence	
	the justices' reasons	
	a certificate of service of the notice of motion	
	as soon as practicable after entering the appeal	FPR 1991, r 8.2(4)
	Citation of judgments must comply with PD	*PD of 9 April 2001*
Directions	By motion to a judge or district judge of the High Court	RSC Ord 55, r 6A; FPR 1991, r 8.2(8)
Powers of the court	The court is not bound to allow the appeal where there has been an improper admission or rejection of evidence, unless there has been substantial wrong or miscarriage of justice	RSC Ord 55, r 7(7); FPR 1991, r 8.2(6)
	The court may:	
	receive further evidence on questions of fact	RSC Ord 55, r 7(2)
	draw inferences of fact which could have been drawn by the court below	RSC Ord 55, r 7(3)
	give any judgment or make any order that could have been made below	RSC Ord 55, r 7(5)
	remit the matter for rehearing	RSC Ord 55, r 7(5)
Appeals	To the Court of Appeal	SCA 1981, s 16; CPR 1998, Pt 52
	If a certificate has been issued under AJA 1969, s 12, to the House of Lords	AJA 1969, s 12; HLPD, Dirs 1.4, 6
	Where the decision is that of the divisional court, leave to appeal is required	SCA 1981, s 18(1)(*e*)
	Where the determination is that of a single judge, he is not a divisional court and leave is not required	SCA 1981, s 66

72: Appeal from a District Judge of the County Court to a Judge of the County Court

Legal background

An appeal from the decision of a district judge of the county court lies to a judge of the same court. If the decision which is the subject of the appeal is a decision made in proceedings under CA 1989, the procedure for such an appeal is prescribed by FPR 1991, r 4.22. If the appeal relates to a decision which is made in family proceedings, but not proceedings under CA 1989, the procedure is prescribed by FPR 1991, r 8.1 and CCR Ord 37, r 1. If the appeal does not fall within either category, the procedure is prescribed by CCR Ord 37, r 6 alone. Such an appeal resembles an appeal to the Court of Appeal, since the judge does not hear the evidence afresh but considers the evidence on paper. The procedure is the same as for an appeal from a judge of the county court to the Court of Appeal (see Guide 75). Where the order was made by consent, it is open to the party seeking its review to commence proceedings to set it aside, or to seek a rehearing under CCR Ord 37, r 1.

Which rules of court
For a detailed examination of the procedural regime applicable to such an appeal see the annotations under FPR 1991, r 1.3 and, in particular, the Table contained therein (and note to Guide 73).

Procedure

Who may appeal	Any party to the hearing	
Procedure on appeal	For CA 1989 proceedings (unless the judge directs otherwise), by a notice of appeal which must be filed and served within 14 days of the decision: unless the appeal relates to an order under s 38(1), in which case the appeal must be filed and served within 7 days	FPR 1991, r 4.22(3)
	Fee payable: £50	
	For family proceedings (except ancillary relief applications under MWPA 1882, MHA 1983 or MCA 1973, ss 27, 35, 36), by a notice of appeal which must be issued within 14 days of the order and served within 14 days before the day fixed for hearing	FPR 1991, r 8.1(4)
	For ancillary relief proceedings, by a notice of appeal which must be served within 14 days of the decision to be appealed against	FPR 1991, r 8.1(2); CCR Ord 37, r 6(2)
	For appeals under FLA 1996, Pt IV, within 14 days of the decision by notice of appeal	FPR 1991, r 8.1A(1)(*a*)
	Fee payable: £50	
Respondents	For CA 1989 proceedings, the parties to the proceedings before the district judge	FPR 1991, r 4.22(2)

Additional persons to be served	For CA 1989 proceedings, any children's guardian appointed	FPR 1991, r 4.22(2)
Documents	For CA 1989 proceedings, the appellant must file and serve: the notice of appeal a copy of the summons or application and order appealed against the reasons given for the decision as soon as practicable after filing and serving the notice of appeal Citation of judgments must comply with PD	FPR 1991, r 4.22(2) *PD of 9 April 2001*
Answer	For CA 1989 proceedings, a respondent's notice may be filed and served within 14 days of receipt of the notice of appeal: unless the appeal relates to an order under s 38(1), in which case no respondent's notice may be filed There is no such provision for other proceedings.	FPR 1991, r 4.22(5), (6)
Powers of the judge	On an appeal under FPR 1991, r 8.1(2), the order under appeal is treated as final for the purposes of CCR Ord 37, r 6; the appeal is limited to a review of the first instance decision unless the judge considers that it would be in the interests of justice to hold a rehearing (whatever the nature of the hearing, fresh evidence may be admitted if it is in the interests of justice to do so) No specific power is defined for appeals under FPR 1991, r 8.1(1).	FPR 1991, r 8.1(3) (as substituted by FP(A)R 2003)
Appeals	To the Court of Appeal	CCA 1984, s 77

73: Appeal from a District Judge of the High Court to a Judge of the High Court

Legal background

An appeal from the decision of a district judge of the High Court lies to a judge of the same court. If the decision which is the subject of the appeal is a decision made in proceedings under CA 1989, the procedure for such an appeal is prescribed by FPR 1991, r 4.22. If not, the procedure is prescribed by RSC Ord 58. Such an appeal, although a rehearing, resembles an appeal to the Court of Appeal, since the judge does not hear the evidence afresh but considers the evidence on paper. Nevertheless, the court is entitled to give "due weight" to the decision and reasons of the district judge.

Which rules of court

As an appeal to the High Court in "family proceedings" (as defined by MFPA 1984, s 32) does not fall within the definition of "civil proceedings" under CPR 1998, r 2.1 and the "old" RSC have not been repealed, it is assumed that they will continue to apply, unamended, to family proceedings (The Civil Procedure (Amendment) Rules 2000 repealed only those parts of RSC which were incorporated in CPR 1998, Sch 1). For a detailed examination of the procedural regime applicable to such an appeal see the annotations under FPR 1991, r 1.3 and, in particular, the Table contained therein.

Procedure

Who may appeal	Any party to the hearing	RSC Ord 58, r 1
Procedure on appeal	For CA 1989 proceedings (unless the judge directs otherwise), by a notice of appeal which must be filed and served within 14 days of the decision: unless the appeal relates to an order under s 38(1), in which case the appeal must be filed and served within 7 days	FPR 1991, r 4.22(3); RSC Ord 58, r 1
	Fee payable: £80	
	For other proceedings, by a notice of appeal which must be issued:	
	within 14 days of the decision under FLA 1996, Pt IV	FPR 1991, r 8.1A(1)
	within 5 days of the decision and served within 5 days thereafter in relation to an appeal from a decision of a district judge of the principal registry	RSC Ord 58, r 1
	within 7 days of the decision and served within 5 days thereafter in relation to an appeal from a decision of any other district judge	RSC Ord 58, r 3
	Fee payable: £80	
Respondents	The parties to the proceedings before the district judge	FPR 1991, r 4.22(2); RSC Ord 58, r 1(2)
Additional persons to be served	For CA 1989 proceedings, any children's guardian appointed	FPR 1991, r 4.22(2)
Documents	For CA 1989 proceedings, the appellant must file and serve:	FPR 1991, 4.22(2)
	the notice of appeal	
	a copy of the summons or application and order appealed against	
	the notes of evidence	
	the reasons given for the decision	
	as soon as practicable after filing and serving the notice of appeal	
	The reports and witness statements filed for the original hearing must also be filed and served	*Re U(T) (A Minor)* [1993] 2 FCR 565

	Citation of judgments must comply with PD	*PD of 9 April 2001*
Answer	For CA 1989 proceedings, a respondent's notice may be filed and served within 14 days of receipt of the notice of appeal: unless the appeal relates to an order under s 38(1), in which case no respondent's notice may be filed There is no such procedure for other proceedings Fee payable for respondent's notice or cross-appeal: £100	FPR 1991, r 4.22(5), (6)
Listing	The appellant, and other parties, must notify the court of the time estimate for the hearing of the appeal	*PD of 22 November 1993*
Appeals	To the Court of Appeal, unless a certificate has been issued under AJA 1969, s 12, in which case an appeal lies to the House of Lords, with leave of the House of Lords	AJA 1969, s 12

74: Appeal from a Judge of the High Court or from the Court of Appeal to the House of Lords

Legal background

An appeal from a decision of a judge of the High Court lies to the Court of Appeal, unless a certificate has been issued by that judge stating that the case merits a "leapfrog" appeal direct to the House of Lords. Where such a certificate is granted, a prospective appellant must seek leave of the House of Lords to appeal direct and, if such leave is refused, he may then appeal to the Court of Appeal (see Administration of Justice Act 1960, s 13). An appeal from a decision of the Court of Appeal must be made to the House of Lords, but only with leave of the Court of Appeal or, if refused, from the House of Lords. The procedure for all appeals to the House of Lords is prescribed by the House of Lords Practice Directions and Standing Orders Applicable to Civil Appeals.

Procedure

Who may appeal	If permission has been granted: any party to a decision of the Court of Appeal any party to a decision of the High Court where a certificate under AJA 1969, s 12 has been granted	AJA 1876, s 3 AJA 1969, s 12
Application for leave	*Appeal from Court of Appeal* Permission must be sought from the Court of Appeal or, if refused, from the House of Lords:	AJ(A)A 1934, s 1; HLPD, Dir 1.2

	within 1 month of the date of the order of the Court of Appeal or	HLPD, Dir 2.1
	within 1 month of the grant of public funding	HLPD, Dir 41
	Appeal from High Court Permission must be sought from the House of Lords:	AJA 1969 s 13; HLPD, Dirs 1.4, 6
	within 1 month of the grant of a certificate under AJA 1969, s 12 (unless extended by the House of Lords) or	HLPD, Dir 2.1
	within 1 month of the grant of public funding	HLPD, Dir 41
	The application for permission will be heard by the Appeal Committee of the House of Lords	HLPD, Dir 4
	Fee payable for presentation of petition: £570	
	Fee payable for entering appeal case: £115	
Procedure on appeal	By a petition of appeal	HLPD, Dir 9.1
	within 3 months of the date of the order appealed or 1 month from the grant of public funding	HLPD, Dir 41
	Otherwise, a petition for permission to appeal out of time must be lodged	HLPD, Dir 7.2
	Fee payable for presentation following leave: £570	
	Alternatively, fee payable for presentation after leave from the court below: £1,140	
Respondents	The parties to the hearing in the court below	HLPD, Dir 1.5
	A respondent may cross-appeal with permission of the Court of Appeal or, if refused, the House of Lords	
	A petition of cross-appeal must be presented within 6 weeks of the original appeal	HLPD, Dir 26.2
	or 6 weeks from the grant of public funding	HLPD, Dir 41
	Any application to intervene in the appeal must be made by petition	HLPD, Dir 36
	Fee payable for entering an appearance: £230	
Lodgment of documents	The appellant must lodge within 6 weeks of the presentation of the appeal:	
	statement of facts and issues	HLPD, Dir 11

	appendix of documents	HLPD, Dir 12
	The appellant must apply to set down the appeal	HLPD, Dir 14
	Fee payable for setting down and lodging statement and appendix: £3,420	
Appellants' and respondents' cases	Must be lodged as soon as setting down, but in any event no later than 2 weeks before the proposed hearing date	HLPD, Dir 15
	Must be exchanged	HLPD, Dir 16
	No later than 1 week before the proposed hearing:	
	the appellant must lodge bound volumes of all the documents	
	the parties must lodge their lists of authorities	HLPD, Dir 17
Order	Draft orders, which must be returned within 1 week, are sent to all who lodged a case for approval	HLPD, Dir 21
	Fee payable for final judgment: £12	

75: Appeal from a Judge of the County Court or the High Court to the Court of Appeal

Legal background

An appeal from a judge of either the High Court or a county court lies to the Court of Appeal (Supreme Court Act 1981, s 16 and County Courts Act 1984, s 77). Appeals from the decision of a district judge of the High Court or a county court lie to the judge of that court (see Guides 73 and 72 respectively). The Court of Appeal is a superior court of record, and has all the authority and jurisdiction of the court from which the appeal is brought (SCA 1981, s 15). As from 2 May 2000, the procedure for all appeals to the Court of Appeal is prescribed by CPR 1998, Pt 52 as supplemented by *Practice Direction – Appeals* (PD 52). Certain decisions of the lower court require leave from that court or, if refused, from the Court of Appeal before an appeal may be made. The provisions that determine whether leave is required are SCA 1981, s 18 and the County Court Appeals Order 1991.

In *Re W, Re A, Re B (Change of Name)* [1999] 2 FLR 930 the Court of Appeal held that the test to be applied by the appellate court in children cases, whether that be the High Court, county court or Court of Appeal, should be the same – ie in accordance with the principles established by *G v G (Minors: Custody Appeal)* [1985] FLR 894 [1985] 1 WLR 647. The House of Lords in *Piglowska v Piglowski* [1999] 2 FLR 763 at 783 gave further guidance to the profession in respect of appeals. Lord Hoffman, referring to *Bellenden v Satterthwaite* [1948] 1 All ER 343, stated that the appellate court must always bear in mind: (i) the advantage that the trial judge has of seeing and hearing the witnesses; (ii) that there is a discretion vested in the trial court; and (iii) that there must be a consideration of proportionality between the amount at stake and the legal resources to be expended.

Procedure

Who may appeal	With permission, any party aggrieved by the decision	SCA 1981, s 16; CCA 1984, s 77
Permission to appeal	Required for all cases apart from where the appeal is against: (*a*) a committal order (*b*) a refusal to grant habeas corpus (*c*) a secure accommodation order; or (*d*) otherwise as provided by practice direction	CPR 1998, r 52.3
	Application should be made to the judge if possible (if not to the Court of Appeal) or, if refused, to the Court of Appeal	CPR 1998, r 52.3(2), (3); PD52, paras 4.6, 4.7
	Permission may be subject to conditions or may limit the issues	CPR 1998, r 52.3(7)
	Fee payable: £100	
Procedure on appeal	Unless otherwise directed Notice of Appeal must be filed within 14 days of the date of the order and served not later than 7 days after filing	CPR 1998, r 52.4
	The appellant must complete the appeal questionnaire sent by the Court of Appeal within 14 days of receipt	PD52, para 6.4
Respondents	All parties to the proceedings who are affected by the appeal and anyone allowed to become a party	CPR 1998, r 52.1(3)
Lodgment of documents	The appellant must file with his notice: (*a*) a copy of his notice for each respondent and the court; (*b*) a copy of his skeleton argument; (*c*) a sealed copy of the order being appealed; and (*d*) witness statements and affidavits in a bundle	PD52, para 5.6
	A bundle of authorities must be filed 28 days before the hearing which must comply with PD	PD52, para 15.11; *PD of 9 April 2001*
Respondent's notice	May be filed but *must* be filed where the respondent seeks to appeal or seeks to uphold the decision for different reasons	CPR 1998, r 52.5

	Unless otherwise directed, must be filed within 14 days of service of the notice of appeal and served as soon as practicable (and in any event within 7 days of filing)	
Powers of the Court of Appeal	To receive fresh evidence	CPR 1998, r 52.11(2)
	To give any judgment and make any order that could have been made by the lower court	CPR 1998, r 52.10(1)
	To order a new trial or hearing	CPR 1998, r 52.10(2)
Appeals	To the House of Lords with leave of either the Court of Appeal or, if refused, the House of Lords	AJA 1876, s 3; AJ(A)A 1934, s 1

75A: Applications for Rehearing, for Leave to Appeal Out of Time and to Set Aside a Court Order

Legal background

The procedural rules on appeals, rehearing and setting aside are to be found variously in CPR 1998, Pt 52 and FPR 1991, Pt VIII (appeals) and CCR 1981, Ord 37 (rehearing and set aside). Applications to set aside in the terms referred to in family proceedings (see definition considered below in *Peek*) seem to be impossible under CPR 1998. Because the application will arise in family proceedings the CCR, in their original style (explained in the annotations under FPR 1991, r 1.3), will apply to these applications.

Terminology
(1) *Rehearing, new trial and set aside* In the High Court application to set aside an order or for a new trial is governed by SCA 1981, s 17. In the county court the application is for a "rehearing where no error of the court at the hearing is alleged" (CCR Ord 37, r 1(1)); though applications can be made to set aside in specific circumstances (CCR Ord 37, rr 2–5: eg an order made in a party's absence).
(2) *Appeal or set aside* The difference between an application to set aside or for a rehearing, and an appeal, as articulated by Lord Merriman P in *Peek v Peek* [1948] P 46 at 60: "... is the allegation which is made against the decision an allegation that the court went wrong on the materials before it, or is it an allegation that the court went wrong because the evidence on a vital matter was concealed from the court?".

If it is the former, a party appeals against the order; but if the latter, he or she applies to set aside (High Court) or for a rehearing (county court).
(3) *Permission to appeal out of time* Where the basis upon which an order was made has been fundamentally altered, application can be made for leave to appeal out of time (*Barder v Barder (Caluori Intervening)* [1988] AC 20, [1987] 2 FLR 480, HL). It is not a conventional appeal out of time, because it cannot be said that the original decision was wrong at the time it was made; nor can a party apply to set aside since, for example, it is not said that facts were not disclosed to the court. The fundamental change has occurred since the order.

Consent order or order after hearing the merits
An appeal against a consent order is a logical impossibility: a party cannot allege that the court went wrong on materials before it, where the materials were not before the court or they were only before it to the limited extent provided for by FPR 1991, r 2.61. The party impliedly agreed to all the facts and wanted the court to make the order. In the county

court the question is put beyond doubt by CCR Ord 37, r 6(1) which expressly prohibits appeals from consent orders.

If there are grounds to apply to set aside, or for a rehearing, it matters not whether the order applied from was a consent order or an order following a hearing on the merits of the case.

Route of the application

In *Benson v Benson (Deceased)* [1996] 1 FLR 692, Bracewell J helpfully reviewed recent case law on procedure in respect of applications to set aside orders and appeals out of time (and see *B-T v B-T (Divorce: Procedure)* [1990] 2 FLR 1, Ward J). Her Ladyship concluded that there are routes which involve separate proceedings – for example a summons to set aside the order (*de Lasala v de Lasala* [1980] AC 546, [1979] 3 WLR 390, HL) – or a party can apply in the family proceedings. Her own preference was for an application in family proceedings and these Guides follow that preference.

On an application to proceed for leave to appeal out of time, it would normally be appropriate for the appellate court to consider the application for permission, since the merits of the appeal are very much part of the first limb of the grounds. If leave is granted, the same court can go on to deal with the appeal.

Application to set aside a court order or for a rehearing

Where "no error of the court at the trial is alleged", application is made for the order to be set aside or for a re-hearing (CCR Ord 37, r 1(1)), ie on grounds of material non-disclosure, fraud, misrepresentation and mistake (but not eg bad legal advice).

(1) *Application to set aside: High Court* The Court of Appeal has power to order a new trial or to set aside an order made in the High Court (SCA 1981, s 17(1)). Application is to the Court of Appeal, probably with permission of that court (*Harris v Manahan* [1997] 1 FLR 205, CA).

(2) *Application for a re-hearing: county court* In the county court application is for a rehearing – not to set aside the order. Application is made under CCR Ord 37, r 1 by notice in the original proceedings. On a rehearing, the court proceeds by consideration, on the papers, of the original evidence. The rules are silent, and the authorities unclear, on how the court receives the fresh evidence on a rehearing (eg of misrepresentation or material non-disclosure). Normally it would be on the papers; but as in the Court of Appeal, it is possible that the county court can arrogate to itself powers to admit further evidence.

Time for application

(1) *Set aside* Application to set aside in the county court must be served fourteen days from the date of the original hearing (CCR Ord 37, r 1(5)). In practice, it may be many months, or even years, before the issue complained of comes to light – such as material non-disclosure (see eg *T v T (Consent Order: Procedure to Set Aside)* [1996] 2 FLR 640, Richard Anelay QC sitting as a deputy judge of the High Court); though the Court of Appeal has urged judges to have careful regard to time limits (*Harris v Manahan* [1997] 1 FLR 205, CA per Ward LJ at 218C–D). Permission to proceed will be needed.

(2) *Permission to appeal out of time: Barder appeals* Where events occur within a relatively short time after an order which fundamentally alters its basis, that order cannot be set aside or application made for a rehearing. However, the court may grant permission to appeal out of time from the original order subject to certain conditions (*Barder v Barder (Caluori Intervening)* [1988] AC 20, [1987] 2 FLR 480, HL at 2 FLR 495C–F):

(i) New events have occurred since the making of the order which invalidate the basis, or a fundamental assumption, on which the order was made, so that, if leave to appeal out of time were to be given, the appeal would be very likely to succeed;

(ii) The new events have occurred a relatively short time after the order (unlikely to be as much as a year; in most cases no more than a few months);

(iii) The application for leave to appeal out of time should be made reasonably promptly;

(iv) The grant of leave to appeal out of time should not prejudice third parties who have acquired property which is the subject matter of the relevant order.

75A(1): Application in the county court in family proceedings for a rehearing ("setting aside an order")

General Note—The rules relating to this application (CCR Ord 37, r 1) are sketchy, and sometimes contradictory. Under CPR 1998 the concept of set aside as it exists in the old civil procedure rules seems to be unknown. No attempt is made in this guide to consider an application to set aside other than in family proceedings.

Procedure

Who may apply	Any party to the hearing which leads to the order	CCR Ord 37, r 1(1)
Application	To the judge or district judge who made the order	CCR Ord 37, r 1(2), (4)
	Application is made on notice to all parties to the original order. This should set out in outline the allegations on which the application is based	CCR Ord 13, r 1(2)
Grounds	Grounds for an application are not closed, but will centre on the question of whether the court was misled because it did not have the full material facts before it: eg because of non-disclosure by one spouse; discovery of material new evidence	*Peek v Peek* [1948] P 46; *Livesey (formerly Jenkins) v Jenkins* [1985] AC 424, [1985] FLR 813, HL
Procedure	There is no specific provision in the rules for an affidavit to support the application; but this should normally be the norm for evidence in support of the application	
Time for application	14 days after the trial	CCR Ord 37, r 1(5); but see note above
Documents	It is suggested that a paginated bundle of documents from the hearing applied from should be available, to include: (*a*) paginated bundle from hearing applied from (*b*) judge's or district judge's note of evidence (or transcript) (*c*) agreed note of judgment (or transcript) (*d*) order applied from (*e*) sworn statements/affidavits and other documents filed in the application (*f*) skeleton arguments	*PD of 10 March 2000*

	(*g*) case summary/chronology where relevant, and in addition to those filed on the original application	
Reply/answer	It may be assumed that the respondent can reply by affidavit or sworn statement	
Disposal available on application	(i) Order for rehearing; with directions for trial, including: adducing evidence of facts giving rise to application permission to call oral evidence (ii) Dismissal (iii) Costs	
Rehearing	Hearing before judge or district judge – according to directions. Evidence: documents before court at original hearing New evidence: per directions; and *quaere* calling oral evidence on the facts giving rise to the application.	

75A(2): Application for permission to appeal out of time (*Barder* appeal)

Procedure

Who may apply	Any party to the hearing which leads to the order from which the appeal is made	
Application	To the judge or district judge who made the order In practice it will be more appropriate to make the application to the appellate court, since it is that court which will try the appeal if permission is granted, ie District judge to judge Judge to Court of Appeal	 FPR 1991, r 8.1 CPR 1998, Pt 52
Grounds	Grounds for an application are:	

	(i) New events have occurred since the making of the order which invalidate the basis, or fundamental assumption, on which the order was made, so that, if permission were to be given, the appeal would be very likely, to succeed. (ii) The new events should have occurred within a relatively short time of the order having been made (probably not more than a year). (iii) The application for permission must be made promptly. (iv) Grant of permission must not prejudice third parties who have acquired property involved in the proceedings	*Barder v Barder (Caluori Intervening)* [1988] AC 20, [1987] 2 FLR 480, HL
Procedure	No procedure is prescribed; and what follows is an amalgam of FPR 1991 procedures and procedures under CPR 1998, Pt 52	
(1) Appeal to Court of Appeal	Where the order was made by a judge, the appeal is to the Court of Appeal and permission is sought there Application for permission is made on Form N161 and must be accompanied by the documents specified in *Practice Direction (Appeals)*: PD52 (also listed in Form N161, Section 11) including, in particular: order below and note of judgment grounds for appeal (Form N161, Section 7) settled by advocate retained on the application affidavit in support of application which will deal fully with the new events on which the application is based skeleton argument documents before the court below	CPR 1998, r 52.3 (and see r 52.6 for "variation of time") CPR 1998, r 52.4; PD52, para 5.6
(2) Appeal to the judge	Where the order was made by a district judge, the appeal is to a circuit judge (in the county court), to a High Court judge in the High Court and in the PRFD (in appropriate cases a direction may be sought that the application for permission be heard by a High Court judge in any event)	*PD of 5 June 1992*

	Application is made by notice in the county court (summons in the High Court) [no form is prescribed]	FPR 1991, r 8.1
	(*a*) setting out grounds for appeal; and	
	(*b*) supported by a sworn statement.	
	Good practice suggests that the application should be accompanied, or there should be available on the hearing or any directions appointment the following:	
	order below and note of judgment	
	the sworn statement in support of application, which will deal fully with the new events on which the application is based	
	documents before the court below	
	all other documents required by the relevant Practice Direction	*PD of 10 March 2000*
Time for application	Within a relatively short time of the order having been made (probably not more than a year)	*Barder* (above)
Documents	See procedure above	
Reply/answer	*Court of Appeal* Respondent's notice (perhaps in draft, but filed pending grant of permission) and affidavit in reply	CPR 1998, r 52.5
	High Court or county court Sworn statement in reply	
Disposal available on application	(i) Permission to appeal	
	(ii) If permission granted, hear appeal	
	(iii) If appeal allowed, set aside or vary original order and rehearing (based on facts as they are at the time of the rehearing): (*a*) by appellate court; or (*b*) upon referral back to first instance court	CPR 1998 r 52.10(2) (powers of appellate court); *Smith v Smith (Smith and ors intervening)* [1992] Fam 69, [1991] 2 FLR 432, CA

76: Proceedings by or against a Party under Disability

Legal background

Court rules define the circumstances in which a person is to be treated as being under a disability in relation to proceedings and the procedure then to be adopted. A person under disability is generally a person under the age of 18 years (variously described as a "minor", an "infant" or a "child") or a "patient" (as defined).

It has long been the case that a person under disability may not:

(i) bring or make a claim in any proceedings;

(ii) acknowledge service, defend, make a counterclaim or intervene in any proceedings; or

(iii) appear in any proceedings under a judgment or order, notice of which has been served on him;

other than by an appointed representative. This has traditionally been *a next friend* for the person bringing proceedings or a *guardian ad litem* for the person defending or responding but the new term *litigation friend* has been introduced by the Civil Procedure Rules 1998 for both categories.

Proceedings commenced or conducted in breach of these requirements will be a nullity (the court may order otherwise under the new rules) and a solicitor who purports to act on the record for a party under disability may become personally liable for the costs of opposing parties.

76A: Family proceedings by or against a minor or a patient

Family proceedings are governed by FPR 1991, but these do not deal with all relevant matters, and FPR 1991, r 1.3 ensures that RSC and CCR (as appropriate) fill any procedural gaps. Those old rules continue to apply in their original form, notwithstanding that they have been replaced with effect from 26 April 1999 as regards civil proceedings generally by the Civil Procedure Rules 1998. Similarly, CCR are not as comprehensive as RSC but, in any case not expressly provided for, the general principles of practice in the High Court may be adopted (County Courts Act 1984, s 76). Thus RSC may be used to fill some lacunae in both CCR and FPR 1991, but not to supplement those rules as to cases provided for by them. This should be borne in mind when reading the following Guide (which relates to *family proceedings* only).

Procedure

Who is under disability	A minor (infant in CCR) or a patient	FPR 1991, r 9.1(1)
Who is a minor	A person who is under the age of 18	FLRA 1969, ss 1, 12
	A minor can bring or defend certain proceedings without a representative	FPR 1991, r 9.2A
	The provisions do not apply to minors who are the subject of applications	FPR 1991, r 9.1(2)
Who is a patient	A person who, by reason of mental disorder within the meaning of the Mental Health Act 1983, is incapable of managing and administering his property and affairs	FPR 1991, r 9.1(1)
What is mental disorder	Mental illness, arrested or incomplete development of mind, psychopathic disorder and any other disorder or disability of mind	MHA 1983, s 1(2)

	Nothing in the definition is to be construed as implying that a person may be dealt with as suffering from mental disorder by reason only of promiscuity, immoral conduct, sexual deviancy or dependence on alcohol or drugs	MHA 1983, s 1(3)
Who is the representative	*Next friend* For petitioner or applicant	FPR 1991, r 9.2(1)
	Guardian ad litem For defendant or respondent	FPR 1991, r 9.2(1)
Who is appointed	Person authorised by the Court of Protection for a patient *or* "proper person" with no adverse interest *or* Official Solicitor	FPR 1991, r 9.2(3), (7)(*c*)(ii)
Is a solicitor required to act	In family proceedings, probably	See FPR 1991, r 9.2(7)
	In the High Court, yes (no provision in CCR)	RSC Ord 80, r 2(3)
Commencement of proceedings	Next friend to be nominated on initiating proceedings	FPR 1991, r 9.2(1)
	There is no procedure for petitioner or applicant under disability to be notified.	
Documents to be filed	Consent Certificate by solicitor	FPR 1991, r 9.2(2), (7)
	An authority by the Court of Protection in respect of a patient is sufficient	FPR 1991, r 9.2(7)
Service	Effected on father or guardian (for infant/minor), or person authorised by Court of Protection (for patient)	RSC Ord 80, r 16(2); CCR Ord 10, r 4(1); FPR 1991, r 9.3(1)
	OR (if no such person)	
	person with whom person under disability resides or in whose care he is	FPR 1991, r 9.3(1)
	Provision exists for deemed service	FPR 1991, r 9.3(1) proviso
	Respondent is only required to be notified in the case of petitions in matrimonial causes	FPR 1991, r 9.3(2)
Defending proceedings	A guardian ad litem must be appointed before the proceedings can continue	FPR 1991, r 9.2(1)
	Query whether the appointment can be made without a court order if not the Official Solicitor	FPR 1991, r 9.2(4)
Documents to be filed	Consent Certificate by solicitor	FPR 1991, r 9.2(7)

	An authority by the Court of Protection in respect of a patient is sufficient	FPR 1991, r 9.3
Appointment by the court	Required when: no response to service;	FPR 1991, r 9.3
	disability arises during proceedings; *or*	RSC Ord 80, r 3(5); CCR, FPR 1991, no provision
	removal or substitution of next friend of guardian	RSC Ord 80, r 3(4); CCR, FPR 1991, no provision
Compromise or settlement	Approval by the court is required	RSC Ord 80, r 10; CCR Ord 10, r 10(1)
	Procedures exist for giving approval – follow these unless some other provision applicable	RSC Ord 80, r 11; CCR Ord 10, r 10(2), (3); FPR 1991, no provision
Control of money recovered	Follow old High Court/county court procedure	FPR 1991, no specific provision, but see r 1.3
	Infant/minor By the court	RSC Ord 80, r 12; CCR Ord 10, r 11
	Patient By the court *or* transfer to the Court of Protection	RSC Ord 80, r 12; CCR Ord 10, r 11
Costs	All costs of a solicitor acting for a person under disability must be assessed or approved by the court	CPR 1998, r 48.5

76B: Non-family proceedings by or against a child or a patient

When dealing with proceedings which are *not* family proceedings it is now necessary to comply with the Civil Procedure Rules 1998 (CPR). Part 21 of the Rules contains special provisions which apply in proceedings involving children and patients (as defined) – the term "under disability" is no longer used. These are supplemented by a *Practice Direction – Children and Patients* (PD 21). Unless the court orders otherwise (in the case of a child) it is necessary for the child or patient to be represented by a *litigation friend.* These special procedures were previously to be found in RSC Ord 80 and CCR Ord 10. The following is an abbreviated version of Procedural Guide 11 contained in *The Civil Court Service* (Jordan Publishing Ltd).

Procedure

Who is a child	A person under 18	CPR 1998, r 21.1(2)(*a*)
Who is a patient	A person who by reason of mental disorder within the meaning of the Mental Health Act 1983 is incapable of managing and administering his own affairs	CPR 1998, r 21.1(2)(*b*); PD 21, para 1.1
What is mental disorder	See Guide 76A (above)	

Requirement for a litigation friend	A **patient** must have a litigation friend to conduct proceedings on his behalf	CPR 1998, r 21.2(1); PD 21, para 1.2
	A **child** must have a litigation friend to conduct proceedings on his behalf unless the court orders otherwise	CPR 1998, r 21.2(2); PD 21, para 1.4
	the court may permit child to conduct proceedings without a litigation friend (for procedure see r 21.2(4))	CPR 1998, r 21.2(3)
	if it subsequently appears desirable for there to be a litigation friend court may so appoint	CPR 1998, r 21.2(5)
Role of litigation friend	To take all steps and decisions for the benefit of the child or patient	PD 21, para 2.1
When must a litigation friend be appointed	A person may not, without permission of the court:	
	(*a*) make an application against a child or patient before proceedings have started; or	
	(*b*) take any step in proceedings except –	
	(i) issuing/serving a claim form; or	
	(ii) applying for the appointment of a litigation friend under r 21.6,	
	until the child or patient has a litigation friend	CPR 1998, r 21.3(2)
	If a party becomes a patient during proceedings, no party may take any step in the proceedings without the permission of the court until the patient has a litigation friend	CPR 1998, r 21.3(3)
	Any step taken before a child or patient has a litigation friend is of no effect, unless the court otherwise orders	CPR 1998, r 21.3(4)
Title to proceedings	"A. B. (a child by .... his litigation friend)" or, if a litigation friend is dispensed with, "C. D. (a child)"	PD 21, para 1.5
	The name of a patient is followed by "(by .... his litigation friend)"	PD 21, para 1.3
Who is appointed (without court order)	A person authorised under MHA 1983, Pt VII to conduct legal proceedings in the name or on behalf of a patient is entitled to be his litigation friend in any proceedings to which his authority extends	CPR 1998, r 21.4(2)
	If nobody has been appointed or authorised, a person may act as a litigation friend if he:	

	can fairly and competently conduct proceedings on behalf of the child or patient; and has no interest adverse to that of the child or patient; and (claim or counterclaim) undertakes to pay any costs which the child or patient may be ordered to pay	CPR 1998, r 21.4(3)
Appointment (without court order)	A person wishing to act as a litigation friend must: (if authorised under MHA 1983, Pt VII) file an official copy of the order or other authorisation; (otherwise) file a certificate of suitability – (claimant) when making the claim; (defendant) when first taking a step in the proceedings	CPR 1998, r 21.5; PD 21, para 2.3
Certificate of suitability	States that proposed litigation friend: consents to act; believes the person to be a child or patient (with reasons/medical evidence); can fairly and competently conduct proceedings on behalf of the person; has no adverse interest; (claimant) undertakes to pay any costs which claimant may be ordered to pay in the proceedings	Form N235; CPR 1998, r 21.4(3); PD 21, para 2.4
	A counterclaim is treated like a claim for the purpose of the costs undertaking	CPR 1998, r 20.3
Service of certificate	The litigation friend must: serve the certificate of suitability on every person on whom the claim form should be served; and file a certificate of service when filing the certificate of suitability	CPR 1998, rr 21.5(6), 6.6
Certificate of service	States that the document has not been returned undelivered and required details of method of service	CPR 1998, r 6.10
Appointment by court	Application for an order appointing litigation friend is made by person wishing to be appointed or a party	

	Claimant must apply where claim against child or patient with no litigation friend and either (i) someone who is not entitled files a defence or (ii) claimant wishes to take some step in the proceedings	CPR 1998, r 21.6; PD 21, paras 3.1–3.6
	Application must be supported by evidence; court to be satisfied that the person appointed is "suitable"	CPR 1998, rr 21.6(4), (5), 21.4(3)
Change of litigation friend	The court may:	
	direct that a person may not act as a litigation friend;	
	terminate the appointment; or appoint a substitute.	
	Application to be supported by evidence; court may not appoint a litigation friend unless satisfied that the person is suitable	CPR 1998, rr 21.4(3), 21.7; PD 21, paras 4.1–4.4
Who is appointed (by court)	On an application court may appoint:	
	person proposed, or	
	any other person who complies with the conditions in r 21.4(3)	CPR 1998, r 21.8(4)
Official Solicitor	May be appointed provided he consents and provision is made for payment of his costs	PD 21, para 3.6
Appointment ceasing (child/patient)	When a child who is not a patient reaches 18 a litigation friend's appointment ceases	CPR 1998, r 21.9(1); PD 21, paras 5.2–5.4
	When a patient recovers, appointment continues until ended by a court order	CPR 1998, r 21.9(2); PD 21, paras 5.7–5.8
Service of claim form (child/patient)	Service of claim form is upon:	
	a parent or guardian or (if none) the person with whom the child resides or in whose care he is	CPR 1998, r 6.6(1)
	the person authorised under MHA 1983, Pt VII or (if none) the person with whom the patient resides or in whose care he is	CPR 1998, r 6.6(1)
Service generally	On litigation friend once appointed (or child allowed to conduct proceedings)	CPR 1998, r 6.6(1), (5)
	The court may by order:	
	permit service on child or patient, or on a specified person; or	CPR 1998, r 6.6(2)
	treat a document as if it had been properly served	CPR 1998, r 6.6(4)
Service of application	Application for order appointing or changing litigation friend served on:	

	every person on whom claim form should be served; and	CPR 1998, r 21.8(1)
	(if appointing) the patient, unless court otherwise orders; or	CPR 1998, r 21.8(2)
	(if changing) the existing and proposed litigation friend	CPR 1998, r 21.8(3)
Compromise or settlement	On a claim or counterclaim by or on behalf of, or against, a child or patient, no settlement, compromise or payment and no acceptance of money paid into court is valid without court approval	CPR 1998, r 21.10(1)
	Procedures are available where the sole purpose of proceedings is to obtain the approval of the court	CPR 1998, r 21.10(2); PD 21, paras 6.1–6.3; Form N292
Control of money recovered	Money recovered on behalf of or for the benefit of a child or patient is dealt with under directions of the court	CPR 1998, r 21.11(1); PD 21, paras 8.1–8.5
	These may provide that the money shall be wholly or partly paid into court and invested; or otherwise dealt with	CPR 1998, r 21.11(2); PD 21, paras 10.1–10.5, 11.1–11.7
	Applications may be made relating to payment out or investment	PD 21, paras 11.2, 12
Guardian of child's estate	The court may appoint the Official Solicitor as a guardian of a child's estate	CPR 1998, r 21.12; PD 21, para 9
Receiver for a patient	The Court of Protection may appoint a receiver for the estate of a patient	PD 21, paras 11.1–11.7
	money of a patient will be transferred	Form CFO 200
	applications for payment out of funds are to the Court of Protection	PD 21, para 12.3
Costs	Costs of solicitor for child or patient must be approved by court	CPR 1998, r 48.5
	Liability of litigation friend continues until:	
	appointment ceases; and	
	former child or patient (or litigation friend) serves notice on other parties	CPR 1998, r 21.9(6); PD 21, para 5.5
Forms	Certificate of Suitability of Litigation Friend	N235
	Order approving terms of a settlement or compromise	N292

77: Scientific Test Direction

Legal background

In any civil proceedings in which an issue as to parentage arises, a party may apply to the court for a direction for the use of scientific tests or bodily samples to determine the issue; or the court may, of its own motion, issue such a direction (Family Law Reform Act 1969, s 20(1)). From this, it follows that such an application cannot be made on a freestanding basis but only in the context of existing proceedings, for example under CA 1989, s 9, CSA 1991, s 27 or MCA 1973, s 1(2)(*a*) (evidence of adultery). The court does not make an order on the application, but issues a direction (see also *Re H (Paternity: Blood Test)* [1996] 2 FLR 65, CA). No sample can therefore be taken without consent (FLRA 1969, s 21(1)), or by direction of the court where a person having care and control of a child refuses consent (FLRA 1969, s 21(3)). A consequence of this is that failure to comply with a direction enables the court to draw such inferences as appear proper in the circumstances of the particular case (FLRA 1969, s 23(1)).

Which rules of court

An application for a scientific test direction depends on its "lead" application for the procedural rules to which it is subject. Consequently, if such a direction is sought in "family proceedings" (eg under CA 1989), RSC Ord 112 and CCR Ord 47, r 5, unrevised, apply. If the application is ancillary to "non-family" civil proceedings (eg under Inheritance (Provision for Family and Dependants) Act 1975), the same rules apply but in their new placement in CPR 1998, Schs 1 and 2. As there is no material difference in the substance of the rules, only changes in some of the language (eg "permission of the court" in place of "leave of the court" in Ord 112 r 2(1)), the text of these rules will be found in the Schedules to the CPR 1998.

Procedure

Who may apply	Any party to the proceedings	
	The court of its own motion can issue a direction	FLRA 1969, s 20(1)
The proceedings	Any proceedings in which parentage is in issue	FLRA 1969, s 20(1)
The application	By summons or on notice	CPR 1998, Sch 1, RSC Ord 112, r 2; CPR 1998, Sch 2, CCR Ord 47, r 5(3)
	In CA 1989 proceedings, *quaere* on Form C2	FPR 1991, r 4.4(1A); FPC(CA 1989)R 1991, r 4(1A)
	The application must specify who is to carry out the tests	FLRA 1969, s 20(1A)
Respondent/Other parties	All other parties to the existing proceedings Anyone else from whom samples may be required	CPR 1998, Sch 1, RSC Ord 112, r 2(1); CPR 1998, Sch 2, CCR Ord 47, r 5(2)
Notice	*Family proceedings* Two clear days before hearing of application	RSC Ord 32, r 3; CCR Ord 13, r 1(2)

	In CA 1989 proceedings, 14 days	FPR 1991, r 4.4(1), App 3; FPC(CA 1989)R 1991, r 4(1), Sch 2
	Non-family proceedings At least 3 days before hearing of application	CPR 1998, r 23.7(1)
Joinder	The court may join as a party any person, not already a party, from whom a sample is directed to be taken	CPR 1998, Sch 1, RSC Ord 112, r 4; CPR 1998, Sch 2, CCR Ord 47, r 5(3)
Direction	Court gives a direction in form proposed in —	*Re H* [1996] 2 FLR 65 at 83
	The name of the tester must be included in the direction	
	On direction being given, the proceedings are adjourned until a report is received on the direction	CPR 1998, Sch 1, RSC Ord 112, r 5; CPR 1998, Sch 2, CCR Ord 47, r 5(5)
Service of direction	By the court on	
	parties to proceedings	CPR 1998, Sch 1, RSC Ord 112, r 5; CPR 1998, Sch 2, CCR Ord 47, r 5(5)
	anyone from whom sample is to be taken	
	any person who is a party to a petition for a declaration under FLA 1986, ss 55A and 56	FLRA 1969, s 20(2A)
Report	Sent to the court by the tester	FLRA 1969, s 20(2)
	Report in form prescribed by Blood Tests (Evidence of Paternity) Regulations 1971	FLRA 1969, s 20(3)
	Served by the court on	
	parties to proceedings	CPR 1998, Sch 1, RSC Ord 112, r 6; CPR 1998, Sch 2, CCR Ord 47, r 5(6)
	anyone from whom sample to be taken	
Fees and costs	Fee for report payable by applicant for direction; but treated as costs in the main proceedings	FLRA 1969, s 20(6)

78: Withdrawal of Treatment in Persistent Vegetative State etc Cases where the Patient is an Adult

Legal background

The withdrawal of artificial feeding and hydration for patients in persistent vegetative state (PVS), or withholding cardio-pulmonary resuscitation and the administration of antibiotics or treatment generally, will require the prior sanction of the High Court. The guidelines and principles to be applied in such cases were set out in *Airedale NHS Trust v Bland* [1993] 1 FLR 1026, and subsequently approved in *Frenchay Healthcare NHS*

Trust v S [1994] 1 FLR 485 and *Re R (Adult Medical Treatment)* [1996] 2 FLR 99. The guidelines issued by the Medical Ethics Committee of the British Medical Association on treatment decisions for patients in PVS should also be considered when seeking to apply for a declaration for the withdrawal of treatment.

The Civil Procedure Rules 1998 do not make any reference to the procedure to be followed in cases where a declaration is sought under the inherent jurisdiction of the High Court. It is submitted that the appropriate procedure is that laid down in CPR 1998, Pt 8, as supplemented by *Practice Direction (Alternative Procedure for Claims)* (PD 8). In view of the fact that the relief sought in such cases is a declaration, it is suggested that instead of using the new terminology of "claimant" and "defendant" it would be more appropriate to use the terms "applicant" and "respondent". The above *Practice Direction/Practice Note of 1 May 2001*, together with the case-law that has developed, will continue to govern these applications until a comprehensive revision is undertaken.

Procedure

Who may apply	Any interested party, usually: next of kin Area Health Authority NHS Trust	*PN of 1 May 2001*; *Re S* [1996] Fam 1; *Re G* [1995] 2 FCR 46
Which court	High Court, Family Division	*PD of 14 December 2001*
Application	Part 8 claim form (Form N208) with sufficient copies for the court and each person to be served	CPR 1998, r 8.1; PD 8, para 2.2
	The claim form should state that it is issued under Pt 8 and should be entitled "in the matter of the Inherent jurisdiction of the court" and must set out the information required under r 8.2	CPR 1998, r 8.2
	The claim form must be verified by a statement of truth	CPR 1998, r 22.1; PD 8, para 2.2
Documents	The applicant must file the written statement/affidavit in support with copies for the court and each party to be served. The evidence must be filed with the claim form	CPR 1998, r 8.5(1), (2)
	The claimant must adduce evidence from: (i) the treating physician (ii) a neurologist or other expert experienced in assessing disturbances of consciousness	*PN of 1 May 2001*, App 2, para 4
Respondent	The patient, by his guardian ad litem (the Official Solicitor), or Any interested party (as above)	*PN of 1 May 2001*, para 9
Fee payable	£120	SCFO 1999, fee 1.2

Service	Acknowledgement of service must be filed within 14 days and served on the applicant and any other party	CPR 1998, rr 8.3(1)(*a*), 10.3
	It must state whether the respondent contests the claim and if a different remedy is sought, set out what that remedy is	CPR 1998, r 8.3
	In urgent cases application should be made to abridge time.	
Evidence in answer	A respondent who wishes to rely on written evidence must file and serve a copy on the other parties when he files his acknowledgement of service	CPR 1998, r 8.5(3), (4); *Re C* [1990] 2 FLR 527; *Re F* [1990] 2 AC 1, [1989] 2 FLR 376
Reply	The applicant may serve further written evidence within 14 days of service of the respondent's evidence on him	CPR 1998, r 8.5(5)
	At least 2 neurological reports	
	Any other medical evidence	
	Evidence (if any) of the previously expressed views of the patient	*Re T* [1992] 2 FLR 458; *Re C* [1994] 1 FLR 31
Directions	A directions hearing may be requested at the time of issuing the claim form	PD 8, para 4.1
	In other cases the court will give directions as soon as practicable before a judge of the Family Division in chambers	PD 8, para 4.2
Final hearing	Parties attend court with their witnesses; judge hears evidence and submissions, and makes a final order or declaration in open court, except in the case of a child.	

79: Costs in Family Proceedings (High Court and County Court)

Legal background

Costs may only be recovered by order of the court (SCA 1981, s 51(3)), save by consent as between the parties. In all family proceedings the factors which affect the award of costs, and the procedure to be followed, are governed by Civil Procedure Rules 1998, Pts 43, 44 (except rr 44.9–44.12), 47 and 48 (see Family Proceedings (Amendment) Rules 2003, r 10.27(1)). These Parts are supplemented by *Practice Direction About Costs (CPR Parts 43–48)* (PD Costs), which is applied to "family proceedings" by *President's Direction of 24 July 2000*, and is specifically referred to in the guides that follow below.

Orders for costs are entirely in the discretion of the court (SCA 1981, s 51(1), which covers the Court of Appeal, the High Court and county courts), subject to "any other enactment and to rules of court". However, there are factors which the court is required to take into account when exercising its discretion whether to award costs (CPR 1998, r 44.3(4), (5)), including letters written "without prejudice save as to costs" (*Calderbank v Calderbank* [1976] Fam 93, (1975) FLR Rep 113, CA; FPR 1991, r 2.69).

Costs awarded to the "successful party"
Civil Procedure Rules 1998, r 44.3(2) provides that where the court decides to make an order as to costs, the general rule is that the "unsuccessful party" should pay the costs of the "successful party", but the court may make a different order (r 44.3(2)(*b*)). This rule does not apply in family proceedings (FP(A)R 2003, r 10.27(1)(*b*)). However, in family courts the judge must have some starting-point which will normally be that costs should be awarded to the "successful party" (*Gojkovic v Gojkovic (No 2)* [1992] Fam 40, [1991] 2 FLR 233, CA). See further Guide 79A.

Costs and children cases
Costs orders will be rare in children cases (*Keller v Keller and Legal Aid Board* [1995] 1 FLR 259, CA), but whilst costs are always entirely in the discretion of the court it has been suggested in *R v R (Costs: Child Case)* [1997] 2 FLR 95, CA, that a criterion for considering an award of costs in children cases might be whether or not a party has been guilty of unreasonable conduct in connection with a case. See further Guide 79A.

Costs in ancillary relief proceedings
A new costs regime for ancillary relief proceedings has been introduced by amendments to FPR 1991. Rule 2.69 gives regulatory approval to the *Calderbank* letter. Rule 2.69B provides that costs "must" be paid to a party who has received an offer which is "more advantageous to him", save where the court considers it unjust. Factors to be taken into account by the court when considering the justice of an order are set out in r 2.69D. See further Guide 79A.

Costs awarded to person acting in a fiduciary capacity
Civil Procedure Rules 1998, r 48.4 provides the court with power to award costs to a trustee, personal representative or other person acting in a fiduciary capacity, from the fund held by him. Where there is any doubt whatsoever in the mind of the trustee or his adviser as to whether the action should be continued on behalf of the beneficiaries of the fund, an application should be made to the court for a *Beddoe* order (*Re Beddoe* [1893] 1 Ch 547). See further Guide 79B.

Wasted costs
Where a legal representative behaves in a manner which is held to be "improper, unreasonable or negligent" (SCA 1981, s 51(7)), a wasted costs order may be made against him or her. These words bear their ordinary meaning; that is to say: (i) "improper" means behaviour which amounts to a significant breach of professional conduct; (ii) "unreasonable" means conduct which does not permit of a reasonable explanation; and (iii) "negligent" means failure to act with the competence to be expected of ordinary members of the profession (*Ridehalgh v Horsefield and ors* [1994] 2 FLR 194, [1994] 3 WLR 462, CA). Conduct of a hopeless or difficult case does not, of itself, justify a finding under s 51(7). See further Guide 79C.

Funded (legal aid) cases
An order for costs may be made against a funded (legally aided) client as against any other party to proceedings; but the amount he can be ordered to pay cannot exceed the amount which it is reasonable for him to pay (AJA 1999, s 11(1)). Where an unassisted party (as defendant/respondent at first instance) cannot obtain costs from a legally aided person he may be able to obtain an order against the Legal Services Commission (AJA 1999, s 11(3); CLS(CP)R 2000, reg 5). The object of the new procedures under AJA 1999, s 11 is to produce a unified scheme where costs are, or would be, awarded against a funded party: first, for assessment of a reasonable amount to be paid (s 11(1), known as "costs protection" – CLS(CP)R 2000, reg 3) and, secondly, for any balance of costs to be paid to a receiving party by the Legal Services Commission. See further Guides 79D and 79E.

Assessment of costs
The court must consider whether to order summary assessment (ie assessment on the day, which will now be much more common than hitherto) or detailed assessment (formerly taxation of costs), in which case assessment will be delayed. Detailed assessment will always occur in a CLS funded case. When assessing the amount of any possible award of costs (either on the indemnity or standard basis) the court should have regard to the various factors set out in CPR 1998, rr 44.4, 44.5. See further Guides 79F, 79G and 79H.

79A: Order for costs against another party to the proceedings

Procedure

Who may apply	Any party to the proceedings	
Time for application	At any stage in the case; and in particular when the court is dealing with an application or makes an order	*PD Costs*, para 8.3
Principles on which orders made	Costs are in the discretion of the court (ie whether, when and how much is to be paid), subject to "any other enactment and to rules of court"	SCA 1981, s 51(1); CPR 1998, r 44.3(1)
Orders for costs	Costs orders may include: (*a*) a proportion of another party's costs; (*b*) a stated amount of those costs; (*c*) costs from or until a certain date; (*d*) costs incurred before issue of proceedings; (*e*) costs relating to particular steps; (*f*) costs relating only to one part of the proceedings; and (*g*) interest on costs from or until a certain date	CPR 1998, r 44.3(6)
	Types of order include: Costs in any event Costs in the case/application Costs reserved (NB means that if no later order is made, costs are in the application) Applicant's/respondent's costs in the application No order as to costs	*PD Costs*, para 8.5

	If a party is not present when an order is made his solicitor must notify him of the order made within 7 days	CPR 1998, r 44.2
When to comply with order for costs	Within 14 days of: (*a*) date of judgment or order (if amount of costs fixed thereby); or (*b*) date of certificate following detailed assessment (see Guide 79G)	CPR 1998, r 44.8
"The general rule"	If the court decides to make an order, the general rule is that the "unsuccessful party" pays the costs of the "successful party"	CPR 1998, r 44.3(2)(*a*)
	This rule does not apply in family proceedings but in such proceedings the court may often use the general rule as a starting-point	FP(A)R 2003, r 10.27(1)(*b*); *Gojkovic v Gojkovic (No 2)* [1991] 2 FLR 233, CA
	It is unusual to order costs in children cases, although it will be appropriate to order costs when a parent (even a litigant in person) goes beyond the limit of what is reasonable in pursuing the application before the court	*R v R (Costs: Child Case)* [1997] 2 FLR 95, CA; *Khatun v Fayez* (unreported) 2 March 1998, CA; *Re B (Costs)* [1999] 2 FLR 221, CA; *Re G (Costs: Child Case)* [1999] 2 FLR 250, CA
Factors in deciding the order for costs: general	All the circumstances of the case, including: (*a*) the conduct of all the parties; (*b*) whether a party has succeeded in only part of his case; and (*c*) any admissible (eg *Calderbank*) offer to settle made by a party which is drawn to the court's attention	CPR 1998, r 44.3(4)
"The conduct of the parties"	Conduct under CPR 1998, r 44.3(4) includes: (*a*) conduct before, as well as during, the proceedings, and in particular the extent to which the parties followed any relevant pre-action protocol; (*b*) whether it was reasonable for a party to raise, pursue or contest a particular allegation or issue; (*c*) the manner in which a party has pursued or defended his case or a particular allegation or issue; and (*d*) whether a claimant who has succeeded in his claim, in whole or in part, exaggerated his claim	CPR 1998, r 44.3(5)

Factors in deciding the order for costs: ancillary relief	(i) Where offeree secures an order which is more advantageous to her than an offer made by the other party, costs may follow the outcome of the proceedings	FPR 1991, r 2.69; CPR 1998, r 44.3(4)(*c*); *Gojkovic v Gojkovic (No 2)* (above)
	(ii) Where order more advantageous to offeror than r 2.69 offer made by either party, court must award costs against offeree, unless it considers it unjust	FPR 1991, r 2.69B
Factors in consideration of whether an order is just or unjust	In deciding whether making an order would be unjust (r 2.69B(2)) the court considers all the circumstances, including: (*a*) the terms of any offer under r 2.69(1) (*b*) the stage in proceedings when the offer was made (*c*) information available to the parties when the offer was made (*d*) conduct of the parties in giving or refusing information required to evaluate the offer (*e*) the means of the parties	FPR 1991, r 2.69D(1)
Payment on account	Discretion to order payment of costs on account pending detailed assessment	CPR 1998, r 44.3(8)
	The court must order how much is to be paid	*PD Costs*, para 8.6(1)
	If nothing is said about time for payment in any order, payment is per r 44.8 (above)	*PD Costs*, para 8.6(2)
Assessment of costs	Summary assessment (see Guide 79F) Detailed assessment (see Guide 79G)	
Basis of assessment	*Standard* (i) Costs assessed on a standard basis are only costs which are proportionate to the matters in issue (ii) Any doubt which the court may have as to whether costs were reasonably incurred or reasonable and proportionate in amount are resolved in favour of the paying party (iii) If no basis for assessment is stated, costs are assessed on the standard basis	CPR 1998, rr 44.4(1)(*a*), (2), (4), 44.5(1)(*a*); *PD Costs*, paras 11.1–11.6

	Indemnity Any doubt as to whether costs were reasonably incurred is resolved in favour of the receiving party	CPR 1998, rr 44.4(1)(*b*), (3), 44.5(1)(*b*); *PD Costs*, paras 11.1–11.6
Factors in defining amount of costs on assessment	(*a*) the conduct of all parties, including in particular: (i) conduct before, and during, the proceedings; and (ii) attempts at mediation (if any) made before and during the proceedings; (*b*) the monetary value of the claim; (*c*) the importance of the case to all parties; (*d*) the complexity of the case or difficulty or novelty of the issues raised; (*e*) the skill, effort, specialised knowledge and responsibility involved; (*f*) the time spent on the case; and (*g*) the place where and circumstances in which work (or part of it) was done	CPR 1998, r 44.5(3)

79B: Application for a *Beddoe* order

Procedure

Who may apply	Trustee, personal representative or person in other fiduciary relationship	*Re Beddoe* [1893] 1 Ch 547
Costs and personal representatives, trustees etc	General rule: costs paid to the trustee etc on an indemnity basis but not if he is held to have acted other than for the benefit of the fund	CPR 1998, r 48.4(2), (3)
Time for application	At any time in proceedings; but in any event where there is a risk of a trustee being criticised by the court for expending the trust fund in costs	
Mode of application	*All types of proceedings* By application in the proceedings [*quaere*: "without serving a copy of the application notice" (ie ex parte)]	CPR 1998, r 23.4(2)

	Family proceedings (i) as above; or (ii) on *ex parte* application interlocutory to the proceedings in question	FPR 1991, r 10.9
Order	That the [trustee etc] be indemnified in any event in respect of costs from [fund concerned; eg name of trust fund/pension fund/bankrupt's estate] in the event of no order being made against another party to the proceedings	

79C: Order for wasted costs

Procedure

Who may apply	Any party to the proceedings The court on its own initiative	SCA 1981, s 51(6); *PD Costs*, para 53.2
Time for application	At any stage in proceedings where an order for costs can be made but normally at the end of "the trial" or final hearing of an application	*PD Costs*, para 53.1
Application	(i) By notice of application (eg per FPR 1991, rr 2.69F(6) and 10.9). The application should be accompanied by evidence of what the legal representative is alleged to have done and specify the costs sought	*PD Costs*, paras 53.3(1), 53.8
	(ii) By making application in the course of hearing (as with any other application for costs)	*PD Costs*, para 53.3(2)
Order	Against legal or other representative, that they pay costs incurred and wasted by another party to the proceedings	SCA 1981, s 51(6), (7); CPR 1998, r 48.7
Factors in making the order	Has the legal representative behaved in a way which is "improper, unreasonable or negligent"; or	SCA 1981, s 51(6)(*a*); cf *Ridehalgh v Horsefield* [1994] 2 FLR 194, CA
	is there expenditure caused by the legal representative which the court considers the other party should not have to pay?	SCA 1981, s 51(6)(*b*)

Procedure	No order can be made unless the legal representative has had a reasonable opportunity to show cause why an order should not be made	CPR 1998, r 48.7(2); *Ridehalgh v Horsfield* (above); *Re A Barrister (Wasted Costs Order) (No 1 of 1991)* [1993] QB 293, CA
Court's directions	The court gives directions as it sees fit for disposal of the application. Directions may include the following:	*PD Costs*, para 53.5; *Ridehalgh v Horsfield* (above)
	(i) Court may direct that privileged documents be disclosed to both itself and to the applicant for wasted costs	CPR 1998, r 48.7(3)
	(ii) Before making an order the court can seek an enquiry from a costs judge or district judge	CPR 1998, r 48.7(6)
	(iii) The court can refer the decision on the issue of an order to a costs judge or district judge	CPR 1998, r 48.7(7)
Court's considerations	(i) Has the lawyer acted improperly, unreasonably or negligently?	
	(ii) If so, has the applicant incurred unnecessary costs as a result?	
	(iii) If so, is it just to require the lawyer to pay the applicant's relevant costs?	*Re A Barrister (Wasted Costs Order)* (above) (approved in *Ridehalgh v Horsefield* at 203H)
	If the court makes an order:	
	it must specify the amount to be paid; or	CPR 1998, r 48.7(4)
	it may ask a costs judge/district judge to report on the amount to be paid	CPR 1998, r 48.7(6)

79D: Costs and CLS funding (legal aid): order for costs against a funded party

General Note—*Practice Direction About Costs (CPR Parts 43–48)* (PD Costs), Sections 21–23 deals with costs under AJA 1999, s 11. It is often misleading, and sometimes wrong. Its sole usefulness seems to be to prescribe the form to be used for an application for costs against the Legal Services Commission under CLS(C)R 2000, regs 17–21 (see Guide 79E). Practitioners are urged, until it is amended, to ignore it and to refer directly to what follows and to the relevant regulations: CLS(C)R 2000, regs 7–12 and CLS(CP)R 2000, regs 3–5.

These provisions apply to all certificates granted since 1 April 2000 (the coming into operation of AJA 1999); and to all pre-1 April 2000 certificates with effect from 5 June 2000 (Administration of Justice Act 1999 (Commencement No 3 Transitional Provisions and Savings) Order, art 8(3)).

Procedure

Time for application	At any stage in proceedings where an order for between parties costs can be made	
Orders for costs	The court has full power to make an order for costs against a funded party; though no order should be made where, but for CLS funding regulations, none would have been made	CLS(C)R 2000, reg 3(*a*), (*b*); *Keller v Keller and Legal Aid Board* [1995] 1 FLR 259
	A costs order (a "section 11(1) costs order") against a CLS funded party may not exceed a reasonable amount for him to pay	AJA 1999, s 11(1); CLS(CP)R 2000, reg 3
	Section 11(1) orders for costs may be expressed by the court as follows – (i) Where an unspecified amount of costs would have been ordered the court may: (*a*) specify the amount to be paid by the funded party if it has sufficient information to determine a reasonable amount (eg in ancillary relief cases) and if that amount is less than the full costs would be; or (*b*) leave the amount unspecified	CLS(C)R 2000, reg 9(2)
	(ii) Where a specified amount would have been ordered the court must specify the full amount to be paid and may: (*a*) specify the amount to be paid if it has sufficient information to determine a reasonable amount; or (*b*) leave the amount unspecified	CLS(C)R 2000, reg 9(3), (4)
	NB: an "unspecified" amount can be determined later (for subsequent or late determination see Guide 79E)	CLS(C)R 2000, regs 10(1), 12(3)
Factors in determination of amount to be paid	In determining a reasonable amount for a funded party to pay the court considers: (*a*) all the circumstances of the case, including (*b*) the financial resources of all parties (*c*) the parties conduct in connection with the dispute	AJA 1999, s 11(1)

	NB: the court can make findings as to conduct for consideration at a later date when an amount to be paid by a funded party is assessed	CLS(C)R 2000, reg 9(6)
Assessment of amount to pay	Assessment of amount to be paid under AJA 1999, s 11(1) is by the court	CLS(C)R 2000, reg 9(1)
	In making the assessment of a reasonable amount the court ignores various of the funded party's resources	AJA 1999, s 11(2); CLS(C)R 2000, reg 7
	Insofar as an order for costs against a funded party is either not specified or is less than the full amount (or likely amount of an order) the receiving party can apply to the court for an order for costs against the Legal Services Commission, for determination of the unspecified amount or for variation of the order (see Guide 79E)	
Forms of court order	If the court decides to make an order for costs	
	(i) It expresses the order in conventional terms under CPR 1998, r 44.3;	
	(ii) It determines, in the usual way, whether to deal with the matter by detailed or summary assessment, and so orders; and if by summary assessment it fixes the amount; and then	CLS(C)R 2000, reg 9(4)
	(iii) It decides whether to fix the amount payable by the funded party under AJA 1999, s 11(1) as follows:	
	(*a*) If the court considers it has enough information to fix an amount payable by the funded party it orders thus:	CLS(C)R 2000, reg 9(2)(*a*), 3(*a*)
	"Upon the court finding that it has sufficient information to fix a reasonable amount for the [applicant] to pay in accordance with Access to Justice Act 1999, s 11(1), the amount payable under the order at paragraph [ ] shall be [nil]/[£x]"	
	NB: '£x' must be less than the amount the court expects the receiving party to receive	CLS(C)R 2000, reg 9(2)(*a*)(ii)
	(*b*) If the court does not consider that it has enough information to fix an amount payable it orders thus:	CLS(C)R 2000, reg 9(2)(*b*), 3(*b*)

	"The court finds that it has insufficient information to fix a reasonable amount for the [applicant] to pay in accordance with Access to Justice Act 1999, s 11(1)"	
	NB There is no need to adjourn the question of costs to another date or judge since it is a matter for the receiving party to decide – *within three months* – whether or not:	
	(i) to proceed with an application for costs against the LSC (see Guide 79E below); or, later still,	CLS(C)R 2000, reg 10(2)
	(ii) to seek determination of the amount of costs payable; or	CLS(C)R 2000, reg 12(3)
	(iii) to seek a variation of the amount ordered	CLS(C)R 2000, reg 12(2)

79E: Costs and CLS funding (legal aid): order for costs against the Legal Services Commission, variation and late determination of orders

General Note—*Practice Direction About Costs (CPR Parts 43–48)* (PD Costs), Sections 21– 23 deals with costs under AJA 1999, s 11. It is often misleading, and sometimes wrong. Its sole usefulness seems to be to prescribe the form to be used for an application for costs against the Legal Services Commission under CLS(C)R 2000, reg 10. Practitioners are urged, until it is amended, to ignore it and to refer directly to what follows and to the relevant regulations: CLS(C)R 2000, regs 7–12 and CLS(CP)R 2000, regs 3–5.

These provisions apply also to certificates granted prior to 1 April 2000 (the coming into operation of AJA 1999).

Determinations of costs considered in this Guide resolve themselves into three aspects (grouped here because the procedure to be followed in each case is often similar or the same):

(1) Assessment of: (*a*) how much (if not dealt with at the time of the s 11(1) order), and (*b*) whether an unfunded party should have his costs paid by the Legal Services Commission where the Commission provided support for a funded party;
(2) Variation of a s 11(1) order made against a funded party; and
(3) Later determination of the amount of costs to be paid by a funded party (if not already dealt with at (1)(*a*) above) where his costs were not determined at the time of a s 11(1) order (Guide 79D).

Procedure

(1) Costs payable by Legal Services Commission	Costs may be paid by the Legal Services Commission to other parties where services have been provided to a funded party by the Commission and the order for costs against a funded party leaves a balance payable to an unfunded party	AJA 1999, s 11(3); CLS(CP)R 2000, reg 5(2)

Time for application	Application for an order against the Commission must be made within three months of the s 11(1) order: ie any order for costs under CLS(C)R 2000, reg 9	CLS(C)R 2000, reg 10(2); CLS(CP)R 2000, reg 5(3)(*b*); *R (Gunn) v Secretary of State for the Home Department* [2001] EWCA Civ 891, [2001] 1 WLR 1634, CA
	whether or not the total amount to be paid by the funded party has been fixed by the court: If not fixed the court will fix it during the reg 10 procedure (see below)	CLS(C)R 2000, reg 9(5)
	NB: only the Legal Services Commission (ie not the court) can extend that time	*Middleton v Middleton* [1994] 1 FLR 557, CA
Pre-requisites for an order against the Commission	(i) Is the intended paying party a funded party?	AJA 1999, s 11(1); CLS(CP)R 2000, reg 5(1)(*a*)
	(ii) Is the applicant for costs (receiving party) an unassisted party?	CLS(CP)R 2000, reg 5(1)(*b*)
	(iii) Were the proceedings finally decided in favour of the unassisted party?	CLS(CP)R 2000, reg 5(1)(*b*)
	(iv) Has a reasonable amount for the funded party to pay been assessed and, if so, is there a balance still to pay to the receiving party?	CLS(CP)R 2000, reg 5(3)(*a*) (and see refs to s 11(1) above)
	(v) In the case of courts of first instance: (*a*) were the proceedings started by the funded party; and (*b*) will the receiving party suffer financial hardship if no order is made?	CLS(CP)R 2000, reg 5(3)(*c*)
	(vi) Is it just and equitable in all the circumstances for the unassisted party's costs to be paid out of the Community Legal Service fund?	CLS(CP)R 2000, reg 5(3)(*d*)
Procedure to be followed on application ("request") for an order	A request is made in application Form N244 by the receiving party and filed at court, accompanied by:	CLS(C)R 2000, reg 9(5); *PD Costs*, para 23.3

	(*a*) the receiving party's bill of costs (as for detailed assessment), save where the costs have already been assessed by the court;	
	(*b*) a statement of resources;	
	(*c*) notice of application (as applicable) for an order against the Commission (no form is prescribed, so in adoption and family proceedings covered by FPR 1991 notice should be per FPR 1991, r 10.9; in family proceedings covered by CPR 1998 application is in accordance with Part 23)	
	NB: the statement of resources must be verified by a statement of truth (per CPR 1998, Pt 22) and must comply with the requirements set out in CLS(C)R 2000, reg 2	See further CLS(C)R 2000, reg 8 and *Jones v Zahedi* [1993] 1 WLR 1445, CA
Service of request	Service of the above is by the receiving party upon:	
	(*a*) the funded party if the amount of costs to be paid has to be determined; and	CLS(C)R 2000, reg 10(4)(*a*)
	(*b*) the Regional Director (quoting the funded party's certificate number: available on notice of issue of certificate) where an assessment of costs from the Commission is sought	CLS(C)R 2000, reg 10(4)(*b*)
	Where Regional Director is served he may appear on the application or give evidence by written statement (with statement of truth)	CLS(C)R 2000, reg 13(1)(*a*), (2), (3)
Funded party's statement of resources	If application is for determination of amount of funded party's costs (per CLS(C)R 2000, reg 10(4)(*a*)) he must prepare and file a statement of resources and serve it on the receiving party (and Regional Director)	CLS(C)R 2000, reg 10(5), (6)
	Time: 21 days from receipt of receiving party's statement of resources	CLS(C)R 2000, reg 10(6)
Points of dispute	(i) The funded party may file points of dispute as to receiving party's bill of costs	CLS(C)R 2000, reg 10(7)
	(ii) There is no specific provision for the Regional Director to serve points of dispute; but by analogy with CLS(C)R 2000, reg 10(7) it seems reasonable that he should be able to do so	cf CPR 1998, r 47.9

Hearing	Court lists for hearing and gives at least 14 days notice to: (*a*) receiving party; (*b*) funded party (unless costs payable by him already fixed); and (*c*) Regional Director, if order may be sought against the Commission	CLS(C)R 2000, reg 10(9)
Costs	The amount to be paid by the funded party or the Commission can include the receiving party's costs of making the request	CLS(C)R 2000, reg 10(11)
(2) Variation of s 11(1) order: application	Application can be made by a receiving party for variation of a s 11(1) costs order where the amount to be paid by the funded party, and the Commission, is less than any costs order ("football pools" order)	CLS(C)R 2000, reg 12(2)
	The Commission can apply where the receiving party was a funded party; and in what follows the Commission is in the position of the receiving party	CLS(C)R 2000, reg 12(8)
Grounds for application	A significant change in the funded party's circumstances	CLS(C)R 2000, reg 12(4)(*a*)
Time for application	Within six years from the date of the s 11(1) costs order	CLS(C)R 2000, reg 12(5)
Procedure on application	Application is in Form N244 accompanied by the receiving party's bill of costs prepared in accordance with CPR 1998, r 47.6 (and *PDCosts*)	CLS(C)R 2000, reg 12(7)(*a*)
	No procedure is specified, so it can be assumed that the application proceeds to final hearing on a similar basis to an application for detailed assessment (see Guide 79G)	
	Where application is by the Legal Services Commission it files a statement of the receiving party's costs or bill of costs (if not yet assessed)	CLS(C)R 2000, reg 12(8)(*a*)
	and the Regional Director may then appear on the application or give evidence by written statement (with statement of truth)	CLS(C)R 2000, reg 13(1)(*c*), (2) (3)
Service	Presumably by the applicant on court having fixed a date: receiving party or Commission	

(3) Late determination of costs under s 11(1) order: application	Application can be made by a receiving party for variation of a s 11(1) costs order where the amount to be paid by the funded party, is less than any costs order and the receiving party has not already applied under CLS(C)R 2000, reg 10(2)	CLS(C)R 2000, reg 12(3)
	The Commission can apply where the receiving party was a funded party; and in what follows the Commission is in the position of the receiving party	CLS(C)R 2000, reg 12(8)
	The Regional Director may then appear on the application or give evidence by written statement (with statement of truth)	CLS(C)R 2000, reg 13(1)(*c*), (2) (3)
Grounds for application	(i) A significant change in the funded party's circumstances; (ii) Material additional information not available at the time of the original reg 10 application; or (iii) Other good reason for the receiving party having failed to apply three month limit under reg 10(2)	CLS(C)R 2000, reg 12(4)(*a*)–(*c*)
Time for application	Within six years from the date of the s 11(1) costs order	CLS(C)R 2000, reg 12(5)
Procedure on application	The regulations are silent as to procedure for an application under reg 10(3). Application may be in Form N244, presumably accompanied by the receiving party's bill of costs prepared in accordance with CPR 1998, r 47.6 (and *PDCosts*). The application may then proceed to final hearing on a similar basis to an application for detailed assessment (see Guide 79G) with the amount to be paid determined at the conclusion	
	Where application is by the Commission it files a statement of the receiving party's costs or bill of costs (if not yet assessed)	CLS(C)R 2000, reg 12(8)(*a*)
Service	Presumably by the applicant on court having fixed a date for hearing: receiving party or Commission	

79F: Summary assessment of costs

Procedure

Stage in proceedings	When a party is ordered to pay costs (for detailed assessment see Guide 79G)	CPR 1998, r 44.7(*a*)
Application	Form N260 should be followed "as closely as possible"	*PD Costs*, paras 3.2, 13.5(3)
Time for summary assessment	Whenever an order for costs is made the court should consider whether to make a summary assessment	*PD Costs*, para 13.1
	NB no summary assessment can be made for a receiving party who is:	
	(i) a legally assisted party or LSC funded party	*PD Costs*, para 13.9
	(ii) a child or patient, unless the child's solicitor waives the right to further costs	*PD Costs*, para 13.11(1)
Factors in deciding on summary assessment	The court should make a summary assessment at the conclusion of a hearing:	
	(i) of less than one day	*PD Costs*, para 13.2(2)
	(ii) in the Court of Appeal where *PD to Part 52*, para 14 (summary assessment in Court of Appeal) applies	*PD Costs*, para 13.2(3)
	unless there is good reason not to do so, eg a substantial dispute as to amount due from the paying party which cannot be resolved immediately; or there is insufficient time	*PD Costs*, para 13.2
Duty of legal representatives	Legal representatives who intend to seek an order for costs must prepare a statement of costs following Form N206 and setting out the detail required by *PD Costs*, para 13.5(2)	*PD Costs*, para 13.5(1)–(3)
Time for filing	The statement of costs should be filed and served not later than "24 hours before the date fixed for the hearing"	*PD Costs*, para 13.5(4)
Failure to comply	Failure ("without reasonable excuse") to comply with *PD Costs*, para 13.5(2)–(4) may be taken into account by the court in considering what order to make, eg no order for costs, costs in claim etc	*PD Costs*, para 13.6; and see *Macdonald v Taree Hldgs Ltd* (2000) *The Times*, 28 December, CA

Factors in deciding basis of award and amount of assessment	See Guide 79A	CPR 1998, rr 44.3, 44.4

79G: Detailed assessment of costs

Procedure

Order for detailed assessment	On ordering a party to pay costs the court may order detailed assessment of costs, instead of making a summary assessment (see Guide 79F)	CPR 1998, r 44.7(*b*)
Time for order	(i) At the conclusion of proceedings	
	(ii) At any other time when the court makes an order for detailed assessment; or	CPR 1998, r 47.1; *PD Costs*, para 28.1(1)
	(iii) When the parties agree	*PD Costs*, para 28.1(3)
	NB An order for detailed assessment is not stayed pending appeal, save where so ordered by the court appealed from, or to which appeal is made	CPR 1998, r 47.2; *PD Costs*, para 29.1
Parties	(i) receiving party	CPR 1998, r 43.2(1)(*f*)
	(ii) paying party	CPR 1998, r 43.2(1)(*g*)
	(iii) other parties ("relevant persons")	CPR 1998, r 47.6(2); *PD Costs*, para 32.10
Notice of commencement of proceedings	Commencement of detailed assessment proceedings occurs upon service by receiving party of the following:	
	(i) notice of commencement (N252)	
	(ii) a copy of the bill of costs	
	(iii) fee notes of counsel, experts etc	
	(iv) evidence of disbursements over £250	
	(v) addresses of persons to be served	*PD Costs*, para 32.3
Service of notice of commencement and other documents	Notice of commencement etc served on:	
	(i) paying party	CPR 1998, r 47.6(1)
	(ii) other parties ("relevant persons")	CPR 1998, r 47.6(2)

Time for commencement of detailed assessment proceedings	(i) Three months from date of judgment, direction or order	
	(ii) If order stayed pending appeal, 3 months from lifting of stay	CPR 1998, r 47.7
	(iii) Other period: as agreed by parties or ordered by the court	*PD Costs*, paras 33.1, 33.2
	NB There is no need for permission to commence out of time (but see CPR 1998, r 47.8 for sanctions for delay in commencement)	*PD Costs*, para 33.4
Costs agreed	Where costs are agreed:	CPR 1998, r 47.10
	(i) The parties may apply (under CPR 1998, r 40.6) for a consent order	*PD Costs*, para 36.1
	(ii) If the receiving party claims the paying party has agreed costs but will not pay or join in a consent order, application can be made under Part 23 (or eg FPR 1991, r 10.9)	*PD Costs*, para 36.3
Points of dispute	Served by paying party and any other party on receiving party and any other party	CPR 1998, r 47.9(1)
	Points of dispute should be succinct and should follow Precedent G	*PD Costs*, para 35.2
	Service: 21 days after receipt of notice of commencement	CPR 1998, r 47.9(2)
	Upon receipt, receiving party can:	
	(i) apply for detailed assessment hearing	CPR 1998, r 47.14(1)
	(ii) serve reply to points of dispute	CPR 1998, r 47.13
Default costs certificate	Receiving party can request if no points of dispute are served within 21 days	CPR 1998, r 47.9(4)
Setting aside a default costs certificate	Where receiving party is not entitled to certificate, court must set aside	CPR 1998, r 47.12(1)
	The court has a discretion to set aside if there is some good reason for detailed assessment proceedings to continue	CPR 1998, r 47.12(2)
	If the notice of commencement is not received by the paying party within 21 days and a default costs certificate is issued, the receiving party must apply to set it aside or seek court directions	CPR 1998, r 47.12(3)

Detailed assessment hearing: application	Upon service of points of dispute the receiving party files a request for a detailed assessment hearing	CPR 1998, r 47.14(1)
	Time for application (i) by receiving party: within 3 months of the expiry of the period for commencement of detailed assessment (see above) or as directed	CPR 1998, r 47.14(2)
	(ii) by paying party: on application to the court to request receiving party to request a hearing	CPR 1998, r 47.14(3), (4)
Procedure for detailed assessment	Request for a detailed assessment must be in Form N258 and must be accompanied by the documents listed in *PD Costs*, para 40.2	*PD Costs*, para 40.2
Parties to detailed assessment	The receiving party, the paying party and any party who has served points of dispute	CPR 1998, r 47.14(6)
Notice of hearing	Notice of hearing is given by the court	*PD Costs*, paras 40.5, 40.6(1)
Interim costs certificate	After the receiving party has applied for a detailed assessment hearing the court may, on a Part 23 application, issue an interim costs certificate (Form N257):	CPR 1998, r 47.15; *PD Costs*, para 41.1
	(i) for costs to be paid; or	
	(ii) for costs to be paid into court	
	NB Where a party is ordered to pay costs he may be required to pay an amount on account before costs are assessed	CPR 1998, r 44.3(8)
Detailed assessment hearing	Only items raised in points of dispute can be raised at the detailed assessment hearing	CPR 1998, r 47.14(7)
Final costs certificate	14 days from the end of the detailed assessment hearing a completed bill of costs must be filed	CPR 1998, r 47.16(1), (2); *PD Costs*, paras 42.3–42.8
	The court then:	
	(i) issues a final costs certificate (Form N256); and	
	(ii) serves it on all parties to the detailed assessment hearing	CPR 1998, r 47.16(3)
Time for payment of costs	Costs are payable 14 days from the date of the costs certificate	CPR 1998, r 44.8(*b*)

Offers to settle	"Without prejudice offers" to settle the detailed assessment proceedings will be taken into account by the court in deciding who is to pay the costs of such assessment	CPR 1998, r 47.19
Costs of detailed assessment	Receiving party is entitled to the costs of the detailed assessment in the absence of any order, rule, practice direction etc which provides otherwise	CPR 1998, r 47.18
Appeals		CPR 1998, rr 47.20–47.26

79H: Detailed assessment: costs payable out of Community Legal Service Fund (legal aid)

Procedure

Request for CLSF detailed assessment	Request in Form N258A filed by funded party's solicitor Documents to be filed with the request are set out in *PD Costs*, para 43.3	CPR 1998, r 47.17(1) *PD Costs*, para 43.3
Notice to funded party (assisted person)	The funded party must be given notice of the request for detailed assessment if their interest has been given to the court in accordance with CLS regulations If the funded party says they want to attend a detailed assessment hearing the court will fix a date	CPR 1998, r 47.17(3); CLA(G)R 1989, reg 119 CPR 1998, r 47.17(4); *PD Costs*, para 43.4
Time for commencement of CLSF detailed assessment	Three months from date when right to detailed assessment arose	CPR 1998, r 47.17(2)
The bill	The form and content of a bill is prescribed by *PD Costs*, Section 4 NB In proceedings covered by LAF(P)R 1991 the "reasonable cost of preparation" of a bill is restricted by the Schs to LAF(P)R 1991; though a further discretionary item may be allowed in the case of a provisional assessment	*PD Costs*, Section 4 *Re C (Legal Aid: Preparation of Bill of Costs)* [2001] 1 FLR 602, CA
Provisional detailed assessment	Notice of provisional assessment is sent to the solicitor in Form N253	CPR 1998, r 47.17(5), (6)

Hearing on CLS funded detailed assessment	If the solicitor requests a hearing following provisional assessment a hearing will be fixed; and if the assisted person has indicated an interest they will be notified	CPR 1998 r 47.17(7); *PD Costs*, para 43.7

80: Application in Respect of the Human Rights Act 1998

Legal background

From 2 October 2000 by virtue of HRA 1998, s 3 all primary and subordinate legislation must be read and given effect in a way which is compatible with the European Convention of Human Rights (as prescribed in HRA 1998, s 1). Where it is not possible to read legislation in this way, an application may be made for a declaration of incompatibility (under s 4). Otherwise, a complaint that there has been a decision by a public authority (court, tribunal, local authority or any person whose functions are of a public nature) which is incompatible with a convention right (under s 6) may be the subject of separate proceedings (pursuant to s 7(1)(*a*)) or brought within existing proceedings (pursuant to s 7(1)(*b*)). A claim pursuant to HRA 1998, s 7(1)(*a*) should be made to the Administrative Court as an application for judicial review (see Guide 69).

Procedure

Who may apply	Any person who is a victim of the action which is the subject of the complaint	HRA 1998, s 7(1)
	A claim under HRA 1998, s 7(1)(*a*) may only be brought within 12 months of the act complained of or such longer period as the court considers equitable	HRA 1998, s 7(5)
Which court	A claim under HRA 1998, s 7(1)(*a*) may be brought in any court in existing or ongoing proceedings	HRA 1998, s 9(1)
	A claim under HRA 1998, s 7(1)(*a*) in respect of a judicial act may only be brought in the High Court (in relation to the actions of an inferior court or tribunal). The procedure is by way of an appeal or judicial review	CPR 1998, r 7.11; HRA 1998, s 9(1)
	A claim under HRA 1998, s 4 for a declaration of incompatibility must be brought in or transferred to the High Court	HRA 1998, s 4
Application	A claim made in existing or continuing proceedings should specify the details in the originating documentation or amend the documentation accordingly setting out:	FPR 1991, r 10.26

	(*a*) the precise details of the Convention right claimed to have been infringed and details; (*b*) specify the relief sought; and (*c*) state whether a declaration of incompatibility is claimed Any application to amend documentation to make a claim should be made as soon as possible any in any event within 28 days, unless otherwise ordered A separate claim (not one made in existing or ongoing proceedings) should be made in accordance with the procedure on an application for judicial review to the Administrative Court Where the claim is for damages in respect of a judicial act, the claim must be set out in the statement of case	
Defendants	The parties to the existing or ongoing proceedings, if the claim is made within those proceedings Otherwise those who are parties to judicial review proceedings	
Additional persons to be served	Where a claim is in respect of damages for a judicial act notice must be given to the Crown (the Lord Chancellor)	CPR 1998, r 19.4A; FPR 1991, r 10.26(18)
	Where a claim for a declaration of incompatibility is made pursuant to HRA 1998, s 4 notice must be given to the Crown, and the Crown or a Minister shall be joined as a party	HRA 1998, s 5; CPR 1998, r 19.4A; FPR 1991, r 10.26 (Family Proceedings); PD19, para 6.1 (Non-Family Proceedings including judicial review and appeals to the Court of Appeal)
Order	The court may make such order as is within its power. Damages or compensation may be awarded only by a court that has power to make such an award	HRA 1998, s 8
	On an application pursuant to HRA 1998, s 4 the court may make a declaration of incompatibility	

PART II

Statutes

PART II: Statutes

Contents

All relevant procedural provisions in the following legislation, as amended and fully annotated, and the principal core substantive provisions:

Access to Justice Act 1999

PART I
LEGAL SERVICES COMMISSION

****

Community Legal Service

****

10 Terms of provision of funded services

(1)–(6) ...

(7) Except so far as regulations otherwise provide, where services have been funded by the Commission for an individual as part of the Community Legal Service –

(*a*) sums expended by the Commission in funding the services (except to the extent that they are recovered under section 11), and

(*b*) other sums payable by the individual by virtue of regulations under this section,

shall constitute a first charge on any property recovered or preserved by him (whether for himself or any other person) in any proceedings or in any compromise or settlement of any dispute in connection with which the services were provided.

(8) ...

Scope of provision—Section 10(7) replaces, and slightly alters, the statutory charge provisions of Legal Aid Act 1988, s 16(6)–(8). It provides that any money paid out by the Commission, save where covered by a funded client's contributions and by orders in his favour under s 11, should be charged on any money or property recovered or retained by the funded client as a result of the proceedings.

The regulations—Community Legal Service (Financial) Regulations 2000 (CLS(F)R 2000), Pt III defines the amount of the charge, exemptions from it, enforcement and postponement and the interest payable. Community Legal Service (Costs) Regulations 2000 (CLS(C)R 2000), regs 17–21 govern the operation of the charge and its postponement where property is to be purchased.

"a first charge on any property recovered or preserved"—Assessment of whether the charge arises turns on the following:

(i) *What are the proceedings?* This refers to the proceedings for which the certificate was issued (*Hanlon v Law Society* [1981] AC 124, [1980] 2 All ER 199, HL).

(ii) *What is the property?* In most matrimonial proceedings "property" will be all the parties' matrimonial assets – ie property owned by both parties whether jointly or individually. For guidance on CLS charge attaching to pension sharing and attachment see note under MCA 1973, s 21A.

(iii) *Was the property in issue?* Whether or not the charge applies to particular property turns on whether or not it was in issue in the proceedings. This is determined by looking at any court order, affidavits or pleadings, and even the correspondence between the parties (*Hanlon v Law Society* (above)).

(iv) *Was the property "recovered or preserved"?* If property is in issue in proceedings then it will have been "recovered or preserved" and the charge applies, subject to any of the statutory exemptions in Community Legal Service (Financial) Regulations 2000, reg 44(1) (eg £2,500 in certain family proceedings; increased to £3000 for post-1/12/2001 certificates). Thus property is recovered if a person takes proceedings to convert it to his own use – eg a property adjustment order or a lump sum order (*Curling v Law Society* [1985] FLR 831, CA); property is preserved if a person successfully resists a claim to his property – eg an order for sale or a property adjustment order (*Parkes v Legal Aid Board* [1997] 1 FLR 77, CA).

"whether for himself or any other person"—The aim of drafting the section in this way was to ensure that the charge arises even though property or money is transferred to a third party, such as a child (see eg *Draskovic v Draskovic* (1981) Fam Law 87, Balcombe J; though in that case the assisted person's solicitors were held to have evaded the charge). The charge will now apply even though the payment is made to the funded client personally.

"in any compromise or settlement of any dispute"—The charge arises even though the liability to costs of the funded client arose as a result of "any compromise or settlement of any dispute". Thus the charge applies, even though the property recovered in the settlement was not the property directly in issue in the proceedings (*Van Hoorn v Law Society* [1985] QB 106, [1984] FLR 203, Balcombe J).

Postponement of the charge—Where a funded client has property which will be subject to the charge, or where there is money which is required to pay for a home in family proceedings (as defined by Community Legal Service (Financial) Regulations 2000, reg 2(1)), then if the client wishes to postpone enforcement of the charge the court must be asked to order that the property (or the property to be purchased) is "to be used as a home for the [funded] client or his dependants" (CLS(F)R 2000, reg 52(1)(*a*)). The court should be asked to so order in the terms of *Practice Direction of 19 August 1991* .

Mediation and the statutory charge—The cost of mediation, both the mediator ("Family Mediation") and the solicitor putting the memorandum of understanding into operation ("Help with Mediation"), are exempt from operation of the charge (Community Legal Service (Financial) Regulations 2000, reg 43(3)).

11 Costs in funded cases

(1) Except in prescribed circumstances, costs ordered against an individual in relation to any proceedings or part of proceedings funded for him shall not exceed the amount (if any) which is a reasonable one for him to pay having regard to all the circumstances including –

(*a*) the financial resources of all the parties to the proceedings, and

(*b*) their conduct in connection with the dispute to which the proceedings relate;

and for this purpose proceedings, or a part of proceedings, are funded for an individual if services relating to the proceedings or part are funded for him by the Commission as part of the Community Legal Service.

(2) In assessing for the purposes of subsection (1) the financial resources of an individual for whom services are funded by the Commission as part of the Community Legal Service, his clothes and household furniture and the tools and implements of his trade shall not be taken into account, except so far as may be prescribed.

(3) Subject to subsections (1) and (2), regulations may make provision about costs in relation to proceedings in which services are funded by the Commission for any of the parties as part of the Community Legal Service.

(4) The regulations may, in particular, make provision –

(*a*) specifying the principles to be applied in determining the amount of any costs which may be awarded against a party for whom services are funded by the Commission as part of the Community Legal Service,

(*b*) limiting the circumstances in which, or extent to which, an order for costs may be enforced against such a party,

(*c*) as to the cases in which, and extent to which, such a party may be required to give security for costs and the manner in which it is to be given,
(*d*) requiring the payment by the Commission of the whole or part of any costs incurred by a party for whom services are not funded by the Commission as part of the Community Legal Service,
(*e*) specifying the principles to be applied in determining the amount of any costs which may be awarded to a party for whom services are so funded,
(*f*) requiring the payment to the Commission, or the person or body by which the services were provided, of the whole or part of any sum awarded by way of costs to such a party, and
(*g*) as to the court, tribunal or other person or body by whom the amount of any costs is to be determined and the extent to which any determination of that amount is to be final.

Scope of provision—Section 11(1) and (2) replace LAA 1988, s 17 and deal with the extent to which costs can be awarded against a funded client. Section 11(3) and (4) replace LAA 1988 s 18 and provide for orders for costs against the Legal Services Commission. The new scheme, in conjunction with the regulations made under s 11 (Community Legal Service (Costs) Regulations 2000 and Community Legal Service (Cost Protection) Regulations 2000) provide a unified system of assessment of a funded client's ability to pay and of a non-funded party's entitlement to costs against the Legal Services Commission.

Costs orders under s 11—In outline the scheme under s 11 is as follows:
(i) *Costs to be awarded* The court decides whether an order for costs should be made in accordance with normal principles (CPR 1998, r 44.3; FPR 1991, rr 2.69B–D; *Gojkovic v Gojkovic (No 2)* [1992] Fam 40, [1991] 2 FLR 233, CA); the fact that a party is funded does not mean that an order should be made where otherwise no order would have followed the proceedings (*Keller v Keller and Legal Aid Board* [1995] 1 FLR 259, CA).
(ii) *Costs against a funded client* If the court decides to make an order against a funded client then it assesses what is reasonable for him to pay or adjourns determination of the amount (CLS(C)R 2000, reg 9).
(iii) *Costs against the Commission* Where a receiving party does not recover all his costs against a funded client then application can be made for costs against the Commission (CLS(C)R 2000, reg 10).

"costs ordered against a [funded client] shall not exceed ..." (s 11(1))—Section 11(1) provides "costs protection" to a funded client as defined by CLS(CP)R 2000 (see especially reg 3), so far as his resources do not make him ineligible for such protection.

"financial resources" (s 11(1), (2))—The resources of a funded client which are disregarded in any computation of what is reasonable for him to pay are specified in two separate sources: see s 11(2) and the definition "prescribed" in CLS(C)R 2000, reg 7 which brings back into account any part of the value (equity value?) of a funded client's dwelling-house over £100,000 and any clothes, tools of trade or furniture of exceptional value.

"a part of proceedings" (s 11(1))—A certificate may be treated as spent where the work done under it, if for only "part of proceedings", has been dealt with (*Littaur v Steggles Palmer* [1986] 1 WLR 287, [1986] 1 All ER 780, CA). Thus the protection available under s 11(1) will come to an end once the certificate is spent, even though the certificate is not finally discharged (*Burridge v Stafford* [2000] 1 WLR 927, CA).

End of cost protection—Cost protection applies from the date on which a certificate is granted (CLS(CP)R 2000, reg 3(3)(*a*)) and comes to an end on one of the following events:
(i) *Discharge of the certificate* Costs protection applies to costs incurred prior to discharge (CLS(CP)R 2000, reg 3(3)(*b*)).
(ii) *Revocation* Where a certificate is revoked, costs protection will be deemed not to have applied at all (CLS(CP)R 2000, reg 3(4)).
(iii) *"Spent certificate"* Where a certificate is treated by the court as spent then it seems unlikely that costs protection will apply.
(iv) *Expired costs limitation* Where a costs limitation expires, either the funded client ceases to be funded, when costs protection cannot apply; or the solicitor continues to act providing that

it has been established that the client remains funded (*R v Legal Aid Board ex parte Burrows* [2001] 2 FLR 998, CA). Presumably, in the latter circumstance, costs protection will apply.

****

PART IV
APPEALS, COURTS, JUDGES AND COURT PROCEEDINGS

Appeals

54 Permission to appeal

(1) Rules of court may provide that any right of appeal to –

(*a*) a county court,
(*b*) the High Court, or
(*c*) the Court of Appeal,

may be exercised only with permission.

(2) This section does not apply to a right of appeal in a criminal cause or matter.

(3) For the purposes of subsection (1) rules of court may make provision as to –

(*a*) the classes of case in which a right of appeal may be exercised only with permission,
(*b*) the court or courts which may give permission for the purposes of this section,
(*c*) any considerations to be taken into account in deciding whether permission should be given, and
(*d*) any requirements to be satisfied before permission may be given,

and may make different provision for different circumstances.

(4) No appeal may be made against a decision of a court under this section to give or refuse permission (but this subsection does not affect any right under rules of court to make a further application for permission to the same or another court).

(5) For the purposes of this section a right to make an application to have a case stated for the opinion of the High Court constitutes a right of appeal.

(6) For the purposes of this section a right of appeal to the Court of Appeal includes –

(*a*) the right to make an application for a new trial, and
(*b*) the right to make an application to set aside a verdict, finding or judgment in any cause or matter in the High Court which has been tried, or in which any issue has been tried, by a jury.

Scope of provision—This section provides the rule making power in relation to the requirement of permission to appeal to the Court of Appeal. CPR 1998, r 52.3 provides that permission to appeal is required in all cases (save for the limited exceptions set out there). Whilst there can be no appeal against the refusal of permission to appeal, r 52.3(3) provides that where the lower court (the court which made the order which is the subject of the proposed appeal) refuses permission to appeal, a further application for permission to appeal may be made to the appeal court. This does not mean that permission to appeal is sought in relation to the refusal to grant permission to appeal, but in relation to the substantive order (see *Bulled v Khayat and Another* [2002] EWCA Civ 804). Procedure for the application for permission to appeal is contained within Practice Direction – Appeals which supplements CPR 1998, Pt 52 (set out in Part V of this work).

55 Second appeals

(1) Where an appeal is made to a county court or the High Court in relation to any matter, and on hearing the appeal the court makes a decision in relation to that matter, no appeal may be made to the Court of Appeal from that decision unless the Court of Appeal considers that –

(*a*) the appeal would raise an important point of principle or practice, or
(*b*) there is some other compelling reason for the Court of Appeal to hear it.

(2) This section does not apply in relation to an appeal in a criminal cause or matter.

Scope of provision—This section imposes a further hurdle in relation to a proposed appeal where the appeal to the Court of Appeal would be a second tier appeal. This further hurdle is in addition to the requirement of permission to appeal (CPR 1998, r 52.13).

56 Power to prescribe alternative destination of appeals

(1) The Lord Chancellor may by order provide that appeals which would otherwise lie to –

(*a*) a county court,
(*b*) the High Court, or
(*c*) the Court of Appeal,

shall lie instead to another of those courts, as specified in the order.

(2) This section does not apply to an appeal in a criminal cause or matter.

(3) An order under subsection (1) –

(*a*) may make different provision for different classes of proceedings or appeals, and
(*b*) may contain consequential amendments or repeals of enactments.

(4) Before making an order under subsection (1) the Lord Chancellor shall consult –

(*a*) the Lord Chief Justice,
(*b*) the Master of the Rolls,
(*c*) the President of the Family Division, and
(*d*) the Vice-Chancellor.

(5) An order under subsection (1) shall be made by statutory instrument.

(6) No such order may be made unless a draft of it has been laid before and approved by resolution of each House of Parliament.

(7) For the purposes of this section an application to have a case stated for the opinion of the High Court constitutes an appeal.

"The Lord Chancellor may by order provide"—No order has been made under this provision.

57 Assignment of appeals to Court of Appeal

(1) Where in any proceedings in a county court or the High Court a person appeals, or seeks permission to appeal, to a court other than the Court of Appeal or the House of Lords –

(*a*) the Master of the Rolls, or

(*b*) the court from which or to which the appeal is made, or from which permission to appeal is sought,

may direct that the appeal shall be heard instead by the Court of Appeal.

(2) The power conferred by subsection (1)(*b*) shall be subject to rules of court.

Scope of provision—Where the county court or High Court is to hear an appeal which would raise an important point of principle or practice or there is some other compelling reason for it to be transferred, that court, or the Master of the Rolls may direct that the appeal be heard by the Court of Appeal. If transferred up in accordance with this provision, the Court of Appeal or the Master of the Rolls may transfer it back for hearing by the original court (CPR 1998, r 52.14(2)).

****

Administration of Justice Act 1960

****

12 Publication of information relating to proceedings in private

(1) The publication of information relating to proceedings before any court sitting in private shall not of itself be contempt of court except in the following cases, that is to say –

(*a*) where the proceedings –
(i) relate to the exercise of the inherent jurisdiction of the High Court with respect to minors;
(ii) are brought under the Children Act 1989; or
(iii) otherwise relate wholly or mainly to the maintenance or upbringing of a minor;

(*b*)–(*e*) ...

(2) Without prejudice to the foregoing subsection, the publication of the text or a summary of the whole or part of an order made by a court sitting in private shall not of itself be contempt of court except where the court (having power to do so) expressly prohibits the publication.

(3) In this section references to a court include references to a judge and to a tribunal and to any person exercising the functions of a court, a judge or a tribunal; and references to a court sitting in private include references to a court sitting in camera or in chambers.

(4) Nothing in this section shall be construed as implying that any publication is punishable as contempt of court which would not be so punishable apart from this section.

Amendments—CA 1989, s 108, Sch 13, para 14.

Scope of provision—This section has the effect of abrogating the strict liability rule of contempt of court, except in certain types of proceedings (ie those mentioned in s 12(1)(*a*), which relate to most types of family proceedings in which children are the focal point). For an exposition of the strict liability rule, reference should be made to specialist works on contempt of court. Section 12 is designed to prevent the publication of information in respect of child law cases which are heard in private. The exceptions set out in s 12(1)(*a*) are not exhaustive. There are situations outside s 12 which require confidentiality to avoid potential prejudice to the proper administration of justice. Family proceedings are not automatically covered by confidentiality even if they are heard in private. The court must look at the application before it and reach a conclusion as to whether the application is covered by s 12, or comes within those recognised categories of cases such as children and ancillary relief issues which are treated as confidential, or because of other factors there would be prejudice to the administration of justice if the proceedings were not to be treated as confidential (*Clibbery v Allan* [2002] EWCA Civ 45, [2002] 1 FLR 565). The word "publication" should be given its ordinary meaning. It does not encompass communication of information between statutory bodies charged with responsibility for child protection (*Re M (Disclosure: Children and Family Reporter* [2002] EWCA Civ 1199, [2002] 2 FLR 893). The section is not designed to cover documents held by social workers which have not been filed at court nor been used in proceedings heard by a court in private. However, such documents are in themselves confidential and are protected from general publication by the doctrine of public interest immunity (*Re W (Disclosure to Police)* [1998] 2 FLR 135). For examples of imposition of restrictions on publication beyond those provided by this section see *Re G (Celebrities: Publicity)* [1999] 1 FLR 409 and *A v M (Family Proceedings: Publicity)* [2000] 1 FLR 562; however, in *Harris v Harris; Attorney-General v Harris* [2001] 2 FLR 895 Munby J indicated that the court should only exercise its powers to restrain publicity under the inherent jurisdiction if the automatic restraints under Administration of Justice Act 1960, s 12, Contempt of Court Act 1981, s 2 and Children Act 1989, s 97(2) were inadequate to protect the child from harm and if the interests of the child could not be adequately protected by an order under Children and Young Persons Act 1933, s 39. For the use of injunctive relief to restrict publicity in wardship see *Kelly v BBC* [2001] 1 FLR 197. See *X v Dempster* [1999] 1 FLR 894 for consideration of this section in a contempt case.

PART II

Prohibition on publication of information relating to proceedings in private (s 12(1)(*a*))—If an application to prohibit the publication of information relating to the proceedings listed in s 12(1)(*a*) is to succeed, the publications to be restrained must relate to the care and upbringing of children over whose welfare the court is exercising a supervisory role; such cases would include those in which the publications might hinder the ability of the carers to carry out their obligations to the court for the care of the child. No child, simply by virtue of being a child, is entitled to a right of privacy or confidentiality (*R v Central Independent Television plc* [1994] Fam 192, [1994] 2 FLR 151). The same principle applies to a ward of court as to any other child. Any element of confidentiality concerning a child in respect of whom the court's jurisdiction is invoked belongs not to the child but to the court. It is imposed to protect the proper functioning of the court's own jurisdiction and will not be imposed to any further extent than is necessary to afford that protection (*Scott v Scott* [1913] AC 417, (1913) FLR Rep 657; *Re F (Orse A) (A Minor) (Publication of Information)* [1977] Fam 58; *Re R (Wardship: Restrictions on Publication)* [1994] Fam 254; *M v British Broadcasting Corporation* [1997] 1 FLR 51 (where an adult involved in Child Support Act proceedings could not use this section to claim protection from the publication of information relating to his own infertility)). The issue of restraint on publicity does not fall to be judged according to the paramountcy of the children's welfare (*Re W (Wardship: Discharge: Publicity)* [1995] 2 FLR 466 at 475H, per Waite LJ). However, when the threatened publication touches matters which are of direct concern to the court in its supervisory role over the care and upbringing of the child, the court must balance the protection of the child against the right of free publication and free speech enjoyed by outside parties (*Re C (A Minor) (No 2) (Wardship: Publication of Information)* [1990] 1 FLR 263, CA – newspaper prevented from identifying child who was terminally ill or her carers; *Re Z (A Minor) (Freedom of Publication)* [1996] 1 FLR 191 – where an injunction was made preventing the mother of a child with special educational needs, about whom there had already been considerable media attention, involving the child in a television broadcast about her treatment). For examples of cases where publication of a story has been permitted on condition that information that could lead to the identification of the children was omitted see *Re M and N (Wards) (Publication of Information)* [1990] 1 FLR 149; *Re W (Wardship: Publication of Information)* [1992] 1 FLR 99; *Re H (Minors) (Injunction: Public Interest)* [1994] 1 FLR 519 and *Re W (Wardship: Discharge: Publicity)* [1995] 2 FLR 466.

In carrying out the balancing exercise, the child's welfare is not paramount unless the court is determining a question with respect to the upbringing of the child: "a question of upbringing is determined whenever the central issue before the court is one which relates to how the child is being reared" (*Re Z (A Minor) (Freedom of Publication)* [1996] 1 FLR 191 at 213G, per Ward LJ). The court has power to direct that such putative statements as a party might make in the future should remain confidential, although any such direction cannot bind, but might influence, future judges in the exercise of their discretion in any subsequent application for the disclosure of evidence (*Cleveland County Council v F* [1995] 1 FLR 797 – where the mother sought a direction in care proceedings that any statement made by or on behalf of the mother to a party in the case or to their representative or to the guardian ad litem should be confidential and not disclosed to anyone other than to a party or to the court; in this particular case, the direction was refused because statements made by the mother were already protected to a certain extent by CA 1989, s 98 and by the hearsay rule, and because the court had to take into account the fact that any direction as to confidentiality must impede the proper exercise of their functions by the agencies concerned).

Proceedings restraining freedom of press to be heard in the High Court—Where an injunction is sought to impose a restraint on the freedom of the press and the media generally, the case should be transferred to the High Court and the Official Solicitor should be invited to act as amicus (*Re H (Minors) (Injunction: Public Interest)* [1994] 1 FLR 519; see also *Practice Note of 2 April 2001* – set out in Part IV of this work).

Power of court to allow disclosure—The court has power to allow disclosure of information which would otherwise be subject to a prohibition on publication (*Re R (MJ) (A Minor) (Publication of Transcript)* [1975] Fam 89; *Re F and Others (Wards) (Disclosure of Material)* [1989] 1 FLR 39; *Re X, Y and Z (Wardship: Disclosure of Material)* [1992] 1 FLR 84; *Re K (Minors) (Disclosure: Criminal Proceedings)* [1994] Fam Law 57, FD). The principles to be applied by the court on considering an application for disclosure are summarised by Balcombe LJ in *Re Manda (Wardship: Disclosure of Evidence)* [1993] 1 FLR 205: (1) the interests of the child concerned will always be the most important factor; (2) where the child is still a minor, the court will decide where his interests lie, although the older the child the more relevant are his own views and wishes; (3) where the child has attained majority, then he alone is entitled to decide what are his best interests; (4) if the material is to be disclosed for use in other proceedings, the public interest in the administration of justice requires that all relevant information should be available for use in those proceedings; (5) if the relevant information has been obtained on an express assurance of confidentiality, then that is a very relevant factor. However, it would be undesirable for an express assurance to be given unless the information could not otherwise be obtained; and (6) where no such express assurance has been given, people who give evidence may normally assume that their evidence will remain confidential, but they are not entitled to assume that it will remain so in all circumstances. Nevertheless, when considering whether leave should be granted, the importance of social workers (and others concerned with the protection of children) performing their duties with candour and frankness, where unnecessary public exposure is likely to do more harm than good, has to be weighed in the balance (*Oxfordshire County Council v L and F* [1997] 1 FLR 235). In exceptional circumstances, confidentiality may in fact be damaging for the child and might not promote his continuing welfare; in such a case, the balance of the interests of the child against legitimate public interest may lead to the reporting of a case, albeit under initials to shield the child's identity (*Re H (Publication of Judgment)* [1995] 2 FLR 542 – where the child was nearly 18 and had developed an obsessive and morally unhealthy enthusiasm for the academy of dancing and performing arts which he attended, the court allowed reporting of the case under initials, as publicity would force the child to face the reality of his behaviour; there was also a legitimate public interest in the sphere of child protection and education). In *R v Cambridge District Health Authority ex parte B (No 2)* [1996] 1 FLR 375, reporting restrictions were removed to allow the identification of a child who had a life-threatening illness; in this case, the child knew details of the proceedings and her illness, her father was seeking to publicise the case to raise funds to seek further treatment, and the maintenance of reporting restrictions could not be justified if it meant the denial of potential therapeutic and life-saving treatment. The original restrictions in this case had been imposed under Children and Young Persons Act 1933, s 39 (power to prohibit publication of certain matters in newspapers), which provides as follows:

"(1) In relation to any proceedings in any court, the court may direct that –

(*a*) no newspaper report of the proceedings shall reveal the name, address, or school, or include particulars calculated to lead to the identification, of any child or young person concerned with the proceedings, either as being the person by or against whom or in respect of whom the proceedings are taken, or as being a witness therein;

(*b*) no picture shall be published in any newspaper as being or including a picture of any child or young person so concerned in the proceedings as aforesaid;

except in so far (if at all) as may be permitted by the direction of the court.

(2) Any person who publishes any matter in contravention of any such direction shall on summary conviction be liable in respect of each offence to a fine not exceeding level 5 on the standard scale."

The possibility that newspaper publication might ease the parents' distress and mitigate their bitterness is not a factor properly to be taken into account in deciding whether to allow publication (*Oxfordshire County Council v L and F* [1997] 1 FLR 235).

Where the claim for disclosure is based on the public interest in the administration of justice, it can only be in exceptional circumstances that the welfare of an individual child will outweigh the public interest. Disclosure has also been ordered where there are, or are about to be, further investigations/proceedings – see **Disclosure for criminal proceedings/investigation** etc under FPR 1991, r 4.23 for the criteria to be applied and examples of disclosure for various proceedings and to other professional bodies. See also **Extent of prohibition on disclosure** under FPR 1991, r 4.23 and FPC(CA 1989)R 1991, r 23.

Power of court to restrict publicity relating to the identity of a ward in criminal proceedings—A judge in wardship proceedings may have power to restrict publicity relating to the identity of a ward in criminal proceedings but, even if he does have such a power, he should not exercise it; any decision as to restraining the publicity relating to the identity of persons concerned in criminal proceedings should be a matter for the discretion of the criminal trial judge (*Re R (Wardship: Restrictions on Publication)* [1994] Fam 254, [1994] 2 FLR 637; *R v Central Criminal Court ex parte Godwin and Crook* [1995] 1 FLR 132 – power of criminal court under Children and Young Persons Act 1933, s 39 to restrict the reporting of information relating to the identification of a child involved in criminal proceedings).

Duration of prohibition on publication (s 12(1)(*a*)(i))—The prohibition on publication is not limited in time, and it thus remains a contempt to publish such information even if wardship proceedings are discharged (*Re E (A Minor) (Child Abuse: Evidence)* [1991] 1 FLR 420 at 455B). Presumably, the same principle applies to the prohibition in s 12(1)(*a*)(ii) and (iii).

Publication of court order (s 12(2))—In *Re G (Celebrities: Publicity)* [1999] 1 FLR 409 the Court of Appeal indicated that it was hard to conceive of circumstances which would justify preventing the media from publishing the bare outcome of a hearing; the court should issue a terse statement approved by the judge and agreed between the parties.

13 Appeal in cases of contempt of court

(1) Subject to the provisions of this section, an appeal shall lie under this section from any order or decision of a court in the exercise of jurisdiction to punish for contempt of court (including criminal contempt); and in relation to any such order or decision the provisions of this section shall have effect in substitution for any other enactment relating to appeals in civil or criminal proceedings.

(2) An appeal under this section shall lie in any case at the instance of the defendant and, in the case of an application for committal or attachment, at the instance of the applicant; and the appeal shall lie –

(*a*) from an order or decision of any inferior court not referred to in the next following paragraph, to the High Court;

(*b*) from an order or decision of a county court or any other inferior court from which appeals generally lie to the Court of Appeal, and from an order or decision (other than a decision on an appeal under this section) of a single judge of the High Court, or of any court having the powers of the High Court or of a judge of that court, to the Court of Appeal;

(*bb*) from an order or decision of the Crown Court to the Court of Appeal;

(*c*) from a decision of a single judge of the High Court on an appeal under this section, from an order or decision of a Divisional Court or the Court of Appeal (including a decision of either of those courts on an appeal under this section), and from an order or decision of the Court of Criminal Appeal or the Courts-Martial Appeal Court, to the House of Lords.

(3) The court to which an appeal is brought under this section may reverse or vary the order or decision of the court below, and make such other orders as may be just; and without prejudice to the inherent powers of any court referred to in subsection (2) of this section, provision may be made by rules of court for authorising the release on bail of an appellant under this section.

(4) Subsections (2) to (4) of section one and section two of this Act shall apply to an appeal to the House of Lords under this section as they apply to an appeal to that House under the said section one, except that so much of the said subsection (2) as restricts the grant of leave to appeal shall apply only where the decision of the court below is a decision on appeal to that court under this section.

(5) In this section "court" includes any tribunal or person having power to punish for contempt; and references in this section to an order or decision of a court in the exercise of jurisdiction to punish for contempt of court include references –

- (*a*) to an order or decision of the High Court, the Crown Court or a county court under any enactment enabling that court to deal with an offence as if it were contempt of court;
- (*b*) to an order or decision of a county court, or of any court having the powers of a county court, under section 14, 92 or 118 of the County Courts Act 1984;
- (*c*) to an order or decision of a magistrates' court under subsection (3) of section 63 of the Magistrates' Courts Act 1980,

but do not include references to orders under section five of the Debtors Act 1869, or under any provision of the Magistrates' Courts Act 1980 or the County Courts Act 1984, except those referred to in paragraphs (*b*) and (*c*) of this subsection and except sections 38 and 142 of the last-mentioned Act so far as those sections confer jurisdiction in respect of contempt of court.

(6) This section does not apply to a conviction or sentence in respect of which an appeal lies under Part I of the Criminal Appeal Act 1968, or to a decision of the criminal division of the Court of Appeal under that Part of that Act.

Amendments—Criminal Appeal Act 1968, s 52(1), Sch 5, Pt I; Courts Act 1971, s 56(1), (4), Sch 8, Pt II, para 40(1), (2), Sch 11, Pt II; Magistrates' Courts Act 1980, s 154, Sch 7, para 37; Supreme Court Act 1981, s 152(4), Sch 7; County Courts Act 1984, s 148(1), Sch 2, para 25; Access to Justice Act 1999, ss 64, 106, Sch 15.

Scope of provision—Proceedings on appeal under this section from an order or decision under Magistrates' Courts Act 1980, s 63(3) (the power to punish for breach of a court order) are assigned to the Family Division of the High Court by Supreme Court Act 1981, s 61(1), (3), Sch 1, para 3(*d*), and the procedure on such appeal is prescribed by FPR 1991, r 8.3. The court has power to punish for an assault on an officer of the court (County Courts Act 1984, s 14), for the rescue of goods seized in execution of process of a county court (CCA 1984, s 92) and for contempt (CCA 1984, s 118).

Committal by district judge—A committal order may now be made in the county court by a district judge (see Attachment of Earnings Act 1971, s 23(11) and CCA 1984, s 118(3)), and an appeal from such a decision appears to be to the judge (see *Marya v Marya* [1995] 2 FLR 911; *King v Read & Slack* (unreported) 18 November 1996, CA).

****

Administration of Justice Act 1969

****

PART II
APPEAL FROM HIGH COURT TO HOUSE OF LORDS

12 Grant of certificate by trial judge

(1) Where on the application of any of the parties to any proceedings to which this section applies the judge is satisfied –

(*a*) that the relevant conditions are fulfilled in relation to his decision in those proceedings, and

(*b*) that a sufficient case for an appeal to the House of Lords under this Part of this Act has been made out to justify an application for leave to bring such an appeal, and

(*c*) that all the parties to the proceedings consent to the grant of a certificate under this section,

the judge, subject to the following provisions of this Part of this Act, may grant a certificate to that effect.

(2) This section applies to any civil proceedings in the High Court which are either –

(*a*) proceedings before a single judge of the High Court, or

(*b*) (*repealed*)

(*c*) proceedings before a Divisional Court.

(3) Subject to any Order in Council made under the following provisions of this section, for the purposes of this section the relevant conditions, in relation to a decision of the judge in any proceedings, are that a point of law of general public importance is involved in that decision and that that point of law either –

(*a*) relates wholly or mainly to the construction of an enactment or of a statutory instrument, and has been fully argued in the proceedings and fully considered in the judgment of the judge in the proceedings, or

(*b*) is one in respect of which the judge is bound by a decision of the Court of Appeal or of the House of Lords in previous proceedings, and was fully considered in the judgments given by the Court of Appeal or the House of Lords (as the case may be) in those previous proceedings.

(4) Any application for a certificate under this section shall be made to the judge immediately after he gives judgment in the proceedings:

Provided that the judge may in any particular case entertain any such application made at any later time before the end of the period of fourteen days beginning with the date on which that judgment is given or such other period as may be prescribed by rules of court.

(5) No appeal shall lie against the grant or refusal of a certificate under this section.

(6) Her Majesty may by Order in Council amend subsection (3) of this section by altering, deleting, or substituting one or more new paragraphs for, either or both of paragraphs (*a*) and (*b*) of that subsection, or by adding one or more further paragraphs.

(7) Any Order in Council made under this section shall be subject to annulment in pursuance of a resolution of either House of Parliament.

(8) In this Part of this Act "civil proceedings" means any proceedings other than proceedings in a criminal cause or matter, and "the judge", in relation to any proceedings to which this section applies, means the judge referred to in paragraph (*a*) of subsection (2) of this section, or the Divisional Court referred to in paragraph (*c*) of that subsection, as the case may be.

Amendments—Courts Act 1971, s 56(4), Sch 11; Supreme Court Act 1981, s 152(4), Sch 7.

Scope of provision—This section allows "leapfrog" appeals from a High Court judge to the House of Lords, thereby providing an exception to the general rule that all appeals to the House of Lords must be from the Court of Appeal (Appellate Jurisdiction Act 1876, s 3) and that appeals from the High Court are to the Court of Appeal (Supreme Court Act 1981, s 16). The judge may grant a certificate if the conditions set out in AJA 1969, s 12(1) are satisfied; see also s 15(3) for an additional requirement where leave to appeal is required in respect of the decision concerned. Where such a certificate is granted, the applicant can apply to the House of Lords for leave to appeal (s 13(2)). If leave is granted, no appeal may then lie to the Court of Appeal (s 13(2), (5)). For cases excluded from this section, see s 15. For a review of the operation of this section, see *Inland Revenue Commissioners v Church Commissioners for England* [1975] 1 WLR 251.

"wholly or mainly" (s 12(3)(*a*))—This phrase means "more than half" (*Fawcett Properties v Buckingham County Council* [1961] AC 636 at 669).

"fourteen days beginning with" (s 12(4))—In computing the period of 14 days, the day from which it runs is to be included (see *Hare v Gocher* [1962] 2 QB 641, [1962] 3 WLR 339; *Trow v Ind Coope (West Midlands)* [1967] 2 QB 899, [1967] 3 WLR 633, CA).

13 Leave to appeal to House of Lords

(1) Where in any proceedings the judge grants a certificate under section 12 of this Act, then, at any time within one month from the date on which that certificate is granted or such extended time as in any particular case the House of Lords may allow, any of the parties to the proceedings may make an application to the House of Lords under this section.

(2) Subject to the following provisions of this section, if on such an application it appears to the House of Lords to be expedient to do so, the House may grant leave for an appeal to be brought directly to the House; and where leave is granted under this section –

(*a*) no appeal from the decision of the judge to which the certificate relates shall lie to the Court of Appeal, but
(*b*) an appeal shall lie from that decision to the House of Lords.

(3) Applications under this section shall be determined without a hearing.

(4) Any order of the House of Lords which provides for applications under this section to be determined by a committee of the House –

(*a*) shall direct that the committee shall consist of or include not less than three of the persons designated as Lords of Appeal in accordance with section 5 of the Appellate Jurisdiction Act 1876, and
(*b*) may direct that the decision of the committee on any such application shall be taken on behalf of the House.

(5) Without prejudice to subsection (2) of this section, no appeal shall lie to the Court of Appeal from a decision of the judge in respect of which a certificate is granted under section 12 of this Act until –

(*a*) the time within which an application can be made under this section has expired, and
(*b*) where such an application is made, that application has been determined in accordance with the preceding provisions of this section.

Defined terms—"judge": s 12(8).

Scope of provision—A judge of the High Court may grant a certificate for a "leapfrog" appeal (s 12). This can be done only with the agreement of all the parties (s 12(1)(*c*)). Once the certificate has been granted, a party may apply to the House of Lords for leave to appeal (s 13(1)). Where leave has been granted, the appeal must be to the House of Lords and cannot to be to the Court of Appeal (s 13(2)). The appeal to the House of Lords thereafter follows the same procedure as an appeal from the Court of Appeal (s 14), and the procedure must be in accordance with the House of Lords Practice Directions and Standing Orders. If leave is refused or an application for leave has not been made within one month from the grant of the certificate, the applicant may appeal to the Court of Appeal (s 13(5)) in accordance with Supreme Court Act 1981, s 16.

"within one month from" (s 13(1))—In computing the period of one month, the day from which it runs is not to be included (see *Goldsmiths' Co v West Metropolitan Ry* [1904] 1 KB 1; *Stewart v Chapman* [1951] 2 KB 792, [1951] 2 All ER 613).

14 Appeal where leave granted

In relation to any appeal which lies to the House of Lords by virtue of subsection (2) of section 13 of this Act –

(*a*) section 4 of the Appellate Jurisdiction Act 1876 (which provides for the bringing of appeals to the House of Lords by way of petition),
(*b*) section 5 of that Act (which regulates the composition of the House for the hearing and determination of appeals), and
(*c*) except in so far as those orders otherwise provide, any orders of the House of Lords made with respect to the matters specified in section 11 of that Act (which relates to the procedure on appeals),

shall have effect as they have effect in relation to appeals under that Act.

Scope of provision—Where the House of Lords grants leave for an appeal to be brought directly from a judge of the High Court (pursuant to ss 12, 13), the appeal must be brought in the same way as an appeal from the Court of Appeal (see further s 13). For procedure see House of Lords Practice Directions.

15 Cases excluded from section 12

(1) No certificate shall be granted under section 12 of this Act in respect of a decision of the judge in any proceedings where by virtue of any enactment, apart from the provisions of this Part of this Act, no appeal would lie from that decision to the Court of Appeal, with or without the leave of the judge or of the Court of Appeal.

(2) No certificate shall be granted under section 12 of this Act in respect of a decision of the judge where –

(*a*) (*repealed*)
(*b*) by virtue of any enactment, apart from the provisions of this Part of this Act, no appeal would (with or without the leave of the Court of Appeal or of the House of Lords) lie from any decision of the Court of Appeal on an appeal from the decision of the judge.

(3) Where by virtue of any enactment, apart from the provisions of this Part of this Act, no appeal would lie to the Court of Appeal from the decision of the judge

PART II

except with the leave of the judge or of the Court of Appeal, no certificate shall be granted under section 12 of this Act in respect of that decision unless it appears to the judge that apart from the provisions of this Part of this Act it would be a proper case for granting such leave.

(4) No certificate shall be granted under section 12 of this Act where the decision of the judge, or any order made by him in pursuance of that decision, is made in the exercise of jurisdiction to punish for contempt of court.

Amendments—Administration of Justice Act 1977, s 32, Sch 5.

Scope of provision—This section has the effect of preventing the procedure for a "leapfrog" appeal from conferring a right of appeal which would not otherwise exist, either from the High Court to the Court of Appeal (s 15(3)) or from the Court of Appeal to the House of Lords (s 15(2)(*b*)).

Administration of Justice Act 1970

****

SCHEDULE 8

MAINTENANCE ORDERS FOR PURPOSES OF 1958 ACT AND PART II OF THIS ACT

1 An order for alimony, maintenance or other payments made, or having effect as if made, under Part II of the Matrimonial Causes Act 1965 (ancillary relief in actions for divorce etc).

2 An order for payments to or in respect of a child being an order made, or having effect as if made, under Part III of the said Act of 1965 (maintenance of children following divorce, etc).

2A An order for periodical or other payments made, or having effect as if made, under Part II of the Matrimonial Causes Act 1973.

3 An order for maintenance or other payments to or in respect of a spouse or child being an order made under Part I of the Domestic Proceedings and Magistrates' Courts Act 1978.

4 An order for periodical or other payments made or having effect as if made under Schedule 1 to the Children Act 1989.

5 (*repealed*)

6 An order –

(*a*) made or having effect as if made under paragraph 23 of Schedule 2 to the Children Act 1989; or

(*b*) made under section 23 of the Ministry of Social Security Act 1966, section 18 of the Supplementary Benefits Act 1976, section 24 of the Social Security Act 1986 or section 106 of the Social Security Administration Act 1992 (various provisions for obtaining contributions from a person whose dependants are assisted or maintained out of public funds).

7 An order under section 43 of the National Assistance Act 1948 (recovery of costs of maintaining assisted person).

8 An order to which section 16 of the Maintenance Orders Act 1950 applies by virtue of subsection (2)(*b*) or (*c*) of that section (that is to say an order made by a court in Scotland or Northern Ireland and corresponding to one of those specified in the foregoing paragraphs) and which has been registered in a court in England and Wales under Part II of that Act.

9 A maintenance order within the meaning of the Maintenance Orders (Facilities for Enforcement) Act 1920 (Commonwealth orders enforceable in the United Kingdom) registered in, or confirmed by, a court in England and Wales under that Act.

10 An order for periodical or other payments made under Part I of the Matrimonial Proceedings and Property Act 1970.

11 A maintenance order within the meaning of Part I of the Maintenance Orders (Reciprocal Enforcement) Act 1972 registered in a magistrates' court under the said Part I.

12 (*repealed*)

13 A maintenance order within the meaning of Part I of the Civil Jurisdiction and Judgments Act 1982, which is registered in a magistrates' court under that Part.

13A A maintenance judgment within the meaning of Council Regulation (EC) No 44/2001 of 22 December 2000 on jurisdiction and the recognition and enforcement of judgments in civil and commercial matters, which is registered in a magistrates' court under that Regulation.

14 An order for periodical or other payments made under Part III of the Matrimonial and Family Proceedings Act 1984.

Amendments—Matrimonial Proceedings and Property Act 1970, s 42(1), Sch 2, para 5; Maintenance Orders (Reciprocal Enforcement) Act 1972, s 22(1), Sch, para 6; Matrimonial Causes Act 1973, s 54(1), Sch 2, para 10(2); Supplementary Benefits Act 1976, s 35(2), Sch 7, para 17; Domestic Proceedings and Magistrates' Courts Act 1978, s 89, Sch 2, para 26; Civil Jurisdiction and Judgments Act 1982, s 15(4), Sch 12, para 5; Matrimonial and Family Proceedings Act 1984, s 46(1), Sch 1, para 8; Social Security Act 1986, s 86, Sch 10, para 42; Family Law Reform Act 1987, s 33(1), Sch 2, para 27, Sch 4; Courts and Legal Services Act

1990, s 116, Sch 16, paras 6, 37; Social Security (Consequential Provisions) Act 1992, s 4, Sch 2, para 7; SI 2001/3929.

Adoption Act 1976

ARRANGEMENT OF SECTIONS

PART I
THE ADOPTION SERVICE

The Adoption Service

PART II
ADOPTION ORDERS

The making of adoption orders

Supplemental

PART III
CARE AND PROTECTION OF CHILDREN AWAITING ADOPTION

Restrictions on removal of children

Protected children

PART IV
STATUS OF ADOPTED CHILDREN

PART V
REGISTRATION AND REVOCATION OF ADOPTION ORDERS AND CONVENTION ADOPTIONS

PART VI
MISCELLANEOUS AND SUPPLEMENTAL

PART I
THE ADOPTION SERVICE

The Adoption Service

1 Establishment of Adoption Service

(1) It is the duty of every local authority to establish and maintain within their area a service designed to meet the needs, in relation to adoption, of –

(*a*) children who have been or may be adopted,
(*b*) parents and guardians of such children, and
(*c*) persons who have adopted or may adopt a child,

and for that purpose to provide the requisite facilities, or secure that they are provided by approved adoption societies.

(2) The facilities to be provided as part of the service maintained under subsection (1) include –

(*a*) temporary board and lodging where needed by pregnant women, mothers or children;
(*b*) arrangements for assessing children and prospective adopters, and placing children for adoption;
(*c*) counselling for persons with problems relating to adoption.

(3) The facilities of the service maintained under subsection (1) shall be provided in conjunction with the local authority's other social services and with approved adoption societies in their area, so that help may be given in a co-ordinated manner without duplication, omission or avoidable delay.

(3A) In this Part, references to adoption are to the adoption of children, wherever they may be habitually resident, effected under the law of any country or territory, whether within or outside the British Islands.

(4) The services maintained by local authorities under subsection (1) may be collectively referred to as "the Adoption Service", and a local authority or approved adoption society may be referred to as an adoption agency.

Amendments—Adoption (Intercountry Aspects) Act 1999, s 9.

2 Local authorities' social services

The social services referred to in section 1(3) are the functions of a local authority which are social services functions within the meaning of the Local Authority Social Services Act 1970, including, in particular but without prejudice to the generality of the foregoing, a local authority's functions –

(*a*) under the Children Act 1989, relating to family assistance orders, local authority support for children and families, care and supervision and emergency protection of children, community homes, voluntary homes and organisations, private children's homes, private arrangements for fostering children, child minding and day care for young children and children accommodated by Health Authorities, Special Health Authorities, Primary Care Trusts, National Health Service trusts and local education authorities or in care homes, independent hospitals or schools; and

(*b*) under the National Health Service Act 1977, relating to the provision of care for expectant and nursing mothers.

Amendments—CA 1989, s 88(1), Sch 10, para 1; National Health Service and Community Care Act 1990, s 66(1), Sch 9, para 17; Health Authorities Act 1995, s 2, Sch 1, para 101; Local Government Act 2000, s 107(1), Sch 5, para 16; SI 2000/90; Care Standards Act 2000, s 116, Sch 4, para 5.

Adoption societies

3 Approval of adoption societies

(1) Subject to regulations under section 9(1), a body which is a voluntary organisation and desires to act as an adoption society or, if it is already an adoption society, desires to continue to act as such may, in the manner specified by regulations made by the Secretary of State, apply to the Secretary of State for his approval to its doing so.

(2) On an application under subsection (1), the Secretary of State shall take into account the matters relating to the applicant specified in subsections (3) to (5) and any other relevant considerations, and if, but only if, he is satisfied that the applicant is likely to make, or, if the applicant is an approved adoption society, is making, an effective contribution to the Adoption Service he shall by notice to the applicant give his approval, which shall be operative from a date specified in the notice or, in the case of a renewal of approval, from the date of the notice.

(3) In considering the application, the Secretary of State shall have regard, in relation to the period for which approval is sought, to the following –

(*a*) the applicant's adoption programme, including, in particular, its ability to make provision for children who are free for adoption,

(*b*) the number and qualifications of its staff,

(*c*) its financial resources, and

(*d*) the organisation and control of its operations.

(4) Where it appears to the Secretary of State that the applicant is likely to operate extensively within the area of a particular local authority he shall ask the authority

whether they support the application, and shall take account of any views about it put to him by the authority.

(5) Where the applicant is already an approved adoption society or, whether before or after the passing of this Act, previously acted as an adoption society, the Secretary of State, in considering the application, shall also have regard to the record and reputation of the applicant in the adoption field, and the areas within which and the scale on which it is currently operating or has operated in the past.

(6) If after considering the application the Secretary of State is not satisfied that the applicant is likely to make or, as the case may be, is making an effective contribution to the Adoption Service, the Secretary of State shall, subject to section 5(1) and (2), by notice inform the applicant that its application is refused.

(7) If not withdrawn earlier under section 4, approval given under this section shall last for a period of three years from the date on which it becomes operative, and shall then expire or, in the case of an approved adoption society whose further application for approval is pending at that time, shall expire on the date that application is granted or, as the case may be, refused.

Amendments—Health and Social Services and Social Security Adjudications Act 1983, s 9, Sch 2, para 29.

4 Withdrawal of approval

(1) If, while approval of a body under section 3 is operative, it appears to the Secretary of State that the body is not making an effective contribution to the Adoption Service he shall, subject to section 5(3) and (4), by notice to the body, withdraw the approval from a date specified in the notice.

(2) If an approved adoption society fails to provide the Secretary of State with information required by him for the purpose of carrying out his functions under subsection (1), or fails to verify such information in the manner required by him, he may by notice to the society withdraw the approval from a date specified in the notice.

(3) Where approval is withdrawn under subsection (1) or (2) or expires the Secretary of State may direct the body concerned to make such arrangements as to children who are in its care and other transitional matters as seem to him expedient.

5 Procedure on refusal to approve, or withdrawal of approval from, adoption societies

(1) Before notifying a body which has applied for approval that the application is refused in accordance with section 3(6) the Secretary of State shall serve on the applicant a notice –

- (*a*) setting out the reasons why he proposes to refuse the application;
- (*b*) informing the applicant that it may make representations in writing to the Secretary of State within 28 days of the date of service of the notice.

(2) If any representations are made by the applicant in accordance with subsection (1), the Secretary of State shall give further consideration to the application taking into account those representations.

(3) The Secretary of State shall, before withdrawing approval of an adoption society in accordance with section 4(1), serve on the society a notice –

- (*a*) setting out the reasons why he proposes to withdraw the approval; and (*b*) informing the society that it may make representations in writing to the Secretary of State within 28 days of the date of service of the notice.

(4) If any representations are made by the society in accordance with subsection (3), the Secretary of State shall give further consideration to the withdrawal of approval under section 4(1) taking into account those representations.

(5) This section does not apply where the Secretary of State, after having considered any representations made by the applicant in accordance with this section, proposes to refuse approval or, as the case may be, to withdraw approval for reasons which have already been communicated to the applicant in a notice under this section.

Welfare of children

6 Duty to promote welfare of child

In reaching any decision relating to the adoption of a child a court or adoption agency shall have regard to all the circumstances, first consideration being given to the need to safeguard and promote the welfare of the child throughout his childhood; and shall so far as practicable ascertain the wishes and feelings of the child regarding the decision and give due consideration to them, having regard to his age and understanding.

Defined terms—"adoption agency": s 1(4), "child": s 72(1); "court": s 62.

"any decision"—This section does not apply to the court's decision on an application to dispense with a parent's consent on the ground that it is being withheld unreasonably under AA 1976, s 16(2)(*b*) (*Re P (An Infant) (Adoption: Parental Consent)* [1977] Fam 25, [1977] 1 All ER 182).

"first consideration"—The welfare principle in CA 1989, s 1 requires the court to give "paramount consideration" to a child's welfare – that approach is materially different from the test in this section (*Re B (Adoption: Child's Welfare)* [1995] 1 FLR 895). The distinction between "first consideration" and "paramount consideration" was drawn by Lord Simon in *Re D (An Infant) (Parent's Consent)* [1977] 1 All ER 145.

Where a court is considering consolidated applications under CA 1989 and AA 1976 relating to more than one child, the welfare of any child who is the subject of a CA 1989 application will have paramountcy over the welfare of a child who is subject only to an application under AA 1976 where there is a conflict of interests between the children (*Re T and E (Proceedings: Conflicting Interests)* [1995] 1 FLR 581).

The balancing exercise required by AA 1976, s 6 does not differ in substance from the exercise undertaken to ensure that a decision is compatible with ECHR Art 8 and represents the court's considered view on proportionality (*Re B (Adoption: Natural Parent)* [2001] UKHL 70, [2002] 1 FLR 196).

Inter-country adoption—In an international case, the court may consider the status of adoption in the home country, questions of immigration status and public policy and the social consequences of adoption (*Re B (Adoption: Child's Welfare)* [1995] 1 FLR 895).

The welfare duty (s 6) is geographically wide-ranging. References in AA 1976, Pt I to "adoption" are to the adoption of children, wherever they may be habitually resident, effected under the law of any country or territory, whether within or outside the British Islands (s 1(3A)).

When considering the adoption of a child who is a foreign national, the court should investigate whether the arrangements culminating in the adoption application are a sham, or made for convenience, and are unsupported by the fundamental foundation of the creation of a psychological relationship between parent and child; such applications will always fail. Soundly based applications, which are tainted by elements of deception, will be judged on their merits (*Re H (Adoption: Non-Patrial)* [1996] 2 FLR 187 as clarified by *Re J (Adoption: Non-Patrial)* [1998] 1 FLR 225). The court cannot ignore the benefits which will accrue to a child as a result of a change of immigration status; such benefits must be taken into account (*Re B (A Minor) (Adoption Order: Nationality)* [1999] 1 FLR 907, HL).

In *Re R (Inter-Country Adoptions: Practice)* [1999] 1 FLR 1042, Bracewell J gave detailed guidance upon the procedure for inter-country adoptions (see relevant annotation under s 16). In such cases there is a duty on the applicants to make full, frank and timely disclosure of any relevant information. The duty imposed on the court by s 6 applies to decisions made at a directions hearing, which may include the summary dismissal of the application. Comprehensive guidance on intercountry adoption is published by the DOH – "*Intercountry Adoption Guide – Practice and Procedures*" – the Guide is available on the Internet at *www.doh.gov.uk/adoption*.

Where an order made in a foreign jurisdiction purports to remove the parental rights of either parent it will be for the courts in England and Wales to determine whether that person no longer has parental responsibility as a consequence of the foreign order. The court will require expert evidence relating to the foreign jurisdiction at an early stage in the proceedings (*Re AMR (Adoption: Procedure)* [1999] 2 FLR 807).

"throughout his childhood"—The court must have regard to the long-term welfare of the child (see *Re D* above) and not just the short-term position which might be considered under CA 1989, s 1 (see *T v T (Minors: Custody Appeal)* [1987] 1 FLR 374). A benefit arising from adoption which might accrue to the child after the age of 18 is a relevant factor to be taken into account in deciding whether to make an adoption order (*Re D (A Minor) (Adoption Order: Validity)* [1991] 2 FLR 66).

"wishes and feelings of the child"—If a child is old enough to understand the broad implications of adoption, the court will require some fairly clear reason to justify proceeding against his expressed wishes and feelings (*Re D (Minors) (Adoption by Step-parent)* (1981) FLR 102 at 105D).

There is no "welfare checklist" included in AA 1976 as there is in CA 1989, s 1; however, the court is required to ascertain, so far as practicable, the child's wishes and feelings and give them due consideration, having regard to his age and understanding. Cases decided under CA 1989 on the weight to be given to a child's wishes and feelings are likely to be relevant in adoption law (see *M v M (Transfer of Custody: Appeal)* [1987] 2 FLR 146; *Re P (A Minor) (Education)* [1992] 1 FLR 316; *Re S (Minors) (Access: Religious Upbringing)* [1992] 2 FLR 313; *Re P (Minors) (Wardship: Care and Control)* [1992] 2 FCR 681).

Parental order under HFEA 1990, s 30—By virtue of the Parental Orders (Human Fertilisation and Embryology) Regulations 1994, the provisions of this section are modified so as to apply to an application for a parental order, thereby emphasising the need for the court to take account of all the circumstances, and to give first consideration to the need to safeguard and promote the welfare of the child who is the subject of the application, notwithstanding the fact that the child will be genetically related to at least one of the applicants. Except in such cases as *Re W (Minors) (Surrogacy)* [1991] 1 FLR 385, which have been awaiting the entry into force of HFEA 1990, s 30, the child in an application for a parental order will generally be too young to express any wish or feelings but, even in relation to a young child, it would be open to the court to infer the child's feelings from evidence concerning the child's reactions to, and relationships with, the applicants/respondents in the case.

7 Religious upbringing of adopted child

An adoption agency shall in placing a child for adoption have regard (so far as is practicable) to any wishes of a child's parents and guardians as to the religious upbringing of the child.

Supplemental

8 Inactive or defunct adoption societies

(1) If it appears to the Secretary of State that an approved adoption society, or one in relation to which approval has been withdrawn under section 4 or has expired, is inactive or defunct he may, in relation to any child who is or was in the care of the society, direct what appears to him to be the appropriate local authority to take any such action as might have been taken by the society or by the society jointly with the authority, and if apart from this section the authority would not be entitled to

take that action, or would not be entitled to take it without joining the society in the action, it shall be entitled to do so.

(2) Before giving a direction under subsection (1) the Secretary of State shall, if practicable, consult both the society and the authority.

9 Regulation of adoption agencies

(1) The Secretary of State may by regulations prohibit unincorporated bodies from applying for approval under section 3; and he shall not approve any unincorporated body whose application is contrary to regulations made under this subsection.

(2) The appropriate Minister may make regulations for any purpose relating to the exercise of its functions by an approved adoption society.

(3) The appropriate Minister may make regulations with respect to the exercise by local authorities of their functions of making or participating in arrangements for the adoption of children.

(4) Any person who contravenes or fails to comply with regulations made under subsection (2) shall be guilty of an offence and liable on summary conviction to a fine not exceeding level 5 on the standard scale.

(5) In this section and section 9A, "the appropriate Minister" means –

(*a*) in relation to England, the Secretary of State,
(*b*) in relation to Wales, the National Assembly for Wales,

and in relation to England and Wales, means the Secretary of State and the Assembly acting jointly.

Amendments—Criminal Justice Act 1982, ss 38, 46; Adoption and Children Act 2002, s 139(2), Sch 4, para 4.

10 (*repealed*)

11 Restriction on arranging adoptions and placing of children

(1) A person other than an adoption agency shall not make arrangements for the adoption of a child, or place a child for adoption, unless –

(*a*) the proposed adopter is a relative of the child, or
(*b*) he is acting in pursuance of an order of the High Court.

(2) An adoption society which is –

(*a*) approved as respects Scotland under section 3 of the Adoption (Scotland) Act 1978; or
(*b*) registered as respects Northern Ireland under Article 4 of the Adoption (Northern Ireland) Order 1987,

but which is not approved under section 3 of this Act, shall not act as an adoption society in England and Wales except to the extent that the society considers it necessary to do so in the interests of a person mentioned in section 1 of the Act of 1978 or Article 3 of the Order of 1987.

(3) A person who –

(*a*) takes part in the management or control of a body of persons which exists wholly or partly for the purpose of making arrangements for the adoption of children and which is not an adoption agency; or

(*b*) contravenes subsection (1) or
(*c*) receives a child placed with him in contravention of subsection (1),

shall be guilty of an offence and liable on summary conviction to imprisonment for a term not exceeding 3 months or to a fine not exceeding level 5 on the standard scale or to both.

(4) In any proceedings for an offence under paragraph (*a*) of subsection (3), proof of things done or of words written, spoken or published (whether or not in the presence of any party to the proceedings) by any person taking part in the management or control of a body of persons, or in making arrangements for the adoption of children on behalf of the body, shall be admissible as evidence of the purpose for which that body exists.

(5) (*repealed*)

Amendments—Criminal Justice Act 1982, ss 38, 46; CA 1989, ss 88(1), 108(7), Sch 10, para 2, Sch 15.

Defined terms—"adoption": s 1(3A); "adoption agency": ss 1(4) and 72(1) (see note to s 57(3A)); "adoption order", "adoption society", "body of persons", "child", "local authority": s 72(1); "making arrangements": s 72(3); "relative": s 72(1).

Scope of provision—References in AA 1976, s 11 to "adoption" are to the adoption of children, wherever they may be habitually resident, effected under the law of any country or territory, whether within or outside the British Islands (s 1(3A)).

General—The courts have developed an approach to "illegal placements" which does not necessarily mean that an adoption application founded on one will fail (see *Re S (Arrangements for Adoption)* [1985] FLR 579; *Gatehouse v Robinson and Robinson* [1986] 1 FLR 504; *Re C (Adoption: Legality)* [1999] 1 FLR 370). A breach of s 11(1) is not an absolute bar to obtaining an adoption order. The court does not have power to give retrospective sanction to an illegal placement. Where an illegal placement has taken place, the court, in deciding whether to make an adoption order, must give first consideration to the welfare of the child, but must also take account of, and balance, all of the circumstances including the public policy consideration of allowing an application which is founded upon the illegal conduct of the applicants (*Re G (Adoption: Illegal Placement)* [1995] 1 FLR 403; *Re C (Adoption: Legality)* [1999] 1 FLR 370).

Where there may have been an illegal placement, the proceedings are "appropriate for determination in the High Court" and should be commenced in, or transferred to, that court (Children (Allocation of Proceedings) Order 1991, art 12; (*Re G (Adoption: Illegal Placement)*, above).

Where a child has not been placed for adoption by an adoption agency, the Schedule 2 report provided to the court by the relevant local authority must give an account of its investigations into whether there has been an illegal placement (AR 1984, r 22(2); MC(A)R 1984, r 22(2)).

Prosecution—All agencies should inform the police in all cases where there is reason to believe that criminal offences under AA 1976, ss 11 and 57 or under Immigration Act 1971, s 25 may have been committed. The AA 1976 offences are summary and must be prosecuted within six months of commission; prompt reporting is therefore essential (*Re R (Inter-Country Adoptions: Practice)* [1999] 1 FLR 1042).

"make arrangements for the adoption of a child" (s 11(1))—A person is deemed to make arrangements for the adoption of a child if he enters into or makes any agreement for, or for facilitating, the adoption of the child by any other person, whether the adoption is effected, or to be effected, in Great Britain or elsewhere, or if he initiates or takes part in any negotiations to conclude an agreement or arrangement for adoption, or if he causes another person to do so, whether the child is in the UK or overseas (s 72(3), (3A); *Flintshire CC v K* [2001] 2 FLR 476). A third party who approaches an adoption agency on behalf of a disabled parent does not act in breach of s 11(1) (*Re W (Arrangements to Place for Adoption)* [1995] 1 FLR 163).

PART II
ADOPTION ORDERS

The making of adoption orders

12 Adoption orders

(1) An adoption order is an order giving parental responsibility for a child to the adopters, made on their application by an authorised court.

(2) The order does not affect parental responsibility so far as it relates to any period before the making of the order.

(3) The making of an adoption order operates to extinguish –

(*a*) the parental responsibility which any person has for the child immediately before the making of the order;

(*aa*) any order under the Children Act 1989; and

(*b*) any duty arising by virtue of an agreement or the order of a court to make payments, so far as the payments are in respect of the child's maintenance or upbringing for any period after the making of the order.

(4) Subsection (3)(*b*) does not apply to a duty arising by virtue of an agreement –

(*a*) which constitutes a trust, or

(*b*) which expressly provides that the duty is not to be extinguished by the making of an adoption order.

(5) An adoption order may not be made in relation to a child who is or has been married.

(6) An adoption order may contain such terms and conditions as the court thinks fit.

(7) An adoption order may be made notwithstanding that the child is already an adopted child.

Amendments—CA 1989, s 88(1), Sch 10, para 3.

Defined terms—"adoption order": s 72(1); "authorised court": s 62(2); "child", "guardian": s 72(1); "parental responsibility": CA 1989, s 3.

Scope of provision—This section describes the legal consequences of the making of an adoption order; prevents the adoption of a child who has been married; permits the attaching of terms and conditions to an adoption order; and makes it clear that a child may be adopted more than once. Once made, an adoption order is irrevocable save in wholly exceptional circumstances (*Re M (Minors) (Adoption)* [1991] 1 FLR 458) or on the child's subsequent legitimation (AA 1976, s 52).

Procedure on the making of an adoption application—The relevant procedure is contained in AR 1984, r 15 and MC(A)R 1984, r 15 (see under AR 1984, r 15). For "authorised court", see under AR 1984, r 4.

"extinguish" (s 12(3))—One effect of this provision is that a natural parent ceases to be regarded as a parent under CA 1989, and can only apply for subsequent s 8 orders with the leave of the court (see CA 1989, ss 9, 10; *M v C and Calderdale Metropolitan Borough Council* [1993] 1 FLR 505). A natural parent will require leave to apply for a contact order post-adoption (see **Meaning of parent** under CA 1989, s 10).

"any order under the Children Act 1989" (s 12(3)(*aa*))—If it is intended that a pre-adoption CA 1989 order (eg a s 8 contact order) is to continue after adoption, a fresh order will have to be made after the adoption order.

"terms and conditions" and CA 1989, s 8 contact orders (s 12(6))—The addition of terms and conditions is subject to the court's duty to give first consideration to the welfare of the child (AA 1976, s 6; *Re C (A Minor) (Adoption Order: Condition)* [1986] 1 FLR 315). The addition of terms and conditions to an adoption order is rare; pre-CA 1989, conditions as to access/contact were sometimes made (see *Re C* (above)), but the better course would seem to be for contact orders to be made in appropriate cases under CA 1989, s 8. Where adopters are willing to agree to contact, it is unnecessary to make an order that binds the adopters to their agreement (*Re T (Adoption: Contact)* [1995] 2 FLR 251).

Any condition imposed must not be inconsistent with the fundamental concept of adoption itself (*Re J (Adoption Order: Conditions)* [1973] Fam 106; *Re C (A Minor) (Wardship and Adoption)* (1981) FLR 177). As a last resort, terms and conditions or injunctions may be enforced by committal proceedings (*Re C (A Minor) (Adoption Order: Condition)* [1986] 1 FLR 315, *Re O (Contempt: Committal)* [1995] 2 FLR 767). Except in exceptional cases, the court should not attach a condition to an adoption order requiring the sending of cards, when this is not a matter agreed by the adopters (*Re D (A Minor) (Adoption Order: Conditions)* [1992] 1 FCR 461). Where the adopters are Jehovah's Witnesses, it is inappropriate to impose a condition, or extract undertakings, concerning the withholding of consent to blood transfusions for the child (*Re S (A Minor) (Blood Transfusion: Adoption Order Conditions)* [1994] 2 FLR 416).

Once an adoption order has been made, a fundamental question such as contact, even if confined to indirect contact, should only be subsequently reopened if there is some fundamental change in circumstances (*Re C (A Minor) (Adopted Child: Contact)* [1993] Fam 210, [1993] 2 FLR 431). In some cases, it may be necessary to transfer the case to the High Court, but that should not be the general rule; an application for leave to apply for contact should be served on the adoption agency (*Re T (Adopted Children: Contact)* [1995] 2 FLR 792). A natural family member, in order to obtain leave to apply for contact, must satisfy the court that any decision of the adopters to oppose contact is sufficiently contrary to the best interests of the child, or sufficiently unreasonable, to warrant the court overriding the discretion concerning contact conferred on the adopters by the adoption order (*Re S (Contact: Application by Sibling)* [1998] 2 FLR 897).

The power to include terms and conditions does not extend to the inclusion of an injunction within the adoption order purporting to control contact between the child and others (*Re D (A Minor) (Adoption Order: Validity)* [1991] Fam 137, [1991] 2 FLR 66). If an injunction is required, it may be achieved under the inherent jurisdiction of the High Court (see, for example, *Re O (Contempt: Committal)* [1995] 2 FLR 767). A non-molestation order may be made in adoption proceedings (FLA 1996, ss 42(2)(*b*), 63(2)).

Effect of adoption—See AA 1976, ss 39–44. The court does not have an inherent power to set aside an adoption order, but an appeal may be allowed in an exceptional case where there has been a breach of natural justice against a natural parent (*Re K (Adoption and Wardship)* [1997] 2 FLR 221; *Re B (Adoption: Jurisdiction to Set Aside)* [1995] 2 FLR 1).

Parental order under HFEA 1990, s 30—By virtue of the Parental Orders (Human Fertilisation and Embryology) Regulations 1994, this provision is modified so as to identify some of the legal consequences of the making of a parental order; see also under s 39. A parental order gives to the husband and wife (ie the commissioning couple) parental responsibility for the child who is the subject of the proceedings, and extinguishes the parental responsibility of the surrogate mother and her husband or partner. It also extinguishes any orders made under CA 1989, s 8 and any duty or liability to provide maintenance for the child. The order cannot be made retrospectively, and has effect from the date when it is made.

13 Child to live with adopters before order is made

(1) Where –

(*a*) the applicant, or one of the applicants, is a parent, step-parent or relative of the child, or

(*b*) the child was placed with the applicants by an adoption agency or in pursuance of an order of the High Court,

an adoption order shall not be made unless the child is at least 19 weeks old and at all times during the preceding 13 weeks had his home with the applicants or one of them.

(2) Where subsection (1) does not apply, an adoption order shall not be made unless the child is at least 12 months old and at all times during the preceding 12 months had his home with the applicants or one of them.

(3) An adoption order shall not be made unless the court is satisfied that sufficient opportunities to see the child with the applicant or, in the case of an application by a married couple, both applicants together in the home environment have been afforded –

(*a*) where the child was placed with the applicant by an adoption agency, to that agency, or
(*b*) in any other case, to the local authority within whose area the home is.

Prospective amendment by Adoption (Intercountry Aspects) Act 1999—By virtue of A(IA)A 1999, s 11 (when in force), insert after subsection (3):

"(4) In relation to –

(*a*) an adoption proposed to be effected by a Convention adoption order; or
(*b*) an adoption of a child habitually resident outside the British Islands which is proposed to be effected by an adoption order other than a Convention adoption order,

subsection (1) shall have effect as if the reference to the preceding 13 weeks were a reference to the preceding six months.".

Defined terms—"adoption agency": ss 1(4), 72(1); "adoption order", "child", "local authority": s 72(1); "months": Interpretation Act 1978, s 5, Sch 1; "parent", "relative": s 72(1).

"had his home with the applicants or one of them" (s 13(1), (2))—The question of where a child has had his home is one of fact. Even if the child is physically absent, he may still be held to have his home with the applicants if they remain in effective parental control of him (*Re CSC (An Infant)* [1960] 1 WLR 304; *Re B (An Infant) (No 2)* [1964] Ch 1; *Re KT (Adoption Application)* (1992) Adoption and Fostering 58). The absence of the child at boarding school or hospital is to be disregarded (AA 1976, s 72(1A)).

"sufficient opportunities to see the child ... in the home environment" (s 13(3))—This requirement, coupled with s 22, means that, where the child has not been placed for adoption by an adoption agency, the applicant must have a "home" within England and Wales (ie within the area of a local authority (defined in s 72(1)). Where the applicant is domiciled in England and Wales but resident abroad, with no home in England and Wales, the court does not have jurisdiction to make an adoption order (*Re Y (Minors) (Adoption: Jurisdiction)* [1986] 1 FLR 152).

14 Adoption by married couple

(1) An adoption order shall not be made on the application of more than one person except in the circumstances specified in subsections (1A) and (1B).

(1A) An adoption order may be made on the application of a married couple where both the husband and the wife have attained the age of 21 years.

(1B) An adoption order may be made on the application of a married couple where –

(*a*) the husband or the wife –
(i) is the father or mother of the child; and
(ii) has attained the age of 18 years;
and
(*b*) his or her spouse has attained the age of 21 years.

(2) An adoption order shall not be made on the application of a married couple unless –

(*a*) at least one of them is domiciled in a part of the United Kingdom, or in the Channel Islands or the Isle of Man, or

(*b*) the application is for a Convention adoption order and section 17 is complied with.

(3) (*repealed*)

Amendments—CA 1989, ss 88(1), 108(7), Sch 10, para 4, Sch 15.

Prospective amendment by Adoption (Intercountry Aspects) Act 1999—By virtue of A(IA)A 1999, s 15(1), Sch 2, para 3(1) (which come into force on 1 June 2003), in subsection (2)(*b*) for "section 17 is" substitute "the requirements of regulations under section 17 are".

Defined terms—"adoption order", "child", "Convention adoption order": s 72(1); "United Kingdom": Interpretation Act 1978, Sch 1.

General—An adoption order may only be made in favour of a sole applicant (see s 15) or a married couple. An order may not be made in favour of an unmarried couple, although one partner in such a relationship may apply as a single applicant. In certain limited circumstances, a married person may apply as a sole applicant (see s 15(1)(*b*)).

"attained the age of ..." (s 14(1A), (1B))—An age is attained at the commencement of the relevant anniversary of the person's date of birth (Family Law Reform Act 1969, s 9(1)).

Each married applicant must have attained the age of 21 years, except where one applicant is the mother or father of the child, in which case the mother or father must have attained the age of 18 years.

"father ... of the child" (s 14(1B))—In this Act, the term "father" includes a natural father who was not married, or deemed to be married, to the child's mother at the time of the child's birth (see "parent" and "relative" in s 72(1)).

Validity of marriage—The validity of the applicant's marriage is a factor which the court will consider. Documentary evidence of their marriage must be filed with the application (AR 1984, r 15(4)). The adoption agency is required to report on the applicant's marital status and the stability of their relationship, together with details of any previous marriages (ibid, Sch 2). The court may make an adoption order in favour of married applicants even where the couple have separated after the adoption application has been issued (*Re WM (Adoption: Non-patrial)* [1997] 1 FLR 132). If an adoption order is made in favour of a couple whose marriage is later found to be bigamous, the adoption order will be regarded as valid until the court makes an order setting it aside (*Re F (Infants) (Adoption Order: Validity)* [1977] Fam 165).

Step-parents (s 14(3))—The repeal of s 14(3) means that there is no longer a requirement for the court to adopt a specific approach to an application by a step-parent. However, this repeal does not imply that earlier cautionary dicta concerning step-parent adoptions no longer apply (*Re PJ (Adoption: Practice on Appeal)* [1998] 2 FLR 252; see also *Re G (Adoption Order)* [1999] 1 FLR 400). It is still considered comparatively unusual for an adoption order to be made in favour of a step-parent in a contested case, particularly where the parents have been married, even where the child consents (*Re B (Adoption: Father's Objections)* [1999] 2 FLR 215). Although a step-parent adoption does amount to an interference with a father's right to family life, the decision falls within the state's margin of appreciation and the adverse affects on the father are not disproportionate to protecting the child's interests. There is no breach of Article 8 of the ECHR (*Söderbäck v Sweden* [1999] 1 FLR 250).

Domicile (s 14(2))—At least one of the married applicants must be domiciled in a part of the UK, the Channel Islands or the Isle of Man, unless the application is for a Convention adoption order (see s 17).

For discussion of "domicile", see under Domicile and Matrimonial Proceedings Act 1973, s 5.

"Child outside Great Britain"—Where the child is not in Great Britain when the application is made (for example in the Isle of Man or Northern Ireland), the application must be made to the High Court (s 62(3)), but in an ordinary case the proceedings should be immediately transferred to a local county court (*Re J (Adoption Procedure: Isle of Man)* [2000] 2 FLR 633).

15 Adoption by one person

(1) An adoption order may be made on the application of one person where he has attained the age of 21 years and –

(*a*) is not married, or

(*b*) is married and the court is satisfied that –

(i) his spouse cannot be found, or

(ii) the spouses have separated and are living apart, and the separation is likely to be permanent, or

(iii) his spouse is by reason of ill-health, whether physical or mental, incapable of making an application for an adoption order.

(2) An adoption order shall not be made on the application of one person unless –

(*a*) he is domiciled in a part of the United Kingdom, or in the Channel Islands or the Isle of Man, or

(*b*) the application is for a Convention adoption order and section 17 is complied with.

(3) An adoption order shall not be made on the application of the mother or father of the child alone unless the court is satisfied that –

(*a*) the other natural parent is dead or cannot be found or, by virtue of section 28 of the Human Fertilisation and Embryology Act 1990, there is no other parent, or

(*b*) there is some other reason justifying the exclusion of the other natural parent,

and where such an order is made the reason justifying the exclusion of the other natural parent shall be recorded by the court.

(4) (*repealed*)

Amendments—CA 1989, s 108(7), Sch 15; Human Fertilisation and Embryology Act 1990, s 49(5), Sch 4, para 4.

Prospective amendment by Adoption (Intercountry Aspects) Act 1999—By virtue of A(IA)A 1999, s 15(1), Sch 2, para 3(2) (which come into force on 1 June 2003), in subsection (2)(*b*) for "section 17 is" substitute "the requirements of regulations under section 17 are".

Defined terms—"adoption order", "child", "Convention adoption order": s 72(1); "United Kingdom": Interpretation Act 1978, Sch 1.

General—See under s 14.

Age (s 15(1))—Any sole adoption applicant must have attained the age of 21 years. If the applicant is the mother or father of the child, the 21-year limit still applies.

Step-parents—See under s 14.

Domicile (s 15(2))—See under s 14.

"father of the child" (s 15(3))—See under s 14.

Adoption by parent (s 15(3))—Where the applicant relies upon "some other reason for excluding the other parent", that reason must be sufficient to outweigh the adverse consequences an adoption order may have by reason of the exclusion of the other parent from the child's life. The other reason, which is likely to be exceptional, and which will depend on the circumstances of each case, does not have to be comparable with the death or disappearance of the other parent. Before making an order, the court must consider alternative orders under CA 1989; an adoption order is not to be used simply to prevent inappropriate intervention by the other parent (*Re B (Adoption: Natural Parent)* [2001] UKHL 70, [2002] 1 FLR 196).

Human Fertilisation and Embryology Act 1990, s 28 (s 15(3))—That section defines the meaning of "father" under that Act.

Unmarried couple—An adoption order may not be made in relation to both partners of an unmarried couple, however, on making an adoption order to one partner, the court may go on to make a joint residence order for both partners (*Re AB (Adoption: Joint Residence)* [1996] 1 FLR 27). A homosexual applicant is not excluded from applying for an adoption order, whether as a sole carer or as one partner in a cohabiting relationship (*Re W (Adoption: Homosexual Adopter)* [1997] 2 FLR 406).

16 Parental agreement

(1) An adoption order shall not be made unless –

(*a*) the child is free for adoption by virtue of an order made –

(i) in England and Wales, under section 18;

(ii) in Scotland, under section 18 of the Adoption (Scotland) Act 1978; or

(iii) in Northern Ireland, under Article 17(1) or 18(1) of the Adoption (Northern Ireland) Order 1987; or

(*b*) in the case of each parent or guardian of the child the court is satisfied that –

(i) he freely, and with full understanding of what is involved, agrees unconditionally to the making of an adoption order (whether or not he knows the identity of the applicants), or

(ii) his agreement to the making of the adoption order should be dispensed with on a ground specified in subsection (2).

(2) The grounds mentioned in subsection (1)(*b*)(ii) are that the parent or guardian –

(*a*) cannot be found or is incapable of giving agreement;

(*b*) is withholding his agreement unreasonably;

(*c*) has persistently failed without reasonable cause to discharge his parental responsibility for the child;

(*d*) has abandoned or neglected the child;

(*e*) has persistently ill-treated the child;

(*f*) has seriously ill-treated the child (subject to subsection (5)).

(3) Subsection (1) does not apply in any case where the child is not a United Kingdom national and the application for the adoption order is for a Convention adoption order.

(4) Agreement is ineffective for the purposes of subsection (1)(*b*)(i) if given by the mother less than six weeks after the child's birth.

(5) Subsection (2)(*f*) does not apply unless (because of the ill-treatment or for other reasons) the rehabilitation of the child within the household of the parent or guardian is unlikely.

Amendments—CA 1989, s 88(1), Sch 10, para 5.

Prospective amendment by Adoption (Intercountry Aspects) Act 1999—By virtue of A(IA)A 1999, s 15, Sch 2, para 3(3), Sch 3 (which come into force on 1 June 2003), subsection (3) is repealed.

Defined terms—"adoption order", "child", "Convention adoption order", "free for adoption", "guardian", "parent": s 72(1); "United Kingdom": Interpretation Act 1978, Sch 1; "United Kingdom national": s 72(1).

Scope of provision—A child may only be adopted if both of his parents or guardians have freely and with full understanding given their unconditional consent to adoption, or the court has dispensed with the need for each such consent on one of the grounds set out in this section. Where a child is freed for adoption (AA 1976, s 18), the question of parental consent will be finalised by the making of the freeing order (s 16(1)); otherwise, the provisions of s 16 must be satisfied before an adoption order is made.

"free for adoption" (s 16(1)(*a*))—See s 18. The provisions in this section apply in relation to parental consent where there is an application to free for adoption as well as to an application for an adoption order where the child has not already been freed for adoption.

"parent"—The definition in s 72(1) covers "any parent who has parental responsibility for the child under CA 1989". The following people are therefore included within the meaning of "parent" for the purposes of AA 1976:

(*a*) the child's natural mother;

(*b*) the child's natural father:

- (i) if he was married to the child's mother at the time of the child's birth;
- (ii) if he subsequently married the child's mother (Legitimacy Act 1976, s 2; Family Law Reform Act 1987);
- (iii) if he has obtained an order granting him parental responsibility with respect to the child (CA 1989, ss 4(1), 11(1));
- (iv) if, before the commencement of CA 1989, he has obtained an order granting him parental rights and duties in respect of the child (under the now repealed FLRA 1987, s 4 and CA 1989, Sch 14, para 4);
- (v) if he has acquired parental responsibility for the child under a parental responsibility agreement made with the mother (CA 1989, s 4(1)(*b*));

(*c*) the child's adoptive parent if he has been the subject of a previous adoption; in those circumstances, the consent of the child's natural parents would not be relevant.

Firm evidence is required to prove that a parent has died (*Re K (Adoption and Wardship)* [1997] 2 FLR 221).

Unmarried father—The consent of the father of a child who was not married to the child's mother, or deemed to be so married, at the time of the child's birth (under FLRA 1987, s 1) is not required within adoption proceedings unless he has obtained parental responsibility for the child (see **"parent"** above).

An unmarried father is not required to be made a respondent to the adoption or freeing application (AR 1984, rr 4(2), 15(2); MC(A)R 1984, rr 4(2), 15(2)); see under AR 1984, r 4.

The child's unmarried father is no longer automatically included in the definition of "guardian" under AA 1976, s 72(1), as amended.

"guardian"—Section 72(1) provides that, unless the context otherwise requires, "guardian" has the same meaning as in the CA 1989 (see CA 1989, ss 5, 105, Sch 10, para 30).

Where a person, or institution, has been appointed to be a child's guardian by an order made in a foreign jurisdiction, it will be for the court in England and Wales (based on legal expert evidence as to the foreign jurisdiction) to determine whether the "guardian" is a guardian under AA 1976 (*Re AMR (Adoption: Procedure)* [1999] 2 FLR 807 and *Re AGN (Adoption: Foreign Adoption)* [2000] 2 FLR 431).

A foreign guardian must either agree to the adoption or their consent must be dispensed with. They must be served with notice of the proceedings (*Re D (Adoption: Foreign Guardianship)* above).

When considering whether a person or authority in another jurisdiction is or is not to be treated as a guardian under AA 1976, s 16, the court should consider:

(i) the extent to which that person's duties, rights and responsibilities equated to those of a person (*a*) who had parental responsibility in English Law and (*b*) whose consent to an adoption order had to be given or dispensed with;

(ii) having particular regard to the purposes of s 16, whether in all the circumstances that person's consent to an adoption order should be given or dispensed with before an adoption order was made.

(*Re J (Adoption: Consent of Foreign Public Authority)* [2002] EWHC 766 (Fam), [2002] 2 FLR 618).

"agrees ... to the making of an adoption order" (s 16(1)(*b*))—In the case of an application to free a child for adoption, the relevant agreement will be to adoption in general. A parent consenting to adoption at the freeing stage must clearly understand that their parental responsibility for, and future involvement with, the child will be extinguished on the making of the freeing order (*Re A* (unreported) 29 November 2000, CA). In the case of an application for adoption, the agreement will be to the particular adoption applied for (whether or not the parent knows the identity of the applicants). The agreement must be to an adoption made in England and Wales (*Re G (Foreign Adoption: Consent)* [1995] 2 FLR 534).

An agreement, once given, may be withdrawn at any stage prior to the making of an adoption or freeing order (*Re F (An Infant)* [1957] 1 All ER 819). However, a later withdrawal may have a significant bearing on the question of dispensation of consent (*Re H (Infants) (Adoption: Parental Consent)* [1977] 2 All ER 339; *Re P (Adoption: Parental Agreement)* [1985] FLR 635; *Re R (A Minor) (Adoption) (No 2)* [1987] FCR 113).

"agrees unconditionally" (s 16(1)(*b*))—The agreement to adoption must be unconditional; however, if the parent or guardian has any wish with regard to the religious upbringing of the child, the adoption agency must have regard to that wish, so far as is practicable, when placing the child (s 7).

Form and proof of agreement—See under AR 1984, rr 8, 20 and MC(A)R 1984, rr 8, 20.

Inter-country adoptions—For detailed guidance on inter-country adoptions, see the Intercountry Adoption (Hague Convention) Regulations 2003, the "*Intercountry Adoption Guide – Practice and Procedures*" published by the DOH (available on the Internet at *www.doh.gov.uk/adoption*) and *Re R (Inter-Country Adoptions: Practice)* [1999] 1 FLR 1042: on being notified of a foreign child's presence a local authority should immediately attempt to contact natural parents to ascertain their views; if it appears that natural parents do not consent, the local authority should immediately inform the DOH and the Home Office; where the applicants cannot produce written parental consent to adoption (and a certified English translation), the application should be transferred to the High Court for urgent directions; there should be personal service on the natural parents (if necessary via the relevant British Embassy); the children's guardian should make early contact with the natural parents; where it appears that the natural parents oppose the adoption the court should consider dismissing the application summarily at an early directions hearing.

Effect of giving agreement—The act of giving consent to adoption materially affects the rights of the parent or guardian and the child's carer. While an application for an adoption order is pending, in a case where a parent or guardian of the child has agreed to the making of an adoption order, the parent or guardian is not entitled, against the will of the person with whom the child has his home, to remove the child from that home without the leave of the court (AA 1976, s 27; see *Re T (A Minor) (Adoption: Parental Consent)* [1986] 1 All ER 817).

Dispensing with agreement (s 16(1)(*b*))—Dispensing with agreement involves the court in a two-stage process:

(*a*) is adoption in the best interests of the child?

(*b*) if so, is a ground, or are grounds, for dispensation proved on the balance of probabilities?

These two stages are separate and must be considered by the court in the sequence set out above (*Re D (A Minor) (Adoption: Freeing Order)* [1991] 1 FLR 48), at the time when the court is considering making a freeing or an adoption order (*Devon County Council v B* [1997] 1 FLR 591).

The Court of Appeal has held that where parental consent is withheld in a case where the child's home is in issue the judge must first consider where the child is to live. In the light of that decision, the question of whether the parent's consent is unreasonably withheld will follow (*Re O (Adoption: Withholding Agreement)* [1999] 1 FLR 451).

Where an order made in a foreign jurisdiction purports to remove the parental rights of either parent, it will be for the courts in England and Wales to determine whether that person no longer has parental responsibility as a consequence of the foreign order. The court will require expert evidence relating to the foreign jurisdiction at an early stage of the proceedings (*Re AMR (Adoption: Procedure)* [1999] 2 FLR 807).

For procedure where an application is made to dispense with consent, see AR 1984, rr 7, 19 and MC(A)R 1984, rr 7, 19.

Dispensing with agreement is a judicial act which has a direct bearing on the propriety and validity of an adoption order and ought therefore to be recorded in the court's order (*S v Huddersfield Borough Council* [1975] Fam 113).

Grounds for dispensing with agreement (s 16(2))—For full discussion of the grounds for dispensing with agreement, see *Children Law and Practice* (Family Law), paras H[118]–[151].

Withholding agreement unreasonably (s 16(2)(*b*))—The leading authority on the test to be applied by the court is the House of Lords' decision in *Re W (An Infant)* [1971] 2 All ER 49. The test as it was cast in *Re W*, and as it has been refined in many subsequent decisions, has a number of important components, each of which must be considered in every case in which this ground is relied on. The components are:

(*a*) the reasonableness of the parent's refusal to consent is judged as at the date of the hearing (*Re W* (above); *Re S (An Infant) (Adoption: Parental Consent)* [1973] 3 All ER 88; *Re L (A Minor) (Adoption: Statutory Criteria)* [1990] 1 FLR 305) and in the light of, and at the conclusion of, all the evidence, but not in the light of the judgment of the court or any findings of fact (*Re M (Adoption or Residence Order)* [1998] 1 FLR 570);

(*b*) the judge must take account of all the circumstances of the case (*Re W* (above); *O'Connor v A and B* [1971] 2 All ER 1230);

(*c*) whilst the welfare of the child must be taken into account, it is not the sole or necessarily paramount criterion (*Re W* (above); *O'Connor v A and B* (above); *Re L (A Minor) (Adoption: Statutory Criteria)* [1990] 1 FLR 305);

(*d*) the test is an objective test – could a reasonable parent in the position of this parent withhold consent? (*Re W (An Infant)* [1971] 2 All ER 49; *Re D (An Infant) (Adoption: Parent's Consent)* [1977] 1 All ER 145, *Re E (Adoption: Freeing Order)* [1995] 1 FLR 382 at 390F);

(*e*) the test is reasonableness and not anything else (*Re W (An Infant)* [1971] 2 All ER 49; *Re El-G (Minors) (Wardship and Adoption)* (1983) FLR 589);

(*f*) the court must be wary not to substitute its own view for that of the reasonable parent (*Re W (An Infant)* [1971] 2 All ER 49; *Re E (A Minor) (Adoption)* [1989] 1 FLR 126; *Re L (A Minor) (Adoption: Statutory Criteria)* [1990] 1 FLR 305) but the court may determine where the child is to live (if in issue) before considering a parent's reasonableness (*Re O (Adoption: Withholding Agreement)* [1999] 1 FLR 451). The court must also be wary of relying too heavily upon the views of the children's guardian (*Re PJ (Adoption: Practice on Appeal)* [1998] 2 FLR 252). However a parent, whose objections to adoption are shared by experienced professionals (for example the children's guardian and a child psychiatrist), cannot be regarded as unreasonable (*Re B (Adoption Order)* [2001] 2 FLR 26);

(*g*) there is a band of differing decisions, each of which may be reasonable in a given case (*Re W (An Infant)* [1971] 2 All ER 49; *Re H and Re W (Adoption: Parental Agreement)* (1983) FLR 614; *Re BA (Wardship and Adoption)* [1985] FLR 1008; *Re E (Adoption: Freeing Order)* [1995] 1 FLR 382).

For full discussion of withholding agreement unreasonably, see *Children Law and Practice* (Family Law) paras H[123]–[145].

In *Re F (Adoption: Freeing Order)* [2000] 2 FLR 505 the Court of Appeal expressly commended the approach described in *Re C (A Minor) (Adoption: Parental Agreement: Contact)* [1993] 2 FLR 260 which suggested that the test may be approached by the judge asking himself whether, having regard to the evidence and applying the current values of our society, the advantages of adoption for the welfare of the child appear sufficiently strong to justify overriding the views and interests of the objecting parent.

17 Convention adoption orders

(1) An adoption order shall be made as a Convention adoption order if the application is for a Convention adoption order and the following conditions are satisfied both at the time of the application and when the order is made.

(2) The child –

(*a*) must be a United Kingdom national or a national of a Convention country, and

(*b*) must habitually reside in British territory or a Convention country.

(3) The applicant or applicants and the child must not all be United Kingdom nationals living in British territory.

(4) If the application is by a married couple, either –

(*a*) each must be a United Kingdom national or a national of a Convention country, and both must habitually reside in Great Britain, or

(*b*) both must be United Kingdom nationals, and each must habitually reside in British territory or a Convention country, and if the applicants are nationals of the same Convention country the adoption must not be prohibited by a specified provision (as defined in subsection (8)) of the internal law of that country.

(5) If the application is by one person, either –

(*a*) he must be a national of a Convention country, and must habitually reside in Great Britain, or

(*b*) he must be a United Kingdom national and must habitually reside in British territory or a Convention country,

and if he is a national of a Convention country the adoption must not be prohibited by a specified provision (as defined in subsection (8)) of the internal law of that country.

(6) If the child is not a United Kingdom national the order shall not be made –

(*a*) except in accordance with the provisions, if any, relating to consents and consultations of the internal law relating to adoption of the Convention country of which the child is a national, and

(*b*) unless the court is satisfied that each person who consents to the order in accordance with that internal law does so with full understanding of what is involved.

(7) The reference to consents and consultations in subsection (6) does not include a reference to consent by and consultation with the applicant and members of the applicant's family (including his or her spouse), and for the purposes of subsection (6) consents may be proved in the manner prescribed by rules and the court shall be treated as the authority by whom, under the law mentioned in subsection (6), consents may be dispensed with and the adoption in question may be effected; and where the provisions there mentioned require the attendance before that authority of any person who does not reside in Great Britain, that requirement shall be treated as satisfied for the purposes of subsection (6) if –

(*a*) that person has been given a reasonable opportunity of communicating his opinion on the adoption in question to the proper officer or clerk of the court, or to an appropriate authority of the country in question, for transmission to the court; and

(*b*) where he has availed himself of that opportunity, his opinion has been transmitted to the court.

(8) In subsections (4) and (5) "specified provision" means a provision specified in an order of the Secretary of State as one notified to the Government of the United Kingdom in pursuance of the provisions of the Convention which relate to prohibitions on an adoption contained in the national law of the Convention country in question.

Prospective amendment by Adoption (Intercountry Aspects) Act 1999—By virtue of A(IA)A 1999, s 3 (which comes into force on 1 June 2003), section 17 is substituted as follows:

"17 Convention adoption orders

An adoption order shall be made as a Convention adoption order if –

(*a*) the application is for a Convention adoption order; and

(*b*) such requirements as may be prescribed by regulations made by the Secretary of State are complied with.".

Defined terms—"adoption order", "British territory", "child", "Convention adoption order": s 72(1); "Great Britain": Interpretation Act 1978, Sch 1; "guardian", "parent": s 72(1); "United Kingdom": IA 1978, Sch 1; "United Kingdom national": s 72(1).

Scope of provision—This section implements in English law the Hague Convention on Jurisdiction, Applicable Law and Recognition of Decrees relating to Adoption (Cmnd 7342), which the UK ratified on 24 August 1978 and which came into force in the UK from 23 October 1978 (Convention Adoption (Austria and Switzerland) Order 1978). The Convention has only been ratified by the UK, Austria and Switzerland. The aim of the Convention is to ease and simplify the application for, and recognition of, adoption orders granted in respect of applicants and children who are nationals or habitual residents of different countries in which the Convention is in force (see DHSS circular LAC (78)19 for a general explanation of the Convention). Very few Convention adoption orders have been made. The relevant procedure is governed by AR 1984, rr 27–36.

When the Adoption (Intercountry Aspects) Act 1999 is brought into force on 1 June 2003, the present law on Convention adoptions will be repealed and replaced by provisions implementing the 1993 Hague Convention on Intercountry Adoption.

Freeing for adoption

18 Freeing child for adoption

(1) Where, on an application by an adoption agency, an authorised court is satisfied in the case of each parent or guardian of the child that –

(*a*) he freely, and with full understanding of what is involved, agrees generally and unconditionally to the making of an adoption order, or

(*b*) his agreement to the making of an adoption order should be dispensed with on a ground specified in section 16(2),

the court shall make an order declaring the child free for adoption.

(2) No application shall be made under subsection (1) unless –

(*a*) it is made with the consent of a parent or guardian of a child, or

(*b*) the adoption agency is applying for dispensation under subsection (1)(*b*) of the agreement of each parent or guardian of the child, and the child is in the care of the adoption agency.

(2A) For the purposes of subsection (2) a child is in the care of an adoption agency if the adoption agency is a local authority and he is in their care.

(3) No agreement required under subsection (1)(*a*) shall be dispensed with under subsection (1)(*b*) unless the child is already placed for adoption or the court is satisfied that it is likely that the child will be placed for adoption.

(4) An agreement by the mother of the child is ineffective for the purposes of this section if given less than 6 weeks after the child's birth.

(5) On the making of an order under this section, parental responsibility for the child is given to the adoption agency, and subsections (2) to (4) of section 12 apply as if the order were an adoption order and the agency were the adopters.

(6) Before making an order under this section, the court shall satisfy itself, in relation to each parent or guardian of the child who can be found, that he has been given an opportunity of making, if he so wishes, a declaration that he prefers not to be involved in future questions concerning the adoption of the child; and any such declaration shall be recorded by the court.

(7) Before making an order under this section in the case of a child whose father does not have parental responsibility for him, the court shall satisfy itself in relation to any person claiming to be the father that –

(*a*) he has no intention of applying for –

(i) an order under section 4(1) of the Children Act 1989, or

(ii) a residence order under section 10 of that Act, or

(*b*) if he did make any such application, it would be likely to be refused.

(8) Subsections (5) and (7) of section 12 apply in relation to the making of an order under this section as they apply in relation to the making of an order under that section.

Amendments—Health and Social Services and Social Security Adjudications Act 1983, s 9, Sch 2, para 31; CA 1989, s 88(1), Sch 10, para 6.

Defined terms—"adoption agency": ss 1(4), 72(1); "adoption order", "authorised court", "child", "Convention adoption order", "guardian", "local authority", "parent", "parental responsibility": s 72(1).

Scope of provision—This section provides for an authorised court to make an order declaring a child to be free for adoption. The principal effect of such an order is that the requirements regarding the parent's or guardian's consent in respect of any subsequent adoption application are satisfied and, subject to a successful application to revoke the order, the parent will have no rights or role in relation to any such adoption application. On the making of a freeing order, parental responsibility for the child is given to the applicant adoption agency. Parental responsibility that vested in any person immediately before the order was made is extinguished. If the child was the subject of a care order, that order ceases to have effect on the making of a freeing for adoption order. A freeing order may be made to facilitate the prospect of an adoption in a foreign jurisdiction (*Re S (Freeing for Adoption)* [2002] EWCA Civ 798, [2002] 2 FLR 681).

"... on an application by an adoption agency ..." (s 18(1))—For procedure, see AR 1984, Pt II and MC(A)R 1984, Pt II.

The application may only be made by an adoption agency, ie a local authority or an adoption society (AA 1976, s 1(4)).

Parental agreement—See under s 16. In a freeing application, the relevant agreement is to adoption generally rather than a particular adoption application. Where there is an issue as to contact, that can be dealt with by the same court that is seised of the freeing application (*Re A (A Minor) (Adoption: Contact Order)* [1993] 2 FLR 645).

Preconditions for a freeing application—An order declaring a child free for adoption may only be made if the following preconditions are satisfied:

(*a*) one of the parents or guardians of the child must consent to the freeing application being made or the child must be subject to a care order (s 18(2));

(*b*) the agreement of each parent or guardian of the child must either be given or dispensed with by the court (s 18(1));

(*c*) if there is an application to dispense with parental consent, the court must be satisfied that the child is already placed for adoption or that it is likely that he will be placed for adoption (s 18(3));

(*d*) each parent or guardian must have been given an opportunity to make a declaration concerning his involvement in future questions about the child (s 18(6));

(*e*) the court must be satisfied that any person claiming to be the father of the child, who does not have parental responsibility, has no intention of applying for a parental responsibility order or a residence order (CA 1989, ss 4, 10), or that, if he did make such an application, it would be likely to be refused (AA 1976, s 18(7)).

"... the court shall make an order declaring the child free for adoption" (s 18(1))—Whilst the wording of this provision suggests that, where the court is satisfied that either the parental consent to adoption is given, or that it should be dispensed with, the court must go on to make a freeing order, it has been held that the welfare test in s 6 applies, and adoption must be seen to be in the child's best interests before the question of the parent's consent is considered (*Re W (A Minor) (Wardship: Jurisdiction)* [1985] 1 All ER 1001; *Re PB (A Minor) (Application to Free for Adoption)* [1985] FLR 394; *Re D (A Minor) (Adoption: Freeing Order)* [1991] 1 FLR 48).

"... the child is in the care of the adoption agency" (s 18(2))—A child is only "in the care of" an adoption agency if the agency is a local authority and he is in its care under a care order or interim care order (s 18(2A); CA 1989, ss 31(11), 105(1)). Thus, adoption societies (or local authorities who are only accommodating a child) may only apply for a freeing order if one of the parents agrees to the making of the freeing application.

"parental responsibility is given to the adoption agency" (s 18(5))—The parental responsibility vested in the applicant adoption agency by a freeing order may subsequently be transferred to another adoption agency under s 21. For procedure, see AR 1984, r 13 and MC(A)R 1984, r 13.

Freeing and contact orders—When making a freeing for adoption order, the court has jurisdiction to make orders for contact under CA 1989, s 8 (CA 1989, ss 8(3), 10(1)). After the conclusion of the proceedings, the court does not retain jurisdiction to make s 8 orders in the absence of continuing "family proceedings", and a local authority is prevented from making an application to vary any s 8 contact order that has been made (*Re C (Contact: Jurisdiction)* [1995] 1 FLR 777). For the potential relevance of continued contact to the question of dispensing with parental consent on a freeing application, see *Re P (Adoption: Freeing Order)* [1994] 2 FLR 1000.

Parental declaration that "he prefers not to be involved in future questions concerning the adoption of the child" (s 18(6))—After a child has been freed for adoption, the former parent or guardian will retain some limited rights under s 19 pending the making of an adoption order. Those rights will not exist if the parent or guardian has made a declaration under s 18(6); see s 19(1). See also under AR 1984, r 5(4).

"a child whose father does not have parental responsibility" (s 18(7))—The position of a natural father without parental responsibility must be considered. The court may direct that he be given notice of the proceedings under AR 1984, r 9(3) or r 21(5) and he may be made a party. As a matter of practice such a father should be informed of the proceedings unless for good reasons the court decides that it is not appropriate to do so. Where a mother refuses to disclose the father's identity, her reasons must be carefully considered and, unless the reasons are cogent, it is wise at an early stage for the adoption agency to consider applying to the court for directions on whether to notify the father (*Re H; Re G (Adoption: Consultation of Unmarried Fathers)* [2001] 1 FLR 646; *Re M (Adoption: Rights of Natural Father)* [2001] 1 FLR 745).

There was no duty on a local authority, children's guardian or the court to inform or consult members of a child's extended family where the family were ignorant of the child's existence and the mother was adamant that she did not wish her relatives to be contacted (*Z County Council v R* [2001] 1 FLR 365).

Application of AA 1976, s 12(5), (7) (s 18(8))—A child who has been married may not subsequently be freed for adoption (s 12(5)). A child who has been previously adopted may be freed for adoption (s 12(7)).

19 Progress reports to former parents

(1) This section and section 20 apply to any person ("the former parent"), who was required to be given an opportunity of making a declaration under section 18(6) but did not do so.

(2) Within the 14 days following the date 12 months after the making of the order under section 18 the adoption agency to which parental responsibility was given on the making of the order, unless it has previously by notice to the former parent informed him that an adoption order has been made in respect of the child, shall by notice to the former parent inform him –

(*a*) whether an adoption order has been made in respect of the child, and (if not)

(*b*) whether the child has his home with a person with whom he has been placed for adoption.

(3) If at the time when the former parent is given notice under subsection (2) an adoption order has not been made in respect of the child, it is thereafter the duty of the adoption agency to give notice to the former parent of the making of an adoption order (if and when made), and meanwhile to give the former parent notice whenever the child is placed for adoption or ceases to have his home with a person with whom he has been placed for adoption.

(4) If at any time the former parent by notice makes a declaration to the adoption agency that he prefers not to be involved in future questions concerning the adoption of the child –

(*a*) the agency shall secure that the declaration is recorded by the court which made the order under section 18, and
(*b*) the agency is released from the duty of complying further with subsection (3) as respects that former parent.

Amendments—CA 1989, s 88(1), Sch 10, para 7.

Defined terms—"adoption agency": ss 1(4), 72(1); "adoption order", "child": s 72(1); "has his home": s 72(1A); "parental responsibility": s 72(1).

Effect of provision—The importance of the provision is that such a former parent has the right to apply for the revocation of the freeing order if, at any time after the first anniversary of its making, no adoption order has been made in respect of the child and the child does not have his home with a person with whom he has been placed for adoption (s 20(1)).

"it is thereafter the duty of the adoption agency ..." (s 19(3))—The adoption agency's duty to give notice to a former parent whenever the child ceases to have his home with a person with whom he has been placed for adoption arises as soon as the quality of the placement changes from that of an adoptive placement, even if the child physically remains living in the same household for the time being (*R v Derbyshire County Council ex parte T* [1990] Fam 164, [1990] 1 FLR 237).

20 Revocation of s 18 order

(1) The former parent, at any time more than 12 months after the making of the order under section 18 when –

(*a*) no adoption order has been made in respect of the child, and
(*b*) the child does not have his home with a person with whom he has been placed for adoption,

may apply to the court which made the order for a further order revoking it on the ground that he wishes to resume parental responsibility.

(2) While the application is pending the adoption agency having parental responsibility shall not place the child for adoption without the leave of the court.

(3) The revocation of an order under section 18 ("a section 18 order") operates –

(*a*) to extinguish the parental responsibility given to the adoption agency under the section 18 order;
(*b*) to give parental responsibility for the child to –
  (i) the child's mother; and
  (ii) where the child's father and mother were married to each other at the time of his birth, the father; and
(*c*) to revive –
  (i) any parental responsibility agreement,
  (ii) any order under section 4(1) of the Children Act 1989, and
  (iii) any appointment of a guardian in respect of the child (whether made by a court or otherwise),

extinguished by the making of the section 18 order.

(3A) Subject to subsection (3)(*c*), the revocation does not –

(*a*) operate to revive –
  (i) any order under the Children Act 1989, or
  (ii) any duty referred to in section 12(3)(*b*),

extinguished by the making of the section 18 order; or

(*b*) affect any person's parental responsibility so far as it relates to the period between the making of the section 18 order and the date of revocation of that order.

(4) Subject to subsection (5), if the application is dismissed on the ground that to allow it would contravene the principle embodied in section 6 –

(*a*) the former parent who made the application shall not be entitled to make any further application under subsection (1) in respect of the child, and

(*b*) the adoption agency is released from the duty of complying further with section 19(3) as respects that parent.

(5) Subsection (4)(*a*) shall not apply where the court which dismissed the application gives leave to the former parent to make a further application under subsection (1), but such leave shall not be given unless it appears to the court that because of a change in circumstances or for any other reason it is proper to allow the application to be made.

Amendments—CA 1989, s 88(1), Sch 10, para 8.

Defined terms—"adoption agency": ss 1(4), 72(1); "child": s 72(1); "court"; s 62; "former parent": s 19(1); "has his home": s 72(1A); "local authority", "order freeing a child for adoption", "parental responsibility", "voluntary organisation": s 72(1).

Scope of provision—Where a child, who has been freed for adoption, has not been subsequently adopted and is not currently placed for adoption, his former parent may apply to revoke the freeing order after a period of 12 months has elapsed following its making. It is the circumstances at the time of the revocation application that are important. While such an application is pending, the adoption agency must not place the child for adoption without the leave of the court.

The approach of the court—In some cases, the legal position following a revocation will meet the needs of the child. In other cases, where, for example, it may be unsafe to return the child to his mother's care, the court is not confined to dealing with the matter solely under AA 1976. If the former parent is not, at the date of revocation, fit to have sole and unfettered responsibility, the court has jurisdiction to make the revocation order provided that the welfare of the child can be protected, whether by making the revocation of the freeing order conditional on such consequential orders as are appropriate under CA 1989 or under the inherent jurisdiction, or in some other way. Where it is proposed to make a care order, the proper course would be to order the revocation of the freeing order, such revocation to take effect on the making of a care order (*Re G (Adoption: Freeing Order)* [1997] 2 FLR 202, HL; *Re P* (*Minors*) (*Breakdown of Adoption Placement*) [1996] 3 FCR 657).

Procedure—On application for revocation, see AR 1984, r 12 and MC(A)R 1984, r 12. On application for leave to place for adoption, see AR 1984, r 47 and MC(A)R 1984, r 27.

Revocation under the inherent jurisdiction—Under the statutory scheme, the only potential applicant for a revocation order is a former parent who has not made a declaration under s 18(6). In all other cases the court may consider revoking a freeing order under the inherent jurisdiction (*Re C (Adoption: Freeing Order)* [1999] 1 FLR 348, FD; *Re J (Freeing for Adoption)* [2000] 2 FLR 58; *Oldham MBC v D* [2000] 2 FLR 382).

Effect of a revocation order (s 20(3), (3A))—If a freeing order is revoked, parental responsibility in relation to the child does not necessarily return to the persons who held it immediately prior to the making of the freeing order. A revocation order operates:

(*a*) to extinguish the parental responsibility given to the adoption agency under the freeing order;

(*b*) to give parental responsibility for the child to:

- (i) the child's mother; and
- (ii) where the parents were married to each other at the time of the child's birth, the father;

(*c*) to revive:

- (i) any parental responsibility agreement;

(ii) any parental responsibility order; and
(iii) any appointment of a guardian in respect of the child, extinguished by the freeing order.

21 Variation of s 18 order so as to substitute one adoption agency for another

(1) On an application to which this section applies, an authorised court may vary an order under section 18 so as to give parental responsibility for the child to another adoption agency ("the substitute agency") in place of the agency for the time being having parental responsibility for the child under the order ("the existing agency").

(2) This section applies to any application made jointly by –

(*a*) the existing agency; and
(*b*) the would-be substitute agency.

(3) Where an order under section 18 is varied under this section, section 19 shall apply as if the substitute agency had been given responsibility for the child on the making of the order.

Amendments—CA 1989, s 88(1), Sch 10, para 9.

Supplemental

22 Notification to local authority of adoption application

(1) An adoption order shall not be made in respect of a child who was not placed with the applicant by an adoption agency unless the applicant has, at least 3 months before the date of the order, given notice to the local authority within whose area he has his home of his intention to apply for the adoption order.

(1A) An application for such an adoption order shall not be made unless the person wishing to make the application has, within the period of two years preceding the making of the application, given notice as mentioned in subsection (1).

(1B) In subsections (1) and (1A) the references to the area in which the applicant or person has his home are references to the area in which he has his home at the time of giving the notice.

(2) On receipt of such a notice the local authority shall investigate the matter and submit to the court a report of their investigation.

(3) Under subsection (2), the local authority shall in particular investigate, –

(*a*) so far as is practicable, the suitability of the applicant, and any other matters relevant to the operation of section 6 in relation to the application; and
(*b*) whether the child was placed with the applicant in contravention of section 11.

(4) A local authority which receive notice under subsection (1) in respect of a child whom the authority know to be looked after by another local authority shall, not more than 7 days after the receipt of the notice, inform that other local authority in writing, that they have received the notice.

Amendments—CA 1989, s 88(1), Sch 10, para 10.

Defined terms—"adoption agency": ss 1(4), 72(1); "adoption order", "child", "local authority": s 72(1).

"notice to the local authority" (s 22(1))—The relevant local authority is the one in whose area the applicant has his home at the time of giving notice. Notice, which must be in writing (s 72), may be given by post (s 69). On notice being given, the child becomes a "protected child" (s 32). Upon receipt of a s 22 notice in relation to a privately fostered child of foreign nationality the local authority should immediately inform the DOH and clarify whether the intention to adopt was disclosed to an immigration officer. If it was not, or if the applicants are not able to produce written evidence of parental consent, or the applicants have not previously obtained a home study report, then any adoption application should be transferred to the High Court and listed for urgent directions before a judge (*Re R (Inter-Country Adoptions: Practice)* [1999] 1 FLR 1042).

23 Reports where child placed by agency

Where an application for an adoption order relates to a child placed by an adoption agency, the agency shall submit to the court a report on the suitability of the applicants and any other matters relevant to the operation of section 6, and shall assist the court in any manner the court may direct.

Report—See **Schedule 2 report** under Adoption Rules 1984, r 4.

24 Restrictions on making adoption orders

(1) The court shall not proceed to hear an application for an adoption order in relation to a child where a previous application for a British adoption order made in relation to the child by the same persons was refused by any court unless –

(*a*) in refusing the previous application the court directed that this subsection should not apply or

(*b*) it appears to the court that because of a change in circumstances or for any other reason it is proper to proceed with the application.

(2) The court shall not make an adoption order in relation to a child unless it is satisfied that the applicants have not, as respects the child, contravened section 57.

Amendments—Health and Social Services and Social Security Adjudications Act 1983, s 9, Sch 2, para 32.

Defined terms—"adoption order", "British adoption order", "child": s 72(1).

Scope of provision—This section deals with two separate matters: first, where a previous adoption application has failed, no subsequent application can be made by the same applicants in respect of the same child, unless the court gives leave to do so either at the time of dismissing the original application, or because there has been a change of circumstances, or some other reason making it proper to proceed; secondly, the section prohibits the making of an adoption order unless the court is satisfied that the applicants have not breached the prohibition on making certain payments in respect of the adoption of the child (under AA 1976, s 57).

Procedure in respect of AA 1976, s 24(1)—The court must conduct a preliminary examination of the application; see under AR 1984, r 16 and MC(A)R 1984, r 16.

Parental order under HFEA 1990, s 30—By virtue of the Parental Orders (Human Fertilisation and Embryology) Regulations 1994, this provision is modified so as to restrict the court from entertaining any subsequent application for a parental order where a previous application has been refused, unless the conditions set out in subsections (1)(*a*) or (*b*) are satisfied. It also reinforces the effect of HFEA 1990, s 30(7), by prohibiting the court from making an order unless it is satisfied that no payment of money or other benefit (other than expenses reasonably incurred) has been given or received by either or both of the applicants or the surrogate mother/parents. Where money or other benefit has changed hands, the court would be required to sanction the breach; see, further, **Payment of money or other benefit** under HFEA 1990, s 30.

25 Interim orders

(1) Where on an application for an adoption order the requirements of sections 16(1) and 22(1) are complied with, the court may postpone the determination of the application and make an order giving parental responsibility for the child to the applicants for a probationary period not exceeding 2 years upon such terms for the maintenance of the child and otherwise as the court thinks fit.

(2) Where the probationary period specified in an order under subsection (1) is less than 2 years, the court may by a further order extend the period to a duration not exceeding 2 years in all.

Amendments—CA 1989, s 88(1), Sch 10, para 11.

Defined terms—"adoption order", "child", "parental responsibility": s 72(1).

Scope of provision—This section allows the court to make an interim order, which is a parental responsibility order in favour of the applicants. It is not an adoption order, but can only be made if the provisions as to parental agreement (s 16) and notification to the local authority (s 22) have been satisfied. Interim orders are rarely made. The purpose of an interim adoption order is wholly different to that of an interim order under CA 1989 (*Re C and F (Adoption: Removal Notice)* [1997] 1 FLR 190).

"probationary period" (s 25(1))—In most cases, where the child has been placed by an adoption agency, the need for a probationary period is unlikely to arise. However, there may be cases where some aspect of the child's welfare requires investigation (see eg *Re AW (Adoption Application)* [1993] 1 FLR 62) where a period of further assessment may be needed. "Probationary" imports a process of investigation or experiment in relation to all the circumstances relevant to the proposed adoption, and not merely the suitability of the applicants (*S v Huddersfield Borough Council* [1975] Fam 113, [1974] 3 All ER 296).

"... giving parental responsibility for the child ..." (s 25(1))—As an alternative to making an interim order, the court has the power to make a residence order at any stage of an adoption application (CA 1989, s 8).

Procedure—See AR 1984, r 25 and MC(A)R 1984, r 25.

26 (*repealed*)

PART III
CARE AND PROTECTION OF CHILDREN AWAITING ADOPTION

Restrictions on removal of children

27 Restrictions on removal where adoption agreed or application made under s 18

(1) While an application for an adoption is pending in a case where a parent or guardian of the child has agreed to the making of the adoption order, (whether or not he knows the identity of the applicant), the parent or guardian is not entitled, against the will of the person with whom the child has his home, to remove the child from the home of that person except with the leave of the court.

(2) While an application is pending for an order freeing a child for adoption and –

(*a*) the child is in the care of the adoption agency making the application, and
(*b*) the application was not made with the consent of each parent or guardian of the child,

no parent or guardian of the child is entitled, against the will of the person with whom the child has his home, to remove the child from the home of that person except with the leave of the court.

(2A) For the purposes of subsection (2) a child is in the care of an adoption agency if the adoption agency is a local authority and he is in their care.

(3) Any person who contravenes subsection (1) or (2) shall be guilty of an offence and liable on summary conviction to imprisonment for a term not exceeding 3 months or a fine not exceeding level 5 on the standard scale or both.

(4), (5) (*repealed*)

Amendments—Criminal Justice Act 1982, ss 38, 46; Health and Social Services and Social Security Adjudications Act 1983, ss 9, 30, Sch 2, para 33, Sch 10, Pt I; CA 1989, s 88(1), Sch 10, paras 12, 13.

Procedure—See AR 1984, r 47; MC(A)R 1984, r 27.

Parental order under HFEA 1990, s 30—By virtue of the Parental Orders (Human Fertilisation and Embryology) Regulations 1994, this section is modified so as to ensure that, where an application for a parental order is pending, the child will not be removed from the care of the applicants except with the leave of the court. For the procedure to be followed when making an application for leave, see FPR 1991, r 4A.10 or FPC(CA 1989)R 1991, r 21J.

28 Restrictions on removal where applicant has provided home for 5 years

(1) While an application for an adoption order in respect of a child made by the person with whom the child has had his home for the 5 years preceding the application is pending, no person is entitled, against the will of the applicant, to remove the child from the applicant's home except with the leave of the court or under authority conferred by any enactment or on the arrest of the child.

(2) Where a person ("the prospective adopter") gives notice to the local authority within whose area he has his home that he intends to apply for an adoption order in respect of a child who for the preceding 5 years has had his home with the prospective adopter, no person is entitled, against the will of the prospective adopter, to remove the child from the prospective adopter's home, except with the leave of a court or under authority conferred by any enactment or on the arrest of the child, before –

(*a*) the prospective adopter applies for the adoption order, or
(*b*) the period of 3 months from the receipt of the notice by the local authority expires,

whichever occurs first.

(2A) The reference in subsections (1) and (2) to any enactment does not include a reference to section 20(8) of the Children Act 1989.

(3) In any case where subsection (1) or (2) applies and –

(*a*) the child was being looked after by a local authority before he began to have his home with the applicant or, as the case may be, the prospective adopter, and
(*b*) the child is still being looked after by a local authority,

the authority which are looking after the child shall not remove him from the home of the applicant or the prospective adopter except in accordance with section 30 or 31 or with the leave of a court.

(4) In subsections (2) and (3) "a court" means a court with jurisdiction to make adoption orders.

(5) A local authority which receive such notice as is mentioned in subsection (2) in respect of a child whom the authority know to be looked after by another local authority shall, not more than 7 days after the receipt of the notice, inform that other authority, in writing, that they have received the notice.

(6) Subsection (2) does not apply to any further notice served by the prospective adopter on any local authority in respect of the same child during the period referred to in paragraph (*b*) of that subsection or within 28 days after its expiry.

(7) Any person who contravenes subsection (1) or (2) shall be guilty of an offence and liable on summary conviction to imprisonment for a term not exceeding 3 months or a fine not exceeding level 5 on the standard scale or both.

(8), (9) (*repealed*)

(10) The Secretary of State may by order amend subsection (1) or (2) to substitute a different period for the period of 5 years mentioned in that subsection (or the period which, by a previous order under this subsection, was substituted for that period).

Amendments—Criminal Justice Act 1982, ss 38, 46; Health and Social Services and Social Security Adjudications Act 1983, ss 9, 30, Sch 2, para 33, Sch 10, Pt I; CA 1989, ss 88(1), 108(7), Sch 10, paras 12, 14, Sch 15.

Procedure—See AR 1984, r 47, MC(A)R 1984, r 27.

29 Return of child taken away in breach of s 27 or 28

(1) An authorised court may, on the application of a person from whose home a child has been removed in breach of –

(*a*) section 27 or 28,
(*b*) section 27 or 28 of the Adoption (Scotland) Act 1978, or
(*c*) Article 28 or 29 of the Adoption (Northern Ireland) Order 1987,

order the person who has so removed the child to return the child to the applicant.

(2) An authorised court may, on the application of a person who has reasonable grounds for believing that another person is intending to remove a child from his home in breach of –

(*a*) section 27 or 28,
(*b*) section 27 or 28 of the Adoption (Scotland) Act 1978, or
(*c*) Article 28 or 29 of the Adoption (Northern Ireland) Order 1987,

by order direct that other person not to remove the child from the applicant's home in breach of any of those provisions.

(3) If, in the case of an order made by the High Court under subsection (1), the High Court or, in the case of an order made by a county court under subsection (1), a county court is satisfied that the child has not been returned to the applicant, the court may make an order authorising an officer of the court to search such premises as may be specified in the order for the child and, if the officer finds the child, to return the child to the applicant.

(4) If a justice of the peace is satisfied by information on oath that there are reasonable grounds for believing that a child to whom an order under subsection (1) relates is in premises specified in the information, he may issue a search

warrant authorising a constable to search the premises for the child; and if a constable acting in pursuance of a warrant under this section finds the child, he shall return the child to the person on whose application the order under subsection (1) was made.

(5) An order under subsection (3) may be enforced in like manner as a warrant for committal.

Amendments—CA 1989, s 88(1), Sch 10, para 15.

Procedure—See AR 1984, r 47, MC(A)R 1984, r 27.

Parental order under HFEA 1990, s 30—By virtue of the Parental Orders (Human Fertilisation and Embryology) Regulations 1994, this provision is modified so as to allow the applicants for a parental order to apply for, and empowers the court to order or issue, a warrant authorising an officer of the court to search premises specified in the order for the child and to remove the child and return him to the applicants. For the procedure to be followed, see FPR 1991, r 4A.10 or FPC(CA 1989)R 1991, r 21J.

30 Return of children placed for adoption by adoption agencies

(1) Subject to subsection (2), at any time after a child has been placed with any person in pursuance of arrangements made by an adoption agency for the adoption of the child by that person, and before an adoption order has been made on the application of that person in respect of the child, –

(*a*) that person may give notice to the agency of his intention not to give the child a home; or

(*b*) the agency may cause notice to be given to that person of their intention not to allow the child to remain in his home.

(2) No notice under paragraph (*b*) of subsection (1) shall be given in respect of a child in relation to whom an application has been made for an adoption order except with the leave of the court to which the application has been made.

(3) Where a notice is given to an adoption agency by any person or by an adoption agency to any person under subsection (1), or where an application for an adoption order made by any person in respect of a child placed with him by an adoption agency is refused by the court or withdrawn, that person shall, within 7 days after the date on which notice was given or the application refused or withdrawn, as the case may be, cause the child to be returned to the agency, who shall receive the child.

(4) Where the period specified in an interim order made under section 25 (whether as originally made or as extended under subsection (2) of that section) expires without an adoption order having been made in respect of the child, subsection (3) shall apply as if the application for an adoption order upon which the interim order was made, had been refused at the expiration of that period.

(5) It shall be sufficient compliance with the requirements of subsection (3) if the child is delivered to, and is received by, a suitable person nominated for the purpose by the adoption agency.

(6) Where an application for an adoption order is refused the court may, if it thinks fit at any time before the expiry of the period of 7 days mentioned in subsection (3), order that period to be extended to a duration, not exceeding 6 weeks, specified in the order.

(7) Any person who contravenes the provisions of this section shall be guilty of an offence and liable on summary conviction to imprisonment for a term not

exceeding 3 months or to a fine not exceeding level 5 on the standard scale or to both; and the court by which the offender is convicted may order the child in respect of whom the offence is committed to be returned to his parent or guardian or to the adoption agency which made the arrangements referred to in subsection (1).

Amendments—Criminal Justice Act 1982, ss 38, 46; CA 1989, s 88(1), Sch 10, para 16.

Procedure—See AR 1984, r 47, MC(A)R 1984, r 27.

Welfare of the child—In considering whether to grant leave for the removal of a child, the court must regard the child's welfare as its first consideration. The court must give most careful consideration to the plan of the local authority, but it is for the court to decide whether the plan should go ahead, or whether the child should remain in his current placement. A genuine application for adoption by a foster-parent with a reasonable prospect of success should normally be determined at a full hearing and not brought to a premature conclusion without a proper investigation (s 6; *Re C (A Minor) (Adoption)* [1994] 2 FLR 513).

Notice of intention to remove (s 30(1)(*b*))—If an adoption agency gives notice of intention to remove the child, and there is no adoption application pending, the court does not have jurisdiction under AA 1976 to intervene to prevent the removal of the child (*Re C and F (Adoption: Removal Notice)* [1997] 1 FLR 190). In such a case, the local authority *may* use the notice procedure under AA 1976, s 30, but is not obliged to do so (*Re C (Adoption: Notice)* [1999] 1 FLR 384).

31 Application of s 30 where child not placed for adoption

(1) Where a person gives notice in pursuance of section 22(1) to the local authority within whose area he has his home of his intention to apply for an adoption order in respect of a child –

(*a*) who is (when the notice is given) being looked after by a local authority; but

(*b*) who was placed with that person otherwise than in pursuance of such arrangements as are mentioned in section 30(1),

that section shall apply as if the child had been placed in pursuance of such arrangements except that where the application is refused by the court or withdrawn the child need not be returned to the local authority in whose care he is unless that authority so require.

(2) Where notice of intention is given as aforesaid in respect of any child who is (when the notice is given) being looked after by a local authority then, until the application for an adoption order has been made and disposed of, any right of the local authority to require the child to be returned to them otherwise than in pursuance of section 30 shall be suspended.

(3) While the child has his home with the person by whom the notice is given no contribution shall be payable (whether under a contribution order or otherwise) in respect of the child by any person liable under Part III of Schedule 2 to the Children Act 1989 to make contributions in respect of him (but without prejudice to the recovery of any sum due at the time the notice is given), unless 12 weeks have elapsed since the giving of the notice without the application being made or the application has been refused by the court or withdrawn.

(4) Nothing in this section affects the right of any person who has parental responsibility for a child to remove him under section 20(8) of the Children Act 1989.

Amendments—CA 1989, s 88(1), Sch 10, para 17.

Protected children

32 Meaning of "protected child"

(1) Where a person gives notice in pursuance of section 22(1) to the local authority within whose area he lives of his intention to apply for an adoption order in respect of a child, the child is for the purposes of this Part a protected child while he has his home with that person.

(2) A child shall be deemed to be a protected child for the purposes of this Part if he is a protected child within the meaning of –

(*a*) section 32 of the Adoption (Scotland) Act 1978; or
(*b*) Article 33 of the Adoption (Northern Ireland) Order 1987.

(3) A child is not a protected child by reason of any such notice as is mentioned in subsection (1) while –

(*a*) he is in the care of any person –
 (i) in any children's home in respect of which a person is registered under Part II of the Care Standards Act 2000;
 (ii) in any school in which he is receiving full-time education;
 (iii) in any health service hospital; or
(*b*) he is –
 (i) suffering from mental disorder within the meaning of the Mental Health Act 1983; and
 (ii) resident in a residential care home, within the meaning of Part I of Schedule 4 to the Health and Social Services and Social Security Adjudications Act 1983; or
(*c*) he is liable to be detained or subject to guardianship under the Mental Health Act 1983; or
(*d*) he is in the care of any person in any home or institution not specified in this subsection but provided, equipped and maintained by the Secretary of State.

(3A) In subsection (3) "children's home", "school" and "health service hospital" have the same meaning as in the Children Act 1989.

(4) A protected child ceases to be a protected child –

(*a*) on the grant or refusal of the application for an adoption order;
(*b*) on the notification to the local authority for the area where the child has his home that the application for an adoption order has been withdrawn;
(*c*) in a case where no application is made for an adoption order, on the expiry of the period of two years from the giving of the notice;
(*d*) on the making of a residence order, a care order or a supervision order under the Children Act 1989 in respect of the child;
(*e*) on the appointment of a guardian for him under that Act;
(*f*) on his attaining the age of 18 years; or
(*g*) on his marriage,

whichever first occurs.

(5) In subsection (4)(*d*) the references to a care order and a supervision order do not include references to an interim care order or interim supervision order.

Amendments—Health and Social Services and Social Security Adjudications Act 1983, s 29, Sch 9, para 19; Mental Health Act 1983, s 148, Sch 4, para 45; CA 1989, s 88(1), Sch 10, para 18; Care Standards Act 2000, s 116, Sch 4, para 5.

"mental disorder" (s 32(3)(*b*)(i))—By virtue of Mental Health Act 1983, s 1(2), this means "mental illness, arrested or incomplete development of mind, psychopathic disorder and any other disorder or disability of mind and 'mentally disordered' shall be construed accordingly". For a full explanation see the note to FPR 1991, r 9.1.

33 Duty of local authorities to secure well-being of protected children

(1) It shall be the duty of every local authority to secure that protected children within their area are visited from time to time by officers of the authority, who shall satisfy themselves as to the well-being of the children and give such advice as to their care and maintenance as may appear to be needed.

(2) Any officer of a local authority authorised to visit protected children may, after producing, if asked to do so, some duly authenticated document showing that he is so authorised, inspect any premises in the area of the authority in which such children are to be or are being kept.

34 (*repealed*)

35 Notices and information to be given to local authorities

(1) Where a person with whom a protected child has his home changes his permanent address he shall, not less than 2 weeks before the change, or, if the change is made in an emergency, not later than one week after the change, give notice specifying the new address to the local authority in whose area his permanent address is before the change, and if the new address is in the area of another local authority, the authority to whom the notice is given shall inform that other local authority and give them such of the following particulars as are known to them, that is to say –

(*a*) the name, sex and date and place of birth of the child;
(*b*) the name and address of every person who is a parent or guardian or acts as a guardian of the child or from whom the child was received.

(2) If a protected child dies, the person with whom he had his home at his death shall within 48 hours give notice of the child's death to the local authority.

Amendments—CA 1989, s 88(1), Sch 10, para 19.

36 Offences relating to protected children

(1) A person shall be guilty of an offence if –

(*a*) being required, under section 35 to give any notice or information, he fails to give the notice within the time specified in that provision or fails to give the information within a reasonable time, or knowingly makes or causes or procures another person to make any false or misleading statement in the notice of information;
(*b*) he refuses to allow the visiting of a protected child by a duly authorised officer of a local authority or the inspection, under the power conferred by section 33(2) of any premises;
(*c*) (*repealed*)

(2) A person guilty of an offence under this section shall be liable on summary conviction to imprisonment for a term not exceeding 3 months or a fine not exceeding level 5 on the standard scale or both.

Amendments—Criminal Justice Act 1982, ss 38, 46; CA 1989, s 108(7), Sch 15.

37 Miscellaneous provisions relating to protected children

(1) (*repealed*)

(2) A person who maintains a protected child shall be deemed for the purposes of the Life Assurance Act 1774 to have no interest in the life of the child.

(3), (4) (*repealed*)

Amendments—CA 1989, s 108(7), Sch 15.

PART IV
STATUS OF ADOPTED CHILDREN

38 Meaning of "adoption" in Part IV

(1) In this Part "adoption" means adoption –

(*a*) by an adoption order;
(*b*) by an order made under the Children Act 1975, the Adoption Act 1958, the Adoption Act 1950 or any enactment repealed by the Adoption Act 1950;
(*c*) by an order made in Scotland, Northern Ireland, the Isle of Man or in any of the Channel Islands;
(*d*) which is an overseas adoption; or
(*e*) which is an adoption recognised by the law of England and Wales and effected under the law of any other country,

and cognate expressions shall be construed accordingly.

(2) The definition of adoption includes, where the context admits, an adoption effected before the passing of the Children Act 1975, and the date of an adoption effected by an order is the date of the making of the order.

Prospective amendment by Adoption (Intercountry Aspects) Act 1999—By virtue of A(IA)A 1999, s 4(1) (which comes into force on 1 June 2003), insert after sub-para (1)(*c*):
"(*cc*) which is a Convention adoption;".

Defined terms—"adoption order": s 72(1); "overseas adoption": s 72(2).

"overseas adoption" (s 38(1)(*d*))—An "overseas adoption" ranks automatically as an adoption order, without the need to institute court proceedings. Specification of overseas adoptions has been made by the Adoption (Designation of Overseas Adoptions) Order 1973, SI 1973/19. The Order covers adoptions made by statute law (and not customary or common law) in any of 39 Commonwealth countries and UK dependent territories or 23 other countries named in the Schedule (not set out here).

"... an adoption recognised by the law of England and Wales ..." (s 38(1)(*e*))—The effect of recognition is that the foreign adoption will rank as an adoption, so far as it relates to the status of the child, as if it had been made by an adoption order in England and Wales. Certain adoptions made in a jurisdiction outside England and Wales are recognised automatically as being adoption orders, without the need to initiate court proceedings either to obtain an adoption order or to establish the status of the adoption order made abroad.

The following are automatically recognised adoption orders:

(*a*) adoption orders made in Scotland, Northern Ireland, Isle of Man or the Channel Islands;
(*b*) "overseas adoptions";
(*c*) Convention adoption orders (see AA 1976, s 17).

Any other adoption order made abroad will only be recognised as valid in England and Wales if it satisfies the criteria for recognition at common law.

A foreign adoption which is neither automatically recognised nor recognised at common law will not be treated as a valid adoption. In those circumstances, it will be necessary for an application for an adoption order to be made in England and Wales.

For explanation of recognition at common law, see *Children Law and Practice* (Family Law), para H[280].

Application to court for declaration as to status of adopted child—Any person whose status as an adopted child of any person depends on whether he has been validly adopted by that person by either an overseas adoption or an adoption recognised at common law may apply to the court for a declaration that the applicant either is or is not, for the purposes of AA 1976, s 39, the adopted child of that person (Family Law Act 1986, s 57(1), (2)). The application is made by petition to the High Court (FPR 1991, rr 3.15, 3.16 (see also under those rules)).

39 Status conferred by adoption

(1) An adopted child shall be treated in law –

(*a*) where the adopters are a married couple, as if he had been born as a child of the marriage (whether or not he was in fact born after the marriage was solemnised);

(*b*) in any other case, as if he had been born to the adopter in wedlock (but not as a child of any actual marriage of the adopter).

(2) An adopted child shall, subject to subsection (3), be treated in law as if he were not the child of any person other than the adopters or adopter.

(3) In the case of a child adopted by one of its natural parents as sole adoptive parent, subsection (2) has no effect as respects entitlement to property depending on relationship to that parent, or as respects anything else depending on that relationship.

(4) It is hereby declared that this section prevents an adopted child from being illegitimate.

(5) This section has effect –

(*a*) in the case of an adoption before 1 January 1976, from that date, and
(*b*) in the case of any other adoption, from the date of the adoption.

(6) Subject to the provisions of this Part, this section –

(*a*) applies for the construction of enactments or instruments passed or made before the adoption or later, and so applies subject to any contrary indication; and

(*b*) has effect as respects things done, or events occurring, after the adoption, or after 31 December 1975, whichever is the later.

Prospective amendment by Adoption (Intercountry Aspects) Act 1999—By virtue of A(IA)A 1999, s 4(2), (3) (which come into force on 1 June 2003), this section is amended as follows:

1 In subsection (2) for "subsection (3)" there is substituted "subsections (3) and (3A)".
2 After subsection (3) there is inserted –

"(3A) Where, in the case of a Convention adoption, the High Court is satisfied, on an application under this subsection –

(*a*) that under the law of the country in which the adoption was effected the adoption is not a full adoption;

(*b*) that the consents referred to in Article 4(*c*) and (*d*) of the Convention have not been given for a full adoption, or that the United Kingdom is not the receiving State (within the meaning of Article 2 of the Convention); and

(*c*) that it would be more favourable to the adopted child for a direction to be given under this subsection,

the Court may direct that subsection (2) shall not apply, or shall not apply to such extent as may be specified in the direction.

In this subsection "full adoption" means an adoption by virtue of which the adopted child falls to be treated in law as if he were not the child of any person other than the adopters or adopter.

(3B) The following provisions of the Family Law Act 1986 –

(*a*) section 59 (provisions relating to the Attorney General); and

(*b*) section 60 (supplementary provision as to declarations),

shall apply in relation to, and to an application for, a direction under subsection (3A) as they apply in relation to, and to an application for, a declaration under Part III of that Act.".

Parental order under HFEA 1990, s 30—By virtue of the Parental Orders (Human Fertilisation and Embryology) Regulations 1994, this section is modified so as to provide that, on the making of a parental order, the child is treated in law as the child of the marriage of the applicants, irrespective of whether the child was born before or after their marriage took place, and he is to be treated as the child of the couple and not of any other person. Thus, the child is not treated as illegitimate. Furthermore, by virtue of subsection (6), these provisions apply to any enactment or instrument (eg a will or other disposition of property etc) which has been passed before the parental order is made.

40 (*repealed*)

41 Adoptive relatives

A relationship existing by virtue of section 39 may be referred to as an adoptive relationship, and –

(*a*) a male adopter may be referred to as the adoptive father;

(*b*) a female adopter may be referred to as the adoptive mother;

(*c*) any other relative of any degree under an adoptive relationship may be referred to as an adoptive relative of that degree,

but this section does not prevent the term "parent", or any other term not qualified by the word "adoptive" being treated as including an adoptive relative.

42 Rules of construction for instruments concerning property

(1) Subject to any contrary indication, the rules of construction contained in this section apply to any instrument, other than an existing instrument, so far as it contains a disposition of property.

(2) In applying section 39(1) to a disposition which depends on the date of birth of a child or children of the adoptive parent or parents, the disposition shall be construed as if –

(*a*) the adopted child had been born on the date of adoption,

(*b*) two or more children adopted on the same date had been born on that date in the order of their actual births,

but this does not affect any reference to the age of a child.

(3) Examples of phrases in wills on which subsection (2) can operate are —

1. Children of A "living at my death or born afterwards".

2. Children of A "living at my death or born afterwards before any one of such children for the time being in existence attains a vested interest and who attain the age of 21 years".
3. As in example 1 or 2, but referring to grandchildren of A instead of children of A.
4. A for life "until he has a child", and then to his child or children.

Note. Subsection (2) will not affect the reference to the age of 21 years in example 2.

(4) Section 39(2) does not prejudice any interest vested in possession in the adopted child before the adoption, or any interest expectant (whether immediately or not) upon an interest so vested.

(5) Where it is necessary to determine for the purposes of a disposition of property effected by an instrument whether a woman can have a child, it shall be presumed that once a woman has attained the age of 55 years she will not adopt a child after execution of the instrument, and, notwithstanding section 39, if she does so that child shall not be treated as her child or as the child of her spouse (if any) for the purposes of the instrument.

(6) In this section, "instrument" includes a private Act settling property, but not any other enactment.

Parental order under HFEA 1990, s 30—By virtue of the Parental Orders (Human Fertilisation and Embryology) Regulations 1994, this section is modified so as to clarify the position in relation to instruments (eg wills under which a disposition of property is made in favour of a child who is the subject of a parental order), by providing that the disposition is construed as if the child had been born on the date of the parental order and not on the date of his actual birth.

43 Dispositions depending on date of birth

(1) Where a disposition depends on the date of birth of a child who was born illegitimate and who is adopted by one of the natural parents as sole adoptive parent, section 42(2) does not affect entitlement under Part II of the Family Law Reform Act 1969 (illegitimate children).

(2) Subsection (1) applies for example where –

(*a*) a testator dies in 1976 bequeathing a legacy to his eldest grandchild living at a specified time,
(*b*) his daughter has an illegitimate child in 1977 who is the first grandchild,
(*c*) his married son has a child in 1978,
(*d*) subsequently the illegitimate child is adopted by the mother as sole adoptive parent,

and in all those cases the daughter's child remains the eldest grandchild of the testator throughout.

44 Property devolving with peerages etc

(1) An adoption does not affect the descent of any peerage or dignity or title of honour.

(2) An adoption shall not affect the devolution of any property limited (expressly or not) to devolve (as nearly as the law permits) along with any peerage or dignity or title of honour.

(3) Subsection (2) applies only if and so far as a contrary intention is not expressed in the instrument, and shall have effect subject to the terms of the instrument.

Parental order under HFEA 1990, s 30—By virtue of the Parental Orders (Human Fertilisation and Embryology) Regulations 1994, this section is modified so as to prevent a child who is the subject of a parental order from inheriting a peerage or other title. It also prevents the child from succeeding to property which is connected to any such peerage or title unless express provision to the contrary is made in the instrument of transfer.

45 Protection of trustees and personal representatives

(1) A trustee or personal representative is not under a duty, by virtue of the law relating to trusts or the administration of estates, to enquire, before conveying or distributing any property, whether any adoption has been effected or revoked if that fact could affect entitlement to the property.

(2) A trustee or personal representative shall not be liable to any person by reason of a conveyance or distribution of the property made without regard to any such fact if he has not received notice of the fact before the conveyance or distribution.

(3) This section does not prejudice the right of a person to follow the property, or any property representing it, into the hands of another person, other than a purchaser, who has received it.

Parental order under HFEA 1990, s 30—By virtue of the Parental Orders (Human Fertilisation and Embryology) Regulations 1994, this section is modified so as to absolve trustees and personal representatives from the duty to enquire, before distributing property, whether a parental order has been made. It also removes from them any liability if property is distributed without knowledge of the existence of a parental order.

46 Meaning of "disposition"

(1) In this Part, unless the context otherwise requires, –

"disposition" includes the conferring of a power of appointment and any other disposition of an interest in or right over property;

"power of appointment" includes any discretionary power to transfer a beneficial interest in property without the furnishing of valuable consideration.

(2) This Part applies to an oral disposition as if contained in an instrument made when the disposition was made.

(3) For the purposes of this Part, the death of the testator is the date at which a will or codicil is to be regarded as made.

(4) For the purposes of this Part, provisions of the law of intestate succession applicable to the estate of a deceased person shall be treated as if contained in an instrument executed by him (while of full capacity) immediately before his death.

(5) (*repealed*)

Amendments—Trusts of Land and Appointment of Trustees Act 1996, s 25(2), Sch 4.

47 Miscellaneous enactments

(1) Section 39 does not apply for the purposes of the table of kindred and affinity in Schedule 1 to the Marriage Act 1949 or sections 10 and 11 (incest) of the Sexual Offences Act 1956.

(2) Section 39 does not apply for the purposes of any provision of –

(*a*) the British Nationality Act 1981,

(*b*) the Immigration Act 1971,

(*c*) any instrument having effect under an enactment within paragraph (*a*) or (*b*), or

(*d*) any other provision of the law for the time being in force which determines British citizenship, British Dependent Territories citizenship, the status of a British National (Overseas) or British Overseas citizenship.

(3)–(5) (*repealed*)

Amendments—British Nationality Act 1981, s 52, Schs 7, 9; Social Security Act 1986, s 86(2), Sch 11; SI 1986/948; Social Security Act 1988, s 16(2), Sch 5.

48 Pensions

Section 39(2) does not affect entitlement to a pension which is payable to or for the benefit of a child and is in payment at the time of his adoption.

49 Insurance

Where a child is adopted whose natural parent has effected an insurance with a friendly society or a collecting society or an industrial insurance company for the payment on the death of the child of money for funeral expenses, the rights and liabilities under the policy shall by virtue of the adoption be transferred to the adoptive parents who shall for the purposes of the enactments relating to such societies and companies be treated as the person who took out the policy.

PART V
REGISTRATION AND REVOCATION OF ADOPTION ORDERS AND CONVENTION ADOPTIONS

50 Adopted Children Register

(1) The Registrar General shall maintain at the General Register Office a register, to be called the Adopted Children Register, in which shall be made such entries as may be directed to be made therein by adoption orders, but no other entries.

(2) A certified copy of an entry in the Adopted Children Register, if purporting to be sealed or stamped with the seal of the General Register Office, shall, without any further or other proof of that entry, be received as evidence of the adoption to which it relates and, where the entry contains a record of the date of the birth or the country or the district and sub-district of the birth of the adopted person, shall also be received as aforesaid as evidence of that date or country or district and sub-district in all respects as if the copy were a certified copy of an entry in the Registers of Births.

(3) The Registrar General shall cause an index of the Adopted Children Register to be made and kept in the General Register Office; and every person shall be entitled to search that index and to have a certified copy of any entry in the Adopted Children Register in all respects upon and subject to the same terms, conditions and regulations as to payment of fees and otherwise as are applicable under the Births and Deaths Registration Act 1953, and the Registration Service Act 1953, in respect of searches in other indexes kept in the General Register

Office and in respect of the supply from that office of certified copies of entries in the certified copies of the Registers of Births and Deaths.

(4) The Registrar General shall, in addition to the Adopted Children Register and the index thereof, keep such other registers and books, and make such entries therein, as may be necessary to record and make traceable the connection between any entry in the Registers of Births which has been marked "Adopted" and any corresponding entry in the Adopted Children Register.

(5) The registers and books kept under subsection (4) shall not be, nor shall any index thereof be, open to public inspection or search, and the Registrar General shall not furnish any person with any information contained in or with any copy or extract from any such registers or books except in accordance with section 51 or under an order of any of the following courts, that is to say –

- (*a*) the High Court;
- (*b*) the Westminster County Court or such other county court as may be prescribed; and
- (*c*) the court by which an adoption order was made in respect of the person to whom the information, copy or extract relates.

(6) In relation to an adoption order made by a magistrates' court, the reference in paragraph (*c*) of subsection (5) to the court by which the order was made includes a reference to a court acting for the same petty sessions area.

(7) Schedule 1 to this Act, which, among other things, provides for the registration of adoptions and the amendment of adoption orders, shall have effect.

Prospective amendment by Adoption (Intercountry Aspects) Act 1999—By virtue of A(IA)A 1999, s 12(1) (which comes into force on 1 June 2003), this section is amended as follows:

1 In subsection (1) "shall be made" and "directed to be made therein by adoption orders, but no other entries" are repealed.

2 At the end of subsection (1) there is inserted –

"(*a*) directed to be made in it by adoption orders, or

(*b*) required to be made under Schedule 1 to this Act,

and no other entries, shall be made.".

Defined terms—"adoption order", "prescribed": s 72(1).

Scope of provision—Every adoption must be registered in the Adopted Children Register by the Registrar General in the prescribed form (see AA 1976, Sch 1, and Forms of Adoption Entry Regulations 1975). The child's entry in the Register of Births must also be marked "adopted". A certified copy of an entry in the Adopted Children Register, if sealed and stamped with the Registrar General's seal, is, without further proof, to be received as evidence of the adoption as if it were a birth certificate.

General Register Office—Smedley Hydro, Trafalgar Road, Birkdale, Southport PR8 2HH.

Disclosure pursuant to court order (s 50(5))—It is quite inappropriate for applications under AA 1976, s 50(5) to be made ex parte, and proper notice should be given to the Registrar General. In the High Court, the application should be issued from the Principal Registry and headed "In the matter of section 50(5) of the Adoption Act 1976", joining the Registrar General as a respondent (*Re H (Adoption: Disclosure of Information)* [1995] 1 FLR 236). In *D v Registrar General* [1997] 1 FLR 715, CA, Sir Stephen Brown P stated obiter that an exceptional need to know the information must be established before a direction would be given under s 50(5). Curiosity on the part of the natural parent is not, on its own, a sufficient reason to justify making an order for disclosure (*D v Registrar General* [1997] 1 FLR 715).

A court does not have the power to edit an entry to be made in the Adopted Children Register; however, the High Court, in the exercise of its inherent jurisdiction, can make an order restricting the disclosure of the details entered on the register (*Re X (A Minor) (Adoption Details: Disclosure)* [1994] Fam 174, [1994] 2 FLR 450; *Re W (Adoption Details: Disclosure)* [1998] 2 FLR 625; *President's Direction of 17 December 1998*).

"Westminster County Court or such other county court as may be prescribed" (s 50(5)(*b*))—The Westminster County Court no longer exists, and jurisdiction does not appear to have been transferred to the Central London County Court which replaced it. No other county court has been prescribed jurisdiction to make such an order.

Parental order under HFEA 1990, s 30—By virtue of the Parental Orders (Human Fertilisation and Embryology) Regulations 1994, this section is modified so as to make provision for the Registrar General to maintain a Parental Order Register at the General Register Office and to provide for a certified copy of an entry to be received as evidence of the birth of the child. The Registrar General is required to keep an index of the Register. Any person is entitled to search the index and to be provided with a certified copy of an entry in the Register. However, any other records kept and maintained linking an entry in the Register of Births with the corresponding entry in the Parental Order Register is not open for public inspection or search. The information contained in such records may be supplied only if authorised by an order of (*a*) the High Court, (*b*) the Westminster County Court or such other county court as may be prescribed, or (*c*) the court by which a parental order was made in respect of the person to whom the information, copy or extract relates.

51 Disclosure of birth records of adopted children

(1) Subject to what follows, the Registrar General shall on an application made in the prescribed manner by an adopted person a record of whose birth is kept by the Registrar General and who has attained the age of 18 years supply to that person on payment of the prescribed fee (if any) such information as is necessary to enable that person to obtain a certified copy of the record of his birth.

(2) On an application made in the prescribed manner by an adopted person under the age of 18 years, a record of whose birth is kept by the Registrar General and who is intending to be married in England or Wales, and on payment of the prescribed fee (if any), the Registrar General shall inform the applicant whether or not it appears from information contained in the registers of live births or other records that the applicant and the person whom he intends to marry may be within the prohibited degrees of relationship for the purposes of the Marriage Act 1949.

(3) Before supplying any information to an applicant under subsection (1), the Registrar General shall inform the applicant that counselling services are available to him –

(*a*) if he is in England and Wales –
- (i) at the General Register Office;
- (ii) from the local authority in whose area he is living;
- (iii) where the adoption order relating to him was made in England and Wales, from the local authority in whose area the court which made the order sat; or
- (iv) from any other local authority;

(*b*) if he is in Scotland –
- (i) from the regional or islands council in whose area he is living;
- (ii) where the adoption order relating to him was made in Scotland, from the council in whose area the court which made the order sat; or
- (iii) from any other regional or islands council;

(*c*) if he is in Northern Ireland –
- (i) from the Board in whose area he is living;
- (ii) where the adoption order relating to him was made in Northern Ireland, from the Board in whose area the court which made the order sat; or
- (iii) from any other Board;

(*d*) if he is in the United Kingdom and his adoption was arranged by an adoption society –
   (i) approved under section 3,
   (ii) approved under section 3 of the Adoption (Scotland) Act 1978,
   (iii) registered under Article 4 of the Adoption (Northern Ireland) Order 1987,

from that society.

(4) Where an adopted person who is in England and Wales –

(*a*) applies for information under –
   (i) subsection (1), or
   (ii) Article 54 of the Adoption (Northern Ireland) Order 1987, or

(*b*) is supplied with information under section 45 of the Adoption (Scotland) Act 1978,

it shall be the duty of the persons and bodies mentioned in subsection (5) to provide counselling for him if asked by him to do so.

(5) The persons and bodies are –

(*a*) the Registrar General;
(*b*) any local authority falling within subsection (3)(*a*)(ii) to (iv);
(*c*) any adoption society falling within subsection (3)(*d*) in so far as it is acting as an adoption society in England and Wales.

(6) If the applicant chooses to receive counselling from a person or body falling within subsection (3), the Registrar General shall send to the person or body the information to which the applicant is entitled under subsection (1).

(7) Where a person –

(*a*) was adopted before 12 November 1975, and
(*b*) applies for information under subsection (1),

the Registrar General shall not supply the information to him unless he has attended an interview with a counsellor arranged by a person or body from whom counselling services are available as mentioned in subsection (3).

(8) Where the Registrar General is prevented by subsection (7) from supplying information to a person who is not living in the United Kingdom, he may supply the information to any body which –

(*a*) the Registrar General is satisfied is suitable to provide counselling to that person, and
(*b*) has notified the Registrar General that it is prepared to provide such counselling.

(9) In this section –

"a Board" means a Health and Social Services Board established under Article 16 of the Health and Personal Social Services (Northern Ireland) Order 1972; and

"prescribed" means prescribed by regulations made by the Registrar General.

Amendments—CA 1989, s 88(1), Sch 10, para 20.

Defined terms—"adoption order", "approved adoption society", "local authority": s 72(1).

Scope of provision—An adopted person, who is over the age of 18 years, may apply to the Registrar General for such information as is necessary to enable the adoptee to obtain a copy of his birth records. The application must be in the form required by the Adopted Persons (Birth

Records) Regulations 1991 (for guidance, see *The Children Act 1989 Guidance and Regulations, Volume 9*, paras 3.9–3.18 and Annex B). In order to assist the adoptee to prepare for receipt of the information, counselling services must be made available for him. This section makes provision for the supply of the information and counselling.

The Registrar General can refuse to allow access to the birth records on grounds of public policy (see *R v Registrar General ex parte Smith* [1990] 2 QB 253, [1990] 2 FLR 79, QBD). The High Court may, under its inherent jurisdiction, attach to an adoption order an order that the Registrar General should not reveal details of an adoption which are recorded in the Adopted Children Register without the leave of the court (*Re X (A Minor) (Adoption Details: Disclosure)* [1994] Fam 174, [1994] 2 FLR 450; *Re W (Adoption Details: Disclosure)* [1998] 2 FLR 625). A local authority is required to obtain leave to make such an application (under CA 1989, s 100(3)) and any application for an order restricting disclosure must be made in, or transferred to, the High Court (*President's Direction of 17 December 1998*).

Parental order under HFEA 1990, s 30—By virtue of the Parental Orders (Human Fertilisation and Embryology) Regulations 1994, this section is modified so as to provide for disclosure of the records of a person who is the subject of a parental order to that person, provided that the person has attained the age of 18. It also imposes on the Registrar General a duty to inform the applicant that counselling services are available. The duty to disclose is mandatory, although it is submitted that the principles laid down in *R v Registrar General ex parte Smith* [1991] 2 QB 393, [1991] 1 FLR 255, CA would operate to impose limitations on that duty on the basis of public policy if the effect of complying with the duty would enable a person to benefit from his crime, or if there were a significant risk that to do so would facilitate the commission of a crime or result in serious danger to the public. Consequently, the duty in such cases is subject to an implied exception on the ground of public policy.

Parental order – procedure for obtaining information—Subsection (1) provides that an application for information must be made in the prescribed manner, and the procedure to be followed by an adopted person is set out in the Adopted Persons (Birth Records) Regulations 1991. Presumably, the same procedure should be followed by a person who is the subject of a parental order.

51A Adoption Contact Register

(1) The Registrar General shall maintain at the General Register Office a register to be called the Adoption Contact register.

(2) The register shall be in two parts –

(*a*) Part I: Adopted Persons; and
(*b*) Part II: Relatives.

(3) The Registrar General shall, on payment of such fee as may be prescribed, enter in Part I of the register the name and address of any adopted person who fulfils the conditions in subsection (4) and who gives notice that he wishes to contact any relative of his.

(4) The conditions are that –

(*a*) a record of the adopted person's birth is kept by the Registrar General; and
(*b*) the adopted person has attained the age of 18 years and –
(i) has been supplied by the Registrar General with information under section 51; or
(ii) has satisfied the Registrar General that he has such information as is necessary to enable him to obtain a certified copy of the record of his birth.

(5) The Registrar General shall, on payment of such fee as may be prescribed, enter in Part II of the register the name and address of any person who fulfils the conditions in subsection (6) and who gives notice that he wishes to contact an adopted person.

(6) The conditions are that –

(*a*) a record of the adopted person's birth is kept by the Registrar General, and
(*b*) the person giving notice under subsection (5) has attained the age of 18 years and has satisfied the Registrar General that –
(i) he is a relative of the adopted person; and
(ii) he has such information as is necessary to enable him to obtain a certified copy of the record of the adopted person's birth.

(7) The Registrar General shall, on receiving notice from any person named in an entry in the register that he wishes the entry to be cancelled, cancel the entry.

(8) Any notice given under this section must be in such form as may be determined by the Registrar General.

(9) The Registrar General shall transmit to an adopted person whose name is entered in Part I of the register the name and address of any relative in respect of whom there is an entry in Part II of the register.

(10) Any entry cancelled under subsection (7) ceases from the time of cancellation to be an entry for the purposes of subsection (9).

(11) The register shall not be open to public inspection or search and the Registrar General shall not supply any person with information entered in the register (whether in an uncancelled or a cancelled entry) except in accordance with this section.

(12) The register may be kept by means of a computer.

(13) In this section –

(*a*) "relative" means any person (other than an adoptive relative) who is related to the adopted person by blood (including half-blood) or marriage;
(*b*) "address" includes any address at or through which the person concerned may be contacted, and
(*c*) "prescribed" means prescribed by the Secretary of State.

Amendments—Inserted by CA 1989, s 88(1), Sch 10, para 21.

Scope of provision—A register to assist those adoptees who wish to trace and have contact with their natural families was created by the CA 1989, which inserted this section into AA 1976. The Adoption Contact Register is divided into two parts: in Part I are details relating to the adopted person; in Part II are details of any relative of the adoptee, by blood, half-blood or marriage (but not adoption), who wishes to make contact with the adoptee. The system operates by the Registrar General transmitting, to the adopted person whose name appears in Part I, the name and address of any relative entered in Part II. A fee is payable for entry on the register (Adopted Persons (Contact Register) (Fees) Rules 1991).

Adoption Contact Register—The Register is held at OPCS, Smedley Hydro, Trafalgar Road, Birkdale, Southport PR8 2HH.

52 Revocation of adoptions on legitimation

(1) Where any person adopted by his father or mother alone has subsequently become a legitimated person on the marriage of his father and mother, the court by which the adoption order was made may, on the application of any of the parties concerned, revoke that order.

(2) Where any person legitimated by virtue of section 1 of the Legitimacy Act 1959, had been adopted by his father and mother before the commencement of that

Act, the court by which the adoption order was made may, on the application of any of the parties concerned, revoke that order.

(3) Where a person adopted by his father or mother alone by virtue of a regulated adoption has subsequently become a legitimated person on the marriage of his father and mother, the High Court may, upon an application under this subsection by the parties concerned, by order revoke the adoption.

(4) In relation to an adoption order made by a magistrates' court, the reference in subsections (1) and (2) to the court by which the order was made includes a reference to a court acting for the same petty sessions area.

Prospective amendment by Adoption (Intercountry Aspects) Act 1999—By virtue of A(IA)A 1999, s 15, Sch 2, para 3(4), Sch 3 (which come into force on 1 June 2003), subsection (3) is repealed.

Defined terms—"adoption order": s 72(1).

Procedure—See AR 1984, rr 37–41 and under those rules; see also AA 1976, s 54.

53 Annulment etc of overseas adoptions

(1) The High Court may, upon an application under this subsection, by order annul a regulated adoption or an adoption effected by a Convention adoption order –

(*a*) on the ground that at the relevant time the adoption was prohibited by a notified provision, if under the internal law then in force in the country of which the adopter was then a national or the adopters were then nationals the adoption could have been impugned on that ground;

(*b*) on the ground that at the relevant time the adoption contravened provisions relating to consents of the internal law relating to adoption of the country of which the adopted person was then a national, if under that law the adoption could then have been impugned on that ground;

(*c*) on any other ground on which the adoption can be impugned under the law for the time being in force in the country in which the adoption was effected.

(2) The High Court may, upon an application under this subsection –

(*a*) order that an overseas adoption or a determination shall cease to be valid in Great Britain on the ground that the adoption or determination is contrary to public policy or that the authority which purported to authorise the adoption or make the determination was not competent to entertain the case;

(*b*) decide the extent, if any, to which a determination has been affected by a subsequent determination.

(3) Any court in Great Britain may, in any proceedings in that court, decide that an overseas adoption or a determination shall, for the purposes of those proceedings, be treated as invalid in Great Britain on either of the grounds mentioned in subsection (2).

(4) An order or decision of the Court of Session on an application under subsection (3) of section 6 of the Adoption Act 1968 shall be recognised and have effect as if it were an order or decision of the High Court on an application under subsection (3) of this section.

(5) Except as provided by this section and section 52(3) the validity of an overseas adoption or a determination shall not be impugned in England and Wales in proceedings in any court.

Amendments—Domestic Proceedings and Magistrates' Courts Act 1978, s 74(2).

Prospective amendment by Adoption (Intercountry Aspects) Act 1999—By virtue of A(IA)A 1999, s 6(1), (2), Sch 3 (which come into force on 1 June 2003), this section is amended as follows:

1 For subsection (1) there is substituted –

"(1) The High Court may, on an application under this subsection, by order annul a Convention adoption or a Convention adoption order on the ground that the adoption or order is contrary to public policy.".

2 In subsection (5) "and section 52(3)" is repealed; and "a Convention adoption, a Convention adoption order," is inserted after "validity of".

Defined terms—"Convention adoption": s 72(1); "overseas adoption": s 72(2).

Procedure—See under s 52.

54 Provisions supplementary to ss 52(3) and 53

(1) Any application for an order under section 52(3) or 53 or a decision under section 53(3) shall be made in the prescribed manner and within such period, if any, as may be prescribed.

(2) No application shall be made under section 52(3) or section 53(1) in respect of an adoption unless immediately before the application is made the person adopted or the adopter habitually resides in England and Wales or, as the case may be, both adopters habitually reside there.

(3) In deciding in pursuance of section 53 whether such an authority as is mentioned in section 59 was competent to entertain a particular case, a court shall be bound by any finding of fact made by the authority and stated by the authority to be so made for the purpose of determining whether the authority was competent to entertain the case.

(4) In section 53 –

"determination" means such a determination as is mentioned in section 59 of this Act;

"notified provision" means a provision specified in an order of the Secretary of State as one in respect of which a notification to or by the Government of the United Kingdom was in force at the relevant time in pursuance of the provisions of the Convention relating to prohibitions contained in the national law of the adopter; and

"relevant time" means the time when the adoption in question purported to take effect under the law of the country in which it purports to have been effected.

Prospective amendment by Adoption (Intercountry Aspects) Act 1999—By virtue of A(IA)A 1999, s 6(3), Sch 3 (which come into force on 1 June 2003), this section is amended as follows:

1 In subsection (1) "52(3) or" is repealed.

2 In subsection (2) "section 52(3) or" is repealed.

3 In subsection (4) the definitions "notified provision" and "relevant time" are repealed.

PART VI
MISCELLANEOUS AND SUPPLEMENTAL

55 Adoption of children abroad

(1) Where on an application made in relation to a child by a person who is not domiciled in England and Wales or Scotland [or Northern Ireland] an authorised court is satisfied that he intends to adopt the child under the law of or within the country in which the applicant is domiciled, the court may, subject to the following provisions of this section, make an order giving him parental responsibility for the child.

(2) The provisions of Part II relating to adoption orders, except sections 12(1), 14(2), 15(2), 17 to 21 and 25, shall apply in relation to orders under this section as they apply in relation to adoption orders subject to the modification that in section 13(1) for "19" and "13" there are substituted "32" and "26" respectively.

(3) Sections 50 and 51 and paragraphs 1 and 2(1) of Schedule 1 shall apply in relation to an order under this section as they apply in relation to an adoption order except that any entry in the Registers of Births, or the Adopted Children Register which is required to be marked in consequence of the making of an order under this section shall, in lieu of being marked with the word "Adopted" or "Re-adopted" (with or without the addition of the words "(Scotland)" or "(Northern Ireland)"), be marked with the words "Proposed foreign adoption" or "Proposed foreign re-adoption", as the case may require.

(4) (*repealed*)

Amendments—CA 1989, ss 88(1), 108(7), Sch 10, para 22, Sch 15.

56 Restriction on removal of children for adoption outside Great Britain

(1) Except under the authority of an order under section 55, section 49 of the Adoption (Scotland) Act 1978 or Article 57 of the Adoption (Northern Ireland) Order 1987 it shall not be lawful for any person to take or send a child who is a British subject or a citizen of the Republic of Ireland out of Great Britain to any place outside the United Kingdom, the Channel Islands and the Isle of Man with a view to the adoption of the child by any person not being a parent or guardian or relative of the child; and any person who takes or sends a child out of Great Britain to any place in contravention of this subsection, or makes or takes part in any arrangements for placing a child with any person for that purpose, shall be guilty of an offence and liable on summary conviction to imprisonment for a term not exceeding 3 months or to a fine not exceeding level 5 on the standard scale or to both.

(2) In any proceedings under this section, a report by a British consular officer of a deposition made before a British consular officer and authenticated under the signature of that officer shall, upon proof that the officer or the deponent cannot be found in the United Kingdom, be admissible as evidence of the matters stated therein, and it shall not be necessary to prove the signature or official character of the person who appears to have signed any such report or deposition.

(3) A person shall be deemed to take part in arrangements for placing a child with a person for the purpose referred to in subsection (1) if –

(*a*) he facilitates the placing of the child with that person; or (*b*) he initiates or takes part in any negotiations of which the purpose or effect is the conclusion of any agreement or the making of any arrangement therefor, and if he causes another person to do so.

Amendments—Criminal Justice Act 1982, ss 38, 46; CA 1989, s 88(1), Sch 10, para 23.

56A Restriction on bringing children into the United Kingdom for adoption

(1) A person habitually resident in the British Islands who at any time brings into the United Kingdom for the purpose of adoption a child who is habitually resident outside those Islands shall be guilty of an offence unless such requirements as may be prescribed by regulations made by the Secretary of State are satisfied either –

(*a*) before that time; or
(*b*) within such period beginning with that time as may be so prescribed.

(2) Subsection (1) does not apply where the child is brought into the United Kingdom for the purpose of adoption by a parent, guardian or relative.

(3) A person guilty of an offence under this section is liable on summary conviction to imprisonment for a term not exceeding three months, or a fine not exceeding level 5 on the standard scale, or both.

(4) Proceedings for an offence under this section may be brought within a period of six months from the date on which evidence sufficient in the opinion of the prosecutor to warrant the proceedings came to his knowledge; but no such proceedings shall be brought by virtue of this subsection more than three years after the commission of the offence.

Amendments—Inserted by Adoption (Intercountry Aspects) Act 1999, s 14.

Defined terms—"parent, guardian or relative": s 72(1).

Requirements to be satisfied (s 56A(1))—The prescribed requirements are set out in Adoption of Children from Overseas Regulations 2001, reg 3(2) (see Adoption of Children from Overseas (Wales) Regulations 2001 for Wales). See also the Intercountry Adoption (Hague Convention) Regulations 2003 (which come into force on 1 June 2003).

57 Prohibition on certain payments

(1) Subject to the provisions of this section, it shall not be lawful to make or give to any person any payment or reward for or in consideration of –

(*a*) the adoption by that person of a child;
(*b*) the grant by that person of any agreement or consent required in connection with the adoption of a child;
(*c*) the handing over of a child by that person, with a view to the adoption of the child; or
(*d*) the making by that person of any arrangements for the adoption of a child.

(2) Any person who makes or gives, or agrees or offers to make or give, any payment or reward prohibited by this section, or who receives or agrees to receive or attempts to obtain any such payment or reward, shall be guilty of an offence and liable on summary conviction to imprisonment for a term not exceeding 3 months or to a fine not exceeding level 5 on the standard scale or to both.

(3) This section does not apply to any payment made to an adoption agency by a parent or guardian of a child or by a person who adopts or proposes to adopt a

child, being a payment in respect of expenses reasonably incurred by the agency in connection with the adoption of the child, or to any payment or reward authorised by the court to which an application for an adoption order in respect of a child is made.

(3A) This section does not apply to –

(*a*) any payment made by an adoption agency to a person who has applied or proposes to apply to a court for an adoption order or an order under section 55 (adoption of children abroad), being a payment of or towards any legal or medical expenses incurred or to be incurred by that person in connection with the application; or

(*b*) any payment made by an adoption agency to another adoption agency in consideration of the placing of a child with any person with a view to the child's adoption; or

(*c*) any payment made by an adoption agency to a voluntary organisation for the time being approved for the purposes of this paragraph by the Secretary of State as a fee for the services of that organisation in putting that adoption agency into contact with another adoption agency with a view to the making of arrangements between the adoption agencies for the adoption of a child.

In paragraph (*c*) "voluntary organisation" means a body, other than a public or local authority, the activities of which are not carried on for profit.

(4)–(10) (*repealed*)

Amendments—Criminal Law Act 1977, s 65, Sch 12; Criminal Justice Act 1982, ss 38, 46; CA 1989, ss 88(1), 108(7), Sch 10, para 24, Sch 15; SI 1989/166.

Defined terms—"adoption agency": s 1(4); "arrangements for the adoption of a child": s 72(3); "child", "guardian", "voluntary organisation": s 72(1).

Scope of provision—Except in certain circumstances listed in this section and s 57A, it is unlawful to make or give to any person any payment or reward for, or in consideration of, an adoption, agreement for adoption, placement for adoption or the making of arrangements for adoption. The court may not make an adoption order unless it is satisfied that the applicants have not breached this section (see s 24(2)). Paying for an assessment report to facilitate adoption of a child from overseas contravenes s 57 (s 72(3A); *Re C (A Minor) (Adoption: Legality)* [1999] Fam 128; *Flintshire CC v K* [2001] 2 FCR 724). There are conflicting first-instance authorities on the question of whether s 57 has extra-territorial effect (*Re An Adoption Application* [1992] 1 FLR 341 (extra-territorial); *Re AW (Adoption Application)* [1993] 1 FLR 62 (not extra-territorial); *Re WM (Adoption: Non-patrial)* [1997] 1 FLR 132 (extra-territorial)). See **Prosecution** under s 11.

"... any payment or reward authorised by the court ..." (s 57(3))—If it considers it appropriate to do so, the court may prospectively or retrospectively sanction a payment that would otherwise be illegal (s 57(3)). In deciding whether to sanction a payment, the court's first consideration will be the child's welfare (*Re An Adoption Application* [1992] 1 FLR 341; *Re AW (Adoption Application)* [1993] 1 FLR 62; *Re C (A Minor) (Adoption Application)* [1993] 1 FLR 87).

"adoption agency" (s 57(3A))—The definition of "adoption agency" (ss 1(4), 72(1)) does not extend to agencies abroad, so that any payment to a foreign agency does not come within the exception and therefore requires sanction from the court (*Re A (Adoption: Placement)* [1988] 2 FLR 133 at 137).

57A Permitted allowances

(1) The Secretary of State may make regulations for the purpose of enabling adoption agencies to pay allowances to persons who have adopted, or intend to adopt, children in pursuance of arrangements made by the agencies.

(2) Section 57(1) shall not apply to any payment made by an adoption agency in accordance with the regulations.

(3) The regulations may, in particular, make provision as to –

- (*a*) the procedure to be followed by any agency in determining whether a person should be paid an allowance;
- (*b*) the circumstances in which an allowance may be paid;
- (*c*) the factors to be taken into account in determining the amount of an allowance;
- (*d*) the procedure for review, variation and termination of allowances; and
- (*e*) the information about allowances to be supplied by any agency to any person who is intending to adopt a child.

(4) Any scheme approved under section 57(4) shall be revoked as from the coming into force of this section.

(5) Section 57(1) shall not apply in relation to any payment made –

- (*a*) in accordance with a scheme revoked under subsection (4) or section 57(5)(*b*); and
- (*b*) to a person to whom such payments were made before the revocation of the scheme.

(6) Subsection (5) shall not apply where any person to whom any payments may lawfully be made by virtue of subsection (5) agrees to receive (instead of such payments) payments complying with regulations made under this section.

Amendments—Inserted by CA 1989, s 88(1), Sch 10, para 25.

58 Restriction on advertisements

(1) It shall not be lawful for any advertisement to be published indicating –

- (*a*) that the parent or guardian of a child desires to cause a child to be adopted; or
- (*b*) that a person desires to adopt a child; or
- (*c*) that any person (not being an adoption agency) is willing to make arrangements for the adoption of a child.

(2) Any person who causes to be published or knowingly publishes an advertisement in contravention of the provisions of this section shall be guilty of an offence and liable on summary conviction to a fine not exceeding level 5 on the standard scale.

Amendments—Criminal Justice Act 1982, ss 38, 46.

58A Information concerning adoption

(1) Every local authority and every approved adoption society shall transmit to the Secretary of State, at such times and in such form as he may direct, such particulars as he may require with respect –

- (*a*) to their performance of all or any of their functions under the enactments mentioned in subsection (2) below; and
- (*b*) to the children and other persons in relation to whom they have exercised those functions.

(2) The enactments referred to in subsection (1) above are –

(*a*) the Adoption Act 1958;
(*b*) Part I of the Children Act 1975; and
(*c*) this Act.

(3) The justices' chief executive for each magistrates' court shall transmit to the Secretary of State, at such times and in such form as he may direct, such particulars as he may require with respect to the proceedings of the court under the enactments mentioned in subsection (2) above.

(4) The Secretary of State shall publish from time to time abstracts of the particulars transmitted to him under subsections (1) and (3) above.

Amendments—Inserted by Health and Social Services and Social Security Adjudications Act 1983, s 9, Sch 2, para 35; amended by Access to Justice Act 1999, s 90, Sch 13, para 88.

59 Effect of determination and orders made in Scotland and overseas in adoption proceedings

(1) Where an authority of a Convention country or any British territory other than the United Kingdom having power under the law of that country or territory –

(*a*) to authorise or review the authorisation of a regulated adoption or a specified order; or
(*b*) to give or review a decision revoking or annulling a regulated adoption, a specified order or a Convention adoption order,

makes a determination in the exercise of that power, then, subject to sections 52(3) and 53 and any subsequent determination having effect under this subsection, the determination shall have effect in England and Wales for the purpose of effecting, confirming or terminating the adoption in question or confirming its termination, as the case may be.

(2) Subsections (2) to (4) of section 12 shall apply in relation to an order freeing a child for adoption (other than an order under section 18) as if it were an adoption order; and, on the revocation in Scotland or Northern Ireland of an order freeing a child for adoption, subsections (3) and (3A) of section 20 shall apply as if the order had been revoked under that section.

(3) Sections 12(3) and (4) and 49 apply in relation to a child who is the subject of an order which is similar to an order under section 55 and is made (whether before or after this Act has effect) in Scotland, Northern Ireland, the Isle of Man or any of the Channel Islands, as they apply in relation to a child who is the subject of an adoption order.

Amendments—CA 1989, s 88(1), Sch 10, para 26.

Prospective amendment by Adoption (Intercountry Aspects) Act 1999—By virtue of A(IA)A 1999, s 6(4), (which comes into force on 1 June 2003), for subsection (1) substitute:

"(1) Where –

(*a*) an authority of a Convention country (other than the United Kingdom) having power under the law of that country –
  (i) to authorise, or review the authorisation of, a Convention adoption; or
  (ii) to give or review a decision revoking or annulling such an adoption or a Convention adoption order; or
(*b*) an authority of any of the Channel Islands, the Isle of Man or any colony having power under the law of that territory –
  (i) to authorise, or review the authorisation of, a Convention adoption or an adoption effected in that territory; or

(ii) to give or review a decision revoking or annulling such an adoption or a Convention adoption order,

makes a determination in the exercise of that power, then, subject to section 53 and any subsequent determination having effect under this subsection, the determination shall have effect in England and Wales for the purpose of effecting, confirming or terminating the adoption in question or confirming its termination as the case may be.".

60 Evidence of adoption in Scotland and Northern Ireland

Any document which is receivable as evidence of any matter –

(*a*) in Scotland under section 45(2) of the Adoption (Scotland) Act 1978; or

(*b*) in Northern Ireland under Article 63(1) of the Adoption (Northern Ireland) Order 1987,

shall also be so receivable in England and Wales.

Amendments—CA 1989, s 88, Sch 10, para 27.

61 Evidence of agreement and consent

(1) Any agreement or consent which is required by this Act to be given to the making of an order or application for an order (other than an order to which section 17(6) applies) may be given in writing, and, if the document signifying the agreement or consent is witnessed in accordance with rules, it shall be admissible in evidence without further proof of the signature of the person by whom it was executed.

(2) A document signifying such agreement or consent which purports to be witnessed in accordance with rules shall be presumed to be so witnessed, and to have been executed and witnessed on the date and at the place specified in the document, unless the contrary is proved.

Prospective amendment by Adoption (Intercountry Aspects) Act 1999—By virtue of A(IA)A 1999, s 15(2), Sch 3 (which come into force on 1 June 2003), in subsection (1) the words "(other than an order to which section 17(6) applies)" are repealed.

Scope of provision—Any agreement or consent required by AA 1976 may be given orally or in writing. This section provides for the agreement or consent to be admissible in evidence if it has been witnessed in accordance with the rules (see AR 1984, rr 8, 20 and Sch 1, Forms 2 and 7, and MC(A)R 1984, rr 8, 20 and Sch 1, Forms 2 and 7). In an inter-country adoption the applicants should supply written evidence of parental agreement together with an authenticated English translation (*Re R (Inter-Country Adoptions: Practice)* [1999] 1 FLR 1042).

Parental order under HFEA 1990, s 30—By virtue of the Parental Orders (Human Fertilisation and Embryology) Regulations 1994, this section is modified so as to deal with the procedure for evidence of consent or agreement to be adduced. The consent or agreement may be given in writing although, by contrast with the provision in relation to adoption, the requirement for a document signifying the agreement or consent witnessed in accordance with the rules is omitted; accordingly, it appears that the agreement or consent may be oral or written. Where the agreement or consent is given in writing, any document signed by the surrogate parent(s) which contains a clear indication that the signatory understood what he was doing and that he has agreed to the making of a parental order can be adduced as evidence of the person's agreement and, in the absence of evidence to the contrary, the court may act upon such a document.

62 Courts

(1) In this Act, "authorised court", as respects an application for an order relating to a child, shall be construed as follows.

(2) Subject to subsections (4) to (6), if the child is in England or Wales when the application is made, the following are authorised courts –

(*a*) the High Court;
(*b*) (*repealed*)
(*c*) any other county court prescribed by rules made under section 75 of the County Courts Act 1984;
(*d*) a magistrates' court within whose area the child is, and, in the case of an application for an order freeing the child for adoption, a magistrates' court within whose area a parent or guardian of the child is.

(3) If, in the case of an application for an adoption order or for an order freeing a child for adoption, the child is not in Great Britain when the application is made, the High Court is the authorised court.

(4) In the case of an application for a Convention adoption order, paragraphs (*b*), (*c*) and (*d*) of subsection (2) do not apply.

(5) Subsection (2) does not apply in the case of an application under section 29 but for the purposes of such an application the following are authorised courts –

(*a*) if there is pending in respect of the child an application for an adoption order or an order freeing him for adoption, the court in which that application is pending;
(*b*) if paragraph (*a*) does not apply and there is no application for an order under –
(i) section 12 or 18 of the Adoption (Scotland) Act 1978; or
(ii) Article 12, 17 or 18 of the Adoption (Northern Ireland) Order 1987,

the High Court, the county court within whose district the applicant lives and the magistrates' court within whose area the applicant lives.

(6) In the case of an order under section 55, paragraph (*d*) of subsection (2) does not apply.

(7) Any court to which the proceedings on an application are transferred under any enactment is, as regards the transferred proceedings, an authorised court if it is not an authorised court under the preceding provisions of this section.

Amendments—County Courts Act 1984, s 148(1), Sch 2, para 58; Matrimonial and Family Proceedings Act 1984, s 46(1), Sch 1, para 20 (not yet fully in force – see **"section 75 of the County Courts Act 1984"** below); CA 1989, s 88, Sch 10, para 28; SI 1994/3138.

Prospective amendment by Adoption (Intercountry Aspects) Act 1999—By virtue of A(IA)A 1999, s 15(1), Sch 2, para 3(5) (which come into force on 1 June 2003), in subsection (4) for "paragraphs (*b*), (*c*) and (*d*) of subsection (2) do not apply" substitute "paragraph (*d*) of subsection (2) does not apply".

Defined terms—"adoption order", "child", "Convention adoption order", "guardian", "order freeing a child for adoption", "parent": s 72(1).

High Court (s 62(2)(*a*))—All causes and matters relating to adoption are assigned to the Family Division of the High Court (Supreme Court Act 1981, s 61 and Sch 1, para 3(*b*)(iii)). The relevant procedure is set out in the Adoption Rules 1984.

County court (s 62(2)(*b*), (*c*))—An application under AA 1976 which is to be commenced in a county court must be commenced in a divorce county court (Children (Allocation of Proceedings) Order 1991, art 14). If an opposed application for an adoption order or a freeing for adoption order is pending in a divorce county court which is not also a family hearing centre, the application must be transferred to a family hearing centre for trial (C(AP)O 1991, art 17). The relevant procedure is set out in the Adoption Rules 1984.

"section 75 of the County Courts Act 1984" (s 62(2)(*c*))—When Matrimonial and Family Proceedings Act 1984, Sch 1, para 20(*a*) is brought into force, the reference to s 75 will be substituted by a reference to AA 1976, s 66(1).

Magistrates' court (s 62(2)(*d*))—Proceedings under AA 1976 are "family proceedings" within the meaning of Magistrates' Courts Act 1980, s 65(1) and will be heard by a family proceedings court. The relevant procedure is set out in the Magistrates' Courts (Adoption) Rules 1984.

Children (Allocation of Proceedings) Order 1991—Proceedings under AA 1976 are subject to the Children (Allocation of Proceedings) Order 1991. Once proceedings have been commenced in an authorised court, they may be transferred to another authorised court under that order.

63 Appeals etc

(1) (*repealed*)

(2) Subject to subsection (3), where on an application to a magistrates' court under this Act the court makes or refuses to make an order, an appeal shall lie to the High Court.

(3) Where an application is made to a magistrates' court under this Act, and the court considers that the matter is one which would more conveniently be dealt with by the High Court, the magistrates' court shall refuse to make an order, and in that case no appeal shall lie to the High Court.

(4) No appeal shall lie to the High Court against an order made under section 34.

Amendments—Matrimonial and Family Proceedings Act 1984, s 46(3), Sch 3; Health and Social Services and Social Security Adjudications Act 1983, ss 9, 30(1), Sch 2, para 36, Sch 10.

General Note—An appeal under this section must be in accordance with RSC Ord 55 rather than FPR 1991.

"more conveniently be dealt with by the High Court" (s 63(3))—This provision is unlikely to be used following the implementation of the Children (Allocation of Proceedings) Order 1991, which provides a more flexible and expeditious procedure for the transfer of a case to the most appropriate court.

"section 34" (s 63(4))—This is a reference to AA 1976, s 34, concerning the removal of a protected child from unsuitable surroundings, which was repealed by CA 1989, Sch 15 with effect from 14 October 1991.

Parental order under HFEA 1990, s 30—By virtue of the Parental Orders (Human Fertilisation and Embryology) Regulations 1994, this section is modified so as to provide that appeals from the family proceedings court will lie to the High Court.

64 Proceedings to be in private

Proceedings under this Act –

(*a*) in the High Court, may be disposed of in chambers;
(*b*) in a county court, shall be heard and determined in camera;
(*c*) (*repealed*)

Amendments—Domestic Proceedings and Magistrates' Courts Act 1978, ss 73(2), 89(2)(*b*), Sch 3.

Scope of provision—This section provides a confusing distinction between practice in the High Court and in the county court. In the High Court, the proceedings "may" (and almost invariably will) be disposed of in chambers. In the county court, the use of the phrase "in camera" suggests that the court will sit in open court, but in private. In practice, all proceedings in the county court relating to adoption are heard in chambers.

Parental order under HFEA 1990, s 30—By virtue of the Parental Orders (Human Fertilisation and Embryology) Regulations 1994, this section is modified so as to provide that an application for a parental order is to be heard in chambers.

65 Duties of officers of the Service

(1) For the purpose of any application for an adoption order or an order freeing a child for adoption or an order under section 20 or 55 rules shall provide for the appointment, in such cases as are prescribed of an officer of the service –

(*a*) to act on behalf of the child upon the hearing of the application, with the duty of safeguarding the interests of the child in the prescribed manner;
(*b*) for the purpose of witnessing agreements to adoption and performing such other duties as the rules may prescribe.

(2) A person who is employed –

(*a*) in the case of an application for an adoption order, by the adoption agency by whom the child was placed; or
(*b*) in the case of an application for an order freeing a child for adoption, by the adoption agency by whom the application was made; or
(*c*) in the case of an application under section 20, by the adoption agency with the parental rights and duties relating to the child,

shall not be appointed to act under subsection (1) for the purposes of the application but, subject to that, the same person may if the court thinks fit act under both paragraphs (*a*) and (*b*) of subsection (1).

(3) Rules of court may make provision as to the assistance which an officer of the Service may be required by the court to give it.

(4) In this section "officer of the Service" has the same meaning as in the Criminal Justice and Court Services Act 2000.

Amendments—Criminal Justice and Court Services Act 2000 s 74, Sch 7, para 52.

Defined terms—"adoption agency": s 1(4), "adoption order", "child", "order freeing a child for adoption": s 72(1).

Scope of provision—This section gives authority for the making of rules. For the relevant rules (and notes thereto), see AR 1984, rr 5, 6, 17 and 18, and MC(A)R 1984, rr 5, 6, 17 and 18.

65A (*repealed*)

66 Rules of procedure

(1) Rules in regard to any matter to be prescribed under this Act and dealing generally with all matters of procedure and incidental matters arising out of this Act and for carrying this Act into effect shall be made by the Lord Chancellor.

(2) Subsection (1) does not apply in relation to proceedings before magistrates' courts, but the power to make rules conferred by section 144 of the Magistrates' Courts Act 1980, shall include power to make provision as to any of the matters mentioned in that subsection.

(3) In the case of –

(*a*) an application for an adoption order in relation to a child who is not free for adoption;
(*b*) an application for an order freeing a child for adoption;

rules shall require every person who can be found and whose agreement or consent to the making of the order is required under this Act to be notified of a date and place where he will be heard on the application and of the fact that, unless he wishes or the court requires, he need not attend.

(4) In the case of an application under section 55, rules shall require every parent and guardian of the child who can be found to be notified as aforesaid.

(5) Rules made as respects magistrates' courts may provide for enabling any fact tending to establish the identity of a child with a child to whom a document relates to be proved by affidavit and for excluding or restricting in relation to any facts that may be so proved the power of a justice of the peace to compel the attendance of witnesses.

(6) This section does not apply in relation to sections 9, 10, 11 and 32 to 37.

Amendments—Magistrates' Courts Act 1980, s 154, Sch 7, para 141.

Rules—The rules made under this section are the Adoption Rules 1984 and the Magistrates' Courts (Adoption) Rules 1984.

67 Orders, rules and regulations

(1) Any power to make orders, rules or regulations conferred by this Act on the Secretary of State, the Lord Chancellor or the Registrar General shall be exercisable by statutory instrument.

(2) A statutory instrument containing rules or regulations made under any provision of this Act, except section 3(1) shall be subject to annulment in pursuance of a resolution of either House of Parliament.

(3) An order under section 28(10) or 57(8) shall not be made unless a draft of the order has been approved by resolution of each House of Parliament.

(4) An order made under any provision of this Act, except section 74, may be revoked or varied by a subsequent order under that provision.

(5) Orders and regulations made under this Act may make different provision in relation to different cases or classes of cases and may exclude certain cases or classes of cases.

(6) The Registrar General shall not make regulations under section 51 or paragraph 1(1) of Schedule 1 except with the approval of the Chancellor of the Exchequer.

Amendments—SI 1996/273.

Prospective amendment by Adoption (Intercountry Aspects) Act 1999—By virtue of A(IA)A 1999, s 15(1), Sch 2, para 3(6) (which come into force on 1 June 2003), in subsection (6) after "paragraph 1(1)" insert "or 3".

68 Offences by bodies corporate

Where an offence under this Act committed by a body corporate is proved to have been committed with the consent or connivance of or to be attributable to any neglect on the part of, any director, manager, member of the committee, secretary or other officer of the body, he as well as the body shall be deemed to be guilty of that offence and shall be liable to be proceeded against and punished accordingly.

PART II

69 Service of notices etc

Any notice or information required to be given under this Act may be given by post.

70 Nationality

(1) If the Secretary of State by order declares that a description of persons specified in the order has, in pursuance of the Convention, been notified to the Government of the United Kingdom as the description of persons who are deemed to possess the nationality of a particular Convention country, persons of that description shall, subject to the following provisions of this section, be treated for the purposes of this Act as nationals of that country.

(2) Subject to section 54(3) and subsection (3) of this section, where it appears to the court in any proceedings under this Act, or to any court by which a decision in pursuance of section 53(3) falls to be given, that a person is or was at a particular time a national of two or more countries, then –

(*a*) if it appears to the said court that he is or was then a United Kingdom national, he shall be treated for the purposes of those proceedings or that decision as if he were or had then been a United Kingdom national only;

(*b*) if, in a case not falling within paragraph (*a*), it appears to the said court that one only of those countries is or was then a Convention country, he shall be treated for those purposes as if he were or had then been a national of that country only;

(*c*) if, in a case not falling within paragraph (*a*), it appears to the said court that two or more of those countries are or were then Convention countries, he shall be treated for those purposes as if he were or had then been a national of such one only of those Convention countries as the said court considers is the country with which he is or was then most closely connected;

(*d*) in any other case, he shall be treated for those purposes as if he were or had then been a national of such one only of those countries as the said court considers is the country with which he is or was then most closely connected.

(3) A court in which proceedings are brought in pursuance of section 17, 52(3) or 53 shall be entitled to disregard the provisions of subsection (2) in so far as it appears to that court appropriate to do so for the purposes of those proceedings; but nothing in this subsection shall be construed as prejudicing the provisions of section 54(3).

(4) Where, after such inquiries as the court in question considers appropriate, it appears to the court in any proceedings under this Act, or to any court by which such a decision as aforesaid falls to be given, that a person has no nationality or no ascertainable nationality, he shall be treated for the purposes of those proceedings or that decision as a national of the country in which he resides or, where that country is one of two or more countries having the same law of nationality, as a national of those countries.

Prospective amendment by Adoption (Intercountry Aspects) Act 1999—By virtue of A(IA)A 1999, ss 15(2), 17, Sch 2, para 3(6), Sch 3 (which come into force on 1 June 2003), section 70 is repealed.

71 Internal law of a country

(1) In this Act "internal law" in relation to any country means the law applicable in a case where no question arises as to the law in force in any other country.

(2) In any case where the internal law of a country falls to be ascertained for the purposes of this Act by any court and there are in force in that country two or more systems of internal law, the relevant system shall be ascertained in accordance with any rule in force throughout that country indicating which of the systems is relevant in the case in question or, if there is no such rule, shall be the system appearing to that court to be most closely connected with the case.

72 Interpretation

(1) In this Act, unless the context otherwise requires –

"adoption agency" in sections 11, 13, 18 to 23 and 27 to 31 includes an adoption agency within the meaning of –

(*a*) section 1 of the Adoption (Scotland) Act 1978; and
(*b*) Article 3 of the Adoption (Northern Ireland) Order 1987;

"adoption order" –

(*a*) means an order under section 12(1); and
(*b*) in sections 12(3) and (4), 18 to 20, 27, 28, and 30 to 32 and in the definition of "British adoption order" in this subsection includes an order under section 12 of the Adoption (Scotland) Act 1978 and Article 12 of the Adoption (Northern Ireland) Order 1987 (Adoption orders in Scotland and Northern Ireland respectively); and
(*c*) in sections 27, 28 and 30 to 32 includes an order under section 55, section 49 of the Adoption (Scotland) Act 1978 and Article 57 of the Adoption (Northern Ireland) Order 1987 (orders in relation to children being adopted abroad);

"adoption society" means a body of persons whose functions consist of or include the making of arrangements for the adoption of children;

"approved adoption society" means an adoption society approved under Part I;

"authorised court" shall be construed in accordance with section 62;

"body of persons" means any body of persons, whether incorporated or unincorporated;

"British adoption order" means –

(*a*) an adoption order as defined in this subsection, and
(*b*) an order under any provision for the adoption of a child effected under the law of any British territory outside the United Kingdom;

"British territory" means, for the purposes of any provision of this Act, any of the following countries, that is to say, Great Britain, Northern Ireland, the Channel Islands, the Isle of Man and a colony, being a country designated for the purposes of that provision by order of the Secretary of State or, if no country is so designated, any of those countries;

"child", except where used to express a relationship, means a person who has not attained the age of 18 years;

"the Convention" means the Convention relating to the adoption of children concluded at the Hague on 15 November 1965 and signed on behalf of the United Kingdom on that date;

"Convention adoption order" means an adoption order made in accordance with section 17(1);

"Convention country" means any country outside British territory, being a country for the time being designated by an order of the Secretary of State as a country in which, in his opinion, the Convention is in force;

"existing" in relation to an enactment or other instrument, means one passed or made at any time before 1 January 1976;

"guardian" has the same meaning as in the Children Act 1989;

"internal law" has the meaning assigned by section 71;

"local authority" means the council of a county (other than a metropolitan county), a metropolitan district, a London borough or the Common Council of the City of London but, in relation to Wales, means the council of a county or county borough;

"notice" means a notice in writing;

"order freeing a child for adoption" means an order under section 18 and in sections 27(2) and 59 includes an order under –

(*a*) section 18 of the Adoption (Scotland) Act 1978; and
(*b*) Article 17 or 18 of the Adoption (Northern Ireland) Act 1987;

"overseas adoption" has the meaning assigned by subsection (2);

"parent" means, in relation to a child, any parent who has parental responsibility for the child under the Children Act 1989;

"parental responsibility" and "parental responsibility agreement" have the same meaning as in the Children Act 1989;

"prescribed" means prescribed by rules;

"regulated adoption" means an overseas adoption of a description designated by an order under subsection (2) as that of an adoption regulated by the Convention;

"relative" in relation to a child means grandparent, brother, sister, uncle or aunt, whether of the full blood or half-blood or by affinity and includes, where the child is illegitimate, the father of the child and any person who would be a relative within the meaning of this definition if the child were the legitimate child of his mother and father;

"rules" means rules made under section 66(1) or made by virtue of section 66(2) under section 144 of the Magistrates' Courts Act 1980;

"specified order" means any provision for the adoption of a child effected under enactments similar to sections 12(1) and 17 in force in any British territory outside the United Kingdom;

"United Kingdom national" means, for the purposes for any provision of this Act, a citizen of the United Kingdom and colonies satisfying such conditions, if any, as the Secretary of State may by order specify for the purposes of that provision;

"upbringing" has the same meaning as in the Children Act 1989;

"voluntary organisation" means a body other than a public or local authority the activities of which are not carried on for profit.

(1A) In this Act, in determining with what person, or where, a child has his home, any absence of the child at a hospital or boarding school and any other temporary absence shall be disregarded.

(1B) In this Act, references to a child who is in the care of or looked after by a local authority have the same meaning as in the Children Act 1989.

(2) In this Act "overseas adoption" means an adoption of such a description as the Secretary of State may by order specify, being a description of adoptions of children appearing to him to be effected under the law of any country outside Great Britain; and an order under this subsection may contain provision as to the manner in which evidence of an overseas adoption may be given.

(3) For the purposes of this Act a person shall be deemed to make arrangements for the adoption of a child if he enters into or makes any agreement for, or for facilitating, the adoption of the child by any other person, whether the adoption is effected, or is intended to be effected, in Great Britain or elsewhere, or if he initiates or takes part in any negotiations of which the purpose or effect is the conclusion of any agreement or the making of any arrangement therefor, and if he causes another person to do so.

(3A) In this Act, in relation to the proposed adoption of a child resident outside the British Islands, references to arrangements for the adoption of a child include references to arrangements for an assessment for the purpose of indicating whether a person is suitable to adopt a child or not.

(4) Except so far as the context otherwise requires, any reference in this Act to an enactment shall be construed as a reference to that enactment as amended by or under any other enactment, including this Act.

(5) In this Act, except where otherwise indicated –

(*a*) a reference to a numbered Part, section or Schedule is a reference to the Part or section of, or the Schedule to, this Act so numbered, and
(*b*) a reference in a section to a numbered subsection is a reference to the subsection of that section so numbered, and
(*c*) a reference in a section, subsection or Schedule to a numbered paragraph is a reference to the paragraph of that section, subsection or schedule so numbered.

Amendments—Magistrates' Courts Act 1980, s 154, Sch 7, para 142; Health and Social Services and Social Security Adjudications Act 1983, s 9, Sch 2, para 37; CA 1989, ss 88, 108(7), Sch 10, para 30, Sch 15; Local Government (Wales) Act 1994, s 22, Sch 10, para 9; Adoption (Intercountry Aspects) Act 1999, s 13.

Prospective amendment by Adoption (Intercountry Aspects) Act 1999—By virtue of A(IA)A 1999, ss 8, 13, 15, Sch 2, para 3(8), Sch 3 (which come into force on 1 June 2003), this section is amended as follows:

1 For the definitions "the Convention", "Convention adoption order" and "Convention country" there are substituted –

""the Convention" means the Convention on Protection of Children and Co-operation in respect of Intercountry Adoption, concluded at the Hague on 29th May 1993;

"Convention adoption" means an adoption effected under the law of a Convention country outside the British Islands, and certified in pursuance of Article 23(1) of the Convention;

"Convention adoption order" means an adoption order made in accordance with section 17;

"Convention country" means any country or territory in which the Convention is in force.".

2 The definitions "regulated adoption" and "specified order" are repealed.

3 In subsection (2) for "Great Britain" substitute "the British Islands".

4 After subsection (3) there is inserted –

"(3B) In this Act, in relation to –

(*a*) an adoption proposed to be effected by a Convention adoption order; or
(*b*) an adoption of a child habitually resident outside the British Islands which is proposed to be effected by an adoption order other than a Convention adoption order,

references to a child placed with any persons by an adoption agency include references to a child who, in pursuance of arrangements made by such an agency, has been adopted by or placed with those persons under the law of a country or territory outside the British Islands.".

"parent" (s 72(1))—The definition is confined to those parents who have parental responsibility for the child under CA 1989 (see CA 1989, ss 2–4 and notes thereto). For full discussion of the meaning of the term "parent", see under AA 1976, s 16.

"relative" (s 72(1))—The definition is in precise terms – a great-uncle does not come within the definition (*Re C (Minors) (Wardship: Adoption)* [1989] 1 FLR 222); however, a step-grandparent *is* within the definition (for example, see *Re U (Application to Free for Adoption)* [1993] 2 FLR 992).

"upbringing" (s 72(1))—This term, in relation to any child, includes the care of the child but not his maintenance (CA 1989, s 105(1)).

"overseas adoption" (s 72(2))—See under s 38.

****

74 Short title, commencement and extent

(1) This Act may be cited as the Adoption Act 1976.

(2) This Act shall come into force on such date as the Secretary of State may by order appoint and different dates may be appointed for different provisions.

(3) This Act extends to England and Wales only.

Amendments—CA 1989, s 88(1), Sch 10, para 31.

****

SCHEDULE 1
REGISTRATION OF ADOPTIONS

1 Registration of adoption orders

(1) Every adoption order shall contain a direction to the Registrar General to make in the Adopted Children Register an entry in such form as the Registrar General may by regulations specify.

(2) The direction contained in a Convention adoption order in pursuance of this paragraph shall include an instruction that the entry made in that register in consequence of the order shall be marked with the words "Convention order".

(3) Where on an application to a court for an adoption order in respect of a child (not being a child who has previously been the subject of an adoption order made by a court in England or Wales under this Act or any enactment at the time in force) there is proved to the satisfaction of the court the identity of the child with a child to whom an entry in the Registers of Births relates, any adoption order made in pursuance of the application shall contain a direction to the Registrar General to cause the entry in the Registers of Births to be marked with the word "Adopted".

(4) Where an adoption order is made in respect of a child who has previously been the subject of an adoption order made by a court in England or Wales under this Act or any enactment at the time in force, the order shall contain a direction to the Registrar General to cause the previous entry in the Adopted Children Register to be marked with the word "Re-adopted".

(5) Where an adoption order is made, the prescribed officer of the court which made the order shall cause the order to be communicated in the prescribed manner to the Registrar General, and upon receipt of the communication the Registrar

General shall cause compliance to be made with the directions contained in the order.

Prospective amendment by Adoption (Intercountry Aspects) Act 1999—By virtue of A(IA)A 1999, ss 12(2), 15(2), Sch 3 (which come into force on 1 June 2003), sub-paragraph (2) is repealed.

2 Registration of adoptions in Scotland, Northern Ireland, the Isle of Man and the Channel Islands

(1) Where the Registrar General is notified by the Registrar General for Scotland that an adoption order has been made by a court in Scotland in respect of a child to whom an entry in the Registers of Births or the Adopted Children Register relates, the Registrar General shall cause the entry to be marked "Adopted (Scotland)" or, as the case may be, "Re-adopted (Scotland)"; and where, after an entry has been so marked, the Registrar General is notified as aforesaid that the adoption order has been quashed, or that an appeal against the adoption order has been allowed, he shall cause the marking to be cancelled.

(2) Where the Registrar General is notified by the authority maintaining a register of adoptions in Northern Ireland, the Isle of Man or any of the Channel Islands that an order has been made in that country authorising the adoption of a child to whom an entry in the Registers of Births or the Adopted Children Register relates, he shall cause the entry to be marked with the word "Adopted" or "Re-adopted", as the case may require, followed by the name, in brackets, of the country in which the order was made.

(3) Where, after an entry has been so marked, the Registrar General is notified as aforesaid that the order has been quashed, that an appeal against the order has been allowed or that the order has been revoked, he shall cause the marking to be cancelled; and a copy or extract of an entry in any register, being an entry the marking of which is cancelled under this sub-paragraph, shall be deemed to be an accurate copy if and only if both the marking and the cancellation are omitted therefrom.

(4) The preceding provisions of this paragraph shall apply in relation to orders corresponding to orders under section 55 as they apply in relation to orders authorising the adoption of a child; but any marking of an entry required by virtue of this sub-paragraph shall consist of the words "proposed foreign adoption" or as the case may require, "proposed foreign re-adoption" followed by the name in brackets of the country in which the order was made.

(5) Without prejudice to sub-paragraphs (2) and (3) where, after an entry in the Registers of Births has been marked in accordance with this paragraph, the birth is re-registered under section 14 of the Births and Deaths Registration Act 1953 (re-registration of births of legitimated children) the entry made on the re-registration shall be marked in the like manner.

3 Registration of overseas adoptions

If the Registrar General is satisfied that an entry in the Registers of Births relates to a person adopted under an overseas adoption and that he has sufficient particulars relating to that person to enable an entry, in the form specified for the purposes of this sub-paragraph in regulations made under paragraph 1(1), to be made in the Adopted Children Register in respect of that person, he shall –

(*a*) make such an entry in the Adopted Children Register; and

PART II

(b) if there is a previous entry in respect of that person in that register, mark the entry (or if there is more than one such entry the last of them) with the word "Re-adopted" followed by the name in brackets of the country in which the adoption was effected; and

(c) unless the entry in the Registers of Births is already marked with the word "Adopted" (whether or not followed by other words), mark the entry with that word followed by the name in brackets of the country aforesaid.

Prospective amendment by Adoption (Intercountry Aspects) Act 1999—By virtue of A(IA)A 1999, ss 12(3), 15(3), Sch 3 (which come into force on 1 June 2003), for paragraph 3 substitute:

"**3 Registration of foreign adoptions**

(1) If the Registrar General is satisfied, on an application under this paragraph, that he has sufficient particulars relating to a child adopted under a registrable foreign adoption to enable an entry to be made in the Adopted Children Register for the child –

(a) he must make the entry accordingly, and

(b) if he is also satisfied that an entry in the Registers of Births relates to the child, he must secure that the entry in those Registers is marked "Adopted" or "Re-adopted", as the case may be, followed by the name in brackets of the country in which the adoption was effected.

(2) An entry made in the Adopted Children Register by virtue of this paragraph must be made in the specified form.

(3) An application under this paragraph must be made, in the specified manner, by a specified person and give the specified particulars.

(4) In this paragraph –

"registrable foreign adoption" means a Convention or overseas adoption which satisfies specified requirements;

"specified" means specified by regulations made by the Registrar General.".

4 Amendment of orders and rectification of Registers

(1) The court by which an adoption order has been made may, on the application of the adopter or of the adopted person, amend the order by the correction of any error in the particulars contained therein, and may –

(a) if satisfied on the application of the adopter or the adopted person that within one year beginning with the date of the order any new name has been given to the adopted person (whether in baptism or otherwise), or taken by him, either in lieu of or in addition to a name specified in the particulars required to be entered in the Adopted Children Register in pursuance of the order, amend the order by substituting or adding that name in those particulars, as the case may require;

(b) if satisfied on the application of any person concerned that a direction for the marking of an entry in the Registers of Births or the Adopted Children Register included in the order in pursuance of sub-paragraph (3) or (4) of paragraph 1 was wrongly so included, revoke that direction.

(2) Where an adoption order is amended or a direction revoked under sub-paragraph (1), the prescribed officer of the court shall cause the amendment to be communicated in the prescribed manner to the Registrar General who shall as the case may require –

(a) cause the entry in the Adopted Children Register to be amended accordingly; or

(b) cause the marking of the entry in the Registers of Births or the Adopted Children Register to be cancelled.

(3) Where an adoption order is quashed or an appeal against an adoption order allowed by any court, the court shall give directions to the Registrar General to cancel any entry in the Adopted Children Register, and any marking of an entry in that Register, or the Registers of Births as the case may be, which was effected in pursuance of the order.

(4) Where an adoption order has been amended, any certified copy of the relevant entry in the Adopted Children Register which may be issued pursuant to subsection (3) of section 50 shall be a copy of the entry as amended, without the reproduction of any note or marking relating to the amendment or of any matter cancelled pursuant thereto; and a copy or extract of an entry in any register, being an entry the marking of which has been cancelled, shall be deemed to be an accurate copy if and only if both the marking and the cancellation are omitted therefrom.

(5) If the Registrar General is satisfied –

(*a*) that a Convention adoption order or an overseas adoption has ceased to have effect, whether on annulment or otherwise; or

(*b*) that any entry or mark was erroneously made in pursuance of paragraph 3 in any register mentioned in that paragraph,

he may cause such alterations to be made in any such register as he considers are required in consequence of the cesser or to correct the error; and where an entry in such a register is amended in pursuance of this sub-paragraph, any copy or extract of the entry shall be deemed to be accurate if and only if it shows the entry as amended but without indicating that it has been amended.

(6) In relation to an adoption order made by a magistrates' court, the reference in sub-paragraph (1) to the court by which the order has been made includes a reference to a court acting for the same petty sessions area.

Prospective amendment by Adoption (Intercountry Aspects) Act 1999—By virtue of A(IA)A 1999, ss 12(4), 15(3), Sch 3 (which come into force on 1 June 2003), in sub-paragraph (5)(*a*) after "that" insert "a Convention adoption".

5 Marking of entries on re-registration of birth on legitimation

(1) Without prejudice to section 52, where, after an entry in the Registers of Births has been marked with the word "Adopted" (with or without the addition of the word "(Scotland)"), the birth is re-registered under section 14 of the Births and Deaths Registration Act 1953 (re-registration of births of legitimated persons) the entry made on the re-registration shall be marked in the like manner.

(2) Without prejudice to paragraph 4(5), where an entry in the Registers of Births is marked in pursuance of paragraph 3 and the birth in question is subsequently re-registered under the said section 14, the entry made on re-registration shall be marked in the like manner.

6 Cancellations in Registers on legitimation

Where an adoption order is revoked under section 52(1) or (2) the prescribed officer of the court shall cause the revocation to be communicated in the prescribed manner to the Registrar General who shall cause to be cancelled –

(*a*) the entry in the Adopted Children Register relating to the adopted person; and (*b*) the marking with the word "Adopted" (or, as the case may be, with that word and the word "(Scotland)") of any entry relating to him in the Registers of Births;

and a copy or extract of an entry in any register, being an entry the marking of which is cancelled under this section, shall be deemed to be an accurate copy if and only if both the marking and the cancellation are omitted therefrom.

Amendments—Domestic Proceedings and Magistrates' Courts Act 1978, ss 74(4), 89(2)(*b*), Sch 3.

****

Adoption (Intercountry Aspects) Act 1999

Guidance—Comprehensive guidance on intercountry adoption is published by the DOH – "*Intercountry Adoption Guide – Practice and Procedures*" – the Guide is available on the Internet at *www.doh.gov.uk/adoption* .

Implementation of Convention

1 Regulations giving effect to Convention

(1) Subject to the provisions of this Act, regulations made by the Secretary of State may make provision for giving effect to the Convention on Protection of Children and Co-operation in respect of Intercountry Adoption, concluded at the Hague on 29th May 1993 ("the Convention").

(2) The text of the Convention (so far as material) is set out in Schedule 1 to this Act.

(3) Regulations under this section may –

(*a*) apply, with or without modifications, any provision of the enactments relating to adoption;

(*b*) provide that any person who contravenes or fails to comply with any provision of the regulations is to be guilty of an offence and liable on summary conviction to imprisonment for a term not exceeding three months, or a fine not exceeding level 5 on the standard scale, or both;

(*c*) make different provision for different purposes or areas; and

(*d*) make such incidental, supplementary, consequential or transitional provision as appears to the Secretary of State to be expedient.

(4) Regulations under this section shall be made by statutory instrument which shall be subject to annulment in pursuance of a resolution of either House of Parliament.

(5) Subject to subsection (6), any power to make subordinate legislation under or for the purposes of the enactments relating to adoption includes power to do so with a view to giving effect to the provisions of the Convention.

(6) Subsection (5) does not apply in relation to any power which is exercisable by the National Assembly for Wales.

Regulations giving effect to the Convention—For procedure see the Intercountry Adoption (Hague Convention) Regulations 2003 which come into force on 1 June 2003.

2 Central Authorities and accredited bodies

(1) The functions under the Convention of the Central Authority are to be discharged –

(*a*) separately in relation to England and Scotland by the Secretary of State; and

(*b*) in relation to Wales by the National Assembly for Wales.

(2) A communication may be sent to the Central Authority in relation to any part of Great Britain by sending it (for forwarding if necessary) to the Central Authority in relation to England.

(3) An approved adoption society is an accredited body for the purposes of the Convention if the approval extends to the provision of facilities in respect of Convention adoptions and adoptions effected by Convention adoption orders.

(4) The functions under Article 9(*a*) to (*c*) of the Convention are to be discharged by local authorities and accredited bodies on behalf of the Central Authority.

(5) In this section in its application to England and Wales, "approved adoption society" has the same meaning as in Part I of the Adoption Act 1976 ("the 1976 Act"); and expressions which are also used in that Act have the same meanings as in that Act.

(6) (*applies to Scotland only*)

****

SCHEDULE 1

CONVENTION ON PROTECTION OF CHILDREN AND CO-OPERATION IN RESPECT OF INTERCOUNTRY ADOPTION

The States signatory to the present Convention.

Recognizing that the child, for the full and harmonious development of his or her personality, should grow up in a family environment, in an atmosphere of happiness, love and understanding,

Recalling that each State should take, as a matter of priority, appropriate measures to enable the child to remain in the care of his or her family of origin,

Recognizing that intercountry adoption may offer the advantage of a permanent family to a child for whom a suitable family cannot be found in his or her State of origin,

Convinced of the necessity to take measures to ensure that intercountry adoptions are made in the best interests of the child and with respect for his or her fundamental rights, and to prevent the abduction, the sale of, or traffic in children,

Desiring to establish common provisions to this effect, taking into account the principles set forth in international instruments, in particular the United Nations Convention on the Rights of the Child, of 20 November 1989, and the United Nations Declaration on Social and Legal Principles relating to the Protection and

Welfare of Children, with Special Reference to Foster Placement and Adoption Nationally and Internationally (General Assembly Resolution 41/85, of 3 December 1986),

Have agreed upon the following provisions –

CHAPTER I
SCOPE OF THE CONVENTION

Article 1

The objects of the present Convention are –

(*a*) to establish safeguards to ensure that intercountry adoptions take place in the best interests of the child and with respect for his or her fundamental rights as recognised in international law;

(*b*) to establish a system of co-operation amongst Contracting States to ensure that those safeguards are respected and thereby prevent the abduction, the sale of, or traffic in children;

(*c*) to secure the recognition in Contracting States of adoptions made in accordance with the Convention.

Article 2

1 The Convention shall apply where a child habitually resident in one Contracting State ("the State of origin") has been, is being, or is to be moved to another Contracting State ("the receiving State") either after his or her adoption in the State of origin by spouses or a person habitually resident in the receiving State, or for the purposes of such an adoption in the receiving State or in the State of origin.

2 The Convention covers only adoptions which create a permanent parent-child relationship.

Article 3

The Convention ceases to apply if the agreements mentioned in Article 17, sub-paragraph (*c*), have not been given before the child attains the age of eighteen years.

CHAPTER II
REQUIREMENTS FOR INTERCOUNTRY ADOPTIONS

Article 4

An adoption within the scope of the Convention shall take place only if the competent authorities of the State of origin –

(*a*) have established that the child is adoptable;

(*b*) have determined, after possibilities for placement of the child within the State of origin have been given due consideration, that an intercountry adoption is in the child's best interests;

(*c*) have ensured that –

(i) the persons, institutions and authorities whose consent is necessary for adoption, have been counselled as may be necessary and duly informed of the effects of their consent, in particular whether or not an adoption will result in the termination of the legal relationship between the child and his or her family of origin,

(ii) such persons, institutions and authorities have given their consent freely, in the required legal form, and expressed or evidenced in writing,

(iii) the consents have not been induced by payment or compensation of any kind and have not been withdrawn, and

(iv) the consent of the mother, where required, has been given only after the birth of the child; and

(*d*) have ensured, having regard to the age and degree of maturity of the child, that –

(i) he or she has been counselled and duly informed of the effects of the adoption and of his or her consent to the adoption, where such consent is required,

(ii) consideration has been given to the child's wishes and opinions,

(iii) the child's consent to the adoption, where such consent is required, has been given freely, in the required legal form, and expressed or evidenced in writing, and

(iv) such consent has not been induced by payment or compensation of any kind.

Article 5

An adoption within the scope of the Convention shall take place only if the competent authorities of the receiving State –

(*a*) have determined that the prospective adoptive parents are eligible and suited to adopt;

(*b*) have ensured that the prospective adoptive parents have been counselled as may be necessary; and

(*c*) have determined that the child is or will be authorised to enter and reside permanently in that State.

CHAPTER III
CENTRAL AUTHORITIES AND ACCREDITED BODIES

Article 6

1 A Contracting State shall designate a Central Authority to discharge the duties which are imposed by the Convention upon such authorities.

2 Federal States, States with more than one system of law or States having autonomous territorial units shall be free to appoint more than one Central Authority and to specify the territorial or personal extent of their functions. Where a State has appointed more than one Central Authority, it shall designate the Central Authority to which any communication may be addressed for transmission to the appropriate Central Authority within that State.

Article 7

1 Central Authorities shall co-operate with each other and promote co-operation amongst the competent authorities in their States to protect children and to achieve the other objects of the Convention.

2 They shall take directly all appropriate measures to –

(*a*) provide information as to the laws of their States concerning adoption and other general information, such as statistics and standard forms;
(*b*) keep one another informed about the operation of the Convention and, as far as possible, eliminate any obstacles to its application.

Article 8

Central Authorities shall take, directly or through public authorities, all appropriate measures to prevent improper financial or other gain in connection with an adoption and to deter all practices contrary to the objects of the Convention.

Article 9

Central Authorities shall take, directly or through public authorities or other bodies duly accredited in their State, all appropriate measures, in particular to –

(*a*) collect, preserve and exchange information about the situation of the child and the prospective adoptive parents, so far as is necessary to complete the adoption;
(*b*) facilitate, follow and expedite proceedings with a view to obtaining the adoption;
(*c*) promote the development of adoption counselling and post-adoption services in their States;
(*d*) provide each other with general evaluation reports about experience with intercountry adoption;
(*e*) reply, in so far as is permitted by the law of their State, to justified requests from other Central Authorities or public authorities for information about a particular adoption situation.

Article 10

Accreditation shall only be granted to and maintained by bodies demonstrating their competence to carry out properly the tasks with which they may be entrusted.

Article 11

An accredited body shall –

(*a*) pursue only non-profit objectives according to such conditions and within such limits as may be established by the competent authorities of the State of accreditation;
(*b*) be directed and staffed by persons qualified by their ethical standards and by training or experience to work in the field of intercountry adoption; and
(*c*) be subject to supervision by competent authorities of that State as to its composition, operation and financial situation.

Article 12

A body accredited in one Contracting State may act in another Contracting State only if the competent authorities of both States have authorised it to do so.

Article 13

The designation of the Central Authorities and, where appropriate, the extent of their functions, as well as the names and addresses of the accredited bodies shall be communicated by each Contracting State to the Permanent Bureau of the Hague Conference on Private International Law.

CHAPTER IV
PROCEDURAL REQUIREMENTS IN INTERCOUNTRY ADOPTION

Article 14

Persons habitually resident in a Contracting State, who wish to adopt a child habitually resident in another Contracting State, shall apply to the Central Authority in the State of their habitual residence.

Article 15

1 If the Central Authority of the receiving State is satisfied that the applicants are eligible and suited to adopt, it shall prepare a report including information about their identity, eligibility and suitability to adopt, background, family and medical history, social environment, reasons for adoption, ability to undertake an intercountry adoption, as well as the characteristics of the children for whom they would be qualified to care.

2 It shall transmit the report to the Central Authority of the State of origin.

Article 16

1 If the Central Authority of the State of origin is satisfied that the child is adoptable, it shall –

(*a*) prepare a report including information about his or her identity, adoptability, background, social environment, family history, medical history including that of the child's family, and any special needs of the child;

(*b*) give due consideration to the child's upbringing and to his or her ethnic, religious and cultural background;

(*c*) ensure that consents have been obtained in accordance with Article 4; and

(*d*) determine, on the basis in particular of the reports relating to the child and the prospective adoptive parents, whether the envisaged placement is in the best interests of the child.

2 It shall transmit to the Central Authority of the receiving State its report on the child, proof that the necessary consents have been obtained and the reasons for its determination on the placement, taking care not to reveal the identity of the mother and the father if, in the State of origin, these identities may not be disclosed.

Article 17

Any decision in the State of origin that a child should be entrusted to prospective adoptive parents may only be made if –

(*a*) the Central Authority of that State has ensured that the prospective adoptive parents agree;

(*b*) the Central Authority of the receiving State has approved such decision, where such approval is required by the law of that State or by the Central Authority of the State of origin;

(*c*) the Central Authorities of both States have agreed that the adoption may proceed; and

(*d*) it has been determined, in accordance with Article 5, that the prospective adoptive parents are eligible and suited to adopt and that the child is or will be authorised to enter and reside permanently in the receiving State.

Article 18

The Central Authorities of both States shall take all necessary steps to obtain permission for the child to leave the State of origin and to enter and reside permanently in the receiving State.

Article 19

1 The transfer of the child to the receiving State may only be carried out if the requirements of Article 17 have been satisfied.

2 The Central Authorities of both States shall ensure that this transfer takes place in secure and appropriate circumstances and, if possible, in the company of the adoptive or prospective adoptive parents.

3 If the transfer of the child does not take place, the reports referred to in Articles 15 and 16 are to be sent back to the authorities who forwarded them.

Article 20

The Central Authorities shall keep each other informed about the adoption process and the measures taken to complete it, as well as about the progress of the placement if a probationary period is required.

Article 21

1 Where the adoption is to take place after the transfer of the child to the receiving State and it appears to the Central Authority of that State that the continued placement of the child with the prospective adoptive parents is not in the child's best interests, such Central Authority shall take the measures necessary to protect the child, in particular –

(*a*) to cause the child to be withdrawn from the prospective adoptive parents and to arrange temporary care;

(*b*) in consultation with the Central Authority of the State of origin, to arrange without delay a new placement of the child with a view to adoption or, if this is not appropriate, to arrange alternative long-term care; an adoption shall not take place until the Central Authority of the State of origin has been duly informed concerning the new prospective adoptive parents;

(*c*) as a last resort, to arrange the return of the child, if his or her interests so require.

2 Having regard in particular to the age and degree of maturity of the child, he or she shall be consulted and, where appropriate, his or her consent obtained in relation to measures to be taken under this Article.

Article 22

1 The functions of a Central Authority under this Chapter may be performed by public authorities or by bodies accredited under Chapter III, to the extent permitted by the law of its State.

2 Any Contracting State may declare to the depositary of the Convention that the functions of the Central Authority under Articles 15 to 21 may be performed in that State, to the extent permitted by the law and subject to the supervision of the competent authorities of that State, also by bodies or persons who –

(*a*) meet the requirements of integrity, professional competence, experience and accountability of that State; and
(*b*) are qualified by their ethical standards and by training or experience to work in the field of intercountry adoption.

3 A Contracting State which makes the declaration provided for in paragraph 2 shall keep the Permanent Bureau of the Hague Conference on Private International Law informed of the names and addresses of these bodies and persons.

4 Any Contracting State may declare to the depositary of the Convention that adoptions of children habitually resident in its territory may only take place if the functions of the Central Authorities are performed in accordance with paragraph 1.

5 Notwithstanding any declaration made under paragraph 2, the reports provided for in Articles 15 and 16 shall, in every case, be prepared under the responsibility of the Central Authority or other authorities or bodies in accordance with paragraph 1.

CHAPTER V
RECOGNITION AND EFFECTS OF THE ADOPTION

Article 23

1 An adoption certified by the competent authority of the State of the adoption as having been made in accordance with the Convention shall be recognised by operation of law in the other Contracting States. The certificate shall specify when and by whom the agreements under Article 17, sub-paragraph (*c*), were given.

2 Each Contracting State shall, at the time of signature, ratification, acceptance, approval or accession, notify the depositary of the Convention of the identity and the functions of the authority or the authorities which, in that State, are competent to make the certification. It shall also notify the depositary of any modification in the designation of these authorities.

Article 24

The recognition of an adoption may be refused in a contracting State only if the adoption is manifestly contrary to its public policy, taking into account the best interests of the child.

Article 25

Any Contracting State may declare to the depositary of the convention that it will not be bound under this Convention to recognise adoptions made in accordance with an agreement concluded by application of Article 39, paragraph 2.

Article 26

1 The recognition of an adoption includes recognition of –

(*a*) the legal parent-child relationship between the child and his or her adoptive parents;
(*b*) parental responsibility of the adoptive parents for the child;
(*c*) the termination of a pre-existing legal relationship between the child and his or her mother and father, if the adoption has this effect in the Contracting State where it was made.

2 In the case of an adoption having the effect of terminating a pre-existing legal parent-child relationship, the child shall enjoy in the receiving State, and in any other Contracting State where the adoption is recognised, rights equivalent to those resulting from adoptions having this effect in each such State.

3 The preceding paragraphs shall not prejudice the application of any provision more favourable for the child, in force in the Contracting State which recognises the adoption.

Article 27

1 Where an adoption granted in the State of origin does not have the effect of terminating a pre-existing legal parent-child relationship, it may, in the receiving State which recognises the adoption under the Convention, be converted into an adoption having such an effect –

(*a*) if the law of the receiving State so permits; and
(*b*) if the consents referred to in Article 4, sub-paragraphs (*c*) and (*d*), have been or are given for the purpose of such an adoption.

2 Article 23 applies to the decision converting the adoption.

CHAPTER VI
GENERAL PROVISIONS

Article 28

The Convention does not affect any law of a State of origin which requires that the adoption of a child habitually resident within that State take place in that State or which prohibits the child's placement in, or transfer to, the receiving State prior to adoption.

Article 29

There shall be no contact between the prospective adoptive parents and the child's parents or any other person who has care of the child until the requirements of Article 4, sub-paragraphs (*a*) to (*c*), and Article 5, sub-paragraph (*a*), have been met, unless the adoption takes place within a family or unless the contact is in compliance with the conditions established by the competent authority of the State of origin.

Article 30

1 The competent authorities of a Contracting State shall ensure that information held by them concerning the child's origin, in particular information concerning the identity of his or her parents, as well as the medical history, is preserved.

2 They shall ensure that the child or his or her representative has access to such information, under appropriate guidance, in so far as is permitted by the law of that State.

Article 31

Without prejudice to Article 30, personal data gathered or transmitted under the Convention, especially data referred to in Articles 15 and 16, shall be used only for the purposes for which they were gathered or transmitted.

Article 32

1 No one shall derive improper financial or other gain from an activity related to an intercountry adoption.

2 Only costs and expenses, including reasonable professional fees of persons involved in the adoption, may be charged or paid.

3 The directors, administrators and employees of bodies involved in an adoption shall not receive remuneration which is unreasonably high in relation to services rendered.

Article 33

A competent authority which finds that any provision of the Convention has not been respected or that there is a serious risk that it may not be respected, shall immediately inform the Central Authority of its State. This Central Authority shall be responsible for ensuring that appropriate measures are taken.

Article 34

If the competent authority of the State of destination of a document so requests, a translation certified as being in conformity with the original must be furnished. Unless otherwise provided, the costs of such translation are to be borne by the prospective adoptive parents.

Article 35

The competent authorities of the contracting States shall act expeditiously in the process of adoption.

Article 36

In relation to a State which has two or more systems of law with regard to adoption applicable in different territorial units –

(*a*) any reference to habitual residence in that State shall be construed as referring to habitual residence in a territorial unit of that State;

(*b*) any reference to the law of that State shall be construed as referring to the law in force in the relevant territorial unit;

(*c*) any reference to the competent authorities or to the public authorities of that State shall be construed as referring to those authorised to act in the relevant territorial unit;

(*d*) any reference to the accredited bodies of that State shall be construed as referring to bodies accredited in the relevant territorial unit.

Article 37

In relation to a State which with regard to adoption has two or more systems of law applicable to different categories of persons, any reference to the law of that State shall be construed as referring to the legal system specified by the law of that State.

Article 38

A State within which different territorial units have their own rules of law in respect of adoption shall not be bound to apply the Convention where a State with a unified system of law would not be bound to do so.

Article 39

1 The convention does not affect any international instrument to which Contracting States are Parties and which contains provisions on matters governed by the Convention, unless a contrary declaration is made by the States parties to such instrument.

2 Any Contracting State may enter into agreements with one or more other Contracting States, with a view to improving the application of the Convention in their mutual relations. These agreements may derogate only from the provisions of Articles 14 to 16 and 18 to 21. The States which have concluded such an agreement shall transmit a copy to the depositary of the Convention.

Article 40

No reservation to the Convention shall be permitted.

Article 41

The Convention shall apply in every case where an application pursuant to Article 14 has been received after the Convention has entered into force in the receiving State and the State of origin.

Article 42

The Secretary General of the Hague Conference on Private International Law shall at regular intervals convene a Special Commission in order to review the practical operation of the Convention.

****

INTERCOUNTRY ADOPTION – HAGUE CONVENTION COUNTRIES

The following lists show the position regarding implementation of the Hague Convention on the Protection of Children and Co-operation in Respect of Intercountry Adoption (The Hague, 29 May 1993). The UK is expected to ratify the Convention on 1 June 2003.

The following States have signed, but not yet ratified the Convention:

Contracting State	*Date of signing*
Belarus	10 December 1997
Belgium	27 January 1999
China	30 November 2000

Contracting State	*Date of signing*
India	9 January 2003
Ireland	19 June 1996
Portugal	26 August 1999
Russian Federation	7 September 2000
Turkey	5 December 2001
United Kingdom	12 January 1994
United States	31 March 1994
Uruguay	1 September 1993

Total number of States having signed, but not yet ratified – 11

The following States have ratified the Convention:

Contracting State	*Date of ratification*	*Entry into force*
Albania	12 September 2000	1 January 2001
Australia	25 August 1998	1 December 1998
Austria	3 June 1999	1 September 1999
Bolivia	12 March 2002	1 July 2002
Brazil	10 March 1999	1 July 1999
Bulgaria	15 May 2002	1 September 2002
Burkina Faso	11 January 1996	1 May 1996
Canada	19 December 1996	1 April 1997
Chile	13 July 1999	1 November 1999
Colombia	13 July 1998	1 November 1998
Costa Rica	30 October 1995	1 February 1996
Cyprus	20 February 1995	1 June 1995
Czech Republic	11 February 2000	1 June 2000
Denmark	2 July 1997	1 November 1997
Ecuador	7 September 1995	1 January 1996
El Salvador	17 November 1998	1 March 1999
Finland	27 March 1997	1 July 1997
France	30 June 1998	1 October 1998
Germany	22 November 2001	1 March 2002
Israel	3 February 1999	1 June 1999
Italy	18 January 2000	1 May 2000
Latvia	9 August 2002	1 December 2002
Luxembourg	5 July 2002	1 November 2002
Mexico	14 September 1994	1 May 1995
Netherlands, The	26 June 1998	1 October 1998
Norway	25 September 1997	1 January 1998
Panama	29 September 1999	1 January 2000
Peru	14 September 1995	1 January 1996

Contracting State	*Date of ratification*	*Entry into force*
Albania	12 September 2000	1 January 2001
Philippines	2 July 1996	1 November 1996
Poland	12 June 1995	1 October 1995
Romania	28 December 1994	1 May 1995
Slovakia	6 June 2001	1 October 2001
Slovenia	24 January 2002	1 May 2002
Spain	11 July 1995	1 November 1995
Sri Lanka	23 January 1995	1 May 1995
Sweden	28 May 1997	1 September 1997
Switzerland	24 September 2002	1 January 2003
Venezuela	10 January 1997	1 May 1997

Total number of ratifications – 38

The following States have acceded to the Convention:

Contracting State	*Date of accession*	*Entry into force*	*Expiry date under Art 44(3)**
Andorra	3 January 1997	1 May 1997	1 August 1997
Burundi	15 October 1998	1 February 1999	15 May 1999
Estonia	22 February 2002	1 June 2002	1 October 2002
Georgia	9 April 1999	1 August 1999	1 November 1999
Guatemala	26 November 2002	1 March 2003	31 July 2003
Iceland	17 January 2000	1 May 2000	15 August 2000
Lithuania	29 April 1998	1 August 1998	1 December 1998
Mauritius	28 September 1998	1 January 1999	15 May 1999
Moldova	10 April 1998	1 August 1998	1 November 1998
Monaco	5 July 1999	1 October 1999	15 January 2000
Mongolia	25 April 2000	1 August 2000	30 November 2000
New Zealand	18 September 1998	1 January 1999	15 April 1999
Paraguay	13 May 1998	1 September 1998	1 December 1998

**In accordance with Article 44(3) of the Convention, the accession has effect only as regards the relations between the acceding State and those Contracting States which have not raised an objection to its accession in the six months following the date on which the depositary gave notice of the accession. The date specified here is the expiry date of that six-month period.*

Total number of accessions – 13

The Convention entered into force on 1 May 1995

Attachment of Earnings Act 1971

ARRANGEMENT OF SECTIONS

Cases in which attachment is available

PART II

Cases in which attachment is available

1 Courts with power to attach earnings

(1) The High Court may make an attachment of earnings order to secure payments under a High Court maintenance order.

(2) A county court may make an attachment of earnings order to secure –

(*a*) payments under a High Court or a county court maintenance order;
(*b*) the payment of a judgment debt, other than a debt of less than £5 or such other sum as may be prescribed by county court rules; or
(*c*) payments under an administration order.

(3) A magistrates' court may make an attachment of earnings order to secure –

(*a*) payments under a magistrates' court maintenance order;
(*b*) the payment of any sum adjudged to be paid by a conviction or treated (by any enactment relating to the collection and enforcement of fines, costs, compensation or forfeited recognisances) as so adjudged to be paid; or
(*c*) the payment of any sum required to be paid by an order under section 17(2) of the Access to Justice Act 1999.

(4) The following provisions of this Act apply, except where otherwise stated, to attachment of earnings orders made, or to be made, by any court.

(5) Any power conferred by this Act to make an attachment of earnings order includes a power to make such an order to secure the discharge of liabilities arising before the coming into force of this Act.

Amendments—Access to Justice Act 1999, s 24, Sch 4, para 8.

Defined terms—"administration order": s 25(1); "judgment debt": s 2(*c*); "maintenance order": s 2(*a*).

Rules—In the High Court, the provisions of RSC Ord 105 governing attachment of earnings applications were revoked on 14 October 1991. The High Court's attachment of earnings jurisdiction is confined to maintenance orders made by that Court. If an application is to be made to the High Court, the county court procedure should be followed with the appropriate modifications; alternatively, advantage may be taken of the county court's power to make an attachment of earnings order to secure a High Court maintenance order.

In county courts, the provisions governing attachment of earnings are contained in CCR Ord 27 as it was immediately before 26 April 1999 (see the annotations under FPR 1991, r 1.3).

In magistrates' courts, the procedure is governed by Magistrates' Courts (Attachment of Earnings) Rules 1971.

"maintenance order"—The Act contains many provisions special to maintenance orders (which expression includes, for example, lump sum orders – see **"maintenance order"** under s 2 below). It is always necessary to bear in mind whether a particular attachment of earnings application or order secures a maintenance order. The same considerations apply equally to CCR Ord 27.

"£5 or such other sum" (s 1(2)(*b*))—The minimum (in the case of a county court judgment debt) is now £50 or the balance under a judgment which was for £50 or more (CCR Ord 27, r 7(9)).

2 Principal definitions

In this Act –

(*a*) "maintenance order" means any order specified in Schedule 1 to this Act and includes such an order which has been discharged if any arrears are recoverable thereunder;

(*b*) "High Court maintenance order", "county court maintenance order" and "magistrates' court maintenance order" mean respectively a maintenance order enforceable by the High Court, a county court and a magistrates' court;

(*c*) "judgment debt" means a sum payable under –

(i) a judgment or order enforceable by a court in England and Wales (not being a magistrates' court);

(ii) an order of a magistrates' court for the payment of money recoverable summarily as a civil debt; or

(iii) an order of any court which is enforceable as if it were for the payment of money so recoverable;

but does not include any sum payable under a maintenance order or an administration order;

(*d*) "the relevant adjudication", in relation to any payment secured or to be secured by an attachment of earnings order, means the conviction, judgment, order or other adjudication from which there arises the liability to make the payment; and

(*e*) "the debtor", in relation to an attachment of earnings order, or to proceedings in which a court has power to make an attachment of earnings order, or to proceedings arising out of such an order, means the person by whom payment is required by the relevant adjudication to be made.

Defined terms—"administration order": s 25(1).

Scope of provision—This section contains the definitions of the expressions which are fundamental to the Act. Other definitions are set out in ss 24 and 25.

"maintenance order" (s 2(*a*))—In addition to periodical payments, the definitions in Sch 1 include "other payments made or having effect as if made under" the provisions there referred to, including, for example, Matrimonial Causes Act 1973, Pt II, which makes provision for lump sum orders and other orders for payment of money which would not normally be thought of as maintenance orders.

"judgment debt" (s 2(*c*))—In family proceedings, the judgment debt most commonly encountered is an order for costs.

3 Application for order and conditions of court's power to make it

(1) The following persons may apply for an attachment of earnings order –

(*a*) the person to whom payment under the relevant adjudication is required to be made (whether directly or through an officer of any court);

(*b*) where the relevant adjudication is an administration order, any one of the creditors scheduled to the order;

(*c*) without prejudice to paragraph (*a*) above, where the application is to a magistrates' court for an order to secure maintenance payments, and there is in force an order under section 59 of the Magistrates' Courts Act 1980, or section 19(2) of the Maintenance Orders Act 1950, that those payments be made to a justices' chief executive, that justices' chief executive;

(*d*) in the following cases the debtor –

(i) where the application is to a magistrates' court; or

(ii) where the application is to the High Court or a county court for an order to secure maintenance payments.

(2) (*repealed*)

(3) Subject to subsection (3A) below for an attachment of earnings order to be made on the application of any person other than the debtor it must appear to the

court that the debtor has failed to make one or more payments required by the relevant adjudication.

(3A) Subsection (3) above shall not apply when the relevant adjudication is a maintenance order.

(3B) Where –

(*a*) a magistrates' court imposes a fine on a person in respect of an offence, and
(*b*) that person consents to an order being made under this subsection,

the court may at the time it imposes the fine, and without the need for an application, make an attachment of earnings order to secure the payment of the fine.

(3C) Where –

(*a*) a magistrates' court makes in the case of a person convicted of an offence an order under section 130 of the Powers of Criminal Courts (Sentencing) Act 2000 (a compensation order) requiring him to pay compensation or to make other payments, and
(*b*) that person consents to an order being made under this subsection,

the court may at the time it makes the compensation order, and without the need for an application, make an attachment of earnings order to secure the payment of the compensation or other payments.

(4) Where proceedings are brought –

(*a*) in the High Court or a county court for the enforcement of a maintenance order by committal under section 5 of the Debtors Act 1869; or
(*b*) in a magistrates' court for the enforcement of a maintenance order under section 76 of the Magistrates' Courts Act 1980 (distress or committal),

then the court may make an attachment of earnings order to secure payments under the maintenance order, instead of dealing with the case under section 5 of the said Act of 1869 or, as the case may be, section 76 of the said Act of 1980.

(5) (*repealed*)

(6) ...

(7) A county court shall not make an attachment of earnings order to secure the payment of a judgment debt if there is in force an order or warrant for the debtor's committal, under section 5 of the Debtors Act 1869, in respect of that debt; but in any such case the court may discharge the order or warrant with a view to making an attachment of earnings order instead.

Amendments—Magistrates' Courts Act 1980, s 154, Sch 7, para 97; Maintenance Enforcement Act 1991, s 11(1), Sch 2, para 1; Criminal Procedure and Investigations Act 1996, s 53; Access to Justice Act 1999, s 90, Sch 13, para 65; Powers of Criminal Courts (Sentencing) Act 2000, s 165, Sch 9, para 44.

Defined terms—"administration order": s 25(1); "debtor": s 2(*e*); "maintenance order": s 2(*a*); "maintenance payments": s 25(1); "relevant adjudication": s 2(*d*).

Application by the debtor (s 3(1)(*d*))—In the High Court or county courts, the debtor may apply only in the case of a maintenance order (on its being made or varied: CCR Ord 27, r 17(4)).

Restriction on order (s 3(3))—No attachment of earnings order may be made (unless it is applied for by the debtor) if the debtor has not defaulted under the judgment or order. This restriction does not apply in the case of a maintenance order (s 3(3A)).

"subsection (3) above shall not apply" (s 3(3A))—Section 3(3) is disapplied from all maintenance orders as defined by s 2(*e*). Where the relevant adjudication is a "qualifying periodical maintenance order" within the meaning of Maintenance Enforcement Act 1991, s 1 (one where money is to be paid periodically (including a lump sum order payable by instalments) and where the payer at the time the order is made is ordinarily resident in England and Wales), wider powers to make an attachment of earnings order exist. In such a case, the High Court and county courts may make an attachment of earnings order on making the relevant maintenance order and, subsequently, on application or of the court's own motion in the course of any proceedings concerning the order (MEA 1991, s 1). In magistrates' courts an attachment of earnings order may be made on the making of the maintenance order, in any enforcement proceedings or, where the court is satisfied that payment has not been made in accordance with the order, on variation (Magistrates' Courts Act 1980, ss 59, 60, 76).

Jurisdiction—The magistrates' court having jurisdiction to make an attachment of earnings order will be the court which enforces payment of the maintenance order (Magistrates' Courts (Attachment of Earnings) Rules 1971, r 4).

Own motion powers (s 3(4))—The court can make an attachment of earnings order, without an application, in lieu of committal or (in magistrates' courts) distress when hearing applications for those remedies, even where the extended powers under MEA 1991, s 1 do not apply.

Administration orders in the county court

4 Extension of power to make administration order

(1) Where, on an application to a county court for an attachment of earnings order to secure the payment of a judgment debt, it appears to the court that the debtor also has other debts, the court –

- (*a*) shall consider whether the case may be one in which all the debtor's liabilities should be dealt with together and that for that purpose an administration order should be made; and
- (*b*) if of opinion that it may be such a case, shall have power (whether or not it makes the attachment of earnings order applied for), with a view to making an administration order, to order the debtor to furnish to the court a list of all his creditors and the amounts which he owes to them respectively.

(2) If, on receipt of the list referred to in subsection (1)(*b*) above, it appears to the court that the debtor's whole indebtedness amounts to not more than the amount which for the time being is the county court limit for the purposes of s 112 of the County Courts Act 1984 (limit of total indebtedness governing county court's power to make administration order on application of debtor), the court may make such an order in respect of the debtor's estate.

(2A) Subsection (2) above is subject to s 112(3) and (4) of the County Courts Act 1984 (which require that, before an administration order is made, notice is to be given to all the creditors and thereafter restrict the right of any creditor to institute bankruptcy proceedings).

(3) (*repealed*)

(4) Nothing in this section is to be taken as prejudicing any right of a debtor to apply, under section 112 of the County Courts Act 1984, for an administration order.

Amendments—Insolvency Act 1976, ss 13, 14(4), Sch 3; County Courts Act 1984, s 148(1), Sch 2, para 40.

Defined terms—"administration order": s 25; "the debtor": s 2(*e*); "judgment debt": s 2(*c*).

Administration orders—CCA 1984, s 112 and CCR Ord 39 make provision for administration orders. CLSA 1990, s 13, amending CCA 1984, s 112, has not been brought into force.

"judgment debt" (s 4(1))—This section does not apply in the case of a maintenance order.

County court limit (s 4(2))—The limit remains at £5,000 for this purpose, notwithstanding the extensive increase in county court jurisdiction which took effect on 1 July 1991.

5 Attachment of earnings to secure payments under administration order

(1) Where a county court makes an administration order in respect of a debtor's estate, it may also make an attachment of earnings order to secure the payments required by the administration order.

(2) At any time when an administration order is in force a county court may (with or without an application) make an attachment of earnings order to secure the payments required by the administration order, if it appears to the court that the debtor has failed to make any such payment.

(3) The power of a county court under this section to make an attachment of earnings order to secure the payments required by an administration order shall, where the debtor is already subject to an attachment of earnings order to secure the payment of a judgment debt, include power to direct that the last-mentioned order shall take effect (with or without variation under section 9 of this Act) as an order to secure the payments required by the administration order.

Defined terms—"administration order": s 25; "the debtor": s 2(*e*); "judgment debt": s 2(*c*).

Consequences of attachment order

6 Effect and contents of order

(1) An attachment of earnings order shall be an order directed to a person who appears to the court to have the debtor in his employment and shall operate as an instruction to that person –

(*a*) to make periodical deductions from the debtor's earnings in accordance with Part I of Schedule 3 to this Act; and

(*b*) at such times as the order may require, or as the court may allow, to pay the amounts deducted to the collecting officer of the court, as specified in the order.

(2) For the purposes of this Act, the relationship of employer and employee shall be treated as subsisting between two persons if one of them, as a principal and not as a servant or agent, pays to the other any sums defined as earnings by section 24 of this Act.

(3) An attachment of earnings order shall contain prescribed particulars enabling the debtor to be identified by the employer.

(4) Except where it is made to secure maintenance payments, the order shall specify the whole amount payable under the relevant adjudication (or so much of that amount as remains unpaid), including any relevant costs.

(5) The order shall specify –

(*a*) the normal deduction rate, that is to say, the rate (expressed as a sum of money per week, month or other period) at which the court thinks it reasonable for the debtor's earnings to be applied to meeting his liability under the relevant adjudication; and

(*b*) the protected earnings rate, that is to say the rate (so expressed) below which, having regard to the debtor's resources and needs, the court thinks it reasonable that the earnings actually paid to him should not be reduced.

(6) In the case of an order made to secure payments under a maintenance order (not being an order for the payment of a lump sum), the normal deduction rate –

(*a*) shall be determined after taking account of any right or liability of the debtor to deduct income tax when making the payments; and

(*b*) shall not exceed the rate which appears to the court necessary for the purpose of –

(i) securing payment of the sums falling due from time to time under the maintenance order, and

(ii) securing payment within a reasonable period of any sums already due and unpaid under the maintenance order.

(7) For the purposes of an attachment of earnings order, the collecting officer of the court shall be (subject to later variation of the order under section 9 of this Act) –

(*a*) in the case of an order made by the High Court, either –

(i) the proper officer of the High Court, or

(ii) the appropriate officer of such county court as the order may specify;

(*b*) in the case of an order made by a county court, the appropriate officer of that court; and

(*c*) in the case of an order made by a magistrates' court, the justices' chief executive for that court or for another magistrates' court specified in the order.

(8) In subsection (7) above "appropriate officer" means an officer designated by the Lord Chancellor.

[*(9) The Lord Chancellor may by order make such provision as he considers expedient (including transitional provision) with a view to providing for the payment of amounts deducted under attachment of earnings orders to be made to such officers as may be designated by the order rather than to collecting officers of the court.*

(10) Any such order may make such amendments in this Act, in relation to functions exercised by or in relation to collecting officers of the court as he considers expedient in consequence of the provision made by virtue of subsection (9) above.

(11) The power to make such an order shall be exercisable by statutory instrument.

(12) Any such statutory instrument shall be subject to annulment in pursuance of a resolution of either House of Parliament.]

Amendments—Administration of Justice Act 1977, s 19(5); CLSA 1990, s 125(2), Sch 17 (not in force – see **Subsections (9)–(12)** below); Access to Justice Act 1999, s 90, Sch 13, para 66.

Defined terms—"the debtor": s 2(*e*); "earnings": s 24; "maintenance order": s 2(*a*); "maintenance payments": s 25(1); "the relevant adjudication": s 2(*d*); "relevant costs": s 25(2).

Employer (s 6(2))—The relationship of employer/employee, for the purposes of this Act, is determined solely by the nature of the payments made by the one to the other. If they fall within the definition in s 24 (and the payer is not merely a servant or agent of another) then the payer is the employer notwithstanding that no other attribute of employment exists.

"prescribed particulars" (s 6(3))—For the prescribed particulars see CCR Ord 27, r 10 and Magistrates' Courts (Attachment of Earnings) Rules 1971, r 7.

"normal deduction rate" (s 6(5)(*a*), (6))—In establishing the normal deduction rate, regard may be had only to the debtor's actual earnings, not to his earning potential, even though this may result in the normal deduction rate being less than the rate of the relevant periodical payments order, on the making of which unrealised earning capacity may have been taken into account (*Pepper v Pepper* [1960] 1 WLR 131, [1960] 1 All ER 529).

"protected earnings rate" (s 6(5)(*b*))—The rate set will not normally be below the income support threshold, though this is not impossible in an appropriate case (*Billington v Billington* [1974] Fam 24, [1974] 2 WLR 53). In practice it will usually be set a little above that threshold so that the debtor is not discouraged from continuing in his employment. The debtor's needs include those of his dependants (s 25(3)).

"right or liability of the debtor to deduct income tax" (s 6(6)(*a*))—Maintenance orders are now paid gross of tax.

Insolvency—The fact that the debtor may become bankrupt does not (if he retains his employment) stay an attachment of earnings application or prevent an attachment of earnings order from being made or continuing to have effect to enforce a judgment or order made in family proceedings. There may be a hiatus in the payments received under an existing attachment of earnings order, since it was held in *Re Green; Official Receiver v Cutting* [1979] 1 WLR 1211, [1979] 1 All ER 832 that deductions made by the employer which have not reached the court when the bankruptcy commences fall into the bankrupt's estate. However, that case was decided under the Bankruptcy Act 1914 and the changed status of family proceedings orders in relation to bankruptcy by virtue of the Insolvency Act 1986 and Insolvency Rules 1986, r 12.3 might lead a court to reach a different conclusion today.

Forms—Form 1 in the Schedule to Magistrates' Courts (Attachment of Earnings) Rules 1971 sets out the form of order to be used by magistrates' courts. In the county court, Form N60 is used.

"The Lord Chancellor may" (s 6(9))—No order has yet been made under this provision (see **Subsections (9)–(12)** below).

Subsections (9)–(12)—CLSA 1990, Sch 17, adding these subsections, has not been brought into force.

7 Compliance with order by employer

(1) Where an attachment of earnings order has been made, the employer shall, if he has been served with the order, comply with it; but he shall be under no liability for non-compliance before seven days have elapsed since the service.

(2) Where a person is served with an attachment of earnings order directed to him and he has not the debtor in his employment, or the debtor subsequently ceases to be in his employment, he shall (in either case), within ten days from the date of service or, as the case may be, the cesser, give notice of that fact to the court.

(3) Part II of Schedule 3 to this Act shall have effect with respect to the priority to be accorded as between two or more attachment of earnings orders directed to a person in respect of the same debtor.

(4) On any occasion when the employer makes, in compliance with the order, a deduction from the debtor's earnings –

(*a*) he shall be entitled to deduct, in addition, five new pence, or such other sum as may be prescribed by order made by the Lord Chancellor, towards his clerical and administrative costs; and (*b*) he shall give to the debtor a statement in writing of the total amount of the deduction.

(5) An order of the Lord Chancellor under subsection (4)(*a*) above –

(*a*) may prescribe different sums in relation to different classes of cases;
(*b*) may be varied or revoked by a subsequent order made under that paragraph; and
(*c*) shall be made by statutory instrument subject to annulment by resolution of either House of Parliament.

Defined terms—"the debtor": s 2(*e*); "the employer": s 25(2).

"seven days" (s 7(1))—The employer is given a period of grace to give effect to the order.

Priority of orders (s 7(3))—There are two categories of attachment of earnings order, namely those which secure judgment debts and administration orders and those which secure other liabilities (including maintenance orders). The latter are usually termed "priority orders" and must be applied to the debtor's earnings first. Within each category, priority follows the dates the orders were made.

Prescribed deduction (s 7(4)(*a*))—The current figure is £1 (prescribed by Attachment of Earnings (Employer's Deduction) Order 1991, SI 1991/356).

8 Interrelation with alternative remedies open to creditor

(1) Where an attachment of earnings order has been made to secure maintenance payments, no order or warrant of commitment shall be issued in consequence of any proceedings for the enforcement of the related maintenance order begun before the making of the attachment of earnings order.

(2) Where a county court has made an attachment of earnings order to secure the payment of a judgment debt –

(*a*) no order or warrant of commitment shall be issued in consequence of any proceedings for the enforcement of the debt begun before the making of the attachment of earnings order; and
(*b*) so long as the order is in force, no execution for the recovery of the debt shall issue against any property of the debtor without the leave of the county court.

(3) An attachment of earnings order made to secure maintenance payments shall cease to have effect upon the making of an order of commitment or the issue of a warrant of commitment for the enforcement of the related maintenance order, or upon the exercise for that purpose of the power conferred on a magistrates' court by section 77(2) of the Magistrates' Courts Act 1980 to postpone the issue of such a warrant.

(4) An attachment of earnings order made to secure the payment of a judgment debt shall cease to have effect on the making of an order of commitment or the issue of a warrant of commitment for the enforcement of the debt.

(5) An attachment of earnings order made to secure any payment specified in section 1(3)(*b*) or (*c*) of this Act shall cease to have effect on the issue of a warrant committing the debtor to prison for default in making that payment.

Amendments—Magistrates' Courts Act 1980, s 154, Sch 7, para 98.

Defined terms—"judgment debt": s 2(*c*); "maintenance order": s 2(*a*); "maintenance payments": s 25(2).

Subsequent proceedings

9 Variation, lapse and discharge of orders

(1) The court may make an order discharging or varying an attachment of earnings order.

(2) Where an order is varied, the employer shall, if he has been served with notice of the variation, comply with the order as varied; but he shall be under no liability for non-compliance before seven days have elapsed since the service.

(3) Rules of court may make provision –

(*a*) as to the circumstances in which an attachment of earnings order may be varied or discharged by the court of its own motion:

(*b*) in the case of an attachment of earnings order made by a magistrates' court, for enabling a single justice, on an application made by the debtor on the ground of a material change in his resources and needs since the order was made or last varied, to vary the order for a period of not more than four weeks by an increase of the protected earnings rate.

(4) Where an attachment of earnings order has been made and the person to whom it is directed ceases to have the debtor in his employment, the order shall lapse (except as respects deduction from earnings paid after the cesser and payment to the collecting officer of amounts deducted at any time) and be of no effect unless and until the court again directs it to a person (whether the same as before or another) who appears to the court to have the debtor in his employment.

(5) The lapse of an order under subsection (4) above shall not prevent its being treated as remaining in force for other purposes.

Defined terms—"the debtor": s 2(*e*); "the employer": s 25(1); "protected earnings rate": s 6(5)(*b*).

"seven days" (s 9(2))—The employer is given a period of grace to give effect to the variation.

"Rules of court" (s 9(3))—For the relevant rules see CCR Ord 27, r 13 and Magistrates' Courts (Attachment of Earnings) Rules 1971, rr 12–14.

"resources and needs" (s 9(3)(*b*))—See **"normal deduction rate"** and **"protected earnings rate"** under s 6.

Lapse of order (s 9(4), (5))—If the debtor loses or changes his employment, this merely creates a temporary hiatus. As soon as the court learns of a new employer, the order will be redirected, and varied as appropriate (CCR Ord 27, r 13(3); MC(AE)R 1971, r 12).

10 Normal deduction rate to be reduced in certain cases

(1) The following provisions shall have effect, in the case of an attachment of earnings order made to secure maintenance payments, where it appears to the collecting officer of the court that –

(*a*) the aggregate of the payments made for the purposes of the related maintenance order by the debtor (whether under the attachment of earnings order or otherwise) exceeds the aggregate of the payments required up to that time by the maintenance order; and

(*b*) the normal deduction rate specified by the attachment of earnings order (or, where two or more such orders are in force in relation to the maintenance order, the aggregate of the normal deduction rates specified by those orders) exceeds the rate of payments required by the maintenance order; and (*c*) no proceedings for the variation or discharge of the attachment of earnings order are pending.

(2) In the case of an order made by the High Court or a county court, the collecting officer shall give the prescribed notice to the person to whom he is required to pay sums received under the attachment of earnings order, and to the debtor; and the court shall make the appropriate variation order, unless the debtor requests it to discharge the attachment of earnings order, or to vary it in some other way, and the court thinks fit to comply with the request.

(3) In the case of an order made by a magistrates' court, the collecting officer shall apply to the court for the appropriate variation order; and the court shall grant the application unless the debtor appears at the hearing and requests the court to discharge the attachment of earnings order, or to vary it in some other way, and the court thinks fit to comply with the request.

(4) In this section, "the appropriate variation order" means an order varying the attachment of earnings order in question by reducing the normal deduction rate specified thereby so as to secure that that rate (or, in the case mentioned in subsection (1)(*b*) above, the aggregate of the rates therein mentioned) –

(*a*) is the same as the rate of payments required by the maintenance order; or
(*b*) is such lower rate as the court thinks fit having regard to the amount of the excess mentioned in subsection (1)(*a*).

Defined terms—"collecting officer": s 6(7); "the debtor": s 2(*e*); "maintenance order": s 2(*a*); "maintenance payments": s 25(1); "normal deduction rate": s 6(5)(*a*).

Restriction (s 10(1)(*c*))—This section does not apply if an application to vary or discharge the maintenance order is pending.

Variation—Arrears having been cleared, the court's response is likely to be to vary the normal deduction rate to the level of the maintenance order, but the debtor may apply for some other variation or for the attachment of earnings order to be discharged.

"prescribed notice" (s 10(2))—In the county court Practice Form N341 is used. The debtor's application for the discharge or other variation of the order must be made within 14 days after the date of this notice (CCR Ord 27, r 17(9)). There is no provision for any application or objection by the creditor.

"the collecting officer shall apply" (s 10(3))—See s 19(4) for service of summons and Magistrates' Courts (Attachment of Earnings) Rules 1971, r 8 for service of notice of the hearing. Any application made by the collecting officer in the magistrates' court (ie the clerk) is deemed to be made on the request of the person in whose favour the order was made (s 18(3)).

11 Attachment order in respect of maintenance payments to cease to have effect on the occurrence of certain events

(1) An attachment of earnings order made to secure maintenance payments shall cease to have effect –

(*a*) upon the grant of an application for registration of the related maintenance order under section 2 of the Maintenance Orders Act 1958 (which provides for the registration in a magistrates' court of a High Court or county court maintenance order, and for registration in the High Court of a magistrates' court maintenance order);
(*b*) where the related maintenance order is registered under Part I of the said Act of 1958, upon the giving of notice with respect thereto under section 5 of that Act (notice with view to cancellation of registration);

(*c*) subject to subsection (3) below, upon the discharge of the related maintenance order while it is not registered under Part I of the said Act of 1958;

(*d*) upon the related maintenance order ceasing to be registered in a court in England or Wales, or becoming registered in a court in Scotland or Northern Ireland, under Part II of the Maintenance Orders Act 1950.

(2) Subsection (1)(*a*) above shall have effect, in the case of an application for registration under section 2(1) of the said Act of 1958, notwithstanding that the grant of the application may subsequently become void under subsection (2) of that section.

(3) Where the related maintenance order is discharged as mentioned in subsection (1)(*c*) above and it appears to the court discharging the order that arrears thereunder will remain to be recovered after the discharge, that court may, if it thinks fit, direct that subsection (1) shall not apply.

Defined terms—"maintenance order": s 2(*a*); "maintenance payments": s 25(1).

Registration and cancellation of registration—If the function of enforcement of the order later passes to another English or Welsh court, a fresh application for an attachment of earnings order may of course be made.

12 Termination of employer's liability to make deductions

(1) Where an attachment of earnings order ceases to have effect under section 8 or 11 of this Act, the proper officer of the prescribed court shall give notice of the cesser to the person to whom the order was directed.

(2) Where, in the case of an attachment of earnings order made other wise than to secure maintenance payments, the whole amount payable under the relevant adjudication has been paid, and also any relevant costs, the court shall give notice to the employer that no further compliance with the order is required.

(3) Where an attachment of earnings order –

(*a*) ceases to have effect under section 8 or 11 of this Act; or

(*b*) is discharged under section 9,

the person to whom the order has been directed shall be under no liability in consequence of his treating the order as still in force at any time before the expiration of seven days from the date on which the notice required by subsection (1) above or, as the case may be, a copy of the discharging order is served on him.

Defined terms—"employer", "maintenance payments": s 25(1); "relevant adjudication": s 2(*d*); "relevant costs": s 25(2).

"proper officer of the prescribed court" (s 12(1))—In the magistrates' court this will be the justices' clerk for the court (Magistrates' Courts (Attachment of Earnings) Rules 1971, r 6).

"seven days" (s 12(3))—The employer is under no liability for a period of grace if he continues to treat the order as in force after service of the relevant notice or copy order.

Administrative provisions

13 Application of sums received by collecting officer

(1) Subject to subsection (3) below, the collecting officer to whom a person makes payments in compliance with an attachment of earnings order shall, after deducting such court fees, if any, in respect of proceedings for or arising out of the order, as

are deductible from those payments, deal with the sums paid in the same way as he would if they had been paid by the debtor to satisfy the relevant adjudication.

(2) Any sums paid to the collecting officer under an attachment of earnings order made to secure maintenance payments shall, when paid to the person entitled to receive those payments, be deemed to be payments made by the debtor (with such deductions, if any, in respect of income tax as the debtor is entitled or required to make) so as to discharge –

(*a*) first, any sums for the time being due and unpaid under the related maintenance order (a sum due at an earlier date being discharged before a sum due at a later date); and

(*b*) secondly, any costs incurred in proceedings relating to the related maintenance order which were payable by the debtor when the attachment of earnings order was made or last varied.

(3) When a county court makes an attachment of earnings order to secure the payment of a judgment debt and also, under section 4(1) of this Act, orders the debtor to furnish to the court a list of his creditors, sums paid to the collecting officer in compliance with the attachment of earnings order shall not be dealt with by him as mentioned in subsection (1) above, but shall be retained by him pending the decision of the court whether or not to make an administration order and shall then be dealt with by him as the court may direct.

Defined terms—“administration order”: s 25(1); “collecting officer”: s 6(7); “the debtor”: s 2(*e*); “maintenance order”: s 2(*a*); “maintenance payments” s 25(1); “relevant adjudication”: s 2(*d*).

Income tax (s 13(2))—Maintenance orders are now paid gross of tax.

14 Power of court to obtain statement of earnings etc

(1) Where in any proceedings a court has the power to make an attachment of earnings order, it may –

(*a*) order the debtor to give to the court, within a specified period, a statement signed by him of –

(i) the name and address of any person by whom earnings are paid to him;

(ii) specified particulars as to his earnings and anticipated earnings, and as to his resources and needs; and

(iii) specified particulars for the purpose of enabling the debtor to be identified by any employer of his;

(*b*) order any person appearing to the court to have the debtor in his employment to give to the court, within a specified period, a statement signed by him or on his behalf of specified particulars of the debtor’s earnings and anticipated earnings.

(2) Where an attachment of earnings has been made, the court may at any time thereafter while the order is in force –

(*a*) make such an order as is described in subsection (1)(*a*) or (*b*) above; and

(*b*) order the debtor to attend before it on a day and at a time specified in the order to give the information described in subsection (1)(*a*) above.

(3) In the case of an application to a magistrates’ court for an attachment of earnings order, or for the variation or discharge of such an order, the power to make an order under subsection (1) or (2) above shall be exercisable also, before the hearing of the application, by a single justice.

(4) Without prejudice to subsections (1) to (3) above, rules of court may provide that where notice of application for an attachment of earnings order is served on the debtor it shall include a requirement that he shall give to the court, within such period and in such manner as may be prescribed, a statement in writing of the matters specified in subsection (1)(*a*) above and of any other prescribed matters which are, or may be, relevant under section 6 of this Act to the determination of the normal deduction rate and the protected earnings rate to be specified in any order made on the application.

(5) In any proceedings in which a court has the power to make an attachment of earnings order, and in any proceedings for the making, variation or discharge of such an order, a document purporting to be a statement given to the court in compliance with an order under subsection (1)(*a*) or (*b*) above, or with any such requirement of a notice of application for an attachment of earnings order as is mentioned in subsection (4) above, shall, in the absence of proof to the contrary, be deemed to be a statement so given and shall be evidence of the facts stated therein.

Amendments—Administration of Justice Act 1982, s 53(1).

Defined terms—"the debtor": s 2(*e*); "earnings": s 24; "employer": s 25(1); "normal deduction rate": s 6(5)(*a*); "protected earnings rate": s 6(5)(*b*).

"in any proceedings" (s 14(1))—The power to order the debtor and apparent employer to provide information may be exercised, for example, in judgment summons proceedings or proceedings in the magistrates court for distress or committal (see s 3(4)) or indeed in any High Court or county court proceedings concerning a qualifying periodical maintenance order within the meaning of Maintenance Enforcement Act 1991, s 1 or enforcement or variation proceedings in the magistrates' court (see **"subsection (3) above shall not apply"** under s 3).

"resources and needs" (s 14(1)(*a*)(ii))—The debtor's needs include those of his dependants (s 25(3)).

"order the debtor to attend" (s 14(2)(*b*))—Unlike a failure to comply with an order to provide information by signed statement made under s 14(1), failure to attend pursuant to an order is not an offence under s 23 and the consequence of non-compliance is *not* committal but a further order to attend under s 23(1), breach of which may lead to committal.

"exercisable ... by a single justice" (s 14(3))—The power may also be exercised by a justices' clerk (Magistrates' Courts (Attachment of Earnings) Rules 1971, r 22).

15 Obligation of debtor and his employers to notify changes of employment and earnings

While an attachment of earnings order is in force –

(*a*) the debtor shall from time to time notify the court in writing of every occasion on which he leaves any employment, or becomes employed or re-employed, not later (in each case) than seven days from the date on which he did so;

(*b*) the debtor shall, on any occasion when he becomes employed or re-employed, include in his notification under paragraph (*a*) above particulars of his earnings and anticipated earnings from the relevant employment; and

(*c*) any person who becomes the debtor's employer and knows that the order is in force and by what court it was made shall, within seven days of his becoming the debtor's employer or of acquiring that knowledge (whichever is the later) notify that court in writing that he is the debtor's employer, and include in his notification a statement of the debtor's earnings and anticipated earnings.

Defined terms—"the debtor": s 2(*e*); "earnings": s 24; "employer": s 25(1).

16 Power of court to determine whether particular payments are earnings

(1) Where an attachment of earnings order is in force, the court shall, on application of a person specified in subsection (2) below, determine whether payments to the debtor of a particular class or description specified by the application are earnings for the purposes of the order; and the employer shall be entitled to give effect to any determination for the time being in force under this section.

(2) The persons referred to in subsection (1) above are –

(*a*) the employer;
(*b*) the debtor;
(*c*) the person to whom payment under the relevant adjudication is required to be made (whether directly or through the officer of any court); and
(*d*) without prejudice to paragraph (*c*) above, where the application is in respect of an attachment of earnings order made to secure payments under a magistrates' court maintenance order, the collecting officer.

(3) Where an application under this section is made by the employer, he shall not incur any liability for non-compliance with the order as respects any payments of the class or description specified by the application which are made by him to the debtor while the application, or any appeal in consequence thereof, is pending; but this subsection shall not, unless the court otherwise orders, apply as respects such payments if the employer subsequently withdraws the application or, as the case may be, abandons the appeal.

Defined terms—"collecting officer": s 6(7); "the debtor": s 2(*e*); "earnings": s 24; "the employer": s 25(1); "magistrates' court maintenance order": s 2(*b*); "the relevant adjudication": s 2(*d*).

Applicant (s 16(2))—An application to determine whether payments are "earnings" may be made by the debtor, the creditor, the employer or in the case of a magistrates' court maintenance order, the collecting officer. In magistrates' courts the application is made by way of complaint (s 19(3)). See s 21 as to the costs of such applications in magistrates' courts.

17 Consolidated attachment orders

(1) The powers of a county court under sections 1 and 3 of this Act shall include power to make an attachment of earnings order to secure the payment of any number of judgment debts; and the powers of a magistrates' court under those sections shall include power to make an attachment of earnings order to secure the discharge of any number of such liabilities as are specified in section 1(3).

(2) An attachment of earnings order made by virtue of this section shall be known as a consolidated attachment order.

(3) The power to make a consolidated attachment order shall be exercised subject to and in accordance with rules of court; and rules made for the purposes of this section may provide –

(*a*) for the transfer from one court to another –

PART II

(i) of an attachment of earnings order, or any proceedings for or arising out of such an order; and

(ii) of functions relating to the enforcement of any liability capable of being secured by attachment of earnings;

(*b*) for enabling a court to which any order, proceedings or functions have been transferred under the rules to vary or discharge an attachment of earnings order made by another court and to replace it (if the court thinks fit) with a consolidated attachment order;

(*c*) for the cases in which any power exercisable under this section or the rules may be exercised by a court of its own motivation or on the application of a prescribed person;

(*d*) for requiring the officer of a court who receives payments made to him in compliance with an attachment of earnings order, instead of complying with section 13 of this Act, to deal with them as directed by the court or the rules; and

(*e*) for modifying or excluding provisions of this Act or Part III of the Magistrates' Courts Act 1980, but only so far as may be necessary or expedient for securing conformity with the operation of rules made by virtue of paragraphs (*a*) to (*d*) of this subsection.

Amendments—Magistrates' Courts Act 1980, s 154, Sch 7, para 99; Access to Justice Act 1999, s 90, Sch 13, para 67.

Defined terms—"judgment debt": s 2(*c*).

Scope of provision—The court is empowered to make one attachment of earnings order to secure payment of a number of debts, but this power does not extend to maintenance orders or, in the county court, to administration orders.

"rules of court" (s 17(3))—In the county court the rules are CCR Ord 27, rr 18–22. In magistrates' courts the rules are Magistrates' Courts (Attachment of Earnings) Rules 1971, rr 15–17.

Special provisions with respect to magistrates' courts

18 Certain action not to be taken by collecting officer except on request

(1) A justices' chief executive who is entitled to receive payments under a maintenance order for transmission to another person shall not –

(*a*) apply for an attachment of earnings order to secure payments under the maintenance order; or

(*b*) except as provided by section 10(3) of this Act, apply for an order discharging or varying such an attachment of earnings order; or

(*c*) apply for a determination under section 16 of this Act,

unless he is requested in writing to do so by a person entitled to receive the payments through him.

(2) Where a justices' chief executive is requested –

(*a*) he shall comply with the request unless it appears to him unreasonable in the circumstances to do so; and

(*b*) the person by whom the request was made shall have the same liabilities for all the costs properly incurred in or about any proceedings taken in pursuance of the request as if the proceedings had been taken by that person.

(3) For the purposes of subsection (2)(*b*) above, any application made by a justices' chief executive as required by section 10(3) of this Act shall be deemed to be made on the request of the person in whose favour the attachment of earnings order in question was made.

Amendments—Access to Justice Act 1999, s 90, Sch 13, para 68.

19 Procedure on applications

(1) Subject to rules of court made by virtue of the following subsection, an application to a magistrates' court for an attachment of earnings order, or an order discharging or varying an attachment of earnings order, shall be made by complaint.

(2) Rules of court may make provision excluding subsection (1) in the case of such an application as is referred to in section 9(3)(*b*) of this Act.

(3) An application to a magistrates' court for a determination under section 16 of this Act shall be made by complaint.

(4) For the purposes of section 51 of the Magistrates' Courts Act 1980 (which provides for the issue of a summons directed to the person against whom an order may be made in pursuance of a complaint) –

(*a*) the power to make an order in pursuance of a complaint by the debtor for an attachment of earnings order, or the discharge or variation of such an order, shall be deemed to be a power to make an order against the person to whom payment under the relevant adjudication is required to be made (whether directly or through an officer of any court); and

(*b*) the power to make an attachment of earnings order, or an order discharging or varying an attachment of earnings order, in pursuance of a complaint by any other person (including a complaint in proceedings to which section 3(4)(*b*) of this Act applies) shall be deemed to be a power to make an order against the debtor.

(5) A complaint for an attachment of earnings order may be heard notwithstanding that it was made within the six months allowed by section 127(1) of the Magistrates' Courts Act 1980.

Amendments—Magistrates' Courts Act 1980, s 154, Sch 7, para 100.

20 Jurisdiction in respect of persons residing outside England and Wales

(1) It is hereby declared that a magistrates' court has jurisdiction to hear a complaint by or against a person residing outside England and Wales for the discharge or variation of an attachment of earnings order made by a magistrates' court to secure maintenance payments; and where such a complaint is made, the following provisions shall have effect.

(2) If the person resides in Scotland or Northern Ireland, section 15 of the Maintenance Orders Act 1950 (which relates to the service of process on persons residing in those countries) shall have effect in relation to the complaint as it has effect in relation to the proceedings therein mentioned.

(3) Subject to the following subsection, if the person resides outside the United Kingdom and does not appear at the time and place appointed for the hearing of the complaint, the court may, if it thinks it reasonable in all the circumstances to do

so, proceed to hear and determine the complaint at the time and place appointed for the hearing, or for any adjourned hearing, in like manner as if the person had then appeared.

(4) Subsection (3) above shall apply only if it is proved to the satisfaction of the court, on oath or in such other manner as may be prescribed, that the complainant has taken such steps as may be prescribed to give to the said person notice of the complaint and of the time and place appointed for the hearing of it.

Defined terms—"maintenance payments": s 25(1).

"such steps as may be prescribed" (s 20(4))—The relevant steps are prescribed by Magistrates' Courts (Attachment of Earnings) Rules 1971, rr 10, 11.

21 Costs on application under s 16

(1) On making a determination under section 16 of this Act, a magistrates' court may in its discretion make such order as it thinks just and reasonable for payment by any of the persons mentioned in subsection (2) of that section of the whole or any part of the costs of the determination (but subject to section 18(2)(*b*) of this Act).

(2) Costs ordered to be paid under this section shall –

(*a*) in the case of costs to be paid by the debtor to the person in whose favour the attachment of earnings order in question was made, be deemed –

(i) if the attachment of earnings order was made to secure maintenance payments, to be a sum due under the related maintenance order, and

(ii) otherwise, to be a sum due to the justices' chief executive for the court; and

(*b*) in any other case, be enforceable as a civil debt.

Amendments—Access to Justice Act 1999, s 90, Sch 13, para 69.

Defined terms—"maintenance order": s 2(*a*); "the debtor": s 2(*e*).

Miscellaneous provisions

22 Persons employed under the Crown

(1) The fact that an attachment of earnings order is made at the suit of the Crown shall not prevent its operation at any time when the debtor is in the employment of the Crown.

(2) Where a debtor is in the employment of the Crown and an attachment of earnings order is made in respect of him, then for the purposes of this Act –

(*a*) the chief officer for the time being of the department, office or other body in which the debtor is employed shall be treated as having the debtor in his employment (any transfer of the debtor from one department, office or body to another being treated as a change of employment); and

(*b*) any earnings paid by the Crown or a Minister of the Crown, or out of the public revenue of the United Kingdom, shall be treated as paid by the said chief officer.

(3) If any question arises, in the proceedings for or arising out of an attachment of earnings order, as to what department, office or other body is concerned for the purposes of this section, or as to who for those purposes is the chief officer thereof, the question shall be referred to and determined by the Minister for the

Civil Service; but that Minister shall not be under any obligation to consider a reference under this subsection unless it is made by the court.

(4) A document purporting to set out a determination of the said Minister under subsection (3) above and to be signed by an official of the Office of Public Service shall, in any such proceedings as are mentioned in that subsection, be admissible in evidence and be deemed to contain an accurate statement of such a determination unless the contrary is shown.

(5) This Act shall have effect notwithstanding any enactment passed before 29 May 1970 and preventing or avoiding the attachment or diversion of sums due to a person in respect of service under the Crown, whether by way of remuneration, pension or otherwise.

Amendments—SI 1992/1296; SI 1995/2985.

Defined terms—"the debtor": s 2(*e*).

"notwithstanding any enactment" (s 22(5))—The protection formerly given to eg the pensions of ex-servicemen is removed; as to servicemen's pay, see s 24(2)(*b*).

23 Enforcement provisions

(1) If, after being served with notice of an application to a county court for an attachment of earnings order or for the variation of such an order or with an order made under section 14(2)(*b*) above, the debtor fails to attend on the day and at the time specified for any hearing of the application or specified in the order, the court may adjourn the hearing and order him to attend at a specified time on another day; and if the debtor –

(*a*) fails to attend at that time on that day; or
(*b*) attends, but refuses to be sworn or give evidence,

he may be ordered by the judge to be imprisoned for not more than fourteen days.

(1A) In any case where the judge has the power to make an order of imprisonment under subsection (1) for failure to attend, he may, in lieu of or in addition to making that order, order the debtor to be arrested and brought to the court either forthwith or at such time as the judge may direct.

(2) Subject to this section, a person commits an offence if –

(*a*) being required by section 7(1) or 9(2) of this Act to comply with an attachment of earnings order, he fails to do so; or
(*b*) being required by section 7(2) of this Act to give a notice for the purposes of that subsection, he fails to give it, or fails to give it within the time required by that subsection; or
(*c*) he fails to comply with an order under section 14(1) of this Act or with any such requirement of a notice of application for an attachment of earnings order as is mentioned in section 14(4), or fails (in either case) to comply within the time required by the order or notice; or
(*d*) he fails to comply with section 15 of this Act; or
(*e*) he gives notice for the purposes of section 7(2) of this Act, or a notification for the purposes of section 15, which he knows to be false in a material particular, or recklessly gives such a notice or notification which is false in a material particular, or
(*f*) in purported compliance with section 7(2) or 15 of this Act, or with an order under section 14(1), or with any such requirement of a notice of application for an attachment of earnings order as is mentioned in section

14(4), he makes any statement which he knows to be false in a material particular, or recklessly makes any statement which is false in a material particular.

(3) Where a person commits an offence under subsection (2) above in relation to proceedings in, or to an attachment of earnings order made by, the High Court or a county court, he shall be liable on summary conviction to a fine of not more than level 2 on the standard scale or he may be ordered by a judge of the High Court or the county court judge (as to the case may be) to pay a fine of not more than £250 or, in the case of an offence specified in subsection (4) below, to be imprisoned for not more than fourteen days; and where a person commits an offence under subsection (2) otherwise than as mentioned above in this subsection, he shall be liable on summary conviction to a fine of not more than level 2 on the standard scale.

(4) The offences referred to above in the case of which a judge may impose imprisonment are –

(*a*) an offence under subsection (2)(*c*) or (*d*), if committed by the debtor; and
(*b*) an offence under subsection (2)(*e*) or (*f*), whether committed by the debtor or any other person.

(5) It shall be a defence –

(*a*) for a person charged with an offence under subsection (2)(*a*) above to prove that he took all reasonable steps to comply with the attachment of earnings order in question;
(*b*) for a person charged with an offence under subsection (2)(*b*) to prove that he did not know, and could not reasonably be expected to know, that the debtor was not in his employment, or (as the case may be) had ceased to be so, and that he gave the required notice as soon as reasonably practicable after the fact came to his knowledge.

(6) Where a person is convicted or dealt with for an offence under subsection (2)(*a*), the court may order him to pay, to whoever is the collecting officer of the court for the purposes of the attachment of earnings order in question, any sums deducted by that person from the debtor's earnings and not already paid to the collecting officer.

(7) Where under this section a person is ordered by a judge of the High Court or a county court judge to be imprisoned, the judge may at any time revoke the order and, if the person is already in custody, order his discharge.

(8) Any fine imposed by a judge of the High Court under subsection (3) above and any sums ordered by the High Court to be paid under subsection (6) above shall be recoverable in the same way as a fine imposed by that court in the exercise of its jurisdiction to punish for contempt of court; section 129 of the County Courts Act 1984 (enforcement of fines) shall apply to payment of a fine imposed by a county court judge under subsection (3) and of any sums ordered by a county court judge to be paid under subsection (6); and any sum ordered by a magistrates' court to be paid under subsection (6) shall be recoverable as a sum adjudged to be paid on a conviction by that court.

(9) For the purposes of section 13 of the Administration of Justice Act 1960 (appeal in cases of contempt of court), subsection (3) above shall be treated as an enactment enabling the High Court or a county court to deal with an offence under subsection (2) above as if it were contempt of court.

(10) In this section references to proceedings in a court are to proceedings in which that court has power to make an attachment of earnings order or has made such an order.

(11) A district judge, assistant district judge or deputy district judge shall have the same powers under this section as a judge of a county court.

Amendments—Contempt of Court Act 1981, s 41(5), Sch 2; Administration of Justice Act 1982, s 53(2); Criminal Justice Act 1982, ss 37, 38, 46; County Courts Act 1984, s 148(1), Sch 2, para 41; Courts and Legal Services Act 1990, s 125(2), Sch 17; Criminal Justice Act 1991, s 17, Sch 4, Pt I.

Defined terms—"the debtor": s 2(*e*).

Offences and penalties—Section 23(2) creates a number of offences which are punishable on summary conviction by a fine. Section 23(1) and (1A) empowers the county court to order the attendance of a debtor who has failed to attend the hearing of an application or pursuant to an order under s 14(2)(*b*); and if he again fails to attend or refuses to be sworn or give evidence then to order either his imprisonment for up to 14 days or his arrest and production to the court or both. Further, s 23(3) empowers the High Court or the county court, in proceedings before it, when one of the offences has been committed, directly to order payment of a fine or, in the cases identified in s 23(4), to order that the offender be imprisoned for up to 14 days.

"level 2 on the standard scale" (s 23(3))—Currently £500 (Criminal Justice Act 1982, s 37(2), as substituted).

Appeal (s 23(9))—An appeal from "any order or decision of a court in the exercise of jurisdiction to punish for contempt of court" lies under Administration of Justice Act 1960, s 13 to the Court of Appeal; orders under s 23(1) or (1A) clearly fall within this description. Section 23(9) applies the same provision to orders dealing with the offences created by s 23(2).

District judge (s 23(11))—The district judge has the same powers in county courts under this section as the judge. Although an appeal from his order will lie direct to the Court of Appeal under Administration of Justice Act 1960, s 13, this does not remove the right of appeal to the judge under CCR Ord 37, r 6 (or, presumably, FPR 1991, r 8.1), and that procedure is to be preferred (*King v Read & Slack* (1996) 18 November, CA).

24 Meaning of "earnings"

(1) For the purposes of this Act, but subject to the following subsection, "earnings" are any sums payable to a person –

(*a*) by way of wages or salary (including any fees, bonus, commission, overtime pay or other emoluments payable in addition to wages or salary or payable under a contract of service);

(*b*) by way of pension (including an annuity in respect of past services, whether or not rendered to the person paying the annuity, and including periodical payments by way of compensation for the loss, abolition or relinquishment, or diminution in emoluments, of any office or employment);

(*c*) by way of statutory sick pay.

(2) The following shall not be treated as earnings –

(*a*) sums payable by any department of the Government of Northern Ireland or of a territory outside the United Kingdom;

(*b*) pay or allowances payable to the debtor as a member of Her Majesty's forces other than pay or allowances payable by his employer to him as a special member of a reserve force (within the meaning of the Reserve Forces Act 1996);

PART II

(*c*) pension, allowances or benefit payable under any enactment relating to social security;
(*d*) pension or allowances payable in respect of disablement or disability;
(*e*) except in relation to a maintenance order wages payable to a person as a seaman, other than wages payable to him as a seaman of a fishing boat;
(*f*) guaranteed minimum pension within the meaning of the Social Security Pensions Act 1975.

(3) In subsection (2)(*e*) above –

"fishing boat" means a vessel of whatever size, and in whatever way propelled, which is for the time being employed in sea fishing or in the sea-fishing service;
"seaman" includes every person (except masters and pilots) employed or engaged in any capacity on board any ship; and
"wages" includes emoluments.

Amendments—Social Security Pensions Act 1975, s 65(1), Sch 4, para 15; Merchant Shipping Act 1979, s 39(1); Social Security Act 1985, s 21, Sch 4, para 1; Social Security Act 1986, s 86(1), Sch 10, Pt VI, para 102; Merchant Shipping Act 1995, s 314(2), Sch 13, para 46; SI 1998/3086.

Defined terms—"maintenance order": s 2(*a*).

Scope of provision—This section defines earnings to include pensions and sick pay but subject to significant exceptions.

Holiday pay (s 24(1)(*a*))—Although holiday pay is not "wages" (*London County Council v Henry Boot & Sons Ltd* [1959] 1 WLR 1609, [1959] 3 All ER 636), it would seem to be caught by "other emoluments payable in addition to wages ... or payable under a contract of service".

Pension (s 24(1)(*b*))—A pension may be attachable under the Act, but the making of the order may breach a prohibition against diversion of the pension contained in the relevant trust deed and so terminate entitlement to pension (see eg *Edmonds v Edmonds* [1965] 2 WLR 58, [1965] 1 All ER 379).

Her Majesty's forces (s 24(2)(*b*))—This exception protects the pay or allowances of a serviceman (but not the pension of an ex-serviceman, as to which see **"notwithstanding any enactment"** under s 22). However, arrangements exist under the Army Act 1955, s 150 (and s 151A), the Air Force Act 1955, s 150 (and s 151A) and the Naval Forces (Enforcement of Maintenance Liabilities) Act 1947 (and the Naval Discipline Act 1957, s 128E) under which relevant authorities may order deductions from the serviceman's pay to meet maintenance orders (and judgment debts) if the serviceman will not comply voluntarily with the judgment or order. The amount of such a deduction is in the discretion of the relevant authority, which is not bound to follow the rate indicated in any order of the court. Any request for such an order should set out the efforts made to secure voluntary compliance, enclose a copy of the judgment or order and set out the state of account under it. The appropriate authorities are:
(*a*) *Navy* All ranks: The Director of Naval Pay and Pensions (Accounts), Ministry of Defence, Room 1043, HMS Centurion, Grange Road, Gosport, Hants. PO13 9XA.
(*b*) *Army* Officers: Ministry of Defence, PF 2d (Army), Lansdowne House, Berkeley Square, London W1X 6AA; other ranks: the appropriate regimental pay office.
(*c*) *RAF* Officers: Ministry of Defence, DPS2 (RAF), Adastral House, Theobalds Road, London WC1X 8RU; other ranks: Ministry of Defence, DGPM (RAF), Eastern Avenue, Barnwood, Gloucester.

"pension or allowances payable in respect of disablement or disability" (s 24(2)(*d*))—This exception does not extend to a pension taken on early retirement due to ill-health (*Miles v Miles* [1979] 1 WLR 371, [1979] 1 All ER 865).

"seaman" (s 24(2)(*e*))—See Home Office Circular No 124/1979 for advice on obtaining information regarding the address of a seaman's employer or a seaman's whereabouts.

25 General interpretation

(1) In this Act, except where the context otherwise requires –

"administration order" means an order made under, and so referred to in, Part VI of the County Courts Act 1984;

"the court", in relation to an attachment of earnings order, means the court which made the order, subject to rules of court as to the venue for, and the transfer of, proceedings in county courts and magistrates' courts;

"debtor" and "relevant adjudication" have the meanings given by section 2 of this Act;

"the employer", in relation to the attachment of earnings order, means the person who is required by the order to make deductions from earnings paid by him to the debtor;

"judgment debt" has the meaning given by section 2 of this Act;

"maintenance order" has the meaning given by section 2 of this Act;

"maintenance payments" means payments required under a maintenance order;

"prescribed" means prescribed by rules of court; and

"rules of court", in relation to a magistrates' court, means rules under section 144 of the Magistrates' Courts Act 1980.

(2) Any reference in this Act to sums payable under a judgment or order, or to the payment of such sums, includes a reference to costs and the payment of them; and the references in sections 6(4) and 12(2) to relevant costs are to any costs of the proceedings in which the attachment of earnings order in question was made, being costs which the debtor is liable to pay.

(3) References in sections 6(5)(*b*), 9(3)(*b*) and 14(1)(*a*) of this Act to the debtor's needs include references to the needs of any person for whom he must, or reasonably may, provide.

(4) (*repealed*)

(5) Any power to make rules which is conferred by this Act is without prejudice to any other power to make rules of court.

(6) This Act, so far as it relates to magistrates' courts, and Part III of the Magistrates' Courts Act 1980 shall be construed as if this Act were contained in that Part.

(7) References in this Act to any enactment include references to that enactment amended by or under any other enactment, including this Act.

Amendments—Magistrates' Courts Act 1980, s 154, Sch 7, para 101; County Courts Act 1984, s 148(1), Sch 2, para 42; Legal Aid Act 1988, Sch 5, para 3; Dock Work Act 1989, Sch 1, Pt I; Access to Justice Act 1999, s 106, Sch 15.

****

SCHEDULE 1

MAINTENANCE ORDERS TO WHICH THIS ACT APPLIES

1 An order for alimony, maintenance or other payments made, or having effect as if made, under Part II of the Matrimonial Causes Act 1965 (ancillary relief in actions for divorce etc).

2 An order for payments to or in respect of a child, being an order made, or having effect as if made, under Part III of the said Act of 1965 (maintenance of children following divorce etc).

3 An order for periodical or other payments made or having effect as if made under Part II of the Matrimonial Causes Act 1973.

4 An order for maintenance or other payments to or in respect of a spouse or child, being an order made under Part I of the Domestic Proceedings and Magistrates' Courts Act 1978.

5 An order for periodical or other payments made or having effect as if made under Schedule 1 to the Children Act 1989.

6 (*repealed*)

7 An order under paragraph 23 of Schedule 2 to the Children Act 1989, section 23 of the Ministry of Social Security Act 1966, section 18 of the Supplementary Benefits Act 1976, section 24 of the Social Security Act 1986, or section 106 of the Social Security Administration Act 1992 (various provisions for obtaining contributions from a person whose dependants are assisted or maintained out of public funds).

8 An order under section 43 of the National Assistance Act 1948 (recovery of costs of maintaining assisted person).

9 An order to which section 16 of the Maintenance Orders Act 1950 applies by virtue of subsection (2)(*b*) or (*c*) of that section (that is to say an order made by a court in Scotland or Northern Ireland and corresponding to one of those specified in the foregoing paragraphs) and which has been registered in a court in England and Wales under Part II of that Act.

10 A maintenance order within the meaning of the Maintenance Orders (Facilities for Enforcement) Act 1920 (Commonwealth orders enforceable in the United Kingdom) registered in, or confirmed in England and Wales under that Act.

11 A maintenance order within the meaning of Part I of the Maintenance Orders (Reciprocal Enforcement) Act 1972 registered in a magistrates' court under the said Part I.

12 An order under section 34(1)(*b*) of the Children Act 1975 (payments of maintenance in respect of a child to his custodian).

13 A maintenance order within the meaning of Part I of the Civil Jurisdiction and Judgments Act 1982 which is registered in a magistrates' court under that Part.

14 A maintenance judgment within the meaning of Council Regulation (EC) No 44/2001 of 22 December 2000 on jurisdiction and the recognition and enforcement of judgments in civil and commercial matters, which is registered in a magistrates' court under that Regulation.

Amendments—Maintenance Order (Reciprocal Enforcement) Act 1972, s 22(1), Sch, para 7; Guardianship Act 1973, s 9; Matrimonial Causes Act 1973, s 53, Sch 2, para 13; Children Act 1975, Sch 3, para 76; Supplementary Benefits Act 1976, s 35(2), Sch 7, para 20; Domestic Proceedings and Magistrates' Courts Act 1978, Sch 2, para 32; Civil Jurisdiction and Judgments Act 1982, s 15(4), Sch 12, para 6; Social Security Act 1986, s 86(1), Sch 10, para 43; Family Law Reform Act 1987, Schs 2, 3; CA 1989, s 108(5), Sch 13, para 29; Courts and Legal Services Act 1990, s 116, Sch 16, para 38; Social Security (Consequential Provisions) Act 1992, s 4, Sch 2, para 7; SI 2001/3929.

Scope of provision—This schedule provides the specific definition of maintenance orders for the purposes of the Act; the definition is not confined to orders for periodical maintenance payments.

****

SCHEDULE 3

DEDUCTIONS BY EMPLOYER UNDER ATTACHMENT OF EARNINGS ORDER

PART I
SCHEME OF DEDUCTIONS

Preliminary definitions

1 The following three paragraphs have effect for defining and explaining, for purposes of this Schedule, expressions used therein.

2 "Pay-day", in relation to earnings paid to a debtor, means an occasion on which they are paid.

3 "Attachable earnings", in relation to a pay-day, are the earnings which remain payable to the debtor on that day after deduction by the employer of –

(*a*) income tax;
(*b*) (*repealed*)
(*bb*) Primary Class I contributions under Part I of the Social Security Act 1975;
(*c*) amounts deductible under any enactment, or in pursuance of a request in writing by the debtor, for the purposes of a superannuation scheme, namely any enactment, rules, deed or other instrument providing for the payment of annuities or lump sums –
  (i) to the persons with respect to whom the instrument has effect on their retirement at a specified age or on becoming incapacitated at some earlier age, or
  (ii) to the personal representatives or the widows, relatives or dependants of such persons on their death or otherwise,
whether with or without any further or other benefits.

4 (1) On any pay-day –

(*a*) "the normal deduction" is arrived at by applying the normal deduction rate (as specified in the relevant attachment of earnings order) with respect to the relevant period; and

(*b*) "the protected earnings" are arrived at by applying the protected earnings rate (as so specified) with respect to the relevant period.

(2) For the purposes of this paragraph the relevant period in relation to any pay-day is the period beginning –

(*a*) if it is the first pay-day of the debtor's employment with the employer, with the first day of employment; or

(*b*) if on the last pay-day earnings were paid in respect of a period falling wholly or partly after that pay-day, with the first day after the end of that period; or

(*c*) in any other case, with the first day after the last pay-day, and ending –

(i) where earnings are paid in respect of a period falling wholly or partly after the pay-day, with the last day of that period; or

(ii) in any other case, with the pay-day.

5 Employer's deduction (judgment debts and administration orders)

In the case of an attachment of earnings order made to secure the payment of a judgment debt or payments under an administration order, the employer shall on any pay-day –

(*a*) if the attachable earnings exceed the protected earnings, deduct from the attachable earnings the amount of the excess or the normal deduction, whichever is the less;

(*b*) make no deduction if the attachable earnings are equal to, or less than, the protected earnings.

6 Employer's deduction (other cases)

(1) The following provision shall have effect in the case of an attachment of earnings order to which paragraph 5 above does not apply.

(2) If on a pay-day the attachable earnings exceed the sum of –

(*a*) the protected earnings; and

(*b*) so much of any amount by which the attachable earnings on any previous pay-day fell short of the protected earnings as has not been made good by virtue of this sub-paragraph on another previous pay-day,

then, in so far as the excess allows, the employer shall deduct from the attachable earnings the amount specified in the following sub-paragraph.

(3) The said amount is the sum of –

(*a*) the normal deduction; and

(*b*) so much of the normal deduction on any previous pay-day as was not deducted on that day and has not been paid by virtue of this sub-paragraph on any other previous pay-day.

(4) No deduction shall be made on any pay-day when the attachable earnings are equal to, or less than, the protected earnings.

PART II
PRIORITY AS BETWEEN ORDERS

7 Where the employer is required to comply with two or more attachment of earnings orders in respect of the same debtor, all or none of which orders are made to secure either the payment of judgment debts or payments under an administration order, then on any pay-day the employer shall, for the purpose of complying with Part I of this Schedule, –

(*a*) deal with the orders according to the respective dates on which they were made, disregarding any later order until an earlier one has been dealt with;

(*b*) deal with any later order as if the earnings to which it relates were the residue of the debtor's earnings after the making of deduction to comply with any earlier order.

8 Where the employer is required to comply with two or more attachment of earnings orders, and one or more (but not all) of those orders are made to secure either the payment of judgment debts or payments under an administration order, then on any pay-day the employer shall, for the purpose of complying with Part I of this Schedule –

(*a*) deal first with any order which is not made to secure the payment of a judgment debt or payments under an administration order (complying with paragraph 7 above if there are two or more such orders); and

(*b*) deal thereafter with any order which is made to secure the payment of a judgment debt or payments under an administration order as if the earnings to which it relates were the residue of the debtor's earnings after the making of any deduction to comply with an order having priority by virtue of sub-paragraph (*a*) above; and

(*c*) if there are two or more orders to which sub-paragraph (*b*) above applies, comply with paragraph 7 above in respect of those orders.

Amendments—Social Security Pensions Act 1975, s 65(3), Sch 5; Social Security (Consequential Provisions) Act 1975, s 1(3), Sch 2, para 43; Administration of Justice Act 1982, s 54; Wages Act 1986, s 32(1), Sch 4, para 4; Employment Rights Act 1996, s 240, Sch 1, para 3.

Priority orders—These are the orders which the employer must deal with first (para 8). If the net pay does not exceed the protected earnings rate sufficiently to allow the entire normal deduction to be made, the shortfall is carried forward and added to the normal deduction on the next pay-day. The shortfall may thus accumulate from pay-day to pay-day (para 6(3)). If in any pay period the net pay is less than the protected earnings rate, the unused protected earnings are similarly carried forward and "rolled up" (para 6(2)).

Other orders—The net pay is the amount left after any deductions have been made for priority orders (para 8(*b*)). The "roll-up" provisions do not apply. Deductions are made whenever the debtor's net pay exceeds the protected earnings rate and are limited to the normal deduction rate without regard to any shortfall (para 5).

The result can be surprising: for example, if a debtor, having a priority order and another order against him, through absence has little or no pay for a time, on his return no deductions will be made under the priority order until his accumulated protected earnings have been used up; thereafter, all of the excess of his pay over the protected earnings rate will be deducted under the priority order until his accumulated normal deductions have been used up. In the meantime, deductions under the other order will recommence as soon as his pay exceeds the protected earnings rate but are likely to cease once the priority order takes effect and resume only after it has been caught up.

****

Charging Orders Act 1979

1 Charging orders

(1) Where, under a judgment or order of the High Court or a county court, a person (the "debtor") is required to pay a sum of money to another person (the "creditor") then, for the purpose of enforcing that judgment or order, the appropriate court may make an order in accordance with the provisions of this Act imposing on any such property of the debtor as may be specified in the order a charge for securing the payment of any money due or to become due under the judgment or order.

(2) The appropriate court is –

- (*a*) in a case where the property to be charged is a fund in court, the court in which that fund is lodged;
- (*b*) in a case where paragraph (*a*) above does not apply and the order to be enforced is a maintenance order of the High Court, the High Court or a county court;
- (*c*) in a case where neither paragraph (*a*) nor paragraph (*b*) above applies and the judgment or order to be enforced is a judgment or order of the High Court for a sum exceeding the county court limit, the High Court or a county court; and
- (*d*) in any other case, a county court.

In this section "county court limit" means the county court limit for the time being specified in an Order in Council under section 145 of the County Courts Act 1984 as the county court limit for the purposes of this section and "maintenance order" has the same meaning as in section 2(*a*) of the Attachment of Earnings Act 1971.

(3) An order under subsection (1) above is referred to in this Act as a "charging order".

(4) Where a person applies to the High Court for a charging order to enforce more than one judgment or order, that court shall be the appropriate court in relation to the application if it would be the appropriate court, apart from this subsection, on an application relating to one or more of the judgments or orders concerned.

(5) In deciding whether to make a charging order the court shall consider all the circumstances of the case and, in particular, any evidence before it as to –

- (*a*) the personal circumstances of the debtor, and
- (*b*) whether any other creditor of the debtor would be likely to be unduly prejudiced by the making of the order.

Amendments—Administration of Justice Act 1982, s 34(3).

"required to pay a sum of money" (s 1(1))—There is no power to make a charging order until the sum is ascertained. Thus, an order for costs to be determined by detailed assessment will not found a charging order until after assessment (*A & M Records Inc v Darakjian* [1975] 1 WLR 1610, [1975] 3 All ER 983).

"to another person" (s 1(1))—A charging order cannot be made to secure an order to pay into court (*Ward v Shakeshaft* [1860] 1 Dr & Sm 269).

"due or to become due" (s 1(1))—A charging order may secure amounts which have not yet fallen due for payment under the judgment, but the court may exercise its discretion not to include such payments in an order (see **"consider all the circumstances"** below).

"maintenance order" (s 1(2)(*b*))—As to the extended meaning of this expression, see Attachment of Earnings Act 1971, Sch 1 and **"expressions used"** under CCR Ord 27, r 1.

County court limit (s 1(2))—The relevant limit is currently £5,000, notwithstanding the increase in the jurisdiction of the county court which took place on 1 July 1991.

"consider all the circumstances" (s 1(5))—The court has a general discretion. A charging order will not lightly be made where the costs of and consequent on doing so (including the costs of discharging the charge in due course) would be disproportionate in comparison with the judgment debt. A charging order will not be made where the creditor would gain security in the face of a pending liquidation or bankruptcy (*Roberts Petroleum Ltd v Bernard Kenny Ltd* [1983] AC 192, [1983] 2 WLR 305).

The position of the debtor's spouse must be considered. In the absence of divorce proceedings, her interests will not prevent the order being made as her beneficial interest is not affected and the creditor will be in no better position than the debtor would be (on, for example, an application under Trusts of Land and Appointment of Trustees Act 1996, s 14); however, the interests of the debtor's resident family must be taken into account (*Lloyds Bank plc v Byrne* [1993] 1 FLR 369). Where a divorce petition has been issued, the spouse's expectation of financial provision and of security of accommodation must be balanced against the creditor's expectation of payment so that it may be appropriate to hear the applications for ancillary relief and for the charging order together (*Harman v Glencross* [1986] Fam 81, [1986] 2 FLR 241; *Austin-Fell v Austin-Fell and Midland Bank* [1989] 2 FLR 497).

If the judgment debt is subject to an instalment order, a charging order should not be made while the payments are up to date when the application is made (*Mercantile Credit Co Ltd v Ellis* (1987) *The Times*, 1 April, where it was also stated obiter that in the county court there is no power to make a charging order in such circumstances). If, after a charging order has been applied for and an order *nisi* (see CCR Ord 31, r 1(4)) has been made, an instalment order is made and complied with, this is simply a factor for the court to take into account in deciding whether to make the order absolute (*Ropaigealach v Allied Irish Bank plc* [2001] EWCA Civ 1790, CA). Similar considerations would no doubt apply to an instalment agreement.

2 Property which may be charged

(1) Subject to subsection (3) below, a charge may be imposed by a charging order only on –

- (*a*) any interest held by the debtor beneficially –
  - (i) in any asset of a kind mentioned in subsection (2) below, or
  - (ii) under any trust; or
- (*b*) any interest held by a person as trustee of a trust ("the trust"), if the interest is in such an asset or is an interest under another trust and –
  - (i) the judgment or order in respect of which a charge is to be imposed was made against that person as trustee of the trust, or
  - (ii) the whole beneficial interest under the trust is held by the debtor unencumbered and for his own benefit, or
  - (iii) in a case where there are two or more debtors all of whom are liable to the creditor for the same debt, they together hold the whole beneficial interest under the trust unencumbered and for their own benefit.

(2) The assets referred to in subsection (1) above are –

- (*a*) land,
- (*b*) securities of any of the following kinds –
  - (i) government stock,
  - (ii) stock of any body (other than a building society) incorporated within England and Wales,
  - (iii) stock of any body incorporated outside England and Wales or of any state or territory outside the United Kingdom, being stock registered in a register kept at any place within England and Wales, or

(*c*) funds in court.

(3) In any case where a charge is imposed by a charging order on any interest in an asset of a kind mentioned in paragraph (*b*) or (*c*) of subsection (2) above, the court making the order may provide for the charge to extend to any interest or dividend payable in respect of the asset.

Defined terms—"building society": s 6(1); "charging order", "debtor": s 1; "dividend", "stock": s 6(1).

Partnerships—A debtor's share in a partnership may also be made the subject of a charging order by virtue of Partnership Act 1890, s 23.

3 Provisions supplementing sections 1 and 2

(1) A charging order may be made absolutely or subject to conditions as to notifying the debtor or as to the time when the charge is to become enforceable, or as to other matters.

(2) The Land Charges Act 1972 and the Land Registration Act 1925 shall apply in relation to charging orders as they apply in relation to other orders or writs issued or made for the purpose of enforcing judgments.

(3) In section 49 of the Land Registration Act 1925 (protection of certain interests by notice) there is inserted at the end of subsection (1) the following paragraph –

> "(*g*) charging orders (within the meaning of the Charging Orders Act 1979) which in the case of unregistered land may be protected by registration under the Land Charges Act 1972 and which, notwithstanding section 59 of this Act, it may be deemed expedient to protect by notice instead of by caution."

(4) Subject to the provisions of this Act, a charge imposed by a charging order shall have the like effect and shall be enforceable in the same courts and in the same manner as an equitable charge created by the debtor by writing under his hand.

(5) The court by which a charging order was made may at any time, on the application of the debtor or of any person interested in any property to which the order relates, make an order discharging or varying the charging order.

(6) Where a charging order has been protected by an entry registered under the Land Charges Act 1972 or the Land Registration Act 1925, an order under subsection (5) above discharging the charging order may direct that the entry be cancelled.

(7) The Lord Chancellor may by order made by statutory instrument amend section 2(2) of this Act by adding to, or removing from, the kinds of asset for the time being referred to there, any asset of a kind which in his opinion ought to be so added or removed.

(8) Any order under subsection (7) above shall be subject to annulment in pursuance of a resolution of either House of Parliament.

Defined terms—"charging order", "debtor": s 1.

"enforceable" (s 3(4))—As to enforcement by order for sale, see RSC Ord 50, r 9A and CCR Ord 31, r 4. A claim for an order for sale must be made outside the family proceedings in which the liability arose and will be governed by CPR 1998, Pt 8.

"person interested" (s 3(5))—The interest need not be a beneficial interest in the property charged (*Harman v Glencross* [1986] Fam 81, [1986] 2 FLR 241).

****

5 Stop orders and notices

(1) In this section –

"stop order" means an order of the court prohibiting the taking, in respect of any of the securities specified in the order, of any of the steps mentioned in subsection (5) below;

"stop notice" means a notice requiring any person or body on whom it is duly served to refrain from taking, in respect of any of the securities specified in the notice, any of those steps without first notifying the person by whom, or on whose behalf, the notice was served; and

"prescribed securities" means securities (including funds in court) of a kind prescribed by rules of court made under this section.

(2) The power to make rules of court under section 1 of, and Schedule 1 to, the Civil Procedure Act 1997 shall include power by any such rules to make provision –

(*a*) for the High Court to make a stop order on the application of any person claiming to be entitled to an interest in prescribed securities; and

(*b*) for the service of a stop notice by any person claiming to be entitled to an interest in prescribed securities.

(3) (*repealed*)

(4) Rules of court made by virtue of subsection (2) above shall prescribe the person or body on whom a copy of any stop order or a stop notice is to be served.

(5) The steps mentioned in subsection (1) above are –

(*a*) the registration of any transfer of the securities;

(*b*) in the case of funds in court, the transfer, sale, delivery out, payment or other dealing with the funds, or of the income thereon;

(*c*) the making of any payment by way of dividend, interest or otherwise in respect of the securities; and

(*d*) in the case of a unit trust, any acquisition of or other dealing with the units by any person or body exercising functions under the trust.

(6) Any rules of court made by virtue of this section may include such incidental, supplemental and consequential provisions as the authority making them consider necessary or expedient, and may make different provision in relation to different cases or classes of case.

Amendments—Supreme Court Act 1981, s 152(1), Sch 5; County Courts Act 1984, s 148(1), Sch 2, para 72; SI 2002/439.

6 Interpretation

(1) In this Act –

"building society" has the same meaning as in the Building Societies Act 1986;

"charging order" means an order made under section 1(1) of this Act;

"debtor" and "creditor" have the meanings given by section 1(1) of this Act;

PART II

"dividend" includes any distribution in respect of any unit of a unit trust;

"government stock" means any stock issued by Her Majesty's government in the United Kingdom or any funds of, or annuity granted by, that government;

"stock" includes shares, debentures and any securities of the body concerned, whether or not constituting a charge on the assets of that body;

"unit trust" means any trust established for the purpose, or having the effect, of providing, for persons having funds available for investment, facilities for the participation by them, as beneficiaries under the trust, in any profits or income arising from the acquisition, holding, management or disposal of any property whatsoever.

(2) For the purposes of section 1 of this Act references to a judgment or order of the High Court or a county court shall be taken to include references to a judgment, order, decree or award (however called) of any court or arbitrator (including any foreign court or arbitrator) which is or has become enforceable (whether wholly or to a limited extent) as if it were a judgment or order of the High Court or a county court.

(3) References in section 2 of this Act to any securities include references to any such securities standing in the name of the Accountant General.

Amendments—Building Societies Act 1986, s 120(1), Sch 18, Pt I, para 14.

****

Child Abduction and Custody Act 1985

ARRANGEMENT OF SECTIONS

PART I
INTERNATIONAL CHILD ABDUCTION

PART II
RECOGNITION AND ENFORCEMENT OF CUSTODY DECISIONS

PART I
INTERNATIONAL CHILD ABDUCTION

1 The Hague Convention

(1) In this Part of this Act "the Convention" means the Convention on the Civil Aspects of International Child Abduction which was signed at The Hague on 25 October 1980.

(2) Subject to the provisions of this Part of this Act, the provisions of that Convention set out in Schedule 1 to this Act shall have the force of law in the United Kingdom.

Object of the Convention—The Hague Convention seeks to protect rights of custody and access and to provide through legal process the expeditious return of any child who is under the age of 16 who has been wrongfully removed or retained in another Contracting State (Sch 1, Arts 3, 4) to the country of its habitual residence. Its first objective is to provide an effective mechanism for the prompt return of children through administrative and judicial procedures so that parents do not resort to self-help and secondary abduction. The second is to ensure that rights of custody and access under the law of one contracting state are effectively respected in the other contracting states. Since this is an international convention to be applied under a variety of systems of law, it must be given a "purposive construction in order to make as effective as possible the machinery set up under it" (see *Re H (Abduction: Rights of Custody)* [2000] 1 FLR 374, [2000] 2 All ER 1, HL). The machinery of the Convention contemplates a summary procedure which can only be operated once (*Re O (Child Abduction: Re-Abduction)* [1997] 2 FLR 712 at 719).

2 Contracting States

(1) For the purposes of the Convention as it has effect under this Part of this Act the Contracting States other than the United Kingdom shall be those for the time being specified by an Order in Council under this section.

(2) An Order in Council under this section shall specify the date of the coming into force of the Convention as between the United Kingdom and any State specified in the Order; and except where the Order otherwise provides, the Convention shall apply as between the United Kingdom and that State only in relation to wrongful removals or retentions occurring on or after that date.

(3) Where the Convention applies, or applies only, to a particular territory or particular territories specified in a declaration made by a Contracting State under Article 39 or 40 of the Convention references to that State in subsections (1) and (2) above shall be construed as references to that territory or those territories.

Defined terms—"the Convention": s 1(1).

"specified by an Order in Council under this section"—See the Child Abduction and Custody (Parties to Conventions) Order 1986 (as amended) which specifies the Contracting States for this purpose. The permanent Bureau of the Hague Conference on Private International Law on its website at *http://www.hcch.net* also gives these details. To facilitate the goal of uniform interpretation it has set up a database (INCADAT) of decisions taken under the Convention, which can be accessed at *www.incadat.com* (see Fam Law [2000] 308 and *Re H (Abduction: Rights of Custody)* (above)).

3 Central Authorities

(1) Subject to subsection (2) below, the functions under the Convention of a Central Authority shall be discharged –

(*a*) in England and Wales and in Northern Ireland by the Lord Chancellor; and
(*b*) in Scotland by the Secretary of State.

(2) Any application made under the Convention by or on behalf of a person outside the United Kingdom may be addressed to the Lord Chancellor as the Central Authority in the United Kingdom.

(3) Where any such application relates to a function to be discharged under subsection (1) above by the Secretary of State it shall be transmitted by the Lord Chancellor to the Secretary of State and where such an application is addressed to the Secretary of State but relates to a function to be discharged under subsection (1) above by the Lord Chancellor the Secretary of State shall transmit it to the Lord Chancellor.

Defined terms—"the Convention": s 1(1).

"functions ... of a Central Authority"—These are specified by Arts 7–11, 15, 21, 26–28 of the Convention.

4 Judicial authorities

The courts having jurisdiction to entertain applications under this Convention shall be –

(*a*) in England and Wales or in Northern Ireland the High Court; and
(*b*) in Scotland the Court of Session.

Defined terms—"the Convention": s 1(1).

"applications under this Convention"—For procedure see FPR 1991, Pt VI. In order to bring about the return of a child who has been wrongfully removed from England and Wales, or who has been wrongfully retained, the applicant should apply to the Lord Chancellor's Department (LCD), which is the Central Authority for England and Wales. The LCD may then apply on behalf of the applicant to the Central Authority in the Contracting State. Where a child has been brought to England and Wales, the Central Authority in the Contracting State which is the country of the child's habitual residence should apply to the LCD for assistance in securing the return of the child. The LCD may then apply to the High Court as the judicial and administrative authority for the purposes of the Convention for assistance in ascertaining the whereabouts of the child and securing its return. It is also open to the applicant to apply directly to the High Court under Art 29.

5 Interim powers

Where an application has been made to a court in the United Kingdom under the Convention, the court may, at any time before the application is determined, give such interim directions as it thinks fit for the purpose of securing the welfare of the child concerned or of preventing changes in the circumstances relevant to the determination of the application.

Defined terms—"the Convention": s 1(1).

Application for interim directions—Application is by summons (FPR 1991, r 6.13). In an emergency it may be made without notice on a sworn statement.

Extent of court's power on interim direction—The court has very wide powers under this section to deal with all interlocutory matters, including taking all appropriate steps to ascertain the whereabouts of the child and to ensure his return (Sch 1, Arts 7 and 10). The court can exercise jurisdiction even before a child's arrival within England and Wales (*A v A (Abduction: Jurisdiction)* [1995] 1 FLR 341). Where appropriate the court will exercise its inherent jurisdiction. It may, for example, make a collection and/or location order, ordering the defendant to deliver the child; and make any necessary order for the disclosure of the child's whereabouts additional to those under s 24A (for the prescribed forms see *Emergency Remedies in the Family Courts* (Family Law, Issue 12)). It can also order any person who has any relevant information about the child, to disclose it (see FPR 1991, r 6.16). A solicitor representing the abductor may be ordered to disclose the whereabouts of the abductor and all documents in his possession relating to the abductor's whereabouts. However, for pragmatic reasons and as a matter of principle, the solicitor cannot properly be ordered to lie to his client or to mislead him. An order forbidding the solicitor to disclose any information relating to the existence of the order may be appropriate until the order is served or comes to the knowledge of the abductor; but thereafter it would be inappropriate to adopt such a course as it is unlikely to assist in the recovery of the child and on balance might stand in the way of the solicitor retaining the confidence of his client and from offering him advice and representation (*Re H (Abduction: Whereabouts Order to Solicitors)* [2000] 1 FLR 766). The court in such cases will strike a balance. It will be mindful of maintaining the privilege of confidentiality which exists between lawyer and client, and of keeping any intrusion into this field to the minimum and only insofar as it is essential (*Re B (Abduction: Disclosure)* [1995] 1 FLR 774). The court also has powers to grant injunctions, to order a CAFCASS reporter to prepare a report (s 9), to give specific directions for trial, and to order publicity (*Re D (A Minor) (Child Abduction)* [1989] 1 FLR 97). The court may dispense with service (FPR 1991, r 6.9), adjourn the hearing for up to 21 days (FPR 1991, r 6.10), and stay the proceedings (FPR 1991, r 6.11).

6 Reports

Where the Lord Chancellor or the Secretary of State is requested to provide information relating to a child under Article 7(*d*) of the Convention he may –

(*a*) request a local authority or an officer of the Service to make a report to him in writing with respect to any matter which appears to him to be relevant;

(*b*) request the Department of Health and Social Services for Northern Ireland to arrange for a suitably qualified person to make such a report to him;

(*c*) request any court to which a written report relating to the child has been made to send him a copy of the report;

and such a request shall be duly complied with.

Amendments—Criminal Justice and Court Services Act 2000 s 74, Sch 7, para 80.

Defined terms—"the Convention": s 1(1); "local authority": s 27(3).

7 Proof of documents and evidence

(1) For the purposes of Article 14 of the Convention a decision or determination of a judicial or administrative authority outside the United Kingdom may be proved by a duly authenticated copy of the decision or determination; and any document purporting to be such a copy shall be deemed to be a true copy unless the contrary is shown.

(2) For the purposes of subsection (1) above a copy is duly authenticated if it bears the seal, or is signed by a judge or officer, of the authority in question.

(3) For the purposes of Articles 14 and 30 of the Convention any such document as is mentioned in Article 8 of the Convention, or a certified copy of any such document, shall be sufficient evidence of anything stated in it.

Defined terms—"the Convention": s 1(1).

8 Declarations by United Kingdom courts

The High Court or Court of Session may, on an application made for the purposes of Article 15 of the Convention by any person appearing to the court to have an interest in the matter, make a declaration or declarator that the removal of any child from, or his retention outside, the United Kingdom was wrongful within the meaning of Article 3 of the Convention.

Defined terms—"the Convention": s 1(1).

Scope of provision—The declaration is often necessary to enable the applicant in proceedings outside the UK to obtain an order for the return of a child who has been wrongly removed or retained. This section contemplates applications being made for the purposes of Art 15 by *any person* appearing to the court to have an interest in the matter and is not limited to the applicant or to the circumstances within the narrow definition of Art 15. In *Re G (Abduction: Rights of Custody)* [2002] 2 FLR 703 an unmarried father, who did not have parental responsibility for the child, and his mother, who had cared for the child, were regarded as having an interest in the child within the terms of s 8. When determining whether to grant the declaration, the court will consider, inter alia, whether the applicant parent had rights of custody according to English law at the time of removal and possible issues of habitual residence and any breach (*Re P (Abduction: Declaration)* [1995] 1 FLR 831).

"wrongful"—See **Wrongful removal or retention** under Sch 1, Art 3.

9 Suspension of court's powers in cases of wrongful removal

The reference in Article 16 of the Convention to deciding on the merits of rights of custody shall be construed as a reference to –

(*a*) making, varying or revoking a custody order, or a supervision order under section 31 of the Children Act 1989 or Article 50 of the Children (Northern Ireland) Order 1995;

(*aa*) enforcing under section 29 of the Family Law Act 1986 a custody order within the meaning of Chapter V of Part I of that Act;

(*b*) registering or enforcing a decision under Part II of this Act;
(*c*) (*repealed*)
(*d*) making, varying or discharging an order under section 86 of the Children (Scotland) Act 1995;
(*e*) (*repealed*)

Amendments—Family Law Act 1986, s 68(1), Sch 1, para 28; CA 1989, s 108(5), Sch 13, para 57(1), Sch 15; Children (Scotland) Act 1995, s 105(4), Sch 4, para 37; SI 1995/756.

Defined terms—"the Convention": s 1(1); "custody order": s 27(1), Sch 3; "rights of custody": Sch 1, Art 5.

Scope of provision—This section supports Art 16 of the Hague Convention (see Sch 1, Art 16) which prevents the court from deciding on the merits of rights of custody until it has determined that a child is not to be returned or unless an application under the Convention is not lodged within a reasonable time after notice of wrongful removal or retention of the child. FPR 1991, r 6.11 provides a procedure which inter alia guards against a court proceeding to determine rights of custody in ignorance of an application under the Convention.

The Magistrates' Courts (Child Abduction and Custody) Rules 1986 also provide inter alia for the family proceedings court: (*a*) to stay all proceedings before it when an application under the Convention is pending in the High Court (r 3); (*b*) to dismiss a complaint pending before it once a decision under Art 12 of the Convention has been made (r 4); and (*c*) to resume any proceedings before it only when it has received notice that the application for the return of the child has been refused by the High Court or Court of Session (r 5).

10 Rules of court

(1) An authority having power to make rules of court may make such provision for giving effect to this Part of this Act as appears to that authority to be necessary or expedient.

(2) Without prejudice to the generality of subsection (1) above, rules of court may make provision –

(*a*) with respect to the procedure on applications for the return of a child and with respect to the documents and information to be furnished and the notices to be given in connection with any such application;
(*b*) for the transfer of any such application between the appropriate courts in the different parts of the United Kingdom;
(*c*) for the giving of notices by or to a court for the purposes of the provisions of Article 16 of the Convention and section 9 above and generally as respects proceedings to which those provisions apply;
(*d*) for enabling a person who wishes to make an application under the Convention in a Contracting State other than the United Kingdom to obtain from any court in the United Kingdom an authenticated copy of any decision of that court relating to the child to whom the application is to relate.

Defined terms—"appropriate court": s 27(2); "the Convention": s 1(1); "part of the United Kingdom": s 27(2).

Rules of court—FPR 1991, Pt VI (rr 6.1–6.16) applies to this Part.

11 Cost of applications

The United Kingdom having made such a reservation as is mentioned in the third paragraph of Article 26 of the Convention, the costs mentioned in that paragraph shall not be borne by any Minister or other authority in the United Kingdom except so far as they fall to be so borne by virtue of –

(*a*) the provision of any service funded by the Legal Services Commission as part of the Community Legal Service, or

(*b*) the grant of legal aid or legal advice and assistance under the Legal Aid (Scotland) Act 1967, Part I of the Legal Advice and Assistance Act 1972 or the Legal Aid Advice and Assistance (Northern Ireland) Order 1981.

Amendments—Legal Aid Act 1988, s 45(1), (3), Sch 5, para 16; Access to Justice Act 1999, s 24, Sch 4, para 31.

Defined terms—"the Convention": s 1(1).

Reservation on costs—The UK is not bound to meet any costs other than those which may be covered by the Legal Services Commission. Article 26 (see Sch 1, Art 26) permits a Contracting State to require the payment of expenses incurred in the return of the child (eg air fare).

Power to order payment of costs and expenses—The court has power, where appropriate, to direct the person who removed or retained the child, or who prevented the exercise of rights of access, to pay necessary expenses incurred by or on behalf of the applicant, including travel expenses, any costs incurred or payment made for locating the child, the costs of legal representation of the applicant and those of returning the child.

PART II
RECOGNITION AND ENFORCEMENT OF CUSTODY DECISIONS

12 The European Convention

(1) In this Part of this Act "the Convention" means the European Convention on Recognition and Enforcement of Decisions concerning Custody of Children and on the Restoration of Custody of Children which was signed in Luxembourg on 20 May 1980.

(2) Subject to the provisions of this Part of this Act, the provisions of that Convention set out in Schedule 2 to this Act (which include Articles 9 and 10 as they have effect in consequence of a reservation made by the United Kingdom under Article 17) shall have the force of law in the United Kingdom.

(3) But those provisions of the Convention are subject to Article 37 of Council Regulation (EC) No 1347/2000 of 29 May 2000 on jurisdiction and the recognition and enforcement of judgments in matrimonial matters and in matters of parental responsibility for children of both spouses (under which the Regulation takes precedence over the Convention), and the provisions of this Part of this Act, and any rules of court made pursuant to section 24 of this Act, shall be construed accordingly.

Amendments—SI 2001/310.

Object of the Convention—The European Convention provides for the registration, recognition and enforcement of decisions relating to custody where there has been an improper removal of a child in breach of such a decision.

13 Contracting States

(1) For the purposes of the Convention as it has effect under this Part of this Act the Contracting States other than the United Kingdom shall be those for the time being specified by an Order in Council under this section.

(2) An Order in Council under this section shall specify the date of the coming into force of the Convention as between the United Kingdom and any State specified in the Order.

(3) Where the Convention applies, or applies only, to a particular territory or particular territories specified by a Contracting State under Article 24 or 25 of the Convention references to that State in subsections (1) and (2) above shall be construed as references to that territory or those territories.

Defined terms—"the Convention": s 12(1).

"specified by an Order in Council under this section"—See the Child Abduction and Custody (Parties to Conventions) Order 1986, as amended, which specifies the Contracting States for this purpose.

14 Central Authorities

(1) Subject to subsection (2) below, the functions under the Convention of a Central Authority shall be discharged –

(*a*) in England and Wales and in Northern Ireland by the Lord Chancellor; and
(*b*) in Scotland by the Secretary of State.

(2) Any application made under the Convention by or on behalf of a person outside the United Kingdom may be addressed to the Lord Chancellor as the Central Authority in the United Kingdom.

(3) Where any such application relates to a function to be discharged under subsection (1) above by the Secretary of State it shall be transmitted by the Lord Chancellor to the Secretary of State and where such an application is addressed to the Secretary of State but relates to a function to be discharged under subsection (1) above by the Lord Chancellor, the Secretary of State shall transmit it to the Lord Chancellor.

Defined terms—"the Convention": s 12(1).

"functions ... of a Central Authority"—These are specified in Arts 7–11, 15, 21, 26–28 of the Convention.

15 Recognition of decisions

(1) Articles 7 and 12 of the Convention shall have effect in accordance with this section.

(2) A decision to which either of those Articles applies which was made in a Contracting State other than the United Kingdom shall be recognised in each part of the United Kingdom as if made by a court having jurisdiction to make it in that part but –

(*a*) the appropriate court in any part of the United Kingdom may, on the application of any person appearing to it to have an interest in the matter, declare on any of the grounds specified in Article 9 or 10 of the Convention that the decision is not to be recognised in any part of the United Kingdom; and
(*b*) the decision shall be enforceable in any part of the United Kingdom unless registered in the appropriate court under section 16 below.

(3) The references in Article 9(1)(*c*) of the Convention to the removal of the child are to his improper removal within the meaning of the Convention.

Defined terms—"appropriate court": s 27(2); "child": Sch 2, Art 1(*a*); "the Convention": s 12(1); "improper removal": Sch 2, Art 1(*d*); "part of the United Kingdom": s 27(2).

16 Registration of decisions

(1) A person on whom any rights are conferred by a decision relating to custody made by an authority in a Contracting State other than the United Kingdom may make an application for the registration of the decision in an appropriate court in the United Kingdom.

(2) The Central Authority in the United Kingdom shall assist a person in making such an application if a request for such assistance is made by him or on his behalf by the Central Authority of the Contracting State in question.

(3) An application under subsection (1) above or a request under subsection (2) above shall be treated as a request for enforcement for the purposes of Articles 10 and 13 of the Convention.

(4) The High Court or Court of Session shall refuse to register a decision if –

(*a*) the court is of the opinion that on any of the grounds specified in Article 9 or 10 of the Convention the decision should not be recognised in any part of the United Kingdom;
(*b*) the court is of the opinion that the decision is not enforceable in the Contracting State where it was made and is not a decision to which Article 12 of the Convention applies;
(*c*) an application in respect of the child under Part I of this Act is pending.

(5) Where the Lord Chancellor is requested to assist in making an application under this section to the Court of Session he shall transmit the request to the Secretary of State and the Secretary of State shall transmit to the Lord Chancellor any such request to assist in making an application to the High Court.

(6) In this section "decision relating to custody" has the same meaning as in the Convention.

Defined terms—"appropriate court": s 27(2); "authority": Sch 2, Art 1(*b*); "Central Authority in the United Kingdom": s 14; "child": Sch 2, Art 1(*a*); "the Convention": s 12(1); "Contracting State": s 13(1); "decision relating to custody": Sch 2, Art 1(*c*).

Procedure on application—The procedure on application is set out in Sch 2, Arts 4 and 13 and FPR 1991, rr 6.2–6.4.

Shall refuse to register—Although the language of s 16(4) is mandatory, see Art 10 of the European Convention (Sch 2) which is permissive and thus gives the court a discretion.

17 Variation and revocation of registered decisions

(1) Where a decision which has been registered under section 16 above is varied or revoked by an authority in the Contracting State in which it was made, the person on whose behalf the application for registration of the decision was made shall notify the court in which the decision is registered of the variation or revocation.

(2) Where a court is notified under subsection (1) above of the revocation of a decision, it shall –

(*a*) cancel the registration, and
(*b*) notify such persons as may be prescribed by rules of court of the cancellation.

(3) Where a court is notified under subsection (1) above of the variation of a decision, it shall –

(*a*) notify such persons as may be prescribed by rules of court of the variation; and

(*b*) subject to any conditions which may be so prescribed, vary the registration.

(4) The court in which a decision is registered under section 16 above may also, on the application of any person appearing to the court to have an interest in the matter, cancel or vary the registration if it is satisfied that the decision has been revoked or, as the case may be, varied by an authority in the Contracting State in which it was made.

Defined terms—"authority": Sch 2, Art 1(*b*); "Contracting State": s 13(1).

Procedure—Where the decision is revoked the court will cancel the registration and will give notice to the parties of the cancellation. There is no provision for the parties to make representations before the cancellation takes place. In a case where the decision has been varied, the court, on receiving notice of the variation, will notify the parties who have the right to make representations before the registration is varied. Although, FPR 1991, r 6.15(4) gives any person who has an interest in the matter the right to apply by summons for the registration, variation or cancellation of a decision, it is silent on the procedure to be followed; for example the filing of evidence and the time for service. In view of Art 6 of the European Convention on Human Rights, before the court takes any steps to cancel, vary or deal with such an application it should give the parties the opportunity to make representations.

18 Enforcement of decisions

Where a decision relating to custody has been registered under section 16 above, the court in which it is registered shall have the same powers for the purpose of enforcing the decision as if it had been made by that court; and proceedings for or with respect to enforcement may be taken accordingly.

19 Interim powers

Where an application has been made to a court for the registration of a decision under section 16 above or for the enforcement of such a decision, the court may, at any time before the application is determined, give such interim directions as it thinks fit for the purpose of securing the welfare of the child concerned or of preventing changes in the circumstances relevant to the determination of the application or, in the case of an application for registration, to the determination of any subsequent application for the enforcement of the decision.

Defined terms—"child": Sch 2, Art 1(*a*).

Application for interim directions—For procedure see FPR 1991, r 6.13.

Extent of court's power on interim directions—The court has broadly similar powers to those described under s 5. See also *T v R* [2002] 2 FLR 544.

20 Suspension of court's powers

(1) Where it appears to any court in which such proceedings as are mentioned in subsection (2) below are pending in respect of a child that –

(*a*) an application has been made for the registration of a decision in respect of the child under section 16 above (other than a decision mentioned in subsection (3) below) or that such a decision is registered; and (*b*) the decision was made in proceedings commenced before the proceedings which are pending,

the powers of the court with respect to the child in those proceedings shall be restricted as mentioned in subsection (2) below unless, in the case of an application for registration, the application is refused.

(2) Where subsection (1) above applies the court shall not –

(*a*) in the case of custody proceedings, make, vary or revoke any custody order, or a supervision order under section 31 of the Children Act 1989 or Article 50 of the Children (Northern Ireland) Order 1995;

(*aa*) in the case of proceedings under section 29 of the Family Law Act 1986 for the enforcement of a custody order within the meaning of Chapter V or Part I of that Act, enforce that order; or

(*b*), (*c*) (*repealed*)

(*d*) in the case of proceedings for, or for the variation or discharge of, a parental responsibilities order under section 86 of the Children (Scotland) Act 1995, make, vary or discharge any such order;

(*e*) (*repealed*)

(2A) Where it appears to the Secretary of State –

(*a*) that an application has been made for the registration of a decision in respect of a child under section 16 above (other than a decision mentioned in subsection (3) below); or

(*b*) that such a decision is registered;

the Secretary of State shall not make, vary or revoke any custody order in respect of the child unless, in the case of an application for registration, the application is refused.

(3) The decision referred to in subsection (1) or (2A) above is a decision which is only a decision relating to custody within the meaning of section 16 of this Act by virtue of being a decision relating to rights of access.

(4) Paragraph (*b*) of Article 10(2) of the Convention shall be construed as referring to custody proceedings within the meaning of this Act.

(5) This section shall apply to a children's hearing (as defined in section 93(1) of the Children (Scotland) Act 1995) as it does to a court.

Amendments—Family Law Act 1986, ss 67(2), (3), 68(1), Sch 1, para 29; CA 1989, s 108(5), Sch 13, para 57(1), Sch 15; Children (Scotland) Act 1995, s 105(4), Sch 4, para 37; SI 1995/756.

Defined terms—"child": Sch 2, Art 1(*a*); "the Convention": s 12(1); "custody order", "custody proceedings": s 27(1), Sch 3.

Scope of provision—See annotation under s 9. This section restricts the court's powers to determine applications for custody when an order is registered under s 16 or an application for registration is pending. FPR 1991, r 6.11 provides a procedure which, inter alia, guards against a court proceeding to determine custody in ignorance of an application under the Convention.

21 Reports

Where the Lord Chancellor or the Secretary of State is requested to make enquiries about a child under Article 15(1)(*b*) of the Convention he may –

(*a*) request a local authority or an officer of the Service to make a report to him in writing with respect to any matter relating to the child concerned which appears to him to be relevant;

(*b*) request the Department of Health and Social Services for Northern Ireland to arrange for a suitably qualified person to make such a report to him;

(*c*) request any court to which a written report relating to the child has been made to send him a copy of the report;

and any such request shall be duly complied with.

Amendments—Criminal Justice and Court Services Act 2000 s 74, Sch 7, para 80.

Defined terms—"child": Sch 2, Art 1(*a*); "the Convention": s 12(1); "local authority": s 27(3).

22 Proof of documents and evidence

(1) In any proceedings under this Part of this Act a decision of an authority outside the United Kingdom may be proved by a duly authenticated copy of the decision; and any document purporting to be such a copy shall be deemed to be a true copy unless the contrary is shown.

(2) For the purpose of subsection (1) above a copy is duly authenticated if it bears the seal, or is signed by a judge or officer, of the authority in question.

(3) In any proceedings under this Part of this Act any such document as is mentioned in Article 13 of the Convention, or a certified copy of any such document, shall be sufficient evidence of anything stated in it.

Defined terms—"authority": Sch 2, Art 1(*b*); "the Convention": s 12(1).

Procedure for obtaining documents etc—The procedure for obtaining an authenticated copy of a family proceedings court order is set out in Magistrates' Courts (Child Abduction and Custody) Rules 1986, r 8.

23 Decisions of United Kingdom courts

(1) Where a person on whom any rights are conferred by a decision relating to custody made by a court in the United Kingdom makes an application to the Lord Chancellor or the Secretary of State under Article 4 of the Convention with a view to securing its recognition or enforcement in another Contracting State, the Lord Chancellor or the Secretary of State may require the court which made the decision to furnish him with all or any of the documents referred to in Article 13(1)(*b*), (*c*) and (*d*) of the Convention.

(2) Where in any custody proceedings a court in the United Kingdom makes a decision relating to a child who has been removed from the United Kingdom, the court may also, on an application made by any person for the purposes of Article 12 of the Convention, declare the removal to have been unlawful if it is satisfied that the applicant has an interest in the matter and that the child has been taken from or sent or kept out of the United Kingdom without the consent of the person (or, if more than one, all the persons) having the right to determine the child's place of residence under the law of the part of the United Kingdom in which the child was habitually resident.

(3) In this section "decision relating to custody" has the same meaning as in the Convention.

Defined terms—"child": Sch 2, Art 1(*a*); "Contracting State": s 13(1); "the Convention": s 12(1); "decision relating to custody": Sch 2, Art 1(*c*); "part of the United Kingdom": s 27(2).

Decision of United Kingdom court relating to custody—Where a court makes a without notice order in proceedings under CA 1989, s 8 of which the abducting parent has notice, the order is both recognised and enforceable for the purposes of Art 9, and the court has jurisdiction to declare the removal unlawful even though the applicant did not possess the appropriate "rights" when the child was removed (*Re S (A Minor) (Child Abduction)* [1996] 3 FCR 115).

"Article 12 of the Convention"—In cases where the provisions of both Conventions may apply, if a custody order existed, for example to a mother whose child has been abducted to France, it would be advisable to obtain a declaration under s 23(2) so that both Conventions may be relied on.

"unlawful"—Where a removal is declared unlawful then the removal is an improper removal (Sch 2, Art 1(*d*)).

Procedure in the family proceedings court—For the procedure to obtain a declaration of unlawful removal of a child, see Magistrates' Courts (Child Abduction and Custody) Rules 1986, r 9.

24 Rules of court

(1) An authority having power to make rules of court may make such provision for giving effect to this Part of this Act as appears to that authority to be necessary or expedient.

(2) Without prejudice to the generality of subsection (1) above, rules of court may make provision –

(*a*) with respect to the procedure on application to a court under any provision of this Part of this Act and with respect to the documents and information to be furnished and the notices to be given in connection with any such application;
(*b*) for the transfer of any such application between the appropriate courts in the different parts of the United Kingdom;
(*c*) for the giving of directions requiring the disclosure of information about any child who is the subject of proceedings under this Part of this Act and for safeguarding its welfare.

Defined terms—"appropriate court": s 27(2); "authority": Sch 2, Art 1(*b*); "child": Sch 2, Art 1(*a*); "part of the United Kingdom": s 27(2).

Rules of court—FPR 1991, Pt VI (rr 6.1–6.16) applies to this Part.

PART III
SUPPLEMENTARY

24A Power to order disclosure of child's whereabouts

(1) Where –

(*a*) in proceedings for the return of a child under Part I of this Act; or
(*b*) on an application for the recognition, registration or enforcement of a decision in respect of a child under Part II of this Act,

there is not available to the court adequate information as to where the child is, the court may order any person who it has reason to believe may have relevant information to disclose it to the court.

(2) A person shall not be excused from complying with an order under subsection (1) above by reason that to do so may incriminate him or his spouse of an offence; but a statement or admission made in compliance with such an order shall not be

admissible in evidence against either of them in proceedings for any offence other than perjury.

Amendments—Inserted by Family Law Act 1986, s 67(4).

Defined terms—"child": Sch 2, Art 1(*a*).

Scope of provision—This section supplements the court's wide powers under its inherent jurisdiction (see *Re D (A Minor) (Child Abduction)* [1989] 1 FLR 97).

Self-incrimination—See under CA 1989, s 98.

Rules—FPR 1991, r 6.16 makes further provision as to orders for disclosure of information on applications under the European Convention.

25 Termination of existing custody orders etc

(1) Where –

(*a*) an order is made for the return of a child under Part I of this Act; or
(*b*) a decision with respect to a child (other than a decision mentioned in subsection (2) below) is registered under section 16 of this Act,

any custody order relating to him shall cease to have effect.

(2) The decision referred to in subsection (1)(*b*) above is a decision which is only a decision relating to custody within the meaning of section 16 of this Act by virtue of being a decision relating to rights of access.

(3)–(7) (*repealed*)

Amendments—CA 1989, s 108(7), Sch 15; Children (Scotland) Act 1995, s 105(4), Sch 4, para 37(1), (4); SI 1995/756.

Defined terms—"child": Sch 2, Art 1(*a*).

26 Expenses

There shall be paid out of money provided by Parliament –

(*a*) any expenses incurred by the Lord Chancellor or the Secretary of State by virtue of this Act; and
(*b*) any increase attributable to this Act in the sums so payable under any other Act.

27 Interpretation

(1) In this Act "custody order" means (unless contrary intention appears) any such order as is mentioned in Schedule 3 to this Act and "custody proceedings" means proceedings in which an order within paragraphs 1, 2, 5, 6, 8 or 9 of that Schedule may be made, varied or revoked.

(2) For the purposes of this Act "part of the United Kingdom" means England and Wales, Scotland or Northern Ireland and "the appropriate court", in relation to England and Wales or Northern Ireland means the High Court and, in relation to Scotland, the Court of Session.

(3) In this Act "local authority" means –

(*a*) in relation to England and Wales, the council of a non-metropolitan county, a metropolitan district, a London borough or the Common Council of the City of London; and
(*b*) in relation to Scotland, a council constituted under section 2 of the Local Government etc (Scotland) Act 1994.

(4) In this Act a decision relating to rights of access in England and Wales or Scotland or Northern Ireland means a decision as to the contact which a child may, or may not, have with any person.

(5) In this Act "officer of the Service" has the same meaning as in the Criminal Justice and Court Services Act 2000.

Amendments—Family Law Act 1986, ss 67(5), 68(1), Sch 1, para 30; CA 1989, s 108(5), Sch 13, para 57(2); Local Government etc (Scotland) Act 1994, s 180(1), Sch 13, para 139; Children (Scotland) Act 1995, s 105(4), Sch 4, para 37(5); SI 1995/756; Criminal Justice and Court Services Act 2000 s 74, Sch 7, para 81.

28 Application as respects British Islands and colonies

(1) Her Majesty may by Order in Council direct that any of the provisions of this Act specified in the Order shall extend, subject to such modifications as may be specified in the Order, to –

(*a*) the Isle of Man,
(*b*) any of the Channel Islands, and
(*c*) any colony.

(2) Her Majesty may by Order in Council direct that this Act shall have effect in the United Kingdom as if any reference in this Act, or in any amendment made by this Act, to any order which may be made, or any proceedings which may be brought or any other thing which may be done in, or in any part of, the United Kingdom included a reference to any corresponding order which may be made or, as the case may be, proceedings which may be brought or other thing which may be done in any of the territories mentioned in subsection (1) above.

(3) An Order in Council under this section may make such consequential, incidental and supplementary provision as Her Majesty considers appropriate.

(4) An Order in Council under this section shall be subject to annulment in pursuance of a resolution of either House of Parliament.

Orders under this section—With effect from 6 December 1994, the Child Abduction and Custody Act 1985 (Isle of Man) Order 1994 (SI 1994/2799) extends the provisions of this Act so as to include the Isle of Man in references to the United Kingdom made in this Act.

With effect from 2 December 1997, by virtue of the Child Abduction and Custody (Cayman Islands) Order 1997 (SI 1997/2574), ss 1–24A, 25(1), (2), 27 and Schs 1–3 of this Act (as modified in the Schedule thereto) extend to the Cayman Islands.

29 Short title, commencement and extent

(1) This Act may be cited as the Child Abduction and Custody Act 1985.

(2) This Act shall come into force on such day as may be appointed by an order made by statutory instrument by the Lord Chancellor and the Lord Advocate; and different days may be so appointed for different provisions.

(3) This Act extends to Northern Ireland.

SCHEDULE 1

CONVENTION ON THE CIVIL ASPECTS OF INTERNATIONAL CHILD ABDUCTION

Article 3

The removal or the retention of a child is to be considered wrongful where –

(*a*) it is in breach of rights of custody attributed to a person, an institution or any other body, either jointly or alone, under the law of the State in which the child was habitually resident immediately before the removal or retention; and

(*b*) at the time of removal or retention those rights were actually exercised, either jointly or alone, or would have been so exercised but for the removal or retention.

The rights of custody mentioned in sub-paragraph (*a*) above, may arise in particular by operation of law or by reason of a judicial or administrative decision, or by reason of an agreement having legal effect under the law of that State.

Defined terms—"rights of custody": Art 5.

Custody rights—A person with whom a child is placed on a long-term placement with the authority to make decisions may acquire "custody rights", as will an unmarried father with no parental responsibility if he lives in the same household and exercises parental rights for a period of time (*Re G (Abduction: Rights of Custody)* [2002] 2 FLR 703 where the child was placed with the paternal grandmother and the father lived with the child and the grandmother for 4 months before the application was made). Where a mother has custody rights and then agrees that the child should reside with the father, the agreement is simply a continuing exercise of the mother's custody rights; the agreement does not revoke her rights (*Re W (Abduction: Procedure)* [1995] 1 FLR 878, which followed *Re H (Minors) (Abduction: Custody Rights)* (below)).

The issue of whether the removal of a child was in contravention of custody rights should be resolved by reference to the Convention law as applied by the English courts, so that when a father had enjoyed equal and separate rights the removal of the child by the mother was found to be in breach of those rights (*Re F (Child Abduction: Risk if Returned)* [1995] 2 FLR 31, which was applied in *S v H (Abduction: Access Rights)* [1997] 1 FLR 971 and see *Re P (Abduction: Declaration)* [1995] 1 FLR 831). See also **"rights of custody"** under Art 5 and *Practice Note of 14 October 1997*.

Wrongful removal or retention—Removal is usually wrongful when it is in breach of someone else's rights (*C v S (A Minor) (Abduction)* [1990] 2 FLR 442, HL). Removal can be wrongful where it is in breach of the defendant's own rights of custody (*Re H (A Minor) (Abduction)* [1990] 2 FLR 439) or where it is in breach of an express court order (*Re C (A Minor)* [1989] 1 FLR 403). Removal is also wrongful within the terms of the Convention where it is in breach of an implied prohibition established on case-law, but not by reason of a court order (*C v C (Minors) (Child Abduction)* [1992] 1 FLR 163). See also *Re H (Minors) (Abduction: Custody Rights)*, *Re S (Minors) (Abduction: Custody Rights)* [1991] 2 AC 476, [1991] 2 FLR 262 and **Scope of provision** under Art 8.

A unilateral decision by one parent not to return a child to the country of the child's habitual residence may constitute wrongful retention (*Re S (Minors) (Abduction: Wrongful Retention)* [1994] Fam 70, [1994] 1 FLR 82; *H v H (Child Abduction: Stay of Domestic Proceedings)* [1994] 1 FLR 530 where, on the basis that there were exceptional circumstances, the court decided to deal with the merits of the application). When construing terms used in the Convention, the court's approach is generally to interpret the Convention purposively and, in so construing "retention", it has been held to be wide enough to comprise not only acts of physical restraint but also juridical orders obtained on the initiative of the offending parent (*Re B (Minors) (Abduction) (No 2)* [1993] 1 FLR 993; *Re AZ (A Minor) (Abduction: Acquiescence)* [1993] 1 FLR 682). Where the retention by one parent has been equivocal pending a determination by the court of the place from where the child has been abducted, a clear finding in that court requiring the return of the child would be sufficient to convert an equivocal retention into an unlawful one (*Re R (Minors) (Abduction)* [1994] 1 FLR 190). On the interpretation of Art 3 in the context of Art 5, see *B v B (Abduction:*

Custody Rights) [1993] Fam 32, [1993] 1 FLR 238. A removal which is not in breach of domestic law may nevertheless be wrongful for the purposes of the Convention (*Re F (Child Abduction: Risk if Returned)* [1995] 2 FLR 31 and *Practice Note of 14 October 1997*). See also *Re S (Custody: Habitual Residence)* [1998] 1 FLR 122, HL where, although the initial removal and retention of the child were not wrongful because the unmarried father had no rights of custody capable of being breached, once he had acquired such rights by virtue of an order giving him care and control, the retention of the child thereafter, contrary to the order and his wishes, became wrongful (notwithstanding the fact that the abductors had obtained an order from the foreign court).

Article 4

The Convention shall apply to any child who was habitually resident in a Contracting State immediately before any breach of custody or access rights. The Convention shall cease to apply when the child attains the age of sixteen years.

Age of the child—The Convention does not apply to a child who, although 15 years of age when the application was issued, is 16 when the application is heard. In such cases, however, the court may consider dealing with the application for the return of the child under its inherent jurisdiction (*Re H (Abduction: Child of 16)* [2000] 2 FLR 51).

Habitual residence—The term "habitual residence" is not defined in the Act or the Convention. It is submitted that this is intended to give the tribunal a free hand in determining the issue in accordance with the circumstances of each particular case. Although reference is made to the terms "ordinarily resident" and "habitually resident" in other statutory provisions relating to the fields of family, revenue and welfare law, these provisions do not identify any specific criteria which need to be satisfied before habitual residence is established. This has resulted in numerous decisions, in different branches of the law and in a variety of factual circumstances, where the terms have received judicial consideration.

Habitual residence is said to have strong similarities with the concept of ordinary residence (*V v B (A Minor) (Abduction)* [1991] 1 FLR 266) but they are not always synonymous (*Nessa v Chief Adjudication Officer* (below)). See also *R v Barnet Borough Council ex parte Shah* [1983] AC 309 and *Inland Revenue Commission v Lysaght* [1928] AC 234. It has been established that there are two features which must be proved to establish "habitual residence"; namely, that the person was present in a place or country (i) voluntarily and (ii) for settled purposes and with a settled intention (see *Re H (Abduction: Habitual Residence: Consent)* [2000] 2 FLR 294 and *Re N (Abduction: Habitual Residence)* [2000] 2 FLR 899 for an example on the issue of "settled intention"). See also *R v Barnet Borough Council* above; *Macrae v Macrae* [1949] P 397; *Kapur v Kapur* [1984] FLR 920 and the cases cited below. The need to establish residence in a place for "an appreciable period of time" was not specifically considered as a necessary ingredient until the decision in *C v S (A Minor) (Abduction)* [1990] 2 FLR 442, HL. In that case Lord Brandon considered the issue of habitual residence and observed:

> "... the question whether a person is or is not habitually resident in a specified country is a question of fact to be decided by reference to all the circumstances of any particular case ... there is a significant difference between a person ceasing to be habitually resident in country A, and his subsequently becoming habitually resident in country B. A person may cease to be habitually resident in country A in a single day if he or she leaves it with a settled intention not to return .... Such a person cannot, however, become habitually resident in country B in a single day. An appreciable period of time and a settled intention will be necessary to enable him or her to become so. During that appreciable period of time the person will have ceased to be habitually resident in country A but not yet have become habitually resident in country B."

Although the reference to the need to establish an elapse of "an appreciable period of time" was obiter, in subsequent cases emphasis has been placed on this requirement as an additional ingredient. Thus, in *A v A (Child Abduction)* [1993] 2 FLR 225, it was held that a person could not become habitually resident in a country in a single day. An appreciable period of time must elapse and a settled intention must be shown. On what would constitute appreciable time, see *Re P(GE) (An Infant)* [1965] Ch 568; *Re E (Child: Abduction)* [1992] 1 FCR 541; *Re R (Wardship: Child Abduction)* [1992] 2 FLR 481; *Re F (A Minor) (Child Abduction)* [1992] 1 FLR 548; *Re R (Wardship: Child Abduction) (No 2)* [1993] 1 FLR 249; *Re B-M (Wardship: Jurisdiction)* [1993] 1 FLR 979; *Re M (Minors) (Residence Order: Jurisdiction)* [1993] 1 FLR 495 and *Re M v M (Abduction: England and Scotland)* [1997] 2 FLR 263. A short period of time spent by a mother in another country with a view to effecting a reconciliation with the father which fails was found to be insufficient for a settled intention to have been formed as to change of residence (*Re B (Child Abduction: Habitual Residence)* [1994] 2 FLR 915). The mere fact of taking a child out of the country is not enough to establish habitual residence (*Re M (Abduction: Habitual Residence)* [1996] 1 FLR 887). A stay in a country for a holiday for more than a few days does not mean that the child is habitually resident in that country (*Re O* [1995] 2 FCR 649). Neither can habitual residence be acquired by a child who is not present in the country concerned (*Re M* (above)). Where a family has two homes, and part of the year is spent in one country and part in another, there is continuity of residence for habitual residence to arise in both countries, but in Convention cases there cannot be habitual residence in more than one place at the same time. The concept of concurrent habitual residence does not fit in with the aims of the Convention. In such cases, the child's habitual residence will be where the child was living at the moment when the wrongful retention or removal occurred (*Re V (Abduction: Habitual Residence)* [1995] 2 FLR 992).

In *Nessa v Chief Adjudication Officer* [1999] 2 FLR 1116, HL (a case concerning a person's entitlement to income support under Income Support (General) Regulations 1987, reg 21(3), Sch 7, para 17) the question whether the elapse of any appreciable period of time is needed to establish "habitual residence" was the key issue. Whilst accepting that there was an overlap between the meaning of "ordinary" and "habitual" residence, the court was not satisfied that they were always synonymous. Each may take a particular meaning from the context and the object/purpose of the legislation. In *Ikimi v Ikimi* [2001] 2 FLR 1288, CA, Thorpe LJ, when deciding this issue in relation to the court's divorce jurisdiction, held that the two adverbs must be synonymous and he opined that it was essential that the same meaning be given to "habitually" wherever it appeared in family law statutes. However, he excluded this interpretation from cases under the Hague Convention on the basis that: "the construction of [this term] is settled and developed within the wider field of international jurisprudence". As a matter of ordinary language, a person could not be said to be habitually resident in any country unless he had taken up residence/lived there for a period and could demonstrate that the residence had become habitual and was likely to continue to be so. However, in other situations it might be appropriate for the purpose of giving effect to particular legislation where it was important that there was no gap (eg for founding jurisdiction) that a person should be habitually or ordinarily resident in a certain state at any one time, or where the person was resuming an habitual residence previously held. Whether habitual residence has been established is a question of fact to be decided on the date when the determination has to be made and in the light of the circumstances of each case. The court must consider all the relevant facts including whether the person has: (i) brought possessions; (ii) a right of abode; (iii) sought to bring family; and (iv) "durable ties" with the country of residence or intended residence. The requisite period is not a fixed one. It will depend on the facts of each case. It might be short as in *Re S (Custody: Habitual Residence)* [1998] 1 FLR 122, HL or might be longer where there are doubts. It is submitted that so far as the family lawyer is concerned, this decision in effect approves the dissenting judgment of Thorpe LJ in the Court of Appeal ([1998] 1 FLR 879).

It is for the applicant initially to satisfy the court that it has jurisdiction (*Re R (Wardship: Child Abduction) (No 2)* [1993] 1 FLR 249). In deciding the issue of habitual residence the court does not need to make a searching and microscopic inquiry. Generally it will suffice for the court to stand back and take a general panoramic view of the evidence (*Re B (Minors) (Abduction) (No 1)* [1993] 1 FLR 988). Once the evidence produced satisfies the court of the applicant's residence, the burden shifts on to the defendant to show that he is not so resident (*Re EW (Wardship: Jurisdiction)* [1992] 2 FCR 441). As to the residence of a child, a child aged four who is in the sole custody of the mother will necessarily have the same habitual residence as the mother (*Re J* (above)). Where parents separate, the child's habitual residence follows that of the parent who has the day-to-day care of the child and with whom the child lives. Uncommunicated reservations and a subsequent change of mind by one party which is not communicated to the other party will not be a relevant consideration (*Re A (Abduction: Habitual Residence)* [1998] 1 FLR 497). Similarly, where the mother alone has parental responsibility for her child, she alone can determine where they should live, and she can change the habitual residence of her child (*Re M (Minors) (Residence Order: Jurisdiction)* [1993] 1 FLR 495). Where parents are living together, the child is habitually resident with both, but where one parent loses his habitual residence with the children and becomes habitually resident elsewhere, the children do not lose their original habitual residence (*Re N (Abduction: Habitual Residence)* [2000] 2 FLR 899). When the parents separate the child's habitual residence will follow that of its principal carer. In the case of a married couple, it is not possible for one parent unilaterally to terminate the habitual residence of a child by removing the child from one jurisdiction to another wrongfully and in breach of the other parent's rights. In *B v H (Habitual Residence: Wardship)* [2002] 1 FLR 388 it was held that a father could not unilaterally change the habitual residence of his children who had been taken from England to Bangladesh, along with the mother, on the pretext of a holiday and then detained there. The

PART II

habitual residence of a new-born baby will be that of the parent who has parental responsibility for and the day-to-day care of the child. The fact that the child is born abroad does not of itself lead to the conclusion that the child is not habitually resident in England. Where there is an agreement between the parents that the child should live abroad and then either parent resiles from the agreement whereby the child became habitually resident abroad, it does not follow that the child will automatically become habitually resident in England, without ever having returned to England (*Re M (A Minor) (Habitual Residence)* [1996] 1 FLR 887). For a change to take effect, the child must be actually transferred into the care of the parent who seeks to establish habitual residence (*Re O (A Minor) (Abduction: Habitual Residence)* [1993] 2 FLR 594). Where the mother has been the sole carer of the child, her death will not immediately strip the child of the habitual residence acquired from her. Nor will the clandestine removal of the child, without a court order or the consent of any interested party, immediately clothe the child with the habitual residence of the person removing him. The issue of whether the child has acquired a new habitual residence will depend upon the facts of each case. The longer the child lives in the new jurisdiction without challenge, the more likely it is that the child will be said to acquire the habitual residence of those who continue to care for him without opposition (*Re G (Abduction: Rights of Custody)* [2002] 2 FLR 703 where the child was said to have acquired the habitual residence of her paternal grandmother and father (without parental responsibility) who were her principal carers; *Re S (Custody: Habitual Residence)* [1998] 1 FLR 122, HL). In *Re S* it was held that a period of 2 days was not sufficient, of itself, to result in the child's existing habitual residence being lost and a new one being acquired. Nor could habitual residence be altered by the courts of the country where the child was retained. Where a parent abducts a baby, fails to comply with any court order for the child's return and successfully goes to ground for many years, there is a powerful argument that it would be an affront to common sense to hold, perhaps 10–12 years later, that the habitual residence of the child was other than the country in which he had spent virtually the whole of his life (*Re B (Abduction: Children's Objection)* [1998] 1 FLR 667). On the issue of the habitual residence of a child born to a surrogate mother with whom she has no biological connection see *W and B v H (Child Abduction: Surrogacy)* [2002] 1 FLR 1008 and *W and W v H (Child Abduction: Surrogacy) No 2* [2002] 2 FLR 252. It is clear from these two decisions that, in appropriate cases, where there is any doubt about proving the habitual residence of a child it would be advisable to seek relief under the Convention and, alternatively under the inherent jurisdiction, to enable the court to exercise the full range of powers available to it.

The habitual residence of a child in England before the abduction will give the High Court inherent jurisdiction to entertain an application in respect of the child. The issue of wardship proceedings, and any orders made by the English court giving interim care and control, will stand, and give both the court and the parent in whose favour the order is made "custody rights" within Art 3 of the Convention, even though an order may have been obtained by the abductors from the foreign court (*Re S* above). The habitual residence of a child of a US serviceman who is posted to a non-Convention country is that country and not the US (*Re A (Abduction: Habitual Residence)* [1996] 1 FLR 1).

It should be noted that Art 4 does not require that, at the time of the application, the child should be habitually resident in the state under which the rights of custody or access arose; it does require, however, that the child should be habitually resident in "a Contracting State" (*Re G (A Minor) (Hague Convention: Access)* [1993] 1 FLR 669; see also *A v A (Child Abduction)* [1993] 2 FLR 225). Art 21 of the Convention, however, only enables the applicant when seeking to enforce an access order to obtain CLS funding and bring the matter before the court through the Central Authority. It does not affect the jurisdiction of the court where the child is habitually resident in England. In such cases, in order to secure rights of contact the application should include an application under CA 1989, s 8.

Article 5

For the purposes of this Convention –

(*a*) "rights of custody" shall include rights relating to the care of the person of the child and, in particular, the right to determine the child's place of residence;

(*b*) "rights of access" shall include the right to take a child for a limited period of time to a place other than the child's habitual residence.

"rights of custody"—Rights of custody include rights relating to the care of the child and, in particular, the right to determine the child's place of residence but not the right to be informed about a decision to change the residence of the child (*Re V-B (Abduction: Custody Rights)* [1999] 2 FLR 192, CA) or his education. See further *C v S (A Minor) (Abduction)* [1990] 2 FLR 442, HL; *Re H (A Minor) (Abduction)* [1990] 2 FLR 439; *Re C (A Minor) (Abduction)* [1989] 1 FLR 403; *Re B (A Minor) (Abduction)* [1994] 2 FLR 249 and the dissenting judgment of Peter Gibson LJ. A father who gives his consent to the children travelling to the mother continues to exercise custody rights (*W v W (Child Abduction: Acquiescence)* [1993] 2 FLR 211). The right of custody may arise by operation of law or by reason of a judicial or administrative decision, or by reason of an agreement having legal effect under the law of that state. It may also arise by reason of an implied prohibition on the removal of a child from a state without the consent of the father or leave of the court (*C v C (Child Abduction)* [1992] 1 FLR 163). A court itself may have a right of custody at the relevant time in the sense that it has a right to determine the child's place of residence, provided that it has acquired "custody rights". It acquires custody rights when its jurisdiction is invoked in respect of matters within the meaning of the Convention. The date on which the court's jurisdiction is invoked is at the latest when the proceedings are served, or in special cases before then (*Re H (Abduction: Rights of Custody)* [2000] 1 FLR 374, HL) and in any event once it has made an interim order (*Re W; Re B (Child Abduction: Unmarried Father)* [1998] 2 FLR 146); or where the court is actively seised of the proceedings to determine custody rights, eg where it has given directions (*Re J (Abduction: Declaration of Wrongful Removal)* [1999] 2 FLR 653); or it has adjourned the hearing for the issue to be resolved by agreement (*Re C (Abduction: Wrongful Removal)* [1999] 2 FLR 859); or where wardship proceedings have been issued (*Re S (Custody: Habitual Residence)* [1998] 1 FLR 122). See also *Practice Note of 14 October 1997* at "'Rights of custody' and pending proceedings".

Where an issue is raised regarding whether the foreign law gives the applicant custody rights or not, the court will determine the issue on expert evidence adduced before it. The court should resist the temptation to make its own findings as to the foreign laws applicable and should be reluctant to allow rights of access to a child to metamorphose into rights of custody. Where the court is faced with conflicting expert evidence, it is for the applicant to prove his rights under the relevant foreign law.

Custody rights and unmarried fathers—See *Re B (A Minor) (Abduction)* [1994] 2 FLR 249 and *Re G (Abduction: Rights of Custody)* [2002] 2 FLR 703 where the unmarried father and the grandmother who had the care of the child were considered as having "custody rights"; *Re C (Abduction: Wrongful Removal)* [1999] 2 FLR 859 and also *Re S (Custody: Habitual Residence)* [1998] 1 FLR 122, HL; and *Re W; Re B (Child Abduction: Unmarried Father)* [1998] 2 FLR 146. It should be noted that the views expressed in *Practice Note of 14 October 1997* were rejected in *Re C*.

Orders made after removal—The view expressed in *Practice Note of 14 October 1997* that an application for parental responsibility does not involve an exercise by the court of "rights of custody" was challenged in *Re C* (above).

"rights of access"—Rights of access include the right to take a child for a limited period of time to a place other than the child's habitual residence. Under Art 21, an application to make arrangements for organising or securing the effective exercise of rights of access may be presented to the Central Authority of a Contracting State in the same way as an application for the return of a child. Article 21 also provides that Central Authorities are bound by the obligations of co-operation in Art 7 to promote the peaceful enjoyment of access rights and the fulfilment of any conditions to which the exercise of those rights may be subject.

****

Article 8

Any person, institution or other body claiming that a child has been removed or retained in breach of custody rights may apply either to the Central Authority of the child's habitual residence or to the Central Authority of any other Contracting State for assistance in securing the return of the child. The application shall contain –

(*a*) information concerning the identity of the applicant, of the child and of the person alleged to have removed or retained the child;

(*b*) where available, the date of birth of the child;

(c) the grounds on which the applicant's claim for return of the child is based;
(d) all available information relating to the whereabouts of the child and the identity of the person with whom the child is presumed to be.

The application may be accompanied or supplemented by –

(e) an authenticated copy of any relevant decision or agreement;
(f) a certificate or an affidavit emanating from a Central Authority or other competent authority of the State of the child's habitual residence, or from a qualified person, concerning the relevant law of that State:
(g) any other relevant document.

Scope of provision—Under this Article a removal may be regarded as wrongful because it is in breach of "custody rights" attributable to "a court" (see further **"rights of custody"** under Art 5).

Procedure on application—See FPR 1991, rr 6.2–6.4 for the manner of application and the documents required to be filed.

****

Article 12

Where a child has been wrongfully removed or retained in terms of Article 3 and, at the date of the commencement of the proceedings before the judicial or administrative authority of the Contracting State where the child is, a period of less than one year has elapsed from the date of the wrongful removal or retention, the authority concerned shall order the return of the child forthwith.

The judicial or administrative authority, even where the proceedings have been commenced after the expiration of the period of one year referred to in the preceding paragraph, shall also order the return of the child, unless it is demonstrated that the child is now settled in its new environment.

Where the judicial or administrative authority in the requested state has reason to believe that the child has been taken to another State, it may stay the proceedings or dismiss the application for the return of the child.

"now settled in its new environment"—Where there has been significant delay in issuing proceedings under the Convention, the proceedings have not been conducted expeditiously and where, as a result of the delay, the children have become settled, the court in appropriate circumstances may regard the continuance of the proceedings as an abuse of the process of the court and strike out the application (*Re G (Abduction: Striking Out Application)* [1995] 2 FLR 410). Furthermore, under FPR 1991, r 6.10, the hearing of the originating summons under which an application under either Convention is made may not be adjourned for a period exceeding 21 days at any one time.

In *Re N (Minors) (Abduction)* [1991] 1 FLR 413 it was held that the word "now" referred to the date when the proceedings were commenced and not the day on which the issue was decided, as otherwise any delay in hearing the case might affect the outcome.

The word settlement has two constituents. First, it involves a physical element of relating to, being established in, a community and an environment. Secondly, it has an emotional constituent denoting security and stability in the sense of permanence. The word "new" encompasses place, home, school, people, friends, activities and opportunities, but not, per se, the relationship with the mother.

Duty to order the return of the child and protection of human rights and fundamental freedoms—Article 20 of the Hague Convention provides that the return of the child under the provisions of Art 12 may be refused if this would not be permitted by the fundamental principles of the requested State relating to the protection of human rights and fundamental freedoms. This Article has not been included in Sch 1 to this Act and does not therefore have the force of law in England and Wales. However, in *Re K (Abduction: Psychological Harm)* [1995] 2 FLR 550, it was raised as an aid to establish that, in considering the issue of whether the return of the child should be ordered under Art 12 and the provisions of Art 13(*b*), the court can and should have regard to the provisions of Art 20 relating to the "protection of human rights"; it was argued that, on the facts of the case, both the child and the mother had been denied their human rights, as the child has the right not to be separated from a parent without that parent (*a*) having been given adequate notice of the hearing at which the issue is to be considered, (*b*) having had advance opportunity to participate in the proceedings, and (*c*) having been given notice of the case which that parent has to meet. See also *Re J (Abduction: Wrongful Removal)* [2000] 1 FLR 78, where the mother raised breach of ECHR, Art 6 on the basis that the orders had been made without notice. Swinton Thomas LJ said:

> "the mother and the father of course have a right to a fair trial, and so also does the child, whose interest must be paramount in family proceedings. Cases concerning children often have to be dealt with as a matter of urgency ... It is always open to an opposing party against whom an order has been made to apply to the court to have it set aside. It is possible that there might be a breach of Art 6 if no opportunity was provided by law to challenge an ex parte order that is made ... Further, and to my mind even more important, the mother did indeed in this case have a full hearing and a full trial".

Duty to order the return of the child after the expiration of 12 months—Where more than 12 months have elapsed, the court has jurisdiction to entertain the application but, in reaching its decision, it will necessarily consider any delay in the making of the application. Where there has been significant delay in instituting the proceedings, and the proceedings have not been conducted expeditiously, the court may regard the application as an abuse of the process of the court (*Re G (Abduction: Striking Out Application)* [1995] 2 FLR 410). An application for an adjournment should be refused where the litigant has delayed or failed to give instructions to his lawyers. Delay will also be a factor which will be taken into account when weighing up the child's objections against the whole policy of the Convention (*Re S (Child Abduction: Delay)* [1998] 1 FLR 651). The reason for the delay in bringing the proceedings and the parties' conduct, particularly that of the abducting parent in concealing the child's whereabouts are relevant factors in determining the issue of settlement and the exercise of the discretion (*Re H (Abduction: Child of 16)* [2000] 2 FLR 51).

Enforcement of order to return—Article 12 places a duty on the court to order the return of the child forthwith. In exercising that duty, the court has jurisdiction to enforce the order for return by issuing a writ of sequestration against the property of a third party, provided it is satisfied so that it is sure that the third party knew of the order requiring the return of the child and that he nevertheless deliberately frustrated the order or aided and abetted the abducting parent in avoiding compliance with the order (*Re S (Abduction: Sequestration)* [1995] 1 FLR 858).

Article 13

Notwithstanding the provisions of the preceding Article, the judicial or administrative authority of the requested State is not bound to order the return of the child if the person, institution or other body which opposes its return establishes that –

(*a*) the person, institution or other body having the care of the person of the child was not actually exercising the custody rights at the time of removal or retention, or had consented to or subsequently acquiesced in the removal or retention; or

(*b*) there is a grave risk that his or her return would expose the child to physical or psychological harm or otherwise place the child in an intolerable situation.

The judicial or administrative authority may also refuse to order the return of the child if it finds that the child objects to being returned and has attained an age and degree of maturity at which it is appropriate to take account of its views.

In considering the circumstances referred to in this Article, the judicial and administrative authorities shall take into account the information relating to the social background of the child provided by the Central Authority or other competent authority of the child's habitual residence.

Consent or acquiescence—As to what constitutes consent or acquiescence, see *Re A and Another (Minors) (Abduction)* [1991] 2 FLR 241 and *Re A (Minors) (Abduction: Acquiescence)* [1992] 2 FLR 14. The evidence to establish consent must be clear, compelling and unequivocal, and is normally required to be in writing or evidenced in documentary form; it cannot be passive, but must be positive consent to the removal of the child (*Re W (Abduction: Procedure)* [1995] 1 FLR 878). Where consent is put in issue, the burden of proof shifts on to the person who is opposed to the return of the child to prove, on the balance of probabilities, that the removal was by consent. The means of proof will vary according to the circumstances of the case, and may include the court receiving oral evidence from the parties. It is possible for consent to be inferred from conduct (*Re M (Abduction: Consent: Acquiescence)* [1999] 1 FLR 171; *Re B (Abduction: Acquiescence)* [1999] 2 FLR 818), but in every case the evidence needed must be clear and cogent (*Re C (Abduction: Consent)* [1996] 1 FLR 414). The leading case on the meaning of consent or acquiescence is *Re H (Abduction: Acquiescence)* [1997] 1 FLR 872, in which the House of Lords laid down the following principles to be adopted when considering the meaning of "acquiescence" within Art 13 of the Convention:

(*a*) The English law concept of acquiescence, which was normally viewed objectively, had no direct application to the proper construction of Art 13. Under the Convention, it must have the same meaning and effect throughout the laws of all the Contracting States. Acquiescence in Art 13 means looking to the subjective state of mind of the wronged parent and asking has he in fact consented to the continued presence of the children in the jurisdiction to which they have been abducted. It is a question of the actual subjective intention of the wronged parent, not the outside world's perception of his intention.

(*b*) Acquiescence is a pure question of fact to be determined by the trial judge on the material before him. In the process of the fact-finding operation to ascertain the subjective intention, the court is more likely to attach weight to the contemporaneous express words and actions of the wronged party than to his subsequent bare assertions in evidence of his intention.

(*c*) The burden of proving that the wronged party has consented to, or acquiesced in, the abduction is on the abducting parent.

(*d*) Judges should be slow to infer an intention to acquiesce from attempts by the wronged parent to effect a reconciliation, or agree a voluntary return of the abducted child.

(*e*) There is only one exception to this general principle. Where the words or actions of the wronged parent clearly and unequivocally lead the other parent to believe that the wronged parent is not asserting or going to assert his right to the summary return of the child and are inconsistent with such return, justice requires that the wronged parent be held to have acquiesced (see *Re D (Abduction: Acquiescence)* [1999] 1 FLR 36).

The acquiescence must be in clear and unequivocal terms (*T v T (Abduction: Consent)* [1999] 2 FLR 912; *Re K (Abduction: Consent)* [1997] 2 FLR 212; *Re R (Child Abduction: Acquiescence)* [1995] 1 FLR 716). See also *Re CT (A Minor) (Abduction)* [1992] 2 FCR 92; *Re AZ (A Minor) (Abduction: Acquiescence)* [1993] 1 FLR 682; *A v A (Child Abduction)* [1993] 2 FLR 225.

The question of whether a purported consent to the child's removal is a valid consent is to be determined according to the circumstances of the case. A consent obtained by fraud or deception is unlikely to be regarded as valid (See *Re B (Abduction: Art 13 Defence)* [1997] 2 FLR 573 and *Re B (A Minor) (Abduction)* [1994] 2 FLR 249). The court should be slow to infer an intention to acquiesce from attempts by the wronged parent to effect a reconciliation or to reach an agreed voluntary return of the child (Arts 7(*c*), 10; *Re I (Abduction: Acquiescence)* [1999] 1 FLR 778 and see *P v P (Abduction: Acquiescence)* [1998] 1 FLR 630, FD, [1998] 2 FLR 835, CA).

Once acquiescence has been established, it is not necessary for the court to consider grave harm. The court can go on to consider what is in the child's best interest and how it should exercise its discretion on whether the child's return should be ordered (see *Re A (Minors) (Abduction: Acquiescence) (No 2)* [1993] 1 FLR 396).

"grave risk"—As to the meaning of "grave risk", see *Re A (A Minor) (Abduction)* [1988] 1 FLR 365, CA: there must be a weighty risk of substantial harm (*Re C (A Minor) (Abduction)* [1989] 1 FLR 403; *Re V v B (A Minor) (Abduction)* [1991] 1 FLR 266; *Re G (A Minor) (Abduction)* [1989] 2 FLR 475). In *Re D (A Minor) (Child Abduction) Note* [1989] 1 FLR 97, Wood J stated that Art 13(*b*) "is likely to apply in the most extreme cases, where evidence of the exposure to physical or psychological harm or otherwise place the child in an intolerable situation". See *Re S (Abduction: Custody Rights)* [2002] 2 FLR 815 where the court considered the risk of harm posed by reason of terrorist attacks and held that the issue was whether there was a risk of specific harm to the particular child and not whether there was a general risk of harm. A person who opposes the peremptory return of a child on the grounds set out in Art 13(*b*) will have to show some exceptional circumstances for the court to justify exercising its discretion (*Re M (Abduction: Peremptory Return Order)* [1996] 1 FLR 478). Such exceptional circumstances may include a situation which demonstrates the risk in the jurisdiction of the habitual residence of persecution, discrimination or some other overt harm, for example that the respondent would be subjected to criminal process or otherwise denied justice. In order to establish such exceptional circumstances, the court may permit expert evidence to be called as to the law and practice in the state of habitual residence, provided it does not lead to undue delay (*Re E-B (Children)* [2002] EWCA Civ 1771). Where the offending party alleges fear of violence from the applicant as a basis to establish grave risk of psychological harm to the children, the court will take into account measures which that party could reasonably be expected to take in the requesting country to protect herself and her children against the applicant (*TB v JB (Abduction: Grave Risk of Harm)* [2001] 2 FLR 515). The evidence will be considered objectively. It has been held that the approach taken will be equivalent to that adopted when considering the hostility of a mother to contact (*Re M (Abduction: Intolerable Situation)* [2000] 1 FLR 930). See also *Re J (A Minor) (Abduction: Ward of Court)* [1990] 1 FLR 276; *Re N (Minors) (Abduction)* [1991] 1 FLR 413; *Re L (Child Abduction: Psychological Harm)* [1993] 2 FLR 401. In *Re M (Abduction: Acquiescence)* [1996] 1 FLR 315, the court found that a fuller investigation of the issue of risk, and the consequent need for protection, needed to be established. In *Re HB (Abduction: Children's Objections)* [1997] 1 FLR 392 the children, who were aged 13 and 11, complained of ill-treatment by their stepfather and mother. The court did not regard this as sufficiently serious to constitute deliberate ill-treatment to bring the case within the ambit of Art 13. Having regard to the report by the Children Act Sub-Committee, which underlined the need for awareness of the effect of domestic violence on children, it remains to be seen whether in future the courts will consider the matters raised in that report, the joint report of Drs Sturge and Glaser ([2000] Fam Law 615) and the guidance given by the Court of Appeal in *Re L (Contact: Domestic Violence); Re V (Contact: Domestic Violence); Re M (Contact: Domestic Violence); Re H (Contact: Domestic Violence)* [2000] 2 FLR 334 as relevant in reaching their rulings in cases under the Convention.

The burden of proof on the defendant to establish that the exception should apply is a very heavy one (*Re E (A Minor) (Abduction)* [1989] 1 FLR 135). The court will require clear and compelling evidence (see *Re M (Child Abduction: Existence of Undertakings)* [2000] 3 FCR 693 and the cases cited therein). For the degree of intolerability that must be established, see *B v B (Abduction: Custody Rights)* [1993] Fam 32, [1993] 1 FLR 238; see also *C v C (Abduction: Jurisdiction)* [1994] 1 FCR 6, [1993] Fam Law 185, where the return of the child to Brazil was refused because of the length of time (ie one year) it would take for the case to be heard in Brazil. That was considered to subject the child to grave risk of being placed in an intolerable situation under Art 13(*b*). Once a prima facie case for applying the exception in Art 13 to the general summary return of the child has been made out, the court has to consider whether to exercise its discretion and it is only in exceptional circumstances that a court should not order summary return (*Re M (Abduction: Psychological Harm)* [1997] 2 FLR 690). Problems which arise from the fact of abduction and are self-induced will not generally suffice (*Re C (Abduction: Grave Risk of Physical or Psychological Harm)* [1999] 2 FLR 478). However, where there is evidence of a grave risk to the children of psychological harm if they are returned, that risk is of greater consequence than the importance of the court marking its disapproval of the abducting parent's behaviour.

The defence of grave risk of exposing the child to physical or psychological harm must be weighed both in the light of the immediate past and in comparative terms. As to the latter, the court is entitled to weigh the risk of psychological harm of return against the psychological consequences of refusing to order the return of the child. Where both risks are substantial, the court must, in exercising its discretion, give due weight to the important primary purpose of the Convention, ie to ensure the swift return of abducted children (*N v N (Abduction: Article 13 Defence)* [1995] 1 FLR 107). See also *Re F (Child Abduction: Risk if Returned)* [1995] 2 FLR 31 and *Re G (Abduction: Psychological Harm)* [1995] 1 FLR 64, where the court declined to order the return of the children. It should be noted, however, that in *Re G* the parents and the children had dual nationality and it was considered that the English court was a satisfactory forum to deal with the issues.

The child's objections—For consideration of the use of the exception relating to the objections of a child of sufficient maturity, see *Re S (A Minor) (Abduction)* [1991] 2 FLR 1; *Re V v B (A Minor) (Abduction)* [1991] 1 FLR 266; *Re C (A Minor) (Abduction)* [1989] 1 FLR 403; *Re G (A Minor) (Abduction)* [1989] 2 FLR 475. In *P v P (Minors) (Child Abduction)* [1992] 1 FLR 155, Waite J said "it will, in every case, be a question of fact and degree for the judge in the requested State whether, on the evidence presented to him, a finding would be justified that the child objects, and is of sufficient age and maturity to have its views taken into account. It will also, in every case, be a matter of discretion for the same court to decide, if the evidence presented to it appears insufficient to enable the court to make any finding one way or other on the issue of objection, age and maturity, whether an investigation into that issue should be made or should not". The exercise of that discretion is not affected by the fact that an order concerning the child has been made, or the fact that proceedings relating to the child are continuing in the requesting State, and nothing in the policy of the Hague Convention requires the court to apply the provisions of Brussels II to the exercise of the discretion. In exercising the discretion, the court will have regard to the conduct of the offending party as well as that of the applicant, particularly where such conduct has led to delay (*Re L (Abduction: Child's Objections to Return)* [2002] EWHC 1864 (Fam), [2002] 2 FLR 1042). In *Re R (A Minor) (Abduction)* [1992] 1 FLR 105 at 108, Bracewell J said "There must be more than a preference expressed by the child. The word 'objects' imports a strength of feeling which goes far beyond the usual ascertainment of the wishes of the child in a custody dispute. Questions must also be addressed as to whether or not the views expressed by the child of appropriate age and maturity and understanding are expressed out of free will and choice, whether or not they are genuine views, or whether they have been influenced by some party or person in contact with the child". See also *Gillick v West Norfolk and Wisbech Area Health Authority* [1986] AC 112, [1986] 1 FLR 224, and *B v K (Child Abduction)* [1993] Fam Law 17, where children aged 9 and 7 years were held to have attained an age and degree of maturity at which it was appropriate to take account of their views. See also *Re T (Abduction: Child's Objection to Return)* [2000] 2 FLR 192, where the child was 11.

Expressed views of the children must be carefully and cautiously assessed, bearing in mind that the wishes and feelings which children express may vary according to mood, adult influence and/or their reaction to the person carrying out the assessment. In general, the younger the child is, the less likely it is that the child would have the maturity which would make it appropriate to take his views into account. Even where the child's views are taken into account, the court is not obliged to give effect to that preference. The decision whether to give effect to it must turn on the particular circumstances of each case (*Re R (Abduction: Hague and European Conventions)* [1997] 1 FLR 663 where the wishes of a 10-year-old were taken into account; *Re R (Child Abduction: Acquiescence)* [1995] 1 FLR 716). See also *Re F (Child Abduction: Risk if Returned)* [1995] 2 FLR 31, where the court declined to order the return of the child.

Where a child's objection to returning arises from a desire to remain with the abducting parent, little or no weight is given to the child's views (*A v A (Child Abduction)* [1993] 2 FLR 225). In *S v S (Child Abduction)* [1992] 2 FLR 31, a child aged 9 but with a mental age of 12 put forward her views which were found to be mature and rational and based on genuine and cogent reasons. At first instance, the court refused to order her return; on appeal ([1993] Fam 242, [1992] 2 FLR 492), whilst confirming the decision, the court said that the scheme of the Convention was that in normal circumstances it is considered to be in the interest of children generally that they should be promptly returned to the country from which they have been wrongfully removed. It was only in exceptional circumstances that the court should have a discretion to refuse to order the child's immediate return. It was a question of fact for the judge whether the child's objections were genuine and whether the child had reached an age and maturity at which it was appropriate to take account of his or her views. See also *Re R (Child Abduction: Acquiescence)* [1995] 1 FLR 716 and *Re B (Abduction: Children's Objections)* [1998] 1 FLR 667.

There is no clear authority on the court's approach where there are siblings who express different views and are of a varying degree of maturity and understanding. Two recent cases contain seemingly conflicting decisions. In *Re HB (Abduction: Children's Objections)* [1997] 1 FLR 392 the older child's objections were not regarded as sufficient to outweigh the policy of the Convention that summary return should be ordered but see [1998] 1 FLR 422, CA and [1998] 1 FLR 564. In *The Ontario Court v M and M (Abduction: Children's Objections)* [1997] 1 FLR 475 the children were aged 10 and 2. The older child raised strong objections to returning to Canada to be cared for by her grandmother whom she disliked and feared. The court considered that to return her would place her in an intolerable situation within Art 13. It may be possible to rationalise the apparent conflict between these two decisions because each case turned on its own facts.

Generally, the child's views and the strength of his or her objections will be adequately represented by one of the parties. This will be assisted by the appointment of a CAFCASS officer to report on the child's degree of maturity and wishes. It is only in exceptional circumstances, where the facts disclose that it would be inappropriate for this method to be used, that the court will consider joining the child as a party to the application and ordering separate representation (*Re M (A Minor) (Abduction: Child's Objections)* [1994] 2 FLR 126). There must also be an arguable case that the discretion under Art 13 should be exercised (*Re S (Abduction: Children: Separate Representation)* [1997] 1 FLR 486).

Intolerable situation—In *C v C (Abduction: Jurisdiction)* [1994] 1 FCR 6 the court found that a delay of a year before the custody application could be determined in Brazil would place the child in an intolerable position. In such cases, however, it will be necessary to establish a high degree of intolerability (*E v E (Child Abduction: Intolerable Situation)* [1998] 2 FLR 980) – hardship or even discomfort or the application of the religious laws or dual system of justice to a parent is insufficient (*Re S (Abduction: Intolerable Situation: Beth Din)* [2000] 1 FLR 454; *B v B (Abduction: Custody Rights)* [1993] Fam 32, [1993] 1 FLR 238, CA). The intolerability complained of must relate to the child. Problems created by the offending party's conduct should not be treated as a basis for raising the defence under Art 13(*b*) (*Re C (Abduction: Grave Risk of Psychological Harm)* [1999] 1 FLR 1145); dependence on welfare benefits is insufficient (*Re M (Abduction: Undertakings)* [1995] 1 FLR 1021; *Re A (Minors) (Abduction: Acquiescence)* [1992] 2 FLR 14). See also *Re O (Child Abduction: Undertakings)* [1994] 2 FLR 349. For the effect of Art 20 on the provisions of Art 13 and, in particular, Art 13(*b*), see *Re K (Abduction: Psychological Harm)* [1995] 2 FLR 550 and **Duty to order. the return of the child and protection of human rights and fundamental freedoms** under Art 12.

PART II

Abduction and the claim for asylum—The court's jurisdiction to order the return of an abducted child is not restricted by the provisions of the Immigration and Asylum Act 1999 and, in particular, the prohibition on removal under s 15 of the 1999 Act is directed at the immigration authorities. It is not intended to circumscribe the duty and discretion of a judge exercising the wardship, Convention or family jurisdiction (*Re S (Child Abduction: Asylum Appeal)* [2002] EWCA Civ 843, [2002] 2 FLR 465).

Art 13 and the welfare test—The court will apply a two-stage process when considering the application of Art 13, namely: (i) establish whether a prima facie case under the Article is made out; and (ii) consider whether or not to order the return of the children. The Art 13 threshold is strictly applied and it is only in exceptional circumstances that the court will consider not returning the children. *Re D (Abduction: Discretionary Return)* [2000] 1 FLR 24 is an example of the robust attitude adopted by the English courts. However, it could also be argued that the decision turned on the particular facts of the case (see further the commentary in *Emergency Remedies in the Family Courts* (Family Law)). See also *Re M (Abduction: Conflict of Jurisdiction)* [2000] 2 FLR 372 for an example of how the High Court seeks to resolve conflicts between the application of two jurisdictions.

Article 14

In ascertaining whether there has been a wrongful removal or retention within the meaning of Article 3, the judicial or administrative authorities of the requested State may take notice directly of the law of, and of judicial or administrative decisions, formally recognised or not in the State of the habitual residence of the child, without recourse to the specific procedures for the proof of that law or for the recognition of foreign decisions which would otherwise be applicable.

Article 15

The judicial or administrative authorities of a Contracting State may, prior to the making of an order for the return of the child, request that the applicant obtain from the authorities of the State of the habitual residence of the child a decision or other determination that the removal or retention was wrongful within the meaning of Article 3 of the Convention, where such a decision or determination may be obtained in that State. The Central Authorities of the Contracting States shall so far as practicable assist applicants to obtain such a decision or determination.

Request by the judicial or administrative authorities of a Contracting State—The provisions of this Article should be read with those of s 8 which contemplates applications for the purposes of Art 15 to be made by any person who appears to have an interest in the matter. Its terms are broader than the limited ones set out in this Article. See *Re P (Abduction: Declaration)* [1995] 1 FLR 831 for an example of where the court applied the provisions of s 8, and proceeded to make a declaration although it involved making a preliminary decision on the issues of habitual residence and breach which were to be decided by the court in the requested State.

Article 16

After receiving notice of a wrongful removal or retention of a child in the sense of Article 3, the judicial or administrative authorities of the Contracting State to which the child has been removed or in which it has been retained shall not decide on the merits of rights of custody until it has been determined that the child is not to be returned under this Convention or unless an application under this Convention is not lodged within a reasonable time following receipt of the notice.

"notice"—This reference is not restricted to notice from any particular source or in any particular form (*R v R (Residence Order: Child Abduction)* [1995] 2 FLR 625). As soon as the court learns that it is concerned with a child who has formerly lived abroad in a Convention country and one parent wishes, or may wish, to return to that country, a possible case under the Hague Convention may arise. If there is any doubt, the matter should be transferred to the High Court. It is the duty of the practitioners involved to draw the attention of the court to the possibility that the Hague Convention may apply (*Re H (Abduction: Habitual Residence: Consent)* [2000] 2 FLR 294).

Application—The machinery of the Convention contemplates a summary procedure, to be operated only once. There cannot be second or subsequent applications under the Convention. This principle also applies where the application has been made and the summary procedure has taken place in another Contracting State (*Re O (Child Abduction: Re-Abduction)* [1997] 2 FLR 712).

Lodging of application within a reasonable time—The question of what is reasonable time must be considered objectively but, unless the court makes a finding that no application has been lodged within a reasonable time, it should refrain from deciding the merits of right of custody and making a residence order including one which is interim (*R v R* (above)).

Procedural steps to be taken by the court—Where the court becomes seised of a matter relating to a child, and it becomes apparent that there has been wrongful removal or retention within the meaning of the Convention, the court has a duty to take steps to secure that the parent in the other State is informed of his rights under the Convention. The English central authority should be requested to inform the central authority of the State from which the child has been removed of the circumstances of the case. The court should also communicate with the parent in that State by means of directions to the effect that he should seek legal advice expeditiously as to his rights, and communicate with the central authority of his State, of which he should be given the name and address.

****

SCHEDULE 2

EUROPEAN CONVENTION ON RECOGNITION AND ENFORCEMENT OF DECISIONS CONCERNING CUSTODY OF CHILDREN

Article 1

For the purposes of this Convention:

(*a*) "child" means a person of any nationality, so long as he is under 16 years of age and has not the right to decide on his own place of residence under the law of his habitual residence, the law of his nationality or the internal law of the State addressed;
(*b*) "authority" means a judicial or administrative authority;
(*c*) "decision relating to custody" means a decision of an authority in so far as it relates to the care of the person of the child, including the right to decide on the place of his residence, or to the right of access to him;

(*d*) "improper removal" means the removal of a child across an international frontier in breach of a decision relating to his custody which has been given in a Contracting State and which is enforceable in such a State; "improper removal" also includes:
  - (i) the failure to return a child across an international frontier at the end of a period of the exercise of the right of access to this child or at the end of any other temporary stay in a territory other than that where the custody is exercised;
  - (ii) a removal which is subsequently declared unlawful within the meaning of Article 12.

Article 4

(1) Any person who has obtained in a Contracting State a decision relating to the custody of a child and who wishes to have that decision recognised or enforced in another Contracting State may submit an application for this purpose to the central authority in any Contracting State.

(2) The application shall be accompanied by the documents mentioned in Article 13.

(3) The central authority receiving the application, if it is not the central authority in the State addressed, shall send the documents directly and without delay to that central authority.

(4) The central authority receiving the application may refuse to intervene where it is manifestly clear that the conditions laid down by this Convention are not satisfied.

(5) The central authority receiving the application shall keep the applicant informed without delay of the progress of his application.

Procedure on application—See FPR 1991, rr 6.2–6.4 for the manner of application and the documents required to be filed.

Determination of application—Determination of the application under the European Convention should not be made while Hague Convention proceedings are pending (*Re R (Abduction: Hague and European Conventions)* [1997] 1 FLR 663).

"decision relating to the custody of a child"—This term refers to a decision of an authority insofar as it relates to the care of the person of the child, including the right to decide on the place of his residence, or to the right of access to him (Art 1(*c*)). Where there is a subsisting order, it is irrelevant that the order was made before the ratification of the European Convention between England and the other Contracting party and, by virtue of Art 7, it is required to be recognised and enforced (*Re L (Child Abduction: European Convention)* [1992] 2 FLR 178).

****

Article 7

A decision relating to custody given in a Contracting State shall be recognised and, where it is enforceable in the State of origin, made enforceable in every other Contracting State.

"decision relating to custody"—Where the abducting parent had notice of the proceedings for a residence and parental responsibility order, an ex parte residence order and an order requiring the abductor to return the child to England are enforceable in other Contracting States, because the recognition and enforcement of such an order could not be refused under the provisions of Art 9 (*Re S (A Minor) (Child Abduction)* [1996] 3 FCR 115).

Article 9

(1) Recognition and enforcement may be refused if:

(*a*) in the case of a decision given in the absence of the defendant or his legal representative, the defendant was not duly served with the document which instituted the proceedings or an equivalent document in sufficient time to enable him to arrange his defence; but such a failure to effect service cannot constitute a ground for refusing recognition or enforcement where service was not effected because the defendant had concealed his whereabouts from the person who instituted the proceedings in the State of origin;

(*b*) in the case of a decision given in the absence of the defendant or his legal representative, the competence of the authority giving the decision was not founded:

(i) on the habitual residence of the defendant; or

(ii) on the last common habitual residence of the child's parents, at least one parent being still habitually resident there, or

(iii) on the habitual residence of the child;

(*c*) the decision is incompatible with a decision relating to custody which became enforceable in the State addressed before the removal of the child, unless the child has had his habitual residence in the territory of the requesting State for one year before his removal.

(3) In no circumstances may the foreign decision be reviewed as to its substance.

Scope of provision—This Article provides for the court to refuse recognition and enforcement on procedural grounds; see *Re G (A Minor) (Child Abduction: Enforcement)* [1990] 2 FLR 325.

Recognition and enforcement—This should be construed disjunctively; thus, a court is entitled to refuse an order which has been registered, eg where it is found that, by reason of changes in the circumstances including the passage of time, the effects of the original decision are manifestly no longer in the interests of the child (*Re H (A Minor) (Foreign Custody Order: Enforcement)* [1994] 1 FLR 512, [1994] 1 All ER 812). Note, however, that the provisions of this Article are not mandatory but discretionary, since the court *may* refuse to recognise and enforce the order (*Re G (A Minor) (Child Abduction: Enforcement)* [1990] 2 FLR 325).

"decision is incompatible with a decision ... enforceable in the State addressed" (Art 9(1)(*c*))—Recognition and enforcement was refused in *Re M (Child Abduction) (European Convention)* [1994] 1 FLR 551.

Review of foreign decision—This Article specifically provides that under no circumstances may the foreign decision be reviewed as to its substance; see also *Re A (Foreign Access Order: Enforcement)* [1996] 1 FLR 561.

Article 10

(1) Recognition and enforcement may also be refused on any of the following grounds –

(*a*) if it is found that the effects of the decision are manifestly incompatible with the fundamental principles of the law relating to the family and children in the State addressed;

(*b*) if it is found that by reason of a change in the circumstances including the passage of time but not including a mere change in the residence of the child after an improper removal, the effects of the original decision are manifestly no longer in accordance with the welfare of the child;

(*c*) if at the time when the proceedings were instituted in the State of origin:

(i) the child was a national of the State addressed or was habitually resident there and no such connection existed with the State of origin;

(ii) the child was a national both of the State of origin and of the State addressed and was habitually resident in the State addressed;

(*d*) if the decision is incompatible with a decision in the State addressed or enforceable in that State after being given in a third State, pursuant to proceedings begun before the submission of the request for recognition or enforcement, and if the refusal is in accordance with the welfare of the child.

(2) Proceedings for recognition or enforcement may be adjourned on any of the following grounds:

(*a*) if an ordinary form of review of the original decision has been commenced;

(*b*) if proceedings relating to the custody of the child, commenced before the proceedings in the State of origin were instituted, are pending in the State addressed;

(*c*) if another decision concerning the custody of the child is the subject of proceedings for enforcement or of any other proceedings concerning the recognition of the decision.

Scope of provision—This Article sets out the substantive ground for refusal of recognition and enforcement. See *Re G (A Minor) (Abduction: Enforcement)* [1990] 2 FLR 325; *Re F (Minors) (Custody: Foreign Order: Enforcement)* [1989] 1 FLR 335; *Re K (A Minor) (Abduction)* [1990] 1 FLR 387. Notwithstanding the mandatory terms of s 16(4), the use of the word "may" in the Article gives the court a discretion. However, if the court permits registration, in view of the provisions of Art 9(3) which prohibit a review of the foreign order, enforcement of that order must follow. Therefore, in exercising its discretion when considering whether to allow registration, the court will also necessarily have to consider the effect on the child of enforcing the order.

"effects of the original decision"—This refers to the effects of the enforcement of the decision, in particular in relation to the welfare of the child, at the date of the determination of the application by the requested State without delay, review or alteration. It does not refer to the effects of taking steps towards its enforcement or the return of the child to the State of origin to enable it to enforce the original order. This flows (per Charles J in *T v R* [2002] 2 FLR 544) from:

"(*a*) the language of the phrase;

(*b*) the underlying purpose of the European Convention which is concerned with the enforcement of existing orders made in the State of origin by the courts of the State addresses;

(*c*) the terms of Art 7;

(*d*) the terms of Art 5(1)(*d*);

(*e*) Art 9(3) which precludes the State addressed from reviewing the substance of the original order; and

(*f*) Art 10(2)(*a*) which provides for the possibility of adjournment if an ordinary review has been commenced".

In considering this issue and any change in the circumstances, the child's views are relevant and should be taken into account in respect of any dispute under Art 10(1)(*b*), unless this is impracticable having regard to the child's age and understanding (Art 15(1)(*a*)). In this regard, a report by a CAFCASS reporter may be ordered to ascertain the child's feelings and views (see also *Re T (Abduction: Appointment of Guardian ad Litem)* below).

"Incompatible with the fundamental principles of family law"—Foreign law relating to the importance of contact and its conclusion that the residence of a child should be changed when a custodial parent opposes and refuses contact with the other parent (which does not reasonably warrant such opposition), is not incompatible with the approach to residence and contact in England having regard to the welfare principle and the application of the welfare checklist (see *T v R* (above) and *Re M (Child Abduction) (European Convention)* [1994] 1 FLR 551).

"improper removal"—For definition see Art 1(*c*) and note that the phrase "decisions relating to custody" includes access. Any action which thwarts such access by the removal of the child to another jurisdiction amounts to improper removal (see *T v R* (above)).

Issues to be determined—The essential task of the court under this Article is to establish what the circumstances were at the time of the original decision. Then it must ascertain whether any or all of the grounds set out in the Article have been proved and whether the original decision can no longer be sustained because it does not accord with the welfare of the child (*Re R (Abduction: Hague and European Conventions)* [1997] 1 FLR 663).

"manifestly no longer in accordance with the welfare of the child"—It is only in circumstances where it is clear that a return of the child would be manifestly against the interest of the child, and that the original decision is manifestly no longer in accordance with the welfare of the child, that the court should exercise its discretion not to comply with the spirit and terms of the Act and Convention. The party who seeks to persuade the court as to this bears a very high burden of proof (*Re L (Child Abduction: European Convention)* [1992] 2 FLR 178). See also *Re A (Foreign Access Order: Enforcement)* [1996] 1 FLR 561, where the decision was found not to come within the exceptions provided by Art 10(2). In appropriate cases a child may be joined as a party to the proceedings and represented by a children's guardian (*Re T (Abduction: Appointment of Guardian Ad Litem)* [1999] 2 FLR 796). Although recognition and enforcement may be refused, the court under its inherent jurisdiction may go on to consider what is the appropriate forum for determining the welfare of the child and any dispute relating to the child's residence and contact and whether, in the circumstances, it would be in the interests of the child to order his/her return whilst the dispute is resolved in the appropriate forum.

Article 11

(1) Decisions on rights of access and provisions of decisions relating to custody which deal with the rights of access shall be recognised and enforced subject to the same conditions as other decisions relating to custody.

(2) However, the competent authority of the State addressed may fix the conditions for the implementation and exercise of the right of access taking into account, in particular, undertakings given by the parties on this matter.

(3) Where no decision on the right of access has been taken or where recognition or enforcement of the decision relating to custody is refused, the central authority of the State addressed may apply to its competent authorities for a decision on the right of access if the person claiming a right of access so requests.

Discretion to fix condition—Article 11(2) gives a court discretion to fix conditions for the implementation and exercise of the right of access. This discretion must be exercised in the light of Art 9(3), which provides that under no circumstances may a foreign decision be reviewed as to its substance (*Re A (Foreign Access Order: Enforcement)* [1996] 1 FLR 561).

Article 12

Where, at the time of the removal of a child across an international frontier, there is no enforceable decision given in a Contracting State relating to his custody, the provisions of this Convention shall apply to any subsequent decision, relating to the custody of that child and declaring the removal to be unlawful, given in a Contracting State at the request of any interested person.

Declaration of unlawful removal—Art 12 prohibits the continued retention of a child when an enforceable decision relating to his custody has been made in a Contracting State. Once the court has found that the child has been wrongfully removed or retained under Art 3 of the Hague Convention, it can give a declaration that he has been unlawfully removed from the jurisdiction contrary to Art 12 (*Re S (Custody: Habitual Residence)* [1998] 1 FLR 122, HL).

"any subsequent decision"—Where the father of an illegitimate child did not have any custody or parental responsibility order in his favour relating to his child who had been unlawfully removed to Denmark, but obtained an ex parte residence order and an order requiring the mother to return the child to the father in England, it was held that the removal of the child was covered by the provisions of s 23(2) and thereby entitled the court to make a declaration under Art 12 that the removal of the child was unlawful (*Re S (A Minor) (Child Abduction)* [1996] 3 FCR 115).

Article 13

(1) A request for recognition or enforcement in another Contracting State of a decision relating to custody shall be accompanied by:

(*a*) a document authorising the central authority of the State addressed to act on behalf of the applicant or to designate another representative for that purpose;

(*b*) a copy of the decision which satisfies the necessary conditions of authenticity;

(*c*) in the case of a decision given in the absence of the defendant or his legal representative, a document which establishes that the defendant was duly served with the document which instituted the proceedings or an equivalent document;

(*d*) if applicable, any document which establishes that, in accordance with the law of the State of origin, the decision is enforceable;

(*e*) if possible, a statement indicating the whereabouts or likely whereabouts of the child in the State addressed;

(*f*) proposals as to how the custody of the child should be restored.

Article 15

(1) Before reaching a decision under paragraph (1)(*b*) of Article 10, the authority concerned in the State addressed:

(*a*) shall ascertain the child's views unless this is impracticable having regard in particular to his age and understanding; and

(*b*) may request that any appropriate enquiries be carried out.

(2) The cost of enquiries in any Contracting State shall be met by the authorities of the State where they are carried out.

Requests for enquiries and the results of enquiries may be sent to the authority concerned through the central authorities.

Article 26

(1) In relation to a State which has in matters of custody two or more systems of law of territorial application:

(*a*) reference of the law of a person's habitual residence or to the law of a person's nationality shall be construed as referring to the system of law determined by the rules in force in that State or, if there are no such rules, to the system of law with which the person concerned is most closely connected;

(*b*) reference to the State of origin or to the State addressed shall be construed as referring, as the case may be, to the territorial unit where the decision was given or to the territorial unit where recognition or enforcement of the decision or restoration of custody is requested.

(2) Paragraph (1)(*a*) of this Article also applies mutatis mutandis to States which have in matters of custody two or more systems of law of personal application.

SCHEDULE 3
CUSTODY ORDERS

PART I
ENGLAND AND WALES

1 The following are the orders referred to in section 27(1) of this Act –

(*a*) a care order under the Children Act 1989 (as defined by section 31(11) of that Act, read with section 105(1) and Schedule 14);
(*b*) a residence order (as defined by section 8 of the Act of 1989); and
(*c*) any order made by a court in England and Wales under any of the following enactments –
(i) section 9(1), 10(1)(*a*) of the Guardianship of Minors Act 1971;
(ii) section 42(1) or (2) or 43(1) of the Matrimonial Causes Act 1973;
(iii) section 2(2)(*b*), (4)(*b*) or (5) of the Guardianship Act 1973 as applied by section 34(5) of the Children Act 1975;
(iv) section 8(2)(*a*), 10(1) or 19(1)(ii) of the Domestic Proceedings and Magistrates' Courts Act 1978;
(v) section 26(1)(*b*) of the Adoption Act 1976.

Amendments—CA 1989, s 108(5), Sch 13, para 57(3).

2 An order made by the High Court in the exercise of its jurisdiction relating to wardship so far as it gives the care and control of a child to any person.

3 (*repealed*)

4 An authorisation given by the Secretary of State under section 26(2) of the Children and Young Persons Act 1969 (except where the relevant order, within the meaning of that section, was made by virtue of the court which made it being satisfied that the child was guilty of an offence).

PART II
SCOTLAND

5 An order made by a court of civil jurisdiction in Scotland under any enactment or rule of law with respect to the residence, custody, care or control of a child or contact with or access to a child, excluding –

(i) an order placing a child under the supervision of a local authority;
(ii) an adoption order under section 12(1) of the Adoption (Scotland) Act 1978;
(ii*a*) an order freeing a child for adoption made under section 18 of the Adoption (Scotland) Act 1978;
(iii) an order relating to the guardianship of a child;
(iv) an order made under section 86 of the Children (Scotland) Act 1995;
(v) an order made, or warrant or authorisation granted, under or by virtue of Chapter 2 or 3 of Part II of the Children (Scotland) Act 1995 to remove the child to a place of safety or to secure accommodation, to keep him at such a place or in such

accommodation, or to prevent his removal from a place where he is being accommodated (or an order varying or discharging any order, warrant or authorisation so made or granted);

(vi) an order made in proceedings under this Act.

Amendments—Family Law Act 1986, s 68(1), Sch 1, para 31; Children (Scotland) Act 1995, s 105(4), Sch 4, para 37(6)(*a*).

6 A supervision requirement made by a children's hearing under section 70 of the Children (Scotland) Act 1995 (whether or not continued under section 73 of that Act) or made by the sheriff under section 51(5)(*c*)(iii) of that Act and any order made by a court in England and Wales or in Northern Ireland if it is an order which, by virtue of section 33(1) of that Act, has effect as if it were such a supervision requirement.

Amendments—Substituted by Children (Scotland) Act 1995, s 105(4), Sch 4, para 37(6)(*b*).

7 (*repealed*)

PART III
NORTHERN IRELAND

8 The following orders –

(*a*) a care order under the Children (Northern Ireland) Order 1995 (as defined by Article 49(1) of that Order read with Article 2(2) and Schedule 8);

(*b*) a residence order (as defined by Article 8 of that Order);

(*c*) any order made by a court in Northern Ireland under any of the following enactments –

(i) section 5 of the Guardianship of Infants Act 1886 (except so far as it relates to costs);

(ii) section 49 of the Mental Health Act (Northern Ireland) 1961;

(iii) Article 45(1) or (2) or 46 of the Matrimonial Causes (Northern Ireland) Order 1978;

(iv) Article 10(2)(*a*), 12(1) or 20(1)(ii) of the Domestic Proceedings (Northern Ireland) Order 1980;

(v) Article 27(1)(*b*) of the Adoption (Northern Ireland) Order 1987.

Amendments—Substituted by SI 1995/756.

9 An order made by the High Court in the exercise of its jurisdiction relating to wardship so far as it gives the care and control of a child to any person.

10 (*repealed*)

Child Support Act 1991

ARRANGEMENT OF SECTIONS

The basic principles

General Note—The Child Support Act 1991 has been substantially amended twice: in 1995 and most recently by the Child Support, Pensions and Social Security Act 2000. The 2000 Act introduced the enabling legislation for the new calculation (replacing "assessment") of child support maintenance (see further annotation to s 4). The new scheme was to have been introduced in April 2002 but is now to be implemented on 3 March 2003 in respect of calculations made *on or after* that date.

1 The duty to maintain

(1) For the purposes of this Act, each parent of a qualifying child is responsible for maintaining him.

(2) For the purposes of this Act, a non-resident parent shall be taken to have met his responsibility to maintain any qualifying child of his by making periodical payments of maintenance with respect to the child of such amount, and at such intervals, as may be determined in accordance with the provisions of this Act.

(3) Where a maintenance calculation made under this Act requires the making of periodical payments, it shall be the duty of the non-resident parent with respect to whom the calculation was made to make those payments.

Amendments—Child Support, Pensions and Social Security Act 2000, s 1(2), Sch 3, para 11(2).

Defined terms—"non-resident parent": s 3(2); "child": s 55(1); "maintenance calculation", "parent": s 54; "periodical payments": s 3(6); "qualifying child": s 3(1).

Scope of provision—This section sets out the basic premise of the Act: that both parents are responsible for maintaining their children, a responsibility which is discharged by the paying of maintenance in accordance with any calculation made under this Act.

"parent" (s 1(1))—The term is defined narrowly at s 54 to comprise only those "in law the mother or father of the child". Adoptive parents are included, but step-parents are not.

"child" (s 1(2))—The term is extensively defined at s 55 in markedly different terms from, for example, "child of the family" in Matrimonial Causes Act 1973, s 52(1) and CA 1989, s 105(1) and "child" in CA 1989, s 105(1).

"periodical payments" and "maintenance" (s 1(2), (3))—The Act at this stage uses these terms more or less interchangeably; but the preferred term is "child support maintenance" (s 3(6)).

"calculation" (s 1(3))—This term has replaced "assessment" or "maintenance assessment" throughout the Child Support Act 1991 (as amended by Child Support, Pensions and Social Security Act 2000). It reflects the fact that the original assessment process has been simplified in the amended Act. Calculation is carried out by the Child Support Agency on behalf of the Secretary of State in accordance with s 11 and Sch 1.

2 Welfare of children: the general principle

Where, in any case which falls to be dealt with under this Act, the Secretary of State is considering the exercise of any discretionary power conferred by this Act, he shall have regard to the welfare of any child likely to be affected by his decision.

Amendments—Social Security Act 1998, s 86, Sch 7, para 18, Sch 8.

Defined terms—"child": s 55(1).

Judicial review: discretion—Where the Secretary of State exercises a discretion there is no appeal. Consequently, a decision of the Secretary of State can only be reconsidered by the courts by means of judicial review (see eg *R v Secretary of State for Social Security ex parte Biggin* [1995] 1 FLR 851, Thorpe J). To succeed in an application for judicial review the applicant must show that one or both of the following apply in relation to the Secretary of State:

(*a*) that he has failed to act in accordance with the rules of natural justice (breach of his duty to act fairly);

(*b*) that the *Wednesbury* principle applies (*Associated Provincial Picture Houses Limited v Wednesbury Corporation* (1947) FLR Rep 44, CA). Is the decision such that the Secretary of State in the performance of his duties, properly directing himself on the relevant law and acting reasonably, could have reached the decision in question?

Procedure for judicial review—Procedure for judicial review is covered by CPR 1998, Pt 54.

"he shall have regard"—That is to say, the welfare of the child is only one of the factors, not the paramount consideration, for the Secretary of State.

"any child"—The reference to "*any* child likely to be affected" (emphasis supplied) makes it clear that it is not only qualifying children who are entitled to be considered; though in practice their welfare may weigh more heavily with the Secretary of State than that of other children. The definition would include children living with the person with care in her household, but it could also include children in the non-resident partner's household who might, for example, be affected by his committal to prison under s 40.

3 Meaning of certain terms used in this Act

(1) A child is a "qualifying child" if –

(*a*) one of his parents is, in relation to him, a non-resident parent; or
(*b*) both of his parents are, in relation to him, non-resident parents.

(2) The parent of any child is a "non-resident parent", in relation to him, if –

(*a*) that parent is not living in the same household with the child; and
(*b*) the child has his home with a person who is, in relation to him, a person with care.

(3) A person is a "person with care", in relation to any child, if he is a person –

(*a*) with whom the child has his home;
(*b*) who usually provides a day to day care for the child (whether exclusively or in conjunction with any other person); and
(*c*) who does not fall within a prescribed category of person.

(4) The Secretary of State shall not, under subsection (3)(*c*), prescribe as a category –

(*a*) parents;
(*b*) guardians;
(*c*) persons in whose favour residence orders under section 8 of the Children Act 1989 are in force;
(*d*) in Scotland, persons with whom a child is to live by virtue of a residence order under section 11 of the Children (Scotland) Act 1995.

(5) For the purposes of this Act there may be more than one person with care in relation to the same qualifying child.

(6) Periodical payments which are required to be paid in accordance with a maintenance calculation are referred to in this Act as "child support maintenance".

(7) Expressions are defined in this section only for the purposes of this Act.

Amendments—Children (Scotland) Act 1995, s 105(4), Sch 4, para 52; Child Support, Pensions and Social Security Act 2000, s 1(2), Sch 3, para 11(2).

Defined terms—"child": s 55(1); "guardian": CA 1989, s 5.

"person with care" (s 3(3))—The person who has care of the child and is therefore entitled to seek a maintenance calculation against the non-resident parent(s). The person with care need not be a parent of the child, nor need they have parental responsibility (within the terms of CA 1989, s 3) for the child.

"prescribed category of person" (s 3(3)(*c*))—Child Support (Maintenance Calculation Procedure) Regulations 2000, reg 21 prescribes, for the purposes of s 3(3)(*c*), local authorities and foster parents with whom a child is placed when looked after by the local authority under CA 1989, s 22, who cannot therefore be a person with care.

4 Child support maintenance

(1) A person who is, in relation to any qualifying child or any qualifying children, either the person with care or the non-resident parent may apply to the Secretary of State for a maintenance calculation to be made under this Act with respect to that child, or any of those children.

(2) Where a maintenance calculation has been made in response to an application under this section the Secretary of State may, if the person with care or non-resident parent with respect to whom the calculation was made applies to him under this subsection, arrange for –

(*a*) the collection of the child support maintenance payable in accordance with the calculation;
(*b*) the enforcement of the obligation to pay child support maintenance in accordance with the calculation.

(3) Where an application under subsection (2) for the enforcement of the obligation mentioned in subsection (2)(*a*) authorises the Secretary of State to take steps to enforce that obligation whenever he considers it necessary to do so, the Secretary of State may act accordingly.

(4) A person who applies to the Secretary of State under this section shall, so far as that person reasonably can, comply with such regulations as may be made by the Secretary of State with a view to the Secretary of State being provided with the information which is required to enable –

(*a*) the non-resident parent to be identified or traced (where that is necessary);
(*b*) the amount of child support maintenance payable by the non-resident parent to be assessed; and
(*c*) that amount to be recovered from the non-resident parent.

(5) Any person who has applied to the Secretary of State under this section may at any time request him to cease acting under this section.

(6) It shall be the duty of the Secretary of State to comply with any request made under subsection (5) (but subject to any regulations made under subsection (8)).

(7) The obligation to provide information which is imposed by subsection (4) –

(*a*) shall not apply in such circumstances as may be prescribed; and
(*b*) may, in such circumstances as may be prescribed, be waived by the Secretary of State.

(8) The Secretary of State may by regulations make such incidental, supplemental or transitional provision as he thinks appropriate with respect to cases in which he is requested to cease to act under this under this section.

(9) No application may be made under this section if there is in force with respect to the person with care and non-resident parent in question a maintenance calculation made in response to an application treated as made under section 6.

(10) No application may be made at any time under this section with respect to a qualifying child or any qualifying children if –

(*a*) there is in force a written maintenance agreement made before 5 April 1993, or a maintenance order made before a prescribed date, in respect of that child or those children and the person who is, at that time, the non-resident parent; or

(*aa*) a maintenance order made on or after the date prescribed for the purposes of paragraph (*a*) is in force in respect of them, but has been so for less than the period of one year beginning with the date on which it was made; or

(*b*) benefit is being paid to, or in respect of, a parent with care of that child or those children.

(11) In subsection (10) "benefit" means any benefit which is mentioned in, or prescribed by regulations under, section 6(1).

Amendments—Child Support Act 1995, s 18; Social Security Act 1998, s 86, Sch 7, para 19, Sch 8; Child Support, Pensions and Social Security Act 2000, ss 1(2), 2, Sch 3, para 11(2), (3).

Defined terms—"non-resident parent": s 3(2); "child": s 55(1); "child support maintenance": s 3(6); "maintenance calculation", "parent": s 54; "periodical payments": s 3(6); "qualifying child": s 3(1).

Outline of new bases for child support calculation—When the amendments introduced by Child Support, Pensions and Social Security Act 2000 come into operation in March 2003 (see CSPSSA 2000, Sch 1 and Child Support (Maintenance Calculations and Special Cases) Regulations 2000, SI 2000/155 (for calculation of child support maintenance) and Child Support (Variations) Regulations 2000, SI 2000/156 (for variations)), calculation of child support maintenance will proceed, in summary, by the following three stages:

1 Based on two data only, ie the number of qualifying children and the net earned income of the non-resident parent, four rates are applicable:
   (i) *Basic rate*: where non-resident parent's weekly net earned income is £200–£2000, he pays 15% of net earned income (1 child), 20% (2 children) and 25% (3+ children).
   (ii) *Reduced rate*: where weekly net earned income is £100–£200, non-resident parent pays £5 on first £100, plus 25%, 35% or 45% on balance between £100–£200.
   (iii) *Flat rate*: £5 per week where weekly net earned income of less than £100.
   (iv) *Nil rate*: for eg non-resident parents who are prisoners or qualifying children themselves.

2 Adjustments based on:
   (i) *Relevant other children* (ie children in non-resident parent's household for whom child benefit is received): net earned income reduced by 15%, 20% or 25% for purposes of calculation of child support maintenance.
   (ii) *Shared care* (ie overnight contact): 52 days contact per annum reduces child support maintenance by 1/7th, 104 days by 2/7ths etc.

3 Variations (formerly departure directions): according to circumstances the non-resident parent or the parent with care can apply for a variation (CSA 1991, ss 28A–28H and Child Support (Variations) Regulations 2000) which may have the effect of notionally increasing or decreasing the non-resident parent's net earned income for calculation purposes.

"either the person with care or the non-resident parent may apply" (s 4(1))—Either the person with care or the non-resident parent of the qualifying children may apply. There may be circumstances where the payment under the pre-March 2003 scheme would have been be less than under the new. Broadly, the non-resident parent whose gross income exceeds £75,000 will pay more under the new scheme than the old.

Termination of application (s 4(5), (6))—Once application has been made under s 4, a request can still be made by the applicant for the application to be withdrawn – for example where terms for periodical payments are agreed privately; and the Secretary of State (ie the Child Support Agency) must comply with any such request.

No application where there is a court order or pre-April 1993 written agreement (s 4(10))—Though amended by the 2000 Act, s 4(10) maintains the position that periodical payments orders, in existence at the coming into operation of the new scheme, and pre-April 1993 written agreements prevent application to the Agency. These can only be varied by the courts, unless discharged, or a parent with care claims a prescribed benefit (under s 6(1)).

"a maintenance order made on or after the date prescribed" (s 4(10)(*aa*))—This provision has been added, providing a fundamental exception to the former s 4(10) scheme. The date "prescribed" for this purpose is 3 March 2003 (see SI 2003/194). Thus, in respect of a court order made *on or after* that date, the prohibition against application to the Agency lasts only for one year following the making of the order. After that, a parent is still entitled to apply to the court for a variation (CSA 1991, s 8(3A); MCA 1973, s 31(1)) but either parent may give notice to the other that they intend to apply to the Agency which will then bring the order to an end. The cost and procedural complexity (the full rigours of FPR 1991, rr 2.53 etc) of applying to court for variation of child periodical payments, as against the nil cost of application to the Agency, should make application to the court of dubious attraction.

****

6 Applications by those claiming or receiving benefit

(1) This section applies where income support, an income-based jobseeker's allowance or any other benefit of a prescribed kind is claimed by or in respect of, or paid to or in respect of, the parent of a qualifying child who is also a person with care of the child.

(2) In this section, that person is referred to as "the parent".

(3) The Secretary of State may –

(*a*) treat the parent as having applied for a maintenance calculation with respect to the qualifying child and all other children of the non-resident parent in relation to whom the parent is also a person with care; and

(*b*) take action under this Act to recover from the non-resident parent, on the parent's behalf, the child support maintenance so determined.

(4) Before doing what is mentioned in subsection (3), the Secretary of State must notify the parent in writing of the effect of subsections (3) and (5) and section 46.

(5) The Secretary of State may not act under subsection (3) if the parent asks him not to (a request which need not be in writing).

(6) Subsection (1) has effect regardless of whether any of the benefits mentioned there is payable with respect to any qualifying child.

(7) Unless she has made a request under subsection (5), the parent shall, so far as she reasonably can, comply with such regulations as may be made by the Secretary of State with a view to the Secretary of State's being provided with the information which is required to enable –

(*a*) the non-resident parent to be identified or traced;

(*b*) the amount of child support maintenance payable by him to be calculated; and

(*c*) that amount to be recovered from him.

(8) The obligation to provide information which is imposed by subsection (7) –

(*a*) does not apply in such circumstances as may be prescribed; and

(*b*) may, in such circumstances as may be prescribed, be waived by the Secretary of State.

(9) If the parent ceases to fall within subsection (1), she may ask the Secretary of State to cease acting under this section, but until then he may continue to do so.

(10) The Secretary of State must comply with any request under subsection (9) (but subject to any regulations made under subsection (11)).

(11) The Secretary of State may by regulations make such incidental or transitional provision as he thinks appropriate with respect to cases in which he is asked under subsection (9) to cease to act under this section.

(12) The fact that a maintenance calculation is in force with respect to a person with care does not prevent the making of a new maintenance calculation with respect to her as a result of the Secretary of State's acting under subsection (3).

Amendments—Substituted by Child Support, Pensions and Social Security Act 2000, s 3.

Defined terms—"non-resident parent": s 3(2); "child": s 55(1); "child support maintenance": s 3(6); "maintenance calculation", "income support", "parent": s 54; "parent" (for this section): s 6(2); "qualifying child": s 3(1).

Scope of provision—This section complements s 4, but deals with parents with care who are receiving state benefit.

"parent of a qualifying child" (s 6(1))—It is important to note that whereas any *person* with care of a qualifying child can apply for a calculation, it is only a *parent* with care who can be required to authorise the Secretary of State to proceed with a calculation and recovery of child support maintenance. Thus, for example, where grandparents or a step-parent are receiving benefit and have care of a child they cannot be required to authorise recovery; though they can, of course, make an application under s 4 if they so wish.

7 (*applies to Scotland only*)

8 Role of the courts with respect to maintenance for children

(1) This subsection applies in any case where the Secretary of State would have jurisdiction to make a maintenance calculation with respect to a qualifying child and a non-resident parent of his on an application duly made (or treated as made) by a person entitled to apply for such a calculation with respect to that child.

(2) Subsection (1) applies even though the circumstances of the case are such that the Secretary of State would not make a calculation if it were applied for.

(3) Except as provided in subsection (3A), in any case where subsection (1) applies, no court shall exercise any power which it would otherwise have to make, vary or revive any maintenance order in relation to the child and non-resident parent concerned.

(3A) Unless a maintenance calculation has been made with respect to the child concerned, subsection (3) does not prevent a court from varying a maintenance order in relation to that child and the non-resident parent concerned –

(*a*) if the maintenance order was made on or after the date prescribed for the purposes of section 4(10)(*a*) or 7(10)(*a*); or

(*b*) where the order was made before then, in any case in which section 4(10) or 7(10) prevents the making of an application for a maintenance calculation with respect to or by that child.

(4) Subsection (3) does not prevent a court from revoking a maintenance order.

(5) The Lord Chancellor or in relation to Scotland the Lord Advocate may by order provide that, in such circumstances as may be specified by the order, this section shall not prevent a court from exercising any power which it has to make a maintenance order in relation to a child if –

(*a*) a written agreement (whether or not enforceable) provides for the making, or securing, by a non-resident parent of the child of periodical payments to or for the benefit of the child; and

(*b*) the maintenance order which the court makes is, in all material respects, in the same terms as that agreement.

(6) This section shall not prevent a court from exercising any power which it has to make a maintenance order in relation to a child if –

(*a*) a maintenance calculation is in force with respect to the child;

(*b*) the non-resident parent's net weekly income exceeds the figure referred to in paragraph 10(3) of Schedule 1 (as it has effect from time to time pursuant to regulations made under paragraph 10A(1)(*b*)); and

(*c*) the court is satisfied that the circumstances of the case make it appropriate for the non-resident parent to make or secure the making of periodical payments under a maintenance order in addition to the child support maintenance payable by him in accordance with the maintenance calculation.

(7) This section shall not prevent a court from exercising any power which it has to make a maintenance order in relation to a child if –

(*a*) the child is, will be or (if the order were to be made) would be receiving instruction at an educational establishment or undergoing training for a trade, profession or vocation (whether or not while in gainful employment); and

(*b*) the order is made solely for the purposes of requiring the person making or securing the making of periodical payments fixed by the order to meet some or all of the expenses incurred in connection with the provision of the instruction or training.

(8) This section shall not prevent a court from exercising any power which it has to make a maintenance order in relation to a child if –

(*a*) a disability living allowance is paid to or in respect of him; or

(*b*) no such allowance is paid but he is disabled,

and the order is made solely for the purpose of requiring the person making or securing the making of periodical payments fixed by the order to meet some or all of any expenses attributable to the child's disability.

(9) For the purposes of subsection (8), a child is disabled if he is blind, deaf or dumb or is substantially and permanently handicapped by illness, injury, mental disorder or congenital deformity or such other disability as may be prescribed.

(10) This section shall not prevent a court from exercising any power which it has to make a maintenance order in relation to a child if the order is made against a person with care of the child.

(11) In this Act "maintenance order", in relation to any child, means an order which requires the making or securing of periodical payments to or for the benefit of the child and which is made under –

(*a*) Part II of the Matrimonial Causes Act 1973;

(*b*) the Domestic Proceedings and Magistrates' Courts Act 1978;

(*c*) Part III of the Matrimonial and Family Proceedings Act 1984;

(*d*) the Family Law (Scotland) Act 1985;

(*e*) Schedule 1 to the Children Act 1989; or

(*f*) any other prescribed enactment,

and includes any order varying or reviving such an order.

Amendments—Child Support Act 1995, s 18; Social Security Act 1998, s 86(1), Sch 7, para 22; Child Support, Pensions and Social Security Act 2000, s 1(2), Sch 3, para 11(2), (5).

Defined terms—"non-resident parent": s 3(2); "child": s 55(1); "child support maintenance": s 3(6); "maintenance calculation": s 54; "parent": s 54; "periodical payments": s 3(6); "person with care": s 3(3); "qualifying child": s 3(1).

"jurisdiction to make a maintenance calculation" (s 8(1))—The jurisdiction of the Secretary of State to make a calculation is provided for by s 44(1).

"no court shall exercise any power" (s 8(3))—Provided the Secretary of State has jurisdiction, and even though no application is made to him, the court has no jurisdiction to hear an application for child periodical payments. This is subject to the following exceptions:

(i) *Applications for top up orders* Where CSA 1991 s 8(5)–(10) applies, application can be made to the court for one or more of the top-up orders therein referred to (though with the upper limit for net income being raised to £2000 per week (Sch 1, para 10(3)) it is unlikely there will be more than a handful of applications under s 8(6)). If application is made within six months of the effective date of the maintenance calculation the order can be back-dated (see eg MCA 1973, s 29(5)–(8)).

(ii) *Variations of existing periodical payments orders* (s 8(3A)) *V v V (Child Maintenance)* [2001] 2 FLR 799, at 804, clarifies that it remains possible for the court to vary existing orders, whether made before or after April 1993, subject to (where the parent with care is on benefit) there being no application for a child support calculation. Additionally, where the parent is on benefit, there is a requirement that notice of the application to vary be given to the Agency (see also **Termination of child periodical payments order** below). A school fees order made before the coming into force of CSA 1995, s 18(6) (on 1 October 1995) is an order which prevents application to the Agency and requires an applicant for further child maintenance to seek variation of that order (*Secretary of State for Social Security v Foster and Foster* [2001] 1 FCR 376, CA).

(iii) *"Segal" orders* The court can make an order for periodical payments for a parent which will later absorb any subsequent child support maintenance calculation (a "Segal" order); but only where the order contains a substantial amount of spousal maintenance (*Dorney-Kingdom v Dorney-Kingdom* [2000] 2 FLR 855, CA).

(iv) *Lump sums for children* A lump sum order can be made for children where the husband withdraws his consent to varying an agreed order (*V v V (Child Maintenance)* [2001] 2 FLR 799, Wilson J); and an interim lump sum paid within the terms of MCA 1973, s 23(3)(*b*) cannot be maintenance within the terms of s 8(3) (*Askew-Page v Page* [2001] Fam Law 794, HH Judge Meston QC; and see *Phillips v Peace* [1996] 2 FLR 230, Johnson J).

See also **Interface with Child Support Act 1991** under MCA 1973, s 23.

Termination of child periodical payments order—Under the new scheme it will be possible for either parent to give notice of termination of a child periodical payments order which was made *on or after* 3 March 2003 (see annotation to s 4(10)(*aa*) above).

FPR 1991—To ensure that applications in respect of qualifying children are not wrongly pursued in the courts, there are procedures in FPR 1991, r 10.24 and Family Proceedings Courts (Child Support Act 1991) Rules 1993, r 7, which require the court to reject such applications.

Jurisdiction of the court—Where the court does have jurisdiction it will be exercised as hitherto under the appropriate statute (eg Matrimonial Causes Act 1973, Pt II or CA 1989, Sch 1; and see the list in s 8(11)).

Written agreements and consent orders (s 8(5))—The Child Maintenance (Written Agreements) Order 1993 gives effect to s 8(5). By art 2, the court retains its powers to make consent orders, even though the Secretary of State would have had jurisdiction and whether or not the written agreement on which the order is to be based postdates the coming into operation of the Act. Where a consent application is submitted, a statement under FPR 1991, r 2.61 is still required in the High Court and county courts; s 8(5) also applies to applications in the magistrates' court for an order for payments agreed between the parties (Domestic Proceedings and Magistrates' Courts Act 1978, s 6; see Family Proceedings Courts (Matrimonial Proceedings etc) Rules 1991, rr 3, 17 for procedure). There is no reason why the consent application dealing with the qualifying children should not be incorporated into an application dealing with other aspects of financial relief, provided that the application is endorsed with the consent of both of the parties themselves so that it can formally be regarded as a written agreement.

"mental disorder" (s 8(9))—By virtue of Mental Health Act 1983, s 1(2), this means "mental illness, arrested or incomplete development of mind, psychopathic disorder and any other disorder or disability of mind and 'mentally disordered' shall be construed accordingly". For a full explanation see the note to FPR 1991, r 9.1.

"any other prescribed enactment" (s 8(11)(*f*))—Child Support (Maintenance Arrangements and Jurisdiction) Regulations 1992, reg 2 (as amended) adds a number of further enactments under which maintenance orders can be dealt with.

Affiliation proceedings—The Affiliation Proceedings Act 1957 is included in the enactments in s 8(11) (Child Support (Maintenance Arrangements and Jurisdiction) Regulations 1992, reg 2). Although the 1957 Act was repealed by Family Law Reform Act 1987, s 17 with effect from 1 April 1989, s 7 remains in force to the extent that it provides for affiliation orders to continue until a child reaches the age of 16. Thus it remains possible, theoretically, for such orders to survive until 2005. In the meantime, such orders are caught by CSA 1991.

9 Agreements about maintenance

(1) In this section "maintenance agreement" means any agreement for the making, or for securing the making, of periodical payments by way of maintenance, or in Scotland aliment, to or for the benefit of any child.

(2) Nothing in this Act shall be taken to prevent any person from entering into a maintenance agreement.

(3) Subject to section 4(10)(*a*) and section 7(10), the existence of a maintenance agreement shall not prevent any party to the agreement, or any other person, from applying for a maintenance calculation with respect to any child to or for whose benefit periodical payments are to be made or secured under the agreement.

(4) Where any agreement contains a provision which purports to restrict the right of any person to apply for a maintenance calculation, that provision shall be void.

(5) Where section 8 would prevent any court from making a maintenance order in relation to a child and a non-resident parent of his, no court shall exercise any power that it has to vary any agreement so as –

(*a*) to insert a provision requiring that non-resident parent to make or secure the making of periodical payments by way of maintenance, or in Scotland aliment, to or for the benefit of that child; or

(*b*) to increase the amount payable under such a provision.

(6) In any case in which section 4(10) or 7(10) prevents the making of an application for a maintenance calculation, and –

(*a*) no parent has been treated under section 6(3) as having applied for a maintenance calculation with respect to the child; or

(*b*) a parent has been so treated but no maintenance calculation has been made,

subsection (5) shall have effect with the omission of paragraph (*b*).

Amendments—Child Support Act 1995, s 18; Child Support, Pensions and Social Security Act 2000, s 1(2), Sch 3, para 11(2), (6).

Defined terms—"non-resident parent": s 3(2); "child": s 55(1); "maintenance calculation", "parent": s 54; "periodical payments": s 3(6).

"maintenance agreement" (s 9(1))—This definition can be contrasted with that in Matrimonial Causes Act 1973, s 34(2) and CSA 1991, s 8(5)(*a*), which state that the agreement must be in writing; however, s 9(1) contemplates the existence of agreements other than in writing (which must beg questions, beyond the scope of this note, as to their enforceability). In any event, whatever the nature of the agreement and the extent of its enforceability, s 9(3) ensures that its existence cannot prevent application being made for a maintenance calculation in respect of the child concerned.

"any child" (s 9(1), (3))—Although the section uses the term "any child", the context – applications for a maintenance calculation, which can only be for qualifying children (ss 4(1) and 6(1)) – makes it clear that it can only apply to qualifying children.

Restriction on the right to apply for maintenance calculation (s 9(4))—Use of the present tense in this section suggests that it must be retroactive, to the extent of being applicable in the same way both to agreements entered into before and after the coming into force of the Act. Any restriction on the right to apply for a maintenance calculation recorded in a consent order would also fail under s 9(4) within the terms of the definition in s 9(1): it may be assumed that the term "maintenance agreement" includes the consent application which would have led to the order.

Alteration of maintenance agreements (s 9(5))—Matrimonial Causes Act 1973, s 35 enables a party to a maintenance agreement to apply to the court for its variation. Section 9(5) prevents this where application is in respect of a qualifying child, save for the following: (i) existing agreements to which s 9(6) applies; and (ii) where the variation is by agreement, in which case it could be made the subject of a consent application to the court, either where matrimonial proceedings are contemplated or are under way (MCA 1973, s 7) or under Domestic Proceedings and Magistrates' Courts Act 1978, s 6. The difference between this arrangement and MCA 1973, s 35 is that the new "agreement" becomes a court order totally separate from the original agreement; whereas under s 35 the whole agreement stands subject only as varied by the court order.

Maintenance agreements (s 9(6))—The effect of this subsection is that the court retains power to vary a maintenance agreement existing prior to 5 April 1993 (see CSA 1991, s 4(1)(*a*)), insofar as it relates to a qualifying child (see eg Matrimonial Causes Act 1973, s 35, which gives the court power to alter maintenance agreements including "the maintenance or education of any child" – see MCA 1973, s 34(2) for the definition of "financial arrangements" under that Act).

Written agreements and consent orders—The Child Maintenance (Written Agreements) Order 1993 gives effect to s 8(5), whereby the court retains its powers to make orders in accordance with a written agreement. This is so even though the Secretary of State would have had jurisdiction and whether or not the written agreement on which the order is to be based postdates the coming into operation of the Act.

10 Relationship between maintenance calculations and certain court orders and related matters

(1) Where an order of a kind prescribed for the purposes of this subsection is in force with respect to any qualifying child with respect to whom a maintenance calculation is made, the order –

(*a*) shall, so far as it relates to the making or securing of periodical payments, cease to have effect to such extent as may be determined in accordance with regulations made by the Secretary of State; or

(*b*) where the regulations so provide, shall, so far as it so relates, have effect subject to such modifications as may be so determined.

(2) Where an agreement of a kind prescribed for the purposes of this subsection is in force with respect to any qualifying child with respect to whom a maintenance calculation is made, the agreement –

(*a*) shall, so far as it relates to the making or securing of periodical payments, be unenforceable to such extent as may be determined in accordance with regulations made by the Secretary of State; or (*b*) where the regulations so provide, shall, so far as it so relates, have effect subject to such modifications as may be so determined.

(3) Any regulations under this section may, in particular, make such provision with respect to –

(*a*) any case where any person with respect to whom an order or agreement of a kind prescribed for the purposes of subsection (1) or (2) has effect applies to the prescribed court, before the end of the prescribed period, for the order or agreement to be varied in the light of the maintenance calculation and of the provisions of this Act;

(*b*) the recovery of any arrears under the order or agreement which fell due before the coming into force of the maintenance calculation,

as the Secretary of State considers appropriate and may provide that, in prescribed circumstances, an application to any court which is made with respect to an order of a prescribed kind relating to the making or securing of periodical payments to or for the benefit of a child shall be treated by the court as an application for the order to be revoked.

(4) The Secretary of State may by regulations make provision for –

(*a*) notification to be given by the Secretary of State concerned to the prescribed person in any case where he considers that the making of a maintenance calculation has affected, or is likely to affect, any order of a kind prescribed for the purposes of this subsection;

(*b*) notification to be given by the prescribed person to the Secretary of State in any case where a court makes an order which it considers has affected, or is likely to affect, a maintenance calculation.

(5) Rules may be made under section 144 of the Magistrates' Courts Act 1980 (rules of procedure) requiring any person who, in prescribed circumstances, makes an application to a magistrates' court for a maintenance order to furnish the court with a statement in a prescribed form, and signed by an officer of the Secretary of State, as to whether or not, at the time when the statement is made, there is a maintenance calculation in force with respect to that person or the child concerned.

In this subsection –

"maintenance order" means an order of a prescribed kind for the making or securing of periodical payments to or for the benefit of a child; and

"prescribed" means prescribed by the rules.

Amendments—Social Security Act 1998, s 86(1), Sch 7, para 23; Child Support, Pensions and Social Security Act 2000, s 1(2).

Defined terms—"child": s 55(1); "child support maintenance": s 3(6); "maintenance calculation", "parent": s 54; "periodical payments": s 3(6); "qualifying child": s 3(1).

Scope of provision—This section deals with the relationship between court orders and maintenance agreements on the one hand, and child maintenance calculations on the other, by providing: that court orders and maintenance agreements shall cease to have effect on the making of the calculation, save as modified; that applications to vary certain orders be treated as applications for revocation once a maintenance calculation has been made; and that certain information be provided as to any maintenance calculation where application is made to the magistrates' court for a maintenance order.

"an order of a kind prescribed" (s 10(1))—The orders prescribed under s 10(1) are the same as those listed in s 8(11) with the addition of an order under the Affiliation Proceedings Act 1957 (Child Support (Maintenance Arrangements and Jurisdiction) Regulations 1992, reg 3(1)).

"an agreement of a kind prescribed" (s 10(2), (3)(*a*))—Maintenance agreements as defined in s 9(1) are those which are prescribed for this subsection (Child Support (Maintenance Arrangements and Jurisdiction) Regulations 1992, reg 4(1)).

Effect of calculation (s 10(1)(*a*), (2)(*a*))—Orders or agreements in respect of any children affected by the maintenance calculation cease to be effective or are unenforceable from the date of the calculation (Child Support (Maintenance Arrangements and Jurisdiction) Regulations 1992, regs 3(2), 4(2)).

Effective date of maintenance calculation—The effective date of a maintenance calculation is the date from which the requirement to pay in accordance with the calculation runs (Child Support (Maintenance Calculation Procedure) Regulations 2000, Pt VII). Where periodical payments are already being paid, the position is as follows:

(*a*) *Existing court orders* Where a court order ceases to be effective as a result of a calculation, the effective date of that calculation is two days after the calculation is complete (Child Support (Maintenance Arrangements and Jurisdiction) Regulations 1992, reg 3(5)). Thus, child support maintenance at the assessed rate is not payable until that date and payments under the original order will remain due until the effective date of the calculation.

(*b*) *Existing agreements to pay maintenance* Where there is an agreement to pay maintenance, that agreement becomes unenforceable from the effective date of the calculation, ie the date on which the maintenance enquiry form is sent out (CS(MAJ)R 1992, reg 4(2)). Paying parents should thus be warned that they should make no more payments under their agreements, since they may not be able to secure credit for such payments from the Child Support Agency.

Orders and agreements ineffective save as modified (s 10(1)(*b*), (2)(*b*))—While the effect of these provisions is that upon the making of a maintenance calculation any existing order or agreement becomes ineffective, regulations can be made to enable the Secretary of State to provide for part of the order – for example, relating to school fees or other particular payments or arrangements – to remain effective. The order or agreement would then continue subject as modified by the calculation. Where the order or agreement is in respect of more than one child and not all of the children are affected by the calculation – perhaps not all are qualifying children – the order or agreement ceases to have effect only so far as it relates to the qualifying children (Child Support (Maintenance Arrangements and Jurisdiction) Regulations 1992, regs 3(2), 4(2)).

****

Reviews and appeals

****

26 Disputes about parentage

(1) Where a person who is alleged to be a parent of the child with respect to whom an application for a maintenance calculation has been made or treated as made ("the alleged parent") denies that he is one of the child's parents, the Secretary of State shall not make a maintenance calculation on the assumption that the alleged parent is one of the child's parents unless the case falls within one of those set out in subsection (2).

(2) The Cases are –

CASE A1

Where –

(*a*) the child is habitually resident in England and Wales;

(*b*) the Secretary of State is satisfied that the alleged parent was married to the child's mother at some time in the period beginning with the conception and ending with the birth of the child; and

(*c*) the child has not been adopted.

CASE A2

Where –

(*a*) the child is habitually resident in England and Wales;

(*b*) the alleged parent has been registered as father of the child under section 10 or 10A of the Births and Deaths Registration Act 1953, or in any register kept under section 13 (register of births and still-births) or section 44 (Register of Corrections Etc) of the Registration of Births, Deaths and Marriages (Scotland) Act 1965, or under Article 14 or 18(1)(*b*)(ii) of the Births and Deaths Registration (Northern Ireland) Order 1976; and

(*c*) the child has not subsequently been adopted.

CASE A3

Where the result of a scientific test (within the meaning of section 27A) taken by the alleged parent would be relevant to determining the child's parentage, and the alleged parent –

(*a*) refuses to take such a test; or

(*b*) has submitted to such a test, and it shows that there is no reasonable doubt that the alleged parent is a parent of the child.

CASE A

Where the alleged parent is a parent of the child in question by virtue of having adopted him.

CASE B

Where the alleged parent is a parent of the child in question by virtue of an order under section 30 of the Human Fertilisation and Embryology Act 1990 (parental orders in favour of gamete donors).

CASE B1

Where the Secretary of State is satisfied that the alleged parent is a parent of the child in question by virtue of section 27 or 28 of that Act (meaning of "mother" and of "father" respectively).

CASE C

Where –

(*a*) either –

(i) a declaration that the alleged parent is a parent of the child in question (or a declaration which has that effect) is in force under section 55A or 56 of the Family Law Act 1986 or Article 32 of the Matrimonial and Family Proceedings (Northern Ireland) Order 1989 (declarations of parentage); or

(ii) a declarator by a court in Scotland that the alleged parent is a parent of the child in question (or a declarator which has that effect) is in force; and

(*b*) the child has not subsequently been adopted.

****

CASE F

Where –

(*a*) the alleged parent has been found, or adjudged, to be the father of the child in question –

(i) in proceedings before any court in England and Wales which are relevant proceedings for the purposes of section 12 of the Civil Evidence Act 1968 or in proceedings before any court in Northern Ireland which are relevant proceedings for the purposes of section 8 of the Civil Evidence Act (Northern Ireland) 1971; or

(ii) in affiliation proceedings before any court in the United Kingdom,

(whether or not he offered any defence to the allegation of paternity) and that finding or adjudication still subsists; and

(*b*) the child has not subsequently been adopted.

(3) In this section –

"adopted" means adopted within the meaning of Part IV of the Adoption Act 1976 or, in relation to Scotland, Part IV of the Adoption (Scotland) Act 1978; and

"affiliation proceedings", in relation to Scotland, means any action of affiliation and aliment.

Amendments—SI 1995/756; Social Security Act 1998, s 86(1), Sch 7, para 31; Child Support, Pensions and Social Security Act 2000, ss 1(2), 15, Sch 3, paras 11(8), 12, Sch 9.

Defined terms—"child": s 55(1); "maintenance calculation", "parent": s 54.

Denial of parentage (s 26(1))—This section provides for an alleged parent's entitlement to deny parentage which brings the application for a calculation to an end, unless one of the presumptions (set out as an expanded list in s 26(2)) apply. If one of the Cases applies, the onus shifts to the putative parent (normally the father) to prove he is not the parent.

Application under Family Law Act 1986, s 55A—The only recourse for a parent caught by one of the s 26(2) presumptions is to apply for a declaration of parentage under FLA 1986, s 55A (see Procedural Guide 42). CSA 1991, s 27 only applies where the person with care or the Secretary of State applies for a declaration.

27 Applications for declaration of parentage under Family Law Act 1986

(1) This section applies where –

(*a*) an application for a maintenance calculation has been made (or is treated as having been made), or a maintenance calculation is in force, with respect to a person ("the alleged parent") who denies that he is a parent of a child with respect to whom the application or calculation was made or treated as made;

(*b*) the Secretary of State is not satisfied that the case falls within one of those set out in section 26(2); and

(*c*) the Secretary of State or the person with care makes an application for a declaration under section 55A of the Family Law Act 1986 as to whether or not the alleged parent is one of the child's parents.

(2) Where this section applies –

(*a*) if it is the person with care who makes the application, she shall be treated as having a sufficient personal interest for the purposes of subsection (3) of that section; and

(*b*) if it is the Secretary of State who makes the application, that subsection shall not apply.

(3) This section does not apply to Scotland.

Amendments—Substituted by Child Support, Pensions and Social Security Act 2000, s 83(5), Sch 8, para 13.

Defined terms—"alleged parent": s 26(1); "child": s 55(1); "maintenance calculation", "parent": s 54; "person with care": s 3(3).

Application under Family Law Act 1986, s 55A—This section brings this aspect of CSA 1991 into line with FLA 1986, s 55A and provides for the Secretary of State, or person with care who applies for another parent to be declared parent of the child, to do so within the terms of s 55A (see Procedural Guide 42).

"sufficient personal interest" (s 27(2)(*a*))—Where the applicant is a person with care she does not have to go through the s 55(3) filter of establishing whether she has a sufficient personal interest in the application. As a parent she will automatically have sufficient personal interest (s 55A(4)), so this section can apply only to persons with care who are not also parents.

27A Recovery of fees for scientific tests

(1) This section applies in any case where –

(*a*) an application for a maintenance calculation has been made or treated as made or a maintenance calculation is in force;

(*b*) scientific tests have been carried out (otherwise than under a direction or in response to a request) in relation to bodily samples obtained from a person who is alleged to be a parent of a child with respect to whom the application or calculation is made or, as the case may be, treated as made;

(*c*) the results of the tests do not exclude the alleged parent from being one of the child's parents; and

(*d*) one of the conditions set out in subsection (2) is satisfied.

(2) The conditions are that –

(*a*) the alleged parent does not deny that he is one of the child's parents;

(*b*) in proceedings under section 55A of the Family Law Act 1986, a court has made a declaration that the alleged parent is a parent of the child in question; or

(*c*) (*applies to Scotland only*)

(3) In any case to which this section applies, any fee paid by the Secretary of State in connection with scientific tests may be recovered by him from the alleged parent as a debt due to the Crown.

(4) In this section –

"bodily sample" means a sample of bodily fluid or bodily tissue taken for the purpose of scientific tests;

"direction" means a direction given by a court under section 20 of the Family Law Reform Act 1969 (tests to determine paternity);

"request" means a request made by a court under section 70 of the Law Reform (Miscellaneous Provisions) (Scotland) Act 1990 (blood and other samples in civil proceedings); and

"scientific tests" means scientific tests made with the object of ascertaining the inheritable characteristics of bodily fluids or bodily tissue.

(5) Any sum recovered by the Secretary of State under this section shall be paid by him into the Consolidated Fund.

Amendments—Inserted by Child Support Act 1995, s 21; amended by Child Support, Pensions and Social Security Act 2000, ss 1(2), 83(5), Sch 3, para 11(9), Sch 8, para 14.

Defined terms—"maintenance calculation", "parent": s 54.

Costs of application for declaration of parentage—Only the fee for the test is covered by s 27A(3), since the costs of any application for a declaration of parentage are provided for by Family Law Reform Act 1969, s 20(6).

****

Collection and enforcement

****

30 Collection and enforcement of other forms of maintenance

(1) Where the Secretary of State is arranging for the collection of any payments under section 29 or subsection (2), he may also arrange for the collection of any periodical payments, or secured periodical payments, of a prescribed kind which are payable to or for the benefit of any person who falls within a prescribed category.

(2) The Secretary of State, except in prescribed cases, may arrange for the collection of any periodical payments, or secured periodical payments, of a prescribed kind which are payable for the benefit of a child even though he is not arranging for the collection of child support maintenance with respect to that child.

(3) Where –

(*a*) the Secretary of State is arranging, under this Act, for the collection of different payments ("the payments") from the same non-resident parent;

(*b*) an amount is collected by the Secretary of State from the non-resident parent which is less than the total amount due in respect of the payments; and

(*c*) the non-resident parent has not stipulated how that amount is to be allocated by the Secretary of State as between the payments,

the Secretary of State may allocate that amount as he sees fit.

(4) In relation to England and Wales, the Secretary of State may by regulations make provision for sections 29 and 31 to 40 to apply, with such modifications (if any) as he considers necessary or expedient, for the purpose of enabling him to enforce any obligation to pay any amount which he is authorised to collect under this section.

(5) In relation to Scotland, the Secretary of State may by regulations make provision for the purpose of enabling him to enforce any obligation to pay any amount which he is authorised to collect under this section –

(*a*) empowering him to bring any proceedings or take any other steps (other than diligence against earnings) which could have been brought or taken by or on behalf of the person to whom the periodical payments are payable;

(*b*) applying sections 29, 31 and 32 with such modifications (if any) as he considers necessary or expedient.

Amendments—Child Support Act 1995, s 30, Sch 3, para 9; Child Support, Pensions and Social Security Act 2000, Sch 3, para 11(2), (15).

Defined terms—"child": s 55(1); "child support maintenance": s 3(6).

"payments under section 29" (s 30(1))—CSA 1991, s 29 makes provision for collection of child support maintenance by the Secretary of State and for the ways in which such maintenance is to be paid.

"periodical payments ... of a prescribed kind" for persons "in a prescribed category" (s 30(1))—Child Support (Collection and Enforcement of Other Forms of Maintenance) Regulations 1992, reg 2 defines the forms of periodical payment which can be collected and enforced under s 30(1) as:
(*a*) payments due under an order within the terms of s 8(6)–(8) (reg 2(*a*));
(*b*) payments due under an order for a spouse or former spouse who is the person with care where collection of child support maintenance has been arranged under s 29 (reg 2(*b*)).

Periodical payments for children (s 30(2))—CS(CEOFM)R 1992, reg 2(*c*) goes on to define the circumstances in which periodical payments for children other than qualifying children can be collected and enforced; that is, where periodical payments are due under an order for a former child of the family of the liable person, where the child is with the person with care (reg 2(*c*)). "Child of the family" here is defined as in Matrimonial Causes Act 1973, s 52 (reg 1(2)). Reference in reg 2(*c*) to a "person with care" implies that there is another qualifying child in the household; though s 30(2) makes no reference to collection also of child support maintenance (as does s 30(1)). The position is unclear; but the inference from the silence of s 30(2) may be preferred, the statute having higher authority than the regulations, with the effect that all maintenance is covered, even though there is not a qualifying child in the household concerned.

"such modifications (if any) as he considers necessary" (s 30(4))—CS(CEOFM)R 1992, reg 3 provides that the Secretary of State's powers to collect and enforce payment of child support maintenance apply also in respect of any of the periodical payments referred to in reg 2; but he cannot collect or enforce payments payable prior to the date on which he notifies the non-resident parent that payments are to be collected by the Child Support Agency.

31 Deduction from earnings orders

(1) This section applies where any person ("the liable person") is liable to make payments of child support maintenance.

(2) The Secretary of State may make an order ("a deduction from earnings order") against a liable person to secure the payment of any amount due under the maintenance calculation in question.

(3) A deduction from earnings order may be made so as to secure the payment of –
- (*a*) arrears of child support maintenance payable under the calculation;
- (*b*) amounts of child support maintenance which will become due under the calculation; or
- (*c*) both such arrears and such future amounts.

(4) A deduction from earnings order –
- (*a*) shall be expressed to be directed at a person ("the employer") who has the liable person in his employment; and
- (*b*) shall have effect from such date as may be specified in the order.

(5) A deduction from earnings order shall operate as an instruction to the employer to –
- (*a*) make deductions from the liable person's earnings; and
- (*b*) pay the amounts deducted to the Secretary of State.

(6) The Secretary of State shall serve a copy of any deduction from earnings order which he makes under this section on –
- (*a*) the person who appears to the Secretary of State to have the liable person in question in his employment; and
- (*b*) the liable person.

(7) Where –

(*a*) a deduction from earnings order has been made; and

(*b*) a copy of the order has been served on the liable person's employer,

it shall be the duty of that employer to comply with the order; but he shall not be under any liability for non-compliance before the end of the period of 7 days beginning with the date on which the copy was served on him.

(8) In this section and in section 32 "earnings" has such meaning as may be prescribed.

Amendments—Child Support, Pensions and Social Security Act 2000, s 1(2).

Defined terms—"child support maintenance": s 3(6); "earnings": s 31(8), Child Support (Collection and Enforcement) Regulations 1992, reg 8(3), (4); "maintenance calculation": s 54.

Scope of provision—This section empowers the Secretary of State to secure payment of child support maintenance from any liable person who is in employment by means of an order which instructs his employer to deduct payments from his earnings (a deduction from earnings order).

Other forms of maintenance—The term "payments of child support maintenance" includes payments of other forms of periodical payments which the Child Support Agency can enforce under s 30 (s 30(4); Child Support (Collection and Enforcement of Other Forms of Maintenance) Regulations 1992, reg 3); and this applies also to arrears and future payments.

"the Secretary of State may make an order" (s 31(2))—The making of a deduction from earnings order is an entirely discretionary remedy. It results in an administrative order with no court involvement in the process (by contrast with orders under Attachment of Earnings Act 1971, s 1 which can only be made on application to the court: s 3). No grounds for imposing the order need be established nor any reasons for it stated.

Challenging the order—

(*a*) *Appeals to the magistrates' courts* Under Child Support (Collection and Enforcement) Regulations 1992, reg 22 limited grounds for appeal against the making of a deduction from earnings order exist: (i) that the order is defective; or (ii) that the payments concerned are not earnings (as defined in reg 8(3)). The magistrates' powers on appeal are limited to quashing the order or stating that the payments in question are not earnings. It is not open to the magistrates to consider the welfare of any children concerned on such an appeal (*R v Secretary of State for Social Security ex parte Biggin* [1995] 1 FLR 851, Thorpe J). At best, this can only be a matter for the Secretary of State, perhaps having regard to his discretion under CSA 1991, s 2. Nor may the magistrates make orders which should have been dealt with by means of review, under s 18, or appeal, under s 20 (*Secretary of State for Social Security v Shotton and Others* [1996] 2 FLR 241, Latham J).

(*b*) *Judicial review* As an administrative decision involving the exercise of discretion, the making of a deduction from earnings order may be susceptible to judicial review in exceptional circumstances and subject to any appeal (where grounds existed) under reg 22 (above); for example, where the liable person's employment may be affected by the order (especially if a child might suffer where he is to lose his job: and see s 2); or if the Secretary of State can be shown to have acted unreasonably or maliciously in imposing the order where other forms of enforcement or collection were available and had been proposed by the liable person.

Procedure on appeal—Appeal is by complaint for an order to the magistrates' courts in accordance with Magistrates' Courts Rules 1981 (for forms of summons and complaint see Magistrates' Courts (Forms) Rules 1981, SI 1981/553). The complaint must be issued within 28 days of "the date on which the matter complained against arose" (reg 22). The procedure on judicial review is covered by CPR 1998, Pt 54.

"earnings" (s 31(8))—A definition of "earnings" has been prescribed by Child Support (Collection and Enforcement) Regulations 1992, reg 8(3)–(5) which is in many respects identical to the definition of "earnings" in Attachment of Earnings Act 1971, s 24. This definition is much narrower than the definition of "earnings" used, for example, in the calculation of maintenance.

****

33 Liability orders

(1) This section applies where –

(*a*) a person who is liable to make payments of child support maintenance ("the liable person") fails to make one or more of those payments; and

(*b*) it appears to the Secretary of State that –

(i) it is inappropriate to make a deduction from earnings order against him (because, for example, he is not employed); or

(ii) although such an order has been made against him, it has proved ineffective as a means of securing that payments are made in accordance with the maintenance calculation in question.

(2) The Secretary of State may apply to a magistrates' court or, in Scotland, to the sheriff for an order ("a liability order") against the liable person.

(3) Where the Secretary of State applies for a liability order, the magistrates' court or (as the case may be) sheriff shall make the order if satisfied that the payments in question have become payable by the liable person and have not been paid.

(4) On an application under subsection (2), the court or (as the case may be) the sheriff shall not question the maintenance calculation under which the payments of child support maintenance fell to be made.

(5) If the Secretary of State designates a liability order for the purposes of this subsection it shall be treated as a judgment entered in a county court for the purposes of section 73 of the County Courts Act 1984 (register of judgments and orders).

(6) Where regulations have been made under section 29(3)(*a*) –

(*a*) the liable person fails to make a payment (for the purposes of subsection (1)(*a*) of this section); and

(*b*) a payment is not paid (for the purposes of subsection (3)),

unless the payment is made to, or through, the person specified in or by virtue of those regulations for the case of the liable person in question.

Amendments—Child Support Act 1995, s 30, Sch 3, para 10; Child Support, Pensions and Social Security Act 2000, s 26, Sch 3, para 11(1), (17).

Defined terms—"child support maintenance": s 3(6); "deduction from earnings order": s 31(2); "maintenance calculation": s 54.

Scope of provision—This section enables the Secretary of State to apply to the magistrates' court for a liability order where a liable person is more than one payment in arrears and a deduction from earnings order is either inappropriate or has proved ineffective.

"the magistrates' court ... shall make the order" (s 33(3))—The role of the magistrates' court in the grant or refusal of a liability order is very limited. The only issue before the court is whether one or more payments are due and, if so, whether they have been paid. If satisfied that payments due have not been paid the court has no discretion but to make the order. It is the Secretary of State, not the magistrates, who decides upon the appropriateness of a deduction from earnings order; or, where a deduction from earnings order had been made, whether or not it was effective (s 33(1)(*b*)). Still less are the magistrates able to query the amount of the maintenance calculation (s 33(4)).

PART II

Effect of a liability order—The consequence of the making of a liability order is that a number of other forms of enforcement are then available: distress (s 35), enforcement in the county courts (s 36) and committal (s 40).

****

36 Enforcement in county courts

(1) Where a liability order has been made against a person, the amount in respect of which the order was made, to the extent that it remains unpaid, shall, if a county court so orders, be recoverable by means of garnishee proceedings or a charging order, as if it were payable under a county court order.

(2) In subsection (1) "charging order" has the same meaning as in section 1 of the Charging Orders Act 1979.

Defined terms—"liability order": s 33(2).

Scope of provision—This section enables payment to be recovered in the county court, once a liability order has been made, by means of garnishee proceedings or a charging order against the liable person's creditors or assets.

"if a county court so orders" (s 36(1))—While the magistrates' court has little discretion but to make a liability order (see s 33(1)), the wording of s 36(1) reflects the wording of CCR Ord 30, r 1(1) and Charging Orders Act 1979, s 1(1) which give the county court a discretion as to whether or not the orders should be made.

Application in the county court—Whereas application for the other means of enforcement (distress or commitment) is by the Secretary of State, s 36 is silent as to who should make the application in the county court. It must therefore be open to the person with care to make her own application.

Jurisdiction of the county court—Applications under s 36(1) are to the county court only (and, in consequence, references below are to CCR only). It is not clear what remedy the applicant under s 36 has if the amount to be enforced is higher than the limit (at present £5,000) imposed for enforcement in the county courts (High Court and County Courts Jurisdiction Order 1991, art 8).

Garnishee proceedings—
(*a*) *Grounds* The grounds for obtaining a garnishee order exist where a third party ("the garnishee") owes money to a judgment debtor and there is a judgment or order against him in favour of a judgment creditor. That creditor can apply for an order that the amount due be paid by the garnishee to her (CCR Ord 30, r 1(1)).
(*b*) *Procedure* The procedure for applying for a garnishee order is set out in CCR Ord 30, rr 2–7 (see also Procedural Guide 31).

Charging orders (s 36(1), (2))—See also under Charging Orders Act 1979.
(*a*) *Grounds* The grounds for applying for a charging order are that, where a debtor is required by a judgment or order to pay money to a creditor, the court may charge the amount owed on any property (as defined by Charging Orders Act 1979, s 2) owned by the debtor (Charging Orders Act 1979, s 1(1)).
(*b*) *Procedure* The procedure for applying for a charging order is set out in CCR Ord 31, rr 1, 2 (see also Procedural Guide 28).

Enforcement of a charging order—Section 36(1) is misleading to the extent that no order can be enforced by a charging order alone (save by waiting till the charged property is sold, if that can even be termed enforcement): other steps by separate originating application for enforcement by order for sale must be taken by the parent with care. In deciding whether to enforce by order for sale the court will exercise its discretion by balancing the needs of the creditor (person with care) against, for example, the interests of the family of the debtor (non-resident parent) (*Harman v Glencross* [1986] Fam 81, [1986] 2 FLR 241, CA; see also *Re Citro* [1991] Ch 142, [1991] 1 FLR 71, CA).

"as if it were payable under a county court order" (s 36(1))—For the purposes of s 36, CCR Ord 30 and Charging Orders Act 1979, s 1(1) can be read as if: (*a*) the (judgment) debtor were the liable person; (*b*) the (judgment) creditor were the person with care; and (*c*) the liability order were the judgment or court order.

****

40 Commitment to prison

(1), (2) (*repealed*)

(3) If, but only if, the court is of the opinion that there has been wilful refusal or culpable neglect on the part of the liable person it may –

(*a*) issue a warrant of commitment against him; or
(*b*) fix a term of imprisonment and postpone the issue of the warrant until such time and on such conditions (if any) as it thinks just.

(4) Any such warrant –

(*a*) shall be made in respect of an amount equal to the aggregate of –
(i) the amount mentioned in section 35(1) or so much of it as remains outstanding; and
(ii) an amount (determined in accordance with regulations made by the Secretary of State) in respect of the costs of commitment; and
(*b*) shall state that amount.

(5) No warrant may be issued under this section against a person who is under the age of 18.

(6) A warrant issued under this section shall order the liable person –

(*a*) to be imprisoned for a specific period; but
(*b*) to be released (unless he is in custody for some other reason) on payment of the amount stated in the warrant.

(7) The maximum period of imprisonment which may be imposed by virtue of subsection (6) shall be calculated in accordance with Schedule 4 to the Magistrates' Courts Act 1980 (maximum periods of imprisonment in default of payment) but shall not exceed six weeks.

(8) The Secretary of State may by regulations make provision for the period of imprisonment specified in any warrant issued under this section to be reduced where there is part payment of the amount in respect of which the warrant was issued.

(9) A warrant issued under this section may be directed to such person or persons as the court issuing it thinks fit.

(10) Section 80 of the Magistrates' Courts Act 1980 (application of money found on defaulter) shall apply in relation to a warrant issued under this section against a liable person as it applies in relation to the enforcement of a sum mentioned in subsection (1) of that section.

(11) The Secretary of State may by regulations make provision –

(*a*) as to the form of any warrant issued under this section;
(*b*) allowing an application under this section to be renewed where no warrant is issued or term of imprisonment is fixed;

PART II

(*c*) that a statement in writing to the effect that wages of any amount have been paid to the liable person during any period, purporting to be signed by or on behalf of his employer, shall be evidence of the facts stated;

(*d*) that, for the purposes of enabling an inquiry to be made as to the liable person's conduct and means, a justice of the peace may issue a summons to him to appear before a magistrates' court and (if he does not obey) may issue a warrant for his arrest;

(*e*) that for the purpose of enabling such an inquiry, a justice of the peace may issue a warrant for the liable person's arrest without issuing a summons;

(*f*) as to the execution of a warrant for arrest.

(12) This section does not apply to Scotland.

Amendments—Child Support, Pensions and Social Security Act 2000, ss 16(2), 17(1), 85, Sch 9, Pt I.

Defined terms—"employer": s 31(4)(*a*); "liable person": s 31(1).

Scope of provision—This section enables the Secretary of State to apply to the magistrates' court for committal to prison of a liable person where the other means of enforcement of a liability order have failed.

Warrant of commitment or imprisonment (s 40(3))—The powers of the magistrates' courts to commit for breach of their own order are provided for by Magistrates' Courts Act 1980, s 76, and their power to postpone issue of a warrant by Magistrates' Courts Act 1980, s 77 (the terminology of which resembles s 40(3)). The justices must make a judgment concerning the conduct of the liable person over his failure to pay and whether that failure constitutes wilful refusal or culpable neglect. If they do so find, and having had regard to his means, they have a discretion as to whether or not to commit to prison immediately. Alternatively they can fix a term of imprisonment but suspend issue of the warrant of commitment to prison on "such conditions as [the court] thinks just".

"such conditions (if any) as [the court] thinks just" (s 40(3)(*b*))—This provision will enable the magistrates, for example, to suspend the warrant on terms that the liable person maintains payments due and pays off the arrears and costs (the amount stated on the warrant: s 40(4)) by fixed periodic instalments (*Fowler v Fowler* (1981) FLR 141).

"costs of commitment" (s 40(4)(*a*)(ii))—The costs of commitment are to be such amount as the court considers "is equal to the costs reasonably incurred" in bringing the application (Child Support (Collection and Enforcement) Regulations 1992, reg 34(2)). No assistance is given to the magistrates by the regulations as to how to determine this figure; nor is there any guidance in the Magistrates' Courts Act 1980, s 64 (powers of the magistrates in their civil jurisdiction to award and enforce orders for costs).

"period of imprisonment … to be reduced where there is part payment" (s 40(8))—Child Support (Collection and Enforcement) Regulations 1992, reg 34(5) provides that where there has been part payment of the amount in the warrant then the period of imprisonment specified in the warrant under s 40(6)(*a*) shall be reduced proportionately in the same proportion as the amount paid off bears the total due. The period of imprisonment will be reduced whether it was suspended or immediate.

Execution of the warrant (s 40(9), (11)(*f*))—Child Support (Collection and Enforcement) Regulations 1992, reg 34(3), (4) deals with execution of the warrant by the person to whom it is addressed, or by the police constable within his area.

"Section 80 of the Magistrates' Courts Act 1980" (s 40(10))—Section 80 enables the court to order that a defaulter, against whom an order for enforcement has been made, be searched (s 80(1)). Any money found on him will be taken to reduce his liability (s 80(2)); unless to remove the money "would be more injurious to his family than would be his detention" (s 80(3)).

Further regulations (s 40(11))—The Child Support (Collection and Enforcement) Regulations 1992 make further provision in accordance with s 40(11):

(*a*) A warrant for commitment is in the form in Sch 3 to the regulations (s 40(11)(*a*); reg 34(1)).

(*b*) Regulation 33(3) is narrower than s 40(11)(*b*); for the regulation provides that, where the magistrates refuse an application to commit, reapplication can only be made where there is a change in the liable person's circumstances. Such change would not be restricted to financial circumstances.

(*c*) Provision for a statement of income from the liable person's employer is in reg 33(2) (s 40(11)(*c*)).

(*d*) To enable an enquiry into the liable person's means to be undertaken reg 33(1) provides for issue of a summons or warrant (s 40(11)(*d*), (*e*)).

****

Jurisdiction

44 Jurisdiction

(1) The Secretary of State shall have jurisdiction to make a maintenance calculation with respect to a person who is –

(*a*) a person with care;
(*b*) a non-resident parent; or
(*c*) a qualifying child,

only if that person is habitually resident in the United Kingdom, except in the case of a non-resident parent who falls within subsection (2A).

(2) Where the person with care is not an individual, subsection (1) shall have effect as if paragraph (*a*) were omitted.

(2A) A non-resident parent falls within this subsection if he is not habitually resident in the United Kingdom, but is –

(*a*) employed in the civil service of the Crown, including Her Majesty's Diplomatic Service and Her Majesty's Overseas Civil Service;
(*b*) a member of the naval, military or air forces of the Crown, including any person employed by an association established for the purposes of Part XI of the Reserve Forces Act 1996;
(*c*) employed by a company of a prescribed description registered under the Companies Act 1985 in England and Wales or in Scotland, or under the Companies (Northern Ireland) Order 1986; or
(*d*) employed by a body of a prescribed description.

(3) (*repealed*)

Amendments—Social Security Act 1998, s 86(1), Sch 7, para 41; Child Support, Pensions and Social Security Act 2000, ss 1(2), 22, Sch 3, para 11(2).

Defined terms—"child": s 55(1); "maintenance calculation": s 54; "maintenance order": s 8(11); "parent": s 54; "qualifying child": s 3(1).

Habitual residence (s 44(1))—The term "habitual residence" is not defined in the Act. Reference may be made to authorities where the applicant seeks to invoke the jurisdiction of the English courts (eg Domicile and Matrimonial Proceedings Act, s 5(2)(*b*) (habitual residence for one year); *Shah v Barnet London Borough Council ex parte Nilish Shah* [1983] 2 AC 942, [1983] 1 All ER 226, HL (residence must be voluntarily adopted and it must be settled)). However, this may be of limited use since, in contrast to the proceedings to which these authorities refer, the object of many litigants under s 44 will be to show that the provisions of the Act do *not* apply to them. A more helpful approach may be to consider "habitually resident" within the terms of Art 4 of the Hague Convention (see further **Habitual residence** under Child Abduction and Custody Act 1985, Sch 1, Art 4), where the term was authoritatively considered by Lord Brandon of Oakbrook in *C v S (A Minor) (Abduction: Illegitimate Child)* [1990] 2 FLR 442 at 454; but see also *Ikimi v Ikimi* [2001] 2 FLR 1288, CA.

Non-resident parent treated as habitually resident (s 44(1), (2A))—The effect of the riders at the end of s 44(1) and (2A) (both added by the 2000 Act) is to bring a number of previously exempt non-resident parents into the Child Support Agency net by providing that those listed in s 44(2A) are comprised within the term "habitually resident" in s 44(1), so as to enable the Secretary of State to assume jurisdiction to make a calculation in respect of them.

Want of jurisdiction—If either the person with care, the qualifying children or the non-resident parent are not habitually resident, or treated as habitually resident, no application for a calculation can be made. Application for periodical payments will then be to the court (subject to any other jurisdictional requirements arising from residence of any of the parties).

Application to court where a maintenance calculation is cancelled—Where a maintenance calculation is cancelled (eg because the Secretary of State lacks jurisdiction under s 44(1)), application can be made to the court for periodical payments for a qualifying child. Provided that such application is made within six months of the cancellation, the court has a discretion to backdate any order it makes to the date on which the calculation was cancelled (Matrimonial Causes Act 1973, s 29(7), Domestic Proceedings and Magistrates' Courts Act 1978, s 5(7) and CA 1989, Sch 1, para 3(7), inserted by Maintenance Orders (Backdating) Order 1993).

45 Jurisdiction of courts in certain proceedings under this Act

(1) The Lord Chancellor or, in relation to Scotland, the Lord Advocate may by order make such provision as he considers necessary to secure that appeals, or such class of appeals as may be specified in the order –

(*a*) shall be made to a court instead of being made to an appeal tribunal; or
(*b*) shall be so made in such circumstances as may be so specified.

(2) In subsection (1), "court" means –

(*a*) in relation to England and Wales and subject to any provision made under Schedule 11 to the Children Act 1989 (jurisdiction of courts with respect to certain proceedings relating to children) the High Court, a county court or a magistrates' court; and
(*b*) in relation to Scotland, the Court of Session or the sheriff.

(3) Schedule 11 to the Act of 1989 shall be amended in accordance with subsections (4) and (5).

(4) The following sub-paragraph shall be inserted in paragraph 1, after sub-paragraph (2) –

"(2A) Sub-paragraphs (1) and (2) shall also apply in relation to proceedings –

(*a*) under section 27 of the Child Support Act 1991 (reference to court for declaration of parentage); or
(*b*) which are to be dealt with in accordance with an order made under section 45 of that Act (jurisdiction of courts in certain proceedings under that Act)".

(5) In paragraphs 1(3) and 2(3), the following shall be inserted after "Act 1976" –

"(*bb*) section 20 (appeals) or 27 (reference to court for declaration of parentage) of the Child Support Act 1991;"

(6) Where the effect of any order under subsection (1) is that there are no longer any appeals which fall to be dealt with by appeal tribunals, the Lord Chancellor after consultation with the Lord Advocate may by order provide for the abolition of those tribunals.

(7) Any order under subsection (1) or (6) may make –

(*a*) such modifications of any provision of this Act or of any other enactment; and

(*b*) such transitional provision,

as the Minister making the order considers appropriate in consequence of any provision made by the order.

Amendments—Social Security Act 1998, s 86(1), Sch 7, para 42.

Defined terms—"child support appeal tribunal": s 21(1).

"shall be made to a court"—Appeals against a Secretary of State decision concerning parentage, which would otherwise have gone to an appeal tribunal, are made to the magistrates' courts in line with applications for declaration of parentage.

"Schedule 11 to the Act of 1989" (s 45(3)–(5))—CA 1989, Sch 11 deals with the jurisdiction of the courts and enables the Lord Chancellor to define the level of court in which proceedings under the Act must be issued. In consequence, to provide for issues under ss 20 and 27 in the magistrates' courts (as referred to above), the Children (Allocation of Proceedings) Order 1991 has been amended by the Children (Allocation of Proceedings) (Amendment) Order 1993.

Miscellaneous and supplemental

****

54 Interpretation

In this Act –

"adjudication officer" has the same meaning as in the benefit Acts;

"appeal tribunal" means an appeal tribunal constituted under Chapter I of Part I of the Social Security Act 1998;

"application for a variation" means an application under section 28A or 28G;

"benefit Acts" means the Social Security Contributions and Benefits Act 1992 and the Social Security Administration Act 1992;

"Chief Adjudication Officer" has the same meaning as in the benefit Acts;

"child benefit" has the same meaning as in the Child Benefit Act 1975;

"child support maintenance" has the meaning given in section 3(6);

"deduction from earnings order" has the meaning given in section 31(2);

"default maintenance decision" has the meaning given in section 12;

"disabled person's tax credit" has the same meaning as in the benefit Acts;

"general qualification" shall be construed in accordance with section 71 of the Courts and Legal Services Act 1990 (qualification for judicial appointments);

"income support" has the same meaning as in the benefit Acts;

"income-based jobseeker's allowance" has the same meaning as in the Jobseekers Act 1995;

"interim maintenance decision" has the meaning given in section 12;

"liability order" has the meaning given in section 33(2);

"maintenance agreement" has the meaning given in section 9(1);

"maintenance calculation" means a calculation of maintenance made under this Act and, except in prescribed circumstances, includes a default maintenance decision and an interim maintenance decision;

"maintenance order" has the meaning given in section 8(11);

"non-resident parent", has the meaning given in section 3(2);

"parent", in relation to any child, means any person who is in law the mother or father of the child;

"parent with care" means a person who is, in relation to a child, both a parent and a person with care;

"parental responsibility", in the application of this Act –

(*a*) to England and Wales, has the same meaning as in the Children Act 1989; and

(*b*) to Scotland, shall be construed as a reference to "parental responsibilities" within the meaning given by section 1(3) of the Children (Scotland) Act 1995;

"person with care" has the meaning given in section 3(3);

"prescribed" means prescribed by regulations made by the Secretary of State;

"qualifying child" has the meaning given in section 3(1);

"voluntary payment" has the meaning given in section 28J;

"working families' tax credit" has the same meaning as in the benefit Acts.

Amendments—Social Security (Consequential Provisions) Act 1992, s 4, Sch 2, para 114; Child Support Act 1995, s 30, Sch 3, para 16; Children (Scotland) Act 1995, s 105(4), Sch 4, para 52; Jobseekers Act 1995, s 41, Sch 2, para 20; Social Security Act 1998, s 86(1), Sch 7, para 47; Tax Credits Act 1999, s 1(2), Sch 1, paras 1, 6(*f*)(ii); Child Support, Pensions and Social Security Act 2000, s 1(2), Sch 3, para 11(2), (20).

55 Meaning of "child"

(1) For the purposes of this Act a person is a child if –

(*a*) he is under the age of 16;

(*b*) he is under the age of 19 and receiving full-time education (which is not advanced education) –

(i) by attendance at a recognised educational establishment; or

(ii) elsewhere, if the education is recognised by the Secretary of State; or

(*c*) he does not fall within paragraph (*a*) or (*b*) but –

(i) he is under the age of 18, and

(ii) prescribed conditions are satisfied with respect to him.

(2) A person is not a child for the purposes of this Act if he –

(*a*) is or has been married;

(*b*) has celebrated a marriage which is void; or

(*c*) has celebrated a marriage in respect of which a decree of nullity has been granted.

(3) In this section –

"advanced education" means education of a prescribed description; and

"recognised educational establishment" means an establishment recognised by the Secretary of State for the purposes of this section as being, or as comparable to, a university, college or school.

(4) Where a person has reached the age of 16, the Secretary of State may recognise education provided for him otherwise than at a recognised educational establishment only if the Secretary of State is satisfied that education was being so provided for him immediately before he reached the age of 16.

(5) The Secretary of State may provide that in prescribed circumstances education is or is not to be treated for the purposes of this section as being full-time.

(6) In determining whether a person falls within subsection (1)(*b*), no account shall be taken of such interruptions in his education as may be prescribed.

(7) The Secretary of State may by regulations provide that a person who ceases to fall within subsection (1) shall be treated as continuing to fall within that subsection for a prescribed period.

(8) No person shall be treated as continuing to fall within subsection (1) by virtue of regulations made under subsection (7) after the end of the week in which he reaches the age of 19.

Regulations and the meaning of "child"—Child Support (Maintenance Calculation Procedure) Regulations 2000, Sch 1 elaborates the definition of "child" under s 55 to include the following:

(*a*) para 1 defines conditions which apply to children under 18 who are to be treated as children within the terms of s 55(1)(*c*), ie where they are registered for work or for training under youth training for a number of specified employers or where they are not in remunerative employment (save of a temporary nature);

(*b*) the meaning of "advanced education", in accordance with s 55(3), is defined by para 2 to include degree and other tertiary level courses and "any other course which is of a standard above that of an ordinary national diploma";

(*c*) for persons under 19, the circumstances in which education is to be treated as full-time for the purposes of s 55(5), and thus bringing them within s 55(1), are defined in terms of time spent in instruction, supervised study, examination and other activities within the course curriculum, where such education exceeds 12 hours per week (para 3);

(*d*) interruptions in education of up to six months, where reasonable, are permitted (s 55(6) and para 4);

(*e*) circumstances in which a person who has ceased full-time education, but remains under 19, may be treated as coming within the terms of s 55(1), and therefore being treated as a "child", are set out in para 5 for the purposes of s 55(7); but where a person is in employment, he cannot be a "child" under s 55(1) (para 5(5)).

****

Children Act 1989

ARRANGEMENT OF SECTIONS

PART I
INTRODUCTORY

PART II
ORDERS WITH RESPECT TO CHILDREN IN FAMILY PROCEEDINGS

General

Financial relief

Family assistance orders

PART III
LOCAL AUTHORITY SUPPORT FOR CHILDREN AND FAMILIES

Provision of services for children and their families

Provision of accommodation for children

Duties of local authorities in relation to children looked after by them

Personal advisers and pathway plans

Advice and assistance for certain children and young persons

Secure accommodation

Supplemental

PART IV
CARE AND SUPERVISION

General

Care orders

Supervision orders

Powers of court

Representation of child

PART V
PROTECTION OF CHILDREN

PART II

PART VI
COMMUNITY HOMES

PART VII
VOLUNTARY HOMES AND VOLUNTARY ORGANISATIONS

PART VIII
REGISTERED CHILDREN'S HOMES

PART IX
PRIVATE ARRANGEMENTS FOR FOSTERING CHILDREN

PART XA
CHILD MINDING AND DAY CARE FOR CHILDREN IN ENGLAND AND WALES

Introductory

Regulations

Registration

Jurisdiction and procedure etc

Search warrants

General

PART I
INTRODUCTORY

1 Welfare of the child

(1) When a court determines any question with respect to –

(*a*) the upbringing of a child; or
(*b*) the administration of a child's property or the application of any income arising from it,

the child's welfare shall be the court's paramount consideration.

(2) In any proceedings in which any question with respect to the upbringing of a child arises, the court shall have regard to the general principle that any delay in determining the question is likely to prejudice the welfare of the child.

(3) In the circumstances mentioned in subsection (4), a court shall have regard in particular to –

(*a*) the ascertainable wishes and feelings of the child concerned (considered in the light of his age and understanding);
(*b*) his physical, emotional and educational needs;
(*c*) the likely effect on him of any change in his circumstances;
(*d*) his age, sex, background and any characteristics of his which the court considers relevant;
(*e*) any harm which he has suffered or is at risk of suffering;
(*f*) how capable each of his parents, and any other person in relation to whom the court considers the question to be relevant, is of meeting his needs;
(*g*) the range of powers available to the court under this Act in the proceedings in question.

(4) The circumstances are that –

(*a*) the court is considering whether to make, vary or discharge a section 8 order, and the making, variation or discharge of the order is opposed by any party to the proceedings; or
(*b*) the court is considering whether to make, vary or discharge an order under Part IV.

(5) Where a court is considering whether or not to make one or more orders under this Act with respect to a child, it shall not make the order or any of the orders unless it considers that doing so would be better for the child than making no order at all.

Defined terms—"child", "upbringing": s 105(1).

Delay generally (s 1(2))—The general principle that delay is harmful applies to any proceedings concerning "the upbringing" of a child, but does not apply where the question at issue is the child's maintenance. Both practitioners and courts have a duty to avoid delay in children cases. The non-adversarial approach to children's litigation means that the solicitors for the parties have a duty, irrespective of whether delay might be tactically advantageous to their client, to ensure that a case does not drift and is resolved with the minimum of delay. Courts have a duty to be proactive in ensuring (through the giving of directions) that applications, once launched, are not allowed to moulder. A children's guardian has a duty to review the file regularly and, if the case is not making satisfactory progress, should take out a summons for directions (*B v B (Minors) (Interviews and Listing Arrangements)* [1994] 2 FLR 489, CA, *Re A and B (Minors) (No 2)* [1995] 1 FLR 351, FD, and *B v B (Child Abuse: Contact)* [1994] 2 FLR 713). The possibility of avoiding delay by arranging for a split hearing should be borne in mind (*Re S (Care Proceedings: Split Hearing)* [1996] 2 FLR 773, FD, considered further under s 31).

However, although delay in legal proceedings is likely to be prejudicial to the welfare of a child, speed itself should not be allowed to become supreme. It is the welfare of the child that is the court's paramount consideration (s 1(1)) and there are bound to be cases in which planned and purposeful delay will improve the chances of meeting the child's needs satisfactorily (for example, where a parent needs time to resolve housing difficulties, or where it is felt that the court would benefit from a full investigation and report from a psychiatrist, or where, as in *C v Solihull MBC* [1993] 1 FLR 290 and *Hounslow LBC v A* [1993] 1 FLR 702, an investigation by the local authority is not yet complete, or where, as in *Re W (Welfare Reports)* [1995] 2 FLR 142, CA, the need to ensure that the court is as fully informed and advised as possible outweighs the disadvantage of delay caused by ordering a court welfare report). For further cases concerning delay occasioned by court welfare reporting, see **Delay occasioned by obtaining welfare report** and **Court differing with recommendations in welfare report** under s 7. For consideration of the difficult problem of when the court should cease to be involved in the case and should hand over to the local authority by making a full care order, see under s 38.

If it is thought appropriate to reserve a case to a particular judge (and continuity of tribunal is important in children cases – see *Re F (Contact: Enforcement: Representation of Child)* [1998] 1 FLR 691, CA), the order should normally say "if available" in order to avoid delay and administrative difficulties (see *Belton v Belton* [1987] 2 FLR 343). See also *Re S (Interim Contact*

Order) [1998] Fam Law 174 where the judge had failed to consider the delay that would be caused by a transfer to the court nearest the children's address.

Delay and pending criminal proceedings—The fact that criminal proceedings are pending does not prevent the court exercising its discretion to proceed to hear a related children's case in order to avoid undesirable delay. The court must balance all the factors involved, taking into account any risk of prejudice to the accused and any risk so far as the child is concerned (*Re TB (Care Proceedings: Criminal Trial)* [1995] 2 FLR 801). Each case must be decided on its merits. The welfare of the child has to take precedence over the detriment to the family facing criminal proceedings. The pending trial of the parents and stepmother in *Re TB* was not of itself a reason to delay care proceedings and, in most cases, care proceedings should not be delayed. *Re B (Agreed Findings of Fact)* [1998] 2 FLR 968, CA is a case with very individual facts. The Court of Appeal permitted the matter to be dealt with upon the basis of the mother's concessions with regard to the threshold criteria and overruled the judge's decision to hold a finding of fact hearing. However, they reaffirmed that, had there been no other matters to put into the balance, it would have been right not to have adjourned that hearing pending the outcome of the criminal proceedings that the mother also faced (see further under CA 1989, s 31). In *Re L (Care: Confidentiality)* [1999] 1 FLR 165, Johnson J took the view that parents who were truthful witnesses would not suffer by cross-examination in the criminal trial as to their statements or admissions in prior care proceedings. He hoped the issue of confidentiality would not be used as a basis for seeking postponement of care proceedings until the conclusion of related criminal proceedings.

Related provisions—The provision as to delay is related to other provisions of the Act, namely s 11 (duty of the court in s 8 proceedings to draw up a timetable and to give appropriate directions) and s 32(1) (corresponding duty in proceedings under s 31 for a care or supervision order). See also the provisions as to timing contained in FPR 1991 and Family Proceedings Courts (Children Act 1989) Rules 1991.

No order (s 1(5))—See further **Form of order** under FPR 1991, r 4.21, and **Form C22 and formal order** under FPC(CA 1989)R 1991, r 21. For an example of the approach being adopted by the courts in relation to the "no order" principle see *Re K (Supervision Orders)* [1999] 2 FLR 303, where Wall J (at 318C) considered that a supervision order under CA 1989, s 31 should only be made if "the children need more protection than can be given voluntarily ... in other words, there must be something in the making or operation of a supervision order which makes it better for the children for an order to be made".

2 Parental responsibility for children

(1) Where a child's father and mother were married to each other at the time of his birth, they shall each have parental responsibility for the child.

(2) Where a child's father and mother were not married to each other at the time of his birth –

(*a*) the mother shall have parental responsibility for the child;

(*b*) the father shall not have parental responsibility for the child, unless he acquires it in accordance with the provisions of this Act.

(3) References in this Act to a child whose father and mother were, or (as the case may be) were not, married to each other at the time of his birth must be read with section 1 of the Family Law Reform Act 1987 (which extends their meaning).

(4) The rule of law that a father is the natural guardian of his legitimate child is abolished.

(5) More than one person may have parental responsibility for the same child at the same time.

(6) A person who has parental responsibility for a child at any time shall not cease to have that responsibility solely because some other person subsequently acquires parental responsibility for the child.

(7) Where more than one person has parental responsibility for a child, each of them may act alone and without the other (or others) in meeting that responsibility; but nothing in this Part shall be taken to affect the operation of any enactment which requires the consent of more than one person in a matter affecting the child.

(8) The fact that a person has parental responsibility for a child shall not entitle him to act in any way which would be incompatible with any order made with respect to the child under this Act.

(9) A person who has parental responsibility for a child may not surrender or transfer any part of that responsibility to another but may arrange for some or all of it to be met by one or more persons acting on his behalf.

(10) The person with whom any such arrangement is made may himself be a person who already has parental responsibility for the child concerned.

(11) The making of any such arrangement shall not affect any liability of the person making it which may arise from any failure to meet any part of his parental responsibility for the child concerned.

3 Meaning of "parental responsibility"

(1) In this Act "parental responsibility" means all the rights, duties, powers, responsibilities and authority which by law a parent of a child has in relation to the child and his property.

(2) It also includes the rights, powers and duties which a guardian of the child's estate (appointed, before the commencement of section 5, to act generally) would have had in relation to the child and his property.

(3) The rights referred to in subsection (2) include, in particular, the right of the guardian to receive or recover in his own name, for the benefit of the child, property of whatever description and wherever situated which the child is entitled to receive or recover.

(4) The fact that a person has, or does not have, parental responsibility for a child shall not affect –

- (*a*) any obligation which he may have in relation to the child (such as a statutory duty to maintain the child); or
- (*b*) any rights which, in the event of the child's death, he (or any other person) may have in relation to the child's property.

(5) A person who –

- (*a*) does not have parental responsibility for a particular child; but
- (*b*) has care of the child,

may (subject to the provisions of this Act) do what is reasonable in all the circumstances of the case for the purpose of safeguarding or promoting the child's welfare.

4 Acquisition of parental responsibility by father

(1) Where a child's father and mother were not married to each other at the time of his birth –

- (*a*) the court may, on the application of the father, order that he shall have parental responsibility for the child; or (*b*) the father and mother may by agreement ("a parental responsibility agreement") provide for the father to have parental responsibility for the child.

(2) No parental responsibility agreement shall have effect for the purposes of this Act unless –

(*a*) it is made in the form prescribed by regulations made by the Lord Chancellor; and

(*b*) where regulations are made by the Lord Chancellor prescribing the manner in which such agreements must be recorded, it is recorded in the prescribed manner.

(3) Subject to section 12(4), an order under subsection (1)(*a*), or a parental responsibility agreement, may only be brought to an end by an order of the court made on the application –

(*a*) of any person who has parental responsibility for the child, or
(*b*) with leave of the court, of the child himself.

(4) The court may only grant leave under subsection (3)(*b*) if it is satisfied that the child has sufficient understanding to make the proposed application.

Defined terms—"child": s 105(1); "parental responsibility": s 3.

Father and mother not married to each other at time of child's birth (s 4(1))—Section 2(3) provides that references in the Act to a child whose father and mother were not married to each other at the time of his birth must be read with Family Law Reform Act 1987, s 1. Consequently, where the child in question is treated as legitimate by virtue of Legitimacy Act 1976, s 1 (legitimacy of children of certain void marriages), is a legitimated person under s 10 of that Act (legitimation in various circumstances such as by subsequent marriage of the child's parents), has been adopted by the parents within the meaning of Adoption Act 1976, Pt IV, or is otherwise treated in law as legitimate, the case does not fall within the provisions of s 4(1) (Family Law Reform Act 1987, s 1(2), (3)). The time of a person's birth must be taken to include any time during the period beginning with the insemination resulting in his birth or, where there was no such insemination, his conception, and ending with his actual birth (Family Law Reform Act 1987, s 1(4)). As to the parents of a child born of in vitro fertilisation, artificial insemination etc see Human Fertilisation and Embryology Act 1990, ss 27–29.

Adoption and Children Act 2002—When ACA 2002, s 111 comes into force it will amend CA 1989, s 4, so that a father who was not married to the mother at the time of the child's birth will have parental responsibility if his name is placed on the birth certificate at registration or re-registration of the birth under the Births and Deaths Registration Act 1953. However, in reality, the unmarried father will not be able to register his name without the consent of the mother. Once the unmarried father acquires parental responsibility by such registration then parental responsibility can only be removed by order of court, on application by any person with parental responsibility for the child or, with leave, on the application of the child himself (provided he has sufficient understanding).

ACA 2002, s 112 will insert a new s 4A into CA 1989 which will enable a step-parent to acquire parental responsibility for a child of his spouse by agreement between the step-parent and the parents who have parental responsibility for the child, or by order of the court. This will be a "parental responsibility agreement" within the definition of CA 1989, s 4(2) and will only be terminated by the court on application by any person with parental responsibility for the child, or, with leave, on application by the child himself.

Parental responsibility order on application of father (s 4(1)(*a*))—Where the parents agree that the father should have parental responsibility, they may enter into a parental responsibility agreement. Where the mother is not prepared to do this or cannot be found, the father will have to apply to the court for a parental responsibility order. The mother cannot apply under s 4 for an order against the father but, if she felt the father was not pulling his weight with regard to the child's upbringing, she would have other remedies open to her, for example a s 8 application or an application under Sch 1 for financial relief for the child. There is nothing illogical in making an order for parental responsibility, even though the father has no prospect of being able to exercise parental rights in the immediate future, or indeed for many years to come. He is entitled to ask the court to recognise his position as the father of the child irrespective of any question of residence or contact. A parental responsibility order confers on the committed father the status of parenthood for which nature has already ordained he must bear responsibility (*Re S (Parental Responsibility)* [1995] 2 FLR 648, CA, which contains a helpful review of the authorities). The court considers the degree of commitment the father has shown towards the child, the degree of attachment between him and the child and the reasons why he is applying for the order but these three requirements, though a starting point, are not intended to be exhaustive and the court must take into account all the relevant circumstances, bearing in mind that CA 1989, s 1 applies and the welfare of the child is therefore paramount (*Re H (Parental Responsibility)* [1998] 1 FLR 855, CA). When considering a father's motivation in applying for parental responsibility there is a presupposition that he is capable of reason. Furthermore, ss 3(1) and 4(1) presuppose that a father who is invested with responsibilities is capable of exercising rights, performing duties and wielding powers in relation to the child. Where a father is unable to exercise such responsibility his application will be refused (*M v M (Parental Responsibility)* [1999] 2 FLR 737).

Where natural unmarried father has not signed Birth Register but wishes to be acknowledged as the parent—Where the natural unmarried father has not signed the Birth Register but wishes to be acknowledged as the parent of his child he may now make an application, either himself or jointly with the mother, to have the birth re-registered so as to show him as the father (Births and Deaths Registration Act 1953, s 10A, as amended by Children Act 1975, s 93(2)). This may be done in one of several ways, by presenting the court with the appropriate declaration, statutory declaration of parentage (as to which see **Statutory declaration of parentage** below), parental responsibility agreement or parental responsibility order in the prescribed form.

Statutory declaration of parentage—Family Law Act 1986, s 55A (as amended by CSPSSA 2000, s 83(1) and (2)), has introduced new provisions for declarations of parentage. Section 55A enables a person to apply to the High Court, a county court or a magistrates' court for a declaration of parentage to confirm whether or not a person named in the application is or was the parent of another person so named (s 55A(1)). This remedies defects in the pre-existing law whereby, for example, a person could seek a declaration that someone else was his parent, but he could not seek confirmation of his own claim that he was a parent. Furthermore, previously it was not possible to obtain a declaration that a named person was *not* the parent of a particular child. There are various restrictions on applications made under s 55A (s 55A(2)), but the general rule is that the applicant must have a sufficient personal interest in the determination of the application (s 55A(3)). Where one of the persons named in the application is a child, the court has a discretion to refuse to hear the application if it considers that the determination of it would not be in the best interests of the child (s 55A(5)). Where a court refuses to hear an application, it may order that the applicant may not apply again for the same declaration without leave of the court (s 55A(6)). Section 55A extends to proceedings which were pending at its date of commencement (1 April 2001).

Parental responsibility where a care order is in force—As to the granting of a parental responsibility order where a care order is in force, see *Re G (A Minor) (Parental Responsibility Order)* [1994] 1 FLR 504 and *Re CB (A Minor) (Parental Responsibility Order)* [1993] 1 FLR 920). Where a care order and a parental responsibility order co-exist, the local authority will also have parental responsibility for the child (s 33(3)(*a*)) and will have the power, subject to the provisions of s 33, to determine the extent to which the father may meet his parental responsibility (s 33(3)(*b*)). A local authority responsible for a child under a care order has no power to prevent the child's mother from entering into a parental responsibility agreement with the child's unmarried father (*Re X (Parental Responsibility Agreement: Children in Care)* [2000] 1 FLR 517 – where the court held that the facility under s 4(1)(*b*) for parents of a non-marital child to enter into a parental responsibility agreement is self-contained and does not depend on the exercise of such responsibility. The local authority's argument, that where a care order is in force it shares parental responsibility by virtue of s 33 and therefore has power to determine the extent to which a parent of a child might meet that responsibility, was rejected because the entry into the agreement by the mother did not amount to an exercise by her of parental responsibility).

Parental responsibility where child is accommodated by local authority—Where a child is simply accommodated by a local authority parental responsibility remains vested in the child's parents (ie is not shared by the local authority, as would be the case if a care order or interim care order were in force) and the local authority has no right to move the child from residential care to the home of foster parents without the consent of the child's parents, since parental responsibility

PART II

includes the right to decide where the child lives (*R v Tameside Metropolitan Borough Council ex parte J* [2000] 1 FLR 942).

Parental responsibility application by mother—Section 4 does not make provision for a mother to apply for parental responsibility. Normally she has no need to do so, having parental responsibility for her child automatically. However, *Re C (Adoption: Freeing Order)* [1999] 1 FLR 348 illustrates the problems that can arise where, upon the making of a freeing order, the mother makes a declaration under Adoption Act 1976, s 18(6) indicating that she does not wish to be involved in future questions concerning the adoption of the child. The freeing order deprives the mother of her parental responsibility for the child and there is no statutory mechanism for her to have the freeing order revoked or to re-acquire parental responsibility should an adoption placement fail to materialise. Mr Justice Wall therefore had recourse to the court's inherent jurisdiction to revoke the freeing order.

Jurisdiction—The jurisdiction of the court to make a parental responsibility order is not limited by the Family Law Act 1986 and can be exercised in relation to a child who is permanently out of the jurisdiction, even if that child was also born out of the jurisdiction (*Re S (Parental Responsibility: Jurisdiction)* [1998] 2 FLR 921, CA).

Parental responsibility – European Convention for the Protection of Human Rights and Fundamental Freedoms 1950—The fact that English law treats unmarried fathers differently from married fathers in relation to the automatic acquisition of parental rights in relation to their children does not amount to a breach of Article 8 of the Convention (*B v UK* [2000] 1 FLR 1).

Automatic parental responsibility order—Where the court makes a residence order in favour of an unmarried father it must also, if he would not otherwise have parental responsibility for the child, make a parental responsibility order (s 12(1)). There may, therefore, be no need for a separate parental responsibility application to be filed if the father is confident of obtaining a residence order.

Parental responsibility agreement to be in prescribed form (s 4(2)(*a*))—The form of agreement is prescribed by Parental Responsibility Agreement Regulations 1991, reg 2 and is set out in the Schedule thereto. It must be signed by both parents and witnessed.

Agreement to be recorded in the prescribed manner (s 4(2)(*b*))—Parental Responsibility Agreement Regulations 1991, reg 3 prescribes the manner in which such agreements must be recorded.

Application to terminate parental responsibility order or agreement (s 4(3))—Anyone with parental responsibility may apply as of right. A child who wishes to apply must first seek leave (in accordance with FPR 1991, r 4.3 where the application is to be made to a county court or to the High Court or under Family Proceedings Courts (Children Act 1989) Rules 1991, r 3 where the application is to a magistrates' court).

Section 1(1) applies when the court is considering whether to terminate parental responsibility (*Re P (Terminating Parental Responsibility)* [1995] 1 FLR 1048, FD). Section 12(4) prevents the court bringing to an end a parental responsibility order made as a consequence of s 12(1) (see **Automatic parental responsibility order** above) at any time while the residence order to which it is linked remains in force.

Leave under s 4(3)(b) not to be given unless child of sufficient understanding (s 4(4))—Although there are no reported authorities considering the question of the child's understanding in the context of an application for leave to seek the discharge of a parental responsibility order, assistance may be gained from authorities in relation to the child's understanding in other contexts within CA 1989. These are gathered together in the annotation **"able ... to give such instructions on his own behalf"** under FPR 1991, r 4.12. The understanding of the child is the factor to which the court's attention is specifically directed, but it is unlikely to be the only relevant factor. Although the checklist of factors in s 1(3) does not apply specifically (see s 1(4)), it indicates the sort of matters that the court might want to consider in an appropriate case. By analogy with leave and other similar applications under other provisions of the Act and rules, the court will no doubt take into account the likelihood of success of the proposed application (see further under s 10). Whether the welfare of the child is paramount on the leave application seems to be a moot point and one which has not yet been considered in the context of s 4(3). See further under **Application for leave by child** under s 10.

Procedure where leave is given—If leave is given, the application proceeds in the normal way save that there is no need for an application form to be filed because the court will already have received a draft with the appropriate number of copies as part of the leave application (FPR 1991, r 4.3(3); FPC(CA 1989)R 1991, r 3(3)).

Family proceedings—Any application under this section is classified as "family proceedings" (s 8(3), (4)).

5 Appointment of guardians

(1) Where an application with respect to a child is made to the court by any individual, the court may by order appoint that individual to be the child's guardian if –

(*a*) the child has no parent with parental responsibility for him; or
(*b*) a residence order has been made with respect to the child in favour of a parent or guardian of his who has died while the order was in force.

(2) The power conferred by subsection (1) may also be exercised in any family proceedings if the court considers that the order should be made even though no application has been made for it.

(3) A parent who has parental responsibility for his child may appoint another individual to be the child's guardian in the event of his death.

(4) A guardian of a child may appoint another individual to take his place as the child's guardian in the event of his death.

(5) An appointment under subsection (3) or (4) shall not have effect unless it is made in writing, is dated and is signed by the person making the appointment or –

(*a*) in the case of an appointment made by a will which is not signed by the testator, is signed at the direction of the testator in accordance with the requirements of section 9 of the Wills Act 1837; or
(*b*) in any other case, is signed at the direction of the person making the appointment, in his presence and in the presence of two witnesses who each attest the signature.

(6) A person appointed as a child's guardian under this section shall have parental responsibility for the child concerned.

(7) Where –

(*a*) on the death of any person making an appointment under subsection (3) or (4), the child concerned has no parent with parental responsibility for him; or
(*b*) immediately before the death of any person making such an appointment, a residence order in his favour was in force with respect to the child,

the appointment shall take effect on the death of that person.

(8) Where, on the death of any person making an appointment under subsection (3) or (4) –

(*a*) the child concerned has a parent with parental responsibility for him; and
(*b*) subsection (7)(*b*) does not apply,

the appointment shall take effect when the child no longer has a parent who has parental responsibility for him.

(9) Subsections (1) and (7) do not apply if the residence order referred to in paragraph (*b*) of those subsections was also made in favour of a surviving parent of the child.

(10) Nothing in this section shall be taken to prevent an appointment under subsection (3) or (4) being made by two or more persons acting jointly.

(11) Subject to any provision made by rules of court, no court shall exercise the High Court's inherent jurisdiction to appoint a guardian of the estate of any child.

(12) Where the rules of court are made under subsection (11) they may prescribe the circumstances in which, and conditions subject to which, an appointment of such a guardian may be made.

(13) A guardian of a child may only be appointed in accordance with the provisions of this section.

Defined terms—"child": s 105(1); "family proceedings": s 8(3); "parental responsibility": s 3; "residence order": s 8(1).

Scope of provision—A guardian appointed under this section will generally take over parental responsibility for the child after the death of a parent and must, of course, be distinguished from a guardian ad litem appointed for the purposes of legal proceedings.

Application by any individual (s 5(1))—Application must be made by the person who wishes to be appointed as guardian. "Individual" is not defined in the Act; it clearly does not include a company or a local authority, or even an "artificial individual" within the local authority such as the director of social services (*Re SH (Care Order: Orphan)* [1995] 1 FLR 746, FD). However, there is nothing to prevent a number of individuals each launching separate applications and this could lead to the appointment of a couple, for example, an aunt and uncle. Although there does not seem to be any bar on an application by a minor, good sense suggests that the court would be unlikely to grant an application by one child to be appointed to act as guardian for another.

"power ... may also be exercised in any family proceedings" (s 5(2))—If it thinks fit, the court may, in any family proceedings, make an order appointing a guardian of its own motion without any formal application having been filed. No doubt such an order will most frequently be prompted at the suggestion of a party to the proceedings or of an interested friend or relative who has been allowed to address the court, or even of the child himself, but there is nothing to prevent the court itself taking the lead in appropriate circumstances.

Date from which the appointment is effective—There may be a delay between a guardian being named (eg in a will or in a court order) and the time when he actually acquires parental responsibility for the child concerned. Although the Act makes no specific provision, it is apparent that the guardian is not regarded as having been appointed in accordance with the provisions of this section until the later stage.

Family proceedings—Any application under this section is classified as "family proceedings" (s 8(3), (4)).

6 Guardians: revocation and disclaimer

(1) An appointment under section 5(3) or (4) revokes an earlier such appointment (including one made in an unrevoked will or codicil) made by the same person in respect of the same child, unless it is clear (whether as the result of an express provision in the later appointment or by any necessary implication) that the purpose of the later appointment is to appoint an additional guardian.

(2) An appointment under section 5(3) or (4) (including one made in an unrevoked will or codicil) is revoked if the person who made the appointment revokes it by a written and dated instrument which is signed –

(*a*) by him; or

(*b*) at his direction, in his presence and in the presence of two witnesses who each attest the signature.

(3) An appointment under section 5(3) or (4) (other than one made in a will or codicil) is revoked if, with the intention of revoking the appointment, the person who made it –

(*a*) destroys the instrument by which it was made; or

(*b*) has some other person destroy that instrument in his presence.

(3A) An appointment under section 5(3) or (4) (including one made in an unrevoked will or codicil) is revoked if the person appointed is the spouse of the person who made the appointment and either –

(*a*) a decree of a court of civil jurisdiction in England and Wales dissolves or annuls the marriage, or

(*b*) the marriage is dissolved or annulled and the divorce or annulment is entitled to recognition in England and Wales by virtue of Part II of the Family Law Act 1986,

unless a contrary intention appears by the appointment.

(4) For the avoidance of doubt, an appointment under section 5(3) or (4) made in a will or codicil is revoked if the will or codicil is revoked.

(5) A person who is appointed as a guardian under section 5(3) or (4) may disclaim his appointment by an instrument in writing signed by him and made within a reasonable time of his first knowing that the appointment has taken effect.

(6) Where regulations are made by the Lord Chancellor prescribing the manner in which such disclaimers must be recorded, no such disclaimer shall have effect unless it is recorded in the prescribed manner.

(7) Any appointment of a guardian under section 5 may be brought to an end at any time by order of the court –

(*a*) on the application of any person who has parental responsibility for the child;

(*b*) on the application of the child concerned, with leave of the court; or

(*c*) in any family proceedings, if the court considers that it should be brought to an end even though no application has been made.

Amendments—Law Reform (Succession) Act 1995, s 4.

Defined terms—"child": s 105(1); "family proceedings": s 8(3); "parental responsibility": s 3.

Scope of provision—This section deals with the ways in which the appointment of a guardian may be brought to an end (ie by revocation, disclaimer or court order). It has now been extended to provide for the revocation of appointment of a guardian, in the absence of any express contrary intention, in the case of an appointment of a former spouse as guardian in the will of a testator dying after 1 January 1996 by dissolution or annulment of the marriage. In practical terms, this will affect appointments made by a testator in favour of his or her former spouse in respect of a child who is not the child of the former spouse. Where the child is the child of both parties, the revocation will not have any practical effect since the former spouse will continue to have parental responsibility for the child.

"Where regulations are made" (s 6(6))—No such regulations have yet been made.

"on the application of any person who has parental responsibility for the child" (s 6(7)(*a*))—As the guardian himself will have acquired parental responsibility for the child under s 5(6), he could apply for an order terminating his own appointment if the circumstances made it inappropriate for him to disclaim under s 6(5).

"on the application of the child concerned, with leave" (s 6(7)(*b*))—Leave must be sought in accordance with FPR 1991, r 4.3, where the application is to a county court or to the High Court or in accordance with Family Proceedings Courts (Children Act 1989) Rules 1991, r 3, where it is to a magistrates' court. As to the circumstances in which leave should be given, see **Leave under s 4(3)(b) not to be given unless child of sufficient understanding** under s 4. As is the case with s 4, the checklist of factors in s 1(3) does not apply specifically but gives examples of factors that may be relevant. The position is also likely to be the same under s 4 and s 6 with regard to the relevance of the chances of success of the proposed application, and there is similar uncertainty with regard to the applicability of s 1(1). One difference between the two provisions is that the court is not, under s 6(7), expressly directed to consider whether the child is of sufficient understanding to make the proposed application, but it will no doubt bear this factor in mind.

Once leave has been given, the application proceeds in the normal way save that there is no 7need for an application form to be filed because the court will already have received a draft with the appropriate number of copies as part of the leave application (FPR 1991, r 4.3(3); FPC(CA 1989)R 1991, r 3(3)).

"in any family proceedings ... even though no application has been made" (s 6(7)(*c*))—If it thinks fit, the court may, in any family proceedings, make an order terminating the appointment of a guardian even though no formal application has been filed. No doubt such an order will most frequently be prompted at the suggestion of a party to the proceedings or of an interested friend or relative who has been allowed to address the court, or even of the child himself, but there is nothing to prevent the court itself taking the lead in appropriate circumstances. Section 6(7)(*c*) could be used by an individual who seeks to replace an existing guardian but who does not have parental responsibility and therefore cannot apply directly for the termination of the existing guardian's appointment. Where such an individual launches an application under s 5(1) for his own appointment (which application is classified as family proceedings), he could then invite the court in the course of that application not only to appoint him as guardian for the child but also to terminate the appointment of the existing guardian.

7 Welfare reports

(1) A court considering any question with respect to a child under this Act may –

- (*a*) ask an officer of the Service; or
- (*b*) ask a local authority to arrange for –
  - (i) an officer of the authority; or
  - (ii) such other person (other than an officer of the Service) as the authority considers appropriate,

to report to the court on such matters relating to the welfare of that child as are required to be dealt with in the report.

(2) The Lord Chancellor may make regulations specifying matters which, unless the court orders otherwise, must be dealt with in any report under this section.

(3) The report may be made in writing, or orally, as the court requires.

(4) Regardless of any enactment or rule of law which would otherwise prevent it from doing so, the court may take account of –

- (*a*) any statement contained in the report; and
- (*b*) any evidence given in respect of the matters referred to in the report,

in so far as the statement or evidence is, in the opinion of the court, relevant to the question which it is considering.

(5) It shall be the duty of the authority or officer of the Service to comply with any request for a report under this section.

Amendments—Criminal Justice and Court Services Act 2000 s 74, Sch 7, para 88.

Defined terms—"child", "local authority": s 105(1); "officer of the Service": Criminal Justice and Court Services Act 2000, s 11(3).

Children and Family Court Advisory and Support Service (CAFCASS)—The Criminal Justice and Court Services Act 2000 has now introduced the Children and Family Court Advisory and Support Service (CAFCASS). CAFCASS combines the family court welfare function provided by the Guardian ad litem and Reporting Officer Service, the Family Court Welfare Service and the Children's Branch of the Official Solicitor's Office within one new unified service under the responsibility of the Lord Chancellor. The central functions of CAFCASS are (i) to safeguard and promote the welfare of children; (ii) to give advice to any court about any application made to it in such proceedings; (iii) to make provision for children to be represented in such proceedings; and (iv) to provide information, advice and other support for children and their families.

References to guardians ad litem, reporting officers and probation officers are subsumed within the Criminal Justice and Court Services Act 2000 as "officers of the service". For details of the new terminology see annotations to CJCSA 2000, s 11.

The FPR 1991 and the FPC(CA 1989)R 1991 are amended by the Family Proceedings (Amendment) Rules 2001 and the Family Proceedings Courts (Children Act 1989) (Amendment) Rules 2001 respectively to set out the principal functions of officers of the service in relation to court proceedings. The rule changes include section 7 reporting undertaken by officers of CAFCASS. The new rules also cover certain children cases currently handled by the Official Solicitor. In future, these will be dealt with by specialist caseworkers in CAFCASS. The rule changes do not generally extend to cover local authority officers reporting under section 7. However, the one exception is that the power of courts to request reports under CA 1989, s 7(1)(*b*) from the local authority is unaffected by the CAFCASS provisions and officers so instructed will still be referred to as "welfare officers".

CAFCASS Practice Note—General guidance in relation to the appointment of a children's guardian is to be found in *Practice Note of March 2001 (Officers of CAFCASS Legal Services and Special Casework: Appointment in Family Proceedings)*, which came into force on 1 April 2001 and supersedes *Practice Note (Official Solicitor: Appointment in Family Proceedings)* (4 December 1998) [1999] 1 FLR 310, issued by the Official Solicitor in relation to the representation of children in family proceedings. It is issued in conjunction with *Practice Note of 2 April 2001 (Official Solicitor: Appointment in Family Proceedings)* (both are set out in Part IV of this work). CAFCASS Legal do not have sufficient resources to deal with the representation of children in every private case in which a judge thinks that this is necessary, as the sheer number of such cases is so high. Increasingly, CAFCASS Legal will concentrate on providing its service in High Court cases and certain unusual county court cases. Less complex county court cases will be dealt with in a different way. With the approval of the President of the Family Division, a letter dated 24 October 2003 has now been circulated by CAFCASS Legal to all Family Division judges and designated circuit judges stipulating that, where the court requires the appointment of a CAFCASS officer as guardian ad litem, all cases should first be referred to CAFCASS Legal in accordance with the *Practice Note* (above) whereupon CAFCASS Legal will make a decision as to whether or not to accept the appointment in any particular case. If CAFCASS Legal decline to provide a guardian (which will happen in most county court cases), either: (i) CAFCASS Legal will liaise with the local CAFCASS office and ensure that a local CAFCASS officer is made available to act as guardian ad litem, with legal representation being provided by a solicitor from the Law Society Children Panel or by CAFCASS Legal; or (ii) the court may decide to appoint some other proper person as guardian ad litem under FPR 1991, r 9.5, such as a practitioner from the National Youth Advocacy Service. Work is proceeding with a view to re-issuing the CAFCASS Legal *Practice Note* (above) later this year in order to clarify the matter.

National Standards for probation service family court welfare work—National standards on family court welfare work have been issued by the Home Office setting out basic standards of good practice which are expected of the family court welfare service (now the Children and Family Court Advisory and Support Service (CAFCASS)). Copies can be obtained from the Family Court Welfare Section, Probation Service Division, Home Office, 50 Queen Anne's Gate, London SW1H 9AT.

Best practice when ordering a children and family reporter's report—Reference should be made to the *Best Practice Note of January 1995* (set out in Part IV of this work) concerning best practice for the judiciary and family proceedings courts and the specimen form for a "welfare report referral" whenever consideration is being given to ordering a welfare report.

Rules as to children and family reporter's duties—FPR 1991, rr 4.11 and 4.11B and Family Proceedings Courts (Children Act 1989) Rules 1991, rr 11 and 11B make provision for the

PART II

children and family reporter's duties as to attending a hearing where his report is to be considered and as to the time and manner of filing the report.

"A court considering any question with respect to a child under this Act" (s 7(1))—The court's power is a very wide one and can be used not only in the traditional way in residence/contact proceedings under s 8 but also, for example, in connection with parental responsibility applications, applications for specific issue orders, applications by children for leave to commence proceedings under the Act, and emergency protection order applications.

Where children's guardian acting—Although there is power both at first instance (CA 1989, s 7) and on appeal to the High Court from the magistrates' court (CA 1989, ss 7 and 94(5)) to appoint a children and family reporter in public law proceedings, only in exceptional circumstances will a welfare report be sought when a children's guardian is already involved (*Re S (A Minor) (Guardian ad litem/Welfare Officer)* [1993] 1 FLR 110). The roles of the children and family reporter and the children's guardian are not identical, in that a children's guardian has an extra duty to represent the child in court and to instruct legal representation for him if necessary, but they are similar in many respects. Therefore, it will usually be a duplication of effort and expense to appoint both in the same proceedings. The general principle in *Re S* was confirmed by the Court of Appeal in *L v L (Minors) (Separate Representation)* [1994] 1 FLR 156 (s 8 case), but the court expressed the hope that the welfare officer (children and family reporter) who had already begun investigations would report despite the subsequent appointment of a guardian ad litem (children's guardian) in that particular difficult case.

Conciliation as an alternative—*Registrar's Direction of 28 July 1986*, as updated by *Practice Direction of 18 October 1991*, provides that, in the principal registry, residence and contact applications under CA 1989, s 8 must be referred for conciliation, and prohibited steps and specific issue order applications can be referred if the applicant so requests. On the conciliation appointment, the district judge is attended by a children and family reporter, and it is essential that both parties and their legal advisers attend. There is an opportunity for the parties to attempt to reach agreement with the assistance of the children and family reporter. If they are able to do so, the district judge will make the appropriate orders; if not, he will give directions for hearing. That district judge and children and family reporter then take no further part in that application. Outside the principal registry, before ordering an inquiry and report by a children and family reporter, a judge or district judge should, where local conciliation facilities exist, consider whether the case is suitable for conciliation; if so, a direction should be given to that effect. If conciliation fails, any report which is ordered must be by a children and family reporter who did not act as a conciliator (see also *Re H (Conciliation: Welfare Reports)* [1986] 1 FLR 476).

When a children and family reporter is reporting as opposed to acting as conciliator, he must investigate and report on the situation, but it is not his role to attempt conciliation although he may encourage the parties to settle their differences if the likelihood of a settlement arises during the course of his enquiries. For an example of a case where it would have been appropriate for the magistrates to adjourn to allow a children and family reporter to mediate between the parents on a parental responsibility application and then report back rather than making no order on the application, see *S v R (Parental Responsibility)* [1993] 1 FCR 331.

Statements made by parties in conciliation meetings are not admissible in evidence, except where the statement clearly indicates that the maker has in the past caused, or is likely in the future to cause, serious harm to the well-being of a child. Even in such a case, the judge has a discretion whether to admit the evidence and should do so only if the public interest in protecting the child outweighs the public interest in the confidentiality of attempted conciliation (*Re D (Minors) (Conciliation: Privilege)* [1993] 1 FLR 932, CA; see also *Practice Direction of 18 October 1991*).

Officer of the Service—Historically, children and family reporters have usually been officers of the Service; however, the court has power to invite a report from the local authority. In this context, the old terminology "welfare officer" remains, since the welfare officer is appointed to report under CA 1989, s 7(1)(*b*) (see under **Children and Family Court Advisory and Support Service (CAFCASS)** (above) and under FPR 1991, r 4.13(1)). It might choose to do so where, for example, the local authority has already become involved with the child following an allegation of abuse by one parent against the other or because of the family's housing difficulties, although there may be situations where, precisely because the local authority has already been involved, it may be open to allegations of bias by one of the parties and, if there is to be only one report, an officer of the Service would be a better choice. The same may also apply where, although the local authority is not at present a party to the proceedings, there is a possibility that it may itself wish to apply for an order at some future date. *Re W (Welfare Reports)* [1995] 2 FLR 142, CA, highlights the different expertise that can be expected from the two classes of reporter. Welfare officers are accustomed to the court process, to interviewing the child and relevant adults, to attending court, to making recommendations orally or in writing and to submitting to questioning by the parties. Social workers are familiar with the reporting routine in the context of preparing reports for use at case conferences and for placing on file for the assistance of other social workers etc. Their knowledge of the court process may be much more limited, and their role will frequently be confined to fact-finding reports and will not involve the making of any recommendations at all.

Despite the fact that paras (*a*) and (*b*) of s 7(1) are expressed as alternatives, it appears that it can be right to order a report from the children and family reporter as well as a report from a social worker (see *Re W (Welfare Reports)* (above) and *Re A and B (Minors) (No 2)* [1995] 1 FLR 351). In *Re A and B*, Wall J described the s 7 report as the principal weapon in the court's armoury in ensuring co-ordination of private law proceedings with statutory local authority child abuse investigations. He envisaged that the first step in a case where there are parallel private law proceedings and local authority investigations would be for the court to require the local authority to provide a report under s 7 on the nature, progress and outcome of the investigation. Although neither s 7 nor the rules refer to a timescale for this report, the court must have power to impose a deadline for it. The report is likely to be in the form of a statement by the social worker allocated to the case, giving details of the local authority's involvement but, in an urgent case, it could be simply a letter from the local authority's legal department setting out the salient facts. Once the report is received, the court will consider the conduct of the case further in the light of it at a directions hearing. The local authority will be expected to make the social worker who writes the s 7 report available to give evidence (which will be at the invitation of the court rather than as a witness for any party) and to be cross-examined at the substantive hearing or at any interim hearing where oral evidence is required and to agree to discovery of relevant documentation underlying the report (as to this, see also *W v Wakefield City Council* [1995] 1 FLR 170). Wall J clearly contemplates that, having received the local authority's report, the court might direct that a further report be prepared, this time by a children and family reporter.

In deciding whether to direct a local authority report under s 7, the alternative of s 37 must, of course, be kept in mind. This entitles the court to direct the local authority to investigate the child's circumstances, provided that it appears that it may be appropriate for a care or supervision order to be made in respect of him. However, Wall J points out in *Re A and B (Minors) (No 2)* (above) that, in most cases, s 37 does not apply and that, in any event, it does not appear appropriate in circumstances where the court is requesting the local authority to provide information about an investigation that has already been undertaken rather than requiring it to embark on an investigation.

For further guidance as to whether a children and family reporter or a local authority should be used, see **Best practice guidance on s 37(1) directions** under CA 1989, s 37, which also provides guidance on the communication to a local authority of a s 7(1) referral and draws attention to the need to fix a new hearing at the time of referral.

"such other person ... as the authority considers appropriate" (s 7(1)(*b*)(ii))—It is not appropriate to use s 7(1)(*b*)(ii) to make an order requiring the local authority to appoint an officer to obtain a report from a child psychiatrist (*Re K (Contact: Psychiatric Report)* [1995] 2 FLR 432, CA). Section 7(1)(*b*)(ii) confers on the local authority discretion as to the other person appointed, and the court has no power to control that appointment or to require the local authority to pay for expert advice. In specified proceedings, a psychiatric report can be obtained independently through a s 41 children's guardian but there can be no such guardian appointed in private law proceedings. The Court of Appeal in *Re K* (which concerned an 8-year-old child who was refusing to have contact with her father) referred to the possibility in certain cases of appointing a solicitor for the child or involving the Official Solicitor, but dismissed these alternatives as impractical there (potential legal aid problems in appointment of solicitor for child, and Official Solicitor's department already over-stretched so that he will only become involved in exceptional cases – see *Practice Note of 2 April 2001 (Official Solicitor: Appointment in Family Proceedings)*. Two alternative methods by which independent psychiatric assistance could be obtained were, however, suggested:

(*a*) by inviting the parties to instruct a psychiatrist jointly; or
(*b*) by invoking RSC Ord 40.

RSC Ord 40 permits the court, on the application of any party, to instruct an independent expert (a "court expert") to report on any question of fact or opinion before the court. However, the provision must be used sparingly and only in really dire circumstances. Guidance can be obtained from *Re K* as to the appropriate form of an order under Ord 40 (an independent child psychiatrist, to be agreed between the parties or, in default of their agreement, to be nominated by the Official Solicitor, to report as court expert pursuant to Ord 40, his or her costs to be at the discretion of the judge).

It appears that, for the time being, the RSC will continue to apply in family cases despite the advent of the Civil Proceedings Rules which, by virtue of CPR 1998, r 2.1, do not apply to family proceedings unless specifically applied by another enactment. There is no such enactment at present.

Delay occasioned by obtaining a welfare report—Obtaining a welfare report will normally take some weeks or months and will not infrequently cause delay in achieving a final resolution of the issues between the parties. In deciding whether to order a report, the court will therefore have to have in mind s 1(2) (the delay principle) and balance any prejudice that there is likely to be to the child through delay against the desirability of obtaining a report, the child's welfare being the paramount consideration. For a case in which it was held to be right for a hearing at least to be commenced without a welfare report, see *Re H (Minors) (Welfare Reports)* [1990] 2 FLR 172, CA. For the position where delay may be occasioned through the need to adjourn proceedings for the children and family reporter to attend to give oral evidence, see **Court differing with recommendations in welfare report** below.

"such matters relating to the welfare of that child as are required" (s 7(1))—Although there is nothing to prevent the court issuing a general request for a report on the child's welfare (in which case, the children and family reporter must simply comply with any regulations in force under s 7(2) and be guided by the National Standards for probation service family court welfare work), it will usually be more efficient for it to indicate which matters should be addressed (see *Practice Direction of 16 July 1981*). This could be a broad request, for example to produce a report relevant to the issue of residence, or a very specific request, for example to visit premises where the child is living to investigate whether or not they present a health risk or to interview the child's teacher with a view to ascertaining his school attendance record and progress. If the children and family reporter becomes concerned about other matters in the course of preparing his report, it would, of course, be entirely proper for him to bring these (and any other relevant factors) to the attention of the court (*Practice Direction of 16 July 1981*). There are circulars governing the obtaining of details of previous convictions of parties, spouses etc from the police: Home Office Circulars 88/1982, 105/1982, 47/1993. As to the desirability of the court knowing of previous convictions of a party, see *Re R (Minors) (Custody)* [1986] 1 FLR 6.

"regulations specifying matters which ... must be dealt with" (s 7(2))—No regulations have yet been made in this respect. The reporter must therefore pay careful attention to any specific directions given by the commissioning court about the scope of the report and derive guidance from authorities and from the National Standards for probation service family court welfare work (see note above). Subject to any limitations expressly imposed by the court it will generally be appropriate to visit the child's home (and, where a change of accommodation is proposed, any proposed new home), to interview the protagonists (mother, father and grandparents if closely involved), local authority social workers with knowledge of the family and anyone else whose view might be of assistance (for example, playgroup leader, teacher or health visitor) and to meet the child (alone and/or in company with parents or carers as appropriate to the application before the court) so as to ascertain, where possible, his wishes and feelings. Cases on the content of welfare reports and the duties of the children and family reporter include *Re W (A Minor) (Custody)* (1983) FLR 492; *Scott v Scott* [1986] 2 FLR 320; *Re R (A Minor) (Court Welfare Report)* [1993] Fam Law 722 (as to the duty to see all relevant parties and, wherever possible, the child with each of the protagonists); *Re P (Welfare Officer: Duty)* [1996] Fam Law 664, FD (welfare report manifestly inadequate where officer had seen children only once at a meeting involving all parties at her office, and report contained no assessment of relationships between children and parents); and *Re T* [1997] 2 FCR 55 (in a stark case where the fundamental issue was whether the father had sexually abused his son, it was not for the children and family reporter to assess the credibility of the adults and he would have been wise to step back from the investigation and predetermination of what was the fundamental issue for the judge).

Duty of local authority or officer of the Service to comply (s 7(5))—In theory, there is no room for argument once the court has made its request for a report; the officer of the Service or local authority chosen has a duty to report as requested. The time for representations about who should be responsible for the report and what it is feasible for it to cover is therefore before the report is commissioned. The problem is that this depends upon a representative of CAFCASS or the local authority being on hand at the relevant time which will not always be the case. In the event that the court's request does cause difficulties, contact should be made with the court explaining the nature of the obstacle and asking for directions to be given under FPR 1991, r 4.14 or Family Proceedings Courts (Children Act 1989) Rules 1991, r 14. If the difficulty is an inability to meet the time-limits set down by the court or, in default of any time-limit set by the court, by the rules (see FPR 1991, r 4.13 and FPC(CA 1989)R 1991, r 13), the court will have to balance the prejudice that there is likely to be to the welfare of the child (see s 1(2)) against the desirability of obtaining a report, the child's welfare being the paramount consideration (*Re H (Minors) (Welfare Reports)* [1990] 2 FLR 172). The power to vary time-limits derives from r 4.14(2)(*a*)/r 14(2)(*a*) where the time-limit is set by the court and r 4.14(2)(*b*)/r 14(2)(*b*) where it is set by the rules. It is not good practice for a case be listed only once the court welfare report is actually available. Normally, the appropriate course is to find out from CAFCASS how long is required for the report and to fix a date in the light of that information so that the report will be available for the fixed hearing (*B v B (Minors) (Interviews and Listing Arrangements)* [1994] 2 FLR 489, CA, *Re A and B (Minors) (No 2)* [1995] 1 FLR 351). In a case which is clearly going to be contested, it is desirable that the direction for a welfare report should, as was pointed out in *Re A and B (Minors) (No 2)*, be given in the context of overall directions for the filing of evidence and a fixed date for final determination, because, whilst it is often useful for the children and family reporter to consider the evidence in the case in the course of his enquiries, there are some cases where it is preferable for him to investigate without the parties having stated their cases in writing, in view of the polarisation and entrenchment that that can engender.

Statements and evidence otherwise inadmissible (s 7(4))—The welfare report and the children and family reporter's evidence will often contain reports of conversations that he has had with third parties (eg relatives, neighbours and teachers) and with the child, and may also contain other statements traditionally viewed as inadmissible. Section 7(4) is a very broad provision enabling the court to disregard all rules of evidence and to take into account any statement or evidence which is relevant to the question in issue. Plainly certain statements or evidence will be more influential than others and the court must decide what weight is appropriate to attach to each (*R v B County Council ex parte P* [1991] 1 FLR 470, [1991] 1 WLR 221; see also the Children (Admissibility of Hearsay Evidence) Order 1993). Where the children and family reporter includes hearsay in his report, he should identify it as such, give the source of it and give any reasons he has for agreeing with any opinions he passes on (*Thompson v Thompson* [1986] Fam 38, [1986] 1 FLR 212). Although it is always difficult for a party to deal with hearsay evidence that is prejudicial to him, this practice will at least alert the court to the deficiencies of the evidence and enable the party who feels himself prejudiced to interview the original author of the statement or opinion with a view to calling him to give evidence if he has been inaccurately reported. It appears that, in accordance with s 7(4)(*b*), once a particular matter has found its way into the welfare report, the court may entertain any relevant evidence with regard to it from any witness (not just the parties and the children and family reporter) with no restrictions as to hearsay.

Guarantees of confidentiality not appropriate—A children and family reporter cannot guarantee confidentiality to a person who makes allegations to him whilst he is investigating the circumstances of the case. It is for the judge to decide whether or not evidence must be disclosed to the parties (*Re G (Minors) (Welfare Report: Disclosure)* [1993] 2 FLR 293). The principles applicable are set out in **Submission of evidence** under FPR 1991, r 4.14.

Court differing with recommendation in welfare report—The final decision as to any question in issue rests with the court, but the welfare report and any recommendations that the children and family reporter makes must be taken into account (*Re P (Custody of Children: Split Custody Order)* [1991] 1 FLR 337). If the court decides not to follow the recommendation of the children and family reporter, it should give its reasons (*Re J (Children) (Residence: Expert Evidence)* [2001] 2 FCR 44). Clearly, it will usually be desirable to set out *in terms* the reasons for differing from the children and family reporter's recommendations, but *Re V (Residence: Review)* [1995] 2 FLR 1010, CA, shows that failure to do so will not necessarily vitiate the decision, provided that the reasons for the decision were sound and either explained or constituted a sound basis for dissenting from the children and family reporter. In *Re CB (Access: Attendance of Court Welfare Officer)* [1995] 1 FLR 622, CA (a case concerning the risk of sexual abuse of a child by a Sch 1 offender), it was said to be a defective exercise of discretion for a judge to reject clear-cut recommendations and warnings in a children and family reporter's report without availing himself of the opportunity of receiving further assistance from the officer by way of oral evidence. The court suggested that where, as in *Re CB*, the children and family reporter is not available in person for some reason, it is open to the judge to adjourn the case and demand his or her presence. He can then put to the children and family reporter the reasons why he, the judge, does not agree with him and obtain from the officer an explanation of the officer's views. However, in *Re C (Section 8 Order: Court Welfare Officer)* [1995] 1 FLR 617, the Court of Appeal pointed out that *Re CB* is not a hard and fast rule of law. Whether to adjourn a case so that the children and family reporter can attend is a matter for the judge's discretion and he must carry out the balancing act which is required by the paramount consideration of the child's welfare and the provisions as to delay in s 1(2). Many factors will have to be taken into account, including how much further assistance the children and family reporter can give, what his attendance is likely to change and the extent to which it would be safe and proper to depart from any recommendations made. Whereas in *Re CB*, the children and family reporter had made clear recommendations and warnings of the most serious kind and it was not proper to reject these in his absence, in *Re C* the report was in reality an account of the interviews that the children and family reporter had had with both parents and with the child and reached conclusions which set out the arguments and considerations very fairly and did not make firm recommendations in any particular directions, although the tenor of the considerations was in favour of the status quo (residence with the mother). In these circumstances, the judge had been entitled to exercise his discretion by refusing the father's application for an adjournment for the children and family reporter to attend. See also *Re L (Residence: Justices' Reasons)* [1995] 2 FLR 445, FD (where welfare report recommended preserving the status quo, but in essence pronounced either home adequate and neither party requested that the children and family reporter give evidence, magistrates could not be criticised for failing to take the initiative and adjourn to hear from her orally before coming to a different conclusion; decision, however, fatally flawed for other reasons, including failure to state with sufficiency why they differed from the children and family reporter) and *Re A (Children: 1959 UN Declaration)* [1998] 1 FLR 354, CA (where the children and family reporter had made a particularly important contribution and the judge had erred in rejecting her recommendation without testing it with her when she gave oral evidence and without giving reasons).

Position of children and family reporter in court—See under CJCSA 2000, s 16.

Independent welfare reports—Although such reports are unusual and, generally speaking, not particularly popular with the courts, independent welfare reports may be admissible. Detailed guidance as to such reports was issued (prior to the Act) in *Practice Direction of 24 March 1983*, which applied in divorce county courts and the Family Division and was influential in magistrates' courts (see *R v Sunderland Juvenile Court ex parte G* [1988] 2 FLR 40, [1988] 1 WLR 398). The principles there set out remain helpful; see also *Re P (A Minor) (Independent Welfare Officer)* [1989] 2 FLR 43; *Re C (A Minor) (Wardship Proceedings)* [1984] FLR 419 and *Re C (Wardship: Independent Social Worker)* [1985] FLR 56. Particular problems were encountered with independent social work reports in *Re S (Expert Evidence)* [1998] Fam Law 594, CA where the court relied upon them, not knowing of certain material matters concerning the independent social worker.

PART II
ORDERS WITH RESPECT TO CHILDREN IN FAMILY PROCEEDINGS

General

8 Residence, contact and other orders with respect to children

(1) In this Act –

"a contact order" means an order requiring the person with whom a child lives, or is to live, to allow the child to visit or stay with the person named in the order, or for that person and the child otherwise to have contact with each other;

"a prohibited steps order" means an order that no step which could be taken by a parent in meeting his parental responsibility for a child, and which is of a kind specified in the order, shall be taken by any person without the consent of the court;

"a residence order" means an order settling the arrangements to be made as to the person with whom a child is to live; and

"a specific issue order" means an order giving directions for the purpose of determining a specific question which has arisen, or which may arise, in connection with any aspect of parental responsibility for a child.

(2) In this Act "a section 8 order" means any of the orders mentioned in subsection (1) and any order varying or discharging such an order.

(3) For the purposes of this Act "family proceedings" means any proceedings –

(*a*) under the inherent jurisdiction of the High Court in relation to children; and

(*b*) under the enactments mentioned in subsection (4),

but does not include proceedings on an application for leave under section 100(3).

(4) The enactments are –

(*a*) Parts I, II and IV of this Act;
(*b*) the Matrimonial Causes Act 1973;
(*c*) (*repealed*)
(*d*) the Adoption Act 1976;
(*e*) the Domestic Proceedings and Magistrates' Courts Act 1978;
(*f*) (*repealed*)
(*g*) Part III of the Matrimonial and Family Proceedings Act 1984;
(*h*) the Family Law Act 1996.
(*i*) sections 11 and 12 of the Crime and Disorder Act 1998.

Amendments—Family Law Act 1996, s 66(1), (3), Sch 8, para 60(1), Sch 10; Crime and Disorder Act 1998, s 119, Sch 8, para 68.

Defined terms—"child": s 105(1); "parental responsibility": s 3.

Scope of provision—The Act seeks to set up a flexible system which enables the court to have as wide a choice of orders as possible so that any question which arises with regard to the welfare of a child can be resolved, whatever the nature of the proceedings before the court. The wide definition of "family proceedings" which is contained in this section facilitates this.

Jurisdiction—See Family Law Act 1986, Part I.

Residence of adult child—Where the local authority felt that an adult child of 17 with a mental age of between 5 and 8 years was at risk of significant harm if she lived at home with her mother, but was too old to be made the subject of a care order, the court held that it had inherent declaratory jurisdiction to keep the "child" in local authority accommodation and to restrict and supervise the child's contact with her family (*Re F (Adult: Court's Jurisdiction)* [2000] 2 FLR 512). The doctrine of necessity could be invoked in such circumstances and the inherent jurisdiction was not excluded by the statutory framework.

Contact with adult child—There is no presumption of a right to contact between a parent and an adult child. Where the adult child is under a disability and is not in a position to consent to contact, the question is whether it is in the adult child's best interests to have contact with her parents (*Re D-R (Adult: Contact)* [1999] 1 FLR 1161). The jurisdictional basis for such an application is unclear, but would not appear to fall within s 8, where the definition of "child" for the purposes of a contact application refers to a child under the age of 18 (see s 105(1)); furthermore, the court is required by CA 1989, s 9(6) not to make any s 8 order which is to have effect for a period that will end after the child has reached the age of 16, unless the circumstances of the case are exceptional.

Contact orders cannot be made in absence of a residence order—Contact orders cannot be made without first determining with whom a child lives, since it is the person who has a residence order in favour of a child who allows the child to stay with the person who has a contact order in their favour (*Re B (A Child)* (2001) LTL 22 November, Extempore (unreported elsewhere) Document No C9900264). An order that shares contact between one parent and the other on a week-by-week basis is a creature unknown in law (*Re B* (above)).

Protocol for referrals of families by judges and magistrates to Child Contact Centres—The National Association of Child Contact Centres (NACC) has issued a Protocol, endorsed by the President of the Family Division, for the referral of families to Child Contact Centres. It provides guidance as to which categories of cases are suitable for this service, the practical steps to be taken in order to get in touch with an appropriate centre and suggested wording for court orders requiring the attendance of parties and children at the centre. The Protocol reads as follows:

"Before making an Order for Contact (whether interim or final) which involves the use of a Child Contact Centre, please check that the matters listed below have been addressed.

Please note in particular that most Child Contact Centres do *not* offer Supervised Contact. The provision which most offer is SUPPORTED CONTACT which is described in the Manual of Guidance produced by the National Association of Child Contact Centres (NACCC) as:

– low vigilance;

– several families at a time in one or a number of rooms;

– volunteers and staff keeping a watchful eye;

– conversations not being monitored.

If you are considering making an Order for contact in a case where domestic violence is an issue, please ensure that you have addressed that issue, and in particular:

(1) that you have considered the effect on the resident parent and the children concerned of any domestic violence you have found or which is alleged and that;
(2) notwithstanding these matters you are satisfied that supported contact is appropriate. If this is *not appropriate*, is supervised contact appropriate and is it available?

Things to check

(1) That the Child Contact Centre Co-ordinator has been contacted and has confirmed:
  (*a*) The referral appears to be suitable for that particular Centre. Child Contact Centres can refuse to accept families if the circumstances appear inappropriate for the Centre.
  (*b*) The intended day and times are available at the particular Centre concerned.
  (*c*) A vacancy is available or a place on a waiting list has been allocated.
(2) That you have directed that a copy of the order is provided to the Centre by one or other of the parties within a specified time together with any other injunctive or relevant Orders on the court file.
(3) That it has been agreed who will have responsibility for completing and returning the Centre's referral form. Solicitors for both parties should agree the contents and it should be forwarded to the Child Contact Centre within 24 hours of the court hearing.
(4) If contact is to be observed at the Child Contact Centre by a family court welfare officer (CAFCASS officer) or other third party, that this is a facility offered by that Centre and that the Centre has agreed to this course of action. (many do not permit such attendance).
(5) That the parties understand whether the Centre offers supported or supervised contact and appreciate the difference.
(6) That it is agreed who is going to tell the children where and when they will see their non-resident parent.
(7) That the Order clearly defines whether or not any other family members are to be a part of the contact visit.
(8) That it has been agreed who will be responsible for informing the Centre when the place is no longer required.
(9) That a date has been set for a review of the contact and any other steps parties have been ordered or undertaken to take which are relevant to the contact issue and for further directions if necessary. Only in exceptional circumstances should use of a Centre be open-ended.

Please also note

(1) The order should be worded "Subject to the parties attendance at a pre-contact meeting (if applicable), the availability of a place and the parties abiding by the rules of the centre ...."

Note: it is a requirement of some Centres that the parents and children attend a pre-contact meeting (parents are seen separately) so that the Centres can follow their own risk assessment procedure. Others will either welcome or insist on a pre-contact visit by the resident parent to acclimatise the child(ren). Non-resident parents are also welcome.

(2) *Ben's Story*, a children's book about visiting a Child Contact Centre is available from NACCC or can be ordered from most good bookshops (ISBN: 0-9536548-0-X). Cost £1.99 plus 35p post and packaging. It is also printed in Welsh – *Stori Ben*.

(3) The Centre or Centres at which you direct contact to take place will very much welcome a visit from you or from your colleagues. It will be greatly appreciated by the volunteer staff if the local judiciary takes a positive interest in its local Centres, and such visits will also help you understand the facilities on offer and thus the type of case which is most suited to contact in the local Child Contact Centre.".

The NACC address is Minerva House, Spaniel Row, Nottingham, NG1 6EP (Tel: 0115 948 4557). See also an article by District Judge John Mitchell "How should contact centres be used" [2001] Fam Law 613 for helpful guidance and a suggested draft contact order.

Contact – European Convention for the Protection of Human Rights and Fundamental Freedoms 1950—The Convention was implemented in this jurisdiction on the coming into force of the Human Rights Act 1998. There are a number of cases in which unmarried fathers have complained that the refusal of the court to grant them contact with their children constitutes a breach of their right to family life, which right is protected by Article 8 of the Convention. The European Court of Human Rights upheld such complaints by unmarried fathers in *Elsholz v Germany* [2000] 2 FLR 486; *Ciliz v The Netherlands* [2000] 2 FLR 469; *Elsholz v Italy* [2000] Fam Law 680, but rejected the father's complaint in *Glaser v UK (Case No 32346/96)* [2001] 1 FLR 153. In *S and G v Italy* [2000] 2 FLR 771 a mother's complaint that the authorities had prevented her having contact with her children was upheld and found to constitute a breach of Art 8. In three cases the ECHR considered the approach of the German courts to contact applications by unmarried fathers. The German law at the time made a distinction between the rights of married and unmarried fathers. The ECHR held that the law amounted to discrimination in breach of Art 14. Furthermore, under Art 8 the ECHR held that consideration of what lies in the best interests of the child is of crucial importance in every case of this kind. A fair balance has to be struck between the interests of each parent and those of the child and in doing so particular importance must be attached to the best interests of the child which, depending on their nature and seriousness, may override those of the parent. A parent's rights are secondary to the child's health and development (*Sahin v Germany; Sommerfeld v Germany; Hoffmann v Germany* [2002] 1 FLR 119).

For the procedure to be followed in making a claim under the Human Rights Act 1998, see annotation thereto and *President's Direction of 24 July 2000*.

Contact – domestic violence—The Court of Appeal in *Re L (Contact: Domestic Violence); Re V (Contact: Domestic Violence); Re M (Contact: Domestic Violence); Re H (Contact: Domestic Violence)* [2000] 2 FLR 334 has laid down useful guidelines as to the way in which courts should approach the hearing of contact applications in which allegations of domestic violence are raised. In the course of the hearing the court considered the report of the *Children Act Sub-Committee of the Advisory Board on Family Law* regarding parental contact in domestic violence cases, and a joint expert report prepared by two child psychiatrists for the Official Solicitor. In each case, a father's application for direct contact had been refused by the judge and all four appeals were dismissed. When hearing contact applications the court should consider:

(*a*) the conduct of both parties towards each other and towards the children;
(*b*) the effect of the violence on the children and on the residential parent;
(*c*) the motivation of the parent seeking contact.

In hearing interim contact applications when allegations of domestic violence have not yet been adjudicated on, the court should give particular consideration to the likely risk of harm to the child, whether physical or emotional, if contact were granted or refused. The court should ensure, so far as possible, that any risk of harm to the child is minimised and that the safety of the child and the residential parent is secured before, during and after any such contact. Where allegations of domestic violence are made which might have an effect on the outcome of the case, those allegations must be adjudicated upon and found proved or not proved. There is no presumption that on proof of domestic violence the offending parent has to surmount a prima facie barrier of no contact, but such violence is a factor in the delicate balancing exercise of discretion carried out by the judge applying the welfare principle and the checklist in CA 1989, s 1(1) and (3). Where domestic violence is proved, the court must weigh the seriousness of the violence, the risks involved and the impact on the child against the positive factors, if any, of contact. The ability of the offending parent to recognise his past conduct, to be aware of the need to change and to make genuine efforts to do so will be an important consideration (see also *Re M (Interim Contact: Domestic Violence)* [2000] 2 FLR 377; *Re G (Domestic Violence: Direct Contact)* [2000] 2 FLR 865; *Re F (A Child) (Contact Order)* [2001] 1 FCR 422).

The President issued further guidance in December 2001 (in the absence of a Practice Direction) to clarify the practical application of the principles in *Re L* (above) in cases where there are allegations of domestic violence, an extract of which reads as follows:

> "Where violence has been alleged, it is a matter for the court to decide whether, if proved, that violence would be relevant to the issue of contact. Where the allegations made may have an effect on the outcome, the court must adjudicate on them and find them proved or not proved. If the allegations would not be serious enough to affect contact, it is not necessary for those allegations to be adjudicated upon.
>
> The CASC report raises the importance of early recognition that the issue of domestic violence may be relevant in a particular case. Where it may be relevant, tightly constructed directions and careful timetabling must be achieved at the earliest possible stage to identify and deal expeditiously with the issues raised. An early exchange of statements may enable the court to determine whether or not the alleged violence may be relevant to the issue of contact with minimum delay.
>
> In either case, the court must suitably instruct the CAFCASS court reporter. It is for the court to decide when a report from CAFCASS is required and to identify the issues which the court wishes the report to address. If the court has determined that the alleged violence is not significant, the court should direct that the CAFCASS officer should make their report notwithstanding the allegations that have been made.
>
> In determining whether or not the alleged violence would be relevant to the issue of contact, regard should be had to the joint report of Dr Sturge and Dr Glaser …" (Susie Barter, Family Division Lawyer, President's Private Office, RCJ).

The joint report of Drs Sturge and Glaser ([2000] Fam Law 615) was referred to and relied upon by the Court of Appeal in *Re L*. It is recommended that practitioners read it in full.

Where the court holds a preliminary hearing to consider the issue of violence in contact disputes it is crucial that the same bench presides over the final hearing, as the case remains part-heard and the view formed by the bench during the inquiry into the domestic violence issues must inform its approach to the remainder of the case (*M v A (Contact: Domestic Violence)* [2002] 2 FLR 921).

Where there is a conflict between the rights and interests of a child and those of a parent, the interests of the child must prevail under European Convention for the Protection of Human Rights and Fundamental Freedoms 1950, Art 8(2) (*Re L* etc (above)). See further **Contact – European Convention for the Protection of Human Rights and Fundamental Freedoms 1950** (above).

Contact disputes – separate representation of children—Should there be an increase in the need for separate representation of a child in private law cases, in part as a result of the Human Rights Act 1998, it may be possible to call on the services of such as the National Youth Advisory Service to represent a child where separate representation is justified (*Re A (Contact: Separate Representation)* [2001] 1 FLR 715 – where the Official Solicitor was invited to act because although there was no doubt that NYAS would in fact act independently, there was a risk that the father would perceive NYAS as acting on the mother's behalf since she had been the first to approach NYAS for representation for the child). As a matter of principle where the court is faced with difficult contact issues, consideration should be given to the children being separately represented (*Re H (Contact Order) (No 2)* [2002] 1 FLR 22; *Re W (A Child)* (2001) LTL 22 November, Extempore (unreported elsewhere)). However, the appointment of a children's guardian and separate representation for a child is still an unusual course to take in private law cases (*Re D (A Child)* (unreported), 8 November 2001, CA). In difficult private law cases where the child does need separate representation, the appropriate course will be to invite CAFCASS Legal to provide a guardian to represent the child and take over the child's case (*Re W (A Child)* (unreported), 22 November 2001, CA; and see further under FPR 1991, r 9.5 and *Practice Note of March 2001 (Officers of CAFCASS Legal Services and Special Casework: Appointment in Family Proceedings)* (set out in Part IV of this work)). However, due to the number of cases in which CAFCASS Legal are asked to represent children in private law cases, a new procedure has been adopted which is described in **CAFCASS Practice Note** under s 7 (above).

"shall be taken by any person" (s 8(1))—In the definition of a prohibited steps order, "any person" includes someone who is not a party to the proceedings (*Re H (Prohibited Steps Order)* [1995] 1 FLR 638, CA – prohibited steps order requiring mother's former cohabitee who was not a party not to have or to seek contact with the children, liberty being given to him to apply on notice to vary or discharge the order under s 11(7)(*d*)).

Change of surname—At birth, a child must be registered in accordance with the Births and Deaths Registration Act 1953. Where the parents are married, the duty to register lies on both the mother and father; where they are not married at the time of the birth, the duty is the mother's alone. The surname entered is to be the one by which at the date of the registration it is intended that the child shall be known. However, it is possible either for the parents jointly or for the mother alone to apply for the name of the father to be entered into the Register of Births, on the production of Statutory Declarations (see Births and Deaths Registration Act 1953, s 10A, as amended by the Children Act 1975, s 93). See further **Where natural unmarried father has not signed Birth Register but wishes to be acknowledged as the parent** under s 4. Once the surname has been registered, there is nothing in the BDRA 1953 to permit it to be changed in the register (see the consideration of the BDRA 1953 in *Dawson v Wearmouth* [1997] 2 FLR 629, CA and [1999] 1 FLR 1167, HL; *Re C (Change of Surname)* [1998] 2 FLR 656, CA and *Re W, Re A, Re B (Change of Name)* [1999] 2 FLR 930). Accordingly, the courts' powers are limited to regulating the name by which a child should be known. However, there is a requirement that the parents of a child who is legitimated by their subsequent marriage must re-register the child's birth within 3 months of the date of the marriage by virtue of which he was legitimated (Legitimacy Act 1976, s 9).

A change of the name by which a child is known can be evidenced by deed poll or, as the cases show tends to happen in practice, can be achieved more informally, by a parent simply arranging for a child to be known on a day-to-day basis by a new surname (for example at school). In each case, there are important pre-conditions for the change of name. The detail varies according to the situation regarding the child but the general principle that must be observed is that "the registration or change of a child's surname is a profound and not a merely formal issue, whatever the age of the child. Any dispute on such an issue must be referred to the court for determination whether or not there is a residence order in force and whoever has or has not parental responsibility. No disputed registration or change should be made unilaterally." (*Dawson v Wearmouth* (above); *Re T (Change of Surname)* [1998] 2 FLR 620). Note the reconsideration by the House of Lords (reported at [1999] 1 FLR 1167, HL) of some aspects of the Court of Appeal's decision in *Dawson v Wearmouth*. The House of Lords reviewed the principles to be applied to a change of name application (including the question of what weight is to be given to the name in which the child has been duly registered) but the procedural aspects of such an application were not the subject of an appeal and were not considered.

It appears that the proper course in all cases in which a change of name is contemplated will be as follows:

(1) There should first be consultation with anyone who has parental responsibility. This should happen whether or not there is a residence order in force (*Re PC (Change of Surname)* [1997] 2 FLR 730, FD).

(2) There remains uncertainty about the extent to which consent of a father who does not have parental responsibility is material to a change of name. Thorpe LJ in *Re T* (above) remarked at p 623B when speaking of the decision in *Re PC* that it was "persuasively indicative of the clear principle that children's names are important and in any situation of dispute, either the consent of the other parent or the leave of the court is an essential pre-requisite, *certainly where both parents have parental responsibility*" (author's emphasis) thus begging the question. Holman J in *Re PC* had, in fact, held (p 739) that where a child is born of parents who are not married to each other and there is no order or agreement for parental responsibility, the mother can lawfully change the child's surname without any other permission or consent. Furthermore, it will be noted that CA 1989, s 13 (which applies where there is a residence order) only refers to the consent of those with parental responsibility and it may be reasonable to infer from this a more general view that a father without parental responsibility should not be entitled to prior consultation about name changes. On the other hand, if a father without parental responsibility learns of, and disagrees with, plans to change his child's name (or wishes to contest a fait accompli), it is clear that he is entitled to bring the matter before the court under s 8 (*Dawson v Wearmouth*, see further below). It may be thought to be somewhat paradoxical that he should have this right but no right to prior consultation. The Court of Appeal in *Re C (Change of Surname)* (above), considering the action of a mother who effected a change of name by deed poll at a time when the father did not have parental responsibility but had made his opposition to the name change known, commented that at the first signs of dispute about a child's name the court should be involved, but expressly left to one side whether that arose as a matter of wisdom, common decency or binding obligation. They were particularly concerned that, because of a lack of frankness on

the part of the mother and her solicitors in disclosing the change of name, the court was considering the question a considerable time after it had taken place.

(3) If consent is forthcoming, it would be prudent in all cases to have it put in writing. Written consent of everyone with parental responsibility is, in any event, a statutory requirement by virtue of CA 1989, s 13(1) where there is a residence order (or a deemed residence order dating from before CA 1989, see *Re B (Change of Surname)* [1996] 1 FLR 791). Written consent will also generally be required if a deed poll is to be enrolled (see below).

(4) If the change of name is disputed, the matter must be referred to the court for determination.

(*a*) Where a residence order (or deemed residence order) is in force, a free-standing application for leave should be made under CA 1989, s 13. An application under s 8 is not appropriate (*Re B (Change of Surname)* (above) as explained in *Dawson v Wearmouth* [1997] 2 FLR 629, CA, undisturbed by the House of Lords decision at [1999] 1 FLR 1167).

(*b*) Where there is no residence order, application should be made under CA 1989, s 8. An application under s 13 is not appropriate (*Dawson v Wearmouth* (above)). Whether the application will be for a specific issue order or for a prohibited steps order may depend upon the circumstances. In both *Dawson v Wearmouth* and *Re T (Change of Surname)* (above), the order sought was a specific issue order; in *Re PC* both specific issue and prohibited steps orders were made.

There looks, technically, to be a difference in the way in which a court should approach s 8 and s 13 applications. Section 1(1) applies in both cases to make the child's welfare the court's paramount consideration but s 1(3) (welfare checklist), whilst applicable to s 8 applications, is not applicable to s 13 applications (see s 1(4)). However, as the Court of Appeal pointed out in *Dawson v Wearmouth*, the distinction is more theoretical than real because the judge entertaining an application under s 13 will invariably have regard, in fact, to the considerations identified in s 1(3) in his search for welfare as the paramount consideration even if under no specific statutory duty so to do. It is anticipated that the review by the House of Lords in *Dawson v Wearmouth* of the approach that should be taken with a s 8 application will accordingly be influential also in s 13 applications. The present position in cases which deal with changing the name of a child is helpfully summarised by Butler-Sloss LJ in *Re W, Re A, Re B (Change of Name)* [1999] 2 FLR 930, with the caveat that the summary only lays down guidelines and does not purport to be exhaustive. Each case must be decided on its own facts, with the welfare of the child the paramount consideration and all the relevant factors weighed in the balance by the court at the time of the hearing. The summary (at 933F) is as follows:

"(*a*) If parents are married, they both have the power and the duty to register their child's names.

(*b*) If they are not married the mother has the sole duty and power to do so.

(*c*) After registration of the child's names, the grant of a residence order obliges any person wishing to change the surname to obtain the leave of the court or the written consent of all those who have parental responsibility.

(*d*) In the absence of a residence order, the person wishing to change the surname from the registered name ought to obtain the relevant written consent or the leave of the court by making an application for a specific issue order.

(*e*) On any application, the welfare of the child is paramount and the judge must have regard to the s 1(3) criteria.

(*f*) Among the factors to which the court should have regard is the registered surname of the child and the reasons for the registration, for instance recognition of the biological link with the child's father. Registration is always a relevant and an important consideration but it is not in itself decisive. The weight to be given to it by the court will depend upon the other relevant factors or valid countervailing reasons which may tip the balance the other way.

(*g*) The relevant considerations should include factors which may arise in the future as well as the present situation.

(*h*) Reasons given for changing or seeking to change a child's name based on the fact that the child's name is or is not the same as the parent making the application do not generally carry much weight.

(*i*) The reasons for an earlier unilateral decision to change a child's name may be relevant.

(*j*) Any changes of circumstances of the child since the original registration may be relevant.

(*k*) In the case of a child whose parents were married to each other, the fact of the marriage is important and I would suggest that there would have to be strong reasons to change the name from the father's surname if the child was so registered.

(*l*) Where the child's parents were not married to each other, the mother has control over registration. Consequently, on an application to change the surname of the child, the degree of commitment of the father to the child, the quality of contact, if it occurs, between father and child, the existence or absence of parental responsibility are all relevant factors to take into account."

A deed poll evidences a change of name in a formal way. It is first executed then enrolled with the Central Office, Filing Department. Enrolment will not be permitted unless certain conditions are complied with. Reference should be made to the Enrolment of Deeds (Change of Name) Regulations 1994 and *Practice Direction* set out at 5PD – 008 of *Civil Procedure*.

Re PC (above) raises (but does not rule upon) the possibility that the position as to name change may be different for an older child, in particular a child of over 16, where the consent of the child *may* be necessary and sufficient.

See also *Re S (Change of Surname)* [1999] 1 FLR 672 (annotated under CA 1989, s 33).

It may be appropriate in certain cases for a child to use the surnames of both his mother and father (*Re R (Surname: Using Both Parents')* [2001] EWCA Civ 1344, [2001] 2 FLR 1358 – where the child was to move to Spain with his mother and the parents were urged to follow the Spanish practice of using both parents' surnames in order to ease the child's adjustment to a life in that culture and to encourage transparency as to his parentage).

There is now provision for anyone to apply to the court for a declaration as to whether or not a person named in the application is or was the parent of another person so named – see FLA 1986, s 55A (which was introduced by CSPSSA 2000, s 83), and Procedural Guide 42.

Change of forenames—The forename(s) given to a child at the registration of his birth are less concrete than the surname, since it is commonplace for a child to receive a statutory registered name and also to receive different given names during the course of family life (*Re H (Child's Name: First Name)* [2002] EWCA Civ 190, [2002] 1 FLR 973, CA – where the father and mother, who were separated, had each registered the child with different forenames; although the father's registration was first in time the mother should be permitted to use the forename she had chosen for the child both at home and when dealing with external authorities).

Sterilisation applications—The question of sterilisation of a minor can be raised under s 8 (specific issue order); however it may be preferable to apply under the inherent jurisdiction of the court because of the procedural and administrative difficulties attached to such an application (see *Practice Note of 2 April 2001 (Official Solicitor: Appointment in Family Proceedings)* and *Practice Note of March 2001 (Officers of CAFCASS Legal Services and Special Casework: Appointment in Family Proceedings)*; both set out in Part IV of this work) which supersede the *Practice Note of June 1996* and the *Practice Note of 26 July 1996*. Applications relating to minors in a persistent vegetative state will also be dealt with under the new *Practice Notes* (above).

"the inherent jurisdiction of the High Court" (s 8(3)(*a*))—The inherent jurisdiction of the High Court was, prior to CA 1989, most commonly exercised in wardship proceedings. The Act has put an end to the majority of wardship applications, but applications are still made under the inherent jurisdiction of the court; see, in particular, under s 100.

"application for leave under section 100(3)" (s 8(3))—This is a reference to an application by a local authority for leave to apply for the exercise of the court's inherent jurisdiction with respect to children.

"Parts I, II and IV of this Act" (s 8(4))—Broadly speaking, this means that most proceedings under the Act are classed as family proceedings but those relating to the protection of children (under Pt V), such as applications for emergency protection orders etc, are not so classified.

Enforcement of s 8 orders—For implementing order, see s 11(7) directions and conditions; for enforcement under Magistrates' Courts Act 1980, s 63(3), see s 14; for penal notices, see FPR 1991, r 4.21A; and for orders for recovery of a child, see Family Law Act 1986, s 34.

9 Restrictions on making section 8 orders

(1) No court shall make any section 8 order, other than a residence order, with respect to a child who is in the care of a local authority.

(2) No application may be made by a local authority for a residence order or contact order and no court shall make such an order in favour of a local authority.

(3) A person who is, or was at any time within the last six months, a local authority foster parent of a child may not apply for leave to apply for a section 8 order with respect to the child unless –

(*a*) he has the consent of the authority;

(*b*) he is a relative of the child; or

(*c*) the child has lived with him for at least three years preceding the application.

(4) The period of three years mentioned in subsection (3)(*c*) need not be continuous but must have begun not more than five years before the making of the application.

(5) No court shall exercise its powers to make a specific issue order or prohibited steps order –

(*a*) with a view to achieving a result which could be achieved by making a residence or contact order; or

(*b*) in any way which is denied to the High Court (by section 100(2)) in the exercise of its inherent jurisdiction with respect to children.

(6) No court shall make any section 8 order which is to have effect for a period which will end after the child has reached the age of sixteen unless it is satisfied that the circumstances of the case are exceptional.

(7) No court shall make any section 8 order, other than one varying or discharging such an order, with respect to a child who has reached the age of sixteen unless it is satisfied that the circumstances of the case are exceptional.

Defined terms—"child": s 105(1); "contact order": s 8(1); "local authority": s 105(1); "local authority foster parent": s 23(3); "relative": s 105(1); "residence order": s 8(1); "section 8 order": s 8(2).

"child who is in the care of a local authority" (s 9(1))—A child who is the subject of a care order as defined in ss 31(11) and 105(1). There is power to make an order under s 34 (parental contact with child in care) as this is not a contact order within the meaning of s 8(1). An order made under s 8 on the application of a child in care for him to have contact with his siblings would be an order in respect of the siblings rather than in respect of the child in care and would not, therefore, fall foul of s 9(1) (*Re F (Contact: Child in Care)* [1995] 1 FLR 510, FD).

No application by a local authority for residence or contact order (s 9(2))—See, for example, *Re C (Contact: Jurisdiction)* [1995] 1 FLR 777, CA (local authority could not apply for contact or variation of contact in relation to children who had been freed for adoption).

"local authority foster parent of a child" (s 9(3))—The mere fact that a person is a local authority foster parent does not bring him within the section. His right to seek leave will be restricted only if he is or has been the foster parent of the particular child who would be the subject of the s 8 application. Prospective adopters who have had a child who is freed for adoption placed with them by a local authority are local authority foster parents and therefore precluded by s 9(3) from applying for leave (*Re C (Adoption: Notice)* [1999] 1 FLR 384, FD). For applications by local authority foster parents, see *JR v Merton London Borough* [1992] 2 FCR 174 reversed on appeal as *Re A and W (Minors) (Residence Order: Leave to Apply)* [1992] 2 FLR 154 and *C v Salford City Council and Others* [1994] 2 FLR 926; for a case in which, unusually, local authority foster parents were joined as parties in care proceedings, see *Re G (Minors) (Interim Care Order)* [1993] 2 FLR 839. The court cannot make a s 8 order in favour of a local authority foster parent of its own motion if s 9(3) would debar that foster parent from applying for leave to apply for such an order. The power to make orders of the court's own motion is subject to the restrictions in s 9 (see CA 1989, s 10(3), but note the exception in *Gloucestershire County Council v P* [1999] 2 FLR 61 which is referred to in **When the court may make a s 8 order** under s 10).

Leave to apply (s 9(3))—Certain people may apply as of right for a s 8 order (see s 10(4), (5), (7)) and a foster parent is not prevented by s 9(3) from making such an application should he fall into any of these categories, for example he may apply for a residence order where the child is in care and the local authority for whom he fosters gives its consent (s 10(5)(*c*)(ii)) or where the child has been living with him for at least three years (s 10(5)(*b*)). In all other situations, leave must be obtained before an application is launched (see s 10(1)–(3)) and s 9(3) restricts the foster parents who may seek leave, as s 10 is expressed to be subject to the restrictions imposed by s 9.

"consent of the authority" (s 9(3)(*a*))—It is the consent of the social services authority accommodating the child which is required where the child is simply accommodated rather than being the subject of a care order (*C v Salford City Council and Others* [1994] 2 FLR 926, FD), just as it appears that it will be the authority that is responsible for the placement of the child with the foster parents that will have to consent where a care order is in force. It is ambiguous whether it is enough for the authority to consent to the foster parent making a leave application or whether the consent must be to the making of the full s 8 application or indeed to the granting of the s 8 order that the foster parent wishes to seek. There is no requirement as to the form of the consent but it would be prudent for it to be given in writing.

"at least three years preceding the application" (s 9(3)(*c*))—The application concerned is plainly the leave application not the application for the s 8 order, but what is not made entirely clear is whether the child must still be living with the applicant immediately prior to the application. Section 10(5)(*b*) is similarly worded to s 9(3)(*c*) (though it is not in identical terms) and s 10(10) (which contains supplementary provisions about the three-year period in s 10(5)(*b*)) is that section's equivalent to s 9(4). It is noteworthy, however, that s 10(10) expressly provides that the three-year period for s 10(5)(*b*) must not have ended more than three months before the making of the application whereas there is no such provision in s 9(4). This would appear to mean that for s 9(3)(*c*) it does not matter when the child last lived with the applicant providing he has lived with him for a total of three out of the last five years. Note that when Adoption and Children Act 2002, s 113 comes into force, CA 1989, s 9(3)(*c*) will be amended so as to reduce the three year period to a minimum of only one year.

Restrictions on specific issue and prohibited steps orders (s 9(5))— Nottinghamshire *County Council v P* [1993] 2 FLR 134, CA, is an example of an attempt by a local authority to obtain a prohibited steps order (instead of proceeding by way of the public law provisions of CA 1989, Pt IV) which failed because it contravened s 9(5). Supervision orders with an order restraining the mother from removing the children from their foster homes are also contrary to ss 9(5) and 100(2)(*b*) (*Re S and D (Children: Powers of Court)* [1995] 2 FLR 456, CA). For further examples of contravention of s 9(5), see *M v C (Children Orders: Reasons)* [1993] 2 FLR 584 (ex parte specific issue order for the return of children to their mother from their father) and *Re H (Prohibited Steps Order)* [1995] 1 FLR 638, CA (prohibited steps order requiring mother to prevent contact between children and former cohabitee contravened s 9(5), but prohibited steps order against former cohabitee requiring him not to have contact was acceptable). *Re M (Care: Leave to Interview Child)* [1995] 1 FLR 825, FD, also illustrates the limitations imposed by s 9(5) (not possible to use specific issue order to deal with question of whether father's solicitor could interview his two sons who were in care for purposes of preparing his defence to criminal charges; inherent jurisdiction of court used instead).

10 Power of court to make section 8 orders

(1) In any family proceedings in which a question arises with respect to the welfare of any child, the court may make a section 8 order with respect to the child if –

- (*a*) an application for the order has been made by a person who –
  - (i) is entitled to apply for a section 8 order with respect to the child; or
  - (ii) has obtained the leave of the court to make the application; or
- (*b*) the court considers that the order should be made even though no such application has been made.

(2) The court may also make a section 8 order with respect to any child on the application of a person who –

(*a*) is entitled to apply for a section 8 order with respect to the child; or
(*b*) has obtained the leave of the court to make the application.

(3) This section is subject to the restrictions imposed by section 9.

(4) The following persons are entitled to apply to the court for any section 8 order with respect to a child –

(*a*) any parent or guardian of the child;
(*b*) any person in whose favour a residence order is in force with respect to the child.

(5) The following persons are entitled to apply for a residence or contact order with respect to a child –

(*a*) any party to a marriage (whether or not subsisting) in relation to whom the child is a child of the family;
(*b*) any person with whom the child has lived for a period of at least three years;
(*c*) any person who –
  (i) in any case where a residence order is in force with respect to the child, has the consent of each of the persons in whose favour the order was made;
  (ii) in any case where the child is in the care of a local authority, has the consent of that authority; or
  (iii) in any other case, has the consent of each of those (if any) who have parental responsibility for the child.

(6) A person who would not otherwise be entitled (under the previous provisions of this section) to apply for the variation or discharge of a section 8 order shall be entitled to do so if –

(*a*) the order was made on his application; or
(*b*) in the case of a contact order, he is named in the order.

(7) Any person who falls within a category of person prescribed by rules of court is entitled to apply for any such section 8 order as may be prescribed in relation to that category of person.

(8) Where the person applying for leave to make an application for a section 8 order is the child concerned, the court may only grant leave if it is satisfied that he has sufficient understanding to make the proposed application for the section 8 order.

(9) Where the person applying for leave to make an application for a section 8 order is not the child concerned, the court shall, in deciding whether or not to grant leave, have particular regard to –

(*a*) the nature of the proposed application for the section 8 order;
(*b*) the applicant's connection with the child;
(*c*) any risk there might be of that proposed application disrupting the child's life to such an extent that he would be harmed by it; and
(*d*) where the child is being looked after by a local authority –
  (i) the authority's plans for the child's future; and
  (ii) the wishes and feelings of the child's parents.

(10) The period of three years mentioned in subsection (5)(*b*) need not be continuous but must not have begun more than five years before, or ended more than three months before, the making of the application.

Defined terms—"child", "child of the family": s 105(1); "contact order": s 8(1); "family proceedings": s 8(3); "guardian", "local authority": s 105(1); "parental responsibility": s 3; "residence order": s 8(1); "section 8 order": s 8(2).

When the court may make a s 8 order—The net effect of s 10(1)–(4) is that (subject to the restrictions set out in s 9) the court may make a s 8 order either:

(*a*) on the application of a person who is entitled to apply as of right, or on the application of a person who can apply with leave and has obtained leave; any such application may be an independent application (s 10(2)) or may be made in the course of existing family proceedings in which a question arises with respect to the welfare of the child (s 10(1)(*a*)); or

(*b*) in any family proceedings in which a question arises with respect to the welfare of a child, where it considers that a s 8 order should be made in respect of the child despite the fact that no application has actually been made (s 10(1)(*b*)).

No doubt the court will normally be prompted to make an order under s 10(1)(*b*) at the suggestion of one of the parties to the proceedings or of an interested friend or relative who has been allowed to address the court, or even at the suggestion of the child himself, but there is nothing to prevent the court itself taking the lead in appropriate circumstances (see eg *Re H (A Minor) (Contact)* [1993] Fam Law 673). The power to make orders of the court's own motion is subject to the restrictions in s 9 (see s 10(3)). However, in *Gloucestershire County Council v P* [1999] 2 FLR 61, the Court of Appeal (Thorpe LJ dissenting) held that although s 10(3) stated that s 10 is subject to the restrictions in s 9, it did not clearly refer to the restriction in s 9(3) which is purely procedural in nature. Therefore, the court did have power under s 10(1)(*b*), on the exceptional facts of the case, to make an order of its own motion, in the interests of the child, unlimited by s 9(3); this meant that the court could grant a residence order to foster-parents even where they were not entitled themselves to seek leave to apply for residence. As to the court's power to make a s 8 order even though it is not in a position to dispose finally of the proceedings before it, see s 11(3).

Application for a s 8 order—For the procedure on an application for a s 8 order, see FPR 1991, r 4.4 and Family Proceedings Courts (Children Act 1989) Rules 1991, r 4. Where an application for leave has already been made, there is no need for an application form to be filed because the court will already have received a draft with the appropriate number of copies as part of the leave application (FPR 1991, r 4.3(3); FPC(CA 1989)R 1991, r 3(3)), but the procedure is otherwise the same as for applications without leave.

"In any family proceedings" (s 10(1))—Where orders of a "final" nature have already been made, care must be taken to ensure that there are extant family proceedings for the purposes of s 10(1); see, for example, *Re C (Contact: Jurisdiction)* [1995] 1 FLR 777, CA.

"a person who ... is entitled to apply for a section 8 order" (s 10(1)(*a*))—Those persons who are entitled to apply for a s 8 order without leave are specified in s 10(4) (those entitled to apply for any s 8 order), s 10(5) (those entitled to apply for a residence or contact order) and s 10(7) (those entitled to apply by virtue of rules of court). Where the child is in care or the proposed applicant is a local authority or a local authority foster parent, the restrictions imposed by s 9 apply (s 10(3)).

Meaning of "parent" (s 10(4))—This term is not defined in the Act. A child's natural mother and father (including, by virtue of Family Law Reform Act 1987, s 1, an unmarried father whether or not he has parental responsibility) are his parents unless he has been adopted, in which case his adoptive mother and father are his parents (Adoption Act 1976, s 39(1)–(3)). A child's natural parents are not parents within the meaning of s 10 once an adoption order has been made in respect of the child (*Re C (A Minor) (Adopted Child: Contact)* [1993] 2 FLR 431) or he has been freed for adoption (*M v C and Calderdale MBC* [1993] 1 FLR 505). A step parent is not a parent but may nevertheless be entitled to apply as of right for a s 8 order by virtue of s 10(5)(*a*). Where a child's mother cohabits with but does not marry a man who is not the child's natural father, that man cannot be classed as a parent of the child (*J v J (A Minor: Property Transfer)* [1993] 2 FLR 56). As to the parents of children born of in vitro fertilisation, artificial insemination etc, see Human Fertilisation and Embryology Act 1990, ss 27–29.

Guardians (s 10(4)(*a*))—There may be a delay between a guardian being named (for example, in a will or in a court order) and the time when he actually acquires parental responsibility for the child concerned (see **Date from which the appointment is effective** under s 5). See also s 6 as to the circumstances in which an appointment can be disclaimed or revoked.

"a residence order is in force" (s 10(4)(*b*))—Although most residence orders are open-ended, a residence order can be made for a specified period of time (s 11(7)), in which case it will cease to be in force at the end of that period. A residence order will also cease to have effect where the court makes a further order to that effect, in certain circumstances where the parents resume cohabitation (see s 11(5)) and, unless the court has expressly ordered to the contrary, when the child concerned reaches 16 (s 9(6)). The person in whose favour a residence order is in force is the person named in the order as the person with whom the child is to live (s 105(13)).

"person with whom the child has lived" (s 10(5)(*b*))—It is usually obvious where a child has been living, but it is less clear to whom the provision applies in cases where he has had more than one base, for example where he has spent weekdays with his aunt and stayed with his grandmother from Friday teatime to Monday morning. In such circumstances, it is submitted that both parties may qualify under s 10(5)(*b*).

"child is in the care of a local authority" (s 10(5)(*c*)(ii))—This refers to a child who is the subject of a care order as defined in ss 31(11) and 105(1).

Form of consent (s 10(5)(*c*)(iii))—Although neither the Act nor any rules stipulate the form in which consent must be expressed, it would be prudent for written consent to be obtained wherever possible and for this to be filed with the application. This will prevent difficulties arising if consent is subsequently withdrawn or the person concerned denies that it was ever given.

Persons not otherwise entitled to apply for variation or discharge (s 10(6))—An order varying or discharging a s 8 order is itself a s 8 order (s 8(2)). Consequently, anyone who may apply for a s 8 order may apply for a variation or discharge as well, with leave where appropriate. Section 10(6) adds two extra categories of person who can apply for variation or discharge, namely the original applicant for the order and, where the application concerns a contact order, any person named in that order. A person who has obtained an order for indirect contact with a child is entitled, by virtue of s 10(6), subsequently to apply for face-to-face contact without leave (*Re W (Application for Leave)* [1996] 3 FCR 337, [1996] Fam Law 665, FD).

Procedure on application for variation or discharge—For the procedure on variation or discharge applications, see FPR 1991, r 4.4 and FPC(CA 1989)R 1991, r 4.

Rules of court entitling persons to apply for a s 8 order (s 10(7))—No rules specifically list additional persons who may apply for a s 8 order; however, *Re HG (Specific Issue Order: Sterilisation)* [1993] 1 FLR 587 held that FPR 1991, r 9.2 does make such a prescription in relation to a child's next friend.

Application by a person requiring leave—If a proposed applicant is not one of those specifically listed in s 10, he will require leave of the court before he can apply. Such applicants could include the child himself, a local authority wishing to apply for a specific issue or prohibited steps order (though note the restrictions on local authority applications imposed by s 9), past carers who cannot establish the requisite period of residence, and relatives other than parents.

Application for leave by child (s 10(8))—Where the child is seeking leave, the only factor to which the court is specifically directed is that in s 10(8). However, the fact that the child has sufficient understanding does not mean that the court is bound to grant leave; it has a discretion. There is no statutory equivalent to s 10(9), and it is a moot point whether s 1(1) applies to make the welfare of the child paramount. Welfare is not paramount where the leave application is by anyone other than the child concerned (*Re A and W (Minors) (Residence Order: Leave to Apply)* [1992] 2 FLR 154, CA), but there is a divergence of opinion as to whether it is paramount where the applicant for leave is the child himself. *Re S (Contact: Application by Sibling)* [1998] 2 FLR 897, FD held that it is not paramount. However, it was held that the child's welfare is paramount in *Re C (A Minor) (Leave to Seek Section 8 Orders)* [1994] 1 FLR 26. As *Re C (Residence: Child's Application for Leave)* [1995] 1 FLR 927 points out, however, even if the welfare of the child is not paramount, the best interests of the child are important in dealing with a leave application. Such applications should be approached cautiously; once a child is a party to proceedings between warring parents, he will be exposed to hearing evidence of the parents which it might be better for him not to hear and may have to be cross-examined. For guidance as to the role that a child applicant is likely to play in the proceedings, see the notes to FPR 1991, r 4.16 and FPC(CA 1989)R 1991, r 16.

The court should also have regard to the likelihood of success of the proposed application (*Re C (Residence: Child's Application for Leave)* and *Re SC (A Minor) (Leave to Seek Residence*

Order) [1994] 1 FLR 96, FD). *Re M (Care: Contact: Grandmother's Application for Leave)* [1995] 2 FLR 86, CA, although a case where leave was sought under CA 1989, s 34, has been taken to provide the most authoritative guidance as to the appropriate test with regard to the prospects of success, see further under **Application for leave by person other than child concerned**. *Re M (Care: Contact: Grandmother's Application)* is fully annotated at CA 1989, s 34 and is helpful also in demonstrating the correct approach to leave applications.

Whilst the checklist in s 1(3) probably does not strictly apply, the matters listed there may be relevant to the court's consideration of whether to grant leave. The court will also consider why the child is seeking to apply for an order to be made in favour of someone else rather than the application being made by that person directly (*Re SC (A Minor) (Leave to Seek Residence Order)* (above) – girl of 14 sought leave to apply for residence order in favour of family friend). As to assessing the understanding of a child, see the annotation **"able ... to give such instructions on his own behalf"** to FPR 1991, r 4.12. As to the possibility of a s 8 application by a child through his next friend when the child does not have sufficient understanding to satisfy s 10(8), see *Re HG (Specific Issue Order: Sterilisation)* [1993] 1 FLR 587 and the comment thereon at [1993] Fam Law 403.

Applications for leave by children should be made in the High Court (*Practice Direction of 22 February 1993*; see further under FPR 1991, r 4.3 and FPC(CA 1989)R 1991, r 3).

Section 10(8) does not make provision for children to be joined as additional respondents to applications; application for that purpose is properly made under FPR 1991, r 4.7 and FPC(CA 1989)R 1991, r 7 (*Re N (A Minor)* (unreported) 25 September 1997, CA).

Application for leave by person other than child concerned (s 10(9))—Section 10(9) applies to any case in which the applicant for leave is not the child who would be the subject of the substantive application, notwithstanding that the leave applicant is himself a child (*Re S (Contact: Application by Sibling)* [1998] 2 FLR 897, FD in which the applicant for leave was a 9-year-old girl who wished to obtain a contact order in relation to her 7-year-old half-brother who had been adopted into another family).

Section 10(9) lists the factors to which the court should have particular regard in deciding an application for leave by someone other than the child himself, but other factors may also be relevant. The s 1(3) checklist does not apply here, nor does s 1(1) (*Re A and Others (Minors) (Residence Order: Leave to Apply)* [1992] Fam 182, CA; *Re T (Adopted Children: Contact)* [1995] 2 FLR 792; *G v F (Contact and Shared Residence: Applications for leave)* [1998] 2 FLR 799, FD; *Re S (Contact: Application by Sibling)* (above).

It is well accepted that the court must have regard to the merits of the proposed application (see *Re A (A Minor) (Residence Order: Leave to Apply)* [1993] 1 FLR 425; *G v Kirklees MBC* [1993] 1 FLR 805; *G v F (Contact and Shared Residence: Applications for leave)* (above) and *Re S (Contact: Application by Sibling)* (above). *Re M (Care: Contact: Grandmother's Application)* [1995] 2 FLR 86, CA, although a case where leave was sought under CA 1989, s 34, has been taken to provide the most authoritative guidance as to the appropriate test with regard to the prospects of success (see *Re G (Child Case: Parental Involvement)* [1996] 1 FLR 857, CA, at 865H and *Re S (Contact: Application by Sibling)* (above) at 906F and see also *Re R (A Minor) (Contact: Leave to Apply)* [1996] 3 FCR 566, CA). It is essential, however, that the court gives proper weight to the statutory criterion and does not place too great an emphasis on the factors in *Re M* (above) (*Re J (Leave to Issue Application for Residence Order)* [2003] Fam Law 27 – where the judge erred in dismissing an application by the maternal grandmother to join contested care proceedings and apply for a residence order in relation to her granddaughter).

In considering the risk of disruption (s 10(9)(*c*)), it is not only the risk of disruption from the making of the substantive application that is relevant but also the disruption that there may be to the child's life if the application succeeds (*Re A (A Minor) (Residence Order: Leave to Apply)* (above) and *Re M (Care: Contact: Grandmother's Application)* (above) at 95H). In *Re M* it was emphasised that the risk of disruption which is primarily contemplated in the subsection is the risk of disruption to the extent that the child would be harmed. By virtue of s 105(1), harm is defined in s 31(9). Ward LJ identified disruption as a factor of crucial significance, a fortiori for a child in care. *Re M (Prohibited Steps Order: Application for Leave)* [1993] 1 FLR 275 exemplifies the application of s 10(9)(*d*)(ii) which specifically requires the court to have regard to the local authority's plans for the child's future (former guardian ad litem of child in emergency protection order proceedings sought leave to apply for a s 8 order). *Re S (Contact: Application by Sibling)* (above) deals with disruption in the context of an adopted child.

The difficulty that natural parents will experience in obtaining leave to seek a s 8 order where their child has been adopted or freed for adoption is illustrated by *Re C (A Minor) (Adopted Child: Contact)* [1993] Fam 210, [1993] 2 FLR 431 and *Re E (Adopted Child: Contact: Leave)* [1995] 1 FLR 57. Applications in relation to siblings who have been adopted will also be subject to special considerations. In *Re S (Contact: Application by Sibling)* (above) the court held that where the

PART II

child who would be the subject of the application was an adopted child, the applicant for leave must satisfy the court that, having regard to the relevant changes of circumstances since the making of the adoption order, the decision of the adopters was sufficiently contrary to the best interests of the child, or sufficiently unreasonable, to warrant the court overriding the discretion conferred on the adopters by the adoption order. Although the application for leave failed in *Re S*, the applicant for leave in *Re T (Adopted Children: Contact)* (above) (a woman who wished to start contact proceedings with regard to her half-siblings who had been adopted by a family who, contrary to their earlier informal agreement, had failed to supply progress reports) was more successful in that the Court of Appeal overturned the first instance decision to refuse her leave and remitted the case to the county court with a direction that if, within a fixed period of time, the adopters gave reasons for their failure to supply the promised report, the court should re-consider the leave application in the light of the reasons but if no reasons were forthcoming, the court should grant the leave application.

The fact that leave has been granted does not create a presumption in favour of a substantive order (*Re A (Section 8 Order: Grandparent Application)* [1995] 2 FLR 153, CA; *G v F (Contact and Shared Residence: Applications for Leave)* (above)) or elevate a person who is not a natural parent to the position of a natural parent (*Re W (Contact: Application by Grandparent)* [1997] 1 FLR 793, FD).

"child ... being looked after by a local authority" (s 10(9)(*d*))—See s 22(1), (2).

Procedure on application for leave—Leave must be sought in accordance with FPR 1991, r 4.3 where the application is made to a county court or the High Court, and in accordance with FPC(CA 1989)R 1991, r 3 where the application is to a magistrates' court.

11 General principles and supplementary provisions

(1) In proceedings in which any question of making a section 8 order, or any other question with respect to such an order, arises, the court shall (in the light of any rules made by virtue of subsection (2)) –

(*a*) draw up a timetable with a view to determining the question without delay; and

(*b*) give such directions as it considers appropriate for the purpose of ensuring, so far as is reasonably practicable, that that timetable is adhered to.

(2) Rules of court may –

(*a*) specify periods within which specified steps must be taken in relation to proceedings in which such questions arise; and

(*b*) make other provision with respect to such proceedings for the purpose of ensuring, so far as is reasonably practicable, that such questions are determined without delay.

(3) Where a court has power to make a section 8 order, it may do so at any time during the course of the proceedings in question even though it is not in a position to dispose finally of those proceedings.

(4) Where a residence order is made in favour of two or more persons who do not themselves all live together, the order may specify the periods during which the child is to live in the different households concerned.

(5) Where –

(*a*) a residence order has been made with respect to a child; and

(*b*) as a result of the order the child lives, or is to live, with one of two parents who each have parental responsibility for him,

the residence order shall cease to have effect if the parents live together for a continuous period of more than six months.

(6) A contact order which requires the parent with whom a child lives to allow the child to visit, or otherwise have contact with, his other parent shall cease to have effect if the parents live together for a continuous period of more than six months.

(7) A section 8 order may –

(*a*) contain directions about how it is to be carried into effect;

(*b*) impose conditions which must be complied with by any person –

(i) in whose favour the order is made;

(ii) who is a parent of the child concerned;

(iii) who is not a parent of his but who has parental responsibility for him; or

(iv) with whom the child is living,

and to whom the conditions are expressed to apply;

(*c*) be made to have effect for a specified period, or contain provisions which are to have effect for a specified period;

(*d*) make such incidental, supplemental or consequential provision as the court thinks fit.

Defined terms—"section 8 order": s 8(2).

Scope of provision—This section contains provisions designed to ensure that any question that arises with regard to a s 8 order is determined without delay (s 11(1) and (2)) and enabling the court to make a s 8 order at any stage during proceedings even where it is not yet ready finally to dispose of the proceedings (s 11(3)). It also contains miscellaneous provisions as to the content and duration of s 8 orders.

Avoidance of delay—Section 11(1) forces the court to take a firm hold of the reins and to lay down a procedural timetable and give appropriate directions (under FPR 1991, r 4.14 or Family Proceedings Courts (Children Act 1989) Rules 1991, r 14) to ensure that any material question is determined without delay. Both practitioners and courts have a duty to avoid delay in children cases. The non-adversarial approach to children's litigation means that the solicitors for the parties have a duty, irrespective of whether delay might be tactically advantageous to their client, to ensure that a case does not drift and is resolved with the minimum of delay. Courts have a duty to be proactive in ensuring (through the giving of precise directions) that applications, once launched, are not allowed to moulder but are brought into court in a fully prepared state at the earliest opportunity. A children's guardian, be he the Official Solicitor or an officer of CAFCASS, has a duty to review the file regularly and, if the case is not making satisfactory progress, should take out a summons for directions (see *B v B (Minors) (Interviews and Listing Arrangements)* [1994] 2 FLR 489, CA, *Re A and B (Minors) (No 2)* [1995] 1 FLR 351, FD, and *B v B (Child Abuse: Contact)* at [1994] 2 FLR 713). It is good practice to avoid the delay that might otherwise be occasioned by awaiting a court welfare report by finding out in advance from the court welfare service how long is required for the report and fixing a date in the light of that information (*B v B (Minors) (Interviews and Listing Arrangements)*, above, and *Re A and B (Minors) (No 2)*, above). Where an assessment is in progress, it may be right to timetable the proceedings to enable them to be concluded as soon as possible once the assessment is completed; the fact that the timetable might need to be revised is not of itself a reason not to timetable (*E v Humberside County Council and S* [1996] Fam Law 444, FD). Although the general principle stated in s 1(2) is that delay is likely to be prejudicial, speed should not be the only consideration in making arrangements for the determination of an issue. The welfare of the child is the paramount consideration when a court determines any question with respect to the upbringing of a child (s 1(1)) and certain cases benefit from the passage of time which can allow tempers to cool, housing arrangements to be sorted out, medical investigations to take place etc. This does not mean that the court needs to let the case drift, merely that it needs to take such matters into account when fixing the timetable and giving directions. For cases approving planned and purposeful delay in the public law sphere, see *C v Solihull MBC* [1993] 1 FLR 290 and *Hounslow LBC v A* [1993] 1 FLR 702, and see also *Re W (Welfare Reports)* [1995] 2 FLR 142, CA, a private law case in which it was proper to call for a welfare report despite the delay that would thereby be occasioned. For the position where there are criminal proceedings pending, see **Delay** under s 1. As Wall J pointed out in *Re A and B (Minors) (No 2)*, above, in such a case the family court will need to be made aware of the current state of the criminal investigation and criminal process (if there is a prosecution) at every stage so that it can make a fully informed decision about the extent to which the duty under s 11 can be fulfilled.

PART II

"proceedings in which any question of making a section 8 order ... arises" (s 11(1))—The court's duty with regard to timetabling and the giving of directions applies whenever any question of making a s 8 order or any other question with respect to such an order arises. It is not therefore confined to applications specifically for a s 8 order.

Shared residence orders (s 11(4))—It is not necessary to show that exceptional circumstances exist before a shared residence order may be granted (*D v D (Shared Residence Order)* [2001] 1 FLR 495). Nor is it probably necessary to show a positive benefit to the child. What is required is a demonstration that the order is in the interests of the child in accordance with the requirements of s 1(1) (*D v D* (above)). In *Re H (A Child)* LTL 20/12/2002 Doc No C9900451 the court held that, although it had power to make an order imposing an arrangement on separated parents so that they shared the same house in order to care for a disabled child, the order was not appropriate on the facts. It is not open to a judge to make a shared residence order as a means of ensuring that there is no resistance to a contact order (*Re W (Children)* (unreported) LTL 22/01/2003 Doc No C9900459, CA).

Making a s 8 order prior to final disposal of proceedings (s 11(3))—Section 11(3) is equivalent to the power to make interim orders. It applies whenever the court has power to make a s 8 order (see s 10 and, as to the restrictions on that power, s 9). It can, of course, be used in the traditional way, for example to grant one parent a temporary residence order pending the final determination of an issue as to residence or to regulate contact pending determination of such an issue. However, given that the court has power to make a s 8 order of its own motion in any family proceedings in which a question arises as to the welfare of a child, and given the wide definition of family proceedings in s 8(3), it could be used in a much wider variety of circumstances as well, for example where an issue arises over the children in the course of pending proceedings under the Family Law Act 1996 or financial proceedings under the Matrimonial Causes Act 1973. For a case in which the father's residence order was left in force to run alongside an interim order placing the children with their mother pending a fuller hearing of the question of residence, see *Re M (Minors)(Interim Residence Order)* [1997] 2 FCR 28, CA.

The object of an interim order should normally be to hold the balance so as to cause the least possible harm to the child; see eg *B v B (Interim Contact with Grandparents)* [1993] Fam Law 393. By analogy with *Re L (Interim Care Order: Power of Court)* [1996] 2 FLR 742, CA, it should not be treated as an indication of how the matter will finally be disposed of; it is not an irreversible decision. Some useful guidance as to the approach to be taken to interim hearings (much of it equally applicable to both the magistrates' courts and the county courts, *Re W (A Minor) (Interim Care Order)* [1994] 2 FLR 892) can be found in *Hampshire County Council v S* [1993] Fam 158, [1993] 1 FLR 559, albeit a public law case (see further under FPC(CA 1989)R 1991, r 21). When a court hears an application for an interim residence order it is not necessary for it to give elaborate consideration to the welfare checklist under CA 1989, s 1(3) (*Re C (A Child)*, LTL 19/9/2001, Document No C0101911, CA). As to the difficulties that may be encountered in persuading the court to make ex parte interim orders, particularly in residence cases, see **Power to make ex parte orders** under FPR 1991, r 4.4. As to the situation in which it may be appropriate to make a residence order on an interim application in pending care proceedings, see *Re RJ (Fostering: Person Disqualified)* [1999] 1 FLR 605, CA (noted under s 38).

Section 11(7)—The tentative view has been expressed in *Re J (A Minor) (Residence)* [1994] 1 FLR 369, FD, that, although magistrates appear to have no power to stay a s 8 order pending appeal, they could achieve a similar result by means of directions under s 11(7) as to when the order is to take effect. Section 11(7)(*d*) can be used to afford liberty to a non-party to apply to vary or discharge a s 8 order (*Re H (Prohibited Steps Order)* [1995] 1 FLR 638, CA – prohibited steps order against mother's former cohabitee, J, requiring him not to have or to seek contact with the children, with liberty to J to apply on notice to vary or discharge the order).

Section 11(7) should not be used to restrict a parent to an area of residence within the United Kingdom save in exceptional circumstances. In *Re H (Children) (Residence Order: Condition)* [2001] EWCA Civ 1338, [2001] 2 FLR 1277 the facts justified a different approach to the general rule, as the medical evidence showed that the effect of the father moving the children away from the area where the mother lived would be devastating and therefore a condition attached to the residence order was justified. Exceptional circumstances justified a similar order in *Re S (A Child)* LTL 4/12/2002 Document No C0104182, where the court imposed a condition on a residence order to prevent the mother from moving her 9-year-old Down's Syndrome child to Cornwall. The court has jurisdiction under s 11(7) to impose any condition that secures the paramountcy of the welfare of the child, but the greater the restriction on the freedom of the parent subject to the condition, the more exceptional the case has to be to justify it (*Re H (A Child)* LTL 20/12/2002

Doc No C9900451 – discussed further under **Shared residence orders** (above)). The court has no power in private law proceedings concerning the residence of a child to use s 11(7) to order a residential assessment of one parent with the child against the wishes of the other parent (*R v R (Private Law Proceedings: Residential Assessment)* [2002] 2 FLR 953; *Birmingham City Council v H* [1992] 2 FLR 323).

Enforcement of s 11(7) directions and conditions—For enforcement under Magistrates' Courts Act 1980, s 63(3), see s 14; for penal notices, see FPR 1991, r 4.21A; and for orders for recovery of a child, see Family Law Act 1986, s 34.

12 Residence orders and parental responsibility

(1) Where the court makes a residence order in favour of the father of a child it shall, if the father would not otherwise have parental responsibility for the child, also make an order under section 4 giving him that responsibility.

(2) Where the court makes a residence order in favour of any person who is not the parent or guardian of the child concerned that person shall have parental responsibility for the child while the residence order remains in force.

(3) Where a person has parental responsibility for a child as a result of subsection (2), he shall not have the right –

(*a*) to consent, or refuse to consent, to the making of an application with respect to the child under section 18 of the Adoption Act 1976;

(*b*) to agree, or refuse to agree, to the making of an adoption order, or an order under section 55 of the Act of 1976, with respect to the child; or

(*c*) to appoint a guardian for the child.

(4) Where subsection (1) requires the court to make an order under section 4 in respect of the father of a child, the court shall not bring that order to an end at any time while the residence order concerned remains in force.

13 Change of child's name or removal from jurisdiction

(1) Where a residence order is in force with respect to a child, no person may –

(*a*) cause the child to be known by a new surname; or

(*b*) remove him from the United Kingdom;

without either the written consent of every person who has parental responsibility for the child or the leave of the court.

(2) Subsection (1)(*b*) does not prevent the removal of a child, for a period of less than one month, by the person in whose favour the residence order is made.

(3) In making a residence order with respect to a child the court may grant the leave required by subsection (1)(*b*), either generally or for specified purposes.

Defined terms—"child": s 105(1); "parental responsibility": s 3; "residence order": s 8(1).

Change of surname (s 13(1)(*a*))—See annotations to s 8.

Method of application for leave (s 13(1)(*a*), (*b*))—The leave application is a freestanding application and not a species of s 8 application (*Re B (Change of Surname)* [1996] 1 FLR 791, CA). It is made in accordance with FPR 1991, r 4.4 or FPC(CA 1989)R 1991, r 4 (and *not* r 4.3 and r 3 respectively, which deal only with applications for leave to commence proceedings). Although the application can be made in any court, where it is for leave to remove a child permanently from the jurisdiction, it should not be heard by magistrates but should be transferred for determination either in the county court or the High Court, depending on the complexity and difficulty of the decision (*MH v GP (Child: Emigration)* [1995] 2 FLR 106, FD).

There is a specific form for the order which FPR 1991, r 4.21(5) and FPC(CA 1989)R 1991, r 21(7) dictate must be used.

Removal from jurisdiction (s 13(1)(*b*))—The Court of Appeal in *Payne v Payne* [2001] EWCA Civ 166, [2001] 1 FLR 1052 has laid down useful guidelines for cases in which leave is sought to remove a child permanently from the jurisdiction (per Butler-Sloss P at 1079):
(*a*) The welfare of the child is always paramount.
(*b*) There is no presumption created by s 13(1)(*b*) in favour of the applicant parent.
(*c*) The reasonable proposals of the parent with a residence order wishing to live abroad carry great weight.
(*d*) Consequently the proposals have to be scrutinised with care and the court needs to be satisfied that there is a genuine motivation for the move and not the intention to bring contact between the child and the other parent to an end.
(*e*) The effect upon the applicant parent and the new family of the child of a refusal of leave is very important.
(*f*) The effect upon the child of the denial of contact with the other parent and in some cases his family is very important.
(*g*) The opportunity for continuing contact between the child and the parent left behind may be very significant.

Note that where there is a residence order in place, the removal of a child from England and Wales to Scotland does not require an application for leave to remove the child from the jurisdiction, since Scotland is part of the United Kingdom (*Re T (A Child)* (2001) 28 June (unreported), CA). *Re X and Y (Leave to Remove from the Jurisdiction: No Order Principle)* [2001] 2 FLR 118 has been disapproved by the Court of Appeal, which confirmed in *Re H (Children) (Residence Order: Condition)* [2001] 2 FLR 1277 that the proper test to be applied is that in *Payne v Payne* (above).

Removal from the jurisdiction – European Convention for the Protection of Human Rights and Fundamental Freedoms 1950—The Convention was implemented in this jurisdiction on the coming into force of the Human Rights Act 1998. There are a number of cases in which non-residential parents have argued that the permanent removal of their child from the jurisdiction by the residential parent constitutes a breach of Article 8 which guarantees the right to family life. The task for the court under Art 8(2) is to balance the right of the non-residential parent to family life (guaranteed by Art 8(1)) against the right of the residential parent to their own right to private life when the two rights are in conflict (*Re A (Permission to Remove Child from Jurisdiction: Human Rights)* [2000] 2 FLR 225; *Payne v Payne* [2001] 1 FLR 1052).

Relocation within the UK—Relocation within the UK can be problematical since whilst the primary carer might not have an obligation to apply under s 13(1)(*b*) he may still have to defeat the challenge of an application for a prohibited steps order under s 8 or for the imposition of a condition to the residence order under s 11(7). In making such decisions, the welfare of the child is always paramount (*Re H (Children) (Residence Order: Condition)* [2001] 2 FLR 1277 – the court made a residence order in favour of the father but attached a condition prohibiting him from removing the children to Northern Ireland). The Court of Appeal in *Re H* (above) held that the test to be applied for external or internal relocation is that laid down in *Payne v Payne* [2001] 1 FLR 1052 (see **Removal from jurisdiction** (above)) and has not been affected by the HRA 1998. The Court of Appeal in *Re H* (above) disapproved *Re X and Y (Leave to Remove from the Jurisdiction: No Order Principle)* [2001] 2 FLR 118. However, the test is less stringent in cases of internal relocation than for cases of external relocation (*Re H* (above); *Re S (A Child) (Residence Order: Condition)* [2001] 3 FCR 154).

14 Enforcement of residence orders

(1) Where –

(*a*) a residence order is in force with respect to a child in favour of any person; and
(*b*) any other person (including one in whose favour the order is also in force) is in breach of the arrangements settled by that order,

the person mentioned in paragraph (*a*) may, as soon as the requirement in subsection (2) is complied with, enforce the order under section 63(3) of the

Magistrates' Courts Act 1980 as if it were an order requiring the other person to produce the child to him.

(2) The requirement is that a copy of the residence order has been served on the other person.

(3) Subsection (1) is without prejudice to any other remedy open to the person in whose favour the residence order is in force.

Defined terms—"residence order": s 8(1).

Scope of provision—This section is intended to allow enforcement of residence orders under the penal procedures of the Magistrates' Courts Act 1980 in addition to any other available procedure for enforcement, eg under Family Law Act 1986, s 34(3). Unlike the High Court or county court, the additional directive requirement under CA 1989, s 11 (for example, to deliver the child to the residential parent) is not required because it may be enforced under MCA 1980, s 63(3) "as if it were an order requiring the other person to produce the child" to the person in whose favour the order was made. There is no need for a specific order requiring when the child should be given up – contrast with FLA 1986, s 34(3).

"section 63(3) of the Magistrates' Courts Act 1980"—MCA 1980, s 63(3) is the penal procedure in magistrates' courts for the enforcement of its orders, and empowers the court to punish for breach of its order. The court may order the contemnor to pay a sum not exceeding £50 for every day during which he is in default or a sum not exceeding £5,000 or to commit him to prison until he has remedied the breach or for a period not exceeding 2 months.

Procedure—Proceedings under MCA 1980, s 63(3) are commenced by complaint (Contempt of Court Act 1981, s 17(2)).

Financial relief

15 Orders for financial relief with respect to children

(1) Schedule 1 (which consists primarily of the re-enactment, with consequential amendments and minor modifications, of provisions of section 6 of the Family Law Reform Act 1969, the Guardianship of Minors Acts 1971 and 1973, the Children Act 1975 and of sections 15 and 16 of the Family Law Reform Act 1987) makes provision in relation to financial relief for children.

(2) The powers of a magistrates' court under section 60 of the Magistrates' Courts Act 1980 to revoke, revive or vary an order for the periodical payment of money and the power of a clerk of a magistrates' court to vary such an order shall not apply in relation to an order made under Schedule 1.

Amendments—Courts and Legal Services Act 1990, s 116, Sch 16, para 10(1); Maintenance Enforcement Act 1991, s 11(1), Sch 2, para 10.

Defined terms—"child": s 105(1); "residence order": s 8(1).

Scope of provision—This section introduces Sch 1 which contains the court's powers to make financial orders for children. Subject to the Child Support Act 1991, which restricts the court's power to order child maintenance (see Procedural Guide 2), Sch 1 covers three situations, namely:

(*a*) orders that a parent pay maintenance or a lump sum or transfer property to children when the first application for such an order is made whilst the child is under the age of 18 (although an order for periodical payments can subsequently be extended if the child is continuing in education or there are special circumstances);

(*b*) orders for periodical payments or a lump sum where the first time an application is made is when the child is aged over 18;

(*c*) alteration, either during the joint lives of the parents or after the death of one of them, of maintenance agreements containing financial provision for a child.

Orders for financial relief against parents—Schedule 1, para 1 essentially re-enacts Guardianship of Minors Act 1971, ss 11B and 11C. An order under para 1 is made either on application or without application at the time a residence order is made, varied or discharged. If the child's parents are married, an alternative way of applying for financial relief for the child is Matrimonial Causes Act 1973, ss 23 and 24, if there are divorce proceedings, or if there are no such proceedings, under s 27. By applying for relief for the child under those sections, the practitioner is able to take advantage of the power under Matrimonial Causes Act 1973, s 37 to restrain anticipated disposals of assets and to set aside past disposals where the intention is to defeat the claim, and the more sophisticated procedural provisions for the effective disposal of a claim for ancillary relief, including, for example, the power to seek information under FPR 1991, r 2.63. If, however, the child's parents are not married, that alternative jurisdiction is not available and the application has to be brought under Sch 1, para 1.

Orders for financial relief for persons aged over 18—Schedule 1, para 2 re-enacts Guardianship of Minors Act 1971, s 11D. It enables a child who has reached 18 and who is continuing in education or to whom special circumstances apply to obtain from his parents an order for periodical payments or a lump sum where his parents are not living with each other in the same household and there was no periodical payments order in force in respect of him before he reached the age of 16. This is the only provision in the Act which permits an original application for relief by a child aged over 18. Paragraph 16(1) of Sch 1 provides that, for this purpose, a person who has reached the age of 18 falls within the meaning of "child". If there was a periodical payments order in force before the child reached the age of 16, the child's remedy is to apply in the proceedings in which that order was made to extend that order. If, however, there was no such order and the applicant's parents are living with each other in the same household, then the applicant has no remedy against his parents. Thus, for instance, the adult child whose parents are living together and for no valid reason are refusing to support him or her through university is in a markedly worse situation than an adult child whose parents have separated.

Alteration of maintenance agreements containing financial provision for a child—Schedule 1, paras 10 and 11 re-enact the powers contained in Family Law Reform Act 1987, ss 15 and 16 to alter agreements made between parents for the maintenance of a child. The jurisdiction is similar to that contained in Matrimonial Causes Act 1973, ss 35 (lifetime variations) and 36 (variation after death), except that ss 35 and 36 apply only where the parents are married. Where the parents are married, the more sophisticated procedural provisions of ss 35 and 36 (including the power to restrain dealings under s 37) make it sensible to bring the application under those sections; where the parents are not married, there is no alternative but to bring the application under Sch 1.

Restriction of magistrates' powers (s 15(2))—Section 15(2) prohibits magistrates' courts from revoking or varying an order for periodical payments made under Sch 1.

Family assistance orders

16 Family assistance orders

(1) Where, in any family proceedings, the court has power to make an order under this Part with respect to any child, it may (whether or not it makes such an order) make an order requiring –

(*a*) an officer of the Service to be made available; or
(*b*) a local authority to make an officer of the authority available,

to advise, assist and (where appropriate) befriend any person named in the order.

(2) The persons who may be named in an order under this section ("a family assistance order") are –

(*a*) any parent or guardian of the child;
(*b*) any person with whom the child is living or in whose favour a contact order is in force with respect to the child;
(*c*) the child himself.

(3) No court may make a family assistance order unless –

(*a*) it is satisfied that the circumstances of the case are exceptional; and
(*b*) it has obtained the consent of every person to be named in the order other than the child.

(4) A family assistance order may direct –

(*a*) the person named in the order; or
(*b*) such of the persons named in the order as may be specified in the order,

to take such steps as may be so specified with a view to enabling the officer concerned to be kept informed of the address of any person named in the order and to be allowed to visit any such person.

(5) Unless it specifies a shorter period, a family assistance order shall have effect for a period of six months beginning with the day on which it is made.

(6) Where –

(*a*) a family assistance order is in force with respect to a child; and
(*b*) a section 8 order is also in force with respect to the child,

the officer concerned may refer to the court the question whether the section 8 order should be varied or discharged.

(7) A family assistance order shall not be made so as to require a local authority to make an officer of theirs available unless –

(*a*) the authority agree; or
(*b*) the child concerned lives or will live within their area.

(8), (9) (*repealed*)

Amendments—Criminal Justice and Court Services Act 2000 s 74, Sch 7, para 89.

Defined terms—"child": s 105(1); "family proceedings": s 8(3); "local authority": s 105(1); "officer of the Service": Criminal Justice and Court Services Act 2000, s 11(3).

Scope of provision—A family assistance order is a short-term order lasting for no more than six months which obliges an officer of the Service or local authority officer to advise, assist and (where appropriate) befriend a named person or persons. Any of the following may be named in the order: a parent or guardian of the child, anyone with whom the child is living or who has a contact order with respect to the child and the child himself (s 16(2)). An order is to be made only where the court is satisfied that the circumstances are exceptional and where every person who is to be named in the order (other than the child) has given consent (s 16(3)). Normally the court will make a family assistance order of its own motion, but although the rules and the Act do not specifically prescribe any procedure for applying for a s 16 order neither do they prohibit such an application and therefore presumably one can be made.

Where there is a concurrent s 8 order, the officer of the Service or local authority officer appointed under this section may refer to the court the question of whether the s 8 order should be varied or discharged (s 16(6)). Such an application is covered by the rules (see FPR 1991, r 4.1(2)(*c*) and App 3, and Family Proceedings Courts (Children Act 1989) Rules 1991, Sch 2).

"order under this Part" (s 16(1))—The orders available under Pt II are: a contact order, a prohibited steps order, a residence order and a specific issue order (all under s 8). It would also seem that an order for financial relief under Sch 1 may be classified as an order under Pt II as Sch 1 derives from s 15. The power to make a family assistance order is not limited to applications for s 8 orders; it may be exercised in any family proceedings where there is power to make an order under Pt II and "family proceedings" is widely defined by s 8(3). It follows that a family assistance order could, for example, be made on an application for a care or supervision order.

Enforcement of family assistance order—In *Re C (Family Assistance Order)* [1996] 1 FLR 424, FD, a family assistance order had been made directed to a local authority. The local authority did not have the resources to implement it and restored the matter before the court. There being no remedy provided in CA 1989 for such a circumstance, the judge supposed that one might make an order directed to the director of social services, endorsed with a penal notice, so that enforcement proceedings could ensue, but commented that that would be totally contrary to the best interests of the child concerned and the child care system as a whole. See also *Re E (Family Assistance Order)* [1999] 2 FLR 512 in which a family assistance order was made against a local authority in spite of the authority's reluctance to submit to it; on the exceptional facts of the case supervised contact between the child and his mother could not have taken place without such an order.

PART III
LOCAL AUTHORITY SUPPORT FOR CHILDREN AND FAMILIES

Provision of services for children and their families

17 Provision of services for children in need, their families and others

(1) It shall be the general duty of every local authority (in addition to the other duties imposed on them by this Part) –

(*a*) to safeguard and promote the welfare of children within their area who are in need; and
(*b*) so far as is consistent with that duty, to promote the upbringing of such children by their families,

by providing a range and level of services appropriate to those children's needs.

(2) For the purpose principally of facilitating the discharge of their general duty under this section, every local authority shall have the specific duties and powers set out in Part I of Schedule 2.

(3) Any service provided by an authority in the exercise of functions conferred on them by this section may be provided for the family of a particular child in need or for any member of his family, if it is provided with a view to safeguarding or promoting the child's welfare.

(4) The Secretary of State may by order amend any provision of Part I of Schedule 2 or add any further duty or power to those for the time being mentioned there.

(5) Every local authority –

(*a*) shall facilitate the provision by others (including in particular voluntary organisations) of services which the authority have power to provide by virtue of this section, or section 18, 20, 23, 23B to 23D, 24A or 24B; and
(*b*) may make such arrangements as they see fit for any person to act on their behalf in the provision of any such service.

(6) The services provided by a local authority in the exercise of functions conferred on them by this section may include giving assistance in kind or, in exceptional circumstances, in cash.

(7) Assistance may be unconditional or subject to conditions as to the repayment of the assistance or of its value (in whole or in part).

(8) Before giving any assistance or imposing any conditions, a local authority shall have regard to the means of the child concerned and of each of his parents.

(9) No person shall be liable to make any repayment of assistance or of its value at any time when he is in receipt of income support, working families' tax credit or disabled person's tax credit under Part VII of the Social Security Contributions and Benefits Act 1992 or of an income-based jobseeker's allowance.

(10) For the purposes of this Part a child shall be taken to be in need if –

(*a*) he is unlikely to achieve or maintain, or to have the opportunity of achieving or maintaining, a reasonable standard of health or development without the provision for him of services by a local authority under this Part;

(*b*) his health or development is likely to be significantly impaired, or further impaired, without the provision for him of such services; or

(*c*) he is disabled,

and "family," in relation to such a child, includes any person who has parental responsibility for the child and any other person with whom he has been living.

(11) For the purposes of this Part, a child is disabled if he is blind, deaf or dumb or suffers from mental disorder of any kind or is substantially and permanently handicapped by illness, injury or congenital deformity or such other disability as may be prescribed; and in this Part –

"development" means physical, intellectual, emotional, social or behavioural development; and

"health" means physical or mental health.

Amendments—Disability Living Allowance and Disability Working Allowance Act 1991, s 7(2), Sch 3, para 13; Social Security (Consequential Provisions) Act 1992, s 4, Sch 2, para 108; Jobseekers Act 1995, s 41, Sch 2, para 19; Tax Credits Act 1999, s 1(2), Sch 1, paras 1, 6(*d*)(i); Children (Leaving Care) Act 2000, s 7(2).

"mental disorder" (s 17(11))—By virtue of Mental Health Act 1983, s 1(2), this means "mental illness, arrested or incomplete development of mind, psychopathic disorder and any other disorder or disability of mind and 'mentally disordered' shall be construed accordingly". For a full explanation see the note to FPR 1991, r 9.1.

Extent of local authority's power to provide accommodation for families—Section 17 gives a local authority the power to provide accommodation for a family where it considers it appropriate to do so. However, the authority may, in the exercise of its discretion, decline to provide such accommodation, provided that it considers each case fairly on its merits (*The Queen on the Application of W v Lambeth London Borough Council* [2002] EWCA Civ 613, [2002] FLR 327).

17A Direct payments

(1) Instead of providing services in the exercise of functions conferred on them by section 17, a local authority may make to a person falling within subsection (2) (if he consents) a payment of such amount as, subject to subsections (5) and (6), they think fit in respect of his securing the provision of any of the services which the local authority would otherwise have provided.

(2) The following fall within this subsection –

(*a*) a person with parental responsibility for a disabled child;

(*b*) a disabled child aged 16 or 17.

(3) A payment under subsection (1) shall be subject to the condition that the person to whom it is made shall not secure the provision of the service to which it relates by a person who is of a prescribed description.

(4) The Secretary of State may by regulations provide that the power conferred by subsection (1) is not to be exercisable in relation to the provision of residential accommodation for any person for a period exceeding a prescribed period.

(5) Except as mentioned in subsection (6) of this section, subsections (2) and (6) of section 1, and subsections (1) and (2) of section 2, of the Community Care

(Direct Payments) Act 1996 apply in relation to payments under subsection (1) as they apply in relation to payments under section 1(1) of that Act, but as if –

(*a*) the reference to "subsection (4)" in section 1(6)(*b*) of that Act were a reference to subsection (3) of this section; and

(*b*) the references to "the relevant community care enactment" in section 2 of that Act were to Part III of the Children Act 1989.

(6) Section 1(2) of the Community Care (Direct Payments) Act 1996 does not apply in relation to payments under subsection (1) to –

(*a*) a person with parental responsibility for a disabled child, other than a parent of such a child under the age of sixteen, in respect of a service which would otherwise have been provided for the child; or

(*b*) any person who is in receipt of income support, working families' tax credit or disabled person's tax credit under Part VII of the Social Security Contributions and Benefits Act 1992 or of an income-based jobseeker's allowance,

and in those cases the amount of any payment under subsection (1) is to be at a rate equal to the local authority's estimate of the reasonable cost of securing the provision of the service concerned.

Amendments—Inserted by Carers and Disabled Children Act 2000, s 7(1).

18 Day care for pre-school and other children

(1) Every local authority shall provide such day care for children in need within their area who are –

(*a*) aged five or under; and

(*b*) not yet attending schools,

as is appropriate.

(2) A local authority may provide day care for children within their area who satisfy the conditions mentioned in subsection (1)(*a*) and (*b*) even though they are not in need.

(3) A local authority may provide facilities (including training, advice, guidance and counselling) for those –

(*a*) caring for children in day care; or

(*b*) who at any time accompany such children while they are in day care.

(4) In this section "day care" means any form of care or supervised activity provided for children during the day (whether or not it is provided on a regular basis).

(5) Every local authority shall provide for children in need within their area who are attending any school such care or supervised activities as is appropriate –

(*a*) outside school hours; or

(*b*) during school holidays.

(6) A local authority may provide such care or supervised activities for children within their area who are attending any school even though those children are not in need.

(7) In this section "supervised activity" means an activity supervised by a responsible person.

19 Review of provision for day care, child minding etc

(1) Every local authority in England and Wales shall review –

(*a*) the provision which they made under section 18;
(*b*) the extent to which the services of child minders are available within their area with respect to children under the age of eight; and
(*c*) the provision for day care within their area made for children under the age of eight by persons other than the authority, required to register under Part XA.

(2) A review under subsection (1) shall be conducted –

(*a*) together with the appropriate local education authority; and
(*b*) at least once in every review period.

(3) Every local authority in Scotland shall, at least once in every review period, review –

(*a*) the provision for day care within their area made for children under the age of eight by the local authority and by persons required to register under section 71(1)(*b*); and
(*b*) the extent to which the services of child minders are available within their area with respect to children under the age of eight.

(4) In conducting any such review, the two authorities or, in Scotland, the authority shall have regard to the provision made with respect to children under the age of eight in relevant establishments within their area.

(5) In this section –

"relevant establishment" means –

(*a*) (*applies to Scotland only*)
(*b*) in relation to England and Wales, any establishment which is mentioned in paragraphs 1 and 2 of Schedule 9A (establishments exempt from the registration requirements which apply in relation to the provision of day care in England and Wales);

"review period" means the period of one year beginning with the commencement of this section and each subsequent period of three years beginning with an anniversary of that commencement.

(6) Where a local authority have conducted a review under this section they shall publish the result of the review –

(*a*) as soon as is reasonably practicable;
(*b*) in such form as they consider appropriate; and
(*c*) together with any proposals they may have with respect to the matters reviewed.

(7) The authorities conducting any review under this section shall have regard to –

(*a*) any representations made to any one of them by any relevant Health Authority, Special Health Authority, Primary Care Trust or health board; and
(*b*) any other representations which they consider to be relevant.

(8) In the application of this section to Scotland, "day care" has the same meaning as in section 79 and "health board" has the same meaning as in the National Health Service (Scotland) Act 1978.

PART II

Amendments—Health Authorities Act 1995, s 2, Sch 1, para 118; SI 2000/90; Care Standards Act 2000, s 116, Sch 4, para 14.

Provision of accommodation for children

20 Provision of accommodation for children: general

(1) Every local authority shall provide accommodation for any child in need within their area who appears to them to require accommodation as a result of –

(*a*) there being no person who has parental responsibility for him;
(*b*) his being lost or having been abandoned; or
(*c*) the person who has been caring for him being prevented (whether or not permanently, and for whatever reason) from providing him with suitable accommodation or care.

(2) Where a local authority provide accommodation under subsection (1) for a child who is ordinarily resident in the area of another local authority, that other local authority may take over the provision of accommodation for the child within –

(*a*) three months of being notified in writing that the child is being provided with accommodation; or
(*b*) such other longer period as may be prescribed.

(3) Every local authority shall provide accommodation for any child in need within their area who has reached the age of sixteen and whose welfare the authority consider is likely to be seriously prejudiced if they do not provide him with accommodation.

(4) A local authority may provide accommodation for any child within their area (even though a person who has parental responsibility for him is able to provide him with accommodation) if they consider that to do so would safeguard or promote the child's welfare.

(5) A local authority may provide accommodation for any person who has reached the age of sixteen but is under twenty-one in any community home which takes children who have reached the age of sixteen if they consider that to do so would safeguard or promote his welfare.

(6) Before providing accommodation under this section, a local authority shall, so far as is reasonably practicable and consistent with the child's welfare –

(*a*) ascertain the child's wishes regarding the provision of accommodation; and
(*b*) give due consideration (having regard to his age and understanding) to such wishes of the child as they have been able to ascertain.

(7) A local authority may not provide accommodation under this section for any child if any person who –

(*a*) has parental responsibility for him; and
(*b*) is willing and able to –
  (i) provide accommodation for him; or
  (ii) arrange for accommodation to be provided for him,

objects.

(8) Any person who has parental responsibility for a child may at any time remove the child from accommodation provided by or on behalf of the local authority under this section.

(9) Subsections (7) and (8) do not apply while any person –

(*a*) in whose favour a residence order is in force with respect to the child; or
(*b*) who has care of the child by virtue of an order made in the exercise of the High Court's inherent jurisdiction with respect to children,

agrees to the child being looked after in accommodation provided by or on behalf of the local authority.

(10) Where there is more than one such person as is mentioned in subsection (9), all of them must agree.

(11) Subsections (7) and (8) do not apply where a child who has reached the age of sixteen agrees to being provided with accommodation under this section.

Local authority has no power to transfer accommodated child out of residential care and into foster care without permission of natural parents—Where a child is being accommodated by a local authority under a voluntary arrangement with her natural parents the local authority has no power to arrange a transfer of the child from a residential institution to foster care without the permission of her natural parents; parental responsibility includes the right to decide where a child lives (*R v Tameside Metropolitan Borough Council ex parte J* [2000] 1 FLR 942).

21 Provision of accommodation for children in police protection or detention or on remand etc

(1) Every local authority shall make provision for the reception and accommodation of children who are removed or kept away from home under Part V.

(2) Every local authority shall receive, and provide accommodation for, children –

(*a*) in police protection whom they are requested to receive under section 46(3)(*f*);
(*b*) whom they are requested to receive under section 38(6) of the Police and Criminal Evidence Act 1984;
(*c*) who are –
  (i) on remand under paragraph 7(5) of Schedule 7 to the Powers of Criminal Courts (Sentencing) Act 2000 or section 23(1) of the Children and Young Persons Act 1969; or
  (ii) the subject of a supervision order imposing a local authority residence requirement under paragraph 5 of Schedule 6 to that Act,

and with respect to whom they are the designated authority.

(3) Where a child has been –

(*a*) removed under Part V; or
(*b*) detained under section 38 of the Police and Criminal Evidence Act 1984,

and he is not being provided with accommodation by a local authority or in a hospital vested in the Secretary of State or a Primary Care Trust or otherwise made available pursuant to arrangements made by a Health Authority or a Primary Care Trust, any reasonable expenses of accommodating him shall be recoverable from the local authority in whose area he is ordinarily resident.

Amendments—Courts and Legal Services Act 1990, s 116, Sch 16, para 11; National Health Service and Community Care Act 1990, s 66(1), Sch 9, para 36; Health Authorities Act 1995, s 2, Sch 1, para 118; SI 2000/90; Powers of Criminal Courts (Sentencing) Act 2000, s 165, Sch 9, para 126.

Duties of local authorities in relation to children looked after by them

22 General duty of local authority in relation to children looked after by them

(1) In this Act, any reference to a child who is looked after by a local authority is a reference to a child who is –

(*a*) in their care; or

(*b*) provided with accommodation by the authority in the exercise of any functions (in particular those under this Act) which are social services functions within the meaning of the Local Authority Social Services Act 1970, apart from functions under sections 23B and 24B.

(2) In subsection (1) "accommodation" means accommodation which is provided for a continuous period of more than 24 hours.

(3) It shall be the duty of a local authority looking after any child –

(*a*) to safeguard and promote his welfare; and

(*b*) to make such use of services available for children cared for by their own parents as appears to the authority reasonable in his case.

(4) Before making any decision with respect to a child whom they are looking after, or proposing to look after, a local authority shall, so far as is reasonably practicable, ascertain the wishes and feelings of –

(*a*) the child;

(*b*) his parents;

(*c*) any person who is not a parent of his but who has parental responsibility for him; and

(*d*) any other person whose wishes and feelings the authority consider to be relevant,

regarding the matter to be decided.

(5) In making any such decision a local authority shall give due consideration –

(*a*) having regard to his age and understanding, to such wishes and feelings of the child as they have been able to ascertain;

(*b*) to such wishes and feelings of any person mentioned in subsection (4)(*b*) to (*d*) as they have been able to ascertain; and

(*c*) to the child's religious persuasion, racial origin and cultural and linguistic background.

(6) If it appears to a local authority that it is necessary, for the purposes of protecting members of the public from serious injury, to exercise their powers with respect to a child whom they are looking after in a manner which may not be consistent with their duties under this section, they may do so.

(7) If the Secretary of State considers it necessary, for the purpose of protecting members of the public from serious injury, to give directions to a local authority with respect to the exercise of their powers with respect to a child whom they are looking after, he may give such directions to the authority.

(8) Where any such directions are given to an authority they shall comply with them even though doing so is inconsistent with their duties under this section.

Amendments—Children (Leaving Care) Act 2000, s 2(1); Local Government Act 2000, s 107(1), Sch 5, para 19.

Duty to ascertain wishes and feelings of the parents (s 22(4)(*b*))—The duty of the local authority to ascertain the wishes and feelings of the parents before making any decision with respect to a looked-after child is directory and not mandatory; the result of any non-compliance with the provisions should be treated as an irregularity (*Re P (Children Act 1989, ss 22 and 26: Local Authority Compliance)* [2000] 2 FLR 910).

23 Provision of accommodation and maintenance by local authority for children whom they are looking after

(1) It shall be the duty of any local authority looking after a child –

(*a*) when he is in their care, to provide accommodation for him; and
(*b*) to maintain him in other respects apart from providing accommodation for him.

(2) A local authority shall provide accommodation and maintenance for any child whom they are looking after by –

(*a*) placing him (subject to subsection (5) and any regulations made by the Secretary of State) with –
(i) a family;
(ii) a relative of his; or
(iii) any other suitable person,
on such terms as to payment by the authority and otherwise as the authority may determine;
(*aa*) maintaining him in an appropriate children's home;
(*b*)–(*e*) (*repealed*)
(*f*) making such other arrangements as –
(i) seem appropriate to them; and
(ii) comply with any regulations made by the Secretary of State.

(2A) Where under subsection (2)(*aa*) a local authority maintains a child in a home provided, equipped and maintained by the Secretary of State under section 82(5), it shall do so on such terms as the Secretary of State may from time to time determine.

(3) Any person with whom a child has been placed under subsection (2)(*a*) is referred to in this Act as a local authority foster parent unless he falls within subsection (4).

(4) A person falls within this subsection if he is –

(*a*) a parent of the child;
(*b*) a person who is not a parent of the child but who has parental responsibility for him; or
(*c*) where the child is in care and there was a residence order in force with respect to him immediately before the care order was made, a person in whose favour the residence order was made.

(5) Where a child is in the care of a local authority, the authority may only allow him to live with a person who falls within subsection (4) in accordance with regulations made by the Secretary of State.

(5A) For the purposes of subsection (5) a child shall be regarded as living with a person if he stays with that person for a continuous period of more than 24 hours.

(6) Subject to any regulations made by the Secretary of State for the purposes of this subsection, any local authority looking after a child shall make arrangements to enable him to live with –

(*a*) a person falling within subsection (4); or

(*b*) a relative, friend or other person connected with him,

unless that would not be reasonably practicable or consistent with his welfare.

(7) Where a local authority provide accommodation for a child whom they are looking after, they shall, subject to the provisions of this Part and so far as is reasonably practicable and consistent with his welfare, secure that –

(*a*) the accommodation is near his home; and
(*b*) where the authority are also providing accommodation for a sibling of his, they are accommodated together.

(8) Where a local authority provide accommodation for a child whom they are looking after and who is disabled, they shall, so far as is reasonably practicable, secure that the accommodation is not unsuitable to his particular needs.

(9) Part II of Schedule 2 shall have effect for the purposes of making further provision as to children looked after by local authorities and in particular as to the regulations that may be made under subsections (2)(*a*) and (*f*) and (5).

(10) In this Act –

"appropriate children's home" means a children's home in respect of which a person is registered under Part II of the Care Standards Act 2000; and
"children's home" has the same meaning as in that Act.

Amendments—Courts and Legal Services Act 1990, s 116, Sch 16, para 12; Care Standards Act 2000, s 116, Sch 4, para 14(3).

Payment of foster allowances (s 23(2)(*a*))—It is unlawful and in breach of Arts 8 and 14 of the ECPHRFF 1950 for a local authority to have a policy whereby it pays its short-term foster carers who are friends or relatives of the child concerned at a different and significantly lower rate than it pays other such foster carers (*The Queen on the Application of L and Others v Manchester City Council; The Queen on the Application of R and Another v Manchester City Council* [2001] EWHC Admin 707, [2002] 1 FLR 43, Munby J, QBD).

23A The responsible authority and relevant children

(1) The responsible local authority shall have the functions set out in section 23B in respect of a relevant child.

(2) In subsection (1) "relevant child" means (subject to subsection (3)) a child who –

(*a*) is not being looked after by any local authority;
(*b*) was, before last ceasing to be looked after, an eligible child for the purposes of paragraph 19B of Schedule 2; and
(*c*) is aged sixteen or seventeen.

(3) The Secretary of State may prescribe –

(*a*) additional categories of relevant children; and
(*b*) categories of children who are not to be relevant children despite falling within subsection (2).

(4) In subsection (1) the "responsible local authority" is the one which last looked after the child.

(5) If under subsection (3)(*a*) the Secretary of State prescribes a category of relevant children which includes children who do not fall within subsection (2)(*b*) (for example, because they were being looked after by a local authority in

Scotland), he may in the regulations also provide for which local authority is to be the responsible local authority for those children.

Amendments—Inserted by Children (Leaving Care) Act 2000, s 2(4).

23B Additional functions of the responsible authority in respect of relevant children

(1) It is the duty of each local authority to take reasonable steps to keep in touch with a relevant child for whom they are the responsible authority, whether he is within their area or not.

(2) It is the duty of each local authority to appoint a personal adviser for each relevant child (if they have not already done so under paragraph 19C of Schedule 2).

(3) It is the duty of each local authority, in relation to any relevant child who does not already have a pathway plan prepared for the purposes of paragraph 19B of Schedule 2 –

- (*a*) to carry out an assessment of his needs with a view to determining what advice, assistance and support it would be appropriate for them to provide him under this Part; and
- (*b*) to prepare a pathway plan for him.

(4) The local authority may carry out such an assessment at the same time as any assessment of his needs is made under any enactment referred to in sub-paragraphs (*a*) to (*c*) of paragraph 3 of Schedule 2, or under any other enactment.

(5) The Secretary of State may by regulations make provision as to assessments for the purposes of subsection (3).

(6) The regulations may in particular make provision about –

- (*a*) who is to be consulted in relation to an assessment;
- (*b*) the way in which an assessment is to be carried out, by whom and when;
- (*c*) the recording of the results of an assessment;
- (*d*) the considerations to which the local authority are to have regard in carrying out an assessment.

(7) The authority shall keep the pathway plan under regular review.

(8) The responsible local authority shall safeguard and promote the child's welfare and, unless they are satisfied that his welfare does not require it, support him by –

- (*a*) maintaining him;
- (*b*) providing him with or maintaining him in suitable accommodation; and
- (*c*) providing support of such other descriptions as may be prescribed.

(9) Support under subsection (8) may be in cash.

(10) The Secretary of State may by regulations make provision about the meaning of "suitable accommodation" and in particular about the suitability of landlords or other providers of accommodation.

(11) If the local authority have lost touch with a relevant child, despite taking reasonable steps to keep in touch, they must without delay –

- (*a*) consider how to re-establish contact; and
- (*b*) take reasonable steps to do so,

and while the child is still a relevant child must continue to take such steps until they succeed.

(12) Subsections (7) to (9) of section 17 apply in relation to support given under this section as they apply in relation to assistance given under that section.

(13) Subsections (4) and (5) of section 22 apply in relation to any decision by a local authority for the purposes of this section as they apply in relation to the decisions referred to in that section.

Amendments—Inserted by Children (Leaving Care) Act 2000, s 2(4).

23C Continuing functions in respect of former relevant children

(1) Each local authority shall have the duties provided for in this section towards –

(*a*) a person who has been a relevant child for the purposes of section 23A (and would be one if he were under eighteen), and in relation to whom they were the last responsible authority; and

(*b*) a person who was being looked after by them when he attained the age of eighteen, and immediately before ceasing to be looked after was an eligible child,

and in this section such a person is referred to as a "former relevant child".

(2) It is the duty of the local authority to take reasonable steps –

(*a*) to keep in touch with a former relevant child whether he is within their area or not; and

(*b*) if they lose touch with him, to re-establish contact.

(3) It is the duty of the local authority –

(*a*) to continue the appointment of a personal adviser for a former relevant child; and

(*b*) to continue to keep his pathway plan under regular review.

(4) It is the duty of the local authority to give a former relevant child –

(*a*) assistance of the kind referred to in section 24B(1), to the extent that his welfare requires it;

(*b*) assistance of the kind referred to in section 24B(2), to the extent that his welfare and his educational or training needs require it;

(*c*) other assistance, to the extent that his welfare requires it.

(5) The assistance given under subsection (4)(*c*) may be in kind or, in exceptional circumstances, in cash.

(6) Subject to subsection (7), the duties set out in subsections (2), (3) and (4) subsist until the former relevant child reaches the age of twenty-one.

(7) If the former relevant child's pathway plan sets out a programme of education or training which extends beyond his twenty-first birthday –

(*a*) the duty set out in subsection (4)(*b*) continues to subsist for so long as the former relevant child continues to pursue that programme; and

(*b*) the duties set out in subsections (2) and (3) continue to subsist concurrently with that duty.

(8) For the purposes of subsection (7)(*a*) there shall be disregarded any interruption in a former relevant child's pursuance of a programme of education or

training if the local authority are satisfied that he will resume it as soon as is reasonably practicable.

(9) Section 24B(5) applies in relation to a person being given assistance under subsection (4)(*b*) as it applies in relation to a person to whom section 24B(3) applies.

(10) Subsections (7) to (9) of section 17 apply in relation to assistance given under this section as they apply in relation to assistance given under that section.

Amendments—Inserted by Children (Leaving Care) Act 2000, s 2(4).

Personal advisers and pathway plans

23D Personal advisers

(1) The Secretary of State may by regulations require local authorities to appoint a personal adviser for children or young persons of a prescribed description who have reached the age of sixteen but not the age of twenty-one who are not –

- (*a*) children who are relevant children for the purposes of section 23A;
- (*b*) the young persons referred to in section 23C; or
- (*c*) the children referred to in paragraph 19C of Schedule 2.

(2) Personal advisers appointed under or by virtue of this Part shall (in addition to any other functions) have such functions as the Secretary of State prescribes.

Amendments—Inserted by Children (Leaving Care) Act 2000, s 3.

23E Pathway plans

(1) In this Part, a reference to a "pathway plan" is to a plan setting out –

- (*a*) in the case of a plan prepared under paragraph 19B of Schedule 2 –
  - (i) the advice, assistance and support which the local authority intend to provide a child under this Part, both while they are looking after him and later; and
  - (ii) when they might cease to look after him; and
- (*b*) in the case of a plan prepared under section 23B, the advice, assistance and support which the local authority intend to provide under this Part,

and dealing with such other matters (if any) as may be prescribed.

(2) The Secretary of State may by regulations make provision about pathway plans and their review.

Amendments—Inserted by Children (Leaving Care) Act 2000, s 3.

Advice and assistance for certain children and young persons

24 Persons qualifying for advice and assistance

(1) In this Part "a person qualifying for advice and assistance" means a person who –

- (*a*) is under twenty-one; and
- (*b*) at any time after reaching the age of sixteen but while still a child was, but is no longer, looked after, accommodated or fostered.

(2) In subsection (1)(*b*), "looked after, accommodated or fostered" means –

(*a*) looked after by a local authority;
(*b*) accommodated by or on behalf of a voluntary organisation;
(*c*) accommodated in a registered children's home;
(*d*) accommodated for a consecutive period of at least three months –
  (i) by any Health Authority, Special Health Authority, Primary Care Trust or local education authority, or
  (ii) in any residential care home, nursing home or mental nursing home or in any accommodation provided by a National Health Service trust; or
(*e*) privately fostered.

(3) Subsection (2)(*d*) applies even if the period of three months mentioned there began before the child reached the age of sixteen.

(4) In the case of a person qualifying for advice and assistance by virtue of subsection (2)(*a*), it is the duty of the local authority which last looked after him to take such steps as they think appropriate to contact him at such times as they think appropriate with a view to discharging their functions under sections 24A and 24B.

(5) In each of sections 24A and 24B, the local authority under the duty or having the power mentioned there ("the relevant authority") is –

(*a*) in the case of a person qualifying for advice and assistance by virtue of subsection (2)(*a*), the local authority which last looked after him; or
(*b*) in the case of any other person qualifying for advice and assistance, the local authority within whose area the person is (if he has asked for help of a kind which can be given under section 24A or 24B).

Amendments—Substituted by Children (Leaving Care) Act 2000, s 4(1).

24A Advice and assistance

(1) The relevant authority shall consider whether the conditions in subsection (2) are satisfied in relation to a person qualifying for advice and assistance.

(2) The conditions are that –

(*a*) he needs help of a kind which they can give under this section or section 24B; and
(*b*) in the case of a person who was not being looked after by any local authority, they are satisfied that the person by whom he was being looked after does not have the necessary facilities for advising or befriending him.

(3) If the conditions are satisfied –

(*a*) they shall advise and befriend him if he was being looked after by a local authority or was accommodated by or on behalf of a voluntary organisation; and
(*b*) in any other case they may do so.

(4) Where as a result of this section a local authority are under a duty, or are empowered, to advise and befriend a person, they may also give him assistance.

(5) The assistance may be in kind or, in exceptional circumstances, in cash.

(6) Subsections (7) to (9) of section 17 apply in relation to assistance given under this section or section 24B as they apply in relation to assistance given under that section.

Amendments—Inserted by Children (Leaving Care) Act 2000, s 4(1).

24B Employment, education and training

(1) The relevant local authority may give assistance to any person who qualifies for advice and assistance by virtue of section 24(2)(*a*) by contributing to expenses incurred by him in living near the place where he is, or will be, employed or seeking employment.

(2) The relevant local authority may give assistance to a person to whom subsection (3) applies by –

(*a*) contributing to expenses incurred by the person in question in living near the place where he is, or will be, receiving education or training; or
(*b*) making a grant to enable him to meet expenses connected with his education or training.

(3) This subsection applies to any person who –

(*a*) is under twenty-four; and
(*b*) qualifies for advice and assistance by virtue of section 24(2)(*a*), or would have done so if he were under twenty-one.

(4) Where a local authority are assisting a person under subsection (2) they may disregard any interruption in his attendance on the course if he resumes it as soon as is reasonably practicable.

(5) Where the local authority are satisfied that a person to whom subsection (3) applies who is in full-time further or higher education needs accommodation during a vacation because his term-time accommodation is not available to him then, they shall give him assistance by –

(*a*) providing him with suitable accommodation during the vacation; or
(*b*) paying him enough to enable him to secure such accommodation himself.

(6) The Secretary of State may prescribe the meaning of "full-time", "further education", "higher education" and "vacation" for the purposes of subsection (5).

Amendments—Inserted by Children (Leaving Care) Act 2000, s 4(1).

24C Information

(1) Where it appears to a local authority that a person –

(*a*) with whom they are under a duty to keep in touch under section 23B, 23C or 24; or
(*b*) whom they have been advising and befriending under section 24A; or
(*c*) to whom they have been giving assistance under section 24B,

proposes to live, or is living, in the area of another local authority, they must inform that other authority.

(2) Where a child who is accommodated –

(*a*) by a voluntary organisation or in a registered children's home;
(*b*) by any Health Authority, Special Health Authority, Primary Care Trust or local education authority; or
(*c*) in any residential care home, nursing home or mental nursing home or any accommodation provided by a National Health Service trust,

ceases to be so accommodated, after reaching the age of sixteen, the organisation, authority or (as the case may be) person carrying on the home shall inform the local authority within whose area the child proposes to live.

(3) Subsection (2) only applies, by virtue of paragraph (*b*) or (*c*), if the accommodation has been provided for a consecutive period of at least three months.

Amendments—Inserted by Children (Leaving Care) Act 2000, s 4(1).

24D Representations: sections 23A to 24B

(1) Every local authority shall establish a procedure for considering representations (including complaints) made to them by –

- (*a*) a relevant child for the purposes of section 23A or a young person falling within section 23C;
- (*b*) a person qualifying for advice and assistance; or
- (*c*) a person falling within section 24B(2),

about the discharge of their functions under this Part in relation to him.

(2) In considering representations under subsection (1), a local authority shall comply with regulations (if any) made by the Secretary of State for the purposes of this subsection.

Amendments—Inserted by Children (Leaving Care) Act 2000, s 5.

Secure accommodation

25 Use of accommodation for restricting liberty

(1) Subject to the following provisions of this section, a child who is being looked after by a local authority may not be placed, and, if placed, may not be kept, in accommodation provided for the purpose of restricting liberty ("secure accommodation") unless it appears –

- (*a*) that –
  - (i) he has a history of absconding and is likely to abscond from any other description of accommodation; and
  - (ii) if he absconds, he is likely to suffer significant harm, or
- (*b*) that if he is kept in any other description of accommodation he is likely to injure himself or other persons.

(2) The Secretary of State may by regulations –

- (*a*) specify a maximum period –
  - (i) beyond which a child may not be kept in secure accommodation without the authority of the court; and
  - (ii) for which the court may authorise a child to be kept in secure accommodation;
- (*b*) empower the court from time to time to authorise a child to be kept in secure accommodation for such further period as the regulations may specify; and
- (*c*) provide that applications to the court under this section shall be made only by local authorities.

(3) It shall be the duty of a court hearing an application under this section to determine whether any relevant criteria for keeping a child in secure accommodation are satisfied in his case.

(4) If a court determines that any such criteria are satisfied, it shall make an order authorising the child to be kept in secure accommodation and specifying the maximum period for which he may be so kept.

(5) On any adjournment of the hearing of an application under this section, a court may make an interim order permitting the child to be kept during the period of the adjournment in secure accommodation.

(6) No court shall exercise the powers conferred by this section in respect of a child who is not legally represented in that court unless, having been informed of his right to apply for representation funded by the Legal Services Commission as part of the Community Legal Service or Criminal Defence Service and having had the opportunity to do so, he refused or failed to apply.

(7) The Secretary of State may by regulations provide that –

(*a*) this section shall or shall not apply to any description of children specified in the regulations;

(*b*) this section shall have effect in relation to children of a description specified in the regulations subject to such modifications as may be so specified;

(*c*) such other provisions as may be so specified shall have effect for the purpose of determining whether a child of a description specified in the regulations may be placed or kept in secure accommodation.

(8) The giving of an authorisation under this section shall not prejudice any power of any court in England and Wales or Scotland to give directions relating to the child to whom the authorisation relates.

(9) This section is subject to section 20(8).

Amendments—Access to Justice Act 1999, s 24, Sch 4, para 45.

Defined terms—"child": s 105(1).

Scope of provision—The Children (Secure Accommodation) Regulations 1991 and the Children (Secure Accommodation) (No 2) Regulations 1991 have been made under this section and reference should also be made to these.

"secure accommodation"—To constitute "secure accommodation" a place does not have to be so designated; each case will depend on its own facts. It is the restriction of liberty which is the essential factor in determining what is secure accommodation, see *A Metropolitan Borough Council v DB* [1997] 1 FLR 767, in which Cazalet J held that a maternity ward was secure accommodation where entrance was only by way of a key or pass. The 17-year-old mother had not been given a key or pass and staff were instructed not to let her leave. However, contrast *Re C (Detention: Medical Treatment)* [1997] 2 FLR 180, where Wall J, whilst agreeing that premises which are not designed as secure accommodation may become such by virtue of the use to which they are put in the particular circumstances of individual cases, held that the more natural meaning of the words "provided for the purpose of restricting liberty" in s 25(1) is "designed for, or having as its primary purpose the restriction of liberty". In *Re C* a clinic for the treatment of anorexia nervosa was held not to be secure accommodation because the primary purpose of the clinic was to achieve treatment, and the restriction of liberty was only incidental to that end. However, a similar result was achieved by invoking the inherent jurisdiction under CA 1989, s 100 to direct that the minor remain an in-patient at the clinic. A secure accommodation order is a deprivation of liberty within the meaning of Art 5 of the European Convention of Human Rights, but is not incompatible with the Convention where it is justified under one of the exceptions in Art 5(1), for example where the order is for the purposes of educational supervision (*Re K (Secure Accommodation Order: Right to Liberty)* [2001] 1 FLR 526, CA).

"being looked after by a local authority" (s 25(1))—See CA 1989, s 22(1) and, as to a child who is bailed with a condition of residence to the local authority, see *Re C (Secure Accommodation: Bail)* [1994] 2 FLR 922.

"may not be placed, and, if placed, may not be kept" (s 25(1))—The legislation does not specify that a child should already have been placed in secure accommodation before an order is sought. The court's authority is not required for the first 72 hours that a child is placed in secure accommodation. While in ordinary cases a child ought to be in secure accommodation at the time of the application, having satisfied either the absconding or injury criterion, exceptional circumstances can justify the making of an application where a child is not already so placed. Neither knowing that the child is absconding nor the lack of suitable accommodation amount to exceptional circumstances (*Re AK (Secure Accommodation Order)* [2000] 1 FLR 317).

Criteria for order (s 25(1)(*a*), (*b*))—The two limbs of s 25(1) should be read disjunctively and not conjunctively. Therefore, the court does not have to find both s 25(1)(*a*) and (*b*) satisfied before making an order, since either is sufficient (*Re D (Secure Accommodation Order) (No 1)* [1997] 1 FLR 197). It is essential that there should be a clear record of facts as found by the court and for which sworn evidence was necessary (*Re AS (Secure Accommodation Order)* [1999] 1 FLR 103). The phrase "likely to abscond" in s 25(1)(*a*)(i) should be construed in the same way as the threshold criteria in s 31. "Likely" is used in the sense of a real possibility, a possibility that cannot be sensibly ignored having regard to the nature and gravity of the feared harm in the particular case (*Re D (Secure Accommodation Order)* [1999] Fam Law 311).

"child who is not legally represented" (s 25(6))—A child who is instructing a solicitor himself (in accordance with FPR 1991, r 4.12 or Family Proceedings Courts (Children Act 1989) Rules 1991, r 12) is obviously legally represented within the meaning of this section. From the wording of the Act and the rules, it is clear that a child is also legally represented where it is his children's guardian who is actually giving instructions to the solicitor (the more normal case since a children's guardian *will* normally be appointed by virtue of s 41(1)). It is implicit that in order for legal representation to be effective it must involve the taking of instructions (*Re AS (Secure Accommodation Order)* [1999] 1 FLR 103 – where an application for a s 25 order was held to be procedurally flawed because the child was not informed of the hearing and a guardian ad litem (children's guardian) was not appointed). However, where the local authority have complied with the service requirements by serving the application on the parents and the solicitor appointed on behalf of the guardian it may still be fair to allow the application to proceed where the child and her own solicitor have only a short time to consult; although in such circumstances it may be preferable to make an interim order and adjourn for a few days to allow the child to respond to the application (*Re C (Secure Accommodation Order: Representation)* [2001] 2 FLR 169).

Attendance of child at hearing—Whilst the court can allow the child who is the subject of the application to attend court, it must always bear in mind that attendance is likely to be harmful to the child and should only permit it if satisfied that it is in the interests of the child (*Re W (Secure Accommodation Order: Attendance at Court)* [1994] 2 FLR 1092, and see further **Use of the power to exclude** under FPR 1991, r 4.16/ FPC(CA 1989)R 1991, r 16). The fact that the child would need to be physically restrained during the hearing in order to control him (as in *Re W (Secure Accommodation Order: Attendance at Court)*, above) would, in itself, be sufficient ground for refusing to allow the child to be in court. Further examples given in *Re W* of situations in which the court would not allow a child to be present are where there is a prospect of disturbance or unruliness in court or the possibility of the child being educationally subnormal or where the child is much younger than the 10-year-old boy in that case. But see *J v Merthyr Tydfil County Borough Council* [1997] Fam Law 522 where a 15-year-old girl successfully appealed the magistrates' decision to exclude her from a hearing, on the grounds that (i) they failed to balance her interests against the risk of her behaving in an unruly manner, (ii) reached the decision to exclude her without hearing from her guardian ad litem (children's guardian) or solicitor, and (iii) refused to allow her solicitor an opportunity of seeing her prior to the hearing.

Role of children's guardian in secure accommodation proceedings—The welfare of the child is not the paramount consideration, and although it remains relevant, CA 1989, s 1 does not apply. The guardian ad litem (children's guardian) has to adapt his general duties to the specific requirements of the application before the court and recommend what he believes to be in the best interests of the child (*Re M (Secure Accommodation Order)* [1995] 1 FLR 418, CA).

Section 25 orders relating to wards—See FPR 1991, r 5.5.

Duration of order—A secure accommodation order runs from the date of the court order and not from the date when the child is actually placed in secure accommodation (*Re B (A Minor) (Secure Accommodation)* [1994] 2 FLR 707, CA). The power to make an interim order is confined to circumstances when the application is adjourned. That power is commonly used where the court lacks sufficient information to justify a finding on the s 25(1) criteria (*Re A (Secure Accommodation Order)* [2001] Fam Law 806). Where an interim order is made, the court, at the adjourned hearing, is still seised of the original application and must take into account the interim period as part of the maximum period of secure accommodation permitted by the regulations (*C v Humberside County Council* [1994] 2 FLR 759, FD). A local authority cannot lawfully keep a child in secure accommodation within the maximum period specified in an order under s 25(4), or the maximum period permitted without the authority of the court, at a time when the local authority itself does not consider the criteria in s 25(1) continue to be met (*LM v Essex County Council* [1999] 1 FLR 988). It is unclear whether the authority can lawfully keep the child in secure accommodation for some further period (provided it is within the maximum period specified in the order) while suitable alternative arrangements are made. There is no provision for discharge of secure accommodation orders within s 25. Once a secure accommodation order has been made, the family proceedings court cannot discharge or set the order aside if the facts subsequently change, nor can a higher court do so under CA 1989, s 94, unless the order has been incorrectly made. Where the criteria no longer apply the remedy is an application for a writ of habeas corpus under RSC Ord 54, r 4 (*LM v Essex County Council* (above)). The court does not have power to make an order under s 25 in respect of someone who is already 16 and being accommodated under s 20(5), but does have power to make an order in respect of a child who is not yet 16, and therefore not yet accommodated under s 20(5), even if the period of the order extends beyond the child's sixteenth birthday and thereafter the child's accommodation will fall under s 20(5) (*Re G (Secure Accommodation)* [2000] 2 FLR 259).

Appropriate court—Where a child has been remanded to local authority accommodation by a youth court pursuant to Criminal Justice Act 1991, s 60(3), any application by the local authority under CA 1989, s 25 should be made to the appropriate youth court rather than the appropriate family court (*Liverpool City Council v B* [1995] 2 FLR 84; *Re G (Secure Accommodation Order)* [2001] 1 FLR 884; and see Children (Secure Accommodation) Regulations 1991, reg 6).

Relationship between secure accommodation orders and refusal of bail—Where magistrates decide that bail is inappropriate in relation to children charged with criminal offences, it does not follow that the court is bound in principle to make a secure accommodation order; it is open to the court to consider other methods of disposal, such as remanding the children to local authority accommodation and imposing conditions on them (*Re W and D (Secure Accommodation)* [1995] 2 FLR 807; and see Children (Secure Accommodation) Regulations 1991, reg 6).

Procedural matters—See FPC(CA 1989)R 1991, r 26.

Supplemental

26 Review of cases and inquiries into representations

(1) The Secretary of State may make regulations requiring the case of each child who is being looked after by a local authority to be reviewed in accordance with the provisions of the regulations.

(2) The regulations may, in particular, make provision –

(*a*) as to the manner in which each case is to be reviewed;

(*b*) as to the considerations to which the local authority are to have regard in reviewing each case;

(*c*) as to the time when each case is first to be reviewed and the frequency of subsequent reviews;

(*d*) requiring the authority, before conducting any review, to seek the views of –

(i) the child;

(ii) his parents;

(iii) any person who is not a parent of his but who has parental responsibility for him; and

(iv) any other person whose views the authority consider to be relevant, including, in particular, the views of those persons in relation to any particular matter which is to be considered in the course of the review;

(*e*) requiring the authority to consider, in the case of a child who is in their care, whether an application should be made to discharge the care order;

(*f*) requiring the authority to consider, in the case of a child in accommodation provided by the authority, whether the accommodation accords with the requirements of this Part;

(*g*) requiring the authority to inform the child, so far as is reasonably practicable, of any steps he may take under this Act;

(*h*) requiring the authority to make arrangements, including arrangements with such other bodies providing services as it considers appropriate, to implement any decision which they propose to make in the course, or as a result, of the review;

(*i*) requiring the authority to notify details of the result of the review and of any decision taken by them in consequence of the review to –

(i) the child;

(ii) his parents;

(iii) any person who is not a parent of his but who has had parental responsibility for him; and

(iv) any other person whom they consider ought to be notified;

(*j*) requiring the authority to monitor the arrangements which they have made with a view to ensuring that they comply with the regulations.

(3) Every local authority shall establish a procedure for considering any representations (including any complaint) made to them by –

(*a*) any child who is being looked after by them or who is not being looked after by them but is in need;

(*b*) a parent of his;

(*c*) any person who is not a parent of his but who has parental responsibility for him;

(*d*) any local authority foster parent;

(*e*) such other person as the authority consider has a sufficient interest in the child's welfare to warrant his representations being considered by them,

about the discharge of the authority of any of their functions under this Part in relation to the child.

(4) The procedure shall ensure that at least one person who is not a member or officer of the authority takes part in –

(*a*) the consideration; and

(*b*) any discussions which are held by the authority about the action (if any) to be taken in relation to the child in the light of the consideration.

(5) In carrying out any consideration of representations under this section a local authority shall comply with any regulations made by the Secretary of State for the purpose of regulating the procedure to be followed.

(6) The Secretary of State may make regulations requiring local authorities to monitor the arrangements that they have made with a view to ensuring that they comply with any regulations made for the purposes of subsection (5).

(7) Where any representation has been considered under the procedure established by a local authority under this section, the authority shall –

(*a*) have due regard to the findings of those considering the representation; and

(*b*) take such steps as are reasonably practicable to notify (in writing) –

(i) the person making the representation;
(ii) the child (if the authority consider that he has sufficient understanding); and
(iii) such other persons (if any) as appear to the authority to be likely to be affected,

of the authority's decision in the matter and their reasons for taking that decision and of any action which they have taken, or propose to take.

(8) Every local authority shall give such publicity to their procedure for considering representations under this section as they consider appropriate.

Section 26 and judicial review—For the potential relevance of the s 26 representation procedure in judicial review proceedings, see under CA 1989, s 84.

Scope of complaints procedure—In deciding not to apply for a care order, the local authority is exercising a function under CA 1989, Pt III and the complaints procedure is applicable to such a decision (*R v East Sussex CC ex parte W* [1998] 2 FLR 1082, QBD).

Duty to consider representations made by a parent—(s 26(3)(*b*))—The duty of the local authority to establish a procedure to consider any representations made to them by the persons named in s 26(3) is directory and not mandatory; the result of any non-compliance with the provisions should be treated as an irregularity (*Re P (Children Act 1989, ss 22 and 26: Local Authority Compliance)* [2000] 2 FLR 910).

Adoption and Children Act 2002 – review of cases of looked-after children—Once ACA 2002, s 118 comes into force a "looked-after children reviewing officer" will be created. Section 118 amends CA 1989, s 26(2)(*e*) (requirement to consider the discharge of a care order) to encompass a review of the care plan and revision of it as necessary. It aims to go some way towards meeting the difficulty now faced by the courts after the rejection by the House of Lords in *Re S (Minors) (Care Order: Implementation of Care Plan)*; *Re W (Minors) (Care Order: Adequacy of Care Plan)* [2002] UKHL 10, [2002] 1 FLR 815 of the suggestion that care plans should contain "starred milestones", a failure to achieve which would have enabled the courts to resume judicial control over the case. Under the current law, once a care order has been made, the responsibility for the child is transferred to the local authority, removing it from the control of the court even in cases where a judge feels that it is necessary for the court to monitor the progress of the child in care.

The ACA 2002 amendment of CA 1989, s 26(2)(e) requires the local authority to appoint a reviewing officer whose functions would be to participate in the review process, monitor the local authority's functions in respect of the review and refer the case to CAFCASS if the reviewer considered it appropriate to do so. The reviewing officer would be a person of a prescribed description in (as yet undrafted) regulations. The Lord Chancellor has power by regulation to extend any functions of CAFCASS officers to meet any referrals made by the reviewing authority. The Government minister who introduced the proposal in the House of Commons on 20 May 2002 suggested that the regulations will require the reviewing officer to be a senior professional with expertise in children's cases who will have the status to ensure that the care plan is implemented. The reviewer would be independent of the line management of the child's case but not necessarily independent of the local authority. The minister proposed that CAFCASS be empowered to take proceedings on behalf of the child. She envisaged that CAFCASS might, for instance, seek to injunct the local authority to prevent, say, removal from an established placement or seek a declaration that the child's human rights were not being met. Whether this amendment will meet the need for reform may depend largely on the detailed regulations that will underpin the day-to-day practice of the regime. Of central concern will be the degree to which the reviewing officer will be independent. The second stage of the amendment depends on action to be taken by CAFCASS but no detail is provided. Regulations will be needed to permit CAFCASS to initiate proceedings. There will need to be provision for the early re-appointment of the solicitor for the child. The minister was of the view that there is already a broad remedy available under HRA 1998, ss 7 and 8. See further **Procedure for raising issues under the Human Rights Act 1998** under CA 1989, s 31, and annotation to HRA 1998.

27 Co-operation between authorities

(1) Where it appears to a local authority that any authority mentioned in subsection (3) could, by taking any specified action, help in the exercise of any of their functions under this Part, they may request the help of that other authority, specifying the action in question.

(2) An authority whose help is so requested shall comply with the request if it is compatible with their own statutory or other duties and obligations and does not unduly prejudice the discharge of any of their functions.

(3) The authorities are –

(*a*) any local authority;
(*b*) any local education authority;
(*c*) any local housing authority;
(*d*) any Health Authority, Special Health Authority, Primary Care Trust or National Health Service trust; and
(*e*) any person authorised by the Secretary of State for the purposes of this section.

(4) (*repealed*)

Amendments—Courts and Legal Services Act 1990, ss 116, 125(7), Sch 16, para 14, Sch 20; Education Act 1993, s 307, Sch 19, para 147; Health Authorities Act 1995, s 2, Sch 1, para 118; SI 2000/90.

28 Consultation with local education authorities

(1) Where –

(*a*) a child is being looked after by a local authority; and
(*b*) the authority propose to provide accommodation for him in an establishment at which education is provided for children who are accommodated there,

they shall, so far as is reasonably practicable, consult the appropriate local education authority before doing so.

(2) Where any such proposal is carried out, the local authority shall, as soon as is reasonably practicable, inform the appropriate local education authority of the arrangements that have been made for the child's accommodation.

(3) Where the child ceases to be accommodated as mentioned in subsection (1)(*b*), the local authority shall inform the appropriate local education authority.

(4) In this section "the appropriate local education authority" means –

(*a*) the local education authority within whose area the local authority's area falls; or
(*b*) where the child has special educational needs and a statement of his needs is maintained under Part IV of the Education Act 1996, the local education authority who maintain the statement.

Amendments—Education Act 1996, s 582(1), Sch 37, Pt I, para 84.

29 Recoupment of cost of providing services etc

(1) Where a local authority provide any service under section 17 or 18, other than advice, guidance or counselling, they may recover from a person specified in subsection (4) such charge for the service as they consider reasonable.

(2) Where the authority are satisfied that that person's means are insufficient for it to be reasonably practicable for him to pay the charge, they shall not require him to pay more than he can reasonably be expected to pay.

(3) No person shall be liable to pay any charge under subsection (1) for a service provided under section 17 or section 18(1) or (5) at any time when he is in receipt of income support, working families' tax credit or disabled person's tax credit under Part VII of the Social Security Contributions and Benefits Act 1992 or of an income-based jobseeker's allowance.

(3A) No person shall be liable to pay any charge under subsection (1) for a service provided under section 18(2) or (6) at any time when he is in receipt of income support under Part VII of the Social Security and Benefits Act 1992 or of an income-based jobseeker's allowance.

(4) The persons are –

- (*a*) where the service is provided for a child under sixteen, each of his parents;
- (*b*) where it is provided for a child who has reached the age of sixteen, the child himself; and
- (*c*) where it is provided for a member of the child's family, that member.

(5) Any charge under subsection (1) may, without prejudice to any other method of recovery, be recovered summarily as a civil debt.

(6) Part III of Schedule 2 makes provision in connection with contributions towards the maintenance of children who are being looked after by local authorities and consists of the re-enactment with modifications of provisions in Part V of the Child Care Act 1980.

(7) Where a local authority provide any accommodation under section 20(1) for a child who was (immediately before they began to look after him) ordinarily resident within the area of another local authority, they may recover from that other authority any reasonable expenses incurred by them in providing the accommodation and maintaining him.

(8) Where a local authority provide accommodation under section 21(1) or (2)(*a*) or (*b*) for a child who is ordinarily resident within the area of another local authority and they are not maintaining him in –

- (*a*) a community home provided by them;
- (*b*) a controlled community home; or
- (*c*) a hospital vested in the Secretary of State or a Primary Care Trust, or any other hospital made available pursuant to arrangements made by a Strategic Health Authority, Health Authority or a Primary Care Trust,

they may recover from that other authority any reasonable expenses incurred by them in providing the accommodation and maintaining him.

(9) Except where subsection (10) applies, where a local authority comply with any request under section 27(2) in relation to a child or other person who is not ordinarily resident within their area, they may recover from the local authority in whose area the child or person is ordinarily resident any reasonable expenses incurred by them in respect of that person.

(10) Where a local authority ("authority A") comply with any request under section 27(2) from another local authority ("authority B") in relation to a child or other person –

- (*a*) whose responsible authority is authority B for the purposes of section 23B or 23C; or (*b*) whom authority B are advising or befriending or to whom they are giving assistance by virtue of section 24(5)(*a*),

authority A may recover from authority B any reasonable expenses incurred by them in respect of that person.

Amendments—Courts and Legal Services Act 1990, s 116, Sch 16, para 15; National Health Service and Community Care Act 1990, s 66(1), Sch 9, para 36(3); Disability Living Allowance and Disability Working Allowance Act 1991, s 7(2), Sch 3, para 14; Social Security (Consequential Provisions) Act 1992, s 4, Sch 2, para 108; Health Authorities Act 1995, s 2, Sch 1, para 118; Jobseekers Act 1995, s 41, Sch 2, para 19; Tax Credits Act 1999, s 1(2), Sch 1, paras 1, 6(*d*)(ii); Children (Leaving Care) Act 2000, s 7; Local Government Act 2000, s 103; SI 2000/90; SI 2002/2469.

30 Miscellaneous

(1) Nothing in this Part shall affect any duty imposed on a local authority by or under any other enactment.

(2) Any question arising under section 20(2), 21(3) or 29(7) to (9) as to the ordinary residence of a child shall be determined by agreement between the local authorities concerned or, in default of agreement, by the Secretary of State.

(3) Where the functions conferred on a local authority by this Part and the functions of a local education authority are concurrent, the Secretary of State may by regulations provide by which authority the functions are to be exercised.

(4) The Secretary of State may make regulations for determining, as respects any local education authority functions specified in the regulations, whether a child who is being looked after by a local authority is to be treated, for purposes so specified, as a child of parents of sufficient resources or as a child of parents without resources.

PART IV
CARE AND SUPERVISION

General

31 Care and supervision orders

(1) On the application of any local authority or authorised person, the court may make an order –

(*a*) placing the child with respect to whom the application is made in the care of a designated local authority; or
(*b*) putting him under the supervision of a designated local authority.

(2) A court may only make a care order or supervision order if it is satisfied –

(*a*) that the child concerned is suffering, or is likely to suffer, significant harm; and
(*b*) that the harm, or likelihood of harm, is attributable to –
  (i) the care given to the child, or likely to be given to him if the order were not made, not being what it would be reasonable to expect a parent to give to him; or
  (ii) the child's being beyond parental control.

(3) No care order or supervision order may be made with respect to a child who has reached the age of seventeen (or sixteen, in the case of a child who is married).

(4) An application under this section may be made on its own or in any other family proceedings.

(5) The court may –

(*a*) on an application for a care order, make a supervision order;
(*b*) on an application for a supervision order, make a care order.

(6) Where an authorised person proposes to make an application under this section he shall –

(*a*) if it is reasonably practicable to do so; and
(*b*) before making the application,

consult the local authority appearing to him to be the authority in whose area the child concerned is ordinarily resident.

(7) An application made by an authorised person shall not be entertained by the court if, at the time when it is made, the child concerned is –

(*a*) the subject of an earlier application for a care order, or supervision order, which has not been disposed of; or
(*b*) subject to –
(i) a care order or supervision order;
(ii) an order under section 63(1) of the Powers of Criminal Courts (Sentencing) Act 2000; or
(iii) a supervision requirement within the meaning of Part II of the Children (Scotland) Act 1995.

(8) The local authority designated in a care order must be –

(*a*) the authority within whose area the child is ordinarily resident; or
(*b*) where the child does not reside in the area of a local authority, the authority within whose area any circumstances arose in consequence of which the order is being made.

(9) In this section –

"authorised person" means –

(*a*) the National Society for the Prevention of Cruelty to Children and any of its officers; and
(*b*) any person authorised by order of the Secretary of State to bring proceedings under this section and any officer of a body which is so authorised;

"harm" means ill-treatment or the impairment of health or development;
"development" means physical, intellectual, emotional, social or behavioural development;
"health" means physical or mental health; and
"ill-treatment" includes sexual abuse and forms of ill-treatment which are not physical.

(10) Where the question of whether harm suffered by a child is significant turns on the child's health or development, his health or development shall be compared with that which could reasonably be expected of a similar child.

(11) In this Act –

"a care order" means (subject to section 105(1)) an order under subsection (1)(*a*) and (except where express provision to the contrary is made) includes an interim care order made under section 38; and

PART II

"a supervision order" means an order under subsection (1)(*b*) and (except where express provision to the contrary is made) includes an interim supervision order made under section 38.

Amendments—Children (Scotland) Act 1995, s 105(4), Sch 4, para 48(1), (2); Criminal Justice and Court Services Act 2000 s 74, Sch 7, para 90; Powers of Criminal Courts (Sentencing) Act 2000, s 165, Sch 9, para 127.

Defined terms—"authorised person": s 31(9); "care order": ss 31(11), 105(1); "child"; s 105(1); "family proceedings": s 8(3); "local authority": s 105(1); "supervision order": s 31(11).

Jurisdiction—Neither the Act nor any other statutory provision sets out the grounds for jurisdiction under s 31. *Re R (Care Orders: Jurisdiction)* [1995] 1 FLR 711, FD, held that the jurisdictional basis for an application under CA 1989, Part IV is effectively the same as that established by the Family Law Act 1986 in relation to s 8 orders. Accordingly, the court will have jurisdiction to entertain a local authority's application if the child concerned is either habitually resident (which Singer J took to mean the same as "ordinarily resident") in England and Wales, or present in England and Wales, when the application is made. In *Re M (Care Orders: Jurisdiction)* [1997] 1 FLR 456, FD, Hale J held that jurisdiction can be founded on the child's presence in England and Wales even if the child is habitually resident elsewhere and raised, but did not decide upon, the question of whether there would be jurisdiction where the child is ordinarily or habitually resident in England and Wales but not present here at the time of the first application. As to the meaning of "habitual residence", see further under CA 1989, s 105(6) and Child Abduction and Custody Act 1985, Sch 1, Art 4.

Care orders – European Convention for the Protection of Human Rights and Fundamental Freedoms 1950—Now that the Human Rights Act 1998 has been implemented in this jurisdiction, the parent may complain that his right to respect for his family life, protected by Article 8(1) of the Convention, has been violated by the making of the care order. In dealing with such a claim the court must consider whether, if there has been such an interference with the right, that interference was justified under Art 8(2) as being necessary in a democratic society for the protection of the health and morals and of the rights and freedoms of others. If such interference is justified the court must also consider whether it is proportionate to the aim of protecting the rights of the child concerned. The task of the domestic court when faced with such a complaint under Art 8(1) is to review under the Convention decisions taken by other public authorities in the exercise of their similar powers and to compare them with the case currently before the court. The width of the discretion allowed to a public authority in each case will vary according to the issues and the interests at stake. Whilst the public authority will have a wide discretion in relation to the actual decision to take a child into care, a stricter scrutiny will be applied to any further steps proposed by the authority which might have the effect of restricting even more tightly the family relations between parents and a young child, for example limits on the amount and/or frequency of contact between the parents and the child in care (*Scott v UK* [2000] 1 FLR 958 – where the child was ultimately freed for adoption since the mother had been unable to overcome a chronic dependence on alcohol). For other examples of the balancing exercise to be carried out by the court see *L v UK* [2000] 2 FLR 322; *K and T v Finland* [2000] 2 FLR 79 (The Chamber decision), [2001] 2 FLR 707 (The Grand Chamber decision); *L v Finland* [2000] 2 FLR 118; *Re C & B (Care Order: Future Harm)* [2001] 1 FLR 611. The Draconian step of removing a baby from its mother shortly after birth must be supported by relevant and sufficient reasons and must be regarded as necessary in a democratic society (*P, C and S v UK* [2002] 2 FLR 631, ECHR). Article 6 of the Convention guarantees the right to a fair hearing and in *L v Finland* (above) it was successfully argued that there was a violation of Art 6 because no oral hearing had been held prior to the decision to take the children concerned into care.

The local authority, when seeking to take a child into care, is under a heavy obligation to ensure that the procedure at all stages is transparent and fair, both in and out of court. In particular, it is vital that a litigant has a proper opportunity in care proceedings to examine and comment on experts' reports and other documents being considered by the court and to cross-examine witnesses interviewed and relied on therein (*Re L (Care: Assessment: Fair Trial)* [2002] EWHC 1379 (Fam), [2002] 2 FLR 730). See further **Disclosure – impact of the European Convention for Human Rights and Fundamental Freedoms 1950** under FPR 1991, r 4.23.

Procedure for raising issues under the Human Rights Act 1998—For the procedure to be followed when raising an issue under the HRA 1998, see the annotation thereto and the *President's Direction of 24 July 2000*. Challenges to care plans and placements of children in care based on allegations that human rights have been breached should be heard in the Family Division of the High Court and, if possible, by judges with experience of sitting in the administrative court (*C v Bury Metropolitan Borough Council* [2002] EWHC 1438 (Fam), [2002] 2 FLR 868).

Need to file care plan—The Adoption and Children Act 2002, s 124 inserts a new s 31A into CA 1989. Once it comes into force it will place a statutory duty on the local authority to prepare a care plan (to be known as a "s 31A care plan") in every case in which it seeks a care order. However, the statutory duty will not apply where the authority seeks only an interim care order. The local authority will be required by statute to keep the care plan under review and to make changes as and when necessary. The current requirement for local authorities to prepare care plans derives from the formal guidance and regulations issued after the implementation of the CA 1989, judicial guidance in reported cases and local authority policy and practice. In *Manchester City Council v F (Note)* [1993] 1 FLR 419, Eastham J accepted the submission that it was the duty of the local authority in all public law cases to file a care plan, and held that such a plan should accord, as far as was reasonably possible, with *The Children Act 1989 Guidance and Regulations* (HMSO), Volume 3, para 2.62. The *Guidance and Regulations* have now been supplemented by Local Authority Circular of 12 August 1999 (LAC(99)29) "*Care Plans and Care Proceedings under The Children Act 1989*" covering practice and policy matters and seeking to improve the consistency between local authorities across the country in relation to the style, format and level of detail set out in care plans. It contains a specific guide to the structure and contents of the care plan and emphasises the need to give reasons as to why a particular placement or course of action has been chosen, since the plan needs to be understood by a range of professionals, the child and the child's family (paras 13–18). The Circular stresses that the care plan must consider "achievable time-scales leading up to specific outcomes for overall implementation" of the plan, as well as for each of the key steps within the plan (para 14). Where care plans are needed at an interim stage in the care proceedings they will not necessarily represent the local authority's confirmed views that will be brought to the final hearing and therefore it is vital that the first page of the plan should distinguish clearly between interim care plans for interim court hearings and the complete care plan for the final hearing (para 17). A separate care plan is needed for each child who is the subject of care proceedings, even though some of the information within the care plans for siblings may be similar or identical (para 19). For discussion of the matters to be considered when it becomes apparent that adoption will be the preferred option set out in the care plan, see **Where adoption is the preferred option** (below). Wherever possible, evidence in support of material parts of the care plan should be available and form part of it (for example, where the plan involves a particular foster placement for the child, it should contain a description of the placement and of the foster carers by a worker who has interviewed them and knows them sufficiently to satisfy the court that the placement is suitable) (*Re J (Minors) (Care: Care Plan)* [1994] 1 FLR 253, FD, in which much further guidance as to the making of a care plan is also to be found). The court will scrutinise the care plan rigorously and if it is not satisfied that it is in the best interests of the child it can refuse to make a care order (*Re J (Minors) (Care: Care Plan)*, above, *Re T (A Minor) (Care Order: Conditions)* [1994] 2 FLR 423, *Re C (Care Order: Appropriate Local Authority)* [1997] 1 FLR 544). The difficult issue of when the court relinquishes control of the case to the local authority by making a full care order as opposed to an interim order is dealt with further under s 38 **Interim care order or full care order?**. Where the care order will designate a local authority other than the applicant local authority, the care plan must be prepared in co-operation between the two authorities (*L v London Borough of Bexley* [1996] 2 FLR 595, FD). Reference should be made to the *Handbook of Best Practice in Children Act cases* produced by the Children Act Advisory Committee (set out in Part IV of this work as *Best Practice Guidance of June 1997*) for advice as to the care plan (see paras 7–12).

Requirement to keep parents properly involved in the planning process—It is essential that the local authority keeps the parents properly involved in the planning process when care proceedings are initiated and the care plan is being formulated (*Re S (Minors) (Care Order: Implementation of Care Plan)*; *Re W (Minors) (Care Order: Adequacy of Care Plan)* [2002] UKHL 10, [2002] 1 FLR 815). A failure to do so may leave it open for the parents of the child concerned to bring an application under HRA 1998, ss 6, 7 and 8 for breaches of ECHRFF 1950, Art 6 (right to a fair trial) and Art 8 (right to respect for private and family life) (*Re C (Care Plan: Human Rights Challenge)* [2002] Fam Law 790). See further **Procedure for raising issues under the Human Rights Act 1998** under CA 1989, s 31 and annotation to HRA 1998. *Re L (Care: Assessment: Fair Trial)* [2002] EWHC 1379 (Fam), [2002] 2 FLR 730 sets out useful guidelines for local authorities and all professionals concerned in care proceedings as to the proper conduct and recording of meetings and the provision of documents; these are considered in more detail in **Disclosure – impact of the European Convention for Human Rights and Fundamental Freedoms 1950** under FPR 1991, r 4.23.

Intervention by court after making of care order—Under the current law, once a care order has been made the responsibility for the child is transferred to the local authority, removing it from the control of the court even in cases where, for example, a judge feels that it is necessary for the court to monitor the progress of the child in care, or where a care plan goes wrong at an early stage. The pressing need for the court to be able to exercise judicial control over the local authority's implementation of, or failure to implement, a care plan was considered by the House of Lords in *Re S (Minors) (Care Order: Implementation of Care Plan)*; *Re W (Minors) (Care Order: Adequacy of Care Plan)* [2002] UKHL 10, [2002] 1 FLR 815 (see also *Re F: F v Lambeth London Borough Council* [2002] 1 FLR 217 – where there were grave and continuing failures by the authority to take effective action or to engage in long-term planning for the children concerned). Their Lordships in *Re S; Re W* rejected the suggestion made by the Court of Appeal that care plans should contain "starred milestones", a failure to achieve which would have enabled the courts to resume judicial control over the case. In an effort to go some way towards meeting the need for a proper review mechanism, Adoption and Children Act 2002, s 118, when it comes into force, will amend CA 1989, s 26(2)(*e*) (requirement to consider the discharge of a care order) to encompass a requirement for the authority to review the care plan and revise it as necessary, together with a route for returning it to the court through the intervention of a CAFCASS officer where appropriate. See further **Adoption and Children Act 2002 – review of cases of looked-after children** under CA 1989, s 26. A remedy also exists under HRA 1998, ss 6, 7 and 8 on the basis that the process adopted by the authority is incompatible with ECHRFF 1950, Art 8 (the right to respect for family life), and Art 6 (right to a fair trial) (*Re S (Minors) (Care Order: Implementation of Care Plan)*; *Re W (Minors) (Care Order: Adequacy of Care Plan)* [2002] UKHL 10, [2002] 1 FLR 815 (above); *Re C (Care Plan: Human Rights Challenge)* [2002] Fam Law 790). See further **Procedure for raising issues under the Human Rights Act 1998** under CA 1989, s 31 and annotation to HRA 1998.

Where adoption is the preferred option—Local authorities must follow the Local Authority Circular of 28 August 1998 (LAC(98)20) "*Adoption – Achieving the Right Balance*", paragraphs 28–33 of which were reissued in an amended form in *Chief Inspector Letter* of June 1999 (CI(99)6). Where adoption is the probable option, the courts will need to be advised of the likely steps and time-scales required to implement the plan. Paragraph 29 of the amended Circular provides that where the choice of placement depends significantly on findings of fact then, even though it may be difficult to effect much preparatory work concerning possible adoptive placement prior to the final hearing, it should still be possible to explain within the care plan the key steps which would need to be taken before an adoptive placement could be made and give estimated time-scales for each of these steps. Even where the facts of the care application are not disputed and the preferred option is adoption, paragraph 30 makes it clear that local authorities must have satisfied themselves that sufficient assessment has taken place in order to rule out rehabilitation or placement with relatives, for example, under a s 8 residence order. In those cases in which the local authority has ruled out rehabilitation or placement with relatives and has confirmed adoption as the preferred option, paragraph 31 sets out the steps which should always have been addressed before the final care hearing, including:

(*a*) the co-ordination of information between the team responsible for the care proceedings application and those responsible for family finding;
(*b*) the completion, as far as possible, of the BAAF Form E giving details about the child;
(*c*) consideration of the case by the adoption panel with a view to making a recommendation on whether adoption is in the child's best interests;
(*d*) the identification by the local authority of the key steps and timetable which would lead to an adoptive placement if the court made a care order;
(*e*) a contingency plan to be used if the preferred option for adoption cannot be achieved;
(*f*) consideration as to whether a freeing application is appropriate.

Paragraph 32 states that it is important to identify as early as possible those care cases with a view to adoption which may also require the child to be freed for adoption, in order that evidence and time-tabling of court hearings can be co-ordinated, to avoid unnecessary stress to all parties concerned, increased expense and delay resulting from a care application followed months later by a freeing application, both of which may be contested. However, paragraph 33 of the amended Circular makes it clear that it is *not* appropriate before the final care hearing for there to have been introductions between the child and the prospective adopters or for the agency to have confirmed the panel's recommendations.

Note that when the Adoption and Children Act 2002 comes into force there will be a new legal process for placing a child for adoption. See **The Adoption and Children Act 2002** (below).

The Adoption and Children Act 2002—When the Adoption and Children Act 2002 comes into force there will be a new legal process for placing a child for adoption. The current process of freeing for adoption will be replaced by one in which the authority applies for a placement order, authorizing it to place a child with prospective adopters (ACA 2002, ss 18–29). ACA 2002, s 1(2) makes the welfare of the child the court's paramount concern in all decisions relating to adoption, bringing it into line with the guiding principle in CA 1989, s 1(1). This means that a court hearing applications for care and placement orders at the same time will be able to hear all the evidence needed for both orders in the course of one hearing and use the paramountcy principle for both applications. Under the current law the court has first to deal with the CA 1989 application, using the paramountcy principle, and then apply different criteria under the Adoption Act 1976 to determine whether, for example, a parent is unreasonably withholding his consent for the purposes of the freeing application.

"Twin track planning" and "Concurrent planning"—In *Re D and K (Care Plan: Twin Track Planning)* [1999] 2 FLR 872 Bracewell J highlighted the problems which arise for the court in cases where the local authority recognises from an early stage that its care plan presents options of rehabilitation within the natural family or permanency outside the family but fails to address the option of an adoptive placement until shortly before the substantive court hearing. The result is that the court is handicapped at the hearing by a lack of information as to the availability of adoptive parents; in the event that the court makes a care order and approves the care plan to place the child outside the natural family in an adoptive placement, there is a substantial delay whilst the child is considered and approved by the adoption and fostering panel and a suitable adoptive placement is identified. Her Ladyship stated that where the local authority are considering two options comprising rehabilitation of the child to his natural family within a strictly limited timescale or adoption outside the family then, particularly in the case of babies or young children, the authority and children's guardian have a duty to seek to prevent delay by clearly identifying the options available to the court by twin track planning as opposed to sequential planning. In such cases, it is vital that the local authority should make it absolutely clear to the natural family as early as possible that it is considering these two options and that inquiries are proceeding on a twin track, so that the court can be presented at the final care hearing with properly researched options in order to prevent delay. See *Handbook of Best Practice in Children Act cases*, paras 7–12 (set out in Part IV of this work as *Best Practice Guidance of June 1997*).

In appropriate cases, the authority may be able to proceed using "concurrent planning". There is a clear distinction between twin track planning and concurrent planning. "Concurrent planning" describes a scheme whereby the local authority choose foster-parents who are trained and willing to foster children on the basis that they work with the natural family towards rehabilitation, but who in the event that rehabilitation is ruled out wish to adopt the children. The scheme has been widely used in the USA over a period of 20 years and is defined as "The process of working towards family reunification, while at the same time establishing an alternative permanent plan". The aim is to reduce the number of moves a child experiences in care, and to reduce temporary placements so that children can achieve permanence, whether rehabilitated with their family or with the foster-family, with minimum disruption. Bracewell J explained in *Re D and K (Care Plan: Twin Track Planning)* (above), at 875C, that "Contact between carers and birth children is encouraged and there is openness between the parties, about the primary aim of rehabilitation with the alternative secondary plan of permanent placement." Therefore, in cases in which concurrent planning takes place it is vital that the two options are clearly explained to the natural family from the outset and that they are re-assured that it in no way pre-empts the outcome of the care proceedings. Her Ladyship emphasised (at 875D) that "Not every case will be suitable for such placement. Generally it is likely to apply to babies or young children where there are some but by no means optimistic prospects in relation to rehabilitation to the natural family". The scheme is currently being used by Bury and Salford local authorities in Manchester. In addition, the Thomas Coram foundation in London is carrying out research on the scheme. Whenever care proceedings are commenced, the court should be pro-active at an early directions hearing, requiring the local authority to establish whether twin track planning and/or concurrent planning is suitable and giving appropriate directions. For an example of the application of concurrent planning in relation to a 15-year-old mother and her baby see *B Metropolitan Borough Council v H (Goodman Project: Concurrent Planning)* [2000] Fam Law 237.

See also annotations **Where adoption is the preferred option** and **The Adoption and Children Act 2002** (above).

Teenage mothers and their children—Following on from the guidance given in **"Twin track planning" and "Concurrent planning"** above, Bracewell J laid down general guidelines in *Re R (Child of a Teenage Mother)* [2000] 2 FLR 660 to be followed by local authorities in the very difficult cases dealing with teenage mothers and their babies, as follows:

(1) There is no general principle that the babies of young teenagers should be adopted.

(2) Each case must turn on its own facts. In the current case, care orders were made, and the care plans approved, by reason of the sad and dysfunctional history of the parenting of the young mother and the risks of her and her baby remaining together.
(3) Where there is united family support of quality for mother and child, at home or elsewhere, the outcome may well be different.
(4) In cases where pregnancy is notified and local authority intervention is a possibility, the local authority has very urgent responsibilities as follows:
  (*a*) Planning for the baby as well as the mother should begin as soon as pregnancy is disclosed. It is not appropriate to concentrate on the welfare of the mother to the exclusion of the needs of the unborn child. In the current case, planning for the baby was left too late, with the consequence that the local authority had to dramatically change their care plan after the birth of the baby, with consequential distress and disruption.
  (*b*) Social work and expert assessments should be completed well before the birth so that effective and timely planning can be undertaken.
  (*c*) If proceedings under CA 1989, s 31 are necessary, they should be issued on the day of birth, and where the mother is very young, the case should be transferred without delay to the High Court, and a separate guardian ad litem (children's guardian) appointed for the mother and for the child immediately.
  (*d*) The baby's interim placement should be determined on evidence by the court at an early hearing as a matter of urgency.
  (*e*) Early final determination is vital, and the case should be time-tabled accordingly, invoking a standby procedure, if necessary, for a judge of the Family Division to hear the case.
  (*f*) Twin-track planning (in relation to which see **"Twin track planning" and "Concurrent planning"** above) is essential for cases in which one of the possible outcomes is an adoptive placement. In the current case, by reason of a misunderstanding by a social worker, no attempt was made to identify and approve a prospective family prior to the hearing. In consequence, the baby would have to undergo two moves, in that a bridging placement was necessary whilst an adoptive family was identified and approved, thereby causing disruption to the baby, and avoidable delay, at a crucial time in her development.

Social work practice—In *Re E (Care Proceedings: Social Work Practice)* [2000] 2 FLR 254 Bracewell J set out guidance in relation to social work practice in the light of lessons learned in the case, which covered a 20-year period of social work intervention with a highly dysfunctional family:
(1) Every social work file should have as the top document a running chronology of significant events kept up-to-date as events unfold.
(2) Lack of co-operation by parents is never a reason to close a file or remove a child from a protection register.
(3) Referrals by professionals such as health visitors and teachers should be investigated and given great weight.
(4) Those with power of decision making should never make a judgment without having full knowledge of the files and consulting those professionals who know the family.
(5) Children who are part of a sibling group should not be considered in isolation, but in the context of the family history.
(6) Cases should be time-limited and an effective timetable laid down within which changes need to be achieved.

See also two very important documents published by the Department of Health in 1999, *Working Together to Safeguard Children – Government Guidance on Inter-Agency Co-operation* and *Framework for the Assessment of Children in Need and their Families*. These replace the 1991 version *Working Together* and the previous guidance on undertaking comprehensive assessments ("The Orange Book"). *Working Together 1999* is issued under Local Authority Social Services Act 1970, s 7. This means that although it does not have the force of statute, generally speaking it must be followed (*R v London Borough of Islington ex parte Rixon* [1997] ELR 66; *R v Cornwall County Council ex parte LH* [2000] 1 FLR 236).

Preparation of public law cases—Important guidance as to the preparation of public law cases by local authorities and other parties is contained in *Re R (Care: Disclosure: Nature of Proceedings)* [2002] 1 FLR 755, where it was held that:
(*a*) those responsible for the preparation should have a proper understanding of the relevant legal principles, the issues in the case and the procedures of the court;

(*b*) there must be a proper examination of the background material and the relevant files;

(*c*) there must be a proper and full discussion with the relevant witnesses, to ensure that, so far as possible, their statements contain a full and proper account of the relevant matters, which include central matters seen or heard by that witness, the sources of hearsay being recorded, and the relevant background to and the circumstances in which the matters set out took place;

(*d*) where appropriate, full consideration should be given to whether there should be disclosure of any contemporaneous notes made by witnesses, including those of the guardian; and

(*e*) there must be a proper consideration of what further information or material should be obtained.

For further useful guidance as to the preparation of public law cases see **Disclosure – impact of the European Convention for Human Rights and Fundamental Freedoms 1950** under FPR 1991, r 4.23, and in particular the judgment of Munby J in *Re L (Care: Assessment: Fair Trial)* [2002] EWHC 1379 (Fam), [2002] 2 FLR 730.

Simultaneous applications for care order and freeing order—Where a court considers an application for a care order together with an application for a freeing order, the former is the primary application. If the judge decides the freeing application first, in which application the child's interest is the first but not the paramount consideration, the judge compromises his application of the paramountcy principle in his subsequent consideration of the care order application (*Re D (Simultaneous Applications for Care Order and Freeing Order)* [1999] 2 FLR 49). See annotation **The Adoption and Children Act 2002** (above) for the changes which the new statute will make to the process of placement for adoption once it is implemented.

"designated local authority" (s 31(8))—Section 31(8) specifies which local authority must be designated. Following a number of conflicting cases in the Family Division dealing with the proper construction of ss 31(8) and 105(6) when deciding which of two or more local authorities should be designated for the purposes of the relevant care order, the Court of Appeal considered the matter in *Northamptonshire CC v Islington LBC* [1999] 2 FLR 881. It held that in designating particular local authorities in care orders, the courts should construe ss 31(8) and 105(6) so as to provide a simple mechanism for designation. To ensure that s 31(8) provided a test applicable in all cases it was legitimate to construe s 31(8)(*b*) as though it read "where the child does not ordinarily reside" in a local authority area, inserting the word "ordinarily". The preferred approach to periods which had to be disregarded under s 105(6) was notionally to extend the child's residence in the authority area where he or she had been ordinarily resident immediately before the commencement of the disregard period. By virtue of ss 31(8)(*a*) and 105(6), this simple test will identify the local authority to be designated in the care order. If there are exceptional circumstances, such as developments affecting the family during the period to be disregarded (eg the movement of the entire family into a different authority area) then these could be considered. If the child has no ordinary residence, the designated local authority will be the one for the principal area in which the primary circumstances that led to the care order being made occurred. Thorpe LJ emphasised that the function of the judge was limited to carrying out a rapid and not over-sophisticated review of the history in order to make a purely factual determination of the child's place of ordinary residence or, if there was no place of ordinary residence, of the place where the case was carried over the s 31 threshold, and to designate a local authority accordingly. It is open to the court to hold that a new-born baby is incapable of ordinary residence apart from the mother, so that the baby's ordinary residence is the same as that of the mother (*C (A Child) v Plymouth County Council* [2000] 1 FLR 875).

Where it is clear that a care order, if made, would designate a local authority other than the applicant authority, full and early liaison needs to take place between the authorities and the care plan must be prepared in co-operation between them. Even if the second authority is not present or represented throughout the hearing, proper arrangements should be made in advance for a representative of the authority to attend court to deal with any issues that might arise and to assure the court and the parents of the authority's commitment to the care plan and its capacity to implement it (*L v London Borough of Bexley* [1996] 2 FLR 595, FD). The arrangements for contact which the court has to consider under s 34(11) before making a care order are the arrangements proposed by the authority into whose care the child would be placed. *Re C (Care Order: Appropriate Local Authority)* (above) endorsed *L v London Borough of Bexley*. It being likely in *Re C* that the children would be ordinarily resident in the area of the second local authority by the final hearing of the care proceedings, Wall J joined that local authority as a party but continued the full involvement of the first local authority as well. Reference should be made to the notes under s 105 and **Habitual residence** under Child Abduction and Custody Act 1985, Sch 1, Art 4.

"ordinarily resident" (s 31(6), (8))—There is a constant trickle of cases concerned with ordinary and habitual residence. Reference should be made to the notes under s 105 (with particular reference to s 105(6)) and **Habitual residence** under Child Abduction and Custody Act 1985, Sch 1, Art 4.

"any person authorised by order of the Secretary of State" (s 31(9))—No person has yet been so authorised.

Extended definition of "harm"—When Adoption and Children Act 2002, s 120 comes into force it will amend s 31(9) to extend the definition of "harm" to include, for example, impairment suffered by hearing or seeing the ill-treatment of another.

Agreed orders—The agreement of the parties cannot deprive the court of its duty to satisfy itself by evidence that the strict criteria for a care order have been fulfilled, but the degree of investigation required of the court will vary from case to case (see, for example, *Re G (A Minor) (Care Proceedings)* [1994] 2 FLR 69). Where the parties are agreed on a care order and also as to the factual substratum underlying the fulfilment of the threshold criteria, the court's duty may be discharged by perusing the documents and approving the agreed order (*Devon County Council v S* [1992] Fam 176, [1992] 2 FLR 244, *Re G (A Minor)*, above).

In some cases parents are prepared to make concessions in relation to the threshold criteria and do not seek to argue as to the disposal of the case, but other parties do not agree that the concessions reflect the nature of the case appropriately. It is a matter for the discretion of the judge as to whether the concessions are sufficient to meet the justice of the matter and the best interests of the children (*Re B (Agreed Findings of Fact)* [1998] 2 FLR 968 – concessions accepted as sufficient; *Re M (Threshold Criteria: Parental Concessions)* [1999] 2 FLR 728 – parents only made anodyne concession and it was necessary for a finding of fact hearing to be held to determine the true factual basis on which the threshold criteria were satisfied; *Re W (Children) (Threshold Criteria: Parental Concessions)* [2001] 1 FCR 139 – parental concessions held to be inadequate because they had not accepted any responsibility for the children's sexualised behaviour and therefore there was no firm basis upon which to deal with future applications by the parents for contact with the children). Where parents agree with the local authority to make concessions, this in no way ties the hands of the judge and arguments by the parents of "issue estoppel" are wholly inappropriate (*Re D (Child: Threshold Criteria)* [2001] 1 FLR 274 – where the experts were unable to advise on issues of child protection without a preliminary judicial determination of the core factual issue).

As the authorities show, in determining whether further investigation is appropriate and deciding upon the extent of that investigation, the court will take into account the circumstances of the case including the interests of the children, whether there is likely to be future litigation in which the disputed facts would be relevant, the relevance of the disputed allegations to the local authority's care plan and management of the case, the time likely to be spent investigating any given issue and the cost to public funds of the investigation, the likely evidential result of the investigation and the emotional toll of the court hearing. For a further case where only some of the parties were agreed upon the threshold, see *Re K (Supervision Orders)* [1999] 2 FLR 303.

In *Re C (A Minor) (Care Order: Appeal)* [1996] 1 FCR 332, FD, it was pointed out that it was unhelpful to have no findings as to the facts underlying the s 31 conditions and that, where the parties agree that the threshold criteria are met, they should at the very least be invited by the court to agree the factual basis for this and to acknowledge it by the signature of the parties or of the legal representatives. Similarly, in *Oxfordshire County Council v L* [1998] 1 FLR 70, FD, it was observed that, even where the s 31 threshold was conceded, it was the court's duty to be satisfied that the circumstances under s 31(2) were met and therefore generally appropriate for the court to record the basis upon which this was so. Sometimes it may do so by making its own findings of fact upon the agreed evidence. Sometimes it may do so by reference to an agreed statement of facts. Without such a statement, it was difficult to know what the basis for making an order had been. In *Stockport MBC v D* (above), Thorpe J expressed the view that, where orders were made without judicial investigation on oral evidence, it would be inappropriate for the court to make findings of fact; he chose to deal with the matter by simply accepting the formal admissions made by the parents and pronouncing the orders sought.

Summary disposal by judge may not be appropriate—In care proceedings where there are issues that require a full investigation and are likely to have a direct impact on the case it is inappropriate for the judge to summarily dismiss them (*Re H (A Child)* LTL, 4 November 2002, CA, Doc No C9600544).

Split hearings—*Re S (Care Proceedings: Split Hearing)* [1996] 2 FLR 773, FD, gives guidance as to split hearings. Consideration should be given to whether questions of fact, such as an allegation of physical or sexual abuse, might need to be determined at a preliminary stage so that the substantive hearing can proceed more speedily and focus on the child's welfare with greater clarity. Local authorities and children's guardians, in particular, should give assistance to the court in identifying cases which are suited to such a split hearing. Where this is appropriate, the court can give early directions for the filing of medical evidence and statements and a hearing as to factual issues, which hearing will sometimes be possible within weeks of the care application being filed. Even where the parents make limited concessions which mean that the threshold criteria are proved, the court still has a discretion, as part of the proper management of the proceedings in the child's best interests, to order that there be a trial in relation to the threshold criteria where this is necessary to resolve a core factual issue without the determination of which the experts involved in the case are unable to advise on child protection (*Re D (Child: Threshold Criteria)* [2001] 1 FLR 274 – where in proceedings relating to her second child the mother accepted that she had failed to supervise her first child, resulting in his admission to hospital for ingestion of substances, but where the issue as to whether such ingestion was due to deliberate abuse or carelessness by the mother remained unresolved. The experts said that they were unable to advise on issues of child protection and care without a determination of this issue). Once findings of fact are made, any further assessments that are necessary can be timetabled. *Re CB and JB (Care Proceedings: Guidelines)* [1998] 2 FLR 211, FD demonstrates how a failure to hold a split hearing (in that case, to resolve who was responsible for the severe shaking of one of the children) can cause obfuscation, delay and the waste of resources and gives valuable guidance as to the procedure to be followed with regard to evidence, assessments etc. where a split hearing is scheduled. Similarly in *Re CD and MD (Care Proceedings: Practice)* [1998] 1 FLR 825 there should have been a split hearing. *Re T (A Minor) (Procedure: Alleged Sexual Abuse) (No 1)* [1996] 2 FCR 370, however, sounds a cautionary note about splitting the evidence on the primary facts as to sexual abuse from the evidence as to what risk there will be in the future if it is established.

Where findings are made on a preliminary issue at a split hearing, there is jurisdiction to hear an appeal if those findings are of crucial importance to the final decision (*Re B (Split Hearings: Jurisdiction)* [2000] 1 FLR 334).

Where there is a split hearing, it is very important that the same judge should hear both limbs of the case if possible. The judge hearing the first part should be requested to ensure that the order at the end of the first part indicates that the second part should be reserved to him or her, if available (*Re G (Care Proceedings: Split Trials)* [2001] 1 FLR 872). Furthermore, where an expert is asked to express an opinion, he must have all the relevant information, including a copy of any judgment given in the case; the summary of a judgment is not sufficient (*Re G (Care Proceedings: Split Trials)* (above)).

Standard and burden of proof—The legal burden of establishing the existence of the threshold conditions in s 31(2) rests on the applicant for a care order. The standard of proof is the ordinary civil standard of balance of probability. When assessing the probabilities, the court will have in mind as a factor, to whatever extent is appropriate in the particular case, that the more serious the allegation the less likely it is that the event occurred and, hence, the stronger should be the evidence before the court concludes that the allegation is established on the balance of probability (*Re H and R (Child Sexual Abuse)* [1996] 1 FLR 80, HL). However, when two people are the possible perpetrators of the child's injuries and their defence is either each to blame the other or to offer no credible explanation, the judge is placed in a similar position to judge and jury in criminal proceedings when trying to determine whether one or both are guilty. In care proceedings the judge applies the elevated civil standard of proof; a degree of heightened cogency is necessary to enable the judge to say that it could not possibly have been one of the parties. There are conflicting decisions of the Court of Appeal on this point. In *Re B (Non-Accidental Injury: Compelling Medical Evidence)* [2002] EWCA Civ 902, [2002] 2 FLR 599, the Court of Appeal held in May 2002 that, where the judge had not given sufficient reasons as to why strong medical evidence indicating that the mother had perpetrated and/or failed to protect her child from serious injuries should be set aside, it was not open to him to exonerate the mother as a perpetrator. However, in *Re O and N (Care: Preliminary Hearing)* [2002] EWCA Civ 1271, [2002] 2 FLR 1167, a differently constituted Court of Appeal, sitting in July 2002 and apparently not referred to the earlier Court of Appeal decision in *Re B* (above), decided that whilst there is an *evidential* burden on the parents to provide some explanation for the injuries to their child which must have happened whilst the child was in the care of either or both of them, that did not amount to a *legal* burden of proof. The Court of Appeal held that, as the local authority had not established on a balance of probabilities that the mother had inflicted any harm at all, the case must proceed on the basis that the child was not harmed by her mother and that there was no risk that the children might suffer physical harm from her. See the useful article "Child Protection in the Court of Appeal" [2002] Fam Law 817 for an analysis of the conflicting decisions.

It is important for the court to hear proper evidence before making a finding of sexual abuse in the face of a complete and consistent denial by the alleged perpetrator (see *Re D (Sexual Abuse Allegations: Evidence of Adult Victim)* [2002] 1 FLR 723 – where the findings of the magistrates were not supported by direct evidence and were overturned on appeal).

The first limb of s 31(2)(*a*) predicates an existing state of affairs: that the child is suffering significant harm. The relevant time for this purpose is the date of the care order application or, if temporary protective arrangements have been continuously in place from an earlier date, the date when those arrangements were initiated (*Re M (A Minor) (Care Order: Threshold Conditions)* [1994] 2 AC 424, [1994] 2 FLR 577. However, the local authority does not have to be in possession of all the information it wishes to rely upon at the date of the application. Evidence gathering continues after proceedings have begun and later acquired information as to the state of affairs at the relevant date can be taken into account (*Re G (Care Proceedings: Threshold Conditions)* [2001] EWCA Civ 968, [2001] 2 FLR 1111). In *Re G* (above), Hale LJ identified three different sets of circumstances where this issue might arise: (i) where information is discovered after the relevant date which throws light on what the facts were at the relevant date; (ii) entirely new events may indicate a completely different risk which did not exist at the relevant date; (iii) where there are new events which may or may not be capable of proving that there was a risk of significant harm at the relevant time. The relevant time for the second limb (likely to suffer significant harm) is the same (*Southwark LBC v B* [1998] 2 FLR 1095, FD). "Likely" means "a real possibility" (*Re H and R* (above)).

Whether either limb of s 31(2)(*a*) is satisfied is an issue to be decided by the court on the basis of the *facts* admitted or proved on the balance of probability before it; suspicion is not sufficient. However, the range of facts that may properly be taken into account is infinite (see *Re H and R (Child Sexual Abuse)* [1996] 1 FLR 80 at 101B for examples), and facts which are minor or even trivial if considered in isolation, when taken together may suffice to satisfy the court of the likelihood of future harm. It follows that the court can conclude that there is a real possibility that the child will suffer harm in the future although harm in the past has not been established.

Once the court is satisfied that the s 31(1) threshold is crossed, and moves on to exercise its discretion as to what order should be made ("the welfare stage"), it can only find that the child has suffered harm or is at risk of suffering harm in the future (s 1(3)(*e*)) on the basis of facts proved on the balance of probabilities, and suspicion is not enough (*Re M and R (Child Abuse: Evidence)* [1996] 2 FLR 195, CA; *Re B and W (Threshold Criteria)* [1999] 2 FLR 833).

Schedule of facts—It should now be routine for the court to direct the local authority to set out a clear schedule of facts upon which it seeks a finding by the court and upon the basis of which it is alleged that the threshold is crossed. This should be lodged with the court and served on the other parties well before the final directions appointment so that the parents know the case they have to meet and have a fair opportunity to do so (*Re R (Care: Disclosure: Nature of Proceedings)* [2002] 1 FLR 755). This exercise helps all parties to focus on the issues involved as early as possible in the proceedings and on the need to identify the evidence, both oral and documentary, on which the local authority rely (*Re R* (above) – where the failure of the local authority properly to marshall its evidence and to identify the facts upon which it wished the court to make findings led to the authority, in the course of the hearing, having to withdraw serious allegations of sexual abuse and rely on other grounds to support its case for care orders).

Care order or supervision order—In deciding whether to make a care order or a supervision order in a particular case where the balance between the two is equal, the court should adopt the least interventionist approach – *Re D (Care or Supervision Order)* [2000] Fam Law 600, where it was held that the court should ask itself whether:

(1) the stronger order is needed to protect the child;
(2) the risks could be met by a supervision order;
(3) there is a need for the speed of action that a care order allows the local authority;
(4) the parent could properly protect the child without sharing parental responsibility with the local authority;
(5) parental co-operation could only be obtained through the more Draconian care order;
(6) the child's needs could be met by advising, assisting and befriending the child rather than by sharing parental responsibility for him;
(7) there have been any improvements seen by objective observers during the current proceedings which would indicate the future; and
(8) the range of powers available under a supervision order, including its duration.

Finally, the court remarked that a local authority should not be burdened with a care order if it was not really necessary, given the pressure on resources to which all local authorities are subject.

In any event, the choice between a care order and a supervision order has to be considered in the light of the Human Rights Act 1998 and the European Convention for the Protection of Human Rights and Fundamental Freedoms 1950. The key in each case is to decide whether a supervision order is proportionate as a response to the risk presented (*Re O (Supervision Order)* [2001] EWCA Civ 16, [2001] 1 FLR 923; *Re C (Care Order or Supervision Order)* [2001] 2 FLR 466). In the light of this, it may be unwise to rely on pre-Human Rights Act 1998 authorities when considering in the course of a post-Human Rights Act 1998 case the choice between a care or supervision order (see *Re O* (above)).

Role of children's guardian continues for duration of supervision order—Where care proceedings under s 31 result in a supervision order, the proceedings are not to be treated as concluded until the order has ceased to have effect so that, unless terminated by the court, the role of the children's guardian continues for the duration of the order (*Re MH (Child) (Care Proceedings: Children's Guardian); Re SB and MB (Children) (Care Proceedings: Children's Guardian)* [2001] 2 FLR 1334).

Undertakings and injunctions—The county court has no jurisdiction to grant injunctions in relation to the exercise by local authorities of their statutory powers in public law proceedings (*D v D (County Court: Jurisdiction: Injunctions)* [1993] 2 FLR 802, CA (no jurisdiction to grant order restraining local authority and police from investigating alleged abuse), *Re S and D (Children: Powers of Court)* [1995] 2 FLR 456, CA (no power to add to a supervision order a provision prohibiting the mother from removing the children from foster parents) and *Devon County Council v B* [1997] 1 FLR 591, CA (no jurisdiction to grant an injunction restraining the mother from entering the town where her child who was in care was living)). The High Court's inherent jurisdiction can only be invoked once leave of that court has been obtained under s 100. For further discussion, see the notes to s 100. However, the powers conferred on the High Court by Supreme Court Act 1981, s 37 are available in support of the rights conferred by CA 1989, s 33, and in particular s 33(3) (the right of the local authority to determine the extent to which a parent may meet his parental responsibility for a child in care) after a care order has been made. Section 100 does not apply to the general statutory power to make injunctions and therefore it is not necessary for the local authority to have leave to apply for such injunctive relief (*Re P (Care Orders: Injunctive Relief)* [2000] 2 FLR 385 – where the local authority sought injunctions ancillary to a care order requiring the parents to allow the child to attend college without interference, and permitting the local authority to monitor the family).

However, note that in *Tameside Metropolitan Borough Council v M (Injunctive Relief: County Courts: Jurisdiction)* [2001] Fam Law 873 the court, in the course of care proceedings, granted an injunction protecting all employees of the local authority who had been in, or who would at any stage come into contact with, members of the children's family in the course of their work, in circumstances where the parents had made a number of attempts to intimidate social workers by way of threatening and violent behaviour. In the *Tameside* case (above) HHJ Wilkinson held that although county courts have no inherent jurisdiction to grant an injunction they have a statutory jurisdiction to do so under the County Courts Act 1984, s 38, when, as in that case, the local authority had established a statutory right, by virtue of the care order granted by the court (see also *D v D (County Court Jurisdiction: Injunctions)* [1993] 2 FLR 802).

In *Re B (Supervision Order: Parental Undertaking)* [1996] 1 FLR 676, the Court of Appeal said that the county court has no inherent jurisdiction to accept undertakings in care proceedings, nor can it accept undertakings as part of a supervision order. The mother's agreement to undergo medical treatment could, however, have been recorded in a preamble to the supervision order.

As to the partial change that the Family Law Act 1996 introduces with regard to undertakings, see under CA 1989, s 38B.

Orders for anonymity of social workers only made in exceptional cases—It has to be recognized that social workers receive threats and actual violence from adults engaged in bitterly contested public law cases at the end of which they face a forced and permanent separation from their children. This is part of their job and it will not generally be possible to obtain an order for anonymity of a social worker involved in such proceedings unless the circumstances are exceptional (*Re W (Children)* LTL, 7 October 2002, Doc No C9600530).

32 Period within which application for order under this Part must be disposed of

(1) A court hearing an application for an order under this Part shall (in the light of any rules made by virtue of subsection (2)) –

(*a*) draw up a timetable with a view to disposing of the application without delay; and

(*b*) give such directions as it considers appropriate for the purpose of ensuring, so far as is reasonably practicable, that that timetable is adhered to.

(2) Rules of court may –

(*a*) specify periods within which specified steps must be taken in relation to such proceedings; and

(*b*) make other provision with respect to such proceedings for the purpose of ensuring, so far as is reasonably practicable, that they are disposed of without delay.

Avoidance of delay—This section forces the court to take a firm hold of the case, to lay down a procedural timetable and give appropriate directions (under FPR 1991, r 4.14 or Family Proceedings Courts (Children Act 1989) Rules 1991, r 14) to ensure that the application in question is determined without delay. Both practitioners and courts have a duty to avoid delay in children cases. The Lord Chancellor's Advisory Committee, jointly chaired by Coleridge J and Munby J, has drafted a protocol which sets out a national model for judicial case management in public law cases; it aims to reduce delay and improve the efficient administration of such cases. See further **Continuity of judge and legal representatives** under FPR 1991, r 4.14. The non-adversarial approach to children's litigation means that the solicitors for the parties have a duty, irrespective of whether delay might be tactically advantageous to their client, to ensure that a case does not drift and is resolved with the minimum of delay. Courts have a duty to be proactive in ensuring (through the giving of precise directions) that applications, once launched, are not allowed to moulder but are brought into court in a fully prepared state at the earliest opportunity. A children's guardian, has a duty to review the file regularly and, if the case is not making satisfactory progress, should take out a summons for directions (*Re A and B (Minors) (No 2)* [1995] 1 FLR 351; *Re O (Care: Delay)* [2001] Fam Law 339). Where an assessment is in progress, it may be right to timetable the proceedings to enable them to be concluded as soon as possible once the assessment is completed; the fact that the timetable might need to be revised is not of itself a reason not to timetable (*E v Humberside County Council and S* [1996] Fam Law 444, FD). In *Re JC (Care Proceedings: Procedure)* [1995] 2 FLR 77, FD, it was stressed that all those who wish to participate in caring for a child need to make their position clear as soon as possible; otherwise, delay can result, for example because the local authority has not been able to assess the suitability of potential carers. The benefits of split hearings in reducing delay must be borne in mind, see *Re S (Care Proceedings: Split Hearing)* [1996] 2 FLR 773 which is considered further at s 31. Although the general principle stated in s 1(2) is that delay is likely to be prejudicial, speed should not be the only consideration in making arrangements for disposal. The welfare of the child is the paramount consideration in many issues that arise in Pt IV applications (s 1(1)) and certain cases benefit from the passage of time to allow housing arrangements to be sorted out, medical and other investigations to take place etc. This does not mean that the court needs to let the case drift, merely that it must take such matters into account when fixing the timetable and giving directions. As to the benefits of planned and purposeful delay, see *C v Solihull MBC* [1993] 1 FLR 290 and *Hounslow LBC v A* [1993] 1 FLR 702. For the position where there are criminal proceedings pending, see **Delay** under s 1. As Wall J pointed out in *Re A and B (Minors) (No 2)*, above, in such a case the family court will need to be made aware of the current state of the criminal investigation and criminal process (if there is a prosecution) at every stage so that it can make a fully informed decision about the extent to which the duty with regard to timetabling can be fulfilled. See **"Twin track planning"/"Concurrent planning"** under CA 1989, s 31 for discussion of twin track planning as a strategy for reducing delay.

Care orders

33 Effect of care order

(1) Where a care order is made with respect to a child it shall be the duty of the local authority designated by the order to receive the child into their care and to keep him in their care while the order remains in force.

(2) Where –

(*a*) a care order has been made with respect to a child on the application of an authorised person; but
(*b*) the local authority designated by the order was not informed that that person proposed to make the application,

the child may be kept in the care of that person until received into the care of the authority.

(3) While a care order is in force with respect to a child, the local authority designated by the order shall –

(*a*) have parental responsibility for the child; and
(*b*) have the power (subject to the following provisions of this section) to determine the extent to which a parent or guardian of the child may meet his parental responsibility for him.

(4) The authority may not exercise the power in subsection (3)(*b*) unless they are satisfied that it is necessary to do so in order to safeguard or promote the child's welfare.

(5) Nothing in subsection (3)(*b*) shall prevent a parent or guardian of the child who has care of him from doing what is reasonable in all the circumstances of the case for the purpose of safeguarding or promoting his welfare.

(6) While a care order is in force with respect to a child, the local authority designated by the order shall not –

(*a*) cause the child to be brought up in any religious persuasion other than that in which he would have been brought up if the order had not been made; or
(*b*) have the right –
(i) to consent or refuse to consent to the making of an application with respect to the child under section 18 of the Adoption Act 1976;
(ii) to agree or refuse to agree to the making of an adoption order, or an order under section 55 of the Act of 1976, with respect to the child; or
(iii) to appoint a guardian for the child.

(7) While a care order is in force with respect to a child, no person may –

(*a*) cause the child to be known by a new surname; or
(*b*) remove him from the United Kingdom,

without either the written consent of every person who has parental responsibility for the child or the leave of the court.

(8) Subsection (7)(*b*) does not –

(*a*) prevent the removal of such a child, for a period of less than one month, by the authority in whose care he is; or
(*b*) apply to arrangements for such a child to live outside England and Wales (which are governed by paragraph 19 of Schedule 2).

(9) The power in subsection (3)(*b*) is subject (in addition to being subject to the provisions of this section) to any right, duty, power, responsibility or authority which a parent or guardian of the child has in relation to the child and his property by virtue of any other enactment.

Defined terms—"authorised person": s 31(9); "care order": ss 31(11), 105(1); "child", "guardian", "local authority": s 105(1); "parental responsibility": ss 3, 105(1).

New surname (s 33(7))—In *Re J (A Minor) (Change of Name)* [1993] 1 FLR 699, an application under s 33(7)(*a*) was dealt with ex parte and without the appointment of a children's guardian, as would normally be required in accordance with s 41.

In *Re M, T, P, K and B (Care: Change of Name)* [2000] 2 FLR 645 the court held that a similar approach should be adopted for public law and private law cases and the principles established in private law change of name cases should not be ignored. On any application to change a child's surname the welfare of the children concerned was paramount. In addition to the welfare checklist factors the court should give very careful consideration to: (i) the wishes, feelings, needs and objectives of the applicant; (ii) the motives and stated objections of the respondents; and (iii) the opinion of the children's guardian. See **Change of surname** under s 8, for details of the private law approach to a change of name.

Method of application for leave under s 33(7)—An application for leave to cause a child to be known by a new surname or to remove him from the United Kingdom should be commenced in a magistrates' court (Children (Allocation of Proceedings) Order 1991, art 3), subject to the exceptions set out in that article and art 4. In *MH v GP (Child: Emigration)* [1995] 2 FLR 106, FD, it was held, however, that a private law application for leave to remove a child permanently from the jurisdiction should not be heard by magistrates but should be transferred for determination either in the county court or the High Court, depending on the complexity and difficulty of the decision; a similar course should no doubt be considered in public law cases. In the exceptional case where an application is made ex parte for a change of surname, the application should be transferred from the magistrates to a higher court (*Re J (A Minor) (Change of Name)* [1993] 1 FLR 699).

The application should be commenced in accordance with FPR 1991, r 4.4 or FPC(CA 1989)R 1991, r 4; although such an application is an application for leave, it is not covered by FPR 1991, r 4.3 and FPC(CA 1989)R 1991, r 3 which deal only with applications for leave to commence proceedings.

34 Parental contact etc with children in care

(1) Where a child is in the care of a local authority, the authority shall (subject to the provisions of this section) allow the child reasonable contact with –

(*a*) his parents;
(*b*) any guardian of his;
(*c*) where there was a residence order in force with respect to the child immediately before the care order was made, the person in whose favour the order was made; and
(*d*) where, immediately before the care order was made, a person had care of the child by virtue of an order made in the exercise of the High Court's inherent jurisdiction with respect to children, that person.

(2) On an application made by the authority or the child, the court may make such order as it considers appropriate with respect to the contact which is to be allowed between the child and any named person.

(3) On an application made by –

(*a*) any person mentioned in paragraph (*a*) to (*d*) of subsection (1); or
(*b*) any person who has obtained the leave of the court to make the application,

the court may make such order as it considers appropriate with respect to the contact which is to be allowed between the child and that person.

(4) On an application made by the authority or the child, the court may make an order authorising the authority to refuse to allow contact between the child and any person who is mentioned in paragraphs (*a*) to (*d*) of subsection (1) and named in the order.

(5) When making a care order with respect to a child, or in any family proceedings in connection with a child who is in the care of a local authority, the court may

make an order under this section, even though no application for such an order has been made with respect to the child, if it considers that the order should be made.

(6) An authority may refuse to allow the contact that would otherwise be required by virtue of subsection (1) or an order under this section if –

(*a*) they are satisfied that it is necessary to do so in order to safeguard or promote the child's welfare; and

(*b*) the refusal –

(i) is decided upon as a matter of urgency; and

(ii) does not last for more than seven days.

(7) An order under this section may impose such conditions as the court considers appropriate.

(8) The Secretary of State may by regulations make provision as to –

(*a*) the steps to be taken by a local authority who have exercised their power under subsection (6);

(*b*) the circumstances in which, and conditions subject to which, the terms of any order under this section may be departed from by agreement between the local authority and the person in relation to whom the order is made;

(*c*) notification by a local authority of any variation or suspension of arrangements made (otherwise than under an order under this section) with a view to affording any person contact with a child to whom this section applies.

(9) The court may vary or discharge any order made under this section on the application of the authority, the child concerned or the person named in the order.

(10) An order under this section may be made either at the same time as the care order itself or later.

(11) Before making a care order with respect such any child the court shall –

(*a*) consider the arrangements which the authority have made, or propose to make, for affording any person contact with a child to whom this section applies; and

(*b*) invite the parties to the proceedings to comment on those arrangements.

Defined terms—"care order": ss 31(11), 105(1); "child": s 105(1); "family proceedings": s 8(3); "guardian", "local authority": s 105(1); "residence order": s 8(1).

"parents" (s 34(1)(*a*))—See **Meaning of "parent"** under s 10.

"person in whose favour the residence order was made" (s 34(1)(*c*))—This refers to the person named in the order as the person with whom the child is to live.

High Court's inherent jurisdiction (s 34(1)(*d*))—The inherent jurisdiction of the High Court was, prior to CA 1989, most commonly exercised in wardship proceedings. The Act has put an end to the majority of wardship applications, but applications are still made under the inherent jurisdiction of the court; see, in particular, under s 100.

Leave to make an application (s 34(3))—For the procedure for seeking leave, where the application is to be made in a county court or the High Court, see FPR 1991, r 4.3; where the application is to be made in a magistrates' court, see Family Proceedings Courts (Children Act 1989) Rules 1991, r 3.

The correct approach to a leave application under s 34 is set out in the Court of Appeal's decision in *Re M (Care: Contact: Grandmother's Application for Leave)* [1995] 2 FLR 86. It was held that the criteria set out in s 10(9) (which relate to an application for leave to apply for an order under CA 1989, s 8) do not strictly apply to an application under s 34 for leave to apply for contact with a child in care but that, nevertheless, the court should still bear those criteria in mind

PART II

in reaching its decision in a leave application under s 34. Accordingly, the court must have regard to all the circumstances of the case, for each case is different, but should always have particular regard at least to the following factors:

(*a*) The nature of the contact sought;
(*b*) The applicant's connection to the child;
(*c*) The risk of the child's life being disrupted by the proposed application to such an extent that the child would be harmed by it;
(*d*) The wishes of the parents and local authority.

In weighing up these factors, the following approach should be adopted:

(*a*) If the application is frivolous, vexatious or an abuse of process, it will fail;
(*b*) If the leave application fails to disclose any real prospect of eventual success (or the prospect is remote so that the application is obviously unsustainable), it must also be dismissed;
(*c*) The applicant must satisfy the court that there is a serious issue to try and must present a good arguable case – is there a real issue which the applicant may reasonably ask the court to try, and has he a case which is better than merely arguable yet not necessarily one which is shown to have a better-than-even chance, a fair chance, of success?

Over-analysis of these "tests" should be avoided and the matter approached "in the loosest way possible, looking at the matter in the round", because it is important that the exercise of discretion by the court is unfettered. (In referring to the report in the Family Law Reports, it should be noted that paragraph (3) should, in fact, end after '... fair chance of success?', and the following passage concerning over-analysis of the tests should be of general application, not only qualifying the test set out in paragraph (3).)

As *Re M* points out, because contact between a child and his family will be assumed to be beneficial by virtue of CA 1989, Sch 2, para 15, a local authority which considers that it is not reasonably practicable or consistent with the child's welfare to promote that contact will need to file evidence to justify its stance.

Interim contact hearing—Interim contact orders are possible (see *West Glamorgan County Council v P (No 1)* [1992] 2 FLR 369 as to interim orders under s 34(4)). For guidance as to how the court should approach an interim hearing, see *Hampshire County Council v S* [1993] 1 FLR 559 and *Re W (A Minor) (Interim Care Order)* [1994] 2 FLR 892, CA (discussed under FPC(CA 1989)R 1991, r 21); with regard to an application for a final order under s 34 heard during the currency of an interim care order, see *A v M and Walsall MBC* [1993] 2 FLR 244.

Review of contact by the court—It is not open to the court to retain control over the issue of contact with a child in care by providing for a general review of the progress of the care plan and of contact arrangements at some date after the making of a care order (*Re B (A Minor) (Care Order: Review)* [1993] 1 FLR 421). See also *Kent County Council v C* [1993] 1 FLR 308 in which Ewbank J held that the court cannot fetter the local authority's plans by adding a direction to a care order that the guardian ad litem (children's guardian) remain involved with the child. What the court *can* do, according to *Re B* (above), is to make what is in effect an interim contact order with a specific provision for a further hearing with a view to making more enduring provision for contact at the subsequent hearing. It may be, however, that *Re S (A Minor) (Care: Contact Order)* [1994] 2 FLR 222 casts doubt on this approach: the Court of Appeal there held that, where the nature and extent of the contact was an integral part of the local authority's care plan, it was not for the court to decide precisely what contact was reasonable. The judge had made a care order, but adjourned the issue of contact for further directions and this was, in effect, providing for a review of the implementation of the care plan which would lead the judge into the forbidden territory of supervising the administration of the local authority's arrangements for rehabilitation. The court has no jurisdiction under s 34 to prohibit a local authority, into whose care a child has been placed, from permitting parental contact with the child; if the court did make such an order it would be unenforceable because, by virtue of Contact with Children Regulations 1991, reg 3, a local authority can, with the parents' agreement, depart from the terms of any order made under s 34 (*Re W (Section 34(2) Orders)* [2000] 1 FLR 502, CA). The whole question of the court relinquishing control of a child's case to the local authority is considered further under s 38 **Interim care order or full care order?**. See also **Adoption and Children Act 2002 – review of cases of looked-after children** under CA 1989, s 26, for a summary of the ways in which it might be possible in future for the circumstances of children subject to care orders to be reviewed by the court once ACA 2002 is implemented, bringing into force amendments to s 26(2)(*e*).

Contact at the discretion of the local authority—*L v London Borough of Bromley* [1998] 1 FLR 709, FD demonstrates how orders for contact at the discretion of the local authority must be interpreted in accordance with CA 1989, s 34(1) and Sch 2, para 15(1). It was not inapt for the magistrates in that case to have indicated the frequency of contact they had in mind for the mother at the same time as ordering that her contact would be at the discretion of the local authority. The judge expressed his view that, notwithstanding the no order principle in s 1(5), in many cases it is beneficial that the court should spell it out when contact with a child is within the discretion of the local authority.

L v London Borough of Bromley should be compared with *Re P (Minors) (Contact with Children in Care)* [1993] 2 FLR 156 in which the judge distinguished between an order for contact with a parent at the discretion of the local authority and an order for reasonable contact.

Contact – European Convention for the Protection of Human Rights and Fundamental Freedoms 1950—The Convention was implemented in this jurisdiction on the coming into force of the Human Rights Act 1998. Litigants were warned in *Re F (Care Proceedings: Contact)* [2000] Fam Law 708 that where care orders have been made together with orders under s 34(4) authorising the local authority to terminate contact with the parents of the child concerned it would be disappointing if the Convention were to be routinely paraded as a make-weight ground of appeal, or if there were in every such case to be extensive citation of authorities from the European Court of Human Rights, particularly where such authorities pre-dated CA 1989. In *Re F* the mother's argument that the decision to terminate contact was an essentially administrative rather than judicial decision failed, and her reliance on *W v UK* (1988) 10 EHHR 29 was misplaced.

Contact with father is just as important as contact with mother—Where a care order was made in relation to children who had suffered serious injuries caused by one of the parents, although the court was unable to say which, and the mother was to continue to have contact, there was no reason to terminate the father's contact. The benefit of keeping the family link alive by way of contact operates just as much for the father as for the mother (*Re G (Children)* [2002] EWCA Civ 761, 20 May 2002, (unreported)).

Contact – Domestic violence—The Court of Appeal in *Re L (Contact: Domestic Violence); Re V (Contact: Domestic Violence); Re M (Contact: Domestic Violence); Re H (Contact: Domestic Violence)* [2000] 2 FLR 334 has laid down useful guidelines as to the way in which courts should approach the hearing of contact applications in which allegations of domestic violence are raised in private law cases. See **Contact – Domestic violence** under s 8. In *Re G (Domestic Violence: Direct Contact)* [2000] 2 FLR 865, the President held that the principles set out in *Re L* (above) were equally applicable in public law cases dealing with contact between the child concerned and his parents. In particular, domestic violence shows a very serious failure in parenting and constitutes a failure to protect the child's carer and a failure to protect the child emotionally.

No order as to contact/no contact order—In *Kent County Council v C* [1993] 1 FLR 308, it was said that, whilst the court has power to make an order for no contact between a parent and child, in the ordinary case it would be better (in the light of the provisions of the Contact with Children Regulations 1991 in respect of departure from a s 34 order), where the court thinks there should be no contact, for the order to say there is no order as to contact (*Re SW (A Minor)* [1993] 2 FLR 609). It is otiose for an order to provide specifically for reasonable contact because s 34(1) obliges the local authority to allow this in any event (*Re S (A Minor) (Care: Contact Order)* [1994] 2 FLR 222, though *L v London Borough of Bromley* [1998] 1 FLR 709 recognises there can be a benefit in spelling things out in certain circumstances; see **Contact at the discretion of the local authority** (above)). If continuing reasonable contact is the intended result, the order can therefore safely remain silent, and reliance can be placed on the local authority's statutory duty. However, if it is intended that the order should provide for there not to be any contact between the applicant and the child, care must clearly be taken to ensure that, in juggling with the phrases "no order as to contact" and "no contact", the draftsman does not arrive at an order which, because it is effectively silent as to contact or because its phraseology is otherwise unfortunate, leaves the local authority with a continuing duty under s 34(1).

Discharge of a s 34(4) "no contact" order—*Re T (Termination of Contact: Discharge of Order)* [1997] 1 FLR 517 establishes that, in order to discharge a s 34(4) order, there must be some material change of circumstances between the making of the order and the application to discharge it. The courts are entitled to screen out disguised appeals against the original order, and should have two considerations in mind: (i) the extent to which circumstances have changed since the original order, and (ii) bearing those changes in mind, the extent to which it is appropriate to reinvestigate the central question. The greater the change in circumstances, the more intensively the court would be prepared to reconsider the desirability of leaving the s 34(4) order in place. The welfare of the child is paramount on a discharge application. As to the power of local authorities to override no contact orders without having further recourse to the court, see the Contact with Children Regulations 1991.

Disclosure of information concerning prospective adopters—As to the question whether information about prospective adopters should be disclosed to a parent where a s 34 application and an adoption application are running concurrently, see *Re S (A Minor) (Adoption)* [1993] 2 FLR 204.

Contact arrangements (s 34(11))—The arrangements for contact which the court has to consider under s 34(11) before making a care order are the arrangements proposed by the authority into whose care the child would be placed. Where this is not the applicant local authority, and if the other authority is not present or represented throughout the hearing, proper arrangements should be made in advance for a representative of the authority to attend court to deal with any issues that might arise and to assure the court and the parents of the authority's commitment to the care plan and its capacity to implement it *L v London Borough of Bexley* [1996] 2 FLR 595, FD).

Supervision orders

35 Supervision orders

(1) While a supervision order is in force it shall be the duty of the supervisor –

(*a*) to advise, assist and befriend the supervised child;

(*b*) to take such steps as are reasonably necessary to give effect to the order; and

(*c*) where –

(i) the order is not wholly complied with; or

(ii) the supervisor considers that the order may no longer be necessary,

to consider whether or not to apply to the court for its variation or discharge.

(2) Parts I and II of Schedule 3 make further provision with respect to supervision orders.

36 Education supervision orders

(1) On the application of any local education authority, the court may make an order putting the child with respect to whom the application is made under the supervision of a designated local education authority.

(2) In this Act "an education supervision order" means an order under subsection (1).

(3) A court may only make an education supervision order if it is satisfied that the child concerned is of compulsory school age and is not being properly educated.

(4) For the purposes of this section, a child is being properly educated only if he is receiving efficient full-time education suitable to his age, ability and aptitude and any special educational needs he may have.

(5) Where a child is –

(*a*) the subject of a school attendance order which is in force under section 437 of the Education Act 1996 and which has not been complied with; or

(*b*) a registered pupil at a school which he is not attending regularly within the meaning of section 444 of that Act,

then, unless it is proved that he is being properly educated, it shall be assumed that he is not.

(6) An education supervision order may not be made with respect to a child who is in the care of a local authority.

(7) The local education authority designated in an education supervision order must be –

(*a*) the authority within whose area the child concerned is living or will live; or

(*b*) where –

(i) the child is a registered pupil at a school; and

(ii) the authority mentioned in paragraph (*a*) and the authority within whose area the school is situated agree,

the latter authority.

(8) Where a local education authority propose to make an application for an education supervision order they shall, before making the application, consult the appropriate local authority.

(9) The appropriate local authority is –

(*a*) in the case of a child who is being provided with accommodation by, or on behalf of, a local authority, that authority; and

(*b*) in any other case, the local authority within whose area the child concerned lives, or will live.

(10) Part III of Schedule 3 makes further provision with respect to education supervision orders.

Amendments—Education Act 1996, s 582(1), Sch 37, Pt I, para 85.

Defined terms—"appropriate local authority": s 36(9); "child": s 105(1); "education supervision order": s 36(2); "local authority", "local education authority": s 105(1).

"designated local education authority"—Section 36(7) specifies which authority must be designated.

"in the care of the local authority" (s 36(6))—This refers to a child who is in the care of a local authority by virtue of a care order (see ss 31(11) and 105(1)).

Powers of court

37 Powers of court in certain family proceedings

(1) Where, in any family proceedings in which a question arises with respect to the welfare of any child, it appears to the court that it may be appropriate for a care or supervision order to be made with respect to him, the court may direct the appropriate authority to undertake an investigation of the child's circumstances.

(2) Where the court gives a direction under this section the local authority concerned shall, when undertaking the investigation, consider whether they should –

(*a*) apply for a care order or for a supervision order with respect to the child;

(*b*) provide services or assistance for the child or his family; or

(*c*) take any other action with respect to the child.

(3) Where a local authority undertake an investigation under this section, and decide not to apply for a care order or supervision order with respect to the child concerned, they shall inform the court of –

(*a*) their reasons for so deciding;

(*b*) any service or assistance which they have provided, or to intend to provide, for the child and his family; and (*c*) any other action which they have taken, or propose to take, with respect to the child.

(4) The information shall be given to the court before the end of the period of eight weeks beginning with the date of the direction, unless the court otherwise directs.

(5) The local authority named in a direction under subsection (1) must be –

(*a*) the authority in whose area the child is ordinarily resident; or

(*b*) where the child is not ordinarily resident in the area of a local authority, the authority within whose area any circumstances arose in consequence of which the direction is being given.

(6) If, on the conclusion of any investigation or review under this section, the authority decide not to apply for a care order or supervision order with respect to the child –

(*a*) they shall consider whether it would be appropriate to review the case at a later date; and

(*b*) if they decide that it would be, they shall determine the date on which that review is to begin.

Amendments—Courts and Legal Services Act 1990, s 116, Sch 16, para 16.

Defined terms—"care order": ss 31(11), 105(1); "child": s 105(1); "family proceedings": s 8(3); "local authority": s 105(1); "supervision order": s 31(11).

Scope of provision—This section empowers the court, of its own motion, to direct a local authority to look into the circumstances of a child with a view to the possibility of taking action with respect to the child, for example by making an application for a care or supervision order or by providing services or assistance for the child and his family. An interim order may be made pending the results of the investigation (s 38(1)). If the local authority decides, after investigating, that it is not going to apply for a care or supervision order, it must inform the court, normally within eight weeks of the court's initial direction (s 37(4)), of its reasons and of any action that it has taken or intends to take with respect to the child (s 37(3)). It must also consider whether to review the case at a later date and, if it decides that a review would be appropriate, fix a date for it (s 37(6)). The court has no power to make a care or supervision order of its own motion, so it cannot override a decision of the local authority not to apply (see eg *Nottinghamshire County Council v P* [1993] 2 FLR 134).

"appropriate authority" (s 37(1))—The appropriate authority is the local authority named in accordance with s 37(5). Reference should be made to the notes to s 31(8), a similar provision in respect of the designation of a local authority for the purposes of a care order, for assistance on the interpretation of s 37(5).

"ordinarily resident" (s 37(5))—See under s 31.

Procedure—For the procedure where a direction is given under s 37 by a county court or the High Court, see FPR 1991, r 4.26; where the direction is given by a magistrates' court, see Family Proceedings Courts (Children Act 1989) Rules 1991, r 27.

Best practice guidance on s 37(1) directions—The Children Act Advisory Committee was concerned about the over-use of the s 37 procedure. In some areas, it appears that s 37 has been adopted as a device to facilitate the appointment of a children's guardian who could not otherwise be appointed in private law proceedings; in other places where the courts face particularly long delays in obtaining a children and family reporter's report, s 37 has apparently been used as an alternative reporting procedure, even though delays have also been experienced in the production of s 37 reports. Accordingly, the Committee published, in its Annual Report 1992/93, *Best Practice Guidance on Section 37(1) Directions* which are to be applied nationally and the text of which is as follows:

(1) A direction under s 37(1) is appropriate where the court desires an investigation because "it appears to the court that it may be appropriate for a care or supervision order to be made" (s 37(1)).

(2) A direction under s 37(1) is not lawful unless it appears to the court that a care or supervision order may be appropriate. Thus, in private law proceedings, a direction under s 37(1) should not be used as a device for the purpose of enabling the court to appoint a guardian ad litem. Unless "it appears to the court that it may be appropriate for a care or supervision order to be made", any referral for a welfare investigation should be made under s 7.

(3) The purpose of a s 37(1) direction is to enable the court to cause the local authority to assess whether a care or supervision order is needed. It is not to obtain a general welfare report. However, the making of a s 37(1) direction will also cause the local authority to consider whether and which child welfare support services should be provided by the local authority, or other action taken, as well as or instead of a care or supervision order: s 37(2), and note the details of the duty of the local authority to report to the court under s 37(3).

(4) Upon a direction under s 37, the local authority must report back within 8 weeks unless the court otherwise directs: s 37(4). The date for the next hearing must be fixed: Family Proceedings Rules 1991, r 4.15(2)(ii), Family Proceedings Courts (Children Act 1989) Rules 1991, r 15(5)(ii). The date for the report should also be specified under FPR 1991, r 4.14(2) or FPC(CA 1989)R 1991, r 14(2).

(5) When a county court which is not a care centre makes a direction under s 37(1), it will facilitate expedition of any proceedings begun by the local authority if the court makes a direction under the Children (Allocation of Proceedings) Order 1991, art 3(2)(*b*) for the application to be made to the appropriate care centre.

Appointment of a panel guardian ad litem

(6) When a court has made a direction under s 37(1), and "has made, or is considering whether to make, an interim care order" (s 41(6)(b)), "the court shall appoint a guardian ad litem for the child concerned unless satisfied that it is not necessary to do so in order to safeguard his interests": s 41(1).

(7) The court cannot appoint a panel guardian unless the proceedings are "specified" within s 41(6). Section 41 does not authorise the court to appoint a guardian ad litem, upon making a s 37(1) direction, if the court has not made and is not considering whether to make an interim care order: s 41(6)(b).

Section 7(1) referrals

(8) Section 7(1) is for cases where the court desires a welfare investigation and report. This might include a child protection issue, for example, abusive interference with a child by a parent or other person who does not have care of the child: in such a case an injunction may be the appropriate remedy.

(9) The reporter under a s 7(1) order is the eyes and ears of the court and is required to investigate and to report to the court on the welfare of the child. The reporter is an independent agent of the court, is not a party to the proceedings and is not legally represented.

(10) Whether an order under s 7(1) should be directed to the court welfare service or the local authority may be affected by:

(i) previous involvement with and knowledge of the family by the local authority, in which case the local authority is likely to be appropriate, particularly if the involvement is recent or continuing;

(ii) local arrangements between the court welfare service and the local authority for distribution or sharing of investigation work.

(11) When considering whether to make a s 7(1) referral or a s 37(1) direction, the court should as far as practicable obtain the available relevant information from any social worker or court welfare officer who is currently involved with the child, or a duty court welfare officer.

(12) Upon making a s 7(1) referral, the date for the next hearing must be fixed: FPR 1991, r 4.15(2)(ii), FPC(CA 1989)R 1991, r 15(5)(ii). The date for the report should also be specified under FPR 1991, r 4.14(2) or FPC(CA 1989)R 1991, r 14(2).

Communication to local authority of s 37(1) direction or s 7(1) referral

(13) It is important that whenever a court makes a s 37(1) direction or a s 7(1) referral to a local authority, the authority should be informed as quickly as possible. An immediate telephone notification should be confirmed in writing. FPR 1991, r 4.26(3) and FPC(CA 1989)R 1991, r 27(3) require that a copy of a s 37(1) direction shall be served on the local authority as soon as practicable. FPR 1991, r 4.26(4) and FPC(CA 1989)R 1991, r 27(4) provide for the court to direct which parts of the documentary evidence should be served on the local authority where a s 37(1) direction has been made.

Authority on s 37—See *Re H (A Minor) (Section 37 Direction)* [1993] 2 FLR 541 ("child's circumstances" under s 37(1) to be widely construed and should include any situation which might have a bearing on the child being likely to suffer significant harm in the future; judge's s 37 order went into detail with regard to investigations to be carried out, and included a time-scale for the investigation). The judge must not, however, seek to fetter the local authority in the execution of its statutory function under s 37 (*Re M (Official Solicitor's Role)* [1998] 2 FLR 815, CA in which the judge wrongly sought to use the Official Solicitor to regulate the s 37 enquiry). In *Re A and B (Minors) (No 2)* [1995] 1 FLR 351, Wall J questioned whether s 37 was appropriate where the local authority had already carried out an investigation and what the court wanted was information about this; he saw s 7 as the better choice (see **Officer of the Service or local authority** under s 7). In *Re D (Residence: Imposition of Conditions)* [1996] 2 FLR 281, CA, a children and family reporter was ordered to investigate the issue of residence, and the local authority (which had recently been involved in the matter) was also invited to report pursuant to s 37. A s 37 investigation is not to be ordered in private law proceedings unless it appears that a public law order might be appropriate (*Re L (Section 37 Direction)* [1999] 1 FLR 984).

Position of children's guardian—Proceedings which become specified by virtue of s 41(6)(*b*) following the making of a s 37 order cease to be specified if the local authority, as a result of its investigation (albeit as yet incomplete), decides not to apply for a care order or supervision order and so informs the court (*Re CE (Section 37 Direction)* [1995] 1 FLR 26, FD). In that case, however, it was in the child's interests for the children's guardian, who had been appointed on the proceedings originally becoming specified, to remain involved until the local authority's final assessment was in place and a final resolution could be ordered or sanctioned by the court. The guardian had consented to her continuing involvement and could be funded as an expert on the child's legal aid certificate, so the court invoked its jurisdiction under FPR 1991, r 9.5 to appoint a guardian in private law proceedings.

It will not always be appropriate to appoint a children's guardian when proceedings have become specified because a s 37 investigation has been directed and the court has made, or is considering whether to make, an interim care order; considerations to be borne in mind are set out in *Re CE (Section 37 Direction)*, above, and are dealt with further under s 41.

Local authority as party—In *F v Cambridgeshire County Council* [1995] 1 FLR 516, FD, it was held that it had been an error to permit a local authority which had carried out a s 37 investigation and decided not to seek a care or supervision order to become a party in private law proceedings by a father against a mother for contact, given the restrictions on local authorities seeking private law orders.

38 Interim orders

(1) Where –

(*a*) in any proceedings on an application for a care order or supervision order, the proceedings are adjourned; or

(*b*) the court gives a direction under section 37(1).

the court may make an interim care order or an interim supervision order with respect to the child concerned.

(2) A court shall not make an interim care order or interim supervision order under this section unless it is satisfied that there are reasonable grounds for believing that circumstances with respect to the child are as mentioned in section 31(2).

(3) Where, in any proceedings on an application for a care order or supervision order, a court makes a residence order with respect to the child concerned, it shall

also make an interim supervision order with respect to him unless satisfied that his welfare will be satisfactorily safeguarded without an interim order being made.

(4) An interim order made under or by virtue of this section shall have effect for such period as may be specified in the order, but shall in any event cease to have effect on whichever of the following events occurs –

(*a*) the expiry of the period of eight weeks beginning with the date on which the order is made;

(*b*) if the order is the second or subsequent such order made with respect to the same child in the same proceedings, the expiry of the relevant period;

(*c*) in a case which falls within subsection (1)(*a*), the disposal of the application;

(*d*) in a case which falls within subsection (1)(*b*), the disposal of an application for a care order or a supervision order made by the authority with respect to the child;

(*e*) in a case which falls within subsection (1)(*b*) and in which –

(i) the court has given a direction under section 37(4), but

(ii) no application for a care order or supervision order has been made with respect to the child,

the expiry of the period fixed by that direction.

(5) In subsection (4)(*b*) "the relevant period" means –

(*a*) the period of four weeks beginning with the date on which the order in question is made; or

(*b*) the period of eight weeks beginning with the date on which the first order was made if that period ends later than the period mentioned in paragraph (*a*).

(6) Where the court makes an interim care order, or interim supervision order, it may give such directions (if any) as it considers appropriate with regard to the medical or psychiatric examination or other assessment of the child; but if the child is of sufficient understanding to make an informed decision he may refuse to submit to the examination or other assessment.

(7) A direction under subsection (6) may be to the effect that there is to be –

(*a*) no such examination or assessment; or

(*b*) no such examination or assessment unless the court directs otherwise.

(8) A direction under subsection (6) may be –

(*a*) given when the interim order is made or at any time while it is in force; and

(*b*) varied at any time on the application of any person falling within any class of person prescribed by rules of court for the purposes of this subsection.

(9) Paragraphs 4 and 5 of Schedule 3 shall not apply in relation to an interim supervision order.

(10) Where a court makes an order under or by virtue of this section it shall, in determining the period for which the order is to be in force, consider whether any party who was, or might have been, opposed to the making of the order was in a position to argue his case against the order in full.

Defined terms—"care order": ss 31(11), 105(1); "child": s 105(1); "relevant period": s 38(5); "residence order": s 8(1); "supervision order": s 31(11).

Nature of interim orders—The object of an interim order should normally be to hold the balance so as to cause the least possible harm to the child; see eg *B v B (Interim Contact with*

Grandparents) [1993] Fam Law 393 (s 8 contact case), *Hampshire County Council v S* [1993] 1 FLR 559 (interim order re contact with child in care). An interim care order is not a step involving any advance judgment of the final issue on the part of the court (see *Re H (A Child)* (unreported) 12/12/2002 LTL Doc No C9500935 – where the Court of Appeal held that an interim hearing could not be a substitute for a full trial of a local authority's concerns about the safety of a child). It can be a neutral and effective way of preserving the status quo, an essentially impartial step favouring neither one side nor the other and affording to no-one, least of all the local authority in whose favour it is made, an opportunity for tactical or adventitious advantage. Parliament intended the regime of an interim care order to operate as a tightly run procedure, closely monitored by the court and affording to all parties an opportunity of frequent review as events unfold during the currency of the order. Therefore, renewals of interim care orders should not be sought routinely by local authorities without any attempt to keep the court up to date with progress, nor should they be granted by the court perfunctorily without the making of any inquiries necessary to eliminate the risk of essential disclosure being lost through administrative lethargy (*Re G (Minors) (Interim Care Order)* [1993] 2 FLR 839). An interim care order is not irreversible either in law or in fact (*Re L (Interim Care Order: Power of Court)* [1996] 2 FLR 742, CA). It does not follow that an interim care order will be made automatically upon the threshold criteria having been met in a particular case (*Re A (Children) (Interim Care Order)* [2001] 3 FCR 402 – although in that case interim care orders were made).

Interim care order or full care order?—It can be difficult to know whether the time has come for the court to make a full care order, handing over responsibility for the child to the local authority, or whether there is still a role for the court and an interim order should be made. In *Re CH (Care or Interim Care Order)* [1998] 1 FLR 402, the Court of Appeal endorsed the approach of Wall J in *Re J (Minors)(Care: Care Plan)* [1994] 1 FLR 253. Wall J had identified a two-stage process that the court must go through before making a care order. Firstly it must be satisfied that the threshold criteria have been met. Secondly it considers whether the making of a care order is better than no order. The court must, as part of the process, carefully scrutinise the care plan and satisfy itself that it is in the child's best interests. If the court is not satisfied of this, it may refuse to make the care order. The court should only pass responsibility to the local authority by a final care order when all the facts are as clearly known as can be hoped. If the court having heard the evidence is not satisfied by material aspects of the plan, it should decline to make the order. On the other hand, the court should be alert to the danger of (wrongly) using an interim care order as a means of exercising the now defunct supervisory role of the court. Wall J's approach had earlier been endorsed by the Court of Appeal in *Re L (Sexual Abuse: Standard of Proof)* [1996] 1 FLR 116, Butler Sloss LJ also agreeing with his view that there are cases in which the making of a full care order involves steps into the unknown but that provided the court is satisfied that the local authority is alert to the difficulties which may arise in the execution of the plan, the function of the court is not to seek to oversee the plan but to entrust its execution to the local authority. As the Court of Appeal held in *Re P (Minors) (Interim Order)* [1993] 2 FLR 742, when current issues regarding care have been determined, it can seldom, if ever, be right for the court to continue to adjourn a case, making interim orders. On the other hand, the fact that a care order is the inevitable eventual outcome should not deflect the judge from using the litigation process to its maximum effect (*Re CH*).

It can be seen that, as the Court of Appeal remarked in *Re L (Sexual Abuse: Standard of Proof)*, the point at which the court withdraws from further control over the child and passes responsibility to the local authority is a matter of the exercise of discretion by the court and will vary with each set of circumstances. Some examples may assist:

(*a*) In *Re CH (Care or Interim Care Order)* (above), the judge wrongly made a full care order before sufficient expert evidence was available. The child had suffered serious injuries, the case was complex and finely balanced and the local authority and the children's guardian differed in their views as to placement, the former cautiously favouring rehabilitation and the latter recommending adoption. The care order was made on the basis that the local authority would instruct a child expert and reconsider placement once that opinion was available. The Court of Appeal pointed out the deficiencies in that course which included the fact that the making of the care order would terminate the guardian's professional role and the fact that there would be no court control over the garnering of the expert evidence.

(*b*) Planned and purposeful delay was helpful in *C v Solihull MBC* [1993] 1 FLR 290 (interim residence order with interim supervision order) and *Hounslow LBC v A* [1993] 1 FLR 702 (interim care order) where the local authority's investigation was not yet complete.

(*c*) In *Re L (Sexual Abuse: Standard of Proof)* (above) findings of sexual abuse were made. There was no dispute that the children could not return to their mother at the conclusion of the hearing and they would be in care for many months to come. The judge found that there was some prospect of rehabilitation to the mother but little prospect of rehabilitation to the father. It was appropriate for the judge to make full care orders.

(*d*) In *Re R (Care Proceedings: Adjournment)* [1998] 2 FLR 390, CA, where the threshold criteria were met and there was no prospect of the mother improving sufficiently as a carer within a suitable time-scale for the baby, there was no realistic alternative to a care order. Compare *Re J (Care: Rehabilitation Plan)* [1998] 2 FLR 498, CA in which further assessment of the rehabilitation prospects was necessary before a final decision was made.

(*e*) Interim care orders were wrongly used in *Kent County Council v C* [1993] 1 FLR 308 and *Re P (Minors) (Interim Order)* [1993] 2 FLR 742 as a means of keeping the progress of rehabilitation under review.

(*f*) The court wrongly tried to keep rehabilitation under review through the issue of contact in *Re S (A Minor) (Care: Contact Order)* [1994] 2 FLR 222.

(*g*) The Court of Appeal made an interim care order in preference to a full care order in *Buckinghamshire County Council v M* [1994] 2 FLR 506, apparently on the basis that a full care order would conflict with the mother's need to feel supported rather than controlled and would leave her vulnerable to the powers vested in the local authority and not subject to periodic court review.

(*h*) It is wrong to make an interim care order to cover the period during which a child is to be the subject of a phased return home if the court has decided that a full care order is inappropriate (*Re B (Care: Expert Witnesses)* [1996] 1 FLR 667, CA in which a residence order with a supervision order was made instead).

(*i*) For the possible use of an interim contact order in conjunction with a full care order, see *Re B (A Minor) (Care Order: Review)* [1993] 1 FLR 421 (noted under **Review of contact by the court** under s 34).

(*j*) Where there is a great deal of flux in the circumstances surrounding a family it is wrong for the court to make a full care order and it should consider whether to make an interim care order whilst further investigations and assessments are carried out (*Re C (A Child) (Care Orders)* [2001] EWCA Civ 810, [2001] 3 FCR 381).

Subject to s 38(6), the court loses control of the manner in which a child is cared for once an interim care order is made and cannot impose conditions; if this is not acceptable, the judge has to decide whether to make an interim residence order subject to supervision instead (*Re L (Interim Care Order: Power of Court* [1996] 2 FLR 742, CA). However, when Adoption and Children Act 2002, s 118 comes into force there will be a mechanism for returning certain cases to the court after a care order has been made in circumstances where, for example, the care plan has not been properly implemented. Section 118 will amend CA 1989, s 26(2)(*e*) (requirement to consider the discharge of a care order) to encompass a requirement for the authority to review the care plan and revise it as necessary, together with a route for returning it to the court through the intervention of a CAFCASS officer where appropriate. See further **Adoption and Children Act 2002 – review of cases of looked-after children** under CA 1989, s 26.

Residence order on interim application in pending care proceedings—There is jurisdiction to make a residence order on an interim application in pending care proceedings (see s 38(3)) but the view was expressed in *Re RJ (Fostering: Disqualified Person)* [1999] 1 FLR 605, CA that where the effect of the interim order would be to alter the status quo, the jurisdiction should only be used in those exceptional cases in which, at the time of the interim application, the court can be confident that, following a substantive hearing, a long-term residence order will be made in favour of the same persons. It is wrong for the court to make residence orders rather than interim care orders pending the final hearing (*Re B (Children)* LTL, 19 July 2002, Doc No C9600520 – where there was strong evidence that returning the children to their mother was plainly exposing them to severe risk of emotional abuse and distorted development).

Conduct of interim hearings—*Hampshire County Council v S* (above) and *Re W (A Minor) (Interim Care Order)* [1994] 2 FLR 892 provide valuable guidance as to the conduct of interim hearings; see further under FPC(CA 1989)R 1991, r 21.

Repeated interim orders (s 38(4), (5))—Provided the time-limits in s 38(4) are observed for each individual interim order, any number of interim orders can be made until such time as the case is ready for effective hearing; the court's power to make interim orders does not expire eight weeks after the original interim order was made (*Gateshead MBC v N* [1993] 1 FLR 811). Each interim application has to be considered independently on its merits in the light of the circumstances existing at the time. It is not right for the court in granting an interim order to attempt to lay down a policy which would or might fetter the discretion of any future sitting to grant or refuse a further interim order (*Re P (Minors) (Interim Order)* [1993] 2 FLR 742). Reference should be made to the *Handbook of Best Practice in Children Act cases* produced by the Children Act Advisory Committee (set out in Part IV of this work as *Best Practice Guidance of June 1997*) which sets out a suggested procedure for the renewal of interim orders, contemplating the possibility of renewal on the attendance of the local authority only, or simply on written application (see "Section 2 – Renewal of interim care orders"). If this approach is to be adopted, the first interim order needs to be drafted accordingly and a specimen is contained in the *Handbook*. A court considering a renewal application for an interim care order has a discretion to limit the scope of the hearing to changes in circumstances since the last hearing (*Re B (Interim Care Orders: Renewal)* [2001] 2 FLR 1217).

Interim orders and split hearings—Where the court conducts a split hearing, it appears to be assumed, in practice, that the period between the preliminary or fact-finding hearing and the final hearing can appropriately be regulated by an interim order.

Directions under s 38(6)—In *Re C (Interim Care Order: Residential Assessment)* [1997] 1 FLR 1, HL, a direction under s 38(6) for a residential assessment of the child and his parents was upheld, the House of Lords holding that s 38(6) and (7) enables the court to order or prohibit any assessment (whether of a type similar to a medical or psychiatric assessment or not) which involves the participation of the child and is directed to providing the court with material which, in the view of the court, is required to enable it to reach a proper decision at the final hearing of the application for a full care order (see *Re O (Interim Care: Removal to Foster-parents for Assessment)* [2000] Fam Law 461; *Re B (Interim Care Order: Directions)* [2002] EWCA Civ 25, [2002] 1 FLR 545). The local authority assumes control of the child once an interim care order has been made, save in specified cases where the court has power to intervene under s 38(6) (*Re B* (above) – it was within the court's jurisdiction to make a direction for residency at a mother and baby unit under s 38(6) even though the local authority objected, since the residential placement was important for assessment purposes). In deciding whether or not it has jurisdiction to make the direction sought, the court must decide whether the programme concerned is truly an assessment within s 38(6) or whether it is really therapeutic. A programme may be an assessment within s 38(6) even if there is an ingredient of ancillary therapy, but a programme which is substantially therapeutic does not fall within s 38(6) even if it involves some element of assessment as it proceeds (*Re B (Psychiatric Therapy for Parents)* [1999] 1 FLR 701; *Re D (Jurisdiction: Programme of Assessment or Therapy)* [1999] 2 FLR 632). In *Re B* (above) the purpose of the proposed programme was to treat the parents' disabilities rather than to assess anything in relation to the child and therefore the court had no jurisdiction to order it. In *Re D* (above) the programme's primary aim was treatment for the mother, not assessment of her parenting abilities, and therefore the court had no jurisdiction to impose such a programme on the local authority. In exercising its discretion whether to order any particular examination or assessment, the court has to take into account the cost of the proposed assessment and the limits on local authority resources. It is important in determining whether to order a local authority to provide residential assessment to give proper weight to the benefits to the children from such an assessment, compared with the wider responsibility of the authority generally (*Re C (Children) (Residential Assessment)* [2001] EWCA Civ 1305, [2001] 3 FCR 164 – where the authority was ordered to provide a residential assessment in spite of the fact that the cost was so high that it would allegedly absorb most of the authority's remaining budget; *B County Council v L and Others* [2002] EWHC 2327 (Fam) (unreported), Charles J, LTL, 12 November 2002, Doc No C0104041 – where the local authority was criticised for terminating an assessment early because of staff commitments and funding problems and a further assessment was ordered before a full care order could be considered). *Re O (Minors) (Medical Examination)* [1993] 1 FLR 860 establishes that directions made under s 38(6) can be appealed under s 94(1). Magistrates are not precluded from granting an application by the children's guardian for a psychological assessment of the child by the fact that an earlier bench had refused a similar application (*Re F (A Minor) (Care Proceedings: Directions)* [1995] 3 FCR 601). In *Re W (Assessment of Child)* [1998] 2 FLR 130, CA, it was held that the court had jurisdiction to direct a particular social worker, as a named employee of the local authority, to carry out a s 38(6) assessment but that applications naming social workers were not to be encouraged. An individual could not be directed to carry out the assessment if unwilling or unable to do so and it should be ascertained in advance that the person concerned was willing and able to act. Account ought to be taken of the resources of the local authority employing the social worker and any difficulties with regard to the authority's responsibility for and duty to supervise him. The court commented that a better direction might be that given in *Berkshire CC v C and Others* [1993] 1 FLR 569 (that assessment should be carried out by a "suitably qualified social worker").

"class of person prescribed by rules of court" (s 38(8))—See FPR 1991, r 4.2(1) (High Court and county courts) and FPC(CA 1989)R 1991, r 2(1) (magistrates' courts).

38A Power to include exclusion requirement in interim care order

(1) Where –

(*a*) on being satisfied that there are reasonable grounds for believing that the circumstances with respect to a child are as mentioned in section 31(2)(*a*) and (*b*)(i), the court makes an interim care order with respect to a child, and

(*b*) the conditions mentioned in subsection (2) are satisfied,

the court may include an exclusion requirement in the interim care order.

(2) The conditions are –

(*a*) that there is reasonable cause to believe that, if a person ("the relevant person") is excluded from a dwelling-house in which the child lives, the child will cease to suffer, or cease to be likely to suffer, significant harm, and

(*b*) that another person living in the dwelling-house (whether a parent of the child or some other person) –

(i) is able and willing to give to the child the care which it would be reasonable to expect a parent to give him, and

(ii) consents to the inclusion of the exclusion requirement.

(3) For the purposes of this section an exclusion requirement is any one or more of the following –

(*a*) a provision requiring the relevant person to leave a dwelling-house in which he is living with the child,

(*b*) a provision prohibiting the relevant person from entering a dwelling-house in which the child lives, and

(*c*) a provision excluding the relevant person from a defined area in which a dwelling-house in which the child lives is situated.

(4) The court may provide that the exclusion requirement is to have effect for a shorter period than the other provisions of the interim care order.

(5) Where the court makes an interim care order containing an exclusion requirement, the court may attach a power of arrest to the exclusion requirement.

(6) Where the court attaches a power of arrest to an exclusion requirement of an interim care order, it may provide that the power of arrest is to have effect for a shorter period than the exclusion requirement.

(7) Any period specified for the purposes of subsection (4) or (6) may be extended by the court (on one or more occasions) on an application to vary or discharge the interim care order.

(8) Where a power of arrest is attached to an exclusion requirement of an interim care order by virtue of subsection (5), a constable may arrest without warrant any person whom he has reasonable cause to believe to be in breach of the requirement.

(9) Sections 47(7), (11) and (12) and 48 of, and Schedule 5 to, the Family Law Act 1996 shall have effect in relation to a person arrested under subsection (8) of this section as they have effect in relation to a person arrested under section 47(6) of that Act.

(10) If, while an interim care order containing an exclusion requirement is in force, the local authority have removed the child from the dwelling-house from which the relevant person is excluded to other accommodation for a continuous period of more than 24 hours, the interim care order shall cease to have effect in so far as it imposes the exclusion requirement.

Amendments—Inserted by Family Law Act 1996, s 52, Sch 6, para 1.

Defined terms—"child": s 105(1); "relevant person": s 38A(2)(*a*).

Scope of provision—Providing the conditions in s 38A(2) are satisfied, the court can safeguard a child by granting an interim care order including a provision excluding from the home the person ("the relevant person") who is putting the child at risk. A power of arrest can be attached to the exclusion requirement.

Interim care order—See s 38.

Procedure—See FPR 1991, r 4.24A and FPC(CA 1989)R 1991, r 25A.

38B Undertakings relating to interim care orders

(1) In any case where the court has power to include an exclusion requirement in an interim care order, the court may accept an undertaking from the relevant person.

(2) No power of arrest may be attached to any undertaking given under subsection (1).

(3) An undertaking given to a court under subsection (1) –

(*a*) shall be enforceable as if it were an order of the court, and
(*b*) shall cease to have effect if, while it is in force, the local authority have removed the child from the dwelling-house from which the relevant person is excluded to other accommodation for a continuous period of more than 24 hours.

(4) This section has effect without prejudice to the powers of the High Court and county court apart from this section.

(5) In this section "exclusion requirement" and "relevant person" have the same meaning as in section 38A.

Amendments—Inserted by Family Law Act 1996, s 52, Sch 6, para 1.

Defined terms—"child": s 105(1); "exclusion requirement": s 38A(3); "relevant person": s 38A(2)(*a*).

Procedure—See under FLA 1996, s 46 for assistance as to procedure which will be the same, albeit that the context is different.

Powers of High Court and county court apart from s 38B (s 38B(4))—As to the question of the county court accepting undertakings in public law proceedings, see **Undertakings and injunctions** under CA 1989, s 31. As to the inherent jurisdiction of the High Court, see CA 1989, s 100.

39 Discharge and variation etc of care orders and supervision orders

(1) A care order may be discharged by the court on the application of –

(*a*) any person who has parental responsibility for the child;

(b) the child himself; or

(c) the local authority designated by the order.

(2) A supervision order may be varied or discharged by the court on the application of –

(a) any person who has parental responsibility for the child;

(b) the child himself; or

(c) the supervisor.

(3) On the application of a person who is not entitled to apply for the order to be discharged, but who is a person with whom the child is living, a supervision order may be varied by the court in so far as it imposes a requirement which affects that person.

(3A) On the application of a person who is not entitled to apply for the order to be discharged, but who is a person to whom an exclusion requirement contained in the order applies, an interim care order may be varied or discharged by the court in so far as it imposes the exclusion requirement.

(3B) Where a power of arrest has been attached to an exclusion requirement of an interim care order, the court may, on the application of any person entitled to apply for the discharge of the order so far as it imposes the exclusion requirement, vary or discharge the order in so far as it confers a power of arrest (whether or not any application has been made to vary or discharge any other provision of the order).

(4) Where a care order is in force with respect to a child the court may, on the application of any person entitled to apply for the order to be discharged, substitute a supervision order for the care order.

(5) When a court is considering whether to substitute one order for another under subsection (4) any provision of this Act which would otherwise require section 31(2) to be satisfied at the time when the proposed order is substituted or made shall be disregarded.

Amendments—Family Law Act 1996, s 52, Sch 6, para 2.

Defined terms—"care order": ss 31(11), 105(1); "child", "exclusion requirement": s 38A(3); "local authority": s 105(1); "parental responsibility': s 3; "relevant person": s 38A(2)(*a*); "supervision order": s 31(11); "supervisor": s 105(1).

"any person who has parental responsibility" (s 39(1), (2))—Parental responsibility may be acquired (and lost) in a number of ways, for example by virtue of being the child's mother or married father (s 2(1)), by a parental responsibility agreement or order under s 4, or by being appointed a child's guardian under s 5(6).

"the child himself" (s 39(1)(*b*))—The child does not require leave to make his application (*Re A (Care: Discharge Application by Child)* [1995] 1 FLR 599, FD). For guidance as to the role that a child applicant should play in the proceedings, see *Re A* (above) and the notes to FPR 1991, r 4.16 and FPC(CA 1989)R 1991, r 16.

Supervision orders imposing a requirement (s 39(3))—The requirements that may be imposed under a supervision order are set out in Sch 3, which applies by virtue of s 35(2).

Applicants for variation/discharge of an exclusion requirement—Section 39(1) establishes three categories of applicant for the discharge of a care order. Section 39(3A) speaks of the discharge of a care order in so far as it imposes an exclusion requirement. It is therefore submitted that s 39(1) entitles a person with parental responsibility, the child himself or the local authority designated in the interim care order to apply for an exclusion requirement to be discharged. Whether an application can be made under s 39(1) for the variation of an exclusion requirement, however, is a moot point. Section 39(3A) appears to draw a distinction between discharge of that part of the interim order which imposes the exclusion requirement and variation of it. A similar distinction between discharge and variation can be found in s 39(2) concerning supervision orders. No doubt the reason that the Act, as originally drafted, was silent as to variation of care orders was that care orders were a bald transfer of responsibility to a local authority and could not, under the statutory scheme, stipulate any particular requirements whereas, in accordance with CA 1989, Sch 3, supervision orders could impose specified obligations. This has, of course, changed with the introduction of the concept of exclusion requirements and it may be that, in the amendment process, the need to extend s 39(1) to provide a right to local authorities etc to apply for a variation of an exclusion requirement, as well as for its discharge, was overlooked. The only person who is secure in his right to apply for a variation of the exclusion requirement is the person to whom it applies (s 39(3A)). This must mean the "relevant person" who has been excluded in accordance with s 38A(1) and (2). Certainly the s 39(3A) right cannot extend to local authorities, the child or those with parental responsibility because they are all entitled to apply for discharge of the order, and therefore expressly excluded by the opening words of the subsection. To what extent the limitation on the categories of applicant really matters in practice remains to be seen. How each case develops will naturally depend on its own particular circumstances. Where the local authority fear for the welfare of the child who is the subject of the interim care order, they can remove him forthwith without further recourse to the court and, if the removal persists for more than 24 hours, s 38A(10) provides that the exclusion requirement ceases to be effective automatically. At the other end of the scale, if time is not of the essence and an application to the court is the most appropriate way forward, the matter can be raised at the next renewal of the interim care order when the court can reconsider the whole picture. Should an earlier application about the exclusion requirement be needed, it seems extremely likely that, whatever the strict technicalities of s 39, an application could legitimately be launched by an interested party (whether for variation or discharge) and that the court would proceed to review the matter broadly.

Applicants for variation or discharge of power of arrest (s 39(3B))—This provision is slightly less unhappily drafted than s 39(3A) and may entitle all those listed in s 39(1), plus the person excluded by the exclusion requirement, to apply for an attendant power of arrest to be varied or discharged.

Burden of proving application—The criterion for deciding on discharge of a care order is the welfare test in CA 1989, s 1(1) and it is the person applying for the care order to be discharged who has the burden of showing that the child's welfare requires the revocation of the order (*Re MD and TD (Minors) (No 2)* [1994] Fam Law 489, and see *Re S (Discharge of Care Order)* [1995] 2 FLR 639, CA).

40 Orders pending appeals in cases about care or supervision orders

(1) Where –

(*a*) a court dismisses an application for a care order; and
(*b*) at the time when the court dismisses the application, the child concerned is the subject of an interim care order,

the court may make a care order with respect to the child to have effect subject to such directions (if any) as the court may see fit to include in the order.

(2) Where –

(*a*) a court dismisses an application for a care order, or an application for a supervision order; and
(*b*) at the time when the court dismisses the application, the child concerned is the subject of an interim supervision order,

the court may make a supervision order with respect to the child to have effect subject to such directions (if any) as the court sees fit to include in the order.

(3) Where a court grants an application to discharge a care order or supervision order, it may order that –

(*a*) its decision is not to have effect; or

(*b*) the care order, or supervision order, is to continue to have effect but subject to such directions as the court sees fit to include in the order.

(4) An order made under this section shall only have effect for such a period, not exceeding the appeal period, as may be specified in the order.

(5) Where –

(*a*) an appeal is made against any decision of a court under this section; or

(*b*) any application is made to the appellate court in connection with a proposed appeal against that decision,

the appellate court may extend the period for which the order in question is to have effect, but not so as to extend it beyond the end of the appeal period.

(6) In this section "the appeal period" means –

(*a*) where an appeal is made against the decision in question, the period between the making of that decision and the determination of the appeal; and

(*b*) otherwise, the period during which an appeal may be made against the decision.

Defined terms—"care order": s 31(11); "child": s 105(1); "the court": s 92(7).

Scope of provision—This section provides the court with power to make a care or supervision order pending an appeal. The power may be exercised when dismissing an application for such an order or granting an application to discharge such an order (if there was an interim order in force beforehand) or on an application to discharge such an order. If the original court refused to make a care order pending appeal, the appeal court has no power to make such an order. The appeal court can only make an interim order pending appeal (*Croydon London Borough Council v A (No 2)* [1992] 2 FLR 348).

Appeal period—An order under this section may be made for up to the appeal period, which means the time within which an appeal can be lodged or, if an appeal is lodged, the order can be made to last until the appeal is determined. Where the appeal relates to an order (or refusal to make an order) in a family proceedings court, the appeal must be lodged within 14 days (FPR 1991, r 4.22(3) for an appeal to the High Court; and CPR 1998, r 52.4 for an appeal to the Court of Appeal). In practice, it would seem that the original court should make an order under this section (if so minded) up to the end of the time within which an appeal can be lodged. To extend the order, application must be made to the appeal court.

Directions—When making an order under this section pending appeal, the court has wide powers to make the order subject to such directions "as the court sees fit". An order under this section is governed by the principles contained in CA 1989, s 1.

Stay—This section does not give the court power to grant a stay of the operation of a care or supervision order pending appeal. A family proceedings court has no power to grant a stay in any event (*Re O (A Minor) (Care Order: Education: Procedure)* [1992] 2 FLR 7) but can give directions pursuant to s 11 as to when the order should come into force (*Re J (A Minor) (Residence)* [1993] 2 FCR 636). Once an appeal has been lodged, the High Court has power to grant a stay (RSC Ord 55, r 3). The county court and High Court have power to grant a stay, and any application should first be made to that court and thereafter to the Court of Appeal (CPR 1998, r 52.7). If the appeal is against the making of an adoption order, an application should be made immediately for a stay of the order (together with an application for an expedited hearing) so as to prevent the children meeting the judge (*Re PJ (Adoption: Practice on Appeal)* [1998] 2 FLR 252, CA).

"appellate court may extend the period" (s 40(5))—In *Re M (A Minor) (Appeal: Interim Order)* [1994] 1 FLR 54, the Court of Appeal held that, where there was an appeal against the refusal to make a care order, an order under this section should be extended by the Court of Appeal unless the appeal is utterly hopeless, so as to preserve the position of the child pending appeal.

Representation of child

41 Representation of child and of his interests in certain proceedings

(1) For the purpose of any specified proceedings, the court shall appoint an officer of the Service for the child concerned unless satisfied that it is not necessary to do so in order to safeguard his interests.

(2) The officer of the Service shall –

(*a*) be appointed in accordance with rules of court; and
(*b*) be under a duty to safeguard the interests of the child in the manner prescribed by such rules.

(3) Where –

(*a*) the child concerned is not represented by a solicitor; and
(*b*) any of the conditions mentioned in subsection (4) is satisfied,

the court may appoint a solicitor to represent him.

(4) The conditions are that –

(*a*) no officer of the Service has been appointed for the child;
(*b*) the child has sufficient understanding to instruct a solicitor and wishes to do so;
(*c*) it appears to the court that it would be in the child's best interests for him to be represented by a solicitor.

(5) Any solicitor appointed under or by virtue of this section shall be appointed, and shall represent the child, in accordance with rules of court.

(6) In this section "specified proceedings" means any proceedings –

(*a*) on an application for a care order or supervision order;
(*b*) in which the court has given a direction under section 37(1) and has made, or is considering whether to make, an interim care order;
(*c*) on an application for the discharge of a care order or the variation or discharge of a supervision order;
(*d*) on an application under section 39(4);
(*e*) in which the court is considering whether to make a residence order with respect to a child who is the subject of a care order;
(*f*) with respect to contact between a child who is the subject of a care order and any other person;
(*g*) under Part V;
(*h*) on an appeal against –
  (i) the making of, or refusal to make, a care order, supervision order or any order under section 34;
  (ii) the making of, or refusal to make, a residence order with respect to a child who is the subject of a care order; or
  (iii) the variation or discharge of, or refusal of an application to vary or discharge, an order of a kind mentioned in sub-paragraph (i) or (ii);
  (iv) the refusal of an application under section 39(4);
  (v) the making of, or refusal to make, an order under Part V; or
(*i*) which are specified for the time being, for the purposes of this section, by rules of court.

(7)–(9) (*repealed*)

(10) Rules of court may make this provision as to –

(*a*) the assistance which any officer of the Service may be required by the court to give to it;

(*b*) the consideration to be given by any officer of the Service, where an order of a specified kind has been made in the proceedings in question, as to whether to apply for the variation or discharge of the order;

(*c*) the participation of officers of the Service in reviews, of a kind specified in the rules, which are conducted by the court.

(11) Regardless of any enactment or rule of law which would otherwise prevent it from doing so, the court may take account of –

(*a*) any statement contained in a report made by an officer of the Service who is appointed under this section for the purpose of the proceedings in question; and

(*b*) any evidence given in respect of the matters referred to in the report,

in so far as the statement or evidence is, in the opinion of the court, relevant to the question which the court is considering.

(12) (*repealed*)

Amendments—Courts and Legal Services Act 1990, s 116, Sch 16, para 17; Criminal Justice and Court Services Act 2000 s 74, Sch 7, para 91.

Defined terms—"care order": ss 31(11), 105(1); "child": s 105(1); "supervision order": s 31(11).

"the child concerned" (s 41(1))—This would appear to mean the child who is the subject of the proceedings and not any other children who may happen to be parties to them (for example, if the mother of a baby in respect of whom a care order was being sought was herself a minor, a children's guardian could not be appointed under s 41 although, in the High Court and county courts, a children's guardian with different powers and duties may be constituted for her under FPR 1991, Pt IX).

"unless satisfied that it is not necessary to do so ..." (s 41(1))—In *Re J (A Minor) (Change of Name)* [1993] 1 FLR 699, an ex parte application was made by the local authority for leave to change the name of a child in its care. Booth J was satisfied that, although the application fell within CA 1989, s 41, it was not necessary to appoint a guardian ad litem (children's guardian) in order to safeguard the interests of the child. In this particular case, the guardian ad litem (children's guardian) could not have said any more than counsel for the local authority, and there was no conflict of interest. See also under **"direction under s 37(1)"** below.

Appointment of Official Solicitor as officer of the Service (s 41(2))—See *Practice Note of 2 April 2001 (Official Solicitor: Appointment in Family Proceedings)* and *Practice Note of March 2001 (Officers of CAFCASS Legal Services and Special Casework: Appointment in Family Proceedings)* (both are set out in Part IV of this work).

Appointment of Official Solicitor as amicus curiae (advocate to the court)—There may arise cases in which the Official Solicitor has initially been appointed to act as guardian ad litem to the child who is subject to the proceedings, but is then removed from his position as guardian ad litem as a result of an application made by the child under FPR 1991, r 9.2A. In such circumstances, it is likely that the Official Solicitor will be invited to remain involved in the case as amicus curiae (advocate to the court) – see *Re H (A Minor) (Role of Official Solicitor)* [1993] 2 FLR 552, FD; see also *Practice Note of 2 April 2001 (Official Solicitor: Appointment in Family Proceedings)*. For further discussion of recent case-law, see under FPR 1991, r 9.2A.

"appointed in accordance with rules of court" (s 41(2)(*a*))—The relevant rules are FPR 1991, r 4.10 and Family Proceedings Courts (Children Act 1989) Rules 1991, r 10.

"safeguard the interests of the child in the manner prescribed by such rules" (s 41(2)(*b*))—The relevant rules are FPR 1991, r 4.11 and FPC(CA 1989)R 1991, r 11.

"court may appoint a solicitor to represent him" (s 41(3))—The power to appoint a solicitor under this section relates only to "specified proceedings" as defined in s 41(6); it does not apply, for example, to proceedings brought under CA 1989, s 8 (*Re W (A Minor) (Contact)* [1994] 1 FLR 843).

"child has sufficient understanding" (s 41(4)(*b*))—See **"able ... to give such instructions on his own behalf"** under FPR 1991, r 4.12.

Appointment of solicitor (s 41(5))—The appointment, removal and role of a solicitor under this section is regulated by FPR 1991, r 4.12 and FPC(CA 1989)R 1991, r 12.

"specified proceedings" (s 41(6))—Proceedings for an education supervision order are *not* specified proceedings within the meaning of s 41(6) and so the court in such proceedings cannot appoint a guardian ad litem (children's guardian) for the child under that section (*Essex County Council v B* [1993] 1 FLR 866). However, in a case where applications were made by the police for disclosure of documents, and by parents for the variation of injunctions restricting publicity in respect of care proceedings which had terminated the day before those applications were made, the court allowed the guardian ad litem (children's guardian) to continue to represent the child's interests despite the fact that, strictly speaking, the proceedings were no longer specified under s 41(6) (*Oxfordshire County Council v L and F* [1997] 1 FLR 235). In *Re W and B; Re W (Care Plan)* [2001] 2 FLR 582 a continuing role for the guardian was envisaged where a full care order was made with a care plan incorporating starred milestones which, if not achieved, could result in a return to court. Pursuant to CJCSA 2000, s 12(5)(*b*), where proceedings under CA 1989, s 31 result in a supervision order the proceedings are not to be treated as concluded until the order has ceased; and, unless terminated by the court, the guardian's role continues. In every case resulting in a supervision order the court, the local authority and the guardian should consider, as part of the care plan, the role (if any) the guardian is to play in the implementation of the supervision order; in the absence of agreement the role of the guardian should be the subject of court directions (*Re MH (A Child) and Re SB and MB (Children)* [2001] 2 FLR 1334). Provision is made in FPR 1991, r 9.5 for the appointment in the High Court or the county court of the Official Solicitor or some other person where it appears to the court that the child should be separately represented. However, that rule is not repeated in the FPC(CA 1989)R 1991, so it appears that the clerk to the justices in the family proceedings court has no power to appoint a children's guardian for a child in non-specified proceedings (see further under FPC(CA 1989)R 1991, r 14).

Hybrid proceedings—In hybrid proceedings, or in any straightforward adoption proceedings, where the wishes and feelings of the child are in conflict with the guardian's assessment of welfare and disposal, it may be necessary to give the child an independent voice through his own legal representation (*Re O (Transracial Adoption: Contact)* [1995] 2 FLR 597 – where the court considered an application for adoption of a child in the care of the local authority together with applications by the mother for discharge of the care order and the making of a residence order in her favour).

"direction under section 37(1)" (s 41(6)(*b*))—Section 37(1) allows the court to direct an investigation of a child's circumstances by the appropriate authority where, in family proceedings in which a question has arisen with respect to his welfare, it appears to the court that it may be appropriate for a care or supervision order to be made. Where the court gives such a direction, an interim care order may be made under s 38(1)(*b*). In *Re CE (Section 37 Direction)* [1995] 1 FLR 26, Wall J made it clear that a guardian should not be appointed automatically at the time at which a s 37 direction is made; the purpose for which a s 37 report is required should be carefully considered. A guardian should be appointed at once if the court decides to make an interim care order under s 38(1)(*b*) at the same time as making a s 37 direction. Otherwise, there must be a prospect that a public law order may be appropriate before a s 37 order can be made in the first place – ss 37 and 41 should not be used to avoid the restrictions on appointing a guardian in private law proceedings. The proceedings cease to be "specified proceedings" if the local authority, as a result of its investigation, decides not to apply for an order. Once a guardian has been appointed, the appointment subsists until terminated by the court (unless the terms of the appointment specify when it is otherwise to come to an end). This remains the case even where the proceedings cease to be "specified". The termination of the guardian's appointment should be by judicial act and must follow the procedure set out in the rules (*Re M (Terminating Appointment of Guardian ad Litem)* [1999] 2 FLR 717; and see FPR 1991, rr 4.10(9), 4.14/FPC(CA 1989)R 1991, rr 10(9), 14). It is good practice for the order making the guardian's appointment to contain a direction that the guardian's continuing involvement be reviewed on completion of the s 37 report (*Re CE (Section 37 Direction)*, above). *Re CE (Section 37 Direction)* [1995] 1 FLR 26, FD, stresses that the appointment of a guardian ad litem (children's guardian) pursuant to s 41(6)(*b*) should not be automatic. The following considerations should be borne in mind:

(*a*) Is it a case in which the court is actually making an interim order as opposed to giving consideration to making one? If so, the circumstances of the case are likely to be serious and unusual, and it may well be appropriate for the appointment of a children's guardian to be made immediately.

(*b*) If the court is only considering making an interim order, what factors are there in the circumstances of the case which require the children's guardian to represent the interests of the child?

(*c*) Given the timescale that the court will set for the investigation, will there in practice be time for the guardian to be informed of the issues in the case and to play a useful role?

(*d*) Is there a specific role for the guardian in the investigation itself, particularly where a very short timescale for it is fixed?

(*e*) Will the child's interests be properly safeguarded in the interim and during the investigation without a guardian?

(*f*) Does the child have his or her own solicitor?

Proceedings which become specified by virtue of s 41(6)(*b*) following the making of a s 37 order cease to be specified if the local authority, as a result of its investigation (albeit as yet incomplete), decides not to apply for a care order or supervision order and so informs the court. A guardian appointed under s 41(6)(*b*) cannot continue as guardian in that capacity, but the appointment has to be terminated by order of the court which should only be made after the court has given the matter due consideration and heard representations from the guardian and the other parties (*Re CE (Section 37 Direction)*, above). Wall J suggested that it should accordingly be the practice, where an appointment is made by virtue of s 41(6)(*b*), for the order making the appointment to contain a direction that the question of the guardian's continuing involvement be reviewed on completion of the s 37 report and for a directions appointment to be fixed for a date shortly after the date on which the s 37 report is due to be received by the court. In *Re CE*, it was in the child's interests for the guardian ad litem (children's guardian), who had been appointed on the proceedings originally becoming specified, to remain involved until the local authority's final assessment was in place and a final resolution could be ordered or sanctioned by the court. The guardian had consented to her continuing involvement and could be funded as an expert on the child's legal aid certificate so, unusually, the court invoked its jurisdiction under FPR 1991, r 9.5 to appoint a guardian in private law proceedings. In *Re S (Contact: Grandparents)* [1996] 1 FLR 158, the guardian ad litem (children's guardian) was appointed in the course of a s 37 investigation which resulted in a decision by the local authority not to take public law proceedings. The guardian was discharged but was later re-appointed, at a time when the proceedings had ceased to be "specified", in order to assist with contact problems. The Court of Appeal held that the reappointment was irregular and should not have occurred and that the proper course would have been to invite the Official Solicitor to act on behalf of the child at that point.

Discharge of a care order and discharge or variation of a supervision order (s 41(6)(*c*))—Discharge and variation of such orders are dealt with in s 39.

"application under section 39(4)" (s 41(6)(*d*), (*h*)(iv))—Section 39(4) provides for an application to substitute a supervision order for a care order which is in force.

"proceedings in which the court is considering whether to make a residence order" (s 41(6)(*e*))—The court may consider making such an order on a specific application for a residence order or in any family proceedings (see s 10(1), (2)).

Contact with a child in care (s 41(6)(*f*))—Applications for contact with a child who is the subject of a care order are made under s 34.

Part V (s 41(6)(*g*), (*h*)(v))—Part V (ss 43–52) provides for proceedings for the protection of children, such as emergency protection orders, child assessment orders and recovery orders.

"specified ... by rules of court" (s 41(6)(*i*))—See FPR 1991, r 4.2(2) and FPC(CA 1989)R 1991, r 2(2).

"regardless of any enactment or rule of law which would otherwise prevent it from doing so" (s 41(11))—Section 41(11) is aimed at the hearsay rule, which would otherwise render a report inadmissible save where the cumbersome procedures laid down under the Civil Evidence Acts are followed. It makes it clear that the court may take account of the contents of a guardian ad litem's (children's guardian's) written report regardless of whether it is otherwise technically admissible as evidence.

PART II

42 Right of officer of the Service to have access to local authority records

(1) Where an officer of the Service has been appointed under section 41 he shall have the right at all reasonable times to examine and take copies of –

(*a*) any records of, or held by, a local authority or an authorised person which were compiled in connection with the making, or proposed making, by any person of any application under this Act with respect to the child concerned;

(*b*) any records of, or held by, a local authority which were compiled in connection with any functions which are social services functions within the meaning of the Local Authority Social Services Act 1970, so far as those records relate to that child; or

(*c*) any records of, or held by, an authorised person which were compiled in connection with the activities of that person, so far as those records relate to that child.

(2) Where an officer of the Service takes a copy of any record which he is entitled to examine under this section, that copy or any part of it shall be admissible as evidence of any matter referred to in any –

(*a*) report which he makes to the court in the proceedings in question; or
(*b*) evidence which he gives in those proceedings.

(3) Subsection (2) has effect regardless of any enactment or rule of law which would otherwise prevent the record in question being admissible in evidence.

(4) In this section "authorised person" has the same meaning as in section 31.

Amendments—Courts and Legal Services Act 1990, ss 116, 125(7), Sch 16, para 18, Sch 20; Criminal Justice and Court Services Act 2000 s 74, Sch 7, para 92; Local Government Act 2000, s 107(1), Sch 5, para 20.

Defined terms—"authorised person": s 31(9); "child", "local authority": s 105(1).

Public interest immunity—Where an issue arises as to whether, because of public interest immunity, certain material (often material in the possession of the local authority) should or should not be disclosed, guidance as to the procedure to be followed can be derived from *Re C (Expert Evidence: Disclosure: Practice)* [1995] 1 FLR 204, noted further at **Public interest immunity** under FPR 1991, r 4.17.

"appointed as a guardian ad litem under this Act" (s 42(1))—The rights granted by this section are available only to the guardians ad litem appointed under s 41 and not those appointed under FPR 1991, Pt IX in non-specified proceedings or for minors who are parties to specified proceedings other than as the subject of those proceedings. For example, the guardian ad litem of a minor mother of a child in respect of whom a care order is being sought will not have a right to inspect the records covered by this section, but the guardian ad litem for her child will have that right.

Local Authority Social Services Act 1970 (s 42(1)(*b*))—Section 2(1) of that Act requires every local authority to establish a social services committee and provides for certain things to stand referred to it. These include all the local authority's functions under the enactments mentioned in Sch 1 to the Act and such other functions as may be designated by the Secretary of State by order. A report of an area child protection committee into a half-brother's death is a document held by the local authority and is compiled in connection with its functions under the Local Authority Social Services Act 1970. The guardian ad litem therefore has a right to see such a report in order to ascertain if there is any material relevant to a child (who is the subject of subsequent proceedings) which may help him to give the appropriate advice and provide the appropriate report to the court. Once the guardian has seen the report, he ought to be very careful as to how the information is further disseminated and, if there are particular concerns, the agency can alert the guardian to its sensitivity or request that the information should not be further disseminated (*Re R (Care Proceedings: Disclosure)* [2000] 2 FLR 751).

Adoption records—In care proceedings, s 42(1)(*b*) entitles a guardian ad litem of the child to see Form F (a case record prepared by the local authority giving detailed information concerning the prospective adopters with whom it is intended to place the child if a care order is granted), and s 42(2)(*a*) entitles him to include the relevant information derived from it in his report in the care proceedings (*Re T (A Minor) (Guardian ad Litem: Case Record)* [1994] 1 FLR 632).

"any enactment or rule of law which would otherwise prevent" (s 42(3))—Section 42(3) is aimed at the hearsay rule, which would otherwise often make a copy of a record inadmissible save where the cumbersome procedures laid down under the Civil Evidence Acts are followed. It has also been held to override the Adoption Agencies Regulations 1983, reg 14 which makes a local authority's Form F concerning prospective adopters a confidential record (*Re T (A Minor) (Guardian ad Litem: Case Record)* [1994] 1 FLR 632).

Limitations of s 42—Section 42 does not entitle a guardian ad litem to see witness statements and similar documents disclosed by the Crown Prosecution Service or the police to the local authority, although their existence is likely to be reflected in the social work records so that, if the guardian feels they are likely to be of particular importance to the parents' case, steps would be taken to determine whether they should be disclosed to the parents (*Nottinghamshire County Council v H* [1995] 1 FLR 115, FD).

Furthermore, s 42 does not entitle a guardian to disclose documents which are covered by public interest immunity. If he finds relevant documents of such a nature when inspecting the social services files pursuant to s 42, the guardian should invite the local authority to disclose them. If the local authority does not wish to do so, the guardian should draw the nature of the documents to the attention of the court and seek directions, only drawing the documents to the attention of the other parties if the court so directs *Re C (Expert Evidence: Disclosure: Practice)* [1995] 1 FLR 204, FD).

Access to materials held by the prosecution authorities in Scotland—Although s 42 gives the guardian ad litem a right to have access to local authority records, there is no corresponding right of access to records held by other agencies, such as the police or prosecution agencies. In practice, there is considerable co-operation between the police and the Crown Prosecution Service with the Official Solicitor and with the guardian ad litem. However, in Scotland the entire prosecution file in any criminal matter is at all stages absolutely confidential. This contrasts with the position in England where it is for the court to decide whether the prosecution is entitled to avoid disclosure of matters contained in criminal proceedings. In *Cheshire County Council v C* [1995] 2 FLR 862, the guardian ad litem appointed in care proceedings in England, and the mother of the children concerned, sought disclosure of various documents and video tapes held by the Scottish prosecution authorities relating to criminal proceedings against the mother's former cohabitant who had sexually abused one child, and against the stepfather of the other child in relation to whom other allegations had been made. The Procurator Fiscal felt obliged to refuse the request. It appeared that a protocol existed within the Scottish Crown Office for the disclosure of certain parts of criminal cases to reporters to the children panel in Scotland. In view of this, Douglas Brown J held that a further application should be made to the Scottish authorities emphasising that it would greatly assist the English court if, without breaching Scottish law, such protocol could be extended to the guardian ad litem in England in order to facilitate the task of properly representing the children concerned.

PART V
PROTECTION OF CHILDREN

43 Child assessment orders

(1) On the application of a local authority or authorised person for an order to be made under this section with respect to a child, the court may make the order if, but only if, it is satisfied that –

(*a*) the applicant has reasonable cause to suspect that the child is suffering, or is likely to suffer, significant harm;

(*b*) an assessment of the state of the child's health or development, or of the way in which he has been treated, is required to enable the applicant to determine whether or not the child is suffering, or is likely to suffer, significant harm; and

(*c*) it is unlikely that such an assessment will be made, or be satisfactory, in the absence of an order under this section.

(2) In this Act "a child assessment order" means an order under this section.

(3) A court may treat an application under this section as an application for an emergency protection order.

(4) No court shall make a child assessment order if it is satisfied –

(*a*) that there are grounds for making an emergency protection order with respect to the child; and

(*b*) that it ought to make such an order rather than a child assessment order.

(5) A child assessment order shall –

(*a*) specify a date by which the assessment is to begin; and

(*b*) have effect for such period, not exceeding 7 days beginning with that date, as may be specified in the order.

(6) Where a child assessment order is in force with respect to a child it shall be the duty of any person who is in a position to produce the child –

(*a*) to produce him to such person as may be named in the order; and

(*b*) to comply with such directions relating to the assessment of the child as the court thinks fit to specify in the order.

(7) A child assessment order authorises any person carrying out the assessment, or any part of the assessment, to do so in accordance with the terms of the order.

(8) Regardless of subsection (7), if the child is of sufficient understanding to make an informed decision he may refuse to submit to a medical or psychiatric examination or other assessment.

(9) The child may only be kept away from home –

(*a*) in accordance with directions specified in the order;

(*b*) if it is necessary for the purposes of the assessment; and

(*c*) for such period or periods as may be specified in the order.

(10) Where the child is to be kept away from home, the order shall contain such directions as the court thinks fit with regard to the contact that he must be allowed to have with other persons while away from home.

(11) Any person making an application for a child assessment order shall take such steps as are reasonably practicable to ensure that notice of the application is given to –

(*a*) the child's parents;

(*b*) any person who is not a parent of his but who has parental responsibility for him;

(*c*) any other person caring for the child;

(*d*) any person in whose favour a contact order is in force with respect to the child;

(*e*) any person who is allowed to have contact with the child by virtue of an order under section 34; and

(*f*) the child,

before the hearing of the application.

(12) Rules of court may make provision as to the circumstances in which –

(*a*) any of the persons mentioned in subsection (11); or
(*b*) such other person as may be specified in the rules,

may apply to the court for a child assessment order to be varied or discharged.

(13) In this section "authorised person" means a person who is an authorised person for the purposes of section 31.

Defined terms—"authorised person": s 43(13); "child": s 105(1); "child assessment order": s 43(2); "contact order": s 8(1); "emergency protection order": s 44(4); "local authority": s 105(1); "parental responsibility": s 3; "significant harm": s 31(10).

"authorised person" (s 43(1))—An authorised person is, according to s 43(13), a person who is authorised for the purposes of s 31, ie the National Society for the Prevention of Cruelty to Children and any of its officers. Any person authorised by order of the Secretary of State to bring proceedings under s 31 would also be an "authorised person" (s 31(9)), but no such order has yet been made.

Persons who are to be given notice of application (s 43(11))—There is a slight difference in terminology between this section and FPR 1991, App 3 and Family Proceedings Courts (Children Act 1989) Rules 1991, Sch 2, which also set out the persons who should be made respondents to a s 43 application or should be given notice of it.

"the child's parents" (s 43(11)(*a*))—The term "parent" is not defined in the Act (see **Meaning of "parent"** under s 10).

"any person ... who has parental responsibility" (s 43(11)(*b*))—Parental responsibility may be acquired in a variety of ways, for example automatically (see s 2), by order or agreement under s 4, or by virtue of being appointed a guardian of the child under s 5(6).

"order under section 34" (s 43(11)(*e*))—An order under s 34 is an order for contact with a child in care.

Rules of court (s 43(12))—See FPR 1991, r 4.2(3) and FPC(CA 1989)R 1991, r 2.3.

44 Orders for emergency protection of children

(1) Where any person ("the applicant") applies to the court for an order to be made under this section with respect to a child, the court may make the order if, but only if, it is satisfied that –

(*a*) there is reasonable cause to believe that the child is likely to suffer significant harm if –
  (i) he is not removed to accommodation provided by or on behalf of the applicant; or
  (ii) he does not remain in the place in which he is then being accommodated;
(*b*) in the case of an application made by the local authority –
  (i) enquiries are being made with respect to the child under section 47(1)(*b*); and
  (ii) those enquiries are being frustrated by access to the child being unreasonably refused to a person authorised to seek access and that the applicant has reasonable cause to believe that access to the child is required as a matter of urgency; or
(*c*) in the case of an application made by an authorised person –
  (i) the applicant has reasonable cause to suspect that a child is suffering, or is likely to suffer, significant harm;

(ii) the applicant is making enquiries with respect to the child's welfare; and

(iii) those enquiries are being frustrated by access to the child being unreasonably refused to a person authorised to seek access and the applicant has reasonable cause to believe that access to the child is required as a matter of urgency.

(2) In this section –

(*a*) "authorised person" means a person who is an authorised person for the purposes of section 31; and

(*b*) "a person authorised to seek access" means –

(i) in the case of an application by a local authority, an officer of the local authority or a person authorised by the local authority to act on their behalf in connection with the enquiries; or

(ii) in the case of an application by an authorised person, that person.

(3) Any person –

(*a*) seeking access to a child in connection with enquiries of a kind mentioned in subsection (1); and

(*b*) purporting to be a person authorised to do so,

shall, on being asked to do so, produce some duly authenticated document as evidence that he is such a person.

(4) While an order under this section ("an emergency protection order") is in force it –

(*a*) operates as a direction to any person who is in a position to do so to comply with any request to produce the child to the applicant;

(*b*) authorises –

(i) the removal of the child at any time to accommodation provided by or on behalf of the applicant and his being kept there; or

(ii) the prevention of the child's removal from any hospital, or other place, in which he was being accommodated immediately before the making of the order; and

(*c*) gives the applicant parental responsibility for the child.

(5) Where an emergency protection order is in force with respect to a child, the applicant –

(*a*) shall only exercise the power given by virtue of subsection (4)(*b*) in order to safeguard the welfare of the child;

(*b*) shall take, and shall only take, such action in meeting his parental responsibility for the child as is reasonably required to safeguard or promote the welfare of the child (having regard in particular to the duration of the order); and

(*c*) shall comply with the requirements of any regulations made by the Secretary of State for the purposes of this subsection.

(6) Where the court makes an emergency protection order, it may give such directions (if any) as it considers appropriate with respect to –

(*a*) the contact which is, or is not, to be allowed between the child and any named person;

(*b*) the medical or psychiatric examination or other assessment of the child.

(7) Where any direction is given under subsection (6)(*b*), the child may, if he is of sufficient understanding to make an informed decision, refuse to submit to the examination or other assessment.

(8) A direction under subsection (6)(*a*) may impose conditions and one under subsection (6)(*b*) may be to the effect that there is to be –

(*a*) no such examination or assessment; or
(*b*) no such examination or assessment unless the court directs otherwise.

(9) A direction under subsection (6) may be –

(*a*) given when the emergency protection order is made or at any time while it is in force; and
(*b*) varied at any time on the application of any person falling within any class of person prescribed by rules of court for the purposes of this subsection.

(10) Where an emergency protection order is in force with respect to a child and –

(*a*) the applicant has exercised the power given by subsection (4)(*b*)(i) but it appears to him that it is safe for the child to be returned; or
(*b*) the applicant has exercised the power given by subsection (4)(*b*)(ii) but it appears to him that it is safe for the child to be allowed to be removed from the place in question,

he shall return the child or (as the case may be) allow him to be removed.

(11) Where he is required by subsection (10) to return the child the applicant shall –

(*a*) return him to the care of the person from whose care he was removed; or
(*b*) if that is not reasonably practicable, return him to the care of –
(i) a parent of his;
(ii) any person who is not a parent of his but who has parental responsibility for him; or
(iii) such other person as the applicant (with the agreement of the court) considers appropriate.

(12) Where the applicant has been required by subsection (10) to return the child, or to allow him to be removed, he may again exercise his powers with respect to the child (at any time while the emergency protection order remains in force) if it appears to him that a change in the circumstances of the case makes it necessary for him to do so.

(13) Where an emergency protection order has been made with respect to a child, the applicant shall, subject to any direction given under subsection (6), allow the child reasonable contact with –

(*a*) his parents;
(*b*) any person who is not a parent of his but who has parental responsibility for him;
(*c*) any person with whom he was living immediately before the making of the order;
(*d*) any person in whose favour a contact order is in force with respect to him;
(*e*) any person who is allowed to have contact with the child by virtue of an order under section 34; and
(*f*) any person acting on behalf of any of those persons.

(14) Wherever it is reasonably practicable to do so, an emergency protection order shall name the child; and where it does not name him it shall describe him as clearly as possible.

(15) A person shall be guilty of an offence if he intentionally obstructs any person exercising the power under subsection (4)(*b*) to remove, or prevent the removal of, a child.

(16) A person guilty of an offence under subsection (15) shall be liable on summary conviction to a fine not exceeding level 3 on the standard scale.

Defined terms—"authorised person": s 44(2)(*a*); "child", "contact order", "harm", "local authority": s 105(1); "parental responsibility": s 3; "person authorised to seek access": s 44(2)(*b*).

"any person falling within any class of person prescribed by rules of court" (s 44(9))—See FPR 1991, r 4.2(4) and FPC(CA 1989)R 1991, r 2(4).

44A Power to include exclusion requirement in emergency protection order

(1) Where –

- (*a*) on being satisfied as mentioned in section 44(1)(*a*), (*b*) or (*c*), the court makes an emergency protection order with respect to a child, and
- (*b*) the conditions mentioned in subsection (2) are satisfied,

the court may include an exclusion requirement in the emergency protection order.

(2) The conditions are –

- (*a*) that there is reasonable cause to believe that, if a person ("the relevant person") is excluded from a dwelling-house in which the child lives, then –
  - (i) in the case of an order made on the ground mentioned in section 44(1)(*a*), the child will not be likely to suffer significant harm, even though the child is not removed as mentioned in section 44(1)(*a*)(i) or does not remain as mentioned in section 44(1)(*a*)(ii), or
  - (ii) in the case of an order made on the ground mentioned in paragraph (*b*) or (*c*) of section 44(1), the enquiries referred to in that paragraph will cease to be frustrated, and
- (*b*) that another person living in the dwelling-house (whether a parent of the child or some other person) –
  - (i) is able and willing to give to the child the care which it would be reasonable to expect a parent to give him, and
  - (ii) consents to the inclusion of the exclusion requirement.

(3) For the purposes of this section an exclusion requirement is any one or more of the following –

- (*a*) a provision requiring the relevant person to leave a dwelling-house in which he is living with the child,
- (*b*) a provision prohibiting the relevant person from entering a dwelling-house in which the child lives, and
- (*c*) a provision excluding the relevant person from a defined area in which a dwelling-house in which the child lives is situated.

(4) The court may provide that the exclusion requirement is to have effect for a shorter period than the other provisions of the order.

(5) Where the court makes an emergency protection order containing an exclusion requirement, the court may attach a power of arrest to the exclusion requirement.

(6) Where the court attaches a power of arrest to an exclusion requirement of an emergency protection order, it may provide that the power of arrest is to have effect for a shorter period than the exclusion requirement.

(7) Any period specified for the purposes of subsection (4) or (6) may be extended by the court (on one or more occasions) on an application to vary or discharge the emergency protection order.

(8) Where a power of arrest is attached to an exclusion requirement of an emergency protection order by virtue of subsection (5), a constable may arrest without warrant any person whom he has reasonable cause to believe to be in breach of the requirement.

(9) Sections 47(7), (11) and (12) and 48 of, and Schedule 5 to, the Family Law Act 1996 shall have effect in relation to a person arrested under subsection (8) of this section as they have effect in relation to a person arrested under section 47(6) of that Act.

(10) If, while an emergency protection order containing an exclusion requirement is in force, the applicant has removed the child from the dwelling-house from which the relevant person is excluded to other accommodation for a continuous period of more than 24 hours, the order shall cease to have effect in so far as it imposes the exclusion requirement.

Amendments—Inserted by Family Law Act 1996, s 52, Sch 6, para 3.

Defined terms—"child": s 105(1); "emergency protection order": s 44(4); "relevant person": s 44A(2)(*a*).

Procedure—See FPR 1991, r 4.24A and FPC(CA 1989)R 1991, r 25A.

44B Undertakings relating to emergency protection orders

(1) In any case where the court has power to include an exclusion requirement in an emergency protection order, the court may accept an undertaking from the relevant person.

(2) No power of arrest may be attached to any undertaking given under subsection (1).

(3) An undertaking given to a court under subsection (1) –

(*a*) shall be enforceable as if it were an order of the court, and

(*b*) shall cease to have effect if, while it is in force, the applicant has removed the child from the dwelling-house from which the relevant person is excluded to other accommodation for a continuous period of more than 24 hours.

(4) This section has effect without prejudice to the powers of the High Court and county court apart from this section.

(5) In this section "exclusion requirement" and "relevant person" have the same meaning as in section 44A.

Amendments—Inserted by Family Law Act 1996, s 52, Sch 6, para 3.

Defined terms—"child": s 105(1); "emergency protection order": s 44(4); "exclusion requirement": s 44A(3); "relevant person": s 44A(2)(*a*).

Procedure—See under FLA 1996, s 46 for assistance as to procedure which will be the same, albeit that the context is different.

Powers of High Court and county court apart from s 44B (s 44B(4))—As to the question of the county court accepting undertakings in public law proceedings, see **Undertakings and injunctions** under CA 1989, s 31. As to the inherent jurisdiction of the High Court, see CA 1989, s 100.

45 Duration of emergency protection orders and other supplemental provisions

(1) An emergency protection order shall have effect for such period, not exceeding eight days, as may be specified in the order.

(2) Where –

(*a*) the court making an emergency protection order would, but for this subsection, specify a period of eight days as the period for which the order is to have effect; but

(*b*) the last of those eight days is a public holiday (that is to say, Christmas Day, Good Friday, a bank holiday or a Sunday),

the court may specify a period which ends at noon on the first later day which is not such a holiday.

(3) Where an emergency protection order is made on an application under section 46(7), the period of eight days mentioned in subsection (1) shall begin with the first day on which the child was taken into police protection under section 46.

(4) Any person who –

(*a*) has parental responsibility for a child as the result of an emergency protection order; and

(*b*) is entitled to apply for a care order with respect to the child,

may apply to the court for the period during which the emergency protection order is to have effect to be extended.

(5) On an application under subsection (4) the court may extend the period during which the order is to have effect by such period, not exceeding seven days, as it thinks fit, but may do so only if it has reasonable cause to believe that the child concerned is likely to suffer significant harm if the order is not extended.

(6) An emergency protection order may only be extended once.

(7) Regardless of any enactment or rule of law which would otherwise prevent it from doing so, a court hearing an application for, or with respect to, an emergency protection order may take account of –

(*a*) any statement contained in any report made to the court in the course of, or in connection with, the hearing; or

(*b*) any evidence given during the hearing,

which is, in the opinion of the court, relevant to the application.

(8) Any of the following may apply to the court for an emergency protection order to be discharged –

(*a*) the child;

(*b*) a parent of his;

(*c*) any person who is not a parent of his but who has parental responsibility for him; or

(*d*) any person with whom he was living immediately before the making of the order.

(8A) On the application of a person who is not entitled to apply for the order to be discharged, but who is a person to whom an exclusion requirement contained in the order applies, an emergency protection order may be varied or discharged by the court in so far as it imposes the exclusion requirement.

(8B) Where a power of arrest has been attached to an exclusion requirement of an emergency protection order, the court may, on the application of any person entitled to apply for the discharge of the order so far as it imposes the exclusion requirement, vary or discharge the order in so far as it confers a power of arrest (whether or not any application has been made to vary or discharge any other provision of the order).

(9) No application for the discharge of an emergency protection order shall be heard by the court before the expiry of the period of 72 hours beginning with the making of the order.

(10) No appeal may be made against –

(*a*) the making of, or refusal to make, an emergency protection order;
(*b*) the extension of, or refusal to extend, the period during which such an order is to have effect;
(*c*) the discharge of, or refusal to discharge, such an order; or
(*d*) the giving of, or refusal to give, any direction in connection with such an order.

(11) Subsection (8) does not apply –

(*a*) where the person who would otherwise be entitled to apply for the emergency protection order to be discharged –
(i) was given notice (in accordance with rules of court) of the hearing at which the order was made; and
(ii) was present at that hearing; or
(*b*) to any emergency protection order the effective period of which has been extended under subsection (5).

(12) A court making an emergency protection order may direct that the applicant may, in exercising any powers which he has by virtue of the order, be accompanied by a registered medical practitioner, registered nurse or registered health visitor, if he so chooses.

Amendments—Courts and Legal Services Act 1990, s 116, Sch 16, para 19; Family Law Act 1996, s 52, Sch 6, para 4.

Defined terms—"care order": s 31(11); "child": s 105(1); "emergency protection order": s 44(4); "parental responsibility": s 3.

"Person with parental responsibility" (s 45(4), (8))—Parental responsibility may be acquired in a variety of ways, for example automatically (see s 2), by order or agreement under s 4, or by virtue of being appointed a guardian under s 5(6). Section s 45(8) encompasses anyone who has parental responsibility whereas s 45(4)(*a*) is restricted to anyone who has parental responsibility as a result of an emergency protection order (ie by virtue of s 44(4)(*c*)). See also Emergency Protection Order (Transfer of Responsibilities) Regulations 1991, SI 1991/1414, which apply where the original applicant for the emergency protection order was not the local authority in whose area the child is ordinarily resident.

"any person who ... is entitled to apply for a care order" (s 45(4)(*b*))—As to who is entitled to apply for a care order, see s 31(1).

"parent" (s 45(8)(*b*))—This term is not defined in the Act (see **Meaning of "parent"** under s 10).

Variation/discharge of exclusion requirement and power of arrest (s 45(8A), (8B))—Section 45(8) lists those who may apply for an emergency protection order to be discharged. Discharge of the order itself would discharge any exclusion requirement or power of arrest attached to it. In addition, by virtue of s 45(8A), discharge/variation of the exclusion requirement element of the order can be sought by the person to whom it applies. That person is also entitled to apply, under s 45(8B), for any attendant power of arrest to be varied or discharged. It is far from clear whether the combined effect of s 45(8) and ss 45(8A), (8B) permits anyone other than the person to whom the exclusion requirement applies to seek a limited order from the court discharging/varying the exclusion requirement or power of arrest, or whether the only application open to these other interested parties (local authority, parent etc) is one for complete discharge (see also **Applicants for variation/discharge of an exclusion requirement under** CA 1989, s 39).

Restrictions on appeal generally (s 45(10))—Magistrates, who adjourned an emergency protection order application on the basis that the mother had not had one clear day's notice of the proceedings and refused to grant an ex parte emergency protection order, had refused to make an order within the meaning of s 45(10) and there was no appeal from their decision (*Essex County Council v F* [1993] 1 FLR 847). If the magistrates had acted unreasonably, the only remedy lay with judicial review proceedings. *Re P (Emergency Protection Order)* [1996] 1 FLR 482, FD, illustrates the dangers of the lack of any appeal procedure, and various devices were there suggested in order to get round the problem (see at 484G).

Prohibition on appeal relating to direction (s 45(10)(*d*))—It is assumed that s 45(10)(*d*) also prohibits an appeal against the outcome of an application under s 44(9)(*b*) for the variation of a s 44(6) direction as to contact with or assessment of the child.

"notice (in accordance with rules of court) of the hearing" (s 45(11)(*a*))—As to the rules concerning notice, see FPR 1991, r 4.4 and Family Proceedings Courts (Children Act 1989) Rules 1991, r 4.

"was present at the hearing" (s 45(11)(*a*))—A person who attends through his legal representative but not in person may nevertheless have been present (see Magistrates' Courts Act 1980, s 122). However, the position in this context is far from clear. See, for example, *Re AS (Secure Accommodation Order)* [1999] 1 FLR 103, FD (annotated under FPR 1991, r 4.16).

46 Removal and accommodation of children by police in cases of emergency

(1) Where a constable has reasonable cause to believe that a child would otherwise be likely to suffer significant harm, he may –

(*a*) remove the child to suitable accommodation and keep him there; or

(*b*) take such steps as are reasonable to ensure that the child's removal from any hospital, or other place, in which he is then being accommodated is prevented.

(2) For the purposes of this Act, a child with respect to whom a constable has exercised his powers under this section is referred to as having been taken into police protection.

(3) As soon as is reasonably practicable after taking a child into police protection, the constable concerned shall –

(*a*) inform the local authority within whose area the child was found of the steps that have been, and are proposed to be, taken with respect to the child under this section and the reasons for taking them;

(*b*) give details to the authority within whose area the child is ordinarily resident ("the appropriate authority") of the place at which the child is being accommodated;

(*c*) inform the child (if he appears capable of understanding) –

(i) of the steps that have been taken with respect to him under this section and of the reasons for taking them; and;

(ii) of the further steps that may be taken with respect to him under this section;

(*d*) take such steps as are reasonably practicable to discover the wishes and feelings of the child;

(*e*) secure that the case is inquired into by an officer designated for the purposes of this section by the chief officer of the police area concerned; and

(*f*) where the child was taken into police protection by being removed to accommodation which is not provided –

(i) by or on behalf of a local authority; or

(ii) as a refuge, in compliance with the requirements of section 51,

secure that he is moved to accommodation which is so provided.

(4) As soon as is reasonably practicable after taking a child into police protection, the constable concerned shall take such steps as are reasonably practicable to inform –

(*a*) the child's parents;

(*b*) every person who is not a parent of his but who has parental responsibility for him; and

(*c*) any other person with whom the child was living immediately before being taken into police protection,

of the steps that he has taken under this section with respect to the child, the reasons for taking them and the further steps that may be taken with respect to him under this section.

(5) On completing any inquiry under subsection (3)(*e*), the officer conducting it shall release the child from police protection unless he considers that there is still reasonable cause for believing that the child would be likely to suffer significant harm if released.

(6) No child may be kept in police protection for more than 72 hours.

(7) While a child is being kept in police protection, the designated officer may apply on behalf of the appropriate authority for an emergency protection order to be made under section 44 with respect to the child.

(8) An application may be made under subsection (7) whether or not the authority know of it or agree to its being made.

(9) While a child is being kept in police protection –

(*a*) neither the constable concerned nor the designated officer shall have parental responsibility for him; but

(*b*) the designated officer shall do what is reasonable in all the circumstances of the case for the purpose of safeguarding or promoting the child's welfare (having regard in particular to the length of the period during which the child will be so protected).

(10) Where a child has been taken into police protection, the designated officer shall allow –

(*a*) the child's parents;

(*b*) any person who is not a parent of the child but who has parental responsibility for him;

(*c*) any person with whom the child was living immediately before he was taken into police protection;

(*d*) any person in whose favour a contact order is in force with respect to the child;

(*e*) any person who is allowed to have contact with the child by virtue of an order under section 34; and

(*f*) any person acting on behalf of any of those persons,

to have such contact (if any) with the child as, in the opinion of the designated officer, is both reasonable and in the child's best interests.

(11) Where a child who has been taken into police protection is in accommodation provided by, or on behalf of, the appropriate authority, subsection (10) shall have effect as if it referred to the authority rather than to the designated officer.

Defined terms—"appropriate authority": s 46(3)(*b*); "child", "contact order": s 105(1); "designated officer": s 46(3)(*e*); "emergency protection order": s 44(4); "police protection": s 46(2).

Designated officer—It is the responsibility of the chief officer of each police area to designate an officer for the purposes of this section (s 46(3)(*e*)).

"on behalf of the appropriate authority" (s 46(7))—The appropriate authority is the local authority within whose area the child is ordinarily resident (s 46(3)(*b*)). For assistance in identifying which local authority this is, see the annotations to s 31. Although only the designated police officer may make an application on behalf of the local authority, any police officer is entitled to apply for an emergency protection order in his own right by virtue of the wide terms of s 44(1).

47 Local authority's duty to investigate

(1) Where a local authority –

(*a*) are informed that a child who lives, or is found, in their area –

(i) is the subject of an emergency protection order; or

(ii) is in police protection; or

(iii) has contravened a ban imposed by a curfew notice within the meaning of Chapter I of Part I of the Crime And Disorder Act 1998; or

(*b*) have reasonable cause to suspect that a child who lives, or is found, in their area is suffering, or is likely to suffer, significant harm,

the authority shall make, or cause to be made, such enquiries as they consider necessary to enable them to decide whether they should take any action to safeguard or promote the child's welfare.

In the case of a child falling within paragraph (*a*)(iii) above, the enquiries shall be commenced as soon as practicable and, in any event, within 48 hours of the authority receiving the information.

(2) Where a local authority have obtained an emergency protection order with respect to a child, they shall make, or cause to be made, such enquiries as they consider necessary to enable them to decide what action they should take to safeguard or promote the child's welfare.

(3) The enquiries shall, in particular, be directed towards establishing –

(*a*) whether the authority should make any application to the court, or exercise any of their other powers under this Act or section 11 of the Crime and Disorder Act 1998 (child safety orders), with respect to the child;

(*b*) whether, in the case of a child –

(i) with respect to whom an emergency protection order has been made; and

(ii) who is not in accommodation provided by or on behalf of the authority,

it would be in the child's best interests (while an emergency protection order remains in force) for him to be in such accommodation; and

(*c*) whether, in the case of a child who has been taken into police protection, it would be in the child's best interests for the authority to ask for an application to be made under section 46(7).

(4) Where enquiries are being made under subsection (1) with respect to a child, the local authority concerned shall (with a view to enabling them to determine what action, if any, to take with respect to him) take such steps as are reasonably practicable –

(*a*) to obtain access to him; or

(*b*) to ensure that access to him is obtained, on their behalf, by a person authorised by them for the purpose,

unless they are satisfied that they already have sufficient information with respect to him.

(5) Where, as a result of any such enquiries, it appears to the authority that there are matters connected with the child's education which should be investigated, they shall consult the relevant local education authority.

(6) Where, in the course of enquiries made under this section –

(*a*) any officer of the local authority concerned; or

(*b*) any person authorised by the authority to act on their behalf in connection with those enquiries –

(i) is refused access to the child concerned; or

(ii) is denied information as to his whereabouts,

the authority shall apply for an emergency protection order, a child assessment order, a care order or a supervision order with respect to the child unless they are satisfied that his welfare can be satisfactorily safeguarded without their doing so.

(7) If, on the conclusion of any enquiries or review made under this section, the authority decide not to apply for an emergency protection order, a care order, a child assessment order or a supervision order they shall –

(*a*) consider whether it would be appropriate to review the case at a later date; and

(*b*) if they decide that it would be, determine the date on which that review is to begin.

(8) Where, as a result of complying with this section, a local authority conclude that they should take action to safeguard or promote the child's welfare they shall take that action (so far as it is both within their power and reasonably practicable for them to do so).

(9) Where a local authority are conducting enquiries under this section, it shall be the duty of any person mentioned in subsection (11) to assist them with those enquiries (in particular by providing relevant information and advice) if called upon by the authority to do so.

(10) Subsection (9) does not oblige any person to assist a local authority where doing so would be unreasonable in all the circumstances of the case.

(11) The persons are –

(*a*) any local authority;

PART II

(*b*) any local education authority;
(*c*) any local housing authority;
(*d*) any Health Authority, Special Health Authority, Primary Care Trust or National Health Service trust; and
(*e*) any person authorised by the Secretary of State for the purposes of this section.

(12) Where a local authority are making enquiries under this section with respect to a child who appears to them to be ordinarily resident within the area of another authority, they shall consult that other authority, who may undertake the necessary enquiries in their place.

Amendments—Courts and Legal Services Act 1990, s 116, Sch 16, para 20; Health Authorities Act 1995, s 2, Sch 1, para 118; Crime and Disorder Act 1998, ss 15(4), 119, Sch 8, para 69; SI 2000/90.

"reasonable cause to suspect" (s 47(1)(*b*))—The threshold contained in s 47 is clearly and deliberately lower than that of "reasonable cause to believe" contained in ss 38, 44 and 46, which all involve a compulsory intervention in the lives of both the child and the family and constitute an interference with family life under Article 6 of the European Convention for the Protection of Human Rights and Fundamental Freedoms 1950, now incorporated into domestic law by the Human Rights Act 1998. By contrast, a s 47 investigation does not generally infringe rights, but merely imposes a duty to conduct investigations necessary for decisions about the child's welfare (*G v Hertfordshire County Council* [2000] Fam Law 883).

48 Powers to assist in discovery of children who may be in need of emergency protection

(1) Where it appears to a court making an emergency protection order that adequate information as to the child's whereabouts –

(*a*) is not available to the applicant for the order; but
(*b*) is available to another person,

it may include in the order a provision requiring that other person to disclose, if asked to do so by the applicant, any information that he may have as to the child's whereabouts.

(2) No person shall be excused from complying with such a requirement on the ground that complying might incriminate him or his spouse of an offence; but a statement of admission made in complying shall not be admissible in evidence against either of them in proceedings for any offence other than perjury.

(3) An emergency protection order may authorise the applicant to enter premises specified by the order and search for the child with respect to whom the order is made.

(4) Where the court is satisfied that there is reasonable cause to believe that there may be another child on those premises with respect to whom an emergency protection order ought to be made, it may make an order authorising the applicant to search for that other child on those premises.

(5) Where –

(*a*) an order has been made under subsection (4);
(*b*) the child concerned has been found on the premises; and
(*c*) the applicant is satisfied that the grounds for making an emergency protection order exist with respect to him,

the order shall have effect as if it were an emergency protection order.

(6) Where an order has been made under subsection (4), the applicant shall notify the court of its effect.

(7) A person shall be guilty of an offence if he intentionally obstructs any person exercising the power of entry and search under subsection (3) or (4).

(8) A person guilty of an offence under subsection (7) shall be liable on summary conviction to a fine not exceeding level 3 on the standard scale.

(9) Where, on an application made by any person for a warrant under this section, it appears to the court –

(*a*) that a person attempting to exercise powers under an emergency protection order has been prevented from doing so by being refused entry to the premises concerned or access to the child concerned; or

(*b*) that any such person is likely to be so prevented from exercising any such powers,

it may issue a warrant authorising any constable to assist the person mentioned in paragraph (*a*) or (*b*) in the exercise of those powers, using reasonable force if necessary.

(10) Every warrant issued under this section shall be addressed to, and executed by, a constable who shall be accompanied by the person applying for the warrant if –

(*a*) that person so desires; and

(*b*) the court by whom the warrant is issued does not direct otherwise.

(11) A court granting an application for a warrant under this section may direct that the constable concerned may, in executing the warrant, be accompanied by a registered medical practitioner, registered nurse or registered health visitor if he so chooses.

(12) An application for a warrant under this section shall be made in the manner and form prescribed by rules of court.

(13) Wherever it is reasonably practicable to do so, an order under subsection (4), an application for a warrant under this section and any such warrant shall name the child; and where it does not name him it shall describe him as clearly as possible.

Defined terms—"child": s 105(1); "emergency protection order": s 44(4).

Authority to search for another child (s 48(4))—The order giving authority should be in Form C27.

Issue of warrants—A warrant may be issued under s 48(9) to authorise a constable to assist in the enforcement of an emergency protection order.

"prescribed by rules of court" (s 48(12))—See FPR 1991, Pt IV and FPC(CA 1989)R 1991. The application for a warrant should be made on Form C1 with the prescribed supplement Form C12. The warrant should be in Form C25.

49 Abduction of children in care etc

(1) A person shall be guilty of an offence if, knowingly and without lawful authority or reasonable excuse, he –

(*a*) takes a child to whom this section applies away from the responsible person;

(*b*) keeps such a child away from the responsible person; or (*c*) induces, assists or incites such a child to run away or stay away from the responsible person.

(2) This section applies in relation to a child who is –

(*a*) in care;
(*b*) the subject of an emergency protection order; or
(*c*) in police protection,

and in this section "the responsible person" means any person who for the time being has care of him by virtue of the care order, the emergency protection order, or section 46, as the case may be.

(3) A person guilty of an offence under this section shall be liable on summary conviction to imprisonment for a term not exceeding six months, or to a fine not exceeding level 5 on the standard scale, or to both.

50 Recovery of abducted children etc

(1) Where it appears to the court that there is reason to believe that a child to whom this section applies –

(*a*) has been unlawfully taken away or is being unlawfully kept away from the responsible person;
(*b*) has run away or is staying away from the responsible person; or
(*c*) is missing,

the court may make an order under this section ("a recovery order").

(2) This section applies to the same children to whom section 49 applies and in this section "the responsible person" has the same meaning as in section 49.

(3) A recovery order –

(*a*) operates as a direction to any person who is in a position to do so to produce the child on request to any authorised person;
(*b*) authorises the removal of the child by any authorised person;
(*c*) requires any person who has information as to the child's whereabouts to disclose that information, if asked to do so, to a constable or an officer of the court;
(*d*) authorises a constable to enter any premises specified in the order and search for the child, using reasonable force if necessary.

(4) The court may make a recovery order on the application of –

(*a*) any person who has parental responsibility for the child by virtue of a care order or emergency protection order; or
(*b*) where the child is in police protection, the designated officer.

(5) A recovery order shall name the child and –

(*a*) any person who has parental responsibility for the child by virtue of a care order or emergency protection order; or
(*b*) where the child is in police protection, the designated officer.

(6) Premises may only be specified under subsection (3)(*d*) if it appears to the court that there are reasonable grounds for believing the child to be on them.

(7) In this section –

"an authorised person" means –

(*a*) any person specified by the court;

(*b*) any constable;

(*c*) any person who is authorised –

(i) after the recovery order is made; and

(ii) by a person who has parental responsibility for the child by virtue of a care order or an emergency protection order,

to exercise any power under a recovery order; and

"the designated officer" means the officer designated for the purposes of section 46.

(8) Where a person is authorised as mentioned in subsection (7)(*c*) –

(*a*) the authorisation shall identify the recovery order; and

(*b*) any person claiming to be so authorised shall, if asked to do so, produce some duly authenticated document showing that he is so authorised.

(9) A person shall be guilty of an offence if he intentionally obstructs an authorised person exercising the power under subsection (3)(*b*) to remove a child.

(10) A person guilty of an offence under this section shall be liable on summary conviction to a fine not exceeding level 3 on the standard scale.

(11) No person shall be excused from complying with any request made under subsection (3)(*c*) on the ground that complying with it might incriminate him or his spouse of an offence; but a statement or admission made in complying shall not be admissible in evidence against either of them in proceedings for an offence other than perjury.

(12)–(14) …

Defined terms—"care order": ss 31(11), 105(1); "child": s 105(1); "designated officer": s 50(7); "emergency protection order": s 44(4); "parental responsibility": s 3; "police protection": s 46(2); "recovery order": s 50(1).

"child to whom this section applies" (s 50(1))—See ss 50(2) and 49(2).

"responsible person" (s 50(1))—See ss 50(2) and 49(2). See also *Re R (Recovery Orders)* [1998] 2 FLR 401, FD.

"any person who has parental responsibility" (s 50(4), (5))—In the case of a care order, the local authority designated by the order (see s 33(3)) will have parental responsibility and, in the case of an emergency protection order, the applicant for the emergency protection order (see s 44(4)(*c*)) will have parental responsibility. Where either the applicant was a designated police officer applying by virtue of s 46(7) on behalf of the local authority or the local authority has taken over the emergency protection order from the original applicant in accordance with the Emergency Protection Order (Transfer of Responsibilities) Regulations 1991, SI 1991/1414, the local authority has parental responsibility.

"designated officer" (s 50(4)(*b*), (5)(*b*))—It is the responsibility of the chief officer for each police area to designate an officer for the purpose of the police protection provisions contained in s 46 (s 46(3)(*e*)).

Procedure—For consideration of the proper procedure where a local authority has replaced a parent or carer as a "responsible person" shortly prior to seeking a recovery order, see *Re R (Recovery Orders)* [1998] 2 FLR 401, FD which also deals with the role the child should play in the proceedings (13-year-old boy's wishes and feelings as to his schooling were properly taken into account even though he was not separately represented at the recovery order hearing).

51 Refuges for children at risk

(1) Where it is proposed to use a voluntary home or private children's home to provide a refuge for children who appear to be at risk of harm, the Secretary of State may issue a certificate under this section with respect to that home.

(2) Where a local authority or voluntary organisation arrange for a foster parent to provide such a refuge, the Secretary of State may issue a certificate under this section with respect to that foster parent.

(3) In subsection (2) "foster parent" means a person who is, or who from time to time is, a local authority foster parent or a foster parent with whom children are placed by a voluntary organisation.

(4) The Secretary of State may by regulations –

(*a*) make provision as to the manner in which certificates may be issued;
(*b*) impose requirements which must be complied with while any certificate is in force; and
(*c*) provide for the withdrawal of certificates in prescribed circumstances.

(5) Where a certificate is in force with respect to a home, none of the provisions mentioned in subsection (7) shall apply in relation to any person providing a refuge for any child in that home.

(6) Where a certificate is in force with respect to a foster parent, none of those provisions shall apply in relation to the provision by him of a refuge for any child in accordance with arrangements made by the local authority or voluntary organisation.

(7) The provisions are –

(*a*) section 49;
(*b*) sections 82 (recovery of certain fugitive children) and 83 (harbouring) of the Children (Scotland) Act 1995, so far as they apply in relation to anything done in England and Wales;
(*c*) section 32(3) of the Children and Young Persons Act 1969 (compelling, persuading, inciting or assisting any person to be absent from detention etc), so far as it applies in relation to anything done in England and Wales;
(*d*) section 2 of the Child Abduction Act 1984.

Amendments—Children (Scotland) Act 1995, s 105(4), Sch 4, para 48(1), (3); Care Standards Act 2000, s 116, Sch 4, para 14(7).

52 Rules and regulations

(1) Without prejudice to section 93 or any other power to make such rules, rules of court may be made with respect to the procedure to be followed in connection with proceedings under this Part.

(2) The rules may in particular make provision –

(*a*) as to the form in which any application is to be made or direction is to be given;
(*b*) prescribing the persons who are to be notified of –
  (i) the making, or extension, of an emergency protection order; or
  (ii) the making of an application under section 45(4) or (8) or 46(7); and
(*c*) as to the content of any such notification and the manner in which, and person by whom, it is to be given.

(3) The Secretary of State may by regulations provide that, where –

(*a*) an emergency protection order has been made with respect to a child;

(*b*) the applicant for the order was not the local authority within whose area the child is ordinarily resident; and

(*c*) that local authority are of the opinion that it would be in the child's best interests for the applicant's responsibilities under the order to be transferred to them,

that authority shall (subject to their having complied with any requirements imposed by the regulations) be treated, for the purposes of this Act, as though they and not the original applicant had applied for, and been granted, the order.

(4) Regulations made under subsection (3) may, in particular, make provision as to –

(*a*) the considerations to which the local authority shall have regard in forming an opinion as mentioned in subsection (3)(*c*); and

(*b*) the time at which responsibility under any emergency protection order is to be treated as having been transferred to a local authority.

PART VI
COMMUNITY HOMES

53 Provision of community homes by local authorities

(1) Every local authority shall make such arrangements as they consider appropriate for securing that homes ("community homes") are available –

(*a*) for the care and accommodation of children looked after by them; and

(*b*) for purposes connected with the welfare of children (whether or not looked after by them),

and may do so jointly with one or more other local authorities.

(2) In making such arrangements, a local authority shall have regard to the need for ensuring the availability of accommodation –

(*a*) of different descriptions; and

(*b*) which is suitable for different purposes and the requirements of different descriptions of children.

(3) A community home may be a home –

(*a*) provided, equipped, maintained and (subject to subsection (3A)) managed by a local authority; or

(*b*) provided by a voluntary organisation but in respect of which a local authority and the organisation –

(i) propose that, in accordance with an instrument of management, the equipment, maintenance and (subject to subsection (3B)) management of the home shall be the responsibility of the local authority; or

(ii) so propose that the management, equipment and maintenance of the home shall be the responsibility of the voluntary organisation.

(3A) A local authority may make arrangements for the management by another person of accommodation provided by the local authority for the purpose of restricting the liberty of children.

(3B) Where a local authority are to be responsible for the management of a community home provided by a voluntary organisation, the local authority may, with the consent of the body of managers constituted by the instrument of management for the home, make arrangements for the management by another person of accommodation provided for the purpose of restricting the liberty of children.

(4) Where a local authority are to be responsible for the management of a community home provided by a voluntary organisation, the authority shall designate the home as a controlled community home.

(5) Where a voluntary organisation are to be responsible for the management of a community home provided by the organisation, the local authority shall designate the home as an assisted community home.

(6) Schedule 4 shall have effect for the purpose of supplementing the provisions of this Part.

Amendments—Criminal Justice and Public Order Act 1994, s 22.

54 (*repealed*)

55 Determination of disputes relating to controlled and assisted community homes

(1) Where any dispute relating to a controlled community home arises between the local authority specified in the home's instrument of management and –

(*a*) the voluntary organisation by which the home is provided; or
(*b*) any other local authority who have placed, or desire or are required to place, in the home a child who is looked after by them,

the dispute may be referred by either party to the Secretary of State for his determination.

(2) Where any dispute relating to an assisted community home arises between the voluntary organisation by which the home is provided and any local authority who have placed, or desire to place, in the home a child who is looked after by them, the dispute may be referred by either party to the Secretary of State for his determination.

(3) Where a dispute is referred to the Secretary of State under this section he may, in order to give effect to his determination of the dispute, give such directions as he thinks fit to the local authority or voluntary organisation concerned.

(4) This section applies even though the matter in dispute may be one which, under or by virtue of Part II of Schedule 4, is reserved for the decision, or is the responsibility, of –

(*a*) the local authority specified in the home's instrument of management; or
(*b*) (as the case may be) the voluntary organisation by which the home is provided.

(5) Where any trust deed relating to a controlled or assisted community home contains provision whereby a bishop or any other ecclesiastical or denominational authority has power to decide questions relating to religious instruction given in the home, no dispute which is capable of being dealt with in accordance with that provision shall be referred to the Secretary of State under this section.

(6) In this Part "trust deed", in relation to a voluntary home, means any instrument (other than an instrument of management) regulating –

(*a*) the maintenance, management or conduct of the home; or
(*b*) the constitution of a body of managers or trustees of the home.

56 Discontinuance by voluntary organisation of controlled or assisted community home

(1) The voluntary organisation by which a controlled or assisted community home is provided shall not cease to provide the home except after giving to the Secretary of State and the local authority specified in the home's instrument of management not less than two years' notice in writing of their intention to do so.

(2) A notice under subsection (1) shall specify the date from which the voluntary organisation intend to cease to provide the home as a community home.

(3) Where such a notice is given and is not withdrawn before the date specified in it, the home's instrument of management shall cease to have effect on that date and the home shall then cease to be a controlled or assisted community home.

(4) Where a notice is given under subsection (1) and the home's managers give notice in writing to the Secretary of State that they are unable or unwilling to continue as its managers until the date specified in the subsection (1) notice, the Secretary of State may by order –

(*a*) revoke the home's instrument of management; and
(*b*) require the local authority who were specified in that instrument to conduct the home until –
(i) the date specified in the subsection (1) notice; or
(ii) such earlier date (if any) as may be specified for the purposes of this paragraph in the order,

as if it were a community home provided by the local authority.

(5) Where the Secretary of State imposes a requirement under subsection (4)(*b*) –

(*a*) nothing in the trust deed for the home shall affect the conduct of the home by the local authority;
(*b*) the Secretary of State may by order direct that for the purposes of any provision specified in the direction and made by or under any enactment relating to community homes (other than this section) the home shall, until the date or earlier date specified as mentioned in subsection (4)(*b*), be treated as a controlled or assisted community home;
(*c*) except in so far as the Secretary of State so directs, the home shall until that date be treated for the purposes of any such enactment as a community home provided by the local authority; and
(*d*) on the date or earlier date specified as mentioned in subsection (4)(*b*) the home shall cease to a community home.

57 Closure by local authority of controlled or assisted community home

(1) The local authority specified in the instrument of management for a controlled or assisted community home may give –

(*a*) the Secretary of State; and
(*b*) the voluntary organisation by which the home is provided,

not less than two years' notice in writing of their intention to withdraw their designation of the home as a controlled or assisted community home.

(2) A notice under subsection (1) shall specify the date ("the specified date") on which the designation is to be withdrawn.

(3) Where –

(*a*) a notice is given under subsection (1) in respect of a controlled or assisted community home;
(*b*) the home's managers give notice in writing to the Secretary of State that they are unable or unwilling to continue as managers until the specified date; and
(*c*) the managers' notice is not withdrawn,

the Secretary of State may by order revoke the home's instrument of management from such date earlier than the specified date as may be specified in the order.

(4) Before making an order under subsection (3), the Secretary of State shall consult the local authority and the voluntary organisation.

(5) Where a notice has been given under subsection (1) and is not withdrawn, the home's instrument of management shall cease to have effect on –

(*a*) the specified date; or
(*b*) where an earlier date has been specified under subsection (3), that earlier date,

and the home shall then cease to be a community home.

58 Financial provisions applicable on cessation of controlled or assisted community home or disposal etc of premises

(1) Where –

(*a*) the instrument of management for a controlled or assisted community home is revoked or otherwise ceases to have effect under section 56(3) or (4)(*a*) or 57(3) or (5); or
(*b*) any premises used for the purposes of such a home are (at any time after 13 January 1987) disposed of, or put to use otherwise than for those purposes,

the proprietor shall become liable to pay compensation ("the appropriate compensation") in accordance with this section.

(2) Where the instrument of management in force at the relevant time relates –

(*a*) to a controlled community home; or
(*b*) to an assisted community home which, at any time before the instrument came into force, was a controlled community home,

the appropriate compensation is a sum equal to that part of the value of any premises which is attributable to expenditure incurred in relation to the premises, while the home was a controlled community home, by the authority who were then the responsible authority.

(3) Where the instrument of management in force at the relevant time relates –

(*a*) to an assisted community home; or
(*b*) to a controlled community home which, at any time before the instrument came into force, was an assisted community home,

the appropriate compensation is a sum equal to that part of the value of the premises which is attributable to the expenditure of money provided by way of grant under section 82, section 65 of the Children and Young Persons Act 1969 or section 82 of the Child Care Act 1980.

(4) Where the home is, at the relevant time, conducted in premises which formerly were used as an approved school or were an approved probation hostel or home, the appropriate compensation is a sum equal to that part of the value of the premises which is attributable to the expenditure –

(*a*) of sums paid towards the expenses of the managers of an approved school under section 104 of the Children and Young Persons Act 1933;

(*b*) of sums paid under section 51(3)(*c*) of the Powers of Criminal Courts Act 1973 or section 20(1)(*c*) of the Probation Service Act 1993 in relation to expenditure on approved probation hostels or homes; or

(*c*) of sums paid under section 3, 5 or 9 of the Criminal Justice and Court Services Act 2000 in relation to expenditure on approved premises (within the meaning of Part I of that Act).

(5) The appropriate compensation shall be paid –

(*a*) in the case of compensation payable under subsection (2), to the authority who were the responsible authority at the relevant time; and

(*b*) in any other case, to the Secretary of State.

(6) In this section –

"disposal" includes the grant of a tenancy and any other conveyance, assignment, transfer, grant, variation or extinguishment of an interest in or right over land, whether made by instrument or otherwise;

"premises" means any premises or part of premises (including land) used for the purposes of the home and belonging to the proprietor;

"the proprietor" means –

(*a*) the voluntary organisation by which the home is, at the relevant time, provided; or

(*b*) if the premises are not, at the relevant time, vested in that organisation, the persons in whom they are vested;

"the relevant time" means the time immediately before the liability to pay arises under subsection (1); and

"the responsible authority" means the local authority specified in the instrument of management in question.

(7) For the purposes of this section an event of a kind mentioned in subsection (1)(*b*) shall be taken to have occurred –

(*a*) in the case of a disposal, on the date on which the disposal was completed or, in the case of a disposal which is effected by a series of transactions, the date on which the last of those transactions was completed;

(*b*) in the case of premises which are put to different use, on the date on which they first begin to be put to their new use.

(8) The amount of any sum payable under this section shall be determined in accordance with such arrangements –

(*a*) as may be agreed between the voluntary organisation by which the home is, at the relevant time, provided and the responsible authority or (as the case may be) the Secretary of State; or

(*b*) in default of agreement, as may be determined by the Secretary of State.

PART II

(9) With the agreement of the responsible authority or (as the case may be) the Secretary of State, the liability to pay any sum under this section may be discharged, in whole or in part, by the transfer of any premises.

(10) This section has effect regardless of –

(*a*) anything in any trust deed for a controlled or assisted community home;
(*b*) the provisions of any enactment or instrument governing the disposition of the property of a voluntary organisation.

Amendments—Probation Service Act 1993, s 32, Sch 3, para 9; Criminal Justice and Court Services Act 2000, s 74, Sch 7, para 93; Care Standards Act 2000, s 117, Sch 6.

PART VII
VOLUNTARY HOMES AND VOLUNTARY ORGANISATIONS

59 Provision of accommodation by voluntary organisations

(1) Where a voluntary organisation provide accommodation for a child, they shall do so by –

(*a*) placing him (subject to subsection (2)) with –
 (i) a family;
 (ii) a relative of his; or
 (iii) any other suitable person,
on such terms as to payment by the organisation and otherwise as the organisation may determine;
(*aa*) maintaining him in an appropriate children's home;
(*b*)–(*e*) (*repealed*)
(*f*) making such other arrangements (subject to subsection (3)) as seem appropriate to them.

(1A) Where under subsection (1)(*aa*) a local authority maintains a child in a home provided, equipped and maintained by the Secretary of State under section 82(5), it shall do so on such terms as the Secretary of State may from time to time determine.

(2) The Secretary of State may make regulations as to the placing of children with foster parents by voluntary organisations and the regulations may, in particular, make provision which (with any necessary modifications) is similar to the provision that may be made under section 23(2)(*f*).

(3) The Secretary of State may make regulations as to the arrangements which may be made under subsection (1)(*f*) and the regulations may in particular make provision which (with any necessary modifications) is similar to the provision that may be made under section 23(2)(*f*).

(4) The Secretary of State may make regulations requiring any voluntary organisation who are providing accommodation for a child –

(*a*) to review his case; and
(*b*) to consider any representations (including any complaint) made to them by any person falling within a prescribed class of person,

in accordance with the provisions of the regulations.

(5) Regulations under subsection (4) may in particular make provision which (with any necessary modifications) is similar to the provision that may be made under section 26.

(6) Regulations under subsections (2) to (4) may provide that any person who, without reasonable excuse, contravenes or fails to comply with a regulation shall be guilty of an offence and liable on summary conviction to a fine not exceeding level 4 on the standard scale.

Amendments—Care Standards Act 2000, s 116, Sch 4, para 14(8).

60 Voluntary homes

(1), (2) (*repealed*)

(3) In this Act "voluntary home" means a children's home which is carried on by a voluntary organisation but does not include a community home.

(4) Schedule 5 shall have effect for the purpose of supplementing the provisions of this Part.

Amendments—Registered Homes (Amendment) Act 1991, s 2(6); Care Standards Act 2000, s 116, Sch 4, para 14(9), Sch 6.

61 Duties of voluntary organisations

(1) Where a child is accommodated by or on behalf of a voluntary organisation, it shall be the duty of the organisation –

(*a*) to safeguard and promote his welfare;
(*b*) to make such use of the services and facilities available for children cared for by their own parents as appears to the organisation reasonable in his case; and
(*c*) to advise, assist and befriend him with a view to promoting his welfare when he ceases to be so accommodated.

(2) Before making any decision with respect to any such child the organisation shall, so far as is reasonably practicable, ascertain the wishes and feelings of –

(*a*) the child;
(*b*) his parents;
(*c*) any person who is not a parent of his but who has parental responsibility for him; and
(*d*) any other person whose wishes and feelings the organisation consider to be relevant,

regarding the matter to be decided.

(3) In making any such decision the organisation shall give due consideration –

(*a*) having regard to the child's age and understanding, to such wishes and feelings of his as they have been able to ascertain;
(*b*) to such other wishes and feelings mentioned in subsection (2) as they have been able to ascertain; and
(*c*) to the child's religious persuasion, racial origin and cultural and linguistic background.

62 Duties of local authorities

(1) Every local authority shall satisfy themselves that any voluntary organisation providing accommodation –

(*a*) within the authority's area for any child; or
(*b*) outside that area for any child on behalf of the authority,

are satisfactorily safeguarding and promoting the welfare of the children so provided with accommodation.

(2) Every local authority shall arrange for children who are accommodated within their area by or on behalf of voluntary organisations to be visited, from time to time, in the interests of their welfare.

(3) The Secretary of State may make regulations –

(*a*) requiring every child who is accommodated within a local authority's area, by or on behalf of a voluntary organisation, to be visited by an officer of the authority –
(i) in prescribed circumstances; and
(ii) on specified occasions or within specified periods; and
(*b*) imposing requirements which must be met by any local authority, or officer of a local authority, carrying out functions under this section.

(4) Subsection (2) does not apply in relation to community homes.

(5) Where a local authority are not satisfied that the welfare of any child who is accommodated by or on behalf of a voluntary organisation is being satisfactorily safeguarded or promoted they shall –

(*a*) unless they consider that it would not be in the best interests of the child, take such steps as are reasonably practicable to secure that the care and accommodation of the child is undertaken by –
(i) a parent of his;
(ii) any person who is not a parent of his but who has parental responsibility for him; or
(iii) a relative of his; and
(*b*) consider the extent to which (if at all) they should exercise any of their functions with respect to the child.

(6) Any person authorised by a local authority may, for the purpose of enabling the authority to discharge their duties under this section –

(*a*) enter, at any reasonable time, and inspect any premises in which children are being accommodated as mentioned in subsection (1) or (2);
(*b*) inspect any children there;
(*c*) require any person to furnish him with such records of a kind required to be kept by regulations made under section 22 of the Care Standards Act 2000 (in whatever form they are held), or allow him to inspect such records, as he may at any time direct.

(7) Any person exercising the power conferred by subsection (6) shall, if asked to do so, produce some duly authenticated document showing his authority to do so.

(8) Any person authorised to exercise the power to inspect records conferred by subsection (6) –

(*a*) shall be entitled at any reasonable time to have access to, and inspect and check the operation of, any computer and any associated apparatus or material which is or has been in use in connection with the records in question; and
(*b*) may require –
(i) the person by whom or on whose behalf the computer is or has been so used; or
(ii) any person having charge of, or otherwise concerned with the operation of, the computer, apparatus or material,

to afford him such assistance as he may reasonably require.

(9) Any person who intentionally obstructs another in the exercise of any power conferred by subsection (6) or (8) shall be guilty of an offence and liable on summary conviction to a fine not exceeding level 3 on the standard scale.

(10) This section does not apply in relation to any voluntary organisation which is an institution within the further education sector, as defined in section 91 of the Further and Higher Education Act 1992, or a school.

Amendments—Care Standards Act 2000, ss 105(5), 116, Sch 4, para 14(10).

PART VIII
REGISTERED CHILDREN'S HOMES

63 Private children's homes etc

(1)–(10) (*repealed*)

(11) Schedule 6 shall have effect with respect to private children's homes.

(12) Schedule 7 shall have effect for the purpose of setting out the circumstances in which a person may foster more than three children without being treated, for the purposes of this Act and the Care Standards Act 2000, as carrying on a children's home.

Amendments—Registered Homes (Amendment) Act 1991, s 2(6); Education Act 1996, s 582(1), Sch 37, Pt I, para 86; Care Standards Act 2000, ss 116, 117, Sch 4, para 14(11), Sch 6.

64 Welfare of children in children's homes

(1) Where a child is accommodated in a private children's home, it shall be the duty of the person carrying on the home to –

(*a*) safeguard and promote the child's welfare;
(*b*) make such use of the services and facilities available for children cared for by their own parents as appears to that person reasonable in the case of the child; and
(*c*) advise, assist and befriend him with a view to promoting his welfare when he ceases to be so accommodated.

(2) Before making any decision with respect to any such child the person carrying on the home shall, so far as is reasonably practicable, ascertain the wishes and feelings of –

(*a*) the child;
(*b*) his parents;
(*c*) any other person who is not a parent of his but who has parental responsibility for him; and
(*d*) any person whose wishes and feelings the person carrying on the home considers to be relevant,

regarding the matter to be decided.

(3) In making any such decision the person concerned shall give due consideration –

(*a*) having regard to the child's age and understanding, to such wishes and feelings of his as he has been able to ascertain;
(*b*) to such other wishes and feelings mentioned in subsection (2) as he has been able to ascertain; and

(*c*) to the child's religious persuasion, racial origin and cultural and linguistic background.

(4) Section 62, except subsection (4), shall apply in relation to any person who is carrying on a private children's home as it applies in relation to any voluntary organisation.

Amendments—Care Standards Act 2000, s 116, Sch 4, para 14(12).

65 Persons disqualified from carrying on, or being employed in, children's homes

(1) A person who is disqualified (under section 68) from fostering a child privately shall not carry on, or be otherwise concerned in the management of, or have any financial interest in, a children's home unless he has –

(*a*) disclosed to the appropriate authority the fact that he is so disqualified; and
(*b*) obtained its written consent.

(2) No person shall employ a person who is so disqualified in a children's home unless he has –

(*a*) disclosed to the appropriate authority the fact that that person is so disqualified; and
(*b*) obtained its written consent.

(3) Where the appropriate authority refuses to give its consent under this section, it shall inform the applicant by a written notice which states –

(*a*) the reason for the refusal;
(*b*) the applicant's right to appeal under section 65A against the refusal to the Tribunal established under section 9 of the Protection of Children Act 1999; and
(*c*) the time within which he may do so.

(4) Any person who contravenes subsection (1) or (2) shall be guilty of an offence and liable on summary conviction to imprisonment for a term not exceeding six months or to a fine not exceeding level 5 on the standard scale or to both.

(5) Where a person contravenes subsection (2) he shall not be guilty of an offence if he proves that he did not know, and had no reasonable grounds for believing, that the person whom he was employing was disqualified under section 68.

(6) In this section and section 65A "appropriate authority" means –

(*a*) in relation to England, the National Care Standards Commission; and
(*b*) in relation to Wales, the National Assembly for Wales.

Amendments—Care Standards Act 2000, s 116, Sch 4, para 14(13).

65A Appeal against refusal of authority to give consent under section 65

(1) An appeal against a decision of an appropriate authority under section 65 shall lie to the Tribunal established under section 9 of the Protection of Children Act 1999.

(2) On an appeal the Tribunal may confirm the authority's decision or direct it to give the consent in question.

Amendments—Inserted by Care Standards Act 2000, s 116, Sch 4, para 14(14).

PART IX
PRIVATE ARRANGEMENTS FOR FOSTERING CHILDREN

66 Privately fostered children

(1) In this Part –

(*a*) "a privately fostered child" means a child who is under the age of sixteen and who is cared for, and provided with accommodation in their own home by, someone other than –

(i) a parent of his;

(ii) a person who is not a parent of his but who has parental responsibility for him; or

(iii) a relative of his; and

(*b*) "to foster a child privately" means to look after the child in circumstances in which he is a privately fostered child as defined by this section.

(2) A child is not a privately fostered child if the person caring for and accommodating him –

(*a*) has done so for a period of less than 28 days; and

(*b*) does not intend to do so for any longer period.

(3) Subsection (1) is subject to –

(*a*) the provisions of section 63; and

(*b*) the exceptions made by paragraphs 1 to 5 of Schedule 8.

(4) In the case of a child who is disabled, subsection (1)(*a*) shall have effect as if for "sixteen" there were substituted "eighteen".

(4A) The Secretary of State may by regulations make provision as to the circumstances in which a person who provides accommodation to a child is, or is not, to be treated as providing him with accommodation in the person's own home.

(5) Schedule 8 shall have effect for the purposes of supplementing the provision made by this Part.

Amendments—Care Standards Act 2000, s 116, Sch 4, para 14(15).

67 Welfare of privately fostered children

(1) It shall be the duty of every local authority to satisfy themselves that the welfare of children who are privately fostered within their area is being satisfactorily safeguarded and promoted and to secure that such advice is given to those caring for them as appears to the authority to be needed.

(2) The Secretary of State may make regulations –

(*a*) requiring every child who is privately fostered within a local authority's area to be visited by an officer of the authority –

(i) in prescribed circumstances; and

(ii) on specified occasions or within specified periods; and

(b) imposing requirements which are to be met by any local authority, or officer of a local authority, in carrying out functions under this section.

(3) Where any person who is authorised by a local authority to visit privately fostered children has reasonable cause to believe that –

(a) any privately fostered child is being accommodated in premises within the authority's area; or
(b) it is proposed to accommodate any such child in any such premises,

he may at any reasonable time inspect those premises and any children there.

(4) Any person exercising the power under subsection (3) shall, if so required, produce some duly authenticated document showing his authority to do so.

(5) Where a local authority are not satisfied that the welfare of any child who is privately fostered within their area is being satisfactorily safeguarded or promoted they shall –

(a) unless they consider that it would not be in the best interests of the child, take such steps as are reasonably practicable to secure that the care and accommodation of the child is undertaken by –
  (i) a parent of his;
  (ii) any person who is not a parent of his but who has parental responsibility for him; or
  (iii) a relative of his; and
(b) consider the extent to which (if at all) they should exercise any of their functions under this Act with respect to the child.

68 Persons disqualified from being private foster parents

(1) Unless he has disclosed the fact to the appropriate local authority and obtained their written consent, a person shall not foster a child privately if he is disqualified from doing so by regulations made by the Secretary of State for the purposes of this section.

(2) The regulations may, in particular, provide for a person to be so disqualified where –

(a) an order of a kind specified in the regulations has been made at any time with respect to him;
(b) an order of a kind so specified has been made at any time with respect to any child who has been in his care;
(c) a requirement of a kind so specified has been imposed at any time with respect to any such child, under or by virtue of any enactment;
(d) he has been convicted of any offence of a kind so specified, or a probation order has been made in respect of him or he has been discharged absolutely or conditionally for any such offence;
(e) a prohibition has been imposed on him at any time under section 69 or under any other specified enactment;
(f) his rights and powers with respect to a child have at any time been vested in a specified authority under a specified enactment.

(3) Unless he has disclosed the fact to the appropriate local authority and obtained their written consent, a person shall not foster a child privately if –

(a) he lives in the same household as a person who is himself prevented from fostering a child by subsection (1); or
(b) he lives in a household at which any such person is employed.

(4) Where an authority refuse to give their consent under this section, they shall inform the applicant by a written notice which states –

(*a*) the reason for the refusal;
(*b*) the applicant's right under paragraph 8 of Schedule 8 to appeal against the refusal; and
(*c*) the time within which he may do so.

(5) In this section –

"the appropriate authority" means the local authority within whose area it is proposed to foster the child in question; and
"enactment" means any enactment having effect, at any time, in any part of the United Kingdom.

Amendments—Criminal Justice and Court Services Act 2000 s 74, Sch 7, para 94.

69 Power to prohibit private fostering

(1) This section applies where a person –

(*a*) proposes to foster a child privately; or
(*b*) is fostering a child privately.

(2) Where the local authority for the area within which the child is proposed to be, or is being, fostered are of the opinion that –

(*a*) he is not a suitable person to foster a child;
(*b*) the premises in which the child will be, or is being, accommodated are not suitable; or
(*c*) it would be prejudicial to the welfare of the child for him to be, or continue to be, accommodated by that person in those premises,

the authority may impose a prohibition on him under subsection (3).

(3) A prohibition imposed on any person under this subsection may prohibit him from fostering privately –

(*a*) any child in any premises within the area of the local authority; or
(*b*) any child in premises specified in the prohibition;
(*c*) a child identified in the prohibition, in premises specified in the prohibition.

(4) A local authority who have imposed a prohibition on any person under subsection (3) may, if they think fit, cancel the prohibition –

(*a*) of their own motion; or
(*b*) on an application made by that person,

if they are satisfied that the prohibition is no longer justified.

(5) Where a local authority impose a requirement on any person under paragraph 6 of Schedule 8, they may also impose a prohibition on him under subsection (3).

(6) Any prohibition imposed by virtue of subsection (5) shall not have effect unless –

(*a*) the time specified for compliance with the requirement has expired; and
(*b*) the requirement has not been complied with.

(7) A prohibition imposed under this section shall be imposed by notice in writing addressed to the person on whom it is imposed and informing him of –

(*a*) the reason for imposing the prohibition;
(*b*) his right under paragraph 8 of Schedule 8 to appeal against the prohibition; and
(*c*) the time within which he may do so.

70 Offences

(1) A person shall be guilty of an offence if –

(*a*) being required, under any provision made by or under this Part, to give any notice or information –
  (i) he fails without reasonable excuse to give the notice within the time specified in that provision; or
  (ii) he fails without reasonable excuse to give the information within a reasonable time; or
  (iii) he makes, or causes or procures another person to make, any statement in the notice or information which he knows to be false or misleading in a material particular;
(*b*) he refuses to allow a privately fostered child to be visited by a duly authorised officer of a local authority;
(*c*) he intentionally obstructs another in the exercise of the power conferred by section 67(3);
(*d*) he contravenes section 68;
(*e*) he fails without reasonable excuse to comply with any requirement imposed by a local authority under this Part;
(*f*) he accommodates a privately fostered child in any premises in contravention of a prohibition imposed by a local authority under this Part;
(*g*) he knowingly causes to be published, or publishes, an advertisement which he knows contravenes paragraph 10 of Schedule 8.

(2) Where a person contravenes section 68(3), he shall not be guilty of an offence under this section if he proves that he did not know, and had no reasonable ground for believing, that any person to whom section 68(1) applied was living or employed in the premises in question.

(3) A person guilty of an offence under subsection (1)(*a*) shall be liable on summary conviction to a fine not exceeding level 5 on the standard scale.

(4) A person guilty of an offence under subsection (1)(*b*), (*c*) or (*g*) shall be liable on summary conviction to a fine not exceeding level 3 on the standard scale.

(5) A person guilty of an offence under subsection (1)(*d*) or (*f*) shall be liable on summary conviction to imprisonment for a term not exceeding six months, or to a fine not exceeding level 5 on the standard scale, or to both.

(6) A person guilty of an offence under subsection (1)(*e*) shall be liable on summary conviction to a fine not exceeding level 4 on the standard scale.

(7) If any person who is required, under any provision of this Part, to give a notice fails to give the notice within the time specified in that provision, proceedings for the offence may be brought at any time within six months from the date when evidence of the offence came to the knowledge of the local authority.

(8) Subsection (7) is not affected by anything in section 127(1) of the Magistrates' Courts Act 1980 (time limit for proceedings).

****

PART II

PART XA
CHILD MINDING AND DAY CARE FOR CHILDREN IN ENGLAND AND WALES

Introductory

79A Child minders and day care providers

(1) This section and section 79B apply for the purposes of this Part.

(2) "Act as a child minder" means (subject to the following subsections) look after one or more children under the age of eight on domestic premises for reward; and "child minding" shall be interpreted accordingly.

(3) A person who –

(*a*) is the parent, or a relative, of a child;
(*b*) has parental responsibility for a child;
(*c*) is a local authority foster parent in relation to a child;
(*d*) is a foster parent with whom a child has been placed by a voluntary organisation; or
(*e*) fosters a child privately,

does not act as a child minder when looking after that child.

(4) Where a person –

(*a*) looks after a child for the parents ("P1"), or
(*b*) in addition to that work, looks after another child for different parents ("P2"),

and the work consists (in a case within paragraph (*a*)) of looking after the child wholly or mainly in P1's home or (in a case within paragraph (*b*)) of looking after the children wholly or mainly in P1's home or P2's home or both, the work is not to be treated as child minding.

(5) In subsection (4), "parent", in relation to a child, includes –

(*a*) a person who is not a parent of the child but who has parental responsibility for the child;
(*b*) a person who is a relative of the child.

(6) "Day care" means care provided at any time for children under the age of eight on premises other than domestic premises.

(7) This Part does not apply in relation to a person who acts as a child minder, or provides day care on any premises, unless the period, or the total of the periods, in any day which he spends looking after children or (as the case may be) during which the children are looked after on the premises exceeds two hours.

(8) In determining whether a person is required to register under this Part for child minding, any day on which he does not act as a child minder at any time between 2 am and 6 pm is to be disregarded.

Amendments—Inserted by Care Standards Act 2000, s 79(1).

79B Other definitions, etc

(1) The registration authority in relation to England is Her Majesty's Chief Inspector of Schools in England (referred to in this Part as the Chief Inspector) and references to the Chief Inspector's area are references to England.

(2) The registration authority in relation to Wales is the National Assembly for Wales (referred to in this Act as "the Assembly").

(3) A person is qualified for registration for child minding if –

(*a*) he, and every other person looking after children on any premises on which he is or is likely to be child minding, is suitable to look after children under the age of eight;
(*b*) every person living or employed on the premises in question is suitable to be in regular contact with children under the age of eight;
(*c*) the premises in question are suitable to be used for looking after children under the age of eight, having regard to their condition and the condition and appropriateness of any equipment on the premises and to any other factor connected with the situation, construction or size of the premises; and
(*d*) he is complying with regulations under section 79C and with any conditions imposed by the registration authority.

(4) A person is qualified for registration for providing day care on particular premises if –

(*a*) every person looking after children on the premises is suitable to look after children under the age of eight;
(*b*) every person living or working on the premises is suitable to be in regular contact with children under the age of eight;
(*c*) the premises are suitable to be used for looking after children under the age of eight, having regard to their condition and the condition and appropriateness of any equipment on the premises and to any other factor connected with the situation, construction or size of the premises; and
(*d*) he is complying with regulations under section 79C and with any conditions imposed by the registration authority.

(5) For the purposes of subsection (4)(*b*) a person is not treated as working on the premises in question if –

(*a*) none of his work is done in the part of the premises in which children are looked after; or
(*b*) he does not work on the premises at times when children are looked after there.

(6) "Domestic premises" means any premises which are wholly or mainly used as a private dwelling and "premises" includes any area and any vehicle.

(7) "Regulations" means –

(*a*) in relation to England, regulations made by the Secretary of State;
(*b*) in relation to Wales, regulations made by the Assembly.

(8) "Tribunal" means the Tribunal established by section 9 of the Protection of Children Act 1999.

(9) Schedule 9A (which supplements the provisions of this Part) shall have effect.

Amendments—Inserted by Care Standards Act 2000, s 79(1).

Regulations

79C Regulations etc governing child minders and day care providers

(1) The Secretary of State may, after consulting the Chief Inspector and any other person he considers appropriate, make regulations governing the activities of registered persons who act as child minders, or provide day care, on premises in England.

(2) The Assembly may make regulations governing the activities of registered persons who act as child minders, or provide day care, on premises in Wales.

(3) The regulations under this section may deal with the following matters (among others) –

- (*a*) the welfare and development of the children concerned;
- (*b*) suitability to look after, or be in regular contact with, children under the age of eight;
- (*c*) qualifications and training;
- (*d*) the maximum number of children who may be looked after and the number of persons required to assist in looking after them;
- (*e*) the maintenance, safety and suitability of premises and equipment;
- (*f*) the keeping of records;
- (*g*) the provision of information.

(4) In relation to activities on premises in England, the power to make regulations under this section may be exercised so as to confer powers or impose duties on the Chief Inspector in the exercise of his functions under this Part.

(5) In particular they may be exercised so as to require or authorise the Chief Inspector, in exercising those functions, to have regard to or meet factors, standards and other matters prescribed by or referred to in the regulations.

(6) If the regulations require any person (other than the registration authority) to have regard to or meet factors, standards and other matters prescribed by or referred to in the regulations, they may also provide for any allegation that the person has failed to do so to be taken into account –

- (*a*) by the registration authority in the exercise of its functions under this Part, or
- (*b*) in any proceedings under this Part.

(7) Regulations may provide –

- (*a*) that a registered person who without reasonable excuse contravenes, or otherwise fails to comply with, any requirement of the regulations shall be guilty of an offence; and
- (*b*) that a person guilty of the offence shall be liable on summary conviction to a fine not exceeding level 5 on the standard scale.

Amendments—Inserted by Care Standards Act 2000, s 79(1).

Registration

79D Requirement to register

(1) No person shall –

- (*a*) act as a child minder in England unless he is registered under this Part for child minding by the Chief Inspector; or (*b*) act as a child minder in Wales unless he is registered under this Part for child minding by the Assembly.

(2) Where it appears to the registration authority that a person has contravened subsection (1), the authority may serve a notice ("an enforcement notice") on him.

(3) An enforcement notice shall have effect for a period of one year beginning with the date on which it is served.

(4) If a person in respect of whom an enforcement notice has effect contravenes subsection (1) without reasonable excuse (whether the contravention occurs in England or Wales), he shall be guilty of an offence.

(5) No person shall provide day care on any premises unless he is registered under this Part for providing day care on those premises by the registration authority.

(6) If any person contravenes subsection (5) without reasonable excuse, he shall be guilty of an offence.

(7) A person guilty of an offence under this section shall be liable on summary conviction to a fine not exceeding level 5 on the standard scale.

Amendments—Inserted by Care Standards Act 2000, s 79(1).

79E Applications for registration

(1) A person who wishes to be registered under this Part shall make an application to the registration authority.

(2) The application shall –

(*a*) give prescribed information about prescribed matters;
(*b*) give any other information which the registration authority reasonably requires the applicant to give.

(3) Where a person provides, or proposes to provide, day care on different premises, he shall make a separate application in respect of each of them.

(4) Where the registration authority has sent the applicant notice under section 79L(1) of its intention to refuse an application under this section, the application may not be withdrawn without the consent of the authority.

(5) A person who, in an application under this section, knowingly makes a statement which is false or misleading in a material particular shall be guilty of an offence and liable, on summary conviction, to a fine not exceeding level 5 on the standard scale.

Amendments—Inserted by Care Standards Act 2000, s 79(1).

79F Grant or refusal of registration

(1) If, on an application by a person for registration for child minding –

(*a*) the registration authority is of the opinion that the applicant is, and will continue to be, qualified for registration for child minding (so far as the conditions of section 79B(3) are applicable); and
(*b*) the applicant pays the prescribed fee,

the authority shall grant the application; otherwise, it shall refuse it.

(2) If, on an application by any person for registration for providing day care on any premises –

(*a*) the registration authority is of the opinion that the applicant is, and will continue to be, qualified for registration for providing day care on those premises (so far as the conditions of section 79B(4) are applicable); and

(*b*) the applicant pays the prescribed fee,

the authority shall grant the application; otherwise, it shall refuse it.

(3) An application may, as well as being granted subject to any conditions the authority thinks necessary or expedient for the purpose of giving effect to regulations under section 79C, be granted subject to any other conditions the authority thinks fit to impose.

(4) The registration authority may as it thinks fit vary or remove any condition to which the registration is subject or impose a new condition.

(5) Any register kept by a registration authority of persons who act as child minders or provide day care shall be open to inspection by any person at all reasonable times.

(6) A registered person who without reasonable excuse contravenes, or otherwise fails to comply with, any condition imposed on his registration shall be guilty of an offence.

(7) A person guilty of an offence under subsection (6) shall be liable on summary conviction to a fine not exceeding level 5 on the standard scale.

Amendments—Inserted by Care Standards Act 2000, s 79(1).

79G Cancellation of registration

(1) The registration authority may cancel the registration of any person if –

(*a*) in the case of a person registered for child minding, the authority is of the opinion that the person has ceased or will cease to be qualified for registration for child minding;

(*b*) in the case of a person registered for providing day care on any premises, the authority is of the opinion that the person has ceased or will cease to be qualified for registration for providing day care on those premises,

or if an annual fee which is due from the person has not been paid.

(2) Where a requirement to make any changes or additions to any services, equipment or premises has been imposed on a registered person under section 79F(3), his registration shall not be cancelled on the ground of any defect or insufficiency in the services, equipment or premises if –

(*a*) the time set for complying with the requirements has not expired; and

(*b*) it is shown that the defect or insufficiency is due to the changes or additions not having been made.

(3) Any cancellation under this section must be in writing.

Amendments—Inserted by Care Standards Act 2000, s 79(1).

79H Suspension of registration

(1) Regulations may provide for the registration of any person for acting as a child minder or providing day care to be suspended for a prescribed period by the registration authority in prescribed circumstances.

PART II

(2) Any regulations made under this section shall include provision conferring on the person concerned a right of appeal to the Tribunal against suspension.

Amendments—Inserted by Care Standards Act 2000, s 79(1).

79J Resignation of registration

(1) A person who is registered for acting as a child minder or providing day care may by notice in writing to the registration authority resign his registration.

(2) But a person may not give a notice under subsection (1) –

(*a*) if the registration authority has sent him a notice under section 79L(1) of its intention to cancel the registration, unless the authority has decided not to take that step; or

(*b*) if the registration authority has sent him a notice under section 79L(5) of its decision to cancel the registration and the time within which an appeal may be brought has not expired or, if an appeal has been brought, it has not been determined.

Amendments—Inserted by Care Standards Act 2000, s 79(1).

79K Protection of children in an emergency

(1) If, in the case of any person registered for acting as a child minder or providing day care –

(*a*) the registration authority applies to a justice of the peace for an order –

(i) cancelling the registration;

(ii) varying or removing any condition to which the registration is subject; or

(iii) imposing a new condition; and

(*b*) it appears to the justice that a child who is being, or may be, looked after by that person, or (as the case may be) in accordance with the provision for day care made by that person, is suffering, or is likely to suffer, significant harm,

the justice may make the order.

(2) The cancellation, variation, removal or imposition shall have effect from the time when the order is made.

(3) An application under subsection (1) may be made without notice.

(4) An order under subsection (1) shall be made in writing.

(5) Where an order is made under this section, the registration authority shall serve on the registered person, as soon as is reasonably practicable after the making of the order –

(*a*) a copy of the order;

(*b*) a copy of any written statement of the authority's reasons for making the application for the order which supported that application; and

(*c*) notice of any right of appeal conferred by section 79M.

(6) Where an order has been so made, the registration authority shall, as soon as is reasonably practicable after the making of the order, notify the local authority in whose area the person concerned acts or acted as a child minder, or provides or provided day care, of the making of the order.

Amendments—Inserted by Care Standards Act 2000, s 79(1).

Procedure – applications without notice—Section 79K authorises without notice applications and where the justice of the peace accedes to such an application he or she must make the order in writing. The with notice procedure in s 79L (below) obviously does not apply to such applications, but it should be used when circumstances permit. It is suggested that it would nevertheless be sensible for the authority, in without notice applications to the court, to follow the procedure in FPC(CA 1989)R 1991, r 4 and to use Form C5 so as to give a written statement of their reasons, indicating at paragraph 2 "**About the Respondent**" that the application will be made without notice. The order should be on Form C41.

There appears, however, to be no requirement for an order made without notice to be served on the person registered; it only has to be served on the registration authority who, in turn, notify the local authority in whose area the person concerned acts as child minder or as a provider of day care. Section 79M provides a right of appeal to the Tribunal against any order made under s 79K.

Under the repealed s 75 there was provision for notice of the order, and a copy of the authority's reasons supporting the application, to be served on the person registered as soon as possible after the making of the order. However, it is suggested that it would constitute good practice for the authority to continue to serve a copy of the order and a copy of the authority's reasons supporting the application for the order on the person registered, as previously required by s 75(4), since the person registered will need this information in order to decide whether to appeal to the Tribunal or, alternatively, whether it is appropriate to pursue redress through judicial review (see *R v St Albans Magistrates' Court ex parte J* [1993] Fam Law 518 for the principles applied under the pre-existing law).

79L Notice of intention to take steps

(1) Not less than 14 days before –

(*a*) refusing an application for registration;
(*b*) cancelling a registration;
(*c*) removing or varying any condition to which a registration is subject or imposing a new condition; or
(*d*) refusing to grant an application for the removal or variation of any condition to which a registration is subject,

the registration authority shall send to the applicant, or (as the case may be) registered person, notice in writing of its intention to take the step in question.

(2) Every such notice shall –

(*a*) give the authority's reasons for proposing to take the step; and
(*b*) inform the person concerned of his rights under this section.

(3) Where the recipient of such a notice informs the authority in writing of his desire to object to the step being taken, the authority shall afford him an opportunity to do so.

(4) Any objection made under subsection (3) may be made orally or in writing, by the recipient of the notice or a representative.

(5) If the authority, after giving the person concerned an opportunity to object to the step being taken, decides nevertheless to take it, it shall send him written notice of its decision.

(6) A step of a kind mentioned in subsection (1)(*b*) or (*c*) shall not take effect until the expiry of the time within which an appeal may be brought under section 79M or, where such an appeal is brought, before its determination.

(7) Subsection (6) does not prevent a step from taking effect before the expiry of the time within which an appeal may be brought under section 79M if the person concerned notifies the registration authority in writing that he does not intend to appeal.

Amendments—Inserted by Care Standards Act 2000, s 79(1).

Procedure – applications with notice—Although s 79K(3) (above) permits an application to be made without notice to the person registered, the with notice procedure in this section should be used when circumstances permit. It would appear that the registration authority alone has the power to grant or refuse the application. Section 79M provides a right of appeal to the Tribunal against any step mentioned in s 79L(1). On an appeal, the Tribunal will be able to (*a*) confirm the taking of the step or the making of the order or direct that it shall not have, or shall cease to have, effect; and (*b*) impose, vary or cancel any condition.

79M Appeals

(1) An appeal against –

(*a*) the taking of any step mentioned in section 79L(1); or
(*b*) an order under section 79K,

shall lie to the Tribunal.

(2) On an appeal, the Tribunal may –

(*a*) confirm the taking of the step or the making of the order or direct that it shall not have, or shall cease to have, effect; and
(*b*) impose, vary or cancel any condition.

Amendments—Inserted by Care Standards Act 2000, s 79(1).

Procedure—It is likely that the procedure to be followed by the Care Standards Tribunal will be a a rehearing rather than a review of the decision which is the subject of appeal (*Tameside Metropolitan Borough Council v Grant* [2002] 1 FLR 318: a decision on the now repealed CA 1989, s 71). Where there is a right of appeal to the Care Standards Tribunal, judicial review is not appropriate (*R(M) v London Borough of Bromley* [2002] EWCA Civ 1113, [2002] 2 FLR 802).

Inspection: England

79N General functions of the Chief Inspector

(1) The Chief Inspector has the general duty of keeping the Secretary of State informed about the quality and standards of child minding and day care provided by registered persons in England.

(2) When asked to do so by the Secretary of State, the Chief Inspector shall give advice or information to the Secretary of State about such matters relating to the provision of child minding or day care by registered persons in England as may be specified in the Secretary of State's request.

(3) The Chief Inspector may at any time give advice to the Secretary of State, either generally or in relation to provision by particular persons or on particular premises, on any matter connected with the provision of child minding or day care by registered persons in England.

(4) The Chief Inspector may secure the provision of training for persons who provide or assist in providing child minding or day care, or intend to do so.

(5) Regulations may confer further functions on the Chief Inspector relating to child minding and day care provided in England.

(6) The annual reports of the Chief Inspector required by subsection (7)(*a*) of section 2 of the School Inspections Act 1996 to be made to the Secretary of State shall include an account of the exercise of the Chief Inspector's functions under this Part, and the power conferred by subsection (7)(*b*) of that section to make

other reports to the Secretary of State includes a power to make reports with respect to matters which fall within the scope of his functions by virtue of this Part.

Amendments—Inserted by Care Standards Act 2000, s 79(1).

79P Early years child care inspectorate

(1) The Chief Inspector shall establish and maintain a register of early years child care inspectors for England.

(2) The register may be combined with the register maintained for England under paragraph 8(1) of Schedule 26 to the School Standards and Framework Act 1998 (register of nursery education inspectors).

(3) Paragraphs 8(2) to (8), 9(1) to (4), 10 and 11 of that Schedule shall apply in relation to the register of early years child care inspectors as they apply in relation to the register maintained for England under paragraph 8(1) of that Schedule, but with the modifications set out in subsection (4).

(4) In the provisions concerned –

(*a*) references to registered nursery education inspectors shall be read as references to registered early years child care inspectors;

(*b*) references to inspections under paragraph 6 of that Schedule shall be read as references to inspections under section 79Q (and references to the functions of a registered nursery education inspector under paragraph 6 shall be interpreted accordingly);

(*c*) references to the registration of a person under paragraph 6 of that Schedule shall be read as references to the registration of a person under subsection (1) (and references to applications made under paragraph 6 shall be interpreted accordingly);

(*d*) ...

(5) Registered early years child care inspectors are referred to below in this Part as registered inspectors.

Amendments—Inserted by Care Standards Act 2000, s 79(1); amended by Education Act 2002, s 155, Sch 14, para 4.

79Q Inspection of provision of child minding and day care in England

(1) The Chief Inspector may at any time require any registered person to provide him with any information connected with the person's activities as a child minder, or provision of day care, which the Chief Inspector considers it necessary to have for the purposes of his functions under this Part.

(2) The Chief Inspector shall at prescribed intervals inspect, or secure the inspection by a registered inspector of, any child minding provided in England by a registered person.

(3) The Chief Inspector shall at prescribed intervals inspect, or secure the inspection by a registered inspector of, any day care provided by a registered person on any premises in England.

(4) The Chief Inspector may comply with subsection (2) or (3) either by organising inspections or by making arrangements with others for them to organise inspections.

(5) In prescribing the intervals mentioned in subsection (2) or (3) the Secretary of State may make provision as to the period within which the first inspection of child minding or day care provided by any person or at any premises is to take place.

(6) A person conducting an inspection under this section shall report on the quality and standards of the child minding or day care provided.

(7) The Chief Inspector may arrange for an inspection conducted by a registered inspector under this section to be monitored by another registered inspector.

Amendments—Inserted by Care Standards Act 2000, s 79(1); amended by Education Act 2002, s 152, Sch 13, para 4.

79R Reports of inspections

(1) A person who has conducted an inspection under section 79Q shall report in writing on the matters inspected to the Chief Inspector within the prescribed period.

(2) The period mentioned in subsection (1) may, if the Chief Inspector considers it necessary, be extended by up to three months.

(3) Once the report of an inspection has been made to the Chief Inspector under subsection (1) he –

(*a*) may send a copy of it to the Secretary of State, and shall do so without delay if the Secretary of State requests a copy;
(*b*) shall send a copy of it, or of such parts of it as he considers appropriate, to any prescribed authorities or persons; and
(*c*) may arrange for the report (or parts of it) to be further published in any manner he considers appropriate.

(4) Subsections (2) to (4) of section 42A of the School Inspections Act 1996 shall apply in relation to the publication of any report under subsection (3) as they apply in relation to the publication of a report under any of the provisions mentioned in subsection (2) of section 42A.

Amendments—Inserted by Care Standards Act 2000, s 79(1).

****

Supplementary

79U Rights of entry etc

(1) Any person authorised for the purposes of this subsection by the registration authority may at any reasonable time enter any premises in England or Wales on which child minding or day care is at any time provided.

(2) Where a person who is authorised for the purposes of this subsection by the registration authority has reasonable cause to believe that a child is being looked after on any premises in contravention of this Part, he may enter those premises at any reasonable time.

(2A) Authorisation under subsection (1) or (2) –

(*a*) may be given for a particular occasion or period;
(*b*) may be given subject to conditions.

(3) A person entering premises under this section may (subject to any conditions imposed under subsection (2A)(*b*)) –

(*a*) inspect the premises;
(*b*) inspect, and take copies of –
  (i) any records kept by the person providing the child minding or day care; and
  (ii) any other documents containing information relating to its provision;
(*c*) seize and remove any document or other material or thing found there which he has reasonable grounds to believe may be evidence of a failure to comply with any condition or requirement imposed by or under this Part;
(*d*) require any person to afford him such facilities and assistance with respect to matters within the person's control as are necessary to enable him to exercise his powers under this section;
(*e*) take measurements and photographs or make recordings;
(*f*) inspect any children being looked after there, and the arrangements made for their welfare;
(*g*) interview in private the person providing the child minding or day care; and
(*h*) interview in private any person looking after children, or living or working, there who consents to be interviewed.

(4) Section 42 of the School Inspections Act 1996 (inspection of computer records for purposes of Part I of that Act) shall apply for the purposes of subsection (3) as it applies for the purposes of Part I of that Act.

(5) (*repealed*)

(6) A person exercising any power conferred by this section shall, if so required, produce some duly authenticated document showing his authority to do so.

(7) It shall be an offence wilfully to obstruct a person exercising any such power.

(8) Any person guilty of an offence under subsection (7) shall be liable on summary conviction to a fine not exceeding level 4 on the standard scale.

(9) In this section –

"documents" and "records" each include information recorded in any form.

Amendments—Inserted by Care Standards Act 2000, s 79(1); amended by Education Act 2002, s 152, Sch 13, para 5.

79V Function of local authorities

Each local authority shall, in accordance with regulations, secure the provision –

(*a*) of information and advice about child minding and day care; and
(*b*) of training for persons who provide or assist in providing child minding or day care.

Amendments—Inserted by Care Standards Act 2000, s 79(1).

PART II

Checks on suitability of persons working with children over the age of seven

79W Requirement for certificate of suitability

(1) This section applies to any person not required to register under this Part who looks after, or provides care for, children and meets the following conditions.

References in this section to children are to those under the age of 15 or (in the case of disabled children) 17.

(2) The first condition is that the period, or the total of the periods, in any week which he spends looking after children or (as the case may be) during which the children are looked after exceeds five hours.

(3) The second condition is that he would be required to register under this Part (or, as the case may be, this Part if it were subject to prescribed modifications) if the children were under the age of eight.

(4) Regulations may require a person to whom this section applies to hold a certificate issued by the registration authority as to his suitability, and the suitability of each prescribed person, to look after children.

(5) The regulations may make provision about –

(*a*) applications for certificates;
(*b*) the matters to be taken into account by the registration authority in determining whether to issue certificates;
(*c*) the information to be contained in certificates;
(*d*) the period of their validity.

(6) The regulations may provide that a person to whom this section applies shall be guilty of an offence –

(*a*) if he does not hold a certificate as required by the regulations; or
(*b*) if, being a person who holds such a certificate, he fails to produce it when reasonably required to do so by a prescribed person.

(7) The regulations may provide that a person who, for the purpose of obtaining such a certificate, knowingly makes a statement which is false or misleading in a material particular shall be guilty of an offence.

(8) The regulations may provide that a person guilty of an offence under the regulations shall be liable on summary conviction to a fine not exceeding level 5 on the standard scale.

Amendments—Inserted by Care Standards Act 2000, s 79(1).

Time limit for proceedings

79X Time limit for proceedings

Proceedings for an offence under this Part or regulations made under it may be brought within a period of six months from the date on which evidence sufficient in the opinion of the prosecutor to warrant the proceedings came to his knowledge; but no such proceedings shall be brought by virtue of this section more than three years after the commission of the offence.

Amendments—Inserted by Care Standards Act 2000, s 79(1).

PART XI
SECRETARY OF STATE'S SUPERVISORY FUNCTIONS AND RESPONSIBILITIES

80 Inspection of children's homes etc by persons authorised by Secretary of State

(1) The Secretary of State may cause to be inspected from time to time any –

(*a*) private children's home;
(*b*) premises in which a child who is being looked after by a local authority is living;
(*c*) premises in which a child who is being accommodated by or on behalf of a local education authority or voluntary organisation is living;
(*d*) premises in which a child who is being accommodated by or on behalf of a Health Authority, Special Health Authority, Primary Care Trust or National Health Service trust is living;
(*e*) premises in which a child is living with a person with whom he has been placed by an adoption agency;
(*f*) premises in which a child who is a protected child is, or will be, living;
(*g*) premises in which a privately fostered child, or child who is treated as a foster child by virtue of paragraph 9 of Schedule 8, is living or in which it is proposed that he will live;
(*h*) premises on which any person is acting as a child minder;
(*i*) premises with respect to which a person is registered under section 71(1)(*b*) or with respect to which a person is registered for providing day care under Part XA;
(*j*) care home or independent hospital used to accommodate children;
(*k*) premises which are provided by a local authority and in which any service is provided by that authority under Part III;
(*l*) school or college providing accommodation for any child.

(2) An inspection under this section shall be conducted by a person authorised to do so by the Secretary of State.

(3) An officer of a local authority shall not be authorised except with the consent of that authority.

(4) The Secretary of State may require any person of a kind mentioned in subsection (5) to furnish him with such information, or allow him to inspect such records (in whatever form they are held), relating to –

(*a*) any premises to which subsection (1) or, in relation to Scotland, subsection (1)(*h*) or (*i*) applies;
(*b*) any child who is living in any such premises;
(*c*) the discharge by the Secretary of State of any of his functions under this Act; or
(*d*) the discharge by any local authority of any of their functions under this Act,

as the Secretary of State may at any time direct.

(5) The persons are any –

(*a*) local authority;
(*b*) voluntary organisation;
(*c*) person carrying on a private children's home;

(*d*) proprietor of an independent school or governing body of any other school;
(*da*) governing body of an institution designated under section 28 of the Further and Higher Education Act 1992;
(*db*) further education corporation;
(*e*) person fostering any privately fostered child or providing accommodation for a child on behalf of a local authority, local education authority, Health Authority, Special Health Authority, Primary Care Trust, National Health Service trust or voluntary organisation;
(*f*) local education authority providing accommodation for any child;
(*g*) person employed in a teaching or administrative capacity at any educational establishment (whether or not maintained by a local education authority) at which a child is accommodated on behalf of a local authority or local education authority;
(*h*) person who is the occupier of any premises in which any person acts as a child minder (within the meaning of Part X) or provides day care for young children (within the meaning of that Part);
(*hh*) person who is the occupier of any premises –
  (i) in which any person required to be registered for child minding under Part XA acts as a child minder (within the meaning of that Part); or
  (ii) with respect to which a person is required to be registered under that Part for providing day care;
(*i*) person carrying on any home of a kind mentioned in subsection (1)(*j*);
(*j*) person carrying on a fostering agency.

(6) Any person inspecting any home or other premises under this section may –

(*a*) inspect the children there; and
(*b*) make such examination into the state and management of the home or premises and the treatment of the children there as he thinks fit.

(7) Any person authorised by the Secretary of State to exercise the power to inspect records conferred by subsection (4) –

(*a*) shall be entitled at any reasonable time to have access to, and inspect and check the operation of, any computer and any associated apparatus or material which is or has been in use in connection with the records in question; and
(*b*) may require –
  (i) the person by whom or on whose behalf the computer is or has been so used; or
  (ii) any person having charge of, or otherwise concerned with the operation of, the computer, apparatus or material,

to afford him such reasonable assistance as he may require.

(8) A person authorised to inspect any premises under this section shall have a right to enter the premises for that purpose, and for any purpose specified in subsection (4), at any reasonable time.

(9) Any person exercising that power shall, if so required, produce some duly authenticated document showing his authority to do so.

(10) Any person who intentionally obstructs another in the exercise of that power shall be guilty of an offence and liable on summary conviction to a fine not exceeding level 3 on the standard scale.

(11) The Secretary of State may by order provide for subsections (1), (4) and (6) not to apply in relation to such homes, or other premises, as may be specified in the order.

(12) Without prejudice to section 104, any such order may make different provision with respect to each of those subsections.

(13) In this section –

"college" means an institution within the further education sector as defined in section 91 of the Further and Higher Education Act 1992;

"fostering agency" has the same meaning as in the Care Standards Act 2000;

"further education corporation" has the same meaning as in the Further and Higher Education Act 1992.

Amendments—National Health Service and Community Care Act 1990, s 66(1), Sch 9, para 36(4); Health Authorities Act 1995, s 2, Sch 1, para 118; Care Standards Act 2000, ss 109, 116, Sch 4, para 14(16); SI 2000/90.

81 Inquiries

(1) The Secretary of State may cause an inquiry to be held into any matter connected with –

(*a*) the functions of a local authority which are social services functions within the meaning of the Local Authority Social Services Act 1970, in so far as those functions relate to children;

(*b*) the functions of an adoption agency;

(*c*) the functions of a voluntary organisation, in so far as those functions relate to children;

(*d*) a private children's home or voluntary home;

(*e*) a care home or independent hospital, so far as it provides accommodation for children;

(*f*) a home provided in accordance with arrangements made by the Secretary of State under section 82(5);

(*g*) the detention of a child under section 92 of the Powers of Criminal Courts (Sentencing) Act 2000.

(2) Before an inquiry is begun, the Secretary of State may direct that it shall be held in private.

(3) Where no direction has been given, the person holding the inquiry may if he thinks fit hold it, or any part of it, in private.

(4) Subsections (2) to (5) of section 250 of the Local Government Act 1972 (powers in relation to local inquiries) shall apply in relation to an inquiry under this section as they apply in relation to a local inquiry under that section.

(5) In this section "functions" includes powers and duties which a person has otherwise than by virtue of any enactment.

Amendments—Courts and Legal Services Act 1990, ss 116, 125(7), Sch 16, para 21, Sch 20; Local Government Act 2000, s 107(1), Sch 5, para 21; Powers of Criminal Courts (Sentencing) Act 2000, s 165, Sch 9, para 128; Care Standards Act 2000, s 116, Sch 4, para 14(17).

82 Financial support by Secretary of State

(1) The Secretary of State may (with the consent of the Treasury) defray or contribute towards –

(*a*) any fees or expenses incurred by any person undergoing approved child care training;

(*b*) any fees charged, or expenses incurred, by any person providing approved child care training or preparing material for use in connection with such training; or

(*c*) the cost of maintaining any person undergoing such training.

(2) The Secretary of State may make grants to local authorities in respect of expenditure incurred by them in providing secure accommodation in community homes other than assisted community homes.

(3) Where –

(*a*) a grant has been made under subsection (2) with respect to any secure accommodation; but

(*b*) the grant is not used for the purpose for which it was made or the accommodation is not used as, or ceases to be used as, secure accommodation,

the Secretary of State may (with the consent of the Treasury) require the authority concerned to repay the grant, in whole or in part.

(4) The Secretary of State may make grants to voluntary organisations towards –

(*a*) expenditure incurred by them in connection with the establishment, maintenance or improvement of voluntary homes which, at the time when the expenditure was incurred –

(i) were assisted community homes; or

(ii) were designated as such; or

(*b*) expenses incurred in respect of the borrowing of money to defray any such expenditure.

(5) The Secretary of State may arrange for the provision, equipment and maintenance of homes for the accommodation of children who are in need of particular facilities and services which –

(*a*) are or will be provided in those homes; and

(*b*) in the opinion of the Secretary of State, are unlikely to be readily available in community homes.

(6) In this Part –

"child care training" means training undergone by any person with a view to, or in the course of –

(*a*) his employment for the purposes of any of the functions mentioned in section 83(9) or in connection with the adoption of children or with the accommodation of children in a care home or independent hospital; or

(*b*) his employment by a voluntary organisation for similar purposes;

"approved child care training" means child care training which is approved by the Secretary of State; and

"secure accommodation" means accommodation provided for the purpose of restricting the liberty of children.

(7) Any grant made under this section shall be of such amount, and shall be subject to such conditions, as the Secretary of State may (with the consent of the Treasury) determine.

Amendments—Care Standards Act 2000, s 116, Sch 4, para 14(18).

83 Research and returns of information

(1) The Secretary of State may conduct, or assist other persons in conducting, research into any matter connected with –

(*a*) his functions, or the functions of local authorities, under the enactments mentioned in subsection (9);
(*b*) the adoption of children; or
(*c*) the accommodation of children in a care home or independent hospital.

(2) Any local authority may conduct, or assist other persons in conducting, research into any matter connected with –

(*a*) their functions under the enactments mentioned in subsection (9);
(*b*) the adoption of children; or
(*c*) the accommodation of children in a care home or independent hospital.

(3) Every local authority shall, at such times and in such form as the Secretary of State may direct, transmit to him such particulars as he may require with respect to –

(*a*) the performance by the local authority of all or any of their functions –
(i) under the enactments mentioned in subsection (9); or
(ii) in connection with the accommodation of children in a care home or independent hospital; and
(*b*) the children in relation to whom the authority have exercised those functions.

(4) Every voluntary organisation shall, at such times and in such form as the Secretary of State may direct, transmit to him such particulars as he may require with respect to children accommodated by them or on their behalf.

(5) The Secretary of State may direct the justices' chief executive for each magistrates' court to which the direction is expressed to relate to transmit –

(*a*) to such person as may be specified in the direction; and
(*b*) at such times and in such form as he may direct,

such particulars as he may require with respect to proceedings of the court which relate to children.

(6) The Secretary of State shall in each year lay before Parliament a consolidated and classified abstract of the information transmitted to him under subsections (3) to (5).

(7) The Secretary of State may institute research designed to provide information on which requests for information under this section may be based.

(8) The Secretary of State shall keep under review the adequacy of the provision of child care training and for that purpose shall receive and consider any information from or representations made by –

(*a*) the Central Council for Education and Training in Social Work;
(*b*) such representatives of local authorities as appear to him to be appropriate; or
(*c*) such other persons or organisations as appear to him to be appropriate,

concerning the provision of such training.

(9) The enactments are –

(*a*) this Act;
(*b*) the Children and Young Persons Acts 1933 to 1969;

(*c*) section 116 of the Mental Health Act 1983 (so far as it relates to children looked after by local authorities);
(*d*) section 10 of the Mental Health (Scotland) Act 1984 (so far as it relates to children for whom local authorities have responsibility).

Amendments—Access to Justice Act 1999, s 90, Sch 13, para 160; Care Standards Act 2000, s 116, Sch 4, para 14(19).

84 Local authority failure to comply with statutory duty: default power of Secretary of State

(1) If the Secretary of State is satisfied that any local authority has failed, without reasonable excuse, to comply with any of the duties imposed on them by or under this Act he may make an order declaring that authority to be in default with respect to that duty.

(2) An order under subsection (1) shall give the Secretary of State's reasons for making it.

(3) An order under subsection (1) may contain such directions for the purpose of ensuring that the duty is complied with, within such period as may be specified in the order, as appear to the Secretary of State to be necessary.

(4) Any such direction shall, on the application of the Secretary of State, be enforceable by mandamus.

Defined terms—"local authority": s 105(1).

Scope of provision—This section does not confer either an express or an implied right on any individual to appeal from a decision by a local authority by which he is aggrieved and, although the existence of a default power such as s 84 can be taken into consideration by the court as an avenue of redress alternative to judicial review, it can be wrong, in view of the particular features of s 84, to treat it as a more suitable remedy for an individual than judicial review (*R v London Borough of Brent ex parte S* [1994] 1 FLR 203, CA).

There exists under s 26(3) a representation procedure which can be used by a person aggrieved by the way in which a local authority has exercised its functions, and this may have relevance as to whether relief will be granted in judicial review proceedings (see *R v London Borough of Brent ex parte S* (above), *R v Royal Borough of Kingston upon Thames ex parte T* [1994] 1 FLR 798, QBD, *R v London Borough of Barnet ex parte B* [1994] 1 FLR 592, QBD, *R v Birmingham City Council ex parte A* [1997] 2 FLR 841, QBD, and *R v East Sussex CC ex parte W* [1998] 2 FLR 1082, QBD).

In *R v Hampshire CC ex parte H* [1999] 2 FLR 359, CA, judicial review was held to be appropriate in relation to a decision of a local authority case conference.

PART XII
MISCELLANEOUS AND GENERAL

Notification of children accommodated in certain establishments

85 Children accommodated by health authorities and local education authorities

(1) Where a child is provided with accommodation by any Health Authority, Special Health Authority, Primary Care Trust, National Health Service trust or local education authority ("the accommodating authority") –

(*a*) for a consecutive period of at least three months; or
(*b*) with the intention, on the part of that authority, of accommodating him for such a period,

the accommodating authority shall notify the responsible authority.

(2) Where subsection (1) applies with respect to a child, the accommodating authority shall also notify the responsible authority when they cease to accommodate the child.

(3) In this section "the responsible authority" means –

(*a*) the local authority appearing to the accommodating authority to be the authority within whose area the child was ordinarily resident immediately before being accommodated; or

(*b*) where it appears to the accommodating authority that a child was not ordinarily resident within the area of any local authority, the local authority within whose area the accommodation is situated.

(4) Where a local authority have been notified under this section, they shall –

(*a*) take such steps as are reasonably practicable to enable them to determine whether the child's welfare is adequately safeguarded and promoted while he is accommodated by the accommodating authority; and

(*b*) consider the extent to which (if at all) they should exercise any of their functions under this Act with respect to the child.

Amendments—National Health Service and Community Care Act 1990, s 66(1), Sch 9, para 36; Health Authorities Act 1995, s 2, Sch 1, para 118; SI 2000/90.

86 Children accommodated in care homes or independent hospitals

(1) Where a child is provided with accommodation in any care home or independent hospital –

(*a*) for a consecutive period of at least three months; or

(*b*) with the intention, on the part of the person taking the decision to accommodate him, of accommodating him for such period,

the person carrying on the home shall notify the local authority within whose area the home is carried on.

(2) Where subsection (1) applies with respect to a child, the person carrying on the home shall also notify that authority when he ceases to accommodate the child in the home.

(3) Where a local authority have been notified under this section, they shall –

(*a*) take such steps as are reasonably practicable to enable them to determine whether the child's welfare is adequately safeguarded and promoted while he is accommodated in the home; and

(*b*) consider the extent to which (if at all) they should exercise any of their functions under this Act with respect to the child.

(4) If the person carrying on any home fails, without reasonable excuse, to comply with this section he shall be guilty of an offence.

(5) A person authorised by a local authority may enter any care home or independent hospital within the authority's area for the purpose of establishing whether the requirements of this section have been complied with.

(6) Any person who intentionally obstructs another in the exercise of the power of entry shall be guilty of an offence.

(7) Any person exercising the power of entry shall, if so required, produce some duly authenticated document showing his authority to do so.

(8) Any person committing an offence under this section shall be liable on summary conviction to a fine not exceeding level 3 on the standard scale.

Amendments—Care Standards Act 2000, s 116, Sch 4, para 14(20).

87 Welfare of children in boarding schools and colleges

(1) Where a school or college provides accommodation for any child, it shall be the duty of the relevant person to safeguard and promote the child's welfare.

(2) Subsection (1) does not apply in relation to a school or college which is a children's home or care home.

(3) Where accommodation is provided for a child by any school or college the appropriate authority shall take such steps as are reasonably practicable to enable them to determine whether the child's welfare is adequately safeguarded and promoted while he is accommodated by the school or college.

(4) Where the Commission are of the opinion that there has been a failure to comply with subsection (1) in relation to a child provided with accommodation by a school or college, they shall –

- (*a*) in the case of a school other than an independent school or a special school, notify the local education authority for the area in which the school is situated;
- (*b*) in the case of a special school which is maintained by a local education authority, notify that authority;
- (*c*) in any other case, notify the Secretary of State.

(4A) Where the National Assembly for Wales are of the opinion that there has been a failure to comply with subsection (1) in relation to a child provided with accommodation by a school or college, they shall –

- (*a*) in the case of a school other than an independent school or a special school, notify the local education authority for the area in which the school is situated;
- (*b*) in the case of a special school which is maintained by a local education authority, notify that authority;

(5) Where accommodation is, or is to be, provided for a child by any school or college, a person authorised by the appropriate authority may, for the purpose of enabling that authority to discharge its duty under this section, enter at any time premises which are, or are to be, premises of the school or college.

(6) Any person exercising the power conferred by subsection (5) may carry out such inspection of premises, children and records as is prescribed by regulations made by the Secretary of State for the purposes of this section.

(7) Any person exercising that power shall, if asked to do so, produce some duly authenticated document showing his authority to do so.

(8) Any person authorised by the regulations to inspect records –

- (*a*) shall be entitled at any reasonable time to have access to, and inspect and check the operation of, any computer and any associated apparatus or material which is or has been in use in connection with the records in question; and
- (*b*) may require –
  - (i) the person by whom or on whose behalf the computer is or has been so used; or

(ii) any person having charge of, or otherwise concerned with the operation of, the computer, apparatus or material,

to afford him such assistance as he may reasonably require.

(9) Any person who intentionally obstructs another in the exercise of any power conferred by this section or the regulations shall be guilty of an offence and liable on summary conviction to a fine not exceeding level 3 on the standard scale.

(10) In this section and sections 87A to 87D –

"the 1992 Act" means the Further and Higher Education Act 1992;

"appropriate authority" means –

(*a*) in relation to England, the National Care Standards Commission;

(*b*) in relation to Wales, the National Assembly for Wales;

"college" means an institution within the further education sector as defined in section 91 of the 1992 Act;

"the Commission" means the National Care Standards Commission;

"further education corporation" has the same meaning as in the 1992 Act;

"local education authority" and "proprietor" have the same meanings as in the Education Act 1996.

(11) In this section and sections 87A and 87D "relevant person" means –

(*a*) in relation to an independent school, the proprietor of the school;

(*b*) in relation to any other school, or an institution designated under section 28 of the 1992 Act, the governing body of the school or institution;

(*c*) in relation to an institution conducted by a further education corporation, the corporation.

(12) Where a person other than the proprietor of an independent school is responsible for conducting the school, references in this section to the relevant person include references to the person so responsible.

Amendments—Registered Homes (Amendment) Act 1991, s 2(6); Education Act 1996, s 582(1), Sch 37, Pt I, para 87; Care Standards Act 2000, s 105.

87A Suspension of duty under section 87(3)

(1) The Secretary of State may appoint a person to be an inspector for the purposes of this section if –

(*a*) that person already acts as an inspector for other purposes in relation to schools or colleges to which section 87(1) applies, and

(*b*) the Secretary of State is satisfied that the person is an appropriate person to determine whether the welfare of children provided with accommodation by such schools or colleges is adequately safeguarded and promoted while they are accommodated by them.

(2) Where –

(*a*) the relevant person enters into an agreement in writing with a person appointed under subsection (1),

(*b*) the agreement provides for the person so appointed to have in relation to the school or college the function of determining whether section 87(1) is being complied with, and

(*c*) the appropriate authority receive from the person mentioned in paragraph (*b*) ("the inspector") notice in writing that the agreement has come into effect, the authority's duty under section 87(3) in relation to the school or college shall be suspended.

(3) Where the appropriate authority's duty under section 87(3) in relation to any school or college is suspended under this section, it shall cease to be so suspended if the appropriate authority receive –

(*a*) a notice under subsection (4) relating to the inspector, or
(*b*) a notice under subsection (5) relating to the relevant agreement.

(4) The Secretary of State shall terminate a person's appointment under subsection (1) if –

(*a*) that person so requests, or
(*b*) the Secretary of State ceases, in relation to that person, to be satisfied that he is such a person as is mentioned in paragraph (*b*) of that subsection,

and shall give notice of the termination of that person's appointment to the appropriate authority.

(5) Where –

(*a*) the appropriate authority's duty under section 87(3) in relation to any school or college is suspended under this section, and
(*b*) the relevant agreement ceases to have effect,

the inspector shall give to the appropriate authority notice in writing of the fact that it has ceased to have effect.

(6) In this section references to the relevant agreement, in relation to the suspension of the appropriate authority's duty under section 87(3) as regards any school or college, are to the agreement by virtue of which the appropriate authority's duty under that provision as regards that school or college is suspended.

Amendments—Substituted by Care Standards Act 2000, s 106(1).

87B Duties of inspectors under section 87A

(1) The Secretary of State may impose on a person appointed under section 87A(1) ("an authorised inspector") such requirements relating to, or in connection with, the carrying out under substitution agreements of the function mentioned in section 87A(2)(*b*) as the Secretary of State thinks fit.

(2) Where, in the course of carrying out under a substitution agreement the function mentioned in section 87A(2)(*b*), it appears to an authorised inspector that there has been a failure to comply with section 87(1) in the case of a child provided with accommodation by the school or college to which the agreement relates, the inspector shall give notice of that fact –

(*a*) in the case of a school other than an independent school or a special school, to the local education authority for the area in which the school is situated;
(*b*) in the case of a special school which is maintained by a local education authority, to that authority;
(*c*) in any other case, to the Secretary of State.

(3) Where, in the course of carrying out under a substitution agreement the function mentioned in section 87A(2)(*b*), it appears to an authorised inspector that a child provided with accommodation by the school or college to which the agreement relates is suffering, or is likely to suffer, significant harm, the inspector shall –

(*a*) give notice of the fact to the local authority in whose area the school is situated, and
(*b*) where the inspector is required to make inspection reports to the Secretary of State, supply that local authority with a copy of the latest inspection report to have been made by the inspector to the Secretary of State in relation to the school.

(4) In this section "substitution agreement" means an agreement by virtue of which the duty of the appropriate authority under section 87(3) in relation to a school or college is suspended.

Amendments—Inserted by Deregulation and Contracting Out Act 1994, s 38; amended by Education Act 1996, s 582(1), Sch 37, Pt I, para 89; Care Standards Act 2000, s 106(2).

87C Boarding schools: national minimum standards

(1) The Secretary of State may prepare and publish statements of national minimum standards for safeguarding and promoting the welfare of children for whom accommodation is provided in a school or college.

(2) The Secretary of State shall keep the standards set out in the statements under review and may publish amended statements whenever he considers it appropriate to do so.

(3) Before issuing a statement, or an amended statement which in the opinion of the Secretary of State effects a substantial change in the standards, the Secretary of State shall consult any persons he considers appropriate.

(4) The standards shall be taken into account –

(*a*) in the making by the appropriate authority of any determination under section 87(4) or (4A);
(*b*) in the making by a person appointed under section 87A(1) of any determination under section 87B(2); and
(*c*) in any proceedings under any other enactment in which it is alleged that the person has failed to comply with section 87(1).

Amendments—Inserted by Care Standards Act 2000, s 107.

87D Annual fee for boarding school inspections

(1) Regulations under subsection (2) may be made in relation to any school or college in respect of which the appropriate authority is required to take steps under section 87(3).

(2) The Secretary of State may by regulations require the relevant person to pay the appropriate authority an annual fee of such amount, and within such time, as the regulations may specify.

(3) A fee payable by virtue of this section may, without prejudice to any other method of recovery, be recovered summarily as a civil debt.

Amendments—Inserted by Care Standards Act 2000, s 108.

****

Criminal care and supervision orders

90 Care and supervision orders in criminal proceedings

(1) The power of a court to make an order under subsection (2) of section 1 of the Children and Young Persons Act 1969 (care proceedings in youth courts) where it is of the opinion that the condition mentioned in paragraph (*f*) of that subsection ("the offence condition") is satisfied is hereby abolished.

(2) The powers of the court to make care orders –

(*a*) under section 7(7)(*a*) of the Children and Young Persons Act 1969 (alteration in treatment of young offenders etc); and
(*b*) under section 15(1) of that Act, on discharging a supervision order made under section 7(7)(*b*) of that Act,

are hereby abolished.

(3) The powers given by that Act to include requirements in supervision orders shall have effect subject to amendments made by Schedule 12.

Amendments—Criminal Justice Act 1991, s 100, Sch 11, para 40.

Effect and duration of orders etc

91 Effect and duration of orders etc

(1) The making of a residence order with respect to a child who is the subject of a care order discharges the care order.

(2) The making of a care order with respect to a child who is the subject of any section 8 order discharges that order.

(3) The making of a care order with respect to a child who is the subject of a supervision order discharges that other order.

(4) The making of a care order with respect to a child who is a ward of court brings that wardship to an end.

(5) The making of a care order with respect to a child who is the subject of a school attendance order made under section 437 of the Education Act 1996 discharges the school attendance order.

(6) Where an emergency protection order is made with respect to a child who is in care, the care order shall have effect subject to the emergency protection order.

(7) Any order made under section 4(1) or 5(1) shall continue in force until the child reaches the age of eighteen, unless it is brought to an end earlier.

(8) Any –

(*a*) agreement under section 4; or
(*b*) appointment under section 5(3) or (4),

shall continue in force until the child reaches the age of eighteen, unless it is brought to an end earlier.

(9) An order under Schedule 1 has effect as specified in that Schedule.

(10) A section 8 order shall, if it would otherwise still be in force, cease to have effect when the child reaches the age of sixteen, unless it is to have effect beyond that age by virtue of section 9(6).

(11) Where a section 8 order has effect with respect to a child who has reached the age of sixteen, it shall, if it would otherwise still be in force, cease to have effect when he reaches the age of eighteen.

(12) Any care order, other than an interim care order, shall continue in force until the child reaches the age of eighteen, unless it is brought to an end earlier.

(13) Any order made under any other provision of this Act in relation to a child shall, if it would otherwise still be in force, cease to have effect when he reaches the age of eighteen.

(14) On disposing of any application for an order under this Act, the court may (whether or not it makes any other order in response to the application) order that no application for an order under this Act of any specified kind may be made with respect to the child concerned by any person named in the order without leave of the court.

(15) Where an application ("the previous application") has been made for –

(*a*) the discharge of a care order;
(*b*) the discharge of a supervision order;
(*c*) the discharge of an education supervision order;
(*d*) the substitution of a supervision order for a care order; or
(*e*) a child assessment order,

no further application of a kind mentioned in paragraphs (*a*) to (*e*) may be made with respect to the child concerned, without leave of the court, unless the period between the disposal of the previous application and the making of the further application exceeds six months.

(16) Subsection (15) does not apply to applications made in relation to interim orders.

(17) Where –

(*a*) a person has made an application for an order under section 34;
(*b*) the application has been refused; and
(*c*) a period of less than six months has elapsed since the refusal,

that person may not make a further application for such an order with respect to the same child, unless he has obtained the leave of the court.

Amendments—Education Act 1996, s 582(1), Sch 37, Pt I, para 90.

Defined terms—"care order": ss 31(11), 105(1); "child": s 105(1); "child assessment order": s 43(2); "education supervision order": s 36(2); "supervision order": s 31(11).

Care order discharges s 8 order (s 91(2))—Where an English court made a care order it had the effect of discharging a Dutch custody order, just as it would discharge a s 8 order (*Oxfordshire County Council v S* [2000] Fam Law 20).

"The making of a care order ... brings that wardship to an end" (s 91(4))—Although an injunction made within wardship proceedings would ordinarily end on the discharge of the wardship, the court has power to order that such an injunction is to continue after the discharge of those proceedings (*Re E (A Minor) (Child Abuse: Evidence)* [1991] 1 FLR 420, per Scott Baker J at 455F). It is probable that the injunction does not subsist beyond the date when the minor achieves majority (*Re D (A Minor) (Adoption Order: Validity)* [1991] 2 FLR 66, per Balcombe LJ at 76E) or the death of the minor during his minority.

"no application ... without leave of the court" (s 91(14))—This subsection has produced many reported decisions concerning the circumstances in which an order restricting future applications should be made. In *Re P (Section 91(14) Guidelines) (Residence and Religious Heritage)* [1999] 2 FLR 573 Butler-Sloss LJ drew up a number of guidelines from the reported cases, while

PART II

indicating that the court always has to carry out a balancing exercise between the welfare of the child and the right of unrestricted access of the litigant to the court. The guidelines are as follows:

1 Section 91(14) should be read in conjunction with s 1(1) which makes the welfare of the child the paramount consideration (see also *B v B (Residence Orders; Restricting Applications)* [1997] 1 FLR 139).

2 The power to restrict applications to the court is discretionary and in the exercise of its discretion the court must weigh in the balance all the relevant circumstances.

3 An important consideration is that to impose a restriction is a statutory intrusion into the right of a party to bring proceedings before the court and to be heard in matters affecting his/her child.

4 The power is therefore to be used with great care and sparingly, the exception and not the rule.

5 It is generally to be seen as a weapon of last resort in cases of repeated and unreasonable applications.

6 In suitable circumstances (and on clear evidence), a court may impose the leave restriction in cases where the welfare of the child requires it, although there is no past history of making unreasonable applications (see also *Re M (Adoption or Residence Order)* [1998] 1 FLR 570; *Re M (Contact: Family Assistance: McKenzie Friend)* [1999] 1 FLR 75; *Re Y (Child Orders: Restricting Applications)* [1994] 2 FLR 699; *Re P (Children Act 1989, ss 22 and 26: Local Authority Compliance)* [2000] 2 FLR 910). A combination of a s 91(14) order and other orders under the Children Act is sometimes preferable to adoption (*Re B (Adoption by one natural parent to exclusion of other)* [2001] 1 FLR 589; *Re B (Adoption Order)* [2001] 2 FLR 26).

7 In cases under para 6 above, the court will need to be satisfied first that the facts go beyond the commonly encountered need for a time to settle to a regime ordered by the court and the all too common situation where there is animosity between the adults in dispute or between the local authority and the family; and secondly that there is a serious risk that, without the imposition of the restriction, the child or the primary carers will be subject to unacceptable strain (see also *Re G (Child Case: Parental Involvement)* [1996] 1 FLR 857; *Re P (Terminating Parental Responsibility)* [1995] 1 FLR 1048; *Re G and M (Child Orders: Restricting Applications)* [1995] 2 FLR 416).

8 A court may impose the restriction on making applications in the absence of a request from any of the parties, subject, of course, to the rules of natural justice such as an opportunity for the parties to be heard on the point (see also *Re S (Contact; Prohibition of Applications)* [1994] 2 FLR 1057; *Re M (Contact: Restrictive Order: Supervision)* [1998] 1 FLR 721). In particular it is wrong in principle, except in exceptional circumstances, to put a litigant in person in the position, at short notice, of having to contest a s 91(14) order (*Re C (Prohibition on Further Applications)*) [2002] EWCA Civ 292, [2002] 1 FLR 1136).

9 A restriction may be imposed with or without limitation of time (see also *Re M (Section 91(14) Order)* [1999] 2 FLR 553).

10 The degree of restriction should be proportionate to the harm it is intended to avoid. Therefore the court imposing the restriction should carefully consider the extent of the restriction to be imposed and specify, where appropriate, the type of application to be restrained and the type of order (see also *Re M (Section 91(14) Order)* (above)).

11 It would be undesirable in other than the most exceptional cases to make the order ex parte.

Furthermore, Butler-Sloss LJ stated that in her view an absolute prohibition on making any application to the court could not be made under s 91(14). Additionally, a s 91(14) order did not infringe the Human Rights Act 1998 or Art 6(1) of the European Convention for the Protection of Human Rights and Fundamental Freedoms 1950 because it did not deny access to the court, only access to an immediate inter partes hearing. An order imposing an absolute prohibition would have to be made under the inherent jurisdiction of the court (see *Re R (Residence: Contact: Restricting Applications)* [1998] 1 FLR 749); where an order is made under the principles of *Grepe v Loam* (1887) 37 Ch D 168 preventing applications by any party without leave, and ordering that any application is to be filed with the court only and dealt with on paper, the guidelines in *Re P* above should apply (*Harris v Harris; Attorney-General v Harris* [2001] 2 FLR 895). It is not appropriate to make a s 91(14) order in contempt proceedings unless there is a contact application before the court (*Heathcote v Crackles* (2002) LTL, 19 February (unreported elsewhere)).

Once a prohibition under s 91(14) has been made, any further applications for leave to bring proceedings should be heard inter partes rather than ex parte; this enables the court to investigate fully whether or not there is a genuine need for further proceedings, since such leave should not be granted lightly (*Re N (Section 91(14) Order)* [1996] 1 FLR 356). The test for granting such leave once a s 91(14) order has been made is whether there is an arguable case and not whether there is a reasonable likelihood that the substantive action would succeed (*Re G (Child Case: Parental Involvement)* [1996] 1 FLR 857 and *Re P (Section 91(14) Guidelines) (Residence and Religious*

Heritage) (above)). However, see also *Re A (Application for Leave)* [1998] 1 FLR 1 where Thorpe LJ held that the simple question for the court is does the application demonstrate that there is any need for renewed judicial investigation? If the answer is yes, then leave should be granted. An application under s 91(14) is a distinct application which should not be subjected to the statutory criteria in s 10(9). The appropriate procedure for applying either for the bar to be discharged in its entirety, or for advancing a lesser application for leave notwithstanding the bar, is to issue the application on Form C2 for a direction in existing family proceedings. If the applicant succeeds, he or she will proceed to issue an application for an order in Form C1 (*Re A (Application for Leave)* (above)).

"order under section 34" (s 91(17)(*a*))—Section 34 provides for various types of order regulating the contact of children in care with their parents and others.

Leave of the court—Where any of the provisions of s 91(14)–(17) requires the leave of the court to be obtained before a particular application under the Act may be made, leave should be sought in accordance with FPR 1991, r 4.3, where the application is to the High Court or a county court, and in accordance with Family Proceedings Courts (Children Act 1989) Rules 1991, r 3 where the application is to a magistrates' court. The application for leave should be made in Form C2 (see FPR 1991, App 1; FPC(CA 1989)R 1991, Sch 1).

Jurisdiction and procedure etc

92 Jurisdiction of courts

(1) The name "domestic proceedings", given to certain proceedings in magistrates' courts, is hereby changed to "family proceedings" and the names "domestic court" and "domestic court panel" are hereby changed to "family proceedings court" and "family panel", respectively.

(2) Proceedings under this Act shall be treated as family proceedings in relation to magistrates' courts.

(3) Subsection (2) is subject to the provisions of section 65(1) and (2) of the Magistrates' Courts Act 1980 (proceedings which may be treated as not being family proceedings), as amended by this Act.

(4) A magistrates' court shall not be competent to entertain any application, or make any order, involving the administration or application of –

(*a*) any property belonging to or held in trust for a child; or
(*b*) the income of any such property.

(5) The powers of a magistrates' court under section 63(2) of the Act of 1980 to suspend or rescind orders shall not apply in relation to any order made under this Act.

(6) Part I of Schedule 11 makes provision, including provision for the Lord Chancellor to make orders, with respect to the jurisdiction of courts and justices of the peace in relation to –

(*a*) proceedings under this Act; and
(*b*) proceedings under certain other enactments.

(7) For the purposes of this Act "the court" means the High Court, a county court or a magistrates' court.

(8) Subsection (7) is subject to the provision made by or under Part I of Schedule 11 and to any express provision as to the jurisdiction of any court made by any other provision of this Act.

(9) The Lord Chancellor may by order make provision for the principal registry of the Family Division of the High Court to be treated as if it were a county court for

PART II

such purposes of this Act, or of any provision made under this Act, as may be specified in the order.

(10) Any order under subsection (9) may make such provision as the Lord Chancellor thinks expedient for the purpose of applying (with or without modifications) provisions which apply in relation to the procedure in county courts to the principal registry when it acts as if it were a county court.

(11) Part II of Schedule 11 makes amendments consequential on this section.

Defined terms—"child": s 105(1).

Jurisdiction under the Act generally—The general scheme of the Act is to give courts as much flexibility as possible so, broadly speaking, most orders may be made by any court. Section 92(4) does however place restrictions on magistrates' courts, which are not competent to deal with the administration or application of any property belonging to or held in trust for a child or the income of any such property; they are also limited in the financial orders which they may make by the provisions of Sch 1, paras 1 and 5. Other restrictions are imposed by the provisions of the Children (Allocation of Proceedings) Order 1991 so that, for example, a local authority's application under Sch 2, para 23 for a contribution order is confined to the magistrates' courts.

As well as ensuring flexibility, another aim in implementing the Act's provisions has been to ensure that the tribunal dealing with a matter has been properly trained for the task. The High Court has full jurisdiction to hear all cases regarding children. In the county courts, the competence of the tribunal is ensured, in the first instance, by establishing a tier system (set up by the Children (Allocation of Proceedings) Order 1991) for county courts: "care centres" are competent to try all cases, but "family hearing centres", "divorce county courts" and other county courts all have restricted jurisdiction. In addition, the Family Proceedings (Allocation to Judiciary) Directions 1999 (as amended) establish different categories of judges and district judges (nominated care judges, nominated family judges etc). In the magistrates' courts, competence is ensured by confining family proceedings (which include the majority of cases under the Act) to family proceedings courts; the magistrates in these courts are all drawn from the family panel, made up of specially trained justices and stipendiary magistrates.

"family proceedings" (s 92(2))—In *Oxfordshire County Council v R* [1992] 1 FLR 648, it was decided that CA 1989, s 25 (secure accommodation) proceedings were, by virtue of s 92(2), to be treated as family proceedings notwithstanding that they are not included in the definition of family proceedings in s 8(3). Accordingly, hearsay evidence was admissible in accordance with the Children (Admissibility of Hearsay Evidence) Order 1991 (as it then was, now the 1993 Order of the same name). It seems extremely unlikely, however, that the s 92(2) provision is intended to override the specific definition of "family proceedings" in s 8(3) when it comes to determining the powers of magistrates' courts to make orders. If it were, magistrates' courts would have wider powers than the High Court or a county court since a wider range of orders is available to a court in family proceedings than in non-family proceedings. Thus, by way of example, with an extended application of s 92(2), a magistrates' court entertaining an application for an emergency protection order would be seised of family proceedings and would be able to make, say, a residence order of its own motion under s 10(1); however, a county court or High Court, limited by the definition of family proceedings in s 8(3) which does not include any proceedings under Part V of the Act, would not.

"section 65(1) and (2) of the Magistrates' Courts Act 1980" (s 92(3))—Magistrates' Courts Act 1980, s 65(1) and (2) lists the proceedings which are generally classed as family proceedings (which list expressly includes proceedings under CA 1989) and creates certain exceptions to the general list (for example, proceedings for the enforcement of an order made under one of the listed enactments). MCA 1980, s 65(2) reduces the impact of the exceptions created by s 65(1) by providing the court with a discretion to order that certain proceedings (for example, proceedings for the enforcement of an order under CA 1989) be treated as family proceedings notwithstanding that they would otherwise be excepted.

"powers of a magistrates' court under s 63(2) of the Act of 1980" (s 92(5))—Magistrates' Courts Act 1980, s 63(2) enables a magistrates' court, by order made on complaint, to suspend or rescind any order requiring either the doing of anything other than the payment of money or prohibiting the doing of anything. Generally, CA 1989 contains its own powers for the variation, suspension and discharge of orders where appropriate, and the procedure provided by the Family

Proceedings Courts (Children Act 1989) Rules 1991 does not involve the use of the complaint procedure.

"provision made by or under Part I of Schedule 11" (s 92(8))—The Children (Allocation of Proceedings) Order 1991, which has the effect of restricting jurisdiction in certain proceedings to magistrates' courts by requiring them to be commenced there and prohibiting their transfer to a county court or the High Court, has been made under this provision.

Principal registry treated as a county court (s 92(9))—C(AP)O 1991, art 19 has been made under this provision.

93 Rules of court

(1) An authority having power to make rules of court may make such provision for giving effect to –

- (*a*) this Act;
- (*b*) the provisions of any statutory instrument made under this Act; or
- (*c*) any amendment made by this Act in any other enactment,

as appears to that authority to be necessary or expedient.

(2) The rules may, in particular, make provision –

- (*a*) with respect to the procedure to be followed in any relevant proceedings (including the manner in which any application is to be made or other proceedings commenced);
- (*b*) as to the persons entitled to participate in any relevant proceedings, whether as parties to the proceedings or by being given the opportunity to make representations to the court;
- (*c*) with respect to the documents and information to be furnished, and notices to be given, in connection with any relevant proceedings;
- (*d*) applying (with or without modification) enactments which govern the procedure to be followed with respect to proceedings brought on a complaint made to a magistrates' court to relevant proceedings in such a court brought otherwise than on a complaint;
- (*e*) with respect to preliminary hearings;
- (*f*) for the service outside England and Wales, in such circumstances and in such manner as may be prescribed, of any notice of proceedings in a magistrates' court;
- (*g*) for the exercise by magistrates' courts, in such circumstances as may be prescribed, of such powers as may be prescribed (even though a party to the proceedings in question is or resides outside England and Wales);
- (*h*) enabling the court, in such circumstances as may be prescribed, to proceed on any application even though the respondent has not been given notice of the proceedings;
- (*i*) authorising a single justice to discharge the functions of a magistrates' court with respect to such relevant proceedings as may be prescribed;
- (*j*) authorising a magistrates' court to order any of the parties to such relevant proceedings as may be prescribed, in such circumstances as may be prescribed, to pay the whole or part of the costs of all or any of the other parties.

(3) In subsection (2) –

"notice of proceedings" means a summons or such other notice of proceedings as is required; and "given", in relation to a summons, means "served",

"prescribed" means prescribed by the rules; and

"relevant proceedings" means any application made, or proceedings brought, under any of the provisions mentioned in paragraphs (*a*) to (*c*) of subsection (1) and any part of such proceedings.

(4) This section and any other power in this Act to make rules of court are not to be taken as in any way limiting any other power of the authority in question to make rules of court.

(5) When making any rules under this section an authority shall be subject to the same requirements as to consultation (if any) as apply when the authority makes rules under its general rule making power.

Amendments—Courts and Legal Services Act 1990, s 116, Sch 16, para 22.

94 Appeals

(1) Subject to any express provisions to the contrary made by or under this Act, an appeal shall lie to the High Court against –

(*a*) the making by a magistrates' court of any order under this Act; or
(*b*) any refusal by a magistrates' court to make such an order.

(2) Where a magistrates' court has power, in relation to any proceedings under this Act, to decline jurisdiction because it considers that the case can more conveniently be dealt with by another court, no appeal shall lie against any exercise by that magistrates' court of that power.

(3) Subsection (1) does not apply in relation to an interim order for periodical payments made under Schedule 1.

(4) On an appeal under this section, the High Court may make such orders as may be necessary to give effect to its determination of the appeal.

(5) Where an order is made under subsection (4) the High Court may also make such incidental or consequential orders as appears to it to be just.

(6) Where an appeal from a magistrates' court relates to an order for the making of periodical payments, the High Court may order that its determination of the appeal shall have effect from such date as it thinks fit to specify in the order.

(7) The date so specified must not be earlier than the earliest date allowed in accordance with rules of court made for the purposes of this section.

(8) Where, on an appeal under this section in respect of an order requiring a person to make periodical payments, the High Court reduces the amount of those payments or discharges the order –

(*a*) it may order the person entitled to the payments to pay to the person making them such sum in respect of payments already made as the High Court thinks fit; and
(*b*) if any arrears are due under the order for periodical payments, it may remit payment of the whole, or part, of those arrears.

(9) Any order of the High Court made on an appeal under this section (other than one directing that an application be re-heard by a magistrates' court) shall, for the purposes –

(*a*) of the enforcement of the order; and
(*b*) of any power to vary, revive or discharge orders,

be treated as if it were an order of the magistrates' court from which the appeal was brought and not an order of the High Court.

(10) The Lord Chancellor may by order make provision as to the circumstances in which appeals may be made against decisions taken by courts on questions arising in connection with the transfer, or proposed transfer, of proceedings by virtue of any order under paragraph 2 of Schedule 11.

(11) Except to the extent provided for in any order made under subsection (10), no appeal may be made against any decision of a kind mentioned in that subsection.

Amendments—Courts and Legal Services Act 1990, s 116, Sch 16, para 23.

Scope of provision—This section provides the machinery for all appeals under CA 1989 from family proceedings courts. The exceptions are that there can be no appeal against a decision to decline jurisdiction (s 94(2)), the making of or refusal to make an emergency protection order or any direction given in connection with such an order (s 45(10), and see *Essex County Council v F* [1993] 1 FLR 847), or an order for interim periodical payments (s 94(3)). On hearing an appeal under this section, the High Court may make any such order as may be necessary to determine the appeal (s 94(4)), and any incidental or consequential orders as appears just (s 94(5)).

Appeals relating to transfer between courts—For appeals against a decision of a magistrates' court to refuse to transfer a case to the county court see Children (Allocation of Proceedings) Order 1991, art 9. For appeals against the order of a district judge to re-transfer a case to the magistrates' court, see the Children (Allocation of Proceedings)(Appeals) Order 1991.

Notes of evidence and reasons—The notice of appeal must be filed and served together with the notes of evidence and reasons. In relation to appeals from magistrates' courts, the justices' clerk must keep a note of the substance of the oral evidence given (Family Proceedings Courts (Children Act 1989) Rules 1991, r 20) and, before making any order, the justices' clerk must record the reasons for the decision and any findings of fact (r 21(5)). These notes should be in legible typescript in order to assist in the disposal of an appeal (*Re W and S* [1992] 2 FCR 665). In *Re U(T) (A Minor) (Care Order Contact)* [1993] 2 FCR 565, Douglas Brown J held that, in addition to filing notes of evidence and reasons, FPR 1991, r 4.22 should be read to include a requirement that reports and witness statements filed for the original hearing should also be filed with the documents on appeal. Although the court should make its decision as soon as practicable (under FPC(CA 1989)R 1991 r 21(4)), the court must be careful to consider its reasons and not make them under pressure of time (see *Oxfordshire County Council v R* [1992] 1 FLR 648). Only those findings of fact and reasons given can be considered on appeal, and they cannot be supplemented later (*Hillingdon London Borough Council v H* [1992] Fam 43, [1992] 2 FLR 372). In *Leicestershire County Council v G* [1994] 2 FLR 329, Stuart-White J said that it would be helpful if the justices' clerk's notes were to include a list identifying any written statements before the magistrates and considered by them, and it would also be helpful if the notes could include information as to which parties were present and whether they were legally represented.

Hearing—The form of appeal is a rehearing, as prescribed under RSC Ord 55, r 3, in the same way as an appeal to the Court of Appeal (under CPR 1998, Pt 52). The court does not hear evidence but considers the matter "on paper". Evidence is admitted only in exceptional circumstances (*Croydon London Borough Council v A (No 1)* [1992] Fam 169, [1992] 2 FLR 341; *Re M (Section 94 Appeals)* [1995] 1 FLR 546; *Y v B (Child Case: Appeal)* [1995] 3 FCR 49; and *Re W, Re A, Re B (Change of Name)* [1999] 2 FLR 930). The High Court has power to make any orders that could have been made by the family proceedings court or, if there has been some error in the hearing itself, may remit the matter for rehearing.

Procedure—The procedure for appeals under this section is governed by FPR 1991, r 4.22. Appeals under FLA 1996, Pt IV (non-molestation and occupation orders) are governed by FLA 1996, s 61 and FPR 1991, r 8.1A. Appeals under the Domestic Proceedings and Magistrates' Courts Act 1978 must be in accordance with FPR 1991, r 8.2 (and RSC Ord 55, subject to r 8.2). Appeals under the Administration of Justice Act 1960, s 13 must be in accordance with FPR 1991, r 8.3. Appeals from the decision of district judges in family proceedings must be in accordance with FPR 1991, r 4.22, and otherwise must be in accordance with RSC Ord 58 (High Court) and FPR 1991, r 8.1 (county court family proceedings), and CCR Ord 37 (other proceedings). To determine the appropriate procedure see FPR 1991, r 4.1(2) for the scope of r 4.22. For guidance on appeal procedure, see *Handbook of Best Practice in Children Act cases* produced by the Children Act Advisory Committee (set out in Part IV of this work as *Best*

Practice Guidance of June 1997) at "Section 6 – Appeals from the family proceedings courts under section 94 of the Children Act 1989".

95 Attendance of child at hearing under Part IV or V

(1) In any proceedings in which a court is hearing an application for an order under Part IV or V, or is considering whether to make any such order, the court may order the child concerned to attend such stage or stages of the proceedings as may be specified in the order.

(2) The power conferred by subsection (1) shall be exercised in accordance with rules of court.

(3) Subsections (4) to (6) apply where –

(*a*) an order under subsection (1) has not been complied with; or
(*b*) the court has reasonable cause to believe that it will not be complied with.

(4) The court may make an order authorising a constable, or such person as may be specified in the order –

(*a*) to take charge of the child and to bring him to the court; and
(*b*) to enter and search any premises specified in the order if he has reasonable cause to believe that the child may be found on the premises.

(5) The court may order any person who is in a position to do so to bring the child to the court.

(6) Where the court has reason to believe that a person has information about the whereabouts of the child it may order him to disclose it to the court.

Defined terms—"child": s 105(1).

"Part IV or V" (s 95(1))—Parts IV and V concern public law orders, such as care and supervision orders, emergency protection orders and child assessment orders.

Court hearing an application or considering making an order (s 95(1))—The court's power to require the attendance of the child is not confined to cases in which there has been an original application for an order under Pt IV or V but may also be exercised where the court is considering making an order of its own motion (for example, where it is entertaining family proceedings and considering making a s 34 contact order of its own motion under s 34(5)).

Use of s 95(1) to compel attendance of child as witness—It is suggested that it may be inappropriate to use the power in s 95(1) to compel the attendance of a child to give evidence and that it would be more appropriate, in the very few instances in which the child's attendance for this reason should be compelled, to use those provisions expressly designed for the purpose (see **Children as witnesses in family proceedings** under s 96).

Rules of court (s 95(2))—The relevant rules of court are FPR 1991, r 4.14 and Family Proceedings Courts (Children Act 1989) Rules 1991, r 14. The provisions as to the representations of the children's guardian, the child's solicitor and, in certain circumstances, the child where the court is considering who should be present or absent are contained in FPR 1991, rr 4.11(4) and 4.16(2) and FPC(CA 1989)R 1991, rr 11(4) and 16(2).

General position as to attendance of child—See **Child at court** under FPR 1991, r 4.16 and FPC(CA 1989)R 1991, r 16.

"reasonable cause to believe" (s 95(3)(*b*), (4)(*b*))—This phrase appears twice in this section and contrasts with the phrase "reason to believe" used in s 95(6). In s 95(3), it is the court which has to have reasonable cause to believe that its s 95(1) order will not be complied with whereas, in s 95(4), it is the constable or other specified person who has to have reasonable cause to believe that the child may be found on any premises before he enters and searches them.

"enter and search any premises specified in the order" (s 95(4))—The court will have to be given some idea of where the child may be because it is not empowered to grant a general authority to enter premises and look for him, only an authority in relation to specified premises. Furthermore, even when authorised to enter and search, the constable or other authorised person will not be able to do so unless *he* has reasonable cause to believe that the child may be found on the premises. He cannot therefore simply rely on the court's order but must give the matter independent thought and satisfy himself, presumably at the time when he is about to enter, that he is entitled to do so.

"reason to believe" (s 95(6))—It is submitted that the phrase "reason to believe" used in s 95(6) denotes a rather lower standard than the phrase "reasonable cause to believe" which is used elsewhere in this section; the s 95(6) terminology mirrors that used in Family Law Act 1986, s 33 which provides for the court to order disclosure of information about the whereabouts of a child in various private law proceedings.

Application for an order under s 95—Although the general tenor of this section suggests that orders will normally be made of the court's own motion, there does not appear to be anything preventing a party applying for such an order in an appropriate case.

96 Evidence given by, or with respect to, children

(1) Subsection (2) applies in any civil proceedings where a child who is called as a witness in any civil proceedings does not, in the opinion of the court, understand the nature of an oath.

(2) The child's evidence may be heard by the court if, in its opinion –

- (*a*) he understands that it is his duty to speak the truth; and
- (*b*) he has sufficient understanding to justify his evidence being heard.

(3) The Lord Chancellor may by order make provision for the admissibility of evidence which would otherwise be inadmissible under any rule of law relating to hearsay.

(4) An order under subsection (3) may only be made with respect to –

- (*a*) civil proceedings in general or such civil proceedings, or class of civil proceedings, as may be prescribed; and
- (*b*) evidence in connection with the upbringing, maintenance or welfare of a child.

(5) An order under subsection (3) –

- (*a*) may, in particular, provide for the admissibility of statements which are made orally or in a prescribed form or which are recorded by any prescribed method of recording;
- (*b*) may make different provision for different purposes and in relation to different descriptions of court; and
- (*c*) may make such amendments and repeals in any enactment relating to evidence (other than in this Act) as the Lord Chancellor considers necessary or expedient in consequence of the provision made by the order.

(6) Subsection (5)(*b*) is without prejudice to section 104(4).

(7) In this section –

"civil proceedings" means civil proceedings, before any tribunal, in relation to which the strict rules of evidence apply, whether as a matter of law or by agreement of the parties, and references to "the court" shall be construed accordingly;

"prescribed" means prescribed by an order under subsection (3).

Amendments—Civil Evidence Act 1995, s 15(1), Sch 1, para 16.

Defined terms—"child": s 105(1).

Scope of provision—Section 96(1) and (2) allows a child who does not understand the oath to give unsworn evidence providing he understands his duty to speak the truth and has sufficient understanding to justify his evidence being heard; s 96(3)–(6) are enabling provisions facilitating the making of orders by the Lord Chancellor as to the admissibility of hearsay evidence (see Children (Admissibility of Hearsay Evidence) Order 1993).

Children as witnesses in family proceedings—A child can give sworn evidence or, if he does not understand the nature of the oath but comes within s 96(2), unsworn evidence. In either of these situations, he is theoretically compellable (*R v B County Council ex parte P* [1991] 1 FLR 470, [1991] 1 WLR 221, [1991] 2 All ER 65). As that case decided, Magistrates' Courts Act 1980, s 97 applies to relevant proceedings in a family proceedings court (see also FPC(CA 1989)R 1991, r 33) and a summons can therefore, technically, be issued to secure the attendance of an unwilling but competent child as a witness (as, presumably, can a witness summons in the county court and a writ of subpoena in the High Court). However, the court said that the use of a s 97 summons (or, by analogy, a witness summons or subpoena) for this purpose is inappropriate in care proceedings in view of the procedure permitting the admission of hearsay evidence in such cases. Accordingly, the court should be very cautious in exercising its discretion to require the attendance of a child and should not issue a summons if:

(*a*) to do so would be inimical to the welfare of the child; or

(*b*) its effect on the child would outweigh the legitimate interest of the person seeking the summons; or

(*c*) the application was made with the object of intimidating the child; or

(*d*) the application was made to procure the attendance of a child whom the applicant for the summons wishes to cross-examine rather than to call as his own witness (though see *Re P (Witness Summons)* [1997] 2 FLR 447, CA below as to this last point).

In *Re P (Witness Summons)*, parties to care proceedings (the mother and step-father) applied for leave to appeal the refusal to permit the issue of a witness summons under CCR Ord 20, r 12 to secure the attendance to give oral evidence and to be cross examined, of N, a 12-year-old child who had made allegations that the step-father had abused her and the child who was the subject of the care proceedings. The principle applicable to the witness summons application was said to be that the judge could decline to issue the summons if to do so would be oppressive. Whether Children and Young Persons Act 1933, s 44(1) applies to oblige the court, in dealing with the child if brought before it under a witness summons, to have regard to her welfare was considered to be an academic question as, in any analysis of whether the issue of the witness summons would be oppressive, the child's welfare would inevitably be of great relevance. However, Wilson J (giving the judgment of the court) expressed the opinion, albeit without having heard full argument, that CA 1989, s 1(1) does not apply where the court is considering whether to issue a witness summons (whether with regard to the child who is the subject of the care proceedings or another child) because that is not a question with respect to the child's upbringing. Wilson J remarked that it is unusual for a child complainant of sexual abuse to give oral evidence in Children Act proceedings but pointed out that the matter must be approached on its merits without preconceptions and, in principle, the older the child, the more arguable will be the application that he or she should give evidence. However, identifying the damage that can be caused by questioning a child complainant, he said that he would expect that, in most cases concerning a child of N's age, or younger, the court would favour the absence of oral evidence despite concomitant weakening, sometimes perhaps fatal weakening, of the evidence against the adult. As to the point which had exercised the Court of Appeal in *R v B County Council ex parte P* (above) concerning the propriety of requiring the attendance of a child for the purposes of cross-examination, Wilson J's judgment suggests that, in the light of the acceptance of the semi-inquisitorial nature of Children Act proceedings and the occasional practice of the court calling a witness so that cross-examination can take place, this consideration may no longer carry the weight attributed to it in that case.

R v B County Council ex parte P and *Re P (Witness Summons)* concern the court's control of the initial issue of a witness summons but, in the High Court, the same principles would presumably apply when the court considers whether to set aside a subpoena which has issued as of right (as it can in the High Court where the proceedings are not in chambers).

As to the undesirability of a child giving evidence, see also *W v W and Hampshire County Council* (1981) FLR 68 and *Re M (Family Proceedings: Affidavits)* [1995] 2 FLR 100, CA. See also *Re A (Care: Discharge Application by Child)* [1995] 1 FLR 599, FD (with regard to the question of a child applicant in public law proceedings giving evidence), and **Child at court** under FPR 1991, r 4.16 and FPC(CA 1989)R 1991, r 16.

In practice in Children Act cases, indirect evidence of what a child has said is often introduced in relation to allegations of child abuse, as the Children (Admissibility of Hearsay Evidence) Order 1993 permits. For example, the adult to whom the child has made an allegation may be called to give evidence of what the child has said, and the children's guardian or children and family reporter may convey to the court the child's wishes and feelings. Because this evidence cannot be tested in cross-examination, the court must, as *R v B County Council ex parte P* (above) stresses, look at it anxiously and consider carefully the extent to which it can be relied on.

There may be a difference of approach where the question is the attendance of a child to give evidence in criminal proceedings, as opposed to family proceedings. Reference should be made to **Grounds for issuing summons** under Magistrates' Courts Act 1980, s 97 and, in particular, to the case of *R v Highbury Corner Magistrates' Court ex parte D* [1997] 1 FLR 683, DC.

Section 95(1) enables the court to require the attendance of the child concerned in a Part IV or Part V application. It is suggested (and this suggestion derives some support from comments in *R v B County Council ex parte P* [1991] 1 FLR 470 at 475, 479) that this procedure may not, however, be appropriate where the attendance of the child *as a witness* is required and that, in such cases, recourse should be had to provisions expressly designed for the purpose. Reference should be made principally to:

(*a*) Magistrates' Courts Act 1980, s 97 as applied by FPC(CA 1989)R 1991, r 33 in relation to magistrates' court proceedings;

(*b*) FPR 1991, r 2.30 in relation to matrimonial causes pending in a divorce county court or the High Court;

(*c*) CCR Ord 20, r 12 as applied by FPR 1991, r 1.3 in relation to non-matrimonial proceedings in the county court;

(*d*) RSC Ord 38, rr 14–19 with regard to non-matrimonial proceedings in the High Court.

It appears that, for the time being, the RSC and CCR will continue to apply in family cases despite the advent of the Civil Proceedings Rules which, by virtue of CPR 1998, r 2.1, do not apply to family proceedings unless specifically applied by another enactment. There is no such enactment at present.

Where a parent wishes to call a willing child to give evidence, he may apparently be prevented from doing so in an appropriate case by means of a specific issue order (see Cousins, "Child's Evidence: Specific Issue Order" [1992] Fam Law 278).

Child understanding the nature of the oath—As to the question of whether a child understands the nature of the oath, see *R v Hayes* [1977] 1 WLR 234, [1977] 2 All ER 288, where it was held that a child could give evidence on oath if he has a sufficient appreciation of the solemnity of the occasion and the added responsibility to tell the truth which is involved in taking the oath, over and above the duty to tell the truth which is an ordinary duty of normal social conduct. The court in *R v Hayes* thought that the dividing line between children who are competent to give sworn evidence and those who are not is normally between the ages of eight and ten. However, under Criminal Justice Act 1988, s 33A, which now governs the competence of children to give evidence in criminal proceedings, the general rule is that under-14s give unsworn evidence and children of 14 and over give sworn evidence.

"sufficient understanding" (s 96(2)(*b*))—The authorities in relation to the child's understanding in various CA 1989 contexts are gathered together in the annotation **"able ... to give such instructions on his own behalf"** under FPR 1991, r 4.12.

Child giving unsworn evidence under s 96(2)—A child who gives unsworn evidence is still liable to be cross-examined.

Compelling attendance of a party to give evidence—A subpoena or witness summons can be issued to compel the attendance of a party to the proceedings to give evidence, irrespective of whether that party is a child or an adult (*R v B County Council ex parte P* [1991] 1 FLR 470).

Judge seeing child privately—See under FPR 1991, r 4.21 and FPC(CA 1989)R 1991, r 21.

97 Privacy for children involved in certain proceedings

(1) Rules made under section 144 of the Magistrates' Courts Act 1980 may make provision for a magistrates' court to sit in private in proceedings in which any powers under this Act may be exercised by the court with respect to any child.

(2) No person shall publish any material which is intended, or likely, to identify –

(*a*) any child as being involved in any proceedings before the High Court, a county court or a magistrates' court in which any power under this Act may be exercised by the court with respect to that or any other child; or

(*b*) an address or school as being that of a child involved in any such proceedings.

(3) In any proceedings for an offence under this section it shall be a defence for the accused to prove that he did not know, and had no reason to suspect, that the published material was intended, or likely, to identify the child.

(4) The court or the Lord Chancellor may, if satisfied that the welfare of the child requires it, by order dispense with the requirements of subsection (2) to such extent as may be specified in the order.

(5) For the purposes of this section –

"publish" includes –

(*a*) include in a programme service (within the meaning of the Broadcasting Act 1990); or

(*b*) cause to be published; and

"material" includes any picture or representation.

(6) Any person who contravenes this section shall be guilty of an offence and liable, on summary conviction, to a fine not exceeding level 4 on the standard scale.

(7) Subsection (1) is without prejudice to –

(*a*) the generality of the rule making power in section 144 of the Act of 1980; or

(*b*) any other power of a magistrates' court to sit in private.

(8) Sections 69 (sittings of magistrates' courts for family proceedings) and 71 (newspaper reports of certain proceedings) of the Act of 1980 shall apply in relation to any proceedings (before a magistrates' court) to which this section applies subject to the provisions of this section.

Amendments—Broadcasting Act 1990, s 203(1), Sch 20, para 53; Courts and Legal Services Act 1990, s 116, Sch 16, para 24; SI 1992/709; Access to Justice Act 1999, s 72.

Defined terms—"child", "school"; s 105(1).

Scope of provision—This section makes provision to ensure that court proceedings in which powers under the Act may be exercised remain confidential. See also Magistrates' Courts Act 1980 and Administration of Justice Act 1960 (contempt by way of publishing information relating to children proceedings).

"Rules made under section 144 of the Magistrates' Courts Act 1980" (s 97(1))—Family Proceedings Courts (Children Act 1989) Rules 1991, r 16(2) and (7) make provision in this respect.

Material which is intended or likely to identify a child (s 97(2))—The prohibition is not an absolute prohibition against publishing material about a child.

Power to dispense with restrictions on publicity (s 97(4))—This power might be used by the court where, for example, a child is missing and press publicity may help in tracing him. It would appear that an order may be made of the court's own motion or on application. If an application is to be made, it may be appropriate to use the directions procedure under Family Proceedings Courts (Children Act 1989) Rules 1991, r 14. As to the attendance of the press at hearings, see *Practice Note of 22 July 1979*. For a recent example of the lifting of restrictions, see *R v*

Cambridge District Health Authority ex parte B (No 2) [1996] 1 FLR 375, CA (reporting restrictions under Children and Young Persons Act 1933, s 39 revoked so that father could raise money to fund child's treatment).

"without prejudice to ... any other power of a magistrates' court to sit in private" (s 97(7)(*b*))—See Magistrates' Courts Act 1980, s 69, which continues to apply, subject to this section.

Magistrates' Courts Act 1980, ss 69 and 71 (s 97(8))—Magistrates' Courts Act 1980, s 69(2) ensures a certain minimum degree of privacy in family proceedings in a magistrates' court by providing that no person shall be present during the hearing and determination of most such proceedings except officers of the court, the parties and their legal representatives, witnesses and other people directly concerned in the case, representatives of the press and news agencies and anyone else whom the court permits. Section 69(4) enables the court, if it thinks it necessary in the interest of the administration of justice or public decency, to exclude anyone who is not an officer of the court, a party or his legal representative or otherwise directly concerned in the case where "indecent evidence" is being taken. Section 69(6) ensures that the court can exclude witnesses until they are called for examination. All the provisions of s 69 are, however, subject to the provisions of Family Proceedings Courts (Children Act 1989) Rules 1991, r 16, which enables the court to restrict attendance at court even further. Under r 16(7), whenever it considers it expedient to do so (and it usually will), the court may hear any "relevant proceedings" (defined in CA 1989, s 93(3) to include all proceedings under CA 1989) in private with only the officers of the court, the parties, their legal representatives and such other persons as may be specified by the court present; under r 16(2) even a party may be excluded if the court considers it in the interests of the child to do so and the party is represented by a children's guardian or solicitor.

Section 71 makes it an offence to publish particulars of family proceedings except as expressly permitted by the section (which, depending on the type of case involved, normally permits publication of such information as names, addresses and occupations of parties and witnesses, submissions on any point of law, the decision of the court etc). It is less restrictive than s 97(2) but, by virtue of s 97(8), s 97(2) prevails wherever it applies.

98 Self-incrimination

(1) In any proceedings in which a court is hearing an application for an order under Part IV or V, no person shall be excused from –

(*a*) giving evidence on any matter; or

(*b*) answering any question put to him in the course of his giving evidence,

on the ground that doing so might incriminate him or his spouse of an offence.

(2) A statement or admission made in such proceedings shall not be admissible in evidence against the person making it or his spouse in proceedings for an offence other than perjury.

Self-incrimination—The general rule, to which this section creates an exception, is that a person is not bound to answer any question if his answer would, in the opinion of the court, tend to expose him to any criminal charge or penalty which the court regards as reasonably likely to be preferred or sued for (*Blunt v Park Lane Hotels* [1942] 2 KB 253).

"Part IV or V" (s 98(1))—Parts IV and V concern public law orders, such as care and supervision orders, emergency protection orders, and child assessment orders.

Ambit of s 98—Ultimately, it will be the criminal court which decides the degree of protection afforded by s 98(2) in any given case. However, there have been a number of views expressed, in the context of family proceedings, about its extent.

(*a*) *Meaning of "statement or admission made in such proceedings"* (s 98(2)) In *Oxfordshire County Council v P* [1995] 1 FLR 552, Ward J considered that s 98(2) provided protection with regard to oral admissions made in advance of care proceedings to a children's guardian. In *Cleveland County Council v F* [1995] 1 FLR 797, Hale J agreed with him and added her view that it extends also to statements made to social workers investigating in a child protection case, at least once the proceedings have begun. *Oxfordshire County Council v P* was referred to without demur in *Oxfordshire County Council v L and F* [1997] 1 FLR 235,

FD. In *Re K and Others (Minors) (Disclosure)* [1994] 1 FLR 377, Booth J (albeit in a different context) may have been expressing a narrower view when she said that it provided "protection to a witness who is required to give evidence in relation to a child when such evidence could incriminate him or his spouse". In *Re G (Social Worker: Disclosure)* [1996] 1 FLR 276, Butler-Sloss LJ, obiter, doubted that s 98(2) could be extended as far as Ward and Hale JJ had suggested.

(*b*) *Meaning of "admissible in evidence"* (s 98(2)) In *Re EC (Disclosure of Material)* [1996] 2 FLR 725, the Court of Appeal decided inter alia that transcripts of an admission made by the father when giving evidence should be disclosed to the police, who would then be free to use it when questioning him. The content of any further interview may, of course, be the subject of submissions as to admissibility in criminal proceedings by virtue of the Police and Criminal Evidence Act 1984, and that would be a matter for the discretion of the trial judge in those proceedings. According to *Re EC* (above), s 98(2) gives protection only against statements being admissible in evidence in criminal proceedings except for an offence of perjury, and does not protect against their use in a police inquiry into the commission of an offence. A judge cannot give a witness in family proceedings any absolute guarantee as to confidentiality, since there is power to order disclosure even of material falling within s 98(2). In *Re EC*, before they gave evidence, the judge had told all members of the child's family who were suspected of causing her injuries that anything they said from the witness-box could not be used in any criminal trial against them relating to the death of the child. The Court of Appeal said that judges may well like to point out to witnesses to whom such a statement is made that guarantees of confidentiality cannot be given; almost certainly legal advisers should do so. As to applications for disclosure of Children Act material for the purposes of criminal proceedings/investigation, see further **Leave under r 4.23(1)** under FPR 1991, r 4.23(1). In *Re L (Care: Confidentiality)* [1999] 1 FLR 165, FD, the parents had submitted that it would not be fair to require them to give evidence in care proceedings which might prejudice their position at their pending criminal trial for murder and sexual assault and they had not given evidence before the family court. The judge held that s 98(2) did not give absolute protection to the parents in the criminal proceedings; putting inconsistent statements to a witness in criminal proceedings in order to challenge his evidence or attack his credibility did not amount to using those statements against them. It was not possible either to draft an injunction that could achieve absolute protection. However, truthful witnesses would not suffer by such cross-examination. The family court would have to consider what inferences to draw from the failure of the parents to give evidence in the family proceedings. It was to be hoped that the issue of confidentiality would not be used as a basis for seeking postponement of the care proceedings until the conclusion of related criminal proceedings. The provisions of s 98(2) do apply to any statement or admission which a parent gives to an expert witness (*A Chief Constable v A County Council, AB (A Child) (By His Children's Guardian SM, DH and RW)* [2002] EWHC 2198 (Fam) (unreported) LTL, 5/11/2002 Doc No C014008 – where Wall J held (at para [134]) that the position of expert witnesses is analogous for these purposes with that of the guardian and therefore a statement made to an expert witness is a statement made in the proceedings and thus entitled to the protection of s 98(2)). Prior to being interviewed by an expert witness, parents should have the terms and purpose of s 98(2) explained to them by their lawyers (*A Chief Constable* (above) at para [134]).

****

100 Restrictions on use of wardship jurisdiction

(1) Section 7 of the Family Law Reform Act 1969 (which gives the High Court power to place a ward of court in the care, or under the supervision, of a local authority) shall cease to have effect.

(2) No court shall exercise the High Court's inherent jurisdiction with respect to children –

(*a*) so as to require a child to be placed in the care, or put under the supervision, of a local authority;

(*b*) so as to require a child to be accommodated by or on behalf of a local authority;

(*c*) so as to make a child who is the subject of a care order a ward of court; or (*d*) for the purpose of conferring on any local authority power to determine any question which has arisen, or which may arise, in connection with any aspect of parental responsibility for a child.

(3) No application for any exercise of the court's inherent jurisdiction with respect to children may be made by a local authority unless the authority have obtained the leave of the court.

(4) The court may only grant leave if it is satisfied that –

(*a*) the result which the authority wish to achieve could not be achieved through the making of any order of a kind to which subsection (5) applies; and

(*b*) there is reasonable cause to believe that if the court's inherent jurisdiction is not exercised with respect to the child he is likely to suffer significant harm.

(5) This subsection applies to any order –

(*a*) made otherwise than in the exercise of the court's inherent jurisdiction; and

(*b*) which the local authority is entitled to apply for (assuming, in the case of any application which may only be made with leave, that leave is granted).

Scope of provision—This section prevents a child from being both in care and a ward of court, and restricts any application by the local authority for the exercise of the court's inherent jurisdiction without leave; see further s 91(4), Sch 14, para 16A and FPR 1991, Pt V. For a recent case where wardship was considered by the Court of Appeal as the preferred option to an application for guardianship under the Mental Health Act 1983 see *Re F (Mental Health Act: Guardianship)* [2000] 1 FLR 192. There have, however, been conflicting decisions on the correct procedure to be followed when the need arises for the court to authorise the administration or withdrawal of medical treatment. In *Re T (Wardship: Medical Treatment)* [1997] 1 FLR 502 the local authority was granted leave under s 100(3) to commence proceedings where the issue before the court were whether it was in the best interests of a baby to undergo liver transplant surgery. The local authority sought permission to perform the operation and an order for the child to be returned to the jurisdiction for the purposes of the surgery. In *Re S (A Minor) (Medical Treatment)* [1993] 1 FLR 376, *Re O (A Minor) (Medical Treatment)* [1993] 2 FLR 149 and *South Glamorgan County Council v W and B* [1993] 1 FLR 574, the court considered that the appropriate procedure was to invoke the inherent jurisdiction of the court. However, in *Re R (A Minor) (Blood Transfusion)* [1993] 2 FLR 757, an application for a specific issue order under s 8 was considered to be appropriate where the application related to blood transfusion. It is submitted that, in cases involving children, a distinction may need to be made between cases where the dispute is between parents, and relates to the administration of ordinary medical treatment which is neither life threatening nor controversial, and those cases which raise issues of public policy. In the former category of cases, an application for a specific issue order may be appropriate, provided the child is not in care and the local authority is not seeking to acquire parental responsibility of the child. In the latter case, however, the appropriate procedure should be to proceed under the inherent jurisdiction of the court. In considering an application by a local authority for leave to invoke the court's inherent jurisdiction, the court's approach should not be too restrictive (*Devon County Council v S and Another* [1994] 1 FLR 355).

In *Re S (Minors) (Inherent Jurisdiction: Ouster)* [1994] 1 FLR 623 and *C v K (Inherent Powers: Exclusion Order)* [1996] 2 FLR 506, it was held that "the inherent jurisdiction is available to exclude a parent from his property indefinitely if there is reasonable cause to believe that the child otherwise would suffer significant harm". Having considered all the relevant authorities, Wall J laid down the following propositions in *C v K*:

"(1) Where judicial interference with the rights of occupation of property, as between spouses, cohabitees or former cohabitees, is specifically governed by statute, the relevant statutory provisions apply.

(2) Leaving on one side the parens patriae jurisdiction of the High Court over children who are specifically its wards, there exists an inherent jurisdiction in both the High Court and the county court to protect children from harm which is exercisable irrespective of the proceedings in which the issue of the need to protect the children arises.

(3) There is a co-existing jurisdiction given in the High Court by s 37 of the Supreme Court Act and in the county court by s 38 of the County Courts Act to grant injunctive relief in support of legal and equitable rights.

(4) The powers exercisable under ss 37 and 38 of the respective statutes may be invoked in support of the rights and duties conferred on a person by a residence order. Thus, in cases where neither the Matrimonial Homes Act 1983 nor the Domestic Violence and Matrimonial Proceedings Act 1976 applies, a non-residential parent may be restrained from interfering with the residential parent's exercise of parental responsibility. The powers of the court in this context extend to orders against molestation and to ouster injunctions.

(5) The powers exercisable by the court under ss 37 and 38 extend to the grant of injunctions against third parties. Thus, a person who is not a parent of the child may be restrained from interfering with the exercise of parental responsibility by a person who has a residence order in relation to the child. The powers of the court to grant injunctive relief include the power to exclude the stranger from property in which he has a beneficial interest.

(6) There is no reported case in which the inherent jurisdiction, unaffected by ss 37 and 38, has been used to exclude anybody who is not a parent from the occupation of property in which he has a proprietary interest. Whilst the power to make such an order may exist, the better course, in my judgment, is to invoke the jurisdiction under ss 37 and 38, since the need to protect the child is then bolstered by the need to protect the rights of the party with parental responsibility to exercise that parental responsibility appropriately.

(7) The powers of the court to exclude a person from property in which he has a proprietary interest should be exercised with extreme caution. By analogy with s 100(4) of the Children Act the jurisdiction is likely only to be exercised where the court is satisfied that if the jurisdiction is not exercised the child is likely to suffer significant harm. In reaching any conclusion the court must look at all the circumstances of the case, including of course the circumstances of each of the parties and the conduct of the parties towards each other and the child. The court must make findings of fact upon which the assessment of likely future harm can be made.

(8) Whilst the jurisdiction exists to make a final order excluding a person from occupation of property in which he has a proprietary interest, without limitation of time, the court cannot by these means vary proprietary interests and must in every such case consider whether an indefinite order is required in order to protect the child from the likelihood of significant harm, and to achieve a result which is just."

It is noted that the decision in *D v D (County Court Jurisdiction: Injunctions)* [1993] 2 FLR 802 established that the county court has no inherent jurisdiction to grant injunctions in relation to the exercise of its statutory powers in children cases, whether under CA 1989 or the Adoption Act 1976. This was reiterated by the Court of Appeal in *Devon County Council v B* [1997] 1 FLR 591. It may thus be argued that, in view of these decisions and particularly the Court of Appeal case, the decision in *C v K* cannot stand. However, it is submitted that *C v K* is distinguishable since, although reference was made in that case to the inherent jurisdiction of the court to protect children, the decision to grant injunctive relief was not made under the inherent jurisdiction of the court: it was based on the court's jurisdiction to grant such relief under SCA 1981, s 37 and CCA 1984, s 38 to protect the rights of the party with parental responsibility to exercise appropriately that parental responsibility, and the rights and duties which that legal responsibility entails.

Where a care order is made in favour of a local authority, the authority has parental responsibility for the child, and it can be argued that the jurisdiction under SCA 1981, s 37 and CCA 1984, s 38 may be invoked to protect their rights to exercise that parental responsibility appropriately and, in particular, to protect the child. It would seem, therefore, that in an appropriate case, where a care order or interim care order is made in favour of a local authority, application may be made for injunctive relief by the local authority against a parent or a third party, pursuant to the power conferred by SCA 1981, s 37 or CCA 1984, s 38 instead of invoking the court's inherent jurisdiction, provided that it can be shown that, if the jurisdiction is not exercised, the child is likely to suffer significant harm. It is also submitted that *C v K* provides a remedy where injunctive relief under any other provision proves impossible, provided it is necessary to protect the child from significant harm, and it is needed to enable the party with parental responsibility to exercise that legal right appropriately and effectively. This view has been confirmed by *Re P (Care Orders: Injunctive Relief)* [2000] 2 FLR 385 where the powers conferred by s 37 were relied on by Charles J to grant ancillary injunctive relief to the local authority.

By virtue of the provisions inserted into CA 1989 by Family Law Act 1996, Sch 6, the court has the power to include an exclusion order and accept an undertaking, in appropriate cases, when an interim care order or emergency protection order is made under ss 38 and 44 respectively. However, the remedy available under ss 38A and 38B, and ss 44A and 44B, is limited in its nature and extent and is subject to the conditions set out in those sections. It is, therefore, submitted that the decision in *C v K* will continue to be of importance to cover both private and public law cases, which do not come within any statutory provisions, to provide relief where it is required to enable a person or body with parental responsibility to exercise those rights and duties.

Inherent jurisdiction and forced marriages—It is submitted that, applying the above principles to the issue of forced marriages and having regard to the need in such cases for urgent, immediate and effective relief, the inherent jurisdiction is the only route available to safeguard and protect a "child" and to prevent the child from suffering significant harm, particularly by removal from the jurisdiction of the court. In such cases, there is often no effective interested party who is able to make the application other than the local authority. Therefore, the local authority should confidently apply for leave to invoke the inherent jurisdiction and the court's approach to such an application should be sympathetic and robust as in *Re A (Wardship: Jurisdiction)* [1995] 1 FLR 767; and *Re KR (Abduction: Forcible Removal by Parents)* [1999] 2 FLR 542. Where the victim of the forced marriage and abduction is an adult the inherent jurisdiction should also be invoked on similar principles as those which apply in cases where the subject of the proceedings is unable to make the application personally due to some incapacity.

101 Effect of orders as between England and Wales and Northern Ireland, the Channel Islands or the Isle of Man

(1) The Secretary of State may make regulations providing –

(*a*) for prescribed orders which –
(i) are made by a court in Northern Ireland; and
(ii) appear to the Secretary of State to correspond in their effect to orders which may be made under any provision of this Act,
to have effect in prescribed circumstances, for prescribed purposes of this Act, as if they were orders of a prescribed kind made under this Act;

(*b*) for prescribed orders which –
(i) are made by a court in England and Wales; and
(ii) appear to the Secretary of State to correspond in their effect to orders which may be made under any provision in force in Northern Ireland,
to have effect in prescribed circumstances, for prescribed purposes of the law of Northern Ireland, as if they were orders of a prescribed kind made in Northern Ireland.

(2) Regulations under subsection (1) may provide for the order concerned to cease to have effect for the purposes of the law of Northern Ireland, or (as the case may be) the law of England and Wales, if prescribed conditions are satisfied.

(3) The Secretary of State may make regulations providing for prescribed orders which –

(*a*) are made by a court in the Isle of Man or in any of the Channel Islands; and
(*b*) appear to the Secretary of State to correspond in their effect to orders which may be made under this Act,

to have effect in prescribed circumstances for prescribed purposes of this Act, as if they were orders of a prescribed kind made under this Act.

(4) Where a child who is in the care of a local authority is lawfully taken to live in Northern Ireland, the Isle of Man or in any of the Channel Islands, the care order in question shall cease to have effect if the conditions prescribed in regulations by the Secretary of State are satisfied.

(5) Any regulations made under this section may –

(a) make such consequential amendments (including repeals) in –
(i) section 25 of the Children and Young Persons Act 1969 (transfers between England and Wales and Northern Ireland); or
(ii) section 26 (transfers between England and Wales and Channel Islands or Isle of Man) of that Act,
as the Secretary of State considers necessary or expedient; and
(b) modify any provision of this Act, in its application (by virtue of the regulations) in relation to an order made otherwise than in England and Wales.

Defined terms—"prescribed": s 105(1).

Scope of provision—This section is intended to give reciprocal effect to orders as between England, Northern Ireland, the Channel Islands and the Isle of Man. It complements the provisions under Sch 2 para 19(2), (3)(*d*) which permit the local authority to arrange for a child in its care to live outside England and Wales. By virtue of s 101(4), if a child who is the subject of a care order is moved to live in Northern Ireland, the Channel Islands or the Isle of Man, the care order may be transferred in accordance with regulations to the public authority there (see Children (Prescribed Orders – Northern Ireland, Guernsey and Isle of Man) Regulations 1991, SI 1991/2032). Where a child is lawfully moved, the care order ceases to have effect if the conditions prescribed in the regulations are satisfied.

Search warrants

102 Power of constable to assist in exercise of certain powers to search for children or inspect premises

(1) Where, on an application made by any person for a warrant under this section, it appears to the court –

(a) that a person attempting to exercise powers under any enactment mentioned in subsection (6) has been prevented from doing so by being refused entry to the premises concerned or refused access to the child concerned; or
(b) that any such person is likely to be so prevented from exercising any such powers,

it may issue a warrant authorising any constable to assist that person in the exercise of those powers, using reasonable force if necessary.

(2) Every warrant issued under this section shall be addressed to, and executed by, a constable who shall be accompanied by the person applying for the warrant if –

(a) that person so desires; and
(b) the court by whom the warrant is issued does not direct otherwise.

(3) A court granting an application for a warrant under this section may direct that the constable concerned may, in executing the warrant, be accompanied by a registered medical practitioner, registered nurse or registered health visitor if he so chooses.

(4) An application for a warrant under this section shall be made in the manner and form prescribed by rules of court.

(5) Where –

(a) an application for a warrant under this section relates to a particular child; and
(b) it is reasonably practicable to do so,

the application and any warrant granted on the application shall name the child; and where it does not name him it shall describe him as clearly as possible.

(6) The enactments are –

(*a*) sections 62, 64, 67, 76, 80, 86 and 87;
(*b*) paragraph 8(1)(*b*) and (2)(*b*) of Schedule 3;
(*c*) section 33 of the Adoption Act 1976 (duty of local authority to secure that protected children are visited from time to time).

Defined terms—"child": s 105(1).

Scope of provision—This section empowers the court to issue a warrant authorising a constable to assist a person seeking to act under one of the specified statutory powers. Section 102(4) and (5) require an application for a warrant under this section to be made in the manner and form prescribed by rules of court and requires any application in respect of a particular child to name him if reasonably practicable, failing which it should give as clear a description of him as possible.

Jurisdiction—Children (Allocation of Proceedings) Order 1991, art 3 requires proceedings under this section to be commenced in a magistrates' court. The only ground for a subsequent transfer to a county court is for consolidation with other related proceedings (art 7(3)).

"manner and form prescribed by rules of court" (s 102(4))—The Family Proceedings Courts (Children Act 1989) Rules 1991 apply generally. Rule 4(4) allows an application under this section to be made ex parte, in which case r 2(5)(*a*) empowers a single justice to determine it. The proceedings are not "specified proceedings" for the purposes of s 41(6). Where the proceedings are transferred to a county court (see **Jurisdiction** above), FPR 1991 apply (in particular Part IV thereof); r 4.4(3)(*e*) allows application to be made ex parte which is presumably only to allow the court to deal with any such application which had been made to a magistrates' court but transferred to a county court before it had been adjudicated on (an unlikely scenario). Form C19 in FPC(CA 1989)R 1991, Sch 1, is the form prescribed (and Form C28 is the warrant itself). No form is prescribed by FPR 1991 as direct application may not be made to a county court or the High Court.

General

103 Offences by bodies corporate

(1) This section applies where any offence under this Act is committed by a body corporate.

(2) If the offence is proved to have been committed with the consent or connivance of or to be attributable to any neglect on the part of any director, manager, secretary or other similar officer of the body corporate, or any person who was purporting to act in any such capacity, he (as well as the body corporate) shall be guilty of the offence and shall be liable to be proceeded against and punished accordingly.

104 Regulations and orders

(1) Any power of the Lord Chancellor or the Secretary of State under this Act to make an order, regulations, or rules, except an order under section 56(4)(*a*), 57(3), 84 or 97(4) or paragraph 1(1) of Schedule 4, shall be exercisable by statutory instrument.

(2) Any such statutory instrument, except one made under section 17(4), 107 or 108(2), shall be subject to annulment in pursuance of a resolution of either House of Parliament.

(3) An order under section 17(4) shall not be made unless a draft of it has been laid before, and approved by a resolution of, each House of Parliament.

(4) Any statutory instrument made under this Act may –

(*a*) make different provision for different cases;
(*b*) provide for exemptions from any of its provisions; and
(*c*) contain such incidental, supplemental and transitional provisions as the person making it considers expedient.

Amendments—Care Standards Act 2000, s 117, Sch 6.

105 Interpretation

(1) In this Act –

"adoption agency" means a body which may be referred to as an adoption agency by virtue of section 1 of the Adoption Act 1976;
"appropriate children's home" has the meaning given by section 23;
"bank holiday" means a day which is a bank holiday under the Banking and Financial Dealings Act 1971;
"care home" has the same meaning as in the Care Standards Act 2000;
"care order" has the meaning given by section 31(11) and also includes any order which by or under any enactment has the effect of, or is deemed to be, a care order for the purposes of this Act; and any reference to a child who is in the care of an authority is a reference to a child who is in their care by virtue of a care order;
"child" means, subject to paragraph 16 of Schedule 1, a person under the age of eighteen;
"child assessment order" has the meaning given by section 43(2);
"child minder" has the meaning given by section 71;
"child of the family", in relation to the parties to a marriage, means –

(*a*) a child of both of those parties;
(*b*) any other child, not being a child who is placed with those parties as foster parents by a local authority or voluntary organisation, who has been treated by both of those parties as a child of their family;

"children's home" has the meaning given by section 23;
"community home" has the meaning given by section 53;
"contact order" has the meaning given by section 8(1);
"day care" (except in Part XA) has the same meaning as in section 18;
"disabled", in relation to a child, has the same meaning as in section 17(11);
"domestic premises" has the meaning given by section 71(12);
"dwelling-house" includes –

(*a*) any building or part of a building which is occupied as a dwelling;
(*b*) any caravan, house-boat or structure which is occupied as a dwelling;

and any yard, garden, garage or outhouse belonging to it and occupied with it;

"education supervision order" has the meaning given in section 36;
"emergency protection order" means an order under section 44;
"family assistance order" has the meaning given in section 16(2);
"family proceedings" has the meaning given by section 8(3);
"functions" includes powers and duties;
"guardian of a child" means a guardian (other than a guardian of the estate of a child) appointed in accordance with the provisions of section 5;

"harm" has the same meaning as in section 31(9) and the question of whether harm is significant shall be determined in accordance with section 31(10);

"Health Authority" means a Health Authority established under section 8 of the National Health Service Act 1977;

"health service hospital" has the same meaning as in the National Health Service Act 1977;

"hospital" (except in Schedule 9A) has the same meaning as in the Mental Health Act 1983, except that it does not include a hospital at which high security psychiatric services within the meaning of that Act are provided;

"ill-treatment" has the same meaning as in section 31(9);

"income-based jobseeker's allowance" has the same meaning as in the Jobseekers Act 1995;

"independent hospital" has the same meaning as in the Care Standards Act 2000;

"independent school" has the same meaning as in the Education Act 1996;

"local authority" means, in relation to England, the council of a county, a metropolitan district, a London Borough or the Common Council of the City of London, in relation to Wales, the council of a county or a county borough and, in relation to Scotland, a local authority within the meaning of section 1(2) of the Social Work (Scotland) Act 1968;

"local authority foster parent" has the same meaning as in section 23(3);

"local education authority" has the same meaning as in the Education Act 1996;

"local housing authority" has the same meaning as in the Housing Act 1985;

"officer of the Service" has the same meaning as in the Criminal Justice and Court Services Act 2000;

"parental responsibility" has the meaning given in section 3;

"parental responsibility agreement" has the meaning given in section 4(1);

"prescribed" means prescribed by regulations made under this Act;

"Primary Care Trust" means a Primary Care Trust established under section 16A of the National Health Service Act 1977;

"private children's home" means a children's home in respect of which a person is registered under Part II of the Care Standards Act 2000 which is not a community home or a voluntary home;

"privately fostered child" and "to foster a child privately" have the same meaning as in section 66;

"prohibited steps order" has the meaning given by section 8(1);

"protected child" has the same meaning as in Part III of the Adoption Act 1976;

"registered pupil" has the same meaning as in the Education Act 1996;

"relative", in relation to a child, means a grandparent, brother, sister, uncle or aunt (whether of the full blood or half blood or by affinity) or step-parent;

"residence order" has the meaning given by section 8(1);

"responsible person", in relation to a child who is the subject of a supervision order, has the meaning given in paragraph 1 of Schedule 3;

"school" has the same meaning as in the Education Act 1996 or, in relation to Scotland, in the Education (Scotland) Act 1980;

"service", in relation to any provision made under Part III, includes any facility;

"signed", in relation to any person, includes the making by that person of his mark;

"special educational needs" has the same meaning as in the Education Act 1996;

"Special Health Authority" means a Special Health Authority established under section 11 of the National Health Service Act 1977;
"specific issue order" has the meaning given by section 8(1);
"Strategic Health Authority" means a Strategic Health Authority established under section 8 of the National Health Service Act 1977;
"supervision order" has the meaning given by section 31(11);
"supervised child" and "supervisor", in relation to a supervision order or an education supervision order, mean respectively the child who is (or is to be) under supervision and the person under whose supervision he is (or is to be) by virtue of the order;
"upbringing", in relation to any child, includes the care of the child but not his maintenance;
"voluntary home" has the meaning given by section 60;
"voluntary organisation" means a body (other than a public or local authority) whose activities are not carried on for profit.

(2) References in this Act to a child whose father and mother were, or (as the case may be) were not, married to each other at the time of his birth must be read with section 1 of the Family Law Reform Act 1987 (which extends the meaning of such references).

(3) References in this Act to –

(*a*) a person with whom a child lives, or is to live, as the result of a residence order; or
(*b*) a person in whose favour a residence order is in force,

shall be construed as references to the person named in the order as the person with whom the child is to live.

(4) References in this Act to a child who is looked after by a local authority have the same meaning as they have (by virtue of section 22) in Part III.

(5) References in this Act to accommodation provided by or on behalf of a local authority are references to accommodation so provided in the exercise of functions of that or any other local authority which are social services functions within the meaning of the Local Authority Social Services Act 1970.

(5A) References in this Act to a child minder shall be construed –

(*a*) in relation to Scotland, in accordance with section 71;
(*b*) in relation to England and Wales, in accordance with section 79A.

(6) In determining the "ordinary residence" of a child for any purpose of this Act, there shall be disregarded any period in which he lives in any place –

(*a*) which is a school or other institution;
(*b*) in accordance with the requirements of a supervision order under this Act or an order under section 63(1) of the Powers of Criminal Courts (Sentencing) Act 2000; or
(*c*) while he is being provided with accommodation by or on behalf of a local authority.

(7) References in this Act to children who are in need shall be construed in accordance with section 17.

(8) Any notice or other document required under this Act to be served on any person may be served on him by being delivered personally to him, or being sent by post to him in a registered letter or by the recorded delivery service at his proper address.

(9) Any such notice or other document required to be served on a body corporate or a firm shall be duly served if it is served on the secretary or clerk of that body or a partner of that firm.

(10) For the purposes of this section, and of section 7 of the Interpretation Act 1978 in its application to this section, the proper address of a person –

(*a*) in the case of a secretary or clerk of a body corporate, shall be that of the registered or principal office of that body;
(*b*) in the case of a partner of a firm, shall be that of the principal office of the firm; and
(*c*) in any other case, shall be the last known address of the person to be served.

Amendments—Registered Homes (Amendment) Act 1991, s 2(6); Local Government (Wales) Act 1994, ss 22, 66, Sch 10, para 13, Sch 18; Health Authorities Act 1995, ss 2, 5 Sch 1, para 118, Sch 3; Jobseekers Act 1995, s 41, Sch 2, para 19; Education Act 1996, s 582(1), Sch 37, Pt I, para 91; Family Law Act 1996, s 52, Sch 6, para 5; Care Standards Act 2000, s 116, Sch 4, para 14(23); Criminal Justice and Court Services Act 2000 s 74, Sch 7, para 95; Local Government Act 2000, s 107(1), Sch 5, para 22; Powers of Criminal Courts (Sentencing) Act 2000, s 165, Sch 9, para 129; SI 2000/90; SI 2002/2469.

"ordinary residence" (s 105(6))—A young child who cannot decide for himself where to live is ordinarily resident in his parents' matrimonial home, and this ordinary residence cannot be changed by one parent without the consent of the other (*Re P (GE) (An Infant)* [1965] Ch 568). If a child's parents are living apart and they have agreed that the child is to live with one of them, he is ordinarily resident in the home of that one and his ordinary residence is not changed just because the other parent removes the child from that home (*Re P* (above)). In *London Borough of Southwark v B* [1993] 2 FLR 559, a young child, in respect of whom the local authority was about to issue care proceedings, was removed from England to Algeria by her mother. It was held that the local authority still had locus standi to apply for a return order. The precipitate way in which she was removed, and the very limited information available as to the nature or permanence of the arrangements for her accommodation in Algeria, gave the judge ample justification for treating the child as being "ordinarily resident" in the area of the authority at the date of the application for the return order.

Subsection 105(6) is closely allied to s 31(8) and the interrelationship between the provisions was considered by the Court of Appeal in *Northamptonshire County Council v Islington County Council* [1999] 2 FLR 881 where Thorpe LJ held that s 31(8) and s 105(6) are to be construed in a way which provides a simple mechanism to determine the question of administration. The subsections are not about child protection or the promotion of child welfare. They are to be read as a simple test to determine which local authority is to be responsible for the care plan and its implementation. It is not appropriate to apply the s 1(3) checklist to this determination. In *C (A Child) v Plymouth County Council* [2000] 1 FLR 875 the Court of Appeal reiterated that the *Northamptonshire* case was not meant to give judges a discretionary exit from the plain application of the statutory mechanisms of ss 31 and 105, but only to indicate that the simple rules of construction should be sufficient to determine all but the most exceptional cases. Where the child is not accommodated by the local authority, because the local authority permits the child to reside at home under an interim care order, s 105(6)(*c*) does not apply and the court is free to apply conventional principles to the definition of "ordinary residence", see *Re C (Care Order: Appropriate Local Authority)* [1997] 1 FLR 544 and also *Re P (Care Proceedings: Designated Authority)* [1998] 1 FLR 80. See also **Habitual residence** under Child Abduction and Custody Act 1985, Sch 1, Art 4.

106 Financial provisions

(1) Any –

(*a*) grants made by the Secretary of State under this Act; and
(*b*) any other expenses incurred by the Secretary of State under this Act,

shall be payable out of money provided by Parliament.

(2) Any sums received by the Secretary of State under section 58, or by way of the repayment of any grant made under section 82(2) or (4) shall be paid into the Consolidated Fund.

107 Application to Channel Islands

Her Majesty may by Order in Council direct that any of the provisions of this Act shall extend to any of the Channel Islands with such exceptions and modifications as may be specified in the Order.

108 Short title, commencement, extent etc

(1) This Act may be cited as the Children Act 1989.

(2) Sections 89 and 96(3) to (7), and paragraph 35 of Schedule 12, shall come into force on the passing of this Act and paragraph 36 of Schedule 12 shall come into force at the end of the period of two months beginning with the day on which this Act is passed but otherwise this Act shall come into force on such date as may be appointed by order made by the Lord Chancellor or the Secretary of State, or by both acting jointly.

(3) Different dates may be appointed for different provisions of this Act in relation to different cases.

(4) The minor amendments set out in Schedule 12 shall have effect.

(5) The consequential amendments set out in Schedule 13 shall have effect.

(6) The transitional provisions and savings set out in Schedule 14 shall have effect.

(7) The repeals set out in Schedule 15 shall have effect.

(8) An order under subsection (2) may make such transitional provisions or savings as appear to the person making the order to be necessary or expedient in connection with the provisions brought into force by the order, including –

(*a*) provisions adding to or modifying the provisions of Schedule 14; and
(*b*) such adaptations –
(i) of the provisions brought into force by the order; and
(ii) of any provisions of this Act then in force,
as appear to him necessary or expedient in consequence of the partial operation of this Act.

(9) The Lord Chancellor may by order make such amendments or repeals, in such enactments as may be specified in the order, as appear to him to be necessary or expedient in consequence of any provision of this Act.

(10) This Act shall, in its application to the Isles of Scilly, have effect subject to such exceptions, adaptations and modifications as the Secretary of State may by order prescribe.

(11) The following provisions of this Act extend to Scotland –

section 19;
section 25(8);
section 50(13);
Part X;
section 80(1)(*h*) and (*i*), (2) to (4), (5)(*a*), (*b*) and (*h*) and (6) to (12);
section 88;

section 104 (so far as necessary);
section 105 (so far as necessary);
subsections (1) to (3), (8) and (9) and this subsection;
in Schedule 2, paragraph 24;
in Schedule 12, paragraphs 1, 7 to 10, 18, 27, 30(*a*) and 41 to 44;
in Schedule 13, paragraphs 18 to 23, 32, 46, 47, 50, 57, 62, 63, 68(*a*), (*b*) and 71;
in Schedule 14, paragraphs 1, 33 and 34;
in Schedule 15, the entries relating to –

(*a*) the Custody of Children Act 1891;
(*b*) the Nurseries and Child Minders Regulation Act 1948;
(*c*) section 53(3) of the Children and Young Persons Act 1963;
(*d*) section 60 of the Health Services and Public Health Act 1968;
(*e*) the Social Work (Scotland) Act 1968;
(*f*) the Adoption (Scotland) Act 1978;
(*g*) the Child Care Act 1980;
(*h*) the Foster Children (Scotland) Act 1984;
(*i*) the Child Abduction and Custody Act 1985; and
(*j*) the Family Law Act 1986.

(12) The following provisions of this Act extend to Northern Ireland –

section 101(1)(*b*), (2) and (5)(*a*)(i);
subsections (1) to (3), (8) and (9) and this subsection;
in Schedule 2, paragraph 24;
in Schedule 12, paragraphs 7 to 10, 18 and 27;
in Schedule 13, paragraphs 21, 22, 46, 47, 57, 62, 63, 68(*c*) to (*e*) and 69 to 71;
in Schedule 14, paragraphs 28 to 30 and 38(*a*); and
in Schedule 15, the entries relating to the Guardianship of Minors Act 1971, the Children Act 1975, the Child Care Act 1980, and the Family Law Act 1986.

Amendments—Courts and Legal Services Act 1990, ss 116, 125(7), Sch 16, para 25, Sch 20.

SCHEDULE 1

FINANCIAL PROVISION FOR CHILDREN

1 Orders for financial relief against parents

(1) On an application made by a parent or guardian of a child, or by any person in whose favour a residence order is in force with respect to a child, the court may –

(*a*) in the case of an application to the High Court or a county court, make one or more of the orders mentioned in sub-paragraph (2);
(*b*) in the case of an application to a magistrates' court, make one or both of the orders mentioned in paragraphs (*a*) and (*c*) of that sub-paragraph.

(2) The orders referred to in sub-paragraph (1) are –

(*a*) an order requiring either or both parents of a child –
  (i) to make to the applicant for the benefit of the child; or
  (ii) to make to the child himself,
such periodical payments, for such term, as may be specified in the order;
(*b*) an order requiring either or both parents of a child –
  (i) to secure to the applicant for the benefit of the child; or

PART II

(ii) to secure to the child himself,

such periodical payments, for such term, as may be so specified;

(*c*) an order requiring either or both parents of a child –

(i) to pay to the applicant for the benefit of the child; or

(ii) to pay to the child himself,

such lump sum as may be so specified;

(*d*) an order requiring a settlement to be made for the benefit of the child, and to the satisfaction of the court, of property –

(i) to which either parent is entitled (either in possession or in reversion); and

(ii) which is specified in the order;

(*e*) an order requiring either or both parents of a child –

(i) to transfer to the applicant, for the benefit of the child; or

(ii) to transfer to the child himself,

such property to which the parent is, or the parents are, entitled (either in possession or in reversion) as may be specified in the order.

(3) The powers conferred by this paragraph may be exercised at any time.

(4) An order under sub-paragraph (2)(*a*) or (*b*) may be varied or discharged by a subsequent order made on the application of any person by or to whom payments were required to be made under the previous order.

(5) Where a court makes an order under this paragraph –

(*a*) it may at any time make a further such order under sub-paragraph (2)(*a*), (*b*) or (*c*) with respect to the child concerned if he has not reached the age of eighteen;

(*b*) it may not make more than one order under sub-paragraph (2)(*d*) or (*e*) against the same person in respect of the same child.

(6) On making, varying or discharging a residence order the court may exercise any of its powers under this Schedule even though no application has been made to it under this Schedule.

(7) Where a child is a ward of court, the court may exercise any of its powers under this Schedule even though no application has been made to it.

Amendments—Courts and Legal Services Act 1990, s 116, Sch 16, para 10(2).

Defined terms—"child", "guardian": s 105(1); "residence order": s 8(1).

Scope of provision—Subject to the Child Support Act 1991, which restricts the court's power to order child maintenance (see Procedural Guide 2), this paragraph enables the High Court and county courts to make a periodical payments, secured periodical payments, lump sum, settlement of property or transfer of property order and enables magistrates' courts to make a periodical payments, secured periodical payments or lump sum order for a child irrespective of whether the child's parents are married. The court may make an order either without an application being made, if a residence order has been made, varied or discharged (para 1(6)), or on an application by the child's parent or guardian or by a holder of a residence order. The child must be aged under 18, but para 3 allows a periodical payments order to be extended for a child over 18 who is or will be undergoing education or where there are special circumstances.

"parent"—This term includes any party to a marriage (whether or not subsisting) in relation to whom the child concerned is a child of the family (para 16(2)). See also **Meaning of "parent"** under s 10.

"property"—In *K v K (Minors: Property Transfer)* [1992] 1 WLR 530, it was held that "property" includes a joint tenancy (see also **"property"** under Matrimonial Causes Act 1973, s 24) and that the words "for the benefit of" do not mean only a financial benefit but cover a welfare benefit as well; thus, a transfer of property can be ordered to oust one parent from the family home by transferring his rights as tenant to the other parent.

2 Orders for financial relief for persons over eighteen

(1) If, on an application by a person who has reached the age of eighteen, it appears to the court –

- (*a*) that the applicant is, will be or (if an order were made under this paragraph) would be receiving instruction at an educational establishment or undergoing training for a trade, profession or vocation, whether or not while in gainful employment; or
- (*b*) that there are special circumstances which justify the making of an order under this paragraph,

the court may make one or both of the orders mentioned in sub-paragraph (2).

(2) The orders are –

- (*a*) an order requiring either or both of the applicant's parents to pay to the applicant such periodical payments, for such term, as may be specified in the order;
- (*b*) an order requiring either or both of the applicant's parents to pay to the applicant such lump sum as may be so specified.

(3) An application may not be made under this paragraph by any person if, immediately before he reached the age of sixteen, a periodical payments order was in force with respect to him.

(4) No order shall be made under this paragraph at a time when the parents of the applicant are living with each other in the same household.

(5) An order under sub-paragraph (2)(*a*) may be varied or discharged by a subsequent order made on the application of any person by or to whom payments were required to be made under the previous order.

(6) In sub-paragraph (3) "periodical payments order" means an order made under –

- (*a*) this Schedule;
- (*b*) (*repealed*)
- (*c*) section 23 or 27 of the Matrimonial Causes Act 1973;
- (*d*) Part I of the Domestic Proceedings and Magistrates' Courts Act 1978, for the making or securing of periodical payments.

(7) The powers conferred by this paragraph shall be exercisable at any time.

(8) Where the court makes an order under this paragraph it may from time to time while that order remains in force make a further such order.

Amendments—Child Support Act 1991, s 58(14).

Scope of provision—Subject to the Child Support Act 1991 (see Procedural Guide 2), this paragraph enables an adult child, whose parents are not living with each other in the same household and in respect of whom there was no periodical payments order in force before he reached the age of 16, to apply for periodical payments or a lump sum if either he is receiving further education or training or there are special circumstances.

"parent"—See **Meaning of "parent"** under s 10.

"periodical payments order" (para 2(3), (6))—The term "periodical payments order" as defined by para 2(6) means an order under (i) this Schedule, (ii) Matrimonial Causes Act 1973, s 23, which provides maintenance in divorce, nullity or judicial separation proceedings, (iii) s 27 of that Act, which provides maintenance on an application for wilful neglect to maintain in the High Court or county court, or (iv) Domestic Proceedings and Magistrates' Courts Act 1978, Pt I in the magistrates' court, on the same ground as in (iii).

Extended meaning of "child"—In this Schedule, an applicant under this paragraph is included within the definition of the term "child" notwithstanding that he has reached the age of 18 (para 16(1)).

3 Duration of orders for financial relief

(1) The term to be specified in an order for periodical payments made under paragraph 1(2)(*a*) or (*b*) in favour of a child may begin with the date of the making of an application for the order in question or any later date or a date ascertained in accordance with sub-paragraph (5) or (6) but –

(*a*) shall not in the first instance extend beyond the child's seventeenth birthday unless the court thinks it right in the circumstances of the case to specify a later date; and
(*b*) shall not in any event extend beyond the child's eighteenth birthday.

(2) Paragraph (*b*) of sub-paragraph (1) shall not apply in the case of a child if it appears to the court that –

(*a*) the child is, or will be or (if an order were made without complying with that paragraph) would be receiving instruction at an educational establishment or undergoing training for a trade, profession or vocation, whether or not while in gainful employment; or
(*b*) there are special circumstances which justify the making of an order without complying with that paragraph.

(3) An order for periodical payments made under paragraph 1(2)(*a*) or 2(2)(*a*) shall, notwithstanding anything in the order, cease to have effect on the death of the person liable to make payments under the order.

(4) Where an order is made under paragraph 1(2)(*a*) or (*b*) requiring periodical payments to be made or secured to the parent of a child, the order shall cease to have effect if –

(*a*) any parent making or securing the payments; and
(*b*) any parent to whom the payments are made or secured,

live together for a period of more than six months.

(5) Where –

(*a*) a maintenance calculation ("the current calculation") is in force with respect to a child; and
(*b*) an application is made for an order under paragraph 1(2)(*a*) or (*b*) of this Schedule for periodical payments in favour of that child –
  (i) in accordance with section 8 of the Child Support Act 1991; and
  (ii) before the end of the period of 6 months beginning with the making of the current calculation,

the term to be specified in any such order made on that application may be expressed to begin on, or at any time after, the earliest permitted date.

(6) For the purposes of subsection (5) above, "the earliest permitted date" is whichever is the later of –

(*a*) the date 6 months before the application is made; or

(*b*) the date on which the current calculation took effect or, where successive maintenance calculations have been continuously in force with respect to a child, on which the first of those calculations took effect.

(7) Where –

(*a*) a maintenance calculation ceases to have effect by or under any provision of the Child Support Act 1991, and

(*b*) an application is made, before the end of the period of 6 months beginning with the relevant date, for an order for periodical payments under paragraph 1(2)(*a*) or (*b*) in favour of a child with respect to whom that maintenance calculation was in force immediately before it ceases to have effect,

the term to be specified in any such order, or in any interim order under paragraph 9, made on that application may begin with the date on which that maintenance calculation ceased to have effect, or any later date.

(8) In sub-paragraph (7)(*b*), –

(*a*) where the maintenance calculation ceased to have effect, the relevant date is the date on which it so ceased; and

(*b*) *(repealed)*

Amendments—SI 1993/623; Child Support, Pensions and Social Security Act 2000, ss 26, 85, Sch 3, para 10, Sch 9.

Defined terms—"child": s 105(1).

Scope of provision—This paragraph is equivalent to Matrimonial Causes Act 1973, s 29(2)–(4) and provides the upper limit for the duration of a periodical payments order. It also provides that any order ceases to have effect if the child's parents live together for more than six months.

"parent"—By para 16(2), "parent" includes any party to a marriage (whether or not subsisting) in relation to whom the child concerned is a child of the family. See also **Meaning of "parent"** under s 10.

"special circumstances" (para 3(2)(*b*))—Compare Matrimonial Causes Act 1973, s 29(3)(*b*). Where there are special circumstances the order can continue beyond 18 years despite Child Support Act 1991, ss 8 and 55. Special circumstances may include physical or other handicap, and the expenses attributed to the child's disability should be taken into account in the broadest sense (*C v F (Disabled Child: Maintenance Orders)* [1998] 2 FLR 1).

4 Matters to which court is to have regard in making orders for financial relief

(1) In deciding whether to exercise its powers under paragraph 1 or 2, and if so in what manner, the court shall have regard to all the circumstances including –

(*a*) the income, earning capacity, property and other financial resources which each person mentioned in sub-paragraph (4) has or is likely to have in the foreseeable future;

(*b*) the financial needs, obligations and responsibilities which each person mentioned in sub-paragraph (4) has or is likely to have in the foreseeable future;

(*c*) the financial needs of the child;

(*d*) the income, earning capacity (if any), property and other financial resources of the child;

(*e*) any physical or mental disability of the child;

(*f*) the manner in which the child was being, or was expected to be, educated or trained.

(2) In deciding whether to exercise its powers under paragraph 1 against a person who is not the mother or father of the child, and if so in what manner, the court shall in addition have regard to –

(*a*) whether that person had assumed responsibility for the maintenance of the child, and, if so, the extent to which and basis on which he assumed that responsibility and the length of the period during which he met that responsibility;
(*b*) whether he did so knowing that the child was not his child;
(*c*) the liability of any other person to maintain the child.

(3) Where the court makes an order under paragraph 1 against a person who is not the father of the child, it shall record in the order that the order is made on the basis that the person against whom the order is made is not the child's father.

(4) The persons mentioned in sub-paragraph (1) are –

(*a*) in relation to a decision whether to exercise its powers under paragraph 1, any parent of the child;
(*b*) in relation to a decision whether to exercise its powers under paragraph 2, the mother and father of the child;
(*c*) the applicant for the order;
(*d*) any other person in whose favour the court proposes to make the order.

Defined terms—"child": s 105(1), Sch 1, para 16(1).

Scope of provision—This paragraph is equivalent to Matrimonial Causes Act 1973, s 25(3) and sets out the circumstances to which the court must have regard when exercising its discretion.

"parent"—This term has the extended meaning given by para 16(2); see also **Meaning of "parent"** under s 10.

5 Provisions relating to lump sums

(1) Without prejudice to the generality of paragraph 1, an order under that paragraph for the payment of a lump sum may be made for the purpose of enabling any liabilities or expenses –

(*a*) incurred in connection with the birth of the child or in maintaining the child; and
(*b*) reasonably incurred before the making of the order,

to be met.

(2) The amount of any lump sum required to be paid by an order made by a magistrates' court under paragraph 1 or 2 shall not exceed £1,000 or such larger amount as the Lord Chancellor may from time to time by order fix for the purposes of this sub-paragraph.

(3) The power of the court under paragraph 1 or 2 to vary or discharge an order for the making or securing of periodical payments by a parent shall include power to make an order under that provision for the payment of a lump sum by that parent.

(4) The amount of any lump sum which a parent may be required to pay by virtue of sub-paragraph (3) shall not, in the case of an order made by a magistrates' court, exceed the maximum amount that may at the time of the making of the order be required to be paid under sub-paragraph (2), but a magistrates' court may make an

order for the payment of a lump sum not exceeding that amount even though the parent was required to pay a lump sum by a previous order under this Act.

(5) An order made under paragraph 1 or 2 for the payment of a lump sum may provide for the payment of that sum by instalments.

(6) Where the court provides for the payment of a lump sum by instalments the court, on an application made either by the person liable to pay or the person entitled to receive that sum, shall have power to vary that order by varying –

(*a*) the number of instalments payable;
(*b*) the amount of any instalment payable;
(*c*) the date on which any instalment becomes payable.

Amendments—SI 1992/709.

Defined terms—"child": s 105(1), Sch 1, para 16(1).

Scope of provision—This paragraph is in part the equivalent of Matrimonial Causes Act 1973, s 23(3) and also imposes a restriction on magistrates' courts to the effect that a lump sum must not exceed £1,000.

"parent"—This term has the extended meaning given by para 16(2); see also **Meaning of "parent"** under s 10.

6 Variation etc of orders for periodical payments

(1) In exercising its powers under paragraph 1 or 2 to vary or discharge an order for the making or securing of periodical payments the court shall have regard to all the circumstances of the case, including any change in any of the matters to which the court was required to have regard when making the order.

(2) The power of the court under paragraph 1 or 2 to vary an order for the making or securing of periodical payments shall include power to suspend any provision of the order temporarily and to revive any provision so suspended.

(3) Where on an application under paragraph 1 or 2 for the variation or discharge of an order for the making or securing of periodical payments the court varies the payments required to be made under that order, the court may provide that the payments as so varied shall be made from such date as the court may specify except that, subject to sub-paragraph (9), the date shall not be earlier than the date of the making of the application.

(4) An application for the variation of an order made under paragraph 1 for the making or securing of periodical payments to or for the benefit of a child may, if the child has reached the age of sixteen, be made by the child himself.

(5) Where an order for the making or securing of periodical payments made under paragraph 1 ceases to have effect on the date on which the child reaches the age of sixteen, or at any time after that date but before or on the date on which he reaches the age of eighteen, the child may apply to the court which made the order for an order for its revival.

(6) If on such an application it appears to the court that –

(*a*) the child is, will be or (if an order were made under this sub-paragraph) would be receiving instruction at an educational establishment or undergoing training for a trade, profession or vocation, whether or not while in gainful employment; or

PART II

(*b*) there are special circumstances which justify the making of an order under this paragraph,

the court shall have power by order to revive the order from such date as the court may specify, not being earlier than the date of the making of the application.

(7) Any order which is revived by an order under sub-paragraph (5) may be varied or discharged under that provision, on the application of any person by whom or to whom payments are required to be made under the revived order.

(8) An order for the making or securing of periodical payments made under paragraph 1 may be varied or discharged, after the death of either parent, on the application of a guardian of the child concerned.

(9) Where –

(*a*) an order under paragraph 1(2)(*a*) or (*b*) for the making or securing of periodical payments in favour of more than one child ("the order") is in force;

(*b*) the order requires payments specified in it to be made to or for the benefit of more than one child without apportioning those payments between them;

(*c*) a maintenance calculation ("the calculation") is made with respect to one or more, but not all, of the children with respect to whom those payments are to be made; and

(*d*) an application is made, before the end of the period of 6 months beginning with the date on which the calculation was made, for the variation or discharge of the order,

the court may, in exercise of its powers under paragraph 1 to vary or discharge the order, direct that the variation or discharge shall take effect from the date on which the calculation took effect or any later date.

Amendments—SI 1993/623; Child Support, Pensions and Social Security Act 2000, s 26, Sch 3, para 10.

Defined terms—"child": s 105(1), Sch 1, para 16(1).

Scope of provision—Subject to the Child Support Act 1991 (see **Interface with Child Support Act 1991** under MCA 1973, s 23 and **Outline of new bases for child support calculation** under CSA 1991, s 4), this paragraph contains the court's powers to vary orders made either under para 1 (order for financial relief for a child against parents) or para 2 (order for financial relief against parents where the child is applying for the first time when the child is over 18).

"parent"—This term has the extended meaning given by para 16(2); see also **Meaning of "parent"** under s 10.

6A Variation of orders for periodical payments etc made by magistrates' courts

(1) Subject to sub-paragraphs (7) and (8), the power of a magistrates' court –

(*a*) under paragraph 1 or 2 to vary an order for the making of periodical payments, or

(*b*) under paragraph 5(6) to vary an order for the payment of a lump sum by instalments,

shall include power, if the court is satisfied that payment has not been made in accordance with the order, to exercise one of its powers under paragraphs (*a*) to (*d*) of section 59(3) of the Magistrates' Courts Act 1980.

(2) In any case where –

(*a*) a magistrates' court has made an order under this Schedule for the making of periodical payments or for the payment of a lump sum by instalments, and

(*b*) payments under the order are required to be made by any method of payment falling within section 59(6) of the Magistrates' Courts Act 1980 (standing order, etc),

any person entitled to make an application under this Schedule for the variation of the order (in this paragraph referred to as "the applicant") may apply to the clerk to the justices for the petty sessions area for which the court is acting for the order to be varied as mentioned in sub-paragraph (3).

(3) Subject to sub-paragraph (5), where an application is made under sub-paragraph (2), the clerk, after giving written notice (by post or otherwise) of the application to any interested party and allowing that party, within the period of 14 days beginning with the date of the giving of that notice, an opportunity to make written representations, may vary the order to provide that payments under the order shall be made to the justices' chief executive for the court.

(4) The clerk may proceed with an application under sub-paragraph (2) notwithstanding that any such interested party as is referred to in sub-paragraph (3) has not received written notice of the application.

(5) Where an application has been made under sub-paragraph (2), the clerk may, if he considers it inappropriate to exercise his power under sub-paragraph (3), refer the matter to the court which, subject to sub-paragraphs (7) and (8), may vary the order by exercising one of its powers under paragraphs (*a*) to (*d*) of section 59(3) of the Magistrates' Courts Act 1980.

(6) Subsection (4) of section 59 of the Magistrates' Courts Act 1980 (power of court to order that account be opened) shall apply for the purposes of sub-paragraphs (1) and (5) as it applies for the purposes of that section.

(7) Before varying the order by exercising one of its powers under paragraphs (*a*) to (*d*) of section 59(3) of the Magistrates' Courts Act 1980, the court shall have regard to any representations made by the parties to the application.

(8) If the court does not propose to exercise its power under paragraph (*c*), (*cc*) or (*d*) of subsection (3) of section 59 of the Magistrates' Courts Act 1980, the court shall, unless upon representations expressly made in that behalf by the applicant for the order it is satisfied that it is undesirable to do so, exercise its power under paragraph (*b*) of that subsection.

(9) None of the powers of the court, or of the clerk to the justices, conferred by this paragraph shall be exercisable in relation to an order under this Schedule for the making of periodical payments, or for the payment of a lump sum by instalments, which is not a qualifying maintenance order (within the meaning of section 59 of the Magistrates' Courts Act 1980).

(10) In sub-paragraphs (3) and (4) "interested party", in relation to an application made by the applicant under sub-paragraph (2), means a person who would be entitled to be a party to an application for the variation of the order made by the applicant under any other provision of this Schedule if such an application were made.

Amendments—Inserted by Maintenance Enforcement Act 1991, s 6; amended by SI 1994/731; Access to Justice Act 1999, s 90, Sch 13, para 161.

PART II

Scope of provision—This paragraph gives to the court the same power to determine method of payment on an application to vary as it has on the making of a new order. In *B v B (Periodical Payments: Transitional Provisions)* [1995] 1 FLR 459, it was held that the court had power to grant an application to vary or discharge a financial provision order made under the Guardianship of Minors Act 1971, despite the repeal of that Act by CA 1989.

7 Variation of orders for secured periodical payments after death of parent

(1) Where the parent liable to make payments under a secured periodical payments order has died, the persons who may apply for the variation or discharge of the order shall include the personal representatives of the deceased parent.

(2) No application for the variation of the order shall, except with the permission of the court, be made after the end of the period of six months from the date on which representation in regard to the estate of that parent is first taken out.

(3) The personal representatives of a deceased person against whom a secured periodical payments order was made shall not be liable for having distributed any part of the estate of the deceased after the end of the period of six months referred to in sub-paragraph (2) on the ground that they ought to have taken into account the possibility that the court might permit an application for variation to be made after that period by the person entitled to payments under the order.

(4) Sub-paragraph (3) shall not prejudice any power to recover any part of the estate so distributed arising by virtue of the variation of an order in accordance with this paragraph.

(5) Where an application to vary a secured periodical payments order is made after the death of the parent liable to make payments under the order, the circumstances to which the court is required to have regard under paragraph 6(1) shall include the changed circumstances resulting from the death of the parent.

(6) In considering for the purposes of sub-paragraph (2) the question when representation was first taken out, a grant limited to settled land or to trust property shall be left out of account and a grant limited to real estate or to personal estate shall be left out of account unless a grant limited to the remainder of the estate has previously been made or is made at the same time.

(7) In this paragraph "secured periodical payments order" means an order for secured periodical payments under paragraph 1(2)(*b*).

"parent"—This term has the extended meaning given by para 16(2); see also **Meaning of "parent"** under s 10.

8 Financial relief under other enactments

(1) This paragraph applies where a residence order is made with respect to a child at a time when there is in force an order ("the financial relief order") made under any enactment other than this Act and requiring a person to contribute to the child's maintenance.

(2) Where this paragraph applies, the court may, on the application of –

(*a*) any person required by the financial relief order to contribute to the child's maintenance; or

(*b*) any person in whose favour a residence order with respect to the child is in force, make an order revoking the financial relief order, or varying it by altering the amount of any sum payable under that order or by substituting the applicant for the person to whom any such sum is otherwise payable under that order.

Defined terms—"child": s 105(1), Sch 1, para 16(1); "residence order": s 8(1).

Scope of provision—Where an order for periodical payments or secured periodical payments for the support of a child made outside Sch 1 (for instance in a divorce suit) already exists and a residence order is then made, this paragraph enables the court to vary that original order by varying the sum payable or the person to whom payment is to be made.

9 Interim orders

(1) Where an application is made under paragraph 1 or 2 the court may, at any time before it disposes of the application, make an interim order –

- (*a*) requiring either or both parents to make such periodical payments, at such times and for such term as the court thinks fit; and
- (*b*) giving any direction which the court thinks fit.

(2) An interim order made under this paragraph may provide for payments to be made from such date as the court may specify except that, subject to paragraph 3(5) and (6), the date shall not be earlier than the date of the making of the application under paragraph 1 or 2.

(3) An interim order made under this paragraph shall cease to have effect when the application is disposed of or, if earlier, on the date specified for the purposes of this paragraph in the interim order.

(4) An interim order in which a date has been specified for the purposes of sub-paragraph (3) may be varied by substituting a later date.

Amendments—SI 1993/623.

Scope of provision—This paragraph enables the court to make interim orders.

"parent"—This term has the extended meaning given by para 16(2); see also **Meaning of "parent"** under s 10.

Alteration of maintenance agreements

10 (1) In this paragraph and in paragraph 11 "maintenance agreement" means any agreement in writing made with respect to a child, whether before or after the commencement of this paragraph, which –

- (*a*) is or was made between the father and mother of the child; and
- (*b*) contains provision with respect to the making or securing of payments, or the disposition or use of any property, for the maintenance or education of the child,

and any such provisions are in this paragraph, and paragraph 11, referred to as "financial arrangements".

(2) Where a maintenance agreement is for the time being subsisting and each of the parties to the agreement is for the time being either domiciled or resident in England and Wales, then, either party may apply for an order under this paragraph.

(3) If the court to which the application is made is satisfied either –

- (*a*) that, by reason of a change in the circumstances in the light of which any financial arrangements contained in the agreement were made (including a change foreseen by the parties when making the agreement), the agreement should be altered so as to make different financial arrangements; or

(*b*) that the agreement does not contain proper financial arrangements with respect to the child,

then that court may by order make such alterations in the agreement by varying or revoking any financial arrangements contained in it as may appear to it to be just having regard to all the circumstances.

(4) If the maintenance agreement is altered by an order under this paragraph, the agreement shall have effect thereafter as if the alteration had been made by agreement between the parties and for valuable consideration.

(5) Where a court decides to make an order under this paragraph altering the maintenance agreement –

(*a*) by inserting provision for the making or securing by one of the parties to the agreement of periodical payments for the maintenance of the child; or

(*b*) by increasing the rate of periodical payments required to be made or secured by one of the parties for the maintenance of the child,

then, in deciding the term for which under the agreement as altered by the order the payments or (as the case may be) the additional payments attributable to the increase are to be made or secured for the benefit of the child, the court shall apply the provisions of sub-paragraphs (1) and (2) of paragraph 3 as if the order were an order under paragraph 1(2)(*a*) or (*b*).

(6) A magistrates' court shall not entertain an application under sub-paragraph (2) unless both the parties to the agreement are resident in England and Wales and at least one of the parties is resident in the commission area for which the court is appointed, and shall not have power to make any order on such an application except –

(*a*) in a case where the agreement contains no provision for periodical payments by either of the parties, an order inserting provision for the making by one of the parties of periodical payments for the maintenance of the child;

(*b*) in a case where the agreement includes provision for the making by one of the parties of periodical payments, an order increasing or reducing the rate of, or terminating, any of those payments.

(7) For the avoidance of doubt it is hereby declared that nothing in this paragraph affects any power of a court before which any proceedings between the parties to a maintenance agreement are brought under any other enactment to make an order containing financial arrangements or any right of either party to apply for such an order in such proceedings.

Amendments—Justices of the Peace Act 1997, s 73(2), Sch 5, para 27; Access to Justice Act 1999, s 106, Sch 15.

Defined terms—"child": s 105(1), Sch 1, para 16(1).

Scope of provision—Subject to the Child Support Act 1991 (see Procedural Guides 2 and 7), this paragraph is equivalent to Matrimonial Causes Act 1973, s 35 and sets out the code for altering maintenance agreements during the lives of the parents. The major difference between this paragraph and MCA 1973, s 35 is that jurisdiction under s 35 depends on the parents being married. By para 10(6), the power of magistrates' courts is limited to inserting provision for periodical payments where none has been made in the maintenance agreement, or, where the agreement does include provision for periodical payments, increasing, reducing or terminating those payments.

11 (1) Where a maintenance agreement provides for the continuation, after the death of one of the parties, of payments for the maintenance of a child and that party dies domiciled in England and Wales, the surviving party or the personal representatives of the deceased party may apply to the High Court or a county court for an order under paragraph 10.

(2) If a maintenance agreement is altered by a court on an application under this paragraph, the agreement shall have effect thereafter as if the alteration had been made, immediately before the death, by agreement between the parties and for valuable consideration.

(3) An application under this paragraph shall not, except with leave of the High Court or a county court, be made after the end of the period of six months beginning with the day on which representation in regard to the estate of the deceased is first taken out.

(4) In considering for the purposes of sub-paragraph (3) the question when representation was first taken out, a grant limited to settled land or to trust property shall be left out of account and a grant limited to real estate or to personal estate shall be left out of account unless a grant limited to the remainder of the estate has previously been made or is made at the same time.

(5) A county court shall not entertain an application under this paragraph, or an application for leave to make an application under this paragraph, unless it would have jurisdiction to hear and determine proceedings for an order under section 2 of the Inheritance (Provision for Family and Dependants) Act 1975 in relation to the deceased's estate by virtue of section 25 of the County Courts Act 1984 (jurisdiction under the Act of 1975).

(6) The provisions of this paragraph shall not render the personal representatives of the deceased liable for having distributed any part of the estate of the deceased after the expiry of the period of six months referred to in sub-paragraph (3) on the ground that they ought to have taken into account the possibility that a court might grant leave for an application by virtue of this paragraph to be made by the surviving party after that period.

(7) Sub-paragraph (6) shall not prejudice any power to recover any part of the estate so distributed arising by virtue of the making of an order in pursuance of this paragraph.

Defined terms—"child": s 105(1), Sch 1, para 16(1); "financial arrangements", "maintenance agreement": para 10(1).

Scope of provision—This paragraph is equivalent to Matrimonial Causes Act 1973, s 36 and enables a maintenance agreement containing provision for a child to be varied on the death of one of the parties to that agreement. MCA 1973, s 36 confers jurisdiction only if the parents are married; this paragraph applies irrespective of whether the parents have been married. The application must be made to the High Court or a county court and not to a magistrates' court.

12 Enforcement of orders for maintenance

(1) Any person for the time being under an obligation to make payments in pursuance of any order for the payment of money made by a magistrates' court under this Act shall give notice of any change of address to such person (if any) as may be specified in the order.

(2) Any person failing without reasonable excuse to give such a notice shall be guilty of an offence and liable on summary conviction to a fine not exceeding level 2 on the standard scale.

(3) An order for the payment of money made by a magistrates' court under this Act shall be enforceable as a magistrates' court maintenance order within the meaning of section 150(1) of the Magistrates' Courts Act 1980.

13 Direction for settlement of instrument by conveyancing counsel

Where the High Court or a county court decides to make an order under this Act for the securing of periodical payments or for the transfer or settlement of property, it may direct that the matter be referred to one of the conveyancing counsel of the court to settle a proper instrument to be executed by all necessary parties.

14 Financial provision for child resident in country outside England and Wales

(1) Where one parent of a child lives in England and Wales and the child lives outside England and Wales with –

(*a*) another parent of his;
(*b*) a guardian of his; or
(*c*) a person in whose favour a residence order is in force with respect to the child,

the court shall have power, on an application made by any of the persons mentioned in paragraphs (*a*) to (*c*), to make one or both of the orders mentioned in paragraph 1(2)(*a*) and (*b*) against the parent living in England and Wales.

(2) Any reference in this Act to the powers of the court under paragraph 1(2) or to an order made under paragraph 1(2) shall include a reference to the powers which the court has by virtue of sub-paragraph (1) or (as the case may be) to an order made by virtue of sub-paragraph (1).

Defined terms—"child": s 105(1), Sch 1, para 16(1); "guardian": s 105(1); "residence order": s 8(1).

Scope of provision—This paragraph enables the court to make a periodical payments or secured periodical payments order against a parent living in England and Wales when the child lives outside England and Wales either with a parent or guardian or with a holder of a residence order.

"parent"—This term has the extended meaning given by para 16(2); see also **Meaning of "parent"** under s 10.

15 Local authority contribution to child's maintenance

(1) Where a child lives, or is to live, with a person as the result of a residence order, a local authority may make contributions to that person towards the cost of the accommodation and maintenance of the child.

(2) Sub-paragraph (1) does not apply where the person with whom the child lives, or is to live, is a parent of the child or the husband or wife of a parent of the child.

Defined terms—"child": s 105(1), Sch 1, para 16(1); "local authority": s 105(1); "residence order": s 8(1).

16 Interpretation

(1) In this Schedule "child" includes, in any case where an application is made under paragraph 2 or 6 in relation to a person who has reached the age of eighteen, that person.

(2) In this Schedule except paragraphs 2 and 15, "parent" includes any party to a marriage (whether or not subsisting) in relation to whom the child concerned is a child of the family; and for this purpose any reference to either parent or both parents shall be construed as references to any parent of his and to all of his parents.

(3) In this Schedule, "maintenance calculation" has the same meaning as it has in the Child Support Act 1991 by virtue of section 54 of that Act as read with any regulations in force under that section.

Amendments—SI 1993/623; Child Support, Pensions and Social Security Act 2000, s 26, Sch 3, para 10.

Defined terms—"child of the family": s 105(1).

SCHEDULE 2
LOCAL AUTHORITY SUPPORT FOR CHILDREN AND FAMILIES

PART I
PROVISION OF SERVICES FOR FAMILIES

1 Identification of children in need and provision of information

(1) Every local authority shall take reasonable steps to identify the extent to which there are children in need within their area.

(2) Every local authority shall –

(*a*) publish information

(i) about services provided by them under sections 17, 18, 20, 23B to 23D, 24A and 24B; and

(ii) where they consider it appropriate, about the provision by others (including, in particular, voluntary organisations) of services which the authority have power to provide under those sections; and

(*b*) take such steps as are reasonably practicable to ensure that those who might benefit from the services receive the information relevant to them.

Amendments—Children (Leaving Care) Act 2000, s 7(4).

1A Children's services plans

(1) Every local authority shall, on or before 31 March 1997 –

(*a*) review their provision of services under sections 17, 20, 21, 23 and 24; and

(*b*) having regard to that review and to their most recent review under section 19, prepare and publish a plan for the provision of services under Part III.

(2) Every local authority –

(*a*) shall, from time to time review the plan prepared by them under sub-paragraph (1)(*b*) (as modified or last substituted under this sub-paragraph), and

(*b*) may, having regard to that review and to their most recent review under section 19, prepare and publish –

(i) modifications (or, as the case may be, further modifications) to the plan reviewed; or
(ii) a plan in substitution for that plan.

(3) In carrying out any review under this paragraph and in preparing any plan or modifications to a plan, a local authority shall consult –

(*a*) every Health Authority and Primary Care Trust the whole or part of whose area lies within the area of the local authority;
(*b*) every National Health Service trust which manages a hospital, establishment or facility (within the meaning of the National Health Service and Community Care Act 1990) in the authority's area;
(*c*) if the local authority is not itself a local education authority, every local education authority the whole or any part of whose area lies within the area of the local authority;
(*d*) any organisation which represents schools in the authority's area which are grant-maintained schools or grant-maintained special schools (within the meaning of the Education Act 1993);
(*e*) the governing body of every such school in the authority's area which is not so represented;
(*f*) such voluntary organisations as appear to the local authority –
(i) to represent the interests of persons who use or are likely to use services provided by the local authority under Part III; or
(ii) to provide services in the area of the local authority which, were they to be provided by the local authority, might be categorised as services provided under that Part;
(*g*) the chief constable of the police force for the area;
(*h*) the probation committee for the area;
(*i*) such other persons as appear to the local authority to be appropriate; and
(*j*) such other persons as the Secretary of State may direct.

(4) Every local authority shall, within 28 days of receiving a written request from the Secretary of State, submit to him a copy of –

(*a*) the plan prepared by them under sub-paragraph (1); or
(*b*) where that plan has been modified or substituted, the plan as modified or last substituted.

Amendments—Inserted by SI 1996/785; amended by SI 2000/90.

2 Maintenance of a register of disabled children

(1) Every local authority shall open and maintain a register of disabled children within their area.

(2) The register may be kept by means of a computer.

3 Assessment of children's needs

Where it appears to a local authority that a child within their area is in need, the authority may assess his needs for the purposes of this Act at the same time as any assessment of his needs is made under –

(*a*) the Chronically Sick and Disabled Persons Act 1970;
(*b*) Part IV of the Education Act 1996;
(*c*) the Disabled Persons (Services, Consultation and Representation) Act 1986; or

(*d*) any other enactment.

Amendments—Education Act 1996, s 582(1), Sch 37, Pt I, para 92.

4 Prevention of neglect and abuse

(1) Every local authority shall take reasonable steps, through the provision of services under Part III of this Act, to prevent children within their area suffering ill-treatment or neglect.

(2) Where a local authority believe that a child who is at any time within their area –

(*a*) is likely to suffer harm; but
(*b*) lives or proposes to live in the area of another local authority they shall inform that other local authority.

(3) When informing that other local authority they shall specify –

(*a*) the harm that they believe he is likely to suffer; and
(*b*) (if they can) where the child lives or proposes to live.

5 Provision of accommodation in order to protect child

(1) Where –

(*a*) it appears to a local authority that a child who is living on particular premises is suffering, or is likely to suffer, ill treatment at the hands of another person who is living on those premises; and
(*b*) that other person proposes to move from the premises,

the authority may assist that other person to obtain alternative accommodation.

(2) Assistance given under this paragraph may be in cash.

(3) Subsections (7) to (9) of section 17 shall apply in relation to assistance given under this paragraph as they apply in relation to assistance given under that section.

6 Provision for disabled children

Every local authority shall provide services designed –

(*a*) to minimise the effect on disabled children within their area of their disabilities; and
(*b*) to give such children the opportunity to lead lives which are as normal as possible.

7 Provision to reduce need for care proceedings etc

Every local authority shall take reasonable steps designed –

(*a*) to reduce the need to bring –
  (i) proceedings for care or supervision orders with respect to children within their area;
  (ii) criminal proceedings against such children;
  (iii) any family or other proceedings with respect to such children which might lead to them being placed in the authority's care; or
  (iv) proceedings under the inherent jurisdiction of the High Court with respect to children;

(*b*) to encourage children within their area not to commit criminal offences; and

(*c*) to avoid the need for children within their area to be placed in secure accommodation.

"reasonable steps" (para 7)—The duty to take "reasonable steps" in relation to the housing needs of an autistic child accommodated by the local authority meant that the council must do its best within the bounds of what is reasonably practicable to secure "not unsuitable" accommodation for the child; the accommodation to be secured was not required to be suitable to the particular needs of the child, only to be "not unsuitable" (*R v London Borough of Brent ex parte S* [1994] 1 FLR 203).

8 Provision for children living with their families

Every local authority shall make such provision as they consider appropriate for the following services to be available with respect to children in need within their area while they are living with their families –

(*a*) advice, guidance and counselling;
(*b*) occupational, social, cultural or recreational activities;
(*c*) home help (which may include laundry facilities);
(*d*) facilities for, or assistance with, travelling to and from home for the purpose of taking advantage of any other service provided under this Act or of any similar service;
(*e*) assistance to enable the child concerned and his family to have a holiday.

9 Family centres

(1) Every local authority shall provide such family centres as they consider appropriate in relation to children within their area.

(2) "Family centre" means a centre at which any of the persons mentioned in sub-paragraph (3) may –

(*a*) attend for occupational, social, cultural or recreational activities;
(*b*) attend for advice, guidance or counselling; or
(*c*) be provided with accommodation while he is receiving advice, guidance or counselling.

(3) The persons are –

(*a*) a child;
(*b*) his parents;
(*c*) any person who is not a parent of his but who has parental responsibility for him;
(*d*) any other person who is looking after him.

10 Maintenance of the family home

Every local authority shall take such steps as are reasonably practicable, where any child within their area who is in need and whom they are not looking after is living apart from his family –

(*a*) to enable him to live with his family; or
(*b*) to promote contact between him and his family,

if, in their opinion, it is necessary to do so in order to safeguard or promote his welfare.

"such steps as are reasonably practicable"—A local authority is not required to contact extended family where a mother wants a child adopted without them being so informed (*Z County Council v R* [2001] 1 FLR 365).

11 Duty to consider racial groups to which children in need belong

Every local authority shall, in making any arrangements –

(*a*) for the provision of day care within their area; or
(*b*) designed to encourage persons to act as local authority foster parents,

have regard to the different racial groups to which children within their area who are in need belong.

PART II
CHILDREN LOOKED AFTER BY LOCAL AUTHORITIES

12 Regulations as to placing of children with local authority foster parents

Regulations under section 23(2)(*a*) may, in particular, make provision –

(*a*) with regard to the welfare of children placed with local authority foster parents;
(*b*) as to the arrangements to be made by local authorities in connection with the health and education of such children;
(*c*) as to the records to be kept by local authorities;
(*d*) for securing that a child is not placed with a local authority foster parent unless that person is for the time being approved as a local authority foster parent by such local authority as may be prescribed;
(*e*) for securing that where possible the local authority foster parent with whom a child is to be placed is –
  (i) of the same religious persuasion as the child; or
  (ii) gives an undertaking that the child will be brought up in that religious persuasion;
(*f*) for securing that children placed with local authority foster parents, and the premises in which they are accommodated, will be supervised and inspected by a local authority and that the children will be removed from those premises if their welfare appears to require it;
(*g*) as to the circumstances in which local authorities may make arrangements for duties imposed on them by the regulations to be discharged, on their behalf.

13 Regulations as to arrangements under section 23(2)(f)

Regulations under section 23(2)(*f*) may, in particular, make provision as to –

(*a*) the persons to be notified of any proposed arrangements;
(*b*) the opportunities such persons are to have to make representations in relation to the arrangements proposed;
(*c*) the persons to be notified of any proposed changes in arrangements;
(*d*) the records to be kept by local authorities;
(*e*) the supervision by local authorities of any arrangements made.

14 Regulations as to conditions under which child in care is allowed to live with parent etc

Regulations under section 23(5) may, in particular, impose requirements on a local authority as to –

(*a*) the making of any decision by a local authority to allow a child to live with any person falling within section 23(4) (including requirements as to those who must be consulted before the decision is made, and those who must be notified when it has been made);
(*b*) the supervision or medical examination of the child concerned;
(*c*) the removal of the child, in such circumstances as may be prescribed, from the care of the person with whom he has been allowed to live;
(*d*) the records to be kept by local authorities.

Amendments—Courts and Legal Services Act 1990, s 116, Sch 16, para 26.

15 Promotion and maintenance of contact between child and family

(1) Where a child is being looked after by a local authority, the authority shall, unless it is not reasonably practicable or consistent with his welfare, endeavour to promote contact between the child and –

(*a*) his parents;
(*b*) any person who is not a parent of his but who has parental responsibility for him; and
(*c*) any relative, friend or other person connected with him.

(2) Where a child is being looked after by a local authority –

(*a*) the authority shall take such steps as are reasonably practicable to secure that
  (i) his parents; and
  (ii) any person who is not a parent of his but who has parental responsibility for him,
are kept informed of where he is being accommodated; and
(*b*) every such person shall secure that the authority are kept informed of his or her address.

(3) Where a local authority ("the receiving authority") take over the provision of accommodation for a child from another local authority ("the transferring authority") under section 20(2) –

(*a*) the receiving authority shall (where reasonably practicable) inform
  (i) the child's parents; and
  (ii) any person who is not a parent of his but who has parental responsibility for him;
(*b*) sub-paragraph (2)(*a*) shall apply to the transferring authority, as well as the receiving authority, until at least one such person has been informed of the change; and
(*c*) sub-paragraph (2)(*b*) shall not require any person to inform the receiving authority of his address until he has been so informed.

(4) Nothing in this paragraph requires a local authority to inform any person of the whereabouts of a child if –

(*a*) the child is in the care of the authority; and
(*b*) the authority has reasonable cause to believe that informing the person would prejudice the child's welfare.

(5) Any person who fails (without reasonable excuse) to comply with sub-paragraph (2)(*b*) shall be guilty of an offence and liable on summary conviction to a fine not exceeding level 2 on the standard scale.

(6) It shall be a defence in any proceedings under sub-paragraph (5) to prove that the defendant was residing at the same address as another person who was the child's parent or had parental responsibility for the child and had reasonable cause to believe that the other person had informed the appropriate authority that both of them were residing at that address.

"local authority shall ... endeavour to promote contact" (para 15(1))—In *Re P (Minors) (Contact with Children in Care)* [1993] 2 FLR 156, Ewbank J dismissed the father's application for the discharge of a care order, but exercised his power under CA 1989, s 34 to order contact between the father and his two daughters. He directed the local authority "to promote and encourage contact", adding that: "The previous practice of access at the discretion of the local authority should not be the regular practice as s 34 provides that reasonable contact should be the norm, not contact at the local authority's discretion which is not the same. 'Reasonable' contact implied agreement with the parents; and if no agreement was possible, contact which was objectively reasonable." How much, or little, contact is "reasonable" must be for the local authority to decide, subject to any order of the court. The local authority's duty to "promote" contact arises only insofar as it perceives this to be consistent with the child's welfare. However, bearing in mind that, even in cases of urgent necessity, s 34(6) only permits refusal of contact for up to 7 days, reasonable contact should not be unduly restricted, unless by agreement or pursuant to a court order applied for by the local authority itself under s 34(2) (*Re T (Termination of Contact)* [1997] 1 FLR 517).

"any relative, friend or other person connected with him" (para 15(1)(*c*))—A person who for a period of time occupies the status of stepfather falls within the ambit of this paragraph, as do half-siblings (*L v London Borough of Bromley*) [1998] 1 FLR 709).

16 Visits to or by children: expenses

(1) This paragraph applies where –

(*a*) a child is being looked after by a local authority; and
(*b*) the conditions mentioned in sub-paragraph (3) are satisfied.

(2) The authority may –

(*a*) make payments to –
(i) a parent of the child;
(ii) any person who is not a parent of his but who has parental responsibility for him; or
(iii) any relative, friend or other person connected with him,
in respect of travelling, subsistence or other expenses incurred by that person in visiting the child; or
(*b*) make payments to the child, or to any person on his behalf, in respect of travelling, subsistence or other expenses incurred by or on behalf of the child in his visiting –
(i) a parent of his;
(ii) any person who has parental responsibility for him; or
(iii) any relative, friend or other person connected with him.

(3) The conditions are that –

(*a*) it appears to the authority that the visit in question could not otherwise be made without undue financial hardship; and
(*b*) the circumstances warrant the making of the payments.

17 Appointment of visitor for child who is not being visited

(1) Where it appears to a local authority in relation to any child that they are looking after that –

(*a*) communication between the child and –

(i) a parent of his, or

(ii) any person who is not a parent of his but who has parental responsibility for him,

has been infrequent; or

(*b*) he has not visited or been visited by (or lived with) any such person during the preceding twelve months,

and that it would be in the child's best interests for an independent person to be appointed to be his visitor for the purposes of this paragraph, they shall appoint such a visitor.

(2) A person so appointed shall –

(*a*) have the duty of visiting, advising and befriending the child; and

(*b*) be entitled to recover from the authority who appointed him any reasonable expenses incurred by him for the purposes of his functions under this paragraph.

(3) A person's appointment as a visitor in pursuance of this paragraph shall be determined if –

(*a*) he gives notice in writing to the authority who appointed him that he resigns the appointment; or

(*b*) the authority give him notice in writing that they have terminated it.

(4) The determination of such an appointment shall not prejudice any duty under this paragraph to make a further appointment.

(5) Where a local authority propose to appoint a visitor for a child under this paragraph, the appointment shall not be made if –

(*a*) the child objects to it; and

(*b*) the authority are satisfied that he has sufficient understanding to make an informed decision.

(6) Where a visitor has been appointed for a child under this paragraph, the local authority shall determine the appointment if –

(*a*) the child objects to its continuing; and

(*b*) the authority are satisfied that he has sufficient understanding to make an informed decision.

(7) The Secretary of State may make regulations as to the circumstances in which a person appointed as a visitor under this paragraph is to be regarded as independent of the local authority appointing him.

18 Power to guarantee apprenticeship deeds etc

(1) While a child is being looked after by a local authority, or is a person qualifying for advice and assistance, the authority may undertake any obligation by way of guarantee under any deed of apprenticeship or articles of clerkship which he enters into.

(2) Where a local authority have undertaken any such obligation under any deed or articles they may at any time (whether or not they are still looking after the person concerned) undertake the like obligation under any supplemental deed or articles.

19 Arrangements to assist children to live abroad

(1) A local authority may only arrange for, or assist in arranging for, any child in their care to live outside England and Wales with the approval of the court.

(2) A local authority may, with the approval of every person who has parental responsibility for the child arrange for, or assist in arranging for, any other child looked after by them to live outside England and Wales.

(3) The court shall not give its approval under sub-paragraph (1) unless it is satisfied that –

(*a*) living outside England and Wales would be in the child's best interests;
(*b*) suitable arrangements have been, or will be, made for his reception and welfare in the country in which he will live;
(*c*) the child has consented to living in that country; and
(*d*) every person who has parental responsibility for the child has consented to his living in that country.

(4) Where the court is satisfied that the child does not have sufficient understanding to give or withhold his consent, it may disregard sub-paragraph (3)(*c*) and give its approval if the child is to live in the country concerned with a parent, guardian, or other suitable person.

(5) Where a person whose consent is required by sub-paragraph (3)(*d*) fails to give his consent, the court may disregard that provision and give its approval if it is satisfied that that person –

(*a*) cannot be found;
(*b*) is incapable of consenting; or
(*c*) is withholding his consent unreasonably.

(6) Section 56 of the Adoption Act 1976 (which requires authority for the taking or sending abroad for adoption of a child who is a British subject) shall not apply in the case of any child who is to live outside England and Wales with the approval of the court given under this paragraph.

(7) Where a court decides to give its approval under this paragraph it may order that its decision is not to have effect during the appeal period.

(8) In sub-paragraph (7) "the appeal period" means –

(*a*) where an appeal is made against the decision, the period between the making of the decision and the determination of the appeal; and
(*b*) otherwise, the period during which an appeal may be made against the decision.

"with the approval of the court" (para 19(1))—An application by a local authority to move children in its care to Northern Ireland was considered in *Re P (Minors) (Interim Order)* [1993] 2 FLR 742. In *Re G (Leave to Appeal: Jurisdiction)* [1999] 1 FLR 771 approval was not necessary because, on an application under Sch 2, para 19, the judge had decided that the best interests of the child were met by making an interim residence order in favour of her father in Scotland. The Court of Appeal held that the court was entitled to dispense with unnecessary procedural difficulties in order to achieve what was in the best interests of the child. In the circumstances of *Flintshire County Council v K* [2001] 2 FLR 476 it was found to be appropriate to order the return of children to the USA under a care order rather than the inherent jurisdiction as it enabled the local authority to manage the arrangements. Paragraph 19 is also a gateway to foreign adoption where a child is in local authority care, in addition to Adoption Act 1976, s 55 (*Re S (Freeing for Adoption)* [2002] EWCA Civ 798, [2002] 2 FLR 681).

"in the child's best interests" (para 19(3)(*a*))—The child's best interests are not paramount in this context; they are merely one of the four specific factors which the court must consider (*Re G (Minors) (Care: Leave to Place Outside Jurisdiction)* [1994] 2 FLR 301).

"is withholding his consent unreasonably" (para 19(5)(*c*))—In determining whether the parent's refusal is within the broad band of reasonable decisions which a responsible parent might take, the court should apply the test set out in *Re W (An Infant)* [1971] AC 682, and regard must be had to the extent of the sacrifice being made by the parent (*Re G (Minors) (Care: Leave to Place Outside Jurisdiction)* [1994] 2 FLR 301; *Re W (Care: Leave to Place Outside Jurisdiction)* [1994] 2 FLR 1087).

Preparation for ceasing to be looked after

19A It is the duty of the local authority looking after a child to advise, assist and befriend him with a view to promoting his welfare when they have ceased to look after him.

Amendments—Inserted by Children (Leaving Care) Act 2000, s 1.

19B (1) A local authority shall have the following additional functions in relation to an eligible child whom they are looking after.

(2) In sub-paragraph (1) "eligible child" means, subject to sub-paragraph (3), a child who –

(*a*) is aged sixteen or seventeen; and
(*b*) has been looked after by a local authority for a prescribed period, or periods amounting in all to a prescribed period, which began after he reached a prescribed age and ended after he reached the age of sixteen.

(3) The Secretary of State may prescribe –

(*a*) additional categories of eligible children; and
(*b*) categories of children who are not to be eligible children despite falling within sub-paragraph (2).

(4) For each eligible child, the local authority shall carry out an assessment of his needs with a view to determining what advice, assistance and support it would be appropriate for them to provide him under this Act –

(*a*) while they are still looking after him; and
(*b*) after they cease to look after him,

and shall then prepare a pathway plan for him.

(5) The local authority shall keep the pathway plan under regular review.

(6) Any such review may be carried out at the same time as a review of the child's case carried out by virtue of section 26.

(7) The Secretary of State may by regulations make provision as to assessments for the purposes of sub-paragraph (4).

(8) The regulations may in particular provide for the matters set out in section 23B(6).

Amendments—Inserted by Children (Leaving Care) Act 2000, s 1.

19C Personal advisers

A local authority shall arrange for each child whom they are looking after who is an eligible child for the purposes of paragraph 19B to have a personal adviser.

Amendments—Inserted by Children (Leaving Care) Act 2000, s 1.

20 Death of children being looked after by local authorities

(1) If a child who is being looked after by a local authority dies, the authority –

(*a*) shall notify the Secretary of State;
(*b*) shall, so far as is reasonably practicable, notify the child's parents and every person who is not a parent of his but who has parental responsibility for him;
(*c*) may, with the consent (so far as it is reasonably practicable to obtain it) of every person who has parental responsibility for the child, arrange for the child's body to be buried or cremated; and
(*d*) may, if the conditions mentioned in sub-paragraph (2) are satisfied, make payments to any person who has parental responsibility for the child, or any relative, friend or other person connected with the child, in respect of travelling, subsistence or other expenses incurred by that person in attending the child's funeral.

(2) The conditions are that –

(*a*) it appears to the authority that the person concerned could not otherwise attend the child's funeral without undue financial hardship; and
(*b*) that the circumstances warrant the making of the payments.

(3) Sub-paragraph (1) does not authorise cremation where it does not accord with the practice of the child's religious persuasion.

(4) Where a local authority have exercised their power under sub-paragraph (1)(*c*) with respect to a child who was under sixteen when he died, they may recover from any parent of the child any expenses incurred by them.

(5) Any sums so recoverable shall, without prejudice to any other method of recovery, be recoverable summarily as a civil debt.

(6) Nothing in this paragraph affects any enactment regulating or authorising the burial, cremation or anatomical examination of the body of a deceased person.

PART III
CONTRIBUTIONS TOWARDS MAINTENANCE OF CHILDREN LOOKED AFTER BY LOCAL AUTHORITIES

21 Liability to contribute

(1) Where a local authority are looking after a child (other than in the cases mentioned in sub-paragraph (7)) they shall consider whether they should recover contributions towards the child's maintenance from any person liable to contribute ("a contributor").

(2) An authority may only recover contributions from a contributor if they consider it reasonable to do so.

(3) The persons liable to contribute are –

(*a*) where the child is under sixteen, each of his parents;

(*b*) where he has reached the age of sixteen, the child himself.

(4) A parent is not liable to contribute during any period when he is in receipt of income support, working families' tax credit or disabled person's tax credit under Part VII of the Social Security Contributions and Benefits Act 1992 or of an income-based jobseeker's allowance.

(5) A person is not liable to contribute towards the maintenance of a child in the care of a local authority in respect of any period during which the child is allowed by the authority (under section 23(5)) to live with a parent of his.

(6) A contributor is not obliged to make any contribution towards a child's maintenance except as agreed or determined in accordance with this Part of this Schedule.

(7) The cases are where the child is looked after by a local authority under –

(*a*) section 21;
(*b*) an interim care order;
(*c*) section 92 of the Powers of Criminal Courts (Sentencing) Act 2000.

Amendments—Disability Living Allowance and Disability Working Allowance Act 1991, s 7(2), Sch 3, para 15; Social Security (Consequential Provisions) Act 1992, s 4, Sch 2, para 108; Jobseekers Act 1995, s 41, Sch 2, para 19; Tax Credits Act 1999, s 1(2), Sch 1, paras 1, 6(*d*)(iii); Powers of Criminal Courts (Sentencing) Act 2000, s 165, Sch 9, para 130.

22 Agreed contributions

(1) Contributions towards a child's maintenance may only be recovered if the local authority have served a notice ("a contribution notice") on the contributor specifying –

(*a*) the weekly sum which they consider that he should contribute; and
(*b*) arrangements for payment.

(2) The contribution notice must be in writing and dated.

(3) Arrangements for payment shall, in particular, include –

(*a*) the date on which liability to contribute begins (which must not be earlier than the date of the notice);
(*b*) the date on which liability under the notice will end (if the child has not before that date ceased to be looked after by the authority); and
(*c*) the date on which the first payment is to be made.

(4) The authority may specify in a contribution notice a weekly sum which is a standard contribution determined by them for all children looked after by them.

(5) The authority may not specify in a contribution notice a weekly sum greater than that which they consider –

(*a*) they would normally be prepared to pay if they had placed a similar child with local authority foster parents; and
(*b*) it is reasonably practicable for the contributor to pay (having regard to his means).

(6) An authority may at any time withdraw a contribution notice (without prejudice to their power to serve another).

(7) Where the authority and the contributor agree –

(*a*) the sum which the contributor is to contribute; and
(*b*) arrangements for payment,

(whether as specified in the contribution notice or otherwise) and the contributor notifies the authority in writing that he so agrees, the authority may recover summarily as a civil debt any contribution which is overdue and unpaid.

(8) A contributor may, by serving a notice in writing on the authority, withdraw his agreement in relation to any period of liability falling after the date of service of the notice.

(9) Sub-paragraph (7) is without prejudice to any other method of recovery.

"reasonably practicable for the contributor to pay (having regard to his means)" (para 22(5)(*a*))—See **"A contribution order ... shall be made with due regard to the contributor's means"** under para 23.

23 Contribution orders

(1) Where a contributor has been served with a contribution notice and has –

(*a*) failed to reach any agreement with the local authority as mentioned in paragraph 22(7) within the period of one month beginning with the day on which the contribution notice was served; or
(*b*) served a notice under paragraph 22(8) withdrawing his agreement,

the authority may apply to the court for an order under this paragraph.

(2) On such an application the court may make an order ("a contribution order") requiring the contributor to contribute a weekly sum towards the child's maintenance in accordance with arrangements for payment specified by the court.

(3) A contribution order –

(*a*) shall not specify a weekly sum greater than that specified in the contribution notice; and
(*b*) shall be made with due regard to the contributor's means.

(4) A contribution order shall not –

(*a*) take effect before the date specified in the contribution notice; or
(*b*) have effect while the contributor is not liable to contribute (by virtue of paragraph 21); or
(*c*) remain in force after the child has ceased to be looked after by the authority who obtained the order.

(5) An authority may not apply to the court under sub-paragraph (1) in relation to a contribution notice which they have withdrawn.

(6) Where –

(*a*) a contribution order is in force;
(*b*) the authority serve another contribution notice; and
(*c*) the contributor and the authority reach an agreement under paragraph 22(7) in respect of that other contribution notice,

the effect of the agreement shall be to discharge the order from the date on which it is agreed that the agreement shall take effect.

(7) Where an agreement is reached under sub-paragraph (6) the authority shall notify the court –

(*a*) of the agreement; and
(*b*) of the date on which it took effect.

(8) A contribution order may be varied or revoked on the application of the contributor or the authority.

(9) In proceedings for the variation of a contribution order, the authority shall specify –

(*a*) the weekly sum which, having regard to paragraph 22, they propose that the contributor should contribute under the order as varied; and

(*b*) the proposed arrangements for payment.

(10) Where a contribution order is varied, the order –

(*a*) shall not specify a weekly sum greater than that specified by the authority in the proceedings for variation; and

(*b*) shall be made with due regard to the contributor's means.

(11) An appeal shall lie in accordance with rules of court from any order made under this paragraph.

Defined terms—"contribution notice": para 22(1); "contributor": para 21(1).

Jurisdiction—Children (Allocation of Proceedings) Order 1991, art 3 requires proceedings under this paragraph to be commenced in a magistrates' court. Articles 5 and 7(2) have the effect of preventing proceedings so commenced from being transferred to a county court; jurisdiction is therefore restricted, in effect, to magistrates' courts.

Rules of court—The Family Proceedings Courts (Children Act 1989) Rules 1991 apply generally; r 30 deals specifically with contribution orders.

"A contribution order ... shall be made with due regard to the contributor's means" (para 23(3)(*b*))—The criteria to be applied in assessing the contribution to be made by a parent in respect of a child who is being accommodated by a local authority are different to those applied when assessing maintenance for a child. The court must assess the contributor's means by reference to the sources of income available to him and to the manner in which he has expended that income; so long as the money was reasonably expended, the court cannot superimpose a value judgment as to priorities for family spending (*Re C (A Minor)(Contribution Notice)* [1994] 1 FLR 111).

24 Enforcement of contribution orders etc

(1) A contribution order made by a magistrates' court shall be enforceable as a magistrates' court maintenance order (within the meaning of section 150(1) of the Magistrates' Courts Act 1980).

(2) Where a contributor has agreed, or has been ordered, to make contributions to a local authority, any other local authority within whose area the contributor is for the time being living may –

(*a*) at the request of the local authority who served the contribution notice; and

(*b*) subject to agreement as to any sum to be deducted in respect of services rendered,

collect from the contributor any contributions due on behalf of the authority who served the notice.

(3) In sub-paragraph (2) the reference to any other local authority includes a reference to –

(*a*) a local authority within the meaning of section 1(2) of the Social Work (Scotland) Act 1968; and (*b*) a Health and Social Services Board established under Article 16 of the Health and Personal Social Services (Northern Ireland) Order 1972.

(4) The power to collect sums under sub-paragraph (2) includes the power to –

(*a*) receive and give a discharge for any contributions due; and
(*b*) (if necessary) enforce payment of any contributions,

even though those contributions may have fallen due at a time when the contributor was living elsewhere.

(5) Any contributions collected under sub-paragraph (2) shall be paid (subject to any agreed deduction) to the local authority who served the contribution notice.

(6) In any proceedings under this paragraph, a document which purports to be –

(*a*) a copy of an order made by a court under or by virtue of paragraph 23; and
(*b*) certified as a true copy by the justices' chief executive for the court,

shall be evidence of the order.

(7) In any proceedings under this paragraph, a certificate which –

(*a*) purports to be signed by the clerk or some other duly authorised officer of the local authority who obtained the contribution order; and
(*b*) states that any sum due to the authority under the order is overdue and unpaid,

shall be evidence that the sum is overdue and unpaid.

Amendments—Access to Justice Act 1999, s 90, Sch 13, para 162.

Defined terms—"contribution notice": para 22(1); "contribution order": para 23(2); "contributor": para 21(1); "local authority": s 105(1).

25 Regulations

The Secretary of State may make regulations –

(*a*) as to the considerations which a local authority must take into account in deciding –
  (i) whether it is reasonable to recover contributions; and
  (ii) what the arrangements for payment should be;
(*b*) as to the procedures they must follow in reaching agreements with –
  (i) contributors (under paragraphs 22 and 23); and
  (ii) any other local authority (under paragraph 23).

SCHEDULE 3

SUPERVISION ORDERS

PART I
GENERAL

1 Meaning of "responsible person"

In this Schedule, "the responsible person", in relation to a supervised child, means –

(*a*) any person who has parental responsibility for the child; and
(*b*) any other person with whom the child is living.

2 Power of supervisor to give directions to supervised child

(1) A supervision order may require the supervised child to comply with any directions given from time to time by the supervisor which require him to do all or any of the following things –

(*a*) to live at a place or places specified in the directions for a period or periods so specified;
(*b*) to present himself to a person or persons specified in the directions at a place or places and on a day or days so specified;
(*c*) to participate in activities specified in the directions on a day or days so specified.

(2) It shall be for the supervisor to decide whether, and to what extent, he exercises his power to give directions and to decide the form of any directions which he gives.

(3) Sub-paragraph (1) does not confer on a supervisor power to give directions in respect of any medical or psychiatric examination or treatment (which are matters dealt with in paragraphs 4 and 5).

Court specifying directions for supervisor to give—See under para 3 below.

3 Imposition of obligations on responsible person

(1) With the consent of any responsible person, a supervision order may include a requirement –

(*a*) that he take all reasonable steps to ensure that the supervised child complies with any direction given by the supervisor under paragraph 2;
(*b*) that he take all reasonable steps to ensure that the supervised child complies with any requirement included in the order under paragraph 4 or 5;
(*c*) that he comply with any directions given by the supervisor requiring him to attend at a place specified in the directions for the purpose of taking part in activities so specified.

(2) A direction given under sub-paragraph (1)(*c*) may specify the time at which the responsible person is to attend and whether or not the supervised child is required to attend with him.

(3) A supervision order may require any person who is a responsible person in relation to the supervised child to keep the supervisor informed of his address, if it differs from the child's.

Court cannot specify directions to be given—In *Re V (Care or Supervision Order)* [1996] 1 FLR 776, the Court of Appeal held that a supervision order cannot have conditions attached (in that case, the judge had wrongly made a supervision order subject to a condition that the child continue as a weekly boarder at a particular school), and that Sch 3 deals only with:
(*a*) directions given by the supervisor (see Sch 3, para 2);
(*b*) requirements which the court can impose with the consent of any responsible person (see Sch 3, para 3); and
(*c*) a detailed regime for psychiatric and medical examination of the child (see Sch 3, paras 4 and 5).

The only sanction for infringement of the terms of a supervision order, or of any directions given under it, is for the supervisor to return to court for the order to be varied or discharged; the ultimate sanction would be the substitution of a care order.

Re V was followed in *Re S (Care or Supervision Order)* [1996] 1 FLR 753, CA; and the following cases are also in line with it: *Re H (Supervision Order)* [1994] 2 FLR 979, FD (no power in court under para 3 to specify that supervisor should impose a particular direction on a responsible person); *Re H (Prohibited Steps Order)* [1995] 1 FLR 638, CA (court cannot impose on supervision order a condition of no contact with mother's former cohabitee); and *Re B (Supervision Order: Parental Undertaking)* [1996] 1 FLR 676, CA. The cases of *Croydon London Borough Council v A (No 3)* [1992] 2 FLR 350, FD, and *Re T (A Minor) (Care Order: Conditions)* [1994] 2 FLR 423, CA, which appear to suggest that conditions (eg of residence in a particular place) *can* be attached to a supervision order by the court, would seem to be wrong. *Re B (Supervision Order: Parental Undertaking)* (above) points out that, even though the county court has no inherent jurisdiction to accept undertakings in care proceedings or as part of a supervision order, a parent's agreement to behave in a particular way (in that case, to undergo medical treatment) could be recorded in a preamble to the order, and any failure to honour this agreement could be brought to the attention of the court in due course.

PART II

4 Psychiatric and medical examinations

(1) A supervision order may require the supervised child –

(*a*) to submit to a medical or psychiatric examination; or
(*b*) to submit to any such examination from time to time as directed by the supervisor.

(2) Any such examination shall be required to be conducted –

(*a*) by, or under the direction of, such registered medical practitioner as may be specified in the order;
(*b*) at a place specified in the order and at which the supervised child is to attend as a non-resident patient; or
(*c*) at –
  (i) a health service hospital; or
  (ii) in the case of a psychiatric examination, a hospital, independent hospital or care home,

at which the supervised child is, or is to attend as, a resident patient.

(3) A requirement of a kind mentioned in sub-paragraph (2)(*c*) shall not be included unless the court is satisfied, on the evidence of a registered medical practitioner, that –

(*a*) the child may be suffering from a physical or mental condition that requires, and may be susceptible to, treatment; and
(*b*) a period as a resident patient is necessary if the examination is to be carried out properly.

(4) No court shall include a requirement under this paragraph in a supervision order unless it is satisfied that –

(*a*) where the child has sufficient understanding to make an informed decision, he consents to its inclusion; and
(*b*) satisfactory arrangements have been, or can be, made for the examination.

Amendments—Care Standards Act 2000, s 116, Sch 4, para 14(24).

5 Psychiatric and medical treatment

(1) Where a court which proposes to make or vary a supervision order is satisfied, on the evidence of a registered medical practitioner approved for the purposes of section 12 of the Mental Health Act 1983, that the mental condition of the supervised child –

(*a*) is such as requires, and may be susceptible to, treatment; but (*b*) is not such as to warrant his detention in pursuance of a hospital order under Part III of that Act,

the court may include in the order a requirement that the supervised child shall, for a period specified in the order, submit to such treatment as is so specified.

(2) The treatment specified in accordance with sub-paragraph (1) must be –

(*a*) by, or under the direction of, such registered medical practitioner as may be specified in the order;
(*b*) as a non-resident patient at such a place as may be so specified; or
(*c*) as a resident patient in a hospital, independent hospital or care home.

(3) Where a court which proposes to make or vary a supervision order is satisfied, on the evidence of a registered medical practitioner, that the physical condition of the supervised child is such as requires, and may be susceptible to, treatment, the court may include in the order a requirement that the supervised child shall, for a period specified in the order, submit to such treatment as is so specified.

(4) The treatment specified in accordance with sub-paragraph (3) must be –

(*a*) by, or under the direction of, such registered medical practitioner as may be specified in the order;
(*b*) as a non-resident patient at such place as may be so specified; or
(*c*) as a resident patient in a health service hospital.

(5) No court shall include a requirement under this paragraph in a supervision order unless it is satisfied –

(*a*) where the child has sufficient understanding to make an informed decision, that he consents to its inclusion; and
(*b*) that satisfactory arrangements have been, or can be, made for the treatment.

(6) If a medical practitioner by whom or under whose direction a supervised person is being treated in pursuance of a requirement included in a supervision order by virtue of this paragraph is unwilling to continue to treat or direct the treatment of the supervised child or is of the opinion that –

(*a*) the treatment should be continued beyond the period specified in the order;
(*b*) the supervised child needs different treatment;
(*c*) he is not susceptible to treatment; or
(*d*) he does not require further treatment,

the practitioner shall make a report in writing to that effect to the supervisor.

(7) On receiving a report under this paragraph the supervisor shall refer it to the court, and on such a reference the court may make an order cancelling or varying the requirement.

Amendments—Care Standards Act 2000, s 116, Sch 4, para 14(24).

PART II
MISCELLANEOUS

6 Life of supervision order

(1) Subject to sub-paragraph (2) and section 91, a supervision order shall cease to have effect at the end of the period of one year beginning with the date on which it was made.

(2) A supervision order shall also cease to have effect if an event mentioned in section 25(1)(*a*) or (*b*) of the Child Abduction and Custody Act 1985 (termination of existing orders) occurs with respect to the child.

(3) Where the supervisor applies to the court to extend, or further extend, a supervision order the court may extend the order for such period as it may specify.

(4) A supervision order may not be extended so as to run beyond the end of the period of three years beginning with the date on which it was made.

Defined terms—"supervision order": s 31(11); "supervisor": s 105(1).

Duration of supervision orders—Normally (subject to s 91 and to Sch 3, para 6(2)), a supervision order lasts for a maximum of one year in the first instance (para 6(1)); there is nothing to preclude an order for less than one year (*M v Warwickshire County Council* [1994] 2 FLR 593). Although para 6(3) facilitates the extension of this period, on more than one occasion if necessary, it nonetheless appears that the effect of para 6(4) is that the longest that the extended order can run is three years from the date of the original order (*Re A (Supervision Order: Extension)* [1995] 1 FLR 335, CA). Thereafter, there would have to be a fresh application under CA 1989, s 31, and the threshold criteria would have to be satisfied.

Test on extension application—To obtain an extension, the applicant must satisfy the court that the welfare of the child requires the supervision order to continue; the s 31 threshold test need not be satisfied again (*Re A (Supervision Order: Extension)* [1995] 1 FLR 335, CA).

CA 1989, s 38 not applicable—CA 1989, s 38 has no application to extension orders. If an application for an extension is made within time and is opposed, and the hearing date will be after the expiry of the original order, the court can make one or more short extension orders pending final determination (*Re A (Supervision Order: Extension)*, above). The court cannot make either a care order or an interim care order on an extension application (ibid).

Procedure—The supervisor must apply for an extension to the court which made the original order (Children (Allocation of Proceedings) Order 1991, art 4(1)) though by virtue of art 4(2) the court has power subsequently to transfer the proceedings in accordance with arts 5–13. FPR 1991, r 4.4 and Family Proceedings Courts (Children Act 1989) Rules 1991, r 4 apply and the appropriate form in App 1 or Sch 1 to the Rules (as the case may be) should be used. For respondents to the application and other persons who must be given written notice, see App 3 or Sch 2 to the rules. As proceedings relating to an extension are "specified proceedings" within the meaning of s 41(6) (s 41(6)(*i*), FPR 1991, r 4.2(2)(*d*) and FPC(CA 1989)R 1991, r 2(2)(*d*)), a children's guardian will normally be appointed.

Alternative applications—The court has a general power under s 39(2) and (3) to vary or discharge a supervision order.

7 (*repealed*)

8 Information to be given to supervisor etc

(1) A supervision order may require the supervised child –

(*a*) to keep the supervisor informed of any change in his address; and
(*b*) to allow the supervisor to visit him at the place where he is living.

(2) The responsible person in relation to any child with respect to whom a supervision order is made shall –

(*a*) if asked by the supervisor, inform him of the child's address (if it is known to him); and

(*b*) if he is living with the child, allow the supervisor reasonable contact with the child.

9 Selection of supervisor

(1) A supervision order shall not designate a local authority as the supervisor unless –

(*a*) the authority agree; or

(*b*) the supervised child lives or will live within their area.

(2)–(5) (*repealed*)

Amendments—Probation Service Act 1993, s 32, Sch 3, para 9; Criminal Justice and Court Services Act 2000 s 74, Sch 7, para 96.

10 Effect of supervision order on earlier orders

The making of a supervision order with respect to any child brings to an end any earlier care or supervision order which –

(*a*) was made with respect to that child; and

(*b*) would otherwise continue in force.

11 Local authority functions and expenditure

(1) The Secretary of State may make regulations with respect to the exercise by a local authority of their functions where a child has been placed under their supervision by a supervision order.

(2) Where a supervision order requires compliance with directions given by virtue of this section, any expenditure incurred by the supervisor for the purposes of the directions shall be defrayed by the local authority designated in the order.

PART III
EDUCATION SUPERVISION ORDERS

Effect of orders

12 (1) Where an education supervision order is in force with respect to a child, it shall be the duty of the supervisor –

(*a*) to advise, assist and befriend, and give directions to –

(i) the supervised child; and

(ii) his parents;

in such a way as will, in the opinion of the supervisor, secure that he is properly educated;

(*b*) where any such directions given to –

(i) the supervised child; or

(ii) a parent of his,

have not been complied with, to consider what further steps to take in the exercise of the supervisor's powers under this Act.

(2) Before giving any directions under sub-paragraph (1) the supervisor shall, so far as is reasonably practicable, ascertain the wishes and feelings of –

(*a*) the child; and
(*b*) his parents;

including, in particular, their wishes as to the place at which the child should be educated.

(3) When settling the terms of any such directions, the supervisor shall give due consideration –

(*a*) having regard to the child's age and understanding, to such wishes and feelings of his as the supervisor has been able to ascertain; and
(*b*) to such wishes and feelings of the child's parents as he has been able to ascertain.

(4) Directions may be given under this paragraph at any time while the education supervision order is in force.

13 (1) Where an education supervision order is in force with respect to a child, the duties of the child's parents under sections 7 and 444 of the Education Act 1996 (duties to secure education of children and to secure regular attendance of registered pupils) shall be superseded by their duty to comply with any directions in force under the education supervision order.

(2) Where an education supervision order is made with respect to a child –

(*a*) any school attendance order –
(i) made under section 437 of the Education Act 1996 with respect to the child; and
(ii) in force immediately before the making of the education supervision order,

shall cease to have effect; and

(*b*) while the education supervision order remains in force, the following provisions shall not apply with respect to the child –
(i) section 437 of that Act (school attendance orders);
(ii) section 9 of that Act (pupils to be educated in accordance with wishes of their parents);
(iii) sections 411 and 423 of that Act (parental preference and appeals against admission decisions);

(*c*) a supervision order made with respect to the child in criminal proceedings, while the education supervision order is in force, may not include an education requirement of the kind which could otherwise be included under paragraph 7 of Schedule 6 to the Powers of Criminal Courts (Sentencing) Act 2000;

(*d*) any education requirement of a kind mentioned in paragraph (*c*), which was in force with respect to the child immediately before the making of the education supervision order, shall cease to have effect.

Amendments—Education Act 1996, s 582(1), Sch 37, Pt I, para 93; Powers of Criminal Courts (Sentencing) Act 2000, s 165, Sch 9, para 131.

14 Effect where child also subject to supervision order

(1) This paragraph applies where an education supervision order and a supervision order, or order under section 63(1) of the Powers of Criminal Courts (Sentencing) Act 2000, are in force at the same time with respect to the same child.

(2) Any failure to comply with a direction given by the supervisor under the education supervision order shall be disregarded if it would not have been reasonably practicable to comply with it without failing to comply with a direction given under the other order.

Amendments—Powers of Criminal Courts (Sentencing) Act 2000, s 165, Sch 9, para 131.

15 Duration of orders

(1) An education supervision order shall have effect for a period of one year, beginning with the date on which it is made.

(2) An education supervision order shall not expire if, before it would otherwise have expired, the court has (on the application of the authority in whose favour the order was made) extended the period during which it is in force.

(3) Such an application may not be made earlier than three months before the date on which the order would otherwise expire.

(4) The period during which an education supervision order is in force may be extended under sub-paragraph (2) on more than one occasion.

(5) No one extension may be for a period of more than three years.

(6) An education supervision order shall cease to have effect on –

(*a*) the child's ceasing to be of compulsory school age; or
(*b*) the making of a care order with respect to the child;

and sub-paragraphs (1) to (4) are subject to this sub-paragraph.

Defined terms—"education supervision order": s 36(2).

Duration of education supervision orders—Normally (subject to para 15(6)) an education supervision order lasts for a maximum of one year in the first instance (para 15(1)). In contrast with para 6(2) and (3), which allow an ordinary supervision order to be extended for no more than three years from the original order, an ESO may be extended for any number of three-year periods until the child ceases to be of compulsory school age or a care order is made and the order expires in accordance with para 15(6). For cases on duration and extension of ordinary supervision orders which may assist with education supervision orders by analogy, see **Duration of supervision orders** under para 6.

"authority in whose favour the order was made" (para 15(2))—Under s 36(1), the designated local education authority is the authority in whose favour the order was made.

16 Information to be given to supervisor etc

(1) An education supervision order may require the child –

(*a*) to keep the supervisor informed of any change in his address; and
(*b*) to allow the supervisor to visit him at the place where he is living.

(2) A person who is the parent of a child with respect to whom an education supervision order has been made shall –

(*a*) if asked by the supervisor, inform him of the child's address (if it is known to him); and
(*b*) if he is living with the child, allow the supervisor reasonable contact with the child.

17 Discharge of orders

(1) The court may discharge any education supervision order on the application of –

(*a*) the child concerned;
(*b*) a parent of his; or
(*c*) the local education authority concerned.

(2) On discharging an education supervision order, the court may direct the local authority within whose area the child lives, or will live, to investigate the circumstances of the child.

Defined terms—"child": s 105(1); "education supervision order": s 36(2); "local authority", "local education authority": s 105(1).

Scope of provision—This paragraph gives the court the option, if it does discharge the order, to require the local authority to investigate the circumstances of the child, no doubt with a view to the local authority seeking a care or supervision order if it considers such action appropriate.

"parent" (para 17(1)(*a*))—By virtue of para 21, for the purposes of Sch 3, Pt III (which includes para 17), "parent" has the same meaning as in the Education Act 1996, ie it includes any person who is not a parent of a child but who has parental responsibility for him or care of him (see Education Act 1996, s 576).

"local education authority concerned" (para 17(1)(*b*))—This refers to the local education authority designated in the order under s 36(1).

Directing local authority investigation (para 17(2))—The wording of para 17(2) contrasts with that of s 37, which is of wider application and empowers the court to direct an investigation in family proceedings. However, a direction under s 37 can only be given where it appears to the court that it may be appropriate for a care or supervision order to be made in respect of the child whereas there is no such restriction under para 17(2). For further detail as to s 37 directions see that section and the annotation **Best practice guidance on s 37(1) directions** thereunder.

18 Offences

(1) If a parent of a child with respect to whom an education supervision order is in force persistently fails to comply with a direction given under the order he shall be guilty of an offence.

(2) It shall be a defence for any person charged with such an offence to prove that –

(*a*) he took all reasonable steps to ensure that the direction was complied with;
(*b*) the direction was unreasonable; or
(*c*) he had complied with –
  (i) a requirement included in a supervision order made with respect to the child; or
  (ii) directions given under such a requirement,

and that it was not reasonably practicable to comply both with the direction and with the requirement or directions mentioned in this paragraph.

(3) A person guilty of an offence under this paragraph shall be liable on summary conviction to a fine not exceeding level 3 on the standard scale.

19 Persistent failure of child to comply with directions

(1) Where a child with respect to whom an education supervision order is in force persistently fails to comply with any direction given under the order, the local education authority concerned shall notify the appropriate local authority.

(2) Where a local authority have been notified under sub-paragraph (1) they shall investigate the circumstances of the child.

(3) In this paragraph "the appropriate local authority" has the same meaning as in section 36.

20 Miscellaneous

The Secretary of State may by regulations make provision modifying, or displacing, the provisions of any enactment about education in relation to any child with respect to whom an education supervision order is in force to such extent as appears to the Secretary of State to be necessary or expedient in consequence of the provision made by this Act with respect to such orders.

21 Interpretation

In this part of this Schedule "parent" has the same meaning as in the Education Act 1996.

Amendments—Education Act 1996, s 582(1), Sch 37, Pt I, para 93.

****

SCHEDULE 7

FOSTER PARENTS: LIMITS ON NUMBER OF FOSTER CHILDREN

1 Interpretation

For the purposes of this Schedule, a person fosters a child if –

(*a*) he is a local authority foster parent in relation to the child;
(*b*) he is a foster parent with whom the child has been placed by a voluntary organisation; or
(*c*) he fosters the child privately.

2 The usual fostering limit

Subject to what follows, a person may not foster more than three children ("the usual fostering limit").

3 Siblings

A person may exceed the usual fostering limit if the children concerned are all siblings with respect to each other.

4 Exemption by local authority

(1) A person may exceed the usual fostering limit if he is exempted from it by the local authority within whose area he lives.

(2) In considering whether to exempt a person, a local authority shall have regard, in particular, to –

(*a*) the number of children whom the person proposes to foster;
(*b*) the arrangements which the person proposes for the care and accommodation of the fostered children;
(*c*) the intended and likely relationship between the person and the fostered children;
(*d*) the period of time for which he proposes to foster the children; and
(*e*) whether the welfare of the fostered children (and of any other children who are or will be living in the accommodation) will be safeguarded and promoted.

(3) Where a local authority exempt a person, they shall inform him by notice in writing –

(*a*) that he is so exempted;
(*b*) of the children, described by name, whom he may foster; and
(*c*) of any condition to which the exemption is subject.

(4) A local authority may at any time by notice in writing –

(*a*) vary or cancel an exemption; or
(*b*) impose, vary or cancel a condition to which the exemption is subject,

and, in considering whether to do so, they shall have regard in particular to the considerations mentioned in sub-paragraph (2).

(5) The Secretary of State may make regulations amplifying or modifying the provisions of this paragraph in order to provide for cases where children need to be placed with foster parents as a matter of urgency.

5 Effect of exceeding fostering limit

(1) A person shall cease to be treated, for the purposes of this Act and the Care Standards Act 2000 as fostering and shall be treated as carrying on a children's home if –

(*a*) he exceeds the usual fostering limit; or
(*b*) where he is exempted under paragraph 4, –
(i) he fosters any child not named in the exemption; and
(ii) in so doing, he exceeds the usual fostering limit.

(2) Sub-paragraph (1) does not apply if the children concerned are all siblings in respect of each other.

Amendments—Care Standards Act 2000, s 116, Sch 4, para 14(25).

6 Complaints etc

(1) Every local authority shall establish a procedure for considering any representations (including any complaint) made to them about the discharge of their functions under paragraph 4 by a person exempted or seeking to be exempted under that paragraph.

(2) In carrying out any consideration of representations under subparagraph (1), a local authority shall comply with any regulations made by the Secretary of State for the purposes of this paragraph.

SCHEDULE 8
PRIVATELY FOSTERED CHILDREN

Exemptions

1 A child is not a privately fostered child while he is being looked after by a local authority.

2 (1) A child is not a privately fostered child while he is in the care of any person –

(*a*) in premises in which any –
  (i) parent of his;
  (ii) person who is not a parent of his but who has parental responsibility for him; or
  (iii) person who is a relative of his and who has assumed responsibility for his care,

is for the time being living;

(*b*) (*repealed*)

(*c*) in accommodation provided by or on behalf of any voluntary organisation;

(*d*) in any school in which he is receiving full-time education;

(*e*) in any health service hospital;

(*f*) in any care home or independent hospital;

(*g*) in any home or institution not specified in this paragraph but provided, equipped and maintained by the Secretary of State.

(2) Sub-paragraph (1)(*c*) to (*g*) does not apply where the person caring for the child is doing so in his personal capacity and not in the course of carrying out his duties in relation to the establishment mentioned in the paragraph in question.

Amendments—Registered Homes (Amendment) Act 1991, s 2(6); Care Standards Act 2000, s 116, Sch 4, para 14(27), (28).

3 A child is not a privately fostered child while he is in the care of any person in compliance with –

(*a*) an order under section 63(1) of the Powers of Criminal Courts (Sentencing) Act 2000; or

(*b*) a supervision requirement within the meaning of Part II of the Children (Scotland) Act 1995.

Amendments—Children (Scotland) Act 1995, s 105(4), Sch 4, para 48(1), (5); Powers of Criminal Courts (Sentencing) Act 2000, s 165, Sch 9, para 132.

4 A child is not a privately fostered child while he is liable to be detained, or subject to guardianship, under the Mental Health Act 1983.

5 A child is not a privately fostered child while –

(*a*) he is placed in the care of a person who proposes to adopt him under arrangements made by an adoption agency within the meaning of –

(i) section 1 of the Adoption Act 1976;

(ii) section 1 of the Adoption (Scotland) Act 1978; or

(iii) Article 3 of the Adoption (Northern Ireland) Order 1987; or

(*b*) he is a protected child.

6 Power of local authority to impose requirements

(1) Where a person is fostering any child privately, or proposes to foster any child privately, the appropriate local authority may impose on him requirements as to –

(*a*) the number, age and sex of the children who may be privately fostered by him;

(*b*) the standard of the accommodation and equipment to be provided for them;

(*c*) the arrangements to be made with respect to their health and safety; and

(*d*) particular arrangements which must be made with respect to the provision of care for them,

and it shall be his duty to comply with any such requirement before the end of such period as the authority may specify unless, in the case of a proposal, the proposal is not carried out.

(2) A requirement may be limited to a particular child, or class of child.

(3) A requirement (other than one imposed under sub-paragraph (1)(*a*)) may be limited by the authority so as to apply only when the number of children fostered by the person exceeds a specified number.

(4) A requirement shall be imposed by notice in writing addressed to the person on whom it is imposed and informing him of –

(*a*) the reason for imposing the requirement;

(*b*) his right under paragraph 8 to appeal against it; and

(*c*) the time within which he may do so.

(5) A local authority may at any time vary any requirement, impose any additional requirement or remove any requirement.

(6) In this Schedule –

(*a*) "the appropriate local authority" means –

(i) the local authority within whose area the child is being fostered; or

(ii) in the case of a proposal to foster a child, the local authority within whose area it is proposed that he will be fostered; and

(*b*) "requirement", in relation to any person, means a requirement imposed on him under this paragraph.

7 Regulations requiring notification of fostering etc

(1) The Secretary of State may by regulations make provision as to –

(*a*) the circumstances in which notification is required to be given in connection with children who are, have been or are proposed to be fostered privately; and

(*b*) the manner and form in which such notification is to be given.

(2) The regulations may, in particular –

(*a*) require any person who is, or proposes to be, involved (whether or not directly) in arranging for a child to be fostered privately to notify the appropriate authority;

(*b*) require any person who is –

(i) a parent of a child; or

(ii) a person who is not a parent of his but who has parental responsibility for a child,

and who knows that it is proposed that the child should be fostered privately, to notify the appropriate authority;

(*c*) require any parent of a privately fostered child, or person who is not a parent of such a child but who has parental responsibility for him, to notify the appropriate authority of any change in his address;

(*d*) require any person who proposes to foster a child privately, to notify the appropriate authority of his proposal;

(*e*) require any person who is fostering a child privately, or proposes to do so, to notify the appropriate authority of –

(i) any offence of which he has been convicted;

(ii) any disqualification imposed on him under section 68; or

(iii) any prohibition imposed on him under section 69;

(*f*) require any person who is fostering a child privately, to notify the appropriate authority of any change in his address;

(*g*) require any person who is fostering a child privately to notify the appropriate authority in writing of any person who begins, or ceases, to be part of his household;

(*h*) require any person who has been fostering a child privately, but has ceased to do so, to notify the appropriate authority (indicating, where the child has died, that that is the reason).

8 Appeals

(1) A person aggrieved by –

(*a*) a requirement imposed under paragraph 6;

(*b*) a refusal of consent under section 68;

(*c*) a prohibition imposed under section 69;

(*d*) a refusal to cancel such a prohibition;

(*e*) a refusal to make an exemption under paragraph 4 of Schedule 7;

(*f*) a condition imposed in such an exemption; or

(*g*) a variation or cancellation of such an exemption,

may appeal to the court.

(2) The appeal must be made within fourteen days from the date on which the person appealing is notified of the requirement, refusal, prohibition, condition, variation or cancellation.

(3) Where the appeal is against –

(*a*) a requirement imposed under paragraph 6;

(*b*) a condition of an exemption imposed under paragraph 4 of Schedule 7; or

(*c*) a variation or cancellation of such an exemption,

the requirement, condition, variation or cancellation shall not have effect while the appeal is pending.

(4) Where it allows an appeal against a requirement or prohibition, the court may, instead of cancelling the requirement or prohibition –

(*a*) vary the requirement, or allow more time for compliance with it; or
(*b*) if an absolute prohibition has been imposed, substitute for it a prohibition on using the premises after such time as the court may specify unless such specified requirements as the local authority had power to impose under paragraph 6 are complied with.

(5) Any requirement or prohibition specified or substituted by a court under this paragraph shall be deemed for the purposes of Part IX (other than this paragraph) to have been imposed by the local authority under paragraph 6 or (as the case may be) section 69.

(6) Where it allows an appeal against a refusal to make an exemption, a condition imposed in such an exemption or a variation or cancellation of such an exemption, the court may –

(*a*) make an exemption;
(*b*) impose a condition; or
(*c*) vary the exemption.

(7) Any exemption made or varied under sub-paragraph (6), or any condition imposed under that sub-paragraph, shall be deemed for the purposes of Schedule 7 (but not for the purpose of this paragraph) to have been made, varied or imposed under that Schedule.

(8) Nothing in sub-paragraph (1)(*e*) to (*g*) confers any right of appeal on –

(*a*) a person who is, or would be if exempted under Schedule 7, a local authority foster parent; or
(*b*) a person who is, or would be if so exempted, a person with whom a child is placed by a voluntary organisation.

Jurisdiction—Children (Allocation of Proceedings) Order 1991, art 3 requires proceedings under Sch 8, para 8 to be commenced in a magistrates' court. Articles 5 and 7(2) have the effect of preventing proceedings so commenced from being transferred to a county court; jurisdiction is therefore restricted, in effect, to magistrates' courts.

"person aggrieved" (para 8(1))—Despite the apparently wide category of potential appellants, the restrictions contained in para 8(8) apply.

"section 68" (para 8(1)(*b*))—Section 68 relates to the need to obtain the consent of the local authority to foster a child privately.

"section 69" (para 8(1)(*c*))—Section 69 empowers a local authority to prohibit private fostering.

"paragraph 4 of Schedule 7" (para 8(1)(*e*))—Schedule 7, para 4 allows a local authority to provide an exemption from the usual fostering limit.

Rules of court—The Family Proceedings Courts (Children Act 1989) Rules 1991 apply generally; r 29(1) requires appeals under para 8(1) to be made by application in accordance with r 4.

9 Extension of Part IX to certain school children during holidays

(1) Where a child under sixteen who is a pupil at a school lives at the school during school holidays for a period of more than two weeks, Part IX shall apply in relation to the child as if –

(*a*) while living at the school, he were a privately fostered child; and
(*b*) paragraphs 2(1)(*c*) and (*d*) and 6 were omitted.

But this sub-paragraph does not apply to a school which is an appropriate children's home.

(2) Sub-paragraph (3) applies to any person who proposes to care for and accommodate one or more children at a school in circumstances in which some or all of them will be treated as private foster children by virtue of this paragraph.

(3) That person shall, not less than two weeks before the first of those children is treated as a private foster child by virtue of this paragraph during the holiday in question, give written notice of his proposal to the local authority within whose area the child is ordinarily resident ("the appropriate authority"), stating the estimated number of the children.

(4) A local authority may exempt any person from the duty of giving notice under sub-paragraph (3).

(5) Any such exemption may be granted for a special period or indefinitely and may be revoked at any time by notice in writing given to the person exempted.

(6) Where a child who is treated as a private foster child by virtue of this paragraph dies, the person caring for him at the school shall, not later than 48 hours after the death, give written notice of it –

(*a*) to the appropriate local authority; and
(*b*) where reasonably practicable, to each parent of the child and to every person who is not a parent of his but who has parental responsibility for him.

(7) Where a child who is treated as a foster child by virtue of this paragraph ceases for any other reason to be such a child, the person caring for him at the school shall give written notice of the fact to the appropriate local authority.

Amendments—Care Standards Act 2000, ss 110, 116, Sch 4, para 14(27).

10 Prohibition of advertisements relating to fostering

No advertisement indicating that a person will undertake, or will arrange for, a child to be privately fostered shall be published, unless it states that person's name and address.

11 Avoidance of insurances on lives of privately fostered children

A person who fosters a child privately and for reward shall be deemed for the purposes of the Life Assurance Act 1774 to have no interest in the life of the child.

****

SCHEDULE 9A

CHILD MINDING AND DAY CARE FOR YOUNG CHILDREN

1 Exemption of certain schools

(1) Except in prescribed circumstances, Part XA does not apply to provision of day care within sub-paragraph (2) for any child looked after in –

(*a*) a maintained school;
(*b*) a school assisted by a local education authority;
(*c*) a school in respect of which payments are made by the Secretary of State or the Assembly under section 485 of the Education Act 1996;

(*d*) an independent school.

(2) The provision mentioned in sub-paragraph (1) is provision of day care made by –

(*a*) the person carrying on the establishment in question as part of the establishment's activities; or
(*b*) a person employed to work at that establishment and authorised to make that provision as part of the establishment's activities.

(3) In sub-paragraph (1) –

"assisted" has the same meaning as in the Education Act 1996;
"maintained school" has the meaning given by section 20(7) of the School Standards and Framework Act 1998.

2 Exemption for other establishments

(1) Part XA does not apply to provision of day care within sub-paragraph (2) for any child looked after –

(*a*) in an appropriate children's home;
(*b*) in a care home;
(*c*) as a patient in a hospital (within the meaning of the Care Standards Act 2000);
(*d*) in a residential family centre.

(2) The provision mentioned in sub-paragraph (1) is provision of day care made by –

(*a*) the department, authority or other person carrying on the establishment in question as part of the establishment's activities; or
(*b*) a person employed to work at that establishment and authorised to make that provision as part of the establishment's activities.

3 Exemption for occasional facilities

(1) Where day care is provided on particular premises on less than six days in any year, that provision shall be disregarded for the purposes of Part XA if the person making it has notified the registration authority in writing before the first occasion on which the premises concerned are so used in that year.

(2) In sub-paragraph (1) "year" means the year beginning with the day (after the commencement of paragraph 5 of Schedule 9) on which the day care in question was or is first provided on the premises concerned and any subsequent year.

Disqualification for registration

4 (1) Regulations may provide for a person to be disqualified for registration for child minding or providing day care.

(2) The regulations may, in particular, provide for a person to be disqualified where –

(*a*) he is included in the list kept under section 1 of the Protection of Children Act 1999;
(*b*) he is included on the grounds mentioned in subsection (6ZA)(*c*) of section 218 of the Education Reform Act 1988 in the list kept for the purposes of regulations made under subsection (6) of that section;

(*c*) an order of a prescribed kind has been made at any time with respect to him;

(*d*) an order of a prescribed kind has been made at any time with respect to any child who has been in his care;

(*e*) a requirement of a prescribed kind has been imposed at any time with respect to such a child, under or by virtue of any enactment;

(*f*) he has at any time been refused registration under Part X or Part XA or any prescribed enactment or had any such registration cancelled;

(*g*) he has been convicted of any offence of a prescribed kind, or has been placed on probation or discharged absolutely or conditionally for any such offence;

(*h*) he has at any time been disqualified from fostering a child privately;

(*j*) a prohibition has been imposed on him at any time under section 69, section 10 of the Foster Children (Scotland) Act 1984 or any prescribed enactment;

(*k*) his rights and powers with respect to a child have at any time been vested in a prescribed authority under a prescribed enactment.

(3) Regulations may provide for a person who lives –

(*a*) in the same household as a person who is himself disqualified for registration for child minding or providing day care; or

(*b*) in a household at which any such person is employed,

to be disqualified for registration for child minding or providing day care.

(4) A person who is disqualified for registration for providing day care shall not provide day care, or be concerned in the management of, or have any financial interest in, any provision of day care.

(5) No person shall employ, in connection with the provision of day care, a person who is disqualified for registration for providing day care.

(6) In this paragraph "enactment" means any enactment having effect, at any time, in any part of the United Kingdom.

5 (1) If any person –

(*a*) acts as a child minder at any time when he is disqualified for registration for child minding; or

(*b*) contravenes any of sub-paragraphs (3) to (5) of paragraph 4,

he shall be guilty of an offence.

(2) Where a person contravenes sub-paragraph (3) of paragraph 4, he shall not be guilty of an offence under this paragraph if he proves that he did not know, and had no reasonable grounds for believing, that the person in question was living or employed in the household.

(3) Where a person contravenes sub-paragraph (5) of paragraph 4, he shall not be guilty of an offence under this paragraph if he proves that he did not know, and had no reasonable grounds for believing, that the person whom he was employing was disqualified.

(4) A person guilty of an offence under this paragraph shall be liable on summary conviction to imprisonment for a term not exceeding six months, or to a fine not exceeding level 5 on the standard scale, or to both.

6 Certificates of registration

(1) If an application for registration is granted, the registration authority shall give the applicant a certificate of registration.

(2) A certificate of registration shall give prescribed information about prescribed matters.

(3) Where, due to a change of circumstances, any part of the certificate requires to be amended, the registration authority shall issue an amended certificate.

(4) Where the registration authority is satisfied that the certificate has been lost or destroyed, the authority shall issue a copy, on payment by the registered person of any prescribed fee.

(5) For the purposes of Part XA, a person is –

(*a*) registered for providing child minding (in England or in Wales); or
(*b*) registered for providing day care on any premises,

if a certificate of registration to that effect is in force in respect of him.

7 Annual fees

Regulations may require registered persons to pay to the registration authority at prescribed times an annual fee of a prescribed amount.

8 Co-operation between authorities

(1) Where it appears to the Chief Inspector that any local authority in England could, by taking any specified action, help in the exercise of any of his functions under Part XA, he may request the help of that authority specifying the action in question.

(2) Where it appears to the Assembly that any local authority in Wales could, by taking any specified action, help in the exercise of any of its functions under Part XA, the Assembly may request the help of that authority specifying the action in question.

(3) An authority whose help is so requested shall comply with the request if it is compatible with their own statutory or other duties and obligations and does not unduly prejudice the discharge of any of their functions.

Amendments—Schedule inserted by Care Standards Act 2000, s 79(2), Sch 3.

****

Civil Jurisdiction and Judgments Act 1982

ARRANGEMENT OF SECTIONS

PART I
IMPLEMENTATION OF THE CONVENTIONS

Main implementing provisions

PART I
IMPLEMENTATION OF THE CONVENTIONS

Main implementing provisions

1 Interpretation of references to the Conventions and Contracting States

(1) In this Act –

"the 1968 Convention" means the Convention on jurisdiction and the enforcement of judgments in civil and commercial matters (including the Protocol annexed to that Convention), signed at Brussels on 27 September 1968;

"the 1971 Protocol" means the Protocol on the interpretation of the 1968 Convention by the European Court, signed at Luxembourg on 3 June 1971;

"the Accession Convention" means the Convention on the accession to the 1968 Convention and the 1971 Protocol of Denmark, the Republic of Ireland and the United Kingdom, signed at Luxembourg on 9 October 1978;

"the 1982 Accession Convention" means the Convention on the accession of the Hellenic Republic to the 1968 Convention and the 1971 Protocol, with the adjustments made to them by the Accession Convention, signed at Luxembourg on 25 October 1982;

"the 1989 Accession Convention" means the Convention on the accession of the Kingdom of Spain and the Portuguese Republic to the 1968 Convention and the 1971 Protocol, with the adjustments made to them by the Accession Convention and the 1982 Accession Convention, signed at Donostia–San Sebastián on 26 May 1989;

"the 1996 Accession Convention" means the Convention on the accession of the Republic of Austria, the Republic of Finland and the Kingdom of Sweden to the 1968 Convention and the 1971 Protocol, with the adjustments made to them by the Accession Convention, the 1982 Accession Convention and the 1989 Accession Convention, signed at Brussels on 29 November 1996;

"the Brussels Conventions" means the 1968 Convention, the 1971 Protocol, the Accession Convention, the 1982 Accession Convention, the 1989 Accession Convention and the 1996 Accession Convention;

"the Lugano Convention" means the Convention on jurisdiction and the enforcement of judgments in civil and commercial matters (including the Protocols annexed to that Convention) opened for signature at Lugano on 16 September 1988 and signed by the United Kingdom on 18 September 1989;

"the Regulation" means Council Regulation (EC) No 44/2001 of 22 December 2000 on jurisdiction and the recognition and enforcement of judgments in civil and commercial matters.

(2) In this Act, unless the context otherwise requires –

(*a*) references to, or to any provision of, the 1968 Convention or the 1971 Protocol are references to that Convention, Protocol or provision as amended by the Accession Convention, the 1982 Accession Convention, the 1989 Accession Convention and the 1996 Accession Convention; and

(*aa*) references to, or to any provision of, the Lugano Convention are references to that Convention as amended on the accession to it of Poland; and

(*b*) any reference in any provision to a numbered article without more is a reference –

(i) to the Article so numbered of the 1968 Convention, in so far as the provision applies in relation to that Convention, and

(ii) to the Article so numbered of the Lugano Convention, in so far as the provision applies in relation to that Convention,

and any reference to a sub-division of a numbered Article shall be construed accordingly.

(3) In this Act –

"Contracting State", without more, in any provision means –

(*a*) in the application of the provision in relation to the Brussels Convention, a Brussels Contracting State; and

(*b*) in the application of the provision in relation to the Lugano Convention, a Lugano Contracting State;

"Brussels Contracting State" means Denmark (which is not bound by the Regulation, but was one of the parties acceding to the 1968 Convention under the Accession Convention);

"Lugano Contracting State" means –

(*a*) one of the original parties to the Lugano Convention, that is to say Austria, Belgium, Denmark, Finland, France, the Federal Republic of Germany, the Hellenic Republic, Iceland, the Republic of Ireland, Italy, Luxembourg, the Netherlands, Norway, Portugal, Spain, Sweden, Switzerland and the United Kingdom; or

(*b*) a party who has subsequently acceded to that Convention, that is to say, Poland

being a State in relation to which that Convention has taken effect in accordance with paragraph 3 or 4 of Article 61.

"Regulation State" in any provision, in the application of that provision in relation to the Regulation, has the same meaning as "Member State" in the Regulation, that is all Member States except Denmark.

(4) ...

Amendments—SI 1989/1346; SI 1990/2591; Civil Jurisdiction and Judgments Act 1991, s 2; SI 2000/1824; SI 2001/3929.

2 The Brussels Conventions to have the force of law

(1) The Brussels Conventions shall have the force of law in the United Kingdom, and judicial notice shall be taken of them.

(2) For convenience of reference there are set out in Schedules 1, 2, 3, 3A, 3B and 3C respectively the English texts of –

(*a*) the 1968 Convention as amended by Titles II and III of the Accession Convention, by Titles II and III of the 1982 Accession Convention, by Titles II and III of, and Annex I(*d*) to, the 1989 Accession Convention and by Titles II and III of the 1996 Accession Convention;

(*b*) the 1971 Protocol as amended by Title IV of the Accession Convention, by Title IV of the 1982 Accession Convention, by Title IV of the 1989 Accession Convention and by Title IV of the 1996 Accession Convention;

(*c*) Titles V and VI of the Accession Convention (transitional and final provisions) as amended by Title V of the 1989 Accession Convention;

(*d*) Titles V and VI of the 1982 Accession Convention (transitional and final provisions), and (*e*) Titles VI and VII of the 1989 Accession Convention (transitional and final provisions),

(*f*) Titles V and VI of the 1996 Accession Convention (transitional and final provisions),

being texts prepared from the authentic English texts referred to in Articles 37 and 41 of the Accession Convention and in Article 17 of the Accession Convention, in Article 34 of the 1989 Accession Convention and in Article 18 of the 1996 Accession Convention.

Amendments—SI 1989/1346; SI 1990/2591; Civil Jurisdiction and Judgments Act 1991, s 3, Sch 2, para 1; SI 2000/1824.

Defined terms—"The Brussels Conventions": s 1(1).

3 Interpretation of the Conventions

(1) Any question as to the meaning or effect of any provision of the Brussels Conventions shall, if not referred to the European Court in accordance with the 1971 Protocol, be determined in accordance with the principles laid down by and any relevant decision of the European Court.

(2) Judicial notice shall be taken of any decision of, or expression of opinion by, the European Court on any such question.

(3) Without prejudice to the generality of subsection (1), the following reports (which are reproduced in the Official Journal of the Communities), namely –

(*a*) the reports by Mr P Jenard on the 1968 Convention and the 1971 Protocol; and

(*b*) the report by Professor Peter Schlosser on the Accession Convention; and

(*c*) the report by Professor Demetrios I Evrigenis and Professor K D Kerameus on the 1982 Accession Convention; and

(*d*) the report by Mr Martinho de Almeida Cruz, Mr Manuel Desantes Real and Mr P Jenard on the 1989 Accession Convention,

may be considered in ascertaining the meaning or effect of any provision of the Brussels Conventions and shall be given such weight as is appropriate in the circumstances.

Amendments—SI 1989/1346; SI 1990/2591; Civil Jurisdiction and Judgments Act 1991, s 3, Sch 2, para 1.

Defined terms—"the Brussels Conventions": s 1(1).

3A The Lugano Convention to have the force of law

(1) The Lugano Convention shall have the force of law in the United Kingdom, and judicial notice shall be taken of it.

(2) For convenience of reference there is set out in Schedule 3C the English text of the Lugano Convention as amended on the accession of Poland to that Convention.

Amendments—Inserted by Civil Jurisdiction and Judgments Act 1991, s 1(1); amended by SI 2000/1824.

Defined terms—"The Lugano Convention": s 1(1).

3B Interpretation of the Lugano Convention

(1) In determining any question as to the meaning or effect of a provision of the Lugano Convention, a court in the United Kingdom shall, in accordance with Protocol No 2 to that Convention, take account of any principles laid down in any relevant decision delivered by a court of any other Lugano Contracting State concerning provisions of the Convention.

(2) Without prejudice to any practice of the courts as to the matters which may be considered apart from this section, the report on the Lugano Convention by Mr P Jenard and Mr G Möller (which is reproduced in the Official Journal of the Communities of 28 July 1990) may be considered in ascertaining the meaning or effect of any provision of the Convention and shall be given such weight as is appropriate in the circumstances.

Amendments—Inserted by Civil Jurisdiction and Judgments Act 1991, s 1(1).

Defined terms—"The Lugano Convention": s 1(1).

Supplementary provisions as to recognition and enforcement of judgments

****

5 Recognition and enforcement of maintenance orders

(1) The function of transmitting to the appropriate court an application under Article 31 for the recognition or enforcement in the United Kingdom of a maintenance order shall be discharged –

(*a*) as respects England and Wales and Northern Ireland, by the Lord Chancellor;

(*b*) as respects Scotland, by the Secretary of State.

In this subsection "the appropriate court" means the magistrates' court or sheriff court having jurisdiction in the matter in accordance with the second paragraph of Article 32.

(2) Such an application shall be determined in the first instance by the prescribed officer of that court.

(3) Where on such an application the enforcement of the order is authorised to any extent, the order shall to that extent be registered in the prescribed manner in that court.

(4) A maintenance order registered under this section shall, for the purposes of its enforcement, be of the same force and effect, the registering court shall have in relation to its enforcement the same powers, and proceedings for or with respect to its enforcement may be taken, as if the order had been originally made by the registering court.

(5) Subsection (4) is subject to Article 39 (restriction on enforcement where appeal pending or time for appeal unexpired), to section 7 and to any provision made by rules of court as to the manner in which and conditions subject to which an order registered under this section may be enforced.

(5A) A maintenance order which by virtue of this section is enforceable by a magistrates' court in England and Wales shall, subject to the modifications of sections 76 and 93 of the Magistrates' Courts Act 1980 specified in subsections (5B) and (5C) below, be enforceable in the same manner as a magistrates' court maintenance order made by that court.

In this subsection "magistrates' court maintenance order" has the same meaning as in section 150(1) of the Magistrates' Courts Act 1980.

(5B) Section 76 (enforcement of sums adjudged to be paid) shall have effect as if for subsections (4) to (6) there were substituted the following subsections –

> "(4) Where proceedings are brought for the enforcement of a magistrates' court maintenance order under this section, the court may vary the order by exercising one of its powers under subsection (5) below.
>
> (5) The powers of the court are –
>
> (*a*) the power to order that payments under the order be made directly to the clerk of the court or the clerk of any other magistrates' court;
>
> (*b*) the power to order that payments under the order be made to the clerk of the court, or to the clerk of any other magistrates' court, by such method of payment falling within section 59(6) above (standing order, etc) as may be specified;
>
> (*c*) the power to make an attachment of earnings order under the Attachment of Earnings Act 1971 to secure payments under the order.
>
> (6) In deciding which of the powers under subsection (5) above it is to exercise, the court shall have regard to any representations made by the debtor (within the meaning of section 59 above).
>
> (7) Subsection (4) of section 59 above (power of court to require debtor to open account) shall apply for the purposes of subsection (5) above as it applies for the purposes of that section but as if for paragraph (*a*) there were substituted –
>
> '(*a*) the court proposes to exercise its power under paragraph (*b*) of section 76(5) below, and'."

(5C) In section 93 (complaint for arrears), subsection (6) (court not to impose imprisonment in certain circumstances) shall have effect as if for paragraph (*b*) there were substituted –

> "(*b*) if the court is of the opinion that it is appropriate –
>
> (i) to make an attachment of earnings order, or
>
> (ii) to exercise its power under paragraph (*b*) of section 76(5) above."

(6) A maintenance order which by virtue of this section is enforceable by a magistrates' court in Northern Ireland shall, subject to the modifications of Article 98 of the Magistrates' Courts (Northern Ireland) Order 1981 specified in subsection (6A) below, be enforceable as an order made by that court to which that Article applies.

(6A) …

(7) The payer under a maintenance order registered under this section in a magistrates' court in England and Wales or Northern Ireland shall give notice of any change of address to the clerk of that court.

A person who without reasonable excuse fails to comply with this subsection shall be guilty of an offence and liable on summary conviction to a fine not exceeding level 2 on the standard scale.

Amendments—Criminal Justice Act 1982, s 46; Family Law Reform Act 1987, s 33(1), Sch 2, para 89; Civil Jurisdiction and Judgments Act 1991, s 3, Sch 2, para 2; Maintenance Enforcement Act 1991, s 10, Sch 1, para 21; SI 1992/709; SI 1993/1576; SI 1995/755.

Defined terms—"maintenance order": s 15(1).

"level 2 on the standard scale" (s 5(7))—Currently £500 (Criminal Justice Act 1982, s 37(2), as substituted).

6 Appeals under Article 37, second paragraph and Article 41

(1) The single further appeal on a point of law referred to in the 1968 Convention and the Lugano Convention in Article 37, second paragraph and Article 41 in relation to the recognition or enforcement of a judgment other than a maintenance order lies –

(*a*) in England and Wales or Northern Ireland, to the Court of Appeal or to the House of Lords in accordance with Part II of the Administration of Justice Act 1969 (appeals direct from the High Court to the House of Lords);
(*b*) (*applies to Scotland only*)

(2) Paragraph (*a*) of subsection (1) has effect notwithstanding section 15(2) of the Administration of Justice Act 1969 (exclusion of direct appeal to the House of Lords in cases where no appeal to that House lies from a decision of the Court of Appeal).

(3) The single further appeal on a point of law referred to in each of those Conventions in Article 37, second paragraph and Article 41 in relation to the recognition or enforcement of a maintenance order lies –

(*a*) in England and Wales, to the High Court by way of case stated in accordance with section 111 of the Magistrates' Courts Act 1980;
(*b*) (*applies to Scotland only*)
(*c*) in Northern Ireland, to the Court of Appeal.

Amendments—Civil Jurisdiction and Judgments Act 1991, s 3, Sch 2, para 3.

Defined terms—"1968 Convention", "the Lugano Convention": s 1(1); "maintenance order": s 15(1).

7 Interest on registered judgments

(1) Subject to subsection (4), where in connection with an application for registration of a judgment under section 4 or 5 the applicant shows –

(*a*) that the judgment provides for the payment of a sum of money; and
(*b*) that in accordance with the law of the Contracting State in which the judgment was given interest on that sum is recoverable under the judgment from a particular date or time,

the rate of interest and the date or time from which it is so recoverable shall be registered with the judgment and, subject to any provision made under subsection (2), the debt resulting, apart from section 4(2), from the registration of the judgment shall carry interest in accordance with the registered particulars.

(2) Provision may be made by rules of court as to the manner in which and the periods by reference to which any interest payable by virtue of subsection (1) is to be calculated and paid, including provision for such interest to cease to accrue as from a prescribed date.

(3) Costs or expenses recoverable by virtue of section 4(2) shall carry interest as if they were the subject of an order for the payment of costs or expenses made by the registering court on the date of registration.

(4) Interest on arrears of sums payable under a maintenance order registered under section 5 in a magistrates' court in England and Wales or Northern Ireland shall not be recoverable in that court, but without prejudice to the operation in relation to any such order of section 2A of the Maintenance Orders Act 1958 or section 11A of the Maintenance and Affiliation Orders Act (Northern Ireland) 1966 (which enable interest to be recovered if the order is re-registered for enforcement in the High Court).

(5) Except as mentioned in subsection (4), debts under judgments registered under section 4 or 5 shall carry interest only as provided by this section.

Defined terms—"Contracting State": s 1(3); "judgment", "maintenance order": s 15(1).

Scope of provision—This section makes limited provision for the enforcement of interest on registered orders. Interest may only be enforced if the original judgment provided for the payment of interest (no more than 6 years' interest may be recovered (*Lowsley and another v Forbes* [1998] 3 All ER 897, HL)).

"shall not be recoverable" (s 7(4))—Interest may not be recovered in a magistrates' court, although re-registration for enforcement in the High Court is possible.

8 Currency of payment under registered maintenance orders

(1) Sums payable in the United Kingdom under a maintenance order by virtue of its registration under section 5, including any arrears so payable, shall be paid in the currency of the United Kingdom.

(2) Where the order is expressed in any other currency, the amounts shall be converted on the basis of the exchange rate prevailing on the date of registration of the order.

(3) For the purposes of this section, a written certificate purporting to be signed by an officer of any bank in the United Kingdom and stating the exchange rate prevailing on a specified date shall be evidence, and in Scotland sufficient evidence, of the facts stated.

Defined terms—"maintenance order": s 15(1).

****

Other supplementary provisions

****

11 Proof of admissibility of certain judgments and related documents

(1) For the purposes of the 1968 Convention and the Lugano Convention –

(*a*) a document, duly authenticated, which purports to be a copy of a judgment given by a court of a Contracting State other than the United Kingdom shall without further proof be deemed to be a true copy, unless the contrary is shown; and (*b*) the original or a copy of any such document as is mentioned in Article 46(2) or 47 (supporting documents to be produced by a party seeking recognition or enforcement of a judgment) shall be evidence, and in Scotland sufficient evidence, of any matter to which it relates.

(2) A document purporting to be a copy of a judgment given by any such court as is mentioned in subsection (1)(*a*) is duly authenticated for the purposes of this section if it purports –

(*a*) to bear the seal of that court; or
(*b*) to be certified by any person in his capacity as a judge or officer of that court to be a true copy of a judgement given by that court.

(3) Nothing in this section shall prejudice the admission in evidence of any document which is admissible apart from this section.

Amendments—Civil Jurisdiction and Judgments Act 1991, s 3, Sch 2, para 6.

Defined terms—"Contracting State": s 1(3); "judgment": s 15(1), "the 1968 Convention", "the Lugano Convention": s 1(1).

12 Provision for issue of copies of, and certificates in connection with, UK judgments

Rules of court may make provision for enabling any interested party wishing to secure under the 1968 Convention or the Lugano Convention the recognition or enforcement in another Contracting State of a judgment given by a court in the United Kingdom to obtain, subject to any conditions specified in the rules –

(*a*) a copy of the judgment; and
(*b*) a certificate giving particulars relating to the judgment and the proceedings in which it was given.

Amendments—Civil Jurisdiction and Judgments Act 1991, s 3, Sch 2, para 7.

Defined terms—"Contracting State": s 1(3); "judgment": s 15(1), "the 1968 Convention", "the Lugano Convention": s 1(1).

Scope of provision—This section provides for rules to be made concerning the issue of copies of, and certificates in connection with, maintenance orders: see Magistrates' Courts (Civil Jurisdiction and Judgments Act 1982) Rules 1986, r 12.

****

15 Interpretation of Part I and consequential amendments

(1) In this Part, unless the context otherwise requires –

"judgment" has the meaning given by Article 25;
"maintenance order" means a maintenance judgment within the meaning of the 1968 Convention or, as the case may be, the Lugano Convention;
"payer", in relation to a maintenance order, means the person liable to make the payments for which the order provides;
"prescribed" means prescribed by rules of court.

(2) References in this Part to a judgment registered under section 4 or 5 include, to the extent of its registration, references to a judgment so registered to a limited extent only.

(3) Anything authorised or required by the 1968 Convention, the Lugano Convention or this Part to be done by, to or before a particular magistrates' court may be done by, to or before any magistrates' court acting for the same petty sessions area (or, in Northern Ireland, petty sessions district) as that court.

(4) The enactments specified in Part I of Schedule 12 shall have effect with the amendments specified there, being amendments consequential on this Part.

Amendments—Civil Jurisdiction and Judgments Act 1991, s 3, Sch 2, para 10.

****

PART IV
MISCELLANEOUS PROVISIONS

Provisions relating to jurisdiction

****

25 Interim relief in England and Wales and Northern Ireland in the absence of substantive proceedings

(1) The High Court in England and Wales or Northern Ireland shall have power to grant interim relief where –

(*a*) proceedings have been or are to be commenced in a Brussels or Lugano Contracting State or a Regulation State other than the United Kingdom or in a part of the United Kingdom other than that in which the High Court in question exercises jurisdiction; and

(*b*) they are or will be proceedings whose subject-matter is within the scope of the Regulation as determined by Article 1 of the Regulation (whether or not the Regulation has effect in relation to the proceedings).

(2) On an application for any interim relief under subsection (1) the court may refuse to grant that relief if, in the opinion of the court, the fact that the court has no jurisdiction apart from this section in relation to the subject-matter of the proceedings in question makes it inexpedient for the court to grant it.

(3) Her Majesty may by Order in Council extend the power to grant interim relief conferred by subsection (1) so as to make it exercisable in relation to proceedings of any of the following descriptions, namely –

(*a*) proceedings commenced or to be commenced otherwise than in a Brussels or Lugano Contracting State or Regulation State;

(*b*) proceedings whose subject-matter is not within the scope of the Regulation as determined by Article 1 of the Regulation;

(*c*) (*repealed*)

(4) An Order in Council under subsection (3) –

(*a*) may confer power to grant only specified descriptions of interim relief;

(*b*) may make different provision for different classes of proceedings, for proceedings pending in different countries or courts outside the United Kingdom or in different parts of the United Kingdom, and for other different circumstances; and (*c*) may impose conditions or restrictions on the exercise of any power conferred by the Order.

(5) (*repealed*)

(6) Any Order in Council under subsection (3) shall be subject to annulment in pursuance of a resolution of either House of Parliament.

(7) In this section "interim relief", in relation to the High Court in England and Wales or Northern Ireland, means interim relief of any kind which that court has power to grant in proceedings relating to matters within its jurisdiction, other than –

(*a*) a warrant for the arrest of property; or
(*b*) provision for obtaining evidence.

Amendments—Civil Jurisdiction and Judgments Act 1991, s 3, Sch 2, para 12; Arbitration Act 1996, s 107(2), Sch 4; SI 2001/3929.

Scope of provision—Where there are proceedings for financial relief outside the United Kingdom, this section enables the court, by injunction or other interim orders, to preserve the assets which are the subject of that overseas litigation. *Credit Suisse Fides Trust SA v Cuoghi* [1997] 3 WLR 871 and *Ryan v Friction Dynamics* (2000) *The Times*, 14 June set out the principles governing the court's jurisdiction to grant interim relief.

****

Provisions relating to recognition and enforcement of judgments

****

36 Registration of maintenance orders in Northern Ireland

(1) Where –

(*a*) a High Court order or a Court of Session order has been registered in the High Court of Justice in Northern Ireland ("the Northern Ireland High Court") under Part II of the Maintenance Orders Act 1950; or
(*b*) a county court order, a magistrates' court order or a sheriff court order has been registered in a court of summary jurisdiction in Northern Ireland under that Part,

an application may be made to the original court for the registration of the order in, respectively, a court of summary jurisdiction in Northern Ireland or the Northern Ireland High Court.

(2) In subsection (1) "the original court", in relation to an order, means the court by which the order was made.

(3) Section 2 (except subsection (6A)) and section 2A of the Maintenance Orders Act 1958 shall have effect for the purposes of an application under subsection (1), and subsections (2), (3), (4) and (4A) of section 5 of that Act shall have effect for the purposes of the cancellation of a registration made on such an application, as if –

(*a*) "registration" in those provisions included registration in the appropriate Northern Ireland court ("registered" being construed accordingly);

(*b*) any reference in those provisions to a High Court order or a magistrates' court order included, respectively, a Court of Session order or a sheriff court order; and

(*c*) any other reference in those provisions to the High Court or a magistrates' court included the Northern Ireland High Court or a court of summary jurisdiction in Northern Ireland.

(*d*) for section 2(6), there were substituted the following subsections –

"(6) Where a magistrates' court order is registered under this Part of this Act in the High Court, then –

(*a*) if payments under the magistrates' court order are required to be made (otherwise than to a collecting officer) by any method of payment falling within Article 85(7) of the Magistrates' Courts (Northern Ireland) Order 1981 (standing order, etc), any order requiring payment by that method shall continue to have effect after registration;

(*b*) any order by virtue of which sums payable under the magistrates' court order are required to be paid to the collecting officer (whether or not by any method of payment falling within Article 85(7) of that Order) on behalf of the person entitled thereto shall cease to have effect.

(6ZA) Where a High Court or county court order is registered under this Part of this Act in a magistrates' court, then –

(*a*) if a means of payment order (within the meaning of Article 96A(7) of the Judgments Enforcement (Northern Ireland) Order 1981) has effect in relation to the order in question, it shall continue to have effect after registration; and

(*b*) in any other case, the magistrates' court shall order that all payments to be made under the order in question (including any arrears accrued before registration) shall be made to the collecting officer.

(6ZB) Any such order as to payment –

(*a*) as is referred to in paragraph (*a*) of subsection (6) of this section may be revoked, suspended, revived or varied by an exercise of the powers conferred by section 13A of the Maintenance and Affiliation Orders Act (Northern Ireland) 1966; and

(*b*) as is referred to in paragraph (*a*) or (*b*) of subsection (6ZA) of this section may be varied or revoked by an exercise of the powers conferred by section 12(2) or 13(2A) or (5A) of that Act of 1966.

(6ZC) Where by virtue of the provisions of this section or any order under subsection (6ZA)(*b*) of this section payments under an order cease to be or become payable to the collecting officer, the person liable to make the payments shall, until he is given the prescribed notice to that effect, be deemed to comply with the order if he makes payments in accordance with the order and any order under subsection (6ZA)(*b*) of this section of which he has received such notice.

(6ZD) In subsections (6), (6ZA) and (6ZC) of this section "collecting officer" means the officer mentioned in Article 85(4) of the Magistrates' Courts (Northern Ireland) Order 1981."

(4) Where an order is registered in Northern Ireland under this section, Part II of the Maintenance and Affiliation Orders Act (Northern Ireland) 1966, except sections 11, 11A and 14(2) and (3), shall apply as if the order had been registered in accordance with the provisions of that Part, as if –

PART II

(*a*) in section 12(2), for modifications of Article 98(8B) to (8D) of the Magistrates' Court (Northern Ireland) Order 1981 specified in that subsection there were substituted the modifications specified in section 18(3ZA) of the Maintenance Orders Act 1950 (enforcement of registered orders); and

(*b*) for section 13(5A), there were substituted the following subsection –

"(5A) Subject to the following provisions of this section, paragraphs (4) to (11) of Article 86 of the Magistrates' Courts (Northern Ireland) Order 1981 (power of clerk and court to vary maintenance orders) shall apply in relation to a registered order as they apply in relation to a maintenance order made by a court of summary jurisdiction (disregarding Article 25(2) of the Domestic Proceedings (Northern Ireland) Order 1980) but –

(*a*) as if for paragraph (4)(*b*) there were substituted –

'(*b*) payments under the order are required to be made to the collecting officer, by any method of payment falling within Article 85(7) (standing order, etc)';

and as if after the words 'petty sessions' there were inserted 'for the petty sessions district for which the court which made the order acts';

(*b*) as if in paragraph (5) for the words 'to the collecting officer' there were substituted 'in accordance with sub-paragraph (*a*) of paragraph (9)';

(*c*) as if in paragraph (7), sub-paragraph (*c*) and the word 'and' immediately preceding it were omitted;

(*d*) as if in paragraph (8) for the words 'sub-paragraphs (*a*) to (*d*) of Article 85(3)' there were substituted 'paragraph (9)';

(*e*) as if for paragraphs (9) and (10) there were substituted the following paragraphs –

'(9) The powers of the court are –

(*a*) the power to order that payments under the order be made directly to the collecting officer;

(*b*) the power to order that payments under the order be made to the collecting officer, by such method of payment falling within Article 85(7) (standing order, etc) as may be specified;

(*c*) the power to make an attachment of earnings order under Part IX to secure payments under the order.

(10) In deciding which of the powers under paragraph (9) above it is to exercise, the court shall have regard to any representations made by the debtor.

(10A) Paragraph (5) of Article 85 (power of court to require debtor to open account) shall apply for the purposes of paragraph (9) as it applies for the purposes of that Article but as if for sub-paragraph (*a*) there were substituted –

"(*a*) the court proposes to exercise its power under sub-paragraph (*b*) of Article 86(9)".'.".

(5) A court of summary jurisdiction in Northern Ireland shall have jurisdiction to hear an application by or against a person residing outside Northern Ireland for the discharge or variation of an order registered in Northern Ireland under this section; and where such an application is made against a person residing outside Northern Ireland, then, if he resides in England and Wales or Scotland, section 15 of the Maintenance Orders Act 1950 (which relates to the service of process on persons

residing in those countries) shall have effect in relation to the application as it has effect in relation to the proceedings therein mentioned.

(5A) Article 165 of the Children (Northern Ireland) Order 1995 (provision which may be made by magistrates' courts rules, etc) shall apply for the purpose of giving effect to subsection (5) above as it applies for the purpose of giving effect to that Order, except that in the application of that Article by virtue of this subsection "relevant proceedings" means any application made, or proceedings brought, by virtue of that subsection and any part of such proceedings.

(6) The enactments specified in Part III of Schedule 12 shall have effect with the amendments specified there, being amendments consequential on this section.

Amendments—SI 1993/1576; SI 1995/755.

****

PART V
SUPPLEMENTARY AND GENERAL PROVISIONS

General

****

50 Interpretation: general

In this Act, unless the context otherwise requires –

"the Accession Convention", "the 1982 Accession Convention", "the 1989 Accession Convention" and "the 1996 Accession Convention" have the meaning given by section 1(1);

"Article" and references to sub-divisions of numbered Articles are to be construed in accordance with section 1(2)(*b*);

"association" means an unincorporated body of persons;

"Brussels Contracting State" has the meaning given by section 1(3);

"the Brussels Conventions" has the meaning given by section 1(1);

"Contracting State" has the meaning given by section 1(3);

"the 1968 Convention" has the meaning given by section 1(1), and references to that Convention and to provisions of it are to be construed in accordance with section 1(2)(*a*);

"corporation" means a body corporate, and includes a partnership subsisting under the law of Scotland;

"court", without more, includes a tribunal;

"court of law", in relation to the United Kingdom, means any of the following courts, namely –

(*a*) the House of Lords,
(*b*) in England and Wales or Northern Ireland, the Court of Appeal, the High Court, the Crown Court, a county court and a magistrates' court,
(*c*) in Scotland, the Court of Session and a sheriff court;

"the Crown" is to be construed in accordance with section 51(2);

"enactment" includes an enactment comprised in Northern Ireland legislation;

"judgment", subject to sections 15(1) and 18(2) and to paragraph 1 of Schedules 6 and 7, means any judgment or order (by whatever name called) given or made by a court in any civil proceedings;

"Lugano Contracting State" has the meaning given by section 1(3);
"the Lugano Convention" has the meaning given by section 1(1);
"magistrates' court", in relation to Northern Ireland, means a court of summary jurisdiction;
"modifications" includes additions, omissions and alterations;
"overseas country" means any country or territory outside the United Kingdom;
"part of the United Kingdom" means England and Wales, Scotland or Northern Ireland;
"the 1971 Protocol" has the meaning given by section 1(1), and references to that Protocol and to provisions of it are to be construed in accordance with section 1(2)(*a*);
"rules of court", in relation to any court, means rules, orders or regulations made by the authority having power to make rules, orders or regulations regulating the procedure of that court, and includes –

(*a*) in Scotland, Acts of Sederunt;
(*b*) in Northern Ireland, Judgment Enforcement Rules;

"statutory provision" means any provision contained in an Act, or in any Northern Ireland legislation, or in –

(*a*) subordinate legislation (as defined in section 21(1) of the Interpretation Act 1978); or
(*b*) any instrument of a legislative character made under any Northern Ireland legislation;

"tribunal" –

(*a*) means a tribunal of any description other than a court of law;
(*b*) in relation to an overseas country, includes, as regards matters relating to maintenance within the meaning of the 1968 Convention, any authority having power to give, enforce, vary or revoke a maintenance order.

Amendments—SI 1990/2591; Civil Jurisdiction and Judgments Act 1991, s 3, Sch 2, para 25; SI 2000/1824.

****

52 Extent

(1) This Act extends to Northern Ireland.

(2) Without prejudice to the power conferred by section 39, Her Majesty may by Order in Council direct that all or any of the provisions of this Act apart from that section shall extend, subject to such modifications as may be specified in the Order, to any of the following territories, that is to say –

(*a*) the Isle of Man;
(*b*) any of the Channel Islands;
(*c*) any colony.

Amendments—SI 1990/2591.

****

Contempt of Court Act 1981

****

11 Publication of matters exempted from disclosure in court

In any case where a court (having power to do so) allows a name or other matter to be withheld from the public in proceedings before the court, the court may give such directions prohibiting the publication of that name or matter in connection with the proceedings as appear to the court to be necessary for the purpose for which it was so withheld.

Directions by the court to protect the position of witnesses and parties in public hearings—The general rule is that hearings are in public (ECHR, Art 6) and that evidence put before the court should be put in public (*Attorney-General v Leveller Magazine* [1979] AC 440). In exceptional cases, which are necessarily rare, s 11 allows the court to give directions which are designed to protect the position of witnesses and parties who are involved in hearings conducted in open court (*Re G (Adult Patient: Publicity)* [1995] 2 FLR 528 – where the court decided that, although the application by the hospital for permission to discontinue life-sustaining treatment for a patient who was in a persistent vegetative state should take place in open court, the very greatest of care should be taken to protect the positions and anonymity of the wife and mother of the patient and the doctors and nurses caring for him). However, the power must be carefully exercised and cannot be used simply to protect privacy or avoid embarrassment (*Attorney-General v Leveller Magazine* [1979] AC 440). The applicant must be able to establish that the failure to grant anonymity would render the attainment of justice really doubtful or impracticable (*Scott v Scott* [1913] AC 417, (1913) FLR Rep 657; *R v Westminster City Council ex parte Castelli; R v Same ex parte Tristran-Garcia* [1996] 1 FLR 534 – where the identity of applicants who were HIV positive had already been revealed at an earlier stage of the proceedings, the court refused to allow their subsequent application that identifying information need not be revealed in the hearing of their later substantive applications for judicial review; considerable publicity had already occurred and their anonymity had already been lost). The court has power to consider at any stage of the hearing whether any particular evidence ought to be given in private (see *Re G (Adult Patient: Publicity)* [1995] 2 FLR 528 at 533A, per Sir Stephen Brown P). Ideally, applications for anonymity and orders under s 11 should be made at the same time as the application for leave. These applications can be heard ex parte and, where appropriate, in camera (*R v Westminster City Council ex parte Castelli; R v Same ex parte Tristran-Garcia* (above)). See also reporting restrictions under Children and Young Persons Act 1933, s 39. Any order needs to be precisely worded (*Briffett v DPP* [2001] EWHC Admin 841, (2001) *The Times*, 26 November).

****

14 Proceedings in England and Wales

(1) In any case where a court has power to commit a person to prison for contempt of court and (apart from this provision) no limitation applies to the period of committal, the committal shall (without prejudice to the power of the court to order his earlier discharge) be for a fixed term, and that term shall not on any occasion exceed two years in the case of committal by a superior court, or one month in the case of committal by an inferior court.

(2) In any case where an inferior court has power to fine a person for contempt of court and (apart from this provision) no limit applies to the amount of the fine, the fine shall not on any occasion exceed £2,500.

(2A) In the exercise of jurisdiction to commit for contempt of court or any kindred offence the court shall not deal with the offender by making an order under section 60 of the Powers of Criminal Courts (Sentencing) Act 2000 (an attendance centre order) if it appears to the court after considering any available evidence, that he is under 17 years of age.

(2A) A fine imposed under subsection (2) above shall be deemed, for the purposes of any enactment, to be a sum adjudged to be paid by a conviction.

(3) (*repealed*)

(4) Each of the superior courts shall have the like power to make a hospital order or guardianship order under section 37 of the Mental Health Act 1983 or an interim hospital order under section 38 of that Act in the case of a person suffering from mental illness or severe mental impairment who could otherwise be committed to prison for contempt of court as the Crown Court has under that section in the case of a person convicted of an offence.

(4A) Each of the superior courts shall have the like power to make an order under section 35 of the said Act of 1983 (remand for report on accused's mental condition) where there is reason to suspect that a person who could be committed to prison for contempt of court is suffering from mental illness or severe mental impairment as the Crown Court has under that section in the case of an accused person within the meaning of that section.

(4A) For the purposes of the preceding provisions of this section a county court shall be treated as a superior court and not as an inferior court.

(5) The enactments specified in Part III of Schedule 2 shall have effect subject to the amendments set out in that Part, being amendments relating to the penalties and procedure in respect of certain offences of contempt in coroners' courts, county courts and magistrates' courts.

Amendments—Criminal Justice Act 1982, ss 77, 78, Sch 14, para 60, Sch 16; Mental Health (Amendment) Act 1982, s 65(1), Sch 3, paras 59, 60; Mental Health Act 1983, s 148, Sch 4, para 57; County Courts (Penalties for Contempt) Act 1983, s 1; SI 1984/447; Criminal Justice Act 1991, s 17, Sch 4, Pt I, Pt V, para 4; Criminal Justice Act 1993, s 65(3), Sch 3, para 6(5); Powers of Criminal Courts (Sentencing) Act 2000, s 165, Sch 9, para 84. Due to an error in drafting, two subsections have been numbered (2A) and (4A) respectively.

Defined terms—"court", "superior court": s 19.

Sentence must be for a fixed term—Once a contemnor has been found guilty of having breached an undertaking or an order, the court has no power to detain him in custody pending consideration of the appropriate sentence to be imposed upon him (*Delaney v Delaney* [1996] 2 WLR 74, [1996] 1 All ER 367, CA).

Contempt in the face of the court—A High Court judge has power to order overnight detention of the alleged contemnor to allow both for a period of reflection and for arrangements to be made for legal representation. If the case cannot be dealt with the next day, detention until the next working day is "the very limit of what could be either lawful or acceptable" (see *Wilkinson v S & anor* (2003) *The Times*, 7 Feb). In the county court, see CCA 1984, s 118.

No breach of ECHR, Art 6 is involved if the judge invokes the summary procedure and deals with the case himself (see *Wilkinson* (above)).

"shall not on any occasion exceed two years in the case of committal by a superior court" (s 14(1))—A court may not, on any single occasion, impose on a contemnor a sentence of imprisonment which exceeds two years, even where it activates a sentence which was previously suspended (*Villiers v Villiers* [1994] 1 FLR 647). Where a contemnor acknowledges his breaches of the relevant order, apologises to the court and thus avoids the need for witnesses to give oral evidence substantiating the breaches, he is entitled to some credit to reduce the length of his total sentence to a period below the maximum of two years' imprisonment (*Re R (A Minor) (Contempt)* [1994] 2 FLR 185).

County court to be treated as superior court (s 14(4A))—County courts may equally impose prison sentences and fines and make hospital orders and guardianship orders.

Powers of inferior courts (s 14(1), (2))—This section imposes a general limit on the powers of inferior courts to punish for contempt, namely one month's imprisonment or a fine of £2,500 or both.

Power of court to order earlier discharge—A court may release a contemnor before the end of his term of imprisonment whether he has purged his contempt or not (*Enfield London Borough Council v Mahoney* [1983] 1 WLR 749, [1983] 2 All ER 901). However, the court does not have power to suspend the remainder of a part-served sentence (*Harris v Harris* [2001] EWCA Civ 1645, [2002] 1 FLR 248, CA).

Review of sentence—The court sends a copy of every committal order and relevant details to the Official Solicitor, who reviews the case and may apply or appeal of his own motion or at the contemnor's request (*Secretary's Circular of 28 September 1981*).

Age (s 14(2A))—A person attains a particular age expressed in years at the commencement of the relevant anniversary of the date of his birth (Family Law Reform Act 1969, s 9). Where a contemnor is aged under 18, there is no power at all to commit to any form of detention (*R v Selby Justices ex parte Frame* [1991] 2 WLR 965, [1991] 2 All ER 344 and Criminal Justice Act 1982, s 9(1)). A person under the age of 21 cannot be sent to prison for contempt but, if he is aged 18 years or more, he can be detained under CJA 1982, s 9(1) (see *R v Selby Justices ex parte Frame* (above); see also *Mason v Lawton* [1991] 2 FLR 50). For further information, see *Emergency Remedies in the Family Courts* (Family Law).

Power of court to order contemnor to attend at attendance centre (s 14(2A))—This section, by implication, contemplates that a contemnor aged at least 17, but less than 21, may be ordered to attend at an attendance centre. However, see arguments to the contrary in *R v Selby Justices ex parte Frame* [1991] 2 WLR 965, [1991] 2 All ER 344, where the Divisional Court upheld a submission by counsel as amicus curiae that, since a person found guilty of contempt had not been "convicted of an offence", it followed that no other means of disposal provided by criminal justice legislation, such as an attendance centre order, was available.

Mentally disordered contemnors (s 14(4), (4A))—Under the Mental Health Act 1983, the court has power to remand a person to a hospital for a report on his mental condition (s 35), to authorise his admission to and detention in hospital, or to place him under the guardianship of a local social services authority or other approved person (s 37), and, where two registered medical practitioners certify that he is suffering from mental illness and that there is reason to suppose that it may be appropriate to make a hospital order, to make an *interim* hospital order (s 38). However, these powers cannot be exercised until the person has been found guilty of contempt. This is clear from the use in s 14(4) and (4A) of the words "a person who could be committed to prison for contempt of court".

Once a person has been found guilty of contempt of court, the High Court or county court has power:

(*a*) if there is reason to suspect that he is suffering from mental illness or severe mental impairment, to remand him in custody for reports under s 35 for not more than 28 days at a time or 12 weeks in all; and

(*b*) if satisfied that he is suffering from mental illness or severe mental impairment, to make either (i) an interim hospital order under s 38 for not more than 12 weeks initially or six months in all, or (ii) a hospital order under s 37.

However, none of these powers can be exercised unless the court has before it the required evidence of the relevant medical practitioner(s) as to the matters set out in Mental Health Act 1983, ss 35, 37 and 38. There is no general power to remand a contemnor before sentence, so the court may have to adjourn until the medical evidence is available. In FLA 1996, Pt IV cases, there is specific power to remand for a medical examination and report (see FLA 1996, s 48).

****

16 Enforcement of fines imposed by certain superior courts

(1) Payment of a fine for contempt of court imposed by a superior court, other than the Crown Court or one of the courts specified in subsection (4) below, may be enforced upon the order of the court –

(*a*) in like manner as a judgment of the High Court for the payment of money; or

(*b*) in like manner as a fine imposed by the Crown Court.

(2) Where payment of a fine imposed by any court falls to be enforced as mentioned in paragraph (*a*) of subsection (1) –

(*a*) the court shall, if the fine is not paid in full forthwith or within such time as the court may allow, certify to Her Majesty's Remembrancer the sum payable;

(*b*) Her Majesty's Remembrancer shall thereupon proceed to enforce payment of that sum as if it were due to him as a judgment debt;

(*c*) (*repealed*)

(3) Where payment of a fine imposed by any court falls to be enforced as mentioned in paragraph (*b*) of subsection (1), the provisions of sections 139 and 140 of the Powers of Criminal Courts (Sentencing) Act 2000 shall apply as they apply to a fine imposed by the Crown Court.

(4) Subsection (1) of this section does not apply to fines imposed by the criminal division of the Court of Appeal or by the House of Lords on appeal from that division.

(5) The Fines Act 1833 shall not apply to a fine to which subsection (1) of this section applies.

(6) (*repealed*)

Amendments—Supreme Court Act 1981, s 152(4), Sch 7; Industrial Tribunals Act 1996, s 45, Sch 3, Pt I; Powers of Criminal Courts (Sentencing) Act 2000, s 165, Sch 9, para 85.

Defined terms—"court", "superior court": s 19.

17 Disobedience to certain orders of magistrates' courts

(1) The powers of a magistrates' court under subsection (3) of section 63 of the Magistrates' Courts Act 1980 (punishment by fine or committal for disobeying an order to do anything other than the payment of money or to abstain from doing anything) may be exercised either of the court's own motion or by order on complaint.

(2) In relation to the exercise of those powers the provisions of the Magistrates' Courts Act 1980 shall apply subject to the modifications set out in Schedule 3 of this Act.

****

19 Interpretation

In this Act –

"court" includes any tribunal or body exercising the judicial power of the State, and "legal proceedings" shall be construed accordingly;

"publication" has the meaning assigned by subsection (1) of section 2, and "publish" (except in section 9) shall be construed accordingly;

"Scottish proceeding" means proceedings before any court, including the Courts-Martial Appeal Court, the Restrictive Practices Court and the Employment Appeal Tribunal, sitting in Scotland, and includes proceedings before the House of Lords in the exercise of any appellate jurisdiction over proceedings in such a court;

"the strict liability rule" has the meaning assigned by section 1;

"superior court" means the Court of Appeal, the High Court, the Crown Court, the Courts-Martial Appeal Court, the Restrictive Practices Court, the Employment Appeal Tribunal and any other court exercising in relation to its proceedings powers equivalent to those of the High Court, and includes the House of Lords in the exercise of its appellate jurisdiction.

Amendments—Cable and Broadcasting Act 1984, s 57(1), Sch 5, para 39(2); Broadcasting Act 1990, s 203(1), (3), Sch 20, para 31, Sch 21.

****

SCHEDULE 3

APPLICATION OF MAGISTRATES' COURTS ACT 1980 TO CIVIL CONTEMPT PROCEEDINGS UNDER SECTION 63(3)

1 (1) Where the proceedings are taken of the court's own motion the provisions of the Act listed in this sub-paragraph shall apply as if a complaint had been made against the person against whom the proceedings are taken, and subject to the modifications specified in sub-paragraphs (2) and (3) below. The enactments so applied are –

section 51 (issue of summons)
section 53(1) and (2) (procedure on hearing)
section 54 (adjournment)
section 55 (non-appearance of defendant)
section 97(1) (summons to witness)
section 101 (onus of proving exceptions etc)
section 121(1) and (3)(*a*) (constitution and place of sitting of court)
section 123 (defect in process).

(2) In section 55, in subsection (1) for the words "the complainant appears but the defendant does not" there shall be substituted the words "the defendant does not appear", and in subsection (2) the words "if the complaint has been substantiated on oath, and" shall be omitted.

(3) In section 123, in subsections (1) and (2) the words "adduced on behalf of the prosecutor or complainant" shall be omitted.

2 Where the proceedings are taken by way of complaint for an order, section 127 of the Act (limitation of time) shall not apply to the complaint.

3 Whether the proceedings are taken of the court's own motion or by way of complaint for an order, subsection (3) of section 55 shall apply as if the following words were added at the end of the subsection –

"or, having been arrested under section 47 of the Family Law Act 1996 in connection with the matter of the complaint, is at large after being remanded under subsection (7)(*b*) or (10) of that section.".

Amendments—Family Law Act 1996, s 66(1), Sch 8, para 50.

"as if a complaint had been made" (para 1(1))—The court acts by order on complaint or as if on complaint. An order for costs in the proceedings appears permissible.

****

County Courts Act 1984

ARRANGEMENT OF SECTIONS

****

PART II
JURISDICTION AND TRANSFER OF PROCEEDINGS

****

25 Jurisdiction under Inheritance (Provision for Family and Dependants) Act 1975

A county court shall have jurisdiction to hear and determine any application for an order under section 2 of the Inheritance (Provision for Family and Dependants) Act 1975 (including any application for permission to apply for such an order and any application made, in the proceedings on an application for such an order, for an order under any other provision of that Act).

Amendments—SI 1991/724.

Transfer of proceedings—CPR 1998, r 30.6 empowers the court to specify the particular court where the trial or some other hearing in the proceedings will take place, without an order for such transfer.

****

38 Remedies available in county courts

(1) Subject to what follows, in any proceedings in a county court the court may make any order which could be made by the High Court if the proceedings were in the High Court.

(2) Any order made by a county court may be –

(*a*) absolute or conditional;
(*b*) final or interlocutory.

(3) A county court shall not have power –

(*a*) to order mandamus, certiorari or prohibition; or
(*b*) to make any order of a prescribed kind.

(4) Regulations under subsection (3) –

(*a*) may provide for any of their provisions not to apply in such circumstances or descriptions of case as may be specified in the regulations;
(*b*) may provide for the transfer of the proceedings to the High Court for the purpose of enabling an order of a kind prescribed under subsection (3) to be made;
(*c*) may make such provision with respect to matters of procedure as the Lord Chancellor considers expedient; and
(*d*) may make provision amending or repealing any provision made by or under any enactment, so far as may be necessary or expedient in consequence of the regulations.

(5) In this section "prescribed" means prescribed by regulations made by the Lord Chancellor under this section.

(6) The power to make regulations under this section shall be exercised by statutory instrument.

(7) No such statutory instrument shall be made unless a draft of the instrument has been approved by both Houses of Parliament.

Amendments—Courts and Legal Services Act 1990, s 3.

Scope of provision—This section provides county courts with the same powers as the High Court, subject to certain exceptions. In particular, a county court may, like the High Court, grant a "freestanding" injunction, ie an injunction in support of a legal right (which legal right is within the jurisdiction of a county court), even though no other remedy is claimed in the proceedings. The power to commit for disobedience of an injunction, or breach of an undertaking, is a power of the High Court which is devolved on the county court by virtue of County Courts Act 1984, s 38. The county court has no inherent jurisdiction to grant injunctions to restrain either a local authority from exercising its statutory powers in relation to children or the police from exercising their statutory or common law powers (*D v D (County Court Jurisdiction: Injunctions)* [1993] 2 FLR 802).

Regulations restricting county courts' powers—The County Court Remedies Regulations 1991, SI 1991/1222, have been made in exercise of the power under s 38(3)(*b*) and (4).

Personal protection injunctions—At common law, "harassment" or "molestation" can be prohibited in proceedings founded in the law of tort, if the conduct complained of amounts to a tort (*Burris v Azadani* [1996] 1 FLR 266). This usually involves proceedings for trespass to the person or trespass to land. However, Protection from Harassment Act 1997, s 3 has, in effect, created a statutory tort of harassment, and proceedings based on that Act will now invariably be a better way of restraining harassment (see notes to that Act). See also Family Law Act 1996, Pt IV and notes thereon.

Form of non-molestation injunction—It is vital, when submitting a draft injunction or undertaking, to use precise and explicit wording. Only an order requiring a person to do an act at or within a specified time, or to abstain from doing an act, can be enforced by committal proceedings (RSC Ord 45, r 5(1); CCR Ord 29, r 1; *Parsons v Nasar* [1990] 2 FLR 103). FPR 1991 contain specimen clauses to be used in orders granted under FLA 1996, Pt IV (see Form FL404). These clauses (set out in FPR 1991, App 1) should be used in cases falling within FLA 1996 but can also be used as precedents and adapted to meet the needs of a case not within FLA 1996.

Power of arrest—There is no power at common law to attach a "power of arrest" to an injunction. A power of arrest can be attached only where authorised by statute, eg FLA 1996, s 47; Housing Act 1996, ss 152 and 153. There is no "power of arrest" available under the Protection from Harassment Act 1997, but see s 3(3) of that Act which provides for a "warrant of arrest".

Penal notice—Before an order can be enforced by committal proceedings, it must be endorsed with a "Notice as to consequences of disobedience to Court Order", often referred to as a "penal notice" (see County Court Prescribed Form N77). If the order has been drawn up without such a notice it can be endorsed on the order subsequently (see CCR Ord 29, r 1(3)). For orders under FLA 1996, Pt IV, see "Notice A" to be endorsed on Form FL404 (set out in FPR 1991, App 1).

Enforcement of injunctions and undertakings—Injunctions and undertakings cannot be enforced by committal proceedings unless the direction or promise is to do or refrain from doing a specific act or acts. An undertaking to pay money is not enforceable by committal save as permitted by Debtors Act 1869, s 5 (*Symmons v Symmons* [1993] 1 FLR 317). In most cases where an order to pay money is made, or an undertaking to pay money is given, the appropriate remedy is by way of judgment summons. For the procedure to be adopted for breach of injunctions and undertakings, see Procedural Guide 38.

Undertakings—A formal undertaking given by the parties and recorded in court is equivalent to an injunction (*Gandolfo v Gandolfo (Standard Chartered Bank, Garnishee)* [1981] QB 359, [1980] 2 WLR 680), save that an undertaking to pay money can only be enforced by committal in very limited circumstances (see **Enforcement of injunctions and undertakings** above). A power of arrest cannot be attached to an undertaking (*Carpenter v Carpenter* [1988] 1 FLR 121; FLA 1996, s 46(2)).

Protection of property injunctions—Property disputes within divorce, judicial separation or nullity proceedings may be settled either under Matrimonial Causes Act 1973 or Married Women's Property Act 1882 or under the inherent jurisdiction of the court (*Roche v Roche* (1981) Fam Law 243). See also the court's powers to include additional provisions in occupation orders under FLA 1996, s 33, 35 or 36 (FLA 1996, s 40).

Injunction under Married Women's Property Act 1882—In order to restrain a sale or disposal of property which is the subject matter of a dispute under Married Women's Property Act 1882, s 17, an injunction may be sought. The injunction must be ancillary or incidental to any relief sought in the s 17 proceedings. The injunction may be granted by a district judge (FPR 1991, r 3.6(9)).

Injunction under Matrimonial Causes Act 1973, s 37—When proceedings for financial relief have been brought by one person against another under the Matrimonial Causes Act 1973, the court may, pursuant to s 37(2)(*a*), grant an injunction to restrain disposal of property. The injunction may be granted by a district judge (FPR 1991, r 2.68). "Property" includes real and personal property and that situated outside the jurisdiction (*Hamlin v Hamlin* [1986] 1 FLR 61, [1985] 3 WLR 629). However a court will not exercise its discretion so as to make an order under s 37 concerning foreign property that cannot be enforced.

Freezing injunctions—Although the County Court Remedies Regulations 1991 removed the power of county courts, other than the patents county court, to grant freezing injunctions, reg 3(3)(*a*) preserves the power for family proceedings. The freezing injunction may be useful in two situations in which an injunction under MCA 1973, s 37 is not available:

(*a*) Where a party is not involved in a disposition to a third party, but is just putting obstacles in the way of the other party from recovering any sum awarded, or is making it difficult for the court to deal with the case, or where there is no evidence of intent to defeat a claim for ancillary relief (see *Shipman v Shipman* [1991] 1 FLR 250, where an injunction was used to restrain the husband from transferring his assets abroad notwithstanding the absence of any intention to avoid his obligations).

(*b*) Where the property is not yet in existence (eg award of damages in a civil action; redundancy payment; maturing insurance policy) but is to be paid at some future date. In the case of *Ghoth v Ghoth* [1992] 2 FLR 300, [1992] 2 All ER 920, the Court of Appeal held that there is jurisdiction to grant freezing injunctions in matrimonial cases, but that the court should be cautious about granting such an injunction in respect of property outside the jurisdiction. The court can only act because it has personal jurisdiction over the respondent. Therefore the order should be limited to restraining the respondent from disposing of those foreign assets, or at least be limited to the extent in which an injunction would be enforced in that foreign court (*Babanaft International Co SA v Bassatne and Another* [1989] 2 WLR 232, [1989] 1 All ER 433). The injunction should not extend beyond the size of the fund necessary to achieve the maximum which the applicant is likely to be awarded in divorce proceedings.

For further detail as to the procedures to be followed and the law and practice involved, see *Emergency Remedies in the Family Courts* (Family Law, 2000). As to the forms and procedures, see **Freezing injunctions** et seq under Supreme Court Act 1981, s 37.

Mareva injunctions—This form of injunction is now known as a "freezing injunction". See *Practice Direction (Interim Injunctions)* (PD 25) and **Freezing injunctions** above.

****

70 Finality of judgments and orders

Every judgment and order of a county court shall, except as provided by this or any other Act or as may be prescribed, be final and conclusive between the parties.

Scope of provision—A judgment or order of the county court is final and cannot be altered by the court, except by consent (*Irving v Askew* (1870) LR 5 QB 208), although the court is entitled to amend the judgment to explain the sense of an ambiguous phrase which might be misunderstood (*Lowery v Walker* [1911] AC 10, [1908-10] All ER 12), and accidental slips and errors may be corrected (*Chessum & Sons v Gordon* [1901] 1 KB 694). A judgment or order may be set aside on appeal to the Court of Appeal (see s 77). CCR Ord 37, r 1 allows a county court to review its own decision where no error of the court is alleged. If an error of the court is alleged, an appeal must be pursued to the Court of Appeal (see **Scope of provision** under s 77).

****

PART IV
APPEALS ETC

Appeals

77 Appeals: general provisions

(1) Subject to the provisions of this section and the following provisions of this Part of this Act and to any order made by the Lord Chancellor under section 56(1) of the Access to Justice Act 1999, if any party to any proceedings in a county court is dissatisfied with the determination of the judge or jury, he may appeal from it to the Court of Appeal in such manner and subject to such conditions as may be provided by Civil Procedure Rules.

(1A) Without prejudice to the generality of the power to make rules of court under section 75, such rules may make provision for any appeal from the exercise by a district judge, assistant district judge or deputy district judge of any power given to him by virtue of any enactment to be to a judge of a county court.

(2)–(4) (*repealed*)

(5) Subject to the provisions of this section and the following provisions of this Part of this Act, where an appeal is brought under subsection (1) in any action, an appeal may be brought under that subsection in respect of any claim or counterclaim in the action notwithstanding that there could have been no such appeal if that claim had been the subject of a separate action.

(6) In proceedings in which either the plaintiff or the defendant is claiming possession of any premises this section shall not confer any right of appeal on any question of fact if by virtue of –

(*a*) section 13(4) of the Landlord and Tenant Act 1954; or
(*b*) Cases III to IX in Schedule 4 to the Rent (Agriculture) Act 1976; or

(*c*) section 98 of the Rent Act 1977, as it applies to Cases 1 to 6 and 8 and 9 in Schedule 15 to that Act, or that section as extended or applied by any other enactment; or

(*d*) section 99 of the Rent Act 1977, as it applies to Cases 1 to 6 and 9 in Schedule 15 to that Act; or

(*e*) section 84(2)(*a*) of the Housing Act 1985; or

(*ee*) section 7 of the Housing Act 1988, as it applies to the grounds in Part II of Schedule 2 to that Act; or

(*f*) any other enactment,

the court can only grant possession on being satisfied that it is reasonable to do so.

(7) This section shall not –

(*a*) confer any right of appeal from any judgment or order where a right of appeal is conferred by some other enactment; or

(*b*) take away any right of appeal from any judgment or order where a right of appeal is so conferred,

and shall have effect subject to any enactment other than this Act.

(8) In this section –

"enactment" means an enactment whenever passed.

Amendments—Housing (Consequential Provisions) Act 1985, s 4, Sch 2, para 57(3); Housing Act 1988, s 140(1), Sch 17, para 35(2); Courts and Legal Services Act 1990, s 125(2), Sch 17, para 15; Civil Procedure Act 1997, s 10, Sch 2, para 2(1), (2), (7); Access to Justice Act 1999, s 106, Sch 15; SI 2000/1071.

Scope of provision—Appeals from the decision of the county court judge lie to the Court of Appeal, in accordance with CPR 1998, Pt 52. Appeals from the decision of the district judge lie to the judge of the county court. Where the decision of the district judge was made in CA 1989 proceedings the appeal must be made in accordance with FPR 1991, r 4.22 or r 8.1. Ancillary relief appeals from the district judge to the judge of the county court must be made in accordance with CCR Ord 37, r 6, applied by FPR 1991, r 8.1(2), as modified by r 8.1(3). For other cases, see FPR 1991, r 8.1. Appeals under FLA 1996, Pt IV (non-molestation and occupation orders) are governed by FLA 1996, s 61 and FPR 1991, r 8.1A.

Permission to appeal—Permission to appeal to the Court of Appeal is required in all cases save for a few limited exceptions as prescribed by CPR 1998, r 52.3.

Rehearing—Where no error of the court is alleged, the proper course is to apply to the county court for a rehearing (under CCR Ord 37, r 1). This does not prevent the Court of Appeal hearing an appeal (see *O'Connor v Dinn* [1997] 1 FLR 226).

****

79 Agreement not to appeal

(1) No appeal shall lie from any judgment, direction, decision or order of a judge of county courts if, before the judgment, direction, decision or order is given or made, the parties agree, in writing signed by themselves or their legal representatives or agents, that it shall be final.

(2) (*repealed*)

Amendments—Statute Law (Repeals) Act 1986; Courts and Legal Services Act 1990, s 125(3), Sch 18, para 49(3).

80 Judge's note on appeal

(1) At the hearing of any proceedings in a county court in which there is a right of appeal or from which an appeal may be brought with leave, the judge shall, at the request of any party, make a note –

(*a*) of any question of law raised at the hearing; and
(*b*) of the facts in evidence in relation to any such question; and
(*c*) of the decision on any such question and of his determination of the proceedings.

(2) Where such a note has been taken, the judge shall (whether notice of appeal has been served or not), on the application of any party to the proceedings, and on payment by that party of such fee as may be prescribed by the fees orders, furnish him with a copy of the note, and shall sign the copy, and the copy so signed shall be used at the hearing of the appeal.

Scope of provision—If the judge refuses to supply a note he may be ordered to do so (*R v Sheffield County Court Judge* (1889) 5 TLR 303). In practice the parties may submit to the judge a note agreed by them for his approval. If an appeal alleges misconduct of the judge the notes should be submitted to the judge with any appeal notes and the judge may comment and communicate those comments to the Court of Appeal and to the parties (*Re R (A Minor) (Adoption: Parental Agreement)* [1987] 1 FLR 391).

"at the request of any party" (s 80(1))—Strictly this means that the request should be made direct to the judge (*Re Lock ex parte Poppleton (No 1)* (1891) 8 Morr 44), but in practice the application is made to the court clerk.

Judge's notes for appeal—It is the duty of the appellant to include in his bundle of documents for the Court of Appeal the judge's signed note of his judgment, or if he has no note of it counsel's (or solicitor's) note (see *Note of judgment* at PD52, para 5.12). It is common practice for recording equipment to be used in the county court and so a transcript can be provided.

81 Powers of Court of Appeal on appeal from county court

(1) On the hearing of an appeal, the Court of Appeal may draw any inference of fact and either –

(*a*) order a new trial on such terms as the court thinks just; or
(*b*) order judgment to be entered for any party; or
(*c*) make a final or other order on such terms as the court thinks proper to ensure the determination on the merits of the real question in controversy between the parties.

(2) Subject to Civil Procedure Rules, on any appeal from a county court the Court of Appeal may reverse or vary, in favour of a party seeking to support the judgment or order of the county court in whole or in part, any determinations made in the county court on questions of fact, notwithstanding that the appeal is an appeal on a point of law only, or any such determinations on points of law, notwithstanding that the appeal is an appeal on a question of fact only.

(3) Subsection (2) shall not enable the Court of Appeal to reverse or vary any determination, unless the party dissatisfied with the determination would have been entitled to appeal in respect of it if aggrieved by the judgment or order.

Amendments—Civil Procedure Act 1997, s 10, Sch 2, para 2(1), (8).

Scope of provision—The Court of Appeal has power to order a new trial (see CPR 1998, r 52.10(2)). It also has power to make or substitute a final order, and, under CPR 1998, r 52.11(2), to admit fresh evidence, where special grounds exist, as to matters that have arisen since the hearing in the court below.

****

Certiorari and prohibition

83 Stay of proceedings in case of certiorari or prohibition

(1) The grant by the High Court of leave to make an application for an order of certiorari or prohibition to a county court shall, if the High Court so directs, operate as a stay of the proceedings in question until the determination of the application, or until the High Court otherwise orders.

(2) Where any proceedings are so stayed, the judge of the county court shall from time to time adjourn the hearing of the proceedings to such day as he thinks fit.

Scope of provision—Where an application is made either to quash a decision of the county court by a quashing order (formerly "certiorari") or to require a county court to make a certain order, by a mandatory order (formerly "mandamus"), the High Court may stay the proceedings which are the subject of judicial review (or relevant to them) until the application for judicial review is determined. This provision is to avoid the effects of an order taking place, possibly undermining the judicial review proceedings, until such an application is determined. An application to quash a decision of the county court is likely to be rare. Where the complaint is against the decision or order, the usual course is to appeal under County Courts Act 1984, s 77. Where it is desired to move the proceedings to the High Court, the application will usually be under County Courts Act 1984, ss 41, 42 or Children (Allocation of Proceedings) Order 1991, art 12 (relating to proceedings under CA 1989 or Adoption Act 1976).

84 Prohibition

(1) Where an application is made to the High Court for an order of prohibition addressed to any county court, the matter shall be finally disposed of by order.

(2) Upon any such application, the judge of the county court shall not be served with notice of it, and shall not, except by the order of a judge of the High Court –

(*a*) be required to appear or be heard; or
(*b*) be liable to any order for the payment of the costs of the application;

but the application shall be proceeded with and heard in the same manner in all respects as an appeal duly brought from a decision of the judge, and notice of the application shall be given to or served upon the same parties as in the case of an order made or refused by a judge in a matter within his jurisdiction.

Scope of provision—Applications for mandatory orders (formerly "mandamus"), quashing orders (formerly "certiorari") and prohibiting orders (formerly "prohibition") are made by way of application for judicial review under CPR 1998, Pt 54. Permission to make such application is required (CPR 1998, r 54.4). A mandatory order is appropriate where a judge, district judge or officer of the county court has improperly refused or declined to perform his ordinary duty under the County Courts Act 1984, but not where he has erred in performing it. Where the complaint is against the decision, the usual course will be an appeal under CCA 1984, s 77 (see *R v Sir Donald Hurst, ex parte Smith* [1960] 2 QB 133, [1960] 2 All ER 385). A prohibiting or quashing order may be granted if a county court acts without jurisdiction or in excess of it. Such orders are rare, and an appeal is more usual; see also CCA 1984, s 83.

PART V
ENFORCEMENT OF JUDGMENTS AND ORDERS

Execution against goods

85 Execution of judgments or orders for payment of money

(1) Subject to article 8 of the High Court and County Courts Jurisdiction Order 1991, any sum of money payable under a judgment or order of a county court may be recovered, in case of default or failure of payment, forthwith or at the time or times and in the manner thereby directed, by execution against the goods of the party against whom the judgment or order was obtained.

(2) The district judge, on the application of the party prosecuting any such judgment or order, shall issue a warrant of execution in the nature of a writ of fieri facias whereby the district judge shall be empowered to levy or cause to be levied by distress and sale of the goods, wherever they may be found within the district of the court, the money payable under the judgment or order and the costs of the execution.

(3) The precise time of the making of the application to the district judge to issue such a warrant shall be entered by him in the record prescribed for the purpose under section 12 and on the warrant.

(4) It shall be the duty of every constable within his jurisdiction to assist in the execution of every such warrant.

Amendments—SI 1991/724.

"Subject to article 8 ..." (s 85(1))—The High Court and County Courts Jurisdiction Order 1991 does not apply to family proceedings (art 12(*a*)).

"application of the party" (s 85(2))—The procedure is contained in CCR Ord 26 as it was immediately before 26 April 1999 (see the annotations under FPR 1991, r 1.3).

"The precise time" (s 85(3))—It is necessary for the court to record the date and time of issue of execution so that if several warrants are issued against a debtor their relevant priority can be determined. See **Considerations affecting issue of warrant**, *Priority* under CCR Ord 26, r 1. Where the debtor's goods are in the district of a court other than the court issuing the warrant, the warrant is sent to that court and the district judge there notes the date and time of receipt for the same purpose (s 103(3)).

86 Execution of orders for payment by instalments

(1) Where the court has made an order for payment of any sum of money by instalments, execution on the order shall not be issued until after default in payment of some instalment according to the order.

(2) Rules of court may prescribe the cases in which execution is to issue if there is any such default and limit the amounts for which and the times at which execution may issue.

(3) Except so far as may be otherwise provided by rules of court made for those purposes, execution or successive executions may issue if there is any such default for the whole of the said sum of money and costs then remaining unpaid or for such part as the court may order either at the time of the original order or at any subsequent time; but except so far as may be otherwise provided by such rules, no execution shall issue unless at the time when it issues the whole or some part of an instalment which has already become due remains unpaid.

Amendments—Civil Procedure Act 1997, s 10, Sch 2, para 2(1), (2).

"execution on the order" (s 86(1))—In *Mercantile Credit Co Ltd v Ellis* (1987) *The Times*, 1 April, the Court of Appeal considered that this provision applied by analogy to an application for a charging order against land. See **"consider all the circumstances"** under Charging Orders Act 1979, s 1.

"rules of court" (s 86(2), (3))—See CCR Ord 26, rr 1(2), (3), 11.

87 Execution to be superseded on payment

(1) In or upon every warrant of execution issued from a county court against the goods of any person, the district judge shall cause to be inserted or indorsed the total amount to be levied, inclusive of the fee for issuing the warrant but exclusive of the fees for its execution.

(2) If the person against whom the execution is issued, before the actual sale of the goods, pays or causes to be paid or tendered to the district judge of the court from which the warrant is issued, or to the bailiff holding the warrant, the amount inserted in, or indorsed upon, the warrant under subsection (1), or such part as the person entitled agrees to accept in full satisfaction, together with the amount stated by the officer of the court to whom the payment or tender is made to be the amount of the fees for the execution of the warrant, the execution shall be superseded, and the goods shall be discharged and set at liberty.

"the total amount to be levied" (s 87(1))—Where the creditor is represented by a solicitor and the warrant is issued for more than £25, a fixed sum of costs (currently £2.00: CCR Ord 38, r 18 and App B, Pt III, Item 3 as it was immediately before 26 April 1999 (see the annotations under FPR 1991, r 1.3)) is endorsed on the warrant in addition to the issue fee.

88 Power to stay execution

If at any time it appears to the satisfaction of the court that any party to any proceedings is unable from any cause to pay any sum recovered against him (whether by way of satisfaction of the claim or counterclaim in the proceedings or by way of costs or otherwise), or any instalment of such a sum, the court may, in its discretion, stay any execution issued in the proceedings for such time and on such terms as the court thinks fit, and so from time to time until it appears that the cause of inability has ceased.

Similar powers—The court may for similar reasons stay the judgment or order itself, s 71(2). Enforcement of a judgment or order may be stayed pending an appeal to the Court of Appeal (CPR 1998, r 52.7) or pending an appeal from the district judge to the judge or other application to set aside a judgment or order (CCR Ord 37, r 8(2)). The High Court's power under RSC Ord 47, r 1(1)(*a*) to stay execution against goods on the ground that there are special circumstances which render it inexpedient to enforce the judgment or order may be exercised by the county court by virtue of ss 38 and 76.

****

Receivers and attachment of debts

107 Receivers

(1) The power of the county court to appoint a receiver by way of equitable execution shall operate in relation to all legal estates and interests in land.

(2) The said power may be exercised in relation to an estate or interest in land whether or not a charge has been imposed on that land under section 1 of the Charging Orders Act 1979 for the purpose of enforcing the judgment, decree, order or award in question, and the said power shall be in addition to and not in derogation of any power of any court to appoint a receiver in proceedings for enforcing such a charge.

(3) Where an order under section 1 of the Charging Orders Act 1979 imposing a charge for the purpose of enforcing a judgment, decree, order or award has been registered under section 6 of the Land Charges Act 1972, subsection (4) of that section (which provides that, amongst other things, an order appointing a receiver and any proceedings pursuant to the order or in obedience to it, shall be void against a purchaser unless the order is for the time being registered under that section) shall not apply to an order appointing a receiver made either in proceedings for enforcing the charge or by way of equitable execution of the judgment, decree, order or award or, as the case may be, of so much of it as requires payment of moneys secured by the charge.

Procedure—As to the appointment of receivers, both under this section and generally, see CCR Ord 32.

108 Attachment of debts

(1) Subject to any order for the time being in force under subsection (4), this section applies to any deposit account, and any withdrawable share account, with a deposit-taker.

(2) In determining whether, for the purposes of the jurisdiction of the county court to attach debts for the purpose of satisfying judgments or orders for the payment of money, a sum standing to the credit of a person in an account to which this section applies is a sum due or accruing to that person and, as such, attachable in accordance with rules of court, any condition mentioned in subsection (3) which applies to the account shall be disregarded.

(3) Those conditions are –

(*a*) any condition that notice is required before any money or share is withdrawn;
(*b*) any condition that a personal application must be made before any money or share is withdrawn;
(*c*) any condition that a deposit book or share-account book must be produced before any money or share is withdrawn; or
(*d*) any other prescribed condition.

(4) The Lord Chancellor may by order make such provision as he thinks fit, by way of amendment of this section or otherwise, for all or any of the following purposes, namely –

(*a*) including in, or excluding from, the accounts to which this section applies accounts of any description specified in the order;
(*b*) excluding from the accounts to which this section applies all accounts with any particular deposit-taker so specified or with any deposit-taker of a description so specified.

(5) An order under subsection (4) shall be made by statutory instrument subject to annulment in pursuance of a resolution of either House of Parliament.

Amendments—Civil Procedure Act 1997, s 10, Sch 2, para 2(1), (2); SI 2001/3649.

"order" (s 108(1), (4), (5))—No such order has been made.

"rules of court" (s 108(2))—As to garnishee proceedings, see CCR Ord 30 as it was immediately before 26 April 1999 (see the annotations under FPR 1991, r 1.3).

109 Administrative and clerical expenses of garnishees

(1) Where an interim third party debt order made in the exercise of the jurisdiction mentioned in subsection (2) of the preceding section is served on a deposit-taker, it may, subject to the provisions of this section, deduct from the relevant debt or debts an amount not exceeding the prescribed sum towards its administrative and clerical expenses in complying with the order; and the right to make a deduction under this subsection shall be exercisable as from the time the interim third party debt order is served on it.

(1A) In subsection (1) "the relevant debt or debts", in relation to an interim third party debt order served on a deposit-taker, means the amount, as at the time the order is served on it, of the debt or debts of which the whole or a part is expressed to be attached by the order.

(1B) A deduction may be made under subsection (1) in a case where the amount referred to in subsection (1A) is insufficient to cover both the amount of the deduction and the amount of the judgment debt and costs in respect of which the attachment was made, notwithstanding that the benefit of the attachment to the creditor is reduced as a result of the deduction.

(2) An amount may not in pursuance of subsection (1) be deducted or, as the case may be, retained in a case where by virtue of section 346 of the Insolvency Act 1986 or section 325 of the Companies Act 1948 or otherwise, the creditor is not entitled to retain the benefit of the attachment.

(3) In this section "prescribed" means prescribed by an order made by the Lord Chancellor.

(4) An order under this section –

(*a*) may make different provision for different cases;
(*b*) without prejudice to the generality of paragraph (*a*) may prescribe sums differing according to the amount due under the judgment or order to be satisfied.
(*c*) may provide for this section not to apply to deposit-takers of any prescribed description.

(5) Any such order shall be made by statutory instrument subject to annulment in pursuance of a resolution of either House of Parliament.

Amendments—Administration of Justice Act 1985, ss 52, 67(2), Sch 8, Pt II; Insolvency Act 1986, s 439(2), Sch 14; SI 2001/3649; SI 2002/439.

"prescribed sum" (s 109(1))—The current sum is £55: SI 1996/3098.

"interim third party debt order"—This expression has been substituted for "order nisi" upon the replacement, for civil proceedings but not (yet) for family proceedings, of garnishee orders by third party debt orders under CPR Part 72. Presumably, in family proceedings, the bank's entitlement to make the deduction when served with a garnishee order nisi is not removed.

Miscellaneous provisions as to enforcement of judgments and orders

110 Penalty for non-attendance on judgment summons

(1) If a debtor summoned to attend a county court by a judgment summons fails to attend on the day and at the time fixed for any hearing of the summons, the judge may adjourn or further adjourn the summons to a specified time on a specified day and order the debtor to attend at that time on that day.

(2) If –

(*a*) a debtor, having been ordered under subsection (1) to attend at a specified time on a specified day, fails to do so;
(*b*) (*repealed*)

the judge may make an order committing him to prison for a period not exceeding 14 days in respect of the failure or refusal.

(3) In any case where the judge has power to make an order of committal under subsection (2) for failure to attend, he may in lieu of or in addition to making that order, order the debtor to be arrested and brought before the court either forthwith or at such time as the judge may direct.

(4) A debtor shall not be committed to prison under subsection (2) for having failed to attend as required by an order under subsection (1) unless there was paid to him at the time of the service of the judgment summons, or paid or tendered to him at the time of the service of the order, such sum in respect of his expenses as may be prescribed for the purposes of this section.

(5) The judge may at any time revoke an order committing a person to prison under this section and, if he is already in custody, order his discharge.

Amendments—SI 2002/439.

Defined terms—"judgment summons": s 147.

"prescribed sum" (s 110(4))—This is "a sum reasonably sufficient to cover his expenses in travelling to and from the court": CCR Ord 28, r 4(2).

****

PART VII
COMMITTALS

118 Power to commit for contempt

(1) If any person –

(*a*) wilfully insults the judge of a county court, or any juror or witness, or any officer of the court during his sitting or attendance in court, or in going to or returning from the court; or
(*b*) wilfully interrupts the proceedings of a county court or otherwise misbehaves in court;

any officer of the court, with or without the assistance of any other person, may, by order of the judge, take the offender into custody and detain him until the rising of the court, and the judge may, if he thinks fit, –

(i) make an order committing the offender for a specified period not exceeding one month to prison; or

(ii) impose upon the offender, for every offence, a fine of an amount not exceeding £2,500,

or may both make such an order and impose such a fine.

(2) The judge may at any time revoke an order committing a person to prison under this section and, if he is already in custody, order his discharge.

(3) A district judge, assistant district judge or deputy district judge shall have the same powers under this section in relation to proceedings before him as a judge.

Amendments—Statute Law (Repeals) Act 1986; Courts and Legal Services Act 1990, s 74(6); Criminal Justice Act 1991, s 17(3)(*a*), Sch 4.

119 Issue and execution of orders of committal

(1) Whenever any order or warrant for the committal of any person to prison is made or issued by a county court (whether in pursuance of this or any other Act or of rules of court), the order or warrant shall be directed to the district judge of the court, who shall thereby be empowered to take the body of the person against whom the order is made or warrant issued.

(2) It shall be the duty of every constable within his jurisdiction to assist in the execution of every such order or warrant.

(3) The governor of the prison mentioned in any such order or warrant shall be bound to receive and keep the person mentioned in it until he is lawfully discharged.

Amendments—Civil Procedure Act 1997, s 10, Sch 2, para 2(1), (2).

****

121 Power of judge to order discharge

If at any time it appears to the satisfaction of a judge of a county court that any debtor arrested or confined in prison by order of the court is unable from any cause to pay any sum recovered against him (whether by way of satisfaction of a claim or counterclaim or by way of costs or otherwise), or any instalment thereof, and ought to be discharged, the judge may order his discharge upon such terms (including liability to re-arrest if the terms are not complied with) as the judge thinks fit.

"unable from any cause to pay"—A debtor will not have been committed unless it was proved that he had the means but neglected or refused to pay (Debtors Act 1869, s 5). Any inability to pay apparent at the time of hearing the judgment summons will have been taken into account in the order made. This section allows the judge to deal with the case where further information comes to light subsequently, for example, where the debtor failed to attend the hearing and the judge proceeded in his absence.

"and ought to be discharged"—There must be some factor in addition to mere inability to pay.

****

PART IX
MISCELLANEOUS AND GENERAL

****

147 Interpretation

(1) In this Act, unless the context otherwise requires –

"action" means any proceedings in a county court which may be commenced as prescribed by plaint;

"Admiralty county court" means a county court appointed to have Admiralty jurisdiction by order under this Act;

"Admiralty proceedings" means proceedings in which the claim would not be within the jurisdiction of a county court but for sections 26 and 27;

"bailiff" includes a district judge;

"the county court limit" means –

(*a*) in relation to any enactment contained in this Act for which a limit is for the time being specified by an Order under section 145, that limit,

(*b*) (*repealed*)

(*c*) in relation to any enactment contained in this Act and not within paragraph (*a*), the county court limit for the time being specified by any other Order in Council or order defining the limit of county court jurisdiction for the purposes of that enactment;

"court" and "county court" mean a court held for a district under this Act;

"deposit-taking institution" means a person who may, in the course of his business, lawfully accept deposits in the United Kingdom;

"district" and "county district" mean a district for which a court is to be held under section 2;

"district judge" and "district judge of a county court" mean a district judge appointed for a district under this Act, or, in a case where two or more district judges are appointed jointly, either or any of those district judges;

"fees orders" means orders made under section 128;

"hearing" includes trial, and "hear" and "heard" shall be construed accordingly;

"hereditament" includes both a corporeal and an incorporeal hereditament;

"judge", in relation to a county court, means a judge assigned to the district of that court under subsection (1) of section 5 and any person sitting as a judge for that district under subsection (3) or (4) of that section;

"judgment summons" means a summons issued on the application of a person entitled to enforce a judgment or order under section 5 of the Debtors Act 1869 requiring a person, or, where two or more persons are liable under the judgment or order, requiring any one or more of them, to attend court;

"landlord", in relation to any land, means the person entitled to the immediate reversion or, if the property therein is held in joint tenancy, any of the persons entitled to the immediate reversion;

"legal representative" means an authorised advocate or authorised litigator, as defined by section 119(1) of the Courts and Legal Services Act 1990;

"matter" means every proceeding in a county court which may be commenced as prescribed otherwise than by plaint;

"officer", in relation to a court, means any district judge, deputy district judge or assistant district judge of that court, and any clerk, bailiff, usher or messenger in the service of that court;

"part-time district judge" and "part-time assistant district judge" have the meaning assigned to them by section 10(3);

"party" includes every person served with notice of, or attending, any proceeding, whether named as a party to that proceeding or not;

"prescribed" means prescribed by rules of court;

"probate proceedings" means proceedings brought in a county court by virtue of section 32 or transferred to that court under section 40;

"proceedings" includes both actions and matters;

"return day" means the day appointed in any summons or proceeding for the appearance of the defendant or any other day fixed for the hearing of any proceedings;

"rules of court" means rules made under section 75;

"ship" includes any description of vessel used in navigation;

"solicitor" means solicitor of the Supreme Court.

(1A) The definition of "deposit-taking institution" in subsection (1) must be read with –

(*a*) section 22 of the Financial Services and Markets Act 2000;
(*b*) any relevant order under that section; and
(*c*) Schedule 2 to that Act.

(2), (3) (*repealed*)

Amendments—Matrimonial and Family Proceedings Act 1984, s 46(3), Sch 3; Banking Act 1987, s 108(1), Sch 6, para 15; Courts and Legal Services Act 1990, s 125(3), Sch 18, para 49(1); SI 1990/776; SI 1991/724; Statute Law (Repeals) Act 1993; Civil Procedure Act 1997, s 10, Sch 2, para 2(1), (2), (9); SI 2001/3649; SI 2002/439.

****

Courts Act 1971

****

52 Award of costs where information or complaint is not proceeded with

(1), (2) (*repealed*)

(3) Where –

(*a*) (*repealed*)
(*b*) a complaint is made to a justice of the peace acting for any area but the complaint is not proceeded with,

a magistrates' court for that area may make such order as to costs to be paid by the complainant to the defendant as it thinks just and reasonable.

(4) An order under subsection (3) above shall specify the amount of the costs ordered to be paid.

(5) For the purpose of enforcement an order under subsection (3) above made in relation to a complaint which is not proceeded with shall be treated as if it were an order made under section 64 of the Magistrates' Courts Act 1980 (power to award, and enforcement of, costs in civil proceedings).

Amendments—Costs in Criminal Cases Act 1973, s 21, Sch 2; Magistrates' Courts Act 1980, s 154, Sch 7, para 96.

Scope of provision—There is no right of appeal to the Crown Court against an order under this section (see *R v Lewes Crown Court ex parte Rogers* [1974] 1 WLR 196).

"not proceeded with" (s 52(3))—For power to order costs where the complaint is proceeded with, see Magistrates' Courts Act 1980, s 64.

****

Courts and Legal Services Act 1990

****

9 Allocation of family proceedings which are within the jurisdiction of county courts

(1) The Lord Chancellor may, with the concurrence of the President of the Family Division, give directions that, in such circumstances as may be specified –

(*a*) any family proceedings which are within the jurisdiction of county courts; or

(*b*) any specified description of such proceedings,

shall be allocated to specified judges or to specified descriptions of judge.

(2) Any such direction shall have effect regardless of any rules of court.

(3) Where any directions have been given under this section allocating any proceedings to specified judges, the validity of anything done by a judge in, or in relation to, the proceedings shall not be called into question by reason only of the fact that he was not a specified judge.

(4) For the purposes of subsection (1) "county court" includes the principal registry of the Family Division of the High Court in so far as it is treated as a county court.

(5) In this section –

"family proceedings" has the same meaning as in the Matrimonial and Family Proceedings Act 1984 and also includes any other proceedings which are family proceedings for the purposes of the Children Act 1989;

"judge" means any person who –

(*a*) is capable of sitting as a judge for a county court district;

(*b*) is a district judge, an assistant district judge or a deputy district judge; or

(*c*) is a district judge of the principal registry of the Family Division of the High Court; and

"specified" means specified in the directions.

10 Family proceedings in magistrates' courts and related matters

(1) In subsection (2) "family proceedings" means proceedings under Part I of the Domestic Proceedings and Magistrates' Courts Act 1978.

(2) Rules made under section 144 of the Magistrates' Courts Act 1980 may make, in relation to any family proceedings, any provision which –

(*a*) falls within subsection (2) of section 93 of the Children Act 1989 (rules of court); and

(*b*) may be made in relation to relevant proceedings under section 93 of the Act of 1989.

(3)–(5) (*repealed*)

Amendments—Maintenance Enforcement Act 1991, s 11(1), Sch 2, para 11; Police and Magistrates' Courts Act 1994, s 93, Sch 9, Pt II.

****

Criminal Justice and Court Services Act 2000

****

CHAPTER II
CHILDREN AND FAMILY COURT ADVISORY AND SUPPORT SERVICE

11 Establishment of the Service

(1) There shall be a body corporate to be known as the Children and Family Court Advisory and Support Service (referred to in this Part as the Service) which is to exercise the functions conferred on it by virtue of this Act and any other enactment.

(2) Schedule 2 (which makes provision about the constitution of the Service, its powers and other matters relating to it) is to have effect.

(3) References in this Act or any other enactment to an officer of the Service are references to –

(*a*) any member of the staff of the Service appointed under paragraph 5(1)(*a*) of that Schedule, and

(*b*) any other individual exercising functions of an officer of the Service by virtue of section 13(2) or (4).

Status of CAFCASS—CAFCASS vested as a non-departmental public body, answerable to Parliament through the Lord Chancellor, on 1 April 2001.

"officer of the Service"—An officer of the Service is a person appointed by the Service under CJCSA 2000, Sch 2, para 5(1)(*a*) or authorised by the Service under s 13(2) or (4) to undertake one or more of the following functions:

(i) As a "children and family reporter", to investigate and provide a welfare report under CA 1989, s 7(1)(*a*);

(ii) As an "officer of the Service" or as a "local authority officer", to implement a family assistance order made under CA 1989, s 16(1)(*a*);

(iii) As a "children's guardian" under CA 1989, s 41(1), (2), to take appropriate steps to safeguard the interests of a child in specified proceedings;
(iv) As a "children's guardian" under Adoption Act 1976, s 65(1) and Adoption Rules 1984, r 6(1) or (2) or r 18(1) or (2), to investigate and report in relation to safeguarding the interests of a child who is the subject of freeing or adoption proceedings;
(v) As a "reporting officer" under AA 1976, s 65(2) and AR 1984, r 5(1) or r 17(1), to investigate and report on the attitude of a parent or guardian of a child who is the subject of freeing or adoption proceedings;
(vi) As a "parental order reporter" under FPR 1991, r 4A.5(1) or FPC(CA 89)R 1991, r 21E(1), to investigate and report on the circumstances relevant under Human Fertilisation and Embryology Act 1990 and to carry out duties under FPR 1991, r 4.11 or FPC(CA 89)R 1991, r 11.

12 Principal functions of the Service

(1) In respect of family proceedings in which the welfare of children is or may be in question, it is a function of the Service to –

(*a*) safeguard and promote the welfare of the children,
(*b*) give advice to any court about any application made to it in such proceedings,
(*c*) make provision for the children to be represented in such proceedings,
(*d*) provide information, advice and other support for the children and their families.

(2) The Service must also make provision for the performance of any functions conferred on officers of the Service by virtue of this Act or any other enactment (whether or not they are exercisable for the purposes of the functions conferred on the Service by subsection (1)).

(3) Regulations may provide for grants to be paid by the Service to any person for the purpose of furthering the performance of any of the Service's functions.

(4) The regulations may provide for the grants to be paid on conditions, including conditions –

(*a*) regulating the purposes for which the grant or any part of it may be used,
(*b*) requiring repayment to the Service in specified circumstances.

(5) In this section, "family proceedings" has the same meaning as in the Matrimonial and Family Proceedings Act 1984 and also includes any other proceedings which are family proceedings for the purposes of the Children Act 1989, but –

(*a*) references to family proceedings include (where the context allows) family proceedings which are proposed or have been concluded, and
(*b*) for the purposes of paragraph (*a*), where a supervision order (within the meaning of the Children Act 1989) is made in family proceedings, the proceedings are not to be treated as concluded until the order has ceased to have effect.

"functions of the Service"—The Service is responsible for fulfilling the requirements of courts in respect of investigations and reporting, and implementing family assistance orders – see annotation to s 11 above.

The Service inherited the functions of the Official Solicitor where he was appointed to act in wardship or other proceedings under the inherent jurisdiction of the High Court; also where he accepted an invitation to investigate and report in a county court. See *Practice Note of 2 April 2001 (Official Solicitor: Appointment in Family Proceedings)* and *Practice Note of March 2001 (Officers of CAFCASS Legal Services and Special Casework: Appointment in Family Proceedings)* (both are set out in Part IV of this work).

The Service also inherited involvement of local Probation Services in additional services such as mediation or pre-court advice for families. The Service is seeking to sustain these for the time being, subject to constraints of budget and to assessment of future viability of such services. Budgetary constraints inhibit significant development of additional services.

13 Other powers of the Service

(1) The Service may make arrangements with organisations under which the organisations perform functions of the Service on its behalf.

(2) Arrangements under subsection (1) may provide for the organisations to designate individuals who may perform functions of officers of the Service.

(3) But the Service may only make an arrangement under subsection (1) if it is of the opinion –

(*a*) that the functions in question will be performed efficiently and to the required standard, and

(*b*) that the arrangement represents good value for money.

(4) The Service may make arrangements with individuals under which they may perform functions of officers of the Service.

(5) The Service may commission, or assist the conduct of, research by any person into matters concerned with the exercise of its functions.

14 Provision of staff or services to other organisations

(1) The Service may make arrangements with an organisation or individual under which staff of the Service may work for the organisation or individual.

(2) The Service may make arrangements with an organisation or individual under which any services provided to the Service by its staff are also made available to the organisation or individual.

(3) The Service may charge for anything done under arrangements under this section.

15 Right to conduct litigation and right of audience

(1) The Service may authorise an officer of the Service of a prescribed description –

(*a*) to conduct litigation in relation to any proceedings in any court,

(*b*) to exercise a right of audience in any proceedings before any court,

in the exercise of his functions.

(2) An officer of the Service exercising a right to conduct litigation by virtue of subsection (1)(*a*) who would otherwise have such a right by virtue of section 28(2)(*a*) of the Courts and Legal Services Act 1990 is to be treated as having acquired that right solely by virtue of this section.

(3) An officer of the Service exercising a right of audience by virtue of subsection (1)(*b*) who would otherwise have such a right by virtue of section 27(2)(*a*) of the Courts and Legal Services Act 1990 is to be treated as having acquired that right solely by virtue of this section.

(4) In this section and section 16, "right to conduct litigation" and "right of audience" have the same meanings as in section 119 of the Courts and Legal Services Act 1990.

"conduct litigation" and "exercise a right of audience"—The legal profession has expressed concern that the power to authorise an officer of the Service to conduct litigation or exercise a right of audience might be used to supplant lawyers by officers of the Service. The Government has disavowed this and stated that the intention was to allow functions previously undertaken by staff of the Official Solicitor to continue to be performed by appropriate officers of the Service.

16 Cross-examination of officers of the Service

(1) An officer of the Service may, subject to rules of court, be cross-examined in any proceedings to the same extent as any witness.

(2) But an officer of the Service may not be cross-examined merely because he is exercising a right to conduct litigation or a right of audience granted in accordance with section 15.

"officer of the Service – witness"—This provision settles the question raised by erroneous dicta in the Court of Appeal that a family court welfare officer was an officer of the court who could not be required to give sworn evidence. An officer of CAFCASS is not an officer of the court. The officer prepares the report and gives evidence as an investigating expert, albeit with authority to perform statutory responsibilities bestowed by the court under the appointment to act in the individual case. Hence, an officer of CAFCASS who exercises a right to conduct litigation or a right of audience under CJCSA 2000, s 15, but does not submit evidence as a reporter, under CJCSA 2000, s 16(2) cannot be cross-examined. This may happen when a representative of the Director of Legal Services of CAFCASS exercises legal service functions which used to be exercised by the Official Solicitor's Office.

A children and family reporter appointed to report under CA 1989, s 16(1)(*a*) and FPR 1991, r 4.11B(2) or FPC(CA 1989)R 1991, r 11B(2) need not attend a hearing unless directed to under FPR 1991, r 4.11B(3) or FPC(CA 1989)R 1991, r 11B(3). A children and family reporter who does attend should give evidence as soon as possible after the case has opened (and in any event on the first day) and be released after giving evidence (*Best Practice Note of January 1995* at (3), para 10). This illustrates the difference of responsibilities between welfare reporting under CA 1989, s 7 and representation of a child by a children's guardian under CA 1989, s 41.

****

Domestic and Appellate Proceedings (Restriction of Publicity) Act 1968

1 Power of court hearing certain appeals and applications to sit in private

(1) Where an appeal is brought against a decision of any of the courts mentioned in subsection (4) below, or an application is made for leave to appeal against a decision of any of those courts, and that court had power to sit in private during the whole or any part of the proceedings in which the decision was given, then, subject to subsections (2) and (3) below, the court hearing the appeal or application shall have power to sit in private during the whole or any part of the proceedings on the appeal or application.

(2) Without prejudice to the next following subsection, the court hearing the appeal or application shall give its decision and the reason for its decision in public

unless there are good and sufficient grounds for giving them in private and in that case the court shall state those grounds in public.

(3) Where the decision of any of the courts mentioned in subsection (4) below against which an appeal is brought –

(*a*) is a conviction, or a sentence or other order made on conviction, or
(*b*) was given in the exercise of jurisdiction to punish for contempt of court,

the court hearing the appeal or any further appeal arising out of the same proceedings shall, notwithstanding that it sat in private during the whole of any part of the proceedings on the appeal, state in open court the order made by it on the appeal.

(4) The courts referred to in subsections (1) and (3) above are the Court of Appeal, the High Court, the Crown Court, the Restrictive Practices Court, a county court and a magistrates' court.

(5) An application to a court to sit in private during the whole of any part of the proceedings on such an appeal or application as is mentioned in subsection (1) above shall be heard in private unless the court otherwise directs.

(6) The powers conferred on a court by this section shall be in addition to any other power of the court to sit in private.

(7) In this section references to a power to sit in private are references to a power to sit in camera or in chambers, but the power conferred by this section on a court which has no power to sit in chambers is a power to sit in camera only.

(8) In this section "appeal" includes appeal by case stated, and references to a court include references to a judge exercising the powers of a court.

Amendments—Courts Act 1971, s 56, Sch 8, para 58, Sch 11, Pt IV.

2 Restriction of publicity for legitimacy proceedings etc and certain proceedings by a wife for maintenance

(1) The following provisions of this section shall have effect with a view to preventing or restricting publicity for –

(*a*) (*repealed*)
(*b*) proceedings under section 22 of that Act (which relates to proceedings by a wife against her husband for maintenance), including any proceedings begun before the said commencement and carried on under that section and any proceedings for the discharge or variation of an order made or deemed to have been made under that section or for the temporary suspension of any provision of any such order or the revival of the operation of any provision so suspended;
(*c*) proceedings under section 27 of the Matrimonial Causes Act 1973 (which relates to proceedings by a wife against her husband, or by a husband against his wife, for financial provision) and any proceedings for the discharge or variation of an order made under that section or for the temporary suspension of any provision of any such order or the revival of the operation of any provision so suspended;
(*d*) proceedings under Part III of the Family Law Act 1986;
(*e*) (*repealed*)

(2) (*repealed*)

(3) Section 1(1)(*b*) of the Judicial Proceedings (Regulation of Reports) Act 1926 (which restricts the reporting of matrimonial causes) shall extend to any such proceedings as are mentioned in subsection (1) above subject, in the case of the proceedings mentioned in subsection (1), (*d*) to the modification that the matters allowed to be printed or published by virtue of sub-paragraph (ii) of the said section 1(1)(*b*) shall be particulars of the declaration sought by a petition (instead of a concise statement of the charges, defences and counter-charges in support of which evidence has been given).

Amendments—Matrimonial Proceedings and Property Act 1970, s 42(1), Sch 2, para 3; Matrimonial Causes Act 1973, ss 53, 54, Sch 1, Sch 2, para 7(1), Sch 3; Family Law Act 1986, s 68, Sch 1, para 9, Sch 2; Family Law Reform Act 1987, s 33, Sch 2, para 19, Sch 4; Child Support, Pensions and Social Security Act 2000, s 85, Sch 9.

****

Domestic Proceedings and Magistrates' Courts Act 1978

ARRANGEMENT OF SECTIONS

PART I
MATRIMONIAL PROCEEDINGS IN MAGISTRATES' COURTS

Powers of court to make orders for financial provision for parties to a marriage and children of the family

PART I
MATRIMONIAL PROCEEDINGS IN MAGISTRATES' COURTS

Powers of court to make orders for financial provision for parties to a marriage and children of the family

1 Grounds of application for financial provision

Either party to a marriage may apply to a magistrates' court for an order under section 2 of this Act on the ground that the other party to the marriage –

(*a*) has failed to provide reasonable maintenance for the applicant; or

(*b*) has failed to provide, or to make a proper contribution towards, reasonable maintenance for any child of the family; or

(*c*) has behaved in such a way that the applicant cannot reasonably be expected to live with the respondent; or

(*d*) has deserted the applicant.

Amendments—Matrimonial and Family Proceedings Act 1984, s 46(1), Sch 1, para 21.

Defined terms—"child", "child of the family": s 88(1); "live with": s 88(2).

Procedure on application—For the procedure to be followed, see Family Proceedings Courts (Matrimonial Proceedings etc) Rules 1991.

"magistrates' court"—Any magistrates' court within the commission area has jurisdiction (Magistrates' Courts Act 1980, s 52).

"behaved" (s 1(*c*))—The date of the behaviour may be relevant (see MCA 1980, s 127 (time-limits)).

Fee payable—See Magistrates' Courts Act 1980, Sch 6.

2 Powers of court to make orders for financial provision

(1) Where on an application for an order under this section the applicant satisfies the court of any ground mentioned in section 1 of this Act, the court may, subject to the provisions of this Part of this Act, make any one or more of the following orders, that is to say –

(*a*) an order that the respondent shall make to the applicant such periodical payments, and for such term, as may be specified in the order;
(*b*) an order that the respondent shall pay to the applicant such lump sum as may be so specified;
(*c*) an order that the respondent shall make to the applicant for the benefit of a child of the family to whom the application relates, or to such a child, such periodical payments, and for such term, as may be so specified;
(*d*) an order that the respondent shall pay to the applicant for the benefit of a child of the family to whom the application relates, or to such a child, such lump sum as may be so specified.

(2) Without prejudice to the generality of subsection (1)(*b*) or (*d*) above, an order under this section for the payment of a lump sum may be made for the purpose of enabling any liability or expenses reasonably incurred in maintaining the applicant, or any child of the family to whom the application relates, before the making of the order to be met.

(3) The amount of any lump sum required to be paid by an order under this section shall not exceed £1,000 or such larger amount as the Lord Chancellor may from time to time by order fix for the purposes of this subsection.

Any order made by the Lord Chancellor under this subsection shall be made by statutory instrument and shall be subject to annulment in pursuance of a resolution of either House of Parliament.

Amendments—SI 1988/1069; SI 1992/709.

Defined terms—"child", "child of the family": s 88(1).

Scope of provision—This section defines the powers of magistrates' courts to order periodical payments and lump sum payments to either party or to a child of the family. Separate but complementary provision for orders for financial provision for children is contained in CA 1989, Sch 1. The courts' powers in respect of child maintenance under this Act and under CA 1989 are subject to the radical restrictions imposed by the Child Support Act 1991.

"the applicant satisfies the court" (s 2(1))—For the procedure where the respondent fails to appear see Magistrates' Courts Act 1980, s 55. The court is entitled to consider written details of the respondent's means where the respondent does not appear and the applicant agrees the details but, if the applicant does not agree with the information supplied in this way, the case should be adjourned and the respondent required to attend (*Whittingstall v Whittingstall* [1990] 2 FLR 368). In *Land v Land* [1949] P 405, [1949] 2 All ER 218, it was held that, where a complaint was withdrawn, a fresh complaint could be made on the same facts provided the complaint was made within the statutory time limit. For power to change the application to an agreed application, see s 6(4). Note the effect of an employer's statement of wages: Magistrates' Courts Act 1980, s 100.

"the court may ... make any one or more of the following orders" (s 2(1))—Although an apparent discretion is given to the court, it has been held that there is a duty to exercise this power where the applicant has proved his case (*Hill v Hill* (1972) 116 Sol Jo 565). Before making an order, the court is obliged under s 26 to consider the possibility of reconciliation.

Form of order—If an order is made, it should include a statement that the complaint is found to be true (*Wilcox v Wilcox* (1902) 66 JP 166; *Dodd v Dodd* [1906] P 189). If there is a finding of desertion, the date of commencement of desertion should be included in the order (*Fengl v Fengl* [1914] P 274). Where the person against whom an order is to be made is a member of Her

Majesty's forces, see the Army Act 1955, ss 144 and 150 to 152, the Air Force Act 1955, ss 144 and 150 to 152 and *Barnish v Barnish* (1976) Fam Law 174. Further guidance is given in Home Office Circulars 251/1970, 12/1982 (Royal Navy and Royal Marines) and 25/1986.

Lump sums (s 2(1)(*b*))—The general power to order payments by instalments appears to apply equally to lump sums (Magistrates' Court Act 1980, s 75; see s 22 for the power to vary the instalments). Even though a payer does not have capital resources, the court may order a lump sum payment provided it has had regard to the payer's ability to pay from income (or potential income).

"a child of the family to whom the application relates" (s 2(1)(*c*))—These words seem to indicate that financial provision for children under this Act is dependent upon an application being made in respect of them and may not be awarded where the application relates only to the applicant spouse.

Method of payment—See Magistrates' Courts Act 1980, s 59 for the requirement for payment to be ordered directly between the parties, through the clerk of a magistrates' court, by standing order (or similar method) or by attachment of earnings.

Court's duty to assist unrepresented party—For the duty of the court to assist an unrepresented party who is unable effectively to examine or cross-examine a witness see Magistrates' Courts Act 1980, s 73.

3 Matters to which the court is to have regard in exercising its powers under s 2

(1) Where an application is made for an order under section 2 of this Act, it shall be the duty of the court, in deciding whether to exercise its powers under that section and, if so, in what manner, to have regard to all the circumstances of the case, first consideration being given to the welfare while a minor of any child of the family who has not attained the age of eighteen.

(2) As regards the exercise of its powers under subsection (1)(*a*) or (*b*) of section 2, the court shall in particular have regard to the following matters –

(*a*) the income, earning capacity, property and other financial resources which each of the parties to the marriage has or is likely to have in the foreseeable future, including in the case of earning capacity any increase in that capacity which it would in the opinion of the court be reasonable to expect a party to the marriage to take steps to acquire;
(*b*) the financial needs, obligations and responsibilities which each of the parties to the marriage has or is likely to have in the foreseeable future;
(*c*) the standard of living enjoyed by the parties to the marriage before the occurrence of the conduct which is alleged as the ground of the application;
(*d*) the age of each party to the marriage and the duration of the marriage;
(*e*) any physical or mental disability of either of the parties to the marriage;
(*f*) the contributions which each of the parties has made or is likely in the foreseeable future to make to the welfare of the family, including any contribution by looking after the home or caring for the family;
(*g*) the conduct of each of the parties, if that conduct is such that it would in the opinion of the court be inequitable to disregard it.

(3) As regards the exercise of its power under subsection (1)(*c*) or (*d*) of section 2, the court shall in particular have regard to the following matters –

(*a*) the financial needs of the child;
(*b*) the income, earning capacity (if any), property and other financial resources of the child;
(*c*) any physical or mental disability of the child;

(*d*) the standard of living enjoyed by the family before the occurrence of the conduct which is alleged as the ground of the application;

(*e*) the manner in which the child was being and in which the parties to the marriage expected him to be educated or trained;

(*f*) the matters mentioned in relation to the parties to the marriage in paragraphs (*a*) and (*b*) of subsection (2) above.

(4) As regards the exercise of its power under section 2 in favour of a child of the family who is not the child of the respondent, the court shall also have regard –

(*a*) to whether the respondent has assumed any responsibility for the child's maintenance and, if he did, to the extent to which, and the basis on which, he assumed that responsibility and to the length of time during which he discharged that responsibility;

(*b*) to whether in assuming and discharging that responsibility the respondent did so knowing that the child was not his own child;

(*c*) to the liability of any other person to maintain the child.

Amendments—Matrimonial and Family Proceedings Act 1984, s 9.

Defined terms—"child of the family": s 88(1).

Scope of provision—This section outlines the matters to which the court is to have regard in making an order under s 2. It follows (with only minor modifications) the guidelines set out in Matrimonial Causes Act 1973 (particularly s 25) and so the principles followed in divorce courts are of equal application in magistrates' courts (*Macey v Macey* (1982) FLR 7).

Maintenance calculations under the Child Support Act 1991 will, in many cases, be substantial. For those cases where jurisdiction is retained by the courts, there is no express duty to apply the Child Support Act 1991 formula to establish a starting-point for maintenance but the likely amount of child support maintenance which would be payable may provide the court with useful and "strongly persuasive" information (*E v C (Child Maintenance)* [1996] 1 FLR 472). There are now three "ranging shots": the prescribed figures set out in the National Foster Care Allowance, in the DSS allowances, and the CSA calculation. The court finds it helpful to know all three figures. Good reasons must exist for any substantial differences between maintenance calculations and maintenance orders.

"shall in particular have regard" (s 3(2))—The procedure to be adopted should be for the court to make a finding upon each of the factors contained in the section. Each of the factors should then be balanced in order to arrive at a just and reasonable order (*Vasey v Vasey* [1985] FLR 596).

4 Duration of orders for financial provision for a party to a marriage

(1) The term to be specified in any order made under section 2(1)(*a*) of this Act shall be such term as the court thinks fit except that the term shall not begin earlier than the date of the making of the application for the order and shall not extend beyond the death of either of the parties to the marriage.

(2) Where the order is made under the said section 2(1)(*a*) and the marriage of the parties affected by the order is subsequently dissolved or annulled but the order continues in force, the order shall, notwithstanding anything in it, cease to have effect on the remarriage of the party in whose favour it was made, except in relation to any arrears due under the order on the date of the remarriage.

Revival of orders—The power to revive an order under s 20(6) is restricted to orders which have been temporarily suspended. An expired term order cannot be revived.

5 Age limit on making orders for financial provision for children and duration of such orders

(1) Subject to subsection (3) below, no order shall be made under section 2(1)(*c*) or (*d*) of this Act in favour of a child who has attained the age of eighteen.

(2) The term to be specified in an order made under section 2(1)(*c*) of this Act in favour of a child may begin with the date of the making of an application for the order in question or any later date or a date ascertained in accordance with subsection (5) or (6) below but –

(*a*) shall not in the first instance extend beyond the date of the birthday of the child next following his attaining the upper limit of the compulsory school age (construed in accordance with section 8 of the Education Act 1996) unless the court considers that in the circumstances of the case the welfare of the child requires that it should extend to a later date; and

(*b*) shall not in any event, subject to subsection (3) below, extend beyond the date of the child's eighteenth birthday.

(3) The court –

(*a*) may make an order under section 2(1)(*c*) or (*d*) of this Act in favour of a child who has attained the age of eighteen, and

(*b*) may include in an order made under section 2(1)(*c*) of this Act in relation to a child who has attained that age a provision for extending beyond the date when the child will attain that age the term for which by virtue of the order any payments are to be made to or for the benefit of that child,

if it appears to the court –

(i) that the child is, or will be, or if such an order or provision were made would be receiving instruction at an educational establishment or undergoing training for a trade, profession or vocation, whether or not he is also, or will also be, in gainful employment; or

(ii) that there are special circumstances which justify the making of the order or provision.

(4) Any order made under section 2(1)(*c*) of this Act in favour of a child shall, notwithstanding anything in the order, cease to have effect on the death of the person liable to make payments under the order.

(5) Where –

(*a*) a maintenance calculation ("the current calculation") is in force with respect to a child; and

(*b*) an application is made for an order under section 2(1)(*c*) of this Act –

(i) in accordance with section 8 of the Child Support Act 1991; and

(ii) before the end of the period of 6 months beginning with the making of the current calculation,

the term to be specified in any such order made on that application may be expressed to begin on, or at any time after, the earliest permitted date.

(6) For the purposes of subsection (5) above, "the earliest permitted date" is whichever is the later of –

(*a*) the date 6 months before the application is made; or

(*b*) the date on which the current calculation took effect or, where successive maintenance calculations have been continuously in force with respect to a child, on which the first of those calculations took effect.

(7) Where –

(*a*) a maintenance calculation ceases to have effect by or under any provision of the Child Support Act 1991; and
(*b*) an application is made, before the end of the period of 6 months beginning with the relevant date, for an order under section 2(1)(*c*) of this Act in relation to a child with respect to whom that maintenance calculation was in force immediately before it ceased to have effect,

the term to be specified in any such order, or in any interim order under section 19 of this Act, made on that application, may begin with the date on which that maintenance calculation ceased to have effect, or any later date.

(8) In subsection (7)(*b*) above –

(*a*) where the maintenance calculation ceased to have effect, the relevant date is the date on which it so ceased
(*b*) (*repealed*)

Amendments—Matrimonial and Family Proceedings Act 1984, s 9(2); SI 1993/623; Education Act 1996, s 582(1), Sch 37, Pt II, para 138; Child Support, Pensions and Social Security Act 2000, ss 26, 85, Sch 3, para 4, Sch 9.

Defined terms—"child": s 88(1).

Scope of provision—This section sets out the permissible duration of an order for financial provision for a child. An existing maintenance calculation terminates when the child ceases to be a "child" under Child Support Act 1991, s 55. A calculation will be cancelled by the Secretary of State in the event that one or more of the person with care, the non-resident parent or the child leaves the jurisdiction (Child Support (Maintenance Arrangements and Jurisdiction) Regulations 1992, reg 7). For power to backdate to the termination or cancellation of the order, see DPMCA 1978, s 5(7). For power to backdate a "top-up" order under Child Support Act 1991, s 8(6), see DPMCA 1978, s 5(5).

Revival of orders—There are limited powers to revive an expired order (see s 20A).

6 Orders for payments which have been agreed by the parties

(1) Either party to a marriage may apply to a magistrates' court for an order under this section on the ground that either the party making the application or the other party to the marriage has agreed to make such financial provision as may be specified in the application and, subject to subjection (3) below, the court on such an application may, if –

(*a*) it is satisfied that the applicant or the respondent, as the case may be, has agreed to make that provision, and
(*b*) it has no reason to think that it would be contrary to the interests of justice to exercise its powers hereunder,

order that the applicant or the respondent, as the case may be, shall make the financial provisions specified in the application.

(2) In this section "financial provision" means the provision mentioned in any one or more of the following paragraphs, that is to say –

(*a*) the making of periodical payments by one party to the other,
(*b*) the payment of a lump sum by one party to the other,
(*c*) the making of periodical payments by one party to a child of the family or to the other party for the benefit of such a child,
(*d*) the payment by one party of a lump sum to a child of the family or to the other party for the benefit of such a child,

and any reference in this section to the financial provision specified in an application made under subsection (1) above or specified by the court under subsection (5) below is a reference to the type of provision specified in the application or by the court, as the case may be, to the amount so specified as the amount of any payment to be made thereunder and, in the case of periodical payments, to the term so specified as the term for which the payments are to be made.

(3) Where the financial provision specified in an application under subsection (1) above includes or consists of provision in respect of a child of the family, the court shall not make an order under that subsection unless it considers that the provision which the applicant or the respondent, as the case may be, has agreed to make in respect of that child provides for, or makes a proper contribution towards, the financial needs of the child.

(4) A party to a marriage who has applied for an order under section 2 of this Act shall not be precluded at any time before the determination of that application from applying for an order under this section; but if an order is made under this section on the application of either party and either of them has also made an application for an order under section 2 of this Act, the application made for the order under section 2 shall be treated as if it had been withdrawn.

(5) Where on an application under subsection (1) above the court decides –

(*a*) that it would be contrary to the interests of justice to make an order for the making of the financial provision specified in the application, or

(*b*) that any financial provision which the applicant or the respondent, as the case may be, has agreed to make in respect of a child of the family does not provide for, or make a proper contribution towards, the financial needs of that child,

but it is of the opinion –

(i) that it would not be contrary to the interests of justice to make an order for the making of some other financial provision specified by the court, and

(ii) that, in so far as that other financial provision contains any provision for a child of the family, it provides for, or makes a proper contribution towards, the financial needs of that child,

then if both the parties agree, the court may order that the applicant or the respondent, as the case may be, shall make that other financial provision.

(6) Subject to subsection (8) below, the provisions of section 4 of this Act shall apply in relation to an order under this section which requires periodical payments to be made to a party to a marriage for his own benefit as they apply in relation to an order under section 2(1)(*a*) of this Act.

(7) Subject to subsection (8) below, the provisions of section 5 of this Act shall apply in relation to an order under this section for the making of financial provision in respect of a child of the family as they apply in relation to an order under section 2(1)(*c*) or (*d*) of this Act.

(8) Where the court makes an order under this section which contains provision for the making of periodical payments and, by virtue of subsection (4) above, an application for an order under section 2 of this Act is treated as if it had been withdrawn, then the term which may be specified as the term for which the payments are to be made may begin with the date of the making of the application for the order under section 2 or any later date.

(9) Where the respondent is not present or represented by counsel or solicitor at the hearing of an application for an order under subsection (1) above, the court shall not make an order under this section unless there is produced to the court such evidence as may be prescribed by rules of –

(*a*) the consent of the respondent to the making of the order,
(*b*) the financial resources of the respondent, and
(*c*) in a case where the financial provision specified in the application includes or consists of provision in respect of a child of the family to be made by the applicant to the respondent for the benefit of the child or to the child, the financial resources of the child.

Amendments—Matrimonial and Family Proceedings Act 1984, s 10.

Defined terms—"child", "child of the family": s 88(1).

Form of application—The form of application and the procedure on application is prescribed by the Family Proceedings Courts (Matrimonial Proceedings etc) Rules 1991.

"either party to a marriage"—The proposed payee or payer may apply for an order under this section.

Method of payment—See under s 2.

Lump sums (s 6(2)(*b*))—The amount of any agreed lump sum is not limited by this section. Contrast the limitation imposed under s 2. The general power to order payment by instalments appears to apply to payment of lump sums under this section (Magistrates' Courts Act 1980, s 75); for the power to vary instalments see s 22.

Relationship with applications under s 2 (s 6(4))—It is possible to make an application under this section while an application under s 2 is outstanding; s 6(4) prescribes the procedure to be adopted in such circumstances.

"such evidence as may be prescribed" (s 6(9))—Family Proceedings Courts (Matrimonial Proceedings etc) Rules 1991, r 17 and Sch 1 prescribe the evidence which must be produced.

Fee payable—See Magistrates' Courts Act 1980, Sch 6.

7 Powers of court where parties are living apart by agreement

(1) Where the parties to a marriage have been living apart for a continuous period exceeding three months, neither party having deserted the other, and one of the parties has been making periodical payments for the benefit of the other party or of a child of the family, that other party may apply to a magistrates' court for an order under this section, and any application made under this subsection shall specify the aggregate amount of the payments so made during the period of three months immediately preceding the date of the making of the application.

(2) Where on an application for an order under this section the court is satisfied that the respondent has made the payments specified in the application, the court may, subject to the provisions of this Part of this Act, make one or both of the following orders, that is to say –

(*a*) an order that the respondent shall make to the applicant such periodical payments, and for such term, as may be specified in the order;
(*b*) an order that the respondent shall make to the applicant for the benefit of a child of the family to whom the application relates, or to such a child, such periodical payments, and for such term, as may be so specified.

(3) The court in the exercise of its powers under this section –

(*a*) shall not require the respondent to make payments which exceed in aggregate during any period of three months the aggregate amount paid by him for the benefit of the applicant or a child of the family during the period of three months immediately preceding the date of the making of the application;

(*b*) shall not require the respondent to make payments to or for the benefit of any person which exceed in amount the payments which the court considers that it would have required the respondent to make to or for the benefit of that person on an application under section 1 of this Act;

(*c*) shall not require payments to be made to or for the benefit of a child of the family who is not a child of the respondent unless the court considers that it would have made an order in favour of that child on an application under section 1 of this Act.

(4) Where on an application under this section the court considers that the orders which it has the power to make under this section –

(*a*) would not provide reasonable maintenance for the applicant, or

(*b*) if the application relates to a child of the family, would not provide, or make a proper contribution towards reasonable maintenance for that child,

the court shall refuse to make an order under this section, but the court may treat the application as if it were an application for an order under section 2 of this Act.

(5) The provisions of section 3 of this Act shall apply in relation to an application for an order under this section as they apply in relation to an application for an order under section 2 of this Act subject to the modification that for the reference in subsection (2)(c) of the said section 3 to the occurrence of the conduct which is alleged as the ground of the application there shall be substituted a reference to the living apart of the parties to the marriage.

(6) The provisions of section 4 of this Act shall apply in relation to an order under this section which requires periodical payments to be made to the applicant for his own benefit as they apply in relation to an order under section 2(1)(*a*) of this Act.

(7) The provisions of section 5 of this Act shall apply in relation to an order under this section for the making of periodical payments in respect of a child of the family as they apply in relation to an order under section 2(1)(*c*) of this Act.

Amendments—Matrimonial and Family Proceedings Act 1984, s 46(1), Sch 1, para 22.

Defined terms—"child of the family": s 88(1); "marriage": s 88(3).

Method of payment—See under s 2.

Fee payable—See Magistrates' Courts Act 1980, Sch 6.

Powers of court as to the custody etc of children

8 Restrictions on making of orders under this Act: welfare of children

Where an application is made by a party to a marriage for an order under section 2, 6 or 7 of this Act, then, if there is a child of the family who is under the age of eighteen, the court shall not dismiss or make a final order on the application until it has decided whether to exercise any of its powers under the Children Act 1989 with respect to the child.

Amendments—CA 1989, s 108(5), Sch 13, para 36.

Defined terms—"child", "child of the family": s 88(1).

"dismiss or make a final order"—An interim order under s 19 is not prohibited.

****

Interim orders

19 Interim orders

(1) Where an application is made for an order under section 2, 6 or 7 of this Act –

(*a*) the magistrates' court at any time before making a final order on, or dismissing the application or on refusing to make an order on the application by virtue of section 27 of this Act, and

(*b*) the High Court on ordering the application to be reheard by a magistrates' court (either after the refusal of an order under section 27 of this Act or on an appeal under section 29 of this Act),

shall, subject to the provisions of this Part of this Act, have the

(i) power to make an order (in this Part of this Act referred to as an "interim maintenance order") which requires the respondent to make to the applicant or to any child of the family who is under the age of eighteen, or to the applicant for the benefit of such a child, such periodical payments as the court thinks reasonable;

(ii) (*repealed*)

(2) (*repealed*)

(3) An interim maintenance order may provide for payments to be made from such date as the court may specify, except that, subject to section 5(5) and (6) of this Act, the date shall not be earlier than the date of the making of the application for an order under section 2, 6 or 7 of this Act; and where such an order made by the High Court on an appeal under section 29 of this Act provides for payments to be made from a date earlier than the date of the making of the order, the interim order may provide that payments made by the respondent under an order made by a magistrates' court shall, to such extent and in such manner as may be provided by the interim order, be treated as having been paid on account of any payment provided for by the interim order.

(3A) Where an application is made for an order under section 6 of this Act by the party to the marriage who has agreed to make the financial provision specified in the application –

(*a*) subsection (1) shall apply as if the reference in paragraph (i) to the respondent were a reference to the applicant and the references to the applicant were references to the respondent; and

(*b*) subsection (3) shall apply accordingly.

(4) (*repealed*)

(5) Subject to subsection (6) below, an interim order made on an application for an order under section 2, 6 or 7 of this Act shall cease to have effect on whichever of the following dates occurs first, that is to say –

(*a*) the date, if any, specified for the purpose in the interim order;

(*b*) the date of the expiration of the period of three months beginning with the date of the making of the interim order;

(*c*) the date on which a magistrates' court either makes a final order on or dismisses the application.

(6) Where an interim order made under subsection (1) above would, but for this subsection, cease to have effect by virtue of subsection (5)(*a*) or (*b*) above, the magistrates' court which made the order or, in the case of an interim order made by the High Court, the magistrates' court by which the application for an order under section 2, 6 or 7 of this Act is to be reheard, shall have power by order to provide that the interim order shall continue in force for a further period, and any order continued in force under this subsection shall cease to have effect on whichever of the following dates occurs first, that is to say –

(*a*) the date, if any specified for the purpose in the order made under this subsection;

(*b*) the date of the expiration of the period of three months beginning with the date of the making of the order under this subsection or, if more than one order has been made under this subsection with respect to the application, beginning with the date of the making of the first of those orders;

(*c*) the date on which the court either makes a final order on, or dismisses, the application.

(7) Not more than one interim maintenance order may be made with respect to any application for an order under section 2, 6 or 7 of this Act, but without prejudice to the powers of the court under this section on any further such application.

(8) No appeal shall lie from the making of or refusal to make, the variation of or refusal to vary, or the revocation of or refusal to revoke, an interim maintenance order.

(9) An interim order made by the High Court under this section on ordering that an application be reheard by a magistrates' court shall for the purpose of its enforcement and for the purposes of section 20 of this Act, be treated as if it were an order of that magistrates' court and not of the High Court.

Amendments—Matrimonial and Family Proceedings Act 1984, s 46(1), Sch 1, para 24; CA 1989, s 108(5), (7), Sch 13, para 37, Sch 15; SI 1993/623.

Defined terms—"child", "child of the family": s 88(1).

"an order" (s 19(1))—Only one interim order may be made with respect to an application (s 19(7)) but there is power under s 19(6) to extend the original interim order for up to a further three months.

"if more than one order has been made" (s 19(6)(*b*))—Whilst only one interim order may be made, a number of extension orders is permissible provided that the aggregate period of extension orders does not exceed three months.

Variation, revocation and cessation of orders etc

20 Variation, revival and revocation of orders for periodical payments

(1) Where a magistrates' court has made an order under section 2(1)(*a*) or (*c*) of this Act for the making of periodical payments the court shall have power, on an application made under this section, to vary or revoke that order and also to make an order under section 2(1)(*b*) or (*d*) of this Act.

(2) Where a magistrates' court has made an order under section 6 of this Act for the making of periodical payments by a party to a marriage the court shall have

power, on an application made under this section, to vary or revoke that order and also to make an order for the payment of a lump sum by that party either –

(*a*) to the other party to the marriage, or

(*b*) to a child of the family or to that other party for the benefit of that child.

(3) Where a magistrates' court has made an order under section 7 of this Act for the making of periodical payments, the court shall have power, on an application made under this section, to vary or revoke that order.

(4) (*repealed*)

(5) Where a magistrates' court has made an interim maintenance order under section 19 of this Act, the court, on an application made under this section, shall have power to vary or revoke that order, except that the court shall not by virtue of this subsection extend the period for which the order is in force.

(6) The power of the court under this section to vary an order for the making of periodical payments shall include power to suspend any provisions thereof temporarily and to revive any provision so suspended.

(7) Where the court has power by virtue of this section to make an order for the payment of a lump sum, the amount of the lump sum shall not exceed the maximum amount that may at that time be required to be paid under section 2(3) of this Act, but the court may make an order for the payment of a lump sum not exceeding that amount notwithstanding that the person required to pay the lump sum was required to pay a lump sum by a previous order under this Part of this Act.

(8) Where the court has power by virtue of subsection (2) above to make an order for the payment of a lump sum and the respondent or the applicant, as the case may be, has agreed to pay a lump sum of an amount exceeding the maximum amount that may at that time be required to be paid under section 2(3) of this Act, the court may, notwithstanding anything in subsection (7) above, make an order for the payment of a lump sum of that amount.

(9) An order made by virtue of this section which varies an order for the making of periodical payments may provide that the payments as so varied shall be made from such date as the court may specify, except that, subject to subsections (9A) and (9B) below, the date shall not be earlier than the date of the making of the application under this section.

(9A) Where –

(*a*) there is in force an order ("the order") –

(i) under section 2(1)(*c*) of this Act,

(ii) under section 6(1) of this Act making provision of a kind mentioned in paragraph (*c*) of section 6(2) of this Act (regardless of whether it makes provision of any other kind mentioned in that paragraph),

(iii) under section 7(2)(*b*) of this Act, or

(iv) which is an interim maintenance order under which the payments are to be made to a child or to the applicant for the benefit of a child;

(*b*) the order requires payments specified in it to be made to or for the benefit of more than one child without apportioning those payments between them;

(*c*) a maintenance calculation ("the calculation") is made with respect to one or more, but not all, of the children with respect to whom those payments are to be made; and (*d*) an application is made, before the end of the period of 6 months beginning with the date on which the calculation was made, for the variation or revocation of the order,

the court may, in exercise of its powers under this section to vary or revoke the order, direct that the variation or revocation shall take effect from the date on which the calculationtook effect or any later date.

(9B) Where –

(*a*) an order ("the child order") of a kind prescribed for the purposes of section 10(1) of the Child Support Act 1991 is affected by a maintenance calculation;

(*b*) on the date on which the child order became so affected there was in force an order ("the spousal order") –

(i) under section 2(1)(*a*) of this Act,

(ii) under section 6(1) of this Act making provision of a kind mentioned in section 6(2)(*a*) of this Act (regardless of whether it makes provision of any other kind mentioned in that paragraph),

(iii) under section 7(2)(*a*) of this Act, or

(iv) which is an interim maintenance order under which the payments are to be made to the applicant (otherwise than for the benefit of a child); and

(*c*) an application is made, before the end of the period of 6 months beginning with the date on which the maintenance calculation was made, for the spousal order to be varied or revoked,

the court may, in exercise of its powers under this section to vary or revoke the spousal order, direct that the variation or revocation shall take effect from the date on which the child order became so affected or any later date.

(9C) For the purposes of subsection (9B) above, an order is affected if it ceases to have effect or is modified by or under section 10 of the Child Support Act 1991.

(10) (*repealed*)

(11) In exercising the powers conferred by this section the court shall, so far as it appears to the court just to do so, give effect to an agreement which has been reached between the parties in relation to the application and, if there is no such agreement or if the court decides not to give effect to the agreement, the court shall have regard to all the circumstances of the case, first consideration being given to the welfare while a minor of any child of the family who has not attained the age of eighteen, and the circumstances of the case shall include any change in any of the matters to which the court was required to have regard when making the order to which the application relates or, in the case of an application for the variation or revocation of an order made under section 6 of this Act or on an appeal under section 29 of this Act, to which the court would have been required to have regard if that order had been made under section 2 of this Act.

(12) An application under this section may be made –

(*a*) where it is for the variation or revocation of an order under section 2, 6, 7 or 19 of this Act for periodical payments, by either party to the marriage in question; and

(*b*) where it is for the variation of an order under section 2(1)(*c*), 6 or 7 of this Act for periodical payments to or in respect of a child, also by the child himself, if he has attained the age of sixteen.

(13) (*repealed*)

PART II

Amendments—Matrimonial and Family Proceedings Act 1984, ss 9(3), 11, 46(1), Sch 1, para 25; Family Law Reform Act 1987, s 33, Sch 4; CA 1989, s 108(5), (7), Sch 13, para 38, Sch 15; SI 1993/623; Child Support, Pensions and Social Security Act 2000, s 26, Sch 3, para 4.

Defined terms—"child", "child of the family": s 88(1).

Variation—The court is required to have regard to all relevant factors under s 3 on an application to vary an order (s 20(11)). The factors must be considered afresh (*Riley v Riley* [1986] 2 FLR 429, (1986) 150 JP 330). The order may not be varied to include periodical payments or a lump sum payment unless the original order contained provision for periodical payments. Section 20(9B) permits an additional power to backdate an order for the variation of a spouse's payment following a child maintenance calculation under the Child Support Act 1991. As to the effect of CSA 1991 on existing orders for child maintenance, see further **Scope of provision** under DPMCA 1978, s 2.

"give effect to any agreement" (s 20(11))—Consent may be given in writing by the party or through the party's solicitor. The court should interfere with an agreement only if a question of injustice to the parties arises (*Whitton v Devizes Justices* [1985] Fam Law 125). See Family Proceedings Courts (Matrimonial Proceedings etc) Rules 1991, r 16 for the application of Magistrates' Courts Act 1980, s 53(3) (orders with the consent of the defendant without hearing evidence) to applications under this section.

Fee payable—See Magistrates' Courts Act 1980, Sch 6.

20ZA Variation of orders for periodical payments: further provisions

(1) Subject to subsections (7) and (8) below, the power of the court under section 20 of this Act to vary an order for the making of periodical payments shall include power, if the court is satisfied that payment has not been made in accordance with the order, to exercise one of its powers under paragraph (*a*) to (*d*) of section 59(3) of the Magistrates' Courts Act 1980.

(2) In any case where –

- (*a*) a magistrates' court has made an order under this Part of this Act for the making of periodical payments, and
- (*b*) payments under the order are required to be made by any method of payment falling within section 59(6) of the Magistrates' Courts Act 1980 (standing order, etc),

an application may be made under this subsection to the clerk of the justices for the petty sessions area for which the court is acting for the order to be varied as mentioned in subsection (3) below.

(3) Subject to subsection (5) below, where an application is made under subsection (2) above, the clerk, after giving written notice (by post or otherwise) of the application to the respondent and allowing the respondent, within the period of 14 days beginning with the date of the giving of that notice, an opportunity to make written representations, may vary the order to provide that payments under the order shall be made to the justices' chief executive for the court.

(4) The clerk may proceed with an application under subsection (2) above notwithstanding that the respondent has not received written notice of the application.

(5) Where an application has been made under subsection (2) above, the clerk may, if he considers it inappropriate to exercise his power under subsection (3) above, refer the matter to the court which, subject to subsections (7) and (8) below, may vary the order by exercising one of its powers under paragraphs (*a*) to (*d*) of section 59(3) of the Magistrates' Courts Act 1980.

(6) Subsection (4) of section 59 of the Magistrates' Courts Act 1980 (power of court to order that account be opened) shall apply for the purposes of subsections (1) and (5) above as it applies for the purposes of that section.

(7) Before varying the order by exercising one of its powers under paragraphs (*a*) to (*d*) of section 59(3) of the Magistrates' Courts Act 1980, the court shall have regard to any representation made by the parties to the application.

(8) If the court does not propose to exercise its power under paragraph (*c*), (*cc*) or (*d*) of subsection (3) of section 59 of the Magistrates' Courts Act 1980, the court shall, unless upon representations expressly made in that behalf by the person to whom payments under the order are required to be made it is satisfied that it is undesirable to do so, exercise its power under paragraph (*b*) of that subsection.

(9) Subsection (12) of section 20 of this Act shall have effect for the purposes of applications under subsection (2) above as it has effect for the purposes of applications under that section.

(10) None of the powers of the court, or of the clerk to the justices, conferred by this section shall be exercisable in relation to an order under this Part of this Act for the making of periodical payments which is not a qualifying maintenance order (within the meaning of section 59 of the Magistrates' Courts Act 1980).

Amendments—Inserted by Maintenance Enforcement Act 1991, s 5; amended by SI 1994/731; Access to Justice Act 1999, s 90, Sch 13, para 91.

"paragraph (a) to (d) of section 59(3) of the Magistrates' Courts Act 1980" (s 20ZA(1))—This subsection permits orders for payments direct between the parties, through the clerk of a court, by standing order (or similar method) or by attachment of earnings.

"paragraph (b) of that subsection" (s 20ZA(8))—This subsection appears to give the payee the right to veto an order for payments direct between the parties.

"qualifying maintenance order" (s 20ZA(10))—A maintenance order will qualify if, at the time the order was made, the debtor was ordinarily resident in England and Wales (Magistrates' Courts Act 1980, s 59(2)).

20A Revival of orders for periodical payments

(1) Where an order made by a magistrates' court under this Part of this Act for the making of periodical payments to or in respect of a child (other than an interim maintenance order) ceases to have effect –

- (*a*) on the date on which the child attains the age of sixteen, or
- (*b*) at any time after that date but before or on the date on which he attains the age of eighteen,

the child may apply to the court which made the order for an order for its revival.

(2) If on such an application it appears to the court that –

- (*a*) the child is, will be or (if an order were made under this subsection) would be receiving instruction at an educational establishment or undergoing training for a trade, profession or vocation, whether or not while in gainful employment, or
- (*b*) there are special circumstances which justify the making of an order under this subsection,

the court shall have power by order to revive the order from such date as the court may specify, not being earlier than the date of the making of the application.

(3) Any order revived under this section may be varied or revoked under section 20 in the same way as it could have been varied or revoked had it continued in being.

Amendments—Inserted by Family Law Reform Act 1987, s 33(1), Sch 2, para 69; amended by CA 1989, s 108(5), Sch 13, para 39.

Scope of provision—This section does not have effect in relation to the revival of orders made under Part I of this Act before April 1989. For the revival of such orders, see s 20.

****

22 Variation of instalments of lump sum

Where in the exercise of its powers under section 75 of the Magistrates' Courts Act 1980 a magistrates' court orders that a lump sum required to be paid under Part of this Act shall be paid by instalments, the court, on an application made by either the person liable to pay or the person entitled to receive that sum, shall have power to vary that order by varying the number of instalments payable, the amount of any instalment payable and the date on which any instalment becomes payable.

Amendments—Magistrates' Courts Act 1980, s 154, Sch 7, para 160.

Payment—See Magistrates' Courts Rules 1981, r 48 for the person to whom payments are to be ordered to be paid.

23 Supplementary provisions with respect to variation and revocation of orders

(1) (*repealed*)

(2) The powers of a magistrates' court to revoke, revive or vary an order for the periodical payment of money and the power of the clerk of a magistrates' court to vary such an order under section 60 of the Magistrates' Courts Act 1980 and the power of a magistrates' court to suspend or rescind certain other orders under section 63(2) of that Act shall not apply in relation to an order made under this Part of this Act.

Amendments—Magistrates' Courts Act 1980, s 154, Sch 7, para 161; Courts and Legal Services Act 1990, s 125(7), Sch 20; Maintenance Enforcement Act 1991, s 11(1), Sch 2, para 2.

24 (*repealed*)

25 Effect on certain orders of parties living together

(1) Where –

(*a*) periodical payments are required to be made to one of the parties to a marriage (whether for his own benefit or for the benefit of a child of the family) by an order made under section 2 or 6 of this Act or by an interim maintenance order made under section 19 of this Act (otherwise than on an application under section 7 of this Act),

(*b*) (*repealed*)

the order shall be enforceable notwithstanding that the parties to the marriage are living with each other at the date of the making of the order or that, although they are not living with each other at that date, they subsequently resume living with each other; but the order shall cease to have effect if after that date the parties continue to live with each other, or resume living with each other, for a continuous period exceeding six months.

(2) Where any of the following orders is made under this Part of this Act, that is to say –

(*a*) an order under section 2 or 6 of this Act which requires periodical payments to be made to a child of the family, or

(*b*) an interim maintenance order under section 19 of this Act (otherwise than on an application under section 7 of this Act) which requires periodical payments to be made to a child of the family,

(*c*), (*d*) *(repealed)*

then, unless the court otherwise directs, the order shall continue to have effect and be enforceable notwithstanding that the parties to the marriage in question are living with each other at the date of the making of the order or that, although they are not living with each other at that date, they subsequently resume living with each other.

(3) Any order made under section 7 of this Act, and any interim maintenance order made on an application for an order under that section, shall cease to have effect if the parties to the marriage resume living with each other.

(4) Where an order made under this Part of this Act ceases to have effect by virtue of subsection (1) or (3) above or by virtue of a direction given under subsection (2) above, a magistrates' court may, on an application made by either party to the marriage, make an order declaring that the first mentioned order ceased to have effect from such date as the court may specify.

Amendments—CA 1989, s 108(5), (7), Sch 13, para 41, Sch 15.

Defined terms—"child", "child of the family": s 88(1); "living with each other": s 88(2).

Scope of provision—This section sets out the effect on orders for financial provision of the parties living with each other. A distinction is drawn between orders payable to one of the parties and orders payable to a child of the family.

Reconciliation

26 Reconciliation

(1) Where an application is made for an order under section 2 of this Act the court, before deciding whether to exercise its powers under that section, shall consider whether there is any possibility of reconciliation between the parties to the marriage in question; and if at any stage of the proceedings on that application it appears to the court that there is a reasonable possibility of such a reconciliation, the court may adjourn the proceedings for such period as it thinks fit to enable attempts to be made to effect a reconciliation.

(2) Where the court adjourns any proceedings under subsection (1) above, it may request an officer of the Service (within the meaning of the Criminal Justice and Court Services Act 2000) or any other person to attempt to effect a reconciliation between the parties to the marriage, and where any such request is made, that officer or other person shall report in writing to the court whether the attempt has been successful or not, but shall not include in that report any other information.

Amendments—Criminal Justice and Court Services Act 2000, s 74, Sch 7, para 57.

"an officer of the Service" (s 26(2))—That is an officer of the Children and Family Court Advisory and Support Service (CAFCASS).

"shall not include in that report any other information" (s 26(2))—The content of the report is restricted to the outcome of the attempt at reconciliation.

Provisions relating to the High Court and county court

27 Refusal of order in case more suitable for High Court

Where on hearing an application for an order under section 2 of this Act a magistrates' court is of the opinion that any of the matters in question between the parties would be more conveniently dealt with by the High Court, the magistrates' court shall refuse to make any order on the application, and no appeal shall lie from that refusal; but if in any proceedings in the High Court relating to or comprising the same subject matter as that application the High Court so orders, the application shall be reheard and determined by a magistrates' court acting for the same petty sessions area as the first mentioned court.

Scope of provision—The power to refuse to deal with an application cannot be exercised in cases where the High Court does not have jurisdiction (*Perks v Perks* [1946] P 1, [1945] 2 All ER 580; *Smyth v Smyth* [1956] P 427, [1956] 3 WLR 210; *Davies v Davies* [1957] P 357, [1957] 3 WLR 34).

"shall refuse to make any order"—The court may nevertheless exercise its power to make an interim order under s 19.

"no appeal shall lie"—This does not exclude a right of appeal on the issue of the High Court's jurisdiction (*Davies v Davies*, above).

28 Powers of High Court and county court in relation to certain orders under Part I

(1) Where after the making by a magistrates' court of an order under this Part of this Act proceedings between, and relating to the marriage of, the parties to the proceedings in which that order was made have been commenced in the High Court or a county court, then, except in the case of an order for the payment of a lump sum, the court in which the proceedings or any application made therein are or is pending may, if it thinks fit, direct that the order made by a magistrates' court shall cease to have effect on such date as may be specified in the direction.

(2) (*repealed*)

(3) Nothing in this section shall be taken as prejudicing the effect of any order made by the High Court or a county court so far as it implicitly supersedes or revokes an order or part of an order made by a magistrates' court.

Amendments—Family Law Act 1996, s 66(3), Sch 10.

Scope of provision—See Home Office Circular 78/1974 and *Registrar's Direction of 11 March 1974* for the requirement to send a copy of the High Court or county court order to the clerk to the magistrates' court which made the original order.

29 Appeals

(1) Subject to section 27 of this Act, where a magistrates' court makes or refuses to make, varies or refuses to vary, revokes or refuses to revoke an order (other than an interim maintenance order) under this Part of this Act, an appeal shall lie to the High Court.

(2) On an appeal under this section the High Court shall have power to make such orders as may be necessary to give effect to its determination of the appeal, including such incidental or consequential orders as appear to the court to be just, and, in the case of an appeal from a decision of a magistrates' court made on an application for or in respect of an order for the making of periodical payments, the High Court shall have power to order that its determination of the appeal shall have effect from such date as the court thinks fit, not being earlier than the date of the making of the application to the magistrates' court or, in a case where there was made to the magistrates' court an application for an order under section 2 and an application under section 6 and the term of the periodical payments was or might have been ordered to begin on the date of the making of the application for an order under section 2, the date of the making of that application.

(3) Without prejudice to the generality of subsection (2) above, where, on an appeal under this section in respect of an order of a magistrates' court requiring any person to make periodical payments, the High Court reduces the amount of those payments or discharges the order, the High Court shall have power to order the person entitled to payments under the order of the magistrates' court to pay to the person liable to make payments under that order such sum in respect of payments already made in compliance with the order as the courts thinks fit and, if any arrears are due under the order of the magistrates' court, the High Court shall have power to remit the payment of those arrears or any part thereof.

(4) (*repealed*)

(5) Any order of the High Court made on an appeal under this section (other than an order directing that an application shall be reheard by a magistrates' court) shall for the purposes of the enforcement of the order and for the purposes of section 20 of this Act be treated as if it were an order of the magistrates' court from which the appeal was brought and not of the High Court.

Amendments—Matrimonial and Family Proceedings Act 1984, s 46(1), Sch 1, para 26; CA 1989, s 108(5), (7), Sch 13, para 42, Sch 15.

Scope of provision—This section is to be construed narrowly and decisions not covered by s 29(1) cannot be appealed against under this section (see for example, *Berry v Berry* [1987] Fam 1, [1987] 1 FLR 105 where an appeal against remission of arrears was held to be excluded). The right to appeal by way of case stated under Magistrates' Courts Act 1980, s 111 is retained for matters excluded from this section. In *P v P (Periodical Payments: Appeals)* [1995] 1 FLR 563, the Divisional Court held that the procedures for appealing under CA 1989, s 94 and this section were entirely different and not interchangeable.

Provisions relating to procedure, jurisdiction and enforcement

30 Provisions as to jurisdiction and procedure

(1) A magistrates' court shall, subject to section 2 of the Family Law Act 1986 and section 70 of the Magistrates' Courts Act 1980 and any determination of a magistrates' courts committee thereunder, have jurisdiction to hear an application for an order under this Part of this Act if at the date of the making of the application either the applicant or the respondent ordinarily resides within the commission area for which the court is appointed.

(2)–(4) (*repealed*)

(5) It is hereby declared that any jurisdiction conferred on a magistrates' court by this Part of this Act is exercisable notwithstanding that any party to the proceedings is not domiciled in England.

Amendments—Magistrates' Courts Act 1980, s 154, Sch 7, para 163; Family Law Act 1986, s 68(1), Sch 1, para 24; Courts and Legal Services Act 1990, s 125(7), Sch 20; Police and Magistrates' Courts Act 1994, s 91, Sch 8, para 29.

Scope of provision—This section sets out the jurisdiction to hear applications under this Act and prescribes the procedures to be adopted. See also Family Proceedings Courts (Matrimonial Proceedings etc) Rules 1991, r 3 and Sch 1.

"ordinarily resides" (s 30(1))—Ordinary residence is established by a person's intention to make a place his or her home for an indefinite period (*Macrae v Macrae* [1949] P 397, [1949] 2 All ER 34; *Stransky v Stransky* [1954] P 428, [1954] 3 WLR 123; *Lewis v Lewis* [1956] 1 WLR 200, [1956] 1 All ER 375).

Respondent in Scotland or Northern Ireland (s 30(3))—Where the respondent resides in Scotland or Northern Ireland, see Maintenance Orders Act 1950, s 15 for endorsement and service of the summons.

31 Constitution of courts

(1) Where the hearing of an application under section 1 of this Act is adjourned after the court has decided that it is satisfied of any ground mentioned in that section, the court which resumes the hearing of that application may include justices who were not sitting when the hearing began if –

(*a*) the parties to the proceedings agree; and

(*b*) at least one of the justices composing the court which resumes the hearing was sitting when the hearing of the application began.

(2) Where, by virtue of subsection (1) above, among the justices composing the court which resumes the hearing of an application under section 1 of this Act there are any justices who were not sitting when the hearing of the application began, the court which resumes the hearing shall before making any order on the application make such inquiry into the facts and circumstances of the case as will enable the justices who were not sitting when the hearing began to be fully acquainted with those facts and circumstances.

32 Enforcement etc of orders for payment of money

(1) An order for the payment of money made by a magistrates' court under this Part of this Act shall be enforceable as a magistrates' court maintenance order.

(2) Without prejudice to section 59 of the Magistrates' Courts Act 1980 (which relates to the power of a magistrates' court to direct periodical payments to be made through a justices' chief executive), a magistrates' court making an order under this Part of this Act for the making of a periodical payment by one person to another may direct that it shall be made to some third party on that other person's behalf instead of directly to that other person; and, for the purposes of any order made under this Part of this Act, the said section 59 shall have effect as if, in subsection (7) thereof, for the words "the person who applied for the maintenance order" there were substituted the words "the person to whom the payments under the order fall to be made".

(3) Any person for the time being under an obligation to make payments in pursuance of any order for the payment of money made under this Part of this Act shall give notice of any change of address to such person, if any, as may be specified in the order; and any person who without reasonable excuse fails to give such a notice shall be liable on summary conviction to a fine not exceeding level 2 on the standard scale.

(4) A person shall not be entitled to enforce through the High Court or any county court the payment of any arrears due under an order made by virtue of this Part of this Act without the leave of that court if those arrears became due more than twelve months before proceedings to enforce the payment of them are begun.

(5) The court hearing an application for the grant of leave under subsection (4) above may refuse leave, or may grant leave subject to such restrictions and conditions (including conditions as to the allowing of time for payment or the making of payment by instalments) as that court thinks proper, or may remit the payment of such arrears or any part thereof.

(6) An application for the grant of leave under subsection (4) above shall be made in such manner as may be prescribed by rules.

Amendments—Magistrates' Courts Act 1980, s 154, Sch 7, para 164; Criminal Justice Act 1982, s 46; Family Law Reform Act 1987, s 33(1), Sch 2, para 70; Maintenance Enforcement Act 1991, s 11(1), Sch 2, para 3; Access to Justice Act 1999, s 90, Sch 13, para 92.

"An order" (s 32(1))—This includes a High Court order made on appeal; see s 29(5) above.

"address" (s 32(3))—See *Practice Direction of 13 February 1989* for disclosure of addresses by government departments.

"level 2 on the standard scale" (s 32(3))—Currently £500 (Criminal Justice Act 1982, s 37(2), as substituted).

****

35 Orders for repayment in certain cases of sums paid after cessation of order by reason of remarriage

(1) Where –

- (*a*) an order made under section 2(1)(*a*), 6 or 7 of this Act has, by virtue of section 4(2) of this Act, ceased to have effect by reason of the remarriage of the party in whose favour it was made, and
- (*b*) the person liable to make payments under the order made payments in accordance with it in respect of a period after the date of that remarriage in the mistaken belief that the order was still subsisting,

no proceedings in respect of a cause of action arising out of the circumstances mentioned in paragraphs (*a*) and (*b*) above shall be maintainable by the person so liable or his personal representatives against the person so entitled or his personal representatives, but on an application made under this section the court may exercise the powers conferred on it by subsection (2) below.

(2) the court may order the respondent to an application made under this section to pay to the applicant a sum equal to the amount of the payments made in respect of the period mentioned in subsection (1)(*b*) above or, if it appears to the court that it would be unjust to make that order, it may either order the respondent to pay to the applicant such lesser sum as it thinks fit or dismiss the application.

(3) An application under this section may be made by the person liable to make payments under the order made under section 2(1)(*a*), 6 or 7 of this Act or his personal representatives and may be made against the person entitled to payments under that order or his personal representatives.

(4) An application under this section shall be made to a county court, except that such an application may be made in proceedings in the High Court or a county

court for leave to enforce, or the enforcement of, the payment of arrears under an order made under section 2(1)(*a*), 6 or 7 of this Act; and accordingly references in this section to the court are references to the High Court or a county court, as the circumstances require.

(5) An order under this section for the payment of any sum may provide for the payment of that sum by instalments of such amount as may be specified in the order.

(6) The jurisdiction conferred on a county court by this section shall be exercisable by a county court notwithstanding that by reason of the amount claimed in an application under this section the jurisdiction would not but for this subsection be exercisable by a county court.

(7) A justices' chief executive to whom any payments under an order made under section 2(1)(*a*), 6 or 7 of this Act are required to be made, and the collecting officer under an attachment of earnings order made to secure payments under the first mentioned order, shall not be liable –

(*a*) in the case of the justices' chief executive, for any act done by him in pursuance of the first mentioned order after the date on which that order ceased to have effect by reason of the remarriage of the person entitled to payments under it, and

(*b*) in the case of the collecting officer, for any act done by him after that date in accordance with any enactment or rule of court specifying how payments made to him in compliance with the attachment of earnings order are to be dealt with,

if, but only if, the act was one which he would have been under a duty to do had the first mentioned order not ceased to have effect by reason of the remarriage and the act was done before notice in writing of the fact that the person so entitled had remarried was given to him by or on behalf of that person, the person liable to make payments under the first mentioned order or the personal representatives of either of those persons.

(8) In this section "collecting officer", in relation to an attachment of earnings order, means the officer of the High Court, the officer designated by the Lord Chancellor or the justices' chief executive to whom a person makes payments in compliance with the order.

Amendments—Access to Justice Act 1999, s 90, Sch 13, para 93.

****

PART V
SUPPLEMENTARY PROVISIONS

****

88 Interpretation

(1) In this Act –

...

"child", in relation to one or both of the parties to a marriage, includes a child whose father and mother were not married to each other at the time of his birth;

"child of the family", in relation to the parties to a marriage, means –

(*a*) a child of both of those parties; and

(*b*) any other child, not being a child who is placed with those parties as foster parents by a local authority or voluntary organisation, who has been treated by both of those parties as a child of their family;

"family proceedings" has the meaning assigned to it by section 65 of the Magistrates' Courts Act 1980;

"local authority" means the council of a county (other than a metropolitan county), of a metropolitan district or of a London borough, or the Common Council of the City of London;

"magistrates' court maintenance order" has the same meaning as in section 150(1) of the Magistrates' Courts Act 1980;

"maintenance calculation has the same meaning as it has in the Child Support Act 1991 by virtue of section 54 of that Act as read with any regulations in force under that section;

"rules" means rules made under section 144 of the Magistrates' Courts Act 1980.

(2) References in this Act to the parties to a marriage living with each other shall be construed as references to their living with each other in the same household.

(3) For the avoidance of doubt it is hereby declared that references in this Act to remarriage include references to a marriage which is by law void or voidable.

(4) Anything authorised or required by this Act to be done by, to or before the magistrates' court by, to or before which any other thing was done, or is to be done, may be done by, to or before any magistrates' court acting for the same petty sessions area as that court.

(5) Any reference in this Act to an enactment shall be construed as a reference to that enactment as amended or extended by or under any subsequent enactment, including this Act.

Amendments—Magistrates' Courts Act 1980, s 154, Sch 7, para 167; Local Government Act 1985, s 12; Family Law Reform Act 1987, Sch 2; CA 1989, ss 92, 108(5), (7), Sch 11, para 6, Sch 13, para 43, Sch 15; SI 1993/623; Justices of the Peace Act 1997, s 73(2), Sch 5, para 18; Access to Justice Act 1999, s 106, Sch 15; Child Support, Pensions and Social Security Act 2000, s 26, Sch 3, para 4.

****

Domicile and Matrimonial Proceedings Act 1973

General Note—From 1 March 2001 the law on domicile in matrimonial causes has changed in relation to divorce, judicial separation and nullity where one party is resident in one of the fourteen EU member states. Instead of the present law, set out in Domicile and Matrimonial Proceedings Act 1973, there is a new scheme (known as "Brussels II") which is derived from the Brussels Convention on Jurisdiction and the Recognition and Enforcement of Judgments in Matrimonial Matters 1998. All petitions are to be drawn in accordance with the provisions of Brussels II which determine the validity of the issue of a petition and the jurisdiction of the issuing court (see Council Regulation (EC) No 1347/2000 – set out in Part VI of this work).

1 Abolition of wife's dependent domicile

(1) Subject to subsection (2) below, the domicile of a married woman as at any time after the coming into force of this section shall, instead of being the same as her husband's by virtue only of marriage, be ascertained by reference to the same factors as in the case of any other individual capable of having an independent domicile.

(2) Where immediately before this section came into force a woman was married and then had her husband's domicile by dependence, she is to be treated as retaining that domicile (as a domicile of choice, if it is not also her domicile of origin) unless and until it is changed by acquisition or revival of another domicile either on or after the coming into force of this section.

(3) This section extends to England and Wales, Scotland and Northern Ireland.

Scope of provision—A court's matrimonial jurisdiction is founded on "domicile" and "habitual residence" (s 5(2)). Originally, a wife shared the domicile of her husband, and domicile alone (as distinct from habitual residence) determined jurisdiction. This position was eased in 1937 and 1949, and, with effect from 1 January 1974, this section ensures that a wife's domicile is decided independently of that of her husband. At the time of the coming into operation of the Act, a woman's domicile of dependence (on her husband) was deemed to become her domicile of choice (s 1(2); see also **Domicile** under s 5).

Domicile—This term is used in the United Kingdom and the Republic of Ireland. Elsewhere, jurisdiction depends on a person being a national of the member state (Council Regulation (EC) No 1347/2000, Art 2).

****

3 Age at which independent domicile can be acquired

(1) The time at which a person first becomes capable of having an independent domicile shall be when he attains the age of sixteen or marries under that age; and in the case of a person who immediately before 1 January 1974 was incapable of having an independent domicile, but had then attained the age of sixteen or been married, it shall be that date.

(2) This section extends to England and Wales and Northern Ireland (but not to Scotland).

4 Dependent domicile of child not living with his father

(1) Subsection (2) of this section shall have effect with respect to the dependent domicile of a child as at any time after the coming into force of this section when his father and mother are alive but living apart.

(2) The child's domicile as at that time shall be that of his mother if –

(*a*) he then has his home with her and has no home with his father; or
(*b*) he has at any time had her domicile by virtue of paragraph (*a*) above and has not since had a home with his father.

(3) As at any time after the coming into force of this section, the domicile of a child whose mother is dead shall be that which she last had before she died if at her death he had her domicile by virtue of subsection (2) above and he has not since had a home with his father.

(4) Nothing in this section prejudices any existing rule of law as to the cases in which a child's domicile is regarded as being, by dependence, that of his mother.

(5) In this section, "child" means a person incapable of having an independent domicile.

(6) This section extends to England and Wales, Scotland and Northern Ireland.

Amendments—Children Act 1975, s 108(1)(*b*), Sch 4, Pt I.

Domicile of dependence on parents—Where a child's parents are together, he has his domicile with them; when they separate or he is not living with either of them, the negative definitions in s 4(2) and (3) suggest that, in the absence of other factors, a child's domicile will be that of his father – for example, if parties share residence arrangements.

"child" (s 4(5))—This refers back to s 3, which defines when a child can have independent domicile.

5 Jurisdiction of High Court and county courts

(1) Subsections (2) to (5) below shall have effect, subject to section 6(3) and (4) of this Act, with respect to the jurisdiction of the court to entertain –

(*a*) proceedings for divorce, judicial separation or nullity of marriage; and
(*b*) proceedings for death to be presumed and a marriage to be dissolved in pursuance of section 19 of the Matrimonial Causes Act 1973.

(1A) In this Part of this Act –

"the Council Regulation" means Council Regulation (EC) No 1347/2000 of 29 May 2000 on jurisdiction and the recognition and enforcement of judgments in matrimonial matters and in matters of parental responsibility for children of both spouses;
"Contracting State" means –

(*a*) one of the original parties to the Council Regulation, that is to say Belgium, Germany, Greece, Spain, France, Ireland, Italy, Luxembourg, the Netherlands, Austria, Portugal, Finland, Sweden and the United Kingdom, and
(*b*) a party which has subsequently adopted the Council Regulation; and

"the court" means the High Court and a divorce county court within the meaning of Part V of the Matrimonial and Family Proceedings Act 1984.

(2) The court shall have jurisdiction to entertain proceedings for divorce or judicial separation if (and only if) –

(*a*) the court has jurisdiction under the Council Regulation; or
(*b*) no court of a Contracting State has jurisdiction under the Council Regulation and either of the parties to the marriage is domiciled in England and Wales on the date when the proceedings are begun.

(3) The court shall have jurisdiction to entertain proceedings for nullity of marriage if (and only if) –

(*a*) the court has jurisdiction under the Council Regulation; or
(*b*) no court of a Contracting State has jurisdiction under the Council Regulation and either of the parties to the marriage –
  (i) is domiciled in England and Wales on the date when the proceedings are begun; or
  (ii) died before that date and either was at death domiciled in England and Wales or had been habitually resident in England and Wales throughout the period of one year ending with the date of death.

(3A) Subsections (2) and (3) above do not give the court jurisdiction to entertain proceedings in contravention of Article 7 of the Council Regulation.

(4) The court shall have jurisdiction to entertain proceedings for death to be presumed and a marriage to be dissolved if (and only if) the petitioner –

(*a*) is domiciled in England and Wales on the date when the proceedings are begun; or
(*b*) was habitually resident in England and Wales throughout the period of one year ending with that date.

(5) The court shall, at any time when proceedings are pending in respect of which it has jurisdiction by virtue of subsection (2) or (3) above (or of this subsection), also have jurisdiction to entertain other proceedings, in respect of the same marriage, for divorce, judicial separation or nullity of marriage, notwithstanding that jurisdiction would not be exercisable under subsection (2) or (3).

(6) Schedule 1 to this Act shall have effect as to the cases in which matrimonial proceedings in England and Wales are to be, or may be, stayed by the court where there are concurrent proceedings elsewhere in respect of the same marriage, and as to the other matters dealt with in that Schedule; but nothing in the Schedule –

(*a*) requires or authorises a stay of proceedings which are pending when this section comes into force; or
(*b*) prejudices any power to stay proceedings which is exercisable by the court apart from the Schedule.

Amendments—Matrimonial and Family Proceedings Act 1984, s 46(1), Sch 1, para 17; SI 2001/310.

Scope of provision—This section provides for the domicile or, failing that, the residence basis for the court to assume jurisdiction in the matrimonial causes set out in s 5(2)–(4). It liberalises the pre-existing law by adding a residential qualification for husbands (who formerly depended on domicile only), and shortens the residential qualification for wives. Furthermore, the section sets out the circumstances in which proceedings should be stayed where there are concurrent matrimonial proceedings in another court.

Domicile—Domicile may be "of origin", "of choice" or "of dependence". Domicile of origin is acquired at birth and from parents. Domicile of dependence is considered under ss 3 and 4. Domicile of choice places a burden of proof on the applicant, and involves persuading the court that a person's domicile has changed: "The burden of establishing a change of domicile – from a domicile of origin to a domicile of choice – is ... a heavy one", per Stephen Brown LJ in *Cramer v Cramer* [1987] 1 FLR 116 at 120. For further discussion of the law relating to domicile, see *Children Law and Practice* (Family Law), para H[271].

Habitual residence—This term is not clearly defined in the Act; however, it was considered in the context of Art 3 of the Hague Convention in *C v S (A Minor) (Abduction)* [1990] 2 FLR 442, HL (see **Habitual residence** under Child Support Act 1991, s 44).

Stay of proceedings (s 5(6))—A petitioner is obliged to state in her petition if there are proceedings in another jurisdiction and whether they concern the marriage or are capable of affecting its validity or subsistence (Sch 1, para 7; FPR 1991, App 2, para 1(*j*)). In the event of reference being made to such proceedings, the court gives consideration to staying the proceedings as follows:

(*a*) *Obligatory* (Sch 1, para 8) Where there are divorce proceedings within the jurisdiction and where certain residence conditions apply, the court has a duty to stay any further proceedings on application by either party to the marriage; or
(*b*) *Discretionary* (Sch 1, para 9) Where there are matrimonial proceedings in another jurisdiction, the question of a stay is discretionary.

Whilst the stay subsists, the court still has powers to make certain financial relief orders and orders under CA 1989, s 8 (Sch 1, para 11). The stay may be discharged if it appears that the other proceedings are stayed or concluded or they have been unreasonably delayed by the party pursuing them (Sch 1, para 10).

****

SCHEDULE 1

STAYING OF MATRIMONIAL PROCEEDINGS (ENGLAND AND WALES)

Interpretation

1 The following five paragraphs have effect for the interpretation of this Schedule.

2 "Matrimonial proceedings" means any proceedings so far as they are one or more of the five following kinds, namely, proceedings for –

divorce,
judicial separation,
nullity of marriage,
a declaration as to the validity of a marriage of the petitioner, and
a declaration as to the subsistence of such a marriage.

3 (1) "Another jurisdiction" means any country outside England and Wales.

(2) "Related jurisdiction" means any of the following countries, namely, Scotland, Northern Ireland, Jersey, Guernsey and the Isle of Man (the reference to Guernsey being treated as including Alderney and Sark).

4 (1) References to the trial or first trial in any proceedings do not include references to the separate trial of an issue as to jurisdiction only.

(2) For purposes of this Schedule, proceedings in the court are continuing if they are pending and not stayed.

5 Any reference in this Schedule to proceedings in another jurisdiction is to proceedings in a court of that jurisdiction, and to any other proceedings in that jurisdiction, which are of a description prescribed for the purposes of this paragraph; and provision may be made by rules of court as to when proceedings of any description in another jurisdiction are continuing for the purposes of this Schedule.

6 "Prescribed" means prescribed by rules of court.

7 Duty to furnish particulars of concurrent proceedings in another jurisdiction

While matrimonial proceedings are pending in the court in respect of a marriage and the trial or first trial in those proceedings has not begun, it shall be the duty of any person who is a petitioner in the proceedings, or is a respondent and has in his answer included a prayer for relief to furnish, in such manner and to such persons and on such occasions as may be prescribed, such particulars as may be prescribed of any proceedings which –

(*a*) he knows to be continuing in another jurisdiction; and
(*b*) are in respect of that marriage or capable of affecting its validity or subsistence.

8 Obligatory stays

(1) Where before the beginning of the trial or first trial in any proceedings for divorce which are continuing in the court it appears to the court on the application of a party to the marriage –

(*a*) that in respect of the same marriage proceedings for divorce or nullity of marriage are continuing in a related jurisdiction; and
(*b*) that the parties to the marriage have resided together after its celebration; and
(*c*) that the place where they resided together when the proceedings in the court were begun or, if they did not then reside together, where they last resided together before those proceedings were begun, is in that jurisdiction; and
(*d*) that either of the said parties was habitually resident in that jurisdiction throughout the year ending with the date on which they last resided together before the date on which the proceedings in the court were begun,

it shall be the duty of the court, subject to paragraph 10(2) below, to order that the proceedings in the court be stayed.

(2) References in sub-paragraph (1) above to the proceedings in the court are, in the case of proceedings which are not only proceedings for divorce, to the proceedings so far as they are proceedings for divorce.

9 Discretionary stays

(1) Where before the beginning of the trial or first trial in any matrimonial proceedings, other than proceedings governed by the Council Regulation, which are continuing in the court it appears to the court –

(*a*) that any proceedings in respect of the marriage in question, or capable of affecting its validity or subsistence, are continuing in another jurisdiction; and
(*b*) that the balance of fairness (including convenience) as between the parties to the marriage is such that it is appropriate for the proceedings in that jurisdiction to be disposed of before further steps are taken in the proceedings in the court or in those proceedings so far as they consist of a particular kind of matrimonial proceedings,

the court may then, if it thinks fit, order that the proceedings in the court be stayed or, as the case may be, that those proceedings be stayed so far as they consist of proceedings of that kind.

(2) In considering the balance of fairness and convenience for the purposes of sub-paragraph (1)(*b*) above, the court shall have regard to all factors appearing to be relevant, including the convenience of witnesses and any delay or expense which may result from the proceedings being stayed, or not being stayed.

(3) In the case of any proceedings so far as they are proceeding for divorce, the court shall not exercise the power conferred on it by sub-paragraph (1) above while an application under paragraph 8 above in respect of the proceedings is pending.

(4) If, at any time after the beginning of the trial or first trial in any matrimonial proceedings which are pending in the court, the court declares by order that it is satisfied that a person has failed to perform the duty imposed on him in respect of the proceedings by paragraph 7 above, sub-paragraph (1) above shall have effect in relation to those proceedings and, to the other proceedings by reference to which the declaration is made, as if the words "before the beginning of the trial or first trial" were omitted; but no action shall lie in respect of the failure of a person to perform such a duty.

Amendments—SI 2001/310.

Supplementary

10 (1) Where an order staying any proceedings is in force in pursuance of paragraph 8 or 9 above, the court may, if it thanks fit, on the application of a party to the proceedings, discharge the order if it appears to the court that the other proceedings by reference to which the order was made are stayed or concluded, or that a party to those other proceedings has delayed unreasonably in prosecuting them.

(2) If the court discharges an order staying any proceedings and made in pursuance of paragraph 8 above, the court shall not again stay those proceedings in pursuance of that paragraph.

11 (1) The provisions of sub-paragraphs (2) and (3) below shall apply (subject to sub-paragraph (4)) where proceedings for divorce, judicial separation or nullity of marriage are stayed by reference to proceedings in a related jurisdiction for divorce, judicial separation of nullity of marriage; and in this paragraph –

"lump sum order" means such an order as is mentioned in paragraph (*f*) of section 23(1) of the Matrimonial Causes Act 1973 (lump sum payment for children), being an order made under section 23(1) or (2)(*a*) or an order made in equivalent circumstances under Schedule 1 to the Children Act 1989 and of a kind mentioned in paragraph 1(2)(*c*) of that Schedule;

"the other proceedings", in relation to any stayed proceedings, means the proceedings in another jurisdiction by reference to which the stay was imposed;

"relevant order" means –

(*a*) an order under section 22 of the Matrimonial Causes Act 1973 (maintenance for spouse pending suit),

(*b*) such an order as is mentioned in paragraph (*d*) or (*e*) of section 23(1) of that Act (periodical payments for children) being an order made under section 23(1) or (2)(*a*) or an order in equivalent circumstances under Schedule 1 to the Children Act 1989 and of a kind mentioned in paragraph 1(2)(*a*) or (*b*) of that Schedule,

(*c*) an order under section 42(1)(*a*) of that Act (orders for the custody and education of children) or a section 8 order under the Children Act 1989, and

(*d*) except for the purposes of sub-paragraph (3) below, any order restraining a person removing a child out of England and Wales or out of the care of another person; and "stayed" means stayed in pursuance of this Schedule.

(2) Where any proceedings are stayed, then, without prejudice to the effect of the stay apart from this paragraph –

(*a*) the court shall not have power to make a relevant order or a lump sum order in connection with the stayed proceedings except in pursuance of paragraph (*c*) below; and

(*b*) subject to paragraph (*c*) below, any relevant order made in connection with the stayed proceedings shall, unless the stay is previously removed or the order previously discharged, cease to have effect on the expiration of the period of three months beginning with the date on which the stay was imposed; but

(*c*) if the court considers that, for the purpose of dealing with circumstances needing to be dealt with urgently, it is necessary during or after that period to make a relevant order or a lump sum order in connection with the stayed proceedings or to extend or further extend the duration of a relevant order made in connection with the stayed proceedings, the court may do so and the order shall not cease to have effect by virtue of paragraph (*b*) above.

(3) Where any proceedings are stayed and at the time when the stay is imposed an order is in force, or at a subsequent time an order comes into force, which was made in connection with the other proceedings and provides for any of the following matters, namely, periodical payments for a spouse of the marriage in question, periodical payments for a child, or any provision which could be made by a section 8 order under the Children Act 1989 then, on the imposition of the stay in a case where the order is in force when the stay is imposed and on the coming into force of the order in any other case –

(*a*) any relevant order made in connection with the stayed proceedings shall cease to have effect in so far as it makes for a spouse or child any provision for any of those matters as respects which the same or different provision for that spouse or child is made by the other order;

(*b*) the court shall not have power in connection with the stayed proceedings to make a relevant order containing for a spouse or child provision for any of those matters as respects which any provision for that spouse or child is made by the other order; and

(*c*) if the other order contains provision for periodical payments for a child, the court shall not have power in connection with the stayed proceedings to make a lump sum order for that child.

(3A) Where any such order as is mentioned in paragraph (*e*) of section 23(1) of the Matrimonial Causes Act 1973, being an order made under section 23(1) or (2)(*a*) of that Act, ceases to have effect by virtue of sub-paragraph (2) or (3) above, any order made under section 24A(1) of the Act which requires the proceeds of sale of property to be used for securing periodical payments under the first mentioned order shall also cease to have effect.

(4) If any proceedings are stayed so far as they consist of matrimonial proceedings of a particular kind but are not stayed so far as they consist of matrimonial proceedings of a different kind, sub-paragraphs (2) and (3) above shall not apply to the proceedings but, without prejudice to the effect of the stay apart from this paragraph, the court shall not have power to make a relevant order or a lump sum order in connection with the proceedings so far as they are stayed; and in this sub-paragraph references to matrimonial proceedings do not include proceedings for a declaration.

(5) Nothing in this paragraph affects any power of the court –

(*a*) to vary or discharge a relevant order so far as the order is for the time being in force; or
(*b*) to enforce a relevant order as respects any period when it is or was in force; or
(*c*) to make a relevant order or a lump sum order in connection with proceedings which were but are no longer stayed.

Amendments—Matrimonial Homes and Property Act 1981, s 8(3); CA 1989, s 108(5), (7), Sch 13, para 33, Sch 15.

Family Law Act 1986

ARRANGEMENT OF SECTIONS

PART I
CHILD CUSTODY

Chapter I. Preliminary

PART I
CHILD CUSTODY

Chapter I. Preliminary

1 Orders to which Part I applies

(1) Subject to the following provisions of this section, in this Part "Part I order" means –

(*a*) a section 8 order made by a court in England and Wales under the Children Act 1989, other than an order varying or discharging such an order;

(*b*) an order made by a court of civil jurisdiction in Scotland under any enactment or rule of law with respect to the residence, custody, care or control of a child, contact with or access to a child or the education or upbringing of a child, excluding –

(i) an order committing the care of a child to a local authority or placing a child under the supervision of a local authority;

(ii) an adoption order as defined in section 12(1) of the Adoption (Scotland) Act 1978;

(iii) an order freeing a child for adoption made under section 18 of the said Act of 1978;

(iv) an order giving parental responsibilities and parental rights in relation to a child made in the course of proceedings for the adoption of the child (other than an order made following the making of a direction under section 53(1) of the Children Act 1975);

(v) an order made under the Education (Scotland) Act 1980;

(vi) an order made under Part II and III of the Social Work (Scotland) Act 1968;

(vii) an order made under the Child Abduction and Custody Act 1985;

(viii) an order for the delivery of a child or other order for the enforcement of a Part I order;

(ix) an order relating to the guardianship of a child;

(*c*) an Article 8 order made by a court in Northern Ireland under the Children (Northern Ireland) Order 1995, other than an order varying or discharging such an order;

(*d*) an order made by a court in England and Wales in the exercise of the inherent jurisdiction of the High Court with respect to children –

(i) so far as it gives care of a child to any person or provides for contact with, or the education of, a child; but

(ii) excluding an order varying or revoking such an order;

(*e*) an order made by the High Court in Northern Ireland in the exercise of its inherent jurisdiction with respect to children –

(i) so far as it gives care of a child to any person or provides for contact with, or the education of, a child; but

(ii) excluding an order varying or discharging such an order;

(*f*) an order made by a court in a specified dependent territory corresponding to an order within paragraphs (*a*) to (*e*) above.

(2) In this Part "Part I order" does not include –

(*a*)–(*c*) (*repealed*)

(3) In this Part, "Part I order" –

(*a*) includes any order which would have been a custody order by virtue of this section in any form in which it was in force at any time before its amendment by the Children Act 1989 or the Children (Northern Ireland) Order 1995, as the case may be; and

(*b*) (subject to sections 32 and 40 of this Act) excludes any order which would have been excluded from being a custody order by virtue of this section in any such form, and

(*c*) excludes any order falling within subsection (1)(*f*) above made before the date specified opposite the name of the territory concerned in Column 2 of Schedule 1 to the Family Law Act 1986 (Dependent Territories) Order 1991, as from time to time in force.

(6) Provision may be made by act of sederunt prescribing, in relation to orders within subsection (1)(*b*) above, what constitutes an application for the purposes of this Part.

Amendments—CA 1989, s 108, Sch 13, paras 62, 63, Sch 15; Age of Legal Capacity (Scotland) Act 1991, s 10(1), Sch 1, para 44; SI 1991/1723; Children (Scotland) Act 1995, s 105(4), Sch 4, para 41; SI 1995/756.

"order made by a court in a specified dependent territory" (s 1(1)(*f*))—See Family Law Act 1986 (Dependent Territories) Order 1991, Sch 3.

"date specified ... Family Law Act 1986 (Dependent Territories) Order 1991" (s 1(3)(*c*))—The only territory currently named in Schedule 1 to that Order is the Isle of Man, and the relevant date specified is 14 October 1991.

Care orders and supervision orders under CA 1989, Part IV—See under s 2.

Chapter II. Jurisdiction of Courts in England and Wales

2 Jurisdiction: general

(1) A court in England and Wales shall not have jurisdiction to make a section 1(1)(*a*) order with respect to a child in or in connection with matrimonial proceedings in England and Wales unless –

(*a*) the child concerned is a child of both parties to the matrimonial proceedings and the court has jurisdiction to entertain those proceedings by virtue of the Council Regulation, or

(*b*) the condition in section 2A of this Act is satisfied.

(2) A court in England and Wales shall not have jurisdiction to make a section 1(1)(*a*) order in a non-matrimonial case (that is to say, where the condition in section 2A of this Act is not satisfied) unless the condition in section 3 of this Act is satisfied.

(3) A court in England and Wales shall not have jurisdiction to make a section 1(1)(*d*) order unless –

(*a*) the condition in section 3 of this Act is satisfied, or

(*b*) the child concerned is present in England and Wales on the relevant date and the court considers that the immediate exercise of its powers is necessary for his protection.

Amendments—CA 1989, s 108(5), Sch 13, para 64; SI 2001/310.

Defined terms—"child": ss 7, 42(4); "corresponding dependent territory order": s 42(1); "matrimonial proceedings", "relevant date": s 7; "specified dependent territory": s 42(1).

Matrimonial proceedings (s 2(1))—In matrimonial proceedings, a court in England and Wales only has jurisdiction to make an order under CA 1989, s 8 (other than an order varying or discharging a s 8 order) where the conditions in FLA 1986, s 2A are satisfied.

Non-matrimonial proceedings (s 2(2))—In non-matrimonial proceedings, a court in England and Wales has jurisdiction to make orders under CA 1989, s 8 (other than an order varying or discharging a s 8 order) only where the child is either habitually resident in England and Wales, or is present in England and Wales and is not habitually resident in any part of the United Kingdom or a specified territory, and the court's jurisdiction is not excluded by FLA 1986, s 3(2). The court has no jurisdiction derived simply from the fact that the child is a British National (*Al Habtoor v Fotheringham* [2001] 1 FLR 951). In *Re S (Residence Order: Forum Conveniens)* [1995] 1 FLR 314, an English court had no jurisdiction to entertain an application for a residence order in respect of a child who was habitually resident in Holland and who had not been present in England and Wales at the date of issue of the application; however, in that case, the court retained jurisdiction to specify or define conditions in a residence order which had been granted prior to the child moving to Holland. See also *D v D (Custody: Jurisdiction)* [1996] 1 FLR 574, which was held to be a non-matrimonial case because, at the relevant date as defined in s 7(*c*) (ie the date on which the s 8 application was made), there were no divorce proceedings in existence anywhere. A court in England and Wales is not excluded from making parental responsibility orders under CA 1989, s 4 in respect of children who are not born in and do not live in the jurisdiction (*Re S (Parental Responsibility: Jurisdiction)* [1998] 2 FLR 921).

Care orders and supervision orders under CA 1989, Part IV—The legislation is silent as to the jurisdictional basis for the making of applications for care orders and supervision orders. However, in *Re R (Care Orders: Jurisdiction)* [1995] 1 FLR 711, Singer J held that the jurisdictional basis for an application under CA 1989, Part IV was the same as that in relation to applications under CA 1989, s 8, namely that, for the court to have jurisdiction to entertain a local authority's application under Part IV, the child concerned should either be habitually resident in England and Wales or present in England and Wales at the relevant time (see FLA 1986, s 3). Singer J's approach was followed by Hale J in *Re M (Care Orders: Jurisdiction)* [1997] 1 FLR 456.

Proceedings under the inherent jurisdiction (s 2(3))—A court in England and Wales has jurisdiction under the inherent jurisdiction (including the wardship jurisdiction) to make orders as to the care of or contact with or education of a child (other than an order varying or revoking such an order) only where:

(*a*) the child is habitually resident in England and Wales (s 3(1)(*a*)); or

(*b*) is present in England and Wales and is not habitually resident in any part of the United Kingdom or a specified dependent territory (s 3(1)(*b*)); and

(*c*) in either (i) and (ii) above, the court's jurisdiction is not excluded by s 3(2) (s 3(1)); or

(*d*) the court considers that the immediate exercise of its powers is necessary for his protection (s 2(3)(*b*); see *B v B (Scottish Contact Order: Jurisdiction to Vary)* [1996] 1 FLR 688, where an application was made under the inherent jurisdiction (ie a s 1(1)(*d*) order) to the English court to vary a Scottish contact order, the children were present in England and Wales, the quantum and not the principle of contact was opposed, and there was no urgency to justify the invocation of the inherent jurisdiction – there was no reason why an application to the Scottish court should not be made). The inclusion of the exercise of the inherent jurisdiction within the orders which can be made in s 1(1)(*d*) gives the English court the jurisdiction to make orders in respect of a child, provided he is habitually resident in England and Wales, even if he is an alien and not physically within the jurisdiction at the start of the proceedings (*Re S (Custody: Habitual Residence)* [1998] 1 FLR 122).

Section 2(3)(*b*) has been used to make mirror orders required for the implementation of orders made in a USA court, in respect of a child resident in the USA, allowing contact to take place in England – see *Re P (A Child: Mirror Orders)* [2000] 1 FLR 435 where Singer J held that it was a very small step from the wording of s 2(3)(*b*) to make an order which expressly only had currency as far as the English courts were concerned while the child was present in the jurisdiction for the purposes of contact. In that context, assistance was to be derived from the general power of the court to make orders in anticipation of the institution of formal process. Singer J indicated that the jurisdiction should be invoked economically, and after appropriate investigation, and should be reserved to judges of the Family Division.

2A Jurisdiction in or in connection with matrimonial proceedings

(1) The condition referred to in section 2(1) of this Act is that the matrimonial proceedings are proceedings in respect of the marriage of the parents of the child concerned and –

(*a*) the proceedings –
(i) are proceedings for divorce or nullity of marriage, and
(ii) are continuing;
(*b*) the proceedings –
(i) are proceedings for judicial separation,
(ii) are continuing,
and the jurisdiction of the court is not excluded by subsection (2) below; or
(*c*) the proceedings have been dismissed after the beginning of the trial but –
(i) the section 1(1)(*a*) order is being made forthwith, or
(ii) the application for the order was made on or before the dismissal.

(2) For the purposes of subsection (1)(*b*) above, the jurisdiction of the court is excluded if, after the grant of a decree of judicial separation, on the relevant date, proceedings for divorce or nullity in respect of the marriage are continuing in Scotland, Northern Ireland or a specified dependent territory.

(3) Subsection (2) above shall not apply if the court in which the other proceedings there referred to are continuing has made –

(*a*) an order under section 13(6) or 19A(4) of this Act (not being an order made by virtue of section 13(6)(*a*)(i)), or a corresponding dependent territory order, or
(*b*) an order under section 14(2) or 22(2) of this Act, or a corresponding dependent territory order, which is recorded as being made for the purpose of enabling Part I proceedings to be taken in England and Wales with respect to the child concerned.

(4) Where a court –

(*a*) has jurisdiction to make a section 1(1)(*a*) order in or in connection with matrimonial proceedings, but
(*b*) considers that it would be more appropriate for Part I matters relating to the child to be determined outside England and Wales,

the court may by order direct that, while the order under this subsection is in force, no section 1(1)(*a*) order shall be made by any court in or in connection with those proceedings.

Amendments—Inserted by CA 1989, s 108(5), Sch 13, para 64; amended by SI 1991/1723; SI 1995/756.

Defined terms—"child": ss 7, 42(4); "corresponding dependent territory order": s 42(1) (and see notes to s 42); "matrimonial proceedings": s 7; "Part I proceedings", "Part I matters": s 42(7); "relevant date": s 7; "specified dependent territory": s 42(1) (and see notes to s 42).

General interpretation—See s 42.

Discretion to make order under s 2A(4)—Where the English court in principle has jurisdiction over the living arrangements for a child by reason of current divorce proceedings between the child's parents, which fact would normally deprive courts in Scotland of jurisdiction, the English court nevertheless has a discretion contained in s 2A(4) to order that it would be more appropriate for matters relating to that child to be decided in Scotland (*Re S (Jurisdiction to Stay Application)* [1995] 1 FLR 1093 – where in reality the child had been looked after in Scotland for many years by her maternal grandmother).

3 Habitual residence or presence of child

(1) The condition referred to in section 2(2) of this Act is that on the relevant date the child concerned –

(*a*) is habitually resident in England and Wales, or
(*b*) is present in England and Wales and is not habitually resident in any part of the United Kingdom or a specified dependent territory,

and, in either case, the jurisdiction of the court is not excluded by subsection (2) below.

(2) For the purposes of subsection (1) above, the jurisdiction of the court is excluded if, on the relevant date, matrimonial proceedings are continuing in a court in Scotland, Northern Ireland or a specified dependent territory in respect of the marriage of the parents of the child concerned.

(3) Subsection (2) above shall not apply if the court in which the other proceedings there referred to are continuing has made –

(*a*) an order under section 13(6) or 19A(4) of this Act (not being an order made by virtue of section 13(6)(*a*)(i)), or a corresponding dependent territory order, or
(*b*) an order under section 14(2) or 22(2) of this Act, or a corresponding dependent territory order, which is recorded as made for the purpose of enabling Part I proceedings with respect to the child concerned to be taken in England and Wales,

and that order is in force.

(4)–(6) (*repealed*)

Amendments—CA 1989, s 108(5), (7) Sch 13, paras 62, 65, Sch 15; SI 1991/1723; SI 1995/756.

Defined terms—"child": ss 7, 42(4); "corresponding dependent territory order": s 42(1); "matrimonial proceedings": s 7; "Part I proceedings", "Part I matters": s 42(7); "relevant date": s 7; "specified dependent territory": s 42(1).

General interpretation—See s 42.

"habitually resident" (s 3(1)(*a*))—There is no statutory definition of habitual residence, and its meaning is essentially a question of fact to be determined by reference to all the circumstances of a particular case. See **Habitual residence** under Child Abduction and Custody Act 1985, Sch 1, Art 4.

****

5 Power of court to refuse application or stay proceedings

(1) A court in England and Wales which has jurisdiction to make a Part I order may refuse an application for the order in any case where the matter in question has already been determined in proceedings outside England and Wales.

(2) Where, at any stage of the proceedings on an application made to a court in England and Wales for a Part I order, or for the variation of a Part I order, other than proceedings governed by the Council Regulation, it appears to the court –

(*a*) that proceedings with respect to the matters to which the application relates are continuing outside England and Wales, or
(*b*) that it would be more appropriate for those matters to be determined in proceedings to be taken outside England and Wales,

the court may stay the proceedings on the application.

(3) The court may remove a stay granted in accordance with subsection (2) above if it appears to the court that there has been unreasonable delay in the taking or prosecution of the other proceedings referred to in that subsection, or that those proceedings are stayed, sisted or concluded.

(4) Nothing in this section shall affect any power exercisable apart from this section to refuse an application or to grant or remove a stay.

Amendments—CA 1989, s 108(5), Sch 13, para 62; SI 2001/310.

Defined terms—"Part I order": ss 1(2), (3), 42(5), (6).

General interpretation—See s 42.

"the court may stay the proceedings" (s 5(2))—In *H v H (Minors) (Forum Conveniens) (Nos 1 and 2)* [1993] 1 FLR 958, an application was made under s 5(2) to stay English proceedings for residence and contact orders because the same issues were being tried in Wisconsin, USA, where the court had already decided that it was the forum conveniens for the residence dispute. Waite J held that:

(*a*) the principles to be applied were those set out in *Spiliada Maritime Corporation v Cansulex Ltd* [1987] AC 460 and those principles were not in any way cut down by the terms of s 5(2);

(*b*) the issue of forum conveniens in relation to proceedings as to child residence was "a question with respect to the upbringing of a child" within CA 1989, s 1(1)(*a*) and therefore the welfare of the child was paramount; (however, Thorpe J reached the opposite conclusion on this point in *Re S (Residence Order: Forum Conveniens)* [1995] 1 FLR 314 (see below));

(*c*) the fact that the children were habitually resident in England was not conclusive of the forum conveniens issue, although it would be persuasive; and

(*d*) s 5(4) made it clear that the inherent jurisdiction of the court, or any other jurisdiction to grant or refuse a stay of proceedings, was to remain unaffected.

This litigation resulted in the court refusing to order a stay under FLA 1986, s 5(2) in relation to proceedings under CA 1989, and coming to the conclusion that the children should reside with their mother in the UK and spend holidays with their father in the USA (*H v H (Minors) (Forum Conveniens) (No 3)* [1994] Fam Law 13).

In *Re S (A Minor) (Stay of Proceedings)* [1993] 2 FLR 912, the Court of Appeal upheld a decision by Ward J to grant a stay of English proceedings instituted by the father for residence and contact orders because similar proceedings were already in existence in Scotland. Furthermore, the Court of Appeal approved his decision to allow the father's application for a parental responsibility order to proceed in England. A parental responsibility order was not within the definition of "Part I order" under FLA 1986 and the statutory provisions did not apply. However, the court still retained an inherent power to stay proceedings in appropriate cases. In *Re S (Residence Order: Forum Conveniens)* [1995] 1 FLR 314 Thorpe J held that the welfare of the child in carrying out a *Spiliada* analysis was an important, but not a paramount, consideration, since a choice between international jurisdictions was not a "question with respect to the upbringing of the child" within the meaning of CA 1989, s 1(1)(*a*) (thus disagreeing with Waite J in *H v H (Minors) (Forum Conveniens) (Nos 1 and 2)* [1993] 1 FLR 958). In conducting the *Spiliada* analysis, Thorpe J held that, in principle, the habitual residence of a child (in this case, in Holland) was an extremely important consideration in determining the forum for a detailed investigation of the child's future needs but that, on the facts of this case, the English court would not at this stage abdicate its jurisdiction in relation to the contact order previously made in England. The father's application for a definition of the contact order's terms could be stayed under s 5(2), although the mother had made no application for such a stay. See also *H v H (A Minor) (No 2) (Forum Conveniens)* [1997] 1 FCR 603 where Bracewell J held that the court could act of its own volition irrespective of whether or not a party had applied for a stay. A stay should not be granted unless it is demonstrated that a more appropriate forum is available elsewhere (*M v B (Residence)* [1994] 2 FLR 819 – where the family was a US family through and through, and its connection with the UK jurisdiction arose only as a consequence of the parents' posting to the UK for the purposes of service, the USA was the appropriate forum; *T v T (Jurisdiction: Forum Conveniens)* [1995] 2 FLR 660 – where the child was resident in Kenya, the assets were situated within that jurisdiction and the husband's income originated in numerous jurisdictions, the English proceedings were stayed in favour of the Kenyan jurisdiction). Where the application for a Part I order is in the context of matrimonial proceedings, see also Domicile and Matrimonial

Proceedings Act 1973, Sch 1, paras 8 and 9. By virtue of FLA 1986, s 5(2) and DMPA 1973, Sch 1, para 9 the court *may* stay proceedings if either FLA 1986, s 5(2)(*a*) or (*b*) is satisfied. However, under DMPA 1973, Sch 1, para 8 the court is obliged to stay proceedings if the parties resided in a related jurisdiction and either of them was habitually resident there for one year before they separated. For further guidance, see *M v M (Abduction: England and Scotland)* [1997] 2 FLR 263, where it was held that the same jurisdiction should deal both with the dissolution of the marriage and the consequential decisions regarding the welfare of the children.

6 Duration and variation of custody orders

(1) If a Part I order made by a court in Scotland, Northern Ireland or a specified dependent territory (or a variation of such an order) comes into force with respect to child at a time when a Part I order made by a court in England and Wales has effect with respect to him, the latter order shall cease to have effect so far as it makes provision for any matter for which the same or different provision is made by (or by the variation of) the order made by the court in Scotland, Northern Ireland or the territory.

(2) Where by virtue of subsection (1) above a Part I order has ceased to have effect so far as it makes provision for any matter, a court in England or Wales shall not have jurisdiction to vary that order so as to make provision for that matter.

(3) A court in England and Wales shall not have jurisdiction to vary a Part I order if, on the relevant date, matrimonial proceedings are continuing in Scotland, Northern Ireland or a specified dependent territory in respect of the marriage of the parents of the child concerned.

(3A) Subsection (3) above shall not apply if –

(*a*) the Part I order was made in or in connection with proceedings for divorce or nullity in England and Wales in respect of the marriage of the parents of the child concerned; and
(*b*) those proceedings are continuing.

(3B) Subsection (3) above shall not apply if –

(*a*) the Part I order was made in or in connection with proceedings for judicial separation in England and Wales;
(*b*) those proceedings are continuing; and
(*c*) the decree of judicial separation has not yet been granted.

(4) Subsection (3) above shall not apply if the court in which the proceedings there referred to are continuing has made –

(*a*) an order under section 13(6) or 19A(4) of this Act (not being an order made by virtue of section 13(6)(*a*)(i)), or a corresponding dependent territory order, or
(*b*) an order under section 14(2) or 22(2) of this Act, or a corresponding dependent territory order, which is recorded as made for the purpose of enabling Part I proceedings with respect to the child concerned to be taken in England and Wales,

and that order is in force.

(5) Subsection (3) above shall not apply in the case of a variation of section 1(1)(*d*) order if the child concerned is present in England and Wales on the relevant date and the court considers that the immediate exercise of its powers is necessary for his protection.

(6) Subsection (7) below applies where a Part I order which is –

(*a*) a residence order (within the meaning of the Children Act 1989) in favour of a person with respect to a child,
(*b*) an order made in the exercise of the High Court's inherent jurisdiction with respect to children by virtue of which a person has care of a child, or
(*c*) an order –
  (i) of a kind mentioned in section 1(3)(*a*) of this Act,
  (ii) under which a person is entitled to the actual possession of a child,

ceases to have effect in relation to that person by virtue of subsection (1) above.

(7) Where this subsection applies, any family assistance order made under section 16 of the Children Act 1989 with respect to the child shall also cease to have effect.

(8) For the purposes of subsection (7) above the references to a family assistance order under section 16 of the Children Act 1989 shall be deemed to include a reference to an order for the supervision of a child made under –

(*a*) section 7(4) of the Family Law Reform Act 1969,
(*b*) section 44 of the Matrimonial Causes Act 1973,
(*c*) section 2(2)(*a*) of the Guardianship Act 1973,
(*d*) section 34(5) or 36(3)(*b*) of the Children Act 1975, or
(*e*) section 9 of the Domestic Proceedings and Magistrates' Courts Act 1978;

but this subsection shall cease to have effect once all such orders for the supervision of children have ceased to have effect in accordance with Schedule 14 to the Children Act 1989.

Amendments—CA 1989, s 108(5), Sch 13, paras 62, 66; SI 1991/1723; SI 1995/756.

Defined terms—"child": ss 7, 42(4); "corresponding dependent territory order": s 42(1); "matrimonial proceedings": s 7; "Part I order": ss 1(2), (3), 42(5), (6); "Part I proceedings", "Part I matters": s 42(7); "relevant date": s 7; "specified dependent territory": s 42(1).

General interpretation—See s 42.

7 Interpretation of Chapter II

In this Chapter –

(*a*) "child" means a person who has not attained the age of eighteen;
(*b*) "matrimonial proceedings" means proceedings for divorce, nullity of marriage or judicial separation;
(*c*) "the relevant date" means in relation to the making or variation of an order –
  (i) where an application is made for an order to be made or varied, the date of the application (or first application, if two or more are determined together), and
  (ii) where no such application is made, the date on which the court is considering whether to make or, as the case may be, vary the order; and
(*d*) "section 1(1)(*a*) order" and "section 1(1)(*d*) order" mean orders falling within section 1(1)(*a*) and (*d*) of this Act respectively.

Amendments—CA 1989, s 108(5), Sch 13, para 67.

"the relevant date" (s 7(*c*))—Presence in the jurisdiction on the "relevant date", for any reason and brought about in any way, is sufficient to give jurisdiction to make a "Part I order" under the Act (ie a s 8 order "other than an order varying or discharging such an order") (*Re F (Residence Order: Jurisdiction)* [1995] 2 FLR 518, but see *Re S (Residence Order: Forum Conveniens)*

[1995] 1 FLR 314, where Thorpe J expressed concern at the possibility of jurisdiction turning on "what might be either chance or strategic manoeuvre" resulting in the child's presence on the date of issue of proceedings). Where no application has been made, the relevant date under s 7(*c*)(ii) is that on which the court is considering whether to make or vary the order (*Re F (Residence Order: Jurisdiction)*, above – where the relevant date was the date of the directions hearing and not the date of the substantive hearing of the abduction issue). Similarly where an application has been made, the relevant date is when the court first addresses its mind to the application and makes directions, even if the order ultimately made is different in terms to that originally sought (*Re J (Abduction: Declaration of Wrongful Removal)* [1999] 2 FLR 653).

Chapter III. Jurisdiction of Courts in Scotland

8 Jurisdiction in independent proceedings

A court in Scotland may entertain an application for a Part I order otherwise than in matrimonial proceedings only if it has jurisdiction under section 9, 10, 12 or 15(2) of this Act.

Amendments—CA 1989, s 108, Sch 13, para 62.

9 Habitual residence

Subject to section 11 of this Act, an application for a Part I order otherwise than in matrimonial proceedings may be entertained by –

(*a*) the Court of Session if, on the date of the application, the child concerned is habitually resident in Scotland;

(*b*) the sheriff if, on the date of the application, the child concerned is habitually resident in the sheriffdom.

Amendments—CA 1989, s 108, Sch 13, para 62.

10 Presence of child

Subject to section 11 of this Act, an application for a Part I order otherwise than in matrimonial proceedings may be entertained by –

(*a*) the Court of Session if, on the date of the application, the child concerned –
  (i) is present in Scotland; and
  (ii) is not habitually resident in any part of the United Kingdom or a specified dependent territory;

(*b*) the sheriff if, on the date of the application, –
  (i) the child is present in Scotland;
  (ii) the child is not habitually resident in any part of the United Kingdom or a specified dependent territory; and
  (iii) either the pursuer or the defender in the application is habitually resident in the sheriffdom.

Amendments—CA 1989, s 108, Sch 13, para 62; SI 1991/1723.

11 Provisions supplementary to sections 9 and 10

(1) Subject to subsection (2) below, the jurisdiction of the court to entertain an application for a Part I order with respect to a child by virtue of section 9, 10 or 15(2) of this Act is excluded if, on the date of the application, matrimonial proceedings are continuing in a court in any part of the United Kingdom or a specified dependent territory in respect of the marriage of the parents of the child.

(2) Subsection (1) above shall not apply in relation to an application for a Part I order if the court in which the matrimonial proceedings are continuing has made one of the following orders, that is to say –

(*a*) an order under section 2A(4), 13(6) or 19A(4) of the Act (not being an order made by virtue of section 13(6)(*a*)(ii) or a corresponding dependent territory order; or

(*b*) an order under section 5(2), 14(2) or 22(2) of this Act, or a corresponding dependent territory order, which is recorded as made for the purpose of enabling Part I proceedings with respect to the child concerned to be taken in Scotland or, as the case may be, in another court in Scotland,

and that order is in force.

Amendments—CA 1989, s 108, Sch 13, paras 62, 68; SI 1991/1723; SI 1995/756.

12 Emergency jurisdiction

Notwithstanding that any other court, whether within or outside Scotland, has jurisdiction to entertain an application for a Part I order, the Court of Session or the sheriff shall have jurisdiction to entertain such an application if –

(*a*) the child concerned is present in Scotland or, as the case may be, in the sheriffdom on the date of the application; and

(*b*) the Court of Session or sheriff considers that, for the protection of the child, it is necessary to make such order immediately.

Amendments—CA 1989, s 108, Sch 13, para 62.

13 Jurisdiction ancillary to matrimonial proceedings

(1) The jurisdiction of a court in Scotland to entertain an application for a Part I order in matrimonial proceedings shall be modified by the following provisions of this section.

(2) A court in Scotland shall not have jurisdiction, after the dismissal of matrimonial proceedings or after decree of absolvitor is granted therein, to entertain an application for a Part I order under section 9(1) of the Matrimonial Proceedings (Children) Act 1958 unless the application therefore was made on or before such dismissal or the granting of the decree of absolvitor.

(3) Where, after a decree of separation has been granted, an application is made in the separation process for a Part I order, the court in Scotland shall not have jurisdiction to entertain that application if, on the date of the application, proceedings for divorce or nullity of marriage in respect of the marriage concerned are continuing in another court in the United Kingdom or a specified dependent territory.

(4) A court in Scotland shall not have jurisdiction to entertain an application for the variation of a Part I order made under section 9(1) of the Matrimonial Proceedings (Children) Act 1958 if, on the date of the application, matrimonial proceedings in respect of the marriage concerned are continuing in another court in the United Kingdom or a specified dependent territory.

(5) Subsections (3) and (4) above shall not apply if the court in which the other proceedings there referred to are continuing has made –

(*a*) an order under section 2A(4) or 19A(4) of this Act or under subsection (6) below (not being an order made by virtue of paragraph (*a*)(ii) of that subsection), or a corresponding dependent territory order, or

(*b*) an order under section 5(2), 14(2) or 22(2) of this Act, or a corresponding dependent territory order, which is recorded as made for the purpose of enabling Part I proceedings with respect to the child concerned to be taken in Scotland or, as the case may be, in another court in Scotland, and that order is in force.

(6) A court in Scotland which has jurisdiction in matrimonial proceedings to entertain an application for a Part I order with respect to a child may make an order declining such jurisdiction if –

(*a*) it appears to the court with respect to that child that –

(i) but for section 11(1) of this Act, another court in Scotland would have jurisdiction to entertain an application for a Part I order, or

(ii) but for section 3(2), 6(3), 20(2) or 23(3) of this Act or a corresponding territory provision, a court in another part of the United Kingdom or a specified dependent territory would have jurisdiction to make a Part I order or an order varying a Part I order; and

(*b*) the court considers that it would be more appropriate for Part I matters relating to that child to be determined in that other court or part.

(7) The court may recall an order made under subsection (6) above.

Amendments—CA 1989, s 108, Sch 13, paras 62, 68; SI 1991/1723; SI 1995/756.

14 Power of court to refuse application or sist proceedings

(1) A court in Scotland which has jurisdiction to entertain an application for a Part I order may refuse the application in any case where the matter in question has already been determined in other proceedings.

(2) Where, at any stage of the proceedings on an application made to a court in Scotland for a Part I order, it appears to the court –

(*a*) that proceedings with respect to the matter to which the application relates are continuing outside Scotland or in another court in Scotland; or

(*b*) that it would be more appropriate for those matters to be determined in proceedings outside Scotland or in another court in Scotland and that such proceedings are likely to be taken there.

the court may sist the proceedings on that application.

Amendments—CA 1989, s 108, Sch 13, para 62.

15 Duration, variation and recall of orders

(1) Where, after the making by a court in Scotland of a Part I order ("the existing order") with respect to a child, –

(*a*) a Part I order, or an order varying a Part I order, competently made by another court in any part of the United Kingdom or in a specified dependent territory with respect to that child; or

(*b*) an order for the custody of that child which is made outside the United Kingdom and any specified dependent territory and recognised in Scotland by virtue of section 26 of this Act, comes into force, the existing order shall cease to have effect so far as it makes provision for any matter for which the same or different provision is made by the order of the other court in the United Kingdom or in the specified dependent territory or, as the case be, the order so recognised.

(2) Subject to sections 11(1) and 13(3) and (4) of this Act, a court in Scotland which has made a Part I order ("the original order") may, notwithstanding that it would no longer have jurisdiction to make the original order, make an order varying or recalling the original order; but if the original order has by virtue of subsection (1) above ceased to have effect so far as it makes provision for any matter, the court shall not have power to vary that order under this subsection so as to make provision for that matter.

(3) In subsection (2) above, an order varying an original order means any Part I order made with respect to the same child as the original order was made.

(4) Where any person who is entitled to the custody of a child under a Part I order made by a court in Scotland ceases to be so entitled by virtue of subsection (1) above, then, if there is in force an order made by a court in Scotland providing for the supervision of that child by a local authority, that order shall cease to have effect.

Amendments—CA 1989, s 108, Sch 13, para 62; SI 1991/1723; Children (Scotland) Act 1995, s 105(5), Sch 5.

Effect in relation to "interim" residence orders (s 15(1))—An "interim" residence order is no different in principle from a residence order, particularly since CA 1989 does not recognise that there is such an order as an interim residence order; instead, the court has power to make a residence order limited in time. Therefore, by the operation of s 15(1), the making of an "interim" residence order by an English court has the consequence that any order previously made by a Scottish court as to the living arrangements for a child no longer has any effect in law, since it makes "provision for any matter for which the same or different provision is made by the order of the other court in the United Kingdom" (*S v S (Custody: Jurisdiction)* [1995] 1 FLR 155; *T v T (Custody: Jurisdiction)* [1992] 1 FLR 43).

16 Tutory and curatory

(1) Subject to subsections (2) and (3) below, an application made after the commencement of this Part for an order relating to the guardianship of a child may be entertained by –

(*a*) the Court of Session if, on the date of the application, the pupil or minor is habitually resident in Scotland;

(*b*) the sheriff if, on the date of the application, the pupil or minor is habitually resident in the sheriffdom.

(2) Subsection (1) above shall not apply to an application for the appointment or removal of a judical factor or of a curator bonis or any application made by such factor or curator.

(3) Subsection (1) above is without prejudice to any other ground of jurisdiction on which the Court of Session or the sheriff may entertain an application mentioned therein.

(4) Provision may be made by act of sederunt prescribing, in relation to orders relating to the guardianship of a child, what constitutes an application for the purposes of this Chapter.

Amendments—Age of Legal Capacity (Scotland) Act 1991, s 10, Sch 1, para 45.

17 Orders for delivery of child

(1) An application by one parent of a child for an order for the delivery of the child from the other parent, where the order is not sought to implement a Part I order, may be entertained by the Court of Session or a sheriff if, but only if, the Court of Session or, as the case may be, the sheriff would have jurisdiction under this Chapter to make a Part I order with respect to the child concerned.

(2) (*repealed*)

(3) Subsection (1) above shall apply to an application by one party to a marriage for an order for the delivery of the child concerned from the other party where the child is the child of one of the parties and has been accepted as one of the family by the other party as it applies to an application by one parent of a child for an order for the delivery of the child from the other parent.

Amendments—CA 1989, s 108, Sch 13, para 62; Children (Scotland) Act 1995, s 105(5), Sch 5.

18 Interpretation of Chapter III

(1) In this Chapter –

"child" means a person who has not attained the age of sixteen;
"matrimonial proceedings" means proceedings for divorce, nullity of marriage or judicial separation.

(2) In this Chapter, "the date of the application" means, where two or more applications are pending, the date of the first of those applications; and, for the purposes of this subsection, an application is pending until a Part I order or, in the case of an application mentioned in section 16(1) of this Act, an order relating to the guardianship of a child, has been granted in pursuance of the application or the court has refused to grant such an order.

Amendments—CA 1989, s 108, Sch 13, para 62; Age of Legal Capacity (Scotland) Act 1991, s 10, Sch 1, para 46.

Chapter IV. Jurisdiction of Courts in Northern Ireland

19 Jurisdiction: general

(1) A court in Northern Ireland shall not have jurisdiction to make a section 1(1)(*c*) order of this Act with respect to a child in or in connection with matrimonial proceedings in Northern Ireland unless –

(*a*) the child concerned is a child of both parties to the matrimonial proceedings and the court has jurisdiction to entertain those proceedings by virtue of the Council Regulation, or

(*b*) the condition in section 19A of this Act is satisfied.

(2) A court in Northern Ireland shall not have jurisdiction to make a section 1(1)(*c*) order in a non-matrimonial case (that is to say, where the condition in section 19A is not satisfied) unless the condition in section 20 of this Act is satisfied.

(3) A court in Northern Ireland shall not have jurisdiction to make a section 1(1)(*e*) order unless –

(*a*) the condition in section 20 of this Act is satisfied; or (*b*) the child concerned is present in Northern Ireland on the relevant date and the court considers that the immediate exercise of its powers is necessary for his protection.

Amendments—Substituted by SI 1995/755; amended by SI 2001/660.

19A Jurisdiction in or in connection with matrimonial proceedings

(1) The condition referred to in section 19(1) of this Act is that the matrimonial proceedings are proceedings in respect of the marriage of the parents of the child concerned and –

(*a*) the proceedings –
  (i) are proceedings for judicial separation, and
  (ii) are continuing;

(*b*) the proceedings –
  (i) are proceedings for divorce or nullity of marriage, and
  (ii) are continuing;

and the jurisdiction of the court is not excluded by subsection (2) below; or

(*c*) the proceedings have been dismissed after the end of the trial but –
  (i) the section 1(1)(*e*) order is being made forthwith, or
  (ii) the application for the order was made on or before the dismissal.

(2) For the purposes of subsection (1)(*b*) above, the jurisdiction of the court is excluded if, after the grant of a decree of judicial separation, on the relevant date, proceedings for divorce or nullity in respect of the marriage are continuing in England and Wales or Scotland.

(3) Subsection (2) above shall not apply if the court in which the other proceedings there referred to are continuing has made –

(*a*) an order under section 2A(4) or 13(6) of this Act (not being an order made by virtue of section 13(6)(*a*)(i)), or

(*b*) an order under section 5(2) or 14(2) of this Act which is recorded as being made for the purpose of enabling Part I proceedings to be taken in Northern Ireland with respect to the child concerned.

(4) Where a court –

(*a*) has jurisdiction to make a section 1(1)(*c*) order in or in connection with matrimonial proceedings, but

(*b*) considers that it would be more appropriate for Part I matters relating to the child to be determined outside Northern Ireland,

the court may by order direct that, while the order under this subsection is in force, no section 1(1)(*c*) order shall be made by any court in or in connection with those proceedings.

Amendments—Inserted by SI 1995/755.

20 Habitual residence or presence of child

(1) The condition referred to in section 19(2) of this Act is that on the relevant date the child concerned –

(*a*) is habitually resident in Northern Ireland, or

(*b*) is present in Northern Ireland and is not habitually resident in any part of the United Kingdom or in a specified dependent territory and, in either case, the jurisdiction of the court is not excluded by subsection (2) below.

(2) For the purposes of subsection (1) above, the jurisdiction of the court is excluded if, on the relevant date, matrimonial proceedings are continuing in a court in England and Wales, Scotland or a specified dependent territory in respect of the marriage of the parents of the child concerned.

(3) Subsection (2) above shall not apply if the court in which the other proceedings there referred to are continuing has made –

(*a*) an order under section 2A(4) or 13(6) of this Act (not being an order made by virtue of section 13(6)(*a*)(i)), or a corresponding dependent territory order, or

(*b*) an order under section 5(2) or 14(2) of this Act, or a corresponding dependent territory order, which is recorded as made for the purpose of enabling Part I proceedings with respect to the child concerned to be taken in Northern Ireland,

and that order is in force.

(4)–(6) (*repealed*)

Amendments—CA 1989, s 108, Sch 13, paras 62, 68, 69; SI 1991/1723; SI 1995/755.

21 (*repealed*)

22 Power of court to refuse application or stay proceedings

(1) A court in Northern Ireland which has jurisdiction to make a Part I order may refuse an application for the order in any case where the matter in question has already been determined in proceedings outside Northern Ireland.

(2) Where, at any stage of the proceedings on an application made to a court in Northern Ireland for a Part I order, or for the variation of a Part I order, other than proceedings governed by the Council Regulation, it appears to the court –

(*a*) that proceedings with respect to the matters to which the application relates are continuing outside Northern Ireland; or

(*b*) that it would be more appropriate for those matters to be determined in proceedings to be taken outside Northern Ireland,

the court may stay the proceedings on the application.

(3) The court may remove a stay granted in accordance with subsection (2) above if it appears to the court that there has been unreasonable delay in the taking or prosecution of the other proceedings referred to in that subsection, or that those proceedings are stayed, sisted or concluded.

(4) Nothing in this section shall affect any power exercisable apart from this section to refuse an application or to grant or remove a stay.

Amendments—CA 1989, s 108, Sch 13, para 62; SI 2001/660.

23 Duration and variation of custody orders

(1) If a Part I order made by a court in England and Wales, Scotland or a specified dependent territory (or a variation of such an order) comes into force with respect to a child at a time when a Part I order made by a court in Northern Ireland has

effect with respect to him, the latter order shall cease to have effect so far as it makes provision for any matter for which the same or different provision is made by (or by the variation of) the order made by the court in England and Wales, Scotland or the territory.

(2) Where by virtue of subsection (1) above a Part I order has ceased to have effect so far as it makes provision for any matter, a court in Northern Ireland shall not have jurisdiction to vary that order so as to make provision for that matter.

(3) A court in Northern Ireland shall not have jurisdiction to vary a Part I order if, on the relevant date, matrimonial proceedings are continuing in England and Wales or Scotland in respect of the marriage of the parents of the child concerned.

(3A) Subsection (3) above shall not apply if –

(*a*) the Part I order was made in or in connection with proceedings for divorce or nullity in Northern Ireland in respect of the marriage of the parents of the child concerned; and
(*b*) those proceedings are continuing.

(3B) Subsection (3) above shall not apply if –

(*a*) the Part I order was made in or in connection with proceedings for judicial separation in Northern Ireland; and
(*b*) those proceedings are continuing;
(*c*) the decree of judicial separation has not yet been granted.

(4) Subsection (3) above shall not apply if the court in which the proceedings there referred to are continuing has made –

(*a*) an order under section 2A(4) or 13(6) of this Act (not being an order made by virtue of section 13(6)(*a*)(i), or a corresponding dependent territory order, or
(*b*) an order under section 5(2) or 14(2) of this Act, or a corresponding dependent territory order, which is recorded as made for the purpose of enabling Part I proceedings with respect to the child concerned to be taken in Northern Ireland,

and that order is in force.

(5) Subsection (3) above shall not apply in the case of a variation of a section 1(1)(*e*) order if the child concerned is present in Northern Ireland on the relevant date and the court considers that the immediate exercise of its powers is necessary for his protection.

(6) Subsection (7) below applies where a Part I order which is –

(*a*) a residence order (within the meaning of the Children (Northern Ireland) Order 1995) in favour of a person with respect to a child,
(*b*) an order made in the exercise of the High Court's inherent jurisdiction with respect to children by virtue of which a person has care of a child, or
(*c*) an order –
  (i) of a kind mentioned in section 1(3)(*a*) of this Act,
  (ii) under which a person is entitled to the actual possession of a child,

ceases to have effect in relation to that person by virtue of subsection (1) above.

(7) Where this subsection applies, any family assistance order made under Article 16 of the Children (Northern Ireland) Order 1995 with respect to a child shall also cease to have effect.

(8) For the purposes of subsection (7) above the reference to a family assistance order under Article 16 of the Children (Northern Ireland) Order 1995 shall be deemed to include a reference to an order for the supervision of a child made under –

(*a*) Article 47 of the Matrimonial Causes (Northern Ireland) Order 1978, or
(*b*) Article 11 of the Domestic Proceedings (Northern Ireland) Order 1980;

but this subsection shall cease to have effect once all such orders for the supervision of children have ceased to have effect in accordance with Schedule 8 to the Children (Northern Ireland) Order 1995.

Amendments—CA 1989, s 108, Sch 13, paras 62, 68, 69; SI 1991/1723; SI 1995/755.

24 Interpretation of Chapter IV

In this Chapter –

(*a*) "child" means a person who has not attained the age of 18;
(*b*) "matrimonial proceedings" means proceedings for divorce, nullity of marriage or judicial separation;
(*c*) "the relevant date" means, in relation to the making or variation of an order –
  (i) where an application is made for an order to be made or varied, the date of the application (or first application, if two or more are determined together), and
  (ii) where no such application is made, the date on which the court is considering whether to make or, as the case may be, vary the order; and
(*d*) "section 1(1)(*c*) order" and "section 1(1)(*e*) order" mean orders falling within section 1(1)(*c*) and (*e*) of this Act respectively.

Amendments—Substituted by SI 1995/755.

Chapter V. Recognition and Enforcement

25 Recognition of custody orders: general

(1) Where a Part I order made by a court in any part of the United Kingdom or in a specified dependent territory is in force with respect to a child who has not attained the age of sixteen, then, subject to subsection (2) below, the order shall be recognised in any other part or, in the case of a dependent territory order, any part of the United Kingdom as having the same effect in that part as if it had been made by the appropriate court in that part and as if that court had had jurisdiction to make it.

(2) Where a Part I order includes provision as to the means by which rights conferred by the order are to be enforced, subsection (1) above shall not apply to that provision.

(3) A court in a part of the United Kingdom in which a Part I order is recognised in accordance with subsection (1) above shall not enforce the order unless it has been registered in that part of the United Kingdom under section 27 of this Act and proceedings for enforcement are taken in accordance with section 29 of this Act.

Amendments—CA 1989, s 108(5), Sch 13, para 62; SI 1991/1723.

Defined terms—"appropriate court": s 32(1) (and see notes to s 32); "part of the United Kingdom": s 42(1).

Scope of provision—Recognition and enforcement are not automatic. The initiative and responsibility for pursuing enforcement proceedings lies with the aggrieved party, not with the court (*Glaser v United Kingdom (Case No 32346/96)* ECHR [2001] 1 FLR 153). An order may be enforced only if it has been registered under s 27 and proceedings for enforcement are taken in accordance with s 29.

"Part I order"—By virtue of ss 1, 32 and 42(5), Pt I orders include those set out in s 1(*a*)–(*f*). FLA 1986 is not retrospective and it does not affect any orders made before the Act came into force, and orders which vary or revoke previous orders are excluded.

"specified dependent territory" (s 25(1))—See Family Law Act 1986 (Dependent Territories) Order 1991, art 2.

****

27 Registration

(1) Any person on whom any rights are conferred by a Part I order may apply to the court which made it for the order to be registered in another part of the United Kingdom under this section, or in a specified dependent territory under a corresponding provision.

(2) An application under this section shall be made in the prescribed manner and shall contain the prescribed information and be accompanied by such documents as may be prescribed.

(3) On receiving an application under this section the court which made the Part I order shall, unless it appears to the court that the order is no longer in force, cause the following documents to be sent to the appropriate court in the part of the United Kingdom or dependent territory specified in the application, namely –

- (*a*) a certified copy of the order, and
- (*b*) where the order has been varied, prescribed particulars of any variation which is in force, and
- (*c*) a copy of the application and of any accompanying documents.

(4) Where the prescribed officer of the appropriate court in any part of the United Kingdom receives a certified copy of a Part I order under subsection (3) above or under a corresponding dependent territory provision, he shall forthwith cause the order, together with particulars of any variation, to be registered in that court in the prescribed manner.

(5) An order shall not be registered under this section in respect of a child who has attained the age of sixteen, and the registration of an order in respect of a child who has not attained the age of sixteen shall cease to have effect on the attainment by the child of that age.

Amendments—CA 1989, s 108(5), Sch 13, para 62; SI 1991/1723.

Defined terms—"appropriate court": s 32(1) (and see notes to s 32); "certified copy", "corresponding dependent territory provision", "corresponding provision", "part of the UK", "prescribed": s 42(1).

General Note—The mere act of registering is not sufficient to cause the enforcement of the order, and a separate application must be made to the registering court to enforce the order.

"Part I order"—See under s 25.

"specified dependent territory" (s 27(1))—See Family Law Act 1986 (Dependent Territories) Order 1991, art 2.

Application (s 27(2))—Application must be made in the prescribed manner as set out in FPR 1991, r 7.8. For application to the family proceedings court, see the Magistrates' Courts (Family Law Act 1986) Rules 1988, as amended.

Documents (s 27(3))—A certified copy and a copy of the original order, any order which has varied any of the terms of the original order and any further orders obtained (eg an additional order under s 33 or 34), together with an affidavit in support and a copy must be filed.

"appropriate court in the part of the United Kingdom specified" (s 27(3))—An order may be registered in any part of the UK to where the child has been or is likely to be abducted and where the order is sought to be enforced. A decision will need to be taken as to the jurisdiction in which the order is required to be registered. In most cases, registration in one jurisdiction will suffice; there may, however, be cases where it is desirable to have the order registered in more than one jurisdiction, particularly where there is a fear that the child may be moved about in order to avoid being traced.

"forthwith" (s 27(4))—The order must be registered as soon as practicable having regard to the circumstances and nature of the act to be done (see *Re Southam ex parte Lamb* (1881) 19 Ch D 169, [1881] 5 All ER 391; *Re Muscovitch ex parte M* [1939] Ch 694, [1939] 1 All ER 135).

"in the prescribed manner" (s 27(4))—Registration in the appropriate court is to be in the prescribed manner. The following rules apply: in England and Wales, FPR 1991, Pt VII, Magistrates' Courts (Family Law Act 1986) Rules 1988, as amended; in Northern Ireland, RSC (Northern Ireland) Ord 90, rr 26–35, CCR (Northern Ireland) Ord 51, rr 6–11, and the Magistrates' Courts (Family Law Act 1986) Rules (Northern Ireland) 1988, SI 1988/113; in Scotland, Court of Session Rules of Court, Act of Sederunt (Rules for the Registration of Custody Orders of the Sheriff Court) 1988 as amended.

28 Cancellation and variation of registration

(1) A court which revokes, recalls or varies an order registered under section 27 of this Act shall cause notice of the revocation, recall or variation to be given in the prescribed manner to the prescribed officer of the court in which it is registered and, on receiving the notice, the prescribed officer –

(*a*) in the case of the revocation or recall of the order, shall cancel the registration, and

(*b*) in the case of the variation of the order, shall cause particulars of the variation to be registered in the prescribed manner.

(2) Where –

(*a*) an order registered under section 27 of this Act ceases (in whole or in part) to have effect in the part of the United Kingdom or in a specified dependent territory in which it was made, otherwise than because of its revocation, recall or variation, or

(*b*) an order registered under section 27 of this Act in Scotland ceases (in whole or in part) to have effect there as a result of the making of an order in proceedings outside the United Kingdom and any specified dependent territory,

the court in which the order is registered may, of its own motion or on the application of any person who appears to the court to have an interest in the matter, cancel the registration (or, if the order has ceased to have effect in part, cancel the registration so far as it relates to the provisions which have ceased to have effect).

Amendments—SI 1991/1723.

Defined terms—"part of the United Kingdom", "prescribed": s 42(1).

Scope of provision—This section makes provision for the cancellation and variation of registration. FPR 1991, rr 7.10 and 7.11 make procedural provision with regard to such cases. The alteration in the register is made by the prescribed officer. Where however the order ceases to have effect otherwise than by revocation or variation, eg by lapse of time or by continued cohabitation or by resumption of cohabitation, or in the case of an order registered in Scotland, as a result of the making of an order in proceedings outside the UK, the cancellation may take place only where the court acts of its own motion or on an application of any person who has an interest in the matter.

"in the prescribed manner" (s 28(1)(*b*))—See under s 27.

"specified dependent territory" (s 28(2))—See Family Law Act 1986 (Dependent Territories) Order 1991, art 2.

29 Enforcement

(1) Where a Part I order has been registered under section 27 of this Act, the court in which it is registered shall have the same powers for the purpose of enforcing the order as it would have if it had itself made the order and had jurisdiction to make it; and proceedings for or with respect to enforcement may be taken accordingly.

(2) Where an application has been made to any court for the enforcement of an order registered in that court under section 27 of this Act, the court may, at any time before the application is determined, give such interim directions as it thinks fit for the purpose of securing the welfare of the child concerned or of preventing changes in the circumstances relevant to the determination of the application.

(3) The references in subsection (1) above to a Part I order do not include references to any provision of the order as to the means by which rights conferred by the order are to be enforced.

Amendments—CA 1989, s 108(5), Sch 13, para 62.

Court's powers to make orders (s 29(1))—Since the court has the same powers for the purposes of enforcement of a registered order as it would if it had itself made the order the court has the power:

(*a*) to order disclosure of the child's whereabouts under s 33 and the discovery of information held by Government departments (see *Practice Direction of 13 February 1989* – it is likely that the Scottish Office and the Northern Ireland Office will co-operate in disclosing addresses);
(*b*) to order the recovery of the child under s 34;
(*c*) to order surrender of passports under s 37;
(*d*) to direct that wardship proceedings be commenced (subject to restrictions on jurisdiction);
(*e*) to grant injunctions and in particular restrain the further removal of the child from the country or from his present address;
(*f*) to order welfare reports and to give directions regarding evidence to be filed;
(*g*) to order the return of the child to the applicant and to his country of origin.

Interim directions (s 29(2))—FPR 1991, r 7.12 provides inter alia that all parties to the proceedings for enforcement, and the applicant for the Part I order if he is not a party, must be made parties to the application for interim directions.

"Part I order"—See under s 25.

Matters to be considered—When considering an application to enforce a custody order made in another part of the UK, an English court is bound to have regard to the principle of comity and not, in effect, purport to act as a court of appeal from the court having jurisdiction in another part of the UK. The English judge should not question the correctness of the procedures and orders of the Scottish court (*Re M (Minors) (Custody: Jurisdiction)* [1992] 2 FLR 382).

30 Staying or sisting of enforcement proceedings

(1) Where in accordance with section 29 of this Act proceedings are taken in any court for the enforcement of an order registered in that court, any person who appears to the court to have an interest in the matter may apply for the proceedings to be stayed or sisted on the ground that he has taken or intends to take other proceedings (in the United Kingdom or elsewhere) as a result of which the order may cease to have effect, or may have a different effect, in the part of the United Kingdom in which it is registered.

(2) If after considering an application under subsection (1) above the court considers that the proceedings for enforcement should be stayed or sisted in order that other proceedings may be taken or concluded, it shall stay or sist the proceedings for enforcement accordingly.

(3) The court may remove a stay or recall a sist granted in accordance with subsection (2) above if it appears to the court –

(*a*) that there has been unreasonable delay in the taking or prosecution of the other proceedings referred to in that subsection, or

(*b*) that those other proceedings are concluded and that the registered order, or a relevant part of it, is still in force.

(4) Nothing in this section shall affect any power exercisable apart from this section to grant, remove or recall a stay or sist.

Defined terms—"part of the United Kingdom": s 42(1).

Procedure—FPR 1991, r 7.13 makes provision for the procedure on an application under this section.

Grounds of application—In addition to the grounds mentioned in this section, where the enforcement proceedings are in Scotland, application may also be made that the court should deal with the application on its merits under s 12.

Stay by reason of other proceedings—See *Re M (Minors) (Custody: Jurisdiction)* [1992] 2 FLR 382 and the effect of Domicile and Matrimonial Proceedings Act 1973, Sch 3, para 8.

31 Dismissal of enforcement proceedings

(1) Where in accordance with section 29 of this Act proceedings are taken in any court for the enforcement of an order registered in that court, any person who appears to the court to have an interest in the matter may apply for those proceedings to be dismissed on the ground that the order has (in whole or in part) ceased to have effect in the part of the United Kingdom or specified dependent territory in which it was made.

(2) Where in accordance with section 29 of this Act proceedings are taken in the Court of Session for the enforcement of an order registered in that court, any person who appears to the court to have an interest in the matter may apply for those proceedings to be dismissed on the ground that the order has (in whole or in part) ceased to have effect in Scotland as a result of the making of an order in proceedings outside the United Kingdom and any specified dependent territory.

(3) If, after considering an application under subsection (1) or (2) above, the court is satisfied that the registered order has ceased to have effect, it shall dismiss the proceedings for enforcement (or, if it is satisfied that the order has ceased to have effect in part, it shall dismiss the proceedings so far as they relate to the enforcement of provisions which have ceased to have effect).

Amendments—SI 1991/1723.

Defined terms—"part of the United Kingdom": s 42(1).

Procedure—FPR 1991, r 7.13 makes provision as to the procedure on an application under this section.

Grounds of application—See annotation under s 30.

32 Interpretation of Chapter V

(1) In this Chapter –

"the appropriate court", in relation to England and Wales or Northern Ireland, means the High Court and, in relation to Scotland, means the Court of Session and, in relation to a specified dependent territory, means the corresponding court in that territory;

"Part I order" includes (except where the context otherwise requires) any order within section 1(3) of this Act which, on the assumptions mentioned in subsection (3) below –

(*a*) could have been made notwithstanding the provisions of this Part or the corresponding dependent territory provisions;
(*b*) would have been a Part I order for the purpose of this Part; and
(*c*) would not have ceased to have effect by virtue of section 6, 15 or 23 of this Act.

(2) In the application of this Chapter to Scotland, "Part I order" also includes (except where the context otherwise requires) any order within section 1(3) of this Act which, on the assumptions mentioned in subsection (3) below –

(*a*) would have been a Part I order for the purpose of this Part; and
(*b*) would not have ceased to have effect by virtue of section 6 or 23 of this Act,

and which, but for the provisions of this Part, would be recognised in Scotland under any rule of law.

(3) The said assumptions are –

(*a*) that this Part or the corresponding dependent territory provisions, as the case may be, had been in force at all material times; and
(*b*) that any reference in section 1 of this Act to any enactment included a reference to any corresponding enactment previously in force.

Amendments—CA 1989, s 108(5), Sch 13, para 62; SI 1991/1723.

Defined terms—"corresponding dependent territory provisions", "specified dependent territory": s 42(1) (and see notes to s 42).

"appropriate court", "corresponding court" (s 32(1))—See also the effect of Family Proceedings (Amendment) (No 3) Rules 1994, SI 1994/2890.

"Part I order"—See under s 25.

Chapter VI. Miscellaneous and Supplemental

33 Power to order disclosure of child's whereabouts

(1) Where in proceedings for or relating to a Part I order in respect of a child there is not available to the court adequate information as to where the child is, the court

may order any person who it has reason to believe may have relevant information to disclose it to the court.

(2) A person shall not be excused from complying with an order under subsection (1) above by reason that to do so may incriminate him or his spouse of an offence; but a statement or admission made in compliance with such an order shall not be admissible in evidence against either of them in proceedings for any offence other than perjury.

(3) A court in Scotland before which proceedings are pending for the enforcement of an order relating to parental responsibilities or parental rights in relation to a child made outside the United Kingdom and any specified dependent territory which is recognised in Scotland shall have the same powers as it would have under subsection (1) above if the order were its own.

Amendments—CA 1989, s 108(5), Sch 13, para 62; SI 1991/1723; Children (Scotland) Act 1995, s 105(4), Sch 4, para 41(1), (7).

Scope of provision—This section provides a power to county courts and family proceedings courts in private law proceedings, as well as to the High Court, similar to an inherent power of the High Court in relation to children. This section also provides for an order for the purpose of giving effect to an order, akin to a CA 1989, s 8 order, made elsewhere in the United Kingdom or in a specified dependent territory, which has been registered in the High Court.

An order under this section may be directed to persons who are not parties to the proceedings, including a legal adviser, the manager of a women's refuge or the police, as well as relatives or friends of a person who may be keeping the child. However, where a mother has taken a child to stay at a women's refuge, the police should not be directed to disclose the address (*Chief Constable of West Yorkshire Police v S* [1998] 2 FLR 973). An order under the inherent jurisdiction of the High Court must be obeyed by a legal adviser and "privilege" is overridden (*Burton v Earl of Darnley* (1869) LR 8 Eq 576; *Ramsbotham v Senior* (1869) LR 8 Eq 575, (1869) FLR Rep 591). The power given by s 33(1) is unqualified and, it is submitted, also overrides privilege.

"Part I order"—See under s 25.

Application for s 33 order—The application may be made at any time during CA 1989, s 8 proceedings and will usually be made ex parte. The application is made in Form C4 (FPR 1991, r 6.17; FPC(CA 1989)R 1991, r 31A). If made ex parte by telephone, as permitted by the rules, the Form C4 must be filed within 24 hours after making the application. Where the court makes an order ex parte, the rules provide that a copy of the application must be served on each respondent within 48 hours after the making of the order. It is impractical to make an application ex parte by telephone to a family proceedings court as there is no provision for the application to be heard by a single justice (FPC(CA 1989)R 1991, rr 2(5), 31A).

Evidence in support of application—The application should be supported by evidence. When the application is made in pending CA 1989, s 8 proceedings, the evidence should be by a statement which complies with FPR 1991, r 4.17(1)(*a*) or FPC(CA 1989)R 1991, r 17(1)(*a*). When the application is made ex parte, leave under r 4.17(1)(*a*) or r 17(1)(*a*) for the statement to be adduced may be sought at the hearing.

Form of order and enforcement—The order is issued in Form C30 (FPR 1991, r 6.17; FPC(CA 1989)R 1991, r 31A). Note that the order directs the person to disclose the information to the court. The order should not purport to direct disclosure to a party to the proceedings (*Chief Constable of West Yorkshire Police v S* [1998] 2 FLR 973). The court will decide what to do with the information. Form C30 incorporates a penal (warning) notice and may be enforced in a county court by application under CCR Ord 29, r 1, or in a family proceedings court under Magistrates' Courts Act 1980, s 63(3).

34 Power to order recovery of child

(1) Where –

(*a*) a person is required by a Part I order, or an order for the enforcement of a Part I order, to give up a child to another person ("the person concerned"), and

(*b*) the court which made the order imposing the requirement is satisfied that the child has not been given up in accordance with the order,

the court may make an order authorising an officer of the court or a constable to take charge of the child and deliver him to the person concerned.

(2) The authority conferred by subsection (1) above includes authority –

(*a*) to enter and search any premises where the person acting in pursuance of the order has reason to believe the child may be found, and

(*b*) to use such force as may be necessary to give effect to the purpose of the order.

(3) Where by virtue of –

(*a*) section 14 of the Children Act 1989, or

(*b*) Article 14 (enforcement of residence orders) of the Children (Northern Ireland) Order 1995,

a Part I order (or a provision of a Part I order) may be enforced as if it were an order requiring a person to give up a child to another person, subsection (1) above shall apply as if the Part I order had included such a requirement.

(4) This section is without prejudice to any power conferred on a court by or under any other enactment or rule of law.

Amendments—CA 1989, s 108(5), Sch 13, paras 62, 70; SI 1995/755.

Scope of provision—This section empowers a county court or a family proceedings court in private law proceedings, as well as the High Court, to authorise the physical taking charge of a child, with the use of such force as may be necessary, and delivery of the child to the person entitled, when a child has not been given up in accordance with an order of the same court. This section also provides for such a power in the High Court in respect of an order, akin to a CA 1989, s 8 order, made elsewhere in the United Kingdom or in a specified dependent territory, which has been registered in the High Court. The power given to county courts and family proceedings courts is similar to, but more restricted than, an inherent power of the High Court in relation to children. Unlike the power of the High Court to direct the tipstaff to take charge of a child even though no previous order has been disobeyed, the power under s 34 cannot be exercised unless the court is satisfied that an order requiring the giving up of the child has been disobeyed. Therefore, on an application for a s 34 order, proof is required that the order to give up the child has been served on, or effectively communicated to, the person bound by the order.

A residence order made in a family proceedings court, by virtue of CA 1989, s 14(1), can be enforced, under Magistrates' Courts Act 1980, s 63(3), against a person on whom the order has been served and who is in breach of the arrangements settled by the order, as if it were an order requiring that person to produce the child. Thus, s 34(3) enables a Part I order made by a family proceedings court to be enforced under s 34(1), even though it does not specifically require the person concerned to give up the child or specify when the child should be given up.

"officer of the court" (s 34(1))—County courts do not have any person who is trained to undertake the functions of the tipstaff of the High Court, and county court bailiffs do not undertake this function.

"Part I order"—See under s 25.

Procedure on application for s 34 order—The application is made in Form C3 (FPR 1991, r 6.17; FPC(CA 1989)R 1991, r 31A). When the application is made to the High Court or a county court which made a CA 1989, s 8 order which has not been complied with, or to the High Court in respect of an order made elsewhere but registered in the High Court, it is submitted that the application may be made within the proceedings in which the order was made or the registration proceedings; the court can make injunctive orders to give effect to a judgment after the trial has concluded, in matrimonial proceedings (*Webb v Webb* [1986] 1 FLR 541, *Lucas v Lucas* [1992] 2 FLR 53) and in civil actions (*Zeeland Navigation Company Ltd v Banque Worms* (1995) *The Times*, 26 December). Where the order was made by a family proceedings court and the proceedings are no longer in motion, a fresh application may be required.

An application should not be made in respect of a county court order unless the order explicitly required the person bound to "give up" the child, preferably specifying when or by when (cf CCR Ord 29, r 1(2)(*b*)), and where, the child was to be given up. If a county court order does not so specify, an order to give up the child (which may be applied for ex parte) should be obtained and served and have been disobeyed, before an application can be made for a s 34 order.

Ex parte or on notice—Application should be made on notice unless there is reason to suppose that the child has been, or is likely to be, removed or hidden, or is likely to suffer significant harm. If made ex parte by telephone, as permitted by the rules, the Form C3 must be filed within 24 hours after making the application. It is impractical to make an application ex parte by telephone to a family proceedings court as there is no provision for the application to be heard by a single justice (FPC(CA 1989)R 1991, rr 2(5), 31A). Where the court makes an order ex parte, the rules provide that a copy of the application must be served on each respondent within 48 hours after the making of the order.

Evidence in support of application—The application should be supported by evidence. When the application is made to the court which made a CA 1989, s 8 order, the statement should comply with FPR 1991, r 4.17(1)(*a*) or FPC(CA 1989)R 1991, r 17(1)(*a*). When an application is made in the High Court in relation to an order made elsewhere in the United Kingdom or in a specified dependent territory, which has been registered in the High Court, the application should be supported by affidavit.

Form of order—The order is issued in Form C31 (FPR 1991, r 6.17; FPC(CA 1989)R 1991, r 31A).

Execution of order—An order under s 34(1) gives authority to an officer of the court or a constable, but it does not direct them to act. Execution of an order under s 34(1) needs to be conducted with discretion, in order to avoid harmful distress to the child. The police are not obliged to assist and may refuse (*R v Chief Constable of Cheshire ex parte K* [1990] 1 FLR 70, [1990] Fam Law 17). Although a solicitor is an officer of the Supreme Court (Solicitors Act 1974, s 50), he is not an officer of either a county court (County Courts Act 1984, s 147) or a family proceedings court.

****

36 Effect of orders restricting removal

(1) This section applies to any order made by a court in the United Kingdom or any specified dependent territory prohibiting the removal of a child from the United Kingdom or from any specified part of it or from any such territory.

(2) An order to which this section applies, made by a court in one part of the United Kingdom or in a specified dependent territory, shall have effect in each other part, or, in the case of an order made in a dependent territory, each part of the United Kingdom –

(*a*) as if it had been made by the appropriate court in that part, and

(*b*) in the case of an order which has the effect of prohibiting the child's removal to that part, as if it had included a prohibition on his further removal to any place except one to which he could be removed consistently with the order.

(3) The references in subsections (1) and (2) above to prohibitions on a child's removal include references to prohibitions subject to exceptions; and in a case where removal is prohibited except with the consent of the court, nothing in subsection (2) above shall be construed as affecting the identity of the court whose consent is required.

(4) In this section "child" means a person who has not attained the age of sixteen; and this section shall cease to apply to an order relating to a child when he attains the age of sixteen.

Amendments—SI 1991/1723.

Defined terms—"appropriate court": ss 40, 32(1) (and see below); "specified dependent territory": s 42(1).

"appropriate court" (s 36(2)(*a*))—In England and Wales, the High Court.

General interpretation—See s 42.

37 Surrender of passports

(1) Where there is in force an order prohibiting or otherwise restricting the removal of a child from the United Kingdom or from any specified part of it or from a specified dependent territory, the court by which the order was in fact made, or by which it is treated under section 36 of this Act as having been made, may require any person to surrender any United Kingdom passport which has been issued to, or contains particulars of, the child.

(2) In this section "United Kingdom passport" means a current passport issued by the Government of the United Kingdom.

Amendments—SI 1991/1723.

Defined terms—"specified dependent territory": s 42(1).

General interpretation—See ss 42, 40, 32(1).

Power to order the surrender of passports—This provision can only be invoked if the court makes an order prohibiting or otherwise restricting the removal of a child from the UK. Its scope is further restricted in that the court can only require the surrender of *any United Kingdom passport* which has been issued *to a child* or contains particulars *of a child*. It does not apply to non-UK passports and passports that do not contain particulars of the child concerned.

"the court ... by which [the order] is treated under section 36 as having been made"—Section 36 enables the appropriate court in each part of the United Kingdom to make an order under s 37 as though it had made the prohibitory order in fact made in another part of the United Kingdom or a specified dependent territory. Note that the "appropriate court" in England and Wales which can exercise the power under s 37 is the High Court.

Other remedies for prevention of removal of a child from the jurisdiction—For arrangements for police to institute a port alert, and for giving notice to the Passport Office that passport facilities should not be provided without the leave of the court, see *Registrar's Direction of 14 April 1986*.

Application for s 37 order—The application may be made by summons or notice in the court which made, or under s 36 is treated as having made, the order. Where the order was made by a family proceedings court, and the proceedings are no longer in motion, a fresh complaint may be required. The application may be made ex parte where removal is thought to be imminent. There is no prescribed form of notice for an application.

38 Automatic restriction on removal of wards of court

(1) The rule of law which (without any order of the court) restricts the removal of a ward of court from the jurisdiction of the court shall, in a case to which this section applies, have effects subject to the modifications in subsection (3) below.

(2) This section applies in relation to a ward of court if –

(*a*) proceedings for divorce, nullity or judicial separation in respect of the marriage of his parents are continuing in a court in another part of the United Kingdom (that is to say, in a part of the United Kingdom outside the jurisdiction of the court of which he is a ward), or in a specified dependent territory, or

(*b*) he is habitually resident in another part of the United Kingdom or in a specified dependent territory,

except where that other part is Scotland and he has attained the age of sixteen.

(3) Where this section applies, the rule referred to in subsection (1) above shall not prevent –

(*a*) the removal of the ward of court, without the consent of any court, to the other part of the United Kingdom or the specified dependent territory mentioned in subsection (2) above, or

(*b*) his removal to any other place with the consent of either the appropriate court in that other part of the United Kingdom or the specified dependent territory or the court mentioned in subsection (2)(*a*) above.

Amendments—SI 1991/1723.

Defined terms—"appropriate court": ss 40, 32(1); "specified dependent territory": s 42(1).

Scope of provision—This section modifies the rule of law which prevents the removal of a ward from the jurisdiction. Subsection (3) creates an exception to the rule in that, if the ward's parents are involved in proceedings for divorce, nullity or judicial separation in a court in another part of the United Kingdom or in a specified dependent territory, or the ward is habitually resident in another part of the United Kingdom (unless it is Scotland and he is over 16), the ward may move to that part of the United Kingdom without leave of the court, or to any other place with leave of the court where the divorce, nullity or judicial separation proceedings are taking place.

General interpretation—See s 42.

"habitually resident" (s 38(2)(*b*))—See under s 3 and **Habitual residence** under Child Support Act 1991, s 44.

39 Duty to furnish particulars of other proceedings

Parties to proceedings for or relating to a Part I order shall, to such extent and in such manner as may be prescribed, give particulars of other proceedings known to them which relate to the child concerned (including proceedings instituted abroad and proceedings which are no longer continuing).

Amendments—CA 1989, s 108(5), Sch 13, para 62.

Defined terms—"Part I order": ss 1(2), (3), 42(5), (6); "prescribed": s 42(1).

General interpretation—See s 42.

"Part I order"—See under s 25.

"to such extent and in such manner as may be prescribed"—Section 42(1) defines "prescribed" in relation to England and Wales as meaning prescribed by rules of court. FPR 1991, r 7.14 contains such provision, as does Magistrates' Courts (Family Law Act 1986) Rules 1988, r 6.

40 Interpretation of Chapter VI

(1) In this Chapter –

"the appropriate court" has the same meaning as in Chapter V;

"Part I order" includes (except where the context otherwise requires) any such order as is mentioned in section 32(1) of this Act.

(2) In the application of this Chapter to Scotland, "Part I order" also includes (except where the context otherwise requires) any such order as is mentioned in section 32(2) of this Act.

Amendments—CA 1989, s 108(5), Sch 13, para 62.

41 Habitual residence after removal without consent etc

(1) Where a child who –

(*a*) has not attained the age of sixteen, and

(*b*) is habitually resident in a part of the United Kingdom or in a specified dependent territory,

becomes habitually resident outside that part of the United Kingdom or that territory in consequence of circumstances of the kind specified in subsection (2) below, he shall be treated for the purposes of this Part as continuing to be habitually resident in that part of the United Kingdom or that territory for the period of one year beginning with the date on which those circumstances arise.

(2) The circumstances referred to in subsection (1) above exist where the child is removed from or retained outside, or himself leaves or remains outside, the part of the United Kingdom or the territory in which he was habitually resident before his change of residence –

(*a*) without the agreement of the person or all the persons having, under the law of that part of the United Kingdom or that territory, the right to determine where he is to reside, or

(*b*) in contravention of an order made by a court in any part of the United Kingdom or in a specified dependent territory.

(3) A child shall cease to be treated by virtue of subsection (1) above as habitually resident in a part of the United Kingdom or a specified dependent territory if, during the period there mentioned –

(*a*) he attains the age of sixteen, or

(*b*) he becomes habitually resident outside that part of the United Kingdom or that territory with the agreement of the person or persons mentioned in subsection (2)(*a*) above and not in contravention of an order made by a court in any part of the United Kingdom or in any specified dependent territory.

Amendments—SI 1991/1723.

Defined terms—"specified dependent territory": s 42(1).

General interpretation—See s 42.

"habitually resident" (s 41(1))—See under s 3 and **Habitual residence** under Child Support Act 1991, s 44.

"agreement of the person or persons mentioned in subsection (2)(a)" (s 41(3)(*b*))—Under s 41(1), if a child under 16 is removed from or retained outside his place of habitual residence without the agreement of everyone having the right to determine where he is to live, he is to be treated as remaining habitually resident there for one year, even if in fact he has become habitually resident elsewhere. Section 41(3) disapplies the one-year rule if everyone who has the right to determine where the child lives agrees that the child's habitual residence should change and the change in residence does not contravene any court order. However, a parent's preliminary or interim views expressed during the course of legal proceedings taken to determine the child's future residence cannot be taken as consent to a change of habitual residence; a parent's participation in such legal proceedings is a sensible course of action and should not be held against the parent (*D v D (Custody: Jurisdiction)* [1996] 1 FLR 574).

PART II

42 General interpretation of Part I

(1) In this Part –

"certified copy", in relation to an order of any court, means a copy certified by the prescribed officer of the court to be a true copy of the order or of the official record of the order;

"corresponding dependent territory order", "corresponding dependent territory provision" and similar expressions, in relation to a specified dependent territory, shall be construed in accordance with Schedule 3 to the Family Law Act 1986 (Dependent Territories) Order 1991 as from time to time in force: "dependent territory" has the meaning given by section 43(2) of this Act;

"parental responsibilities" and "parental rights" have the meanings respectively given by sections 1(3) and 2(4) of the Children (Scotland) Act 1995;

"part of the United Kingdom" means England and Wales, Scotland or Northern Ireland;

"prescribed" means prescribed by rules of court or act of sederunt;

"specified dependent territory" means a dependent territory for the time being specified in Schedule 1 to the said order of 1991.

"the Council Regulation" means Council Regulation (EC) No 1347/2000 of 29 May 2000 on jurisdiction and the recognition and enforcement of judgments in matrimonial matters and in matters of parental responsibility for children of both spouses.

(2) For the purposes of this Part proceedings in England and Wales, Northern Ireland or a specified dependent territory for divorce, nullity or judicial separation in respect of the marriage of the parents of a child shall, unless they have been dismissed, be treated as continuing until the child concerned attains the age of eighteen (whether or not a decree has been granted and whether or not, in the case of a decree of divorce or nullity of marriage, that decree has been made absolute).

(3) For the purposes of this Part, matrimonial proceedings in a court in Scotland which has jurisdiction in those proceedings to make a Part I order with respect to a child shall, unless they have been dismissed or decree of absolvitor has been granted therein, be treated as continuing until the child concerned attains the age of sixteen.

(4) Any reference in this Part to proceedings in respect of the marriage of the parents of a child shall, in relation to a child who, although not a child of both parties to the marriage, is a child of the family of those parties, be construed as a reference to proceedings in respect of that marriage; and for this purpose "child of the family" –

(*a*) if the proceedings are in England and Wales, means any child who has been treated by both parties as a child of their family, except a child who is placed with those parties as foster parents by a local authority or a voluntary organisation;

(*b*) if the proceedings are in Scotland, means any child who has been treated by both parties as a child of their family, except a child who has been placed with those parties as foster parents by a local authority or a voluntary organisation;

(*c*) if the proceedings are in Northern Ireland, means any child who has been treated by both parties as a child of their family, except a child who is placed with those parties as foster parents by an authority within the meaning of the Children (Northern Ireland) Order 1995;

(*d*) if the proceedings are in a specified dependent territory, means any child who has been treated by both parties as a child of their family, except a child who has been placed with those parties as foster parents by a public authority in that territory.

(5) References in this Part to Part I orders include (except where the context otherwise requires) references to Part I orders as varied.

(6) For the purposes of this Part each of the following orders shall be treated as varying the Part I order to which it relates –

(*a*) an order which provides for a person to be allowed contact with or to be given access to a child who is the subject of a Part I order, or which makes provision for the education of such a child,

(*b*)–(*e*) (*repealed*)

(7) In this Part –

(*a*) references to Part I proceedings in respect of a child are references to any proceedings for a Part I order or an order corresponding to a Part I order and include, in relation to proceedings outside the United Kingdom and any specified dependent territory, references to proceedings before a tribunal or other authority having power under the law having effect there to determine Part I matters; and

(*b*) references to Part I matters are references to matters that might be determined by a Part I order or an order corresponding to a Part I order.

Amendments—CA 1989, s 108(5), (7), Sch 13, paras 62, 71, Sch 15; SI 1991/1723; Children (Scotland) Act 1995, s 105(4), Sch 4, para 41(1), (9); SI 1995/756; SI 2001/310; SI 2001/660.

"corresponding dependent territory order" etc—In relation to the Isle of Man, see Family Law Act 1986 (Dependent Territories) Order 1991, Sch 3 for specific interpretation.

"specified dependent territory"—See also Family Law Act 1986 (Dependent Territories) (Amendment) Order 1994, SI 1994/2800, and FPR 1991, r 7.7(1), as amended.

****

PART II
RECOGNITION OF DIVORCES, ANNULMENTS AND LEGAL SEPARATIONS

Divorces, annulments and judicial separations granted in the British Islands

44 Recognition in United Kingdom of divorces, annulments and judicial separations granted in the British Islands

(1) Subject to section 52(4) and (5)(*a*) of this Act, no divorce or annulment obtained in any part of the British Islands shall be regarded as effective in any part of the United Kingdom unless granted by a court of civil jurisdiction.

(2) Subject to section 51 of this Act, the validity of any divorce, annulment or judicial separation granted by a court of civil jurisdiction in any part of the British Islands shall be recognised throughout the United Kingdom.

Defined terms—"annulment", "part of the United Kingdom": s 54(1).

Overseas divorces, annulments and legal separations

45 Recognition in the United Kingdom of overseas divorces, annulments and legal separations

(1) Subject to subsection (2) of this section and to sections 51 and 52 of this Act, the validity of a divorce, annulment or legal separation obtained in a country outside the British Islands (in this Part referred to as an overseas divorce, annulment or legal separation) shall be recognised in the United Kingdom if, and only if, it is entitled to recognition –

(*a*) by virtue of sections 46 to 49 of this Act, or
(*b*) by virtue of any enactment other than this Part.

(2) Subsection (1) and the following provisions of this Part do not apply to an overseas divorce, annulment or legal separation as regards which provision as to recognition is made by Articles 14 to 20 of the Council Regulation.

Amendments—SI 2001/310.

Defined terms—"annulment": s 54(1); "country": s 54(2).

46 Grounds for recognition

(1) The validity of an overseas divorce, annulment or legal separation obtained by means of proceedings shall be recognised if –

(*a*) the divorce, annulment or legal separation is effective under the law of the country in which it was obtained; and
(*b*) at the relevant date either party to the marriage –
  (i) was habitually resident in the country in which the divorce, annulment or legal separation was obtained; or
  (ii) was domiciled in that country; or
  (iii) was a national of that country.

(2) The validity of an overseas divorce, annulment or legal separation obtained otherwise than by means of proceedings shall be recognised if –

(*a*) the divorce, annulment or legal separation is effective under the law of the country in which it was obtained;

(*b*) at the relevant date –

(i) each party to the marriage was domiciled in that country; or

(ii) either party to the marriage was domiciled in that country and the other party was domiciled in a country under whose law the divorce, annulment or legal separation is recognised as valid; and

(*c*) neither party to the marriage was habitually resident in the United Kingdom throughout the period of one year immediately preceding that date.

(3) In this section "the relevant date" means –

(*a*) in the case of an overseas divorce, annulment or legal separation obtained by means of proceedings, the date of the commencement of the proceedings;

(*b*) in the case of an overseas divorce, annulment or legal separation obtained otherwise than by means of proceedings, the date on which it was obtained.

(4) Where in the case of an overseas annulment, the relevant date fell after the death of either party to the marriage, any reference in subsection (1) or (2) above to that date shall be construed in relation to that party as a reference to the date of death.

(5) For the purpose of this section, a party to a marriage shall be treated as domiciled in a country if he was domiciled in that country either according to the law of that country in family matters or according to the law of the part of the United Kingdom in which the question of recognition arises.

Defined terms—"annulment": s 54(1); "country": s 54(2); "part of the United Kingdom", "proceedings" s 54(1).

"effective under the law of the country in which it was obtained" (s 46(1)(*a*))—Where a husband had applied for a divorce to a tribunal in Ghana and had made his wife's mother a defendant to the proceedings, but where his wife had no knowledge of the proceedings and there was no evidence that her mother had voluntarily submitted to the jurisdiction of the tribunal, or that the tribunal had made adequate efforts by adjourning the case to hear the wife's side of the case, Wall J held that the order dissolving the marriage was not effective since the High Court in Ghana would not have upheld the decree on a judicial review. Even if this were not the case, Family Law Act 1986, s 51(3)(*a*)(i) gives the court a wide discretion to refuse what would otherwise be mandatory recognition afforded under s 46 by applying the English concept of what would constitute "reasonable steps" to give notice of the proceedings to the wife (*D v D (Recognition of Foreign Divorce)* [1994] 1 FLR 38). For an example of a case under s 46(2)(*a*) see *Wicken v Wicken* [1999] 1 FLR 293 where expert evidence called by both parties established that a divorce letter was, as a matter of substantive law, effective under the law of The Gambia to dissolve the marriage. There was a requirement that in the event of a dispute in The Gambia the authenticity of the document be proved by the testimony of two righteous male witnesses. However, that requirement was a matter of evidence and not substantive law, and as the dispute as to authenticity arose in England, the rules of evidence of England and Wales applied. Applying those rules, the letter was held to be authentic and therefore valid under Gambian law.

Ordinarily, a talaq is not the product of judicial or other proceedings but is the product of a simple pronouncement. However, where Lebanese law required a talaq to be recorded with the Sharia court, that registration process was properly described as "proceedings" for the purposes of s 46(1), even though no judicial decision was required (*El Fadl v El Fadl* [2000] 1 FLR 175). However, a bare talaq pronounced in England between nationals of Saudi Arabia did not dissolve a marriage, even if it was subsequently registered with the Sharia court in Saudi Arabia, because divorces obtained in the UK other than by proceedings in a court of civil jurisdiction are not recognised (s 44(1)). Furthermore, neither was it an overseas divorce within the meaning of s 45 (1)(*a*) as it was obtained in the UK not Saudi Arabia (*Sulaiman v Juffali* [2002] 1 FLR 479).

"Effective" connotes a less rigorous standard than "valid". "Effective" can mean a decree which, although invalid per se in the granting state, is none the less to be treated as valid by virtue of some supervening legal decision or equitable principle such as estoppel (*Kellman v Kellman* [2000] 1 FLR 785).

"habitually resident" (s 46(1)(*b*)(i), (2)(*c*))—See under s 3 and **Habitual residence** under Child Support Act 1991, s 44.

Transnational divorces (s 46(3))—FLA 1986 contemplates that the proceedings by which the "overseas divorce" has been obtained should have been commenced and concluded in the same place. The mere fact that a divorce was pronounced or finalised in one country does not entitle the court to overlook the fact that part of the proceedings has been conducted elsewhere. The word "obtained" connotes a process rather than a single act. Where an important step in the proceedings leading to the divorce has taken place in England rather than in the jurisdiction in which the divorce was pronounced, that divorce is properly to be regarded not as an "overseas divorce" but rather as a transnational divorce. If the divorce has not been terminated by means of "overseas proceedings", it cannot be recognised in England and Wales under FLA 1986 (*Berkovits v Grinberg (Attorney-General Intervening)* [1995] Fam 142).

47 Cross-proceedings and divorces following legal separations

(1) Where there have been cross-proceedings, the validity of an overseas divorce, annulment or legal separation obtained either in the original proceedings or in the cross-proceedings shall be recognised if –

(*a*) the requirements of section 46(1)(*b*)(i), (ii) or (iii) of this Act are satisfied in relation to the date of the commencement either of the original proceedings or of the cross-proceedings, and

(*b*) the validity of the divorce, annulment or legal separation is otherwise entitled to recognition by virtue of the provisions of this Part.

(2) Where a legal separation, the validity of which is entitled to recognition by virtue of the provisions of section 46 of this Act or of subsection (1) above is converted, in the country in which it was obtained, into a divorce which is effective under the law of that country, the validity of the divorce shall be recognised whether or not it would itself be entitled to recognition by virtue of those provisions.

Defined terms—"annulment": s 54(1); "country": s 54(2); "proceedings": s 54(1).

48 Proof of facts relevant to recognition

(1) For the purpose of deciding whether an overseas divorce, annulment or legal separation obtained by means of proceedings is entitled to recognition by virtue of section 46 and 47 of this Act, any finding of fact made (whether expressly or by implication) in the proceedings and on the basis of which jurisdiction was assumed in the proceedings shall –

(*a*) if both parties to the marriage took part in the proceedings, be conclusive evidence of the fact found; and

(*b*) in any other case, be sufficient proof of that fact unless the contrary is shown.

(2) In this section "finding of fact" includes a finding that either party to the marriage –

(*a*) was habitually resident in the country in which the divorce, annulment or legal separation was obtained; or

(*b*) was under the law of that country domiciled there; or

(*c*) was a national of that country.

(3) For the purposes of subsection (1)(*a*) above, a party to the marriage who has appeared in judicial proceedings shall be treated as having taken part in them.

Defined terms—"annulment": s 54(1); "country": s 54(2); "proceedings": s 54(1).

"habitually resident" (s 48(2)(*a*))—See under s 3 and **Habitual residence** under Child Support Act 1991, s 44.

Supplemental

49 Modifications of Part II in relation to countries comprising territories having different systems of law

(1) In relation to a country comprising territories in which different systems of law are in force in matters of divorce, annulment or legal separation, the provisions of this Part mentioned in subsections (2) to (5) below shall have effect subject to the modifications there specified.

(2) In the case of a divorce, annulment or legal separation the recognition of the validity of which depends on whether the requirements of subsection (1)(*b*)(i) or (ii) of section 46 of this Act are satisfied, that section and, in the case of a legal separation, section 47(2) of this Act shall have effect as if each territory were a separate country.

(3) In the case of a divorce, annulment or legal separation the recognition of the validity of which depends on whether the requirements of subsection (1)(*b*)(iii) of section 46 of this Act are satisfied –

(*a*) that section shall have effect as if for paragraph (*a*) of subsection (1) there were substituted the following paragraph –

"(*a*) the divorce, annulment or legal separation is effective throughout the country in which it was obtained;"; and

(*b*) in the case of a legal separation, section 47(2) of this Act shall have effect as if for the words "is effective under the law of that country" there were substituted the words "is effective throughout that country".

(4) In the case of a divorce, annulment or legal separation the recognition of the validity of which depends on whether the requirements of subsection (2)(*b*) of section 46 of this Act are satisfied, that section and section 52(3) and (4) of this Act and, in the case of a legal separation, section 47(2) of this Act shall have effect as if each territory were a separate country.

(5) Paragraphs (*a*) and (*b*) of section 48(2) of this Act shall each have effect as if each territory were a separate country.

Defined terms—"annulment": s 54(1); "country": s 54(2).

50 Non-recognition of divorce or annulment in another jurisdiction no bar to remarriage

Where, in any part of the United Kingdom –

(*a*) a divorce or annulment has been granted by a court of civil jurisdiction, or

(*b*) the validity of a divorce or annulment is recognised by virtue of this Part,

the fact that the divorce or annulment would not be recognised elsewhere shall not preclude either party to the marriage from re-marrying in that part of the United

Kingdom or cause the remarriage of either party (wherever the re-marriage takes place) to be treated as invalid in that part.

Defined terms—"annulment", "part of the United Kingdom": s 54(1).

51 Refusal of recognition

(1) Subject to section 52 of this Act, recognition of the validity of –

(*a*) a divorce, annulment or judicial separation granted by a court of civil jurisdiction in any part of the British Islands, or

(*b*) an overseas divorce, annulment or legal separation,

may be refused in any part of the United Kingdom if the divorce, annulment or separation was granted or obtained at a time when it was irreconcilable with a decision determining the question of the subsistence or validity of the marriage of the parties previously given (whether before or after the commencement of this Part) by a court of civil jurisdiction in that part of the United Kingdom or by a court elsewhere and recognised or entitled to be recognised in that part of the United Kingdom.

(2) Subject to section 52 of this Act, recognition of the validity of –

(*a*) a divorce or judicial separation granted by a court of civil jurisdiction in any part of the British Islands, or

(*b*) an overseas divorce or legal separation,

may be refused in any part of the United Kingdom if the divorce or separation was granted or obtained at a time when, according to the law of that part of the United Kingdom (including its rules of private international law and the provisions of this Part), there was no subsisting marriage between the parties.

(3) Subject to section 52 of this Act, recognition by virtue of section 45 of this Act of the validity of an overseas divorce, annulment or legal separation may be refused if –

(*a*) in the case of a divorce, annulment or legal separation obtained by means of proceedings, it was obtained –

(i) without such steps having been taken for giving notice of the proceedings to a party to the marriage as, having regard to the nature of the proceedings and all the circumstances, should reasonably have been taken; or

(ii) without a party to the marriage having been given (for any reason other than lack of notice) such opportunity to take part in the proceedings as, having regard to those matters, he should reasonably have been given; or

(*b*) in the case of a divorce, annulment or legal separation obtained otherwise than by means of proceedings –

(i) there is no official document certifying that the divorce, annulment or legal separation is effective under the law of the country in which it was obtained; or

(ii) where either party to the marriage was domiciled in another country at the relevant date, there is no official document certifying that the divorce, annulment or legal separation is recognised as valid under the law of that other country; or

(*c*) in either case, recognition of the divorce, annulment or legal separation would be manifestly contrary to public policy.

(4) In this section –

PART II

"official", in relation to a document certifying that a divorce, annulment or legal separation is effective, or is recognised as valid, under the law of any country, means issued by a person or body appointed or recognised for the purpose under that law;

"the relevant date" has the same meaning as in section 46 of this Act;

and subsection (5) of that section shall apply for the purposes of this section as it applies for the purposes of that section.

(5) Nothing in this Part shall be construed as requiring the recognition of any finding of fault made in any proceedings for divorce, annulment or separation or of any maintenance, custody or other ancillary order made in any such proceedings.

Defined terms—"annulment": s 54(1); "country": s 54(2); "part of the United Kingdom", "proceedings": s 54(1).

"without such steps having been taken for giving notice of the proceedings to a party to the marriage" (s 51(3)(*a*)(i))—A foreign divorce may be refused even where the requirements of Family Law Act 1986, s 46 are satisfied if it was obtained "without such steps being taken for giving notice of the proceedings to a party to the marriage as, having regard to the nature of the proceedings and all the circumstances, should reasonably have been taken" (*D v D (Recognition of Foreign Divorce)* [1994] 1 FLR 38: divorce obtained in Ghana not recognised in England). See also **"effective under the law of the country in which it was obtained"** under s 46.

"manifestly contrary to public policy" (s 51(3)(*c*))—The discretion to refuse recognition on the grounds that it would be manifestly contrary to public policy is one to be exercised sparingly – see *El Fadl v El Fadl* [2000] 1 FLR 175 and *Kellman v Kellman* [2000] 1 FLR 785. The motive for the divorce is generally irrelevant to the exercise of that discretion. Whilst fraud is not a ground for refusal of recognition, there may be exceptional circumstances where one party may have deceived the other and the foreign court which may be relevant to the exercise of the discretion. In *Eroglu v Eroglu* [1994] 2 FLR 287, where the petitioner participated with the respondent in a ruse to obtain a Turkish divorce which was designed to achieve material advantage for the respondent, and which material advantage was enjoyed and shared by the petitioner, the petitioner fell far short of persuading the court that the recognition of the Turkish divorce would be manifestly contrary to public policy. A divorce granted by a state that is not recognised by the Government of the United Kingdom can be recognised, provided that it was obtained in accordance with the relevant conditions applicable within the area and that the provisions under ss 46–54 have been complied with. However, such recognition must never be inconsistent with foreign policy or the diplomatic stance of the government and therefore when the court is asked to recognise the acts of an unrecognised state or its courts, it should, where possible, be assisted by representations on behalf of the Attorney General (*Emin v Yeldag (Attorney-General and Secretary of State for Foreign and Commonwealth Affairs Intervening)* [2002] 1 FLR 956).

52 Provisions as to divorces, annulments etc obtained before commencement of Part II

(1) The provisions of this Part shall apply –

(*a*) to a divorce, annulment or judicial separation granted by a court of civil jurisdiction in the British Islands before the date of the commencement of this Part, and

(*b*) to an overseas divorce, annulment or legal separation obtained before that date,

as well as to one granted or obtained on or after that date.

(2) In the case of such a divorce, annulment or separation as is mentioned in subsection (1)(*a*) or (*b*) above, the provisions of this Part shall require or, as the case may be, preclude the recognition of its validity in relation to any time before that date as well as in relation to any subsequent time, but those provisions shall not –

(*a*) affect any property to which any person became entitled before that date, or

(*b*) affect the recognition of the validity of the divorce, annulment or separation if that matter has been decided by any competent court in the British Islands before that date.

(3) Subsections (1) and (2) above shall apply in relation to any divorce or judicial separation granted by a court of civil jurisdiction in the British Islands before the date of the commencement of this Part whether granted before or after the commencement of section 1 of the Recognition of Divorces and Legal Separations Act 1971.

(4) The validity of any divorce, annulment or legal separation mentioned in subsection (5) below shall be recognised in the United Kingdom whether or not it is entitled to recognition by virtue of any of the foregoing provisions of this Part.

(5) The divorces, annulments and legal separations referred to in subsection (4) above are –

(*a*) a divorce which was obtained in the British Islands before 1 January 1974 and was recognised as valid under rules of law applicable before that date;

(*b*) an overseas divorce which was recognised as valid under the Recognition of Divorces and Legal Separations Act 1971 and was not affected by section 16(2) of the Domicile and Matrimonial Proceedings Act 1973 (proceedings otherwise than in a court of law where both parties resident in the United Kingdom);

(*c*) a divorce of which the decree was registered under section 1 of the Indian and Colonial Divorce Jurisdiction Act 1926;

(*d*) a divorce or annulment which was recognised as valid under section 4 of the Matrimonial Causes (War Marriages) Act 1944; and

(*e*) an overseas legal separation which was recognised as valid under the Recognition of Divorces and Legal Separations Act 1971.

Defined terms—"annulment": s 54(1).

****

54 Interpretation of Part II

(1) In this Part –

"annulment" includes any decree or declarator of nullity of marriage, however expressed;

"the Council Regulation" means Council Regulation (EC) No 1347/2000 of 29 May 2000 on jurisdiction and the recognition and enforcement of judgments in matrimonial matters and in matters of parental responsibility for children of both spouses;

"part of the United Kingdom" means England and Wales, Scotland or Northern Ireland;

"proceedings" means judicial or other proceedings.

(2) In this Part "country" includes a colony or other dependent territory of the United Kingdom but for the purposes of this Part a person shall be treated as a national of such a territory only if it has a law of citizenship or nationality separate

from that of the United Kingdom and he is a citizen or national of that territory under that law.

Amendments—SI 2001/310.

PART III
DECLARATIONS OF STATUS

55 Declarations as to marital status

(1) Subject to the following provisions of this section, any person may apply to the High Court or a county court for one or more of the following declarations in relation to a marriage specified in the application, that is to say –

(*a*) a declaration that the marriage was at its inception a valid marriage;
(*b*) a declaration that the marriage subsisted on a date specified in the application;
(*c*) a declaration that the marriage did not subsist on a date so specified;
(*d*) a declaration that the validity of a divorce, annulment or legal separation obtained in any country outside England and Wales in respect of the marriage is entitled to recognition in England and Wales;
(*e*) a declaration that the validity of a divorce, annulment or legal separation so obtained in respect of the marriage is not entitled to recognition in England and Wales.

(2) A court shall have jurisdiction to entertain an application under subsection (1) above if, and only if, either of the parties to the marriage to which the application relates –

(*a*) is domiciled in England and Wales on the date of the application, or
(*b*) has been habitually resident in England and Wales throughout the period of one year ending with that date, or
(*c*) died before that date and either –
 (i) was at death domiciled in England and Wales, or
 (ii) had been habitually resident in England and Wales throughout the period of one year ending with the date of death.

(3) Where an application under subsection (1) above is made to a court by any person other than a party to the marriage to which the application relates, the court shall refuse to hear the application if it considers that the applicant does not have a sufficient interest in the determination of that application.

Amendments—Child Support, Pensions and Social Security Act 2000, s 83, Sch 8, para 4.

"habitually resident" (s 55(2)(*b*), (*c*)(i))—See under s 3 and **Habitual residence** under Child Support Act 1991, s 44.

Procedure—See Procedural Guide 14.

55A Declarations of parentage

(1) Subject to the following provisions of this section, any person may apply to the High Court, a county court or a magistrates' court for a declaration as to whether or not a person named in the application is or was the parent of another person so named.

(2) A court shall have jurisdiction to entertain an application under subsection (1) above if, and only if, either of the persons named in it for the purposes of that subsection –

(*a*) is domiciled in England and Wales on the date of the application, or
(*b*) has been habitually resident in England and Wales throughout the period of one year ending with that date, or
(*c*) died before that date and either –
  (i) was at death domiciled in England and Wales, or
  (ii) had been habitually resident in England and Wales throughout the period of one year ending with the date of death.

(3) Except in a case falling within subsection (4) below, the court shall refuse to hear an application under subsection (1) above unless it considers that the applicant has a sufficient personal interest in the determination of the application (but this is subject to section 27 of the Child Support Act 1991).

(4) The excepted cases are where the declaration sought is as to whether or not –

(*a*) the applicant is the parent of a named person;
(*b*) a named person is the parent of the applicant; or
(*c*) a named person is the other parent of a named child of the applicant.

(5) Where an application under subsection (1) above is made and one of the persons named in it for the purposes of that subsection is a child, the court may refuse to hear the application if it considers that the determination of the application would not be in the best interests of the child.

(6) Where a court refuses to hear an application under subsection (1) above it may order that the applicant may not apply again for the same declaration without leave of the court.

(7) Where a declaration is made by a court on an application under subsection (1) above, the prescribed officer of the court shall notify the Registrar General, in such a manner and within such period as may be prescribed, of the making of that declaration.

Amendments—Inserted by Child Support, Pensions and Social Security Act 2000, s 83(1), (2).

Procedure—See Procedural Guide 42.

56 Declarations as to legitimacy or legitimation

(1) Any person may apply to the High Court or a county court for a declaration –

(*a*) (*repealed*)
(*b*) that he is the legitimate child of his parents.

(2) Any person may apply to the court for one (or for one or, in the alternative, the other) of the following declarations, that is to say –

(*a*) a declaration that he has become a legitimated person;
(*b*) a declaration that he has not become a legitimated person.

(3) A court shall have jurisdiction to entertain an application under this section if, and only if, the applicant –

(*a*) is domiciled in England and Wales on the date of the application, or
(*b*) has been habitually resident in England and Wales throughout the period of one year ending with that date.

(4) Where a declaration is made by a court on an application under subsection (1) above, the prescribed officer of the court shall notify the Registrar General, in such a manner and within such period as may be prescribed, of the making of that declaration.

(5) In this section "legitimated person" means a person legitimated or recognised as legitimated –

(*a*) under section 2 or 3 of the Legitimacy Act 1976; or
(*b*) under section 1 or 8 of the Legitimacy Act 1926; or
(*c*) by a legitimation (whether or not by virtue of the subsequent marriage of his parents) recognised by the law of England and Wales and effected under the law of another country.

Amendments—Family Law Reform Act 1987, s 22; Child Support, Pensions and Social Security Act 2000, s 83, Sch 8, para 5, Sch 9.

"habitually resident" (s 56(3)(*b*))—See under s 3 and **Habitual residence** under Child Support Act 1991, s 44.

Procedure—See Procedural Guide 41.

57 Declarations as to adoptions effected overseas

(1) Any person whose status as an adopted child of any person depends on whether he has been adopted by that person by either –

(*a*) a overseas adoption as defined by section 72(2) of the Adoption Act 1976, or
(*b*) an adoption recognised by the law of England and Wales and effected under the law of any country outside the British Islands,

may apply to the High Court or a county court for one (or for one or, in the alternative, the other) of the declarations mentioned in subsection (2) below.

(2) The said declarations are –

(*a*) a declaration that the applicant is for the purposes of section 39 of the Adoption Act 1976 the adopted child of that person;
(*b*) a declaration that the applicant is not for the purposes of that section the adopted child of that person.

(3) A court shall have jurisdiction to entertain an application under subsection (1) above if, and only if, the applicant –

(*a*) is domiciled in England and Wales on the date of the application, or
(*b*) has been habitually resident in England and Wales throughout the period of one year ending with that date.

(4) Until the Adoption Act 1976 comes into force –

(*a*) subsection (1) above shall have effect as if for the reference to section 72(2) of that Act there were substituted a reference to section 4(3) of the Adoption Act 1968; and
(*b*) subsection (2) above shall have effect as if for the reference to section 39 of that Act there were substituted a reference to Part II of Schedule I to the Children Act 1975.

Amendments—Child Support, Pensions and Social Security Act 2000, s 83, Sch 8, para 6.

58 General provisions as to the making and effect of declarations

(1) Where on an application to a court for a declaration under this Part the truth of the proposition to be declared is proved to the satisfaction of the court, the court shall make that declaration unless to do so would manifestly be contrary to public policy.

(2) Any declarations made under this Part shall be binding on Her Majesty and all other persons.

(3) A court, on the dismissal of an application for a declaration under this Part, shall not have power to make any declaration for which an application has not been made.

(4) No declaration which may be applied for under this Part may be made otherwise than under this Part by any court.

(5) No declaration may be made by any court, whether under this Part or otherwise –

(*a*) that a marriage was at its inception void;
(*b*) (*repealed*)

(6) Nothing in this section shall affect the powers of any court to grant a decree of nullity of marriage.

Amendments—Child Support, Pensions and Social Security Act 2000, s 83(3), Sch 8, para 7, Sch 9.

59 Provisions relating to the Attorney-General

(1) On an application to a court for a declaration under this Part the court may at any stage of the proceedings, of its own motion or on the application of any party to the proceedings, direct that all necessary papers in the matter be sent to the Attorney-General.

(2) The Attorney-General, whether or not he is sent papers in relation to an application to a court for a declaration under this Part, may –

(*a*) intervene in the proceedings on that application in such manner as he thinks necessary or expedient, and
(*b*) argue before the court any question in relation to the application which the court considers it necessary to have fully argued.

(3) Where any costs are incurred by the Attorney-General in connection with any application to a court for a declaration under this Part, the court may make such order as it considers just as to the payment of those costs by parties to the proceedings.

Amendments—Child Support, Pensions and Social Security Act 2000, s 83(3), Sch 8, para 8.

****

Family Law Act 1996

ARRANGEMENT OF SECTIONS

PART IV
FAMILY HOMES AND DOMESTIC VIOLENCE

****

PART IV
FAMILY HOMES AND DOMESTIC VIOLENCE

Rights to occupy matrimonial home

30 Rights concerning matrimonial home where one spouse has no estate etc

(1) This section applies if –

(*a*) one spouse is entitled to occupy a dwelling-house by virtue of –

(i) a beneficial estate or interest or contract; or

(ii) any enactment giving that spouse the right to remain in occupation; and

(*b*) the other spouse is not so entitled.

(2) Subject to the provisions of this Part, the spouse not so entitled has the following rights ("matrimonial home rights") –

(*a*) if in occupation, a right not to be evicted or excluded from the dwelling-house or any part of it by the other spouse except with the leave of the court given by an order under section 33;

(*b*) if not in occupation, a right with the leave of the court so given to enter into and occupy the dwelling-house.

(3) If a spouse is entitled under this section to occupy a dwelling-house or any part of a dwelling-house, any payment or tender made or other thing done by that spouse in or towards satisfaction of any liability of the other spouse in respect of rent, mortgage payments or other outgoings affecting the dwelling-house shall, whether or not it is made or done in pursuance of an order under section 40, be as good as if made or done by the other spouse.

(4) A spouse's occupation by virtue of this section –

(*a*) is to be treated, for the purposes of the Rent (Agriculture) Act 1976 and the Rent Act 1977 (other than Part V and sections 103 to 106 of that Act), as occupation by the other spouse as the other spouse's residence, and (*b*) if the spouse occupies the dwelling-house as that spouse's only or principal home, is to be treated, for the purposes of the Housing Act 1985, Part I of the Housing Act 1988 and Chapter I of Part V of the Housing Act 1996, as occupation by the other spouse as the other spouse's only or principal home.

(5) If a spouse ("the first spouse") –

(*a*) is entitled under this section to occupy a dwelling-house or any part of a dwelling-house, and

(*b*) makes any payment in or towards satisfaction of any liability of the other spouse ("the second spouse") in respect of mortgage payments affecting the dwelling-house,

the person to whom the payment is made may treat it as having been made by that other spouse, but the fact that that person has treated any such payment as having been so made does not affect any claim of the first spouse against the second spouse to an interest in the dwelling-house by virtue of the payment.

(6) If a spouse is entitled under this section to occupy a dwelling-house or part of a dwelling-house by reason of an interest of the other spouse under a trust, all the provisions of subsections (3) to (5) apply in relation to the trustees as they apply in relation to the other spouse.

(7) This section does not apply to a dwelling-house which has at no time been, and which was at no time intended by the spouses to be, a matrimonial home of theirs.

(8) A spouse's matrimonial home rights continue –

(*a*) only so long as the marriage subsists, except to the extent that an order under section 33(5) otherwise provides; and

(*b*) only so long as the other spouse is entitled as mentioned in subsection (1) to occupy the dwelling-house, except where provision is made by section 31 for those rights to be a charge on an estate or interest in the dwelling-house.

(9) It is hereby declared that a spouse –

(*a*) who has an equitable interest in a dwelling-house or in its proceeds of sale, but

(*b*) is not a spouse in whom there is vested (whether solely or as joint tenant) a legal estate in fee simple or a legal term of years absolute in the dwelling-house,

is to be treated, only for the purpose of determining whether he has matrimonial home rights, as not being entitled to occupy the dwelling-house by virtue of that interest.

Amendments—SI 1997/74.

Defined terms—"dwelling-house": s 63(1), (4); "mortgage": s 63(1).

Scope of provision—This section provides that where one spouse has the right to occupy a dwelling-house, either because he owns it or has a contractual tenancy or is a statutory tenant of it, the other party has matrimonial home rights. Those rights are, if in occupation, not to be evicted without leave of the court or, if not in occupation, the right, with leave of the court, to return. The provision mirrors Matrimonial Homes Act 1983, s 1 but is different in three respects: first, the rights are now known as "matrimonial home rights" instead of rights of occupation; secondly, by virtue of s 63(1), a "dwelling-house" includes a caravan or houseboat; and thirdly, under ss 30(7) and 33(1)(*b*), a dwelling-house which has not yet been, but is intended to be, a matrimonial home is included.

Occupation orders – general—See under s 33.

Duration of matrimonial home rights (s 30(8))—Matrimonial home rights subsist only for the duration of the marriage unless an order is made under s 33(5) before the marriage is ended by death or decree of divorce or nullity.

Treatment of one spouse's rights and obligations as those of the other spouse (s 30(3)–(5))—These subsections provide that payment of rent or mortgage by the spouse who does not have an interest or tenancy in the property is as good as payment by the other, and that the occupation of one spouse is to be treated as occupation by the other. Thus, if there is a statutory tenancy, even though the statutory tenant has left, the remaining spouse's occupation is as good as that of the statutory tenant. This protection lasts only so long as the status of the spouse is not ended by decree absolute. In s 30(4)(*b*) the references to the Housing Act 1985, the Housing Act 1988, Pt I and Housing Act 1996 are respectively to occupation by virtue of a secure tenancy, an assured tenancy/assured shorthold tenancy and an introductory tenancy (in effect a shorthold tenancy in the private sector).

Prevention of unilateral termination of tenancy—As set out in Procedural Guide 12, a tenancy in the other spouse's name or in joint names can be destroyed unilaterally by surrender or notice to quit. Consideration should therefore be given to applying for an injunction to prevent such action.

"matrimonial home" (s 30(7))—There is no definition of this term, although it includes a dwelling-house which has not yet been but is intended to be a matrimonial home, and a caravan or houseboat (see **Scope of provision** above). However, for the purpose of certain sections, a caravan and a houseboat are *not* within the definition of dwelling-house (see s 63(4)). Whether a dwelling-house is or is intended to be a matrimonial home is a question of fact, having regard to any periods of time spent living there and any agreement between the parties as to whether a property is to be treated as their present or intended matrimonial home (*King v King* [1941] 2 All ER 103).

31 Effect of matrimonial home rights as charge on dwelling-house

(1) Subsections (2) and (3) apply if, at any time during a marriage, one spouse is entitled to occupy a dwelling-house by virtue of a beneficial estate or interest.

(2) The other spouse's matrimonial home rights are a charge on the estate or interest.

(3) The charge created by subsection (2) has the same priority as if it were an equitable interest created at whichever is the latest of the following dates –

(*a*) the date on which the spouse so entitled acquires the estate or interest;
(*b*) the date of the marriage; and
(*c*) 1st January 1968 (the commencement date of the Matrimonial Homes Act 1967).

(4) Subsections (5) and (6) apply if, at any time when a spouse's matrimonial home rights are a charge on an interest of the other spouse under a trust, there are, apart from either of the spouses, no persons, living or unborn, who are or could become beneficiaries under the trust.

(5) The rights are a charge also on the estate or interest of the trustees for the other spouse.

(6) The charge created by subsection (5) has the same priority as if it were an equitable interest created (under powers overriding the trusts) on the date when it arises.

(7) In determining for the purposes of subsection (4) whether there are any persons who are not, but could become, beneficiaries under the trust, there is to be disregarded any potential exercise of a general power of appointment exercisable

by either or both of the spouses alone (whether or not the exercise of it requires the consent of another person).

(8) Even though a spouse's matrimonial home rights are a charge on an estate or interest in the dwelling-house, those rights are brought to an end by –

(*a*) the death of the other spouse, or
(*b*) the termination (otherwise than by death) of the marriage,

unless the court directs otherwise by an order made under section 33(5).

(9) If –

(*a*) a spouse's matrimonial home rights are a charge on an estate or interest in the dwelling-house, and
(*b*) that estate or interest is surrendered to merge in some other estate or interest expectant on it in such circumstances that, but for the merger, the person taking the estate or interest would be bound by the charge,

the surrender has effect subject to the charge and the persons thereafter entitled to the other estate or interest are, for so long as the estate or interest surrendered would have endured if not so surrendered, to be treated for all purposes of this Part as deriving title to the other estate or interest under the other spouse or, as the case may be, under the trustees for the other spouse, by virtue of the surrender.

(10) If the title to the legal estate by virtue of which a spouse is entitled to occupy a dwelling-house (including any legal estate held by trustees for that spouse) is registered under the Land Registration Act 1925 or any enactment replaced by that Act –

(*a*) registration of a land charge affecting the dwelling-house by virtue of this Part is to be effected by registering a notice under that Act; and
(*b*) a spouse's matrimonial home rights are not an overriding interest within the meaning of that Act affecting the dwelling-house even though the spouse is in actual occupation of the dwelling-house.

(11) A spouse's matrimonial home rights (whether or not constituting a charge) do not entitle that spouse to lodge a caution under section 54 of the Land Registration Act 1925.

(12) If –

(*a*) a spouse's matrimonial home rights are a charge on the estate of the other spouse or of trustees of the other spouse, and
(*b*) that estate is the subject of a mortgage,

then if, after the date of the creation of the mortgage ("the first mortgage"), the charge is registered under section 2 of the Land Charges Act 1972, the charge is, for the purposes of section 94 of the Law of Property Act 1925 (which regulates the rights of mortgagees to make further advances ranking in priority to subsequent mortgages), to be deemed to be a mortgage subsequent in date to the first mortgage.

(13) It is hereby declared that a charge under subsection (2) or (5) is not registrable under subsection 10 or under section 2 of the Land Charges Act 1972 unless it is a charge on a legal estate.

Defined terms—"dwelling-house": s 63(1), (4); "matrimonial home rights": s 30(2); "mortgage": s 63(1).

Taking precautions—To give protection against third parties such as mortgagees or purchasers, it is essential that the charge is registered under either the Land Registration Act 1925 or the Land

Charges Act 1972, as appropriate. It should be registered as soon as the legal adviser is informed that the marriage is in difficulty (*Miles v Bull* [1969] 1 QB 258 at 260). From May 2001 the Land Registration Rules 2001 provide that notice of the charge is automatically given to the owner. Protection ends with the termination of the marriage. Therefore, immediately prior to decree absolute, an application should be made for ancillary relief, including a claim for a property adjustment order. The "Class F land charge" must be replaced with a "Pending Action Land Charge/Caution Against Dealings" in respect of the pending application for a property adjustment order (*Perez-Adamson v Perez-Rivas* [1987] 3 WLR 500).

Existing all moneys charges need extra precautions. The registration of a Class F land charge/pending action/caution merely gives notice to future purchasers or lenders. An informed commentator suggests that where there is already an existing all moneys charge, the party seeking protection should send to the bank details of his/her potential claims together with the charge, notice or caution and a request to lend no further sum. See "Cautions and the Reviewable Disposition" [2001] Fam Law 437.

PART II

Bank's obligation before taking a charge over joint property for benefit of one owner—The House of Lords in *Royal Bank of Scotland Plc v Etridge (No 2)* [2001] 2 FLR 1364, [2001] UKHL 44 gave important practical guidelines when a lender took a charge over a property owned by two people in a personal relationship and where the money was being advanced to one of them. For the future, it is no longer sufficient for a solicitor acting for the party charging the property as security to the other to inform the bank that he has brought home the risks. The bank must, in a private meeting, explain the risks and urge the party to take legal advice. Their Lordships explained the core minimum of what that advice should contain and the information to be given to the legal adviser.

Removing a "Class F land charge"—If the charge under s 31 has been improperly registered, for example where the applicant is not in occupation of home and does not wish to enter (*Barnett v Hassett* [1982] 1 WLR 1385), the court can set aside the charge or injunct its removal. It is submitted, by analogy with *Poon v Poon* [1994] 2 FLR 857 (where it was held that a matrimonial court rather than a companies court should deal with the future of a company, by injunction if need be), that where a respondent is caused severe prejudice by registration of the charge, by for instance a bank refusing further borrowing, and the merits justify his application, the matrimonial court can set aside the charge.

32 Further provisions relating to matrimonial home rights

Schedule 4 re-enacts with consequential amendments and minor modifications provisions of the Matrimonial Homes Act 1983.

Scope of provision—This section relegates to FLA 1996, Sch 4 the technical conveyancing provisions formerly contained in Matrimonial Homes Act 1983, ss 3–6.

Occupation orders

33 Occupation orders where applicant has estate or interest etc or has matrimonial home rights

(1) If –

(*a*) a person ("the person entitled") –

(i) is entitled to occupy a dwelling-house by virtue of a beneficial estate or interest or contract or by virtue of any enactment giving him the right to remain in occupation, or

(ii) has matrimonial home rights in relation to a dwelling-house, and

(*b*) the dwelling-house –

(i) is or at any time has been the home of the person entitled and of another person with whom he is associated, or

(ii) was at any time intended by the person entitled and any such other person to be their home, the person entitled may apply to the court for an order containing any of the provisions specified in subsections (3), (4) and (5).

(2) If an agreement to marry is terminated, no application under this section may be made by virtue of section 62(3)(*e*) by reference to that agreement after the end of the period of three years beginning with the date on which it is terminated.

(3) An order under this section may –

(*a*) enforce the applicant's entitlement to remain in occupation as against the other person ("the respondent");

(*b*) require the respondent to permit the applicant to enter and remain in the dwelling-house or part of the dwelling-house;

(*c*) regulate the occupation of the dwelling-house by either or both parties;

(*d*) if the respondent is entitled as mentioned in subsection (1)(*a*)(i), prohibit, suspend or restrict the exercise by him of his right to occupy the dwelling-house;

(*e*) if the respondent has matrimonial home rights in relation to the dwelling-house and the applicant is the other spouse, restrict or terminate those rights;

(*f*) require the respondent to leave the dwelling-house or part of the dwelling-house; or

(*g*) exclude the respondent from a defined area in which the dwelling-house is included.

(4) An order under this section may declare that the applicant is entitled as mentioned in subsection (1)(*a*)(i) or has matrimonial home rights.

(5) If the applicant has matrimonial home rights and the respondent is the other spouse, an order under this section made during the marriage may provide that those rights are not brought to an end by –

(*a*) the death of the other spouse; or

(*b*) the termination (otherwise than by death) of the marriage.

(6) In deciding whether to exercise its powers under subsection (3) and (if so) in what manner, the court shall have regard to all the circumstances including –

(*a*) the housing needs and housing resources of each of the parties and of any relevant child;

(*b*) the financial resources of each of the parties;

(*c*) the likely effect of any order, or of any decision by the court not to exercise its powers under subsection (3), on the health, safety or well-being of the parties and of any relevant child; and

(*d*) the conduct of the parties in relation to each other and otherwise.

(7) If it appears to the court that the applicant or any relevant child is likely to suffer significant harm attributable to conduct of the respondent if an order under this section containing one or more of the provisions mentioned in subsection (3) is not made, the court shall make the order unless it appears to the court that –

(*a*) the respondent or any relevant child is likely to suffer significant harm if the order is made; and

(*b*) the harm likely to be suffered by the respondent or child in that event is as great as, or greater than, the harm attributable to conduct of the respondent which is likely to be suffered by the applicant or child if the order is not made.

(8) The court may exercise its powers under subsection (5) in any case where it considers that in all the circumstances it is just and reasonable to do so.

(9) An order under this section –

(*a*) may not be made after the death of either of the parties mentioned in subsection (1); and

(*b*) except in the case of an order made by virtue of subsection (5)(*a*), ceases to have effect on the death of either party.

(10) An order under this section may, in so far as it has continuing effect, be made for a specified period, until the occurrence of a specified event or until further order.

Defined terms—"associated": s 62(3); "relevant child": s 62(2).

Occupation orders – general—Sections 33 to 41 deal with occupation orders. Occupation orders can be made under five different sections, namely ss 33, 35, 36, 37 and 38. Under each section the court can make orders to regulate occupation of the home, to exclude the respondent from the home and the vicinity of the home and to prohibit, terminate or restrict the exercise of the respondent's occupation rights, as appropriate. The court's powers, the factors to which regard is to be had in deciding what, if any, order to make, and the maximum duration of orders, differ from section to section, each representing a self-contained code. It is therefore important that the order is made under the correct section.

Scope of provision—Section 33 is the only section under which occupation orders can be made which does not distinguish between spouses and cohabitants. Applications can be made under this section if three conditions are satisfied (s 33(1)), namely that the applicant "is entitled to occupy"; the respondent is "associated"; and the house was, is, or was intended to be their home. Thus the majority of occupation orders will be made under this section as most spouses will be entitled to occupy within s 33(1) by virtue of their interest in the property or matrimonial home rights. Many cohabitants too will be "entitled to occupy".

"matrimonial home rights"—See s 30.

Court's powers—These are set out in s 33(3) and include the power (previously referred to as an "ouster order") in s 33(3)(*f*) to require the respondent to leave the dwelling-house. There is no maximum duration for an order under s 33 (s 33(10)).

Criteria—The criteria to be applied by the court in deciding whether to exercise its powers are prescribed in s 33(6) but note also the "balance of harm" test in s 33(7).

The "balance of harm" test—Making or not making an order under s 33(3) inevitably causes some harm, and s 33(7) requires the court to balance the harm caused by not making an order against the harm that would be caused by making one. The wording of the section is important but, in summary, if it appears that the applicant or any relevant child is likely to suffer significant harm, attributable to conduct of the respondent, if an order is not made, then the court *shall* make the order unless it appears that the respondent or any relevant child is likely to suffer significant harm if the order is made and that harm is as great as, or greater than, the harm likely to be suffered by the applicant or child if the order is not made. The balance of harm test may well prove decisive in many cases and require the court to make the order in the applicant's favour. Even if the test is not decisive (because, for example, the harm would be equal) the court still could make the order having regard to the criteria in s 33(6). The court must consider s 33(7) before s 33(6) (*Chalmers v Johns* [1999] 1 FLR 392).

Extension of matrimonial home rights—The court has power to issue declarations under s 33(4) and to extend matrimonial home rights beyond death or dissolution (s 33(5), subject to s 33(8)). Save where a declaration has been made under s 33(5)(*a*), an order ceases to have effect on the death of either party (s 33(9)).

Form of order—See specimen clauses 1–12 in Form FL404 (set out in FPR 1991, App 1).

34 Effect of order under s 33 where rights are charge on dwelling-house

(1) If a spouse's matrimonial home rights are a charge on the estate or interest of the other spouse or of trustees for the other spouse –

(*a*) any order under section 33 against the other spouse has, except so far as a contrary intention appears, the same effect against persons deriving title under the other spouse or under the trustees and affected by the charge, and

(*b*) subsections 33(1), (3), (4) and (10) and 30(3) to (6) apply in relation to any person deriving title under the other spouse or under the trustees and affected by the charge as they apply in relation to the other spouse.

(2) The court may make an order under section 33 by virtue of subsection (1)(*b*) if it considers that in all the circumstances it is just and reasonable to do so.

35 One former spouse with no existing right to occupy

(1) This section applies if –

(*a*) one former spouse is entitled to occupy a dwelling-house by virtue of a beneficial estate or interest or contract, or by virtue of any enactment giving him the right to remain in occupation;

(*b*) the other former spouse is not so entitled; and

(*c*) the dwelling-house was at any time their matrimonial home or was at any time intended by them to be their matrimonial home.

(2) The former spouse not so entitled may apply to the court for an order under this section against the other former spouse ("the respondent").

(3) If the applicant is in occupation, an order under this section must contain provision –

(*a*) giving the applicant the right not to be evicted or excluded from the dwelling-house or any part of it by the respondent for the period specified in the order; and

(*b*) prohibiting the respondent from evicting or excluding the applicant during that period.

(4) If the applicant is not in occupation, an order under this section must contain provision –

(*a*) giving the applicant the right to enter into and occupy the dwelling-house for the period specified in the order; and

(*b*) requiring the respondent to permit the exercise of that right.

(5) An order under this section may also –

(*a*) regulate the occupation of the dwelling-house by either or both of the parties;

(*b*) prohibit, suspend or restrict the exercise by the respondent of his right to occupy the dwelling-house;

(*c*) require the respondent to leave the dwelling-house or part of the dwelling-house; or

(*d*) exclude the respondent from a defined area in which the dwelling-house is included.

(6) In deciding whether to make an order under this section containing provision of the kind mentioned in subsection (3) or (4) and (if so) in what manner, the court shall have regard to all the circumstances including –

(*a*) the housing needs and housing resources of each of the parties and of any relevant child;

(*b*) the financial resources of each of the parties;

(*c*) the likely effect of any order, or of any decision by the court not to exercise its powers under subsection (3) or (4), on the health, safety or well-being of the parties and of any relevant child;

(*d*) the conduct of the parties in relation to each other and otherwise;

(*e*) the length of time that has elapsed since the parties ceased to live together;

(*f*) the length of time that has elapsed since the marriage was dissolved or annulled; and

(*g*) the existence of any pending proceedings between the parties –

(i) for an order under section 23A or 24 of the Matrimonial Causes Act 1973 (property adjustment orders in connection with divorce proceedings etc);

(ii) for an order under paragraph 1(2)(*d*) or (*e*) of Schedule 1 to the Children Act 1989 (orders for financial relief against parents); or

(iii) relating to the legal or beneficial ownership of the dwelling-house.

(7) In deciding whether to exercise its power to include one or more of the provisions referred to in subsection (5) ("a subsection (5) provision") and (if so) in what manner, the court shall have regard to all the circumstances including the matters mentioned in subsection (6)(*a*) to (*e*).

(8) If the court decides to make an order under this section and it appears to it that, if the order does not include a subsection (5) provision, the applicant or any relevant child is likely to suffer significant harm attributable to conduct of the respondent, the court shall include the subsection (5) provision in the order unless it appears to the court that –

(*a*) the respondent or any relevant child is likely to suffer significant harm if the provision is included in the order; and

(*b*) the harm likely to be suffered by the respondent or child in that event is as great as or greater than the harm attributable to conduct of the respondent which is likely to be suffered by the applicant or child if the provision is not included.

(9) An order under this section –

(*a*) may not be made after the death of either of the former spouses; and

(*b*) ceases to have effect on the death of either of them.

(10) An order under this section must be limited so as to have effect for a specified period not exceeding six months, but may be extended on one or more occasions for a further specified period not exceeding six months.

(11) A former spouse who has an equitable interest in the dwelling-house or in the proceeds of sale of the dwelling-house but in whom there is not vested (whether solely or as joint tenant) a legal estate in fee simple or a legal term of years absolute in the dwelling-house is to be treated (but only for the purpose of determining whether he is eligible to apply under this section) as not being entitled to occupy the dwelling-house by virtue of that interest.

(12) Subsection (11) does not prejudice any right of such a former spouse to apply for an order under section 33.

(13) So long as an order under this section remains in force, subsections (3) to (6) of section 30 apply in relation to the applicant –

(*a*) as if he were the spouse entitled to occupy the dwelling-house by virtue of that section; and

(*b*) as if the respondent were the other spouse.

Occupation orders – general—See under s 33.

Scope of provision—Section 35 applies only to former spouses. There are three conditions (s 35(1), (2)): the applicant former spouse is not entitled to occupy; the respondent former spouse is entitled to occupy; and the dwelling-house in question was, or was intended to be, their matrimonial home.

Declarations—An order under s 35 must contain a declaration pursuant to s 35(3) or s 35(4), as appropriate.

Subsection (5) provisions—In addition to the appropriate declaration, an order may also contain any of the provisions referred to in s 35(5). This includes a provision requiring the respondent to leave the dwelling-house.

Criteria—The criteria are prescribed in subsections (6), (7) and (8). Section 35(6)(*a*), (*b*), (*c*) and (*d*) are the same as s 33(6)(*a*), (*b*), (*c*) and (*d*) but s 35(6)(*e*), (*f*) and (*g*) are additional factors. Section 35(7) limits the factors to be considered in deciding whether or not to include a "subsection (5) provision".

The "balance of harm" test—The "balance of harm" test in s 35(8) differs from the "balance of harm" test in s 33(7). For s 35(8) to apply, the court must first decide to make an order but is then required to "include a subsection (5) provision" if (in summary) not doing so would cause greater harm attributable to conduct of the respondent than doing so.

Duration—Section 35 orders can only be for a specified period not exceeding 6 months (s 35(10)) but can be extended on one or more occasions for a maximum of 6 months each time.

Form of order—See specimen clauses 13–18 in Form FL404 (set out in FPR 1991, App 1).

36 One cohabitant or former cohabitant with no existing right to occupy

(1) This section applies if –

(*a*) one cohabitant or former cohabitant is entitled to occupy a dwelling-house by virtue of a beneficial estate or interest or contract or by virtue of any enactment giving him the right to remain in occupation;

(*b*) the other cohabitant or former cohabitant is not so entitled; and

(*c*) that dwelling-house is the home in which they live together as husband and wife or a home in which they at any time so lived together or intended so to live together.

(2) The cohabitant or former cohabitant not so entitled may apply to the court for an order under this section against the other cohabitant or former cohabitant ("the respondent").

(3) If the applicant is in occupation, an order under this section must contain provision –

(*a*) giving the applicant the right not to be evicted or excluded from the dwelling-house or any part of it by the respondent for the period specified in the order, and

(*b*) prohibiting the respondent from evicting or excluding the applicant during that period.

(4) If the applicant is not in occupation, an order under this section must contain provision –

(*a*) giving the applicant the right to enter into and occupy the dwelling-house for the period specified in the order; and
(*b*) requiring the respondent to permit the exercise of that right.

(5) An order under this section may also –

(*a*) regulate the occupation of the dwelling-house by either or both of the parties;
(*b*) prohibit, suspend or restrict the exercise by the respondent of his right to occupy the dwelling-house;
(*c*) require the respondent to leave the dwelling-house or part of the dwelling-house; or
(*d*) exclude the respondent from a defined area in which the dwelling-house is included.

(6) In deciding whether to make an order under this section containing provision of the kind mentioned in subsection (3) or (4) and (if so) in what manner, the court shall have regard to all the circumstances including –

(*a*) the housing needs and housing resources of each of the parties and of any relevant child;
(*b*) the financial resources of each of the parties;
(*c*) the likely effect of any order, or of any decision by the court not to exercise its powers under subsection (3) or (4), on the health, safety or well-being of the parties and of any relevant child;
(*d*) the conduct of the parties in relation to each other and otherwise;
(*e*) the nature of the parties' relationship;
(*f*) the length of time during which they have lived together as husband and wife;
(*g*) whether there are or have been any children who are children of both parties or for whom both parties have or have had parental responsibility;
(*h*) the length of time that has elapsed since the parties ceased to live together; and
(*i*) the existence of any pending proceedings between the parties –
  (i) for an order under paragraph 1(2)(*d*) or (*e*) of Schedule 1 to the Children Act 1989 (orders for financial relief against parents), or
  (ii) relating to the legal or beneficial ownership of the dwelling-house.

(7) In deciding whether to exercise its powers to include one or more of the provisions referred to in subsection (5) ("a subsection (5) provision") and (if so) in what manner, the court shall have regard to all the circumstances including –

(*a*) the matters mentioned in subsection (6)(*a*) to (*d*); and
(*b*) the questions mentioned in subsection (8).

(8) The questions are –

(*a*) whether the applicant or any relevant child is likely to suffer significant harm attributable to conduct of the respondent if the subsection (5) provision is not included in the order; and
(*b*) whether the harm likely to be suffered by the respondent or child if the provision is included is as great as or greater than the harm attributable to conduct of the respondent which is likely to be suffered by the applicant or child if the provision is not included.

(9) An order under this section –

(*a*) may not be made after the death of either of the parties; and
(*b*) ceases to have effect on the death of either of them.

(10) An order under this section must be limited so as to have effect for a specified period not exceeding six months, but may be extended on one occasion for a further specified period not exceeding six months.

(11) A person who has an equitable interest in the dwelling-house or in the proceeds of sale of the dwelling-house but in whom there is not vested (whether solely or as joint tenant) a legal estate in fee simple or a legal term of years absolute in the dwelling-house is to be treated (but only for the purpose of determining whether he is eligible to apply under this section) as not being entitled to occupy the dwelling-house by virtue of that interest.

(12) Subsection (11) does not prejudice any right of such a person to apply for an order under section 33.

(13) So long as the order remains in force, subsections (3) to (6) of section 30 apply in relation to the applicant –

(*a*) as if he were a spouse entitled to occupy the dwelling-house by virtue of that section; and
(*b*) as if the respondent were the other spouse.

Occupation orders – general—See under s 33.

Scope of provision—Section 36 applies only to cohabitants and former cohabitants. (Applicants should first consider if they are eligible to apply under s 33.) There are three conditions for an application under s 36: namely that the applicant cohabitant, or former cohabitant, is not entitled to occupy; the respondent cohabitant, or former cohabitant, is entitled to occupy; and the dwelling-house in question is the home in which they live, did live or intended to live as husband and wife (s 36(1)).

Mandatory provisions—If the court does make an order under s 36 it must contain a provision under s 36(3) or s 36(4), as appropriate.

Discretionary provisions—The order may also contain any of the provisions in s 36(5). This includes requiring the respondent to leave the dwelling-house.

Criteria—The criteria are prescribed in s 36(6), (7) and (8).

"nature of the parties' relationship"(s 36(6)(*e*))—See also s 41 which may affect the court's decision whether or not to make an order, or as to the duration of any order made.

The "balance of harm" test—Note that the "balance of harm" test in s 36(8) is quite different from that in s 33(7) and s 35(8) as it imposes no duty on the court to make the order but merely requires the court to consider the questions posed.

Duration—A s 36 order is limited in time to 6 months and can be extended once only for a further period not exceeding 6 months (s 36(10)).

Form of order—See specimen clauses 13–18 in Form FL404 (set out in FPR 1991, App 1).

37 Neither spouse entitled to occupy

(1) This section applies if –

(*a*) one spouse or former spouse and the other spouse or former spouse occupy a dwelling-house which is or was the matrimonial home; but
(*b*) neither of them is entitled to remain in occupation –
(i) by virtue of a beneficial estate or interest or contract; or

(ii) by virtue of any enactment giving him the right to remain in occupation.

(2) Either of the parties may apply to the court for an order against the other under this section.

(3) An order under this section may –

(*a*) require the respondent to permit the applicant to enter and remain in the dwelling-house or part of the dwelling-house;
(*b*) regulate the occupation of the dwelling-house by either or both of the spouses;
(*c*) require the respondent to leave the dwelling-house or part of the dwelling-house; or
(*d*) exclude the respondent from a defined area in which the dwelling-house is included.

(4) Subsections (6) and (7) of section 33 apply to the exercise by the court of its powers under this section as they apply to the exercise by the court of its powers under subsection (3) of that section.

(5) An order under this section must be limited so as to have effect for a specified period not exceeding six months, but may be extended on one or more occasions for a further specified period not exceeding six months.

Occupation orders – general—See under s 33.

Scope of provision—An application under s 37 can be made if three conditions are satisfied: namely that the applicant is a spouse or former spouse; the respondent is the spouse or former spouse; and neither of them is entitled to occupy the dwelling-house which is or was the matrimonial home.

Applications under s 37 will be relatively rare but can be made, for example, where the parties occupy under a bare licence and the property is owned by trustees, or even where applicant and respondent are squatters.

Court's powers—The orders which the court can make are specified in s 37(3). This includes power to require the respondent to leave the dwelling-house.

Criteria—The criteria are the same as those set out in s 33(6).

The "balance of harm" test—The balance of harm test in s 33(7) applies (s 37(4)).

Duration—Orders can be for a maximum period of 6 months but can be extended on one or more occasions each for 6 months (s 37(5)).

Form of order—See specimen clauses 20–23 in Form FL404 (set out in FPR 1991, App 1).

38 Neither cohabitant or former cohabitant entitled to occupy

(1) This section applies if –

(*a*) one cohabitant or former cohabitant and the other cohabitant or former cohabitant occupy a dwelling-house which is the home in which they live or lived together as husband and wife; but
(*b*) neither of them is entitled to remain in occupation –
(i) by virtue of a beneficial estate or interest or contract; or
(ii) by virtue of any enactment giving him the right to remain in occupation.

(2) Either of the parties may apply to the court for an order against the other under this section.

PART II

(3) An order under this section may –

(*a*) require the respondent to permit the applicant to enter and remain in the dwelling-house or part of the dwelling-house;
(*b*) regulate the occupation of the dwelling-house by either or both of the parties;
(*c*) require the respondent to leave the dwelling-house or part of the dwelling-house; or
(*d*) exclude the respondent from a defined area in which the dwelling-house is included.

(4) In deciding whether to exercise its powers to include one or more of the provisions referred to in subsection (3) ("a subsection (3) provision") and (if so) in what manner, the court shall have regard to all the circumstances including –

(*a*) the housing needs and housing resources of each of the parties and of any relevant child;
(*b*) the financial resources of each of the parties;
(*c*) the likely effect of any order, or of any decision by the court not to exercise its powers under subsection (3), on the health, safety or well-being of the parties and of any relevant child;
(*d*) the conduct of the parties in relation to each other and otherwise; and
(*e*) the questions mentioned in subsection (5).

(5) The questions are –

(*a*) whether the applicant or any relevant child is likely to suffer significant harm attributable to conduct of the respondent if the subsection (3) provision is not included in the order; and
(*b*) whether the harm likely to be suffered by the respondent or child if the provision is included is as great as or greater than the harm attributable to conduct of the respondent which is likely to be suffered by the applicant or child if the provision is not included.

(6) An order under this section shall be limited so as to have effect for a specified period not exceeding six months, but may be extended on one occasion for a further specified period not exceeding six months.

Occupation orders – general—See under s 33.

Scope of provision—An application can be made under s 38 if the applicant is a cohabitant or former cohabitant, the respondent is the other cohabitant or former cohabitant and neither of them is entitled to occupy the dwelling-house which is the home in which they live or lived together as husband and wife.

Court's powers—The court's powers are in s 38(3). This includes power to require the respondent to leave the dwelling-house.

Criteria—The criteria to be applied are in s 38(4) and (5).

The "balance of harm" test—The "balance of harm" test in s 38(5) imposes no duty on the court to make the order (unlike s 33(7) and s 35(8)) and the balancing of the harm caused by making or not making the order is merely a factor to be considered.

Duration—Orders under s 38 can be for a maximum duration of 6 months only and can be extended once only (s 38(6)).

Form of order—See specimen clauses 20–23 in Form FL404 (set out in FPR 1991, App 1).

39 Supplementary provisions

(1) In this Part an "occupation order" means an order under section 33, 35, 36, 37 or 38.

(2) An application for an occupation order may be made in other family proceedings or without any other family proceedings being instituted.

(3) If –

(*a*) an application for an occupation order is made under section 33, 35, 36, 37 or 38, and

(*b*) the court considers that it has no power to make the order under the section concerned, but that it has power to make an order under one of the other sections,

the court may make an order under that other section.

(4) The fact that a person has applied for an occupation order under sections 35 to 38, or that an occupation order has been made, does not affect the right of any person to claim a legal or equitable interest in any property in any subsequent proceedings (including subsequent proceedings under this Part).

Scope of provision—Applications for occupation orders can be free-standing or ancillary to other family proceedings (s 39(2)). In either case the procedure is the same. Form FL401 is used to make the application (see Procedural Guide 10). Occupation orders often have to be sought at short notice where solicitors have to act on prima facie instructions, often given when the client is under emotional stress. It is inevitable, therefore, that despite every effort to proceed under the correct section, it may transpire at the hearing that the application has in fact been made under the wrong section. Section 39(3) prevents the court having to dismiss the application and gives it power to make the order as if the application had been made under the correct section.

Section 39(4) avoids an applicant being estopped from asserting an interest in the property. A misinformed applicant claiming a legal or beneficial interest will not be prejudiced by the fact that an application for an occupation order initially stated that the applicant had no interest in the property.

40 Additional provisions that may be included in certain occupation orders

(1) The court may on, or at any time after, making an occupation order under section 33, 35 or 36 –

(*a*) impose on either party obligations as to –

(i) the repair and maintenance of the dwelling-house; or

(ii) the discharge of rent, mortgage payments or other outgoings affecting the dwelling-house;

(*b*) order a party occupying the dwelling-house or any part of it (including a party who is entitled to do so by virtue of a beneficial estate or interest or contract or by virtue of any enactment giving him the right to remain in occupation) to make periodical payments to the other party in respect of the accommodation, if the other party would (but for the order) be entitled to occupy the dwelling-house by virtue of a beneficial estate or interest or contract or by virtue of any such enactment;

(*c*) grant either party possession or use of furniture or other contents of the dwelling-house;

(*d*) order either party to take reasonable care of any furniture or other contents of the dwelling-house;

(*e*) order either party to take reasonable steps to keep the dwelling-house and any furniture or other contents secure.

(2) In deciding whether and, if so, how to exercise its powers under this section, the court shall have regard to all the circumstances of the case including –

(*a*) the financial needs and financial resources of the parties; and

(*b*) the financial obligations which they have, or are likely to have in the foreseeable future, including financial obligations to each other and to any relevant child.

(3) An order under this section ceases to have effect when the occupation order to which it relates ceases to have effect.

Scope of provision—This section contains ancillary provisions which need to be considered in every case where an occupation order is sought under s 33, 35 or 36. Section 40(1)(*a*)(ii) enables the court, at the initial or a subsequent application, to order that rent or mortgage payments should be paid. It will sometimes be better, and certainly quicker, to obtain an order under this provision rather than, for example, making a separate application for maintenance pending suit. Under s 40(3) the additional provision cannot last longer than the occupation order itself. See **Duration** in the commentary to the relevant section. Unfortunately s 40 is seriously defective in that there is no procedure for enforcing compliance: "it was clear that orders under s 40 ... were unenforceable and of no value to the spouse or cohabitee remaining in occupation. That was a serious omission which required urgent alteration" (per Butler-Sloss P in (*Nwogbe v Nwogbe* [2000] 2 FLR 744). Thus s 40 is only of value if the respondent is likely to comply without the need for enforcement.

41 Additional considerations if parties are cohabitants or former cohabitants

(1) This section applies if the parties are cohabitants or former cohabitants.

(2) Where the court is required to consider the nature of the parties' relationship, it is to have regard to the fact that they have not given each other the commitment involved in marriage.

Scope of provision—This section only applies if the parties are cohabitants or former cohabitants. The "nature of the parties' relationship" is mentioned in s 36(6)(*e*) and does not appear in any of the other sections dealing with occupation orders. Arguably, therefore, s 41(2) is confined to applications under s 36.

Non-molestation orders

42 Non-molestation orders

(1) In this Part a "non-molestation order" means an order containing either or both of the following provisions –

(*a*) provision prohibiting a person ("the respondent") from molesting another person who is associated with the respondent;

(*b*) provision prohibiting the respondent from molesting a relevant child.

(2) The court may make a non-molestation order –

(*a*) if an application for the order has been made (whether in other family proceedings or without any other family proceedings being instituted) by a person who is associated with the respondent; or

(*b*) if in any family proceedings to which the respondent is a party the court considers that the order should be made for the benefit of any other party to the proceedings or any relevant child even though no such application has been made.

(3) In subsection (2) "family proceedings" includes proceedings in which the court has made an emergency protection order under section 44 of the Children Act 1989

which includes an exclusion requirement (as defined in section 44A(3) of that Act).

(4) Where an agreement to marry is terminated, no application under subsection (2)(*a*) may be made by virtue of section 62(3)(*e*) by reference to that agreement after the end of the period of three years beginning with the day on which it is terminated.

(5) In deciding whether to exercise its powers under this section and, if so, in what manner, the court shall have regard to all the circumstances including the need to secure the health, safety and well-being –

(*a*) of the applicant or, in a case falling within subsection (2)(*b*), the person for whose benefit the order would be made; and
(*b*) of any relevant child.

(6) A non-molestation order may be expressed so as to refer to molestation in general, to particular acts of molestation, or to both.

(7) A non-molestation order may be made for a specified period or until further order.

(8) A non-molestation order which is made in other family proceedings ceases to have effect if those proceedings are withdrawn or dismissed.

Defined terms—"associated": s 62(3); "relevant child": s 62(2).

Scope of provision—All non-molestation orders are now made under s 42.

"Molesting"—The term "molesting" is not defined in FLA 1996 and consequently pre-Act case-law continues to apply. "Molesting" has been judicially defined. "Molest" has been considered synonymous with "pester" (*Vaughan v Vaughan* [1973] 1 WLR 1159, [1973] 3 All ER 449) where the court considered the definition of molestation in the *Shorter Oxford Dictionary*, namely "to cause trouble; to vex; to annoy; to put to inconvenience". It has been held to include conduct which does not amount to violent behaviour (*Davis v Johnson* [1979] AC 264 at 334). The term "molest" applies to any conduct which can properly be regarded as constituting such a degree of harassment as to call for the intervention of the court (*Horner v Horner* [1982] Fam 96, (1983) FLR 50; *C v C* [2001] EWCA Civ 1625). Repeated telephoning can amount to molestation (*Burnett v George* [1992] 1 FLR 525). The court has a wide discretion whether to grant or refuse the relief sought (see *C v C (Non-Molestation Order: Jurisdiction)* [1998] 1 FLR 554 and *Chechi v Bashier* [1999] 2 FLR 489, both cases where injunctions under s 42 were refused). Form FL404 contains specimen clauses for use in non-molestation orders (set out in FPR 1991, App 1). These orders do not in fact use the term "molest" but prefer the term "harass". It has been suggested that the term "harass" is more readily understood by the respondents to whom orders are addressed and that the term "molest" has unfortunate sexual connotations.

Criteria—The criteria for the making of a non-molestation order are in s 42(5), namely "all the circumstances including the need to secure the health, safety and well-being of the applicant or of any relevant child". The following three principles should be considered when deciding whether to grant a non-molestation injunction:

(*a*) there must be evidence of molestation (*Spindlow v Spindlow* [1979] Fam 52, (1980) FLR 133; *C v C (Non-Molestation Order: Jurisdiction)* [1998] 1 FLR 554);
(*b*) the applicant (or child) must need protection; and
(*c*) the judge must be satisfied on the balance of probabilities that judicial intervention is required to control the behaviour which is the subject of the complaint (see eg *C v C* [2001] EWCA Civ 1625).

Form of order—The order can refer to molestation in general, particular acts of molestation or both (s 42(6)). See specimen clauses 38–41 in Form FL404 (set out in FPR 1991, App 1).

Ex parte applications—See notes to s 45.

PART II

Duration—By virtue of s 42(7) the order can be for a specified period or until further order. An injunction made "until further order" will last until such time as either the applicant or respondent applies to discharge it (see s 49): such orders are made only in exceptional cases, eg where there is a history of expired injunctions. It is established practice to stipulate a time-limit in the majority of cases. Obsolete Practice Notes issued under the old law suggested that "a period of up to three months is likely to suffice". Three months should be regarded as a minimum but experience shows that an order as short as this is often insufficient (see eg *Research Findings No 46 – Home Office Research and Statistics Directorate*). Orders are frequently made for six months, a year or longer duration where the case so requires (see eg *Galan v Galan* [1985] FLR 905; *Horgan v Horgan* [2002] All ER (D) 95). Application can be made to vary, extend, or discharge an order (see FPR 1991, r 3.9(8)).

Forms—The form of application is Form FL401, and the order is in Form FL404.

Power of arrest—See under s 47.

Undertakings—See notes to s 46.

Service of application—Not less than two clear days before the hearing date unless otherwise ordered (FPR 1991, r 3.8(6)).

Service of order—Both orders made ex parte and at an inter partes hearing must be served on the respondent personally (FPR 1991, r 3.9(2), (4)).

Further provisions relating to occupation and non-molestation orders

43 Leave of court required for applications by children under sixteen

(1) A child under the age of sixteen may not apply for an occupation order or a non-molestation order except with the leave of the court.

(2) The court may grant leave for the purposes of subsection (1) only if it is satisfied that the child has sufficient understanding to make the proposed application for the occupation order or non-molestation order.

Scope of provision—Applications for leave under this section must be made to a High Court judge. The application is made in the usual way in Form FL401 (there is a misprint in the relevant rule which refers to form FLA401 – there is no such form) but the application is treated in the first instance as an application for leave (FPR 1991, r 3.8(2)).

44 Evidence of agreement to marry

(1) Subject to subsection (2) the court shall not make an order under section 33 or 42 by virtue of section 62(3)(*e*) unless there is produced to it evidence in writing of the existence of the agreement to marry.

(2) Subsection (1) does not apply if the court is satisfied that the agreement to marry was evidenced by –

(*a*) the gift of an engagement ring by one party to the agreement to the other in contemplation of their marriage, or

(*b*) a ceremony entered into by the parties in the presence of one or more other persons assembled for the purpose of witnessing the ceremony.

Scope of provision—Engaged couples are "associated persons" within the definition in s 62(3)(*e*). However, s 44 requires this to be a formal engagement and defines the required evidence.

45 Ex parte orders

(1) The court may, in any case where it considers that it is just and convenient to do so, make an occupation order or a non-molestation order even though the respondent has not been given such notice of the proceedings as would otherwise be required by rules of court.

(2) In determining whether to exercise its powers under subsection (1), the court shall have regard to all the circumstances including –

(*a*) any risk of significant harm to the applicant or a relevant child, attributable to conduct of the respondent, if the order is not made immediately;

(*b*) whether it is likely that the applicant will be deterred or prevented from pursuing the application if an order is not made immediately; and

(*c*) whether there is reason to believe that the respondent is aware of the proceedings but is deliberately evading service and that the applicant or a relevant child will be seriously prejudiced by the delay involved –

(i) where the court is a magistrates' court, in effecting service of proceedings; or

(ii) in any other case, in effecting substituted service.

(3) If the court makes an order by virtue of subsection (1) it must afford the respondent an opportunity to make representations relating to the order as soon as just and convenient at a full hearing.

(4) If, at a full hearing, the court makes an occupation order ("the full order"), then –

(*a*) for the purposes of calculating the maximum period for which the full order may be made to have effect, the relevant section is to apply as if the period for which the full order will have effect began on the date on which the initial order first had effect; and

(*b*) the provisions of section 36(10) or 38(6) as to the extension of orders are to apply as if the full order and the initial order were a single order.

(5) In this section –

"full hearing" means a hearing of which notice has been given to all the parties in accordance with rules of court;

"initial order" means an occupation order made by virtue of subsection (1); and

"relevant section" means section 33(10), 35(10), 36(10), 37(5) or 38(6).

Scope of provision—It has long been established practice to make orders on an ex parte basis where the circumstances of the case justify this exceptional course. Under s 45 the court can only make an ex parte order where it is "just and convenient" and, although s 45(1) enables the court to make either an occupation order or a non-molestation order even though the respondent has not been served, there is an important difference of approach between these two different types of order. It is recognised that victims of domestic violence often need immediate protection which can be effectively granted only on an ex parte basis. As the respondent has no legal right to inflict or threaten violence, it follows that his legal rights are not infringed by a non-molestation order. This may be quite different in the case of an occupation order and it will be extremely unusual to deprive a respondent of his home on an ex parte basis. Unlike non-molestation orders, occupation orders override proprietary rights (*Chalmers v Johns* [1999] 1 FLR 392). In *G v G (Ouster: Ex parte application)* [1990] 1 FLR 395 and *Masich v Masich* (1977) Fam Law 245 it was stated that ouster or exclusion orders should seldom be granted ex parte. This still applies to occupation orders, and although the court clearly has power under s 45(1) to make an ex parte occupation order, this is reserved for exceptional cases only. An application on notice requires only 2 days' notice (FPR 1991, r 3.8(6)) and the court has power to abridge time (r 3.8(7)). Even though the court may not feel able to grant an ex parte occupation order, it will invariably grant an ex parte non-molestation order pending the hearing of the application for an occupation order on notice.

Full hearing—Whenever an order has been made ex parte there must be a full hearing as soon as just and convenient thereafter. This will normally take place within a week.

The Act does not in fact require the ex parte order to be limited in time. However, any ex parte order must contain a specific date for a full hearing and it would not, for example, be a sufficient compliance with s 45(3) for an ex parte order to be made for twelve months merely giving the respondent liberty to apply to vary or revoke it. Most judges now take the view that an ex parte order should be for a period of (say) six months provided that the order is reconsidered promptly at a full inter partes hearing. This practice has the advantage that, if no change is required in the terms of the order (as often proves to be the case), no further order needs to be made, drawn up and served, thus saving time and costs. It is submitted that this practice is preferable to making an order for, say, just 14 days. However, if such a short order is made the ex parte order should at least extend beyond the date of the full hearing, as otherwise there is a risk of the applicant being left without protection during the gap between expiry of the ex parte order and service of the inter partes order. In *Horgan v Horgan* [2002] All ER (D) 95 the Court of Appeal, commenting on an ex parte order, stated that it was just to make the order run for one year.

46 Undertakings

(1) In any case where the court has power to make an occupation order or non-molestation order, the court may accept an undertaking from any party to the proceedings.

(2) No power of arrest may be attached to any undertaking given under subsection (1).

(3) The court shall not accept an undertaking under subsection (1) in any case where apart from this section a power of arrest would be attached to the order.

(4) An undertaking given to a court under subsection (1) is enforceable as if it were an order of the court.

(5) This section has effect without prejudice to the powers of the High Court and the county court apart from this section.

Scope of provision—Where an undertaking is given it may be enforced as if it were an injunction (s 46(4)), ie as a contempt of court punishable by committal proceedings. An undertaking is a promise by the respondent to the court, not to the other party. Powers of arrest cannot be attached to undertakings (s 46(2)).

Procedure—The following procedural points arise in connection with undertakings:

(*a*) *Recording of undertaking* The undertaking should be in Form N117. It should be explained to the respondent by the judge and the respondent asked to sign it.

(*b*) *Mutual undertakings* Where both parties give undertakings, two separate forms must be used.

(*c*) *Service of undertakings* The court must provide a copy of the undertaking to the person who has given it and it is good practice to provide a copy also to the applicant. This may be effected by handing a copy to him before he leaves the court building, by posting him a copy, through his solicitor or, if none of these is practical, by personal service (CCR Ord 29, r 1A). The better practice is for a copy of the undertaking to be given to both parties before they leave the court building. In any event the court clerk must record the way in which delivery was effected in the relevant box on the back of Form N117.

(*d*) *Judge's responsibility* Where an undertaking is to be given, the judge has the following responsibilities:

- (i) to approve the terms of the proposed promises.
- (ii) to ensure that the giver of the undertaking understands what has been promised and the consequences of breach.
- (iii) to consider whether the signature of the giver should be included in the box on the back of Form N117 in order to avoid argument about what happened when the undertaking was given; and
- (iv) where an undertaking is given in the absence of the giver through his advocate, to ensure that the advocate has been given specific instructions to give the undertaking and that the giver understands the consequences of breach. (In practice it is rare for undertakings to be taken in the absence of the giver.)

Restriction on undertakings (s 46(3))—By virtue of s 46(3) the court is prohibited from accepting an undertaking in any case where a power of arrest would be attached to the order. In fact the requirement to impose a power of arrest is "almost mandatory" (per Butler-Sloss LJ in *Chechi v Bashier* [1999] 2 FLR 489 at 495, commenting on s 47). It follows that powers of arrest are the rule rather than the exception and that undertakings are the exception rather than the rule.

PART II

47 Arrest for breach of order

(1) In this section "a relevant order" means an occupation order or a non-molestation order.

(2) If –

(*a*) the court makes a relevant order; and
(*b*) it appears to the court that the respondent has used or threatened violence against the applicant or a relevant child,

it shall attach a power of arrest to one or more provisions of the order unless the court is satisfied that in all the circumstances of the case the applicant or child will be adequately protected without such a power of arrest.

(3) Subsection (2) does not apply in any case where the relevant order is made by virtue of section 45(1), but in such a case the court may attach a power of arrest to one or more provisions of the order if it appears to it –

(*a*) that the respondent has used or threatened violence against the applicant or a relevant child; and
(*b*) that there is a risk of significant harm to the applicant or child, attributable to conduct of the respondent, if the power of arrest is not attached to those provisions immediately.

(4) If, by virtue of subsection (3), the court attaches a power of arrest to any provisions of a relevant order, it may provide that the power of arrest is to have effect for a shorter period than the other provisions of the order.

(5) Any period specified for the purposes of subsection (4) may be extended by the court (on one or more occasions) on an application to vary or discharge the relevant order.

(6) If, by virtue of subsection (2) or (3), a power of arrest is attached to certain provisions of an order, a constable may arrest without warrant a person whom he has reasonable cause for suspecting to be in breach of any such provision.

(7) If a power of arrest is attached under subsection (2) or (3) to certain provisions of the order and the respondent is arrested under subsection (6) –

(*a*) he must be brought before the relevant judicial authority within the period of 24 hours beginning at the time of his arrest; and
(*b*) if the matter is not then disposed of forthwith, the relevant judicial authority before whom he is brought may remand him.

In reckoning for the purposes of this subsection any period of 24 hours, no account is to be taken of Christmas Day, Good Friday or any Sunday.

(8) If the court has made a relevant order but –

(*a*) has not attached a power of arrest under subsection (2) or (3) above to any provisions of the order, or
(*b*) has attached that power only to certain provisions of the order,

then, if at any time the applicant considers that the respondent has failed to comply with the order, he may apply to the relevant judicial authority for the issue of a warrant for the arrest of the respondent.

(9) The relevant judicial authority shall not issue a warrant on an application under subsection (8) unless –

(*a*) the application is substantiated on oath; and
(*b*) the relevant judicial authority has reasonable grounds for believing that the respondent has failed to comply with the order.

(10) If a person is brought before a court by virtue of a warrant issued under subsection (9) and the court does not dispose of the matter forthwith, the court may remand him.

(11) Schedule 5 (which makes provision corresponding to that applying in magistrates' courts in civil cases under sections 128 and 129 of the Magistrates' Courts Act 1980) has effect in relation to the powers of the High Court and a county court to remand a person by virtue of this section.

(12) If a person remanded under this section is granted bail (whether in the High Court or a county court under Schedule 5 or in a magistrates' court under section 128 or 129 of the Magistrates' Courts Act 1980), he may be required by the relevant judicial authority to comply, before release on bail or later, with such requirements as appear to that authority to be necessary to secure that he does not interfere with witnesses or otherwise obstruct the course of justice.

Powers of arrest—There is no inherent power to attach a power of arrest. The power of arrest was initially introduced in a restrictive way by Domestic Violence and Matrimonial Proceedings Act 1976 but s 47 is in much wider terms than the old law. The requirement to impose a power of arrest is "almost mandatory". "Although the court has a wide discretion whether to grant or refuse the relief sought, it does not have the same flexibility whether to attach a power of arrest if the facts come within s 47(2)(*b*) where the respondent has used or threatened violence. This appears to be deliberate policy." (per Butler-Sloss LJ in *Chechi v Bashier* [1999] 2 FLR 489 at 495). The court is required to attach a power of arrest unless satisfied that in all the circumstances the applicant or child will be adequately protected without it (which would be a matter for evidence, not just submissions). Therefore, powers of arrest are now the rule rather than the exception and are attached to virtually all non-molestation orders.

Ex parte orders—A power of arrest can be attached to an ex parte order. The criteria are set out in s 47(3). The court has to be satisfied that the respondent has used or threatened violence and that there is a risk of significant harm if a power of arrest is not attached. The power of arrest must be announced in open court: see *President's Direction of 17 December 1997 (Family Law Act 1996, Part IV)*.

Order—The clauses of an injunction to which a power of arrest is attached must be separate from non-arrestable clauses. The relevant provisions to which a power of arrest is attached must be set out in Form FL406, and the form must include *only* those provisions to which a power of arrest has been attached (FPR 1991, r 3.9A).

Duration—Section 47(4) expressly enables the court when attaching a power of arrest to an ex parte order to provide that the power of arrest is to have effect for a shorter period than the other provisions of the order. This provision is rarely used and a more pressing question has been whether the court has a similar power in the case of full orders. For example, if the court makes an injunction to last "until further order" (see s 42) can it attach a power of arrest to last for (say) two years? The Court of Appeal has answered this question affirmatively (see *Re B-J (Power of Arrest)* [2000] 2 FLR 443, overruling *M v W (Non-Molestation Order: Duration)* [2000] 1 FLR 107). Hale LJ commented that: "anecdote suggests that such orders are not uncommon" and held that s 47(2) is wide enough to permit it.

Delivery to police station—By virtue of FPR 1991, r 3.9A(1)(*b*) a copy of Form FL406 must be delivered to the officer for the time being in charge of any police station for the applicant's address or of such other police station as the court may specify. The form must be accompanied by a statement showing that the respondent has been served with the order or informed of its terms (whether by being present when the order was made or by telephone or otherwise). Thus the police must only be notified of the power of arrest after the respondent has been notified. Where the relevant police authority has a Domestic Violence Unit which deals with all domestic violence cases within its area, it may be sensible to specify the address of the police station where the unit is located as the appropriate police station to be served with the FL406, rather than the police station for the applicant's address.

Arrest without warrant—The significance of a power of arrest is that, pursuant to s 47(6), a constable may arrest without warrant any person whom he has reasonable cause for suspecting to be in breach of the order to which the power has been attached. Any person arrested must then be brought before the relevant judicial authority within 24 hours. Where a person arrested under a power of arrest cannot conveniently be brought to a courtroom, he may be brought before the relevant judicial authority at any convenient place: see *President's Direction of 17 December 1997 (Family Law Act 1996, Part IV)*. If the person arrested is not dealt with immediately the court has power to remand under Sch 5. Remand can be on bail or in custody.

Warrant of arrest—Section 47(8) provides a procedure which involves the police even in cases where no power of arrest has been attached. As an alternative to applying for an order for committal under CCR Ord 29 the applicant can apply to the court for a warrant for arrest. The police will then arrest the respondent and bring him before the court.

Unfortunately the useful provisions relating to warrants are restricted. It is clear from the wording of s 47(8) that a warrant cannot be applied for in a case where the order does contain a power of arrest but where the respondent has not in fact been arrested pursuant to it. In such circumstances the applicant must apply to commit by notice to show cause in Form N78. It is uncertain whether a warrant of arrest can be issued to enforce an undertaking. Section 47(8) refers to "a relevant order" which is defined in s 47(1) where undertakings are not mentioned. Although s 46(4) provides that an undertaking can be enforced "as if it were an order of the court", that may be limited to the court's powers to commit. Orders are enforced by committal. Arrest is not a method of enforcement but rather a means of bringing an alleged contemnor before the court for the purpose of enforcement. The alternative argument is that the court can only accept an undertaking where it "has power to make an occupation order or non-molestation order" (s 46(1)) and that each of these is "a relevant order" within s 47(1) and therefore must be enforceable by warrants of arrest pursuant to s 47(8). Certainly the draftsman of Form FL407 (application for a warrant of arrest) considers that a warrant can be issued to enforce both orders and undertakings. As any arrest which is not "in accordance with a procedure prescribed by law" is a breach of European Convention on Human Rights, Art 5 (incorporated directly into English law by Human Rights Act 1998), the better view is the former, ie a warrant of arrest will not be issued to enforce an undertaking.

Remand—Magistrates' courts have power to remand in civil cases under Magistrates' Courts Act 1980, ss 128, 129. FLA 1996, Sch 5 gives a similar power to the High Court and county courts.

48 Remand for medical examination and report

(1) If the relevant judicial authority has reason to consider that a medical report will be required, any power to remand a person under section 47(7)(*b*) or (10) may be exercised for the purpose of enabling a medical examination and report to be made.

(2) If such a power is so exercised, the adjournment must not be for more than 4 weeks at a time unless the relevant judicial authority remands the accused in custody.

(3) If the relevant judicial authority so remands the accused, the adjournment must not be for more than 3 weeks at a time.

(4) If there is reason to suspect that a person who has been arrested –

(*a*) under section 47(6), or
(*b*) under a warrant issued on an application made under section 47(8),

is suffering from mental illness or severe mental impairment, the relevant judicial authority has the same power to make an order under section 35 of the Mental Health Act 1983 (remand for report on accused's mental condition) as the Crown Court has under section 35 of the Act of 1983 in the case of an accused person within the meaning of that section.

Remand—Remands in custody are normally limited to 8 days (Sch 5, para 2(5)). Section 48 enables remands in custody to be for up to three weeks if the remand is for the purpose of a medical report. The section is silent on the question of who is to pay for the medical report. If the person to be medically examined is publicly funded, the Legal Services Commission will pay pursuant to the order of the court. If he is not publicly funded, no doubt, in an appropriate case, a party can be ordered to pay but quaere whether the prison to which he is remanded can be required to obtain the medical report and/or the court service be required to fund it.

For the powers of the court to make a hospital order once the medical report has been obtained see Contempt of Court Act 1981, s 14 and the sections of the Mental Health Act 1983 there referred to. See also FPR 1991, r 3.9A.

49 Variation and discharge of orders

(1) An occupation order or non-molestation order may be varied or discharged by the court on an application by –

(*a*) the respondent, or
(*b*) the person on whose application the order was made.

(2) In the case of a non-molestation order made by virtue of section 42(2)(*b*), the order may be varied or discharged by the court even though no such application has been made.

(3) If a spouse's matrimonial home rights are a charge on the estate or interest of the other spouse or of trustees for the other spouse, an order under section 33 against the other spouse may also be varied or discharged by the court on an application by any person deriving title under the other spouse or under the trustees and affected by the charge.

(4) If, by virtue of section 47(3), a power of arrest has been attached to certain provisions of an occupation order or non-molestation order, the court may vary or discharge the order under subsection (1) in so far as it confers a power of arrest (whether or not any application has been made to vary or discharge any other provision of the order).

Enforcement powers of magistrates' courts

50 Power of magistrates' court to suspend execution of committal order

(1) If, under section 63(3) of the Magistrates' Courts Act 1980, a magistrates' court has power to commit a person to custody for breach of a relevant requirement, the court may by order direct that the execution of the order of committal is to be suspended for such period or on such terms and conditions as it may specify.

(2) In subsection (1) "a relevant requirement" means –

(*a*) an occupation order or non-molestation order;
(*b*) an exclusion requirement included by virtue of section 38A of the Children Act 1989 in an interim care order made under section 38 of that Act; or

(*c*) an exclusion requirement included by virtue of section 44A of the Children Act 1989 in an emergency protection order under section 44 of that Act.

51 Power of magistrates' court to order hospital admission or guardianship

(1) A magistrates' court shall have the same power to make a hospital order or guardianship order under section 37 of the Mental Health Act 1983 or an interim hospital order under section 38 of that Act in the case of a person suffering from mental illness or severe mental impairment who could otherwise be committed to custody for breach of a relevant requirement as a magistrates' court has under those sections in the case of a person convicted of an offence punishable on summary conviction with imprisonment.

(2) In subsection (1) "a relevant requirement" has the meaning given by section 50(2).

****

Transfer of tenancies

53 Transfer of certain tenancies

Schedule 7 makes provision in relation to the transfer of certain tenancies on divorce etc or on separation of cohabitants.

Defined terms—"cohabitants": s 62(1).

Scope of provision—This section and FLA 1996, Sch 7 (which re-enact Matrimonial Homes Act 1983, s 7 and Sch 1) provide the court with the power to transfer tenancies, including statutory tenancies. By virtue of Matrimonial Causes Act 1973, s 24, the court has jurisdiction to transfer a contractual tenancy where there is no covenant against assignment, but it has no power to transfer a statutory tenancy because that is not within the definition of property. Under Sch 7 the court has jurisdiction to transfer a contractual tenancy and may do so even where there is a covenant against assignment (although whether the court will, in its discretion, exercise its jurisdiction to transfer when there is such a covenant remains to be seen). It also has jurisdiction under Sch 7 to transfer a statutory tenancy. However, in contrast to the old provisions of MHA 1983, Sch 1, Sch 7 contains two new powers: first, tenancies of cohabitants can be transferred; and secondly, the party to whom the tenancy is being transferred can be ordered to make a payment to the other.

Prevention of unilateral termination of tenancy—As set out in Procedural Guide 12, a tenancy in the other spouse's name or in joint names can be destroyed unilaterally by surrender or notice to quit. Once the tenancy is surrendered it is lost and therefore a party should ask the other tenant for an undertaking not to surrender it. If the undertaking is given, it should be served on the landlord. If it is not given, application should be made for an injunction to prevent the tenancy being surrendered and, once made, the injunction order should be served on the landlord (*Bater v Greenwich London Borough Council* [1999] 2 FLR 993).

Dwelling-house subject to mortgage

54 Dwelling-house subject to mortgage

(1) In determining for the purposes of this Part whether a person is entitled to occupy a dwelling-house by virtue of an estate or interest, any right to possession of the dwelling-house conferred on a mortgagee of the dwelling-house under or by virtue of his mortgage is to be disregarded.

(2) Subsection (1) applies whether or not the mortgagee is in possession.

(3) Where a person ("A") is entitled to occupy a dwelling-house by virtue of an estate or interest, a connected person does not by virtue of –

(*a*) any matrimonial home rights conferred by section 30, or
(*b*) any rights conferred by an order under section 35 or 36,

have any larger right against the mortgagee to occupy the dwelling-house than A has by virtue of his estate or interest and of any contract with the mortgagee.

(4) Subsection (3) does not apply, in the case of matrimonial home rights, if under section 31 those rights are a charge, affecting the mortgagee, on the estate or interest mortgaged.

(5) In this section "connected person", in relation to any person, means that person's spouse, former spouse, cohabitant or former cohabitant.

Defined terms—"cohabitant", "former cohabitant": s 62(1); "dwelling-house": s 63(1), (4); "matrimonial home rights": s 30.

55 Actions by mortgagees: joining connected persons as parties

(1) This section applies if a mortgagee of land which consists of or includes a dwelling-house brings an action in any court for the enforcement of his security.

(2) A connected person who is not already a party to the action is entitled to be made a party in the circumstances mentioned in subsection (3).

(3) The circumstances are that –

(*a*) the connected person is enabled by section 30(3) or (6) (or by section 30(3) or (6) as applied by section 35(13) or 36(13)), to meet the mortgagor's liabilities under the mortgage;
(*b*) he has applied to the court before the action is finally disposed of in that court; and
(*c*) the court sees no special reason against his being made a party to the action and is satisfied –
 (i) that he may be expected to make such payments or do such other things in or towards satisfaction of the mortgagor's liabilities or obligations as might affect the outcome of the proceedings; or
 (ii) that the expectation of it should be considered under section 36 of the Administration of Justice Act 1970.

(4) In this section "connected person" has the same meaning as in section 54.

Defined terms—"cohabitant", "former cohabitant": s 62(1); "dwelling-house": s 63(1), (4); "matrimonial home rights": s 30.

Scope of provision—This section which is based on Matrimonial Homes Act 1983, s 8(2) entitles the spouse, cohabitant, former spouse or former cohabitant to be made a party in mortgage possession proceedings.

56 Actions by mortgagees: service of notice on certain persons

(1) This section applies if a mortgagee of land which consists, or substantially consists, of a dwelling-house brings an action for the enforcement of his security, and at the relevant time there is –

(*a*) in the case of unregistered land, a land charge of Class F registered against the person who is the estate owner at the relevant time or any person who, where the estate owner is a trustee, preceded him as trustee during the subsistence of the mortgage; or

(*b*) in the case of registered land, a subsisting registration of –

(i) a notice under section 31(10);

(ii) a notice under section 2(8) of the Matrimonial Homes Act 1983; or

(iii) a notice or caution under section 2(7) of the Matrimonial Homes Act 1967.

(2) If the person on whose behalf –

(*a*) the land charge is registered, or

(*b*) the notice or caution is entered,

is not a party to the action, the mortgagee must serve notice of the action on him.

(3) If –

(*a*) an official search has been made on behalf of the mortgagee which would disclose any land charge of Class F, notice or caution within subsection (1)(*a*) or (*b*),

(*b*) a certificate of the result of the search has been issued, and

(*c*) the action is commenced within the priority period,

the relevant time is the date of the certificate.

(4) In any other case the relevant time is the time when the action is commenced.

(5) The priority period is, for both registered and unregistered land, the period for which, in accordance with section 11(5) and (6) of the Land Charges Act 1972, a certificate on an official search operates in favour of a purchaser.

Defined terms—"dwelling-house": s 63(1), (4); "mortgage": s 63(1).

Jurisdiction and procedure etc

57 Jurisdiction of courts

(1) For the purposes of this Act "the court" means the High Court, a county court or a magistrates' court.

(2) Subsection (1) above is subject to the provision made by or under the following provisions of this section, to section 59 and to any express provision as to the jurisdiction of any court made by any other provision of this Part.

(3) The Lord Chancellor may by order specify proceedings under this Act which may only be commenced in –

(*a*) a specified level of court;

(*b*) a court which falls within a specified class of court; or

(*c*) a particular court determined in accordance with, or specified in, the order.

(4) The Lord Chancellor may by order specify circumstances in which specified proceedings under this Part may only be commenced in –

(*a*) a specified level of court;

(*b*) a court which falls within a specified class of court; or

(*c*) a particular court determined in accordance with, or specified in, the order.

(5) The Lord Chancellor may by order provide that in specified circumstances the whole, or any specified part of any specified proceedings under this Part shall be transferred to –

(*a*) a specified level of court;

(*b*) a court which falls within a specified class of court; or
(*c*) a particular court determined in accordance with, or specified in, the order.

(6) An order under subsection (5) may provide for the transfer to be made at any stage, or specified stage, of the proceedings and whether or not the proceedings, or any part of them, have already been transferred.

(7) An order under subsection (5) may make provision as the Lord Chancellor thinks appropriate for excluding specified proceedings from the operation of section 38 or 39 of the Matrimonial and Family Proceedings Act 1984 (transfer of family proceedings) or any other enactment which would otherwise govern the transfer of those proceedings, or any part of them.

(8) For the purposes of subsections (3), (4) and (5), there are three levels of court –

(*a*) the High Court;
(*b*) any county court; and
(*c*) any magistrates' court.

(9) The Lord Chancellor may by order make provision for the principal registry of the Family Division of the High Court to be treated as if it were a county court for specified purposes of this Part, or of any provision made under this Part.

(10) Any order under subsection (9) may make such provision as the Lord Chancellor thinks expedient for the purpose of applying (with or without modifications) provisions which apply in relation to the procedure in county courts to the principal registry when it acts as if it were a county court.

(11) In this section "specified" means specified by an order under this section.

Family Law Act 1996 (Part IV) (Allocation of Proceedings) Order 1997—This Order ("the 1997 Order") was made by the Lord Chancellor pursuant to this section, and came into force on 1 October 1997.

Applications under FLA 1996, Pt IV are family proceedings and are governed by FPR 1991. Thus non-molestation injunctions and occupation orders cannot be obtained in all county courts but only in divorce county courts (designated under Matrimonial and Family Proceedings Act 1984, s 33), family hearing centres (set out in Children (Allocation of Proceedings) Order 1991, Sch 1) and care centres (set out in C(AP)O 1991, Sch 2). Furthermore, not all magistrates' courts will have jurisdiction but only those that are family proceedings courts so constituted in accordance with Magistrates' Courts Act 1980, s 67.

The 1997 Order provides for transfer both vertically (in both directions) and horizontally. The Principal Registry of the Family Division is treated for the purposes of the 1997 Order as if it were a divorce county court, a family hearing centre and a care centre. Further, art 17 of the 1997 Order provides that Part IV proceedings may be commenced in, transferred to or tried in Lambeth, Shoreditch or Woolwich County Courts.

58 Contempt proceedings

The powers of the court in relation to contempt of court arising out of a person's failure to comply with an order under this Part may be exercised by the relevant judicial authority.

Defined terms—"relevant judicial authority": s 63.

"contempt of court"—The term is of ancient origin and has been in use since at least the 13th century. The court's powers to punish for contempt of court are in the Contempt of Court Act 1981. Committal must be for a specified (not sine die) period not exceeding two years. Proceedings for committal for contempt of court in a civil action are civil proceedings. Nevertheless the appropriate standard of proof to be applied in committal proceedings is the criminal standard of proof (*Dean v Dean* [1987] 1 FLR 517). An order of committal must be made in a courtroom open to the public or announced in open court at the earliest opportunity: see *President's Direction of 17 December 1997 (Family Law Act 1996, Part IV).*

59 Magistrates' courts

(1) A magistrates' court shall not be competent to entertain any application, or make any order, involving any disputed question as to a party's entitlement to occupy any property by virtue of a beneficial estate or interest or contract or by virtue of any enactment giving him the right to remain in occupation, unless it is unnecessary to determine the question in order to deal with the application or make the order.

(2) A magistrates' court may decline jurisdiction in any proceedings under this Part if it considers that the case can more conveniently be dealt with by another court.

(3) The powers of a magistrates' court under section 63(2) of the Magistrates' Courts Act 1980 to suspend or rescind orders shall not apply in relation to any order made under this Part.

****

61 Appeals

(1) An appeal shall lie to the High Court against –

(*a*) the making by a magistrates' court of any order under this Part, or
(*b*) any refusal by a magistrates' court to make such an order,

but no appeal shall lie against any exercise by a magistrates' court of the power conferred by section 59(2) of this Act.

(2) On an appeal under this section, the High Court may make such orders as may be necessary to give effect to its determination of the appeal.

(3) Where an order is made under subsection (2), the High Court may also make such incidental or consequential orders as appear to it to be just.

(4) Any order of the High Court made on an appeal under this section (other than one directing that an application be re-heard by a magistrates' court) shall, for the purposes –

(*a*) of the enforcement of the order, and
(*b*) of any power to vary, revive or discharge orders,

be treated as if it were an order of the magistrates' court from which the appeal was brought and not an order of the High Court.

(5) The Lord Chancellor may by order make provision as to the circumstances in which appeals may be made against decisions taken by courts on questions arising in connection with the transfer, or proposed transfer, of proceedings by virtue of any order under section 57(5).

(6) Except to the extent provided for in any order made under subsection (5), no appeal may be made against any decision of a kind mentioned in that subsection.

Scope of provision—This section provides the machinery for all appeals in relation to non-molestation and occupation orders. The procedure is contained within FPR 1991, r 8.1A. The exception is that there can be no appeal against a decision of magistrates to decline jurisdiction on the basis that the matter should be dealt with by another court (ss 61(1)(*b*), 59(2)). Decisions concerning the transfer of proceedings between courts are regulated by Family Law Act 1996 (Part IV) (Allocation of Proceedings) Order 1997, and not by way of appeal under this section (s 61(6)).

Procedure—The procedure for appeals under this section is governed by FPR 1991, r 8.1A (and RSC Ord 55). Appeals under CA 1989 are governed by CA 1989, s 94 and FPR 1991, r 4.22 (see the notes thereto for reference to other appeals).

Hearing—The form of appeal is a re-hearing by a High Court judge (FPR 1991, r 8.1A(6)) in chambers (r 8.1(5)). The judge is not bound to allow the appeal because of a misdirection or improper reception or rejection of evidence unless there has been a substantial wrong or miscarriage of justice occasioned (r 8.2(6)).

General

62 Meaning of "cohabitants", "relevant child" and "associated persons"

(1) For the purposes of this Part –

(*a*) "cohabitants" are a man and a woman who, although not married to each other, are living together as husband and wife; and

(*b*) "former cohabitants" is to be read accordingly, but does not include cohabitants who have subsequently married each other.

(2) In this Part, "relevant child", in relation to any proceedings under this Part, means –

(*a*) any child who is living with or might reasonably be expected to live with either party to the proceedings;

(*b*) any child in relation to whom an order under the Adoption Act 1976 or the Children Act 1989 is in question in the proceedings; and

(*c*) any other child whose interests the court considers relevant.

(3) For the purposes of this Part, a person is associated with another person if –

(*a*) they are or have been married to each other;

(*b*) they are cohabitants or former cohabitants;

(*c*) they live or have lived in the same household, otherwise than merely by reason of one of them being the other's employee, tenant, lodger or boarder;

(*d*) they are relatives;

(*e*) they have agreed to marry one another (whether or not that agreement has been terminated);

(*f*) in relation to any child, they are both persons falling within subsection (4); or

(*g*) they are parties to the same family proceedings (other than proceedings under this Part).

(4) A person falls within this subsection in relation to a child if –

(*a*) he is a parent of the child; or

(*b*) he has or has had parental responsibility for the child.

(5) If a child has been adopted or has been freed for adoption by virtue of any of the enactments mentioned in section 16(1) of the Adoption Act 1976, two persons are also associated with each other for the purpose of this Part if –

(*a*) one is a natural parent of the child or a parent of such a natural parent, and

(*b*) the other is the child or any person –

(i) who had become a parent of the child by virtue of an adoption order or has applied for an adoption order, or

(ii) with whom the child has at any time been placed for adoption.

(6) A body corporate and another person are not, by virtue of subsection (3)(*f*) or (*g*), to be regarded for the purposes of this Part as associated with each other.

Defined terms—"relative": s 63.

Associated persons (s 62(3))—Only "associated persons" and "a relevant child" can apply for a non–molestation order under s 42. Further, for the purposes of an occupation order under s 33, the respondent must be associated with the applicant.

The effect of this definition is to widen considerably the list of persons who can seek the court's protection in family proceedings. Originally, such protection was available only to spouses. In 1976 it was extended to cohabitants and now it is extended in effect to virtually all family members. However, if the family relationship is merely incidental – eg to a dispute over land which other civil proceedings would have to resolve – an order under FLA 1996 may be refused (*Chechi v Bashier* [1999] 2 FLR 489).

Section 62(3)(*a*) and (*b*) enable former spouses and former cohabitants to seek the court's protection under FLA 1996, Pt IV, no matter how long ago the relationship ended. See *G v F (Non-Molestation Order: Jurisdiction)* [2000] 2 FLR 533 where a finding that the parties were not "associated" was reversed on appeal. The Act is to be given a purposive construction. Section 62(3)(*c*) is wide enough to cover same-sex relationships.

A notable omission from the definition is, as the equivalent American statute puts it, "persons who are or have been dating". Such persons, if not within any other paragraph of s 62(3) will have to sue in tort under, eg Protection from Harassment Act 1997.

63 Interpretation of Part IV

(1) In this Part –

"adoption order" has the meaning given by section 72(1) of the Adoption Act 1976;

"associated", in relation to a person, is to be read with section 62(3) to (6);

"child" means a person under the age of eighteen years;

"cohabitant" and "former cohabitant" have the meaning given by section 62(1);

"the court" is to be read with section 57;

"development" means physical, intellectual, emotional, social or behavioural development;

"dwelling-house" includes (subject to subsection (4)) –

(*a*) any building or part of a building which is occupied as a dwelling,

(*b*) any caravan, house-boat or structure which is occupied as a dwelling,

and any yard, garden, garage or outhouse belonging to it and occupied with it;

"family proceedings" means any proceedings –

(*a*) under the inherent jurisdiction of the High Court in relation to children; or

(*b*) under the enactments mentioned in subsection (2),

"harm" –

(*a*) in relation to a person who has reached the age of eighteen years, means ill-treatment or the impairment of health; and

(*b*) in relation to a child, means ill-treatment or the impairment of health or development;

"health" includes physical or mental health;

"ill-treatment" includes forms of ill-treatment which are not physical and, in relation to a child, includes sexual abuse;

"matrimonial home rights" has the meaning given by section 30;

"mortgage", "mortgagor" and "mortgagee" have the same meaning as in the Law of Property Act 1925;

"mortgage payments" includes any payments which, under the terms of the mortgage, the mortgagor is required to make to any person;

"non-molestation order" has the meaning given by section 42(1);

"occupation order" has the meaning given by section 39;

"parental responsibility" has the same meaning as in the Children Act 1989;

"relative", in relation to a person, means –

(*a*) the father, mother, stepfather, stepmother, son, daughter, stepson, stepdaughter, grandmother, grandfather, grandson or granddaughter of that person or of that person's spouse or former spouse, or

(*b*) the brother, sister, uncle, aunt, niece or nephew (whether of the full blood or of the half blood or by affinity) of that person or of that person's spouse or former spouse,

and includes, in relation to a person who is living or has lived with another person as husband or wife, any person who would fall within paragraph (*a*) or (*b*) if the parties were married to each other;

"relevant child", in relation to any proceedings under this Part, has the meaning given by section 62(2);

"the relevant judicial authority", in relation to any order under this Part, means –

(*a*) where the order was made by the High Court, a judge of that court;

(*b*) where the order was made by a county court, a judge or district judge of that or any other county court; or

(*c*) where the order was made by a magistrates' court, any magistrates' court.

(2) The enactments referred to in the definition of "family proceedings" are –

(*a*) Part II;

(*b*) this Part;

(*c*) the Matrimonial Causes Act 1973;

(*d*) the Adoption Act 1976;

(*e*) the Domestic Proceedings and Magistrates' Court Act 1978;

(*f*) Part III of the Matrimonial and Family Proceedings Act 1984;

(*g*) Parts I, II and IV of the Children Act 1989;

(*h*) section 30 of the Human Fertilisation and Embryology Act 1990.

(3) Where the question of whether harm suffered by a child is significant turns on the child's health or development, his health or development shall be compared with that which could reasonably be expected of a similar child.

(4) For the purposes of sections 31, 32, 53 and 54 and such other provisions of this Part (if any) as may be prescribed, this Part is to have effect as if paragraph (*b*) of the definition of "dwelling-house" were omitted.

(5) It is hereby declared that this Part applies as between the parties to a marriage even though either of them is, or has at any time during the marriage been, married to more than one person.

****

SCHEDULE 4
PROVISIONS SUPPLEMENTARY TO SECTIONS 30 AND 31

1 Interpretation

(1) In this Schedule –

(*a*) any reference to a solicitor includes a reference to a licensed conveyancer or a recognised body, and
(*b*) any reference to a person's solicitor includes a reference to a licensed conveyancer or recognised body acting for that person.

(2) In sub-paragraph (1) –

"licensed conveyancer" has the meaning given by section 11(2) of the Administration of Justice Act 1985;
"recognised body" means a body corporate for the time being recognised under section 9 (incorporated practices) or section 32 (provision of conveyancing by recognised bodies) of that Act.

2 Restriction on registration where spouse entitled to more than one charge

Where one spouse is entitled by virtue of section 31 to a registrable charge in respect of each of two or more dwelling-houses, only one of the charges to which that spouse is so entitled shall be registered under section 31(10) or under section 2 of the Land Charges Act 1972 at any one time, and if any of those charges is registered under either of those provisions the Chief Land Registrar, on being satisfied that any other of them is so registered, shall cancel the registration of the charge first registered.

3 Contract for sale of house affected by registered charge to include term requiring cancellation of registration before completion

(1) Where one spouse is entitled by virtue of section 31 to a charge on an estate in a dwelling-house and the charge is registered under section 31(10) or section 2 of the Land Charges Act 1972, it shall be a term of any contract for the sale of that estate whereby the vendor agrees to give vacant possession of the dwelling-house on completion of the contract that the vendor will before such completion procure the cancellation of the registration of the charge at his expense.

(2) Sub-paragraph (1) shall not apply to any such contract made by a vendor who is entitled to sell the estate in the dwelling-house freed from any such charge.

(3) If, on the completion of such a contract as is referred to in sub-paragraph (1), there is delivered to the purchaser or his solicitor an application by the spouse entitled to the charge for the cancellation of the registration of that charge, the term of the contract for which sub-paragraph (1) provides shall be deemed to have been performed.

(4) This paragraph applies only if and so far as a contrary intention is not expressed in the contract.

(5) This paragraph shall apply to a contract for exchange as it applies to a contract for sale.

(6) This paragraph shall, with the necessary modifications, apply to a contract for the grant of a lease or underlease of a dwelling-house as it applies to a contract for the sale of an estate in a dwelling-house.

4 Cancellation of registration after termination of marriage etc

(1) Where a spouse's matrimonial home rights are a charge on an estate in the dwelling-house and the charge is registered under section 31(10) or under section 2 of the Land Charges Act 1972, the Chief Land Registrar shall, subject to sub-paragraph (2), cancel the registration of the charge if he is satisfied –

(*a*) by the production of a certificate or other sufficient evidence, that either spouse is dead, or

(*b*) by the production of an official copy of a decree or order of a court, that the marriage in question has been terminated otherwise than by death, or

(*c*) by the production of an order of the court, that the spouse's matrimonial home rights constituting the charge have been terminated by the order.

(2) Where –

(*a*) the marriage in question has been terminated by the death of the spouse entitled to an estate in the dwelling-house or otherwise than by death, and

(*b*) an order affecting the charge of the spouse not so entitled had been made under section 35(5),

then if, after the making of the order, registration of the charge was renewed or the charge registered in pursuance of sub-paragraph (3), the Chief Land Registrar shall not cancel the registration of the charge in accordance with sub-paragraph (1) unless he is also satisfied that the order has ceased to have effect.

(3) Where such an order has been made, then, for the purposes of sub-paragraph (2), the spouse entitled to the charge affected by the order may –

(*a*) if before the date of the order the charge was registered under section 31(10) or under section 2 of the Land Charges Act 1972, renew the registration of the charge, and

(*b*) if before the said date the charge was not so registered, register the charge under section 31(10) or under section 2 of the Land Charges Act 1972.

(4) Renewal of the registration of a charge in pursuance of sub-paragraph (3) shall be effected in such manner as may be prescribed, and an application for such renewal or for registration of a charge in pursuance of that sub-paragraph shall contain such particulars of any order affecting the charge made under section 33(5) as may be prescribed.

(5) The renewal in pursuance of sub-paragraph (3) of the registration of a charge shall not affect the priority of the charge.

(6) In this paragraph "prescribed" means prescribed by rules made under section 16 of the Land Charges Act 1972 or section 144 of the Land Registration Act 1925, as the circumstances of the case require.

5 Release of matrimonial home rights

(1) A spouse entitled to matrimonial home rights may by a release in writing release those rights or release them as respects part only of the dwelling-house affected by them.

(2) Where a contract is made for the sale of an estate or interest in a dwelling-house, or for the grant of a lease or underlease of a dwelling-house, being (in either case) a dwelling-house affected by a charge registered under section 31(10) or under section 2 of the Land Charges Act 1972, then, without prejudice to sub-paragraph (1), the matrimonial home rights constituting the charge shall be deemed to have been released on the happening of whichever of the following events first occurs –

(*a*) the delivery to the purchaser or lessee, as the case may be, or his solicitor on completion of the contract of an application by the spouse entitled to the charge for the cancellation of the registration of the charge; or

(*b*) the lodging of such an application at Her Majesty's Land Registry.

General note—Irrespective of this provision allowing voluntary release of matrimonial home rights, the court retains jurisdiction to set aside the registration of matrimonial home rights where they have been improperly registered or where the registration is causing severe prejudice to the other party (see **Removing a "Class F land charge"** under s 31).

6 Postponement of priority of charge

A spouse entitled by virtue of section 31 to a charge on an estate or interest may agree in writing that any other charge on, or interest in, that estate or interest shall rank in priority to the charge to which that spouse is so entitled.

SCHEDULE 5

POWERS OF HIGH COURT AND COUNTY COURT TO REMAND

1 Interpretation

In this Schedule "the court" means the High Court or a county court and includes –

(*a*) in relation to the High Court, a judge of that court, and

(*b*) in relation to a county court, a judge or district judge of that court.

2 Remand in custody or on bail

(1) Where a court has power to remand a person under section 47, the court may –

(*a*) remand him in custody, that is to say, commit him to custody to be brought before the court at the end of the period of remand or at such earlier time as the court may require, or

(*b*) remand him on bail –

(i) by taking from him a recognizance (with or without sureties) conditioned as provided in sub-paragraph (3), or

(ii) by fixing the amount of the recognizances with a view to their being taken subsequently in accordance with paragraph 4 and in the meantime committing the person to custody in accordance with paragraph (*a*).

(2) Where a person is brought before the court after remand, the court may further remand him.

(3) Where a person is remanded on bail under sub-paragraph (1), the court may direct that his recognizance be conditioned for his appearance –

(*a*) before that court at the end of the period of remand, or
(*b*) at every time and place to which during the course of the proceedings the hearing may from time to time be adjourned.

(4) Where a recognizance is conditioned for a person's appearance in accordance with sub-paragraph (1)(*b*), the fixing of any time for him next to appear shall be deemed to be a remand; but nothing in this sub-paragraph or sub-paragraph (3) shall deprive the court of power at any subsequent hearing to remand him afresh.

(5) Subject to paragraph 3, the court shall not remand a person under this paragraph for a period exceeding 8 clear days, except that –

(*a*) if the court remands him on bail, it may remand him for a longer period if he and the other party consent, and
(*b*) if the court adjourns a case under section 48(1), the court may remand him for the period of the adjournment.

(6) Where the court has power under this paragraph to remand a person in custody it may, if the remand for a period not exceeding 3 clear days, commit him to the custody of a constable.

Scope of provision—Schedule 5 introduces a remand scheme for the High Court and county courts. Magistrates' courts already have power to remand in civil cases pursuant to Magistrates' Courts Act 1980, ss 128, 129, and Sch 5 is clearly modelled on the magistrates' powers. It is part of the philosophy of the Act to have common terminology and common powers in all courts.

Persons alleged to be in breach of injunctions will appear before the court in one of three ways:
(*a*) persons arrested pursuant to a power of arrest under s 47(6);
(*b*) persons arrested pursuant to a warrant of arrest issued under s 47(8);
(*c*) persons brought before the court under an application to show cause why they should not be committed under CCR Order 29.

In all cases the court would prefer to deal with the matter at the first hearing. However, before dealing with the person for contempt of court, the court must record findings of fact and therefore the facts have to be either admitted or proved by evidence. If the facts are not admitted and the evidence is not before the court, the court will not be able to deal with the matter properly. This may arise, for example, where the respondent has been arrested pursuant to a power of arrest but the person who has the benefit of the injunction is not before the court to give evidence (the arresting officer is not usually required to attend: see *President's Direction of 9 December 1999*). In such circumstances, as an alternative to merely adjourning, the court can now remand and has to decide whether the remand should be in custody or on bail. A remand in custody cannot be for a period exceeding eight clear days (three clear days, if in the custody of a constable).

Although Sch 5 clearly envisages conditional bail, it is submitted that this in practice is not necessary. The injunction will still be in force and therefore imposing similar terms as a condition of bail achieves no purpose. The injunction itself could still be enforced whereas there is no procedure for enforcing breach of bail conditions. It is respectfully submitted that the Schedule has overlooked the fundamental distinction between bail in criminal matters and bail in civil matters. Bail in a criminal case is primarily to ensure that the defendant is before the court when his case comes up for trial. The criminal trial will invariably have to be adjourned, and a bench warrant issued, if the defendant does not answer to his bail. The situation is wholly different in a civil matter whereby, provided the court is satisfied that the respondent has notice of the hearing date, the court can, and frequently does, proceed in the absence of a party. Thus no practical purpose is served by conditional bail in the context of civil cases. Indeed, it is submitted that bail itself, conditional or not, serves no practical purpose in the context of injunction cases. If the court is unable to deal with the alleged breach of the injunction at the first hearing and has decided that a remand in custody is not necessary, how does a remand on bail differ from an adjournment, given that the injunction itself is still in force? An adjournment without a remand on bail is adequate, and if conditions are required to protect the applicant they could be in the form of an amended or expanded injunction, with a power of arrest. However, the term "bail" is widely understood, and perhaps a remand on bail, following arrest, could have a psychological impact, given that the court's main purpose will be to secure future compliance with its order. If the court does remand a person on bail it is obliged to take from him a recognizance (para 2(1)(*b*)(i)).

Contempt of court—The court's powers to commit for contempt of court are in the Contempt of Court Act 1981.

3 Further remand

(1) If the court is satisfied that any person who has been remanded under paragraph 2 is unable by reason of illness or accident to appear or be brought before the court at the expiration of the period for which he was remanded, the court may, in his absence, remand him for a further time; and paragraph 2(5) shall not apply.

(2) Notwithstanding anything in paragraph 2(1), the power of the court under sub-paragraph (1) to remand a person on bail for a further time may be exercised by enlarging his recognizance and those of any sureties for him to a later time.

(3) Where a person remanded on bail under paragraph 2 is bound to appear before the court at any time and the court has no power to remand him under sub-paragraph (1), the court may in his absence enlarge his recognizance and those of any sureties for him to a later time; and the enlargement of his recognizance shall be deemed to be a further remand.

4 Postponement of taking of recognizance

Where under paragraph 2(1)(*b*)(ii) the court fixes the amount in which the principal and his sureties, if any, are to be bound, the recognizance may thereafter be taken by such person as may be prescribed by rules of court, and the same consequences shall follow as if it had been entered into before the court.

"prescribed by rules of court"—The relevant rule is FPR 1991, r 3.10(4). The persons prescribed are a district judge, a justice of the peace, a justices' clerk, a police officer of at least the rank of inspector or in charge of a police station, and (where the person making the application is in his custody) the governor or keeper of a prison.

****

SCHEDULE 7

TRANSFER OF CERTAIN TENANCIES ON DIVORCE ETC OR ON SEPARATION OF COHABITANTS

Scope of Schedule—Taking into account the matters set out in para 5, including the suitability of the parties as tenants (the landlord has the right to be heard by virtue of para 14), the court can transfer a range of tenancies including statutory tenancies held by one or both spouses or former spouses (provided there is a decree nisi or a decree of judicial separation (para 2(2)) and the applicant has not remarried (para 13)) or cohabitants who no longer live together as husband and wife (para 3). The transferee can be ordered to pay compensation to the transferor (para 10). If immediate payment of the compensation causes the transferee greater financial hardship than the transferor, payment can be deferred or be by instalments. The court can direct that both be liable under the obligations of the tenancy and that one indemnify the other (para 11). If jurisdiction is founded on a decree of divorce or nullity, the order cannot take effect until the decree is absolute (para 12).

PART I
GENERAL

Interpretation

1 In this Schedule –

"cohabitant", except in paragraph 3, includes (where the context requires) former cohabitant,

"the court" does not include a magistrates' court,

"landlord" includes –

(*a*) any person from time to time deriving title under the original landlord; and

(*b*) in relation to any dwelling-house, any person other than the tenant who is, or (but for Part VII of the Rent Act 1977 or Part II of the Rent (Agriculture) Act 1976) would be, entitled to possession of the dwelling-house;

"Part II order" means an order under Part II of this Schedule;

"a relevant tenancy" means –

(*a*) a protected tenancy or statutory tenancy within the meaning of the Rent Act 1977;

(*b*) a statutory tenancy within the meaning of the Rent (Agriculture) Act 1976;

(*c*) a secure tenancy within the meaning of section 79 of the Housing Act 1985;

(*d*) an assured tenancy or assured agricultural occupancy within the meaning of Part I of the Housing Act 1988; or

(*e*) an introductory tenancy within the meaning of Chapter I of Part V of the Housing Act 1996;

"spouse", except in paragraph 2, includes (where the context requires) former spouse; and

"tenancy" includes sub-tenancy.

Amendments—SI 1997/74.

Defined terms—"cohabitant": s 62(1).

Cases in which court may make order

2 (1) This paragraph applies if one spouse is entitled, either in his own right or jointly with the other spouse, to occupy a dwelling-house by virtue of a relevant tenancy.

(2) On granting a decree of divorce, a decree of nullity of marriage or a decree of judicial separation or at any time thereafter (whether, in the case of a decree of divorce or nullity of marriage, before or after the decree is made absolute), the court may make a Part II order.

Amendments—SI 1997/1892.

"dwelling-house"—In contrast to s 30, 33 et seq, this term is restricted so that it does not include a caravan or houseboat (see s 63(1), (4)). Additionally, by virtue of para 4 below, a court may only make an order in respect of a dwelling-house which is or was a matrimonial home, as opposed to one intended to be a matrimonial home.

3 (1) This paragraph applies if one cohabitant is entitled, either in his own right or jointly with the other cohabitant, to occupy a dwelling-house by virtue of a relevant tenancy.

(2) If the cohabitants cease to live together as husband and wife, the court may make a Part II order.

Note—The court cannot transfer a tenancy to one cohabitant if that tenancy is held jointly by the other cohabitant with a third party. Nor can it do so if it is a statutory tenancy whose security has been lost by the tenant being out of occupation (*Gay v Sheeran* [1999] 2 FLR 519).

4 The court shall not make a Part II order unless the dwelling-house is or was –

(*a*) in the case of spouses, a matrimonial home; or
(*b*) in the case of cohabitants, a home in which they lived together as husband and wife.

PART II

Matters to which the court must have regard

5 In determining whether to exercise its powers under Part II of this Schedule and, if so, in what manner, the court shall have regard to all the circumstances of the case including –

(*a*) the circumstances in which the tenancy was granted to either or both of the spouses or cohabitants or, as the case requires, the circumstances in which either or both of them became tenant under the tenancy;
(*b*) the matters mentioned in section 33(6)(*a*), (*b*) and (*c*) and, where the parties are cohabitants and only one of them is entitled to occupy the dwelling-house by virtue of the relevant tenancy, the further matters mentioned in section 36(6)(*e*), (*f*), (*g*) and (*h*); and
(*c*) the suitability of the parties as tenants.

PART II
ORDERS THAT MAY BE MADE

References to entitlement to occupy

6 References in this Part of this Schedule to a spouse or a cohabitant being entitled to occupy a dwelling-house by virtue of a relevant tenancy apply whether that entitlement is in his own right or jointly with the other spouse or cohabitant.

Protected, secure or assured tenancy or assured agricultural occupancy

7 (1) If a spouse or cohabitant is entitled to occupy the dwelling-house by virtue of a protected tenancy within the meaning of the Rent Act 1977, a secure tenancy within the meaning of the Housing Act 1985, an assured tenancy or assured agricultural occupancy within the meaning of Part I of the Housing Act 1988 or an introductory tenancy within the meaning of Chapter I of Part V of the Housing Act 1996, the court may by order direct that, as from such date as may be specified in the order, there shall, by virtue of the order and without further assurance, be transferred to, and vested in, the other spouse or cohabitant –

(*a*) the estate or interest which the spouse or cohabitant so entitled had in the dwelling-house immediately before that date by virtue of the lease or agreement creating the tenancy and any assignment of that lease or agreement, with all rights, privileges and appurtenances attaching to that estate or interest but subject to all covenants, obligations, liabilities and incumbrances to which it is subject; and

(*b*) where the spouse or cohabitant so entitled is an assignee of such lease or agreement, the liability of that spouse or cohabitant under any covenant of indemnity by the assignee express or implied in the assignment of the lease or agreement to that spouse or cohabitant.

(2) If an order is made under this paragraph, any liability or obligation to which the spouse or cohabitant so entitled is subject under any covenant having reference to the dwelling-house in the lease or agreement, being a liability or obligation falling due to be discharged or performed on or after the date so specified, shall not be enforceable against that spouse or cohabitant.

(3) If the spouse so entitled is a successor within the meaning of Part IV of the Housing Act 1985, his former spouse or former cohabitant (or, in the case of judicial separation, his spouse) shall be deemed also to be a successor within the meaning of that Part.

(3A) If the spouse or cohabitant so entitled is a successor within the meaning of section 132 of the Housing Act 1996, his former spouse or former cohabitant (or, if a separation order is in force, his spouse) shall be deemed also to be a successor within the meaning of that section.

(4) If the spouse or cohabitant so entitled is for the purpose of section 17 of the Housing Act 1988 a successor in relation to the tenancy or occupancy, his former spouse or former cohabitant (or, in the case of judicial separation, his spouse) is to be deemed to be a successor in relation to the tenancy or occupation for the purposes of that section.

(5) If the transfer under sub-paragraph (1) is of an assured agricultural occupancy, then, for the purposes of Chapter III of Part I of the Housing Act 1988 –

(*a*) the agricultural worker condition is fulfilled with respect to the dwelling-house while the spouse or cohabitant to whom the assured agricultural occupancy is transferred continues to be the occupier under that occupancy, and

(*b*) that condition shall be treated as so fulfilled by virtue of the same paragraph of Schedule 3 to the Housing Act 1988 as was applicable before the transfer.

(6) (*omitted*)

Amendments—SI 1997/74; SI 1997/1892.

Interrelation with Matrimonial Causes Act 1973, s 24 where parties are married—By virtue of MCA 1973, s 24, the court can transfer a tenancy but not a statutory tenancy, as it is not property. The advantages of applying for a transfer of a tenancy under this Schedule as opposed to the MCA 1973 are:

(*a*) the court order operates as the transfer "without further assurance" so that, in the case of a reluctant transferor, there is no need to apply for the district judge to execute the transfer on his behalf;

(*b*) if there is a covenant against assignment, an order under MCA, s 24 is a breach of that covenant (except in the case of a secured tenancy under Housing Act 1985, s 91(3)). However, under Sch 7, para 7(1), the transfer operates to vest the interest as it existed immediately before the date of the transfer, so on the literal wording of this provision no assignment has taken place.

Statutory tenancy within the meaning of the Rent Act 1977

8 (1) This paragraph applies if the spouse or cohabitant is entitled to occupy the dwelling-house by virtue of a statutory tenancy within the meaning of the Rent Act 1977.

(2) The court may by order direct that, as from the date specified in the order –

(*a*) that spouse or cohabitant is to cease to be entitled to occupy the dwelling-house; and
(*b*) the other spouse or cohabitant is to be deemed to be the tenant or, as the case may be, the sole tenant under that statutory tenancy.

(3) The question whether the provisions of paragraphs 1 to 3, or (as the case may be) paragraphs 5 to 7 of Schedule 1 to the Rent Act 1977, as to the succession by the surviving spouse of a deceased tenant, or by a member of the deceased tenant's family, to the right to retain possession are capable of having effect in the event of the death of the person deemed by an order under this paragraph to be the tenant or sole tenant under the statutory tenancy is to be determined according as those provisions have or have not already had effect in relation to the statutory tenancy.

Statutory tenancy within the meaning of the Rent (Agriculture) Act 1976

9 (1) This paragraph applies if the spouse or cohabitant is entitled to occupy the dwelling-house by virtue of a statutory tenancy within the meaning of the Rent (Agriculture) Act 1976.

(2) The court may by order direct that, as from such date as may be specified in the order –

(*a*) that spouse or cohabitant is to cease to be entitled to occupy the dwelling-house; and
(*b*) the other spouse or cohabitant is to be deemed to be the tenant or, as the case may be, the sole tenant under that statutory tenancy.

(3) A spouse or cohabitant who is deemed under this paragraph to be the tenant under a statutory tenancy is (within the meaning of that Act) a statutory tenant in his own right, or a statutory tenant by succession, according as the other spouse or cohabitant was a statutory tenant in his own right or a statutory tenant by succession.

PART III
SUPPLEMENTARY PROVISIONS

Compensation

10 (1) If the court makes a Part II order, it may by the order direct the making of a payment by the spouse or cohabitant to whom the tenancy is transferred ("the transferee") to the other spouse or cohabitant ("the transferor").

(2) Without prejudice to that, the court may, on making an order by virtue of sub-paragraph (1) for the payment of a sum –

(*a*) direct that payment of that sum or any part of it is to be deferred until a specified date or until the occurrence of a specified event, or
(*b*) direct that that sum or any part of it is to be paid by instalments.

(3) Where an order has been made by virtue of sub-paragraph (1), the court may, on the application of the transferee or the transferor –

(*a*) exercise its powers under sub-paragraph (2), or
(*b*) vary any direction previously given under that sub-paragraph,

at any time before the sum whose payment is required by the order is paid in full.

(4) In deciding whether to exercise its powers under this paragraph and, if so, in what manner, the court shall have regard to all the circumstances including –

(*a*) the financial loss that would otherwise be suffered by the transferor as a result of the order;
(*b*) the financial needs and financial resources of the parties; and
(*c*) the financial obligations which the parties have, or are likely to have in the foreseeable future, including financial obligations to each other and to any relevant child.

(5) The court shall not give any direction under sub-paragraph (2) unless it appears to it that immediate payment of the sum required by the order would cause the transferee financial hardship which is greater than any financial hardship that would be caused to the transferor if the direction were given.

Liabilities and obligations in respect of the dwelling-house

11 (1) If the court makes a Part II order, it may by the order direct that both spouses or cohabitants are to be jointly and severally liable to discharge or perform any or all of the liabilities and obligations in respect of the dwelling-house (whether arising under the tenancy or otherwise) which –

(*a*) have at the date of the order fallen due to be discharged or performed by one only of them; or
(*b*) but for the direction, would before the date specified as the date on which the order is to take effect fall due to be discharged or performed by one only of them.

(2) If the court gives such a direction, it may further direct that either spouse or cohabitant is to be liable to indemnify the other in whole or in part against any payment made or expenses incurred by the other in discharging or performing any such liability or obligation.

Date when order made between spouses is to take effect

12 (1) In the case of a decree of divorce or nullity of marriage, the date specified in a Part II order as the date on which the order is to take effect must not be earlier than the date on which the decree is made absolute.

(2) (*omitted*)

Amendments—SI 1997/1892.

Remarriage of either spouse

13 (1) If after the grant of a decree dissolving or annulling a marriage either spouse remarries, that spouse is not entitled to apply, by reference to the grant of that decree, for a Part II order.

(2) For the avoidance of doubt it is hereby declared that the reference in sub-paragraph (1) to remarriage includes a reference to a marriage which is by law void or voidable.

Amendments—SI 1997/1892.

Rules of court

14 (1) Rules of court shall be made requiring the court, before it makes an order under this Schedule, to give the landlord of the dwelling-house to which the order will relate an opportunity of being heard.

(2) Rules of court may provide that an application for a Part II order by reference to an order or decree may not, without the leave of the court by which that order was made or decree was granted, be made after the expiration of such period from the order or grant as may be prescribed by the rules.

Scope of provision—FPR 1991, r 3.8 makes provision for proceedings under the Act. In particular, r 3.8(12) provides for the landlord to be served and entitled to be heard (see **Code for applying for occupation and non-molestation orders** under r 3.8). No rules have been made under para 14(2) prohibiting the application if not made within a specific time, although para 13 provides that an application must be made before remarriage.

Saving for other provisions of Act

15 (1) If a spouse is entitled to occupy a dwelling-house by virtue of a tenancy, this Schedule does not affect the operation of sections 30 and 31 in relation to the other spouse's matrimonial home rights.

(2) If a spouse or cohabitant is entitled to occupy a dwelling-house by virtue of a tenancy, the court's powers to make orders under this Schedule are additional to those conferred by sections 33, 35 and 36.

****

Family Law Reform Act 1969

ARRANGEMENT OF SECTIONS

PART I

REDUCTION OF AGE OF MAJORITY AND RELATED PROVISIONS

PART III

PROVISIONS FOR USE OF SCIENTIFIC TESTS IN DETERMINING PATERNITY

PART I
REDUCTION OF AGE OF MAJORITY AND RELATED PROVISIONS

1 Reduction of age of majority from 21 to 18

(1) As from the date on which this section comes into force a person shall attain full age on attaining the age of eighteen instead of on attaining the age of twenty-one; and a person shall attain full age on that date if he has then already attained the age of eighteen but not the age of twenty-one.

(2) The foregoing subsection applies for the purposes of any rule of law, and, in the absence of a definition or of any indication of a contrary intention, for the construction of "full age", "infant", "infancy", "minor", "minority" and similar expressions in –

(*a*) any statutory provision, whether passed or made before, on or after the date on which this section comes into force; and

(*b*) any deed, will or other instrument of whatever nature (not being a statutory provision) made on or after that date.

(3) In the statutory provisions specified in Schedule 1 to this Act for any reference to the age of twenty-one years there shall be substituted a reference to the age of eighteen years; but the amendment by this subsection of the provisions specified in Part II of that Schedule shall be without prejudice to any power of amending or revoking those provisions.

(4) This section does not affect the construction of any such expression as is referred to in subsection (2) of this section in any of the statutory provisions described in Schedule 2 to this Act, and the transitional provisions and savings contained in Schedule 3 to this Act shall have effect in relation to this section.

(5) The Lord Chancellor may by order made by statutory instrument amend any provision in any local enactment passed on or before the date on which this section comes into force (not being a provision described in paragraph 2 of Schedule 2 to this Act) by substituting a reference to the age of eighteen years for any reference therein to the age of twenty-one years; and any statutory instrument containing an order under this subsection shall be subject to annulment in pursuance of a resolution of either House of Parliament.

(6) In this section "statutory provision" means any enactment (including, except where the context otherwise requires, this Act) and any order, rule, regulation, byelaw or other instrument made in the exercise of a power conferred by any enactment.

(7) Notwithstanding any rule of law, a will or codicil executed before the date on which this section comes into force shall not be treated for the purposes of this section as made on or after that date by reason only that the will or codicil is confirmed by a codicil executed on or after that date.

****

8 Consent by persons over 16 to surgical, medical and dental treatment

(1) The consent of a minor who has attained the age of sixteen years to any surgical, medical or dental treatment which, in the absence of consent, would constitute a trespass to his person, shall be as effective as it would be if he were of full age; and where a minor has by virtue of this section given an effective consent to any treatment it shall not be necessary to obtain any consent for it from his parent or guardian.

(2) In this section "surgical, medical or dental treatment" includes any procedure undertaken for the purposes of diagnosis, and this section applies to any procedure (including, in particular, the administration of an anaesthetic) which is ancillary to any treatment as it applies to that treatment.

(3) Nothing in this section shall be construed as making ineffective any consent which would have been effective if this section had not been enacted.

Scope of provision—This section gives to minors who have attained the age of 16 a right to consent to surgical, medical or dental treatment. The effect of consent to treatment by the minor, or someone else with authority to give it, is limited to protecting the medical or dental practitioner from claims for damages for trespass to the person. Such consent cannot be overridden by those with parental responsibility for the minor, although it can be overridden by the court. This statutory right does not extend to the donation of blood or organs (*Re W (A Minor) (Consent to Medical Treatment)* [1993] 1 FLR 1). This section is of no significance where the case concerns the effect of a *refusal* as distinct from a *consent* to treatment. The court or any person with parental responsibility can override the refusal of any minor who is under or over 16 years to consent to medical treatment, although the minor's wishes are a crucial consideration to be taken into account. In *Re W (A Minor) (Consent to Medical Treatment)* (above), a 16-year-old girl suffering from anorexia nervosa opposed the plans of the local authority to move her to a new treatment unit and to give her medical treatment without her consent. The local authority applied under CA 1989, s 100(3) for leave of the court to carry out its plans. The Court of Appeal held that the only purpose of FLRA 1969, s 8 was to enable a 16-year-old to consent to medical treatment which, in the absence of consent by the child or its parents, would constitute a trespass to the person; further, as the section was silent on the question whether a minor of 16 had an absolute right to refuse medical treatment, it could not be construed to confer such a right. There was no overriding limitation to preclude the exercise by the court of its inherent jurisdiction over minors to act in the minor's best interests. The court authorised the plans of the local authority.

Guidance where children are nearly 16 years of age—Useful guidance in this area is to be found in the conclusions set out by Lord Donaldson MR in *Re R (A Minor) (Wardship: Consent to Treatment)* [1992] Fam 11, [1992] 1 FLR 190, where the court considered the case of a 15-year-old girl who refused medication for her psychotic state. The court found that, due to her mental state, she was not "*Gillick* competent" within the guidelines set out in *Gillick v West Norfolk and Wisbech Area Health Authority and Another* [1986] AC 112, [1986] 1 FLR 224, HL. The court authorised the proposed treatment, holding as follows:

(*a*) No doctor could be *required* to treat a child since the decision to do so was a matter for his own professional judgement, subject only to obtaining, where necessary, the consent of someone with the authority to give that consent. In forming that judgement, the wishes of the child were a factor whose importance increases with the increase in the child's intelligence and understanding.

(*b*) There can be concurrent powers to consent. If more than one body or person has a power to consent, only a failure to, or refusal of, consent by all having that power will create a veto.

(*c*) A "*Gillick*-competent" child or a child over the age of 16 will have a power to consent, but that will be concurrent with that of a parent or guardian.

(*d*) "*Gillick* competence" is a developmental concept and will not be lost or acquired on a day-to-day or a week-by-week basis. In the case of mental disability, that disability must also be taken into account, particularly where it is fluctuating in its effect.

(*e*) The court, in the exercise of its wardship or statutory jurisdiction, has power to override the decisions of a "*Gillick*-competent" child as much as those of parents or guardians.

See also *Re E (A Minor) (Wardship: Medical Treatment)* [1993] 1 FLR 386, where the parents of a 15-year-old boy suffering from leukaemia refused to consent to blood transfusions being given to him as they were Jehovah's Witnesses. The hospital authority made the boy a ward of court. Although the boy was nearly 16 and in spite of this section, Ward J decided that the court in wardship should order that the child's welfare, assessed objectively, required leave to be given for the transfusion to take place. Where a 15-year-old girl suffered a long-term illness requiring monthly blood transfusions, but after attending meetings of Jehovah's Witnesses with her mother had decided to refuse further transfusions, the court held that she was not "*Gillick*-competent" because, inter alia, she appeared not to understand the full implications of what would happen if treatment were discontinued. The court exercised its discretion so as to override the patient's wishes and to give authority for the treatment to be carried out (*Re S (A Minor) (Consent to Medical Treatment)* [1994] 2 FLR 1065).

9 Time at which a person attains a particular age

(1) The time at which a person attains a particular age expressed in years shall be the commencement of the relevant anniversary of the date of his birth.

(2) This section applies only where the relevant anniversary falls on a date after that on which this section comes into force, and, in relation to any enactment, deed, will or other instrument, has effect subject to any provision therein.

****

PART III
PROVISIONS FOR USE OF SCIENTIFIC TESTS IN DETERMINING PATERNITY

20 Power of court to require use of scientific tests

(1) In any civil proceedings in which the parentage of any person falls to be determined, the court may, either of its own motion or on an application by any party to the proceedings, give a direction –

(*a*) for the use of scientific tests to ascertain whether such tests show that a party to the proceedings is or is not the father or mother of that person; and

(*b*) for the taking, within a period specified in the direction, of bodily samples from all or any of the following, namely, that person, any party who is alleged to be the father or mother of that person and any other party to the proceedings;

and the court may at any time revoke or vary a direction previously given by it under this subsection.

(1A) Tests required by a direction under this section may only be carried out by a body which has been accredited for the purposes of this section by –

(*a*) the Lord Chancellor, or
(*b*) a body appointed by him for the purpose.

(2) The individual carrying out scientific tests in pursuance of a direction under subsection (1) above ("the tester") shall make to the court a report in which he shall state –

(*a*) the results of the tests;
(*b*) whether the party to whom the report relates is or is not excluded by the results from being the father or mother of the person whose parentage is to be determined; and

(*c*) in relation to any party who is not so excluded, the value, if any, of the results in determining whether that party is the father or mother of that person;

and the report shall be received by the court as evidence in the proceedings of the matters stated in it.

(2A) Where the proceedings in which the parentage of any person falls to be determined are proceedings on an application under section 55A or 56 of the Family Law Act 1986, any reference in subsection (1) or (2) of this section to any party to the proceedings shall include a reference to any person named in the application.

(3) A report under subsection (2) of this section shall be in the form prescribed by regulations made under section 22 of this Act.

(4) Where a report has been made to a court under subsection (2) of this section, any party may, with the leave of the court, or shall, if the court so directs, obtain from "the tester" a written statement explaining or amplifying any statement made in the report, and that statement shall be deemed for the purposes of this section (except subsection (3) thereof) to form part of the report made to the court.

(5) Where a direction is given under this section in any proceedings, a party to the proceedings, unless the court otherwise directs, shall not be entitled to call as a witness the tester, or any other person by whom any thing necessary for the purpose of enabling those tests to be carried out was done, unless within fourteen days after receiving a copy of the report he serves notice on the other parties to the proceedings, or on such of them as the court may direct, of his intention to call the tester, or that other person; and where the tester or any such person is called as a witness the party who called him shall be entitled to cross-examine him.

(6) Where a direction is given under this section the party on whose application the direction is given shall pay the cost of taking and testing bodily samples for the purpose of giving effect to the direction (including any expenses reasonably incurred by any person in taking any steps required of him for the purpose), and of making a report to the court under this section, but the amount paid shall be treated as costs incurred by him in the proceedings.

Amendments—Family Law Reform Act 1987, ss 23(1), 33(1), Sch 2, para 21; CA 1989, s 89; Courts and Legal Services Act 1990, s 116, Sch 16, para 3; Child Support, Pensions and Social Security Act 2000, s 82(1), (2), Sch 8, para 9.

Defined terms—"bodily samples", "scientific tests", "excluded": s 25.

"the parentage of any person falls to be determined" (s 20(1))—This section now adopts the terminology of Family Law Act 1986, s 55A and enables the court to give a direction designed to show whether or not a person is the parent of the child ("the person") concerned. Section 55A enables a free-standing application to be made for parentage. However, a free-standing application for a direction only cannot be made: there must be other civil proceedings in which the issue of parentage arises.

Making the direction (s 20(1))—The direction can be made by the court of its own initiative or on the application of a party to the proceedings. Procedure is covered by RSC Ord 112 and CCR 1981 Ord 47, r 5 (as set out in CPR 1998, Schs 1 and 2 for proceedings not covered by FPR 1991).

"party to the proceedings" (s 20(1), (2A))—In proceedings under FLA 1986, ss 55A and 56, individuals may be named in a petition brought thereunder (see FPR 1991, rr 3.13 and 3.14). If so named in the petition, the individual becomes a party for the purposes of a direction under s 20(1).

PART II

Interests of justice—The interests of justice in terms of exercise of the discretion whether to make a direction was explained by Thorpe LJ in *Re H and A (Paternity: Blood Tests)* [2002] EWCA Civ 383, [2002] 1 FLR 1145, CA at [29] as follows:

> "The points of principle to be drawn from [recent cases are]: first, that the interests of justice are best served by the ascertainment of the truth and, secondly, that the court should be furnished with the best available science and not confined to such unsatisfactory alternatives as presumptions and inferences."

Discretion to direct—The direction of a blood test is a discretionary remedy and should only be made if in the interests of the child concerned (*S v S, W v Official Solicitor* [1972] AC 24, [1970] 3 All ER 107, HL; and see *Re F (A Minor) (Paternity Test)* [1993] 1 FLR 598, CA). In *Re H (Paternity: Blood Test)* [1996] 2 FLR 65, CA, Ward LJ explained fully the factors to be borne in mind when the court exercises its discretion, and concluded:

(1) A parent's refusal to comply with a direction was not determinative of the issue of whether or not a direction should be made;
(2) The welfare of the child is a relevant but not paramount factor in deciding whether or not to make a direction; the interests of other persons may also be involved (and see *S v S, W v Official Solicitor* (above));
(3) The outcome of the proceedings in which the direction is sought is not a factor in deciding whether to make a direction: the paternity question was a free-standing application entitled to its own considerations; and
(4) A child's welfare generally demands that it know the truth about his or her parentage.

The direction—In *Re H (Paternity: Blood Test)* [1996] 2 FLR 65, CA, Ward LJ stressed the fact that the court is required to make a direction, and not an order, since the court cannot order the taking of samples against a person's consent (s 21(1)). He proposed (at 83D) a form of words for the direction as follows:

> "It is directed pursuant to s 20(1) of the Family Law Reform Act 1969:
>
> (*a*) that blood tests (including DNA tests) be used to ascertain whether such tests show that [Mr A] is or is not excluded form being the father of [child B] born on [ ]; and
>
> (*b*) that for that purpose blood samples be taken on or before [ ] from the following persons: [Mr A], [Mrs X (mother of child B)] and [child B]; and
>
> (*c*) that the person appearing to the court to have care and control of [child B], who is under the age of 16, is [Mrs X];
>
> (*d*) that such tests be carried out by [Mr CD of]."

"any party" (s 20(1))—An intervener would be included in this definition as would, for example, a non-parent who had obtained leave (pursuant to CA 1989, s 10) to apply for a CA 1989, s 8 order. Where a person not already a party to the proceedings is made the subject of a direction the court may at any time direct that he be made a party to the proceedings (RSC Ord 112, r 4).

Two or more putative fathers—In *Re A (A Minor) (Paternity: Refusal of Blood Test)* [1994] 2 FLR 463, CA, Waite LJ left open the issue of whether or not a mother could make successive claims, leading to further applications under s 20, against two or more putative fathers where a first or subsequent claim had failed, although he felt that to deny her the ability to do this would be illogical.

"regulations made under section 22" (s 20(3))—The regulations are the Blood Tests (Evidence of Paternity) Regulations 1971, SI 1971/1861.

"report ... in the form prescribed" (s 20(3))—The form prescribed is defined by BT(EP)R 1971, reg 10 and is prepared by the tester who has been appointed to carry out tests. When received by the court it must be sent to every party and to anyone else involved in giving a sample (RSC Ord 112, r 6; CCR Ord 47, r 5(6)).

Oral evidence from testers (s 20(5))—The time-limits for a party availing himself of the oral evidence of a tester are short; but where he is called he appears in a capacity analogous to that of a court expert and can be cross-examined by the party who sought that he be called (cf RSC Ord 40, r 4).

"treated as costs incurred by him in the proceedings" (s 20(6))—In the first instance the applicant for the direction bears liability for the cost of the tests; if ultimately his costs are ordered to be paid by another party the cost of the test will be included.

21 Consents etc required for taking of bodily samples

(1) Subject to the provisions of subsections (3) and (4) of this section, a bodily sample which is required to be taken from any person for the purpose of giving effect to a direction under section 20 of this Act shall not be taken from that person except with his consent.

(2) The consent of a minor who has attained the age of sixteen years to the taking from himself of a bodily sample shall be as effective as it would be if he were of full age; and where a minor has by virtue of this subsection given an effective consent to the taking of a bodily sample it shall not be necessary to obtain any consent for it from any other person.

(3) A bodily sample may be taken from a person under the age of sixteen years, not being such a person as is referred to in subsection (4) of this section –

- (*a*) if the person who has the care and control of him consents; or
- (*b*) where that person does not consent, if the court considers that it would be in his best interests for the sample to be taken.

(4) A bodily sample may be taken from a person who is suffering from mental disorder within the meaning of the Mental Health Act 1983 and is incapable of understanding the nature and purpose of scientific tests if the person who has the care and control of him consents and the medical practitioner in whose care he is has certified that the taking of a bodily sample from him will not be prejudicial to his proper care and treatment.

(5) The foregoing provisions of this section are without prejudice to the provisions of section 23 of this Act.

Amendments—Mental Health Act 1983, s 148, Sch 4, para 25; Family Law Reform Act 1987, s 33(1), Sch 2, para 22; Child Support, Pensions and Social Security Act 2000, s 82(1), (3).

Defined terms—"bodily sample": s 25.

"consent" (s 21(1))—The effect of failing to comply with a direction which, by virtue of s 23(3), is implicit in refusing to consent, is dealt with in s 23.

Direction where court considers that it is in a child's best interests for sample to be taken (s 21(3))—The amendment to s 21(3), by the addition of s 21(3)(*b*), enables the court to direct tests where a person having care and control of the child does *not* consent. This reverses the decision in *Re O and J (Paternity: Blood Tests)* [2000] 1 FLR 418, Wall J. In considering whether to make such a direction the court will, in appropriate cases, want to take account of *Gillick v West Norfolk and Wisbech Area Health Authority* [1986] AC 112, [1986] 1 FLR 224 and CA 1989 (see in particular ss 38(6), 43(8), 44(7): children, if of sufficient understanding, may refuse to submit to medical examination or other assessment). Balanced against the interests of a child's mother and her husband it may, nevertheless, be in a child's interests to have a test against the wishes of the person with care and control (*Re T (Paternity: Ordering Blood Tests)* [2001] 2 FLR 1190, Bodey J).

"mental disorder" (s 21(4))—By virtue of Mental Health Act 1983, s 1(2), this means "mental illness, arrested or incomplete development of mind, psychopathic disorder and any other disorder or disability of mind and 'mentally disordered' shall be construed accordingly". For a full explanation see the note to FPR 1991, r 9.1.

22 Power to provide for manner of giving effect to direction for use of scientific tests

(1) The Lord Chancellor may by regulations make provision as to the manner of giving effect to directions under section 20 of this Act and, in particular, any such regulations may –

- (*a*) provide that bodily samples shall not be taken except by registered medical practitioners or members of such professional bodies as may be prescribed by the regulations;
- (*aa*) prescribe the bodily samples to be taken;
- (*b*) regulate the taking, identification and transport of bodily samples;
- (*c*) require the production at the time when a bodily sample is to be taken of such evidence of the identity of the person from whom it is to be taken as may be prescribed by the regulations;
- (*d*) require any person from whom a bodily sample is to be taken, or, in such cases as may be prescribed by the regulations, such other person as may be so prescribed, to state in writing whether he or the person from whom the sample is to be taken, as the case may be, has during such period as may be specified in the regulations suffered from any such illness or condition or undergone any such treatment as may be so specified or received a transfusion of blood;
- (*e*) prescribe conditions which a body must meet in order to be eligible for accreditation for the purposes of section 20 of this Act;
- (*f*) prescribe the scientific tests to be carried out and the manner in which they are to be carried out;
- (*g*) regulate the charges that may be made for the taking and testing of bodily samples and for the making of a report to a court under section 20 of this Act;
- (*h*) make provisions for securing that so far as practicable the bodily samples to be tested for the purpose of giving effect to a direction under section 20 of this Act are tested by the same person;
- (*i*) prescribe the form of the report to be made to a court under section 20 of this Act;
- (*j*) make different provision for different cases or for different descriptions of case.

(2) The power to make regulations under this section shall be exercisable by statutory instrument which shall be subject to annulment in pursuance of a resolution of either House of Parliament.

Amendments—Family Law Reform Act 1987, s 33(1), Sch 2, para 23; SI 1992/709; Child Support, Pensions and Social Security Act 2000, s 82(1), (4).

Defined terms—"bodily sample", "scientific test": s 25.

Regulations—The regulations are the Blood Tests (Evidence of Paternity) Regulations 1971, SI 1971/1861, as amended by SIs 1989/776, 1990/359, 1991/839.

23 Failure to comply with direction for taking scientific tests

(1) Where a court gives a direction under section 20 of this Act and any person fails to take any step required of him for the purpose of giving effect to the direction, the court may draw such inferences, if any, from that fact as appear proper in the circumstances.

(2) Where in any proceedings in which the parentage of any person falls to be determined by the court hearing the proceedings there is a presumption of law that that person is legitimate, then if –

(*a*) a direction is given under section 20 of this Act in those proceedings, and
(*b*) any party who is claiming any relief in the proceedings and who for the purpose of obtaining that relief is entitled to rely on the presumption fails to take any step required of him for the purpose of giving effect to the direction,

the court may adjourn the hearing for such period as it thinks fit to enable that party to take that step, and if at the end of that period he has failed without reasonable cause to take it the court may, without prejudice to subsection (1) of this section, dismiss his claim for relief notwithstanding the absence of evidence to rebut the presumption.

(3) Where any person named in a direction under section 20 of this Act fails to consent to the taking of a bodily sample from himself or from any person named in the direction of whom he has the care and control, he shall be deemed for the purposes of this section to have failed to take a step required of him for the purpose of giving effect to the direction.

Amendments—Family Law Reform Act 1987, s 33(1), Sch 2, para 24.

Defined terms—"scientific test": s 25.

"the court may draw such inference" (s 23(1))—Where a sample is refused, the court is entitled to infer that this corroborates the applicant's case (see eg *McV v B* [1988] 2 FLR 67, Wood J). The fact that more than one man might also be the father of the child, and none of those men was being proceeded against, did not entitle a respondent father to avoid the consequences of refusing to consent to a test (*Re A (A Minor) (Paternity: Refusal of Blood Test)* [1994] 2 FLR 463, CA).

Refusal of tests—If an inference is to be drawn from the refusal of a test, such inference can be drawn, even though a direction has not been made, if a parent clearly indicates an intention not to comply with any direction made by the court (*Re H (Paternity: Blood Test)* [1996] 2 FLR 65, CA).

"presumption of law" (s 23(2))—There is a presumption that a child born in wedlock is legitimate. If, in reliance on this, application is made to the court and paternity is challenged, the applicant must submit to any tests directed. If he does not, he risks having his application dismissed even though there is no evidence to rebut the presumption which would otherwise operate in his favour. For example, a person over 18 can apply for his parent to provide financial relief (CA 1989, s 15, Sch 1, para 2). If he applies against his mother's estranged husband, who then challenges his paternity, he will have to submit to a test if one is directed; and if he does not comply with the direction, the court has a discretion to dismiss his application.

"deemed ... to have failed to take a step required" (s 23(3))—This subsection refers back to consent under s 21(3) and involves children under 16.

24 Penalty for personating another, etc, for purpose of providing bodily sample

If for the purpose of providing a bodily sample for a test required to give effect to a direction under section 20 of this Act any person personates another, or proffers a child knowing that it is not the child named in the direction, he shall be liable –

(*a*) on conviction on indictment, to imprisonment for a term not exceeding two years, or
(*b*) on summary conviction, to a fine not exceeding the prescribed sum.

Amendments—Magistrates' Courts Act 1980, s 32(2); Family Law Reform Act 1987, s 33(1), Sch 2, para 25.

Defined terms—"bodily sample": s 25.

25 Interpretation of Part III

In this Part of this Act the following expressions have the meanings hereby respectively assigned to them, that is to say –

"bodily sample" means a sample of bodily fluid or bodily tissue taken for the purpose of scientific tests;

"excluded" means excluded subject to the occurrence of mutation to section 27 of the Family Law Reform Act 1987 and to sections 27 to 29 of the Human Fertilisation and Embryology Act 1990;

"scientific tests" means scientific tests carried out under this Part of this Act and made with the object of ascertaining the inheritable characteristics of bodily fluids or bodily tissue.

Amendments—Family Law Reform Act 1987, s 23(2); Human Fertilisation and Embryology Act 1990, s 49(5), Sch 4, para 1.

PART IV
MISCELLANEOUS AND GENERAL

26 Rebuttal of presumption as to legitimacy and illegitimacy

Any presumption of law as to the legitimacy or illegitimacy of any person may in any civil proceedings be rebutted by evidence which shows that it is more probable than not that that person is illegitimate or legitimate, as the case may be, and it shall not be necessary to prove that fact beyond reasonable doubt in order to rebut the presumption.

Standard of proof—For a discussion of the subject of "standard of proof", see *Cross and Tapper on Evidence* (8th Edn) (Butterworths), at 156 et seq. The "civil standard" is required here, although it has been suggested that the standard should reflect the seriousness of the question in issue, namely the parentage of a child (*Serio v Serio* (1983) FLR 756), summarised by Waite LJ in (*Re A (A Minor) (Paternity: Refusal of Blood Test)* [1994] 2 FLR 463, CA (at 470B) as follows:

> "(1) The question raised by an issue of paternity is a serious one – more serious in the scale of gravity than, for example, proof of debt or minor negligence.
>
> (2) The balance of probability has to be established to a degree of sureness in the mind of the court which matches the seriousness of the issue.
>
> (3) The weighing process involved in (2) must not however be overelaborate. The court should not attempt, in a precise – almost mathematical – way to determine precisely what degree of probability is appropriate to the gravity of the issue. There is still ample scope for the influence of common sense and the insight gained from first impression."

****

Family Law Reform Act 1987

1 General principle

(1) In this Act and enactments passed and instruments made after the coming into force of this section, references (however expressed) to any relationship between two persons shall, unless the contrary intention appears, be construed without regard to whether or not the father and mother of either of them, or the father and mother of any person through whom the relationship is deduced, have or had been married to each other at any time.

(2) In this Act and enactments passed after the coming into force of this section, unless the contrary intention appears –

(*a*) references to a person whose father and mother were married to each other at the time of his birth include; and

(*b*) references to a person whose father and mother were not married to each other at the time of his birth do not include,

references to any person to whom subsection (3) below applies, and cognate references shall be construed accordingly.

(3) This subsection applies to any person who –

(*a*) is treated as legitimate by virtue of section 1 of the Legitimacy Act 1976;

(*b*) is a legitimated person within the meaning of section 10 of that Act;

(*c*) is an adopted child within the meaning of Part IV of the Adoption Act 1976; or

(*d*) is otherwise treated in law as legitimate.

(4) For the purpose of construing references falling within subsection (2) above, the time of a person's birth shall be taken to include any time during the period beginning with –

(*a*) the insemination resulting in his birth; or

(*b*) where there was no such insemination, his conception,

and (in either case) ending with his birth.

****

18 Succession on intestacy

(1) In Part IV of the Administration of Estates Act 1925 (which deals with the distribution of the estate of an intestate), references (however expressed) to any relationship between two persons shall be construed in accordance with section 1 above.

(2) For the purposes of subsection (1) above and that Part of that Act, a person whose father and mother were not married to each other at the time of his birth shall be presumed not to have been survived by his father, or by any person related to him only through his father, unless the contrary is shown.

(3) In section 50(1) of that Act (which relates to the construction of documents), the reference to Part IV of that Act, or to the foregoing provisions of that Part, shall in relation to an instrument inter vivos made, or a will or codicil coming into operation, after the coming into force of this section (but not in relation to

PART II

instruments inter vivos made or wills or codicils coming into operation earlier) be construed as including references to this section.

(4) This section does not affect any rights under the intestacy of a person dying before the coming into force of this section.

19 Dispositions of property

(1) In the following dispositions, namely –

(*a*) dispositions inter vivos made on or after the date on which this section comes into force; and

(*b*) dispositions by will or codicil where the will or codicil is made on or after that date,

references (whether express or implied) to any relationship between two persons shall be construed in accordance with section 1 above.

(2) It is hereby declared that the use, without more, of the word "heir" or "heirs" or any expression purporting to create an entailed interest in real or personal property does not show a contrary intention for the purposes of section 1 as applied by subsection (1) above.

(3) In relation to the dispositions mentioned in subsection (1) above, section 33 of the Trustee Act 1925 (which specifies the trust implied by a direction that income is to be held on protective trusts for the benefit of any person) shall have effect as if any reference (however expressed) to any relationship between two persons were construed in accordance with section 1 above.

(4) Where under any disposition of real or personal property, any interest in such property is limited (whether subject to any preceding limitation or charge or not) in such a way that it would, apart from this section, devolve (as nearly as the law permits) along with a dignity or title of honour, then –

(*a*) whether or not the disposition contains an express reference to the dignity or title of honour; and

(*b*) whether or not the property or some interest in the property may in some event become severed from it,

nothing in this section shall operate to sever the property or any interest in it from the dignity or title, but the property or interest shall devolve in all respects as if this section had not been enacted.

(5) This section is without prejudice to section 42 of the Adoption Act 1976 (construction of dispositions in cases of adoption).

(6) In this section "disposition" means a disposition, including an oral disposition, of real or personal property whether inter vivos or by will or codicil.

(7) Notwithstanding any rule of law, a disposition made by will or codicil executed before the date on which this section comes into force shall not be treated for the purposes of this section as made on or after that date by reason only that the will or codicil is confirmed by a codicil executed on or after that date.

Amendments—Trusts of Land and Appointment of Trustees Act 1996, s 25(1), Sch 3, para 25.

20 No special protection for trustees and personal representatives

Section 17 of the Family Law Reform Act 1969 (which enables trustees and personal representatives to distribute property without having ascertained that no person whose parents were not married to each other at the time of his birth, or who claims through such a person, is or may be entitled to an interest in the property) shall cease to have effect.

21 Entitlement to grant probate etc

(1) For the purpose of determining the person or persons who would in accordance with probate rules be entitled to a grant of probate or administration in respect of the estate of a deceased person, the deceased shall be presumed, unless the contrary is shown, not to have been survived –

(*a*) by any person related to him whose father and mother were not married to each other at the time of his birth; or

(*b*) by any person whose relationship with him is deduced through such a person as is mentioned in paragraph (*a*) above.

(2) In this section "probate rules" means rules of court made under section 127 of the Supreme Court Act 1981.

(3) This section does not apply in relation to the estate of a person dying before the coming into force of this section.

****

27 Artificial insemination

(1) Where after the coming into force of this section a child is born in England and Wales as the result of the artificial insemination of a woman who –

(*a*) was at the time of the insemination a party to a marriage (being a marriage which had not at that time been dissolved or annulled); and

(*b*) was artificially inseminated with the semen of some person other than the other party to that marriage,

then, unless it is proved to the satisfaction of any court by which the matter has to be determined that the other party to that marriage did not consent to the insemination, the child shall be treated in law as the child of the parties to that marriage and shall not be treated as the child of any person other than the parties to that marriage.

(2) Any reference in this section to a marriage includes a reference to a void marriage if at the time of the insemination resulting in the birth of the child both or either of the parties reasonably believed that the marriage was valid; and for the purposes of this section it shall be presumed, unless the contrary is shown, that one of the parties so believed at that time that the marriage was valid.

(3) Nothing in this section shall affect the succession to any dignity or title of honour or render any person capable of succeeding to or transmitting a right to succeed to any such dignity or title.

Scope of provision—This section came into force on 4 April 1988 and provides that a child born to a married woman after 4 April 1988 as a result of artificial insemination with the semen of someone other than her husband should be treated in law as legitimate provided her husband had consented to the insemination. However, the section ceased to have effect on 1 August 1991 when the Human Fertilisation and Embryology Act 1990 came into force. It therefore does not have any

PART II

effect in relation to children carried by a woman as a result of artificial insemination after the commencement of HFEA 1990, ss 27–29 (HFEA 1990, s 49(3), (4)).

****

Human Fertilisation and Embryology Act 1990

ARRANGEMENT OF SECTIONS

Principal terms used

Principal terms used

1 Meaning of "embryo", "gamete" and associated expressions

(1) In this Act, except where otherwise stated –

(*a*) embryo means a live human embryo where fertilisation is complete, and
(*b*) references to an embryo include an egg in the process of fertilisation, and, for this purpose, fertilisation is not complete until the appearance of a two cell zygote.

(2) This Act, so far as it governs bringing about the creation of an embryo, applies only to bringing about the creation of an embryo outside the human body; and in this Act –

(*a*) references to embryos the creation of which was brought about in vitro (in their application to those where fertilisation is complete) are to those where fertilisation began outside the human body whether or not it was completed there, and
(*b*) references to embryos taken from a woman do not include embryos whose creation was brought about in vitro.

(3) This Act, so far as it governs the keeping or use of an embryo, applies only to keeping or using an embryo outside the human body.

(4) References in this Act to gametes, eggs or sperm, except where otherwise stated, are to live human gametes, eggs or sperm but references below in this Act to gametes or eggs do not include eggs in the process of fertilisation.

"embryo"—Human embryos created by cell nuclear replacement fall within the definition of embryo in s 1(1) and are subject to regulation under the 1990 Act (*R (Quintavelle) v Secretary of State for Health* [2002] EWCA Civ 29, [2002] 2 WLR 550, CA).

2 Other terms

(1) In this Act –

"the Authority" means the Human Fertilisation and Embryology Authority established under section 5 of this Act,
"directions" means directions under section 23 of this Act,
"licence" means a licence under Schedule 2 to this Act and, in relation to a licence, "the person responsible" has the meaning given by section 17 of this Act, and
"treatment services" means medical, surgical or obstetric services provided to the public or a section of the public for the purpose of assisting women to carry children.

(2) References in this Act to keeping, in relation to embryos or gametes, include keeping while preserved, whether preserved by cryopreservation or in any other way; and embryos or gametes so kept are referred to in this Act as "stored" (and "store" and "storage" are to be interpreted accordingly).

(3) For the purposes of this Act, a woman is not to be treated as carrying a child until the embryo has become implanted.

Activities governed by the Act

3 Prohibitions in connection with embryos

(1) No person shall –

(*a*) bring about the creation of an embryo, or
(*b*) keep or use an embryo,

except in pursuance of a licence.

(2) No person shall place in a woman –

(*a*) a live embryo other than a human embryo, or
(*b*) any live gametes other than human gametes.

(3) A licence cannot authorise –

(*a*) keeping or using an embryo after the appearance of the primitive streak,
(*b*) placing an embryo in any animal,
(*c*) keeping or using an embryo in any circumstances in which regulations prohibit its keeping or use, or
(*d*) replacing a nucleus of a cell of an embryo with a nucleus taken from a cell of any person, embryo or subsequent development of an embryo.

(4) For the purposes of subsection (3)(*a*) above, the primitive streak is to be taken to have appeared in an embryo not later than the end of the period of 14 days beginning with the day when the gametes are mixed, not counting any time during which the embryo is stored.

"placing in a woman a human embryo"—The Human Reproductive Cloning Act 2001 makes it an offence to place in a woman a human embryo which has been created otherwise than by fertilisation (which on conviction on indictment carries a maximum sentence of 10 years or a fine or both).

3A Prohibition in connection with germ cells

(1) No person shall, for the purpose of providing fertility services for any woman, use female germ cells taken or derived from an embryo or a foetus or use embryos created by using such cells.

(2) In this section –

"female germ cells" means cells of the female germ line and includes such cells at any stage of maturity and accordingly includes eggs; and
"fertility services" means medical, surgical or obstetric services provided for the purpose of assisting women to carry children.

Amendment—Inserted by Criminal Justice and Public Order Act 1994, s 156(1), (2).

4 Prohibitions in connection with gametes

(1) No person shall –

(*a*) store any gametes, or
(*b*) in the course of providing treatment services for any woman, use the sperm of any man unless the services are being provided for the woman and the man together or use the eggs of any other woman, or
(*c*) mix gametes with the live gametes of any animal,

except in pursuance of a licence.

(2) A licence cannot authorise storing or using gametes in any circumstances in which regulations prohibit their storage or use.

(3) No person shall place sperm and eggs in a woman in any circumstances specified in regulations except in pursuance of a licence.

(4) Regulations made by virtue of subsection (3) above may provide that, in relation to licences only to place sperm and eggs in a woman in such circumstances, sections 12 to 22 of this Act shall have effect with such modifications as may be specified in the regulations.

(5) Activities regulated by this section or section 3 of this Act are referred to in this Act as "activities governed by this Act".

Defined terms—"treatment services": Sch 2, para 1.

"provided for the woman and the man together"—See annotation to s 28. Treatment cannot be regarded as being provided for a woman and man together once the man who provided the sperm has died (*R v Human Fertilisation and Embryology Authority ex parte Blood* [1997] 2 FLR 742, [1997] 2 All ER 687); but see the effect of Arts 59 and 60 of the EC Treaty regarding the infringement of the right to receive medical treatment in another member state if the Authority refused to authorise the export of sperm for treatment abroad. In *Centre for Reproductive Medicine v U* [2002] FLR 927, where consent for the posthumous use of sperm had been withdrawn as a result of pressure being brought to bear upon the man, the court would not accede to his widow's wish to have the opportunity to use the sperm of her deceased husband in an attempt to bear his child posthumously.

The Human Fertilisation and Embryology Authority, its functions and procedure

5 The Human Fertilisation and Embryology Authority

(1) There shall be a body corporate called the Human Fertilisation and Embryology Authority.

(2) The Authority shall consist of –

- (*a*) a chairman and deputy chairman, and
- (*b*) such number of other members as the Secretary of State appoints.

(3) Schedule 1 to this Act (which deals with the membership of the Authority, etc.) shall have effect.

****

Scope of licences

11 Licences for treatment, storage and research

(1) The Authority may grant the following and no other licences –

- (*a*) licences under paragraph 1 of Schedule 2 to this Act authorising activities in the course of providing treatment services,
- (*b*) licences under that Schedule authorising the storage of gametes and embryos, and
- (*c*) licences under paragraph 3 of that Schedule authorising activities for the purposes of a project of research.

(2) Paragraph 4 of that Schedule has effect in the case of all licences.

"providing treatment services"—See under s 4.

Licence conditions

12 General conditions

The following shall be conditions of every licence granted under this Act –

(*a*) that the activities authorised by the licence shall be carried on only on the premises to which the licence relates and under the supervision of the person responsible,

(*b*) that any member or employee of the Authority, on production, if so required, of a document identifying the person as such, shall at all reasonable times be permitted to enter those premises and inspect them (which includes inspecting any equipment or records and observing any activity),

(*c*) that the provisions of Schedule 3 to this Act shall be complied with,

(*d*) that proper records shall be maintained in such form as the Authority may specify in directions,

(*e*) that no money or other benefit shall be given or received in respect of any supply of gametes or embryos unless authorised by directions,

(*f*) that, where gametes or embryos are supplied to a person to whom another licence applies, that person shall also be provided with such information as the Authority may specify in directions, and

(*g*) that the Authority shall be provided, in such form and at such intervals as it may specify in directions, with such copies of or extracts from the records, or such other information, as the directions may specify.

13 Conditions of licences for treatment

(1) The following shall be conditions of every licence under paragraph 1 of Schedule 2 to this Act.

(2) Such information shall be recorded as the Authority may specify in directions about the following –

(*a*) the persons for whom services are provided in pursuance of the licence,

(*b*) the services provided for them,

(*c*) the persons whose gametes are kept or used for the purposes of services provided in pursuance of the licence or whose gametes have been used in bringing about the creation of embryos so kept or used,

(*d*) any child appearing to the person responsible to have been born as a result of treatment in pursuance of the licence,

(*e*) any mixing of egg and sperm and any taking of an embryo from a woman or other acquisition of an embryo, and

(*f*) such other matters as the Authority may specify in directions.

(3) The records maintained in pursuance of the licence shall include any information recorded in pursuance of subsection (2) above and any consent of a person whose consent is required under Schedule 3 to this Act.

(4) No information shall be removed from any records maintained in pursuance of the licence before the expiry of such period as may be specified in directions for records of the class in question.

(5) A woman shall not be provided with treatment services unless account has been taken of the welfare of any child who may be born as a result of the treatment (including the need of that child for a father), and of any other child who may be affected by the birth.

(6) A woman shall not be provided with any treatment services involving –

(*a*) the use of any gametes of any person, if that person's consent is required under paragraph 5 of Schedule 3 to this Act for the use in question,

(*b*) the use of any embryo the creation of which was brought about in vitro, or

(*c*) the use of any embryo taken from a woman, if the consent of the woman from whom it was taken is required under paragraph 7 of that Schedule for the use in question,

unless the woman being treated and, where she is being treated together with a man, the man have been given a suitable opportunity to receive proper counselling about the implications of taking the proposed steps, and have been provided with such relevant information as is proper.

(7) Suitable procedures shall be maintained –

(*a*) for determining the persons providing gametes or from whom embryos are taken for use in pursuance of the licence, and

(*b*) for the purpose of securing that consideration is given to the use of practices not requiring the authority of a licence as well as those requiring such authority.

"unless account has been taken of the welfare of any child" (s 13(5))—See Code of Practice (4th Edition, 1998), laid down by the Human Fertilisation and Embryology Authority, with which licence holders must comply. See also DHSS Circular (LAC(85)12) which draws attention to the need to be aware of possible risks to the child in such circumstances and the duty to investigate.

14 Conditions of storage licences

(1) The following shall be conditions of every licence authorising the storage of gametes or embryos –

(*a*) that gametes of a person or an embryo taken from a woman shall be placed in storage only if received from that person or woman or acquired from a person to whom a licence applies and that an embryo the creation of which has been brought about in vitro otherwise than in pursuance of that licence shall be placed in storage only if acquired from a person to whom a licence applies,

(*b*) that gametes or embryos which are or have been stored shall not be supplied to a person otherwise than in the course of providing treatment services unless that person is a person to whom a licence applies,

(*c*) that no gametes or embryos shall be kept in storage for longer than the statutory storage period and, if stored at the end of the period, shall be allowed to perish, and

(*d*) that such information as the Authority may specify in directions as to the persons whose consent is required under Schedule 3 to this Act, the terms of their consent and the circumstances of the storage and as to such other matters as the Authority may specify in directions shall be included in the records maintained in pursuance of the licence.

(2) No information shall be removed from any records maintained in pursuance of such a licence before the expiry of such period as may be specified in directions for records of the class in question.

(3) The statutory storage period in respect of gametes is such period not exceeding ten years as the licence may specify.

(4) The statutory storage period in respect of embryos is such period not exceeding five years as the licence may specify.

(5) Regulations may provide that subsection (3) or (4) above shall have effect as if for ten years or, as the case may be, five years there were substituted –

(*a*) such shorter period, or
(*b*) in such circumstances as may be specified in the regulations, such longer period,

as may be specified in the regulations.

****

Status

27 Meaning of "mother"

(1) The woman who is carrying or has carried a child as a result of the placing in her of an embryo or of sperm and eggs, and no other woman, is to be treated as the mother of the child.

(2) Subsection (1) above does not apply to any child to the extent that the child is treated by virtue of adoption as not being the child of any person other than the adopter or adopters.

(3) Subsection (1) above applies whether the woman was in the United Kingdom or elsewhere at the time of placing in her of the embryo or the sperm and eggs.

Defined terms—"carrying or has carried a child": s 2(3); "eggs": s 1(4); "embryo": s 1(1); "sperm": s 1(4).

Scope of provision—This section follows the recommendations of the Warnock Committee: *Report of Inquiry into Human Fertilisation and Embryology* (1984). The effect is that the woman who carries the child is treated as the child's mother, ie the gestational mother not the genetic mother is treated as the mother of the child. Thus, where an infertile woman receives donated egg or embryo which she carries to full term, she will be regarded as the mother and, in the case of surrogacy, it is the surrogate mother who will be treated as the child's mother.

28 Meaning of "father"

(1) This section applies in the case of a child who is being or has been carried by a woman as the result of the placing in her of an embryo or of sperm and eggs or her artificial insemination.

(2) If –

(*a*) at the time of the placing in her of the embryo or the sperm and eggs or of her insemination, the woman was a party to a marriage, and
(*b*) the creation of the embryo carried by her was not brought about with the sperm of the other party to the marriage,

then, subject to subsection (5) below, the other party to the marriage shall be treated as the father of the child unless it is shown that he did not consent to the placing in her of the embryo or the sperm and eggs or to her insemination (as the case may be).

(3) If no man is treated, by virtue of subsection (2) above, as the father of the child but –

(*a*) the embryo or the sperm and eggs were placed in the woman, or she was artificially inseminated, in the course of treatment services provided for her and a man together by a person to whom a licence applies, and (*b*) the creation of the embryo carried by her was not brought about with the sperm of that man,

then, subject to subsection (5) below, that man shall be treated as the father of the child.

(4) Where a person is treated as the father of the child by virtue of subsection (2) or (3) above, no other person is to be treated as the father of the child.

(5) Subsections (2) and (3) above do not apply –

(*a*) in relation to England and Wales and Northern Ireland, to any child who, by virtue of the rules of common law, is treated as the legitimate child of the parties to a marriage,

(*b*) (*applies to Scotland only*), or

(*c*) to any child to the extent that the child is treated by virtue of adoption as not being the child of any person other than the adopter or adopters.

(6) Where –

(*a*) the sperm of a man who had given such consent as is required by paragraph 5 of Schedule 3 to this Act was used for a purpose for which such consent was required, or

(*b*) the sperm of a man, or any embryo the creation of which was brought about with his sperm, was used after his death,

he is not to be treated as the father of the child.

(7) The references in subsection (2) above to the parties to a marriage at the time there referred to –

(*a*) are to the parties to a marriage subsisting at that time, unless a judicial separation was then in force, but

(*b*) include the parties to a void marriage if either or both of them reasonably believed at that time that the marriage was valid; and for the purposes of this subsection it shall be presumed, unless the contrary is shown, that one of them reasonably believed at that time that the marriage was valid.

(8) This section applies whether the woman was in the United Kingdom or elsewhere at the time of the placing in her of the embryo or the sperm and eggs or her artificial insemination.

(9) In subsection (7)(*a*) above, "judicial separation" includes a legal separation obtained in a country outside the British Islands and recognised in the United Kingdom.

Defined terms—"carried by a woman": s 2(3); "eggs": s 1(4); "embryo": s 1(1); "licence": s 2(1); "sperm": s 1(4); "treatment services": s 2(1).

Scope of provision—This section replaces the Family Law Reform Act 1987, s 27 in relation to surrogacy arrangements. It is more extensive in that it covers additional reproductive techniques involving the use of donated embryos or sperm and eggs.

Receiving "treatment services ... together" (s 28(3)(*a*))—For the meaning of this phrase, see *Re B (Parentage)* [1996] 2 FLR 15; *Re Q (Parental Order)* [1996] 1 FLR 369; *R v Human Fertilisation and Embryology Authority ex parte Blood* [1997] 2 FLR 742, [1997] 2 All ER 687 and *Leeds Teaching Hospitals NHS Trust v Mr and Mrs A and Others* (2003) *The Times*, 28 February. Where treatment is requested by a man and a woman as a couple, then notwithstanding the absence of any physical role by the man in such treatment, it is nevertheless provided for the couple "together" (*U v W (Attorney-General Intervening)* (No 2) [1997] 2 FLR 282, FD). See also *In re R (Parental responsibilty: IVF baby)* (2003) *The Times*, 19 February, LTL 19/02/2003, Doc No C0104560, CA, where the mother misled the medical authority by falsely representing that her

PART II

relationship with her partner was ongoing. The Court of Appeal held that where embryos resulting in a successful pregnancy are placed in the mother after she has separated from the father he is *not* the legal father of the child within the meaning of s 28(3), since they are no longer being provided with treatment services "together" at the relevant time.

Unmarried couples (s 28(3))—In the case of an unmarried couple where treatment services were provided to the man and the woman together, but not with the sperm of that man, the man is treated as the father of the child even though he is not the genetic father. The effect of this provision is to extend the benefit of infertility treatment to unmarried couples and to impose on the man the responsibility for the care of the child as in the case of a married couple. The man will be liable to maintain the child, and the woman may apply for financial relief for the child. Where the treatment is administered abroad and therefore by a non-licence holder, s 28(3) cannot apply to confer paternity on the man, particularly where there is uncertainty regarding whether the treatment has been provided "together" and whether the man has been warned of the consequences and given a full opportunity to make an informed choice.

Where, however, the embryo or the sperm and eggs are placed in an unmarried surrogate woman and the man whose sperm led to its creation is a donor for the purpose of licensed treatment, the donor of the sperm is not treated as the father as he is excluded under s 28(6). The husband of the commissioning couple too cannot be treated as the father pursuant to s 28(3) because the husband cannot be regarded as a man for whom treatment services were provided by the licence holder together with the carrying woman (see *Re Q (Parental Order)* [1996] 1 FLR 369).

Preservation of presumptions (s 28(5))—The presumptions of legitimacy and paternity are preserved by s 28(5), even in cases where the husband can show that he did not consent to his wife receiving treatment. In such cases, the husband must disprove paternity, eg by DNA testing.

Parental responsibility—Where a man is to be treated as the father of the child, he may apply for parental responsibility for the child under CA 1989, s 4.

Exceptions—Where the man gives his consent to the use of his sperm for the purposes of licensed treatment services under the provisions of Sch 3, para 5, the donor is not to be treated as the child's father (s 28(5)). In such cases the child is fatherless. Where treatment is received as a result of unlicensed activities, the donor is treated as the father with all the rights and responsibilities of a putative father. Where the sperm of a man is used or any embryo created after his death, he cannot be treated as the child's father; for example, where a child is born to a woman as a result of the use, after his death, of her deceased husband's frozen sperm or embryo, he is not treated as the child's father, and the child is fatherless.

29 Effect of sections 27 and 28

(1) Where by virtue of section 27 or 28 of this Act a person is to be treated as the mother or father of a child, that person is to be treated in law as the mother or, as the case may be, father of the child for all purposes.

(2) Where by virtue of section 27 or 28 of this Act a person is not to be treated as the mother or father of a child, that person is to be treated in law as not being the mother or, as the case may be, father of the child for any purpose.

(3) Where subsection (1) or (2) above has effect, references to any relationship between two people in any enactment, deed or other instrument or document (whenever passed or made) are to be read accordingly.

(4) In relation to England and Wales and Northern Ireland, nothing in the provisions of section 27(1) or 28(2) to (4), read with this section, affects –

(*a*) the succession to any dignity or title of honour or renders any person capable of succeeding to or transmitting a right to succeed to any such dignity or title, or

(*b*) the devolution of any property limited (expressly or not) to devolve (as nearly as the law permits) along with the dignity or title of honour.

(5) (*applies to Scotland only*).

Scope of provision—Where pursuant to ss 27 and 28 a person is to be treated as the parent of the child, rules relating to incest and prohibited relationship will apply. The child is entitled to all the rights and benefits which flow from and through the parents. Thus the child is entitled to inherit, save for the exception on inheritance of titles laid down under s 29(4), from his parents (cf Adoption Act 1976, s 44(1), under which an adoption order does not affect the descent of any peerage or dignity or title of honour).

"for all purposes" (s 29(1))—This entitles the person who has no biological links with the child, but is treated as a father, to apply for orders under CA 1989, s 8 (*Re R (Contact: Human Fertilisation and Embryology Act 1990)* [2001] 1 FLR 247).

30 Parental orders in favour of gamete donors

(1) The court may make an order providing for a child to be treated in law as the child of the parties to a marriage (referred to in this section as "the husband" and "the wife") if –

(*a*) the child has been carried by a woman other than the wife as the result of the placing in her of an embryo or sperm and eggs or her artificial insemination,
(*b*) the gametes of the husband or the wife, or both, were used to bring about the creation of the embryo, and
(*c*) the conditions in subsections (2) to (7) below are satisfied.

(2) The husband and the wife must apply for the order within six months of the birth of the child or, in the case of a child born before the coming into force of this Act, within six months of such coming into force.

(3) At the time of the application and of the making of the order –

(*a*) the child's home must be with the husband and the wife, and
(*b*) the husband or the wife, of both of them, must be domiciled in a part of the United Kingdom or in the Channel Islands or the Isle of Man.

(4) At the time of the making of the order both the husband and the wife must have attained the age of eighteen.

(5) The court must be satisfied that both the father of the child (including a person who is the father by virtue of section 28 of this Act), where he is not the husband, and the woman who carried the child have freely, and with full understanding of what is involved, agreed unconditionally to the making of the order.

(6) Subsection (5) above does not require the agreement of a person who cannot be found or is incapable of giving agreement and the agreement of the woman who carried the child is ineffective for the purposes of that subsection if given by her less than six weeks after the child's birth.

(7) The court must be satisfied that no money or other benefit (other than for expenses reasonably incurred) has been given or received by the husband or the wife for or in consideration of –

(*a*) the making of the order,
(*b*) any agreement required by subsection (5) above,
(*c*) the handing over of the child to the husband and the wife, or
(*d*) the making of any arrangements with a view to the making of the order,

unless authorised by the court.

(8) For the purposes of an application under this section –

(*a*) in relation to England and Wales, section 92(7) to (10) of, and Part I of Schedule 11 to, the Children Act 1989 (jurisdiction of courts) shall apply for the purposes of this section to determine the meaning of "the court" as they apply for the purposes of that Act and proceedings on the application shall be "family proceedings" for the purposes of that Act,

(*b*) (*applies to Scotland only*), and

(*c*) in relation to Northern Ireland, "the court" means the High Court or any county court within whose division the child is.

(9) Regulations may provide –

(*a*) for any provision of the enactments about adoption to have effect, with such modifications (if any) as may be specified in the regulations, in relation to orders under this section, and applications for such orders, as it has effect in relation to adoption, and applications for adoption orders, and

(*b*) for references in any enactment to adoption, an adopted child or an adoptive relationship to be read (respectively) as references to the effect of an order under this section, a child to whom such an order applies and a relationship arising by virtue of the enactments about adoption, as applied by the regulations, and for similar expressions in connection with adoption to be read accordingly,

and the regulations may include such incidental or supplemental provision as appears to the Secretary of State necessary or desirable in consequence of any provision made by virtue of paragraph (*a*) or (*b*) above.

(10) In this section "the enactments about adoption" means the Adoption Act 1976, the Adoption (Scotland) Act 1978 and the Adoption (Northern Ireland) Order 1987.

(11) Subsection (1)(*a*) above applies whether the woman was in the United Kingdom or elsewhere at the time of the placing in her of the embryo or the sperm and eggs or her artificial insemination.

Defined terms—"eggs": s 1(4); "embryo": s 1(1); "family proceedings": CA 1989, s 8(3); "gametes": s 1(4); "parties to a marriage": s 28(7); "sperm": s 1(4).

Scope of provision—This section came into force on 1 November 1994 (SI 1994/1776), and provides for the making of a parental order on an application by the commissioning couple in respect of a child who is born to a surrogate mother, and the gametes used are those of one or other of the commissioning couple. The effect of the order is to transfer parenthood to the commissioning couple, with the effect that the child is for all purposes treated in law as a child of the parties to a marriage. This section sets out the conditions to be satisfied by the applicants before a parental order can be made.

An example of a case concerning a child who is genetically the child of the husband or wife or both but is carried by a surrogate is *Re W (Minors) (Surrogacy)* [1991] 1 FLR 385, where the court was asked to make a declaration as to parentage in favour of the genetic parents. In view of the effect of s 30, the court confirmed the wardship but adjourned all other applications on the genetic parents undertaking to apply under s 30(2) for a parental order. This section is limited in its application; it applies only to married couples and not to those who are cohabiting as husband and wife (cf s 28(3) and Adoption Act 1976, s 14(1), whereby cohabiting couples are not permitted to make a joint application for adoption). It should be stressed that the placing of sperm and eggs in a woman by any person, save in pursuance of a licence, is prohibited (HFEA 1990, s 4).

Limitation of time (s 30(2))—An application under this section must be made within six months of the birth of the child or within six months of the section coming into force.

Age of applicant (s 30(4))—Both the husband and the wife must have attained the age of 18 years.

Consent (s 30(5))—The unconditional agreement of the father of the child and the surrogate mother, given freely and with full understanding of what the making of the order involves, must be proved (cf Adoption Act 1976, s 16(1)(*b*)(i)). Unlike the case of adoption, there is no provision for dispensation of consent. Pursuant to the Parental Orders (Human Fertilisation and Embryology) Regulations 1994, certain provisions of the Adoption Act 1976 apply to applications under s 30 for a parental order, and FPR 1991, Pt IVA sets out the procedure to be followed. However, there are no specific provisions for signifying the consent of the father of the child and the surrogate mother (see **Parental order under HFEA 1990, s 30** under Adoption Act 1976, s 61). It is suggested that Form 2 (see Adoption Rules 1984, Sch 1) should be used with appropriate modification. Under FPR 1991, Pt IVA, in contrast to AR 1984, r 5, the parental order reporter is not specifically required to ensure that any agreement to the making of an order is given freely, unconditionally and with a full understanding of what is involved. The parental order reporter appointed for proceedings under s 30 is merely required to "investigate" and does not have to witness the signature by the parent evidencing written agreement to the making of an order.

Where the child was carried by an unmarried mother who had had placed in her an egg of the wife fertilised by the sperm of a donor (who was not the husband of the wife), who donated his sperm for the purpose of licensed treatment and was therefore not the father by virtue of s 28(6) of the Act, there was no man who could be treated as the father and whose consent was necessary to the making of a parental order. Accordingly, the consent of the husband was not required under s 30(5) (*Re Q (Parental Order)* [1996] 1 FLR 369).

Payment of money or other benefit (s 30(7))—Save for expenses reasonably incurred, payment of money or other benefit to the surrogate is prohibited unless sanctioned by the court. The meaning of "expenses reasonably incurred" is not defined. It should cover expenses associated with the expense of bearing a child but payments which exceed these are often made (as occurred in *Re C (A Child)* [2002] EWHC 157 (Fam)). However, Wall J warned that couples and surrogate mothers should be made aware for the need for transparency in the definition and true extent of expenses reasonably incurred. Notwithstanding this decision, it is submitted that there is need for a review of this provision to provide a clear definition; reference may be made to Adoption Act 1976, ss 24(2) and 57, and the following cases where payment was agreed and made as part of a surrogacy agreement: *Re Adoption Application (Payment for Adoption)* [1987] Fam 81, [1987] 2 FLR 291; *Re P (Minors) (Wardship: Surrogacy)* [1987] 2 FLR 421; *Re C (A Minor) (Wardship: Surrogacy)* [1985] FLR 846. This provision should be read in conjunction with s 36, which inserts s 1A into the Surrogacy Arrangements Act 1985, thereby making surrogacy arrangements unenforceable. Thus, a surrogate mother cannot enforce any agreement for payment to her for expenses, although such payments are permitted under s 30(7), nor can the commissioning couple demand the child to be handed over under the terms of the agreement. In cases where there are difficulties over the conditions necessary to obtain a parental order under this section, the parties will have to resort to the provisions of CA 1989 and wardship.

Family proceedings (s 30(8)(*a*))—Applications under this section are to be treated as family proceedings and therefore the principles of CA 1989 apply and the court is free to make orders under s 8 if it considers any such order to be more appropriate.

Regulations (s 30(9))—Provision is made under s 30(9) for secondary legislation to provide for any provision of the enactments relating to adoption to apply to proceedings under the Act. The Parental Orders (Human Fertilisation and Embryology) Regulations 1994 introduce, with modifications, certain provisions of the Adoption Act 1976 to have effect in relation to parental orders, and the effect of these modifications is noted under the relevant sections of the 1976 Act.

Part IVA of the FPR 1991 (inserted by SI 1994/2165) and Part IIA of the Family Proceedings Courts (Children Act 1989) Rules 1991 (inserted by SI 1994/2166) set out the procedure to be followed in an application for a parental order and for related applications within the substantive application.

****

34 Disclosure in interests of justice

(1) Where in any proceedings before a court the question whether a person is or is not the parent of a child by virtue of sections 27 to 29 of this Act falls to be

determined, the court may on the application of any party to the proceedings make an order requiring the Authority –

(*a*) to disclose whether or not any information relevant to that question is contained in the register kept in pursuance of section 31 of this Act, and

(*b*) if it is, to disclose so much of it as is specified in the order,

but such an order may not require the Authority to disclose any information falling within section 31(2)(*b*) of this Act.

(2) The court must not make an order under subsection (1) above unless it is satisfied that the interests of justice require it to do so, taking into account –

(*a*) any representations made by any individual who may be affected by the disclosure, and

(*b*) the welfare of the child, if under 18 years old, and of any other person under that age who may be affected by the disclosure.

(3) If the proceedings before the court are civil proceedings, it –

(*a*) may direct that the whole or any part of the proceedings on the application for an order under subsection (2) above shall be heard in camera, and

(*b*) if it makes such an order, may then or later direct that the whole or any part of any later stage of the proceedings shall be heard in camera.

(4) An application for a direction under subsection (3) above shall be heard in camera unless the court otherwise directs.

Defined terms—"the Authority": s 2(1).

"register" (s 34(1)(*a*))—A register is required to be maintained by the Authority under s 31 containing information relating to the provision of treatment services for any identifiable individual or the keeping or use of any gametes of any identifiable individual or of an embryo taken from any identifiable woman or information showing that any identifiable individual was, or may have been, born as a consequence of treatment services.

"information falling within section 31(2)(b)" (s 34(1))—This is information obtained by any member or employee of the Authority on terms or in circumstances requiring it to be held in confidence.

35 Disclosure in interests of justice: congenital disabilities etc

(1) Where for the purpose of instituting proceedings under section 1 of the Congenital Disabilities (Civil Liability) Act 1976 (civil liability to child born disabled) it is necessary to identify a person who would or might be the parent of a child but for sections 27 to 29 of this Act, the court may, on the application of the child, make an order requiring the Authority to disclose any information contained in the register kept in pursuance of section 31 of this Act identifying that person.

(2) ...

(3) Subsections (2) to (4) of section 34 of this Act apply for the purposes of this section as they apply for the purposes of that.

(4) ...

****

SCHEDULE 2

ACTIVITIES FOR WHICH LICENCES MAY BE GRANTED

1 Licences for treatment

(1) A licence under this paragraph may authorise any of the following in the course of providing treatment services –

(*a*) bringing about the creation of embryos in vitro,
(*b*) keeping embryos,
(*c*) using gametes,
(*d*) practices designed to secure that embryos are in a suitable condition to be placed in a woman or to determine whether embryos are suitable for that purpose,
(*e*) placing any embryo in a woman,
(*f*) mixing sperm with the egg of a hamster, or other animal specified in directions, for the purpose of testing the fertility or normality of the sperm, but only where anything which forms is destroyed when the test is complete and, in any event, not later than the two cell stage, and
(*g*) such other practices as may be specified in, or determined in accordance with, regulations.

(2) Subject to the provisions of this Act, a licence under this paragraph may be granted subject to such conditions as may be specified in the licence and may authorise the performance of any of the activities referred to in sub-paragraph (1) above in such manner as may be so specified.

(3) A licence under this paragraph cannot authorise any activity unless it appears to the Authority to be necessary or desirable for the purpose of providing treatment services.

(4) A licence under this paragraph cannot authorise altering the genetic structure of any cell while it forms part of an embryo.

(5) A licence under this paragraph shall be granted for such period not exceeding five years as may be specified in the licence.

****

SCHEDULE 3

CONSENTS TO USE OF GAMETES OR EMBRYOS

Consent

1 A consent under this Schedule must be given in writing and, in this Schedule, "effective consent" means a consent under this Schedule which has not been withdrawn.

"consent"—Where sperm was taken whilst the donor was in a coma at the request of the donor's wife and where no consent had been previously given by the donor for the sperm to be stored, it was held that the Authority was correct in refusing a licence for treatment involving the use of the sperm in the UK, as to do so would be contrary to the provisions of s 4(1) and Sch 3 (*R v Human Fertilisation and Embryology Authority ex parte Blood* [1997] 2 FLR 742, [1997] 2 All ER 687).

2 (1) A consent to the use of any embryo must specify one or more of the following purposes –

(*a*) use in providing treatment services to the person giving consent, or that person and another specified person together,
(*b*) use in providing treatment services to persons not including the person giving consent, or
(*c*) use for the purposes of any project of research,

and may specify conditions subject to which the embryo may be so used.

(2) A consent to the storage of any gametes or any embryo must –

(*a*) specify the maximum period of storage (if less than the statutory storage period), and
(*b*) state what is to be done with the gametes or embryo if the person who gave the consent dies or is unable because of incapacity to vary the terms of the consent or to revoke it,

and may specify conditions subject to which the gametes or embryo may remain in storage.

(3) A consent under this Schedule must provide for such other matters as the Authority may specify in directions.

(4) A consent under this Schedule may apply –

(*a*) to the use or storage of a particular embryo, or
(*b*) in the case of a person providing gametes, to the use or storage of any embryo whose creation may be brought about using those gametes,

and in the paragraph (*b*) case the terms of the consent may be varied, or the consent may be withdrawn, in accordance with this Schedule either generally or in relation to a particular embryo or particular embryos.

3 Procedure for giving consent

(1) Before a person gives consent under this Schedule –

(*a*) he must be given a suitable opportunity to receive proper counselling about the implications of taking the proposed steps, and
(*b*) he must be provided with such relevant information as is proper.

(2) Before a person gives consent under this Schedule he must be informed of the effect of paragraph 4 below.

4 Variation and withdrawal of consent

(1) The terms of any consent under this Schedule may from time to time be varied, and the consent may be withdrawn, by notice given by the person who gave the consent to the person keeping the gametes or embryo to which the consent is relevant.

(2) The terms of any consent to the use of any embryo cannot be varied, and such consent cannot be withdrawn, once the embryo has been used –

(*a*) in providing treatment services, or
(*b*) for the purposes of any project of research.

5 Use of gametes for treatment of others

(1) A person's gametes must not be used for the purposes of treatment services unless there is an effective consent by that person to their being so used and they are used in accordance with the terms of the consent.

(2) A person's gametes must not be received for use for those purposes unless there is an effective consent by that person to their being so used.

(3) This paragraph does not apply to the use of a person's gametes for the purpose of that person, or that person and another together, receiving treatment services.

6 In vitro fertilisation and subsequent use of embryo

(1) A person's gametes must not be used to bring about the creation of any embryo in vitro unless there is an effective consent by that person to any embryo the creation of which may be brought about with the use of those gametes being used for one or more of the purposes mentioned in paragraph 2(1) above.

(2) An embryo the creation of which was brought about in vitro must not be received by any person unless there is an effective consent by each person whose gametes were used to bring about the creation of the embryo to the use for one or more of the purposes mentioned in paragraph 2(1) above of the embryo.

(3) An embryo the creation of which was brought about in vitro must not be used for any purpose unless there is an effective consent by each person whose gametes were used to bring about the creation of the embryo to the use for that purpose of the embryo and the embryo is used in accordance with those consents.

(4) Any consent required by this paragraph is in addition to any consent that may be required by paragraph 5 above.

7 Embryos obtained by lavage, etc

(1) An embryo taken from a woman must not be used for any purpose unless there is an effective consent by her to the use of the embryo for that purpose and it is used in accordance with the consent.

(2) An embryo taken from a woman must not be received by any person for use for any purpose unless there is an effective consent by her to the use of the embryo for that purpose.

(3) This paragraph does not apply to the use, for the purpose of providing a woman with treatment services, of an embryo taken from her.

8 Storage of gametes and embryos

(1) A person's gametes must not be kept in storage unless there is an effective consent by that person to their storage and they are stored in accordance with the consent.

(2) An embryo the creation of which was brought about in vitro must not be kept in storage unless there is an effective consent, by each person whose gametes were used to bring about the creation of the embryo, to the storage of the embryo and the embryo is stored in accordance with those consents.

(3) An embryo taken from a woman must not be kept in storage unless there is an effective consent by her to its storage and it is stored in accordance with the consent.

****

Human Rights Act 1998

ARRANGEMENT OF SECTIONS

Introduction

1 The Convention Rights

(1) In this Act "the Convention rights" means the rights and fundamental freedoms set out in –

(*a*) Articles 2 to 12 and 14 of the Convention,
(*b*) Articles 1 to 3 of the First Protocol, and
(*c*) Articles 1 and 2 of the Sixth Protocol,

as read with Articles 16 to 18 of the Convention.

(2) Those Articles are to have effect for the purposes of this Act subject to any designated derogation or reservation (as to which see sections 14 and 15).

(3) The Articles are set out in Schedule 1.

(4) The Lord Chancellor may by order make such amendments to this Act as he considers appropriate to reflect the effect, in relation to the United Kingdom, of a protocol.

(5) In subsection (4) "protocol" means a protocol to the Convention –

(*a*) which the United Kingdom has ratified; or
(*b*) which the United Kingdom has signed with a view to ratification.

(6) No amendment may be made by an order under subsection (4) so as to come into force before the protocol concerned is in force in relation to the United Kingdom.

Amendments—2001/3500.

Scope of provision—It is important to note that *only* those Articles of the European Convention listed are to be read into domestic law (see under s 3 (below)). Articles not listed are specifically excluded.

2 Interpretation of Convention rights

(1) A court or tribunal determining a question which has arisen in connection with a Convention right must take into account any –

(*a*) judgment, decision, declaration or advisory opinion of the European Court of Human Rights,
(*b*) opinion of the Commission given in a report adopted under Article 31 of the Convention,
(*c*) decision of the Commission in connection with Article 26 or 27(2) of the Convention, or
(*d*) decision of the Committee of Ministers taken under Article 46 of the Convention,

whenever made or given, so far as, in the opinion of the court or tribunal, it is relevant to the proceedings in which that question has arisen.

(2) Evidence of any judgment, decision, declaration or opinion of which account may have to be taken under this section is to be given in proceedings before any court or tribunal in such manner as may be provided by rules.

(3) In this section "rules" means rules of court or, in the case of proceedings before a tribunal, rules made for the purposes of this section –

(*a*) by the Lord Chancellor or the Secretary of State, in relation to any proceedings outside Scotland;
(*b*) by the Secretary of State, in relation to proceedings in Scotland; or
(*c*) by a Northern Ireland department, in relation to proceedings before a tribunal in Northern Ireland –
(i) which deals with transferred matters; and
(ii) for which no rules made under paragraph (*a*) are in force.

"a question which has arisen" (s 2(1))—A question may arise in ongoing proceedings, in which case the issue must be determined (if possible) within those proceedings (see annotations to s 7). Alternatively, a question may arise as a freestanding issue where there are no current proceedings. In this case, an application may be made by way of judicial review to determine the question (see annotations to s 7).

"Evidence of any judgment ..." (s 2(2))—By *President's Direction of 24 July 2000* ("Human Rights Act 1998") the President has directed that when an authority is to be cited at a hearing, the authority must be an authoritative and complete report and copies of the report, with a list of authorities, must be filed in accordance with *President's Direction of 10 March 2000*, or otherwise not less than two days before the hearing. The *President's Direction* states that these must be copies of the complete original text issued by the European Court and Commission (either paper-based or through HUDOC which is available on the internet at *www.echr.coe.int/hudoc*).

Legislation

3 Interpretation of legislation

(1) So far as it is possible to do so, primary legislation and subordinate legislation must be read and given effect in a way which is compatible with the Convention rights.

(2) This section –

(*a*) applies to primary legislation and subordinate legislation whenever enacted;
(*b*) does not affect the validity, continuing operation or enforcement of any incompatible primary legislation; and
(*c*) does not affect the validity, continuing operation or enforcement of any incompatible subordinate legislation if (disregarding any possibility of revocation) primary legislation prevents removal of the incompatibility.

Scope of provision—This section is described as the "lynch-pin" of the Act (see *Swindells et al – Family Law and the Human Rights Act 1998* (Family Law, 1999), at p 9). It requires that all primary and subordinate legislation must, as far as possible, be read and given effect in a way which is compatible with Convention rights.

4 Declaration of incompatibility

(1) Subsection (2) applies in any proceedings in which a court determines whether a provision of primary legislation is compatible with a Convention right.

(2) If the court is satisfied that the provision is incompatible with a Convention right, it may make a declaration of that incompatibility.

(3) Subsection (4) applies in any proceedings in which a court determines whether a provision of subordinate legislation, made in the exercise of a power conferred by primary legislation, is compatible with a Convention right.

(4) If the court is satisfied –

(*a*) that the provision is incompatible with a Convention right, and
(*b*) that (disregarding any possibility of revocation) the primary legislation concerned prevents removal of the incompatibility,

it may make a declaration of that incompatibility.

(5) In this section "court" means –

(*a*) the House of Lords;
(*b*) the Judicial Committee of the Privy Council;
(*c*) the Courts-Martial Appeal Court;
(*d*) in Scotland, the High Court of Justiciary sitting otherwise than as a trial court or the Court of Session;
(*e*) in England and Wales or Northern Ireland, the High Court or the Court of Appeal.

(6) A declaration under this section ("a declaration of incompatibility") –

(*a*) does not affect the validity, continuing operation or enforcement of the provision in respect of which it is given; and
(*b*) is not binding on the parties to the proceedings in which it is made.

Scope of provision—This section provides the higher courts (as defined in s 4(4)) with power to make a "declaration of incompatibility" if satisfied that a provision of primary or subordinate legislation is incompatible with the Convention. Such a declaration is not binding upon the parties and it does not change the law, which the court is required to continue to apply. The court therefore cannot set aside the primary legislation but, it appears, can set aside subordinate legislation unless the terms of the enabling statute make this impossible (see *Swindells et al – Family Law and the Human Rights Act 1998* (Family Law, 1999), at p 10). Such a declaration should have the effect of prompting the government to change the law.

Procedure—A claim for a declaration of incompatibility must be made on a claim form. The procedure for an application under s 4 is contained within FPR 1991, r 10.26. 21 days' notice of a s 4 application must be given to the Crown, or otherwise such notice as the court directs (CPR 1998, r 19.4A and FPR 1991, r 10.26(4)) .

PART II

5 Right of Crown to intervene

(1) Where a court is considering whether to make a declaration of incompatibility, the Crown is entitled to notice in accordance with rules of court.

(2) In any case to which subsection (1) applies –

(*a*) a Minister of the Crown (or a person nominated by him),
(*b*) a member of the Scottish Executive,
(*c*) a Northern Ireland Minister,
(*d*) a Northern Ireland department,

is entitled, on giving notice in accordance with rules of court, to be joined as a party to the proceedings.

(3) Notice under subsection (2) may be given at any time during the proceedings.

(4) A person who has been made a party to criminal proceedings (other than in Scotland) as the result of a notice under subsection (2) may, with leave, appeal to the House of Lords against any declaration of incompatibility made in the proceedings.

(5) In subsection (4) –

"criminal proceedings" includes all proceedings before the Courts-Martial Appeal Court; and

"leave" means leave granted by the court making the declaration of incompatibility or by the House of Lords.

Scope of provision—Where consideration is being given to a "declaration of incompatibility", the Crown should be notified and allowed to become a party to the proceedings. A court may not make a declaration unless 21 days' notice has been given to the Crown (CPR 1998, r 19.4A and FPR 1991, r 10.26(4)). Where such notice has been given, a Minister, on giving notice to the court, will be joined as a party (CPR 1998, r 19.4A(2) and FPR 1991, r 10.26(5)).

Public authorities

6 Acts of public authorities

(1) It is unlawful for a public authority to act in a way which is incompatible with a Convention right.

(2) Subsection (1) does not apply to an act if –

(*a*) as the result of one or more provisions of primary legislation, the authority could not have acted differently; or
(*b*) in the case of one or more provisions of, or made under, primary legislation which cannot be read or given effect in a way which is

compatible with the Convention rights, the authority was acting so as to give effect to or enforce those provisions.

(3) In this section "public authority" includes –

(*a*) a court or tribunal, and
(*b*) any person certain of whose functions are functions of a public nature,

but does not include either House of Parliament or a person exercising functions in connection with proceedings in Parliament.

(4) In subsection (3) "Parliament" does not include the House of Lords in its judicial capacity.

(5) In relation to a particular act, a person is not a public authority by virtue only of subsection (3)(*b*) if the nature of the act is private.

(6) "An act" includes a failure to act but does not include a failure to –

(*a*) introduce in, or lay before, Parliament a proposal for legislation; or
(*b*) make any primary legislation or remedial order.

Scope of provision—It is unlawful for a public authority (meaning, inter alia, a court, tribunal or local authority) to act in a way which is incompatible with Convention rights unless it could not have acted differently because of primary legislation or the primary legislation (or subordinate legislation) could not be read in a manner compatible with Convention rights. Where the provision cannot be read as compatible, an application can be made for a declaration of incompatibility (pursuant to s 4).

7 Proceedings

(1) A person who claims that a public authority has acted (or proposes to act) in a way which is made unlawful by section 6(1) may –

(*a*) bring proceedings against the authority under this Act in the appropriate court or tribunal, or
(*b*) rely on the Convention right or rights concerned in any legal proceedings,

but only if he is (or would be) a victim of the unlawful act.

(2) In subsection (1)(*a*) "appropriate court or tribunal" means such court or tribunal as may be determined in accordance with rules; and proceedings against an authority include a counterclaim or similar proceeding.

(3) If the proceedings are brought on an application for judicial review, the applicant is to be taken to have a sufficient interest in relation to the unlawful act only if he is, or would be, a victim of that act.

(4) If the proceedings are made by way of a petition for judicial review in Scotland, the applicant shall be taken to have title and interest to sue in relation to the unlawful act only if he is, or would be, a victim of that act.

(5) Proceedings under subsection (1)(*a*) must be brought before the end of –

(*a*) the period of one year beginning with the date on which the act complained of took place; or
(*b*) such longer period as the court or tribunal considers equitable having regard to all the circumstances,

but that is subject to any rule imposing a stricter time limit in relation to the procedure in question.

(6) In subsection (1)(*b*) "legal proceedings" includes –

(*a*) proceedings brought by or at the instigation of a public authority; and
(*b*) an appeal against the decision of a court or tribunal.

(7) For the purposes of this section, a person is a victim of an unlawful act only if he would be a victim for the purposes of Article 34 of the Convention if proceedings were brought in the European Court of Human Rights in respect of that act.

(8) Nothing in this Act creates a criminal offence.

(9) In this section "rules" means –

(*a*) in relation to proceedings before a court or tribunal outside Scotland, rules made by the Lord Chancellor or the Secretary of State for the purposes of this section or rules of court,
(*b*) in relation to proceedings before a court or tribunal in Scotland, rules made by the Secretary of State for those purposes,
(*c*) in relation to proceedings before a tribunal in Northern Ireland –
(i) which deals with transferred matters; and
(ii) for which no rules made under paragraph (*a*) are in force,
rules made by a Northern Ireland department for those purposes,

and includes provision made by order under section 1 of the Courts and Legal Services Act 1990.

(10) In making rules, regard must be had to section 9.

(11) The Minister who has power to make rules in relation to a particular tribunal may, to the extent he considers it necessary to ensure that the tribunal can provide an appropriate remedy in relation to an act (or proposed act) of a public authority which is (or would be) unlawful as a result of section 6(1), by order add to –

(*a*) the relief or remedies which the tribunal may grant; or
(*b*) the grounds on which it may grant any of them.

(12) An order made under subsection (11) may contain such incidental, supplemental, consequential or transitional provision as the Minister making it considers appropriate.

(13) "The Minister" includes the Northern Ireland department concerned.

Scope of provision—This section provides the mechanism for complaints about acts which are unlawful, being incompatible with Convention rights. There are two routes: under s 7(1)(*b*) in legal proceedings in any court or tribunal in which the proceedings are brought by or at the instigation of a public authority, or constitute an appeal against the decision of a court or tribunal (s 7(6)). The other route is a separate claim under s 7(1)(*a*) in the High Court (or Administrative Court) for judicial review. Where the claim under s 7(1)(*a*) relates to a judicial act, the claim must be way of judicial review or by way of an appeal (HRA 1998, s 9).

Where the complaint is in relation to a local authority care plan, the application under this provision should be heard in the Family Division of the High Court, if possible by a judge with experience of sitting in the Administrative Court. Oral evidence may be heard and this should be determined at a directions hearing (*C v Bury Metropolitan Borough Council* [2002] EWHC 1438 (Fam) [2002] 2 FLR 868).

"victim"—A claim of breach of Convention rights can only be made by a victim or prospective victim.

"public authority"—A claim under section 7(1)(*a*) in relation to a judicial act must be brought in the High Court. Otherwise a claim in relation to an act of a public authority may be brought in any court (CPR 1998, r 7.11) in ongoing proceedings. The more usual procedure in relation to a claim concerning a judicial act will be by way of appeal from the decision made.

8 Judicial remedies

(1) In relation to any act (or proposed act) of a public authority which the court finds is (or would be) unlawful, it may grant such relief or remedy, or make such order, within its powers as it considers just and appropriate.

(2) But damages may be awarded only by a court which has power to award damages, or to order the payment of compensation, in civil proceedings.

(3) No award of damages is to be made unless, taking account of all the circumstances of the case, including –

(*a*) any other relief or remedy granted, or order made, in relation to the act in question (by that or any other court), and
(*b*) the consequences of any decision (of that or any other court) in respect of that act,

the court is satisfied that the award is necessary to afford just satisfaction to the person in whose favour it is made.

(4) In determining –

(*a*) whether to award damages, or
(*b*) the amount of an award,

the court must take into account the principles applied by the European Court of Human Rights in relation to the award of compensation under Article 41 of the Convention.

(5) A public authority against which damages are awarded is to be treated –

(*a*) in Scotland, for the purposes of section 3 of the Law Reform (Miscellaneous Provisions) (Scotland) Act 1940 as if the award were made in an action of damages in which the authority has been found liable in respect of loss or damage to the person to whom the award is made;
(*b*) for the purposes of the Civil Liability (Contribution) Act 1978 as liable in respect of damage suffered by the person to whom the award is made.

(6) In this section –

"court" includes a tribunal;
"damages" means damages for an unlawful act of a public authority; and
"unlawful" means unlawful under section 6(1).

Scope of provision—This section does not grant additional powers. Damages can only be awarded by a court with jurisdiction to do so. This means that, as it is doubtful that a court in family proceedings can award damages (though, theoretically, the inherent jurisdiction is limitless), such a claim will have to be made in civil "freestanding" proceedings or within judicial review proceedings, where damages may be awarded (see SCA 1981, s 31 and CPR 1998, Pt 54).

9 Judicial acts

(1) Proceedings under section 7(1)(*a*) in respect of a judicial act may be brought only –

(*a*) by exercising a right of appeal;
(*b*) on an application (in Scotland a petition) for judicial review; or
(*c*) in such other forum as may be prescribed by rules.

(2) That does not affect any rule of law which prevents a court from being the subject of judicial review.

(3) In proceedings under this Act in respect of a judicial act done in good faith, damages may not be awarded otherwise than to compensate a person to the extent required by Article 5(5) of the Convention.

(4) An award of damages permitted by subsection (3) is to be made against the Crown; but no award may be made unless the appropriate person, if not a party to the proceedings, is joined.

(5) In this section –

"appropriate person" means the Minister responsible for the court concerned, or a person or government department nominated by him;

"court" includes a tribunal;

"judge" includes a member of a tribunal, a justice of the peace and a clerk or other officer entitled to exercise the jurisdiction of a court;

"judicial act" means a judicial act of a court and includes an act done on the instructions, or on behalf, of a judge; and

"rules" has the same meaning as in section 7(9).

Scope of provision—Where there are freestanding proceedings in which a complaint is made of a judicial act, the appropriate procedure is to appeal. Where the judicial act is not within existing proceedings or there is no right of appeal, the appropriate procedure is by way of an application for judicial review under CPR 1998, Pt 54.

****

21 Interpretation, etc

(1) In this Act –

"amend" includes repeal and apply (with or without modifications);

"the appropriate Minister" means the Minister of the Crown having charge of the appropriate authorised government department (within the meaning of the Crown Proceedings Act 1947);

"the Commission" means the European Commission of Human Rights;

"the Convention" means the Convention for the Protection of Human Rights and Fundamental Freedoms, agreed by the Council of Europe at Rome on 4th November 1950 as it has effect for the time being in relation to the United Kingdom;

"declaration of incompatibility" means a declaration under section 4;

"Minister of the Crown" has the same meaning as in the Ministers of the Crown Act 1975;

"Northern Ireland Minister" includes the First Minister and the deputy First Minister in Northern Ireland;

"primary legislation" means any –

(*a*) public general Act;
(*b*) local and personal Act;
(*c*) private Act;
(*d*) Measure of the Church Assembly;
(*e*) Measure of the General Synod of the Church of England;
(*f*) Order in Council –
 (i) made in exercise of Her Majesty's Royal Prerogative;
 (ii) made under section 38(1)(*a*) of the Northern Ireland Constitution Act 1973 or the corresponding provision of the Northern Ireland Act 1998; or
 (iii) amending an Act of a kind mentioned in paragraph (*a*), (*b*) or (*c*);

and includes an order or other instrument made under primary legislation (otherwise than by the National Assembly for Wales, a member of the Scottish Executive, a Northern Ireland Minister or a Northern Ireland department) to the extent to which it operates to bring one or more provisions of that legislation into force or amends any primary legislation;

"the First Protocol" means the protocol to the Convention agreed at Paris on 20th March 1952;

"the Sixth Protocol" means the protocol to the Convention agreed at Strasbourg on 28th April 1983;

"the Eleventh Protocol" means the protocol to the Convention (restructuring the control machinery established by the Convention) agreed at Strasbourg on 11th May 1994;

"remedial order" means an order under section 10;

"subordinate legislation" means any –

(*a*) Order in Council other than one –

(i) made in exercise of Her Majesty's Royal Prerogative;

(ii) made under section 38(1)(*a*) of the Northern Ireland Constitution Act 1973 or the corresponding provision of the Northern Ireland Act 1998; or

(iii) amending an Act of a kind mentioned in the definition of primary legislation;

(*b*) Act of the Scottish Parliament;

(*c*) Act of the Parliament of Northern Ireland;

(*d*) Measure of the Assembly established under section 1 of the Northern Ireland Assembly Act 1973;

(*e*) Act of the Northern Ireland Assembly;

(*f*) order, rules, regulations, scheme, warrant, byelaw or other instrument made under primary legislation (except to the extent to which it operates to bring one or more provisions of that legislation into force or amends any primary legislation);

(*g*) order, rules, regulations, scheme, warrant, byelaw or other instrument made under legislation mentioned in paragraph (*b*), (*c*), (*d*) or (*e*) or made under an Order in Council applying only to Northern Ireland;

(*h*) order, rules, regulations, scheme, warrant, byelaw or other instrument made by a member of the Scottish Executive, a Northern Ireland Minister or a Northern Ireland department in exercise of prerogative or other executive functions of Her Majesty which are exercisable by such a person on behalf of Her Majesty;

"transferred matters" has the same meaning as in the Northern Ireland Act 1998; and

"tribunal" means any tribunal in which legal proceedings may be brought.

(2) The references in paragraphs (*b*) and (*c*) of section 2(1) to Articles are to Articles of the Convention as they had effect immediately before the coming into force of the Eleventh Protocol.

(3) The reference in paragraph (*d*) of section 2(1) to Article 46 includes a reference to Articles 32 and 54 of the Convention as they had effect immediately before the coming into force of the Eleventh Protocol.

(4) The references in section 2(1) to a report or decision of the Commission or a decision of the Committee of Ministers include references to a report or decision made as provided by paragraphs 3, 4 and 6 of Article 5 of the Eleventh Protocol (transitional provisions).

(5) Any liability under the Army Act 1955, the Air Force Act 1955 or the Naval Discipline Act 1957 to suffer death for an offence is replaced by a liability to imprisonment for life or any less punishment authorised by those Acts; and those Acts shall accordingly have effect with the necessary modifications.

****

SCHEDULE 1

THE ARTICLES

PART I
THE CONVENTION

Rights and Freedoms

Article 2 – Right to Life

1 Everyone's right to life shall be protected by law. No one shall be deprived of his life intentionally save in the execution of a sentence of a court following his conviction of a crime for which this penalty is provided by law.

2 Deprivation of life shall not be regarded as inflicted in contravention of this Article when it results from the use of force which is no more than absolutely necessary:

(*a*) in defence of any person from unlawful violence;
(*b*) in order to effect a lawful arrest or to prevent the escape of a person lawfully detained;
(*c*) in action lawfully taken for the purpose of quelling a riot or insurrection.

****

Article 5 – Right to liberty and security

1 Everyone has the right to liberty and security of person. No one shall be deprived of his liberty save in the following cases and in accordance with a procedure prescribed by law –

(*a*) the lawful detention of a person after conviction by a competent court;
(*b*) the lawful arrest or detention of a person for non-compliance with the lawful order of a court or in order to secure the fulfilment of any obligation prescribed by law;
(*c*) the lawful arrest or detention of a person effected for the purpose of bringing him before the competent legal authority on reasonable suspicion of having committed an offence or when it is reasonably considered necessary to prevent his committing an offence or fleeing after having done so;
(*d*) the detention of a minor by lawful order for the purpose of educational supervision or his lawful detention for the purpose of bringing him before the competent legal authority;
(*e*) the lawful detention of persons for the prevention of the spreading of infectious diseases, of persons of unsound mind, alcoholics or drug addicts or vagrants;

(*f*) the lawful arrest or detention of a person to prevent his effecting an unauthorised entry into the country or of a person against whom action is being taken with a view to deportation or extradition.

2 Everyone who is arrested shall be informed promptly, in a language which he understands, of the reasons for his arrest and of any charge against him.

3 Everyone arrested or detained in accordance with the provisions of paragraph 1(*c*) of this Article shall be brought promptly before a judge or other officer authorised by law to exercise judicial power and shall be entitled to trial within a reasonable time or to release pending trial. Release may be conditioned by guarantees to appear for trial.

4 Everyone who is deprived of his liberty by arrest or detention shall be entitled to take proceedings by which the lawfulness of his detention shall be decided speedily by a court and his release ordered if the detention is not lawful.

5 Everyone who has been the victim of arrest or detention in contravention of the provisions of this Article shall have an enforceable right to compensation.

Article 6 – Right to a fair trial

1 In the determination of his civil rights and obligations or of any criminal charge against him, everyone is entitled to a fair and public hearing within a reasonable time by an independent and impartial tribunal established by law. Judgment shall be pronounced publicly but the press and public may be excluded from all or part of the trial in the interest of morals, public order or national security in a democratic society, where the interests of juveniles or the protection of the private life of the parties so require, or to the extent strictly necessary in the opinion of the court in special circumstances where publicity would prejudice the interests of justice.

2 Everyone charged with a criminal offence shall be presumed innocent until proved guilty according to law.

3 Everyone charged with a criminal offence has the following minimum rights –

(*a*) to be informed promptly, in a language which he understands and in detail, of the nature and cause of the accusation against him;
(*b*) to have adequate time and facilities for the preparation of his defence;
(*c*) to defend himself in person or through legal assistance of his own choosing or, if he has not sufficient means to pay for legal assistance, to be given it free when the interests of justice so require;
(*d*) to examine or have examined witnesses against him and to obtain the attendance and examination of witnesses on his behalf under the same conditions as witnesses against him;
(*e*) to have the free assistance of an interpreter if he cannot understand or speak the language used in court.

****

Article 8 – Right to respect for private and family life

1 Everyone has the right to respect for his private and family life, his home and his correspondence.

2 There shall be no interference by a public authority with the exercise of this right except such as is in accordance with the law and is necessary in a democratic

society in the interests of national security, public safety or the economic well-being of the country, for the prevention of disorder or crime, for the protection of health or morals, or for the protection of the rights and freedoms of others.

****

Article 12 – Right to marry

Men and women of marriageable age have the right to marry and to found a family, according to the national laws governing the exercise of this right.

Article 14 – Prohibition of discrimination

The enjoyment of the rights and freedoms set forth in this Convention shall be secured without discrimination on any ground such as sex, race, colour, language, religion, political or other opinion, national or social origin, association with a national minority, property, birth or other status.

****

Inheritance (Provision for Family and Dependants) Act 1975

ARRANGEMENT OF SECTIONS

Powers of court to order financial provision from deceased's estate

Powers of court to order financial provision from deceased's estate

1 Application for financial provision from deceased's estate

(1) Where after the commencement of this Act a person dies domiciled in England and Wales and is survived by any of the following persons –

(*a*) the wife or husband of the deceased;
(*b*) a former wife or former husband of the deceased who has not remarried;
(*ba*) any person (not being a person included in paragraph (*a*) or (*b*) above) to whom subsection (1A) below applies;
(*c*) a child of the deceased;
(*d*) any person (not being a child of the deceased) who, in the case of any marriage to which the deceased was at any time a party, was treated by the deceased as a child of the family in relation to that marriage;
(*e*) any person (not being a person included in the foregoing paragraphs of this subsection) who immediately before the death of the deceased was being maintained, either wholly or partly, by the deceased;

that person may apply to the court for an order under section 2 of this Act on the ground that the disposition of the deceased's estate affected by his will or the law relating to intestacy, or the combination of his will and that law, is not such as to make reasonable financial provision for the applicant.

(1A) This subsection applies to a person if the deceased died on or after 1 January 1996 and, during the whole of the period of two years ending immediately before the date when the deceased died, the person was living –

(*a*) in the same household as the deceased, and
(*b*) as the husband or wife of the deceased.

(2) In this Act "reasonable financial provision" –

(*a*) in the case of an application made by virtue of subsection (1)(*a*) above by the husband or wife of the deceased (except where the marriage with the deceased was the subject of a decree of judicial separation and at the date of death the decree was in force and the separation was continuing), means such financial provision as it would be reasonable in all the circumstances of the case for a husband or wife to receive, whether or not that provision is required for his or her maintenance;

(*b*) in the case of any other application made by virtue of subsection (1) above, means such financial provision as it would be reasonable in all the circumstances of the case for the applicant to receive for his maintenance.

(3) For the purposes of subsection (1)(*e*) above, a person shall be treated as being maintained by the deceased, either wholly or partly, as the case may be, if the deceased, otherwise than for full valuable consideration, was making a substantial contribution in money or money's worth towards the reasonable needs of that person.

Amendments—Law Reform (Succession) Act 1995, s 2.

Defined terms—"former wife", "former husband": s 25(1).

"wife or husband of the deceased" (s 1(1)(*a*))—This includes reference to a person who in good faith entered into a void marriage with the deceased unless either the marriage of the deceased and that person was dissolved or annulled during the lifetime of the deceased and the dissolution or annulment is recognised by the law of England and Wales, or that person has during the lifetime of the deceased entered into a later marriage (s 25(4)). The meaning of a void marriage under s 25(4) is the same as in MCA 1973, s 11. For a ceremony of marriage to create a void marriage it has to at least purport to be a marriage contemplated by the Marriage Acts and it must have been entered into in good faith (*Gandhi v Patel* [2002] 1 FLR 603). By virtue of the Matrimonial Proceedings (Polygamous Marriages) Act 1972, a party to a polygamous marriage is a spouse of the deceased (*Re Sehota (dec'd), Kaur v Kaur* [1978] 1 WLR 1506, [1978] 3 All ER 385). Where the marriage is polygamous and the deceased has more than one wife, each of the wives would become a widow on his death. However, their entitlement to financial provision may vary (*Bibi v Chief Adjudication Officer* [1998] 1 FLR 375). Furthermore, where, within 12 months from the date on which a decree of divorce or nullity of marriage has been made absolute or a decree of judicial separation has been granted, a party to the marriage dies and either no application for a financial provision order under Matrimonial Causes Act 1973, s 23 or s 24 has been made by the other party to that marriage or such an application has been made but the proceedings thereon have not been determined at the time of death of the deceased, then, if an application under s 2 is made, the court has power, notwithstanding anything in ss 1 and 3, to treat that person as if he or she were a spouse of the deceased (s 14).

Former spouse of the deceased—In *Barrass v Harding and Newman* [2001] 1 FLR 138, where the ancillary relief proceedings were concluded 32 years before the death of the deceased and in the intervening years there was no ongoing relationship between the deceased and his first wife (but as a result of an improvement in the relationship between the deceased and his son, the deceased had given him some modest financial assistance), the Court of Appeal held that there was no basis on which an order under the Act could be justified.

"child of the deceased" (s 1(1)(*c*))—A child of the deceased includes an illegitimate child and a child en ventre sa mère at the death of the deceased (s 25(1)). A child who is adopted after his parent's death but before he makes his application is not a child of the deceased because, by virtue of Adoption Act 1976, s 39(2), an adopted child is treated in law as the child of the adopters. The Adoption Act 1976 does not confer on such an applicant an interest expectant as he merely has a right to apply to the court for relief (*Re Collins (dec'd)* [1990] Fam 56, [1990] 2 FLR 72). The Legitimacy Act 1976, as amended, provides that a child of a void marriage whenever born is, subject to s 2 of and Sch 1 to the Act, to be treated as a legitimate child of his parents if, at the time of the insemination resulting in the birth or, where there was no such insemination, the child's conception (or at the time of the celebration of the marriage, if later), both parties to the marriage or either of them reasonably believed that the marriage was valid. See also *Re Spence (dec'd)* [1990] 2 FLR 278, [1990] 2 WLR 1430. See further the provisions of the Family Law Reform Act 1987 and the Human Fertilisation and Embryology Act 1990, to determine who can now be treated as the "father" and "mother" of a child, and the decisions in *Re B (Minors) (Parentage)* [1996] 2 FLR 15; *Re Q (Parental Order)* [1996] 1 FLR 369; and *R v Human Fertilisation and Embryology Authority ex parte Blood* [1997] 2 FLR 742.

Pursuant to regulations made under the Human Fertilisation and Embryology Act 1990, where a parental order has been made under s 30 of the Act, the provisions of AA 1976, s 39(1)(*a*), (2), (4), and (6) will apply, with the appropriate modification. The effect of these provisions is that a child who is the subject of a parental order will be treated as the child of the marriage of the couple in whose favour the parental order is made, and the child will not be regarded as illegitimate. These provisions will apply to enactments and instruments, such as wills and other dispositions of property or inheritance of title, effective before the parental order was made. The provisions of AA 1976, s 42 apply also to children who are the subject of a parental order.

Cohabitant of the deceased (s 1(1)(*ba*), (1A))—The categories of person who may apply for financial provision now include a cohabitant of the deceased. Previously, such an applicant would have had to bring himself or herself within the ambit of s 1(1)(*e*) and overcome the hurdle of proving "dependency" in order to succeed. Although, in recent years, the courts had tended to adopt a broad and commonsense approach to such cases, there were some instances where the applicant's care of the deceased was not regarded as going beyond the normal exchange of support (see **Other persons** below). The provision is limited in that it will apply only if: (i) the deceased dies on or after 1 January 1996; (ii) the applicant has lived in the same household as the deceased and as the husband/wife of the deceased; and (iii) such cohabitation has been for a period of two years immediately preceding the deceased's death. Where these conditions are not satisfied, the applicant will have to rely on s 1(1)(*e*). The question whether a person falls within s 1(1A) should be determined by asking whether in the opinion of a reasonable person with normal perceptions, it could be said that the two people in question were living together as husband and wife (*Re Watson (Deceased)* [1999] 1 FLR 878). This raises the issue of whether this provision extends to same-sex cohabitation. "Cohabitant" is not defined in the Act, in contrast to Family Law Act 1996, s 62 where it is given the meaning "a man and woman who are living together as husband and wife". In *Fitzpatrick v Sterling Housing Association Limited* [2000] 1 FLR 271, the House of Lords held that the word "spouse" in Rent Act 1977, Sch 1, para 2(2) did not apply to same-sex partners. The words were gender specific, connoting a relationship between a man and woman. The decision in *Fitzpatrick* turned on the construction of the word "spouse" as used in the Rent Act 1977. In this sense it could only be interpreted as referring to heterosexual relationships and could not form a basis for providing the true construction of the word "cohabitant". Furthermore, it is submitted that the definition clause in the Family Law Act 1996 cannot provide the answer because had Parliament intended to restrict the meaning of "cohabitant" to that defined in FLA 1996 it would have so provided when it amended the provisions of the 1975 Act to extend it to cohabitants. It is suggested that, having regard to the judgment of Neuberger J in *Watson* and the strong dissenting judgment of Ward LJ in *Fitzpatrick* [1998] Ch 304, [1997] 4 All ER 991, CA, it is arguable that "cohabitant" could extend to same-sex relationships.

"child of the family" (s 1(1)(*d*))—There is no definition of "child of the family" nor any guidance in the Act as to when a person is regarded as having been treated as a child of the family. The treatment need not have occurred during the marriage provided it was "in relation to the marriage" (*Re Debenham (dec'd)* [1986] 1 FLR 404). An adult child is included. The nature of the relationship between the deceased and the applicant is the relevant factor (*Re Callaghan (dec'd)* [1985] Fam 1, [1985] FLR 116; *Re Leach, Leach v Lindeman* [1986] Ch 226, [1984] FLR 590 where the treatment by a stepmother of an adult stepchild before and after the death of the child's father was taken into account). In each case the question will be judged by an objective test on the basis of all the facts, so that where grandparents had assumed primary responsibility for their grandchild for the forseeable future the grandchild was a "child of the family" (*Re A (Child of the Family)* [1998] 1 FLR 347).

"court"—Pursuant to Courts and Legal Services Act 1990, s 1, County Courts Act 1984, s 25 and High Court and County Courts Jurisdiction Order 1991, art 2(1), unlimited jurisdiction is now conferred on the county court in respect of claims under the Inheritance (Provision for Family and Dependants) Act 1975. However, under art 7 of the 1991 Order, subject to the criteria set out in art 7(5), any action where the value of the claim (the sum which the applicant has reasonable expectancy of recovering) is less than £25,000 must be tried in the county court. Where the value of the claim is £50,000 or more, the action must be tried in the High Court unless it is commenced in the county court and the court does not consider it ought to be transferred up to the High Court. Similarly, if the action has been commenced in the High Court, that court may transfer the action down to the county court.

Other persons (s 1(1)(*e*))—An applicant under s 1(1)(*e*) must establish that he or she was being maintained, either wholly or partly, by the deceased immediately before the deceased's death (s 1(1)(*e*)). The applicant must establish some sort of obligation to be maintained by the deceased beyond the fact of a relationship (*Williams v Johns* [1988] 2 FLR 475). A person is treated as being so maintained if the deceased, otherwise than for valuable consideration, was making a substantial contribution in money or money's worth towards the reasonable needs of that person (s 1(3)). For the purposes of the Act, "valuable consideration" does not include marriage or a promise of marriage (s 25(1)). In determining whether the applicant had been maintained by the deceased, the court is required to have regard to the extent to which, the basis upon which and the length of time for which the deceased discharged that responsibility (s 3(4)). The court will look at the problem in the round, applying a commonsense approach, avoiding fine balancing computations involving the value of normal exchanges of support in the domestic sense (*Bishop v Plumley* [1991] 1 FLR 121, [1991] 1 WLR 582; see also *Rees v Newbery and the Institute of Cancer Research* [1998] 1 FLR 1041; *Graham v Murphy and Another* [1997] 1 FLR 860 where a male applicant succeeded in his claim, made before 1 January 1996, for financial provision from the estate of his cohabitant; *Re Wilkinson, Neale v Newell* [1978] Fam 22, [1977] 3 WLR 514, where the applicant who had left her employment at the age of 61 to look after her brother succeeded in her claim; *Re Haig, Powers v Haig* (1979) 129 NLJ 420, where a mistress's claim was upheld; *Harrington v Gill* (1983) FLR 265, where eight years' cohabitation with the deceased was held sufficient evidence of dependency; *Re Viner, Kreeger v Cooper* [1978] CLY 3091, where a weekly payment of £5 for six months before death was considered sufficient). In *Beaumont, Martin v Midland Bank Trust Co Ltd* [1980] Ch 444, [1979] 3 WLR 818, the claim failed because the applicant had regularly paid the outgoings and other expenses.

It is the settled basis or general arrangement between the parties as regards maintenance during the lifetime of the deceased which has to be looked at, not the actual, perhaps fluctuating, variations of it which exist immediately before his or her death. The court has to consider whether the deceased was in fact making a substantial contribution in money or money's worth towards the reasonable needs of the applicant which was either in force immediately before the deceased's death or would have lasted until death but for the approach of death and the consequent inability of either party to continue to carry out the arrangement (*Jelley v Illife* [1981] Fam 128, [1981] 2 WLR 801). "Whether one person makes a substantial gratuitous contribution to another person's needs is essentially a question of fact, and the benefactor's motives or intentions are irrelevant except so far as s 3(4) makes them relevant to the court's task in deciding whether to make provision for the claimant, and if so in what form and on what scale. Even when s 3(4) is taken into account this court has taken the view that actions speak louder than words" (per Robert Walker LJ in *Bouette v Rose* [2000] 1 FLR 363).

"immediately before the death" (s 1(1)(*e*))—See *Re Beaumont, Martin v Midland Bank Trust Ltd*; *Kourkgy v Lusher* (1983) FLR 65, where the claim failed because cohabitation came to an end nine days before the deceased's death; and *Layton v Martin* [1986] 2 FLR 227, where cohabitation had ended two years before death.

Reasonable financial provision (s 1(2)(*a*), (*b*))—The Act does not distinguish between claims made by a surviving wife or husband of the deceased. In cases decided before the 1975 Act, the courts had shown a disinclination to grant relief to a surviving husband save in exceptional circumstances. In view of the decisions in *White v White* [2000] 2 FLR 981, HL and *Cowan v Cowan* [2001] EWCA Civ 679, [2001] 2 FLR 192, there is no place for discrimination based on gender. In defining reasonable financial provision, the Act distinguishes between a surviving spouse and the other categories of applicants. In the case of a surviving spouse, it need not be an amount required for maintenance (*Jessop v Jessop* [1992] 1 FLR 591, where it was held to be unreasonable for the widow not to be given some part of the capital sum as a capital reserve for future contingencies, but see *Davis v Davis* [1993] 1 FLR 54, where the deceased prior to his death had provided his widow with a substantial capital sum together with all his chattels and a life interest in real estate, and it was held that it could not be said that he had failed to make reasonable financial provision for her). In *Re Besterman (dec'd), Besterman v Grusin* [1984] Ch 458, [1984] FLR 503, under the will the wife received a life interest in war stocks, which produced an income of £3,500 per annum, and the principal beneficiary was Oxford University, the wife succeeded on appeal in being awarded a lump sum of £378,000. However, all the circumstances must be considered. The test of "reasonable requirements" as a tool for assessing the needs of a spouse was disapproved of in *White v White* (above). The objective must be to achieve a fair outcome. In *Adams v Adams* [2001] WLR 493 the court considered that the provisions of MCA 1973, s 25 were the most important factor. It is submitted that there is nothing in the 1975 Act to suggest that this factor should be given more weight than the other factors referred to in s 3 of the Act: in *Re Rowlands (dec'd)* [1984] FLR 813 the widow was 90, had been separated from the deceased for 47 years and was unable to formulate what her needs were and what she would do if a substantial sum was awarded to her; she received £3,000. See also *Re Bunning (dec'd), Bunning v Salmon* [1984] Ch 480, [1985] FLR 1 and *Re Gregory, Gregory v Goodenough* [1970] 1 WLR 1465, [1971] 1 All ER 497. Where the former husband and wife settle their financial claims on divorce without a court order, the court will be slow to order further provision under the Act (*Re Fullard* [1982] Fam 42). In *Benson v Benson (Deceased)* [1996] 1 FLR 692, however, the husband of the deceased, who died six months after a consent order for financial relief had been made on their divorce, sought to have the order set aside and reviewed on

PART II

the grounds that it was still executory by appealing against the order. The court, when dismissing the appeal, held that the death of the wife was not a contemplated event when the order was made and was therefore a new event, but the application to appeal, which had been made over a year after the wife's death, had not been made promptly, and the court would not interfere with a consent order which was clear, unambiguous and for good consideration and reached when both sides were appropriately represented.

In respect of any other applicant, including a judicially separated or divorced spouse and a cohabitant as defined by s 1(1A), reasonable financial provision is limited to what would be reasonable in all the circumstances for the applicant to receive *for his maintenance*. See *Re Abram (Deceased)* [1996] 2 FLR 379 and *Rhodes v Dean* [1996] 7 CL 593, where the court held that it was reasonable for the testator to have made no provision in his will for his cohabitant who had received the sum of £36,000 held in a joint account. In *Graham v Murphy and Another* [1997] 1 FLR 860 it was held that, in the circumstances, the deceased's intestacy had resulted in a lack of reasonable provision for the applicant, who was the cohabitant of the deceased; however, on the facts it was decided that reasonable financial provision did not mean that the applicant should be provided for on a lavish scale, such as would relieve him from the need to earn a living or provide himself with a home. The application in this case predated 1 January 1996 and would now be governed by Law Reform (Succession) Act 1995, s 2. An adult child, towards whom the deceased failed to discharge his responsibility, is not entitled to make a claim where he is in comfortable circumstances, in order to maintain his standard of living (*Re Jennings (deceased)*; *Harlow v National Westminster Bank plc and Others* [1994] 1 FLR 536; *Re Hancock (dec'd)* [1998] 2 FLR 346; *Re Abram (dec'd)* [1996] 2 FLR 379). A former spouse would need to establish exceptional circumstances to succeed (see *Re Fullard (dec'd)* [1981] 3 WLR 743, [1981] 2 All ER 796); for examples of exceptional circumstances see *Talbot v Talbot* [1962] 1 WLR 111, [1962] 3 All ER 174; *Eyre v Eyre* [1962] 1 WLR 530, [1968] 1 All ER 968; *Lusternik v Lusternik* [1972] Fam 125, [1972] 2 WLR 203; *Re Bellman* [1963] P 239, [1963] 2 WLR 314; *Re Crawford (dec'd)* (1983) FLR 273; and *Re Farrow (dec'd)* [1987] 1 FLR 205. Where a former wife's claims in divorce proceedings had been compromised by a consent order in full and final settlement her claim under the Act failed (*Brill v Proud* [1984] Fam Law 59). See also *Cameron v Treasury Solicitor* [1996] 2 FLR 716, where a former wife's claim under the Act failed even though, on intestacy, the testator's estate devolved as bona vacantia on the Crown.

The court must have regard to all the matters set out under s 3. It is not necessary in every case for the applicant to establish "a moral obligation". For a discussion of this issue see *Re Coventry, Coventry v Coventry* [1980] Ch 461, (1979) FLR Rep 142; *Re Jennings (deceased)* (above); *Re Pearce (deceased)* [1998] 2 FLR 705; and *Re Hancock (dec'd)* (above). One particular issue which has to be addressed and considered is whether the financial resources of the claimant should include means-tested benefits. There are no clear decisions on this particular point. In *Re Collins* [1990] Fam 56, [1990] 2 FLR 72, the applicant, the daughter of the deceased, received £5,000 although she was on state benefits. Hollins J said "I do not consider that the fact of support from the DSS precludes consideration of whether the intestacy has or has not made reasonable financial provision for her." It is submitted that the decision in that case turned on its own facts. Furthermore, the case considered only the claim to social security benefits. It did not consider cases of funding or means-tested local authority provisions. Consideration must be given in each individual case where the applicant is on state benefit to whether an award under the Act would benefit the applicant or merely have the effect of removing entitlement to state benefit and thereby reducing the applicant's standard of living. See also *Re E, E v E* [1966] 1 WLR 709, [1966] 2 All ER 44, where it was stated that if the estate is so small and the means of the applicant so exiguous that the only effect of making provision for the applicant would be to relieve the national insurance fund, there might well be no point in making provision for the applicant. See also *Re Watkins, Hayward v Chatterton* [1949] 1 All ER 695.

2 Powers of court to make orders

(1) Subject to the provisions of this Act, where an application is made for an order under this section, the court may, if it is satisfied that the disposition of the deceased's estate effected by his will or the law relating to intestacy, or the combination of his will and that law, is not such as to make reasonable financial provision for the applicant, make any one or more of the following orders –

(*a*) an order for the making to the applicant out of the net estate of the deceased of such periodical payments and for such term as may be specified in the order;

(*b*) an order for the payment to the applicant out of that estate of a lump sum of such amount as may be so specified;

(*c*) an order for the transfer to the applicant of such property comprised in that estate as may be so specified;

(*d*) an order for the settlement for the benefit of the applicant of such property comprised in that estate as may be so specified;

(*e*) an order for the acquisition out of property comprised in that estate of such property as may be so specified and for the transfer of the property so acquired to the applicant or for the settlement thereof for his benefit;

(*f*) an order varying any ante-nuptial or post-nuptial settlement (including such a settlement made by will) made on the parties to a marriage to which the deceased was one of the parties, the variation being for the benefit of the surviving party to that marriage, or any child of that marriage, or any person who was treated by the deceased as a child of the family in relation to that marriage.

(2) An order under subsection (1)(*a*) above providing for the making out of the net estate of the deceased of periodical payments may provide for –

(*a*) payments of such amount as may be specified in the order,

(*b*) payments equal to the whole of the income of the net estate or of such portion thereof as may be so specified,

(*c*) payments equal to the whole of the income of such part of the net estate as the court may direct to be set aside or appropriated for the making out of the income thereof of payments under this section,

or may provide for the amount of the payments or any of them to be determined in any other way the court thinks fit.

(3) Where an order under subsection (1)(*a*) above provides for the making of payments of an amount specified in the order, the order may direct that such part of the net estate as may be so specified shall be set aside or appropriated for the making out of the income thereof of those payments; but no larger part of the net estate shall be so set aside or appropriated than is sufficient, at the date of the order, to produce by the income thereof the amount required for the making of those payments.

(4) An order under this section may contain such consequential and supplemental provisions as the court thinks necessary or expedient for the purpose of giving effect to the order or for the purpose of securing that the order operates fairly as between one beneficiary of the estate of the deceased and another and may, in particular, but without prejudice to the generality of this subsection –

(*a*) order any person who holds any property which forms part of the net estate of the deceased to make such payment or transfer such property as may be specified in the order;

(*b*) vary the disposition of the deceased's estate effected by the will or the law relating to intestacy, or by both the will and the law relating to intestacy, in such manner as the court thinks fair and reasonable having regard to the provisions of the order and all the circumstances of the case;

(*c*) confer on the trustees of any property which is the subject of an order under this section such powers as appear to the court to be necessary or expedient.

"net estate"—Defined in s 25, and see ss 8, 9. See also *Jessop v Jessop* [1992] 1 FLR 591, where it was held that a severable share in property in which the deceased held a joint tenancy may be treated as part of the net estate pursuant to s 9.

Periodical payments (s 2(1)(*a*))—Unless an application has been made for an interim order, the order for periodical payments will normally be made from the date of the deceased's death, even where the applicant has been in receipt of state benefits (*Re Goodwin, Goodwin v Goodwin* [1969] 1 Ch 283, [1968] 3 WLR 558). The matter is one for the discretion of the court. The court may specify the amount to be paid under the order, express the amount to be paid to be such sum as is equivalent to the whole or a specified portion of the income of the net estate, direct that a specified part of the net estate be appropriated or set aside for meeting periodical payments and express the amount of such periodical payments to be equivalent to the whole of the income of such part of the net estate or provide for the amount of the payment to be determined in any other way it thinks fit (s 2(2)).

Lump sum (s 2(1)(*b*))—In the case of a lump sum order, particularly where the capital sum is provided to produce an income, the fact that the applicant will not be able to return to the court for further orders means that in assessing the amount the court should make allowances for inflation and possible future contingencies (*Re Besterman* [1984] Ch 458, [1984] FLR 503); but see *A v A (Financial Provision)* [1998] 2 FLR 180, a case concerning an application for financial provision under the Matrimonial Causes Act 1973, where it was held that the concept of awarding a lump sum as a cushion had not survived the introduction of *Duxbury* calculations). However, it is submitted that where the estate is large, and therefore a choice arises, the matter should be resolved in favour of the applicant. The fact that a lump sum order enables the applicant to provide for someone else must not govern the amount (*Preston v Preston* (1981) FLR 331, [1981] 3 WLR 619). A lump sum may also be made on an application for a variation of periodical payments order under s 6. The court has the power to order that the lump sum payment be made by instalments and may vary the number of instalments payable, the amount of the instalments and the date on which any instalment becomes payable (s 7(2)).

Settlement of property and the mentally disabled (s 2(1)(*d*))—It is not unusual to find that parents refrain from making provision for a mentally disabled child, particularly an adult child, in the belief that the child will be provided for adequately by the state and any benefit under a testamentary provision will have the effect of reducing the benefit. With the increasing tendency of care for such persons being provided within the community, some financial support could make a difference to the quality of life of that person. Although there are no decided cases on the subject it is submitted that under the wide powers given to the court by s 2, and in particular s 2(4), the court could make an order for the settlement of property for the benefit of a mentally handicapped claimant by setting up a discretionary trust so as to permit the whole or any part of the income of the trust fund to be applied for the maintenance, care and benefit of the claimant as the trustees in their absolute discretion deem fit. For further information on the provisions which may be included in the trust, see *Butterworths Wills, Probate and Administration Service* and Ashton and Ward, *Mental Handicap and the Law* (Sweet & Maxwell, 1992).

3 Matters to which the court is to have regard in exercising powers under s 2

(1) Where an application is made for an order under section 2 of this Act, the court shall, in determining whether the disposition of the deceased's estate effected by his will or the law relating to intestacy, or the combination of his will and that law, is such as to make reasonable financial provision for the applicant and, if the court considers that reasonable financial provision has not been made, in determining whether and in what manner it shall exercise its powers under that section, have regard to the following matters, that is to say –

- (*a*) the financial resources and financial needs which the applicant has or is likely to have in the foreseeable future;
- (*b*) the financial resources and financial needs which any other applicant for an order under section 2 of this Act has or is likely to have in the foreseeable future;
- (*c*) the financial resources and financial needs which any beneficiary of the estate of the deceased has or is likely to have in the foreseeable future;

(*d*) any obligations and responsibilities which the deceased had towards any applicant for an order under the said section 2 or towards any beneficiary of the estate of the deceased;

(*e*) the size and nature of the net estate of the deceased;

(*f*) any physical or mental disability of any applicant for an order under the said section 2 or any beneficiary of the estate of the deceased;

(*g*) any other matter, including the conduct of the applicant or any other person, which in the circumstances of the case the court may consider relevant.

(2) Without prejudice to the generality of paragraph (*g*) of subsection (1) above, where an application for an order under section 2 of this Act is made by virtue of section 1(1)(*a*) or 1(1)(*b*) of this Act, the court shall, in addition to the matters specifically mentioned in paragraphs (*a*) to (*f*) of that subsection, have regard to –

(*a*) the age of the applicant and the duration of the marriage;

(*b*) the contribution made by the applicant to the welfare of the family of the deceased, including any contribution made by looking after the home or caring for the family;

and, in the case of an application by the wife or husband of the deceased, the court shall also, unless at the date of death a decree of judicial separation was in force and the separation was continuing, have regard to the provision which the applicant might reasonably have expected to receive if on the day on which the deceased died the marriage, instead of being terminated by death, had been terminated by a decree of divorce.

(2A) Without prejudice to the generality of paragraph (*g*) of subsection (1) above, where an application for an order under section 2 of this Act is made by virtue of section 1(1)(*ba*) of this Act, the court shall, in addition to the matters specifically mentioned in paragraphs (*a*) to (*f*) of that subsection, have regard to –

(*a*) the age of the applicant and the length of the period during which the applicant lived as the husband or wife of the deceased and in the same household as the deceased;

(*b*) the contribution made by the applicant to the welfare of the family of the deceased, including any contribution made by looking after the home or caring for the family.

(3) Without prejudice to the generality of paragraph (*g*) of subsection (1) above, where an application for an order under section 2 of this Act is made by virtue of section 1(1)(*c*) or 1(1)(*d*) of this Act, the court shall, in addition to the matters specifically mentioned in paragraphs (*a*) to (*f*) of that subsection, have regard to the manner in which the applicant was being or in which he might expect to be educated or trained, and where the application is made by virtue of section 1(1)(*d*) the court shall also have regard –

(*a*) to whether the deceased had assumed any responsibility for the applicant's maintenance and, if so, to the extent to which and the basis upon which the deceased assumed that responsibility and to the length of time for which the deceased discharged that responsibility;

(*b*) to whether in assuming and discharging that responsibility the deceased did so knowing that the applicant was not his own child;

(*c*) to the liability of any other person to maintain the applicant.

(4) Without prejudice to the generality of paragraph (*g*) of subsection (1) above, where an application for an order under section 2 of this Act is made by virtue of section 1(1)(*e*) of this Act, the court shall, in addition to the matters specifically

PART II

mentioned in paragraphs (*a*) to (*f*) of that subsection, have regard to the extent to which and the basis upon which the deceased assumed responsibility for the maintenance of the applicant, and to the length of time for which the deceased discharged that responsibility.

(5) In considering the matters to which the court is required to have regard under this section, the court shall take into account the facts as known to the court at the date of the hearing.

(6) In considering the financial resources of any person for the purposes of this section the court shall take into account his earning capacity and in considering the financial needs of any person for the purposes of this section the court shall take into account his financial obligations and responsibilities.

Amendments—Law Reform (Succession) Act 1995, s 2.

Matters to be considered in determining reasonable financial provision (s 3(1))—See **Reasonable financial provision** under s 1. It should be noted that, in the case of an application by a cohabitant, the further specific matters that the court is required to take into account under s 3(2A) are identical to those which apply in the case of a spouse or former spouse who has not married.

"financial resources and financial needs" (s 3(1)(*b*))—"Financial needs" means reasonable requirements and, in assessing this factor, the court may take into account the standard of living enjoyed by the applicant during the lifetime of the deceased and the extent to which the deceased contributed to that standard (*Harrington v Gill* (1983) FLR 265). The court may also restrict the distribution of the liquid assets of the estate to ensure the preservation of the capital of the estate to cover unforeseen circumstances (*Stead v Stead* [1985] FLR 16; see also *Malone v Harrison* [1979] 1 WLR 1353). In considering the applicant's claim the court may need to balance the applicant's needs and those of the beneficiaries (*Kusminow v Barclay's Bank Trust Co Ltd and Sokolow and Sitnikova* [1989] Fam Law 66).

Obligations and responsibilities—"Obligations and responsibilities" in s 3(1)(*d*) extends beyond legal obligation and the deceased's obligations are not to be construed too narrowly, but in a broad sense (*Espinosa v Bourke* [1999] 1 FLR 747). The court is entitled to have regard to the entire estate, including foreign property, when considering whether the estate made reasonable provision for the applicant and assessing the financial resources and needs of any beneficiary of the estate (*Bheekhun v Williams* [1999] 2 FLR 229, CA). The deceased's moral obligation and the morality of the applicant's claim may be relevant. In *Re Goodchild (Deceased) and Another* [1997] 2 FLR 644, CA, the testator and his first wife, who predeceased him, had made simultaneous wills in identical terms with reference to property which the testator held jointly with his first wife. The first wife had made the will on the understanding that the testator would honour what she believed to be their mutual intention. The court held that this gave rise to a moral though not a legal obligation to that part of the estate which was attributable to her asset and which should be made available to meet the applicant son's claim (see also *Re Debenham (dec'd)* [1986] 1 FLR 404). The applicant must establish some sort of a moral claim to be maintained by the deceased beyond the mere fact of blood relationship (*Re Coventry (dec'd), Coventry v Coventry* [1980] Ch 461, (1979) FLR Rep 142 and *Re Abram (Deceased)* [1996] 2 FLR 379). In *Re Debenham (dec'd)* [1986] 1 FLR 404, the court found that, although the deceased did not have any legal obligation to the applicant, she owed her a moral obligation; in *Re Jennings (deceased), Harlow v National Westminster Bank plc and Others* [1994] 1 FLR 536, a claim made by an adult son of the deceased, which was based on the fact that the deceased had failed to discharge his responsibilities to the son during his minority, failed; see also *Re Wood, Wood v Wood* (1982) LS Gaz 774 and *Re Rowlands (dec'd)* [1984] FLR 813.

Size and nature of the net estate—Where the size of the estate is limited, the court will be slow to deprive the deceased of his freedom to dispose of his estate as he willed (*Re Gregory, Gregory v Goodenough* [1970] 1 WLR 1455, [1971] 1 All ER 497).

Physical and mental disability—See final paragraph of **Reasonable financial provision** under s 1 and **Settlement of property and the mentally handicapped** under s 2.

Conduct—In *Re Snoek (dec'd)* [1983] Fam Law 18, Wood J said that he could see no reason why conduct under s 3 should be understood differently from that under MCA 1973, s 25. In *Talbot v Talbot* [1962] 3 All ER 174, the court had regard to the applicant's unchastity, but not as a decisive factor since the deceased had continued to pay maintenance with knowledge of the child born to her. Concealment by the applicant widow of her true financial position after her marriage had broken down and had been dissolved, resulting in her continuing to receive maintenance at a much higher level than she would have been entitled to, was taken into account in *Re Harker-Thomas* [1969] P 28, [1968] 3 All ER 17. In *Re W (dec'd)* (1975) 119 SJ 439, the deceased's conduct in being secretive about his financial position was taken into account. The conduct of the deceased in encouraging the applicant to believe that the applicant would acquire an interest in the estate and, on that belief, allowing her to act to her detriment can give rise to an estoppel on which a claim to family assets may be based (*Re Basham* [1987] 2 FLR 264). Where the applicant has unlawfully killed the deceased, the forfeiture rule applies (see below).

Deceased's reason—The Act does not specifically provide for the deceased's reason for making or not making any provision to be considered, but the section is wide enough for the court to consider his reasons and can infer his intention from all the circumstances and weigh these against all other factors which the court is required to take into account (see *Re Coventry (dec'd), Coventry v Coventry* [1980] Ch 461, (1979) FLR Rep 142; *Re Leach (dec'd), Leach v Linderman* [1986] Ch 226; [1984] FLR 590).

Any other matter—See *Re Wood, Wood v Wood* (1982) LS Gaz 774.

Forfeiture rule—This rule disentitles a person from acquiring a benefit from the estate of another whom he has unlawfully killed. However, it does not preclude that person from making a claim under this Act since the Forfeiture Act 1982 gives the court a discretion to modify the application of the rule if it takes the view that the moral culpability of the applicant is such that it would be unjust to deny him any benefit (*Re K* [1985] Ch 85, [1985] FLR 558; *Re S (Deceased) (Forfeiture Rule)* [1996] 1 FLR 910). This is subject to the proviso that an application in respect of the unlawful killing is made within 3 months of the applicant's conviction and that the effect of the rule has been to preclude the applicant from acquiring an interest in property (as defined in the Forfeiture Act 1982). When applying the forfeiture rule, and in exercising its discretion, the court does not draw any distinction between murder and manslaughter. In both cases the assailant remains criminally responsible for his actions (*Jones v Roberts* [1995] 2 FLR 422 and *Re Jones (Deceased), Jones v Midland Bank Trust Co Ltd and Others* [1997] Fam Law 660, [1998] 1 FLR 246). The rule also applies to offences under the Suicide Act 1961, including aiding and abetting a suicide in pursuance of a suicide pact. Where one of the parties to a suicide pact succeeded in taking his life and the other survived, public policy would not normally require forfeiture by the survivor (*Dunbar v Plant* [1998] 1 FLR 157). It is submitted that the decision whether to exercise the discretion, and in what manner, will depend upon the facts of each case. In *Dunbar v Plant* (above) the circumstances of the suicide were extremely tragic and the events which occurred were horrific for the parties involved in the suicide pact and their families.

Provision which the deceased's spouse might have expected to receive on divorce—Any disposition by the deceased with the intention of defeating the spouse's claim would be a relevant factor (*Re Dawkins, Dawkins v Judd* [1986] 2 FLR 360), as is the length of the marriage and the contribution made by the applicant (*Kusminow v Barclay's Bank Trust Co Ltd and Sokolow and Sitnikova* [1989] Fam Law 66). However, it is not the duty of the court to alter the disposition so as to make an equitable redistribution of the available assets. Furthermore, the provision which the spouse might reasonably have expected to receive on divorce is only one of the matters which the court is required to consider. The major element is what is reasonable in all the circumstances of the case (*Re Krubert (Deceased)* [1997] 1 FLR 42).

Responsibility assumed for maintenance—The court is required to have regard to (*a*) the extent to which the deceased assumed responsibility for the applicant, (*b*) the basis on which the responsibility had been assumed, and (*c*) the length of time for which he had maintained the applicant. In *Rhodes v Dean* [1996] 7 CL 593, where the responsibility did not include the daily living expenses, the relationship was not like a marriage, and the applicant, who had cohabited with the deceased, was entitled to capital held in a joint account; thus, the application failed. See also **Other persons** and **"immediately before the death"** under s 1.

4 Time-limit for applications

An application for an order under section 2 of this Act shall not, except with the permission of the court, be made after the end of the period of six months from the date on which representation with respect to the estate of the deceased is first taken out.

Time-limit—An application cannot be made if no grant is taken out (*Re McBroom (Deceased)* [1992] 2 FLR 49). Provided the application is issued within six months of the grant, there is no time-limit for service (*Re Miller, Miller v De Courcey* [1969] 1 WLR 583, [1968] 3 All ER 844; *Re Kay, Kay v West* [1965] 1 WLR 1463, [1965] 3 All ER 724 and *Re Chittenden, Chittenden v Doe* [1970] 1 WLR 1618, [1970] 3 All ER 562). The period of six months begins to run from the grant in common form (*Re Miller*). Where a grant of probate is replaced by letters of administration, time begins to run from the date of the grant of letters of administration and vice versa (*Re Freeman (dec'd), Weston v Freeman* [1985] FLR 543, [1984] 1 WLR 1419). An application is not rendered invalid if it is issued before the date on which representation is taken out (*Re Searle, Searle v Siems* [1949] Ch 73, [1948] 2 All ER 426).

Standing searches—In order to gain protection against the possibility that a grant may be issued without its existence coming to the attention of an interested party, facilities are available for a standing search to be made at the principal registry or sub-registry (see *Practice Note of 26 September 1991*). An application for such a search is made in accordance with the Non-Contentious Probate Rules 1987, r 43 by completing the notice in Form 2 and paying the appropriate £5 fee (Fee 5 of the Non-Contentious Probate Fees Order 1999). Furthermore, the name and date of death of the deceased, as recorded in the Register of Deaths, must be included in the notice lodged for a standing search and in any case where the name of the deceased differs from that recorded in the Register, that name shall also be included in the oath or the notice, as appropriate (see *Practice Direction of 12 January 1999*). The court will then make an entry and acknowledge it. Once an entry is made the applicant for a standing search will receive an office copy of any grant which tallies with the particulars given and which either has been issued not more than 12 months before the receipt of the application for the search or is issued within a period of six months thereafter. An application for the search to be extended may be made within the last month of the six months' period by completing a request in the following form and lodging it or sending it by post to the registry or sub-registry at which the standing search was entered:

"I Hereby request that the above standing search be extended for a further period of six months from the date on which it is due to expire. I enclose the further fee.

Signed .... Dated ...."

Application out of time—The court's power to extend time is discretionary. Where an applicant wishes the court to exercise its discretion by extending the time for making an application for an order, such relief must be expressly asked for in the claim form and the grounds on which the court's leave to entertain the application is sought must be included in the supporting witness statement or affidavit. If the application is opposed, the defendant must file an affidavit in answer, setting out the grounds upon which the application is opposed and the personal representative is required to file a witness statement or affidavit in answer setting out the matters required by CPR 1998, r 57.16(5) and PD 57, para 16. In exercising its discretion the court will look at all the circumstances and consider whether extension of time is required in the interests of justice (*Re Ruttie, Ruttie v Saul* [1970] 1 WLR 89, [1969] 3 All ER 1633). In *Re Salmon (dec'd), Coard v National Westminster Bank Ltd and Others* [1981] Ch 167, [1980] 3 WLR 748, Sir Robert Megarry VC considered *Re Ruttie* and gave a full account of the matters which might be considered material on an application for permission to apply out of time.

Examples of cases where leave was granted are *Re Trott, Trott v Miles* [1958] 1 WLR 604, [1958] 2 All ER 296, where the widow gave posthumous birth to a child; *Re McNare, McNare v McNare* [1964] 1 WLR 1255, [1964] 3 All ER 373, where the widow, who was blind, crippled and aged 71, was unaware of the husband's death until five months after probate had been granted and had no information regarding the deceased's assets. Leave was refused in *Longley, Longley and Longley v Longley* [1981] CLY 2885 (but cf *Adams v Schofeld* [1983] CLY 594) and *Escritt v Escritt* (1982) FLR 280, where there was a delay of over three years.

The crucial factor in deciding whether to grant leave to apply out of time is the balance of prejudice over and above that which is inherent in the granting or withholding of leave (*Bouette v*

Rose [1999] 2 FLR 466). In considering the application, the court will look at all the circumstances of the case, including whether it is in the interest of justice to allow an extension of time. The court will have regard, in particular, to: the reasons for the delay; what efforts have been made to mitigate any effects of the delay; whether any negotiations are being carried out; whether the estate has been distributed before notice of the claim is given; whether the applicant would have a claim against the solicitors if the application were refused; whether refusal would cause hardship and operate unfairly against the applicant and, in particular, whether it would leave the applicant without redress against anyone; and whether the applicant has an arguable case (*Re Salmon (dec'd), Coard v National Westminster Bank* [1981] Ch 167, [1980] 3 All ER 532, *Re C (Deceased) (Leave to Apply for Provision)* [1995] 2 FLR 24 (where an 8-year-old illegitimate child of the deceased was granted leave, although her mother had taken no steps to make a claim for two and a half years). Similarly, in *Re W (A Minor) (Claim from Deceased's Estate)* [1995] 2 FCR 689, an application on behalf of a child out of time was allowed on the basis that the child would suffer due to the default of another against whom the child would not have a claim. Furthermore, in view of the circumstances of the mother and the applicant child, the likelihood was that the court would make an order under the Act. See also *Stock v Brown* [1994] 1 FLR 840 (where the time-limit had been exceeded by six years)).

PART II

5 Interim orders

(1) Where on an application for an order under section 2 of this Act it appears to the court –

(*a*) that the applicant is in immediate need of financial assistance, but it is not yet possible to determine what order (if any) should be made under that section; and

(*b*) that property forming part of the net estate of the deceased is or can be made available to meet the need of the applicant;

the court may order that, subject to such conditions or restrictions, if any, as the court may impose and to any further order of the court, there shall be paid to the applicant out of the net estate of the deceased such sum or sums and (if more than one) at such intervals at the court thinks reasonable; and the court may order that, subject to the provisions of this Act, such payments are to be made until such date as the court may specify, not being later than the date on which the court either makes an order under the said section 2 or decides not to exercise its powers under that section.

(2) Subsections (2), (3) and (4) of section 2 of this Act shall apply in relation to an order under this section as they apply in relation to an order under that section.

(3) In determining what order, if any, should be made under this section the court shall, so far as the urgency of the case admits, have regard to the same matters as those to which the court is required to have regard under section 3 of this Act.

(4) An order made under section 2 of this Act may provide that any sum paid to the applicant by virtue of this section shall be treated to such an extent and in such manner as may be provided by that order as having been paid on account of any payment provided for by that order.

Procedure—The rules do not prescribe the procedure for such an application. Since the application is made in the main proceedings, it should be made by summons in those proceedings and supported by affidavit. The applicant must show that the conditions in s 5(1)(*a*) and (*b*) are satisfied.

Sanctioning interim payments—Personal representatives may find themselves in difficulties when such an application is made, particularly when the parties are on bad terms. In such cases "they should form their own view, with the assistance, of course of their legal advisers, as to the payments which can properly be made, and if they are not prepared to make such payments on their own responsibility they should ask the parties who might conceivably be affected – whether applicant or residuary legatee – for their consent. If such consent is not forthcoming the executors can apply to the court for leave to make the payment in question, and the court, if it thinks that withholding of consent was unreasonable, could throw the costs of the application on the party to blame. It is, of course, impossible to lay down precise rules covering every case" (per Cross J in *Re Ralphs, Ralphs v District Bank* [1968] 1 WLR 1522, [1968] 3 All ER 285).

6 Variation, discharge, etc of orders for periodical payments

(1) Subject to the provisions of this Act, where the court has made an order under section 2(1)(*a*) of this Act (in this section referred to as "the original order") for the making of periodical payments to any person (in this section referred to as "the original recipient"), the court, on an application under this section, shall have power by order to vary or discharge the original order or to suspend any provision of it temporarily and to revive the operation of any provision so suspended.

(2) Without prejudice to the generality of subsection (1) above, an order made on an application for the variation of the original order may –

- (*a*) provide for the making out of any relevant property of such periodical payments and for such term as may be specified in the order to any person who has applied, or would but for section 4 of this Act be entitled to apply, for an order under section 2 of this Act (whether or not, in the case of any application, an order was made in favour of the applicant);
- (*b*) provide for the payment out of any relevant property of a lump sum of such amount as may be so specified to the original recipient or to any such person as is mentioned in paragraph (*a*) above;
- (*c*) provide for the transfer of the relevant property, or such part thereof as may be so specified, to the original recipient or to any such person as is so mentioned.

(3) Where the original order provides that any periodical payments payable thereunder to the original recipient are to cease on the occurrence of an event specified in the order (other than the remarriage of a former wife or former husband) or on the expiration of a period so specified, then, if, before the end of the period of six months from the date of the occurrence of that event or of the expiration of that period, an application is made for an order under this section, the court shall have power to make any order which it would have had power to make if the application had been made before that date (whether in favour of the original recipient or any such person as is mentioned in subsection (2)(*a*) above and whether having effect from that date or from such later date as the court may specify).

(4) Any reference in this section to the original order shall include a reference to an order made under this section and any reference in this section to the original recipient shall include a reference to any person to whom periodical payments are required to be made by virtue of an order under this section.

(5) An application under this section may be made by any of the following persons, that is to say –

- (*a*) any person who by virtue of section 1(1) of this Act has applied, or would but for section 4 of this Act be entitled to apply, for an order under section 2 of this Act,
- (*b*) the personal representatives of the deceased,
- (*c*) the trustees of any relevant property, and
- (*d*) any beneficiary of the estate of the deceased.

(6) An order under this section may only affect –

(*a*) property the income of which is at the date of the order applicable wholly or in part for the making of periodical payments to any person who has applied for an order under this Act, or

(*b*) in the case of an application under subsection (3) above in respect of payments which have ceased to be payable on the occurrence of an event or the expiration of a period, property the income of which was so applicable immediately before the occurrence of that event or the expiration of that period, as the case may be,

and any such property as is mentioned in paragraph (*a*) or (*b*) above is in subsections (2) and (5) above referred to as "relevant property".

(7) In exercising the powers conferred by this section the court shall have regard to all the circumstances of the case, including any change in any of the matters to which the court was required to have regard when making the order to which the application relates.

(8) Where the court makes an order under this section, it may give such consequential directions as it thinks necessary or expedient having regard to the provisions of the order.

(9) No such order as is mentioned in section 2(1)(*d*), (*e*) or (*f*), 9, 10 or 11 of this Act shall be made on an application under this section.

(10) For the avoidance of doubt it is hereby declared that, in relation to an order which provides for the making of periodical payments which are to cease on the occurrence of an event specified in the order (other than the remarriage of a former wife or former husband) or on the expiration of a period so specified, the power to vary an order includes power to provide for the making of periodical payments after the expiration of that period or the occurrence of that event.

7 Payment of lump sums by instalments

(1) An order under section 2(1)(*b*) or 6(2)(*b*) of this Act for the payment of a lump sum may provide for the payment of that sum by instalments of such amount as may be specified in the order.

(2) Where an order is made by virtue of subsection (1) above, and court shall have power, on an application made by the person to whom the lump sum is payable, by the personal representatives of the deceased or by the trustees of the property out of which the lump sum is payable, to vary that order by varying the number of instalments payable, the amount of any instalment and the date on which any instalment becomes payable.

Property available for financial provision

8 Property treated as part of "net estate"

(1) Where a deceased person has in accordance with the provisions of any enactment nominated any person to receive any sum of money or other property on his death and that nomination is in force at the time of his death, that sum of money, after deducting therefrom any capital transfer tax payable in respect thereof, or that other property, to the extent of the value thereof at the date of the death of the deceased after deducting therefrom any capital transfer tax so payable, shall be treated for the purposes of this Act as part of the net estate of the deceased; but this subsection shall not render any person liable for having paid that sum or transferred that other property to the person named in the nomination in accordance with the directions given in the nomination.

PART II

(2) Where any sum of money or other property is received by any person as a donatio mortis causa made by a deceased person, that sum of money, after deducting therefrom any capital transfer tax payable thereon, or that other property, to the extent of the value thereof at the date of the death of the deceased after deducting therefrom any capital transfer tax so payable, shall be treated for the purposes of this Act as part of the net estate of the deceased; but this subsection shall not render any person liable for having paid that sum or transferred that other property in order to give effect to that donatio mortis causa.

(3) The amount of capital transfer tax to be deducted for the purpose of this section shall not exceed the amount of that tax which has been borne by the person nominated by the deceased or, as the case may be, the person who has received a sum of money or other property as a donatio mortis causa.

Defined terms—"net estate": s 25(1) (see also under s 2).

"property"—This term includes a chose in action (s 25(1)).

"donatio mortis causa"—Land is capable of passing through a donatio mortis causa (*Sen v Headley* [1991] Ch 425, [1991] 2 FLR 449).

9 Property held on a joint tenancy

(1) Where a deceased person was immediately before his death beneficially entitled to a joint tenancy of any property, then, if, before the end of the period of six months from the date on which representation with respect to the estate of the deceased was first taken out, an application is made for an order under section 2 of this Act, the court for the purpose of facilitating the making of financial provision for the applicant under this Act may order that the deceased's severable share of that property, at the value thereof immediately before his death, shall, to such extent as appears to the court to be just in all the circumstances of the case, be treated for the purposes of this Act as part of the net estate of the deceased.

(2) In determining the extent to which any severable share is to be treated as part of the net estate of the deceased by virtue of any order under subsection (1) above, the court shall have regard to any capital transfer tax payable in respect of that severable share.

(3) Where an order is made under subsection (1) above, the provisions of this section shall not render any person liable for anything done by him before the order was made.

(4) For the avoidance of doubt it is hereby declared that for the purposes of this section there may be a joint tenancy of a chose in action.

Defined terms—"net estate": s 25(1).

"joint tenancy of any property" (s 9(1))—In *Jessop v Jessop* [1992] 1 FLR 591, the court ordered the deceased's severable share of his cohabitee's house which had been jointly owned prior to the deceased's death, to be treated as part of the net estate of the deceased and ordered the cohabitee to pay a lump sum to the widow. In *Re Crawford* (1983) FLR 273, a lump sum received by the deceased on his retirement had been paid into an account held jointly with his second wife. The court made an order under s 9 that the deceased's share of the lump sum should be treated as part of his estate. Where the deceased's net estate consists of a beneficial half share to a joint tenancy of property which is subject to a mortgage secured by a collateral endowment insurance policy the value of the deceased's net estate is determined for the purposes of s 9(1) at the time immediately before his death (*Powell v Osbourne* [1993] 1 FLR 1001). Where a deceased person's estate is found to be insolvent, administration takes place under Insolvency Act 1986, s 421 and the matter is governed by the Administration of Insolvent Estates of Deceased Persons Order 1986. However, the making of an insolvency administration order does not relate back to sever the deceased's beneficial interest in property owned by the deceased and his wife immediately before the deceased's death, as the deceased's interest in the property passes to the widow by survivorship at the moment of death (*Re Palmer (Deceased) (Insolvent Estate)* [1994] 2 FLR 609). Where, on an application for ancillary relief following a divorce, an agreement is reached between the parties for the sale of the former matrimonial home and the division of the proceeds of sale, the joint tenancy is severed so that, if one of the parties dies before the agreement is approved by the court and an order made, the joint tenancy remains severed by the agreement. The agreement does not have to be enforceable, provided it indicates a common intention to sever (*Hunter v Babbage* [1994] 2 FLR 806).

"for the purpose of facilitating the making of financial provision" (s 9(1))—This should not be understood to narrow the broad discretionary power given by s 9 (*Kourkgy v Lusher* (1983) FLR 65), but the broad discretionary power is no more than a power to facilitate the making of an order under s 2 (*Jessop v Jessop* [1992] 1 FLR 591).

Powers of court in relation to transactions intended to defeat applications for financial provision

10 Dispositions intended to defeat applications for financial provision

(1) Where an application is made to the court for an order under section 2 of this Act, the applicant may, in the proceedings on that application, apply to the court for an order under subsection (2) below.

(2) Where on an application under subsection (1) above the court is satisfied –

- (*a*) that, less than six years before the date of the death of the deceased, the deceased with the intention of defeating an application for financial provision under this Act made a disposition, and
- (*b*) that full valuable consideration for that disposition was not given by the person to whom or for the benefit of whom the disposition was made (in this section referred to as "the donee") or by any other person, and
- (*c*) that the exercise of the powers conferred by this section would facilitate the making of financial provision for the applicant under this Act,

then, subject to the provisions of this section and of sections 12 and 13 of this Act, the court may order the donee (whether or not at the date of the order he holds any interest in the property disposed of to him or for his benefit by the deceased) to provide, for the purpose of the making of that financial provision, such sum of money or other property as may be specified in the order.

(3) Where an order is made under subsection (2) above as respects any disposition made by the deceased which consisted of the payment of money to or for the benefit of the donee, the amount of any sum of money or the value of any property orders to be provided under that subsection shall not exceed the amount of the payment made by the deceased after deducting therefrom any capital transfer tax borne by the donee in respect of that payment.

(4) Where an order is made under subsection (2) above as respects any disposition made by the deceased which consisted of the transfer of property (other than a sum of money) to or for the benefit of the donee, the amount of any sum of money or the value of any property ordered to be provided under that subsection shall not exceed the value at the date of the death of the deceased of the property disposed of by him to or for the benefit of the donee (or if that property has been disposed of by the person to whom it was transferred by the deceased, the value at the date of that disposal thereof) after deducting therefrom any capital transfer tax borne by the donee in respect of the transfer of that property by the deceased.

(5) Where an application (in this subsection referred to as "the original application") is made for an order under subsection (2) above in relation to any disposition, then, if on an application under this subsection by the donee or by any applicant for an order under section 2 of this Act the court is satisfied –

(*a*) that, less than six years before the date of the death of the deceased, the deceased with the intention of defeating an application for financial provision under this Act made a disposition other than the disposition which is the subject of the original application, and

(*b*) that full valuable consideration for that other disposition was not given by the person to whom or for the benefit of whom that other disposition was made or by any other person,

the court may exercise in relation to the person to whom or for the benefit of whom that other disposition was made the powers which the court would have had under subsection (2) above if the original application had been made in respect of that other disposition and the court had been satisfied as to the matters set out in paragraphs (*a*), (*b*) and (*c*) of that subsection; and where any application is made under this subsection, any reference in this section (except in subsection (2)(*b*)) to the donee shall include a reference to the person to whom or for the benefit of whom that other disposition was made.

(6) In determining whether and in what manner to exercise its powers under this section, the court shall have regard to the circumstances in which any disposition was made and any valuable consideration which was given therefor, the relationship, if any, of the donee to the deceased, the conduct and financial resources of the donee and all the other circumstances of the case.

(7) In this section "disposition" does not include –

(*a*) any provision in a will, any such nomination as is mentioned in section 8(1) of this Act or any donatio mortis causa, or

(*b*) any appointment of property made, otherwise than by will, in the exercise of a special power of appointment,

but, subject to these exceptions, includes any payment of money (including the payment of a premium under a policy of assurance) and any conveyance, assurance, appointment or gift of property of any description, whether made by an instrument or otherwise.

(8) The provisions of this section do not apply to any disposition made before the commencement of this Act.

Defined terms—"valuable consideration": s 25.

Avoidance of disposition intended to defeat a claim—An applicant who applies for an order under s 2 may also apply for an order that the donee of a disposition made less than six years before the deceased's death with the intention of defeating a claim under the Act and without full valuable consideration should provide such sum or property as may be necessary for the making of reasonable financial provision for the applicant. The court's power under this section is subject to the matters referred to in ss 12 and 13.

See *Clifford v Tanner* [1987] CLY 3881, where it was held that a deed releasing a donee from a covenant allowing the donor and his wife to occupy a house, which was the subject of a gift to the donee, is a disposition within s 10(7).

"intention of defeating an application" (s 10(2)(*a*), (5)(*a*))—It is not essential to show that the deceased had the provision of the Act in mind when the transaction in issue was made, but the evidence must show that he intended to defeat a claim against his estate made after his death (*Re Kennedy (dec'd)* [1980] CLY 2820).

11 Contracts to leave property by will

(1) Where an application is made to a court for an order under section 2 of this Act, the applicant may, in the proceedings on that application, apply to the court for an order under this section.

(2) Where on an application under subsection (1) above the court is satisfied –

(*a*) that the deceased made a contract by which he agreed to leave by his will a sum of money or other property to any person or by which he agreed that a sum of money or other property would be paid or transferred to any person out of his estate, and

(*b*) that the deceased made that contract with the intention of defeating an application for financial provision under this Act, and

(*c*) that when the contract was made full valuable consideration for that contract was not given or promised by the person with whom or for the benefit of whom the contract was made (in this section referred to as "the donee") or by any other person, and

(*d*) that the exercise of the powers conferred by this section would facilitate the making of financial provision for the applicant under this Act,

then, subject to the provisions of this section and of sections 12 and 13 of this Act, the court may make any one or more of the following orders, that is to say –

(i) if any money has been paid or any other property has been transferred to or for the benefit of the donee in accordance with the contract, an order directing the donee to provide, for the purpose of the making of that financial provision, such sum of money or other property as may be specified in the order;

(ii) if the money or all the money has not been paid or the property or all the property has not been transferred in accordance with the contract, an order directing the personal representatives not to make any payment or transfer any property, or not to make any further payment or transfer any further property, as the case may be, in accordance therewith or directing the personal representatives only to make such payment or transfer such property as may be specified in the order.

(3) Notwithstanding anything in subsection (2) above, the court may exercise its powers thereunder in relation to any contract made by the deceased only to the extent that the court considers that the amount of any sum of money paid or to be paid or the value of any property transferred or to be transferred in accordance with the contract exceeds the value of any valuable consideration given or to be given for that contract, and for this purpose the court shall have regard to the value of property at the date of the hearing.

(4) In determining whether and in what manner to exercise its powers under this section, the court shall have regard to the circumstances in which the contract was made, the relationship, if any, of the donee to the deceased, the conduct and financial resources of the donee and all the other circumstances of the case.

(5) Where an order has been made under subsection (2) above in relation to any contract, the rights of any person to enforce that contract or to recover damages or to obtain other relief for the breach thereof shall be subject to any adjustment made by the court under section 12(3) of this Act and shall survive to such extent only as is consistent with giving effect to the terms of that order.

(6) The provision of this section do not apply to a contract made before the commencement of this Act.

Avoidance of contracts to leave property by will—An applicant who applies for an order under s 2 may also apply for an order directing the donee under a contract which was made with the intention of defeating a claim under the Act and without full valuable consideration to provide such sum of money or other property as may be necessary for the making of reasonable financial provision for the applicant. Where the sum of money or the property has not been transferred, the order should direct that the personal representatives must not make the payment or transfer the property, or make any further payment or transfer any further property, or that they may make only such payment or transfer as the court may direct. Under this section the court has power to make such further consequential directions as it thinks fit for giving effect to any order it makes.

12 Provisions supplementary to ss 10 and 11

(1) Where the exercise of any of the powers conferred by section 10 or 11 of this Act is conditional on the court being satisfied that a disposition or contract was made by a deceased person with the intention of defeating an application for financial provision under this Act, that condition shall be fulfilled if the court is of the opinion that, on a balance of probabilities, the intention of the deceased (though not necessarily his sole intention) in making the disposition or contract was to prevent an order for financial provision being made under this Act or to reduce the amount of the provision which might otherwise be granted by an order thereunder.

(2) Where an application is made under section 11 of this Act with respect to any contract made by the deceased and no valuable consideration was given or promised by any person for that contract then, notwithstanding anything in subsection (1) above, it shall be presumed, unless the contrary is shown, that the deceased made that contract with the intention of defeating an application for financial provision under this Act.

(3) Where the court makes an order under section 10 or 11 of this Act it may give such consequential directions as it thinks fit (including directions requiring the making of any payment or the transfer of any property) for giving effect to the order or for securing a fair adjustment of the rights of the persons affected thereby.

(4) Any power conferred on the court by the said section 10 or 11 to order the donee, in relation to any disposition or contract, to provide any sum of money or other property shall be exercisable in like manner in relation to the personal representative of the donee, and –

(*a*) any reference in section 10(4) to the disposal of property by the donee shall include a reference to disposal by the personal representative of the donee, and

(*b*) any reference in section 10(5) to an application by the donee under that subsection shall include a reference to an application by the personal representative of the donee;

but the court shall not have power under the said section 10 or 11 to make an order in respect of any property forming part of the estate of the donee which has been distributed by the personal representative; and the personal representative shall not be liable for having distributed any such property before he has notice of the making of an application under the said section 10 or 11 on the ground that he ought to have taken into account the possibility that such an application would be made.

13 Provisions as to trustees in relation to ss 10 and 11

(1) Where an application is made for –

(*a*) an order under section 10 of this Act in respect of a disposition made by the deceased to any person as a trustee, or

(*b*) an order under section 11 of this Act in respect of any payment made or property transferred, in accordance with a contract made by the deceased, to any person as a trustee,

the powers of the court under the said section 10 or 11 to order that trustee to provide a sum of money or other property shall be subject to the following limitation (in addition, in a case of an application under section 10, to any provision regarding the deduction of capital transfer tax) namely, that the amount of any sum of money or the value of any property ordered to be provided –

(i) in the case of an application in respect of a disposition which consisted of the payment of money or an application in respect of the payment of money in accordance with a contract, shall not exceed the aggregate of so much of that money as is at the date of the order in the hands of the trustee and the value at that date of any property which represents that money or is derived therefrom and is at that date in the hands of the trustee;

(ii) in the case of an application in respect of a disposition which consisted of the transfer of property (other than a sum of money) or an application in respect of the transfer of property (other than a sum of money) in accordance with a contract, shall not exceed the aggregate of the value at the date of the order of so much of that property as is at that date in the hands of the trustee and the value at that date of any property which represents the first mentioned property or is derived therefrom and is at that date in the hands of the trustee.

(2) Where any such application is made in respect of a disposition made to any person as a trustee or in respect of any payment made or property transferred in pursuance of a contract to any person as a trustee, the trustee shall not be liable for having distributed any money or other property on the ground that he ought to have taken into account the possibility that such an application would be made.

(3) Where any such application is made in respect of a disposition made to any person as a trustee or in respect of any payment made or property transferred in accordance with a contract to any person as a trustee, any reference in the said section 10 or 11 to the donee shall be construed as including a reference to the trustee or trustees for the time being of the trust in question and any reference in subsection (1) or (2) above to a trustee shall be construed in the same way.

Special provisions relating to cases of divorce, separation etc

14 Provision as to cases where no financial relief was granted in divorce proceedings etc

(1) Where, within twelve months from the date on which a decree of divorce or nullity of marriage has been made absolute or a decree of judicial separation has been granted, a party to the marriage dies and –

(*a*) an application for a financial provision order under section 23 of the Matrimonial Causes Act 1973 or a property adjustment order under section 24 of that Act has not been made by the other party to that marriage, or

(*b*) such an application has been made but the proceedings thereon have not been determined at the time of the death of the deceased,

then, if an application for an order under section 2 of this Act is made by that other party, the court shall, notwithstanding anything in section 1 or section 3 of this Act, have power, if it thinks it just to do so, to treat that party for the purposes of that application as if the decree of divorce or nullity of marriage had not been made absolute or the decree of judicial separation had not been granted, as the case may be.

(2) This section shall not apply in relation to a decree of judicial separation unless at the date of the death of the deceased the decree was in force and the separation was continuing.

Defined terms—"financial provision": Matrimonial Causes Act 1973, s 23; "property adjustment order": MCA 1973, s 24.

15 Restriction imposed in divorce proceedings etc on application under this Act

(1) On the grant of a decree of divorce, a decree of nullity of marriage or a decree of judicial separation or at any time thereafter the court, if it considers it just to do so, may, on the application of either party to the marriage, order that the other party to the marriage shall not on the death of the applicant be entitled to apply for an order under section 2 of this Act.

In this subsection "the court" means the High Court or, where a county court has jurisdiction by virtue of Part V of the Matrimonial and Family Proceedings Act 1984, a county court.

(2) In the case of a decree of divorce or nullity of marriage an order may be made under subsection (1) above before or after the decree is made absolute, but if it is made before the decree is made absolute it shall not take effect unless the decree is made absolute.

(3) Where an order made under subsection (1) above on the grant of a decree of divorce or nullity of marriage has come into force with respect to a party to a marriage, then, on the death of the other party to that marriage, the court shall not entertain any application for an order under section 2 of this Act made by the first-mentioned party.

(4) Where an order made under subsection (1) above on the grant of a decree of judicial separation has come into force with respect to any party to a marriage, then, if the other party to that marriage dies while the decree is in force and the separation is continuing, the court shall not entertain any application for an order under section 2 of this Act made by the first-mentioned party.

Amendments—Matrimonial and Family Proceedings Act 1984, s 8(1).

"if it considers it just to do so"—See *Whiting v Whiting* [1988] 2 FLR 189, where it was held that before a court makes such an order there must be evidence of what the estate is likely to consist of and of the persons who may have a prior claim against the estate.

15A Restriction imposed in proceedings under Matrimonial and Family Proceedings Act 1984 on application under this Act

(1) On making an order under section 17 of the Matrimonial and Family Proceedings Act 1984 (orders for financial provision and property adjustment) the court, if it considers it just to do so, may, on the application of either party to the marriage, order that the other party to the marriage shall not on the death of the applicant be entitled to apply for an order under section 2 of this Act.

In this subsection "the court" means the High Court or, where a county court has jurisdiction by virtue of Part V of the Matrimonial and Family Proceedings Act 1984, a county court.

(2) Where an order under subsection (1) above has been made with respect to a party to a marriage which has been dissolved or annulled, then, on the death of the other party to that marriage, the court shall not entertain an application under section 2 of this Act made by the first-mentioned party.

(3) Where an order under subsection (1) above has been made with respect to a party to a marriage the parties to which have been legally separated, then, if the other party to the marriage dies while the legal separation is in force, the court shall not entertain an application under section 2 of this Act made by the first-mentioned party.

Amendments—Inserted by Matrimonial and Family Proceedings Act 1984, s 25.

16 Variation and discharge of secured periodical payments orders made under Matrimonial Causes Act 1973

(1) Where an application for an order under section 2 of this Act is made to the court by any person who was at the time of the death of the deceased entitled to payments from the deceased under a secured periodical payments order made under the Matrimonial Causes Act 1973, then, in the proceedings on that application, the court shall have power, if an application is made under this section by that person or by the personal representative of the deceased, to vary or discharge that periodical payments order or to revive the operation of any provision thereof which has been suspended under section 31 of that Act.

(2) In exercising the powers conferred by this section the court shall have regard to all the circumstances of the case, including any order which the court proposes to make under section 2 or section 5 of this Act and any change (whether resulting from the death of the deceased or otherwise) in any of the matters to which the court was required to have regard when making the secured periodical payments order.

(3) The powers exercisable by the court under this section in relation to an order shall be exercisable also in relation to any instrument executed in pursuance of the order.

Defined terms—"secured periodical payments": Matrimonial Causes Act 1973, s 23.

17 Variation and revocation of maintenance agreements

(1) Where an application for an order under section 2 of this Act is made to the court by any person who was at the time of the death of the deceased entitled to payments from the deceased under a maintenance agreement which provided for the continuation of payments under the agreement after the death of the deceased, then, in the proceedings on that application, the court shall have power, if an

application is made under this section by that person or by the personal representative of the deceased, to vary or revoke that agreement.

(2) In exercising the powers conferred by this section the court shall have regard to all the circumstances of the case, including any order which the court proposes to make under section 2 or section 5 of this Act and any change (whether resulting from the death of the deceased or otherwise) in any of the circumstances in the light of which the agreement was made.

(3) If a maintenance agreement is varied by the court under this section the like consequences shall ensue as if the variation had been made immediately before the death of the deceased by agreement between the parties and for valuable consideration.

(4) In this section "maintenance agreement", in relation to a deceased person, means any agreement made, whether in writing or not and whether before or after the commencement of this Act, by the deceased with any person with whom he entered into marriage, being an agreement which contained provisions governing the rights and liabilities towards one another when living separately of the parties to that marriage (whether or not the marriage has been dissolved or annulled) in respect of the making or securing of payments or the disposition or use of any property, including such rights and liabilities with respect to the maintenance or education of any child, whether or not a child of the deceased or a person who was treated by the deceased as a child of the family in relation to that marriage.

Scope of provision—The court had powers, similar to those under s 16, to vary or revoke a maintenance agreement which provided for the continuation of payment under the agreement after the death of the deceased. Matrimonial Causes Act 1973, s 36 also provides for an application to be made for the alteration of a maintenance agreement after the death of one of the spouses, and FPR 1991, r 3.3 prescribes the procedure that must be followed. When making an application under this section it is suggested that the affidavit in support should include the matters set out in the FPR 1991, r 3.3(2).

18 Availability of court's powers under this Act in applications under ss 31 and 36 of the Matrimonial Causes Act 1973

(1) Where –

(*a*) a person against whom a secured periodical payments order was made under the Matrimonial Causes Act 1973 has died and an application is made under section 31(6) of that Act for the variation or discharge of that order or for the revival of the operation of any provision thereof which has been suspended, or

(*b*) a party to a maintenance agreement within the meaning of section 34 of that Act has died, the agreement being one which provides for the continuation of payments thereunder after the death of one of the parties, and an application is made under section 36(1) of that Act for the alteration of the agreement under section 35 thereof,

the court shall have power to direct that the application made under the said section 31(6) or 36(1) shall be deemed to have been accompanied by an application for an order under section 2 of this Act.

(2) Where the court gives a direction under subsection (1) above it shall have power, in the proceedings on the application under the said section 31(6) or 36(1), to make any order which the court would have had power to make under the provisions of this Act if the application under the said section 31(6) or 36(1), as the case may be, had been made jointly with an application for an order under the said section 2; and the court shall have power to give such consequential directions as

may be necessary for enabling the court to exercise any of the powers available to the court under this Act in the case of an application for an order under section 2.

(3) Where an order made under section 15(1) of this Act is in force with respect to a party to a marriage, the court shall not give a direction under subsection (1) above with respect to any application made under the said section 31(6) or 36(1) by that party on the death of the other party.

Miscellaneous and supplementary provisions

19 Effect, duration and form of orders

(1) Where an order is made under section 2 of this Act then for all purposes, including the purposes of the enactments relating to inheritance tax, the will or the law relating to intestacy, or both the will and the law relating to intestacy, as the case may be, shall have effect and be deemed to have had effect as from the deceased's death subject to the provisions of the order.

(2) Any order made under section 2 or 5 of this Act in favour of –

(*a*) an applicant who was the former husband or former wife of the deceased, or

(*b*) an applicant who was the husband or wife of the deceased in a case where the marriage with the deceased was the subject of a decree of judicial separation and at the date of death the decree was in force and the separation was continuing,

shall, in so far as it provides for the making of periodical payments, cease to have effect on the remarriage of the applicant, except in relation to any arrears due under the order on the date of the remarriage.

(3) A copy of every order made under this Act other than an order made under section 15(1) of this Act shall be sent to the principal registry of the Family Division for entry and filing, and a memorandum of the order shall be endorsed on, or permanently annexed to, the probate or letters of administration under which the estate is being administered.

Amendments—Administration of Justice Act 1982, s 52.

****

25 Interpretation

(1) In this Act –

"beneficiary", in relation to the estate of a deceased person, means –

(*a*) a person who under the will of the deceased or under the law relating to intestacy is beneficially interested in the estate or would be so interested if an order had not been made under this Act, and

(*b*) a person who has received any sum of money or other property which by virtue of section 8(1) or (2) of this Act is treated as part of the net estate of the deceased or would have received that sum or other property if an order had not been made under this Act;

"child" includes an illegitimate child and a child en ventre sa mere at the death of the deceased;

"the court" means, unless the context otherwise requires, the High Court, or where a county court has jurisdiction by virtue of section 22 of this Act, a county court;

"former wife" or "former husband" means a person whose marriage with the deceased was during the lifetime of the deceased either –

(*a*) dissolved or annulled by a decree of divorce or a decree of nullity of marriage granted under the law of any part of the British Islands, or

(*b*) dissolved or annulled in any country or territory outside the British Islands by a divorce or annulment which is entitled to be recognised as valid by the law of England and Wales;

"net estate", in relation to a deceased person, means –

(*a*) all property of which the deceased had power to dispose by his will (otherwise than by virtue of a special power of appointment) less the amount of his funeral, testamentary and administration expenses, debts and liabilities, including any capital transfer tax payable out of his estate on his death;

(*b*) any property in respect of which the deceased held a general power of appointment (not being a power exercisable by will) which has not been exercised;

(*c*) any sum of money or other property which is treated for the purposes of this Act as part of the net estate of the deceased by virtue of section 8(1) or (2) of this Act;

(*d*) any property which is treated for the purposes of this Act as part of the net estate of the deceased by virtue of an order made under section 9 of the Act;

(*e*) any sum of money or other property which is, by reason of a disposition or contract made by the deceased, ordered under section 10 or 11 of this Act to be provided for the purpose of the making of financial provision under this Act;

"property" includes any chose in action;

"reasonable financial provision" has the meaning assigned to it by section 1 of this Act;

"valuable consideration" does not include marriage or a promise of marriage;

"will" includes codicil.

(2) For the purposes of paragraph (*a*) of the definition of "net estate" in subsection (1) above a person who is not of full age and capacity shall be treated as having power to dispose by will of all property of which he would have had power to dispose by will if he had been of full age and capacity.

(3) Any references in this Act to provision out of the net estate of a deceased person includes a reference to provision extending to the whole of that estate.

(4) For the purposes of this Act any reference to a wife or husband shall be treated as including a reference to a person who in good faith entered into a void marriage with the deceased unless either –

(*a*) the marriage of the deceased and that person was dissolved or annulled during the lifetime of the deceased and the dissolution or annulment is recognised by the law of England and Wales, or

(*b*) that person has during the lifetime of the deceased entered into a later marriage.

(5) Any reference in this Act to remarriage or to a person who has remarried includes a reference to a marriage which is by law void or voidable or to a person who has entered into such a marriage, as the case may be, and a marriage shall be

treated for the purposes of this Act as a remarriage, in relation to any party thereto, notwithstanding that the previous marriage of that party was void or voidable.

(6) Any reference in this Act to an order or decree made under the Matrimonial Causes Act 1973 or under any section of that Act shall be construed as including a reference to an order or decree which is deemed to have been made under that Act or under that section thereof, as the case may be.

(7) Any reference in this Act to any enactment is a reference to that enactment as amended by or under any subsequent enactment.

****

Judicial Proceedings (Regulation of Reports) Act 1926

1 Restriction on publication of reports of judicial proceedings

(1) It shall not be lawful to print or publish, or cause or procure to be printed or published –

(*a*) in relation to any judicial proceedings any indecent matter or indecent medical, surgical or physiological details being matter or details the publication of which would be calculated to injure public morals;

(*b*) in relation to any judicial proceedings for dissolution of marriage, for nullity of marriage, or for judicial separation, or for restitution of conjugal rights, any particulars other than the following, that is to say:

(i) the names, addresses and occupations of the parties and witnesses;

(ii) a concise statement of the charges, defences and countercharges in support of which evidence has been given;

(iii) submissions on any point of law arising in the course of the proceedings, and the decision of the court thereon;

(iv) the summing-up of the judge and the finding of the jury (if any) and the judgment of the court and observations made by the judge in giving judgment.

Provided that nothing in this part of this subsection shall be held to permit the publication of anything contrary to the provisions of paragraph (*a*) of this subsection.

(2) If any person acts in contravention of the provisions of this Act, he shall in respect of each offence be liable, on summary conviction, to imprisonment for a term not exceeding four months, or to a fine not exceeding level 5 on the standard scale, or to both such imprisonment and fine:

Provided that no person, other than a proprietor, editor, master printer or publisher, shall be liable to be convicted under this Act.

(3) No prosecution for an offence under this Act shall be commenced in England and Wales by any person without the sanction of the Attorney-General.

(4) Nothing in this section shall apply to the printing of any pleading, transcript of evidence or other document for use in connection with any judicial proceedings or the communication thereof to persons concerned in the proceedings, or to the printing or publishing of any notice or report in pursuance of the directions of the court; or to the printing or publishing of any matter in any separate volume or part of any bone fide series of law reports which does not form part of any other publication and consists solely of reports of proceedings in courts of law, or in any publication of a technical character bona fide intended for circulation among members of the legal or medical professions.

(5) (*applies to Scotland only*)

Amendments—Criminal Justice Act 1982, s 46(1). See also under **Extension of s 1(1)(b)** below.

General Note—The fact that a hearing takes place in chambers does not determine whether it should be regarded as subject to a ban on publication. Hearings relating to children and ancillary relief are covered by privacy and secrecy; information about such cases cannot be disclosed without leave of the court. Other family proceedings are not so protected. Whether or not they are protected depends on the applicability of Administration of Justice Act 1960, s 12 or the existence of other circumstances which make disclosure prejudicial to the administration of justice, including consideration of the requirement of Contempt of Court Act 1981, s 11 (*Clibbery v Allan and Another* [2002] EWCA Civ 45, [2002] 1 FLR 565).

"in relation to any judicial proceedings for dissolution of marriage" (s 1(1)(*b*))—Proceedings are not concluded finally until any question arising as to the validity of any decree or order which might have been made is finally resolved; thus, proceedings concerning an application to render a decree of divorce null and void were covered by the 1926 Act and the evidence given at the hearing cannot be reported (*Moynihan v Moynihan (Nos 1 and 2)* [1997] 1 FLR 59). However, Sir Stephen Brown P indicated (at 62G) that "there would appear to be ample scope in the context of the subparagraphs of subpara (*b*) for clear and full details to be given, though not necessarily a line-by-line account of what a particular witness says at any particular time".

Extension of s 1(1)(b)—Although this section has not been amended textually, it has been extended, by virtue of amendments made to Domestic and Appellate Proceedings (Restriction of Publicity) Act 1968, s 2(3) by the Family Law Act 1986 and Family Law Reform Act 1987, to cover proceedings under Matrimonial Causes Act 1973, s 27 (failure to maintain), proceedings under FLA 1986, Pt III (as from 4 April 1988), and applications for a declaration under FLA 1986, s 56(1) (as from 4 April 1988). The particulars specified in s 1(1)(*b*) are modified in their application to allow publication of the particulars of the declaration sought instead of a concise statement of charges, defences and coutercharges. See further under DAP(RP)A 1968, s 2.

Procedure—See *Emergency Remedies in the Family Courts* (Family Law).

Law Reform (Miscellaneous Provisions) Act 1970

1 Engagements to marry not enforceable at law

(1) An agreement between two persons to marry one another shall not under the law of England and Wales have effect as a contract giving rise to legal rights and no action shall lie in England and Wales for breach of such an agreement, whatever the law applicable to the agreement.

(2) This section shall have effect in relation to agreements entered into before it comes into force, except that it shall not affect any action commenced before it comes into force.

2 Property of engaged couples

(1) Where an agreement to marry is terminated, any rule of law relating to the rights of husbands and wives in relation to property in which either or both has or have a beneficial interest, including any such rule as explained by section 37 of the Matrimonial Proceedings and Property Act 1970, shall apply, in relation to any property in which either or both of the parties to the agreement had a beneficial interest while the agreement was in force, as it applies in relation to property in which a husband or wife has a beneficial interest.

(2) Where an agreement to marry is terminated, section 17 of the Married Women's Property Act 1882 and section 7 of the Matrimonial Causes (Property and Maintenance) Act 1958 (which sections confer power on a judge of the High Court or a county court to settle disputes between husband and wife about property) shall apply, as if the parties were married, to any dispute between, or claim by, one of them in relation to property in which either or both had a beneficial interest while the agreement was in force; but an application made by virtue of this section to the judge under the said section 17, as originally enacted or as extended by the said section 7, shall be made within three years of the termination of the agreement.

3 Gifts between engaged couples

(1) A party to an agreement to marry who makes a gift of property to the other party to the agreement on the condition (express or implied) that it shall be returned if the agreement is terminated shall not be prevented from recovering the property by reason only of his having terminated the agreement.

(2) The gift of an engagement ring shall be presumed to be an absolute gift; this presumption may be rebutted by proving that the ring was given on the condition, express or implied, that it should be returned if the marriage did not take place for any reason.

****

Legitimacy Act 1976

ARRANGEMENT OF SECTIONS

1 Legitimacy of children of certain void marriages

(1) The child of a void marriage, whenever born, shall, subject to subsection (2) below and Schedule 1 to this Act, be treated as the legitimate child of his parents if at the time of the insemination resulting in the birth or, where there was no such insemination, the child's conception (or at the time of the celebration of the marriage if later) both or either of the parties reasonably believed that the marriage was valid.

(2) This section only applies where the father of the child was domiciled in England and Wales at the time of the birth or, if he died before the birth, was so domiciled immediately before his death.

(3) It is hereby declared for the avoidance of doubt that subsection (1) above applies notwithstanding that the belief that the marriage was valid was due to a mistake as to law.

(4) In relation to a child born after the coming into force of section 28 of the Family Law Reform Act 1987, it shall be presumed for the purposes of subsection (1) above, unless the contrary is shown, that one of the parties to the void marriage reasonably believed at the time of the insemination resulting in the birth or, where there was no such insemination, the child's conception (or at the time of the celebration of the marriage if later) that the marriage was valid.

Amendments—Family Law Reform Act 1987, s 28.

Defined terms—"void marriage": s 10(1).

"child of a void marriage"—The decision in *Spence, Spence v Dennis* [1990] Ch 652, [1990] 2 FLR 278 suggests that this definition includes only a child who would be born *in wedlock* if the marriage were valid; there is a distinction between a child of a void marriage and a child legitimated by the subsequent marriage of its parents (see s 2). In the case of a child born *after* a void marriage, the child will be treated as a legitimate child, but a child born *before* the void marriage will be treated as illegitimate (see also *F and F v AG and F* [1980] Fam Law 60).

2 Legitimation by subsequent marriage of parents

Subject to the following provisions of this Act, where the parents of an illegitimate person marry one another, the marriage shall, if the father of the illegitimate person is at the date of marriage domiciled in England and Wales, render that person, if living, legitimate from the date of the marriage.

3 Legitimation by extraneous law

Subject to the following provisions of this Act, where the parents of an illegitimate person marry one another and the father of the illegitimate person is not at the time of the marriage domiciled in England and Wales but is domiciled in a country by the law of which the illegitimate person became legitimated by virtue of such subsequent marriage, that person, if living, shall in England and Wales be recognised as having been so legitimated from the date of the marriage notwithstanding that, at the time of his birth, his father was domiciled in a country the law of which did not permit legitimation by subsequent marriage.

4 Legitimation of adopted child

(1) Section 39 of the Adoption Act 1976 does not prevent an adopted child being legitimated under section 2 or 3 above if either natural parent is the sole adoptive parent.

(2) Where an adopted child (with a sole adoptive parent) is legitimated –

(*a*) subsection (2) of the said section 39 shall not apply after the legitimation to the natural relationship with the other natural parent, and
(*b*) revocation of the adoption order in consequence of the legitimation shall not affect section 39, 41 or 42 of the Adoption Act 1976 as it applies to any instrument made before the date of legitimation.

Amendments—Adoption Act 1976, s 73(2), Sch 3, para 23.

5 Rights of legitimated persons and others to take interests in property

(1) Subject to any contrary indication, the rules of construction contained in this section apply to any instrument other than an existing instrument, so far as the instrument contains a disposition of property.

(2) For the purposes of this section, provisions of the law of intestate succession applicable to the estate of a deceased person shall be treated as if contained in an instrument executed by him (while of full capacity) immediately before his death.

(3) A legitimated person, and any other person, shall be entitled to take any interest as if the legitimated person had been born legitimate.

(4) A disposition which depends on the date of birth of a child or children of the parent or parents shall be construed as if –

(*a*) a legitimated child had been born on the date of legitimation,
(*b*) two or more legitimated children legitimated on the same date had been born on that date in the order of their actual births,

but this does not affect any reference to the age of a child.

(5) Examples of phrases in wills on which subsection (4) above can operate are –

1 Children of A "living at my death or born afterwards".
2 Children of A "living at my death or born afterwards before any one of such children for the time being in existence attains a vested interest, and who attain the age of 21 years".
3 As in example 1 or 2, but referring to grandchildren of A, instead of children of A.
4 A for life "until he has a child" and then to his child or children.

Note. Subsection (4) above will not affect the reference to the age of 21 years in example 2.

(6) If an illegitimate person or a person adopted by one of his natural parents dies, or has died before the commencement of this Act, and –

(*a*) after his death his parents marry or have married; and
(*b*) the deceased would, if living at the time of the marriage, have become a legitimated person,

this section shall apply for the construction of the instrument so far as it relates to the taking of interests by, or in succession to, his spouse, children and remoter issue as if he had been legitimated by virtue of the marriage.

(7) In this section "instrument" includes a private Act settling property, but not any other enactment.

Defined terms—"disposition", "legitimated person": s 10(1).

6 Dispositions depending on date of birth

(1) Where a disposition depends on the date of birth of a child who was born illegitimate and who is legitimated (or, if deceased, is treated as legitimated), section 5(4) above does not affect entitlement under Part II of the Family Law Reform Act 1969 (illegitimate children).

(2) Where a disposition depends on the date of birth of an adopted child who is legitimated (or, if deceased, is treated as legitimated) section 5(4) above does not affect entitlement by virtue of section 42(2) of the Adoption Act 1976.

(3) This section applies for example where –

(*a*) a testator dies in 1976 bequeathing a legacy to his eldest grandchild living at a specified time,

(*b*) a daughter has an illegitimate child in 1977 who is the first grandchild,

(*c*) his married son has a child in 1978,

(*d*) subsequently the illegitimate child is legitimated,

and in all those cases the daughter's child remains the eldest grandchild of the testator throughout.

Amendments—Adoption Act 1976, s 73(2), Sch 3, para 24.

7 Protection of trustees and personal representatives

(1) A trustee or personal representative is not under a duty, by virtue of the law relating to trusts or the administration of estates, to enquire, before conveying or distributing any property, whether any person is illegitimate or has been adopted by one of his natural parents, and could be legitimated (or if deceased be treated as legitimated), if that fact could affect entitlement to the property.

(2) A trustee or personal representative shall not be liable to any person by reason of a conveyance or distribution of the property made without regard to any such fact if he has not received notice of the fact before the conveyance or distribution.

(3) This section does not prejudice the right of a person to follow the property, or any property representing it, into the hands of another person, other than a purchaser, who has received it.

8 Personal rights and obligations

A legitimated person shall have the same rights, and shall be under the same obligations in respect of the maintenance and support of himself or of any other person as if he had been born legitimate, and, subject to the provisions of this Act, the provisions of any Act relating to claims for damages, compensation, allowance, benefit or otherwise by or in respect of a legitimate child shall apply in like manner in the case of a legitimated person.

9 Re-registration of birth of legitimated person

(1) It shall be the duty of the parents of a legitimated person or, in cases where re-registration can be effected on information furnished by one parent and one of

the parents is dead, of the surviving parent to furnish to the Registrar General information with a view to obtaining the re-registration of the birth of that person within 3 months after the date of the marriage by virtue of which he was legitimated.

(2) The failure of the parents or either of them to furnish information as required by subsection (1) above in respect of any legitimated person shall not affect the legitimation of that person.

(3) This section does not apply in relation to a person who was legitimated otherwise than by virtue of the subsequent marriage of his parents.

(4) Any parent who fails to give information as required by this section shall be liable on summary conviction to a fine not exceeding level 1 on the standard scale.

Amendments—Criminal Justice Act 1982, ss 38, 46.

10 Interpretation

(1) In this Act, except where the context otherwise requires, –

"disposition" includes the conferring of a power of appointment and any other disposition of an interest in or right over property;

"existing", in relation to an instrument, means one made before 1 January 1976;

"legitimated person" means a person legitimated or recognised as legitimated –

(*a*) under section 2 or 3 above; or

(*b*) under section 1 or 8 of the Legitimacy Act 1926; or

(*c*) except in section 8, by a legitimation (whether or not by virtue of the subsequent marriage of his parents) recognised by the law of England and Wales and effected under the law of any other country:

and cognate expressions shall be construed accordingly;

"power of appointment" includes any discretionary power to transfer a beneficial interest in property without the furnishing of valuable consideration;

"void marriage" means a marriage, not being voidable only, in respect of which the High Court has or had jurisdiction to grant a decree of nullity, or would have or would have had such jurisdiction if the parties were domiciled in England and Wales.

(2) For the purposes of this Act "legitimated person" includes, where the context admits, a person legitimated, or recognised as legitimated, before the passing of the Children Act 1975.

(3) For the purpose of this Act, except where the context otherwise requires, –

(*a*) the death of the testator is the date at which a will or codicil is to be regarded as made;

(*b*) an oral disposition of property shall be deemed to be contained in an instrument made when the disposition was made.

(4) (*repealed*)

(5) Except in so far as the context otherwise requires, any reference in this Act to an enactment shall be construed as a reference to that enactment as amended by or under any other enactment, including this Act.

Amendments—Trusts of Land and Appointment of Trustees Act 1996, s 25(2), (4), (5), Sch 4.

****

Magistrates' Courts Act 1980

ARRANGEMENT OF SECTIONS

PART II
CIVIL JURISDICTION AND PROCEDURE

Jurisdiction to issue summons and deal with complaints

PART VII
MISCELLANEOUS AND SUPPLEMENTARY

Constitution and place of sitting of magistrates' courts

Appearance by a legal representative

Process

Limitation of time

Remand

Restrictions on imprisonment

Fees, fines, forfeitures etc

Clerks to justices

Power to alter sums specified in certain provisions

Rules

Interpretation

****

PART II
CIVIL JURISDICTION AND PROCEDURE
Jurisdiction to issue summons and deal with complaints

51 Issue of summons on complaint

Subject to the provisions of this Act, where a complaint is made to a justice of the peace acting for any petty sessions area upon which a magistrates' court acting for that area has power to make an order against any person, the justice may issue a summons directed to that person requiring him to appear before a magistrates' court acting for that area to answer to the complaint.

Defined terms—"petty sessions area": s 150(1).

Scope of provision—The power may also be exercised, by virtue by the Justices' Clerks Rules 1999, by a justices' clerk provided the complaint is not made on oath.

"may issue"—The decision whether to issue a summons is a judicial decision and may not be delegated (*R v Manchester Stipendiary Magistrate ex parte Hill* [1983] 1 AC 328, [1982] 2 All ER 963). The justice of the peace or the justices' clerk must apply his mind to the complaint and decide whether or not the summons should be issued. See *R v Brentford Justices ex parte Catlin* [1975] QB 455, [1975] 2 WLR 506.

52 Jurisdiction to deal with complaints

Where no express provision is made by any Act or the rules specifying what magistrates' courts shall have jurisdiction to hear a complaint, a magistrates' court shall have such jurisdiction if the complaint relates to anything done within the commission area for which the court is appointed or anything left undone that ought to have been done there, or ought to have been done either there or elsewhere, or relates to any other matter arising within that area.

Amendments—Justices of the Peace Act 1997, s 73(2), Sch 5, para 19; Access to Justice Act 1999, s 106, Sch 15.

Hearing of complaint

53 Procedure on hearing

(1) On the hearing of a complaint, the court shall, if the defendant appears, state to him the substance of the complaint.

(2) The court, after hearing the evidence and the parties, shall make the order for which the complaint is made or dismiss the complaint.

(3) Where a complaint is for an order for the payment of a sum recoverable summarily as a civil debt, or for the variation of the rate of any periodical payments ordered by a magistrates' court to be made, or for such other matter as may be prescribed, the court may make the order with the consent of the defendant without hearing evidence.

Orders made without hearing evidence—See, for example, *R v King's Lynn Magistrates' Court ex parte M* [1988] 2 FLR 79.

54 Adjournment

(1) A magistrates' court may at any time, whether before or after beginning to hear a complaint, adjourn the hearing, and may do so, notwithstanding anything in this Act, when composed of a single justice.

(2) The court may when adjourning either fix the time and place at which the hearing is to be resumed or, unless it remands the defendant under section 55 below, leave the time and place to be determined later by the court; but the hearing shall not be resumed at that time and place unless the court is satisfied that the parties have had adequate notice thereof.

Defined terms—"magistrates' court": s 148(1).

Scope of provision—Under the Justices' Clerks Rules 1999, a justices' clerk is permitted to adjourn the hearing with the consent of the parties.

"adequate notice"—The service of a summons and other documents is governed by Magistrates' Courts Rules 1981, r 99. The same rule applies to the service of an adjournment notice (*Unitt v Unitt* (1981) FLR 89).

55 Non-appearance of defendant

(1) Where at the time and place appointed for the hearing or adjourned hearing of a complaint the complainant appears but the defendant does not, the court may, subject to subsection (3) below, proceed in his absence.

(2) Where the court, instead of proceedings in the absence of the defendant, adjourns, or further adjourns, the hearing, the court may, if the complaint has been substantiated on oath, and subject to the following provisions of this section, issue a warrant for his arrest.

(3) The court shall not begin to hear the complaint in the absence of the defendant or issue a warrant under this section unless either it is proved to the satisfaction of the court, on oath or in such other manner as may be prescribed, that the summons was served on him within what appears to the court to be a reasonable time before the hearing or adjourned hearing or the defendant has appeared on a previous occasion to answer to the complaint.

(4) Where the defendant fails to appear at an adjourned hearing, the court shall not issue a warrant under this section unless it is satisfied that he has had adequate notice of the time and place of the adjourned hearing.

(5) Where the defendant is arrested under a warrant issued under this section, the court may, on any subsequent adjournment of the hearing, but subject to the provisions of subsection (6) below, remand him.

(6) The court shall not issue a warrant or remand a defendant under this section or further remand him by virtue of section 128(3) below after he has given evidence in the proceedings.

(7) Where the court remands the defendant, the time fixed for the resumption of the hearing shall be that at which he is required to appear to be brought before the court in pursuance of the remand.

(8) A warrant under this section shall not be issued in any proceedings for the recovery or enforcement of a sum recoverable summarily as a civil debt or in proceedings in any matter of bastardy.

Scope of provision—This section sets out the powers and duties of the court where the complainant appears for the hearing or adjourned hearing of the complaint but the defendant does not.

Issue of warrant for arrest (s 55(2))—The warrant may be endorsed with bail under s 117. The Bail Act 1976 does not apply to civil proceedings, and a recognizance must be set (see s 117(2)(*b*)).

56 Non-appearance of complainant

Where at the time and place appointed for the hearing or adjourned hearing of a complaint the defendant appears but the complainant does not, the court may dismiss the complaint or, if evidence has been received on a previous occasion, proceed in the absence of the complainant.

57 Non-appearance of both parties

Where at the time and place appointed for the hearing or adjourned hearing of a complaint neither the complainant nor the defendant appears, the court may dismiss the complaint.

Civil debt

58 Money recoverable summarily as civil debt

(1) A magistrates' court shall have power to make an order on complaint for the payment of any money recoverable summarily as a civil debt.

(2) Any sum payment of which may be ordered by a magistrates' court shall be recoverable summarily as a civil debt except –

(*a*) a sum recoverable on complaint for a magistrates' court maintenance order; or

(*b*) a sum that may be adjudged to be paid by a summary conviction or by an order enforceable as if it were a summary conviction.

Amendments—Family Law Reform Act 1987, s 33(1), Sch 2, para 80.

Scope of provision—This section gives magistrates the power to order the payment of a sum as a civil debt but provides that that power shall not apply to certain sums. The power of recovery is restricted by s 96 and Magistrates' Courts Rules 1981, rr 53, 54, and 58, which impose procedural requirements before committal for civil debt. Other restrictions include the protection under the Reserve and Auxiliary Forces (Protection of Civil Interests) Act 1951, Insolvency Act 1986, ss 264 (bankruptcy order) and 268 (bankruptcy notice) and County Courts Act 1984, s 112 (administration order).

Orders for periodical payment

59 Orders for periodical payment: means of payment

(1) In any case where a magistrates' court orders money to be paid periodically by one person (in this section referred to as "the debtor") to another (in this section referred to as "the creditor"), then –

(*a*) if the order is a qualifying maintenance order, the court shall at the same time exercise one of its powers under paragraphs (*a*) to (*d*) of subsection (3) below;

(*b*) if the order is not a maintenance order, the court shall at the same time exercise one of its powers under paragraphs (*a*) and (*b*) of that subsection.

(2) For the purposes of this section a maintenance order is a "qualifying maintenance order" if, at the time it is made, the debtor is ordinarily resident in England and Wales.

(3) The powers of the court are –

(*a*) the power to order that payments under the order be made directly by the debtor to the creditor;

(*b*) the power to order that payments under the order be made to a justices' chief executive;

(*c*) the power to order that payments under the order be made by the debtor to the creditor by such method of payment falling within subsection (6) below as may be specified;

(*cc*) the power to order that payments under the order be made in accordance with arrangements made by the Secretary of State for their collection;

(*d*) the power to make an attachment of earnings order under the Attachment of Earnings Act 1971 to secure payments under the order.

(3A) No order made by a magistrates' court under paragraphs (*a*) to (*d*) of subsection (3) above (other than one made under paragraph (*cc*)) shall have effect at any time when the Secretary of State is arranging for the collection of payments under the qualifying maintenance order concerned.

(4) In any case where –

(*a*) the court proposes to exercise its power under paragraph (*c*) of subsection (3) above, and

(*b*) having given the debtor an opportunity of opening an account from which payments under the order may be made in accordance with the method of payment proposed to be ordered under that paragraph, the court is satisfied that the debtor has failed, without reasonable excuse, to open such an account.

the court in exercising its power under that paragraph may order that the debtor open such an account.

(5) In deciding, in the case of a maintenance order, which of the powers under paragraphs (*a*) to (*d*) of subsection (3) above (other than paragraph (*cc*)) it is to exercise, the court having (if practicable) given them an opportunity to make representations shall have regard to any representations made –

(*a*) by the debtor,

(*b*) by the creditor, and

(*c*) if the person who applied for the maintenance order is a person other than the creditor, by that other person.

(6) The methods of payment referred to in subsection (3)(*c*) above are the following, that is to say –

(*a*) payment by standing order; or

(*b*) payment by any other method which requires one person to give his authority for payments of a specific amount to be made from an account of his to an account of another's on specific dates during the period for which the authority is in force and without the need for any further authority from him.

(7) Where the maintenance order is an order –

(*a*) under the Guardianship of Minors Acts 1971 and 1973,

(*b*) under Part I of the Domestic Proceedings and Magistrates' Courts Act 1978, or

(*c*) under, or having effect as if made under, Schedule 1 to the Children Act 1989,

and the court does not propose to exercise its powers under paragraph (*c*), (*cc*) or (*d*) of subsection (3) above, the court shall, unless upon representations expressly made in that behalf by the person who applied for the maintenance order it is satisfied that it is undesirable to do so, exercise its power under paragraph (*b*) of that subsection.

(8) The Lord Chancellor may by regulations confer on magistrates' courts, in addition to their powers under paragraphs (*a*) to (*d*) of subsection (3) above, the power (the "additional power") to order that payments under a qualifying maintenance order be made by the debtor to the creditor or a justices' chief executive (as the regulations may provide) by such method of payment as may be specified in the regulations.

(9) Any reference in any enactment to paragraphs (*a*) to (*d*) of subsection (3) above (but not a reference to any specific paragraph of that subsection) shall be taken to include a reference to the additional power, and the reference in subsection (10) below to the additional power shall be construed accordingly.

(10) Regulations under subsection (8) above may make provision for any enactment concerning, or connected with, payments under maintenance orders to apply, with or without modifications, in relation to the additional power.

(11) The power of the Lord Chancellor to make regulations under subsection (8) above shall be exercisable by statutory instrument and any such statutory instrument shall be subject to annulment in pursuance of a resolution of either House of Parliament.

(12) For the purposes of this section –

(*a*) the reference in subsection (1) above to money paid periodically by one person to another includes, in the case of a maintenance order, a reference to a lump sum paid by instalments by one person to another; and

(*b*) references to arrangements made by the Secretary of State for the collection of payments are to arrangements made by him under section 30 of the Child Support Act 1991 and regulations made under that section.

Amendments—Maintenance Enforcement Act 1991, s 2; SI 1992/709; SI 1994/731; Access to Justice Act 1999, s 90, Sch 13, para 99.

Defined terms—"magistrates' court": s 148(1).

Scope of provision—Where the order is not a maintenance order, the court is restricted to ordering direct payments or payments through any magistrates' court.

For the duties of the clerk and justices' chief executive where a means of payment order has been made, see Magistrates' Courts Rules 1981, r 39.

59A Orders for periodical payment: proceedings by justices' chief executive

(1) Where payments under a relevant UK order are required to be made periodically –

(*a*) to or through a justices' chief executive, or

(*b*) by any method of payment falling within section 59(6) above, and any sums payable under the order are in arrear, the relevant justices' chief executive shall, if the person for whose benefit the payments are required to be made so requests in writing, and unless it appears to that justices' chief executive that it is unreasonable in the circumstances to do so, proceed in his own name for the recovery of those sums.

(2) Where payments under a relevant UK order are required to be made periodically to or through a justices' chief executive, the person for whose benefit the payments are required to be made may, at any time during the period in which the payments are required to be so made, give authority in writing to the relevant justices' chief executive for him to proceed as mentioned in subsection (3) below.

(3) Where authority under subsection (2) above is given to the relevant justices' chief executive, he shall, unless it appears to him that it is unreasonable in the circumstances to do so, proceed in his own name for the recovery of any sums payable to or through him under the order in question which, on or after the date of the giving of the authority, fall into arrear.

(4) In any case where –

(*a*) authority under subsection (2) above has been given to a justices' chief executive, and

(*b*) the person for whose benefit the payments are required to be made gives notice in writing to the justices' chief executive cancelling the authority,

the authority shall cease to have effect and, accordingly, the justices' chief executive shall not continue any proceedings already commenced by virtue of the authority.

(5) The person for whose benefit the payments are required to be made shall have the same liability for all the costs properly incurred in or about proceedings taken under subsection (1) above at his request or under subsection (3) above by virtue of his authority (including any costs incurred as a result of any proceedings commenced not being continued) as if the proceedings had been taken by him.

(6) Nothing in subsection (1) or (3) above shall affect any right of a person to proceed in his own name for the recovery of sums payable on his behalf under an order of any court.

(7) In this section –

"the relevant justices' chief executive", in relation to an order, means –

(*a*) in a case where payments under the order are required to be made to or through a justices' chief executive, that justices' chief executive;

(*b*) in a case where such payments are required to be made by any method of payment falling within section 59(6) above and the order was made by a magistrates' court, the justices' chief executive for that magistrates' court; and

(*c*) in a case where such payments are required to be made by any method of payment falling within section 59(6) above and the order was not made by a magistrates' court, the justices' chief executive for the magistrates' court in which the order is registered;

"relevant UK order" means –

(*a*) an order made by a magistrates' court, other than an order made by virtue of Part II of the Maintenance Orders (Reciprocal Enforcement) Act 1972;

(*b*) an order made by the High Court or a county court (including an order deemed to be made by the High Court by virtue of section 1(2) of the

Maintenance Orders Act 1958) and registered under Part I of that Act of 1958 in a magistrates' court; or

(*c*) an order made by a court in Scotland or Northern Ireland and registered under Part II of the Maintenance Orders Act 1950 in a magistrates' court;

and any reference to payments required to be made periodically includes, in the case of a maintenance order, a reference to instalments required to be paid in respect of a lump sum payable by instalments.

Amendments—Inserted by Maintenance Enforcement Act 1991, s 3; amended by Access to Justice Act 1999, s 90, Sch 13, para 100.

Defined terms—"maintenance order": s 150(1).

Scope of provision—Under Justices of the Peace Act 1997, s 41A, the justices' chief executive is designated as the collecting officer of the magistrates' court. This section requires the justices' chief executive to proceed to recover any arrears under a relevant UK order where payment has been ordered through a magistrates' court or by standing order on the written authority of the person entitled to payment. Liability to costs may be incurred by the person who gives the written authority to enforce. The justices' chief executive has a discretion not to take proceedings and, if the justices' chief executive chooses not to do so, the person entitled to payment may proceed in his own name under s 59A(6).

"in arrear" (s 59A(1))—The justices' chief executive is required by Magistrates' Courts Rules 1981, r 40 to notify arrears to the person entitled to payment.

59B Maintenance orders: penalty for breach

(1) In any case where –

(*a*) payments under a relevant English maintenance order are required to be made periodically in the manner mentioned in paragraph (*a*) or (*b*) of section 59A(1) above, and

(*b*) the debtor fails, on or after the date of commencement of this section, to comply with the order in so far as the order relates to the manner of payment concerned,

the person for whose benefit the payments are required to be made may make a complaint to a relevant justice giving details of the failure to comply.

(2) If the relevant justice is satisfied that the nature of the alleged failure to comply may be such as to justify the relevant court in exercising its power under subsection (3) below, he shall issue a summons directed to the debtor requiring him to appear before the relevant court to answer the complaint.

(3) On the hearing of the complaint, the relevant court may order the debtor to pay a sum not exceeding £1,000.

(4) Any sum ordered to be paid under subsection (3) above shall for the purposes of this Act be treated as adjudged to be paid by a conviction of a magistrates' court.

(5) In this section –

"debtor" has the same meaning as it has in section 59 above;
"the relevant court" has the same meaning as it has in section 59A above;
"relevant English maintenance order" means –

(*a*) a maintenance order made by a magistrates' court, other than an order made by virtue of Part II of the Maintenance Orders (Reciprocal Enforcement) Act 1972; or

(*b*) an order made by the High Court or a county court (other than an order deemed to be made by the High Court by virtue of section 1(2) of the Maintenance Orders Act 1958) and registered under Part I of that Act of 1958 in a magistrates' court;

"relevant justice", in relation to a relevant court, means a justice of the peace for the petty sessions area for which the relevant court is acting;

and any reference to payments required to be made periodically includes a reference to instalments required to be paid in respect of a lump sum payable by instalments.

Amendments—Inserted by Maintenance Enforcement Act 1991, s 3.

Defined terms—"maintenance order": s 150(1).

60 Revocation, variation etc of orders for periodical payment

(1) Where a magistrates' court has made an order for money to be paid periodically by one person to another, the court may, by order on complaint, revoke, revive or vary the order.

(2) The power under subsection (1) above to vary an order shall include power to suspend the operation of any provision of the order temporarily and to revive the operation of any provision so suspended.

(3) Where the order mentioned in subsection (1) above is a maintenance order, the power under that subsection to vary the order shall include power, if the court is satisfied that payment has not been made in accordance with the order, to exercise one of its powers under paragraphs (*a*) to (*d*) of section 59(3) above.

(4) In any case where –

(*a*) a magistrates' court has made a maintenance order, and

(*b*) payments under the order are required to be made by any method of payment falling within section 59(6) above,

an interested party may apply in writing to the clerk of the court for the order to be varied as mentioned in subsection (5) above.

(5) Subject to subsection (8) below, where an application has been made under subsection (4) above, the clerk, after giving written notice (by post or otherwise) of the application to any other interested party and allowing that party, within the period of 14 days beginning with the date of the giving of that notice, an opportunity to make written representations, may vary the order to provide that payments under the order shall be made to the justices' chief executive for the court.

(6) The clerk may proceed with an application under subsection (4) above notwithstanding that any such interested party as is referred to in subsection (5) above has not received written notice of the application.

(7) In subsections (4) to (6) above "interested party", in relation to a maintenance order, means –

(*a*) the debtor;

(*b*) the creditor; and

(*c*) if the person who applied for the maintenance order is a person other than the creditor, that other person.

(8) Where an application has been made under subsection (4) above, the clerk may, if he considers it inappropriate to exercise his power under subsection (5) above, refer the matter to the court which may vary the order by exercising one of its powers under paragraphs (*a*) to (*d*) of section 59(3) above.

(9) Subsections (4), (5) and (7) of section 59 above shall apply for the purposes of subsections (3) and (8) above as they apply for the purposes of that section.

(10) None of the powers of the court, or of the clerk of the court, conferred by subsections (3) to (9) above shall be exercisable in relation to a maintenance order which is not a qualifying maintenance order (with the meaning of section 59 above).

(11) For the purposes of this section –

(*a*) "creditor" and "debtor" have the same meaning as they have in section 59 above; and

(*b*) the reference in subsection (1) above to money paid periodically by one person to another includes, in the case of a maintenance order, a reference to a lump sum paid by instalments by one person to another.

Amendments—Substituted by Maintenance Enforcement Act 1991, s 4; amended by Access to Justice Act 1999, s 90, Sch 13, para 101.

Defined terms—"maintenance order": s 150(1).

Scope of provision—This section provides for the revocation, revival or variation of orders for periodical payments. For the procedure to be followed, see Magistrates' Courts Rules 1981, rr 41 and 106. This section does not apply to orders made under the Domestic Proceedings and Magistrates' Courts Act 1978 (see instead ss 20–24 of that Act), to orders with a foreign element (see eg Maintenance Orders (Reciprocal Enforcement) Act 1972, ss 5, 32) or to registered High Court or county court orders (see Maintenance Orders Act 1958, s 4).

Special powers of variation relating to payments methods are conferred under subsections (4) to (10).

"complaint" (s 60(1))—Any person entitled to recover the sum payable under the order for his own benefit is entitled to make complaint (*Moore v Ball* [1984] Fam 41, [1984] FLR 555).

"revoke" (s 60(1))—This does not include the power to revoke a finding of paternity (*R v Copestake, ex parte Wilkinson* [1927] 1 KB 468).

"section 59(6)" (s 60(4))—This refers to payment by standing order or similar method, but does not include payment by direct debit.

"subsections (4), (5) and (7) of section 59" (s 60(9))—This refers to the power to apply for the variation of an order for payment by standing order to payment to the justices' chief executive. See also Magistrates' Courts Rules 1981, r 39.

Fee payable—See Magistrates' Courts Act 1980, Sch 6.

61 Periodical payments payable by one person under more than one order

(1) The power to make rules conferred by section 144 below shall, without prejudice to the generality of subsection (1) of that section, include power to make provision –

(*a*) for enabling a person to make one complaint for the recovery of payments required to be made to him by another person under more than one periodical payments order; and

(*b*) for apportioning between two or more periodical payments orders, in such manner as may be prescribed by the rules, any sum paid to a justices' chief executive on any date by the person liable to make payments under the orders which is less than the total sum required to be paid on that date to that justices' chief executive by that person in respect of those orders (being orders one of which requires payments to be made for the benefit of a child to that person with whom the child has his home and one or more of which requires payments to be made to that person either for his own benefit or for the benefit of another child who has his home with him).

(2) In this section –

"child" means a person who has not attained the age of 18;

"periodical payments order" means an order made by a magistrates' court, or registered in a magistrates' court under Part II of the Maintenance Orders Act 1950 or Part I of the Maintenance Orders Act 1958, which requires the making of periodical payments,

and any payments required under a periodical payments order to be made to a child shall for the purposes of subsection (1) above be treated as if they were required to be made to the person with whom the child has his home.

Amendments—Access to Justice Act 1999, s 90, Sch 13, para 102.

Scope of provision—This rule provides for rules to be made for a number of periodical payments to be enforced in one complaint and for the apportionment of payments between two or more periodical payments orders, see Magistrates' Courts Rules 1981, r 60.

Payments to children

62 Provisions as to payments required to be made to a child etc

(1) Where –

(*a*) periodical payments are required to be made, or a lump sum is required to be paid, to a child under an order made by a magistrates' court, or

(*b*) periodical payments are required to be made to a child under an order which is registered in a magistrates' court,

any sum required under the order to be paid to the child may be paid to the person with whom the child has his home, and that person –

(i) may proceed in his own name for the variation, revival or revocation of the order, and

(ii) may either proceed in his own name for the recovery of any sum required to be paid under the order or request or authorise the justices' chief executive for the magistrates' court under subsection (1) or subsection (2) respectively of section 59A above to proceed for the recovery of that sum.

(2) Where a child has a right under any enactment to apply for the revival of an order made by a magistrates' court which provided for the making of periodical payments to or for the benefit of the child, the person with whom the child has his home may proceed in his own name for the revival of that order.

(3) Where any person by whom periodical payments are required to be paid to a child under an order made by or registered in a magistrates' court makes a

complaint for the variation or revocation of that order, the person with whom the child has his home may answer the complaint in his own name.

(4) Nothing in subsections (1) and (2) above shall affect any right of a child to proceed in his own name for the variation, revival or revocation of an order or for the recovery of any sum payable thereunder.

(5) In this section references to the person with whom a child has his home –

- (*a*) in the case of any child who is being looked after by a local authority (within the meaning of section 22 of the Children Act 1989), are references to that local authority; and
- (*b*) in any other case, are references to the person who, disregarding any absence of the child at a hospital or boarding school and any other temporary absence, has care of the child.

(6) In this section any reference to an order registered in a magistrates' court is a reference to an order registered in a magistrates' court under Part II of the Maintenance Orders Act 1950 or Part I of the Maintenance Orders Act 1958.

(7) In this section "child" means a person who has not attained the age of 18.

Amendments—CA 1989, s 108(5), Sch 13, para 44(2); Maintenance Enforcement Act 1991, s 11(1), Sch 2, para 5; Access to Justice Act 1999, s 90, Sch 13, para 103.

Defined terms—"child": s 62(7); "magistrates' court": s 148(1).

Orders other than for payment of money

63 Orders other than for payment of money

(1) Where under any Act passed after 31 December 1879 a magistrates' court has power to require the doing of anything other than the payment of money, or to prohibit the doing of anything, any order of the court for the purpose of exercising that power may contain such provisions for the manner in which anything is to be done, for the time within which anything is to be done, or during which anything is not to be done, and generally for giving effect to the order, as the court thinks fit.

(2) The court may by order made on complaint suspend or rescind any such order as aforesaid.

(3) Where any person disobeys an order of a magistrates' court made under an Act passed after 31 December 1879 to do anything other than the payment of money or to abstain from doing anything the court may –

- (*a*) order him to pay a sum not exceeding £50 for every day during which he is in default or a sum not exceeding £5,000; or
- (*b*) commit him to custody until he has remedied his default or for a period not exceeding 2 months;

but a person who is ordered to pay a sum for every day during which he is in default or who is committed to custody until he has remedied his default shall not by virtue of this section be ordered to pay more than £1,000 or be committed for more than 2 months in all for doing or abstaining from doing the same thing contrary to the order (without prejudice to the operation of this section in relation to any subsequent default).

(4) Any sum ordered to be paid under subsection (3) above shall for the purposes of this Act be treated as adjudged to be paid by a conviction of a magistrates' court.

(5) The preceding provisions of this section shall not apply to any order for the enforcement of which provision is made by any other enactment.

Amendments—Criminal Justice Act 1991, s 17(3)(*a*), Sch 4, Pt I.

Defined terms—"commit him to custody": s 150(1).

Scope of provision—This section provides for the enforcement of orders of magistrates' courts other than those for the payment of money and can be used to enforce non-molestation orders and occupation orders made under Family Law Act 1996, Pt IV and orders for contact with a child (*P v W (Access Order: Breach)* [1984] Fam 32, [1984] 2 WLR 439). The proceedings are not family proceedings unless the court treats them as family proceedings under s 65(2) or unless s 65(3) applies. Failure to obey orders may amount to contempt (see Contempt of Court Act 1981, s 17 and Sch 3).

Power to suspend or rescind (s 63(2))—Domestic Proceedings and Magistrates' Courts Act 1978, s 23(2) disapplies s 63(2) in respect of orders made under Part I of the 1978 Act.

"disobeys" (s 63(3))—An unintentional breach is not sufficient. The breach must be deliberate and wilful. For the approach to be adopted when enforcing a contact order, see *T v T* (1984) *The Times*, 19 July.

"the court may" (s 63(3))—For the procedure to be followed, see Contempt of Court Act 1981, Sch 3. Where the breach is proved, the court has a discretion to take no action, impose a financial penalty or commit to custody. Where payment of a sum is ordered, time to pay or payment by instalments may be allowed (s 75). A committal under this section may not be suspended (*B(BPM) v B(MM)* [1969] P 103, [1969] 2 WLR 862).

Appeal against order or committal (s 63(3))—Under Administration of Justice Act 1960, s 13, appeal lies to a Divisional Court of the High Court. For procedure on appeal, see CPR 1998, Sch 1, RSC Ord 109, r 2.

Remedying default (s 63(3))—No procedure is prescribed for notifying the prison that the default has been remedied or for ending the daily penalty. Natural justice would seem to require that the original applicant should be given an opportunity to make representations and some sort of hearing appears necessary. Following committal for breach of a non-molestation order and/or an occupation order, FPC(MP etc)R 1991, r 20(15) makes specific provision for such a hearing, with notice to the original applicant, upon the contemnor's application to purge his contempt. The difficulty arises only where committal or a daily penalty is ordered until the default is remedied. Where a period of committal is ordered for a past breach of the order, there does not appear to be any power of review.

Use of s 63—In order for contact to be enforced under this provision, it must be precisely defined as an active rather than a passive order; s 63 should be used only as a last resort, and is to be approached with the utmost caution. The question of punishment for past behaviour, or of damage to the dignity of the court if the order is disobeyed, should not enter into consideration (*Re H (Contact: Enforcement)* [1996] 1 FLR 614).

Enforcement of payment (s 63(4))—The sum is treated as adjudged to be paid by a conviction; the provisions as to enforcement are contained in ss 75 to 91.

Costs

64 Power to award costs and enforcement of costs

(1) On the hearing of a complaint, a magistrates' court shall have power in its discretion to make such order as to costs –

(*a*) on making the order for which the complaint is made, to be paid by the defendant to the complainant;
(*b*) on dismissing the complaint, to be paid by the complainant to the defendant,

as it thinks just and reasonable; but if the complaint is for an order for the periodical payment of money, or for the revocation, revival or variation of such an order, or for the enforcement of such an order, the court may, whatever adjudication it makes, order either party to pay the whole or any part of the other's costs.

(2) The amount of any sum ordered to be paid under subsection (1) above shall be specified in the order, or order of dismissal, as the case may be.

(3) Subject to subsection (4) below, costs ordered to be paid under this section shall be enforceable as a civil debt.

(4) Any costs awarded on a complaint for a maintenance order, or for the enforcement, variation, revocation, discharge or revival of such an order, against the person liable to make payments under the order shall be enforceable as a sum ordered to be paid by a magistrates' court maintenance order.

(5) The preceding provisions of this section shall have effect subject to any other Act enabling a magistrates' court to order a successful party to pay the other party's costs.

Amendments—Family Law Reform Act 1987, s 33(1), Sch 2, para 81.

Defined terms—"enforceable as a civil debt": s 150(1).

Scope of provision—The power to order costs where the complaint is not proceeded with is contained in Courts Act 1971, s 52(3).

"On the hearing of a complaint" (s 64(1))—This section does not empower the court to make orders for costs when an application is dealt with (*R v Salisbury and Tisbury and Mere Combined Juvenile Court ex parte Ball* [1986] 1 FLR 1).

"just and reasonable" (s 64(1))—The order should not be for more than the proper costs incurred. The costs order is not a penalty (*R v Highgate Justices ex parte Petrou* [1954] 1 WLR 485, [1954] 1 All ER 406). However, the court has a wide discretion to order costs and, in *R v Southend Stipendiary Magistrates ex parte Rochford DC* [1994] TLR 257, a sum of £75,000 was upheld.

"the amount ... shall be specified" (s 64(2))—The amount of the costs order must be fixed by the court. It is not permissible to make a non-specific order and to delegate the task of taxation to the justices' clerk. Contrast the position in criminal cases.

"enforceable as a civil debt" (s 64(3))—See under s 58.

Family proceedings

65 Meaning of family proceedings

(1) In this Act "family proceedings" means proceedings under any of the following enactments, that is to say –

(*a*) the Maintenance Orders (Facilities for Enforcement) Act 1920;
(*b*) section 43 of the National Assistance Act 1948;
(*c*) section 3 of the Marriage Act 1949;
(*d*), (*e*) (*repealed*)
(*ee*) section 35 of the Matrimonial Causes Act 1973;
(*f*) Part I of the Maintenance Orders (Reciprocal Enforcement) Act 1972;
(*g*) (*repealed*)
(*h*) the Adoption Act 1976, except proceedings under section 34 of that Act;
(*i*) section 18 of the Supplementary Benefits Act 1976;
(*j*) Part I of the Domestic Proceedings and Magistrates' Courts Act 1978;

(*k*) (*repealed*)
(*l*) section 60 of this Act;
(*m*) Part I of the Civil Jurisdiction and Judgments Act 1982, so far as that Part relates to the recognition or enforcement of maintenance orders;
(*mm*) section 55A of the Family Law Act 1986;
(*n*) the Children Act 1989;
(*n*) section 106 of the Social Security Administration Act 1992;
(*o*) section 20 (so far as it provides, by virtue of an order under section 45, for appeals to be made to a court) of the Child Support Act 1991;
(*p*) Part IV of the Family Law Act 1996;
(*q*) sections 11 and 12 of the Crime and Disorder Act 1998;
(*r*) Council Regulation (EC) No 44/2001 of 22 December 2000 on jurisdiction and the recognition and enforcement of judgments in civil and commercial matters, so far as that Regulation relates to the recognition or enforcement of maintenance orders;

except that, subject to subsection (2) below, it does not include –

(i) proceedings for the enforcement of any order made, confirmed or registered under any of those enactments;
(ii) proceedings for the variation of any provision for the periodical payment of money contained in an order made, confirmed or registered under any of those enactments; or
(iii) proceedings on an information in respect of the commission of an offence under any of these enactments.

(2) The court before which there fall to be heard any of the following proceedings, that is to say –

(*a*) proceedings (whether under this Act or any other enactment) for the enforcement of any order made, confirmed or registered under any of the enactments specified in paragraphs (*a*) to (*k*), (*m*), (*n*), (*p*) and (*r*) of subsection (1) above;
(*b*) proceedings (whether under this Act or any other enactment) for the variation of any provision for the making of periodical payments contained in an order made, confirmed or registered under any of those enactments;
(*c*) proceedings for an attachment of earnings order to secure maintenance payments within the meaning of the Attachment of Earnings Act 1971 or for the discharge or variation of such an order; or
(*d*) proceedings for the enforcement of a maintenance order which is registered in a magistrates' court under Part II of the Maintenance Orders Act 1950 or Part I of the Maintenance Orders Act 1958 or for the variation of the rate of payments specified by such an order,
(*e*) proceedings under section 20 (so far as it provides, by virtue of an order under section 45, for appeals to be made to a court) of the Child Support Act 1991,

may if it thinks fit order that those proceedings and any other proceedings being heard therewith shall, notwithstanding anything in subsection (1) above, be treated as family proceedings for the purposes of this Act.

(3) Where the same parties are parties –

(*a*) to proceedings which are family proceedings by virtue of subsection (1) above, and
(*b*) to proceedings which the court has power to treat as family proceedings by virtue of subsection (2) above,

and the proceedings are heard together by a magistrates' court, the whole of those proceedings shall be treated as family proceedings for the purposes of this Act.

(4) No appeal shall lie from the making of, or refusal to make, an order under subsection (2) above.

(5), (6) ...

Amendments—Civil Jurisdiction and Judgments Act 1982, s 15(4), Sch 12, para 7; Matrimonial and Family Proceedings Act 1984, s 44; Social Security Act 1986, Sch 10; Family Law Reform Act 1987, s 33(4), Sch 4; CA 1989, ss 92(11), 108(7), Sch 11, para 8, Sch 15; Courts and Legal Services Act 1990, s 125(7), Sch 20; Social Security (Consequential Provisions) Act 1992, ss 3, 4, Schs 1, 2, para 60; Family Law Act 1996, s 66(1), Sch 8, para 49; SI 1997/1898; Crime and Disorder Act 1998, s 119, Sch 8, para 42; Child Support, Pensions and Social Security Act 2000, s 83(5), Sch 8, para 2, Sch 9; SI 2001/3929.

Scope of provision—Proceedings included in s 65(1) are always family proceedings, while proceedings included in s 65(2) and proceedings being heard at the same time may be treated as family proceedings by the court.

Section 65(1)(mm)—Under Family Law Act 1986, s 55A (inserted by Child Support, Pensions and Social Security Act 2000, s 83) free-standing applications for a declaration of parentage may be made by any individual to a family proceedings court, county court or the High Court.

Section 65(1)(n)—Two paragraphs lettered (*n*) have been added to s 65(1) by CA 1989 and the Social Security (Consequential Provisions) Act 1992.

Section 65(1)(q)—Child safety orders are a new form of order available to local authority social services departments, upon application to a family proceedings court. The purpose of such an order is to prevent a child under the age of 10 from becoming involved in crime. A pilot phase began in October 1998 for a period of 18 months and these orders are only available at present in selected, notified areas; namely the London Boroughs of Hammersmith and Fulham, Kensington and Chelsea and City of Westminster (jointly), the London Borough of Lewisham, Hampshire, Southampton, Portsmouth and the Isle of Wight (jointly), Wolverhampton, Sheffield, Luton and Bedfordshire (jointly), Devon, St Helen's and Sunderland.

66 Composition of magistrates' courts for family proceedings: general

(1) A magistrates' court when hearing family proceedings shall be composed of –

(*a*) two or three lay justices; or
(*b*) a District Judge (Magistrates' Courts) as chairman and one or two lay justices;

or, if it is not practicable for such a court to be so composed, a District Judge (Magistrates' Courts) sitting alone.

(2) Except where such a court is composed of a District Judge (Magistrates' Courts) sitting alone, it shall, so far as practicable, include both a man and a woman.

(3) In this section and section 67 below "lay justices" means justices of the peace who are not District Judges (Magistrates' Courts).

Amendments—Substituted by Access to Justice Act 1999, s 78, Sch 11, para 27.

Defined terms—"family proceedings": s 65.

PART II

67 Family proceedings courts and panels

(1) Magistrates' courts constituted in accordance with the provisions of this section and sitting for the purpose of hearing family proceedings shall be known as family proceedings courts.

(2) A justice shall not be qualified to sit as a member of a family proceedings court unless –

(*a*) he is a District Judge (Magistrates' Courts) nominated by the Lord Chancellor to do so; or

(*b*) he is a member of a family panel, that is to say a panel of lay justices specially appointed to deal with family proceedings.

(3) Without prejudice to the generality of the power to make rules under section 144 below relating to the procedure and practice to be followed in magistrates' courts, provision may be made by such rules with respect to any of the following matters, that is to say –

(*a*) the formation and revision of family panels and the eligibility of justices to be members of such panels;
(*b*) the appointment of persons as chairman of family proceedings courts; and
(*c*) the composition of family proceedings courts.

(4) Any provision made by rules by virtue of subsection (3) above for the formation of family panels shall include provision for the formation of at least one family panel for each commission area, but provision shall not be made by the rules for the formation of more than one family panel for any petty sessions area.

(5) Rules made by virtue of subsection (3) above may confer powers on the Lord Chancellor with respect to any of the matters specified in the rules and may, in particular, provide for the appointment of family panels by him and for the removal from a family panel of any justice who, in his opinion, is unsuitable to serve on a family proceedings court.

(6) Rules made by virtue of subsection (3) above may make different provision in relation to different areas for which family panels are formed; and in the application of this section to the counties of Greater Manchester, Merseyside and Lancashire for any reference in subsection (5) above to the Lord Chancellor there shall be substituted a reference to the Chancellor of the Duchy of Lancaster.

(7) (*repealed*)

(8) Nothing in this section shall require the formation of a family panel for the City of London.

Amendments—CA 1989, s 92(11), Sch 11, para 8; Justices of the Peace Act 1997, s 73(2), Sch 5, para 19; Access to Justice Act 1999, ss 78, 106, Sch 11, para 28, Sch 15.

Defined terms—"family proceedings": s 65.

Rules—The relevant rules are contained in the Family Proceedings Courts (Constitution) Rules 1991 and the Family Proceedings Courts (Constitution) (Metropolitan Areas) Rules 1991.

68 Combined family panels

(1) Where the Lord Chancellor considers –

(*a*) that a combined family panel should be formed for 2 or more petty sessions areas, or (*b*) that any combined family panel which has been so formed should be dissolved,

he may direct the magistrates' courts committee for the area concerned to review the functioning of family proceedings courts in their area and on completion of the review to submit a report to the Lord Chancellor.

(2) Where the Lord Chancellor gives a direction under subsection (1) above, then –

(*a*) after consideration of any report submitted to him under that subsection, or
(*b*) if the committee fail to comply with the direction within 6 months from the giving thereof, after the expiration of that period of 6 months,

the Lord Chancellor may, if he thinks fit, make an order for the formation of a combined family panel for the petty sessions areas concerned or, as the case may be, for the dissolution of the combined family panel concerned.

(3) Where the Lord Chancellor proposes to make an order under subsection (2) above, he shall send a copy of the proposed order to the magistrates' courts committee for any area the whole or part of which is concerned and to any family panel which is concerned.

(4) Where a copy of the proposed order is required to be sent under subsection (3) above to any committee or panel, the Lord Chancellor shall, before making an order, consider any representations made to him by the committee or panel within one month from the time the copy of the proposed order was sent.

(5) An order of the Lord Chancellor under subsection (2) above shall be made by statutory instrument and may be revoked or varied by a subsequent order thereunder.

(6) Any order made under subsection (2) above may contain supplementary, incidental and consequential provisions.

(7) (*repealed*)

Amendments—CA 1989, s 92(11), Sch 11, para 8; SI 1992/709; Police and Magistrates' Courts Act 1994, s 93, Sch 9.

Defined terms—"family proceedings courts": s 67(1); "family panel": s 67(2).

69 Sittings of magistrates' courts for family proceedings

(1) The business of magistrates' courts shall, so far as is consistent with the due dispatch of business, be arranged in such manner as may be requisite for separating the hearing and determination of family proceedings from other business.

(2) In the case of family proceedings in a magistrates' court other than proceedings under the Adoption Act 1976, no person shall be present during the hearing and determination by the court of the proceedings except –

(*a*) officers of the court;
(*b*) parties to the case before the court, their legal representatives, witnesses and other persons directly concerned in the case;
(*c*) representatives of newspapers or news agencies;
(*d*) any other person whom the court may in its discretion permit to be present, so, however, that permission shall not be withheld from a person who appears to the court to have adequate grounds for attendance.

(3) In relation to any family proceedings under the Adoption Act 1976, subsection (2) above shall apply with the omission of paragraphs (*c*) and (*d*).

(4) When hearing family proceedings, a magistrates' court may, if it thinks it necessary in the interest of the administration of justice or of public decency, direct that any persons, not being officers of the court or parties to the case, the parties' legal representatives, or other persons directly concerned in the case, be excluded during the taking of any indecent evidence.

(5) The powers conferred on a magistrates' court by this court by this section shall be in addition and without prejudice to any other powers of the court to hear proceedings in camera.

(6) Nothing in this section shall affect the exercise by a magistrates' court of the power to direct that witnesses shall be excluded until they are called for examination.

(7) ...

Amendments—CA 1989, s 92(11), Sch 11, para 8; Courts and Legal Services Act 1990, s 125(3), Sch 18, para 25.

Defined terms—"family proceedings": s 65; "legal representative": s 150(1).

70 Jurisdiction of magistrates' courts in inner London for family proceedings

(1) A relevant court for an inner London petty sessions area shall, in addition to hearing proceedings which (apart from subsection (2) below) may be heard by a relevant court for that area, have jurisdiction to hear proceedings which could be heard before a relevant court for any other such area, but shall not exercise the jurisdiction conferred by this subsection except in such cases or classes of case as may be determined by the magistrates' courts committee whose area consists of or includes that petty sessions area.

(2) A magistrates' court for an inner London petty sessions area shall not hear any family proceedings if the magistrates' courts committee whose area consists of or includes that petty sessions area so determine.

(3) In this section –

"relevant court" means a magistrates' court when composed for the purpose of exercising jurisdiction to hear family proceedings;

"inner London petty sessions area" means any petty sessions area falling wholly or partly within the area consisting of the inner London boroughs and the City of London.

Amendments—CA 1989, s 92(11), Sch 11, para 8; Police and Magistrates' Courts Act 1994, s 91, Sch 8, para 30; Access to Justice Act 1999, s 76(2), Sch 10, para 34.

Defined terms—"family proceedings": s 65.

71 Newspaper reports of family proceedings

(1) In the case of family proceedings in a magistrates' court (other than proceedings under the Adoption Act 1976) it shall not be lawful for a person to whom this subsection applies –

(*a*) to print or publish, or cause or procure to be printed or published, in a newspaper or periodical, or (*b*) to include, or cause or procure to be included, in a programme included in a programme service (within the meaning of the Broadcasting Act 1990) for reception in Great Britain,

any particulars of the proceedings other than such particulars as are mentioned in subsection (1A) below.

(1A) The particulars referred to in subsection (1) above are –

(*a*) the names, addresses and occupations of the parties and witnesses;
(*b*) the grounds of the application, and a concise statement of the charges, defences and counter-charges in support of which evidence has been given;
(*c*) submissions on any point of law arising in the course of the proceedings and the decision of the court on the submissions;
(*d*) the decision of the court, and any observations made by the court in giving it.

(1B) Subsection (1) above applies –

(*a*) in relation to paragraph (*a*) of that subsection, to the proprietor, editor or publisher of the newspaper or periodical, and
(*b*) in relation to paragraph (*b*) of that subsection, to any body corporate which provides the service in which the programme is included and to any person having functions in relation to the programme corresponding to those of an editor of a newspaper.

(2) In the case of family proceedings in a magistrates' court under the Adoption Act 1976, subsection (1A) above shall apply with the omission of paragraphs (*a*) and (*b*) and the reference in that subsection to the particulars of the proceedings shall, in relation to any child concerned in the proceedings, include –

(*a*) the name, address or school of the child,
(*b*) any picture as being, or including, a picture of the child, and
(*c*) any other particulars calculated to lead to the identification of the child.

(3) Any person acting in contravention of this section shall be liable on summary conviction to a fine not exceeding level 4 on the standard scale.

(4) No prosecution for an offence under this section shall be begun without the consent of the Attorney General.

(5) Nothing in this section shall prohibit the printing or publishing of any matter in a newspaper or periodical of a technical character bona fide intended for circulation among members of the legal or medical professions.

(6) ...

Amendments—Criminal Justice Act 1982, ss 38, 46; CA 1989, s 92(11), Sch 11, para 8; Broadcasting Act 1990, s 203, Sch 20, para 29.

Defined terms—"family proceedings": s 65.

"level 4 on the standard scale" (s 71(3))—Currently £2,500 (Criminal Justice Act 1982, s 37(2), as substituted).

Attorney General (s 71(4))—The Solicitor General may act with the authority of the Attorney General or if the office of the Attorney General is vacant or if he is ill or absent (Law Officers Act 1944, s 1).

72 (*repealed*)

73 Examination of witnesses by court

Where in any family proceedings, or in any proceedings for the enforcement or variation of an order made in family proceedings, it appears to a magistrates' court that any party to the proceedings who is not legally represented is unable effectively to examine or cross-examine a witness, the court shall ascertain from that party what are the matters about which the witness may be able to depose or on which the witness ought to be cross-examined, as the case may be, and shall put, or cause to be put, to the witness such questions in the interests of that party as may appear to the court to be proper.

Amendments—CA 1989, s 92(11), Sch 11, para 8.

Defined terms—"family proceedings": s 65.

Scope of provision—This section imposes a statutory duty upon the court to assist an unrepresented party, where necessary, to examine or cross-examine a witness. The section does not apply to legally represented parties (*Ratcliff v Ratcliff* [1964] 1 WLR 1098, [1964] 3 All ER 351). The cross-examination must be justified (*Brewster v Brewster* [1971] 1 WLR 1102, [1971] 2 All ER 993).

"unable effectively"—The duty will also arise where a party is not present and writes a letter to the court containing his case (*Marjoram v Marjoram* [1955] 1 WLR 520, [1955] 2 All ER 1).

74 Reasons for decisions in family proceedings

(1) The power to make rules conferred by section 144 below shall, without prejudice to the generality of subsection (1) of that section, include power to make provision for the recording by a magistrates' court, in such manner as may be prescribed by the rules, of reasons for a decision made in such family proceedings or class of family proceedings as may be so prescribed, and for making available a copy of any record made in accordance with those rules of the reasons for a decision of a magistrates' court to any person who requests a copy thereof for the purposes of an appeal against that decision or for the purpose of deciding whether or not to appeal against that decision.

(2) A copy of any record made by virtue of this section of the reasons for a decision of a magistrates' court shall, if certified by such officer of the court as may be prescribed, be admissible as evidence of those reasons.

Amendments—CA 1989, s 92(11), Sch 11, para 8.

Defined terms—"family proceedings": s 65.

Scope of provision—Family Proceedings Courts (Children Act 1989) Rules 1991, r 21(5), (6) makes provision for recording and stating findings of fact and reasons in all cases heard under CA 1989. Similar provision is made in Family Proceedings Courts (Matrimonial Proceedings etc) Rules 1991, r 12(5), (6) in respect of cases heard under DPMCA 1978 and FLA 1996, Pt IV. Although there is no requirement to state reasons prior to or when making an order in proceedings concerning periodical payments orders made in the High Court or a county court and subsequently registered in the magistrates' courts, it is good practice for reasons to be recorded (*Hackshaw v Hackshaw* [1999] 2 FLR 876; see also *Stray v Stray* [1999] 2 FLR 610).

PART III
SATISFACTION AND ENFORCEMENT

General provisions

75 Power to dispense with immediate payment

(1) A magistrates' court by whose conviction or order a sum is adjudged to be paid may, instead of requiring immediate payment, allow time for payment, or order payment by instalments.

(2) Where a magistrates' court has allowed time for payment, the court may, on application by or on behalf of the person liable to make the payment, allow further time or order payment by instalments.

(2A) An order under this section that a lump sum required to be paid under a maintenance order shall be paid by instalments (a "maintenance instalments order") shall be treated for the purposes of section 59, 59B and 60 above as a maintenance order.

(2B) Subsections (5) and (7) of section 59 above (including those sub-sections as they apply for the purposes of section 60 above) shall have effect in relation to a maintenance instalments order –

- (*a*) as if in subsection (5), paragraph (*c*) and the word "and" immediately preceding it were omitted; and
- (*b*) as if in subsection (7) –
  - (i) the reference to the maintenance order were a reference to the maintenance order in respect of which the maintenance instalments order in question is made;
  - (ii) for the words "the person who applied for the maintenance order" there were substituted "the debtor".

(2C) Section 60 above shall have effect in relation to a maintenance instalments order as if in subsection (7), paragraph (*c*) and the word "and" immediately preceding it were omitted.

(3) Where a court has ordered payment by instalments and default is made in the payment of any one instalment, proceedings may be taken as if the default had been made in the payment of all the instalments then unpaid.

Amendments—Maintenance Enforcement Act 1991, s 11(1), Sch 2, para 6.

Scope of provision—A decision to allow time or further time must be recorded in the court register or in a separate record kept for that purpose (Magistrates' Courts Rules 1981, rr 62, 65). See also s 86 for power to fix a day when the defaulter must appear before the court.

"the court" (s 75(2))—By Justices' Clerks Rules 1999, Sch, para 30, the justices clerk also has this power.

"on application" (s 75(2))—The application may be in writing (Magistrates' Courts Rules 1981, r 51).

"section 59" (s 75(2A), (2B))—This section provides for means of payments orders to be made for the payment of periodical payments.

"section 59B" (s 75(2A))—This section provides a penalty for failure to pay a relevant English maintenance order where payment is ordered to or through the clerk of a magistrates' court or by standing order.

"section 60" (s 75(2A), (2B), (2C))—This section provides for the variation of periodical payments.

76 Enforcement of sums adjudged to be paid

(1) Subject to the following provisions of this Part of this Act, and to section 132 below, where default is made in paying a sum adjudged to be paid by a conviction or order of a magistrates' court, the court may issue a warrant of distress for the purpose of levying the sum or issue a warrant committing the defaulter to prison.

(2) A warrant of commitment may be issued as aforesaid either –

(*a*) where it appears on the return to a warrant of distress that the money and goods of the defaulter are insufficient to satisfy the sum with the costs and charges of levying the sum; or
(*b*) instead of a warrant of distress.

(3) The period for which a person may be committed to prison under such a warrant as aforesaid shall not, subject to the provisions of any enactment passed after 31st December 1879, exceed the period applicable to the case under Schedule 4 to this Act.

(4) Where proceedings are brought for the enforcement of a magistrates' court maintenance order under this section, the court may vary the order by exercising one of its powers under paragraphs (*a*) to (*d*) of section 59(3) above.

(5) Subsections (4), (5) and (7) of section 59 above shall apply for the purposes of subsection (4) above as they apply for the purposes of that section.

(6) Subsections (4) and (5) above shall not have effect in relation to a maintenance order which is not a qualifying maintenance order (within the meaning of section 59 above).

Amendments—Criminal Justice Act 1982, s 78, Sch 16; Maintenance Enforcement Act 1991, s 7.

Scope of provision—The section is subject to the restrictions imposed by ss 92, 96 and Sch 4 and to the additional procedural requirements of Maintenance Orders Act 1958, s 18. For issue and execution of distress warrants see Magistrates' Courts Rules 1981, r 54.

"section 132" (s 76(1))—The minimum period of imprisonment is five days.

"the court may issue" (s 76(1))—A discretion arises and the justices must have regard to the means of the defaulter and to the assets which may be available for distress. For exercise of the discretion see *R v Swindon Justices* (1878) 42 JP 407 (duty to enforce order improperly made but within jurisdiction and not appealed from) and *R v Gravesend Justices ex parte Doodney* [1971] 1 WLR 818, [1971] 2 All ER 364 (availability of enforcement proceedings even where the creditor lived out of the jurisdiction and could not be served with summons to vary the order).

"warrant committing" (s 76(1))—Section 92 restricts the exercise of the power to commit to prison, but excludes magistrates' court maintenance orders from this particular restriction. Section 96 makes special provision for the enforcement by committal of civil debts. Complaints for arrears of maintenance must be made under s 93.

Warrant of distress—If there is a reasonable likelihood that the debtor has sufficient goods to satisfy the debt, the court should issue a distress warrant rather than commit to prison (*R v Birmingham Justices ex parte Bennett* [1983] 1 WLR 114). Special protection against execution is given by the Reserve and Auxiliary Forces (Protection of Civil Interests) Act 1951.

Warrant of commitment (s 76(2))—See s 125 for general provisions as to warrants and s 126 for execution of warrants outside England and Wales.

77 Postponement of issue of warrant

(1) Where a magistrates' court has power to issue a warrant of distress under this Part of this Act, it may, if it thinks it expedient to do so, postpone the issue of the warrant until such time and on such conditions, if any, as the court thinks just.

(2) Where a magistrates' court has power to issue a warrant of commitment under this Part of this Act, it may, if it thinks it expedient to do so, fix a term of imprisonment or detention under section 108 of the Powers of Criminal Courts (Sentencing) Act 2000 (detention of persons aged 18 to 20 for default) and postpone the issue of the warrant until such time and on such conditions, if any, as the court thinks just.

(3) A magistrates' court shall have power at any time to do either or both of the following –

(*a*) to direct that the issue of the warrant of commitment shall be postponed until a time different from that to which it was previously postponed;

(*b*) to vary any of the conditions on which its issue is postponed,

but only if it thinks it just to do so having regard to a change of circumstances since the relevant time.

(4) In this section "the relevant time" means –

(*a*) where neither of the powers conferred by subsection (3) above has been exercised previously, the date when the issue of the warrant was postponed under subsection (2) above; and

(*b*) in any other case, the date of the exercise or latest exercise of either or both of the powers.

(5) Without prejudice to the generality of subsection (3) above, if on an application by a person in respect of whom issue of a warrant has been postponed it appears to a justice of the peace acting for the petty sessions area in which the warrant has been or would have been issued that since the relevant time there has been a change of circumstances which would make it just for the court to exercise one or other or both of the powers conferred by that subsection, he shall refer the application to the court.

(6) Where such an application is referred to the court –

(*a*) the clerk of the court shall fix a time and place for the application to be heard; and

(*b*) the justices' chief executive for the court shall give the applicant notice of that time and place.

(7) Where such a notice has been given but the applicant does not appear at the time and place specified in the notice, the court may proceed with the consideration of the application in his absence.

(8) If a warrant of commitment in respect of the sum adjudged to be paid has been issued before the hearing of the application, the court shall have power to order that the warrant shall cease to have effect and, if the applicant has been arrested in pursuance of it, to order that he shall be released, but it shall only make an order under this subsection if it is satisfied that the change of circumstances on which the applicant relies was not put before the court when it was determining whether to issue the warrant.

Amendments—Criminal Justice Act 1982, s 77, Sch 14, para 50; Criminal Justice Act 1988, s 61; Powers of Criminal Courts (Sentencing) Act 2000, s 165, Sch 9, para 66; SI 2001/618.

PART II

Scope of provision—See Maintenance Orders Act 1958, s 18 for the duty to review the issue of the postponed warrant.

"this Part" (s 77(1))—Part III covers sums adjudged to be paid by conviction or order (s 76), civil debt (s 96) and maintenance orders (s 93).

Conditional postponement of warrant of commitment (s 77(2))—Whilst it is good practice when postponing the issue of a committal warrant in relation to a maintenance order to make it a condition that the debtor pays the current order together with an amount off the arrears (*Fowler v Fowler* (1981) FLR 141), the court collecting officer is obliged to apply all amounts paid first to the arrears in respect of which the committal order was made (*R v Miskin Lower Justices ex parte Young* [1953] 1 QB 533, [1953] 2 WLR 409). If the debtor fails to comply with the terms of the postponement, the warrant may be issued but arrears which have accrued since the warrant was ordered may not be added to the warrant (*R v Bedford Prison (Governor) ex parte Ames* [1953] 1 WLR 607, [1953] 1 All ER 1002).

78 Defect in distress warrant and irregularity in its execution

(1) A warrant of distress issued for the purpose of levying a sum adjudged to be paid by the conviction or order of a magistrates' court shall not, if it states that the sum has been so adjudged to be paid, be held void by reason of any defect in the warrant.

(2) A person acting under a warrant of distress shall not be deemed to be a trespasser from the beginning by reason only of any irregularity in the execution of the warrant.

(3) Nothing in this section shall prejudice the claim of any person for special damages in respect of any loss caused by a defect in the warrant or irregularity in its execution.

(4) If any person removes any goods marked in accordance with the rules as articles impounded in the execution of a warrant of distress, or defaces or removes any such mark, he shall be liable on summary conviction to a fine not exceeding level 1 on the standard scale.

(5) If any person charged with the execution of a warrant of distress wilfully retains from the proceeds of a sale of the goods on which distress is levied, or otherwise exacts, any greater costs and charges than those properly payable, or makes any improper charge, he shall be liable on summary conviction to a fine not exceeding level 1 on the standard scale.

Amendments—Criminal Justice Act 1982, ss 38, 46.

Rules (s 78(4))—For the relevant rules, see Magistrates' Courts Rules 1981, r 58.

"level 1 on the standard scale" (s 78(4), (5))—Currently £200 (Criminal Justice Act 1982, s 37(2), as substituted).

79 Release from custody and reduction of detention on payment

(1) Where imprisonment or other detention has been imposed on any person by the order of a magistrates' court in default of payment of any sum adjudged to be paid by the conviction or order of a magistrates' court or for want of sufficient distress to satisfy such a sum, then, on the payment of the sum, together with the costs and charges, if any, of the commitment and distress, the order shall cease to have effect; and if the person has been committed to custody he shall be released unless he is in custody for some other cause.

(2) Where, after a period of imprisonment or other detention has been imposed on any person in default of payment of any sum adjudged to be paid by the conviction or order of a magistrates' court or for want of sufficient distress to satisfy such a sum, payment is made in accordance with the rules of part of the sum, the period of detention shall be reduced by such number of days as bears to the total number of days in that period less one day the same proportion as the amount so paid bears to so much of the said sum, and the costs and charges of any distress levied to satisfy that sum, as was due at the time the period of detention was imposed.

(3) In calculating the reduction required under subsection (2) above any fraction of a day shall be left out of account.

Scope of provision—This section defines the effect of payment on the imprisonment or detention of a person for default in making payments under Part II. See Magistrates' Courts Rules 1981, r 55 for the persons authorised to receive payments and for the duties imposed upon them.

80 Application of money found on defaulter to satisfy sum adjudged

(1) Where a magistrates' court has adjudged a person to pay a sum by a conviction or has ordered the enforcement of a sum due from a person under a magistrates' court maintenance order, the court may order him to be searched.

(2) Any money found on the arrest of a person adjudged to pay such a sum as aforesaid, or on a search as aforesaid, or on his being taken to a prison or other place of detention in default of payment of such a sum or for want of sufficient distress to satisfy such a sum, may, unless the court otherwise directs, be applied towards payment of the said sum; and the balance, if any, shall be returned to him.

(3) A magistrates' court shall not allow the application as aforesaid of any money found on a person if it is satisfied that the money does not belong to him or that the loss of the money would be more injurious to his family than would be his detention.

Amendments—Family Law Reform Act 1987, s 33(1), Sch 2, para 83.

Defined terms—"magistrates' court maintenance order": s 150(1).

"unless the court otherwise directs" (s 80(2))—There is a general discretion to give a direction but if the circumstances under s 80(3) are found, the discretion does not arise and the money may not be applied to satisfy the sum adjudged.

****

Sums adjudged to be paid by an order

92 Restriction on power to impose imprisonment for default

(1) A magistrates' court shall not exercise its power under section 76 above to issue a warrant to commit to prison a person who makes default in paying a sum adjudged to be paid by an order of such a court except where the default is under –

(*a*) a magistrates' court maintenance order;

(*b*) an order under section 17(2) of the Access to Justice Act 1999 (payment by individual in respect of cost of his defence in a criminal case); or

(*c*) an order for the payment of any of the taxes, contributions, premiums or liabilities specified in Schedule 4 to the Administration of Justice Act 1970.

(2) This section does not affect the power of a magistrates' court to issue such a warrant as aforesaid in the case of default in paying a sum adjudged to be paid by a conviction, or treated (by any enactment relating to the collection or enforcement of fines, costs, compensation or forfeited recognizances) as so adjudged to be paid.

(3) (*repealed*)

Amendments—Family Law Reform Act 1987, s 33(4), Sch 4; Legal Aid Act 1988, s 45, Sch 5, para 9; Access to Justice Act 1999, s 24, Sch 4, paras 15, 17.

"magistrates' court maintenance order" (s 92(1)(*a*))—This term is defined in s 150(1), and includes orders made under the following provisions: Domestic Proceedings and Magistrates' Courts Act 1978, Pt I; National Assistance Act 1948, s 43; Supplementary Benefits Act 1976, s 18; Social Security Act 1986, s 24; Maintenance Orders Act 1958; Maintenance Orders Act 1950, Pt II; Maintenance Orders (Facilities for Enforcement) Act 1920; Maintenance Orders (Reciprocal Enforcement) Act 1972; Matrimonial Proceedings (Magistrates' Courts) Act 1960 and CA 1989, Sch 1.

93 Complaint for arrears

(1) Where default is made in paying a sum ordered to be paid by a magistrates' court maintenance order, the court shall not enforce payment of the sum under section 76 above except by an order made on complaint.

(2) A complaint under this section shall be made not earlier than the fifteenth day after the making of the order for the enforcement of which it is made; but subject to this such a complaint may be made at any time notwithstanding anything in this or any other Act.

(3) In relation to complaints under this section, section 55 above shall not apply and section 56 above shall have effect as if the words "if evidence has been received on a previous occasion" were omitted.

(4) Where at the time and place appointed for the hearing or adjourned hearing of a complaint under this section the complainant appears but the defendant does not, the court may proceed in his absence; but the court shall not begin to hear the complaint in the absence of the defendant unless either it is proved to the satisfaction of the court, on oath or in such other manner as may be prescribed, that the summons was served on him within what appears to the court to be a reasonable time before the hearing or adjourned hearing or the defendant has appeared on a previous occasion to answer the complaint.

(5) If a complaint under this section is substantiated on oath, any justice of the peace acting for the same petty sessions area as a court having jurisdiction to hear the complaint may issue a warrant for the defendant's arrest, whether or not a summons has been previously issued.

(6) A magistrates' court shall not impose imprisonment in respect of a default to which a complaint under this section relates unless the court has inquired in the presence of the defendant whether the default was due to the defendant's wilful refusal or culpable neglect, and shall not impose imprisonment as aforesaid if it is of opinion that the default was not so due; and, without prejudice to the preceding provisions of this subsection, a magistrates' court shall not impose imprisonment as aforesaid –

(*a*) in the absence of the defendant; or
(*b*) in a case where the court has power to do so, if it is of the opinion that it is appropriate –
 (i) to make an attachment of earnings order; or

(ii) to order that payments under the order be made by any method of payment falling within section 59(6) above; or

(*c*) where the sum to which the default relates comprises only interest which the defendant has been ordered to pay by virtue of section 94A(1) below.

(7) Notwithstanding anything in section 76(3) above, the period for which a defendant may be committed to prison under a warrant of commitment issued in pursuance of a complaint under this section shall not exceed 6 weeks.

(8) The imprisonment or other detention of a defendant under a warrant of commitment issued as aforesaid shall not operate to discharge the defendant from his liability to pay the sum in respect of which the warrant was issued.

Amendments—Family Law Reform Act 1987, s 33(1), Sch 2, para 84; Maintenance Enforcement Act 1991, s 11(1), Sch 2, para 7.

Defined terms—"magistrates' court maintenance order": s 150(1).

Scope of provision—For enforcement of an order against members of the armed forces, see Army Act 1955, ss 150 and 151, Air Force Act 1955, ss 150 and 151 and Naval Forces (Enforcement of Maintenance Liabilities) Act 1947.

"shall not enforce" (s 93(1))—The obligation to serve a copy of the order before enforcement which applies to civil debt does not apply to enforcement of orders under this section.

"proved ... in such other manner as may be prescribed" (s 93(4))—The procedure is prescribed by Magistrates' Courts Rules 1981, r 67.

Imposition of imprisonment (s 93(6))—The obligation to inform the defendant of a right to legal aid which applies to the imposition of imprisonment in criminal proceedings does not apply to proceedings under this section (*R v Cardiff Justices ex parte Salter* [1986] 1 FLR 162).

"wilful refusal or culpable neglect" (s 93(6))—The onus of proving that default is not due to wilful refusal or culpable neglect is on the debtor (*R v Cardiff Magistrates' Court ex parte Czech* [1999] 1 FLR 95). Clear evidence and a full means enquiry are required to justify the debtor's immediate committal to prison on a finding of culpable neglect (*R v Slough Magistrates' Court ex parte Lindsay* [1997] 1 FLR 695). The receipt of benefits from the DSS is only a factor in reaching a decision as to whether conduct amounts to wilful refusal or culpable neglect and is not a conclusive factor (*R v Cardiff Justices ex parte Salter* (above)).

"section 59(6) above" (s 93(6))—This section provides for the making of periodical payments by standing order or similar methods (but not by way of direct debit).

"make an attachment of earnings order" (s 93(6))—See Attachment of Earnings Act 1971.

Warrant of commitment (s 93(8))—For execution of the warrant outside England and Wales see s 126. Enforcement of imprisonment may be used only once in respect of the same arrears.

94 Effect of committal on arrears

Where a person is committed to custody under this Part of this Act for failure to pay a sum due under a magistrates' court maintenance order, then, unless the court that commits him otherwise directs, no arrears shall accrue under the order while he is in custody.

Amendments—Family Law Reform Act 1987, s 33(1), Sch 2, para 85.

Defined terms—"magistrates' court maintenance order": s 150(1).

Scope of provision—A direction may be inappropriate where the defendant was committed to custody on the basis of culpable neglect, but see *Starkey v Starkey* [1954] P 449 at 454, [1954] 1

All ER 1036 at 1039 where it was indicated that a direction may be appropriate for wilful refusal to pay.

"while he is in custody"—See Magistrates' Courts Rules 1981, r 63 for the duty of the prison governor to notify the clerk of the court of details of the dates of reception and discharges.

94A Interest on arrears

(1) The Lord Chancellor may by order provide that a magistrates' court, on the hearing of a complaint for the enforcement, revocation, revival, variation or discharge of an English maintenance order, may order that interest of an amount calculated at the prescribed rate shall be paid on so much of the sum due under the order as they may determine.

(2) In subsection (1) above "the prescribed rate" means such rate of interest as the Lord Chancellor may by order prescribe.

(3) An order under this section may make provision for the manner in which and the periods by reference to which interest is to be calculated.

(4) Where, by virtue of subsection (1) above, a magistrates' court orders the payment of interest on any sum due under a maintenance order –

(*a*) then if it orders that the whole or any part of the interest be paid by instalments that order shall be regarded as an instalments order for the purposes of section 95 below and that section shall accordingly apply in relation to it; and

(*b*) the whole of the interest shall be enforceable as a sum adjudged to be paid by the maintenance order.

(5) In this section –

"English maintenance order" means –

(*a*) a qualifying maintenance order made by a magistrates' court, other than an order made by virtue of Part II of the Maintenance Orders (Reciprocal Enforcement) Act 1972; or

(*b*) an order made by the High Court or a county court (other than an order deemed to be made by the High Court by virtue of section 1(2) of the Maintenance Orders Act 1958) and registered under Part I of that Act of 1958 in a magistrates' court;

"qualifying maintenance order" has the same meaning as it has in section 59 above.

(6) The power of the Lord Chancellor to make an order under this section shall be exercisable by statutory instrument made with the concurrence of the Treasury and any such statutory instrument shall be subject to annulment in pursuance of a resolution of either House of Parliament.

Amendments—Inserted by Maintenance Enforcement Act 1991, s 8; amended by SI 1992/709.

"may by order prescribe"—No such order has yet been made.

95 Remission of arrears and manner in which arrears to be paid

(1) On the hearing of a complaint for the enforcement, revocation, revival, variation or discharge of a magistrates' court maintenance order, a magistrates' court may remit the whole or any part of the sum due under the order.

(2) If, on the hearing of a complaint for the enforcement, revocation, revival, variation or discharge of a magistrates' court maintenance order, a magistrates' court orders that the whole or any part of the sum due under the order be paid by instalments (an "instalments order"), then –

(*a*) if the maintenance order is an English maintenance order, the court shall at the same time exercise one of its powers under paragraphs (*a*) to (*d*) of section 59(3) above in relation to the instalments orders;

(*b*) if the maintenance order is a non-English maintenance order, the court shall at the same time exercise one of its powers under subsection (3) below in relation to the instalments order.

(3) The powers of the court referred to in subsection (2)(*b*) above are –

(*a*) the power to order that payments under the order be made directly to a justices' chief executive;

(*b*) the power to order that payments under the order be made to a justices' chief executive, by such method of payment falling within section 59(6) above as may be specified;

(*c*) the power to make an attachment of earnings order under the Attachment of Earnings Act 1971 to secure payments under the order.

(4) The court may in the course of any proceedings concerning an instalments order or the magistrates' court maintenance order to which it relates vary the instalments order by exercising –

(*a*) in respect of an English maintenance order, one of the powers referred to in subsection (2)(*a*) above;

(*b*) in respect of a non-English maintenance order, one of its powers under subsection (3) above.

(5) In respect of an English maintenance order, subsections (4), (5) and (7) of section 59 above shall apply for the purposes of subsections (2)(*a*) and (4)(*a*) above as they apply for the purposes of that section.

(6) In respect of a non-English maintenance order –

(*a*) subsection (4) of section 59 above shall apply for the purposes of subsections (2)(*b*) and (4)(*b*) above as it applies for the purposes of that section but as if for paragraph (*a*) there were substituted –

"(*a*) the court proposes to exercise its power under paragraph (*b*) of section 95(3) below;"; and

(*b*) in deciding which of the powers under subsection (3) above it is to exercise the court shall have regard to any representations made by the debtor (within the meaning of section 59 above).

(7) In this section –

"English maintenance order" has the same meaning as it has in section 94A above;

"non-English maintenance order" means –

(*a*) a maintenance order registered in, or confirmed, by, a magistrates' court –

(i) under the Maintenance Orders (Facilities for Enforcement) Act 1920;

(ii) under Part II of the Maintenance Orders Act 1950;

(iii) under Part I of the Maintenance Orders (Reciprocal Enforcement) Act 1972;

(iv) under Part I of the Civil Jurisdiction and Judgments Act 1982; or

PART II

(v) under Council Regulation (EC) No 44/2001 of 22 December 2000 on jurisdiction and the recognition and enforcement of judgments in civil and commercial matters;

(*b*) an order deemed to be made by the High Court by virtue of section 1(2) of the Maintenance Orders Act 1958 and registered under Part I of that Act in a magistrates' court; or

(*c*) a maintenance order made by a magistrates' court by virtue of Part II of the Maintenance Orders (Reciprocal Enforcement) Act 1972.

Amendments—Maintenance Enforcement Act 1991, s 11(1), Sch 2, para 8; Access to Justice Act 1999, s 90, Sch 13, para 110; SI 2001/3929.

Defined terms—"English maintenance order": s 94A; "magistrates' court maintenance order": s 150(1); "non-English maintenance order": s 95(7).

Remission of sum due—As a general rule and in the absence of special circumstances, arrears which have accrued more than a year before the complaint for enforcement will not be enforced (see, for example, *Bernstein v O'Neill* [1989] 2 FLR 1 and *B v C (Enforcement: Arrears)* [1995] 1 FLR 467). The court may not, on discharge, remit monies paid before the date of complaint (*Fildes (formerly Simkin) v Simkin* [1960] P 70, [1960] 2 WLR 1). Courts should act cautiously and only if the evidence justifies it, when basing decisions not to remit arrears upon anticipated changes in circumstances (*C v S (Maintenance Order : Enforcement)* [1997] 1 FLR 298). The court may not order the refund of monies paid without the knowledge that a divorced wife had remarried (*Young v Young (No 2)* [1962] P 218, [1961] 3 WLR 1041). The payment by a husband of his wife's debts is not a ground for remittal of arrears payable to the children (*Parry v Meugens* [1986] 1 FLR 125). Remission of arrears is not a penalty (*R v Halifax Justices ex parte Woolverton* (1981) FLR 369).

For the duty to give notice and to consider representations see Magistrates' Courts Rules 1981, r 44. Appeal against the order is by way of case stated.

"paragraphs (a) to (d) of section 59(3) above" (s 95(2))—This section provides for periodical payments to be made direct between the debtor and creditor, to the justices' chief executive, by standing order (or similar method but not by direct debit) or by attachment of earnings. Payment by one of these means can be applied to the original order and to any instalment payment of arrears under the order.

96 Civil debt: complaint for non-payment

(1) A magistrates' court shall not commit any person to prison or other detention in default of payment of a sum enforceable as a civil debt or for want of sufficient distress to satisfy such a sum except by an order made on complaint and on proof to the satisfaction of the court that that person has, or has had since the date on which the sum was adjudged to be paid, the means to pay the sum or any instalment of it on which he has defaulted, and refuses or neglects or, as the case may be, has refused or neglected to pay it.

(2) A complaint under this section may be made at any time notwithstanding anything in this or any other Act.

(3) Where on any such complaint the defendant is committed to custody, such costs incurred by the complainant in proceedings for the enforcement of the sum as the court may direct shall be included in the sum on payment of which the defendant may be released from custody.

Defined terms—"committed to custody": s 150(1); "sum enforceable as a civil debt": s 150(1).

Scope of provision—This section provides for the making of a complaint for the enforcement of a sum enforceable as a civil debt and, in conjunction with s 92, limits the use of committal to custody for non-payment. Some protection is afforded by the Reserve and Auxiliary Forces (Protection of Civil Interests) Act 1951.

Committal to prison (s 96(1))—The maximum period of committal is six weeks (Sch 4, para 3). If the court has allowed time to pay, a summons to show cause is required before committal can be ordered (*Kinnings Case* (1847) 10 QB 730). For the execution of the warrant outside England and Wales see s 126.

"order made on complaint" (s 96(1))—See Magistrates' Courts Rules 1981, r 58 for the requirement to serve a judgment summons and the requirement for three days to elapse between service and hearing except with the debtor's consent.

Application of other sections to civil debt enforcement—Section 76 (distraint) applies to civil debt enforcement but neither s 88 (money payments supervision order) nor s 95 (remission of arrears etc) applies to civil debts enforceable under this section.

Costs (s 96(3))—Section 64 (power to award costs) applies to costs awarded under this section.

96A Application of Part III to persons aged 18 to 20

This Part of this Act shall have effect in relation to a person aged 18 or over but less than 21 as if any reference to committing a person to prison, or fixing a term of imprisonment for a default, were a reference to committing the person to, or, as the case may be, to fixing a term of, detention under section 108 of the Powers of Criminal Courts (Sentencing) Act 2000; and any reference to warrants of commitment, or to periods of imprisonment imposed for default, shall be construed accordingly.

Amendments—Inserted by Criminal Justice Act 1982, s 77, Sch 14, para 54; amended by Criminal Justice Act 1991, s 68, Sch 8, para 6; Powers of Criminal Courts (Sentencing) Act 2000, s 165, Sch 9, para 70.

PART IV
WITNESSES AND EVIDENCE

Procuring attendance of witness

97 Summons to witness and warrant for his arrest

(1) Where a justice of the peace for any commission area is satisfied that any person in England or Wales is likely to be able to give material evidence, or produce any document or thing likely to be material evidence, at the summary trial of an information or hearing of a complaint by a magistrates' court for that commission area and that that person will not voluntarily attend as a witness or will not voluntarily produce the document or thing, the justice shall issue a summons directed to that person requiring him to attend before the court at the time and place appointed in the summons to give evidence or to produce the document or thing.

(2) If a justice of the peace is satisfied by evidence on oath of the matters mentioned in subsection (1) above, and also that it is probable that a summons under that subsection would not procure the attendance of the person in question, the justice may instead of issuing a summons issue a warrant to arrest that person and bring him before such a court as aforesaid at a time and place specified in the warrant; but a warrant shall not be issued under this subsection where the attendance is required for the hearing of a complaint.

(2A) A summons may also be issued under subsection (1) above if the justice is satisfied that the person in question is outside the British Islands but no warrant shall be issued under subsection (2) above unless the justice is satisfied by evidence on oath that the person in question is in England or Wales.

(2B) A justice may refuse to issue a summons under subsection (1) above in relation to the summary trial of an information if he is not satisfied that an application for the summons was made by a party to the case as soon as reasonably practicable after the accused pleaded not guilty.

(2C) In relation to the summary trial of an information, subsection (2) above shall have effect as if the reference to the matters mentioned in subsection (1) above included a reference to the matter mentioned in subsection (2B) above.

(3) On the failure of any person to attend before a magistrates' court in answer to a summons under this section, if –

(*a*) the court is satisfied by evidence on oath that he is likely to be able to give material evidence or produce any document or thing likely to be material evidence in the proceedings; and

(*b*) it is proved on oath, or in such other manner as may be prescribed, that he has been duly served with the summons, and that a reasonable sum has been paid or tendered to him for costs and expenses; and

(*c*) it appears to the court that there is no just excuse for the failure.

the court may issue a warrant to arrest him and bring him before the court at a time and place specified in the warrant.

(4) If any person attending or brought before a magistrates' court refuses without just excuse to be sworn or give evidence, or to produce any document or thing, the court may commit him to custody until the expiration of such period not exceeding one month as may be specified in the warrant or until he sooner gives evidence or produces the document or thing or impose on him a fine not exceeding £2,500 or both.

(5) A fine imposed under subsection (4) above shall be deemed, for the purposes of any enactment, to be a sum adjudged to be paid by a conviction.

Amendments—Contempt of Court Act 1981, Sch 2; SI 1984/447; Criminal Justice (International Co-operation) Act 1990, s 31(1), Sch 4, para 2; Criminal Justice Act 1991, s 17(3), Sch 4, Pt I, Pt V, para 2; Criminal Justice Act 1993, s 65(3), Sch 3, para 6(3); Criminal Procedure and Investigations Act 1996, ss 47, 51(1), (2), 80, Sch 1, Pt I, paras 1, 7, Sch 5(10); SI 1996/674; SI 1996/675.

Scope of provision—This section provides for the issue of a witness summons to a person likely to be able to give material evidence or produce a document or thing. A witness warrant under s 97(2) may only be issued in criminal proceedings.

"justice of the peace" (s 97(1))—By virtue of Justices' Clerks Rules 1999, Sch, para 42, this power may also be exercised by a justices' clerk or a specifically authorised court clerk (see Family Proceedings Courts (Children Act 1989) Rules 1991, r 32).

Grounds for issuing summons (s 97(1))—The court should enquire into the nature of the evidence. The evidence should be material to the party making application for the summons (*R v Peterborough Magistrates' Court, ex parte Willis and Amos* (1987) 151 JP 785). The evidence of a hostile witness is not material to the applicant party (*R v Marylebone Magistrates' Court ex parte Gatting and Emburey* (1990) 154 JP 549). See also *R v Hove Justices ex parte Donne* [1967] 2 All ER and *R v Cheltenham Justices ex parte Secretary of State for Trade* [1977] 1 WLR 95, [1977] 1 All ER 460. An application for a witness summons should not be a "fishing expedition" (*R v Tower Bridge Magistrates' Court ex parte DPP* [1988] Crim LR 693). If a court considers that, for reasons of a child's welfare, the child should not be called as a witness, it would be inappropriate to issue the summons (*R v B County Council ex parte P* [1991] 1 FLR 470). This case, where the prospective child witness was already before the court, was distinguished where the prospective child witness was not before the court when the summons was applied for, and it was held that it was premature to balance the welfare of the child against possible harm in giving evidence, at the stage of issuing the summons. It should be left to the court of trial to decide if the summoned child should actually give evidence (*R v Highbury Corner Magistrates' Court ex parte*

D [1997] 1 FLR 683). However, when considering a witness summons against a child, the child's welfare is of great relevance: the older the child, the more likely the application is to succeed (*Re P (A Minor) (Care Proceedings: Witness Summons)* [1997] 2 FLR 447). A witness summons should not be allowed to produce a record of instructions to solicitors where the witness had not waived legal professional privilege (*R v Derby Magistrates' Court ex parte B* [1995] 3 WLR 681, HL). There is a discretion to refuse a witness summons where to issue would be oppressive (*Re P (A Minor) (Care Proceedings: Witness Summons)* (above)).

Production of documents (s 97(1))—If production of a number of documents is sought, the relevance of each document must be considered individually (*R v Greenwich Juvenile Court ex parte Greenwich London Borough Council* (1977) 76 LGR 99). An order for the production of a privileged document should not be made (see, for example, *R v Bournemouth Justices ex parte Grey* [1987] 1 FLR 36.

"duly served" (s 97(3)(*b*))—See Magistrates' Courts Rules 1981, r 99(6) for method of service.

"may issue a warrant to arrest him" (s 97(3))—A warrant may be issued under s 97(3) in civil proceedings after the failure of the witness summons. A warrant should be issued only where the evidence sought is critical to the case (*R v Bradford Justices ex parte Wilkinson* [1990] 1 WLR 692, [1990] 2 All ER 833). Before issuing a warrant, the court should be satisfied that the evidence is really critical (*R v Nottingham Justices ex parte Fraser* [1995] JP Rep 613).

"refuses without just excuse" (s 97(4))—Duress may amount to a defence (*R v K* (1983) 148 JP 410).

****

Evidence generally

98 Evidence on oath

Subject to the provisions of any enactment or rule of law authorising the reception of unsworn evidence, evidence given before a magistrates' court shall be given on oath.

99 Proof of non-payment of sum adjudged

Where a magistrates' court has ordered one person to pay to another any sum of money, and proceedings are taken before that or any other magistrates' court to enforce payment of that sum, then –

- (*a*) if the person to whom the sum is ordered to be paid is a justices' chief executive, a certificate purporting to be signed by the justices' chief executive that the sum has not been paid to him; and
- (*b*) in any other case a document purporting to be a statutory declaration by the person to whom the sum is ordered to be paid that the sum has not been paid to him,

shall be admissible as evidence that the sum has not been paid to him, unless the court requires the justices' chief executive or other person to be called as a witness.

Amendments—Access to Justice Act 1999, s 90, Sch 13, para 112.

100 Statement of wages to be evidence

A statement in writing to the effect that wages of any amount have been paid to a person during any period, purporting to be signed by or on behalf of his employer, shall be evidence of the facts therein stated in any proceedings taken before a magistrates' court –

(*a*) for enforcing payment by the person to whom the wages are stated to have been paid of a sum adjudged to be paid by a summary conviction or order; or

(*b*) on any application made by or against that person for the making of a magistrates' court maintenance order, or for the variation, revocation, discharge or revival of such an order.

Amendments—Family Law Reform Act 1987, s 33(1), Sch 2, para 87.

****

Offences

****

107 False statements in declaration proving service etc

If, in any solemn declaration, certificate or other writing made or given for the purpose of its being used in pursuance of the rules as evidence of the service of any document or the handwriting or seal of any person, a person makes a statement that he knows to be false in a material particular, or recklessly makes any statement that is false in a material particular, he shall be liable on summary conviction to imprisonment for a term not exceeding 6 months or a fine not exceeding level 3 on the standard scale or both.

Amendments—Criminal Justice Act 1982, ss 38, 46.

Scope of provision—This section makes it an offence to make a false statement in a solemn declaration or certificate as to service under Magistrates' Courts Rules 1981, r 67. Proceedings under the Perjury Act 1911 remain an alternative course of action (see s 16(3) of that Act).

"level 3 on the standard scale"—Currently £1,000 (Criminal Justice Act 1982, s 37(2), as substituted).

****

PART VI
RECOGNIZANCES

****

Other provisions

117 Warrant endorsed for bail

(1) A justice of the peace on issuing a warrant for the arrest of any person may grant him bail by endorsing the warrant for bail, that is to say, by endorsing the warrant with a direction in accordance with subsection (2) below.

(2) A direction for bail endorsed on a warrant under subsection (1) above shall –

(*a*) in the case of bail in criminal proceedings, state that the person arrested is to be released on bail subject to a duty to appear before such magistrates' court and at such time as may be specified in the endorsement;

(*b*) in the case of bail otherwise than in criminal proceedings, state that the person arrested is to be released on bail on his entering into such a recognizance (with or without sureties) conditioned for his appearance before a magistrates' court as may be specified in the endorsement;

and the endorsement shall fix the amounts in which any sureties and, in a case falling within paragraph (*b*) above, that person is or are to be bound.

(3) Where a warrant has been endorsed for bail under subsection (1) above –

(*a*) where the person arrested is to be released on bail on his entering into a recognizance without sureties, it shall not be necessary to take him to a police station, but if he is so taken, he shall be released from custody on his entering into the recognizance; and

(*b*) where he is to be released on his entering into a recognizance with sureties, he shall be taken to a police station on his arrest, and the custody officer there shall (subject to his approving any surety tendered in compliance with the endorsement) release him from custody as directed in the endorsement.

Amendments—Police and Criminal Evidence Act 1984, s 47(8).

"custody officer" (s 117(3)(*b*))—Custody officers are appointed under Police and Criminal Evidence Act 1984, s 36.

118 Varying or dispensing with requirement as to sureties

(1) Subject to subsection (2) below, where a magistrates' court has committed a person to custody in default of finding sureties, the court may, on application by or on behalf of the person committed, and after hearing fresh evidence, reduce the amount in which it is proposed that any surety should be bound or dispense with any of the sureties or otherwise deal with the case as it thinks just.

(2) Subsection (1) above does not apply in relation to a person granted bail in criminal proceedings.

119 Postponement of taking recognizance

(1) Where a magistrates' court has power to take any recognizance, the court may, instead of taking it, fix the amount in which the principal and his sureties, if any, are to be bound; and thereafter the recognizance may be taken by any such person as may be prescribed.

(2) Where, in pursuance of this section, a recognizance is entered into otherwise than before the court that fixed the amount of it, the same consequences shall follow as if it had been entered into before that court; and references in this or any other Act to the court before which a recognizance was entered into shall be construed accordingly.

(3) Nothing in this section shall enable a magistrates' court to alter the amount of a recognizance fixed by the High Court or the Crown Court.

Amendments—Criminal Justice Act 1982, s 77, Sch 14, para 55.

Scope of provision—This section permits recognizances to be fixed and for them to be taken subsequently. See Magistrates' Courts Rules 1981, rr 86–89 for persons prescribed for the taking of recognizances and for taking recognizances out of court.

120 Forfeiture of recognizance

(1) This section applies where –

(*a*) a recognizance to keep the peace or to be of good behaviour has been entered into before a magistrates' court; or
(*b*) any recognizance is conditioned for the appearance of a person before a magistrates' court, or for his doing any other thing connected with a proceeding before a magistrates' court.

(1A) If, in the case of a recognizance which is conditioned for the appearance of an accused before a magistrates' court, the accused fails to appear in accordance with the condition, the court shall –

(*a*) declare the recognizance to be forfeited;
(*b*) issue a summons directed to each person bound by the recognizance as surety, requiring him to appear before the court on a date specified in the summons to show cause why he should not be adjudged to pay the sum in which he is bound;

and on that date the court may proceed in the absence of any surety if it is satisfied that he has been served with the summons.

(2) If, in any other case falling within subsection (1) above, the recognizance appears to the magistrates' court to be forfeited, the court may –

(*a*) declare the recognizance to be forfeited; and
(*b*) adjudge each person bound by it, whether as principal or surety, to pay the sum in which he is bound;

but in a case falling within subsection (1)(*a*) above, the court shall not declare the recognizance to be forfeited except by order made on complaint.

(3) The court which declares the recognizance to be forfeited may, instead of adjudging any person to pay the whole sum in which he is bound, adjudge him to pay part only of the sum or remit the sum.

(4) Payment of any sum adjudged to be paid under this section, including any costs awarded against the defendant, may be enforced, and any such sum shall be applied, as if it were a fine and as if the adjudication were a summary conviction of an offence not punishable with imprisonment and so much of section 85(1) above as empowers a court to remit fines shall not apply to the sum but so much thereof as relates to remission after a term of imprisonment has been imposed shall so apply; but at any time before the issue of a warrant of commitment to enforce payment of the sum, or before the sale of goods under a warrant of distress to satisfy the sum, the court may remit the whole or any part of the sum either absolutely or on such conditions as the court thinks just.

(5) A recognizance such as is mentioned in this section shall not be enforced otherwise than in accordance with this section, and accordingly shall not be transmitted to the Crown Court nor shall its forfeiture be certified to that Court.

Amendments—Crime and Disorder Act 1998, s 55.

Defined terms—"fine": s 150(1).

Procedure—No procedure is prescribed under s 120(2) for attendance of any surety before the court but it is good practice to give the surety notice of the court's intention before estreating a recognisance and it is likely that the court will adopt the procedure set out in s 120(1A)(*b*) irrespective of whether or not that subsection applies in the case before it.

"appears to the magistrates' court to be forfeited" (s 120(2))—The civil standard of proof applies (*R v Marlow Justices ex parte O'Sullivan* [1984] QB 381, [1984] 2 WLR 107). It is generally accepted that jurisdiction to declare forfeiture is confined to the petty sessional area which set the recognizance.

Power to remit or order payment of part only (s 120(3))—The culpability of the person bound must be considered and certiorari will be available where the court has failed to do so (*R v Southampton Justices ex parte Green* [1976] 1 QB 11, [1975] 3 WLR 277).

PART VII
MISCELLANEOUS AND SUPPLEMENTARY

Constitution and place of sitting of magistrates' courts

121 Constitution and place of sitting of court

(1) A magistrates' court shall not try an information summarily or hear a complaint except when composed of at least 2 justices unless the trial or hearing is one that by virtue of any enactment may take place before a single justice.

(2) A magistrates' court shall not hold an inquiry into the means of an offender for the purposes of section 82 above or determine under that section at a hearing at which the offender is not present whether to issue a warrant of commitment except when composed of at least 2 justices.

(3) A magistrates' court shall not–

(*a*) try summarily an information for an indictable offence or hear a complaint except when sitting in a petty-sessional court-house;

(*b*) try an information for a summary offence or hold an inquiry into the means of an offender for the purposes of section 82 above, or impose imprisonment, except when sitting in a petty-sessional court-house or an occasional courthouse.

(4) Subject to the provisions of any enactment to the contrary, where a magistrates' court is required by this section to sit in a petty-sessional or occasional court-house, it shall sit in open court.

(5) A magistrates' court composed of a single justice, or sitting in an occasional courthouse, shall not impose imprisonment for a period exceeding 14 days or order a person to pay more than £1.

(6) Subject to the provisions of subsection (7) below, the justices composing the court before which any proceedings take place shall be present during the whole of the proceedings; but, if during the course of the proceedings any justice absents himself, he shall cease to act further therein and, if the remaining justices are enough to satisfy the requirements of the preceding provisions of this section, the proceedings may continue before a court composed of those justices.

(7) Where the trial of an information is adjourned after the accused has been convicted and before he is sentenced or otherwise dealt with, the court which sentences or deals with him need not be composed of the same justices as that which convicted him; but, where among the justices composing the court which sentences or deals with an offender there are any who were not sitting when he was convicted, the court which sentences or deals with the offender shall before doing so make such inquiry into the facts and circumstances of the case as will enable the justices who were not sitting when the offender was convicted to be fully acquainted with those facts and circumstances.

(8) This section shall have effect subject to the provisions of this Act relating to family proceedings.

Amendments—Criminal Justice Act 1988, s 61; CA 1989, s 92(11), Sch 11, para 8.

Defined terms—"family proceedings": s 65.

Appearance by a legal representative

122 Appearance by a legal representative

(1) A party to any proceedings before a magistrates' court may be represented by a legal representative.

(2) Subject to subsection (3) below, an absent party so represented shall be deemed not to be absent.

(3) Appearance of a party by a legal representative shall not satisfy any provision of any enactment or any condition of a recognizance expressly requiring his presence.

Amendments—Courts and Legal Services Act 1990, s 125(3), Sch 18, para 25.

Defined terms—"legal representative": s 150(1).

Scope of provision—This section will not operate to excuse a person's presence when it is required as a matter of law, for example as under s 93(6) or in answer to bail.

Process

123 Defect in process

(1) No objection shall be allowed to any information or complaint, or to any summons or warrant to procure the presence of the defendant, for any defect in it in substance or in form, or for any variance between it and the evidence adduced on behalf of the prosecutor or complainant at the hearing of the information or complaint.

(2) If it appears to a magistrates' court that any variance between a summons or warrant and the evidence adduced on behalf of the prosecutor or complainant is such that the defendant has been misled by the variance, the court shall, on the application of the defendant, adjourn the hearing.

Scope of provision—This section is designed to prevent the dismissal of informations and complaints on the basis of minor defects where no injustice is done to the defendant.

"No objection shall be allowed" (s 123(1))—There is little case-law regarding the application of this section to complaints, whereas a considerable line of cases has examined the application of the section to alleged defects in informations: see, for example *Garfield v Maddocks* [1974] QB 7, [1973] 2 All ER 303 (circumstances in which the prosecution may be required to amend the information); *Lawrence v Same* [1968] 2 QB 93, [1968] 1 All ER 1191 (circumstances in which a fresh information must be laid). The general principles seem to be the same, and it appears that amendment is allowed, provided no injustice is caused to the defendant thereby.

"the court shall" (s 123(2))—If the court finds that the defendant has been misled by any variance between a summons (or warrant) and the evidence adduced by the complainant, there is no discretion to refuse an application for an adjournment by the defendant.

124 Process valid notwithstanding death etc of justice

A warrant or summons issued by a justice of the peace shall not cease to have effect by reason of his death or his ceasing to be a justice.

125 Warrants

(1) A warrant of arrest issued by a justice of the peace shall remain in force until it is executed or withdrawn or it ceases to have effect in accordance with the rules.

(2) A warrant of arrest, warrant of commitment, warrant of detention, warrant of distress or search warrant issued by a justice of the peace may be executed anywhere in England and Wales by any person to whom it is directed or by any constable within his police area.

This subsection does not apply to a warrant of commitment or a warrant of distress issued under Part VI of the General Rate Act 1967.

(3), (4) (*repealed*)

Amendments—Police and Criminal Evidence Act 1984, s 33; Criminal Justice Act 1988, s 65(1); Courts and Legal Services Act 1990, s 125(2), Sch 17, para 11; Reserve Forces Act 1996, s 131(1), Sch 10, para 18; SI 1997/1898; Crime and Disorder Act 1998, s 119, Sch 8, para 44; Access to Justice Act 1999, s 95(1), Sch 15; Youth Justice and Criminal Evidence Act 1999, s 67, Sch 4, para 8; Powers of Criminal Courts (Sentencing) Act 2000, s 165, Sch 9, para 73.

"A warrant ... shall remain in force" (s 125(1))—A warrant remains in force even if the document is lost or mislaid. If satisfied of such circumstances, a justice may issue a duplicate warrant (*R v Leigh Justices ex parte Kara* (1980) 72 Cr App Rep 327); it is good practice to mark all such warrants as duplicates.

"ceases to have effect in accordance with the rules" (s 125(1))—As provided in Magistrates' Courts Rules 1981, r 96(5).

"any person to whom it is directed" (s 125(2))—The persons to whom a warrant may be directed are specified in Magistrates' Courts Rules 1981, rr 54, 96 and 97.

****

126 Execution of certain warrants outside England and Wales

Sections 12 to 14 of the Indictable Offences Act 1848 (which relate, among other things, to the execution in Scotland, Northern Ireland, the Isle of Man and the Channel Islands of warrants of arrest for the offences referred to in those sections) shall, so far as applicable, apply to –

(*a*) warrants of arrest issued under section 1 above for offences other than those referred to in the said sections 12 to 14;
(*b*) warrants of arrest issued under section 13 above;
(*c*) warrants of arrest issued under section 97 above other than warrants issued in bastardy proceedings to arrest a witness;
(*cc*) warrants of arrest issued under section 97A above;
(*d*) warrants of commitment issued under this Act;
(*e*) warrants of arrest issued under paragraph 4 of Schedule 3 to the Crime and Disorder Act 1998; and
(*f*) warrants of arrest issued under paragraph 3(2) of Schedule 1 to the Powers of Criminal Courts (Sentencing) Act 2000 (offender referred to court by youth offender panel).

Amendments—Crime and Disorder Act 1998, s 119, Sch 8, para 45; Youth Justice and Criminal Evidence Act 1999, s 67, Sch 4, para 9; Powers of Criminal Courts (Sentencing) Act 2000, s 165, Sch 9, para 74.

Limitation of time

127 Limitation of time

(1) Except as otherwise expressly provided by any enactment and subject to subsection (2) below, a magistrates' court shall not try an information or hear a complaint unless the information was laid, or the complaint made, within 6 months from the time when the offence was committed, or the matter of complaint arose.

(2) Nothing in –

(*a*) subsection (1) above; or

(*b*) subject to subsection (4) below, any other enactment (however framed or worded) which, as regards any offence to which it applies, would but for this section impose a time-limit on the power of a magistrates' court to try an information summarily or impose a limitation on the time for taking summary proceedings,

shall apply in relation to any indictable offence.

(3) Without prejudice to the generality of paragraph (*b*) of subsection (2) above, that paragraph includes enactments which impose a time-limit that applies only in certain circumstances (for example, where the proceedings are not instituted by or with the consent of the Director of Public Prosecutions or some other specified authority).

(4) Where, as regards any indictable offence, there is imposed by any enactment (however framed or worded, and whether falling within subsection (2)(*b*) above or not) a limitation on the time for taking proceedings on indictment for that offence no summary proceedings for that offence shall be taken after the latest time for taking proceedings on indictment.

Scope of provision—This section does not apply where it is specifically excluded by statute (for example in civil contempt proceedings under s 63(3): see Contempt of Court Act 1981, Sch 3).

Remand

128 Remand in custody or on bail

(1) Where a magistrates' court has power to remand any person, then, subject to section 4 of the Bail Act 1976 and to any other enactment modifying that power, the court may –

(*a*) remand him in custody, that is to say, commit him to custody to be brought before the court, subject to subsection (3A) below, at the end of the period of remand or at such earlier time as the court may require; or

(*b*) where it is inquiring into or trying an offence alleged to have been committed by that person or has convicted him of an offence, remand him on bail in accordance with the Bail Act 1976, that is to say, by directing him to appear as provided in subsection (4) below; or

(*c*) except in a case falling within paragraph (*b*) above, remand him on bail by taking from him a recognizance (with or without sureties) conditioned as provided in that subsection;

and may, in a case falling within paragraph (*c*) above, instead of taking recognizances in accordance with that paragraph, fix the amount of the recognizances with a view to their being taken subsequently in accordance with section 119 above.

(1A)–(1C) ...

(2) Where the court fixes the amount of a recognizance under subsection (1) above or section 8(3) of the Bail Act 1976 with a view to its being taken subsequently the court shall in the meantime commit the person so remanded to custody in accordance with paragraph (*a*) of the said subsection (1).

(3) Where a person is brought before the court after remand, the court may further remand him.

(3A)–(3E) ...

(4) Where a person is remanded on bail under subsection (1) above the court may, where it remands him on bail in accordance with the Bail Act 1976 direct him to appear or, in any other case, direct that his recognizance be conditioned for his appearance –

(*a*) before that court at the end of the period of remand; or
(*b*) at every time and place to which during the course of the proceedings the hearing may be from time to time adjourned;

and, where it remands him on bail conditionally on his providing a surety during an inquiry into an offence alleged to have been committed by him, may direct that the recognizance of the surety be conditioned to secure that the person so bailed appears –

(*c*) at every time and place to which during the course of the proceedings the hearing may be from time to time adjourned and also before the Crown Court in the event of the person so bailed being committed for trial there.

(5) Where a person is directed to appear or a recognizance is conditioned for a person's appearance in accordance with paragraph (*b*) or (*c*) of subsection (4) above, the fixing at any time of the time for him next to appear shall be deemed to be a remand; but nothing in this subsection or subsection (4) above shall deprive the court of power at any subsequent hearing to remand him afresh.

(6) Subject to the provisions of section 129 below, a magistrates' court shall not remand a person for a period exceeding 8 clear days, except that –

(*a*) if the court remands him on bail, it may remand him for a longer period if he and the other party consent;

(*b*), (*c*) ...

(7), (8) ...

Amendments—Criminal Justice Act 1982, s 59, Sch 9, paras 2–4.

Defined terms—"commit to custody": s 150(1); "magistrates' court": s 148(1).

Scope of provision—This section defines the power of the court to remand in custody or on bail. In civil proceedings, the power to remand arises under s 55. The reception of evidence on oath is not a precondition to a remand in custody (*R v Guest ex parte Metropolitan Police Commissioner* [1961] 3 All ER 1118).

"8 clear days" (s 128(6))—The day of the remand and the day of the return to court are excluded from the period of eight days.

****

129 Further remand

(1) If a magistrates' court is satisfied that any person who has been remanded is unable by reason of illness or accident to appear or be brought before the court at the expiration of the period for which he was remanded, the court may, in his absence, remand him for a further time; and section 128(6) above shall not apply.

(2) Notwithstanding anything in section 128(1) above, the power of a court under subsection (1) above to remand a person on bail for a further time –

(*a*) where he was granted bail in criminal proceedings, includes power to enlarge the recognizance of any surety for him to a later time;

(*b*) where he was granted bail otherwise than in criminal proceedings, may be exercised by enlarging his recognizance and those of any sureties for him to a later time.

(3) Where a person remanded on bail is bound to appear before a magistrates' court at any time and the court has no power to remand him under subsection (1) above, the court may in his absence –

(*a*) where he was granted bail in criminal proceedings, appoint a later time as the time at which he is to appear and enlarge the recognizances of any sureties for him at that time;

(*b*) where he was granted bail otherwise than in criminal proceedings, enlarge his recognizance and those of any sureties for him to a later time;

and the appointment of the time or the enlargement of his recognizance shall be deemed to be a further remand.

(4) Where a magistrates' court commits a person for trial on bail and the recognizance of any surety for him has been conditioned in accordance with paragraph (*a*) of subsection (4) of section 128 above the court may, in the absence of the surety, enlarge his recognizance so that he is bound to secure that the person so committed for trial appears also before the Crown Court.

****

Restrictions on imprisonment

132 Minimum term

A magistrates' court shall not impose imprisonment for less than 5 days.

****

Fees, fines, forfeitures etc

137 Fees

(1) Subject to the provisions of this section, the court fees set out in Part I of Schedule 6 to this Act, and no others, shall be chargeable by justices' chief executives; and any enactment providing for the payment of any fees for the payment of which provision is made in the said Part I shall have effect accordingly.

(2) No fee shall be chargeable by a justices' chief executive in respect of any matter specified in Part II of the said Schedule.

(3) Nothing in this section shall affect the fees chargeable in respect of the matters specified in Part III of the said Schedule.

(4) The Lord Chancellor may from time to time by order make such variations in Part I of the said Schedule as may seem to him proper.

(5) The power to make an order under subsection (4) above shall be exercisable by statutory instrument; and a draft of any such statutory instrument shall be laid before Parliament.

(6) (*repealed*)

Amendments—SI 1992/709; Access to Justice Act 1999, s 106, Sch 13, para 114, Sch 15.

Scope of provision—This section provides for certain fees to be charged by justices' chief executives. Fees cannot be recovered before the justices – an action for recovery in the county court is required, and it may be that a more efficient method of collection may be to withhold the document or to decline to take action until the fee is paid. No fee may be charged except as provided by statute. Reference to the fee payable is made under each of the sections creating the power to issue process.

PART II

138 Remission of fees

A magistrates' court may on the ground of poverty or for other reasonable cause remit in whole or in part any fee payable in proceedings before the court.

"magistrates' court"—The power to remit may only be exercised by the court; this is in contrast to the duty to charge fees, which is exercisable by the justices' chief executive. In view of the difficulties of enforcement noted under s 137, an applicant may be required to persuade the justices' chief executive to defer the imposition of the fee until the matter is before the court in order to preserve the court's discretion to remit.

"poverty or other reasonable cause"—Persons in receipt of public funding, income-based jobseeker's allowance or working families' tax credit are already exempt from the requirement to pay a fee (Sch 6, note (*a*)). If an applicant would qualify on grounds of means for legal aid, but it has been refused for some other reason, this may be an appropriate ground for remission of fees. The discretion is wide.

****

Clerks to justices

141 Clerks to justices

(1) Any reference in this Act to a clerk of any magistrates' court shall be construed as a reference to the clerk to the justices for the petty sessions area for which the court is acting, or was acting at the relevant time.

(2) Where there is more than one clerk to the justices for any petty sessions area, anything that this Act requires or authorises to be done by or to the clerk to the justices shall or may be done by or to any of the clerks or by or to such of the clerks as the magistrates' courts committee having power over the appointment of clerks to justices for that area generally or in any particular case or cases may direct.

(3) (*repealed*)

Amendments—Police and Magistrates' Courts Act 1994, s 93, Sch 9.

Defined terms—"petty sessions area": s 150(1).

****

Power to alter sums specified in certain provisions

143 Power to alter sums specified in certain provisions

(1) If it appears to the Secretary of State that there has been a change in the value of money since the relevant date, he may by order substitute for the sum or sums for the time being specified in any provision mentioned in subsection (2) below such other sum or sums as appear to him justified by the change.

(2) The said provisions are –

(*a*) section 22(1) above;
(*aa*) section 24(3) and (4) above;
(*b*) the definition of "the prescribed sum" in section 32(9) above;
(*c*) paragraph (*a*) of section 33(1) above;
(*ca*) section 34(3)(*b*) above;
(*cb*) section 131(1) of the Powers of Criminal Courts (Sentencing) Act 2000 (limit on compensation order of magistrates' court);
(*d*) section 135 of that Act (limit on fine imposed on young offender by magistrates' court);
(*dd*) section 59B(3) above;
(*e*) the Table in paragraph 1 of Schedule 4 to this Act;
(*f*) any provision mentioned in Schedule 6A to this Act;
(*g*) paragraph 11(2) of Schedule 5A to the Army Act 1955 and to the Air Force Act 1955 (compensation orders);
(*h*) paragraph 14(1) of that Schedule and paragraph 14(1) of Schedule 4A to the Naval Discipline Act 1957 (recognizance from parents and guardians);
(*i*) (*repealed*)
(*j*) the Table in section 139(4) of the Powers of Criminal Courts (Sentencing) Act 2000;
(*k*) section 8(1)(*b*) of the Armed Forces Act 1976 (maximum fine awarded by Standing Civilian Courts);
(*l*)–(*n*) (*repealed*)
(*o*) section 37(2) of the Criminal Justice Act 1982;
(*p*) section 150(2) and (3) of the Powers of Criminal Courts (Sentencing) Act 2000 (recognizance from parents or guardians);
(*q*) column 5 or 6 of Schedule 4 to the Misuse of Drugs Act 1971 so far as the column in question relates to the offences under provisions of that Act specified in column 1 of that Schedule in respect of which the maximum fines were increased by Part II of Schedule 8 to the Criminal Justice and Public Order Act 1994.

(3) In subsection (1) above "the relevant date" means –

(*a*) the date of the coming into force of section 17 of the Criminal Justice Act 1991 (increase of certain maxima); or
(*b*) where the sums specified in a provision mentioned in subsection (2) above have been substituted by an order under subsection (1) above, the date of that order.

(4), (5) (*repealed*)

(6) An order under subsection (1) above –

(*a*) shall be made by statutory instrument subject to annulment in pursuance of a resolution of either House of Parliament and may be revoked by a subsequent order thereunder; and
(*b*) shall not affect the punishment for an offence committed before that order comes into force.

Amendments—Criminal Justice Act 1982, s 48(1); Criminal Justice Act 1988, s 170(2), Sch 16; CA 1989, s 108(7), Sch 15; Criminal Justice Act 1991, s 100, Sch 11, para 7; Maintenance Enforcement Act 1991, s 11(1), Sch 2, para 9; Criminal Justice and Public Order Act 1994, s 157(6); Powers of Criminal Courts (Sentencing) Act 2000, s 165, Sch 9, para 79.

Rules

144 Rule committee and rules of procedure

(1) The Lord Chancellor may appoint a rule committee for magistrates' courts, and may on the advice of or after consultation with the rule committee make rules for regulating and prescribing the procedure and practice to be followed in magistrates' courts and by justices' clerks and justices' chief executives.

(2) The rule committee shall consist of the Lord Chief Justice, the President of the Family Division of the High Court, the Senior District Judge (Chief Magistrate) and such number of other persons appointed by the Lord Chancellor as he may determine.

(3) Among the members of the committee appointed by the Lord Chancellor there shall be at least –

(*a*) one justices' clerk;

(*b*) one person who has a Supreme Court qualification (within the meaning of section 71 of the Courts and Legal Services Act 1990); and

(*c*) one person who has been granted by an authorised body, under Part II of that Act, the right to conduct litigation in relation to all proceedings in the Supreme Court.

(4) The power to make rules conferred by this section shall be exercisable by statutory instrument which shall be subject to annulment by resolution of either House of Parliament.

(5) In this section the expression "justices' clerk" means a clerk to the justices for a petty sessions area.

Amendments—Courts and Legal Services Act 1990, s 125(3), Sch 18, para 25; Access to Justice Act 1999, s 78, Sch 11, para 29, Sch 13, para 116.

145 Rules: supplementary provisions

(1) The power to make rules conferred by section 144 above shall, without prejudice to the generality of subsection (1) of that section, include power to make provision –

(*a*) as to the practice and procedure of justices in exercising functions preliminary or incidental to proceedings before a magistrates' court;

(*b*) as to the service and execution of process issued by or for the purposes of a magistrates' court, including the service and execution in England and Wales of process issued in other parts of the United Kingdom;

(*c*) as to the keeping of records of proceedings before magistrates' courts and the manner in which things done in the course of, or as preliminary or incidental to, any such proceedings, or any proceedings on appeal from a magistrates' court to the Crown Court, may be proved in any legal proceedings;

(*d*), (*e*) (*repealed*)

(*f*) as to the furnishing by any person having custody of the depositions of copies thereof, and of copies of the information if it is in writing, to a person committed for trial;

(*g*) as to what magistrates' court shall have jurisdiction to hear any complaint;

(*h*) as to the matters additional to those specified in section 53 above on complaint for which a magistrates' court shall have power to make an order with the consent of the defendant without hearing evidence;

(*i*) as to any other matters as to which immediately before the coming into force of section 15 of the Justices of the Peace Act 1949 provision was or could have been made by virtue of the enactments and parts of enactments repealed by Part II of Schedule 7 to the said Act of 1949.

(2) Where any Act expressly confers jurisdiction on any magistrates' court to hear a complaint, rules made under subsection (1)(*g*) above shall not take away that jurisdiction, but may extend it to any other magistrates' court.

(3) Any Act passed before 16th December 1949, in so far as that Act relates to matters about which rules may be made under section 144 above, shall have effect subject to any rules so made and may be amended or repealed by the rules accordingly; but nothing in the said section shall authorise the rules to reduce the number of justices required for any purpose by any Act.

(4) No provision included in rules under section 144 above which dispenses with the need to prove that a summons issued under section 1 above and served in accordance with the rules has come to the knowledge of the accused shall apply to a summons for an indictable offence.

(5) Any rules, directions, forms or other instrument having effect immediately before this subsection comes into force as if contained in rules made under section 15 of the Justices of the Peace Act 1949 by virtue of section 15(8) of that Act (rules etc which previously had effect under the enactments repealed by Part II of Schedule 7 to that Act) shall have effect as if contained in rules made under section 144 above.

Amendments—Courts and Legal Services Act 1990, s 125(3), Sch 18, para 25; Police and Magistrates' Courts Act 1994, ss 91, 93, Sch 8, para 31, Sch 9; Criminal Procedure and Investigations Act 1996, ss 65(3), 80, Sch 5(6).

145A Rules: costs order against legal representative

(1) In any civil proceedings, a magistrates' court may disallow or (as the case may be) order the legal or other representative concerned to meet the whole of any wasted costs or such part of them as may be determined in accordance with rules.

(2) In subsection (1), "wasted costs" means any costs incurred by a party –

(*a*) as a result of any improper, unreasonable or negligent act or omission on the part of any legal or other representative or any employee of such a representative; or

(*b*) which, in the light of any such act or omission occurring after they were incurred, the court considers it is unreasonable to expect that party to pay.

(3) In this section "legal or other representative", in relation to any proceedings, means any person who is exercising a right of audience, or a right to conduct litigation, on behalf of any party to the proceedings.

(4) Rules made by virtue of this section may, in particular, make provision as to the destination of any payment required to be made under the rules (including provision for the reimbursement of sums paid by the Legal Services Commission).

(5) Rules made by virtue of this section –

(*a*) shall require a magistrates' court which proposes to act under the rules against a legal or other representative to allow him a reasonable opportunity to appear before it and show cause why it should not do so,

(*b*) shall provide that action may be taken under the rules either on the application of any party to the proceedings or on the motion of the court;

(*c*) shall provide that no such action shall be taken after the end of the period of six months beginning with the date on which the proceedings are disposed of by the court; and

(*d*) shall provide that a legal or other representative against whom action is taken under the rules may appeal to the Crown Court.

Amendments—Inserted by Courts and Legal Services Act 1990, s 112; amended by Access to Justice Act 1999, s 24, Sch 4, para 19.

****

Interpretation

148 "Magistrates' court"

(1) In this Act the expression "magistrates' court" means any justice or justices of the peace acting under any enactment or by virtue of his or their commission or under the common law.

(2) Except where the contrary is expressed, anything authorised or required by this Act to be done by, to or before the magistrates' court by, to or before which any other thing was done, or is to be done, may be done by, to or before any magistrates' court acting for the same petty sessions area as that court.

149 Isles of Scilly

For the purposes of this Act the Isles of Scilly form part of the county of Cornwall.

150 Interpretation of other terms

(1) In this Act, unless the context otherwise requires, the following expressions have the meaning hereby assigned to them, that is to say –

"Act" includes local Act;

"bail in criminal proceedings" has the same meaning as in the Bail Act 1976;

"commit to custody" means commit to prison or, where any enactment authorises or requires committal to some other place of detention instead of committal to prison, to that other place;

"committal proceedings" means proceedings before a magistrates' court acting as examining justices;

"family proceedings" has the meaning assigned to it by section 65 above;

"enactment" includes an enactment contained in a local Act or in any order, regulation or other instrument having effect by virtue of an Act;

"fine", except for the purposes of any enactment imposing a limit on the amount of any fine, includes any pecuniary penalty or pecuniary forfeiture or pecuniary compensation payable under a conviction;

"impose imprisonment" means pass a sentence of imprisonment or fix a term of imprisonment for failure to pay any sum of money, or for want of sufficient distress to satisfy any sum of money, or for failure to do or abstain from doing anything required to be done or left undone;

"legal representative" means an authorised advocate or authorised litigator, as defined by section 119(1) of the Courts and Legal Services Act 1990;

"magistrates' court maintenance order" means a maintenance order enforceable by a magistrates' court;

"maintenance order" means any order specified in Schedule 8 to the Administration of Justice Act 1970 and includes such an order which has been discharged, if any arrears are recoverable thereunder;

"petty-sessional court-house" means any of the following, that is to say –

(*a*) a court-house or place at which justices are accustomed to assemble for holding special or petty sessions or for the time being appointed as a substitute for such a court-house or place (including, where justices are accustomed to assemble for either special or petty sessions at more than one court-house or place in a petty sessions area, any such court-house or place);

(*b*) a court-house or place at which a District Judge (Magistrates' Courts) is authorised by law to do alone any act authorised to be done by more than one justice of the peace;

"prescribed" means prescribed by the rules;

"the register" means the register of proceedings before a magistrates' court required by the rules to be kept by the clerk of the court;

"the rules" means rules made under section 144 above;

"sentence" does not include a committal in default of payment of any sum of money, or for want of sufficient distress to satisfy any sum of money, or for failure to do or abstain from doing anything required to be done or left undone;

"sum enforceable as a civil debt" means –

(*a*) any sum recoverable summarily as a civil debt which is adjudged to be paid by the order of a magistrates' court;

(*b*) any other sum expressed by this or any other Act to be so enforceable;

"transfer of fine order" has the meaning assigned to it by section 89 above.

(2) Except where the contrary is expressed or implied, anything required or authorised by this Act to be done by justices may, where two or more justices are present, be done by one of them on behalf of the others.

(3) Any reference in this Act to a sum adjudged to be paid by a conviction or order of a magistrates' court shall be construed as including a reference to any costs, damages or compensation adjudged to be paid by the conviction or order of which the amount is ascertained by the conviction or order; but this subsection does not prejudice the definition of "sum adjudged to be paid by a conviction" contained in subsection (8) of section 81 above for the purposes of that section.

(4) Where the age of any person at any time is material for the purposes of any provision of this Act regulating the powers of a magistrates' court, his age at the material time shall be deemed to be or to have been that which appears to the court after considering any available evidence to be or to have been his age at that time.

(5) Except where the context otherwise requires, any reference in this Act to an offence shall be construed as including a reference to an alleged offence; and any reference in this Act to an offence committed, completed or begun anywhere shall be construed as including a reference to an offence alleged to have been committed, completed or begun there.

(6) References in this Act to an offence punishable with imprisonment or punishable on summary conviction with imprisonment shall be construed without

regard to any prohibition or restriction imposed by or under this or any other Act on imprisonment of young offenders.

(7) The provisions of this Act authorising a magistrates' court on conviction of an offender to pass a sentence or make an order instead of dealing with him in any other way shall not be construed as taking away any power to order him to pay costs, damages or compensation.

Amendments—Local Government Act 1985, s 12; Family Law Reform Act 1987, s 33, Sch 2, para 88, Sch 4; CA 1989, s 92(11), Sch 11, para 8; Courts and Legal Services Act 1990, s 125(3), Sch 18, para 25; SI 1996/674; SI 1996/675; Justices of the Peace Act 1997, s 73(2), Sch 5, para 19; Access to Justice Act 1999, ss 76(2), 78, 106, Sch 10, para 36, Sch 11, para 30, Sch 15.

****

SCHEDULE 4

MAXIMUM PERIODS OF IMPRISONMENT IN DEFAULT OF PAYMENT

1 Subject to the following provisions of this Schedule, the periods set out in the second column of the following Table shall be the maximum periods applicable respectively to the amounts set out opposite thereto, being amounts due at the time the imprisonment or detention is imposed.

TABLE

An amount not exceeding £200	7 days
An amount exceeding £200 but not exceeding £500	14 days
An amount exceeding £500 but not exceeding £1,000	28 days
An amount exceeding £1,000 but not exceeding £2,500	45 days
An amount exceeding £2,500 but not exceeding £5,000	3 months
An amount exceeding £5,000 but not exceeding £10,000	6 months
An amount exceeding £10,000	12 months

2 (1) Where the amount due at the time imprisonment or detention is imposed is so much of a sum adjudged to be paid by a summary conviction as remains due after part payment, then, subject to sub-paragraph (2) below, the maximum period applicable to the amount shall be the period applicable to the whole sum reduced by such number of days as bears to the total number of days therein the same proportion as the part paid bears to the whole sum.

(2) In calculating the reduction required under sub-paragraph (1) above any fraction of a day shall be left out of account and the maximum period shall not be reduced to less than 7 days.

3 The maximum period applicable to a sum of any amount enforceable as a civil debt shall be 6 weeks.

Amendments—Criminal Justice Act 1982, s 77, Sch 14, para 59: SI 1984/447; Criminal Justice Act 1988, s 60; Criminal Justice Act 1991, ss 23, 100, Sch 11, para 28.

****

SCHEDULE 6

FEES TO BE TAKEN BY JUSTICES' CHIEF EXECUTIVES

****

	£
...	
Case for the opinion of High Court (s 111 of this Act)	
Drawing case, copies, taking recognizance as required by s 114 of this Act and enlargements and renewals thereof (composite fee), where the application to state a case is made on or after 1 April 1992	382.00
Certificate of refusal of case, where the application is so made	8.00
Certificate	
Every certificate not otherwise charged	8.00
Child Support Act 1991	
Application for a liability order (each child)	0.70

Note: This fee is payable on the making of the application.

Paternity application (each child) (sections 20 and 27 of the Act)	30.00
Appeal against a deduction from earnings order	10.00
Complaint or application and summons	10.00
Warrant of arrest	10.00
Commitment order	40.00

Note: The fee for a commitment order is payable on the making of the order.

...

Copy	
First photocopy or 90 word folio of any document	1.10
Each folio of succeeding 90 words	0.55
Each additional photocopy	0.10

Note: No fee shall be charged in pursuance hereof for a copy of a summons, of an order or of a warrant in a case in which, as hereafter provided, a fee is authorised for the summons, the order or, as the case may be, the warrant and a copy thereof. For the purposes hereof, a reference to a photocopy includes a reference to any other facsimile copy, however made.

Duplicate	
For the duplicate of any document	5.00
Family proceedings	
Applications under Parts I or II of the Children Act 1989, section 30 of the Human Fertilisation and Embryology Act 1990, Part I of the Domestic Proceedings and Magistrates' Courts Act 1978, except under section 16 of that Act for the protection of a spouse or child from violence, the Adoption Act 1976, except under section 21 of that Act, and all applications for financial orders (excluding applications to vary or discharge such orders or in respect of claims for maintenance or maintenance orders made to the benefit of, or against, a person residing outside the United Kingdom)	30.00

Applications under section 31 (care or supervision order), 36 (education supervision order) or 43 (child assessment order) of the Children Act 1989 — 50.00

Applications –
- (*a*) to vary, extend or discharge an order;
- (*b*) for contact or refusal of contact with a child in care, to change a child's surname or remove the child from the jurisdiction; and — 20.00
- (*c*) under section 21 of the Adoption Act 1976

Applications under Part XA (affecting the registration of a child minder or day carer including appeals against cancellation or varying the conditions of the registration) of, and paragraph 8(1) of Schedule 8 (appeals concerning foster parenting) to, the Children Act 1989 — 50.00

Note: When an application requires leave of the court, the relevant fee applies where leave is sought but no further fee may be charged if leave is granted and the application is made.

Licences

For every licence, consent or authority not otherwise provided for, to include registration when necessary — 8.00

Application for the revocation of a licence not otherwise provided for — 30.00

Oaths

Attestation of constable — 8.00

Every oath, affirmation or solemn declaration not otherwise charged (no fee is payable for the swearing in of witnesses in civil proceedings or in any case where an Act of Parliament directs that no fee shall be taken) — 8.00

Other civil proceedings

Complaint or application	3.50
Summons and copy	3.50
Order and copy	16.50
Warrant and copy	6.50

...

Note: 1 Nothing in this Part shall be construed as authorising –

(*a*) the collection of any fee from any person who is receiving services funded by the Legal Services Commission as part of the Community Legal Service or is in receipt of income support or working families' tax credit under sections 124 and 128 of the Social Security Contributions and Benefits Act 1992 or of an income-based jobseeker's allowance (payable under the Jobseekers Act 1995); or

(*b*) where, in family proceedings, a fee is payable, as herebefore provided, in respect of an application for any order, the demand of a fee in respect of any action which may subsequently be taken in relation to the enforcement of the order in question.

...

Amendments—SI 1993/1889; SI 1994/3250; Jobseekers Act 1995, s 41, Sch 2, para 4; Access to Justice Act 1999, s 24, Sch 4, para 20, Sch 13, para 117; Tax Credits Act 1999, s 1(2), Sch 1, paras 1, 6(*a*); Care Standards Act 2000, s 116, Sch 4, para 7.

****

Maintenance Enforcement Act 1991

1 Maintenance orders in the High Court and county courts: means of payment, attachment of earnings and revocation, variation, etc

(1) Where the High Court or a county court makes a qualifying periodical maintenance order, it may at the same time exercise either of its powers under subsection (4) below in relation to the order, whether of its own motion or on an application made under this subsection by an interested party.

(2) For the purposes of this section, a periodical maintenance order is an order –

(*a*) which requires money to be paid periodically by one person ("the debtor") to another ("the creditor"); and
(*b*) which is a maintenance order;

and such an order is a "qualifying periodical maintenance order" if, at the time it is made, the debtor is ordinarily resident in England and Wales.

(3) Where the High Court or a county court has made a qualifying periodical maintenance order, it may at any later time –

(*a*) on an application made under this subsection by an interested party, or
(*b*) of its own motion, in the course of any proceedings concerning the order,

exercise either of its powers under subsection (4) below in relation to the order.

(4) The powers mentioned in subsections (1) and (3) above are –

(*a*) the power to order that payments required to be made by the debtor to the creditor under the qualifying periodical maintenance order in question shall be so made by such a method of payment falling within subsection (5) below as the court may specify in the particular case; or
(*b*) the power, by virtue of this section, to make an attachment of earnings order under the Attachment of Earnings Act 1971 to secure payments under the qualifying periodical maintenance order in question.

(5) The methods of payment mentioned in subsection (4)(*a*) above are –

(*a*) payment by standing order; or
(*b*) payment by any other method which requires the debtor to give his authority for payments of a specific amount to be made from an account of his to an account of the creditor's on specific dates during the period for which the authority is in force and without the need for any further authority from the debtor.

(6) In any case where –

(*a*) the court proposes to exercise its power under paragraph (*a*) of subsection (4) above, and
(*b*) having given the debtor an opportunity of opening an account from which payments under the order may be made in accordance with the method of payment proposed to be ordered under that paragraph, the court is satisfied that the debtor has failed, without reasonable excuse, to open such an account,

the court in exercising its power under that paragraph may order that the debtor open such an account.

(7) Where in the exercise of its powers under subsection (1) or (3) above, the High Court or a county court has made in relation to a qualifying periodical maintenance

order such an order as is mentioned in subsection (4)(*a*) above (a "means of payment order"), it may at any later time –

(*a*) on an application made under this subsection by an interested party, or

(*b*) of its own motion, in the course of any proceedings concerning the qualifying periodical maintenance order,

revoke, suspend, revive or vary the means of payment order.

(8) In deciding whether to exercise any of its powers under this section the court in question having (if practicable) given every interested party an opportunity to make representations shall have regard to any representations made by any such party.

(9) Nothing in this section shall be taken to prejudice –

(*a*) any power under the Attachment of Earnings Act 1971 which would, apart from this section, be exercisable by the High Court or a county court; or

(*b*) any right of any person to make any application under that Act;

and subsection (7) above is without prejudice to any other power of the High Court or a county court to revoke, suspend, revive or vary an order.

(10) For the purposes of this section –

"debtor" and "creditor" shall be construed in accordance with subsection (2) above;

"interested party" means any of the following, that is to say –

(*a*) the debtor;

(*b*) the creditor; and

(*c*) in a case where the person who applied for the qualifying periodical maintenance order in question is a person other than the creditor, that other person;

"maintenance order" means any order specified in Schedule 8 to the Administration of Justice Act 1970 and includes any such order which has been discharged, if any arrears are recoverable under it;

"qualifying periodical maintenance order" shall be construed in accordance with subsection (2) above, and the references to such an order in subsections (3) and (7) above are references to any such order, whether made before or after the coming into force of this section;

and the reference in subsection (2) above to an order requiring money to be paid periodically by one person to another includes a reference to an order requiring a lump sum to be paid by instalments by one person to another.

Defined terms—"creditor", "debtor": s 1(2); "interested party", "maintenance order": s 1(10); "qualifying maintenance order": s 1(2), (10).

"qualifying periodical maintenance order" (s 1(2))—The powers created or extended by this section apply only on making such an order or in relation to such an order already made.

"application ... by an interested party" (s 1(3)(*a*))—The expression "interested party" includes both the person who applied for the qualifying periodical maintenance order and, if different, the person entitled to receive the payments. Thus it would appear that the latter, though not a party, can apply directly and presumably would not need leave to intervene in the main proceedings or cause. The debtor is also an interested party; in the case of a qualifying periodical maintenance order s 1(3)(*a*) seems to enable the debtor to apply for an attachment of earnings order at any time, not only on the maintenance order being made or varied under CCR Ord 27, r 17(4).

"of its own motion" (s 1(3)(*b*))—The court may exercise its powers in the course of any proceedings relating to the qualifying periodical maintenance order. This provision is general so,

PART II

for example, the powers may be exercised not only on an application to vary or discharge but also on an enforcement application or an application by the debtor to suspend a warrant of execution. Since the powers include the power to make an attachment of earnings order, s 1(3) has the effect of extending to such an occasion the powers to require information given by Attachment of Earnings Act 1971, s 14.

"order that payments ... shall be made by such a method" (s 1(4)(*a*))—It would seem that such an order (if served endorsed with a "penal" notice) would be enforceable by committal under RSC Ord 52, r 1 or CCR Ord 29, r 1. However if the essence of the complaint was that the debtor had failed to maintain the payments under the underlying order it appears unlikely that the court would impose a penalty in circumstances where it would not make a committal order on a judgment summons under Debtors Act 1869, s 5.

Methods of payment (s 1(5))—It is perhaps unlikely that banks would accept a direct debit authority in favour of a personal maintenance creditor, but this power might be used where the person entitled to receive the payments had authorised an institution or Government department to collect them on his behalf.

"opportunity to make representations" (s 1(8))—This requirement will be satisfied if the debtor is present at the hearing at which the question is considered or if he has been given notice of the intention to apply for the order. Otherwise, the court must adjourn and cause notice to be given to him that it is minded to make the order.

Lump sums (s 1(10))—Although a lump sum order is a maintenance order, it is not a qualifying periodical maintenance order unless the lump sum has been ordered to be paid by instalments.

Rules and forms—If an attachment of earnings order is sought in the county court the procedure described in CCR Ord 27 should normally be followed. Otherwise an interlocutory summons or notice of application may be used, or the court may permit the application to be made orally if proceedings concerning the maintenance order are already before it.

Maintenance Orders Act 1950

ARRANGEMENT OF SECTIONS

PART I
JURISDICTION

PART II
ENFORCEMENT

PART III
GENERAL

PART I
JURISDICTION

****

4 Contributions under the Children and Young Persons Act 1933, and National Assistance Act 1948

(1) A court of summary jurisdiction in England shall have jurisdiction in proceedings against a person residing in Scotland or Northern Ireland –

(*a*) (*repealed*)
(*b*) for an order under section forty-three of the National Assistance Act 1948 (which provides for the recovery from spouses or parents of sums in respect of assistance given under that Act)
(*c*) for an order under section 18 of the Supplementary Benefits Act 1976 (which provides for the recovery of expenditure on supplementary benefits from persons liable for maintenance)
(*d*) for an order under section 106 of the Social Security Administration Act 1992 (which provides for the recovery of expenditure on income support from such persons).

(2) A court in England by which an order has been made under the said section forty-three or the said section 18 or the said section 106 shall have jurisdiction in proceedings by or against a person residing in Scotland or Northern Ireland for the revocation, revival or variation of that order.

Amendments—Supplementary Benefits Act 1976, s 35(2), Sch 7, para 8; Child Care Act 1980, s 89(3), Sch 6; Social Security Act 1986, s 86(1), Sch 10, para 35; Social Security (Consequential Provisions) Act 1992, s 4, Sch 2, para 3.

"revocation, revival or variation" (s 1(2))—Magistrates' Courts Act 1980, s 60 applies to such proceedings.

****

15 Service of process

(1) Where –

(*a*) proceedings are begun in a court having jurisdiction under or by virtue of the following, namely –
(i) this Part of this Act; or
(ii) sections 24(1) and 30(3) of the Domestic Proceedings and Magistrates' Courts Act 1978;
(iii) section 92 of and Schedule 11 to the Children Act 1989; or

(iv) section 93(2)(*g*) of that Act (including that provision as applied in relation to Northern Ireland by section 116(3) of the Courts and Legal Services Act 1990; or

(v) Article 164 of and Schedule 7 to the Children (Northern Ireland) Order 1995 or Article 165(2)(*g*) of that Order; or

(vi) Article 5(2) of Schedule 4 to the Civil Jurisdiction and Judgments Act 1982; or

(*b*) an action which contains a conclusion for aliment not falling within the scope of paragraph (*a*)(i) above is commenced in a sheriff court in Scotland,

and the person against whom the action or other proceedings is or are brought resides in another part of the United Kingdom, any summons or initial writ addressed to him in the proceedings may, if endorsed in accordance with the provisions of this section in that part of the United Kingdom, be served within that part of the United Kingdom as if it had been issued or authorised to be served, as the case may be, by the endorsing authority.

(2) A summons or writ may be endorsed under this section, in England by a justice of the peace, in Scotland by a sheriff, and in Northern Ireland by a resident magistrate; and the endorsement shall be made in the form numbered 1 in the Second Schedule to this Act, or any form to the like effect.

(3) In any proceedings in which a summons or writ is served under this section, the service may be proved by means of a declaration made in the form numbered 2 in the Second Schedule to this Act, or any form to the like effect, before a justice of the peace, sheriff, or resident magistrate, as the case may be.

(4) Nothing in this section shall be construed as authorising the service of a summons or writ otherwise than personally.

(5) Section four of the Summary Jurisdiction (Process) Act 1881 shall not apply to any process which may be served under this section; and nothing in this section or in any other enactment shall be construed as authorising the execution in one part of the United Kingdom of a warrant for the arrest of a person who fails to appear in answer to any such process issued in another part of the United Kingdom.

Amendments—Children Act 1975, s 108(1), Sch 3, para 10; Administration of Justice Act 1977, s 3, Sch 3, para 11; Domestic Proceedings and Magistrates' Courts Act 1978, s 89(2)(*a*), Sch 2, para 12; Child Care Act 1980, s 89, Sch 5, para 2; SI 1980/564; Civil Jurisdiction and Judgments Act 1982, ss 16(5), 23(2), Sch 12, para 2; Courts and Legal Services Act 1990, s 116, Sch 16, para 34; SI 1995/756.

"declaration" (s 15(3))—For proof of declarations, see s 26.

PART II
ENFORCEMENT

16 Application of Part II

(1) Any order to which this section applies (in this Part of this Act referred to as a maintenance order) made by a court in any part of the United Kingdom may, if registered in accordance with the provisions of this Part of this Act in a court in another part of the United Kingdom, be enforced in accordance with those provisions in that other part of the United Kingdom.

(2) This section applies to the following orders, that is to say –

(*a*) an order for alimony, maintenance or other payments made or deemed to be made by a court in England under any of the following enactments –
  (i) sections 15 to 17, 19 to 22, 30, 34 and 35 of the Matrimonial Causes Act 1965 and sections 22, 23(1), (2) and (4) and 27 of the Matrimonial Causes Act 1973 and section 14 or 17 of the Matrimonial and Family Proceedings Act 1984;
  (ii) Part I of the Domestic Proceedings and Magistrates' Courts Act 1978;
  (iii) Schedule 1 to the Children Act 1989;
  (iv) (*repealed*)
  (v) paragraph 23 of Schedule 2 to the Children Act 1989 or section 43 of the National Assistance Act 1948;
  (vi) section 18 of the Supplementary Benefits Act 1976;
  (vii) (*repealed*)
  (viii) section 106 of the Social Security Administration Act 1992;

(*b*) a decree for payment of aliment granted by a court in Scotland, including –
  (i) an order for the payment of an annual or periodical allowance under section two of the Divorce (Scotland) Act 1938 or an order for the payment of a periodical allowance or a capital sum under section 26 of the Succession (Scotland) Act 1964 or section 5 of the Divorce (Scotland) Act 1976 or an order for financial provision in the form of a monetary payment under s 8 of the Family Law (Scotland) Act 1985;
  (ii) an order for the payment of weekly or periodical sums under subsection (2) of section 3 or subsection (4) of section 5 of the Guardianship of Infants Act 1925;
  (iii) an order for the payment of sums in respect of aliment under subsection (3) of section 1 of the Illegitimate Children (Scotland) Act 1930;
  (iv) a decree for payment of aliment under section 44 of the National Assistance Act 1948, or under section 26 of the Children Act 1948; and
  (v) an order under section 43 of the National Assistance Act 1948;
  (vi) a contribution order under section 80 of, or a decree or an order made under section 81 of, the Social Work (Scotland) Act 1968;
  (vii) an order for the payment of weekly or other periodical sums under subsection (3) of section 11 of the Guardianship Act 1973;
  (viii) an order made on an application under section 18 or section 19(8) of the Supplementary Benefits Act 1976;
  (ix) an order made on an application under section 106 of the Social Security Administration Act 1992;

(*c*) an order for alimony, maintenance or other payments made by a court in Northern Ireland under or by virtue of any of the following enactments: –
  (i) subsection (2) of section 17, subsections (2) to (7) of section 19, subsection (2) of section 20, section 22 or subsection (1) of section 28 of the Matrimonial Causes Act (Northern Ireland) 1939;
  (ii) Schedule 1 to the Children (Northern Ireland) Order 1995;
  (iii) (*repealed*)
  (iv) Article 41 of the Children (Northern Ireland) Order 1995 or Article 101 of the Health and Personal Social Services (Northern Ireland) Order 1972;
  (v) any enactment of the Parliament of Northern Ireland containing provisions corresponding with section 22(1), 34 or 35 of the

Matrimonial Causes Act 1965, with section 22, 23(1), (2) or (4) or 27 of the Matrimonial Causes Act 1973;

(vi) Article 23 or 24 of the Supplementary Benefits (Northern Ireland) Order 1977;

(vii) the Domestic Proceedings (Northern Ireland) Order 1980;

(viii) any enactment applying in Northern Ireland and corresponding to section 106 of the Social Security Administration Act 1992;

(ix) Articles 18 or 21 of the Matrimonial and Family Proceedings (Northern Ireland) Order 1989.

Amendments—Social Work (Scotland) Act 1968, s 95(1), Sch 8, para 34; Guardianship of Minors Act 1971, s 18(1), Sch 1; Guardianship Act 1973, ss 9(3), 14, 15(3), Sch 5, para 4; Matrimonial Causes Act 1973, s 54, Sch 2, para 3(1); Children Act 1975, s 108(1), Sch 3, para 11; Supplementary Benefits Act 1976, s 35(2), Sch 7, para 13; Divorce (Scotland) Act 1976, s 12(1), Sch 1, para 1; Administration of Justice Act 1977, s 3, Sch 3, para 12; SI 1977/2158; Domestic Proceedings and Magistrates' Courts Act 1978, s 89(2), Sch 2, para 13; Child Care Act 1980, s 89, Sch 5, para 3; SI 1980/564; Social Security and Housing Benefit Act 1982, s 48(5), Sch 4, para 2; Civil Jurisdiction and Judgments Act 1982, s 54, Sch 14; Matrimonial and Family Proceedings Act 1984, s 46(1), Sch 1, para 1; Family Law (Scotland) Act 1985, s 28(1), Sch 1, para 3; Social Security Act 1986, Sch 10; Family Law Reform Act 1987, Schs 2 and 4; SI 1989/678; Courts and Legal Services Act 1990, Schs 16 and 20; Social Security (Consequential Provisions) Act 1992, s 4, Sch 2, para 3; SI 1995/756.

17 Procedure for registration of maintenance orders

(1) An application for the registration of a maintenance order under this Part of this Act shall be made in the prescribed manner to the appropriate authority, that is to say –

(*a*) where the maintenance order was made by a court of summary jurisdiction in England, a justice or justices for the same place as the court which made the order;

(*b*) where the maintenance order was made by a court of summary jurisdiction in Northern Ireland, a resident magistrate acting for the same petty sessions district as the court which made the order;

(*c*) in every other case, the prescribed officer of the court which made the order.

(2) If upon application made as aforesaid by or on behalf of the person entitled to payments under a maintenance order it appears that the person liable to make those payments resides in another part of the United Kingdom, and that it is convenient that the order should be enforceable there, the appropriate authority shall cause a certified copy of the order to be sent to the prescribed officer of a court in that part of the United Kingdom in accordance with the provisions of the next following subsection.

(3) The court to whose officer the certified copy of a maintenance order is sent under this section shall be –

(*a*) where the maintenance order was made by a superior court, the Supreme Court of Judicature in England, the Court of Session or the Supreme Court of Judicature of Northern Ireland, as the case may be;

(*b*) in any other case, a court of summary jurisdiction acting for the place in England or Northern Ireland in which the defendant appears to be, or, as the case may be, the sheriff court in Scotland within the jurisdiction of which he appears to be.

(4) Where the prescribed officer of any court receives a certified copy of a maintenance order sent to him under this section, he shall cause the order to be

registered in that court in the prescribed manner, and shall give notice of the registration in the prescribed manner to the prescribed officer of the court which made the order.

(5) The officer to whom any notice is given under the last foregoing subsection shall cause particulars of the notice to be registered in his court in the prescribed manner.

(6) Where the sums payable under a maintenance order, being an order made by a court of summary jurisdiction in England or Northern Ireland, are payable to or through an officer of any court, that officer shall, if the person entitled to the payments so requests, make an application on behalf of that person for the registration of the order under this Part of this Act; but the person at whose request the application is made shall have the same liability for costs properly incurred in or about the application as if the application had been made by him.

(7) An order which is for the time being registered under this Part of this Act in any court shall not be registered thereunder in any other court.

Scope of provision—The registration in magistrates' courts of orders made by the Court of Session or High Court in Northern Ireland which were first registered in the High Court is validated by Administration of Justice Act 1977, Sch 3, para 10.

"maintenance order" (s 17(1))—See s 16(2).

"prescribed manner" (s 17(1))—The manner of application is prescribed, for cases in the High Court or county court, in FPR 1991, rr 7.18–7.21 and, for cases in the magistrates' court, in the Maintenance Orders Act 1950 (Summary Jurisdiction) Rules 1950.

18 Enforcement of registered orders

(1) Subject to the provisions of this section, a maintenance order registered under this Part of this Act in a court in any part of the United Kingdom may be enforced in that part of the United Kingdom in all respects as if it had been made by that court and as if that court had had jurisdiction to make it; and proceedings for or with respect to the enforcement of any such order may be taken accordingly.

(1A) A maintenance order registered under this Part of this Act in a court of summary jurisdiction in England or Northern Ireland shall not carry interest; but where a maintenance order so registered is registered in the High Court under Part I of the Maintenance Orders Act 1958 or section 36 of the Civil Jurisdiction and Judgments Act 1982, this subsection shall not prevent any sum for whose payment the order provides from carrying interest in accordance with section 2A of the said Act of 1958 or section 11A of the Maintenance and Affiliation Orders Act (Northern Ireland) 1966.

(1B) A maintenance order made in Scotland which is registered under this Part of this Act in the Supreme Court in England or Northern Ireland shall, if interest is by the law of Scotland recoverable under the order, carry the like interest in accordance with subsection (1) of this section.

(2) Every maintenance order registered, under this Part of this Act in a magistrates' court in England and Wales shall, subject to the modifications of sections 76 and 93 of the Magistrates' Courts Act 1980 specified in subsections (2ZA) and (2ZB) of this section, be enforceable as a magistrates' court maintenance order within the meaning of section 150(1) of the Magistrates' Courts Act 1980.

(2ZA) Section 76 (enforcement of sums adjudged to be paid) shall have effect as if for subsections (4) to (6) there were substituted the following subsections –

"(4) Where proceedings are brought for the enforcement of a magistrates' court maintenance order under this section, the court may vary the order by exercising one of its powers under subsection (5) below.

(5) The powers of the court are –

(*a*) the power to order that payments under the order be made directly to a justices' chief executive;

(*b*) the power to order that payments under the order be made to a justices' chief executive by such method of payment falling within section 59(6) above (standing order, etc) as may be specified;

(*c*) the power to make an attachment of earnings order under the Attachment of Earnings Act 1971 to secure payments under the order.

(6) In deciding which of the powers under subsection (5) above it is to exercise, the court shall have regard to any representations made by the debtor (within the meaning of section 59 above).

(7) Subsection (4) of section 59 above (power of court to require debtor to open account) shall apply for the purposes of subsection (5) above as it applies for the purposes of that section but as if for paragraph (*a*) there were substituted –

'(*a*) the court proposes to exercise its power under paragraph (b) of section 76(5) below, and'."

(2ZB) In section 93 (complaint for arrears), subsection (6) (court not to impose imprisonment in certain circumstances) shall have effect as if for paragraph (*b*) there were substituted –

"(*b*) if the court is of the opinion that it is appropriate –

(i) to make an attachment of earnings order; or

(ii) to exercise its power under paragraph (*b*) of section 76(5) above."

(2A) Any person under an obligation to make payments under a maintenance order registered under this Part of this Act in a court of summary jurisdiction in England or Northern Ireland shall give notice of any change of address to the proper officer of the court; and any person who without reasonable excuse fails to give such a notice shall be liable on summary conviction to a fine not exceeding level 2 on the standard scale.

(2B) In subsection (2A) of this section "proper officer" means –

(*a*) in relation to a court of summary jurisdiction in England and Wales, the justices' chief executive for the court; and

(*b*) in relation to a court of summary jurisdiction in Northern Ireland, the clerk of the court.

(3) Every maintenance order registered under this Part of this Act in a court of summary jurisdiction in Northern Ireland shall be enforceable as an order made by that court to which Article 98 of the Magistrates' Courts (Northern Ireland) Order 1981 applies, subject to the modifications of that Article specified in subsection (3ZA) of this section.

(3ZA) Article 98 (enforcement of sums adjudged to be paid) shall have effect –

(*a*) as if for paragraph (7)(*a*) there were substituted the following sub-paragraph –

"(*a*) if the court is of the opinion that it is appropriate –
(i) to make an attachment of earnings order; or
(ii) to exercise its power under paragraph (8C)(*b*)";

(*b*) as if for paragraphs (8B) to (8D) there were substituted the following paragraphs –

"(8B) Upon the appearance of a person or proof of service of the summons on him as mentioned in paragraph (4) for the enforcement of an order to which this Article applies, the court or resident magistrate may vary the order by exercising one of the powers under paragraph (8C).

(8C) The powers mentioned in paragraph (8B) are –

(*a*) the power to order that payments under the order be made directly to the collecting officer;

(*b*) the power to order that payments under the order be made to the collecting officer by such method of payment falling within Article 85(7) (standing order, etc) as may be specified;

(*c*) the power to make an attachment of earnings order under Part IX to secure payments under the order.

(8D) In deciding which of the powers under paragraph (8C) is to be exercised, the court or, as the case may be, a resident magistrate shall have regard to any representations made by the debtor (within the meaning of Article 85).

(8E) Paragraph (5) of Article 85 (power of court to require debtor to open account) shall apply for the purposes of paragraph (8C) as it applies for the purposes of that Article but as if for sub-paragraph (*a*) there were substituted –

'(*a*) the court proposes to exercise its power under sub-paragraph (*b*) of Article 98(8C), and'.".

(3A) Notwithstanding subsection (1) above, no court in England in which a maintenance, order is registered under this Part of this Act shall enforce that order to the extent that it is for the time being registered in another court in England under Part I of the Maintenance Orders Act 1958.

(3B) Notwithstanding subsection (1) above, no court in Northern Ireland in which a maintenance order is registered under this Part of this Act shall enforce that order to the extent that it is for the time being registered in another court in Northern Ireland under section 36 of the Civil Jurisdiction and Judgments Act 1982.

(4), (5) (*repealed*)

(6) Except as provided by this section, no proceedings shall be taken for or with respect to the enforcement of a maintenance order which is for the time being registered in any court under this Part of this Act.

Amendments—Ministry of Social Security Act 1966, s 39(3), Sch 8; Administration of Justice Act 1977, s 3, Sch 3, para 6; SI 1981/1675; Civil Jurisdiction and Judgments Act 1982, ss 36(6), 37(1), Sch 11, paras 1, 5, Sch 12, para 1; Matrimonial and Family Proceedings Act 1984, s 46(1), Sch 1, para 2; Family Law Reform Act 1987, Sch 2; SI 1989/678; Maintenance Enforcement Act 1991, s 10, Sch 1, para 3; Statute Law (Repeals) Act 1993; SI 1993/1577; SI 1995/756; Access to Justice Act 1999, s 90, Sch 13, para 13.

Scope of provision—For the duties of the justices' chief executive when a method of payments order is made under s 18(2ZA) see Maintenance Orders Act 1950 (Summary Jurisdiction) Rules 1950, r 9B.

"proceedings ... may be taken" (s 18(1))—In magistrates' courts in England and Northern Ireland, enforcement proceedings may be taken by the court on behalf of the person entitled to payment. In Scotland, the sheriff's court will not act on behalf of the person entitled to payment, and legal representation is therefore advisable.

"standing order, etc" (s 18(2ZA), (3ZA))—The methods of payment which may be required do not include payment by direct debit.

"level 2 on the standard scale" (s 18(2A))—Currently £500 (Criminal Justice Act 1982, s 37(2), as substituted).

19 Functions of collecting officer etc

(1) Where a maintenance order made in England or Northern Ireland by a court of summary jurisdiction is registered in any court under this Part of this Act, any provision of the court by virtue of which sums payable thereunder are required to be paid through or to any officer or person on behalf of the person entitled thereto shall be of no effect so long as the order is so registered.

(2) Where a maintenance order is registered under this Part of this Act in a court of summary jurisdiction in England or Northern Ireland, the court shall order that all payments to be made under the maintenance order (including any arrears accrued before the date of the registration) shall be made through the collecting officer of the court or the collecting officer of some other court of summary jurisdiction in England or Northern Ireland, as the case may be.

(3) An order made under subsection (2) of this section –

- (*a*) by a court of summary jurisdiction in England may be varied or revoked by an exercise of the powers conferred by virtue of section 18(2ZA) or section 22(1A) or (1E) of this Act;
- (*b*) by a court of summary jurisdiction in Northern Ireland may be varied or revoked by an exercise of the powers conferred by virtue of section 18(3ZA) or section 22(1F) or (1J) of this Act.

(4) Where by virtue of the provisions of this section or any order made thereunder payments under a maintenance order cease to be or become payable through or to any officer or person, the person liable to make the payments shall, until he is given the prescribed notice to that effect, be deemed to comply with the maintenance order if he makes payments in accordance with the maintenance order and any order under this section of which he had received such notice.

(5) (*repealed*)

Amendments—SI 1981/1675; Maintenance Enforcement Act 1991, s 10, Sch 1, para 4; SI 1993/1577.

Scope of provision—This section prescribes the duties of court collecting officers in relation to the enforcement of orders registered under the Act. See, however, **"proceedings ... may be taken"** under s 18.

20 Arrears under registered maintenance orders

(1) Where application is made for the registration of a maintenance order under this Part of this Act, the applicant may lodge with the appropriate authority –

- (*a*) if the payments under the order are required to be made to or through an officer of any court, a certificate in the prescribed form, signed by that officer, as to the amount of any arrears due under the order;
- (*b*) in any other case, a statutory declaration or affidavit as to the amount of those arrears;

and if a certified copy of the maintenance order is sent to the prescribed officer of any court in pursuance of the application, the certificate, declaration or affidavit shall also be sent to that officer.

(2) In any proceedings for or with respect to the enforcement of a maintenance order which is for the time being registered in any court under this Part of this Act, a certificate, declaration or affidavit sent under this section to the appropriate officer of that court shall be evidence, and in Scotland sufficient evidence, of the facts stated therein.

(3) Where a maintenance order made by a court in England or Northern Ireland is registered in a court in Scotland, a person shall not be entitled, except with the leave of the last-mentioned court, to enforce, whether by diligence or otherwise, the payment of any arrears accrued and due under the order before the commencement of this Act; and on any application for leave to enforce the payment of any such arrears, the court may refuse leave, or may grant leave subject to such restrictions and conditions (including conditions as to the allowing of time for payment or the making of payment by instalments) as the court thinks proper, or may remit the payment of such arrears or of any part thereof.

"appropriate authority" (s 20(1))—See s 17(1).

"prescribed form" (s 20(1))—See Maintenance Orders Act 1950 (Summary Jurisdiction) Rules 1950, Form 3.

21 Discharge and variation of maintenance orders registered in superior courts

(1) The registration of a maintenance order in a superior court under this Part of this Act shall not confer on that court any power to vary or discharge the order, or affect any jurisdiction of the court in which the order was made to vary or discharge the order.

(2) Where a maintenance order made in Scotland is for the time being –

(*a*) registered under this Part of this Act in a superior court and not registered under Part I of the Maintenance Orders Act 1958 or under section 36 of the Civil Jurisdiction and Judgments Act 1982, or

(*b*) registered in a court in England under that Part of that Act of 1958 by virtue of section 1(2) of that Act of 1958,

(*c*) registered in a court in Northern Ireland under section 36 of the Civil Jurisdiction and Judgments Act 1982,

the person liable to make payments under the order may, upon application made to that court in the prescribed manner, adduce before that court any evidence upon which he would be entitled to rely in any proceedings brought before the court by which the order was made for the variation or discharge of the order.

(3) A court before which evidence is adduced in accordance with the foregoing subsection shall cause a transcript or summary of that evidence, signed by the deponent, to be sent to the prescribed officer of the court by which the order was made; and in any proceedings before the last-mentioned court for the variation or discharge of the order, the transcript or summary shall be evidence of the facts stated therein.

Amendments—Administration of Justice Act 1977, s 3, Sch 3, para 7; Civil Jurisdiction and Judgments Act 1982, s 36(6), Sch 12, Pt III, para 1(3).

"prescribed manner" (s 21(2))—See FPR 1991, rr 7.18–7.21.
"prescribed officer" (s 21(3))—See FPR 1991, r 7.20(4).

22 Discharge and variation of maintenance orders registered in summary or sheriff courts

(1) Where a maintenance order is for the time being registered under this Part of this Act in a court of summary jurisdiction or sheriff court, that court may, upon application made in the prescribed manner by or on behalf of the person liable to make periodical payments under the order or the person entitled to those payments, by order make such variation as the court thinks fit in the rate of the payments under the maintenance order; but no such variation shall impose on the person liable to make payments under the maintenance order a liability to make payments in excess of the maximum rate (if any) authorised by the law for the time being in force in the part of the United Kingdom in which the maintenance order was made.

(1A) The power of a magistrates' court in England and Wales to vary a maintenance order under subsection (1) of this section shall include power, if the court is satisfied that payment has not been made in accordance with the order, to vary the order by exercising one of its powers under subsection (1B) of this section.

(1B) The powers of the court are –

- (*a*) the power to order that payments under the order be made directly to a justices' chief executive;
- (*b*) the power to order that payments under the order be made to a justices' chief executive, by such method of payment falling within section 59(6) of the Magistrates' Courts Act 1980 (standing order etc) as may be specified;
- (*c*) the power to make an attachment of earnings order under the Attachment of Earnings Act 1971 to secure payments under the order.

(1C) In deciding which of the powers under subsection (1B) of this section it is to exercise, the court shall have regard to any representations made by the person liable to make payments under the order.

(1D) Subsection (4) of section 59 of the Magistrates' Courts Act 1980 (power of court to require debtor to open account) shall apply for the purposes of subsection (1B) of this section as it applies for the purposes of that section but as if for paragraph (*a*) there were substituted –

> "(*a*) the court proposes to exercise its power under paragraph (*b*) of section 22(1B) of the Maintenance Orders Act 1950, and".

(1E) Subsections (4) to (11) of section 60 of the Magistrates' Courts Act 1980 (power of clerk and court to vary maintenance order) shall apply in relation to a maintenance order for the time being registered under this Part of this Act in a magistrates' court in England and Wales as they apply in relation to a maintenance order made by a magistrates' court in England and Wales but –

- (*a*) as if in subsection (4) for paragraph (*b*) there were substituted –
  "(*b*) payments under the order are required to be made to a justices' chief executive by any method of payment falling within section 59(6) above (standing order, etc)";
- (*b*) as if in subsection (5) for the words "to the justices' chief executive for the court" there were substituted "in accordance with paragraph (*a*) of section 22(1B) of the Maintenance Orders Act 1950";

(*c*) as if in subsection (7), paragraph (*c*) and the word "and" immediately preceding it were omitted;

(*d*) as if in subsection (8) for the words "paragraphs (*a*) to (*d*) of section 59(3) above" there were substituted "section 22(1B) of the Maintenance Orders Act 1950";

(*e*) as if for subsections (9) and (10) there were substituted the following subsections –

"(9) In deciding which of the powers under section 22(1B) of the Maintenance Orders Act 1950 it is to exercise, the court shall have regard to any representations made by the debtor.

(10) Subsection (4) of section 59 above (power of court to require debtor to open account) shall apply for the purposes of subsection (8) above as it applies for the purposes of that section but as if for paragraph (*a*) there were substituted –

'(*a*) the court proposes to exercise its power under paragraph (*b*) of section 22(1B) of the Maintenance Orders Act 1950, and'."

(1F) The power of a court of summary jurisdiction in Northern Ireland to vary a maintenance order under subsection (1) of this section shall include power, if the court is satisfied that payment has not been made in accordance with the order, to vary the order by exercising one of its powers under subsection (1G) of this section.

(1G) The powers of the court are –

(*a*) the power to order that payments under the order be made directly to the collecting officer;

(*b*) the power to order that payments under the order be made to the collecting officer by such method of payment falling within Article 85(7) of the Magistrates' Courts (Northern Ireland) Order 1981 (standing order, etc) as may be specified;

(*c*) the power to make an attachment of earnings order under Part IX of the Order of 1981 to secure payments under the order;

and in this subsection "collecting officer" means the officer mentioned in Article 85(4) of the Order of 1981.

(1H) In deciding which of the powers under subsection (1G) of this section it is to exercise, the court shall have regard to any representations made by the person liable to make payments under the order.

(1I) Paragraph (5) of Article 85 of the Magistrates' Courts (Northern Ireland) Order 1981 (power of court to require debtor to open account) shall apply for the purposes of subsection (1G) of this section as it applies for the purposes of that Article but as if for sub-paragraph (*a*) there were substituted –

"(*a*) the court proposes to exercise its power under paragraph (*b*) of section 22(1G) of the Maintenance Orders Act 1950, and".

(1J) Paragraphs (4) to (11) of Article 86 of the Magistrates' Courts (Northern Ireland) Order 1981 (power of clerk and court to vary maintenance order) shall apply in relation to a maintenance order for the time being registered under this Part of this Act in a court of summary jurisdiction in Northern Ireland as they apply in relation to a maintenance order made by a court of summary jurisdiction in Northern Ireland but –

(*a*) as if in paragraph (4) for sub-paragraph (*b*) there were substituted –

PART II

"(*b*) payments under the order are required to be made to the collecting officer by any method of payment falling within Article 85(7) (standing order, etc)";

and as if after the words "petty sessions" there were inserted "for the petty sessions district for which the court which made the order acts";

(*b*) as if in paragraph (5) for the words "to the collecting officer" there were substituted "in accordance with paragraph (*a*) of section 22(1G) of the Maintenance Orders Act 1950";

(*c*) as if in paragraph (7), sub-paragraph (*c*) and the word "and" immediately preceding it were omitted;

(*d*) as if in paragraph (8) for the words "sub-paragraphs (*a*) to (*d*) of Article 85(3)" there were substituted "section 22(1G) of the Maintenance Orders Act 1950";

(*e*) as if for paragraphs (9) and (10) there were substituted the following paragraphs –

"(9) In deciding which of the powers under section 22(1G) of the Maintenance Orders Act 1950 it is to exercise, the court shall have regard to any representations made by the debtor.

(10) Paragraph (5) of Article 85 (power of court to require debtor to open account) shall apply for the purposes of paragraph (8) as it applies for the purposes of that Article but as if for sub-paragraph (*a*) there were substituted –

'(*a*) the court proposes to exercise its power under paragraph (*b*) of section 22(1G) of the Maintenance Orders Act 1950, and'.".

(2) For the purposes of subsection (1) of this section, a court in any part of the United Kingdom may take notice of the law in force in any other part of the United Kingdom.

(3) Section 15 of this Act shall apply to the service of process for the purposes of this section as it applies to the service of process in proceedings begun in a court having jurisdiction by virtue of Part I of this Act.

(4) Except as provided by subsection (1) of this section, no variation shall be made in the rate of the payments under a maintenance order which is for the time being registered under this Part of this Act in a court of summary jurisdiction or sheriff court, but without prejudice to any power of the court which made the order to discharge it or vary it otherwise than in respect of the rate of the payments thereunder.

(5) Where a maintenance order is for the time being registered under this Part of this Act in a court of summary jurisdiction or sheriff court –

(*a*) the person entitled to payments under the order or the person liable to make payments under the order may, upon application made in the prescribed manner to the court by which the order was made, or in which the order is registered, as the case may be, adduce in the prescribed manner before the court in which the application is made any evidence on which he would be entitled to rely in proceedings for the variation or discharge of the order;

(*b*) the court in which the application is made shall cause a transcript or summary of that evidence, signed by the deponent, to be sent to the prescribed officer of the court in which the order is registered or of the court by which the order was made, as the case may be; and in any proceedings for the variation or discharge of the order the transcript or summary shall be evidence of the facts stated therein.

Amendments—Domestic Proceedings and Magistrates' Courts Act 1978, s 89(2), Sch 2, para 14; Maintenance Enforcement Act 1991, s 10, Sch 1, para 5; SI 1993/1577; Access to Justice Act 1999, s 90, Sch 13, para 14, Sch 15.

Scope of provision—For the duties of the justices' chief executive when a method of payments order is made under s 22(1A), s 22(1E) or s 22(1F) see Maintenance Orders Act 1950 (Summary Jurisdiction) Rules 1950, r 9B.

"prescribed manner" (s 22(1), (5))—The manner of application is prescribed in Maintenance Orders Act 1950 (Summary Jurisdiction) Rules 1950, rr 8 and 9.

"standing order etc" (s 22(1B), (1E), (1G))—This does not include the power to order payment by direct debit.

23 Notice of variation etc

(1) Where a maintenance order registered under this Part of this Act is discharged or varied by any court, the prescribed officer of that court shall give notice of the discharge or variation in the prescribed manner –

(*a*) to the prescribed officer of any court in which the order is registered; and

(*b*) if the order was made by another court, to the prescribed officer of that court.

(2) Any officer to whom a notice is given under this section shall cause particulars of the notice to be registered in his court in the prescribed manner.

Amendments—Administration of Justice Act 1977, s 3, Sch 3, para 8.

"prescribed manner" (s 23(1))—See FPR 1991, rr 7.19(4), 7.20(4) and Maintenance Orders Act 1950 (Summary Jurisdiction) Rules 1950, rr 4 and 10.

"prescribed officer" (s 23(1)(*a*))—See FPR 1991, r 7.20(4).

24 Cancellation of registration

(1) At any time while a maintenance order is registered under this Part of this Act in any court, an application for the cancellation of the registration may be made in the prescribed manner to the prescribed officer of that court by or on behalf of the person entitled to payments under the order; and upon any such application that officer shall (unless proceedings for the variation of the order are pending in that court), cancel the registration, and thereupon the order shall cease to be registered in that court.

(2) Where, after a maintenance order has been registered under this Part of this Act in a court of summary jurisdiction in England or Northern Ireland or a sheriff court in Scotland, it appears to the appropriate authority (as defined by section seventeen of this Act), upon application made in the prescribed manner by or on behalf of the person liable to make payments under the order, that the person has ceased to reside in England, Northern Ireland or Scotland, as the case may be, the appropriate authority may cause a notice to that effect to be sent to the prescribed officer of any court in which the order is registered; and where such a notice is sent the prescribed officer shall cancel the registration of the maintenance order, and thereupon the order shall cease to be registered in that court.

(3) Where the prescribed officer of any court cancels the registration of a maintenance order under this section, he shall give notice of the cancellation in the prescribed manner –

(*a*) to the prescribed officer of the court by which the order was made; and (*b*) to the prescribed officer of any court in which it is registered under Part I of the Maintenance Orders Act 1958 or section 36 of the Civil Jurisdiction and Judgments Act 1982.

(3A) On receipt of a notice under subsection 3 above –

(*a*) any such officer as is mentioned in paragraph (*a*) of that subsection shall cause particulars of the notice to be registered in his court in the prescribed manner; and

(*b*) any such officer as is mentioned in paragraph (*b*) of that subsection shall cause particulars of the notice to be registered in his court in the prescribed manner and shall cancel the registration of the order.

(4) Except as provided by subsection (5) of this section, the cancellation of the registration of a maintenance order shall not affect anything done in relation to the maintenance order while it was registered.

(5) On the cancellation of the registration of a maintenance order, any order made in relation thereto under subsection (2) of section 19 of this Act shall cease to have effect; but until the person liable to make payments under the maintenance order receives the prescribed notice of the cancellation, he shall be deemed to comply with the maintenance order if he makes payments in accordance with any order under the said subsection (2) which was in force immediately before the cancellation.

(5A) On the cancellation of the registration of a maintenance order registered in a magistrates' court in England and Wales, any order –

(*a*) made in relation thereto by virtue of the powers conferred by section 18(2ZA) or section 22(1A) or (1E) of this Act, and

(*b*) requiring payment to a justices' chief executive (whether or not by any method of payment falling within section 59(6) of the Magistrates' Courts Act 1980),

shall cease to have effect; but until the person liable to make payments under the maintenance order receives the prescribed notice of the cancellation, he shall be deemed to comply with the maintenance order if he makes payments in accordance with any such order which was in force immediately before the cancellation.

(5B) On the cancellation of the registration of a maintenance order registered in a court of summary jurisdiction in Northern Ireland, any order –

(*a*) made in relation thereto by virtue of the powers conferred by section 18(3ZA) or section 22(1F) or (1J) of this Act, and

(*b*) requiring payment to the collecting officer in Northern Ireland (whether or not by any method of payment falling within Article 85(7) of the Magistrates' Court (Northern Ireland) Order 1981),

shall cease to have effect; but until the person liable to make payments under the maintenance order receives the prescribed notice of the cancellation, he shall be deemed to comply with the maintenance order if he makes payments in accordance with any such order which was in force immediately before the cancellation.

(6) Where, by virtue of an order made under subsection (2) of section nineteen of this Act, sums payable under a maintenance order registered in a court of summary jurisdiction in England or Northern Ireland are payable through the collecting officer of any court, that officer shall, if the person entitled to the payments so requests, make an application on behalf of that person for the cancellation of the registration.

Amendments—Administration of Justice Act 1977, s 3, Sch 3, para 9; Civil Jurisdiction and Judgments Act 1982, s 36(6), Sch 12, para 1; Maintenance Enforcement Act 1991, s 10, Sch 1, para 6; SI 1993/1577; Access to Justice Act 1999, s 90, Sch 13, para 15.

"prescribed manner" (s 24(1), (3), (5))—For the High Court and county courts, see FPR 1991, r 7.19; for magistrates' courts, see Maintenance Orders Act 1950 (Summary Jurisdiction) Rules 1950, rr 5, 6, 11 and 12 and Form 4.

25 Rules as to procedure of courts of summary jurisdiction

(1) The power of the Lord Chancellor to make rules under section 144 of the Magistrates' Courts Act 1980 shall include power to make rules for regulating the practice to be followed in courts of summary jurisdiction in England under this Part of this Act.

(2) Rules made under section 23 of the Magistrates' Courts Act (Northern Ireland) 1964 may regulate the practice to be followed in courts of summary jurisdiction in Northern Ireland under this Part of this Act.

(2A) Without prejudice to the generality of the power to make rules under Article 13 of the Magistrates' Courts (Northern Ireland) Order 1981, for the purposes of giving effect to this Part of this Act such rules may make, in relation to any proceedings brought under or by virtue of this Part of this Act, any provision not covered by subsection (2) above which –

- (*a*) falls within paragraph (2) of Article 165 of the Children (Northern Ireland) Order 1995, and
- (*b*) may be made in relation to relevant proceedings under that Article.

(3) Rules made for the purposes of this Part of this Act may require that any order or other matter required under this Part of this Act to be registered in a court of summary jurisdiction in England or Northern Ireland shall be registered –

- (*a*) in England, by means of a memorandum entered and signed by the prescribed officer of the court in the register kept pursuant to section 22 of the Summary Jurisdiction Act 1879;
- (*b*) in Northern Ireland, by means of an entry made and signed by the prescribed officer of the court in the order book kept pursuant to magistrates' courts rules made under section 23(4) of the Magistrates' Courts Act (Northern Ireland) 1964.

Amendments—SI 1977/2158; Judicature (Northern Ireland) Act 1978, s 122(1), Sch 5, Pt II; Magistrates' Courts Act 1980, s 154, Sch 7, para 8; SI 1995/756.

Duty to keep the register—The register is now kept in pursuance of a duty imposed by Magistrates' Courts Rules 1981, r 66.

PART III
GENERAL

26 Proof of declarations etc

(1) Any document purporting to be a declaration made under section 15 of this Act, or to be a certified copy, statutory declaration, affidavit, certificate, transcript or summary made for the purposes of this Act or of any rules made thereunder shall, unless the contrary is shown, be deemed without further proof to be the document which it purports to be, and to have been duly certified, made or signed

by or before the person or persons by or before whom it purports to have been certified, made or signed.

(2) Paragraph 7 of the Second Schedule to the Emergency Laws (Miscellaneous Provisions) Act 1947 (which relates to the proof of affiliation orders and maintenance orders and of orders for the discharge or variation of such orders), shall apply to the registration of orders under Part II of this Act, and to the cancellation of such registration, as it applies to the variation of orders; and for the purposes of that paragraph –

(*a*) a maintenance order registered under the said Part II in a court of summary jurisdiction; and

(*b*) any proceedings under the said Part II relating to a maintenance order made by or registered in such a court, being a proceeding of which a memorandum is required to be entered in the register kept by the clerk of that court pursuant to section 22 of the Summary Jurisdiction Act 1879,

shall be deemed to be an order made by that court.

****

Maintenance Orders Act 1958

ARRANGEMENT OF SECTIONS

PART I
REGISTRATION, ENFORCEMENT AND VARIATION OF CERTAIN MAINTENANCE ORDERS

PART III
MISCELLANEOUS AND SUPPLEMENTAL

Miscellaneous

Supplemental

PART I
REGISTRATION, ENFORCEMENT AND VARIATION OF CERTAIN MAINTENANCE ORDERS

1 Application of Part I

(1) The provisions of this Part of this Act shall have effect for the purpose of enabling maintenance orders to which this Part of this Act applies to be registered –

(*a*) in the case of an order made by the High Court or a county court, in a magistrates' court; and

(*b*) in the case of an order made by a magistrates' court, in the High Court,

and, subject to those provisions, while so registered –

(i) to be enforced in like manner as an order made by the court of registration; and

(ii) in the case of an order registered in a magistrates' court, to be varied by a magistrates' court.

(1A) In the following provisions of this Act "maintenance order" means any order specified in Schedule 8 to the Administration of Justice Act 1970.

(2) For the purposes of subsection (1) above, a maintenance order made by a court in Scotland or Northern Ireland and registered in England under Part II of the Maintenance Orders Act 1950 shall be deemed to have been made by the court in England in which it is so registered.

(2A) This Part of this Act applies –

(*a*) to maintenance orders made by the High Court or a county court or a magistrates' court, other than orders registered in Scotland or Northern Ireland under Part II of the Maintenance Orders Act 1950, and

(*b*) to maintenance orders made by a court in Scotland or Northern Ireland and registered in England under Part II of the Maintenance Orders Act 1950.

(3) Without prejudice to the provisions of section 21 of this Act, in this Part of this Act, unless the context otherwise requires, the following expressions have the following meanings –

"High court order", "county court order" and "magistrates' court order" mean an order made by the High Court, a county court or a magistrates' court, as the case may be;

"order" means a maintenance order to which this Part of this Act applies;

"original court" and "court of registration", in relation to an order mean the court by which the order was made or, as the case may be, the court in which the order is registered;

"registered" means registered in accordance with the provisions of this Part of this Act, and "registration" shall be construed accordingly;

and for the purposes of this Part of this Act an order for the payment by the defendant of any costs incurred in proceedings relating to a maintenance order, being an order for the payment of costs made while the maintenance order is not registered, shall be deemed to form part of that maintenance order.

(4) For the purposes of this section a maintenance order which is registered in a magistrates' court under Part I of the Maintenance Orders (Reciprocal Enforce-ment) Act 1972 or Part I of the Civil Jurisdiction and Judgments Act 1982 or Council Regulation (EC) No 44/2001 of 22 December 2000 on jurisdiction and

the recognition and enforcement of judgments in civil and commercial matters shall be deemed to be a maintenance order made by that court.

Amendments—Administration of Justice Act 1970, s 27(3); Maintenance Orders (Reciprocal Enforcement) Act 1972, s 22(1), Sch, para 4; Administration of Justice Act 1977, s 3, Sch 3, para 1; Civil Jurisdiction and Judgments Act 1982, s 15(4), Sch 12, para 3; SI 2001/3929.

Defined terms—"costs": s 21(4); "defendant", "England": s 21(1).

2 Registration of orders

(1) A person entitled to receive payments under a High Court or county court order may apply for the registration of the order to the original court, and the court may, if it thinks fit, grant the application.

(2) Where an application for the registration of such an order is granted –

(*a*) no proceedings shall be begun, and no writ, warrant or other process shall be issued, for the enforcement of the order before the registration of the order or the expiration of the prescribed period from the grant of the application, whichever first occurs; and

(*b*) the original court shall, on being satisfied within the period aforesaid by the person who made the application that no such proceedings or process begun or issued before the grant of the application remain pending or in force, cause a certified copy of the order to be sent to the justices' chief executive for the magistrates' court acting for the petty sessions area in which the defendant appears to be;

but if at the expiration of the period aforesaid the original court has not been so satisfied, the grant of the application shall become void.

(3) A person entitled to receive payments under a magistrates' court order who considers that the order could be more effectively enforced if it were registered may apply for the registration of the order to the original court, and the court may, if it thinks fit, grant the application.

(3A) Without prejudice to subsection (3) of this section, where a magistrates' court order provides both for the payment of a lump sum and for the making of periodical payments, a person entitled to receive a lump sum under the order who considers that, so far as it relates to that sum, the order could be more effectively enforced if it were registered may apply to the original court for the registration of the order so far as it so relates, and the court may, if it thinks fit, grant the application.

(3B) Where an application under subsection (3A) of this section is granted in the case of a magistrates' court order, the provisions of this Part of this Act shall have effect in relation to that order as if so far as it relates to the payment of a lump sum it were a separate order.

(4) Where an application for the registration of a magistrates' court order is granted –

(*a*) no proceedings for the enforcement of the order shall be begun before the registration takes place and no warrant or other process for the enforcement thereof shall be issued in consequence of any such proceedings begun before the grant of the application; and

(*b*) (*repealed*)

(*c*) the original court shall, on being satisfied in the prescribed manner that no process for the enforcement of the order issued before the grant of the application remains in force, cause a certified copy of the order to be sent to the prescribed officer of the High Court.

(5) The officer of, or justices' chief executive for, a court who receives a certified copy of an order sent to him under this section shall cause the order to be registered in that court.

(6) Where a magistrates' court order is registered under this Part of this Act in the High Court, then –

(*a*) if payments under the magistrates' court order are required to be made (otherwise than to a justices' chief executive) by any method of payment falling within section 59(6) of the Magistrates' Courts Act 1980 (standing order, etc), any order requiring payment by that method shall continue to have effect after registration;

(*b*) any order by virtue of which sums payable under the magistrates' court order are required to be paid to a justices' chief executive (whether or not by any method of payment falling within section 59(6) of that Act) on behalf of the person entitled thereto shall cease to have effect.

(6ZA) Where a High Court or county court order is registered under this Part of this Act in a magistrates' court, then –

(*a*) if a means of payment order (within the meaning of section 1(7) of the Maintenance Enforcement Act 1991) has effect in relation to the order in question, it shall continue to have effect after registration; and

(*b*) in any other case, the magistrates' court shall order that all payments to be made under the order in question (including any arrears accrued before registration) shall be made to a justices' chief executive.

(6ZB) Any such order as to payment –

(*a*) as is referred to in paragraph (*a*) of subsection (6) of this section may be revoked, suspended, revived or varied by an exercise of the powers conferred by section 4A of this Act; and

(*b*) as is referred to in paragraph (*a*) or (*b*) of subsection (6ZA) of this section may be varied or revoked by an exercise of the powers conferred by section 3(2A) or (2B) or section 4(2A), (5A) or (5B) of this Act.

(6ZC) Where by virtue of the provisions of this section or any order under subsection (6ZA)(*b*) of this section payments under an order cease to be or become payable to a justices' chief executive, the person liable to make the payments shall, until he is given the prescribed notice to that effect, be deemed to comply with the order if he makes payments in accordance with the order and any order under subsection (6ZA)(*b*) of this section of which he has received such notice.

(6A) In this section –

"High Court order" includes a maintenance order deemed to be made by the High Court by virtue of section 1(2) above, and

"magistrates' court order" includes a maintenance order deemed to be made by a magistrates' court by virtue of that subsection.

(7) In this section "certified copy" in relation to an order of a court means a copy certified by the proper officer of the court to be a true copy of the order or of the official record thereof.

Amendments—Administration of Justice Act 1977, s 3, Sch 3, para 2; Civil Jurisdiction and Judgments Act 1982, s 37(1), Sch 11, para 2; Maintenance Enforcement Act 1991, s 10, Sch 1, para 7; Access to Justice Act 1999, s 90, Sch 13, para 26, Sch 15.

Defined terms—"certified copy": s 2(7); "county court order": s 1(3); "defendant": s 21(1); "High Court order": s 1(3); "magistrates' court": s 21(1); "magistrates' court order", "original court": s 1(3); "person entitled to receive payments": s 21(2); "petty sessions area": s 21(1); "registered": s 1(3).

Scope of provision—For the duties of the justices' chief executive when a means of payment order is made, see Magistrates' Courts (Maintenance Orders Act 1958) Rules 1959, r 5A.

"the court may" (s 2(1))—The registration of nominal or interim orders is discouraged (*Practice Direction of 10 March 1980*).

"The officer or clerk ... shall" (s 2(5))—If the original court has granted the application, the recipient court cannot decline to effect the registration.

"prescribed period" (s 2(2))—The prescribed period is 14 days (FPR 1991, r 7.23(2)).

"person entitled to receive payments" (s 2(3))—Although this expression includes a court collecting officer, he or she is prevented from applying for registration except in accordance with the provisions of s 20.

"prescribed officer of the High Court" (s 2(4))—At the principal registry or such district registry as may be specified by the applicant (Magistrates' Courts (Maintenance Orders Act 1958) Rules 1959, rr 3, 25).

"standing order, etc" (s 2(6)(*a*))—This does not include payment by direct debit.

2A Interest on sums recoverable under certain orders registered in the High Court

(1) Where, in connection with an application under section 2(3) of this Act for the registration of a magistrates' court order, the applicant shows in accordance with rules of court –

(*a*) that the order, though deemed for the purposes of section 1 of this Act to have been made by a magistrates' court in England, was in fact made in another part of the United Kingdom or in a country or territory outside the United Kingdom, and

(*b*) that, as regards any sum for whose payment the order provides, interest on that sum at a particular rate is, by the law of that part or of that country or territory, recoverable under the order from a particular date or time,

then, if the original court grants the application and causes a certified copy of the order to be sent to the prescribed officer of the High Court under section 2(4)(*c*) of this Act, it shall also cause to be sent to him a certificate in the prescribed form showing, as regards that sum, the rate of interest so recoverable and the date or time from which it is so recoverable.

(2) The officer of the court who receives a certificate sent to him under the preceding subsection shall cause the certificate to be registered in that court together with the order to which it relates.

(3) Where an order is registered together with a certificate under this section, then, subject to any provision made under the next following subsection, sums payable under the order shall carry interest at the rate specified in the certificate from the date or time so specified.

(4) Provision may be made by rules of court as to the manner in which and the periods by reference to which any interest payable by virtue of subsection (3) is to be calculated and paid, including provision for such interest to cease to accrue as from a prescribed date.

(5) Except as provided by this section sums payable under registered orders shall not carry interest.

Amendments—Inserted by Civil Jurisdiction and Judgments Act 1982, s 37(1), Sch 11, para 6.

Defined terms—"certified copy": s 2(7); "magistrates' court": s 21(1); "magistrates' court order", "registered": s 1(3).

"rules of court"—Magistrates' Courts (Maintenance Orders Act 1958) Rules 1959, r 2A.

3 Enforcement of registered orders

(1) Subject to the provisions of section 2A of this Act and this section, a registered order shall be enforceable in all respects as it if had been made by the court of registration and as if that court had had jurisdiction to make it; and proceedings for or with respect to the enforcement of a registered order may be taken accordingly.

(2) Subject to the provisions of subsections (2A) to (3) of this section, an order registered in a magistrates' court shall be enforceable as a magistrates' court maintenance order within the meaning of section 150(1) of the Magistrates' Courts Act 1980.

(2A) Where an order registered in a magistrates' court is an order other than one deemed to be made by the High Court by virtue of section 1(2) of this Act, section 76 of the Magistrates' Courts Act 1980 (enforcement of sums adjudged to be paid) shall have effect as if for subsections (4) to (6) there were substituted the following subsections –

"(4) Where proceedings are brought for the enforcement of a magistrates' court maintenance order under this section, the court may vary the order by exercising one of its powers under paragraphs (*a*) to (*d*) of section 59(3) above.

(5) In deciding which of the powers under paragraphs (*a*) to (*d*) of section 59(3) above it is to exercise, the court shall have regard to any representations made by the debtor and the creditor (which expressions have the same meaning as they have in section 59 above).

(6) Subsection (4) of section 59 above shall apply for the purposes of subsection (4) above as it applies for the purposes of that section."

(2B) Where an order registered in a magistrates' court is an order deemed to be made by the High Court by virtue of section 1(2) of this Act, sections 76 and 93 of the Magistrates' Courts Act 1980 (enforcement of sums adjudged to be paid and complaint for arrears) shall have effect subject to the modifications specified in subsections (2ZA) and (2ZB) of section 18 of the Maintenance Orders Act 1950 (enforcement of registered orders).

(3) Where an order remains or becomes registered after the discharge of the order, no proceedings shall be taken by virtue of that registration except in respect of arrears which were due under the order at the time of the discharge and have not been remitted.

(3A) Any person under an obligation to make payments under an order registered in a magistrates' court shall give notice of any change of address to the justices' chief executive for the court; and any person who without reasonable excuse fails to give such a notice shall be liable on summary conviction to a fine not exceeding level 2 on the standard scale.

(4) Except as provided by this section, no proceedings shall be taken for or with respect to the enforcement of a registered order.

Amendments—Civil Jurisdiction and Judgments Act 1982, Sch 11; Matrimonial and Family Proceedings Act 1984, Sch 1; Family Law Reform Act 1987, Sch 2; Maintenance Enforcement Act 1991, s 10, Sch 1, para 8; Statute Law (Repeals) Act 1993; Access to Justice Act 1999, s 90, Sch 13, para 27.

Defined terms—"court of registration": s 1(3); "magistrates' court": s 21(1); "registered": s 1(3).

"paragraphs (a) to (d) of section 59(3)" (s 3(2A))— Section 59(3) of the Magistrates' Courts Act 1980 permits orders for payments direct between the parties, through a clerk of a magistrates' court, by standing order (or similar method but not by direct debit) or by attachment of earnings.

"subsection (2ZA)" (s 3(2B))—This permits the full range of means of payments orders to be used on enforcement of an order.

"subsection (2ZB)" (s 3(2B))—This prevents the use of imprisonment for enforcement of an order if the court is of opinion that an attachment of earnings order or an order for payment by standing order is appropriate. For the duties of the justices' chief executive when a means of payment order is made, see Magistrates' Court (Maintenance Orders Act 1958) Rules 1959, r 5A.

"shall be enforceable" (s 3(1))—For enforcement, see Magistrates' Courts Act 1980, ss 76 and 93.

"level 2 on the standard scale" (s 3(3A))—Currently £500 (Criminal Justice Act 1982, s 37(2), as substituted).

4 Variation of orders registered in magistrates' courts

(1) The provisions of this section shall have effect with respect to the variation of orders registered in magistrates' courts, and references in this section to registered orders shall be construed accordingly.

(2) Subject to the following provisions of this section –

(*a*) the court of registration may exercise the same jurisdiction to vary any rate of payments specified by a registered order (other than jurisdiction in a case where a party to the order is not present in England when the application for variation is made) as is exercisable, apart from this subsection, by the original court; and

(*b*) a rate of payments specified by a registered order shall not be varied except by the court of registration or any other magistrates' court to which the jurisdiction conferred by the foregoing paragraph is extended by rules of court.

(2A) The power of a magistrates' court to vary a registered order under subsection (2) of this section shall include power, if the court is satisfied that payment has not been made in accordance with the order, to vary the order by exercising one of its powers under paragraphs (*a*) to (*d*) of section 59(3) of the Magistrates' Courts Act 1980.

(2B) Subsection (4) of section 59 of that Act shall apply for the purposes of subsection (2A) of this section as it applies for the purposes of that section.

(2C) In deciding which of the powers under paragraphs (*a*) to (*d*) of section 59(3) of that Act it is to exercise, the court shall have regard to any representations made by the debtor and the creditor (which expressions have the same meaning as they have in section 59 of that Act).

(3) (*repealed*)

(4) If it appears to the court to which an application is made by virtue of subsection (2) of this section for the variation of a rate of payments specified by a registered order that it is for any reason appropriate to remit the application to the original court, the first-mentioned court shall so remit the application, and the original court shall thereupon deal with the application as if the order were not registered.

(5) Nothing in subsection (2) of this section shall affect the jurisdiction of the original court to vary a rate of payments specified by a registered order if an application for the variation of that rate is made to that court –

(*a*) in proceedings for a variation of provisions of the order which do not specify a rate of payments; or
(*b*) at a time when a party to the order is not present in England.

(5A) Subject to the following provisions of this section, subsections (4) to (11) of section 60 of the Magistrates' Courts Act 1980 (power of clerk and court to vary maintenance orders) shall apply in relation to a registered order (other than one deemed to be made by the High Court by virtue of section 1(2) of this Act) as they apply in relation to a maintenance order made by a magistrates' court (disregarding section 23(2) of the Domestic Proceedings and Magistrates' Courts Act 1978 and section 15(2) of the Children Act 1989) but –

(*a*) as if in subsection (8) after the words "the court which may" there were inserted "subject to subsection (10) below"; and
(*b*) as if for subsections (9) and (10) there were substituted the following subsections –

"(9) Subsection (4) of section 59 above shall apply for the purposes of subsection (8) above as it applies for the purposes of that section.

(10) In deciding which of the powers under paragraphs (*a*) to (*d*) of section 59(3) above it is to exercise, the court shall have regard to any representations made by the debtor and the creditor."

(5B) Subject to the following provisions of this section, subsections (4) to (11) of section 60 of the Magistrates' Courts Act 1980 (power of clerk and court to vary maintenance orders) shall apply in relation to a registered order deemed to be made by the High Court by virtue of section 1(2) of this Act as they apply in relation to a maintenance order made by a magistrates' court (disregarding section 23(2) of the Domestic Proceedings and Magistrates' Courts Act 1978 and section 15(2) of the Children Act 1989) but –

(*a*) as if in subsection (4) for paragraph (*b*) there were substituted –
"(*b*) payments under the order are required to be made to a justices' chief executive, by any method of payment falling within section 59(6) above (standing order, etc)";
(*b*) as if in subsection (5) for the words "to the justices' chief executive for the court" there were substituted "in accordance with paragraph (*a*) of subsection (9) below";
(*c*) as if in subsection (7), paragraph (*c*) and the word "and" immediately preceding it were omitted;
(*d*) as if in subsection (8) for the words "paragraphs (*a*) to (d) of section 59(3) above" there were substituted "subsection (9) below";
(*e*) as if for subsections (9) and (10) there were substituted the following subsections –

"(9) The powers of the court are –

(*a*) the power to order that payments under the order be made directly to a justices' chief executive;

(*b*) the power to order that payments under the order be made to a justices' chief executive, by such method of payment falling within section 59(6) above (standing order, etc) as may be specified;

(*c*) the power to make an attachment of earnings order under the Attachment of Earnings Act 1971 to secure payments under the order.

(10) In deciding which of the powers under subsection (9) above it is to exercise, the court shall have regard to any representations made by the debtor.

(10A) Subsection (4) of section 59 above (power of court to require debtor to open account) shall apply for the purposes of subsection (9) above as it applies for the purposes of that section but as if for paragraph (*a*) there were substituted –

'(*a*) the court proposes to exercise its powers under paragraph (*b*) of section 60(9) below'."

(6) No application for any variation of a registered order shall be made to any court while proceedings for any variation of the order are pending in any other court.

(6A) Except as provided by subsection (5B) of this section no application for any variation in respect of a registered order shall be made to any court in respect of an order made by the Court of Session or the High Court in Northern Ireland and registered in that court in accordance with the provisions of this Part of this Act by virtue of section 1(2) above.

(6B) No application for any variation of a registered order shall be made to any court in respect of an order for periodical or other payments made under Part III of the Matrimonial and Family Proceedings Act 1984.

(7) Where a magistrates' court, in exercise of the jurisdiction conferred by subsection (2) of this section, varies or refuses to vary a registered order, an appeal from the variation or refusal shall lie to the High Court.

Amendments—Administration of Justice Act 1970, s 48, Sch 11; Administration of Justice Act 1977, ss 3, 32, Schs 3, 5; Matrimonial and Family Proceedings Act 1984, s 46(1), Sch 1, para 5; Maintenance Enforcement Act 1991, s 10, Sch 1, para 9; Access to Justice Act 1999, s 90, Sch 13, para 28, Sch 15.

Defined terms—"court of registration": s 1(3); "England", "magistrates' court": s 21(1); "original court", "registered": s 1(3).

Scope of provision—This section provides for the variation of the rate of payment under registered orders. The section does not allow the revocation or revival of registered orders, or the extension (after expiry) of a child periodical payments order where the child remains dependent. The section also allows the making of a means of payment order if satisfied that payment has not been made in accordance with the order. See FPR 1991, r 7.27 and Magistrates' Courts (Maintenance Orders Act 1958) Rules 1959, r 7.

Variation—In exercising the power of variation, the court must apply the same principles as the court which made the original order (*Miller v Miller* [1961] P 1, [1960] 3 WLR 658). Where the application is made a short time after the original order and there is no change of circumstances, the court should refuse the application (*Bromiley v Bromiley* [1987] 2 FLR 207). The variation of the order may be backdated to the date of complaint (*Moon v Moon* (1980) FLR 115). The prohibition on variation in s 4(2) is subject to the exceptions contained in s 4(5).

"section 59(3)" (s 4(2A))—The court may exercise its power under Magistrates' Courts Act 1980, s 59(3) to make a means of payment order. There is no power to order payment by direct debit.

Remittal of the application (s 4(4))—For the principles upon which the power to remit should be exercised see *Gsell v Gsell* [1971] 1 WLR 225, [1971] 1 All ER 559. The matters to be taken into account include the length of the case, the consideration of a large number of documents or the need to exercise one of the special powers of the High Court (eg the power to order discovery).

Appeals (s 4(7))—Appeal lies to the Family Division (FPR 1991, r 7.28). An appeal against a decision on the remission of arrears, however, must be made by way of case stated under Magistrates' Courts Act 1980, s 111 (*Berry v Berry* [1987] Fam 1, [1987] 1 FLR 105).

4A Variation etc of orders registered in the High Court

(1) The provisions of this section shall have effect with respect to orders registered in the High Court other than maintenance orders deemed to be made by a magistrates' court by virtue of section 1(4) of this Act, and the reference in subsection (2) of this section to a registered order shall be construed accordingly.

(2) The High Court may exercise the same powers in relation to a registered order as are exercisable by the High Court under section 1 of the Maintenance Enforcement Act 1991 in relation to a qualifying periodical maintenance order (within the meaning of that section) which has been made by the High Court, including the power under subsection (7) of that section to revoke, suspend, revive or vary –

(*a*) any such order as is referred to in paragraph (*a*) of section 2(6) of this Act which continues to have effect by virtue of that paragraph; and
(*b*) any means of payment order (within the meaning of section 1(7) of that Act of 1991) made by virtue of the provisions of this section.

Amendments—Inserted by Maintenance Enforcement Act 1991, s 10, Sch 1, para 10.

Defined terms—"magistrates' court": s 21(1); "registered": s 1(3).

5 Cancellation of registration

(1) If a person entitled to receive payments under a registered order desires the registration to be cancelled, he may give notice under this section.

(2) Where the original court varies or discharges an order registered in a magistrates' court, the original court may, if it thinks fit, give notice under this section.

(3) Where the original court discharges an order registered in the High Court and it appears to the original court whether by reason of the remission of arrears by that court or otherwise, that no arrears under the order remain to be recovered, the original court shall give notice under this section.

(4) Notice under this section shall be given to the court of registration; and where such notice is given –

(*a*) no proceedings for the enforcement of the registered order shall be begun before the cancellation of the registration and no writ, warrant or other process for the enforcement thereof shall be issued in consequence of any such proceedings begun before the giving of the notice; and
(*b*) (*repealed*)
(*c*) the court of registration shall cancel the registration on being satisfied in the prescribed manner –
  (i) that no process for the enforcement of the registered order issued before the giving of the notice remains in force; and

(ii) in the case of an order registered in a magistrates' court, that no proceedings for the variation of the order are pending in a magistrates' court.

(4A) For the purposes of a notice under subsection (2) or (3) above –

"court of registration" includes any court in which an order is registered under Part II of the Maintenance Orders Act 1950, and

"registration" includes registration under that Act.

(5) On the cancellation of the registration of a High Court or county court order –

(*a*) any order which requires payments under the order in question to be made (otherwise than to a justices' chief executive) by any method of payment falling within section 59(6) of the Magistrates' Courts Act 1980 or section 1(5) of the Maintenance Enforcement Act 1991 (standing order, etc) shall continue to have effect; and

(*b*) any order made under section 2(6ZA)(*b*) of this Act or by virtue of the powers conferred by section 3(2A) or (2B) or section 4(2A), (5A) or (5B) of this Act and which requires payments under the order in question to be made to a justices' chief executive (whether or not by any method of payment falling within section 59(6) of the Magistrates' Courts Act 1980) shall cease to have effect;

but, in a case falling within paragraph (*b*) of this subsection, until the defendant receives the prescribed notice of the cancellation he shall be deemed to comply with the High Court or county court order if he makes payment in accordance with any such order as is referred to in paragraph (*b*) of this subsection which was in force immediately before the cancellation and of which he has notice.

(6) On the cancellation of the registration of a magistrates' court order –

(*a*) any order which requires payments under the magistrates' court order to be made by any method of payment falling within section 59(6) of the Magistrates' Courts Act 1980 or section 1(5) of the Maintenance Enforcement Act 1991 (standing order, etc) shall continue to have effect; and

(*b*) in any other case, payments shall become payable to the justices' chief executive for the original court;

but, in a case falling within paragraph (*b*) of this subsection, until the defendant receives the prescribed notice of the cancellation he shall be deemed to comply with the magistrates' court order if he makes payments in accordance with any order which was in force immediately before the cancellation and of which he has notice.

(7) In subsection (5) and (6) of this section "High Court order" and "magistrates' court order" shall be construed in accordance with section 2(6A) of this Act.

Amendments—Administration of Justice Act 1977, s 3, Sch 3, para 4; Maintenance Enforcement Act 1991, s 10, Sch 1, para 11; Access to Justice Act 1999, s 90, Sch 13, para 29, Sch 15.

Defined terms—"court of registration": ss 1(3), 5(4A); "defendant", "magistrates' court", "original court": s 21(1); "person entitled to receive payments": s 21(2).

Scope of provision—This section enables the person entitled to receive the payments or the original court to cancel the registration; and sets out the procedure for and the consequences of cancellation, see FPR 1991, r 7.29. For notices to be given on cancellation, see Magistrates' Courts (Maintenance Orders Act 1958) Rules 1959, r 7.

"person entitled to receive payments" (s 5(1))—The court collecting officer is included within this description, but the officer's power to give notice is restricted by s 20(1).

"prescribed notice" (s 5(5))—See Magistrates' Courts (Maintenance Orders Act 1958) Rules 1959, r 2.

****

PART III
MISCELLANEOUS AND SUPPLEMENTAL

Miscellaneous

17 Prohibition of committal more than once in respect of same arrears

Where a defendant has been imprisoned or otherwise detained under an order or warrant of commitment issued in respect of his failure to pay a sum due under a maintenance order, then, notwithstanding anything in this Act, no such order or warrant (other than a warrant of which the issue has been postponed under paragraph (ii) of subsection (5) of the next following section) shall thereafter be issued in respect of that sum or any part thereof.

Defined terms—"defendant": s 21(1).

18 Power of magistrates to review committals etc

(1) Where, for the purpose of enforcing a maintenance order, a magistrates' court has exercised its power under subsection 2 of section 77 of the Magistrates' Courts Act 1980, or this section to postpone the issue of a warrant of commitment and under the terms of the postponement the warrant falls to be issued, then –

(*a*) the warrant shall not be issued except in pursuance of subsection (2) or paragraph (*a*) of subsection (3) of this section; and

(*b*) the justices' chief executive for the court shall give notice to the defendant stating that if the defendant considers there are grounds for not issuing the warrant he may make an application to the court in the prescribed manner requesting that the warrant shall not be issued and stating those grounds.

(2) If no such application is received by the justices' chief executive for the court within the prescribed period, any justice of the peace acting for the same petty sessions area as the court may issue the warrant of commitment at any time after the expiration of that period; and if such an application is so received any such justice may, after considering the statements contained in the application –

(*a*) if he is of opinion that the application should be further considered, refer it to the court;

(*b*) if he is not of that opinion, issue the warrant forthwith;

and when an application is referred to the court under this subsection, the justices' chief executive for the court shall give to the defendant and the person in whose favour the maintenance order in question was made notice of the time and place appointed for the consideration of the application by the court.

(3) On considering an application referred to it under the last foregoing subsection the court shall, unless in pursuance of subsection (6) of this section it remits the

whole of the sum in respect of which the warrant could otherwise be issued, either –

(*a*) issue the warrant; or
(*b*) further postpone the issue thereof until such time and on such conditions, if any, as the court thinks just; or
(*c*) if in consequence of any change in the circumstances of the defendant the court considers it appropriate so to do, order that the warrant shall not be issued in any event.

(4) A defendant who is for the time being imprisoned or otherwise detained under a warrant of commitment issued by a magistrates' court for the purpose of enforcing a maintenance order, and who is not detained otherwise than for the enforcement of such an order, may make an application to the court in the prescribed manner requesting that the warrant shall be cancelled and stating the grounds of the application; and thereupon any justice of the peace acting for the same petty sessions area as the court may, after considering the statements contained in the application –

(*a*) if he is of opinion that the application should be further considered refer it to the court;
(*b*) if he is not of that opinion, refuse the application;

and when an application is referred to the court under this subsection, the justices' chief executive for the court shall give to the person in charge of the prison or other place in which the defendant is detained and the person in whose favour the maintenance order in question was made notice of the time and place appointed for the consideration of the application by the court.

(5) On considering an application referred to it under the last foregoing subsection, the court shall, unless in pursuance of the next following subsection it remits the whole of the sum in respect of which the warrant was issued or such part thereof as remains to be paid, either –

(*a*) refuse the application; or
(*b*) if the court is satisfied that the defendant is unable to pay, or to make any payment or further payment towards, the sum aforesaid and if it is of opinion that in all the circumstances of the case the defendant ought not to continue to be detained under the warrant, order that the warrant shall cease to have effect when the person in charge of the prison or other place aforesaid is informed of the making of the order;

and where the court makes an order under paragraph (*b*) of this subsection, it may if it thinks fit also –

(i) fix a term of imprisonment in respect of the sum aforesaid or such part thereof as remains to be paid, being a term not exceeding so much of the term of the previous warrant as, after taking into account any reduction thereof by virtue of the next following subsection, remained to be served at the date of the order; and
(ii) postpone the issue of a warrant for the commitment of the defendant for that term until such time and on such conditions, if any, as the court thinks just.

(6) On considering an application under this section in respect of a warrant or a postponed warrant, the court may, if the maintenance order in question is an affiliation order or an order enforceable as an affiliation order, remit the whole or any part of the sum due under the order; and where the court remits the sum or part of the sum in respect of which the warrant was issued or the postponed warrant

could have been issued section 79 of the Magistrates' Courts Act 1980 (which provides that on payment of the sum for which imprisonment has been ordered by a magistrates' court the order shall cease to have effect and that on payment of part of that sum the period of detention shall be reduced proportionately) shall apply as if payment of that sum or part had been made as therein mentioned.

(7) Where notice of the time and place appointed for the consideration of an application is required by this section to be given to the defendant or the person in whose favour the maintenance order in question was made and the defendant or, as the case may be, that person does not appear at that time and place, the court may proceed with the consideration of the application in his absence.

(8) A notice required by this section to be given by the justices' chief executive for a magistrates' court to any person shall be deemed to be given to that person if it is sent by registered post addressed to him at his last known address, notwithstanding that the notice is returned as undelivered or is for any other reason not received by that person.

Amendments—Magistrates' Courts Act 1980, s 154, Sch 7, para 23; Access to Justice Act 1999, s 90, Sch 13, para 30.

Defined terms—"defendant": s 21(1).

"shall give notice" (s 18(1))—Notice is to be served by registered post or, under the Recorded Delivery Service Act 1962, by recorded delivery. Delivery is not required provided the notice was addressed to the defendant at his last known address (s 18(8)). Separate notice is required on each occasion that the court is considering the issue of the warrant of committal (*Slater v Calder Justices* [1984] FLR 719).

"prescribed manner" (s 18(1), (4))—See Magistrates' Courts (Maintenance Orders Act 1958) Rules 1959, r 22.

"prescribed period" (s 18(2))—The period prescribed by Magistrates' Courts (Maintenance Orders Act 1958) Rules 1959, r 22(3) is eight days beginning with the day the clerk sends notice to the defendant.

"refer" (s 18(2), (4))—The justices' discretion is limited to referring the application to the court or issuing the warrant forthwith. Where there is, prima facie, a change in circumstances, the justice should refer the application to the court (*Wood v Warley Justices* (1974) Fam Law 130).

"order enforceable as an affiliation order" (s 18(6))—This includes an order registered under s 3.

****

Supplemental

20 Special provisions as to magistrates' courts

(1) Notwithstanding anything in this Act, a justices' chief executive who is entitled to receive payments under a maintenance order for transmission to another person shall not apply for the registration of the maintenance order under Part I of this Act or give notice in relation to the order in pursuance of subsection (1) of section five thereof unless he is requested in writing to do so by a person entitled to receive the payments through him; and where a justices' chief executive is requested as aforesaid –

(i) he shall comply with the request unless it appears to him unreasonable in the circumstances to do so;

(ii) the person by whom the request was made shall have the same liabilities for all the costs properly incurred in or about any proceedings taken in pursuance of the request as if the proceedings had been taken by that person.

(2) An application to a magistrates' court by virtue of subsection (2) of section four of this Act for the variation of a maintenance order shall be made by complaint.

(3)–(7) ...

(8) For the avoidance of doubt it is hereby declared that a complaint may be made to enforce payment of a sum due and unpaid under a maintenance order notwithstanding that a previous complaint has been made in respect of that sum or a part thereof and whether or not an order was made in pursuance of the previous complaint.

Amendments—Attachment of Earnings Act 1971, Sch 5; Magistrates' Courts Act 1980, s 154, Sch 9; Access to Justice Act 1999, s 90, Sch 13, para 31.

Defined terms—"magistrates' court": s 21(1).

21 Interpretation etc

(1) In this Act, unless the context otherwise requires, the following expressions have the following meanings –

"magistrates' court" has the meaning assigned to it by the Magistrates' Courts Act 1980 and the reference to that Act in subsection (2) of section 148 thereof shall be construed as including a reference to this Act;

"defendant", in relation to a maintenance order or a related attachment of earnings order, means the person liable to make payments under the maintenance order;

"England" includes Wales;

"prescribed" means prescribed by rules of court;

"rules of court", in relation to a magistrates' court, means rules under section fifteen of the Justices of the Peace Act 1949.

(2) Any reference in this Act to a person entitled to receive payments under a maintenance order is a reference to a person entitled to receive such payments either directly or through another person or for transmission to another person.

(3) Any reference in this Act to proceedings relating to an order includes a reference to proceedings in which the order may be made.

(4) Any reference in this Act to costs incurred in proceedings relating to a maintenance order shall be construed, in the case of a maintenance order made by the High Court, as a reference to such costs as are included in an order for costs relating solely to that maintenance order.

(5) (*repealed*)

(6) Any reference in this Act to any enactment is a reference to that enactment as amended by or under any subsequent enactment.

Amendments—Administration of Justice Act 1970, s 54(3), Sch 11; Magistrates' Courts Act 1980, s 154, Sch 7, para 24; Family Law Reform Act 1987, s 33(4), Sch 4; Access to Justice Act 1999, s 76, Sch 10, para 22, Sch 15.

****

Maintenance Orders (Facilities for Enforcement) Act 1920

ARRANGEMENT OF SECTIONS

1 Enforcement in England and Ireland of maintenance orders made in His Majesty's dominions outside the United Kingdom

(1) Where a maintenance order has, whether before or after the passing of this Act, been made against any person by any court in any part of His Majesty's dominions outside the United Kingdom to which this Act extends, and a certified copy of the order has been transmitted by the governor of that part of His Majesty's dominions to the Lord Chancellor, the Lord Chancellor shall send a copy of the order to the prescribed officer of a court in England or Ireland for registration; and on receipt thereof the order shall be registered in the prescribed manner, and shall, from the date of such registration, be of the same force and effect, and, subject to the provisions of this Act, all proceedings may be taken on such order as if it had been an order originally obtained in the court in which it is so registered, and that court shall have power to enforce the order accordingly.

(2) The Court in which an order is to be so registered as aforesaid shall, if the court by which the order was made was a court of superior jurisdiction, be the Family Division of the High Court, or in Ireland the King's Bench Division (Matrimonial) of the High Court of Justice in Ireland, and, if the court was not a court of superior jurisdiction, be a court of summary jurisdiction.

Amendments—Administration of Justice Act 1970, s 1(6), Sch 2, para 2; SI 1992/709.

Defined terms—"certified copy", "maintenance order": s 10.

Areas to which the Act extends—The Act remains in force only for Commonwealth countries which are not designated as reciprocating countries under the Maintenance Orders (Reciprocal Enforcement) Act 1972. Although the 1972 Act provides for the repeal of the whole of this Act, that provision (s 22(2) of the 1972 Act) has been brought into force only as regards such designated countries. This Act currently applies to:

(*a*) *Africa* Botswana, Lesotho, Malawi, Mauritius, Nigeria, Seychelles, Sierra Leone, Swaziland Protectorate, The Gambia, Uganda, Zambia, Zanzibar.

(*b*) *America* Antigua, Bahamas, Belize, Cayman Islands, Dominica, Grenada, Guyana, Jamaica, Montserrat, St Christopher and Nevis, St Lucia, St Vincent, Trinidad and Tobago, Virgin Islands, Yukon Territory.
(*c*) *Asia* Cyprus, Malaysia, Sri Lanka.
(*d*) *Australasia* British Solomon Islands Protectorate, Territory of Cocos (Keeling) Islands, Territory of Christmas Island (Indian Ocean), Gilbert and Ellice Islands.
(*e*) *Europe* Guernsey, Jersey.

See also s 12.

"shall be registered" (s 1(1))—For procedure in the High Court and county court, see FPR 1991, r 7.17 and, in magistrates' courts, see Maintenance Orders (Facilities for Enforcement) Rules 1922, rr 1, 3 and 5, and Home Office Circular 469, 726/4 (15 June 1925). Registration is an administrative and not a judicial act, and the payer cannot object to or appeal against registration (*Pilcher v Pilcher* [1955] P 318, [1955] 3 WLR 231).

Date from which order takes effect—An order registered under this section takes effect from the date specified in the original order or from the date of the original order. Contrast the position for the confirmation of provisional orders under s 4.

Payment of monies collected—Monies collected are to be sent to the court which made the order, except for the following countries and territories: Guernsey, Jersey, Christmas Island (Indian Ocean), Cocos (Keeling) Islands, Yukon Territory. Monies collected for these countries and territories are to be sent to the Crown Agents for overseas governments and administration at 4 Millbank, London, SW1. See Maintenance Orders (Facilities for Enforcement) Rules 1922, r 6.

"power to enforce" (s 1(1))—This does not include the power to vary or discharge the order (see *Pilcher v Pilcher* (above) and *R v Rose ex parte McGibbon* (1959) 123 JP 374).

2 Transmission of maintenance orders made in England or Ireland

Where a court in England or Ireland has, whether before or after the commencement of this Act, made a maintenance order against any person, and it is proved to that court that the person against whom the order was made is resident in some part of His Majesty's dominions outside the United Kingdom to which this Act extends, the court shall send to the Lord Chancellor for transmission to the governor of that part of His Majesty's dominions a certified copy of the order.

Amendments—SI 1992/709.

Defined terms—"certified copy", "maintenance order": s 10.

Scope of provision—Application in the High Court or county court is made to a district judge; for procedure, see FPR 1991, r 7.17.

3 Power to make provisional orders of maintenance against persons resident in His Majesty's dominions outside the United Kingdom

(1) Where an application is made to a court of summary jurisdiction in England or Ireland for a maintenance order against any person, and it is proved that that person is resident in a part of His Majesty's dominions outside the United Kingdom to which this Act extends, the court may, in the absence of that person, if after hearing the evidence it is satisfied of the justice of the application, make any such order as it might have made if that person had been resident in England and Wales, had received reasonable notice of the date of the hearing of the application and had failed to appear at the hearing, but in such case the order shall be provisional only, and shall have no effect unless and until confirmed by a competent court in such part of His Majesty's dominions as aforesaid.

(2) The evidence of any witness who is examined on any such application shall be put into writing, and such deposition shall be read over to and signed by him.

(3) Where such an order is made, the court shall send to the Lord Chancellor for transmission to the governor of the part of His Majesty's dominions in which the person against whom the order is made is alleged to reside the depositions so taken and a certified copy of the order, together with a statement of the grounds on which the making of the order might have been opposed if the person against whom the order is made had been resident in England and Wales, had received reasonable notice of the date of the hearing and had appeared at the hearing, and such information as the court possesses for facilitating the identification of that person, and ascertaining his whereabouts.

(4) Where any such provisional order has come before a court in a part of His Majesty's dominions outside the United Kingdom to which this Act extends for confirmation, and the order has by that court been remitted to the court of summary jurisdiction which made the order for the purpose of taking further evidence, that court or any other court of summary jurisdiction appointed for the same commission area shall, after the prescribed notice, proceed to take the evidence in like manner and subject to the like conditions as the evidence in support of the original application.

If upon the hearing of such evidence it appears to the court that the order ought not to have been made, the court may revoke the order, but in any other case the depositions shall be sent to the Lord Chancellor and dealt with in like manner as the original depositions.

(5) The confirmation of an order made under this section shall not affect any power of a court of summary jurisdiction to vary or revoke that order:

Provided that on the making of a varying or revoking order the court shall send a certified copy thereof to the Lord Chancellor for transmission to the governor of the part of His Majesty's dominions in which the original order was confirmed, and that in the case of an order varying the original order the order shall not have any effect unless and until confirmed in like manner as the original order.

(6) The applicant shall have the same right of appeal, if any, against a refusal to make a provisional order as he would have had against a refusal to make the order had the person against whom the order is sought to be made been resident in England and Wales and received reasonable notice of the date of the hearing of the application.

(7) Where subsection (1) of section 60 of the Magistrates' Courts Act 1980 (revocation, variation etc of orders for periodical payment) applies in relation to an order made under this section which has been confirmed, that subsection shall have effect as if for the words "by order on complaint", there were substituted "on an application being made, by order".

(8) In this section "revoke" includes discharge.

Amendments—Domestic Proceedings and Magistrates' Courts Act 1978, s 89(2), Sch 2, para 2; Justices of the Peace Act 1979, s 71, Sch 2, para 1; Maintenance Orders (Reciprocal Enforcement) Act 1992, s 1, Sch 1, para 1; SI 1992/709; Justices of the Peace Act 1997, s 73(2), Sch 5, para 2; Access to Justice Act 1999, s 106, Sch 15.

Application to court of summary jurisdiction (s 3(1))—Jurisdiction is based on the residence of the applicant (see Domestic Proceedings and Magistrates' Courts Act 1978, s 30 and *Collister v Collister* [1972] 1 WLR 54, [1972] 1 All ER 334). For procedure, see Maintenance Orders (Facilities for Enforcement) Rules 1922, Sch 2.

"the order shall be provisional only" (s 3(1))—Liability to make payments cannot precede the date of registration.

"deposition" (s 3(2))—See 86 JP Jo 225 for a form of deposition.

Statement of grounds (s 3(3))—See Home Office Circular 469, 726/4, (15 June 1925) and 86 JP Jo 225 for a form for such a statement.

"prescribed notice" (s 3(4))—The notice should specify the further evidence required and the date, time and place fixed for taking the evidence. The notice should be sent by the clerk to the person who applied for the provisional order.

"right of appeal" (s 3(6))—As to the right of appeal, see Domestic Proceedings and Magistrates' Courts Act 1978, s 29.

4 Power of court of summary jurisdiction to confirm maintenance order made out of the United Kingdom

(1) Where a maintenance order has been made by a court in a part of His Majesty's dominions outside the United Kingdom to which this Act extends, and the order is provisional only and has no effect unless and until confirmed by a court of summary jurisdiction in England or Ireland, and a certified copy of the order, together with the depositions of witnesses and a statement of the grounds on which the order might have been opposed has been transmitted to the Lord Chancellor, and it appears to the Lord Chancellor that the person against whom the order was made is resident in England or Ireland, the Lord Chancellor may send the said documents to the prescribed officer of a court of summary jurisdiction, with a requisition that a notice be served on the person informing him that he may attend a hearing at the time and place specified in the notice to show cause why that order should not be confirmed, and upon receipt of such documents and requisition the court shall cause such a notice to be served upon such a person.

(2) A notice required to be served under this section may be served by post.

(3) At the hearing it shall be open to the person on whom the notice was served to oppose the confirmation of the order on any grounds on which he might have opposed the making of the order in the original proceedings had he been a party to them, but on no other grounds, and the certificate from the court which made the provisional order stating the grounds on which the making of the order might have been opposed if the person against whom the order was made had been a party to the proceedings shall be conclusive evidence that those grounds are grounds on which objection may be taken.

(4) If at the hearing the person served with the notice does not appear or, on appearing, fails to satisfy the court that the order ought not to be confirmed, the court may confirm the order either without modification or with such modifications as to the court after hearing the evidence may seem just.

(5) If the person served with the notice appears at the hearing and satisfies the court that for the purpose of establishing any grounds on which he opposes the confirmation of the order it is necessary to remit the case to the court which made the provisional order for the taking of any further evidence, the court may so remit the case and adjourn the proceedings for the purpose.

(5A) Where a magistrates' court confirms a provisional order under this section, it shall at the same time exercise one of its powers under subsection (5B).

(5B) The powers of the court are –

(*a*) the power to order that payments under the order be made directly to a justices' chief executive;

(*b*) the power to order that payments under the order be made to a justices' chief executive by such method of payment falling within section 59(6) of the Magistrates' Courts Act 1980 (standing order, etc) as may be specified;

(*c*) the power to make an attachment of earnings order under the Attachment of Earnings Act 1971 to secure payments under the order.

(5C) In deciding which of the powers under subsection (5B) it is to exercise, the court shall have regard to any representations made by the person liable to make payments under the order.

(5D) Subsection (4) of section 59 of the Magistrates' Courts Act 1980 (power of court to require debtor to open account) shall apply for the purposes of subsection (5B) as it applies for the purposes of that section but as if for paragraph (*a*) there were substituted –

"(*a*) the court proposes to exercise its power under paragraph (*b*) of section 4(5B) of the Maintenance Orders (Facilities for Enforcement) Act 1920, and".

(6) Subject to subsection (6A), where a provisional order has been confirmed under this section, it may be varied or revoked in like manner as if it had originally been made by the confirming court.

(6A) Where the confirming court is a magistrates' court, section 60 of the Magistrates' Courts Act 1980 (revocation, variation etc of orders for periodical payment) shall have effect in relation to a provisional order confirmed under this section –

(*za*) as if in subsection (1) for the words "by order on complaint" there were substituted "on an application being made, by order";

(*a*) as if in subsection (3) for the words "paragraphs (*a*) to (*d*) of section 59(3) above" there were substituted "section 4(5B) of the Maintenance Orders (Facilities for Enforcement) Act 1920";

(*b*) as if in subsection (4) for paragraph (*b*) there were substituted –

"(*b*) payments under the order are required to be made to a justices' chief executive by any method of payment falling within section 59(6) above (standing order, etc)";

(*c*) as if in subsection (5) for the words "to the justices' chief executive for the court" there were substituted "in accordance with paragraph (*a*) of section 4(5B) of the Maintenance Orders (Facilities for Enforcement) Act 1920";

(*d*) as if in subsection (7), paragraph (*c*) and the word "and" immediately preceding it were omitted;

(*e*) as if in subsection (8) for the words "paragraphs (*a*) to (*d*) of section 59(3) above" there were substituted "section 4(5B) of the Maintenance Orders (Facilities for Enforcement) Act 1920";

(*f*) as if for subsections (9) and (10) there were substituted the following subsections –

"(9) In deciding, for the purposes of subsection (3) and (8) above, which of the powers under section 4(5B) of the Maintenance Orders (Facilities for Enforcement) Act 1920 it is to exercise, the court shall have regard to any representations made by the debtor.

(10) Subsection (4) of section 59 above (power of court to require debtor to open account) shall apply for the purposes of subsections (3) and (8) above as

PART II

it applies for the purposes of that section but as if for paragraph (*a*) there were substituted –

'(*a*) the court proposes to exercise its powers under paragraph (*b*) of section 4(5B) of the Maintenance Orders (Facilities for Enforcement) Act 1920, and'."

(6B) Where on an application for variation or revocation the confirming court is satisfied that it is necessary to remit the case to the court which made the order for the purpose of taking any further evidence, the court may so remit the case and adjourn the proceedings for the purpose.

(7) Where an order has been so confirmed the person bound thereby shall have the same right of appeal, if any, against the confirmation of the order as he would have had against the making of the order had the order been an order made by the court confirming the order.

Amendments—Maintenance Enforcement Act 1991, s 10, Sch 1, para 1; Maintenance Orders (Reciprocal Enforcement) Act 1992, s 1, Sch 1, para 2; SI 1992/709; Access to Justice Act 1999, s 90, Sch 13, para 7, Sch 15.

Scope of provision—If the relevant law of the foreign court permits the making of an order for custody and maintenance, this may also be confirmed under the Act. For the duties of the justices' chief executive when a method of payments order is made, see Maintenance Orders (Facilities for Enforcement) Rules 1922, r 5A.

"prescribed officer" (s 4(1))—See Maintenance Orders (Facilities for Enforcement) Rules 1922, rr 1 to 4 for the duties of the justices' chief executive.

Defences which may be raised (s 4(3))—Although the certificate is said to be conclusive as to the grounds of objection which may be taken, other defences have been allowed; in *Harris v Harris* [1949] 2 All ER 318, a challenge on the grounds of want of jurisdiction was allowed (see also *Re Wheat* [1932] 2 KB 716).

"standing order, etc" (s 4(5B))—This does not include the power to order payment by direct debit.

"right of appeal" (s 4(7))—As to the right of appeal, see Domestic Proceedings and Magistrates' Courts Act 1978, s 29.

Conversion to sterling—The order, on confirmation, should be converted to sterling (see Home Office Circular 469, 726/4). It is suggested that the rate of exchange applicable on the date of registration should apply throughout the life of the order.

4A Variation and revocation of maintenance orders

(1) This section applies to –

(*a*) any maintenance order made by virtue of section 3 of this Act which has been confirmed as mentioned in that section; and

(*b*) any maintenance order which has been confirmed under section 4 of this Act.

(2) Where the respondent to an application for the variation or revocation of a maintenance order to which this section applies is residing in a part of Her Majesty's dominions outside the United Kingdom to which this Act extends, a magistrates' court in England and Wales shall have jurisdiction to hear the application (where it would not have such jurisdiction apart from this subsection) if that court would have had jurisdiction to hear it had the respondent been residing in England and Wales.

(3) Where the respondent to an application for the variation or revocation of a maintenance order to which this section applies is residing in a part of Her Majesty's dominions outside the United Kingdom to which this Act extends, a court of summary jurisdiction in Northern Ireland shall have jurisdiction to hear the application (where it would not have such jurisdiction apart from this subsection) if that court would have had jurisdiction to hear it had the respondent been residing in Northern Ireland.

(4) Where –

(*a*) the respondent to an application for the variation or revocation of a maintenance order to which this section applies does not appear at the time and place appointed for the hearing of the application by a magistrates' court in England and Wales, and

(*b*) the court is satisfied that the respondent is residing in a part of Her Majesty's dominions outside the United Kingdom to which this Act extends,

the court may proceed to hear and determine the application at the time and place appointed for the hearing or for any adjourned hearing in like manner as if the respondent had appeared at that time and place.

(5) Subsection (4) shall apply to Northern Ireland with the following modifications –

(*a*), (*b*) (*repealed*)

(*c*) for the words "a magistrates' court in England and Wales" there shall be substituted "a court of summary jurisdiction in Northern Ireland".

(6) In this section "revocation" includes "discharge".

Amendments—Inserted by Maintenance Orders (Reciprocal Enforcement) Act 1992, s 1, Sch 1, para 3; amended by SI 1995/755.

5 Power of Lord Chancellor to make regulations for facilitating communications between courts

The Lord Chancellor may make regulations as to the manner in which a case can be remitted by a court authorised to confirm a provisional order to the court which made the provisional order, and generally for facilitating communications between such courts.

Amendments—SI 1992/709.

Regulations—No regulations have yet been made in exercise of this power.

6 Mode of enforcing orders

(1) A court of summary jurisdiction in which an order has been registered under this Act or by which an order has been confirmed under this Act, and the officers of such court, shall take all such steps for enforcing the order as may be prescribed.

(2) Every such order shall be enforceable in like manner as if the order were for the payment of a civil debt recoverable summarily;

Provided that, if the order is of such a nature that if made by the court in which it is so registered, or by which it is so confirmed, it would be enforceable in like manner as an order of affiliation, the order shall, subject to the modifications of sections 76 and 93 of the Magistrates' Courts Act 1980 (enforcement of sums

PART II

adjudged to be paid and complaint for arrears) specified in subsections (2ZA) and (2ZB) of section 18 of the Maintenance Orders Act 1950 (enforcement of registered orders), be so enforceable.

(3) A warrant of distress or commitment issued by a court of summary jurisdiction for the purpose of enforcing any order so registered or confirmed may be executed in any part of the United Kingdom in the same manner as if the warrant had been originally issued or subsequently endorsed by a court of summary jurisdiction having jurisdiction in the place where the warrant is executed.

Amendments—Maintenance Enforcement Act 1991, s 10, Sch 1, para 2.

"subsections (2ZA) and (2ZB) of section 18 of the Maintenance Orders Act 1950" (s 6(2))—These sections modify the means of payments orders available on variation and restrict the use of imprisonment for enforcement where the court is of the view that it is appropriate to make an attachment of earnings order or an order for payment by standing order.

7 Application of Summary Jurisdiction Acts

(1) The Summary Jurisdiction Acts shall apply to proceedings before courts of summary jurisdiction under this Act in like manner as they apply to proceedings under those Acts.

(2) Without prejudice to the generality of the power to make rules under section 144 of the Magistrates' Courts Act 1980 (magistrates' courts rules), for the purpose of giving effect to this Act such rules may make, in relation to any proceedings brought under or by virtue of this Act, any provision which –

(*a*) falls within subsection (2) of section 93 of the Children Act 1989, and
(*b*) may be made in relation to relevant proceedings under that section.

Amendments—Justices of the Peace Act 1949, s 46(2), Sch 7, Pt II; Maintenance Orders (Reciprocal Enforcement) Act 1992, s 1, Sch 1, para 4.

8 Proof of documents signed by officers of court

Any documents purporting to be signed by a judge or officer of a court outside the United Kingdom shall, until the contrary is proved, be deemed to have been so signed without proof of the signature or judicial or official character of the person appearing to have signed it, and the officer of a court by whom a document is signed shall, until the contrary is proved, be deemed to have been the proper officer of the court to sign the document.

9 Depositions to be evidence

Depositions taken in a court in a part of His Majesty's dominions outside the United Kingdom to which this Act extends for the purposes of this Act, may be received in evidence in proceedings before courts of summary jurisdiction under this Act.

10 Interpretation

For the purposes of this Act, the expression "maintenance order" means an order other than an order of affiliation for the periodical payment of sums of money towards the maintenance of the wife or other dependants of the person against whom the order is made, and the expression "dependants" means such persons as that person is, according to the law in force in the part of His Majesty's dominions in which the maintenance order was made, liable to maintain; the expression "certified copy" in relation to an order of a court means a copy of the order certified by the proper officer of the court to be a true copy, and the expression "prescribed" means prescribed by rules of court.

"rules of court"—The rules of court for the purposes of the Act are FPR 1991, r 7.17 and the Maintenance Orders (Facilities for Enforcement) Rules 1922.

****

12 Extent of Act

(1) Where His Majesty is satisfied that reciprocal provisions have been made by the legislature of any part of His Majesty's dominions outside the United Kingdom for the enforcement within that part of maintenance orders made by courts within England and Ireland, His Majesty may by Order in Council extend this Act to that part, and thereupon that part shall become a part of His Majesty's dominions to which this Act extends.

(2) His Majesty may by Order in Council extend this Act to any British protectorate and where so extended this Act shall apply as if any such protectorate was a party of His Majesty's dominions to which this Act extends.

"dominions to which this Act extends"—See **Areas to which the Act extends** under s 1.

****

Maintenance Orders (Reciprocal Enforcement) Act 1972

ARRANGEMENT OF SECTIONS

PART I

RECIPROCAL ENFORCEMENT OF MAINTENANCE ORDERS MADE IN UNITED KINGDOM OR RECIPROCATING COUNTRY

Designation of reciprocating countries

Orders made by courts in reciprocating countries

Appeals

Evidence

Supplemental

Amendments, repeals and transitional provisions

PART II

RECIPROCAL ENFORCEMENT OF CLAIMS FOR THE RECOVERY OF MAINTENANCE

Convention countries

Application by person in the United Kingdom for recovery etc of maintenance in Convention country

Application by person in Convention country for recovery of maintenance in England, Wales or Northern Ireland

PART I
RECIPROCAL ENFORCEMENT OF MAINTENANCE ORDERS MADE IN UNITED KINGDOM OR RECIPROCATING COUNTRY

Designation of reciprocating countries

1 Orders in Council designating reciprocating countries

(1) Her Majesty, if satisfied that, in the event of the benefits conferred by this Part of this Act being applied to, or to particular classes of, maintenance orders made

by the courts of any country or territory outside the United Kingdom, similar benefits will in that country or territory be applied to, or to those classes of, maintenance orders made by the courts of the United Kingdom, may by Order in Council designate that country or territory as a reciprocating country for the purposes of this Part of this Act; and, subject to subsection (2) below, in this Part of this Act "reciprocating country" means a country or territory that is for the time being so designated.

(2) A country or territory may be designated under subsection (1) above as a reciprocating country either as regards maintenance orders generally, or as regards maintenance orders other than those of any specified class, or as regards maintenance orders of one or more specified classes only; and a country or territory which is for the time being so designated otherwise than as regards maintenance orders generally shall for the purposes of this Part of this Act be taken to be a reciprocating country only as regards maintenance orders of the class to which the designation extends.

Defined terms—"court", "maintenance order": s 21(1); "reciprocating country": s 1(1).

"may by Order in Council designate" (s 1(1))—The Reciprocal Enforcement of Maintenance Orders (Designation of Reciprocating Countries) Order 1974 has been made for this purpose.

Orders made by courts in the United Kingdom

2 Transmission of maintenance order made in United Kingdom for enforcement in reciprocating country

(1) Subject to subsection (2) below, where the payer under a maintenance order made, whether before or after the commencement of this Part of this Act, by a court in the United Kingdom is residing or has assets in a reciprocating country, the payee under the order may apply for the order to be sent to that country for enforcement.

(2) Subsection (1) above shall not have effect in relation to a provisional order or to an order made by virtue of a provision of Part II of this Act.

(3) Every application under this section shall be made in the prescribed manner to the prescribed officer of the court which made the maintenance order to which the application relates.

(4) If, on an application duly made under this section to the prescribed officer of a court in the United Kingdom, that officer is satisfied that the payer under the maintenance order to which the application relates is residing or has assets in a reciprocating country, the following documents, that is to say –

- (*a*) a certified copy of the maintenance order;
- (*b*) a certificate signed by that officer certifying that the order is enforceable in the United Kingdom;
- (*c*) a certificate of arrears so signed;
- (*d*) a statement giving such information as the officer possesses as to the whereabouts of the payer and the nature and location of his assets in that country;
- (*e*) a statement giving such information as the officer possesses for facilitating the identification of the payer; and
- (*f*) where available, a photograph of the payer;

shall be sent by that officer to the Lord Chancellor with a view to their being transmitted by the Lord Chancellor to the responsible authority in the reciprocating country if he is satisfied that the statement relating to the whereabouts of the payer and the nature and location of his assets in that country gives sufficient information to justify that being done.

(5) Nothing in this section shall be taken as affecting any jurisdiction of a court in the United Kingdom with respect to a maintenance order to which this section applies, and any such order may be enforced, varied or revoked accordingly.

Amendments—Civil Jurisdiction and Judgments Act 1982, s 37(1), Sch 11, para 9; SI 1992/709.

Defined terms—"certificate of arrears", "certified copy", "court", "maintenance order", "payee", "payer", "provisional order": s 21(1); "reciprocating country": s 1(1).

"reciprocating country"—For Ireland, see Reciprocal Enforcement of Maintenance Orders (Republic of Ireland) Order 1993; for Hague Convention country, see Reciprocal Enforcement of Maintenance Orders (Hague Convention Countries) Order 1993; for specified States of the United States of America, see Reciprocal Enforcement of Maintenance Orders (United States of America) Order 1995.

"prescribed manner" (s 2(3))—See FPR 1991, r 7.31 and Magistrates' Courts (Reciprocal Enforcement of Maintenance Orders) Rules 1974, r 4.

"prescribed officer" (s 2(3), (4))—See MC(REMO)R 1974, r 3.

3 Power of magistrates' court to make provisional maintenance order against person residing in reciprocating country

(1) Where an application is made to a magistrates' court for a maintenance order against a person residing in a reciprocating country and the court would have jurisdiction to determine the application under the Domestic Proceedings and Magistrates' Courts Act 1978 or the Children Act 1989 if that person –

(*a*) were residing in England and Wales, and
(*b*) received reasonable notice of the date of the hearing of the application,

the court shall (subject to subsection (2) below) have jurisdiction to determine the application.

(2) A maintenance order made by virtue of this section shall be a provisional order.

(3) (*repealed*)

(4) No enactment (or provision made under an enactment) requiring or enabling –

(*a*) a court to transfer proceedings from a magistrates' court to a county court or the High Court, or
(*b*) a magistrates' court to refuse to make an order on an application on the ground that any matter in question is one that would be more conveniently dealt with by the High Court,

shall apply in relation to an application to which subsection (1) above applies.

(5) Where a court makes a maintenance order which is by virtue of this section a provisional order, the following documents, that is to say –

(*a*) a certified copy of the maintenance order;
(*b*) a document, authenticated in the prescribed manner, setting out or summarising the evidence given in the proceedings;
(*c*) a certificate signed by the prescribed officer of the court certifying that the grounds stated in the certificate are the grounds on which the making of the order might have been opposed by the payer under the order;

PART II

(*d*) a statement giving such information as was available to the court as to the whereabouts of the payer;
(*e*) a statement giving such information as the officer possesses for facilitating the identification of the payer, and
(*f*) where available, a photograph of the payer;

shall be sent by that officer to the Lord Chancellor with a view to their being transmitted by the Lord Chancellor to the responsible authority in the reciprocating country in which the payer is residing if he is satisfied that the statement relating to the whereabouts of the payer gives sufficient information to justify that being done.

(6) A maintenance order made by virtue of this section which has been confirmed by a competent court in a reciprocating country shall be treated for all purposes as if the magistrates' court which made the order had made it in the form in which it was confirmed and as if the order had never been a provisional order, and subject to section 5 of this Act, any such order may be enforced, varied or revoked accordingly.

(7) In the application of this section to Northern Ireland –

(*a*) for subsection (1) there shall be substituted –

"(1) Where an application is made to a magistrates' court against a person residing in a reciprocating country and the court would have jurisdiction to determine the application under the Domestic Proceedings (Northern Ireland) Order 1980 or the Children (Northern Ireland) Order 1995 if that person –

(*a*) were residing in Northern Ireland, and
(*b*) received reasonable notice of the date of the hearing of the application,

the court shall (subject to subsection (2) below) have jurisdiction to determine the application.";

(*b*) in subsection (4), for references to the High Court there shall be substituted references to the High Court of Justice in Northern Ireland.

Amendments—Family Law Reform Act 1987, s 33(4), Sch 4; Maintenance Orders (Reciprocal Enforcement) Act 1992, s 1, Sch 1, para 6; SI 1992/709; SI 1995/755.

Defined terms—"certified copy", "court": s 21(1); "jurisdiction": s 47(3); "maintenance order", "payer", "provisional order": s 21(1); "reciprocating country": s 1(1); "responsible authority": s 21(1).

"reciprocating country"—For Ireland, see Reciprocal Enforcement of Maintenance Orders (Republic of Ireland) Order 1993; for Hague Convention country, see Reciprocal Enforcement of Maintenance Orders (Hague Convention Countries) Order 1993.

"prescribed manner" (s 3(5)(*b*))—See MC(REMO)R 1974, r 5.

Certificate of grounds of opposition (s 3(5)(*c*))—In Manitoba and Ontario, a copy of the legislation rather than a certificate of possible grounds of opposition is required (see Home Office Circular No 89/1984).

"prescribed officer" (s 3(5))—See MC(REMO)R 1974, r 3.

****

5 Variation and revocation of maintenance order made in United Kingdom

(1) This section applies to a maintenance order a certified copy of which has been sent to a reciprocating country in pursuance of section 2 of this Act and to a maintenance order made by virtue of section 3 or 4 thereof which has been confirmed by a competent court in such a country.

(2) A court in the United Kingdom having power to vary a maintenance order to which this section applies shall have power to vary that order by a provisional order.

(3) Where the court hearing an application for the variation of a maintenance order to which this section applies proposes to vary it by increasing the rate of the payments under the order then, unless either –

(*a*) both the payer and the payee under the order appear in the proceedings, or
(*b*) the applicant appears and the appropriate process has been duly served on the other party,

the order varying the order shall be a provisional order.

(3A) Where subsection (1) of section 60 of the Magistrates' Courts Act 1980 (revocation, variation etc of orders for periodical payment) applies in relation to a maintenance order to which this section applies, that subsection shall have effect as if for the words "by order on complaint", there were substituted "on an application being made, by order".

(3B) Where paragraph (1) of Article 86 of the Magistrates' Courts (Northern Ireland) Order 1981 applies in relation to a maintenance order to which this section applies, that paragraph shall have effect as if for the words "by order on complaint," there were substituted "on an application being made, by order".

(4) Where a court in the United Kingdom makes a provisional order varying a maintenance order to which this section applies, the prescribed officer of the court shall send in the prescribed manner to the court in a reciprocating country having power to confirm the provisional order a certified copy of the provisional order together with a document, authenticated in the prescribed manner, setting out or summarising the evidence given in the proceedings.

(5) Where a certified copy of a provisional order made by a court in a reciprocating country, being an order varying or revoking a maintenance order, to which this section applies, together with a document, duly authenticated, setting out or summarising the evidence given in the proceedings in which the provisional order was made, is received by the court in the United Kingdom which made the maintenance order, that court may confirm or refuse to confirm the provisional order and, if that order is an order varying the maintenance order, confirm it either without alteration or with such alterations as it thinks reasonable.

(6) For the purpose of determining whether a provisional order should be confirmed under subsection (5) above, the court shall proceed as if an application for the variation or revocation, as the case may be, of the maintenance order in question, had been made to it.

(7) Where a maintenance order to which this section applies has been varied by an order (including a provisional order which has been confirmed) made by a court in the United Kingdom or by a competent court in a reciprocating country, the maintenance order shall, as, from the date on which under the provisions of the order the variation is to take effect, have effect as varied by that order and, where

that order was a provisional order, as if that order had been made in the form in which it was confirmed, and as if it had never been a provisional order.

(8) Where a maintenance order to which this section applies has been revoked by an order made by a court in the United Kingdom or by a competent court in a reciprocating country, including a provisional order made by the last-mentioned court which has been confirmed by a court in the United Kingdom, the maintenance order shall, as from the date on which under the provisions of the order the revocation is to take effect, be deemed to have ceased to have effect except as respects any arrears due under the maintenance order at that date.

(9) Where before a maintenance order made by virtue of section 3 or 4 of this Act is confirmed a document, duly authenticated, setting out or summarising evidence taken in a reciprocating country for the purpose of proceedings relating to the confirmation of the order is received by the court in the United Kingdom which made the order, or that court, in compliance with a request made to it by a court in such a country, takes the evidence of a person residing in the United Kingdom for the purpose of such proceedings, the court in the United Kingdom which made the order shall consider that evidence and if, having done so, it appears to it that the order ought not to have been made –

(*a*) it shall, in such manner as may be prescribed, give to the person on whose application the maintenance order was made an opportunity to consider that evidence, to make representations with respect to it and to adduce further evidence; and

(*b*) after considering all the evidence and any representations made by that person, it may revoke the maintenance order.

(10) ...

Amendments—Domestic Proceedings and Magistrates' Courts Act 1978, s 54; Maintenance Orders (Reciprocal Enforcement) Act 1992, s 1, Sch 1, para 7; SI 1995/755.

Defined terms—"certified copy", "court", "maintenance order", "payee", "payer", "provisional order": s 21(1); "reciprocating country": s 1(1).

"reciprocating country"—For Ireland, see Reciprocal Enforcement of Maintenance Orders (Republic of Ireland) Order 1993; for Hague Convention country, see Reciprocal Enforcement of Maintenance Orders (Hague Convention Countries) Order 1993; for specified States of the United States of America, see Reciprocal Enforcement of Maintenance Orders (United States of America) Order 1995.

"prescribed officer" (s 5(4))—See FPR 1991, r 7.32 and MC(REMO)R 1974, r 3.

"prescribed manner" (s 5(4))—See FPR 1991, rr 7.32, 7.35, 7.36 and MC(REMO)R 1974, r 5.

"court may confirm or refuse to confirm" (s 5(5))—The discretion is as wide as if the application had been made to that court (*Horn v Horn* [1985] FLR 984).

"prescribed" (s 5(9)(*a*))—See MC(REMO)R 1974, r 7.

Orders made by courts in reciprocating countries

6 Registration in United Kingdom court of maintenance order made in reciprocating country

(1) This section applies to a maintenance order made, whether before or after the commencement of this Part of this Act, by a court in a reciprocating country, including such an order made by such a court which has been confirmed by a court

in another reciprocating country but excluding a provisional order which has not been confirmed.

(2) Where a certified copy of an order to which this section applies is received by the Lord Chancellor from the responsible authority in a reciprocating country, and it appears to the Lord Chancellor that the payer under the order is residing or has assets in the United Kingdom, he shall send the copy of the order to the prescribed officer of the appropriate court.

(3) Where the prescribed officer of the appropriate court receives from the Lord Chancellor a certified copy of an order to which this section applies, he shall, subject to subsection (4) below, register the order in the prescribed manner in that court.

(4) Before registering an order under this section an officer of a court shall take such steps as he thinks fit for the purpose of ascertaining whether the payer under the order is residing or has assets within the jurisdiction of the court, and if after taking those steps he is satisfied that the payer is not residing and has no assets within the jurisdiction of the court he shall return the certified copy of the order to the Lord Chancellor with a statement giving such information as he possesses as to the whereabouts of the payer and the nature and location of his assets.

Amendments—Civil Jurisdiction and Judgments Act 1982, s 37(1), Sch 11, para 10; SI 1992/709.

Defined terms—"appropriate court", "certified copy", "court", "maintenance order", "payer", "provisional order": s 21(1); "reciprocating country": s 1(1); "responsible authority": s 21(1).

"reciprocating country"—See note under s 5.

"prescribed officer" (s 6(2))—See Magistrates' Courts (Reciprocal Enforcement of Maintenance Orders) Rules 1974, r 3.

"prescribed manner" (s 6(3))—See MC(REMO)R 1974, r 8.

7 Confirmation by United Kingdom court of provisional maintenance order made in reciprocating country

(1) This section applies to a maintenance order made, whether before or after the commencement of this Part of this Act, by a court in a reciprocating country being a provisional order.

(2) Where a certified copy of an order to which this section applies together with –

- (*a*) a document, duly authenticated, setting out or summarising the evidence given in the proceedings in which the order was made; and
- (*b*) a statement of the grounds on which the making of the order might have been opposed by the payer under the order,

is received by the Lord Chancellor from the responsible authority in a reciprocating country, and it appears to the Lord Chancellor that the payer under the order is residing in the United Kingdom, he shall send the copy of the order and documents which accompanied it to the prescribed officer of the appropriate court, and that court shall –

- (i) if the payer under the order establishes any grounds on which he might have opposed the making of the order in the proceedings in which the order was made, refuse to confirm the order; and
- (ii) in any other case, confirm the order either without alteration or with such alterations as it thinks reasonable.

(3) In any proceedings for the confirmation under this section of a provisional order the statement received from the court which made the order of the grounds on which the making of the order might have been opposed by the payer under the order shall be conclusive evidence that the payer might have opposed the making of the order on any of those grounds.

(4) For the purpose of determining whether a provisional order should be confirmed under this section a magistrates' court in Northern Ireland shall proceed as if an application for a maintenance order against the payer under the provisional order had been made to it.

(5) The prescribed officer of a court having power under this section to confirm a provisional order shall, if the court confirms the order, register the order in the prescribed manner in that court, and shall, if the court refuses to confirm the order, return the certified copy of the order and the documents which accompanied it to the Lord Chancellor.

(5A) Where a magistrates' court in England and Wales confirms a provisional order under this section, it shall at the same time exercise one of its powers under subsection (5B) below.

(5B) The powers of the court are –

- (*a*) the power to order that payments under the order be made directly to a justices' chief executive;
- (*b*) the power to order that payments under the order be made to a justices' chief executive by such method of payment falling within section 59(6) of the Magistrates' Courts Act 1980 (standing order, etc) as may be specified;
- (*c*) the power to make an attachment of earnings order under the Attachment of Earnings Act 1971 to secure payments under the order.

(5C) In deciding which of the powers under subsection (5B) above it is to exercise, the court shall have regard to any representations made by the payer under the order.

(5D) Subsection (4) of section 59 of the Magistrates' Courts Act 1980 (power of court to require debtor to open account) shall apply for the purposes of subsection (5B) above as it applies for the purposes of that section but as if for paragraph (*a*) there were substituted –

> "(*a*) the court proposes to exercise its power under paragraph (*b*) of section 7(5B) of the Maintenance Orders (Reciprocal Enforcement) Act 1972, and".

(5E) Where a court of summary jurisdiction in Northern Ireland confirms a provisional order under this section, it shall at the same time exercise one of its powers under subsection (5F) below.

(5F) The powers of the court are –

- (*a*) the power to order that payments under the order be made directly to the collecting officer;
- (*b*) the power to order that payments under the order be made to the collecting officer, by such method of payment falling within Article 85(7) of the Magistrates' Court (Northern Ireland) Order 1981 (standing order, etc) as may be specified;
- (*c*) the power to make an attachment of earnings order under Part IX of the Order of 1981 to secure payments under the order;

and in this subsection "collecting officer" means the officer mentioned in Article 85(4) of the Order of 1981.

(5G) In deciding which of the powers under subsection (5F) above it is to exercise, the court shall have regard to any representations made by the payer under the order.

(5H) Paragraph (5) of Article 85 of the Magistrates' Courts (Northern Ireland) Order 1981 (power of court to require debtor to open account) shall apply for the purposes of subsection (5F) above as it applies for the purposes of that Article but as if for sub-paragraph (*a*) there were substituted –

"(*a*) the court proposes to exercise its powers under paragraph (*b*) of section 7(5F) of the Maintenance Orders (Reciprocal Enforcement) Act 1972, and".

(6) If notice of the proceedings for the confirmation of the provisional order cannot be duly served on the payer under that order the officer by whom the certified copy of the order was received shall return that copy and the documents which accompanied it to the Lord Chancellor with a statement giving such information as he possesses as to the whereabouts of the payer.

(7) ...

(8) (*repealed*)

Amendments—Maintenance Enforcement Act 1991, s 10, Sch 1, para 12; Maintenance Orders (Reciprocal Enforcement) Act 1992, s 1, Sch 1, para 8; SI 1992/709; SI 1993/1576; SI 1995/755; Access to Justice Act 1999, s 90, Sch 13, para 72.

Defined terms—"court", "maintenance order", "payer", "provisional order": s 21(1); "reciprocating country": s 1(1); "responsible authority": s 21(1).

"prescribed officer" (s 7(2), (5))—See MC(REMO)R 1974.

Alteration of order (s 7(2)(ii))—The laws of the reciprocating country are to be applied to the making of the order (*Peagram v Peagram* [1926] 2 KB 165; *Harris v Harris* [1949] 2 All ER 318).

"statement ... shall be conclusive evidence" (s 7(3))—The statement of possible grounds of opposition received from the reciprocating country does not prevent other defences being raised (*Re Wheat* [1932] 2 KB 716; see also *Harris v Harris* (above), where the payer was permitted to raise the issue of jurisdiction).

"prescribed manner" (s 7(5))—See MC(REMO)R 1974, r 8.

"standing order, etc" (s 7(5B)(*b*), (5E)(*b*))—The methods of payment available do not include power to order payment by direct debit.

8 Enforcement of maintenance order registered in United Kingdom court

(1) Subject to subsection (2) below, a registered order may be enforced in the United Kingdom as if it had been made by the registering court and as if that court had had jurisdiction to make it; and proceedings for or with respect to the enforcement of any such order may be taken accordingly.

(2) Subsection (1) above does not apply to an order which is for the time being registered in the High Court under Part I of the Maintenance Orders Act 1958 or to an order which is for the time being registered in the High Court of Justice in

Northern Ireland under Part II of the Maintenance and Affiliation Orders Act (Northern Ireland) 1966.

(3) Any person for the time being under an obligation to make payments in pursuance of a registered order shall give notice of any change of address to the clerk of the registering court, and any person failing without reasonable excuse to give such a notice shall be liable on summary conviction to a fine not exceeding level 2 on the standard scale.

(3A) ...

(4) An order which by virtue of this section is enforceable by a magistrates' court shall subject to the modifications of sections 76 and 93 of the Magistrates' Courts Act 1980 specified in subsections (4A) and (4B) below be enforceable as if it were a magistrates' court maintenance order made by that court.

In this subsection "magistrates' court maintenance order" has the same meaning as in s 150(1) of the Magistrates' Courts Act 1980.

(4A) Section 76 (enforcement of sums adjudged to be paid) shall have effect as if for subsections (4) to (6) there were substituted the following subsections –

"(4) Where proceedings are brought for the enforcement of a magistrates' court maintenance order under this section, the court may vary the order by exercising one of its powers under subsection (5) below.

(5) The powers of the court are –

(*a*) the power to order that payments under the order be made directly to a justices' chief executive;

(*b*) the power to order that payments under the order be made to a justices' chief executive by such method of payment falling within section 59(6) above (standing order, etc) as may be specified;

(*c*) the power to make an attachment of earnings order under the Attachment of Earnings Act 1971 to secure payments under the order.

(6) In deciding which of the powers under subsection (5) above it is to exercise, the court shall have regard to any representations made by the debtor (within the meaning of section 59 above).

(7) Subsection (4) of section 59 above (power of court to require debtor to open account) shall apply for the purposes of subsection (5) above as it applies for the purposes of that section but as if for paragraph (*a*) there were substituted –

'(*a*) the court proposes to exercise its power under paragraph (*b*) of section 76(5) below, and'."

(4B) In section 93 (complaint for arrears), subsection (6) (court not to impose imprisonment in certain circumstances) shall have effect as if for paragraph (*b*) there were substituted –

"(*b*) if the court is of the opinion that it is appropriate –

(i) to make an attachment of earnings order; or

(ii) to exercise its power under paragraph (*b*) of section 76(5) above."

(5) The magistrates' court by which an order is enforceable by virtue of this section, and the officers thereof, shall take all such steps for enforcing the order as may be prescribed.

(6) In any proceedings for or with respect to the enforcement of an order which is for the time being registered in any court under this Part of this Act a certificate of arrears sent to the prescribed officer of the court shall be evidence of the facts stated therein.

(7) Subject to subsection (8) below, sums of money payable under a registered order shall be payable in accordance with the order as from the date on which they are required to be paid under the provisions of the order.

(8) The court having power under section 7 of this Act to confirm a provisional order may, if it decides to confirm the order, direct that the sums of money payable under it shall be deemed to have been payable in accordance with the order as from the date on which they are required to be paid under the provisions of the order or such later date as it may specify; and subject to any such direction, a maintenance order registered under the said section 7 shall be treated as if it had been made in the form in which it was confirmed and as if it had never been a provisional order.

(9) ...

(10) (*repealed*)

Amendments—Domestic Proceedings and Magistrates' Courts Act 1978, s 54; SI 1981/1675; Criminal Justice Act 1982, s 46; Civil Jurisdiction and Judgments Act 1982, s 37(1), Sch 11, para 11; Family Law Reform Act 1987, s 33(1), Sch 2, para 45; Maintenance Enforcement Act 1991, s 10, Sch 1, para 13; Access to Justice Act 1999, s 90, Sch 13, para 73.

Defined terms—"certificate of arrears", "maintenance order", "provisional order", "registered order", "registering court": s 21(1).

Application to Northern Ireland—Enforcement in Northern Ireland is effected under a modified Magistrates' Court (Northern Ireland) Order 1981. The provisions are similar to the powers outlined here but reference should be made to the Family Law (Northern Ireland) Order 1993.

"reciprocating country"—See note under s 5.

"standing order, etc" (s 8(4A))—The methods of payment available do not include power to order payment by direct debit.

"prescribed" (s 8(5))—See MC(REMO)R 1974, r 9.

"prescribed officer" (s 8(6))—See MC(REMO)R 1974, r 3.

9 Variation and revocation of maintenance order registered in United Kingdom court

(1) Subject to the provisions of this section, the registering court –

(*a*) shall have the like power, on an application made by the payer or payee under a registered order, to vary or revoke the order as if it had been made by the registering court and as if that court had had jurisdiction to make it; and

(*b*) shall have power to vary or revoke a registered order by a provisional order.

(1ZA) Where the registering court is a magistrates' court in England and Wales, section 60 of the Magistrates' Courts Act 1980 (revocation, variation etc of orders for periodical payment) shall have effect in relation to the registered order –

(*za*) as if in subsection (1) for the words "by order on complaint", there were substituted "on an application being made, by order";

(*a*) as if in subsection (3) for the words "paragraphs (*a*) to (*d*) of section 59(3) above" there were substituted "subsection (3A) below" and after that subsection there were inserted –

"(3A) The powers of the court are –

(*a*) the power to order that payments under the order be made directly to a justices' chief executive;

(*b*) the power to order that payments under the order be made to a justices' chief executive by such method of payment falling within section 59(6) above (standing order, etc) as may be specified;

(*c*) the power to make an attachment of earnings order under the Attachment of Earnings Act 1971 to secure payments under the order.";

(*b*) as if in subsection (4) for paragraph (*b*) there were substituted –

"(*b*) payments under the order are required to be made to a justices' chief executive by any method of payment falling within section 59(6) above (standing order, etc)";

(*c*) as if in subsection (5) for the words "to the justices' chief executive for the court" there were substituted "in accordance with paragraph (*a*) of subsection (3A) above";

(*d*) as if in subsection (7), paragraph (*c*) and the word "and" immediately preceding it were omitted;

(*e*) as if in subsection (8) for the words "paragraphs (*a*) to (*d*) of section 59(3) above" there were substituted "subsection (3A) above";

(*f*) as if for subsections (9) and (10) there were substituted the following subsections –

"(9) In deciding, for the purposes of subsections (3) and (8) above, which of the powers under subsection (3A) above it is to exercise, the court shall have regard to any representations made by the debtor.

(10) Subsection (4) of section 59 above (power of court to require debtor to open account) shall apply for the purposes of subsection (3A) above as it applies for the purposes of that section but as if for paragraph (*a*) there were substituted –

'(*a*) the court proposes to exercise its power under paragraph (*b*) of section 60(3A) below, and'."

(1ZB) Where the registering court is a court of summary jurisdiction in Northern Ireland, Article 86 of the Magistrates' Courts (Northern Ireland) Order 1981 (revocation, variation etc, of orders for periodical payment) shall have effect in relation to the registered order –

(*za*) as if in paragraph (1) for the words "by order on complaint," there were substituted "on an application being made, by order";

(*a*) as if in paragraph (3) for the words "sub-paragraphs (*a*) to (*d*) of Article 85(3)" there were substituted "paragraph (3A)" and after that paragraph there were inserted –

"(3A) The powers of the court are –

(*a*) the power to order that payments under the order be made directly to the collecting officer;

(*b*) the power to order that payments under the order be made to the collecting officer by such method of payment falling within Article 85(7) (standing order, etc) as may be specified;

(*c*) the power to make an attachment of earnings order under Part IX to secure payments under the order.";

(*b*) as if in paragraph (4) for sub-paragraph (*b*) there were substituted –

"(*b*) payments under the order are required to be made to the collecting officer by any method of payment falling within Article 85(7) (standing order, etc)";

and as if after the words "petty sessions" there were inserted "for the petty sessions district for which the court which made the order acts";

(*c*) as if in paragraph (5) for the words "to the collecting officer" there were substituted "in accordance with sub-paragraph (*a*) of paragraph (3A)";

(*d*) as if in paragraph (7), sub-paragraph (*c*) and the word "and" immediately preceding it were omitted;

(*e*) as if in paragraph (8) for the words "sub-paragraphs (*a*) to (*d*) of Article 85(3)" there were substituted "paragraph (3A)";

(*f*) as if for paragraphs (9) and (10) there were substituted the following paragraphs –

"(9) In deciding, for the purposes of paragraphs (3) and (8), which of the powers under paragraph (3A) it is to exercise, the court shall have regard to any representations made by the debtor.

(10) Paragraph (5) of Article 85 (power of court to require debtor to open account) shall apply for the purposes of paragraph (3A) as it applies for the purposes of that Article but as if for sub-paragraph (*a*) there were substituted –

'(*a*) the court proposes to exercise its powers under sub-paragraph (*b*) of Article 86(3A), and'.".

(2) The registering court shall not vary a registered order otherwise than by a provisional order unless –

(*a*) both the payer and the payee under the registered order are for the time being residing in the United Kingdom; or

(*b*) the application is made by the payee under the registered order; or

(*c*) the variation consists of a reduction in the rate of the payments under the registered order and is made solely on the ground that there has been a change in the financial circumstances of the payer since the registered order was made or, in the case of an order registered under section 7 of this Act, since the registered order was confirmed, and the courts in the reciprocating country in which the maintenance order in question was made do not have power, according to the law in force in that country, to confirm provisional orders varying maintenance orders.

(3) The registering court shall not revoke a registered order otherwise than by a provisional order unless both the payer and the payee under the registered order are for the time being residing in the United Kingdom.

(4) On an application for the revocation of a registered order the registering court shall, unless both the payer and the payee under the registered order are for the time being residing in the United Kingdom, apply the law applied by the reciprocating country in which the registered order was made; but where by virtue of this subsection the registering court is required to apply that law, that court may make a provisional order if it has reason to believe that the ground on which the application is made is a ground on which the order could be revoked according to the law applied by the reciprocating country, notwithstanding that it has not been established that it is such a ground.

(5) Where the registering court makes a provisional order varying or revoking a registered order the prescribed officer of the court shall send in the prescribed manner to the court in the reciprocating country which made the registered order a

certified copy of the provisional order together with a document, authenticated in the prescribed manner, setting out or summarising the evidence given in the proceedings.

(6) Where a certified copy of a provisional order made by a court in a reciprocating country, being an order varying a registered order, together with a document, duly authenticated, setting out or summarising the evidence given in the proceedings in which the provisional order was made, is received by the registering court, that court may confirm the order either without alteration or with such alterations as it thinks reasonable or refuse to confirm the order.

(7) For the purpose of determining whether a provisional order should be confirmed under subsection (6) above the court shall proceed as if an application for the variation of the registered order had been made to it.

(8) Where a registered order has been varied by an order (including a provisional order which has been confirmed) made by a court in the United Kingdom or by a competent court in a reciprocating country, the registered order shall, as from the date on which under the provisions of the order the variation is to take effect, have effect as varied by that order and, where that order was a provisional order, as if that order had been made in the form in which it was confirmed and as if it had never been a provisional order.

(9) Where a registered order has been revoked by an order made by a court in the United Kingdom or by a competent court in a reciprocating country, including a provisional order made by the first-mentioned court which has been confirmed by a competent court in a reciprocating country, the registered order shall, as from the date on which under the provisions of the order the revocation is to take effect, be deemed to have ceased to have effect except as respects any arrears due under the registered order at that date.

(10) The prescribed officer of the registering court shall register in the prescribed manner any order varying a registered order other than a provisional order which is not confirmed.

(11) ...

Amendments—Domestic Proceedings and Magistrates' Courts Act 1978, s 54; Civil Jurisdiction and Judgments Act 1982, s 37(1), Sch 11, paras 4, 12; Maintenance Enforcement Act 1991, s 10, Sch 1, para 14; Maintenance Orders (Reciprocal Enforcement) Act 1992, s 1, Sch 1, para 9; SI 1993/1576; SI 1995/755; Access to Justice Act 1999, s 90, Sch 13, para 74, Sch 15.

Defined terms—"payee", "payer", "provisional order": s 21(1); "reciprocating country": s 1(1); "registered order", "registering court": s 21(1).

"reciprocating country"—See note under s 5.

"standing order, etc" (s 9(1ZA))—See under s 7.

"prescribed officer" (s 9(5), (10))—See MC(REMO)R 1974, r 3.

"prescribed manner" (s 9(10))—See MC(REMO)R 1974, r 12.

10 Cancellation of registration and transfer of order

(1) Where –

(*a*) a registered order is revoked by an order made by the registering court; or (*b*) a registered order is revoked by a provisional order made by that court which has been confirmed by a court in a reciprocating country and notice of the confirmation is received by the registering court; or

(*c*) a registered order is revoked by an order made by a court in such a country and notice of the revocation is received by the registering court,

the prescribed officer of the registering court shall cancel the registration; but any arrears due under the registered order at the date when its registration is cancelled by virtue of this subsection shall continue to be recoverable as if the registration had not been cancelled.

(2) Where the prescribed officer of the registering court is of opinion that the payer under a registered order is not residing within the jurisdiction of that court and has no assets within that jurisdiction against which the order can be effectively enforced, he shall cancel the registration of the order and, subject to subsection (3) below, shall send the certified copy of the order to the Lord Chancellor.

(3) Where the prescribed officer of the registering court, being a magistrates' court, is of opinion that the payer is residing or has assets within the jurisdiction of another magistrates' court in that part of the United Kingdom in which the registering court is, he shall transfer the order to that other court by sending the certified copy of the order to the prescribed officer of that other court.

(4) On the transfer of the order under subsection (3) above the prescribed officer of the court to which it is transferred shall, subject to subsection (6) below, register the order in the prescribed manner in that court.

(5) Where the certified copy of an order is received by the Lord Chancellor under this section and it appears to him that the payer under the order is residing or has assets in the United Kingdom, he shall transfer the order to the appropriate court by sending the certified copy of the order together with the related documents to the prescribed officer of the appropriate court and, subject to subsection (6) below, that officer shall register the order in the prescribed manner in that court.

(6) Before registering an order in pursuance of subsection (4) or (5) above an officer of a court shall take such steps as he thinks fit for the purpose of ascertaining whether the payer is residing or has assets within the jurisdiction of the court, and if after taking those steps he is satisfied that the payer is not residing and has no assets within the jurisdiction of the court he shall send the certified copy of the order to the Lord Chancellor.

(7) The officer of a court who is required by any of the foregoing provisions of this section to send to the Lord Chancellor or to the prescribed officer of another court the certified copy of an order shall send with that copy –

(*a*) a certificate of arrears signed by him;

(*b*) a statement giving such information as he possesses as to the whereabouts of the payer and the nature and location of his assets; and

(*c*) any relevant documents in his possession relating to the case.

(8) ...

Amendments—Civil Jurisdiction and Judgments Act 1982, s 37(1), Sch 11, para 13; SI 1992/709.

Defined terms—"certified copy", "court": s 21(1); "jurisdiction": s 47(3); "provisional order": s 21(1); "reciprocating country": s 1(1); "registered order", "registering court": s 21(1).

"reciprocating country"—See note under s 5.

PART II

"prescribed officer" (s 10(1), (2), (3))—See Magistrates' Courts (Reciprocal Enforcement of Maintenance Orders) Rules 1974, r 3.

"prescribed manner" (s 10(4), (5))—See MC(REMO)R 1974, r 8.

11 Steps to be taken by Lord Chancellor where payer under certain orders is not residing in the United Kingdom

(1) If at any time it appears to the Lord Chancellor that the payer under a maintenance order, a certified copy of which has been received by him from a reciprocating country, is not residing and has no assets in the United Kingdom, he shall send to the responsible authority in that country or, if having regard to all the circumstances he thinks it proper to do so, to the responsible authority in another reciprocating country –

- (*a*) the certified copy of the order in question and a certified copy of any order varying that order;
- (*b*) if the order has at any time been a registered order, a certificate of arrears signed by the prescribed officer;
- (*c*) a statement giving such information as the Lord Chancellor possesses as to the whereabouts of the payer and the nature and location of his assets; and
- (*d*) any other relevant documents in his possession relating to the case.

(2) Where the documents mentioned in subsection (1) above are sent to the responsible authority in a reciprocating country other than that in which the order in question was made, the Lord Chancellor shall inform the responsible authority in the reciprocating country in which that order was made of what he has done.

Amendments—Civil Jurisdiction and Judgments Act 1982, s 37(1), Sch 11, para 13; SI 1992/709.

Defined terms—"certified copy", "maintenance order", "payer": s 21(1); "reciprocating country": s 1(1); "registered order", "responsible authority": s 21(1).

"reciprocating country"—See note under s 5.

"prescribed officer" (s 11(1))—See Magistrates' Courts (Reciprocal Enforcement of Maintenance Orders) Rules 1974, r 3.

Appeals

12 Appeals

(1) No appeal shall lie from a provisional order made in pursuance of any provision of this Part of this Act by a court in the United Kingdom.

(2) Where in pursuance of any such provision any such court confirms or refuses to confirm a provisional order made by a court in a reciprocating country, whether a maintenance order or an order varying or revoking a maintenance order, the payer or payee under the maintenance order shall have the like right of appeal (if any) from the confirmation of, or refusal to conform, the provisional order as he would have if that order were not a provisional order and the court which confirmed or refused to confirm it had made or, as the case may be, refused to make it.

(3) Where in pursuance of any such provision any such court makes, or refuses to make, an order varying or revoking a maintenance order made by a court in a reciprocating country, then, subject to subsection (1) above, the payer or payee under the maintenance order shall have the like right of appeal (if any) from that

order or from the refusal to make it as he would have if the maintenance order had been made by the first-mentioned court.

(4) Nothing in this section (except subsection (1)) shall be construed as affecting any right of appeal conferred by any other enactment.

Defined terms—"court", "payee", "payer", "provisional order": s 21(1); "reciprocating country": s 1(1).

"reciprocating country"—See note under s 5.

Evidence

13 Admissibility of evidence given in reciprocating country

(1) A statement contained in –

(*a*) a document, duly authenticated, which purports to set out or summarise evidence given in proceedings in a court in a reciprocating country; or

(*b*) a document, duly authenticated, which purports to set out or summarise evidence taken in such a country for the purpose of proceedings in a court in the United Kingdom under this Part of this Act, whether in response to a request made by such a court or otherwise; or

(*c*) a document, duly authenticated, which purports to have been received in evidence in proceedings in a court in such a country or to be a copy of a document so received,

shall in any proceedings in a court in the United Kingdom relating to a maintenance order to which this Part of this Act applies be admissible as evidence of any fact stated therein to the same extent as oral evidence of that fact is admissible in those proceedings.

(2) A document purporting to set out or summarise evidence given as mentioned in subsection (1)(*a*) above, or taken as mentioned in subsection (1)(*b*) above, shall be deemed to be duly authenticated for the purposes of that subsection if the document purports to be certified by the judge, magistrate or other person before whom the evidence was given, or, as the case may be, by whom it was taken, to be the original document containing or recording, or, as the case may be, summarising, that evidence or a true copy of that document.

(3) A document purporting to have been received in evidence as mentioned in subsection (1)(*c*) above, or to be a copy of a document so received, shall be deemed to be duly authenticated for the purposes of that subsection if the document purports to be certified by a judge, magistrate or officer of the court in question to have been, or to be a true copy of a document which has been, so received.

(4) It shall not be necessary in any such proceedings to prove the signature or official position of the person appearing to have given such a certificate.

(5) Nothing in this section shall prejudice the admission in evidence of any document which is admissible in evidence apart from this section.

Defined terms—"court", "maintenance order": s 21(1); "reciprocating country": s 1(1).

"reciprocating country"—See note under s 5.

PART II

14 Obtaining of evidence needed for purpose of certain proceedings

(1) Where for the purpose of any proceedings in a court in a reciprocating country relating to a maintenance order to which this Part of this Act applies a request is made by or on behalf of that court for the taking in the United Kingdom of the evidence of a person residing therein relating to matters specified in the request, such court in the United Kingdom as may be prescribed shall have power to take that evidence and, after giving notice of the time and place at which the evidence is to be taken to such persons and in such manner as it thinks fit, shall take the evidence in such manner as may be prescribed.

Evidence taken in compliance with such a request shall be sent in the prescribed manner by the prescribed officer of the court to the court in the reciprocating country by or on behalf of which the request was made.

(2) Where any person, not being the payer or the payee under the maintenance order to which the proceedings in question relate, is required by virtue of this section to give evidence before a court in the United Kingdom, the court may order that there shall be paid –

(*a*) if the court is a court in England, Wales or Scotland, out of moneys provided by Parliament; and
(*b*) if the court is a court in Northern Ireland, out of moneys provided by Parliament,

such sums as appear to the court reasonably sufficient to compensate that person for the expense, trouble or loss of time properly incurred in or incidental to his attendance.

(3) Section 97(1), (3) and (4) of the Magistrates' Courts Act 1980 (which provide for compelling the attendance of witnesses, etc) shall apply in relation to a magistrates' court having power under subsection (1) above to take the evidence of any person as if the proceedings in the court in a reciprocating country for the purpose of which a request for the taking of the evidence has been made were proceedings in the magistrates' court and had been begun by complaint.

(4) ...

(5) A court in the United Kingdom may for the purpose of any proceedings in that court under this Part of this Act relating to a maintenance order to which this Part of this Act applies request a court in a reciprocating country to take or provide evidence relating to such matters as may be specified in the request and may remit the case to that court for that purpose.

(6) In the application of this section to Northern Ireland, in subsection (3), for the reference to section 97(1), (3) and (4) of the Magistrates' Courts Act 1980 there shall be substituted a reference to Articles 118(1), (3) and (4), 119 and 120 of the Magistrates' Courts (Northern Ireland) Order 1981.

Amendments—SI 1973/2163; Magistrates' Courts Act 1980, s 154, Sch 7, para 105; SI 1981/1675.

Defined terms—"court", "maintenance order": s 21(1); "reciprocating country": s 1(1).

"reciprocating country"—See note under s 5.

"such court ... as may be prescribed" (s 14(1))—See FPR 1991, r 7.34 and Magistrates' Courts (Reciprocal Enforcement of Maintenance Orders) Rules 1974, r 10.

"prescribed manner" (s 14(1))—See FPR 1991, r 7.34 and MC(REMO)R 1974, r 10.

"prescribed officer" (s 14(1))—See FPR 1991, r 7.34 and MC(REMO)R 1974, r 3.

15 Order etc made abroad need not be proved

For the purposes of this Part of this Act, unless the contrary is shown –

(*a*) any order made by a court in a reciprocating country purporting to bear the seal of that court or to be signed by any person in his capacity as a judge, magistrate or officer of the court, shall be deemed without further proof to have been duly sealed or, as the case may be, to have been signed by that person;

(*b*) the person by whom the order was signed shall be deemed without further proof to have been a judge, magistrate or officer, as the case may be, of that court when he signed it and, in the case of an officer, to have been authorised to sign it; and

(*c*) a document purporting to be a certified copy of an order made by a court in a reciprocating country shall be deemed without further proof to be such a copy.

Defined terms—"certified copy", "court": s 21(1); "reciprocating country": s 1(1).

"reciprocating country"—See note under s 5.

Supplemental

16 Payment of sums under orders made abroad: conversion of currency

(1) Payment of sums due under a registered order shall, while the order is registered in a court in England, Wales or Northern Ireland, be made in such manner and to such person as may be prescribed.

(2) Where the sums required to be paid under a registered order are expressed in a currency other than the currency of the United Kingdom, then, as from the relevant date, the order shall be treated as if it were an order requiring the payment of such sums in the currency of the United Kingdom as, on the basis of the rate of exchange prevailing at that date, are equivalent to the sums so required to be paid.

(3) Where the sum specified in any statement, being a statement of the amount of any arrears due under a maintenance order made by a court in a reciprocating country is expressed in a currency other than the currency of the United Kingdom, that sum shall be deemed to be such sum in the currency of the United Kingdom as, on the basis of the rate of exchange prevailing at the relevant date, is equivalent to the sum so specified.

(4) For the purposes of this section a written certificate purporting to be signed by an officer of any bank in the United Kingdom certifying that a specified rate of exchange prevailed between currencies at a specified date and that at such rate a specified sum in the currency of the United Kingdom is equivalent to a specified sum in another specified currency shall be evidence of the rate of exchange so prevailing on that date and of the equivalent sums in terms of the respective currencies.

(5) In this section "the relevant date" means –

(*a*) in relation to a registered order or to a statement of arrears due under a maintenance order made by a court in a reciprocating country, the date on which the order first becomes a registered order or (if earlier) the date on which it is confirmed by a court in the United Kingdom;

(*b*) in relation to a registered order which has been varied, the date on which the last order varying that order is registered in a court in the United Kingdom or (if earlier) the date on which the last order varying that order is confirmed by such a court.

(6) ...

Defined terms—"maintenance order", "registered order": s 21(1); "reciprocating country": s 1(1).

"reciprocating country"—See note under s 5.

"to such person as may be prescribed" (s 16(1))—See Magistrates' Courts (Reciprocal Enforcement of Maintenance Orders) Rules 1974, r 9.

17 Proceedings in magistrates' courts

(1)–(3) (*repealed*)

(4) Anything authorised or required by this Part of this Act to be done by, to or before the magistrates' court by, to or before which any other thing was done may be done by, to or before any magistrates' court acting for the same petty sessions area (or, in Northern Ireland, petty sessions district) as that court.

(5) (*repealed*)

(5A) Where the respondent to an application for the variation or revocation of –

(*a*) a maintenance order made by a magistrates' court in England and Wales, being an order to which section 5 of this Act applies; or

(*b*) a registered order which is registered in such a court,

is residing in a reciprocating country, a magistrates' court in England and Wales shall have jurisdiction to hear the application (where it would not have such jurisdiction apart from this subsection) if it would have had jurisdiction to hear it had the respondent been residing in England and Wales.

(6) Where the respondent to an application for the variation or revocation of –

(*a*) a maintenance order made by a magistrates' court in Northern Ireland, being an order to which section 5 of this Act applies; or

(*b*) a registered order which is registered in such a court,

is residing in a reciprocating country, a magistrates' court in Northern Ireland shall have jurisdiction to hear the application (where it would not have jurisdiction apart from this subsection) if it would have had jurisdiction to hear it had the respondent been residing in Northern Ireland.

(7) Where the respondent to an application for the variation or revocation –

(*a*) of a maintenance order made by a magistrates' court, being an order to which section 5 of this Act applies; or

(*b*) of a registered order registered in a magistrates' court,

does not appear at the time and place appointed for the hearing of the application, but the court is satisfied that the respondent is residing in a reciprocating country, the court may proceed to hear and determine the application at the time and place appointed for the hearing or for any adjourned hearing in like manner as if the respondent had appeared at that time and place.

(7A), (8) (*repealed*)

Amendments—Domestic Proceedings and Magistrates' Courts Act 1978, s 89(2), Sch 3; SI 1981/1675; Maintenance Orders (Reciprocal Enforcement) Act 1992, s 1, Sch 1, para 10 ; SI 1995/755.

Defined terms—"maintenance order": s 21(1); "reciprocating country": s 1(1); "registered order": s 21(1).

"reciprocating country"—See note under s 5.

18 Magistrates' courts rules

(1) Without prejudice to the generality of the power to make rules under section 144 of the Magistrates' Courts Act 1980 (magistrates' courts rules), provision may be made by such rules with respect to any of the following matters, namely –

(*a*) the circumstances in which anything authorised or required by this Part of this Act to be done by, to or before a magistrates' court acting for a particular petty sessions area or by, to or before an officer of that court may be done by, to or before a magistrates' court acting for such other petty sessions area as the rules may provide or by, to or before an officer of that court;

(*b*) the orders made, or other things done, by a magistrates' court, or an officer of such a court, under this Part of this Act, or by a court in a reciprocating country, notice of which is to be given to such persons as the rules may provide and the manner in which such notice shall be given;

(*c*) the cases and manner in which courts in reciprocating countries are to be informed of orders made, or other things done, by a magistrates' court under this Part of this Act;

(*d*) the cases and manner in which a justices' clerk may take evidence needed for the purpose of proceedings in a court in a reciprocating country relating to a maintenance order to which this Part of this Act applies;

(*e*) the circumstances and manner in which cases may be remitted by magistrates' courts to courts in reciprocating countries;

(*f*) the circumstances and manner in which magistrates' courts may for the purposes of this Part of this Act communicate with courts in reciprocating countries.

(1A) For the purpose of giving effect to this Part of this Act, rules made under section 144 of the Magistrates' Courts Act 1980 may make, in relation to any proceedings brought under or by virtue of this Part of this Act, any provision not covered by subsection (1) above which –

(*a*) falls within subsection (2) of section 93 of the Children Act 1989, and

(*b*) may be made in relation to relevant proceedings under that section.

(2) Rules with respect to the matter mentioned in subsection (1) above may be made in accordance with Article 13 of the Magistrates' Courts (Northern Ireland) Order 1981 in relation to proceedings or matters in magistrates' courts in Northern Ireland under this Part of this Act.

(2A) For the purpose of giving effect to this Part of this Act, rules made in accordance with Article 13 of the Magistrates' Courts (Northern Ireland) Order 1981 may make, in relation to any proceedings brought under or by virtue of this Part of this Act, any provision not covered by subsection (2) above which –

(*a*) falls within paragraph (2) of Article 165 of the Children (Northern Ireland) Order 1995, and

(*b*) may be made in relation to relevant proceedings under that Article.

Amendments—Magistrates' Courts Act 1980, s 154, Sch 7, para 106; SI 1981/1675; Maintenance Orders (Reciprocal Enforcement) Act 1992, s 1, Sch 1, para 11; SI 1995/755.

Defined terms—"maintenance order": s 21(1); "reciprocating country": s 1(1).

Scope of provision—This section provides for the making of rules for the application of Pt I. The Magistrates' Courts (Reciprocal Enforcement of Maintenance Orders) Rules 1974 have been made for this purpose.

"reciprocating country"—See note under s 5.

****

20 Restriction on enforcement of arrears under maintenance order registered in Scotland

Where a maintenance order is for the time being registered in the sheriff court under this Part of this Act, a person shall not be entitled, except with the leave of the sheriff, to enforce, whether by diligence or otherwise, the payment of any arrears due under the order, if either –

(*a*) the sheriff has made a provisional order under section 9 of this Act revoking the said maintenance order and the arrears accrued after the making of the said provisional order, or

(*b*) the arrears accrued before the commencement of this Part of this Act;

and on any application for leave to enforce the payment of any such arrears, the sheriff may refuse leave, or may grant leave subject to such restrictions and conditions (including conditions as to the allowing of time for payment or the making of payment by instalments) as he thinks appropriate, or may remit the payment of such arrears or of any part thereof.

Defined terms—"maintenance order", "provisional order": s 21(1).

21 Interpretation of Part I

(1) In this Part of this Act –

"affiliation order" means an order (however described) adjudging, finding or declaring a person to be the father of a child, whether or not it also provides for the maintenance of the child;

"the appropriate court" in relation to a person residing or having assets in England and Wales or in Northern Ireland means a magistrates' court, and in relation to a person residing or having assets in Scotland means a sheriff court, within the jurisdiction of which that person is residing or has assets;

"certificate of arrears", in relation to a maintenance order, means a certificate certifying that the sum specified in the certificate is to the best of the information or belief of the officer giving the certificate the amount of the arrears due under the order at the date of the certificate or, as the case may be, that to the best of his information or belief there are no arrears due thereunder at that date;

"certified copy", in relation to an order of a court, means a copy of the order certified by the proper officer of the court to be a true copy;

"court" includes any tribunal or person having power to make, confirm, enforce, vary or revoke a maintenance order;

...

"maintenance order" means an order (however described) of any of the following descriptions, that is to say –

(*a*) an order (including an affiliation order or order consequent upon an affiliation order) which provides for the payment of a lump sum on the making of periodical payments towards the maintenance of any person, being a person whom the person liable to make payments under the order is, according to the law applied in the place where the order was made, liable to maintain; and

(*b*) an affiliation order or order consequent upon an affiliation order, being an order which provides for the payment by a person adjudged, found or declared to be a child's father of expenses incidental to the child's birth or, where the child has died, of his funeral expenses,

and, in the case of a maintenance order which has been varied, means that order as varied;

...

"payee", in relation to a maintenance order, means the person entitled to the payments for which the order provides;

"payer", in relation to a maintenance order, means the person liable to make payments under the order;

"prescribed", in relation to a magistrates' court in England and Wales or in Northern Ireland, means prescribed by rules made under section 144 of the Magistrates' Courts Act 1980 or by rules made in accordance with Article 13 of the Magistrates' Courts (Northern Ireland) Order 1981, as the case may be, and in relation to any other court means prescribed by rules of court;

"provisional order" means (according to the context) –

(*a*) an order made by a court in the United Kingdom which is provisional only and has no effect unless and until confirmed, with or without alteration, by a competent court in a reciprocating country; or

(*b*) an order made by a court in a reciprocating country which is provisional only and has no effect unless and until confirmed, with or without alteration, by a court in the United Kingdom having power under this Part of this Act to confirm it;

"reciprocating country" has the meaning assigned to it by section 1 of this Act;

"registered order" means a maintenance order which is for the time being registered in a court in the United Kingdom under this Part of this Act;

"registering court", in relation to a registered order, means the court in which that order is for the time being registered under this Part of this Act;

"the responsible authority", in relation to a reciprocating country, means any person who in that country has functions similar to those of the Lord Chancellor under this Part of this Act;

"revoke" and "revocation" include discharge.

(2) For the purposes of this Part of this Act an order shall be taken to be a maintenance order so far (but only so far) as it relates to the payment of a lump sum on the making of periodical payments as mentioned in paragraph (*a*) of the definition of "maintenance order" in subsection (1) above or to the payment by a person adjudged, found or declared to be a child's father of any such expenses as are mentioned in paragraph (*b*) of that definition.

(3) Any reference in this Part of this Act to the payment of money for the maintenance of a child shall be construed as including a reference to the payment of money for the child's education.

Amendments—Magistrates' Courts Act 1980, s 154, Sch 7, para 107; SI 1981/1675; Civil Jurisdiction and Judgments Act 1982, s 37(1), Sch 11, paras 4, 15; Maintenance Orders (Reciprocal Enforcement) Act 1992, s 1, Sch 1, para 12; SI 1992/709.

Amendments, repeals and transitional provisions

22 Amendments and repeals

(1) The enactments mentioned in the Schedule to this Act shall have effect subject to the minor and consequential amendments specified therein.

(2) The following are hereby repealed –

(*a*) the Maintenance Orders (Facilities for Enforcement) Act 1920;
(*b*) (*repealed*)
(*c*) in the Maintenance Orders Act 1958, section 19 and, in section 23(2), the words "section nineteen";
(*d*) (*repealed*)

Amendments—Magistrates' Courts Act 1980, s 154, Sch 9; South Africa Act 1995, s 1, Sch, para 7(2).

23 Maintenance order registered in High Court under the Maintenance Orders etc Act 1920

(1) Where a country or territory, being a country or territory to which at the commencement of section 1 of this Act the Maintenance Orders (Facilities for Enforcement) Act 1920 extended becomes a reciprocating country, then, if immediately before the Order in Council made under section 12 of that Act extending that Act to that country or territory was revoked any maintenance order made by a court in that country or territory was registered in the High Court under section 1 of that Act, the High Court may, on an application by the payer or the payee under the order or of its own motion, transfer the order to such magistrates' court as having regard to the place where the payer is residing and to all the circumstances it thinks most appropriate, with a view to the order being registered in that court under this Part of this Act.

(2) Where the High Court transfers an order to a magistrates' court under this section it shall –

(*a*) cause a certified copy of the order to be sent to the appropriate officer of that court, and
(*b*) cancel the registration of the order in the High Court.

(3) The appropriate officer of the court who receives a certified copy of an order sent to him under this section shall register the order in the prescribed manner in that court.

(4) On registering a maintenance order in the magistrates' court by virtue of this section the appropriate officer of the court shall, if the order is registered in that court under Part I of the Maintenance Orders Act 1958 cancel that registration.

(5) In the application of this section to Northern Ireland, for references to the High Court there shall be substituted references to the High Court of Justice in Northern Ireland.

(6) ...

Amendments—Access to Justice Act 1999, s 90, Sch 13, para 75.

Defined terms—"certified copy", "court", "maintenance order", "payee", "payer": s 21(1); "reciprocating country": s 1(1).

"prescribed manner" (s 23(3))—See Magistrates' Courts (Reciprocal Enforcement of Maintenance Orders) Rules 1974, r 8.

24 Application of Part I to certain orders and proceedings under the Maintenance Orders etc Act 1920

Where Her Majesty proposes by an Order in Council under section 1 of this Act to designate as a reciprocating country a country or territory to which at the commencement of that section the Maintenance Orders (Facilities for Enforcement) Act 1920 extended, that Order in Council may contain such provisions as Her Majesty considers expedient for the purpose of securing –

(*a*) that the provisions of this Part of this Act apply, subject to such modifications as may be specified in the Order, to maintenance orders, or maintenance orders of a specified class –

(i) made by a court in England, Wales or Northern Ireland against a person residing or having assets in that country or territory, or

(ii) made by a court in that country or territory against a person residing or having assets in England, Wales or Northern Ireland,

being orders to which immediately before the date of the coming into operation of the Order in Council the said Act of 1920 applied, except any order which immediately before that date is registered in the High Court or the High Court of Justice in Northern Ireland under section 1 of that Act;

(*b*) that any maintenance order, or maintenance order of a specified class, made by a court in that country or territory which has been confirmed by a court in England, Wales or Northern Ireland under section 4 of the said Act of 1920 and is in force immediately before that date is registered under section 7 of this Act;

(*c*) that any proceedings brought under or by virtue of a provision of the said Act of 1920 in a court in England, Wales or Northern Ireland which are pending at that date, being proceedings affecting a person resident in that country or territory, are continued as if they had been brought under or by virtue of the corresponding provision of this Part of this Act.

Amendments—Civil Jurisdiction and Judgments Act 1982, s 37(1), Sch 11, para 16.

Defined terms—"court", "maintenance order": s 21(1); "reciprocating country": s 1(1).

PART II
RECIPROCAL ENFORCEMENT OF CLAIMS FOR THE RECOVERY OF MAINTENANCE

Convention countries

25 Convention countries

(1) Her Majesty may by Order in Council declare that any country or territory specified in the Order, being a country or territory outside the United Kingdom to which the Maintenance Convention extends, is a Convention country for the purposes of this Part of this Act.

(2) In this section "the Maintenance Convention" means the United Nations Convention on the Recovery Abroad of Maintenance done at New York on 20 June 1956.

Scope of provision—This section provides that a country or territory may be declared a Convention country for the purposes of Pt II by Order in Council. The Recovery Abroad of Maintenance (Convention Countries) Order 1975 and the Recovery of Maintenance (United States of America) Order 1993 have been made for this purpose. For guidance on the application of Pt II, see Home Office Circular No 54/1975. See also the Magistrates' Courts (Recovery Abroad of Maintenance) Rules 1975.

Application by person in the United Kingdom for recovery etc of maintenance in Convention country

26 Application by person in United Kingdom for recovery etc of maintenance in Convention country

(1) Where a person in the United Kingdom ("the applicant") claims to be entitled to recover in a Convention country maintenance from another person, and that other person is for the time being subject to the jurisdiction of that country, the applicant may apply to the Lord Chancellor, in accordance with the provisions of this section, to have his claim for the recovery of maintenance from that other person transmitted to that country.

(2) Where the applicant seeks to vary any provision made in a Convention country for the payment by any other person of maintenance to the applicant, and that other person is for the time being subject to the jurisdiction of that country, the applicant may apply to the Lord Chancellor, in accordance with the provisions of this section, to have his application for the variation of that provision transmitted to that country.

(3) An application to the Lord Chancellor under subsection (1) or (2) above shall be made through the appropriate officer, and that officer shall assist the applicant in completing an application which will comply with the requirements of the law applied by the Convention country and shall send the application to the Lord Chancellor, together with such other documents, if any, as are required by that law.

(4) On receiving an application from the appropriate officer the Lord Chancellor shall transmit it, together with any accompanying documents, to the appropriate authority in the Convention country, unless he is satisfied that the application is not made in good faith or that it does not comply with the requirements of the law applied by that country.

(5) The Lord Chancellor may request the appropriate officer to obtain from the court of which he is an officer such information relating to the application as may be specified in the request, and it shall be the duty of the court to furnish the Lord Chancellor with the information he requires.

(6) ...

Amendments—SI 1992/709.

Defined terms—"Convention country": s 25(1).

Application by person in Convention country for recovery of maintenance in England, Wales or Northern Ireland

27 *(repealed)*

27A Applications for recovery of maintenance in England and Wales

(1) This section applies to any application which –

(*a*) is received by the Lord Chancellor from the appropriate authority in a Convention country, and

(*b*) is an application by a person in that country for the recovery of maintenance from another person who is for the time being residing in England and Wales.

(2) Subject to sections 27B to 28B of this Act, an application to which this section applies shall be treated for the purposes of any enactment as if it were an application for a maintenance order under the relevant Act, made at the time when the application was received by the Lord Chancellor.

(3) In the case of an application for maintenance for a child (or children) alone, the relevant Act is the Children Act 1989.

(4) In any other case, the relevant Act is the Domestic Proceedings and Magistrates' Courts Act 1978.

(5) In subsection (3) above, "child" means the same as in Schedule 1 to the Children Act 1989.

Amendments—Inserted by Maintenance Orders (Reciprocal Enforcement) Act 1992, s 1, Sch 1, para 13.

Defined terms—"Convention country": s 25(1).

27B Sending application to the appropriate magistrates' court

(1) On receipt of an application to which section 27A of this Act applies, the Lord Chancellor shall send it, together with any accompanying documents, to the justices' chief executive for a magistrates' court acting for the petty sessions area in which the respondent is residing.

(2) Subject to subsection (4) below, if notice of the hearing of the application by a magistrates' court having jurisdiction to hear it cannot be duly served on the respondent, the justices' chief executive for the court shall return the application and the accompanying documents to the Lord Chancellor with a statement giving such information as he possesses as to the whereabouts of the respondent.

(3) If the application is returned to the Lord Chancellor under subsection (2) above, then, unless he is satisfied that the respondent is not residing in the United Kingdom, he shall deal with it in accordance with subsection (1) above or section 28D(1) of this Act or send it to the Secretary of State to be dealt with in accordance with section 31 of this Act (as the circumstances of the case require).

(4) If the justices' chief executive for a court to whom the application is sent under this section is satisfied that the respondent is residing within the petty sessions area for which another magistrates' court acts, he shall send the application and accompanying documents to the justices' chief executive for that other court and shall inform the Lord Chancellor that he has done so.

PART II

(5) If the application is sent to the justices' chief executive for a court under subsection (4) above, he shall proceed as if it had been sent to him under subsection (1) above.

Amendments—Inserted by Maintenance Orders (Reciprocal Enforcement) Act 1992, s 1, Sch 1, para 13; SI 1995/756; amended by Access to Justice Act 1999, s 90, Sch 13, para 77.

Defined terms—"jurisdiction": s 47(3).

27C Applications to which section 27A applies: general

(1) This section applies where a magistrates' court makes an order on an application to which section 27A of this Act applies.

(2) Section 59 of the Magistrates' Courts Act 1980 (orders for periodical payment: means of payment) shall not apply.

(3) The court shall, at the same time that it makes the order, exercise one of its powers under subsection (4) below.

(4) Those powers are –

(*a*) the power to order that payment under the order be made directly to a justices' chief executive;

(*b*) the power to order that payments under the order be made to a justices' chief executive in England and Wales, by such method of payment falling within section 59(6) of the Magistrates' Courts Act 1980 (standing order, etc) as may be specified;

(*c*) the power to make an attachment of earnings order under the Attachment of Earnings Act 1971 to secure payments under the order.

(5) In deciding which of the powers under subsection (4) above it is to exercise, the court shall have regard to any representations made by the person liable to make payments under the order.

(6) Subsection (4) of section 59 of the Magistrates' Courts Act 1980 (power of court to require debtor to open account) shall apply for the purposes of subsection (4) above as it applies for the purposes of that section, but as if for paragraph (*a*) there were substituted –

"(*a*) the court proposes to exercise its power under paragraph (*b*) of section 27C(4) of the Maintenance Orders (Reciprocal Enforcement) Act 1972, and".

(7) The justices' chief executive for the court shall register the order in the prescribed manner in the court.

Amendments—Inserted by Maintenance Orders (Reciprocal Enforcement) Act 1992, s 1, Sch 1, para 13; amended by Access to Justice Act 1999, s 90, Sch 13, para 78.

28 Applications by spouses under the Domestic Proceedings and Magistrates' Courts Act 1978

(1) The magistrates' court hearing an application which by virtue of section 27A of this Act is to be treated as if it were an application for a maintenance order under the Domestic Proceedings and Magistrates' Courts Act 1978 may make any order on the application which it has power to make under section 2 or 19(1) of that Act.

(2) Part I of that Act shall apply in relation to such an application, and to any order made on such an application, with the following modifications –

(*a*) sections 6 to 8, 16 to 18, 20ZA, 25 to 27 and 28(2) shall be omitted,
(*b*) in section 30(1), for the words "either the applicant or the respondent ordinarily resides" there shall be substituted "the respondent resides", and
(*c*) section 32(2) shall be omitted.

(3) Subsections (1) and (2) above do not apply where section 28A of this Act applies.

Amendments—Maintenance Orders (Reciprocal Enforcement) Act 1992, s 1, Sch 1, para 13.

28A Applications by former spouses under the Domestic Proceedings and Magistrates' Courts Act 1978

(1) This section applies where in the case of any application which by virtue of section 27A of this Act is to be treated as if it were an application for a maintenance order under the Domestic Proceedings and Magistrates' Courts Act 1978 ("the 1978 Act") –

(*a*) the applicant and respondent were formerly married,
(*b*) their marriage was dissolved or annulled in a country or territory outside the United Kingdom by a divorce or annulment which is recognised as valid by the law of England and Wales,
(*c*) an order for the payment of maintenance for the benefit of the applicant or a child of the family has, by reason of the divorce or annulment, been made by a court in a Convention country, and
(*d*) where the order for the payment of maintenance was made by a court of a different country from that in which the divorce or annulment was obtained, either the applicant or the respondent was resident in the Convention country whose court made that order at the time that order was applied for.

(2) Any magistrates' court that would have jurisdiction to hear the application under section 30 of the 1978 Act (as modified in accordance with subsection (6) below) if the applicant and the respondent were still married shall have jurisdiction to hear it notwithstanding the dissolution or annulment of the marriage.

(3) If the magistrates' court hearing the application is satisfied that the respondent has failed to comply with the provisions of any order such as is mentioned in subsection (1)(*c*) above, it may (subject to subsections (4) and (5) below) make any order which it has power to make under section 2 or 19(1) of the 1978 Act.

(4) The court shall not make an order for the making of periodical payments for the benefit of the applicant or any child of the family unless the order made in the Convention country provides for the making of periodical payments for the benefit of the applicant or, as the case may be, that child.

(5) The court shall not make an order for the payment of a lump sum for the benefit of the applicant or any child of the family unless the order made in the Convention country provides for the payment of a lump sum to the applicant or, as the case may be, to that child.

(6) Part I of the 1978 Act shall apply in relation to the application, and to any order made on the application, with the following modifications –

(*a*) section 1 shall be omitted,

(*b*) for the reference in section 2(1) to any ground mentioned in section 1 of that Act there shall be substituted a reference to non-compliance with any such order as is mentioned in subsection (1)(*c*) of this section,

(*c*) for the references in section 3(2) and (3) to the occurrence of the conduct which is alleged as the ground of the application there shall be substituted references to the breakdown of the marriage,

(*d*) the reference in section 4(2) to the subsequent dissolution or annulment of the marriage of the parties affected by the order shall be omitted,

(*e*) sections 6 to 8, 16 to 18, 20ZA and 25 to 28 shall be omitted,

(*f*) in section 30(1), for the words "either the applicant or the respondent ordinarily resides" there shall be substituted "the respondent resides", and

(*g*) section 32(2) shall be omitted.

(7) A divorce or annulment obtained in a country or territory outside the United Kingdom shall be presumed for the purposes of this section to be one the validity of which is recognised by the law of England and Wales, unless the contrary is proved by the respondent.

(8) In this section, "child of the family" has the meaning given in section 88 of the 1978 Act.

Amendments—Inserted by Maintenance Orders (Reciprocal Enforcement) Act 1992, s 1, Sch 1, para 13.

Defined terms—"Convention country": s 25(1); "jurisdiction": s 47(3).

28B Applications under the Children Act 1989

No provision of an order made under Schedule 11 to the Children Act 1989 requiring or enabling a court to transfer proceedings from a magistrates' court to a county court or the High Court shall apply in relation to an application which by virtue of section 27A of this Act is to be treated as if it were an application for a maintenance order under that Act.

Amendments—Inserted by Maintenance Orders (Reciprocal Enforcement) Act 1992, s 1, Sch 1, para 13.

28C Applications for recovery of maintenance in Northern Ireland

(1) This section applies to any application which –

(*a*) is received by the Lord Chancellor from the appropriate authority in a convention country, and

(*b*) is an application by a person in that country for the recovery of maintenance from another person who is for the time being residing in Northern Ireland.

(2) Subject to sections 28D to 29B of this Act, an application to which this section applies shall be treated for the purposes of any enactment as if it were an application for a maintenance order under the relevant Order, made at the time when the application was received by the Lord Chancellor.

(3) In the case of an application for maintenance for a child (or children) alone, the relevant Order is the Children (Northern Ireland) Order 1995.

(4) In any other case, the relevant Order is the Domestic Proceedings (Northern Ireland) Order 1980.

(5) In subsection (3) above, "child" means the same as in Schedule 1 to the Children (Northern Ireland) Order 1995.

Amendments—Inserted by Maintenance Orders (Reciprocal Enforcement) Act 1992, s 1, Sch 1, para 13; substituted by SI 1995/755.

Defined terms—"Convention country": s 25(1).

28D Sending application to the appropriate magistrates' court

(1) On receipt of an application to which section 28C of this Act applies, the Lord Chancellor shall send it, together with any accompanying documents, to the clerk of a magistrates' court acting for the petty sessions district in which the respondent is residing.

(2) Subject to subsection (4) below, if notice of the hearing of the application by a magistrates' court having jurisdiction to hear it cannot be duly served on the respondent, the clerk of the court shall return the application and the accompanying documents to the Lord Chancellor with a statement giving such information as he possesses as to the whereabouts of the respondent.

(3) If the application is returned to the Lord Chancellor under subsection (2) above, then, unless he is satisfied that the respondent is not residing in the United Kingdom, he shall deal with it in accordance with subsection (1) above or section 27B of this Act or send it to the Secretary of State to be dealt with in accordance with section 31 of this Act (as the circumstances of the case require).

(4) If the clerk of a court to whom the application is sent under this section is satisfied that the respondent is residing within the petty sessions district for which another magistrates' court acts, he shall send the application and accompanying documents to the clerk of that other court and shall inform the Lord Chancellor that he has done so.

(5) If the application is sent to the clerk of a court under subsection (4) above, he shall proceed as if it had been sent to him under subsection (1) above.

Amendments—Inserted by SI 1995/755.

28E Applications to which section 28C applies: general

(1) This section applies where a magistrates' court makes an order on an application to which section 28C of this Act applies.

(2) Article 85 of the Magistrates' Courts (Northern Ireland) Order 1981 ("the 1981 Order") (orders for periodical payment: means of payment) shall not apply.

(3) The court shall, at the same time that it makes the order, exercise one of its powers under subsection (4) below.

(4) Those powers are –

- (*a*) the power to order that payments under the order be made directly to the collecting officer;
- (*b*) the power to order that payments under the order be made to the collecting officer, by such method of payment falling within Article 85(7) of the 1981 Order (standing order, etc.) as may be specified;
- (*c*) the power to make an attachment of earnings order under Part IX of the 1981 Order to secure payments under the order;

and in this subsection "collecting officer" means the officer mentioned in Article 85(4) of the 1981 Order.

(5) In deciding which of the powers under subsection (4) above it is to exercise, the court shall have regard to any representation made by the person liable to make payments under the order.

(6) Paragraph (5) of Article 85 of the 1981 Order (power of court to require debtor to open account) shall apply for the purposes of subsection (4) above as it applies for the purposes of that Article, but as if for sub-paragraph (*a*) there were substituted –

"(*a*) the court proposes to exercise its power under paragraph (*b*) of section 28E(4) of the Maintenance Orders (Reciprocal Enforcement) Act 1972, and".

(7) The clerk of the court shall register the order in the prescribed manner in the court.

Amendments—Inserted by SI 1995/755.

****

Transfer, enforcement, variation and revocation of registered orders

32 Transfer of orders

(1) Where the prescribed officer of the registering court is of opinion that the payer under a registered order has ceased to reside within the jurisdiction of that court, then, unless he is of opinion that the payer has ceased to reside in the United Kingdom, he shall, subject to subsection (2) below, send a certified copy of the order and the related documents to the Lord Chancellor, and if he is of opinion that the payer has ceased to reside in the United Kingdom he shall send a notice to that effect to the Lord Chancellor.

(2) Where the appropriate officer of the registering court, being a magistrates' court, is of opinion that the payer is residing within the jurisdiction of another magistrates' court in that part of the United Kingdom in which the registering court is, he shall transfer the order to that other court by sending a certified copy of the order and the related documents to the appropriate officer of that other court and, subject to subsection (4) below, the appropriate officer shall register the order in the prescribed manner in that court.

(2A) ...

(3) Where a certified copy of an order is received by the Lord Chancellor under this section and it appears to him that the payer under the order is still residing in the United Kingdom, he shall transfer the order to the appropriate court by sending the copy of the order and the related documents to the prescribed officer of the appropriate court and subject to subsection (4) below, that officer shall register the order in the prescribed manner in that court.

(4) Before registering an order in pursuance of subsection (2) or (3) above an officer of a court shall take such steps as he thinks fit for the purpose of ascertaining whether the payer under the order is residing within the jurisdiction of the court, and if after taking those steps he is satisfied that the payer is not so residing he shall return the certified copy of the order and the related documents to the officer of the court or the Lord Chancellor, as the case may be, from whom he

received them, together with a statement giving such information as he possesses as to the whereabouts of the payer.

(5) Where a certified copy of an order is received by the Lord Chancellor under this section and it appears to him that the payer under the order has ceased to reside in the United Kingdom he shall return the copy of the order and the related documents to the registering court.

(6) An officer of a court on registering an order in the court in pursuance of subsection (2) or (3) above shall give notice of the registration in the prescribed manner to the prescribed officer of the court in which immediately before its registration under this section the order was registered.

(7) The officer to whom notice is given under subsection (6) above shall on receiving the notice cancel the registration of the order in that court.

(7A), (7B) ...

(8) In this section –

"the appropriate court", in relation to a person residing in England and Wales or in Northern Ireland, means a magistrates' court within the jurisdiction of which that person is residing;

"certificate of arrears" and "certified copy" have the same meanings respectively as in Part I of this Act;

"payer", in relation to a registered order, means the person liable to make payments under the order; and

"related documents" means –

(*a*) the application on which the order was made;

(*b*) a certificate of arrears signed by the prescribed officer of the registering court;

(*c*) a statement giving such information as he possesses as to the whereabouts of the payer; and

(*d*) any relevant documents in his possession relating to the case.

(9) ...

Amendments—SI 1992/709; Access to Justice Act 1999, s 90, Sch 13, para 79.

Defined terms—"certificate of arrears", "certified copy": s 21(1); "jurisdiction": s 47(3); "part of the United Kingdom": s 47(2); "registered order", "registering court": s 39.

33 Enforcement of orders

(1) Subject to subjection (2) below, a registered order which is registered in a court other than the court by which the order was made may be enforced as if it had been made by the registered court and as if that court had had jurisdiction to make it; and proceedings for or with respect to the enforcement of any such order may be taken in accordance with this subsection but not otherwise.

(2) Subsection (1) above does not apply to an order which is for the time being registered in the High Court under Part I of the Maintenance Orders Act 1958 or to an order which is for the time being registered in the High Court of Justice in Northern Ireland under Part II of the Maintenance and Affiliation Orders Act (Northern Ireland) 1966.

(3) An order which by virtue of subsection (1) above is enforceable by a magistrates' court shall, subject to the modifications of sections 76 and 93 of the Magistrates' Courts Act 1980 (enforcement of sums adjudged to be paid and

PART II

complaint for arrears) specified in subsections (4A) and (4B) of section 8 of this Act, be enforceable as if it were a magistrates' court maintenance order made by that court.

In this subsection "magistrates' court maintenance order" has the same meaning as in section 150(1) of the Magistrates' Courts Act 1980.

(3A) Where, by virtue of being registered in the magistrates' court in which it was made, a registered order is enforceable as a magistrates' court maintenance order, sections 76 and 93 of the Magistrates' Courts Act 1980 shall have effect subject to the modifications specified in subsections (4A) and (4B) of section 8 of this Act.

(4) A magistrates' court in which an order is registered under this Part of this Act, and the officers thereof, shall take all such steps for enforcing the order as may be prescribed.

(5) In any proceedings for or with respect to the enforcement of an order which is for the time being registered in any court under this Part of this Act a certificate of arrears sent under section 32 of this Act to the prescribed officer of the court shall be evidence of the facts stated therein.

(6) Part II of the Maintenance Orders Act 1950 (enforcement of certain orders throughout the United Kingdom) shall not apply to a registered order.

(7) ...

Amendments—Family Law Reform Act 1987, s 33, Sch 2, para 50; Maintenance Enforcement Act 1991, s 10, Sch 1, para 18.

Defined terms—"certificate of arrears": s 21(1); "registered order", "registering court": s 39.

Application to Northern Ireland—In Northern Ireland, subsection (3) is modified and an additional subsection (3B) is added by Family Law (Northern Ireland) Order 1993 and Children (Northern Ireland) Order 1995.

34 Variation and revocation of orders

(1) Subject to subsection (3A) below and section 34A of this Act, where a registered order is registered in a court other than the court by which the order was made, the registering court shall have the like power to vary or revoke the order as if it had been made by the registering court and as if that court had had jurisdiction to make it; and no court other than the registering court shall have power to vary or revoke a registered order.

(2) Where the registering court revokes a registered order it shall cancel the registration.

(3) Where the Lord Chancellor receives from the appropriate authority in a Convention country an application by a person in that country for the variation of a registered order, he shall, if the registering court is a magistrates' court, send the application together with any documents accompanying it to –

(*a*) the justices' chief executive for the court, if the court is in England and Wales; or

(*b*) the clerk of the court, if the court is in Northern Ireland.

(3A) Where subsection (1) of section 60 of the Magistrates' Courts Act 1980 (revocation, variation etc of orders for periodical payment) applies in relation to a registered order, that subsection shall have effect as if for the words "by order on complaint", there were substituted "on an application being made, by order".

(4) Where a court in a part of the United Kingdom makes, or refuses to make, an order varying or revoking a registered order made by a court in another part thereof, any person shall have the like right of appeal (if any) against the order or refusal as he would have if the registered order had been made by the first-mentioned court.

(5) ...

Amendments—Maintenance Enforcement Act 1991, s 10, Sch 1, para 19(1); Maintenance Orders (Reciprocal Enforcement) Act 1992, s 1, Sch 1, para 14; SI 1992/709; Access to Justice Act 1999, s 90, Sch 13, para 80.

Defined terms—"Convention country": s 25(1); "part of the United Kingdom": s 47(2); "registered order", "registering court": s 39.

Application to Northern Ireland—See note under s 33.

34A Variation of orders by magistrates' courts in England and Wales

(1) The provisions of this section shall have effect in relation to a registered order which is registered in a magistrates' court in England and Wales (whether or not the court made the order) in place of the following enactments, that is to say –

(*a*) subsections (3) to (11) of section 60 of the Magistrates' Courts Act 1980;
(*b*) section 20ZA of the Domestic Proceedings and Magistrates' Courts Act 1978; and
(*c*) paragraph 6A of Schedule 1 to the Children Act 1989.

(2) The power of a magistrates' court in England and Wales to vary a registered order shall include power, if the court is satisfied that payment has not been made in accordance with the order, to exercise one of its powers under subsection (3) below.

(3) The powers of the court are –

(*a*) the power to order that payments under the order be made directly to a justices' chief executive;
(*b*) the power to order that payments under the order be made to a justices' chief executive by such method of payment falling within section 59(6) of the Magistrates' Courts Act 1980 (standing order, etc) as may be specified;
(*c*) the power to make an attachment of earnings order under the Attachment of Earnings Act 1971 to secure payments under the order.

(4) In any case where –

(*a*) a registered order is registered in a magistrates' court in England and Wales, and
(*b*) payments under the order are required to be made to a justices' chief executive by any method of payment falling within section 59(6) of the Magistrates' Courts Act 1980 (standing order, etc),

an interested party may apply in writing to the clerk of the court in which the order is registered for the order to be varied as mentioned in subsection (5) below.

(5) Subject to subsection (8) below, where an application has been made under subsection (4) above, the clerk, after giving written notice (by post or otherwise) of the application to any other interested party and allowing that party, within the period of 14 days beginning with the date of the giving of that notice, an opportunity to make written representations, may vary the order to provide that

payments under the order shall be made in accordance with paragraph (*a*) of subsection (3) above.

(6) The clerk may proceed with an application under subsection (4) above notwithstanding that any such interested party as is referred to in subsection (5) above has not received written notice of the application.

(7) In subsections (4) to (6) above "interested party", in relation to an order, means the debtor or the creditor.

(8) Where an application has been made under subsection (4) above, the clerk may, if he considers it inappropriate to exercise his power under subsection (5) above, refer the matter to the court which may vary the order by exercising one of its powers under subsection (3) above.

(9) In deciding, for the purposes of subsections (2) and (8) above, which of the powers under subsection (3) above it is to exercise, the court shall have regard to any representations made by the debtor.

(10) Subsection (4) of section 59 of the Magistrates' Courts Act 1980 (power of court to require debtor to open account) shall apply for the purposes of subsection (3) above as it applies for the purposes of that section but as if for paragraph (*a*) there were substituted –

"(*a*) the court proposes to exercise its power under paragraph (*b*) of section 34A(3) of the Maintenance Orders (Reciprocal Enforcement) Act 1972, and".

(11) In this section "creditor" and debtor" have the same meaning as they have in section 59 of the Magistrates' Courts Act 1980.

Amendments—Inserted by Maintenance Enforcement Act 1991, s 10, Sch 1, para 19(2); amended by Access to Justice Act 1999, s 90, Sch 13, para 81.

Defined terms—"registered order": s 39.

"standing order, etc" (s 34A(3)(*b*))—The methods of payment available do not include power to order payment by direct debit.

34B Variation of orders by courts of summary jurisdiction in Northern Ireland

(1) The provisions of this section shall have effect in relation to a registered order which is registered in a court of summary jurisdiction in Northern Ireland (whether or not the court made the order) in place of the following enactments, that is to say –

(*a*) paragraphs (3) to (11) of Article 86 of the Magistrates' Courts (Northern Ireland) Order 1981; and

(*b*) Article 22A of the Domestic Proceedings (Northern Ireland) Order 1980.

(2) The power of a court of summary jurisdiction in Northern Ireland to vary a registered order shall include power, if the court is satisfied that payment has not been made in accordance with the order, to exercise one of its powers under subsection (3) below.

(3) The powers of the court are –

(*a*) the power to order that payments under the order be made directly to the collecting officer;

(*b*) the power to order that payments under the order be made to the collecting officer by such method of payment falling within Article 85(7) of the Magistrates' Courts (Northern Ireland) Order 1981 (standing order, etc) as may be specified;

(*c*) the power to make an attachment of earnings order under Part IX of the Order of 1981 to secure payments under the order;

and in this subsection "collecting officer" means the officer mentioned in Article 85(4) of the Order of 1981.

(4) In any case where –

(*a*) a registered order is registered in a court of summary jurisdiction in Northern Ireland, and

(*b*) payments under the order are required to be made to the collecting officer in Northern Ireland, by any method of payment falling within Article 85(7) of the Magistrates' Courts (Northern Ireland) Order 1981 (standing order, etc),

an interested party may apply in writing to the clerk of petty sessions in which the order is registered for the order to be varied as mentioned in subsection (5) below.

(5) Subject to subsection (8) below, where an application has been made under subsection (4) above, the clerk, after giving written notice (by post or otherwise) of the application to any other interested party and allowing that party, within the period of 14 days beginning with the date of the giving of that notice, an opportunity to make written representations, may vary the order to provide that payments under the order shall be made in accordance with paragraph (*a*) of subsection (3) above.

(6) The clerk may proceed with an application under subsection (4) above notwithstanding that any such interested party as is referred to in subsection (5) above has not received written notice of the application.

(7) In subsections (4) to (6) above "interested party", in relation to an order, means the debtor or the creditor.

(8) Where an application has been made under subsection (4) above, the clerk may, if he considers it inappropriate to exercise his power under subsection (5) above, refer the matter to the court which may vary the order by exercising one of its powers under subsection (3) above.

(9) In deciding, for the purposes of subsections (2) and (8) above, which of the powers under subsection (3) above it is to exercise, the court shall have regard to any representations made by the debtor.

(10) Paragraph (5) of Article 85 of the Magistrates' Courts (Northern Ireland) Order 1981 (power of court to require debtor to open account) shall apply for the purposes of subsection (3) above as it applies for the purposes of that Article but as if for sub-paragraph (*a*) there were substituted –

"(*a*) the court proposes to exercise its power under paragraph (*b*) of section 34B(3) of the Maintenance Orders (Reciprocal Enforcement) Act 1972, and".

(11) In this section "creditor" and "debtor" have the same meaning as they have in Article 85 of the Magistrates' Courts (Northern Ireland) Order 1981.

Amendments—Inserted by SI 1993/1576.

35 Further provisions with respect to variation etc of orders by magistrates' courts in England and Wales

(1) Notwithstanding anything in section 28(2) or 28A(6)(*e*) of this Act, a magistrates' court in England and Wales shall have jurisdiction to hear an application –

(*a*) for the variation or revocation of a registered order registered in that court, and

(*b*) made by the person against whom or on whose application the order was made,

notwithstanding that the person by or against whom the application is made is residing outside England and Wales.

(2) None of the powers of the court, or of the clerk of the court, under section 34A of this Act shall be exercisable in relation to such an application.

(3) Where the respondent to an application for the variation or revocation of a registered order which is registered in a magistrates' court in England and Wales does not appear at the time and place appointed for the hearing of the application, but the court is satisfied –

(*a*) that the respondent is residing outside England and Wales, and

(*b*) that the prescribed notice of the making of the application and of the time and place appointed for the hearing has been given to the respondent in the prescribed manner,

the court may proceed to hear and determine the application at the time and place appointed for the hearing or for any adjourned hearing in like manner as if the respondent had appeared at that time and place.

Amendments—Maintenance Orders (Reciprocal Enforcement) Act 1992, s 1, Sch 1, para 16.

Defined terms—"registered order": s 39.

Scope of provision—A means of payment order may not be made under this section.

35A Further provisions with respect to variation etc of orders by magistrates' courts in Northern Ireland

(1) Notwithstanding anything in section 29(2) or 29A(6)(*e*) of this Act, a magistrates' court in Northern Ireland shall have jurisdiction to hear an application –

(*a*) for the variation or revocation of a registered order registered in that court, and

(*b*) made by the person against whom or on whose application the order was made,

notwithstanding that the person by or against whom the application is made is residing outside Northern Ireland.

(2) None of the powers of the court, or of the clerk, under section 34B of this Act shall be exercisable in relation to such an application.

(3) Where the respondent to an application for the variation or revocation of a registered order which is registered in a magistrates' court in Northern Ireland does not appear at the time and place appointed for the hearing of the application, but the court is satisfied –

(*a*) that the respondent is residing outside Northern Ireland, and

(*b*) that the prescribed notice of the making of the application and of the time and place appointed for the hearing has been given to the respondent in the prescribed manner,

the court may proceed to hear and determine the application at the time and place appointed for the hearing or for any adjourned hearing in like manner as if the respondent had appeared at that time and place.

Amendments—Inserted by Maintenance Orders (Reciprocal Enforcement) Act 1992, s 1, Sch 1, para 16; substituted by SI 1995/755.

Defined terms—"registered order": s 39.

Scope of provision—A means of payment order may not be made under this section.

PART II

Supplemental

36 Admissibility of evidence given in Convention country

(1) A statement contained in –

(*a*) a document, duly authenticated, which purports to set out or summarise evidence given in proceedings in a court in a Convention country; or

(*b*) a document, duly authenticated, which purports to set out or summarise evidence taken in such a country for the purpose of proceedings in a court in the United Kingdom under this Part of this Act, whether in response to a request made on behalf of such a court or otherwise; or

(*c*) a document, duly authenticated, which purports to have been received in evidence in proceedings in a court in such a country, or to be a copy of a document so received,

shall, in any proceedings in a magistrates' court or in, or remitted from, a sheriff court arising out of an application to which section 27A(1) of this Act applies, an application to which section 28C(1) of this Act applies, an application received by the Secretary of State as mentioned in section 31(1) of this Act or an application made by any person for the variation or revocation of a registered order or in proceedings on appeal from any such proceedings, be admissible as evidence of any fact stated therein to the same extent as oral evidence of that fact is admissible in those proceedings.

(2) A document purporting to set out or summarise evidence given as mentioned in subsection (1)(*a*) above, or taken as mentioned in subsection (1)(*b*) above, shall be deemed to be duly authenticated for the purposes of that subsection if the document purports to be certified by the judge, magistrate or other person before whom the evidence was given or, as the case may be, by whom it was taken, to be the original document containing or recording, or, as the case may be, summarising, that evidence or a true copy of that document.

(3) A document purporting to have been received in evidence as mentioned in subsection (1)(*c*) above, or to be a copy of a document so received, shall be deemed to be duly authenticated for the purposes of that subsection if the document purports to be certified by a judge, magistrate or officer of the court in question to have been, or to be a true copy of a document which has been, so received.

(4) It shall not be necessary in any such proceedings to prove the signature or official position of the person appearing to have given such a certificate.

(5) Nothing in this section shall prejudice the admission in evidence of any document which is admissible in evidence apart from this section.

Amendments—Domestic Proceedings and Magistrates' Courts Act 1978, s 60(3); Maintenance Orders (Reciprocal Enforcement) Act 1992, s 1, Sch 1, para 17; SI 1992/709; SI 1995/755.

Defined terms—"Convention country": s 25(1); "registered order": s 39.

37 Obtaining of evidence for purpose of proceedings in United Kingdom court

(1) A court in the United Kingdom may for the purpose of any proceedings in that court under this Part of this Act arising out of an application received by the Lord Chancellor from a Convention country request the Lord Chancellor to make to the appropriate authority or court in the Convention country a request for the taking in that country of the evidence of a person residing therein relating to matters connected with the application.

(2) A request made by a court under this section shall –

- (*a*) give details of the application in question;
- (*b*) state the name and address of the person whose evidence is to be taken; and
- (*c*) specify the matters relating to which the evidence of that person is required.

(3) If the Lord Chancellor is satisfied that a request made to him under this section contains sufficient information to enable the evidence of the person named in the request relating to the matters specified therein to be taken by a court or person in the Convention country, he shall transmit the request to the appropriate authority or court in that country.

Amendments—SI 1992/709.

Defined terms—"Convention country": s 25(1).

38 Taking of evidence at request of court in Convention country

(1) Where a request is made to the Lord Chancellor by or on behalf of a court in a Convention country to obtain the evidence of a person residing in the United Kingdom relating to matters connected with an application to which section 26 of this Act applies, the Lord Chancellor shall request such court, or such officer of a court, as he may determine to take the evidence of that person relating to such matters connected with that application as may be specified in the request.

(2) The court by which or officer by whom a request under subsection (1) above is received from the Lord Chancellor shall have power to take the evidence and, after giving notice of the time and place at which the evidence is to be taken to such persons and in such manner as it or he thinks fit, shall take the evidence of the person named in the request relating to the matters specified therein in such manner as may be prescribed; and the evidence so taken shall be sent in the prescribed manner by the prescribed officer to the court in the Convention country by or on behalf of which the request referred to in subsection (1) above was made.

(3) Where any person, not being the person by whom the application mentioned in subsection (1) above was made, is required by virtue of this section to give evidence before a court in the United Kingdom, the court may order that there shall be paid –

(*a*) if the court is a court in England, Wales or Scotland, out of moneys provided by Parliament; and

(*b*) if the court is a court in Northern Ireland, out of moneys provided by Parliament,

such sums as appear to the court reasonably sufficient to compensate that person for the expense, trouble or loss of time properly incurred in or incidental to his attendance.

(4) Section 97(1), (3) and (4) of the Magistrates' Courts Act 1980 (which provide for compelling the attendance of witnesses, etc) shall apply in relation to a magistrates' court to which a request under subsection (1) above is made as if the application to which the request relates were a complaint to be heard by that court.

(5) ...

(6) In the application of this section to Northern Ireland, in subsection (4), for the reference to section 97(1), (3) and (4) of the Magistrates' Courts Act 1980 there shall be substituted a reference to Articles 118(1), (3) and (4), 119 and 120 of the Magistrates' Courts (Northern Ireland) Order 1981.

Amendments—SI 1973/2163; Magistrates' Courts Act 1980, s 154, Sch 7, para 109; SI 1981/1675; SI 1992/709.

Defined terms—"Convention country": s 25(1).

38A Magistrates' courts rules

(1) Without prejudice to the generality of the power to make rules under section 144 of the Magistrates' Courts Act 1980 (magistrates' courts rules), such rules may make provision with respect to the orders made or other things done by a magistrates' court, or an officer of such a court, by virtue of this Part of this Act, notice of which is to be given to such persons as the rules may provide and the manner in which such notice shall be given.

(2) For the purpose of giving effect to this Part of this Act, rules made under section 144 of the Magistrates' Courts Act 1980 may make, in relation to any proceedings brought under or by virtue of this Part of this Act, any provision not covered by subsection (1) above which –

(*a*) falls within subsection (2) of section 93 of the Children Act 1989, and

(*b*) may be made in relation to relevant proceedings under that section.

(3) In the application of this section to Northern Ireland –

(*a*) in subsection (1), for the reference to section 144 of the Magistrates' Courts Act 1980 there shall be substituted a reference to Article 13 of the Magistrates' Courts (Northern Ireland) Order 1981, and

(*b*) (*repealed*)

(4) For the purpose of giving effect to this Part of this Act, rules made under Article 13 of the Magistrates' Courts (Northern Ireland) Order 1981 may make, in relation to any proceedings brought under or by virtue of this Part of this Act, any provision not covered by subsection (1) above which –

(*a*) falls within paragraph (2) of Article 165 of the Children (Northern Ireland Order) 1995, and

(*b*) may be made in relation to relevant proceedings under that Article.

Amendments—Inserted by Maintenance Orders (Reciprocal Enforcement) Act 1992, s 1, Sch 1, para 18; amended by SI 1995/755.

39 Interpretation of Part II

In this Part of this Act –

...

"maintenance order" has the same meaning as in Part I of this Act;

"prescribed" has the same meaning as in Part I of this Act;

"registered order" means an order which is for the time being registered in a court in the United Kingdom under this Part of this Act;

"registering court", in relation to a registered order, means the court in which that order is for the time being registered under this Part of this Act;

"revoke" and "revocation" include "discharge".

Amendments—Maintenance Orders (Reciprocal Enforcement) Act 1992, s 1, Sch 1, para 19.

PART III
MISCELLANEOUS AND SUPPLEMENTAL

Further provisions relating to enforcement of maintenance orders and to applications for recovery of maintenance

40 Power to apply Act to maintenance orders and applications for recovery of maintenance made in certain countries

Where Her Majesty is satisfied –

(*a*) that arrangements have been or will be made in a country or territory outside the United Kingdom to ensure that maintenance orders made by courts in the United Kingdom can be enforced in that country or territory or that applications by persons in the United Kingdom for the recovery of maintenance from persons in that country or territory can be entertained by courts in that country or territory; and

(*b*) that in the interest of reciprocity it is desirable to ensure that maintenance orders made by courts in that country or territory can be enforced in the United Kingdom or, as the case may be, that applications by persons in that country or territory for the recovery of maintenance from persons in the United Kingdom can be entertained by courts in the United Kingdom,

Her Majesty may by Order in Council make provision for applying the provisions of this Act, with such exceptions, adaptations and modifications as may be specified in the Order, to such orders or applications as are referred to in paragraph (*a*) or (*b*) above and to maintenance and other orders made in connection with such applications by courts in the United Kingdom or in that country or territory.

Amendments—Civil Jurisdiction and Judgments Act 1982, ss 37(1), 54, Sch 11, para 17, Sch 14.

Scope of provision—This section allows the application of the Act to be extended to other countries by Order in Council, with such modifications as may be necessary. The following Orders, set out in this work, have been made under this section: Recovery of Maintenance Orders (United States of America) Order 1993; Reciprocal Enforcement of Maintenance Orders (Hague Convention Countries) Order 1993; Reciprocal Enforcement of Maintenance Orders (Republic of Ireland) Order 1993; Reciprocal Enforcement of Maintenance Orders (United States of America) Order 1995. Reference should also be made to Procedural Guide 25 (Reciprocal Enforcement) in Part I of this work.

****

Provisions with respect to certain orders of magistrates' courts

42 Provisional order for maintenance of party to marriage made by magistrates' court to cease to have effect on remarriage of party

(1) Where a magistrates' court has, by virtue of section 3 of this Act, made a provisional maintenance order consisting of, or including, a provision such as is mentioned in section 2(1)(*a*) of the Domestic Proceedings and Magistrates' Courts Act 1978 (making of periodical payments by husband or wife) or Article 4(1)(*a*) of the Domestic Proceedings (Northern Ireland) Order 1980 and the order has been confirmed by a competent court in a reciprocating country, then, if after the making of that order the marriage of the parties to the proceedings in which the order was made is dissolved or annulled but the order continues in force, that order or, as the case may be, that provision thereof shall cease to have effect on the remarriage of the party in whose favour it was made, except in relation to any arrears due under it on the date of such remarriage and shall not be capable of being revived.

(2) For the avoidance of doubt it is hereby declared that reference in this section to remarriage include references to a marriage which is by law void and voidable.

(3) ...

Amendments—Domestic Proceedings and Magistrates' Courts Act 1978, s 89(2), Sch 2, para 37; SI 1980/564.

****

Supplemental provisions

44 Exclusion of certain enactments relating to evidence

(1) Section 20 of the Family Law Reform Act 1969 (power of court hearing certain proceedings to require use of blood tests to determine paternity) and any corresponding enactment of the Parliament of Northern Ireland shall not apply to any proceedings under this Act, but the foregoing provision is without prejudice to the power of a court to allow the report of any person who has carried out such tests to be given in evidence in those proceedings.

(2) The Evidence (Proceedings in Other Jurisdictions) Act 1975 shall not apply to the taking of evidence in the United Kingdom for the taking of which section 14 or section 38 of this Act provides.

Amendments—Evidence (Proceedings in Other Jurisdictions) Act 1975, s 8(1), Sch 1.

****

47 Interpretation: general

(1) In this Act –

"enactment" includes an enactment of the Parliament of Northern Ireland;

"magistrates' court", in relation to Northern Ireland, means a court of summary jurisdiction within the meaning of Article 2(2)(*a*) of the Magistrates' Courts (Northern Ireland) Order 1981.

(2) References in this Act to a part of the United Kingdom are references to England and Wales, to Scotland, or to Northern Ireland.

PART II

(3) Any reference in this Act to the jurisdiction of a court, where the reference is to assets being located or to a person residing within the jurisdiction of a court, shall be construed in relation to a magistrates' court in England and Wales as a reference to the petty sessions area, and in relation to a magistrates' court in Northern Ireland as a reference to the petty sessions district, for which the court acts.

(4) Any reference to this Act to any other enactment is a reference thereto as amended, and includes a reference thereto as extended or applied, by or under any other enactment.

Amendments—SI 1981/1675; Civil Jurisdiction and Judgments Act 1982, ss 37(1), 54, Sch 11, para 18, Sch 14.

****

Married Women's Property Act 1882

****

17 Questions between husband and wife as to property to be decided in summary way

In any question between husband and wife as to the title to or possession of property, either party may apply by summons or otherwise in a summary way to the High Court or such county court as may be prescribed and the court may, on such an application (which may be heard in private), make such order with respect to the property as it thinks fit.

In this section "prescribed" means prescribed by rules of court and rules made for the purposes of this section may confer jurisdiction on county courts whatever the situation or value of the property in dispute.

Amendments—Statute Law (Repeals) Act 1969; Matrimonial and Family Proceedings Act 1984, s 43.

Scope of provision—This section enables the court to declare and enforce the proprietary rights of each party as they are found to exist in accordance with trust and common law principles. It does not give the court power to adjust those rights to produce a fair allocation of capital and income in the way that is done on an application for financial provision and property adjustment orders under Matrimonial Causes Act 1973, s 25. Where there is or will be an application for financial relief under MCA 1973 it is, generally speaking, a waste of time and money to apply under this section (*Fielding v Fielding* [1977] 1 WLR 1146, [1978] 1 All ER 267). Two situations where s 17 still has a useful purpose are:

(*a*) where it is believed that one party may shortly become bankrupt, a declaration as to each party's respective beneficial interests in an asset may be of some value against any claim that a trustee in bankruptcy may subsequently mount; and

(*b*) where it is desired to obtain a sale prior to the final ancillary relief hearing.

As explained in **Extension of court's powers** below, s 17 contains a power of sale. In *Wicks v Wicks* [1998] 1 FLR 470 the Court of Appeal suggested that an application under s 17, combined with an application under FLA 1996, Pt IV if possession was required, allowed the court to order a sale prior to the final ancillary relief hearing.

"property"—Property is defined by s 24 to include a thing in action. The Matrimonial Causes (Property and Maintenance) Act 1958, an Act which enables the court to make orders in respect of property which a party has had in his possession or control, defines "property" (in s 8) to mean any real or personal property, any money, any negotiable instrument, debt or other chose in action and any other right or interest whether in possession or not.

"such county court as may be prescribed"—The county court jurisdiction in respect of this section is prescribed by FPR 1991, rr 3.6 and 3.7.

Extension of court's powers—Matrimonial Causes (Property and Maintenance) Act 1958, s 7 extends this section to enable the court to make orders where money or property has ceased to be in the possession or under the control of one of the parties. In such a case the court is able to order one party to pay to the other the value of the applicant's interest in the asset that has been disposed of or to transfer to the applicant any property which can be traced to the original asset. Section 7(7) of that Act confirms the court's power to order a sale of property but a sale may be ordered only if there is some question between the parties as to the title to or possession of the property other than the issue of whether the property should be sold (*Rawlings v Rawlings* [1964] P 398, [1964] 3 WLR 294).

Engaged parties—Law Reform (Miscellaneous Provisions) Act 1970, s 2(2) provides that an application under this section may be made by parties who have been engaged but not married. Jurisdiction exists even if the agreement to marry is unenforceable at common law, eg because it was made at a time when one of the parties was already married (*Shaw v Fitzgerald* [1992] 1 FLR 357).

Polygamous marriages—The reference to "husband and wife" includes parties to a polygamous or potentially polygamous marriage (*Chaudhry v Chaudhry* [1976] Fam 148, [1976] 1 WLR 221).

Time-limit for making application—Under Matrimonial Proceedings and Property Act 1970, s 39, a husband or wife must apply within three years of decree absolute. Engaged parties must apply within three years after the termination of the engagement (Law Reform (Miscellaneous Provisions) Act 1970, s 2(2)).

Court's powers—The court's jurisdiction to declare and enforce proprietary rights includes the power to restrain by injunction one party from disposing of a matrimonial home whilst the other wishes to live in it (*Lee v Lee* [1952] 2 QB 489, [1952] 1 All ER 1299; *Halden v Halden* [1966] 1 WLR 1481, [1966] 3 All ER 412), and the power to assess the monetary value of a party's interest in an asset and to order the other party to pay a lump sum in that amount (*Bothe v Amos* [1976] Fam 46, [1975] 2 WLR 838).

****

Married Women's Property Act 1964

1 Money and property derived from housekeeping allowance

If any question arises as to the right of a husband or wife to money derived from any allowance made by the husband for the expenses of the matrimonial home or for similar purposes, or to any property acquired out of such money, the money or

property shall, in the absence of any agreement between them to the contrary, be treated as belonging to the husband and the wife in equal shares.

****

Matrimonial and Family Proceedings Act 1984

ARRANGEMENT OF SECTIONS

PART III
FINANCIAL RELIEF IN ENGLAND AND WALES AFTER OVERSEAS DIVORCE ETC

Applications for financial relief

PART V
FAMILY BUSINESS: DISTRIBUTION AND TRANSFER

Preliminary

Jurisdiction of county courts in matrimonial causes and matters

Distribution and transfer of family business and proceedings

Rules of court and fees

County court proceedings in principal registry

****

PART III
FINANCIAL RELIEF IN ENGLAND AND WALES AFTER OVERSEAS DIVORCE ETC

Applications for financial relief

12 Applications for financial relief after overseas divorce etc

(1) Where –

(*a*) a marriage has been dissolved or annulled, or the parties to a marriage have been legally separated, by means of judicial or other proceedings in an overseas country, and

(*b*) the divorce, annulment or legal separation is entitled to be recognised as valid in England and Wales,

either party to the marriage may apply to the court in the manner prescribed by rules of court for an order for financial relief under this Part of this Act.

(2) If after a marriage has been dissolved or annulled in an overseas country one of the parties to the marriage remarries that party shall not be entitled to make an application in relation to that marriage.

(3) For the avoidance of doubt it is hereby declared that the reference in subsection (2) above to remarriage includes a reference to a marriage which is by law void or voidable.

(4) In this Part of this Act except sections 19, 23, and 24 "order for financial relief" means an order under section 17 or 22 below of a description referred to in that section.

Defined terms—"order for financial relief": s 12(4); "overseas country": s 27.

Scope of provision—This section enables a party whose marriage has been ended by proceedings taken overseas (including by talaq) which are recognised as valid in accordance with Family Law Act 1986, Pt II to apply for financial relief in this country. The orders by way of financial relief to which a party may be entitled are practically identical to the orders which may be made under Matrimonial Causes Act 1973, ss 22 to 24A and Matrimonial Homes Act 1983, Sch 1 except that, where the only ground conferring jurisdiction is the existence of a matrimonial home within the jurisdiction, special rules apply. Remarriage bars an application in the same way as under MCA 1973, s 28(3).

13 Leave of the court required for applications for financial relief

(1) No application for an order for financial relief shall be made under this Part of this Act unless the leave of the court has been obtained in accordance with rules of court; and the court shall not grant leave unless it considers that there is substantial ground for the making of an application for such an order.

(2) The court may grant leave under this section notwithstanding that an order has been made by a court in a country outside England and Wales requiring the other party to the marriage to make any payment or transfer any property to the applicant or a child of the family.

(3) Leave under this section may be granted subject to such conditions as the court thinks fit.

Defined terms—"child of the family": s 27; "order for financial relief": s 12(4).

Scope of provision—The procedure to obtain permission is set out at FPR 1991, r 3.17. The grounds conferring jurisdiction are set out in s 15. The factors relevant to whether the court should in its discretion exercise jurisdiction to grant leave are set out in s 16.

14 Interim orders for maintenance

(1) Where leave is granted under section 13 above for the making of an application for an order for financial relief and it appears to the court that the applicant or any child of the family is in immediate need of financial assistance, the court may make an interim order for maintenance, that is to say, an order requiring the other party to the marriage to make to the applicant or to the child such periodical payments, and for such term, being a term beginning not earlier than the date of the grant of leave and ending with the date of the determination of the application for an order for financial relief, as the court thinks reasonable.

(2) If it appears to the court that the court has jurisdiction to entertain the application for an order for financial relief by reason only of paragraph (*c*) of section 15(1) below the court shall not make an interim order under this section.

(3) An interim order under subsection (1) above may be made subject to such conditions as the court thinks fit.

Defined terms—"child of the family": s 27; "order for financial relief": s 12(4).

Scope of provision—Except where jurisdiction arises only through ownership of a matrimonial home within the jurisdiction, in which case the court may make capital orders only up to the value of that asset, this section enables the court to make an interim order for maintenance for the applicant and/or the children of the family pending the final hearing of the application.

15 Jurisdiction of the court

(1) Subject to subsection (2) below, the court shall have jurisdiction to entertain an application for an order for financial relief if any of the following jurisdictional requirements are satisfied that is to say –

(*a*) either of the parties to the marriage was domiciled in England and Wales on the date of the application for leave under section 13 above or was so domiciled on the date on which the divorce, annulment or legal separation obtained in the overseas country took effect in that country; or

(*b*) either of the parties to the marriage was habitually resident in England and Wales throughout the period of one year ending with the date of the application for leave or was so resident throughout the period of one year ending with the date on which the divorce, annulment or legal separation obtained in the overseas country took effect in that country; or

(*c*) either or both of the parties to the marriage had at the date of the application for leave a beneficial interest in possession in a dwelling-house situated in England or Wales which was at some time during the marriage a matrimonial home of the parties to the marriage.

(2) Where the jurisdiction of the court to entertain proceedings under this Part of this Act would fall to be determined by reference to the jurisdictional requirements imposed by virtue of Part I of the Civil Jurisdiction and Judgments Act 1982 (implementation of certain European conventions) or by virtue of Council Regulation (EC) No 44/2001 of 22 December 2000 on jurisdiction and the recognition and enforcement of judgments in civil and commercial matters then –

(*a*) satisfaction of the requirements of subsection (1) above shall not obviate the need to satisfy the requirements imposed by virtue of that Regulation or Part I of that Act; and

(*b*) satisfaction of the requirements imposed by virtue of that Regulation or Part I of that Act shall obviate the need to satisfy the requirements of subsection (1) above;

and the court shall entertain or not entertain the proceedings accordingly.

Amendments—SI 2001/3929.

Defined terms—"dwelling-house": s 27; "order for financial relief": s 12(4); "overseas country", "possession": s 27.

"matrimonial home" (s 15(1)(*c*))—Whether a property has been a matrimonial home is a question of fact, evidenced by any period of time spent living there or any agreement to so treat it (*King v King* [1941] 2 All ER 103).

Civil Jurisdiction and Judgments Act 1982, Pt I (s 15(2))—The 1982 Act applies only where the respondent is domiciled in a contracting state. With the exception of Greece, all the contracting states are in Western Europe; they include Belgium, Germany, France, Italy, Luxembourg, The Netherlands, Denmark, Republic of Ireland and United Kingdom. By Sch 1, Art 1, the 1982 Act does not apply to rights in property arising out of a matrimonial relationship, but subject to that exception the basic theme of the 1982 Act, Pt I is that if a proposed respondent is domiciled in a contracting state he must be sued there. There is one further exception, namely that in matters relating to maintenance even though the respondent is domiciled in a contracting state he may nevertheless be sued in the courts of the country where the maintenance creditor is either domiciled or habitually resident. In summary, if the proposed respondent is resident outside the contracting states, Civil Jurisdiction and Judgments Act, Pt I is irrelevant. If the respondent is resident within a contracting state, careful attention should be paid to the provisions of Pt I.

16 Duty of the court to consider whether England and Wales is appropriate venue for application

(1) Before making an order for financial relief the court shall consider whether in all the circumstances of the case it would be appropriate for such an order to be made by a court in England and Wales, and if the court is not satisfied that it would be appropriate, the court shall dismiss the application.

(2) The court shall in particular have regard to the following matters –

(*a*) the connection which the parties to the marriage have with England and Wales;

(*b*) the connection which those parties have with the country in which the marriage was dissolved or annulled or in which they were legally separated;

(*c*) the connection which those parties have with any other country outside England and Wales;

(*d*) any financial benefit which the applicant or a child of the family has received or is likely to receive, in consequence of the divorce, annulment or legal separation, by virtue of any agreement or the operation of the law of a country outside England and Wales,

(*e*) in a case where an order has been made by a court in a country outside England and Wales requiring the other party to the marriage to make any payment or transfer any property for the benefit of the applicant or a child of the family, the financial relief given by the order and the extent to which the order has been complied with or is likely to be complied with;

(*f*) any right which the applicant has, or has had, to apply for financial relief from the other party to the marriage under the law of any country outside England and Wales and if the applicant has omitted to exercise that right the reason for that omission;

(*g*) the availability in England and Wales of any property in respect of which an order under this Part of this Act in favour of the applicant could be made;

(*h*) the extent to which any order made under this Part of this Act is likely to be enforceable;

(*i*) the length of time which has elapsed since the date of the divorce, annulment or legal separation.

Defined terms—"child of the family": s 27; "order for financial relief": s 12(4).

Scope of provision—This section sets out the factors which the court will consider when exercising its discretion to grant or refuse leave (see also *Holmes v Holmes* [1989] 2 FLR 364; *M v M (Financial Provision after Foreign Divorce)* [1994] 1 FLR 399; *Hewitson v Hewitson* [1995] 1 FLR 241; *N v N (Foreign Divorce: Financial Relief)* [1997] 1 FLR 900; *E v E* [1997] Fam Law 637). The burden of establishing that leave should be granted rests on the applicant (*Z v Z (Financial Provision: Overseas Divorce)* [1992] 2 FLR 291). An application that has as its sole objective the enforcement of a foreign order is unlikely to succeed, unless the enforcement remedies of the foreign court and the specific enforcement remedies under the Maintenance Orders (Reciprocal Enforcement) Act 1972 or under common law are inadequate or have been exhausted (*Jordan v Jordan* [1999] 2 FLR 1069, CA).

Orders for financial provision and property adjustment

17 Orders for financial provision and property adjustment

(1) Subject to section 20 below, on an application by a party to a marriage for an order for financial relief under this section, the court may –

(a) make any one or more of the orders which it could make under Part II of the 1973 Act if a decree of divorce, a decree of nullity of marriage or a decree of judicial separation in respect of the marriage had been granted in England and Wales, that is to say –

(i) any order mentioned in section 23(1) of the 1973 Act (financial provision orders); and

(ii) any order mentioned in section 24(1) of that Act (property adjustment orders); and

(b) if the marriage has been dissolved or annulled, make one or more orders each of which would, within the meaning of that Part of that Act, be a pension sharing order in relation to the marriage.

(2) Subject to section 20 below, where the court makes a secured periodical payments order, an order for the payment of a lump sum or a property adjustment order under subsection (1) above, then, on making that order or at any time thereafter, the court may make any order mentioned in section 24A(1) of the 1973 Act (orders for sale of property) which the court would have power to make if the order under subsection (1) above had been made under Part II of the 1973 Act.

Amendments—Welfare Reform and Pensions Act 1999, s 84(1), Sch 12, para 3.

Defined terms—"order for financial relief": s 12(4); "property adjustment order", "secured periodical payments order": s 27.

Scope of provision—Subject to the Child Support Act 1991, which restricts the court's power to order child maintenance (see Procedural Guide 21), this section equates the court's power after an overseas divorce to make orders for financial provision, including pension attachment and pension sharing, property adjustment and sale to those made under Matrimonial Causes Act 1973, ss 23–24B following a divorce in this country. Section 20 restricts the court's power where jurisdiction is based solely on the existence of a matrimonial home in this country.

Pension Sharing/Pension Attachment—For an overview of pension sharing and pension attachment see the annotations to MCA 1973, s 21.

18 Matters to which the court is to have regard in exercising its powers under s 17

(1) In deciding whether to exercise its powers under section 17 above and, if so, in what manner the court shall act in accordance with this section.

(2) The court shall have regard to all the circumstances of the case, first consideration being given to the welfare while a minor of any child of the family who has not attained the age of eighteen.

(3) As regards the exercise of those powers in relation to a party to the marriage, the court shall in particular have regard to the matters mentioned in section 25(2)(a) to (h) of the 1973 Act and shall be under duties corresponding with those imposed by section 25A(1) and (2) of the 1973 Act where it decides to exercise under section 17 above powers corresponding with the powers referred to in those subsections.

(3A) The matters to which the court is to have regard under subsection (3) above –

(a) so far as relating to paragraph (a) of section 25(2) of the 1973 Act, include any benefits under a pension arrangement which a party to the marriage has or is likely to have (whether or not in the foreseeable future), and

(b) so far as relating to paragraph (h) of that provision, include any benefits under a pension arrangement which, by reason of the dissolution or

PART II

annulment of the marriage, a party to the marriage will lose the chance of acquiring.

(4) As regards the exercise of those powers in relation to a child of the family, the court shall in particular have regard to the matters mentioned in section 25(3)(*a*) to (*e*) of the 1973 Act.

(5) As regards the exercise of those powers against a party to the marriage in favour of a child of the family who is not the child of that party, the court shall also have regard to the matters mentioned in section 25(4)(*a*) to (*c*) of the 1973 Act.

(6) Where an order has been made by a court outside England and Wales for the making of payments or the transfer of property by a party to the marriage, the court in considering in accordance with this section the financial resources of the other party to the marriage or a child of the family shall have regard to the extent to which that order has been complied with or is likely to be complied with.

(7) In this section –

(*a*) "pension arrangement" has the meaning given by section 25D(3) of the 1973 Act, and

(*b*) references to benefits under a pension arrangement include any benefits by way of pension, whether under a pension arrangement or not.

Amendments—Welfare Reform and Pensions Act 1999, s 22(2), (3).

Defined terms—"child of the family": s 27.

Scope of provision—This section incorporates the principles of Matrimonial Causes Act 1973, ss 25 and 25A, including the obligation to consider whether a clean break is appropriate, where the court is considering whether and in what manner to exercise its powers under the Act.

19 Consent orders for financial provision or property adjustment

(1) Notwithstanding anything in section 18 above, on an application for a consent order for financial relief the court may, unless it has reason to think that there are other circumstances into which it ought to inquire, make an order in the terms agreed on the basis only of the prescribed information furnished with the application.

(2) Subsection (1) above applies to an application for a consent order varying or discharging an order for financial relief as it applies to an application for an order for financial relief.

(3) In this section –

"consent order", in relation to an application for an order, means an order in the terms applied for to which the respondent agrees;

"order for financial relief" means an order under section 17 above; and

"prescribed" means prescribed by rules of court.

20 Restriction of powers of court where jurisdiction depends on matrimonial home in England or Wales

(1) Where the court has jurisdiction to entertain an application for an order for financial relief by reason only of the situation in England or Wales of a dwelling-house which was a matrimonial home of the parties, the court may make under section 17 above any one or more of the following orders (but no other) –

(*a*) an order that either party to the marriage shall pay to the other such lump sum as may be specified in the order;

(*b*) an order that a party to the marriage shall pay to such person as may be so specified for the benefit of a child of the family, or to such a child, such lump sum as may be so specified;

(*c*) an order that a party to the marriage shall transfer to the other party, to any child of the family or to such person as may be so specified for the benefit of such a child, the interest of the first-mentioned party in the dwelling-house or such part of that interest as may be so specified;

(*d*) an order that a settlement of the interest of a party to the marriage in the dwelling-house, or such part of that interest as may be so specified, be made to the satisfaction of the court for the benefit of the other party to the marriage and of the children of the family or either or any of them;

(*e*) an order varying for the benefit of the parties to the marriage and of the children of the family or either or any of them any ante-nuptial or post-nuptial settlement (including such a settlement made by will or codicil) made on the parties to the marriage so far as that settlement relates to an interest in the dwelling-house;

(*f*) an order extinguishing or reducing the interest of either of the parties to the marriage under any such settlement so far as that interest is an interest in the dwelling-house;

(*g*) an order for the sale of the interest of a party to the marriage in the dwelling-house.

(2) Where, in the circumstances mentioned in subsection (1) above, the court makes an order for the payment of a lump sum by a party to the marriage, the amount of the lump sum shall not exceed, or where more than one such order is made the total amount of the lump sums shall not exceed in aggregate, the following amount, that is to say –

(*a*) if the interest of that party in the dwelling-house is sold in pursuance of an order made under subsection (1)(*g*) above, the amount of the proceeds of the sale of that interest after deducting therefrom any costs incurred in the sale thereof;

(*b*) if the interest of that party is not so sold, the amount which in the opinion of the court represents the value of that interest.

(3) Where the interest of a party to the marriage in the dwelling-house is held jointly or in common with any other person or persons –

(*a*) the reference in subsection (1)(*g*) above to the interest of a party to the marriage shall be construed as including a reference to the interest of that other person, or the interest of those other persons in the dwelling-house, and

(*b*) the reference in subsection (2)(*a*) above to the amount of the proceeds of a sale ordered under subsection (1)(*g*) above shall be construed as a reference to that part of those proceeds which is attributable to the interest of that party to the marriage in the dwelling-house.

Defined terms—"child of the family", "dwelling-house": s 27; "order for financial relief": s 12(4).

Scope of provision—Where the only fact establishing jurisdiction is the existence of a matrimonial home in this country, the court cannot make any maintenance order and it must not make a capital order which exceeds the monetary value of the matrimonial home.

21 Application to orders under ss 14 and 17 of certain provisions of Part II of Matrimonial Causes Act 1973

(1) The following provisions of Part II of the 1973 Act (financial relief for parties to marriage and children of family) shall apply in relation to an order under section 14 or 17 above as they apply in relation to a like order under that Part of that Act, that is to say –

(*a*) section 23(3) (provisions as to lump sums);

(*b*) section 24A(2), (4), (5) and (6) (provisions as to orders for sale);

(*ba*) section 24B(3) to (5) (provisions about pension sharing orders in relation to divorce and nullity);

(*bb*) section 24C (duty to stay pension sharing orders);

(*bc*) section 24D (apportionment of pension sharing charges);

(*bd*) section 25B(3) to (7B) (power, by financial provision order, to attach payments under a pension arrangement, or to require the exercise of a right of commutation under such an arrangement);

(*be*) section 25C (extension of lump sum powers in relation to death benefits under a pension arrangement);

(*c*) section 28(1) and (2) (duration of continuing financial provision orders in favour of party to marriage);

(*d*) section 29 (duration of continuing financial provision orders in favour of children, and age limit on making certain orders in their favour);

(*e*) section 30 (direction for settlement of instrument for securing payments or effecting property adjustment), except paragraph (*b*);

(*f*) section 31 variation, discharge etc of certain orders for financial relief), except subsection (2)(*e*) and subsection (4);

(*g*) section 32 (payment of certain arrears unenforceable without the leave of the court);

(*h*) section 33 (orders for repayment of sums paid under certain orders);

(*i*) section 38 (orders for repayment of sums paid after cessation of order by reason of remarriage);

(*j*) section 39 (settlements etc made in compliance with a property adjustment order may be avoided on bankruptcy of settlor); and

(*k*) section 40 (payments etc under order made in favour of person suffering from mental disorder).

(*l*) section 40A (appeals relating to pension sharing orders which have taken effect).

(2) Subsection (1)(*bd*) and (*be*) above shall not apply where the court has jurisdiction to entertain an application for an order for financial relief by reason only of the situation in England or Wales of a dwelling-house which was a matrimonial home of the parties.

(3) Section 25D(1) of the 1973 Act (effect of transfers on orders relating to rights under a pension arrangement) shall apply in relation to an order made under section 17 above by virtue of subsection (1)(*bd*) or (*be*) above as it applies in relation to an order made under section 23 of that Act by virtue of section 25B or 25C of the 1973 Act.

(4) The Lord Chancellor may by regulations make for the purposes of this Part of this Act provision corresponding to any provision which may be made by him under subsections (2) to (2B) of section 25D of the 1973 Act.

(5) Power to make regulations under this section shall be exercisable by statutory instrument which shall be subject to annulment in pursuance of a resolution of either House of Parliament.

Amendments—Welfare Reform and Pensions Act 1999, ss 22(4), (5), 84(1), Sch 12, para 4, Sch 13, Pt II.

Scope of provision—Subject to the Child Support Act 1991, which restricts the court's power to order child maintenance (see Procedural Guide 21), this section imports into the provisions for providing financial relief following an overseas divorce the vast majority of the powers of the court which apply where a financial application is brought following a divorce in this country. The three conspicuous absentees are the power to award interest on a lump sum under Matrimonial Causes Act 1973, s 23(6), the power to make a direction under s 25A(3) that there may be no further application for a periodical payments or secured periodical payments order, and the prohibition from applying to extend the term of a maintenance order under s 28(1A).

"mental disorder" (s 21(*k*))—By virtue of Mental Health Act 1983, s 1(2), this means "mental illness, arrested or incomplete development of mind, psychopathic disorder and any other disorder or disability of mind and 'mentally disordered' shall be construed accordingly". For a full explanation see the note to FPR 1991, r 9.1.

Orders for transfer of tenancies

22 Powers of the court in relation to certain tenancies of dwelling-houses

(1) This section applies if –

(*a*) an application is made by a party to a marriage for an order for financial relief; and

(*b*) one of the parties is entitled, either in his own right or jointly with the other party, to occupy a dwelling-house situated in England or Wales by virtue of a tenancy which is a relevant tenancy within the meaning of Schedule 7 to the Family Law Act 1996 (certain statutory tenancies).

(2) The court may make in relation to that dwelling-house any order which it could make under Part II of that Schedule if a decree of divorce, a decree of nullity of marriage or a decree of judicial separation has been granted in England and Wales in respect of the marriage.

(3) The provisions of paragraphs 10, 11 and 14(1) in Part III of that Schedule apply in relation to any order under this section as they apply to any order under Part II of that Schedule.

Amendments—Substituted by Family Law Act 1996, s 66(1), Sch 8, para 52; amended by SI 1997/1892.

Defined terms—"dwelling-house": s 27; "order for financial relief": s 12(4).

Avoidance of transactions intended to prevent or reduce financial relief

23 Avoidance of transactions intended to defeat applications for financial relief

(1) For the purposes of this section "financial relief" means relief under section 14 or 17 above and any reference to defeating a claim by a party to a marriage for financial relief from being granted is a reference to preventing financial relief from being granted or reducing the amount of relief which might be granted, or frustrating or impeding the enforcement of any order which might be or has been made under either of those provisions at the instance of that party.

(2) Where leave is granted under section 13 above for the making by a party to a marriage of an application for an order for financial relief under section 17 above, the court may, on an application by that party –

(*a*) if it is satisfied that the other party to the marriage is, with the intention of defeating the claim for financial relief, about to make any disposition or to transfer out of the jurisdiction or otherwise deal with any property, make such order as it thinks fit for restraining the other party from so doing or otherwise for protecting the claim;

(*b*) if it is satisfied that the other party has, with that intention, made a reviewable disposition and that if the disposition were set aside financial relief or different financial relief would be granted to the applicant, make an order setting aside the disposition.

(3) Where an order for financial relief under section 14 or 17 above has been made by the court at the instance of a party to a marriage, then, on an application made by that party, the court may, if it is satisfied that the other party to the marriage has, with the intention of defeating the claim for financial relief, made a reviewable disposition, make an order setting aside the disposition.

(4) Where the court has jurisdiction to entertain the application for an order for financial relief by reason only of paragraph (*c*) of section 15(1) above, it shall not make any order under subsection (2) or (3) above in respect of any property other than the dwelling-house concerned.

(5) Where the court makes an order under subsection (2)(*b*) or (3) above setting aside a disposition it shall give such consequential directions as it thinks fit for giving effect to the order (including directions requiring the making of any payments or the disposal of any property).

(6) Any disposition made by the other party to the marriage (whether before or after the commencement of the application) is a reviewable disposition for the purposes of subsections (2)(*b*) and (3) above unless it was made for valuable consideration (other than marriage) to a person who, at the time of the disposition, acted in relation to it in good faith and without notice of any intention on the part of the other party to defeat the applicant's claim for financial relief.

(7) Where an application is made under subsection (2) or (3) above with respect to a disposition which took place less than three years before the date of the application or with respect to a disposition or other dealing with property which is about to take place and the court is satisfied –

(*a*) in a case falling within subsection (2)(*a*) or (*b*) above, that the disposition or other dealing would (apart from this section) have the consequence, or

(*b*) in a case falling within subsection (3) above, that the disposition has had the consequence,

of defeating a claim by the applicant for financial relief, it shall be presumed unless the contrary is shown, that the person who disposed of or is about to dispose of or deal with the property did so or, as the case may be, is about to do so, with the intention of defeating the applicant's claim for financial relief.

(8) In this section "disposition" does not include any provision contained in a will or codicil but, with that exception, includes any conveyance, assurance or gift of property of any description, whether made by an instrument or otherwise.

(9) The preceding provisions of this section are without prejudice to any power of the High Court to grant injunctions under section 37 of the Supreme Court Act 1981.

Defined terms—"dwelling-house": s 27.

Scope of provision—This section is the equivalent of Matrimonial Causes Act 1973, s 37. It enables an applicant who has been granted leave to apply for financial relief to restrain future, and set aside past, disposals made with the intention of defeating the claim.

24 Prevention of transactions intended to defeat prospective applications for financial relief

(1) Where, on an application by a party to a marriage, it appears to the court –

(*a*) that the marriage has been dissolved or annulled, or that the parties to the marriage have been legally separated, by means of judicial or other proceedings in an overseas country; and

(*b*) that the applicant intends to apply for leave to make an application for an order for financial relief under section 17 above as soon as he or she has been habitually resident in England and Wales for a period of one year; and

(*c*) that the other party to the marriage is, with the intention of defeating a claim for financial relief, about to make any disposition or to transfer out of the jurisdiction or otherwise deal with any property,

the court may make such order as it thinks fit for restraining the other party from taking such action as is mentioned in paragraph (*c*) above.

(2) For the purposes of an application under subsection (1) above –

(*a*) the reference to defeating a claim for financial relief shall be construed in accordance with subsection (1) of section 23 above (omitting the reference to any order which has been made); and

(*b*) subsections (7) and (8) of section 23 above shall apply as they apply for the purposes of an application under that section.

(3) The preceding provisions of this section are without prejudice to any power of the High Court to grant injunctions under section 37 of the Supreme Court Act 1981.

Defined terms—"the court", "overseas country": s 27.

Scope of provision—Although the major restraining provisions, equivalent to Matrimonial Causes Act 1973, s 37, are contained in s 23, this provides a remedy, equivalent to that contained in MCA 1973, s 37(2)(*a*), for an applicant who has not yet obtained leave but who intends to do so as soon as there has been one year's habitual residence. Without prejudice to the court's power under Supreme Court Act 1981, s 37, this section enables an applicant to restrain anticipated dealings made with the intention of defeating the claim.

****

Interpretation

27 Interpretation of Part III

In this Part of this Act –

"the 1973 Act" means the Matrimonial Causes Act 1973;

"child of the family" has the meaning as in section 52(1) of the 1973 Act;

"the court" means the High Court or, where a county court has jurisdiction by virtue of Part V of this Act, a county court;

"dwelling-house" includes any building or part thereof which is occupied as a dwelling, and any yard, garden, garage or outhouse belonging to the dwelling-house and occupied therewith;

"order for financial relief" has the meaning given by section 12(4) above;
"overseas country" means a country or territory outside the British Islands;
"possession" includes receipt of, or the right to receive, rents and profits;
"property adjustment order" means such an order as is specified in section 24(1)(*a*), (*b*), (*c*) or (*d*) of the 1973 Act;
"rent" does not include mortgage interest;
"secured periodical payments order" means such an order as is specified in section 23(1)(*b*) or (*e*) of the 1973 Act.

"where a county court has jurisdiction by virtue of Part V of this Act"—This is a reference to a divorce county court.

****

PART V
FAMILY BUSINESS: DISTRIBUTION AND TRANSFER

Preliminary

32 What is family business

In this Part of this Act –

"family business" means business of any description which in the High Court is for the time being assigned to the Family Division and to no other Division by or under section 61 of (and Schedule 1 to) the Supreme Court Act 1981;
"family proceedings" means proceedings which are family business;
"matrimonial cause" means an action for divorce, nullity of marriage or judicial separation;

and "the 1973 Act" means the Matrimonial Causes Act 1973.

Amendments—Family Law Act 1986, s 68(1), Sch 1, para 27.

Jurisdiction of county courts in matrimonial causes and matters

33 Jurisdiction of county courts in matrimonial causes

(1) The Lord Chancellor may by order designate any county court as a divorce county court and any court so designated shall have jurisdiction to hear and determine any matrimonial cause, except that it shall have jurisdiction to try such a cause only if it is also designated in the order as a court of trial.

In this Part of this Act "divorce county court" means a county court so designated.

(2) The jurisdiction conferred by this section on a divorce county court shall be exercisable throughout England and Wales, but rules of court may provide for a matrimonial cause pending in one such court to be heard and determined in another or partly in that and partly in another.

(3) Every matrimonial cause shall be commenced in a divorce county court and shall be heard and determined in that or another such court unless or except to the extent it is transferred to the High Court under section 39 below or section 41 of the County Courts Act 1984 (transfer to High Court by order of High Court).

(4) The Lord Chancellor may by order designate a divorce county court as a court for the exercise of jurisdiction in matrimonial matters arising under Part III of this Act.

(5) The power to make an order under subsection (1) to (4) above shall be exercisable by statutory instrument.

34 Jurisdiction of divorce county courts as respects financial relief and protection of children

(1) Subject to subsections (2) and (3) below, a divorce county court shall have the following jurisdiction, namely –

(*a*) a jurisdiction to exercise any power exercisable under Part II or Part III of the 1973 Act in connection with any petition, decree or order pending in or made by such a court and to exercise any power under section 27 or 35 of that Act;

(*b*) if designated by an order under section 33(4) above, jurisdiction to exercise any power under Part III of this Act.

(2) Any proceedings for the exercise of a power which a divorce county court has jurisdiction to exercise by virtue of subsection (1)(*a*) or (*b*) above shall be commenced in such divorce county court as may be prescribed by rules of court.

(3) A divorce county court shall not by virtue of subsection (1)(*a*) above have jurisdiction to exercise any power under section 32, 33, 36 or 38 of the 1973 Act; but nothing in this section shall prejudice the exercise by a county court of any jurisdiction conferred on county courts by any of those sections.

(4) Nothing in this section shall affect the jurisdiction of a magistrates' court under section 35 of the 1973 Act.

35 Consideration of agreements or arrangements

Any provision to be made by rules of court for the purposes of section 7 of the 1973 Act with respect to any power exercisable by the court on an application made before the presentation of a petition shall confer jurisdiction to exercise the power on divorce county courts.

36 Assignment of Circuit judges to matrimonial proceedings

The jurisdiction conferred by the preceding provisions of this Part of this Act on divorce county courts, so far as it is exercisable by judges of such courts, shall be exercised by such Circuit judges as the Lord Chancellor may direct.

Distribution and transfer of family business and proceedings

37 Directions as to distribution and transfer of family business and proceedings

The President of the Family Division may, with the concurrence of the Lord Chancellor, give directions with respect to the distribution and transfer between the High Court and county courts of family business and family proceedings.

38 Transfer of family proceedings from High Court to county court

(1) At any stage in any family proceedings in the High Court the High Court may, if the proceedings are transferable under this section, either of its own motion or on the application of any party to the proceedings, order the transfer of the whole or any part of the proceedings to a county court.

(2) The following family proceedings are transferable to a county court under this section, namely –

(*a*) all family proceedings commenced in the High Court which are within the jurisdiction of a county court or divorce county court;
(*b*) wardship proceedings, except applications for an order that a minor be made, or cease to be, a ward of court or any other proceedings which relate to the exercise and the inherent jurisdiction of the High Court with respect to minors; and
(*c*) all family proceedings transferred from a county court to the High Court under section 39 below or section 41 of the County Courts Act 1984 (transfer to High Court by order of High Court); and
(*d*) all matrimonial causes and matters transferred from a county court otherwise than as mentioned in paragraph (*c*) above.

(3) Proceedings transferred under this section shall be transferred to such county court or, in the case of a matrimonial cause or matter within the jurisdiction of a divorce county court only, such divorce county court as the High Court directs.

(4) The transfer shall not affect any right of appeal from the order directing the transfer, or the right to enforce in the High Court any judgment signed, or order made, in that Court before the transfer.

(5) Where proceedings are transferred to a county court under this section, the county court –

(*a*) if it has no jurisdiction apart from this paragraph, shall have jurisdiction to hear and determine those proceedings;
(*b*) shall have jurisdiction to award any relief which could have been awarded by the High Court.

Amendments—Matrimonial Proceedings (Transfer) Act 1988, s 1(1); CA 1989, s 108(5), Sch 13, para 51.

39 Transfer of family proceedings to High Court from county court

(1) At any stage in any family proceedings in a county court, the county court may, if the proceedings are transferable under this section, either of its own motion or on the application of any party to the proceedings, order the transfer of the whole or any part of the proceedings to the High Court.

(2) The following family proceedings are transferable to the High Court under this section, namely –

(*a*) all family proceedings commenced in a county court or divorce county court; and
(*b*) all family proceedings transferred from the High Court to a county court or divorce county court under section 38 above.

Rules of court and fees

40 Family proceedings rules

(1) Subject to subsection (2) below, the power to make rules of court for the purposes of family proceedings in the High Court or county courts shall be exercisable by the Lord Chancellor together with any four or more of the following persons, namely –

(*a*) the President of the Family Division,
(*b*) one puisne judge attached to that Division,
(*c*) one district judge of the principal registry of that Division,
(*d*) two Circuit Judges,
(*e*) one district judge appointed under the County Courts Act 1984,
(*f*) two persons who have a Supreme Court qualification (within the meaning of section 71 of the Courts and Legal Services Act 1990), and
(*g*) two persons who have been granted by an authorised body, under Part II of that Act, the right to conduct litigation in relation to all proceedings in the Supreme Court.

(2) Subsection (1) above is without prejudice to the powers of the following authorities to make rules in respect of the matters referred to below and rules in respect of those matters shall continue to be made by those authorities and shall not be made by the authority constituted by subsection (1) above.

The rules and rule-making authorities are –

(*a*) adoption rules made by the Lord Chancellor under section 9(3) of the Adoption Act 1958, section 12(1) of the Adoption Act 1968 or section 66(1) of the Adoption Act 1976;
(*b*) probate rules made by the President of the Family Division with the concurrence of the Lord Chancellor under section 127 of the Supreme Court Act 1981.

(3) The persons to act in pursuance of subsection (1) above with the Lord Chancellor, other than the President of the Family Division, shall be appointed by the Lord Chancellor for such time as he may think fit.

(3A) Rules made under this section may make different provision for different cases or different areas, including different provision –

(*a*) for a specific court, or
(*b*) for specific proceedings, or a specific jurisdiction,

specified in the rules.

(4) Rules made under this section may –

(*a*) modify or exclude the application of any provision of the County Courts Act 1984; and
(*b*) provide for the enforcement in the High Court of orders made in a divorce county court.

(5) Rules of court under this section shall be made by statutory instrument subject to annulment in pursuance of a resolution of either House of Parliament; and the Statutory Instrument Act 1946 shall apply to a statutory instrument containing such rules as if the rules had been made by a Minister of the Crown.

Amendments—Civil Procedure Act 1997, s 10, Sch 2, para 3.

41 Fees in family proceedings

The fees to be taken in any family proceedings in the High Court or any county court shall be such as the Lord Chancellor with the concurrence of the Treasury may prescribe from time to time by order made by statutory instrument.

County court proceedings in principal registry

42 County court proceedings in principal registry of Family Division

(1) Sections 33 to 35 above shall not prevent the commencement of any proceedings in the principal registry except where rules of court under section 34(2) above otherwise provide; and the following provisions of this section shall have effect for the purposes of enabling proceedings to be dealt with in that registry as in a divorce county court.

(2) The jurisdiction in matrimonial causes or matters conferred by sections 33, 34 and 35 above on divorce county courts shall be exercised in the principal registry –

(*a*) so far as it is exercisable by judges of such courts, at such sittings and in such places as the Lord Chancellor may direct; and
(*b*) so far as it is exercisable by registrars of such courts, by such registrars or by registrars and other officers of the principal registry according as rules of court may provide;

and rules of court may make provision for treating, for any purposes specified in the rules, matrimonial causes and matters pending in the registry with respect to which that jurisdiction is exercisable as pending in a divorce county court and for the application of section 74(3) of the Solicitors Act 1974 (costs) with respect to proceedings so treated.

(3) Where, by virtue of rules under subsection (2) above, a matrimonial cause is pending in the registry as in a divorce county court, any ancillary or related proceedings which could be taken in a divorce county court and which are not of a description excluded by the rules from the operation of this subsection may be taken and dealt with in the registry as in a divorce county court.

(4) The principal registry shall be treated as a divorce county court –

(*a*) for the purposes of any provision to be made by rules of court under section 33(2) above;
(*b*) for the purpose of any provision to be made under section 34(2) above prescribing the county court in which any proceedings are to be commenced; and
(*c*) for the purpose of any transfer of family proceedings under section 38 or 39 above between the High Court and a divorce county court.

(4A) Where a district judge of the principal registry is exercising jurisdiction in any matrimonial cause or matter which could be exercised by a district judge of a county court, he shall have the same powers in relation to those proceedings as if he were a district judge of a county court and the proceedings were in a county court.

(5) Rules of court shall make provision for securing, with respect to family proceedings dealt with under this section, that, as nearly as may be, the same consequences shall follow –

(*a*) as regards service of process, as if proceedings commenced in the principal registry had been commenced in a divorce county court; and (*b*) as regards enforcement of orders, as if orders made in that registry in the exercise of the family jurisdiction conferred by sections 33, 34 and 35 above on divorce county courts were orders made by such a court.

(6) In this section "the principal registry" means the principal registry of the Family Division of the High Court and, for the purposes of subsection (3) above, proceedings are "ancillary" to a matrimonial cause if they are connected with the cause and are "related" to a matrimonial cause if they are for protecting or otherwise relate to any rights, or the exercise of any rights, of the parties to the marriage as husband and wife or any children of the family.

Amendments—Courts and Legal Services Act 1990, ss 74(7), 125(3), Sch 18, para 50.

****

Matrimonial Causes Act 1973

ARRANGEMENT OF SECTIONS

PART I
DIVORCE, NULLITY AND OTHER MATRIMONIAL SUITS

Divorce

Nullity

Other matrimonial suits

General

PART II

FINANCIAL RELIEF FOR PARTIES TO MARRIAGE AND CHILDREN OF FAMILY

Financial provision and property adjustment orders

Ancillary relief in connection with divorce proceedings etc

Financial provision in case of neglect to maintain

Additional provisions with respect to financial provision and property adjustment orders

Variation, discharge and enforcement of certain orders etc

PART I
DIVORCE, NULLITY AND OTHER MATRIMONIAL SUITS

Divorce

1 Divorce on breakdown of marriage

(1) Subject to section 3 below, a petition for divorce may be presented to the court by either party to a marriage on the ground that the marriage has broken down irretrievably.

(2) The court hearing a petition for divorce shall not hold the marriage to have broken down irretrievably unless the petitioner satisfies the court of one or more of the following facts, that is to say –

(*a*) that the respondent has committed adultery and the petitioner finds it intolerable to live with the respondent;
(*b*) that the respondent has behaved in such a way that the petitioner cannot reasonably be expected to live with the respondent;
(*c*) that the respondent has deserted the petitioner for a continuous period of at least two years immediately preceding the presentation of the petition;
(*d*) that the parties of the marriage have lived apart for a continuous period of at least two years immediately preceding the presentation of the petition

(hereafter in this Act referred to as "two years' separation") and the respondent consents to a decree being granted;

(*e*) that the parties to the marriage have lived apart for a continuous period of at least five years immediately preceding the presentation of the petition (hereafter in this Act referred to as "five years' separation").

(3) On a petition for divorce it shall be the duty of the court to inquire, so far as it reasonably can, into the facts alleged by the petitioner and into any facts alleged by the respondent.

(4) If the court is satisfied on the evidence of any such fact as is mentioned in subsection (2) above, then, unless it is satisfied on all the evidence that the marriage has not broken down irretrievably, it shall, subject to section 5 below, grant a decree of divorce.

(5) Every decree of divorce shall in the first instance be a decree nisi and shall not be made absolute before the expiration of six months from its grant unless the High Court by general order from time to time fixes a shorter period, or unless in any particular case the court in which the proceedings are for the time being pending from time to time by special order fixes a shorter period than the period otherwise applicable for the time being by virtue of this subsection.

Amendments—Matrimonial and Family Proceedings Act 1984, s 46(1), Sch 1, para 10.

Defined terms—"the court": s 52.

Scope of provision—This section defines the ground for divorce and sets out the facts which must be proved to establish that ground. Procedurally, it places on the court the duty to inquire into the fact alleged and to grant a decree – initially a decree nisi followed by a decree absolute – if the fact is proved; unless the court is not satisfied as to irretrievable breakdown.

Procedure—Procedure for divorce and most other matrimonial causes is covered by FPR 1991, rr 2.1–2.51; see also Procedural Guides 15 and 16.

"duty of the court to inquire ... into the facts alleged" (s 1(3))—The court's duty is usually performed by the district judge under the special procedure (FPR 1991, r 2.24(3)), but it may be performed under the standard procedure in open court if the petition is defended or the district judge is not prepared to sign his certificate under the special procedure.

"facts alleged by the petitioner [or] by the respondent" (s 1(3))—Where an answer has been filed with a cross-prayer, there will be cases where a decree is granted solely on the fact(s) in the answer. The respondent is therefore the spouse who has obtained the decree nisi.

"decree of divorce"(s 1(4), (5))—In the first instance, a decree nisi is issued (FPR 1991, r 2.43). This decree can be made absolute on application by the spouse who obtained the decree (FPR 1991, r 2.49) or, failing that, by the other spouse.

Time for application for decree absolute (s 1(5))—The time for application for a decree absolute is as follows:

(*a*) *Expedited decree* Occasionally, application may be made to the court to "fix a shorter period" (s 1(5)); see also **Application to expedite decree absolute** under FPR 1991, r 2.49.

(*b*) *Application by party who obtained the decree nisi* Application can be made by the party who obtained the decree in accordance with FPR 1991, r 2.49. The period for applying has been shortened to six weeks by the Matrimonial Causes (Decree Absolute) Order 1972, as amended.

(*c*) *Application by spouse against whom decree pronounced* The party against whom the decree was obtained can apply for a decree absolute on notice three months after the other spouse could have applied (MCA 1973, s 9(2); FPR 1991, r 2.50).

2 Supplemental provisions as to facts raising presumption of breakdown

(1) One party to a marriage shall not be entitled to rely for the purposes of section 1(2)(*a*) above on adultery committed by the other if, after it became known to him that the other had committed that adultery, the parties have lived with each other for a period exceeding, or periods together exceeding, six months.

(2) Where the parties to a marriage have lived with each other after it became known to one party that the other had committed adultery, but subsection (1) above does not apply, in any proceedings for divorce in which the petitioner relies on that adultery the fact that the parties have lived with each other after that time shall be disregarded in determining for the purposes of section 1(2)(*a*) above whether the petitioner finds it intolerable to live with the respondent.

(3) Where in any proceedings for divorce the petitioner alleges that the respondent has behaved in such a way that the petitioner cannot reasonably be expected to live with him, but the parties to the marriage have lived with each other for a period or periods after the date of the occurrence of the final incident relied on by the petitioner and held by the court to support his allegation, that fact shall be disregarded in determining for the purposes of section 1(2)(*b*) above whether the petitioner cannot reasonably be expected to live with the respondent if the length of that period or of those periods together was six months or less.

(4) For the purposes of section 1(2)(*c*) above the court may treat a period of desertion as having continued at a time when the deserting party was incapable of continuing the necessary intention if the evidence before the court is such that, had that party not been so incapable, the court would have inferred that his desertion continued at that time.

(5) In considering for the purposes of section 1(2) above whether the period for which the respondent has deserted the petitioner or the period for which the parties to a marriage have lived apart has been continuous, no account shall be taken of any one period (not exceeding six months) or of any two or more periods (not exceeding six months in all) during which the parties resumed living with each other, but no period during which the parties lived with each other shall count as part of the period of desertion or of the period for which the parties to the marriage lived apart, as the case may be.

(6) For the purposes of section 1(2)(*d*) and (*e*) above and this section a husband and wife shall be treated as living apart unless they are living with each other in the same household, and references in this section to the parties to a marriage living with each other shall be construed as references to their living with each other in the same household.

(7) Provision shall be made by rules of court for the purpose of ensuring that where in pursuance of section 1(2)(*d*) above the petitioner alleges that the respondent consents to a decree being granted the respondent has been given such information as will enable him to understand the consequences to him of his consenting to a decree being granted and the steps which he must take to indicate that he consents to the grant of a decree.

Defined terms—"the court": s 52.

Scope of provision—This section sets out a variety of provisions (s 2(1)–(5)) which have the effect of enabling the parties to live together for six months, or periods totalling six months, without jeopardising the evidence on which they may ultimately wish to found a divorce petition. It defines living apart as a state of not living together in the same household, and requires rules to

PART II

be made which will ensure that the respondent to a petition based on s 1(2)(*d*) is properly able to give informed consent.

Rules of court to ensure respondent's consent under s 1(2)(d) (s 2(7))—A rule to cover this requirement is set out in FPR 1991, r 2.10.

3 Bar on petitions for divorce within one year of marriage

(1) No petition for divorce shall be presented to the court before the expiration of the period of one year from the date of the marriage.

(2) Nothing in this section shall prohibit the presentation of a petition based on matters which occurred before the expiration of that period.

Amendments—Matrimonial and Family Proceedings Act 1984, s 1.

Defined terms—"the court": s 52.

"matters which occurred before" (s 3(2))—Facts arising prior to the one-year period can be pleaded as a basis for a divorce petition.

Judicial separation—Section 3 is no bar, for example, to a petition for judicial separation. Most other forms of relief under MCA 1973 (eg financial relief) are thus available to a petitioner, even though her marriage cannot be dissolved. If dissolution is subsequently sought, leave to present a petition is not necessary (FPR 1991, r 2.6(4) proviso); however, leave is required to file a fresh petition even if the facts relied on predate the one-year period and no decree in the judicial separation proceedings has been granted (*Butler v Butler, The Queen's Proctor Intervening* [1990] 1 FLR 114).

4 Divorce not precluded by previous judicial separation

(1) A person shall not be prevented from presenting a petition for divorce, or the court from granting a decree of divorce, by reason only that the petitioner or respondent has at any time, on the same facts or substantially the same facts as those proved in support of the petition, been granted a decree of judicial separation or an order under, or having effect as if made under, the Matrimonial Proceedings (Magistrates' Courts) Act 1960 or Part I of the Domestic Proceedings and Magistrates' Courts Act 1978 or any corresponding enactments in force in Northern Ireland, the Isle of Man or any of the Channel Islands.

(2) On a petition for divorce in such a case as is mentioned in subsection (1) above, the court may treat the decree or order as sufficient proof of any adultery, desertion or other fact by reference to which it was granted, but shall not grant a decree of divorce without receiving evidence from the petitioner.

(3) Where a petition for divorce in such a case follows a decree of judicial separation or (subject to subsection (5) below) an order containing a provision exempting one party to the marriage from the obligation to cohabit with the other, for the purposes of that petition a period of desertion immediately preceding the institution of the proceedings for the decree or order shall, if the parties have not resumed cohabitation and the decree or order has been continuously in force since it was granted, be deemed immediately to precede the presentation of the petition.

(4) For the purposes of section 1(2)(*c*) above the court may treat as a period during which the respondent has deserted the petitioner any of the following periods, that is to say –

(*a*) any period during which there is in force an injunction granted by the High Court or a county court which excludes the respondent from the matrimonial home;

(*b*) any period during which there is in force an order made by the High Court or a county court under section 1 or 9 of the Matrimonial Homes Act 1983 which prohibits the exercise by the respondent of the right to occupy a dwelling-house in which the applicant and the respondent have or at any time have had a matrimonial home;

(*c*) any period during which there is in force an order made by a magistrates' court under section 16(3) of the Domestic Proceedings and Magistrates' Courts Act 1978 which requires the respondent to leave the matrimonial home or prohibits the respondent from entering the matrimonial home.

(5) Where –

(*a*) a petition for divorce is presented after the date on which Part I of the Domestic Proceedings and Magistrates' Courts Act 1978 comes into force, and

(*b*) an order made under the Matrimonial Proceedings (Magistrates' Courts) Act 1960 containing a provision exempting the petitioner from the obligation to cohabit with the respondent is in force on that date,

then, for the purpose of section 1(2)(*c*) above, the court may treat a period during which such a provision was included in that order (whether before or after that date) as a period during which the respondent has deserted the petitioner.

Amendments—Domestic Proceedings and Magistrates' Courts Act 1978, ss 62, 89(2)(*a*), Sch 2, para 38; Matrimonial Homes Act 1983, s 12, Sch 2.

Defined terms—"the court": s 52.

Scope of provision—This section enables a spouse who has obtained a decree of judicial separation to seek a divorce on substantially the same facts and relying on findings in the previous proceedings. The section also sets out a number of factors which do not prevent the petitioner from seeking a decree under s 1(2)(*c*) (desertion).

Petition for divorce after decree of judicial separation (s 4(1))—If a decree of divorce is sought by a petitioner who has, or who is proceeding with, a judicial separation petition where the parties have not been married for a year, it is necessary to file a fresh petition (*Butler v Butler, The Queen's Proctor Intervening* [1990] 1 FLR 114); however, if the petition is presented after the one-year period has expired, it may be amended, provided no decree has already been granted (see **Supplemental and amended petitions contrasted** under FPR 1991, r 2.11).

No decree "without receiving evidence from the petitioner" (s 4(2))—Not only is a fresh petition needed where there has already been a decree, but the petitioner will also need to prove formally that the facts have already been found by a court. For example, it should be sufficient to recite in the petition the fact of the decree based on unreasonable behaviour and then to exhibit the previous petition and decree of judicial separation to a special procedure affidavit, or to give evidence concerning it in open court (as necessary).

Desertion (s 4(3)–(5))—Given the relative rarity with which decrees are now sought under s 1(2)(*c*), these provisions are likely to be rarely used. They are designed to ensure that, for the purposes of decree proceedings based on the fact of desertion for two years prior to the presentation of the petition (s 1(2)(*c*)), the time can run even though the respondent might not otherwise be regarded technically as in desertion.

5 Refusal of decree in five year separation cases on grounds of grave hardship to respondent

(1) The respondent to a petition for divorce in which the petitioner alleges five years' separation may oppose the grant of a decree on the ground that the dissolution of the marriage will result in grave financial or other hardship to him and that it would in all the circumstances be wrong to dissolve the marriage.

(2) Where the grant of a decree is opposed by virtue of this section, then –

(*a*) if the court finds that the petitioner is entitled to rely in support of his petition on the fact of five years' separation and makes no such finding as to any other fact mentioned in section 1(2) above, and

(*b*) if apart from this section the court would grant a decree on the petition,

the court shall consider all the circumstances, including the conduct of the parties to the marriage and the interests of those parties and of any children or other persons concerned, and if of opinion that the dissolution of the marriage will result in grave financial or other hardship to the respondent and that it would in all the circumstances be wrong to dissolve the marriage it shall dismiss the petition.

(3) For the purposes of this section hardship shall include the loss of the chance of acquiring any benefit which the respondent might acquire if the marriage were not dissolved.

Scope of provision—This section enables the respondent to a petition under s 1(2)(*e*) (five years' living apart), if no other fact under s 1(2) is pleaded by the petitioner, to oppose the grant of a decree on the grounds that divorce will cause grave financial hardship and that it would in all the circumstances be wrong to dissolve the marriage. If, after consideration of all the circumstances including those in s 5(2)(*b*), the court finds the grounds established by the respondent then the petition must be dismissed. Proceedings under this section are to be distinguished from those under s 10(2)–(4), where the court's power is limited to delaying the grant of a decree absolute.

Procedure—To oppose the grant of a decree under this section the respondent must file an answer within 28 days of service of the petition (FPR 1991, r 2.12(1)(*c*)). The answer must plead details of the financial hardship which the respondent will suffer and the circumstances which it is alleged would make it wrong to dissolve the marriage. The answer should conclude with a prayer that the petition be dismissed. The petitioner may wish to consider filing a reply, although if he does not, on seeking directions for trial he will be deemed to have denied factual allegations in the answer (FPR 1991, r 2.13(2)). The cause then proceeds as a defended cause: directions for trial must be sought (FPR 1991, r 2.24), place of trial must be determined (FPR 1991, r 2.25), provisions as to evidence apply (FPR 1991, rr 2.28–2.31), and, unless otherwise directed, the cause will be heard in open court by a judge (FPR 1991, r 2.32(1)).

Financial provision for the respondent—Whilst the petition subsists the respondent may seek maintenance pending suit; but upon "determination of the suit" (which includes dismissal of the petition under s 5(2)(*b*)) the maintenance pending suit ceases (s 22). If the respondent seeks continuing financial provision and the petitioner has failed to provide her with reasonable maintenance, application may be made under s 27. The respondent may seek to have such an application consolidated with the petition and tried immediately thereafter in the event of dismissal (RSC Ord 4, r 9; CCR Ord 13, r 9); if the petition is dismissed many of the factors considered by the court in its dismissal will be similar to those in a consideration of the respondent's financial circumstances under ss 25(2) and 27(3) (RSC Ord 4, r 9(1)(*a*); CCR Ord 13, r 9(1)(*a*)).

"grave financial or other hardship" (s 5(1))—The hardship, whether financial or otherwise, must be caused by the dissolution, as opposed to the breakdown, of the marriage. The usual case of financial hardship is where dissolution will result in one of the parties (usually the wife) losing a widow's pension (contingent upon her husband's death), the pension often being index-linked. In such a case, she must set out her case in her answer (probably referring to the Value of Lost Pension Table in *At A Glance*) and it is then for the husband in his reply to set out his proposals, if any, for compensating the wife for that financial hardship, for example by offering to fund a policy providing the wife with a lump sum should he predecease her, offering to agree a pension sharing order or, so as to cover the death in benefit lump sum, a pension attachment order – although both forms of relief may not be given against the same pension scheme. Additionally, he will point out that, whilst on decree absolute the wife will lose the chance of obtaining a widow's pension under the terms of his employer's scheme, the realisation of that chance depends on her outliving him and, by virtue of the divorce, she can rely on his national insurance contributions during the marriage, whereby she will receive the certainty of a State retirement pension at age 60 (for women who attain that age by 2010 and under the Government's current equalisation proposals staggered to age 65 up to 2020, and age 65 for those who attain that age after that date) whereas she would otherwise receive a much lesser amount by way of State retirement pension, ie the difference between a married couple's pension and a single person's pension. Pound for pound compensation for loss of contingent widow's pension rights is not appropriate (*Le Marchant v Le Marchant* [1977] 1 WLR 559, [1977] 3 All ER 610). Hardship other than financial hardship, such as being regarded as a social outcast in one's own community (*Banik v Banik* (1973) FLR Rep 65), must also be pleaded in the answer but is very difficult to establish. If, for example, a wife petitions for divorce on the ground of the husband's behaviour and the husband then cross-petitions on the ground of five years' separation the wife is estopped from pleading that dissolution will result in grave financial or other hardship (*Grenfell v Grenfell* [1978] Fam 128, [1977] 3 WLR 738). If the party who is losing pension rights has substantial capital, grave financial hardship is unlikely to be made out (*Archer v Archer* [1999] 1 FLR 327).

6 Attempts at reconciliation of parties to marriage

(1) Provision shall be made by rules of court for requiring the solicitor acting for a petitioner for divorce to certify whether he has discussed with the petitioner the possibility of a reconciliation and given him the names and addresses of persons qualified to help effect a reconciliation between parties to a marriage who have become estranged.

(2) If at any stage of proceedings for divorce it appears to the court that there is a reasonable possibility of a reconciliation between the parties to the marriage, the court may adjourn the proceedings for such period as it thinks fit to enable attempts to be made to effect such a reconciliation.

The power conferred by the foregoing provision is additional to any other power of the court to adjourn proceedings.

Defined terms—"the court": s 52.

Scope of provision—This section provides for any solicitor acting for a petitioner to certify that reconciliation has been discussed with his client, and enables the court to adjourn proceedings if reconciliation appears to be a possibility. As worded, it applies to divorce proceedings only, although s 17(3) applies it to judicial separation proceedings as well.

"Provision shall be made by rules of court" (s 6(1))—Such provision is made by FPR 1991, r 2.6(3), which requires the solicitor acting for a petitioner in divorce proceedings to file with her petition a certificate concerning reconciliation in Form M3, set out in FPR 1991, App 1.

"If ... it appears to the court" (s 6(2))—This little-used provision is not mentioned in the rules. As drafted, it can be invoked by the court of its own motion but, presumably, it could also be used by a spouse to test the possibility of reconciliation by making application to the court, by summons in the High Court or on notice in the county court (FPR 1991, r 10.9).

7 Consideration by the court of certain agreements or arrangements

Provision may be made by rules of court for enabling the parties to a marriage, or either of them, on application made either before or after the presentation of a petition for divorce, to refer to the court any agreement or arrangement made or proposed to be made between them, being an agreement or arrangement which relates to, arises out of, or is connected with, the proceedings for divorce which are contemplated or, as the case may be, have begun, and for enabling the court to express an opinion, should it think it desirable to do so, as to the reasonableness of the agreement or arrangement and to give such directions, if any, in the matter as it thinks fit.

Defined terms—"the court": s 52.

Rules of court—No rules have been made under this section, but practices have developed which have given some effect to what is proposed here:

(*a*) *Pounds v Pounds* [1994] 1 FLR 775, [1994] 1 WLR 1535, CA Where a consent application (see FPR 1991, r 2.61) is lodged prior to decree, but after the filling of a petition, this can be made the subject of an order effective on grant of decree nisi.

(*b*) *Agreement between the parties* In *Smith v McInerney* [1994] 2 FLR 1077, Thorpe J (following *Edgar v Edgar* (1981) FLR 19, [1980] 1 WLR 1410, CA) held that parties should be required to adhere to any "contract (sic)" entered into by them at the time of separation:

> "As a matter of general policy I think it is very important that what the parties themselves agree at the time of separation should be upheld by the courts unless there are overwhelmingly strong considerations for interference." (at 1081A).

However, see also **Prohibition of any restriction on right to apply** under MCA 1973, s 34.

8 Intervention of Queen's Proctor

(1) In the case of a petition for divorce –

(*a*) the court may, if it thinks fit, direct all necessary papers in the matter to be sent to the Queen's Proctor, who shall under the directions of the Attorney-General instruct counsel to argue before the court any question in relation to the matter which the court considers it necessary or expedient to have fully argued;

(*b*) any person may at any time during the progress of the proceedings or before the decree nisi is made absolute give information to the Queen's Proctor on any matter material to the due decision of the case, and the Queen's Proctor may thereupon take such steps as the Attorney-General considers necessary or expedient.

(2) Where the Queen's Proctor intervenes or shows cause against a decree nisi in any proceedings for divorce, the court may make such order as may be just as to the payment by other parties to the proceedings of the costs incurred by him in so doing or as to the payment by him of any costs incurred by any of those parties by reason of his so doing.

(3) The Queen's Proctor shall be entitled to charge as part of the expenses of his office –

(*a*) the costs of any proceedings under subsection (1)(*a*) above;

(*b*) where his reasonable costs of intervening or showing cause as mentioned in subsection (2) above are not fully satisfied by any order under that subsection, the amount of the difference;

(*c*) if the Treasury so directs, any costs which he pays to any parties under an order made under subsection (2).

Defined terms—"the court": s 52.

Divorce and nullity—As worded, this section applies to divorce proceedings only, although s 15 applies it to nullity proceedings as well.

Procedure (s 8(1))—Despite the breadth of s 8(1), the rules apply only to an application by the Queen's Proctor to show cause against a decree nisi being made absolute (FPR 1991, r 2.46).

9 Proceedings after decree nisi: general powers of court

(1) Where a decree of divorce has been granted but not made absolute, then, without prejudice to section 8 above, any person (excluding a party to the proceedings other than the Queen's Proctor) may show cause why the decree

should not be made absolute by reason of material facts not having been brought before the court; and in such a case the court may –

(*a*) notwithstanding anything in section 1(5) above (but subject to sections 10(2) to (4) and 41 below) make the decree absolute; or
(*b*) rescind the decree; or
(*c*) require further inquiry; or
(*d*) otherwise deal with the case as it thinks fit.

(2) Where a decree of divorce has been granted and no application for it to be made absolute has been made by the party to whom it was granted, then, at any time after the expiration of three months from the earliest date on which that party could have made such an application, the party against whom it was granted may make an application to the court, and on that application the court may exercise any of the powers mentioned in paragraphs (*a*) to (*d*) of subsection (1) above.

Defined terms—"the court": s 52.

Divorce and nullity—As worded, this section applies to divorce proceedings only, although s 15 applies it to nullity proceedings as well.

Application to show cause (s 9(1))—The procedure for applying to show cause why a decree nisi should not be made absolute is set out in FPR 1991, r 2.47.

Application for decree absolute by spouse against whom the decree nisi was obtained (s 9(2))—The procedure for the spouse who did not obtain the decree nisi to apply for a decree absolute is set out in FPR 1991, r 2.50(2).

"at any time after the expiration of three months" (s 9(2))—An application for a decree nisi to be made absolute which is made before the time-limit of three months renders void (as distinct from voidable) a decree made on that application, and the decree must be set aside (*Manchanda v Manchanda* [1995] 2 FLR 590, CA).

10 Proceedings after decree nisi: special protection for respondent in separation cases

(1) Where in any case the court has granted a decree of divorce on the basis of a finding that the petitioner was entitled to rely in support of his petition on the fact of two years' separation coupled with the respondent's consent to a decree being granted and has made no such finding as to any other fact mentioned in section 1(2) above, the court may, on an application made by the respondent at any time before the decree is made absolute, rescind the decree if it is satisfied that the petitioner misled the respondent (whether intentionally or unintentionally) about any matter which the respondent took into account in deciding to give his consent.

(2) The following provisions of this section apply where –

(*a*) the respondent to a petition for divorce in which the petitioner alleged two years' or five years' separation coupled, in the former case, with the respondent's consent to a decree being granted, has applied to the court for consideration under subsection (3) below of his financial position after the divorce; and
(*b*) the court has granted a decree on the petition on the basis of a finding that the petitioner was entitled to rely in support of his petition on the fact of two years' or five years' separation (as the case may be) and has made no such finding as to any other fact mentioned in section 1(2) above.

(3) The court hearing an application by the respondent under subsection (2) above shall consider all the circumstances, including the age, health, conduct, earning

capacity, financial resources and financial obligations of each of the parties, and the financial position of the respondent as, having regard to the divorce, it is likely to be after the death of the petitioner should the petitioner die first; and, subject to subsection (4) below, the court shall not make the decree absolute unless it is satisfied –

(*a*) that the petitioner should not be required to make any financial provision for the respondent, or

(*b*) that the financial provision made by the petitioner for the respondent is reasonable and fair or the best that can be made in the circumstances.

(4) The court may if it thinks fit make the decree absolute notwithstanding the requirements of subsection (3) above if –

(*a*) it appears that there are circumstances making it desirable that the decree should be made absolute without delay, and

(*b*) the court has obtained a satisfactory undertaking from the petitioner that he will make such financial provision for the respondent as the court may approve.

Defined terms—"the court": s 52(1); "financial provision": s 21; "five years' separation": s 1(2)(*e*); "two years' separation": s 1(2)(*d*).

Scope of provision—This section contains two distinct provisions. Firstly, s 10(1) enables a respondent who claims to have been misled when giving his consent to seek rescission of a decree of divorce, but not judicial separation, under MCA 1973, s 1(2)(*d*) (two years' living apart with consent), provided that no other fact in MCA 1973, s 1(2) was proved by the petitioner. It makes no difference whether the petitioner misled him intentionally or unintentionally. The second aspect of the section is contained in s 10(2)–(4) which is a half-way house between the full defence to the grant of a decree nisi on the ground of financial (or other) hardship under s 5 and the range of income and capital orders available under ss 23 and 24. Where there is a loss of widow's pension rights, before issuing a s 10(2) application consideration should be given as to whether an application for a pension attachment and/or sharing order (although the two forms of relief may not be granted in respect of the same pension scheme) will meet the requirements of the applicant. In *Garcia v Garcia* [1992] Fam 83, this section was successfully used when the petitioner was in breach of a past obligation to contribute equally to the maintenance of a child.

Procedure for application under s 10(1)—FPR 1991, r 2.44 applies. It is probable that a decree under MCA 1973, s 1(2)(*d*) obtained on a respondent's answer would also be covered by this procedure (see under FPR 1991, r 2.44).

Procedure for application under s 10(2)—For applications made before 5 June 2000 see Procedural Guide 17 in *The Family Court Practice 1999*. For applications made after that date, Form B should be used followed by Form E (see FPR 1991, rr 2.45 and 2.51A–2.70).

Effect of s 10(2) application—Making the application has the effect that the decree cannot be made absolute until the application has been heard, unless there are both circumstances making it desirable for the decree to be made absolute before hearing the application and the petitioner has given an undertaking to make suitable financial provision. The undertaking must contain concrete specific proposals and not merely be a general undertaking to carry out whatever the court may consider appropriate at some future time (see *Grigson v Grigson* [1974] 1 WLR 228, [1974] 1 All ER 478).

10A Proceedings after decree nisi: religious marriage

(1) This section applies if a decree of divorce has been granted but not made absolute and the parties to the marriage concerned –

(*a*) were married in accordance with –

(i) the usages of the Jews, or

(ii) any other prescribed religious usages; and

(*b*) must co-operate if the marriage is to be dissolved in accordance with those usages.

(2) On the application of either party, the court may order that a decree of divorce is not to be made absolute until a declaration made by both parties that they have taken such steps as are required to dissolve the marriage in accordance with those usages is produced to the court.

(3) An order under subsection (2) –

(*a*) may be made only if the court is satisfied that in all the circumstances of the case it is just and reasonable to do so; and

(*b*) may be revoked at any time.

(4) A declaration of a kind mentioned in subsection (2) –

(*a*) must be in a specified form;

(*b*) must, in specified cases, be accompanied by such documents as may be specified; and

(*c*) must, in specified cases, satisfy such other requirements as may be specified.

(5) The validity of a decree of divorce made by reference to such a declaration is not to be affected by any inaccuracy in that declaration.

(6) "Prescribed" means prescribed in an order made by the Lord Chancellor and such an order –

(*a*) must be made by statutory instrument;

(*b*) shall be subject to annulment in pursuance of a resolution of either House of Parliament.

(7) "Specified" means specified in rules of court.

Amendments—Inserted by Divorce (Religious Marriages) Act 2002, s 1.

Procedure—FPR 1991, rr 2.45A and 2.45B (inserted by FP(A)R 2003) set out, respectively, the procedure upon application for an order for stay pending a declaration and the content of the declaration itself (see s 10A(4)); and see Procedural Guide 15A.

Nullity

11 Grounds on which a marriage is void

A marriage celebrated after 31 July 1971 shall be void on the following grounds only, that is to say –

(*a*) that it is not a valid marriage under the provisions of the Marriage Acts 1949 to 1986 (that is to say where –

(i) the parties are within the prohibited degrees of relationship;

(ii) either party is under the age of sixteen; or

(iii) the parties have intermarried in disregard of certain requirements as to the formation of marriage);

(*b*) that at the time of the marriage either party was already lawfully married;

(*c*) that the parties are not respectively male and female;

(*d*) in the case of a polygamous marriage entered into outside England and Wales, that either party was at the time of the marriage domiciled in England and Wales.

For the purposes of paragraph (*d*) of this subsection a marriage is not polygamous if at its inception neither party has any spouse additional to the other.

Amendments—Marriage (Prohibited Degrees of Relationship) Act 1986, s 6(4); Private International Law (Miscellaneous Provisions) Act 1995, s 8, Sch, para 2.

Procedure—The procedure for petitions for nullity of marriage are, as for divorce, set out in FPR 1991, rr 2.1–2.51.

12 Grounds on which a marriage is voidable

A marriage celebrated after 31 July 1971 shall be voidable on the following grounds only, that is to say –

(*a*) that the marriage has not been consummated owing to the incapacity of either party to consummate it;
(*b*) that the marriage has not been consummated owing to the wilful refusal of the respondent to consummate it;
(*c*) that either party to the marriage did not validly consent to it, whether in consequence of duress, mistake, unsoundness of mind or otherwise;
(*d*) that at the time of the marriage either party, though capable of giving a valid consent, was suffering (whether continuously or intermittently) from mental disorder within the meaning of the Mental Health Act 1983 of such a kind or to such an extent as to be unfitted for marriage;
(*e*) that at the time of the marriage the respondent was suffering from venereal disease in a communicable form;
(*f*) that at the time of the marriage the respondent was pregnant by some person other than the petitioner.

Amendments—Mental Health Act 1983, s 148, Sch 4, para 34.

Procedure—The procedure for petitions for nullity of marriage is dealt with in FPR 1991, rr 2.1–2.51. FPR 1991, rr 2.22 and 2.23 contain particular rules for medical evidence where the allegation is that a spouse has been incapable of consummating the marriage (s 12(*a*)).

"mental disorder" (s 12(*d*))—By virtue of Mental Health Act 1983, s 1(2), this means "mental illness, arrested or incomplete development of mind, psychopathic disorder and any other disorder or disability of mind and 'mentally disordered' shall be construed accordingly". For a full explanation see the note to FPR 1991, r 9.1.

13 Bars to relief where marriage is voidable

(1) The court shall not, in proceedings instituted after 31 July 1971, grant a decree of nullity on the ground that a marriage is voidable if the respondent satisfies the court –

(*a*) that the petitioner, with knowledge that it was open to him to have the marriage avoided, so conducted himself in relation to the respondent as to lead the respondent reasonably to believe that he would not seek to do so; and
(*b*) that it would be unjust to the respondent to grant the decree.

(2) Without prejudice to subsection (1) above, the court shall not grant a decree of nullity by virtue of section 12 above on the grounds mentioned in paragraph (*c*), (*d*), (*e*) or (*f*) of that section unless –

(*a*) it is satisfied that proceedings were instituted within the period of three years from the date of marriage, or
(*b*) leave for the institution of proceedings after the expiration of that period has been granted under subsection (4) below.

(3) Without prejudice to subsections (1) and (2) above, the court shall not grant a decree of nullity by virtue of section 12 above on the grounds mentioned in paragraph (*e*) or (*f*) of that section unless it is satisfied that the petitioner was at the time of the marriage ignorant of the facts alleged.

(4) In the case of proceedings for the grant of a decree of nullity by virtue of section 12 above on the grounds mentioned in paragraph (*c*), (*d*), (*e*) or (*f*) of that section, a judge of the court may, on an application made to him, grant leave for the institution of proceedings after the expiration of the period of three years from the date of the marriage if –

(*a*) he is satisfied that the petitioner has at some time during that period suffered from mental disorder within the meaning of the Mental Health Act 1983, and

(*b*) he considers that in all the circumstances of the case it would be just to grant leave for the institution of proceedings.

(5) An application for leave under subsection (4) above may be made after the expiration of the period of three years from the date of the marriage.

Amendments—Matrimonial and Family Proceedings Act 1984, s 2.

Defined terms—"the court": s 52.

Application for leave after three years (s 13(4))—No procedure is prescribed for application under this provision. The process is similar to an application for leave under the pre-1984 s 3 (petition within three years on grounds of hardship or depravity) or, to some extent, an application for leave to omit an address (see **"Unless otherwise directed"** under FPR 1991, r 2.3). Thus, an application should be made ex parte (by summons in the High Court) to the judge, with an affidavit in support containing the following:

(*a*) a draft petition;
(*b*) the medical evidence on which the petitioner relies in support of her contention that she was a patient;
(*c*) a statement of the background to the marriage and application; and
(*d*) a statement of why the petitioner believes the interests of justice require that she be granted leave.

"mental disorder" (s 13(4)(*a*))—By virtue of Mental Health Act 1983, s 1(2), this means "mental illness, arrested or incomplete development of mind, psychopathic disorder and any other disorder or disability of mind and 'mentally disordered' shall be construed accordingly". For a full explanation see the note to FPR 1991, r 9.1.

"at some time during that period" (s 13(4)(*a*))—The disorder may have existed at the time of the marriage, or may have developed during the three years since the marriage.

14 Marriages governed by foreign law or celebrated abroad under English law

(1) Where, apart from this Act, any matter affecting the validity of a marriage would fall to be determined (in accordance with the rules of private international law) by reference to the law of a country outside England and Wales, nothing in section 11, 12 or 13(1) above shall –

(*a*) preclude the determination of that matter as aforesaid; or

(*b*) require the application to the marriage of the grounds or bar there mentioned except so far as applicable in accordance with those rules.

(2) In the case of a marriage which purports to have been celebrated under the Foreign Marriage Acts 1892 to 1947 or has taken place outside England and Wales and purports to be a marriage under common law, section 11 above is without

prejudice to any ground on which the marriage may be void under those Acts or, as the case may be, by virtue of the rules governing the celebration of marriages outside England and Wales under common law.

15 Application of ss 1(5), 8 and 9 to nullity proceedings

Sections 1(5), 8 and 9 above shall apply in relation to proceedings for nullity of marriage as if for any reference in those provisions to divorce there were substituted a reference to nullity of marriage.

16 Effect of decree of nullity in case of voidable marriage

A decree of nullity granted after 31 July 1971 in respect of a voidable marriage shall operate to annul the marriage only as respects any time after the decree has been made absolute, and the marriage shall, notwithstanding the decree, be treated as if it had existed up to that time.

Scope of provision—This section provides that a voidable marriage (ie covered by one or more of the grounds under s 12) only becomes void on decree absolute and is deemed to subsist until that time.

Other matrimonial suits

17 Judicial separation

(1) A petition for judicial separation may be presented to the court by either party to a marriage on the ground that any such fact as is mentioned in section 1(2) above exists, and the provisions of section 2 above shall apply accordingly for the purposes of a petition for judicial separation alleging any such fact, as they apply in relation to a petition for divorce alleging that fact.

(2) On a petition for judicial separation it shall be the duty of the court to inquire, so far as it reasonably can, into the facts alleged by the petitioner and into any facts alleged by the respondent, but the court shall not be concerned to consider whether the marriage has broken down irretrievably, and if it is satisfied on the evidence of any such fact as is mentioned in section 1(2) above it shall, subject to section 41 below, grant a decree of judicial separation.

(3) Sections 6 and 7 above shall apply for the purpose of encouraging the reconciliation of parties to proceedings for judicial separation and of enabling the parties to a marriage to refer to the court for its opinion an agreement or arrangement relevant to actual or contemplated proceedings for judicial separation, as they apply in relation to proceedings for divorce.

Defined terms—"the court": s 52.

Procedure—The procedure for judicial separation is covered by FPR 1991, rr 2.1–2.51; see also Procedural Guides 15 and 16.

"duty of the court to inquire ... into the facts alleged" (s 17(2))—The court's duty is usually performed by the district judge under the special procedure (FPR 1991, r 2.24(3)), but it may be performed under the standard procedure in open court if the petition is defended or the district judge is not prepared to sign his certificate under the special procedure.

"decree of judicial separation" (s 17(2))—In the case of judicial separation only a single decree is issued, but this cannot be granted until after the court has dealt with any issues which may arise under s 41 (arrangements for the children of the family).

18 Effects of judicial separation

(1) Where the court grants a decree of judicial separation it shall no longer be obligatory for the petitioner to cohabit with the respondent.

(2) If while a decree of judicial separation is in force and the separation is continuing either of the parties to the marriage dies intestate as respects all or any of his or her real or personal property, the property as respects which he or she died intestate shall devolve as if the other party to the marriage had then been dead.

(3) Notwithstanding anything in section 2(1)(*a*) of the Matrimonial Proceedings (Magistrates' Courts) Act 1960, a provision in force under an order made, or having effect as if made, under that section exempting one party to a marriage from the obligation to cohabit with the other shall not have effect as a decree of judicial separation for the purposes of subsection (2) above.

Defined terms—"the court": s 52.

Divorce after judicial separation—If divorce is sought where there are judicial separation proceedings not yet disposed of by dismissal or decree, leave to present a further petition is necessary (FPR 1991, r 2.6(4)); save where the petition follows a judicial separation petition filed within one year of the marriage and the new petition is based on the same facts as the old (FPR 1991, proviso to r 2.6(4)).

19 Presumption of death and dissolution of marriage

(1) Any married person who alleges that reasonable grounds exist for supposing that the other party to the marriage is dead may present a petition to the court to have it presumed that the other party is dead and to have the marriage dissolved, and the court may, if satisfied that such reasonable grounds exist, grant a decree of presumption of death and dissolution of the marriage.

(2) (*repealed*)

(3) In any proceedings under this section the fact that for a period of seven years or more the other party to the marriage has been continually absent from the petitioner and the petitioner has no reason to believe that the other party has been living within that time shall be evidence that the other party is dead until the contrary is proved.

(4) Sections 1(5), 8 and 9 above shall apply to a petition and a decree under this section as they apply to a petition for divorce and a decree of divorce respectively.

(5) (*repealed*)

(6) It is hereby declared that neither collusion nor any other conduct on the part of the petitioner which has at any time been a bar to relief in matrimonial proceedings constitutes a bar to the grant of a decree under this section.

Amendments—Domicile and Matrimonial Proceedings Act 1973, ss 6(4), 17(2), Sch 6.

Defined terms—"the court": s 52.

Scope of provision—The fact that a spouse has been continually absent for seven years and the petitioner has no reason to believe him to be alive during that time creates a rebuttable presumption of the death of that spouse.

Procedure—The procedure for seeking a decree of presumption of death is covered by FPR 1991, rr 2.1–2.51. However, the procedure for a petition under this section is different in a number of respects:

(*a*) *The petition* A petition seeking a decree of presumption of death is the same as a petition for divorce, except that the facts required by FPR 1991, App 2, para 3 must also be pleaded;

(*b*) *Statement of arrangements* It is not necessary to file a statement of arrangements for the minor children of the family when filing a petition for presumption of death (FPR 1991, r 2.2(2));
(*c*) *Service of the petition* By definition, there is no other spouse to serve, although FPR 1991, r 2.9 is silent as to whether the court automatically dispenses with any attempt at service, thereby relieving the petitioner from the need to make an application to dispense with service under FPR 1991, r 2.9(11);
(*d*) *Special procedure* The special procedure under FPR 1991, r 2.24(3) is not available for petitions for presumption of death, which must therefore be heard in open court;
(*e*) *Consideration of arrangements for the children of the family* There is no need for the court to consider the arrangements for any children of the family (s 41(1)).

"the court may, if satisfied" (s 19(1))—These words impose on the court a duty equivalent to "duty of the court to inquire ... into the facts alleged" under ss 1(3) and 17(2).

Decree of presumption of death and dissolution of marriage (s 19(4))—The reference to s 1(5) applies a procedure for decrees in the case of presumption of death similar to that for decrees of divorce.

General

20 Relief for respondent in divorce proceedings

If in any proceedings for divorce the respondent alleges and proves any such fact as is mentioned in subsection (2) of section 1 above (treating the respondent as the petitioner and the petitioner as the respondent for the purposes of that subsection) the court may give to the respondent the relief to which he would have been entitled if he had presented a petition seeking that relief.

Defined terms—"the court": s 52.

"the court may give to the respondent the relief"—This situation may arise, for example, where a respondent files an answer to a petition and the suit proceeds on the prayer in his answer instead of on the prayer in the petition. In such a case, the court may grant a decree (with costs, as appropriate) to the respondent. That decree will have the effect of dissolving the marriage in the same way as if the decree were based on the prayer in the petition.

PART II
FINANCIAL RELIEF FOR PARTIES TO MARRIAGE AND CHILDREN OF FAMILY

Financial provision and property adjustment orders

21 Financial provision and property adjustment orders

(1) The financial provision orders for the purposes of this Act are the orders for periodical or lump sum provision available (subject to the provisions of this Act) under section 23 below for the purpose of adjusting the financial position of the parties to a marriage and any children of the family in connection with proceedings for divorce, nullity of marriage or judicial separation and under section 27(6) below on proof of neglect by one party to a marriage to provide, or to make a proper contribution towards, reasonable maintenance for the other or a child of the family, that is to say –

(*a*) any order for periodical payments in favour of a party to a marriage under section 23(1)(*a*) or 27(6)(*a*) or in favour of a child of the family under section 23(1)(*d*), (2) or (4) or 27(6)(*d*);

(*b*) any order for secured periodical payments in favour of a party to a marriage under section 23(1)(*b*) or 27(6)(*b*) or in favour of a child of the family under section 23(1)(*e*), (2) or (4) or 27(6)(*e*); and

(*c*) any order for lump sum provision in favour of a party to a marriage under section 23(1)(*c*) or 27(6)(*c*) or in favour of a child of the family under section 23(1)(*f*), (2) or (4) or 27(6)(*f*);

and references in this Act (except in paragraphs 17(1) and 23 of Schedule 1 below) to periodical payments orders, secured periodical payments orders, and orders for the payment of a lump sum are references to all or some of the financial provision orders requiring the sort of financial provision in question according as the context of each reference may require.

(2) The property adjustment orders for the purposes of this Act are the orders dealing with property rights available (subject to the provisions of this Act) under section 24 below for the purpose of adjusting the financial position of the parties to a marriage and any children of the family on or after the grant of a decree of divorce, nullity of marriage or judicial separation, that is to say –

(*a*) any order under subsection (1)(*a*) of that section for a transfer of property;

(*b*) any order under subsection (1)(*b*) of that section for a settlement of property; and

(*c*) any order under subsection (1)(*c*) or (*d*) of that section for a variation of settlement.

Defined terms—"child of the family": s 52(1).

21A Pension sharing orders

(1) For the purposes of this Act, a pension sharing order is an order which –

(*a*) provides that one party's –

(i) shareable rights under a specified pension arrangement, or

(ii) shareable state scheme rights,

be subject to pension sharing for the benefit of the other party, and

(*b*) specifies the percentage value to be transferred.

(2) In subsection (1) above –

(*a*) the reference to shareable rights under a pension arrangement is to rights in relation to which pension sharing is available under Chapter I of Part IV of the Welfare Reform and Pensions Act 1999, or under corresponding Northern Ireland legislation,

(*b*) the reference to shareable state scheme rights is to rights in relation to which pension sharing is available under Chapter II of Part IV of the Welfare Reform and Pensions Act 1999, or under corresponding Northern Ireland legislation, and

(*c*) "party" means a party to a marriage.

Amendments—Inserted by Welfare Reform and Pensions Act 1999, s 19, Sch 3, para 2.

Defined terms—"Pension arrangement": s 25D(3).

"Shareable rights under a pension arrangement"—Widely defined in Welfare Reform and Pensions Act 1999, ss 19–46 to include all pension arrangements and unfunded public service pensions except for:

(i) The Great Offices of State;

(ii) Those arising from being the widow, widower or other dependant of a deceased person (Pension Sharing (Valuation) Regulations 2000 (SI 2000/1052)).

PART II

"Shareable State Scheme rights"—Defined by Welfare Reform and Pensions Act 1999, s 47 as earnings related additional pension and shared additional pension, ie SERPS but Basic State Retirement Pension is excluded from definition.

Scope of provision—Welfare Reform and Pensions Act 1999, ss 19–51 provide that a pension sharing order operates by debiting from the person with pension rights a percentage of the value of his fund and transferring that percentage to the credit of the other party to the marriage. The valuation is based on the cash equivalent transfer value on a date between one year prior to the petition and the date of the order. The CETV is calculated on the basis of the benefits earned to date. In unfunded public service schemes, only an internal transfer is possible. Otherwise, dependent on the position of the person responsible for managing the pension arrangements, there will be either an internal transfer within the scheme or an external transfer to some other pension arrangement. In either case, the applicant receives an indefeasible pension fund in her own right which does not end on remarriage and (subject to a limited exception) is not capable of variation. Broadly speaking, the charges are met by the parties and not by the pension provider.

Inter-Relation of Pension Sharing, Pension Attachment and *Brooks v Brooks* Variation of Settlement

Pension Sharing: ss 24B–D

(1) Only applies to post-1 December 2000 petitions but rescission of decree nisi by agreement possible – see **Scope of provision** under MCA 1973, s 24B.
(2) Does not apply to judicial separation.
(3) Percentage of cash equivalent transfer value.
(4) Applicant receives fund carved out of other party's pension. Whilst if it is an internal transfer she is bound by the rules of the scheme (ie if husband could only take pension before 65 if substantial discount for accelerated payment she will also be bound by that rule) she can choose when and how to take the benefit. Not capable of variation unless application made before order takes effect and before decree absolute. Not affected by wife's remarriage or husband's death.
(5) Not available if there is or has been pension sharing for this pension arrangement in respect of this marriage for this pension arrangement. Not available if there is an attachment order for this or any other marriage.
(6) Periodical payments element taxable in the hands of the person to whom the transfer of pension rights has been made.
(7) Community Legal Service statutory charge will not bite against the pension fund either as regards the periodical payments or lump sum element (see [2002] Fam Law 710).

Pension Attachment (previously known as earmarking): ss 23 and 25A–D

(1) Applies to post-1 July 1996 petitions.
(2) Applies to all forms of relief including judicial separation.
(3) Attaches a percentage of –
 (*a*) member's pension in retirement;
 (*b*) lump sum payable on retirement and lump sum payable on death after retirement;
 (*c*) lump sum payable on death in service, after leaving service but before retirement and after retirement.
 No power to attach spouse's pension on member's death.
(4) Court cannot order husband to take pension benefits on any specific date. As a species of periodical payments, attachment orders end on remarriage and can be varied at any time. A pension attachment lump sum order can be varied prior to either party's death.
(5) Not available if pension arrangement is or has been subject to pension sharing between parties to this marriage.
(6) Periodical payments element taxable in the hands of the person with pension rights.
(7) Statutory charge crystallises on lump sum element only of pension fund attached (see [2002] Fam Law 710).

***Brooks v Brooks* variations: s 24(1)(*c*) and (*d*)**

(1) Only available if pre-1 December 2000 petition (Welfare Reform and Pensions Act 1999, s 85(4)).
(2) Operates to carve out benefits for wife out of husband's pension scheme.

Necessity of service on person responsible for managing pension arrangements—For an effective order to be made in pension sharing pension attachment or *Brooks v Brooks* variation the person responsible for the pension arrangement must be served and given at least 21 days' notice of the application.

Ancillary relief in connection with divorce proceedings etc

22 Maintenance pending suit

On a petition for divorce, nullity of marriage or judicial separation, the court may make an order for maintenance pending suit, that is to say, an order requiring either party to the marriage to make to the other such periodical payments for his or her maintenance and for such term, being a term beginning not earlier than the date of the presentation of the petition and ending with the date of the determination of the suit, as the court thinks reasonable.

Mode of application—The procedure on an application for maintenance pending suit made by Form A after 5 June 2000 is set out in FPR 1991, rr 2.52–2.70 (the rules, as amended, are set out in this edition providing for a new procedural code governed by the Family Proceedings (Amendment No 2) Rules 1999). For applications made before that date see Procedural Guide 18 or 19 in *The Family Court Practice 1999*.

Conversion to final order—The procedure for converting a maintenance pending suit order into a periodical payments order on decree absolute is prescribed by FPR 1991, r 2.67.

Legal costs element of maintenance pending suit—Although the court will be cautious in including a costs element in maintenance pending suit, s 22 empowers it to include an element towards the payee's costs where it is reasonable to do so (*A v A (Maintenance Pending Suit: Provision for Legal Fees)* [2001] 1 FLR 377).

23 Financial provision orders in connection with divorce proceedings etc

(1) On granting a decree of divorce, a decree of nullity of marriage or a decree of judicial separation or at any time thereafter (whether, in the case of a decree of divorce or of nullity of marriage, before or after the decree is made absolute), the court may make any one or more of the following orders, that is to say –

(*a*) an order that either party to the marriage shall make to the other such periodical payments, for such term, as may be specified in the order;

(*b*) an order that either party to the marriage shall secure to the other to the satisfaction of the court such periodical payments, for such term, as may be so specified;

(*c*) an order that either party to the marriage shall pay to the other such lump sum or sums as may be so specified;

(*d*) an order that a party to the marriage shall make to such person as may be specified in the order for the benefit of a child of the family, or to such a child, such periodical payments, for such term, as may be so specified;

(*e*) an order that a party to the marriage shall secure to such person as may be so specified for the benefit of such a child, or to such a child, to the satisfaction of the court, such periodical payments, for such term, as may be so specified;

(*f*) an order that a party to the marriage shall pay to such person as may be so specified for the benefit of such a child, or to such a child, such lump sum as may be so specified;

subject, however, in the case of an order under paragraph (*d*), (*e*) or (*f*) above, to the restrictions imposed by section 29(1) and (3) below on the making of financial provision orders in favour of children who have attained the age of eighteen.

(2) The court may also, subject to those restrictions, make any one or more of the orders mentioned in subsection (1)(*d*), (*e*) and (*f*) above –

(*a*) in any proceedings for divorce, nullity of marriage or judicial separation, before granting a decree; and
(*b*) where any such proceedings are dismissed after the beginning of the trial, either forthwith or within a reasonable period after the dismissal.

(3) Without prejudice to the generality of subsection (1)(*c*) or (*f*) above –

(*a*) an order under this section that a party to a marriage shall pay a lump sum to the other party may be made for the purpose of enabling that other party to meet any liabilities or expenses reasonably incurred by him or her in maintaining himself or herself or any child of the family before making an application for an order under this section in his or her favour;
(*b*) an order under this section for the payment of a lump sum to or for the benefit of a child of the family may be made for the purpose of enabling any liabilities or expenses reasonably incurred by or for the benefit of that child before the making of an application for an order under this section in his favour to be met; and
(*c*) an order under this section for the payment of a lump sum may provide for the payment of that sum by instalments of such amount as may be specified in the order and may require the payment of the instalments to be secured to the satisfaction of the court.

(4) The power of the court under subsection (1) or (2)(*a*) above to make an order in favour of a child of the family shall be exercisable from time to time; and where the court makes an order in favour of a child under subsection (2)(*b*) above, it may from time to time, subject to the restrictions mentioned in subsection (1) above, make a further order in his favour of any of the kinds mentioned in subsection (1)(*d*), (*e*) or (*f*) above.

(5) Without prejudice to the power to give a direction under section 30 below for the settlement of an instrument by conveyancing counsel, where an order is made under subsection (1)(*a*), (*b*) or (*c*) above on or after granting a decree of divorce or nullity of marriage, neither the order nor any settlement made in pursuance of the order shall take effect unless the decree has been made absolute.

(6) Where the court –

(*a*) makes an order under this section for the payment of a lump sum; and
(*b*) directs –
  (i) that payment of that sum or any part of it shall be deferred; or
  (ii) that the sum or any part of it shall be paid by instalments,

the court may order that the amount deferred or the instalments shall carry interest at such rate as may be specified by the order from such date, not earlier than the date of the order, as may be so specified, until the date when payment of it is due.

Amendments—Administration of Justice Act 1982, s 16.

Defined terms—"child", "child of the family": s 52(1).

Mode of application—Applications by Form A after 5 June 2000 are governed by FPR 1991, rr 2.51A–2.70 as printed in this edition. For pre-5 June 2000 applications see Procedural Guide 18 or 19 in *The Family Court Practice 1999*.

Timing of application—If an order is made before there has been a decree, it is made without jurisdiction and cannot be validated either under the slip rule or the inherent jurisdiction of the court (*Board (Board Intervening) v Checkland* [1987] 2 FLR 257), save in the case of a pure clerical error (*Pounds v Pounds* [1994] 1 FLR 775, CA). Further, by s 23(5), the order only takes effect on the decree being made absolute.

Although there is no jurisdiction to make an order under this section (or s 24) before decree nisi, in view of the time it will take to get the application ready for a final hearing, the application should normally be made as soon after the filing of the petition as possible. There is no statute of limitation in the matrimonial jurisdiction so that, for example, the fact that an application for a lump sum order is made 17 years after a maintenance order is no bar (*Twiname v Twiname* [1991] Fam Law 520).

Number of applications for periodical payments (s 23(1)(*a*))—A party to the marriage may make any number of applications for a periodical payments order (but see **Power to prevent further application** under s 25A). The earliest date on which the order can commence is the date when the claim is made (see FPR 1991, r 2.53); the order can continue until the death of either of the parties or the remarriage of the recipient, whichever is the earlier (see s 28(1)(*a*)).

Duration and form of periodical payments order—The order is usually expressed as "during the parties' joint lives the [petitioner's] earlier remarriage or further Order".

Number of applications for secured periodical payments (s 23(1)(*b*))—Any number of applications may be made for a secured periodical payments order in the absence of a direction under s 25A(3) (see **Power to prevent further application** under s 25A).

Duration and form of secured periodical payments order—The earliest date on which a secured periodical payments order can commence is the date when the claim is made but, by s 28(1)(*b*), it can be defined to continue beyond the death of the payer.

Number of applications for lump sum order (s 23(1)(*c*))—Only one lump sum order may be made for a party to the marriage (*Coleman v Coleman* [1973] Fam 10, [1972] 3 WLR 681; *Banyard v Banyard* [1984] FLR 643). Lump sums to children are not subject to the same restriction (see s 23(4)).

Rollover of statutory charge—For a suggested form of wording for a lump sum order which is to be adopted to allow for rollover of the Legal Services Commission's statutory charge where the lump sum is to be used for home purchase, see *Practice Direction of 19 August 1991* .

Interface with Child Support Act 1991—The Child Support Act 1991 (see further annotations thereunder) limits the courts jurisdiction to order maintenance for a child to situations where:
(i) The child, one or both non-resident parents or the person with care is not habitually resident in the United Kingdom (s 44).
(ii) The child is married, over 19 or over 16 and not in advanced education (s 55).
(iii) The parties seek a consent order in the terms of a written agreement (s 8(5)), a top-up order following a child support calculation (s 8(6)), a school fees order (s 8(7)), or expenses for a disabled child (s 8(8)).
(iv) The claim is against parents with care (s 8(10)) or against a step-parent.
(v) The parents have not yet separated.

The court has jurisdiction to make periodical payments or capitalised periodical payments for children as follows:
(i) *Periodical payments*
 (*a*) Where spousal maintenance includes an element of child support, by making a global order to be reduced pro tanto if a child support calculation is paid: a "Segal Order" (*Dorney-Kingdom v Dorney-Kingdom* [2000] 2 FLR 855).
 (*b*) Where there is a consent order for child periodical payments (which may be nominal) and an application is filed returnable at the final hearing to vary the order in accordance with the merits. An application for a consent order accompanied by a written agreement can be made for 5p per annum at the outset of a final hearing, a perfected order made and notice of application then made to vary that order at the end of the hearing – although sometimes not all of these formalities are complied with (*V v V (Child Maintenance)* [2001] 2 FLR 799).
(ii) *Capitalised periodical payments by way of lump sum*
 (*a*) If a child support calculation is in place (no matter how unreasonable it may seem) the court will not circumvent the Child Support Act's embargo on its jurisdiction by making a lump sum order for capitalising the proper level of child periodical payments (*Phillips v Peace* [1996] 2 FLR 230). But if no child support calculation is applied for,

it has the power to capitalise periodical payments by way of a lump sum. See *V v V* (above) where the husband had withdrawn his consent to varying an agreed order.

(*b*) A lump sum can be ordered to the spouse to meet past expenses for a child (*Askew-Page v Page* [2001] Fam Law 794). See **Interim orders** below.

Outline of new bases for child support calculation—See under Child Support Act 1991, s 4.

Duration and form of child periodical payments order (s 23(1)(*d*), (*e*))—Unless there are special circumstances (such as physical or mental disability), or the child remains in education, an order for child periodical payments should cease when the child reaches 18 (s 29(1),(3)). By s 29(2)(*a*), the order should in the first instance be expressed not to extend beyond the age of 17. It is now usual to use the following words: "until the said child attains the age of 17 years or ceases full-time education whichever is the later or further order".

School fees—A suggested form of wording for a school fees order is:

"As from the Petitioner/Respondent do pay or cause to be paid to the Respondent/Petitioner for the benefit of until he/she shall attain the age of 17 years or cease full-time secondary education if later or further order periodical payments of an amount equivalent to the school fees (but not extras/including the following extras) at the school the said child shall from time to time attend by way of three payments at the start of each term and it is further directed that the school fees shall be paid to the headmaster/bursar/school secretary as agent for the Respondent/Petitioner and the receipt of that payee shall be sufficient discharge."

Assignment of pensions by service personnel—Pensions Act 1995, s 166 provides that the statutory provisions which prohibit service personnel from assigning their pensions do not prevent a divorce court from making orders in respect of those pension benefits, thus overruling the line of cases, such as *Walker v Walker* [1983] Fam 68, which had previously prevented the court from exercising jurisdiction in respect of terminal grants and other pension rights. Section 166(4)–(6) provides as follows:

"(4) Nothing in the provisions mentioned in subsection (5) applies to a court exercising its powers under section 23 of the Matrimonial Causes Act 1973 (financial provision orders in connection with divorce proceedings etc) in respect of any benefits under a pension scheme (within the meaning of section 25B of the Matrimonial Causes Act 1973) which a party to the marriage has or is likely to have.

(5) The provisions referred to in subsection (4) are:

(*a*) section 203(1) and (2) of the Army Act 1955, s 203(1) and (2) of the Air Force Act 1955, s 128G(1) and (2) of the Naval Discipline Act 1957 or s 159(4) or (4A) of the Pension Schemes Act 1993 (which prevent assignment, or orders being made restraining a person from receiving anything which he is prevented from assigning),

(*b*) section 91 of this Act,

(*c*) any provision of any Act (whether passed or made before or after this Act is passed) corresponding to any of the enactments mentioned in paragraphs (*a*) and (*b*), and

(*d*) any provision in the scheme in question corresponding to any of those enactments.

(6) Subsections (3) to (7) of section 25B and section 25C of the Matrimonial Causes Act 1973, as inserted by this section, do not affect the powers of the court under section 31 of that Act (variation, discharge etc) in relation to any order made before the commencement of this section.".

Interim orders—Whilst the court can make a maintenance pending suit order, it does not have power to make an interim lump sum order under s 23 (*Bolsom v Bolsom* (1983) FLR 21; *Barry v Barry* [1992] 2 FLR 233), except under s 23(3)(*a*) for meeting expenses for maintaining an applicant or child before applying for an order under s 23(1)(*c*); but this limited type of order can not be applied for before decree nisi and does not take effect until decree absolute. In *Wicks v Wicks* [1998] 1 FLR 470 the Court of Appeal held that the court does not have an administrative power of appropriation which it may exercise before the substantive hearing by allocating a particular asset, thus overruling *Barry v Barry* [1992] 2 FLR 233. See **No power to make interim capital order** under FPR 1991, r 2.64. To obtain a sale prior to the final ancillary relief hearing, there appear to be two alternatives:

(i) an application under the Married Women's Property Act 1882 with, if an order for possession is required, an application under FLA 1996, Pt IV (see Procedural Guide 4); or

(ii) an application under the Trusts of Land and Appointment of Trustees Act 1996 (see Procedural Guide 5).

Interest—Section 23(6) was added by Administration of Justice Act 1982, s 16 and provides that, where payment of the lump sum is deferred or is to be made in instalments, the court may, at the time of making the lump sum order but not afterwards (*L v L (Lump Sum: Interest)* [1994] 2 FLR 324), order interest between the date of the order and the date when it is due to be paid. If the payer is late in paying, there is no jurisdiction under s 23(6) to order interest. However, at the date when it is due to be paid, it becomes a judgment debt and, if the order is made in the High Court, it will carry interest as a judgment debt under the Judgments Act 1838 at the current rate of 8 per cent; in the case of a county court order for £5,000 or more, interest will be payable as from the date when the sum is due by virtue of the County Courts (Interest on Judgment Debts) Order 1991. In order to obtain interest on a county court order for a lump sum of less than £5,000 the judgment should be transferred to the High Court for enforcement and, once transferred, interest will automatically accrue. There is no minimum amount for a transfer, except that High Court and County Courts Jurisdiction Order 1991, art 8(1) states that the amount must be more than £600 where it is sought to enforce wholly or partially by execution against goods. The Queen's Bench Masters' Practice Direction (32) provides for the procedure for transfer as follows: (i) the applicant obtains from the county court a certificate of judgment in accordance with CCR Ord 22, r 8; and (ii) the applicant attends the Action Department (Judgments) appropriate to the applicant's name with a sealed certificate of judgment and copy. No fee is payable. The original certificate is then date sealed and returned to the applicant with interest running from the date of the certificate.

24 Property adjustment orders in connection with divorce proceedings etc

(1) On granting a decree of divorce, a decree of nullity of marriage or a decree of judicial separation or at any time thereafter (whether, in the case of a decree of divorce or of nullity of marriage, before or after the decree is made absolute), the court may make any one or more of the following orders, that is to say –

(*a*) an order that a party to the marriage shall transfer to the other party, to any child of the family or to such person as may be specified in the order for the benefit of such a child such property as may be so specified, being property to which the first-mentioned party is entitled, either in possession or reversion;

(*b*) an order that a settlement of such property as may be so specified, being property to which a party to the marriage is so entitled, be made to the satisfaction of the court for the benefit of the other party to the marriage and of the children of the family or either or any of them;

(*c*) an order varying for the benefit of the parties to the marriage and of the children of the family or either or any of them any ante-nuptial or post-nuptial settlement (including such a settlement made by will or codicil) made on the parties to the marriage, other than one in the form of a pension arrangement (within the meaning of section 25D below);

(*d*) an order extinguishing or reducing the interest of either of the parties to the marriage under any such settlement, other than one in the form of a pension arrangement (within the meaning of section 25D below);

subject, however, in the case of an order under paragraph (*a*) above, to the restrictions imposed by section 29(1) and (3) below on the making of orders for a transfer of property in favour of children who have attained the age of eighteen.

(2) The court may make an order under subsection (1)(*c*) above notwithstanding that there are no children of the family.

(3) Without prejudice to the power to give a direction under section 30 below for the settlement of an instrument by conveyancing counsel, where an order is made under this section on or after granting a decree of divorce or nullity of marriage,

neither the order nor any settlement made in pursuance of the order shall take effect unless the decree has been made absolute.

Amendments—Welfare Reform and Pensions Act 1999, s 19, Sch 3, para 3.

Defined terms—"child", "child of the family": s 52(1).

Scope of provision—This section defines the court's power to make a property adjustment order for a party to the marriage or to any children. As regards children there is no jurisdiction to make an order under s 24(1)(*a*) if the child is over 18 unless there are special circumstances such as disability or continuing education. The jurisdiction to make an order under this section arises only if there is a decree.

Mode of application—Applications by Form A after 5 June 2000 are governed by FPR 1991, rr 2.51A–2.70 as printed in this edition. For pre-5 June 2000 applications see Procedural Guide 18 or 19 in *The Family Court Practice 1999*.

"property"—Property includes a council tenancy (*Newlon Housing Trust v Alsulaimen* [1998] 2 FLR 690) and a contractual weekly tenancy (*Hale v Hale* [1975] 1 WLR 931, [1975] 2 All ER 1090). As the court may make an order under s 37 to restrain dealing with property outside the jurisdiction (*Hamlin v Hamlin* [1986] Fam 11, [1986] 1 FLR 61) it has by implication power to make a property adjustment order in respect of overseas property. Where property in issue is a tenancy, an alternative way of obtaining a transfer is under Family Law Act 1996, Sch 7. Where there is a covenant against assignment, such an application is the preferred option (see under Sch 7, para 7 of that Act).

"settlement"—Settlement means any provision (other than an absolute gift) made for the benefit of the parties to the marriage by either one or both of them or by a third party (*Ulrich v Ulrich and Felton* [1968] 1 WLR 180, [1968] 1 All ER 67). It includes a pension fund, although the court will not exercise jurisdiction to vary if the interests of third parties, including the Inland Revenue, will be prejudiced (*Brooks v Brooks* [1995] 2 FLR 13, HL). A *Brooks v Brooks* variation of a pension fund settlement is now permissible only if made in proceedings commenced by petition prior to the 1 December 2000 (Welfare Reform and Pensions Act 1999, s 85(4) and Sch 3, para 3).

Number of applications—In general terms, the fact that an order has been made under one subsection of this section does not preclude a later application for an order under another subsection (*Carson v Carson* (1981) FLR 352, [1983] 1 WLR 285 per Sheldon J). However, on the subsequent application, any earlier order and any admissible material relating to it should be examined to establish whether it was intended as a final and conclusive financial settlement (either overall or in relation to a particular property). If it was intended to be a once and for all settlement of all claims any further claim under this section is precluded. It follows that if the earlier order was intended as a once and for all settlement in respect of one property only, a second application in respect of another property may be made (*Dinch v Dinch* [1987] 2 FLR 162, [1987] 1 WLR 252; *Sandford v Sandford* [1986] 1 FLR 412).

No power to make interim property adjustment order—The court does not have power to make an interim property adjustment order, and the line of authority starting in *Barry v Barry* [1992] 2 FLR 233 that it may make an order to a similar effect under its administrative power of appropriation has been overruled by *Wicks v Wicks* [1998] 1 FLR 470. See **No power to make interim capital order** under FPR 1991, r 2.64.

Timing of application—An order under this section does not take effect until decree absolute, but there is good reason to make the application and prepare it for hearing as soon as the petition is filed. There is no time-limit for making an application. For greater detail see **Timing of application** under s 23.

Rollover of statutory charge—For a suggested form of wording for an order which is to be adopted to allow for rollover of the Legal Services Commission's statutory charge where property is to be used as a home, see *Practice Direction of 19 August 1991*.

Rights of third parties—Whereas s 24A (in the context of applying for an order for sale where a property is owned by a party to the marriage and a third party) expressly provides for that third party to be served with the application so that he can be heard on it, there is no similar express provision on an application under this section where the property is owned jointly with another or is subject to third party rights. Two points should be noted:

(*a*) The court cannot adversely affect third party rights unless those third parties have been given notice of the proceedings and the opportunity to intervene, in which case they will be bound by the court's decision (*Tebbutt v Haynes* [1981] 2 All ER 238).

(*b*) Where a third party does have such an interest the district judge should be asked to direct that Forms A and E be served in accordance with the concluding words of FPR 1991, r 2.59(3).

Pension sharing—See **Inter-Relation of Pension Sharing, Pension Attachment etc** under MCA 1973, s 21A.

24A Orders for sale of property

(1) Where the court makes under section 23 or 24 of this Act a secured periodical payments order, an order for the payment of a lump sum or a property adjustment order, then, on making that order or at any time thereafter, the court may make a further order for the sale of such property as may be specified in the order, being property in which or in the proceeds of sale of which either or both of the parties to the marriage has or have a beneficial interest, either in possession or reversion.

(2) Any order made under subsection (1) above may contain such consequential or supplementary provisions as the court thinks fit and, without prejudice to the generality of the foregoing provision, may include –

(*a*) provision requiring the making of a payment out of the proceeds of sale of the property to which the order relates, and

(*b*) provision requiring any such property to be offered for sale to a person, or class of persons, specified in the order.

(3) Where an order is made under subsection (1) above on or after the grant of a decree of divorce or nullity of marriage, the order shall not take effect unless the decree has been made absolute.

(4) Where an order is made under subsection (1) above, the court may direct that the order, or such provision thereof as the court may specify, shall not take effect until the occurrence of an event specified by the court or the expiration of a period so specified.

(5) Where an order under subsection (1) above contains a provision requiring the proceeds of sale of the property to which the order relates to be used to secure periodical payments to a party to the marriage, the order shall cease to have effect on the death or re-marriage of that person.

(6) Where a party to a marriage has a beneficial interest in any property, or in the proceeds of sale thereof, and some other person who is not a party to the marriage also has a beneficial interest in that property or in the proceeds of sale thereof, then, before deciding whether to make an order under this section in relation to that property, it shall be the duty of the court to give that other person an opportunity to make representations with respect to the order; and any representations made by that other person shall be included among the circumstances to which the court is required to have regard under section 25(1) below.

Amendments—Inserted by Matrimonial Homes and Property Act 1981, s 7; amended by Matrimonial and Family Proceedings Act 1984, s 46(1), Sch 1, para 11.

Defined terms—"lump sum order", "secured periodical payments order": ss 21(1), 23(1); "property adjustment order": ss 21(2), 24(1).

Scope of provision—This section gives the court jurisdiction to make an order for sale if there has been a lump sum or property adjustment order (which, by implication and by s 24A(3), can only take effect on decree absolute). Consequently, there is no jurisdiction under this section to order a sale until the final hearing of the claims for ancillary relief.

Interim orders—For a discussion as to why FPR 1991 has probably not given the court jurisdiction under RSC Ord 31, r 1 to order a sale pending the final hearing of ancillary relief claims, see **Power to make interim orders** under FPR 1991, r 2.64. However, subject to suitable undertakings to maintain the full flexible powers of the court at the final hearing, the court's administrative power of appropriation allows the net proceeds of sale of an asset to be invested in a new property pending the final hearing (*Barry v Barry* [1992] 2 FLR 233, [1992] 2 WLR 799).

Property jointly owned with third parties (s 24A(6))—Section 24(6) requires that a third party who has a beneficial interest in the property which it is proposed be sold must be given the opportunity to be heard on whether there should be a sale.

Mode of application—Although an order under s 24A does not come within the definition of "ancillary relief" (see FPR 1991, r 1.2(1)), with the result that FPR 1991, rr 2.52–2.69E do not literally apply to it, common sense suggests that the application should be made and pursued in the same way as an application for ancillary relief was formerly made, namely:
(*a*) filing of Form M11 plus supporting affidavit;
(*b*) filing by respondent of affidavit in reply;
(*c*) disclosure of relevant documents;
(*d*) if a third party is a joint owner, service of Form M11 plus supporting affidavit on joint owner informing him of right to apply to intervene;
(*e*) directions appointment (if appropriate);
(*f*) set down before district judge.

24B Pension sharing orders in connection with divorce proceedings etc

(1) On granting a decree of divorce or a decree of nullity of marriage or at any time thereafter (whether before or after the decree is made absolute), the court may, on an application made under this section, make one or more pension sharing orders in relation to the marriage.

(2) A pension sharing order under this section is not to take effect unless the decree on or after which it is made has been made absolute.

(3) A pension sharing order under this section may not be made in relation to a pension arrangement which –

(*a*) is the subject of a pension sharing order in relation to the marriage, or
(*b*) has been the subject of pension sharing between the parties to the marriage.

(4) A pension sharing order under this section may not be made in relation to shareable state scheme rights if –

(*a*) such rights are the subject of a pension sharing order in relation to the marriage, or
(*b*) such rights have been the subject of pension sharing between the parties to the marriage.

(5) A pension sharing order under this section may not be made in relation to the rights of a person under a pension arrangement if there is in force a requirement imposed by virtue of section 25B or 25C below which relates to benefits or future benefits to which he is entitled under the pension arrangement.

Amendments—Inserted by Welfare Reform and Pensions Act 1999, s 19, Sch 3, para 4.

Defined terms—"pension sharing order": s 21A – an order transferring a percentage of shareable rights under a pension arrangement or state scheme.

Scope of provision—This section empowers the court in proceedings for divorce or nullity, but not judicial separation, to make on or at any time after a decree one or more pension sharing orders. It appears that, provided orders at different points of time relate to different schemes, the court, having made one pension sharing order, can subsequently make another. The order does not take effect unless there is a decree absolute. Pension sharing is only available if the petition was filed on or after 1 December 2000 – see Welfare Reform and Pensions Act 1999, s 85(3)(*a*). An answer and cross petition filed after 1/12/2000 to a pre-1/12/2000 petition does not give jurisdiction for pension sharing (*W v W (Divorce Proceedings: withdrawal of consent after perfection of order)* [2002] EWHC 1826, [2002] 2 FLR 1225). In *S v S (Rescission of Decree Nisi: Pension Sharing Provision)* [2002] 1 FLR 457 Singer J, whilst stressing the embargo on making pension sharing orders on pre-December 2000 petitions, rescinded a decree nisi in circumstances where the respondent husband supported the application, so as to permit a fresh petition to found jurisdiction to make a pension sharing order. If one party refuses consent, rescission is refused (*Rye v Rye* [2002] EWHC 956 (Fam), [2002] 2 FLR 981). See further annotation under FPR 1991, r 2.48.

Prohibition if other pension sharing or attachment orders made (s 24B(iii)–(v))—An order for pension sharing against a particular scheme cannot be made if there either is or has been a pension sharing order made in relation to the marriage before the court against that scheme – but if a pension sharing order has been made for the benefit of one of the parties in proceedings relating to a previous marriage it *can* be made, as that is a fund which the party has in his own right. An attachment (formerly called earmarking) order which is in force for this or any previous marriage prevents a pension sharing order.

Valuations—The valuation of the pension benefits is prescribed by Pensions on Divorce etc (Provision of Information) Regulations 2000, reg 3 as the cash equivalent transfer value of the benefits acquired to date, on the assumption that the member ceased employment on the date of the valuation. As set out in the annotations to the Pensions on Divorce etc (Provision of Information) Regulations, the CETV does not include the value of the death in service package nor past service reserve.

Divorce etc (Pensions) Regulations 2000, reg 3 provides for the point in time when the CETV is to be valued. Regulation 3(1)(*a*) provides for the benefits to be valued at a date to be specified by the court not earlier than 1 year before the date of the petition and not later than the date of the court order. Regulation 3(1)(*b*) and (*c*) provide that when determining the date, the court should have regard to the date of the CETV.

The court can only order a percentage of the CETV and must take a date of valuation within the time-frame outlined above. Thus, if the court wishes to take into account a substantial period of separation it can only do so by adjusting the percentage.

Regulation 3(1) reads as follows:

"3 Valuation

(1) For the purposes of the court's functions in connection with the exercise of any of its powers under Part II of the Matrimonial Causes Act 1973, benefits under a pension arrangement shall be calculated and verified in the manner set out in regulation 3 of the Pensions on Divorce etc (Provision of Information) Regulations 2000, and –

(*a*) the benefits shall be valued as at a date to be specified by the court (being not earlier than one year before the date of the petition and not later than the date on which the court is exercising its power);

(*b*) in determining that value the court may have regard to information furnished by the person responsible for the pension arrangement pursuant to any of the provisions set out in paragraph (2); and

(*c*) in specifying a date under sub-paragraph (*a*) above the court may have regard to the date specified in any information furnished as mentioned in sub-paragraph (*b*) above."

24C Pension sharing orders: duty to stay

(1) No pension sharing order may be made so as to take effect before the end of such period after the making of the order as may be prescribed by regulations made by the Lord Chancellor.

PART II

(2) The power to make regulations under this section shall be exercisable by statutory instrument which shall be subject to annulment in pursuance of a resolution of either House of Parliament.

Amendments—Inserted by Welfare Reform and Pensions Act 1999, s 19, Sch 3, para 4.

Scope of provision—A pension sharing order cannot take effect until, as provided by Divorce etc (Pensions) Regulations 2000, reg 9, seven days have elapsed after the time for filing notice of appeal (14 days). The period is therefore 21 days.

Regulation 9 reads as follows:

> **"9 Pension sharing order not to take effect pending appeal**
>
> (1) No pension sharing order under section 24B or variation of a pension sharing order under section 31 shall take effect earlier than 7 days after the end of the period for filing notice of appeal against the order.
>
> (2) The filing of a notice of appeal within the time allowed for doing so prevents the order taking effect before the appeal has been dealt with."

24D Pension sharing orders: apportionment of charges

If a pension sharing order relates to rights under a pension arrangement, the court may include in the order provision about the apportionment between the parties of any charge under section 41 of the Welfare Reform and Pensions Act 1999 (charges in respect of pension sharing costs), or under corresponding Northern Ireland legislation.

Amendments—Inserted by Welfare Reform and Pensions Act 1999, s 19, Sch 3, para 4.

Scope of provision—This section enables the court to order who should pay the charges of the person responsible for the pension arrangement. The core points of Welfare Reform and Pensions Act 1999, s 41 and the Pensions on Divorce (Charging) Regulations (SI 2000/1049) are as follows:

(i) There is no charge for providing the valuation of the CETV provided that only one valuation is given in 12 months.

(ii) Provided that the person responsible for the pension arrangement has stated his costs in writing in advance and that those costs are reasonable, the parties must pay for the cost of implementing the pension sharing and pension attachment orders.

(iii) If the court's order is silent as to who should pay the charges, the costs fall on the transferor (Welfare Reform and Pensions Act 1999, s 41(3)(*b*)).

The National Association of Pension Funds in a booklet "Pension Sharing on Divorce" (obtainable by telephoning 020-7808-1300) recommends that, on the basis of no undue complications, the bracket of charges of the person responsible for the pension arrangement in complying with a pension sharing order should be £750–£1000.

25 Matters to which court is to have regard in deciding how to exercise its powers under ss 23, 24 and 24A

(1) It shall be the duty of the court in deciding whether to exercise its powers under section 23, 24, 24A or 24B above and, if so, in what manner, to have regard to all the circumstances of the case, first consideration being given to the welfare while a minor of any child of the family who has not attained the age of eighteen.

(2) As regards the exercise of the powers of the court under section 23(1)(*a*), (*b*) or (*c*), 24, 24A or 24B above in relation to a party to the marriage, the court shall in particular have regard to the following matters –

(*a*) the income, earning capacity, property and other financial resources which each of the parties to the marriage has or is likely to have in the foreseeable future, including in the case of earning capacity any increase in that capacity which it would in the opinion of the court be reasonable to expect a party to the marriage to take steps to acquire;

(*b*) the financial needs, obligations and responsibilities which each of the parties to the marriage has or is likely to have in the foreseeable future;

(*c*) the standard of living enjoyed by the family before the breakdown of the marriage;

(*d*) the age of each party to the marriage and the duration of the marriage;

(*e*) any physical or mental disability of either of the parties to the marriage;

(*f*) the contributions which each of the parties has made or is likely in the foreseeable future to make to the welfare of the family, including any contribution by looking after the home or caring for the family;

(*g*) the conduct of each of the parties, if that conduct is such that it would in the opinion of the court be inequitable to disregard it;

(*h*) in the case of proceedings for divorce or nullity of marriage, the value to each of the parties to the marriage of any benefit which, by reason of the dissolution or annulment of the marriage, that party will lose the chance of acquiring.

(3) As regards the exercise of the powers of the court under section 23(1)(*d*), (*e*) or (*f*), (2) or (4), 24 or 24A above in relation to a child of the family, the court shall in particular have regard to the following matters –

(*a*) the financial needs of the child;

(*b*) the income, earning capacity (if any), property and other financial resources of the child;

(*c*) any physical or mental disability of the child;

(*d*) the manner in which he was being and in which the parties to the marriage expected him to be educated or trained;

(*e*) the considerations mentioned in relation to the parties to the marriage in paragraphs (*a*), (*b*), (*c*) and (*e*) of subsection (2) above.

(4) As regards the exercise of the powers of the court under section 23(1)(*d*), (*e*) or (*f*), (2) or (4), 24 or 24A above against a party to a marriage in favour of a child of the family who is not the child of that party, the court shall also have regard –

(*a*) to whether that party assumed any responsibility for the child's maintenance, and, if so, to the extent to which, and the basis upon which, that party assumed such responsibility and to the length of time for which that party discharged such responsibility;

(*b*) to whether in assuming and discharging such responsibility that party did so knowing that the child was not his or her own;

(*c*) to the liability of any other person to maintain the child.

Amendments—Matrimonial and Family Proceedings Act 1984, s 3; Pensions Act 1995, s 166; Welfare Reform and Pensions Act 1999, s 19, Sch 3, para 5.

Defined terms—"child", "child of the family": s 52(1).

Scope of provision—This section and s 25A ("the clean break section") contain the statutory criteria for determining how claims by a party to the marriage for income and capital should be determined.

Obtaining office copy entries and registration of protective charges—Land Registration Act 1925, s 112 (as amended) permits inspection and copying of entries on the register. At each stage in the proceedings, before and after decree absolute, the practitioner should check that he has registered the appropriate charge against the property subject to the claim. Thus, on decree absolute, any Class F land charge should be replaced by a pending action land charge or its registered land equivalent, ie a caution or restriction against dealings.

25A Exercise of court's powers in favour of party to marriage on decree of divorce or nullity of marriage

(1) Where on or after the grant of a decree of divorce or nullity of marriage the court decides to exercise its powers under section 23(1)(*a*), (*b*) or (*c*), 24, 24A or 24B above in favour of a party to the marriage, it shall be the duty of the court to consider whether it would be appropriate so to exercise those powers that the financial obligations of each party towards the other will be terminated as soon after the grant of the decree as the court considers just and reasonable.

(2) Where the court decides in such a case to make a periodical payments or secured periodical payments order in favour of a party to the marriage, the court shall in particular consider whether it would be appropriate to require those payments to be made or secured only for such term as would in the opinion of the court be sufficient to enable the party in whose favour the order is made to adjust without undue hardship to the termination of his or her financial dependence on the other party.

(3) Where on or after the grant of a decree of divorce or nullity of marriage an application is made by a party to the marriage for a periodical payments or secured periodical payments order in his or her favour, then, if the court considers that no continuing obligation should be imposed on either party to make or secure periodical payments in favour of the other, the court may dismiss the application with a direction that the applicant shall not be entitled to make any future application in relation to that marriage for an order under section 23(1)(*a*) or (*b*) above.

Amendments—Inserted by Matrimonial and Family Proceedings Act 1984, s 3; amended by Welfare Reform and Pensions Act 1999, s 19, Sch 3, para 6.

Defined terms—"periodical payments order", "secured periodical payments order": s 21(1).

Scope of provision—This is the "clean break" section. As regards the parties' long-term responsibilities, there are three possibilities.

(*a*) There is no clean break and a continuing obligation to pay periodical payments exists (subject to the right of both parties, since 1 November 1998, to apply subsequent to the original ancillary relief order for the right to maintenance to be terminated in return for a capital sum. See **Further capital order now possible on application of either party for clean break on variation application** under MCA 1973, s 31).

(*b*) The claim for maintenance is dismissed either immediately or at a defined time in the future under s 25A(1) but there is no order under s 28(1A) preventing the applicant applying to extend the term of the periodical payments order, and no prohibition under s 25A(3) against the applicant making a further application under s 23(1)(*a*) or (*b*).

(*c*) There is dismissal of the claim either immediately or at a defined point in time in the future with directions under ss 25A(3) and 28(1A). Such an order must expressly state that the applicant is excluded from applying to extend the term (*Richardson v Richardson* [1994] 1 FLR 286). As a subsequent pension sharing order is possible, the wording of the clean break should specifically bar such an application.

The second course is of doubtful advantage to the person seeking a clean break because the applicant is always able to return to make another application. The person who wants a clean break should, particularly in negotiations leading to a consent order, make every effort to obtain agreement that there should be directions under ss 25A(3) and 28(1A).

Power to prevent further application (s 25A(3))—Although the headnote of *Minton v Minton* [1979] AC 593, (1978) FLR Rep 461 suggests that the House of Lords decided that after an applicant's claim for periodical payments had been dismissed the court could not entertain a second application, that headnote is an incorrect summary of that decision (per Ormrod LJ in *Carter v Carter* (1980) FLR 271, [1980] 1 WLR 390 and Roskill LJ in *Dipper v Dipper* (1980) FLR 286, [1980] 3 WLR 626) which was, per Roskill LJ, that, where an application is dismissed by consent, there is no power to entertain a second application. Section 25A was introduced in order to enable the court to prevent further applications where the clean break was non-consensual.

Clean break inapplicable to judicial separation suit—The duty under s 25A(1) to consider whether there should be a clean break and the power under s 25A(3) to prevent further applications apply only to divorce and nullity and not to judicial separation.

25B Pensions

(1) The matters to which the court is to have regard under section 25(2) above include –

(*a*) in the case of paragraph (*a*), any benefits under a pension arrangement which a party to the marriage has or is likely to have, and

(*b*) in the case of paragraph (*h*), any benefits under a pension arrangement which, by reason of the dissolution or annulment of the marriage, a party to the marriage will lose the chance of acquiring,

and, accordingly, in relation to benefits under a pension arrangement, section 25(2)(*a*) above shall have effect as if "in the foreseeable future" were omitted.

(2) (*repealed*)

(3) The following provisions apply where, having regard to any benefits under a pension arrangement, the court determines to make an order under section 23 above.

(4) To the extent to which the order is made having regard to any benefits under a pension arrangement, the order may require the person responsible for the pension arrangement in question, if at any time any payment in respect of any benefits under the arrangement becomes due to the party with pension rights, to make a payment for the benefit of the other party.

(5) The order must express the amount of any payment required to be made by virtue of subsection (4) above as a percentage of the payment which becomes due to the party with pension rights.

(6) Any such payment by the person responsible for the arrangement –

(*a*) shall discharge so much of his liability to the party with pension rights as corresponds to the amount of the payment, and

(*b*) shall be treated for all purposes as a payment made by the party with pension rights in or towards the discharge of his liability under the order.

(7) Where the party with pension rights has a right of commutation under the arrangement, the order may require him to exercise it to any extent; and this section applies to any payment due in consequence of commutation in pursuance of the order as it applies to other payments in respect of benefits under the arrangement.

(7A) The power conferred by subsection (7) above may not be exercised for the purpose of commuting a benefit payable to the party with pension rights to a benefit payable to the other party.

(7B) The power conferred by subsection (4) or (7) above may not be exercised in relation to a pension arrangement which –

(*a*) is the subject of a pension sharing order in relation to the marriage, or

(*b*) has been the subject of pension sharing between the parties to the marriage.

PART II

(7C) In subsection (1) above, references to benefits under a pension arrangement include any benefits by way of pension, whether under a pension arrangement or not.

Amendments—Inserted by Pensions Act 1995, s 166; amended by Welfare Reform and Pensions Act 1999, ss 21, 88, Sch 4, para 1, Sch 13, Pt II.

Scope of provision—This section, taken together with the following two sections, incorporates the following eight points of pension attachment, formerly known as pension earmarking (which for the reasons set out in **Inter-Relation of Pension Sharing, Pension Attachment etc** under MCA 1973, s 21A is less favoured by applicants than pension sharing):

1 The court can order that a percentage of the benefits under a pension arrangement be paid to the other party. The order must be expressed as a percentage rather than a cash amount.

2 For the order to be effective the person responsible for the pension arrangement must be given notice of the proceedings, order and subsequent changes of address of the applicant after the order is made.

3 Orders can be made if, at any time, any payment in respect of any benefits becomes due to the party with pension rights in respect of part (or all) of the following:
   (*a*) member's pension in retirement (s 25B(4));
   (*b*) lump sum payable on retirement and lump sum payable on death after retirement (s 25B(7) – court can require commutation); or
   (*c*) lump sum payable on death (i) in service; (ii) after leaving service but before retirement; and (iii) after retirement (s 25C – court can require trustees to exercise discretion as regards lump sum or can require respondent to nominate for the benefit).

4 There is no power to attach the spouse's pension on the member's death.

5 The court must have regard to the benefits of all pension schemes, not just those in the foreseeable future (s 25B(1)), thus abrogating the rule in *Priest v Priest* (1980) FLR 189, that pension schemes whose benefits could only be taken many years ahead were not in the foreseeable future.

6 A deferred periodical payments order ends on remarriage and can be varied at any time. A deferred lump sum order can be varied prior to either party's death (s 31(2)(*dd*)).

7 Armed services pensions are now amenable to s 23 orders (s 25D(5)), whose full text is set out in **Assignment of pensions by service personnel** under s 23.

8 A pension attachment order cannot be made if it is or has been subject to a pension sharing order in relation to this marriage.

T v T (Financial Relief: Pensions) [1998] 1 FLR 1072, which comprehensively reviews these sections, suggests at 1086G that the court cannot require a party to take their pension at a specific time (eg by directing commutation of the benefits under s 25B(7) on a specific date).

Commencement—This provision applies to petitions filed after 1 July 1996, in cases where an application is made after 1 August 1996, or where the application is made between 1 and 31 July 1996 and Form M11 is amended to include an application under s 25B or 25C. The Act does not apply to answers or cross-petitions filed after 1 July 1996 in the context of pre-l July 1996 divorce suits (SI 1996/1675, art 4).

Pension sharing—See **Inter-Relation of Pension Sharing, Pension Attachment etc** under MCA 1973, s 21A.

25C Pensions: lump sums

(1) The power of the court under section 23 above to order a party to a marriage to pay a lump sum to the other party includes, where the benefits which the party with pension rights has or is likely to have under a pension arrangement include any lump sum payable in respect of his death, power to make any of the following provision by the order.

(2) The court may –

(*a*) if the person responsible for the pension arrangement in question has power to determine the person to whom the sum, or any part of it, is to be paid, require him to pay the whole or part of that sum, when it becomes due, to the other party, (*b*) if the party with pension rights has power to nominate the person to whom the sum, or any part of it, is to be paid, require the party with pension rights to nominate the other party in respect of the whole or part of that sum,

(*c*) in any other case, require the person responsible for the pension arrangement in question to pay the whole or part of that sum, when it becomes due, for the benefit of the other party instead of to the person to whom, apart from the order, it would be paid.

(3) Any payment by the person responsible for the pension arrangement under an order made under section 23 above by virtue of this section shall discharge so much of his liability in respect of the party with pension rights as corresponds to the amount of the payment.

(4) The powers conferred by this section may not be exercised in relation to a pension arrangement which –

(*a*) is the subject of a pension sharing order in relation to the marriage, or

(*b*) has been the subject of pension sharing between the parties to the marriage.

Amendments—Inserted by Pensions Act 1995, s 166; amended by Welfare Reform and Pensions Act 1999, s 21, Sch 4, para 2.

Scope of provision—This section, except where there is or has been a pension sharing order in relation to this marriage, enables the court to attach the lump sum payable if the person with pension benefits dies before taking his benefits. Lump sums defined as a multiple of pensionable salary are common in public service and occupational pension schemes. The terms of most personal pension and retirement annuity contracts allow for the return of the fund in the event of the member's death before taking his retirement benefits.

25D Pensions: supplementary

(1) Where –

(*a*) an order made under section 23 above by virtue of section 25B or 25C above imposes any requirement on the person responsible for a pension arrangement ("the first arrangement") and the party with pension rights acquires rights under another pension arrangement ("the new arrangement") which are derived (directly or indirectly) from the whole of his rights under the first arrangement, and

(*b*) the person responsible for the new arrangement has been given notice in accordance with regulations made by the Lord Chancellor,

the order shall have effect as if it had been made instead in respect of the person responsible for the new arrangement.

(2) The Lord Chancellor may by regulations –

(*a*) in relation to any provision of sections 25B or 25C above which authorises the court making an order under section 23 above to require the person responsible for a pension arrangement to make a payment for the benefit of the other party, make provision as to the person to whom, and the terms on which, the payment is to be made,

(*ab*) make, in relation to payment under a mistaken belief as to the continuation in force of a provision included by virtue of section 25B or 25C above in an order under section 23 above, provision about the rights or liabilities of the payer, the payee or the person to whom the payment was due, (*b*) require notices to be given in respect of changes of circumstances relevant to such orders which include provision made by virtue of sections 25B and 25C above,

(*ba*) make provision for the person responsible for a pension arrangement to be discharged in prescribed circumstances from a requirement imposed by virtue of section 25B or 25C above,

(*c*), (*d*) (*repealed*)

(*e*) make provision about calculation and verification in relation to the valuation of –

(i) benefits under a pension arrangement, or

(ii) shareable state scheme rights,

for the purposes of the court's functions in connection with the exercise of any of its powers under this Part of this Act.

(2A) Regulations under subsection (2)(*e*) above may include –

(*a*) provision for calculation or verification in accordance with guidance from time to time prepared by a prescribed person, and

(*b*) provision by reference to regulations under section 30 or 49(4) of the Welfare Reform and Pensions Act 1999.

(2B) Regulations under subsection (2) above may make different provision for different cases.

(2C) Power to make regulations under this section shall be exercisable by statutory instrument which shall be subject to annulment in pursuance of a resolution of either House of Parliament.

(3) In this section and sections 25B and 25C above –

"occupational pension scheme" has the same meaning as in the Pension Schemes Act 1993;

"the party with pension rights" means the party to the marriage who has or is likely to have benefits under a pension arrangement and "the other party" means the other party to the marriage;

"pension arrangement" means –

(*a*) an occupational pension scheme,

(*b*) a personal pension scheme,

(*c*) a retirement annuity contract,

(*d*) an annuity or insurance policy purchased, or transferred, for the purpose of giving effect to rights under an occupational pension scheme or a personal pension scheme, and

(*e*) an annuity purchased, or entered into, for the purpose of discharging liability in respect of a pension credit under section 29(1)(*b*) of the Welfare Reform and Pensions Act 1999 or under corresponding Northern Ireland legislation;

"personal pension scheme" has the same meaning as in the Pension Schemes Act 1993;

"prescribed" means prescribed by regulations;

"retirement annuity contract" means a contract or scheme approved under Chapter III of Part XIV of the Income and Corporation Taxes Act 1988;

"shareable state scheme rights" has the same meaning as in section 21A(1) above; and

"trustees or managers", in relation to an occupational pension scheme or a personal pension scheme, means –

(*a*) in the case of a scheme established under a trust, the trustees of the scheme, and

(*b*) in any other case, the managers of the scheme.

(4) In this section and sections 25B and 25C above, references to the person responsible for a pension arrangement are –

(*a*) in the case of an occupational pension scheme or a personal pension scheme, to the trustees or managers of the scheme,

(*b*) in the case of a retirement annuity contract or an annuity falling within paragraph (*d*) or (*e*) of the definition of "pension arrangement" above, the provider of the annuity, and

(*c*) in the case of an insurance policy falling within paragraph (*d*) of the definition of that expression, the insurer.

Amendments—Inserted by Pensions Act 1995, s 166; amended by Welfare Reform and Pensions Act 1999, ss 21, 88, Sch 4, para 3, Sch 13, Pt II.

Scope of provision—In addition to providing that notice of the attachment order is given to the person responsible for a pension arrangement, any subsequent transfer takes place subject to that attachment. This section defines various terms and provides for regulations to be made, particularly for enabling pension benefits to be valued. As outlined in the annotations to MCA 1973, s 24B the method of calculating the value of the cash equivalent transfer value is prescribed by Pensions on Divorce etc (Provision of Information) Regulations 2000, reg 3 and the date of the valuation is specified by Divorce etc (Pensions) Regulations 2000, reg 3 (to be between 1 year prior to the petition and the date of the order). The prescribed method of valuation is calculated on the basis that the member's service ends at the date of valuation. For the constituent elements of the cash equivalent transfer value and the fact that the death in service benefit is excluded, as are past service reserves, see annotations to the Pensions on Divorce etc (Provision of Information) Regulations 2000.

The only regulations that the reader need have a working knowledge of are the Pensions on Divorce etc (Provision of Information) Regulations 2000 (SI 2000/1048) and the Sharing of State Scheme Rights (Provision of Information and Valuations) Regulations 2000 (SI 2000/2693), both of which are set out in full in Part III of this work.

26 Commencement of proceedings for ancillary relief etc

(1) Where a petition for divorce, nullity of marriage or judicial separation has been presented, then, subject to subsection (2) below, proceedings for maintenance pending suit under section 22 above, for a financial provision order under section 23 above, or for a property adjustment order may be begun, subject to and in accordance with rules of court, at any time after the presentation of the petition.

(2) Rules of court may provide, in such cases as may be prescribed by the rules –

(*a*) that applications for any such relief as is mentioned in subsection (1) above shall be made in the petition or answer; and

(*b*) that applications for any such relief which are not so made, or are not made until after the expiration of such period following the presentation of the petition or filing of the answer as may be so prescribed, shall be made only with the leave of the court.

"Rules of court may provide" (s 26(2))—The relevant rules are FPR 1991, rr 2.52–2.68.

Financial provision in case of neglect to maintain

27 Financial provision orders etc in case of neglect by party to marriage to maintain other party or child of the family

(1) Either party to a marriage may apply to the court for an order under this section on the ground that the other party to the marriage (in this section referred to as the respondent) –

(*a*) has failed to provide reasonable maintenance for the applicant, or
(*b*) has failed to provide, or to make a proper contribution towards, reasonable maintenance for any child of the family.

(2) The court shall not entertain an application under this section unless –

(*a*) the applicant or the respondent is domiciled in England and Wales on the date of the application; or
(*b*) the applicant has been habitually resident there throughout the period of one year ending with that date; or
(*c*) the respondent is resident there on that date.

(3) Where an application under this section is made on the ground mentioned in subsection (1)(*a*) above, then, in deciding –

(*a*) whether the respondent has failed to provide reasonable maintenance for the applicant, and
(*b*) what order, if any, to make under this section in favour of the applicant,

the court shall have regard to all the circumstances of the case including the matters mentioned in section 25(2) above, and where an application is also made under this section in respect of a child of the family who has not attained the age of eighteen, first consideration shall be given to the welfare of the child while a minor.

(3A) Where an application under this section is made on the ground mentioned in subsection (1)(*b*) above then, in deciding –

(*a*) whether the respondent has failed to provide, or to make a proper contribution towards, reasonable maintenance for the child of the family to whom the application relates, and
(*b*) what order, if any, to make under this section in favour of the child,

the court shall have regard to all the circumstances of the case including the matters mentioned in section 25(3)(*a*) to (*e*) above, and where the child of the family to whom the application relates is not the child of the respondent, including also the matters mentioned in section 25(4) above.

(3B) In relation to an application under this section on the ground mentioned in subsection (1)(*a*) above, section 25(2)(*c*) above shall have effect as if for the reference therein to the breakdown of the marriage there were substituted a reference to the failure to provide reasonable maintenance for the applicant, and in relation to an application under this section on the ground mentioned in subsection (1)(*b*) above, section 25(2)(*c*) above (as it applies by virtue of section 25(3)(*e*) above) shall have effect as if for the reference therein to the breakdown of the marriage there were substituted a reference to the failure to provide, or to make a proper contribution towards, reasonable maintenance for the child of the family to whom the application relates.

(4) (*repealed*)

(5) Where on an application under this section it appears to the court that the applicant or any child of the family to whom the application relates is in immediate need of financial assistance, but it is not yet possible to determine what order, if any, should be made on the application, the court may make an interim order for maintenance, that is to say, an order requiring the respondent to make to the applicant until the determination of the application such periodical payments as the court thinks reasonable.

(6) Where on an application under this section the applicant satisfies the court of any ground mentioned in subsection (1) above, the court may make any one or more of the following orders, that is to say –

- (*a*) an order that the respondent shall make to the applicant such periodical payments, for such term, as may be specified in the order;
- (*b*) an order that the respondent shall secure to the applicant, to the satisfaction of the court, such periodical payments, for such term, as may be so specified;
- (*c*) an order that the respondent shall pay to the applicant such lump sum as may be so specified;
- (*d*) an order that the respondent shall make to such person as may be specified in the order for the benefit of the child to whom the application relates, or to that child, such periodical payments, for such term, as may be so specified;
- (*e*) an order that the respondent shall secure to such person as may be so specified for the benefit of that child, or to that child, to the satisfaction of the court, such periodical payments, for such term, as may be so specified;
- (*f*) an order that the respondent shall pay to such person as may be so specified for the benefit of that child, or to that child, such lump sum as may be so specified;

subject, however, in the case of an order under paragraph (*d*), (*e*) or (*f*) above, to the restrictions imposed by section 29(1) and (3) below on the making of financial provision orders in favour of children who have attained the age of eighteen.

(6A) An application for the variation under section 31 of this Act of a periodical payments order or secured periodical payments order made under this section in favour of a child may, if the child has attained the age of sixteen, be made by the child himself.

(6B) Where a periodical payments order made in favour of a child under this section ceases to have effect on the date on which the child attains the age of sixteen or at any time after that date but before or on the date on which he attains the age of eighteen, then, if at any time before he attains the age of twenty-one an application is made by the child for an order under this subsection, the court shall have power by order to revive the first-mentioned order from such date as the court may specify, not being earlier than the date of the making of the application, and to exercise its powers under section 31 of this Act in relation to any order so revived.

(7) Without prejudice to the generality of subsection (6)(*c*) or (*f*) above, an order under this section for the payment of a lump sum –

- (*a*) may be made for the purpose of enabling any liabilities or expenses reasonably incurred in maintaining the applicant or any child of the family to whom the application relates before the making of the application to be met;
- (*b*) may provide for the payment of that sum by instalments of such amount as may be specified in the order and may require the payment of the instalments to be secured to the satisfaction of the court.

(8) (*repealed*)

Amendments—Domicile and Matrimonial Proceedings Act 1973, s 6(1); Domestic Proceedings and Magistrates' Courts Act 1978, ss 63, 89(2)(*b*), Sch 3; Matrimonial and Family Proceedings Act 1984, ss 4, 46(1), Sch 1, para 12; Family Law Reform Act 1987, s 33(1), Sch 2, para 52.

Defined terms—"child", "child of the family": s 52(1); "lump sum orders", "periodical payments order", "secured periodical payments order": s 21(1).

Scope of provision—Subject to the Child Support Act 1991, which restricts the court's power to order child maintenance (see further **Interface with Child Support Act 1991** under MCA 1973, s 23 and **Outline of new bases for child support calculation** under CSA 1991, s 4), this section enables an applicant (once he has established the domicile/residence requirement under s 27(2) and the fact that the other party has failed to provide reasonable maintenance) to obtain a financial provision order (ie periodical payments, secured periodical payments or lump sum) for herself/himself and any children of the family without petitioning. The same principles apply to an application under this section as to an application for ancillary relief where a petition has been filed.

Interim orders—An interim order for periodical payments or secured periodical payments may be made under this section. However, only one lump sum order may be made, so an interim lump sum order cannot be made (see **Interim orders** under s 23).

Mode of application—FPR 1991, r 3.1 specifies the procedure for applications under this section.

Additional provisions with respect to financial provision and property adjustment orders

28 Duration of continuing financial provision orders in favour of party to marriage, and effect of remarriage

(1) Subject in the case of an order made on or after the grant of a decree of a divorce or nullity of marriage to the provisions of sections 25A(2) above and 31(7) below, the term to be specified in a periodical payments or secured periodical payments order in favour of a party to a marriage shall be such term as the court thinks fit, except that the term shall not begin before or extend beyond the following limits, that is to say –

(*a*) in the case of a periodical payments order, the term shall begin not earlier than the date of the making of an application for the order, and shall be so defined as not to extend beyond the death of either of the parties to the marriage or, where the order is made on or after the grant of a decree of divorce or nullity of marriage, the remarriage of the party in whose favour the order is made; and

(*b*) in the case of a secured periodical payments order, the term shall begin not earlier than the date of the making of an application for the order, and shall be so defined as not to extend beyond the death or, where the order is made on or after the grant of such a decree, the remarriage of the party in whose favour the order is made.

(1A) Where a periodical payments or secured periodical payments order in favour of a party to a marriage is made on or after the grant of a decree of divorce or nullity of marriage, the court may direct that that party shall not be entitled to apply under section 31 below for the extension of the term specified in the order.

(2) Where a periodical payments or secured periodical payments order in favour of a party to a marriage is made otherwise than on or after the grant of a decree of divorce or nullity of marriage, and the marriage in question is subsequently dissolved or annulled but the order continues in force, the order shall,

notwithstanding anything in it, cease to have effect on the remarriage of that party, except in relation to any arrears due under it on the date of the remarriage.

(3) If after the grant of a decree dissolving or annulling a marriage either party to that marriage remarries whether at any time before or after the commencement of this Act, that party shall not be entitled to apply, by reference to the grant of that decree, for a financial provision order in his or her favour, or for a property adjustment order, against the other party to that marriage.

Amendments—Matrimonial and Family Proceedings Act 1984, s 5.

Defined terms—"financial provision order", "periodical payments order": s 21(1); "property adjustment order": s 20(1), (2); "secured periodical payments order": s 21(1).

Maximum term of periodical payments order and secured periodical payments order (s 28(1))—This section is the source of the important difference that, whilst a periodical payments order must end on the death of the payer (or earlier remarriage of the payee), a secured periodical payments order can continue after the payer's death.

Power to prohibit extension of term (s 28(1A))—Section 28(1A) enables the court to prohibit a person who has the benefit of a maintenance order from applying to extend its term. See **Scope of provision** under s 25A for the crucial importance of inserting this prohibition in an order where a complete clean break is required. A s 28(1A) direction is inappropriate where there are young children (*Mawson v Mawson* [1994] 2 FLR 985). If the applicant's right to extend the term is to be excluded, the order must expressly state that fact (*Richardson v Richardson* [1994] 1 FLR 286). Even if a court order does not contain this prohibition against applying to extend the term, any application to extend must be made before the order has expired. An order for periodical payments which ceased on a determined event cannot be varied after that event (*T v T (Financial Provision)* [1988] 1 FLR 480). The application for variation must be made in the life of the order but the fact that the order has expired at the time of the hearing of the application to vary does not prevent jurisdiction (*Jones v Jones* [2000] 2 FLR 307).

"to apply" (s 28(1A), (3))—The term "to apply" means to make an application in accordance with FPR 1991, r 2.53.

Prohibition on application after remarriage (s 28(3))—Section 28(3) imposes an absolute bar on the court's jurisdiction to entertain an application made after remarriage. If the application is made before remarriage but is then proceeded with after remarriage, there is no jurisdictional problem, although the remarriage will be relevant on the merits. The prohibition is against a husband or wife making an application for their own benefit; applications for children are not affected. The fact that the other party has made an application for property adjustment does not enable the court to make an order in favour of the party who has not applied (*Robin v Robin* (1983) 4 FLR 632).

The application has to be made either in the petition or answer (if it is an answer claiming relief) or by notice in Form A (with leave if the application ought to have been made in the petition or answer) in accordance with procedure specified in FPR 1991, r 2.53. In *Nixon v Fox (formerly Nixon)* [1978] Fam 173, [1978] 3 WLR 565, the wife, who had made an application for maintenance for the children before her remarriage on what is now Form A, unsuccessfully tried after her remarriage to amend her Form A to include a lump sum and s 24 application for herself. Had she claimed, say, periodical payments for herself before her marriage, there may have been jurisdiction to amend that notice of application after her remarriage to seek a lump sum or property adjustment order, but the contention that she could so amend after her remarriage an application made on the children's behalf before her remarriage was rejected. In *Doherty v Doherty* [1976] Fam 71, [1975] 3 WLR 1, an application for a property adjustment order was considered wide enough to include a lump sum order, and the court stressed that it retained its power to allow a claim for one type of relief to be amended to include another even if there had been remarriage, but see *Wilson v Wilson* [1976] Fam 142, [1975] 3 WLR 537 where the other party had been lulled into a false sense of security. In *Hargood (formerly Jenkins) v Jenkins* [1978] Fam 148, [1978] 2 WLR 969, it was held that an answer in an acknowledgement of service did not amount to an application for ancillary relief.

It is therefore wise practice, in order to avoid the effect of this prohibition, always to include in the petition (or answer claiming relief) the full range of ancillary relief or, in the case of a

PART II

respondent who has not filed an answer claiming relief, to file a Form A claiming the full range of relief as soon as possible.

29 Duration of continuing financial provision orders in favour of children, and age limit on making certain orders in their favour

(1) Subject to subsection (3) below, no financial provision order and no order for a transfer of property under section 24(1)(*a*) above shall be made in favour of a child who has attained the age of eighteen.

(2) The term to be specified in a periodical payments or secured periodical payments order in favour of a child may begin with the date of the making of an application for the order in question or any later date or a date ascertained in accordance with subsection (5) or (6) below but –

(*a*) shall not in the first instance extend beyond the date of the birthday of the child next following his attaining the upper limit of the compulsory school age (that is to say, the age that is for the time being that limit by virtue of section 35 of the Education Act 1944 together with any Order in Council made under that section) unless the court considers that in the circumstances of the case the welfare of the child requires that it should extend to a later date; and

(*b*) shall not in any event, subject to subsection (3) below, extend beyond the date of the child's eighteenth birthday.

(3) Subsection (1) above, and paragraph (*b*) of subsection (2), shall not apply in the case of a child, if it appears to the court that –

(*a*) the child is, or will be, or if an order were made without complying with either or both of those provisions would be, receiving instruction at an educational establishment or undergoing training for a trade, profession or vocation, whether or not he is also, or will also be, in gainful employment; or

(*b*) there are special circumstances which justify the making of an order without complying with either or both of those provisions.

(4) Any periodical payments order in favour of a child shall, notwithstanding anything in the order, cease to have effect on the death of the person liable to make payments under the order, except in relation to any arrears due under the order on the date of the death.

(5) Where –

(*a*) a maintenance calculation ("the current calculation") is in force with respect to a child; and

(*b*) an application is made under Part II of this Act for a periodical payments or secured periodical payments order in favour of that child –

(i) in accordance with section 8 of the Child Support Act 1991, and

(ii) before the end of the period of 6 months beginning with the making of the current calculation,

the term to be specified in any such order made on that application may be expressed to begin on, or at any time after, the earliest permitted date.

(6) For the purposes of subsection (5) above, "the earliest permitted date" is whichever is the later of –

(*a*) the date 6 months before the application is made; or

(*b*) the date on which the current calculation took effect or, where successive maintenance calculations have been continuously in force with respect to a child, on which the first of those calculations took effect.

(7) Where –

(*a*) a maintenance calculation ceases to have effect by or under any provision of the Child Support Act 1991; and

(*b*) an application is made, before the end of the period of 6 months beginning with the relevant date, for a periodical payments or secured periodical payments order in favour of a child with respect to whom that maintenance calculation was in force immediately before it ceased to have effect,

the term to be specified in any such order made on that application may begin with the date on which that maintenance calculation ceased to have effect, or any later date.

(8) In subsection (7)(*b*) above, –

(*a*) where the maintenance calculation ceased to have effect, the relevant date is the date on which it so ceased

(*b*) (*repealed*)

Amendments—Matrimonial and Family Proceedings Act 1984, s 5; SI 1993/623; Child Support, Pensions and Social Security Act 2000, ss 26, 85, Sch 3, para 3, Sch 9.

Defined terms—"child": s 52(1); "financial provision order", "periodical payments order", "secured periodical payments order": s 21(1).

Scope of provision—This section provides that no financial provision order and no property adjustment order shall be made for children who have reached the age of 18 unless either they are continuing in education or there are special circumstances such as physical or mental disability. It also provides that in the first instance a child maintenance order should be specified to extend to the age of 17. The standard wording is "until the said child shall attain the age of 17 years or ceases full time education if later or further order".

"special circumstances" (s 29(3)(*b*))—Compare CA 1989, Sch 1, para 3(2)(*b*). Where there are special circumstances the order can continue beyond 18 years despite Child Support Act 1991, ss 8 and 55. Special circumstances may include physical or other handicap, and the expenses attributed to the child's disability should be taken into account in the broadest sense (*C v F (Disabled Child: Maintenance Orders)* [1998] 2 FLR 1).

30 Direction for settlement of instrument for securing payments or effecting property adjustment

Where the court decides to make a financial provision order requiring any payments to be secured or a property adjustment order –

(*a*) it may direct that the matter be referred to one of the conveyancing counsel of the court for him to settle a proper instrument to be executed by all necessary parties; and

(*b*) where the order is to be made in proceedings for divorce, nullity of marriage or judicial separation it may, if it thinks fit, defer the grant of the decree in question until the instrument has been duly executed.

Defined terms—"financial provision order": s 21(1); "property adjustment order": s 21(2).

Scope of provision—This section provides for the relatively rare event of instructing conveyancing counsel. For the standard wording of a secured periodical payments order see **Duration and form of secured periodical payments order** under s 23.

Variation, discharge and enforcement of certain orders etc

31 Variation, discharge etc of certain orders for financial relief

(1) Where the court has made an order to which this section applies, then, subject to the provisions of this section and of section 28(1A) above, the court shall have power to vary or discharge the order or to suspend any provision thereof temporarily and to revive the operation of any provision so suspended.

(2) This section applies to the following orders, that is to say –

(*a*) any order for maintenance pending suit and any interim order for maintenance;
(*b*) any periodical payments order;
(*c*) any secured periodical payments order;
(*d*) any order made by virtue of section 23(3)(*c*) or 27(7)(*b*) above (provision for payment of a lump sum by instalments);
(*dd*) any deferred order made by virtue of section 23(1)(*c*) (lump sums) which includes provision made by virtue of –
(i) section 25B(4), or
(ii) section 25C,
(provision in respect of pension rights);
(*e*) any order for a settlement of property under section 24(1)(*b*) or for a variation of settlement under section 24(1)(*c*) or (*d*) above, being an order made on or after the grant of a decree of judicial separation;
(*f*) any order made under section 24A(1) above for the sale of property.
(*g*) a pension sharing order under section 24B above which is made at a time before the decree has been made absolute.

(2A) Where the court has made an order referred to in subsection (2)(*a*), (*b*) or (*c*) above, then, subject to the provisions of this section, the court shall have power to remit the payment of any arrears due under the order or of any part thereof.

(2B) Where the court has made an order referred to in subsection (2)(*dd*)(ii) above, this section shall cease to apply to the order on the death of either of the parties to the marriage.

(3) The powers exercisable by the court under this section in relation to an order shall be exercisable also in relation to any instrument executed in pursuance of the order.

(4) The court shall not exercise the powers conferred by this section in relation to an order for a settlement under section 24(1)(*b*) or for a variation of settlement under section 24(1)(*c*) or (*d*) above except on an application made in proceedings –

(*a*) for the rescission of the decree of judicial separation by reference to which the order was made, or
(*b*) for the dissolution of the marriage in question.

(4A) In relation to an order which falls within paragraph (*g*) of subsection (2) above ("the subsection (2) order") –

(*a*) the powers conferred by this section may be exercised –
(i) only on an application made before the subsection (2) order has or, but for paragraph (*b*) below, would have taken effect; and
(ii) only if, at the time when the application is made, the decree has not been made absolute; and
(*b*) an application made in accordance with paragraph (*a*) above prevents the subsection (2) order from taking effect before the application has been dealt with.

(4B) No variation of a pension sharing order shall be made so as to take effect before the decree is made absolute.

(4C) The variation of a pension sharing order prevents the order taking effect before the end of such period after the making of the variation as may be prescribed by regulations made by the Lord Chancellor.

(5) Subject to subsections (7A) to (7G) below and without prejudice to any power exercisable by virtue of subsection (2)(*d*), (*dd*), (*e*) or (*g*) above or otherwise than by virtue of this section, no property adjustment order or pension sharing order shall be made on an application for the variation of a periodical payments or secured periodical payments order made (whether in favour of a party to a marriage or in favour of a child of the family) under section 23 above, and no order for the payment of a lump sum shall be made on an application for the variation of a periodical payments or secured periodical payments order in favour of a party to a marriage (whether made under section 23 or under section 27 above).

(6) Where the person liable to make payments under a secured periodical payments order has died, an application under this section relating to that order (and to any order made under section 24A(1) above which requires the proceeds of sale of property to be used for securing those payments) may be made by the person entitled to payments under the periodical payments order or by the personal representatives of the deceased person, but no such application shall, except with the permission of the court, be made after the end of the period of six months from the date on which representation in regard to the estate of that person is first taken out.

(7) In exercising the powers conferred by this section the court shall have regard to all the circumstances of the case, first consideration being given to the welfare while a minor of any child of the family who has not attained the age of eighteen, and the circumstances of the case shall include any change in any of the matters to which the court was required to have regard when making the order to which the application relates, and –

(*a*) in the case of a periodical payments or secured periodical payments order made on or after the grant of a decree of divorce or nullity of marriage, the court shall consider whether in all the circumstances and after having regard to any such change it would be appropriate to vary the order so that payments under the order are required to be made or secured only for such further period as will in the opinion of the court be sufficient (in the light of any proposed exercise by the court, where the marriage has been dissolved, of its powers under subsection (7B) below) to enable the party in whose favour the order was made to adjust without undue hardship to the termination of those payments;

(*b*) in a case where the party against whom the order was made has died, the circumstances of the case shall also include the changed circumstances resulting from his or her death.

(7A) Subsection (7B) below applies where, after the dissolution of a marriage, the court –

(*a*) discharges a periodical payments order or secured periodical payments order made in favour of a party to the marriage; or

(*b*) varies such an order so that payments under the order are required to be made or secured only for such further period as is determined by the court.

(7B) The court has power, in addition to any power it has apart from this subsection, to make supplemental provision consisting of any of –

(*a*) an order for the payment of a lump sum in favour of a party to the marriage;
(*b*) one or more property adjustment orders in favour of a party to the marriage;
(*ba*) one or more pension sharing orders;
(*c*) a direction that the party in whose favour the original order discharged or varied was made is not entitled to make any further application for –
(i) a periodical payments or secured periodical payments order, or
(ii) an extension of the period to which the original order is limited by any variation made by the court.

(7C) An order for the payment of a lump sum made under subsection (7B) above may –

(*a*) provide for the payment of that sum by instalments of such amount as may be specified in the order; and
(*b*) require the payment of the instalments to be secured to the satisfaction of the court.

(7D) Section 23(6) above applies where the court makes an order for the payment of a lump sum under subsection (7B) above as it applies where the court makes such an order under section 23 above.

(7E) If under subsection (7B) above the court makes more than one property adjustment order in favour of the same party to the marriage, each of those orders must fall within a different paragraph of section 21(2) above.

(7F) Sections 24A and 30 above apply where the court makes a property adjustment order under subsection (7B) above as they apply where it makes such an order under section 24 above.

(7G) Subsections (3) to (5) of section 24B above apply in relation to a pension sharing order under subsection (7B) above as they apply in relation to a pension sharing order under that section.

(8) The personal representatives of a deceased person against whom a secured periodical payments order was made shall not be liable for having distributed any part of the estate of the deceased after the expiration of the period of six months referred to in subsection (6) above on the ground that they ought to have taken into account the possibility that the court might permit an application under this section to be made after that period by the person entitled to payments under the order; but this subsection shall not prejudice any power to recover any part of the estate so distributed arising by virtue of the making of an order in pursuance of this section.

(9) In considering for the purposes of subsection (6) above the question when representation was first taken out, a grant limited to settled land or to trust property shall be left out of account and a grant limited to real estate or to personal estate shall be left out of account unless a grant limited to the remainder of the estate has previously been made or is made at the same time.

(10) Where the court, in exercise of its powers under this section, decides to vary or discharge a periodical payments or secured periodical payments order, then, subject to section 28(1) and (2) above, the court shall have power to direct that the variation or discharge shall not take effect until the expiration of such period as may be specified in the order.

(11) Where –

(*a*) a periodical payments or secured periodical payments order in favour of more than one child ("the order") is in force;

(*b*) the order requires payments specified in it to be made to or for the benefit of more than one child without apportioning those payments between them;

(*c*) a maintenance calculation ("the calculation") is made with respect to one or more, but not all, of the children with respect to whom those payments are to be made; and

(*d*) an application is made, before the end of the period of 6 months beginning with the date on which the assessment was made, for the variation or discharge of the order,

the court may, in exercise of its powers under this section to vary or discharge the order, direct that the variation or discharge shall take effect from the date on which the calculation took effect or any later date.

(12) Where –

(*a*) an order ("the child order") of a kind prescribed for the purposes of section 10(1) of the Child Support Act 1991 is affected by a maintenance calculation;

(*b*) on the date on which the child order became so affected there was in force a periodical payments or secured periodical payments order ("the spousal order") in favour of a party to a marriage having the care of the child in whose favour the child order was made; and

(*c*) an application is made, before the end of the period of 6 months beginning with the date on which the maintenance calculation was made, for the spousal order to be varied or discharged,

the court may, in exercise of its powers under this section to vary or discharge the spousal order, direct that the variation or discharge shall take effect from the date on which the child order became so affected or any later date.

(13) For the purposes of subsection (12) above, an order is affected if it ceases to have effect or is modified by or under section 10 of the Child Support Act 1991.

(14) Subsections (11) and (12) above are without prejudice to any other power of the court to direct that the variation of discharge of an order under this section shall take effect from a date earlier than that on which the order for variation or discharge was made.

(15) The power to make regulations under subsection (4C) above shall be exercisable by statutory instrument which shall be subject to annulment in pursuance of a resolution of either House of Parliament.

Amendments—Matrimonial Homes and Property Act 1981, s 8(2); Administration of Justice Act 1982, s 51; Matrimonial and Family Proceedings Act 1984, s 6; SI 1993/623; Pensions Act 1995, s 166; Family Law Act 1996, Sch 8, para 16(5)(*a*), (6)(*b*), (7) (as modified by SI 1998/2572); Welfare Reform and Pensions Act 1999, s 19, Sch 3, para 7; Child Support, Pensions and Social Security Act 2000, s 26, Sch 3, para 3.

Defined terms—"child", "child of the family": s 52(1); "interim order for maintenance": s 27(5); "lump sum order": s 21(1); "maintenance pending suit": s 22; "periodical payments order": s 21(1); "property adjustment order": s 21(2); "secured periodical payments order": s 21(1).

Scope of provision—This section gives the court power to vary its financial orders; the power to vary agreements is contained in ss 35 and 36.

Mode of application—A variation application comes within the definition of "ancillary relief". An application made by Form A after 5 June 2000 is governed by FPR 1991, rr 2.51A–2.70 as printed in this edition. For pre-5 June 2000 applications to vary see Procedural Guides 19 and 20 in *The Family Court Practice 1999*.

Varying child periodical payments—*V v V (Child Maintenance)* [2001] 2 FLR 799 clarifies that the court has power to vary a child maintenance order even where the order is a consent nominal order. However, if the parent with care is on benefit the court only has power to vary if there is no application for a child support calculation, and further notice of the application to vary should be given to the Child Support Agency. See **Interface with Child Support Act 1991** under MCA 1973, s 23 and **Outline of new bases for child support calculation** under CSA 1991, s 4.

Extent of court's power to vary—The court's wide powers (including the power to remit arrears) apply only to orders requiring the payment of income to another and orders for sale of property so that the court has no jurisdiction to vary a capital order subject to four limited exceptions. The first is where the order is for a lump sum payable by instalments (*Penrose v Penrose* [1994] 2 FLR 621). The second is where a settlement of property or variation of settlement order has been made in the course of judicial separation proceedings and there is a subsequent application either for a divorce or a rescission of the decree of judicial separation. The third is where a pension attachment lump sum order under s 25B(4) or 25C has been made. The fourth is where a pension sharing order has been made and the application to vary is made both before the order has taken effect and before the decree has been made absolute. Nevertheless, the court has power to extend time to pay a lump sum under its inherent power to regulate its executory orders, provided that the application to extend time does not strike at the heart of the order (*Masefield v Alexander (Lump Sum: Extension of Time)* [1995] 1 FLR 100).

Extending the term of a periodical payments order—The application for variation must be made in the life of the order and the fact that the order has expired at the time of the hearing of the application to vary does not prevent jurisdiction (*Jones v Jones* [2000] 2 FLR 307).

Further capital order now possible on application of either party for clean break on variation application (s 31(5), (7A)–(7G))—Section 31(5) prohibits the making of a property adjustment or lump sum order on an application for variation of maintenance. There are two exceptions to this prohibition:

(*a*) if a lump sum or property adjustment order has not already been made, then an application (with leave if necessary) for a lump sum or property adjustment order may be made and heard at the same time as a variation application (*Pearce v Pearce* (1980) FLR 261);

(*b*) from 1 November 1998 the court can, on an application made by either party for an immediate or deferred clean break, order a lump sum or make a further property adjustment order. This power applies to all petitions including those filed before 1 November 1998. See *Harris v Harris* [2001] 1 FCR 68.

From 1 December 2000 the court can make a pension sharing order. This power applies only to those petitions filed after 1 December 2000. See Welfare Reform and Pensions Act 1999, s 85(3)(*b*).

This reverses the previous practice as set out in *S v S* [1986] Fam 189, [1987] 1 FLR 71 that it was only the payer and not the payee who had the right to apply for capitalised periodical payments on a variation application.

Principles on which the court will act (s 31(7))—Section 31(7) sets out the statutory criteria governing the exercise of the court's discretion. For the importance, where a complete clean break is desired, of obtaining a prohibition against the other party making a further application for (secured) periodical payments or applying to extend the term, see **Scope of provision** under s 25A.

Variation due to death (s 31(6), (8), (9))—If an application to vary a secured periodical payments order arises because of the payer's death then the application to vary must be made with leave if it is made later than six months from the grant of probate or letters of administration. The personal representatives will not be liable for distributing the estate prior to an application being made if it is made after the six-month period has elapsed.

The eight big points of pension sharing—See note under MCA 1973, s 21.

32 Payment of certain arrears unenforceable without the leave of the court

(1) A person shall not be entitled to enforce through the High Court or any county court the payment of any arrears due under an order for maintenance pending suit,

an interim order for maintenance or any financial provision order without the leave of that court if those arrears became due more than twelve months before proceedings to enforce the payment of them are begun.

(2) The court hearing an application for the grant of leave under this section may refuse leave, or may grant leave subject to such restrictions and conditions (including conditions as to the allowing of time for payment or the making of payment by instalments) as that court thinks proper, or may remit the payment of the arrears or of any part thereof.

(3) An application for the grant of leave under this section shall be made in such manner as may be prescribed by rules of court.

Defined terms—"financial provision order": s 21(1); "interim order for maintenance": s 27(5); "maintenance pending suit": s 22.

Mode of application—When applying for the issue of a judgment summons, the form prescribed by FPR 1991, r 7.4(3) (Form M16) gives the option of including an application for leave under this section; and, where such an application is included, the judgment summons itself (Form M17) gives the debtor notice of it. In such a case the application for leave will be decided by the judge hearing the judgment summons. Otherwise no procedure is specially prescribed and the position is governed by FPR 1991, r 10.9. The application must be made to the district judge, in the High Court by summons and in the county court in accordance with CCR Ord 13, r 1.

Where an attachment of earnings order is sought, it may be convenient to issue the summons or notice of application under this section simultaneously with and returnable on the same date as the attachment of earnings application. The same practice may be adopted on an application for the appointment of a receiver by way of equitable execution or on an application for a means of payment order under Maintenance Enforcement Act 1991, s 1(4)(*a*). In the case of execution, and in the case of applications for garnishee or charging orders where relief is given initially on an ex parte application, leave must be sought under this section as a preliminary step.

"may refuse leave, or may grant leave" (s 32(2))—There is no presumption that leave should be granted only in special circumstances (*Lumsden v Lumsden* 11 November 1998, CA).

33 Orders for repayment in certain cases of sums paid under certain orders

(1) Where on an application made under this section in relation to an order to which this section applies it appears to the court that by reason of –

(*a*) a change in the circumstances of the person entitled to, or liable to make, payments under the order since the order was made, or
(*b*) the changed circumstances resulting from the death of the person so liable,

the amount received by the person entitled to payments under the order in respect of a period after those circumstances changed or after the death of the person liable to make payments under the order, as the case may be, exceeds the amount which the person so liable or his or her personal representatives should have been required to pay, the court may order the respondent to the application to pay to the applicant such sum, not exceeding the amount of the excess, as the court thinks just.

(2) This section applies to the following orders, that is to say –

(*a*) any order for maintenance pending suit and any interim order for maintenance;
(*b*) any periodical payments order; and
(*c*) any secured periodical payments order.

(3) An application under this section may be made by the person liable to make payments under an order to which this section applies or his or her personal

PART II

representatives and may be made against the person entitled to payments under the order or her or his personal representatives.

(4) An application under this section may be made in proceedings in the High Court or a county court for –

(*a*) the variation or discharge of the order to which this section applies, or
(*b*) leave to enforce, or the enforcement of, the payment of arrears under that order;

but when not made in such proceedings shall be made to a county court, and accordingly references in this section to the court are references to the High Court or a county court, as the circumstances require.

(5) The jurisdiction conferred on a county court by this section shall be exercisable notwithstanding that by reason of the amount claimed in the application the jurisdiction would not but for this subsection be exercisable by a county court.

(6) An order under this section for the payment of any sum may provide for the payment of that sum by instalments of such amount as may be specified in the order.

Defined terms—"interim order for maintenance": s 27(5); "maintenance pending suit": s 22; "periodical payments order", "secured periodical payments order": s 21(1).

Scope of provision—This section empowers the court to order the party who has received maintenance to repay monies that have been received where there has been a change in circumstances of the payee or a change of circumstances which results from the payer's death. The power to order repayment relates to the period before the order is varied and is distinct from the court's powers to remit arrears and to vary the order itself. Section 38 covers the situation where payments have been made at a time when the order no longer existed because it had been determined by, for instance, the remarriage of the payee.

No repayment in respect of capital orders (s 33(2))—The power to order repayment applies only to orders for maintenance pending suit and periodical payments orders and not to capital orders. For the impeachability of a capital order where there has been a drastic change of circumstances, on the principles established by the House of Lords in *Barder v Barder* [1988] AC 20, [1987] 2 FLR 480, see under FPR 1991, r 8.1.

Mode of application (s 33(4), (5))—Where application is made under this section, the county court's jurisdiction is unlimited. Normally the party applying will be seeking a discharge of the order and it is likely that there will be a linked application to vary the order so that the procedure set out in FPR 1991, rr 2.51A–2.69 applies. If there are no variation proceedings and the application stands on its own, no form of application is specified by FPR 1991. It is suggested that the application should be in Form M11 in the existing suit supported by affidavit and in other respects should be in accordance with FPR 1991, rr 2.51A–2.69.

Consent orders

33A Consent orders for financial provision on property adjustment

(1) Notwithstanding anything in the preceding provisions of this Part of this Act, on an application for a consent order for financial relief the court may, unless it has reason to think that there are other circumstances into which it ought to inquire, make an order in the terms agreed on the basis only of the prescribed information furnished with the application.

(2) Subsection (1) above applies to an application for a consent order varying or discharging an order for financial relief as it applies to an application for an order for financial relief.

(3) In this section –

"consent order", in relation to an application for an order, means an order in the terms applied for to which the respondent agrees;

"order for financial relief" means an order under any of sections 23, 24, 24A, 24B or 27 above; and

"prescribed" means prescribed by rules of court.

Amendments—Inserted by Matrimonial and Family Proceedings Act 1984, s 7; amended by Welfare Reform and Pensions Act 1999, s 19, Sch 3, para 8.

Scope of provision—This section empowers the court to make a consent order without a full investigation and without hearing oral evidence. The court cannot exercise its mandatory duties under ss 25 and 25A without up to date information of the salient facts (*Jenkins v Livesey (formerly Jenkins)* [1985] AC 424, [1985] FLR 813).

Mode of application—FPR 1991, r 2.61 applies to applications under this section.

Maintenance agreements

34 Validity of maintenance agreements

(1) If a maintenance agreement includes a provision purporting to restrict any right to apply to a court for an order containing financial arrangements, then –

(*a*) that provision shall be void; but

(*b*) any other financial arrangements contained in the agreement shall not thereby be rendered void or unenforceable and shall, unless they are void or unenforceable for any other reason (and subject to sections 35 and 36 below), be binding on the parties to the agreement.

(2) In this section and in section 35 below –

"maintenance agreement" means any agreement in writing made, whether before or after the commencement of this Act, between the parties to a marriage, being –

(*a*) an agreement containing financial arrangements, whether made during the continuance or after the dissolution or annulment of the marriage; or

(*b*) a separation agreement which contains no financial arrangements in a case where no other agreement in writing between the same parties contains such arrangements;

"financial arrangements" means provisions governing the rights and liabilities towards one another when living separately of the parties to a marriage (including a marriage which has been dissolved or annulled) in respect of the making or securing of payments or the disposition or use of any property, including such rights and liabilities with respect to the maintenance or education of any child, whether or not a child of the family.

Defined terms—"child", "child of the family": s 52(1).

Prohibition of any restriction on right to apply (s 34(1))—Section 34(1) provides that it is not possible for an agreement to restrict either party's right to apply for income or capital relief from the court. However, whilst it is impossible to restrict the theoretical right to apply, the fact that parties have come to an agreement carefully arrived at with the benefit of legal advice (in the absence of a vitiating factor such as set out in *Edgar v Edgar* [1980] 1 WLR 1410 at 1417C, [1980] 3 All ER 887 893B) will be an important factor but only one ingredient within a complex equation in determining whether the court should in fact make financial provision and property adjustment orders in identical terms to those that had been agreed (*Smith v Smith* [2000] 3 FCR 374).

"maintenance agreement" (s 34(2))—This term is defined as either an agreement containing financial arrangements made at any time or a separation agreement which contains no such financial arrangements.

35 Alteration of agreements by court during lives of parties

(1) Where a maintenance agreement is for the time being subsisting and each of the parties to the agreement is for the time being either domiciled or resident in England and Wales, then, subject to subsection (3) below, either party may apply to the court or to a magistrates' court for an order under this section.

(2) If the court to which the application is made is satisfied either –

(*a*) that by reason of a change in the circumstances in the light of which any financial arrangements contained in the agreement were made or, as the case may be, financial arrangements were omitted from it (including a change foreseen by the parties when making the agreement), the agreement should be altered so as to make different, or, as the case may be, so as to contain, financial arrangements, or

(*b*) that the agreement does not contain proper financial arrangements with respect to any child of the family,

then subject to subsections (3), (4) and (5) below, that court may by order make such alterations in the agreement –

(i) by varying or revoking any financial arrangements contained in it, or

(ii) by inserting in it financial arrangements for the benefit of one of the parties to the agreement or of a child of the family,

as may appear to that court to be just having regard to all the circumstances, including, if relevant, the matters mentioned in section 25(4) above; and the agreement shall have effect thereafter as if any alteration made by the order had been made by agreement between the parties and for valuable consideration.

(3) A magistrates' court shall not entertain an application under subsection (1) above unless both the parties to the agreement are resident in England and Wales and at least one of the parties is resident within the commission area for which the court is appointed, and shall not have power to make any order on such an application except –

(*a*) in a case where the agreement includes no provision for periodical payments by either of the parties, an order inserting provision for the making by one of the parties of periodical payments for the maintenance of the other party or for the maintenance of any child of the family;

(*b*) in a case where the agreement includes provision for the making by one of the parties of periodical payments, an order increasing or reducing the rate of, or terminating, any of those payments.

(4) Where a court decides to alter, by order under this section, an agreement by inserting provision for the making or securing by one of the parties to the agreement of periodical payments for the maintenance of the other party or by increasing the rate of the periodical payments which the agreement provides shall be made by one of the parties for the maintenance of the other, the term for which the payments or, as the case may be, the additional payments attributable to the increase are to be made under the agreement as altered by the order shall be such term as the court may specify, subject to the following limits, that is to say –

(*a*) where the payments will not be secured, the term shall be so defined as not to extend beyond the death of either of the parties to the agreement or the remarriage of the party to whom the payments are to be made;

(*b*) where the payments will be secured, the term shall be so defined as not to extend beyond the death or remarriage of that party.

(5) Where a court decides to alter, by order under this section, an agreement by inserting provision for the making or securing by one of the parties to the agreement of periodical payments for the maintenance of a child of the family or by increasing the rate of the periodical payments which the agreement provides shall be made or secured by one of the parties for the maintenance of such a child, then, in deciding the term for which under the agreement as altered by the order the payments, or as the case may be, the additional payments attributable to the increase are to be made or secured for the benefit of the child, the court shall apply the provisions of section 29(2) and (3) above as to age limits as if the order in question were a periodical payments or secured periodical payments order in favour of the child.

(6) For the avoidance of doubt it is hereby declared that nothing in this section or in section 34 above affects any power of a court before which any proceedings between the parties to a maintenance agreement are brought under any other enactment (including a provision of this Act) to make an order containing financial arrangements or any right of either party to apply for such an order in such proceedings.

Amendments—Matrimonial and Family Proceedings Act 1984, s 46(1), Sch 1, para 13; Justices of the Peace Act 1997, s 73(2), Sch 5, para 14; Access to Justice Act 1999, s 106, Sch 15.

Defined terms—"child of the family": s 52(1); "financial arrangements", "maintenance agreement": s 34(2).

Scope of provision—Subject to the Child Support Act 1991 (see **Interface with Child Support Act 1991** under MCA 1973, s 23), this section empowers the court to alter a maintenance agreement during the lives of the parties. The power arises if either there is a change in circumstances or there are no proper financial arrangements for the children. This is the only section within Part II where jurisdiction is vested not only in the High Court and county courts but magistrates' courts as well.

Mode of application—FPR 1991, r 3.2 specifies the procedure on an application under this section to the High Court or a county court. In magistrates' courts, application is by way of complaint (Magistrates' Courts Rules 1981, r 105).

36 Alteration of agreements by court after death of one party

(1) Where a maintenance agreement within the meaning of section 34 above provides for the continuation of payments under the agreement after the death of one of the parties and that party dies domiciled in England and Wales, the surviving party or the personal representatives of the deceased party may, subject to subsections (2) and (3) below, apply to the High Court or a county court for an order under section 35 above.

(2) An application under this section shall not, except with the permission of the High Court or a county court, be made after the end of the period of six months from the date on which representation in regard to the estate of the deceased is first taken out.

(3) A county court shall not entertain an application under this section, or an application for permission to make an application under this section, unless it would have jurisdiction by virtue of section 22 of the Inheritance (Provision for

Family and Dependants) Act 1975 (which confers jurisdiction on county courts in proceedings under that Act if the value of the property mentioned in that section does not exceed £5,000 or such larger sum as may be fixed by order of the Lord Chancellor) to hear and determine proceedings for an order under section 2 of that Act in relation to the deceased's estate.

(4) If a maintenance agreement is altered by a court on an application made in pursuance of subsection (1) above, the like consequences shall ensue as if the alteration had been made immediately before the death by agreement between the parties and for valuable consideration.

(5) The provisions of this section shall not render the personal representatives of the deceased liable for having distributed any part of the estate of the deceased after the expiration of the period of six months referred to in subsection (2) above on the ground that they ought to have taken into account the possibility that a court might permit an application by virtue of this section to be made by the surviving party after that period; but this subsection shall not prejudice any power to recover any part of the estate so distributed arising by virtue of the making of an order in pursuance of this section.

(6) Section 31(9) above shall apply for the purposes of subsection (2) above as it applies for the purposes of subsection (6) of section 31.

(7) Subsection (3) of section 22 of the Inheritance (Provision for Family and Dependants) Act 1975 (which enables rules of court to provide for the transfer from a county court to the High Court or from the High court to a county court of proceedings for an order under section 2 of that Act) and paragraphs (*a*) and (*b*) of subsection (4) of that section (provisions relating to proceedings commenced in county court before coming into force of order of the Lord Chancellor under that section) shall apply in relation to proceedings consisting of any such application as is referred to in subsection (3) above as they apply in relation to proceedings for an order under section 2 of that Act.

Amendments—Inheritance (Provision for Family and Dependants) Act 1975, s 26(1).

Defined terms—"maintenance agreement": s 34(2).

Six-month time-limit (s 36(2))—Leave to apply is required if the application is made later than six months from the grant of probate or letters of administration.

County court jurisdiction (s 36(3))—County courts have the same jurisdiction under this section as under the Inheritance (Provision for Family and Dependants) Act 1975. By art 2 of the High Court and County Courts Jurisdiction Order 1991, SI 1991/724, county court jurisdiction under this section is unlimited.

Mode of application—FPR 1991, r 3.3 sets out the procedure for an application under this section.

Miscellaneous and supplemental

37 Avoidance of transactions intended to prevent or reduce financial relief

(1) For the purposes of this section "financial relief" means relief under any of the provisions of sections 22, 23, 24, 24B, 27, 31 (except subsection (6)) and 35 above, and any reference in this section to defeating a person's claim for financial relief is a reference to preventing financial relief from being granted to that person, or to that person for the benefit of a child of the family, or reducing the amount of any financial relief which might be so granted, or frustrating or impeding the

enforcement of any order which might be or has been made at his instance under any of those provisions.

(2) Where proceedings for financial relief are brought by one person against another, the court may, on the application of the first-mentioned person –

(*a*) if it is satisfied that the other party to the proceedings is, with the intention of defeating the claim for financial relief, about to make any disposition or to transfer out of the jurisdiction or otherwise deal with any property, make such order as it thinks fit for restraining the other party from so doing or otherwise for protecting the claim;

(*b*) if it is satisfied that the other party has, with that intention, made a reviewable disposition and that if the disposition were set aside financial relief or different financial relief would be granted to the applicant, make an order setting aside the disposition;

(*c*) if it is satisfied, in a case where an order has been obtained under any of the provisions mentioned in subsection (1) above by the applicant against the other party, that the other party has, with that intention, made a reviewable disposition, make an order setting aside the disposition;

and an application for the purposes of paragraph (*b*) above shall be made in the proceedings for the financial relief in question.

(3) Where the court makes an order under subsection (2)(*b*) or (*c*) above setting aside a disposition it shall give such consequential directions as it thinks fit for giving effect to the order (including directions requiring the making of any payments or the disposal of any property).

(4) Any disposition made by the other party to the proceedings for financial relief in question (whether before or after the commencement of those proceedings) is a reviewable disposition for the purposes of subsection (2)(*b*) and (*c*) above unless it was made for valuable consideration (other than marriage) to a person who, at the time of the disposition, acted in relation to it in good faith and without notice of any intention on the part of the other party to defeat the applicant's claim for financial relief.

(5) Where an application is made under this section with respect to a disposition which took place less than three years before the date of the application or with respect to a disposition or other dealing with property which is about to take place and the court is satisfied –

(*a*) in a case falling within subsection (2)(*a*) or (*b*) above, that the disposition or other dealing would (apart from this section) have the consequence, or

(*b*) in a case falling within subsection (2)(*c*) above, that the disposition has had the consequence,

of defeating the applicant's claim for financial relief, it shall be presumed, unless the contrary is shown, that the person who disposed of or is about to dispose of or deal with the property did so or, as the case may be, is about to do so, with the intention of defeating the applicant's claim for financial relief.

(6) In this section "disposition" does not include any provision contained in a will or codicil but, with that exception, includes any conveyance, assurance or gift of property of any description, whether made by an instrument or otherwise.

(7) This section does not apply to a disposition made before 1 January 1968.

Amendments—Welfare Reform and Pensions Act 1999, s 19, Sch 3, para 9.

Defined terms—"child of the family": s 52(1).

Scope of provision—This section has two separate functions. First, it empowers the court to restrain the future disposal of or future dealings with property in order to protect the applicant's pending claims (s 37(2)(*a*)). The court's inherent jurisdiction and its jurisdiction under Supreme Court Act 1981, s 37(3) to freeze assets are in addition to the jurisdiction under this section (see Procedural Guide 19). Secondly, it empowers the court to set aside dispositions which have already been made where if the disposition were set aside different financial relief would be granted to the applicant (s 37(2)(*b*)) or where following an order of the court a disposition has been made which impedes the enforcement of an order (s 37(2)(*c*)). In all cases the applicant has to show the existence of an intention to defeat the claim for financial relief.

Essential preconditions (s 37(2), (5), (6))—Before an order may be made under this section, there must be proceedings for financial relief in existence. (Section 37(1) defines "financial relief" to mean an order for maintenance pending suit, financial provision, property adjustment, wilful neglect to maintain or a variation application.) Thus, there must be a valid notice of application either in the petition or in Form M11 (see FPR 1991, r 2.53).

The applicant must also show that the act complained of was made with the intention of defeating the claim for financial relief. If the act complained of took place less than three years before the application (or is anticipated at the time of the application) then it shall be presumed until the contrary is shown that the person who disposed (will dispose) of the asset had (will have) the necessary intention if the disposition has (will have) the effect of reducing the amount of any financial relief which might be granted or frustrating or impeding the enforcement of any order. Otherwise, proving the necessary intention is a question of fact.

The definition of "disposition" is wide but any provision in a will is excluded. The meaning of "property" is not defined but it is not restricted to property in England and Wales and includes real and personal property situated abroad (*Hamlin v Hamlin* [1986] Fam 11, [1986] 1 FLR 61).

Mode of application—To restrain an anticipated disposal under s 37(2)(*a*) file notice of application supported by a sworn statement (an affidavit) in accordance with FPR 1991 r 2.68.

To set aside a disposition that has already taken place, if the application is made by Form A after 5 June 2000, apply in accordance with FPR 1991, rr 2.51A–2.69D as printed in this edition. If the application is made before 5 June 2000 see Procedural Guide 19 or 22 in *The Family Court Practice 1999*.

Restraining surrender of a tenancy—The surrender of a tenancy is not a disposition so, once made, it cannot be set aside under s 37(2)(*b*) or (*c*). If it is believed that a tenancy or joint tenancy is about to be surrendered then, in the absence of any undertaking, there should be an application under s 37(2)(*a*) to restrain the surrender. The undertaking/order should be served on the landlord (*Bater v Greenwich London Borough Council* [1999] FLR 993).

Assignment of pensions by service personnel—Pensions Act 1995, s 166 now enables the court to exercise jurisdiction in respect of terminal grants and other pension rights; see further under s 23 of this Act.

38 Orders for repayment in certain cases of sums paid after cessation of order by reason of remarriage

(1) Where –

(*a*) a periodical payments or secured periodical payments order in favour of a party to a marriage (hereafter in this section referred to as "a payments order") has ceased to have effect by reason of the remarriage of that party, and

(*b*) the person liable to make payments under the order or his or her personal representatives made payments in accordance with it in respect of a period after the date of the remarriage in the mistaken belief that the order was still subsisting,

the person so liable or his or her personal representatives shall not be entitled to bring proceedings in respect of a cause of action arising out of the circumstances mentioned in paragraphs (*a*) and (*b*) above against the person entitled to payments under the order or her or his personal representatives, but may instead make an application against that person or her or his personal representatives under this section.

(2) On an application under this section the court may order the respondent to pay to the applicant a sum equal to the amount of the payments made in respect of the period mentioned in subsection (1)(*b*) above or, if it appears to the court that it would be unjust to make that order, it may either order the respondent to pay to the applicant such lesser sum as it thinks fit or dismiss the application.

(3) An application under this section may be made in proceedings in the High Court or a county court for leave to enforce, or the enforcement of, payment of arrears under the order in question, but when not made in such proceedings shall be made to a county court; and accordingly references in this section to the court are references to the High Court or a county court, as the circumstances require.

(4) The jurisdiction conferred on a county court by this section shall be exercisable notwithstanding that by reason of the amount claimed in the application the jurisdiction would not but for this subsection be exercisable by a county court.

(5) An order under this section for the payment of any sum may provide for the payment of that sum by instalments of such amount as may be specified in the order.

(6) A justices' chief executive to whom any payments under a payments order are required to be made, and the collecting officer under an attachment of earnings order made to secure payments under a payments order, shall not be liable –

(*a*) in the case of the justices' chief executive, for any act done by him in pursuance of the payments order after the date on which that order ceased to have effect by reason of the remarriage of the person entitled to payments under it, and

(*b*) in the case of the collecting officer, for any act done by him after that date in accordance with any enactment or rule of court specifying how payments made to him in compliance with the attachment of earnings order are to be dealt with,

if, but only if, the act was one which he would have been under a duty to do had the payments order not so ceased to have effect and the act was done before notice in writing of the fact that the person so entitled had remarried was given to him by or on behalf of that person, the person liable to make payments under the payments order or the personal representatives of either of those persons.

(7) In this section "collecting officer", in relation to an attachment of earnings order, means the officer of the High Court, the district judge of a county court or a justices' chief executive to whom a person makes payments in compliance with the order.

Amendments—Access to Justice Act 1999, s 90, Sch 13, para 82.

Defined terms—"periodical payments order", "secured periodical payments order": s 21(1).

Scope of provision—This section empowers the court to order repayment of a maintenance order when payments have been made under it after the order had in fact ceased (eg because the payee has remarried without informing the payer of that fact). Section 33 will apply if the reason for seeking repayment arises from a change of circumstances such as, for instance, steady cohabitation. The jurisdiction of county courts under this section is unlimited.

Mode of application—Usually the application will be linked with an application to vary or discharge the order and should therefore be made in the same way as a variation application, ie on Form M11 with a supporting affidavit as set out in FPR 1991, rr 2.52–2.67. If it is not combined with any other application, no procedure is prescribed except that it should be made to a county court. It is suggested that the application should be made in the suit by Form M11 plus supporting affidavit.

39 Settlement etc made in compliance with a property adjustment order may be avoided on bankruptcy of settlor

The fact that a settlement or transfer of property had to be made in order to comply with a property adjustment order shall not prevent that settlement or transfer from being a transaction in respect of which an order may be made under section 339 or 340 of the Insolvency Act 1986 (transfers at an undervalue and preferences).

Amendments—Insolvency Act 1985, s 235(1), Sch 8, para 23; Insolvency Act 1986, s 439(2), Sch 14.

Defined terms—"property adjustment order": s 21(2); "settlement", "transfer of property": s 24.

Scope of provision—This section provides that the fact that a settlement or transfer of property is made pursuant to a property adjustment order does not prevent it from being attacked by a trustee in bankruptcy. A declaration of solvency as a recital to a property adjustment order may deter the trustee in bankruptcy from attacking the transfer. Since this section was amended in 1986, the ability of the trustee in bankruptcy to set aside an order made in matrimonial proceedings seems to be reduced.

"section 339 or 340 of the Insolvency Act 1986"—In essence, s 339 enables a transaction to be set aside on the application of a trustee in bankruptcy where an individual has been adjudged bankrupt and he has in the five years prior to the bankruptcy made a gift of property or transferred it at an undervalue. As s 339 requires a bankrupt individual to have entered into a transaction at an undervalue, it is difficult to see how this section would enable the trustee in bankruptcy to set aside a property adjustment order after genuinely contested proceedings. Insolvency Act 1986, s 340 enables a transaction to be set aside where a bankrupt individual does something or allows something to be done within two years of his bankruptcy which has the effect of putting one of his creditors into a better position than he otherwise would have been. Again, particularly after contested proceedings, it will be difficult for the trustee in bankruptcy to set aside a transfer of property which flows from the court exercising its mandatory duties under s 25.

40 Payments etc under order made in favour of person suffering from mental disorder

Where the court makes an order under this Part of this Act requiring payments (including a lump sum payment) to be made, or property to be transferred, to a party to a marriage and the court is satisfied that the person in whose favour the order is made is incapable, by reason of mental disorder within the meaning of the Mental Health Act 1959, of managing and administering his or her property and affairs then, subject to any order, direction or authority made or given in relation to that person under Part VIII of that Act, the court may order the payments to be made, or as the case may be, the property to be transferred, to such persons having charge of that person as the court may direct.

Mental Health Act—This reference would now be to Mental Health Act 1983, Pt VII and should be construed accordingly.

"mental disorder"—By virtue of Mental Health Act 1983, s 1(2), this means "mental illness, arrested or incomplete development of mind, psychopathic disorder and any other disorder or disability of mind and 'mentally disordered' shall be construed accordingly". For a full explanation see the note to FPR 1991, r 9.1.

"property and affairs"—This is restricted to property and financial affairs (*Re W* [1970] 2 All ER 502).

"order, direction or authority"—This is a reference to the powers of the Court of Protection pursuant to Mental Health Act 1983, Pt VII. The jurisdiction of that Court is based upon the same criteria as set out here, namely: "incapable by reason of mental disorder of managing and administering his property and affairs".

"persons having charge"—This may include an officer of the local social services authority or other guardian when the individual is under a guardianship order, or the district health authority when the individual has been compulsorily admitted to hospital under the Mental Health Act 1983. There are few, if any, other provisions under which somebody may legally be "in charge of" an incapacitated adult, although it might be argued that this situation arises under the Community Care legislation when the individual is in residential care funded by a local authority. However, it is likely that the courts, in construing this phrase, will take a practical approach to the relationship rather than examine the legal basis thereof, although such an approach could be open to question. This would enable maintenance to be paid direct to an informal carer, whether or not another member of the family.

Use of this provision—This provision leaves considerable discretion to the court as to the future management of the financial provision but it will not always be appropriate to exercise the power conferred thereby (see notes below). The power will be useful where the incapacitated recipient has no capital or savings, only periodical payments are involved and there is an established carer who can receive and expend the money on his or her behalf. In that situation, any social security benefits will usually be dealt with under the appointeeship procedure and the person who is appointee may be suitable to handle additional weekly maintenance. But there will be no continuing supervision and it may be difficult to deal with a subsequent change of carer. Query whether this power might be used to direct payments to the local authority where the incapacitated recipient is in residential care funded by that authority.

Role of the Court of Protection—If the incapacitated party in whose favour an order is made already has income or assets which need to be administered, or if substantial provision is to be made, the Court of Protection should be left to administer the entire financial affairs. The jurisdiction of the county court or High Court under this provision should not be allowed to conflict with that of the Court of Protection (see generally notes to RSC Ord 80, r 12 and CCR Ord 10, r 11).

Enduring Powers of Attorney Act 1985—Where there is a registered enduring power of attorney, it would normally be appropriate for the attorney who is managing the affairs to receive all payments or property pursuant to the financial provision order, if the terms of the power are capable of extending to this.

Implications on the proceedings—A party who is "incapable by reason of mental disorder of managing and administering his property and affairs" within this provision will be a "patient" for whom a next friend or guardian ad litem must be appointed. See generally FPR 1991, Pt IX (Disability).

40A Appeals relating to pension sharing orders which have taken effect

(1) Subsections (2) and (3) below apply where an appeal against a pension sharing order is begun on or after the day on which the order takes effect.

(2) If the pension sharing order relates to a person's rights under a pension arrangement, the appeal court may not set aside or vary the order if the person responsible for the pension arrangement has acted to his detriment in reliance on the taking effect of the order.

(3) If the pension sharing order relates to a person's shareable state scheme rights, the appeal court may not set aside or vary the order if the Secretary of State has acted to his detriment in reliance on the taking effect of the order.

(4) In determining for the purposes of subsection (2) or (3) above whether a person has acted to his detriment in reliance on the taking effect of the order, the appeal court may disregard any detriment which in its opinion is insignificant.

(5) Where subsection (2) or (3) above applies, the appeal court may make such further orders (including one or more pension sharing orders) as it thinks fit for the purpose of putting the parties in the position it considers appropriate.

(6) Section 24C above only applies to a pension sharing order under this section if the decision of the appeal court can itself be the subject of an appeal.

(7) In subsection (2) above, the reference to the person responsible for the pension arrangement is to be read in accordance with section 25D(4) above.

Amendments—Inserted by Welfare Reform and Pensions Act 1999, s 19, Sch 3, para 10.

General Note—As set out in MCA 1973, s 24 a pension sharing order does not take effect until 7 days after the time for appealing has expired.

PART III
PROTECTION, CUSTODY ETC OF CHILDREN

41 Restrictions on decrees for dissolution, annulment or separation affecting children

(1) In any proceedings for a decree of divorce or nullity of marriage, or a decree of judicial separation, the court shall consider –

(*a*) whether there are any children of the family to whom this section applies; and

(*b*) where there are any such children, whether (in the light of the arrangements which have been, or are proposed to be, made for their upbringing and welfare) it should exercise any of its powers under the Children Act 1989 with respect to any of them.

(2) Where, in any case to which this section applies, it appears to the court that –

(*a*) the circumstances of the case require it, or are likely to require it, to exercise any of its powers under the Act of 1989 with respect to any such child;

(*b*) it is not in a position to exercise that power or (as the case may be) those powers without giving further consideration to the case; and

(*c*) there are exceptional circumstances which make it desirable in the interests of the child that the court should give a direction under this section,

it may direct that the decree of divorce or nullity is not to be made absolute, or that the decree of judicial separation is not to be granted, until the court orders otherwise.

(3) This section applies to –

(*a*) any child of the family who has not reached the age of sixteen at the date when the court considers the case in accordance with the requirements of this section; and

(*b*) any child of the family who has reached that age at that date and in relation to whom the court directs that this section shall apply.

Amendments—CA 1989, s 108(4), Sch 12, para 31.

Defined terms—"child", "child of the family", "the court": s 52(1).

Scope of provision—This section imposes on the court a duty in decree proceedings to consider whether there are any children of the family (as defined by s 52 and applied by s 41(3)); and, if so, to consider whether the court should exercise any of its powers under CA 1989. If the court considers that it may need so to exercise its powers and exceptional circumstances make such action desirable, the court can stay the grant of a decree absolute of divorce or nullity or a decree of judicial separation.

Procedure—The procedure for complying with s 41 is set out in FPR 1991, r 2.39 and, unlike the pre-CA 1989 procedure, is dealt with by the district judge as a solely paper exercise, save where s 41(1)(*b*) or (2) applies. Thus, consistent with the philosophy behind CA 1989, s 1(5) and subject to the limited powers of the court under s 41(2), to any applications under CA 1989, Pt II and to its power to order a report under CA 1989, s 37(1), the court has no power to intervene concerning a child of the family.

"powers under the Children Act 1989" (s 41(1)(*b*))—For practical purposes, the powers which the court may exercise are:
(*a*) to make an order under s 8, whether of its own motion or on application under s 10;
(*b*) to make a family assistance order under s 16;
(*c*) to make a direction for investigation by the local authority under s 37(1).

"exceptional circumstances" (s 41(2)(*c*))—In addition to the other factors in s 41(2), the district judge must be satisfied that "exceptional circumstances" exist before he can stay the grant of any decree. Thus, for example, the fact that an application for an order under CA 1989, s 8 is pending should not preclude the grant of a decree absolute. However, if care proceedings are pending, it is conceivable, but not inevitable, that a stay would be appropriate.

"child of the family" (s 41(3))—This limitation on the age of a child of the family is in contrast to, for example, the age for matrimonial financial relief (no order above 18, save where child is in full-time education or there are special circumstances: MCA 1973, s 29(1), (3)), orders under CA 1989, s 8 (no order above 16, save in exceptional circumstances: CA 1989, s 9(6)) and for child support maintenance (up to 16, and then up to 19 if in full-time or other prescribed education: CSA 1991, s 55).

****

PART IV
MISCELLANEOUS AND SUPPLEMENTAL

47 Matrimonial relief and declarations of validity in respect of polygamous marriages

(1) A court in England and Wales shall not be precluded from granting matrimonial relief or making a declaration concerning the validity of a marriage by reason only that either party to the marriage is, or has during the subsistence of the marriage been, married to more than one person.

(2) In this section "matrimonial relief" means –

(*a*) any decree under Part I of this Act;
(*b*) a financial provision order under section 27 above;
(*c*) an order under section 35 above altering a maintenance agreement;
(*d*) an order under any provision of this Act which confers a power exercisable in connection with, or in connection with proceedings for, such decree or order as is mentioned in paragraphs (*a*) to (*c*) above;
(*dd*) an order under Part III of the Matrimonial and Family Proceedings Act 1984;
(*e*) an order under Part I of the Domestic Proceedings and Magistrates' Courts Act 1978.

(3) In this section "a declaration concerning the validity of a marriage" means any declaration under Part III of the Family Law Act 1986 involving a determination as to the validity of a marriage.

(4) Provision may be made by rules of court –

- (*a*) for requiring notice of proceedings brought by virtue of this section to be served on any additional spouse of a party to the marriage in question; and
- (*b*) for conferring on any such additional spouse the right to be heard in the proceedings,

in such cases as may be specified in the rules.

Amendments—Domestic Proceedings and Magistrates' Courts Act 1978, s 89(2)(*a*), Sch 2, para 39; Matrimonial and Family Proceedings Act 1984, s 46(1), Sch 1, para 15; Family Law Act 1986, s 68(1), Sch 1, para 14; Private International Law (Miscellaneous Provisions) Act 1995, s 8, Sch, para 2.

Defined terms—"the court": s 52.

"provision may be made by rules of court" (s 47(4))—FPR 1991, r 3.11 makes provision for proceedings for matrimonial relief, as defined by s 47(2). FPR 1991, r 3.11(3) requires the court to give notice to any additional spouse and to order that spouse to be made a party to the proceedings if the court considers it appropriate. Rule 3.11 only covers proceedings in the High Court and county courts under s 47(2)(*a*)–(*dd*); for the magistrates' courts, it is by no means clear that the provisions of the Family Proceedings Courts (Matrimonial Proceedings etc) Rules 1991 cover proceedings concerning polygamous marriages within the terms of s 47(2)(*e*); nor is there any provision in FPC(MP etc)R 1991 equivalent to FPR 1991, r 3.11.

48 Evidence

(1) The evidence of a husband or wife shall be admissible in any proceedings to prove that marital intercourse did or did not take place between them during any period.

(2) In any proceedings for nullity of marriage, evidence on the question of sexual capacity shall be heard in camera unless in any case the judge is satisfied that in the interests of justice any such evidence ought to be heard in open court.

Scope of provision—This section enables the admission of a spouse's evidence as to whether or not intercourse took place, and requires evidence of sexual capacity to be heard in camera unless otherwise directed by the judge.

"evidence of a husband or wife" (s 48(1))—A husband and wife can give evidence against one another in all circumstances (Evidence Amendment Act 1853, s 1), including in respect of adultery and marital intercourse, or lack of it.

"shall be heard in camera" (s 48(2))—Hearings should only be held in camera if the administration of justice would not be impeded (*Scott v Scott* [1913] AC 417, (1913) FLR Rep 657, HL). This section reverses the normal presumption that justice requires cases to be heard in open court, and places on the judge the duty to say why the interests of justice would be served by the cause being heard in open court.

49 Parties to proceedings under this Act

(1) Where in a petition for divorce or judicial separation, or in any other pleading praying for either form of relief, one party to a marriage alleges that the other has committed adultery, he or she shall make the person alleged to have committed adultery with the other party to the marriage a party to the proceedings unless excused by the court on special grounds from doing so.

(2) Rules of court may, either generally or in such cases as may be prescribed by the rules, exclude the application of subsection (1) above where the person alleged to have committed adultery with the other party to the marriage is not named in the petition or other pleading.

(3) Where in pursuance of subsection (1) above a person is made a party to proceedings for divorce or judicial separation, the court may, if after the close of the evidence on the part of the person making the allegation of adultery it is of opinion that there is not sufficient evidence against the person so made a party, dismiss him or her from the suit.

(4) Rules of court may make provision, in cases not falling within subsection (1) above, with respect to the joinder as parties to proceedings under this Act of persons involved in allegations of adultery or other improper conduct made in those proceedings, and with respect to the dismissal from such proceedings of any parties so joined; and rules of court made by virtue of this subsection may make different provision for different cases.

(5) In every case in which adultery with any party to a suit is alleged against any person not made a party to the suit or in which the court considers, in the interest of any person not already a party to the suit, that that person should be made a party to the suit, the court may if it thinks fit allow that person to intervene upon such terms, if any, as the court thinks just.

Defined terms—"the court": s 52.

Scope of provision—This section requires a person against whom adultery is alleged in any proceedings for divorce or judicial separation to be made a party to those proceedings, although rules may exempt this provision where the person is not named. If there is insufficient evidence against a party, that party may be dismissed from the suit. Others involved in allegations of adultery or other improper conduct may be joined as parties, and a person alleged to have committed adultery but not joined may be permitted by the court to intervene.

Rules and procedure—FPR 1991, r 2.7 deals with parties to a matrimonial cause: in particular, r 2.7(1)(*a*) enables a petitioner to omit the name of the alleged adulterer.

****

52 Interpretation

(1) In this Act –

"child", in relation to one or both of the parties to a marriage, includes an illegitimate child of that party or, as the case may be, of both parties;

"child of the family", in relation to the parties to a marriage, means –

(*a*) a child of both of those parties; and

(*b*) any other child, not being a child who is placed with those parties as foster parents by a local authority or voluntary organisation, who has been treated by both of those parties as a child of their family;

"the court" (except where the context otherwise requires) means the High Court or, where a county court has jurisdiction by virtue of Part V of the Matrimonial and Family Proceedings Act 1984, a county court;

"education" includes training;

"maintenance calculation" has the same meaning as it has in the Child Support Act 1991 by virtue of section 54 of that Act as read with any regulations in force under that section.

(2) In this Act –

(*a*) references to financial provision orders, periodical payments and secured periodical payments orders and orders for the payment of a lump sum, and references to property adjustment orders, shall be construed in accordance with section 21 above;

(*aa*) references to pension sharing orders shall be construed in accordance with section 21A above; and

(*b*) references to orders for maintenance pending suit and to interim orders for maintenance shall be construed respectively in accordance with section 22 and section 27(5) above.

(3) For the avoidance of doubt it is hereby declared that references in this Act to remarriage include references to a marriage which is by law void or voidable.

(4) Except where the contrary intention is indicated, references in this Act to any enactment include references to that enactment as amended, extended or applied by or under any subsequent enactment, including this Act.

Amendments—Children Act 1975, s 108(1)(*b*), Sch 4; Matrimonial and Family Proceedings Act 1984, s 46(1), Sch 1, para 16; CA 1989, s 108(4), (7), Sch 12, para 33, Sch 15; SI 1993/623; Welfare Reform and Pensions Act 1999, s 19, Sch 3, para 11; Child Support, Pensions and Social Security Act 2000, s 26, Sch 3, para 3.

****

Matrimonial Proceedings and Property Act 1970

****

30 Order for maintenance of party to marriage made by magistrates' court to cease to have effect on remarriage of that party

(1) (*repealed*)

(2) Section 4(2) of the Domestic Proceedings and Magistrates' Courts Act 1978 shall apply in relation to an order consisting of or including a provision such as is mentioned in section 2(1)(*a*) of that Act made by a magistrates' court and confirmed in accordance with section 3 of the Maintenance Orders (Facilities for Enforcement) Act 1920 (which enables a magistrates' court to make a maintenance order against a person resident in a part of Her Majesty's dominions outside the United Kingdom but provides that the order shall have no effect unless and until confirmed by a competent court in that part) as it applies in relation to an order made under section 2(1)(*a*) of the Domestic Proceedings and Magistrates' Courts Act 1978.

Amendments—Maintenance Orders (Reciprocal Enforcement) Act 1972, s 42(3); Domestic Proceedings and Magistrates' Courts Act 1978, s 89(2), Sch 2, para 28, Sch 3.

****

37 Contributions by spouse in money or money's worth to the improvement of property

It is hereby declared that where a husband or wife contributes in money or money's worth to the improvement of real or personal property in which or in the proceeds of sale of which either or both of them has or have a beneficial interest, the husband or wife so contributing shall, if the contribution is of a substantial nature and subject to any agreement between them to the contrary express or implied, be treated as having then acquired by virtue of his or her contribution a share or an enlarged share, as the case may be, in that beneficial interest of such an extent as may have been then agreed or, in default of such agreement, as may seem in all the circumstances just to any court before which the question of the existence or extent of the beneficial interest of the husband or wife arises (whether in proceedings between them or in any other proceedings).

****

39 Extension of s 17 of Married Women's Property Act 1882

An application may be made to the High Court or a county court under section 17 of the Married Women's Property Act 1882 (powers of the court in disputes between husband and wife about property) (including that section as extended by section 7 of the Matrimonial Causes (Property and Maintenance) Act 1958) by either of the parties to a marriage notwithstanding that their marriage has been dissolved or annulled so long as the application is made within the period of three years beginning with the date on which the marriage was dissolved or annulled; and references in the said section 17 and the said section 7 to a husband or a wife shall be construed accordingly.

****

Protection from Harassment Act 1997

England and Wales

1 Prohibition of harassment

(1) A person must not pursue a course of conduct –

(*a*) which amounts to harassment of another, and
(*b*) which he knows or ought to know amounts to harassment of the other.

(2) For the purposes of this section, the person whose course of conduct is in question ought to know that it amounts to harassment of another if a reasonable person in possession of the same information would think the course of conduct amounted to harassment of the other.

(3) Subsection (1) does not apply to a course of conduct if the person who pursued it shows –

(*a*) that it was pursued for the purpose of preventing or detecting crime, (*b*) that it was pursued under any enactment or rule of law or to comply with any condition or requirement imposed by any person under any enactment, or

(*c*) that in the particular circumstances the pursuit of the course of conduct was reasonable.

"harassment"—This term includes, but is not restricted to, "alarming the person" and "causing the person distress" (s 7(2)). "Harassment ... includes within it an element of intent, intent to cause distress or harm" per Lord Donaldson in *Johnson v Walton* [1990] 1 FLR 350 at 352H.

"course of conduct"—Harassment is a "course of conduct" (s 1(1)) which "must involve conduct on at least two occasions" (s 7(3)). However proceedings can be brought based on an "apprehended breach of section 1" (see under s 3(1)). "'Conduct' includes speech" (s 7(4)). In *R v Hills* [2001] 1 FLR 580, CA it was held that assaults in April and October were not a "course of conduct", particularly since the parties had been reconciled. On the facts, a charge of assault might have been more appropriate. As to the distance between incidents, see also *Lau v DPP* [2000] 1 FLR 799. Note the new s 7(3A) which is relevant where the harasser acts through an accomplice.

2 Offence of harassment

(1) A person who pursues a course of conduct in breach of section 1 is guilty of an offence.

(2) A person guilty of an offence under this section is liable on summary conviction to imprisonment for a term not exceeding six months, or a fine not exceeding level 5 on the standard scale, or both.

(3) ...

3 Civil remedy

(1) An actual or apprehended breach of section 1 may be the subject of a claim in civil proceedings by the person who is or may be the victim of the course of conduct in question.

(2) On such a claim, damages may be awarded for (among other things) any anxiety caused by the harassment and any financial loss resulting from the harassment.

(3) Where –

(*a*) in such proceedings the High Court or a county court grants an injunction for the purpose of restraining the defendant from pursuing any conduct which amounts to harassment, and

(*b*) the plaintiff considers that the defendant has done anything which he is prohibited from doing by the injunction,

the plaintiff may apply for the issue of a warrant for the arrest of the defendant.

(4) An application under subsection (3) may be made –

(*a*) where the injunction was granted by the High Court, to a judge of that court, and

(*b*) where the injunction was granted by a county court, to a judge or district judge of that or any other county court.

(5) The judge or district judge to whom an application under subsection (3) is made may only issue a warrant if –

(*a*) the application is substantiated on oath, and

(*b*) the judge or district judge has reasonable grounds for believing that the defendant has done anything which he is prohibited from doing by the injunction.

(6) Where –

(*a*) the High Court or a county court grants an injunction for the purpose mentioned in subsection (3)(*a*), and

(*b*) without reasonable excuse the defendant does anything which he is prohibited from doing by the injunction,

he is guilty of an offence.

(7) Where a person is convicted of an offence under subsection (6) in respect of any conduct, that conduct is not punishable as a contempt of court.

(8) A person cannot be convicted of an offence under subsection (6) in respect of any conduct which has been punished as a contempt of court.

(9) A person guilty of an offence under subsection (6) is liable –

(*a*) on conviction on indictment, to imprisonment for a term not exceeding five years, or a fine, or both, or

(*b*) on summary conviction, to imprisonment for a term not exceeding six months, or a fine not exceeding the statutory maximum, or both.

Scope of provision—This section creates the statutory tort of harassment. In *Tuppen and anor v Microsoft Corporation Ltd and anor* (2000) *The Times*, 15 November it was held, after referring to *Hansard*, that the Act was directed at the prevention of stalking, anti-social behaviour by neighbours and racial harassment. The Act cannot be used to stifle litigation.

"claim in civil proceedings", "damages"—A claim for damages is not necessary if all the applicant seeks is an injunction. A free standing application for an injunction can be made in a county court in proceedings founded on any matter within the jurisdiction of a county court: County Courts Act 1984, s 38. However, in many cases it will be appropriate to seek damages and the court is given express power to award damages for anxiety and any financial loss (see s 3(2)).

Procedure—Proceedings under PHA 1997 are civil proceedings and are thus governed by CPR 1998 and not FPR 1991. See further Procedural Guide 11.

"apprehended breach of section 1"—Although the tort is incomplete until the course of conduct involves "conduct on at least two occasions" (s 7(3)), an application for an injunction can be brought for a threatened tort, provided the evidence justifies a finding that commission of the tort is likely (*South Carolina Insurance Co v Assurantie Maatschappij 'De Zeven Provincien' NV* [1987] AC 24; *Khorasandjian v Bush* [1993] 2 FLR 66).

Ambit of injunction—An injunction can forbid the defendant from entering a defined area around the applicant's home, where this is needed to make the injunction effective (*Burris v Azadani* [1996] 1 FLR 266), and presumably also around the applicant's place of work.

"warrant of arrest"—A warrant of arrest can be obtained for the purpose of arresting the defendant and bringing him before the court following a breach of the injunction. See further Procedural Guide 38. Note that it is not possible for a power of arrest (see FLA 1996, s 47) to be attached to the injunction itself.

"guilty of an offence"—By virtue of s 3(6)–(7), where the defendant has disobeyed an injunction forbidding harassment, he may be convicted of an offence, in which case contempt proceedings are no longer permissible. Where he has been punished for the contempt, criminal proceedings are no longer permissible (s 3(8)).

4 Putting people in fear of violence

(1) A person whose course of conduct causes another to fear, on at least two occasions, that violence will be used against him is guilty of an offence if he knows or ought to know that his course of conduct will cause the other so to fear on each of those occasions.

(2) For the purposes of this section, the person whose course of conduct is in question ought to know that it will cause another to fear that violence will be used against him on any occasion if a reasonable person in possession of the same information would think the course of conduct would cause the other so to fear on that occasion.

(3) It is a defence for a person charged with an offence under this section to show that –

(*a*) his course of conduct was pursued for the purpose of preventing or detecting crime,
(*b*) his course of conduct was pursued under any enactment or rule of law or to comply with any condition or requirement imposed by any person under any enactment, or
(*c*) the pursuit of his course of conduct was reasonable for the protection of himself or another or for the protection of his or another's property.

(4) A person guilty of an offence under this section is liable –

(*a*) on conviction on indictment, to imprisonment for a term not exceeding five years, or a fine, or both, or
(*b*) on summary conviction, to imprisonment for a term not exceeding six months, or a fine not exceeding the statutory maximum, or both.

(5) If on the trial on indictment of a person charged with an offence under this section the jury find him not guilty of the offence charged, they may find him guilty of an offence under section 2.

(6) The Crown Court has the same powers and duties in relation to a person who is by virtue of subsection (5) convicted before it of an offence under section 2 as a magistrates' court would have on convicting him of the offence.

5 Restraining orders

(1) A court sentencing or otherwise dealing with a person ("the defendant") convicted of an offence under section 2 or 4 may (as well as sentencing him or dealing with him in any other way) make an order under this section.

(2) The order may, for the purpose of protecting the victim of the offence, or any other person mentioned in the order, from further conduct which –

(*a*) amounts to harassment, or
(*b*) will cause a fear of violence,

prohibit the defendant from doing anything described in the order.

(3) The order may have effect for a specified period or until further order.

(4) The prosecutor, the defendant or any other person mentioned in the order may apply to the court which made the order for it to be varied or discharged by a further order.

(5) If without reasonable excuse the defendant does anything which he is prohibited from doing by an order under this section, he is guilty of an offence.

(6) A person guilty of an offence under this section is liable –

(*a*) on conviction on indictment, to imprisonment for a term not exceeding five years, or a fine, or both, or

(*b*) on summary conviction, to imprisonment for a term not exceeding six months, or a fine not exceeding the statutory maximum, or both.

****

7 Interpretation of this group of sections

(1) This section applies for the interpretation of sections 1 to 5.

(2) References to harassing a person include alarming the person or causing the person distress.

(3) A "course of conduct" must involve conduct on at least two occasions.

(3A) A person's conduct on any occasion shall be taken, if aided, abetted, counselled or procured by another –

(*a*) to be conduct on that occasion of the other (as well as conduct of the person whose conduct it is); and

(*b*) to be conduct in relation to which the other's knowledge and purpose, and what he ought to have known, are the same as they were in relation to what was contemplated or reasonably foreseeable at the time of the aiding, abetting, counselling or procuring.

(4) "Conduct" includes speech.

Amendments—Criminal Justice and Police Act 2001, s 44.

****

Social Security Administration Act 1992

ARRANGEMENT OF SECTIONS

****

78 Recovery of social fund awards

(1)–(5) ...

(6) For the purposes of this section –

(*a*) a man shall be liable to maintain his wife and any children of whom he is the father;

(*b*) a woman shall be liable to maintain her husband and any children of whom she is the mother;

(*c*) a person shall be liable to maintain another person throughout any period in respect of which the first-mentioned person has, on or after 23 May 1980 (the date of the passing of the Social Security Act 1980) and either alone or jointly with a further person, given an undertaking in writing in pursuance of immigration rules within the meaning of the Immigration Act 1971 to be responsible for the maintenance and accommodation of the other person; and

(*d*) "child" includes a person who has attained the age of 16 but not the age of 19 and in respect of whom either parent, or some person acting in the place of either parent, is receiving income support or an income-based jobseeker's allowance.

(7) Any reference in subsection (6) above to children of whom the man or the woman is the father or the mother shall be construed in accordance with section 1 of the Family Law Reform Act 1987.

(8) Subsection (7) above does not apply in Scotland, and in the applications of subsection (6) above to Scotland any reference to children of whom the man or the woman is the father or the mother shall be construed as a reference to any such children whether or not their parents have ever been married to one another.

(9) A document bearing a certificate which –

(*a*) is signed by a person authorised in that behalf by the Secretary of State; and

(*b*) states that the document apart from the certificate is, or is a copy of, such an undertaking as is mentioned in subsection (6)(*c*) above,

shall be conclusive of the undertaking in question for the purposes of this section; and a certificate purporting to be so signed shall be deemed to be so signed until the contrary is proved.

Amendments—Jobseekers Act 1995, s 41, Sch 2, para 51.

****

106 Recovery of expenditure on benefit from person liable for maintenance

(1) Subject to the following provisions of this section, if income support is claimed by or in respect of a person whom another person is liable to maintain or paid to or in respect of such a person, the Secretary of State may make a complaint against the liable person to a magistrates' court for an order under this section.

(2) On the hearing of a complaint under this section the court shall have regard to all the circumstances and, in particular, to the income of the liable person, and may order him to pay such sum, weekly or otherwise, as it may consider appropriate, except that in a case falling within section 78(6)(*c*) above that sum shall not

include any amount which is not attributable to income support (whether paid before or after the making of the order).

(3) In determining whether to order any payments to be made in respect of income support for any period before the complaint was made, or the amount of any such payments, the court shall disregard any amount by which the liable person's income exceeds the income which was his during that period.

(4) Any payments ordered to be made under this section shall be made –

- (*a*) to the Secretary of State in so far as they are attributable to any income support (whether paid before or after the making of the order);
- (*b*) to the person claiming income support or (if different) the dependant; or
- (*c*) to such other person as appears to the court expedient in the interests of the dependant.

(5) As order under this section shall be enforceable as a magistrates' court maintenance order within the meaning of section 150(1) of the Magistrates' Courts Act 1980.

(6) In the application of this section to Scotland, subsection (5) above shall be omitted and for the references to a complaint and to a magistrates' court there shall be substituted respectively references to an application and to the sheriff.

(7) On an application under subsection (1) above a court in Scotland may make a finding as to the parentage of a child for the purpose of establishing whether a person is, for the purposes of section 105 above and this section, liable to maintain him.

Defined terms—"child", "liable to maintain": s 78(6).

107 Recovery of expenditure on income support: additional amounts and transfer of orders

(1) In any case where –

- (*a*) the claim for income support referred to in section 106(1) above is or was made by the parent of one or more children in respect of both himself and those children; and
- (*b*) the other parent is liable to maintain those children but, by virtue of not being the claimant's husband or wife, is not liable to maintain the claimant,

the sum which the court may order that other parent to pay under subsection (2) of that section may include an amount, determined in accordance with regulations, in respect of any income support paid to or for the claimant by virtue of such provisions as may be prescribed.

(2) Where the sum which a court orders a person to pay under section 106 above includes by virtue of subsection (1) above an amount (in this section referred to as a "personal allowance element") in respect of income support by virtue of paragraph 1(2) of schedule 2 to the Income Support (General) Regulations 1987 (personal allowance for lone parent) the order shall separately identify the amount of the personal allowance element.

(3) In any case where –

- (*a*) there is in force an order under subsection (2) of section 106 above made against a person ("the liable parent") who is the parent of one or more children, in respect of the other parent or the children; and

PART II

(*b*) payments under the order fall to be made to the Secretary of State by virtue of subsection (4)(*a*) of that section; and

(*c*) that other parent ("the dependent parent") ceases to claim income support,

the Secretary of State may, by giving notice in writing to the court which made the order and to the liable parent and the dependent parent, transfer to the dependent parent the right to receive the payments under the order, exclusive of any personal allowance element, and to exercise the relevant rights in relation to the order, except so far as relating to that element.

(4) Notice under subsection (3) above shall not be given (and if purportedly given, shall be of no effect) at a time when there is in force a maintenance order made against the liable parent –

(*a*) in favour of the dependent parent or one or more of the children; or

(*b*) in favour of some other person for the benefit of the dependent parent or one or more of the children;

and if such a maintenance order is made at any time after notice under that subsection has been given, the order under section 106(2) above shall cease to have effect.

(5) In any case where –

(*a*) notice is given to a magistrates' court under subsection (3) above,

(*b*) payments under the order are required to be made by any method of payment falling within section 59(6) of the Magistrates' Courts Act 1980 (standing order, etc), and

(*c*) the clerk to the justices for the petty sessions area for which the court is acting decides that payment by that method is no longer possible,

the clerk shall amend the order to provide that payments under the order shall be made by the liable parent to the justices' chief executive for the court.

(6) Except as provided by subsections (8) and (12) below, where the Secretary of State gives notice under subsection (3) above, he shall cease to be entitled –

(*a*) to receive any payment under the order in respect of any personal allowance element; or

(*b*) to exercise the relevant rights, so far as relating to any such element,

notwithstanding that the dependent parent does not become entitled to receive any payment in respect of that element or to exercise the relevant rights so far as so relating.

(7) If, in a case where the Secretary of State gives notice under subsection (3) above, a payment under the order is or has been made to him wholly or partly in respect of the whole or any part of the period beginning with the day on which the transfer takes effect and ending with the day on which the notice under subsection (3) above is given to the liable parent, the Secretary of State shall –

(*a*) repay to or for the liable parent so much of the payment as is referable to any personal allowance element in respect of that period or, as the case may be, the part of it in question; and

(*b*) pay to or for the dependent parent so much of any remaining balance of the payment as is referable to that period or part;

and a payment under paragraph (*b*) above shall be taken to discharge, to that extent, the liability of the liable parent to the dependent parent under the order in respect of that period or part.

(8) If, in a case where the Secretary of State has given notice under subsection (3) above, the dependent parent makes a further claims for income support, then –

(*a*) the Secretary of State may, by giving a further notice in writing to the court which made the order and to the liable parent and the dependent parent, transfer back from the dependent parent to himself the right to receive the payments and to exercise the relevant rights; and

(*b*) that transfer shall revive the Secretary of State's right to receive payment under the order in respect of any personal allowance element and to exercise the relevant rights so far as relating to any such element.

(9) Subject to subsections (10) and (11) below, in any case where –

(*a*) notice is given to a magistrates' court under subsection (8) above, and

(*b*) the method of payment under the order which subsists immediately before the day on which the transfer under subsection (8) above takes effect differs from the method of payment which subsisted immediately before the day on which the transfer under subsection (3) above (or, if there has been more than one such transfer, the last such transfer) took effect,

the clerk to the justices for the petty sessions area for which the court is acting shall amend the order by reinstating the method of payment under the order which subsisted immediately before the day on which the transfer under subsection (3) above (or, as the case may be, the last such transfer) took effect.

(10) The clerk shall not amend the order under subsection (9) above if the Secretary of State gives notice in writing to the clerk, on or before the day on which the notice under subsection (8) above is given, that the method of payment under the order which subsists immediately before the day on which the transfer under subsection (8) above takes effect is to continue.

(11) In any case where –

(*a*) notice is given to a magistrates' court under subsection (8) above,

(*b*) the method of payment under the order which subsisted immediately before the day on which the transfer under subsection (3) above (or, if there has been more than one such transfer, the last such transfer) took effect was any method of payment falling within section 59(6) of the Magistrates' Courts Act 1980 (standing order etc), and

(*c*) the clerk decides that payment by that method is no longer possible,

the clerk shall amend the order to provide that payments under the order shall be made by the liable parent to the justices' chief executive for the court.

(12) A transfer under subsection (3) or (8) above does not transfer or otherwise affect the right of any person –

(*a*) to receive a payment which fell due to him at a time before the transfer took effect; or

(*b*) to exercise the relevant rights in relation to any such payment;

and, where notice is given under subsection (3), subsection (6) above does not deprive the Secretary of State of his right to receive such a payment in respect of any personal allowance element or to exercise the relevant rights in relation to such a payment.

(13) For the purposes of this section –

(*a*) a transfer under subsection (3) above takes effect on the day on which the dependent parent ceases to be in receipt of income support in consequence of the cessation referred to in paragraph (*c*) of that subsection, and

(*b*) a transfer under subsection (8) above takes effect on –
(i) the first day in respect of which the dependent parent receives income support after the transfer under subsection (3) above took effect, or
(ii) such later day as may be specified for the purpose in the notice under subsection (8),

irrespective of the day on which notice under the subsection in question is given.

(14) Any notice required to be given to the liable parent under subsection (3) or (8) above shall be taken to have been given if it has been sent to his last known address.

(15) In this section –

"child" means a person under the age of 16, notwithstanding section 78(6)(*d*) above;
"court" shall be construed in accordance with section 106 above;
"maintenance order" –

(*a*) in England and Wales, means –
(i) any order for the making periodical payments or for the payment of a lump sum which is, or has at any time been, a maintenance order within the meaning of the Attachment of Earnings Act 1971;
(ii) any order under Part III of the Matrimonial and Family Proceedings Act 1984 (overseas divorce) for the making of periodical payments or for the payment of a lump sum;
(*b*) in Scotland, has the meaning assigned by section 106 of the Debtors (Scotland) Act 1987, but disregarding paragraph (*h*) (alimentary bond or agreement);

"the relevant rights", in relation to an order under section 106(2) above, means the right to bring any proceedings, take any steps or do any other thing under or in relation to the order which the Secretary of State could have brought, taken or done apart from any transfer under this section.

Amendments—Access to Justice Act 1999, s 90, Sch 13, para 168.

Defined terms—"child": s 107(15); "claim": s 191; "court": s 107(15); "liable to maintain": s 78(6); "relevant rights": s 107(15).

Scope of provision—This section provides that the order may include an element for the support of a child's parent even though the person liable to maintain the child is not liable to maintain the parent. The section also makes provision for the transfer of the right to receive the payments between the Secretary of State and the dependent parent.

For the purpose of this section, the definition of "child" in s 78(6)(*d*) is replaced by the definition in s 107(15).

108 Reduction of expenditure on income support: certain maintenance orders to be enforceable by the Secretary of State

(1) This section applies where –

(*a*) a person ("the claimant") who is the parent of one or more children is in receipt of income support either in respect of those children or in respect of both himself and those children; and
(*b*) there is in force a maintenance order made against the other parent ("the liable person") –
(i) in favour of the claimant or one or more of the children, or

(ii) in favour of some other person for the benefit of the claimant or one or more of the children;

and in this section "the primary recipient" means the person in whose favour that maintenance order was made.

(2) If, in a case where this section applies, the liable person fails to comply with any of the terms of the maintenance order –

(*a*) the Secretary of State may bring any proceedings or take any other steps to enforce the order that could have been brought or taken by or on behalf of the primary recipient; and

(*b*) any court before which proceedings are brought by the Secretary of State by virtue of paragraph (*a*) above shall have the same powers in connection with those proceedings as it would have had if they had been brought by the primary recipient.

(3) The Secretary of State's powers under this section are exercisable at his discretion and whether or not the primary recipient or any other person consents to their exercise; but any sums recovered by virtue of this section shall be payable to or for the primary recipient, as if the proceedings or steps in question had been brought or taken by him or on his behalf.

(4) The powers conferred on the Secretary of State by subsection (2)(*a*) above include power –

(*a*) to apply for the registration of the maintenance order under –

(i) section 17 of the Maintenance Orders Act 1950;

(ii) section 2 of the Maintenance Orders Act 1958;

(iii) the Civil Jurisdiction and Judgments Act 1982; or

(iv) Council Regulation (EC) No 44/2001 of 22 December 2000 on jurisdiction and the recognition and enforcement of judgments in civil and commercial matters; and

(*b*) to make an application under section 2 of the Maintenance Orders (Reciprocal Enforcement) Act 1972 (application for enforcement in reciprocating country).

(5) Where this section applies, the prescribed person shall in prescribed circumstances give the Secretary of State notice of any application –

(*a*) to alter, vary, suspend, discharge, revoke, revive or enforce the maintenance order in question; or

(*b*) to remit arrears under that maintenance order;

and the Secretary of State shall be entitled to appear and be heard on the application.

(6) Where, by virtue of this section, the Secretary of State commences any proceedings to enforce a maintenance order, he shall, in relation to those proceedings, be treated for the purposes of any enactment or instrument relating to maintenance orders as if he were a person entitled to payment under the maintenance order in question (but shall not thereby become entitled to any such payment).

(7) Where, in any proceedings under this section in England and Wales, the court makes an order for the whole or any part of the arrears due under the maintenance order in question to be paid as a lump sum, the Secretary of State shall inform the Legal Services Commission of the amount of that lump sum if he knows –

(*a*) that the primary recipient either –

PART II

(i) received legal aid under the Legal Aid Act 1974 in connection with the proceedings in which the maintenance order was made, or

(ii) was an assisted party, within the meaning of the Legal Aid Act 1988, in those proceedings, or

(iii) received services funded by the Legal Services Commission as part of the Community Legal Service; and

(*b*) that a sum remains unpaid on account of the contribution required of the primary recipient –

(i) under section 9 of the Legal Aid Act 1974 in respect of those proceedings, or

(ii) under section 16 of the Legal Aid Act 1988 in respect of the costs of his being represented under Part IV of that Act in those proceedings, or

(iii) by virtue of section 10 of the Access to Justice Act 1999 in respect of services funded by the Legal Services Commission as part of the Community Legal Service,

as the case may be.

(8) In this section "maintenance order" has the same meaning as it has in section 107 above but does not include any such order for the payment of a lump sum.

Amendments—Access to Justice Act 1999, s 24, Sch 4, para 48; SI 2001/3929.

Defined terms—"claimant": s 191.

****

116 Legal proceedings

(1) Any person authorised by the Secretary of State in that behalf may conduct any proceedings under any provision of this Act other than section 114 or under any provision of the Jobseekers Act 1995 before a magistrates' court although not a barrister or solicitor.

(2)–(7) ...

Amendments—Jobseekers Act 1995, s 41, Sch 2, para 56; Social Security Contributions (Transfer of Functions, etc) Act 1999, s 1(1), Sch 1, para 21.

"authorised by the Secretary of State" (s 116(1))—An officer may prove his authority to conduct proceedings by producing a certified copy of the original authority. The Documentary Evidence Act 1868 is applied by Secretary of State for Social Services Order 1968, art 5(3).

****

191 Interpretation – general

In this Act, unless the context otherwise requires –

...

"claim" is to be construed in accordance with "claimant";

"claimant" (in relation to contributions under Part I and to benefit under Parts II to IV of the Contributions and Benefits Act) means –

(*a*) a person whose right to be excepted from liability to pay, or to have his liability deferred for, or to be credited with, a contribution, is in question;

(*b*) a person who has claimed benefit;

and includes, in relation to an award or decision a beneficiary under the award or affected by the decision;

"claimant" (in relation to industrial injuries benefit) means a person who has claimed such a benefit and includes –

(*a*) an applicant for a declaration under section 44 above that an accident was or was not an industrial accident; and

(*b*) in relation to an award or decision, a beneficiary under the award or affected by the decision;

...

****

Summary Jurisdiction (Process) Act 1881

4 Service of process of English court in Scotland and of Scotch court in England

Subject to the provisions of this Act, any process issued under the Summary Jurisdiction Acts may, if issued by a court of summary jurisdiction in England and endorsed by a court of summary jurisdiction in Scotland, or issued by a court of summary jurisdiction in Scotland and endorsed by a court of summary jurisdiction in England, be served and executed within the jurisdiction of the endorsing court in like manner as it may be served and executed in the jurisdiction of the issuing court, and that by an officer either of the issuing or of the endorsing court.

For the purposes of this Act –

(1) Any process may be issued and endorsed under the hand of any such person as is declared by this Act to be a court of summary jurisdiction, and may be endorsed upon proof alone of the handwriting of the person issuing it, and such proof may be either on oath or by such solemn declaration as is mentioned in section forty-one of the Summary Jurisdiction Act 1879, or by any like declaration taken in Scotland before a sheriff, justice of the peace, or other magistrate having the authority of a justice of the peace. Such indorsement may be in the form contained in the schedule to this Act annexed, or in a form to the like effect:

(2) Where any process requiring the appearance of a person to answer any information or complaint has been served in pursuance of this section, the court, before issuing a warrant for the apprehension of such person for failure so to appear, shall be satisfied on oath that there is sufficient prima facie evidence in support of such information or complaint:

(3) If the process is to procure the attendance of a witness, the court issuing the process shall be satisfied on oath of the probability that the evidence of such witness will be material, and that the witness will not appear voluntarily without such process, and the witness shall not be subject to any liability for not obeying the process, unless a reasonable amount for his expenses has been paid or tendered to him:

(4) This Act shall not apply to any process requiring the appearance of a person to answer a complaint if issued by an English court of summary jurisdiction for the recovery of a sum of money which is a civil debt within the meaning of the Summary Jurisdiction Act 1879, or if issued by a Scotch court in a case which falls within the definition of "civil jurisdiction" contained in the Summary Procedure Act 1864.

Scope of provision—This section makes provision for reciprocal service of process in England and Scotland. Service of process in relation to maintenance orders is excluded (as separate provision is made by Maintenance Orders Act 1950, s 15). The Act does, however, have application to process for non-molestation orders and occupation orders (Family Law Act 1996, Pt IV) and enforcement of non-monetary orders (Magistrates' Courts Act 1980, s 63).

"form contained in the schedule to this Act" (s 4(1))—A revised form of the indorsement set out in the Schedule (not reproduced here) is as follows:

> Proof by solemn declaration or oath having been produced before me that the name of [*name*] subscribed to this summons (or warrant or order etc) is of the handwriting of the justice of the peace (or sheriff) mentioned in it,
>
> I authorise [ ] to effect the service or execution of it within the county of [ ].
>
> Dated [ ]
>
> [*Signature of Justice of the Peace*]
> Justice of the Peace
> for [ ]

5 Provision as to execution of process

Where a person is apprehended under any process executed in pursuance of this Act, such person shall be forthwith taken to some place within the jurisdiction of the court issuing the process, and be there dealt with as if he had been there apprehended.

A warrant of distress issued in England when endorsed in pursuance of this Act shall be executed in Scotland as if it were a Scotch warrant of poinding and sale, and a Scotch warrant of poinding and sale when endorsed in pursuance of this Act shall be executed in England as if it were an English warrant of distress, and the enactments relating to the said warrants respectively shall apply accordingly, except that any account of the costs and charges in connexion with the execution, or of the money levied thereby or otherwise relating to the execution, shall be made, and any money raised by the execution shall be dealt with in like manner as if the warrant had been executed within the jurisdiction of the court issuing the warrant.

Defined terms—"process": s 8.

****

7 Saving

This Act shall be in addition to and not in derogation of any power existing under any other Act relating to the execution of any warrant or other process in England and Scotland respectively.

8 Definitions

In this Act, unless the context otherwise requires, – The expression "process" includes any summons or warrant of citation to appear either to answer any information or complaint, or as a witness; also any warrant of commitment, any warrant of imprisonment, any warrant of distress, any warrant of poinding and sale, also any order or minute of a court of summary jurisdiction or copy of such order or minute, also an extract decree, and any other document or process, other than a warrant of arrestment, required for any purpose connected with a court of summary jurisdiction to be served or executed.

The expression "sheriff" shall include sheriff substitute.

The expression "court of summary jurisdiction" means any justice of the peace, also any officer or other magistrate having the authority in England or Scotland of a justice of the peace, also in Scotland the sheriff.

The expression "officer of a court of summary jurisdiction" means the constable, officer, or person to whom any process issued by the court is directed, or who is by law required or authorised to serve or execute any process issued by the court.

Amendments—Statute Law Revision Act 1894.

****

Supreme Court Act 1981

ARRANGEMENT OF SECTIONS

PART II
JURISDICTION

****

PART II
JURISDICTION

THE COURT OF APPEAL

15 General jurisdiction of Court of Appeal

(1) The Court of Appeal shall be a superior court of record.

(2) Subject to the provisions of this Act, there shall be exercisable by the Court of Appeal –

(*a*) all such jurisdiction (whether civil or criminal) as is conferred on it by this or any other Act; and
(*b*) all such other jurisdiction (whether civil or criminal) as was exercisable by it immediately before the commencement of this Act.

(3) For all purposes of or incidental to –

(*a*) the hearing and determination of any appeal to the civil division of the Court of Appeal; and
(*b*) the amendment, execution and enforcement of any judgment or order made on such an appeal,

the Court of Appeal shall have all the authority and jurisdiction of the court or tribunal from which the appeal was brought.

(4) It is hereby declared that any provision in this or any other Act which authorises or requires the taking of any steps for the execution or enforcement of a judgment or order of the High Court applies in relation to a judgment or order of the civil division of the Court of Appeal as it applies in relation to a judgment or order of the High Court.

Scope of provision—This section establishes the general jurisdiction of the Court of Appeal. For the procedural regime governing appeals to the Court of Appeal see Procedural Guide 75.

"for all purposes of or incidental to" (s 15(3))—In relation to the hearing and determination of an appeal, this does not include maintenance pending suit where the appeal is subsequent to decree absolute (see *Cavendish-Bentinck v Cavendish-Bentinck* [1949] P 203, [1948] 2 All ER 285, CA).

"all the authority and jurisdiction" (s 15(3))—This includes a power conferred on the High Court after the order being appealed was made (see *Attorney-General v Vernazza* [1960] AC 965, [1960] 3 WLR 466).

PART II

16 Appeals from High Court

(1) Subject as otherwise provided by this or any other Act (and in particular to the provision in section 13(2)(*a*) of the Administration of Justice Act 1969 excluding appeals to the Court of Appeal in cases where leave to appeal from the High Court directly to the House of Lords is granted under Part II of that Act), or as provided by any order made by the Lord Chancellor under section 56(1) of the Access to Justice Act 1999 the Court of Appeal shall have jurisdiction to hear and determine appeals from any judgment or order of the High Court.

(2) An appeal from a judgment or order of the High Court when acting as a prize court shall not be to the Court of Appeal, but shall be to Her Majesty in Council in accordance with the Prize Acts 1864 to 1944.

Amendments—SI 2000/1071.

Scope of provision—Subject to certain exceptions, this section gives the Court of Appeal power to hear any appeal from a High Court judgment or order; for the procedure governing appeals to the Court of Appeal, see CPR 1998, Pt 52. This section must be read in conjunction with CPR 1998, r 52.3 which require permission (leave) to appeal for all appeals save for a few limited exceptions.

"judgment or order"—This phrase includes a decree (Supreme Court Act 1981, s 151(1)), and a decree absolute of nullity (*Whitehead v Whitehead* [1962] 3 WLR 884, [1962] 3 All ER 800). Dismissal of an application to postpone a trial may be appealed, but will require permission (*Maxwell v Keun* [1928] 1 KB 645). The grant or refusal of an adjournment is peculiarly a matter for the discretion of the judge with which the Court of Appeal is unlikely to interfere (*Re C (Abused Children: Orders)* [1992] FCR 57, but see also *Re C (Minors) (Parental Rights)* [1992] 2 All ER 86). An appeal cannot be pursued against the reasons for a decision, only against the judgment or order (*Lake v Lake* [1955] P 336, [1955] WLR 145), but it is possible to appeal findings of fact made after a split trial (*Re B (Split Hearings: Jurisdiction* [2000] 1 FLR 334). Appeals against ex parte orders should not be made as they are provisional and expected to be revisited by the court (*WEA Records Ltd v Visions Channel 4 Ltd* [1983] 1 WLR 721, [1983] 2 All ER 589).

17 Applications for new trial

(1) Where any cause or matter, or any issue in any cause or matter, has been tried in the High Court, any application for a new trial thereof, or to set aside a verdict, finding or judgment therein, shall be heard and determined by the Court of Appeal except where rules of court made in pursuance of subsection (2) provide otherwise.

(2) As regards cases where the trial was by a judge alone and no error of the court at the trial is alleged, or any prescribed class of such cases, rules of court may provide that any such application as is mentioned in subsection (1) shall be heard and determined by the High Court.

(3) Nothing in this section shall alter the practice in bankruptcy.

Scope of provision—CPR 1998, r 52.10 sets out the powers of the Court of Appeal on hearing an appeal and specifically provides the power to order a new trial or hearing (r 52.10(2)). No rules have been made pursuant to s 17(2). Therefore any application for a new trial must be made to the Court of Appeal (see also *B-T v B-T (Divorce: Procedure)* [1990] 2 FLR 1). It is important to distinguish between orders which are capable of review by the original court: for example ex parte orders (see notes to SCA 1981, s 18), interim orders and orders where there has been an error on the face (which may be corrected in accordance with CPR 1998, r 40.12); and those orders which are covered by this section, where an appeal must be made to obtain a fresh hearing. For the purpose of considering the requirement of permission to appeal under Access to Justice Act 1999, s 54, an application for a new trial is treated as an appeal to the Court of Appeal.

18 Restrictions on appeals to Court of Appeal

(1) No appeal shall lie to the Court of Appeal –

(*a*) except as provided by the Administration of Justice Act 1960, from any judgment of the High Court in any criminal cause or matter;

(*b*) from any order of the High Court or any other court or tribunal allowing an extension of time for appealing from a judgment or order;

(*c*) from any order, judgment or decision of the High Court or any other court or tribunal which, by virtue of any provision (however expressed) of this or any other Act, is final;

(*d*) from a decree absolute of divorce or nullity of marriage, by a party who, having had time and opportunity to appeal from the decree nisi on which that decree was founded, has not appealed from the decree nisi;

(*e*), (*f*) (*repealed*)

(*g*) except as provided by Part I of the Arbitration Act 1996, from any decision of the High Court under that Part;

(*h*) (*repealed*)

(1A)–(2) (*repealed*)

Amendments—CA 1989, s 108(5), Sch 13, para 45(1); Courts and Legal Services Act 1990, s 7(1)–(3), Sch 20; Arbitration Act 1996, s 107(1), Sch 3, para 37(2); Civil Procedure Act 1997, s 10, Sch 2, para 1(1), (2); Access to Justice Act 1999, s 106, Sch 15.

Scope of provision—This section sets out the restrictions which apply to the apparently wide-ranging right of appeal provided by s 16. In most cases, an appeal may be made only with permission (see CPR 1998, r 52.3). There is no appeal against the refusal of permission to appeal by a court below (where the court below would have been exercising an appellate jurisdiction, for example a judge from a district judge, see *Bulled v Khayat and Another* [2002] EWCA Civ 804 and *Slot v Isaac* [2002] EWCA Civ 481, [2002] All ER (D) 197 (Apr)).

"extension of time for appealing" (s 18(1)(*b*))—There is no appeal against an order allowing an extension of time for appealing, but the Court of Appeal does have jurisdiction to hear an appeal against the refusal of an application for an extension of time (*Rickards v Rickards* [1990] Fam 194, [1989] 3 WLR 748).

"decree absolute" (s 18(1)(*d*))—A decree absolute should not be made if there is an appeal pending (*Lloyd-Davies v Lloyd-Davies* [1947] P 53, [1947] 1 All ER 161; *Everitt v Everitt* [1948] 2 All ER 545).

Costs—The Court of Appeal may interfere on an order for costs where the judge has not acted judicially, without exercising his discretion at all or without material with which to exercise his discretion (see *Jones v McKie* [1964] 1 WLR 960, [1964] 2 All ER 842; *Hellyer v Sheriff of Yorkshire* [1975] Ch 16, [1974] 2 WLR 844; *Alltrans Express Ltd v CVA Holdings Ltd* [1984] 1 WLR 394, [1984] 1 All ER 685; *Scherer v Counting Instruments Ltd* [1986] 1 WLR 615, [1986] 2 All ER 529; *Taylor v UKF Fertilisers Ltd and Harvey Plant Ltd* (1988) *The Independent*, 14 November). There is a right of appeal where the appeal is genuinely as to other issues (*Crystall v Crystall* [1963] 1 WLR 564 [1963] 2 All ER 330), even where the outcome to those other issues is unsuccessful (*Wheeler v Somerfield* [1966] 2 QB 94, [1966] 2 WLR 1006).

Ex parte orders—The Court of Appeal will not entertain appeals against ex parte orders; the proper course is to apply, if possible to the same judge, to vary or discharge the order (*WEA Records Ltd v Visions Channel 4 Ltd* [1983] 1 WLR 721, [1983] 2 All ER 589; *Re P (A Minor) (Ex Parte Interim Residence Order)* [1993] 1 FLR 915).

Consent orders—In *Re R (Contact: Consent Order)* [1995] 1 FLR 123, the Court of Appeal held that, where a mother gave co… to an order for contact after the judge had warned of a risk of costs being ordered agai… this (being a criticism of the trial judge), such an order was for the Court of Appeal, and … the court of first instance, to set aside (distinguishing *Re F (A Minor) (Custody: Conse…der: Procedure)* [1992] 1 FLR 561). Bad advice is not a good basis to appeal a co…er (*Tibbs v Dick* [1998] 2 FLR 1118).

Pe…on to appeal—By virtue of Access to Justice Act 1999, s 54, permission to appeal to the … of Appeal is required in all cases, save for a few limited exceptions (as prescribed by CPR …98, r 52.3). The application for permission should normally be made to the trial judge and, if refused, thereafter to the Court of Appeal. Full details of the procedure are contained within *Practice Direction – Appeals* which supplements CPR 1998, Pt 52 (set out in Part V of this work).

THE HIGH COURT

General jurisdiction

19 General jurisdiction of High Court

(1) The High Court shall be a superior court of record.

(2) Subject to the provisions of this Act, there shall be exercisable by the High Court –

- (*a*) all such jurisdiction (whether civil or criminal) as is conferred on it by this or any other Act; and
- (*b*) all such other jurisdiction (whether civil or criminal) as was exercisable by it immediately before the commencement of this Act (including jurisdiction conferred on a judge of the High Court by any statutory provision).

(3) Any jurisdiction of the High Court shall be exercised only by a single judge of that court, except in so far as it is –

- (*a*) by or by virtue of rules of court or any other statutory provision required to be exercised by a divisional court; or
- (*b*) by rules of court made exercisable by a master, district judge or other officer of the court, or by any other person.

(4) The specific mention elsewhere in this Act of any jurisdiction covered by subsection (2) shall not derogate from the generality of that subsection.

Scope of provision—Subject to the provisions of this Act, s 19(2) prescribes in general terms the jurisdiction of the High Court by defining its statutory and non-statutory jurisdiction. By virtue of s 19(2)(*a*), the High Court is empowered to exercise all the jurisdiction conferred by this Act or any Act passed after it. Thus, the High Court has jurisdiction as a court of first instance and as a court of appeal from decisions of family proceedings courts. The High Court may hear and determine family proceedings commenced in the High Court or transferred to the High Court from the county court in accordance with the Children (Allocation of Proceedings) Order 1991, and may hear and determine family proceedings appeals from family proceedings courts (see s 28). FPR 1991, r 4.22 governs appeals from a district judge to High Court judge in family proceedings. Other appeals from a district judge must be made in accordance with RSC Ord 58.

High Court—For the constitution and divisions of the High Court, see s 4 et seq.

PART II

"all such other jurisdiction ..." (s 19(2)(*b*))—Subject to the provisions of this Act, the High Court has retained all such jurisdiction, whether statutory or otherwise, which was exerciseable by it immediately before the commencement of this Act. This includes the "inherent jurisdiction" of the court, which has been exerciseable by the superior court from the earliest days of the common law.

Inherent jurisdiction—The exercise of the court's powers under its inherent jurisdiction is unrestricted and unlimited, except where it has been specifically curtailed by statute. It is derived from the very nature of the court as a superior court of law and not from any statute or rule of law. It invests the court with power to maintain its authority and, as a residual source of power, to deal with and act effectively on any matter when it is just and equitable to do so. It can be exercised summarily, and may be invoked by or against any person, irrespective whether they are party to the proceedings. Examples of situations where, in recent years, the court has assumed and exercised its inherent jurisdiction and made orders and declarations, and given directions, include cases relating to the administration or withdrawal of medical treatment, particularly in cases where the sterilisation of an adult mentally disabled person is considered necessary, and in cases of persistent vegetative state (PVS).

Writ ne exeat regno—The provisions of s 19(2)(*b*) subsume the High Court's jurisdiction to grant this prerogative writ, whereby a person may be prevented from leaving the jurisdiction of the court. Before the writ may be granted, the conditions set out in Debtors Act 1869, s 6 must be satisfied, and may be summarised as follows: (*a*) the action must be one in which, if brought before 1869, the defendant would have been liable for arrest; (*b*) the applicant must show that he has a good cause of action against the defendant for at least £50; (*c*) there must be strong evidence for believing that the defendant is about to leave England unless he is arrested; and (*d*) there must be evidence that the defendant's absence would materially prejudice the applicant in the prosecution of his case. It should be noted, however, that the issue of the writ is discretionary, and the standard and burden of proof imposed on the applicant is extremely high. The court will require convincing evidence, so that it can be sure that it is right to grant the writ. It will not generally be granted as an ancillary remedy to enforce a *Mareva* injunction or an *Anton Piller* order (see *Allied Arab Bank Ltd v Hajjar* [1988] QB 787 and *Al Nahkel for Contracting and Trading v Lowe* [1986] QB 235). Although the relief was granted in *Thaha v Thaha* [1987] 2 FLR 142 by reason of the particular facts of the case, it is submitted that the writ is unlikely to be issued for the purpose of supporting or pursuing ancillary relief in matrimonial proceedings or for the purpose of enforcing an injunction obtained under Matrimonial Causes Act 1973, s 37(1). For a fuller consideration of the issue concerning the writ, see *Felton v Callis* [1969] 1 QB 200 and *Emergency Remedies in the Family Courts* (Family Law).

****

Other particular fields of jurisdiction

****

29 Orders of mandamus, prohibition and certiorari

(1) Subject to subsection (3A), the High Court shall have jurisdiction to make orders of mandamus, prohibition and certiorari in those classes of cases in which it had power to do so immediately before the commencement of this Act.

(2) Every such order shall be final, subject to any right of appeal therefrom.

(3), (3A) ...

(4) The power of the High Court under any enactment to require justices of the peace or a judge or officer of a county court to do any act relating to the duties of their respective offices, or to require a magistrates' court to state a case for the opinion of the High Court, in any case where the High Court formerly had by virtue of any enactment jurisdiction to make a rule absolute, or an order, for any of those purposes, shall be exercisable by order of mandamus.

(5), (6) ...

Scope of provision—The procedure for an application for judicial review is contained within CPR 1998, Pt 54. In judicial review proceedings, the court can grant a mandatory order (formerly mandamus), a prohibiting order (formerly prohibition) or a quashing order (formerly certiorari) (Supreme Court Act 1981, s 31(1), CPR 1998, r 54.2); it also has power to grant declarations and injunctions (SCA 1981, s 31, CPR 1998, r 54.3). Under SCA 1981, s 31 and CPR 1998, r 54.3, an application for a mandatory order, a prohibiting order or a quashing order must be by way of an application for judicial review; however, a declaration or injunction may be obtained in proceedings for judicial review or in other proceedings.

30 Injunctions to restrain persons from acting in offices in which they are not entitled to act

(1) Where a person not entitled to do so acts in an office to which this section applies, the High Court may –

(*a*) grant an injunction restraining him from so acting; and
(*b*) if the case so requires, declare the office to be vacant.

(2) This section applies to any substantive office of a public nature and permanent character which is held under the Crown or which has been created by any statutory provision or royal charter.

Scope of provision—An application under this section must be made by way of judicial review in accordance with the provisions of CPR 1998, Pt 54. The application may be made in conjunction with an application for any prerogative order, ie a mandatory, prohibiting or quashing order (CPR 1998, r 54.3).

31 Application for judicial review

(1) An application to the High Court for one or more of the following forms of relief, namely –

(*a*) an order of mandamus, prohibition or certiorari;
(*b*) a declaration or injunction under subsection (2); or
(*c*) an injunction under section 30 restraining a person not entitled to do so from acting in an office to which that section applies,

shall be made in accordance with rules of court by a procedure to be known as an application for judicial review.

(2) A declaration may be made or an injunction granted under this subsection in any case where an application for judicial review, seeking that relief, has been made and the High Court considers that, having regard to –

(*a*) the nature of the matters in respect of which relief may be granted by orders of mandamus, prohibition or certiorari;
(*b*) the nature of the persons and bodies against whom relief may be granted by such orders; and
(*c*) all the circumstances of the case,

it would be just and convenient for the declaration to be made or for the injunction to be granted, as the case may be.

(3) No application for judicial review shall be made unless the leave of the High Court has been obtained in accordance with rules of court; and the court shall not grant leave to make such an application unless it considers that the applicant has a sufficient interest in the matter to which the application relates.

(4) On an application for judicial review the High Court may award damages to the applicant if –

(*a*) he has joined with his application a claim for damages arising from any matter to which the application relates; and

(*b*) the court is satisfied that, if the claim had been made in an action begun by the applicant at the time of making his application, he would have been awarded damages.

(5) If, on an application for judicial review seeking an order of certiorari, the High Court quashes the decision to which the application relates, the High Court may remit the matter to the court, tribunal or authority concerned, with a direction to reconsider it and reach a decision in accordance with the findings of the High Court.

(6) Where the High Court considers that there has been undue delay in making an application for judicial review, the court may refuse to grant –

(*a*) leave for the making of the application; or

(*b*) any relief sought on the application,

if it considers that the granting of the relief sought would be likely to cause substantial hardship to, or substantially prejudice the rights of, any person or would be detrimental to good administration.

(7) Subsection (6) is without prejudice to any enactment or rule of court which has the effect of limiting the time within which an application for judicial review may be made.

Scope of provision—All applications for judicial review must be made in accordance with CPR 1998, Pt 54. CPR 1998, r 54.2 states that the procedure of judicial review must be used where the claimant is seeking a mandatory order (mandamus), a prohibiting order (prohibition), a quashing order (certiorari), or an injunction (under SCA 1981 restraining a person acting in an office in which he is not entitled). Further, r 54.3 provides that judicial review may also be used to claim a declaration or an injunction. The remedies, other than damages, may be claimed as alternatives or in addition to any other relief (CPR 1998, r 54.3). An application for judicial review may proceed only after permission has been granted (SCA 1981, s 31; CPR 1998, r 54.4).

There is an overlap between the supervisory jurisdiction of the High Court in judicial review proceedings and the inherent jurisdiction of the High Court to make orders in respect of children and incompetent adults. Where the court's task is to come to a decision for and on behalf of the child or incompetent adult, their welfare should be the court's paramount consideration and hence the inherent jurisdiction rather than judicial review would be the most appropriate procedure (*A (A Patient) v A Health Authority* [2002] EWHC 18, [2002] 1 FLR 845 at para [113]).

Where there is a right of appeal to the Care Standards Tribunal, judicial review is not appropriate (*R(M) v London Borough of Bromley* [2002] EWCA Civ 1113, [2002] 2 FLR 802). Judicial review is limited to a review of the local authority decision and not to a detailed examination of the evidence.

"just and convenient" (s 31(2))—The High Court has power to grant a declaration or injunction on an application for judicial review. Unlike the prerogative orders (mandatory, prohibiting or quashing orders), a declaration or injunction is available not only on an application for judicial review, but may also be obtained in other proceedings (CPR 1998, r 54.3).

"sufficient interest" (s 31(3))—The applicant for judicial review must have sufficient interest in the matter to which the application relates in order to proceed. "Mere busybodies do not have sufficient interest" (*Inland Revenue Commissioners v Federation of Self-employed and Small Businesses Ltd* [1981] 2 All ER 93 at 108B; see also *Council of Civil Service Unions v Minister for the Civil Service* [1984] 3 All ER 935 at 949F).

"undue delay" (s 31(6))—If the court considers that there has been undue delay in making the application, it may refuse leave to move for judicial review. This provision must be read in conjunction with the time limitations imposed by CPR 1998, r 54.5, namely that the application must be made promptly and in any event within three months from the date when the grounds for the application first arose and the time limit cannot be extended by agreement of the parties.

****

Powers

****

37 Powers of High Court with respect to injunctions and receivers

(1) The High Court may by order (whether interlocutory or final) grant an injunction or appoint a receiver in all cases in which it appears to the court to be just and convenient to do so.

(2) Any such order may be made either unconditionally or on such terms and conditions as the court thinks just.

(3) The power of the High Court under subsection (1) to grant an interlocutory injunction restraining a party to any proceedings from removing from the jurisdiction of the High Court, or otherwise dealing with, assets located within that jurisdiction shall be exercisable in cases where that party is, as well as in cases where he is not, domiciled, resident or present within that jurisdiction.

(4), (5) ...

"whether interlocutory or final" (s 37(1))—These words confirm the practice which existed before the Act, and do not restrict the power to grant an injunction after judgment to assist in the process of enforcement. Thus, in family cases, an injunction can be obtained to prevent a respondent from disposing of assets to defeat enforcement (see *Orwell Steel (Erection and Fabrication) Ltd v Asphalt and Tarmac (UK) Ltd* [1984] 1 WLR 1097, [1985] 3 All ER 747; *Roche v Roche* (1981) Fam Law 243; *Shipman v Shipman* [1991] 1 FLR 250).

Civil Procedure Act 1997, s 7—This section provides as follows:

"7 Power of courts to make orders for preserving evidence, etc

(1) The court may make an order under this section for the purpose of securing, in the case of any existing or proposed proceedings in the court –

(*a*) the preservation of evidence which is or may be relevant, or
(*b*) the preservation of property which is or may be the subject-matter of the proceedings or as to which any question arises or may arise in the proceedings.

(2) A person who is, or appears to the court likely to be, a party to proceedings in the court may make an application for such an order.

(3) Such an order may direct any person to permit any person described in the order, or secure that any person so described is permitted –

(*a*) to enter premises in England and Wales, and
(*b*) while on the premises, to take in accordance with the terms of the order any of the following steps.

(4) Those steps are –

(*a*) to carry out a search for or inspection of anything described in the order, and
(*b*) to make or obtain a copy, photograph, sample or other record of anything so described.

(5) The order may also direct the person concerned –

(*a*) to provide any person described in the order, or secure that any person so described is provided, with any information or article described in the order, and
(*b*) to allow any person described in the order, or secure that any person so described is allowed, to retain for safe keeping anything described in the order.

(6) An order under this section is to have effect subject to such conditions as are specified in the order.

(7) This section does not affect any right of a person to refuse to do anything on the ground that to do so might tend to expose him or his spouse to proceedings for an offence or for the recovery of a penalty.

(8) In this section –

"court" means the High Court, and
"premises" includes any vehicle;

and an order under this section may describe anything generally, whether by reference to a class or otherwise."

This section does no more than clarify the statutory basis of the court's power to grant "Freezing injunctions" and "Search orders". Most judges took the view that SCA 1981, s 37 was sufficient but, for the avoidance of doubt and because of the Draconian nature of these orders, it was considered necessary to clarify the statutory basis: hence CPA 1997, s 7.

"Search order"—A search order is provided for by CPR 1998, r 25.1(1)(*h*) and was formerly often referred to as an *Anton Piller* order. It is an interlocutory order which achieves disclosure and protection of documentary and real evidence. It has been described by Lord Denning MR as a "search warrant" (*Anton Piller KG v Manufacturing Processes Ltd* [1976] Ch 55, [1976] 1 All ER 779). It is a drastic order and will only be granted in the most exceptional circumstances where there is an extremely strong prima facie case of vital evidence being destroyed or otherwise disposed of and thus causing prejudice to the applicant's case and defeating justice. It is normally granted ex parte. The form of the order is mandatory and is designed for immediate execution. The search order is usually accompanied by a freezing injunction freezing the defendant's bank accounts and restraining him from making any disposition of his assets (see **Freezing injunctions** below). In matrimonial proceedings, it is very much an order of last resort, where all other methods of seeking the necessary information have failed. For example, where a wife maintained that her husband had failed to make full disclosure of his financial position and that he was a man of substantial means and had secreted his assets abroad, the court was prepared to make a search order (*Kepa v Kepa* (1983) FLR 515). Where a party to matrimonial proceedings seeks documents which are not themselves the subject matter of the proceedings, the Family Division still has jurisdiction to grant a search order provided that the applicant has a strong prima facie case that the relevant documents are essential for his case and are at serious risk of being removed or destroyed (*Emanuel v Emanuel* [1982] 1 WLR 669). The order may permit a search of the defendant's premises and seizure of documents or other items found there which might form evidence in the applicant's action or proposed action against the defendant. The procedure must not be used oppressively. In *Burgess v Burgess* [1996] 2 FLR 34, the husband obtained a search order, but the search yielded no relevant evidence; he was ordered to pay the wife's costs on the indemnity basis, and the court reiterated that, in family proceedings, search orders are to be used only in extreme or exceptional circumstances; see also *A v A* [1997] Fam Law 301, in which the application was refused.

Procedure for Search order—CPR 1998, r 25.3(1) provides that the court can grant an interim remedy on an application made without notice if it appears that there are good reasons for not giving notice. See further PD25, para 4. Application is to the High Court and in family cases should be in the Family Division. A county court (save for the Patents county court) has no power to make a search order (County Courts Remedies Regulations 1991, reg 3(2)(*b*)). If in the county court, an application for a search order (which can be made at any stage of the proceedings) becomes necessary, those proceedings should be transferred to the High Court. The procedure is now governed by CPR 1998, Pt 25. See *Practice Direction – Interim Injunctions* (PD25), set out in Part V of this work.

Effect of Search order—The search order is a draconian remedy and should be used with the utmost caution. An order made without notice must be given the earliest practicable return day. The court considering whether or not to make the order must strike a balance between the applicant's need for a remedy for a breach of his civil rights and the requirements of justice that a defendant should not be deprived of his property without being heard (*Columbia Picture Industries v Robinson* [1987] Ch 38, [1986] 3 WLR 542). The order must contain a provision for the defendant to apply to vary or discharge the order, even though this will be of little value because, when the order is served, he is under an obligation to allow entry and search of his premises and removal of the documents and items specified in the order. If he fails to comply, he risks the sanction of a committal order for contempt of court (*Wardle Fabrics Ltd v G Myristis Ltd* [1984] FSR 263). For the form of search order see the Annex to PD25.

Duty of disclosure—The applicant is under a duty to make a full and frank disclosure to the court in his affidavit in support of an application for a search order (*Lock International plc v Beswick* [1989] 1 WLR 1268, [1989] 3 All ER 373), even where the material comes to his knowledge after the order was obtained (*O'Regan v Iambic Productions Ltd* (1989) 139 NLJ 1378). Failure to do so is likely to lead to the order being discharged without consideration of the merits (*Manor Electronics Ltd v Dickson* [1988] RPC 618).

Safeguards for interests of defendant—See PD25. The order must be served by a "supervising solicitor" and carried out in his presence and under his supervision. The supervising solicitor should be an experienced solicitor, having some familiarity with the operation of search orders, who is not a member or employee of the firm acting for the applicant. The evidence in support of the application should include the identity and experience of the proposed supervising solicitor.

Search and seizure of documents and articles—Where a search order is executed at business premises, it should be conducted by the supervising solicitor named in the order, and it should be carried out in the presence of the defendant or a person appearing to be a responsible employee of the defendant. The order may only be served on a weekday between 9.30 am and 5.30 pm. When the supervising solicitor and the applicant's solicitor attend at the premises to execute the order, the defendant (or any other person appearing to be in control of the premises) may seek legal advice, and may apply to the court to vary or discharge the order, provided that he does so at once. See further PD25.

Discharge of Search order—An application for variation or discharge of a search order must be made immediately to the court which made the order (see the form of order in PD25). It should not be made ex parte. The applicant must be given notice (*Hallmark Cards Inc v Image Arts Ltd* [1977] FSR 150). The application should be accompanied by sworn evidence. So far as practicable, any application for the discharge or variation of the order should be dealt with effectively on the inter partes return date. If the order is discharged on the return date, the judge should always consider whether it is appropriate that he should assess damages at once and direct immediate payment by the applicant. It is not possible to appeal against the order until the application to set aside has been made and refused (*WEA Records Ltd v Visions Channel 4 Ltd* [1983] 1 WLR 721, [1983] 3 All ER 589).

Jurisdiction (s 37(3))—Interlocutory applications for freezing injunctions and directions as to dealing with assets outside the jurisdiction should generally be dealt with in the High Court. However, county courts do have jurisdiction to grant freezing injunctions when exercising jurisdiction in family proceedings (County Court Remedies Regulations 1991, reg 3(3)) and application can therefore be made to a divorce county court if the nature of the issues raised are suitable.

Freezing injunctions (s 37(3))—The term "freezing injunction" is the modern term for a "Mareva injunction"; see CPR 1998, r 25.1(*f*). Section 37(3) embodies in statute the practice explained in *Mareva Compania Naviera SA v International Bulk Carriers SA* [1980] 1 All ER 213. Initially, the practice was confined to cases where there was a risk of assets being transferred abroad but the practice of granting freezing injunctions has been extended to cover any situation where there are grounds for believing that the defendant may transfer or dissipate assets, whether inside or outside the jurisdiction, with a view to defeating the applicant's claim.

Procedure for Freezing injunctions—An application for a freezing injunction is made without notice, supported by an affidavit (CPR 1998, Pt 25 and PD25). It should be accompanied by the divorce petition (if there is one) and the documents set out in FPR 1991, r 2.6(3) and (5). The affidavit should be concise and set out the material facts to justify the claim; it should not contain detailed arguments as to the merits of the claim. The application should be issued in the High Court unless the subject matter of the application makes it more suitable for disposal in a county court. It may be made in proposed or pending divorce proceedings, followed by an application inter partes. The without notice application is heard before a judge in chambers. Where practicable, the papers to be used on the application should be lodged with the judge at least two hours before the hearing (see PD25, para 4.3). The applicant and any supporting witnesses will usually attend the hearing, but the judge will normally rely on the affidavit evidence. Examples of freezing injunctions are annexed to PD25. In practice it is essential to draft the order being sought for consideration by the judge. A date will then be fixed for an inter partes return day, which must be at least three clear days after the date of service of the application on the respondent (CPR 1998, r 23.7). Personal service is required in respect of any without notice injunction order granted (CPR 1998, Sch 1, RSC Ord 45, r 7); personal service is not required in respect of the application for the injunction, but judges are reluctant to grant an injunction unless they are satisfied that the respondent has been served. It is good practice to serve the respondent with all the accompanying documents at the same time as service of the without notice order, such as the affidavit in support of the application. It is also wise to serve the without notice order on all relevant parties, eg banks and building societies. The parties should attend at court for the inter partes hearing, together with any witnesses. The hearing is before a judge in open court. So far as practicable, any application for the discharge or variation of the order should be dealt with effectively on the return date for the inter partes hearing. The court will prepare the injunction order and penal notice and deliver them to the applicant for service on the respondent (FPR 1991, r 2.43(1)). The order should be served on all relevant parties, such as banks and building societies. The injunction order should be personally served on the respondent (CPR 1998, Sch 1, RSC Ord 45, r 7). The applicant should file in court an affidavit of service, including exhibits, since although it is not strictly required at this stage, it is required for enforcement proceedings (CPR 1998, Sch 1, RSC Ord 41, r 9). If the court accepts an undertaking from the respondent rather than making an injunction, the undertaking should be recorded on Form D787.

Principles on which a Freezing injunction is made—The principles on which a freezing injunction is made were set out by Lord Denning MR in *Third Chandris Shipping Corporation v Unimarine SA* [1979] QB 645, [1979] 2 All ER 972. They include a duty on the applicant to make full and frank disclosure of all matters in his knowledge which are material for the judge to know. If material non-disclosure is established at a later stage, the court has a discretion to discharge the order. The applicant must make proper inquiries before making the application, and this duty applies to any additional facts he would have known if he had made such inquiries (*Bank Mellat v Nikpour* [1985] FSR 87). The applicant must give particulars of his claim against the respondent, stating his grounds and the amount involved, and fairly state the points made against the applicant by the respondent. The applicant must depose to some grounds for believing that there is a risk of the assets being removed or dissipated before the judgment or award is satisfied (*Z Ltd v A-Z and AA-LL* [1982] QB 558, [1982] 1 All ER 556). The applicant must give an undertaking in damages in case he fails in his claim or the injunction turns out to have been unjustified. The undertakings to be given by the applicant are set out in the Annex to PD25. An applicant should be required, in an appropriate case, to support his cross-undertaking in damages by a payment into court or the provision of a bond by an insurance company. Alternatively, the judge may order a payment by way of such security to the applicant's solicitor to be held by the solicitor as an officer of the court pending further order. If a freezing injunction is discharged on the return date, the judge should always consider whether it is appropriate for him to assess damages at once and direct immediate payment by the applicant). A legally aided person may be granted an injunction although his undertaking may be of little value (*Allen v Jambo Holdings Ltd* [1980] 2 All ER 502). Where the injunction affects third parties, the applicant may have to give an undertaking to indemnify those third parties against all expenses reasonably incurred in complying with the order.

Form of Freezing injunction—PD 25 sets out specimen orders for freezing injunctions. The injunction may, in its widest form, include an order that the respondent disclose all his assets, which include chattels and choses in action (*CBS UK Ltd v Lambert* [1983] Ch 37, [1982] 3 All ER 237; *Z Ltd v A-Z and AA-LL* [1982] QB 558), but at the inter partes hearing the court may consider whether the disclosure order against the respondent should be discharged (*Arab Monetary Fund v Hashim* [1989] 3 All ER 466). Where appropriate, and especially where the injunction relates to the rights of third parties, the injunction should extend to the specified maximum amount claimed by the applicant. Where there is a risk of the respondent disposing of money owed to him, the court may, with the approval of the creditor, order that sum to be paid into court or into an account frozen by the injunction (*Bank Mellat v Kazmi* [1989] 2 WLR 613, [1989] 1 All ER 925). The injunction takes effect, from the moment it is made, in respect of every asset of the respondent covered by the order. It is desirable to fix a return date when the continuation can be considered inter partes and third parties can have the opportunity to be heard. The order must be carefully drafted so as to make clear the date on which the order begins and ends. Where the court is concerned with injunctions imposing serious restrictions on the activities of litigants, the "slip rule" will be invoked to remedy a defect in the order only in exceptional circumstances (*Langley v Langley* [1994] 1 FLR 383).

Notice of Freezing injunction—Notice of the injunction should be given to banks and other financial institutions, where it is believed that the respondent has assets, and they must do what they can to preserve such assets; otherwise, they risk being in contempt of court. The applicant

must give to the bank as much detail as possible about the account number, branch number and so forth. The specimen order set out in PD25 contains a clause which provides that the injunction does not prevent any bank from exercising any right of set-off it may have in respect of any facility which it gave to the respondent before it was notified of the order, and this proviso should be included where appropriate (*Oceanica Castelana Armadora SA v Mineralimportexport, The Theotokos* [1983] 1 WLR 1302, [1983] 2 All ER 65). The bank is entitled to apply for a variation to enable it to exercise any right of facilities granted before it receives notice of the injunction and, in order to save court time, a proviso to that effect should be included in the injunction (*Oceanica Castelana Armadora SA v Mineralimportexport, The Theotokos* [1983] 1 WLR 1302, [1983] 2 All ER 65).

Respondent's access to assets—The respondent should be allowed access to sums for his normal living expenses, and the injunction should specify these. Those sums may include sums for medical expenses and legal expenses where appropriate.

Assets outside the jurisdiction—By virtue of Civil Jurisdiction and Judgments Act 1982, s 25(1), it is clear that a freezing injunction can cover assets worldwide, even though the respondent is outside the jurisdiction (*Babanaft International Co SA v Bassatne* [1989] 2 WLR 232, [1989] 1 All ER 433; *Republic of Haiti and Others v Duvaliers and Others* [1989] 2 WLR 261, [1989] 1 All ER 456), provided that the personal effect of such an order is limited to the particular respondents against whom it was granted. A worldwide injunction will only be granted in exceptional circumstances and should be subject to strict undertakings and provisos to prevent the injunction from being more oppressive to the respondent than beneficial to the applicant. The specimen order contained in PD25 should be used for an injunction to prevent the disposal of assets worldwide. The specimen order contains the undertakings to be given to the court by the applicant.

In matrimonial disputes, an injunction should not extend to all the assets of the other party. In a case where the petitioner would not be awarded all the assets of the other party, the injunction should be limited to the size of the fund the petitioner could reasonably regard as being in issue (*Ghoth v Ghoth* [1992] 2 FLR 300). An injunction should be limited to the extent to which it is enforceable.

Limitations—A freezing injunction should not be granted unless the applicant can show a substantial case for saying that, unless it is granted, there will be a serious risk of the assets which might otherwise be available to meet judgment being dissipated (*Behbehani v Salem (Note)* [1989] 1 WLR 723).

No jurisdiction to grant Freezing injunctions in support of enforcement of assessments under Child Support Act 1991—The High Court has no jurisdiction to grant a freezing injunction in support of, and as ancillary to, the enforcement procedure for maintenance assessments provided for by the Child Support Act 1991 (*Department of Social Security v Butler* [1996] 1 FLR 65).

"or otherwise dealing with" (s 37(3))—These words include disposing of, selling or charging (see *CBS UK Ltd v Lambert* [1983] Ch 37, [1982] 3 All ER 237).

Writ ne exeat regno—This writ cannot be issued for the purpose of enforcing a freezing injunction (see further under s 19 above).

Appeals—Permission to appeal to the Court of Appeal from an order granting or refusing an interlocutory injunction is required pursuant to CPR 1998, r 52.3.

****

39 Execution of instrument by person nominated by High Court

(1) Where the High Court has given or made a judgment or order directing a person to execute any conveyance, contract or other document, or to indorse any negotiable instrument, then, if that person –

(*a*) neglects or refuses to comply with the judgment or order; or
(*b*) cannot after reasonable inquiry be found,

the High Court may, on such terms and conditions, if any, as may be just, order that the conveyance, contract or other document shall be executed, or that the negotiable instrument shall be indorsed, by such person as the court may nominate for that purpose.

(2) A conveyance, contract, document or instrument executed or indorsed in pursuance of an order under this section shall operate, and be for all purposes available, as if it had been executed or indorsed by the person originally directed to execute or indorse it.

"directing a person to execute" (s 39(1))—The person must of course be identified in the order, and he must have been ordered to execute a document, not merely (for example) to transfer a property. If an order has been made in the latter form, it is necessary first to secure an order requiring execution of the relevant document before an order can be made under this section.

"neglects or refuses" (s 39(1)(*a*))—In the case of neglect or refusal, this section provides a cheaper, more effective and less draconian remedy than an application to commit. If this ground is relied on it must be shown that the Respondent is aware of the order but personal service is not mandatory. It is normally required that he has been given the opportunity to execute the document, but not if it is patent that he refuses and will continue to refuse to do so (*Savage v Norton* [1908] 1 Ch 290).

"such person as the court may nominate" (s 39(1))—Any person may be nominated, but it is frequently the district judge (who may, it seems, nominate himself). The nominee signs not "on behalf of" the respondent but merely pursuant to the order.

"as if it had been executed ... by the person originally directed" (s 39(2))—The nominee assumes no personal liability under the document.

County court—The same power is exercised by the county court by virtue of County Courts Act 1984, s 38.

Procedure—Normally the application is made by summons or on notice to the district judge (FPR 1991, r 10.9). If the respondent cannot be found (and has no solicitor on record), the application will usually be made without notice, unless (rarely) the court directs substituted service (eg by advertisement).

Alternative procedure—Where what is sought to be achieved is the transfer of a property from one party to another, it may be possible to avoid the expense and inconvenience of preparing a document for signature, obtaining an order that the transferor sign it, obtaining an order under this section and then having the document signed by the named person. The court can be asked instead to make an order under Trustee Act 1925, s 44(vii), vesting the property in the transferee. If such an order is available, it may particularly be appropriate where the whereabouts of the transferor are unknown or his co-operation otherwise seems unlikely.

40 Attachment of debts

(1) Subject to any order for the time being in force under subsection (4), this section applies to the following accounts, namely –

(*a*) any deposit account with a bank or other deposit-taking institution; and
(*b*) any withdrawable share account with any deposit-taking institution.

(2) In determining whether, for the purposes of the jurisdiction of the High Court to attach debts for the purpose of satisfying judgments or orders for the payment of money, a sum standing to the credit of a person in an account to which this section applies is a sum due or accruing to that person and, as such, attachable in accordance with rules of court, any condition mentioned in subsection (3) which applies to the account shall be disregarded.

(3) Those conditions are –

(*a*) any condition that notice is required before any money or share is withdrawn;

(*b*) any condition that a personal application must be made before any money or share is withdrawn;

(*c*) any condition that a deposit book or share-account book must be produced before any money or share is withdrawn; or

(*d*) any other prescribed condition.

(4) The Lord Chancellor may by order make such provision as he thinks fit, by way of amendment of this section or otherwise, for all or any of the following purposes, namely –

(*a*) including in, or excluding from, the accounts to which this section applies accounts of any description specified in the order;

(*b*) excluding from the accounts to which this section applies all accounts with any particular deposit-taking institution so specified or with any deposit-taking institution of a description so specified.

(5) Any order under subsection (4) shall be made by statutory instrument subject to annulment in pursuance of a resolution of either House of Parliament.

(6) In this section "deposit-taking institution" means any person carrying on a business which is a deposit-taking business for the purposes of the Banking Act 1987.

Amendments—Banking Act 1987, s 108(1), Sch 6, para 11.

Scope of provision—This section extends the availability of garnishee proceedings to bank and building society accounts which would otherwise not be vulnerable to such an order because of conditions attached to their operation (see RSC Ord 49).

40A Administrative and clerical expenses of garnishees

(1) Where an interim third party debt order made in the exercise of the jurisdiction mentioned in subsection (2) of the preceding section is served on any deposit-taking institution, the institution may, subject to the provision of this section, deduct from the relevant debt or debts an amount not exceeding the prescribed sum towards the administrative and clerical expenses of the institution in complying with the order; and the right of an institution to make a deduction under this subsection shall be exercisable as from the time the order nisi is served on it.

(1A) In subsection (1) "the relevant debt or debts", in relation to an interim third party debt order served on any such institution as is mentioned in that subsection, means the amount, as at the time the order is served on the institution, of the debt or debts of which the whole or a part is expressed to be attached by the order.

(1B) A deduction may be made under subsection (1) in a case where the amount referred to in subsection (1A) is insufficient to cover both the amount of the deduction and the amount of the judgment debt and costs in respect of which the attachment was made, notwithstanding that the benefit of the attachment to the creditor is reduced as a result of the deduction.

(2) An amount may not in pursuance of subsection (1) be deducted or, as the case may be, retained in a case where, by virtue of section 346 of the Insolvency Act 1986 or section 183 of the Insolvency Act 1986 or otherwise, the creditor is not entitled to retain the benefit of the attachment.

(3) In this section –

"deposit-taking institution" has the meaning assigned to it by section 40(6); and

"prescribed" means prescribed by an order made by the Lord Chancellor.

(4) An order under this section –

(*a*) may make different provision for different cases;

(*b*) without prejudice to the generality of paragraph (*a*) of this subsection, may prescribe sums differing according to the amount due under the judgment or order to be satisfied;

(*c*) may provide for this section not to apply to deposit-taking institutions of any prescribed description.

(5) Any such order shall be made by statutory instrument subject to annulment in pursuance of a resolution of either House of Parliament.

Amendments—Inserted by Administration of Justice Act 1982, s 55, Sch 4, Pt I; amended by Administration of Justice Act 1985, s 52; Companies Consolidation (Consequential Provisions) Act 1985, s 30, Sch 2; Insolvency Act 1986, s 439(2), Sch 14; SI 2002/439.

"the prescribed sum" (s 40A(1))—The current sum is £55: SI 1996/3098.

"interim third party debt order"—This expression has been substituted for "order nisi" upon the replacement, for civil proceedings but not (yet) for family proceedings, of garnishee orders by third party debt orders under CPR Part 72. Presumably, in family proceedings, the bank's entitlement to make the deduction when served with a garnishee order nisi is not removed.

41 Wards of court

(1) Subject to the provisions of this section, no minor shall be made a ward of court except by virtue of an order to that effect made by the High Court.

(2) Where an application is made for such an order in respect of a minor, the minor shall become a ward of court on the making of the application, but shall cease to be a ward of court at the end of such period as may be prescribed unless within that period an order has been made in accordance with the application.

(2A) Subsection (2) does not apply with respect to a child who is the subject of a care order (as defined by section 105 of the Children Act 1989).

(3) The High Court may, either upon an application in that behalf or without such an application, order that any minor who is for the time being a ward of court shall cease to be a ward of court.

Amendments—CA 1989, s 108(5), Sch 13, para 45(2).

Defined terms—"minor": Family Law Reform Act 1969, s 1.

Applications without notice—It is on the issue of the originating summons that a child becomes a ward. The court however, has the power to grant injunctions and emergency orders before the summons is issued (*Re N (Infants) (No 2)* [1967] Ch 512, [1967] 2 WLR 691). Applications without notice before the issue of proceedings should be used only as a matter of emergency (*Re O (Proposed Wardship Proceedings)* [1990] FCR 599). Where an application without notice is made before the issue of the originating summons on undertakings given to file the process, it is essential that the court is asked at that stage to confirm the wardship because it is not uncommon for the applicant to overlook the need to obtain the first appointment within the set time-limits, particularly if the emergency which occasioned the issue of the wardship has been adequately protected by the judge's order or the emergency has passed.

****

GENERAL PROVISIONS

Law and equity

49 Concurrent administration of law and equity

(1) Subject to the provisions of this or any other Act, every court exercising jurisdiction in England or Wales in any civil cause or matter shall continue to administer law and equity on the basis that, wherever there is any conflict or variance between the rules of equity and the rules of the common law with reference to the same matter, the rules of equity shall prevail.

(2) Every such court shall give the same effect as hitherto –

(*a*) to all equitable estates, titles, rights, reliefs, defences and counterclaims, and to all equitable duties and liabilities; and
(*b*) subject thereto, to all legal claims and demands and all estates, titles, rights, duties, obligations and liabilities existing by the common law or by any custom or created by any statute,

and, subject to the provisions of this or any other Act, shall so exercise its jurisdiction in every cause or matter before it as to secure that, as far as possible, all matters in dispute between the parties are completely and finally determined, and all multiplicity of legal proceedings with respect to any of those matters is avoided.

(3) Nothing in this Act shall affect the power of the Court of Appeal or the High Court to stay any proceedings before it, where it thinks fit to do so, either of its own motion or on the application of any person, whether or not a party to the proceedings.

Scope of provision—This section provides for courts to act as courts of law and equity. The principle that equity prevails relates to substantive law and not practice (*La Grange v McAndrew* (1879) 4 QBD 210). The court has an inherent jurisdiction to stay any proceedings which are an abuse of its powers (see *Hinckley and South Leicestershire Permanent Benefit Building Society v Freeman* [1941] Ch 32).

****

Costs

51 Costs in civil division of Court of Appeal, High Court and county courts

(1) Subject to the provisions of this or any other enactment and to rules of court, the costs of and incidental to all proceedings in –

(*a*) the civil division of the Court of Appeal;
(*b*) the High Court; and
(*c*) any county court,

shall be in the discretion of the court.

(2) Without prejudice to any general power to make rules of court, such rules may make provision for regulating matters relating to the costs of those proceedings including, in particular, prescribing scales of costs to be paid to legal or other representatives.

(3) The court shall have full power to determine by whom and to what extent the costs are to be paid.

(4) In subsections (1) and (2) "proceedings" includes the administration of estates and trusts.

(5) Nothing in subsection (1) shall alter the practice in any criminal cause, or in bankruptcy.

(6) In any proceedings mentioned in subsection (1), the court may disallow, or (as the case may be) order the legal or other representative concerned to meet, the whole of any wasted costs or such part of them as may be determined in accordance with rules of court.

(7) In subsection (6), "wasted costs" means any costs incurred by a party –

(*a*) as a result of any improper, unreasonable or negligent act or omission on the part of any legal or other representative or any employee of such a representative; or

(*b*) which, in the light of any such act or omission occurring after they were incurred, the court considers it is unreasonable to expect that party to pay.

(8) Where –

(*a*) a person has commenced proceedings in the High Court; but

(*b*) those proceedings should, in the opinion of the court, have been commenced in a county court in accordance with any provision made under section 1 of the Courts and Legal Services Act 1990 or by or under any other enactment,

the person responsible for determining the amount which is to be awarded to that person by way of costs shall have regard to those circumstances.

(9) Where, in complying with subsection (8), the responsible person reduces the amount which would otherwise be awarded to the person in question –

(*a*) the amount of that reduction shall not exceed 25 per cent; and

(*b*) on any taxation of the costs payable by that person to his legal representative, regard shall be had to the amount of the reduction.

(10) The Lord Chancellor may by order amend subsection (9)(*a*) by substituting, for the percentage for the time being mentioned there, a different percentage.

(11) Any such order shall be made by statutory instrument and may make such transitional or incidental provision as the Lord Chancellor considers expedient.

(12) No such statutory instrument shall be made unless a draft of the instrument has been approved by both Houses of Parliament.

(13) In this section "legal or other representative", in relation to a party to proceedings, means any person exercising a right of audience or right to conduct litigation on his behalf.

Amendments—Courts and Legal Services Act 1990, s 4(1).

Rules of Court—The general rule, prescribed by CPR 1998, r 44.3 is that the unsuccessful party pays the costs of the successful party. This provision is specifically disapplied in relation to family appeals (by CPR 1998, r 44.3(3)). The court has a discretion as to costs and when exercising that discretion must have regard to the conduct of the parties, the success of the appeal and attempts or offers to settle the matter (r 44.3).

Wasted costs orders—These orders are dealt with by CPR 1998, r 44.14.

****

PART III
PRACTICE AND PROCEDURE

****

THE COURT OF APPEAL

Composition of court

54 Court of civil division

(1) This section relates to the civil division of the Court of Appeal; and in this section "court", except where the context otherwise requires, means a court of that division.

(2) Subject as follows, a court shall be duly constituted for the purpose of exercising any of its jurisdiction if it consists of one or more judges.

(3) The Master of the Rolls may, with the concurrence of the Lord Chancellor, give (or vary or revoke) directions about the minimum number of judges of which a court must consist if it is to be duly constituted for the purpose of any description of proceedings.

(4) The Master of the Rolls, or any Lord Justice of Appeal designated by him, may (subject to any directions under subsection (3)) determine the number of judges of which a court is to consist for the purpose of any particular proceedings.

(4A) The Master of the Rolls may give directions as to what is to happen in any particular case where one or more members of a court which has partly heard proceedings are unable to continue.

(5) Where –

- (*a*) an appeal has been heard by a court consisting of an even number of judges; and
- (*b*) the members of the court are equally divided, the case shall, on the application of any party to the appeal, be re-argued before and determined by an uneven number of judges not less than three, before any appeal to the House of Lords.

(6), (7) (*repealed*)

(8) Subsections (1) and (2) of section 70 (assessors in the High Court) shall apply in relation to causes and matters before the civil division of the Court of Appeal as they apply in relation to causes and matters before the High Court.

(9) Subsections (3) and (4) of section 70 (scientific advisers to assist the Patents Court in proceedings under the Patents Act 1949 and the Patents Act 1977) shall apply in relation to the civil division of the Court of Appeal and proceedings on appeal from any decision of the Patents Court in proceedings under those Acts as they apply in relation to the Patents Court and proceedings under those Acts.

(10) (*repealed*)

Amendments—Courts and Legal Services Act 1990, s 7(4); Access to Justice Act 1999, ss 59, 106, Sch 15.

Procedure—For procedure on appeal, see CPR 1998, Pt 52.

****

THE HIGH COURT

****

67 Proceedings in court and in chambers

Business in the High Court shall be heard and disposed of in court except in so far as it may, under this or any other Act, under rules of court or in accordance with the practice of the court, be dealt with in chambers.

Exercise of the court's discretion as to whether a hearing should take place in open court or in chambers—This section does not provide a statutory basis for making a direction that a particular hearing should be held in chambers. However, it was held in *Scott v Scott* [1913] AC 417, (1913) FLR Rep 657 that, although business conducted in the High Court should normally be by way of public hearing to secure that justice is done, the court has jurisdiction in matrimonial proceedings to decide whether or not a particular hearing should be in chambers or in open court, where the case falls within the three exceptions identified by Viscount Haldane LC, that is to say: (i) wards; (ii) lunatics (in each of which the court is sitting primarily to safeguard the interests of the ward or lunatic); and (iii) litigation in respect of a secret process where the effect of publicity would be to destroy the subject matter. However, *Scott* (above) cannot be taken to prevent or restrict the enactment of rules for regulating the trial of family proceedings and there is no objection to hearing family cases in private and excluding the public where the rules permit it (*Clibbery v Allan and Another* [2002] EWCA Civ 45, [2002] 1 FLR 565, CA). In exercising its discretion in this matter, the court must conduct a balancing exercise between the genuine public interest in the case in holding the hearing in open court, and the competing interest of those people concerned in the case who seek the protection of a hearing in chambers (*Re G (Adult Patient: Publicity)* [1995] 2 FLR 528 – where an adult patient was maintained on life support machines in a persistent vegetative state, the court decided that the genuine public interest in the decision as to whether or not to allow the hospital to discontinue the life-sustaining treatment required that the hearing should be held in open court, but with safeguards to protect the positions and anonymity of the relatives, doctors and nursing staff involved). The general rule is that it is not a contempt of court to report what happened in a hearing in chambers unless Administration of Justice Act 1960, s 12 applies, or the case comes within the recognised categories of children or ancillary relief cases, or the administration of justice would otherwise be impeded or prejudiced by publication (*Clibbery v Allan and Another* [2002] EWCA Civ 45, [2002] 1 FLR 565, CA). See further under Contempt of Court Act 1981, s 11 and Administration of Justice Act 1960, s 12.

****

151 Interpretation of this Act, and rules of construction for other Acts and documents

(1) In this Act, unless the context otherwise requires –

"action" means any civil proceedings commenced by writ or in any other manner prescribed by rules of court;

"appeal", in the context of appeals to the civil division of the Court of Appeal, includes –

(*a*) an application for a new trial, and

(*b*) an application to set aside a verdict, finding or judgment in any cause or matter in the High Court which has been tried, or in which any issue has been tried, by a jury;

"arbitration agreement" has the same meaning as it has in Part I of the Arbitration Act 1996;

"cause" means any action or any criminal proceedings;

"Division", where it appears with a capital letter, means a division of the High Court;

"judgment" includes a decree;

"jurisdiction" includes powers;

"matter" means any proceedings in court not in a cause;

"party", in relation to any proceedings, includes any person who pursuant to or by virtue of rules of court or any other statutory provision has been served with notice of, or has intervened in, those proceedings;

"prescribed" means –

(*a*) except in relation to fees, prescribed by rules of court; and

(*b*) in relation to fees, prescribed by an order under section 130;

"senior judge", where the reference is to the senior judge of a Division, means –

(*a*) in the case of the Chancery Division, the Vice-Chancellor;

(*b*) in any other case, the president of the Division in question;

"solicitor" means a solicitor of the Supreme Court;

"statutory provision" means any enactment, whenever passed, or any provision contained in subordinate legislation (as defined in section 21(1) of the Interpretation Act 1978), whenever made;

"this or any other Act" includes an Act passed after this Act.

(2) Section 128 contains definitions of expressions used in Part V and in the other provisions of this Act relating to probate causes and matters.

(3) Any reference in this Act to rules of court under section 84 includes a reference to rules of court in relation to the Supeme Court under any provision of this or any other Act which confers on the Civil Procedure Rule Committee or the Crown Court Rule Committee power to make rules of court.

(4) Except where the context otherwise requires, in this or any other Act –

"Criminal Appeal Rules" means rules of court made by the Crown Court Rule Committee in relation to the criminal division of the Court of Appeal;

"Crown Court Rules" means rules of court made by the Crown Court Rule Committee in relation to the Crown Court;

"divisional court" (with or without capital letters) means a divisional court constituted under section 66;

"judge of the Supreme Court" means –

(*a*) a judge of the Court of Appeal other than an ex-officio judge within paragraph (*b*) or (*c*) of section 2(2), or

(*b*) a judge of the High Court,

and accordingly does not include, as such, a judge of the Crown Court;

"official referees' business" has the meaning given by section 68(6);

(5) The provisions of Schedule 4 (construction of references to superseded courts and officers) shall have effect.

Amendments—Courts and Legal Services Act 1990, s 125(3), Sch 18, para 41; Arbitration Act 1996, s 107(1), Sch 3, para 37(1), (3); Civil Procedure Act 1997, s 10, Sch 2, para 2(1), (7).

PART II

SCHEDULE 1

DISTRIBUTION OF BUSINESS IN HIGH COURT

****

3 Family Division

To the Family Division are assigned –

(*a*) all matrimonial causes and matters (whether at first instance or on appeal);

(*b*) all causes and matters (whether at first instance or on appeal) relating to –

(i) legitimacy;

(ii) the exercise of the inherent jurisdiction of the High Court with respect to minors, the maintenance of minors and any proceedings under the Children Act 1989, except proceedings solely for the appointment of a guardian of a minor's estate;

(iii) adoption;

(iv) non-contentious or common form probate business;

(*c*) applications for consent to the marriage of a minor or for a declaration under section 27B(5) of the Marriage Act 1949;

(*d*) proceedings on appeal under section 13 of the Administration of Justice Act 1960 from an order or decision made under section 63(3) of the Magistrates' Courts Act 1980 to enforce an order of a magistrates' court made in matrimonial proceedings or proceedings under Part IV of the Family Law Act 1996 or with respect to the guardianship of a minor;

(*e*) applications under Part III of the Family Law Act 1986;

(*e*) proceedings under the Children Act 1989;

(*f*) all proceedings under –

(i) Part IV of the Family Law Act 1996;

(ii) the Child Abduction and Custody Act 1985;

(iii) the Family Law Act 1986;

(iv) section 30 of the Human Fertilisation and Embryology Act 1990; and

(*fa*) all proceedings relating to a debit or credit under section 29(1) or 49(1) of the Welfare Reform and Pensions Act 1999;

(*g*) all proceedings for the purpose of enforcing an order made in any proceedings of a type described in this paragraph;

(*h*) all proceedings under the Child Support Act 1991.

Amendments—Marriage (Prohibited Degrees of Relationship) Act 1986, s 5; Family Law Act 1986, s 68(1), Sch 1, para 26; Family Law Reform Act 1987, s 33(4), Sch 4; CA 1989, ss 92(11), 108(5), Sch 11, para 9, Sch 13, para 45(3); SI 1991/1210; SI 1993/622; Family Law Act 1996, s 66(1), Sch 8, para 51; Welfare Reform and Pensions Act 1999, s 84(1), Sch 12, para 1.

Two sub-paragraphs (e)—A sub-paragraph (*e*) was inserted by the Family Law Act 1986, but the draftsman of the insertion made by CA 1989 seems to have been unaware of it; it is submitted that the words of amendment in CA 1989, Sch 11, para 9 ("In paragraph 3 ... the following sub-paragraph shall be added at the end – (*e*)") mean that the second (*e*) has not inadvertently been substituted for the first (*e*), but merely added after it, so that both paragraphs (*e*) are fully effective, albeit that they inconveniently have the same name.

Two references to CA 1989—CA 1989 is referred to in both (*b*)(ii) and (the second) (*e*). This seems to have been simply a proverbial case of the "left hand and the right hand", as the two references were inserted by different provisions of CA 1989 (Sch 13, para 45 and Sch 11, para 9, respectively). The result is overkill but nothing more; although (*b*)(ii) more obviously includes appeals from proceedings under the Act, it would seem that the effect of each reference is identical.

****

Surrogacy Arrangements Act 1985

1 Meaning of "surrogate mother", "surrogacy arrangement" and other terms

(1) The following provisions shall have effect for the interpretation of this Act.

(2) "Surrogate mother" means a woman who carries a child in pursuance of an arrangement –

- (*a*) made before she began to carry the child, and
- (*b*) made with a view to any child carried in pursuance of it being handed over to, and parental responsibility being met (so far as practicable) by, another person or other persons.

(3) An arrangement is a surrogacy arrangement if, were a woman to whom the arrangement relates to carry a child in pursuance of it, she would be a surrogate mother.

(4) In determining whether an arrangement is made with such a view as is mentioned in subsection (2) above regard may be had to the circumstances as a whole (and, in particular, where there is a promise or understanding that any payment will or may be made to the woman or for her benefit in respect of the carrying of any child in pursuance of the arrangement, to that promise or understanding).

(5) An arrangement may be regarded as made with such a view though subject to conditions relating to the handing over of any child.

(6) A woman who carries a child is to be treated for the purposes of subsection (2)(*a*) above as beginning to carry it at the time of the insemination or of the placing in her of an embryo, of an egg in the process of fertilisation or of sperm and eggs as the case may be, that results in her carrying the child.

(7) "Body of persons" means a body of persons corporate or unincorporate.

(8) "Payment" means payment in money or money's worth.

(9) This Act applies to arrangements whether or not they are lawful.

Amendments—CA 1989, s 108(5), Sch 13, para 56; Human Fertilisation and Embryology Act 1990, s 36; SI 1995/755.

1A Surrogacy arrangements unenforceable

No surrogacy arrangement is enforceable by or against any of the persons making it.

Amendments—Inserted by Human Fertilisation and Embryology Act 1990, s 36.

PART II

2 Negotiating surrogacy arrangements on a commercial basis etc

(1) No person shall on a commercial basis do any of the following acts in the United Kingdom, that is –

(*a*) initiate or take part in any negotiations with a view to the making of a surrogacy arrangement,
(*b*) offer or agree to negotiate the making of a surrogacy arrangement, or
(*c*) compile any information with a view to its use in making, or negotiating the making of, surrogacy arrangements;

and no person shall in the United Kingdom knowingly cause another to do any of those acts on a commercial basis.

(2) A person who contravenes subsection (1) above is guilty of an offence; but it is not a contravention of that subsection –

(*a*) for a woman, with a view to becoming a surrogate mother herself, to do any act mentioned in that subsection or to cause such an act to be done, or
(*b*) for any person, with a view to a surrogate mother carrying a child for him, to do such an act or to cause such an act to be done.

(3) For the purposes of this section, a person does an act on a commercial basis (subject to subsection (4) below) if –

(*a*) any payment is at any time received by himself or another in respect of it, or
(*b*) he does it with a view to any payment being received by himself or another in respect of making, or negotiating or facilitating the making of, any surrogacy arrangement.

In this subsection "payment" does not include payment to or for the benefit of a surrogate mother or prospective surrogate mother.

(4) In proceedings against a person for an offence under subsection (1) above, he is not to be treated as doing an act on a commercial basis by reason of any payment received by another in respect of the act if it is proved that –

(*a*) in a case where the payment was received before he did the act, he did not do the act knowing or having reasonable cause to suspect that any payment had been received in respect of the act; and
(*b*) in any other case, he did not do the act with a view to any payment being received in respect of it.

(5) Where –

(*a*) a person acting on behalf of a body of persons takes any part in negotiating or facilitating the making of a surrogacy arrangement in the United Kingdom, and
(*b*) negotiating or facilitating the making of surrogacy arrangements is an activity of the body,

then, if the body at any time receives any payment made by or on behalf of –

(i) a woman who carries a child in pursuance of the arrangement,
(ii) the person or persons for whom she carries it, or
(iii) any person connected with the woman or with that person or those persons, the body is guilty of an offence.

For the purposes of this subsection, a payment received by a person connected with a body is to be treated as received by the body.

(6) In proceedings against a body for an offence under subsection (5) above, it is a defence to prove that the payment concerned was not made in respect of the arrangement mentioned in paragraph (*a*) of that subsection.

(7) A person who in the United Kingdom takes part in the management or control –

(*a*) of any body of persons, or
(*b*) of any of the activities of any body of persons,

is guilty of an offence if the activity described in subsection (8) below is an activity of the body concerned.

(8) The activity referred to in subsection (7) above is negotiating or facilitating the making of surrogacy arrangements in the United Kingdom, being –

(*a*) arrangements the making of which is negotiated or facilitated on a commercial basis, or
(*b*) arrangements in the case of which payments are received (or treated for the purposes of subsection (5) above as received) by the body concerned in contravention of subsection (5) above.

(9) In proceedings against a person for an offence under subsection (7) above, it is a defence to prove that he neither knew nor had reasonable cause to suspect that the activity described in subsection (8) above was an activity of the body concerned; and for the purposes of such proceedings any arrangement falling within subsection (8)(*b*) above shall be disregarded if it is proved that the payment concerned was not made in respect of the arrangement.

3 Advertisements about surrogacy

(1) This section applies to any advertisement containing an indication (however expressed) –

(*a*) that any person is or may be willing to enter into a surrogacy arrangement or to negotiate or facilitate the making of a surrogacy arrangement, or
(*b*) that any person is looking for a woman willing to become a surrogate mother or for persons wanting a woman to carry a child as a surrogate mother.

(2) Where a newspaper or periodical containing an advertisement to which this section applies is published in the United Kingdom, any proprietor, editor or publisher of the newspaper or periodical is guilty of an offence.

(3) Where an advertisement to which this section applies is conveyed by means of a telecommunication system so as to be seen or heard (or both) in the United Kingdom, any person who in the United Kingdom causes it to be so conveyed knowing it to contain such an indication as is mentioned in subsection (1) above is guilty of an offence.

(4) A person who publishes or causes to be published in the United Kingdom an advertisement to which this section applies (not being an advertisement contained in a newspaper or periodical or conveyed by means of a telecommunication system) is guilty of an offence.

(5) A person who distributes or causes to be distributed in the United Kingdom an advertisement to which this section applies (not being an advertisement contained in a newspaper or periodical published outside the United Kingdom or an advertisement conveyed by means of a telecommunication system) knowing it to

PART II

contain such an indication as is mentioned in subsection (1) above is guilty of an offence.

(6) In this section "telecommunication system" has the same meaning as in the Telecommunications Act 1984.

4 Offences

(1) A person guilty of an offence under this Act shall be liable on summary conviction –

(*a*) in the case of an offence under section 2 to a fine not exceeding level 5 on the standard scale or to imprisonment for a term not exceeding 3 months or both,

(*b*) in the case of an offence under section 3 to a fine not exceeding level 5 on the standard scale.

(2) No proceedings for an offence under this Act shall be instituted –

(*a*) in England and Wales, except by or with the consent of the Director of Public Prosecutions; and

(*b*) in Northern Ireland, except by or with the consent of the Director of Public Prosecutions for Northern Ireland.

(3) Where an offence under this Act committed by a body corporate is proved to have been committed with the consent or connivance of, or to be attributable to any neglect on the part of, any director, manager, secretary or other similar officer of the body corporate or any person who was purporting to act in any such capacity, he as well as the body corporate is guilty of the offence and is liable to be proceeded against and punished accordingly.

(4) Where the affairs of a body corporate are managed by its members, subsection (3) above shall apply in relation to the acts and defaults of a member in connection with his functions of management as if he were a director of the body corporate.

(5) In any proceedings for an offence under section 2 of this Act, proof of things done or of words written, spoken or published (whether or not in the presence of any party to the proceedings) by any person taking part in the management or control of a body of persons or of any of the activities of the body, or by any person doing any of the acts mentioned in subsection (1)(*a*) to (*c*) of that section on behalf of the body, shall be admissible as evidence of the activities of the body.

(6) In relation to an offence under this Act, section 127(1) of the Magistrates' Courts Act 1980 (information must be laid within six months of commission of offence), section 136(1) of the Criminal Procedure (Scotland) Act 1995 (proceedings must be commenced within that time) and Article 19(1) of the Magistrates' Courts (Northern Ireland) Order 1981 (complaint must be made within that time) shall have effect as if for the reference to six months there were substituted a reference to two years.

Amendments—Statute Law (Repeals) Act 1993; Criminal Procedure (Consequential Provisions) (Scotland) Act 1995, ss 4, 5, Sch 4, para 57.

****

Trusts of Land and Appointment of Trustees Act 1996

****

13 Exclusion and restriction of right to occupy

(1) Where two or more beneficiaries are (or apart from this subsection would be) entitled under section 12 to occupy land, the trustees of land may exclude or restrict the entitlement of any one or more (but not all) of them.

(2) Trustees may not under subsection (1) –

(*a*) unreasonably exclude any beneficiary's entitlement to occupy land, or

(*b*) restrict any such entitlement to an unreasonable extent.

(3) The trustees of land may from time to time impose reasonable conditions on any beneficiary in relation to his occupation of land by reason of his entitlement under section 12.

(4) The matters to which trustees are to have regard in exercising the powers conferred by this section include –

(*a*) the intentions of the person or persons (if any) who created the trust,

(*b*) the purposes for which the land is held, and

(*c*) the circumstances and wishes of each of the beneficiaries who is (or apart from any previous exercise by the trustees of those powers would be) entitled to occupy the land under section 12.

(5) The conditions which may be imposed on a beneficiary under subsection (3) include, in particular, conditions requiring him –

(*a*) to pay any outgoings or expenses in respect of the land, or

(*b*) to assume any other obligation in relation to the land or to any activity which is or is proposed to be conducted there.

(6) Where the entitlement of any beneficiary to occupy land under section 12 has been excluded or restricted, the conditions which may be imposed on any other beneficiary under subsection (3) include, in particular, conditions requiring him to –

(*a*) make payments by way of compensation to the beneficiary whose entitlement has been excluded or restricted, or

(*b*) forgo any payment or other benefit to which he would otherwise be entitled under the trust so as to benefit that beneficiary.

(7) The powers conferred on trustees by this section may not be exercised –

(*a*) so as to prevent any person who is in occupation of land (whether or not by reason of an entitlement under section 12) from continuing to occupy the land, or

(*b*) in a manner likely to result in any such person ceasing to occupy the land,

unless he consents or the court has given approval.

(8) The matters to which the court is to have regard in determining whether to give approval under subsection (7) include the matters mentioned in subsection (4)(*a*) to (*c*).

Scope of provision—This section provides that, where beneficiaries are entitled under s 12 to occupy land (s 12 defines entitlement to occupy land as arising when a beneficiary is entitled to an interest in possession, and the purpose of the trust is to make the land available for his occupation), the trustees of land may exclude a beneficiary's entitlement to occupy, provided they act reasonably. The trustees can impose conditions (including apportioning occupation – *Rodway v Landy* [2001] EWCA Civ 471, [2001] Ch 703) and can compensate the beneficiary who has been excluded. A checklist of factors to be taken into account is set out; and the trustees cannot exclude without the person's consent or the court's approval.

Powers of court

14 Applications for order

(1) Any person who is a trustee of land or has an interest in property subject to a trust of land may make an application to the court for an order under this section.

(2) On an application for an order under this section the court may make any such order –

(*a*) relating to the exercise by the trustees of any of their functions (including an order relieving them of any obligation to obtain the consent of, or to consult, any person in connection with the exercise of any of their functions), or

(*b*) declaring the nature or extent of a person's interest in property subject to the trust,

as the court thinks fit.

(3) The court may not under this section make any order as to the appointment or removal of trustees.

(4) The powers conferred on the court by this section are exercisable on an application whether it is made before or after the commencement of this Act.

Scope of provision—Any trustee, or anyone who has an interest in property subject to a trust of land (which, by virtue of s 17(2), includes a beneficiary in the proceeds of sale of land), may apply for an order relating to the exercise by the trustees of any of their functions (including the power to exclude or the power of sale) or may apply for an order declaring the nature or extent of a person's interest in the trust of land. The court's powers under this section are wide, but do not encompass the appointment or removal of trustees, which is provided for in ss 19–21.

15 Matters relevant in determining applications

(1) The matters to which the court is to have regard in determining an application for an order under section 14 include –

(*a*) the intentions of the person or persons (if any) who created the trust,

(*b*) the purposes for which the property subject to the trust is held,

(*c*) the welfare of any minor who occupies or might reasonably be expected to occupy any land subject to the trust as his home, and

(*d*) the interests of any secured creditor of any beneficiary.

(2) In the case of an application relating to the exercise in relation to any land of the powers conferred on the trustees by section 13, the matters to which the court is to have regard also include the circumstances and wishes of each of the beneficiaries who is (or apart from any previous exercise by the trustees of those powers would be) entitled to occupy the land under section 12.

(3) In the case of any other application, other than one relating to the exercise of the power mentioned in section 6(2), the matters to which the court is to have regard also include the circumstances and wishes of any beneficiaries of full age

and entitled to an interest in possession in property subject to the trust or (in case of dispute) of the majority (according to the value of their combined interests).

(4) This section does not apply to an application if section 335A of the Insolvency Act 1986 (which is inserted by Schedule 3 and relates to applications by a trustee of a bankrupt) applies to it.

Scope of provision—This section sets out the criteria to be applied on an application under s 14. The use of the word "include" demonstrates that the four listed factors are not exhaustive; children are now a consideration in their own right. Compared with the repealed Law of Property Act 1925, s 30, this section gives the court more discretion in favour of families and against banks and other chargees (*Mortgage Corporation v Shaire* [2000] 1 FLR 973), although whether a creditor is receiving proper recompense for being kept out of his money remains a powerful consideration (*Bank of Ireland Home Mortgages Ltd v Bell* [2001] 2 FLR 809).

Application by trustee in bankruptcy—If the applicant under s 14 is a trustee in bankruptcy, s 15 does not apply. Section 25 of, and Sch 3 to, this Act insert s 335A into the Insolvency Act 1986, which provides that any application by a trustee in bankruptcy under s 14 for an order for sale of land must be made to the court having jurisdiction in relation to the bankruptcy. On such application, the court will make such order as it thinks just and reasonable, having regard to: (*a*) the interests of the creditors; (*b*) where the application is made in respect of land which includes a dwelling house which is, or has been, the home of the bankrupt or the bankrupt's spouse or former spouse, (i) the conduct of the spouse or former spouse in terms of contributing to the bankruptcy, (ii) the needs and financial resources of the spouse or former spouse, and (iii) the needs of any children; and (*c*) all the circumstances of the case other than the needs of the bankrupt. Further, where such an application is made more than a year after the vesting of the bankrupt's estate in the trustee, the court is entitled to assume, unless the circumstances of the case are exceptional, that the interests of the bankrupt's creditors outweigh all other considerations.

****

PART III

Statutory Instruments

PART III: Statutory Instruments

Contents

All relevant procedural provisions in the following legislation, as amended and fully annotated:

PART III

Adoption Rules 1984, SI 1984/265

ARRANGEMENT OF RULES

PART I
INTRODUCTORY

PART II
FREEING FOR ADOPTION

PART III
ADOPTION ORDERS

PART IV
CONVENTION PROCEEDINGS

Additional provisions for cases where child is not a United Kingdom national

PART III

Proceedings under sections 52 or 53 of the Act

Supplementary

PART V
MISCELLANEOUS

PART I
INTRODUCTORY

1 Citation and commencement

These rules may be cited as the Adoption Rules 1984 and shall come into operation on 27 May 1984.

"These rules ..."—The rules, which were made before the commencement of the Adoption Act 1976, have effect as if made under Adoption Act 1976, s 66 (AA 1976, s 73(1), Sch 2, para 1). They govern the procedure for proceedings for adoption or freeing for adoption in the High Court and county courts. Procedure in magistrates' courts is governed by the Magistrates' Courts (Adoption) Rules 1984. The rules consolidate, with amendments, the Adoption (High Court) Rules 1976, SI 1976/1645, the Adoption (County Court) Rules 1976, SI 1976/1644 and the Convention Adoption Rules 1978, SI 1978/417. Each of the earlier sets of rules is revoked (r 54).

2 Interpretation

(1) In these rules, unless the context otherwise requires –

"the Act" means the Adoption Act 1976;

"adoption agency" means a local authority or approved adoption society; "the child" means the person whom the applicant for an adoption order or an order authorising a proposed foreign adoption proposes to adopt, or, as the case may be, the person the adoption agency proposes should be freed for adoption;

"children's guardian" means an officer of the service appointed to act on behalf of the child in accordance with section 65(1)(*a*) of the 1976 Act;

"Convention proceedings" means proceedings in the High Court on an application for a Convention adoption order and proceedings in the High Court under the Act;

"the court" means the High Court and any county court falling within the class specified for the commencement of proceedings under the Act by an Order under Part I of Schedule 11 to the Children Act 1989;

"interim order" means an order under section 25 of the Act;

"order authorising a proposed foreign adoption" means an order under section 55 of the Act;

"process" means, in the High Court, a summons and, in a county court, an application;

"proper officer" means, in the High Court, a district judge of the Principal Registry of the Family Division and, in a county court, the person defined as "proper officer" by Order 1(3) of the County Court Rules 1981;

"regular armed forces of the Crown" means the Royal Navy, the Regular Armed Forces as defined by section 225 of the Army Act 1955, the Regular Air Force as defined by section 223 of the Air Force Act 1955, the Queen Alexandra's Royal Naval Nursing Service and the Women's Royal Naval Service;

"reporting officer" means an officer of the service appointed in accordance with section 65(1)(*b*) of the Act.

(2) Except where a contrary intention appears, a word or phrase used in these rules shall have the same meaning as in the Children Act 1989 or, where the word or phrase does not appear in that Act, as in the Act.

(3) In these rules a form referred to by number means the form so numbered in Schedule 1 to these rules, or a form substantially to the like effect, with such variations, as the circumstances may require.

Amendments—SI 1991/1880; SI 2001/819.

Prospective amendment by Adoption (Amendment) Rules 2003—By virtue of A(A)R 2003, r 3, which comes into force on 1 June 2003:

(*a*) after the definition of "adoption agency" insert –

""CA of the receiving State" means, in relation to a Convention country other than the United Kingdom, the Central Authority of the receiving State;

"CA of the State of origin" means, in relation to a Convention country other than the United Kingdom, the Central Authority of the State of origin;

"Central Authority" means, in relation to England, the Secretary of State for Health, and in relation to Wales, the National Assembly for Wales;";

(*b*) after the definition of "children's guardian" insert –

""Convention" means the Convention on Protection of Children and Co-operation in respect of Intercountry Adoption, concluded at the Hague on 29 May 1993;";

(*c*) for the definition of "Convention proceedings" substitute –

""Convention proceedings" means proceedings in the High Court or a county court for a Convention adoption order or in connection with a Convention adoption order or a Convention adoption;";

(*d*) after the definition of "the court" insert –

""Hague Convention Regulations" means the Intercountry Adoption (Hague Convention) Regulations 2003;";

(*e*) after the definition of "proper officer" insert –

PART III

""receiving State" means the state in which it is proposed that the child will become habitually resident;";

(*f*) in the definition of "reporting officer" for "Act." insert "Act; and"; and

(*g*) after the definition of "reporting officer" insert –

""State of origin" means the state in which the child is habitually resident.".

Defined terms—"adoption agency": see Adoption Act 1976, s 1(4); "approved adoption society": AA 1976, s 72(1); "child": CA 1989, s 105(1); "Convention adoption order": AA 1976, ss 17(1), 72(1); "local authority": CA 1989, s 105(1).

Adoption agency (r 2(1))—The activities of adoption agencies are governed by the Adoption Agency Regulations 1983, SI 1983/1964.

"Order under Part I of Schedule 11 to the Children Act 1989" (r 2(1))—The relevant order is the Children (Allocation of Proceedings) Order 1991 which governs the allocation and transfer of adoption proceedings.

Proper officer in a county court (r 2(1))—In a county court, the "proper officer" is the district judge but, in relation to any task of a formal or administrative character which is not by statute the responsibility of the district judge, the task may be undertaken by the chief clerk or any person acting on his behalf (CCR Ord 1, r 3). Thus, functions of a judicial or quasi-judicial character may not be delegated to a clerical officer.

Children Act 1989 (r 2(2))—Definitions contained in CA 1989 prevail over definitions in AA 1976, unless a contrary intention appears or there is no appropriate definition in CA 1989 (see **Parent** under r 4).

3 Extent and application of other rules

(1) These rules shall apply to proceedings in the High Court and in a county court under the Act, and Part IV of these rules shall apply to Convention proceedings, commenced on or after 27 May 1984.

(2) Subject to the provisions of these rules and to any enactment, the Rules of the Supreme Court 1965 and the County Court Rules 1981 in force immediately before 26th April 1999 shall continue to apply, with any necessary modifications, to proceedings in the High Court or a county court under the Act, and any reference in these rules to those rules shall be construed accordingly.

(3) For the purposes of paragraph (2) any provision of these rules authorising or requiring anything to be done shall be treated as if it were a provision of the Rules of the Supreme Court 1965 or the County Court Rules 1981 as the case may be.

(4) Unless the contrary intention appears, any power which by these rules may be exercised by the court may be exercised by the proper officer.

Amendments—SI 1991/1880; SI 1999/1477.

Prospective amendment by Adoption (Amendment) Rules 2003—By virtue of A(A)R 2003, r 4, which comes into force on 1 June 2003:
(*a*) in para (1) omit "27 May 1984" and substitute "1 June 2003"; and
(*b*) after para (3) insert –

"(3A) In any proceedings concerning an adoption in accordance with the Convention relating to Adoption concluded at the Hague on 15 November 1965, the Adoption Rules 1984 in force immediately before 1 June 2003 shall continue to apply, with any necessary modifications, to proceedings in the High Court.".

Defined terms—"Convention proceedings": AA 1976, ss 17, 72(1); "proper officer": r 2(1).

Scope of provision—This rule provides that adoption proceedings in the High Court or a county court will be governed by these rules. The Civil Procedure Rules 1998 do not apply to adoption proceedings, save with respect to appeals and costs (AR 1984, r 51(2)). If the AR 1984 are silent on a particular point, the RSC 1965 and CCR 1981 in force immediately before 26 April 1999 will continue to apply, with any necessary modifications.

Power of the proper officer (r 3(4))—These rules expressly exclude the following powers from the jurisdiction of the proper officer:

(*a*) the hearing of an application to free a child for adoption, which must be listed before a judge (r 9(1));
(*b*) the hearing of an application to revoke a freeing order, which must be listed before a judge (r 12(3));
(*c*) the hearing of an application for an adoption order, which must be listed before a judge (r 21(1)); a district judge may give directions (Family Proceedings (Allocation to Judiciary) Directions 1999), but does not have the power to approve uncontested adoption applications;
(*d*) when an interim order has been made, the case must be relisted before a judge prior to the expiry of the order (r 25);
(*e*) an order for costs, which may be made only by a judge (r 51).

PART II
FREEING FOR ADOPTION

4 Commencement of proceedings

(1) Proceedings to free a child for adoption shall be commenced –

(*a*) by originating summons in Form 1 issued out of the Principal Registry of the Family Division; or
(*b*) by filing in the office of a county court an originating application in Form 1.

(2) The applicant shall be the adoption agency and the respondents shall be –

(*a*) each parent or guardian of the child;
(*b*) any local authority or voluntary organisation which has parental responsibility for, is looking after, or is caring for, the child;
(*f*) any person liable by virtue of any order or agreement to contribute to the maintenance of the child; and
(*g*) in the High Court, the child.

(3) The court may at any time direct that any other person or body be made a respondent to the process.

(4) On filing the originating process the applicant shall pay the appropriate fee and supply three copies of –

(*a*) Form 1, together with any other documents required to be supplied, and
(*b*) a report in writing covering all the relevant matters specified in Schedule 2 to these rules.

Amendments—SI 1991/1880; SI 2001/819.

Defined terms—"adoption agency": r 2(1) (see also Adoption Act 1976, s 1(4)); "caring for child": CA 1989, s 105(1); "free a child for adoption": AA 1976, s 18; "guardian": CA 1989, s 105(1); "local authority": CA 1989, s 105(1); "looking after": CA 1989, s 22(1); "parental responsibility": CA 1989, s 3; "voluntary organisation": CA 1989, s 105(1).

Scope of provision—This rule sets out the procedure for the commencement of proceedings under Part II, which governs the procedure on an application to free a child for adoption. The relevant substantive law is AA 1976, ss 18 to 21.

Commencement of an application to free for adoption—An application to free a child for adoption may be made only where the parent or guardian of the child consents or where an adoption agency is applying to dispense with the consent of each parent or guardian (under AA 1976, s 16(2)) and the child is in the care of the adoption agency (which is a local authority) under a care order (AA 1976, ss 18(2), (2A), 72(1B); CA 1989, s 105(1)). Only an adoption agency may apply to free a child for adoption (r 4(2)). Where the child is a ward of court, it is necessary to obtain the prior leave of the wardship court before freeing proceedings are commenced.

Adoption application made while freeing proceedings pending—An adoption application can be made while proceedings for freeing the same child are pending – see under r 15.

Choice of application where child already placed for adoption—Once a child has been placed for adoption, a free-standing freeing application is rarely appropriate (*President's Guidelines of 1 October 2001 (Adoption Proceedings: A New Approach)* – set out in Part IV of this work; *Re H (A Minor) (Freeing Order)* [1993] 2 FLR 325).

Application to dispense with parental consent—Where the applicant intends to request the court to dispense with parental consent under AA 1976, s 16(2), the request must, unless otherwise directed, be made in the originating process, or, if made subsequently, by notice to the proper officer (r 7(1)).

High Court or county court (r 4(1))—Where the child is not in Great Britain but is elsewhere in the UK, Channel Islands or Isle of Man the application must be made in the High Court, but in an ordinary case the proceedings should be immediately transferred to a local county court (*Re J (Adoption Procedure: Isle of Man)* [2000] 2 FLR 633). If the child is not in Great Britain when the application is made, the application may be brought only in the High Court (AA 1976, s 62(3)). If the child is in England and Wales when the application is made, it may be commenced in:

(*a*) the Principal Registry of the Family Division (AA 1976, s 62(2)(*a*)); cases may be transferred from London for hearing at a provincial centre;
(*b*) the divorce county court within whose district the child is, or any divorce county court within whose district a parent or guardian of the child is (AA 1976, s 62(2)(*b*) and Children (Allocation of Proceedings) Order 1991, art 14);
(*c*) a magistrates' court within whose area the child is, or within whose area a parent or guardian of the child is (AA 1976, s 62(2)(*c*) – for magistrates' court procedure, see Magistrates' Courts (Adoption) Rules 1984).

Transfer between courts—The Children (Allocation of Proceedings) Order 1991 applies to adoption proceedings; transfers and active case management should be undertaken in accordance with the *President's Guidelines of 1 October 2001 (Adoption Proceedings: A New Approach)* (set out in Part IV of this work).

Parties (r 4(2))—The applicant will be the adoption agency. In the county court the application must be made in the name of an officer of the agency who has been authorised to do so (Sch 1, Form 1). The respondents will be those listed in r 4(2). The court may at any time direct that any other person or body be joined as a respondent (r 4(3)).

Parent (r 4(2)(*a*))—A natural father who does not have parental responsibility is not someone who has to be made a respondent (*Re C (Adoption: Parties)* [1995] 2 FLR 483). See **"a child whose father does not have parental responsibility"** under AA 1976, s 18.

Child (r 4(2)(*g*), 4(3))—In the High Court the child who is the subject of the application must be made a respondent and in a county court the subject child may be made a respondent. The child will be represented by a children's guardian (see under r 6). The major advantage in joining the child as a party is that he can be legally represented. Prior to 2001 it was not possible to join the child as a party in the county court, and the practice developed of joining the children's guardian as a respondent in an appropriate case. Such a course is now unlikely to be required if the child himself is a party. Previous guidance on the appropriateness of separate representation for the child is likely to remain of use: in cases which are finely balanced or evidentially complex, the child's interests should be fully represented so that the court may be guided and directed on the relevant issues (*Re G (A Minor) (Adoption: Parental Agreement)* [1990] 2 FLR 429).

Documents to be filed (r 4(4)(*a*))—In any proceedings to free a child for adoption in the High Court or a county court, the applicant must pay the fee prescribed by Family Proceedings Fees Order 1999 and file three copies of the following documents with the court:
(*a*) the originating process in Form 1;
(*b*) a written report prepared in accordance with Sch 2;
(*c*) the birth certificate or certificate of previous adoption, which should be attached to the application (see notes to Form 1);
(*d*) if a parent or guardian has agreed to the making of an adoption order, any document signifying that agreement (which may be, but need not necessarily be, in Form 2: see r 8). If that agreement has been signified in a document executed outside England and Wales, the document must be filed with the application (r 8);
(*e*) where the child is a ward of court, it is usual to attach a copy of the wardship orders giving leave to commence proceedings for adoption or freeing for adoption, together with any ancillary directions;
(*f*) where the application requests the court to dispense with the agreement of a parent or guardian, a statement of facts must be filed in support of that request (r 7).

Schedule 2 report (r 4(4)(*b*))—The applicant must file with the originating process three copies of a written report covering all the relevant matters set out in Sch 2 of these rules (see also AA 1976, s 23). This report, which is generally known as a "Schedule 2 report", should be comprehensive, and is influential as it covers in detail every aspect of the circumstances and history of the application, and the parties to it. The Schedule 2 report is not automatically disclosed to the parents or guardians or to their representative (see **Confidential reports** under r 5). For a useful guide to compiling such reports, see BAAF Practice Note 15: *Schedule 2 reports under the Adoption Rules 1984* (1989).

Where a man is unaware that he has fathered a child, and if the consequences of him becoming aware of the child's existence would be detrimental to the child, the court will be prepared to say that seeking his wishes for the Schedule 2 report is not practicable (*Re P (Adoption) (Natural Father's Rights)* [1994] 1 FLR 771).

5 Appointment and duties of reporting officer

(1) As soon as practicable after the originating process has been filed or at any stage thereafter, if it appears that a parent or guardian of the child is willing to agree to the making of an adoption order and is in England and Wales, the proper officer, shall appoint a reporting officer in respect of that parent or guardian, and shall send to him a copy of the originating process and any documents attached thereto and of the report supplied by the applicant.

(2) The same person may be appointed as reporting officer in respect of two or more parents or guardians of the child.

(3) The reporting officer shall not be a member or employee of the applicant or any respondent body nor have been involved in the making of any arrangements for the adoption of the child.

(4) The reporting officer shall –

(*a*) ensure so far as is reasonably practicable that any agreement to the making of an adoption order is given freely and unconditionally and with full understanding of what is involved;

(*b*) confirm that the parent or guardian has been given an opportunity of making a declaration under section 18(6) of the Act that he prefers not be involved in future questions concerning the adoption of the child;

(*c*) witness the signature by the parent or guardian of the written agreement to the making of an adoption order;

(*d*) investigate all the circumstances relevant to that agreement and any such declaration;

(*e*) where it is proposed to free for adoption a child whose parents were not married to each other at the time of his birth and whose father is not his guardian, interview any person claiming to be the father in order to be able to advise the court on the matters listed in section 18(7) of the Act; but if more than one reporting officer has been appointed, the proper officer shall nominate one of them to conduct the interview; and

(*f*) on completing his investigations make a report in writing to the court, drawing attention to any matters which, in his opinion, may be of assistance to the court in considering the application.

(5) With a view to obtaining the directions of the court on any matter, the reporting officer may at any time make such interim report to the court as appears to him to be necessary and, in particular, the reporting officer shall make a report if a parent or guardian of the child is unwilling to agree to the making of an adoption order, and in such a case the proper officer shall notify the applicant.

(6) The court may, at any time before the final determination of the application, require the reporting officer to perform such further duties as the court considers necessary.

(7) The reporting officer shall attend any hearing of the application if so required by the court.

(8) Any report made to the court under this rule shall be confidential.

Amendments—SI 1991/1880; SI 2001/819.

Defined terms—"person whose father and mother were not married to each other at the time of his birth": Family Law Reform Act 1987, s 1; "proper officer": r 2(1).

Scope of provision—This rule is made under Adoption Act 1976, s 65. A reporting officer is appointed in every application for a freeing order where a parent or guardian who is in England and Wales appears willing to consent to the making of an adoption order (including step-parent cases). It is consent to an adoption order, rather than the freeing order, that is relevant. The focus of the reporting officer's work is the parent or guardian in respect of whom the appointment is made.

Appointment of reporting officer—The appointment is made by the proper officer and must be made as soon as practicable after the application has been made. The same person may be appointed as reporting officer in respect of two or more parents or guardians (r 5(2)), and the same officer may also be acting as children's guardian in respect of the child who is the subject of the application (r 6(3)).

Parent—See under r 4.

Written agreement (r 5(4)(*a*), (*c*))—The relevant agreement is to the eventual adoption of the child by virtue of an adoption order made in England and Wales. It must be given freely and unconditionally, whether or not the parent knows the identity of the eventual adopters (AA 1976, s 16(1)(*b*)). An agreement that seeks to contain conditions is invalid.

The agreement may be given in writing or orally to the court. A written agreement should be in Form 2 (AR 1984, Sch 1). Whilst other, non-standard, written agreements may be accepted by the court, it is clearly essential that they purport to express the agreement in terms wide enough to satisfy AA 1976, ss 16, 18 and 61 (see *Re LW (Written Agreement)* [1991] 1 FCR 867). The Court of Appeal has criticised the potential for confusion in Form 2; a parent consenting to adoption at the freeing stage must clearly understand that their parental responsibility for, and future involvement with, the child will be extinguished on the making of the freeing order (*Re A (Adoption: Agreement: Procedure)* [2001] 2 FLR 455).

If the document is witnessed in accordance with r 8, it will be admissible without further proof as to the parent's signature (AA 1976, s 61(1)) and there will be a rebuttable presumption that it is validly witnessed (AA 1976, s 61(2)).

The reporting officer must carry out his duty of witnessing parental agreement personally. He may not delegate his duty (DHSS Circular LAC (84)10).

Declaration under AA 1976, s 18(6) (r 5(4)(*b*))—Before making a freeing order, the court must satisfy itself, in relation to each of the child's parents or guardians who can be found, that each parent or guardian has been given an opportunity of making a declaration that he or she prefers not to be involved in future questions concerning the adoption of the child. There is provision, within Form 2, paras 6 and 7, for the parent or guardian either to make, or decline to make, the declaration. If the parent or guardian does not make such a declaration, the parent or guardian, as a "former parent", retains the right to receive progress reports (AA 1976, s 19) and to apply for the revocation of the freeing order (AA 1976, s 20). Where a declaration under s 18(6) has been made prior to the issue of the originating process, the declaration should be attached to the process when it is filed (AR 1984, Sch 1, Form 1).

Parent or guardian unwilling to agree to adoption (r 5(5))—If a parent or guardian is unwilling to agree to adoption, the reporting officer must report that fact to the court and notify the applicant. If the applicant decides to continue with the application, an application must be made to dispense with the consent of that parent or guardian (AA 1976, s 16(2)). In such a case the reporting officer will cease to function as such in respect of that parent or guardian and a children's guardian will be appointed. The children's guardian will often be the person who was the reporting officer (r 6(3)).

Confidential reports (r 5(8))—A party who is an individual and who is referred to in a confidential report supplied to the court may inspect, for the purposes of the hearing, that Part of the report which refers to him, subject to any directions given by the court restricting or extending the parts of the report which may be disclosed to him or restricting disclosure to his legal advisers only (r 53(2)). The House of Lords has defined the test to be applied when considering disclosure under r 53(2) (*Re D (Adoption Reports: Confidentiality)* [1996] AC 593, [1995] 2 FLR 687) but the test is not confined to r 53(2) disclosure (*Re K (Adoption: Disclosure of Information)* [1997] 2 FLR 74). A court must consider:

(1) whether disclosure would involve a real possibility of significant harm to the child; if so, then
(2) whether the overall interests of the child would benefit from non-disclosure, weighing on the one hand the interests of the child in having the material properly tested, and on the other both the magnitude of the risk of harm that will occur and the gravity of the harm if it did occur;
(3) if the interests of the child point towards non-disclosure, the court must weigh that consideration, and its strength in the circumstances of the case, against the interests of the party seeking disclosure in having an opportunity to see and respond to the material, taking account of the importance of the material to the issues in the case.

Non-disclosure should be the exception and not the rule. The court should be rigorous in its examination of the risk and the gravity of the feared harm, and should order non-disclosure only when the case for doing so is compelling.

Compatibility with ECHR Art 8 may require the privacy rights of adult parties, witnesses or victims to be considered in addition to those of the child (*Re X (Adoption: Confidentiality Procedure)* [2002] EWCA Civ 828, [2002] 2 FLR 476, para 14). In *Re X* Hale LJ stated that the disclosure issue "comes down to striking a fair balance between the various interests involved: the interests of all parties, but particularly the birth parents and the children themselves, in a fair trial of the issues, in which the evidence on each side can be properly tested and the relevant arguments properly advanced before the court; the interests of the children, their birth family and their prospective adoptive family, in protecting their family and private lives from unjustified interference; and the interests of the children in being protected from harm and damage to their welfare, whether in the short, medium or longer term".

The court should consider the extent of the inspection to be allowed far enough in advance of the hearing for instructions to be taken and any necessary evidence prepared for the hearing (*Re S (A Minor) (Adoption or Custodianship)* [1987] 2 WLR 977). A parent's right to oppose an adoption application does not entitle him to receive information about the prospective adopters (*Re S (A Minor) (Adoption)* [1993] 2 FLR 204). There is no rule in adoption proceedings requiring that notice of an application not to disclose information should always be given to a party (*Re K (Adoption: Disclosure of Information)* [1997] 2 FLR 74).

6 Appointment and duties of children's guardian

(1) As soon as practicable after the originating process has been filed, or after receipt of the statement of facts supplied under rule 7, if it appears that a parent or guardian of the child is unwilling to agree to the making of an adoption order, the proper officer shall appoint a children's guardian of the child and shall send to him a copy of the originating process, together with any documents attached thereto, the statement of facts and the report supplied by the applicant.

(2) Where there are special circumstances and it appears to the court that the welfare of the child requires it, the court may at any time appoint a children's guardian of the child, and where such an appointment is made the court shall indicate any particular matters which it requires the children's guardian to investigate, and the proper officer shall send the children's guardian a copy of the originating process together with any documents attached thereto and the report supplied by the applicant.

(3) The same person may be appointed as reporting officer under rule 5(1) in respect of a parent or guardian who appears to be willing to agree to the making of an adoption order, and as children's guardian of the child under this rule, and, whether or not so appointed as reporting officer, the children's guardian may be appointed as reporting officer in respect of a parent or guardian of the child who originally was unwilling to agree to the making of an adoption order but who later signifies his or her agreement.

(4) (*repealed*)

(5) The children's guardian shall not be a member or employee of the applicant or any respondent body nor have been involved in the making of any arrangements for the adoption of the child.

(6) With a view to safeguarding the interests of the child before the court, the children's guardian shall, so far as is reasonably practicable –

(*a*) investigate –
- (i) so far as he considers necessary, the matters alleged in the originating process, the report supplied by the applicant and, where appropriate, the statement of facts supplied under rule 7, and
- (ii) any other matters which appear to him to be relevant to the making of an order freeing the child for adoption;

(*b*) advise whether, in his opinion, the child should be present at the hearing of the process; and

(*c*) perform such other duties as appear to him to be necessary or as the court may direct.

(7) On completing his investigations the children's guardian shall make a report in writing to the court, drawing attention to any matters which, in his opinion, may be of assistance to the court in considering the application.

(8) With a view to obtaining the directions of the court on any matter, the children's guardian may at any time make such interim report to the court as appears to him to be necessary.

(9) The court may, at any time before the final determination of the application, require the children's guardian to perform such further duties as the court considers necessary.

(10) The children's guardian shall attend any hearing of the application unless the court otherwise orders.

(11) Any report made to the court under this rule shall be confidential.

Amendments—SI 1991/1880; SI 2001/819.

Defined terms—"children's guardian": r 2(1); "proper officer": r 2(1); "statement of facts": r 7.

Scope of provision—This rule is made under Adoption Act 1976, s 65. Where a parent or guardian is unwilling to give his consent to adoption, the court must appoint a children's guardian of the child. The children's guardian's duties in adoption proceedings are governed by these rules and not by FPR 1991, r 4.11. The focus of the children's guardian's work is to act on the child's behalf in the proceedings with a view to safeguarding the interests of the child before the court. In particular, the children's guardian conducts a thorough investigation of the child's circumstances relevant to the issues of adoption and consent.

"report supplied by the applicant" (r 6(1))—The report referred to is the Schedule 2 report supplied under r 4(4).

Parent—See under r 4.

Appointment of children's guardian (r 6(1), (2))—Where parental consent to adoption is being withheld a children's guardian must be appointed (r 6(1)). In any other case, where there are special circumstances and the child's welfare requires it, the court may appoint a children's guardian at any time (r 6(2)). The person appointed as children's guardian must be a CAFCASS officer (r 2(1)). Where adoption proceedings are pending in, or transferred to, the High Court, the case should be referred to CAFCASS Legal Section to consider the appropriate representation for the child (*Practice Note of March 2001 (Officers of CAFCASS Legal Services and Special Casework: Appointment in Family Proceedings)* – set out in Part IV of this work). In cases where a person has acted as a children's guardian in previous proceedings, and in the absence of any evidence of bias, the judge has the discretion to re-appoint the same person in subsequent adoption proceedings. There is likely to be a benefit both to the court and to the child if a children's guardian with previous familiarity of a case can be re-appointed (*Re J (Adoption: Appointment of Guardian ad Litem)* [1999] 2 FLR 86).

Legal representation of the children's guardian—In the High Court the children's guardian must be legally represented (RSC Ord 80, r 2(3)). The county court may join the child or the children's guardian as a respondent (r 4(3)). See **"Child"** under r 4.

Confidential reports (r 6(11))—See under r 5.

7 Statement of facts in dispensation cases

(1) Where the adoption agency applying for an order freeing a child for adoption intends to request the court to dispense with the agreement of a parent or guardian of the child on any of the grounds specified in section 16(2) of the Act, the request shall, unless otherwise directed, be made in the originating process, or, if made subsequently, by notice to the proper officer and there shall be attached to the originating process or notice three copies of the statement of facts on which the applicant intends to rely.

(2) Where the applicant has been informed by a person with whom the child has been placed for adoption that he wishes his identity to remain confidential, the statement of facts supplied under paragraph (1) shall be framed in such a way as not to disclose the identity of that person.

(3) Where a statement of facts has been supplied under paragraph (1), the proper officer shall, where and as soon as practicable, inform the parent or guardian of the request to dispense with his agreement and shall send to him a copy of the statement supplied under paragraph (1).

(4) The proper officer shall also send a copy of the statement supplied under paragraph (1) to the children's guardian and to the reporting officer if a different person.

Amendments—SI 1991/1880; SI 2001/819.

Defined terms—"adoption agency": r 2(1) (see also Adoption Act 1976, s 1(4)); "proper officer": r 2(1).

Scope of provision—Where the court is to determine whether the consent to adoption given by a parent or guardian should be dispensed with under AA 1976, s 16, the applicant agency must file a statement of the facts on which it intends to rely in support of its contention that consent should be dispensed with.

Statement of facts—The statement of facts should specify the grounds under AA 1976, s 16(2) on which the applicant will rely. As a matter of practice, the statement of facts will be of most use if it sets out in numbered paragraphs the detailed factual history relied on by the applicant.

Parent—See under r 4.

Children's guardian—For the appointment and duties of the children's guardian, see r 6.

Reporting officer—For the appointment and duties of the reporting officer, see r 5.

8 Agreement

(1) Any document signifying the agreement of a person to the making of an adoption order may be in Form 2, and, if executed by a person outside England and Wales before the commencement of the proceedings, shall be filed with the originating process.

(2) If the document is executed in Scotland it shall be witnessed by a Justice of the Peace or a Sheriff.

(3) If the document is executed in Northern Ireland it shall be witnessed by a Justice of the Peace.

(4) If the document is executed outside the United Kingdom it shall be witnessed by one of the following persons –

(*a*) any person for the time being authorised by law in the place where the document is executed to administer an oath for any judicial or other legal purpose;

(*b*) a British consular officer;

(*c*) a notary public; or

(*d*) if the person executing the document is serving in any of the regular armed forces of the Crown, an officer holding a commission in any of those forces.

Defined terms—"United Kingdom": Interpretation Act 1978, Sch 1.

Scope of provision—The agreement to adoption of a parent or guardian may be given in writing or orally to the court. This rule sets out the formal requirements for the form of agreement, witnessing of the signature and filing of the resulting document. A written agreement which does not conform with this provision may nevertheless be accepted by the court. Where a document purports to be witnessed in accordance with this rule, there is a rebuttable presumption that it is validly witnessed (Adoption Act 1976, s 61(2)).

Effect of giving agreement—Where a parent or guardian has given oral or written agreement to an adoption application and an application for an adoption order is pending, the parent or guardian is not entitled to remove the child from the home of the person with whom he has his home, unless that person consents or he obtains a court order (AA 1976, s 27).

Parent—See under r 4.

9 Notice of hearing

(1) As soon as practicable after receipt of the originating process, the proper officer shall list the case for hearing by a judge, and shall serve notice of the hearing on all the parties, the reporting officer and the children's guardian (if appointed) in Form 3.

(2) The reporting officer and the children's guardian (if appointed), but no other person, shall be served with a copy of the originating process and the report supplied by the applicant, and that report shall be confidential.

(3) If, at any stage before the hearing of the process, it appears to the court that directions for the hearing are required, the court may give such directions as it considers necessary and, in any event, the court shall, not less than four weeks before the date fixed for the hearing under paragraph (1), consider the documents relating to the process with a view to giving such further directions for the hearing as appear to the court to be necessary.

Amendments—SI 2001/819.

Defined terms—"proper officer": r 2(1).

Service (r 9(1))—The rule requiring service is mandatory. It is fundamental to the making of an adoption order that the natural parent should be informed of the application. The court may dispense with service, but in adoption proceedings the court should not be inclined to cut corners (*Re G (Foreign Adoption: Consent)* [1995] 2 FLR 534).

Reporting officer—For the appointment and duties of the reporting officer, see r 5.

Children's guardian—For the appointment and duties of the children's guardian, see r 6.

Confidential reports—See under r 5.

Directions—Although the rule requires the court to consider the papers in the case at least four weeks before the final hearing, in practice the court will consider giving directions within a short time after the filing of the originating process and after the filing of any report from the reporting officer or the children's guardian. The *President's Guidelines of 1 October 2001 (Adoption Proceedings: A New Approach)* (see Part IV of this work) set out a detailed list of matters to be considered at the first directions hearing.

Procedure in the High Court—The court gives notice to the natural parent, asking if he or she wishes to be heard in the proceedings. If no acknowledgement is received within 21 days, the court informs the applicant's solicitors and they must then serve the parent with a notice in the form set out in *Practice Direction of 24 March 1986*.

10 The hearing

(1) On the hearing of the process, any person upon whom notice is required to be served under rule 9 may attend and be heard on the question whether an order freeing the child for adoption should be made.

(2) Any member or employee of a party which is a local authority, adoption agency or other body may address the court if he is duly authorised in that behalf.

(3) Where the court has been informed by the applicant that the child has been placed with a person (whether alone or jointly with another) for adoption and that person wishes his identity to remain confidential, the proceedings shall be conducted with a view to securing that any such person is not seen by or made known to any respondent who is not already aware of his identity except with his consent.

(4) Subject to paragraph (5), the judge shall not make an order freeing the child for adoption except after the personal attendance before him of a representative of the applicant duly authorised in that behalf and of the child.

(5) If there are special circumstances which, having regard to the report of the children's guardian (if any), appear to the court to make the attendance of the child unnecessary, the court may direct that the child need not attend.

(6) If there are special circumstances which appear to the court to make the attendance of any party necessary, the court may direct that that party shall attend.

Amendments—SI 2001/819.

Defined terms—"adoption agency": r 2(1) (see also Adoption Act 1976, s 1(4)).

Scope of provision—This rule makes a number of specific provisions with regard to the hearing of a freeing application. In the absence of specific provision, the hearing will be conducted, at the discretion of the judge, in accordance with the general rules of procedure and evidence.

Hearing in private—In the High Court, the hearing "may be disposed of in chambers" (AA 1976, s 64(*a*)). In the county court, the proceedings "shall be heard and determined in camera" (AA 1976, s 64(*b*)).

Procedure in contested case—The question of whether a child should be freed for adoption (or adopted), and the question of whether a parent's agreement to adoption should be dispensed with, should be determined at the same hearing (*Re K (A Minor) (Adoption: Procedure)* [1986] 1 FLR 295; *Re LS (A Minor) (Adoption: Procedure)* [1986] 1 FLR 302).

The assistance of legal representation for a parent at a contested freeing or adoption hearing (where the parent wishes to be legally represented) is "an indispensable requirement' of the ECHR Art 6 right to a fair trial. Failure to adjourn a final hearing to enable a parent to be represented is likely to breach ECHR rights under both Arts 6 and 8 (*P, C and S v UK* [2002] 2 FLR 631). In addition, where the final adoption (or freeing hearing) proceeds almost immediately following contested care proceedings, the lack of any real lapse of time may also contribute to a breach of the parent's interests under Art 8 (*P, C and S v UK* (above)).

Evidence—The general law of evidence will apply. In an uncontested case, after the court has read the reports it may not require any formal evidence to be given at the hearing itself. Alternatively, short confirmatory evidence may be required to be given on behalf of the applicant. In a contested case, where the applicant seeks the dispensation of parental consent, the court must deal with the matter in a proper judicial hearing. All the evidence must be on oath, with both (or all) parties being given an opportunity to cross-examine each witness and with the court taking a proper note (*Re C (Adoption Application: Hearing)* (1982) FLR 95).

The Children (Admissibility of Hearsay Evidence) Order 1993 applies to proceedings under AA 1976.

"attend and be heard" (r 10(1))—The parties, the reporting officer and the children's guardian may attend and be heard on the question of whether a freeing order should be made. The children's guardian must attend the hearing unless the court directs otherwise (r 6(10)).

Member or employee of adoption agency (r 10(2))—The applicant agency may be represented by a non-lawyer member or employee who is duly authorised to address the court.

Attendance of the child (r 10(5))—In most cases, in practice, the court will direct that the child need not attend the hearing. The underlying purpose of the provision is to ensure that a child in respect of whom an adoption order is about to be made understands fully, as far as he or she can, the nature of the order (*Re P (Minors) (Adoption)* [1989] 1 FLR 1).

Children's guardian—For the appointment and duties of the children's guardian, see r 6.

11 Proof of identity of child etc

(1) Where the child who is the subject of the proceedings is identified in the originating process by reference to a birth certificate which is the same, or relates to the same entry in the Registers of Births, as a birth certificate exhibited to a form of agreement, the child so identified shall be deemed, unless the contrary appears, to be the child to whom the form of agreement refers.

(2) Where the child has previously been adopted, paragraph (1) shall have effect as if for the references to a birth certificate and to Registers of Births there were

substituted respectively references to a certified copy of an entry in the Adopted Children Register and to that Register.

(3) Where the precise date of the child's birth is not proved to the satisfaction of the court, the court shall determine the probable date of his birth and the date so determined may be specified in the order freeing the child for adoption as the date of his birth.

(4) Where the place of birth of the child cannot be proved to the satisfaction of the court but it appears probable that the child was born in the United Kingdom, the Channel Islands or the Isle of Man, he may be treated as having been born in the registration district and sub-district in which the court sits, and in any other case (where the country of birth is not proved) the particulars of the country of birth may be omitted from the order freeing the child for adoption.

Defined terms—"Adopted Children Register": Adoption Act 1976, s 50; "United Kingdom": Interpretation Act 1978, Sch 1.

12 Application for revocation of order freeing a child for adoption

(1) An application by a former parent for an order revoking an order freeing the child for adoption shall be made in Form 4 in the proceedings commenced under rule 4.

(2) Notice of the proceedings shall be served on all parties and on any adoption agency which has parental responsibility for the child by virtue of section 21 of the Act, save that notice shall not be served on a party to the proceedings who was joined as a party by virtue of rule 4(2)(*b*).

(3) As soon as practicable after receipt of the application, the proper officer shall list the case for hearing by a judge and shall appoint a children's guardian of the child in accordance with rule 6(4) or (5) and shall send to him a copy of the application and any documents attached thereto.

(4) The children's guardian shall have the same duties as if he had been appointed under rule 6 but as if in that rule –

(*a*) the reference to an order freeing the child for adoption was a reference to the revocation of an order freeing the child for adoption; and

(*b*) each reference to the report supplied by the applicant was omitted.

Amendments—SI 1991/1880; SI 2001/819.

Defined terms—"adoption agency": r 2(1) (see also Adoption Act 1976, s 1(4)); "former parent": AA 1976, s 19(1); "parental responsibility": CA 1989, s 3; "proper officer": r 2(1).

Scope of provision—A former parent who has not made a declaration under AA 1976, s 18(6) (ie that he prefers not to be involved in future questions concerning the adoption of the child – see **Declaration under AA 1976, s 18(6)** under r 5) may, in certain limited circumstances, apply for the freeing order to be revoked under AA 1976, s 20.

Application to be made in original freeing proceedings (r 12(1))—This rule and the text of Form 4 make it plain that the application for revocation must be made to the court that made the original freeing order.

Parties (r 12(2))—Notice must be served on all the parties to the original proceedings, other than any local authority or voluntary organisation which was made a party only because, at the time of the original application, it was looking after, or caring for, the child (r 4(2)(*b*)). Additionally, where parental responsibility for the child has been transferred to another adoption agency under AA 1976, s 21, that substitute agency must also be served with notice.

Children's guardian (r 12(3), (4))—For the appointment and duties of the children's guardian, see r 6.

Schedule 2 report (r 12(4)(*b*))—See generally under r 4. No fresh Schedule 2 report is required on an application to revoke a freeing order. The adoption agency will normally be required to file a report describing the placement arrangements following the making of the original order and the plans for the future placement of the child.

13 Substitution of one adoption agency for another

(1) An application under section 21(1) of the Act shall be made in Form 5 in the proceedings commenced under rule 4.

(2) Notice of any order made under section 21 of the Act shall be sent by the court to the court which made the order under section 18 of the Act (if a different court) and to any former parent (as defined in section 19(1) of the Act) of the child.

Amendments—SI 1991/1880.

Scope of provision—Under Adoption Act 1976, s 21, the court may vary the original freeing order under s 18 by giving parental responsibility for the child to another adoption agency ("the substitute agency") in place of the agency for the time being having parental responsibility for the child under the s 18 order ("the existing agency").

Joint application—An application for substitution under AA 1976, s 21 must be made jointly by the existing agency and the would-be substitute agency (AA 1976, s 21(2)).

Application to original court or in magistrates' court—Rule 13(1) states that the application should be made in the original s 18 proceedings. However, Children (Allocation of Proceedings) Order 1991, art 3 states that an application under AA 1976, s 21 must be commenced in a magistrates' court (art 3(1)(*r*)). An exception to art 3 is provided by art 4 which states that an application to vary an order must be made to the court that made the original order. It may be said that any AA 1976, s 21 application has the effect of varying the original freeing order and that therefore the application should be made to the original court; however, if this reasoning applied, there would have been no need for AA 1976, s 21 applications to have been included in art 3.

Form 5—The application must be made in accordance with Form 5, which provides for the joint application by the two adoption agencies. The application must state the reasons why the transfer would be in the best interests of the child, together with the reasons which make the transfer administratively desirable.

Notice—Although the application must be made in the original s 18 proceedings, there is no requirement to serve the application on the parties to those proceedings (contrast r 12(2)). The only requirement is that any "former parent" (see AA 1976, s 19(1)) must be informed of the making of the application (Form 5, para 4).

PART III
ADOPTION ORDERS

14 Application for a serial number

If any person proposing to apply to the court for an adoption order wishes his identity to be kept confidential, he may, before commencing proceedings, apply to the proper officer for a serial number to be assigned to him for the purposes of identifying him in the proposed process and a number shall be assigned to him accordingly.

Defined terms—"adoption order": Adoption Act 1976, s 12(1); "proper officer": r 2(1).

Scope of provision—If an applicant for an adoption order wishes his identity to be kept confidential, he may apply for a serial number to be assigned to him. If a serial number has been assigned, the proceedings must be conducted with a view to ensuring that the applicant is neither seen by, nor made known to, any respondent who is not already aware of his identity (r 23(3)). Ultimately the court retains the power to order disclosure of the identity of the adopters; that power should be exercised in the manner applicable to disclosure of other confidential material (*Re X (Adoption: Confidentiality Procedure)* [2002] EWCA Civ 828, [2002] 2 FLR 476) (see **Confidential reports** under r 5).

15 Commencement of proceedings

(1) Proceedings for an adoption order shall be commenced –

(*a*) by originating summons in Form 6 issued out of the Principal Registry of the Family Division; or
(*b*) by filing in the office of a county court an originating application in Form 6.

(2) The applicant shall be the proposed adopter and the respondents shall be –

(*a*) each parent or guardian (not being an applicant) of the child, unless the child is free for adoption;
(*b*) any adoption agency having parental responsibility for the child by virtue of sections 18 or 21 of the Act;
(*c*) any adoption agency named in the application or in any form of agreement to the making of the adoption order as having taken part in the arrangements for the adoption of the child;
(*d*) any local authority to whom the applicant has given notice under section 22 of the Act of his intention to apply for an adoption order;
(*e*) any local authority or voluntary organisation which has parental responsibility for, is looking after, or is caring for, the child;
(*f*), (*g*) (*revoked*)
(*h*) any person liable by virtue of any order or agreement to contribute to the maintenance of the child;
(*i*) (*revoked*)
(*j*) where the applicant proposes to rely on section 15(1)(*b*)(ii) of the Act, the spouse of the applicant; and
(*k*) in the High Court, the child.

(3) The court may at any time direct that any other person or body be made a respondent to the process.

(4) On filing the originating process the applicant shall pay the appropriate fee and supply three copies of –

(*a*) Form 6, together with any other documents required to be supplied, and
(*b*) where the child was not placed for adoption with the applicant by an adoption agency, save where the applicant or one of the applicants is a parent of the child, reports by a registered medical practitioner made not more than three months earlier on the health of the child and of each applicant, covering the matters specified in Schedule 3 to these rules.

Amendments—SI 1991/1880; SI 2001/819.

Defined terms—"adoption agency": r 2(1) (see also Adoption Act 1976, s 1(4)); "caring for", "child": CA 1989, s 105(1), AA 1976, s 72(1B); "guardian", "local authority": CA 1989, s 105(1); "looking after": CA 1989, s 22(1); "parental responsibility": CA 1989, ss 3, 105(1); "voluntary organisation": CA 1989, s 105(1).

Substantive law—The relevant substantive law is AA 1976, ss 12–16.

PART III

High Court or county court (r 15(1))—See generally under r 4. If the applicants are seeking ratification of a prohibited private placement (AA 1976, s 11(1)), the application must be made to the High Court (*Re K (A Minor) (Adoption and Wardship)* (1983) Fam Law 146).

Transfer between courts—The Children (Allocation of Proceedings) Order 1991 applies to adoption proceedings.

Adoption application made while freeing proceedings pending—An adoption application can be made while proceedings for freeing the same child are pending. The court can proceed with the adoption application, treating the freeing application as obsolete, but the court can revert to and proceed with the freeing application if, for some reason, this later becomes appropriate (*Re B (Minors) (Freeing for Adoption)* [1992] 2 FLR 37. See also **Choice of application where child already placed for adoption** under r 4.

Application to dispense with parental consent—Where the applicant intends to request the court to dispense with parental consent under AA 1976, s 16(2), the request must, unless otherwise directed, be made in the originating process, or, if made subsequently, by notice to the proper officer (r 19(1)).

"applicant" (r 15(2))—The applicant will be the proposed adopter or adopters. In a case where the child has been placed with the proposed adopter by an adoption agency, the agency will normally support the applicant by funding legal representation, providing access to its files for the preparation of a statement of facts in a contested case and by making its workers available to give evidence in support of the application.

Respondents (r 15(2), (3))—Each of the persons referred to in r 15(2)(*a*)–(*k*) must be made a respondent to the application (*Re K (Adoption and Wardship)* [1997] 2 FLR 221). It is the adoption applicant, rather than any adoption agency, that is responsible for ensuring that those who should be respondents are properly joined in the proceedings (*Re L (A Minor) (Adoption: Procedure)* [1991] 1 FLR 171). Any other person or body may be joined as a respondent by the court.

Parent (r 15(2)(*a*))—See under r 4.

Child (r 15(2)(*k*))—See under r 4.

Documents to be filed with application (r 15(4))—At the commencement of the proceedings, the applicant must pay the fee prescribed by the Family Proceedings Fees Order 1999 and supply the court with three copies of the following documents:
(*a*) the originating process (Form 6);
(*b*) if there are two applicants who are married to each other, their marriage certificate;
(*c*) in any other case, documentary evidence of marital status should be supplied; if a married applicant is applying alone, the applicant should attach any documentary evidence in support of the application being granted without the non-applicant spouse (AA 1976, s 15(1)(*b*));
(*d*) a medical report on the health of each applicant and on the child made during the three months prior to the application (in accordance with AR 1984, Sch 3), but no medical report is required if the child was placed for adoption by an adoption agency or is the child of one of the applicants;
(*e*) either the child's birth certificate or, if appropriate, a copy of the entry in the Adopted Children Register relating to his previous adoption;
(*f*) if the child has been freed for adoption, a copy of the freeing order and any order transferring parental responsibility to another adoption agency under AA 1976, s 21;
(*g*) any document executed outside England and Wales before the commencement of the proceedings which signifies that the parent or guardian has given his agreement to the making of an adoption order;
(*h*) where the application includes a request for the court to dispense with the agreement of a parent, the statement of facts relied on in support of that request;
(*i*) where the child is a ward of court, it is usual to attach a copy of the wardship orders giving leave to commence adoption proceedings, together with any ancillary directions.

Inter-country adoptions—Where an application is made to adopt a foreign national, who is not a relative of the applicant(s), regard must be had to the Intercountry Adoption (Hague Convention) Regulations 2003, the "*Intercountry Adoption Guide – Practice and Procedures*" published by the DOH (available on the Internet at *www.doh.gov.uk/adoption*) and to the extensive procedural guidance given by Bracewell J in *Re R (Inter-Country Adoptions: Practice)* [1999] 1 FLR 1042. In particular: there is a duty upon the applicants to make full, frank and timely disclosure of all relevant information; the court should never accept documents which are not translated into English; in cases where there is doubt about parental consent, or proper pre-application procedure, the case should be transferred to the High Court for an urgent directions hearing (see under r 21).

Notice to Home Office—Where it is possible that the object of the application is simply to enable the child to acquire British citizenship, it is desirable for the court to add the Home Secretary as a respondent (*Re H (A Minor) (Adoption: Non-patrial)* (1983) FLR 85). Where a British citizen applies to adopt a foreign child, the applicant should give notice to the Home Office, so that the Home Secretary has the opportunity to apply to become a respondent (*Re W (A Minor) (Adoption: Non-patrial)* [1986] 1 FLR 179; *Re K (Adoption and Wardship)* [1997] 2 FLR 221). It is the applicant, and not the court, that is required to give the notice. The court must ensure that the notice has been given, and the applicant will require evidence of service of the notice and of the fact that the Home Secretary does not wish to intervene. The Secretary of State, if joined as a party to the proceedings, has a right of appeal; that right is not excluded by British Nationality Act 1981, s 1(6) (*Re K (A Minor) (Adoption Order: Nationality)* [1994] 2 FLR 557).

16 Preliminary examination of application

If it appears to the proper officer on receipt of the originating process for an adoption order that the court –

(*a*) may be precluded, by virtue of section 24(1) of the Act, from proceeding to hear the application, or

(*b*) may for any other reason appearing in the process have no jurisdiction to make an adoption order,

he shall refer the process to the judge or district judge for directions.

Amendments—SI 1991/1880.

Defined terms—"proper officer": r 2(1).

Scope of provision—The court must conduct a preliminary examination of the application to determine whether there are any potential issues as to jurisdiction.

Adoption Act 1976, s 24(1)—The court must not proceed to hear an application for an adoption order in relation to a child where a previous application for a British adoption order made in relation to the child by the same person or persons was refused by any court, unless when refusing the application the court ordered that s 24(1) would not apply, or it appears to the court that because of a change of circumstances, or some other reason, it is proper to proceed.

17 Appointment and duties of reporting officer

(1) As soon as practicable after the originating process has been filed or at any stage thereafter, if the child is not free for adoption and if it appears that a parent or guardian of the child is willing to agree to the making of an adoption order and is in England and Wales, the proper officer shall appoint a reporting officer in respect of that parent or guardian, and shall send him a copy of the originating process and any documents attached thereto.

(2) The same person may be appointed as reporting officer in respect of two or more parents or guardians of the child.

(3) The reporting officer shall not be a member or employee of the applicant or any respondent body (except where a local authority is made a respondent only under rule 15(2)(*d*)) nor have been involved in the making of any arrangements for the adoption of the child.

(4) The reporting officer shall –

(*a*) ensure so far as is reasonably practicable that any agreement to the making of the adoption order is given freely and unconditionally and with full understanding of what is involved;

(*b*) witness the signature by the parent or guardian of the written agreement to the making of the adoption order;

(*c*) investigate all the circumstances relevant to that agreement; and

(*d*) on completing his investigations make a report in writing to the court, drawing attention to any matters which, in his opinion, may be of assistance to the court in considering the application.

(5) Paragraphs (5) to (8) of rule 5 shall apply to a reporting officer appointed under this rule as they apply to a reporting officer appointed under that rule.

Amendments—SI 1991/1880; SI 2001/819.

Defined terms—"free for adoption": Adoption Act 1976, s 18.

Scope of provision—This rule is made under AA 1976, s 65. A reporting officer is appointed in every application for an adoption order where a parent or guardian who is in England and Wales appears willing to consent to the making of an adoption order (including step-parent cases). The focus of the reporting officer's work is the agreement of the parent or guardian in respect of whom he is appointed rather than the welfare of the child.

Appointment of reporting officer (r 17(1))—See under r 5.

Parent—See under r 4.

Written agreement (r 17(4)(*a*), (*b*))—See under r 5.

Parent or guardian unwilling to agree to adoption (r 17(5))—See under r 5.

Confidential reports (r 17(5))—See under r 5.

18 Appointment and duties of children's guardian

(1) As soon as practicable after the originating process has been filed, or after receipt of the statement of facts supplied under rule 19, if the child is not free for adoption and if it appears that a parent or guardian of the child is unwilling to agree to the making of the adoption order, the proper officer shall appoint a children's guardian of the child and shall send him a copy of the originating process together with any documents attached thereto.

(2) Where there are special circumstances and it appears to the court that the welfare of the child requires it, the court may at any time appoint a children's guardian of the child and where such an appointment is made the court shall indicate any particular matters which it requires the children's guardian to investigate, and the proper officer shall send to the children's guardian a copy of the originating process together with any documents attached thereto.

(3) The same person may be appointed as reporting officer under rule 17(1) in respect of a parent or guardian who appears to be willing to agree to the making of the adoption order, and as children's guardian of the child under this rule, and, whether or not so appointed as reporting officer, the children's guardian may be appointed as reporting officer in respect of a parent or guardian of the child who originally was unwilling to agree to the making of an adoption order but who later signifies his or her agreement.

(4) (*repealed*)

(5) The children's guardian shall not be a member or employee of the applicant or any respondent body (except where a local authority is made a respondent only under rule 15(2)(*d*)) nor have been involved in the making of any arrangements for the adoption of the child.

(6) With a view to safeguarding the interests of the child before the court the children's guardian shall, so far as is reasonably practicable –

(*a*) investigate –

(i) so far as he considers necessary, the matters alleged in the originating process, any report supplied under rule 22(1) or (2) and, where appropriate, the statement of facts supplied under rule 19;

(ii) any other matters which appear to him to be relevant to the making of an adoption order;

(*b*) advise whether, in his opinion, the child should be present at the hearing of the process; and

(*c*) perform such other duties as appear to him to be necessary or as the court may direct.

(7) Paragraphs (7) to (11) of rule 6 shall apply to a children's guardian appointed under this rule as they apply to a children's guardian appointed under that rule.

Amendments—SI 1991/1880; SI 2001/819.

Prospective amendment by Adoption (Amendment) Rules 2003—By virtue of A(A)R 2003, r 5, which comes into force on 1 June 2003:

(*a*) in para (2) for "Where" substitute "Subject to paragraph (2A), where";

(*b*) after para (2) insert –

"(2A) Where an application is made for a Convention adoption order under rule 28, the proper officer shall as soon as possible appoint a children's guardian of the child and shall send him a copy of the originating process together with any documents attached thereto.";

(*c*) in para (6)(*a*)(i) after "22(1) or (2)" insert ", any reports filed under the Convention or Hague Convention Regulations"; and

(*d*) in para (6)(*a*)(ii) after "adoption order" insert "/Convention adoption order".

Defined terms—"proper officer": r 2(1); "statement of facts": r 19.

Scope of provision—This rule is made under Adoption Act 1976, s 65. Where a parent or guardian is unwilling to give his consent to adoption, the court must appoint a children's guardian of the child. The children's guardian's duties in adoption proceedings are governed by these rules and not by FPR 1991, r 4.11. The focus of the children's guardian's work is to act on the child's behalf in the proceedings with a view to safeguarding the interests of the child before the court. In particular, the children's guardian conducts a thorough investigation of the child's circumstances relevant to the issues of adoption and consent.

Parent—See under r 4.

Appointment of children's guardian where consent is not being withheld (r 18(2))—See under r 6. In any case where it is clear that further investigations will be required (for example an international case) a children's guardian should be appointed (*Re K (Adoption and Wardship)* [1997] 2 FLR 221).

Confidential reports (r 18(7))—See under r 5.

Inter-country adoptions—In an inter-country adoption it is essential that the children's guardian recognises the importance of making contact with the natural family as a matter of priority. The children's guardian should seek an early directions hearing in such cases and full disclosure of any social services or adoption agency files relating to the applicants (*Re R (Inter-Country Adoptions: Practice)* [1999] 1 FLR 1042).

PART III

19 Statement of facts in dispensation cases

(1) Where the child is not free for adoption and the applicant for the adoption order intends to request the court to dispense with the agreement of a parent or guardian of the child on any of the grounds specified in section 16(2) of the Act, the request shall, unless otherwise directed, be made in the originating process or, if made subsequently, by notice to the proper officer and there shall be attached to the originating process or notice three copies of the statement of facts on which the applicant intends to rely.

(2) Where a serial number has been assigned to the applicant under rule 14, the statement of facts supplied under paragraph (1) shall be framed in such a way as not to disclose the identity of the applicant.

(3) Where a statement of facts has been supplied under paragraph (1), the proper officer shall, where and as soon as practicable, inform the parent or guardian of the request to dispense with his agreement and shall send to him a copy of the statement supplied under paragraph (1).

(4) The proper officer shall also send a copy of the statement supplied under paragraph (1) to the children's guardian and to the reporting officer if a different person.

Amendments—SI 1991/1880; SI 2001/819.

Defined terms—"free for adoption": Adoption Act 1976, s 18; "proper officer": r 2(1).

Scope of provision—Where the court is to determine whether the consent to adoption of a parent or guardian should be dispensed with under AA 1976, s 16, the applicant must file a statement of the facts on which he intends to rely in support of his contention that consent should be dispensed with.

Statement of facts—See under r 7.

Children's guardian—For the appointment and duties of the children's guardian, see r 18.

Reporting officer—For the appointment and duties of the reporting officer, see r 17.

20 Agreement

(1) Any document signifying the agreement of a person to the making of the adoption order may be in Form 7, and, if executed by a person outside England and Wales before the commencement of the proceedings, shall be filed with the originating process.

(2) If the document is executed outside England and Wales it shall be witnessed by one of the persons specified in rule 8(2), (3) or (4), according to the country in which it is executed.

Scope of provision—The agreement to adoption of a parent or guardian may be given in writing or orally to the court. This rule sets out the formal requirements for the form of agreement, witnessing of the signature and filing of the resulting document. A written agreement which does not conform with this provision may nevertheless be accepted by the court. Where a document purports to be witnessed in accordance with this rule, there is a rebuttable presumption that it is validly witnessed (Adoption Act 1976, s 61(2)).

21 Notice of hearing

(1) Subject to paragraph (4), the proper officer shall list the case for hearing by a judge as soon as practicable after the originating process has been filed, and shall

serve notice of the hearing on all the parties, the reporting officer and the children's guardian (if appointed) in Form 8.

(2) In a case where section 22 of the Act applies, the proper officer shall send a copy of the originating process and, where appropriate, of the report supplied under rule 15(4), to the local authority to whom notice under that section was given.

(3) No person other than the reporting officer, the children's guardian (if appointed) and, in cases where section 22 of the Act applies, the local authority to whom notice under that section was given, shall be served with a copy of the originating process.

(4) Where section 22 of the Act applies, the proper officer shall list the case for hearing on a date not less than three months from the date of the notice given to the local authority under that section.

(5) If, at any stage before the hearing of the process, it appears to the court that directions for the hearing are required, the court may give such directions as it considers necessary and, in any event, the court shall, not less than four weeks before the date fixed for the hearing under paragraph (1), consider the documents relating to the process with a view to giving such further directions for the hearing as appear to the court to be necessary.

PART III

Amendments—SI 1991/1880; SI 2001/819.

Defined terms—"proper officer": r 2(1).

Service (r 21(1))—See under r 9.

AA 1976, s 22 (r 21(2)–(4))—An adoption order cannot be made in respect of a child who was not placed with the applicant by an adoption agency, unless the applicant has, at least three months before the date of the order, given notice to the local authority within whose area he has his home of his intention to apply for the adoption order. The application must be made within a period of two years following the giving of that notice (AA 1976, s 22(1A)).

Originating process not to be served on parents (r 21(3))—The originating process (Form 6), which, in every case, contains details of the applicant, is to be served only on the reporting officer, the children's guardian and a local authority to whom notice has been given. The parents will not be served with a copy of the originating process, but will be served with the notice of hearing (Form 8) and, in a contested case, with a copy of the statement of facts.

Reporting officer—For the appointment and duties of the reporting officer, see r 17.

Children's guardian—For the appointment and duties of the children's guardian, see r 18.

Directions—See under r 9.

Procedure in the High Court—See under r 9.

Inter-country adoptions—Guidance given in *Re R (Inter-Country Adoptions: Practice)* [1999] 1 FLR 1042 regarding inter-country adoption includes:

(*a*) drawing up a timetable to determine the application without delay;
(*b*) never accepting documents which do not have an English translation;
(*c*) early transfer to the High Court where there is a doubt concerning parental consent or adherence to proper pre-application procedures;
(*d*) prior to the directions hearing, the applicant should be directed to file and serve an affidavit setting out full details of the circumstances of the application;
(*e*) cross-examination of the applicants may take place at the directions hearing;
(*f*) directions should be given for personal service on the natural parents within 28 days, including the provision of information about the role of the children's guardian and Legal Aid availability;

(*g*) further directions should be fixed before a judge within six weeks, with provision for filing an interim report from the children's guardian;

(*h*) at the next directions hearing, if it appears that the natural parents never consented and now seek the return of the child, the court should consider whether to dismiss the adoption application summarily and consider proceeding in wardship.

22 Reports by adoption agency or local authority

(1) Where the child was placed for adoption with the applicant by an adoption agency, that agency shall supply, within six weeks of receipt of the notice of hearing under rule 21, three copies of a report in writing covering the matters specified in Schedule 2 to these rules.

(2) Where the child was not placed for adoption with the applicant by an adoption agency, the local authority to whom the notice under section 22 of the Act was given shall supply, within six weeks of receipt of the notice of hearing under rule 21, three copies of a report in writing covering the matters specified in Schedule 2 to these rules.

(3) The court may request a further report under paragraph (1) or (2) and may indicate any particular matters it requires such a further report to cover.

(4) The proper officer shall send a copy of any report supplied under paragraph (1) or (2) to the reporting officer and to the children's guardian (if appointed).

(5) No other person shall be supplied with a copy of any report supplied under paragraph (1) or (2) and any such report shall be confidential.

Amendments—SI 1991/1880; SI 2001/819.

Defined terms—"adoption agency": r 2(1) (see also Adoption Act 1976, s 1(4)); "proper officer": r 2(1).

Scope of provision—In every adoption case, whether the child's parents are in agreement or not, the relevant local authority or adoption agency must compile a written report covering all the relevant matters set out in Sch 2 to these rules (see **Schedule 2 report** under r 4).

Timing and authorship of report (r 22(1), (2))—If the child was placed for adoption with the applicant by an adoption agency, the Schedule 2 report need not be filed with the originating process, but it must be filed within six weeks of the agency receiving notice of the hearing issued under r 21.

In the case of a non-agency placement, the report must be compiled by the local authority to whom notice has been given under AA 1976, s 22, and must also be filed within six weeks of the local authority receiving notice of the hearing issued under r 21.

Reporting officer—For the appointment and duties of the reporting officer, see r 17.

Children's guardian—For the appointment and duties of the children's guardian, see r 18.

Confidential reports—See under r 5.

23 The hearing

(1) On the hearing of the process, any person upon whom notice is required to be served under rule 21 may attend and be heard on the question whether an adoption order should be made.

(2) Any member or employee of a party which is a local authority, adoption agency or other body may address the court if he is duly authorised in that behalf.

(3) If a serial number has been assigned to the applicant under rule 14, the proceedings shall be conducted with a view to securing that he is not seen by or made known to any respondent who is not already aware of the applicant's identity except with his consent.

(4) Subject to paragraphs (5) and (7), the judge shall not make an adoption order or an interim order except after the personal attendance before him of the applicant and the child.

(5) If there are special circumstances which, having regard to the report of the children's guardian (if any), appear to the court to make the attendance of the child unnecessary, the court may direct that the child need not attend.

(6) If there are special circumstances which appear to the court to make the attendance of any other person necessary, the court may direct that that party shall attend.

(7) In the case of an application under section 14(1A) or (1B) of the Act, the judge may in special circumstances make an adoption order or an interim order after the personal attendance of one only of the applicants, if the originating process is verified by an affidavit sworn by the other applicant or, if he is outside the United Kingdom, by a declaration made by him and witnessed by any of the persons specified in rule 8(4).

Amendments—SI 1991/1880; SI 2001/819.

Defined terms—"adoption agency": r 2(1) (see also Adoption Act 1976, s 1(4)).

Hearing in private—See under r 10.

Procedure in contested case—See under r 10.

Evidence—See under r 10.

"attend and be heard" (r 23(1))—The parties, the reporting officer and the children's guardian may attend and be heard on the question whether an adoption order should be made. The children's guardian must attend the hearing unless the court directs otherwise (rr 6(10), 18(7)).

Member or employee of adoption agency (r 23(2))—See under r 10.

Serial number case (r 23(3))—The operation of this rule will inevitably mean that the applicant and those who do not know the applicant's identity may not be in the courtroom at the same time. The normal approach of courts is to conduct most of the hearing in the absence of the applicant. In some cases, particularly in the High Court, arrangements can be made for the absent applicant to listen to the proceedings without being present in the courtroom. If the applicant is called to give evidence, the roles are reversed and those who do not know the applicant's identity will leave the courtroom.

Personal attendance of the applicant and the child (r 23(4)–(7))—The requirement for the attendance of the applicant and the child applies whether or not the application is contested. Attendance in an uncontested case will not normally involve giving evidence. In practice, most High Court judges dispense with this requirement.

24 Proof of identity of child etc

(1) Where the child who is the subject of the proceedings is identified in the originating process by reference to a birth certificate which is the same, or relates to the same entry in the Registers of Births, as a birth certificate exhibited to a form of agreement, the child so identified shall be deemed, unless the contrary appears, to be the child to whom the form of agreement refers.

(2) Where the child has previously been adopted, paragraph (1) shall have effect as if for the references to a birth certificate and to the Registers of Births there were substituted respectively references to a certified copy of an entry in the Adopted Children Register and to that Register.

(3) Subject to paragraph (5), where the precise date of the child's birth is not proved to the satisfaction of the court, the court shall determine the probable date of birth and the date so determined may be specified in the adoption order as the date of his birth.

(4) Subject to paragraph (5), where the place of birth of the child cannot be proved to the satisfaction of the court but it appears probable that the child was born in the United Kingdom, the Channel Islands or the Isle of Man, he may be treated as having been born in the registration district and sub-district in which the court sits, and in any other case (where the country of birth is not proved) the particulars of the country of birth may be omitted from the adoption order.

(5) Where the child is free for adoption, any order made identifying the probable date and place of birth of the child in the proceedings under section 18 of the Act shall be sufficient proof of the date and place of birth of the child in proceedings to which this rule applies.

Amendments—SI 1991/1880.

Defined terms—"Adopted Children Register": Adoption Act 1976, s 50; "United Kingdom": Interpretation Act 1978, Sch 1.

Scope of provision—This rule allows the identity of the child to be presumed proved where the birth certificate relied upon in the application relates to the certificate filed with a written form of agreement. The rule also allows the court to determine the child's date or place of birth where there is no precise evidence available.

25 Further proceedings after interim order

Where the court has made an interim order, the proper officer shall list the case for further hearing by a judge on a date before the order expires and shall send notice in Form 8 of the date of the hearing to all the parties and to the children's guardian (if appointed) not less than one month before that date.

Defined terms—"interim order": Adoption Act 1976, s 25; "proper officer": r 2(1).

Scope of provision—An interim order is an order, made on an application for an adoption order, whereby the court postpones the determination of the application and makes an order giving parental responsibility for the child to the applicant for a probationary period not exceeding two years (AA 1976, s 25). This rule provides for the relisting of the case before a judge prior to the expiry of the probationary period.

Children's guardian—For the appointment and duties of the children's guardian, see r 18.

****

PART IV
CONVENTION PROCEEDINGS

General Note—When Adoption (Intercountry Aspects) Act 1999, s 3 comes into force on 1 June 2003, AA 1976, s 17 will be replaced by a new provision which relates to "Convention" adoptions under the 1993 Hague Convention on Intercountry Adoption. On the same date, Part IV of these rules will also be substantially amended by the Adoption (Amendment) Rules 2003 (see Prospective amendment notes below for the text of these revisions).

27 Introductory

(1) This Part of these rules shall apply to Convention proceedings and, subject to the provisions of this Part of these rules, Parts I, III and V of these rules shall apply, with the necessary modifications, to Convention proceedings as they apply to proceedings in the High Court under the Act.

(2) Any reference in this Part of these rules to the nationality of a person who is not solely a United Kingdom national means that person's nationality as determined in accordance with section 70 of the Act.

Amendments—SI 1991/1880.

Prospective amendment by Adoption (Amendment) Rules 2003—By virtue of A(A)R 2003, r 6, which comes into force on 1 June 2003:
(*a*) in para (1) after "High Court" insert "or a county court"; and
(*b*) omit para (2).

Defined terms—"Convention proceedings": Adoption Act 1976, s 17.

Scope of provision—Rules 27 to 36 apply to Convention adoptions. The number of Convention applications is extremely small, and so detailed annotations have been omitted from this Part of the rules. See also AA 1976, s 17.

28 Originating process

(1) An applicant for a Convention adoption order shall state in his originating process that he is applying for a Convention adoption order.

(2) The originating process –

(*a*) need not contain paragraphs corresponding to paragraphs 2, 24 or 25 of Form 6, but

(*b*) shall contain the additional information required by Schedule 4 to these rules.

29 Evidence as to nationality

(1) Any document (or copy of a document) which is to be used for the purposes of satisfying the court as to the nationality of the applicant or of the child shall be attached to the originating process.

(2) Where the applicant claims that for the purposes of section 17(2)(*a*), (4)(*a*) or (5)(*a*) of the Act he or the child is a national of a Convention country, he shall attach to the originating process a statement by an expert as to the law of that country relating to nationality applicable to that person.

Amendments—SI 1991/1880.

Prospective amendment by Adoption (Amendment) Rules 2003—By virtue of A(A)R 2003, r 7, which comes into force on 1 June 2003, rule 29 is revoked.

30 Statement at hearing

The requirement that the conditions in section 17(2), (3) and (4) or (5) of the Act are satisfied immediately before the order is made may be established by –

PART III

(*a*) oral evidence at the hearing of an application for a Convention adoption order, or

(*b*) a document executed by the applicant containing a statement to that effect attested in accordance with rule 44 and such a statement shall be admissible in evidence without further proof of the signature of the applicant.

Amendments—SI 1991/1880.

Prospective amendment by Adoption (Amendment) Rules 2003—By virtue of A(A)R 2003, r 8, which comes into force on 1 June 2003, for rule 30 substitute:

> "**30** The requirements prescribed by regulations 21 and 32 of the Hague Convention Regulations may be established by a document executed by the applicant containing a statement to that effect attested in accordance with rule 44 and such a statement shall be admissible in evidence without further proof of the signature of the applicant.".

31 Orders

Within 7 days after a Convention adoption order has been drawn up, the proper officer shall by notice to the Registrar General request him to send the information to the designated authorities of any Convention country –

(*a*) of which the child is a national;
(*b*) in which the child was born;
(*c*) in which the applicant habitually resides; or
(*d*) of which the applicant is a national.

Prospective amendment by Adoption (Amendment) Rules 2003—By virtue of A(A)R 2003, r 9, which comes into force on 1 June 2003, rule 31 is revoked.

Additional provisions for cases where child is not a United Kingdom national

32 Scope of Rules 33 to 36

Rules 33 to 36 shall apply to any case where the child is not a United Kingdom national, and in such a case –

(*a*) the provisions in Part III of these rules, other than rules 17 and 20 (agreement to adoption), and

(*b*) paragraphs 9 to 14 of Form 6,

shall apply with the necessary modifications to take account of section 17(6)(*a*) of the Act.

Amendments—SI 1991/1880.

Prospective amendment by Adoption (Amendment) Rules 2003—By virtue of A(A)R 2003, r 9, which comes into force on 1 June 2003, rule 32 is revoked.

Scope of provision—Rules 32 to 36 are solely concerned with Convention adoptions under Adoption Act 1976, s 17 where the child concerned is not a United Kingdom national. For a description of the scope of the Convention, see AA 1976, s 17.

33 Evidence as to foreign law relating to consents and consultations

The applicant shall file, with his originating process, a statement by an expert as to the provisions relating to consents and consultations of the internal law relating to adoption of the Convention country of which the child is a national.

Prospective amendment by Adoption (Amendment) Rules 2003—By virtue of A(A)R 2003, r 9, which comes into force on 1 June 2003, rule 33 is revoked.

34 Form of consent etc

(1) Any document signifying the consent of a person to, or otherwise containing the opinion of a person on the making of, the Convention adoption order shall be in a form which complies with the internal law relating to adoption of the Convention country of which the child is a national: provided that where the court is not satisfied that a person consents with full understanding of what is involved, it may call for further evidence.

(2) A document referred to in paragraph (1) shall, if sufficiently witnessed, be admissible as evidence of the consent or opinion contained therein without further proof of the signature of the person by whom it is executed.

(3) A document referred to in paragraph (1) shall, if executed before the date of the applicant's originating process referred to in rule 28(2), be attached to that process.

Prospective amendment by Adoption (Amendment) Rules 2003—By virtue of A(A)R 2003, r 10, which comes into force on 1 June 2003, in para (1) for "a national" substitute "habitually resident".

35 Notice of hearing

(1) When serving notice of the hearing on the persons specified in rule 21, the proper officer shall also serve notice on any person –

(*a*) whose consent to the making of the order is required, not being an applicant, or

(*b*) who, in accordance with the internal law relating to adoption of the Convention country of which the child is a national, has to be consulted about, but does not have to consent to, the adoption.

(2) Any person served or required to be served with notice under this rule shall be treated as if he had been served or was required to be served with notice under rule 21.

Prospective amendment by Adoption (Amendment) Rules 2003—By virtue of A(A)R 2003, r 10, which comes into force on 1 June 2003, in para (1)(*b*) for "a national" substitute "habitually resident".

36 Proper officer to receive opinions on adoption

For the purposes of this rule and of section 17(7)(*a*) of the Act, the Senior District Judge of the Principal Registry of the Family Division is the proper officer of the court to whom any person whose consent is required under or who is consulted in pursuance of the internal law relating to adoption of the Convention country of which the child is a national may communicate his consent or other opinion on the adoption.

Amendments—SI 1991/1880.

Prospective amendment by Adoption (Amendment) Rules 2003—By virtue of A(A)R 2003, r 11, which comes into force on 1 June 2003, rule 36 is revoked.

PART III

Proceedings under sections 52 or 53 of the Act

37 Application to annul or revoke adoption

(1) An application for an order under sections 52(1) or 53(1) of the Act shall be made by originating process issued out of the Principal Registry of the Family Division in Form 9; and the person filing the process shall be described as the applicant and the adopted person and any adopted, not being the applicant, shall be described as a respondent.

(2) An application under section 53(1) of the Act shall not, except with the leave of the court, be made later than 2 years after the date of the adoption to which it relates.

Amendments—SI 1991/1880.

Scope of provision—By Adoption Act 1976, s 52, where a person who has been adopted by his mother or father alone becomes a legitimated person on the marriage of his father and mother, the court by which the adoption order was made may, on the application of any of the parties concerned, revoke the adoption order. By AA 1976, s 53, the High Court may by order annul a regulated overseas adoption or an adoption effected by a Convention adoption order.

Rules 37 to 41 provide for the procedure which applies to such applications.

High Court only (r 37(1))—Applications under AA 1976, s 52(1) or 53(1) may be made only to the High Court and must be issued out of the Principal Registry of the Family Division in London.

Prospective amendment by Adoption (Amendment) Rules 2003—By virtue of A(A)R 2003, r 12, which comes into force on 1 June 2003, after rule 37 insert:

"37A Application to annul Convention adoption or Convention adoption order

(1) An application for the annulment of a Convention adoption or a Convention adoption order under section 53(1) of the Act shall be made by originating process issued out of the Principal Registry of the Family Division in Form 9, and may be made by –

(*a*) the adopter or adopters, or
(*b*) the adopted person, or
(*c*) the relevant Central Authority, or
(*d*) the adoption agency, or
(*e*) the local authority to whom notice under section 22 of the Act was given (if different), or
(*f*) the Secretary of State for the Home Department.

(2) The adopted person and any adopter, not being the applicant, shall be respondents and the court may require notice of the application to be served on such other persons as it thinks fit.

37B Application for directions where a full adoption has not been made

(1) An application for a direction under section 39(3A) of the Act –

(*a*) may be made by the adopted child, the adopter or adopters or the birth parents of the child; and
(*b*) shall be made by originating process issued out of the Principal Registry of the Family Division in Form 15A.

(2) The person filing the process shall be described as the applicant.

(3) The respondents shall be –

(*a*) the adopter or adopters (if not the applicant),
(*b*) the birth parents (if not the applicant),
(*c*) the adoption agency,
(*d*) the local authority to whom notice under section 22 of the Act was given (if different),
(*e*) the Attorney-General

and the court may require notice of the application to be served on such other persons as it thinks fit including the child, having regard to the child's age and degree of maturity.

(4) Any direction given in accordance with section 39(3A) of the Act shall be in Form 15B.".

38 Application to declare adoption invalid or determination invalid or affected

An application for an order or decision under section 53(2) of the Act shall be made by originating process issued out of the Principal Registry of the Family Division in Form 10; and the person filing the process shall be described as the applicant and the adopted person and any adopter, not being the applicant, shall be described as a respondent.

Amendments—SI 1991/1880.

Scope of provision—Under Adoption Act 1976, s 53(2), the High Court may, on an application being made, order that an overseas adoption (see Adoption (Designation of Overseas Adoptions) Order 1973, SI 1973/19) or a determination ceases to be valid in Great Britain on the ground that the adoption or determination is contrary to public policy or that it was made by an authority that was not competent to do so. This rule provides the basic procedure for such an application.

PART III

39 Evidence in support of application

(1) Evidence in support of an application under sections 52 or 53 of the Act shall be given by means of an affidavit in Form 11 which shall be filed within 14 days after the issue of the originating process.

(2) Where the application is made under section 53 of the Act there shall be exhibited to the affidavit a statement of the facts and, subject to rule 42, there shall be filed with the affidavit expert evidence of any provision of foreign law relating to adoption on which the applicant intends to rely.

(3) The court may order any deponent to give oral evidence concerning the facts stated in, or exhibited to, his affidavit.

Amendments—SI 1991/1880.

Prospective amendment by Adoption (Amendment) Rules 2003—By virtue of A(A)R 2003, r 13, which comes into force on 1 June 2003, in para (2) omit ", subject to rule 42,".

Scope of provision—This rule provides for the filing of evidence in support of an application under Adoption Act 1976, s 52 or 53.

40 Children's guardian

Where the adopted person is under the age of 18 on the date on which an application under sections 52 or 53 of the Act is made, rule 18(2) and (4) to (7) shall apply to the application as it applies to an application for an adoption order as if the references in rule 18 to the making of an adoption order were references to the granting of an application under sections 52 or 53 of the Act.

Amendments—SI 1991/1880; SI 2001/819.

Prospective amendment by Adoption (Amendment) Rules 2003—By virtue of A(A)R 2003, r 14, which comes into force on 1 June 2003:
(*a*) after "18(2)" insert ", (2A)"; and
(*b*) after "adoption order" wherever it appears insert "/Convention adoption order".

Scope of provision—This rule provides for the appointment of a children's guardian in respect of an adopted person who is under the age of 18 years on the date that an application is made under AA 1976, s 52 or 53.

41 Notice of order made under sections 52 or 53

(1) Where under section 52 or 53 of the Act the court has ordered that an adoption be annulled or revoked or that an adoption or a determination shall cease to be valid in Great Britain, the proper officer shall serve notice of the order on the Registrar General, and shall state in the notice –

(*a*) the date of the adoption;
(*b*) the name and address of the authority which granted the adoption; and
(*c*) the names of the adopted or adopters and of the adopted person as given in the affidavit referred to in rule 39.

(2) A notice under paragraph (1) in respect of the annulment or revocation of an adoption shall request the Registrar General to send the information to the designated authorities of any Convention country –

(*a*) in which the adoption was granted;
(*b*) of which the adopted person is a national; or
(*c*) in which the adopted person was born.

(3) (*revoked*)

Amendments—SI 1991/1880.

Prospective amendment by Adoption (Amendment) Rules 2003—By virtue of A(A)R 2003, r 15, which comes into force on 1 June 2003:
(*a*) in para (1) after "Registrar General" insert "and, where it relates to a Convention adoption order or a Convention adoption, the relevant Central Authority"; and
(*b*) omit para (2).

Defined terms—"proper officer": r 2(1).

Supplementary

42 Evidence as to specified or notified provisions

(1) Where the applicant seeks to satisfy the court as to any question which has arisen or is likely to arise concerning a provision –

(*a*) of the internal law of the Convention country of which the applicant or any other person is or was a national,
(*b*) which has been specified in an order –
  (i) under section 17(8) of the Act (a "specified provision") or
  (ii) under section 54(4) of the Act (a "notified provision"),

expert evidence of the specified or notified provision shall, where practicable, be attached to the originating process.

(2) Paragraph (1) shall apply, in the case of a person who is or was a United Kingdom national, for the purposes of a notified provision in respect of a specified country as it applies for the purposes of a notified provision in respect of a Convention country of which a person is or was a national.

Amendments—SI 1991/1880.

Prospective amendment by Adoption (Amendment) Rules 2003—By virtue of A(A)R 2003, r 16, which comes into force on 1 June 2003, rule 42 is revoked.

Defined terms—"Convention country": Adoption Act 1976, s 72(1); "internal law": AA 1976, s 71(1); "notified provision": AA 1976, s 54(4), SI 1978/1431, SI 1978/1432; "specified provision": AA 1976, s 17(8) (see also SI 1978/1431, SI 1978/1432); "United Kingdom": Interpretation Act 1978, Sch 1.

Choice between different internal law systems—Where two or more systems of internal law are in force in a country, the system of internal law that is relevant to the application will be ascertained in accordance with any rule in force throughout the relevant country which determines the choice between the conflicting systems. If no such rule applies, the court will look to the system of internal law which appears to be most closely connected with the case (AA 1976, s 71(2)).

43 Interim order

Where the applicant is a national or both applicants are nationals of a Convention country, the court shall take account of any specified provision (as defined in section 17(8) of the Act) of the internal law of that country before any decision is made to postpone the determination of the application and to make an interim order.

Amendments—SI 1991/1880.

Prospective amendment by Adoption (Amendment) Rules 2003—By virtue of A(A)R 2003, r 16, which comes into force on 1 June 2003, rule 43 is revoked.

Defined terms—"Convention country": Adoption Act 1976, s 72(1); "interim order": r 2(1); "internal law": AA 1976, s 71(1): "specified provision": AA 1976, s 17(8) (see also SI 1978/1431, SI 1978/1432).

44 Witnessing of documents

A document shall be sufficiently attested for the purposes of this Part of these rules if it is witnessed by one of the following persons –

(*a*) if it is executed in England and Wales, the reporting officer, a Justice of the Peace, an officer of a county court appointed for the purposes of section 58(1)(*c*) of the County Courts Act 1984 or a justices' clerk within the meaning of section 70 of the Justices of the Peace Act 1979; or

(*b*) if it is executed elsewhere, any person specified in rule 8(2), (3) or (4), according to the country in which it is executed.

Amendments—SI 1991/1880.

Scope of provision—This rule sets out the formal requirements of attestation of a document in relation to Convention adoption proceedings and proceedings under Adoption Act 1976, ss 52 and 53.

45 Service of documents

(1) Any document to be served for the purposes of this Part of these rules may be served out of the jurisdiction without leave of the court.

(2) Any document served out of the jurisdiction in a country in which English is not an official language shall be accompanied by a translation of the document in the official language of that country in which service is to be effected or, if there is more than one official language of the country, in any one of those languages which is appropriate to the place in that country where service is to be effected.

46 Translation of documents

Where a translation of any document is required for the purposes of Convention proceedings, the translation shall, unless otherwise directed, be provided by the applicant.

PART III

PART V
MISCELLANEOUS

47 Application for removal, return etc of child

(1) An application –

(*a*) for leave under section 27 or 28 of the Act to remove a child from the home of a person with whom the child lives,
(*b*) under section 29(2) of the Act for an order directing a person not to remove a child from the home of a person with whom the child lives,
(*c*) under section 29(1) of the Act for an order for the return of a child who has been removed from the home of a person with whom the child lives,
(*d*) under section 30(2) of the Act for leave to give notice of an intention not to give a home to a child or not to allow a child to remain in a person's home, or
(*e*) under section 20(2) of the Act for leave to place a child for adoption,

shall be made in accordance with paragraph (2).

(2) The application under paragraph (1) shall be made –

(*a*) if an application for an adoption order or an order under sections 18 or 20 of the Act is pending, by process on notice in those proceedings; or
(*b*) if no such application is pending, by filing an originating process in the court.

(3) (*revoked*)

(4) Any respondent to the originating process made under paragraph (2)(*b*) who wishes to claim relief shall do so by means of an answer to the process which shall be made within 7 days of the service of the copy of the process on the respondent.

(5) Subject to paragraph (6), the proper officer shall serve a copy of the process, and of any answer thereto, and a notice of the date of the hearing –

(*a*) in a case where proceedings for an adoption order or an order under sections 18 or 20 of the Act are pending (or where such proceedings have subsequently been commenced), on all the parties to those proceedings and on the reporting officer and children's guardian, if any;
(*b*) in any other case, on any person against whom an order is sought in the application and on the local authority to whom the prospective adopter has given notice under section 22 of the Act; and
(*c*) in any case, on such other person or body, not being the child, as the court thinks fit.

(6) If in any application under this rule a serial number has been assigned to a person who has applied or who proposes to apply for an adoption order, or such a person applies to the proper officer in that behalf before filing the originating process and a serial number is assigned accordingly –

(*a*) the proper officer shall ensure that the documents served under paragraph (5) do not disclose the identity of that person to any other party to the application under this rule who is not already aware of that person's identity, and
(*b*) the proceedings on the application under this rule shall be conducted with a view to securing that he is not seen by or made known to any party who is not already aware of his identity except with his consent.

(7) Unless otherwise directed, any prospective adopter who is served with a copy of an application under this rule and who wishes to oppose the application shall file his process for an adoption order within 14 days or before or at the time of the hearing of the application under this rule, whichever is the sooner.

(8) The court may at any time give directions, and if giving directions under paragraph (7) shall give further directions, as to the conduct of any application under this rule and in particular as to the appointment of a children's guardian of the child.

(9) Where an application under paragraph (1)(*a*) or (*d*) is granted or an application under paragraph (1)(*b*) or (*c*) is refused, the judge may thereupon, if process for an adoption order has been filed, treat the hearing of the application as the hearing of the process for an adoption order and refuse an adoption order accordingly.

(10) Where an application under this rule is determined the proper officer shall serve notice of the effect of the determination on all the parties.

(11) Paragraphs (6) to (10) shall apply to an answer made under this rule as they apply to an originating process made under this rule as if the answer were the originating process.

Amendments—SI 1991/1880; SI 2001/819.

Defined terms—"proper officer": r 2(1).

Originating process (r 47(2))—If there are adoption, freeing or revocation applications pending, the ancillary application must be made within those proceedings. Where there is no main application pending, the ancillary application must be made by filing an originating summons in the High Court or an originating application in a county court. There is no standard form for such an application.

Respondents (r 47(5))—Unlike the rules applicable to an adoption application or an application to free a child for adoption, it is the responsibility of the court to ensure that potential respondents are served with a copy of the application.

Reporting officer—For the appointment and duties of the reporting officer, see r 17.

Children's guardian—For the appointment and duties of the children's guardian, see r 18.

Serial number (r 47(6))—See generally under r 14. If there is no adoption application pending, a prospective adopter may apply for a serial number under this rule to preserve anonymity.

Issue of adoption application (r 47(7))—This provision provides that, where no adoption application is pending, the prospective adopter must issue his application for adoption within 14 days of receipt of an application under this rule.

Prospective amendment by Adoption (Amendment) Rules 2003—By virtue of A(A)R 2003, r 17, which comes into force on 1 June 2003, after rule 47 insert:

"47A Application for removal, return etc, of child in Convention proceedings

(1) Paragraph (2) shall apply where –

(*a*) a notice under regulation 18(1) of the Hague Convention Regulations has been given but has not been complied with; or

(*b*) before such a notice was given an application for a Convention adoption order has been made and not disposed of.

(2) Where this paragraph applies an application for the return of the child shall be made by the local authority to whom notice under section 22 of the Act was given by filing an originating process in the court or, where paragraph (1)(*b*) applies, by process on notice in the existing proceedings.

(3) The respondents shall be –

(*a*) the prospective adopter or adopters,
(*b*) the children's guardian,
(*c*) the adoption agency

and the court may require notice of the application to be served on such other persons as it thinks fit, including the child, having regard to the child's age and degree of maturity.

(4) Any respondent who wishes to contest the notice shall, within 7 days of service of the notice upon him, file and serve an answer.

(5) The proper officer shall list the case for hearing on a date not more than 21 days from the date the application under paragraph (2) was submitted to the court.

47B Specific applications in Convention proceedings

(1) Where a Convention adoption order is to be or has been sought and has not been disposed of the applicant or proposed applicant may apply to the court for an order –

(*a*) permitting the child to be known by a new surname, or
(*b*) permitting the child to be removed from the United Kingdom for a period of one month or more.

(2) The application under paragraph (1) shall be made –

(*a*) if an application for a Convention adoption order under section 17 of the Act is pending, by process on notice in those proceedings; or
(*b*) if no such application is pending, by filing an originating process in the court.

(3) The proper officer shall serve a copy of the process and a notice of the date of the hearing –

(a) in a case where proceedings for an adoption order are pending on all the parties to those proceedings and on the children's guardian; and
(b) in any other case, on the adoption agency and the local authority to whom notice under section 22 of the Act was given (if different).".

48 Proposed foreign adoption proceedings

(1) Proceedings for an order authorising a proposed foreign adoption shall be commenced –

(*a*) by originating summons in Form 6 issued out of the Principal Registry of the Family Division; or
(*b*) by filing in the office of the county court within whose district the child is an originating application in Form 6.

(2) Subject to paragraph (3), Part III of these rules except rule 15(1) and Part V except rule 52(1)(*d*) shall apply to an application for an order authorising a proposed foreign adoption as if such an order were an adoption order.

(3) An applicant for an order authorising a proposed foreign adoption shall provide expert evidence of the law of adoption in the country in which he is domiciled and an affidavit as to that law sworn by such a person as is mentioned in section 4(1) of the Civil Evidence Act 1972 (that is to say a person who is suitably qualified on account of his knowledge or experience to give evidence as to that law) shall be admissible in evidence without notice.

Scope of provision—Under Adoption Act 1976, s 55, the court may make an order giving an applicant parental responsibility for a child where the court is satisfied that the applicant is domiciled outside the United Kingdom, and that he intends to adopt the child under the law of, or within the country of, his domicile. The purpose of the order is to facilitate the foreign adoption. In the absence of such an order, it is an offence to take or send a child who is a British citizen or a citizen of the Republic of Ireland out of Great Britain to any place outside the United Kingdom, the Channel Islands or the Isle of Man with a view to adoption by any person not being a parent, guardian or relative of the child (AA 1976, s 56(1)).

49 Amendment and revocation of orders

(1) An application under paragraph 4 of Schedule 1 of the Act for the amendment of an adoption order or the revocation of a direction to the Registrar General, or under section 52 of the Act for the revocation of an adoption order, may be made ex parte in the first instance, but the court may require notice of the application to be served on such persons as it thinks fit.

(2) Where the application is granted, the proper officer shall send to the Registrar General a notice specifying the amendments or informing him of the revocation and shall give sufficient particulars of the order to enable the Registrar General to identify the case.

Amendments—SI 1991/1880.

Defined terms—"proper officer": r 2(1).

Scope of provision—Under Adoption Act 1976, Sch 1, para 4, the court which made an adoption order may, on the application of the adopter or the adopted person, amend the order by the correction of any error in the particulars contained within it. The adopted child's name may be changed within one year of the making of the adoption order. This rule makes provision for the procedure for the amendment of orders and the rectification of registers. The procedure also applies to applications for the revocation of adoptions on a subsequent legitimation under AA 1976, s 52.

49A Power of court to limit cross examination

The court may limit the issues on which a children's guardian or a reporting officer may be cross-examined.

Amendments—Inserted by SI 2001/819.

50 Service of documents

(1) Subject to rule 45 and unless otherwise directed, any document under these rules may be served –

(*a*) on a corporation or body of persons, by delivering it at, or sending it by post to, the registered or principal office of the corporation or body;

(*b*) on any other person, by delivering it to him, or by sending it by post to him at his usual or last known address.

(2) The person effecting service of any document under these rules shall make, sign and file a certificate showing the date, place and mode of service. If he has failed to effect service of any document, he shall make, sign and file a certificate of non-service showing the reason why service has not been effected.

Defined terms—"body of persons": Adoption Act 1976, s 72(1).

Scope of provision—This rule governs the service of documents in all proceedings in the High Court and county courts under the Adoption Act 1976, with the exception of proceedings within Part IV of the rules which relate to Convention adoption orders and AA 1976, ss 52 and 53. The more detailed provisions for service contained in FPR 1991, Pt X apply to proceedings under AA 1976; those rules permit, inter alia, service by facsimile or via document exchange.

Rule 45 (r 50(1))—Rule 45 of these rules governs the service of documents in respect of proceedings within Part IV of the rules relating to Convention adoptions and orders under AA 1976, ss 52 and 53.

Post (r 50(1))—The class of post is not specified. If first-class post is used, service is deemed to have been achieved on the second business day after posting.

51 Costs

(1) On the determination of proceedings to which these rules apply or on the making of an interim order, the judge may make such order as to the costs as he thinks just and, in particular, may order the applicant to pay –

(*a*) the expenses incurred by the reporting officer and the children's guardian (if appointed),
(*b*) the expenses incurred by any respondent in attending the hearing,

or such Part of those expenses as the judge thinks proper.

(2) Order 62 of the Rules of the Supreme Court 1965 and Order 38 of the County Court Rules 1981 shall not apply to costs in proceedings under the Act and Parts 43, 44 (except rules 44.9 to 44.12), 47 and 48 of the Civil Procedure Rules 1998 shall apply to costs in those proceedings with the following modifications –

(*a*) in rule 43.2(1)(*c*)(ii) of the Civil Procedure Rules, "district judge" includes a district judge of the Principal Registry of the Family Division; and
(*b*) rule 44.3(2) of the Civil Procedure Rules (costs follow the event) shall not apply.

(3) Except in the case of an appeal against a decision of an authorised court officer (to which rules 47.20 to 47.23 of the Civil Procedure Rules apply), an appeal against a decision in assessment proceedings relating to costs in proceedings under the Act shall be dealt with in accordance with the following paragraphs of this rule.

(4) An appeal within paragraph (3) shall lie as follows –

(*a*) where the decision appealed against was made by a district judge of the High Court or a costs judge (as defined by rule 43.2(1)(*b*) of the Civil Procedure Rules), to a judge of the High Court; or
(*b*) where the decision appealed against was made by a district judge of a county court, to a judge of that court.

(5) Part 52 of the Civil Procedure Rules applies to every appeal within paragraph (3), and any reference in Part 52 to a judge or a district judge shall be taken to include a district judge of the Principal Registry of the Family Division.

(6) The Civil Procedure Rules shall apply to an appeal to which Part 52 or rules 47.20 to 47.23 of those Rules apply in accordance with paragraph (3) in the same way as they apply to any other appeal within Part 52 or rules 47.20 to 47.23 as the case may be; accordingly the Rules of the Supreme Court 1965 and the County Court Rules 1981 shall not apply to any such appeal.

Amendments—SI 1999/1477; SI 2001/819; SI 2003/183.

Scope of provision—Although the power to order costs is available, it is rarely exercised in adoption proceedings.

52 Notice and copies of orders etc

(1) In proceedings to which these rules apply orders shall be made in the form indicated in this paragraph –

Description of order	*Form*
(*a*) Order under section 18 of the Act	12
(*b*) Order under section 20 of the Act	13
(*c*) Interim order	14
(*d*) Adoption order	15

(*e*) Convention adoption order	15 (with the word "Convention" inserted where appropriate)
(*f*) Order authorising a proposed foreign adoption	15 (with the words "order authorising a proposed foreign adoption" substituted for the words "adoption order" wherever they appear).

(2) Where an adoption order is made by a court sitting in Wales in respect of a child who was born in Wales (or is treated under rule 24(4) as having been born in the registration district and sub-district in which that court sits) and the adopter so requests before the order is drawn up, the proper officer shall obtain a translation into Welsh of the particulars set out in the order.

(3) Within 7 days of the making of an order in proceedings to which these rules apply, the proper officer shall send a copy of the order (and of any translation into Welsh obtained under paragraph (2)) to the applicant.

(4) Within 7 days of the making of an order to which paragraph (1)(*d*), (*e*) or (*f*) applies, the proper officer shall send a copy of the order (and of any translation into Welsh obtained under paragraph (2)) to the Registrar General and, in the case of a Convention adoption order, shall comply with rule 31; where a translation into Welsh under paragraph (2) has been obtained, the English text shall prevail.

(5) Where an order to which paragraph (1)(*a*), (*b*), (*d*), (*e*) or (*f*) applies is made or refused or an order to which paragraph (1)(*c*) applies is made, the proper officer shall serve notice to that effect on every respondent.

(6) (*revoked*)

(7) The proper officer shall serve notice of the making of an order to which paragraph (1)(*a*), (*b*), (*d*), (*e*) or (*f*) applies on any court in Great Britain which appears to him to have made any such order as is referred to in section 12(8) of the Act (orders relating to parental responsibility for, and maintenance of, the child).

(8) A copy of any order may be supplied to the Registrar General at his request.

(9) A copy of any order may be supplied to the applicant.

(10) A copy of any order may be supplied to any other person with the leave of the court.

Amendments—SI 1991/1880.

Prospective amendment by Adoption (Amendment) Rules 2003—By virtue of A(A)R 2003, r 19, which comes into force on 1 June 2003:

(*a*) in para (4) –

(i) after "Registrar General and," insert "where paragraph (*e*) applies, to the Central Authority;"; and

(ii) omit "in the case of a Convention adoption order, shall comply with rule 31;";

(*b*) after para (10) insert –

"(11) Within 7 days of the making of an order to annul a Convention adoption order or a Convention adoption, the proper officer shall send a copy of the order to the applicant, every respondent, the relevant Central Authority and the Registrar General.".

Defined terms—"Convention adoption order": Adoption Act 1976, s 17; "proper officer": r 2(1).

Scope of provision—This rule makes provision for the drafting of orders in proceedings under AA 1976. Orders must be drawn in accordance with the appropriate form in Sch 1.

53 Custody, inspection and disclosure of documents and information

(1) All documents relating to proceedings under the Act (or under any previous enactment relating to adoption) shall, while they are in the custody of the court, be kept in a place of special security.

(2) A party who is an individual and is referred to in a confidential report supplied to the court by an adoption agency, a local authority, a reporting officer or a children's guardian may inspect, for the purposes of the hearing, that Part of any such report which refers to him, subject to any direction given by the court that –

(*a*) no Part of one or any of the reports shall be revealed to that party, or
(*b*) the Part of one or any of the reports referring to that party shall be revealed only to that party's legal advisers, or
(*c*) the whole or any other Part of one or any of the reports shall be revealed to that party.

(3) Any person who obtains any information in the course of, or relating to, any proceedings mentioned in paragraph (1) shall treat that information as confidential and shall only disclose it if –

(*a*) the disclosure is necessary for the proper exercise of his duties, or
(*b*) the information is requested –
  (i) by a court or public authority (whether in Great Britain or not) having power to determine adoptions and related matters, for the purpose of the discharge of its duties in that behalf, or
  (ii) by the Registrar General, or a person authorised in writing by him where the information requested relates only to the identity of any adoption agency which made the arrangements for placing the child for adoption in the actual custody of the applicants, and of any local authority which was notified of the applicant's intention to apply for an adoption order in respect of the child, or
  (iii) by a person who is authorised in writing by the Secretary of State to obtain the information for the purposes of research.

(3A) Nothing in this rule shall prevent the disclosure of a document prepared by an officer of the service for the purpose of –

(*a*) enabling a person to perform functions required under section 62(3A) of the Justices of the Peace Act 1997; and
(*b*) assisting an officer of the service who is appointed by the court under any enactment to perform his functions.

(3B) Nothing in this rule shall prevent the disclosure of any document relating to proceedings by an officer of the service to any other officer of the service unless that other officer is involved in the same proceedings but on behalf of a different party.

(4) Save as required or authorised by a provision of any enactment or of these rules or with the leave of the court, no document or order held by or lodged with the court in proceedings under the Act (or under any previous enactment relating to adoption) shall be open to inspection by any person, and no copy of any such document or order, or of an extract from any such document or order, shall be taken by or issued to any person.

Amendments—SI 1991/1880; SI 2001/819.

Defined terms—"adoption agency": r 2(1) (see also Adoption Act 1976, s 1(4)).

Inspection by an individual (r 53(2))—See **Confidential reports** under r 5.

Reporting officer—For the appointment and duties of the reporting officer, see rr 5 and 17.

Children's guardian—For the appointment and duties of the children's guardian, see rr 6 and 18.

Confidential information (r 53(3))—Each of the reports supplied to the court is rendered confidential by other rules (rr 5(8), 6(11), 22(5)). An adoption agency must maintain the confidentiality of any adoption information, case records and related indexes (Adoption Agencies Regulations 1983, reg 6). Documents that are held by a local authority, and have never been in the control of the court, are nevertheless within the confidentiality provisions of this rule (*Re H (Criminal Proceedings: Disclosure of Adoption Records)* [1995] 1 FLR 964).

This rule establishes the basic position that all information obtained by a person in the course of, or relating to, any proceedings under AA 1976 must be treated as confidential. This rule goes on to create exceptions relating to the discharge of a person's duties and to certain other legitimate disclosures. It is a contempt of court to breach a direction which prevents the disclosure of reports (*Re G (A Minor) (Welfare Officer's Reports)* [1989] Fam Law 475). Where the interests of justice outweigh the need for confidentiality, the court for which a report was prepared can give leave for the report to be used in other proceedings (*B v M (Disclosure of Welfare Reports)* [1990] 2 FLR 46).

A court hearing a CA 1989, s 8 application arising out of adoption proceedings, that are already before the same court, is unlikely to require the High Court to give leave before the report is released into the s 8 proceedings (*Re C (A Minor) (Disclosure of Adoption Reports)* [1994] 2 FLR 525).

Criminal proceedings—Where information which is confidential to the adoption proceedings may be relevant in criminal proceedings, the proper course is to issue an originating summons in the High Court to determine whether disclosure should be made (*Re An Adoption Application* [1990] 1 FLR 412; *Practice Note of 4 January 1990*). The High Court is likely to refer any decision relating to disclosure to the judge having conduct of the criminal trial, who, in determining the issue, should have regard to the high degree of confidentiality attaching to adoption proceedings (*Re H (Criminal Proceedings: Disclosure of Adoption Records)* [1995] 1 FLR 964).

****

SCHEDULE 2

MATTERS TO BE COVERED IN REPORTS SUPPLIED UNDER RULES 4(4), 22(1) OR 22(2)

So far as is practicable, the report supplied by the adoption agency or, in the case of a report supplied under rule 22(2), the local authority shall include all the following particulars –

1 The Child

(*a*) Name, sex, date and place of birth and address;
(*b*) whether the child's parents were married to each other at the time of his birth and, if not, whether he was subsequently legitimated;
(*c*) nationality;
(*d*) physical description;
(*e*) personality and social development;
(*f*) religion, including details of baptism, confirmation or equivalent ceremonies;
(*g*) details of any wardship proceedings and of any court orders relating to parental responsibility for the child or to maintenance and residence;

(*h*) details of any brothers and sisters, including dates of birth, arrangements concerning with whom they are to live and whether any brother or sister is the subject of a parallel application;
(*i*) extent of contact with members of the child's natural family and, if the child's parents were not married to each other at the time of his birth, his father, and in each case the nature of the relationship enjoyed;
(*j*) if the child has been in the care of a local authority or voluntary organisation, or is in such care, or is being, or has been, looked after by such an authority or organisation details (including dates) of any placements with foster parents, or other arrangements in respect of the care of the child, including particulars of the persons with whom the child has had his home and observations on the care provided;
(*k*) date and circumstances of placement with prospective adopter;
(*l*) names, addresses and types of schools attended, with dates, and educational attainments;
(*m*) any special needs in relation to the child's health (whether physical or mental) and his emotional and behavioural development and whether he is subject to a statement under the Education Act 1981;
(*n*) what, if any, rights to or interest in property or any claim to damages, under the Fatal Accidents Act 1976 or otherwise, the child stands to retain or lose if adopted;
(*o*) wishes and feelings in relation to adoption and the application, including any wishes in respect of religious and cultural upbringing; and
(*p*) any other relevant information which might assist the court.

Prospective amendment by Adoption (Amendment) Rules 2003—By virtue of A(A)R 2003, r 27, which comes into force on 1 June 2003, in para 1(*k*) after "prospective adopter" insert "and where a Convention adoption is proposed, details of the arrangements which were made for the transfer of the child to the UK and that they were in accordance with regulation 12(8) of the Hague Convention Regulations;".

2 Each Natural Parent

(*a*) Name, date and place of birth and address;
(*b*) marital status and date and place of marriage (if any);
(*c*) past and present relationship (if any) with the other natural parent, including comments on its stability;
(*d*) physical description;
(*e*) personality;
(*f*) religion;
(*g*) educational attainments;
(*h*) past and present occupations and interests;
(*i*) so far as available, names and brief details of the personal circumstances of the parents and any brothers and sisters of the natural parent, with their ages or ages at death;
(*j*) wishes and feelings in relation to adoption and the application, including any wishes in respect of the child's religious and cultural upbringing;
(*k*) reasons why any of the above information is unavailable; and
(*l*) any other relevant information which might assist the court.

3 Guardian(s)

Give the details required under paragraph 2(*a*), (*f*), (*j*) and (*l*).

4 Prospective Adopter(s)

(*a*) Name, date and place of birth and address;
(*b*) relationship (if any) to the child;
(*c*) marital status, date and place of marriage (if any) and comments on stability of relationship;
(*d*) details of any previous marriage;
(*e*) if a parent and step-parent are applying, the reasons why they prefer adoption to a residence order;
(*f*) if a natural parent is applying alone, the reasons for the exclusion of the other parent;
(*g*) if a married person is applying alone, the reasons for this;
(*h*) physical description;
(*i*) personality;
(*j*) religion, and whether willing to follow any wishes of the child or his parents or guardian in respect of the child's religious and cultural upbringing;
(*k*) educational attainments;
(*l*) past and present occupations and interests;
(*m*) particulars of the home and living conditions (and particulars of any home where the prospective adopter proposes to live with the child, if different);
(*n*) details of income and comments on the living standards of the household;
(*o*) details of other members of the household (including any children of the prospective adopter even if not resident in the household);
(*p*) details of the parents and any brothers or sisters of the prospective adopter, with their ages or ages at death;
(*q*) attitudes to the proposed adoption of such other members of the prospective adopter's household and family as the adoption agency or, as the case may be, the local authority considers appropriate;
(*r*) previous experience of caring for children as step-parent, foster parent, child-minder or prospective adopter and assessment of ability in this respect, together where appropriate with assessment of ability in bringing up the prospective adopter's own children;
(*s*) reasons for wishing to adopt the child and extent of understanding of the nature and effect of adoption;
(*t*) any hope and expectations for the child's future;
(*u*) assessment of ability to bring up the child throughout his childhood;
(*v*) details of any adoption allowance payable;
(*w*) confirmation that any referees have been interviewed, with a report of their views and opinion of the weight to be placed thereon; and
(*x*) any other relevant information which might assist the court.

5 Actions of the adoption agency or local authority supplying the report

(*a*) Reports under rules 4(4) or 22(1) –
(i) brief account of the agency's actions in the case, with particulars and dates of all written information and notices given to the child, his natural parents and the prospective adopter;
(ii) details of alternatives to adoption considered;
(iii) reasons for considering that adoption would be in the child's best interests (with date of relevant decision); and
(iv) reasons for considering that the prospective adopter would be suitable to be an adoptive parent and that he would be suitable for this child (with dates of relevant decisions) or, if the child has not

yet been placed for adoption, reasons for considering that he is likely to be so placed.

OR

(*b*) Reports under rule 22(2) –

(i) confirmation that notice was given under section 22 of the Act, with the date of that notice;

(ii) brief account of the local authority's actions in the case; and

(iii) account of investigations whether child was placed in contravention of section 11 of the Act.

6 Generally

(*a*) Whether any respondent appears to be under the age of majority or under a mental disability; and

(*b*) whether, in the opinion of the body supplying the report, any other person should be made a respondent (for example, a person claiming to be the father of a child whose parents were not married to each other at the time of his birth, a spouse or ex-spouse of a natural parent, a relative of a deceased parent, or a person with parental responsibility).

Prospective amendment by Adoption (Amendment) Rules 2003—By virtue of A(A)R 2003, r 27, which comes into force on 1 June 2003, after para 6 insert –

"6A Further information to be provided in proceedings relating to a Convention adoption/foreign adoption

(*a*) where the UK is the State of origin confirmation that an order has been made under section 18(1) of the Act, section 18 of the Adoption (Scotland) Act 1978 or Article 17(1) or 18(1) of the Adoption Northern Ireland Order 1987;

(*b*) where the UK is the State of origin confirmation that, after possibilities for placement of the child within the UK have been given due consideration, an intercountry adoption is in the child's best interests;

(*c*) confirmation that, in the case of a foreign adoption, the requirements of regulations made under section 56A of the Adoption Act 1976 have been complied with and, in the case of a Convention adoption, that the requirements of the Intercountry Adoption (Hague Convention) Regulations 2003 have been complied with; and

(*d*) for the Convention adoption where the United Kingdom is either the State of origin or the receiving State confirmation that the Central Authorities of both States have agreed that the adoption may proceed. The documents supplied by the CA of the State of origin should be attached to the report together with a translation if necessary.".

7 Conclusions

(This Part of the report should contain more than a simple synopsis of the information above. As far as possible, the court should be given a fuller picture of the child, his natural parents and, where appropriate, the prospective adopter.)

(*a*) Except where the applicant or one of them is a parent of the child, a summary by the medical adviser to the body supplying the report, of the health history and state of health of the child, his natural parents and, if appropriate, the prospective adopter, with comments on the implications for the order sought and on how any special health needs of the child might be met;

(*b*) opinion on whether making the order sought would be in the child's best long-term interests, and on how any special emotional, behavioural and educational needs of the child might be met;

(*c*) opinion on the effect on the child's natural parents of making the order sought;

(*d*) if the child has been placed for adoption, opinion on the likelihood of full integration of the child into the household, family and community of the prospective adopter, and on whether the proposed adoption would be in the best long-term interests of the prospective adopter;

(*e*) opinion, if appropriate, on the relative merits of adoption and a residence order; and

(*f*) final conclusions and recommendations whether the order sought should be made (and, if not, alternative proposals).

Amendments—SI 1991/1880.

SCHEDULE 3

REPORTS ON THE HEALTH OF THE CHILD AND OF THE APPLICANT(S)

This information is required for reports on the health of a child and of his prospective adopter(s). Its purpose is to build up a full picture of their health history and current state of health, including strengths and weaknesses. This will enable the local authority's medical adviser to base his advice to the court on the fullest possible information, when commenting on the health implications of the proposed adoption. The reports made by the examining doctor should cover, as far as practicable, the following matters.

1 The Child

Name, date of birth, sex, weight and height.

(*a*) A health history of each natural parent, so far as is possible, including –

(i) name, date of birth, sex, weight and height;

(ii) a family health history, covering the parents, the brothers and sisters and the other children of the natural parent, with details of any serious physical or mental illness and inherited and congenital disease;

(iii) past health history, including details of any serious physical or mental illness, disability, accident, hospital admission or attendance at an out-patient department, and in each case any treatment given;

(iv) a full obstetric history of the mother, including any problems in the ante-natal, labour and post-natal periods, with the results of any tests carried out during or immediately after pregnancy.

(v) details of any present illness including treatment and prognosis;

(vi) any other relevant information which might assist the medical adviser; and

(vii) the name and address of any doctor(s) who might be able to provide further information about any of the above matters.

(*b*) A neo-natal report on the child, including –

(i) details of the birth, and any complications;

(ii) results of a physical examination and screening tests;

(iii) details of any treatment given;

(iv) details of any problem in management and feeding;

(v) any other relevant information which might assist the medical adviser; and

(vi) the name and address of any doctor(s) who might be able to provide further information about any of the above matters.

(*c*) A full health history and examination of the child, including –

(i) details of any serious illness, disability, accident, hospital admission or attendance at an out-patient department, and in each case any treatment given;

(ii) details and dates of immunisations;

(iii) a physical and developmental assessment according to age, including an assessment of vision and hearing and of neurological, speech and language development and any evidence of emotional disorder;

(iv) for a child over five years of age, the school health history (if available);

(v) any other relevant information which might assist the medical adviser; and

(vi) the name and address of any doctor(s) who might be able to provide further information about any of the above matters.

(*d*) The signature, name, address and qualifications of the registered medical practitioner who prepared the report, and the date of the report and of the examinations carried out.

2 The Applicant

(If there is more than one applicant, a report on each applicant should be supplied covering all the matters listed below).

(*a*) (i) name, date of birth, sex, weight and height;

(ii) a family health history, covering the parents, the brothers and sisters and the children of the applicant, with details of any serious physical or mental illness and inherited and congenital disease;

(iii) marital history, including (if applicable) reasons for inability to have children;

(iv) past health history, including details of any serious physical or mental illness, disability, accident, hospital admission or attendance at an out-patient department, and in each case any treatment given;

(v) obstetric history (if applicable);

(vi) details of any present illness, including treatment and prognosis;

(vii) a full medical examination;

(viii) details of any daily consumption of alcohol, tobacco and habit-forming drugs;

(ix) any other relevant information which might assist the medical adviser; and

(x) the name and address of any doctor(s) who might be able to provide further information about any of the above matters.

(*b*) The signature, name, address and qualifications of the registered medical practitioner who prepared the report, and the date of the report and of the examinations carried out.

****

Adoption of Children from Overseas Regulations 2001, SI 2001/1251

1 Citation, commencement and extent

(1) These Regulations may be cited as the Adoption of Children from Overseas Regulations 2001 and shall come into force on 30 April 2001.

(2) This regulation and regulations 2 and 3 extend to England and Wales; regulation 4 extends to England only.

Guidance—Regard should be had to the "*Intercountry Adoption Guide – Practice and Procedures*" published by the DOH (available on the Internet at *www.doh.gov.uk/adoption*).

2 Interpretation

In these Regulations –

"the 1976 Act" means the Adoption Act 1976;
"the 1983 Regulations" means the Adoption Agencies Regulations 1983;
"adoption panel" has the same meaning as in the 1983 Regulations;
"prospective adopter" means a person habitually resident in the British Islands who at any time brings into the United Kingdom for the purpose of adoption (other than adoption by a parent, guardian or relative) a child who is habitually resident outside those Islands.

3 Requirements applying to prospective adopters

(1) The requirements which a prospective adopter must satisfy before bringing a child into the United Kingdom are those prescribed in paragraph (2).

(2) The requirements are that –

(*a*) the prospective adopter has applied to an adoption agency for assessment of his suitability to be an adoptive parent and has followed such procedure and provided such information to the agency as it may request in order to enable it to undertake such an assessment;
(*b*) an adoption agency has notified the prospective adopter in writing of a decision to approve him as suitable to be an adoptive parent; and
(*c*) the Secretary of State for Health has notified the prospective adopter in writing that he is prepared to issue a certificate confirming to the relevant overseas authority that the prospective adopter has been assessed and approved as suitable to be an adoptive parent and that the child will be authorised to reside permanently within the British Islands, if entry clearance is granted and an adoption order is made.

(3) A prospective adopter must also within the period of fourteen days beginning with the date on which he brings the child into the United Kingdom give notice to the local authority within whose area he has his home of –

(*a*) his intention to apply for an adoption order, in accordance with section 22 of the 1976 Act; or
(*b*) his intention not to give the child a home.

(4) In this regulation –

"adoption agency" includes an adoption agency within the meaning of section 1 of the Adoption (Scotland) Act 1978 and Article 3 of the Adoption (Northern Ireland) Order 1987;

"the relevant overseas authority" means a person or body performing functions in the country in which the child is habitually resident which correspond to the functions of an adoption agency;

"entry clearance" has the same meaning as in the Immigration Act 1971.

4 Duties of an adoption agency and adoption panel functions in respect of a prospective adopter

(1) This regulation applies to –

(*a*) a local authority to which a prospective adopter has applied for assessment in accordance with regulation 3(2)(*a*); and

(*b*) an approved adoption society which has agreed to assess a prospective adopter who has applied to it in accordance with that regulation.

(2) The adoption agency shall assess a prospective adopter in accordance with regulations 8 (adoption agency's duties in respect of a prospective adopter) and 8A (criminal conviction of a prospective adopter) of the 1983 Regulations.

(3) An adoption panel to which the case of a prospective adopter is referred shall consider the case and make a recommendation to the referring adoption agency as to whether the prospective adopter is suitable to be an adoptive parent, in accordance with regulation 10 (adoption panel functions) of those Regulations.

(4) The adoption agency shall –

(*a*) make a decision as to the suitability of the prospective adopter to be an adoptive parent and notify him of its decision, in accordance with regulation 11A (adoption agency decisions and notifications – prospective adopters) of the 1983 Regulations; and

(*b*) where the agency has decided to approve the prospective adopter as suitable to be an adoptive parent, notify the Secretary of State in writing of that decision and provide to him –

(i) all information considered by the adoption panel before making a recommendation to the agency as to whether the prospective adopter is suitable to be an adoptive parent; and

(ii) such other information relating to the prospective adopter's case as he may require.

Child Abduction and Custody (Parties to Conventions) Order 1986, SI 1986/1159

1 This Order may be cited as the Child Abduction and Custody (Parties to Conventions) Order 1986, and shall come into operation on 1 August 1986.

2 (1) In this Article of, and in Schedule 1 to, this Order "the Convention" means the Convention on the Civil Aspects of International Child Abduction which was signed at The Hague on 25 October 1980.

(2) (*a*) The Contracting States to the Convention shall be as specified in the first column of Schedule 1 to this Order.

(*b*) Where the Convention applies, or applies only, to a particular territory or particular territories specified in a declaration made by a Contracting State under Article 39 or 40 of the Convention, the territory or territories in question shall be as specified in the second column of Schedule 1 to this Order.

(*c*) The date of the coming into force of the Convention as between the United Kingdom and any State or territory so specified shall be as specified in the third column of Schedule 1 to this Order.

3 (1) In this Article of, and in Schedule 2 to, this Order "the Convention" means the European Convention on Recognition and Enforcement of Decisions concerning Custody of Children and on the Restoration of Custody of Children which was signed in Luxembourg on 20 May 1980.

(2) (*a*) The Contracting States to the Convention shall be as specified in the first column of Schedule 2 to this Order.

(*b*) Where the Convention applies, or applies only, to a particular territory or particular territories specified by a Contracting State under Article 24 or 25 of the Convention, the territory or territories in question shall be as specified in the second column of Schedule 2 to this Order.

(*c*) The date of the coming into force of the Convention as between the United Kingdom and any State or territory so specified shall be as specified in the third column of Schedule 2 to this Order.

SCHEDULE 1

CONVENTION ON THE CIVIL ASPECTS OF INTERNATIONAL CHILD ABDUCTION, THE HAGUE, 25TH OCTOBER 1980

Contracting States to the Convention	*Territories specified in Declarations under Article 39 or 40 of the Convention*	*Date of Coming into Force as between the United Kingdom and the State or Territory*
Argentina	—	1st June 1991
Australia	Australian States and mainland Territories	1st January 1987
Austria	—	1st October 1988
The Bahamas	—	1st January 1994
Belgium	—	1st May 1999
Belize	—	1st October 1989
Bosnia and Herzegovina	—	7th April 1992
Burkina	—	1st August 1992
Canada	Ontario	1st August 1986
	New Brunswick	1st August 1986
	British Columbia	1st August 1986
	Manitoba	1st August 1986
	Nova Scotia	1st August 1986

Contracting States to the Convention	*Territories specified in Declarations under Article 39 or 40 of the Convention*	*Date of Coming into Force as between the United Kingdom and the State or Territory*
	Newfoundland	1st August 1986
	Prince Edward Island	1st August 1986
	Quebec	1st August 1986
	Yukon Territory	1st August 1986
	Saskatchewan	1st November 1986
	Alberta	1st February 1987
	Northwest Territories	1st April 1988
Chile	—	1st May 1994
China	Hong Kong Special Administrative Region	1st September 1997
	Macau Special Administrative Region	1st March 1999
Columbia	—	1st March 1996
Croatia	—	1st December 1991
Cyprus	—	1st February 1995
Czech Republic	—	1st March 1998
Denmark	—	1st July 1991
Ecuador	—	1st April 1992
The Federal Republic of Yugoslavia	—	27th April 1992
Finland	—	1st August 1994
France	—	1st August 1986
Georgia	—	1st October 1997
Germany	—	1st December 1990
Greece	—	1st June 1993
Honduras	—	1st March 1994
Hungary	—	1st September 1986
Iceland	—	1st November 1996
Republic of Ireland	—	1st October 1991
Israel	—	1st December 1991
Italy	—	1st May 1995
Luxembourg	—	1st January 1987
Macedonia	—	1st December 1991
Malta	—	1st March 2002
Mauritius	—	1st June 1993
Mexico	—	1st September 1991
Monaco	—	1st February 1993
Netherlands	—	1st September 1990
New Zealand	—	1st August 1991
Norway	—	1st April 1989
Panama	—	1st December 1991
Poland	—	1st November 1992
Portugal	—	1st August 1986
Romania	—	1st February 1993
Slovakia	—	1st February 2001
Slovenia	—	1st June 1994
South Africa	—	1st October 1997
Spain	—	1st September 1987
St Kitts and Nevis	—	1st August 1994
Sweden	—	1st June 1989

Contracting States to the Convention	*Territories specified in Declarations under Article 39 or 40 of the Convention*	*Date of Coming into Force as between the United Kingdom and the State or Territory*
Switzerland	—	1st August 1986
Turkey	—	1st August 2001
Turkmenistan	—	1st March 1998
United States	—	1st July 1988
Venezuela	—	1st January 1997
Zimbabwe	—	1st July 1995

Amendments—Schedule last substituted by SI 2001/3923.

SCHEDULE 2

EUROPEAN CONVENTION ON RECOGNITION AND ENFORCEMENT OF DECISIONS CONCERNING CUSTODY OF CHILDREN AND ON THE RESTORATION OF CUSTODY OF CHILDREN, LUXEMBOURG, 20TH MAY 1980

Contracting States to the Convention	*Territories specified in Declarations under Article 24 or 25 of the Convention*	*Date of Coming into Force of Convention as between the United Kingdom and the State or Territory*
Austria	—	1st August 1986
Belgium	—	1st August 1986
Cyprus	—	1st October 1986
Czech Republic	—	1st July 2000
Denmark	—	1st August 1991
Finland	—	1st August 1994
France	—	1st August 1986
Germany	—	1st February 1991
Greece	—	1st July 1993
The Republic of Ireland	—	1st October 1991
Iceland	—	1st November 1996
Italy	—	1st June 1995
Liechtenstein	—	1st August 1997
Luxembourg	—	1st August 1986
Malta	—	1st February 2000
Netherlands	—	1st September 1990
Norway	—	1st May 1989
Poland	—	1st March 1996
Portugal	—	1st August 1986
Spain	—	1st August 1986
Sweden	—	1st July 1989
Switzerland	—	1st August 1986
Turkey	—	1st June 2000

Amendments—Schedule last substituted by SI 2001/3923.

Child Maintenance (Written Agreements) Order 1993, SI 1993/620

1 This Order may be cited as the Child Maintenance (Written Agreements) Order 1993 and shall come into force on 5 April 1993.

2 Section 8 shall not prevent a court from exercising any power which it has to make a maintenance order in relation to a child in any circumstances in which paragraphs (*a*) and (*b*) of section 8(5) apply.

Scope of provision—This Order gives effect to Child Support Act 1991, s 8(5) and provides that, where there is a written agreement, the court still has power to make an order for child periodical payments (see also **Written agreements and consent orders** under CSA 1991, s 8).

Child Support (Collection and Enforcement of Other Forms of Maintenance) Regulations 1992, SI 1992/2643

1 Citation, commencement and interpretation

(1) These Regulations may be cited as the Child Support (Collection and Enforcement of Other Forms of Maintenance) Regulations 1992 and shall come into force on 5 April 1993.

(2) In these Regulations –

"the Act" means the Child Support Act 1991;
"child of the family" has the same meaning as in the Matrimonial Causes Act 1973 or, in Scotland, the Family Law (Scotland) Act 1985; and
"periodical payments" includes secured periodical payments.

2 Periodical payments and categories of person prescribed for the purposes of section 30 of the Act

The following periodical payments and categories of persons are prescribed for the purposes of section 30(1) of the Act –

(*a*) payments under a maintenance order made in relation to a child in accordance with the provisions of section 8(6) (periodical payments in addition to child support maintenance), 8(7) (periodical payments to meet expenses incurred in connection with the provision of instruction or training) or 8(8) of the Act (periodical payments to meet expenses attributable to disability);

(*b*) any periodical payments under a maintenance order or, in Scotland, registered minutes of agreement which are payable to or for the benefit of a spouse or former spouse who is the person with care of a child who is a qualifying child in respect of whom a child support maintenance calculation is in force in accordance with which the Secretary of State has arranged for the collection of child support maintenance under section 29 of the Act; and

(*c*) any periodical payments under a maintenance order payable to or for the benefit of a former child of the family of the person against whom the order is made, that child having his home with the person with care.

Amendments—SI 1993/913; SI 2001/162.

Defined terms—"the Act": reg 1(2); "child of the family": reg 1(2), MCA 1973, s 52; "maintenance order": s 8(11); "periodical payments": reg 1(2).

"prescribed for the purposes of section 30(1)"—Child Support Act 1991, s 30 enables the Secretary of State to prescribe certain forms of periodical payments which the child support officer can then arrange to collect and enforce for prescribed persons.

"payments under a maintenance order"/"any periodical payments"—Although CSA 1991, s 30(2) seems to imply that any periodical payment can be collected for a child even in cases where child support maintenance is not also involved, this regulation restricts payments which can be collected at this stage to payments for persons with care (but including children who are not qualifying children, so long as they are living with a person with care: reg 2(*c*)). See also **Periodical payments for children** under CSA 1991, s 30.

3 Collection and enforcement – England and Wales

In relation to England and Wales, sections 29(2) and (3) and 31 to 40B of the Act, and any regulations made under those sections, shall apply for the purpose of enabling the Secretary of State to enforce any obligation to pay any amount which he is authorised to collect under section 30 of the Act, with the modification that any reference in those sections or regulations to child support maintenance shall be read as a reference to any of the periodical payments mentioned in regulation 2 above, and any reference to a maintenance calculation shall be read as a reference to any of the maintenance orders mentioned in that regulation.

Amendments—SI 2001/162.

Defined terms—"the Act": reg 1(2); "child support maintenance": CSA 1991, s 3(6); "periodical payments": reg 1(2).

****

5 Collection and enforcement – supplementary

Nothing in Regulations 3 or 4 applies to any periodical payment which falls due before the date specified by the Secretary of State by a notice in writing to the non-resident parent that he is arranging for those payments to be collected, and that date shall be not earlier than the date the notice is given.

Amendments—SI 2001/162.

Defined terms—"absent parent": CSA 1991, s 3(2); "periodical payments": reg 1(2).

Child Support (Maintenance Arrangements and Jurisdiction) Regulations 1992, SI 1992/2645

1 Citation, commencement and interpretation

(1) These Regulations may be cited as the Child Support (Maintenance Arrangements and Jurisdiction) Regulations 1992 and shall come into force on 5 April 1993.

(2) In these Regulations –

"the Act" means the Child Support Act 1991;

"Maintenance Calculation Procedure Regulations" means the Child Support (Maintenance Calculation Procedure) Regulations 2000;

"Maintenance Calculations and Special Cases Regulations" means the Child Support (Maintenance Calculations and Special Cases) Regulations 2000;

"effective date" means the date on which a maintenance calculation takes effect for the purposes of the Act;

"maintenance order" has the meaning given in section 8(11) of the Act.

(3) In these Regulations, unless the context otherwise requires, a reference –

(*a*) to a numbered regulation is to the regulation in these Regulations bearing that number;

(*b*) in a regulation to a numbered paragraph is to the paragraph in that regulation bearing that number;

(*c*) in a paragraph to a lettered or numbered sub-paragraph is to the sub-paragraph in that paragraph bearing that letter or number.

Amendments—SI 1995/1045; SI 2001/161.

"effective date" (reg 1(2))—In most cases, the effective date, ie the date from which a new calculation runs, is defined by Child Support (Maintenance Calculation Procedure) Regulations 2000, regs 25–29; however, see under reg 3 for the situation where the calculation replaces an existing maintenance order or agreement.

2 Prescription of enactments for the purposes of section 8(11) of the Act

The following enactments are prescribed for the purposes of section 8(11)(*f*) of the Act –

(*a*) the Conjugal Rights (Scotland) Amendment Act 1861;
(*b*) the Court of Session Act 1868;
(*c*) the Sheriff Courts (Scotland) Act 1907;
(*d*) the Guardianship of Infants Act 1925;
(*e*) the Illegitimate Children (Scotland) Act 1930;
(*f*) the Children and Young Persons (Scotland) Act 1932;
(*g*) the Children and Young Persons (Scotland) Act 1937;
(*h*) the Custody of Children (Scotland) Act 1939;
(*i*) the National Assistance Act 1948;
(*j*) the Affiliation Orders Act 1952;
(*k*) the Affiliation Proceedings Act 1957;
(*l*) the Matrimonial Proceedings (Children) Act 1958;
(*m*) the Guardianship of Minors Act 1971;
(*n*) the Guardianship Act 1973;
(*o*) the Children Act 1975;

(*p*) the Supplementary Benefits Act 1976;
(*q*) the Social Security Act 1986;
(*r*) the Social Security Administration Act 1992.

Amendments—Substituted by SI 1995/1045.

Defined terms—"the Act": reg 1(2).

Scope of provision—Child Support Act 1991, s 8 prevents courts from making, varying or reviving maintenance orders for children, save in certain defined circumstances. The enactments under which such orders are made are listed in s 8(11), and this regulation adds orders under the statutes set out above to that list.

3 Relationship between maintenance calculations and certain court orders

(1) Orders made under the following enactments are of a kind prescribed for the purposes of section 10(1) of the Act –

(*a*) the Conjugal Rights (Scotland) Amendment Act 1861;
(*b*) the Court of Session Act 1868;
(*c*) the Sheriff Courts (Scotland) Act 1907;
(*d*) the Guardianship of Infants Act 1925;
(*e*) the Illegitimate Children (Scotland) Act 1930;
(*f*) the Children and Young Persons (Scotland) Act 1932;
(*g*) the Children and Young Persons (Scotland) Act 1937;
(*h*) the Custody of Children (Scotland) Act 1939;
(*i*) the National Assistance Act 1948;
(*j*) the Affiliation Orders Act 1952;
(*k*) the Affiliation Proceedings Act 1957;
(*l*) the Matrimonial Proceedings (Children) Act 1958;
(*m*) the Guardianship of Minors Act 1971;
(*n*) the Guardianship Act 1973;
(*o*) Part II of the Matrimonial Causes Act 1973;
(*p*) the Children Act 1975;
(*q*) the Supplementary Benefits Act 1976;
(*r*) the Domestic Proceedings and Magistrates' Courts Act 1978;
(*s*) Part III of the Matrimonial and Family Proceedings Act 1984;
(*t*) the Family Law (Scotland) Act 1985;
(*u*) the Social Security Act 1986;
(*v*) Schedule 1 to the Children Act 1989;
(*w*) the Social Security Administration Act 1992.

(2) Subject to paragraphs (3) and (4), where a maintenance calculation is made with respect to –

(*a*) all of the children with respect to whom an order falling within paragraph (1) is in force; or
(*b*) one or more but not all of the children with respect to whom an order falling within paragraph (1) is in force and where the amount payable under the order to or for the benefit of each child is separately specified,

that order shall, so far as it relates to the making or securing of periodical payments to or for the benefit of the children with respect to whom the maintenance calculation has been made, cease to have effect on the effective date of the maintenance calculation.

(3) The provisions of paragraph (2) shall not apply where a maintenance order has been made in accordance with section 8(7) or (8) of the Act.

(4) In Scotland, where –

(*a*) an order has ceased to have effect by virtue of the provisions of paragraph (2) to the extent specified in that paragraph; and
(*b*) the Secretary of State no longer has jurisdiction to make a maintenance calculation with respect to a child with respect to whom the order ceased to have effect,

that order shall, so far as it relates to that child, again have effect from the date the Secretary of State no longer has jurisdiction to make a maintenance calculation with respect to that child.

(5)–(8) ...

Amendments—SI 1995/123; SI 1995/1045; SI 1995/3261; SI 1999/1510; SI 2001/161.

Defined terms—"the Act": reg 1(2); "effective date": reg 1(2); "maintenance calculation": s 54; "maintenance order": reg 1(2) and s 8(11).

Scope of provision—Child Support Act 1991, s 10 deals with the relationship between maintenance calculations and continuing court orders. This regulation deals with the effect of a calculation on such orders, namely that, insofar as the order affects a child, it ceases to have effect except to the extent that s 8(7) and (8) apply.

Consequences of a calculation pursuant to CSA 1991, s 10(3) (reg 3(1), (2))—Where there is an existing court order, the effect of a maintenance calculation is as follows: it ceases to have effect on the making of the calculation, except as modified by the calculation (s 10(1), (2)); and applications to vary certain orders are treated as applications for revocation once a maintenance calculation has been made (s 10(3)).

"periodical payments" (reg 3(2))—Although the term is not defined in CSA 1991, it is clear from the definition in s 8(11) that the terms "periodical payments" and "maintenance" are used interchangeably.

"cease to have effect" (reg 3(2))—CSA 1991, s 10(1) and this regulation use the term "cease to have effect" which can now be taken to mean that the order is discharged and that it cannot be revived (*Askew Page v Page* [2001] Fam Law 794, HH Judge Meston QC).

"section 8(7) or (8) of the Act" (reg 3(3))—These provisions enable courts to continue to make orders for maintenance for children if the maintenance is for educational expenses or the child is disabled; reg 3(3) exempts such orders from the effects of reg 3(2).

4 Relationship between maintenance calculations and certain agreements

(1) Maintenance agreements within the meaning of section 9(1) of the Act are agreements of a kind prescribed for the purposes of section 10(2) of the Act.

(2) Where a maintenance calculation is made with respect to –

(*a*) all of the children with respect to whom an agreement falling within paragraph (1) is in force; or
(*b*) one or more but not all of the children with respect to whom an agreement falling within paragraph (1) is in force and where the amount payable under the agreement to or for the benefit of each child is separately specified,

that agreement shall, so far as it relates to the making or securing of periodical payments to or for the benefit of the children with respect to whom the maintenance calculation has been made, become unenforceable from the effective date of the calculation.

(3) Where an agreement becomes unenforceable under the provisions of paragraph (2) to the extent specified in that paragraph, it shall remain unenforceable in relation to a particular child until such date as the Secretary of State no longer has jurisdiction to make a maintenance calculation with respect to that child.

Amendments—SI 1999/1510; SI 2001/161.

Defined terms—"the Act": reg 1(2); "effective date": reg 1(2); "maintenance agreement": s 8(11); "maintenance calculation": s 54.

Scope of provision—Child Support Act 1991, s 10(2) deals with the relationship between new maintenance calculations and existing maintenance agreements. This regulation deals with the effect of a calculation on such agreements, namely that the agreement ceases to be enforceable to the extent that it concerns a qualifying child.

"become unenforceable" (reg 4(2))—This expression concerning maintenance agreements has a similar effect to "ceases to have effect" has for maintenance orders; however, reg 4(3) goes on expressly to provide that the agreement is only unenforceable for so long as the Secretary of State has jurisdiction.

5 Notifications by the Secretary of State

(1) Where the Secretary of State is aware that an order of a kind prescribed in paragraph (2) is in force and considers that the making of a maintenance calculation has affected, or is likely to affect, that order, he shall notify the persons prescribed in paragraph (3) in respect of whom that maintenance calculation is in force, and the persons prescribed in paragraph (4) holding office in the court where the order in question was made or subsequently registered, of the calculation and its effective date.

(2) The prescribed orders are those made under an enactment mentioned in regulation 3(1).

(3) The prescribed persons in respect of whom the maintenance calculation is in force are –

(*a*) a person with care;
(*b*) a non-resident parent;
(*c*) a person who is treated as a non-resident parent under regulation 8 of the Maintenance Calculations and Special Cases Regulations;
(*d*) a child who has made an application for a maintenance calculation under section 7 of the Act.

(4) The prescribed person holding office in the court where the order in question was made or subsequently registered is –

(*a*) in England and Wales –
  (i) in relation to the High Court, the senior district judge of the principal registry of the Family Division or, where proceedings were instituted in a district registry, the district judge;
  (ii) in relation to a county court, the proper officer of that court within the meaning of Order 1, Rule 3 of the County Court Rules 1981;
  (iii) in relation to a magistrates' court, the justices' chief executive for that court;
(*b*) in Scotland –
  (i) in relation to the Court of Session, the Deputy Principal Clerk of Session;

(ii) in relation to a sheriff court, the sheriff clerk.

Amendments—SI 1999/1510; SI 2001/161.

Defined terms—"the Act": reg 1(2); "effective date": reg 1(2); "maintenance calculation": s 54.

6 Notification by the court

(1) Where a court is aware that a maintenance calculation is in force and makes an order mentioned in regulation 3(1) which it considers has affected, or is likely to affect, that calculation, the person prescribed in paragraph (2) shall notify the Secretary of State to that effect.

(2) The prescribed person is the person holding the office specified below in the court where the order in question was made or subsequently registered –

(*a*) in England and Wales –

(i) in relation to the High Court, the senior district judge of the principal registry of the Family Division or, where proceedings were instituted in a district registry, the district judge;

(ii) in relation to a county court, the proper officer of that court within the meaning of Order 1, Rule 3 of the County Court Rules 1981;

(iii) in relation to a magistrates' court, the justices' chief executive for that court;

(*b*) in Scotland –

(i) in relation to the Court of Session, the Deputy Principal Clerk of Session;

(ii) in relation to a sheriff court, the sheriff clerk.

Amendments—SI 2001/161.

Defined terms—"maintenance calculation": s 54.

****

8 Maintenance calculations and maintenance orders made in error

(1) Where –

(*a*) at the time that a maintenance calculation with respect to a qualifying child was made a maintenance order was in force with respect to that child;

(*aa*) the maintenance order has ceased to have effect by virtue of the provisions of regulation 3;

(*b*) the non-resident parent has made payments of child support maintenance due under that calculation; and

(*c*) the Secretary of State revises the decision as to the maintenance calculation under section 16 of the Act and decides that no child support maintenance was payable on the ground that the previous decision was made in error,

the payments of child support maintenance shall be treated as payments under the maintenance order and that order shall be treated as having continued in force.

(2) Where –

(*a*) at the time that a maintenance order with respect to a qualifying child was made a maintenance calculation was in force with respect to that child;

(*aa*) the maintenance calculation ceases to have effect;

(*b*) the non-resident parent has made payments of maintenance due under that order; and

(*c*) the maintenance order is revoked by the court on the grounds that it was made in error,

the payments under the maintenance order shall be treated as payments of child support maintenance and the maintenance calculation shall be treated as not having ceased to have effect.

Amendments—SI 1993/913; SI 1999/1510; SI 2001/161.

Defined terms—"non-resident parent": CSA 1991, s 3(2); "child support maintenance": s 3(6); "maintenance calculation": s 54; "maintenance order": reg 1(2); "qualifying child": s 3(1).

9 Cases in which application may be made under section 4 or 7 of the Act

The provisions of section 4(10) or 7(10) of the Act shall not apply to prevent an application being made under those sections after 22 January 1996 where a decision has been made by the relevant court either that it has no power to vary or that it has no power to enforce a maintenance order in a particular case.

Amendments—Added by SI 1995/3261.

Scope of provision—CSA 1991, s 4(10) prevents an application being made for a calculation where there is in force a written maintenance agreement (made before 5 April 1993) or a maintenance order. Thus, if application has been made unsuccessfully to vary the order, or a court has decided that it has no power to enforce an order, application can be made under CSA 1991, s 4 for a calculation.

"relevant court"—This term is not defined in these regulations, so may be taken to apply to the courts with power to vary periodical payments orders for children, namely the High Court, county courts and magistrates' courts.

Children (Admissibility of Hearsay Evidence) Order 1993, SI 1993/621

1 Citation and commencement

This Order may be cited as the Children (Admissibility of Hearsay Evidence) Order 1993 and shall come into force on 5 April 1993.

2 Admissibility of hearsay evidence

In –

(*a*) civil proceedings before the High Court or a county court; and

(*b*) (i) family proceedings, and

(ii) civil proceedings under the Child Support Act 1991 in a magistrates' court, evidence given in connection with the upbringing, maintenance or welfare of a child shall be admissible notwithstanding any rule of law relating to hearsay.

Defined terms—"child": CA 1989, s 105(1).

"civil proceedings"—This term is not defined for the purposes of the Order but will not usually cause any difficulty. The Civil Evidence Act 1968 contains a definition of civil proceedings but only for the purpose of clarifying the position of proceedings before tribunals and arbitrations, which do not arise in relation to the scope of this Order, and excluding certain proceedings from the strict rules of evidence, which is immaterial for the purposes of this Order as it imposes no preconditions for admissibility.

"family proceedings ... in a magistrates' court"—This concept is not defined by the Order. CA 1989, s 8(3) defines "family proceedings" for the purposes of the Act, but s 92(2) provides that "proceedings under this Act shall be treated as family proceedings in relation to magistrates' courts". This is, in context, clearly a reference to the concept of "family proceedings" as defined by Magistrates' Courts Act 1980, s 65, ie the former "domestic proceedings" which were renamed by CA 1989, s 92(1). In *Oxfordshire County Council v R* [1992] 1 FLR 648, Douglas Brown J seems to have regarded the s 92(2) definition as bringing all proceedings under CA 1989 within the scope of the Children (Admissibility of Hearsay Evidence) Order 1991, which was revoked by this Order, and which contained reference to "family proceedings in a magistrates' court". This would seem to indicate that the definition in MCA 1980 is the one that applies for this purpose. It is, however, arguable that the effect of Interpretation Act 1978, s 11 (which attributes to expressions used in a statutory instrument the meaning which they bear in the Act which confers the power under which the instrument is made, unless the contrary intention appears) is to attract the s 8(3) definition, which does not include proceedings under CA 1989, Pt V within its definition (see also CA 1989, s 105, which refers back to s 8(3)). Section 92(2) relates to the unconnected concept of the meaning of family proceedings for the purposes of MCA 1980, which is consequentially amended under s 92(11) and Sch 11.

"civil proceedings under the Child Support Act 1991"—The relevant proceedings in a magistrates' court are under s 20 (appeals from a child support officer where made in accordance with the Child Support Appeals (Jurisdiction of Courts) Order 2002, ie on an issue of parentage), s 26 (reference to court for declaration of parentage), and certain proceedings on enforcement under ss 33–40.

"in connection with the upbringing, maintenance or welfare of a child"—This is a flexible form of words which will need to be applied in relation to each individual case. The concept of a question with respect to the upbringing of a child is also one of the triggers for activating the principle that the court should treat the child's welfare as its paramount consideration (CA 1989, s 1(1)). "In connection with" leaves some uncertainty about what it is that should relate to the "upbringing etc". It is submitted that if the proceedings are about the child's upbringing, maintenance or welfare, eg s 8 proceedings, it is not necessary to determine whether particular things that are sought to be proved in those proceedings so relate; if the proceedings so relate, every piece of evidence allowed to be adduced will necessarily be relevant to the outcome and thus within the scope of the Order, even though the evidence itself may not directly relate to any of the three things specified in the Order. For example, in proceedings for child maintenance the respondent's income is clearly relevant and, although his wage slips do not relate directly to the maintenance of the child, they are relevant to the issue of how much child maintenance should be ordered and are therefore admissible under the Order. Where proceedings consist of more than one aspect not all of which relate to any of the three issues, it will be necessary to analyse whether the fact sought to be admitted by virtue of the Order relates to any of those issues.

The Order clearly applies to contempt proceedings which take place as part of "family proceedings". For hearsay evidence to be admissible under the Order, the onus lies on the applicant seeking to rely on the hearsay evidence to show that the evidence has a "substantial connection with the upbringing, maintenance or welfare of a child". If the injunctive relief is being granted to protect a child, evidence from the child of any breach of the injunction is likely to have a "substantial connection" with his welfare. However, if the injunction was granted in a parental dispute to protect one parent, the evidence of a child as to a breach of that injunction, where he himself was not directly affected by it, would be unlikely to show a "substantial connection" with his welfare (*C v C (Contempt: Evidence)* [1993] 1 FLR 220). The decision as to admissibility will be for the judge to consider on the particular facts of each case. Where this Order does not apply, hearsay evidence may nevertheless be admissible following the ruling in *Savings and Investment*

Bank Ltd v Gasco Investments (Netherlands) BV (No 2) [1988] 1 All ER 975, in relation to which, see Fricker and Bean *Enforcement of Injunctions and Undertakings* (Jordans, 1991), para 11.10.

"shall be admissible"—The effect of this Order is to render hearsay evidence admissible. Thus, a local authority is entitled to adduce in evidence the written and videotaped record of a child's interview in which allegations of sexual abuse are made, and can decline to call her to give oral evidence. In *Re P (Witness Summons)* [1997] 2 FLR 447 it was observed that the only way in which another party could secure the child's attendance to give evidence was to issue a witness summons against the child under CCR Ord 20, r 12, and that the judge had a discretion whether to issue such a summons. In *Re P* it was held that the question of whether to issue a witness summons against a child was not a question with respect to upbringing and therefore CA 1989, s 1(1) did not apply (though the case provides useful guidance on the factors to be considered in the exercise of the discretion).

As to the right approach to hearsay evidence in care proceedings see *Re H (Care: Change in Care Plan)* [1998] 1 FLR 193 where the Court of Appeal accepted that even an unsworn allegation was capable of constituting a very serious cause for concern which a court could accept provided it was evaluated against testimony on oath. What weight should be attached to the particular piece of hearsay evidence is a question for the court to decide (*F v Child Support Agency* [1999] 2 FLR 244).

"rule of law relating to hearsay"—Hearsay evidence is, at common law, inadmissible save in certain circumstances. The number of exceptions to the rule against hearsay has been increased by or under statute over the years. This Order may be relied on in preference to other exceptions which may also apply and which are less attractive because they have preconditions; for example, if evidence is admissible under the Order, no notice need be served in accordance with the exception created by the Civil Evidence Act 1968.

3 Revocation

The Children (Admissibility of Hearsay Evidence) Order 1991 is hereby revoked.

Children (Allocation of Proceedings) Order 1991, SI 1991/1677

ARRANGEMENT OF ARTICLES

1 Citation, commencement and interpretation

(1) This Order may be cited as the Children (Allocation of Proceedings) Order 1991 and shall come into force on 14 October 1991.

(2) In this Order, unless the context otherwise requires –

"child" –

(*a*) means, subject to sub-paragraph (*b*), a person under the age of 18 with respect to whom proceedings are brought, and
(*b*) where the proceedings are under Schedule 1, also includes a person who has reached the age of 18,

"London commission area" has the meaning assigned to it by section 2(1) of the Justices of the Peace Act 1979;
"petty sessions area" has the meaning assigned to it by section 4 of the Justices of the Peace Act 1979; and
"the Act" means the Children Act 1989, and a section, Part or Schedule referred to by number alone means the section, Part or Schedule so numbered in that Act.

"Schedule 1" (art 1(2))—The reference to Sch 1 is to CA 1989, Sch 1, by virtue of which the definition of child is extended because "children" who are aged over 18 may claim maintenance from their parents where Sch 1, para 2 applies (see also the definition in para 16(1)).

"section 2(1) of the Justices of the Peace Act 1979" (art 1(2))— Section 2(1) of the 1979 Act lists those areas of Greater London which form the "London commission areas", subject to their variation by Order in Council under s 2(2) of that Act.

"section 4 of the Justices of the Peace Act 1979" (art 1(2))— Section 4 of the 1979 Act divides England and Wales into petty sessions areas by reference to various types of local government area and petty sessional divisions.

Other sources of definitions—As the order was made under CA 1989, expressions used in the order will bear any meaning which they have in that Act, unless the contrary intention appears (Interpretation Act 1978, s 11).

2 Classes of county court

For the purposes of this Order there shall be the following classes of county court –

(*a*) divorce county courts, being those courts designated for the time being as divorce county courts by an order under section 33 of the Matrimonial and Family Proceedings Act 1984;
(*b*) family hearing centres, being those courts set out in Schedule 1 to this Order;
(*c*) care centres, being those courts set out in column (ii) of Schedule 2 to this Order.

Divorce county courts (art 2(*a*))—Certain county courts are designated as divorce county courts by the Lord Chancellor under the provision cited for the purpose of exercising jurisdiction in matrimonial causes.

Family hearing centres (art 2(*b*))—Family hearing centres are created by the order; they comprise the county courts listed in Sch 1. The concentration of hearings in these centres is designed to facilitate the availability of nominated members of the judiciary to whom proceedings of the types covered by the order are allocated by the Family Proceedings (Allocation to Judiciary) Directions 1999.

Care centres (art 2(*c*))—The concept of care centres is created by the order. It is said to comprise "the courts" listed in column (ii) of Sch 2. In fact, that column also includes the Principal Registry of the Family Division, which is not a court as such although it is part of the High Court. There are fewer care centres than there are family hearing centres and this reflects the fact that fewer judges may deal with care and related proceedings than may deal with other proceedings under CA 1989 and adoption proceedings.

Commencement of proceedings

3 Proceedings to be commenced in magistrates' court

(1) Subject to paragraphs (2) and (3) and to article 4, proceedings under any of the following provisions shall be commenced in a magistrates' court –

(*a*) section 25 (use of accommodation for restricting liberty);
(*b*) section 31 (care and supervision orders);
(*c*) section 33(7) (leave to change name of or remove from United Kingdom child in care);
(*d*) section 34 (parental contact);
(*e*) section 36 (education supervision orders);
(*f*) section 43 (child assessment orders);
(*g*) section 44 (emergency protection orders);
(*h*) section 45 (duration of emergency protection orders etc);
(*i*) section 46(7) (application for emergency protection order by police officer);
(*j*) section 48 (powers to assist discovery of children etc);
(*k*) section 50 (recovery orders);
(*l*) section 75 (protection of children in an emergency);
(*m*) section 77(6) (appeal against steps taken under section 77(1));
(*n*) section 102 (powers of constable to assist etc);
(*o*) paragraph 19 of Schedule 2 (approval of arrangements to assist child to live abroad);
(*p*) paragraph 23 of Schedule 2 (contribution orders);
(*q*) paragraph 8 of Schedule 8 (certain appeals);
(*r*) section 21 of the Adoption Act 1976;
(*s*) (*revoked*)

PART III

(*t*) section 20 of the Child Support Act 1991 (appeals) where the appeals are to be dealt with in accordance with the Child Support Appeals (Jurisdiction of Courts) Order 1993;

(*u*) section 30 of the Human Fertilisation and Embryology Act 1990 (parental orders in favour of gamete donors).

(2) Notwithstanding paragraph (1) and subject to paragraph (3), proceedings of a kind set out in sub-paragraph (*b*), (*e*), (*f*), (*g*), (*i*) or (*j*) of paragraph (1), and which arise out of an investigation directed, by the High Court or a county court, under section 37(1), shall be commenced –

(*a*) in the court which directs the investigation, where that court is the High Court or a care centre, or

(*b*) in such care centre as the court which directs the investigation may order.

(3) Notwithstanding paragraphs (1) and (2), proceedings of a kind set out in sub-paragraph (*a*) to (*k*), (*n*) or (*o*) of paragraph (1) shall be commenced in a court in which are pending other proceedings, in respect of the same child, which are also of a kind set out in those sub-paragraphs.

Amendments—SI 1993/624; SI 1994/2164; SI 2001/775.

Defined terms—"care centre": art 2(*c*); "child", "section": art 1(2).

Structure of art 3—Article 3(1) provides for 18 types of proceedings under CA 1989 to be commenced only in a magistrates' court, subject to the exceptions in arts 3(2), 3(3) and 4. Article 3(2) makes an exception in relation to six of those types of proceedings by requiring them to be made to the county court or the High Court if the application arises out of a s 37(1) direction made by that court (unless the direction was made by a county court which was not a care centre, in which case that court must specify the care centre in which the application is to be made). Article 3(3) makes an exception in relation to 13 types of proceedings by allowing them to be commenced in a court where other proceedings of one of those types are already pending in relation to the child in question. The proceedings affected by this article are all in the public law sphere.

Restriction of commencement—Where this article applies, it restricts the choice of forum which would otherwise exist by reason of the fact that CA 1989 confers jurisdiction in each of the relevant types of proceedings on "the court", which is defined by s 92(7) to mean the High Court, a county court or a magistrates' court.

Leave to change name etc (art 3(1)(*c*))—Although under this article an application for leave pursuant to s 33(7) should be commenced in the family proceedings court, an application properly made ex parte by a local authority without notice to the child's parents for a change of the child's name should be transferred for consideration by a higher court (*Re J (A Minor) (Change of Name)* [1993] 1 FLR 699 per Booth J).

"section 21 of the Adoption Act 1976" (art 3(1)(*r*))—AA 1976, s 21 provides for the variation of an order freeing a child for adoption (made under AA 1976, s 18), so as to substitute the adoption agency named in the order for another adoption agency.

"section 37(1)" (art 3(2))—CA 1989, s 37(1) allows the court, in general family proceedings, to direct that the appropriate authority carry out an investigation of the child's circumstances, where it appears to the court that it may be appropriate for a care or supervision order to be made. Article 3(2)(*b*) is necessary because the directing court may not itself be a care centre. The policy of restricting care proceedings to care centres prevails over that of consolidation, but it will still be necessary to keep any such resulting proceedings within the county court system when it is desirable for the same judge to deal with them as has dealt with the proceedings from which they derive.

"proceedings ... which arise out of" (art 3(2))—This is not a precise expression. It is suggested that it would only cover an application made after the end of the period of eight weeks mentioned in CA 1989, s 37(4) if it resulted directly from a review of a type mentioned in s 37(6).

Procedure—The making of applications under CA 1989 in magistrates' courts is governed by Family Proceedings Courts (Children Act 1989) Rules 1991, r 4.

4 Application to extend, vary or discharge order

(1) Subject to paragraphs (2) and (3), proceedings under the Act, or under the Adoption Act 1976 –

(*a*) to extend, vary or discharge an order, or
(*b*) the determination of which may have the effect of varying or discharging an order,

shall be commenced in the court which made the order.

(2) Notwithstanding paragraph (1), an application for an order under section 8 which would have the effect of varying or discharging an order made, by a county court, in accordance with section 10(1)(*b*) shall be made to a divorce county court.

(3) Notwithstanding paragraph (1), an application to extend, vary or discharge an order made, by a county court, under section 38, or for an order which would have the effect of extending, varying or discharging such an order, shall be made to a care centre.

(4) A court may transfer proceedings commenced in accordance with paragraph (1) to any other court in accordance with the provisions of articles 5 to 13.

Amendments—SI 1993/624.

Defined terms—"care centre": art 2(*c*); "divorce county court": art 2(*a*).

Override of art 3—Where art 4 applies, its requirements override any inconsistent requirement which art 3(1) would otherwise have produced (see the opening words of art 3(1)).

"section 10(1)(b)" (art 4(2))—CA 1989, s 10(1)(*b*) gives the court power to make section 8 orders of its own motion.

"section 38" (art 4(3))—CA 1989, s 38 allows the court to make interim care and interim supervision orders.

Procedure—The making of applications under CA 1989 in magistrates' courts is governed by the Family Proceedings Courts (Children Act 1989) Rules 1991, r 4. The making of applications under the Adoption Act 1976 is governed by the Adoption Rules 1984 (for applications in the High Court and county courts) and the Magistrates' Courts (Adoption) Rules 1984 (for applications in magistrates' courts).

Transfer of proceedings

5 Disapplication of enactments about transfer

Sections 38 and 39 of the Matrimonial and Family Proceedings Act 1984 shall not apply to proceedings under the Act or under the Adoption Act 1976.

MFPA 1984, ss 38, 39—Section 38 allows the High Court to transfer to a county court any family proceedings which are within that county court's jurisdiction. Section 39 allows a county court to transfer family proceedings to the High Court. The effect of their disapplication is that the order contains the only provisions enabling proceedings under CA 1989 or AA 1976 to be transferred between the High Court and county courts. The general transfer provisions of County Courts Act 1984, ss 40, 41 and 42 do not apply to family proceedings within the meaning of MFPA 1984, Pt V.

6 Transfer from one magistrates' court to another

(1) A magistrates' court (the "transferring court") shall transfer proceedings to which this article applies to another magistrates' court (the "receiving court") where –

(*a*) having regard to the principle set out in section 1(2), the transferring court considers that the transfer is in the interests of the child –
  (i) because it is likely significantly to accelerate the determination of the proceedings,
  (ii) because it would be appropriate for those proceedings to be heard together with other family proceedings which are pending in the receiving court, or
  (iii) for some other reason, and

(*b*) the receiving court, by its justices' clerk (as defined by rule 1(2) of the Family Proceedings Courts (Children Act 1989) Rules 1991), consents to the transfer.

(2) This article applies to proceedings –

(*a*) under the Act;
(*b*) under the Adoption Act 1976;
(*c*) of the kind mentioned in sub-paragraph (*t*) or (*u*) of article 3(1) and under section 55A of the Family Law Act 1986;
(*d*) under section 11 of the Crime and Disorder Act 1998 (child safety orders).

Amendments—SI 1993/624; SI 1994/2164; SI 1998/2166; SI 2001/775.

Defined terms—"child": art 1(2); "family proceedings": CA 1989, s 8(3).

"magistrates' court"—The jurisdiction of a magistrates' court to transfer proceedings to which this article applies may be exercised by a justices' clerk (Justices' Clerks Rules 1999, Sch, para 38) or, where the proceedings are under CA 1989, by court clerks authorised under Family Proceedings Courts (Children Act 1989) Rules 1991, r 32.

"principle set out in section 1(2)" (art 6(1)(*a*))—"In any proceedings in which any question with respect to the upbringing of a child arises, the court shall have regard to the general principle that any delay in determining the question is likely to prejudice the welfare of the child".

Family Proceedings Courts (Children Act 1989) Rules 1991, r 1(2) (art 6(1)(*b*))—FPC(CA 1989)R 1991, r 1(2) defines "justices' clerk" by attracting the definition in the Justices of the Peace Act 1979, s 70 (which defines a "justices' clerk" as a clerk to the justices for a petty sessions area) and providing that justices' clerk also includes any person who performs a justices' clerk's functions by reason of r 32 (which enables certain other court clerks to be authorised to perform various functions).

Procedure—In relation to proceedings under CA 1989, the procedure as to transfer is set out in FPC(CA 1989)R 1991, rr 6, 14. There is no relevant procedural provision relating to transfer with respect to adoption proceedings.

7 Transfer from magistrates' court to county court by magistrates' court

(1) Subject to paragraphs (2), (3) and (4) and to articles 15 to 18, a magistrates' court may, upon application by a party or of its own motion, transfer to a county court proceedings of any of the kinds mentioned in article 3(1) or proceedings under section 55A of the Family Law Act 1986 where it considers it in the interests of the child to do so having regard, first, to the principle set out in section 1(2) and, secondly, to the following questions –

(*a*) whether the proceedings are exceptionally grave, important or complex, in particular –

(i) because of complicated or conflicting evidence about the risks involved to the child's physical or moral well-being or about other matters relating to the welfare of the child;

(ii) because of the number of parties;

(iii) because of a conflict with the law of another jurisdiction;

(iv) because of some novel and difficult point of law; or

(v) because of some question of general public interest;

(*b*) whether it would be appropriate for those proceedings to be heard together with other family proceedings which are pending in another court; and

(*c*) whether transfer is likely significantly to accelerate the determination of the proceedings, where –

(i) no other method of doing so, including transfer to another magistrates' court, is appropriate, and

(ii) delay would seriously prejudice the interests of the child who is the subject of the proceedings.

(2) Notwithstanding paragraph (1), proceedings of the kind mentioned in sub-paragraphs (*g*) to (*j*), (*l*), (*m*), (*p*) or (*q*) of article 3(1) should not be transferred from a magistrates' court.

(3) Notwithstanding paragraph (1), proceedings of the kind mentioned in sub-paragraph (*a*) or (*n*) of article 3(1) shall only be transferred from a magistrates' court to a county court in order to be heard together with other family proceedings which arise out of the same circumstances as gave rise to the proceedings to be transferred and which are pending in another court.

(4) Notwithstanding paragraphs (1) and (3), proceedings of the kind mentioned in article 3(1)(*a*) shall not be transferred from a magistrates' court which is not a family proceedings court within the meaning of section 92(1).

Amendments—SI 2001/775.

Defined terms—"child": art 1(2); "family proceedings": CA 1989, s 8(3).

Proceedings within scope of art 7 (art 7(1), (2))—The combination of the reference, in art 7(1), to the list of proceedings in art 3(1) and the exclusion achieved by art 7(2) is that the following are, in principle, transferable under the article: proceedings under CA 1989, s 25 (use of accommodation for restricting liberty), s 31 (care and supervision orders), s 33(7) (leave to change name or remove from United Kingdom), s 34 (parental contact), s 36 (education supervision order), s 43 (child assessment order), s 50 (recovery orders), s 102 (powers of constable to assist etc), Sch 2, para 19 (approval of arrangements to assist child to live abroad) and Adoption Act 1976, s 21 (substitution of one adoption agency for another).

"magistrates' court" (art 7(1))—See under art 6.

Restrictions in arts 15–18 (art 7(1))—Articles 15–18 restrict the type of county court to which proceedings may be transferred in certain circumstances. In fact, arts 15 and 16 have no application to the transfer of proceedings under art 7. Article 17(2) requires that proceedings under Adoption Act 1976, s 21 which are to be transferred to a county court must be transferred to a divorce county court. Article 18(3) requires all other proceedings that are transferable under art 7, except for proceedings under s 102, to be transferred to the relevant care centre (or, by virtue of art 19, the Principal Registry of the Family Division).

"grave, important or complex" (art 7(1)(*a*))—The types of case which should generally be transferred upwards from the magistrates' court include the following: where there is a conflict of expert medical evidence (*Essex County Council v L (Minors)* [1993] Fam Law 458); where there is complex and conflicting evidence on ability of a disturbed 15-year-old to instruct a solicitor (*Re H (A Minor) (Care Proceedings: Child's Wishes)* [1993] 1 FLR 440); where there have been

PART III

serious non-accidental injuries to young children for which the parents offer no proper explanation and where there is conflicting expert medical evidence as to the risk of leaving the children in the home (*C v Solihull Metropolitan Borough Council* [1993] 1 FLR 290; *S v Oxfordshire County Council* [1993] 1 FLR 452); where the case is likely to last for more than two or three days (*Re H (A Minor) (Care Proceedings: Child's Wishes)* [1993] 1 FLR 440; *Essex County Council v L (Minors)* [1993] Fam Law 458); where the case has an international element, eg consideration of the Hague Convention on the Civil Aspects of International Child Abduction 1980 (*R v R (Residence Order: Child Abduction)* [1995] 2 FLR 625).

Where a party seeks leave of the court to withhold information from another party, the question of principle involved is such that the proceedings should be transferred to the High Court *(Re C (Disclosure)* [1996] 1 FLR 797); where an issue about the release of confidential information involves difficult points of law, or where the disclosure of documentation involves a difficult or sensitive exercise of discretion, it may be advisable to transfer the proceedings (or the issue itself) to the High Court (*Re EC (Disclosure of Material)* [1996] 2 FLR 123).

Reducing delay (art 7(1)(*c*))—Delay is only one of the factors relevant to the assessment of whether a case is suitable for upwards transfer. The test is "whether the interests of the child demanded that the proceedings be transferred", and all factors bearing on the interests of that child in that case must be considered (*R v South East Hampshire Family Proceedings Court ex parte D* [1994] 2 FLR 190, Ewbank J). In *L v Berkshire CC* [1992] 1 FCR 481, a magistrates' court had heard an application for a care order on eight non-consecutive days over a period of four weeks. On appeal, Sir Stephen Brown P said that, when faced with a lengthy hearing, magistrates' courts should consider transferring the case upwards. In *Essex CC v L* [1993] Fam Law 458 Bracewell J indicated that justices should transfer a care application to a county court when told that the estimated length of hearing was more than two days or, at the most, three days. In *Re H (A Minor) (Care Proceedings: Child's Wishes)* [1993] 1 FLR 440, Thorpe J commented that it was appropriate for justices, when faced with a lengthy hearing in excess of two or at the most three days, to consider the option of transferring the matter to a higher court. However, where magistrates do proceed to hear a long case, their inappropriate refusal to transfer the case upwards does not invalidate the decision reached (*Re A* [1993] Fam Law 619). Time estimates given to the court in any case must make provision for the following: judicial reading time; length of opening; realistic calculation of the likely time to be taken in respect of the evidence of each witness; the points of law or procedure likely to arise and the length of time they will take to argue; the number and likely length of closing speeches; and time for an extempore judgment (*Re MD and TD (Minors) (Time Estimates)* [1994] 2 FLR 336 (set out in Part IV of this work as *Practice Note of 2 February 1994)* and *President's Direction of 22 November 1993*).

Proceedings under s 25 or 102 transferable for consolidation only (art 7(3))—Article 7(3) achieves the result that proceedings under CA 1989, s 25 (use of accommodation for restricting liberty) or s 102 (warrant for constable to assist) may be transferred under the article only in order to be heard together with other family proceedings which arise out of the same circumstances.

No transfer from a magistrates' court which is not a family proceedings court (art 7(4))—Article 7(4) affects proceedings to authorise the use of secure accommodation under CA 1989, s 25. Such proceedings are referred to in Magistrates' Courts Act 1980, s 65(1)(*n*) and are thus family proceedings which, by virtue of s 67 of that Act, are to be heard by a family proceedings court. However, this is subject to an exception made by Criminal Justice Act 1991, s 60(3), which provides for applications under CA 1989, s 25 to be made to a youth court or a magistrates' court (ie an adult court convened to deal with criminal business) in certain circumstances. Article 7(4) restricts the scope of the article to proceedings under s 25 which are family proceedings; proceedings arising in the general magistrates' court or the youth court will not be so transferred.

Timing of application—In many cases, an application for transfer will be made soon after the proceedings are commenced. Where this does not happen (or where an initial transfer application is rejected) and it later becomes apparent that the case is more complex than had originally been anticipated, it is essential that action is taken swiftly to transfer it to the appropriate level of court (*Re H (A Minor) (Care Proceedings) (Child's Wishes)* [1993] 1 FLR 440).

Procedure—In relation to proceedings under CA 1989, the procedure as to transfer is contained in Family Proceedings Courts (Children Act 1989) Rules 1991, rr 6 and 14. There is no relevant procedural provision relating to transfer with respect to adoption proceedings.

8 Subject to articles 15 to 18, a magistrates' court may transfer to a county court proceedings under the Act or under the Adoption Act 1976, being proceedings to which article 7 does not apply, where, having regard to the principle set out in section 1(2), it considers that in the interests of the child the proceedings can be dealt with more appropriately in that county court.

Defined terms—"child": art 1(2).

Scope of provision—This article allows magistrates' courts to transfer proceedings under CA 1989 or the Adoption Act 1976 to a county court in certain cases where art 7 does not apply. There is a distinction between public law cases and private law cases in relation to transfer from the magistrates' court to a county court. Article 7 deals with public law cases and provides that a magistrates' court can transfer a case to a county court on an application by a party, or of its own motion, if it considers it to be in the interests of the child having regard, first, to the principle set out in CA 1989, s 1(2) ("the delay principle") and, second, to the gravity, importance and complexity of the case. Article 8 deals with the transfer of private law cases and it contains no reference to who may make an application for transfer or whether the court can make a transfer of its own motion. There is no reference to any appeal of an order made under art 8. There is no possibility of applying to a care centre to overrule the refusal of a magistrates' court to transfer a private law case to a county court (contrast the position with public law proceedings in art 9). Therefore, the only remedy available to challenge such a refusal in relation to private law proceedings is by way of judicial review (*R v South East Hampshire Family Proceedings Court ex parte D* [1994] 2 FLR 190).

"proceedings to which article 7 does not apply"—This would seem to refer to those proceedings which are not listed anywhere in art 3(1), on the basis that art 7 applies even to those which are not transferable under it by virtue of the exclusion in art 7(2).

Restrictions in arts 15–18—Articles 15–18 restrict the type of county court to which proceedings may be transferred in certain circumstances. Article 15(1) and (3) requires proceedings under CA 1989, Pt I or II or Sch 1 to be transferred to a divorce county court (or, by virtue of art 19, the Principal Registry of the Family Division). Article 17(2) requires proceedings under the Adoption Act 1976 to be transferred to a divorce county court (or, by virtue of art 19, the Principal Registry of the Family Division). Article 18(3) requires proceedings under CA 1989, Pt III, IV or V to be transferred to the relevant care centre (or, by virtue of art 19, the Principal Registry of the Family Division).

"magistrates' court"—See under art 6.

"having regard to the principle set out in section 1(2)"—These words form a subordinate clause to the main clause, so that, although the court must have regard to the question of delay (as is required by CA 1989, s 1(2)), its main function is to consider the interests of the child and to decide whether the proceedings can be more appropriately dealt with in a county court than in a magistrates' court (*R v South East Hampshire Family Proceedings Court ex parte D* [1994] 2 FLR 190 – a magistrates' court fell into error when it limited itself to the question of delay and precluded itself from considering the interests of the child on an application for upwards transfer). See also under art 6.

Procedure—In relation to proceedings under CA 1989, the procedure as to transfer is contained in FPC(CA 1989)R 1991, rr 6 and 14. There is no relevant procedural provision relating to transfer with respect to adoption proceedings.

9 Transfer from magistrates' court following refusal of magistrates' court to transfer

(1) Where a magistrates' court refuses to transfer proceedings under article 7, a party to those proceedings may apply to the care centre listed in column (ii) of Schedule 2 to this Order against the entry in column (i) for the petty sessions area or London commission area in which the magistrates' court is situated for an order under paragraph (2).

PART III

(2) Upon hearing an application under paragraph (1) the court may transfer the proceedings to itself where, having regard to the principle set out in section 1(2) and the questions set out in article 7(1)(*a*) to (*c*), it considers it in the interests of the child to do so.

(3) Upon hearing an application under paragraph (1) the court may transfer the proceedings to the High Court where, having regard to the principle set out in section 1(2), it considers –

(*a*) that the proceedings are appropriate for determination in the High Court, and

(*b*) that such determination would be in the interests of the child.

(4) This article shall apply (with the necessary modifications) to proceedings brought under Parts I and II as it applies where a magistrates' court refuses to transfer proceedings under article 7.

Amendments—SI 1997/1897.

Defined terms—"care centre": art 2(*c*); "child", "London commission area", "petty sessions area": art 1(2).

Scope of provision—Where a magistrates' court has refused to transfer the proceedings to a county court under art 7, art 9 allows a party to apply to a care centre for the proceedings to be transferred to the care centre or to the High Court. In addition, where the magistrates' court has refused to transfer private law proceedings to the county court a party may, under art 9(4), apply to a county court for the proceedings to be transferred to a county court or the High Court. The application is heard afresh, and not as an appeal from the decision of the magistrates' court, notwithstanding that the applicant is necessarily seeking to reverse that decision.

"principle set out in section 1(2)" (art 9(2), (3))—See under art 6.

Procedure—In relation to proceedings under CA 1989 to which Pt IV of FPR 1991 applies, FPR 1991, r 4.6(1)–(4) sets out the procedure to be followed and allows a district judge to make the order. There is no relevant procedural provision relating to transfer with respect to adoption proceedings.

10 Transfer from one county court to another

(1) Subject to articles 15 to 17, a county court (the "transferring court") shall transfer proceedings to which this article applies to another county court (the "receiving court") where –

(*a*) the transferring court, having regard to the principle set out in section 1(2), considers the transfer to be in the interests of the child, and

(*b*) the receiving court is –

(i) of the same class or classes, within the meaning of article 2, as the transferring court, or

(ii) to be presided over by a judge or district judge who is specified by directions under section 9 of the Courts and Legal Services Act 1990, for the same purposes as the judge or district judge presiding over the transferring court.

(2) This article applies to proceedings –

(*a*) under the Act;

(*b*) under the Adoption Act 1976;

(*c*) of the kind mentioned in sub-paragraph (*t*) or (*u*) of article 3(1) and under section 55A of the Family Law Act 1986.

Amendments—SI 1993/624; SI 1994/2164; SI 2001/775.

Defined terms—"child": art 1(2).

Restrictions in arts 15–17—Articles 15–17 restrict the type of county court to which proceedings may be transferred in certain circumstances. Articles 15(3) and 16(3) apply but say nothing meaningful in this context. Article 16(1) requires contested s 8 proceedings to be transferred to a family hearing centre for trial (or, by virtue of art 19, the Principal Registry of the Family Division); and art 17(1) makes broadly similar provision in relation to proceedings under Adoption Act 1976, ss 12 and 18.

"principle set out in section 1(2)" (art 10(*a*))—See under art 6.

"directions under section 9 of the Courts and Legal Services Act 1990" (art 10(*b*)(ii))—The directions referred to are the Family Proceedings (Allocation to Judiciary) Directions 1999.

Procedure—In relation to proceedings under CA 1989 to which FPR 1991, Pt IV applies, FPR 1991, r 4.14(2)(*h*) allows the transfer to be ordered in the form of a direction and r 4.14(3)–(10) regulates the procedural framework within which that can be done. The reference to "court" in r 4.14(2) allows a district judge to make the transfer order (see the definition in r 1.2(2)). No other procedures are provided by FPR 1991 or CCR in relation to transfer under this article except FPR 1991, r 4.6(5), which requires the court to notify the parties of any transfer under art 10. It would therefore seem that a district judge would have jurisdiction to make an order under this article only as a direction under r 4.14.

There is no relevant procedural provision relating to transfer with respect to adoption proceedings.

PART III

11 Transfer from county court to magistrates' court by county court

(1) A county court may transfer to a magistrates' court before trial proceedings which were transferred under article 7(1) where the county court, having regard to the principle set out in section 1(2) and the interests of the child, considers that the criterion cited by the magistrates' court as the reason for transfer –

(*a*) in the case of the criterion in article 7(1)(*a*), does not apply,
(*b*) in the case of the criterion in article 7(1)(*b*), no longer applies, because the proceedings with which the transferred proceedings were to be heard have been determined,
(*c*) in the case of the criterion in article 7(1)(*c*), no longer applies.

(2) Paragraph (1) shall apply (with the necessary modifications) to proceedings under Parts I and II brought in, or transferred to, a county court as it applies to proceedings transferred to a county court under article 7(1).

Amendments—SI 1997/1897.

Defined terms—"child": art 1(2).

Scope of provision—This article allows a county court, in certain circumstances, to retransfer to a magistrates' court proceedings which had earlier been transferred the other way under art 7(1). The county court is also able to transfer to the magistrates' court private law proceedings which have been commenced in the county court and to retransfer to the magistrates' court private law proceedings which were transferred to it under art 7.

Circumstances in which a retransfer may be ordered—This article reads rather opaquely, but the principles involved are simple. The criterion will depend on which of the three criteria was relied on by the magistrates' court when it transferred the proceedings to the county court: where art 7(1)(*a*) was the basis for the original transfer, art 11(1)(*a*) enables the county court to send the proceedings back if it considers that that criterion does not apply (either because of a change in the circumstances or because the county court disagrees with the magistrates' court); where art 7(1)(*b*)) was relied on, art 11(1)(*b*) allows a retransfer only where the pending county court proceedings which had activated the criterion have been concluded (presumably the magistrates' court will seldom be mistaken about whether there are such proceedings pending, but, where that does happen, it would seem that there is no scope for the county court to send the proceedings back when the misapprehension is discovered); and where art 7(1)(*c*) was relied upon (avoidance of seriously prejudicial delay), art 11(1)(*c*) allows a retransfer only where the county court considers that the factual basis for the conclusion no longer applies. There is no scope for the county court simply to disagree with the view of the magistrates' court; the decision can only arise as a result of changed circumstances, such as a reduction in the magistrates' courts' waiting times or a reduction of the need for urgency in the particular case.

In applying each of the tests for retransfer set out in art 11(1)(*a*)–(*c*), the county court is required by the preliminary words of art 11 to have regard to the principle set out in CA 1989, s 1(2) and the interests of the child. The preliminary words also provide that a retransfer may only be ordered "before trial", which presumably means before the trial has begun. It is implicit that, where the original transfer had been ordered under more than one of the criteria set out in art 7(1)(*a*)–(*c*), each of the corresponding grounds for retransfer must apply before the proceedings can be retransferred.

"principle set out in section 1(2)"—See under art 6.

Procedure—In relation to proceedings under CA 1989 to which Pt IV of the FPR 1991 applies, art 11 is governed by FPR 1991, r 4.6(6) and (7) (technically (5) as well, but it is less detailed than (7) and adds nothing to it). The justices' clerk must first be consulted (r 4.6(6)). FPR 1991, r 4.14(2)(*h*) allows the transfer to be ordered in the form of a direction, and r 4.14(3)–(10) regulates the procedural framework in which that can be done. The reference to "court" in r 4.14(2) allows a district judge to make the transfer order (see the definition in r 1.2(2)). Even where the issue arises in the context of directions, r 4.6(6) and (7) must be complied with. It seems that a district judge would have jurisdiction to order a transfer under this article only as a direction under r 4.14.

There is no relevant procedural provision relating to transfer with respect to adoption proceedings.

12 Transfer from county court to High Court by county court

(1) A county court may transfer proceedings to which this article applies to the High Court where, having regard to the principle set out in section 1(2), it considers –

(*a*) that the proceedings are appropriate for determination in the High Court, and

(*b*) that such determination would be in the interests of the child.

(2) This article applies to proceedings –

(*a*) under the Act;

(*b*) under the Adoption Act 1976;

(*c*) of the kind mentioned in sub-paragraph (*t*) or (*u*) of article 3(1) and under section 55A of the Family Law Act 1986.

Amendments—SI 1993/624; SI 1994/2164; SI 2001/775.

Defined terms—"child": art 1(2).

Scope of provision—This article allows proceedings under CA 1989 or the Adoption Act 1976 to be transferred by a county court from itself to the High Court where the proceedings are appropriate to be determined there and it is in the interests of the child for that to happen, having regard to the general dangers of delay amongst other relevant factors. The High Court also has power to transfer an application to itself from a county court (County Courts Act 1984, s 41).

"principle set out in section 1(2)"—See under art 6.

"appropriate for determination in the High Court" (art 12(1)(*a*))—Where a child was placed for adoption in contravention of Adoption Act 1976, s 11(1), the Court of Appeal said the order could still be made, but only in the High Court; such proceedings were therefore "appropriate for determination in the High Court" (*Re G (Adoption: Illegal Placement)* [1995] 1 FLR 403).

Procedure—In relation to proceedings under CA 1989 to which Pt IV of FPR 1991 applies, FPR 1991, r 4.6(4) applies where the proceedings have been transferred to the county court in question by a magistrates' court. Rule 4.14(2)(*h*) allows the transfer to be ordered in the form of a direction, and r 4.14(3)–(10) regulates the procedural framework within which that can be done. The reference to "court" in r 4.14(2) allows a district judge to make the transfer order (see the definition in r 1.2(2)), and it would seem that a district judge has jurisdiction to order a transfer only as a direction under r 4.14. There is no relevant procedural provision relating to transfer with respect to adoption proceedings. Where a case is transferred to the High Court and the hearing is estimated to take five days or more, an early directions hearing should be sought before a High Court judge (*Practice Direction of 5 March 1993*; *Re MD and TD (Minors) (Time Estimates)* [1994] 2 FLR 336 (set out in Part IV of this work as *Practice Note of 2 February 1994*); *President's Direction of 22 November 1993*; *Re M (Minors) (Care Proceedings: Child's Wishes)* [1994] 1 FLR 749).

Adoption where child's place of origin is outside the United Kingdom—In Adoption Act 1976 proceedings relating to a child whose place of origin is outside the United Kingdom, guidance on the question of whether the proceedings should be transferred from the county court to the High Court may still be derived from *N and L (Minors) (Adoption Proceedings: Venue)* [1987] 1 WLR 829 (see *Practice Direction of 23 November 1993*; *Re K (Adoption and Wardship)* [1997] 2 FLR 221). Transfer should be limited to those cases giving rise to issues of complexity, difficulty or gravity. Orders for transfer should not be made of the court's own motion without the parties and the children's guardian (if appointed) having the opportunity to make representations on the question of transfer. It will usually be possible for the necessary inquiries to be made by letter and for the matter to be determined without a hearing. In those cases where there is an issue as to transfer, a hearing for determination of the issue should be fixed, with notice of the date, time and place of hearing given to the parties and the children's guardian. It will usually be impracticable to obtain the views of the natural parents or for them to be given notice of any hearing.

13 Transfer from High Court to county court

(1) Subject to articles 15, 16 and 18, the High Court may transfer to a county court proceedings to which this article applies where, having regard to the principle set out in section 1(2), it considers that the proceedings are appropriate for determination in such a court and that such determination would be in the interests of the child.

(2) This article applies to proceedings –

(*a*) under the Act;
(*b*) under the Adoption Act 1976;
(*c*) of the kind mentioned in sub-paragraph (*t*) or (*u*) of article 3(1) and under section 55A of the Family Law Act 1986.

Amendments—SI 1993/624; SI 1994/2164; SI 2001/775.

Defined terms—"child": art 1(2).

Scope of provision—This article allows the High Court to transfer proceedings under CA 1989 and the Adoption Act 1976 to a county court where the proceedings are appropriate to be determined there and it is in the interests of the child for that to happen (having regard to the general dangers of delay amongst other relevant factors). For guidance on the procedure to be adopted when prospective adopters who are resident on the Isle of Man wish to apply for an adoption order see *Re J (Adoption Procedure: Isle of Man)* [2000] 2 FLR 633 where it was said that unless there is some complication of law or fact such cases should be transferred to the county court. However, a transfer should not be made unless there is sufficient information to ensure that it is appropriate. In *Leicestershire County Council v G* [1994] 2 FLR 329, Stuart-White J considered that the High Court did not have power, under CA 1989, s 94(4) and (5), to order, on appeal, the transfer of care proceedings from the family proceedings court to the county court, so that any application for such transfer should be made to the family proceedings court under art 7. However, the matter was not fully argued and it does not appear that art 13 was considered in that case. By contrast, in *Suffolk County Council v C* [1999] 1 FLR 259 Holman J held that the High Court *did* have the power to order such a transfer, under a combination of s 94(4) and (5) and arts

13 and 18(2). His Lordship distinguished the *Leicestershire* decision on the ground that it concerned interim orders, whereas the *Suffolk* case involved an appeal against final orders where he had decided that the matter should be remitted for a fresh hearing of the substantive applications themselves.

"Subject to articles 15, 16 and 18"—Articles 15, 16 and 18 restrict the categories of county court to which proceedings of particular types may be transferred in certain circumstances. Article 15(2) requires proceedings under CA 1989, Pt I or II or Sch 1 to be transferred to a divorce county court (or, by virtue of art 19, the Principal Registry of the Family Division) except where consolidation is the reason for the transfer. Article 16(2) requires s 8 applications to be transferred to a family hearing centre (or, by virtue of art 19, the Principal Registry of the Family Division). Article 18(2) requires applications under Pt III, IV or V to be transferred to a care centre (or, by virtue of art 19, the Principal Registry of the Family Division).

"principle set out in section 1(2)"—See under art 6.

Procedure—In relation to proceedings under CA 1989 to which Pt IV of FPR 1991 applies, FPR 1991, r 4.14(2)(*h*) allows the transfer to be ordered in the form of a direction, and r 4.14(3)–(10) regulates the procedural framework within which that can be done. The reference to "court" in r 4.14(2) allows a district judge to make the transfer order (see the definition in r 1.2(2)). Where the High Court wishes to order a transfer under this article otherwise than as a direction under r 4.14, RSC Ord 107, r 2(1) applies and requires it to give the parties the opportunity of being heard before making such an order (unless they consent to the order).

There is no relevant procedural provision relating to transfer with respect to adoption proceedings.

Allocation of proceedings to particular county courts

14 Commencement

Subject to articles 18, 19 and 20 and to rule 2.40 of the Family Proceedings Rules 1991 (Application under Part I or II of the Children Act 1989 where matrimonial cause is pending), an application under the Act or under the Adoption Act 1976 which is to be made to a county court shall be made to a divorce county court.

Amendments—SI 1993/624.

Defined terms—"divorce county court": art 2(*a*).

Scope of provision—This article requires applications under CA 1989 or the Adoption Act 1976 which are to be made to a county court to be made to a divorce county court, subject to certain exceptions.

Exceptions—The following exceptions apply:

(*a*) art 18 requires applications under Pt III, IV or V to be made to a care centre;

(*b*) art 19 puts the Principal Registry of the Family Division in the same position as a divorce county court for this purpose;

(*c*) art 20 allows such applications to be commenced, where otherwise appropriate, in Lambeth County Court or in Woolwich County Court despite the fact that they are not divorce county courts; and

(*d*) FPR 1991, r 2.40 requires any application under CA 1989, Pt I or II to be made in the course of any pending matrimonial cause.

Procedure—Commencement of proceedings under CA 1989 to which FPR 1991, Pt IV applies is governed by FPR 1991, r 4.4. Commencement of proceedings in the county court under the Adoption Act 1976 is governed by Adoption Rules 1984, r 4 (freeing for adoption) and r 15 (adoption).

15 Proceedings under Part I or II or Schedule 1

(1) Subject to paragraph (3), where an application under Part I or II or Schedule 1 is to be transferred from a magistrates' court to a county court, it shall be transferred to a divorce county court.

(2) Subject to paragraph (3), where an application under Part I or II or Schedule 1, other than an application for an order under section 8, is to be transferred from the High Court to a county court, it shall be transferred to a divorce county court.

(3) Where an application under Part I or II or Schedule 1, other than an application for an order under section 8, is to be transferred to a county court for the purpose of consolidation with other proceedings, it shall be transferred to the court in which those other proceedings are pending.

Defined terms—"divorce county court": art 2(*a*).

Consolidation (art 15(3))—Article 15(3) seems to be an obvious proposition, but the way the article is structured makes it technically necessary to exclude such cases from the requirement in art 15(1) that the application be made to a divorce county court: the attracting proceedings may be pending in a county court which is not a divorce county court.

16 Orders under section 8 of the Children Act 1989

(1) An application for an order under section 8 in a divorce county court, which is not also a family hearing centre, shall, if the court is notified that the application will be opposed, be transferred for trial to a family hearing centre.

(2) Subject to paragraph (3), where an application for an order under section 8 is to be transferred from the High Court to a county court it shall be transferred to a family hearing centre.

(3) Where an application for an order under section 8 is to be transferred to a county court for the purpose of consolidation with other proceedings, it may be transferred to the court in which those other proceedings are pending whether or not it is a family hearing centre; but paragraph (1) shall apply to the application following the transfer.

Defined terms—"divorce county court": art 2(*a*): "family hearing centre": art 2(*b*).

Procedure—FPR 1991, r 4.14(2)(*h*) allows the transfer to be ordered in the form of a direction and r 4.14(3)–(10) regulates the procedural framework in which that can be done. The reference to "court" in r 4.14(2) allows a district judge to make the transfer order (see the definition in r 1.2(2)) and it would seem that a district judge would have jurisdiction to order a transfer only as a direction under r 4.14.

17 Application for adoption or freeing for adoption

(1) Subject to article 22, proceedings in a divorce county court, which is not also a family hearing centre, under section 12 or 18 of the Adoption Act 1976 shall, if the court is notified that the proceedings will be opposed, be transferred for trial to a family hearing centre.

(2) Where proceedings under the Adoption Act 1976 are to be transferred from a magistrates' court to a county court, they shall be transferred to a divorce county court.

Defined terms—"divorce county court": art 2(*a*); "family hearing centre": art 2(*b*).

Scope of provision—This article provides that any contested proceedings for an adoption order or to free a child for adoption (Adoption Act 1976, ss 12 and 18, respectively) must be transferred for trial to a family hearing centre. In addition, in line with the requirement that all proceedings commenced in a county court under the Adoption Act 1976 should start in a divorce county court (art 14), this article requires a case that is transferred from a magistrates' court to be sent to a divorce county court.

"Subject to article 22" (art 17(1))—Article 22 makes transitional provision for proceedings under the Adoption Act 1976 which were commenced in a county court prior to 14 October 1991. Such proceedings may continue in the county court in which they are pending.

"notified that the proceedings will be opposed" (art 17(1))—The court will normally be aware, from the application form filed at the start of the proceedings, that a parent is withholding consent to adoption (see Adoption Rules 1984, Sch 1, Forms 1, 6). Some parents who do not consent may not actively oppose the proceedings. The meaning of this article requires clarification on the question whether all proceedings where the parent's consent is in issue must be transferred to a family hearing centre, or whether the rule is confined to those cases where the parent is actively opposing the application.

18 Applications under Part III, IV or V

(1) An application under Part III, IV or V, if it is to be made to a county court, shall be made to a care centre.

(2) An application under Part III, IV or V which is to be transferred from the High Court to a county court shall be transferred to a care centre.

(3) An application under Part III, IV or V which is to be transferred from a magistrates' court to a county court shall be transferred to the care centre listed against the entry in column (i) of Schedule 2 to this Order for the petty sessions area or London commission area in which the relevant magistrates' court is situated.

Amendments—SI 1993/624.

Defined terms—"care centre": art 2(*c*); "London commission area", "petty sessions area": art 1(2).

CA 1989, Parts III to V—Pt III deals with local authority support for children and families, and includes the authorisation of secure accommodation; Pt IV deals with care and supervision; and Pt V deals with the protection of children and includes child assessment orders, emergency protection orders and recovery orders.

19 Principal Registry of the Family Division

The principal registry of the Family Division of the High Court shall be treated, for the purposes of this Order, as if it were a divorce county court, a family hearing centre and a care centre listed against every entry in column (i) of Schedule 2 to this Order (in addition to the entries against which it is actually listed).

Defined terms—"care centre": art 2(*c*); "divorce county court": art 2(*a*); "family hearing centre": art 2(*b*).

Scope of provision—This article deems the Principal Registry of the Family Division to be a divorce county court, family hearing centre and care centre for the purposes of this Order, and enables any magistrates' courts to transfer "care centre" business to it even though it is not the care centre listed in the appropriate entry in Sch 2 for the magistrates' court in question. A district judge sitting in the Principal Registry has the same powers as a county court judge and is empowered to grant orders placing children in the care of the local authority (*Re S (Appeal from Principal Registry: Procedure)* [1997] 2 FLR 856).

20 Lambeth, Shoreditch and Woolwich County Courts

Notwithstanding articles 14, 16 and 17, an application for an order under section 4 or 8 or under the Adoption Act 1976 may be made to and tried in Lambeth, Shoreditch or Woolwich County Court.

Amendments—Substituted by SI 1997/1897.

Miscellaneous

21 Contravention of provisions of this Order

Where proceedings are commenced or transferred in contravention of a provision of this Order, the contravention shall not have the effect of making the proceedings invalid; and no appeal shall lie against the determination of proceedings on the basis of such contravention alone.

****

SCHEDULE 1

FAMILY HEARING CENTRES

Midland Circuit

Birmingham County Court
Derby County Court
Leicester County Court
Mansfield County Court
Nottingham County Court
Stoke-on-Trent County Court
Walsall County Court
Worcester County Court
Coventry County Court
Dudley County Court
Lincoln County Court
Northampton County Court
Stafford County Court
Telford County Court
Wolverhampton County Court

Northern Circuit

Blackburn County Court
Carlisle County Court
Liverpool County Court
Oldham County Court
Bolton County Court
Lancaster County Court
Manchester County Court
Stockport County Court

North Eastern Circuit

Barnsley County Court
Darlington County Court
Doncaster County Court
Grimsby County Court
Harrogate County Court
Keighley County Court
Leeds County Court
Pontefract County Court
Scarborough County Court
Skipton County Court
Teesside County Court
York County Court
Bradford County Court
Dewsbury County Court
Durham County Court
Halifax County Court
Huddersfield County Court
Kingston-upon-Hull County Court
Newcastle-upon-Tyne County Court
Rotherham County Court
Sheffield County Court
Sunderland County Court
Wakefield County Court

South Eastern Circuit

PART III

Barnet County Court
Bow County Court
Brighton County Court
Cambridge County Court
Chelmsford County Court
Colchester and Clacton County Court
Dartford County Court
Guildford County Court
Ilford County Court
King's Lynn County Court
Luton County Court
Medway County Court
Norwich County Court
Peterborough County Court
Romford County Court
Southend County Court
Watford County Court
Bedford County Court
Brentford County Court
Bromley County Court
Canterbury County Court
Chichester County Court
Croydon County Court
Edmonton County Court
Hitchin County Court
Ipswich County Court
Kingston-upon-Thames County Court
Maidstone County Court
Milton Keynes County Court
Oxford County Court
Reading County Court
Slough County Court
Wandsworth County Court
Willesden County Court

Wales and Chester Circuit
Aberystwyth County Court
Cardiff County Court
Chester County Court
Haverfordwest County Court
Macclesfield County Court
Newport (Gwent) County Court
Rhyl County Court
Warrington County Court
Wrexham County Court
Caernarfon County Court
Carmarthen County Court
Crewe County Court
Llangefni County Court
Merthyr Tydfil County Court
Pontypridd County Court
Swansea County Court
Welshpool and Newtown County Court

Western Circuit
Barnstaple County Court
Bath County Court
Bristol County Court
Gloucester County Court
Portsmouth County Court
Southampton County Court
Taunton County Court
Weymouth County Court
Basingstoke County Court
Bournemouth County Court
Exeter County Court
Plymouth County Court
Salisbury County Court
Swindon County Court
Truro County Court
Yeovil County Court

Amendments—SI 1994/3138; SI 1995/1649; SI 1997/1897; SI 1999/524; SI 2000/2670; SI 2001/775; SI 2001/1656.

SCHEDULE 2
CARE CENTRES

(i) **Petty Sessions Areas**	(ii) **Care Centres**
	Midland Circuit
Aldridge and Brownhills	Wolverhampton County Court
Alfreton and Belper	Derby County Court
Ashby-De-La-Zouch	Leicester County Court

(i) **Petty Sessions Areas**	(ii) **Care Centres**
Atherstone and Coleshill	Coventry County Court
Bewdley and Stourport	Worcester County Court
Birmingham	Birmingham County Court
Boston	Lincoln County Court
Bourne and Stamford	Lincoln County Court
Bridgnorth	Telford County Court
Bromsgrove	Worcester County Court
Burton-upon-Trent	Derby County Court
Caistor	Lincoln County Court
Cannock	Wolverhampton County Court
Cheadle	Stoke-on-Trent County Court
Chesterfield	Derby County Court
City of Hereford	Worcester County Court
Congleton	Stoke-on-Trent County Court
Corby	Northampton County Court
Coventry	Coventry County Court
Crewe and Nantwich	Stoke-on-Trent County Court
Daventry	Northampton County Court
Derby and South Derbyshire	Derby County Court
Drayton	Telford County Court
Dudley	Wolverhampton County Court
East Retford	Nottingham County Court
Eccleshall	Stoke-on-Trent County Court
Elloes	Lincoln County Court
Gainsborough	Lincoln County Court
Glossop	Derby County Court
Grantham	Lincoln County Court
Halesowen	Wolverhampton County Court
High Peak	Derby County Court
Ilkeston	Derby County Court
Kettering	Northampton County Court
Kidderminster	Worcester County Court
Leek	Stoke-on-Trent County Court
Leicester (City)	Leicester County Court
Leicester (County)	Leicester County Court
Lichfield	Stoke-on-Trent County Court
Lincoln District	Lincoln County Court
Loughborough	Leicester County Court
Louth	Lincoln County Court
Ludlow	Telford County Court
Lutterworth	Leicester County Court
Malvern Hills	Worcester County Court
Mansfield	Nottingham County Court
Market Bosworth	Leicester County Court
Market Harborough	Leicester County Court
Market Rasen	Lincoln County Court
Melton and Belvoir	Leicester County Court
Mid-Warwickshire	Coventry County Court
Mid-Worcestershire	Worcester County Court
Newark and Southwell	Nottingham County Court
Newcastle-under-Lyme	Stoke-on-Trent County Court

(i) Petty Sessions Areas	(ii) Care Centres
Northampton	Northampton County Court
North Herefordshire	Worcester County Court
Nottingham	Nottingham County Court
Nuneaton	Coventry County Court
Oswestry	Telford County Court
Pirehill North	Stoke-on-Trent County Court
Redditch	Worcester County Court
Rugby	Coventry County Court
Rugeley	Wolverhampton County Court
Rutland	Leicester County Court
Seisdon	Wolverhampton County Court
Sleaford	Lincoln County Court
Shrewsbury	Telford County Court
Solihull	Birmingham County Court
South Herefordshire	Worcester County Court
South Warwickshire	Coventry County Court
Spilsby and Skegness	Lincoln County Court
Stoke-on-Trent	Stoke-on-Trent County Court
Stone	Stoke-on-Trent County Court
Stourbridge	Wolverhampton County Court
Sutton Coldfield	Birmingham County Court
Tamworth	Stoke-on-Trent County Court
Telford	Telford County Court
Towcester	Northampton County Court
Uttoxeter	Stoke-on-Trent County Court
Vale of Evesham	Worcester County Court
Warley	Wolverhampton County Court
Walsall	Wolverhampton County Court
Wellingborough	Northampton County Court
West Bromwich	Wolverhampton County Court
West Derbyshire	Derby County Court
Wolds	Lincoln County Court
Wolverhampton	Wolverhampton County Court
Worcester City	Worcester County Court
Worksop	Nottingham County Court
	Northern Circuit
Appleby	Carlisle County Court
Ashton-under-Lyne	Manchester County Court
Barrow with Bootle	Lancaster County Court
Blackburn	Blackburn County Court
Blackpool	Lancaster County Court
Bolton	Manchester County Court
Burnley	Blackburn County Court
Bury	Manchester County Court
Carlisle	Carlisle County Court
Chorley	Blackburn County Court
Darwen	Blackburn County Court
Eccles	Manchester County Court
Fylde	Lancaster County Court
Hyndburn	Blackburn County Court

(i) Petty Sessions Areas	(ii) Care Centres
Kendal and Lonsdale	Lancaster County Court
Keswick	Carlisle County Court
Knowsley	Liverpool County Court
Lancaster	Lancaster County Court
Leigh	Manchester County Court
Liverpool	Liverpool County Court
Manchester	Manchester County Court
Middleton and Heywood	Manchester County Court
North Lonsdale	Lancaster County Court
North Sefton	Liverpool County Court
Oldham	Manchester County Court
Ormskirk	Liverpool County Court
Pendle	Blackburn County Court
Penrith and Alston	Carlisle County Court
Preston	Blackburn County Court
Ribble Valley	Blackburn County Court
Rochdale	Manchester County Court
Rossendale	Blackburn County Court
St Helens	Liverpool County Court
Salford	Manchester County Court
South Lakes	Lancaster County Court
South Ribble	Blackburn County Court
South Sefton	Liverpool County Court
South Tameside	Manchester County Court
Stockport	Manchester County Court
Trafford	Manchester County Court
West Allerdale	Carlisle County Court
Whitehaven	Carlisle County Court
Wigan	Liverpool County Court
Wigton	Carlisle County Court
Wirral	Liverpool County Court
Wyre	Lancaster County Court
	North Eastern Circuit
Bainton Beacon	Kingston-upon-Hull County Court
Barnsley	Sheffield County Court
Batley and Dewsbury	Leeds County Court
Berwick-upon-Tweed	Newcastle-upon-Tyne County Court
Beverley	Kingston-upon-Hull County Court
Blyth Valley	Newcastle-upon-Tyne County Court
Bradford	Leeds County Court
Brighouse	Leeds County Court
Calder	Leeds County Court
Chester-le-Street	Newcastle-upon-Tyne County Court
Claro	York County Court
Coquetdale	Newcastle-upon-Tyne County Court
Darlington	Teesside County Court
Derwentside	Newcastle-upon-Tyne County Court
Dickering	Kingston-upon-Hull County Court
Doncaster	Sheffield County Court
Durham	Newcastle-upon-Tyne County Court

(i) Petty Sessions Areas	(ii) Care Centres
Easington	Sunderland County Court
Easingwold	York County Court
Gateshead	Newcastle-upon-Tyne County Court
Grimsby and Cleethorpes	Kingston-upon-Hull County Court
Goole and Howdenshire	Kingston-upon-Hull County Court
Hartlepool	Teesside County Court
Holme Beacon	Kingston-upon-Hull County Court
Houghton-le-Spring	Sunderland County Court
Huddersfield	Leeds County Court
Keighley	Leeds County Court
Kingston-upon-Hull	Kingston-upon-Hull County Court
Langbaurgh East	Teesside County Court
Leeds	Leeds County Court
Middle Holderness	Kingston-upon-Hull County Court
Morley	Leeds County Court
Morpeth Ward	Newcastle-upon-Tyne County Court
Newcastle-upon-Tyne	Newcastle-upon-Tyne County Court
Northallerton	Teesside County Court
North Holderness	Kingston-upon-Hull County Court
North Lincolnshire	Kingston-upon-Hull County Court
North Tyneside	Newcastle-upon-Tyne County Court
Pontefract	Leeds County Court
Pudsey and Otley	Leeds County Court
Richmond	Teesside County Court
Ripon Liberty	York County Court
Rotherham	Sheffield County Court
Ryedale	York County Court
Scarborough	York County Court
Sedgefield	Newcastle-upon-Tyne County Court
Selby	York County Court
Sheffield	Sheffield County Court
Skyrack and Wetherby	Leeds County Court
South Holderness	Kingston-upon-Hull County Court
South Hunsley Beacon	Kingston-upon-Hull County Court
South Tyneside	Sunderland County Court
Staincliffe	Leeds County Court
Sunderland	Sunderland County Court
Teesdale and Wear Valley	Newcastle-upon-Tyne County Court
Teesside	Teesside County Court
Todmorden	Leeds County Court
Tynedale	Newcastle-upon-Tyne County Court
Wakefield	Leeds County Court
Wansbeck	Newcastle-upon-Tyne County Court
Whitby Strand	Teesside County Court
Wilton Beacon	Kingston-upon-Hull County Court
York	York County Court
	South Eastern Circuit
Abingdon	Oxford County Court
Ampthill	Luton County Court
Arundel	Brighton County Court

(i)	(ii)
Petty Sessions Areas	**Care Centres**
Ashford and Tenterden	Canterbury County Court
Aylesbury	Milton Keynes County Court
Barnet	Principal Registry of the Family Division
Barking and Dagenham	Principal Registry of the Family Division
Basildon	Chelmsford County Court
Battle and Rye	Brighton County Court
Beccles	Ipswich County Court
Bedford	Luton County Court
Bexhill	Brighton County Court
Bexley	Principal Registry of the Family Division
Bicester	Oxford County Court
Biggleswade	Luton County Court
Bishop's Stortford	Watford County Court
Brent	Principal Registry of the Family Division
Brentwood	Chelmsford County Court
Brighton	Brighton County Court
Bromley	Principal Registry of the Family Division
Buckingham	Milton Keynes County Court
Burnham	Milton Keynes County Court
Cambridge	Peterborough County Court
Canterbury and St Augustine	Canterbury County Court
Chelmsford	Chelmsford County Court
Chertsey	Guildford County Court
Cheshunt	Watford County Court
Chichester and District	Brighton County Court
Chiltern	Milton Keynes County Court
Colchester	Chelmsford County Court
Crawley	Brighton County Court
Cromer	Norwich County Court
Crowborough	Brighton County Court
Croydon	Principal Registry of the Family Division
Dacorum	Watford County Court
Dartford	Medway County Court
Didcot and Wantage	Oxford County Court
Diss	Norwich County Court
Dorking	Guildford County Court
Dover and East Kent	Canterbury County Court
Downham Market	Norwich County Court
Dunmow	Chelmsford County Court
Dunstable	Luton County Court
Ealing	Principal Registry of the Family Division
Eastbourne	Brighton County Court
East Dereham	Norwich County Court
East Oxfordshire	Oxford County Court
Ely	Peterborough County Court
Enfield	Principal Registry of the Family Division
Epping and Ongar	Chelmsford County Court
Epsom	Guildford County Court
Esher and Walton	Guildford County Court
Fakenham	Norwich County Court
Farnham	Guildford County Court

(i)	(ii)
Petty Sessions Areas	**Care Centres**
Faversham and Sittingbourne	Medway County Court
Felixstowe	Ipswich County Court
Folkestone and Hythe	Canterbury County Court
The Forest	Reading County Court
Freshwell and South Hinckford	Chelmsford County Court
Godstone	Guildford County Court
Guildford	Guildford County Court
Gravesham	Medway County Court
Great Yarmouth	Norwich County Court
Hailsham	Brighton County Court
Halstead and Hedingham	Chelmsford County Court
Harlow	Chelmsford County Court
Harrow Gore	Principal Registry of the Family Division
Haringey	Principal Registry of the Family Division
Harwich	Chelmsford County Court
Hastings	Brighton County Court
Havering	Principal Registry of the Family Division
Henley	Oxford County Court
Hertford and Ware	Watford County Court
Hillingdon	Principal Registry of the Family Division
Horsham	Brighton County Court
Hounslow	Principal Registry of the Family Division
Hove	Brighton County Court
Hunstanton	Norwich County Court
Huntingdon	Peterborough County Court
Ipswich	Ipswich County Court
King's Lynn	Norwich County Court
Kingston-upon-Thames	Principal Registry of the Family Division
Leighton Buzzard	Luton County Court
Lewes	Brighton County Court
Lowestoft	Ipswich County Court
Luton	Luton County Court
Maidenhead	Reading County Court
Maidstone	Medway County Court
Maldon and Witham	Chelmsford County Court
Medway	Medway County Court
Merton	Principal Registry of the Family Division
Mid-Hertfordshire	Watford County Court
Mid-Sussex	Brighton County Court
Mildenhall	Ipswich County Court
Milton Keynes	Milton Keynes County Court
Newham	Principal Registry of the Family Division
Newmarket	Ipswich County Court or Peterborough County Court
North Hertfordshire	Watford County Court
North Oxfordshire and Chipping Norton	Oxford County Court
North Walsham	Norwich County Court
North Witchford	Peterborough County Court
Norwich	Norwich County Court
Oxford	Oxford County Court

(i) Petty Sessions Areas	(ii) Care Centres
Peterborough	Peterborough County Court
Reading and Sonning	Reading County Court
Redbridge	Principal Registry of the Family Division
Reigate	Guildford County Court
Richmond-upon-Thames	Principal Registry of the Family Division
Risbridge	Ipswich County Court
Rochford and Southend-on-Sea	Chelmsford County Court
Saffron Walden	Chelmsford County Court
St Albans	Watford County Court
St Edmundsbury	Ipswich County Court
Saxmundham	Ipswich County Court
Sevenoaks	Medway County Court
Slough	Reading County Court
South Mimms	Watford County Court
Staines and Sunbury	Guildford County Court
Stevenage	Watford County Court
Steyning	Brighton County Court
Stow	Ipswich County Court
Sudbury and Cosford	Ipswich County Court
Sutton	Principal Registry of the Family Division
Swaffham	Norwich County Court
Tendring	Chelmsford County Court
Thanet	Canterbury County Court
Thetford	Norwich County Court
Thurrock	Chelmsford County Court
Tonbridge and Malling	Medway County Court
Toseland	Peterborough County Court
Tunbridge Wells and Cranbrook	Medway County Court
Waltham Forest	Principal Registry of the Family Division
Watford	Watford County Court
West Berkshire	Reading County Court
Windsor	Reading County Court
Wisbech	Peterborough County Court
Witney	Oxford County Court
Woking	Guildford County Court
Woodbridge	Ipswich County Court
Woodstock	Oxford County Court
Worthing	Brighton County Court
Wycombe	Milton Keynes County Court
Wymondham	Norwich County Court
	Wales and Chester Circuit
Ardudwy-is-Artro	Caernarfon County Court
Ardudwy-uwch-Artro	Caernarfon County Court
Bangor	Caernarfon County Court
Bedwellty	Newport (Gwent) County Court
Berwyn	Rhyl County Court
Brecon	Pontypridd County Court
Caernarfon and Gwyrfai	Caernarfon County Court
Cardiff	Cardiff County Court

(i) Petty Sessions Areas	(ii) Care Centres
Carmarthen North	Swansea County Court
Carmarthen South	Swansea County Court
Ceredigion Ganol	Swansea County Court
Chester	Chester County Court
Cleddau	Swansea County Court
Colwyn	Rhyl County Court
Congleton	Stoke-on-Trent County Court
Conwy and Llandudno	Caernarfon County Court
Crewe and Nantwich	Stoke-on-Trent County Court
Cynon Valley	Pontypridd County Court
De Ceredigion	Swansea County Court
Dinefwr	Swansea County Court
Dyffryn Clywd	Rhyl County Court
East Gwent	Newport (Gwent) County Court
Eifionydd	Caernarfon County Court
Ellesmere Port and Neston	Chester County Court
Estimaner	Caernarfon County Court
Flint	Rhyl County Court
Gogledd Ceredigion	Swansea County Court
Gogledd Preseli	Swansea County Court
Halton	Warrington County Court
Hawarden	Rhyl County Court
Llandrindod Wells	Pontypridd County Court
Llanelli	Swansea County Court
Lliw Valley	Swansea County Court
Lower Rhymney Valley	Cardiff County Court
Macclesfield	Warrington County Court
Machynlleth	Chester County Court
Merthyr Tydfil	Pontypridd County Court
Miskin	Pontypridd County Court
Mold	Rhyl County Court
Nant Conwy	Caernarfon County Court
Neath	Swansea County Court
Newcastle and Ogmore	Cardiff County Court
Newport	Newport (Gwent) County Court
Newtown	Chester County Court
North Anglesey	Caernarfon County Court
Penllyn	Caernarfon County Court
Port Talbot	Swansea County Court
Pwllheli	Caernarfon County Court
Rhuddlan	Rhyl County Court
South Anglesey	Caernarfon County Court
South Pembrokeshire	Swansea County Court
Swansea	Swansea County Court
Talybont	Caernarfon County Court
Upper Rhymney Valley	Pontypridd County Court
Vale of Glamorgan	Cardiff County Court
Vale Royal	Chester County Court
Warrington	Warrington County Court
Welshpool	Chester County Court
Wrexham Maelor	Rhyl County Court

(i) Petty Sessions Areas	(ii) Care Centres
Ystradgynlais	Swansea County Court
	Western Circuit
Alton	Portsmouth County Court
Andover	Portsmouth County Court
Axminster	Taunton County Court
Barnstaple	Taunton County Court
Basingstoke	Portsmouth County Court
Bath and Wansdyke	Bristol County Court
Bideford and Great Torrington	Taunton County Court
Blandford and Sturminster	Bournemouth County Court
Bodmin	Truro County Court
Bournemouth	Bournemouth County Court
Bristol	Bristol County Court
Bridport	Bournemouth County Court
Cheltenham	Bristol County Court
Christchurch	Bournemouth County Court
Cirencester, Fairford and Tetbury	Swindon County Court
Cullompton	Taunton County Court
Dorchester	Bournemouth County Court
Droxford	Portsmouth County Court
Dunheved and Stratton	Truro County Court
Eastleigh	Portsmouth County Court
East Penwith	Truro County Court
East Powder	Truro County Court
Exeter	Plymouth County Court
Exmouth	Plymouth County Court
Falmouth and Kerrier	Truro County Court
Fareham	Portsmouth County Court
Forest of Dean	Bristol County Court
Gloucester	Bristol County Court
Gosport	Portsmouth County Court
Havant	Portsmouth County Court
Honiton	Taunton County Court
Hythe	Bournemouth County Court
Isle of Wight	Portsmouth County Court
Isles of Scilly	Truro County Court
Kennet	Swindon County Court
Kingsbridge	Plymouth County Court
Long Ashton	Bristol County Court
Lymington	Bournemouth County Court
Mendip	Taunton County Court
North Avon	Bristol County Court
North Cotswold	Bristol County Court
North Wiltshire	Swindon County Court
Odiham	Portsmouth County Court
Okehampton	Plymouth County Court
Penwith	Truro County Court
Petersfield	Portsmouth County Court
Plymouth	Plymouth County Court
Plympton	Plymouth County Court

(i) Petty Sessions Areas	(ii) Care Centres
Portsmouth	Portsmouth County Court
Poole	Bournemouth County Court
Pydar	Truro County Court
Ringwood	Bournemouth County Court
Romsey	Bournemouth County Court
Salisbury	Swindon County Court
Sedgemoor	Taunton County Court
Shaftesbury	Bournemouth County Court
Sherborne	Bournemouth County Court
Southampton	Portsmouth County Court
South East Cornwall	Plymouth County Court
South Gloucestershire	Bristol County Court
South Molton	Taunton County Court
South Somerset	Taunton County Court
Swindon	Swindon County Court
Taunton Deane	Taunton County Court
Tavistock	Plymouth County Court
Teignbridge	Plymouth County Court
Tewkesbury	Bristol County Court
Tiverton	Taunton County Court
Torbay	Plymouth County Court
Totnes	Plymouth County Court
Totton and New Forest	Bournemouth County Court
Truro and South Powder	Truro County Court
Wareham and Swanage	Bournemouth County Court
West Somerset	Taunton County Court
Weston-Super-Mare	Bristol County Court
West Wiltshire	Swindon County Court
Weymouth and Portland	Bournemouth County Court
Wimborne	Bournemouth County Court
Winchester	Portsmouth County Court
Wonford	Plymouth County Court

(i) London Commission Area	(ii) Care Centre
Inner London Area and City of London	Principal Registry of the Family Division

Amendments—SI 1994/2164; SI 1994/3138; SI 1995/1649; SI 1997/1897; SI 2001/775.

Defined terms—"care centre": art 2(*c*); "London commission area", "petty sessions area": art 1(2).

Principal Registry of the Family Division—Although the principal registry is expressly listed as the relevant care centre for certain areas, art 19 has the effect of deeming it to be listed for every area. Presumably, this means that the transferring magistrates' court will have a choice of whether to transfer proceedings covered by Sch 2 to the local care centre expressly listed or to the principal registry.

London commission area—The City of London is referred to under this heading but it is not a London commission area within the meaning of art 1(2) (see Justices of the Peace Act 1979, ss 2, 3(1)); it is, however, a petty sessions area within the meaning of Justices of the Peace Act 1979, s 4(2)(*f*). As all the references to Sch 2 in the body of the Order refer to petty sessions areas listed in column (ii) as well as London commission areas, the misdescription in the heading would not seem to matter.

Children (Allocation of Proceedings) (Appeals) Order 1991, SI 1991/1801

1 Citation, commencement and interpretation

(1) This Order may be cited as the Children (Allocation of Proceedings) (Appeals) Order 1991 and shall come into force on 14 October 1991.

(2) In this Order –

"district judge" includes an assistant district judge and a deputy district judge; and

"circuit judge" means any person who is capable of sitting as a judge for a county court district and who is allocated to hear appeals permitted by this Order in accordance with directions given under section 9 of the Courts and Legal Services Act 1990.

Scope of provision—This Order provides a limited right of appeal from a decision of a district judge to transfer proceedings back to the magistrates' court which were transferred up to the county court. Proceedings may be transferred to the county court from the magistrates' court in accordance with Children (Allocation of Proceedings) Order 1991, art 7, and transferred back under art 11 (if the criterion for transfer no longer applies). This Order allows an appeal against the decision to retransfer under art 11. For transfer of proceedings under FLA 1996, Pt IV (non-molestation and occupation orders), see the Family Law Act 1996 (Part IV) (Allocation of Proceedings) Order 1997.

2 Appeals

Where a district judge orders the transfer of proceedings to a magistrates' court in accordance with article 11 of the Children (Allocation of Proceedings) Order 1991 an appeal may be made against that decision –

(*a*) to a judge of the Family Division of the High Court, or
(*b*) except where the order was made by a district judge or deputy district judge of the principal registry of the Family Division, to a circuit judge.

Scope of provision—The power of the district judge to transfer proceedings to the family proceedings court under C(AP)O 1991, art 11 relates only to proceedings transferred to the county court. There is no power to transfer proceedings that were commenced in the county court.

PART III

Children (Secure Accommodation) Regulations 1991, SI 1991/1505

****

3 Approval by Secretary of State of secure accommodation in a children's home

Accommodation in a children's home shall not be used as secure accommodation unless it has been approved by the Secretary of State for such use and approval shall be subject to such terms and conditions as he sees fit.

Amendments—SI 1995/1398.

4 Placement of a child aged under 13 in secure accommodation in a children's home

A child under the age of 13 years shall not be placed in secure accommodation in a children's home without the prior approval of the Secretary of State to the placement of that child and such approval shall be subject to such terms and conditions as he sees fit.

Amendments—SI 1992/2117; SI 1995/1398.

5 Children to whom section 25 of the Act shall not apply

(1) Section 25 of the Act shall not apply to a child who is detained under any provision of the Mental Health Act 1983 or in respect of whom an order has been made under section 90 or 91 of the Powers of the Criminal Courts (Sentencing) Act 2000 (detention at Her Majesty's pleasure or for specified period).

(2) Section 25 of the Act shall not apply to a child –

(*a*) to whom section 20(5) of the Act (accommodation of persons over 16 but under 21) applies and who is being accommodated under that section,

(*b*) in respect of whom an order has been made under section 43 of the Act (child assessment order) and who is kept away from home pursuant to that order.

Amendments—SI 2002/546.

6 Detained and remanded children to whom section 25 of the Act shall have effect subject to modifications

(1) Subject to regulation 5, section 25 of the Act shall have effect subject to the modification specified in paragraph (2) in relation to children who are being looked after by a local authority and are of the following descriptions –

(*a*) children detained under section 38(6) of the Police and Criminal Evidence Act 1984 (detained children), and

(*b*) children remanded to local authority accommodation under section 23 of the Children and Young Persons Act 1969 (remand to local authority accommodation) but only if –

(i) the child is charged with or has been convicted of a violent or sexual offence, or of an offence punishable in the case of an adult with imprisonment for a term of 14 years or more, or

(ii) the child has a recent history of absconding while remanded to local authority accommodation, and is charged with or has been convicted of an imprisonable offence alleged or found to have been committed while he was so remanded.

(2) The modification referred to in paragraph (1) is that, for the words "unless it appears" to the end of subsection (1), there shall be substituted the following words –

"unless it appears that any accommodation other than that provided for the purpose of restricting liberty is inappropriate because –

(*a*) the child is likely to abscond from such other accommodation, or

(*b*) the child is likely to injure himself or other people if he is kept in any such other accommodation".

Amendments—SI 1992/2117.

Regulation 6(1)(*b*)—Where a child is remanded into the care of the local authority under Children and Young Persons Act 1969, s 23, and the child's criminal record exhibits one of the features referred to in reg 6(1)(*b*)(i) or (ii) the Youth Court has power to make a secure accommodation order even if the s 25 criteria are not met, provided that the criteria in reg 6(2) are met. Where the conditions in reg 6(1)(*b*) are not met, the Youth Court can nonetheless make a secure accommodation order if the s 25(1) criteria are met (*Re G (Secure Accommodation Order)* [2001] 1 FLR 884).

7 Children to whom section 25 of the Act shall apply and have effect subject to modifications

(1) Subject to regulation 5 and paragraphs (2) and (3) of this regulation section 25 of the Act shall apply (in addition to children looked after by a local authority) –

(*a*) to children, other than those looked after by a local authority, who are accommodated by health authorities, Primary Care Trusts, National Health Service trusts established under section 5 of the National Health Service and Community Care Act 1990 or local education authorities, and

(*b*) to children, other than those looked after by a local authority, who are accommodated in care homes or independent hospitals.

(2) In relation to the children of a description specified in paragraph (1)(*a*) section 25 of the Act shall have effect subject to the following modifications –

(*a*) for the words "who is being looked after by a local authority" in subsection (1) there shall be substituted the words "who is being provided with accommodation by a health authority, a Primary Care Trust, a National Health Service trust established under section 5 of the National Health Service and Community Care Act 1990 or a local education authority".

(*b*) for the words "local authorities" in subsection (2)(*c*) there shall be substituted the words "health authorities, Primary Care Trusts, National Health Service trusts or local education authorities".

(3) In relation to the children of a description specified in paragraph (1)(*b*), section 25 of the Act shall have effect subject to the following modifications –

PART III

(*a*) for the words "who is being looked after by a local authority" in subsection (1) there shall be substituted the words "who is being provided with accommodation in a care home or an independent hospital"; and

(*b*) for the words "local authorities" in subsection (2)(*c*) there shall be substituted the words "persons carrying on care homes or independent hospitals".

Amendments—SI 2000/694; SI 2002/546.

8 Applications to court

Subject to section 101 of the Local Government Act 1972 or to provisions in or under sections 14 to 20 of the Local Government Act 2000, applications to a court under section 25 of the Act in respect of a child shall be made only by the local authority which are looking after that child.

Amendments—SI 2001/2237.

"local authority which are looking after that child"—See CA 1989, s 22(1) and, as to a child who is bailed with a condition of residence to the local authority, see *Re C (Secure Accommodation: Bail)* [1994] 2 FLR 922.

****

10 Maximum period in secure accommodation without court authority

(1) Subject to paragraphs (2) and (3), the maximum period beyond which a child to whom section 25 of the Act applies may not be kept in secure accommodation without the authority of a court is an aggregate of 72 hours (whether or not consecutive) in any period of 28 consecutive days.

(2) Where authority of a court to keep a child in secure accommodation has been given, any period during which the child has been kept in such accommodation before the giving of that authority shall be disregarded for the purposes of calculating the maximum period in relation to any subsequent occasion on which the child is placed in such accommodation after the period authorised by court has expired.

(3) Where a child is in secure accommodation at any time between 12 midday on the day before and 12 midday on the day after a public holiday or a Sunday, and

(*a*) during that period the maximum period specified in paragraph (1) expires, and

(*b*) the child had, in the 27 days before the day on which he was placed in secure accommodation, been placed and kept in such accommodation for an aggregate of more than 48 hours,

the maximum period does not expire until 12 midday on the first day, which is not itself a public holiday or a Sunday, after the public holiday or Sunday.

11 Maximum initial period of authorisation by a court

Subject to regulations 12 and 13 the maximum period for which a court may authorise a child to whom section 25 of the Act applies to be kept in secure accommodation is three months.

12 Further periods of authorisation by a court

Subject to regulation 13 a court may from time to time authorise a child to whom section 25 of the Act applies to be kept in secure accommodation for a further period not exceeding six months at any one time.

****

14 Duty to inform parents and others in relation to children in secure accommodation in a children's home

Where a child to whom section 25 of the Act applies is kept in secure accommodation in a children's home and it is intended that an application will be made to a court to keep the child in that accommodation, the local authority which are looking after the child shall if practicable inform of that intention as soon as possible –

(*a*) his parents,
(*b*) any person who is not a parent of his but who has parental responsibility for him,
(*c*) the child's independent visitor, if one has been appointed, and
(*d*) any other person who that local authority consider should be informed.

Amendments—SI 1995/1398.

****

PART III

Children (Secure Accommodation) (No 2) Regulations 1991, SI 1991/2034

1 Citation and commencement

(1) These Regulations may be cited as the Children (Secure Accommodation) (No 2) Regulations 1991 and shall come into force on 14 October 1991 immediately after the Children (Secure Accommodation) Regulations 1991.

2 Applications to court – special cases

(1) Applications to a court under section 25 of the Children Act 1989 in respect of a child provided with accommodation by a health authority, a Primary Care Trust, a National Health Service trust established under section 5 of the National Health Service and Community Care Act 1990 or a local education authority shall, unless the child is looked after by a local authority, be made only by the health authority, Primary Care Trust, National Health Service trust or local education authority providing accommodation for the child.

(2) Applications to a court under section 25 of the Children Act 1989 in respect of a child provided with accommodation in a care home or independent hospital shall,

unless the child is looked after by a local authority, be made only by the person carrying on the home in which accommodation is provided for the child.

Amendments—SI 2000/694; SI 2002/546.

"looked after by a local authority"—See CA 1989, s 22(1) and, as to a child who is bailed with a condition of residence to the local authority, see *Re C (Secure Accommodation: Bail)* [1994] 2 FLR 922.

Civil Procedure Rules 1998, SI 1998/3132

ARRANGEMENT OF RULES

PART 1
OVERRIDING OBJECTIVE

PART 2
APPLICATION AND INTERPRETATION OF THE RULES

PART 3
THE COURT'S CASE MANAGEMENT POWERS

PART 6
SERVICE OF DOCUMENTS

PART 7
HOW TO START PROCEEDINGS – THE CLAIM FORM

PART III

PART 21
CHILDREN AND PATIENTS

PART 22
STATEMENTS OF TRUTH

PART 23
GENERAL RULES ABOUT APPLICATIONS FOR COURT ORDERS

PART 25
INTERIM REMEDIES AND SECURITY FOR COSTS

PART 30
TRANSFER

PART 31
DISCLOSURE AND INSPECTION OF DOCUMENTS

PART 32
EVIDENCE

PART 33
MISCELLANEOUS RULES ABOUT EVIDENCE

PART 34
WITNESSES, DEPOSITIONS AND EVIDENCE FOR FOREIGN COURTS

I Witnesses and Depositions

PART 35
EXPERTS AND ASSESSORS

PART 39
MISCELLANEOUS PROVISIONS RELATING TO HEARINGS

PART 40
JUDGMENTS, ORDERS, SALE OF LAND ETC

PART 43
SCOPE OF COST RULES AND DEFINITIONS

PART 44
GENERAL RULES ABOUT COSTS

PART 47
PROCEDURE FOR DETAILED ASSESSMENT OF COSTS AND DEFAULT PROVISIONS

Section I – General Rules about Detailed Assessment

Section II – Costs Payable by One Party to Another – Commencement of Detailed Assessment Proceedings

Section III – Costs Payable by One Party to Another – Default Provisions

Section IV – Costs Payable by One Party to Another – Procedure where Points of Dispute are Served

Section V – Interim Costs Certificate and Final Costs Certificate

PART III

PART 1
OVERRIDING OBJECTIVE

1.1 The overriding objective

(1) These Rules are a new procedural code with the overriding objective of enabling the court to deal with cases justly.

(2) Dealing with a case justly includes, so far as is practicable –

- (*a*) ensuring that the parties are on an equal footing;
- (*b*) saving expense;
- (*c*) dealing with the case in ways which are proportionate –
  - (i) to the amount of money involved;
  - (ii) to the importance of the case;
  - (iii) to the complexity of the issues; and
  - (iv) to the financial position of each party;
- (*d*) ensuring that it is dealt with expeditiously and fairly; and
- (*e*) allotting to it an appropriate share of the court's resources, while taking into account the need to allot resources to other cases.

Scope of the Civil Procedure Rules—The CPR 1998, in force from 26 April 1999, are a new procedural code which have replaced both the RSC and the CCR for civil proceedings issued on or after that date (but see **Effect of CPR 1998 on family proceedings** under CPR 1998, r 2.1).

1.2 Application by the court of the overriding objective

The court must seek to give effect to the overriding objective when it –

- (*a*) exercises any power given to it by the Rules; or
- (*b*) interprets any rule.

"interprets any rule"—The overriding objective applies to every rule and therefore applies to those Parts of the CPR which apply in family proceedings, eg costs (Pts 43–48), experts in ancillary relief (Pt 35).

1.3 Duty of the parties

The parties are required to help the court to further the overriding objective.

1.4 Court's duty to manage cases

(1) The court must further the overriding objective by actively managing cases.

(2) Active case management includes –

- (*a*) encouraging the parties to co-operate with each other in the conduct of the proceedings;
- (*b*) identifying the issues at an early stage;
- (*c*) deciding promptly which issues need full investigation and trial and accordingly disposing summarily of the others;
- (*d*) deciding the order in which issues are to be resolved;

(*e*) encouraging the parties to use an alternative dispute resolution(GL) procedure if the court considers that appropriate and facilitating the use of such procedure;
(*f*) helping the parties to settle the whole or part of the case;
(*g*) fixing timetables or otherwise controlling the progress of the case;
(*h*) considering whether the likely benefits of taking a particular step justify the cost of taking it;
(*i*) dealing with as many aspects of the case as it can on the same occasion;
(*j*) dealing with the case without the parties needing to attend at court;
(*k*) making use of technology; and
(*l*) giving directions to ensure that the trial of a case proceeds quickly and efficiently.

PART 2
APPLICATION AND INTERPRETATION OF THE RULES

Practice Direction—See *Practice Direction (Court Offices)* and *Practice Direction (Allocation of Cases to Levels of Judiciary)* which supplement this Part generally; both are set out in Section 2 of the *Civil Court Service* (Jordan Publishing Ltd).

2.1 Application of the Rules

(1) Subject to paragraph (2), these Rules apply to all proceedings in –

(*a*) county courts;
(*b*) the High Court; and
(*c*) the Civil Division of the Court of Appeal.

(2) These Rules do not apply to proceedings of the kinds specified in the first column of the following Table (proceedings for which rules may be made under the enactments specified in the second column) except to the extent that they are applied to those proceedings by another enactment –

Proceedings	Enactments
1. Insolvency proceedings	Insolvency Act 1986, ss 411 and 412
2. Non-contentious or common form probate proceedings	Supreme Court Act 1981, s 127
3. Proceedings in the High Court when acting as a Prize Court	Prize Courts Act 1894, s 3
4. Proceedings before the judge within the meaning of Part VII of the Mental Health Act 1983	Mental Health Act 1983, s 106
5. Family proceedings	Matrimonial and Family Proceedings Act 1984, s 40
6. Adoption proceedings	Adoption Act 1976, s 66

Amendments—SI 1999/1008.

Effect of CPR 1998 on family proceedings—Rule 2.1(2) provides that the new rules do not apply to "family proceedings". Neither the RSC or the CCR are expressly repealed but both cease to have practical relevance for all civil proceedings as from 25 April 2000. FPR 1991, r 1.3 applies the CCR and the RSC to family proceedings "with the necessary modifications" and "subject to the provisions of" the FPR. Family Proceedings (Miscellaneous Amendments) Rules

1999, r 3 confirms that references in FPR 1991 to the CCR and the RSC "are references to [such rules] in force immediately before 26 April 1999". Thus, where the FPR are incomplete or silent on any matter they must continue to be supplemented where necessary by either the CCR or RSC, as hitherto (see further annotations under FPR 1991, r 1.3). However, Family Proceedings (Amendment) Rules 2003, r 10.27(1) does apply the new costs rules to family proceedings. Thus, CPR 1998, Pts 43, 44 (except rr 44.9–44.12), 47 and 48 apply to the assessment of costs and not CCR Ord 38 or RSC Ord 62. All assessments of costs are now governed by CPR 1998 but no costs for work done before 26 April 1999 will be disallowed if they would have been allowed before that date.

From 5 June 2000, CPR 1998, rr 35.1–35.14 relating to expert evidence, except rr 35.5(2) and 35.8(4)(*b*), apply to all ancillary relief applications (FPR 1991, r 2.61C).

Reform of the FPR 1991—Following the implementation of the CPR 1998, the current state of the FPR 1991 must be regarded as unsatisfactory. Though many of the concepts contained in the CPR are already familiar to family lawyers, there is no doubt that the CPR have "leapfrogged" the FPR and the latter now need to be completely revised. The FPR are a gloss on the RSC and CCR and the Rules Committee should decide whether to re-write the FPR as a gloss on the CPR or as a self-contained code.

2.2 The glossary

(1) The glossary at the end of these Rules is a guide to the meaning of certain legal expressions used in the Rules, but is not to be taken as giving those expressions any meaning in the Rules which they do not have in the law generally.

(2) Subject to paragraph (3), words in these Rules which are included in the glossary are followed by '(GL)'.

(3) The words "counterclaim", "damages", "practice form" and "service", which appear frequently in the Rules, are included in the glossary but are not followed by '(GL)'.

2.3 Interpretation

(1) In these Rules –

"child" has the meaning given by rule 21.1(2);

"claim for personal injuries" means proceedings in which there is a claim for damages in respect of personal injuries to the claimant or any other person or in respect of a person's death, and "personal injuries" includes any disease and any impairment of a person's physical or mental condition;

"claimant" means a person who makes a claim;

"CCR" is to be interpreted in accordance with Part 50;

"court officer" means a member of the court staff;

"defendant" means a person against whom a claim is made;

"defendant's home court" means –

(*a*) if the claim is proceeding in a county court, the county court for the district in which the defendant resides or carries on business; and

(*b*) if the claim is proceeding in the High Court, the district registry for the district in which the defendant resides or carries on business or, where there is no such district registry, the Royal Courts of Justice;

(Rule 6.5 provides for a party to give an address for service)

"filing", in relation to a document, means delivering it, by post or otherwise, to the court office;

"judge" means, unless the context otherwise requires, a judge, Master or district judge or a person authorised to act as such;

"jurisdiction" means, unless the context requires otherwise, England and Wales and any part of the territorial waters of the United Kingdom adjoining England and Wales;

"legal representative" means a barrister or a solicitor, solicitor's employee or other authorised litigator (as defined in the Courts and Legal Services Act 1990) who has been instructed to act for a party in relation to a claim.

"litigation friend" has the meaning given by Part 21;

"patient" has the meaning given by rule 21.1(2);

"RSC" is to be interpreted in accordance with Part 50;

"statement of case" –

(*a*) means a claim form, particulars of claim where these are not included in a claim form, defence, Part 20 claim, or reply to defence; and

(*b*) includes any further information given in relation to them voluntarily or by court order under rule 18.1;

"statement of value" is to be interpreted in accordance with rule 16.3;

"summary judgment" is to be interpreted in accordance with Part 24.

(2) A reference to a "specialist list" is a reference to a list(GL) that has been designated as such by a rule or practice direction.

(3) Where the context requires, a reference to "the court" means a reference to a particular county court, a district registry, or the Royal Courts of Justice.

Amendments—SI 2000/2092; SI 2001/4015.

****

2.8 Time

(1) This rule shows how to calculate any period of time for doing any act which is specified –

(*a*) by these Rules;

(*b*) by a practice direction; or

(*c*) by a judgment or order of the court.

(2) A period of time expressed as a number of days shall be computed as clear days.

(3) In this rule "clear days" means that in computing the number of days –

(*a*) the day on which the period begins; and

(*b*) if the end of the period is defined by reference to an event, the day on which that event occurs

are not included.

Examples

(i) Notice of an application must be served at least 3 days before the hearing.
An application is to be heard on Friday 20 October.
The last date for service is Monday 16 October.

(ii) The court is to fix a date for a hearing.
The hearing must be at least 28 days after the date of notice.
If the court gives notice of the date of the hearing on 1 October, the earliest date for the hearing is 30 October.

(iii) Particulars of claim must be served within 14 days of service of the claim form.

PART III

The claim form is served on 2 October.
The last day for service of the particulars of claim is 16 October.

(4) Where the specified period –

(*a*) is 5 days or less; and
(*b*) includes –
(i) a Saturday or Sunday; or
(ii) a Bank Holiday, Christmas Day or Good Friday,

that day does not count.

Example
Notice of an application must be served at least 3 days before the hearing.

An application is to be heard on Monday 20 October.

The last date for service is Tuesday 14 October.

(5) When the period specified –

(*a*) by these Rules or a practice direction; or
(*b*) by any judgment or court order,

for doing any act at the court office ends on a day on which the office is closed, that act shall be in time if done on the next day on which the court office is open.

****

PART 3
THE COURT'S CASE MANAGEMENT POWERS

3.1 The court's general powers of management

(1) The list of powers in this rule is in addition to any powers given to the court by any other rule or practice direction or by any other enactment or any powers it may otherwise have.

(2) Except where these Rules provide otherwise, the court may –

(*a*) extend or shorten the time for compliance with any rule, practice direction or court order (even if an application for extension is made after the time for compliance has expired);
(*b*) adjourn or bring forward a hearing;
(*c*) require a party or a party's legal representative to attend the court;
(*d*) hold a hearing and receive evidence by telephone or by using any other method of direct oral communication;
(*e*) direct that part of any proceedings (such as a counterclaim) be dealt with as separate proceedings;
(*f*) stay(GL) the whole or part of any proceedings or judgment either generally or until a specified date or event;
(*g*) consolidate proceedings;
(*h*) try two or more claims on the same occasion;
(*i*) direct a separate trial of any issue;
(*j*) decide the order in which issues are to be tried;
(*k*) exclude an issue from consideration;
(*l*) dismiss or give judgment on a claim after a decision on a preliminary issue;

(*m*) take any other step or make any other order for the purpose of managing the case and furthering the overriding objective.

(3) When the court makes an order, it may –

(*a*) make it subject to conditions, including a condition to pay a sum of money into court; and
(*b*) specify the consequence of failure to comply with the order or a condition.

(4) Where the court gives directions it may take into account whether or not a party has complied with any relevant pre-action protocol(GL).

(5) The court may order a party to pay a sum of money into court if that party has, without good reason, failed to comply with a rule, practice direction or a relevant pre-action protocol.

(6) When exercising its power under paragraph (5) the court must have regard to –

(*a*) the amount in dispute; and
(*b*) the costs which the parties have incurred or which they may incur.

(6A) Where a party pays money into court following an order under paragraph (3) or (5), the money shall be security for any sum payable by that party to any other party in the proceedings, subject to the right of a defendant under rule 37.2 to treat all or part of any money paid into court as a Part 36 payment.

(Rule 36.2 explains what is meant by a Part 36 payment)

(7) A power of the court under these Rules to make an order includes a power to vary or revoke the order.

Amendments—SI 1999/1008.

3.2 Court officer's power to refer to a judge

Where a step is to be taken by a court officer –

(*a*) the court officer may consult a judge before taking that step;
(*b*) the step may be taken by a judge instead of the court officer.

3.3 Court's power to make order of its own initiative

(1) Except where a rule or some other enactment provides otherwise, the court may exercise its powers on an application or of its own initiative.

(Part 23 sets out the procedure for making an application)

(2) Where the court proposes to make an order of its own initiative –

(*a*) it may give any person likely to be affected by the order an opportunity to make representations; and
(*b*) where it does so it must specify the time by and the manner in which the representations must be made.

(3) Where the court proposes –

(*a*) to make an order of its own initiative; and
(*b*) to hold a hearing to decide whether to make the order,

it must give each party likely to be affected by the order at least 3 days' notice of the hearing.

PART III

(4) The court may make an order of its own initiative, without hearing the parties or giving them an opportunity to make representations.

(5) Where the court has made an order under paragraph (4) –

(*a*) a party affected by the order may apply to have it set aside(GL), varied or stayed(GL); and

(*b*) the order must contain a statement of the right to make such an application.

(6) An application under paragraph (5)(*a*) must be made –

(*a*) within such period as may be specified by the court; or

(*b*) if the court does not specify a period, not more than 7 days after the date on which the order was served on the party making the application.

(CCR Ord 42, in Schedule 2, sets out the circumstances when the court may not make an order of its own initiative against the Crown)

****

PART 6
SERVICE OF DOCUMENTS

Practice Direction—See *Practice Direction (Service)* which supplements this Part generally, set out in Section 2 of the *Civil Court Service* (Jordan Publishing Ltd).

****

6.6 Service of documents on children and patients

(1) The following table shows the person on whom a document must be served if it is a document which would otherwise be served on a child or a patient –

Type of document	Nature of party	Person to be served
Claim form	Child who is not also a patient	One of the child's parents or guardians; or if there is no parent or guardian, the person with whom the child resides or in whose care the child is.
Claim form	Patient	The person authorised under Part VII of the Mental Health Act 1983 to conduct the proceedings in the name of the patient or on his behalf; or if there is no person so authorised, the person with whom the patient resides or in whose care the patient is.

Type of document	Nature of party	Person to be served
Application for an order appointing a litigation friend, where a child or patient has no litigation friend	Child or patient	See rule 21.8.
Any other document	Child or patient	The litigation friend who is conducting proceedings on behalf of the child or patient.

(2) The court may make an order permitting a document to be served on the child or patient, or on some person other than the person specified in the table in this rule.

(3) An application for an order under paragraph (2) may be made without notice.

(4) The court may order that, although a document has been served on someone other than the person specified in the table, the document is to be treated as if it had been properly served.

(5) This rule does not apply where the court has made an order under rule 21.2(3) allowing a child to conduct proceedings without a litigation friend.

(Part 21 contains rules about the appointment of a litigation friend)

Scope of provision—The general principle is that a document in proceedings cannot be served on a patient as if he were not a patient, and if it is so served the proceedings based on it are invalid (*Cutbush v Cutbush* (1893) 37 Sol Jo 685). The principle is likely to apply also to a child. This rule makes special provision for service upon a child or a patient. Service is effected in the normal way upon the category of person specified.

"child"; "patient" (r 6.6 generally)—See the notes to r 21.1.

Person to be served—Where there is no parent or guardian (for a child) or person authorised (for a patient – see r 21.4(2)), the claim form is to be served on "the person with whom he resides or in whose care he is". Once a litigation friend has been appointed (r 21.2), service of documents will be on that person, or the solicitor on the record instructed by that person (if any), in the usual way unless it is an application relating to the appointment of the litigation friend (r 21.8).

"the person with whom [the child or patient] resides or in whose care [the child or patient] is" (r 6.6(1))—See note under CCR Ord 10, r 4.

Communication to person under disability—See note under CCR Ord 10, r 4.

Deemed service—The provision for deemed service enables the court to proceed with the appointment of a litigation friend when service is not otherwise possible.

6.7 Deemed service

(1) A document which is served in accordance with these rules or any relevant practice direction shall be deemed to be served on the day shown in the following table –

Method of service	Deemed day of service
First class post	The second day after it was posted.

Method of service	Deemed day of service
Document exchange	The second day after it was left at the document exchange.
Delivering the document to or leaving it at a permitted address	The day after it was delivered to or left at the permitted address.
Fax	If it is transmitted on a business day before 4 p.m, on that day; or in any other case, on the business day after the day on which it is transmitted.
Other electronic method	The second day after the day on which it is transmitted.

(Rule 2.8 excludes a Saturday, Sunday, a Bank Holiday, Christmas Day or Good Friday from calculations of periods of 5 days or less)

(2) If a document is served personally –

(*a*) after 5 pm, on a business day; or
(*b*) at any time on a Saturday, Sunday or a Bank Holiday,

it will be treated as being served on the next business day.

(3) In this rule –

"business day" means any day except Saturday, Sunday or a bank holiday; and "bank holiday" includes Christmas Day and Good Friday.

Amendments—SI 2000/221.

****

6.10 Certificate of service

Where a rule, practice direction or court order requires a certificate of service, the certificate must state –

(*a*) that the document has not been returned undelivered; and
(*b*) the details set out in the following table –

Method of service	Details to be certified
Post	Date of posting
Personal	Date of personal service
Document exchange	Date of delivery to the document exchange

Delivery of document to or leaving it at a permitted place	Date when the document was delivered or left at the permitted place
Fax	Date and time of transmission
Other electronic means	Date of transmission and the means used
Alternative method permitted by the court	As required by the court

****

PART 7
HOW TO START PROCEEDINGS – THE CLAIM FORM

Practice Direction—See *Practice Direction (How to Start Proceedings – The Claim Form)* which supplements this Part generally, set out in Part V of this work.

7.1 Where to start proceedings

Restrictions on where proceedings may be started are set out in the relevant practice direction.

7.2 How to start proceedings

(1) Proceedings are started when the court issues a claim form at the request of the claimant.

(2) A claim form is issued on the date entered on the form by the court.

(A person who seeks a remedy from the court before proceedings are started or in relation to proceedings which are taking place, or will take place, in another jurisdiction must make an application under Part 23)

(Part 16 sets out what the claim form must include)

(The costs practice direction sets out the information about a funding arrangement to be provided with the claim form where the claimant intends to seek to recover an additional liability.)

("Funding arrangements" and "additional liability" are defined in rule 43.2.)

Amendments—SI 2000/1317.

7.3 Right to use one claim form to start two or more claims

A claimant may use a single claim form to start all claims which can be conveniently disposed of in the same proceedings.

7.4 Particulars of claim

(1) Particulars of claim must –

(*a*) be contained in or served with the claim form; or
(*b*) subject to paragraph (2) be served on the defendant by the claimant within 14 days after service of the claim form.

(2) Particulars of claim must be served on the defendant no later than the latest time for serving a claim form.

(Rule 7.5 sets out the latest time for serving a claim form)

(3) Where the claimant serves particulars of claim separately from the claim form in accordance with paragraph (1)(*b*), he must, within 7 days of service on the defendant, file a copy of the particulars together with a certificate of service.

(Part 16 sets out what the particulars of claim must include)

(Part 22 requires particulars of claim to be verified by a statement of truth)

(Rule 6.10 makes provision for a certificate of service)

7.5 Service of a claim form

(1) After a claim form has been issued, it must be served on the defendant.

(2) The general rule is that a claim form must be served within 4 months after the date of issue.

(3) The period for service is 6 months where the claim form is to be served out of the jurisdiction.

7.6 Extension of time for serving a claim form

(1) The claimant may apply for an order extending the period within which the claim form may be served.

(2) The general rule is that an application to extend the time for service must be made –

(*a*) within the period for serving the claim form specified by rule 7.5; or
(*b*) where an order has been made under this rule, within the period for service specified by that order.

(3) If the claimant applies for an order to extend the time for service of the claim form after the end of the period specified by rule 7.5 or by an order made under this rule, the court may make such an order only if –

(*a*) the court has been unable to serve the claim form; or
(*b*) the claimant has taken all reasonable steps to serve the claim form but has been unable to do so; and,
(*c*) in either case, the claimant has acted promptly in making the application.

(4) An application for an order extending the time for service –

(*a*) must be supported by evidence; and
(*b*) may be made without notice.

7.7 Application by defendant for service of claim form

(1) Where a claim form has been issued against a defendant, but has not yet been served on him, the defendant may serve a notice on the claimant requiring him to serve the claim form or discontinue the claim within a period specified in the notice.

(2) The period specified in a notice served under paragraph (1) must be at least 14 days after service of the notice.

(3) If the claimant fails to comply with the notice, the court may, on the application of the defendant –

- (*a*) dismiss the claim; or
- (*b*) make any other order it thinks just.

7.8 Form for defence etc must be served with particulars of claim

(1) When particulars of claim are served on a defendant, whether they are contained in the claim form, served with it or served subsequently, they must be accompanied by –

- (*a*) a form for defending the claim;
- (*b*) a form for admitting the claim; and
- (*c*) a form for acknowledging service.

(2) Where the claimant is using the procedure set out in Part 8 (alternative procedure for claims) –

- (*a*) paragraph (1) does not apply; and
- (*b*) a form for acknowledging service must accompany the claim form.

****

7.11 Human Rights

(1) A claim under section 7(1)(*a*) of the Human Rights Act 1998 in respect of a judicial act may be brought only in the High Court.

(2) Any other claim under section 7(1)(*a*) of that Act may be brought in any court.

Amendments—Inserted by SI 2000/2092.

Scope of provision—Where a claim is made in relation to a human rights issue in ongoing proceedings, that issue should be determined by the court in which the proceedings are being heard. This rule provides the general rule and the exception that, where the issue raised concerns a judicial act, this must be dealt with in the High Court. HRA 1998, s 9(1) provides that proceedings under s 7(1)(*a*) in relation to a judicial act may be brought only by way of judicial review or on appeal.

PART 8
ALTERNATIVE PROCEDURE FOR CLAIMS

Practice Direction—See *Practice Direction (Alternative Procedure for Claims)* (PD 8) which supplements this Part generally, set out in Part V of this work; see also *Practice Direction (How to Make Claims in the Schedule Rules and Other Claims)* (PD 8B), set out in Section 2 of the *Civil Court Service* (Jordan Publishing Ltd).

Scope of Part—Part 8 procedure is appropriate to all free standing applications relating to adults under the inherent jurisdiction of the High Court. These proceedings are not classified as "family proceedings" within the definition provided in the Matrimonial and Family Proceedings Act 1984, s 32 and therefore FPR 1991 do not apply. These applications invariably seek declaratory orders and the court's decision is sought on questions which do not involve substantial issues of fact. See also the provisions of *Practice Direction (Alternative Procedure for Claims)* (PD 8).

8.1 Types of claim in which Part 8 procedure may be followed

(1) The Part 8 procedure is the procedure set out in this Part.

(2) A claimant may use the Part 8 procedure where –

(*a*) he seeks the court's decision on a question which is unlikely to involve a substantial dispute of fact; or
(*b*) paragraph (6) applies.

(3) The court may at any stage order the claim to continue as if the claimant had not used the Part 8 procedure and, if it does so, the court may give any directions it considers appropriate.

(4) Paragraph (2) does not apply if a practice direction provides that the Part 8 procedure may not be used in relation to the type of claim in question.

(5) Where the claimant uses the Part 8 procedure he may not obtain default judgment under Part 12.

(6) A rule or practice direction may, in relation to a specified type of proceedings –

(*a*) require or permit the use of the Part 8 procedure; and
(*b*) disapply or modify any of the rules set out in this Part as they apply to those proceedings.

(Rule 8.9 provides for other modifications to the general rules where the Part 8 procedure is being used)

8.2 Contents of the claim form

Where the claimant uses the Part 8 procedure the claim form must state –

(*a*) that this Part applies;
(*b*) (i) the question which the claimant wants the court to decide; or
(ii) the remedy which the claimant is seeking and the legal basis for the claim to that remedy;
(*c*) if the claim is being made under an enactment, what that enactment is;
(*d*) if the claimant is claiming in a representative capacity, what that capacity is; and
(*e*) if the defendant is sued in a representative capacity, what that capacity is.

(Part 22 provides for the claim form to be verified by a statement of truth)

(Rule 7.5 provides for service of the claim form)

(The costs practice direction sets out the information about a funding arrangement to be provided with the claim form where the claimant intends to seek to recover an additional liability.)

("Funding arrangement" and "additional liability" are defined in rule 43.2.)

Amendments—SI 2000/1317.

****

8.3 Acknowledgment of service

(1) The defendant must –

(*a*) file an acknowledgment of service in the relevant practice form not more than 14 days after service of the claim form; and
(*b*) serve the acknowledgment of service on the claimant and any other party.

(2) The acknowledgment of service must state –

(*a*) whether the defendant contests the claim; and
(*b*) if the defendant seeks a different remedy from that set out in the claim form, what that remedy is.

(3) The following rules of Part 10 (acknowledgment of service) apply –

(*a*) rule 10.3(2) (exceptions to the period for filing an acknowledgment of service); and
(*b*) rule 10.5 (contents of acknowledgment of service).

(4) (*revoked*)

(The costs practice direction sets out the information about a funding arrangement to be provided with the claim form where the claimant intends to seek to recover an additional liability.)

("Funding arrangement" and "additional liability" are defined in rule 43.2.)

Amendments—SI 2000/1317; SI 2001/4015.

8.4 Consequence of not filing an acknowledgment of service

(1) This rule applies where –

(*a*) the defendant has failed to file an acknowledgment of service; and
(*b*) the time period for doing so has expired.

(2) The defendant may attend the hearing of the claim but may not take part in the hearing unless the court gives permission.

8.5 Filing and serving written evidence

(1) The claimant must file any written evidence on which he intends to rely when he files his claim form.

(2) The claimant's evidence must be served on the defendant with the claim form.

(3) A defendant who wishes to rely on written evidence must file it when he files his acknowledgment of service.

(4) If he does so, he must also, at the same time, serve a copy of his evidence on the other parties.

(5) The claimant may, within 14 days of service of the defendant's evidence on him, file further written evidence in reply.

PART III

(6) If he does so, he must also, within the same time limit, serve a copy of his evidence on the other parties.

(7) The claimant may rely on the matters set out in his claim form as evidence under this rule if the claim form is verified by a statement of truth.

8.6 Evidence – general

(1) No written evidence may be relied on at the hearing of the claim unless –

(*a*) it has been served in accordance with rule 8.5; or
(*b*) the court gives permission.

(2) The court may require or permit a party to give oral evidence at the hearing.

(3) The court may give directions requiring the attendance for cross-examination(GL) of a witness who has given written evidence.

(Rule 32.1 contains a general power for the court to control evidence)

8.7 Part 20 claims

Where the Part 8 procedure is used, Part 20 (counterclaims and other additional claims) applies except that a party may not make a Part 20 claim (as defined by rule 20.2) without the court's permission.

8.8 Procedure where defendant objects to use of the Part 8 procedure

(1) Where the defendant contends that the Part 8 procedure should not be used because –

(*a*) there is a substantial dispute of fact; and
(*b*) the use of the Part 8 procedure is not required or permitted by a rule or practice direction,

he must state his reasons when he files his acknowledgment of service.

(Rule 8.5 requires a defendant who wishes to rely on written evidence to file it when he files his acknowledgment of service)

(2) When the court receives the acknowledgment of service and any written evidence it will give directions as to the future management of the case.

(Rule 8.1(3) allows the court to make an order that the claim continue as if the claimant had not used the Part 8 procedure)

8.9 Modifications to the general rules

Where the Part 8 procedure is followed –

(*a*) provision is made in this Part for the matters which must be stated in the claim form and the defendant is not required to file a defence and therefore –
  (i) Part 16 (statements of case) does not apply;
  (ii) Part 15 (defence and reply) does not apply;
  (iii) any time limit in these Rules which prevents the parties from taking a step before a defence is filed does not apply;
  (iv) the requirement under rule 7.8 to serve on the defendant a form for defending the claim does not apply;

(*b*) the claimant may not obtain judgment by request on an admission and therefore –
  (i) rules 14.4 to 14.7 do not apply; and
  (ii) the requirement under rule 7.8 to serve on the defendant a form for admitting the claim does not apply; and

(*c*) the claim shall be treated as allocated to the multi-track and therefore Part 26 does not apply.

PART 9
RESPONDING TO PARTICULARS OF CLAIM – GENERAL

9.1 Scope of this Part

(1) This Part sets out how a defendant may respond to particulars of claim.

(2) Where the defendant receives a claim form which states that particulars of claim are to follow, he need not respond to the claim until the particulars of claim have been served on him.

9.2 Defence, admission or acknowledgment of service

When particulars of claim are served on a defendant, the defendant may –

(*a*) file or serve an admission in accordance with Part 14;
(*b*) file a defence in accordance with Part 15,

(or do both, if he admits only part of the claim); or

(*c*) file an acknowledgment of service in accordance with Part 10.

(RSC Order 15 r 12A in Schedule 1 makes special provision where the defendant in a derivative claim responds to particulars of claim)

PART 10
ACKNOWLEDGMENT OF SERVICE

Practice Direction—See *Practice Direction (Acknowledgment of Service)* which supplements this Part generally, set out in Section 2 of the *Civil Court Service* (Jordan Publishing Ltd).

****

10.3 The period for filing an acknowledgment of service

(1) The general rule is that the period for filing an acknowledgment of service is –

(*a*) where the defendant is served with a claim form which states that particulars of claim are to follow, 14 days after service of the particulars of claim; and
(*b*) in any other case, 14 days after service of the claim form.

(2) The general rule is subject to the following rules –

(*a*) rule 6.22 (which specifies how the period for filing an acknowledgment of service is calculated where the claim form is served out of the jurisdiction); and
(*b*) rule 6.16(4) (which requires the court to specify the period for responding to the particulars of claim when it makes an order under that rule).

PART III

Amendments—SI 2000/940.

****

PART 12
DEFAULT JUDGMENT

Practice Direction—See *Practice Direction (Default Judgment)* which supplements this Part generally, set out in Section 2 of the *Civil Court Service* (Jordan Publishing Ltd).

****

12.3 Conditions to be satisfied

(1) The claimant may obtain judgment in default of an acknowledgment of service only if –

(*a*) the defendant has not filed an acknowledgment of service or a defence to the claim (or any part of the claim); and
(*b*) the relevant time for doing so has expired.

(2) Judgment in default of defence may be obtained only –

(*a*) where an acknowledgment of service has been filed but a defence has not been filed;
(*b*) in a counterclaim made under rule 20.4, where a defence has not been filed,

and, in either case, the relevant time limit for doing so has expired.

(Rules 10.3 and 15.4 deal respectively with the period for filing an acknowledgment of service and the period for filing a defence)

(Rule 20.4 makes general provision for a defendant's counterclaim against a claimant, and rule 20.4(3) provides that Part 10 (acknowledgment of service) does not apply to a counterclaim made under that rule)

(3) The claimant may not obtain a default judgment if –

(*a*) the defendant has applied –
(i) to have the claimant's statement of case struck out under rule 3.4; or
(ii) for summary judgment under Part 24,

and, in either case, that application has not been disposed of;
(*b*) the defendant has satisfied the whole claim (including any claim for costs) on which the claimant is seeking judgment; or
(*c*) (i) the claimant is seeking judgment on a claim for money; and
(ii) the defendant has filed or served on the claimant an admission under rule 14.4 or 14.7 (admission of liability to pay all of the money claimed) together with a request for time to pay.

(Part 14 sets out the procedure where a defendant admits a money claim and asks for time to pay)

(Rule 6.14 provides that, where the claim form is served by the claimant, he may not obtain default judgment unless he has filed a certificate of service)

(Article 19(4) of Council Regulation (EC) No 1348/2000 of 29 May 2000 on the service in the Member States of judicial and extrajudicial documents in civil or commercial matters applies in relation to judgment in default where the claim form is served in accordance with that Regulation)

Amendments—SI 2000/221; SI 2001/1388.

****

PART 15
DEFENCE AND REPLY

Practice Direction—See *Practice Direction (Defence and Reply)* which supplements this Part generally, set out in Section 2 of the *Civil Court Service* (Jordan Publishing Ltd).

****

15.4 The period for filing a defence

(1) The general rule is that the period for filing a defence is –

(*a*) 14 days after service of the particulars of claim; or
(*b*) if the defendant files an acknowledgment of service under Part 10, 28 days after service of the particulars of claim.

(Rule 7.4 provides for the particulars of claim to be contained in or served with the claim form or served within 14 days of service of the claim form)

(2) The general rule is subject to the following rules –

(*a*) rule 6.23 (which specifies how the period for filing a defence is calculated where the claim form is served out of the jurisdiction);
(*b*) rule 11 (which provides that, where the defendant makes an application disputing the court's jurisdiction, he need not file a defence before the hearing);
(*c*) rule 24.4(2) (which provides that, if the claimant applies for summary judgment before the defendant has filed a defence, the defendant need not file a defence before the summary judgment hearing); and
(*d*) rule 6.16(4) (which requires the court to specify the period for responding to the particulars of claim when it makes an order under that rule).

Amendments—SI 2000/940.

****

PART 16
STATEMENTS OF CASE

Practice Direction—See *Practice Direction (Statements of Case)* which supplements this Part generally, set out in Part V of this work.

16.1 Part not to apply where claimant uses Part 8 procedure

This Part does not apply where the claimant uses the procedure set out in Part 8 (alternative procedure for claims).

16.2 Contents of the claim form

(1) The claim form must –

(*a*) contain a concise statement of the nature of the claim;
(*b*) specify the remedy which the claimant seeks;
(*c*) where the claimant is making a claim for money, contain a statement of value in accordance with rule 16.3; and
(*d*) contain such other matters as may be set out in a practice direction.

(2) If the particulars of claim specified in rule 16.4 are not contained in, or are not served with the claim form, the claimant must state on the claim form that the particulars of claim will follow.

(3) If the claimant is claiming in a representative capacity, the claim form must state what that capacity is.

(4) If the defendant is sued in a representative capacity, the claim form must state what that capacity is.

(5) The court may grant any remedy to which the claimant is entitled even if that remedy is not specified in the claim form.

(Part 22 requires a claim form to be verified by a statement of truth)

(The costs practice direction sets out the information about a funding arrangement to be provided with the claim form where the claimant intends to seek to recover an additional liability.)

("Funding arrangement" and "additional liability" are defined in rule 43.2.)

Amendments—SI 2000/1317.

16.3 Statement of value to be included in the claim form

(1) This rule applies where the claimant is making a claim for money.

(2) The claimant must, in the claim form, state –

(*a*) the amount of money which he is claiming;
(*b*) that he expects to recover –
  (i) not more than £5,000;
  (ii) more than £5,000 but not more than £15,000; or
  (iii) more than £15,000; or
(*c*) that he cannot say how much he expects to recover.

(3)–(7) …

16.4 Contents of the particulars of claim

(1) Particulars of claim must include –

(*a*) a concise statement of the facts on which the claimant relies;
(*b*) if the claimant is seeking interest, a statement to that effect and the details set out in paragraph (2);
(*c*) if the claimant is seeking aggravated damages(GL) or exemplary damages(GL), a statement to that effect and his grounds for claiming them;
(*d*) if the claimant is seeking provisional damages, a statement to that effect and his grounds for claiming them; and
(*e*) such other matters as may be set out in a practice direction.

(2) If the claimant is seeking interest he must –

(*a*) state whether he is doing so –
(i) under the terms of a contract;
(ii) under an enactment and if so which; or
(iii) on some other basis and if so what that basis is; and
(*b*) if the claim is for a specified amount of money, state –
(i) the percentage rate at which interest is claimed;
(ii) the date from which it is claimed;
(iii) the date to which it is calculated, which must not be later than the date on which the claim form is issued;
(iv) the total amount of interest claimed to the date of calculation; and
(v) the daily rate at which interest accrues after that date.

(Part 22 requires particulars of claim to be verified by a statement of truth)

****

PART 18
FURTHER INFORMATION

Practice Direction—See *Practice Direction (Further Information)* which supplements this Part generally, set out in Part V of this work.

18.1 Obtaining further information

(1) The court may at any time order a party to –

(*a*) clarify any matter which is in dispute in the proceedings; or
(*b*) give additional information in relation to any such matter,

whether or not the matter is contained or referred to in a statement of case.

(2) Paragraph (1) is subject to any rule of law to the contrary.

(3) Where the court makes an order under paragraph (1), the party against whom it is made must –

(*a*) file his response; and
(*b*) serve it on the other parties,

within the time specified by the court.

(Part 22 requires a response to be verified by a statement of truth)

(Part 53 (defamation) restricts requirements for providing further information about sources of information in defamation claims)

Amendments—SI 2000/221.

18.2 Restriction on the use of further information

The court may direct that information provided by a party to another party (whether given voluntarily or following an order made under rule 18.1) must not be used for any purpose except for that of the proceedings in which it is given.

(RSC Order 82, in Schedule 1, provides for circumstances in which further information is not allowed in defamation claims)

PART 19
PARTIES AND GROUP LITIGATION

****

19.4A Human Rights

Section 4 of the Human Rights Act 1998

(1) The court may not make a declaration of incompatibility in accordance with section 4 of the Human Rights Act 1998 unless 21 days' notice, or such other period of notice as the court directs, has been given to the Crown.

(2) Where notice has been given to the Crown a Minister, or other person permitted by that Act, shall be joined as a party on giving notice to the court.

(Only courts specified in section 4 of the Human Rights Act 1998 can make a declaration of incompatibility)

Section 9 of the Human Rights Act 1998

(3) Where a claim is made under that Act for damages in respect of a judicial act –

(*a*) that claim must be set out in the statement of case or the appeal notice; and
(*b*) notice must be given to the Crown.

(4) Where paragraph (3) applies and the appropriate person has not applied to be joined as a party within 21 days, or such other period as the court directs, after the notice is served, the court may join the appropriate person as a party.

(A practice direction makes provision for these notices)

Amendments—Inserted by SI 2000/2092.

Scope of provision—In any proceedings where a human rights point is raised and there is either an issue as to whether a declaration of incompatibility of domestic legislation to ECHR should be made (as detailed in HRA 1998, s 1) or there has been a potential breach of a provision of the ECHR by virtue of a judicial act, it is necessary to give notice to the Crown with a view to joinder (see also CPR 1998, r 7.11 and FPR 1991, r 10.26).

****

19.7 Representation of interested persons who cannot be ascertained etc

(1) This rule applies to claims about –

(*a*) the estate of a deceased person;
(*b*) property subject to a trust; or
(*c*) the meaning of a document, including a statute.

(2) The court may make an order appointing a person to represent any other person or persons in the claim where the person or persons to be represented –

(*a*) are unborn;
(*b*) cannot be found;
(*c*) cannot easily be ascertained; or
(*d*) are a class of persons who have the same interest in a claim and –
  (i) one or more members of that class are within sub-paragraphs (*a*), (*b*) or (*c*); or

(ii) to appoint a representative would further the overriding objective.

(3) An application for an order under paragraph (2) –

(*a*) may be made by –

(i) any person who seeks to be appointed under the order; or

(ii) any party to the claim; and

(*b*) may be made at any time before or after the claim has started.

(4) An application notice for an order under paragraph (2) must be served on –

(*a*) all parties to the claim, if the claim has started;

(*b*) the person sought to be appointed, if that person is not the applicant or a party to the claim; and

(*c*) any other person as directed by the court.

(5) The court's approval is required to settle a claim in which a party is acting as a representative under this rule.

(6) The court may approve a settlement where it is satisfied that the settlement is for the benefit of all the represented persons.

(7) Unless the court otherwise directs, any judgment or order given in a claim in which a party is acting as a representative under this rule –

(*a*) is binding on all persons represented in the claim; but

(*b*) may only be enforced by or against a person who is not a party to the claim with the permission of the court.

Amendments—Inserted by SI 2000/221.

19.7A Representation of beneficiaries by trustees etc

(1) A claim may be brought by or against trustees, executors or administrators in that capacity without adding as parties any persons who have a beneficial interest in the trust or estate ("the beneficiaries").

(2) Any judgment or order given or made in the claim is binding on the beneficiaries unless the court orders otherwise in the same or other proceedings.

Amendments—Inserted by SI 2002/2058.

****

PART 21
CHILDREN AND PATIENTS

Practice Direction—See *Practice Direction (Children and Patients)* which supplements this Part generally, set out in Part V of this work.

21.1 Scope of this Part

(1) This Part –

(*a*) contains special provisions which apply in proceedings involving children and patients; and

(*b*) sets out how a person becomes a litigation friend.

(2) In this Part –

(*a*) "child" means a person under 18; and

(*b*) "patient" means a person who by reason of mental disorder within the meaning of the Mental Health Act 1983 is incapable of managing and administering his own affairs.

(Rule 6.6 contains provisions about the service of documents on children and patients)

(Rule 48.5 deals with costs where money is payable by or to a child or patient)

Scope of provision—This Part, which has no application to family proceedings, makes special provision in civil proceedings for those litigants who were previously described as being "persons under disability". There are two distinct categories: "child" and "patient" (as defined). FPR 1991 will apply instead to family proceedings but there are situations in the family context in which reliance may have to be placed on this Part of the CPR (eg an application under the Protection from Harassment Act 1997 or for a personal protection injunction based in tort against or on behalf of a person under disability).

"child" or "patient" (r 21.1(2))—It is possible for a child also to be a patient and this may be relevant if that condition will continue to subsist on ceasing to be a child (eg in regard to the disposal of money awarded to the child). Thus a child who has severe learning disabilities will continue to be a patient even after attaining the age of 18.

"litigation friend" (r 21.1(1)(*b*))—This expression replaces both next friend and guardian ad litem used in previous rules.

"mental disorder" (r 21.1(2)(*b*))—By virtue of Mental Health Act 1983, s 1(2), this means "mental illness, arrested or incomplete development of mind, psychopathic disorder and any other disorder or disability of mind and 'mentally disordered' shall be construed accordingly". For a full explanation see the note to FPR 1991, r 9.1.

"patient" (r 21.1(2)(*b*))—A person who by reason of mental disorder within the meaning of the Mental Health Act 1983 is incapable of managing and administering his own affairs (the former RSC and CCR concluded "... property and affairs" but it is not thought that there is any material difference). For a further explanation see **"patients"** under FPR 1991, r 9.1.

Assessing capacity—See generally the note under FPR 1991, r 9.1.

Doubt about capacity—The rules make no express provision for the situation where it is unclear whether a party to litigation is a patient. However, the court may order an inquiry to be made in the proceedings to determine any such issue. This inquiry would normally be heard before the district judge who can compel the attendance of witnesses (including medical attendants and the claimant or defendant himself) and the production of documents. Where there are practical difficulties in obtaining medical evidence the Official Solicitor may be consulted. The court can also direct the Official Solicitor to make inquiries and to report about such matters as the Court thinks fit (*Harbin v Masterman* [1896] 1 Ch 351, CA).

Human rights—See note under FPR 1991, r 9.1.

21.2 Requirement for litigation friend in proceedings by or against children and patients

(1) A patient must have a litigation friend to conduct proceedings on his behalf.

(2) A child must have a litigation friend to conduct proceedings on his behalf unless the court makes an order under paragraph (3).

(3) The court may make an order permitting the child to conduct proceedings without a litigation friend.

(4) An application for an order under paragraph (3) –

(*a*) may be made by the child;
(*b*) if the child already has a litigation friend, must be made on notice to the litigation friend; and
(*c*) if the child has no litigation friend, may be made without notice.

(5) Where –

(*a*) the court has made an order under paragraph (3); and
(*b*) it subsequently appears to the court that it is desirable for a litigation friend to conduct the proceedings on behalf of the child,

the court may appoint a person to be the child's litigation friend.

Verification that a party is a child or patient—The Rules assume that it is known whether the party is a child or a patient. *Practice Direction (Children and Patients)*, para 2.3 (set out in Part V of this work) requires the litigation friend to state in the "certificate of suitability" that he consents to act and knows or believes the party to be a child or patient. The grounds for this belief must be stated and if based upon medical opinion, this document must be attached. It is unlikely to be difficult to ascertain the age of a party, but there may be doubt as to whether a party is a patient and in that event a preliminary issue as to capacity should be tried with notice being given to that party who may wish to make representations.

Even where the issue does not seem to be contentious, a district judge who is responsible for case management will generally require the assistance of a medical report before being able to be satisfied that incapacity exists. An admission by a person alleged to lack capacity will carry little weight. It may assist for the judge to see the person alleged to lack capacity (*Masterman-Lister v Brutton & Co and Jewell & Home Counties Dairies* [2002] EWCA Civ 1889, [2002] All ER (D) 297 (Dec)).

Notification to the child or patient—Neither the Rules nor Practice Directions actually provide that a child or patient must be given notice of the proceedings unless the court is involved in the appointment of the litigation friend, so it is possible for proceedings in the name of a child or patient to be commenced or defended without the personal knowledge of that party. Reliance is placed on the certificate of suitability (see above) and upon service on the parent or guardian of the child, or the person with whom the patient resides or in whose care he is (see notes to CCR Ord 10, r 4 for detailed consideration of this). Reference should also be made to *Practice Direction (Children and Patients)* at para 2.4. It cannot be assumed that this person will inform the patient in every situation where this would be prudent.

Child as a party—The court may now authorise a child to conduct proceedings, but will only do so when satisfied that the child has the required capacity.

Patient as a party—An adult who has the necessary capacity will not be a patient even if mentally disordered, so there is no need for a comparable provision whereby the court may authorise a patient to conduct proceedings. However, there may now be a departure from the general rule in so far as the court may permit proceedings to continue (to a limited extent) even though a litigation friend has not been appointed (see r 21.3).

Duty of litigation friend—The duty of a litigation friend is set out in *Practice Direction (Children and Patients)*. It is "fairly and competently to conduct proceedings on behalf of a child or patient. He must have no interest in the proceedings adverse to that of the child or patient and all steps and decisions he takes in the proceedings must be taken for the benefit of the child or patient".

Status of litigation friend—The powers of the litigation friend are not expressly set out but as the appointment is to "conduct proceedings on behalf of" the child or patient it may be assumed that, subject to the provisions of the rules, any act which in the ordinary conduct of any proceedings is required or authorised to be done by a party shall or may be done by the litigation friend. Unless the litigation friend is also a receiver appointed by the Court of Protection or an attorney under a registered enduring power of attorney, he will have no status in regard to the affairs of the patient outside the proceedings in which he is appointed. It follows that if money is awarded to a child or patient the litigation friend has no authority to receive or expend that money. The money may only be dealt with pursuant to the directions of the court and in this respect reference must be made to r 21.11. Similarly, any settlement or compromise will have to be approved by the court under r 21.10.

Statement of truth—Part 22 makes provision for certain documents to be verified by a "statement of truth". If a party is a child or a patient it will be the litigation friend who makes and signs this statement (see r 22.1(5), (6)).

Need for a solicitor—Unlike the former RSC it appears that there is no requirement for a solicitor to act on behalf of a child or patient whose proceedings are being conducted by a litigation friend.

21.3 Stage of proceedings at which a litigation friend becomes necessary

(1) This rule does not apply where the court has made an order under rule 21.2(3).

(2) A person may not, without the permission of the court –

(*a*) make an application against a child or patient before proceedings have started; or

(*b*) take any step in proceedings except –

(i) issuing and serving a claim form; or

(ii) applying for the appointment of a litigation friend under rule 21.6,

until the child or patient has a litigation friend.

(3) If a party becomes a patient during proceedings, no party may take any step in the proceedings without the permission of the court until the patient has a litigation friend.

(4) Any step taken before a child or patient has a litigation friend, shall be of no effect unless the court otherwise orders.

Scope of provision—Under RSC and CCR any proceedings conducted in the absence of a next friend or guardian ad litem were of no effect if a party was under a disability. This caused problems where the disability was not realised by the other parties or their solicitors or arose during the proceedings without their knowledge, and liabilities could arise in respect of abortive costs. The court now has a discretion under the CPR to permit specified steps to be taken or retrospectively to approve any steps that have been taken in breach or ignorance of the general rule. This is a useful provision though it is unlikely to be relied upon where prejudice would be caused to the child or patient or to a party not at fault.

Provided everyone has acted in good faith and there has been no manifest disadvantage to the party subsequently found to have been a patient at the relevant time it is likely that the court will regularise the position retrospectively (*Masterman-Lister v Brutton & Co and Jewell & Home Counties Dairies* [2002] EWCA Civ 1889, [2002] All ER (D) 297 (Dec)).

Effect on timetable—Until there is a litigation friend no party may take any step in the proceedings so it is assumed that any timetable is suspended. When the court appoints the litigation friend it may be prudent to consider further directions as to the future conduct of the proceedings.

21.4 Who may be a litigation friend without a court order

(1) This rule does not apply if the court has appointed a person to be a litigation friend.

(2) A person authorised under Part VII of the Mental Health Act 1983 to conduct legal proceedings in the name of a patient or on his behalf, is entitled to be the litigation friend of the patient in any proceedings to which his authority extends.

(3) If nobody has been appointed by the court or, in the case of a patient, authorised under Part VII, a person may act as a litigation friend if he –

(*a*) can fairly and competently conduct proceedings on behalf of the child or patient; and
(*b*) has no interest adverse to that of the child or patient; and
(*c*) where the child or patient is a claimant, undertakes to pay any costs which the child or patient may be ordered to pay in relation to the proceedings, subject to any right he may have to be repaid from the assets of the child or patient.

Scope of provision—This rule sets out the procedural steps for the appointment of a litigation friend otherwise than by a court order.

Authorised person—Any person authorised under Mental Health Act 1983, Pt VII (ie as a receiver appointed by the Court of Protection – see generally s 96(1)) to conduct legal proceedings in the name or on behalf of a patient is entitled to become the litigation friend in accordance with such authority. An office copy of the order or other authorisation sealed with the official seal of the Court of Protection should be filed. It is not clear if the court has power to appoint someone else, but this situation is unlikely to arise. A registered attorney of a patient under an enduring power of attorney is not specifically mentioned but would be an obvious person to appoint as litigation friend because he will control the financial affairs.

Official Solicitor—The Official Solicitor should be approached in case of difficulty and may be appointed if he consents but in practice he will only consent if there is no-one else suitable and willing to act. It is not necessary to approach him in all cases and the court will not be concerned to ascertain whether he has declined to consent before appointing someone else. He should not be appointed without his consent which will not be forthcoming until provision is made for payment of his costs (see *Practice Direction (Children and Patients)*, para 3.6 – set out in Part V of this work). Save in the most urgent of cases, it is unlikely that he will be able to complete his enquiries in less than three months. Accordingly, a lengthy adjournment of the proceedings might become necessary and a substantive hearing should not be fixed within such period of his initial appointment without consulting him. Where the circumstances of the case justify the involvement of the Official Solicitor, a completed questionnaire, and a copy of the order appointing him (subject to his consent) and the court file should be sent to his office. The Official Solicitor to the Supreme Court is provided for by Supreme Court Act 1981, s 90 and may be contacted at 81 Chancery Lane, London WC2A 1DD; Tel: 0171-911-7127, Fax: 0171-911-7105.

Suitability—There can be no doubt as to the suitability of a person authorised by the Court of Protection. The rule helpfully sets out the criteria whereby other persons may be regarded as suitable for appointment as litigation friend (r 21.4(3)). These criteria feature throughout Pt 21 and the court must be satisfied that they are complied with before appointing a litigation friend. They may be relied upon where there is a dispute as to who should be appointed. Apart from this there is no restriction on who may be a litigation friend save that (in practice) the person appointed should normally be within the jurisdiction and must not be a patient. If the court becomes aware of the person's unsuitability, it may remove him under r 21.7 below and substitute another person as litigation friend, but there is no express duty to monitor the situation.

Undertaking as to costs—As the litigation friend is in effect required to provide an indemnity he will wish to be in control of adequate funds held by the child or patient or otherwise protected by a Legal Aid Certificate, unless willing to fund the action. If not acting under a registered enduring power of attorney this will involve applying to the Court of Protection for appointment as a receiver. Further difficulties arise in regard to conditional fee arrangements. The requirement for this undertaking imposes a severe limitation upon the ability of a child or patient to bring a claim although "after the event" (ATE) indemnity insurance may be available. Query whether it amounts to discrimination against a person with a mental disability contrary to the Disability Discrimination Act 1995.

21.5 How a person becomes a litigation friend without a court order

(1) If the court has not appointed a litigation friend, a person who wishes to act as a litigation friend must follow the procedure set out in this rule.

(2) A person authorised under Part VII of the Mental Health Act 1983 must file an official copy[(GL)] of the order or other document which constitutes his authorisation to act.

(3) Any other person must file a certificate of suitability stating that he satisfies the conditions specified in rule 21.4(3).

(4) A person who is to act as a litigation friend for a claimant must file –

(*a*) the authorisation; or
(*b*) the certificate of suitability,

at the time when the claim is made.

(5) A person who is to act as a litigation friend for a defendant must file –

(*a*) the authorisation; or
(*b*) the certificate of suitability,

at the time when he first takes a step in the proceedings on behalf of the defendant.

(6) The litigation friend must –

(*a*) serve the certificate of suitability on every person on whom, in accordance with rule 6.6 (service on parent, guardian etc), the claim form should be served; and
(*b*) file a certificate of service when he files the certificate of suitability.

(Rule 6.10 sets out the details to be contained in a certificate of service)

No need for court appointment of next friend—A litigation friend may be appointed simply by filing the relevant documents. It is strange that there is no requirement for the child or patient to be personally notified that proceedings are being brought in his name because he may wish to make representations as to who the litigation friend should be or dispute that he is a patient (see generally the provisions as to service). The Court of Appeal has recommended a change in the rules so that a person cannot be categorised as a patient without knowing what is going on (*Masterman-Lister v Brutton & Co and Jewell & Home Counties Dairies* [2002] EWCA Civ 1889, [2002] All ER (D) 297 (Dec)). It would therefore be good practice to ensure that the patient is notified and the court may require confirmation of this.

"certificate of suitability"—This document confirms that the person to be appointed meets the criteria whereby a person may be regarded as suitable for appointment as a litigation friend (see r 21.4(3)). As to suitability see note under r 21.4 above. The certificate is a pre-requisite for appointment without a court order but will not be conclusive in the event of a dispute as to suitability.

"certificate of service"—*Practice Direction (Children and Patients)*, para 2.4 (set out in Part V of this work) clarifies the persons on whom the certificate of suitability must be served in accordance with the stated rule. The (alleged) patient is not included (but see note above).

21.6 How a person becomes a litigation friend by court order

(1) The court may make an order appointing a litigation friend.

(2) An application for an order appointing a litigation friend may be made by –

(*a*) a person who wishes to be the litigation friend; or
(*b*) a party.

(3) Where –

(*a*) a person makes a claim against a child or patient;
(*b*) the child or patient has no litigation friend;

(*c*) the court has not made an order under rule 21.2(3) (order that a child can act without a litigation friend); and

(*d*) either –

(i) someone who is not entitled to be a litigation friend files a defence; or

(ii) the claimant wishes to take some step in the proceedings,

the claimant must apply to the court for an order appointing a litigation friend for the child or patient.

(4) An application for an order appointing a litigation friend must be supported by evidence.

(5) The court may not appoint a litigation friend under this rule unless it is satisfied that the person to be appointed complies with the conditions specified in rule 21.4(3).

Scope of provision—This rule sets out the procedural steps for the appointment of a litigation friend by a court order. These provisions will apply where it has not been possible to appoint a litigation friend without an order pursuant to r 21.5. The court must be satisfied that the person to be appointed is suitable for appointment in accordance with the criteria set out in r 21.4(3).

Service—See r 21.8(1) and (2). *Practice Direction (Children and Patients)*, at para 3.3 clarifies who should be served (set out in Part V of this work). The application must be served on the (alleged) patient "unless the court otherwise orders".

Evidence—*Practice Direction (Children and Patients)*, at para 3.4 clarifies the evidence required. This will presumably include evidence that the party is a child or patient although this is not expressly stated.

Suitability—See note to r 21.4 above. The court may appoint the person proposed or any other person who complies with the conditions specified in r 21.4(3) (see r 21.8(4)).

21.7 Court's power to change litigation friend and to prevent person acting as litigation friend

(1) The court may –

(*a*) direct that a person may not act as a litigation friend;

(*b*) terminate a litigation friend's appointment;

(*c*) appoint a new litigation friend in substitution for an existing one.

(2) An application for an order under paragraph (1) must be supported by evidence.

(3) The court may not appoint a litigation friend under this rule unless it is satisfied that the person to be appointed complies with the conditions specified in rule 21.4(3).

Scope of provision—This rule enables the court to prevent a person from being a litigation friend or replace a litigation friend during the course of proceedings. The court must be satisfied that the person to be appointed is suitable for appointment in accordance with the criteria set out in r 21.4(3).

Service—See r 21.8(1) and (3). *Practice Direction (Children and Patients)*, at para 4.4 clarifies who should be served. Although this does not include the patient it may be good practice to consult this person as capacity is not an "all or nothing" concept.

Evidence—*Practice Direction (Children and Patients)*, at paras 4.2 and 4.3 clarifies the evidence required (set out in Part V of this work).

Suitability—See note to r 21.4 above. The court may appoint the person proposed or any other person who complies with the conditions specified in r 21.4(3) (see r 21.8(4)). The Rules express no limit on the power to terminate the appointment, and if the litigation friend acts manifestly contrary to the child or patient's best interests, the court will remove him, even though neither his good faith nor his diligence is in issue (*Re A (Conjoined Twins: Medical Treatment) (No 2)* [2001] 1 FLR 267, CA).

21.8 Appointment of litigation friend by court order – supplementary

(1) An application for an order under rule 21.6 or 21.7 must be served on every person on whom, in accordance with rule 6.6 (service on parent, guardian etc), the claim form should be served.

(2) Where an application for an order under rule 21.6 is in respect of a patient, the application must also be served on the patient unless the court orders otherwise.

(3) An application for an order under rule 21.7 must also be served on –

(*a*) the person who is the litigation friend, or who is purporting to act as the litigation friend, when the application is made; and

(*b*) the person who it is proposed should be the litigation friend, if he is not the applicant.

(4) On an application for an order under rule 21.6 or 21.7, the court may appoint the person proposed or any other person who complies with the conditions specified in rule 21.4(3).

Scope of provision—This rule makes provision for service where a party is a child or patient and supplements r 6.6 in that respect. It also provides that when an application is made to appoint or change a litigation friend the court is not obliged to appoint the person proposed.

Service—Service on the parent or guardian of the child, or the person with whom the patient resides or in whose care he is, is required in all cases (see notes to CCR Ord 10, r 4 for detailed consideration of this). Note that the application under r 21.6 must be served on the patient but this is not a universal provision. Where it is proposed to change the litigation friend both the existing and intended litigation friend must be served.

Who is appointed—The court may decide to appoint any other person who meets the criteria set out in r 21.4(3) and is willing to act.

21.9 Procedure where appointment of litigation friend ceases

(1) When a child who is not a patient reaches the age of 18, a litigation friend's appointment ceases.

(2) When a party ceases to be a patient, the litigation friend's appointment continues until it is ended by a court order.

(3) An application for an order under paragraph (2) may be made by –

(*a*) the former patient;
(*b*) the litigation friend; or
(*c*) a party.

(4) The child or patient in respect of whom the appointment to act has ceased must serve notice on the other parties –

(*a*) stating that the appointment of his litigation friend to act has ceased;
(*b*) giving his address for service; and
(*c*) stating whether or not he intends to carry on the proceedings.

(5) If he does not do so within 28 days after the day on which the appointment of the litigation friend ceases the court may, on application, strike out[GL] any claim or defence brought by him.

(6) The liability of a litigation friend for costs continues until –

(*a*) the person in respect of whom his appointment to act has ceased serves the notice referred to in paragraph (4); or

(*b*) the litigation friend serves notice on the parties that his appointment to act has ceased.

Child—Clearly there will be no need for a litigation friend when the child attains 18 (unless the child is also a patient) and the appointment then ceases automatically. If this party does not then continue the proceedings they may be struck out.

Patient—The position is different in respect of a patient who recovers capacity. This is an unlikely occurrence when the incapacity arises by reason of learning disability, senility or brain damage but it can arise in the case of mental illness. The litigation friend will only be removed by court order following an application and evidence will be required as to capacity. But notice must still be served by the former patient or the proceedings may be struck out.

Costs—The litigation friend of a claimant will have given an indemnity as to costs. This liability continues until notice is served on the other parties either by the claimant or the former litigation friend. It is not clear whether, when discharged, the litigation friend is released from all liability for costs or only costs incurred from that date although it is probably the latter.

21.10 Compromise etc by or on behalf of child or patient

(1) Where a claim is made –

(*a*) by or on behalf of a child or patient; or

(*b*) against a child or patient,

no settlement, compromise or payment and no acceptance of money paid into court shall be valid, so far as it relates to the claim by, on behalf of or against the child or patient, without the approval of the court.

(2) Where –

(*a*) before proceedings in which a claim is made by or on behalf of, or against a child or patient (whether alone or with any other person) are begun, an agreement is reached for the settlement of the claim; and

(*b*) the sole purpose of proceedings on that claim is to obtain the approval of the court to a settlement or compromise of the claim,

the claim must –

(i) be made using the procedure set out in Part 8 (alternative procedure for claims); and

(ii) include a request to the court for approval of the settlement or compromise.

(Rule 48.5 contains provisions about costs where money payable to a child or patient)

Scope of provision—This provision ensures that compromises and settlements negotiated in any proceedings on behalf of children or patients are approved by the court. Without this approval the settlement, compromise or payment of any claim is wholly invalid and unenforceable, and is made entirely at the risk of the parties and their solicitors. It would be an abuse of the process of the court for the parties and their solicitors in any subsisting proceedings to make or act on any such settlement, compromise or payment without the court's approval. This does not prevent the settlement of small claims (eg under £1,000) by payment to parents or carers on the basis of their indemnity and that may be appropriate to avoid disproportionate costs, but there are risks especially if the true value of the claim was not recognised.

Appeals—A decision not to appeal, where permission has been obtained on the express understanding that the possible appellant needs time to consider the matter, and with no consideration moving from the possible respondents, is not a "compromise" and does not require the approval of the court (*Re A (Conjoined Twins: Medical Treatment) (No 2)* [2001] 1 FLR 267, CA).

Role of the Court of Protection—These provisions apply even where the proceedings are being conducted by the patient's receiver as litigation friend under the authority of the Court of Protection, but in that event the approval of the Court of Protection should also be obtained as a pre-requisite to application to the court for approval under this rule.

21.11 Control of money recovered by or on behalf of child or patient

(1) Where in any proceedings –

(*a*) money is recovered by or on behalf of or for the benefit of a child or patient; or

(*b*) money paid into court is accepted by or on behalf of a child or patient, the money shall be dealt with in accordance with directions given by the court under this rule and not otherwise.

(2) Directions given under this rule may provide that the money shall be wholly or partly paid into court and invested or otherwise dealt with.

Scope of provision—This rule ensures that there is supervision of money awarded to or recovered by a child or patient. Further guidance is to be found in *Practice Direction (Children and Patients)* which supplements CPR Part 21 generally (set out in Part V of this work).

Control of money—This subject generally is beyond the scope of this volume. The court will control funds held on behalf of a child but in the case of a patient reference must usually be made to the Court of Protection pursuant to Mental Health Act 1983, Pt VII. If there is a registered attorney under an enduring power it may be appropriate to release the fund to such attorney. The powers of the litigation friend are restricted to the conduct of the proceedings and do not extend to dealing with the financial affairs of the infant or patient.

Monies are usually held in the Court Funds Office which until April 2001 was a division of the Public Trust Office but has now been transferred to the Court Service. The Public Trust Office has itself ceased to exist, with its mental incapacity functions (protection and receivership) being taken over by the new Public Guardianship Office which is the administrative arm of the Court of Protection.

Need for Court of Protection involvement—Someone who is treated as a patient and has a litigation friend does not necessarily need to become a patient of the Court of Protection as that jurisdiction is only exercised when, after considering medical evidence, a nominated judge is satisfied as to the person's incapacity. That judge must consider the totality of the property and affairs of the alleged patient. In civil proceedings a judge does not have to consider medical evidence, or be satisfied as to incapacity, before a person can be treated as a patient and it is only the immediate affairs that are considered (*Masterman-Lister v Brutton & Co and Jewell & Home Counties Dairies* [2002] EWCA Civ 1889, [2002] All ER (D) 297 (Dec)). Conversely, a patient of the Court of Protection will require a litigation friend for civil proceedings.

Additional powers: infant—The court will control funds held on behalf of an infant but under r 21.12 (see below) may appoint the Official Solicitor as guardian of that child's estate.

21.12 Appointment of guardian of child's estate

(1) The court may appoint the Official Solicitor to be a guardian of a child's estate where –

(*a*) money is paid into court on behalf of the child in accordance with directions given under rule 21.11 (control of money received by a child or patient);
(*b*) the Criminal Injuries Compensation Board or the Criminal Injuries Compensation Authority notifies the court that it has made or intends to make an award to the child;
(*c*) a court or tribunal outside England and Wales notifies the court that it has ordered or intends to order that money be paid to the child;
(*d*) the child is absolutely entitled to the proceeds of a pension fund; or
(*e*) in any other case, such an appointment seems desirable to the court.

(2) The court may not appoint the Official Solicitor under this rule unless –

(*a*) the persons with parental responsibility (within the meaning of section 3 of the Children Act 1989) agree; or
(*b*) the court considers that their agreement can be dispensed with.

(3) The Official Solicitor's appointment may continue only until the child reaches 18.

Official Solicitor—The expression means the Official Solicitor to the Supreme Court provided for by Supreme Court Act 1981, s 90. The Official Solicitor may be contacted at 81 Chancery Lane, London WC2A 1DD; Tel: 0171-911-7127, Fax: 0171-911-7105.

PART III

PART 22
STATEMENTS OF TRUTH

Practice Direction—See *Practice Direction (Statements of Truth)* which supplements this Part generally, set out in Section 2 of the *Civil Court Service* (Jordan Publishing Ltd).

22.1 Documents to be verified by a statement of truth

(1) The following documents must be verified by a statement of truth –

(*a*) a statement of case;
(*b*) a response complying with an order under rule 18.1 to provide further information;
(*c*) a witness statement;
(*d*) an acknowledgment of service in a claim begun by way of the Part 8 procedure;
(*e*) a certificate stating the reasons for bringing a possession claim or a landlord and tenant claim in the High Court in accordance with rules 55.3(2) and 56.2(2); and
(*f*) any other document where a rule or practice direction requires.

(2) Where a statement of case is amended, the amendments must be verified by a statement of truth unless the court orders otherwise.

(Part 17 provides for amendments to statements of case)

(3) If an applicant wishes to rely on matters set out in his application notice as evidence, the application notice must be verified by a statement of truth.

(4) Subject to paragraph (5), a statement of truth is a statement that –

(*a*) the party putting forward the document; or
(*b*) in the case of a witness statement, the maker of the witness statement,

believes the facts stated in the document are true.

(5) If a party is conducting proceedings with a litigation friend, the statement of truth in –

(*a*) a statement of case;
(*b*) a response; or
(*c*) an application notice,

is a statement that the litigation friend believes the facts stated in the document being verified are true.

(6) The statement of truth must be signed by –

(*a*) in the case of a statement of case, a response or an application –
(i) the party or litigation friend; or
(ii) the legal representative on behalf of the party or litigation friend; and
(*b*) in the case of a witness statement, the maker of the statement.

(7) A statement of truth which is not contained in the document which it verifies, must clearly identify that document.

(8) A statement of truth in a statement of case may be made by –

(*a*) a person who is not a party; or
(*b*) by two parties jointly,

where this is permitted by a relevant practice direction.

Amendments—SI 2001/256; SI 2001/1388; SI 2001/1769; SI 2001/4015.

****

PART 23
GENERAL RULES ABOUT APPLICATIONS FOR COURT ORDERS

Practice Direction—See *Practice Direction (Applications)* which supplements this Part generally, set out in Part V of this work.

23.1 Meaning of "application notice" and "respondent"

In this Part –

"application notice" means a document in which the applicant states his intention to seek a court order; and
"respondent" means –

(*a*) the person against whom the order is sought; and
(*b*) such other person as the court may direct.

23.2 Where to make an application

(1) The general rule is that an application must be made to the court where the claim was started.

(2) If a claim has been transferred to another court since it was started, an application must be made to the court to which the claim has been transferred.

(3) If the parties have been notified of a fixed date for the trial, an application must be made to the court where the trial is to take place.

(4) If an application is made before a claim has been started, it must be made to the court where it is likely that the claim to which the application relates will be started unless there is good reason to make the application to a different court.

(5) If an application is made after proceedings to enforce judgment have begun, it must be made to any court which is dealing with the enforcement of the judgment unless any rule or practice direction provides otherwise.

23.3 Application notice to be filed

(1) The general rule is that an applicant must file an application notice.

(2) An applicant may make an application without filing an application notice if –

(*a*) this is permitted by a rule or practice direction; or
(*b*) the court dispenses with the requirement for an application notice.

23.4 Notice of an application

(1) The general rule is that a copy of the application notice must be served on each respondent.

(2) An application may be made without serving a copy of the application notice if this is permitted by –

(*a*) a rule;
(*b*) a practice direction; or
(*c*) a court order.

(Rule 23.7 deals with service of a copy of the application notice)

23.5 Time when an application is made

Where an application must be made within a specified time, it is so made if the application notice is received by the court within that time.

23.6 What an application notice must include

An application notice must state –

(*a*) what order the applicant is seeking; and
(*b*) briefly, why the applicant is seeking the order.

(Part 22 requires an application notice to be verified by a statement of truth if the applicant wishes to rely on matters set out in his application notice as evidence)

23.7 Service of a copy of an application notice

(1) A copy of the application notice –

(*a*) must be served as soon as practicable after it is filed; and
(*b*) except where another time limit is specified in these Rules or a practice direction, must in any event be served at least 3 days before the court is to deal with the application.

(2) If a copy of the application notice is to be served by the court, the applicant must, when he files the application notice, file a copy of any written evidence in support.

PART III

(3) When a copy of an application notice is served it must be accompanied by –

(*a*) a copy of any written evidence in support; and
(*b*) a copy of any draft order which the applicant has attached to his application.

(4) If –

(*a*) an application notice is served; but
(*b*) the period of notice is shorter than the period required by these Rules or a practice direction,

the court may direct that, in the circumstances of the case, sufficient notice has been given and hear the application.

(5) This rule does not require written evidence –

(*a*) to be filed if it has already been filed; or
(*b*) to be served on a party on whom it has already been served.

(Part 6 contains the general rules about service of documents including who must serve a copy of the application notice)

23.8 Applications which may be dealt with without a hearing

The court may deal with an application without a hearing if –

(*a*) the parties agree as to the terms of the order sought;
(*b*) the parties agree that the court should dispose of the application without a hearing, or
(*c*) the court does not consider that a hearing would be appropriate.

23.9 Service of application where application made without notice

(1) This rule applies where the court has disposed of an application which it permitted to be made without service of a copy of the application notice.

(2) Where the court makes an order, whether granting or dismissing the application, a copy of the application notice and any evidence in support must, unless the court orders otherwise, be served with the order on any party or other person –

(*a*) against whom the order was made; and
(*b*) against whom the order was sought.

(3) The order must contain a statement of the right to make an application to set aside(GL) or vary the order under rule 23.10.

23.10 Application to set aside or vary order made without notice

(1) A person who was not served with a copy of the application notice before an order was made under rule 23.9, may apply to have the order set aside (GL) or varied.

(2) An application under this rule must be made within 7 days after the date on which the order was served on the person making the application.

Amendments—SI 2000/221.

23.11 Power of the court to proceed in the absence of a party

(1) Where the applicant or any respondent fails to attend the hearing of an application, the court may proceed in his absence.

(2) Where –

(*a*) the applicant or any respondent fails to attend the hearing of an application; and
(*b*) the court makes an order at the hearing,

the court may, on application or of its own initiative, re-list the application.

(Part 40 deals with service of orders)

****

PART 25
INTERIM REMEDIES AND SECURITY FOR COSTS

Practice Direction—See *Practice Direction (Interim Injunctions)* which supplements this Part generally, set out in Part V of this work.

25.1 Orders for interim remedies

(1) The court may grant the following interim remedies –

(*a*) an interim injunction(GL);
(*b*) an interim declaration;
(*c*) an order –
  (i) for the detention, custody or preservation of relevant property;
  (ii) for the inspection of relevant property;
  (iii) for the taking of a sample of relevant property;
  (iv) for the carrying out of an experiment on or with relevant property;
  (v) for the sale of relevant property which is of a perishable nature or which for any other good reason it is desirable to sell quickly; and
  (vi) for the payment of income from relevant property until a claim is decided;
(*d*) an order authorising a person to enter any land or building in the possession of a party to the proceedings for the purposes of carrying out an order under sub-paragraph (*c*);
(*e*) an order under section 4 of the Torts (Interference with Goods) Act 1977 to deliver up goods;
(*f*) an order (referred to as a "freezing injunction(GL)") –
  (i) restraining a party from removing from the jurisdiction assets located there; or
  (ii) restraining a party from dealing with any assets whether located within the jurisdiction or not;
(*g*) an order directing a party to provide information about the location of relevant property or assets or to provide information about relevant property or assets which are or may be the subject of an application for a freezing injunction(GL);
(*h*) an order (referred to as a "search order") under section 7 of the Civil Procedure Act 1997 (order requiring a party to admit another party to premises for the purpose of preserving evidence etc);

(*i*) an order under section 33 of the Supreme Court Act 1981 or section 52 of the County Courts Act 1984 (order for disclosure of documents or inspection of property before a claim has been made);

(*j*) an order under section 34 of the Supreme Court Act 1981 or section 53 of the County Courts Act 1984 (order in certain proceedings for disclosure of documents or inspection of property against a non-party);

(*k*) an order (referred to as an order for interim payment) under rule 25.6 for payment by a defendant on account of any damages, debt or other sum (except costs) which the court may hold the defendant liable to pay;

(*l*) an order for a specified fund to be paid into court or otherwise secured, where there is a dispute over a party's right to the fund;

(*m*) an order permitting a party seeking to recover personal property to pay money into court pending the outcome of the proceedings and directing that, if he does so, the property shall be given up to him;

(*n*) an order directing a party to prepare and file accounts relating to the dispute;

(*o*) an order directing any account to be taken or inquiry to be made by the court.

(Rule 34.2 provides for the court to issue a witness summons requiring a witness to produce documents to the court at the hearing or on such date as the court may direct)

(2) In paragraph (1)(*c*) and (*g*), "relevant property" means property (including land) which is the subject of a claim or as to which any question may arise on a claim.

(3) The fact that a particular kind of interim remedy is not listed in paragraph (1) does not affect any power that the court may have to grant that remedy.

(4) The court may grant an interim remedy whether or not there has been a claim for a final remedy of that kind.

Amendments—SI 2002/2058.

25.2 Time when an order for an interim remedy may be made

(1) An order for an interim remedy may be made at any time, including –

(*a*) before proceedings are started; and

(*b*) after judgment has been given.

(Rule 7.2 provides that proceedings are started when the court issues a claim form)

(2) However –

(*a*) paragraph (1) is subject to any rule, practice direction or other enactment which provides otherwise;

(*b*) the court may grant an interim remedy before a claim has been made only if –

(i) the matter is urgent; or

(ii) it is otherwise desirable to do so in the interests of justice; and

(*c*) unless the court otherwise orders, a defendant may not apply for any of the orders listed in rule 25.1(1) before he has filed either an acknowledgment of service or a defence.

(Part 10 provides for filing an acknowledgment of service and Part 15 for filing a defence)

(3) Where the court grants an interim remedy before a claim has been commenced, it may give directions requiring a claim to be commenced.

(4) In particular, the court need not direct that a claim be commenced where the application is made under section 33 of the Supreme Court Act 1981 or section 52 of the County Courts Act 1984 (order for disclosure, inspection etc before commencement of a claim).

25.3 How to apply for an interim remedy

(1) The court may grant an interim remedy on an application made without notice if it appears to the court that there are good reasons for not giving notice.

(2) An application for an interim remedy must be supported by evidence, unless the court orders otherwise.

(3) If the applicant makes an application without giving notice, the evidence in support of the application must state the reasons why notice has not been given.

(Part 3 lists general powers of the court)

(Part 23 contains general rules about making an application)

25.4 Application for an interim remedy where there is no related claim

(1) This rule applies where a party wishes to apply for an interim remedy but –

(*a*) the remedy is sought in relation to proceedings which are taking place, or will take place, outside the jurisdiction; or

(*b*) the application is made under section 33 of the Supreme Court Act 1981 or section 52 of the County Courts Act 1984 (order for disclosure, inspection etc before commencement) before a claim has been commenced.

(2) An application under this rule must be made in accordance with the general rules about applications contained in Part 23.

(The following provisions are also relevant –

- Rule 25.5 (inspection of property before commencement or against a non-party)
- Rule 31.16 (orders for disclosure of documents before proceedings start)
- Rule 31.17 (orders for disclosure of documents against a person not a party))

****

25.10 Interim injunction to cease if claim is stayed

If –

(*a*) the court has granted an interim injunction(GL) other than a freezing injunction; and

(*b*) the claim is stayed(GL) other than by agreement between the parties, the interim injunction(GL) shall be set aside(GL) unless the court orders that it should continue to have effect even though the claim is stayed.

Amendments—SI 2001/4015.

25.11 Interim injunction to cease after 14 days if claim struck out

(1) If –

(*a*) the court has granted an interim injunction(GL); and
(*b*) the claim is struck out under rule 3.7 (sanctions for non-payment of certain fees),

the interim injunction(GL) shall cease to have effect 14 days after the date that the claim is struck out unless paragraph (2) applies.

(2) If the claimant applies to reinstate the claim before the interim injunction ceases to have effect under paragraph (1), the injunction shall continue until the hearing of the application unless the court orders otherwise.

Amendments—Inserted by SI 1999/1008.

****

PART 30
TRANSFER

Practice Direction—See *Practice Direction (Transfer)* which supplements this Part generally, set out in Section 2 of the *Civil Court Service* (Jordan Publishing Ltd).

30.1 Scope of this Part

This Part deals with the transfer of proceedings between county courts, between the High Court and the county courts and within the High Court.

(Rule 26.2 provides for automatic transfer in certain cases)

30.2 Transfer between county courts and within the High Court

(1) A county court may order proceedings before that court, or any part of them (such as a counterclaim or an application made in the proceedings), to be transferred to another county court if it is satisfied that –

(*a*) an order should be made having regard to the criteria in rule 30.3; or
(*b*) proceedings for –
  (i) the detailed assessment of costs; or
  (ii) the enforcement of a judgment or order,

could be more conveniently or fairly taken in that other county court.

(2) If proceedings have been started in the wrong county court, a judge of the county court may order that the proceedings –

(*a*) be transferred to the county court in which they ought to have been started;
(*b*) continue in the county court in which they have been started; or
(*c*) be struck out.

(3) An application for an order under paragraph (1) or (2) must be made to the county court where the claim is proceeding.

(4) The High Court may, having regard to the criteria in rule 30.3, order proceedings in the Royal Courts of Justice or a district registry, or any part of such proceedings (such as a counterclaim or an application made in the proceedings) to be transferred –

- (*a*) from the Royal Courts of Justice to a district registry; or
- (*b*) from a district registry to the Royal Courts of Justice or to another district registry.

(5) A district registry may order proceedings before it for the detailed assessment of costs to be transferred to another district registry if it is satisfied that the proceedings could be more conveniently or fairly taken in that other district registry.

(6) An application for an order under paragraph (4) or (5) must, if the claim is proceeding in a district registry, be made to that registry.

(7) Where some enactment, other than these Rules, requires proceedings to be started in a particular county court, neither paragraphs (1) nor (2) give the court power to order proceedings to be transferred to a county court which is not the court in which they should have been started or to order them to continue in the wrong court.

(8) Probate proceedings may only be transferred under paragraph (4) to the Chancery Division at the Royal Courts of Justice or to one of the Chancery district registries.

30.3 Criteria for a transfer order

(1) Paragraph (2) sets out the matters to which the court must have regard when considering whether to make an order under –

- (*a*) section 40(2), 41(1) or 42(2) of the County Courts Act 1984 (transfer between the High Court and a county court);
- (*b*) rule 30.2(1) (transfer between county courts); or
- (*c*) rule 30.2(4) (transfer between the Royal Courts of Justice and the district registries).

(2) The matters to which the court must have regard include –

- (*a*) the financial value of the claim and the amount in dispute, if different;
- (*b*) whether it would be more convenient or fair for hearings (including the trial) to be held in some other court;
- (*c*) the availability of a judge specialising in the type of claim in question;
- (*d*) whether the facts, legal issues, remedies or procedures involved are simple or complex;
- (*e*) the importance of the outcome of the claim to the public in general;
- (*f*) the facilities available at the court where the claim is being dealt with and whether they may be inadequate because of any disabilities of a party or potential witness;
- (*g*) whether the making of a declaration of incompatibility under section 4 of the Human Rights Act 1998 has arisen or may arise.

Amendments—SI 2000/2092.

30.4 Procedure

(1) Where the court orders proceedings to be transferred, the court from which they are to be transferred must give notice of the transfer to all the parties.

(2) An order made before the transfer of the proceedings shall not be affected by the order to transfer.

****

30.6 Power to specify place where hearings are to be held

The court may specify the place (for instance, a particular county court) where the trial or some other hearing in any proceedings is to be held and may do so without ordering the proceedings to be transferred.

****

PART 31
DISCLOSURE AND INSPECTION OF DOCUMENTS

Practice Direction—See *Practice Direction (Disclosure and Inspection)* which supplements this Part generally, set out in Part V of this work.

31.1 Scope of this Part

(1) This Part sets out rules about the disclosure and inspection of documents.

(2) This Part applies to all claims except a claim on the small claims track.

31.2 Meaning of disclosure

A party discloses a document by stating that the document exists or has existed.

31.3 Right of inspection of a disclosed document

(1) A party to whom a document has been disclosed has a right to inspect that document except where –

(*a*) the document is no longer in the control of the party who disclosed it;
(*b*) the party disclosing the document has a right or a duty to withhold inspection of it; or
(*c*) paragraph (2) applies.

(Rule 31.8 sets out when a document is in the control of a party)

(Rule 31.19 sets out the procedure for claiming a right or duty to withhold inspection)

(2) Where a party considers that it would be disproportionate to the issues in the case to permit inspection of documents within a category or class of document disclosed under rule 31.6(*b*) –

(*a*) he is not required to permit inspection of documents within that category or class; but
(*b*) he must state in his disclosure statement that inspection of those documents will not be permitted on the grounds that to do so would be disproportionate.

(Rule 31.6 provides for standard disclosure)

(Rule 31.10 makes provision for a disclosure statement)

(Rule 31.12 provides for a party to apply for an order for specific inspection of documents)

Duty of disclosure—The duty to disclose only arises where the court orders disclosure (r 31.5), though the parties may themselves arrange disclosure and inspection in accordance with their duty to further the overriding objective (eg see rr 1.1(2)(*d*) and 1.4(2)(*a*)). Such disclosure will always be subject to further review by the court. Where a party seeks specific disclosure or inspection of documents, application is made under r 31.12, and when he seeks to rely on public interest immunity, application is made under r 31.19.

"duty to withhold inspection" (r 31.3(1)(*b*))—This expression refers to public interest immunity, for which see **Application to withhold disclosure or inspection (public interest immunity)** under r 31.19 below.

Privilege: the "right ... to withhold inspection' (r 31.3(1)(*b*))—This is a reference to the doctrine of "privilege", a word not used in Pt 31, but one recognised by CPR 1998 and defined in the glossary as:

> "The right of a party to refuse to disclose a document or produce a document or to refuse to answer questions on the ground of some special interest recognised by law."

Privilege: categorisation—For a detailed examination of the various forms of privilege see **"documents privileged from production"** under RSC 1965 Ord 24, r 5.

"a party considers that it would be disproportionate to the issues ..." (r 31.3(2))—In the first instance it is for the disclosing party to take a view on whether or not inspection of particular documents is disproportionate. Rule 31.12(3) enables the party who seeks inspection of the documents to apply for an order for "specific inspection".

The position under RSC 1965 Ord 24, r 8 is that discovery sought on application should be refused if the court considers that it is "not necessary either for disposing fairly of the cause or matter or for saving costs". This rule can be equated broadly with the rule of evidence that only material which is relevant to an issue before the court is admissible (Lord Hailsham in his speech in *Livesey (formerly Jenkins) v Jenkins* [1985] AC 424, [1985] FLR 813, HL preferred the term "full relevant disclosure" to the now more common "full and frank disclosure"). The various terminology is considered as follows:

(1) **Relevance** The question of whether or not disclosure should be ordered on grounds of relevance may be regarded as a broader ground than "proportionality". It has been applied to family proceedings, for example, to deny disclosure of documents and information considered to be irrelevant to the issue before the court (*Thyssen-Bornemisza v Thyssen-Bornemisza (No 2)* [1985] FLR 1069, CA: millionaire's defence; the issue before the court was the reasonable needs of the wife not the means of the husband; held he need not disclose) or to refuse disclosure which was regarded by the court as oppressive (*Hildebrand v Hildebrand* [1992] 1 FLR 244, Waite J).

(2) **Standard disclosure** Standard disclosure is defined in rr 31.5 and 31.6. Use of the term "standard" and the setting out of the specific documents referred to in r 31.6 provide for a more restrictive approach to disclosure than the old rules of discovery. If more than standard disclosure is sought, the court will expect a party to go beyond merely establishing the relevance of the documents required. It is likely that the court will need to be satisfied to a higher standard, namely is the request, and compliance with it, proportionate to the issues before the court?

(3) **Proportionality** At this stage, the party disclosing documents will have in mind the principle of "proportionality" within the terms of r 1.1(2)(*c*); in particular "the importance of the case", "the complexity of the issues" involved and the cost to the parties (in the context of the case) of disclosure and inspection of the documents concerned.

31.4 Meaning of document

In this Part –

"document" means anything in which information of any description is recorded; and "copy", in relation to a document, means anything onto which information recorded in the document has been copied, by whatever means and whether directly or indirectly.

"document"—The term "document" includes not only information on paper but also information stored on computer or recorded on video. See further **"documents"** under RSC 1965 Ord 24, r 3.

31.5 Disclosure limited to standard disclosure

(1) An order to give disclosure is an order to give standard disclosure unless the court directs otherwise.

(2) The court may dispense with or limit standard disclosure.

(3) The parties may agree in writing to dispense with or to limit standard disclosure.

(The court may make an order requiring standard disclosure under rule 28.3 which deals with directions in relation to cases on the fast track and under rule 29.2 which deals with case management in relation to cases on the multi-track)

Standard disclosure—Unless otherwise directed by the court, an order "to give disclosure" is to give standard disclosure (as defined by r 31.6). This may be dispensed with or limited by the court and the parties may, themselves, dispense with disclosure.

"parties may agree ... to dispense with or to limit standard disclosure" (r 31.5(3))—In a discretionary jurisdiction, eg as is the case with proceedings under Inheritance (Provision for Family and Dependants) Act 1975, s 3(1) ("the court shall ... have regard to the following matters ..."), the judge is directed by statute to consider certain factors. Thus, it would seem that r 31.5(3) cannot enable the parties to prevent the court, of its own motion, directing them (despite their previous agreement) to produce documents which it needs to see; just as no agreement in the matrimonial ancillary relief jurisdiction can oust the jurisdiction of the court (*Hyman v Hyman* [1929] AC 601, HL). Given this duty, it is likely that the judge would expect to retain ultimate control of disclosure. See also **Discovery in a discretionary jurisdiction** under RSC 1965 Ord 24, r 1.

31.6 Standard disclosure – what documents are to be disclosed

Standard disclosure requires a party to disclose only –

(*a*) the documents on which he relies; and
(*b*) the documents which –
   (i) adversely affect his own case;
   (ii) adversely affect another party's case; or
   (iii) support another party's case; and
(*c*) the documents which he is required to disclose by a relevant practice direction.

Scope of provision—Standard disclosure is limited to the documents set out in this rule. It is further limited to documents "which are or have been in a party's control" (r 31.8). However, a party must make a "reasonable search" for documents which adversely affect his case (r 31.7(1)).

31.7 Duty of search

(1) When giving standard disclosure, a party is required to make a reasonable search for documents falling within rule 31.6(*b*) or (*c*).

(2) The factors relevant in deciding the reasonableness of a search include the following –

(*a*) the number of documents involved;
(*b*) the nature and complexity of the proceedings;
(*c*) the ease and expense of retrieval of any particular document; and
(*d*) the significance of any document which is likely to be located during the search.

(3) Where a party has not searched for a category or class of document on the grounds that to do so would be unreasonable, he must state this in his disclosure statement and identify the category or class of document.

(Rule 31.10 makes provision for a disclosure statement)

31.8 Duty of disclosure limited to documents which are or have been in party's control

(1) A party's duty to disclose documents is limited to documents which are or have been in his control.

(2) For this purpose a party has or has had a document in his control if –

(*a*) it is or was in his physical possession;
(*b*) he has or has had a right to possession of it; or
(*c*) he has or has had a right to inspect or take copies of it.

Scope of provision—This rule restricts disclosure to those documents which are or have been in a party's control and should be read alongside r 31.6 which defines those documents which should be produced. It was intended that this would achieve disclosure "in a more limited form" (*Access to Justice: Final Report* by Lord Woolf MR, (July 1996, HMSO) Section III para 37, p 124) than under RSC 1965 Ord 24, r 1(1) ("documents which are or have been in [a party's] possession, custody or power").

31.9 Disclosure of copies

(1) A party need not disclose more than one copy of a document.

(2) A copy of a document that contains a modification, obliteration or other marking or feature –

(*a*) on which a party intends to rely; or
(*b*) which adversely affects his own case or another party's case or supports another party's case;

shall be treated as a separate document.

(Rule 31.4 sets out the meaning of a copy of a document)

31.10 Procedure for standard disclosure

(1) The procedure for standard disclosure is as follows.

(2) Each party must make, and serve on every other party, a list of documents in the relevant practice form.

(3) The list must identify the documents in a convenient order and manner and as concisely as possible.

(4) The list must indicate –

(*a*) those documents in respect of which the party claims a right or duty to withhold inspection; and
(*b*) (i) those documents which are no longer in the party's control; and

(ii) what has happened to those documents.

(Rule 31.19(3) and (4) require a statement in the list of documents relating to any documents inspection of which a person claims he has a right or duty to withhold)

(5) The list must include a disclosure statement.

(6) A disclosure statement is a statement made by the party disclosing the documents –

(*a*) setting out the extent of the search that has been made to locate documents which he is required to disclose;
(*b*) certifying that he understands the duty to disclose documents; and
(*c*) certifying that to the best of his knowledge he has carried out that duty.

(7) Where the party making the disclosure statement is a company, firm, association or other organisation, the statement must also –

(*a*) identify the person making the statement; and
(*b*) explain why he is considered an appropriate person to make the statement.

(8) The parties may agree in writing –

(*a*) to disclose documents without making a list; and
(*b*) to disclose documents without the disclosing party making a disclosure statement.

(9) A disclosure statement may be made by a person who is not a party where this is permitted by a relevant practice direction.

Scope of provision—Each party must prepare and serve on other parties (but not file at court) a list in the prescribed form, indicating which documents he has and which he claims the right or duty not to disclose. If necessary, the reasons why documents are no longer in a party's control must be explained. The list must have a signed disclosure statement. Parties may agree to disclose without making a list.

"a list of documents in the relevant practice form" (r 31.10(2))—The relevant form is PF N265.

"right or duty to withhold inspection" (r 31.10(4)(*a*))—See commentary on this subject under rr 31.3 and 31.19. If a party wishes to claim the right to withhold he must set out the grounds for so doing (*Practice Direction (Disclosure and Inspection)*, para 4.5).

"disclosure statement" (r 31.10(5)–(7))—A disclosure statement which complies with r 31.10(6) and (7) is set out in the Annex to *Practice Direction (Disclosure and Inspection)*, and certain other requirements are set out in paras 4.2–4.6 of the *Practice Direction*.

31.11 Duty of disclosure continues during proceedings

(1) Any duty of disclosure continues until the proceedings are concluded.

(2) If documents to which that duty extends come to a party's notice at any time during the proceedings, he must immediately notify every other party.

"until the proceedings are concluded" (r 31.11(1))—The reference to the conclusion of proceedings may be taken to include the completion of any appeal (*Vernon v Bosley (No 2)* [1998] 1 FLR 304, [1997] 3 WLR 683, CA – this case also deals with the important duty of legal advisers and of the parties themselves not to mislead the court by their failure to disclose).

Supplemental list—Where documents within the terms of this rule come to light a supplemental list must be prepared (*Practice Direction (Disclosure and Inspection)*, para 3.3) unless such a list can be dispensed with under r 31.10(8).

31.12 Specific disclosure or inspection

(1) The court may make an order for specific disclosure or specific inspection.

(2) An order for specific disclosure is an order that a party must do one or more of the following things –

(*a*) disclose documents or classes of documents specified in the order;
(*b*) carry out a search to the extent stated in the order;
(*c*) disclose any documents located as a result of that search.

(3) An order for specific inspection is an order that a party permit inspection of a document referred to in rule 31.3(2).

(Rule 31.3(2) allows a party to state in his disclosure statement that he will not permit inspection of a document on the grounds that it would be disproportionate to do so)

Application for specific disclosure or inspection—An application for an order for specific disclosure/inspection is made in accordance with Pt 23. The application should state the order applied for (r 23.6(*a*) – ie one or more of the orders set out in r 31.12(2) and (3)) and must be supported by a statement of evidence (and see *Practice Direction (Applications)*, para 9.1 which reminds parties that "the court will often need to be satisfied by evidence of the facts that are relied on in support of or for opposing the application"). Grounds for the application may be in the application notice but a statement of evidence should also be filed setting out which documents are sought and why (*Practice Direction (Disclosure and Inspection)*, para 5.3). In particular, an application for specific inspection will need to deal with the respondent's assertion that inspection is "disproportionate to the issues" (r 31.3(2)).

Proportionality and relevance—All orders for disclosure are governed by the overriding objective in Pt 1 (*Practice Direction (Disclosure and Inspection)*, para 5.4). The court should bear in mind the need for "saving expense" (r 1.1(2)(*b*)) and that orders for disclosure or inspection should be proportionate "to the complexity of the issues" in the case (r 1.1(2)(*c*)(iii)). Disclosure and inspection will always be subject to the fundamental rule of evidence that material is only admissible where relevant to the issues before the court (*Thyssen-Bornemisza v Thyssen-Bornemisza (No 2)* [1985] FLR 1069, CA). The court retains its equitable jurisdiction to refuse disclosure or inspection on the ground that to order it would be oppressive (*Hildebrand v Hildebrand* [1992] 1 FLR 244, Waite J). In considering disclosure under this rule, Lord Woolf suggested (*Access to Justice: Final Report* by Lord Woolf MR, (July 1996, HMSO) Section III para 40, p 125):

"When ordering extra disclosure, the court would have to be satisfied not only that it was necessary to do justice but that the cost of such disclosure would not be disproportionate to the benefit and that a party's ability to continue the litigation would not be impaired by an order for specific disclosure against him."

31.13 Disclosure in stages

The parties may agree in writing, or the court may direct, that disclosure or inspection or both shall take place in stages.

31.14 Documents referred to in statements of case etc

(1) A party may inspect a document mentioned in –

(*a*) a statement of case;
(*b*) a witness statement;
(*c*) a witness summary; or
(*d*) an affidavit(GL).
(*e*) (*revoked*)

(2) Subject to rule 35.10(4), a party may apply for an order for inspection of any document mentioned in an expert's report which has not already been disclosed in the proceedings.

(Rule 35.10(4) makes provision in relation to instructions referred to in an expert's report)

Amendments—SI 2001/4015.

31.15 Inspection and copying of documents

Where a party has a right to inspect a document –

(*a*) that party must give the party who disclosed the document written notice of his wish to inspect it;

(*b*) the party who disclosed the document must permit inspection not more than 7 days after the date on which he received the notice; and

(*c*) that party may request a copy of the document and, if he also undertakes to pay reasonable copying costs, the party who disclosed the document must supply him with a copy not more than 7 days after the date on which he received the request.

(Rule 31.3 and 31.14 deal with the right of a party to inspect a document)

****

31.19 Claim to withhold inspection or disclosure of a document

(1) A person may apply, without notice, for an order permitting him to withhold disclosure of a document on the ground that disclosure would damage the public interest.

(2) Unless the court orders otherwise, an order of the court under paragraph (1) –

(*a*) must not be served on any other person; and
(*b*) must not be open to inspection by any person.

(3) A person who wishes to claim that he has a right or a duty to withhold inspection of a document, or part of a document must state in writing –

(*a*) that he has such a right or duty; and
(*b*) the grounds on which he claims that right or duty.

(4) The statement referred to in paragraph (3) must be made –

(*a*) in the list in which the document is disclosed; or
(*b*) if there is no list, to the person wishing to inspect the document.

(5) A party may apply to the court to decide whether a claim made under paragraph (3) should be upheld.

(6) For the purpose of deciding an application under paragraph (1) (application to withhold disclosure) or paragraph (3) (claim to withhold inspection) the court may –

(*a*) require the person seeking to withhold disclosure or inspection of a document to produce that document to the court; and
(*b*) invite any person, whether or not a party, to make representations.

(7) An application under paragraph (1) or paragraph (5) must be supported by evidence.

(8) This Part does not affect any rule of law which permits or requires a document to be withheld from disclosure or inspection on the ground that its disclosure or inspection would damage the public interest.

Scope of provision—This rule deals both with the withholding of disclosure and the withholding of inspection of documents. A party may apply, without notice, to withhold disclosure on the ground that it would damage the public interest (public interest immunity). Any order made is not to be served on another party or to be open to inspection, unless the court so orders. Any claim to withhold inspection must be included in the party's list of documents, with grounds set out, and any such claim may be referred to the court for verification. The judge may require production of the documents to the court.

Application to withhold disclosure or inspection (public interest immunity) (r 31.19(1), (5))—An application for an order to withhold disclosure on grounds of public interest immunity or to withhold inspection is made under Pt 23. The application should state the order applied for (r 23.6(*a*) – ie an order under either r 31.19(1) or r 31.19(5)). In either case, the application must be supported by evidence (r 31.19(7)) and state the reasons for asserting public interest immunity or any other ground why documents are considered to be exempt from inspection.

Public interest immunity: the test for disclosure—See **Disclosure injurious to public interest** under RSC 1965 Ord 24, r 5.

PART III

31.20 Restriction on use of a privileged document inspection of which has been inadvertently allowed

Where a party inadvertently allows a privileged(GL) document to be inspected, the party who has inspected the document may use it or its contents only with the permission of the court.

31.21 Consequence of failure to disclose documents or permit inspection

A party may not rely on any document which he fails to disclose or in respect of which he fails to permit inspection unless the court gives permission.

31.22 Subsequent use of disclosed documents

(1) A party to whom a document has been disclosed may use the document only for the purpose of the proceedings in which it is disclosed, except where –

(*a*) the document has been read to or by the court, or referred to, at a hearing which has been held in public;
(*b*) the court gives permission; or
(*c*) the party who disclosed the document and the person to whom the document belongs agree.

(2) The court may make an order restricting or prohibiting the use of a document which has been disclosed, even where the document has been read to or by the court, or referred to, at a hearing which has been held in public.

(3) An application for such an order may be made –

(*a*) by a party; or
(*b*) by any person to whom the document belongs.

31.23 False disclosure statements

(1) Proceedings for contempt of court may be brought against a person if he makes, or causes to be made, a false disclosure statement, without an honest belief in its truth.

(2) Proceedings under this rule may be brought only –

(*a*) by the Attorney-General; or
(*b*) with the permission of the court.

Amendments—Inserted by SI 2000/221.

PART 32
EVIDENCE

Practice Direction—See *Practice Direction (Written Evidence)* which supplements this Part generally, set out in Part V of this work.

32.1 Power of court to control evidence

(1) The court may control the evidence by giving directions as to –

(*a*) the issues on which it requires evidence;
(*b*) the nature of the evidence which it requires to decide those issues; and
(*c*) the way in which the evidence is to be placed before the court.

(2) The court may use its power under this rule to exclude evidence that would otherwise be admissible.

(3) The court may limit cross-examination(GL).

"The court may control the evidence" (r 32.1(1))—It is doubtful whether the court has power to control evidence in the way described here, other than by reference to its powers under the overriding objective.

"its power under this rule to exclude evidence" (r 32.1(2))—This sub-rule is arguably *ultra vires*, if it is intended to enable the court to exclude admissible evidence (which is what it appears to say). The nearest the Civil Procedure Act 1997 (under which these rules are made) comes to a provision which could confer a power to enact this rule is Sch 1, para 4 which reads: "Civil Procedure Rules may modify the rules of evidence as they apply to proceedings in any court within the scope of the rules". To modify rules of evidence is one thing. To deny a party their right to adduce admissible evidence (subject to proportionality and permission in the case of expert evidence) is quite another. The *vires* of the rule can be challenged before the individual court, should the need arise.

"may limit cross-examination" (r 32.1(3))—The court probably has power to limit time spent in cross-examination, but to limit it altogether would be *ultra vires*. There is no provision in the Civil Procedure Act 1997 conferring a power to make rules which completely exclude cross-examination.

32.2 Evidence of witnesses – general rule

(1) The general rule is that any fact which needs to be proved by the evidence of witnesses is to be proved –

(*a*) at trial, by their oral evidence given in public; and
(*b*) at any other hearing, by their evidence in writing.

(2) This is subject –

(*a*) to any provision to the contrary contained in these Rules or elsewhere; or (*b*) to any order of the court.

Scope of provision—This rule mirrors RSC Ord 38, r 1 and gives prominence to oral evidence in open court at trial. This, however, is the "general rule" and may be displaced by court order. At all other hearings (eg under Pt 23), the general rule is that evidence should be in writing (and see r 32.6 below).

"evidence ... at trial ... given in public' (r 32.2(1)(*a*))—Rule 39.2 deals with hearings in public and the circumstances where a hearing may be held in private. In *Clibbery v Allan* [2002] EWCA Civ 45, [2002] 1 FLR 565, the Court of Appeal explained the different circumstances in which the court might hold family proceedings in open court, in private and in secret (now "confidential"): see Table set out at the front of this work, following the calendars.

"evidence in writing" (r 32.2(1)(*b*))—Evidence at hearings other than the trial (eg at interim hearings or Pt 23 applications) will be in writing, ie statements of case and witness statements, which must be accompanied by a statement of truth (Pt 22) and affidavits. This is the general rule, and therefore may be displaced by order of the court (and see r 32.2(2)(*b*)).

32.3 Evidence by video link or other means

The court may allow a witness to give evidence through a video link or by other means.

Video link and the overriding objective—This rule is consistent with the overriding objective; see r 1.4(2)(*k*) which provides that case management includes "making use of technology" and r 3.1(2)(*d*) which enables the court to "receive evidence by telephone or by using any other method of direct oral communication".

32.4 Requirement to serve witness statements for use at trial

(1) A witness statement is a written statement signed by a person which contains the evidence which that person would be allowed to give orally.

(2) The court will order a party to serve on the other parties any witness statement of the oral evidence which the party serving the statement intends to rely on in relation to any issues of fact to be decided at the trial.

(3) The court may give directions as to –

(*a*) the order in which witness statements are to be served; and
(*b*) whether or not the witness statements are to be filed.

Witness statements—Witness statements, as stipulated by r 32.8, must comply with the requirements of *Practice Direction (Written Evidence)*, paras 17.1–22.2. Hearsay evidence in witness statements is dealt with in r 33.2.

32.5 Use at trial of witness statements which have been served

(1) If –

(*a*) a party has served a witness statement; and
(*b*) he wishes to rely at trial on the evidence of the witness who made the statement,

he must call the witness to give oral evidence unless the court orders otherwise or he puts the statement in as hearsay evidence.

(Part 33 contains provisions about hearsay evidence)

PART III

(2) Where a witness is called to give oral evidence under paragraph (1), his witness statement shall stand as his evidence in chief (GL) unless the court orders otherwise.

(3) A witness giving oral evidence at trial may with the permission of the court –

(*a*) amplify his witness statement; and
(*b*) give evidence in relation to new matters which have arisen since the witness statement was served on the other parties.

(4) The court will give permission under paragraph (3) only if it considers that there is good reason not to confine the evidence of the witness to the contents of his witness statement.

(5) If a party who has served a witness statement does not –

(*a*) call the witness to give evidence at trial; or
(*b*) put the witness statement in as hearsay evidence,

any other party may put the witness statement in as hearsay evidence.

Scope of provision—Witnesses who have filed a statement must be available for cross-examination unless the court otherwise directs or the statement is put in as hearsay. The statement stands as their evidence-in-chief, though it can be elaborated upon and updated with the court's permission. Where a witness is not called, another party can use the statement as hearsay evidence.

"statement in as hearsay evidence" (r 32.5(1))—Hearsay notices are dealt with in r 33.2.

32.6 Evidence in proceedings other than at trial

(1) Subject to paragraph (2), the general rule is that evidence at hearings other than the trial is to be by witness statement unless the court, a practice direction or any other enactment requires otherwise.

(2) At hearings other than the trial, a party may rely on the matters set out in –

(*a*) his statement of case; or
(*b*) his application notice,

if the statement of case or application notice is verified by a statement of truth.

Amendments—SI 2000/221.

"hearings other than the trial" (r 32.6(1), (2))—This refers primarily to Pt 23 applications. Interim remedy applications under Pt 25 will, by definition, be hearings other than the trial (and see *Practice Direction (Interim Injunctions)*, paras 3.1–3.3).

Committal applications—Such applications must be supported by affidavit evidence. However, a respondent may give oral evidence (in which case he may be cross-examined) and may call oral evidence from a witness (*Practice Direction (Committal Applications)*, paras 3.3, 3.4).

32.7 Order for cross-examination

(1) Where, at a hearing other than the trial, evidence is given in writing, any party may apply to the court for permission to cross-examine the person giving the evidence.

(2) If the court gives permission under paragraph (1) but the person in question does not attend as required by the order, his evidence may not be used unless the court gives permission.

32.8 Form of witness statement

A witness statement must comply with the requirements set out in the relevant practice direction.

(Part 22 requires a witness statement to be verified by a statement of truth)

"requirements set out in the relevant practice direction"—See *Practice Direction (Written Evidence)*, paras 17.1–19.2 which deal with such matters as how the statement should be set out, formalities as to the content thereof etc.

32.9 Witness summaries

(1) A party who –

(*a*) is required to serve a witness statement for use at trial; but
(*b*) is unable to obtain one,

may apply, without notice, for permission to serve a witness summary instead.

(2) A witness summary is a summary of –

(*a*) the evidence, if known, which would otherwise be included in a witness statement; or
(*b*) if the evidence is not known, the matters about which the party serving the witness summary proposes to question the witness.

(3) Unless the court orders otherwise, a witness summary must include the name and address of the intended witness.

(4) Unless the court orders otherwise, a witness summary must be served within the period in which a witness statement would have had to be served.

(5) Where a party serves a witness summary, so far as practicable, rules 32.4 (requirement to serve witness statements for use at trial), 32.5(3) (amplifying witness statements), and 32.8 (form of witness statement) shall apply to the summary.

32.10 Consequence of failure to serve witness statement or summary

If a witness statement or a witness summary for use at trial is not served in respect of an intended witness within the time specified by the court, then the witness may not be called to give oral evidence unless the court gives permission.

32.11 Cross-examination on a witness statement

Where a witness is called to give evidence at trial, he may be cross-examined on his witness statement, whether or not the statement or any part of it was referred to during the witness's evidence in chief[(GL)].

32.12 Use of witness statements for other purposes

(1) Except as provided by this rule, a witness statement may be used only for the purpose of the proceedings in which it is served.

(2) Paragraph (1) does not apply if and to the extent that –

(*a*) the witness gives consent in writing to some other use of it;
(*b*) the court gives permission for some other use; or

(*c*) the witness statement has been put in evidence at a hearing held in public.

Scope of provision—In general, a witness statement may only be used in the proceedings to which it relates. However, a witness may agree, or the court direct, that the statement be used for another purpose. Once a trial has taken place, the statement is in the public domain but if a case settles, or a witness is not called, the statement cannot be used for other purposes, save where r 32.12(2)(*a*) and (*b*) apply.

32.13 Availability of witness statements for inspection

(1) A witness statement which stands as evidence in chief(GL) is open to inspection during the course of the trial unless the court otherwise directs.

(2) Any person may ask for a direction that a witness statement is not open to inspection.

(3) The court will not make a direction under paragraph (2) unless it is satisfied that a witness statement should not be open to inspection because of –

(*a*) the interests of justice;
(*b*) the public interest;
(*c*) the nature of any expert medical evidence in the statement;
(*d*) the nature of any confidential information (including information relating to personal financial matters) in the statement; or
(*e*) the need to protect the interests of any child or patient.

(4) The court may exclude from inspection words or passages in the statement.

Amendments—SI 2001/256.

32.14 False statements

(1) Proceedings for contempt of court may be brought against a person if he makes, or causes to be made, a false statement in a document verified by a statement of truth without an honest belief in its truth.

(Part 22 makes provision for a statement of truth)

(2) Proceedings under this rule may be brought only –

(*a*) by the Attorney General; or
(*b*) with the permission of the court.

32.15 Affidavit evidence

(1) Evidence must be given by affidavit(GL), instead of or in addition to a witness statement if this is required by the court, a provision contained in any other Rule, a practice direction or any other enactment.

(2) Nothing in these Rules prevents a witness giving evidence by affidavit(GL) at a hearing other than the trial if he chooses to do so in a case where paragraph (1) does not apply, but the party putting forward the affidavit(GL) may not recover the additional cost of making it from any other party unless the court orders otherwise.

Scope of provision—The object of the rules is to make the use of affidavits less frequent than before. However, particular applications may require affidavit evidence – eg applications for freezing injunctions/search orders (*Practice Direction (Interim Injunctions)*, para 3.1) and applications for committal (*Practice Direction (Committal Applications)*, para 3.1).

32.16 Form of affidavits

An affidavit(GL) must comply with the requirements set out in the relevant practice direction.

"relevant practice direction"—See *Practice Direction (Written Evidence)*, paras 2–10.2.

32.17 Affidavit made outside the jurisdiction

A person may make an affidavit(GL) outside the jurisdiction in accordance with –

(*a*) this Part; or
(*b*) the law of the place where he makes the affidavit(GL).

32.18 Notice to admit facts

(1) A party may serve notice on another party requiring him to admit the facts, or the part of the case of the serving party, specified in the notice.

(2) A notice to admit facts must be served no later than 21 days before the trial.

(3) Where the other party makes any admission in response to the notice the admission may be used against him only –

(*a*) in the proceedings in which the notice to admit is served; and
(*b*) by the party who served the notice.

(4) The court may allow a party to amend or withdraw any admission made by him on such terms as it thinks just.

Scope of provision—This rule, derived broadly from RSC Ord 27, r 2 and CCR Ord 20, r 2, enables a party to give notice to another to admit facts. Any admission can only be used in the proceedings to which it relates and cannot create any form of estoppel. An admission can be amended or withdrawn on such terms as the court directs.

Costs consequences of failing to admit facts later proved—RSC Ord 62, r 6(7) provided that costs followed automatically where a notice to admit facts did not draw an admission, and the party giving notice then had to prove the facts alleged in the notice. Rule 44.3 (factors to be taken into account by the court when exercising its discretion as to the award of costs) is by no means as categoric in this regard and the party who serves the notice can only ask that the non-admission be taken into account by the court as an aspect of conduct, ie "the manner in which a party has ... defended his case or a particular allegation or issue" (r 44.3(5)(*c*)).

32.19 Notice to admit or produce documents

(1) A party shall be deemed to admit the authenticity of a document disclosed to him under Part 31 (disclosure and inspection of documents) unless he serves notice that he wishes the document to be proved at trial.

(2) A notice to prove a document must be served –

(*a*) by the latest date for serving witness statements; or
(*b*) within 7 days of disclosure of the document,

whichever is later.

Scope of provision—The heading to this rule is misleading, since the rule provides for a presumption that a party admits that any disclosed document is authentic unless notice is given for the document to be produced at trial within the time limits set out in r 32.19(2).

PART 33
MISCELLANEOUS RULES ABOUT EVIDENCE

Practice Direction—See *Practice Direction (Civil Evidence Act 1995)* which supplements this Part generally, set out in Section 2 of the *Civil Court Service* (Jordan Publishing Ltd).

33.1 Introductory

In this Part –

(*a*) "hearsay" means a statement, made otherwise than by a person while giving oral evidence in proceedings, which is tendered as evidence of the matters stated; and

(*b*) references to hearsay include hearsay of whatever degree.

Definition of "hearsay"—This definition is taken verbatim from Civil Evidence Act 1995, s 1(2). Hearsay evidence in children proceedings is dealt with by Children (Admissibility of Hearsay Evidence) Order 1993.

33.2 Notice of intention to rely on hearsay evidence

(1) Where a party intends to rely on hearsay evidence at trial and either –

(*a*) that evidence is to be given by a witness giving oral evidence; or

(*b*) that evidence is contained in a witness statement of a person who is not being called to give oral evidence;

that party complies with section 2(1)(*a*) of the Civil Evidence Act 1995 by serving a witness statement on the other parties in accordance with the court's order.

(2) Where paragraph (1)(*b*) applies, the party intending to rely on the hearsay evidence must, when he serves the witness statement –

(*a*) inform the other parties that the witness is not being called to give oral evidence; and

(*b*) give the reason why the witness will not be called.

(3) In all other cases where a party intends to rely on hearsay evidence at trial, that party complies with section 2(1)(*a*) of the Civil Evidence Act 1995 by serving a notice on the other parties which –

(*a*) identifies the hearsay evidence;

(*b*) states that the party serving the notice proposes to rely on the hearsay evidence at trial; and

(*c*) gives the reason why the witness will not be called.

(4) The party proposing to rely on the hearsay evidence must –

(*a*) serve the notice no later than the latest date for serving witness statements; and

(*b*) if the hearsay evidence is to be in a document, supply a copy to any party who requests him to do so.

Intention to rely on hearsay evidence—Notice of an intention to rely on hearsay evidence in a statement can be given by a party serving the statement. Where the witness is not to be called to give evidence, this must be stated when the statement is served and reasons should be given for the non-appearance. If hearsay is to be adduced by other means, notice is given by identifying the evidence, stating that it is to be relied upon and giving reasons for the non-appearance of any witness. The notice must be served no later than the latest time at which a statement could be served. A copy of any relevant document should be provided if requested.

Civil Evidence Act 1995, s 2(1)(*a*)—This provision deals with notice to adduce hearsay evidence. Section 2(1) requires a party who intends to rely on hearsay evidence to give notice of that fact and "on request to give such particulars of or relating to the evidence, as is reasonable and practicable in the circumstances".

"in accordance with the court's order" (r 33.2(1))—Rule 32.4(2) provides the court with the power to order the stage in proceedings at which statements are to filed and served.

Document—Hearsay evidence may be included in a document, in which case a copy of it must be produced if requested (r 33.2(4)(*b*)). By virtue of Civil Evidence Act 1995, s 13 "document" is defined as including "anything in which information of any description is recorded". It is reasonable to assume that courts will adopt a similar definition for documents in Pt 33. It is not easy to imagine any form of hearsay, other that oral evidence, which could be included in any medium other than a document as defined by s 13. If hearsay is contained in a film or a video recording this will be a document and the party who seeks to rely on it must be prepared to supply a copy, if requested to do so by another party (r 33.2(4)(*b*)).

Weight of hearsay evidence—Even where notice is correctly given in accordance with Civil Evidence Act 1995, s 2(1) and this rule, it remains the case that the court must consider the cogency of any hearsay evidence. Accordingly, CEA 1995, s 4(1) provides that "the court shall have regard to any circumstances from which any inference can reasonably be drawn as to the reliability or otherwise of the evidence", and s 4(2) provides a checklist for the court in its consideration of the weight to be accorded to the evidence.

PART III

33.3 Circumstances in which notice of intention to rely on hearsay evidence is not required

Section 2(1) of the Civil Evidence Act 1995 (duty to give notice of intention to rely on hearsay evidence) does not apply –

(*a*) to evidence at hearings other than trials;
(*aa*) to an affidavit or witness statement which is to be used at trial but which does not contain hearsay evidence;
(*b*) to a statement which a party to a probate action wishes to put in evidence and which is alleged to have been made by the person whose estate is the subject of the proceedings; or
(*c*) where the requirement is excluded by a practice direction.

Amendments—SI 1999/1008.

Scope of provision—This rule is made pursuant to Civil Evidence Act 1995, s 2(2) which enables rules to be made "specifying classes of proceedings or evidence to which [s 2(1)] does not apply".

"hearings other than trials" (r 33.3(*a*))—It will not be necessary to give notice of an intention to rely on hearsay evidence at a hearing other than the trial, ie interlocutory (Pt 23) and interim remedies (Pt 25) applications. Even though notice need not be given, the court will still need to have regard to the cogency of the evidence (and see under r 33.2 (above)).

33.4 Power to call witness for cross-examination on hearsay evidence

(1) Where a party –

(*a*) proposes to rely on hearsay evidence; and
(*b*) does not propose to call the person who made the original statement to give oral evidence,

the court may, on the application of any other party, permit that party to call the maker of the statement to be cross-examined on the contents of the statement.

(2) An application for permission to cross-examine under this rule must be made not more than 14 days after the day on which a notice of intention to rely on the hearsay evidence was served on the applicant.

Scope of provision—Pursuant to Civil Evidence Act 1995, s 3, this rule enables a party, with the court's permission, to cross-examine the maker of a statement containing hearsay even though the other party does not intend to call the witness before the court. Cross-examination is limited to "the contents of the statement".

33.5 Credibility

(1) Where a party –

(*a*) proposes to rely on hearsay evidence; but

(*b*) does not propose to call the person who made the original statement to give oral evidence; and

(*c*) another party wishes to call evidence to attack the credibility of the person who made the statement,

the party who so wishes must give notice of his intention to the party who proposes to give the hearsay statement in evidence.

(2) A party must give notice under paragraph (1) not more than 14 days after the day on which a hearsay notice relating to the hearsay evidence was served on him.

Scope of provision—Where a party intends to question the credibility of the maker of a statement containing hearsay, that party must give notice of his intention so to do. Presumably the party who served the statement has the option, where possible, to call the witness whose credibility is attacked.

33.6 Use of plans, photographs and models as evidence

(1) This rule applies to evidence (such as a plan, photograph or model) which is not –

(*a*) contained in a witness statement, affidavit(GL) or expert's report;

(*b*) to be given orally at trial; or

(*c*) evidence of which prior notice must be given under rule 33.2.

(2) This rule includes documents which may be received in evidence without further proof under section 9 of the Civil Evidence Act 1995.

(3) Unless the court orders otherwise the evidence shall not be receivable at a trial unless the party intending to put it in evidence has given notice to the other parties in accordance with this rule.

(4) Where the party intends to use the evidence as evidence of any fact then, except where paragraph (6) applies, he must give notice not later than the latest date for serving witness statements.

(5) He must give notice at least 21 days before the hearing at which he proposes to put in the evidence, if –

(*a*) there are not to be witness statements; or

(*b*) he intends to put in the evidence solely in order to disprove an allegation made in a witness statement.

(6) Where the evidence forms part of expert evidence, he must give notice when the expert's report is served on the other party.

(7) Where the evidence is being produced to the court for any reason other than as part of factual or expert evidence, he must give notice at least 21 days before the hearing at which he proposes to put in the evidence.

(8) Where a party has given notice that he intends to put in the evidence, he must give every other party an opportunity to inspect it and to agree to its admission without further proof.

33.7 Evidence of finding on question of foreign law

(1) This rule sets out the procedure which must be followed by a party who intends to put in evidence a finding on a question of foreign law by virtue of section 4(2) of the Civil Evidence Act 1972.

(2) He must give any other party notice of his intention.

(3) He must give the notice –

(*a*) if there are to be witness statements, not later than the latest date for serving them; or
(*b*) otherwise, not less than 21 days before the hearing at which he proposes to put the finding in evidence.

(4) The notice must –

(*a*) specify the question on which the finding was made; and
(*b*) enclose a copy of a document where it is reported or recorded.

33.8 Evidence of consent of trustee to act

A document purporting to contain the written consent of a person to act as trustee and to bear his signature verified by some other person is evidence of such consent.

33.9 Human Rights

(1) This rule applies where a claim is –

(*a*) for a remedy under section 7 of the Human Rights Act 1998 in respect of a judicial act which is alleged to have infringed the claimant's Article 5 Convention rights; and
(*b*) based on a finding by a court or tribunal that the claimant's Convention rights have been infringed.

(2) The court hearing the claim –

(*a*) may proceed on the basis of the finding of that other court or tribunal that there has been an infringement but it is not required to do so, and
(*b*) may reach its own conclusion in the light of that finding and of the evidence heard by that other court or tribunal.

Amendments—Inserted by SI 2000/2092.

PART 34
WITNESSES, DEPOSITIONS AND EVIDENCE FOR FOREIGN COURTS

Practice Direction—See *Practice Direction (Depositions and Court Attendance by Witnesses)* which supplements this Part generally, set out in Section 2 of the *Civil Court Service* (Jordan Publishing Ltd).

I Witnesses and Depositions

34.1 Scope of this Part

(1) This Section of this Part provides –

(*a*) for the circumstances in which a person may be required to attend court to give evidence or to produce a document; and
(*b*) for a party to obtain evidence before a hearing to be used at the hearing.

(2) In this Section, reference to a hearing includes a reference to the trial.

Amendments—SI 2002/2058.

34.2 Witness summonses

(1) A witness summons is a document issued by the court requiring a witness to –

(*a*) attend court to give evidence; or
(*b*) produce documents to the court.

(2) A witness summons must be in the relevant practice form.

(3) There must be a separate witness summons for each witness.

(4) A witness summons may require a witness to produce documents to the court either –

(*a*) on the date fixed for a hearing; or
(*b*) on such date as the court may direct.

(5) The only documents that a summons under this rule can require a person to produce before a hearing are documents which that person could be required to produce at the hearing.

Witness summons—This is the terminology employed in the rules in preference to "subpoena".

Documents—A witness may be required to produce documents. By virtue of Civil Evidence Act 1995, s 13 "document" is defined as "anything in which information of any description is recorded". It is reasonable to assume (subject to the overriding objective and the consideration of whether production of a document is proportionate to the issues) that the courts will adopt a similar definition for documents in Pt 34.

"requiring a witness to ... attend court ... or produce documents" (r 34.2(1))—A witness summons issues as of right (cf RSC Ord 32, r 7 which required leave to issue a subpoena in respect of High Court hearings conducted in chambers – ie the majority of hearings in the Family Division). A witness summons can be set aside or varied (r 34.3(4) (below)).

"produce documents to the court" (r 34.2(1)(*b*), (4))—These provisions replace the former "subpoena duces tecum" and enable the summons to require a witness to produce the documents at the hearing/trial, or on such other date as the court directs. Permission is required before a witness can be required to attend court to produce documents at a date prior to the trial (r 34.3(2) (below)).

"only documents ... which that person could be required to produce at the hearing" (r 34.2(5))—The summons can only bring forward the time at which a witness is required to produce documents for a hearing (*Frary v Frary and anor* [1993] 2 FLR 696, CA – the husband was living with a wealthy woman who had been ordered to produce documents prior to an ancillary relief hearing, supposedly under FPR 1991 r 2.62(7) which is equivalent in effect to r 34.2(4)(*b*)):

> "The effect of r 2.62(7) ... is to bring forward the time at which a witness may be required to attend ... Thus, if [but only if] the court would issue a subpoena duces tecum or make an order for the production of documents at trial, it can make that order for production at a production appointment under the rule." – per Ralph Gibson LJ at 702H-703A.

34.3 Issue of a witness summons

(1) A witness summons is issued on the date entered on the summons by the court.

(2) A party must obtain permission from the court where he wishes to –

(*a*) have a summons issued less than 7 days before the date of the trial;
(*b*) have a summons issued for a witness to attend court to give evidence or to produce documents on any date except the date fixed for the trial; or
(*c*) have a summons issued for a witness to attend court to give evidence or to produce documents at any hearing except the trial.

(3) A witness summons must be issued by –

(*a*) the court where the case is proceeding; or
(*b*) the court where the hearing in question will be held.

(4) The court may set aside(GL) or vary a witness summons issued under this rule.

Scope of provision—A witness summons is issued on the date which the court enters on the summons. Permission to issue a summons is required where issue is less than seven days before a hearing and where the witness is required to give evidence or produce documents prior to the final hearing. A summons may be set aside or varied.

The court does not have power to require a witness to attend for the purpose of *taking* evidence prior to the hearing (other than in the unusual circumstances of evidence being taken on deposition under r 34.8). Rule 34.2(1) makes it clear that a witness summons may only be issued for a person to "attend court to give evidence" and that adducing evidence from a witness on a date prior to the final hearing is limited to production of documents. A witness summons could be issued for the attendance of a witness at the hearing of an application (Pts 23 or 25) or on a committal application.

Witness summons for trial of a preliminary issue—Where the resolution of a factual issue before trial might assist resolution of the case, a witness could be required to attend the hearing of the trial of such a preliminary issue. By virtue of r 1.4(2), "active case management" includes identification of issues at an early stage and deciding promptly which issues need to be fully investigated by the court. Rule 3.1(2)(*i*) gives the court a discretion to "direct a separate trial of any issue" (this rule may be said to be equivalent to RSC Ord 33, r 4(2) and CCR Ord 13, r 2). The omission from the rules of a provision to enable oral evidence to be heard prior to the final hearing can be rectified if a suitable preliminary issue, or issues, can be identified to be tried separately, and the court is willing to so order.

"a summons issued for a witness ... to produce documents on any date except the date fixed for the trial" (r 34.3(2)(*b*))—This is the equivalent of the *Khanna* appointment (*Khanna v Lovell White Durrant (a Firm)* [1995] 1 WLR 121, Sir Donald Nicholls; and see under RSC Ord 38, r 14) and, like the inspection appointment under FPR 1991, r 2.62(7)–(9), it enables a party to see documents in advance of a final hearing (for a recent reference to this power of the court see *Roker International Properties Inc and anor v Couveras and Wolf* [2000] 2 FLR 976, Wilson J).

"The court may set aside or vary a witness summons" (r 34.3(4))—Though not explicitly stated in r 34.3, such an application should be made by the witness to a district judge. Since the power to issue a subpoena was derived from the equitable jurisdiction, the court always had a discretion to set it aside, whether it required attendance in person or production of documents – eg see *Morgan v Morgan* [1977] Fam 122, (1976) FLR Rep 473, Watkins J following *Senior v Holdsworth ex parte Independent Television News Ltd* [1976] QB 23, CA, where (at p 35) Lord Denning MR refused to order production of a film by ITN on the grounds that:

> "'The court should exercise [its] power only when it is likely that the film will have a direct and important place in the determination of the issues before the court. The mere assertion that the film may have some bearing will not be enough. If the judge considers that the request is irrelevant, or fishing, or speculative, or oppressive, he should refuse it."

The witness summons and proportionality—In deciding: (i) whether to give permission to issue a summons for the purposes set out in r 34.3(2); and (ii) whether a summons should be set aside or varied (r 34.3(4)), the court should consider the overriding objective in Pt 1. In particular, the judge will evaluate whether the need to adduce the evidence, or to have the documents produced, is proportionate to the issues before the court (r 1.1(2)(*c*)). In cases of doubt, the question to be addressed is whether the evidence will "have a direct and important place in the determination of the issues before the court" (*Senior v Holdsworth ex parte Independent Television News Ltd* (above) per Lord Denning MR).

34.4 Witness summons in aid of inferior court or of tribunal

(1) The court may issue a witness summons in aid of an inferior court or of a tribunal.

(2) The court which issued the witness summons under this rule may set it aside.

(3) In this rule, "inferior court or tribunal" means any court or tribunal that does not have power to issue a witness summons in relation to proceedings before it.

34.5 Time for serving a witness summons

(1) The general rule is that a witness summons is binding if it is served at least 7 days before the date on which the witness is required to attend before the court or tribunal.

(2) The court may direct that a witness summons shall be binding although it will be served less than 7 days before the date on which the witness is required to attend before the court or tribunal.

(3) A witness summons which is –

(*a*) served in accordance with this rule; and
(*b*) requires the witness to attend court to give evidence,

is binding until the conclusion of the hearing at which the attendance of the witness is required.

Witness summons issued less than seven days before hearing—If a witness summons is to be binding in such circumstances, permission must be granted for its issue (r 34.3(2)(*a*)).

34.6 Who is to serve a witness summons

(1) A witness summons is to be served by the court unless the party on whose behalf it is issued indicates in writing, when he asks the court to issue the summons, that he wishes to serve it himself.

(2) Where the court is to serve the witness summons, the party on whose behalf it is issued must deposit, in the court office, the money to be paid or offered to the witness under rule 34.7.

Service of the witness summons—Where the court serves a document, it should decide the method of service under r 6.2 (r 6.3(2)). Postal service by first class post is likely to be the preferred means.

34.7 Right of witness to travelling expenses and compensation for loss of time

At the time of service of a witness summons the witness must be offered or paid –

(*a*) a sum reasonably sufficient to cover his expenses in travelling to and from the court; and

(*b*) such sum by way of compensation for loss of time as may be specified in the relevant practice direction.

"compensation for loss ... specified in the relevant practice direction" (r 34.7(*b*))—*Practice Direction (Depositions and Court Attendance by Witnesses)*, paras 3.2 and 3.3 (set out in Section 2 of the *Civil Court Service* (Jordan Publishing Ltd)) define the sums to be paid.

34.8 Evidence by deposition

(1) A party may apply for an order for a person to be examined before the hearing takes place.

(2) A person from whom evidence is to be obtained following an order under this rule is referred to as a "deponent" and the evidence is referred to as a "deposition".

(3) An order under this rule shall be for a deponent to be examined on oath before –

(*a*) a judge;

(*b*) an examiner of the court; or

(*c*) such other person as the court appoints.

(Rule 34.15 makes provision for the appointment of examiners of the court)

(4) The order may require the production of any document which the court considers is necessary for the purposes of the examination.

(5) The order must state the date, time and place of the examination.

(6) At the time of service of the order the deponent must be offered or paid –

(*a*) a sum reasonably sufficient to cover his expenses in travelling to and from the place of examination; and

(*b*) such sum by way of compensation for loss of time as may be specified in the relevant practice direction.

(7) Where the court makes an order for a deposition to be taken, it may also order the party who obtained the order to serve a witness statement or witness summary in relation to the evidence to be given by the person to be examined.

(Part 32 contains the general rules about witness statements and witness summaries)

Evidence by deposition and alternatives—The taking of evidence by deposition is likely to be rare and will occur only where a witness is not available on the date of trial, or cannot attend because of disability. A less expensive way of dealing with the evidence, where possible, would be to arrange for it to be dealt with by telephone or video link. Active case management includes "making use of technology" (r 1.4(2)(*k*)) and receiving "evidence by telephone or by using any other method of direct oral communication" (r 3.1(2)(*d*)).

****

PART 35
EXPERTS AND ASSESSORS

General Note—From 5 June 2000, by virtue of FPR 1991, r 2.61C, all ancillary relief applications will be subject to CPR 1998, rr 35.1–35.14, save for rr 35.5(2) and 35.8(4)(*b*) (which apply only to fast-track claims and payments into court in respect of expert's fees and expenses).

Practice Direction—See *Practice Direction (Experts and Assessors)* which supplements this Part generally, set out in Part V of this work.

35.1 Duty to restrict expert evidence

Expert evidence shall be restricted to that which is reasonably required to resolve the proceedings.

"Expert evidence"—It is the expert's ability to express an opinion based on expertise, not the expertise itself, which makes such evidence different from other evidence and calls for particular rules governing it. The common law rule is that a witness gives evidence only as to fact. Expert evidence is an exception. Thus, Civil Evidence Act 1972, s 3(1) provides that "where a person is called as a witness in any civil proceedings, his opinion on any relevant matter on which he is qualified to give expert evidence shall be admissible in evidence".

"restricted to that which is reasonably required"—The court must decide what expert evidence is "reasonably required", though whether it is the court or the party whose reasonable requirements are to be met is unclear. When exercising the requirement to restrict expert evidence, the overriding objective in Pt 1 (and FPR 1991, r 2.51B) should be borne in mind. Given the expense of adducing expert evidence and the time involved in the hearing of further evidence, the court is likely to be concerned to ensure that such evidence is proportionate to the issues before it (r 1.1(2)(*b*) and (*c*)(iii); FPR 1991, r 2.51B(2)).

Issues not calling for expertise—The court will not allow expert evidence to be called where the point at issue can be resolved without reference to such evidence (*Brown v Gold and Swayn* (1996, unreported), CA).

Issues calling for expertise—The court will be wary of making assumptions where expert evidence is available (eg as to valuation of property: see *Martin (BH) v Martin (D)* [1978] Fam 12, (1977) FLR Rep 444, CA cited with approval by Lord Hoffman in *Piglowska v Piglowski* [1999] 1 WLR 1360, [1999] 2 FLR 763, HL at 782B–C). "The court has no expertise of its own, other than legal expertise ... The expert advises, but the judge decides." – per Ward LJ in *Re B (Care: Expert Witnesses)* [1996] 1 FLR 667, CA at 670C–D.

35.2 Interpretation

A reference to an "expert" in this Part is a reference to an expert who has been instructed to give or prepare evidence for the purpose of court proceedings.

35.3 Experts – overriding duty to the court

(1) It is the duty of an expert to help the court on the matters within his expertise.

(2) This duty overrides any obligation to the person from whom he has received instructions or by whom he is paid.

Scope of provision—This rule defines the expert's duty, which is to the court rather than to the party by whom he is instructed or paid. Consequently, *Practice Direction (Experts and Assessors)*, para 2.1 requires the expert's report to "be addressed to the court and not to the party" who has instructed him, though in practice the report will be sent to the instructing solicitors for them to file at court and serve on other parties.

"duty overrides any obligation" (r 35.3(2))—The essence of expert evidence is its impartiality (see *Access to Justice: Final Report* by Lord Woolf MR, (July 1996, HMSO)) and this should be so, whoever instructs the expert (see eg *Whitehouse v Jordan* [1981] 1 WLR 246, HL and *Vernon v Bosley (Expert Evidence) (Note)* [1998] 1 FLR 297, CA). The expert must not join in the adversarial process and should provide the court with information in respect of both facts which support, and facts which do not support, the case of the person who commissioned the evidence. If an expert advances a hypothesis which he knows to be controversial he must tell the court and put forward any material which contradicts his hypothesis (*Re A and B (Minors) (No 2)* [1995] 1 FLR 351, Wall J).

Forensic report—Legal representatives must not confuse the role of the medical expert who treats an individual with the role of the expert who provides a forensic report ("to treat is not to be muddled with the role of the expert to report": per Thorpe LJ in *Re B (Sexual abuse: Expert's Report)* [2000] 1 FLR 871 at 873D, CA).

Duties of the expert witness—In *The Ikarian Reefer* [1993] 2 Lloyd's Rep 69 at 81, Cresswell J (drawing on *Re R (A Minor) (Experts' Evidence) (Note)* [1991] 1 FLR 291, Cazalet J – set out in Part IV of this work as *Practice Note of 27 July 1990*) summarised the duties and responsibilities of the expert as follows:

(i) Expert evidence should be the independent product of the expert uninfluenced as to form or content by the surrounding litigation;
(ii) An expert should provide independent assistance to the court by means of objective opinion on matters within his expertise, without assuming the role of advocate for a point of view or for a party to the proceedings;
(iii) An expert should state the facts or assumptions on which his opinions are based, and should not omit facts which could detract from his stated opinion;
(iv) An expert should state when a question falls outside his expertise;
(v) Where an opinion is based on provisional data, or the opinion is qualified in any way, the expert must say so;
(vi) If an expert changes his mind on reading another expert's report he should say so as soon as possible, through legal representatives.

Aspects of expert's impartiality

(1) *Employed expert*—Provided that the expert understands the need for objectivity in giving evidence, he is not disqualified from giving opinion evidence merely because he is employed by a party to the proceedings; eg a social worker or medical witness in children proceedings (*Field v Leeds City Council* (2000) *The Times*, 18 January, CA). This principle will apply regardless of whether or not proceedings are covered by CPR 1998, since r 35.3 restates the common law position on opinion evidence.
(2) *Relationship with a party*—Just because one party may regard a witness as lacking impartiality it does not necessarily mean that his evidence will be excluded, since it may be disproportionate to do so (*R (Factortame Ltd) v Secretary of State for Transport (No 8)* [2002] EWCA Civ 932, [2002] 3 WLR 1104, CA; but see a contrary view in *Liverpool Roman Catholic Trustees v Goldberg (No 3)* [2001] 1 WLR 2337, Evans-Lombe J).

35.4 Court's power to restrict expert evidence

(1) No party may call an expert or put in evidence an expert's report without the court's permission.

(2) When a party applies for permission under this rule he must identify –

(*a*) the field in which he wishes to rely on expert evidence; and
(*b*) where practicable the expert in that field on whose evidence he wishes to rely.

(3) If permission is granted under this rule it shall be in relation only to the expert named or the field identified under paragraph (2).

(4) The court may limit the amount of the expert's fees and expenses that the party who wishes to rely on the expert may recover from any other party.

Scope of provision—This rule is equivalent to RSC Ord 38, r 36 but is much more prescriptive since it does not allow the parties to agree expert evidence. Expert evidence may only be adduced with permission of the court. Where leave is sought, the field of expertise and, if possible, a named expert must be identified. The court can limit the fees which a party can recover from another party if an order for costs is made.

Directions for expert evidence—In cases governed by CPR 1998, directions for expert evidence are likely to be included in any case management directions, or application for permission can be made specifically under Pt 23. Under the ancillary relief rules, the district judge at the First Appointment is specifically required to consider directions as to expert evidence (FPR 1991, r 2.61D(2)(*b*)).

35.5 General requirement for expert evidence to be given in a written report

(1) Expert evidence is to be given in a written report unless the court directs otherwise.

(2) ...

Content of report—*Practice Direction (Experts and Assessors)*, paras 2.2–2.5 set out the matters which must be included in an expert's report; and see r 35.10 for the contents of the report. The report must be verified by a statement of truth in the form set out at para 2.4.

35.6 Written questions to experts

(1) A party may put to –

(*a*) an expert instructed by another party; or
(*b*) a single joint expert appointed under rule 35.7,

written questions about his report.

(2) Written questions under paragraph (1) –

(*a*) may be put once only;
(*b*) must be put within 28 days of service of the expert's report; and
(*c*) must be for the purpose only of clarification of the report;

unless in any case,

(i) the court gives permission; or
(ii) the other party agrees.

(3) An expert's answers to questions put in accordance with paragraph (1) shall be treated as part of the expert's report.

(4) Where –

(*a*) a party has put a written question to an expert instructed by another party in accordance with this rule; and
(*b*) the expert does not answer that question,

the court may make one or both of the following orders in relation to the party who instructed the expert –

(i) that the party may not rely on the evidence of that expert; or
(ii) that the party may not recover the fees and expenses of that expert from any other party.

Questions to other party's solicitors—*Practice Direction (Experts and Assessors)*, para 5.2 provides that where questions are raised with an expert and the instructing party is represented by solicitors, they should be sent a copy of the questions. Courtesy would suggest that unrepresented parties should also be sent the questions but the *Practice Direction* is silent on this.

Questions of jointly instructed expert—If one party, for good reason, is discontented with the report of a jointly instructed expert, he can put questions to the expert (*Daniels v Walker* [2000] 1 WLR 1382, CA (and see r 35.8 below)).

35.7 Court's power to direct that evidence is to be given by a single joint expert

(1) Where two or more parties wish to submit expert evidence on a particular issue, the court may direct that the evidence on that issue is to given by one expert only.

(2) The parties wishing to submit the expert evidence are called "the instructing parties".

(3) Where the instructing parties cannot agree who should be the expert, the court may –

(*a*) select the expert from a list prepared or identified by the instructing parties; or

(*b*) direct that the expert be selected in such other manner as the court may direct.

Scope of provision—Where parties want to adduce expert evidence on a particular issue, the court has a discretion to direct that the evidence be given by one witness only. The court can select the witness, or direct the manner of his/her selection. This rule is more prescriptive than RSC Ord 40 which permits one or other party to apply for appointment of an independent court expert.

35.8 Instructions to a single joint expert

(1) Where the court gives a direction under rule 35.7 for a single joint expert to be used, each instructing party may give instructions to the expert.

(2) When an instructing party gives instructions to the expert he must, at the same time, send a copy of the instructions to the other instructing parties.

(3) The court may give directions about –

(*a*) the payment of the expert's fees and expenses; and

(*b*) any inspection, examination or experiments which the expert wishes to carry out.

(4) The court may, before an expert is instructed –

(*a*) limit the amount that can be paid by way of fees and expenses to the expert; and

(*b*) ...

(5) Unless the court otherwise directs, the instructing parties are jointly and severally liable(GL) for the payment of the expert's fees and expenses.

Joint or individual instructions (r 35.8(1))—Once a direction is given under r 35.7 "*each* instructing party may give instructions to the expert" (r 35.8(1) – emphasis added), though parties should try to agree the instructions (*Daniels v Walker* (below) at 1383H). A copy of the instruction letter must be sent to other parties (r 35.8(2)).

Further report—The fact that the court has directed joint instruction of an expert does not prevent one party "for reasons which are not fanciful" seeking another report (*Daniels v Walker* [2000] 1 WLR 1382, CA at 1387E); for list of relevant factors permitting own report see *Cosgrove v Pattison* (2001) *The Times*, 13 February noted under FPR 1991, r 2.61C. In *Daniels v Walker* Lord Woolf MR (at 1387E–H) proposed the following steps in the instruction of an expert (or experts) where the court has ordered a joint approach:

(*a*) parties endeavour to instruct on the basis of an agreed letter;

(*b*) failing that, parties write separately;
(*c*) if one party, for reasonable reasons, is discontented with the report, he can put questions to the expert;
(*d*) if that does not resolve the position, then one or both parties may seek a direction as to the calling of further evidence. Such a direction will be considered on the basis of proportionality to the issues and money involved.

"limit the amount that can be paid" (r 35.8(4)(*a*))—Any party who anticipates that there is an issue on which a joint instruction may be ordered would be prudent to discover the fee of a suitable expert before a directions appointment. This sub-rule should be distinguished from r 35.4(4) which enables the court to restrict the costs which can be recovered from another party if an order for costs is made.

Best Practice Guidance—*Best Practice Guidance of November 2002 (Instructing a Single Joint Expert)* has been issued by the President's Ancillary Relief Advisory Group (set out in Part IV of this work). It is dedicated to the promotion of "efficiency, effectiveness and economy ... when instructions are given jointly to experts in applications for ancillary relief". Notwithstanding this laudable aim, it does not fully parallel the equivalent provisions of CPR 1998, Pt 35. Thus:
(i) The requirement of para 6(*d*) that the court direct a "jointly agreed letter" is more restrictive than the rule and its rationale. Lord Woolf MR recognised (in *Daniels v Walker* (above)) that, in the event that such a letter cannot be agreed quickly, it is more economical and time-efficient to send in separate instructions.
(ii) The requirement of para 6(*g*), which seeks to define a date by which questions must be answered, is redundant: r 35.6(2)(*b*) provides a time-limit, namely 28 days from receipt of the report (seemingly not variable by the court).
(iii) It is suggested that para 4(1)(*g*), which stipulates that an expert be asked in publicly funded cases whether he will accept instructions, is unnecessary. Provided that the Legal Services Commission accepts the fee proposed by the expert (and its authority to instruct will always be limited in financial scope), there is no differential in fees for experts as between the private and the funded client. Were there to be, r 35.8(5) would be contravened in all cases between a private and a publicly funded party.

35.9 Power of court to direct a party to provide information

Where a party has access to information which is not reasonably available to the other party, the court may direct the party who has access to the information to –

(*a*) prepare and file a document recording the information; and
(*b*) serve a copy of that document on the other party.

"information"—CPR 1998, r 1.1(2)(*a*) (and FPR 1991, r 2.51B(2)) provide that "dealing with a case justly includes ... ensuring that the parties are on an equal footing". Though r 35.9 does not explicitly say so, it is intended to overcome the concern (see *Access to Justice: Final Report* by Lord Woolf MR, (July 1996, HMSO), at p 146) that in some cases one party (eg in the family law sphere, a local authority) may have access to expertise or other specialist information which other parties do not have. This rule is intended to compel the party with such expertise or particular information to produce it and *Practice Direction (Experts and Assessors)*, para 3 requires that such a document should set out "sufficient details of all the facts, tests, experiments and assumptions which underlie any part of the information to enable the party on whom it is served to make ... an assessment of its significance" (ie the information should be produced in a form which can be understood by a non-expert).

35.10 Contents of report

(1) An expert's report must comply with the requirements set out in the relevant practice direction.

(2) At the end of an expert's report there must be a statement that –

(*a*) the expert understands his duty to the court; and
(*b*) he has complied with that duty.

(3) The expert's report must state the substance of all material instructions, whether written or oral, on the basis of which the report was written.

(4) The instructions referred to in paragraph (3) shall not be privileged(GL) against disclosure but the court will not, in relation to those instructions –

(*a*) order disclosure of any specific document; or

(*b*) permit any questioning in court, other than by the party who instructed the expert,

unless it is satisfied that there are reasonable grounds to consider the statement of instructions given under paragraph (3) to be inaccurate or incomplete.

Content of the report—*Practice Direction (Experts and Assessors)*, para 2.2 sets out details of the formal requirements of the report. These include the following:

(i) The report must contain a statement of "the substance of all material instructions" received by the expert (r 35.10(3)) which should include a summary of all instructions and facts referred to therein which are relevant to the report or any opinion expressed in it (para 2.2(3));

(ii) The report is required to have both a statement that the expert understands his/her duty to the court and has complied with that duty (see r 35.3), in addition to a form of statement of truth prescribed by para 2.4.

"instructions [are not] privileged against disclosure" (r 35.10(4))—Instructions to an expert are no longer covered by any form of privilege, though a party will not be entitled to disclosure (discovery), save where there is a doubt as to whether the summary of the instructions given (ie apparently not the instructions themselves) is accurate or complete. In these circumstances, disclosure of the instructions may be ordered with the court's permission and the expert may be cross-examined "where it appears to be in the interests of justice to do so" (*Practice Direction (Experts and Assessors)*, para 4).

35.11 Use by one party of expert's report disclosed by another

Where a party has disclosed an expert's report, any party may use that expert's report as evidence at the trial.

35.12 Discussions between experts

(1) The court may, at any stage, direct a discussion between experts for the purpose of requiring the experts to –

(*a*) identify and discuss the expert issues in the proceedings; and

(*b*) where possible, reach an agreed opinion on those issues.

(2) The court may specify the issues which the experts must discuss.

(3) The court may direct that following a discussion between the experts they must prepare a statement for the court showing –

(*a*) those issues on which they agree; and

(*b*) those issues on which they disagree and a summary of their reasons for disagreeing.

(4) The content of the discussion between the experts shall not be referred to at the trial unless the parties agree.

(5) Where experts reach agreement on an issue during their discussions, the agreement shall not bind the parties unless the parties expressly agree to be bound by the agreement.

Amendments—SI 2001/4015.

"The court may ... direct a discussion" (r 35.12(1))—The usefulness of discussions between experts has been referred to in a number of family cases (see eg *Evans v Evans* [1990] 1 FLR 319, Booth J and *Re C (Expert Evidence: Disclosure: Practice)* [1995] 1 FLR 204, Cazalet J). In *Re S (Care Proceedings: Split Hearing)* [1996] 2 FLR 773, Bracewell J suggested that it should be a condition of the appointment of experts in similar fields of expertise that they meet (or discuss) the areas of agreement between them.

"at any stage" (r 35.12(1))—This power enables the court to direct that experts should engage in discussion at an early stage in proceedings. In many cases, there may be value in holding such discussion before reports are prepared, eg to ensure experts are working from similar instructions or considering the same issues.

"discussion between experts" (r 35.12(1))—The term "discussion" has been used deliberately in preference to the expression "meeting" (found in RSC Ord 38, r 38) in order to enable experts to use, if they so wish, telephone conferencing facilities, video conferencing, etc.

"must prepare a statement" (r 35.12(3))—This provision goes further than RSC Ord 38, r 38 which left it to the experts to decide whether they prepared a report identifying the parts of the evidence in issue. Now experts can be directed to file a statement dealing with points on which they agree and the areas of their disagreement (supported with reasons).

35.13 Consequence of failure to disclose expert's report

A party who fails to disclose an expert's report may not use the report at the trial or call the expert to give evidence orally unless the court gives permission.

Scope of provision—Rule 35.4 requires a party to obtain the permission of the court if he is to adduce expert evidence but it does not require expert evidence, once obtained, to be disclosed. This rule provides that a party who wishes to rely on expert evidence which has not been disclosed cannot do so without the court's permission.

35.14 Expert's right to ask court for directions

(1) An expert may file a written request for directions to assist him in carrying out his function as an expert.

(2) An expert must, unless the court orders otherwise, provide a copy of any proposed request for directions under paragraph (1) –

(*a*) to the party instructing him, at least 7 days before he files the request; and
(*b*) to all other parties, at least 4 days before he files it.

(3) The court, when it gives directions, may also direct that a party be served with a copy of the directions.

Amendments—SI 2001/4015.

"request for directions" (r 35.14(1))—Rules 35.8(3)(*b*) and 35.12(2) enable the court to give directions to experts as to how they should prepare their reports and the framework for their discussions. Rule 35.6 gives the parties the right to put questions to an expert. The expert's duty is to the court (r 35.3) and it therefore follows that he should have a direct means of access to the court, either to clarify or amend instructions, or to seek directions (eg as to the extent to which he is bound to answer enquiries raised by a party to the proceedings).

****

PART 39
MISCELLANEOUS PROVISIONS RELATING TO HEARINGS

Practice Direction—See *Practice Direction (Miscellaneous Provisions Relating to Hearings)* and *Practice Direction (Court Sittings)* which supplement this Part generally; both are set out in Section 2 of the *Civil Court Service* (Jordan Publishing Ltd).

39.1 Interpretation

In this Part, reference to a hearing includes a reference to the trial.

39.2 General rule – hearing to be in public

(1) The general rule is that a hearing is to be in public.

(2) The requirement for a hearing to be in public does not require the court to make special arrangements for accommodating members of the public.

(3) A hearing, or any part of it, may be in private if –

(*a*) publicity would defeat the object of the hearing;
(*b*) it involves matters relating to national security;
(*c*) it involves confidential information (including information relating to personal financial matters) and publicity would damage that confidentiality;
(*d*) a private hearing is necessary to protect the interests of any child or patient;
(*e*) it is a hearing of an application made without notice and it would be unjust to any respondent for there to be a public hearing;
(*f*) it involves uncontentious matters arising in the administration of trusts or in the administration of a deceased person's estate; or
(*g*) the court considers this to be necessary, in the interests of justice.

(4) The court may order that the identity of any party or witness must not be disclosed if it considers non-disclosure necessary in order to protect the interests of that party or witness.

(RSC Ord 52, in Schedule 1, provides that a committal hearing may be in private)

****

39.5 Trial bundles

(1) Unless the court orders otherwise, the claimant must file a trial bundle containing documents required by –

(*a*) a relevant practice direction; and
(*b*) any court order.

(2) The claimant must file the trial bundle not more than 7 days and not less than 3 days before the start of the trial.

****

PART 40
JUDGMENTS, ORDERS, SALE OF LAND ETC

Practice Direction—See *Practice Direction (Judgments and Orders)* (PD 40B) which supplements this Part generally, set out in Part V of this work.

****

40.3 Drawing up and filing of judgments and orders

(1) Every judgment or order will be drawn up by the court unless –

(*a*) the court orders a party to draw it up;
(*b*) a party, with the permission of the court, agrees to draw it up;
(*c*) the court dispenses with the need to draw it up; or
(*d*) it is a consent order under rule 40.6.

(2) The court may direct that –

(*a*) a judgment or an order drawn up by a party must be checked by the court before it is sealed(GL); or
(*b*) before a judgment or an order is drawn up by the court, the parties must file an agreed statement of its terms.

(3) Where a judgment or an order is to be drawn up by a party –

(*a*) he must file it no later than 7 days after the date on which the court ordered or permitted him to draw it up so that it can be sealed(GL) by the court; and
(*b*) if he fails to file it within that period, any other party may draw it up and file it.

40.4 Service of judgments and orders

(1) Where a judgment or an order has been drawn up by a party and is to be served by the court –

(*a*) the party who drew it up must file a copy to be retained at court and sufficient copies for service on him and on the other parties; and
(*b*) once it has been sealed(GL), the court must serve a copy of it on each party to the proceedings.

(2) Unless the court directs otherwise, any order made otherwise than at trial must be served on –

(*a*) the applicant and the respondent; and
(*b*) any other person on whom the court orders it to be served.

(Rule 6.3 specifies who must serve judgments and orders)

Amendments—SI 2002/2058.

40.5 Power to require judgment or order to be served on a party as well as his solicitor

Where the party on whom a judgment or order is to be served is acting by a solicitor, the court may order the judgment or order to be served on the party as well as on his solicitor.

40.6 Consent judgments and orders

(1) This rule applies where all the parties agree the terms in which a judgment should be given or an order should be made.

(2) A court officer may enter and seal(GL) an agreed judgment or order if –

- (*a*) the judgment or order is listed in paragraph (3);
- (*b*) none of the parties is a litigant in person; and
- (*c*) the approval of the court is not required by these Rules, a practice direction or any enactment before an agreed order can be made.

(3) The judgments and orders referred to in paragraph (2) are –

- (*a*) a judgment or order for –
  - (i) the payment of an amount of money (including a judgment or order for damages or the value of goods to be decided by the court); or
  - (ii) the delivery up of goods with or without the option of paying the value of the goods or the agreed value.
- (*b*) an order for –
  - (i) the dismissal of any proceedings, wholly or in part;
  - (ii) the stay(GL) of proceedings on agreed terms, disposing of the proceedings, whether those terms are recorded in a schedule to the order or elsewhere;
  - (iii) the stay(GL) of enforcement of a judgment, either unconditionally or on condition that the money due under the judgment is paid by instalments specified in the order;
  - (iv) the setting aside under Part 13 of a default judgment which has not been satisfied;
  - (v) the payment out of money which has been paid into court;
  - (vi) the discharge from liability of any party;
  - (vii) the payment, assessment or waiver of costs, or such other provision for costs as may be agreed.

(4) Rule 40.3 (drawing up and filing of judgments and orders) applies to judgments and orders entered and sealed(GL) by a court officer under paragraph (2) as it applies to other judgments and orders.

(5) Where paragraph (2) does not apply, any party may apply for a judgment or order in the terms agreed.

(6) The court may deal with an application under paragraph (5) without a hearing.

(7) Where this rule applies –

- (*a*) the order which is agreed by the parties must be drawn up in the terms agreed;
- (*b*) it must be expressed as being "By Consent";
- (*c*) it must be signed by the legal representative acting for each of the parties to whom the order relates or, where paragraph (5) applies, by the party if he is a litigant in person.

40.7 When judgment or order takes effect

(1) A judgment or order takes effect from the day when it is given or made, or such later date as the court may specify.

(2) This rule applies to all judgments and orders except those to which rule 40.10 (judgment against a State) applies.

PART III

40.8 Time from which interest begins to run

(1) Where interest is payable on a judgment pursuant to section 17 of the Judgments Act 1838 or section 74 of the County Courts Act 1984, the interest shall begin to run from the date that judgment is given unless –

(*a*) a rule in another Part or a practice direction makes different provision; or
(*b*) the court orders otherwise.

(2) The court may order that interest shall begin to run from a date before the date that judgment is given.

****

40.12 Correction of errors in judgments and orders

(1) The court may at any time correct an accidental slip or omission in a judgment or order.

(2) A party may apply for a correction without notice.

****

PART 43
SCOPE OF COST RULES AND DEFINITIONS

Practice Direction—*Practice Direction about Costs* (PDCosts) now covers Pts 43–48 as a whole. It must be read with caution: on occasions it attempts to summarise or restate the law, but inaccurately (paras 22.5–22.7); on other occasions it is wrong (para 22.9 and 23.5); and on further occasions (see eg paras 13.9–13.11, 23.4) it seeks to state the law without providing any statutory authority. That said, it provides much of the only available guidance on such matters as summary assessment and the procedure for detailed assessment.

43.1 Scope of this Part

This Part contains definitions and interpretation of certain matters set out in the rules about costs contained in Parts 44 to 48.

(Part 44 contains general rules about costs; Part 45 deals with fixed costs; Part 46 deals with fast track trial costs; Part 47 deals with the detailed assessment of costs and related appeals and Part 48 deals with costs payable in special cases)

43.2 Definitions and application

(1) In Parts 44 to 48, unless the context otherwise requires –

(*a*) "costs" includes fees, charges, disbursements, expenses, remuneration, reimbursement allowed to a litigant in person under rule 48.6, any additional liability incurred under a funding arrangement and any fee or reward charged by a lay representative for acting on behalf of a party in proceedings allocated to the small claims track;
(*b*) "costs judge" means a taxing master of the Supreme Court;
(*c*) "costs officer" means –
  (i) a costs judge;
  (ii) a district judge; and
  (iii) an authorised court officer;
(*d*) "authorised court officer" means any officer of –

(i) a county court;
(ii) a district registry;
(iii) the Principal Registry of the Family Division; or
(iv) the Supreme Court Costs Office;

whom the Lord Chancellor has authorised to assess costs.

(*e*) "fund" includes any estate or property held for the benefit of any person or class of person and any fund to which a trustee or personal representative is entitled in his capacity as such;
(*f*) "receiving party" means a party entitled to be paid costs;
(*g*) "paying party" means a party liable to pay costs;
(*h*) "assisted person" means an assisted person within the statutory provisions relating to legal aid;
(*i*) "LSC funded client" means an individual who receives services funded by the Legal Services Commission as part of the Community Legal Service within the meaning of Part I of the Access to Justice Act 1999;
(*j*)–(*o*) ...

(2) The costs to which Parts 44 to 48 apply include –

(*a*) the following costs where those costs may be assessed by the court –
(i) costs of proceedings before an arbitrator or umpire;
(ii) costs of proceedings before a tribunal or other statutory body; and
(iii) costs payable by a client to his solicitor; and
(*b*) costs which are payable by one party to another party under the terms of a contract, where the court makes an order for an assessment of those costs.

Amendments—SI 2000/1317.

"district judge" (r 43.2(1)(*c*)(ii))—This includes a district judge of the Principal Registry of the Family Division (see Family Proceedings (Amendment) Rules 2003, r 10.27(1)(*a*)).

43.3 Meaning of summary assessment

"Summary assessment" means the procedure by which the court, when making an order about costs, orders payment of a sum of money instead of fixed costs or "detailed assessment".

43.4 Meaning of detailed assessment

"Detailed assessment" means the procedure by which the amount of costs is decided by a costs officer in accordance with Part 47.

PART 44
GENERAL RULES ABOUT COSTS

44.1 Scope of this Part

This Part contains general rules about costs and entitlement to costs.

(The definitions contained in Part 43 are relevant to this Part)

44.2 Solicitor's duty to notify client

Where –

(*a*) the court makes a costs order against a legally represented party; and
(*b*) the party is not present when the order is made,

the party's solicitor must notify his client in writing of the costs order no later than 7 days after the solicitor receives notice of the order.

44.3 Court's discretion and circumstances to be taken into account when exercising its discretion as to costs

(1) The court has discretion as to –

(*a*) whether costs are payable by one party to another;
(*b*) the amount of those costs; and
(*c*) when they are to be paid.

(2) If the court decides to make an order about costs –

(*a*) the general rule is that the unsuccessful party will be ordered to pay the costs of the successful party; but
(*b*) the court may make a different order.

(3) The general rule does not apply to the following proceedings –

(*a*) proceedings in the Court of Appeal on an application or appeal made in connection with proceedings in the Family Division; or
(*b*) proceedings in the Court of Appeal from a judgment, direction, decision or order given or made in probate proceedings or family proceedings.

(4) In deciding what order (if any) to make about costs, the court must have regard to all the circumstances, including –

(*a*) the conduct of all the parties;
(*b*) whether a party has succeeded on part of his case, even if he has not been wholly successful; and
(*c*) any payment into court or admissible offer to settle made by a party which is drawn to the court's attention (whether or not made in accordance with Part 36).

(Part 36 contains further provisions about how the court's discretion is to be exercised where a payment into court or an offer to settle is made under that Part)

(5) The conduct of the parties includes –

(*a*) conduct before, as well as during, the proceedings and in particular the extent to which the parties followed any relevant pre-action protocol;
(*b*) whether it was reasonable for a party to raise, pursue or contest a particular allegation or issue;
(*c*) the manner in which a party has pursued or defended his case or a particular allegation or issue; and
(*d*) whether a claimant who has succeeded in his claim, in whole or in part, exaggerated his claim.

(6) The orders which the court may make under this rule include an order that a party must pay –

(*a*) a proportion of another party's costs;
(*b*) a stated amount in respect of another party's costs;
(*c*) costs from or until a certain date only;
(*d*) costs incurred before proceedings have begun;
(*e*) costs relating to particular steps taken in the proceedings;
(*f*) costs relating only to a distinct part of the proceedings; and

(*g*) interest on costs from or until a certain date, including a date before judgment.

(7) Where the court would otherwise consider making an order under paragraph (6)(*f*), it must instead, if practicable, make an order under paragraph (6)(*a*) or (*c*).

(8) Where the court has ordered a party to pay costs, it may order an amount to be paid on account before the costs are assessed.

(9) Where a party entitled to costs is also liable to pay costs the court may assess the costs which that party is liable to pay and either –

(*a*) set off the amount assessed against the amount the party is entitled to be paid and direct him to pay any balance; or
(*b*) delay the issue of a certificate for the costs to which the party is entitled until he has paid the amount which he is liable to pay.

Defined terms—"assessment of costs": Pt 47; "costs": r 43.2(1)(*a*); "Part 36 offer": r 36.5.

Court's discretion on costs (r 44.3(1))—Rule 44.3(1) gives regulatory effect to Supreme Court Act 1981, s 51(3); namely that costs can only be recovered by order of the court and that orders for costs are in the court's discretion (SCA 1981, s 51(1)). The rule prescribes bases upon which the court is to exercise its discretion.

"the amount of those costs" (r 44.3(1)(*b*))—The court's discretion as to the amount of costs "includes its discretion to decide whether some or all of the costs awarded should be on a standard or indemnity basis" (*Reid Minty (a firm) v Taylor* [2002] EWCA Civ 1723, [2002] 1 WLR 2800 per May LJ at [27]); and see note under r 44.4 on standard and indemnity costs.

Practice Direction—*Practice Direction about Costs*, para 8.5 draws attention to a "non-exhaustive list" of "certain costs orders which the court will commonly make". The following should be particularly noted:

(*a*) *Respondent's costs* A wholly successful respondent should normally be awarded his costs unless he has brought about the proceedings or has done something in connection with the institution or conduct of the proceedings intended to prolong them or cause unnecessary expense (*Ritter v Godfrey* [1920] KB 47; r 44.3(5)).

(*b*) *"Costs in the cause" or "Costs in the application"* Where proceedings are discontinued or withdrawn (eg domestic violence injunction proceedings where applicant does not pursue application beyond initial order) the defendant or respondent does not automatically have an order for costs in his favour where there is an order for "costs in the cause [or] application": the court retains its discretion as to costs, since no judgment on the issues has yet been given (*Barretts & Baird (Wholesale) Ltd v Institution of Professional Civil Servants* [1987] IRLR 3).

(*c*) *"Costs reserved"* A party in whose favour an order for costs is made will be awarded costs in respect of any "costs reserved" order, unless some other order is made. The former exception of family proceedings, where the converse applied, has not been preserved. Thus, where costs are reserved at an interlocutory hearing and, at the final hearing, costs either (i) are not awarded at all or (ii) are awarded to one or other party, it will be necessary to seek a specific order for the prior hearing, in respect of which costs were reserved, at that final hearing. A party who fails to seek, at the final hearing, an order for the costs which were reserved at an earlier hearing, can cure the omission by making a separate application (*S v S (Reserved Costs Order)* [1995] 1 FLR 739, Michael Horowitz QC sitting as a deputy High Court judge).

"the general rule" (r 44.3(2)(*a*))—This rule replaces RSC Ord 62, r 3(3) which provided that "costs should follow the event", unless some other order seemed appropriate, save in the Family Division (Ord 62, r 3(5)). The previous position is mirrored by the disapplication of r 44.3(2) in respect of family proceedings (see Family Proceedings (Amendment) Rules 2003, r 10.27(1)(*b*)). However, in *Gojkovic v Gojkovic (No 2)* [1992] Fam 40, [1991] 2 FLR 233, Butler-Sloss LJ held that in family courts the judge must have some starting-point which should normally be that "costs follow the event". It seems likely, therefore, that this tenet will continue to apply in family proceedings, with the proviso that it can be more easily displaced in such proceedings (eg applications in respect of children or where the parties' assets are minimal).

"In deciding what order (if any) to make about costs" (r 44.3(4))—The exercise of the court's discretion was considered by Nourse LJ in the Court of Appeal in *Re Elgindata Ltd (No 2)* [1992] 1 WLR 1207, at 1214A–C (cited with approval as applicable to a financial relief application by Thorpe LJ in *Dart v Dart* [1996] 2 FLR 286, CA). In that case Nourse LJ set out the main principles on which he considered that an order for costs should be awarded:

(*a*) costs are in the discretion of the court (SCA 1981, s 51(1));

(*b*) orders for costs should "follow the event" (ie should be paid to the "successful party": see r 44.3(2)(*a*)), unless the court considers that in the circumstances of the case some other order should be made (r 44.3(2)(*b*));

(*c*) these general rules do not cease to apply because a party raises issues on which he is not successful, although if, in raising those issues, he substantially lengthens the trial he may lose part or all of his costs;

(*d*) where a successful party raises issues or makes allegations improperly or unreasonably, the court may deprive him of his costs (and see r 44.3(4)(*a*) and (5)) and order him to pay the unsuccessful party's costs (SCA 1981, s 51(6)).

"the conduct of all the parties" (r 44.3(4)(*a*), (5))—In the exercise of its discretion, the court will be required to pay particular attention to the conduct of the parties and r 44.3(5) provides an inclusive check-list of the factors for consideration when assessing conduct.

"whether a party has succeeded" (r 44.3(4)(*b*))—This is the terminology used to replace costs following "the event" as considered by the Court of Appeal in *Gojkovic v Gojkovic (No 2)* [1992] Fam 40, [1991] 2 FLR 233, CA.

"admissible offer to settle ... (whether or not made in accordance with Part 36)" (r 44.3(4)(*c*))—Part 36 is not directly relevant to family proceedings, though it has similarities in some respects with *Calderbank* correspondence (cf FPR 1991, rr 2.69-2.69C).

Calderbank letters—*Calderbank* letters set out proposals for settlement of any issue in proceedings (*Calderbank v Calderbank* [1976] Fam 93, (1975) FLR Rep 113, CA; and see CPR 1998, r 36.5(2)). In *Gojkovic v Gojkovic (No 2)* [1991] 2 FLR 233, at 238F, Butler-Sloss LJ expressed the view that "*Calderbank* offers are required to have teeth in order for them to be effective". The following are the essential aspects of a *Calderbank* offer:

(*a*) *Full disclosure a prerequisite* A *Calderbank* offer cannot be effective until there has been full disclosure by the offeror. By extension, this also applies to an open offer (*H v H (Clean Break: Non-disclosure: Costs)* [1994] 2 FLR 309).

(*b*) *Response to offer* An applicant may risk failure on an application for costs where no counter-offer is made (*S v S (Financial Provision)* [1990] 2 FLR 252, CA: W awarded £435,000 but after she failed to respond to offer of £400,000; Court of Appeal upheld judge's refusal to award costs), but not where the offer is made very late in the proceedings (*Gojkovic v Gojkovic (No 2)* (above)). Where the response to an offer comes very late then, even if beaten, it may attract an order for costs against the respondent to the offer (*A v A (Costs: Appeal)* [1996] 1 FLR 14, where Singer J suggested three weeks as a reasonable period for response to a *Calderbank* offer; and see CPR 1998, r 36.5(6)).

"whether a claimant .... exaggerated his claim" (r 44.3(5)(*d*))—Whilst an applicant is obliged to respond to an offer (*A v A (Costs: Appeal)* [1996] 1 FLR 14, Singer J; and see above) there is no need for her to set out proposals at any stage in the proceedings. However, if she does so, it is important to ensure that these are moderate; for if the claim is exaggerated then r 44.3(5)(*d*) may be pleaded (and see *Phillips v Peace* [1996] 2 FLR 230, Johnson J, where a claim for costs was reduced by one-third because of the applicant's immoderate proposals for settlement).

Costs against local authority in public law children proceedings—Where the local authority unsuccessfully argues an application in respect of a child, it should not normally pay a party's costs (*Re M (Local Authority's Costs)* [1995] 1 FLR 533, Cazalet J – father's successful opposition to a local authority's application to terminate contact).

Official Solicitor's costs—The costs of the Official Solicitor are entirely a matter for the discretion of the judge (*B v Croydon Health Authority (No 2)* [1996] 1 FLR 253, CA). It may be appropriate to order a party to pay one half of the Official Solicitor's costs (*Re G (Minors) (Wardship: Costs)* [1982] 1 WLR 438, [1982] 2 All ER 32, CA) or, where the Official Solicitor has become involved because of the position the parties find themselves in, he might be expected to bear his own costs (see comments of the then Master of the Rolls in *Northampton Health*

Authority v The Official Solicitor and the Governors of St Andrews Hospital [1994] 1 FLR 162, CA).

Appeals against orders for costs—In family proceedings to which FPR 1991 apply, the terms of FPR 1991, r 8.1(2) and (3) make it possible to appeal against an order for costs only, as distinct from appealing against the order as a whole (*A v A (Costs: Appeal)* [1996] 1 FLR 14, Singer J).

****

44.4 Basis of assessment

(1) Where the court is to assess the amount of costs (whether by summary or detailed assessment) it will assess those costs –

(*a*) on the standard basis; or
(*b*) on the indemnity basis,

but the court will not in either case allow costs which have been unreasonably incurred or are unreasonable in amount.

(Rule 48.3 sets out how the court decides the amount of costs payable under a contract)

(2) Where the amount of costs is to be assessed on the standard basis, the court will –

(*a*) only allow costs which are proportionate to the matters in issue; and
(*b*) resolve any doubt which it may have as to whether costs were reasonably incurred or reasonable and proportionate in amount in favour of the paying party.

(Factors which the court may take into account are set out in rule 44.5)

(3) Where the amount of costs is to be assessed on the indemnity basis, the court will resolve any doubt which it may have as to whether costs were reasonably incurred or were reasonable in amount in favour of the receiving party.

(4) Where –

(*a*) the court makes an order about costs without indicating the basis on which the costs are to be assessed; or
(*b*) the court makes an order for costs to be assessed on a basis other than the standard basis or the indemnity basis,

the costs will be assessed on the standard basis.

(5) (*revoked*)

(6) …

Amendments—SI 2000/1317.

Defined terms—"costs": r 43.2(1)(*a*); "costs officer": r 43.2(1)(*c*); "detailed assessment": r 43.4; "summary assessment": r 43.3.

Assessment of costs—Rule 44.4 deals with the basis of the assessment of costs (standard or indemnity) which the court awards; r 44.5 deals with the factors to be taken into account when undertaking that assessment; and r 44.6 deals with the procedure (detailed or summary) by which the assessment is to take place.

Indemnity or standard basis (r 44.4(1))—An award of costs on the indemnity basis is only justified where a paying party has been responsible for conduct which is unreasonable to a high

PART III

degree: not "merely wrong or misguided in hindsight" (*Kiam v MGN Ltd (No 2)* [2002] EWCA Civ 66, [2002] 1 WLR 2810, CA per Simon Brown LJ at [12]). Where one party makes a sensible attempt at settlement and the other party resists, the latter party puts himself at risk of an indemnity order (*Reid Minty (a firm) v Taylor* [2002] EWCA Civ 1723, [2002] 1 WLR 2800 per Kay LJ at [37]). Implicit disapproval of the way the litigation was conducted may be reflected by such an order.

44.5 Factors to be taken into account in deciding the amount of costs

(1) The court is to have regard to all the circumstances in deciding whether costs were –

(*a*) if it is assessing costs on the standard basis –
(i) proportionately and reasonably incurred; or
(ii) were proportionate and reasonable in amount, or

(*b*) if it is assessing costs on the indemnity basis –
(i) unreasonably incurred; or
(ii) unreasonable in amount.

(2) In particular the court must give effect to any orders which have already been made.

(3) The court must also have regard to –

(*a*) the conduct of all the parties, including in particular –
(i) conduct before, as well as during, the proceedings; and
(ii) the efforts made, if any, before and during the proceedings in order to try to resolve the dispute;

(*b*) the amount or value of any money or property involved;

(*c*) the importance of the matter to all the parties;

(*d*) the particular complexity of the matter or the difficulty or novelty of the questions raised;

(*e*) the skill, effort, specialised knowledge and responsibility involved;

(*f*) the time spent on the case; and

(*g*) the place where and the circumstances in which work or any part of it was done.

(Rule 35.4(4) gives the court power to limit the amount that a party may recover with regard to the fees and expenses of an expert)

Defined terms—"costs": r 43.2(1)(*a*); "indemnity basis": r 44.4(1)(*b*); "standard basis": r 44.4(1)(*a*).

"proportionate and reasonable in amount" (r 44.5(1)(*a*)(ii))—In assessing what is "proportionate and reasonable" the court considers, in its assessment on a standard basis, what costs should be awarded if "the litigation had been appropriately conducted". A reasonable sum should be awarded for the work which was carried out and was necessary (*Lownds v Home Office (Practice Note)* [2002] EWCA Civ 365, [2002] 1 WLR 2450, CA per Lord Woolf CJ at [32] and [38]).

"conduct of all the parties" (r 44.5(3)(*a*))—In assessing one party's costs and their conduct of the dispute, the conduct of the other party is highly relevant. A co-operative opponent can contain costs: by being unco-operative he can increase costs and make work necessary which would otherwise be unnecessary (*Lownds v Home Office* (above) at [38]).

"efforts made … in order to try to resolve the dispute" (r 44.5(3)(*a*)(ii))—Orders for costs can relate to work done prior to the issue of proceedings and to proposals for settlement made prior to issue (*Butcher v Wolfe and Wolfe* [1999] 1 FLR 334, CA).

"the circumstances in which work or any part of it was done" (r 44.5(3)(*g*))—The court may allow variable rates of remuneration according to the nature of the work done at each stage (*Re Children Act 1989 (Taxation of Costs)* [1994] 2 FLR 934, Cazalet J; and see under LAFP(R)R 1991, reg 3).

****

44.7 Procedure for assessing costs

Where the court orders a party to pay costs to another party (other than fixed costs) it may either –

(*a*) make a summary assessment of the costs; or
(*b*) order detailed assessment of the costs by a costs officer,

unless any rule, practice direction or other enactment provides otherwise.

(The costs practice direction sets out the factors which will affect the court's decision under this rule)

Defined terms—"costs": r 43.2(1)(*a*); "costs officer": r 43.2(1)(*c*); "detailed assessment": r 43.4; "summary assessment": r 43.3.

Summary assessment—*Practice Direction about Costs,* Section 13 replaces, with only minor amendments, the former PD on summary assessment. Though it is said that practice directions cannot create law (*Re C (Legal Aid: Preparation of Bill of Costs)* [2001] 1 FLR 602, CA), this section of the *Practice Direction* provides an important mainstay to the operation of such very limited rules as there are on summary assessment. Thus:

(*a*) *Duty to consider costs* In general the court should consider whether to order summary assessment (para 13.1) where the hearing has lasted for not more than one day (para 13.2(2)); and see *Q v Q (Costs: Summary Assessment)* (below).
(*b*) *Parties duties to assist with summary assessment* Parties must provide a written statement of costs following Form N260 (para 13.5(1)–(3)).
(*c*) *Time for filing statement* The statement of costs should be filed "not less than 24 hours before the date fixed for the hearing" (para 13.5(4)), which in most courts seems to mean 24 hours before the hearing.
(*d*) *Failure to comply with provisions* Failure, "without reasonable excuse", to comply with this practice direction will be taken into account when any order is made (para 13.6), though failure to comply need not be fatal (*Macdonald v Taree Holdings Ltd* (2000) *The Times*, 28 December, Neuberger J).

Summary assessment: public funding and children or patients—Without citing any authority for the propositions, the *Practice Direction* states that the court "will not make a summary assessment" where the receiving party is a funded client (para 13.9) or a child or patient (para 13.11(1)). In principle, and in the absence of statutory authority, there seems to be no reason why a summary assessment of costs for a funded client receiving party should not be made: certainly that was the position which pertained before CPR 1998 came into operation.

Summary assessment and the *Leary* order—In *Leary v Leary* [1987] 1 FLR 384, Booth J made an order that a husband pay a sum of costs which she assessed summarily at the end of the hearing. This approach was subsequently approved by the Court of Appeal. It was thought that *Practice Direction about Costs*, para 13.2(2) might have brought to an end the *Leary* order. In *Q v Q (Costs: Summary Assessment)* [2002] 2 FLR 668, Wilson J drew attention to para 13.1 of the *Practice Direction* which specifies that the court "should [always] consider whether to make a summary assessment". In *Q v Q* he stated (at [34]) that the need for the parties to avoid "expense, delay and aggravation" (per Purchas LJ in *Leary*) and get on with their lives, not least of all for the benefit of the child concerned, dictated summary assessment.

44.8 Time for complying with an order for costs

A party must comply with an order for the payment of costs within 14 days of –

(*a*) the date of the judgment or order if it states the amount of those costs;
(*b*) if the amount of those costs (or part of them) is decided later in accordance with Part 47, the date of the certificate which states the amount; or
(*c*) in either case, such later date as the court may specify.

(Part 47 sets out the procedure for detailed assessment of costs)

Amendments—SI 2000/1317.

****

44.13 Special situations

(1) Where the court makes an order which does not mention costs –

(*a*) the general rule is that no party is entitled to costs in relation to that order; but
(*b*) this does not affect any entitlement of a party to recover costs out of a fund held by him as trustee or personal representative, or pursuant to any lease, mortgage or other security.

(2) The court hearing an appeal may, unless it dismisses the appeal, make orders about the costs of the proceedings giving rise to the appeal as well as the costs of the appeal.

(3) Where proceedings are transferred from one court to another, the court to which they are transferred may deal with all the costs, including the costs before the transfer.

(4) Paragraph (3) is subject to any order of the court which ordered the transfer.

Amendments—SI 2001/4015.

44.14 Court's powers in relation to misconduct

(1) The court may make an order under this rule where –

(*a*) a party or his legal representative, in connection with a summary or detailed assessment, fails to comply with a rule, practice direction or court order; or
(*b*) it appears to the court that the conduct of a party or his legal representative, before or during the proceedings which gave rise to the assessment proceedings, was unreasonable or improper.

(2) Where paragraph (1) applies, the court may –

(*a*) disallow all or part of the costs which are being assessed; or
(*b*) order the party at fault or his legal representative to pay costs which he has caused any other party to incur.

(3) Where –

(*a*) the court makes an order under paragraph (2) against a legally represented party; and
(*b*) the party is not present when the order is made,

the party's solicitor must notify his client in writing of the order no later than 7 days after the solicitor receives notice of the order.

(Other rules about costs can be found –

(*a*) in Schedule 1, in the following RSC Ord 45 (court may order act to be done at the expense of disobedient party); Ord 47 (writ of fieri facias to enforce payment of costs); and

(*b*) in Schedule 2, in the following CCR Ord 27 (attachment of earnings – judgment creditor's entitlement to costs); Ord 28 (costs on judgment summons); Ord 30 (garnishee proceedings – judgment creditor's entitlement to costs); Ord 49 (costs incurred in making a payment in under section 63 of the Trustee Act 1925 to be assessed by the detailed procedure))

Amendments—SI 2000/1317.

Defined terms—"costs": r 43.2(1)(*a*); "costs officer": r 43.2(1)(*c*); "detailed assessment": r 43.4.

"unreasonable or improper" (r 44.14(1)(*b*))—These bases for judging conduct of a party or his representative must be distinguished from the more serious "wasted costs" criteria set out in Supreme Court Act 1981, s 51(7) (see further under r 48.7). The purpose of r 44.14 is to enable the court to exercise its discretion to disallow a party's costs and to order him to pay another party's costs (see eg *Langley v North West Water Authority* [1991] 1 WLR 697, [1991] 3 All ER 610 – solicitors ordered to pay costs on their failure to comply with directions; and *R v Nottinghamshire County Council* [1993] 1 FCR 576, [1993] Fam Law 625 – local authority ordered to pay costs where adjournment was necessary because of their delay).

****

44.17 Application of costs rules

This Part and Part 45 (fixed costs), Part 46 (fast track trial costs, Part 47 (procedure for detailed assessment of costs and default provisions) and Part 48 (special cases), do not apply to the assessment of costs in proceedings to the extent that –

(*a*) section 11 of the Access to Justice Act 1999, and the provisions made under that Act; or

(*b*) regulations made under the Legal Aid Act 1988;

make different provision.

(The costs practice direction sets out the procedure to be followed where a party was wholly or partially funded by the Legal Services Commission.)

Amendments—Inserted by SI 2000/1317.

****

PART 47
PROCEDURE FOR DETAILED ASSESSMENT OF COSTS AND DEFAULT PROVISIONS

(The definitions contained in Part 43 are relevant to this Part)

Section I – General Rules about Detailed Assessment

47.1 Time when detailed assessment may be carried out

The general rule is that the costs of any proceedings or any part of the proceedings are not to be assessed by the detailed procedure until the conclusion of the proceedings but the court may order them to be assessed immediately.

(The costs practice direction gives further guidance about when proceedings are concluded for the purpose of this rule)

Defined terms —"costs": r 43.2(1)(*a*).

Scope of provision—"Detailed assessment", as distinct from "summary assessment", is the terminology preferred under CPR 1998 for what was formerly known as taxation of costs under both the old rules governing civil procedure and in legal aid legislation.

47.2 No stay of detailed assessment where there is an appeal

Detailed assessment is not stayed pending an appeal unless the court so orders.

47.3 Powers of an authorised court officer

(1) An authorised court officer has all the powers of the court when making a detailed assessment, except –

(*a*) power to make a wasted costs order as defined in rule 48.7;
(*b*) power to make an order under –
 (i) rule 44.14 (powers in relation to misconduct);
 (ii) rule 47.8 (sanction for delay in commencing detailed assessment proceedings);
 (iii) paragraph (2) (objection to detailed assessment by authorised court officer); and
(*c*) power to make a detailed assessment of costs payable to a solicitor by his client, unless the costs are being assessed under rule 48.5 (costs where money is payable to a child or patient).

(2) Where a party objects to the detailed assessment of costs being made by an authorised court officer, the court may order it to be made by a costs judge or a district judge.

(The costs practice direction sets out the relevant procedure)

Defined terms—"authorised court officer": r 43.2(1)(*d*); "costs": r 43.2(1)(*a*); "costs judge": r 43.2(1)(*b*); "detailed assessment": r 43.4; "wasted costs": SCA 1981, s 51(7).

47.4 Venue for detailed assessment proceedings

(1) All applications and requests in detailed assessment proceedings must be made to or filed at the appropriate office.

(The costs practice direction sets out the meaning of 'appropriate office' in any particular case)

(2) The court may direct that the appropriate office is to be the Supreme Court Costs Office.

(3) A county court may direct that another county court is to be the appropriate office.

(4) A direction under paragraph (3) may be made without proceedings being transferred to that court.

(Rule 30.2 makes provision for any county court to transfer the proceedings to another county court for detailed assessment of costs)

Section II – Costs Payable by One Party to Another – Commencement of Detailed Assessment Proceedings

47.5 Application of this Section

This section of Part 47 applies where a costs officer is to make a detailed assessment of costs which are payable by one party to another.

47.6 Commencement of detailed assessment proceedings

(1) Detailed assessment proceedings are commenced by the receiving party serving on the paying party –

(*a*) notice of commencement in the relevant practice form; and
(*b*) a copy of the bill of costs.

(Rule 47.7 sets out the period for commencing detailed assessment proceedings)

(2) The receiving party must also serve a copy of the notice of commencement and the bill on any other relevant persons specified in the costs practice direction.

(3) A person on whom a copy of the notice of commencement is served under paragraph (2) is a party to the detailed assessment proceedings (in addition to the paying party and the receiving party).

(The costs practice direction deals with –

- other documents which the party must file when he requests detailed assessment;
- the court's powers where it considers that a hearing may be necessary;
- the form of a bill;
- the length of notice which will be given if a hearing date is fixed).

Defined terms—"costs": r 43.2(1)(*a*); "detailed assessment": r 43.4; "paying party": r 43.2(1)(*g*); "receiving party": r 43.2(1)(*f*).

"any other relevant persons" (r 47.6(2))—*Practice Direction about Costs*, para 32.10 defines a "relevant person" for the purposes of Pt 47. This definition includes a non-party who may be required to pay costs (and see r 48.2), a trustee out of whose trust fund costs might, unusually, be paid, but not a legally assisted person (see r 47.17) and probably not a legal representative under a wasted costs order (since costs should be defined by the court at the time of the order: r 48.7(4)). The Legal Services Commission will become a relevant person where r 47.8(4) applies, as indeed it will on its own application under CLS(C)R 2000, reg 12 (and see further Procedural Guide 79E).

The client as "relevant person"—The party in respect of whom the costs are to be paid is not a relevant person, save where application is made by him to be joined as a party to assessment proceedings (*Practice Direction about Costs*, para 32.10(3)). A person can apply to be made a party under Pt 19. This will give a legally aided assisted person the right to apply to be heard on taxation of their bill, whereas, in the past, such a person's standing as a party to the taxation process was unclear. These provisions will be of greater significance where costs orders are made for differing amounts, for proportions etc. Practitioners will need to be aware that their interests may be in conflict with those of their client.

47.7 Period for commencing detailed assessment proceedings

The following table shows the period for commencing detailed assessment proceedings.

Source of right to detailed assessment	Time by which detailed assessment proceedings must be commenced
Judgment, direction, order, award or other determination	3 months after the date of the judgment etc Where detailed assessment is stayed pending an appeal, 3 months after the date of the order lifting the stay.
Discontinuance under Part 38	3 months after the date of service of notice of discontinuance under rule 38.3; or 3 months after the date of the dismissal of application to set the notice of discontinuance aside under rule 38.4
Acceptance of an offer to settle or a payment into court under Part 36	3 months after the date when the right to costs arose.

47.8 Sanction for delay in commencing detailed assessment proceedings

(1) Where the receiving party fails to commence detailed assessment proceedings within the period specified –

(*a*) in rule 47.7; or
(*b*) by any direction of the court,

the paying party may apply for an order requiring the receiving party to commence detailed assessment proceedings within such time as the court may specify.

(2) On an application under paragraph (1), the court may direct that, unless the receiving party commences detailed assessment proceedings within the time specified by the court, all or part of the costs to which the receiving party would otherwise be entitled will be disallowed.

(3) If –

(*a*) the paying party has not made an application in accordance with paragraph (1); and
(*b*) the receiving party commences the proceedings later than the period specified in rule 47.7,

the court may disallow all or part of the interest otherwise payable to the receiving party under –

(i) section 17 of the Judgments Act 1838; or
(ii) section 74 of the County Courts Act 1984,

but must not impose any other sanction except in accordance with rule 44.14 (powers in relation to misconduct).

(4) Where the costs to be assessed in a detailed assessment are payable out of the Community Legal Service Fund, this rule applies as if the receiving party were the solicitor to whom the costs are payable and the paying party were the Legal Services Commission.

Amendments—SI 2000/1317.

Defined terms—"costs": r 43.2(1)(*a*); "detailed assessment": r 43.4; "paying party": r 43.2(1)(*g*); "receiving party": r 43.2(1)(*f*).

Scope of provision—It is not necessary to obtain court permission to start detailed assessment proceedings out of time but, where proceedings are not commenced, a paying party, including for this purpose the Legal Services Commission, can seek an order to require the receiving party to do so. Thereafter, failure to commence proceedings within the requisite period of time may attract an order that all or part of the costs be disallowed. By contrast, failure to commence in accordance with the r 44.7 time-limits may only be penalised by (i) an order that interest be awarded for a shorter period and (ii) an award of costs against the legal representative on the basis of misconduct under r 44.14.

"period specified" (r 47.8(1))—See r 47.7.

"interest otherwise payable to the receiving party" (r 47.8(3))—Rule 44.3(6)(*g*) provides that an order for payment of interest on costs due can be made by the court at the same time as any order for costs is made.

47.9 Points of dispute and consequence of not serving

(1) The paying party and any other party to the detailed assessment proceedings may dispute any item in the bill of costs by serving points of dispute on –

(*a*) the receiving party; and
(*b*) every other party to the detailed assessment proceedings.

(2) The period for serving points of dispute is 21 days after the date of service of the notice of commencement.

(3) If a party serves points of dispute after the period set out in paragraph (2), he may not be heard further in the detailed assessment proceedings, unless the court gives permission.

(The costs practice direction sets out requirements about the form of points of dispute)

(4) The receiving party may file a request for a default costs certificate if –

(*a*) the period set out in rule 47.9(2) for serving points of dispute has expired; and
(*b*) he has not been served with any points of dispute.

(5) If any party (including the paying party) serves points of dispute before the issue of a default costs certificate the court may not issue the default costs certificate.

(Section IV of this Part sets out the procedure to be followed after points of dispute have been filed)

Defined terms—"costs": r 43.2(1)(*a*); "default costs certificate": r 47.11; "detailed assessment": r 43.4; "paying party": r 43.2(1)(*g*); "receiving party": r 43.2(1)(*f*).

Scope of provision—At this stage in the detailed assessment process the court is still not involved (subject to any order under r 47.8). The paying party who wishes to dispute any item on the detailed assessment bill does so by sending points of dispute, 21 days after service of the bill, to the receiving party and to anyone else interested in the assessment. Failure to send points of dispute within that time (i) prevents the paying party being heard on the detailed assessment except with the court's permission and (ii) enables the receiving party to apply to the court for a default costs certificate.

"points of dispute" (r 47.9(1))—*Practice Direction about Costs*, para 35.1 et seq provide for points of dispute and the consequences of non-service. Points of dispute should be briefly set out in accordance with para 35.3.

"21 days after the date of service of the notice" (r 47.9(2))—See r 6.7 for details of deemed service periods.

47.10 Procedure where costs are agreed

(1) If the paying party and the receiving party agree the amount of costs, either party may apply for a costs certificate (either interim or final) in the amount agreed.

(Rule 47.15 and Rule 47.16 contain further provisions about interim and final costs certificates respectively)

(2) An application for a certificate under paragraph (1) must be made to the court which would be the venue for detailed assessment proceedings under rule 47.4.

Amendments—SI 2000/1317.

Defined terms—"costs": r 43.2(1)(*a*); "default costs certificate": r 47.11; "detailed assessment": r 43.4; "paying party": r 43.2(1)(*g*); "receiving party": r 43.2(1)(*f*).

Section III – Costs Payable by One Party to Another – Default Provisions

47.11 Default costs certificate

(1) Where the receiving party is permitted by rule 47.9 to obtain a default costs certificate, he does so by filing a request in the relevant practice form.

(The costs practice direction deals with the procedure by which the receiving party may obtain a default costs certificate)

(2) A default costs certificate will include an order to pay the costs to which it relates.

(3) Where a receiving party obtains a default costs certificate, the costs payable to him for the commencement of detailed assessment proceedings shall be the sum set out in the costs practice direction.

Amendments—SI 1999/1008.

Procedure—Practice and procedure governing the application are dealt with in *Practice Direction about Costs*, paras 37.1–37.8.

47.12 Setting aside default costs certificate

(1) The court must set aside a default costs certificate if the receiving party was not entitled to it.

(2) In any other case, the court may set aside or vary a default costs certificate if it appears to the court that there is some good reason why the detailed assessment proceedings should continue.

(3) Where –

(*a*) the receiving party has purported to serve the notice of commencement on the paying party;
(*b*) a default costs certificate has been issued; and
(*c*) the receiving party subsequently discovers that the notice of commencement did not reach the paying party at least 21 days before the default costs certificate was issued;

the receiving party must –

(i) file a request for the default costs certificate to be set aside; or
(ii) apply to the court for directions.

(4) Where paragraph (3) applies, the receiving party may take no further step in –

(*a*) the detailed assessment proceedings; or
(*b*) the enforcement of the default costs certificate,

until the certificate has been set aside or the court has given directions.

(The costs practice direction contains further details about the procedure for setting aside a default costs certificate and the matters which the court must take into account)

Procedure—Practice and procedure for setting aside the certificate are dealt with in *Practice Direction about Costs*, paras 38.1–38.4.

Section IV – Costs Payable by One Party to Another – Procedure where Points of Dispute are Served

47.13 Optional reply

(1) Where any party to the detailed assessment proceedings serves points of dispute, the receiving party may serve a reply on the other parties to the assessment proceedings.

(2) He may do so within 21 days after service on him of the points of dispute to which his reply relates.

(The costs practice direction sets out the meaning of reply.)

Amendments—SI 2000/1317.

Defined terms—"detailed assessment": r 43.4; "points of dispute": r 47.9; "receiving party": r 43.2(1)(*f*).

Scope of provision—A receiving party who is served with points of dispute may serve a reply. This is entirely voluntary but if no reply is filed it may be reflected in a later order for costs on the detailed assessment. If a receiving party accepts a point raised in dispute, it might be prudent to indicate this in a reply under r 47.13. However, merely to re-argue points already raised in the bill would seem to be sterile and might risk the receiving party losing the costs so incurred.

47.14 Detailed assessment hearing

(1) Where points of dispute are served in accordance with this Part, the receiving party must file a request for a detailed assessment hearing.

(2) He must file the request within 3 months of the expiry of the period for commencing detailed assessment proceedings as specified –

(*a*) in rule 47.7; or
(*b*) by any direction of the court.

(3) Where the receiving party fails to file a request in accordance with paragraph (2), the paying party may apply for an order requiring the receiving party to file the request within such time as the court may specify.

(4) On an application under paragraph (3), the court may direct that, unless the receiving party requests a detailed assessment hearing within the time specified by the court, all or part of the costs to which the receiving party would otherwise be entitled will be disallowed.

(5) If –

(*a*) the paying party has not made an application in accordance with paragraph (3); and

(*b*) the receiving party files a request for a detailed assessment hearing later than the period specified in paragraph (2),

the court may disallow all or part of the interest otherwise payable to the receiving party under –

(i) section 17 of the Judgments Act 1838; or
(ii) section 74 of the County Courts Act 1984,

but must not impose any other sanction except in accordance with rule 44.14 (powers in relation to misconduct).

(6) No party other than –

(*a*) the receiving party;
(*b*) the paying party; and
(*c*) any party who has served points of dispute under rule 47.9,

may be heard at the detailed assessment hearing unless the court gives permission.

(7) Only items specified in the points of dispute may be raised at the hearing, unless the court gives permission.

(The costs practice direction specifies other documents which must be filed with the request for hearing and the length of notice which the court will give when it fixes a hearing date)

Amendments—SI 1999/1008; SI 2002/2058.

Defined terms—"costs": r 43.2(1)(*a*); "default costs certificate": r 47.11; "detailed assessment": r 43.4; "paying party": r 43.2(1)(*g*); "points of dispute": r 47.9; "receiving party": r 43.2(1)(*f*).

Scope of provision—Once points of dispute are served, the receiving party must file a request for a detailed assessment within three months. If the receiving party is out of time for filing the request, the paying party can ask the court to specify a date for filing. In default of this requirement, all or part of the costs may be allowed and if both paying and receiving parties delay in applying under this rule, interest on costs due may be disallowed. Only the paying party, the receiving party and any other party who has filed points of dispute may be heard at the detailed assessment hearing(s). Where matters have not been raised in the points of dispute, a party will be estopped from raising them unless the court gives permission.

Practice and procedure—*Practice Direction about Costs*, paras 40.1 et seq set out specific requirements which need to be complied with in the request for a detailed assessment hearing. Applications in the assessment proceedings are made under Pt 23.

Document giving the right to detailed assessment—This document is defined in *Practice Direction about Costs*, para 40.4 and is crucial to the process of detailed assessment since it underlines the fact that there is a right to proceed with such an assessment. The list contained in para 40.4 is intended to be exhaustive but it appears to have omitted the entitlement to legal aid detailed assessment (see further r 47.17 below), hitherto available to a solicitor as of right on termination of his retainer where the client was legally aided (except under Civil Legal Aid (General) Regulations 1989, reg 82; see para 4.5(*h*)).

"request for a detailed assessment hearing" (r 47.14(1))—The request must be in Form N258 (*Practice Direction about Costs*, para 40.2).

"any party who has served points of dispute under rule 47.9" (r 47.14(6)(*c*))—Points of dispute may also be served by every other party to the detailed assessment proceedings (r 47.9(1)(*b*)); only those "other parties" who have served points of dispute can be heard.

Section V – Interim Costs Certificate and Final Costs Certificate

47.15 Power to issue an interim certificate

(1) The court may at any time after the receiving party has filed a request for a detailed assessment hearing –

(*a*) issue an interim costs certificate for such sum as it considers appropriate;
(*b*) amend or cancel an interim certificate.

(2) An interim certificate will include an order to pay the costs to which it relates, unless the court orders otherwise.

(3) The court may order the costs certified in an interim certificate to be paid into court.

Defined terms—"costs": r 43.2(1)(*a*); "detailed assessment": r 43.4; "receiving party": r 43.2(1)(*f*).

Scope of provision—Once the receiving party has applied under r 47.14 for a detailed assessment hearing, the court may issue an interim certificate or may cancel or amend such a certificate. Costs of the application will normally be included in the certificate and an order may be made that such costs be paid into court.

Procedure for application—In accordance with *Practice Direction about Costs*, para 41.1, application for a certificate (and for its cancellation and amendment) is in accordance with Pt 23 (applications for interlocutory orders).

"issue an interim costs certificate" (r 47.15(1)(*a*))—This power appears to be additional to the power under r 44.3(8) to order costs to be paid on account before they are assessed, although any payment made under the latter rule will doubtless be taken into account when the amount to be paid under the interim costs certificate is quantified.

47.16 Final costs certificate

(1) In this rule a completed bill means a bill calculated to show the amount due following the detailed assessment of the costs.

(2) The period for filing the completed bill is 14 days after the end of the detailed assessment hearing.

(3) When a completed bill is filed the court will issue a final costs certificate and serve it on the parties to the detailed assessment proceedings.

(4) Paragraph (3) is subject to any order made by the court that a certificate is not to be issued until other costs have been paid.

(5) A final costs certificate will include an order to pay the costs to which it relates, unless the court orders otherwise.

(The costs practice direction deals with the form of a final costs certificate)

Amendments—SI 1999/1008.

Defined terms—"costs": r 43.2(1)(*a*); "detailed assessment": r 43.4; "receiving party": r 43.2(1)(*f*).

Scope of provision—Not more than two weeks after completion of all detailed assessment hearings, the receiving party should lodge a final bill showing the amount due following such assessment. The court then issues a final costs certificate which includes an order to the paying party to discharge the liability for costs, unless otherwise ordered (eg because the receiving party has an outstanding liability to make payment of a lump sum or costs to the paying party). *Practice Direction about Costs*, paras 42.1 et seq deal with practice and procedure in relation to obtaining a final certificate.

Section VI – Detailed Assessment Procedure for Costs of a LSC Funded Client or an Assisted Person where Costs are Payable out of the Community Legal Service Fund

47.17 Detailed assessment procedure for costs of a LSC funded client or an assisted person where costs are payable out of the Community Legal Service Fund

(1) Where the court is to assess costs of a LSC funded client or an assisted person which are payable out of the Community Legal Service Fund, that person's solicitor may commence detailed assessment proceedings by filing a request in the relevant practice form.

(2) A request under paragraph (1) must be filed within 3 months after the date when the right to detailed assessment arose.

(3) The solicitor must also serve a copy of the request for detailed assessment on the LSC funded client or the assisted person, if notice of that person's interest has been given to the court in accordance with community legal service or legal aid regulations.

(4) Where the solicitor has certified that the LSC funded client or the assisted person wishes to attend an assessment hearing, the court will, on receipt of the request for assessment, fix a date for the assessment hearing.

(5) Where paragraph (3) does not apply, the court will, on receipt of the request for assessment provisionally assess the costs without the attendance of the solicitor, unless it considers that a hearing is necessary.

(6) After the court has provisionally assessed the bill, it will return the bill to the solicitor.

(7) The court will fix a date for an assessment hearing if the solicitor informs the court, within 14 days after he receives the provisionally assessed bill, that he wants the court to hold such a hearing.

Amendments—SI 2000/1317; SI 2000/2092.

Defined terms—"assisted person": r 43.2(1)(*h*); "costs": r 43.2(1)(*a*); "detailed assessment": r 43.4; "request for detailed assessment": r 47.14(1).

Scope of provision—Civil Legal Aid (General) Regulations 1989, reg 107 provides for taxation of an assisted person's solicitor's bill of costs, in accordance with court order or the provisions of that regulation. This rule now applies the process of detailed assessment to such bills. It seems that any request for detailed assessment of a legal aid fund bill should be served on the assisted person, where he has an interest in such assessment, in accordance with CLA(G)R 1989, reg 119. If the assisted person so requests, the court will fix a detailed assessment hearing at which that person will be entitled to attend. *Practice Direction about Costs*, paras 43.1–43.9 deal with LSC funded (legal aid) detailed assessment.

47.17A Detailed assessment procedure where costs are payable out of a fund other than the Community Legal Service Fund

(1) Where the court is to assess costs which are payable out of a fund other than the Community Legal Service Fund, the receiving party may commence detailed assessment proceedings by filing a request in the relevant practice form.

(2) A request under paragraph (1) must be filed within 3 months after the date when the right to detailed assessment arose.

(3) The court may direct that the party seeking assessment serve a copy of the request on any person who has a financial interest in the outcome of the assessment.

(4) The court will, on receipt of the request for assessment, provisionally assess the costs without the attendance of the receiving party, unless it considers that a hearing is necessary.

(5) After the court has provisionally assessed the bill, it will return the bill to the receiving party.

(6) The court will fix a date for an assessment hearing if the party informs the court, within 14 days after he receives the provisionally assessed bill, that he wants the court to hold such a hearing.

Amendments—Inserted by SI 2000/1317.

Section VII – Costs of Detailed Assessment Proceedings

47.18 Liability for costs of detailed assessment proceedings

The receiving party is entitled to his costs of the detailed assessment proceedings except where –

- (*a*) the provisions of any Act, any of these Rules or any relevant practice direction provide otherwise; or
- (*b*) the court makes some other order in relation to all or part of the costs of the detailed assessment proceedings.

(2) In deciding whether to make some other order, the court must have regard to all the circumstances, including –

- (*a*) the conduct of all the parties;
- (*b*) the amount, if any, by which the bill of costs has been reduced; and
- (*c*) whether it was reasonable for a party to claim the costs of a particular item or to dispute that item.

47.19 Offers to settle without prejudice save as to costs of the detailed assessment proceedings

(1) Where –

- (*a*) a party (whether the paying party or the receiving party) makes a written offer to settle the costs of the proceedings which gave rise to the assessment proceedings; and
- (*b*) the offer is expressed to be without prejudice(GL) save as to the costs of the detailed assessment proceedings,

the court will take the offer into account in deciding who should pay the costs of those proceedings.

(2) The fact of the offer must not be communicated to the costs officer until the question of costs of the detailed assessment proceedings falls to be decided.

(The costs practice direction provides that rule 47.19 does not apply where the receiving party is a LSC funded client or an assisted person, unless the court orders otherwise)

Amendments—SI 2000/1317; SI 2002/2058.

Section VIII – Appeals from Authorised Court Officers in Detailed Assessment Proceedings

47.20 Right to appeal

(1) Any party to detailed assessment proceedings may appeal against a decision of an authorised court officer in those proceedings.

(2) For the purposes of this Section, a LSC funded client or an assisted person is not a party to the detailed assessment proceedings.

(Part 52 sets out general rules about appeals.)

Amendments—Substituted by SI 2000/940; amended by SI 2000/1317.

47.21 Court to hear appeal

An appeal against a decision of an authorised court officer is to a costs judge or a district judge of the High Court.

Amendments—Substituted by SI 2000/940.

47.22 Appeal procedure

(1) The appellant must file an appeal notice within 14 days after the date of the decision he wishes to appeal against.

(2) On receipt of the appeal notice, the court will –

(*a*) serve a copy of the notice on the parties to the detailed assessment proceedings; and
(*b*) give notice of the appeal hearing to those parties.

Amendments—Substituted by SI 2000/940; amended by SI 2000/1317.

47.23 Powers of the court on appeal

On an appeal from an authorised court officer the court will –

(*a*) re-hear the proceedings which gave rise to the decision appealed against; and
(*b*) make any order and give any directions as it considers appropriate.

Amendments—Substituted by SI 2000/940.

PART 48
COSTS – SPECIAL CASES

(The definitions contained in Part 43 are relevant to this Part)

Section I – Costs Payable by or to Particular Persons

48.1 Pre-commencement disclosure and orders for disclosure against a person who is not a party

(1) This paragraph applies where a person applies –

(*a*) for an order under –
(i) section 33 of the Supreme Court Act 1981; or

(ii) section 52 of the County Courts Act 1984,

(which give the court powers exercisable before commencement of proceedings); or

(*b*) for an order under –

(i) section 34 of the Supreme Court Act 1981; or

(ii) section 53 of the County Courts Act 1984,

(which give the court power to make an order against a non-party for disclosure of documents, inspection of property etc).

(2) The general rule is that the court will award the person against whom the order is sought his costs –

(*a*) of the application; and

(*b*) of complying with any order made on the application.

(3) The court may however make a different order, having regard to all the circumstances, including –

(*a*) the extent to which it was reasonable for the person against whom the order was sought to oppose the application; and

(*b*) whether the parties to the application have complied with any relevant pre-action protocol.

48.2 Costs orders in favour of or against non-parties

(1) Where the court is considering whether to exercise its power under section 51 of the Supreme Court Act 1981 (costs are in the discretion of the court) to make a costs order in favour of or against a person who is not a party to proceedings –

(*a*) that person must be added as a party to the proceedings for the purposes of costs only; and

(*b*) he must be given a reasonable opportunity to attend a hearing at which the court will consider the matter further.

(2) This rule does not apply –

(*a*) where the court is considering whether to –

(i) make an order against the Legal Services Commission;

(ii) make a wasted costs order (as defined in 48.7); and

(*b*) in proceedings to which rule 48.1 applies (pre-commencement disclosure and orders for disclosure against a person who is not a party).

Amendments—SI 2000/1317.

Defined terms—"costs": r 43.2(1)(*a*).

Scope of provision—This rule is framed pursuant to SCA 1981, s 51(3), which gives the court discretion "to determine by whom and to what extent costs are to be paid". This includes costs against a third party. Such a party must be given an opportunity to attend a hearing when, presumably, he will have the opportunity to make representations prior to any order against him being made. The rule does not apply where the third party against whom the order is sought is involved as a legal representative, in which case the wasted costs jurisdiction applies (see r 48.7).

"costs order in favour of or against a person who is not a party to proceedings" (r 48.2(1))—Guidelines for the ordering of costs against a third party were laid down by the Court of Appeal in *Symphony Group plc v Hodgson* [1994] QB 179; and see *Sarra v Sarra* [1994] 2 FLR 880, Thorpe J (costs sought against accountant called as expert witness by one party) for an example of a case in the ancillary relief jurisdiction.

48.3 Amount of costs where costs are payable pursuant to a contract

(1) Where the court assesses (whether by the summary or detailed procedure) costs which are payable by the paying party to the receiving party under the terms of a contract, the costs payable under those terms are, unless the contract expressly provides otherwise, to be presumed to be costs which –

(*a*) have been reasonably incurred; and

(*b*) are reasonable in amount;

and the court will assess them accordingly.

(The costs practice direction sets out circumstances where the court may order otherwise)

(2) This rule does not apply where the contract is between a solicitor and his client.

48.4 Limitations on court's power to award costs in favour of trustee or personal representative

(1) This rule applies where –

(*a*) a person is or has been a party to any proceedings in the capacity of trustee or personal representative; and

(*b*) rule 48.3 does not apply.

(2) The general rule is that he is entitled to be paid the costs of those proceedings, insofar as they are not recovered from or paid by any other person, out of the relevant trust fund or estate.

(3) Where he is entitled to be paid any of those costs out of the fund or estate, those costs will be assessed on the indemnity basis.

Amendments—SI 1999/1008; SI 2001/4015.

Defined terms—"costs": r 43.2(1)(*a*); "indemnity basis": r 44.4(1)(*b*).

Indemnity basis—This rule re-states the general principle that a person acting in a representative capacity should have his costs paid on an indemnity basis and, as seems likely, on the basis that those costs are paid in any event (see r 44.4 and, by analogy, RSC Ord 62 r 6(2)).

***Beddoe* orders**—Part 44 introduces much more flexibility when ordering costs. Those acting in a fiduciary capacity should be aware of the need, where necessary, to seek a *Beddoe* order (*Re Beddoe* [1893] 1 Ch 547); eg personal representatives in proceedings under I(PFD)A 1975, trustees joined in ancillary relief proceedings (see *T v T and ors (Joinder of Third Parties)* [1996] 2 FLR 357, Wilson J), pension fund trustees, trustees in bankruptcy (cf *Albert v Albert* [1997] 2 FLR 791, CA) and building society (not bank) mortgagees who respond when served in ancillary relief proceedings. In many instances, such an application is likely to be inappropriate but in cases of doubt, where a trustee thinks there is any risk of his being criticised by the court for expending the trust, or other (eg pension) fund, application should be made for an order.

Procedure on application for a *Beddoe* order—The procedure for such an application has never been clear. The family practitioner finds himself faced with a potentially hybrid procedure since the costs jurisdiction is under CPR 1998, but his application (other than under I(PFD)A 1975) is likely to be under FPR 1991 and therefore governed by those rules alone (see Procedural Guide 79B). It seems arguable that in family proceedings (as defined by MFPA, s 32), the applicant has a choice either to:

(*a*) apply on notice with an affidavit in support (FPR 1991, r 10.9); or

(*b*) apply for an order under CPR 1998, Pt 23 (which deals with applications during proceedings, ie interlocutory applications).

48.5 Costs where money is payable by or to a child or patient

(1) This rule applies to any proceedings where a party is a child or patient and –

(*a*) money is ordered or agreed to be paid to, or for the benefit of, that party; or

(*b*) money is ordered to be paid by him or on his behalf.

("Child" and "patient" are defined in rule 2.3)

(2) The general rule is that –

(*a*) the court must order a detailed assessment of the costs payable by any party who is a child or patient to his solicitor; and

(*b*) on an assessment under paragraph (*a*), the court must also assess any costs payable to that party in the proceedings, unless the court has issued a default costs certificate in relation to those costs under rule 47.11.

(3) The court need not order detailed assessment of costs in the circumstances set out in the costs practice direction.

(4) Where –

(*a*) a claimant is a child or patient; and

(*b*) a detailed assessment has taken place under paragraph (2)(*a*),

the only amount payable by the child or patient to his solicitor is the amount which the court certifies as payable.

(This rule applies to a counterclaim by or on behalf of a child or patient by virtue of rule 20.3)

****

Section II – Costs Relating to Solicitors and Other Legal Representatives

48.7 Personal liability of legal representative for costs – wasted costs orders

(1) This rule applies where the court is considering whether to make an order under section 51(6) of the Supreme Court Act 1981 (court's power to disallow or (as the case may be) order a legal representative to meet, "wasted costs").

(2) The court must give the legal representative a reasonable opportunity to attend a hearing to give reasons why it should not make such an order.

(3) (*revoked*)

(4) When the court makes a wasted costs order, it must –

(*a*) specify the amount to be disallowed or paid; or

(*b*) direct a costs judge or a district judge to decide the amount of costs to be disallowed or paid.

(5) The court may direct that notice must be given to the legal representative's client, in such manner as the court may direct –

(*a*) of any proceedings under this rule; or

(*b*) of any order made under it against his legal representative.

(6) Before making a wasted costs order, the court may direct a costs judge or a district judge to inquire into the matter and report to the court.

PART III

(7) The court may refer the question of wasted costs to a costs judge or a district judge, instead of making a wasted costs order.

Amendments—SI 2000/1317; SI 2002/2058.

Defined terms—"costs": r 43.2(1)(*a*); "costs judge": r 43.2(1)(*c*); "legal representative": SCA 1981, s 51(13); "privileged": Glossary; "wasted costs": SCA 1981, s 51(7).

Jurisdiction—This rule derives from SCA 1981, s 51(6). Where there has been an improper, negligent or unreasonable act by a legal representative, the rule gives the court a discretion to make a wasted costs order against that legal representative personally. The court must give the representative notice of any such application.

Guidance on the court's jurisdiction—In *Ridehalgh v Horsefield, and Watson v Watson (Wasted Costs Order)* [1994] 2 FLR 194, the Court of Appeal fully considered the wasted costs jurisdiction and proposed guidelines as to its exercise. Accordingly, the court must balance two, often conflicting, questions of public interest. On the one hand, lawyers should not be deterred from pursuing their clients' interests for fear of incurring personal liability for costs; on the other hand, litigants need to be protected from financial prejudice caused by the unjustifiable conduct of lawyers. The jurisdiction is one which is entirely discretionary. "Just because an application [in this case, to discharge a care order] is plainly doomed to failure it is not necessarily an improper application for a solicitor to advise a party to proceed with" (*Re O (A Minor) (Wasted Costs Application)* [1994] 2 FLR 842 per Connell J at 846H), and it therefore follows that such conduct should not attract an order for wasted costs.

Meaning of "improper, unreasonable or negligent"—These words from SCA 1981, s 51(7), were considered fully in *Ridehalgh v Horsefield* (above):

(*a*) *"Improper"* This word covers conduct which might lead to disbarment, striking off or other serious professional penalty; however, it is not restricted to this and might include other conduct stigmatised by the court in appropriate circumstances.

(*b*) *"Unreasonable"* This term includes conduct which is vexatious or harasses other parties, but it does not include an approach which merely leads to an unsuccessful result or which a more cautious representative might not have adopted.

(*c*) *"Negligent"* Essentially, this term is to be approached in a non-technical way. A legal representative may come within the definition by failing to act with the competence reasonably to be expected of a member of the legal profession.

A legal representative is not to be regarded as acting improperly, unreasonably or negligently where pursuing a hopeless case for the client, providing this does not represent an abuse of the court's process. It is the responsibility of a lawyer to present the case and of the court to judge it.

Warnings on unarguable appeals—In *Re G (A Minor) (Role of the Appellate Court)* [1987] 1 FLR 164 at 168, May LJ, firmly echoed by Nourse LJ, issued a warning to legal representatives that the court would not shrink from "investigating how public money has come to be spent in [unarguable appeals] and to make all appropriate orders to ensure that it has not been wasted".

Procedure on wasted costs orders—In *Ridehalgh v Horsefield* (above) the Court of Appeal made comments on the procedure for seeking an order. These comments have been overlaid with more detail by *Practice Direction about Costs*:

(1) Procedure after *Ridehalgh* Any procedure should be as simple and summary as possible, while remaining consistent with fairness to the respondent legal representative. In *Ridehalgh v Horsefield* Sir Thomas Bingham MR (as he then was) approved the procedure in *Re A Barrister (Wasted Costs Order) (No 1 of 1991)* [1993] QB 293; namely:

(*a*) Where the court intends to exercise the wasted costs jurisdiction it must set out clearly and concisely the complaint and grounds upon which the order is to be made. These measures are draconian and, as with contempt proceedings, the grounds must be clear and particularised.

(*b*) A three-stage test would apply: (i) Had there been an improper, unreasonable or negligent act or omission? (ii) As a result had any costs been incurred by a party? (iii) If the answers to both questions was "yes", should the court make an order; and if so what specific sum should be considered?

(*c*) The court should formally state its complaint, in chambers, and invite comments from the representative. After comments have been heard from any other party, the court should give a formal ruling.

(*d*) The court must specify the sum to be disallowed.

(2) Procedure under the *Practice Direction about Costs*—Under the *Practice Direction* it becomes clear that there can be two routes to an order (paras 53.3 and 53.4): (i) the application by a party and (ii) the order by the court of its own initiative. Hitherto, the first route has been the more usual but the procedure proposed by *Re A Barrister (Wasted Costs Order) (No 1 of 1991)* suggested that it could only be the court which would frame the claim against the legal representative. Now the party seeking a wasted costs order must state a complaint. Paragraph 53.3 of the *Practice Direction* requires that the party who wishes to apply for a wasted costs order must give notice of such application in accordance with Part 23 or by making an oral application in the course of any hearing. Under Part 23 the application notice must set out "what the legal representative is alleged to have done or failed to do", accompanied by details of precisely what costs are sought against him.

"legal representative" (r 48.7(1), (2), (5))—Supreme Court Act 1981, s 51(13) defines "legal or other representative" as "in relation to a party to proceedings, any person exercising a right of audience or right to conduct litigation on his behalf". Rule 48.7 uses "legal representative" as synonymous with that definition. Courts and Legal Services Act 1990, s 119(1) defines "right of audience" as "the right to exercise any of the functions of appearing before and addressing a court including the calling and examining of witnesses"; it defines "right to conduct litigation" as being the right to issue process and to perform ancillary functions in relation to proceedings. This definition of legal representative applies also to members of the bar as advocates (see eg *Re G, S and M (Wasted Costs)* [2000] 1 FLR 52, Wall J: care proceedings where time was wasted because expert witnesses had not seen relevant documents before giving evidence – resulted in wasted costs order against counsel for local authority). A wasted costs order cannot be made against a party's former legal representative who neither issued proceedings nor did anything ancillary to the conduct of litigation (*Byrne v Sefton Health Authority* [2001] EWCA Civ 1904, (2001) *The Times*, 28 November, CA).

PART III

Wasted costs, proportionality and disclosure of documents—Where a party's solicitors press another party, especially a local authority, for wide-ranging disclosure which may be of dubious relevance to the case, their attention may be drawn to the case of *R v Reading Justices ex parte Berkshire County Council* [1996] 1 FLR 149, in which disclosure of documents from criminal proceedings was limited to "material evidence" (MCA 1980, s 97(1)). If the solicitors persist in seeking extensive disclosure, they risk a wasted costs order (*R v M (Wasted Costs Order)* [1996] 1 FLR 750). With greater court control of disclosure under CPR 1998 these comments will become less relevant but they remain noteworthy whilst the majority of those Rules do not apply to family proceedings.

Privilege and wasted costs—Where a paying party has refused to waive privilege in respect of documents relevant to assessment of wasted costs, the court must be particularly wary of making an order against a legal representative (*Medcalf v Weatherhill* [2002] 3 WLR 272, HL).

CLS funding (Legal aid)—Nothing in these rules, or in Supreme Court Act 1981, s 51(6), affects the power of the court on taxation of legal aid costs to disallow or reduce wasted costs (Civil Legal Aid (General) Regulations 1989, reg 109(1), which adopts the same definition of "wasted costs" as does SCA 1981, s 51(7); and see reg 102, which enables a legal aid area committee to defer part or all of a solicitor's costs where he has failed to comply with any regulation/condition and as a result the fund suffers loss). The court retains its inherent jurisdiction to order solicitors to repay costs to the legal aid fund where there has been a serious dereliction of duty, and presumably now where costs have been wasted, but this applies only where the Legal Services Commission pursues its remedy promptly (*Clark v Clark (No 2)* [1991] 1 FLR 179).

48.8 Basis of detailed assessment of solicitor and client costs

(1) This rule applies to every assessment of a solicitor's bill to his client except a bill which is to be paid out of the Community Legal Service Fund under the Legal Aid Act 1988 or the Access to Justice Act 1999.

(1A) Section 74(3) of the Solicitors Act 1974 applies unless the solicitor and client have entered into a written agreement which expressly permits payment to the solicitor of an amount of costs greater than that which the client could have recovered from another party to the proceedings.

(2) Subject to paragraph (1A), costs are to be assessed on the indemnity basis but are to be presumed –

(*a*) to have been reasonably incurred if they were incurred with the express or implied approval of the client;

(*b*) to be reasonable in amount if their amount was expressly or impliedly approved by the client;

(*c*) to have been unreasonably incurred if –

(i) they are of an unusual nature or amount; and

(ii) the solicitor did not tell his client that as a result he might not recover all of them from the other party.

(3), (4) ...

Amendments—SI 1999/1008; SI 2000/1317; SI 2001/256.

****

PART 50
APPLICATION OF THE SCHEDULES

50 (1) The Schedules to these Rules set out, with modifications, certain provisions previously contained in the Rules of the Supreme Court 1965 and the County Court Rules 1981.

(2) These Rules apply in relation to the proceedings to which the Schedules apply subject to the provisions in the Schedules and the relevant practice directions.

(3) A provision previously contained in the Rules of the Supreme Court 1965 –

(*a*) is headed "RSC";

(*b*) is numbered with the Order and rule numbers it bore as part of the RSC; and

(*c*) unless otherwise stated in the Schedules or the relevant practice direction, applies only to proceedings in the High Court.

(4) A provision previously contained in the County Court Rules 1981 –

(*a*) is headed "CCR";

(*b*) is numbered with the Order and rule numbers it bore as part of the CCR; and

(*c*) unless otherwise stated in the Schedules or the relevant practice direction, applies only to proceedings in the county court.

(5) A reference in a Schedule to a rule by number alone is a reference to the rule so numbered in the Order in which the reference occurs.

(6) A reference in a Schedule to a rule by number prefixed by "CPR" is a reference to the rule with that number in these Rules.

(7) In the Schedules, unless otherwise stated, "the Act" means –

(*a*) in a provision headed "RSC", the Supreme Court Act 1981; and

(*b*) in a provision headed "CCR", the County Courts Act 1984.

****

PART 52
APPEALS

I General Rules about Appeals

52.1 Scope and interpretation

(1) The rules in this Part apply to appeals to –

(*a*) the civil division of the Court of Appeal;
(*b*) the High Court; and
(*c*) a county court.

(2) This Part does not apply to an appeal in detailed assessment proceedings against a decision of an authorised court officer.

(Rules 47.21 to 47.26 deal with appeals against a decision of an authorised court officer in detailed assessment proceedings)

(3) In this Part –

(*a*) "appeal" includes an appeal by way of case stated;
(*b*) "appeal court" means the court to which an appeal is made;
(*c*) "lower court" means the court, tribunal or other person or body from whose decision an appeal is brought;
(*d*) "appellant" means a person who brings or seeks to bring an appeal;
(*e*) "respondent" means –
  (i) a person other than the appellant who was a party to the proceedings in the lower court and who is affected by the appeal; and
  (ii) a person who is permitted by the appeal court to be a party to the appeal; and
(*f*) "appeal notice" means an appellant's or respondent's notice.

(4) This Part is subject to any rule, enactment or practice direction which sets out special provisions with regard to any particular category of appeal.

Amendments—Inserted by SI 2000/221; amended by SI 2000/2092.

Scope of Part 52—This Part applies to all appeals to the Court of Appeal and to appeals to the High Court which are not defined as family proceedings under MFPA 1984, s 40. It applies to non-family appeals to the High Court which were previously covered by RSC Ords 55 and 58. This Part also provides, in addition to appeals to the Court of Appeal, the power of the High Court or the county court on appeal to transfer a case for determination by the Court of Appeal where it is thought that that appeal raises an important point of practice, or there is some other compelling reason (r 52.14).

For the general jurisdiction of the Court of Appeal, see SCA 1981, ss 15–18. For restriction of appeals to the Court of Appeal, see SCA 1981, ss 16, 18.

Appeal—An appeal is an application to set aside or vary a decision of the court below on the ground that it was wrongly made. Appeals against ex parte orders are discouraged (see **Ex parte orders** under SCA 1981, s 18), as are appeals against interim orders (see *G v G (Interim Custody: Appeal)* (1983) FLR 327; *Edwards v Edwards* [1986] 1 FLR 205). To challenge an order that has been made by consent where the basis of the order has been frustrated by one party, the aggrieved party may appeal or should preferably return to the court which made the order (*Middleton v Middleton* [1998] 2 FLR 821; see also notes to FPR 1991, r 8.1).

Appeals against Decree Nisi—PD52, para 21.1 makes special provision for such appeals.

Contempt appeals—PD52, para 21.4 makes special provision for such appeals.

52.2 Parties to comply with the practice direction

All parties to an appeal must comply with the relevant practice direction.

Amendments—Inserted by SI 2000/221.

"the relevant practice direction"—See *Practice Direction (Appeals)* (PD52) which supplements this Part generally, set out in Part V of this work.

52.3 Permission

(1) An appellant or respondent requires permission to appeal –

(*a*) where the appeal is from a decision of a judge in a county court or the High Court, except where the appeal is against –
(i) a committal order;
(ii) a refusal to grant habeas corpus; or
(iii) a secure accommodation order made under section 25 of the Children Act 1989; or

(*b*) as provided by the relevant practice direction.

(Other enactments may provide that permission is required for particular appeals)

(2) An application for permission to appeal may be made –

(*a*) to the lower court at the hearing at which the decision to be appealed was made; or
(*b*) to the appeal court in an appeal notice.

(Rule 52.4 sets out the time limits for filing an appellant's notice at the appeal court. Rule 52.5 sets out the time limits for filing a respondent's notice at the appeal court. Any application for permission to appeal to the appeal court must be made in the appeal notice (see rules 52.4(1) and 52.5(3))

(Rule 52.13(1) provides that permission is required from the Court of Appeal for all appeals to that court from a decision of a county court or the High Court which was itself made on appeal)

(3) Where the lower court refuses an application for permission to appeal, a further application for permission to appeal may be made to the appeal court.

(4) Where the appeal court, without a hearing, refuses permission to appeal, the person seeking permission may request the decision to be reconsidered at a hearing.

(5) A request under paragraph (4) must be filed within seven days after service of the notice that permission has been refused.

(6) Permission to appeal will only be given where –

(*a*) the court considers that the appeal would have a real prospect of success; or
(*b*) there is some other compelling reason why the appeal should be heard.

(7) An order giving permission may –

(*a*) limit the issues to be heard; and
(*b*) be made subject to conditions.

(Rule 3.1(3) also provides that the court may make an order subject to conditions)

(Rule 25.15 provides for the court to order security for costs of an appeal)

Amendments—Inserted by SI 2000/221.

Scope of provision—Save for those limited exceptions set out here, permission to appeal is required in all cases. The application should usually be made to the judge whose decision is to be appealed, at the time the decision is made (see PD52, para 4.6) and, if refused, thereafter to the Court of Appeal. An application directly to the Court of Appeal, whilst permissible within the terms of the rule (see PD52, para 4.7), is unusual. If there has been a "paper" refusal by the Court of Appeal (see PD52, para 4.11), there may be a renewal of the application before a Lord Justice (see PD52, para 4.13). It is necessary to show a "real prospect" of success or "some other compelling reason" (r 52.3(6)). There is no appeal from the decision at the oral hearing (see PD52, para 4.8). Where the appeal to the Court of Appeal is a second appeal (ie an appeal from a decision of the High Court on appeal from the family proceedings court) there is an additional hurdle to overcome (see r 52.13), namely the requirement to establish an important point of principle or practice or some other compelling reason to grant permission. On a second appeal, the application for permission to appeal must be made to the Court of Appeal (see PD52, para 4.9).

Limited permission—It is possible for there to be a grant of permission to appeal in relation to a limited issue (r 52.3(7)). The court should normally refuse permission on the other grounds (see PD52, para 4.18) and those issues may then not be raised at the appeal hearing without the court's permission (PD52, para 4.18). Where a party has been present at the hearing to determine permission to appeal, he cannot apply to limit the scope of the appeal (see r 52.9).

Consent orders—In relation to a consent order, consideration must be given to whether the matter should be returned to the judge who heard the matter for a rehearing rather than to appeal. This seems to be the preferred course in relation to orders made as a result of fraud, mistake or material non-disclosure, or where there has been a new event to invalidate the basis of the order (see *Re C (Financial Provision: Leave to Appeal)* [1993] 2 FLR 799 and *Benson v Benson (Deceased)* [1996] 1 FLR 692). This route is the more appropriate where there are issues of fact to be determined or a substitute order is sought. Bad advice cannot found the basis for an appeal against the making of a consent order (*Tibbs v Dick* [1998] 2 FLR 1118).

52.4 Appellant's notice

(1) Where the appellant seeks permission from the appeal court it must be requested in the appellant's notice.

(2) The appellant must file the appellant's notice at the appeal court within –

(*a*) such period as may be directed by the lower court; or

(*b*) where the court makes no such direction, 14 days after the date of the decision of the lower court that the appellant wishes to appeal.

(3) Unless the appeal court orders otherwise, an appeal notice must be served on each respondent –

(*a*) as soon as practicable; and

(*b*) in any event not later than 7 days,

after it is filed.

Amendments—Inserted by SI 2000/221.

Scope of provision—A notice of appeal must be filed (unless otherwise ordered) within 14 days of the decision to be appealed. PD52, para 5.19 states that the prescribed period should not normally exceed 28 days. The Notice must be served as soon as practicable thereafter and in any event not later than 7 days thereafter. The respondent need do nothing until notification of the grant of permission to appeal (PD52, para 5.22).

Where the appeal is out of time, it seems that a composite application for permission to appeal must be made in order to comply with the general requirement of permission and because the time for appealing has expired. In those circumstances, the Notice of Appeal should seek permission to appeal and an extension of time for filing the Notice of Appeal (see PD52, para 5.2).

PART III

Procedure following the grant of permission—PD52, para 5.6 sets out the documents that the appellant is required to file with the Notice of Appeal. A skeleton argument must also accompany the Notice (see PD52, para 5.9). Once permission to appeal has been granted, copies of all the documents filed must be served upon the respondents within 7 days of receiving the order granting permission to appeal (PD52, para 6.2). The Court of Appeal send the parties notification of the period of time in which the appeal is likely to be heard, together with a questionnaire (PD52, para 6.4). This requires the appellant to give a time estimate for the hearing of the appeal.

52.5 Respondent's notice

(1) A respondent may file and serve a respondent's notice.

(2) A respondent who –

(*a*) is seeking permission to appeal from the appeal court; or
(*b*) wishes to ask the appeal court to uphold the order of the lower court for reasons different from or additional to those given by the lower court,

must file a respondent's notice.

(3) Where the respondent seeks permission from the appeal court it must be requested in the respondent's notice.

(4) A respondent's notice must be filed within –

(*a*) such period as may be directed by the lower court; or
(*b*) where the court makes no such direction, 14 days, after the date in paragraph (5).

(5) The date referred to in paragraph (4) is –

(*a*) the date the respondent is served with the appellant's notice where –
(i) permission to appeal was given by the lower court; or
(ii) permission to appeal is not required;
(*b*) the date the respondent is served with notification that the appeal court has given the appellant permission to appeal; or
(*c*) the date the respondent is served with notification that the application for permission to appeal and the appeal itself are to be heard together.

(6) Unless the appeal court orders otherwise a respondent's notice must be served on the appellant and any other respondent –

(*a*) as soon as practicable; and
(*b*) in any event not later than 7 days,

after it is filed.

Amendments—Inserted by SI 2000/221.

Scope of provision—Unless the respondent wishes to cross-appeal or justify the order for different reasons, there is no need to provide a Notice. If the respondent wishes to file a Notice, he must do so within 14 days unless otherwise directed (r 52.5(4)) and serve it as soon as practicable and in any event within 7 days thereafter (r 52.5(6)). An appeal by a respondent will also require permission (see PD52, para 7.1). A respondent must file and serve a skeleton argument. It may be lodged as part of the Respondent's Notice. If there is no Respondent's Notice, the skeleton argument must be lodged and served within 21 days of receipt of the appellant's skeleton argument (PD52, para 7.7).

52.6 Variation of time

(1) An application to vary the time limit for filing an appeal notice must be made to the appeal court.

(2) The parties may not agree to extend any date or time limit set by –

(*a*) these Rules;
(*b*) the relevant practice direction; or
(*c*) an order of the appeal court or the lower court.

(Rule 3.1(2)(*a*) provides that the court may extend or shorten the time for compliance with any rule, practice direction or court order (even if an application for extension is made after the time for compliance has expired))

(Rule 3.1(2)(*b*) provides that the court may adjourn or bring forward a hearing)

Amendments—Inserted by SI 2000/221.

52.7 Stay(GL)

Unless –

(*a*) the appeal court or the lower court orders otherwise; or
(*b*) the appeal is from the Immigration Appeal Tribunal,

an appeal shall not operate as a stay of any order or decision of the lower court.

Amendments—Inserted by SI 2000/221.

Scope of provision—An appeal (meaning an application for permission or following the grant of permission) does not automatically operate to stop the order which is the subject of the appeal taking effect. An application must be made for a stay of the order. A stay should normally be sought at the time of the application for permission to appeal, if not immediately following the decision which is to be appealed. An application for a stay must be determined by a judge and is usually heard by a single Lord Justice (see r 52.16).

52.8 Amendment of appeal notice

An appeal notice may not be amended without the permission of the appeal court.

Amendments—Inserted by SI 2000/221.

52.9 Striking out(GL) appeal notices and setting aside or imposing conditions on permission to appeal

(1) The appeal court may –

(*a*) strike out the whole or part of an appeal notice;
(*b*) set aside(GL) permission to appeal in whole or in part;
(*c*) impose or vary conditions upon which an appeal may be brought.

(2) The court will only exercise its powers under paragraph (1) where there is a compelling reason for doing so.

(3) Where a party was present at the hearing at which permission was given he may not subsequently apply for an order that the court exercise its powers under sub-paragraphs (1)(*b*) or (1)(*c*).

Amendments—Inserted by SI 2000/221.

Scope of provision—See notes to r 52.3 (above).

52.10 Appeal court's powers

(1) In relation to an appeal the appeal court has all the powers of the lower court.

(Rule 52.1(4) provides that this Part is subject to any enactment that sets out special provisions with regard to any particular category of appeal – where such an enactment gives a statutory power to a tribunal, person or other body it may be the case that the appeal court may not exercise that power on an appeal)

(2) The appeal court has power to –

(*a*) affirm, set aside or vary any order or judgment made or given by the lower court;
(*b*) refer any claim or issue for determination by the lower court;
(*c*) order a new trial or hearing;
(*d*) make orders for the payment of interest;
(*e*) make a costs order.

(3) In an appeal from a claim tried with a jury the Court of Appeal may, instead of ordering a new trial –

(*a*) make an order for damages(GL); or
(*b*) vary an award of damages made by the jury.

(4) The appeal court may exercise its powers in relation to the whole or part of an order of the lower court.

(Part 3 contains general rules about the court's case management powers)

Amendments—Inserted by SI 2000/221.

Scope of provision—Like the High Court, the Court of Appeal is a Superior Court of Record (SCA 1981, s 15) and has all the authority and jurisdiction of the court from which the appeal is brought. Having decided that the decision of the lower court was wrong, the Court of Appeal may set aside the order and order a new trial, substitute an order and make such order as the case may require. This includes a power to make interim orders pending a re-hearing (*Re R (Minors) (Custody)* [1986] 1 FLR 6). Supreme Court Act 1981, s 17 provides that any application for a new trial in the High Court must be made to the Court of Appeal.

"all the powers of the lower court" (r 52.10(1))—This includes the power to re-hear the matter (see r 52.11). This is a power seldom used (see r 52.11). The appeal is determined in accordance with the principles of *G v G (Minors: Custody Appeal)* [1985] FLR 894 [1985] 1 WLR 647. The appeal court does not hear the evidence and does not exercise a discretion afresh but must consider whether the court that heard the evidence erred in principle or was otherwise plainly wrong (see *Re W, Re A, Re B* [1999] 2 FLR 930 and *Re C (Leave to remove from jurisdiction)* [2000] 2 FCR 40).

Fresh evidence—There is a presumption that the Court of Appeal will determine the appeal on the basis of the evidence that was before the lower court. Fresh evidence will not be admitted without an order to that effect. Fresh evidence may be evidence of events since the decision which was the subject of the appeal or evidence relating to matters prior to the hearing that is the subject of the appeal but was not available at the hearing in the lower court. There is no specific requirement to be satisfied in respect of an application to admit fresh evidence. The former requirements laid down in *Ladd v Marshall* [1954] 1 WLR 1489, [1954] 3 All ER 745 are relevant as matters which should be considered in an exercise of the discretion whether to allow an appellant to rely on evidence not before the court below. These factors are:
(*a*) the evidence could not have been obtained with reasonable diligence at the trial;
(*b*) the evidence must be such that, if given, it would probably have had an important influence on the result of the case, though it need not be decisive; and
(*c*) the evidence must be such as would presumably be believed, or in other words, it must be apparently credible though it need not be incontrovertible (see *Hickey v Marks* (2000) 6 July, (unreported), CA and *Gillingham v Gillingham* [2001] EWCA Civ 906, [2001] All ER 52). There are dicta to suggest that in any case involving the welfare of a child fresh evidence

would be admitted (*M v M (Transfer of Custody: Appeal)* [1987] 2 FLR 146 at 150B; *Re B (Minors) (Custody)* [1991] 1 FLR 137 at 149B; but see also *B v P (Access)* [1992] 2 FCR 576).

These conditions do not apply to evidence in relation to matters that have occurred after the trial or where there was no trial on the facts. In such a situation the question of receiving the new evidence is a matter for the discretion of the Court of Appeal. In deciding whether to admit fresh evidence as to events since the date of the trial, the Court of Appeal will consider the matter without the benefit of the fresh evidence and, if the decision was wrong in accordance with the principles of *G v G (Minors: Custody Appeal)* [1985] FLR 894, [1985] 1 WLR 647, the court will consider the evidence and consider what weight to attach to it (*M v M (Transfer of Custody: Appeal)* [1987] 2 FLR 146 and *Re G (A Minor) (Wardship: Access)* [1988] 1 FLR 305).

Hopeless appeals—See notes to FPR 1991, r 8.1.

52.11 Hearing of appeals

(1) Every appeal will be limited to a review of the decision of the lower court unless –

(*a*) a practice direction makes different provision for a particular category of appeal; or

(*b*) the court considers that in the circumstances of an individual appeal it would be in the interests of justice to hold a re-hearing.

(2) Unless it orders otherwise, the appeal court will not receive –

(*a*) oral evidence; or

(*b*) evidence which was not before the lower court.

(3) The appeal court will allow an appeal where the decision of the lower court was –

(*a*) wrong; or

(*b*) unjust because of a serious procedural or other irregularity in the proceedings in the lower court.

(4) The appeal court may draw any inference of fact which it considers justified on the evidence.

(5) At the hearing of the appeal a party may not rely on a matter not contained in his appeal notice unless the appeal court gives permission.

Amendments—Inserted by SI 2000/221.

Listing—Following the grant of permission to appeal, the Court of Appeal will send a questionnaire to the appellant requesting a time estimate and giving the period of time in which the appeal is likely to be heard (see PD52, para 6.1). There are seven different lists held in respect of cases in the Court of Appeal (see PD52, para 15.8). A further category entitled the "special fixtures list" was added by *Practice Note of 20 February 2001* . *Practice Note of 4 July 2001* gives details of the hear-by date listing windows, within which time it is expected that the Court of Appeal will hear an appeal. In respect of family cases, the hear-by date window is 3–4 months in relation to children cases and 6–9 months in respect of other family appeals. An application to expedite or delay a hearing must be made to a Master or single Lord Justice.

Expediting an appeal—In *Unilever plc v Chefaro Proprietaries Ltd* [1995] 1 WLR 243, the Court of Appeal set out the approach to applications for expedition of the hearing of an appeal (to be included in the "expedited list"). It was stated that, in the following cases, justice could be done only if the appeal was heard immediately or within a matter of days:

(*a*) committal appeals, particularly if there were adverse findings or the sentence was short;

(*b*) where children were likely to suffer extraordinary prejudice beyond that inevitably involved in the proceedings;

(*c*) Hague Convention cases;

(*d*) asylum appeals;

(*e*) execution of a possession order;
(*f*) where an irrevocable decision is to be implemented;
(*g*) publication of allegedly unlawful material;
(*h*) judicial decisions in the course of proceedings.

Further, the court recognised the need to try and arrange an expedited hearing where otherwise:
(*a*) a party might lose its livelihood;
(*b*) the appeal would become futile;
(*c*) the resolution of other similar cases awaiting the outcome of the appeal would be delayed;
(*d*) a widespread divergence of practice would continue;
(*e*) there would be serious detriment to public administration.

52.12 Non-disclosure of Part 36 offers and payments

(1) The fact that a Part 36 offer or Part 36 payment has been made must not be disclosed to any judge of the appeal court who is to hear and finally determine an appeal until all questions (other than costs) have been determined.

(2) Paragraph (1) does not apply if the Part 36 offer or Part 36 payment is relevant to the substance of the appeal.

(3) Paragraph (1) does not prevent disclosure in any application in the appeal proceedings if disclosure of the fact that a Part 36 offer or Part 36 payment has been made is properly relevant to the matter to be decided.

Amendments—Inserted by SI 2000/221.

II Special Provisions applying to the Court of Appeal

52.13 Second appeals to the court

(1) Permission is required from the Court of Appeal for any appeal to that court from a decision of a county court or the High Court which was itself made on appeal.

(2) The Court of Appeal will not give permission unless it considers that –

(*a*) the appeal would raise an important point of principle or practice; or
(*b*) there is some other compelling reason for the Court of Appeal to hear it.

Amendments—Inserted by SI 2000/221.

Scope of provision—Where it is proposed to appeal the decision of the county court or the High Court which itself was a determination of an appeal, there is an additional hurdle to overcome in obtaining permission to appeal. The proposed appellant must show that there is some compelling reason or some important point of principle. It is possible that rather than determining the appeal itself, the lower court, having considered that there is some important point of principle or there is some other compelling reason may transfer the appeal to be heard by the Court of Appeal (see r 52.14). Permission to appeal may be sought in relation to the substantive order but there can be no appeal in relation to the refusal (of the lower court) to grant permission to appeal (see Access to Justice Act 1999, s 54; *Bulled v Khayat and Another* [2002] EWCA Civ 804 and *Slot v Isaac* [2002] EWCA Civ 481, [2002] All ER (D) 197 (Apr)).

52.14 Assignment of appeals to the Court of Appeal

(1) Where the court from or to which an appeal is made or from which permission to appeal is sought ("the relevant court") considers that –

(*a*) an appeal which is to be heard by a county court or the High Court would raise an important point of principle or practice; or
(*b*) there is some other compelling reason for the Court of Appeal to hear it,

the relevant court may order the appeal to be transferred to the Court of Appeal.

(The Master of the Rolls has the power to direct that an appeal which would be heard by a county court or the High Court should be heard instead by the Court of Appeal – see section 57 of the Access to Justice Act 1999)

(2) The Master of the Rolls or the Court of Appeal may remit an appeal to the court in which the original appeal was or would have been brought.

Amendments—Inserted by SI 2000/221.

Scope of provision—Where an appeal is to be heard in the county court or the High Court, that court may transfer the appeal to be heard by the Court of Appeal. If that court (the county court or High Court) hears and determines the appeal, there can be an appeal to the Court of Appeal from that decision only if there is some important point of principle or other compelling reason (see r 52.13).

52.15 Judicial review appeals

(1) Where permission to apply for judicial review has been refused at a hearing in the High Court, the person seeking that permission may apply to the Court of Appeal for permission to appeal.

(2) An application in accordance with paragraph (1) must be made within 7 days of the decision of the High Court to refuse to give permission to apply for judicial review.

(3) On an application under paragraph (1), the Court of Appeal may, instead of giving permission to appeal, give permission to apply for judicial review.

(4) Where the Court of Appeal gives permission to apply for judicial review in accordance with paragraph (3), the case will proceed in the High Court unless the Court of Appeal orders otherwise.

Amendments—Inserted by SI 2000/221.

52.16 Who may exercise the powers of the Court of Appeal

(1) A court officer assigned to the Civil Appeals Office who is –

(*a*) a barrister; or
(*b*) a solicitor

may exercise the jurisdiction of the Court of Appeal with regard to the matters set out in paragraph (2) with the consent of the Master of the Rolls.

(2) The matters referred to in paragraph (1) are –

(*a*) any matter incidental to any proceedings in the Court of Appeal;
(*b*) any other matter where there is no substantial dispute between the parties; and
(*c*) the dismissal of an appeal or application where a party has failed to comply with any order, rule or practice direction.

(3) A court officer may not decide an application for –

(*a*) permission to appeal;
(*b*) bail pending an appeal;
(*c*) an injunction (GL);

(*d*) a stay(GL) of any proceedings, other than a temporary stay of any order or decision of the lower court over a period when the Court of Appeal is not sitting or cannot conveniently be convened.

(4) Decisions of a court officer may be made without a hearing.

(5) A party may request any decision of a court officer to be reviewed by the Court of Appeal.

(6) At the request of a party, a hearing will be held to reconsider a decision of –

(*a*) a single judge; or
(*b*) a court officer,

made without a hearing.

(7) A single judge may refer any matter for a decision by a court consisting of two or more judges.

(Section 54(6) of the Supreme Court Act 1981 provides that there is no appeal from the decision of a single judge on an application for permission to appeal)

(Section 58(2) of the Supreme Court Act 1981 provides that there is no appeal to the House of Lords from decisions of the Court of Appeal that –

(*a*) are taken by a single judge or any officer or member of staff of that court in proceedings incidental to any cause or matter pending before the civil division of that court; and
(*b*) do not involve the determination of an appeal or of an application for permission to appeal,

and which may be called into question by rules of court. Rules 52.16(5) and (6) provide the procedure for the calling into question of such decisions)

Amendments—Inserted by SI 2000/221.

****

PART 54
JUDICIAL REVIEW

Practice Direction—See *Practice Direction (Judicial Review)* which supplements this Part generally, set out in Part V of this work.

54.1 Scope and interpretation

(1) This Part contains rules about judicial review.

(2) In this Part –

(*a*) a "claim for judicial review" means a claim to review the lawfulness of –
  (i) an enactment; or
  (ii) a decision, action or failure to act in relation to the exercise of a public function.
(*b*) an order of mandamus is called a "mandatory order";
(*c*) an order of prohibition is called a "prohibiting order";
(*d*) an order of certiorari is called a "quashing order";
(*e*) "the judicial review procedure" means the Part 8 procedure as modified by this Part;

(*f*) "interested party" means any person (other than the claimant and defendant) who is directly affected by the claim; and

(*g*) "court" means the High Court, unless otherwise stated.

(Rule 8.1(6)(*b*) provides that a rule or practice direction may, in relation to a specified type of proceedings, disapply or modify any of the rules set out in Part 8 as they apply to those proceedings)

Amendments—Inserted by SI 2000/2092.

Scope of provision—This rule provides the procedure for an application to the Administrative Court for judicial review. A claim for judicial review means a claim to review the lawfulness of an enactment or a decision, action or failure to act in relation to the exercise of a public function. The procedure must be used where the claimant is seeking a mandatory order (formerly known as an order of mandamus), a prohibiting order (formerly known as an order of prohibition) and a quashing order (formerly known as an order of certiorari) (see r 52.2). The procedure may also be used to obtain a declaration or injunction or an order for damages (see r 52.3 and Supreme Court Act 1981, s 31).

The Administrative Court—All applications for judicial review in England must be made to the Administrative Court, The Royal Courts of Justice, The Strand, WC2A 2LL. Where a judicial review application is proceeding in Wales (because there is a devolution issue arising out of the Government of Wales Act 1998 or an issue concerning the National Assembly of Wales, the Welsh executive, or any Welsh public body) an application may be lodged at the Royal Courts of Justice in London or at the Law Courts, Cathays Park, Cardiff, CF10 3PG (see also PD54, para 3.1). Neither the court or the Administrative Court has power to grant public funding (legal aid), which must be obtained from the Legal Services Commission.

54.2 When this Part must be used

The judicial review procedure must be used in a claim for judicial review where the claimant is seeking –

(*a*) a mandatory order;

(*b*) a prohibiting order;

(*c*) a quashing order; or

(*d*) an injunction under section 30 of the Supreme Court Act 1981 (restraining a person from acting in any office in which he is not entitled to act).

Amendments—Inserted by SI 2000/2092.

Scope of provision—Part 54 provides the only method of seeking the orders set out (see also Supreme Court Act 1981, ss 29–31; County Courts Act 1984, s 38).

54.3 When this Part may be used

(1) The judicial review procedure may be used in a claim for judicial review where the claimant is seeking –

(*a*) a declaration; or

(*b*) an injunction[(GL)].

(Section 31(2) of the Supreme Court Act 1981 sets out the circumstances in which the court may grant a declaration or injunction in a claim for judicial review)

(Where the claimant is seeking a declaration or injunction in addition to one of the remedies listed in rule 54.2, the judicial review procedure must be used)

(2) A claim for judicial review may include a claim for damages but may not seek damages alone.

(Section 31(4) of the Supreme Court Act sets out the circumstances in which the court may award damages on a claim for judicial review)

Amendments—Inserted by SI 2000/2092.

Scope of provision—Part 54 provides the method of seeking the orders set out (see also Supreme Court Act 1981, ss 29–31). A declaration or injunction may also be obtained in other proceedings (under the inherent jurisdiction of the High Court; see Supreme Court Act 1981, s 37 and County Courts Act 1984, s 38 for injunctions).

54.4 Permission required

The court's permission to proceed is required in a claim for judicial review whether started under this Part or transferred to the Administrative Court.

Amendments—Inserted by SI 2000/2092.

Scope of provision—There is a filter process for all applications for judicial review. Permission to apply must be obtained. This is usually considered, in the first instance without a hearing (see PD54, para 8.4). The decision of the judge (Form JRJ) will be served upon the claimant, the defendant and any other person named on the claim form. If permission is granted, the claimant must lodge the application fee (£120) with the Administrative Office within 7 days of service of the judge's decision upon him. If permission is refused or granted subject to conditions or on certain grounds, the claimant may request an oral hearing. Such a request must be filed within 7 days after service of the notification of the decision (see r 54.12 and PD54, para 8.5). At the oral hearing the claimant is allocated 20 minutes of court time. If this is considered insufficient, the claimant must file a written estimate and request a special fixture. It is not necessary for the defendant or any interested party to attend, but they may do so (see PD54, para 8.5). An appeal may be made to the Court of Appeal in respect of the judge's decision, following an oral hearing (see r 52.15).

Documents—The claimant must file a claim form in accordance with CPR 1998, Pt 8 as modified by this rule. The standard form N461 should be used, which may be obtained from the Administrative Office or on the Court Service website (*www.courtservice.gov.uk*). The following documents must be filed with the claim form (PD54, para 5.6). The claimant must lodge two copies of a paginated and indexed bundle containing the claim form, which must include or be accompanied by:

(1) a detailed statement of the claimant's grounds for bringing the claim for judicial review;
(2) a statement of the facts relied on;
(3) any application to extend the time limit for filing the claim form;
(4) any application for directions; and
(5) a time estimate for the hearing.

In addition, the claim form must be accompanied by:

(i) any written evidence in support of the claim or application to extend time;
(ii) a copy of any order that the claimant seeks to have quashed;
(iii) where the claim for judicial review relates to a decision of a court or tribunal, an approved copy of the reasons for reaching that decision;
(iv) copies of any documents on which the claimant proposes to rely;
(v) copies of any relevant statutory material;
(vi) a list of essential documents for advance reading by the court (with page references to the passages relied on).

Where it is not possible to file all the above documents, the claimant must indicate which documents have not been filed and the reasons why they are not currently available (see PD54, para 5.6).

Human rights issues—Where the claimant is seeking to raise any human rights issue the claim form must include the information specified in PD16, para 15.1, namely:

(*a*) give details of the alleged convention right infringed;
(*b*) specify the relief sought;

(*c*) state if the relief sought includes a declaration of incompatibility or damages in respect of a judicial act;
(*d*) where there is a claim for a declaration of incompatibilty, give details of the legislative provision;
(*e*) where the claim relates to unlawfulness by another court or tribunal, give details of the finding;
(*f*) where the claim relates to a judicial act, provide details of the act complained of and the court or tribunal concerned.

54.5 Time limit for filing claim form

(1) The claim form must be filed –

(*a*) promptly; and
(*b*) in any event not later than 3 months after the grounds to make the claim first arose.

(2) The time limit in this rule may not be extended by agreement between the parties.

(3) This rule does not apply when any other enactment specifies a shorter time limit for making the claim for judicial review.

Amendments—Inserted by SI 2000/2092.

54.6 Claim form

(1) In addition to the matters set out in rule 8.2 (contents of the claim form) the claimant must also state –

(*a*) the name and address of any person he considers to be an interested party;
(*b*) that he is requesting permission to proceed with a claim for judicial review; and
(*c*) any remedy (including any interim remedy) he is claiming.

(Part 25 sets out how to apply for an interim remedy)

(2) The claim form must be accompanied by the documents required by the relevant practice direction.

Amendments—Inserted by SI 2000/2092.

Scope of provision—See notes to r 54.4 (above).

54.7 Service of claim form

The claim form must be served on –

(*a*) the defendant; and
(*b*) unless the court otherwise directs, any person the claimant considers to be an interested party,

within 7 days after the date of issue.

Amendments—Inserted by SI 2000/2092.

Scope of provision—Once permission to apply for judicial review has been granted, the application will be issued by the Administrative Court. Within 7 days of the date of issue, the claimant must serve the defendant and any interested party with the claim form and accompanying documents. Once service has been effected, the claimant must lodge a certificate of service in the Administrative Court Office within 7 days of service. The Administrative Court will not effect service (see PD54, para 6.1).

54.8 Acknowledgment of service

(1) Any person served with the claim form who wishes to take part in the judicial review must file an acknowledgment of service in the relevant practice form in accordance with the following provisions of this rule.

(2) Any acknowledgment of service must be –

(*a*) filed not more than 21 days after service of the claim form; and
(*b*) served on –
(i) the claimant; and
(ii) subject to any direction under rule 54.7(*b*), any other person named in the claim form,

as soon as practicable and, in any event, not later than 7 days after it is filed.

(3) The time limits under this rule may not be extended by agreement between the parties.

(4) The acknowledgment of service –

(*a*) must –
(i) where the person filing it intends to contest the claim, set out a summary of his grounds for doing so; and
(ii) state the name and address of any person the person filing it considers to be an interested party; and
(*b*) may include or be accompanied by an application for directions.

(5) Rule 10.3(2) does not apply.

Amendments—Inserted by SI 2000/2092.

Scope of provision—Any person served with a claim form who wishes to take part in the proceedings must file in the Administrative Court Office an acknowledgment of service on Form N462 (available from the Office or the Court Service website on *www.courtservice.gov.uk*) within 21 days of service. The acknowledgment of service must state whether the defendant intends to contest the claim and whether he seeks a different remedy (CPR 1998, r 8.3(2)). The acknowledgment must be served upon the claimant within 7 days of it being filed. The court, if requested, will serve this (the defendant must provide the copies for service). The acknowledgment of service may only be amended or withdrawn with permission of the court (see PD10, para 5.4).

54.9 Failure to file acknowledgment of service

(1) Where a person served with the claim form has failed to file an acknowledgment of service in accordance with rule 54.8, he –

(*a*) may not take part in a hearing to decide whether permission should be given unless the court allows him to do so; but
(*b*) provided he complies with rule 54.14 or any other direction of the court regarding the filing and service of –
(i) detailed grounds for contesting the claim or supporting it on additional grounds; and
(ii) any written evidence,

may take part in the hearing of the judicial review.

(2) Where that person takes part in the hearing of the judicial review, the court may take his failure to file an acknowledgment of service into account when deciding what order to make about costs.

(3) Rule 8.4 does not apply.

Amendments—Inserted by SI 2000/2092.

54.10 Permission given

(1) Where permission to proceed is given the court may also give directions.

(2) Directions under paragraph (1) may include a stay[GL] of proceedings to which the claim relates.

(Rule 3.7 provides a sanction for the non-payment of the fee payable when permission to proceed has been given)

Amendments—Inserted by SI 2000/2092.

Scope of provision—Upon the granting of permission to proceed, directions may be made about serving the claim form/evidence on any other person and the need for expedition.

Human Rights issues—Where a claim relates to a human rights issue, a direction may be made for giving notice to the Crown or joining it as a party to the proceedings. By virtue of CPR 1998, r 19.4A the court is not entitled to make a declaration of incompatibility in accordance with HRA 1998, s 4 unless 21 days' notice (or such other period as the court may direct) has been given to the Crown. Where notice has been given to the Crown, a Minister or other person permitted by the Act must be joined as a party. There is a similar provision where the claim under HRA 1998, s 9 seeks damages and notice must be given to the Crown.

54.11 Service of order giving or refusing permission

The court will serve –

(*a*) the order giving or refusing permission; and
(*b*) any directions,

on –

(i) the claimant;
(ii) the defendant; and
(iii) any other person who filed an acknowledgment of service.

Amendments—Inserted by SI 2000/2092.

54.12 Permission decision without a hearing

(1) This rule applies where the court, without a hearing –

(*a*) refuses permission to proceed; or
(*b*) gives permission to proceed –
  (i) subject to conditions; or
  (ii) on certain grounds only.

(2) The court will serve its reasons for making the decision when it serves the order giving or refusing permission in accordance with rule 54.11.

(3) The claimant may not appeal but may request the decision to be reconsidered at a hearing.

(4) A request under paragraph (3) must be filed within 7 days after service of the reasons under paragraph (2).

(5) The claimant, defendant and any other person who has filed an acknowledgment of service will be given at least 2 days' notice of the hearing date.

Amendments—Inserted by SI 2000/2092.

Scope of provision—The court will generally, in the first instance, consider the question of permission without a hearing (PD54, para 8.4). Where permission has been refused or granted with conditions or on a limited basis, the claimant may seek an oral hearing for reconsideration of the decision (see notes to r 54.4).

54.13 Defendant etc may not apply to set aside(GL)

Neither the defendant nor any other person served with the claim form may apply to set aside(GL) an order giving permission to proceed.

Amendments—Inserted by SI 2000/2092.

54.14 Response

(1) A defendant and any other person served with the claim form who wishes to contest the claim or support it on additional grounds must file and serve –

(*a*) detailed grounds for contesting the claim or supporting it on additional grounds; and
(*b*) any written evidence,

within 35 days after service of the order giving permission.

(2) The following rules do not apply –

(*a*) rule 8.5(3) and 8.5(4) (defendant to file and serve written evidence at the same time as acknowledgment of service); and
(*b*) rule 8.5(5) and 8.5(6) (claimant to file and serve any reply within 14 days).

Amendments—Inserted by SI 2000/2092.

Scope of provision—A party who has been served with a claim form may contest the claim. To do so they must, within 35 days of service of the order granting permission, file and serve their grounds and written evidence in a paginated bundle (PD54, para 10.1).

54.15 Where claimant seeks to rely on additional grounds

The court's permission is required if a claimant seeks to rely on grounds other than those for which he has been given permission to proceed.

Amendments—Inserted by SI 2000/2092.

54.16 Evidence

(1) Rule 8.6(1) does not apply.

(2) No written evidence may be relied on unless –

(*a*) it has been served in accordance with any –
(i) rule under this Part; or
(ii) direction of the court; or
(*b*) the court gives permission.

Amendments—Inserted by SI 2000/2092; amended by SI 2002/2058.

Scope of provision—The provisions for filing evidence in judicial review proceedings are contained within this rule, as Pt 8 is disapplied. When the claim form is lodged, it should be accompanied by written evidence (see notes to r 54.4). If the claimant seeks to rely on further evidence permission must be obtained to do so.

Skeleton arguments—The claimant must file and serve a skeleton argument not less than 21 days before the hearing (or the warned date) (PD54, para 15.1; for documents to be filed see notes to r 54.4). The skeleton argument must contain:

(1) a time estimate for the complete hearing, including delivery of judgment;
(2) a list of issues;
(3) a list of the legal points to be taken (together with any relevant authorities with page references to the passages relied on);
(4) a chronology of events, with page references to the bundle of documents (see para 16.1);
(5) a list of essential documents for the advance reading of the court, with page references to the passages relied on (if different from that filed with the claim form) and a time estimate for that reading; and
(6) a list of persons referred to.

Any defendant or interested party must file a skeleton argument not less than 14 days before the hearing.

Documents—The claimant must file a paginated and indexed bundle of all relevant documents required for the hearing of the judicial review when he files his skeleton argument. The bundle must also include those documents required by the defendant and any other party who is to make representations at the hearing (PD54, para 16).

54.17 Court's powers to hear any person

(1) Any person may apply for permission –

(*a*) to file evidence; or
(*b*) make representations at the hearing of the judicial review.

(2) An application under paragraph (1) should be made promptly.

Amendments—Inserted by SI 2000/2092.

Scope of provision—Where the parties consent, the court may deal with an application to file evidence without a hearing. Permission to file evidence may be given on conditions or with directions (PD54, para 13).

54.18 Judicial review may be decided without a hearing

The court may decide the claim for judicial review without a hearing where all the parties agree.

Amendments—Inserted by SI 2000/2092.

54.19 Court's powers in respect of quashing orders

(1) This rule applies where the court makes a quashing order in respect of the decision to which the claim relates.

(2) The court may –

(*a*) remit the matter to the decision-maker; and
(*b*) direct it to reconsider the matter and reach a decision in accordance with the judgment of the court.

(3) Where the court considers that there is no purpose to be served in remitting the matter to the decision-maker it may, subject to any statutory provision, take the decision itself.

(Where a statutory power is given to a tribunal, person or other body it may be the case that the court cannot take the decision itself)

Amendments—Inserted by SI 2000/2092.

Scope of provision—The court is entitled to quash a decision and direct there be a further consideration, or make the decision itself.

54.20 Transfer

The court may –

(*a*) order a claim to continue as if it had not been started under this Part; and
(*b*) where it does so, give directions about the future management of the claim.

(Part 30 (transfer) applies to transfers to and from the Administrative Court)

Amendments—Inserted by SI 2000/2092.

Scope of provision—Under CPR 1998, r 30.5 the High Court may transfer proceedings from one Division to another. Any application to transfer should be made to the Judge of the Administrative Court for a matter to proceed in that court. In deciding whether to transfer to the Administrative Court, the court will consider whether the case contains issues of public law (PD54, para 14.2).

****

PART 57
PROBATE AND INHERITANCE

Practice Direction—See *Practice Direction (Probate)* (PD 57) which supplements this Part generally, set out in Part V of this work.

57.1 Scope of this Part and definitions

(1) This Part contains rules about –

(*a*) probate claims;
(*b*) claims for the rectification of wills;
(*c*) claims and applications to –
(i) substitute another person for a personal representative; or
(ii) remove a personal representative; and
(*d*) claims under the Inheritance (Provision for Family and Dependants) Act 1975.

(2) In this Part:

(*a*) "probate claim" means a claim for –
(i) the grant of probate of the will, or letters of administration of the estate, of a deceased person;
(ii) the revocation of such a grant; or
(iii) a decree pronouncing for or against the validity of an alleged will;
not being a claim which is non-contentious (or common form) probate business;

(Section 128 of the Supreme Court Act 1981 defines non-contentious (or common form) probate business.)

(*b*) "relevant office" means –
(i) in the case of High Court proceedings in a Chancery district registry, that registry;

(ii) in the case of any other High Court proceedings, Chancery Chambers at the Royal Courts of Justice, Strand, London, WC2A 2LL; and

(iii) in the case of county court proceedings, the office of the county court in question;

(*c*) "testamentary document" means a will, a draft of a will, written instructions for a will made by or at the request of, or under the instructions of, the testator, and any document purporting to be evidence of the contents, or to be a copy, of a will which is alleged to have been lost or destroyed;

(*d*) "will" includes a codicil.

Amendments—Inserted by SI 2001/1388; amended by SI 2002/2058.

****

IV Claims under the Inheritance (Provision for Family and Dependants) Act 1975

57.14 Scope of this Section

This Section contains rules about claims under the Inheritance (Provision for Family and Dependants) Act 1975 ("the Act").

Amendments—Inserted by SI 2002/2058.

57.15 Proceedings in the High Court

(1) Proceedings in the High Court under the Act shall be issued in either –

(*a*) the Chancery Division; or
(*b*) the Family Division.

(2) The Civil Procedure Rules apply to proceedings under the Act which are brought in the Family Division, except that the provisions of the Family Proceedings Rules 1991 relating to the drawing up and service of orders apply instead of the provisions in Part 40 and its practice direction.

Amendments—Inserted by SI 2002/2058.

Jurisdiction—See **"court"** under I(PFD)A 1975, s 1. As to the jurisdiction of the county court, see also under County Courts Act 1984, s 25. For transfer of proceedings to a county court and from a county court, see CPR 1998, Pt 30.

Transfer of proceedings—The criteria to which the court must have regard include those set out in CPR 1998, r 30.3(2). Where there are existing related proceedings, these may make transfer appropriate and it may also be appropriate where, for example, the application involves the taking of complicated accounts, for which facilities exist in the Chancery Division.

57.16 Procedure for claims under section 1 of the Act

(1) A claim under section 1 of the Act must be made by issuing a claim form in accordance with Part 8.

(2) Rule 8.3 (acknowledgment of service) and rule 8.5 (filing and serving written evidence) apply as modified by paragraphs (3) to (5) of this rule.

(3) The written evidence filed and served by the claimant with the claim form must have exhibited to it an official copy of –

(*a*) the grant of probate or letters of administration in respect of the deceased's estate; and

(*b*) every testamentary document in respect of which probate or letters of administration were granted.

(4) The time within which a defendant must file and serve –

(*a*) an acknowledgment of service; and

(*b*) any written evidence,

is not more than 21 days after service of the claim form on him.

(5) A defendant who is a personal representative of the deceased must file and serve written evidence, which must include the information required by the practice direction.

Amendments—Inserted by SI 2002/2058.

Time for application—Save with the leave of the court, an application under the Inheritance (Provision for Family and Dependants) Act 1975 may not be made after the end of the period of six months from the date on which representation with respect to the estate is first taken out (I(PFD)A 1975, s 4). Where an extension of time is sought this must be applied for specifically in the claim form.

Procedure on application—The claim is issued in the case of High Court proceedings either in London (in Chancery Chambers at the Royal Courts of Justice, Strand, London WC2A 2LL or the Principal Registry of the Family Division) or in any district registry of the High Court. In the case of county court proceedings, the office of the county court in question. The claimant must file any written statement or an affidavit in support of the claim when he files the claim form and serve a copy on the defendant with the claim form. It should be intituled "In the matter of [the estate in which the claim arises] and in the matter of the Inheritance (Provision for Family and Dependants) Act 1975". It must set out concisely the relief or remedy which is claimed in the proceedings.

"claim under section 1"—An application under s 1 of the 1975 Act is an application for financial provision from a deceased's estate. The relief claimed will generally be that available under ss 2, 5, 10–13, 16 and 17 of the Act.

Subsequent application—Where an order has been made under s 1 of the Act any subsequent applications, for instance under ss 6 and 7 of the Act for variation, discharge or suspension of an order under s 2(1) for periodical payments and a lump sum by instalment, whether by a party to the proceedings or by any other person should be made by the issue of an application on notice in accordance with Part 23. Such an application is by "application notice" in the proceedings and must be supported by a witness statement/affidavit. It is submitted that since the application is akin to an application for a variation of an order in matrimonial proceedings the procedure laid down under FPR 1991, Pt III should be followed.

Claimants—See PD 57, para 17. Where it is discovered that there may be conflicting interests between two or more claimants, eg between mother and a child, the court will have to consider what directions to give. In such cases, the court may direct that the claimants be separately represented or that some of the claimants be made defendants, direct that separate applications be issued and then make an order consolidating all the applications.

Witness statement/affidavit in support—This rule and r 8.5 refer to written evidence being filed without referring to the form in which that evidence should be given. It is suggested that the evidence should either take the form of a written statement with the appropriate declaration or an affidavit. This rule does not prescribe the contents of the applicant's witness statement/affidavit but clearly the statement/affidavit must set out facts which establish the right to apply and exhibit to it an official copy of the grant of probate or letters of administration in respect of the deceased's estate and any other testamentary document in respect of which probate or letters of administration was granted. In the case of a spouse the marriage certificate should be exhibited; where there has been a divorce, or a decree of nullity or judicial separation a certified copy of the decree should be exhibited. A certified copy of the death certificate should always be exhibited. The applicant should also set out the basis upon which the claim is made. Where seeking to transfer proceedings between county courts, within the High Court or between the High Court and a county court, the attention of practitioners is also drawn to the importance of setting out particulars of any known proceedings relevant to the application and any other matter referred to in CPR 1998, r 30.3. Such proceedings will often be material to the question whether the application ought to be transferred from the Family Division to the Chancery Division or vice versa. Where the application seeks an order for the avoidance of a disposition, the witness statement/affidavit must show that the conditions set out in ss 10 and 11 are satisfied. In a case where the application seeks the variation of a maintenance agreement, the provisions of FPR 1991, r 3.3(2) should be used as a guide.

Defendants—The personal representatives and the beneficiaries under the will or on intestacy are the defendants to an application under I(PFD)A 1975. Where the defendant is a child or under disability, the usual procedure for the appointment of a litigation friend should be followed. RSC Ord 99, r 4 provided that the court could direct any person to be added to the proceedings or that notice of the proceedings be served on any person. It also provided that CPR, r 19.7 should apply to proceedings under the Act. CPR, Pt 57 is silent on this issue. However it is submitted that CPR, r 19.7 continues to apply because that rule provides that it applies to "claims about the estate of a deceased person". Thus, where there are possible claimants under the deceased's will or intestacy who cannot be ascertained or found, or it appears to the court expedient for the purpose of saving costs, the Official Solicitor can be appointed under this rule to represent the missing beneficiaries or possible claimants. Where the proceedings raise issues of disputed facts, it is not appropriate to order a third party, such as the Official Solicitor, to represent the missing defendant/s (*Cotton v Official Solicitor* [1989] 6 CL 385). This rule is not however confined to cases of missing claimants or defendants. The court may use its power to join a person for example where there is a mentally handicapped person who may have a possible claim against the estate. In such an instance the person may be joined by his litigation friend, in which case the usual procedure for the appointment of a litigation friend may be followed. Where however, there is a possibility of conflict arising, and it is difficult to appoint a suitable person to act for the mentally handicapped person it may be more appropriate to invite the Official Solicitor to act.

Acknowledgement of service by personal representative—See PD 57, para 15.

Personal representative's statement/affidavit—For contents of the statement/affidavit see PD 57, para 16. It is mandatory for the personal representative to file a statement/affidavit in answer within 21 days of service (including the day of service). The information required to be particularised in the statement/affidavit is that contained in r 5(2). With reference to r 5(2)(*d*), the facts which might be relevant to the exercise of the court's powers depend on the circumstances of each case. I(PFD)A 1975, s 3(1)(*g*) requires the court to have regard to "any other matter ... which in the circumstances of the case the court may consider relevant". This provision is wide enough to include, for example, the deceased's reasons for making or not making any provision in his will for the applicant. The deceased's reasons may have been given orally, in writing or otherwise, and may be very relevant. Provision is made under I(PFD)A 1975, s 21 for a statement made by the deceased, whether orally or in a document or otherwise, to be admissible under Civil Evidence Act 1968, s 2 "as evidence of any fact stated therein in like manner as if the statement were a statement falling within section 2(1) of that Act" or "given or proposed to be given in evidence under section 2". For cases where the deceased's reasons were found to be relevant, see *Re Coventry (dec'd); Coventry v Coventry* [1980] Ch 461, (1979) FLR Rep 142; *Re Leach (dec'd); Leach v Lindeman* [1986] Ch 226, [1985] FLR 1120.

****

GLOSSARY

Scope

This glossary is a guide to the meaning of certain legal expressions as used in these Rules, but it does not give the expressions any meaning in the Rules which they do not otherwise have in the law.

PART III

Expression	**Meaning**
Affidavit	A written, sworn statement of evidence.
Alternative dispute resolution	Collective description of methods of resolving disputes otherwise than through the normal trial process.
Base rate	The interest rate set by the Bank of England which is used as the basis for other banks' rates.
Contribution	A right of someone to recover from a third person all or part of the amount which he himself is liable to pay.
Counterclaim	A claim brought by a defendant in response to the claimant's claim, which is included in the same proceedings as the claimant's claim.
Cross-examination (and see "evidence in chief")	Questioning of a witness by a party other than the party who called the witness.
Damages	A sum of money awarded by the court as compensation to the claimant.
– aggravated damages	Additional damages which the court may award as compensation for the defendant's objectionable behaviour.
– exemplary damages	Damages which go beyond compensating for actual loss and are awarded to show the court's disapproval of the defendant's behaviour.
Defence of tender before claim	A defence that, before the claimant started proceedings, the defendant unconditionally offered to the claimant the amount due or, if no specified amount is claimed, an amount sufficient to satisfy the claim.
Evidence in chief (and see "cross-examination")	The evidence given by a witness for the party who called him.
Indemnity	A right of someone to recover from a third party the whole amount which he himself is liable to pay.
Injunction	A court order prohibiting a person from doing something or requiring a person to do something.

Joint liability (and see "several liability")	Parties who are jointly liable share a single liability and each party can be held liable for the whole of it.
Limitation period	The period within which a person who has a right to claim against another person must start court proceedings to establish that right. The expiry of the period may be a defence to the claim.
List	Cases are allocated to different lists depending on the subject matter of the case. The lists are used for administrative purposes and may also have their own procedures and judges.
Official copy	A copy of an official document, supplied and marked as such by the office which issued the original.
Practice form	Form to be used for a particular purpose in proceedings, the form and purpose being specified by a practice direction.
Pre-action protocol	Statements of understanding between legal practitioners and others about pre-action practice and which are approved by a relevant practice direction.
Privilege	The right of a party to refuse to disclose a document or produce a document or to refuse to answer questions on the ground of some special interest recognised by law.
Seal	A seal is a mark which the court puts on a document to indicate that the document has been issued by the court.
Service	Steps required by rules of court to bring documents used in court proceedings to a person's attention.
Set aside	Cancelling a judgment or order or a step taken by a party in the proceedings.
Several liability (and see "joint liability")	A person who is severally liable with others may remain liable for the whole claim even where judgment has been obtained against the others.
Stay	A stay imposes a halt on proceedings, apart from taking any steps allowed by the Rules or the terms of the stay. Proceedings can be continued if a stay is lifted.

Strike out	Striking out means the court ordering written material to be deleted so that it may no longer be relied upon.
Without prejudice	Negotiations with a view to a settlement are usually conducted "without prejudice" which means that the circumstances in which the content of those negotiations may be revealed to the court are very restricted.

SCHEDULE 1

****

RSC ORDER 45
ENFORCEMENT OF JUDGMENTS AND ORDERS: GENERAL

1–4

Set out in original Rules of the Supreme Court 1965.

5 Enforcement of judgment to do or abstain from doing any act (RSC Ord 45, r 5)

(1) Where –

(*a*) a person required by a judgment or order to do an act within a time specified in the judgment or order refuses or neglects to do it within that time or, as the case may be, within that time as extended or abridged under [a court order or CPR rule 2.11] [*Order 3, rule 5*]; or

(*b*) a person disobeys a judgment or order requiring him to abstain from doing an act,

then, subject to the provisions of these rules, the judgment or order may be enforced by one or more of the following means, that is to say –

(i) with the [permission] [*leave*] of the Court, a writ of sequestration against the property of that person;

(ii) where that person is a body corporate, with the [permission] [*leave*] of the Court, a writ of sequestration against the property of any director or other officer of the body;

(iii) subject to the provisions of the Debtors Act 1869 and 1878, an order of committal against that person or, where that person is a body corporate, against any such officer.

(2) Where a judgment or order requires a person to do an act within a time therein specified and an order is subsequently made under rule 6 requiring the act to be done within some other time, references in paragraph (1) of this rule to a judgment or order shall be construed as references to the order made under rule 6.

(3) Where under any judgment or order requiring the delivery of any goods the person liable to execution has the alternative of paying the assessed value of the goods, the judgment or order shall not be enforceable by order of committal under paragraph (1), but the Court may, on the application of the person entitled to

enforce the judgment or order, make an order requiring the first mentioned person to deliver the goods to the applicant within a time specified in the order, and that order may be so enforced.

General Note—Modifications to this rule, set out above in its re-enacted form, are highlighted by the addition of square brackets. The words in italics are those employed in the original version of the RSC (which continue to govern enforcement in "family proceedings"). For further examination of this issue see **Which rules of court** in the Legal background to Procedural Guide 38 and the annotations under FPR 1991, r 1.3.

"may be enforced" (r 5(1))—Refusal or neglect to do an act specified in an injunctive order (see below), or doing an act prohibited by an injunctive order, is a civil contempt of court and the court has power to enforce the order or punish the contempt by imprisonment, fine, sequestration, authorisation of work being done at the expense of the disobedient party (r 8) and other means of enforcement. An injunctive order which is irregular or thought to be oppressive must be obeyed unless or until it is set aside (*Isaac v Robertson* [1985] AC 97, [1984] 3 WLR 705). Application to set aside an order made ex parte should be made to the court which granted the order, not by appeal (*Hadkinson v Hadkinson* [1952] P 285, [1952] 2 All ER 567; *G v G (Ouster: Ex parte Application)* [1990] 1 FLR 395). An injunction which is unfairly oppressive may be reviewed by the court which granted it (*Jordan v Norfolk CC* [1994] 1 WLR 1353). For extended discussion of the powers for enforcement, see the annotations to CPR 1998, Sch 2, CCR Ord 29. For procedure, see CPR 1998, Sch 1, RSC Ord 45, rr 6, 7.

Injunctive order—Not all orders which provide for an act to be done or abstained from are injunctive. A declaratory order, eg a pattern of defined contact under CA 1989, s 8, should not have a warning notice attached under FPR 1991, r 4.21A unless a specific direction to hand over the child has been added under CA 1989, s 11(7), although in a family proceedings court this is not required by virtue of CA 1989, s 14(1). Further, with limited exceptions, orders for payment of money are not enforceable as contempts; see **Debtors Acts 1869 and 1878** below.

Debtors Acts 1869 and 1878 (r 5(1)(iii))—Subject to certain exceptions, an order for committal may not be made for disobedience to an order for payment of money. The only provision of these Acts which is likely to be of interest in family proceedings is Debtors Act 1869, s 5 (see FPR 1991, rr 7.4, 7.5 (judgment summons on non-payment of maintenance order)).

"writ of sequestration" (r 5(1)(i), (ii))—See rr 6–8 and Ord 46, r 5.

"order of committal" (r 5(1)(iii))—See rr 6 to 8 and Ord 52.

Undertaking enforceable as if it were an order—An undertaking to the court to do something, or to refrain from doing something, is enforceable as if it were an order (*Gandolfo v Gandolfo (Standard Chartered Bank, Garnishee)* [1981] QB 359). The court can require the giver to sign a statement to the effect that he understands the terms of his undertaking and the consequences of failure to comply with it (*Practice Direction (Judgments and Orders)* (PD 40B), para 9.3).

Undertaking to pay money—An order to pay money in general is not enforceable as a civil contempt under Ord 45, r 5, but may be enforced by judgment summons under Debtors Act 1869, s 5, if it is a maintenance order (Administration of Justice Act 1970, s 11). An undertaking to pay money may not be enforced by committal except as permitted under Debtors Act 1869, s 5 (*Buckley v Crawford* [1893] 1 QB 105). An undertaking can be enforced as if it were an order (*Gandolfo v Gandolfo (Standard Bank, Garnishee)* [1981] QB 359). In *Mubarak v Mubarak* [2001] 1 FLR 698 the judgment summons procedure was held to be incompatible with the European Convention on Human Rights. However, FPR 1991 have been amended with effect from 24 February 2003 to remove that incompatibility.

6 Judgment, etc requiring act to be done: order fixing time for doing it (RSC Ord 45, r 6)

(1) Notwithstanding that a judgment or order requiring a person to do an act specifies a time within which the act is to be done, the Court shall, [*without prejudice to Order 3, rule 5,*] have power to make an order requiring the act to be

done within another time, being such time after service of that order, or such other time, as may be specified therein.

(2) Where [, *notwithstanding Order 42, rule 2(1) or by reason of Order 42, rule 2(2)*] a judgment or order requiring a person to do an act does not specify a time within which the act is to be done, the Court shall have power subsequently to make an order requiring the act to be done within such time after service of that order, or such other time, as may be specified therein.

(3) An application for an order under this rule must be made [in accordance with CPR Part 23 and the application notice must] [*by summons and the summons must, notwithstanding anything in Order 65, rule 9*], be served on the person required to do the act in question.

General Note—Modifications to this rule, set out above in its re-enacted form, are highlighted by the addition of square brackets. The words in italics are those employed in the original version of the RSC (which continue to govern enforcement in "family proceedings"). For further examination of this issue see **Which rules of court** in the Legal background to Procedural Guide 38 and the annotations under FPR 1991, r 1.3.

Scope of provision—This rule empowers the court to change (or fix) the time for doing an act required by an earlier order. *Practice Direction (Judgments and Orders)* (PD 40B), para 8.1 also requires the date to be fixed.

Order 42, r 2 (r 6(2))—An order for delivery of goods, for possession of land or for payment of money will not usually specify a time for compliance, although it may do so, and any other order should do so.

"notwithstanding anything in Order 65, rule 9" (r 6(3))—But for this provision, this rule would excuse service on a defendant who had not filed an acknowledgement of service or who otherwise did not have an address for service.

Undertakings – variation of time specified—An undertaking is given voluntarily, and the time within which an undertaking is to be complied with can be varied upon application by the giver. The court should not vary the time promised by the giver, unless the giver agrees.

Specifying a time—Any order made under this rule must be precise and clear as to the time fixed. Unless reference to a period after service of the order is necessary, it is preferable to refer to a calendar date than to an interval. It is best to avoid the need to refer to other orders or documents to interpret the order made.

7 Service of copy of judgment, etc, prerequisite to enforcement under r 5 (RSC Ord 45, r 7)

(1) In this rule references to an order shall be construed as including references to a judgment.

(2) Subject to [*Order 24, rule 16(3), Order 26, rule 6(3), and*] paragraphs (6) and (7) of this rule, an order shall not be enforced under rule 5 unless –

- (*a*) a copy of the order has been served personally on the person required to do or abstain from doing the act in question; and
- (*b*) in the case of an order requiring a person to do an act, the copy has been so served before the expiration of the time within which he was required to do the act.

(3) Subject as aforesaid, an order requiring a body corporate to do or abstain from doing an act shall not be enforced as mentioned in rule 5(1)(*b*)(ii) or (iii) unless –

(*a*) a copy of the order has also been served personally on the officer against whose property [permission] [*leave*] is sought to issue a writ of sequestration or against whom an order of committal is sought; and
(*b*) in the case of an order requiring the body corporate to do an act, the copy has been so served before the expiration of the time within which the body was required to do the act.

(4) There must be prominently displayed on the front of the copy of an order served under this rule a warning to the person on whom the copy is served that disobedience to the order would be a contempt of court punishable by imprisonment, or (in the case of an order requiring a body corporate to do or abstain from doing an act) punishable by sequestration of the assets of the body corporate and by imprisonment of any individual responsible.

(5) With the copy of an order required to be served under this rule, being an order requiring a person to do an act, there must also be served a copy of any order [or agreement under CPR rule 2.11] [*made under Order 3, rule 5,*] extending or abridging the time for doing the act and, where the first-mentioned order was made under rule 5(3) or 6 of this Order, a copy of the previous order requiring the act to be done.

(6) An order requiring a person to abstain from doing an act may be enforced under rule 5 notwithstanding that service of a copy of the order has not been effected in accordance with this rule if the Court is satisfied that pending such service, the person against whom or against whose property is sought to enforce the order has had notice thereof either –

(*a*) by being present when the order was made; or
(*b*) by being notified of the terms of the order, whether by telephone, telegram or otherwise.

(7) [*Without prejudice to its powers under Order 65, rule 4,*] The Court may dispense with service of a copy of an order under this rule if it thinks it just to do so.

General Note—Modifications to this rule, set out above in its re-enacted form, are highlighted by the addition of square brackets. The words in italics are those employed in the original version of the RSC (which continue to govern enforcement in "family proceedings"). For further examination of this issue see **Which rules of court** in the Legal background to Procedural Guide 38 and the annotations under FPR 1991, r 1.3.

Ord 24, r 16(3), Ord 26, r 6(3) (r 7(2))—Orders to discover documents and answer interrogatories are, subject to certain safeguards, required to have been served only on the solicitor for the party concerned.

"served personally", "pending such service", and "dispense with service" (r 7(2)(*a*), (3)(*a*), (6), (7) and *Practice Direction (Committal Applications)*, para 2.6)—An order which is capable of enforcement by committal must, in general, be served personally on the respondent to make it enforceable. In the case of a mandatory injunctive order, which directs an act to be done, the order incorporating the penal warning must be served in reasonable time before the time fixed by the order for the act to be done (r 7(2)(*b*)), unless the court dispenses with service under r 7(7). An order dispensing with service must normally have been made before the time by or at which the act is directed to be done. In an exceptional case, where the court is satisfied that the order can be adequately communicated without personal service, the court might provide for some form of alternative notification or service. The fundamental point is that contempt is not established without proof that the contemnor knew what he was directed to do or abstain from doing. An order dispensing with personal service of an injunction can be made in proceedings for breach of the injunction, even if the injunction was mandatory and thus directing an act to be done (*Davy International and others v Tazzyman and others* [1997] 3 All ER 183). However, this will be appropriate only where the court is satisfied that the respondent knew that the court had made the injunctive order. In *Davy International* (above) the court dispensed with service when the injunction had been served but was deficient in that no penal notice appeared on the face of it. Further, if the order is only a restraining order prohibiting conduct "pending such service", the court does have power to commit, provided that the respondent knew about the order by being present when it was made (r 7(6)(*a*)) or had been adequately notified of it (r 7(6)(*b*)). This power to commit can be exercised where an order is served which does not incorporate a penal notice (*Sofroniou v Szigetti* [1990] TLR 618).

Form of injunctive order and warning notice (r 7(4))—A non-molestation or occupation order made under FLA 1996, Pt IV should be drawn in Form FL404, which incorporates on the front a warning notice which complies with the requirement in r 7(4). The form of words for the warning notice in proceedings under CPR 1998 is set out in *Practice Direction (Judgments and Orders)* (PD 40B), para 9.1.

Where a directive order is made under CA 1989, s 8 in a county court, eg for a child to be handed over at a specific time and place, a warning notice cannot be put on the order without the leave of a judge or district judge (FPR 1991, r 4.21A). This requirement is not included in RSC, but directions should be sought as a matter of good practice.

Undertakings—This rule, unlike CPR 1998, Sch 2, CCR Ord 29, r 1A, does not include provision for undertakings. However, under *Practice Direction (Judgments and Orders)* (PD 40B), para 9.3 the court can require the giver of an undertaking to sign a statement that he understands the terms of his undertaking and the consequences of failure to comply with it. It is the giving of an undertaking, and the acceptance of it by the court, which makes it binding and enforceable (*Hussain v Hussain* [1986] Fam 134, [1986] 2 FLR 271). However in *Hussain* it was made clear that it is desirable that the undertaking be recorded in a document, which includes a warning notice and is provided to the giver of the undertaking, so that he cannot credibly excuse himself by asserting that he did not understand what had been promised or the consequences of a breach. In the Principal Registry, Form D787 should be used.

8–12

Set out in original Rules of the Supreme Court 1965.

****

RSC ORDER 50
CHARGING ORDERS, STOP ORDERS, ETC

****

9A Enforcement of charging order by sale (RSC Ord 50, r 9A)

(1) Proceedings for the enforcement of a charging order by sale of the property charged must be begun by a claim form issued out of Chancery Chambers or out of one of the Chancery District Registries.

(2) The provisions of Order 88 shall apply to all such proceedings.

Defined terms—"charging order": Charging Orders Act 1979, s 1(3).

Scope of provision—This rule requires an application for an order for sale to be made by separate proceedings. See **"sale of the property charged"** and **Criteria applied** under CPR 1998, Sch 2, CCR Ord 31, r 4.

Procedure—The claim is made under Pt 8 as modified by *Practice Direction (How to Make Claims in the Schedule Rules and Other Claims)*, Section A (claims made in the county court for such orders are governed by Section B). See *Civil Court Service* (Jordan Publishing Ltd) for a Procedural Guide to such claims.

****

RSC ORDER 52
COMMITTAL

Practice Direction—See *Practice Direction (Committal Applications)* which supplements this Order generally, set out in Part V of this work.

1 Committal for contempt of court (RSC Ord 52, r 1)

(1) The power of the High Court or Court of Appeal to punish for contempt of court may be exercised by an order of committal.

(2) Where contempt of court –

(*a*) is committed in connection with –

(i) any proceedings before a Divisional Court of the Queen's Bench Division; or

(ii) criminal proceedings, except where the contempt is committed in the face of the court or consists of disobedience to an order of the court or a breach of an undertaking to the court; or

(iii) proceedings in an inferior court; or

(*b*) is committed otherwise than in connection with any proceedings,

then, subject to paragraph (4), an order of committal may be made only by a Divisional Court of the Queen's Bench Division.

This paragraph shall not apply in relation to contempt of the Court of Appeal.

(3) Where contempt of court is committed in connection with any proceedings in the High Court, then, subject to paragraph (2), an order of committal may be made by a single judge of the Queen's Bench Division except where the proceedings were assigned or subsequently transferred to some other Division, in which case the order may be made only by a single judge of that other Division.

The reference in this paragraph to a single judge of the Queen's Bench Division shall, in relation to proceedings in any court the judge or judges of which are, when exercising the jurisdiction of that court, deemed by virtue of any enactment to constitute a court of the High Court, be construed as a reference to a judge of that court.

(4) Where by virtue of any enactment the High Court has power to punish or take steps for the punishment of any person charged with having done anything in relation to a court, tribunal or person which would, if it had been done in relation to the High Court, have been a contempt of that Court, an order of committal may be made –

(*a*) on an application under section 88 of the Charities Act 1993, by a single judge of the Chancery Division; and

(*b*) in any other case, by a single judge of the Queen's Bench Division.

Amendments—SI 2002/2058.

Scope of provision—This rule identifies the court's general power to punish contempt by committal. Rule 1(1) and (3) applies in connection with the enforcement of orders made in family proceedings.

Procedure—*Practice Direction (Committal Applications)* (set out in Part V of this work) regulates the mode of application for committals under CPR 1998 including the requirement that each allegation be identified, separately and numerically in the form of application, the period of 14 days for service in such proceedings, the form of evidence, case management and conduct of the hearing. This *Practice Direction* also applies to family proceedings (see *President's Direction of 16 March 2001* – set out in Part IV of this work).

"order of committal" (r 1(1))—Under an order of committal the contemnor's person is seized by the tipstaff, or by a police officer as his assistant, and taken to prison. A fixed term of imprisonment must be imposed, which may not exceed two years (Contempt of Court Act 1981, s 14(1)). Consecutive terms may be imposed if more than one contempt is proved (*Lee v Walker* [1985] QB 1191, [1985] FLR 701), though not totalling more than two years on any one occasion (s 14(1); *Villiers v Villiers* [1994] 1 FLR 647). The sentence may be suspended (*Brewer v Brewer* [1989] 2 FLR 251). The terms of the suspension must be clearly set out.

The court sends a copy of every committal order and relevant details to the Official Solicitor, who reviews the case and may apply or appeal of his own motion or at the contemnor's request (*Secretary's Circular of 28 September 1981*).

Other remedies—On hearing the application, the court may fine the contemnor instead of (or as well as) committing him, or may require him to give security for his future good behaviour (see r 9). There is no limit to the amount of the fine which may be imposed. For a case where, in family proceedings, a fine was imposed in lieu of committal even though the contemnor was in breach of an earlier suspended committal order, see *Banton v Banton* [1990] 2 FLR 465.

Contempt may be met by sequestration (see Ord 46, r 5), which is likely to be appropriate in family proceedings only where the assets are substantial, but in such a case sequestration may be a preferable and indeed more effective remedy. In a suitable case the court may authorise the breach of an order to be remedied by the applicant at the contemnor's expense under Ord 45, r 8.

Contempt proceedings should not be brought to enforce an order which may be adequately enforced by writ of execution (eg writ of possession or writ of delivery) or other means (eg appointment of a person to execute a document under Supreme Court Act 1981, s 39 or a vesting order under the Trustee Act 1925) (*Clements v Erlanger* (1877) 46 LJ Ch 382; *Danchevsky v Danchevsky* [1975] Fam 17, [1974] 3 WLR 709).

Orders which may be enforced by committal—As to the types of orders, and undertakings, which may be enforced by committal, see Ord 45, rr 5–7.

Generally—For further information, see under CCR Ord 29, r 1.

Form—Order of committal: RSC, App A, Form No 85. The Court of Appeal has repeatedly stressed the need for detail and accuracy in drawing the order. Although in family proceedings it will be drawn up by the court, the applicant's solicitor should seek the opportunity of checking it before it is perfected as any significant defect may result in its being quashed. The order breached and the breaches of it must be clearly stated so that the contemnor knows the reason for the committal from the face of the order (*Parra v Rones* [1986] Fam Law 262; *Linkleter v Linkleter* [1988] 1 FLR 360; *Langley v Langley* [1994] 1 FLR 383). Allegations of which the contemnor was not given notice must not be referred to (*Tabone v Seguna* [1986] 1 FLR 591). The order must accord with the oral judgment given (*Re C (Contempt: Committal Order)* [1989] 1 FLR 288, CA), but a minor irregularity may not be fatal (*Nicholls v Nicholls* [1997] 1 FLR 649; see **The importance of abiding by correct procedure** in commentary under CPR 1998, Sch 2, CCR Ord 29, r 1).

****

4 Application to Court other than Divisional Court (RSC Ord 52, r 4)

(1) Where an application for an order of committal may be made to a court other than a Divisional Court, the application must be made by [claim form or application notice] [*motion*] and be supported by an affidavit.

(2) Subject to paragraph (3) the [claim form or application notice] [*notice of motion*], stating the grounds of the application and accompanied by a copy of the

affidavit in support of the application, must be served personally on the person sought to be committed.

(3) Without prejudice to its powers under [Part 6 of the CPR] [*Order 65, rule 4*], the Court may dispense with service [*of the notice of motion*] under this rule if it thinks it just to do so.

(4) This rule does not apply to [committal applications which under rules 1(2) and 3(1) should be made to a Divisional Court but which, in vacation, have been properly made to a single judge in accordance with RSC Order 64, rule 4] [*proceedings brought before a single judge by virtue of Order 64, rule 4*].

General Note—Modifications to this rule, set out above in its re-enacted form, are highlighted by the addition of square brackets. The words in italics are those employed in the original version of the RSC (which continue to govern enforcement in "family proceedings"). For further examination of this issue see **Which rules of court** in the Legal background to Procedural Guide 38 and the annotations under FPR 1991, r 1.3.

Scope of provision—Derived from the former RSC Ord 44, r 2(3), this rule gives the procedure by which an application to commit is made. Reference should be made to Ord 45, rr 5–7 as to the steps which must have been taken before this stage is reached.

Manner of application (r 4(1), (2))—In family proceedings the application is not made by claim form or application notice but by summons (FPR 1991, r 7.2(1)). The affidavit in support should identify the terms of the order said to have been breached and set out the facts relied on as constituting the breach. It may be an affidavit of information and belief (*Savings & Investment Bank Ltd v Gasco Investments (Netherlands) BV (No 2)* [1988] Ch 422, [1988] 2 WLR 1212).

"the grounds of the application" (r 4(2))—It is not enough merely to refer to the affidavit (*Harmsworth v Harmsworth* [1988] 1 FLR 349, [1987] 1 WLR 1676). The grounds for the application (which constitute the charge faced by the respondent) must be set out in the summons itself or at least in a schedule annexed to it and forming part of it. The grounds must be sufficiently particularised to enable the respondent to meet the charge (*Chiltern District Council v Keane* [1985] 1 WLR 619, [1985] 2 All ER 118).

"must be served personally" (r 4(2))—At least two clear days' notice must be given (Ord 32, r 3). The court may abridge the time for service or may order substituted service, but it will be slow to do so when the respondent's liberty is at stake. Even when an order for substituted service has been complied with, a committal order may be set aside and a new trial ordered if the contemnor did not have actual notice of the hearing (*Duo v Osborne (formerly Duo)* [1992] 2 FLR 425, [1992] 3 All ER 121, CA). If the application is adjourned, notice of the adjourned hearing must be similarly served (*Chiltern District Council v Keane* (above)).

Dispensing with service (r 4(3))—To dispense with service of the summons (ie to hear an application to commit ex parte) "is a wholly exceptional course to take and one which can only be justified if no other course is open either to uphold the authority of the court or to protect the applicant" (*Wright v Jess* [1987] 2 FLR 373, [1987] 1 WLR 1070). An order made ex parte is provisional (*R v R (Contempt of Court)* [1988] Fam Law 388). The contemnor is entitled to apply for its discharge (*Wright v Jess* (above)), which will in effect mean a complete rehearing (*Aslam v Singh* [1987] 1 FLR 122), though no greater sentence can then be imposed than was originally imposed (*Lamb v Lamb* [1984] FLR 278).

Standard of proof—The appropriate standard of proof in committal proceedings is the criminal standard (*Dean v Dean* [1987] 1 FLR 517).

5 Saving for power to commit without application for purpose (RSC Ord 52, r 5)

Nothing in the foregoing provisions of this Order shall be taken as affecting the power of the High Court or Court of Appeal to make an order of committal of its own initiative against a person guilty of contempt of court.

Scope of provision—The court retains the power to commit a contemnor of its own motion. This power is exercised to deal with contempt in the face of the court. Very rarely it has been used to punish blatant disregard of an order, for example in wardship cases (see *Warwick Corporation v Russell* [1964] 1 WLR 613, [1964] 2 All ER 337).

6 Provisions as to hearing (RSC Ord 52, r 6)

(1) Subject to paragraph (2), the Court hearing an application for an order of committal may sit in private in the following cases, that is to say –

(*a*) where the application arises out of proceedings relating to the wardship or adoption of an infant or wholly or mainly to the guardianship, custody, maintenance or upbringing of an infant, or rights of access to an infant;

(*b*) where the application arises out of proceedings relating to a person suffering or appearing to be suffering from mental disorder within the meaning of the Mental Health Act 1983;

(*c*) where the application arises out of proceedings in which a secret process, discovery or invention was in issue;

(*d*) where it appears to the Court that in the interests of the administration of justice or for reasons of national security the application should be heard in private;

but, except as aforesaid, the application shall be heard in [public] [*open court*].

(2) If the Court hearing an application in private by virtue of paragraph (1) decides to make an order of committal against the person sought to be committed, it shall in [public] [*open court*] state –

(*a*) the name of that person;

(*b*) in general terms the nature of the contempt of Court in respect of which the order of committal is being made; and

(*c*) the length of the period for which he is being committed.

(3) Except with the [permission] [*leave*] of the Court hearing an application for an order of committal, no grounds shall be relied upon at the hearing except the grounds set out in the statement under rule 2 or, as the case may be, in the [claim form or application notice] [*notice of motion*] under rule 4.

[*The foregoing provision is without prejudice to the powers of the Court under Order 20, rule 8*]

(4) If on the hearing of the application the person sought to be committed expresses a wish to give oral evidence on his own behalf, he shall be entitled to do so.

Amendments—SI 1999/1008.

General Note—Modifications to this rule, set out above in its re-enacted form, are highlighted by the addition of square brackets. The words in italics are those employed in the original version of the RSC (which continue to govern enforcement in "family proceedings"). For further examination of this issue see **Which rules of court** in the Legal background to Procedural Guide 38 and the annotations under FPR 1991, r 1.3.

"wholly or mainly" (r 6(1)(*a*))—Rule 6(1)(*a*) would not cover, for example, proceedings for ancillary relief generally on divorce in which a periodical payments order for a child was one of the reliefs sought; but presumably it would cover such proceedings if the only provision sought was for children.

"Order 20, rule 8" (r 4(3))—The court may, on proper terms, allow the grounds to be amended by virtue of Ord 20, r 8.

Remedying irregularity—If, in wardship proceedings, the name of the person committed, the nature of the contempt and the length of sentence are not stated in open court, in breach of r 6(2), the court may remedy the situation by making a subsequent statement in open court of the particulars required (Ord 2, r 1). However, the Court of Appeal has a discretion to set aside the order (*Re C (A Minor)* (1988) *The Times*, 16 November).

7 Power to suspend execution of committal order (RSC Ord 52, r 7)

(1) The Court by whom an order of committal is made may by order direct that the execution of the order of committal shall be suspended for such period or on such terms or conditions as it may specify.

(2) Where execution of an order of committal is suspended by an order under paragraph (1), the applicant for the order of committal must, unless the Court otherwise directs, serve on the person against whom it was made a notice informing him of the making and terms of the order under that paragraph.

"for such period or on such terms ..." (r 7(1))—The court has an unfettered discretion as to the period of the suspension and the terms or conditions of the suspension. The power is commonly exercised in the case of a matrimonial injunction; in such a case, the conditions of the suspension will normally be that there be no further breach and that the committal order cease to have effect at the end of the suspension period. The order may be, and usually is, suspended for a definite period. However, in *Griffin v Griffin* [2000] 2 FLR 44, the Court of Appeal (Simon Brown and Hale LJJ) upheld the validity of a committal order suspended so long as the contemnor complied with the terms of an order expressed to last "until further order" (see **Duration** in commentary under FLA 1996, s 42), even though the effect was to suspend the sentence of imprisonment indefinitely.

"the applicant ... must ... serve ... a notice" (r 7(2))—There is no requirement for personal service but, if there should be an application to activate the sentence for breach of the terms, the court will require to be satisfied that the contemnor had notice of them.

"unless the court otherwise directs" (r 7(2))—For example, if the terms are straightforward and the contemnor is present to hear the order made.

8 Discharge of person committed (RSC Ord 52, r 8)

(1) The Court may, on the application of any person committed to prison for any contempt of Court, discharge him.

(2) Where a person has been committed for failing to comply with a judgment or order requiring him to deliver any thing to some other person or to deposit it in Court or elsewhere, and a writ of sequestration has also been issued to enforce that judgment or order, then, if the thing is in the custody or power of the person committed, the commissioners appointed by the writ of sequestration may take possession of it as if it were the property of that person and, without prejudice to the generality of paragraph (1), the Court may discharge the person committed and may give such directions for dealing with the thing taken by the commissioners as it thinks fit.

(RSC Order 46, rule 5 contains rules relating to writs of sequestration)

Scope of provision—This rule enables the court to discharge a contemnor before the end of the term for which he was imprisoned. On an application to purge, the court must grant or refuse the application: it cannot suspend the remainder of the sentence (*Harris v Harris* [2001] EWCA Civ 1645, [2002] 1 FLR 248, CA).

Procedure on application—The general practice is to apply by motion. The special provision in family proceedings requiring an application to commit to be made by summons does not apply to an application to discharge. However, where no judge is conveniently available to hear the application, it may be made to the district judge (FPR 1991, r 7.2(2)(*a*)). The district judge may, if

PART III

satisfied as to the urgency of the matter and that it is expedient to do so, make any order which the judge could have made. If not so satisfied, he will no doubt adjourn the application to the judge. Generally, an application to purge is best made to the judge who passed the sentence.

Attendance on hearing—In family proceedings the contemnor should be present to hear the outcome of his application unless, in his solicitor's view, his mental condition makes that undesirable (*Practice Direction of 25 July 1983*).

Court's discretion—Discharge is subject to the discretion of the court. Even if the order has not been fully complied with, the contemnor may be released where it is clear that further imprisonment will not secure compliance, provided he has been sufficiently punished for his disobedience (*Re Barrell Enterprises* [1973] 1 WLR 19, [1972] 3 All ER 631).

9 Saving for other powers (RSC Ord 52, r 9)

Nothing in the foregoing provisions of this Order shall be taken as affecting the power of the Court to make an order requiring a person guilty of contempt of court, or a person punishable by virtue of any enactment in like manner as if he had been guilty of contempt of the High Court, to pay a fine or to give security for his good behaviour, and those provisions, so far as applicable, and with the necessary modifications, shall apply in relation to an application for such an order as they apply in relation to an application for an order of committal.

Scope of provision—This rule has the effect of confirming the retention of the court's power to require payment of a fine or the giving of security for good behaviour (see **Other remedies** under r 1).

****

RSC ORDER 94
APPLICATIONS AND APPEALS TO HIGH COURT UNDER VARIOUS ACTS: QUEEN'S BENCH DIVISION

****

16 Proceedings under the Protection from Harassment Act 1997 (RSC Ord 94, r 16)

(1) In this rule, "the Act" means the Protection from Harassment Act 1997.

(2) This rule shall apply to injunctions granted on or after 1st September 1998 and injunctions granted before that date shall be treated as if this rule had not come into force.

(3) Proceedings in the High Court under section 3 of the Act shall be assigned to the Queen's Bench Division.

(4) An application for the issue of a warrant for the arrest of the defendant under section 3(3) of the Act shall –

(*a*) state that it is an application for the issue of a warrant for the arrest of the defendant;

(*b*) set out the grounds for making the application and be supported by an affidavit or evidence on oath;

(*c*) state whether the claimant has informed the police of the defendant's conduct as described in sub-paragraph (*b*); and (*d*) state whether, to the claimant's knowledge, criminal proceedings are being pursued.

(5) The Court before whom a person is brought following his arrest may –

(*a*) determine whether the facts, and the circumstances which led to the arrest, amounted to disobedience of the injunction, or

(*b*) adjourn the proceedings and, where such an order is made, the arrested person shall be released and –

(i) may be dealt with within 14 days of the day on which he was arrested; and

(ii) be given not less than 2 days' notice of the adjourned hearing.

(6) This rule applies to proceedings under section 3 of the Act in a county court with the following modifications –

(*a*) Such proceedings in a county court shall be begun –

(i) in the court for the district in which the claimant resides or carries on business; or

(ii) in the court for the district in which the defendant resides or carries on business.

(*b*) Where a county court –

(i) grants an injunction under section 3 of the Act; or

(ii) issues a warrant for the arrest of the defendant,

the injunction or warrant shall be issued in the appropriate prescribed form.

Amendments—Inserted by SI 1999/1008.

****

RSC ORDER 112
APPLICATIONS FOR USE OF SCIENTIFIC TESTS IN DETERMINING PATERNITY

1 Interpretation (RSC Ord 112, r 1)

In this Order –

"the Act" means Part III of the Family Law Reform Act 1969;

"bodily samples" and "scientific tests" have the meanings assigned to them by section 25 of the Act;

"direction" means a direction for the use of scientific tests under section 20(1) of the Act;

"the [court] [*proper*] officer" means the officer of the court who draws up a direction.

Amendments—SI 2001/256.

General Note—Modifications to this rule, set out above in its re-enacted form, are highlighted by the addition of square brackets. The words in italics are those employed in the original version of the RSC (which continue to govern applications for scientific tests in "family proceedings"). For further examination of this issue see **Which rules of court** in the Legal background to Procedural Guide 77 and the annotations under FPR 1991, r 1.3.

Scope of Order—Order 112 provides the regulatory framework where application is made in the High Court for tests in accordance with FLRA 1969, s 20. An application must be on notice to every party to the proceedings (save with leave of the court) and anyone not a party who is to be served must be served personally (r 2). In respect of a child under 16, or a person suffering from a mental disorder, the person who has care of them is the person to be served with the application (r 3). Where a third party is to be tested, the court may join him as a party (r 4). Where a direction is given, this must be served by the court on anyone from whom a sample is to be taken; and, until there is a report in accordance with the direction, the proceedings in which the direction is made stand adjourned (r 5). Once received by the court, a copy of the report is sent to all parties to the proceedings and to anyone else from whom a sample has been taken (r 6).

"direction"—A form for the direction was proposed by Ward LJ in *Re H (Paternity: Blood Test)* [1996] 2 FLR 65, CA, and is set out in **The direction** under FLRA 1969, s 20.

Arrangements for testing—In the Family Division and the county court, it is the responsibility of the solicitor acting on behalf of the applicant for the direction to make arrangements for the testing in accordance with *Practice Direction of 17 February 1972*.

2 Application for direction (RSC Ord 112, r 2)

(1) Except with the [permission] [*leave*] of the court, an application in any proceedings for a direction shall be [in accordance with CPR Part 23 and a copy of the application notice shall be served on] [*made on notice to*] every party to the proceedings (other than the applicant) and to any other person from whom the direction involves the taking of bodily samples.

[*(2) If the application is made otherwise than at the hearing of the proceedings it shall be made by summons.*]

(3) Any notice [*or summons*] required by this rule to be served on a person who is not a party to the proceedings shall be served on him personally.

Amendments—SI 2001/256.

General Note—Modifications to this rule, set out above in its re-enacted form, are highlighted by the addition of square brackets. The words in italics are those employed in the original version of the RSC (which continue to govern applications for scientific tests in "family proceedings"). For further examination of this issue see **Which rules of court** in the Legal background to Procedural Guide 77 and the annotations under FPR 1991, r 1.3.

Scope of provision—See **Scope of Order** under r 1.

"in accordance with CPR Part 23" (r 2(1))—Part 23 enables the court to make orders in the course of proceedings (interlocutory applications). Such applications are made in Form N244 and are governed by *Practice Direction (Applications)* which supplements Pt 23 generally.

3 Applications involving [children under 16 and patients] [*persons under disability*] (RSC Ord 112, r 3)

Where an application is made for a direction in respect of a person [*(in this rule referred to as a person under disability)*] who is either –

(*a*) under 16, or

(*b*) suffering from a mental disorder within the meaning of the Mental Health Act 1983 and incapable of understanding the nature and purpose of scientific tests,

the [application notice or claim form] [*notice of application or summons*] shall state the name and address of the person having the care and control of the person under disability and shall be served on him instead of on the person under disability.

Amendments—SI 2001/256.

General Note—Modifications to this rule, set out above in its re-enacted form, are highlighted by the addition of square brackets. The words in italics are those employed in the original version of the RSC (which continue to govern applications for scientific tests in "family proceedings"). For further examination of this issue see **Which rules of court** in the Legal background to Procedural Guide 77 and the annotations under FPR 1991, r 1.3.

Scope of provision—See generally **Scope of Order** under r 1. This rule contains provisions to regulate the service of applications in the High Court for scientific tests in respect of an individual who is not a party to the proceedings but is a "person under disability" (as specifically defined in the rule). It applies, subject to the provisions of FPR 1991, and with the necessary modifications, to family proceedings in the High Court by virtue of FPR 1991, r 1.3. In the county court, reference should be made to CCR Ord 47, r 5(4). The provisions may overlap with FPR 1991, Pt IX which deals with the conduct of proceedings where a party is under a disability (defined in different terms, see below).

"person under disability"—To come within this definition a person over the age of 16 must suffer from a mental disorder *and* be incapable of understanding the nature and purpose of scientific tests, but there is no requirement that the incapacity be related to the mental disorder. The definition is unique to this rule, being decision specific in regard to capacity to understand the nature and purpose of scientific tests. It differs materially from that generally used in respect of capacity to conduct proceedings, which is that the person is by reason of mental disorder incapable of managing and administering his property and affairs (see CPR 1998, Pt 21; FPR 1991, Pt IX; RSC Ord 80; CCR Ord 10). It is possible that an individual may come within one definition but not the other. For a further explanation see **Assessment of capacity** under FPR 1991, r 9.1.

"mental disorder"—Defined by Mental Health Act 1983, s 1(3) as "mental illness, arrested or incomplete development of mind, psychopathic disorder and any other disorder or disability of mind". For a further explanation see **"mental disorder"** under FPR 1991, r 9.1.

"the person having the care and control of the person under disability"—It by no means follows that a person who meets this specific definition is under the care and control of some other person, so situations may arise where service under this rule is technically impossible. Service on a proper officer of the local social services authority or other guardian when the patient is under a guardianship order, or the district health authority when the patient has been compulsorily admitted to hospital under the Mental Health Act 1983, may be sufficient. Such service is only required (ie under Ord 112, r 2) where the person is not already a party to the proceedings, so if a next friend or guardian ad litem has already been appointed, such representative would have to be served in the usual way.

Mode of service of the application—It is not clear if personal service of the notice of application is required on the person having the care and control of the person under disability, but that may be the effect of r 2(3).

Service of other documents—This provision for substituted service of the notice of application upon a carer does not apply to service of any direction of the court under r 5, or to a copy of the report pursuant to r 6. Such documents are to be served on the "person from whom the direction involved the taking of bodily samples" in the usual way.

Communication to person under disability—Service of the notice of application upon the person alleged to be under disability is not required, notwithstanding that he may be capable of intervening in the proceedings and/or may wish to dispute the suggestion that he does not understand "the nature and purpose of scientific tests". The person in whose care he is (if there is such a person) may not wish him to do so, perhaps because of an adverse interest in the application, so there is no certainty that he will be informed at that stage, although it seems (see above) that subsequent directions and reports will have to be served on him.

Implications—If the person to be tested becomes a party to the proceedings and is a person under disability in relation to the proceedings pursuant to CPR 1998, Pt 21 or FPR 1991, Pt IX (as appropriate), the proceedings will have to be stayed until a guardian ad litem has been appointed. In default, any continuing proceedings will be a nullity.

4 [Addition as a party] [*Joinder*] of person to be tested (RSC Ord 112, r 4)

Where an application is made for a direction involving the taking of bodily samples from a person who is not a party to the proceedings in which the application is made, the court may at any time direct that person to be made a party to the proceedings.

Amendments—SI 2001/256.

General Note—Modifications to this rule, set out above in its re-enacted form, are highlighted by the addition of square brackets. The words in italics are those employed in the original version of the RSC (which continue to govern applications for scientific tests in "family proceedings"). For further examination of this issue see **Which rules of court** in the Legal background to Procedural Guide 77 and the annotations under FPR 1991, r 1.3.

Scope of provision—See **Scope of Order** under r 1.

5 Service of direction and adjournment of proceedings (RSC Ord 112, r 5)

Where the court gives a direction in any proceedings, the [court] [*proper*] officer shall send a copy to every party to the proceedings and to every other person from whom the direction involves the taking of bodily samples and, unless otherwise ordered, further consideration of the proceedings shall [be] [*stand*] adjourned until the court receives a report pursuant to the direction.

General Note—Modifications to this rule, set out above in its re-enacted form, are highlighted by the addition of square brackets. The words in italics are those employed in the original version of the RSC (which continue to govern applications for scientific tests in "family proceedings"). For further examination of this issue see **Which rules of court** in the Legal background to Procedural Guide 77 and the annotations under FPR 1991, r 1.3.

Amendments—SI 2001/256.

Scope of provision—See **Scope of Order** under r 1.

6 Service of copy report (RSC Ord 112, r 6)

On receipt by the court of a report made pursuant to a direction, the proper officer shall send a copy to every party to the proceedings and to every other person from whom the direction involved the taking of bodily samples.

Amendments—SI 2001/256.

Scope of provision—See **Scope of Order** under r 1.

****

SCHEDULE 2

****

CCR ORDER 29
COMMITTAL FOR BREACH OF ORDER OR UNDERTAKING

Practice Direction—See *Practice Direction (Committal Applications)* which supplements this Order generally, set out in Part V of this work.

1 Enforcement of judgment to do or abstain from doing any act (CCR Ord 29, r 1)

(1) Where a person required by a judgment or order to do an act refuses or neglects to do it within the time fixed by the judgment or order or any subsequent order, or where a person disobeys a judgment or order requiring him to abstain from doing an act, then, subject to the Debtors Acts 1869 and 1878 and to the provisions of these rules, the judgment or order may be enforced, by order of the judge, by a committal order against that person or, if that person is a body corporate, against any director or other officer of the body.

(2) Subject to paragraphs (6) and (7), a judgment or order shall not be enforced under paragraph (1) unless –

(*a*) a copy of the judgment or order has been served personally on the person required to do or abstain from doing the act in question and also, where that person is a body corporate, on the director or other officer of the body against whom a committal order is sought; and

(*b*) in the case of a judgment or order requiring a person to do an act, the copy has been so served before the expiration of the time within which he was required to do the act and was accompanied by a copy of any order, made between the date of the judgment or order and the date of service, fixing that time.

(3) Where a judgment or order enforceable by committal order under paragraph (1) has been given or made, the [court] [*proper*] officer shall, if the judgment or order is in the nature of an injunction, at the time when the judgment or order is drawn up, and in any other case on the request of the judgment creditor, issue a copy of the judgment or order, indorsed with or incorporating a notice as to the consequences of disobedience, for service in accordance with paragraph (2).

(4) If the person served with the judgment or order fails to obey it, [the judgment creditor may issue a claim form or, as the case may be, an application notice seeking the committal for contempt of court of that person] [*the proper officer shall at the request of the judgment creditor, issue a notice warning him that an application will be made for him to be committed,*] and subject to paragraph (7), the [claim form or application notice] [*notice*] shall be served on him personally.

(4A) [The claim form or application notice (as the case may be)] [*The request for issue of the notice under paragraph (4)*] shall –

(*a*) identify the provisions of the injunction or undertaking which it is alleged have been disobeyed or broken;

(*b*) list the ways in which it is alleged that the injunction has been disobeyed or the undertaking has been broken;

(*c*) be supported by an affidavit stating the grounds on which the application is made,

and unless service is dispensed with under paragraph (7), a copy of the affidavit shall be served with the [claim form or application notice] [*notice*].

(5) If a committal order is made, the order shall be for the issue of a warrant of committal and, unless the judge otherwise orders –

(*a*) a copy of the order shall be served on the person to be committed either before or at the time of the execution of the warrant; or
(*b*) where the warrant has been signed by the judge, the order for issue of the warrant may be served on the person to be committed at any time within 36 hours after the execution of the warrant.

(6) A judgment or order requiring a person to abstain from doing an act may be enforced under paragraph (1) notwithstanding that service of a copy of the judgment or order has not been effected in accordance with paragraph (2) if the judge is satisfied that, pending such service, the person against whom it is sought to enforce the judgment or order has had notice thereof either –

(*a*) by being present when the judgment or order was given or made; or
(*b*) by being notified of the terms of the judgment or order whether by telephone, telegram or otherwise.

(7) Without prejudice to its powers under [Part 6 of the CPR] [*Order 7, rule 8*], the court may dispense with service of a copy of a judgment or order under paragraph (2) or a [claim form or application notice] [*notice*] under paragraph (4) if the court thinks it just to do so.

(8) Where service of [the claim form or application notice has been] [*a notice to show cause is*] dispensed with under paragraph (7) and a committal order is made in the absence of the respondent, the judge may [on his own initiative] [*of his own motion*] fix a date and time when the person to be committed is to be brought before him or before the court.

General Note—Modifications to this rule, set out above in its re-enacted form, are highlighted by the addition of square brackets. The words in italics are those employed in the original version of the CCR (which continue to govern enforcement in "family proceedings"). For further examination of this issue see **Which rules of court** in the Legal background to Procedural Guide 38 and the annotations under FPR 1991, r 1.3.

Disobedience of an order as a contempt of court – "refuses ... neglects ... disobeys" (r 1(1))—This rule regulates an enforcement procedure in respect of an order directing a person, or an undertaking promising, to do an act at or within a specified time (such as an occupation order for a person to leave the family home), or to abstain from doing an act (such as a non-molestation order or an order forbidding torts). Disobedience of a directive order capable of enforcement by committal, or an undertaking to like effect, is a civil contempt of court. Refusal, neglect and disobedience are all forms of contempt. The purpose of the powers available on proof of such contempt is enforcement – to compel obedience (*Lightfoot v Lightfoot* [1989] 1 FLR 414), to punish (*Martin v Bannister* (1899) 4 QBD 491) and to deter disobedience by others (*James v Cliffe* (1987) *The Times*, 16 June). Contempt consists of "actus reus" and "mens rea". This means a deliberate act, or neglect to act, by the respondent who knew what the order was (*Re the Supply of Ready Mixed Concrete (No 2)* [1995] 1 AC 456). It is not necessary to prove that the respondent's purpose was to breach the order or undertaking.

Power to enforce injunctive orders and undertakings—The power to commit, and the other forms of enforcement available in the High Court for disobedience of an injunctive order or breach of an undertaking, are bestowed on county courts by County Courts Act 1984, s 38(1). By virtue of s 38(1), county courts are granted the inherent powers of the High Court to enforce orders.

Approach of court when selecting disposal—A useful summary of the appropriate approach to choosing a disposal, after proof or admission of a contempt, appears in *Hale v Tanner* [2000] 2 FLR 879.

Immediate committal—Any order for imprisonment, whether immediate or suspended, must be for a fixed term, and the maximum period which may be imposed on one occasion is two years (Contempt of Court Act 1981, s 14(1); *Villiers v Villiers* [1994] 1 FLR 647; *Re R (A Minor) (Contempt)* [1994] 2 FLR 185). Consecutive sentences can be imposed where more than one breach is proved (*Lee v Walker* [1985] QB 1191, [1985] FLR 701), provided that the total does not exceed two years (*Villiers v Villiers* above). A contemnor under the age of 21 cannot be sent to prison (Criminal Justice Act 1982, s 14(1)), but if he is aged 18 or more he may be detained in a young offenders' institution, provided that the court is of the opinion that no other way of dealing with him is appropriate (CJA 1982, ss 1(5), 9(1); *R v Selby Justices ex parte Frame* [1992] QB 72; *Mason v Lawton* [1991] 2 FLR 50). A contemnor aged less than 18 cannot be committed to any form of detention (*R v Selby Justices ex parte Frame* above). "The heresy that there could in any cases of domestic violence be what Lord Donaldson in *Jordan v Jordan* [1993] 1 FLR 169 called 'one free breach' was scotched in that case". See, to like effect, *Neil v Ryan* [1998] 2 FLR 1069.

Suspended committal—A committal (which must be for a fixed term not exceeding two years) may be suspended (*Brewer v Brewer* [1989] 2 FLR 251: see also commentary to CPR Sch 1, RSC Ord 52, r 7; *Griffin v Griffin* (2000) *The Times*, 28 April and *Loseby v Newman* [1995] 2 FLR 754).

Adjournment of consideration of penalty—The court may, where disobedience of an injunctive order or breach of an undertaking has been proved, adjourn consideration of the penalty. If this is done, the terms which are required to be obeyed and breach of which may result in imposition of a penalty, and the period during which such conduct may so result, must be specified in the order (CC Form N79 and see *Pidduck v Molloy* [1992] 2 FLR 202).

Fines—Although fines are not mentioned in this rule, the House of Lords held in *Heatons Transport (St Helens) Ltd v TGWU* [1973] AC 15 at 109 that the High Court may impose a fine in lieu of, or in addition to, committal; county courts also have this power (*Rose v Laskington* [1990] 1 QB 562 at 567). For an example of this provision, see *Banton v Banton* [1990] 2 FLR 465; there is no statutory limit to such a fine.

Sequestration—Although no county court rule makes provision for sequestration as an alternative response to contempt, it has been held that the remedy is available in a county court (*Richardson v Richardson* [1990] 1 FLR 186). In practice, its expense confines it to the larger cases, and the ease with which most county court orders made in family proceedings may be transferred to the High Court for enforcement under FPR 1991, r 7.3 means that any such application will usually be made to that court. If an application for sequestration is to be made to a county court, the High Court practice should be followed as nearly as may be. See RSC Ord 45, rr 5–7 and RSC Ord 46, r 5.

Other remedies—In *Danchevsky v Danchevsky* [1975] Fam 17 at 22A, [1974] 3 All ER 934 at 937H, Lord Denning MR said "Whenever there is a reasonable alternative available instead of committal to prison, that alternative must be taken". The power to authorise an act to be done at the respondent's expense under RSC Ord 45, r 8 is available in a county court by virtue of County Courts Act 1984, ss 38 and 76. Similarly, the High Court's power to nominate a person to execute a document when the respondent having been so ordered neglects or refuses to do so or cannot be found is available (see Supreme Court Act 1981, s 39).

Residence or contact orders under CA 1989, s 8 which contain orders to "give up" a child may be enforceable, in an appropriate case, by an application under Family Law Act 1986, s 34.

Undertaking (r 1(4A))—See under r 1A.

Enforcement of orders or undertakings to pay money—An order to pay money, or an undertaking to do so, cannot be enforced by committal proceedings, except in the very limited circumstances permitted under Debtors Act 1869, s 5, as limited by Administration of Justice Act 1970, s 11 and Sch 8 (*Symmons v Symmons* [1993] 1 FLR 317). If such an order is made, or undertaking given, in ancillary relief proceedings, the appropriate remedy is by way of judgment summons. Although in *Mubarak v Mubarak* [2001] 1 FLR 698 the Court of Appeal held that the judgment summons procedure was not compatible with the European Convention on Human Rights, the FPR 1991 have been amended with effect from 24 February 2003 to remove the incompatibility.

"subject to ... these rules" (r 1(1))—The principal special cases are:

(*a*) *Attachment of earnings* Specific powers to deal with disobedience of orders in such proceedings are contained in Attachment of Earnings Act 1971, s 23, and are governed by CCR Ord 27.

(*b*) *Orders to obtain information from judgment debtors* (formerly known as "oral examination") See now CPR 1998, Pt 71.

PART III

(*c*) *Judgment summonses* Specific powers and a procedure similar to that which applies in attachment of earnings cases are created by CCA 1984, s 112 and CCR Ord 28. Criticism of the procedure in *Mubarak v Mubarak* [2001] 1 FLR 698 has been addressed. The FPR 1991 have been amended with effect from 24 February 2003 to remove the incompatibility.

"notice as to the consequences of disobedience" (r 1(3))—An injunctive order capable of enforcement by committal may be thus enforced, subject to the requirements as to service, if it has on it a penal notice warning the respondent of the consequences of breach. Prescribed Form FL404 (see FPR 1991, App 1), which includes the menus for non-molestation and directive occupation orders, and county court injunction Form N78, have a penal notice incorporated in the text. The person who has the benefit of a non-molestation order, a directive occupation order, or an injunction order against torts, is entitled to have the order issued with a penal notice incorporated or endorsed on it (FL404, Notice A in the case of an order which includes a non-molestation requirement) (r 1(3), FPR 1991, r 3.9A(5)). Where an occupation order is made, which does not have a non-molestation order included, the court has a discretion as to whether to authorise a penal notice (FL404, Notice B). A warning notice cannot be added to an order under CA 1989, s 8 without the leave of a judge (FPR 1991, r 4.21A).

"served personally", "pending such service", and "dispense with service" (r 1(2)(*a*), (6) and (7))—An order which is capable of enforcement by committal must, in general, be served personally on the respondent to make it enforceable. In the case of a mandatory injunctive order, which directs an act to be done, the order incorporating the penal warning must be served in reasonable time, before the time fixed by the order for the act to be done (r 1(2)(*b*)), unless the court dispenses with service under r 1(7). An order dispensing with service must normally have been made before the time by or at which the act is directed to be done. In an exceptional case, where the court is satisfied that the order can be adequately communicated without personal service, the court may provide for some form of alternative notification or service. The fundamental point is that contempt is not established without proof that the contemnor knew what he was being directed to do, or abstain from doing. An order dispensing with personal service of an injunction can be made in proceedings for breach of the injunction, even if the injunction was mandatory and thus directing an act to be done (*Davy International and others v Tazzyman and others* [1997] 3 All ER 183). However, this will be appropriate only where the court is satisfied that the respondent knew that the court had made the injunctive order. In *Davy International* (above) the court dispensed with service when the injunction had been served, but was deficient, in that no penal notice appeared on the face of it. Further, if the order is only a restraining order prohibiting conduct "pending such service", the court does have power to commit, provided that the respondent knew about the order by being present when it was made (r 1(6)(*a*)), or had been adequately notified of it (r 1(6)(*b*)). This power to commit can be exercised where an order is served which does not incorporate a penal notice (*Sofroniou v Szigetti* [1990] TLR 618).

Issue of the "Notice to show good reason" and evidence in support—Penal enforcement under Ord 29, r 1 is initiated on request by the applicant ("judgment creditor") for the issue of Form N78, entitled "Notice to show good reason why you should not be committed to prison" (r 1(4)), supported by an affidavit stating the grounds relied upon (r 1(4A)(*c*)). There is no separate form for the request for issue. County court practice is that the applicant drafts and submits Form N78, which is treated as the request for issue, and the court revises it only if it appears to be defective.

Drafting the "Notice to show good reason" and the affidavit or statement in support—The precise requirements for the request for issue are prescribed in r 1(4A). The specific allegations relied on as amounting to the breaches must be listed sufficiently clearly to enable the respondent to know the case that he has to answer (*Harmsworth v Harmsworth* [1988] 1 FLR 349 and see *Practice Direction (Committal Applications)*, para 2.5(2) (set out in Part V of this work)). The affidavit or statement in support is to narrate the events, not to specify the allegations. If the particulars of the alleged breaches have not been included in Form N78, but are adequately particularised in the evidence in support, the court should be asked for leave to amend the Notice before the hearing begins. The court must not act on allegations of which notice has not been given, unless exceptional circumstances justify an application being made ex parte (*Tabone v Seguna* [1986] 1 FLR 591; *Wright v Jess* [1987] 2 FLR 373, [1987] 2 All ER 1067).

Service of Notice in Form N78 and affidavit in support (r 1(4))—The Notice instructs the respondent to attend the hearing of the application for an order of committal and, together with the affidavit in support, must be served personally on the respondent (r 1(4), (4A)) unless service is dispensed with under r 1(7), or an order has been made for substituted service. In family proceedings two court office days' (CCR Ord 1, r 9(4)) notice must be given (Ord 13, r 1(2)), unless this is abridged by order (Ord 13, r 4(1)). In proceedings under CPR 1998, 14 clear days from service is required (*Practice Direction (Committal Applications)*, para 4.2).

Procedural requirements—*Practice Direction (Committal Applications)* (set out in Part V of this work) regulates the mode of application for committals under CPR 1998 including the requirement that each allegation be identified, separately and numerically in the form of application, the period of 14 days for service in such proceedings, the form of evidence, case management and conduct of the hearing.

Service of notice of adjourned hearing in "Notice to show good reason"—The respondent must be personally served with notice of an adjourned hearing, unless he was present when the adjournment was granted and was given the new date (*Chiltern District Council v Keane* [1985] 1 WLR 619, [1985] 2 All ER 118).

Dispensing with service of "Notice to show good reason" and ex parte committal (r 1(7), (8))—Proceeding ex parte by dispensation with service of the Notice is exceptional, but may be allowed by the court where the respondent is shown to be evading service (*Wright v Jess* [1987] 2 FLR 373). If this course is taken and an order of committal is made, the court should provide for the respondent to be brought before it at the earliest opportunity after he has been arrested (r 1(8); *Lamb v Lamb* [1984] FLR 278). The respondent is entitled to a complete rehearing (*Aslam v Singh* [1987] 1 FLR 122) and the court cannot impose a sentence greater than was ordered at the ex parte hearing (*Lamb v Lamb* above). An order made ex parte is provisional (*R v R (Contempt of Court)* [1988] Fam Law 388), and the contemnor is entitled to apply for it to be discharged (*Wright v Jess* above).

Production in court of person arrested under FLA 1996, s 47 and attendance of the victim—A person arrested by virtue of a power of arrest under s 47(6) must be brought before the court within 24 hours of the arrest (s 47(7)(*a*)). A warrant of arrest authorises the immediate arrest of the respondent for failing to comply with the provisions of a non-molestation or occupation order but, unlike the requirement in s 47(7)(*a*), there is no provision that a person arrested on a warrant must be brought before the court within 24 hours of the arrest. In practice, a person arrested under a warrant will be produced before the court as soon as reasonably practicable, regard being given to enabling the applicant to attend, unless the respondent is arrested some distance from the court which issued the warrant. When an arrested respondent is brought before the court, the attendance of the applicant will almost always be needed to enable the court to deal with the alleged breach, and if she is not available within a reasonable time the court may have to adjourn the matter, and consider whether to remand the respondent.

Procedural powers of court when person arrested under FLA 1996, s 47 is brought before court—When a respondent is brought before the court following arrest, whether under a power of arrest or a warrant, the court may hear and deal with the alleged breach, or adjourn the hearing. The court may adjourn without having determined whether a breach has been proved, or after finding a breach proved. If the hearing is adjourned, the arrested person may be (i) released without remand, in which case additional injunctive directions may be appropriate; (ii) remanded in custody under s 47(7)(*b*) or s 47(10), and s 47(11) and Sch 5, para 2(1)(*a*); (iii) remanded on bail under s 47(7)(*b*) or s 47(10), and s 47(11) and (12) and Sch 5, para 2(1)(*b*); or (iv) remanded for the purpose of enabling a medical examination to be made under s 48(1) or for a report on his mental condition under s 48(4). The procedures available when a person is arrested upon a power of arrest (not upon a warrant of arrest) are provided in FPR 1991, r 3.9A(4), which enables the court either (i) to deal with an arrested person forthwith, without issue of, or dispensation with, a "Notice to show good reason" or (ii) to adjourn, with or without remand of the arrested person, and deal with the matter within 14 days, without a "Notice to show good reason". If the court does deal with the matter forthwith, or at an adjourned hearing within 14 days, it is restricted to considering the matter on which the person was arrested, and cannot deal with other alleged breaches. If the court does not deal with the matter by virtue of the respondent being brought before it by arrest or adjournment following arrest, the victim can apply later upon a "Notice to show good reason".

Remand under FLA 1996, s 47(7)(*b*), (10), (11) or s 48—A person arrested and brought before the court can be remanded under s 47(7)(*b*) or s 47(10), and s 47(11), (12) and Sch 5, in custody or on bail, or remanded for a medical report under s 48, in custody or on bail (s 47(11), (12) and Sch 5).

PART III

Bail under FLA 1996, Sch 5—FPR 1991, r 3.10 provides for an application for bail by an arrested person, which may be with or without a surety. The following prescribed forms should be referred to for the requirements of bail: recognizance of the person making an application (FL411); recognizance of a surety (FL411); and bail notice (FL412).

Warrant of arrest for breach of an injunction under the Protection from Harassment Act 1997—PHA 1997, s 3(3) provides for issue of a warrant for the arrest of a defendant. A warrant of arrest may be issued by a judge or a district judge (but not a deputy district judge) upon an application substantiated on oath, if the court concludes that the defendant has done anything which he is prohibited from doing by the injunction. PHA 1997 makes no provision for remand of a defendant. Therefore, it appears that the court before which the defendant is brought must either deal with him for the alleged breach, or adjourn and release the defendant. Consequently, the defendant should usually be brought before the court at the earliest reasonable time at which the claimant can attend and give evidence. If the defendant is released, the claimant can issue a "Notice to show good reason" in Form N78.

Further arrest where the respondent fails to appear at an adjourned hearing after being released following arrest by virtue of a power of arrest under FLA 1996, s 47—Where a person has been arrested by virtue of a power of arrest under s 47, and the case has been adjourned but the respondent fails to appear for the adjourned hearing following his remand or release, the court cannot grant a warrant of arrest under s 47(8) (unless the power of arrest was only attached to some of the terms of the non-molestation order). However, it is arguable that the respondent can be re-arrested under the original power of arrest, provided that he is again brought before a judge within 24 hours of the second arrest. In *Wheeldon v Wheeldon* [1998] 1 FLR 463 the Court of Appeal held that, where a person had been arrested for a criminal offence of assault and released on bail, he was validly re-arrested under a power of arrest for domestic violence, and brought before a judge within 24 hours of the second arrest, although the "spirit (of the statutory power of arrest) requires that he be brought before the judge within 24 hours of the initial arrest where the circumstances clearly indicate two reasons for the arrest prevail" (per Ward LJ at 468G); thus a power of arrest is a procedural device which can be used for detaining the respondent and bringing him before the court even though the breach of the injunction is not continuing. In practice, re-arrest is rare. As with any civil case, provided that the court is satisfied that the absent party has been served, and is aware of the trial date, the court can simply proceed in his absence.

Warrant of arrest where the respondent fails to appear at an adjourned hearing, having appeared at the first hearing of a "Notice to show good reason" for breach of an order under FLA 1996, Pt IV—Where a person appears in answer to a "Notice to show good reason", and the case is adjourned and/or the respondent bailed, if he subsequently fails to appear at the adjourned hearing, and no power of arrest has been attached to the non-molestation order, a warrant for arrest under FLA 1996 can be granted in respect of the order (s 47(8), (9)). If a power of arrest was attached to all of the terms of the order, and a warrant of arrest cannot be granted because there are no terms of the original injunction to which the power of arrest was not attached, it is arguable that the respondent can be arrested under the original power of arrest. Alternatively, as with any civil case, provided that the court is satisfied that the absent party has been served, and is aware of the trial date, the court can simply proceed in his absence.

Hearing where respondent fails to attend despite having been given due "Notice to show good reason"—If the contemnor fails to attend, having been given due Notice, the committal hearing can proceed in his absence and committal or a penalty can be imposed (*Payne v Payne* (1979) CAT 209).

Committal hearing while criminal proceedings pending—Where criminal proceedings are pending in respect of the conduct alleged to be a contempt, the court has a discretion whether to proceed with the application for committal (*M v M (Contempt: Committal)* [1997] 1 FLR 762).

Unrepresented contemnors—The court has no power to grant public funding (legal aid) to an unrepresented contemnor (the limited power to grant legal representation in contempt cases applies only to a contempt in the face of the court: Access to Justice Act 1999, s 12(2), Sch 3). However, it is desirable that an alleged contemnor be represented. Accordingly, the court may adjourn (and in FLA 1996 cases, remand) to enable the contemnor to be represented. Alternatively, the judge will often require a member of the court staff to arrange for a solicitor to provide "Help at Court". If a hearing proceeds without the contemnor being represented, the judge should ensure that he understands his right to cross-examine, give evidence and call witnesses (*Shoreditch County Court Bailiffs v Madeiros* (1988) *The Times*, 24 February).

The importance of abiding by correct procedure—The Court of Appeal has stressed in several cases that, because committal for contempt of court is concerned with offences of a quasi-criminal nature and the liberty of the subject is at stake, the relevant rules of court must be complied with and the prescribed forms must be used. However, *Practice Direction (Committal Applications)*, para 10 provides that "Any procedural defect in the commencement or conduct by the applicant of a committal application may be waived by the court if satisfied that no injustice has been caused to the respondent by the defect". In *Nicholls v Nicholls* [1997] 1 FLR 649, Lord Woolf MR, giving the judgment of the Court of Appeal, stated (at 655D) that "While the ... requirements of Ord 29, r 1 are there to be observed, in the absence of authority to the contrary, even though the liberty of the subject is involved, we would not expect the requirements to be mandatory, in the sense that any non-compliance with the rule means that a committal for contempt is irredeemably invalid." Lord Woolf gave the following guidance (at 661E):

> "(1) As committal orders involve the liberty of the subject it is particularly important that the relevant rules are duly complied with. It remains the responsibility of the judge when signing the committal order to ensure that it is properly drawn and that it adequately particularises the breaches which have been proved and for which the sentence has been imposed.
>
> (2) As long as the contemnor has had a fair trial and the order has been made on valid grounds the existence of a defect either in the application to commit or in the committal order served will not result in the order being set aside except insofar as the interests of justice require this to be done.
>
> (3) Interests of justice will not require an order to be set aside where there is no prejudice caused as the result or errors in the application to commit or in the order to commit. When necessary the order can be amended.
>
> (4) When considering whether to set aside the order, the court should have regard to the interests of any other party and the need to uphold the reputation of the justice system.
>
> (5) If there has been a procedural irregularity or some other defect in the conduct of the proceedings which has occasioned injustice, the court will consider exercising its powers to order a new trial unless there are circumstances which indicate that it would not be just to do so."

Committal hearing procedure—In general terms, hearings of committal proceedings are in many respects similar to hearings of criminal charges. The burden of proof rests on the person making the allegation of contempt. The standard of proof is the criminal standard (*Re C (A Minor) (Contempt)* [1986] 1 FLR 578 at 588). The respondent must be allowed to cross-examine witnesses and to call evidence. The respondent is entitled to submit that there is no case to answer (*Savings and Investment Bank v Gasco Investments (Netherlands)* (1986) 136 NLJ 657). If a contempt is found proved, the contemnor must be allowed to address the court by way of mitigation or seeking to purge his contempt (*Stilwell v Williamson* (1986) *The Times*, 1 September). Autrefois acquit and autrefois convict apply.

Evidence and witnesses at hearing—An alleged contemnor is not a compellable witness (*Comet Products UK Ltd v Hawkex Plastics Ltd* [1971] 2 QB 67, [1971] 2 WLR 361). The court can issue a witness summons to a person who witnessed an alleged contempt to attend committal proceedings although no application has been made by a party (*Yianni v Yianni* [1966] 1 WLR 120, [1966] 1 All ER 231n). Hearsay evidence is admissible but caution should be exercised (*Savings and Investment Bank v Gasco Investments (Netherlands) BV (No 2)* [1988] Ch 422, [1988] 2 WLR 1212). Respondents to a motion to commit can be required by the court to swear, file and serve affidavits, or produce statements of witnesses of fact upon which they might wish to rely before the hearing, in order to enable proper preparation of the evidence in reply (*Re B (Contempt: Evidence)* [1996] 1 FLR 239, Wall J). However, the applicant must prove his case on the evidence filed in support of the application, supplemented by any admissions made by the alleged contemnor upon which the applicant was entitled to rely, and the applicant can make no use of the respondent's evidence until it has been deployed by the respondent. A respondent who complies with a direction from the court in the foregoing terms is not in peril of cross-examination until such time as he deploys the evidence in his own case (*Re B (Contempt: Evidence)*, above).

Form N79 committal order and Form N80 committal warrant (r 1(5))—Form N79, the prescribed form for a committal order in county courts, can be relied on as a checklist for committal procedures, and incorporates most of the usual orders which can be made on proof of disobedience of an injunctive order or breach of an undertaking. The court should complete the relevant parts of Form N79 and delete the parts not required. The most important requirements are that the contempt(s) found proved must have been alleged in the "Notice to show good reason" (*Tabone v Seguna* [1986] 1 FLR 591), must accord with the evidence accepted by the judge (*Re C (Contempt: Committal Order)* [1989] 1 FLR 288), and must be clearly and precisely recited (*Parra v Rones* [1986] Fam Law 262; *Linkleter v Linkleter* [1988] 1 FLR 360; *C v Hackney London Borough Council* [1995] 2 FLR 681). The precise details of the orders made must be entered. The committal warrant is in Form N80.

1A Undertaking given by party (CCR Ord 29, r 1A)

Rule 1 (except paragraph (6)) shall apply to undertakings as it applies to orders with the necessary modifications and as if –

(*a*) for paragraph (2) of that rule there were substituted the following –

"(2) A copy of the document recording the undertaking shall be delivered by the [court] [*proper*] officer to the party giving the undertaking –

(*a*) by handing a copy of the document to him before he leaves the court building; or
(*b*) where his place of residence is known, by posting a copy to him at his place of residence; or
(*c*) through his solicitor,

and, where delivery cannot be effected in this way, the [court] [*proper*] officer shall deliver a copy of the document to the party for whose benefit the undertaking is given and that party shall cause it to be served personally as soon as is practicable".

(*b*) in paragraph (7), the words from "a copy of" to "paragraph (2) or" were omitted.

General Note—Modifications to this rule, set out above in its re-enacted form, are highlighted by the addition of square brackets. The words in italics are those employed in the original version of the CCR (which continue to govern enforcement in "family proceedings"). For further examination of this issue see **Which rules of court** in the Legal background to Procedural Guide 38 and the annotations under FPR 1991, r 1.3.

Undertaking to pay money—An order to pay money in general is not enforceable as a civil contempt under Ord 29, r 1, but may be enforced by judgment summons under Debtors Act 1869, s 5, if it is a maintenance order (Administration of Justice Act 1970, s 11). An undertaking to pay money may not be enforced by committal, except as permitted under Debtors Act 1869, s 5 (*Buckley v Crawford* [1893] 1 QB 105). An undertaking can be enforced as if it were an order (*Gandolfo v Gandolfo (Standard Bank, Garnishee)* [1981] QB 359). Arguably, an undertaking which is part of an ancillary relief order can be enforced by judgment summons (*Symmons v Symmons* [1993] 1 FLR 317, [1993] Fam Law 135). As from 25 March 2002, CPR Sch 2, CCR Ord 28 has been amended to remove incompatibility with the European Convention on Human Rights (see further annotation under "old-style" CCR Ord 28).

Form N117 general form of undertaking—Following *Hussain v Hussain* [1986] Fam 134, [1986] 2 FLR 271, r 1A was introduced, in addition to Form N117, to provide for delivery, usually by the court, of a copy of the form of undertaking to the giver. This was to redress the problem identified in *Hussain v Hussain* (above) that if, upon answering to a "Notice to show good reason", the giver of an undertaking asserts that he did not adequately understand the promises given to the court, or the consequences of breach, it is difficult for the court to be sure what occurred when the undertaking was given. It is good practice for the judge to require the giver to sign the acknowledgement of giving the undertaking, in the box provided on the back of Form N117. The court can require the giver of an undertaking to sign a statement that he understands the terms of his undertaking and the consequences of failure to comply with it (*Practice Direction (Judgments and Orders)* (PD 40B), para 9.3).

Personal attendance of giver of the undertaking generally essential—Form N117 provides for the court to accept the undertaking, having explained its meaning and the consequences of failing to keep the promises. The giver should normally be required to sign the acknowledgement on the back of Form N117. The court may accept an undertaking in the absence of the giver (see *Practice Direction (Judgments and Orders)* (PD 40B), para 9.4), provided that it is satisfied that he understands the promises and the consequences of a breach. This should happen only where an appropriately worded document is given to the judge, or where the advocate satisfies the court that he is adequately instructed to give the undertaking on behalf of his absent client.

"shall be delivered by the proper officer to the party giving the undertaking" (r 1A(*a*))—An undertaking duly given to the court (recorded in county court Form N117), in promised terms which are within its powers, by a person who has been told what the consequences of breach may be, is enforceable as soon as it has been given (*D v A & Co* [1900] 1 Ch 484; *Hussain v Hussain* [1986] Fam 134). The rules specify that the form shall be "delivered", not served, because delivery is an administrative act, and it is the giving of the undertaking which makes it enforceable, not delivery of the copy. Where the court accepts an undertaking from the giver who is absent, the proper officer must ensure that the document recording the undertaking, which should be in the form of an order or a suitably amended N117, is posted to the giver at his place of residence, or delivered through the giver's solicitor.

"where delivery cannot be effected in this way ... served personally as soon as is practicable"—This provision should only apply very rarely, for example where a giver of the undertaking is not represented by a solicitor and, with his address unknown, leaves the court before receiving a copy of the undertaking.

PART III

2 Solicitor's undertaking (CCR Ord 29, r 2)

(1) An undertaking given by a solicitor in relation to any proceeding in a county court may be enforced, by order of the judge of that court, by committal order against the solicitor.

(2) Where it appears to the judge that a solicitor has failed to carry out any such undertaking, he may of his own [initiative] [*motion*] direct the court officer to issue a notice calling on the solicitor to show cause why he should not be committed to prison.

(3) Where any party to the proceedings desires to have the undertaking enforced by committal order, the [court] [*proper*] officer shall, on the application of the party supported by an affidavit setting out the facts on which the application is based, issue such a notice as is referred to in paragraph (2).

[*(4) A notice to show cause issued under paragraph (2) or (3) shall be served on the solicitor personally, together with a copy of any affidavit filed under paragraph (3), but rule 1(5) and (7) shall apply in relation to the notice as they apply in relation to a notice to show cause issued under rule 1(4).*]

General Note—Modifications to this rule, set out above in its re-enacted form, are highlighted by the addition of square brackets. The words in italics are those employed in the original version of the CCR (which continue to govern enforcement in "family proceedings"). For further examination of this issue see **Which rules of court** in the Legal background to Procedural Guide 38 and the annotations under FPR 1991, r 1.3.

Enforceability of undertakings (r 2(1))—To be enforceable against the solicitor, the undertaking must have been given in his capacity as solicitor (*United Mining and Finance Corporation Ltd v Becher* [1910] 2 KB 276), and personally, not merely as agent for his client (*Burnett v Proois* (1870) 22 LT 543). If the solicitor is not accepting personal responsibility, it is for him to make this clear (*Re Marchant* [1908] 1 KB 998).

Forms—The form of notice to show cause is Form N81; the form of committal order is Form N82.

3 Discharge of person in custody (CCR Ord 29, r 3)

(1) Where a person in custody under a warrant or order, other than a warrant of committal to which Order 27, rule 8, or Order 28, rule 4 or 14, relates, desires to apply to the court for his discharge, he shall make his application in writing attested by the governor of the prison (or any other officer of the prison not below the rank of principal officer) showing that he has purged or is desirous of purging his contempt and shall, not less than one day before the application is made, serve notice of it on the party, if any, at whose instance the warrant or order was issued.

(2) If the committal order –

(*a*) does not direct that any application for discharge shall be made to a judge; or

(*b*) was made by the district judge under section 118 of the Act,

any application for discharge may be made to the district judge.

(3) Nothing in paragraph (1) shall apply to an application made by the Official Solicitor in his official capacity for the discharge of a person in custody.

Scope of provision—A person committed to prison for contempt is entitled to apply to purge his contempt and to be discharged from prison (r 3(1); FPR 1991, r 7.2(2); Form N79). This rule provides a simple procedure for the prisoner to apply for his discharge, whether committed under the preceding rules of this order or, where there is no separate procedure, otherwise. It should be noted that Contempt of Court Act 1981, s 14(1) expressly saves the court's power to order a prisoner's early discharge. In *Enfield London Borough Council v Mahoney* [1983] 1 WLR 749, [1983] 2 All ER 901, it was held that a contemnor may be released, even though he has not purged his contempt, where he has been sufficiently punished by the term already served and further imprisonment will have no coercive effect.

"Order 27, rule 8, or Order 28, rule 4 or 14" (r 3(1))—As in the case of the committal proceedings themselves, separate procedures exist for debtors committed in oral examination, attachment of earnings and judgment summons proceedings to seek their discharge.

Attendance on hearing—The contemnor should be present to hear the outcome of his application unless, in his solicitor's view, his mental condition makes that undesirable (*Practice Direction of 25 July 1983*).

Forms—No form of application is prescribed but Form N244 may be used; the form of order for discharge is Form N83.

****

CCR ORDER 31
CHARGING ORDERS

****

4 Enforcement of charging order by sale (CCR Ord 31, r 4)

(1) Proceedings in a county court for the enforcement of a charging order by sale of the property charged shall be commenced by a claim form, which shall be filed in the appropriate court, together with a witness statement or affidavit and a copy thereof –

(*a*) identifying the charging order sought to be enforced and the subject matter of the charge;

(*b*) specifying the amount in respect of which the charge was imposed and the balance outstanding at the date of the application;
(*c*) verifying, so far as known, the debtor's title to the property charged;
(*d*) identifying any prior incumbrances on the property charged, with, so far as known, the names and addresses of the incumbrancers and the amounts owing to them; and
(*e*) giving an estimate of the price which would be obtained on sale of the property.

(2) The appropriate court shall be –
(*a*) if the charging order was made by a county court, that court;
(*b*) in any other case, the court for the district in which the debtor resides or carries on business or, if there is no such district, the court for the district in which the judgment creditor resides or carries on business.

(3) A copy of the witness statement or affidavit filed under paragraph (1) shall be served on the respondent with a copy of the claim form and a notice to each respondent of the date of the hearing.

(4) The proceedings may be heard and determined by a district judge.

(5) The net proceeds of sale, after discharging any prior incumbrances and deducting the amount referred to in paragraph (1)(*b*) and the costs of the sale, shall be paid into court.

Defined terms—"charging order": Charging Orders Act 1979, s 1(3); "debtor": s 1(1).

Jurisdiction—A charging order is equated by Charging Orders Act 1979, s 3(4) to an equitable charge, both as to its effect and as to its enforcement. An order for sale is the most obvious method of enforcement. If such an order is sought in the county court, the procedure set by this rule must be used; otherwise, application may be made to the High Court. The county court's jurisdiction arises from County Courts Act 1984, s 23(*c*) and is limited to cases where the debt secured does not exceed £30,000.

Procedure—The claim is made under Pt 8 as modified by *Practice Direction (How to Make Claims in the Schedule Rules and Other Claims)*, Section B (claims made in the High Court for such orders are governed by Section A). See *Civil Court Service* (Jordan Publishing Ltd) for a Procedural Guide to such claims.

"sale of the property charged" (r 4(1))—If the debtor's interest which is charged is merely a beneficial share, a sale of the whole property cannot be ordered under this rule, although theoretically a sale of that share might be ordered. However, the chargee has sufficient standing to make application under Trusts of Land and Appointment of Trustees Act 1996, s 14 for an order for the sale of the property (*Midland Bank plc v Pike* [1988] 2 All ER 434). This rule would not apply to such an application; see the annotations to TLATA 1996, ss 14, 15 and Procedural Guide 5.

Criteria applied (r 4(4))—In the case of the debtor's home, it is a draconian step to require a sale to satisfy a simple debt. It is rarely done, except in response to the debtor's contumelious neglect or refusal to pay; even then, the order will often be suspended on terms as to payment. It may be otherwise in the case of investment property. Where the order to be enforced is a maintenance order, the debtor's resources will have been taken into account when it was made and his neglect or refusal may thus be easier to demonstrate.

Forms—The form of order for sale is Form N436. However, this practice form is barely adequate and reference should be made to the forms of order employed in the Chancery Division for sale under an equitable charge.

****

PART III

CCR ORDER 47
DOMESTIC AND MATRIMONIAL PROCEEDINGS

****

5 Family Law Reform Act 1969 (CCR Ord 47, r 5)

(1) In this rule –

"bodily samples" and "scientific tests" have the meanings assigned to them by section 25 of the Family Law Reform Act 1969, and

"direction" means a direction for the use of scientific tests under section 20(1) of that Act.

(2) Except with the [permission] [*leave*] of the court, an application in any proceedings for a direction shall be made on notice to every party to the proceedings (other than the applicant) and to any other person from whom the direction involves the taking of bodily samples.

(3) Where an application is made for a direction involving the taking of bodily samples from a person who is not a party to the proceedings in which the application is made, the [application notice] [*notice of application*] shall be served on him personally and the court may at any time direct him to be made a party to the proceedings.

(4) Where an application is made for a direction in respect of a person (in this paragraph referred to as a person under disability) who is either –

(*a*) under 16, or

(*b*) suffering from mental disorder within the meaning of the Mental Health Act 1983 and incapable of understanding the nature and purpose of scientific tests,

the notice of application shall state the name and address of the person having the care and control of the person under disability and shall be served on him instead of on the person under disability.

(5) Where the court gives a direction in any proceedings, the [court] [*proper*] officer shall send a copy to every party to the proceedings and to every other person from whom the direction involves the taking of bodily samples and, unless otherwise ordered, the proceedings shall stand adjourned until the court receives a report pursuant to the direction.

(6) On receipt by the court of a report made pursuant to a direction, the [court] [*proper*] officer shall send a copy to every party to the proceedings and to every other person from whom the direction involved the taking of bodily samples.

Amendments—SI 2001/256.

General Note—Modifications to this rule, set out above in its re-enacted form, are highlighted by the addition of square brackets. The words in italics are those employed in the original version of the CCR (which continue to govern applications for scientific tests in "family proceedings"). For further examination of this issue see **Which rules of court** in the Legal background to Procedural Guide 77 and the annotations under FPR 1991, r 1.3.

"person under disability" (r 5(4))—To come within this definition a person over the age of 16 must suffer from a mental disorder *and* be incapable of understanding the nature and purpose of scientific tests, but there is no requirement that the incapacity be related to the mental disorder. The definition is unique to this rule, being decision specific in regard to capacity to understand the nature and purpose of scientific tests. It differs materially from that generally used in respect of capacity to conduct proceedings, which is that the person is by reason of mental disorder incapable of managing and administering his property and affairs (see FPR 1991, Pt IX; CCR Ord 10). It is possible that an individual may come within one definition but not the other. For a further explanation see **Assessment of capacity** under FPR 1991, r 9.1.

"mental disorder"—Defined by Mental Health Act 1983, s 1(3) as "mental illness, arrested or incomplete development of mind, psychopathic disorder and any other disorder or disability of mind". For a further explanation see **"mental disorder"** under FPR 1991, r 9.1.

Service on a person under disability—The rule provides for substituted service of the notice of application upon a carer where it involves taking bodily samples from a person under disability who is not a party to the proceedings. For the implications of this, see **Mode of service of the application** and **Service of other documents** under RSC Ord 112 (which repeats CCR Ord 47, r 5 in almost identical terms).

Implications—If the person to be tested becomes a party to the proceedings and is a person under disability in relation to the proceedings pursuant to FPR 1991, Pt IX, the proceedings will have to be stayed until a guardian ad litem has been appointed. In default, any continuing proceedings will be a nullity.

"direction"—A form for the direction was proposed by Ward LJ in *Re H (Paternity: Blood Test)* [1996] 2 FLR 65, CA, and is set out in **The direction** under FLRA 1969, s 20.

****

Community Legal Service (Cost Protection) Regulations 2000, SI 2000/824

1 Citation and commencement

These Regulations may be cited as the Community Legal Service (Cost Protection) Regulations 2000 and shall come into force on 1 April 2000.

****

3 Cost protection

(1) Cost protection shall not apply in relation to such parts of proceedings, or prospective proceedings, as are funded for the client by way of –

(*a*) Help at Court or Litigation Support;

(*b*) Investigative Support, except where any proceedings in respect of which the Investigative Support was given are not pursued (whether or not as funded proceedings) after the certificate for Investigative Support is discharged;

(*c*) subject to paragraph (2), Legal Help.

(2) Subject to paragraph (4), where the client receives Legal Help, but later receives Legal Representation or Approved Family Help in respect of the same dispute, cost protection shall apply, both in respect of –

(*a*) the costs incurred by the receiving party before the commencement of proceedings which, as regards the client, are funded proceedings by virtue of the client's receipt of Legal Help, and

(*b*) the costs incurred by the receiving party in the course of proceedings which, as regards the client, are funded proceedings by virtue of the client's receipt of Legal Representation or Approved Family Help.

(3) Subject to paragraph (4), cost protection shall apply only to costs incurred by the receiving party in relation to proceedings which, as regards the client, are funded proceedings, and –

(*a*) where work is done before the issue of a certificate, cost protection shall (subject to paragraphs (2) and (5)) apply only to costs incurred after the issue of the certificate;

(*b*) where funding is withdrawn by discharging the client's certificate, cost protection shall apply only to costs incurred before the date when funded services under the certificate ceased to be provided.

(4) Where funding is withdrawn by revoking the client's certificate, cost protection shall not apply, either in respect of work done before or after the revocation.

(5) Cost protection shall apply to work done immediately before the grant of an emergency certificate if –

(*a*) no application for such a certificate could be made because the Commission's office was closed; and

(*b*) the client's solicitor applies for an emergency certificate at the first available opportunity, and the certificate is granted.

****

5 Costs order against Commission

(1) The following paragraphs of this regulation apply where –

(*a*) funded services are provided to a client in relation to proceedings;

(*b*) those proceedings are finally decided in favour of a non-funded party; and

(*c*) cost protection applies.

(2) The court may, subject to the following paragraphs of this regulation, make an order for the payment by the Commission to the non-funded party of the whole or any part of the costs incurred by him in the proceedings (other than any costs that the client is required to pay under a section 11(1) costs order).

(3) An order under paragraph (2) may only be made if all the conditions set out in sub-paragraphs (*a*), (*b*), (*c*) and (*d*) are satisfied –

(*a*) a section 11(1) costs order is made against the client in the proceedings, and the amount (if any) which the client is required to pay under that costs order is less than the amount of the full costs;

(*b*) unless there is a good reason for the delay, the non-funded party makes a request under regulation 10(2) of the Community Legal Service (Costs) Regulations 2000 within three months of the making of the section 11(1) costs order;

(*c*) as regards costs incurred in a court of first instance, the proceedings were instituted by the client, the non-funded party is an individual, and the court is satisfied that the non-funded party will suffer financial hardship unless the order is made; and

(*d*) in any case, the court is satisfied that it is just and equitable in the circumstances that provision for the costs should be made out of public funds.

(3A) An order under paragraph (2) may be made –

(*a*) in relation to proceedings in the House of Lords, by the Clerk to the Parliaments;

(*b*) in relation to proceedings in the Court of Appeal, High Court or a county court, by a costs judge or a district judge;

(*c*) in relation to proceedings in a magistrates' court, by a single justice or by the justices' clerk;

(*d*) in relation to proceedings in the Employment Appeal Tribunal, by the Registrar of that tribunal.".

(4) Where the client receives funded services in connection with part only of the proceedings, the reference in paragraph (2) to the costs incurred by the non-funded party in the relevant proceedings shall be construed as a reference to so much of those costs as is attributable to the part of the proceedings which are funded proceedings.

(5) Where a court decides any proceedings in favour of the non-funded party and an appeal lies (with or without permission) against that decision, any order made under this regulation shall not take effect –

(*a*) where permission to appeal is required, unless the time limit for applications for permission to appeal expires without permission being granted;

(*b*) where permission to appeal is granted or is not required, unless the time limit for appeal expires without an appeal being brought.

(6) Subject to paragraph (7), in determining whether the conditions in paragraph (3)(*c*) and (*d*) are satisfied, the court shall have regard to the resources of the non-funded party and of his partner.

(7) The court shall not have regard to the resources of the partner of the non-funded party if the partner has a contrary interest in the funded proceedings.

(8) Where the non-funded party is acting in a representative, fiduciary or official capacity and is entitled to be indemnified in respect of his costs from any property, estate or fund, the court shall, for the purposes of paragraph (3), have regard to the value of the property, estate or fund and the resources of the persons, if any, including that party where appropriate, who are beneficially interested in that property, estate or fund.

Amendments—SI 2001/823; SI 2001/3812.

****

Community Legal Service (Costs) Regulations 2000, SI 2000/441

PART I
GENERAL

1 Citation and commencement

These Regulations may be cited as the Community Legal Service (Costs) Regulations 2000 and shall come into force on 1 April 2000.

2 Interpretation

In these Regulations –

"the Act" means the Access to Justice Act 1999;

"certificate" means a certificate issued under the Funding Code certifying a decision to fund services for the client;

"client" means an individual who receives funded services;

"Commission" means the Legal Services Commission established under section 1 of the Act;

"costs judge" has the same meaning as in the CPR;

"costs order" means an order that a party pay all or part of the costs of proceedings;

"costs order against the Commission" means an order, made under regulation 5 of the Community Legal Service (Cost Protection) Regulations 2000 (but not one under regulation 6 of those Regulations), that the Commission pay all or part of the costs of a party to proceedings who has not received funded services in relation to those proceedings under a certificate, other than a certificate which has been revoked;

"cost protection" means the limit on costs awarded against a client set out in section 11(1) of the Act;

"court" includes any tribunal having the power to award costs in favour of, or against, a party;

"CPR" means the Civil Procedure Rules 1998, and a reference to a Part or rule, prefixed by "CPR", means the Part or rule so numbered in the CPR;

"Financial Regulations" means the Community Legal Service (Financial) Regulations 2000;

"Funding Code" means the code approved under section 9 of the Act;

"full costs" means, where a section 11(1) costs order is made against a client, the amount of costs which that client would, but for section 11(1) of the Act, have been ordered to pay;

"funded services" means services which are provided directly for a client and funded for that client by the Commission as part of the Community Legal Service under sections 4 to 11 of the Act;

"partner", in relation to a party to proceedings, means a person with whom that party lives as a couple, and includes a person with whom the party is not currently living but from whom he is not living separate and apart;

"proceedings" include proceedings in any tribunal which is a court, as defined, in this paragraph;

"receiving party" means a party in favour of whom a costs order is made;

"Regional Director" means any Regional Director appointed by the Commission in accordance with the Funding Code and any other person authorised to act on his behalf, except a supplier;

"rules of court", in relation to a tribunal, means rules or regulations made by the authority having power to make rules or regulations regulating the practice and procedure of that tribunal and, in relation to any court, includes practice directions;

"section 11(1) costs order" means a costs order against a client where cost protection applies;

"solicitor" means solicitor or other person who is an authorised litigator within the meaning of section 119(1) of the Courts and Legal Services Act 1990;

"statement of resources" means –

(*a*) a statement, verified by a statement of truth, made by a party to proceedings setting out:

(i) his income and capital and financial commitments during the previous year and, if applicable, those of his partner;

(ii) his estimated future financial resources and expectations and, if applicable, those of his partner; and

(iii) a declaration that he and, if applicable, his partner, has not deliberately foregone or deprived himself of any resources or expectations, particulars of any application for funding made by him in connection with the proceedings, and any other facts relevant to the determination of his resources; or

(*b*) a statement, verified by a statement of truth, made by a client receiving funded services, setting out the information provided by the client under regulation 6 of the Financial Regulations, and stating that there has been no significant change in the client's financial circumstances since the date on which the information was provided or, as the case may be, details of any such change;

"statement of truth" has the same meaning as in CPR Part 22;

"supplier" means any person or body providing funded services to the client, including any authorised advocate (within the meaning of section 119(1) of the Courts and Legal Services Act 1990) engaged by the client's solicitor to act in proceedings.

PART III

3 Effect of these Regulations

Nothing in these Regulations shall be construed, in relation to proceedings where one or more parties are receiving, or have received, funded services, as –

(*a*) requiring a court to make a costs order where it would not otherwise have made a costs order; or

(*b*) affecting the court's power to make a wasted costs order against a legal representative.

****

PART II
COSTS ORDERS AGAINST CLIENT AND AGAINST COMMISSION

5 Application of regulations 6 to 13

Regulations 6 to 13 apply only where cost protection applies.

****

7 Assessment of resources

(1) The first £100,000 of the value of the client's interest in the main or only dwelling in which he resides shall not be taken into account in having regard to the client's resources for the purposes of section 11(1) of the Act.

(2) Where, but only to the extent that, the court considers that the circumstances are exceptional, having regard in particular to the quantity or value of the items concerned, the court may take into account the value of the client's clothes and household furniture, or the tools and implements of his trade, in having regard to the client's resources for the purposes of section 11(1) of the Act.

(3) Subject to paragraph (4), in having regard to the resources of a party for the purposes of section 11(1) of the Act, the resources of his partner shall be treated as his resources.

(4) The resources of a party's partner shall not be treated as that party's resources if the partner has a contrary interest in the dispute in respect of which the funded services are provided.

(5) Where a party is acting in a representative, fiduciary or official capacity, the court shall not take the personal resources of the party into account for the purposes of section 11(1) of the Act, but shall have regard to the value of any property or estate, or the amount of any fund out of which he is entitled to be indemnified, and may also have regard to the resources of the persons, if any, including that party where appropriate, who are beneficially interested in that property, estate or fund.

8 Statements of resources

(1) Any person who is a party to proceedings in which another party is a client may make a statement of resources, and file it with the court.

(2) A person making and filing a statement of resources under paragraph (1) shall serve a copy of it on the client.

(3) Where a copy of a statement of resources has been served under paragraph (2) not less than seven days before the date fixed for a hearing at which the amount to be paid under a section 11(1) costs order falls, or may fall, to be decided, the client shall also make a statement of resources, and shall produce it at that hearing.

9 Procedures for ordering costs against client and Commission

(1) Where the court is considering whether to make a section 11(1) costs order, it shall consider whether, but for cost protection, it would have made a costs order against the client and, if so, whether it would, on making the costs order, have specified the amount to be paid under that order.

(2) If the court considers that it would have made a costs order against the client, but that it would not have specified the amount to be paid under it, the court shall, when making the section 11(1) costs order –

(*a*) specify the amount (if any) that the client is to pay under that order if, but only if:

(i) it considers that it has sufficient information before it to decide what amount is, in that case, a reasonable amount for the client to pay, in accordance with section 11(1) of the Act; and

(ii) it is satisfied that, if it were to determine the full costs at that time, they would exceed the amount referred to in sub-paragraph (i);

(*b*) otherwise, it shall not specify the amount the client is to pay under the costs order.

(3) If the court considers that it would have made a costs order against the client, and that it would have specified the amount to be paid under it, the court shall, when making the section 11(1) costs order –

(*a*) specify the amount (if any) that the client is to pay under that order if, but only if, it considers that it has sufficient information before it to decide what amount is, in that case, a reasonable amount for the client to pay, in accordance with section 11(1) of the Act;

(*b*) otherwise, it shall not specify the amount the client is to pay under the costs order.

(4) Any order made under paragraph (3) shall state the amount of the full costs.

(5) The amount (if any) to be paid by the client under an order made under paragraph (2)(*b*) or paragraph (3)(*b*), and any application for a costs order against the Commission, shall be determined in accordance with regulation 10, and at any such determination following an order made under paragraph (2)(*b*), the amount of the full costs shall also be assessed.

(6) Where the court makes a section 11(1) costs order that does not specify the amount which the client is to pay under it, it may also make findings of fact, as to the parties' conduct in the proceedings or otherwise, relevant to the determination of that amount, and those findings shall be taken into consideration in that determination.

Amendments—SI 2001/822.

10 (1) The following paragraphs of this regulation apply where the amount to be paid under a section 11(1) costs order, or an application for a costs order against the Commission, is to be determined under this regulation, by virtue of regulation 9(5).

(2) The receiving party may, within three months after a section 11(1) costs order is made, request a hearing to determine the costs payable to him.

(3) A request under paragraph (2) shall be accompanied by –

(*a*) if the section 11(1) costs order does not state the full costs, the receiving party's bill of costs, which shall comply with any requirements of relevant rules of court relating to the form and content of a bill of costs where the court is assessing a party's costs;

(*b*) a statement of resources; and

(*c*) if the receiving party is seeking, or, subject to the determination of the amount to be paid under the section 11(1) costs order, may seek, a costs order against the Commission, written notice to that effect.

PART III

(4) The receiving party shall file the documents referred to in paragraph (3) with the court and at the same time serve copies of them –

(*a*) on the client, if a determination of costs payable under section 11(1) of the Act is sought; and
(*b*) on the Regional Director, if notice has been given under paragraph (3)(*c*).

(5) Where documents are served on the client under paragraph (4)(*a*), the client shall make a statement of resources.

(6) The client shall file the statement of resources made under paragraph (5) with the court, and serve copies of it on the receiving party and, if notice has been given under paragraph (3)(*c*), on the Regional Director, not more than 21 days after the client receives a copy of the receiving party's statement of resources.

(7) The client may, at the same time as filing and serving a statement of resources under paragraph (6), file, and serve on the same persons, a statement setting out any points of dispute in relation to the bill of costs referred to in paragraph (3)(*a*).

(8) If the client, without good reason, fails to file a statement of resources in accordance with paragraph (6), the court shall determine the amount which the client shall be required to pay under the section 11(1) costs order (and, if relevant, the full costs), having regard to the statement made by the receiving party, and the court need not hold an oral hearing for such determination.

(9) If the client files a statement of resources in accordance with paragraph (6), or the period for filing such notice expires, or if the costs payable by the client have already been determined, the court shall set a date for the hearing and, at least 14 days before that date, serve notice of it on –

(*a*) the receiving party;
(*b*) the client (unless the costs payable by the client have already been determined); and
(*c*) if a costs order against the Commission is or may be sought, the Regional Director.

(10) The court's functions under this regulation may be exercised –

(*a*) in relation to proceedings in the House of Lords, by the Clerk to the Parliaments;
(*b*) in relation to proceedings in the Court of Appeal, High Court or a county court, a costs judge or a district judge;
(*c*) in relation to proceedings in a magistrates' court, by a single justice or by the justices' clerk;
(*d*) in relation to proceedings in the Employment Appeal Tribunal, by the Registrar of that Tribunal.

(11) The amount of costs to be determined under this regulation may include the costs incurred in relation to a request made under this regulation.

"within three months" (reg 10(2))—It is essential that the hearing be requested within the three month period referred to in the rule (*R (Gunn) v Secretary of State for the Home Department* [2001] EWCA Civ 891, [2001] 1 WLR 1634, CA). The court cannot extend this time-limit (*Middleton v Middleton* [1994] 1 FLR 557, CA).

10A (1) Subject to paragraph (2), where the court makes a section 11(1) costs order but does not specify the amount which the client is to pay under it, the court may order the client to pay an amount on account of the costs which are the subject of the order.

(2) The court may order a client to make a payment on account of costs under this regulation only if it has sufficient information before it to decide the minimum amount which the client is likely to be ordered to pay on a determination under regulation 10.

(3) The amount of the payment on account of costs shall not exceed the minimum amount which the court decides that the client is likely to be ordered to pay on such a determination.

(4) Where the court orders a client to make a payment on account of costs –

- (*a*) it shall order the client to make the payment into court; and
- (*b*) the payment shall remain in court unless and until the court –
  - (i) makes a determination under regulation 10 of the amount which the client should pay to the receiving party under the section 11(1) costs order, and orders the payment on account or part of it to be paid to the receiving party in satisfaction or part satisfaction of the client's liability under that order; or
  - (ii) makes an order under paragraph (5)(*b*) or (5)(*c*) of this regulation that the payment on account or part of it be repaid to the client.

(5) Where a client has made a payment on account of costs pursuant to an order under paragraph (1) of this regulation –

- (*a*) the receiving party shall request a hearing under regulation 10 to determine the amount of costs payable to him;
- (*b*) if the receiving party fails to request such a hearing within the time permitted by regulation 10(2), the payment on account shall be repaid to the client;
- (*c*) if upon the hearing under regulation 10 the amount of costs which it is determined that the client should pay is less than the amount of the payment on account, the difference shall be repaid to the client.

Amendments—Inserted by SI 2001/822.

****

12 Variation and late determination of amount of costs

(1) The following paragraphs of this regulation apply where the court makes a section 11(1) costs order.

(2) Where the amount (if any) which the client is required to pay under the section 11(1) costs order, together with the amount which the Commission is required to pay under any costs order against the Commission, is less than the full costs, the receiving party may, on the ground set out in paragraph (4)(*a*), apply to the court for an order varying the amount which the client is required to pay under the section 11(1) costs order.

(3) Where the court has not specified the amount to be paid under the section 11(1) costs order, and the receiving party has not, within the time limit in regulation 10(2), applied to have that amount determined in accordance with regulation 10, the receiving party may, on any of the grounds set out in paragraph (4), apply for a determination of the amount that the client is required to pay.

(4) The grounds referred to in paragraphs (2) and (3) are the grounds that –

- (*a*) there has been a significant change in the client's circumstances since the date of the order;

(*b*) material additional information as to the client's financial resources is available, and that information could not with reasonable diligence have been obtained by the receiving party in time to make an application in accordance with regulation 10; or

(*c*) there were other good reasons justifying the receiving party's failure to make an application within the time limit in regulation 10(2).

(5) Any application under paragraph (2) or (3) shall be made by the receiving party within six years from the date on which the section 11(1) costs order is first made.

(6) On any application under paragraph (2), the order may be varied as the court thinks fit, but the amount of costs ordered (excluding any costs ordered to be paid under paragraph (9)) shall not exceed the amount of the full costs as stated in any previous order of the court.

(7) When the amount which the client is required to pay under the section 11(1) costs order has been determined under regulation 9(2)(*a*), and the receiving party applies under paragraph (2) for an order varying that amount –

(*a*) the receiving party shall file with the application under paragraph (2) his bill of costs, which shall comply with any requirements of relevant rules of court relating to the form and content of a bill of costs where the court is assessing a party's costs; and

(*b*) the court shall, when determining the application, assess the full costs.

(8) Where the receiving party has received funded services in relation to the proceedings, the Commission may make an application under paragraph (2) or paragraph (3), and –

(*a*) when making the application the Commission shall file with the court a statement of the receiving party's costs or, if those costs have not been assessed, the receiving party's bill of costs; and

(*b*) paragraphs (4) to (6) shall apply to that application as if "the Commission" were substituted for "the receiving party" in those paragraphs.

(9) The amount of costs to be determined under this regulation may include the costs incurred in relation to an application made under this regulation.

13 Rights to appear

(1) The Regional Director may appear at –

(*a*) any hearing in relation to which notice has been given under regulation 10(3)(*c*);

(*b*) the hearing of any appeal under regulation 11(4); or

(*c*) the hearing of any application under regulation 12(8).

(2) The Regional Director may, instead of appearing under paragraph (1), give evidence in the form of a written statement to the court, verified by a statement of truth.

(3) The Regional Director shall file with the court any statement under paragraph (2), and serve a copy on the receiving party, not less than seven days before the hearing to which it relates.

****

Community Legal Service (Funding) (Counsel in Family Proceedings) Order 2001, SI 2001/1077

ARRANGEMENT OF ARTICLES

PART I
GENERAL

PART II
RULES REGARDING FEES

General Note—These regulations define the level of counsel's entitlement to charge fees in funded family proceedings.

(i) The term "family proceedings" is defined widely, as with all funded proceedings (art 2: cf the narrower definition in Legal Aid in Family Proceedings (Remuneration) Regulations 1991) and may catch a variety of forms of process not normally associated with family courts (eg applications which proceed under CPR 1998 such as TLATA 1996 and PHA 1997: possibly even lender/guarantor undue influence proceedings where the relationship of dependence is also a family relationship).

(ii) Article 4(6) provides the Bar's equivalent of an exception from the indemnity rule permissible in legal aid (funded) cases. Counsel's clerk, in all cases, should be asked to quote both a private rate and a rate under these regulations; and both figures should then appear in Form H.

(iii) Claims for fees are submitted by counsel directly to the Regional Director of the Commission (art 17). This takes counsel's fees out of the legal aid detailed assessment process. There is provision for a client with a financial interest (eg because the statutory charge arises) to make representations (art 19(2)); though the Order is silent as to whom these representations are to be addressed.

PART I
GENERAL

1 Citation and commencement

This Order may be cited as the Community Legal Service (Funding) (Counsel in Family Proceedings) Order 2001 and shall come into force on 1 May 2001.

2 Interpretation

In this Order –

"the Act" means the Access to Justice Act 1999;

"assessment of costs" means the determination of all costs and disbursements due under the relevant certificate in relation to proceedings in which counsel has submitted a claim for payment under this Order;

"certificate" means a certificate issued under the Funding Code certifying a decision to fund services for the client;

"client" means an individual who receives funded services from the Commission as part of the Community Legal Service under sections 4 to 11 of the Act;

"the Commission" means the Legal Services Commission established under section 1 of the Act;

"Cost Appeals Committee" means a committee appointed by the Commission for the purpose of considering appeals from the Costs Committee;

"Costs Committee" means a committee appointed by the Commission for the purpose of considering appeals in relation to costs, whether under this Order or generally;

"counsel" means a barrister in independent practice;

"family proceedings" means proceedings, other than proceedings for judicial review, which arise out of family relationships, including proceedings in which the welfare of children is determined, and including all proceedings under one or more of the following:

(*a*) the Matrimonial Causes Act 1973;
(*b*) the Inheritance (Provision for Family and Dependants) Act 1975;
(*c*) the Adoption Act 1976;
(*d*) the Domestic Proceedings and Magistrates' Courts Act 1978;
(*e*) Part III of the Matrimonial and Family Proceedings Act 1984;
(*f*) Parts I to V of the Children Act 1989;
(*g*) Part IV of the Family Law Act 1996; and
(*h*) the inherent jurisdiction of the High Court in relation to children;

"function F1" means all work, other than conferences:

(*a*) which is carried out prior to the issue of proceedings; or
(*b*) which does not fall within functions F2 to F5;

"function F2" means all work carried out in connection with a hearing relating to injunctive relief or enforcement procedures, other than work which falls within function F5, including but not limited to preparation, advocacy, advising and drafting;

"function F3" means all work carried out in connection with a hearing, other than work which falls within function F2 or F5, including but not limited to preparation, advocacy, advising and drafting;

"function F4" means all work carried out in connection with a conference (including a telephone or video conference), other than any conference which takes place on the same day as a hearing for which payment is claimed under function F5, including but not limited to preparation and advice;

"function F5" means all work carried out in connection with the main hearing, including but not limited to preparation, advocacy, advising and drafting;

"Funding Code" means the code approved under section 9 of the Act;

"Funding Review Committee" means a committee appointed by the Commission for the purpose of considering appeals in relation to the discharge or revocation of a certificate, whether under this Order or generally;

"the main hearing" means the hearing at which the substantive issues are listed to be determined and are considered by the court;

"the primary hearing unit" means the first day of the main hearing;

"Regional Director" means any Regional Director appointed by the Commission under the Funding Code and includes any person authorised to act on his behalf, other than a solicitor authorised by contract to determine applications on behalf of the Commission; and

"the secondary hearing unit" means any day of the main hearing other than the first.

3 Transitional provisions

This Order applies to all fees mentioned in article 4(2) payable to counsel under a certificate granted on or after 1 May 2001, and such fees payable under a certificate granted before that date shall be treated as if this Order had not been made.

4 Scope

(1) In respect of proceedings to which this Order applies, the Commission shall fund services as part of the Community Legal Service in accordance with the provisions of the following articles.

(2) Subject to article 3 and paragraphs (3) to (6), and to any limitations on the relevant certificate, this Order applies to counsel's fees in respect of all family proceedings in the High Court, county courts and magistrates' courts.

(3) This Order does not apply to proceedings where the length of the main hearing exceeds 10 days.

(4) This Order does not apply to appeals to –

(*a*) the Divisional Court of the High Court;
(*b*) the Court of Appeal; or
(*c*) the House of Lords.

(5) Where the Commission issues a High Cost Case Contract under the Funding Code, this Order applies except to the extent that the terms of such contract provide otherwise.

(6) Nothing in this Order shall affect any determination of the amount of costs payable under an order or agreement which provides that another party to proceedings or prospective proceedings shall pay all or part of the costs of a client.

5 Graduated fees

(1) The amount of the graduated fee for counsel shall be the base fee or the hearing unit fee, as appropriate, in respect of the function for which the fee is

claimed, which is specified in the Schedules to this Order as applicable to the category of proceedings and the counsel instructed, increased by any –

(*a*) settlement supplement ("SS") or additional payment;
(*b*) special issue payment ("SIP"); and
(*c*) court bundle payment;

so specified.

(2) The total graduated fee, as set out in paragraph (1), shall be increased by 33% in respect of all work carried out while the proceedings are in the High Court.

6 Mixed and multiple claims

(1) Only one base fee may be claimed in respect of each of functions F1 and F4 in relation to any single set of proceedings.

(2) Where counsel carries out work relating to more than one category of proceedings within the same function in a single set of proceedings, he may claim the fee for one category only.

(3) Counsel shall specify the category of proceedings upon which the fee payable under this Order is to be based when he submits his claim for payment.

(4) For the purposes of this Order, applications to the court constitute a single set of proceedings irrespective of whether they are made separately or together, where they are –

(*a*) heard together or consecutively; and
(*b*) treated by the court as a single set of proceedings.

7 Representation of more than one party

Subject to article 9(1)(*c*), where counsel represents more than one party in the same set of proceedings, payment shall be made as if counsel represented a single party.

PART II
RULES REGARDING FEES

8 Hearing units

(1) Where –

(*a*) preparatory work for a hearing is carried out but that hearing does not take place; or
(*b*) preparatory work for the main hearing is carried out but counsel is prevented from representing his client because –
  (i) he has withdrawn from the proceedings with the permission of the court because of his professional code of conduct or to avoid embarrassment in the exercise of his profession; or
  (ii) he has been dismissed by his client

one half of the relevant hearing unit fee, without special issue payments or court bundle payments, shall be paid.

(2) For the purpose of functions F2 and F3 –

(*a*) one hearing unit fee shall be paid for each period of two and a half hours or less for which the hearing continues;

(*b*) the hearing shall –

(i) commence at the time at which it is listed to begin or at the time at which counsel is specifically directed by the court to attend for that particular hearing, whichever is earlier;

(ii) end when it concludes or at 5pm, whichever is earlier; and

(iii) take no account of any luncheon adjournment; and

(*c*) where a hearing continues after 5pm and concludes on that same day, an additional one half of the hearing unit fee shall be paid in respect of the time on that day after 5pm.

(3) For the purpose of function F5 –

(*a*) where the hearing takes place on one day, the primary hearing unit fee shall be paid for the period from the time at which the hearing begins until 5pm on that day;

(*b*) where the hearing takes place over more than one day, whether by reason of being adjourned, split or otherwise –

(i) the hearing on the first day shall be paid at the primary hearing unit rate; and

(ii) the hearing on any subsequent date shall be paid at the secondary hearing unit rate; and

(*c*) where a hearing continues after 5pm and ends on that same day, an additional one half of the appropriate hearing unit fee (whether primary or secondary) shall be paid in respect of the time on that day after 5pm.

9 Special issue payments

(1) A special issue may arise where the proceedings involve, or, with regard to sub-paragraphs (*e*) to (*g*), are alleged to involve –

(*a*) a litigant in person;

(*b*) more than two parties;

(*c*) representation of more than one child by counsel submitting a claim for payment under this Order;

(*d*) more than one expert;

(*e*) a relevant foreign element;

(*f*) relevant assets which are not or may not be under the exclusive control of any of the parties; or

(*g*) a party who has or may have been involved in the following –

(i) conduct by virtue of which a child who is the subject of the proceedings has, may have or might suffer very significant harm; or

(ii) intentional conduct which has, could have or might significantly reduce the assets available for distribution by the court.

(2) The judge hearing the case shall, at the conclusion of the relevant hearing, certify on a form provided for that purpose any special issues mentioned in paragraph (1)(*a*) to (*c*), and any mentioned in paragraph (1)(*d*) to (*g*) which were of substance and relevant to any of the issues before the court.

(3) The decision of the judge under paragraph (2) shall be final save on a point of law.

(4) Subject to paragraph (7) –

(*a*) a special issue payment shall be made for each special issue certified in relation to functions F2, F3 and F5;

(*b*) such payment shall equate to the percentage of the single hearing unit fee applicable to the function in which the issue arises which is specified in Schedule 1 for that special issue.

(5) Subject to paragraph (8) –

(*a*) counsel may, when he submits his claim for payment, claim a special issue payment in respect of any special issue which arises in relation to functions F1 and F4;

(*b*) such payment shall equate to the percentage of the single base fee applicable to the function in which the issue arises which is specified in Schedule 1 for that special issue.

(6) The Regional Director shall, in considering any claim made under paragraph (5), consider whether the work in question was reasonably carried out and, in respect of any special issues mentioned in paragraph (1)(*d*) to (*g*), whether the issue was of substance and relevant to any of the issues before the court.

(7) With regard to functions F2 and F3, where more than one hearing has taken place in a single set of proceedings, a special issue payment shall be made only in respect of one such hearing in relation to any special issue certified in respect of that hearing, and counsel shall specify in respect of which hearing in each function it shall be made.

(8) With regard to function F4, where more than one conference has taken place counsel shall specify in respect of which single conference the special issue payment shall be made.

10 Financial Dispute Resolution hearing payments

In respect of a set of proceedings which include proceedings for ancillary relief, an additional payment shall be paid at a rate of £150 in respect of Queen's Counsel, and £60 in respect of counsel other than Queen's Counsel, in respect of the Financial Dispute Resolution hearing in function F3.

11 Court bundle payments

(1) A court bundle payment shall be made –

(*a*) where the court bundle comprises between 176 and 350 pages;
(*b*) where the court bundle comprises between 351 and 700 pages; and
(*c*) as a special preparation fee in accordance with article 16 where the court bundle comprises more than 700 pages.

(2) Where there is no court bundle, equivalent provisions to those in paragraph (1) shall apply to counsel's brief.

12 Early settlement payments

(1) Subject to paragraphs (2) and (3), one settlement supplement shall be paid, as a percentage of the base fee or the hearing unit fee, as appropriate, applicable to the function in which the settlement takes place, where a settlement takes place which leads to the resolution of the set of proceedings.

(2) Subject to paragraph (3), no settlement supplement shall be paid in respect of a settlement which takes place in –

(*a*) function F1;
(*b*) function F4;

(c) the primary hearing unit of function F5 where the proceedings have been listed for less than 2 days; or

(d) the secondary hearing unit of function F5.

(3) In respect of a set of proceedings which include proceedings for ancillary relief, an additional payment shall be paid at a rate of £171.88 in respect of Queen's Counsel, and £68.75 in respect of counsel other than Queen's Counsel, where a settlement takes place in function F1 which leads to the resolution of the set of proceedings.

13 Incidental items

An incidental item payment may be claimed, where it was reasonably and necessarily incurred, in respect of the following –

(a) listening to or viewing evidence recorded on tape, disc or video cassette, once in respect of each item, at a rate of £10.90 per 10 minutes running time; and

(b) except where the court is within 40 kilometres from Charing Cross or where there is a local Bar which the Commission considers to be sufficiently specialist in, or within 40 kilometres of, the court town:

(i) time spent travelling, at an hourly rate of £13.60;

(ii) incurring travel expenses at a mileage rate of 45p per mile or at the rate of the cheapest second class fare reasonably available, as appropriate; and

(iii) incurring hotel expenses at an overnight subsistence rate of £85.25 in respect of hotels situated within the London Region of the Commission and £55.25 elsewhere.

14 Replacement counsel

Where one counsel replaces another during the course of a function, payment shall be made to the replacement counsel and shall be divided by agreement between them.

15 Applications after the main hearing

(1) Claims for payment in respect of work carried out after the main hearing shall be paid at the appropriate function rate.

(2) For the purposes of this Order, an appeal from a District Judge to a Circuit Judge or a High Court Judge, and all work relating thereto including but not limited to an advice on appeal, shall be treated as the commencement of a new set of proceedings.

16 Special preparation fee

(1) Where this article applies, counsel may claim a special preparation fee in addition to the graduated fee payable under this Order.

(2) This article applies where –

(a) the proceedings to which the relevant certificate relates involve exceptionally complex issues of law or fact; or

(b) in public law children proceedings, in relation to work carried out within the secondary hearing unit of function F5, where the main hearing is split so that a period of at least four months elapses between its commencement and the time at which it resumes

such that it has been necessary for counsel to carry out work by way of preparation substantially in excess of the amount normally carried out for proceedings of the same type; or

(*c*) the court bundle comprises more than 700 pages.

(3) The amount of the special preparation fee shall be calculated by multiplying the number of hours of preparation in excess of the amount normally carried out for proceedings of the same type, by an hourly rate of £100.50 in respect of Queen's Counsel, and £40.20 in respect of counsel other than Queen's Counsel.

(4) Where counsel claims a special preparation fee for work carried out within functions F1 and F4, or within functions F2, F3 and F5 where no hearing takes place, he shall, when submitting his claim for payment, supply such information and documents as may be required by the Regional Director as proof of the complexity of the relevant issues of law or fact and of the number of hours of preparation, and the Regional Director shall decide what special preparation fee, if any, shall be paid.

(5) Where counsel claims a special preparation fee for work carried out within functions F2, F3 and F5 he shall apply accordingly to the judge hearing the case at the relevant hearing, who shall decide what additional fee, if any, shall be paid, and whose decision shall be final save on a point of law.

17 Claims for payment

(1) Claims for payment in respect of work to which this Order applies shall be submitted to the Regional Director and shall contain full details of the claim and copies of all relevant documents.

(2) Counsel may submit a claim for payment –

(*a*) when the proceedings to which the certificate relates are concluded;
(*b*) when the certificate under which the work has been carried out is discharged or revoked and any review by the Commission or the Funding Review Committee has been completed;
(*c*) when he has completed all work in respect of which he has been instructed up to and including function F2 or F3, as appropriate;
(*d*) when he has completed all work in respect of which he has been instructed in function F5; and
(*e*) where he has received no instructions from the instructing solicitor for a period of 3 months.

(3) Only one claim for payment may be submitted under paragraph (2)(*c*) in respect of any one set of proceedings.

(4) Only one claim for payment may be submitted in respect of function F4 in respect of any one set of proceedings.

(5) Any claim for payment may include a claim in respect of all work carried out in the proceedings for which counsel has not previously submitted a claim.

(6) Counsel shall submit his claim for payment within 3 months of the discharge or revocation of the certificate to which it relates and, if he fails to do so, the Regional Director may reduce the amount payable under this Order; provided that the amount payable shall not be reduced unless counsel has been allowed a

reasonable opportunity to show cause in writing why the amount should not be reduced.

(7) Any claim for payment shall include a claim in respect of all special issue payments, court bundle payments, settlement supplements and additional payments in respect of any functions for which the base fee or hearing unit fee, as appropriate, has been claimed and no later claim may be made in this respect.

(8) The Regional Director shall consider claims for payment under this Order and all relevant information and shall pay counsel such sums as are properly and reasonably due under this Order for work carried out within the scope of any relevant certificate or contract.

(9) No claims for payment on account of sums payable under this Order may be made.

18 Appeals

(1) If counsel is dissatisfied with any decision of the Regional Director with regard to the assessment of his fees under this Order, he may, within 21 days of the date of the assessment, (or such longer period as the Regional Director may allow) make written representations to the Costs Committee by way of an appeal.

(2) In any appeal under paragraph (1) the Costs Committee shall review the assessment and shall confirm, increase or decrease the amount assessed.

(3) If counsel is dissatisfied with the decision of the Costs Committee he may, within 21 days of the date of the reviewed assessment, apply to that Committee to certify a point of principle of general importance.

(4) Where the Costs Committee certifies a point of principle of general importance, counsel may, within 21 days of the date of the certification, appeal in writing to the Cost Appeals Committee against the reviewed assessment.

(5) If the Regional Director is dissatisfied with any reviewed assessment under paragraph (2), he may, within 21 days of the date of such reviewed assessment, certify a point of principle of general importance and appeal in writing to the Cost Appeals Committee.

(6) In any appeal under paragraph (5) the Regional Director shall serve notice of the appeal on counsel who may, within 21 days of the date of such notice, make written representations to the Cost Appeals Committee.

(7) In any appeal under paragraph (4) or (5) the Cost Appeals Committee shall review the decision of the Costs Committee and shall confirm, increase or decrease the reviewed assessment.

19 Review of payments

(1) Subject to the provisions of this article and article 4, payments under this Order shall be final payments.

(2) Nothing in this Order shall affect any right of a client with a financial interest in an assessment of costs to make representations after the conclusion of the set of proceedings with regard to such payments.

(3) Representations under paragraph (2) above may include representations as to the use of counsel in proceedings and as to the sums payable to counsel under this Order.

(4) Where a contract entered into by the Commission in accordance with section 6(3)(*a*) of the Act includes rules for the assessment of costs in proceedings in which fees have been paid or are payable to counsel under this Order, and such costs are to be assessed by the court, the court shall carry out such assessment in accordance with those rules.

(5) Where in any assessment of costs it appears that payments made to counsel are in excess of the amount properly and reasonably due to counsel under this Order or any relevant certificate, counsel's fees shall be reduced accordingly.

(6) Where in any assessment of costs payment to counsel under this Order alone would exceed any limit set by the Commission on the total costs payable under the relevant certificate or contract, counsel's fees shall be reduced accordingly.

(7) Counsel shall be informed of any reduction in his fees under this article and shall have the same rights to make representations with regard to any such reduction as would a solicitor, in accordance with the relevant rules of court, contract and regulations, as applicable.

(8) Where payment has been made under this Order which is in excess of the amount properly and reasonably due to counsel, the Commission may recover the excess payment either by way of repayment by counsel or by way of deduction from any other sum which may be due to him.

SCHEDULE 1
TABLES OF FEES

1 In respect of the proceedings mentioned in paragraph 1 of Schedule 2, the amount of the graduated fee shall be as follows:

(*a*) in respect of Queen's Counsel:

	Base fee	*Hearing unit fee*	*SS*	*CBP(1)*	*CBP(2)*
F1	£150	–	–	£40	£79
F2	–	£287.50	100%	£47	£94
F4	£125	–	–	£33	£67
F5 primary	–	£800	10%	£221	£442
F5 secondary	–	£550	–	£135	£271
Special Issue Payments					
Litigant in person		5%			
More than two parties		5%			
More than one child		5%			
More than one expert		10%			
Foreign		0%			
Assets		0%			
Conduct		0%			

(1) where the court bundle comprises between 176 and 350 pages.

(2) where the court bundle comprises between 351 and 700 pages.

(*b*) in respect of counsel other than Queen's Counsel:

	Base fee	*Hearing unit fee*	*SS*	*CBP(1)*	*CBP(2)*
F1	£60	–	–	£16	£32
F2	–	£115	100%	£19	£37.50
F4	£50	–	–	£13	£27
F5 primary	–	£320	10%	£88	£177
F5 secondary	–	£220	–	£54	£108
Special Issue Payments					
Litigant in person		5%			
More than two parties		5%			
More than one child		5%			
More than one expert		10%			
Foreign		0%			
Assets		0%			
Conduct		0%			

(1) where the court bundle comprises between 176 and 350 pages.

(2) where the court bundle comprises between 351 and 700 pages.

2 In respect of the proceedings mentioned in paragraph 2 of Schedule 2, the amount of the graduated fee shall be as follows:

(*a*) in respect of Queen's Counsel:

	Base fee	*Hearing unit fee*	*SS*	*CBP(1)*	*CBP(2)*
F1	£175	–	–	£40	£79
F2	–	£212.50	100%	£47	£94
F3	–	£412.50	100%	£82	£165
F4	£150	–	–	£33	£67
F5 primary	–	£1075	20%	£221	£442
F5 secondary	–	£575	–	£135	£271
Special Issue Payments					
Litigant in person		40%			
More than two parties		40%			
More than one child		5%			

	Base fee	*Hearing unit fee*	*SS*	*CBP(1)*	*CBP(2)*
More than one expert		20%			
Foreign		30%			
Assets		0%			
Conduct		50%			

(1) where the court bundle comprises between 176 and 350 pages.

(2) where the court bundle comprises between 351 and 700 pages.

(*b*) in respect of counsel other than Queen's Counsel:

	Base fee	*Hearing unit fee*	*SS*	*CBP(1)*	*CBP(2)*
F1	£70	–	–	£16	£32
F2	–	£85	100%	£19	£37.50
F3	–	£165	100%	£33	£66
F4	£60	–	–	£13	£27
F5 primary	–	£430	20%	£88	£177
F5 secondary	–	£230	–	£54	£108
Special Issue Payments					
Litigant in person		40%			
More than two parties		40%			
More than one child		5%			
More than one expert		20%			
Foreign		30%			
Assets		0%			
Conduct		50%			

(1) where the court bundle comprises between 176 and 350 pages.

(2) where the court bundle comprises between 351 and 700 pages.

3 In respect of the proceedings mentioned in paragraph 3 of Schedule 2, the amount of the graduated fee shall be as follows:

(*a*) in respect of Queen's Counsel:

	Base fee	*Hearing unit fee*	*SS*	*CBP(1)*	*CBP(2)*
F1	£150	–	–	£40	£79
F2	–	£187.50	100%	£47	£94
F3	–	£300	100%	£82	£165
F4	£125	–	–	£33	£67

	Base fee	*Hearing unit fee*	*SS*	*CBP(1)*	*CBP(2)*
F5 primary	–	£812.50	10%	£221	£442
F5 secondary	–	£550	–	£135	£271
Special Issue Payments					
Litigant in person		30%			
More than two parties		30%			
More than one child		5%			
More than one expert		50%			
Foreign		30%			
Assets		0%			
Conduct		50%			

(1) where the court bundle comprises between 176 and 350 pages.

(2) where the court bundle comprises between 351 and 700 pages.

(*b*) in respect of counsel other than Queen's Counsel:

	Base fee	*Hearing unit fee*	*SS*	*CBP(1)*	*CBP(2)*
F1	£60	–	–	£16	£32
F2	–	£75	100%	£19	£37.50
F3	–	£120	100%	£33	£66
F4	£50	–	–	£13	£27
F5 primary	–	£325	10%	£88	£177
F5 secondary	–	£220	–	£54	£108
Special Issue Payments					
Litigant in person		30%			
More than two parties		30%			
More than one child		5%			
More than one expert		50%			
Foreign		30%			
Assets		0%			
Conduct		50%			

(1) where the court bundle comprises between 176 and 350 pages.

(2) where the court bundle comprises between 351 and 700 pages.

4 In respect of the proceedings mentioned in paragraph 4 of Schedule 2, the amount of the graduated fee shall be as follows:

(*a*) in respect of Queen's Counsel:

	Base fee	*Hearing unit fee*	*SS*	*CBP(1)*	*CBP(2)*
F1	£150	–	–*	£40	£79
F2	–	£162.50	50%	£47	£94
F3	–	£300	50%	£82	£165
F4	£125	–	–	£33	£67
F5 primary	–	£812.50	10%	£221	£442
F5 secondary	–	£550	–	£135	£271
Special Issue Payments					
Litigant in person		10%			
More than two parties		10%			
More than one child		5%			
More than one expert		10%			
Foreign		25%			
Assets		50%			
Conduct		50%			

* see article 12(3).

(1) where the court bundle comprises between 176 and 350 pages.

(2) where the court bundle comprises between 351 and 700 pages.

(*b*) in respect of counsel other than Queen's Counsel:

	Base fee	*Hearing unit fee*	*SS*	*CBP(1)*	*CBP(2)*
F1	£60	–	–*	£16	£32
F2	–	£65	50%	£19	£37.50
F3	–	£120	50%	£33	£66
F4	£50	–	–	£13	£27
F5 primary	–	£325	10%	£88	£177
F5 secondary	–	£220	–	£54	£108
Special Issue Payments					
Litigant in person		10%			
More than two parties		10%			
More than one child		5%			
More than one expert		10%			
Foreign		25%			

	Base fee	*Hearing unit fee*	*SS*	*CBP(1)*	*CBP(2)*
Assets		50%			
Conduct		50%			

* see article 12(3).

(1) where the court bundle comprises between 176 and 350 pages.

(2) where the court bundle comprises between 351 and 700 pages.

SCHEDULE 2
CATEGORIES OF PROCEEDINGS

1 Category of proceedings: family injunctions.

Family proceedings (other than those for ancillary relief) for an injunction, committal order, or other order for the protection of a person (other than proceedings for the protection of children within paragraph 2).

2 Category of proceedings: public law children.

Family proceedings under Parts III, IV or V of the Children Act 1989, adoption proceedings (including applications to free for adoption), and other family proceedings within the inherent jurisdiction of the High Court concerning the welfare of children (other than proceedings for ancillary relief).

3 Category of proceedings: private law children.

Family proceedings between individuals concerning the welfare of children (other than those for ancillary relief or within paragraph 2).

4 Category of proceedings: ancillary relief and all other family proceedings.

All other family proceedings not within paragraphs 1 to 3.

County Court Rules 1981, SI 1981/1687

ARRANGEMENT OF RULES

ORDER 1
CITATION, APPLICATION AND INTERPRETATION

ORDER 3
COMMENCEMENT OF PROCEEDINGS

ORDER 27
ATTACHMENT OF EARNINGS

Part I. General

Part II. Consolidated Attachment of Earnings Orders

ORDER 28
JUDGMENT SUMMONSES

ORDER 29
COMMITTAL FOR BREACH OF ORDER OR UNDERTAKING

ORDER 47
DOMESTIC AND MATRIMONIAL PROCEEDINGS

* 1560

ORDER 1
CITATION, APPLICATION AND INTERPRETATION

****

3 Definitions (Ord 1, r 3)

In these rules, unless the context otherwise requires –

"the Act" means the County Courts Act 1984;

"address for service" means the address of a place at or to which any document may be delivered or sent for the party giving the address, being –

(*a*) in the case of a party in person, his place of residence or business or, if he has no such place within England or Wales, the address of a place within England or Wales at or to which documents for him may be delivered or sent,

(*b*) where the party is represented by a solicitor, the business address of the solicitor;

"defendant" includes respondent;

"document exchange" means any document exchange for the time being approved by the Lord Chancellor;

"filed" has the meaning assigned to it by Order 2, rule 4;

"foreign court" means the court to which process is sent by another court;

"hire-purchase agreement" has the same meaning as in the Consumer Credit Act 1974;

"home court" means the court from which process is originally issued;

"judgment" means the final decision of the court in an action;

"mental patient" means a person who, by reason of mental disorder within the meaning of the Mental Health Act 1983, is incapable of managing and administering his property and affairs;

"order" means the final decision of the court in a matter and also any decision of the court other than a final decision in any proceedings;

"originating process" means –

(*a*) the summons in a default, fixed date or admiralty action or

(*b*) in relation to a garnishee, an order nisi under Order 30, rule 2, or

(*c*) an interpleader summons or notice under Order 33, rule 4, 7 or 8, or

(*d*) an originating application, petition or request for the entry of an appeal to a county court;

"person under disability" means a person who is a minor or a mental patient;

"plaintiff" includes applicant, petitioner and appellant;

"pre-trial review" means the preliminary consideration of an action or matter under Order 17;

"proper officer" means the district judge or –

(*a*) in relation to any act of a formal or administrative character which is not by statute the responsibility of the district judge, and

(*b*) in

(i) Order 9, rule 3(3),

(ii) Order 13, rule 2(3A),

PART III

(iii) Order 22, rules 7A and 10,
(iv) Order 25, rules 2, 3(1), 8 and 12,
(v) Order 27, rules 7, 7A, 7B, 19(3C) and 20,
(vi) Order 39, rule 5, and
(vii) Order 48B, rule 4,

the court manager or any other officer of the court acting on his behalf in accordance with directions given by the Lord Chancellor;

"records of the court" means such records of and in relation to proceedings in the court as the Lord Chancellor may by regulations prescribe;

"recovery of land" means the recovery or delivery of possession of land;

"residence", in relation to a body corporate, means the registered or principal office of the body;

"senior master" means the senior master of the Queen's Bench Division.

"trial centre" means a county court designated by the Lord Chancellor for the hearing of trials.

"value", in relation to an action or claim, shall be considered in accordance with Articles 9 and 10 of the High Court and County Courts Jurisdiction Order 1991.

Amendments—SI 1982/1140; SI 1983/1716; SI 1984/878; SI 1985/566; SI 1986/636; SI 1991/1126; SI 1991/1328; SI 1993/711; SI 1993/2150; SI 1994/2403; SI 1996/2810; SI 1997/1837.

****

ORDER 3
COMMENCEMENT OF PROCEEDINGS

****

6 Appeals to county court (Ord 3, r 6)

(1) Where by or under any Act an appeal lies to a county court from any order, decision or award of any tribunal or person, then, subject to any special provision made by or under that Act, the provisions of this rule shall apply.

(2) The appellant shall, within 21 days after the date of the order, decision or award, file –

(*a*) a request for the entry of the appeal, stating the names and addresses of the persons intended to be served (in this rule called "respondents") and the appellant's address for service, together with as many copies of the request as there are respondents; and

(*b*) a copy of the order, decision or award appealed against.

(3) Where the provision under which the appeal lies requires the appellant to give to the other parties notice in writing of his intention to appeal and of the grounds of his appeal, the appellant shall file a copy of such notice with the request, and in any other case he shall include in his request a statement of the grounds of the appeal.

(4) On the filing of the documents mentioned in paragraphs (2) and (3) the proper officer shall –

(*a*) enter the appeal in the records of the court and fix the return day;

(*b*) prepare a notice to each respondent of the day on which the appeal will be heard and annex each copy of the request for the entry of the appeal to a copy of the notice; and

(*c*) deliver a plaint note to the appellant.

(5) The return day shall be a day fixed for the hearing of the appeal by the judge (or, if the district judge has jurisdiction to hear the appeal, by the district judge) or, if the court so directs, a day fixed for a pre-trial review.

(6) Rule 3(2)(*d*)(ii) of this Order and the provisions of Order 7 shall apply, with the necessary modifications, to the service of the request for the entry of the appeal as if the notice of the day of hearing were a fixed date summons.

Scope of provision—This rule makes provision for appeals to the county court from some other tribunal or person, so that it does not apply to an appeal to the judge from the district judge which is provided for in CCR Ord 37, r 6 and FPR 1991, rr 4.22, 8.1.

****

ORDER 7
SERVICE OF DOCUMENTS

****

8 Substituted service (Ord 7, r 8)

(1) If it appears to the court that it is impracticable for any reason to serve a document in any manner prescribed by these rules, for the service of that document, the court may, upon an affidavit showing grounds, make an order (in this rule called "an order for substituted service") giving leave for such steps to be taken as the court directs to bring the document to the notice of the person to be served.

(2) Where a document is to be served by bailiff, the proper officer of the bailiff's court shall, if so requested, take such steps as may be necessary to provide evidence on which an order for substituted service may be made.

"affidavit showing grounds" (r 8(1))—The affidavit should contain sufficient details (*Re De Cespedes. The Debtor v Petitioning Creditor and Official Receiver* [1937] 2 All ER 572). The affidavit should give full details of the failed attempts to effect service by the usual methods, and state specifically which form of substituted service is contended for, eg service by post at an employer's address, service by advertisement in a particular publication, personal service on a named person, or any other method which is appropriate on the particular facts.

"substituted service" (r 8(2))—Substituted service may take the form of service by letter, advertisement or otherwise as may seem just (*Porter v Freudenberg* [1915] KB 857 at 887).

Procedure—The application can be made to a district judge (*Petersen v Petersen* [1989] 5 CL 322).

Effect of order—Once there has been substituted service in the manner prescribed, it has all the effects of personal service (*Watt v Barnett* (1878) 3 QBD 183 at 186 and 366), but see *Duo v Duo* [1992] 1 WLR 611, [1992] 3 All ER 121, CA, where substituted service of an application to commit was not relied on.

PART III

Forms—The form of order for substituted service is Form N217.

****

ORDER 10
PERSONS UNDER DISABILITY

Scope of Order—Until 26 April 1999 this Order contained provisions to regulate the conduct of proceedings by and against a "person under disability" in the county court. These provisions ensured that a mental patient was represented by a next friend or guardian ad litem (as appropriate), that compromises and settlements were approved by the court, and that there was supervision of money recovered by a person under disability. In the High Court reference was made instead to RSC Ord 80 and in any case not expressly provided for by the CCR the general principles of practice in the High Court might be adopted (County Courts Act 1984, s 76; CCR Ord 1, r 6 assists with interpretation). Thus RSC could be used to fill some lacunae in CCR but not to supplement those rules as to cases provided for by them.

From 26 April 1999 CCR Ord 10 has been replaced as regards *civil proceedings* by Civil Procedure Rules 1998, Pt 21 but continues to apply, subject to the provisions of the FPR 1991 and with the necessary modifications, to *family proceedings* in the county court by virtue of FPR 1991, r 1.3. Most of its provisions are replaced by FPR 1991, Pt IX but there are circumstances in which reference must still be made to parts of Ord 10 and where necessary such reference may also be made to RSC Ord 80.

Person under disability—Defined by Ord 1, r 3 as a "person who is a minor or a mental patient". It is possible for a minor also to be a (mental) patient and this may be relevant if that condition will continue to subsist on ceasing to be a minor (eg in regard to the disposal of money awarded to the minor). Thus a minor who has severe learning disabilities will continue to be under disability even after attaining majority.

"minor"—A minor is defined by the Family Law Reform Act 1969, ss 1 and 12 as a person who is under the age of 18 – see generally note to FPR 1991, r 9.1. The term "infant" is adopted by RSC and "child" by the CPR 1998, but there is no distinction.

"mental patient"—A person who, by reason of mental disorder within the meaning of the Mental Health Act 1983, is incapable of managing and administering his property and affairs (Ord 1, r 3). The term used in FPR 1991 is "patient" but there is no significance in the different terminology. For a further explanation see **"patients"** under FPR 1991, r 9.1.

"mental disorder"—By virtue of Mental Health Act 1983, s 1(2), this means "mental illness, arrested or incomplete development of mind, psychopathic disorder and any other disorder or disability of mind and 'mentally disordered' shall be construed accordingly". For a full explanation see the note to FPR 1991, r 9.1.

"next friend", "guardian ad litem"—These terms are also used by FPR 1991 and relate respectively to the person bringing the proceedings and the person responding, but the term used in CPR 1998 in both cases is litigation friend.

****

4 Service on person under disability (Ord 10, r 4)

(1) Where a defendant is a person under disability, the summons shall be served –

(*a*) in the case of a minor who is not also a mental patient, on one of his parents or his guardian or, if he has no parent or guardian, on the person with whom he resides or in whose care he is;

(*b*) in the case of a mental patient, on the person (if any) who is authorised under Part VII to conduct in the name of the mental patient or on his behalf the proceedings in connection with which the summons is to be served or, if there is no person so authorised, on the person with whom he resides or in whose care he is,

and shall be served on the person to be served in the manner required by these rules with respect to the summons in question.

(2) Notwithstanding anything in paragraph (1), the court may order that any summons which has been, or is to be, served on the person under disability or on a person other than a person mentioned in that paragraph shall be deemed to be duly served on the person under disability.

Amendments—SI 1983/1716.

Defined terms—"person under disability": Ord 1, r 3 (see note above).

Scope of provision—The general principle is that a document in proceedings cannot be served on a patient as if he were not a patient, and if it is so served the proceedings based on it are invalid (*Cutbush v Cutbush* (1893) 37 Sol Jo 685). The principle is likely to apply also to an infant. This rule makes special provision for service upon a person under disability in the county court. Service is effected in the normal way upon the category of person specified or, in default, on "the person with whom he resides or in whose care he is". Once a next friend or guardian ad litem has been appointed, service of documents will be on that person, or the solicitor on the record instructed by that person (if any), in the usual way.

PART III

Application to family proceedings—The provision for service upon a person under disability in FPR 1991 (r 9.3) only relates to the service of a petition in matrimonial proceedings. Accordingly, the above rule must be relied upon in regard to the service of other family proceedings in the county court upon a person under disability. It relates to the summons (ie the document initiating the proceedings); once a next friend or guardian ad litem has been appointed service of documents will be on that person, or the solicitor on the record instructed by that person (if any), in the usual way.

"the person ... in whose care he is" (r 4(1)(*a*), (*b*))—The purpose of this provision is to reach a responsible adult who will be concerned to ensure that the party under a disability is properly represented in the proceedings and will initiate the appointment of a guardian ad litem. There will seldom be a problem in the case of a minor. In cases of difficulty involving a patient, in addition to attempts at formal service, it may be prudent to communicate with any person concerned as to the welfare of the patient, in the hope that a suitable representative will emerge. A person cannot be in the care of someone who is himself under a disability, so where several such persons share a home (eg under supervision) it will be necessary to look beyond the occupants of the home (eg to the persons who provide the supervision). Occupants of a residential care or nursing home will be in the care of the registered proprietor who should bring the proceedings to the attention of any concerned person. If such care is funded by the local authority it would be appropriate to involve the social services department which will have carried out a Community Care assessment of need. Service on a proper officer of the local social services authority or other guardian when the patient is under a guardianship order, or the district health authority when the patient has been compulsorily admitted to hospital under the Mental Health Act 1983, may be sufficient. Where no-one can be identified it is possible to resort to the provision for deemed service (see note below) thereby ensuring that the problem is brought before the court. When there is no response to due service the need for a guardian ad litem will have to be addressed by the court in any event. Reference may be made to the Official Solicitor in case of continuing difficulty as he may need to be appointed (see notes to FPR 1991 r 9.2).

Communication to person under disability—There is no requirement for service on the person alleged to be under disability, nor for the court to be satisfied that the proceedings have been brought to the attention of that person (unlike FPR 1991, r 9.3(2)). This is surprising, because this individual may wish to dispute being a mental patient or alert some particular person to take steps on his behalf (eg seek appointment as guardian ad litem). The proceedings may be conducted without a solicitor or the knowledge of the party considered to be a mental patient, notwithstanding that no evidence of mental disorder or incapacity is required, and the court will not have enquired into this. It seems that the prospect of an indemnity by the next friend or guardian ad litem (and the fact that the proceedings may be a nullity) is regarded as sufficient, but this is little reassurance to any of those involved, especially in relation to the uncertainty that so often arises as to whether or not an individual is to be treated as a mental patient. In case of doubt, it would be prudent to serve that person also. (See further comment under CPR 1998, r 21.5).

Mode of service—Unlike the equivalent rule for matrimonial causes (FPR 1991, r 2.9(2)(*a*)), there is no restriction as to the mode of service.

Deemed service (r 4(2))—The provision for deemed service enables the court to proceed with the appointment of a guardian ad litem when service is not otherwise possible.

****

7 Appointment of guardian ad litem at hearing (Ord 10, r 7)

Where a defendant attends the hearing of an action and it appears that he is a minor who has no guardian ad litem, then –

(*a*) if the defendant names a person as his guardian ad litem who consents to act, that person shall be appointed guardian;

(*b*) if the defendant does not name a guardian ad litem, the court may appoint as guardian any person present who is willing to act or, in default of any such person, the court may appoint the district judge to act.

Scope of provision—This provision deals with the specific situation where a defendant attends court and proves to be a minor. It may presumably be relied upon in family proceedings in a county court in the case of a respondent.

"the court may appoint"—The court has a discretion, and will only wish to appoint someone who is suitable to represent the minor and who does not have a conflict of interest. However, it appears from paragraph (*a*) that, if the minor attends and nominates someone as guardian, that person must be appointed.

Appointment of district judge—In practice it is unlikely that a district judge would accept the appointment, and no funding is available for that purpose. The appropriate course when there is no suitable person available is to approach the Official Solicitor. The option of appointing a district judge has not been repeated in the CPR 1998.

****

9 Guardian not liable for costs (Ord 10, r 9)

A guardian ad litem of a person under disability shall not be personally liable for any costs not occasioned by his personal negligence or misconduct.

Scope of provision—There is no provision regarding costs in FPR 1991, so this provision may be assumed to apply to family proceedings.

10 Compromise etc by person under disability (Ord 10, r 10)

(1) Where in any proceedings money is claimed by or on behalf of a person under disability, no settlement, compromise or payment and no acceptance of money paid into court, whenever entered into or made, shall so far as it relates to that person's claim be valid without the approval of the court.

(2) Where the sole object of an action in which a claim for money is made by or on behalf of a person under disability is to obtain the approval of the court to a settlement or compromise of the claim, the particulars of claim shall contain a brief statement of the cause of action together with a request for the approval of the settlement or compromise.

(3) Whatever the amount involved, the approval of the court may be given either by the judge or by the district judge and either in chambers or in open court.

Scope of provision—There is no provision in FPR 1991 for the settlement of claims in family proceedings (eg ancillary relief proceedings) made by or on behalf of persons under disability, so reliance must be placed on the CCR pursuant to FPR 1991, r 1.3. This rule deals with the approval of the court to any such settlement, and provides that no settlement or compromise is valid without that approval. It applies with such modifications as are necessary, so a cause or application may be treated as an action or claim, and the reference to a payment into court has no relevance. The rule corresponds to RSC Ord 80, rr 10 and 11.

Role of the Court of Protection—These provisions apply even where the proceedings are being conducted by the patient's receiver as next friend or guardian ad litem under the authority of the Court of Protection, but in that event the approval of the Court of Protection should also be obtained as a pre-requisite to an application to the county court.

Procedure—Where the compromise or settlement is reached after the proceedings have been commenced, approval is sought by way of an application in the course of those proceedings. An affidavit may be required in support of the application.

11 Control of money recovered by person under disability (Ord 10, r 11)

(1) Where in any proceedings –

(*a*) money is recovered by or on behalf of, or adjudged or ordered or agreed to be paid to, or for the benefit of, a person under disability, or

(*b*) money paid into court is accepted by or on behalf of a person under disability,

then, unless the court otherwise directs, the money shall not be paid to the person under disability or to his next friend, guardian ad litem or his solicitor but shall be paid into or remain in court.

(2) The money and any interest thereon shall be invested, applied or otherwise dealt with as the court may from time to time direct.

(3) An application to the court as to the mode of dealing with the money and any interest thereon may be made by or on behalf of any person interested.

(4) Unless the court otherwise directs, the costs payable to his solicitor by any plaintiff in the proceedings shall be taxed as between solicitor and own client and no costs shall be payable to the plaintiff's solicitor except the amount allowed on taxation.

(5) On the taxation of a solicitor's bill to any plaintiff in accordance with paragraph (4), the district judge shall also tax any costs payable to that plaintiff in the proceedings and shall certify –

(*a*) the amount (if any) by which the amount allowed on the taxation of the solicitor's bill exceeds the amount allowed on the taxation of the costs payable to that plaintiff in the proceedings, and

(*b*) where necessary, the proportion of the amount of the excess payable by or out of any money belonging to any party to the proceedings who is a person under disability.

(6) …

Amendments—SI 1984/878.

Scope of provision—This rule ensures that there is supervision of money awarded to or recovered by a person under disability. There is no similar provision in FPR 1991 so reliance must be placed on this rule pursuant to FPR 1991, r 1.3, unless the court exercises its additional powers (see notes below).

Control of money—This subject generally is beyond the scope of this volume, but the procedures adopted in regard to the award of damages will apply and are initiated by this rule (or in the High Court by RSC Ord 80, r 12). The court will control funds held on behalf of a minor but in the case of a patient reference must usually be made to the Court of Protection pursuant to Mental Health Act 1983, Pt VII. If there is a registered attorney under an enduring power it may be appropriate to release the fund to such attorney.

Additional powers: patient—Where a party in whose favour an order is made for financial provision is incapable by reason of mental disorder of managing and administering his property and affairs, the court has power under Matrimonial Causes Act 1973, s 40 to direct that any maintenance or lump sum be paid (or property be transferred) to a person "having charge of that party". This leaves considerable discretion to the court as to the future management of the financial provision. If the incapacitated party in whose favour an order is made already has income or assets which need to be administered, or if substantial provision is to be made, it is best that the Court of Protection be left to administer the entire affairs. Where, however, there is a registered enduring power of attorney it would normally be appropriate for the attorney who is managing the affairs to receive all payments or property pursuant to the financial provision order.

Authority of the next friend or guardian ad litem—See r 12 below and the notes thereto.

Costs—Unless the court otherwise directs, the costs payable in any proceedings by any plaintiff under disability to his solicitor must be taxed (assessed) as between solicitor and own client, and no costs are payable to the solicitor except the amount allowed on taxation (Ord 10, r 11(4)). Provision is made for the taxation of the costs payable by the plaintiff under disability to his solicitor, as well as the costs recovered by him (r 5). If the costs are agreed between the plaintiff's solicitors and the defendant, and the solicitors agree to waive any claim to further costs, the district judge may waive formal taxation if satisfied with the amount notified to him, but will usually require a breakdown of the profit costs, VAT and disbursements.

Need for Court of Protection involvement—See note under CPR 1998, r 21.11.

12 Authority of next friend or guardian (Ord 10, r 12)

Subject to the provisions of these rules, any act which in the ordinary conduct of any proceedings is required or authorised by a provision of these rules to be done by a party to the proceedings shall or may, if the party is a person under disability, be done by his next friend or guardian ad litem.

Scope of provision—There is no provision in FPR 1991 defining the authority of the next friend or guardian ad litem, but this rule may be relied on pursuant to FPR 1991, r 1.3. It corresponds to RSC Ord 80, r 2(2). The next friend or guardian has no authority beyond the conduct of the proceedings. The CCR do not require a next friend or guardian ad litem to act by a solicitor (contrast RSC Ord 80, r 2(3) and, for family proceedings, see under FPR 1991, r 9.2).

Extent of authority—The powers of the next friend or guardian ad litem are restricted to the conduct of the proceedings and do not extend to dealing with the financial affairs of the minor or patient (*Leather v Kirby* [1965] 3 All ER 927). The person who was the next friend or guardian ad litem may of course have a sufficient continuing interest (eg as a parent) for the court to involve that person in the application of the funds in court on behalf of the minor or patient under r 11 (see above).

****

ORDER 13
APPLICATIONS AND ORDERS IN THE COURSE OF PROCEEDINGS

1 General provisions (Ord 13, r 1)

(1) Except as otherwise provided, the following paragraphs of this rule shall have effect in relation to any application authorised by or under any Act or rule to be made in the course of an action or matter before or after judgment.

(2) Unless allowed or authorised to be made ex parte, the application shall be made on notice, which shall be filed and served on the opposite party not less than two days before the hearing of the application.

(3) Where the application is made ex parte, notice of the application shall be filed a reasonable time before the application is heard, unless the court otherwise directs.

(4) Unless allowed or authorised to be made otherwise, every application shall be heard in chambers.

(5) Where a party to the application fails to attend on the hearing the court may proceed in his absence if, having regard to the nature of the application, the court thinks it expedient to do so.

(6) The jurisdiction of the court to hear and determine the application may be exercised by the district judge and the applicant shall, unless the judge otherwise directs, make the application to the district judge in the first instance.

(7) Where the application is made to the district judge, he may refer to the judge any matter which he thinks should properly be decided by the judge, and the judge may either dispose of the matter or refer it back to the district judge with such directions as he thinks fit.

(8) The court may, as a condition of granting any application, impose such terms and conditions as it thinks fit, including a term or condition requiring any party to –

(*a*) give security,
(*b*) give an undertaking,
(*c*) pay money into court,
(*d*) pay all or any part of the costs of the proceedings, or
(*e*) give a power of re-entry.

(9) Unless the court otherwise directs, the costs of the application shall not be taxed until the general taxation of the costs of the action or matter and, where an earlier taxation is directed, Order 38 shall apply as if the word "claimed" were substituted for the word "recovered" wherever it appears.

(10) An appeal shall lie to the judge from any order made by the district judge on the application and the appeal shall be disposed of in chambers unless the judge otherwise directs.

(11) An appeal under paragraph (10) shall be made on notice, which shall be filed and served on the opposite party within 5 days after the order appealed from or such further time as the judge may allow.

"authorised by or under any Act or rule" (r 1(1))—The general authority to give interlocutory relief is confirmed by County Courts Act 1984, s 38.

Notice (r 1(2))—It is provided that the other party shall give notice (not less than two clear days) unless the application is allowed or authorised to be made ex parte. The notice of application for an interlocutory injunction should be made in Form N16A. Form N16A should be used whether the application is made ex parte or on notice.

Ex parte applications—If a party who intends to make an ex parte application notifies the other party, that party is entitled to attend the hearing.

Hearing in chambers (r 1(4))—Rule 1(4) requires the hearing to be in chambers, unless allowed or authorised otherwise. In urgent cases, this would appear to allow a hearing to take place in the judge's home or elsewhere.

"appeal" (r 1(10), (11))—These paragraphs do not apply in family proceedings, in which such appeals are governed by FPR 1991, r 8.1.

****

4 Extension or abridgment of time (Ord 13, r 4)

(1) Except as otherwise provided, the period within which a person is required or authorised by these rules or by any judgment, order or direction to do any act in any proceedings may be extended or abridged by consent of all the parties or by the court on the application of any party.

(2) Any such period may be extended by the court although the application for extension is not made until after the expiration of the period.

Power to abridge time for service of notice—The power to abridge time for service of notice of an application should be exercised on application before the service of the notice. Service too late to satisfy the period of notice stipulated by the Rules is defective and cannot be retrospectively validated. However, "informal notice" (ie less than the period stipulated by the rules) is sometimes better than no notice at all (*G v G (Ouster: Ex Parte Application)* [1990] 1 FLR 395). On an ex parte application being made, the court should consider whether it would be more appropriate to require service of notice and to abridge time under Ord 13, r 4(1) rather than to proceed ex parte.

****

6 Application for injunction (Ord 13, r 6)

(1) An application for the grant of an injunction may be made by any party to an action or matter before or after the trial or hearing, whether or not a claim for the injunction was included in that party's particulars of claim, originating application, petition, counterclaim or third party notice, as the case may be.

(2) Except where the district judge has power under Order 21, rule 5 or otherwise to hear and determine the proceedings in which the application is made, the application shall be made to the judge and rule 1(6) shall not apply.

(3) The application shall be made in the appropriate prescribed form and shall –

(*a*) state the terms of the injunction applied for; and

(*b*) be supported by an affidavit in which the grounds for making the application are set out,

and a copy of the affidavit and a copy of the application shall be served on the party against whom the injunction is sought not less than 2 days before the hearing of the application.

(3A) Where an order is sought ex parte before a copy of the application has been served on the other party, the affidavit shall explain why the application is so made and a copy of any order made ex parte shall be served with the application and affidavit in accordance with paragraph (3).

(4) An application may not be made before the issue of the summons, originating application or petition by which the action or matter is to be commenced except where the case is one of urgency, and in that case –

(*a*) the affidavit in support of the application shall show that the action or matter is one which the court to which the application is made has jurisdiction to hear and determine, and

(*b*) the injunction applied for shall, if granted, be on terms providing for the issue of the summons, originating application or petition in the court granting the application and on such other terms, if any, as the court thinks fit.

(4A) Paragraph (4)(*a*) and (*b*) shall apply, with the necessary modifications, where an application for an injunction is made by a defendant in a case of urgency before issuing a counterclaim or cross-application.

(5) Unless otherwise directed, every application not made ex parte shall be heard in open court.

(6) Except where the case is one of urgency, a draft of the injunction shall be prepared beforehand by the party making an application to the judge under paragraph (1) and, if the application is granted, the draft shall be submitted to the judge by whom the application was heard and shall be settled by him.

(7) The injunction, when settled, shall be forwarded to the proper officer for filing.

Amendments—SI 1991/525; SI 1991/1126.

Scope of provision—This provision deals with applications for interlocutory injunctions. The applicant must state in his notice of application the terms of the injunction applied for. The notice of application should be made in Form N16A. Form N16A should be used whether the application is made ex parte or on notice. The applicant must also set out in his supporting affidavit the grounds on which his application is made. It is the responsibility of the applicant to prepare a draft order setting out the terms of the injunction applied for, so that it may be submitted to the judge who hears the application. The draft order should comply with the requirements of Form N16. The application will be heard in open court, except where it is made ex parte, unless the court otherwise directs.

Injunctions generally—The general power of the High Court to grant injunctions is devolved on the county court by County Courts Act 1984, s 38 (see further under CCA 1984, s 38).

Ex parte applications (r 6(3A))—An application for an injunction should not be made, or granted, ex parte unless there is a real immediate danger of serious injury or irreparable damage (*Beese v Woodhouse* [1970] 1 WLR 586, [1970] 1 All ER 769). The principle that both sides must be heard can be displaced only where it appears to the court that injustice would be caused if the court does not act at once (*Re First Express Ltd* [1991] BCC 782). In domestic violence cases courts recognise that victims require immediate protection which can be effectively granted only on an ex parte basis (see FLA 1996, s 45 and commentary thereon). On an ex parte application, the court should consider whether it would be more appropriate to require service and to abridge time under CCR Ord 13, r 4(1) rather than to proceed ex parte (*G v G (Ouster: Ex Parte Application)* [1990] 1 FLR 395). Those who seek relief ex parte are under a duty to make the fullest, most candid and frank disclosure of all the relevant circumstances known to them (see *Re S (Ex Parte Orders)* [2001] 1 FLR 308). Ex parte applications are usually heard by a judge in chambers, whereas an application on notice is generally heard in open court, unless otherwise directed.

Non-molestation and occupation orders—Such orders are sought under FLA 1996, Pt IV and are now governed by FPR 1991. Rule 3.8 requires applications to be made in Form FL401 supported by a "sworn statement". Rule 3.8 does not specifically require a draft order. However, it is established practice, both in the High Court and county courts, for an applicant seeking an injunction to prepare a draft of the order sought. It is submitted that CCR Ord 13, r 6(6) should be followed by virtue of FPR 1991, r 1.3. Therefore, even in applications under FPR 1991, r 3.8 pursuant to FLA 1996, Pt IV, a draft order should be submitted to the judge in Form FL404 based on the specimen clauses set out in FPR 1991, App 1.

Freezing injunction—See under County Courts Act 1984, s 38 and Supreme Court Act 1981, s 37.

Search order—See under Supreme Court Act 1981, s 37.

****

ORDER 20
EVIDENCE

****

10 Form and contents of affidavit (Ord 20, r 10)

(1) Subject to the following paragraphs of this rule, the provisions of the RSC with respect to –

(*a*) the form and contents of an affidavit;
(*b*) the making of an affidavit by two or more deponents or by a blind or illiterate deponent;
(*c*) the use of any affidavit which contains an interlineation, erasure or other alteration or is otherwise defective;
(*d*) the striking out of any matter which is scandalous, irrelevant or otherwise oppressive;
(*e*) the insufficiency of an affidavit sworn before any agent, partner or clerk of a party's solicitor; and
(*f*) the making and marking of exhibits to an affidavit,

shall apply in relation to an affidavit for use in a county court as they apply in relation to an affidavit for use in the High Court.

(2) Before any affidavit is used in evidence it must be filed, but in an urgent case the court may make an order upon the undertaking of a party to file, within such time as the court may require, any affidavit used by him before it is filed.

(3) Every affidavit must be marked in the top right hand corner of the first page and in the top right hand corner of the back sheet with –

(*a*) the party on whose behalf the affidavit is filed;
(*b*) the initials and surname of the deponent;
(*c*) the number of the affidavit in relation to the deponent;
(*d*) the date on which it is sworn, and
(*e*) the date on which it is filed.

(4) Unless the court otherwise orders, an affidavit may be used notwithstanding that it contains statements of information or belief.

(5) Every affidavit shall state which of the facts deposed to are within the deponent's knowledge and which are based on information or belief and shall give, in the former case, his means of knowledge and, in the latter case, the sources and grounds of the information or belief.

Amendments—SI 1991/525.

Scope of provision—This rule incorporates the relevant provisions as to affidavits found in RSC Ord 41. The technical requirements of affidavits are important, and care is needed when drafting affidavits to ensure they are observed.

Statements of information and belief (r 10(4))—Where an affidavit contains statements of information or belief, it is a matter for the court as to what weight should be attached to such statements (see r 9(1)). Evidence which is irrelevant, and therefore inadmissible, should not be adduced by affidavit (*Savings and Investment Bank Ltd v Gasco Investments (Netherlands) BV* [1984] 1 WLR 271, [1984] 1 All ER 296).

Form—For the general form of affidavit, see Form N285.

Sworn statement—FPR 1991, r 3.8 requires applications for non-molestation or occupation orders under FLA 1996, Pt IV to be in Form FL401 supported by "a statement which is signed by the applicant and is sworn to be true". Clearly an affidavit complying with CCR Ord 20, r 10 is also a "sworn statement" complying with FPR 1991, r 3.8.

Presentation of affidavits—Note the requirement for the marking of affidavits in CCR Ord 20, r 10(3). There is a similar requirement in the High Court by virtue of *Practice Note of 21 July 1983*. It is submitted that this marking requirement should also be applied to a sworn statement required by FPR 1991, r 3.8.

****

12 Witness summons (Ord 20, r 12)

(1) Where a party to an action or matter desires a person to be summoned as a witness to give oral evidence or to produce a document in his possession, custody or power, the proper officer shall, on an application made by a party in accordance with paragraph (2), issue a witness summons, together with a copy.

(2) The applicant shall file a request for the issue of the summons and, if the summons is to be served by an officer of the court, deposit in the court office the money to be paid or tendered under paragraph (7).

(3) The summons shall contain the name of one witness only but may, as regards such name, be issued in blank.

(4) (*a*) The summons shall be issued not less than 7 days before the date upon which attendance before the court is required unless the judge or district judge otherwise directs and shall be served on the witness not less than 4 days before the date upon which attendance before the court is required unless the judge or district judge otherwise directs.

(*b*) Service under this paragraph shall, subject to paragraph (5), be effected by delivering the summons to the witness personally.

(5) Where the applicant or his solicitor gives a certificate for postal service, the summons shall, unless the district judge otherwise directs, be served on the witness by an officer of the court sending it to him by first-class post at the address stated in the request for the summons and, unless the contrary is shown, the date of service shall be deemed to be the seventh day after the date on which the summons was sent to the witness.

(6) Where the summons has been served by post, the witness shall not be fined for failing to appear on the return day unless the judge is satisfied that –

(*a*) the summons came to his knowledge in sufficient time for him to appear on that day, and (*b*) the money to be paid or tendered under paragraph (7) was sent to him with the summons.

(7) At the time of service of the summons there shall be paid or tendered to the witness the sum of £6 for a police officer and £8.50 for any other person and, in addition, a sum reasonably sufficient to cover his expenses in travelling to and from the court.

(8) No summons shall be issued to require a witness to give evidence at a hearing in chambers for directions without leave of the judge or district judge, the application for which shall be made ex parte.

Amendments—SI 1989/236.

****

ORDER 22
JUDGMENTS AND ORDERS

****

3 Time for complying with other judgments (Ord 22, r 3)

Every judgment or order requiring any person to do an act other than the payment of money shall state the time within which the act is to be done.

Scope of provision—This provision is important for purposes of enforcement. An order to do an act cannot be enforced unless and until a date for the act to be done is fixed (Ord 29, r 1(1)). If a period of time is incorporated, the order should state the date from which the period of time is to run. It is better practice to nominate a day and time by which an act is to be done. Sufficient time should be allowed for the order to be sealed and served, and, thereafter, for compliance.

Calculation of time—Any period of time which is fixed is calculated in accordance with Ord 1, r 9.

****

ORDER 25
ENFORCEMENT OF JUDGMENTS AND ORDERS: GENERAL

CPR 1998—Where the order to be enforced was obtained in proceedings which are not "family proceedings", Ords 25–35 will apply in the modified form in which they are set out in CPR 1998, Sch 2. See the annotations to FPR 1991, r 1.3.

1 Judgment creditor and debtor (Ord 25, r 1)

In this Order and Orders 26 to 29 "judgment creditor" means the person who has obtained or is entitled to enforce a judgment or order and "debtor" means the person against whom it was given or made.

2 Transfer of proceedings for enforcement (Ord 25, r 2)

(1) Where, with a view to enforcing a judgment or order obtained by him in a county court, a judgment creditor desires to apply for –

(*a*) the oral examination of the debtor,
(*b*) a charging order under section 1 of the Charging Orders Act 1979,
(*c*) an attachment of earnings order, or
(*d*) the issue of a judgment summons,

and the application is required by any provision of these rules to be made to another county court, the judgment creditor shall make a request in writing to the proper officer of the court in which the judgment or order was obtained for the transfer of the action or matter to the other court.

(2) On receipt of a request under paragraph (1), the proper officer shall make an order transferring the action or matter to the court and shall –

(*a*) make an entry of the transfer in the records of his court; and
(*b*) send to the proper officer of the court to which the action or matter has been transferred a certificate of the judgment or order, stating the purpose for which it has been issued, and, if requested by that officer, all the documents in his custody relating to the action or matter.

(3) When the action or matter has been transferred to the other court –

(*a*) the proper officer of that court shall give notice of the transfer to the judgment creditor and the debtor,
(*b*) any payment which, by or under these rules or the Court Funds Rules 1987, is authorised or required to be made into court shall be made into that court, and
(*c*) subject to sub-paragraph (*d*), any subsequent proceedings in the action or matter shall be taken in that court, but
(*d*) any application or appeal under Order 37 shall be made to the court in which the judgment or order was obtained.

(4) If the judgment creditor desires to make a subsequent application for any of the remedies mentioned in paragraph (1)(*a*) to (*d*) and the application is required to be made to another court, he may make a request under paragraph (1) to the court to which the action or matter has been transferred and paragraphs (2) and (3) shall apply with the necessary modifications.

Amendments—SI 1989/1838; SI 1994/2403.

Application of rule to family proceedings—This rule is not observed in family proceedings, although no other provision appears to exclude it. Indeed, if it were followed it could result in some cases in, for example, a divorce cause being transferred to a non-divorce county court.

3 Oral examination of debtor (Ord 25, r 3)

(1) Where a person has obtained a judgment or order in a county court for the payment of money or where an order has been made under rule 12 of this Order, the proper officer of the appropriate court may, on an application made ex parte by the judgment creditor, order the debtor or, if the debtor is a body corporate, an officer thereof to attend before the proper officer and be orally examined as to the debtor's means of satisfying the judgment or order, and may also order the person to be examined to produce at the time and place appointed for the examination any books or documents in his possession relevant to the debtor's means.

(1A) An application under paragraph (1) shall certify the amount of money remaining due under the judgment, order or award (as that word is defined by rule 12(1) of this Order).

PART III

(2) The appropriate court for the purposes of paragraph (1) shall be the court for the district in which the person to be examined (or, if there are more such persons than one, any of them) resides or carries on business.

(3) The order shall be served in the same manner as a default summons.

(4) If the person to be examined fails to attend at the time and place fixed for the examination, the court may adjourn the examination and make a further order for his attendance and any such order shall direct that any such payments made thereafter shall be paid into court and not direct to the judgment creditor.

(5) Nothing in Order 29, rule 1(2) to (7) shall apply to an order made under paragraph (4), but Order 27, rules 7B and 8, shall apply, with the necessary modifications, as they apply to orders made under section 23(1) of the Attachment of Earnings Act 1971 except that for the period of 5 days specified in paragraph (1) of Order 27, rule 8 there shall be substituted a period of 10 days.

(5A) Where an examination has been adjourned, the judgment creditor, if requested to do so by the person to be examined not less than 7 days before the day fixed for the adjourned examination, shall pay to him a sum reasonably sufficient to cover his expenses in travelling to and from the court unless such a sum was paid to him at the time of service of the order for oral examination.

(5B) The judgment creditor shall, not more than 4 days before the day fixed for the adjourned examination, file a certificate stating either that no request has been made under paragraph (5A) or that a sum has been paid in accordance with such a request.

(5C) Where the person to be examined has made a request under paragraph (5A), he shall not be committed to prison under Order 29, rule 1(1) for having failed to attend at the time and place fixed for the adjourned examination unless the judgment creditor has paid to him a sum reasonably sufficient to cover the travelling expenses before the day fixed for the adjourned examination.

(6) Order 20, rule 13, shall apply with the necessary modifications, to an examination under this rule as it applies to an examination under that rule.

(7) Nothing in this rule shall be construed as preventing the court, before deciding whether to make an order under paragraph (1), from giving the person to be examined an opportunity of making a statement in writing or an affidavit as to the debtor's means.

Amendments—SI 1984/878; SI 1988/278; SI 1989/1838; SI 1989/2426; SI 1994/2403; SI 1995/2838; SI 1997/1837.

Defined terms—"debtor", "judgment creditor": r 1, "proper officer": Ord 1, r 3.

Application (r 3(1))—The application is made ex parte by filing in the appropriate county court (see **Venue** below) an affidavit (in family proceedings only, see FPR 1991, r 7.1(5)(*b*)) verifying the amount due and giving the grounds of the application. A copy of the judgment or order must be exhibited if the application is made to a court other than the one which gave it but it is good practice to do so in all cases. In practice the application will be granted unless the court regards it as abusive (eg when it follows a recent similar examination).

Venue—In family proceedings, r 3(2) does not apply and the application is made to such divorce county court (which includes the principal registry) as in the opinion of the applicant is nearest to the place where the debtor resides or carries on business (FPR 1991, r 7.1(5)(*a*)).

High Court judgment—Proceedings under this rule are not available where the judgment or order was obtained in the High Court. In such a case, application may be made to the High Court under the equivalent rule (RSC Ord 48, r 1). The fact that the cause may have been transferred to the county court subsequently under Matrimonial and Family Proceedings Act 1984, s 38 does not affect the position as, unlike County Courts Act 1984, s 40 (which does not apply to family proceedings), s 38 preserves the character of the judgment as a High Court judgment.

Order (r 3(1), (7))—The order may require the debtor to attend before an authorised court officer or the district judge (see the definition of "proper officer" in Ord 1, r 3). In an appropriate case (eg where the order to be enforced is merely an order for costs), the court may invite the debtor to lodge a statement or affidavit of his means and, if he complies, decline to make the order. If made, the order is in Form N37.

Service (r 3(3))—The order is served as a default summons used before 26 April 1999 to be served, ie by the court posting it. The rule makes no particular provision as to the period of notice to be given, but 21 days will be allowed by analogy with the equivalent rule in civil proceedings: CPR 1998, Sch 2, CCR Ord 25, r 3 (applying Sch 2, CCR Ord 3, r 6).

Non-compliance (r 3(4), (5))—The order is not directly enforceable by committal. If the debtor fails to attend, the examination may be adjourned and a further order may be made requiring the debtor to attend the adjourned hearing. That further order (in Form N39) must require future payments made by the debtor to be made to the court (although the prescribed form appears merely to permit this). It must be personally served at least 10 days before the new return date. Unless paid at the time of service, the debtor may at least seven days before the return date request a sum for his travelling expenses to and from court. The judgment creditor must certify no more than four days before the return date that the expenses have been paid or have not been requested. Form N39 informs the debtor that the expenses paid will be added to the judgment debt but, although this may well be the usual outcome, there is no express provision in the rules which overrides the court's usual discretion. If the debtor fails to attend the adjourned hearing, then (unless he has requested but has not been paid the expenses) a committal order may be made by the judge. No further hearing is required as Ord 29, r 1(2)–(7) is disapplied and the judge relies on the certificate of the officer or district judge before whom the examination was to take place that the debtor failed to attend. In practice, the committal order is often suspended under Ord 27, r 7B on terms that the debtor attend a further "last opportunity" appointment to undergo examination, and it will usually be discharged if he does so.

The examination—The judgment creditor may cross-examine the debtor rigorously (*Republic of Costa Rica v Strousberg* (1880) 16 Ch D 8) as to his assets, including those overseas (*Interpool Ltd v Galani* [1987] 3 WLR 1042, [1987] 2 All ER 981), and as to other means by which the judgment may be satisfied, but not for some other purpose (*Watkins v Ross* (1893) 68 LT 423).

Other powers—If the proceedings concern a "qualifying periodical maintenance order" within the meaning of Maintenance Enforcement Act 1991, s 1, the court may of its own motion make a "means of payment order" under s 1(4)(*a*) of that Act or an attachment of earnings order by virtue of s 1(4)(*b*). These are not powers which a court officer can exercise. If it is thought that their use may be needed, the creditor should ask that the examination be conducted by the district judge.

Costs—The order for the examination usually provides that the costs of the application and of the examination be in the discretion of the district judge. If the examination does not produce any useful information then costs will not be allowed. If they are allowed then in practice in a simple case the district judge will usually allow a sum equal to the fixed costs on a judgment summons or attachment of earnings application (CCR App B, Pt III, Item 6) as well as disbursements, but assessed costs are allowed when appropriate.

4 Examination of debtor under judgment not for money (Ord 25, r 4)

Where any difficulty arises in or in connection with the enforcement of any judgment or order for some relief other than the payment of money, the court may make an order under rule 3 for the attendance of the debtor and for his examination on such questions as may be specified in the order, and that rule shall apply accordingly with the necessary modifications.

Defined terms—"debtor": r 1.

Scope of provision—This rule extends the oral examination procedure to non-monetary judgments. The same practice is followed as under r 3, mutatis mutandis.

Affidavit—As the order will identify the matters on which the "debtor" is to be examined, care must be taken to set these out in the affidavit applying for the order.

5 Production of plaint note and other information (Ord 25, r 5)

(1) The requests and applications mentioned in paragraph (2) are –

(*a*) a request for a warrant of execution, delivery or possession,
(*b*) a request for a judgment summons or warrant of committal,
(*c*) an application for a garnishee order under Order 30, rule 1, and
(*d*) an application for a charging order.

(2) Where the judgment creditor has filed any request or application referred to in paragraph (1) or is seeking to enforce a judgment or order by making an application under rule 3 or under Order 27 or 32, he shall forthwith notify the proper officer of any payment received from the debtor in respect of the judgment to be enforced after the date of the application and before –

(*a*) the final return to the warrant of execution, delivery or possession; or
(*b*) in any other case, the date fixed for the hearing of the application.

(3) Without prejudice to rule 8(9), where the judgment creditor applies to re-issue enforcement proceedings, he shall file a request in that behalf certifying the amount of money remaining due under the judgment or order and that the whole or part of any instalment due remains unpaid and stating why re-issue is necessary.

Amendments—SI 1989/1838; SI 1991/1882.

Defined terms—"charging order": Charging Orders Act 1979, s 1(3); "debtor", "judgment creditor": r 1; "judgment summons": County Courts Act 1984, s 147; "proper officer": Ord 1, r 3; "warrant of delivery": Ord 26, r 16; "warrant of execution": CCA 1984, s 85(2); "warrant of possession": Ord 26, r 17.

Notification of payments received (r 5(2))—The creditor must keep the court informed of any payments made by the debtor while the enforcement process is pending.

"re-issue" (r 5(3))—The requirement imposed by FPR 1991, r 7.1(1) that an affidavit be filed applies on re-issue as on the original issue of enforcement process. The information required by r 5(3) should be included in that affidavit.

5A Interest on judgment debts (Ord 25, r 5A)

Where the judgment creditor claims interest pursuant to the County Courts (Interest on Judgment Debts) Order 1991 and takes proceedings to enforce payment under the relevant judgment (within the meaning of article 4(1) of that Order), any request or application for enforcement made in those proceedings shall be accompanied by two copies of a certificate giving details of –

(*a*) the amount of interest claimed and the sum on which it is claimed,
(*b*) the dates from and to which interest has accrued, and
(*c*) the rate of interest which has been applied and, where more than one rate of interest has been applied, the relevant dates and rates.

Amendments—Inserted by SI 1991/1328.

Defined terms—"judgment creditor": r 1.

Certificate—FPR 1991, r 7.1(1) in any event requires a judgment creditor in family proceedings to file an affidavit showing the calculation of the amount due (ie including the information required by this rule). It will be convenient either to incorporate the information in the text of the affidavit and file a copy or to exhibit one of the two copies of the required certificate to the affidavit.

County Courts (Interest on Judgment Debts) Order 1991—The terms of the order are not without difficulty but the general purport is that interest runs at the rate prescribed for the High Court from the date when payment is due under a judgment or order for at least £5,000. If a lump sum financial provision order is made for less than £5,000, any interest ordered to be paid under Matrimonial Causes Act 1973, s 23(6) will not bring the judgment debt under this rule even though the total due may exceed £5,000. Interest will remain payable where a payment on account reduces the balance below £5,000. Interest ceases to accrue as soon as any enforcement step is taken, including an application for oral examination but excluding an application for a charging order, if the step produces any payment at all from the debtor. No more than 6 years' interest may be recovered (*Lowsley and another v Forbes* [1998] 3 All ER 897, HL).

Rate of interest—The rate is 8% per annum (Judgment Debts (Rate of Interest) Order 1993, SI 1993/564).

6 Description of parties (Ord 25, r 6)

Where the name or address of the judgment creditor or the debtor as given in the request for the issue of a warrant of execution or delivery, judgment summons or warrant of committal differs from his name or address in the judgment or order sought to be enforced and the judgment creditor satisfies the proper officer that the name or address as given in the request is applicable to the person concerned, the judgment creditor or the debtor, as the case may be, shall be described in the warrant or judgment summons as "C.D. of [*name and address as given in the request*] suing [*or sued*] as A.D. of [*name and address in the judgment or order*]".

Defined terms—"debtor", "judgment creditor": r 1; "judgment summons": County Courts Act 1984, s 147; "proper officer": Ord 1, r 3; "warrant of execution": CCA 1984, s 85(2).

7 Recording and giving information as to warrants and orders (Ord 25, r 7)

(1) Subject to paragraph (1A), every district judge by whom a warrant or order is issued or received for execution shall from time to time state in the records of his court what has been done in the execution of the warrant or order.

(1A) Where a warrant of execution is sent to another court for execution, paragraph (1) shall not apply to the district judge of the home court, but when such a warrant is returned to the proper officer of the home court under paragraph (7), the proper officer of the home court shall state in the records of his court what has been done in the execution of the warrant or order.

(2) If the warrant or order has not been executed within one month from the date of its issue or receipt by him, the proper officer of the court responsible for its execution shall, at the end of that month and every subsequent month during which the warrant remains outstanding, send notice of the reason for non-execution to the judgment creditor and, if the warrant or order (other than a warrant of execution) was received from another court, to the proper officer of that court.

(3) The district judge responsible for executing a warrant or order shall give such information respecting it as may reasonably by required by the judgment creditor and, if the warrant or order was received by him from another court, by the district judge of that court.

(4) Where money is received in pursuance of a warrant of execution or committal sent by one court to another court, the proper officer of the foreign court shall, subject to paragraph (5) and to section 346 of the Insolvency Act 1986 and section 326 of the Companies Act 1948, send the money to the judgment creditor in the manner prescribed by the County Court Funds Rules and, where the money is received in pursuance of a warrant of committal, make a return to the proper officer of the home court.

(5) Where interpleader proceedings are pending, the proper officer shall not proceed in accordance with paragraph (4) until the interpleader proceedings are determined and the district judge shall then make a return showing how the money is to be disposed of and, if any money is payable to the judgment creditor, the proper officer shall proceed in accordance with paragraph (4).

(6) Where a warrant of committal has been received from another court, the proper officer of the foreign court shall, on the execution of the warrant, send notice thereof to the proper officer of the home court.

(7) Where a warrant of execution has been received from another court, either

- (*a*) on the execution of the warrant or,
- (*b*) if the warrant is not executed –
  - (i) on the making of a final return to the warrant; or
  - (ii) on suspension of the warrant under rule 8 (suspension of judgment or execution) or Order 26, rule 10 (withdrawal and suspension of warrant at creditor's request),

the proper officer of the foreign court shall return the warrant to the proper officer of the home court.

Amendments—SI 1982/1794; SI 1986/2001; SI 1995/969.

Defined terms—"interpleader": Ord 33, r 4; "judgment creditor": Ord 25, r 1; "proper officer": Ord 1, r 3; "warrant of execution": County Courts Act 1984, s 85(2).

"such information ... as may reasonably be required" (r 7(3))—Rule 7(3) has to be read subject to the constraints of practicability (*Polentz v Roberts* (1900) 110 LT Jo 376). Resources expended on dealing with enquiries are necessarily diverted from dealing with the process itself.

8 Suspension of judgment or execution (Ord 25, r 8)

(1) The power of the court to suspend or stay a judgment or order or to stay execution of any warrant may be exercised by the district judge or, in the case of the power to stay execution of a warrant of execution and in accordance with the provisions of this rule, by the proper officer.

(2) An application by the debtor to stay execution of a warrant of execution shall be in the appropriate form stating the proposed terms, the grounds on which it is made and including a signed statement of the debtor's means.

(3) Where the debtor makes an application under paragraph (2), the proper officer shall –

- (*a*) send the judgment creditor a copy of the debtor's application (and statement of means); and
- (*b*) require the creditor to notify the court in writing, within 14 days of service of notification upon him, giving his reasons for any objection he may have to the granting of the application.

(4) If the judgment creditor does not notify the court of any objection within the time stated, the proper officer may make an order suspending the warrant on terms of payment.

(5) Upon receipt of a notice by the judgment creditor under paragraph (3), the proper officer may, if the judgment creditor objects only to the terms offered, determine the date and rate of payment and make an order suspending the warrant on terms of payment.

(6) Any party affected by an order made under paragraph (5) may, within 14 days of service of the order on him and giving his reasons, apply on notice for the order to be reconsidered and the proper officer shall fix a day for the hearing of the application before the district judge and give to the judgment creditor and the debtor not less than 8 days' notice of the day so fixed.

(7) On hearing an application under paragraph (6), the district judge may confirm the order or set it aside and make such new order as he thinks fit and the order so made shall be entered in the records of the court.

(8) Where the judgment creditor states in his notice under paragraph (3)(*b*) that he wishes the bailiff to proceed to execute the warrant, the proper officer shall fix a day for a hearing before the district judge of the debtor's application and give to the judgment creditor and to the debtor not less than 2 days' notice of the day so fixed.

(9) Subject to any directions given by the district judge, where a warrant of execution has been suspended, it may be re-issued on the judgment creditor's filing a request pursuant to rule 5(3) showing that any condition subject to which the warrant was suspended has not been complied with.

(10) Where an order is made by the district judge suspending a warrant of execution, the debtor may be ordered to pay the costs of the warrant and any fees or expenses incurred before its suspension and the order may authorise the sale of a sufficient portion of any goods seized to cover such costs, fees and expenses and the expenses of sale.

(11) In this rule "proper officer" does not include the district judge.

Amendments—SI 1991/1126.

Defined terms—"debtor", "judgment creditor": r 1; "proper officer": Ord 1, r 3; "warrant of execution": County Courts Act 1984, s 85(2).

"power of the court to suspend or stay" (r 8(1))—Power to stay a judgment on terms is given by County Courts Act 1984, s 71(2) and that to stay execution by s 88. In each case the ground is the debtor's inability to pay. The proper officer's authority does not extend to applications to stay on any other ground as he can make an order suspending the warrant only on terms as to payment.

"may make an order" (r 8(4))—The proper officer is not obliged to exercise his powers under this rule. If he declines to do so, the application will be listed before a district judge in the same way as an application where the creditor opposes any suspension.

Other powers—If the proceedings concern a "qualifying periodical maintenance order" within the meaning of MEA 1991, s 1, the court (ie the district judge, not the proper officer) may of its own motion make a "means of payment order" under s 1(4)(*a*) of that Act or an attachment of earnings order under s 1(4)(*b*).

Costs (r 8(10))—The proper officer has no power to deal with the question of costs. Where it seems that an order for costs may be appropriate, the application will be listed for hearing before a district judge.

****

11 Enforcement of High Court judgment (Ord 25, r 11)

(1) A judgment creditor who desires to enforce a judgment or order of the High Court, or a judgment, order, decree or award of any court or arbitrator which is or has become enforceable as if it were a judgment or order of the High Court, shall file in the appropriate court (with such documents as are required to be filed for the purpose of enforcing a judgment or order of a county court) –

- (*a*) an office copy of the judgment or order or, in the case of a judgment, order, decree or award of a court other than the High Court or an arbitrator, such evidence of the judgment, order, decree or award and of its enforceability as a judgment of the High Court as the district judge may require;
- (*b*) a certificate verifying the amount due under the judgment, order, decree or award; and
- (*c*) where a writ of execution has been issued to enforce it, a copy of the sheriff's return to the writ;
- (*d*) a copy of the order to transfer the proceedings to the county court.

(2) In this rule the "appropriate court" means the county court in which the relevant enforcement proceedings might, by virtue of these rules, be brought if the judgment or order had been obtained in proceedings commenced in a county court.

Provided that if under these rules the court in which the relevant enforcement proceedings might be brought is identified by reference to the court in which the judgment or order has been obtained the appropriate court shall be the court for the district in which the debtor resides or carries on business.

(3) The provisions of this rule are without prejudice to Order 26, rule 2.

Amendments—SI 1984/878; SI 1994/2403.

Defined terms—"debtor", "judgment creditor": r 1.

Availability—High Court judgments may be enforced in the county court under Debtors Act 1869, s 5, Charging Orders Act 1979, s 1 and Attachment of Earnings Act 1971, s 1(2). County Courts Act 1984, s 105, which enabled High Court judgments generally to be so enforced, was repealed on 1 July 1991 and, as regards family proceedings, has not been replaced.

"order to transfer" (r 11(1)(*d*))—This is a reference to orders (to transfer proceedings to enforce High Court judgments) made under County Courts Act 1984, s 40, which does not apply to family proceedings. A High Court judgment or order may be enforced in a county court by judgment summons, attachment of earnings application or charging order without the proceedings being transferred. As these are the only remedies available in the county court to enforce a High Court family proceedings order, no such order is needed or made in such proceedings.

Establishing the appropriate court (r 11(2))—In the case of a judgment summons under the Debtors Act 1869, s 5, the choice of court is governed by FPR 1991, r 7.4(2); otherwise it will usually be the debtor's home court (see Ord 27, r 3 and Ord 31, r 1(1)). There is no general requirement in family proceedings that the documents be filed in a divorce county court.

Interest—A High Court family proceedings order enforced in the county court continues to have the character of a High Court order. Interest continues to run as on any High Court judgment or order.

Form—The affidavit should be in Form N321.

****

ORDER 26
WARRANTS OF EXECUTION, DELIVERY AND POSSESSION

1 Application for warrant of execution (Ord 26, r 1)

(1) A judgment creditor desiring a warrant of execution to be issued shall file a request in that behalf certifying –

(*a*) the amount remaining due under the judgment or order, and
(*b*) where the order made is for payment of a sum of money by instalments,
 (i) that the whole or part of any instalment due remains unpaid, and
 (ii) the amount for which the warrant is to be issued.

(1A) The proper officer shall discharge the functions –

(*a*) under section 85(2) of the Act of issuing a warrant of execution; and
(*b*) under section 85(3) of the Act of entering in the record mentioned in that subsection and on the warrant the precise time of the making of the application to issue the warrant, and
(*c*) under section 103(1) of the Act of sending the warrant of execution to another county court.

(2) Where the court has made an order for payment of a sum of money by instalments and default has been made in payment of such an instalment, a warrant of execution may be issued for the whole of the said sum of money and costs then remaining unpaid or, subject to paragraph (3), for such part as the judgment creditor may request, not being in the latter case less than £50 or the amount of one monthly instalment or, as the case may be, four weekly instalments, whichever is the greater.

(3) In any case to which paragraph (2) applies no warrant shall be issued unless at the time when it is issued –

(*a*) the whole or part of an instalment which has already become due remains unpaid, and
(*b*) any warrant previously issued for part of the said sum of money and costs has expired or has been satisfied or abandoned.

(4) Where a warrant is issued for the whole or part of the said sum of money and costs, the proper officer shall, unless the district judge responsible for execution of the warrant directs otherwise, send a warning notice to the person against whom the warrant is issued and, where such a notice is sent, the warrant shall not be levied until 7 days thereafter.

(5) Where judgment is given or an order made for payment otherwise than by instalments of a sum of money and costs to be taxed and default is made in payment of the sum of money before the costs have been taxed, a warrant of execution may issue for recovery of the sum of money and a separate warrant may issue subsequently for the recovery of the costs if default is made in payment of them.

Amendments—SI 1983/1716; SI 1989/1838; SI 1996/2181.

PART III

Defined terms—"judgment creditor": Ord 25, r 1; "warrant of execution": County Courts Act 1984, s 85(2).

Considerations affecting issue of warrant—The power to enforce judgments by execution against goods and to issue a warrant of execution to the like effect as a writ of fieri facias is given by County Courts Act 1984, s 85 and controlled by ss 86 to 104. Practical considerations include:

(*a*) *Priority* The court records the time the warrant is applied for (s 85(3)) and the warrant "binds the property in the goods" (and therefore has priority over later executions) from that time (s 99(1)), unless it is used to levy on goods in another county court district, in which case the time of its receipt by that county court is recorded and governs its priority as regards those goods (s 103(2)).

(*b*) *Instalment judgments* Execution may not be issued unless the debtor is in arrear (s 86).

(*c*) *Suspension* The court may suspend or stay the execution (on terms if it thinks fit) if the debtor is unable to pay (s 88 – see also Ord 25, r 8). Where the warrant has been sent to another court, both courts have this power (s 103(5)). If the proceedings concern (ie if the application is to suspend a warrant issued to enforce) a "qualifying periodical maintenance order" within the meaning of Maintenance Enforcement Act 1991, s 1, the court may of its own motion make a "means of payment order" under s 1(4)(*a*) of that Act or an attachment of earnings order by virtue of s 1(4)(*b*).

(*d*) *Goods* Section 89 exempts certain goods from execution. Cash and valuable securities may be taken in the execution of the warrant.

(*e*) *Rescue* The rescue by any person of goods seized in execution is punishable by up to one month's imprisonment or a fine of up to £1,000 (s 92).

(*f*) *Sale* Goods seized must be sold by public auction unless the court otherwise orders (s 97 – see also r 15).

Availability of warrant of execution—The High Court and County Courts Jurisdiction Order 1991, art 8 prohibits enforcement by execution of county court judgments for £5,000 or more in the county court or under £2,000 in the High Court, but the order does not apply to family proceedings. Thus any judgment or order made in family proceedings in the county court may be enforced by execution in the county court, irrespective of amount. It does not seem now to be possible to enforce a High Court judgment or order made in family proceedings by execution in the county court following the repeal of the former County Courts Act 1984, s 105. County Courts Act 1984, s 40 (which enables proceedings for enforcement of High Court judgments to be transferred to the county court) does not apply to family proceedings (s 40(9)).

Insolvency of debtor—Insolvency Act 1986, s 285(3), which prevents enforcement of debts against a bankrupt, applies only to creditors with provable debts and so does not restrict the family proceedings creditor. The court does however retain a discretionary power to stay enforcement process (s 285(1), (2)). See also **Insolvency Act 1986** under r 8.

"file a request" (r 1(1))—Although Form N323 is merely a practice form and the required information could well be included in the affidavit required by FPR 1991, r 7.1(1), it is helpful to use Form N323 in addition to the affidavit as the print contains space for information to be recorded by the court staff.

Warning notice (r 1(4))—The usual form of warning notice is set out in practice form N326, which informs the debtor that extra costs may be incurred if goods are seized and sold and that further interest will accrue (if the judgment is for more than £5,000) unless the warrant and any balance of the judgment debt are paid off. Courts' practices on sending this notice vary. If there is any particular reason to fear that the debtor may hide goods if warned, the court should be advised of this at the time of issue and requested not to use the notice.

****

3 Execution against farmer (Ord 26, r 3)

If after the issue of a warrant of execution the district judge for the district in which the warrant is to be executed has reason to believe that the debtor is a farmer, the execution creditor shall, if so required by the district judge, furnish him with an official certificate, dated not more than three days beforehand, of the result of a search at the Land Registry as to the existence of any charge registered against the debtor under the Agricultural Credits Act 1928.

Defined terms—"debtor": Ord 25, r 1; "warrant of execution": County Courts Act 1984, s 85(2).

Scope of provision—This rule enables the court to call for a search under the Agricultural Credits Act 1928 where the debtor is a farmer. It is unlikely to do so unless goods are in fact seized. The search will reveal whether a charge over the farmer's assets exists under the Act. If there is a charge, the chargee is informed of the levy in case he wishes to claim the goods on the ground that the charge has crystallised.

4 Concurrent warrants (Ord 26, r 4)

Two or more warrants of execution may be issued concurrently for execution in different districts, but –

(*a*) no more shall be levied under all the warrants together than is authorised to be levied under one of them, and
(*b*) the costs of more than one such warrant shall not be allowed against the debtor except by order of the court.

Defined terms—"debtor": Ord 25, r 1; "warrant of execution": County Courts Act 1984, s 85(2).

Costs—The fixed costs of one warrant only will be allowed against the debtor unless the creditor, on application to the district judge, can justify the use of concurrent warrants.

5 Leave to issue certain warrants (Ord 26, r 5)

(1) A warrant of execution shall not issue without the leave of the court where –

(*a*) six years or more have elapsed since the date of the judgment or order;
(*b*) any change has taken place, whether by death or otherwise in the parties entitled to enforce the judgment or order or liable to have it enforced against them;
(*c*) the judgment or order is against the assets of a deceased person coming to the hands of his executors or administrators after the date of the judgment or order and it is sought to issue execution against such assets; or
(*d*) any goods to be seized under a warrant of execution are in the hands of a receiver appointed by a court.

(2) An application for leave shall be supported by an affidavit establishing the applicant's right to relief and may be made ex parte in the first instance but the court may direct notice of the application to be served on such persons as it thinks fit.

(3) Where, by reason of one and the same event, a person seeks leave under paragraph (1)(*b*) to enforce more judgments or orders than one, he may make one application only, specifying in a schedule all the judgments or orders in respect of which it is made, and if notice is directed to be given to any person, it need set out only such part of the application as affects him.

(4) Paragraph (1) is without prejudice to any enactment, rule or direction by virtue of which a person is required to obtain the leave of the court for the issue of a warrant or to proceed to execution or otherwise to the enforcement of a judgment or order.

Defined terms—"warrant of execution": County Courts Act 1984, s 85(2).

PART III

"six years ... have elapsed" (r 5(1)(*a*))—The court will require the applicant to show good reason before permitting execution on a stale judgment and will take into account any prejudice to the debtor caused by the delay.

Change of party (r 5(1)(*b*))—The alternative is to apply to change the party under Ord 5, r 11. It is not thought that following an order under that rule leave would also be required under this rule. An order under Ord 5, r 11 would still be needed before other enforcement proceedings were taken following (presumably abortive) execution issued with leave under this rule. A mere change of description does not call for leave under this rule if the proper officer is satisfied under Ord 25, r 6.

Procedure (r 5(2))—The application may be made ex parte by affidavit. In practice, one affidavit may be used containing the application and grounds and the information required by FPR 1991, r 7.1(1). The district judge may however require notice to be given (and indeed must do so in the case of an application under r 5(1)(*c*): *Re Shephard* (1890) 43 Ch D 131). In a case where he clearly will so require, time may be saved by making the application on notice (supported by affidavit) in the first instance.

Duration of leave—In the High Court leave to issue execution (whether granted under the equivalent rule or in any other case where leave is required) ceases to have effect if the authorised process is not issued within one year (RSC Ord 46, r 2(3)). The High Court practice applies in the county court by virtue of County Courts Act 1984, s 76.

Other cases where leave is required (r 5(4))—Leave is required where it is sought to enforce arrears under a financial provision order which accrued more than 12 months beforehand (Matrimonial Causes Act 1973, s 32(1)) and, in the case of periodical payments arrears, where a variation application is pending (FPR 1991, r 7.1(2)). In those cases the application must be made on notice to the debtor, not under this rule.

6 Duration and renewal of warrant (Ord 26, r 6)

(1) A warrant of execution shall, for the purpose of execution, be valid in the first instance for 12 months beginning with the date of its issue, but if not wholly executed, it may be renewed from time to time, by order of the court, for a period of 12 months at any one time, beginning with the day next following that on which it would otherwise expire, if an application for renewal is made before that day or such later day (if any) as the court may allow.

(2) A note of any such renewal shall be indorsed on the warrant and it shall be entitled to priority according to the time of its original issue or, where appropriate, its receipt by the district judge responsible for its execution.

Defined terms—"warrant of execution": County Courts Act 1984, s 85(2).

Extension—The extension covers the period of 12 months immediately following the original period of validity (or previous extension). Only one extension may be granted at a time. An extension may be granted after a warrant has expired, but the period of 12 months will run from the expiry date, not from the date of the order (the converse of the position in the High Court: see RSC Ord 46, r 8(2)). Thus an extension given more than 12 months after expiry would be ineffective and will not be granted (cf *Rolph v Zolan* [1993] 1 WLR 1305, CA).

Priority—Rule 6(2) preserves the existing priority of the warrant (see **Considerations affecting issue of warrant**, *Priority* under r 1). Extension therefore prejudices any other execution creditors who would have achieved a higher priority on the expiry of the applicant's warrant.

Procedure for application for renewal—No special procedure is prescribed for the application, consequently, it is made in accordance with Ord 13, r 1. In practice, courts often allow the application to be made ex parte by letter. The grounds of the application, including any reason for allowing the warrant to expire, should be given. The High Court practice is to extend only if priority is important (as fresh execution can be issued if it is not) and accordingly to require the applicant to identify any other execution creditors and give them the opportunity to make representations. In the county court, the delay will usually have occurred because the warrant has been suspended (with consequent loss of priority) and, in such a case, the court will be the more ready to extend. Nevertheless, if it appears to the proper officer that other execution creditors would be significantly prejudiced, he may require the application to be made on notice to them, by analogy with the High Court practice.

7 Notice of levy (Ord 26, r 7)

Any bailiff upon levying execution shall deliver to the debtor or leave at the place where execution is levied a notice of the warrant.

Form—A form of notice is incorporated into the warrant document as a slip to be torn off and handed to the debtor. Similar information is provided to the debtor in the warning notice Form N326 (see r 1), if used.

8 Bankruptcy or winding up of debtor (Ord 26, r 8)

(1) Where the district judge responsible for the execution of a warrant is required by any provision of the Insolvency Act 1986 or any other enactment relating to insolvency to retain the proceeds of sale of goods sold under the warrant or money paid in order to avoid a sale, the proper officer shall, as soon as practicable after the sale or the receipt of the money, send notice to the execution creditor and, if the warrant issued out of another court, to the proper officer of that court.

(2) Where the district judge responsible for the execution of a warrant –

(*a*) receives notice that a bankruptcy order has been made against the debtor or, if the debtor is a company, that a provisional liquidator has been appointed or that an order has been made or a resolution passed for the winding up of the company, and

(*b*) withdraws from possession of goods seized or pays over to the official receiver or trustee in bankruptcy or, if the debtor is a company, to the liquidator the proceeds of sale of goods sold under the warrant or money paid in order to avoid a sale or seized or received in part satisfaction of the warrant,

the proper officer shall send notice to the execution creditor and, if the warrant issued out of another court, to the proper officer of that court.

(3) Where the proper officer of a court to which a warrant issued out of another court has been sent for execution receives any such notice as is referred to in paragraph (2)(*a*) after he has sent to the proper officer of the home court any money seized or received in part satisfaction of the warrant, he shall forward the notice to the proper officer of that court.

Amendments—SI 1986/2001; SI 1989/236.

Defined terms—"proper officer": Ord 1, r 3.

Insolvency Act 1986 (r 8(1))—At the time when a bankruptcy order is made, Insolvency Act 1986, s 346(1) passes to the trustee in bankruptcy the benefit of execution against goods (or payment made to avoid it) begun before the bankruptcy order was made, unless the goods are seized and sold (or the payment is made) before then. Further, where execution against goods is issued but before it is completed the bailiff receives notice that a bankruptcy order has been made against the debtor, s 346(2) requires him to pass the fruits of the execution to the trustee in bankruptcy. Where the amount levied for (not the amount of the judgment: *Re Grubb ex parte Sims* (1877) 5 Ch D 375; *Re Hinks ex parte Berthier* (1878) 7 Ch D 882) exceeds £500, the bailiff within 14 days after sale or payment receives notice that a bankruptcy petition has been presented against the debtor, and a bankruptcy order is made on it, then again the proceeds go to the bankrupt's estate. Accordingly, the bailiff is required to retain the amount received for 14 days in case such a notice is received. However s 346(6) enables the bankruptcy court to set aside the

PART III

trustee's rights under s 346; there is no relevant authority on the use of s 346(6), but the fact that a family proceedings creditor cannot prove the debt in the bankruptcy would clearly be a factor for the court to consider; just as such a creditor's special position must be considered in relation to an Insolvent Voluntary Arrangement under that Act (*Re a Debtor* No 488 IO of 1996, 12 November 1998, Ch D).

****

10 Withdrawal and suspension of warrant at creditor's request (Ord 26, r 10)

(1) Where an execution creditor requests the district judge responsible for executing a warrant to withdraw from possession, he shall, subject to the following paragraphs of this rule, be treated as having abandoned the execution, and the proper officer shall mark the warrant as withdrawn by request of the execution creditor.

(2) Where the request is made in consequence of a claim having been made under Order 33, rule 1, to goods seized under the warrant, the execution shall be treated as being abandoned in respect only of the goods claimed.

(3) If the district judge responsible for executing a warrant is requested by the execution creditor to suspend it in pursuance of an arrangement between him and the debtor, the proper officer shall mark the warrant as suspended by request of the execution creditor and the execution creditor may subsequently apply to the district judge holding the warrant for it to be re-issued and, if he does so, the application shall be deemed for the purpose of section 85(3) of the Act to be an application to issue the warrant.

(4) Nothing in this rule shall prejudice any right of the execution creditor to apply for the issue of a fresh warrant or shall authorise the re-issue of a warrant which has been withdrawn or has expired or has been superseded by the issue of a fresh warrant.

Amendments—SI 1984/878.

Defined terms—"proper officer": Ord 1, r 3.

Scope of provision—A distinction must be made between withdrawal or abandonment of a warrant by the creditor on the one hand and its suspension by him on the other. This rule deals with the consequences of both.

Suspension by court—This rule does not apply to suspension by the court; Ord 25, r 8 applies in such circumstances.

Priority—The effect of r 10(3) is that on suspension the priority of the warrant is lost and on re-issue it is accorded priority as if issued on the re-issue date, or presumably its re-delivery to the foreign court (see **Considerations affecting issue of warrant**, *Priority* under r 1). It is otherwise if the bailiff maintains the levy, by taking "walking possession", for example so as to allow the debtor time to raise money to pay. However the creditor is not entitled to require the bailiff to proceed thus, and in view of the heavy burden which it places upon the court he may well decline to maintain "walking possession" for any great length of time.

11 Suspension of part warrant (Ord 26, r 11)

Where a warrant issued for part of a sum of money and costs payable under a judgment or order is suspended on payment of instalments, the judgment or order shall, unless the court otherwise directs, be treated as suspended on those terms as respects the whole of the sum of money and costs then remaining unpaid.

Scope of provision—A "part warrant" may be issued only if there is already an instalment order in force (see r 1(2)). This rule sets out the position where such a warrant is itself suspended on instalments; the underlying instalment order is treated as varied in the same terms (unless otherwise ordered). This rule is taken to apply only to suspensions by order (see Ord 25, r 8), not those effected by arrangement under r 10(3). Presumably the "arrangement" between creditor and debtor will provide for payment of the whole debt, not merely the amount recoverable under the part warrant.

12 Inventory and notice where goods removed (Ord 26, r 12)

(1) Where goods seized in execution are removed, the proper officer shall forthwith deliver or send to the debtor a sufficient inventory of the goods removed and shall, not less than 4 days before the time fixed for the sale, give him notice of the time and place at which the goods will be sold.

(2) The inventory and notice shall be given to the debtor by delivering them to him personally or by sending them to him by post at his place of residence or, if his place of residence is not known, by leaving them for him, or sending them to him by post, at the place from which the goods were removed.

Defined terms—"debtor": Ord 25, r 1; "proper officer": Ord 1, r 3.

13 Account of sale (Ord 26, r 13)

Where goods are sold under an execution, the proper officer shall furnish the debtor with a detailed account in writing of the sale and of the application of the proceeds.

Defined terms—"debtor": Ord 25, r 1; "proper officer": Ord 1, r 3.

14 Notification to foreign court of payment made (Ord 26, r 14)

Where, after a warrant has been sent to a foreign court for execution but before a final return has been made to the warrant, the home court is notified of a payment made in respect of the sum for which the warrant is issued, the proper officer of the home court shall send notice of the payment to the proper officer of the foreign court.

Amendments—SI 1989/1838; SI 1989/2426.

Defined terms—"proper officer": Ord 1, r 3.

15 Order for private sale (Ord 26, r 15)

(1) Subject to paragraph (6), an order of the court under section 97 of the Act that a sale under an execution may be made otherwise than by public auction may be made on the application of the execution creditor or the debtor or the district judge responsible for the execution of the warrant.

(2) Where he is not the applicant for an order under this rule the district judge responsible for the execution of the warrant shall, on the demand of the applicant, furnish him with a list containing the name and address of every execution creditor under any other warrant or writ of execution against the goods of the debtor of which the district judge has notice, and where the district judge is the applicant, he shall prepare such a list.

(3) Not less than 4 days before the day fixed for the hearing of the application, the applicant shall give notice of the application to each of the other persons by whom

PART III

the application might have been made and to every person named in the list referred to in paragraph (2).

(4) The applicant shall produce the list to the court on the hearing of the application.

(5) Every person to whom notice of the application was given may attend and be heard on the hearing of the application.

(6) Where the district judge responsible for the execution of the warrant is the district judge by whom it was issued and he has no notice of any other warrant or writ of execution against the goods of the debtor, an order under this rule may be made by the court of its own motion with the consent of the execution creditor and the debtor or after giving them an opportunity of being heard.

Amendments—SI 1984/878.

Defined terms—"debtor": Ord 25, r 1.

Scope of provision—County Courts Act 1984, s 97 requires a sale of goods seized in execution to be by public auction (if the execution is for more than £20) unless the court otherwise orders. This rule provides the procedure for making such an order.

"court" (r 15(1))—The order must be made by the court which issued the warrant. In family proceedings this will normally be the court in which the cause or matter is proceeding. The warrant may of course have been sent to some other (possibly non-divorce) county court for execution.

Applicant (r 15(2))—The application may be made by either party or (in effect) by the bailiff.

Procedure—Notice must be given to any party who is not the applicant and to any other known execution creditor. Only if there is no such other creditor can the order be made without a hearing, provided the parties consent or, having been given an opportunity to be heard, do not object.

Private sale—The advantage of seeking a private sale is that a better price may be obtained than at auction, to the benefit of both debtor and creditors. It is preferable for the order to authorise a particular sale, and the application should be specific as to the actual sale proposed. The purchaser may be the execution creditor (*Ex parte Villars* (1874) LR 9 Ch 432). If the point is contentious the applicant must be prepared to compare the proposed sale price with what is likely to be achieved at auction. The procedure may be particularly useful where the creditor has an intimate knowledge of the debtor's leviable assets, and therefore some idea of the best market for them, as may sometimes occur in family proceedings.

16 Warrant of delivery (Ord 26, r 16)

(1) Except where by any Act or rule it is otherwise provided, a judgment or order for the delivery of any goods shall be enforceable by warrant of delivery, in accordance with this rule.

(2) If the judgment or order does not give the person against whom it was given or made the alternative of paying the value of the goods, it may be enforced by a warrant of specific delivery, that is to say, a warrant to recover the goods without alternative provision for recovery of their value.

(3) If the judgment or order is for the delivery of the goods or payment of their value, it may be enforced by a warrant of delivery to recover the goods or their value.

(4) Where a warrant of delivery is issued, the judgment creditor shall be entitled, by the same or a separate warrant, to execution against the debtor's goods for any

money payable under the judgment or order which is to be enforced by the warrant of delivery.

(4A) Where a judgment or order is given or made for the delivery of goods or payment of their value and a warrant is issued to recover the goods or their value, money paid into court under the warrant shall be appropriated first to any sum of money and costs awarded.

(5) The foregoing provisions of this Order, so far as applicable, shall have effect, with the necessary modifications, in relation to warrants of delivery as they have effect in relation to warrants of execution.

Amendments—SI 1989/1838.

Defined terms—"debtor", "judgment creditor": Ord 25, r 1; "warrant of execution": County Courts Act 1984, s 85(2).

Form of warrant (r 16(2), (3))—There are two forms of warrant, one requires the return of the goods or payment of their value (Form N48) and the other simply requires delivery of the goods (Form N46). In the case of the former, the bailiff will levy execution for the value if the goods cannot be found; in the case of the latter, if the bailiff cannot recover the goods, application may be made for the order to be enforced by committal (see **Delivery of goods** under r 18). It is therefore important to seek at the hearing the form of order appropriate to the case. In either case the warrant may provide also for execution for any money judgment or order and will provide for execution for the costs of the warrant.

Application of other rules to warrants of delivery (r 16(5))—Rules 1 to 15 apply, so far as applicable, to delivery warrants as they apply to warrants of execution.

17 Warrant of possession (Ord 26, r 17)

(1) A judgment or order for the recovery of land shall be enforceable by warrant of possession.

(2) Without prejudice to paragraph (3A), the person desiring a warrant of possession to be issued shall file a request in that behalf certifying that the land has not been vacated in accordance with the judgment or order for the recovery of the said land.

(3) Where a warrant of possession is issued, the judgment creditor shall be entitled, by the same or a separate warrant, to execution against the debtor's goods for any money payable under the judgment or order which is to be enforced by the warrant of possession.

(3A) In a case to which paragraph (3) applies or where an order for possession has been suspended on terms as to payment of a sum of money by instalments, the judgment creditor shall in his request certify –

(*a*) the amount of money remaining due under the judgment or order, and
(*b*) that the whole or part of any instalment due remains unpaid.

(4) A warrant of restitution may be issued, with the leave of the court, in aid of any warrant of possession.

(5) An application for leave under paragraph (4) may be made ex parte and shall be supported by evidence of wrongful re-entry into possession following the execution of the warrant of possession and of such further facts as would, in the High Court, enable the judgment creditor to have a writ of restitution issued.

(6) Rules 5 and 6 shall apply, with the necessary modifications, in relation to a warrant of possession and any further warrant in aid of such a warrant as they apply in relation to a warrant of execution.

Amendments—SI 1989/1838; SI 1992/793.

Defined terms—"debtor", "judgment creditor": Ord 25, r 1; "recovery of land": Ord 1, r 3; "warrant of execution": County Courts Act 1984, s 85(2).

Use in family proceedings—A warrant of possession is appropriate to enforce an occupation order made under Family Law Act 1996, Pt IV (*Danchevsky v Danchevsky* [1975] Fam 17, [1974] 3 WLR 709; *Larkman v Lindsell* [1989] Fam Law 229; *C v C (Contempt: Committal)* [1989] Fam Law 477). It may of course also be used in any other case where the court has ordered possession of land to be given up.

Issue—The warrant cannot be issued until the date for possession in the order has passed; however, where the order requires possession "forthwith", the warrant can be issued immediately. Normal administrative processes mean that several weeks may elapse between the issue and execution of a warrant, but courts will have regard to the urgency which often exists when an "ouster" order is made and give priority accordingly. If it is thought necessary, a direction to this effect should be sought from the judge either when the order is made or subsequently.

Effect—When enforcing a warrant of possession, the bailiff need not remove chattels (County Courts Act 1984, s 111(1)) but may evict any person on the premises even though not a party (*R v Wandsworth County Court ex parte London Borough of Wandsworth* [1975] 1 WLR 1314, [1975] 3 All ER 390). An occupier who claims the right to stay may apply to be added as a defendant (Ord 15, r 3) in order to apply for the judgment to be set aside.

Warrant of restitution (r 17(4), (5))—If after possession has been recovered the land or premises are re-occupied, application may be made ex parte for a warrant of restitution to eject the occupier. There must be a sufficient connection between the original eviction and the re-occupation, but it may be that restitution is effective against someone other than those originally evicted (*Wiltshire County Council v Frazer* [1986] 1 WLR 109, [1986] 1 All ER 65, where however there had been a summary order for possession against trespassers).

Application of other rules to warrants of possession (r 17(6))—Only rr 5 (leave to issue certain warrants) and 6 (duration and renewal of warrant) apply to possession warrants.

18 Saving for enforcement by committal (Ord 26, r 18)

Nothing in rule 16 or 17 shall prejudice any power to enforce a judgment or order for the delivery of goods or the recovery of land by an order of committal.

Delivery of goods—By analogy with the High Court practice (see RSC Ord 45, r 4), an order for delivery of goods or their value will not be enforced by committal. However, County Courts Act 1984, s 76 no doubt enables the court in a proper case to apply RSC Ord 45, r 5(3) and in effect substitute a specific delivery order, which would be enforceable by committal.

Committal generally—The court will be reluctant to commit where the order could well have been enforced by the less draconian (and much less expensive) option of a warrant (*Danchevsky v Danchevsky* [1975] Fam 17, [1974] 3 All ER 934). The applicant for committal should therefore be prepared to show that a warrant has been issued but has proved ineffective or that that method of enforcement is for some reason inappropriate.

ORDER 27
ATTACHMENT OF EARNINGS

Part I. General

1 Interpretation (Ord 27, r 1)

(1) In this Order –

"the Act of 1971" means the Attachment of Earnings Act 1971 and, unless the context otherwise requires, expressions used in that Act have the same meanings as in that Act;

"proper officer" does not include the district judge.

(2) Order 1, rule 8 shall apply in relation to any power conferred by the Act of 1971 as it applies in relation to any power conferred by these rules.

Scope of provision—This rule and Ord 27 generally provide a code, largely delegated to court staff, for attachment of earnings applications to enforce judgment debts, while reserving to the district judge attachment of earnings applications to enforce maintenance orders.

Defined terms—"proper officer": Ord 1, r 3 (see also Ord 27, r 1(1)).

"Order 1, rule 8" (r 1(2))—Order 1, r 8 sets out the extent to which the jurisdiction of the court may be exercised by the district judge.

"expressions used" (r 1(1))—AEA 1971, ss 2, 24, 25 define the expressions used therein. Note in particular the extended meaning of "maintenance order" given in s 2(*a*) (ie order specified in Sch 1 to the Act). As well as orders for periodical maintenance payments, such orders include orders for lump sums and other capital amounts which therefore do not create "judgment debts" for the purposes of this order. Costs awarded on the making of "maintenance orders" are treated as part of the maintenance orders (s 25(2)). Orders for costs made, for example, on pronouncement of a decree would not be within Sch 1 and would be "judgment debts".

2 Index of orders (Ord 27, r 2)

(1) The proper officer of every court shall keep a nominal index of the debtors residing within the district of his court in respect of whom there are in force attachment of earnings orders which have been made by that court or of which the proper officer has received notice from another court.

(2) Where a debtor in respect of whom a court has made an attachment of earnings order resides within the district of another court, the proper officer of the first-mentioned court shall send a copy of the order to the proper officer of the other court for entry in his index.

(3) The proper officer of a court shall, on the request of any person having a judgment or order against a person believed to be residing within the district of the court, cause a search to be made in the index of the court and issue a certificate of the result of the search.

Defined terms—"debtor": AEA 1971, s 2(*e*); "proper officer": Ord 1, r 3 (see also Ord 27, r 1(1)).

"notice from another court" (r 2(1))—The High Court and magistrates' courts notify any attachment of earnings orders which they make to the appropriate county court, which thus maintains a comprehensive index.

Search of the index (r 2(3))—The index is not open to public inspection but may be searched by anyone who has a judgment or order against a person believed to reside within the district of the court.

Form—The form of search and result is Form N336.

3 Appropriate court (Ord 27, r 3)

(1) Subject to paragraphs (2) and (3), an application for an attachment of earnings order may be made to the court for the district in which the debtor resides.

(2) If the debtor does not reside within England or Wales, or the creditor does not know where he resides, the application may be made to the court in which, or for the district in which, the judgment or order sought to be enforced was obtained.

(3) Where the creditor applies for attachment of earnings orders in respect of two or more debtors jointly liable under a judgment or order, the application may be made to the court for the district in which any of the debtors resides, so however that if the judgment or order was given or made by any such court, the application shall be made to that court.

Defined terms—"debtor": AEA 1971, s 2(*e*).

Scope of provision—This rule determines the venue of the application in the case of a judgment debt. It does not apply in the case of a maintenance order (r 17(2)).

"the court for the district in which the debtor resides" (r 3(1))—The court to which application is made need not be a divorce county court. No special rule exists as to venue in family proceedings, except in the case of a maintenance order. It is not, however, the practice to transfer the cause or matter in which the judgment or order was made (see **Application of rule to family proceedings** under Ord 25, r 2) whether it is proceeding in the High Court or another county court.

4 Mode of applying (Ord 27, r 4)

(1) A judgment creditor who desires to apply for an attachment of earnings order shall file his application certifying the amount of money remaining due under the judgment or order and that the whole or part of any instalment due remains unpaid and, where it is sought to enforce an order of a magistrates' court –

(*a*) a certified copy of the order, and

(*b*) an affidavit verifying the amount due under the order or, if payments under the order are required to be made to the clerk to the magistrates' court, a certificate by that clerk to the same effect.

(2) On the filing of the documents mentioned in paragraph (1) the proper officer shall where the order to be enforced is a maintenance order fix a day for the hearing of the application.

Amendments—SI 1982/1140; SI 1989/1838; SI 1991/1126.

Defined terms—"judgment creditor": Ord 25, r 1; "maintenance order": AEA 1971, s 2(*a*); "proper officer": Ord 1, r 3 (see also Ord 27, r 1(1)).

Form of application (r 4(1))—Form N337 should be used which, in family proceedings, must be accompanied by an affidavit under FPR 1991, r 7.1(1). If the cause or matter is not proceeding in the county court to which the attachment of earnings application is being made, a copy of the judgment or order should be exhibited.

"fix a day for the hearing" (r 4(2))—A hearing date is fixed only if the judgment or order is a maintenance order.

Debtor's application—This rule does not apply when the debtor applies for an attachment of earnings order on the making or variation of a maintenance order (r 17(4)).

5 Service and reply (Ord 27, r 5)

(1) Notice of the application, together with a form of reply in the appropriate form, shall be served on the debtor in the manner prescribed by these rules for the service of a default summons.

(2) The debtor shall, within 8 days after service on him of the documents mentioned in paragraph (1), file a reply in the form provided, and the instruction to that effect in the notice to the debtor shall constitute a requirement imposed by virtue of section 14(4) of the Act of 1971:

Provided that no proceedings shall be taken for an offence alleged to have been committed under section 23(2)(*c*) or (*f*) of the Act of 1971 in relation to the requirement unless the said documents have been served on the debtor personally or the court is satisfied that they came to his knowledge in sufficient time for him to comply with the requirement.

(2A) Nothing in paragraph (2) shall require a defendant to file a reply if, within the period of time mentioned in that paragraph, he pays to the judgment creditor the money remaining due under the judgment or order and, where such payment is made, the judgment creditor shall so inform the proper officer.

(3) On receipt of a reply the proper officer shall send a copy to the applicant.

Amendments—SI 1982/1140; SI 1991/1126.

Defined terms—"debtor": AEA 1971, s 2(*e*); "judgment creditor": Ord 25, r 1; "proper officer": Ord 1, r 3 (see also Ord 27, r 1(1)).

"service of a default summons" (r 5(1))—Usually the notice will be served by the court sending it by first class post to the debtor's address given on the application but it may be served by the creditor delivering it personally if he so requests (Ord 7, r 10). The practice of "serving" the notice by posting to the debtor "care of" the employer is not supported by the rules, save where it has been authorised by an order for substituted service under Ord 7, r 8. In the case of a maintenance order, r 17(3A) substitutes "fixed date summons" for "default summons" as the notice specifies a hearing date. The debtor must thus be given 21 days' notice of the hearing.

"the money remaining due" (r 5(2A))—Rule 5(2A) does not apply in the case of maintenance orders (r 17(3A)). The hearing fixed in the case of a maintenance order is not vacated by payment of the arrears and the district judge may still proceed to make an attachment of earnings order if appropriate and to deal with the costs of the application. In other cases, the payment will have included the issue fee, which is added into the "amount due" on the Form N55, and in most cases no further action will be taken.

Debtor's application—This rule does not apply when the debtor applies for an attachment of earnings order on the making or variation of a maintenance order (r 17(4)).

Forms—Notice of the application is given to the debtor by the court in either Form N55 (judgment debt) or Form N55(1) (maintenance order); the form of reply is Form N56.

6 Notice to employer (Ord 27, r 6)

Without prejudice to the powers conferred by section 14(1) of the Act of 1971, the proper officer may, at any stage of the proceedings, send to any person appearing to have the debtor in his employment a notice requesting him to give to the court, within such period as may be specified in the notice, a statement of the debtor's earnings and anticipated earnings with such particulars as may be so specified.

Amendments—SI 1991/1126.

Defined terms—"debtor": AEA 1971, s 2(*e*); "proper officer": Ord 1, r 3 (see also Ord 27, r 1(1)).

"notice requesting"—There is no compulsion on the employer to comply with the request but, if he does not do so, the court may decide to make an order under AEA 1971, s 14(1); failure to comply with such an order would be an offence (s 23(2)(*c*)).

Form—The form of notice is Form N338.

7 Hearing of application (Ord 27, r 7)

(1) On receipt of the debtor's reply, the proper officer may, if he has sufficient information to do so, make an attachment of earnings order and a copy of the order shall be sent to the parties and to the debtor's employer.

(2) Where an order is made under paragraph (1), the judgment creditor or the debtor may, within 14 days of service of the order on him and giving his reasons, apply on notice for the order to be re-considered and the proper officer shall fix a day for the hearing of the application and give to the judgment creditor and the debtor not less than 2 days' notice of the day so fixed.

(3) On hearing an application under paragraph (2), the district judge may confirm the order or set it aside and make such new order as he thinks fit and the order so made shall be entered in the records of the court.

(4) Where an order is not made under paragraph (1), the proper officer shall refer the application to the district judge who shall, if he considers that he has sufficient information to do so without the attendance of the parties, determine the application.

(5) Where the district judge does not determine the application under paragraph (4), he shall direct that a day be fixed for the hearing of the application whereupon the proper officer shall fix such a day and give to the judgment creditor and the debtor not less than 8 days' notice of the day so fixed.

(6) Where an order is made under paragraph (4), the judgment creditor or the debtor may, within 14 days of service of the order on him and giving his reasons, apply on notice for the order to be re-considered; and the proper officer shall fix a day for the hearing of the application and give to the judgment creditor and the debtor not less than 2 days' notice of the day so fixed.

(7) On hearing an application under paragraph (6), the district judge may confirm the order or set it aside and make such new order as he thinks fit and the order so made shall be entered in the records of the court.

(8) If the creditor does not appear at the hearing of the application under paragraph (5) but –

(*a*) the court has received an affidavit of evidence from him, or
(*b*) the creditor requests the court in writing to proceed in his absence,

the court may, notwithstanding anything in Order 21, rule 1, proceed to hear the application and to make an order thereon.

(9) An attachment of earnings order may be made to secure the payment of a judgment debt if the debt is –

(*a*) of not less than £50, or
(*b*) for the amount remaining payable under a judgment for a sum of not less than £50.

Amendments—SI 1991/1126.

Defined terms—"debtor": AEA 1971, s 2(*e*); "judgment creditor": Ord 25, r 1; "proper officer": Ord 1, r 3 (see also Ord 27, r 1(1)).

Scope of provision—This rule gives the procedure when the application is to enforce a judgment debt (usually, in family proceedings, an order for costs). It does not apply in the case of a maintenance order, including a lump sum order (see "**expressions used**" under r 1), as r 7(1)–(8) is replaced by a straightforward provision that the application may be heard by the district judge in chambers (r 17(5)) and r 7(9) has no application.

Procedure—If the debtor files a reply under r 5(2), a senior member of the court staff may (though he need not) make an attachment of earnings order on the information before him without a hearing. Otherwise, the application is referred to the district judge, who similarly may make an attachment of earnings order on the information before him without a hearing. Either the debtor or the creditor may apply on notice to the other for any order so made to be reconsidered by the district judge. On the hearing he may confirm the order or make a different one.

If neither of those procedures is followed, the application itself is listed for hearing before the district judge. In that event, the creditor need not attend if he either files an affidavit of evidence or writes asking the court to proceed in his absence.

Restriction (r 7(9))—An attachment of earnings order cannot be made on a judgment debt unless it is (or was when the judgment or order was made) at least £50.

Form—An attachment of earnings order should be in Form N60.

7A Failure by debtor (Ord 27, r 7A)

(1) If the debtor has failed to comply with rule 5(2) or to make payment to the judgment creditor, the proper officer may issue an order under section 14(1) of the Act of 1971 which shall –

(*a*) be indorsed with or incorporate a notice warning the debtor of the consequences of disobedience to the order,

(*b*) be served on the debtor personally, and

(*c*) direct that any payments made thereafter shall be paid into the court and not direct to the judgment creditor.

(2) Without prejudice to rule 16, if the person served with an order made pursuant to paragraph (1) fails to obey it or to file a statement of his means or to make payment, the proper officer shall issue a notice calling on that person to show good reason why he should not be imprisoned and any such notice shall be served on the debtor personally not less than 5 days before the hearing.

(3) Order 29, rule 1 shall apply, with the necessary modifications and with the substitution of references to the district judge for references to the judge, where a notice is issued under paragraph (2) as it applies where a notice is issued under paragraph (4) of that rule.

(4) In this rule "statement of means" means a statement given under section 14(1) of the Act of 1971.

Amendments—Inserted by SI 1991/1126.

Defined terms—"debtor": AEA 1971, s 2(*e*); "judgment creditor": Ord 25, r 1; "proper officer": Ord 1, r 3 (see also Ord 27, r 1(1)).

"an order under section 14(1)" (r 7A(1))—See Form N61, which specifies the information required by attaching a further print of Form N56 and specifies a period of eight days from service for the debtor to provide it. Failure to comply with such an order is an offence under AEA 1971, s 23(2). If the debtor does comply then (in the case of a judgment debt) the procedure under r 7 applies.

"rule 16" (r 7A(2))—Rule 16 provides the alternative procedure of a summons for an offence under s 23(2).

"notice to show good reason" (r 7A(2))—The notice is contained in Form N63.

"Order 29, rule 1" (r 7A(3))—Order 29, r 1 governs the procedure relating to committal for breach of an order of the court.

Maintenance orders—This rule does apply where the application relates to a maintenance order, but it is perhaps unlikely to be used as a hearing will have been fixed at which the district judge will have wider powers available, in particular the power to order the debtor to attend an adjourned hearing under AEA 1971, s 23(1) and, if he still fails to respond, either to have him arrested and brought to court or to make a suspended or outright committal order (see rr 7B and 8). If Form N61 or Form N63 is used in the case of a maintenance order, it will need some adaptation to fit the case.

7B Suspended committal order (Ord 27, r 7B)

(1) If the debtor fails to attend at an adjourned hearing of an application for an attachment of earnings order and a committal order is made, the judge or district judge may direct that the committal order shall be suspended so long as the debtor attends at the time and place specified in the committal order and paragraphs (2), (4) and (5) of Order 28, rule 7 shall apply, with the necessary modifications, where such a direction is given as they apply where a direction is given under paragraph (1) of that rule.

(2) Where a committal order is suspended under paragraph (1) and the debtor fails to attend at the time and place specified under paragraph (1), a certificate to that effect given by the proper officer shall be sufficient authority for the issue of a warrant of committal.

Amendments—Inserted by SI 1994/2403.

Defined terms—"debtor": AEA 1971, s 2(*e*); "proper officer": Ord 1, r 3 (see also Ord 27, r 1(1)).

8 Failure by debtor – maintenance orders (Ord 27, r 8)

(1) An order made under section 23(1) of the Act of 1971 for the attendance of the debtor at an adjourned hearing of an application for an attachment of earnings order to secure payments under a maintenance order shall –

(*a*) be served on the debtor personally not less than 5 days before the day fixed for the adjourned hearing; and

(*b*) direct that any payments made thereafter shall be paid into the court and not direct to the judgment creditor.

(2) An application by a debtor for the revocation of an order committing him to prison and, if he is already in custody, for his discharge under subsection (7) of the said section 23 shall be made to the judge or district judge ex parte in writing showing the reasons for the debtor's failure to attend the court or his refusal to be sworn or to give evidence, as the case may be, and containing an undertaking by the debtor to attend the court or to be sworn or to give evidence when next ordered or required to do so.

(3) The application shall, if the debtor has already been lodged in prison, be attested by the governor of the prison (or any other officer of the prison not below the rank of principal officer) and in any other case be made on affidavit.

(4) Before dealing with the application the judge or district judge may, if he thinks fit, cause notice to be given to the judgment creditor that the application has been made and of a day and hour when he may attend and be heard.

Amendments—SI 1989/1838; SI 1991/1126; SI 1994/2403.

Defined terms—"debtor": AEA 1971, s 2(*e*); "judgment creditor": Ord 25, r 1; "proper officer": Ord 1, r 3 (see also Ord 27, r 1(1)).

Maintenance orders—The requirements of personal service and five days' notice appear to be mandatory only in the case of a maintenance order. However in those (probably few) cases where an application for an attachment of earnings order to secure a judgment debt is listed for hearing under r 7(5) and in cases where (an attachment of earnings order being already in existence) the debtor is ordered to attend under AEA 1971, s 14(2)(*b*), the same powers under s 23(1) exist. In such cases no doubt the provisions of this paragraph would be applied by analogy.

"adjourned hearing" (r 8(1))—The alternative to a committal order is an order that the debtor be arrested and brought before the court under AEA 1971, s 23(1A). Whether this is a practical course of action will depend on the sitting arrangements at, and the resources available to, the particular court. Hence the paragraph provides the further alternative of committal suspended on the debtor's attendance at a place (presumably the court office) and time specified.

Forms—The form of order to attend adjourned hearing is Form N58; the form of warrant of committal is N59; and the form of order to arrest and bring before the court is Form N112.

9 Costs (Ord 27, r 9)

(1) Where costs are allowed to the judgment creditor on an application for an attachment of earnings order, there may be allowed –

(*a*) a charge of a solicitor for attending the hearing and, if the court so directs, for serving the application;
(*b*) if the court certifies that the case is fit for counsel, a fee to counsel and
(*c*) the court fee on the issue of the application.

(2) For the purposes of paragraph (1)(*a*) a solicitor who has prepared on behalf of the judgment creditor an affidavit or request under rule 7(5) shall be treated as having attended the hearing.

(3) The costs may be fixed and allowed without taxation and the scale shall be determined by the amount payable under the relevant adjudication (or so much of that amount as remains unpaid), including any relevant costs.

Defined terms—"judgment creditor": Ord 25, r 1; "relevant adjudication": AEA 1971, s 2(*d*).

"may be fixed and allowed without taxation" (r 9(3))—Fixed costs are set at £7.50 for each hearing attended (plus the court fee paid) by Ord 38, App B, Pt III, Item 6 in the form in which it was immediately before 26 April 1999. However, the rule is permissive only and the court may award costs summarily assessed or to be determined by detailed assessment (CPR 1998, r 44.7). It will usually take one of these courses in a maintenance order case where the creditor has had to be represented on a hearing in order to secure an attachment of earnings order.

"amount payable" (r 9(3))—In the case of a maintenance order, this means the arrears due (r 17(6)).

10 Contents and service of order (Ord 27, r 10)

(1) An attachment of earnings order shall contain such of the following particulars relating to the debtor as are known to the court, namely –

(*a*) his full name and address,

(*b*) his place of work and
(*c*) the nature of his work and his works number, if any,

and those particulars shall be the prescribed particulars for the purposes of section 6(3) of the Act of 1971.

(2) An attachment of earnings order and any order varying or discharging such an order shall be served on the debtor and on the person to whom the order is directed, and Order 7, rule 1, shall apply with the modification contained in Order 22, rule 1(5), and with the further modification that where the order is directed to a corporation which has requested the court that any communication relating to the debtor or to the class of persons to whom he belongs shall be directed to the corporation at a particular address, service may, if the district judge thinks fit, be effected on the corporation at that address.

(3) Where an attachment of earnings order is made to enforce a judgment or order of the High Court or a magistrates' court, a copy of the attachment of earnings order and of any order discharging it shall be sent by the proper officer of the county court to the proper officer of the High Court or, as the case may be, the clerk of the magistrates' court.

Defined terms—"debtor": AEA 1971, s 2(*e*); "proper officer": Ord 1, r 3 (see also Ord 27, r 1(1)).

Suspended order—The court will sometimes direct that the order be not served on the employer so long as the debtor complies with certain terms as to payment. This practice is not referred to in this Order but is thought to be authorised by CCA 1984, s 71(2) and/or Ord 13, r 1(8). The prescribed forms used are Form N64 and Form N64A.

Service (r 10(2))—The order is served in the same manner as any other order for which no special provision is made (ie by first class post), save that the fact that a solicitor is on record may be ignored and that the court may send the order to some address other than the employer's "residence" if the employer, being a corporation, has so requested (eg to a wages department).

Period of payment—To ease the burden on employers it is usual to express the normal deduction rate and protected earnings rate by reference to the periods for which the debtor is paid, even where instalments under the judgment or order, or payments under the maintenance order, may have been defined in relation to some other period.

Forms—Form N60 is to be used in the case of judgment debts. It contains notice to the parties of their right to object under r 7(2) or (6); the words are deleted where the paragraphs do not apply, if, for example, the application has been heard under r 7(5). Form N65 is used in the case of maintenance orders; the form is appropriate to a periodical maintenance order, but if the "maintenance order" is for a lump sum a hybrid form will need to be prepared.

11 Application to determine whether particular payments are earnings (Ord 27, r 11)

An application to the court under section 16 of the Act of 1971 to determine whether payments to the debtor of a particular class or description are earnings for the purpose of an attachment of earnings order may be made to the district judge in writing and the proper officer shall thereupon fix a date and time for the hearing of the application by the court and give notice thereof to the persons mentioned in the said section 16(2)(*a*), (*b*) and (*c*).

Defined terms—"debtor": AEA 1971, s 2(*e*); "proper officer": Ord 1, r 3 (see also Ord 27, r 1(1)).

Procedure—The normal procedure under Ord 13, r 1 is slightly modified in that no formal notice of the application is required, no particular period of notice of the hearing is specified and the court (rather than the applicant) gives notices of the hearing to the applicant and the other parties.

****

13 Variation and discharge by court of own motion (Ord 27, r 13)

(1) Subject to paragraph (9), the powers conferred by section 9(1) of the Act of 1971 may be exercised by the court of its own motion in the circumstances mentioned in the following paragraphs.

(2) Where it appears to the court that a person served with an attachment of earnings order directed to him has not the debtor in his employment, the court may discharge the order.

(3) Where an attachment of earnings order which has lapsed under section 9(4) of the Act of 1971 is again directed to a person who appears to the court to have the debtor in his employment, the court may make such consequential variations in the order as it thinks fit.

(4) Where, after making an attachment of earnings order, the court makes or is notified of the making of another such order in respect of the same debtor which is not to secure the payment of a judgment debt or payments under an administration order, the court may discharge or vary the first-mentioned order having regard to the priority accorded to the other order by paragraph 8 of Schedule 3 to the Act of 1971.

(5) Where, after making an attachment of earnings order, the court makes an order under section 4(1)(*b*) of the Act of 1971 or makes an administration order, the court may discharge the attachment of earnings order or, if it exercises the power conferred by section 5(3) of the said Act, may vary the order in such manner as it thinks fit.

(6) On making a consolidated attachment of earnings order the court may discharge any earlier attachment of earnings order made to secure the payment of a judgment debt by the same debtor.

(7) Where it appears to the court that a bankruptcy order has been made against a person in respect of whom an attachment of earnings order is in force to secure the payments of a judgment debt, the court may discharge the attachment of earnings order.

(8) Where an attachment of earnings order has been made to secure the payment of a judgment debt and the court grants leave to issue execution for the recovery of the debt, the court may discharge the order.

(9) Before varying or discharging an attachment of earnings order of its own motion under any of the foregoing paragraphs of this rule, the court shall, unless it thinks it unnecessary in the circumstances to do so, give the debtor and the person on whose application the order was made an opportunity of being heard on the question whether the order should be varied or discharged, and for that purpose the proper officer may give them notice of a date, time and place at which the question will be considered.

Amendments—SI 1986/2001.

Defined terms—"administration order": AEA 1971, s 25(1); "consolidated attachment of earnings order": s 17(2); "debtor": s 2(*e*); "judgment debt": s 2(*c*); "proper officer": Ord 1, r 3 (see also Ord 27, r 1(1)).

Priority (r 13(4))—When a priority order is made at a time when a non-priority order is already in existence, the court may discharge or vary the non-priority order. As to the priority of orders, see AEA 1971, Sch 3.

Administration orders (r 13(5))—AEA 1971, s 5(3) enables the court to adopt an existing attachment of earnings order into an administration order.

Maintenance orders—In relation to maintenance orders, this rule has effect as if r 13(5), (6) and (7) were omitted and a new r 13(4) substituted (r 17(10)).

Forms—The notice of discharge is in Form N339.

14 Transfer of attachment order (Ord 27, r 14)

(1) Where the court by which the question of making a consolidated attachment order falls to be considered is not the court by which any attachment of earnings order has been made to secure the payment of a judgment debt by the debtor, the district judge of the last-mentioned court shall, at the request of the district judge of the first-mentioned court, transfer to that court the matter in which the attachment of earnings order was made.

(2) Without prejudice to paragraph (1), if in the opinion of the judge or district judge of any court by which an attachment of earnings order has been made, the matter could more conveniently proceed in some other court, whether by reason of the debtor having become resident in the district of that court or otherwise, he may order the matter to be transferred to that court.

(3) The court to which proceedings arising out of an attachment of earnings order are transferred under this rule shall have the same jurisdiction in relation to the order as if it had been made by that court.

Defined terms—"the debtor": AEA 1971, s 2(*e*); judgment debt": s 2(*c*).

"consolidated attachment order" (r 14(1))—See rr 18 to 22. Such an order may include a judgment debt incurred in family proceedings but not a maintenance order.

Family proceedings—While r 14(1) refers to "the matter in which" the attachment of earnings order was made, it is in practice often applied to the attachment of earnings matter itself so that the cause or matter remains untransferred: see **"the court for the district in which the debtor resides"** under r 3. If there is a question of transferring the cause or matter then it will not in practice be transferred to a non-divorce county court.

15 Exercise of power to obtain statement of earnings etc (Ord 27, r 15)

(1) An order under section 14(1) of the Act of 1971 shall be indorsed with or incorporate a notice warning the person to whom it is directed of the consequences of disobedience to the order and shall be served on him personally.

(2) Order 34, rule 2, shall apply, with the necessary modifications, in relation to any penalty for failure to comply with an order under the said section 14(1) or, subject to the proviso to rule 5(2), any penalty for failure to comply with a requirement mentioned in that rule, as it applies in relation to a fine under section 55 of the County Courts Act 1984.

Amendments—SI 1984/878.

"section 14(1)" (r 15(1))—AEA 1971, s 14(1) gives the court power to order the debtor or the apparent employer to supply information. Non-compliance is an offence under AEA 1971, s 23(2)(*c*).

"the consequences of disobedience" (r 15(1))—A fine of up to £500 or up to level 2 on the standard scale or (in the cases mentioned in AEA 1971, s 23(4)) up to 14 days' imprisonment.

"Order 34, r 2" (r 15(2))—The procedure which applies to disobedience to a witness summons is adopted as regards any penalty not merely a fine. In practice a "notice to show cause" will always be served before imprisonment is ordered and the safeguards set out in Ord 29, r 1 will be observed.

Forms—The form of notice is to be found in Form N61.

16 Offences (Ord 27, r 16)

(1) Where it is alleged that a person has committed any offence mentioned in section 23(2)(*a*), (*b*), (*d*), (*e*) or (*f*) of the Act of 1971 in relation to proceedings in, or to an attachment of earnings order made by, a county court, the district judge shall, unless it is decided to proceed against the alleged offender summarily, issue a summons calling upon him to show cause why he should not be punished for the alleged offence.

The summons shall be served on the alleged offender personally not less than 14 days before the return day.

(2) Order 34, rules 3 and 4, shall apply, with the necessary modifications, to proceedings for an offence under section 23(2) of the Act of 1971 as they apply to proceedings for offences under the County Courts Act 1984.

Amendments—SI 1984/878.

"any offence" (r 16(1))—AEA 1971, s 23(2) gives the exact definitions but the offences may be summarised as follows: employer failing to comply with an attachment of earnings order or variation order (s 23(2)(*a*)); employer failing to tell the court that the debtor is not in, or has left, his employment (s 23(2)(*b*)); debtor failing to tell the court of a change in his employment or new employer, who is aware of the order, failing to report the new employment to the court (s 23(2)(*c*)); giving false information to the court (s 23(2)(*e*), (*f*)).

Form—The form of summons to show cause is Form N62.

17 Maintenance orders (Ord 27, r 17)

(1) The foregoing rules of this Order shall apply in relation to maintenance payments as they apply in relation to a judgment debt, subject to the following paragraphs.

(2) An application for an attachment of earnings order to secure payments under a maintenance order made by a county court shall be made to that county court.

(3) Any application under section 32 of the Matrimonial Causes Act 1973 for leave to enforce the payment of arrears which became due more than 12 months before the application for an attachment of earnings order shall be made in that application.

(3A) Rule 5(1) shall apply as if for the reference to a default summons there were substituted a reference to a fixed date summons and rule 5(2A) shall not apply.

(4) An application by the debtor for an attachment of earnings order to secure payments under a maintenance order may be made on the making of the

PART III

maintenance order or an order varying the maintenance order, and rules 4 and 5 shall not apply.

(5) Rule 7 shall have effect as if for paragraphs (1) to (8) there were substituted the following paragraph –

"(1) An application for an attachment of earnings order may be heard and determined by the district judge, who shall hear the application in chambers.".

(6) Rule 9 shall apply as if for the reference to the amount payable under the relevant adjudication there were substituted a reference to the arrears due under the related maintenance order.

(7) Where an attachment of earnings order made by the High Court designates the proper officer of a county court as the collecting officer, that officer shall, on receipt of a certified copy of the order from the proper officer of the High Court, send to the person to whom the order is directed a notice as to the mode of payment.

(8) Where an attachment of earnings order made by a county court to secure payments under a maintenance order ceases to have effect and –

(*a*) the related maintenance order was made by that court, or
(*b*) the related maintenance order was an order of the High Court and –
  (i) the proper officer of the county court has received notice of the cessation from the proper officer of the High Court, or
  (ii) a committal order has been made in the county court for the enforcement of the related maintenance order,

the proper officer of the county court shall give notice of the cessation to the person to whom the attachment of earnings order was directed.

(9) Where an attachment of earnings order has been made by a county court to secure payments under a maintenance order, notice under section 10(2) of the Act of 1971 to the debtor and to the person to whom the district judge is required to pay sums received under the order shall be in the form provided for that purpose, and if the debtor wishes to request the court to discharge the attachment of earnings order or to vary it otherwise than by making the appropriate variation, he shall apply to the court, within 14 days after the date of the notice, for the relief desired.

(10) Rule 13 shall have effect as if for paragraphs (4) to (7) there were substituted the following paragraph –

"(4) Where it appears to the court by which an attachment of earnings order has been made that the related maintenance order has ceased to have effect, whether by virtue of the terms of the maintenance order or under section 28 of the Matrimonial Causes Act 1973 or otherwise, the court may discharge or vary the attachment of earnings order.".

(11) (*revoked*)

Amendments—SI 1991/1126.

Defined terms—"appropriate variation": AEA 1971, s 10; "debtor": s 2(*e*); "judgment debt": s 2(*c*); "maintenance order": s 2(*a*); "maintenance payments": s 25(1); "proper officer": Ord 1, r 3 (see also Ord 27, r 1(1)); "relevant adjudication": s 2(*d*).

"heard and determined" (r 17(5))—Rule 7(8), which enables the court to proceed in the absence of the applicant, does not apply in the case of a maintenance order. It is necessary to attend and prove the exact and up-to-date amount of the arrears. If the proceedings concern a "qualifying periodical maintenance order" within the meaning of Maintenance Enforcement Act 1991, s 1, the court may make a "means of payment order" under s 1(4)(*a*) of that Act. This might occur where it appears that the debtor is self-employed.

Forms—An attachment of earnings order relating to maintenance is in Form N65; Form N340 is used for notice to pay (High Court attachment of earnings order); and Form N341 for proposals to vary under AEA 1971, s 10(2).

Part II. Consolidated Attachment of Earnings Orders

18 Cases in which consolidated order may be made (Ord 27, r 18)

Subject to the provisions of rules 19 to 21, the court may make a consolidated attachment order where –

(*a*) two or more attachment of earnings orders are in force to secure the payment of judgment debts by the same debtor, or

(*b*) on an application for an attachment of earnings order to secure the payment of a judgment debt, or for a consolidated attachment order to secure the payment of two or more judgment debts, it appears to the court that an attachment of earnings order is already in force to secure the payment of a judgment debt by the same debtor.

Defined terms—"consolidated attachment order": AEA 1971, s 17(2); "debtor": s 2(*e*); "judgment debt": s 2(*c*).

Maintenance orders—Maintenance orders, as defined by AEA 1971, s 2(*a*) and Sch 1 (see **"expressions used"** under r 1), are not "judgment debts" and cannot be included in consolidated attachment of earnings orders.

19 Application for consolidated order (Ord 27, r 19)

(1) An application for a consolidated attachment order may be made –

(*a*) by the debtor in respect of whom the order is sought, or

(*b*) by any person who has obtained or is entitled to apply for an attachment of earnings order to secure the payments of a judgment debt by that debtor.

(2) An application under paragraph (1) may be made in the proceedings in which any attachment of earnings order (other than a priority order) is in force and rules 3, 4 and 5 of this Order shall not apply.

(3) Where the judgment which it is sought to enforce was not given by the court which made the attachment of earnings order, the judgment shall be automatically transferred to the court which made the attachment of earnings order.

(3A) An application under paragraph (1)(*b*) shall certify the amount of money remaining due under the judgment or order and that the whole or part of any instalment due remains unpaid.

(3B) Where an application for a consolidated attachment of earnings order is made, the proper officer shall –

(*a*) notify any party who may be affected by the applications of its terms; and

(*b*) require him to notify the court in writing, within 14 days of service of notification upon him, giving his reasons for any objection he may have to the granting of the application.

(3C) If notice of any objection is not given within the time stated, the proper officer shall make a consolidated attachment of earnings order.

(3D) If any party objects to the making of a consolidated attachment of earnings order, the proper officer shall refer to the application to the district judge who may grant the application after considering the objection made and the reasons given.

(3E) In the foregoing paragraphs of this rule, a party affected by the application means –

(*a*) where the application is made by the debtor, the creditor in the proceedings in which the application is made and any other creditor who has obtained an attachment of earnings order which is in force to secure the payment of a judgment debt by the debtor;

(*b*) where the application is made by the judgment creditor, the debtor and every person who, to the knowledge of the applicant, has obtained an attachment of earnings order which is in force to secure the payment of a judgment debt by the debtor.

(4) A person to whom two or more attachment of earnings orders are directed to secure the payment of judgment debts by the same debtor may request the court in writing to make a consolidated attachment order to secure the payment of those debts, and on receipt of such a request paragraphs (3B) to (3E) shall apply, with the necessary modifications, as if the request were an application by the judgment creditor.

Amendments—SI 1991/1126.

Defined terms—"consolidated attachment order": AEA 1971, s 17(2); "debtor": s 2(*e*); "judgment debt": s 2(*c*); "proper officer": Ord 1, r 3 (see also Ord 27, r 1(1)).

Maintenance orders—See under r 18.

20 Making of consolidated order by court of its own motion (Ord 27, r 20)

Where an application is made for an attachment of earnings order to secure the payment of a judgment debt by a debtor in respect of whom an attachment of earnings order is already in force to secure the payment of another judgment debt and no application is made for a consolidated attachment order, the proper officer may make such an order of his own motion after giving all persons concerned an opportunity of submitting written objections.

Amendments—SI 1991/1126; SI 1991/1328.

Defined terms—"consolidated attachment order": AEA 1971, s 17(2); "debtor": s 2(*e*); "judgment debt": s 2(*c*); "proper officer": Ord 1, r 3 (see also Ord 27, r 1(1)).

Maintenance orders—See under r 18.

21 Extension of consolidated order (Ord 27, r 21)

(1) Where a consolidated attachment order is in force to secure the payment of two or more judgment debts, any creditor to whom another judgment debt is owed by the same judgment debtor may apply to the court by which the order was made for it to be extended so as to secure the payment of that debt as well as the first-mentioned debts and, if the application is granted, the court may either vary the order accordingly or may discharge it and make a new consolidated attachment order to secure payment of all the aforesaid judgment debts.

(2) An application under this rule shall be treated for the purposes of rules 19 and 20 as an application for a consolidated attachment order.

Defined terms—"consolidated attachment order": AEA 1971, s 17(2); "judgment debt": s 2(*c*).

Maintenance orders—See under r 18.

22 Payments under consolidated order (Ord 27, r 22)

Instead of complying with section 13 of the Act of 1971, a proper officer who receives payments made to him in compliance with a consolidated attachment order shall, after deducting such court fees, if any, in respect of proceedings for or arising out of the order as are deductible from those payments, deal with the sums paid as he would if they had been paid by the debtor to satisfy the relevant adjudications in proportion to the amounts payable thereunder, and for that purpose dividends may from time to time be declared and distributed among the creditors entitled thereto.

Defined terms—"consolidated attachment order": AEA 1971, s 17(2); "debtor": s 2(*e*); "proper officer": Ord 1, r 3 (see also Ord 27, r 1(1)).

Maintenance orders—See under r 18.

ORDER 28
JUDGMENT SUMMONSES

Effect of FPR 1991—This Order is extensively modified, in relation to family proceedings, by FPR 1991, rr 7.4 and 7.6. Only the surviving provisions relevant to family proceedings are reproduced.

****

3 Time for service (Ord 28, r 3)

(1) A judgment summons shall be served not less than 14 days before the day fixed for the hearing.
(2) ...

(3) Order 7, rules 19 and 20, shall apply, with the necessary modifications, to a judgment summons as they apply to a fixed date summons.

Defined terms—"judgment summons": FPR 1991, r 7.4(1).

"14 days" (r 3(1))—There is a conflict between this requirement and FPR 1991, r 7.4(5) which specifies a period of 10 days. Since this rule is expressly applied by FPR 1991, r 7.4(6) (and this paragraph of it is not disapplied), the safer course is to allow the longer period.

"Order 7, rules 19 and 20" (r 3(3))—Rule 19 (with the omission of r 19(2) in the case of family proceedings) enables successive judgment summonses to be issued on the strength of the original request, as a continuation of the original judgment summons, if the debtor is not served in time. Rule 20 limits the time for service to four months from the issue of the (original) judgment summons but enables the court to extend the period.

4 Enforcement of debtor's attendance (Ord 28, r 4)

(1) Order 27, rules 7B and 8, shall apply, with the necessary modifications, to an order made under section 110(1) of the Act for the attendance of the debtor at an

adjourned hearing of a judgment summons as they apply to an order made under section 23(1) of the Attachment of Earnings Act 1971 for the attendance of the debtor at an adjourned hearing of an application for an attachment of earnings order.

(2) At the time of service of the order there shall be paid or tendered to the debtor a sum reasonably sufficient to cover his expenses in travelling to and from the court, unless such a sum was paid to him at the time of service of the judgment summons.

Amendments—SI 1984/878; SI 1994/2403.

Defined terms—"debtor", "judgment summons": FPR 1991, r 7.4(1).

Order for attendance (r 4(1))—The consequence of failure to attend on the original hearing is not that the court may commit the debtor but that, pursuant to CCA 1984, s 110(1), it may order his attendance at an adjourned hearing. Failure to comply with that order is punishable by committal for up to 14 days (s 110(2)). There is also a power to order the debtor to be arrested and brought before the court (s 110(3)). Conduct money must have been paid or tendered (s 110(4)) and there is power to revoke or discharge the committal (s 110(5)). There is a close parallel with the procedure on failure to attend an attachment of earnings application, but in the case of a judgment summons the court's powers are not exercisable by the district judge. In family proceedings, both the judgment summons (FPR 1991, r 7.4(5)) and the order to attend (FPR 1991, r 7.4(7A)(*b*)) must be served personally. Now that it has been held (in *Mubarak v Mubarak* [2001] 1 FLR 698, CA) that the debtor cannot be compelled to give evidence, there may be cases where the creditor sees little value in seeking an order compelling his attendance.

"paid or tendered" (r 4(2))—In family proceedings, the sum will have been paid or tendered when the judgment summons was served (FPR 1991, r 7.4(5)). Note that if it was merely tendered then, it must be paid or tendered again when the order is served.

Forms—The order to attend is in Form N69; the form of committal for failure to attend is Form N70; the order revoking such committal is Form N71; and the order for arrest is Form N112.

****

7 Suspension of committal order (Ord 28, r 7)

(1) If on the hearing of a judgment summons a committal order is made, the judge may direct execution of the order to be suspended to enable the debtor to pay the amount due.

(2) A note of any direction given under paragraph (1) shall be entered in the records of the court and notice of the suspended committal order shall be sent to the debtor.

(3) ...

(4) Where execution of a committal order is suspended under paragraph (1) and the debtor subsequently desires to apply for a further suspension, the debtor shall attend at or write to the court office and apply for the suspension he desires, stating the reasons for his inability to comply with the terms of the original suspension, and the proper officer shall fix a day for the hearing of the application by the judge and give at least 3 days' notice thereof to the judgment creditor and the debtor.

(5) The district judge may suspend execution of the committal order pending the hearing of an application under paragraph (4).

Defined terms—"debtor", "judgment creditor", "judgment summons": FPR 1991, r 7.4(1); "proper officer": Ord 1, r 3.

"to enable the debtor to pay" (r 7(1))—This provision is in effect superseded by FPR 1991, r 7.4(10), at least in the case of arrears under a periodical payments order, as FPR 1991, r 7.4(10) expressly authorises terms requiring the debtor to pay the amount due "in addition to any sums accruing due under the original order". Payments are then attributed first to those sums and secondly to that amount (FPR 1991, r 7.4(12)(*a*)).

Forms—The notice of suspended committal order is in Form N72.

8 New order on judgment summons (Ord 28, r 8)

(1) Where on the hearing of a judgment summons, the judge makes a new order for payment of the amount of the judgment debt remaining unpaid, there shall be included in the amount payable under the order for the purpose of any enforcement proceedings, otherwise than by judgment summons, any amount in respect of which a committal order has already been made and the debtor imprisoned.

(2) No judgment summons under the new order shall include any amount in respect of which the debtor was imprisoned before the new order was made, and any amount subsequently paid shall be appropriated in the first instance to the amount due under the new order.

Defined terms—"debtor", "judgment summons": FPR 1991, r 7.4(1).

New order—The making of a simple instalment order is authorised by Debtors Act 1869, s 5 itself and by FPR 1991, r 7.4(9), which presumably limits the exercise of the statutory power to the cases there mentioned.

No judgment summons under the new order—Debtors Act 1869, s 5 permits a term of imprisonment in respect of any debt or instalment under any judgment or order, and this means one term only (*Evans v Wills* (1876) 1 CPD 229). This rule prohibits a second judgment summons for the same debt or instalment notwithstanding that it has become due under a different order, namely the new order.

Forms—A new order on a judgment summons is in Form N73.

9 Notification of order on judgment of High Court (Ord 28, r 9)

(1) Notice of the result of the hearing of a judgment summons on a judgment or order of the High Court shall be sent by the proper officer of the county court to the proper officer of the High Court.

(2) ...

Defined terms—"judgment summons": FPR 1991, r 7.4(1); "proper officer": Ord 1, r 3.

Forms—The form of notice to the High Court is Form N343.

Effect of FPR 1991—The rule applies in the case of a judgment or order not only of the High Court but also of any other court (FPR 1991, r 7.6(2)).

10 Costs on judgment summons (Ord 28, r 10)

(1) No costs shall be allowed to the judgment creditor on the hearing of a judgment summons unless –

- (*a*) a committal order is made, or
- (*b*) the sum in respect of which the judgment summons was issued is paid before the hearing.

(2) Where costs are allowed to the judgment creditor,

(*a*) there may be allowed–
   (i) a charge of the judgment creditor's solicitor for attending the hearing and, if the judge so directs, for serving the judgment summons;
   (ii) a fee to counsel if the court certifies that the case is fit for counsel;
   (iii) any travelling expenses paid to the debtor, and
   (iv) the court fee on the issue of the judgment summons;
(*b*) the costs may be fixed and allowed without taxation; and
(*c*) the scale shall be determined by the sum in respect of which the judgment summons was issued.

(3) ...

Amendments—SI 1982/1794.

Defined terms—"debtor", "judgment creditor", "judgment summons": FPR 1991, r 7.4(1).

"No costs shall be allowed ... unless" (r 10(1))—Not only is the creditor deprived of costs if the debt is not paid and no committal order is made, he is also at risk as to the debtor's costs if he fails to prove means and refusal or neglect. The request for the judgment summons (Form M16) includes an acknowledgement of this risk.

"may be fixed and allowed without taxation" (r 10(2)(*b*))—Fixed costs are set at £7.50 for each hearing attended (plus the court fee paid) by Ord 38, App B, Pt III, Item 6 in the form in which it was immediately before 26 April 1999. However, the rule is permissive only and the court may award costs summarily assessed or to be determined by detailed assessment (CPR 1998, r 44.7). It will usually take one of these courses in anything but the simplest case.

Amount of costs—See App C, Pt III, Item 6.

11 Issue of warrant of committal (Ord 28, r 11)

(1) A judgment creditor desiring a warrant to be issued pursuant to a committal order shall file a request in that behalf.

(2) Where two or more debtors are to be committed in respect of the same judgment or order, a separate warrant of committal shall be issued for each of them.

(3) Where a warrant of committal is sent to a foreign court for execution, the proper officer of that court shall indorse on it a notice as to the effect of section 122(3) of the Act addressed to the governor of the prison of that court.

Amendments—SI 1984/878.

Defined terms—"debtor": FPR 1991, r 7.4(1); "foreign court": Ord 1, r 3; "judgment creditor": FPR 1991, r 7.4(1); "proper officer": Ord 1, r 3.

Affidavit of default—In the case of a suspended committal order, an affidavit of default must be filed by the creditor so that the order may be issued before the warrant is applied for (FPR 1991, r 7.4(12)(*c*)).

Nature of warrant—The warrant requires the district judge to take the body of the person against whom it is issued, the police to assist the district judge and the governor of the prison to receive and keep the person until discharged (CCA 1984, s 119).

Forms—The request for warrant is in Form N344; the warrant in Form N74; and the indorsement to a foreign court is in Form N75.

12 Notification to foreign court of part payment before debtor lodged in prison (Ord 28, r 12)

Where, after a warrant of committal has been sent to a foreign court for execution but before the debtor is lodged in prison, the home court is notified that an amount which is less than the sum on payment of which the debtor is to be discharged has been paid, the proper officer of the home court shall send notice of the payment to the proper officer of the foreign court.

Amendments—SI 1989/1838.

Defined terms—"debtor": FPR 1991, r 7.4(1); "foreign court", "proper officer": Ord 1, r 3.

Forms—The form of notification is Form N335.

13 Payment after debtor lodged in prison (Ord 28, r 13)

(1) Where, after the debtor has been lodged in prison under a warrant of committal, payment is made of the sum on payment of which the debtor is to be discharged, then –

(*a*) if the payment is made to the proper officer of the court responsible for the execution of the warrant, he shall make and sign a certificate of payment and send it by post or otherwise to the gaoler;
(*b*) if the payment is made to the proper officer of the court which issued the warrant of committal after the warrant has been sent to a foreign court for execution, the proper officer of the home court shall send notice of the payment to the proper officer of the foreign court, who shall make and sign a certificate of payment and send it by post or otherwise to the gaoler;
(*c*) if the payment is made to the gaoler, he shall sign a certificate of payment and send the amount to the proper officer of the court which made the committal order.

(2) Where, after the debtor has been lodged in prison under a warrant of committal, payment is made of an amount less than the sum on payment of which the debtor is to be discharged, then, subject to paragraph (3), paragraph (1)(*a*) and (*b*) shall apply with the substitution of references to a notice of payment for the references to a certificate of payment and paragraph (1)(*c*) shall apply with the omission of the requirement to make and sign a certificate of payment.

(3) Where, after the making of a payment to which paragraph (2) relates, the balance of the sum on payment of which the debtor is to be discharged is paid, paragraph (1) shall apply without the modifications mentioned in paragraph (2).

Defined terms—"debtor": FPR 1991, r 7.4(1); "foreign court", "proper officer": Ord 1, r 3.

Discharge—The purpose of this seemingly cumbersome and obvious rule is to provide the mechanism for discharge on payment which is required by Debtors Act 1869, s 5.

Forms—The certificate of payment is Form N345.

14 Discharge of debtor otherwise than on payment (Ord 28, r 14)

(1) Where the judgment creditor lodges with the district judge a request that a debtor lodged in prison under a warrant of committal may be discharged from custody, the district judge shall make an order for the discharge of the debtor in respect of the warrant of committal and the proper officer shall send the gaoler a certificate of discharge.

(2) Where a debtor who has been lodged in prison under a warrant of committal desires to apply for his discharge under section 121 of the Act, the application shall be made to the judge ex parte in writing showing the reasons why the debtor alleges that he is unable to pay the sum in respect of which he has been committed and ought to be discharged and stating any offer which he desires to make as to the terms on which his discharge is to be ordered, and Order 27, rule 8(3) and (4), shall apply, with the necessary modifications, as it applies to an application by a debtor for his discharge from custody under section 23(7) of the Attachment of Earnings Act 1971.

(3) If in a case to which paragraph (2) relates the debtor is ordered to be discharged from custody on terms which include liability to re-arrest if the terms are not complied with, the judge may, on the application of the judgment creditor if the terms are not complied with, order the debtor to be re-arrested and imprisoned for such part of the term of imprisonment as remained unserved at the time of discharge.

(4) Where an order is made under paragraph (3), a duplicate warrant of committal shall be issued, indorsed with a certificate signed by the proper officer as to the order of the judge.

Amendments—SI 1984/878.

Defined terms—"debtor", "judgment creditor": FPR 1991, r 7.4(1); "proper officer": Ord 1, r 3.

"section 121 of the Act"—CCA 1984, s 121 provides that while a committal order may be made if it is proved that the debtor *has had* the means to pay, the judge may order his discharge if satisfied that he is now unable to pay (and that he ought to be discharged).

Forms—The form of creditor's request to discharge is Form N346; the form of certificate of discharge on the creditor's request is Form N347; the certificate of discharge following the debtor's application is Form N348; and the form of indorsement on the duplicate committal warrant is Form N76.

ORDER 29
COMMITTAL FOR BREACH OF ORDER OR UNDERTAKING

* Set out in Civil Procedure Rules 1998, Sch 2.

ORDER 30
GARNISHEE PROCEEDINGS

1 Attachment of debt due to judgment debtor (Ord 30, r 1)

(1) Where a person (in this Order called "the judgment creditor") has obtained in a county court a judgment or order for the payment of a sum of money amounting in value to at least £50 by some other person ("the judgment debtor") and any person within England and Wales ("the garnishee") is indebted to the judgment debtor, that court may, subject to the provisions of this Order and of any enactment, order the garnishee to pay the judgment creditor the amount of any debt due or accruing due from the garnishee to the judgment debtor or so much thereof as is sufficient to satisfy the judgment or order against the judgment debtor and the costs of the garnishee proceedings.

(2) An order under this rule shall in the first instance be an order to show cause, specifying the place and time for the further consideration of the matter (in this

Order called "the return day") and in the meantime attaching the debt due or accruing due from the garnishee or so much thereof as is sufficient for the purpose aforesaid.

(3) Among the conditions mentioned in section 108(3) of the Act (which enables any sum standing to the credit of a person in certain types of account to be attached notwithstanding that certain conditions applicable to the account in question have not been satisfied) there shall be included any condition that a receipt for money deposited in the account must be produced before any money is withdrawn.

(4) (*revoked*)

(5) An order under this rule shall not require a payment which would reduce below £1 the amount standing in the name of the judgment debtor in an account with a building society or a credit union.

Amendments—SI 1982/436; SI 1984/878; SI 1991/1328; SI 1996/3218.

"obtained in a county court" (r 1(1))—In family proceedings, no mechanism currently exists under which a High Court judgment may be enforced in a county court under this rule.

"is indebted" (r 1(1))—There must be in existence something recognised in law as a debt, notwithstanding that it may be payable on a future date (*O'Driscoll v Manchester Insurance Committee* [1915] 3 KB 499). Thus a cause of action in damages is not attachable (*Johnson v Diamond* (1855) 11 Exch 73), until judgment is pronounced (*Holtby v Hodgson* (1889) 24 QBD 103). The distinction, often subtle, between an expectation of payment which is a debt and one which is not is best understood by consideration of the very many cases on the point referred to in *Civil Procedure* in the note to RSC Ord 49, r 1. Once a garnishee order is made, a subsequent cross-claim by the garnishee against the judgment debtor does not reduce the garnishee's liability under the order (*Wolfe v Marshall and Harding (Garnishee)*, 25 March 1997, CA).

"that court may ... order" (r 1(1))—The court has a discretion whether to make the order nisi, and may decline to do so where, for example, the judgment debt is so small that the costs would be disproportionately burdensome (see **Court's discretion to make order** under r 7).

"in the first instance" (r 1(2))—There is but one garnishee order, which initially is provisional but is then confirmed (or discharged) on the return day. If the garnishee was not indebted when the order nisi was served on him, it will not avail the creditor on the return day if a debt has since come into existence.

"conditions mentioned in section 108(3)" (r 1(3))—If a liability is conditional then there may be no debt if the condition is not satisfied. In the case of balances held for the debtor by banks, building societies and the like this difficulty is removed by County Courts Act 1984, s 108, which provides that requirements as to the giving of notice, personal application and the production of a pass-book are to be disregarded; r 1(3) effectively extends the effect of s 108.

The Crown—This procedure is not available against the Crown as garnishee. An equivalent procedure is provided by the Crown Proceedings Act 1947, s 27 and CCR Ord 42, r 14. This restriction also applies in respect of the National Savings Bank. Although Supreme Court Act 1981, s 139(2) enables the Lord Chancellor to make an order removing the restriction in relation to inter alia that bank, no such order has been made.

2 Application for order (Ord 30, r 2)

An application for an order under rule 1 may be made ex parte by filing an affidavit –

(*a*) stating the name and last known address of the judgment debtor;

(*b*) identifying the judgment or order to be enforced and stating the amount of such judgment or order;

(*c*) stating that, to the best of the information or belief of the deponent, the garnishee (giving his name and address) is indebted to the judgment debtor;

(*d*) where the garnishee is a deposit-taking institution having more than one place of business, giving the name and address of the branch at which the judgment debtor's account is believed to be held and the number of that account or, if it be the case, that all or part of this information is unknown to the deponent; and

(*e*) certifying the amount of money remaining due under the judgment or order and that the whole or part of any instalment due remains unpaid.

Amendments—SI 1982/436; SI 1989/1838.

Defined terms—"deposit-taking institution": County Courts Act 1984, s 147; "garnishee", "judgment debtor": r 1.

"certifying the amount ... remaining due" (r 2(*e*))—The judgment debt is not "due" until the date by which it is to be paid. A garnishee order is analogous to execution against goods and will not be made where such execution would not issue (*White, Son & Pill v Stennings* [1911] 2 KB 418).

Forms—Practice form N349 is to be used but will need minor adaptation if the judgment or order to be enforced is a periodical payments order.

3 Preparation, service and effect of order to show cause (Ord 30, r 3)

(1) An order under rule 1 to show cause shall be drawn up by the proper officer with sufficient copies for service under this rule.

(2) Unless otherwise directed, a copy of the order shall be served –

(*a*) on the garnishee in the same manner as a fixed date summons at least 15 days before the return day, and

(*b*) on the judgment debtor in accordance with Order 7, rule 1, at least 7 days after a copy has been served on the garnishee and at least 7 days before the return day,

and as from such service on the garnishee the order shall bind in his hands any debt due or accruing due from the garnishee to the judgment debtor, or so much thereof as is sufficient to satisfy the judgment or order obtained by the judgment creditor against the judgment debtor, and the costs entered on the order to show cause.

Amendments—SI 1982/436.

Defined terms—"garnishee", "judgment creditor", "judgment debtor": r 1; "proper officer": Ord 1, r 3; "return day": r 1.

"as a fixed date summons" (r 3(2)(*a*))—The rules which, before 26 April 1999, provided for service of a fixed date summons (Ord 7, rr 10–20) allowed it to be effected in the case of a body corporate at the relevant trading address (Ord 7, r 14(2)). It remains the case that, as to a deposit-taking institution, only the branch identified in the affidavit need be served. In the case of a partnership, where there is a possibility that a partner may be outside England and Wales, it is safer not to rely on postal service by the court – see r 14.

Effect of order nisi—The garnishee's debt to the debtor is not transferred to the judgment creditor by virtue of the order but an equitable charge is created so that (to the extent stated in the order nisi) a garnishee who has been served with the order and makes payment otherwise than to the judgment creditor risks having to pay twice (*Galbraith v Grimshaw & Baxter* [1910] AC 508). The judgment creditor can be in no better position against the garnishee than was the judgment debtor (*Levene v Maton* (1907) 51 SJ 532). If, for example, the judgment debtor assigned the debt to a third party before the order nisi was made there will be no debt due to him to which the order nisi may attach, even where the order was served before the garnishee had notice of the assignment (*Holt v Heatherfield* [1942] 2 KB 1). If the garnishee is aware that a third party claims the debt, he must so inform the court; otherwise, the fact that he paid the judgment creditor under a garnishee order will not provide a defence to that person's claim (*The Leader* (1868) LR 2 A&E 314) (see also **"question at issue"** under r 9). The garnishee is not protected if he pays the judgment creditor upon receipt of the order nisi but before it is made absolute (*Re Webster* [1907] 1 KB 623).

Forms—The form of order nisi is Form N84.

****

5 Notice by deposit-taking institution denying indebtedness (Ord 30, r 5)

Where the garnishee being a deposit-taking institution alleges that it does not hold any money to the credit of the judgment debtor, the garnishee may, at any time before the return day, give notice to that effect to the proper officer and to the judgment creditor and thereupon, subject to rule 8, the proceedings against the garnishee shall be stayed.

Amendments—SI 1982/436.

Defined terms—"deposit-taking institution": County Courts Act 1984, s 147; "garnishee", "judgment creditor", "judgment debtor": r 1; "proper officer": Ord 1, r 3; "return day": r 1.

Scope of provision—This rule effectively removes the need for a deposit-taking institution to attend on the return day if it writes to the court and the creditor stating that no balance is held for the debtor.

"subject to rule 8"—Where the deposit-taking institution gives notice under this rule, the return day is not vacated and the creditor may then dispute the deposit-taking institution's denial, whereupon directions will be given.

****

7 Order where no notice given etc (Ord 30, r 7)

(1) Where the garnishee –

(*a*) does not give notice under rule 5, and

(*b*) does not on the return day appear or dispute the debt due or claimed to be due from him to the judgment debtor,

then, if the judgment debtor does not appear or show cause to the contrary, the court may, if it thinks fit, make an order absolute under rule 1 against the garnishee.

(2) An order absolute under rule 1 may be enforced in the same manner as any other order for the payment of money.

Amendments—SI 1989/1838.

Defined terms—"garnishee", "judgment debtor", "return day": r 1.

Court's discretion to make order (r 7(1))—There is a general discretion whether to make the order. Relevant considerations will include the size of the judgment debt and the existence of any instalment order in respect of it, the size of the debt due from the garnishee and the existence of any instalment order or agreement in respect of it, and the burden of costs resulting from an order. The interests of any other creditors of the judgment debtor are also material (*Roberts Petroleum Ltd v Bernard Kenny Ltd* [1983] 2 AC 192, [1983] 2 WLR 305). If there is doubt whether the judgment debtor is solvent the court may order the garnishee to pay the money into court pending its decision (*George Lee & Sons (Builders) Ltd v Olink* [1972] 1 WLR 214, [1972] 1 All ER 359). If the proceedings concern a "qualifying periodical maintenance order" within the meaning of Maintenance Enforcement Act 1991, s 1 then the court may of its own motion make a "means of payment order" under s 1(4)(*a*) of that Act or an attachment of earnings order by virtue of s 1(4)(*b*).

Forms—The order absolute is Form N85.

8 Directions where dispute as to notice under rule 5 (Ord 30, r 8)

Where the garnishee in a notice given under rule 5 makes an allegation which the judgment creditor disputes, the court shall on the return day give directions for the determination of the question at issue.

Amendments—SI 1989/1838.

Defined terms—"garnishee", "judgment creditor", "return day": r 1.

9 Determination of liability in other cases (Ord 30, r 9)

Where in a case in which no notice has been given under rule 5 the garnishee on the return day disputes liability to pay the debt due or claimed to be due from him to the judgment debtor, the court may summarily determine the question at issue or order that any question necessary for determining the liability of the garnishee be tried in any manner in which any question or issue in an action may be tried.

Amendments—SI 1989/1838.

Defined terms—"garnishee", "judgment debtor", "return day": r 1.

"question at issue"—Primarily, the issue is between the judgment creditor and the garnishee, and so the debtor is not a party to it. However, if there is a question whether a third party is interested in or entitled to the fund, that third party may be joined into the proceedings (RSC Ord 49, r 6, applied by County Courts Act 1984, s 76). If the judgment creditor prefers not to contest the issue raised, he may of course abandon his application, but he will thereupon be liable in costs (*Wintle v Williams* (1858) 3 H&N 288).

10 Transfer of proceedings (Ord 30, r 10)

A garnishee who does not reside or carry on business within the district of the court in which the garnishee proceedings have been commenced and who desires to dispute liability for the debt due or claimed to be due from him to the judgment debtor may apply ex parte in writing to that court for an order transferring the action in which the judgment or order sought to be enforced was obtained to the court for the district in which the garnishee resides or carries on business, and the court applied to may, if it thinks fit, grant the application after considering any representations which it may give the judgment creditor and the judgment debtor an opportunity of making.

Defined terms—"garnishee", "judgment creditor", "judgment debtor": r 1.

"the action in which the judgment ... was obtained"—The rule authorises transfer of the action, not merely the garnishee proceedings. In family proceedings it will often be inconvenient to transfer the cause or matter under this rule. An alternative may be to direct that the trial take place at the location best suited to the parties' convenience.

11 Discharge of garnishee (Ord 30, r 11)

Any payment made by a garnishee in compliance with an order absolute in garnishee proceedings, and any execution levied against him in pursuance of such an order, shall be a valid discharge of his liability to the judgment debtor to the extent of the amount paid or levied (otherwise than in respect of any costs ordered to be paid by the garnishee personally), notwithstanding that the garnishee proceedings are subsequently set aside or the judgment or order from which they arose is reversed.

Amendments—SI 1989/1838.

Defined terms—"garnishee", "judgment debtor": r 1.

Scope of provision—This rule provides that to the extent that the garnishee has made payment under the order absolute (not the order nisi), he is discharged from his former liability to the judgment debtor. Where the garnishee has been ordered to bear costs personally, payments against that liability do not of course have this effect.

12 Money in court (Ord 30, r 12)

(1) Where money is standing to the credit of the judgment debtor in any county court, the judgment creditor shall not be entitled to take garnishee proceedings in respect of the money but may apply to the court on notice for an order that the money or so much thereof as is sufficient to satisfy the judgment or order sought to be enforced and the costs of the application be paid to the judgment creditor.

(2) On receipt of notice of an application under paragraph (1) the proper officer shall retain the money in court until the application has been determined.

(3) The court hearing an application under paragraph (1) may make such order with respect to the money in court as it thinks just.

Amendments—SI 1982/1140.

Defined terms—"judgment creditor", "judgment debtor": r 1.

13 Costs of judgment creditor (Ord 30, r 13)

Any costs allowed to the judgment creditor on an application for an order under rule 1 or 12 which in the former case are not ordered to be paid by the garnishee personally shall, unless the court otherwise directs, be retained by the judgment creditor out of the money recovered by him under the order in priority to the amount due under the judgment or order obtained by him against the judgment debtor.

Defined terms—"garnishee", "judgment creditor", "judgment debtor": r 1.

Scope of provision—This rule provides that the judgment debt is reduced by only the net fruits of the garnishee proceedings, save that the risk of the garnishee not paying costs which he has been ordered to pay personally is borne by the creditor not the debtor.

Amount of costs—Ord 38, r 18 and App B, Pt III, Item 7 in the form in which they were immediately before 26 April 1999 provide for fixed costs of £41.75 (or, if the amount recovered is less than £70, one half of the amount recovered), together with the court fee; unless the court orders otherwise – ie by assessing summarily or ordering detailed assessment. (The reference in

App B, Pt I, para 1(*b*) to a sum to be shown on the order nisi for the purpose only of Ord 30, r 4 should be ignored, that rule having been revoked.)

Garnishee's expenses—County Courts Act 1984, s 109 authorises a deposit-taking institution to deduct from the account a sum (currently £55) in respect of its expenses, even if the amount recovered under the order is thereby reduced.

14 Attachment of debt owed by firm (Ord 30, r 14)

(1) An order may be made under rule 1 in relation to a debt due or accruing due from a firm carrying on business within England and Wales, notwithstanding that one or more members of the firm may be resident out of England and Wales.

(2) An order to show cause under rule 1 relating to such a debt shall be served on a member of the firm within England and Wales or on some other person having the control or management of the partnership business.

Scope of provision—A garnishee order cannot generally be made against a garnishee who is out of the jurisdiction (r 1(1)). This rule creates an exception in the case of a firm one or more of whose partners are out of the jurisdiction, provided that the firm carries on business within the jurisdiction.

Service—The order nisi must not only be served within the jurisdiction, but it must also be served on a partner or other person having control or management of the business. This differs from the general case, where the order nisi may be served in the same manner as a fixed date summons (r 3(2)(*a*)), which would include posting by the court to the address stated in the application (Ord 7, r 13(1)(*b*)).

15 Powers of district judge (Ord 30, r 15)

The powers conferred on the court by any provision of this Order may be exercised by the judge or district judge.

ORDER 31
CHARGING ORDERS

1 Application for charging order (Ord 31, r 1)

(1) An application to a county court for a charging order under section 1 of the Charging Orders Act 1979 may be made –

(*a*) if the order is sought in respect of a fund in court, to the court where the money is lodged;

(*b*) subject to (*a*), if the judgment or order sought to be enforced is that of a county court, to the court in which the judgment or order was obtained or, if the action or matter has been transferred to another court under Order 16, rule 1(*d*) or (*e*), or Order 25, rule 2, the court to which it has been transferred;

(*c*) subject to (*a*) and (*b*), to the court for the district in which the debtor resides or carries on business or, if there is no such district, to the court for the district in which the judgment creditor resides or carries on business.

(1A) ...

(2) The application may be made ex parte by filing an affidavit –

(*a*) stating the name and address of the debtor and, if known, of every creditor of his whom the applicant can identify;

(*aa*) certifying the amount of money remaining due under the judgment or order and that the whole or part of any instalment due remains unpaid;

(*b*) identifying the subject matter of the intended charge;

(*c*) either verifying the debtor's beneficial ownership of the asset to be charged or, where the asset is held by one or more trustees (including where the asset is land which is jointly owned) and the applicant relies on paragraph (*b*) of section 2(1) of the said Act of 1979, stating on which of the three grounds appearing in that paragraph the application is based and verifying the material facts;

(*d*) stating, in the case of securities other than securities in court, the name and address of the person or body to be served for the purpose of protecting the intended charge;

(*e*) stating, where the subject matter is an interest under a trust, or held by a trustee, the names and addresses of such trustees and beneficiaries as are known to the applicant.

Where the judgment or order to be enforced is a judgment or order of the High Court or a judgment, order, decree or award of a court or arbitrator which is or has become enforceable as if it were a judgment or order of the High Court, the applicant shall file with his affidavit the documents mentioned in Order 25, rule 11(*a*) and (*c*), and the affidavit shall verify the amount unpaid at the date of the application.

(3) Subject to paragraph (1), an application may be made for a single charging order in respect of more than one judgment or order against a debtor.

(4) Upon the filing of the affidavit mentioned in paragraph (2), the application shall be entered in the records of the court, and if, in the opinion of the district judge, a sufficient case for such an order is made in the affidavit, the district judge shall make a charging order nisi fixing a day for the further consideration of the matter by the court.

(5) A copy of the order shall be sent by the proper officer to the judgment creditor and, where funds in court are to be charged, shall be served by the proper officer on the Accountant-General at the Court Funds Office.

(6) Copies of the order and of the affidavit shall be served by the judgment creditor on –

(*a*) the debtor,

(*b*) the other creditors named in the affidavit (unless the district judge otherwise directs), and

(*c*) where a trust is involved, on any trustee holding the asset to be charged, where the applicant relies on paragraph (*b*) of section 2(1) of the said Act of 1979 and on such other trustees and beneficiaries as the district judge may direct.

(7) Where an interest in securities not in court is to be charged, copies of the order nisi shall be served by the judgment creditor on the person or body required to be served in like circumstances by RSC Order 50, rule 2(1)(*b*).

(8) The documents required by the foregoing paragraphs to be served shall be served in accordance with Order 7, rule 1, not less than 7 days before the day fixed for the further consideration of the matter.

(9) Upon further consideration of the matter service required under paragraph (6) or (7) shall be proved by affidavit.

Amendments—SI 1989/236; SI 1989/1838; SI 1991/1328; SI 1993/3273; SI 1994/2403.

Defined terms—"charging order", "debtor": Charging Orders Act 1979, s 1.

"debtor's beneficial ownership" (r 1(2)(*c*))—If the debtor is the sole owner of land, it is usual to seek to charge his legal and beneficial interests so that the position will be clear to the Land Registry. If he is a co-owner with someone who is not a joint debtor, only the debtor's beneficial interest can be charged. That beneficial interest is an interest in the proceeds of sale (*National Westminster Bank Ltd v Stockman* [1981] 1 WLR 67, [1981] 1 All ER 800); accordingly, the charge cannot be registered under the Land Charges Act 1925 (*Perry v Phoenix Assurance plc* [1988] 1 WLR 940, [1988] 3 All ER 60). Service on the trustees will afford protection where they can be relied on to discharge their duties – but not (eg, when they are the debtor and his wife) where there is a risk that the trustees might sell or mortgage, overreaching the charge, and dispose of the proceeds in breach of trust. In such a case, application might also be made under TLATA 1996 for the appointment of new trustees or the sale of the trust property (see Procedural Guide 5) and the position protected by registering that application as a pending action. On the other hand, if the interests of all the beneficial owners are to be charged and the requirements of this rule are complied with, a charging order may be made over the property itself (*Clark v Chief Land Registrar* [1993] 2 WLR 141, [1993] 2 All ER 936).

"where the asset is held by one or more trustees" (r 1(2)(*c*))—If joint debtors hold the whole beneficial interest in land, then the legal estate held by the trustees (usually the debtors themselves) may also be charged under Charging Orders Act 1979, s 2(1)(*b*)(iii).

"beneficiaries" (r 1(2)(*e*))—Even though not on the title, the debtor's spouse or other cohabitee may have some beneficial interest in the matrimonial home. Where the debtor's home is the property to be charged, the spouse should therefore be identified if possible. Similarly, if the debtor is known to have a cohabitee, he or she should be identified.

High Court (r 1(2))—In order to secure a High Court judgment, application is made to the county court under Charging Orders Act 1979, s 1(1). This does not imply that the High Court judgment or action is transferred to the county court.

"a sufficient case" (r 1(4))—An order nisi is not granted automatically. It will be refused not only if the affidavit fails to satisfy r 1(2) but also if the debt is too small to justify the remedy or the application appears otherwise oppressive, for example where there is a pending application to vary the maintenance order sought to be enforced (compare FPR 1991, r 7.1(2)). Nor will an order nisi be made where the debt is subject to an instalment order and the payments are up to date (*Mercantile Credit Co Ltd v Ellis* (1987) *The Times*, 1 April, CA; *Ropaigealach v Allied Irish Bank plc* [2001] EWCA Civ 1790, CA).

Charging order nisi (r 1(4))—Charging Orders Act 1979, s 1 authorises the making of just one charging order. It is made initially in the form of an order nisi, to be confirmed or discharged on the return day. Any Land Registry notice or caution or Land Charges Registry entry is properly effected pursuant to COA 1979, s 3(2) and (3) on the making of the order nisi and should not be repeated when the order is made absolute. Any such notice, caution or entry should be removed promptly if the order is discharged.

Service (r 1(6))—It is for the applicant, not the court, to effect service. Service on prior chargees is sometimes dispensed with on the basis that they cannot be prejudiced by the making of the order. Although the debtor's spouse or other cohabitee is not mentioned in the rule, he or she should also be served as he or she may be a "beneficiary" or if in occupation will have rights to be considered (*Harman v Glencross* [1986] Fam 81, [1986] 2 FLR 241).

"Order 7, rule 1" (r 1(8))—Service under Ord 7, r 1 is usually by first class post.

"proved by affidavit" (r 1(9))—Rule 1(9) seems to admit of no discretion as to the method of proving service, even though, for example, the debtor may have written to acknowledge the papers.

Forms—The form of order nisi is Form N86.

2 Order on further consideration of application for charging order (Ord 31, r 2)

(1) On the day fixed under rule 1(4) for the further consideration of the matter, the court shall either make the order absolute, with or without modifications, or discharge it.

(2) If an order absolute is made, a copy shall be served by the proper officer, in accordance with Order 7, rule 1, on each of the following persons, namely –

(*a*) the debtor,
(*b*) the applicant for the order,
(*c*) where funds in court are charged, the Accountant General at the Court Funds Office, and
(*d*) unless otherwise directed, any person or body on whom a copy of the order nisi was served pursuant to rule 1(7).

(3) Every copy of an order served on a person or body under paragraph (2)(*d*) shall contain a stop notice.

Defined terms—"debtor": Charging Orders Act 1979, s 6(1); "proper officer": Ord 1, r 3; "stop notice": COA 1979, s 5.

Effect of order absolute (r 2(1))—Although the order is fully effective only from the return day, the charge is effective from the day the order nisi was made (*Haley v Barry* (1868) 3 Ch App 452).

"with ... modifications" (r 2(1))—As there is but one charging order, it cannot when made absolute be modified to extend to property which it did not charge in the order nisi form.

Discharge of order (r 2(1))—The order should be discharged if the debtor had no interest in the property when the order nisi was made, or if he has since parted with it to someone who would not be affected by a mere equitable charge, such as a bona fide purchaser for value without notice (*Howell v Montey* (1990) *The Times*, 17 March). If there is some dispute as to whether the debtor has an interest, the court may direct a trial of the issue. The onus is on the debtor and the third party to show why the order should not be made absolute (*Rosseel NV v Oriental Commercial and Shipping (UK) Ltd and Others* (1991) *The Times*, 11 October). Any registered notice, caution or Land Charges entry should be removed promptly when the order is discharged. See also **"consider all the circumstances"** under Charging Orders Act 1979, s 1.

Adjournment—Any adjournment should be to a fixed date as a general adjournment will leave the charge in place indefinitely in the order nisi form. It is usual when adjourning to direct that the order nisi continue in the meantime.

Conditions—Charging Orders Act 1979, s 3(1) enables the order to be made subject to conditions.

Other powers—If the proceedings concern a "qualifying periodical maintenance order" within the meaning of Maintenance Enforcement Act 1991, s 1, the court may of its own motion make a "means of payment order" under s 1(4)(*a*) of that Act or an attachment or earnings order by virtue of s 1(4)(*b*). Those powers may be exercised, in an appropriate case, in addition to making the charging order absolute.

Costs—Ord 38, App B, Pt III, Item 8 (as it was immediately before 26 April 1999) fixes the costs at £63.50 and the court fee. The court may also allow search and registration fees. However, the court may direct otherwise, ie by assessing summarily or directing detailed assessment.

Forms—The order absolute is Form N87.

PART III

3 Effect of charging order etc (Ord 31, r 3)

(1) Where a charging order nisi or a charging order absolute has been made and served in accordance with rule 1 or 2, it shall have the same effect as an order made and served in like circumstances under RSC Order 50.

(2) The court may vary or discharge a charging order in the like circumstances and in accordance with the same procedure, with the necessary modifications, as a like order made by the High Court.

(3) The powers of the court under rule 2 or the last preceding paragraph, except the power to vary an order made by the judge, may be exercised by the district judge.

4 Enforcement of charging order by sale (Ord 31, r 4)

General Note—This rule requires separate proceedings to be taken to seek an order for sale. Such a claim will be governed by CPR 1998. See those rules, Sch 2, CCR Ord 31, r 4 and the annotations thereto.

ORDER 32
RECEIVERS

1 Application for appointment (Ord 32, r 1)

(1) An application for the appointment of a receiver may be made before, at or after the trial or hearing of any proceedings.

(2) An application for an injunction ancillary or incidental to an order appointing a receiver may be joined with the application for such an order.

(3) Where the applicant wishes to apply for the immediate grant of such an injunction pending the hearing of his application for the appointment of a receiver, he may do so ex parte on affidavit.

(4) The power to make an order for the appointment of a receiver shall be exercisable by the court and, without prejudice to Order 21, rule 5, the district judge shall have power to grant an injunction if, and only so far as, it is ancillary or incidental to an order for the appointment of a receiver by way of execution.

In this paragraph "receiver by way of execution" means a receiver appointed by way of equitable execution in relation either to an equitable interest or to a legal estate or interest in land.

Scope of provision—This and the following two rules deal generally with the appointment of receivers. In family proceedings their most common use will be by way of enforcement of a judgment or order.

"receiver by way of execution" (r 1(4))—Given the broadened powers of the district judge under CCR Ord 13, r 6 since 1 July 1991, this paragraph may now take effect to limit the district judge's powers rather than (as before that date) extend them. This limitation applies only to the district judge's power under this rule to grant an ancillary injunction.

"interest in land" (r 1(4))—County Courts Act 1984, s 107 expressly extends the power of the county court to appoint a receiver by way of equitable execution to interests in land, whether or not a charging order has been made. It also provides that, where a charging order has been registered under the Land Charges Act 1972, the further registration of the receiver's appointment is unnecessary.

Partnership share—Partnership Act 1890, s 23(2) enables a county court, having made a charging order in respect of the debtor's interest in a partnership, to appoint a receiver of profits and other money payable in respect of it.

Other assets—The above-mentioned statutory provisions merely extend the court's general powers (that is, the High Court's powers enjoyed by the county court through County Courts Act 1984, s 38) by means of the appointment of a receiver to enable a judgment creditor to reach interests of the debtor which cannot be taken in execution by other process (*Levermore v Levermore* [1979] 1 WLR 1277, [1980] 1 All ER 1). It is equitable relief granted because execution strictly so-called cannot be had and it will not be "just and convenient" to grant it (see Supreme Court Act 1981, s 37) when such execution is in fact available (*Re Shephard* (1890) Ch D 131). There must be an asset to which the receivership is directed. Thus a receiver cannot be appointed of the debtor's future salary (*Holmes v Millage* [1893] 1 QB 551), a disputed insurance claim (*Pearce v Johns* (1987) 41 Sol Jo 661), or his property generally (*Hamilton v Brogden* (1891) 35 Sol Jo 206). Otherwise, the discretion is wide; for example, receivers may be appointed not only of the rents and profits of land vested in the debtor but of his undivided share under a trust for sale, his entitlement out of the estate of a deceased person, his interest under a trust (including a life interest), his entitlement under an annuity or the profits of his business.

Discretion—The appointment of a receiver may be expensive, as security will usually be required of him and he will usually require to be remunerated; accordingly, it will not be ordered where the judgment debt or the amount likely to be recovered is small.

Forms—The form of appointment of a receiver by way of equitable execution of land is Form N356. In other cases, reference to forms N353 and N354 may assist in adapting Form N356 to suit the circumstances.

PART III

2 Receiver to give security (Ord 32, r 2)

Unless the court otherwise orders, a person other than an officer of the court who is appointed a receiver shall not act as such until he has given security duly to account for what he receives and to deal with it as the court directs.

Defined terms—"officer": County Courts Act 1984, s 147.

Security—Usually, where security is required, it is provided in the form of a guarantee given by a bank or insurance company. Where the amounts involved are not large and the duration of the receivership will be short, a solicitor's undertaking may be offered. In a small case, the judgment creditor himself (or, presumably therefore, his solicitor) may be appointed receiver, and security may be dispensed with (*Fuggle v Bland* (1883) 11 QBD 711).

3 Application of RSC (Ord 32, r 3)

(1) Subject to the following paragraphs of this rule, the provisions of the RSC with regard to –

(*a*) the remuneration of receivers,
(*b*) service of an order appointing a receiver,
(*c*) receivers' accounts,
(*d*) payments into court by receivers,
(*e*) default by receivers, and
(*f*) directions to receivers,

shall apply in relation to a receiver appointed by a county court as they apply in relation to a receiver appointed by the High Court.

(2) The application of RSC Order 30, rule 4 by paragraph (1)(*b*) shall have effect with the modification that the reference in that rule to the party having conduct of the proceedings shall be construed as a reference to the proper officer.

(3) (*revoked*)

(4) Where the order for the appointment of a receiver was made by the judge, the power on any default by the receiver to direct his discharge and the appointment of another receiver shall be exercised only by the judge.

Amendments—SI 1984/878.

Defined terms—"proper officer": Ord 1, r 3.

Scope of provision—The provisions of RSC (particularly RSC Ord 30) as they were immediately before 26 April 1999 are applied to the conduct of the receivership, save that the court rather than the judgment creditor serves the order appointing the receiver. The provisions are summarised under RSC Ord 51, r 3.

****

ORDER 35
ENFORCEMENT OF COUNTY COURT JUDGMENTS OUTSIDE ENGLAND AND WALES

Part I. Enforcement outside United Kingdom

1 Interpretation of Part I (Ord 35, r 1)

In this Part of this Order "the Act of 1933" means the Foreign Judgments (Reciprocal Enforcement) Act 1933, "the Act of 1982" means the Civil Jurisdiction and Judgments Act 1982 and expressions which are defined in those Acts have the same meaning in this Part of this order as they have in those Acts.

Amendments—SI 1985/1269.

2 Application under s 10 of the Act of 1933 for certified copy of county court judgment (Ord 35, r 2)

(1) An application under section 10 of the Act of 1933 for a certified copy of a judgment of a county court may be made by filing an affidavit, made by a solicitor of the party entitled to enforce the judgment, or by the party himself, if he is acting in person.

(2) An affidavit by which an application under section 10 of the Act of 1933 is made must –

(*a*) give particulars of the proceedings in which the judgment was obtained,
(*b*) have annexed to it evidence of service on the defendant of the summons or other process by which the proceedings were begun (where service was effected otherwise than through the court), copies of the pleadings, if any, and a statement of the grounds on which the judgment was based,
(*c*) state whether the defendant did or did not object to the jurisdiction, and, if so, on what grounds,
(*d*) show that the judgment is not subject to any stay of execution,
(*e*) state that the time for appealing or applying for a re-hearing has expired, or, as the case may be, the date on which it will expire and in either case whether notice of appeal against the judgment has been given or an application for a re-hearing has been made, and
(*f*) state whether interest is recoverable on the judgment or part thereof and, if so, the rate and period in respect of which it is recoverable.

(3) The certified copy of the judgment shall be a sealed copy indorsed with a certificate signed by the district judge certifying that the copy is a true copy of a judgment obtained in the county court and that it is issued in accordance with section 10 of the Act of 1933.

(4) There shall also be issued a sealed certificate signed by the district judge and having annexed to it a copy of the summons or other process by which the proceedings were begun and stating –

(*a*) the manner in which the summons or other process was served on the defendant or that the defendant has delivered to the court an admission, defence or counterclaim,
(*b*) what objections, if any, were made to the jurisdiction,
(*c*) what pleadings, if any, were filed,
(*d*) the grounds on which the judgment was based,
(*e*) that the time for appealing or applying for a re-hearing has expired or, as the case may be, the date on which it will expire,
(*f*) whether notice of appeal against the judgment has been given or an application for a re-hearing has been made,
(*g*) whether interest is recoverable on the judgment or part thereof and, if such be the case, the rate of interest, the date from which interest is recoverable, and the date on which interest ceases to accrue, and
(*h*) such other particulars as it may be necessary to give the court in the foreign country in which it is sought to obtain execution of the judgment.

Amendments—SI 1985/1269.

Scope of provision—This rule sets out the requirements to obtain a certified copy of a money judgment (other than a maintenance order) for the purpose of its enforcement in one of the countries to which the Foreign Judgments (Reciprocal Enforcement) Act 1933 has been applied (see Procedural Guide 25, letter 'K' in the Table).

3 Application under s 12 of the Act of 1982 for certified copy of county court judgment (Ord 35, r 3)

(1) An application under section 12 of the Act of 1982 for a certified copy of a judgment of a county court may be made by filing an affidavit made by a solicitor of the party entitled to enforce the judgment, or by the party himself, if he is acting in person.

(2) An affidavit by which an application under section 12 of the Act of 1982 is made must –

(*a*) give particulars of the proceedings in which the judgment was obtained,
(*b*) have annexed to it evidence of service on the defendant of the summons or other process by which the proceedings were begun (where service was effected otherwise than through the court), copies of the pleadings, if any, and a statement of the grounds on which the judgment was based together with, where appropriate, any document under which the applicant is entitled to legal aid or assistance by way of representation for the purposes of the proceedings,
(*c*) state whether the defendant did or did not object to the jurisdiction and, if so, on what grounds,
(*d*) show that the judgment has been served in accordance with Order 22, rule 1 and is not subject to any stay of execution,
(*e*) state that the time for appealing or applying for a re-hearing has expired, or, as the case may be, the date on which it will expire and in either case

whether notice of appeal against the judgment has been given or an application for a re-hearing has been made, and

(*f*) state –

(i) whether the judgment provides for the payment of a sum or sums of money,

(ii) whether interest is recoverable on the judgment or part thereof and, if such be the case, the rate of interest, the date from which interest is recoverable, and the date on which interest ceases to accrue.

(3) The certified copy of the judgment shall be a sealed copy and there shall be issued with the copy of the judgment a sealed certificate signed by the district judge and having annexed to it a copy of the summons or other process by which the proceedings were begun.

Amendments—SI 1985/1269.

Scope of provision—This rule sets out the requirements to obtain a certified copy of money judgment or other order (but not a maintenance order) for the purpose of its enforcement in one of the European Union or European Free Trade Area countries (see Procedural Guide 25, letter 'M' in the Table).

Part II. Enforcement in other parts of the United Kingdom

4 Interpretation of Part II (Ord 35, r 4)

In this Part of the Order –

"the Act of 1982" means the Civil Jurisdiction and Judgments Act 1982,

"money provision" means a provision in any judgment to which section 18 of the Act 1982 applies for the payment of one or more sums of money,

"non-money provision" means a provision in any judgment to which section 18 of the Act of 1982 applies for any relief or remedy not requiring payment of a sum of money.

Amendments—SI 1985/1269.

5 Application for certificate of money provision (Ord 35, r 5)

(1) A certificate in respect of any money provision contained in a judgment of the county court may be obtained by filing an affidavit made by the solicitor of the party entitled to enforce the judgment, or by the party himself if he is acting in person, together with a form of certificate.

(2) An affidavit by which an application under paragraph (1) is made must –

(*a*) give particulars of the judgment, stating the rate of payment, if any, specified under the money provisions contained in the judgment, the sum or aggregate of sums (including any costs or expenses) remaining unsatisfied, the rate of interest, if any, applicable and the date or time from which any such interest began to accrue,

(*b*) verify that the time for appealing against the judgment or for applying for a re-hearing has expired, or that any appeal or re-hearing has been finally disposed of and that enforcement of the judgment is not stayed or suspended, and

(*c*) state to the best of the information or belief of the deponent the usual or last known address of the party entitled to enforce the judgment and of the party liable to execution on it.

(3) The proper officer shall enter on the certificate –

(*a*) the number of the action,
(*b*) the amount remaining due under the judgment,
(*c*) the rate of interest payable on the judgment debt, and the date or time from which any such interest began to accrue,
(*d*) a note of the costs, if any, allowed for obtaining the certificate, and
(*e*) the date on which the certificate is issued.

Amendments—SI 1985/1269.

Note—This procedure is not appropriate to enforce a maintenance order. See FPR 1991, r 7.19(1).

6 Application for certified copy of judgment containing non-money provision (Ord 35, r 6)

(1) A certified copy of a judgment of a county court which contains any non-money provision may be obtained by filing an affidavit made by the solicitor of the party entitled to enforce the judgment, or by the party himself, if he is acting in person.

(2) The requirements in paragraph (2) of rule 5 shall apply with the necessary modifications to an affidavit made in an application under paragraph (1) of this rule.

(3) The certified copy of a judgment shall be a sealed copy to which shall be annexed a certificate signed by the proper officer and stating that the conditions specified in paragraph (3)(*a*) and (*b*) of Schedule 7 to the Act of 1982 are satisfied in relation to the judgment.

Amendments—SI 1985/1269.

****

ORDER 37
REHEARING, SETTING ASIDE AND APPEAL FROM DISTRICT JUDGE

1 Rehearing (Ord 37, r 1)

(1) In any proceedings tried without a jury the judge shall have power on application to order a rehearing where no error of the court at the hearing is alleged.

(2) Unless the court otherwise orders, any application under paragraph (1) shall be made to the judge by whom the proceedings were tried.

(3) A rehearing may be ordered on any question without interfering with the finding or decision or any other question.

(4) Where the proceedings were tried by the district judge, the powers conferred on the judge by paragraphs (1) and (3) shall be exercisable by the district judge and paragraph (2) shall not apply.

(5) Any application for a rehearing under this rule shall be made on notice stating the grounds of the application and the notice shall be served on the opposite party not more than 14 days after the day of the trial and not less than 7 days before the day fixed for the hearing of the application.

PART III

(6) On receipt of the notice, the proper officer shall, unless the court otherwise orders, retain any money in court until the application had been heard.

Scope of provision—This rule provides an exception to the provision of County Courts Act 1984, s 70, which provides that every judgment or order of the county court shall be treated as final and conclusive between the parties. It gives the county court power to review its own decision where no error of the court is alleged. This is wider than the powers available to the High Court under Supreme Court Act 1981, s 17, which in effect requires an application for a new trial to made to the Court of Appeal under CPR 1998, r 52.10(2)(*c*). A judge, or district judge (r 1(4)), may order a rehearing. This means that the judge or district judge will consider the evidence at the original hearing together with the fresh evidence. Where the complaint is that a party was not present at the hearing an application should be made under r 2. An order made by consent may be varied under the terms of this rule (and FPR 1991, r 8.1) – see under FPR 1991, r 8.1. This provision, whilst being the more appropriate course, does not preclude an appeal (see *O'Connor v Din* [1997] 1 FLR 226).

No error of the court—An application for a rehearing may be made under this rule where no error of the court is alleged. The test to be applied is "Is the allegation which is made against the decision an allegation that the court went wrong on the materials before it, or is it an allegation that the court went wrong because evidence on a vital matter was concealed from the court?" (*Peek v Peek* [1948] 2 All ER 297). If the allegation is that the court went wrong (ie an error of the court) on the information before it, the remedy is an appeal. If material on a vital matter was not before the court, an application should be made under this rule. The most common grounds for an application are:
(*a*) where there has been default or misconduct by an officer of the court or a party;
(*b*) where fresh evidence has been discovered or the judgment has been obtained by fraud;
(*c*) where there has been an irregularity during the course of the trial, eg during speeches the judge was misled or there was perjury or a mistake by a witness;
(*d*) where there is an allegation of material non-disclosure (see eg *Livesey (formerly Jenkins) v Jenkins* [1985] AC 424, [1985] FLR 813, HL; *T v T (Consent Order: Procedure to Set Aside)* [1996] 2 FLR 640, Richard Anelay QC sitting as a deputy High Court judge).

2 Setting aside judgment given in party's absence (Ord 37, r 2)

(1) Any judgment or order obtained against a party in his absence at the hearing may be set aside by the court on application by that party on notice.

(2) The application shall be made to the judge if the judgment or order was given or made by the judge and in any other case shall be made to the district judge.

3 Setting aside on failure of postal service (Ord 37, r 3)

(1) Where in an action or matter the originating process has been sent to the defendant or inserted in his letter-box in accordance with Order 7, rule 10(1)(*b*) or (4)(*a*) or 13(1)(*b*) or (4), and after judgment has been entered or given or an order has been made it appears to the court that the process did not come to the knowledge of the defendant in due time, the court may of its own motion set aside the judgment or order and may give any such directions as the court thinks fit.

(2) The proper officer shall give notice of the plaintiff of the setting aside of any judgment or order under this rule.

Amendments—SI 1983/1716.

Scope of provision—This rule gives the court a specific power to set aside a judgment or order where postal service has not been effective. See also the requirements for service in relation to family proceedings under FPR 1991, rr 4.8, 10.2, 10.3, 10.4, 10.5 and Family Proceedings Courts (Children Act 1989) Rules 1991, r 8.

****

5 Non-compliance with rules (Ord 37, r 5)

(1) Where there has been a failure to comply with any requirement of these rules, the failure shall be treated as an irregularity and shall not nullify the proceedings, but the court may set aside the proceedings wholly or in part or exercise its powers under these rules to allow any such amendments and to give any such directions as it thinks fit.

(2) No application to set aside any proceedings for irregularity shall be granted unless made within a reasonable time, nor if the party applying has taken any step in the proceedings after knowledge of the irregularity.

(3) Where any such application is made, the grounds of objection shall be stated in the notice.

(4) The expression "proceedings" in paragraph (1), and where it first occurs in paragraph (2), includes any step taken in the proceedings and any document, judgment or order therein.

6 Appeal from district judge (Ord 37, r 6)

(1) Any party affected by a judgment or final order of the district judge may, except where he has consented to the terms thereof, appeal from the judgment or order to the judge, who may, upon such terms as he thinks fit, –

- (*a*) set aside or vary the judgment or order or any part thereof, or
- (*b*) give any other judgment or make any other order in substitution for the judgment or order appealed from, or
- (*c*) remit the action or matter or any question therein to the district judge for rehearing or further consideration, or
- (*d*) order a new trial to take place before himself or another judge of the court on a day to be fixed.

(2) The appeal shall be made on notice, which shall state the grounds of the appeal and be served within 14 days after the day on which judgment or order appealed from was given or made.

Amendments—SI 1991/1882.

Scope of provision—This rule provides the county court judge with the power to set aside or vary the order of a district judge (r 6(1)(*a*)) and substitute another order (r 6(1)(*b*)), or order a retrial by the district judge (r 6(1)(*c*)) or by a judge (r 6(1)(*d*)). An appeal under this rule is akin to an appeal to the Court of Appeal, meaning that the judge will not hear all the evidence again but will consider the appeal, meaning the evidence and the course of the trial on paper (see under CPR 1998, r 52.11).

An appeal against a consent order is not permitted under this rule. The solution is either to apply to the district judge under CCR Ord 37, r 1 to rehear the matter and set aside the order, or to seek a transfer to the High Court (pursuant to Matrimonial and Family Proceedings Act 1984, s 39) for the appeal to be heard pursuant to RSC Ord 58, rr 1 and 3, which does not have the restriction relating to consent orders (*Benson v Benson* [1996] 1 FLR 692; see also *Re C (Financial Provision: Leave to Appeal)* [1993] 2 FLR 799). For consent orders, see CCR Ord 37, r 1.

Relationship with FPR—A proposed appellant must examine the provisions of FPR 1991 which also give the right of appeal from the decision of a district judge in family proceedings. If the proceedings are those set out in FPR 1991, r 4.1(2), an appeal from a district judge is governed by r 4.22. If the proceedings are family proceedings but not included within r 4.1(2), the appeal is governed by the provisions of r 8.1. If the proceedings are not family proceedings, this rule governs the procedure. This rule applies to any appeal from the decision of a district judge which is a judgment or final order, but, in appropriate cases subject to the provisions of FPR 1991 (see also **Appeals from the district judge** under FPR 1991, r 4.22 and **Relationship with FPR 1991, r 4.22** under FPR 1991, r 8.1).

****

8 Imposition of terms and stay of execution (Ord 37, r 8)

(1) An application to the judge or district judge under any of the foregoing rules may be granted on such terms as he thinks reasonable.

(2) Notice of any such application shall not of itself operate as a stay of execution on the judgment or order to which it relates but the court may order a stay of execution pending the hearing of the application or any rehearing or new trial ordered on the application.

(3) If a judgment or order is set aside under any of the foregoing rules, any execution issued on the judgment or order shall cease to have effect unless the court otherwise orders.

ORDER 47
DOMESTIC AND MATRIMONIAL PROCEEDINGS

* For r 5, see Civil Procedure Rules 1998, Sch 2.

****

County Court Remedies Regulations 1991, SI 1991/1222

1 These Regulations may be cited as the County Court Remedies Regulations 1991 and shall come into force on 1 July 1991.

2 In these Regulations, "prescribed relief" means relief of any of the following kinds –

(*a*) an order requiring a party to admit any other party to premises for the purpose of inspecting or removing documents or articles which may provide evidence in any proceedings, whether or not the proceedings have been commenced;

(*b*) an interlocutory injunction –

(i) restraining a party from removing from the jurisdiction of the High Court assets located within that jurisdiction; or

(ii) restraining a party from dealing with assets whether located within the jurisdiction of the High Court or not.

3 (1) Subject to the following provisions of this regulation, a county court shall not grant prescribed relief or vary or revoke an order made by the High Court granting such relief.

(2) Paragraph (1) shall not apply to –

(*a*) any county court held by a judge of the Court of Appeal or judge of the High Court sitting as a judge for any county court district;
(*b*) a patents county court held by a person nominated under section 291 of the Copyright, Designs and Patents Act 1988 to sit as a judge of that court.

(3) A county court may grant relief of a kind referred to in regulation 2(*b*) –

(*a*) when exercising jurisdiction in family proceedings within the meaning of Part V of the Matrimonial and Family Proceedings Act 1984;
(*b*) for the purpose of making an order for the preservation, custody or detention of property which forms or may form the subject matter of proceedings,
(*c*) in aid of execution of a judgment or order made in proceedings in a county court to preserve assets until execution can be levied upon them, or
(*d*) where the proceedings are to be or are included in the Central London County Court Mercantile List and the application is made to a Circuit judge nominated by the Senior Presiding Judge.

(3A) In paragraph (3)(*d*) –

"the Central London County Court Mercantile List" means the Mercantile Court established at the Central London County Court pursuant to Part 59 of the Civil Procedure Rules 1998; and
"the Senior Presiding Judge" means the judge appointed as such under section 72(2) of the Courts and Legal Services Act 1990.

(4) Paragraph (1) shall not –

(*a*) affect or modify powers expressly conferred on a county court by or under any enactment other than section 38 of the County Courts Act 1984; or
(*b*) prevent a county court from varying an order granting prescribed relief where all the parties are agreed on the terms of the variation.

Amendments—SI 1995/206; SI 2002/439.

Freezing injunctions—Although county courts generally have no power to grant such injunctions, the power is expressly preserved in family proceedings by reg 3(3)(*a*). Similarly, such injunctions can be obtained in aid of a judgment or order made to preserve assets until execution can be levied (reg 3(3)(*c*)).

4 An application to the High Court for relief of a kind referred to in regulation 2(*a*) in county court proceedings shall be deemed to include an application for transfer of the proceedings to the High Court.

5 (1) After an application for prescribed relief has been disposed of by the High Court, the proceedings shall, unless the High Court orders otherwise, be transferred to a county court if –

(*a*) they were transferred to the High Court; or
(*b*) apart from these Regulations, they should have been commenced in a county court.

(2) Where an order is made on an ex parte application, the application shall not be treated as disposed of for the purposes of paragraph (1) until any application to set aside or vary the order has been heard, or until the expiry of 28 days (or such other period as the Court may specify) during which no such application has been made.

Family Law Act 1986 (Dependent Territories) Order 1991, SI 1991/1723

1 This Order may be cited as the Family Law Act 1986 (Dependent Territories) Order 1991 and shall come into force on 14 October 1991.

2 In this Order –

"the Act" means the Family Law Act 1986;

"specified dependent territory" means a dependent territory specified in column 1 of Schedule 1 to this Order;

"Part I order" has the meaning given by section 1(1) of the Act;

"part of the United Kingdom" has the meaning given by section 42(1) of the Act.

3 (1) This Order applies in relation to a specified dependent territory from the date specified opposite the name of that territory in column 2 of Schedule 1 to this Order.

(2) Part I of the Act shall apply, for the purpose of regulating, as between any specified dependent territory and any part of the United Kingdom, the jurisdiction of courts to make Part I orders, and the recognition and enforcement of orders corresponding to such orders, with the modifications specified in Schedule 2 to this Order.

(3) Each Part of Schedule 3 to this Order shall have effect for the construction of Part I of the Act as modified by this Order in relation to the specified dependent territory named in the heading to that Part of that Schedule.

4 This Order does not extend to any territory outside the United Kingdom.

SCHEDULE 1

SPECIFIED DEPENDENT TERRITORIES

Dependent Territory	*Date from which this Order applies*
The Isle of Man	14 October 1991

****

SCHEDULE 3

INTERPRETATION OF CERTAIN EXPRESSIONS IN PART I OF THE FAMILY LAW ACT 1986 AS MODIFIED BY SCHEDULE 2 TO THIS ORDER

PART I
THE ISLE OF MAN

1 In section 1(1)(*f*) "an order made by the court in a specified dependent territory corresponding to an order within paragraphs (*a*) to (*e*) above" means –

(*a*) an order under section 9 of the Family Law Act 1991 (an Act of Tynwald) or any of the following enactments (being enactments repealed by that Act) –

(i) section 3(5) of the Guardianship of Infants Act 1953 (an Act of Tynwald), so far as it relates to the custody of infants;

(ii) section 4(1) of that Act, except so far as it relates to costs, but including that section as applied by section 3(1) of the Legitimacy Act 1962 (an Act of Tynwald);

(iii) section 42(1) or (2) of the Judicature (Matrimonial Causes) Act 1976 (an Act of Tynwald);

(iv) section 8(2) or 18(1)(ii) of the Domestic Proceedings Act 1983 (an Act of Tynwald);

(v) section 34(1) of that Act;

(vi) section 49(1) of that Act, so far as it relates to the custody of or access to a child;

(*b*) an order made by the High Court of Justice of the Isle of Man in the exercise of its jurisdiction relating to wardship or its inherent jurisdiction with respect to children –

(i) so far as it gives care of a child to any person or provides for contact with or access to, or the education of, a child but

(ii) excluding an order varying or revoking such an order, or an order relating to a child of whom care or control is (immediately after the making of the order) vested in a public authority in the Isle of Man.

2 In each of sections 2A(3), 3(3), 6(4), 11(2), 13(5), 20(3), 21(4) and 23(4) –

(*a*) in paragraph (*a*) "corresponding dependent territory order" means an order under section 3(3) of the Child Custody Act 1987 (an Act of Tynwald);

(*b*) in paragraph (*b*) "corresponding dependent territory order" means an order under section 4(2) of that Act.

3 In section 13(6)(*a*)(ii), "corresponding dependent territory provision" means section 2(2) or 5(3) of the Child Custody Act 1987 (an Act of Tynwald).

4 (1) In section 27(1) "corresponding provision" means section 7 of the Child Custody Act 1987 (an Act of Tynwald).

(2) In section 27(4) "corresponding dependent territory provision" means section 12(3) of that Act.

5 (1) In section 32(1) "the corresponding court" means the High Court of Justice of the Isle of Man.

(2) In section 32(1) and (3)(*a*) "the corresponding dependent territory provisions" means Part I of the Child Custody Act 1987 (an Act of Tynwald).

6 In section 42(6)(*e*) "corresponding dependent territory provision" means –

(*a*) section 42(6) or (7) of the Judicature (Matrimonial Causes) Act 1976 (an Act of Tynwald);

(*b*) section 18(6) of the Domestic Proceedings Act 1983 (an Act of Tynwald).

Family Law Act 1996 (Part IV) (Allocation of Proceedings) Order 1997, SI 1997/1896

1 (1) This Order may be cited as the Family Law Act 1996 (Part IV) (Allocation of Proceedings) Order 1997 and shall come into force on 1st October 1997.

(2) In this Order, unless the context otherwise requires –

"county court" means a county court of one of the classes specified in article 2;

"family proceedings" has the meaning assigned by section 63 and includes proceedings which are family business within the meaning of section 32 of the Matrimonial and Family Proceedings Act 1984;

"family proceedings court" has the meaning assigned by article 3;

"the Act" means the Family Law Act 1996 and a section, Part or Schedule referred to by number alone means the section, Part or Schedule so numbered in that Act.

"family proceedings" (art 1(2))—Defined in FLA 1996, s 63 as any proceedings under: the inherent jurisdiction of the High Court in relation to children; FLA 1996, Pts II and IV; Matrimonial Causes Act 1973; Adoption Act 1976; Domestic Proceedings and Magistrates' Courts Act 1978; Matrimonial and Family Proceedings Act 1984, Pt III; CA 1989, Pts I, II and IV; and Human Fertilisation and Embryology Act 1990, s 30.

"family business" (art 1(2))—Defined in Matrimonial and Family Proceedings Act 1984, s 32(2) as business of any description which is for the time being assigned to the Family Division, and no other Division, by or under Supreme Court Act 1981, s 61 and Sch 1.

2 Classes of county court

The classes of county court specified for the purposes of this Order are –

(*a*) divorce county courts, being those courts designated for the time being as divorce county courts by an order under section 33 of the Matrimonial and Family Proceedings Act 1984;

(*b*) family hearing centres, being those courts set out in Schedule 1 to the Children (Allocation of Proceedings) Order 1991; and

(*c*) care centres, being those courts set out in column (ii) of Schedule 2 to that Order.

Scope of provision—This article defines three classes of county court for the purposes of the Order.

"divorce county courts" (art 2(*a*))—Certain county courts are designated as divorce county courts by the Lord Chancellor, under Matrimonial and Family Proceedings Act 1984, s 33, for the purpose of exercising jurisdiction in matrimonial causes.

"family hearing centres" (art 2(*b*))—Family hearing centres were created under the provisions of the Children (Allocation of Proceedings) Order 1991 and comprise the county courts listed in Sch 1 to that Order. The concentration of hearings in these centres is designed to facilitate the availability of nominated members of the judiciary to whom proceedings of the types covered by the Order are allocated by the Family Proceedings (Allocation to Judiciary) Directions 1997.

"care centres" (art 2(*c*))—The concept of care centres was created by the Children (Allocation of Proceedings) Order 1991. The relevant courts are listed in column (ii) of Sch 2 to that Order.

3 Classes of magistrates' court

The classes of magistrates' court specified for the purposes of this Order are family proceedings courts, being those courts constituted in accordance with section 67 of the Magistrates' Courts Act 1980.

"section 67 of the Magistrates' Courts Act 1980"—Section 67 governs the constitution of family proceedings courts and formation of family panels.

Commencement of proceedings

4 Commencement of proceedings

(1) Subject to section 59, paragraph 1 of Schedule 7 and the provisions of this article, proceedings under Part IV may be commenced in a county court or in a family proceedings court.

(2) An application –

(*a*) under Part IV brought by an applicant who is under the age of eighteen; and

(*b*) for the grant of leave under section 43 (Leave of court required for applications by children under sixteen),

shall be commenced in the High Court.

(3) Where family proceedings are pending in a county court or a family proceedings court, an application under Part IV may be made in those proceedings.

Defined terms—"county court": art 1(2); "family proceedings": art 1(2); "family proceedings court": art 3.

Scope of provision—This article specifies in which forum proceedings under FLA 1996, Pt IV should be commenced. There is a unified system of courts and there is a free choice between a county court (limited to divorce county courts, care centres and family hearing centres) and a family proceedings court, subject to the exceptions set out in art 4(2). However, a magistrates' court is not competent to entertain any application or make any order involving a disputed question as to a party's entitlement to occupy any property by virtue of any beneficial estate or interest or contract, unless it is unnecessary to determine the question in order to deal with the application or make the order (FLA 1996, s 59(1)). A magistrates' court may decline jurisdiction if it considers that the case can more conveniently be dealt with by another court (FLA 1996, s 59(2)). Proceedings which involve the transfer of certain tenancies may not be commenced in a magistrates' court (FLA 1996, Sch 7, Pt I).

5 Application to extend, vary or discharge order

(1) Proceedings under Part IV –

(*a*) to extend, vary or discharge an order, or
(*b*) the determination of which may have the effect of varying or discharging an order,

shall be made to the court which made the order.

(2) A court may transfer proceedings made in accordance with paragraph (1) to any other court in accordance with the provisions of articles 6 to 14.

Transfer of proceedings

6 Disapplication of enactments about transfer

Sections 38 and 39 of the Matrimonial and Family Proceedings Act 1984 shall not apply to proceedings under Part IV.

Scope of provision—This article disapplies the transfer provisions of the Matrimonial and Family Proceedings Act 1984, ss 38, 39 in the case of proceedings under FLA 1996, Pt IV.

"sections 38 and 39 of the Matrimonial and Family Proceedings Act 1984"—Section 38 allows the High Court to transfer to the county court:
(*a*) family proceedings commenced in the High Court which are within the jurisdiction of a county court or a divorce county court;
(*b*) certain applications in wardship proceedings, or any other proceedings which relate to the exercise of the inherent jurisdiction of the High Court with respect to minors;
(*c*) all family proceedings transferred to the High Court under s 39 (see below) or County Courts Act 1984, s 41 (transfer to the High Court by order of the High Court); and
(*d*) all matrimonial causes and matters transferred from a county court, otherwise than as mentioned in (*c*) above.

Section 39 allows the county court to transfer to the High Court:
(*a*) all family proceedings commenced in the county court and divorce county court; and
(*b*) all family proceedings transferred from the High Court to a county court or a divorce county court under s 38 above.

The effect of their disapplication is that this order contains the only provisions enabling proceedings under FLA 1996, Pt IV to be transferred between the High Court and the county court.

7 Transfer from one family proceedings court to another

A family proceedings court ("the transferring court") shall (on application or of its own motion) transfer proceedings under Part IV to another family proceedings court ("the receiving court") where –

(*a*) the transferring court considers that it would be appropriate for those proceedings to be heard together with other family proceedings which are pending in the receiving court; and
(*b*) the receiving court, by its justices' clerk (as defined by rule 1(2) of the Family Proceedings Courts (Children Act 1989) Rules 1991), consents to the transfer.

Defined terms—"family proceedings": art 1(2); "family proceedings court": arts 1(2), 3.

"rule 1(2) of the Family Proceedings Courts (Children Act 1989) Rules 1991"—Rule 1(2) defines "justices' clerk" by reference to the definition in Justices of the Peace Act 1979, s 70 (which defines a "justices' clerk" as a clerk to the justices for a petty sessions area) and by further providing that justices' clerk also includes any person who performs a justices' clerk's functions by reason of r 32 (which enables certain other court clerks to be authorised to perform various functions).

8 Transfer from family proceedings court to county court

(1) A family proceedings court may, on application or of its own motion, transfer proceedings under Part IV to a county court where it considers that –

(*a*) it would be appropriate for those proceedings to be heard together with other family proceedings which are pending in that court; or

(*b*) the proceedings involve –

(i) a conflict with the law of another jurisdiction;

(ii) some novel and difficult point of law;

(iii) some question of general public interest; or

(*c*) the proceedings are exceptionally complex.

(2) A family proceedings court must transfer proceedings under Part IV to a county court where –

(*a*) a child under the age of eighteen is the respondent to the application or wishes to become a party to the proceedings; or

(*b*) a party to the proceedings is a person who, by reason of mental disorder within the meaning of the Mental Health Act 1983, is incapable of managing and administering his property and affairs.

(3) Except where transfer is ordered under paragraph (1)(*a*), the proceedings shall be transferred to the nearest county court.

Defined terms—"county court": arts 1(2), 2; "family proceedings": art 1(2).

"Mental Health Act 1983"—MHA 1983, s 1 defines "mental disorder" as mental illness, arrested or incomplete development of mind, psychopathic disorder and any other disorder or disability of mind.

"nearest county court"—Such a court must be designated as a divorce county court, family hearing centre or care centre within the ambit of art 2.

9 Transfer from family proceedings court to High Court

A family proceedings court may, on application or of its own motion, transfer proceedings under Part IV to the High Court where it considers that it would be appropriate for those proceedings to be heard together with other family proceedings which are pending in that Court.

10 Transfer from one county court to another

A county court may, on application or of its own motion, transfer proceedings under Part IV to another county court where –

(*a*) it considers that it would be appropriate for those proceedings to be heard together with other family proceedings which are pending in that court;

(*b*) the proceedings involve the determination of a question of a kind mentioned in section 59(1) and the property in question is situated in the district of another county court; or

(*c*) it seems necessary or expedient so to do.

Defined terms—"county court": arts 1(2), 2; "family proceedings": art 1(2).

PART III

"section 59(1)"—FLA 1996, s 59(1) refers to any disputed question as to a party's entitlement to occupy any property by virtue of a beneficial estate or interest or contract, or by virtue of any enactment giving him the right to remain in occupation.

11 Transfer from county court to family proceedings court

A county court may, on application or of its own motion, transfer proceedings under Part IV to a family proceedings court where –

(*a*) it considers that it would be appropriate for those proceedings to be heard together with other family proceedings which are pending in that court; or

(*b*) it considers that the criterion

(i) in article 8(1)(*a*) no longer applies because the proceedings with which the transferred proceedings were to be heard have been determined;

(ii) in article 8(1)(*b*) or (*c*) does not apply.

Defined terms—"county court": arts 1(2), 2; "family proceedings court": arts 1(2), 3.

Circumstances in which a retransfer may be ordered—Retransfer under art 11(*b*) will depend on which of the three criteria was relied upon by the family proceedings court when it transferred the proceedings to the county court. Where art 8(1)(*a*) was the basis for the original transfer, art 11(*b*)(i) allows a retransfer only where the pending county court proceedings which had activated the criterion have been concluded (presumably the family proceedings court will seldom be mistaken about whether there are such proceedings pending, but where that does happen, it would seem that there is no scope for the county court to send the proceedings back, when the misapprehension is discovered). Where art 8(1)(*b*) or (*c*) was the basis for the original transfer, art 11(*b*)(ii) enables the county court to send the proceedings back if it considers that either criterion does not apply (either because of a change in the circumstances or because the county court disagrees with the family proceedings court).

12 Transfer from county court to High Court

A county court may, on application or of its own motion, transfer proceedings under Part IV to the High Court where it considers that the proceedings are appropriate for determination in the High Court.

Defined terms—"county court": arts 1(2), 2.

Note—The High Court also has power to direct transfer of an application from a county court to itself (County Courts Act 1984, s 41).

13 Transfer from High Court to family proceedings court

The High Court may, on application or of its own motion, transfer proceedings under Part IV to a family proceedings court where it considers that it would be appropriate for those proceedings to be heard together with other family proceedings which are pending in that court.

Defined terms—"family proceedings": art 1(2); "family proceedings court": arts 1(2), 3.

14 Transfer from High Court to county court

The High Court may, on application or of its own motion, transfer proceedings under Part IV to a county court where it considers that –

(*a*) it would be appropriate for those proceedings to be heard together with other family proceedings which are pending in that court;

(*b*) the proceedings are appropriate for determination in a county court; or (*c*) it is appropriate for an application made by a child under the age of eighteen to be heard in a county court.

Defined terms—"county court": arts 1(2), 2; "family proceedings": art 1(2).

15 Disposal following arrest

Where a person is brought before –

(*a*) a relevant judicial authority in accordance with section 47(7)(*a*), or
(*b*) a court by virtue of a warrant issued under section 47(9),

and the matter is not disposed of forthwith, the matter may be transferred to be disposed of by the relevant judicial authority or court which issued the warrant or, as the case may be, which attached the power of arrest under section 47(2) or (3), if different.

Defined terms—"court": FLA 1996, ss 57(1), 63; "relevant judicial authority": FLA 1996, s 63(1).

Scope of provision—This article allows a relevant judicial authority or a court before whom a person is brought in accordance with FLA 1996, s 47(7)(*a*), or by virtue of a warrant issued under FLA 1996, s 47(9), to transfer the matter back to the original judicial authority or court which issued the warrant or attached the power of arrest, if the matter cannot be disposed of forthwith. In respect of an order made by a High Court judge the relevant judicial authority is any judge of that court; in respect of an order made by a county court judge or district judge the relevant judicial authority is any equivalent judge; and in respect of any magistrates' court the relevant authority is any magistrates' court (FLA 1996, s 63(1)). Thus, a person who was made subject to a power of arrest by a county court judge in Leeds could be arrested and brought before a judge in Lincoln who could either deal with the matter, or transfer it back to Leeds under this article.

Miscellaneous

16 Principal Registry of the Family Division

(1) The principal registry of the Family Division of the High Court shall be treated, for the purposes of this Order, as if it were a divorce county court, a family hearing centre and a care centre.

(2) Without prejudice to article 10, the principal registry may transfer an order made in proceedings which are pending in the principal registry to the High Court for enforcement.

Defined terms—"care centre": art 2(*c*); "divorce county court": art 2(*a*); "family hearing centre": art 2(*b*).

17 Lambeth, Shoreditch and Woolwich County Courts

Proceedings under Part IV may be commenced in, transferred to and tried in Lambeth, Shoreditch or Woolwich County Court.

18 Contravention of provisions of this Order

Where proceedings are commenced or transferred in contravention of a provision of this Order, the contravention shall not have the effect of making the proceedings invalid.

Scope of provision—This article prevents a breach of the requirements of the Order affecting the validity of any proceedings which are, as a result, dealt with in the wrong court.

Family Proceedings Rules 1991, SI 1991/1247

ARRANGEMENT OF RULES

PART I
PRELIMINARY

PART II
MATRIMONIAL CAUSES

Evidence

Trial etc

Decrees and orders

Ancillary relief

PART III
OTHER MATRIMONIAL ETC PROCEEDINGS

PART IV
PROCEEDINGS UNDER THE CHILDREN ACT 1989

PART I
PRELIMINARY

1.1 Citation and commencement

These rules may be cited as the Family Proceedings Rules 1991 and shall come into force on 14 October 1991.

1.2 Interpretation

(1) In these rules, unless the context otherwise requires –

"the Act of 1973" means the Matrimonial Causes Act 1973;
"the Act of 1984" means the Matrimonial and Family Proceedings Act 1984;
"the Act of 1986" means the Family Law Act 1986;
"the Act of 1989" means the Children Act 1989;
"the Act of 1991" means the Child Support Act 1991;
"ancillary relief" means –

(*a*) an avoidance of disposition order,
(*b*) a financial provision order,
(*c*) an order for maintenance pending suit,
(*d*) a property adjustment order,
(*e*) a variation order, or
(*f*) a pension sharing order;

"avoidance of disposition order" means an order under section 37(2)(*b*) or (*c*) of the Act of 1973;

"business day" has the meaning assigned to it by rule 1.5(6);

"cause" means a matrimonial cause as defined by section 32 of the Act of 1984 or proceedings under section 19 of the Act of 1973 (presumption of death and dissolution of marriage);

"child" and "child of the family" have, except in Part IV, the meanings respectively assigned to them by section 52(1) of the Act of 1973;

"consent order" means an order under section 33A of the Act of 1973;

"Contracting State" means –

(*a*) one of the original parties to the Council Regulation, that is to say Belgium, Germany, Greece, Spain, France, Ireland, Italy, Luxembourg, the Netherlands, Austria, Portugal, Finland, Sweden and the United Kingdom, and

(*b*) a party which has subsequently adopted the Council Regulation;

"the Council Regulation" means Council Regulation (EC) No 1347/2000 of 29 May 2000 on jurisdiction and the recognition and enforcement of judgments in matrimonial matters and in matters of parental responsibility for children of both spouses;

"court" means a judge or the district judge;

"court of trial" means a divorce county court designated by the Lord Chancellor as a court of trial pursuant to section 33(1) of the Act of 1984 and, in relation to matrimonial proceedings pending in a divorce county court, the principal registry shall be treated as a court of trial having its place of sitting at the Royal Courts of Justice;

"defended cause" means a cause not being an undefended cause;

"district judge", in relation to proceedings in the principal registry, a district registry or a county court, means the district judge or one of the district judges of that registry or county court, as the case may be;

"district registry", except in rule 4.22(2A), means any district registry having a divorce county court within its district;

"divorce county court" means a county court so designated by the Lord Chancellor pursuant to section 33(1) of the Act of 1984;

"divorce town", in relation to any matrimonial proceedings, means a place at which sittings of the High Court are authorised to be held outside the Royal Courts of Justice for the hearing of such proceedings or proceedings of the class to which they belong;

"document exchange" means any document exchange for the time being approved by the Lord Chancellor;

"family proceedings" has the meaning assigned to it by section 32 of the Act of 1984;

"financial provision order" means any of the orders mentioned in section 21(1) of the Act of 1973 except an order under section 27(6) of that Act;

"financial relief" has the same meaning as in section 37 of the Act of 1973;

"judge" does not include a district judge;

"notice of intention to defend" has the meaning assigned to it by rule 10.8;

"officer of the service" has the same meaning as in the Criminal Justice and Court Services Act 2000;

"order for maintenance pending suit" means an order under section 22 of the Act of 1973;

"person named" includes a person described as "passing under the name of A.B.";

PART III

"the President" means the President of the Family Division or, in the case of his absence or incapacity through illness or otherwise or of a vacancy in the office of President, the senior puisne judge of that Division;
"principal registry" means the Principal Registry of the Family Division;
"proper officer" means –

(*a*) in relation to the principal registry, the family proceedings department manager, and
(*b*) in relation to any other court or registry, the court manager,
or other officer of the court or registry acting on his behalf in accordance with directions given by the Lord Chancellor;
"property adjustment order" means any of the orders mentioned in section 21(2) of the Act of 1973;
"registry for the divorce town" shall be construed in accordance with rule 2.32(6);
"Royal Courts of Justice", in relation to matrimonial proceedings pending in a divorce county court, means such place, being the Royal Courts of Justice or elsewhere, as may be specified in directions given by the Lord Chancellor pursuant to section 42(2)(*a*) of the Act of 1984;
"senior district judge" means the senior district judge of the Family Division or, in his absence from the principal registry, the senior of the district judges in attendance at the registry;
"special procedure list" has the meaning assigned to it by rule 2.24(3);
"undefended cause" means –
(i) a cause in which no answer has been filed or any answer filed has been struck out, or
(ii) a cause which is proceeding only on the respondent's answer and in which no reply or answer to the respondent's answer has been filed or any such reply or answer has been struck out, or
(iii) a cause to which rule 2.12(4) applies and in which no notice has been given under that rule or any notice so given has been withdrawn, or
(iv) a cause in which an answer has been filed claiming relief but in which no pleading has been filed opposing the grant of a decree on the petition or answer or any pleading or part of a pleading opposing the grant of such relief has been struck out, or
(v) any cause not within (i) to (iv) above in which a decree has been pronounced;
"variation order" means an order under section 31 of the Act of 1973.

(2) Unless the context otherwise requires, a cause begun by petition shall be treated as pending for the purposes of these rules notwithstanding that a final decree or order has been made on the petition.

(3) Unless the context otherwise requires, a rule or Part referred to by number means the rule or Part so numbered in these rules.

(4) In these rules a form referred to by number means the form so numbered in Appendix 1 or 1A to these rules with such variation as the circumstances of the particular case may require.

(5) In these rules any reference to an Order and rule is –

(*a*) if prefixed by the letters "CCR", a reference to that Order and rule in the County Court Rules 1981, and
(*b*) if prefixed by the letters "RSC", a reference to that Order and rule in the Rules of the Supreme Court 1965.

(5A) In these rules a reference to a Part or rule, if prefixed by the letters "CPR", is a reference to that Part or rule in the Civil Procedure Rules 1998.

(6) References in these rules to a county court shall, in relation to matrimonial proceedings, be construed as references to a divorce county court.

(7) In this rule and in rule 1.4, "matrimonial proceedings" means proceedings of a kind with respect to which divorce county courts have jurisdiction by or under section 33, 34 or 35 of the Act of 1984.

Amendments—SI 1992/2067; SI 1993/295; SI 1997/1056; SI 1999/3491; SI 2000/2267; SI 2001/821.

"matrimonial cause" (r 1.2(1))—The term "cause" is used to extend "matrimonial cause" (defined by MFPA 1984, s 32 as "an action for divorce, nullity of marriage or judicial separation") to include also petitions for presumption of death or dissolution of marriage.

"child" and "child of the family" (r 1.2(1))—The definition of "child" for the purposes of Pt IV, excluded from this definition, is at r 4.1(1).

"family proceedings" (r 1.2(1))—Nowhere in these rules (or elsewhere) is the term "family proceedings" fully defined, save by reference to SCA 1981, Sch 1, para 3. Thus, non-contentious probate business is included in the term, whilst proceedings under I(PFD)A 1975 and PHA 1997 are not "family proceedings" within the definition of r 1.2(1).

"matrimonial proceedings" (r 1.2(1), (6), (7))—Rule 1.2(7) restricts use of "matrimonial proceedings" only to this rule and to r 1.4. By reference to MFPA 1984, ss 33 and 34 (the reference to s 32 is redundant), the term is applied only to proceedings pending in the county courts.

"a cause begun by petition shall be treated as pending" (r 1.2(2))—The main significance of this rule is its applicability to financial relief proceedings which can be commenced ancillary to a matrimonial cause even though there is a final decree. In the case of children proceedings, the cause remains pending for one year since "the last hearing or judicial intervention in the cause" (r 2.40(3)).

"the County Court Rules 1981", "the Rules of the Supreme Court 1965" (r 1.2(5))—This refers to the CCR/RSC in force immediately before 26 April 1999 and subsequent references to provisions of those Rules in FPR 1991 should be read accordingly (see Family Proceedings (Miscellaneous Amendments) Rules 1999, r 3).

1.3 Application of other rules

(1) Subject to the provisions of these rules and of any enactment the County Court Rules 1981 and the Rules of the Supreme Court 1965 shall continue to apply, with the necessary modifications, to family proceedings in a county court and the High Court respectively.

(2) For the purposes of paragraph (1) any provision of these rules authorising or requiring anything to be done in family proceedings shall be treated as if it were, in the case of proceedings pending in a county court, a provision of the County Court Rules 1981 and, in the case of proceedings pending in the High Court, a provision of the Rules of the Supreme Court 1965.

Amendments—SI 1999/1012.

Defined terms—"family proceedings": r 1.2(1).

CCR and RSC "shall continue to apply" (r 1.3(1))—The application of CCR and RSC in their original form (ie those rules in force immediately before 26 April 1999) is mandatory in the absence of other, or inconsistent, provision in these rules or in any other enactment. Thus, for example, the provisions of RSC Ord 38 and CCR Ord 20, concerning evidence (especially leave to

PART III

adduce expert evidence: RSC Ord 38, r 36 and CCR Ord 20, r 27) apply in family proceedings (but see **Expert evidence in ancillary relief proceedings** below).

"family proceedings" (r 1.3(1), (2))—See **"family proceedings"** under r 1.2.

Civil Procedure Rules 1998—With effect from 26 April 1999 the Civil Procedure Rules 1998 came into operation for all civil proceedings save for "family proceedings" as defined by Matrimonial and Family Proceedings Act 1984, s 32 (CPR 1998, r 2.1(2)). The result of this is that there will be three regimes for the various forms of family process referred to in *Family Court Practice* (see **Table** below) namely:

(*a*) the original RSC and CCR which continue to govern family proceedings (but see **Costs in family proceedings** and **Expert evidence in ancillary relief proceedings** below) for as long as CPR 1998 do not apply directly to family proceedings within the meaning of MFPA 1984, s 32;

(*b*) various of the existing RSC and CCR (as modified to bring them into line with CPR 1998 and set out in Schs 1 and 2 thereto) continue to apply (such as the rules relating to enforcement of orders); and

(*c*) the Civil Procedure Rules 1998 are applicable to proceedings under Inheritance (Provision for Family and Dependants) Act 1975, Protection from Harassment Act 1997, Trusts of Land and Appointment of Trustees Act 1996, s 14, judicial review and appeals to the Court of Appeal.

Thus, references to RSC Ord 31, r 1 (see FPR 1991, r 2.64(3)) and CCR Ord 29 (see FPR 1991, r 3.9A(4)) will continue to refer to the original unamended procedural rules. All proceedings covered by FPR 1991 and, for example, Adoption Rules 1984 will be subject to the provisions of the unamended RSC/CCR.

Costs in family proceedings—With effect from 26 April 1999, the new costs regime contained in CPR 1998, Pts 43, 44 (except rr 44.9–44.12), 47 and 48 was specifically applied (subject to appropriate modifications) to family proceedings (see now Family Proceedings (Amendment) Rules 2003, r 10.27(1)). Thereafter, RSC Ord 62 and CCR Ord 38 ceased to apply to the assessment of costs in such proceedings and the Family Proceedings (Costs) Rules 1991 were revoked (see Procedural Guide 79 and annotations to CPR 1998, Pt 44 et seq for further detailed commentary). However, as a general rule, no costs for work done before that date should be disallowed if they would have been allowed on taxation before that date.

Expert evidence in ancillary relief proceedings—From 5 June 2000, CPR 1998, rr 35.1–35.14 relating to expert evidence, except rr 35.5(2) and 35.8(4)(*b*), apply to all ancillary relief applications (FPR 1991, r 2.61C).

Table

(1) *Family process*

Form of family process	(*a*) **Original RSC/CCR**	(*b*) **Modified RSC/CCR (set out in CPR 1998, Schs 1, 2)**	(*c*) **CPR 1998**
Adoption Act 1976	*		
Child Abduction and Custody Act 1985	*		
Child Support Acts – appeals	*		
Children Act 1989	*		
Domestic Proceedings and Magistrates' Courts Act 1978[1]	–	–	–
Family Law Act 1986	*		
Family Law Act 1996, Pt IV	*		

Form of family process	(*a*) Original RSC/CCR	(*b*) Modified RSC/CCR (set out in CPR 1998, Schs 1, 2)	(*c*) CPR 1998
Human Fertilisation and Embryology Act 1990, s 30	*		
Inheritance (Provision for Family and Dependants) Act 1975			*
Injunctions in inherent jurisdiction (free-standing)		*	*
Judicial review in family proceedings			*
Married Women's Property Act 1882	*		
Matrimonial Causes Act 1973	*		
Matrimonial and Family Proceedings Act 1984, Pt III	*		
Protection from Harassment Act 1997		*	*
Trusts of Land and Appointment of Trustees Act 1996, s 14			*
Wardship and the inherent jurisdiction	*		

(2) *Ancillary processes*

Note: the following proceedings (with the exception of costs), ancillary to other applications, will depend on their "lead" application for the procedural rules to which they are subject. Thus, an application for enforcement of a lump sum order by charging order will be family proceedings and therefore subject to the existing, "old style", CCR; whilst an application for a blood test in Inheritance (Provision for Family and Dependants) Act 1975 proceedings will be governed by the modified, "new style", RSC/CCR (set out in CPR 1998, Schs 1, 2). Accordingly, in the former case, leave to adduce valuation evidence should be sought under "old style" CCR 1981, Ord 20, r 27(1)(*a*); by contrast, in the latter scenario, permission will be required under CPR 1998, r 35.4(1).

Form of family process	(*a*) Original RSC/CCR	(*b*) Modified RSC/CCR (set out in CPR 1998, Schs 1, 2)	(*c*) CPR 1998
Scientific tests under Family Law Reform Act 1969[2]	*	*	
Enforcement of orders	*	*	*
Costs			*
Appeals			
(i) District judge to circuit judge in family proceedings (as defined by MPPA 1984, s 32)	*		
(ii) Judge to Court of Appeal			*
(iii) Family proceedings court to High Court judge	*		

PART III

1 Proceedings in the family proceedings court are not in any event "civil proceedings" (Civil Procedure Act 1997, s 1(1)); but see *Cordle v Cordle* [2001] EWCA Civ 1791, [2002] 1 FLR 207, CA.

2 For the purposes of FLRA 1969, s 1, family proceedings are "civil proceedings".

1.4 County court proceedings in principal registry

(1) Subject to the provisions of these rules, matrimonial proceedings pending at any time in the principal registry which, if they had been begun in a divorce county court, would be pending at that time in such a court, shall be treated, for the purposes of these rules and of any provision of the County Court Rules 1981 and the County Courts Act 1984, as pending in a divorce county court and not in the High Court.

(2) Unless the context otherwise requires, any reference to a divorce county court in any provision of these rules which relates to the commencement or prosecution of proceedings in a divorce county court, or the transfer of proceedings to or from such a court, includes a reference to the principal registry.

Defined terms—"divorce county court": r 1.2(1); "matrimonial proceedings": r 1.2(7); "pending": r 1.2(2); "principal registry": r 1.2(1).

"the County Court Rules 1981" (r 1.4(1))—This refers to the CCR in force immediately before 26 April 1999 and subsequent references to provisions of those Rules in FPR 1991 should be read accordingly (see Family Proceedings (Miscellaneous Amendments) Rules 1999, r 3).

1.5 Computation of time

(1) Any period of time fixed by these rules, or by any rules applied by these rules, or by any decree, judgment, order or direction for doing any act shall be reckoned in accordance with the following provisions of this rule.

(2) Where the act is required to be done not less than a specified period before a specified date, the period starts immediately after the date on which the act is done and ends immediately before the specified date.

(3) Where the act is required to be done within a specified period after or from a specified date, the period starts immediately after that date.

(4) Where, apart from this paragraph, the period in question, being a period of seven days or less, would include a day which is not a business day, that day shall be excluded.

(5) Where the time so fixed for doing an act in the court office expires on a day on which the office is closed, and for that reason the act cannot be done on that day, the act shall be in time if done on the next day on which the office is open.

(6) In these rules "business day" means any day other than –

(*a*) a Saturday, Sunday, Christmas Day or Good Friday; or

(*b*) a bank holiday under the Banking and Financial Dealings Act 1971, in England and Wales.

Extension of time—RSC Ord 3, r 5 and CCR Ord 13, r 4 provide for the court to extend or abridge time on application or by consent of the parties (save that, in the High Court, consent applies only to the service, filing or amendment of documents). Application, where applicable or otherwise necessary, should be made on notice (or may be ex parte in cases of abridgement) to the district judge with an affidavit, giving reasons for the application and for any delay. RSC Ord 3, r 5 and CCR Ord 13, r 4 are disapplied in CA 1989 proceedings by r 4.15(1) to the extent that parties cannot themselves consent to the extending of time otherwise directed by the court or prescribed by the rules.

PART II
MATRIMONIAL CAUSES

2.1 Application of Part II

This Part applies –

(*a*) to causes;
(*b*) to applications under Part II of the Act of 1973, except sections 27, 32, 33, 35, 36 and 38; and
(*c*) for specifying the procedure for complying with the requirements of section 41 of the Act of 1973.

Defined terms—"cause": r 1.2(1).

"causes" (r 2.1(*a*))—Defined in r 1.2(1) by reference to Matrimonial and Family Proceedings Act 1984, s 32 and Matrimonial Causes Act 1973, s 19, causes are actions for divorce, nullity of marriage, judicial separation and presumption of death and dissolution. Rules 2.2 to 2.51, excluding r 2.45, deal with causes (ie the main suit) from filing of the petition to grant of decree absolute.

"Part II of the Act of 1973" (r 2.1(*b*))—MCA 1973, Pt II deals with applications for financial relief for parties to a marriage and children of the family. Rules 2.52 to 2.68 deal with these applications when ancillary to a matrimonial cause.

"section 41 of the Act of 1973" (r 2.1(*c*))—MCA 1973, s 41 deals with consideration of the arrangements for the children of the family and is considered in detail in rr 2.38, 2.39.

Commencement etc of proceedings

2.2 Cause to be begun by petition

(1) Every cause shall be begun by petition.

(2) Where a petition for divorce, nullity or judicial separation discloses that there is a minor child of the family who is under 16 or who is over that age and is receiving instruction at an educational establishment or undergoing training for a trade or profession, the petition shall be accompanied by a statement, signed by the petitioner personally and if practicable agreed with the respondent, containing the information required by Form M4, to which shall be attached a copy of any medical report mentioned therein.

Amendments—SI 1992/2067.

Defined terms—"cause", "child of the family": r 1.2(1); "minor": Family Law Reform Act 1969, ss 1(2), 12.

"instruction at an educational establishment or undergoing training for a trade or profession" (r 2.2(2))—These terms are not clearly defined in this context, and petitioners have been left to adopt their own approach. By virtue of the Child Support Act 1991, more clarity will be needed since, if a minor is not a "child" within the definition in that Act (s 55 and Child Support (Maintenance Calculation Procedure) Regulations 2000, Sch 1), it may still be possible to obtain periodical payments for the child in family proceedings (Matrimonial Causes Act 1973, s 23 or CA 1989, Sch 1).

"if practicable agreed with the respondent" (r 2.2(2))—The extent to which court offices issuing petitions insist on adherence to this requirement of the rules is not clear. The following should be borne in mind by them and by respondents:

(*a*) court staff and district judges are asked to spare a thought for the practicality of a petitioner obtaining the consent of a reluctant or hostile respondent;

(*b*) when he signs the acknowledgement of service, the respondent will be asked to say whether or not he agrees with the proposals in the statement of arrangements (question 7(*c*) on Form M6);

(*c*) although the opportunity is rarely used, the respondent is entitled to file his own statement, setting out his views on the arrangements for the children (r 2.38); this rule may be of use to a respondent who does not agree with the petitioner's statement.

Form M4—It should be noted that r 2.2(2) does not require the form itself to be used but only that the information in it should be provided to the court.

2.3 Contents of petition

Unless otherwise directed, every petition shall contain the information required by Appendix 2 to these rules.

The petition—The use of forms issued by the courts or law stationers is acceptable but not obligatory. Many practitioners will have their petitions typed or word-processed.

"Unless otherwise directed"—Information prescribed by FPR 1991, App 2 may be omitted, but only if leave of the court to do so is obtained. Application is most commonly made to exclude the petitioner's private address, although application may be made to exclude other information.

(*a*) *Private address* Despite the terms of r 10.21 (which specifically excludes r 2.3), it remains necessary for the petitioner to seek the court's leave to omit her address. Procedure for this is governed by *Practice Direction of 8 May 1975* as follows:

(i) the petition is filed, omitting the petitioner's address, accompanied by an application (summons in the High Court) to the district judge (r 10.9) which is made ex parte (para 1);

(ii) whether this need be supported by an affidavit is a matter for the district judge's discretion. Any such affidavit should state the petitioner's address (para 2);

(iii) if leave is given that the petitioner stands with the address omitted, a note of the petitioner's address should be deposited in an envelope with the court file. The order granting leave should record that the petitioner's affidavit or note of her address be sealed up and not opened without leave (para 3). If leave to omit is refused, the petition is amended to show the address (para 4);

(iv) the order granting leave is served with the petition (para 3);

(v) the court file is marked that leave for non-disclosure has been given (para 3). Thereafter, care must be taken not to nullify the effect of the order, eg by showing the petitioner's public funding (legal aid) certificate to anyone inspecting the file (para 3); and affidavits should be suitably amended to omit the address (para 5).

(*b*) *Other information* To exclude other particulars, the petition should be filed with those particulars (eg details of another child or of previous proceedings which the petitioner does not wish to disclose) left blank. At the same time, application should be made to the district judge ex parte, with an affidavit in support explaining the reason for seeking the omission. If the application is refused, the petition will be amended to include the particulars (*Practice Direction of 11 April 1968*).

"information required by Appendix 2"—All petitions, except those for declarations as to marital status (r 3.12), of parentage (r 3.13), of legitimacy or legitimation (r 3.14) or as to adoption overseas (r 3.15), must contain the information set out in App 2, in relation to which the following points arise:

(*a*) *Names of the parties and date and place of marriage* (App 2, para 1(*a*)) These details should be taken precisely from the marriage certificate except that, in most instances, the wife will have taken her husband's surname. Any other change of name should be shown by supplying the new name followed in brackets by the former name.

(*b*) *Domicile or habitual residence* (para 1(*c*), (*d*)) Bearing in mind Domicile and Matrimonial Proceedings Act 1973, s 5 and the provisions of "Brussels II" (see Council Regulation (EC) No 1347/2000 – set out in Part VI of this work), the petitioner must ensure that details are set out fully so that the basis for claiming the court's jurisdiction is made clear (see further under DMPA 1973).

(*c*) *Children of the family* (para 1(*f*)) The following must be included:
(i) any living children of the family (as defined by MCA 1973, s 52(1));
(ii) in respect of each, the full name (including present surname) and date of birth (if under 18) or statement that he is over 18;
(iii) in respect of a child over 16 but under 18, a statement whether he is still at school or undergoing training for a trade, profession or vocation;
(iv) indication of the existence of any dispute as to whether a child is a child of the family (para 1(*h*)).

(*d*) *Other children* (para 1(*g*)) Details of other children born to the wife during the marriage must be given.

(*e*) *Previous proceedings* (para 1(*i*)) This includes not only proceedings with reference to the marriage, but also proceedings concerning (i) marital property (eg under Trusts of Land and Appointment of Trustees Act 1996, s 14) and (ii) children of the family (eg care or adoption proceedings).

(*f*) *Child Support Act 1991 details* (para 1(*ia*)) This addition to App 2 requires that the petition include information as to whether or not any applications have been made under CSA 1991 and, if so, further details concerning the calculation. An additional paragraph in the standard form of petition is included for this. It will not be clear from the face of the petition whether or not children of the family are qualifying children (see CSA 1991, s 3(1)), but see information in Pt 1, para 2 of the statement of arrangements for the children.

(*g*) *Financial agreements in proceedings under MCA 1973, s 1(2)(e)* (para 1(*k*)) In proceedings based on five years' living apart, if a petitioner wishes to say that agreement has been reached between the parties or to put forward proposals (rarely an advisable course), particular care will be needed in drafting this paragraph. An agreement between spouses cannot oust the jurisdiction of the courts (*Hyman v Hyman* [1929] AC 601, (1929) FLR Rep 342, HL) or the child support officer (CSA 1991, s 9(3)). The courts will be slow to upset an agreement freely reached between spouses (*Edgar v Edgar* (1981) FLR 19, [1980] 3 All ER 887, CA); but see also *Smith v Smith* [2000] 3 FCR 374.

(*h*) *Irretrievable breakdown* (para 1(*l*)) This must only be pleaded in a petition for divorce.

(*i*) *Facts under MCA 1973, s 1(2) for divorce or judicial separation* (para 1(*m*)) These should be stated succinctly and will be elaborated on (as necessary) in the particulars (see (*k*) below).

(*j*) *Grounds for other petitions* (paras 1(*m*), 2) These should be stated succinctly and elaborated on (as necessary) in the particulars (see (*k*) below). Nullity petitions under MCA 1973, s 12(*e*) or (*f*) (respondent suffering from venereal disease or pregnancy *per alium*) must state whether, at the time of the marriage, the petitioner was ignorant of the facts.

(*k*) *Particulars* (para 1(*m*)) The particulars to be relied on in support of the fact or ground alleged, but not the evidence in support, are to be pleaded briefly. In drafting these, it will be necessary to bear in mind any dates relevant for the purposes of MCA 1973, s 2 (resumption or continuation of living together).
(i) *Adultery* (MCA 1973, s 1(2)(*a*)) The approximate date when the adultery commenced should be stated (if known). If the parties are still living in the same household, it should be stated that the adultery is continuing (if that is the case) or the date when the petitioner first knew of it (cf MCA 1973, s 2(1)). The name of the co-respondent need not be stated (r 2.7(1)) but, if an order for costs is sought against him, his name must be included and he will be served with the petition.
(ii) *Unreasonable behaviour* (MCA 1973, s 1(2)(*b*)) Other than in very "weak" petitions, it will rarely be necessary to plead more than five or six instances of unreasonable behaviour, since "brief particulars" are stipulated. Dates or approximate dates should be given if possible and, where the parties remain in the same household, the last allegation must be less than six months prior to the date of the petition (MCA 1973, s 2(3)). If an answer is filed, application can be made for leave to amend the petition to give further particulars (r 2.11(1)); see also *Butterworth v Butterworth* [1997] 2 FLR 336, CA.
(iii) *Desertion* (MCA 1973, s 1(2)(*c*)) The particulars must show that the separation was against the petitioner's wishes.
(iv) *Civil Evidence Act 1968* If evidence is to be relied on under this Act, the particulars must plead this (see r 2.4).

(*l*) *Prayer in the petition* (para 4(*a*)) The prayer in the petition sets out the relief sought by the petitioner, including:
(i) a decree of divorce, judicial separation, nullity or as the case may be;
(ii) any application concerning the children, although the court will be slow to make orders in respect of children (CA 1989, s 1(5); see also r 2.39);
(iii) any claim for costs;
(iv) any claims for ancillary relief: despite the fact that these need not be particularised precisely, it is important that they are alluded to (r 2.53(1)) or it will be necessary for the

petitioner to seek leave to pursue an application for ancillary relief (r 2.53(2)); exact particulars of any property sought to be adjusted need not be given, only that the petitioner seeks "a property adjustment order": this avoids committing the petitioner to unforeseen consequences and avoids the public funding (legal aid) statutory charge (*Jones v The Law Society* (1983) FLR 733).

Petitioner "fee exempt"—Where the petitioner is "fee exempt" (Family Proceedings Fees Order 1999, art 4), she may give her solicitor's name and address for service if he agrees (App 2, para 4(*c*)). In practice, this arrangement is normally shown on court documents by putting "c/o" before the solicitor's address.

Service personnel—Para 4(*c*) requires the petitioner to give an address for service "in England and Wales"; however, where a member of the Services serving overseas, or a civilian employee of the Ministry of Defence, is a petitioner acting in person, she may give her address for service as a British Forces Post Office (BFPO) number (*Practice Direction of 22 August 1978*).

2.4 Petitioner relying on section 11 or 12 of the Civil Evidence Act 1968

(1) A petitioner who, in reliance on section 11 or 12 of the Civil Evidence Act 1968, intends to adduce evidence that a person –

(*a*) was convicted of an offence by or before a court in the United Kingdom or by a court-martial there or elsewhere, or

(*b*) was found guilty of adultery in matrimonial proceedings or to be the father of a child in relevant proceedings before any court in England and Wales, or was adjudged to be the father of a child in affiliation proceedings before a court in the United Kingdom,

must include in his petition a statement of his intention with particulars of –

(i) the conviction, finding or adjudication and the date thereof,

(ii) the court or court-martial which made the conviction, finding or adjudication and, in the case of a finding or adjudication, the proceedings in which it was made, and

(iii) the issue in the proceedings to which the conviction, finding or adjudication is relevant.

(2) In this rule "matrimonial proceedings", "relevant proceedings" and "affiliation proceedings" have the same meaning as in the said section 12.

"petitioner who ... intends to adduce evidence" (r 2.4(1))—This includes a respondent in his answer: r 2.15(6).

"section 11 or 12 of the Civil Evidence Act 1968" (r 2.4(1))—CEA 1968, s 11 enables a court hearing civil proceedings to accept as evidence of the conviction a certificate thereof (s 11(3)), where to do so is relevant to those proceedings and provided that the offence is not "spent" (s 11(1)). CEA 1968, s 12(1) enables a court hearing civil proceedings to admit as evidence of adultery or paternity a finding in other matrimonial, affiliation or relevant proceedings (see below for definitions). Rule 2.4(1)(*a*), (*b*) adopts similar wording to ss 11 and 12 but, if evidence on this basis is to be adduced, the respondent must be given notice in the petition and the further information required by r 2.4(1) must also be set out in the petition. In this rule, "matrimonial proceedings" means any matrimonial cause in the High Court or a county court in England and Wales or in the High Court in Northern Ireland, any consistorial action in Scotland, or any appeal arising out of any such cause or action; "affiliation proceedings" means, in relation to Scotland, any action of affiliation and aliment (s 12(5)).

2.5 Signing of petition

Every petition shall be signed by counsel if settled by him or, if not, by the petitioner's solicitor in his own name or the name of his firm, or by the petitioner if he sues in person.

"signed by counsel"—It is sufficient for counsel or the solicitor to sign the draft petition, provided his name is reproduced on the filed petition (*Practice Direction of 24 April 1947* unreported).

Solicitor's signature—In practice, the signature will normally be in the name of the firm, but it may be by the solicitor who settled the petition. The object of the rule is to place the solicitor under a duty to ensure that the petition is in order.

Petitioner acting in person—The petitioner signs the petition if acting in person; if the petitioner is "fee exempt" (Family Proceedings Fees Order 1999, art 4), she must sign the petition personally.

2.6 Presentation of petition

(1) A petition may be presented to any divorce county court.

(2) Unless otherwise directed on an application made ex parte, a certificate of the marriage to which the cause relates shall be filed with the petition.

(3) Where a solicitor is acting for a petitioner for divorce or judicial separation, a certificate in Form M3 shall be filed with the petition, unless otherwise directed on an application made ex parte.

(4) Where there is before a divorce county court or the High Court a petition which has not been dismissed or otherwise disposed of by a final order, another petition by the same petitioner in respect of the same marriage shall not be presented without leave granted on an application made in the pending proceedings:

Provided that no such leave shall be required where it is proposed, after the expiration of the period of one year from the date of the marriage, to present a petition for divorce alleging such of the facts mentioned in section 1(2) of the Act of 1973 as were alleged in a petition for judicial separation presented before the expiration of that period.

(5) The petition shall be presented by filing it, together with any statement and report required by rule 2.2(2) in the court office, with as many copies of the petition as there are persons to be served and a copy of the statement and report required by rule 2.2(2) for service on the respondent.

(6) CCR Order 3, rule 4(2) (which, as applied by rule 5 of that Order, deals with the filing and service of petitions) shall not apply, but on the filing of the petition the proper officer shall annex to every copy of the petition for service a notice in Form M5 with Form M6 attached and shall also annex to the copy petition for service on a respondent the copy of any statement and report filed pursuant to paragraph (5) of this rule.

Defined terms—"cause", "divorce county court", "proper officer": r 1.2(1).

"any divorce county court" (r 2.6(1))—The petition may be filed in any divorce county court (listed in Civil Courts Order 1983 (as amended)), which includes the principal registry (r 1.4(2)). This applies regardless of where the petitioner lives within the jurisdiction and subject only to the requirements as to domicile and residence of the Domicile and Matrimonial Proceedings Act 1973, s 5.

Filing of the petition and accompanying documents (r 2.6(2), (3), (5))—When filed, the petition must be accompanied by the following:

(*a*) as many copies of the petition as there are parties to be served (r 2.6(5)) (cf statement of arrangements, where only a copy for the other spouse is needed);

(*b*) parties' marriage certificate, or certified copy obtained from the appropriate register office (r 2.6(2)); if the certificate cannot be produced at the time of filing of the petition (eg because not yet obtained from the register office) but it is urgent that the petition be filed, application may be made ex parte to the district judge for the filing of the petition without the certificate. Such application will normally be by affidavit (by the proposed petitioner or his solicitor) with a brief explanation of the reason why the certificate is not available and why the petition needs to be filed urgently. It may be granted if the petitioner or his solicitor undertakes to file the certificate subsequently. NB foreign certificates (see also r 10.14) should be accompanied by a translation authenticated by a notary (r 10.14(2));

(*c*) certificate regarding reconciliation in Form M3 (see App 1 and MCA 1973, s 6(2)) where, in divorce or judicial separation proceedings, the petitioner is represented by a solicitor. The certificate need not be filed where the petitioner is acting in person or where she is "fee exempt" (see (*f*) below), even if she has received advice from a solicitor whose address is on the record;

(*d*) statement of arrangements for the children of the family (with any report referred to therein), as required by r 2.2(2), with a copy of each for service on the other spouse;

(*e*) petitioner's public funding (legal aid) certificate, if such funding has been granted at this stage, with notice of issue thereof (Funding Code Procedures, Section C16);

(*f*) court fee (see Family Proceedings Fees Order 1999), except where the petitioner is "fee exempt" under that Order, in which case the petitioner files a statement to that effect; the petitioner is "fee exempt" in the following circumstances:
   (i) where he is receiving Legal Help in accordance with the Funding Code: 1999 Order, art 4(*a*);
   (ii) where he is receiving income support or working families' tax credit: art 4(*b*);
   (iii) where the Lord Chancellor remits or reduces the fee because its payment would cause undue hardship owing to the exceptional circumstances of the case: art 5.

Leave to file another petition (r 2.6(4))—Subject to the proviso to the rule, where an earlier petition by the same petitioner remains undisposed of (whether by dismissal or final decree) that petitioner must, in order to file a further petition, have leave. Application should be made to the district judge ex parte on the filing of an affidavit by the petitioner in the original proceedings. If leave is granted, reference to the original proceedings must be made in the further petition (App 2, para 1(*i*)). Examples of where an earlier petition might justifiably be left extant while a second proceeds are: where the respondent consents to a decree under MCA 1973, s 1(2)(*d*) (two years apart with consent) in place of a petition under MCA 1973, s 1(2)(*b*) (unreasonable behaviour), the petitioner may prefer to keep the original petition alive until decree absolute in case the respondent withdraws his consent; or where the parties are reconciled after the filing of the first petition but the reconciliation fails, if the petitioner cannot proceed on a supplemental petition, she may need to file a fresh petition but wishes to keep the first alive because of interim relief obtained therein.

Filing of petition by respondent—This provision applies only to a petitioner, but the respondent to a petition is not precluded from filing his own contemporaneous petition and does not need leave to do so.

Judicial separation petition filed within one year of marriage (r 2.6(4), proviso)—The proviso to the rule applies only in the limited circumstances of a judicial separation petition having been filed within one year of marriage when a petitioner may, without leave, file a divorce petition alleging the same fact or facts as in the petition for judicial separation. Although it is necessary to rely on the same fact(s) (ie adultery or unreasonable behaviour), it does not seem necessary to rely on the same particulars in support. Thus it would appear that, for example, further allegations of unreasonable behaviour could be included in the further petition. However, it is necessary to file a further petition rather than to amend the existing judicial separation petition (*Butler v Butler, The Queen's Proctor Intervening* [1990] 1 FLR 114).

"CCR Order 3, rule 4(2) ... shall not apply" (r 2.6(6))—The effect of CCR Ord 3, rr 4(2), 5 is to provide generally for the contents of a petition issued in the county court; however, since this is already dealt with in FPR 1991, App 2 with regard to matrimonial causes petitions, the CCR provisions are redundant.

"a notice in Form M5 with Form M6 attached" (r 2.6(6))—Forms M5 and M6 are to be found in FPR 1991, App 1 and are issued by the court. After they have been sealed by the court, the petition and accompanying documents are ready for service (see r 2.9).

2.7 Parties

(1) Subject to paragraph (2), where a petition alleges that the respondent has committed adultery, the person with whom the adultery is alleged to have been committed shall be made a co-respondent in the cause unless –

(*a*) that person is not named in the petition, or
(*b*) the court otherwise directs.

(2) Where a petition alleges that the respondent has been guilty of rape upon a person named, then, notwithstanding anything in paragraph (1) that person shall not be made a co-respondent in the cause unless the court so directs.

(3) Where a petition alleges that the respondent has been guilty of an improper association (other than adultery) with a person named, the court may direct that the person named be made co-respondent in the cause, and for that purpose the district judge may require the proper officer to give notice to the petitioner and to any other party who has given notice of intention to defend of a date, time and place at which the court will consider giving such a direction.

(4) An application for directions under paragraph (1) may be made ex parte if no notice of intention to defend has been given.

(5) Paragraphs (1) and (3) of this rule do not apply where the person named has died before the filing of the petition.

Defined terms—"cause", "court", "district judge": r 1.2(1); "notice of intention to defend": rr 1.2(1), 10.8; "person named": r 1.2(1); "proper officer": rr 1.2(1), 2.32(6).

Parties to the proceedings—In all matrimonial causes, the parties will be the spouses, as petitioner and respondent. The respondent remains so called, even though he files an answer and the cause proceeds on the prayer in that answer (see also r 2.12). Others may be joined as co-respondent (see below) or as party cited (r 2.16), and others may apply to intervene (see eg MCA 1973, s 49(5) and FPR 1991, rr 2.40, 2.60) or be ordered to be joined (see eg r 2.7(3); cf RSC Ord 15, r 6 and CCR Ord 15, r 1). However, the mere service of proceedings (eg under r 2.60(1)) does not make the person served a party to proceedings unless the person is formally joined as a party by the court (*Re T (Divorce: Interim Maintenance: Discovery)* [1990] 1 FLR 1).

Co-respondent named in petition (r 2.7(1))—The person with whom the respondent is alleged to have committed adultery is required to be joined as co-respondent unless he is not named or the court otherwise directs (MCA 1973, s 49(1); cf a person "guilty of an improper association", where the court has a discretion to make him a co-respondent: r 2.7(3). If rape on a person named is alleged, that person also need not be named as a co-respondent (r 2.7(2)).

"that person is not named in the petition" (r 2.7(1)(*a*))—The effect of this wording is to enable a petition to proceed under MCA 1973, s 1(2)(*a*) where the petitioner alleges adultery without the co-respondent being named, whether or not the petitioner knows his identity (see also MCA 1973, s 49(2)).

"the court otherwise directs" (r 2.7(1)(*b*))—When the allegation is of adultery with a girl under the age of 16, application should be made to the district judge as to whether she should be joined as a co-respondent (*Practice Note of 15 December 1960*). Application is made on notice (by summons in the High Court) to the district judge (r 10.9). It may be made ex parte at the time of filing the petition and before service on the respondent.

"improper association (other than adultery)" (r 2.7(3))—The district judge will consider of his own motion whether a third party against whom an improper association is alleged should be joined as a co-respondent. The district judge may fix an appointment, of which notice will be

PART III

given to the petitioner and anyone who has given notice of intention to defend (ie not just an acknowledgement of service of the petition). The district judge will want to consider such matters as how old and how serious the allegations are, how likely they are to be true and whether the person concerned has since married. It should rarely be necessary or desirable to serve a third party in these circumstances, and this difficulty would be avoided if the third party's name were omitted altogether.

Death of co-respondent (r 2.7(5))—If the person named as adulterer, or against whom an allegation of improper association is made, has died before the filing of the petition, that person may be named; the fact of the death should be stated in the petition, and that person is not joined as co-respondent. If a co-respondent dies during the course of proceedings and service has not been effected, application for an order to dispense with service should be made (r 2.9(11). On the granting of such an order, the court may direct that the name be struck from the suit (*Walpole v Walpole and Chamberlain* [1901] P 86). In special procedure cases, it should be sufficient to produce a copy of the co-respondent's death certificate to the petitioner's special procedure affidavit, with a request to dispense with service briefly stated in the affidavit.

Intervention in a suit—Wherever adultery is alleged against anyone not made a party, or where the court considers it appropriate in the interests of a person to be joined, the court may allow such a person to intervene and become a party on such terms as the court thinks fit (MCA 1973, s 49(5); see also eg FPR 1991, rr 2.40, 2.60).

Dismissal of a party from the suit—Where, having heard all the evidence, the court considers that there is insufficient evidence against a co-respondent to justify his inclusion as a party to proceedings, it may dismiss him from the suit (MCA 1973, s 49(3)).

2.8 Discontinuance of cause before service of petition

Before a petition is served on any person, the petitioner may file a notice of discontinuance and the cause shall thereupon stand dismissed.

Defined terms—"cause": r 1.2(1).

"notice of discontinuance"—The effect of filing a notice of discontinuance is that the petition is dismissed and thus nullified. However, it does not prevent the petitioner from filing a subsequent petition on the same facts, since there has been no adjudication on the original petition. If the petition has been served, the petitioner applies on notice (by summons in the High Court) to the district judge (r 10.9) for dismissal of the petition.

Discontinuance—This term should be distinguished from: (*a*) *striking out*, which may occur, for example, for want of prosecution, if the petitioner fails to attend a hearing, or if a petition is held to be frivolous, vexatious or an abuse of the court process (RSC Ord 18, r 19), and (*b*) *stay of proceedings*, where the cause remains in being but can only be proceeded with if leave of the court is granted. The court has a discretionary power to order a stay of proceedings at any time (Supreme Court Act 1981, s 49(3), County Courts Act 1984, s 38.

Service of petition etc

2.9 Service of petition

(1) Subject to the provisions of this rule and rules 9.3 and 10.6, a copy of every petition shall be served personally or by post on every respondent or co-respondent.

(2) Service may be effected –

(*a*) where the party to be served is a person under disability within the meaning of rule 9.1, through the petitioner, and

(*b*) in any other case, through the court or, if the petitioner so requests, through the petitioner.

(3) Personal service shall in no case be effected by the petitioner himself.

(4) A copy of any petition which is to be served through the court shall be served by post by an officer of the court or, if on a request by the petitioner the district judge so directs, by a bailiff delivering a copy of the petition to the party personally.

(5) For the purposes of the foregoing paragraphs, a copy of a petition shall be deemed to be duly served if –

(*a*) an acknowledgement of service in Form M6 is signed by the party to be served or by a solicitor on his behalf and is returned to the court office, and

(*b*) where the form purports to be signed by the respondent, his signature is proved at the hearing or, where the cause is undefended, in the affidavit filed by the petitioner under rule 2.24(3).

(6) Where a copy of a petition has been sent to a party and no acknowledgment of service has been returned to the court office, the district judge, if satisfied by affidavit or otherwise that the party has nevertheless received the document, may direct that the document shall be deemed to have been duly served on him.

(6A) Paragraph (6) shall not apply in cases where –

(*a*) the petition alleges two years' separation coupled with the respondent's consent to a decree being granted; and

(*b*) none of the other facts mentioned in section 1(2) of the Act of 1973 is alleged,

unless the petitioner produces to the court a written statement containing the respondent's consent to the grant of a decree.

(7) Where a copy of a petition has been served on a party personally and no acknowledgement of service has been returned to the court office, service shall be proved by filing an affidavit of service (or, in the case of service by bailiff, an indorsement of service under CCR Order 7, rule 6) showing, in the case of a respondent, the server's means of knowledge of the identity of the party served.

(8) Where an acknowledgement of service is returned to the court office, the proper officer shall send a photographic copy thereof to the petitioner.

(9) An application for leave to substitute some other mode of service for the modes of service prescribed by paragraph (1) or to substitute notice of the proceedings by advertisement or otherwise, shall be made ex parte by lodging an affidavit setting out the grounds on which the application is made; and the form of any advertisement shall be settled by the district judge:

Provided that no order giving leave to substitute notice of the proceedings by advertisement shall be made unless it appears to the district judge that there is a reasonable probability that the advertisement will come to the knowledge of the person concerned.

(10) CCR Order 7, rule 8 shall apply in relation to service by bailiff under this rule as it applies to service of a summons by bailiff in accordance with rule 10 of that Order.

(11) Where in the opinion of the district judge it is impracticable to serve a party in accordance with any of the foregoing paragraphs or it is otherwise necessary or expedient to dispense with service of a copy of a petition on the respondent or on any other person, the district judge may make an order dispensing with such service.

An application for an order under this paragraph shall be made in the first instance ex parte by lodging an affidavit setting out the grounds of the application, but the district judge may, if he thinks fit, require the attendance of the petitioner on the application.

Amendments—SI 1997/1893.

Defined terms—"district judge": r 1.2(1); "officer" (including "bailiff"): CCA 1984, s 147(1); "person under disability": r 9.1(1); "proper officer": r 1.2(1).

Scope of provision—This rule defines the variety of ways that a petition, or answer (r 2.16(1)), can be served, the essence being to ensure so far as possible that a respondent or other party has had notice of the proceedings; see also RSC Ord 65 and CCR Ord 7 as to service of documents.

Service of the petition—Rule 2.9 deals with service of a petition. General rules as to service of other documents are provided for in rr 10.2 to 10.6. The rules about service apply to both respondent and co-respondent (r 2.9(1)), and also to any party cited (r 2.16(1)).

"personally or by post" (r 2.9(1))—In the first instance, the petition will normally be served by post. The requirement to serve personally is provided for as an alternative to postal service and is not obligatory (see CCR Ord 7, r 1(1)(*a*) which also sets out personal and postal service as alternatives, but cf RSC Ord 65, r 1 which requires personal service only where there is express provision or where the court orders it).

Service on a person under disability (r 2.9(2)(*a*))—Service on a person under a disability, a minor or mental health patient (r 9.3(1)), must be "*through* the petitioner" (emphasis supplied) and not by the petitioner (see r 2.9(3)). This is understood to mean that the petitioner's solicitor or a process server must arrange service. Service on a person under disability is governed by r 9.3.

Service out of the jurisdiction—This is governed by r 10.6.

"through the court" (r 2.9(2)(*b*), (4))—Unless the petitioner otherwise requests, and save in the case of a person under disability, the court serves the petition. Service will be by post, whereupon the court officer complies with r 10.5(1). If the district judge so directs, on application by the petitioner, service may be by court bailiff (see below). Service may be effected on a party acting in person in accordance with r 10.3, or a solicitor may be instructed to accept service when the petition can be sent to him.

Forms M5 and M6—Forms M5 (notice of proceedings) and M6 (acknowledgement of service) are substantially amended by Family Proceedings (Amendment) Rules 1993, rr 11, 12. The acknowledgement of service has been revised to take account of the provisions of "Brussels II" (see **General Note** under Domicile and Matrimonial Proceedings Act 1973).

Deemed service (r 2.9(5), (6))—There are two means by which service may be deemed under r 2.9:

(*a*) *Acknowledgement of service exhibited to special procedure affidavit* (r 2.9(5)) This is the means by which service is most commonly proved. The acknowledgement of service (in Form M6) is signed by the respondent or his solicitor. If signed by the respondent, the acknowledgement of service is exhibited to the petitioner's special procedure affidavit, and the petitioner's identification of his signature enables the district judge to deem service (see also r 2.24(3)).

(*b*) *Court satisfied on other evidence* (r 2.9(6)) If no acknowledgement of service is returned to the court but the district judge is satisfied as to service on other evidence, he may deem the petition to have been served. A common example of deemed service is by production of a letter from the respondent's solicitors which states that the petition was brought to them by the respondent. Such a letter can be exhibited to the petitioner's special procedure affidavit with an extra paragraph asking the district judge to deem service of the petition in view of the contents of the letter.

Personal service (r 2.9(7))—If service is effected personally (other than by bailiff) and no acknowledgement of service is returned to the court, an affidavit of service must be filed. If, as is generally the case, the respondent is not known to the server, his means of identifying the respondent must be described in one of the following ways: eg (*a*) by means of a photograph, (*b*) by personal knowledge of the process server or other person identifying the respondent, or (*c*) by admission of the person served; in (*b*) or (*c*), corroborative evidence will be necessary. (In the first instance, the process server should be asked to seek the respondent's signature on the acknowledgement of service obviating the need for an affidavit of service.) In no circumstances may the petitioner effect personal service (r 2.9(3)).

Bailiff service (r 2.9(4), (7))—The petitioner can request the district judge to direct that personal service be by the court bailiff. A reason for the request will be expected and postal service should normally have been attempted. A form of request can be obtained from the court and a fee is payable (Family Proceedings Fees Order 1999). Proof of service is by means of indorsement of service under CCR Ord 7, r 6(*a*). If the bailiff has secured the respondent's signature on this indorsement, the petitioner can prove the signature by exhibiting the indorsement to his special procedure affidavit.

Substituted service (r 2.9(9), (10))—Application can be made ex parte to the district judge for some other mode of service such as by advertisement or by posting to an address where the petition might be expected to come to the respondent's attention. Before making an order for substituted service, or for deemed service (r 2.9(11)), the district judge will need to be satisfied that full enquiries as to the whereabouts of the respondent (or other party to be served) have been made.

Service of petition based on MCA 1973, s 1(2)(d) (r 2.9(6A))—The only way in which consent to a petition based solely on s 1(2)(*d*) (two years living apart with consent) can be evidenced is by production of the acknowledgement of service or other written evidence of the respondent's consent to a decree; see also r 2.10 for the form of the consent.

Enquiries as to respondent's whereabouts—Enquiries should be made of at least the following people or organisations, where appropriate:

(*a*) *Relatives, friends, neighbours, former employers* The district judge will want to know that, at the very least, letters have been sent to such of these as might know of the respondent's whereabouts.

(*b*) *Bank, accountant, former solicitors, doctor, dentist etc* Any of these may be willing to forward a stamped envelope containing the petition to a (former) customer/client, even though they will not reveal his address.

(*c*) *Government departments generally* In the case of applications concerning financial provision or tracing a child, certain government departments may be requested to provide a party's or a child's address (*Practice Direction of 13 February 1989*). Requests for such information must be made officially by the district judge. A petition containing a prayer for financial relief would satisfy the Practice Direction's requirement enabling an address to be requested. The departments concerned are the Department of Social Security, the Office of Population Censuses and Surveys (which administers the National Health Service Central Register), the Passport Office and the Ministry of Defence. The district judge asks the applicant to provide as much as possible of the information set out in the Practice Direction; the Passport Office and the Ministry of Defence require, in addition to the request, an undertaking that the information will be used only for the purposes of service of court process.

(*d*) *Department of Social Security* In addition to the facilities available under the Practice Direction (see (*c*) above), this department, if able to identify the respondent, will forward the petition to him. Application may be made direct by the petitioner to: Department of Social Security, NICB, Special Section A, Newcastle-upon-Tyne, NE98 1YU. As much information as possible about the respondent, by reference to the Practice Direction, should be given.

"some other mode of service" (r 2.9(9))—An order for some other mode of service will only be made if the district judge is satisfied that all other modes of service prescribed in the rule are impracticable (see RSC Ord 65, r 4(1)) and that there is some prospect of the documents coming to the attention of the respondent by another means of service, such as by posting it to the respondent's bank, a relative or employer.

Advertisement—To make an order for substituted service by advertisement, the district judge must be satisfied that there is a "reasonable probability" that the advertisement will come to the attention of the person sought to be served (proviso to r 2.9(9)). In most cases, the district judge is likely to prefer other modes of substituted service or to deem service rather than putting a party (or public funds) to the expense of advertising. If the order is made, the district judge settles the form of the advertisement, although he may ask the petitioner to submit a draft.

Effect of order for substituted service—If validly obtained, such an order cannot be challenged, even if the party intended to be served did not receive the documents; however, the order cannot be said to have been validly obtained if the district judge is not given all the necessary information relevant to the application (for example that, in the past, the respondent had a solicitor acting for him) (*Clifford v Clifford* [1985] FLR 732, CA).

Application for substituted service (r 2.9(9))—Application for the order is made ex parte to the district judge. The grounds on which the application is made must be set out, bearing in mind the relevant criterion above, ie service by other means impracticable or, in the case of advertisement, reasonable probability of coming to the respondent's attention. The affidavit should set out information as to the efforts made to serve and a statement with reasons as to why the proposed method of substituted service might ensure service. The affidavit may be sworn by the petitioner or by his solicitor.

Affidavit of substituted service—If substituted service is effected, an affidavit to this effect will need to be filed to satisfy the district judge as to service when directions for trial are requested (r 2.24(1)(*a*)). It may be possible to incorporate sufficient information about substituted service in the petitioner's special procedure affidavit.

Dispensing with service (r 2.9(11))—To dispense with service of a petition, the district judge must be satisfied either (i) that it is "impracticable" to serve a party by any of the other means available under r 2.9, or (ii) that it is "otherwise necessary or expedient" for service to be dispensed with. The district judge will need to be satisfied that full enquiries as to the respondent's whereabouts have been made (see above). By dispensing with service, the district judge accepts that a party cannot be served and, in doing so, he balances the need for the court to be satisfied that a party to proceedings has had notice of them against the petitioner's wish or need to proceed with a petition. The needs of any children involved might be a factor in the district judge's considerations.

Application to dispense with service (r 2.9(11))—The application to dispense with service is made ex parte to the district judge, setting out the grounds (a standard form of affidavit which incorporates most, if not all, of the questions to which the district judge will want the petitioner to have addressed himself is available from the court). This may be sworn by the petitioner or his solicitor. The district judge will need to be satisfied that full enquiries as to the respondent's whereabouts have been made, and he may ask for the personal attendance of the petitioner before him, perhaps to clarify points in the affidavit in support of the application.

2.10 Consent to grant of decree

(1) Where, before the hearing of a petition alleging two years' separation coupled with the respondent's consent to a decree being granted, the respondent wishes to indicate to the court that he consents to the grant of a decree, he shall do so by filing a notice to that effect signed by the respondent personally.

For the purposes of this paragraph an acknowledgement of service containing a statement that the respondent consents to the grant of a decree shall be treated as such a notice if the acknowledgement is signed –

(*a*) in the case of a respondent acting in person, by the respondent, or
(*b*) in the case of a respondent represented by a solicitor, by the respondent as well as by the solicitor.

(2) A respondent to a petition which alleges any such fact as is mentioned in paragraph (1) may give notice to the court either that he does not consent to a decree being granted or that he withdraws any consent which he has already given.

Where any such notice is given and none of the other facts mentioned in section 1(2) of the Act of 1973 is alleged, the proceedings on the petition shall be stayed and the proper officer shall thereupon give notice of the stay to all parties.

Defined terms—"proper officer": r 1.2(1).

Notice of consent (r 2.10(1))—MCA 1973, s 1(2)(*d*) is the only fact which requires a respondent's consent to a decree. Thus the court needs to know not only that the respondent has received the petition but also that he consents to a decree. The acknowledgement of service (Form M6) asks, at question 6, if the respondent consents to a decree being granted. Consent will be given if the respondent answers this affirmatively and signs the form personally. Any other form of notice filed at court by the respondent and indicating his consent would appear to suffice.

No consent or withdrawal of consent (r 2.10(2))—A respondent may indicate to the court that he does not consent or that he withdraws his consent, although no date by which this is to be done is specified in the rule. Once a decree nisi has been obtained withdrawal of consent is unlikely to be effective (unless a respondent can successfully apply for rehearing (r 2.42) or for rescission of the decree (r 2.44)). Further, once the district judge has signed his certificate under the special procedure, it may be difficult to set up the withdrawal (*Day v Day* [1980] Fam 29, (1980) FLR 341, CA: registrar's certificate held to be tantamount to a decree nisi).

Stay on proceedings (r 2.10(2))—When the respondent gives an indication of no consent or withdrawal of consent, the petition is stayed. It remains on file and can be proceeded with only if leave is granted by the court. If there is no consent, the petitioner will be unable to proceed since consent is an essential component for proof of the fact under MCA 1973, s 1(2)(*d*). However, where the respondent withdraws consent, the court may be able to resurrect the original consent when considering an application to remove the stay (*N v N (Divorce: Agreement not to Defend)* [1992] 1 FLR 266: husband who agreed not to defend was held to his original agreement). Application for removal is made on notice (by summons in the High Court) to the district judge (r 10.9), and the decision whether to remove the stay is discretionary.

Pleadings and amendment

2.11 Supplemental petition and amendment of petition

(1) Subject to rule 2.14 –

(*a*) a supplemental petition may be filed without leave at any time before an answer is filed but thereafter only with leave; and

(*b*) a petition may be amended without leave at any time before an answer is filed but thereafter only with leave.

(2) Subject to paragraph (3) an application for leave under this rule –

(*a*) may if every opposite party consents in writing to the supplemental petition being filed or the petition being amended, be made by lodging in the court office the supplemental petition or a copy of the petition as proposed to be amended; and

(*b*) shall, in any other case, be made on notice (or in the High Court by summons) to be served, unless otherwise directed, on every opposite party.

(3) The district judge may, if he thinks fit, require an application for leave to be supported by an affidavit.

(4) An order granting leave shall –

(*a*) where any party has given notice of intention to defend, fix the time within which his answer must be filed or amended;

(*b*) where the order is made after directions for trial have been given, provide for a stay of the hearing until after the directions have been renewed.

(5) An amendment authorised to be made under this rule shall be made by filing a copy of the amended petition.

(6) Rules 2.5 and 2.7 shall apply to a supplemental or amended petition as they apply to the original petition.

(7) Unless otherwise directed, a copy of a supplemental or amended petition, together with a copy of the order (if any) made under this rule shall be served on

every respondent and co-respondent named in the original petition or in the supplemental or amended petition.

(8) The petitioner shall file the documents required by paragraph (7) to be served on any person and thereupon, unless otherwise directed, rules 2.6(6) and 2.9 shall apply in relation to that person as they apply in relation to a person required to be served with an original petition.

Defined terms—"district judge": r 1.2(1); "notice of intention to defend": rr 1.2(1), 10.8.

Supplemental and amended petitions contrasted—A petition can be amended where the further particulars alleged occurred before the date of the petition. If a petitioner wishes to rely on particulars which occurred after the date of the petition, a supplemental petition must be filed. A supplemental petition is not another petition, but merely supplements an existing one. Thus, if a period of separation or desertion were not complete at the time of filing of the original petition, a new petition and not a supplemental one would be needed: accordingly, the original petition could be discontinued (r 2.8) or leave may be sought to file a further petition (r 2.6(4)). Similar considerations apply to the amendment of a petition, in that the petition still dates from its filing. As a result, it is not possible, for example, to amend a petition under MCA 1973, s 1(2)(*b*) (unreasonable behaviour) to one under s 1(2)(*d*) (two years' living apart with consent) if the two-year period had not elapsed at the time of filing of the petition to be amended. Similarly, a judicial separation petition filed before the parties have been married for a year may not be amended to one for divorce (*Butler v Butler, The Queen's Proctor Intervening* [1990] 1 FLR 114; see also r 2.6(4)).

Filing without leave (r 2.11(1))—At any time before an answer is filed, either a supplemental or an amended petition may be filed. If directions for trial have been given, leave will be needed (r 2.14).

Filing with leave (r 2.11(1)–(3))—If an answer has been filed leave of the court is required for the filing of a supplemental petition or to amend a petition. Such leave may be sought in one of the following ways:

(*a*) *With consent* (r. 2.11(2)(*a*)) If all parties consent to the filing of the supplemental petition or to amendment of the petition, the application for leave can be made by filing the proposed supplemental or amended petition (with, presumably, the document indicating the consent of all parties);

(*b*) *On notice* (r 2.11(2)(*b*), (3)) If consent has not been obtained, the application is made on notice (by summons in the High Court) to the district judge (r 10.9). The proposed supplemental or amended petition should accompany the application. Although it may be desirable to do so, it does not seem essential to file an affidavit in support of the application, since r 2.11(3) enables the district judge to require an application, after filing, to be supported by affidavit, if he so directs.

Further directions for trial—The petitioner will need to seek further directions on the supplemental or amended petition. In view of the definition of "undefended cause" in r 1.2(1), it seems unlikely, where an answer to the original petition has been filed, that the petitioner would be able to proceed under the special procedure even where no answer to the supplemental or amended petition is filed. On giving leave, the district judge may direct that, in the event of no answer to the supplemental or amended petition being filed, the original answer be struck out (see (i) under definition of "undefended cause" in r 1.2(1)).

Filing and service of supplemental or amended petition (r 2.11(5)–(8))—The amended petition is filed at court (r 2.11(5)). A supplemental or amended petition proceeds in much the same way as an ordinary petition (r 2.11(6), (8)): signing of petition (r 2.5), parties to be joined (r 2.7), service (r 2.9) after attachment of the notice of proceedings and acknowledgement of service (r 2.6(6)). The only variation from the standard procedure is that, in the case of service, the district judge may direct that a party should not be served (r 2.11(7)). This would be by analogy with r 2.7(1) and, if an order dispensing with service on a party had already been obtained, the district judge might be willing to dispense with service on that party of the supplemental or amended petition.

Amendment of petition on birth of child after filing of petition—A petition may be amended to show the birth of a child of the marriage subsequently to the date thereof, if it is so desired, and re-service of a petition, so amended, should be a matter for the discretion of the district judge (*Practice Note of 14 December 1939* unreported).

2.12 Filing of answer to petition

(1) Subject to paragraph (2) and to rules 2.10, 2.14 and 2.37, a respondent or co-respondent who –

(*a*) wishes to defend the petition or to dispute any of the facts alleged in it,

(*b*) being the respondent wishes to make in the proceedings any charge against the petitioner in respect of which the respondent prays for relief, or

(*c*) being the respondent to a petition to which section 5(1) of the Act of 1973 applies, wishes to oppose the grant of a decree on the ground mentioned in that subsection,

shall, within 21 days after the expiration of the time limited for giving notice of intention to defend, file an answer to the petition.

(2) An answer may be filed notwithstanding that the person filing the answer has not given notice of intention to defend.

(3) Any reference in these rules to a person who has given notice of intention to defend shall be construed as including a reference to a person who has filed an answer without giving notice of intention to defend.

(4) Where in a cause in which relief is sought under section 12(*d*) of the Act of 1973 the respondent files an answer containing no more than a simple denial of the facts stated in the petition, he shall, if he intends to rebut the charges in the petition, give the court notice to that effect when filing his answer.

Defined terms—"notice of intention to defend": rr 1.2(1), 10.8.

Answer by respondent, co-respondent or party cited—It is generally a respondent who files an answer, but a co-respondent or party cited (to whom this rule also applies: r 2.16(2)) may also wish to file an answer. The following description refers predominantly to "respondent", but that term can be taken to include "co-respondent" and "party cited", where appropriate. Drafting and the contents of the answer are considered in r 2.15.

"Subject to ... rules 2.10, 2.14 and 2.37" (r 2.12(1))—These exceptions are included for the following reasons:

(*a*) *Rule 2.10* A respondent to a petition under MCA 1973, s 1(2)(*d*) (two years' living apart with consent) can withdraw his consent, which would have the effect of making any answer unnecessary, and the petition would be stayed (r 2.10(2)).

(*b*) *Rule 2.14* Once directions for trial have been given, no pleading, which includes an answer, may be filed without leave of the court.

(*c*) *Rule 2.37* Despite the fact that no answer has been filed, a party to proceedings may be heard on the issue of costs. Thus a party who wishes only to be heard on costs need not file an answer.

Circumstances in which an answer must be filed (r 2.12(1))—An answer should be filed by a respondent (or exceptionally a co-respondent or party cited) in the following circumstances:

(*a*) *Defending petition or disputing facts in it* (r 2.12(1)(*a*)) If a respondent wishes to oppose the grant of a decree, or a co-respondent or party cited wishes to dispute facts in a petition, he must file an answer. If a respondent accepts that the marriage has irretrievably broken down but disputes certain of the particulars, he may wish to file an answer; however, if the purpose of doing so is to answer allegations which might be raised again in children or ancillary relief proceedings, it may be sufficient for him to write to the petitioner or her solicitors, at the time of filing his acknowledgement of service, in the following terms: "The respondent accepts that the marriage has irretrievably broken down but does not accept certain of the allegations in the petition. He reserves the right to reply to those allegations if raised in any subsequent proceedings relating to the children or for ancillary relief." In any event, public funding (legal aid) is only rarely available for respondents to defend proceedings where it is admitted that the marriage has irretrievably broken down.

(*b*) *Respondent wishing to make "any charge against the petitioner"* (r 2.12(1)(*b*)) If a respondent wishes to make allegations against a petitioner and to cross-apply for a decree on facts which he alleges, he must file an answer. It is not necessary to file an answer if the respondent seeks relief other than a decree (see below).

(*c*) *Respondent under MCA 1973, s 5(1) wishing to oppose grant of decree* (r 2.12(1)(*c*)) Where the respondent to a petition under MCA 1973, s 1(2)(*e*) (five years' living apart) wishes to oppose the grant of a decree on grounds that it will result in grave financial or other hardship, she must file an answer containing particulars of the hardship alleged.

Circumstances where filing of answer not required—There is no need to file an answer where the respondent seeks or opposes an order in respect of children (r 2.40), seeks an order or to be heard on ancillary relief (r 2.52) or where a party wishes to be heard on a question of costs (r 2.37).

Time-limit for filing an answer (r 2.12(1))—The effect of this rule, in view of the amendment to Form M5 (notice of proceedings) pursuant to Family Proceedings (Amendment) Rules 1993, r 11(*a*), is to require the filing of the answer within 28 days of service. It is not clear whether leave is necessary for this. The rule is expressed in mandatory terms, implying that leave may be necessary. Further, there are a number of cases in the early 1970s which suggest that leave is indeed necessary (see eg *Huxford v Huxford* [1972] 1 WLR 210, [1972] 1 All ER 330; *Spill v Spill* [1972] 1 WLR 793, [1972] 3 All ER 9; *Rogers v Rogers* [1974] 1 WLR 709, [1974] 2 All ER 361).

Filing an answer where directions for trial are given (r 2.12(1))—Once directions for trial have been given, it is beyond doubt that leave is required to file an answer (r 2.14). If directions for trial are given under the special procedure (r 2.24(3)), this may make it difficult for the respondent to obtain leave (*Day v Day* [1980] Fam 29, (1980) FLR 341, CA; see also r 2.42).

No notice of intention to defend (r 2.12(2), (3))—An answer can be filed, even though no notice of intention to defend has been filed (r 2.12(2)). A respondent in these circumstances is included in any reference to "a person who has given notice of intention to defend" (r 2.12(3)).

2.13 Filing of reply and subsequent pleadings

(1) A petitioner may file a reply to an answer within 14 days after he has received a copy of the answer pursuant to rule 2.17.

(2) If the petitioner does not file a reply to an answer, he shall, unless the answer prays for a degree, be deemed, on making a request for directions for trial, to have denied every material allegation of fact made in the answer.

(3) No pleading subsequent to a reply shall be filed without leave.

Time-limit for filing reply (r 2.13(1))—Rule 2.17 provides for service of further pleadings by the court. If the petitioner intends to file a reply, he must do so within 14 days of receiving the answer.

Deemed denial of facts (r 2.13(2))—Unless the answer seeks a decree, the petitioner need not file a reply if he intends solely to deny allegations of fact in the answer: he will be deemed to do so on filing a request for directions for trial (r 2.24).

Leave of the court (r 2.13(3))—If leave is sought, application is made on notice (by summons in the High Court) to the district judge (r 10.9).

2.14 Filing and amendment of pleadings after directions for trial

No pleading shall be filed or amended without leave after directions for trial have been given.

Leave of the court—If leave is sought, application is made on notice (by summons in the High Court) to the district judge (r 10.9). The additional pleading sought to be filed should be available at the hearing of the application.

Amendment of pleadings—For procedure on amendment of a petition see r 2.11; for procedure on amendment of an answer and other pleadings see r 2.18.

Directions for trial—See r 2.24.

2.15 Contents of answer and subsequent pleadings

(1) Where an answer, reply or subsequent pleading contains more than a simple denial of the facts stated in the petition, answer or reply, as the case may be, the pleading shall set out with sufficient particularity the facts relied on but not the evidence by which they are to be proved and, if the pleading is filed by the husband or wife, it shall, in relation to those facts, contain the information required in the case of a petition by paragraph 1(*k*) of Appendix 2.

(2) Unless otherwise directed, an answer by a husband or wife who disputes any statement required by paragraphs 1(*f*), (*g*) and (*h*) of Appendix 2 to be included in the petition shall contain full particulars of the facts relied on.

(3) Paragraph 4(*a*) of Appendix 2 shall, where appropriate, apply with the necessary modifications, to a respondent's answer as it applies to a petition:

Provided that it shall not be necessary to include in the answer any claim for costs against the petitioner.

(4) Where an answer to any petition contains a prayer for relief, it shall contain the information required by paragraph 1(*j*) of Appendix 2 in the case of the petition in so far as it has not been given by the petitioner.

(5) Where a party's pleading includes such a statement as is mentioned in rule 2.4, then if the opposite party –

- (*a*) denies the conviction, finding or adjudication to which the statement relates, or
- (*b*) alleges that the conviction, finding or adjudication was erroneous, or
- (*c*) denies that the conviction, finding or adjudication is relevant to any issue in the proceedings,

he must make the denial or allegation in his pleading.

(6) Rules 2.4 and 2.5 shall apply, with the necessary modifications, to a pleading other than a petition as they apply to a petition.

"simple denial of the facts" (r 2.15(1))—An answer or reply may contain a simple denial, without explanation or amplification, but parties must be wary that the denial itself cannot be regarded as an assertion of fact (eg where many of the allegations in a petition are expressed in the negative). As a result, the party making the assertions in the petition or other pleading must prove them. If a respondent wishes to raise allegations himself or to cross-apply he must do so, since a bare denial raises no issue triable on the respondent's suit (*Haque v Haque* [1977] 1 WLR 888, [1977] 3 All ER 667).

"sufficient particularity" (r 2.15(1))—This wording is similar to that of App 2, para 1(*m*), which deals with allegations in a petition and requires that the answer, reply or other pleading should set out clearly the allegations on which it is based, but without setting out the evidence on which those allegations are to be proved.

Answer seeking decree on ground of five years' separation (r 2.15(1))—If the respondent cross-prays for a decree under Matrimonial Causes Act 1973, s 1(2)(*e*), he must include the information required by App 2, para 1(*k*) (ie whether there is any agreement or arrangement for the financial support of the petitioner or any child of the family).

Dispute concerning children of the family (r 2.15(2))—If a respondent wishes to dispute a petitioner's statement in her petition concerning a child of the family (App 2, para 1(*f*)), or to dispute a statement as to other children born to the wife (App 2, para 1(*g*)) or to set up a dispute as to whether a child is a child of the family (App 2, para 1(*h*)), his answer must contain "full particulars of the facts relied on" unless he obtains a direction to the contrary.

"Unless otherwise directed" (r 2.15(2))—If a respondent seeks a direction not to include particulars of a dispute concerning children, where, for example, the facts were particularly distasteful and their proof or otherwise would serve no useful purpose, or the facts relate to events which happened many years before, an application is made ex parte to the district judge. An affidavit should be submitted exhibiting the draft answer with the particulars omitted and explaining the reason for seeking to exclude them.

"Paragraph 4(a) of Appendix 2 shall, where appropriate, apply" (r 2.15(3))—If a respondent wishes to cross-pray for relief he must do so in his answer, whether for divorce, judicial separation or nullity; if a reply is filed, the respondent must also include any applications he intends to make concerning children (under CA 1989, Pts I and II), or for ancillary relief (App 2, para 4(*a*)). It is not necessary to include a claim for costs in the answer (proviso to r 2.15(3); see also r 2.37). Nor is it necessary to file an answer if the only relief sought is an application relating to the children or for ancillary relief (see discussion under r 2.12).

Cross-prayer—Once filed, an answer with a cross-prayer is treated as a petition, and any amendment of it is dealt with by r 2.17. As with a petition, it cannot be amended, for example, to seek a decree based on two years' living apart where the two-year period had not expired at the time the answer was filed (see also r 2.11 on amendment of petitions). If a respondent obtains a decree on the prayer in his answer, the court can grant him the relief claimed as if he were the petitioner (MCA 1973, s 20). Thus it would appear that a respondent in his answer can cross-pray for and obtain a decree of judicial separation (in the absence of a decree being obtained on the petition).

Particulars of proceedings outside the jurisdiction (r 2.15(4))—An answer which contains a cross-prayer for relief must also include particulars of proceedings continuing outside the jurisdiction which relate to the marriage or are capable of affecting its validity or subsistence (as set out in App 2, para 1(*j*)), but such particulars need only be given insofar as they are not already included in the petition.

"Rule 2.4 ... shall apply" (r 2.15(6))—Any relevant allegation of conviction or finding of adultery must be included in an answer, reply or other pleading, as in a petition in accordance with r 2.4.

Signing of further pleadings (r 2.15(6))—An answer, reply or other pleading must be signed by counsel or the party's solicitor, or the party himself if in person, as with a petition in accordance with r 2.5.

2.16 Allegation against third person in pleading

(1) Rules 2.7 and 2.9 shall apply, with the necessary modifications, to a pleading other than a petition as they apply to a petition, so however that for the references in those rules to a co-respondent there shall be substituted references to a party cited.

(2) Rule 2.12 shall apply, with the necessary modifications, to a party cited as it applies to a co-respondent.

"party cited" (r 2.16(1))—Where adultery or an improper association is alleged by a respondent in his answer, the person against whom the allegation is made becomes a party to the proceedings and is referred to as "a party cited". This is subject to the court directing otherwise (r 2.7(1)(*b*)) and the other exceptions contained in r 2.7. A party cited is thus in the same position in regard to the answer as is a co-respondent to a petition.

Adulterer not named (r 2.16(1))—By analogy with r 2.7(1)(*a*), it should be possible for a respondent, if he so wishes, to omit the name of the adulterer; however, the adulterer should be named and served if an order for costs is sought against him.

Answer of party cited (r 2.16(2))—A party cited may answer allegations in an answer in the same way as a co-respondent (see r 2.12(1)(*a*)), subject to the same time-limits for filing (ie 28 days). The party cited need not file an answer if he wishes to be heard only on the question of costs (r 2.37).

2.17 Service of pleadings

A party who files an answer, reply or subsequent pleading shall at the same time file a copy for service on every opposite party, and thereupon the proper officer shall annex to every copy for service on a party cited in the pleading a notice in Form M5 with Form M6 attached and shall send a copy to every other opposite party.

Defined terms—"proper officer": r 1.2(1).

Documents for service—Sufficient copies for service on all other parties must be filed at court. If public funding has been granted to the respondent or other party, the public funding (legal aid) certificate with notice of issue should also be filed.

Forms M5 and M6 for party cited—Only the party cited, as a new party to the proceedings, must be served with notice of proceedings (Form M5) and acknowledgement of service (Form M6).

"send a copy to every other opposite party"—The court is responsible for service in the first instance. Where that fails, alternatives for service of petitions are available (r 2.16(1) applying r 2.9 to an answer, reply or other pleading).

2.18 Supplemental answer and amendment of pleadings

Rule 2.11 shall apply, with the necessary modifications, to the filing of a supplemental answer, and the amendment of a pleading or other document not being a petition, as it applies to the filing of a supplemental petition and the amendment of a petition.

2.19 Particulars

(1) A party on whom a pleading has been served may in writing request the party whose pleading it is to give particulars of any allegation or other matter pleaded and, if that party fails to give the particulars within a reasonable time, the party requiring them may apply for an order that the particulars be given.

(2) The request or order in pursuance of which particulars are given shall be incorporated with the particulars, each item of the particulars following immediately after the corresponding item of the request or order.

(3) A party giving particulars, whether in pursuance of an order or otherwise, shall at the same time file a copy of them.

Request for particulars (r 2.19(1))—A party to proceedings is entitled to know sufficient particulars of allegations against him, or of other matters pleaded, to enable him to meet the case against him. "[E]very pleading must contain, and contain only, a statement in a summary form of the material facts on which the party pleading relies for his claim or defence, as the case may be, ... and the statement must be as brief as the nature of the case admits" (RSC Ord 18, r 7(1)). Further, "every pleading must contain the necessary particulars of any claim, defence or other matter pleaded" (RSC Ord 18, r 12(1); see also eg *Butterworth v Butterworth* [1997] 2 FLR 336, CA).

PART III

Preparations for trial

2.20 Discovery of documents in defended cause

(1) RSC Order 24 (discovery and inspection of documents) shall apply to a defended cause begun by petition whether pending in the High Court or county court as it applies to an action begun by writ, with the following modifications –

(*a*) the second paragraph of rule 2(1) and rules 2(2) to (4), rules 4(2), 6 and 7A shall be omitted,
(*b*) in rule 16(1) the words from "including" to the end shall be omitted,
(*c*) in rule 2(7) for the words "the summons for directions in the action is taken out" there shall be substituted the words "directions for trial are given".

(2) For the purposes of RSC Order 24, rule 2(1) as applied by paragraph (1) of this rule, pleadings shall be deemed to be closed at the expiration of 14 days after service of the answer, and are deemed to be closed then notwithstanding that any request or order for particulars previously made has not been complied with.

(3) The petitioner and any party who has filed an answer shall be entitled to have a copy of any list of documents served on any other party under RSC Order 24 as applied by paragraph (1) of this rule, and such copy shall, on request, be supplied to him free of charge by the party who served the list.

In this paragraph "list of documents" includes an affidavit verifying the list.

Defined terms—"defended cause": r 1.2(1).

Scope of provision—This rule imports RSC Ord 24 (with certain modifications) into the rules in defended causes (whether in the High Court or county court). RSC Ord 24 provides for discovery of documents by list (whether with or without an order), and for inspection, production and copying of documents.

"pleadings shall be deemed to be closed" (r 2.20(2))—Pleadings are deemed to be closed 14 days after service of the answer. Thus a petitioner wishing to serve a reply, or any other party filing a reply, to the answer will find that his list of documents must be served before his reply, ie 14 days and 28 days respectively (r 2.16(2) applying r 2.12(1)). There is also potential for uncertainty in this provision: since the court serves the answer (r 2.17), the respondent will not know when service has been effected, and thus when time starts to run, unless in every case the court notifies the respondent when the answer has been sent to the petitioner, but there appears to be no requirement for this in the rules.

2.21 Discovery by interrogatories in defended cause

(1) RSC Order 26 (which deals with discovery by interrogatories) shall apply to a defended cause begun by petition and pending in the High Court as it applies to a cause within the meaning of that Order, but with the omission of –

(*a*) rule 2(1)(*b*),
(*b*) in rule 4(1) the words "or the notice under Order 25, rule 7," and
(*c*) in rule 6(1) the words from "including" to the end.

(2) A copy of the proposed interrogatories shall be filed when they are served under RSC Order 26, rule 3(1) or when a summons for an order under RSC Order 26, rule 1(2) is issued.

(3) Where a defended cause is pending in a divorce county court RSC Order 26 as applied by CCR Order 14, rule 11, shall apply, and references in this rule to provisions of the said Order 26 shall be construed as references to those provisions as so applied.

Defined terms—"defended cause", "divorce county court": r 1.2(1).

Scope of provision—This rule applies RSC Ord 26 (with certain modifications) to defended causes proceeding in the High Court and divorce county courts. Ord 26 deals with discovery by interrogatories.

2.22 Medical examination in proceedings for nullity

(1) In proceedings for nullity on the ground of incapacity to consummate the marriage the petitioner shall, subject to paragraph (2), apply to the district judge to determine whether medical inspectors should be appointed to examine the parties.

(2) An application under paragraph (1) shall not be made in an undefended cause –

(*a*) if the husband is the petitioner, or

(*b*) if the wife is the petitioner and –

(i) it appears from the petition that she was either a widow or divorced at the time of the marriage in question, or

(ii) it appears from the petition or otherwise that she has borne a child, or

(iii) a statement by the wife that she is not a virgin is filed;

unless, in any such case, the petitioner is alleging his or her own incapacity.

(3) References in paragraphs (1) and (2) to the petitioner shall, where the cause is proceeding only on the respondent's answer or where the allegation of incapacity is made only in the respondent's answer, be construed as references to the respondent.

(4) An application under paragraph (1) by the petitioner shall be made –

(*a*) where the respondent has not given notice of intention to defend, after the time limited for giving the notice has expired;

(*b*) where the respondent has given notice of intention to defend, after the expiration of the time allowed for filing his answer or, if he has filed an answer, after it has been filed;

and an application under paragraph (1) by the respondent shall be made after he has filed an answer.

(5) Where the party required to make an application under paragraph (1) fails to do so within a reasonable time, the other party may, if he is prosecuting or defending the cause, make an application under that paragraph.

(6) In proceedings for nullity on the ground that the marriage has not been consummated owing to the wilful refusal of the respondent, either party may apply to the district judge for the appointment of medical inspectors to examine the parties.

(7) If the respondent has not given notice of intention to defend, an application by the petitioner under paragraph (1) or (6) may be made ex parte.

(8) If the district judge hearing an application under paragraph (1) or (6) considers it expedient to do so, he shall appoint a medical inspector or, if he thinks it necessary, two medical inspectors to examine the parties and report to the court the result of the examination.

(9) At the hearing of any such proceedings as are referred to in paragraph (1) the court may, if it thinks fit, appoint a medical inspector or two medical inspectors to

examine any party who has not been examined or to examine further any party who has been examined.

(10) The party on whose application an order under paragraph (8) is made or who has the conduct of proceedings in which an order under paragraph (9) has been made for the examination of the other party, shall serve on the other party notice of the date, time and place appointed for his or her examination.

Defined terms—"cause", "district judge": r 1.2(1); "notice of intention to defend": rr 1.2(1), 10.8; "undefended cause": r 1.2(1).

"the petitioner shall, subject to paragraph (2), apply" (r 2.22(1))—Where a nullity decree is sought on the ground that the marriage has not been consummated due to the incapacity of either party to consummate it (MCA 1973, s 12(*a*)), there is an obligation on the petitioner to apply to the district judge to determine whether a medical inspector should be appointed (r 2.22(1)). This obligation is subject to the exceptions contained in r 2.22(2), which is itself subject to the discretion of the court under r 2.22(9) to appoint a medical inspector.

Cause proceeding on respondent's answer (r 2.22(3))—If the cause is proceeding on the respondent's answer alone or solely on a prayer in his answer under MCA 1973, s 12(*a*), it is the respondent who must make the application under r 2.22(1).

Time for application under r 2.22(1) (r 2.22(4))—The time for making the application to the district judge under r 2.22(1) is computed by reference to the time for giving notice of intention to defend or for filing an answer. If no notice of intention to defend is filed, application is made seven days after service of the petition (ie the time-limit for filing notice to defend: rr 2.22(4)(*a*), 10.8(2)(*a*)). If notice of intention is given, the application is taken out 28 days after service of the petition (ie the time-limit for filing an answer (r 2.12(1)). If an answer is filed earlier, the application is taken out at that time (r 2.22(4)(*b*)).

Other party's application (r 2.22(5))—If the party required to make the application under r 2.22(1) has not done so "within a reasonable time", the other party may make the application. The rules do not specify what is a reasonable time, but 14 days may be considered appropriate, especially since the cause cannot proceed until the application under r 2.22(1) has been disposed of.

"either party may apply" (r 2.22(6))—It will be noted that, in contrast to r 2.22(1), either party has a discretion whether or not to apply where the petition is based on the ground that the marriage has not been consummated owing to the wilful refusal of the respondent to consummate it (MCA 1973, s 12(*b*)).

The application (r 2.22(7))—The application under r 2.22(1) or (6) is on notice (by summons in the High Court) to the district judge; however, if no notice of intention to defend has been filed, the application can be ex parte (r 2.22(7)). There appears to be no obligation to support the application by affidavit but, if the applicant intends to request an order that there be no medical report, it may be thought prudent to set out the reasons for such request.

The appointment (r 2.22(8), (9))—Only one inspector will normally be appointed unless there is good reason for appointing two (r 2.22(8)), for example where the wife exercises her right to request an examination by a woman doctor. A wife's solicitor should advise her of this right and satisfy the district judge that he has done so (*Practice Direction of 19 February 1963*). A man is not to be examined by a woman doctor (*Practice Direction* above). At the hearing, the judge has a discretion to appoint a medical inspector, or two if appropriate (r 2.22(9)), but such appointment would presumably be subject to the requirements of the Practice Direction.

Notice of the examination (r 2.22(10))—Responsibility for service of notice of the appointment for examination rests with the party on whose application the order was made, if by the district judge, or on the party conducting the proceedings if the order is made by the judge.

2.23 Conduct of medical examination

(1) Every medical examination under rule 2.22 shall be held at the consulting room of the medical inspector or, as the case may be, of one of the medical inspectors appointed to conduct the examination:

Provided that the district judge may, on the application of a party, direct that the examination of that party shall be held at the court office or at such other place as the district judge thinks convenient.

(2) Every party presenting himself for examination shall sign, in the presence of the inspector or inspectors, a statement that he is the person referred to as the petitioner or respondent, as the case may be, in the order for the examination, and at the conclusion of the examination the inspector or inspectors shall certify on the statement that it was signed in his or their presence by the person who has been examined.

(3) Every report made in pursuance of rule 2.22 shall be filed and either party shall be entitled to be supplied with a copy on payment of the prescribed fee.

(4) In an undefended cause it shall not be necessary for the inspector or inspectors to attend and give evidence at the trial unless so directed.

(5) In a defended cause, if the report made in pursuance of rule 2.22 is accepted by both parties, notice to that effect shall be given by the parties to the district judge and to the inspector or inspectors not less than seven clear days before the date fixed for the trial; and where such notice is given, it shall not be necessary for the inspector or inspectors to attend and give evidence at the trial.

(6) Where pursuant to paragraphs (4) or (5) the evidence of the inspector or inspectors is not given at the trial, his or their report shall be treated as information furnished to the court by a court expert and be given such weight as the court thinks fit.

The examination and inspectors' fees—The duties of medical inspectors are set out in *Practice Direction of 5 July 1971*. Liability for payment of the fee rests with the party at whose instigation the inspector was appointed (*Practice Direction of 18 November 1968*).

"on payment of the prescribed fee" (r 2.23(3))—The fee for a copy of the report is £1 per page (Family Proceedings Fees Order 1999, Sch 1, fee 7.1).

Attendance at trial of undefended cause (r 2.23(4))—The direction to attend may come from: the district judge on giving directions for trial in accordance with r 2.24(1)(*e*); the judge on the trial; or on application to the district judge by one of the parties. By analogy with RSC Ord 38, r 37, the court will want to do everything in its power to avoid the expense of calling experts.

"treated as information furnished ... by a court expert" (r 2.23(6))—The court will thus treat the medical inspector's opinion as admissible on any relevant matter including an issue in the cause (see further RSC Ord 38, rr 36–39).

Fee for attending court—Liability for payment of fees of a medical inspector who attends court remains with the party who instigated the report (*Practice Direction of 18 November 1968*), regardless of who required the inspector's attendance at court; however, this is presumably subject to the court's overriding discretion on costs.

2.24 Directions for trial

(1) On the written request of the petitioner or of any party who is defending a cause begun by petition the district judge shall give directions for the trial of the cause if he is satisfied –

(*a*) that a copy of the petition (including any supplemental or amended petition) and any subsequent pleading has been duly served on every party required to be served and, where that party is a person under disability, that an affidavit required by rule 9.3(2) has been filed;

(*b*) if no notice of intention to defend has been given by any party entitled to give it, that the time limited for giving such notice has expired;

(*c*) if notice of intention to defend has been given by any party, that the time allowed him for filing an answer has expired;

(*d*) if an answer has been filed, that the time allowed for filing any subsequent pleadings has expired;

(*e*) in proceedings for nullity –

(i) that any application required by rule 2.22(1) has been made, and

(ii) where an order for the examination of the parties has been made on an application under rule 2.22, that the notice required by paragraph (10) of that rule has been served and that the report of the inspector or inspectors has been filed.

(2) Subject to paragraph (3), where the cause is pending in a divorce county court other than the principal registry and is to be tried at that court, the district judge shall, if he considers it practicable to do so, give directions for trial.

(3) Where the cause is an undefended cause for divorce or judicial separation and, in a case to which section 1(2)(*d*) of the Act of 1973 applies, the respondent has filed a notice under rule 2.10(1) that he consents to the grant of a decree, then, unless otherwise directed, there shall be filed with the request for directions for trial an affidavit by the petitioner –

(*a*) containing the information required by Form M7(*a*), (*b*), (*c*), (*d*), or (*e*) (whichever is appropriate) as near as may be in the order there set out, together with any corroborative evidence on which the petitioner intends to rely, and

(*b*) verifying, with such amendments as the circumstances may require, the contents of any statement of arrangements filed by the petitioner under rule 2.2(2),

and the district judge shall give directions for trial by entering the cause in a list to be known as the special procedure list.

(4) In the case of a defended cause the district judge may treat the request for directions for trial as a summons or application for directions so as to enable him to give such directions with regard to –

(*a*) the future course of the cause,

(*b*) any application made therein for ancillary relief or for an order relating to a child, and

(*c*) the provision of evidence relating to the arrangements or proposed arrangements for the children of the family,

as appear to be necessary or desirable for securing the just, expeditious and economical disposal of the cause or application; and the proper officer shall give the parties notice of a date, time and place at which the request will be considered.

(5) In any other case the district judge shall give directions for trial by requiring the proper officer to set the cause down for trial and give notice that he has done so to every party to the cause.

(6) Except where evidence has been provided under paragraph (3)(*b*), directions for trial under this rule shall, unless the court orders otherwise, include a direction to the petitioner to file an affidavit verifying, with such amendments as the

circumstances may require, the contents of any statement of arrangements filed by the petitioner under rule 2.2(2).

(7) In the case of an undefended cause proceeding on the respondent's answer, paragraphs (3) and (6) shall have effect as if for the references to the petitioner and respondent there were substituted references to the respondent and the petitioner respectively.

Defined terms—"ancillary relief", "cause", "child", "child of the family", "defended cause", "district judge", "divorce county court": r 1.2(1); "notice of intention to defend": rr 1.2(1), 10.8(1); "principal registry", "proper officer": r 1.2(1); "special procedure list": rr 1.2(1), 2.24(3); "undefended cause": r 1.2(1).

"written request of the petitioner or of any party" (r 2.24(1))—The form of request for directions will depend on whether or not the cause is to be dealt with under the special procedure, ie undefended divorce and judicial separation proceedings (r 2.24(3) below). In that case, the request for directions is on Form D84 (obtainable from county courts, and often sent out by the courts when the acknowledgement of service is sent in accordance with r 2.9(8)). In relation to "any other case" (ie defended divorces and as referred to below), the request for directions is made on Form D21 (Form D267 in the principal registry). In addition to the petitioner, any other party who is defending a cause may apply for directions. Some courts require only a letter by way of request.

"the district judge shall give directions for the trial" (r 2.24(1))—The district judge is required to give directions for trial if he is satisfied as to the matters set out in the rule:

(*a*) that the petition and other documents have been served in accordance with rr 2.9 (petitions) and 2.16(1) (answers and other pleadings);

(*b*) that relevant time-limits have expired: ie for filing notice of intention to defend, seven days from service (r 10.8(2)(*a*)); for filing an answer where notice of intention to defend has been given, 28 days from service (rr 2.12(1), 10.8(2)(*a*)); for filing of other pleadings where an answer has been filed, 14 days after service of the answer in the case of a petitioner (r 2.13(1)) and 28 days in the case of a party cited who has filed notice of intention to defend (rr 2.12(1), 2.16(2));

(*c*) that questions of medical examination have been dealt with in the case of the nullity petitions referred to in r 2.22(1).

Amendment of pleadings—Once directions for trial have been given, no further pleadings can be filed nor any pleading amended without leave of the court (r 2.14).

"shall ... give directions for trial" (r 2.24(2))—Save in the case of undefended divorce or judicial separation proceedings where the special procedure applies (r 2.24(3)), the district judge must give directions, if he considers it practicable to do so, on considering the request under r 2.24(1). Directions as to place of trial are governed by r 2.25 and mode and time of trial by r 2.32.

Undefended causes in the special procedure list (r 2.24(3))—The special procedure, directions for which are dealt with in r 2.24(3), applies to undefended causes for divorce and judicial separation only, and it applies whether the cause is proceeding on the prayer in the petition or in the respondent's answer (r 2.24(7)). The disposal of causes entered in the special procedure list is dealt with in r 2.36.

"corroborative evidence" (r 2.24(3)(*a*))—Corroborative evidence will be needed in the case of an adultery petition, usually by means of the petitioner identifying the respondent's signature on the acknowledgement of service, if filed, admitting adultery and exhibiting this to the affidavit in Form M7(*a*). (Form M7(*a*) enables a confession statement to be exhibited, but this should rarely be necessary, especially where the respondent admits adultery in the acknowledgement of service.) District judges are frequently alerted by adultery petitions which complain of adultery with persons unknown, at places unknown and at times unknown. FPR 1991 do not change the law, and the court retains a solemn duty to ensure that the ground is made out before the marriage is dissolved. Thus petitioners would be well advised to provide background information in the affidavit by detailing when and how the adultery was first suspected, or admitted. Failure to observe this simple measure may result in delay following the district judge's request for further information; at worst, it may result in removal from the special procedure list.

Where a medical report is available, this can be exhibited to the affidavit in the case of an unreasonable behaviour petition, Form M7(*b*). In the case of living apart for two years with consent, the acknowledgement of service, or other document indicating consent, must be exhibited to the affidavit in Form M7(*d*), and the petitioner must identify the respondent's signature.

"verifying ... the contents of any statement of arrangements" (r 2.24(3)(*b*))—This provision has been added to the rules and Forms M7 have been extended accordingly. It enables the district judge to deal with the provisions of MCA 1973, s 41, as substituted, (satisfaction concerning arrangements for children of the family), within the terms of CA 1989, s 1(5) and in accordance with r 2.39 (and see further rr 2.2(2), 2.36(1)(*a*)).

Directions in defended causes (r 2.24(4))—In defended causes, the district judge can treat the request for directions as an application (summons in the High Court) for directions. The parties must be told by the court when the district judge will give directions. He can give directions at that stage, not only as to the progress of the main suit (r 2.24(4)(*a*)) but also concerning any applications which may have been issued for ancillary relief or in respect of the children, eg for residence or contact (r 2.24(4)(*b*)). It has been held that where decisions about the matrimonial home and about children impinge on one another, it is desirable to have both dealt with together (*Re B (A Minor: Custody)* [1991] 2 FLR 405, CA). It is not easy to envisage circumstances where the court would wish to try issues of property or children and the main suit together, although it may be desirable to have the main suit tried first, with other issues tried by the same judge immediately afterwards if a decree nisi has been obtained in the main suit.

Transfer to the High Court—Most defended causes will remain in the county court, but they may be transferred to the High Court in the light of the complexity, gravity or difficulty of the issues involved (*Practice Direction of 5 June 1992*).

"provision of evidence relating to ... the children of the family" (r 2.24(4)(*c*))—This provision recognises the fact that the district judge now deals with questions of satisfaction concerning arrangements for the children of the family (see also r 2.39(1)).

"In any other case" (r 2.24(5))—Where the cause is not defended and is not in the special procedure list (or has been removed from it: see r 2.36(1)(*b*)), the district judge gives directions on his own motion as to the setting down of the cause and the court gives notice to the parties that he has done so. Apart from causes removed from the special procedure list, examples of causes which might be dealt with in this way are petitions for nullity (see also rr 2.22, 2.23), petitions for a decree of presumption of death and dissolution (MCA 1973, s 19) and proceedings to be begun by petition under FPR 1991, Pt III (eg declarations as to marital status, parentage etc).

Direction to verify statement of arrangements for children (r 2.24(6))—This paragraph applies where no special procedure affidavit (Form M7) is filed. The district judge deals with satisfaction concerning the arrangements for the children of the family (MCA 1973, s 41; see also r 2.39). At this stage, he will also want affidavit evidence confirming, with any amendments, the statement of arrangements for the children. Where the cause is proceeding on the prayer in the respondent's answer, the affidavit must be sworn by him (r 2.24(7)).

2.25 Determination of place of trial

(1) Directions for trial, except where given under rule 2.24(3), shall determine the place of trial.

(2) In the case of an undefended cause to which rule 2.24(3) does not apply, the request for directions shall state –

(*a*) the place of trial desired,

(*b*) the place where the witnesses whom it is proposed to call at the trial reside,

(*c*) an estimate of the probable length of trial, and

(*d*) any other fact which may be relevant for determining the place of trial.

(3) In the case of a defended cause, the party intending to make a request for directions shall, not less than eight days before making his request, give notice of

the place of trial desired to every other party who has given notice of intention to defend and, if the party intending to make the request is the respondent, to the petitioner.

The notice shall state the number of witnesses to be called on behalf of the party giving the notice and the places where he and his witnesses reside.

(4) If any party to whom notice is given under paragraph (3) does not consent to the place of trial specified in the notice, he may, within eight days after receiving it, apply to the district judge to direct trial at some other place; and if he does consent to the place so specified, he shall within that period send to the party by whom the notice was given a statement signed by his solicitor (or by him, if he is acting in person) indicating that the notice has been received and specifying the number of witnesses to be called on his behalf and the places where he and his witnesses reside.

(5) Where no application for trial at some other place is made under paragraph (4) within the period specified in that paragraph, the party making the request for directions shall state in his request –

- (*a*) the place of trial desired;
- (*b*) the number of witnesses to be called on his behalf and the places where he and his witnesses reside;
- (*c*) if it be the case, that no statement has been received from any party (naming him) to whom notice was given under paragraph (3); and
- (*d*) an estimate of the probable length of trial;

and shall file with the request any statement sent to him by any other party in accordance with paragraph (4).

(6) If circumstances arise tending to show that the estimate of the probable length of the trial given under paragraph (2)(*c*) or (5)(*d*) or made on an application under paragraph (4) is inaccurate, a further estimate shall be filed.

(7) In determining the place of trial the district judge shall have regard to all the circumstances of the case so far as it is possible for him to do so on the basis of the information available to him, including the convenience of the parties and their witnesses, the costs likely to be incurred, the date on which the trial can take place and the estimated length of the trial.

(8) Directions determining the place of trial of any cause may be varied by the district judge of the court or registry in which the cause is proceeding on the application of any party to the cause.

Defined terms—"cause", "defended cause", "district judge": r 1.2(1); "notice of intention to defend": rr 1.2(1), 10.8(1).

2.26 Directions as to allegations under section 1(2)(b) of Act of 1973

(1) Where in a defended cause the petitioner alleges that the respondent has behaved in such a way that the petitioner cannot reasonably be expected to live with the respondent, the district judge may, of his own motion on giving directions for trial or on the application of any party made at any time before the trial, order or authorise the party who has made the request for or obtained such directions to file a schedule of the allegations and counter-allegations made in the pleadings or particulars.

(2) Where such an order is made or authority given, the allegations and counter-allegations shall, unless otherwise directed, be listed concisely in

chronological order, each counter-allegation being set out against the allegation to which it relates, and the party filing the schedule shall serve a copy of it on any other party to the cause who has filed a pleading.

Defined terms—"defended cause", "district judge": r 1.2(2).

"the district judge may ... order or authorise" (r 2.26(1))—The rule appears to envisage a party either being ordered to file the schedule or applying for authority to file; it does not seem open to one party to seek an order requiring another party to file a schedule, nor does the rule specifically deal with causes proceeding defended on the prayer in a respondent's answer. However, it is envisaged that, in appropriate cases, few district judges would feel inhibited from making an order under this rule. The district judge can make the order of his own motion or he may make it on application by the party seeking to file the schedule.

2.27 Stay under Domicile and Matrimonial Proceedings Act 1973

(1) An application to the court by the petitioner or respondent in proceedings for divorce for an order under paragraph 8 of Schedule 1 to the Domicile and Matrimonial Proceedings Act 1973 (in this rule referred to as "Schedule 1") shall be made to the district judge, who may determine the application or refer the application, or any question arising thereon, to a judge for his decision as if the application were an application for ancillary relief.

(2) An application for an order under paragraph 9 of Schedule 1 shall be made to a judge.

(3) Where, on giving directions for trial, it appears to the district judge from any information given in pursuant to paragraph 1(*j*) of Appendix 2 or rule 2.15(4) or paragraph (4) of this rule that any proceedings which are in respect of the marriage in question or which are capable of affecting its validity or subsistence are continuing in any country outside England and Wales and he considers that the question whether the proceedings on the petition should be stayed under paragraph 9 of Schedule 1 ought to be determined by the court, he shall fix a date, time and place for the consideration of that question by a judge and give notice thereof to all parties.

In this paragraph "proceedings continuing in any country outside England and Wales" has the same meaning as in paragraph 1(*j*) of Appendix 2.

(4) Any party who makes a request for directions for trial in matrimonial proceedings within the meaning of paragraph 2 of Schedule 1 shall, if there has been a change in the information given pursuant to paragraph 1(*j*) of Appendix 2 and rule 2.15(4) file a statement giving particulars of the change.

(5) An application by a party to the proceedings for an order under paragraph 10 of Schedule 1 may be made to the district judge, and he may determine the application or may refer the application, or any question arising thereon, to a judge as if the application were an application for ancillary relief.

Defined terms—"court", "district judge", "judge": r 1.2(2).

Scope of provision—This rule deals with the procedure by which the district judge imposes an obligatory stay on pending divorce proceedings, or the judge exercises his discretion to impose a stay on any matrimonial proceedings, where other proceedings are pending outside the jurisdiction. Domicile and Matrimonial Proceedings Act 1973, s 5(6) gives the court power to stay matrimonial proceedings (as defined in Sch 1, para 2) where there are concurrent proceedings in another jurisdiction in respect of the same marriage. By FPR 1991, App 2, para 1(*j*), a petitioner, or respondent in his answer (r 2.15(4)), is required to give information as to any proceedings continuing outside England and Wales which relate to the marriage or are capable of affecting its validity or subsistence.

Application for an obligatory stay (r 2.27(1))—Either the petitioner or the respondent can apply to the district judge for a stay of divorce proceedings where there are proceedings for divorce or nullity in a related jurisdiction (ie Scotland, Northern Ireland, the Isle of Man or the Channel Islands), provided also that the residence conditions set out in the paragraph are met (DMPA 1973, Sch 1, para 8). The application is made on notice (by summons in the High Court) to the district judge (r 10.9) and should state the grounds on which the stay is sought.

Referral to the judge (r 2.27(1))—The district judge may refer the application, or a question arising from it, to a judge for his decision, in the same way as under r 2.65 (reference of applications for ancillary relief to the judge). Applications so referred are dealt with in the same way as applications for ancillary relief under r 2.66: the court fixes a date for a hearing in chambers, at which the judge has the same powers as a district judge to give directions and of adjudication.

Application for a discretionary stay (r 2.27(2))—An application for a discretionary stay under DMPA 1973, Sch 1, para 9 is heard by a judge. Application is made on notice (by summons in the High Court) to the judge (r 10.9) and should state as clearly as possible the grounds for seeking a stay. If a party seeks to persuade the court on the basis that another jurisdiction is the more appropriate or convenient for deciding the issue ("forum non conveniens"), it is important that the application be made at the outset of proceedings, or at the first opportunity, before steps have been taken in the cause and costs incurred (*Mansour v Mansour* [1989] 1 FLR 418, CA; *Krenge v Krenge* [1999] 1 FLR 969, Holman J).

Referral at time of giving directions for trial (r 2.27(3), (4))—If, on giving directions, the district judge considers that there is information in the petition or answer or in a statement made under r 2.27(4) (giving new particulars) referring to other proceedings relating to the marriage or capable of affecting its validity or subsistence which might lead to a discretionary stay, he must fix an appointment before the judge and give notice of this to the parties.

"matrimonial proceedings" (r 2.27(4))—Matrimonial proceedings within the meaning of DMPA 1973, Sch 1, para 2 consist of: divorce, judicial separation, nullity and declarations as to the validity or subsistence of marriage.

Stay during the trial—If a party fails to provide particulars of other proceedings as required by the rules and the Act, the court can stay proceedings even after the start of the trial (DMPA 1973, Sch 1, para 9(4)).

Removal of stay (r 2.27(5))—An application for removal of a stay can be made on grounds that the other proceedings are stayed or concluded, or that a party has delayed unreasonably in prosecuting them (DMPA 1973, Sch 1, para 10(1)). The application is made on notice (by summons in the High Court) to the district judge (r 10.9) who can deal with the application or refer it to a judge (see **Referral to the judge** above). The application should state the grounds on which removal of the stay is sought.

2.27A Stay under the Council Regulation

(1) An application for an order under Article 11 of the Council Regulation shall be made to a district judge, who may determine the application or refer the application, or any question arising thereon, to a judge for his decision as if the application were an application for ancillary relief.

(2) Where at any time after the presentation of a petition, it appears to the court that, under Articles 9, 10 or 11 of the Council Regulation, the court does not have jurisdiction to hear the petition and is required or may be required to stay the proceedings, the Court shall stay the proceedings and fix a date for a hearing to determine the questions of jurisdiction and whether there should be a stay or other order and shall serve notice of the hearing on the parties to the proceedings.

(3) The court must give reasons for its decision under Articles 9, 10 or 11 of the Council Regulation and, where it makes a finding of fact, state such finding of fact.

(4) An order under Article 9 of the Council Regulation that the court has no jurisdiction over the proceedings shall be recorded by the court or the proper officer in writing.

(5) The court may, if all parties agree, deal with any question about the jurisdiction of the court without a hearing.

Amendments—Inserted by SI 2001/821.

Evidence

2.28 Evidence at trial of cause

(1) Subject to the provisions of this rule and rules 2.29, 2.36 and 10.14 and of the Civil Evidence Act 1995 and any other enactment, any fact required to be proved by the evidence of witnesses at the trial of a cause begun by petition shall be proved by the examination of the witnesses orally and in open court.

(2) Nothing in this rule and rules 2.29 and 10.14 shall affect the power of the judge at the trial to refuse to admit any evidence if in the interest of justice he thinks fit to do so.

(3) The court may order –

(*a*) that the affidavit of any witnesses may be read at the trial on such conditions as the court thinks reasonable;

(*b*) that the evidence of any particular fact shall be given at the trial in such manner as may be specified in the order and in particular –

(i) by statement on oath of information or belief, or

(ii) by the production of documents or entries in books, or

(iii) by copies of documents or entries in books, or

(iv) in the case of a fact which is or was a matter of common knowledge either generally or in a particular district, by the production of a specified newspaper containing a statement of that fact; and

(*c*) that not more than a specified number of expert witnesses may be called.

(4) An application to the district judge for an order under paragraph (3) shall –

(*a*) if no notice of intention to defend has been given, or

(*b*) if the petitioner and every party who has given notice of intention to defend consents to the order sought, or

(*c*) if the cause is undefended and directions for trial have been given, be made ex parte by filing an affidavit stating the grounds on which the application is made.

(5) Where an application is made before the trial for an order that the affidavit of a witness may be read at the trial or that evidence of a particular fact may be given at the trial by affidavit, the proposed affidavit or a draft thereof shall be submitted with the application; and where the affidavit is sworn before the hearing of the application and sufficiently states the ground on which the application is made, no other affidavit shall be required under paragraph (4).

Amendments—SI 1997/1056.

Defined terms—"cause", "court", "judge": r 1.2(2); "notice of intention to defend": rr 1.2(2), 10.8.

"the evidence of witnesses at the trial" (r 2.28(1))—This rule is derived from RSC Ord 38, r 1 and states one of the general rules of the law of evidence, requiring witnesses in a cause begun by petition to give their evidence orally and in open court whether the cause is defended or undefended (unless, where undefended, it is entered in the special procedure list). The general rule is subject to a number of exceptions as follows:

(*a*) the court's powers to order evidence by other means in accordance with r 2.28(3);

(*b*) the discretion of the court to order the obtaining of evidence by deposition (r 2.29);

(*c*) the provisions for evidence where the cause is entered in the special procedure list (rr 2.24(4), 2.36(1));

(*d*) that proof of a foreign marriage whose existence and validity is not disputed may be by means of a certificate of that marriage (r 10.14(1)); and

(*e*) exceptions contained in the Civil Evidence Act 1995: evidence is not inadmissible on grounds that it is hearsay (Civil Evidence Act 1995, s 1) provided that notice to adduce such evidence has been given (s 2); and it is still open to the court to regard such evidence as less cogent than first-hand evidence (s 4). Without notice being served, the court retains a discretion to admit the evidence (s 4(4)); though its cogency may be adversely affected by the lack of notice (s 4(4)(*b*)).

Evidence and proof—A respondent is entitled to have the allegations against him in a petition properly proved, and proved to the civil standard of the balance of probabilities (*Butterworth v Butterworth* [1997] 2 FLR 336, CA).

Judge's power to refuse to admit evidence (r 2.28(2))—The judge has an overriding discretion to refuse to admit any evidence at the trial if he considers that it is in the interests of justice to do so.

"The court may order" (r 2.28(3))—This rule is derived from RSC Ord 38, rr 2–4 and enables parties to seek leave of the court to adduce evidence other than by means of witnesses giving oral evidence. In the first instance, the application should be to the district judge on notice (by summons in the High Court) (r 10.9), except in the circumstances set out in r 2.28(4), where the application may be made ex parte with an affidavit in support stating the grounds for the application. If there is a summons or application for directions for trial, the application may be dealt with at that time (see r 2.24(4)). Application on notice or by summons may be made to the judge in appropriate cases. By analogy with RSC Ord 38, rr 2(1), 3(1) (which enable applications to be made at the trial), applications under r 2.28(3) can be made at the trial in exceptional circumstances. In considering any application, the court will be concerned to achieve expedition and save costs, but not so as to cause prejudice to a party or to derogate from the interests of justice.

Application to adduce evidence on affidavit—The party seeking to adduce evidence by affidavit must annex the affidavit or a draft to his application. In the essentially non-controversial cases described in r 2.28(4), if the affidavit has been sworn and states the ground for the application there is no need to submit a further affidavit in support of the ex parte application (r 2.28(5)).

Contents of affidavits—Affidavits must comply with RSC Ord 41 and CCR Ord 20, r 10. In particular, the following points should be noted: affidavits should contain only such facts as the deponent can prove from his own knowledge (RSC Ord 41, r 5(1)), although CCR Ord 20, r 10(4), (5) allows for statements of information or belief to be deposed to if indicated as such. The court may order the striking-out of an affidavit which is scandalous, irrelevant or otherwise oppressive (RSC Ord 41, r 6 and CCR Ord 20, r 10(1)(*d*)). *Practice Note of 21 July 1983* [1983] 1 WLR 922, [1983] 3 All ER 33 contains directions concerning affidavits and their exhibits and, in particular, requires that every affidavit on its first page and back-sheet must have endorsed on it a note showing (i) on whose behalf it is filed (CCR Ord 20, r 10(3)), (ii) the initials and surname of the deponent, (iii) the number of the affidavit in relation to the deponent and (iv) the date of swearing, eg "Petitioner/ P. F. Smith/ 2nd/ 27.2.95" (RSC Ord 41, r 9(5)).

Evidence of particular facts (r 2.28(3)(*b*))—This rule is intended to be drawn widely to enable evidence to be given in any appropriate way, such as by videotape or video-link, by tape-recording and so on. By use of the words "in particular", it is clear that the list of means of adducing evidence is not intended to be exhaustive. The court is more likely to order evidence to be given in this way if it is non-controversial.

Expert evidence (r 2.28(3)(*c*))—This rule merely enables the court to restrict the number of experts to be called. The question of disclosure of evidence by experts, and reliance on their reports, is covered by RSC Ord 38, rr 35–44 and CCR Ord 20, rr 27, 28. Expert evidence may only be relied on where it has been disclosed pursuant to court direction, where all parties agree or where the evidence is by affidavit and a direction under r 2.28(3)(*a*) has been obtained.

2.29 Evidence by deposition

The court may, on the application of any party to a cause begun by petition, make an order under CCR Order 20, rule 13, or (if the cause is pending in the High Court) under RSC Order 39, rule 1, for the examination on oath of any person; and CCR Order 20, rule 13 or (if the cause is pending in the High Court) RSC Order 38, rule 9, and Order 39, rules 1 to 14 (which regulate the procedure where evidence is to be taken by deposition) shall have effect accordingly with the appropriate modifications.

Amendments—SI 1997/1893.

Defined terms—"court": r 1.2(1).

Court order on application—Either a judge or a district judge may make the order on application by any party to a cause begun by petition. Application is made on notice (by summons in the High Court) to the district judge (or judge where appropriate) (r 10.9). The application or summons should be supported by an affidavit setting out in as much detail as possible the reasons why examination is required, why the witnesses cannot attend the trial and the names of the witnesses sought to be examined. The application or summons can be dealt with on any hearing of the application for directions or on a separate application.

Grounds for ordering examination—To make an order, the court must be satisfied that the examination "appears necessary for the purposes of justice" (RSC Ord 39, r 1(1); CCR Ord 20, r 13(1)). The exercise of the power is discretionary and, in exercising it, the court will have regard to the cost involved and the prejudice to a party if the order were refused. Examples of the grounds on which orders are made (often by consent) are that the witness is too old to attend trial or might die before the trial, that he is too ill to attend the trial, that he is planning to leave the country before the trial or, if the witness is female, that she may be on the point of delivery of a child at the time of the trial.

2.30 Issue of witness summons or subpoena

(1) A witness summons in a cause pending in a divorce county court may be issued in that court or in the court of trial at which the cause is to be tried.

(2) A writ of subpoena in a cause pending in the High Court may issue out of –

- (*a*) the registry in which the cause is proceeding; or
- (*b*) if the cause is to be tried at the Royal Courts of Justice, the principal registry; or
- (*c*) if the cause is to be tried at a divorce town, the registry for that town.

Defined terms—"cause", "court of trial", "divorce county court": r 1.2(1).

Scope of provision—This rule provides for compelling the attendance of witnesses at court and should be read in conjunction with the relevant Rules of the Supreme Court and County Court Rules considered below.

Witness summons in the county court (r 2.30(1))—The procedure for issue and service of a witness summons is dealt with by CCR Ord 20, r 12. Witness summonses issue as of right on presentation of the necessary request (Form N286; Ord 20, r 12(2)), except that leave is needed to require attendance of a witness on the hearing of directions in chambers (Ord 20, r 12(8)). The summons may be for a person to give evidence or to produce documents (Ord 20, r 12(1)). The request for issue can be made in the court where the cause is proceeding or, if different, in the court where the cause is to be tried.

Subpoena in the High Court (r 2.30(2))—The procedure for issue and service of writs of subpoena is dealt with in RSC Ord 38, rr 14–19. A subpoena issues as of right on filing of a praecipe seeking issue (Ord 38, r 14(5)) except that, in the case of any proceedings to be heard in chambers, leave of the court is required for issue of a subpoena (Ord 37, r 7; cf in the county court (above) where leave is required only for a witness summons for attendance at directions appointments). The subpoena may be for a person to give evidence or to produce documents (Ord 38, r 14(1)). The subpoena may issue out of the registry in which the cause is proceeding, the principal registry (where the cause is proceeding in the Royal Courts of Justice) or the registry of the divorce town if the cause is to be tried there.

Court's power to order attendance of witnesses—The court itself may not call evidence without the consent of the parties, and the court cannot dictate to a party what evidence he is to call (*Tay Bok Choon v Tahansan SDN BHD* [1987] 1 WLR 413, PC).

2.31 (*revoked*)

Trial etc

2.32 Mode and place of trial

(1) Unless otherwise directed and subject to rule 2.36 every cause and any issue arising therein shall be tried by a judge without a jury.

(2) Any cause begun by petition (except one entered in the special procedure list) which is pending in a divorce county court may be tried at any court of trial.

(3) Any cause begun by petition which is pending in the High Court may be tried at the Royal Courts of Justice or at any divorce town.

(4) A judge or the district judge of the registry for the divorce town at which any cause has been set down for trial may, where it appears to him that the cause cannot conveniently be tried at that town, order that it be tried at some other divorce town; and rule 10.10(4) and (5) shall apply to such an order as it applies to an order under paragraph (1) of that rule.

(5) As soon as practicable after a cause pending in a divorce county court has been set down for trial, the proper officer of the court of trial shall fix the date, place and, as nearly as may be, the time of the trial and give notice thereof to every party to the cause.

(6) In these rules any reference to the registry for the divorce town at which a cause is to be tried shall, in relation to a divorce town in which there is no district registry, be construed as a reference to such district registry as the Lord Chancellor may designate for the purpose or, if the divorce town is not situated within the district of any district registry, as a reference to the principal registry.

Defined terms—"cause", "court of trial", "district judge", "district registry", "divorce county court", "divorce town", "judge": r 1.2(1); "registry for the divorce town": rr 1.2(1), 2.32(6); "special procedure list": rr 1.2(1), 2.24(3).

Trial—Setting down for trial is dealt with at r 2.24 and determination of place of trial at r 2.25.

"Unless otherwise directed" (r 2.32(1))—Modes of trial fall into the following categories (and see *Clibbery v Allan* [2002] EWCA Civ 45, [2002] 1 FLR 565, CA and consideration of modes of trial in the Table set out at the front of this work, following the calendars):

(*a*) *Open court* The general rule is that all matrimonial proceedings should be heard in open court (r 2.28(1)). This applies to the main suit, but is subject to exception in respect of most other matrimonial proceedings.

(*b*) *Chambers* Applications for ancillary relief, concerning children and other applications and summonses are heard in chambers (RSC Ord 32, r 1; CCR Ord 13, r 1(4)), including hearings for ancillary relief before a judge (r 2.66(2)).

(*c*) *Hearings in camera* Where it is shown that the administration of justice would otherwise be impeded, a trial may be ordered in camera (*Scott v Scott* [1913] AC 417, (1913) FLR Rep 657, HL). This will only rarely be ordered and not, for example, solely to save embarrassment to a suitor or to avoid awkward publicity. In proceedings for nullity of marriage, evidence as to sexual capacity must be heard in camera unless the judge considers that, in the interests of justice, such evidence should be heard in open court (Matrimonial Causes Act 1973, s 48(2)).

2.33 Trial of issue

Where directions are given for the separate trial of any issue and those directions have been complied with, the district judge shall –

(*a*) if the issue arises on an application for ancillary relief or an application with respect to any child or alleged child of the family, proceed as if the issue were a question referred to a judge on an application for ancillary relief and rule 2.65 shall apply accordingly;

(*b*) in any other case, set the issue down for trial and thereupon rule 2.32(5) and (6) shall apply as if the issue were a cause.

Defined terms—"ancillary relief", "cause", "child of the family", "district judge", "judge": r 1.2(1).

Scope of provision—Derived from Matrimonial Causes Rules 1977, r 45, this rule enables the district judge to refer to a judge preliminary issues in the cause or issues arising in connection with applications for ancillary relief or concerning a child, or alleged child, of the family. [MCR 1977, r 45(*a*) applied MCR 1977, r 82 to itself, the equivalent rule of FPR 1991 to MCR 1977, r 82 being FPR 1991, r 2.66. It would seem more logical to import FPR 1991, r 2.66 into this rule, and therefore the reference to FPR 1991, r 2.65 in FPR 1991, r 2.33(*a*) can perhaps be assumed to be a misprint.]

"Where directions are given for the separate trial"—Where an issue arises, for example concerning jurisdiction or paternity, it may be necessary or desirable to try this separately to the main issue. The court may order the trial of a separate or preliminary issue of its own motion or on application by one of the parties (RSC Ord 33, rr 3, 4(2); CCR Ord 13, r 2). The application is made to the district judge on notice (on summons in the High Court) (r 10.9) and should state the issue to be tried separately (*Practice Direction of 11 November 1975*). The question of whether an issue should be tried separately is broadly decided according to whether the separate trial could (*a*) assist in reducing delay and expense, or (*b*) isolate an issue, such as jurisdiction or a point of law or fact, which could dispose of the whole action. On hearing the application, the district judge will give directions and, once satisfied that the directions have been complied with, will set the separate issue down for trial.

Mode of trial—The order directing trial should state the mode of trial, ie whether the hearing should be in open court or in chambers (*Practice Direction of 11 November 1975*, para 2). Unless otherwise directed, hearings concerning children or ancillary relief will be in chambers (rr 2.33(*a*), 2.66(2)). All other issues will be heard in open court, unless otherwise directed (r 2.28(1); see also r 2.32(1)).

2.34 Exercise of district judge's jurisdiction in causes set down for trial

(1) The district judge of the registry for the divorce town at which a cause has been set down for trial, or, in the case of a cause set down for a trial at the Royal Courts of Justice, a district judge of the principal registry may, if it appears to him to be desirable having regard to the proximity of the date of trial or otherwise, exercise in the cause any jurisdiction of the district judge of the registry in which the cause is proceeding.

(2) RSC Order 34, rule 5(3) shall apply, with the necessary modifications, to a defended cause pending in the High Court as it applies to an action begun by writ.

Defined terms—"cause", "defended cause", "district judge", "principal registry": r 1.2(1); "registry for the divorce town": rr 1.2(1), 2.32(6); "Royal Courts of Justice": r 1.2(1).

Scope of provision—This rule applies to causes proceeding in the High Court and enables a district judge of the registry where a cause has been set down for trial, where this is not the court in which the cause is proceeding, to exercise any jurisdiction available to the district judge of the original court. It also enables the court to call on parties to state the extent of their readiness for trial.

2.35 Further provisions as to date of trial

Except with the consent of the parties or by leave of a judge, no cause, whether defended or undefended, shall be tried until after the expiration of 10 days from the date on which directions for trial were given:

Provided that nothing in this rule shall apply to a cause entered in the special procedure list.

Defined terms—"cause", "judge": r 1.2(1); "special procedure list": rr 1.2(1), 2.24(3).

2.36 Disposal of causes in special procedure list

(1) As soon as practicable after a cause has been entered in the special procedure list, the district judge shall consider the evidence filed by the petitioner and –

(*a*) if he is satisfied that the petitioner has sufficiently proved the contents of the petition and is entitled to a decree the district judge shall so certify;

(*b*) if he is not so satisfied he may either give the petitioner an opportunity of filing further evidence or remove the cause from the special procedure list whereupon rule 2.24(3) shall cease to apply.

(2) On the making of a certificate under paragraph (1) a date shall be fixed for the pronouncement of a decree by a judge or district judge in open court and the proper officer shall send to each party notice of the date and place so fixed and a copy of the certificate, but subject to paragraph (3) it shall not be necessary for any party to appear on that occasion.

(3) Where the district judge makes a certificate under paragraph (1) and the petition contains a prayer for costs, the district judge may –

(*a*) if satisfied that the petitioner is entitled to such costs, include in his certificate a statement to that effect;

(*b*) if not so satisfied, give to any party who objects to paying such costs notice that, if he wishes to proceed with his objection, he must attend before the court on the date fixed pursuant to paragraph (2).

(4) Within 14 days after the pronouncement of a decree in accordance with a certificate under paragraph (1) any person may inspect the certificate and the evidence filed under rule 2.24(3) (except the statement of arrangements) and may bespeak copies on payment of the prescribed fee.

Amendments—SI 1997/1893.

Defined terms—"cause", "district judge", "judge", "proper officer": r 1.2(1); "special procedure list": rr 1.2(1), 2.24(3).

"after a cause has been entered in the special procedure list" (r 2.36(1))—The cause, if undefended and for divorce or judicial separation, will have been entered in the special procedure list at the time when the petitioner, or respondent (see below and r 2.24(7)), seeks directions for trial and files his special procedure affidavit (r 2.24(3)). Before he gives directions and thus before the cause can be entered in the special procedure list, the district judge must be satisfied as to the factors listed in r 2.24(1)).

Respondent filing evidence (r 2.36(1))—Although the rule refers throughout to the "petitioner" and his "petition", it must be assumed that the rule also applies to causes proceeding undefended on the prayer in the respondent's answer, since such causes can be entered in the special procedure list on the respondent filing a request for directions and the appropriate special procedure affidavit (r 2.24(7)). In the remainder of this note, references to a "petition" or "petitioner" can be taken to include references to a respondent or cause proceeding on a respondent's answer in accordance with r 2.24(7).

"the district judge shall consider the evidence" (r 2.36(1))—In the performance of this duty, the district judge considers the petition and the special procedure affidavit filed under r 2.24(3). Having considered the evidence, the district judge has the following options:

(*a*) *Signing his certificate* (r 2.36(1)(*a*)) If the district judge is satisfied that the petitioner has "*sufficiently* proved the contents of the petition" (emphasis supplied) and is entitled to a decree, he signs a certificate to this effect. By use of the word "sufficiently", the rule does not envisage a high standard of proof. An object of the special procedure is simplicity, speed and economy. The essentials of the petition and proof of its contents must be satisfied, but there should be no room for over-meticulousness and over-technicality of approach by district judges (*R v Nottinghamshire County Court ex parte Byers* [1985] FLR 695). Once signed, the certificate has been held to be tantamount to a decree nisi which may only be set aside on similar bases to an application for rehearing after decree nisi (*Day v Day* [1980] Fam 29, (1980) FLR 341, CA; see also **Setting aside the district judge's certificate** below).

(*b*) *Give an opportunity to file further evidence* (r 2.36(1)(*b*)) If not satisfied as to the evidence, the district judge can offer the petitioner an opportunity to file further evidence, which would normally be filed on affidavit. It is to be hoped that if the district judge requires satisfying on a particular point he would so indicate when offering a petitioner the opportunity to file further evidence. It will be rare for the district judge to hear oral evidence, but it may sometimes be possible to arrange a directions appointment at which matters can be clarified for him.

(*c*) *Remove the cause from the special procedure list* (r 2.36(1)(*b*)) As an alternative to (*b*) above, or if the district judge remains dissatisfied after offering an opportunity to file further evidence, he removes the cause from the special procedure list. The parties must then seek directions for trial of the cause in accordance with rr 2.24, 2.25(2).

District judge's refusal to sign his certificate—If the district judge refuses to sign his certificate, the likelihood is that he will remove the cause from the special procedure list and the petitioner can seek directions for trial. Alternatively, the petitioner may appeal either if the district judge refuses to sign his certificate or if he makes an order for the removal of the cause from the special procedure list, since the refusal to sign his certificate constitutes the making of an order (*R v Nottinghamshire County Court ex parte Byers* [1985] FLR 695). The advantage of an appeal is that, by means of a relatively simple process in chambers, the question of whether or not the certificate should have been signed can be heard by the judge and it is to be hoped that, if there are any irregularities on the pleadings, they can be resolved. The alternative is a process involving directions being given followed by the ordeal of a hearing in open court for the petitioner. (For procedure on appeals from district judge to judge see r 8.1.)

Setting aside the district judge's certificate—Once directions for trial have been given, an answer cannot be filed without leave (r 2.14). Thus if a respondent has failed to file an answer within 28 days of service of the petition (r 2.12(1)) and the petitioner has obtained a certificate under the special procedure or if, after the certificate has been signed, the respondent decides that he wants to defend the proceedings, application must be made to the district judge to set aside his certificate and give leave to file an answer out of time. The application should be supported by affidavit giving reasons, eg for the delay in filing or for the change of mind, and should exhibit a draft answer. It is a matter for the district judge's discretion whether he sets aside his certificate. The certificate should not be set aside unless the respondent can show that there are substantial grounds for believing that a decree, if obtained, would be contrary to the justice of the case (*Owen v Owen* [1964] P 277, [1964] 2 All ER 58); however the court must be alert to the particular problems encountered by respondents under the special procedure in that they are not given notice of when the district judge will be considering his certificate (*Day v Day* [1980] Fam 29, (1980) FLR 341, CA). Where a respondent can show that he was not served or was in some way deceived about the proceedings, the certificate should be set aside almost automatically; and where, for example, an adviser failed to act on the respondent's instructions or where through ignorance the respondent failed to take the necessary procedural steps to file an answer, the grounds for setting aside the certificate might exist (*Mitchell v Mitchell* [1984] Fam 1, [1984] FLR 50, CA). In the latter instance, the court must also be satisfied that, if the certificate were not set aside, the respondent would be prevented from putting forward a case which might lead to there being no decree. Once a decree nisi has been granted, the respondent may apply to set it aside and seek a rehearing (r 2.42) or appeal against the decree (r 8.1).

Pronouncement of decree by judge or district judge (r 2.36(2))—After the certificate has been signed, the court office fixes a date for pronouncement of decree nisi and sends the parties notification of this and of the certificate (in practice, this is generally on the same document). The decree is pronounced in open court by either a judge or a district judge. Save in connection with costs, it is not necessary for any party to attend court for this pronouncement.

Petition containing a prayer for costs (r 2.36(3))—The wording of r 2.36(3)(*a*) suggests that there is a presumption that the district judge will award costs to a petitioner unless he receives information (ie more than a bare denial in the acknowledgement of service) from the respondent or co-respondent why an order should not be made. If he is not satisfied that an order should be made, the district judge will refer the issue to be heard in open court where the party opposing an order for costs must attend to pursue his objection; in addition, he may order the party objecting to file and serve reasons for his objection (r 2.37(1)). The dilemma for the petitioner's representative must be whether to robe and attend court on this hearing with the possibility that a respondent will not attend. In the first instance, it may be thought sufficient to write to the court asking that an order for costs be made but that, if the respondent or co-respondent makes out a case to answer against such an order, the judge should fix a further short appointment for the question to be considered further on appearance by the petitioner. (For the right to be heard on costs see generally r 2.37.)

"any person may inspect" (r 2.36(4))—The provision that any person, not just a party to proceedings, can examine the certificate and evidence in the special procedure affidavit is consistent with the fact that, but for the special procedure, the main suit (as distinct from the decree alone) would have been heard in open court. For other family proceedings, the rule is that documents can only be inspected by third parties by leave of the court (r 10.20(3); but cf CCR Ord 22, r 8 and CCR Ord 50, r 10). It does not seem to be open to anyone to have a copy of the petition, even though its contents will be referred to in the special procedure affidavit and much of the evidence in it would have been given in open court but for the special procedure. Similarly, there is no provision for a party to prevent the obtaining of copies. It is submitted that the only way that this could be done would be on application to the judge or district judge who is to pronounce the decree on grounds analogous to those enabling the court to hold hearings in camera (see r 2.32(1)).

"on payment of the prescribed fee" (r 2.36(4))—The fee for a copy of the certificate and evidence is £1 per page (Family Proceedings Fees Order 1999, Sch 1, fee 7.1).

2.37 Right to be heard on question of costs

(1) A respondent, co-respondent or party cited may, without filing an answer, be heard on any question as to costs, but the court may at any time order any party objecting to a claim for costs to file and serve on the party making the claim a written statement setting out the reasons for his objection.

(2) A party shall be entitled to be heard on any question pursuant to paragraph (1) whether or not he has returned to the court office an acknowledgment of service stating his wish to be heard on that question.

(3) In proceedings after a decree nisi of divorce or a decree of judicial separation no order the effect of which would be to make a co-respondent or party cited liable for costs which are not directly referable to the decree shall be made unless the co-respondent or party cited is a party to such proceedings or has been given notice of the intention to apply for such an order.

Defined terms—"court": r 1.2(1).

Application of the rule—Rule 2.37 applies equally to petitions in the special procedure list and to those proceeding undefended. In the case of causes in the special procedure list, the rule enlarges the powers available to the district judge under r 2.36(3)(*b*)).

PART III

"without filing an answer" or acknowledgement of service (r 2.37(1), (2))—This rule preserves the position of a respondent, co-respondent or party cited to be heard on questions of costs even though they have not filed an answer to the petition or lodged at court an acknowledgement of service stating a wish to be heard on this question. If an acknowledgement has been lodged indicating opposition (see question 9 in Form M6), the court will know of the party's opposition to the claim. If no acknowledgement is returned, the party will need to indicate objection in some other way, such as by letter or formal notice of application. The rules are silent as to how the objection is registered and no requirement for a formal application is indicated.

"statement setting out the reasons for his objection" (r 2.37(1))—Once notified of a party's objection to a claim for costs, the judge or district judge may order the party objecting to file and serve on the party claiming costs a statement setting out his reasons for objecting. It will be seen that the acknowledgement of service (question 9 in Form M6) provides for this but leaves very little space for setting out grounds for objecting (although these may be elaborated upon on a separate sheet of paper). The objections will be before the court on the hearing of the decree proceedings, and the party objecting should attend court to answer questions on the objections, if any are raised.

Costs in discretion of the court—See the notes to CPR 1998, r 44.3.

2.38 Respondent's statement as to arrangements for children

(1) A respondent on whom there is served a statement in accordance with rule 2.2(2) may, whether or not he agreed that statement, file in the court office a written statement of his views on the present and proposed arrangements for the children, and on receipt of such a statement from the respondent the proper officer shall send a copy to the petitioner.

(2) Any such statement of the respondent's views shall, if practicable, be filed within the time limited for giving notice of intention to defend and in any event before the district judge considers the arrangements or proposed arrangements for the upbringing and welfare of the children of the family under section 41(1) of the Act of 1973.

Defined terms—"district judge": r 1.2(1); "notice of intention to defend": rr 1.2(1), 10.8; "proper officer": r 1.2(1).

2.39 Procedure for complying with section 41 of Act of 1973

(1) Where no such application as is referred to in rule 2.40(1) is pending the district judge shall, after making his certificate under rule 2.36(1)(*a*) or after the provision of evidence pursuant to a direction under rule 2.24(4), as the case may be, proceed to consider the matters specified in section 41(1) of the Act of 1973 in accordance with the following provisions of this rule.

(2) Where, on consideration of the relevant evidence, including any further evidence or report provided pursuant to this rule and any statement filed by the respondent under rule 2.38, the district judge is satisfied that –

(*a*) there are no children of the family to whom section 41 of the Act of 1973 applies, or

(*b*) there are such children but the court need not exercise its powers under the Act of 1989 with respect to any of them or give any direction under section 41(2) of the Act of 1973,

the district judge shall certify accordingly and, in a case to which sub-paragraph (*b*) applies, the petitioner and the respondent shall each be sent a copy of the certificate by the proper officer.

(3) Where the district judge is not satisfied as mentioned in paragraph (2) above he may, without prejudice to his powers under the Act of 1989 or section 41(2) of the Act of 1973, give one or more of the following directions –

(*a*) that the parties, or any of them, shall file further evidence relating to the arrangements for the children (and the direction shall specify the matters to be dealt with in further evidence);

(*b*) that a welfare report on the children, or any of them, be prepared;

(*c*) that the parties, or any of them, shall attend before him at the date, time and place specified in the direction;

and the parties shall be notified accordingly.

(4) Where the court gives a direction under section 41(2) of the Act of 1973, notice of the direction shall be given to the parties.

(5) In this rule "parties" means the petitioner, the respondent and any person who appears to the court to have the care of the child.

Defined terms—"the Act of 1973", "the Act of 1989": r 1.2(1); "children of the family": r 1.2(1), MCA 1973, s 52(1); "district judge": r 1.2(1); "parties": r 2.39(5); "proper officer": r 1.2(1).

"such application as is referred to in rule 2.40(1)" (r 2.39(1))—This refers to applications under CA 1989, Part I or II in relation to a child of the family.

"certificate under rule 2.36(1)(a)" (r 2.39(1))—Such certificate states that the district judge is satisfied that the petitioner has sufficiently proved the contents of the petition and is entitled to a decree (under the special procedure).

"direction under rule 2.24(4)" (r 2.39(1))—Such direction may be given in defended causes with regard to the provision of evidence relating to the arrangements or proposed arrangements for the children of the family.

Undefended cause not in special procedure list (r 2.39(1))—The terms of r 2.39(1) suggest that the provision does not apply to undefended nullity proceedings, or to undefended divorce or judicial separation proceedings which have been stood out of the special procedure list under r 2.36(1)(*b*), because there will never be a certificate under r 2.36(1)(*a*) or any directions under r 2.24(4). In those circumstances, the direction-giving power under r 2.39(1) would seem not to be available.

"section 41(1) of the Act of 1973" (r 2.39(1))—The subsection requires the court to consider: (*a*) whether there are any children of the family to whom the section applies; and (*b*) where there are any such children, whether (in the light of the arrangements which have been, or are proposed to be, made for their upbringing and welfare) it should exercise any of its powers under CA 1989 with respect to any of them. MCA 1973, s 41(3) provides that the section applies to (*a*) any child of the family who has not reached the age of 16 at the date when the court considers the case in accordance with the requirements of the section, and (*b*) any child of the family who has reached that age at that date and in relation to whom the court directs that the section will apply.

"children of the family to whom section 41 of the Act of 1973 applies" (r 2.39(2)(*a*))—See note on s 41(1) above.

Court's powers under CA 1989 (r 2.39(2)(*b*), (3))—For most practical purposes, the powers under CA 1989 which the court may exercise of its own motion are those of making s 8 orders CA 1989, s 10(1)(*b*) and giving a direction under s 37(1).

Certification by district judge (r 2.39(2))—This is usually effected by completing Practice Form D84B.

"sent" (r 2.39(2))—Method of sending is governed by FPR 1991, r 10.2 where the recipient is acting by a solicitor and r 10.3 where he is acting in person.

PART III

Direction under MCA 1973, s 41(2) (r 2.39(3), (4))— Section 41(2) provides that, in any case where s 41 applies (see note above), if it appears to the court that: (*a*) the circumstances of the case require it, or are likely to require it, to exercise any of its powers under the CA 1989 in respect of any such child; (*b*) it is not in a position to exercise that power or (as the case may be) those powers without giving further consideration to the case; and (*c*) there are exceptional circumstances which make it desirable in the interests of the child that the court should give a direction under the section, it may direct that the decree of divorce or nullity is not to be made absolute, or that the decree of judicial separation is not to be granted, until the court orders otherwise. Where a direction is given, it is usually in Practice Form D66.

Filing (r 2.39(3)(*a*))—See under r 2.38.

Notice of the direction (r 2.39(4))—The mode of giving such a notice is governed by FPR 1991, r 10.7.

2.40 Applications relating to children of the family

(1) Where a cause is pending, an application by a party to the cause or by any other person for an order under any provision of Part I or Part II of the Act of 1989 in relation to a child of the family shall be made in the cause; and where the applicant is not a party and has obtained such leave as is required under the Act of 1989 to make the application, no leave to intervene in the cause shall be necessary.

(2) If, while a cause is pending, proceedings relating to any child of the family are begun in any other court, a concise statement of the nature of the proceedings shall forthwith be filed by the person beginning the proceedings or, if he is not a party to the cause, by the petitioner.

(3) A cause shall be treated as pending for the purposes of this rule for a period of one year after the last hearing or judicial intervention in the cause and rule 1.2(2) shall not apply.

Amendments—SI 1997/1893.

Defined terms—"the Act of 1989", "cause", "child of the family": r 1.2(1).

Children Act 1989: "family proceedings"—A matrimonial cause constitutes "family proceedings" for the purposes of CA 1989 (CA 1989, s 8(3)).

Non-application of rule where child is ward of court (r 2.40(1))—This rule does not apply in circumstances where the child has already been made a ward of court, since the High Court assumes control of a ward and no important step in the life of the ward can be taken without the consent of that court (*Re E (A Minor) (Wardship: Court's Duty)* [1984] FLR 457; *Re S (Infants)* [1967] 1 All ER 202). Where the child of the family is a ward, any application made in relation to that child under CA 1989, Pt I or II should be made within the wardship proceedings.

"rule 1.2(2) shall not apply" (r 2.40(3))—FPR 1991, r 1.2(2) provides that proceedings begun by petition are regarded as pending indefinitely. For a period of one year from the last judicial involvement in the case, proceedings relating to children of the family can only be issued in the court in which the petition is pending. After that period, children proceedings can be issued in such court as an applicant may choose (Children (Allocation of Proceedings) Order 1991).

"judicial intervention" (r 2.40(3))—A consideration of the arrangements for the children of the family under Matrimonial Causes Act 1973, s 41 and of the cause under the special procedure (r 2.36) can be regarded as a "judicial intervention", though whether a routine decree nisi hearing or grant of decree absolute on notice (r 2.49) can be so regarded must be more questionable.

Part I or II of the 1989 Act (r 2.40(1))—These Parts cover the "private law" relating to the care and upbringing of children and include applications for parental responsibility, guardianship and s 8 orders.

Requirement for leave to intervene is unnecessary—The rule expressly provides that leave to intervene is unnecessary where the applicant has obtained "such leave as is required under the Act" to make the application in question. It is submitted that this should be construed as including cases where the person making the application is not required to obtain leave under the Act at all (eg those within CA 1989, s 10(4) or (5)).

Filing of statement by the petitioner (r 2.40(2))—The petitioner may not be aware of the subsequent proceedings: for example where the petitioner was the stepfather of the child concerned he may, after the divorce, lose touch and he is unlikely to be a respondent to any subsequent application by someone else in relation to the child; this is exacerbated by the artificially prolonged meaning of "pending" for this purpose. It is submitted that the requirement only arises implicitly where the petitioner is aware that there are proceedings to report. It would be good practice for the respondent to notify the court of the new proceedings in which she is involved but knows that the petitioner is not involved and may not know of the proceedings.

Filing (r 2.40(2))—See under r 2.38.

2.41 Restoration of matters adjourned at the hearing

Where at the trial of a cause any application is adjourned by the court for hearing in chambers, it may be restored –

(*a*) in the High Court, by notice without a summons;

(*b*) in a divorce county court, on notice under CCR Order 13, rule 1 (which deals with applications in the course of proceedings); or

(*c*) in the High Court or a divorce county court, by notice given by the district judge when in his opinion the matter ought to be further considered;

and the notice shall state the date, time and place for the hearing of the restored application and be served on every party concerned.

Defined terms—"cause", "court", "district judge", "divorce county court": r 1.2(1).

"adjourned by the court"—Most adjourned applications will relate to children (see r 2.40 and rr 4.1–4.28) and to ancillary relief see r 2.59 et seq) and may be restored by notice either in the High Court or the county court for hearing before the district judge, unless otherwise directed by the judge (CCR Ord 13, r 1(6)). In the first instance, the hearing is likely to be for directions unless any existing directions have been complied with and the court has an accurate time estimate.

"notice given by the district judge" (r 2.41(*c*))—If the judge fails to give directions on adjourning an issue relating to children which was likely to be contested, the district judge will be aware of the need to bring children cases on for hearing as soon as possible (CA 1989, s 1(2); see also r 4.14).

2.42 Application for re-hearing

(1) An application for re-hearing of a cause tried by a judge alone (whether in the High Court or a divorce county court) where no error of the court at the hearing is alleged, shall be made to a judge.

(2) Unless otherwise directed, the application shall be made to the judge by whom the cause was tried and shall be heard in open court.

(3) The application shall be made –

(*a*) in the High Court, by a notice to attend before the judge on a day specified in the notice, and

(*b*) in the county court, on notice in accordance with CCR Order 13, rule 1 (which deals with applications in the course of proceedings),

and the notice shall state the grounds of the application.

(4) Unless otherwise directed, the notice must be issued within six weeks after the judgment and served on every other party to the cause not less than 14 days before the day fixed for the hearing of the application.

(5) The applicant shall file a certificate that the notice has been duly served on each person required to be served therewith.

(6) The application shall be supported by an affidavit setting out the allegations on which the applicant relies or exhibiting a copy of any pleading which he proposes to file if the application is granted, and a copy of the affidavit shall be served on every other party to the cause.

(7) Not less than seven days before the application is heard the applicant shall file a copy of a transcript of so much as is relevant of any official shorthand note of the proceedings at the trial.

(8) Where a party wishes to appeal against a decree absolute of divorce or nullity of marriage, the question whether he has had the time and opportunity to appeal from the decree nisi on which the decree absolute was founded shall be determined on an application for a re-hearing under this rule.

(9) Any other application for re-hearing shall be made by way of appeal to the Court of Appeal.

(10) This rule shall apply, with the necessary modifications, to a cause disposed of under rule 2.36 as it applies to a cause tried by a judge alone, save that where in such a case the decree was pronounced by a district judge the application shall be made to a district judge.

Defined terms—"cause", "district judge", "divorce county court", "judge": r 1.2(1).

Concept of "re-hearing"—This should be distinguished from setting aside an order, setting aside a district judge's certificate, rescission of a decree (MCA 1973, s 10(1) and rr 2.44, 2.48) and an appeal against an order (rr 2.42(9), 8.1). See further the helpful analysis of this subject by Ward J in *B-T v B-T (Divorce: Procedure)* [1990] 2 FLR 1 where his Lordship held that the power of the county court to order a rehearing is limited to cases where there has been non-disclosure of material information which a party had a duty to place before the court. If information becomes available later, this should be a matter for appeal.

"re-hearing of a cause" (r 2.42(1))—This rule relates to decrees granted in causes, ie decrees of divorce, nullity of marriage, judicial separation or presumption of death and dissolution of marriage (r 1.2(1)). Special rules apply to decrees absolute of divorce or nullity of marriage (r 2.42(8)).

"application for re-hearing of a cause" (r 2.42(1))—A rehearing may be ordered provided the applicant is not alleging any error on the part of the court. The test to be applied is whether the allegation is that (*a*) the court erred on the basis of the materials before it, or (*b*) it erred because evidence on a vital matter was concealed from it so that a trial of the real issue between the parties was not possible (*Peek v Peek* [1948] P 46, [1947] 2 All ER 578, affirmed [1948] 2 All ER 297, CA; see also *B-T v B-T (Divorce: Procedure)* [1990] 2 FLR 1 at 17). If (*a*) above is alleged, a rehearing would be inappropriate and the applicant should appeal to the Court of Appeal (see also r 2.42(9)). If (*b*) is alleged, an application may be made for a rehearing: for example, where a party has been wrongly advised and failed to attend at a hearing or failed to file an answer (eg *Nash v Nash* [1968] P 597, [1967] 1 All ER 535), where one party has misled the other (*Montague v Montague* [1968] P 604, [1967] 1 All ER 802, CA) or where there is evidence which, if before the court, might lead to a different result (*Mitchell v Mitchell* [1984] Fam 1, [1984] FLR 50, CA). Further principles applicable to the ordering of a rehearing include the fact that, in exceptional circumstances, fresh evidence has come to light since the decree, failure of the respondent, for good reason, to attend the trial or the fact that a witness perjured himself or was mistaken in the giving of evidence (see also CCR Ord 37, r 1).

Effect of order for rehearing on decree—The order sought under r 2.42 is for a rehearing and not for the setting aside of the decree, although this may in fact be the result of a successful rehearing. CCR Ord 37 clearly distinguishes between the terms "rehearing" (Ord 37, r 1) and "setting aside" (Ord 37, rr 2–7). If the application is successful, it may be desirable to seek to attach terms to the order for rehearing. The county court can order a rehearing on such terms as it thinks reasonable (Ord 37, r 8(1)). Amongst the terms for any rehearing could be a stay on the decree. The notice of application itself (like a notice of appeal to the Court of Appeal) does not operate as a stay on the decree although, pending the hearing of the application, the court can order a stay on any order (CCR Ord 37, r 8(2)). The High Court does not have powers to set aside orders or to order a rehearing similar to those available in the county court, and a party aggrieved must apply to the Court of Appeal (SCA 1981, s 17(1)). However, an exception to the rule under s 17(1) is contained in FPR 1991, r 2.42 (r 2.42(3) and see Ward J's assessment of the rule in *B-T v B-T (Divorce: Procedure)* [1990] 2 FLR 1 at 9). The High Court's powers to order a rehearing are not clear and if, for example, a stay pending the hearing is sought, it may need to resort to its inherent jurisdiction.

Hearing of application by judge who tried the cause (r 2.42(2), (10))—The application should, where possible, be heard by the judge (or district judge: r 2.42(10)) who granted the original decree. Where evidence has been heard by the judge, his consideration of the application would clearly be desirable but, if he is not available, the court (ie another judge or the district judge on directions) can direct a hearing by another judge. Where the decree was pronounced by a judge or district judge in the special procedure list, the routine nature of the pronouncement removes the necessity for the same judge or district judge to hear the application for rehearing.

"shall be heard in open court" (r 2.42(2))—An application for rehearing must be heard in open court, despite the normal rule that applications made in the course of proceedings are heard in chambers (CCR Ord 13, r 1(4)). A hearing of the application might exceptionally be ordered in camera (see note to r 2.32(1)).

"in accordance with CCR Order 13, rule 1" (r 2.42(3)(*b*))—CCR Ord 13, r 1 deals generally with applications in the course of proceedings, but it is difficult to see why this reference has been included since most of the provisions of r 2.42 either contradict the provisions of Ord 13, r 1 or render them redundant.

"state the grounds of the application" (r 2.42(3))—The application should state the grounds, having regard to the factors considered under **"application for re-hearing of a cause"** above. Grounds should be stated concisely and will be elaborated on in the affidavit required by r 2.42(6).

Time-limit for issue of notice (r 2.42(4))—Practice on seeking an extension of time is governed by RSC Ord 3, r 5 and CCR Ord 13, r 4. The application for extension of time should be made to the judge or district judge who will hear the main application, and both applications can be included in the same document. The affidavit in support of the application will need to explain fully the reasons for the delay in making the application.

"affidavit setting out the allegations" (r 2.42(6))—The application must be supported by an affidavit setting out as fully as possible the matters on which the applicant relies. Any pleading sought to be filed if the application is successful, such as an answer to the petition, should be exhibited to the affidavit in draft. If a party seeks to rely on fresh evidence, at the very least a proof of that evidence should be available, and the applicant will need to explain why the evidence could not be adduced at the first trial and he must show that its absence was due to no failure on his part (*Ladd v Marshall* (1954) FLR Rep 422, CA). If the applicant claims that the court might have reached a different decision if it had heard his evidence, he must say why, and reasons for delay in serving pleadings must be fully explained.

Appeal from decree absolute (r 2.42(8), (9))—Rule 2.42(8) should be read in conjunction with r 2.42(4), and bearing in mind the fact that an application for decree absolute cannot be made until six weeks after decree nisi (MCA 1973, s 1(5) and Matrimonial Causes (Decree Absolute) General Order 1972, dated 20 July 1972, as amended). Thus leave to proceed out of time will be needed (r 2.42(4)). No appeal lies to the Court of Appeal from a decree absolute where there was time to seek a rehearing of the decree nisi (SCA 1981, s 18(1)(*d*); see also *Note: Clark v Clark* [1995] 2 FLR 487, CA).

Appeal from decree absolute out of time (r 2.42(8))—Where a party is out of time for appealing against the decree absolute, and where he did not appeal against the decree nisi and had no opportunity so to appeal, he then applies to the court which granted the decree (High Court or county court) to determine whether or not he had time and opportunity to appeal (*Note: Clark v Clark* [1995] 2 FLR 487, CA).

"Any other application for re-hearing" (r 2.42(9))—In any case not covered above and, in particular, where the applicant alleges that the court was in error within the terms of r 2.42(1) (see **"application for re-hearing of a cause"** and *Peek v Peek* above), he should appeal to the Court of Appeal in the case of a decree granted by the judge (for procedure in the Court of Appeal see CPR 1998, Pt 52 and CCA 1984, s 77 et seq). Appeals from a district judge's grant of a decree following the special procedure (see r 2.36(2)) are to a judge, in accordance with r 8.1 (*Marya v Marya* [1995] 2 FLR 911, CA).

"a cause disposed of under rule 2.36" (r 2.42(10))—Rule 2.36 deals with the special procedure under which a district judge may now grant a decree nisi (r 2.36(2)). Consequently, for the rehearing of a decree granted by a district judge, the application is made to him in accordance with the provisions of r 2.42(1)–(6).

Decrees and orders

2.43 Decrees and orders

(1) Except in a case to which rule 2.61 (consent orders) applies, every decree, every order made in open court and every other order which is required to be drawn up shall be drawn up –

(*a*) in the case of a decree or order made at a divorce county court, by the proper officer of that court;
(*b*) in the case of a decree or order made at the Royal Courts of Justice, by the proper officer of the principal registry;
(*c*) in the case of a decree or order made at a divorce town, by the proper officer of the registry for that town.

(2) CCR Order 22, rule 7 (which deals among other things with the settlement of judgments) shall not apply to a decree made in a cause pending in a divorce county court.

Defined terms—"cause", "divorce county court", "divorce town", "principal registry", "proper officer": r 1.2(1); "registry for the divorce town": rr 1.2(1), 2.32(6).

"CCR Order 22, rule 7 ... shall not apply" (r 2.43(2))—CCR Ord 22, r 7 enables the district judge, where he considers it desirable to do so, to require that an order be settled in the presence of the parties. Exclusion of CCR Ord 22, r 7 ensures that there will never be any necessity for this in the case of the drawing up of a decree.

Polygamous marriages—A decree in respect of a polygamous marriage must be stated to be granted by virtue of Matrimonial Causes Act 1973, s 47 (*Registrar's Direction of 14 May 1973*, para 5).

2.44 Application for rescission of decree

(1) An application by a respondent under section 10(1) of the Act of 1973 for the rescission of a decree of divorce shall be made to a judge and shall be heard in open court, save that where the decree was pronounced by a district judge the application shall be made to a district judge.

(2) Paragraphs (3) and (5) of rule 2.42 shall apply to an application under this rule as they apply to an application under that rule.

(3) Unless otherwise directed, the notice of the application shall be served on the petitioner not less than 14 days before the day fixed for the hearing of the application.

(4) The application shall be supported by an affidavit setting out the allegations on which the applicant relies and a copy of the affidavit shall be served on the petitioner.

Defined terms—"district judge", "judge": r 1.2(1).

Scope of provision—This rule provides the procedure by which a respondent applies for rescission of a decree under MCA 1973, s 1(2)(*d*) (provided that no other fact under MCA 1973, s 1(2) was also proved) where he alleges, within the terms of MCA 1973, s 10(1), that he has been misled by the petitioner in giving his consent.

Application to judge or district judge (r 2.44(1)–(4))—This rule has many features in common with r 2.42(1)–(6) (applications for rehearing), to which reference should be made.

Grounds of application and affidavit in support (r 2.44(2), (4))—In the drafting of grounds, it is necessary to have regard to MCA 1973, s 10(1), namely that the respondent was misled by the petitioner, whether intentionally or unintentionally. The factors which influenced the respondent in consenting can be elaborated on in his affidavit in support of the application. If intentional misleading is alleged, it must be borne in mind that this is a serious allegation and, as a result, the court is likely to require a high standard of proof from the respondent. Since this is essentially an application to set aside a consent order (a decree obtained on the basis of the respondent's consent), consideration must be given to the particular difficulties of such applications (see eg *Jenkins v Livesey (formerly Jenkins)* [1985] AC 424, [1985] FLR 813, HL).

2.45 Application under section 10(2) of Act of 1973

(1) An application by a respondent to a petition for divorce for the court to consider the financial position of the respondent after the divorce shall be made by notice in Form B.

(2), (3) (*revoked*)

(4) The powers of the court on hearing the application may be exercised by the district judge.

(5) Where the petitioner has relied on the fact of two or five years' separation and the court has granted a decree nisi without making any finding as to any other fact mentioned in section 1(2) of the Act of 1973, rules 2.51B to 2.70 and 10.10 shall apply as if the application were an application for ancillary relief and, unless the context otherwise requires, those rules shall be read as if all references to Form A were references to Form B.

(6) A statement of any of the matters mentioned in section 10(3) of the Act of 1973 with respect to which the court is satisfied, or, where the court has proceeded under section 10(4), a statement that the conditions for which that subsection provides have been fulfilled, shall be entered in the records of the court.

Amendments—SI 1999/3491.

Defined terms—"Act of 1973", "court", "district judge": r 1.2(1).

Post-5 June 2000 applications—For applications started by filing Form B after 5 June 2000, procedure is governed by FPR 1991, rr 2.51B–2.70. The key stages are: (i) filing Form B; (ii) 5 weeks before first appointment, disclosing means in Form E; (iii) first appointment; (iv) financial dispute resolution appointment; and (v) final hearing (see further Procedural Guide 17). The factor determining whether the application is made before or after 5 June 2000 is not the date of the petition but the date of filing Form M12/B.

Effect of making s 10(2) application—Decree absolute cannot be pronounced until the application is heard (*Registrar's Direction of 7 November 1973*).

Rule 10.10—Rule 10.10 relates to transfers between courts, both transfers between different registries and different county courts and transfers from county court to High Court and vice versa.

Pre-5 June 2000 applications—Where the application has been started (by filing a notice in Form M12, which may be done at any time after the petition is served but must be done before decree absolute) the relevant procedure is governed by the pre-5 June 2000 text of FPR 1991 (as summarised in Procedural Guides 17 and 19 of the *Family Court Practice 1999*).

2.45A Application under section 10A(2) of the Act of 1973

(1) This rule applies to an application under section 10A(2) of the Act of 1973 for an order that the decree of divorce is not to be made absolute until a declaration made by both parties that they have taken such steps as are required to dissolve the marriage in accordance with the relevant religious usages is produced to the court.

(2) Paragraphs (3) and (5) of rule 2.42 shall apply to an application under this rule as they apply to an application under that rule.

(3) The application shall be supported by an affidavit setting out the grounds on which the applicant seeks the order and a copy of the affidavit shall be served with the notice on the other parties.

Amendments—Inserted by SI 2003/184.

Context of provision—MCA 1973, s 10A(1) provides that, where a couple were married in accordance with "the usages of the Jews" or other religious usages and these prescribe final dissolution, an application can be made under s 10A(2) for an order which stays the grant of a decree absolute. The stay will continue until the court is satisfied by a declaration of both parties that the marriage is also dissolved in accordance with "those [Jewish or other] usages". Rules 2.45A and 2.45B provide the regulatory framework for an application under s 10A(2).

"rule 2.42 [(3) and (5)] shall apply" (r 2.45A(2))—Rule 2.42(3) provides that the application should be made on notice, setting out grounds; and r 2.42(5) requires a certificate of service of the notice to be filed at court.

Timing of application—MCA 1973, s 10A(1) is engaged as soon as "a decree of divorce has been granted" (ie upon decree nisi, but not before). This will demand vigilance from practitioners, since the importance of s 10A(2) to a Jewish wife will be lost if the decree nisi is made absolute. An early return date will be needed (for a respondent wife, before the end of the six week period for decree absolute). If a husband manages to persuade the court to expedite a decree absolute, it is possible that little can be done, unless he has in some way misled the court.

2.45B Order under section 10A(2) of the Act of 1973

(1) Where the court has made an order under section 10A(2) of the Act of 1973 the declaration referred to in that section shall –

(*a*) be made and signed by both parties;
(*b*) give particulars of the proceedings in which the order under section 10A(2) of the Act of 1973 was obtained;
(*c*) confirm that such steps as are required to dissolve the marriage in accordance with the religious usages, appropriate to the parties, referred to in section 10A(1)(*a*) of the Act of 1973 have been taken;
(*d*) unless the court orders otherwise, be accompanied by a certificate from a relevant religious authority that all such steps have been taken; and
(*e*) be filed at the court either before or together with an application to make the decree absolute under rules 2.49 or 2.50.

(2) For the purposes of paragraph (1)(*d*), a religious authority is "relevant" if the party who made the application for the order under section 10A(2) of the Act of 1973 considers that authority competent to confirm that the steps referred to in paragraph (1)(*c*) have been taken.

(3) Where the certificate referred to in paragraph (1)(*d*) is not in English the declaration must also be accompanied by a translation of that certificate into English, certified by a notary public or authenticated by affidavit.

(4) If the court dispenses with the need for a certificate under paragraph (1)(*d*), it may direct the parties to file other documents showing that the relevant steps have been taken and may refuse to make the decree absolute until that direction has been complied with.

Amendments—Inserted by SI 2003/184.

"the party who made the application" (r 2.45B(2))—The effect of this paragraph is to make the applicant for the declaration the arbiter of what constitutes a "relevant religious authority", with no apparent appeal from her decision on this point.

2.46 Intervention to show cause by Queen's Proctor

(1) If the Queen's Proctor wishes to show cause against a decree nisi being made absolute, he shall give notice to that effect to the court and to the party in whose favour it was pronounced.

(2) Within 21 days after giving notice under paragraph (1) the Queen's Proctor shall file his plea setting out the grounds on which he desires to show cause, together with a copy for service on the party in whose favour the decree was pronounced and every other party affected by the decree.

(3) The proper officer shall serve a copy of the plea on each of the persons mentioned in paragraph (2).

(4) Subject to the following provisions of this rule, these rules shall apply to all subsequent pleadings and proceedings in respect of the plea as if it were a petition by which a cause is begun.

(5) If no answer to the plea is filed within the time limited or, if an answer is filed and struck out or not proceeded with, the Queen's Proctor may apply forthwith by motion for an order rescinding the decree and dismissing the petition.

(6) Rule 2.24 shall apply to proceedings in respect of a plea by the Queen's Proctor as it applies to the trial of a cause, so however that if all the charges in the plea are denied in the answer the application for directions shall be made by the Queen's Proctor and in any other case it shall be made by the party in whose favour the decree nisi has been pronounced.

Defined terms—"cause", "court", "proper officer": r 1.2(1).

Amendments—SI 1992/456.

Show cause against decree nisi—This rule is limited to the occasions where the Queen's Proctor seeks to show cause in respect of a decree nisi; the circumstances in which the court refers a question to the Queen's Proctor are covered by MCA 1973, s 8(1)(*a*).

Treatment of plea (r 2.46(4))—By providing that the plea of the Queen's Proctor is to be regarded as a petition, the rules import into the Queen's Proctor's application rr 2.11 to 2.14, rr 2.16 to 2.21 and rr 2.28 to 2.35, insofar as any of these rules is applicable. An answer to the plea may be filed by any party, and not only the party who obtained the decree. The Queen's Proctor can file a reply to the answer(s), by analogy with r 2.13. The plea then proceeds as a defended cause, so that discovery of documents and by interrogatories can apply (rr 2.20, 2.21), and the rules concerning evidence (rr 2.28–2.31) and trial (rr 2.32–2.35) also apply.

Time-limit for filing an answer (r 2.46(5))—Although the rule states "*the* time limited" (emphasis supplied), the term is not clearly defined. This is alarming in view of the consequences of failure to file in time; for example, the Queen's Proctor can apply "forthwith" for an order that the decree be rescinded and the petition dismissed. Consideration must first be given to r 2.12(1) which applies to the answer (r 2.46(4)): r 2.12(1) provides that an answer must be filed 21 days after the time for filing notice of intention to defend. Rule 2.46(3) does not appear to require the court to serve with the plea a notice in Form M5 and M6 (including an acknowledgement of service: cf r 2.6(6)). Thus no notice of intention to defend will be given. In these circumstances, the party in whose favour the decree was pronounced may regard the 21-day limit in r 2.12(1) as appropriate, with time running from the date of service of the Queen's Proctor's plea.

Hearing of the plea—No specific provision is made in r 2.46 for hearing of the plea. Thus r 2.32(1) would appear to apply, with the result that the hearing is in open court before a judge without jury. Since the plea is similar to a rehearing, it might be thought that the hearing of a plea in respect of a decree nisi granted by the district judge might be heard before him (r 2.42(10)). If this is the case, it seems likely that the district judge would refer the plea to a judge (rr 2.33, 2.66) and, although the requirement to transfer causes in which the Queen's Proctor intervenes to the High Court was removed in 1986, it may still be thought appropriate in certain cases so to transfer (Matrimonial and Family Proceedings Act 1984, s 39 and r 10.10(6)). See also *Practice Direction of 5 June 1992*.

Consequences of the plea—The consequences of a plea by the Queen's Proctor are not defined, but it may be assumed that they are analogous to MCA 1973, s 9(1). This section includes making the decree nisi absolute, rescission of the decree or other order, which could include dismissal of the petition. If the court orders rescission, it does not necessarily mean that the petition must be dismissed (*Newman v Newman (Queen's Proctor Intervening)* [1984] FLR 835). The Queen's Proctor's costs are provided for by MCA 1973, s 8(2), (3).

2.47 Intervention to show cause by person other than Queen's Proctor

(1) If any person other than the Queen's Proctor wishes to show cause under section 9 of the Act of 1973 against a decree nisi being made absolute, he shall file an affidavit stating the facts on which he relies and a copy shall be served on the party in whose favour the decree was pronounced.

(2) A party on whom a copy of the affidavit has been served under paragraph (1) may, within 14 days after service, file an affidavit in answer and, if he does so, a copy thereof shall be served on the person showing cause.

(3) The person showing cause may file an affidavit in reply within 14 days after service of the affidavit in answer and, if he does so, a copy shall be served on each party who was served with a copy of his original affidavit.

(4) No affidavit after an affidavit in reply shall be served without leave.

(5) Any person who files an affidavit under paragraphs (1), (2) or (3) shall at the same time file a copy for service on each person required to be served therewith and the proper officer shall thereupon serve the copy on that person.

(6) A person showing cause shall apply to the judge (or, where a district judge has pronounced the decree nisi, a district judge) for directions within 14 days after expiry of the time allowed for filing an affidavit in reply or, where an affidavit in answer has been filed, within 14 days after the expiry of the time allowed for filing such an affidavit.

(7) If the person showing cause does not apply under paragraph (6) within the time allowed, the person in whose favour the decree was pronounced may do so.

Defined terms—"district judge", "judge", "proper officer": r 1.2(1).

"any person" (r 2.47(1))—This term must be read in conjunction with MCA 1973, s 9(1) which makes it clear that parties to the proceedings as well as the Queen's Proctor are intended to be excluded.

Application to judge or district judge for directions (r 2.47(6), (7))—This rule provides for either party to apply for directions, but it is silent as to arrangements for a hearing. The application proceeds on affidavit evidence and might be thought more appropriate for hearing in chambers (see r 10.9 and CCR Ord 13, r 1(4)); however, it is similar to an application for a rehearing, at which one of the court's options is rescission of the decree (MCA 1973, s 9(1)(*b*)), and such applications are held in open court unless otherwise directed (r 2.42(2)). The application will presumably be heard by judge or district judge, according to who granted the decree nisi (r 2.47(6), and by analogy with r 2.42(2), (10)).

Consequences of the application—The consequences are provided for by MCA 1973, s 9(1) (see also **Consequences of the plea** under r 2.46).

PART III

2.48 Rescission of decree nisi by consent

(1) Where a reconciliation has been effected between the petitioner and the respondent –

(*a*) after a decree nisi has been pronounced but before it has been made absolute, or

(*b*) after a decree of judicial separation has been pronounced,

either party may apply for an order rescinding the decree by consent.

(2) Where the cause is pending in a divorce county court, the application shall be made on notice to the other spouse and to any other party against whom costs have been awarded or who is otherwise affected by the decree, and where the cause is pending in the High Court a copy of the summons by which the application is made shall be served on every such person.

(3) The application shall be made to a district judge and may be heard in chambers.

Defined terms—"cause", "district judge", "divorce county court": r 1.2(1).

Rescission by consent where parties not reconciled—Rule 2.48 applies only where a couple are reconciled. If rescission by consent is sought where there has been no reconciliation and no decree absolute obtained, the court does have the power to mitigate any stalemate which then arises (*S v S (Rescission of Decree Nisi: Pension Sharing Provision)* [2002] 1 FLR 457, Singer J). If one party refuses consent, rescission will be refused (*Rye v Rye* [2002] EWHC 956).

Application where no reconciliation—Application by consent should be to a judge at the same level of the court hierarchy as the judge who granted the decree (normally a district judge) (*S v S* (above)). The original petition can be stayed and leave granted to file another, so that the original petition will be dismissed on the pronouncement of decree in the second.

2.49 Decree absolute on lodging notice

(1) Subject to rule 2.50(1) an application by a spouse to make absolute a decree nisi pronounced in his favour may be made by lodging with the court a notice in Form M8.

(2) On the lodging of such a notice, the district judge shall cause the records of the court to be searched, and if he is satisfied –

(*a*) that no application for rescission of the decree or for re-hearing of the cause and no appeal against the decree or the dismissal of an application for re-hearing of the cause is pending;
(*b*) that no order has been made by the court extending the time for making an application for re-hearing of the cause or by the Court of Appeal extending the time for appealing against the decree or the dismissal of an application for re-hearing of the cause or, if any such order has been made, that the time so extended has expired;
(*c*) that no application for such an order as is mentioned in sub-paragraph (*b*) is pending;
(*d*) that no intervention under rule 2.46 or 2.47 is pending;
(*e*) that the court has complied with section 41(1) of the Act of 1973 and has not given any direction under section 41(2);
(*f*) where a certificate has been granted under section 12 of the Administration of Justice Act 1969 in respect of the decree –
 (i) that no application for leave to appeal directly to the House of Lords is pending;
 (ii) that no extension of the time to apply for leave to appeal directly to the House of Lords has been granted or, if any such extension has been granted, that the time so extended has expired; and
 (iii) that the time for any appeal to the Court of Appeal has expired;
(*g*) that the provisions of section 10(2) to (4) of the Act of 1973 do not apply or have been complied with; and
(*h*) that any order under section 10A(2) of the Act of 1973 has been complied with

the district judge shall make the decree absolute:

Provided that if the notice is lodged more than 12 months after the decree nisi there shall be lodged with the notice an explanation in writing:

(*a*) giving reasons for the delay;
(*b*) stating whether the parties have lived with each other since the decree nisi and, if so, between what dates; and
(*c*) stating whether the applicant being the wife has, or being the husband has reason to believe that his wife has, given birth to any child since the decree nisi and, if so, stating the relevant facts and whether or not it is alleged that the child is or may be a child of the family;

and the district judge may require the applicant to file an affidavit verifying the said explanation and may make such order on the application as he thinks fit.

Amendments—SI 2003/184.

Defined terms—"child of the family", "district judge": r 1.2(1).

"Subject to rule 2.50(1)" (r 2.49(1))—Rule 2.50(1) provides for certain circumstances in which an application should be made to the judge; otherwise, application is made to the district judge.

Application by spouse in whose favour decree pronounced (r 2.49(1))—In the first instance, the application can only be by the spouse who obtained the decree nisi. After the final date for applying has passed (see **Time-limit for application** below), the other spouse can apply.

"notice in Form M8" (r 2.49(1))—The notice in Form M8 is set out in FPR 1991, App 1 and is available from most court offices. It is signed by the applicant's solicitor, except where the applicant acts in person or where he is "fee exempt", in which case it is signed by the applicant (ie the petitioner, unless the respondent has obtained a decree on the prayer in his answer).

Time-limit for application—The time-limit for application by the party who obtained the decree nisi is six weeks (MCA 1973, s 1(5), as varied by the Matrimonial Causes (Decree Absolute) General Order 1972 (as amended)). Three months from the expiry of that period, the other spouse may apply (MCA 1973, s 9(2); see r 2.50(2) for procedure). Such application gives the district judge a discretion, inter alia, to grant a decree absolute to the other spouse, although he may refuse to exercise discretion in appropriate circumstances (*Smith v Smith* [1990] 1 FLR 438). The decree will not be made absolute if the refusal to do so is the only way to ensure that a party complies with an ancillary relief order (*Wickler v Wickler* [1998] 2 FLR 326).

District judge's request for search of court records (r 2.49(2))—In practice, the search will be by the member of the county court staff who receives the application. The purpose of this search is to check that there is no outstanding application or question affecting the decree nisi or preventing the grant of the decree absolute, and in particular:

(*a*) *No appeal, application for rescission or for re-hearing pending* (r 2.49(2)(*a*)) As to application for rescission see r 2.48; for rehearing, see r 2.42. Appeals against the decree will be rare (see r 2.42(8), and the court need be satisfied only that no appeal is pending against dismissal of an application for rehearing, and not that time for such appeal has expired (cf r 2.49(2)(*f*)(iii) below which applies only where a certificate under AJA 1969, s 12 has been issued).

(*b*) *Time extended for appeal* (r 2.49(2)(*b*)) The reference to the court extending time for application for rehearing is curious since neither r 2.42 nor CCR Ord 13, r 1 provides the means for the court to do this. The Court of Appeal undoubtedly has the powers described in the rule (see eg SCA 1981, s 18(1)(*b*) and RSC Ord 51, r 10(1)).

(*c*) *"no intervention under rule 2.46 or 2.47"* (r 2.49(2)(*d*)) The search must ensure that there is no intervention to show cause has been filed by the Queen's Proctor (r 2.46) or by a person other than a party to the suit (r 2.47).

(*d*) *Compliance with MCA 1973, s 41* (r 2.49(2)(*e*)) In proceedings for divorce, nullity or judicial separation, the court must consider whether there are children of the family and, if so, whether it needs to exercise its powers under CA 1989 in relation to them (MCA 1973, s 41(1), as substituted by CA 1989, s 92, Sch 12, para 31). A stay on the decree being made absolute until satisfaction has been expressed by the judge is no longer available, but MCA 1973, s 41(2) (as substituted by CA 1989) enables the court in the instances set out in the subsection to stay the grant of a decree until further order (see also r 2.45).

(*e*) *"section 12 of the Administration of Justice Act 1969"* (r 2.49(2)(*f*)) AJA 1969, s 12 deals with the very rare instance of a certificate being given by a single High Court judge or the Divisional Court to enable a case to "leap-frog" to the House of Lords where a point of law of general public importance is involved.

(*f*) *"the provisions of section 10(2) to (4) of the Act of 1973"* (r 2.49(2)(*g*)) MCA 1973, s 10(2)–(4) concerns applications for consideration of the respondent's financial position in divorce proceedings under MCA 1973, s 1(2)(*d*), (*e*) (two years' living apart with consent and five years' living apart), and enables the court to delay the decree absolute (MCA 1973, s 10(3)), subject to the provisions of MCA 1973, s 10(4).

"the district judge shall make the decree absolute" (r 2.49(2))—The district judge is required to make the decree nisi absolute if he is satisfied that none of the factors listed in the rule applies, subject to the proviso (considered below) where the application is made 12 months after decree nisi.

Where notice is lodged more than 12 months after decree nisi (proviso to r 2.49(2))—Where application is made more than 12 months after decree nisi, an explanation in writing must be provided to the district judge. This could be by letter from the applicant (if acting in person) or his solicitor. The district judge can call for an affidavit by the applicant to verify the explanation, for example where he has doubts as to the explanation or where an unusual state of affairs is described. The explanation must deal with the factors mentioned in the proviso, including the following:

(*a*) *"whether the parties have lived with each other"* Living with each other means living together in the same household and sharing a common life (MCA 1973, s 2(6); see also eg *Mouncer v Mouncer* [1972] 1 WLR 321, [1972] 1 All ER 289). If the parties have lived together for less than six months during the previous 12 months, it may be safe to assume that the district judge will ignore this by analogy with MCA 1973, s 2(5); however, where the parties have lived together for longer than six months during that period, there is likely to be a presumption that the marriage has not irretrievably broken down, a decree absolute may be refused and the decree nisi rescinded (*Biggs v Biggs and Wheatley* [1977] Fam 1, [1977] 1 All ER 20).

PART III

(*b*) *"relevant facts" concerning any child born to the wife* Such facts would include the date of birth and the child's parentage and, if the parties are the parents, they will need to give an even fuller explanation concerning cohabitation, if any. If the child is a child of the family, the district judge will need to deal with him under MCA 1973, s 41 (see also r 2.39) before he can consider the question of granting a decree absolute.

"the district judge ... may make such order ... as he thinks fit"—The district judge has an absolute discretion as to the order he makes: whether to grant a decree absolute; to refuse a decree (in which case he is likely to consider rescinding the decree nisi and, where appropriate, dismissing the petition); or to make any other order. The orders available to the court can perhaps be regarded as analogous to MCA 1973, s 9(1) (see **Consequences of the plea** under r 2.46). If the decree nisi was granted by a judge and the district judge is contemplating rescission, he may refer the application to the judge; likewise, in any other case, it is open to him to refer the application to a judge (r 2.33; RSC Ord 33, rr 3, 4(2); CCR Ord 13, r 1(7); see also r 2.50(1)(*b*)).

Hearing of the application—Under r 2.49, there seems to be no obligation on the court to arrange a hearing where the judge or district judge contemplates refusing the application; however, where this happens, it should be recalled that the order is an ex parte order and thus covered by the fundamental rule of practice that any party affected by an ex parte order can apply to the court to discharge it (RSC Ord 32, r 6). Thus it is submitted that, if a judge or district judge contemplates refusing an application, he should fix an appointment in chambers (CCR Ord 13, r 1(4)) for representations to be heard on the grant of the application or for any other order to be made.

Application to expedite decree absolute—In special procedure cases, an application to expedite the decree absolute should be made to a judge on notice with evidence in support (eg an affidavit exhibiting a medical certificate as to date of birth of an expected child), and the court should arrange an appointment as soon as possible after the decree nisi hearing (*Practice Direction of 15 June 1977*). Notice of the application should be given to all parties. Although the decree nisi hearing will be in open court, this, as an application in the course of proceedings, should be heard in chambers (CCR Ord 13, r 1(4)). In causes not proceeding under the special procedure, application should, where possible, be made for an earlier hearing; where this fails, application should be made to the trial judge at the hearing of the cause with the information needed for the judge to make a decision. If events after decree nisi necessitate an application, this should be made to a judge in chambers (*Practice Direction of 19 November 1964*).

2.50 Decree absolute on application

(1) In the following cases an application for a decree nisi to be made absolute shall be made to a judge, that is to say –

(*a*) where the Queen's Proctor gives to the court and to the party in whose favour the decree was pronounced a notice that he requires more time to decide whether to show cause against the decree being made absolute and the notice has not been withdrawn, or

(*b*) where there are other circumstances which ought to be brought to the attention of the court before the decree nisi is made absolute.

Unless otherwise directed, the summons by which the application is made (or, where the cause is pending in a divorce county court, notice of the application) shall be served on every party to the cause (other than the applicant) and, in a case to which sub-paragraph (*a*) applies, on the Queen's Proctor.

(2) An application by a spouse for a decree nisi pronounced against him to be made absolute may be made to a judge or the district judge, and the summons by which the application is made (or, where the cause is pending in a divorce county court, notice of the application) shall be served on the other spouse not less than four clear days before the day on which the application is heard.

(3) An order granting an application under this rule shall not take effect until the district judge has caused the records of the court to be searched and is satisfied as to the matters mentioned in rule 2.49(2).

Defined terms—"cause", "court", "district judge", "divorce county court", "judge": r 1.2(1).

"other circumstances" (r 2.50(1)(*b*))—The rule does not define "other circumstances", but they might include more difficult issues under the proviso to r 2.49(2). The advantage of applying to the judge under this rule, rather than to the district judge under the proviso to r 2.49(2), is that the application is on notice and the applicant is thus guaranteed a hearing (cf **Hearing of the application** under r 2.49). Since this is an application in the course of proceedings, the hearing is in chambers (CCR Ord 13, r 1(4)).

Application for decree absolute by spouse against whom decree nisi obtained (r 2.50(2))—This rule provides the procedure by which an application for a decree absolute under MCA 1973, s 9(2) can be made by the spouse against whom a decree nisi has been obtained. The procedure for such a spouse differs greatly from that applicable to the spouse who obtained the decree nisi (see r 2.49(1)). Application is made on notice (by summons in the High Court) to the judge or district judge (r 10.9), both of whom have a discretion as to whether or not to grant the application (MCA 1973, s 9(2); *Smith v Smith* [1990] 1 FLR 438). The decree will not be made absolute if the refusal to do so is the only way to ensure that a party complies with an ancillary relief order (*Wickler v Wickler* [1998] 2 FLR 326). There appears to be nothing in r 2.49(2) to prevent the spouse who obtained the decree applying herself under r 2.49(1), on receiving notice of the application under this rule (unless 12 months have elapsed since the date of the decree nisi). If that happens, the spouse applying under r 2.50(2) should maintain his application if he wishes to seek an order for costs against the spouse who obtained the decree nisi.

"shall be served on the other spouse" (r 2.50(2))—Failure to serve on the petitioner an application (or summons) pursuant to MCA 1973, s 9(2) for pronouncement of a decree absolute renders the decree absolute void, and the decree must therefore be set aside (*Manchanda v Manchanda* [1995] 2 FLR 590, CA).

Time for application under MCA 1973, s 9(2)—Application under s 9(2) is made not earlier than three months from the date when the petitioner can first apply for a decree absolute; that will generally be six weeks from the grant of a decree nisi (MCA 1973, s 1(5): see **Time-limit for application** under r 2.49). Where the district judge gives a direction pursuant to FPR 1991, r 2.39(3) (non-satisfaction concerning arrangements for the children), and satisfaction is not expressed until after the six-week period has elapsed, the three-month period nevertheless runs from the normal six-week date (*Griffiths v Griffiths* (1976, unreported)).

2.51 Indorsement and certificate of decree absolute

(1) Where a decree nisi is made absolute, the proper officer shall make an indorsement to that effect on the decree, stating the precise time at which it was made absolute.

(2) On a decree nisi being made absolute, the proper officer shall send to the petitioner and the respondent a certificate in Form M9 or M10 whichever is appropriate, authenticated by the seal of the divorce county court or registry from which it is issued.

(3) A central index of decrees absolute shall be kept under the control of the principal registry and any person shall be entitled to require a search to be made therein, and to be furnished with a certificate of the result of the search, on payment of the prescribed fee.

(4) A certificate in Form M9 or M10 that a decree nisi has been made absolute shall be issued to any person requiring it on payment of the prescribed fee.

Defined terms—"divorce county court", "principal registry", "proper officer": r 1.2(1).

"certificate in Form M9 or M10" (r 2.51(2))—Forms M9 (in the case of divorce) and M10 (nullity) are to be found in FPR 1991, App 1.

Public availability of documents (r 2.51(3), (4))—Both the index of decrees absolute and the decree itself are public documents, and any person is entitled to see the index and to have copies of entries therein and copies of the certificate making the decree nisi absolute. The prescribed fee is £1 per page (Family Proceedings Fees Order 1999, Sch 1, fee 7.1).

Polygamous marriages—A decree in respect of a polygamous marriage must be stated to be granted by virtue of Matrimonial Causes Act 1973, s 47 (*Registrar's Direction of 14 May 1973*, para 5).

Ancillary relief

2.51A Application of ancillary relief rules

(1) The procedures set out in rules 2.51B to 2.70 ("the ancillary relief rules") apply to any ancillary relief application and to any application under section 10(2) of the Act of 1973.

(2) In the ancillary relief rules, unless the context otherwise requires:

"applicant" means the party applying for ancillary relief;

"respondent" means the respondent to the application for ancillary relief;

"FDR appointment" means a Financial Dispute Resolution appointment in accordance with rule 2.61E.

Amendments—Inserted by SI 1999/3491.

Defined terms—"ancillary relief": r 1.2(1).

Scope of provision: "5 June 2000 Watershed"—Applications for ancillary relief and applications under MCA 1973, s 10(2) which were commenced by Form M11 or M12 before 5 June 2000 are governed by the pre-5 June 2000 procedure but by virtue of Family Proceedings (Amendment No 2) Rules 1999, r 1(3) the court may, if it considers it just to do so, direct that the new procedure shall apply to those proceedings. The determining factor of whether the proceedings are pre or post-5 June 2000 is the date of filing Form M11/M12 or Form A/B and not the date of the petition. In respect of pre-5 June 2000 proceedings see Procedural Guide 18 in *The Family Court Practice 1999* for proceedings outside what were then pilot scheme courts and Procedural Guide 19 for proceedings in pilot scheme courts. The pre-June 2000 version of FPR 1991, rr 2.52–2.69 is printed in earlier editions of *The Family Court Practice*.

Non-ancillary relief—FPR 1991, rr 2.51A–2.70 as printed in this edition apply only to claims under MCA 1973, s 10(2) and ancillary relief claims, ie applications for maintenance pending suit, financial provision or property adjustment, pension sharing, avoidance of disposition or variation under MCA 1973, s 31. The new rules do not therefore apply to applications for financial relief for a child under Children Act 1989, Sch 1, the Married Women's Property Act 1882, the Trusts of Land and Appointment of Trustees Act 1996, failure to provide reasonable maintenance under MCA 1973, s 27, variation of a maintenance agreement under MCA 1973, s 35 or 36, the Inheritance (Provision for Family and Dependants) Act 1975 or a tenancy transfer under Family Law Act 1996, Pt IV. These applications have their own codes but where they draw upon FPR 1991, r 2.52 et seq they refer to the version of those rules as printed in earlier editions of *The Family Court Practice*. Their broad thrust is not substantially different from the version of those rules printed in this edition which apply to such claims; namely rr 2.52–2.62, 2.64–2.66. The original version also includes r 2.63 which enables a party to request from the other further information concerning any matter contained in any affidavit or any other relevant matter, or to furnish a list of relevant documents to allow inspection and, in default of compliance, to apply to the district judge for directions.

2.51B The overriding objective

(1) The ancillary relief rules are a procedural code with the overriding objective of enabling the court to deal with cases justly.

(2) Dealing with a case justly includes, so far as is practicable –

(*a*) ensuring that the parties are on an equal footing;
(*b*) saving expense;
(*c*) dealing with the case in ways which are proportionate –
  (i) to the amount of money involved;
  (ii) to the importance of the case;
  (iii) to the complexity of the issues; and
  (iv) to the financial position of each party;
(*d*) ensuring that it is dealt with expeditiously and fairly; and
(*e*) allotting to it an appropriate share of the court's resources, while taking into account the need to allot resources to other cases.

(3) The court must seek to give effect to the overriding objective when it –

(*a*) exercises any power given to it by the ancillary relief rules; or
(*b*) interprets any rule.

(4) The parties are required to help the court to further the overriding objective.

(5) The court must further the overriding objective by actively managing cases.

(6) Active case management includes –

(*a*) encouraging the parties to co-operate with each other in the conduct of the proceedings;
(*b*) encouraging the parties to settle their disputes through mediation, where appropriate;
(*c*) identifying the issues at an early date;
(*d*) regulating the extent of disclosure of documents and expert evidence so that they are proportionate to the issues in question;
(*e*) helping the parties to settle the whole or part of the case;
(*f*) fixing timetables or otherwise controlling the progress of the case;
(*g*) making use of technology; and
(*h*) giving directions to ensure that the trial of a case proceeds quickly and efficiently.

Amendments—Inserted by SI 1999/3491.

Scope of provision: The overriding objective—Following *Practice Direction of 31 January 1995* (court will exercise its discretion to limit discovery, oral evidence and issues) and *Practice Direction of 16 June 1997* (purpose of what was then the pilot scheme, and is now the procedure in all courts, to provide the court with more effective control over the proceedings), the overriding objective, which essentially mirrors CPR 1998, Pt 1, sets out the means by which the court will actively manage the case, from the time that the application is made until the order is carried out, so as to avoid unnecessary cost, delay and complexity. The parties, working in partnership with the court and co-operating with each other will be expected to adhere to timetables. Disclosure will be limited to that which is really necessary. Expert evidence will only be admissible with the court's permission. As envisaged by *Practice Direction of 31 January 1995*, only relevant issues will be investigated and the court can limit the time for examination and cross-examination. The relevance of old civil procedural authorities has been doubted in the light of the overriding objective contained in CPR 1998, Pt 1 (*Biguzzi v Rank Leisure plc* [1999] 1 WLR 1926; *NatWest Lombard Factors Ltd v Arbis* (1999) *The Times*, 10 December).

PART III

2.52 Right to be heard on ancillary questions

A respondent may be heard on any question of ancillary relief without filing an answer and whether or not he has returned to the court office an acknowledgement of service stating his wish to be heard on that question.

Defined terms—"ancillary relief": r 1.2(1).

2.53 Application by petitioner or respondent for ancillary relief

(1) Any application by a petitioner, or by a respondent who files an answer claiming relief, for –

(*a*) an order for maintenance pending suit,
(*b*) a financial provision order,
(*c*) a property adjustment order,
(*d*) a pension sharing order

shall be made in the petition or answer, as the case may be.

(2) Notwithstanding anything in paragraph (1), an application for ancillary relief which should have been made in the petition or answer may be made subsequently –

(*a*) by leave of the court, either by notice in Form A or at the trial, or
(*b*) where the parties are agreed upon the terms of the proposed order, without leave by notice in Form A.

(3) An application by a petitioner or respondent for ancillary relief, not being an application which is required to be made in the petition or answer, shall be made by notice in Form A.

Amendments—SI 1999/3491; SI 2000/2267.

Defined terms—"ancillary relief": r 1.2(1); "financial provision order": Matrimonial Causes Act 1973, ss 21(1), 23; "maintenance pending suit": MCA 1973, s 22; "property adjustment order": MCA 1973, ss 21(2), 23.

Scope of provision—This rule provides that the first procedural step in a claim for ancillary relief by a party to the marriage is that there must be an application for it (r 2.54 sets out who may apply when the claim is for a child). If there is no application there is no jurisdiction to make an order (*Robin v Robin* (1983) FLR 632). For the importance of a validly constituted notice of application see **Prohibition on application after remarriage** under MCA 1973, s 28.

The application (r 2.53(1))—The application, if made by the petitioner, should be claimed in the petition and, if made by a respondent who files an answer which claims relief, should be made in the answer. The claim is made in the prayer of the petition/answer.

Making an application which has been omitted from the petition or answer (r 2.53(2))—Rule 2.53(2) provides the two ways by which a claim for ancillary relief may be made if it has been omitted from the petition or answer. In the absence of consent to the terms of the proposed order, the applicant needs leave. If decree nisi has not yet been pronounced, the application is made to the district judge for leave to amend the petition by including the claim for ancillary relief, and the amended petition should then be re-served on the respondent. *Registrar's Direction of 5 March 1957* [1957] 1 All ER 860 specifies the procedure on such an application. The application must be supported by what in the last century was called an affidavit but is now better called a sworn statement. The notice of application and sworn statement must be served on the respondent to the application.

If the application is made after decree nisi has been pronounced then it is made in Form A and should be supported by a sworn statement setting out the reasons why the claim was omitted.

Application made by a party who has not filed a petition or answer claiming relief (r 2.53(3))—A respondent who has filed no answer or has filed an answer which merely denies the charges made in the petition without claiming relief should make application by filing notice in Form A. Subject to the remarriage bar (see **Prohibition on application after remarriage** under MCA 1973, s 28), there is no time-limit as to when the application may be filed.

Pension Sharing and Attachment—The rule requires an application for pension sharing or attachment (formerly known as earmarking and included within the definition of a financial provision order) to be made in the petition or answer.

No statute of limitation—Subject to the remarriage bar (see **Prohibition on application after remarriage** under MCA 1973, s 28), there is no jurisdictional bar on the court entertaining an application made many years after the divorce (*Twiname v Twiname* [1991] Fam Law 520).

Applying against oneself—It is not an abuse of process for one party to seek an order making provision for the other (*Dart v Dart* [1996] 2 FLR 286 at 296).

2.54 Application by parent, guardian etc for ancillary relief in respect of children

(1) Any of the following persons, namely –

(*a*) a parent or guardian of any child of the family,
(*b*) any person in whose favour a residence order has been made with respect to a child of the family, and any applicant for such an order,
(*c*) any other person who is entitled to apply for a residence order with respect to a child,
(*d*) a local authority, where an order has been made under section 30(1)(*a*) of the Act of 1989 placing a child in its care,
(*e*) the Official Solicitor, if appointed the guardian ad litem of a child of the family under rule 9.5, and
(*f*) a child of the family who has been given leave to intervene in the cause for the purpose of applying for ancillary relief,

may apply for an order for ancillary relief as respects that child by notice in Form A.

(2) In this rule "residence order" has the meaning assigned to it by section 8(1) of the Act of 1989.

Amendments—SI 1999/3491.

Defined terms—"ancillary relief": r 1.2(1); "child of the family"; Matrimonial Causes Act 1973, s 52(1); "residence order": CA 1989, s 8(1).

Scope of provision—A party may apply for ancillary relief for a child notwithstanding that the appropriate prayer does not appear in the petition. If one of his parents is not prepared to do so on his behalf, a child who, for example, is at university and requiring maintenance, may apply to intervene in the suit (*Downing v Downing* [1976] 3 WLR 335) and then apply for ancillary relief under r 2.54(1)(*f*).

2.55, 2.56 (*revoked*)

2.57 Children to be separately represented on certain applications

(1) Where an application is made to the High Court or a divorce county court for an order for a variation of settlement, the court shall, unless it is satisfied that the proposed variation does not adversely affect the rights or interests of any children concerned, direct that the children be separately represented on the application,

PART III

either by a solicitor or by a solicitor and counsel, and may appoint the Official Solicitor or other fit person to be guardian ad litem of the children for the purpose of the application.

(2) On any other application for ancillary relief the court may give such a direction or make such appointment as it is empowered to give or make by paragraph (1).

(3) Before a person other than the Official Solicitor is appointed guardian ad litem under this rule there shall be filed a certificate by the solicitor acting for the children that the person proposed as guardian has no interest in the matter adverse to that of the children and that he is a proper person to be such guardian.

Defined terms—"ancillary relief": r 1.2(1); "child": Matrimonial Causes Act 1973, s 52(1); "variation of settlement": MCA 1973, s 24.

Scope of provision—This rule provides that where there is an application to vary a settlement of property then, unless that variation does not prejudice any children concerned, the children must be separately represented. In all other applications for ancillary relief the district judge has a discretion to direct that the children be separately represented.

2.58 (*revoked*)

2.59 Evidence on application for property adjustment or avoidance of disposition order

(1) (*revoked*)

(2) Where an application for a property adjustment order or an avoidance of disposition order relates to land, the notice in Form A shall identify the land and –

(*a*) state whether the title to the land is registered or unregistered and, if registered, the Land Registry title number; and

(*b*) give particulars, so far as known to the applicant, of any mortgage of the land or any interest therein.

(3) Copies of Form A and of Form E completed by the applicant, shall be served on the following persons as well as on the respondent to the application, that is to say –

(*a*) in the case of an application for an order for a variation of settlement, the trustees of the settlement and the settlor if living;

(*b*) in the case of an application for an avoidance of disposition order, the person in whose favour the disposition is alleged to have been made;

and such other persons, if any, as the district judge may direct.

(4) In the case of an application to which paragraph (2) refers, a copy of Form A shall be served on any mortgagee of whom particulars are given pursuant to that paragraph; any person so served may apply to the court in writing, within 14 days after service, for a copy of the applicant's Form E.

(5) Any person who –

(*a*) is served with copies of Forms A and E pursuant to paragraph (3), or

(*b*) receives a copy of Form E following an application made in accordance with paragraph (4),

may, within 14 days after service or receipt, as the case may be, file a statement in answer.

(6) A statement filed under paragraph (5) shall be sworn to be true.

Amendments—SI 1992/456; SI 1999/3491.

Defined terms—"avoidance of disposition order": r 1.2(1); "disposition": Matrimonial Causes Act 1973, s 37(6); "settlement of property", "transfer", "variation of settlement": MCA 1973, s 24.

Contents of Form A when order sought relates to land/variation of settlement/avoidance of disposition order—Form A is a tick box form. The applicant should add the following information to it where applying for a property adjustment or avoidance of disposition order relating to land:

(*a*) whether the title to the land is unregistered or registered and, if so, the Land Registry title number (Land Registration Act 1925, s 112 (as amended) now permits inspection and copying of entries on the Register);
(*b*) details of any mortgage including the name and address of the mortgagee; and
(*c*) details of any interest therein, ie of any interest which any third party may have in the property concerned.

Service on third parties including mortgagees—Rule 2.59(3) and (4) impose a duty on the applicant to serve Forms A and E on: (i) the mortgagee; (ii) if applying for a variation of settlement, the trustees and the settlor; and (iii) if applying for an avoidance of disposition order, the person in whose favour the disposition has been made. Further, the concluding words of r 2.59(3) give a discretion to the district judge to direct that Forms A and E should be served on any other third party, eg someone who alleges that he has a beneficial interest in the property concerned. The service of a notice of application on a third party does not of itself make that person a party to the litigation with the attendant duty to give disclosure (*Re T (Divorce: Interim Maintenance: Discovery)* [1990] 1 FLR 1). However, if the third party is served and declines to play a part in the proceedings, he is bound by the court's findings as to the extent of his interest (*Tebbutt v Haynes* [1981] 2 All ER 238).

Service on pension provider of application for pension attachment or sharing—The pension provider must be served with Form A which requests a pension attachment (formerly earmarking) or pension sharing order as set out in r 2.70(6), (7).

2.60 Service of statement in answer

(1) Where a form or other document filed with the court contains an allegation of adultery or of an improper association with a named person ("the named person"), the court may direct that the party who filed the relevant form or document serve a copy of all or part of that form or document on the named person, together with Form F.

(2) If the court makes a direction under paragraph (1), the named person may file a statement in answer to the allegations.

(3) A statement under paragraph (2) shall be sworn to be true.

(4) Rule 2.37(3) shall apply to a person served under paragraph (1) as it applies to a co-respondent.

Amendments—Substituted by SI 1999/3491.

2.61 Information on application for consent order for financial relief

(1) Subject to paragraphs (2) and (3), there shall be lodged with every application for a consent order under any of sections 23, 24 or 24A of the Act of 1973 two copies of a draft of the order in the terms sought, one of which shall be indorsed with a statement signed by the respondent to the application signifying his agreement, and a statement of information (which may be made in more than one document) which shall include –

(*a*) the duration of the marriage, the age of each party and of any minor or dependent child of the family;

(*b*) an estimate in summary form of the approximate amount of value or the capital resources and net income of each party and of any minor child of the family;

(*c*) what arrangements are intended for the accommodation of each of the parties and any minor child of the family;

(*d*) whether either party has remarried or has any present intention to marry or to cohabit with another person;

(*dd*) where the order includes provision to be made under section 24B, 25B or 25C of the Act of 1973, a statement confirming that the person responsible for the pension arrangement in question has been served with the documents required by rule 2.70(11) and that no objection to such an order has been made by that person within 14 days from such service;

(*e*) where the terms of the order provide for a transfer of property, a statement confirming that any mortgagee of that property has been served with notice of the application and that no objection to such a transfer has been made by the mortgagee within 14 days from such service; and

(*f*) any other especially significant matters.

(2) Where an application is made for a consent order varying an order for periodical payments paragraph (1) shall be sufficiently complied with if the statement of information required to be lodged with the application includes only the information in respect of net income mentioned in paragraph (1)(*b*) (and, where appropriate, a statement under paragraph (1)(*dd*)), and an application for a consent order for interim periodical payments pending the determination of an application for ancillary relief may be made in like manner.

(3) Where all or any of the parties attend the hearing of an application for financial relief the court may dispense with the lodging of a statement of information in accordance with paragraph (1) and give directions for the information which would otherwise be required to be given in such a statement to be given in such a manner as it sees fit.

Amendments—SI 1996/1674; SI 2000/2267.

Scope of provision—This rule provides for the information that the court must be given to enable it to exercise its discretion under Matrimonial Causes Act 1973, s 25 by making an order in accordance with the terms agreed between the parties. Without full and frank disclosure of both parties' circumstances as at the time that the court order is made (as opposed to when the proceedings started) the court cannot lawfully exercise its powers (*Jenkins v Livesey (formerly Jenkins)* [1985] AC 424, [1985] FLR 813) and the order is at risk of being subsequently set aside. This rule requires two copies of the proposed consent order to be lodged, one of which should be endorsed by the respondent to the application signifying his agreement. To minimise the scope for the applicant (or respondent) subsequently saying, genuinely or otherwise, that distress at the time prevented him or her from understanding the terms of the settlement, it is a wise precaution to insert at the end of the proposed order a statement that each party has read and understood the terms of the proposed consent order and to ensure that the parties sign the proposed consent order themselves, as opposed to it being signed by solicitors on their behalf.

Where the parties have reached a "Xydhias Accord" (typically at the conclusion of the FDR – see **Steps to be taken if agreement reached** under r 2.61E), the first stage is for the heads of agreement to be set out in writing in simple terms and signed by both parties and their legal advisers and the second stage is to formulate those heads of agreement in the language of the court (*Xydhias v Xydhias* [1999] 1 FLR 683).

The terms of any capital clean break clause should cover whether it is intended that either party may subsequently seek any further pension sharing order.

Where the agreed provisions contain terms going outside that which the court is able to order under the Matrimonial Causes Act 1973, those terms should be set out as recitals to the order and the body of the order should state that the court approves the recitals and directs that they are made a rule of court and filed as such. The effect of this is to enable the terms to be summarily enforced in the suit without the necessity of bringing a separate action (*Hall v Hall* (1972) *The Times*, 30 June, *Graves v Graves* (1893) LT 420).

Pension Sharing and Attachment—An essential pre-condition of an effective consent pension sharing or attachment (formerly earmarking) order is that the person responsible for the pension arrangement has been served with the Form A and has had sufficient time to object and has not done so. Although this rule states the time for a pension provider to object to a pension attachment order is 14 days, FPR 1991, r 2.70(12) states 21 and it is therefore suggested that 21 days' notice should be given.

Inheritance Act Clean Break Information—Where a clean break order under the Inheritance (Provision for Family and Dependants) Act 1975, s 15 is sought, brief details of the testamentary intention of the party who is seeking the order are required (*Whiting v Whiting* [1988] 2 FLR 189, [1988] 1 WLR 565); ie simply a concise statement of who are the likely beneficiaries.

"varying an order for periodical payments" (r 2.61(2))—A variation order is an order under MCA 1973, s 31.

Consent application for interim periodical payments order or for an order varying a periodical payments order (r 2.61(2))—The only information required on the r 2.61 statement in such cases is the net income of each party and the children.

Dispensing with r 2.61 statement (r 2.61(3))—If a consent order is made when both or either of the parties attend the hearing, the court has discretion to dispense with the statement of information. It is likely to exercise that discretion where there are current sworn statements or the current financial position of both parties is adequately documented.

Agreements prior to decree nisi—Such agreements can be made the subject of a consent order on the basis of the procedure in this rule, subject to validation on decree nisi (*Pounds v Pounds* [1994] 1 FLR 775, CA).

2.61A Application for ancillary relief

(1) A notice of intention to proceed with an application for ancillary relief made in the petition or answer or an application for ancillary relief must be made by notice in Form A.

(2) The notice must be filed:

(*a*) if the case is pending in a divorce county court, in that court; or
(*b*) if the case is pending in the High Court, in the registry in which it is proceeding.

(3) Where the applicant requests an order for ancillary relief that includes provision to be made by virtue of section 24B, 25B or 25C of the Act of 1973 the terms of the order requested must be specified in the notice in Form A.

(4) Upon the filing of Form A the court must:

(*a*) fix a first appointment not less than 12 weeks and not more than 16 weeks after the date of the filing of the notice and give notice of that date;
(*b*) serve a copy on the respondent within 4 days of the date of the filing of the notice.

(5) The date fixed under paragraph (4) for the first appointment, or for any subsequent appointment, must not be cancelled except with the court's permission and, if cancelled, the court must immediately fix a new date.

Amendments—Inserted by SI 1999/3491; amended by SI 2000/2267.

Defined terms—"ancillary relief": r 1.2(1).

Scope of provision—After entering cost effective and issue based pre-action disclosure of information and negotiations as required by the Pre-Application Protocol (see *President's Direction of 25 May 2000*), this rule establishes that the filing of Form A is the first step to be taken under the new procedural code. The applicant, if applying for a property adjustment order, avoidance of disposition order or variation of settlement order, must add the information required by r 2.59 to the basic tick box structure of Form A, and if applying for a pension sharing or pension attachment (formerly earmarking) order must set out the terms of the requested order. No sworn statement (ie affidavit) is required at this stage.

Service, including pension sharing and attachment application—The court should serve the respondent within 4 days. *Practice Direction of 13 February 1989* sets out how the Department of Social Security, the National Health Service Central Register, the Passport Office or, if the person whom it is sought to trace has recently been serving in HM Forces, the Ministry of Defence will assist in tracing the respondent where service proves difficult. The applicant serves, as required by r 2.59(3) and (4): (i) the mortgagee; (ii) if a variation of settlement application, the trustees and the settlor; (iii) if an avoidance of disposition application, the person in whose favour the disposition is alleged to have been made; (iv) any other person who the court directs to be served as having an interest in the property; and (v) by virtue of r 2.70(6) and (7), the person responsible for managing the pension arrangement in respect of which the applicant seeks either a pension sharing or a pension attachment (formerly earmarking) order.

Obtaining the Form E documents—This is the appropriate time to obtain the documents to be attached to Form E (see further under r 2.61B below).

Court (not parties) in control of timetable—The other party's consent to an adjournment of a hearing date is insufficient. The court's permission must be obtained and a new date will be fixed.

2.61B Procedure before the first appointment

(1) Both parties must, at the same time, exchange with each other, and each file with the court, a statement in Form E, which –

(*a*) is signed by the party who made the statement;
(*b*) is sworn to be true, and
(*c*) contains the information and has attached to it the documents required by that Form.

(2) Form E must be exchanged and filed not less than 35 days before the date of the first appointment.

(3) Form E must have attached to it:

(*a*) any documents required by Form E;
(*b*) any other documents necessary to explain or clarify any of the information contained in Form E; and
(*c*) any documents furnished to the party producing the form by a person responsible for a pension arrangement, either following a request under rule 2.70(2) or as part of a "relevant valuation" as defined in rule 2.70(4).

(4) Form E must have no documents attached to it other than the documents referred to in paragraph (3).

(5) Where a party was unavoidably prevented from sending any document required by Form E, that party must at the earliest opportunity:

(*a*) serve copies of that document on the other party, and
(*b*) file a copy of that document with the court, together with a statement explaining the failure to send it with Form E.

(6) No disclosure or inspection of documents may be requested or given between the filing of the application for ancillary relief and the first appointment, except –

(*a*) copies sent with Form E, or in accordance with paragraph (5); or (*b*) in accordance with paragraph (7).

(7) At least 14 days before the hearing of the first appointment, each party must file with the court and serve on the other party –

(*a*) a concise statement of the issues between the parties;
(*b*) a chronology;
(*c*) a questionnaire setting out by reference to the concise statement of issues any further information and documents requested from the other party or a statement that no information and documents are required;
(*d*) a notice in Form G stating whether that party will be in a position at the first appointment to proceed on that occasion to a FDR appointment.

(8) (*revoked*)

(9) At least 14 days before the hearing of the first appointment, the applicant must file with the court and serve on the respondent, confirmation of the names of all persons served in accordance with rule 2.59(3) and (4), and that there are no other persons who must be served in accordance with those paragraphs.

Amendments—Inserted by SI 1999/3491; amended by SI 2000/2267.

Scope of provision—This is the second step under the new procedural rules. First, the parties simultaneously exchange full disclosure of their means with certain documents attached by Form E. Secondly, no disclosure of documents (other than required by Form E – see below) may be asked for or given between the filing of Form A and the first appointment. Thirdly, two weeks before the first appointment each party must exchange and file five documents: (*a*) a statement of issues; (*b*) a chronology; (*c*) a questionnaire and request for documents; (*d*) Form G (which states whether or not, with reasons, a party is ready to treat the first appointment as an FDR appointment; and (*e*) confirmation that all relevant parties, including mortgagees and pension providers, have been served (rr 2.59(3), (4) and 2.70(6), (7)).

Form E—Form E is a printed 20 page document divided into the following four sections: (i) general information; (ii) assets of all descriptions including capital pension and income; (iii) income and capital requirements; and (iv) other information (including standard of living, contributions and details of requested order). Each party confirms that the information given is full, frank, clear and accurate. A party who does not give full and frank disclosure is at risk of a subsequent application being made to set the order aside (*Jenkins v Livesey (formerly Jenkins)* [1985] AC 424, [1985] FLR 813).

Documents to be attached to Form E—The following documents (and no others) must be attached to Form E:

1 (Box 2.1 and 2.2) Any valuation obtained in the last six months of the matrimonial home or any other land or property plus latest mortgage statement.
2 (Box 2.3) Bank and building society statements for the last 12 months.
3 (Box 2.5) Surrender value of any life policy.
4 (Box 2.14) Last 2 years' accounts of any company and any document relied on for any valuation of that company.
5 (Box 2.16) Cash equivalent transfer value in last 12 months of each pension arrangement or letter of request asking for that valuation.
6 (Box 2.18) Last 3 pay slips and latest P60.
7 (Box 2.20) If self-employed, accounts for the last 2 years.

Box 1.13 requires an estimate of the likely CSA calculation (obtainable from Bird, *Practitioner's Child Support Calculation Pack* (Family Law)).

Pension information to be obtained on notification of first appointment—Anyone with benefits under a pension arrangement (whether or not a pension sharing or attachment order is claimed) must within 7 days after receiving the date of the first appointment ask the person responsible for each of his pension arrangements for a CETV (unless he already has one not more than 12 months old) and within 7 days of receiving the CETV send it to the other party with the address of the pension provider (r 2.70(1)–(5)).

PART III

Prohibition on disclosure being given voluntarily (r 2.61B(6))—No disclosure of documents can be requested or given between the filing of Form A and the first appointment.

Filing and exchange of documents 2 weeks before the first appointment (r 2.61B(7))—The parties must file and exchange a statement of issues, a chronology, a questionnaire and request for documents, notice in Form G and (applicant only) confirmation that mortgagees and pension providers have been served.

The millionaire's defence to disclosure—If a respondent to an application for ancillary relief concedes that his wealth is such as to enable him to pay any order that might reasonably be made, the court has a discretion to decline to require him to provide full disclosure (*Dart v Dart* [1996] 2 FLR 286 at 293) although a certain minimum amount of information (*Van G v Van G (Financial Provision: Millionaires' Defence)* [1995] 1 FLR 328) and information intended to establish the broad realities of the case and illuminate past dealings will be required (*F v F (Ancillary Relief: Substantial Assets)* [1995] 2 FLR 45). The rationale for the millionaire's defence is that it is disproportionate to permit substantial disclosure where the claim is based on the applicant's reasonable needs. *White v White* [2000] 2 FLR 981 and *Lambert v Lambert* [2002] EWCA Civ 1685, [2003] 1 FLR 139 may well have limited the relevance of this defence, subject to disclosure being given proportionately having regard to the overriding objective.

2.61C Expert evidence

CPR rules 35.1 to 35.14 relating to expert evidence (with appropriate modifications), except CPR rules 35.5(2) and 35.8(4)(*b*), apply to all ancillary relief proceedings.

Amendments—Inserted by SI 1999/3491.

Scope of provision—Expert evidence is now governed by CPR 1998, Pt 35, the main points of which are:

(i) Expert evidence (whether written or oral) is not allowed unless permission has been given (CPR 1998 r 35.4). Permission will not be given unless the evidence is reasonably required (CPR 1998, r 35.1) and justified in the light of the overriding objective (FPR 1991, r 2.51B).

(ii) The expert evidence must be in a written report and oral expert evidence is not permitted unless the court directs otherwise (CPR 1998, r 35.5).

(iii) The court can direct that evidence be given by a single jointly instructed expert (to be agreed between the parties or in default of agreement selected by a third party – usually the president of the professional body concerned). The parties are initially equally liable for the expert's fees (CPR 1998, rr 35.7 and 35.8). Whether it is desirable for there to be a single joint expert is determined by the criteria of the overriding objective set out in FPR 1991, r 2.51B. Expert evidence should be given by a single jointly instructed expert where possible (*Best Practice Guidance of November 2002*). If a party is dissatisfied with a jointly instructed expert's report he may be at liberty to commission his own report, although whether that report will be admitted will be dependent upon proportionality and the overriding objective (*Daniels v Walker* [2000] 1 WLR 1382). *Cosgrove v Pattison* (2001) *The Times*, 13 February identifies relevant factors as the nature and number of issues between the parties, the reason for wishing to call one's own expert, the amount at stake, any delay in making the application and whether the hearing will be delayed or otherwise affected. See also **Further report** under CPR 1998, r 35.8.

(iv) Written questions can be put once within 28 days of receiving an expert's report, whether the expert is instructed jointly or by the other party (CPR 1998, r 35.6).

(v) The court can direct a discussion between experts to narrow the issues (CPR 1998, r 35.12).

Form of expert reports—The court's fundamental concern is to make a break with the past when, on occasion, experts have been partisan. The expert's duty to help the court overrides his obligation to the person who pays him (CPR 1998, r 35.3). By virtue of CPR 1998, r 35.10, the expert's report must be in the format prescribed by *Practice Direction (Experts and Assessors)* (set out in Part V of this work), and contain a statement that he understands his duty to the court, that the facts and opinions stated are true and summarising the substance of all material instructions.

Business valuations—The following points should be noted:

(1) Where a business has some capital value but there is no intention to realise the business in the foreseeable future, the fact that at retirement the owner will receive a capital sum can in some circumstances be sufficiently dealt with in Form E. If a valuation is obtained, all that is needed is a short report from a business transfer agent, ie a person who sells businesses of the type in question, stating what the business is likely to fetch.

(2) Where the business is of substantial value (relative to the general means of the parties) and (i) there is a real possibility of a sale in the near future; (ii) there are substantial assets within the business that can be sold without affecting the viability of the core business; or (iii) the business should, for some other good reason, be sold, a broad valuation is clearly needed and the consideration set out in the overriding objective in FPR 1991, r 2.51B will determine whether the valuation should be joint. The expert report will need to consider (*a*) valuation; and (*b*) ability to raise funds to pay the claimant a lump sum.

(3) Where both parties have shares in the company and it is proposed that one should transfer his shares to the other, the court will usually try to transfer the shares of the party who is not running the business, and may do so for no consideration. Unless the transfer is made before 5 April of the year of separation, a charge for capital gains tax will arise on the person who is transferring the shares. An accurate estimate of how the Inland Revenue is likely to treat the value of the shares transferred should be obtained. Otherwise, the party transferring the shareholding may find that the sum paid in capital gains tax exceeds the lump sum that the court has awarded.

(4) Where assets will be subject to capital gains tax, the amount of tax should be quantified so that the court is given the net value of the asset after capital gains tax and costs of sale (*White v White* [2000] 2 FLR 981 at 996).

Pension Valuations—As set out in the annotations to MCA 1973, s 24B and the Pensions on Divorce etc (Provision of Information) Regulations 2000, the method prescribed for valuing the cash equivalent transfer value of a pension benefit is based on the pension member leaving service today. No regard is had to past service reserves. The CETV does not include the death in service benefit.

Further, as a woman's life expectancy is longer than a man's, equal division of pension assets does not lead to equality of benefits. Expert evidence will only be permitted to clarify the above point if it is both reasonably necessary and justified in the light of the overriding objective.

PART III

2.61D The first appointment

(1) The first appointment must be conducted with the objective of defining the issues and saving costs.

(2) At the first appointment the district judge –

(*a*) must determine –

(i) the extent to which any questions seeking information under rule 2.61B must be answered, and

(ii) what documents requested under rule 2.61B must be produced,

and give directions for the production of such further documents as may be necessary;

(*b*) must give directions about –

(i) the valuation of assets (including, where appropriate, the joint instruction of joint experts);

(ii) obtaining and exchanging expert evidence, if required; and

(iii) evidence to be adduced by each party and, where appropriate, about further chronologies or schedules to be filed by each party;

(*c*) must, unless he decides that a referral is not appropriate in the circumstances, direct that the case be referred to a FDR appointment;

(*d*) must, where he decides that a referral to a FDR appointment is not appropriate, direct one or more of the following:

(i) that a further directions appointment be fixed;

(ii) that an appointment be fixed for the making of an interim order;

(iii) that the case be fixed for final hearing and, where that direction is given, the district judge must determine the judicial level at which the case should be heard;

(iv) that the case be adjourned for out-of-court mediation or private negotiation or, in exceptional circumstances, generally;

(*e*) must consider whether, having regard to all the circumstances (including the extent to which each party has complied with this Part, and in particular the requirement to send documents with Form E), to make an order about the costs of the hearing; and

(*f*) may –

(i) make an interim order where an application for it has been made in accordance with rule 2.69F returnable at the first appointment;

(ii) having regard to the contents of Form G filed by the parties, treat the appointment (or part of it) as a FDR appointment to which rule 2.61E applies;

(iii) in a case where an order for ancillary relief is requested that includes provision to be made under section 25B or 25C of the Act of 1973, require any party to request a valuation under regulation 4 of the Divorce etc (Pensions) Regulations 1996 from the trustees or managers of any pension scheme under which the party has, or is likely to have, any benefits.

(3) After the first appointment, a party is not entitled to production of any further documents except in accordance with directions given under paragraph (2)(*a*) above or with the permission of the court.

(4) At any stage:

(*a*) a party may apply for further directions or a FDR appointment;

(*b*) the court may give further directions or direct that the parties attend a FDR appointment.

(5) Both parties must personally attend the first appointment unless the court orders otherwise.

Amendments—Inserted by SI 1999/3491; amended by SI 2003/184.

Scope of provision—The third stage under the new procedural rules is the first appointment at which the court will, in pursuance of the overriding objective of r 2.51B, actively manage the case (issues, disclosure, expert evidence and extent of other evidence) and order the next hearing (usually an FDR). The parties must attend the first appointment personally. An up-to-date estimate of costs must be produced. After the first appointment there is no further disclosure of documents except as ordered at that appointment or with permission.

Active case management: The answer to questionnaires and requests for documents, expert evidence and other evidence—All aspects of case management are conducted in the light of the overriding objective at r 2.51B.

(i) *Questionnaire seeking information* The criteria of the overriding objective may suggest that only information that is really necessary will be ordered. A party may be ordered to use his best endeavours to obtain from a third party a document not yet in existence, eg a letter from a partnership secretary confirming earnings (*G v-G (Financial Provision: Discovery)* [1992] 1 FLR 40).

(ii) *Disclosure of documents* Similarly, the criteria of the overriding objective may suggest that only documents that are really necessary will be ordered to be produced.

(iii) *Valuation of assets and expert evidence* Expert evidence, whether written or oral, is only allowed with permission. *President's Direction of 25 May 2000* encourages the use of a single joint expert. The expert's report must bear a statement that he understands his duty to the court and a statement of truth. See further annotations under r 2.61C.

(iv) *Other evidence* Either at this juncture (or at the conclusion of the FDR if, for instance, this course is more cost effective) the court will give directions as to what other evidence may be called and the form that evidence should take. An affidavit as to the historical background and each party's contributions may be ordered after the Financial Dispute Resolution (*W v W (Ancillary Relief: Practice)* [2000] Fam Law 473). See r 2.62 and the annotations thereunder for detailed examination of the following issues:

(*a*) no power to order a sworn statement (previously known as an affidavit) from third party;
(*b*) disclosure and inspection of documents of third party;
(*c*) securing attendance of witness;
(*d*) notices to admit and hearsay notices.

Fixing the next stage—The court will usually fix an FDR appointment but can fix a final hearing, a further directions appointment, treat the hearing as an FDR and/or adjourn for mediation or negotiation.

Interim applications—See FPR 1991, r 2.69F.

No further production of documents without permission—Rule 2.63 (request for further information at any time) has been revoked. The request for information and documents made fourteen days before the first appointment is intended as a one-window opportunity for disclosure and permission is needed for further disclosure of documents after the first appointment (sought by separate application on notice for a directions appointment under r 2.61D(4)(*a*)).

Enforcement of order to provide information or documents—If the order for information or documents is not complied with it is suggested that an application should be made ex parte to the district judge by letter (with a copy to the other party) for a penal notice to be added to the order. The order, endorsed with the penal notice, should be served by enquiry agent on the person ordered to provide the information or document. If the information is then not delivered within the period set out, application may be made to commit.

Power to order provision of copies and payment for copies—Rule 2.61D is silent as to who should pay for the cost of copying documents. RSC Ord 24, r 11A and CCR Ord 14, r 5A provide for the party who has requested the document to pay the cost of copying. It is suggested that by virtue of FPR 1991, r 1.3 these rules apply to family proceedings. CPR 1998, r 31.15 provides that where a party has a right to inspect a document he may request a copy of it, provided he also undertakes to pay the reasonable copying costs. It is submitted that the party requesting the documents is under an obligation to pay the copying charges.

Bank statements—Under the Data Protection Act 1984 a bank may not charge more than £10 per request for bank statements, even though a large number of pages are requested (this upper limit ceases to be applicable if the information is transferred to manual microfiche; also, where a request relates to more than one area of registration, ie for copies of credit card as well as bank statements, a further £10 fee will be charged). The following formula is suggested to bring the request within the Act (see "Bank Charges Made for Duplicate Statements" [1997] Fam Law 583):

> "Section 21(1)(*b*) of the Data Protection Act 1984 states that an individual is entitled to be supplied by any data user with a copy of the information constituting any such personal data held by him. A data user is not obliged to supply such information except in response to a request in writing and on payment of such fee not exceeding the prescribed maximum as he may required. This is currently £10 (Data Protection (Subject Access) Fees Regulations 1987 (SI 1987/1507), reg 2). This is so regardless of the number of pages. Accordingly we confirm that we will pay £10."

Self help—Where non-disclosure is reasonably anticipated, a party may take photocopies of such of the other party's documents as can be located without the use of force. The use of force to obtain documents, the interception of mail and the retention of original documents are disapproved and will be taken into account when considering costs (*T v T (Interception of Documents)* [1994] 2 FLR 1083).

Pension sharing and attachment

(i) If a pension sharing or attachment (formerly earmarking) order, has person responsible for pension arrangement been served under FPR 1991, r 2.70(6) and (7) and does he object?
(ii) If either party has the benefit of a pension arrangement, has information as to its CETV etc been provided as required by FPR 1991, r 2.70(3)? If either has applied for pension attachment or sharing of a state scheme (ie other than the basic state pension) has information

as to its CETV etc been provided? If not, court can order under FPR 1991, r 2.62(4) the person with pension benefit to provide the information both as to the pension arrangement and the shareable state scheme rights under. The court can order the pension provider to provide information as to the pension arrangement under Pensions on Divorce etc (Provision of Information) Regulations 2000, reg 2(5) and can order the Secretary of State to provide the information on shareable state scheme rights under Sharing of State Scheme Rights (Provision of Information and Valuation) Regulations 2000, reg 2(1). Has the person who has no pension rights other than basic state retirement pension applied for retirement benefit forecast by sending BR19 to Benefits Agency, RPFA Unit, Pensions & Overseas Benefit Directorate, Newcastle Upon Tyne, NE98 1YX?

(iii) Should there be expert evidence by an actuary or independent financial adviser?

2.61E The FDR appointment

(1) The FDR appointment must be treated as a meeting held for the purposes of discussion and negotiation and paragraphs (2) to (9) apply.

(2) The district judge or judge hearing the FDR appointment must have no further involvement with the application, other than to conduct any further FDR appointment or to make a consent order or a further directions order.

(3) Not later than 7 days before the FDR appointment, the applicant must file with the court details of all offers and proposals, and responses to them.

(4) Paragraph (3) includes any offers, proposals or responses made wholly or partly without prejudice, but paragraph (3) does not make any material admissible as evidence if, but for that paragraph, it would not be admissible.

(5) At the conclusion of the FDR appointment, any documents filed under paragraph (3), and any filed documents referring to them, must, at the request of the party who filed them, be returned to him and not retained on the court file.

(6) Parties attending the FDR appointment must use their best endeavours to reach agreement on the matters in issue between them.

(7) The FDR appointment may be adjourned from time to time.

(8) At the conclusion of the FDR appointment, the court may make an appropriate consent order, but otherwise must give directions for the future course of the proceedings, including, where appropriate, the filing of evidence and fixing a final hearing date.

(9) Both parties must personally attend the FDR appointment unless the court orders otherwise.

Amendments—Inserted by SI 1999/3491.

Scope of provision—The Financial Dispute Resolution (FDR) appointment is the fourth step in the new procedure. The court expects both parties to place their cards face up on the table. All offers, whether open, "without prejudice" or *Calderbank*, must be disclosed so that the district judge can, if appropriate, advise the parties that the costs implications make it sensible to examine how the gap between them can be bridged. In order that the parties are able to approach conciliation openly and without reserve, anything said at the FDR appointment is inadmissible in any subsequent proceedings, except where an offence is committed at the appointment (*President's Direction of 25 May 2000*). The district judge who conducts the appointment has no further involvement.

Requirement to file details of offers—A week before the appointment, the applicant files a schedule of all offers and counter-offers. At the end of the appointment the parties should request the return of the schedule of offers and proposals and any other privileged documents that they have submitted during the course of the FDR.

Costs estimate and personal attendance—Each party should file a costs estimate and personally attend the appointment.

Active case management—Rule 2.61E(8) provides that if the FDR does not result in a consent order the court will fix a date for the final hearing and give all necessary case management directions (see annotations under r 2.61D). An affidavit setting out the broader presentation of the historical background or other relevant evidence may be ordered, at any rate in cases of greater wealth (*W v W (Ancillary Relief: Practice)* [2000] Fam Law 473).

Steps to be taken if agreement reached—If at all possible, a consent order signed by both parties and their legal representatives should be handed to the judge so that an order can be made immediately. If time does not permit a consent order to be drawn up, written heads of agreement signed by the parties and their legal representatives should be submitted to the judge and he should be asked to approve the heads of agreement so that the proposed order is approved by the court. The judge should order the date by which the perfected minuted order should be filed and fix a further hearing to resolve any outstanding points. A form of order appears at [2002] Fam Law 910. If the judge is not handed written heads of agreement, he should in any event be told the core terms of the agreement and asked to approve that agreement so that the order ceases to be a contractual agreement and instead becomes an unperfected order of the court (*Rose v Rose* [2002] EWCA Civ 208, [2002] 1 FLR 978).

2.61F Costs

(1) At every court hearing or appointment each party must produce to the court an estimate in Form H of the costs incurred by him up to the date of that hearing or appointment.

(2) The parties' obligation under paragraph (1) is without prejudice to their obligations under paragraph 4.1 to 4.11 of the Practice Direction relating to CPR Part 44.

Amendments—Inserted by SI 1999/3491.

Scope of provision—This rule provides first that at every hearing each party must produce a costs estimate of the costs incurred to date and secondly that where a party is applying for a summary assessment of his costs in respect of a hearing he must provide a written statement of those costs.

Summary assessment of costs under CPR 1998, Pt 44 and its supplementary Practice Direction—*President's Direction of 22 April 1999* applies the costs provisions of CPR 1998, Pts 43–48 to family proceedings. "Pay as you go" is one of the principles of those rules so that the court can order a summary assessment of costs at the end of the hearing or, if it does not do so, can order a payment on account (CPR 1998, r 44.3(8)). *Practice Direction about Costs* (set out in Part V of this work) establishes the principles of summary assessment and of payment on account. The general rule is that a summary assessment will be made if the hearing has lasted less than one day where there is an order that one party pays the other party's costs. A summary assessment will not be made when the order is costs in the case. Such an assessment can be made against a legally aided paying party; however, it cannot be made in favour of a legally aided receiving party. The costs estimate must be served at least 24 hours before the hearing on the other party and the court and should be in Form 1 of the Schedule of Costs Forms. It must state that the costs estimated do not exceed the costs which the solicitor's own client is liable to pay and must be signed by the party's solicitor. If a party is appearing in person, on an assessment of his costs, he is entitled to payment of his disbursements (which include the cost of obtaining legal advice). As regards his own time, if he has incurred financial loss he is entitled to up to two-thirds of the costs which would be chargeable by a legal representative. If he has not incurred financial loss, his time is remunerated at £9.25 per hour (CPR 1998, r 48.6). Failure to serve a costs schedule 24 hours before the hearing will not necessarily be fatal to a costs application but may lead the court exercising discretion as to the amount of costs in favour of the paying party or standing the matter over for a detailed assessment, or a summary assessment at a later date or in writing (*Macdonald v Taree Holdings Ltd* (2000) *The Times*, 28 December, CA).

2.62 Investigation by district judge of application for ancillary relief

(1) (*revoked*)

(2) An application for an avoidance of disposition order shall, if practicable, be heard at the same time as any related application for financial relief.

(3) (*revoked*)

(4) At the hearing of an application for ancillary relief the district judge shall, subject to rules 2.64, 2.65 and 10.10 investigate the allegations made in support of and in answer to the application, and may take evidence orally and may at any stage of the proceedings, whether before or during the hearing, order the attendance of any person for the purpose of being examined or cross-examined and order the disclosure and inspection of any document or require further statements.

(4A) A statement filed under paragraph (4) shall be sworn to be true.

(5), (6) (*revoked*)

(7) Any party may apply to the court for an order that any person do attend an appointment (an "inspection appointment") before the court and produce any documents to be specified or described in the order, the inspection of which appears to the court to be necessary for disposing fairly of the application for ancillary relief or for saving costs.

(8) No person shall be compelled by an order under paragraph (7) to produce any document at an inspection appointment which he could not be compelled to produce at the hearing of the application for ancillary relief.

(9) The court shall permit any person attending an inspection appointment pursuant to an order under paragraph (7) above to be represented at the appointment.

Amendments—SI 1999/3491.

Defined terms—"ancillary relief", "avoidance of disposition order", "proper officer": r 1.2(1).

No power to order a third party to file a sworn statement—The court has no power under this or any other rule, in the absence of consent, to order any other person to file a sworn statement, formerly called an affidavit (*Wynne v Wynne and Jeffers* [1980] 1 WLR 69). Thus, as a co-respondent is not a party to the application for ancillary relief, the court cannot order a sworn statement from such a person.

Inspection appointment: the disclosure of a third party's documents—The court's power to order a third party to produce any relevant document is contained in r 2.62(7)–(9). *Frary v Frary* [1993] 2 FLR 696 held that these rules do not change the law but merely bring forward to a date earlier than the final hearing the time at which a witness might be required to attend court to produce a document. Procedure is in part governed by the consideration that a third party is entitled to respect for the privacy of his documents. Thus, it is oppressive to apply ex parte, unless there is good reason to do so. The first stage is to apply on notice to the other party with supporting sworn statement, but not on notice to the person who is to produce the documents (*B v B (Production Appointment: Procedure)* [1995] 1 FLR 913) for an order that the document be produced. The application should be supported by a sworn statement setting out: (i) the nature of the proceedings; (ii) the necessity for the production of the documents; (iii) the precise documents sought; and (iv) whether the applicant intends to call the witness at the hearing. This application should, it is suggested, be made either at the time of the first appointment or at the conclusion of the FDR. At that stage, the district judge will weed out any unnecessary or oppressive application. Upon granting the order, the third party will be ordered to attend an appointment, bringing the documents which he has been ordered to produce. At this second stage, the person producing the documents has the right to be represented and object to their production. The court has to balance the interests of the parties to the suit against the interests of privacy of the third party, having regard to the principles set out in *Morgan v Morgan* [1977] Fam 122, (1976) FLR Rep 473 (where an application for a wife's wealthy father to disclose his testamentary intentions was refused). Each exercise of discretion depends on its own facts. In *H v H (Disclosure by Third Party)* (1981) FLR 303, the chairman of the company in which the wife held 3 per cent of the shares was ordered to produce the documents showing the rent payable to the company so that its assets, and hence the wife's shareholding, could be valued. In *Frary v Frary* (above) disclosure of the documents (P60 and accounts, bank and credit card statements etc) was refused against the respondent's cohabitee with whom he shared a house under a cohabitation agreement. If an order is made for documents to be inspected, it appears that the producer may be required or permitted to give evidence (*Frary v Frary*). The statement contained in *The Family Court Practice 1999* that there is no power, in the absence of agreement, for copies of the documents to be taken must be critically re-considered in the light of the overriding objective at r 2.51B.

Right to discretionary trust documents—Ordinarily, a trustee will be compelled to disclose to a beneficiary documents showing the state of the funds of the trust, such as the annual accounts, but will be entitled not to disclose any document showing the reasons for exercising a discretionary power, such as the minutes of meetings (*Re Londonderry's Settlement* [1965] 2 WLR 229, CA). In *Re Rabiotti's Settlements* [2001] Fam Law 808 the Royal Court of Jersey, whilst confirming that a beneficiary is ordinarily not entitled to see a letter of wishes, allowed disclosure because the letter supported the assertion advanced by the discretionary beneficiary in the English matrimonial court that his interest in the settlement was limited.

Right of third party to documents in ancillary relief proceedings—The application should be made in the matrimonial court, not in the court of another action (*Nayler and Boyle v Beard* [2001] 2 FLR 1346). See note under FPR 1991 r 10.20.

Securing the attendance of witnesses—Rule 2.62(4) empowers the court to order the attendance of any person to give evidence, whether or not that person is a party or has filed a sworn statement. Alternatively, the same result can be obtained by issuing in the High Court (with leave) a writ of subpoena ad testificandum (to give oral evidence) or a writ of subpoena duces tecum (to produce documents which should be specified) or, in the county court (without leave) a witness summons to give oral evidence or to produce specific documents. The CPR 1998 equivalent is rr 34.2–34.7. The principles on which a witness can set aside the summons are the same as those entitling him to object to the inspection of his documents; see **Inspection appointment** (above).

Form of evidence, notices to admit and hearsay notices—Subject to the directions given at the first appointment/FDR as to what further evidence may be called and the time by which sworn statements (previously called affidavits) must be served and filed, the courts' previous practice has been that a party who wishes to call a witness to give oral evidence must, at the very least, have submitted a proof of evidence well in advance of the final hearing (*Krywald v Krywald* [1988] 2 FLR 401).

CPR 1998, r 32.18 – the RSC/CCR equivalents are RSC Ord 27, r 2 (plus Practice Form 58) and CCR Ord 20, r 2 (plus Form N281) – enables a party to serve a notice requiring the other to admit facts, and if the other does not do so, the costs of proving the facts are, unless the court otherwise directs, borne by the other party.

The hearsay rule has been practically abolished by the Civil Evidence Act 1995, which came into force on 31 January 1997. However, s 2 requires a party wishing to adduce hearsay evidence to give the other notice of that fact (a "hearsay notice") and although failure to give a hearsay notice does not affect admissibility, it may be taken into account in assessing the weight given to the hearsay and in deciding any issue in respect of an adjournment or costs. By virtue of CPR 1998, r 33.2 (the RSC/CCR equivalents are RSC Ord 38, r 21 and CCR Ord 20, r 15), a hearsay notice must state that it is such, identify the hearsay evidence and the person who made the statement, state why that person will not be called and, if the evidence is contained in a witness statement, refer to the part where it is set out.

Paginated Bundle of Documents—*President's Direction of 10 March 2000* (set out in Part IV of this work) provides that, with effect from 2 May 2000 in all family proceedings, hearings of any duration in the High Court and in the Royal Courts of Justice and for those with a time estimate of half a day or more elsewhere, there must be a paginated and indexed bundle of documents delivered, if practicable, two clear days before the hearing. The bundle should start with a summary of the background, the issues, the order sought, with chronologies and skeleton arguments dependent on the complexity of the issues. The bundle should be divided into three separate sections:

(*a*) applications and orders;

(*b*) statements and affidavits;
(*c*) experts reports.

If the *Practice Direction* is not complied with fees may be disallowed (*Re CH (A minor) (Court Bundles: Disallowance of Fees)* (2000) *The Times*, 6 June).

2.63 (*revoked*)

Pre-5 June 2000 rules—The rule applicable to ancillary relief claims started before 5 June 2000 and non-ancillary relief claims started at any time (see annotation under r 2.51A) is as follows:

"2.63* Request for further information etc

Any party to an application for ancillary relief may by letter require any other party to give further information concerning any matter contained in any affidavit filed by or on behalf of that other party or any other relevant matter, or to furnish a list of relevant documents or to allow inspection of any such document, and may, in default of compliance by such other party, apply to the district judge for directions."

2.64 Order on application for ancillary relief

(1) Subject to rule 2.65 the district judge shall, after completing his investigation under rule 2.62, make such order as he thinks just.

(2) Pending the final determination of the application, and subject to rule 2.69F, the district judge may make an interim order upon such terms as he thinks just.

(3) RSC Order 31, rule 1 (power to order sale of land) shall apply to applications for ancillary relief as it applies to causes and matters in the Chancery Division.

Amendments—SI 1999/3491.

Defined terms—"ancillary relief": r 1.2(1).

Final order (r 2.64(1))—For the form of a periodical payments or secured periodical payments order or a child periodical payments order see under Matrimonial Causes Act 1973, s 23. For the form of a property adjustment order or lump sum order where it is desired to roll over the Legal Services Commission's statutory charge see *Practice Direction of 19 August 1991*.

No power to make interim capital orders (r 2.64(2))—The court, under MCA 1973, ss 22, 23 and 31, has an unfettered power to make interim periodical payments orders for a spouse and/or the children. It is suggested that the court has no power to make interim capital orders:
(*a*) The power under RSC Ord 29, rr 9–12 and CCR Ord 13, r 12 to make an order for interim payment in respect of a claim for the payment of a sum of money probably does not apply to an application for a lump sum order or property adjustment order because it is a pre-condition of an interim payment under those rules that a writ or summons must have been served.
(*b*) *Wicks v Wicks* [1998] 1 FLR 470 has overruled the line of authority of *Barry v Barry* [1992] 2 FLR 233 and *F v F (Ancillary Relief: Substantial Assets)* [1995] 2 FLR 45 which had previously held that the court had jurisdiction to make interim orders under its administrative power to appropriate assets.

Wicks v Wicks suggested that if an order for the sale of matrimonial assets is required prior to a final ancillary relief hearing, the application should be made under the Married Women's Property Act 1882 (see Procedural Guide 4) linked, if an order for possession is required, with an application under FLA 1996, Pt IV. Alternatively, it is suggested that an application could be made under the Trusts of Land and Appointment of Trustees Act 1996 (see Procedural Guide 5).

Power to order sale of land with vacant possession (r 2.64(3))—RSC Ord 31, r 1 provides that, in appropriate circumstances, the court has power to order that land is sold, and any party bound by the order may be compelled to deliver up possession to the purchaser or to whomever the court directs; this rule therefore reverses the effect of *Crosthwaite v Crosthwaite* [1989] 2 FLR 86, where it was held that the court had no power under MCA 1973, s 24A to direct that one of the joint owners of a property which had been ordered to be sold should leave the property so as to give vacant possession.

2.65 Reference of application to judge

The district judge may at any time refer an application for ancillary relief, or any question arising thereon, to a judge for his decision.

Defined terms—"ancillary relief": r 1.2(1).

Scope of provision—This rule enables a district judge to direct that an application be heard by a judge.

2.66 Arrangements for hearing of application etc by judge

(1) Where an application for ancillary relief or any question arising thereon has been referred or adjourned to a judge, the proper officer shall fix a date, time and place for the hearing of the application or the consideration of the question and give notice thereof to all parties.

(2) The hearing or consideration shall, unless the court otherwise directs, take place in chambers.

(3) Where the application is proceeding in a divorce county court which is not a court of trial or is pending in the High Court and proceedings in a district registry which is not in a divorce town, the hearing or consideration shall take place at such court of trial or divorce town as in the opinion of the district judge is the nearest or most convenient.

For the purposes of this paragraph the Royal Courts of Justice shall be treated as a divorce town.

(4) In respect of any application referred to him under this rule, a judge shall have the same powers to make directions as a district judge has under these rules.

Amendments—SI 1999/3491.

Defined terms—"district judge", "district registry", "proper officer": r 1.2(1).

2.67 Request for periodical payments order at same rate as order for maintenance pending suit

(1) Where at or after the date of a decree nisi of divorce or nullity of marriage an order for maintenance pending suit is in force, the party in whose favour the order was made may, if he has made an application for an order for periodical payments for himself in his petition or answer, as the case may be, request the district judge in writing to make such an order (in this rule referred to as a "corresponding order") providing for payments at the same rate as those provided for by the order for maintenance pending suit.

(2) Where such a request is made, the proper officer shall serve on the other spouse a notice in Form I requiring him, if he objects to the making of a corresponding order, to give notice to that effect to the court and to the applicant within 14 days after service of the notice on Form I.

(3) If the other spouse does not give notice of objection within the time aforesaid, the district judge may make a corresponding order without further notice to that spouse and without requiring the attendance of the applicant or his solicitor, and shall in that case serve a copy of the order on the applicant as well as on the other spouse.

Amendments—SI 1999/3491.

Defined terms—"maintenance pending suit": Matrimonial Causes Act 1973, s 22; "periodical payments": MCA 1973, ss 21(1), 23.

2.68 Application for order under section 37(2)(a) of Act of 1973

(1) An application under section 37(2)(*a*) of the Act of 1973 for an order restraining any person from attempting to defeat a claim for financial provision or otherwise for protecting the claim may be made to the district judge.

(2) Rules 2.65 and 2.66 shall apply, with the necessary modifications, to the application as if it were an application for ancillary relief.

Scope of provision—An essential requirement for restraining an anticipated disposal is that the applicant must have filed an application for ancillary relief. The application for a restraint order is made by filing a notice of application supported by sworn statement. The initial application is usually made ex parte; the order should provide both for a return date and for the respondent to be at liberty, on two days' notice, to apply to discharge the order.

2.69 Offers to settle

(1) Either party to the application may at any time make a written offer to the other party which is expressed to be "without prejudice except as to costs" and which relates to any issue in the proceedings relating to the application.

(2) Where an offer is made under paragraph (1), the fact that such an offer has been made shall not be communicated to the court, except in accordance with rule 2.61E(3), until the question of costs falls to be decided.

Amendments—Substituted by SI 1999/3491.

Scope of provision—This rule gives statutory authority to the practice approved in *Calderbank v Calderbank* [1976] Fam 93, [1995] FLR 113 of making an offer in a letter headed "Without prejudice except as to costs".

2.69A (*revoked*)

2.69B Judgment or order more advantageous than an offer made by the other party

(1) This rule applies where the judgment or order in favour of the applicant or respondent is more advantageous to him than an offer made under rule 2.69(1) by the other party.

(2) The court must, unless it considers it unjust to do so, order that other party to pay any costs incurred after the date beginning 28 days after the offer was made.

Amendments—Inserted by SI 1999/3491.

Scope of provision—The general rules as to how the court will exercise its discretion on costs in family proceedings. and the factors to be taken into account, are set out in CPR 1998, r 44.3(1), (4) and (5). Although the general rule set out in r 44.3(2), that the unsuccessful party will pay unless the court makes a different order, does not apply to family proceedings (FPR 1991, r 10.27(1)(*b*)), the judge's starting-point will normally be that costs should be awarded to the successful party, success being judged by whether a *Calderbank* offer has been exceeded (*Gojkovic v Gojkovic (No 2)* [1992] Fam 40, [1991] 2 FLR 233).

This rule confirms the approach in *Gojkovic* by providing that, where a party obtains an order more favourable than the other party has proposed in a *Calderbank* letter, that party is entitled to his costs for the period from four weeks after the offer was made, unless it would be unjust to make such an order.

With effect from 24 February 2003, the rule formerly contained in r 2.69C, that if a party beat both his own and the other party's offer he was entitled to indemnity costs and interest at up to 10% above base rate on the award and costs, has been revoked. The power to order costs on an indemnity basis under CPR 1998, r 44.4 and interest on costs under r 44.3 is unaffected by the revocation. For power to order interest on the award see **Interest** under MCA 1973, s 23.

2.69C *(revoked)*

2.69D Factors for court's consideration under rule 2.69B

(1) In considering whether it would be unjust, or whether it would be just, to make the order referred to in rule 2.69B, the court must take into account all the circumstances of the case, including –

(*a*) the terms of any offers made under rule 2.69(1);

(*b*) the stage in the proceedings when any offer was made;

(*c*) the information available to the parties at the time when the offer was made;

(*d*) the conduct of the parties with regard to the giving or refusing to give information for the purposes of enabling the offer to be made or evaluated: and

(*e*) the respective means of the parties.

(2) *(revoked)*

Amendments—Inserted by SI 1999/3491; amended by SI 2003/184.

Scope of provision—This rule sets out the criteria for deciding whether it is unjust for a party to receive his costs under r 2.69B. A crucial consideration is whether all cards have been placed face up on the table when the offer was made (*Gojkovic v Gojkovic (No 2)* [1992] Fam 40, [1991] 2 FLR 233).

2.69E Open proposals

(1) Not less than 14 days before the date fixed for the final hearing of an application for ancillary relief, the applicant must (unless the court directs otherwise) file with the court and serve on the respondent an open statement which sets out concise details, including the amounts involved, of the orders which he proposes to ask the court to make.

(2) Not more than 7 days after service of a statement under paragraph (1), the respondent must file with the court and serve on the applicant an open statement which sets out concise details, including the amounts involved, of the orders which he proposes to ask the court to make.

Amendments—Inserted by SI 1999/3491.

2.69F Application for interim orders

(1) A party may apply at any stage of the proceedings for an order for maintenance pending suit, interim periodical payments or an interim variation order.

(2) An application for such an order must be made by notice of application and the date fixed for the hearing of the application must be not less than 14 days after the date the notice of application is issued.

(3) The applicant shall forthwith serve the respondent with a copy of the notice of application.

PART III

(4) Where an application is made before a party has filed Form E, that party must file with the application and serve on the other party, a draft of the order requested and a short sworn statement explaining why the order is necessary and giving the necessary information about his means.

(5) Not less than 7 days before the date fixed for the hearing, the respondent must file with the court and serve on the other party, a short sworn statement about his means, unless he has already filed Form E.

(6) A party may apply for any other form of interim order at any stage of the proceedings with or without notice.

(7) Where an application referred to in paragraph (6) is made with notice, the provisions of paragraphs (1) to (5) apply to it.

(8) Where an application referred to in paragraph (6) is made without notice, the provisions of paragraph (1) apply to it.

Amendments—Inserted by SI 1999/3491.

Scope of provision—The lapse of time between filing Form A and the final hearing will probably be 8 months to a year. This rule allows either party at any stage to apply for maintenance pending suit, interim periodical payments or any other form of interim order.

Form of application for maintenance pending suit etc—The application for maintenance pending suit, interim periodical payments or interim variation order is made by notice of application (giving 14 days' notice) and if made before Form E is filed, should be supported by a draft order and sworn statement disclosing means. If the respondent has not filed his Form E he must file, 7 days before the hearing, a sworn statement disclosing his means.

Application for other forms of interim relief—This may be made with or without notice. Evidence, usually in the form of a sworn statement, should be filed to support the case.

Paginated bundle of documents—As noted under r 2.62 in any hearing in the High Court or Royal Courts of Justice of any length of time and in any hearing elsewhere with a time estimate of half a day or more, an indexed and paginated bundle of documents must be filed, if practical, 2 clear days prior to the hearing.

2.70 Pensions

(1) This rule applies where an application for ancillary relief has been made, or notice of intention to proceed with the application has been given, in Form A, or an application has been made in Form B, and the applicant or respondent has or is likely to have any benefits under a pension arrangement.

(2) When the court fixes a first appointment as required by rule 2.61A(4)(*a*), the party with pension rights shall, within seven days after receiving notification of the date of that appointment, request the person responsible for each pension arrangement under which he has or is likely to have benefits to furnish the information referred to in regulation 2(2) and (3)(*b*) to (*f*) of the Pensions on Divorce etc (Provision of Information) Regulations 2000.

(3) Within seven days of receiving information under paragraph (2) the party with pension rights shall send a copy of it to the other party, together with the name and address of the person responsible for each pension arrangement.

(4) A request under paragraph (2) above need not be made where the party with pension rights is in possession of, or has requested, a relevant valuation of the pension rights or benefits accrued under the pension arrangement in question.

(5) In this rule, a relevant valuation means a valuation of pension rights or benefits as at a date not more than twelve months earlier than the date fixed for the first appointment which has been furnished or requested for the purposes of any of the following provisions –

(*a*) the Pensions on Divorce etc (Provision of Information) Regulations 2000;
(*b*) regulation 5 of and Schedule 2 to the Occupational Pension Schemes (Disclosure of Information) Regulations 1996 and regulation 11 of and Schedule 1 to the Occupational Pension Schemes (Transfer Value) Regulations 1996;
(*c*) section 93A or 94(1)(*a*) or (*aa*) of the Pension Schemes Act 1993;
(*d*) section 94(1)(*b*) of the Pension Schemes Act 1993 or paragraph 2(*a*) (or, where applicable, 2(*b*)) of Schedule 2 to the Personal Pension Schemes (Disclosure of Information) Regulations 1987.

(6) Upon making or giving notice of intention to proceed with an application for ancillary relief including provision to be made under section 24B (pension sharing) of the Act of 1973, or upon adding a request for such provision to an existing application for ancillary relief, the applicant shall send to the person responsible for the pension arrangement concerned a copy of Form A.

(7) Upon making or giving notice of intention to proceed with an application for ancillary relief including provision to be made under section 25B or 25C (pension attachment) of the Act of 1973, or upon adding a request for such provision to an existing application for ancillary relief, the applicant shall send to the person responsible for the pension arrangement concerned –

(*a*) a copy of Form A;
(*b*) an address to which any notice which the person responsible is required to serve on the applicant under the Divorce etc (Pensions) Regulations 2000 is to be sent;
(*c*) an address to which any payment which the person responsible is required to make to the applicant is to be sent; and
(*d*) where the address in sub-paragraph (*c*) is that of a bank, a building society or the Department of National Savings, sufficient details to enable payment to be made into the account of the applicant.

(8) A person responsible for a pension arrangement on whom a copy of a notice under paragraph (7) is served may, within 21 days after service, require the applicant to provide him with a copy of section 2.16 of the statement in Form E supporting his application; and the applicant must then provide that person with the copy of that section of the statement within the time limited for filing it by rule 2.61B(2), or 21 days after being required to do so, whichever is the later.

(9) A person responsible for a pension arrangement who receives a copy of section 2.16 of Form E as required pursuant to paragraph (8) may within 21 days after receipt send to the court, the applicant and the respondent a statement in answer.

(10) A person responsible for a pension arrangement who files a statement in answer pursuant to paragraph (9) shall be entitled to be represented at the first appointment, and the court must within 4 days of the date of filing of the statement in answer give the person notice of the date of the first appointment.

(11) Where the parties have agreed on the terms of an order including provision under section 25B or 25C (pension attachment) of the Act of 1973, then unless service has already been effected under paragraph (7), they shall serve on the person responsible for the pension arrangement concerned –

(*a*) the notice of application for a consent order under rule 2.61(1);

(*b*) a draft of the proposed order under rule 2.61(1), complying with paragraph (13) below; and

(*c*) the particulars set out in sub-paragraphs (*b*), (*c*) and (*d*) of paragraph (7) above.

(12) No consent order under paragraph (11) shall be made unless either –

(*a*) the person responsible has not made any objection within 21 days after the service on him of such notice; or

(*b*) the court has considered any such objection

and for the purpose of considering any objection the court may make such direction as it sees fit for the person responsible to attend before it or to furnish written details of his objection.

(13) An order for ancillary relief, whether by consent or not, including provision under section 24B (pension sharing), 25B or 25C (pension attachment) of the Act of 1973, shall –

(*a*) in the body of the order, state that there is to be provision by way of pension sharing or pension attachment in accordance with the annex or annexes to the order; and

(*b*) be accompanied by an annex containing the information set out in paragraph (14) or paragraph (15) as the case may require; and if provision is made in relation to more than one pension arrangement there shall be one annex for each pension arrangement.

(14) Where provision is made under section 24B (pension sharing) of the Act of 1973, the annex shall state –

(*a*) the name of the court making the order, together with the case number and the title of the proceedings;

(*b*) that it is a pension sharing order made under Part IV of the Welfare Reform and Pensions Act 1999;

(*c*) the names of the transferor and the transferee;

(*d*) the national insurance number of the transferor;

(*e*) sufficient details to identify the pension arrangement concerned and the transferor's rights or benefits from it including the name and address of the person responsible for the pension arrangement and a policy reference number;

(*f*) the specified percentage, or where appropriate the specified amount, required in order to calculate the appropriate amount for the purposes of section 29(1) of the Welfare Reform and Pensions Act 1999 (creation of pension debits and credits);

(*g*) how the pension sharing charges are to be apportioned between the parties or alternatively that they are to be paid in full by the transferor;

(*h*) that the person responsible for the pension arrangement has furnished the information required by regulation 4 of the Pensions on Divorce etc (Provision of Information) Regulations 2000 and that it appears from that information that there is power to make an order including provision under section 24B (pension sharing) of the Act of 1973;

(*i*) the day on which the order or provision takes effect; and

(*j*) that the person responsible for the pension arrangement concerned must discharge his liability in respect of the pension credit within a period of 4 months beginning with the day on which the order or provision takes effect or, if later, with the first day on which the person responsible for the pension arrangement concerned is in receipt of –

(i) the order for ancillary relief, including the annex;

(ii) the decree of divorce or nullity of marriage; and

(iii) the information prescribed by regulation 5 of the Pensions on Divorce etc (Provision of Information) Regulations 2000;

provided that if the court knows that the implementation period is different from that stated in sub-paragraph (*j*) by reason of regulations under section 34(4) or 41(2)(*a*) of the Welfare Reform and Pensions Act 1999, the annex shall contain details of the implementation period as determined by those regulations instead of the statement in sub-paragraph (*j*).

(15) Where provision is made under section 25B or 25C (pension attachment) of the Act of 1973, the annex shall state –

(*a*) the name of the court making the order, together with the case number and the title of the proceedings;

(*b*) that it is an order making provision under section 25B or 25C, as the case may be, of the Act of 1973;

(*c*) the names of the party with pension rights and the other party;

(*d*) the national insurance number of the party with pension rights;

(*e*) sufficient details to identify the pension arrangement concerned and the rights or benefits from it to which the party with pension rights is or may become entitled including the name and address of the person responsible for the pension arrangement and a policy reference number;

(*f*) in the case of an order including provision under section 25B(4) of the Act of 1973, what percentage of any payment due to the party with pension rights is to be paid for the benefit of the other party;

(*g*) in the case of an order including any other provision under section 25B or 25C of the Act of 1973, what the person responsible for the pension arrangement is required to do;

(*h*) the address to which any notice which the person responsible for the pension arrangement is required to serve on the other party under the Divorce etc (Pensions) Regulations 2000 is to be sent, if not notified under paragraph (7)(*b*);

(*i*) an address to which any payment which the person responsible for the pension arrangement is required to make to the other party is to be sent, if not notified under paragraph (7)(*c*);

(*j*) where the address in sub-paragraph (*i*) is that of a bank, a building society or the Department of National Savings, sufficient details to enable payment to be made into the account of the other party, if not notified under paragraph (7)(*d*); and

(*k*) where the order is made by consent, that no objection has been made by the person responsible for the pension arrangement, or that an objection has been received and considered by the court, as the case may be.

(16) A court which makes, varies or discharges an order including provision under section 24B (pension sharing), 25B or 25C (pension attachment) of the Act of 1973, shall send to the person responsible for the pension arrangement concerned –

(*a*) a copy of the decree of divorce, nullity of marriage or judicial separation;

(*b*) in the case of divorce or nullity of marriage, a copy of the certificate under rule 2.51 that the decree has been made absolute; and

(*c*) a copy of that order, or as the case may be of the order varying or discharging that order, including any annex to that order relating to that pension arrangement but no other annex to that order.

PART III

(17) The documents referred to in paragraph (16) shall be sent within 7 days after the making of the relevant order, or within 7 days after the decree absolute of divorce or nullity or decree of judicial separation, whichever is the later.

(18) In this rule –

(*a*) all words and phrases defined in sections 25D(3) and (4) of the Act of 1973 have the meanings assigned by those subsections;

(*b*) all words and phrases defined in section 46 of the Welfare Reform and Pensions Act 1999 have the meanings assigned by that section.

Amendments—Substituted by SI 2000/2267; amended by SI 2001/821; SI 2003/184.

Scope of provision—This rule governs the procedure for pension sharing and pension attachment (formerly earmarking) as well as the disclosure of a party with benefits under a pension arrangement, whether or not pension sharing or earmarking is applied for where the proceedings have been commenced by petition on or after 1 December 2000. If a Form A applying for earmarking has been filed before that date, Family Proceedings (Amendment) Rules 2000, r 2(2), (3) provide that the regime governing that attachment application is the unamended version of r 2.70 which is set out in earlier editions of *The Family Court Practice*.

Outline of Procedural Framework for Pensions Sharing/Attachment Applications

1 *The application* is made in the petition (r 2.53(1)) and the claim made in Form A (r 2.61A).

2 The person with pension benefits within 7 days of notice of the first appointment *must apply for a CETV* unless there is already one in existence less than a year old (r 2.72(2)).

3 The person responsible for the pension arrangement *must be served and given 21 days to object*.

4 *The form of the order* must be:

(i) expressed as a *percentage* (MCA 1973, s 21A) of the *cash equivalent transfer value* calculated in accordance with Pensions on Divorce etc (Provision of Information) Regulations 2000, reg 3 *on a date specified by the court* not earlier than one year prior to the petition and not later than the date of the order (Divorce etc (Pensions) Regulations 2000, reg 3);

(ii) in the form of an annex (which is prescribed) to the order which should specify who is paying the charges (r 2.70(13) and (14)). It must not take effect until 7 days after the time has expired for appealing (MCA 1973, s 24C).

5 The final stage is *implementation.* The court serves the order (r 2.70 (16)–(18)). The information needed from the parties for implementation to take place is set out in Pensions on Divorce etc (Provision of Information) Regulations 2000, reg 5 et seq.

Provision of Information (r 2.70(1)–(5))—These sub-rules provide that if one party has benefits under a pension arrangement (as opposed to shareable state scheme rights) then, irrespective of whether a pension sharing or pension attachment order is being sought or not, that person must within seven days of being notified of the date of the first appointment apply to the pension provider for information about the scheme. That information, as set out in Divorce etc (Provision for Information) Regulations 2000, reg 2(2) and (3) is, in summary, the cash equivalent transfer value, a statement saying how it is calculated, what benefits are included in the valuation, whether an internal transfer will be offered and what the charges will be. As regards shareable state scheme rights (ie sharing the state pension apart from basic pension, these rules do not require similar information as to the CETV etc to be obtained). It is suggested that it is good practice to obtain the information at this stage. Sharing of State Scheme Rights (Provision for Information and Valuation) Regulations 2000, reg 2 requires the Secretary of State to provide the person with shareable state scheme rights on request or the court with a valuation of that person's shareable state scheme rights and an explanation of how a pension sharing order will affect that person and his spouse.

Service and objection by pension provider (r 2.70(6)–(12))—The pension provider (ie the person responsible for running the pension scheme or, with shareable state scheme rights, the Secretary of State) must be given notice for a pension sharing or attachment order to be effective. As regards a pension sharing order, r 2.70(6) sets out the requirement on the applicant to send Form A to the pension provider. But no specific provision is given for the pension provider to require further information about the claim or take any part in the proceedings. As regards pension attachment, r 2.70(7)–(12) provide: (i) a detailed code for the service of Form A (together with the applicant's address for service and details of his bank account); (ii) for the pension provider within 21 days after service to require the applicant to supply a copy of the r 2.16 statement in the applicant's Form E; and (iii) thereafter for the pension provider to file a statement in answer and appear at the first appointment. These sub-rules, as regards a pension attachment order, stipulate that an order by consent or otherwise cannot be made without the pension provider having 21 days to object. It is unclear why a detailed procedural code for objection has been provided for a pension attachment order with no corresponding code for objection for a pension sharing order. In the absence of express provision, it is suggested, as a matter of good practice, that the procedural code provided for a pension attachment objection should be applied if there is an objection to a pension sharing order and that in both cases the pension provider should be given 21 days to object (although r 2.61(1)(*dd*) suggests the period of 14 days for both a consent, sharing and attachment order).

Form of the order (r 2.70(13)–(15))—These sub-rules set out the formalities of the form of the pension sharing or attachment order. The order is in the form of a prescribed annex (a copy of which can be obtained from the court office). Important points are that:

(i) the order is expressed as a percentage (MCA 1973, s 21A) of the cash equivalent transfer value calculated in accordance with Pensions on Divorce etc (Provision of Information) Regulations 2000, reg 3 (or in respect of shareable state scheme rights as provided under Sharing of State Scheme Rights (Provision of Information and Valuation) Regulations 2000, reg 2);

(ii) the date of the valuation of the cash equivalent transfer value is as specified by the court between one year prior to the petition and the date of the order (Divorce etc (Pensions) Regulations 2000, reg 3). Responsibility between the parties for payment of the charges must be set out. If the order is silent the transferor will pay (Welfare Reform and Pensions Act 1999, s 41(3)(*b*));

(iii) the order must not take effect until the expiry of 7 days after the time for appealing has elapsed (see annotation to MCA 1973, s 24C).

Service of order and implementation (r 2.70 (16), (17))—Within one week of the order or decree absolute, whichever is the later, the court sends to the pension provider the order and a copy of the decree.

Both parties must provide the pension provider with the formal information (date of birth, national insurance number, etc) set out Pensions in Divorce etc (Provision of Information) Regulations 2000, reg 5. Service by the court of the order and provision by the parties of the above formal information triggers the start of the 4 month period which the pension provider has to implement the order (WRPA 1999, s 34(1)). The pension provider must, if he has not already done so, provide details of the charges within 3 weeks of receiving the order and must issue a notice of discharge within 3 weeks of him implementing the order (Pensions on Divorce etc (Provision of Information) Regulations 2000, regs 7 and 8).

2.71–2.77 (*revoked*)

PART III
OTHER MATRIMONIAL ETC PROCEEDINGS

3.1 Application in case of failure to provide reasonable maintenance

(1) Every application under section 27 of the Act of 1973 shall be made by originating application in Form M19.

(2) The application may be made to any divorce county court and there shall be filed with the application an affidavit by the applicant and also a copy of the application and of the affidavit for service on the respondent.

(3) The affidavit shall state –

(*a*) the same particulars regarding the marriage, the court's jurisdiction, the children and the previous proceedings as are required in the case of a petition by sub-paragraphs (*a*), (*c*), (*d*), (*f*) and (*i*) of paragraph 1 of Appendix 2;

(*b*) particulars of the respondent's failure to provide reasonable maintenance for the applicant, or, as the case may be, of the respondent's failure to provide, or to make a proper contribution towards, reasonable maintenance for the children of the family; and

(*c*) full particulars of the applicant's property and income and of the respondent's property and income, so far as may be known to the applicant.

(4) A copy of the application and of the affidavit referred to in paragraph (2) shall be served on the respondent, together with a notice in Form M20 with Form M6.

(5) Subject to paragraph (6), the respondent shall, within 14 days after the time allowed for sending the acknowledgement of service, file an affidavit stating –

(*a*) whether the alleged failure to provide, or to make proper contribution towards, reasonable maintenance is admitted or denied, and, if denied, the grounds on which he relies;

(*b*) any allegation which he wishes to make against the applicant; and

(*c*) full particulars of his property and income, unless otherwise directed.

(6) Where the respondent challenges the jurisdiction of the court to hear the application he shall, within 14 days after the time allowed for sending the acknowledgement of service, file an affidavit setting out the grounds of the challenge; and the obligation to file an affidavit under paragraph (5) shall not arise until 14 days after the question of jurisdiction has been determined and the court has decided that the necessary jurisdiction exists.

(7) Where the respondent's affidavit contains an allegation of adultery or of an improper association with a person named, the provisions of rule 2.60 (which deal with service on, and filing of a statement in answer by, a named person) shall apply.

(8) If the respondent does not file an affidavit in accordance with paragraph (5), the court may order him to file an affidavit containing full particulars of his property and income, and in that case the respondent shall serve a copy of any such affidavit on the applicant.

(9) Within 14 days after being served with a copy of any affidavit filed by the respondent, the applicant may file a further affidavit as to means and as to any fact in the respondent's affidavit which is disputed, and in that case the applicant shall serve a copy on the respondent.

No further affidavit shall be filed without leave.

(10) Rules 2.61 to 2.66 and rule 10.10 shall apply, with such modifications as may be appropriate, to an application for an order under section 27 of the Act of 1973 as if the application were an application for ancillary relief.

Amendments—SI 1999/3491.

Defined terms—"ancillary relief": r 1.2(1); "child", "court": Matrimonial Causes Act 1973, s 52(1); "divorce county court": r 1.2(1).

Scope of provision—This rule regulates the format and conduct of an application under MCA 1973, s 27 for periodical payments, secured periodical payments and/or a lump sum for a party to the marriage or the children of the family. The procedure largely follows that which is applicable on a claim made before 5 June 2000 for ancillary relief.

General Note—The Family Proceedings (Amendment No 2) Rules 1999 have amended FPR 1991, rr 2.52–2.77 in respect of claims for ancillary relief started on or after 5 June 2000. The amended version of the rules is printed in this edition. A claim for failure to provide reasonable maintenance is not a claim for ancillary relief. Family Proceedings (Amendment No 2) Rules 1999, r 20 provides that the unamended version of those rules applies to a claim for failure to provide reasonable maintenance. The unamended version is printed in earlier editions of *The Family Court Practice*. See **non-ancillary relief** under r 2.51A.

The application and supporting affidavit (r 3.1(1)–(4))—The originating application should be supported by a lead affidavit which should contain:
(*a*) the formal details required for a petition by Appendix 2, para 1;
(*b*) full disclosure of means;
(*c*) the facts relied on to establish the applicant's and the children's entitlement.

Respondent's affidavit in answer (r 3.1(5)–(8))—Except where jurisdiction is challenged (because the domicile/residence requirement in MCA 1973, s 27(2) is in issue), the respondent must file an affidavit disclosing his means and stating his case within 28 days of service of the originating application on him.

If the respondent (or applicant) alleges adultery or an improper association with a named person, the court may direct as set out in r 2.60, that the affidavit is served on the person against whom the allegation is made.

"time allowed for sending the acknowledgement of service" (r 3.1(5), (7))—The time allowed is 14 days.

Further affidavits (r 3.1(9))—Apart from the right of the applicant to file an affidavit in reply, leave is necessary for any further affidavits.

Procedure following filing of affidavits (r 3.1(10))—Rule 3.1(10) provides that, following the filing of affidavits, the procedure is identical to that for an application for a financial provision or property adjustment order. It applies the following provisions from Pt II to applications under MCA 1973, s 27:
(*a*) r 2.61 (information to be given on application for consent order);
(*b*) r 2.63 (request/order for further information and documents);
(*c*) r 2.62 (directions, power to order the parties to produce documents and conduct of the final hearing including ordering the attendance of non-parties);
(*d*) r 2.64 (interim orders); and
(*e*) r 2.65 and 2.66 (district judge referring application to a judge).

3.2 Application for alteration of maintenance agreement during lifetime of parties

(1) An application under section 35 of the Act of 1973 for the alteration of a maintenance agreement shall be made by originating application containing, unless otherwise directed, the information required by Form M21.

(2) The application may be made to any divorce county court and may be heard and determined by the district judge.

(3) There shall be filed with the application an affidavit by the applicant exhibiting a copy of the agreement and verifying the statements in the application and also a copy of the application and of the affidavit for service on the respondent.

(4) A copy of the application and of the affidavit referred to in paragraph (3) shall be served on the respondent, together with a notice in Form M20 with Form M6 attached.

(5) The respondent shall, within 14 days after the time limited for giving notice of intention to defend, file an affidavit in answer to the application containing full particulars of his property and income and, if he does not do so, the court may order him to file an affidavit containing such particulars.

PART III

(6) A respondent who files an affidavit under paragraph (5) shall at the same time file a copy which the proper officer shall serve on the applicant.

Defined terms—"district judge", "divorce county court": r 1.2(1); "maintenance agreement": Matrimonial Causes Act 1973, s 34; "proper officer": r 1.2(1).

3.3 Application of alteration of maintenance agreement after death of one party

(1) An application under section 36 of the Act of 1973 for the alteration of a maintenance agreement after the death of one of the parties shall be made –

- (*a*) in the High Court, by originating summons out of the principal registry or any district registry, or
- (*b*) in a county court, by originating application,

in Form M22.

(2) There shall be filed in support of the application an affidavit by the applicant exhibiting a copy of the agreement and an official copy of the grant of representation to the deceased's estate and of every testamentary document admitted to proof and stating –

- (*a*) whether the deceased died domiciled in England and Wales;
- (*b*) the place and date of the marriage between the parties to the agreement and the name and status of the wife before the marriage;
- (*c*) the name of every child of the family and of any other child for whom the agreement makes financial arrangements, and –
  - (i) the date of birth of each such child who is still living (or, if it be the case, that he has attained 18) and the place where and the person with whom any such minor child is residing,
  - (ii) the date of death of any such child who has died since the agreement was made;
- (*d*) whether there have been in any court any, and if so what, previous proceedings with reference to the agreement or to the marriage or to the children of the family or any other children for whom the agreement makes financial arrangements, and the date and effect of any order or decree made in such proceedings;
- (*e*) whether there have been in any court any proceedings by the applicant against the deceased's estate under the Inheritance (Provision for Family and Dependants) Act 1975 or any Act repealed by that Act and the date and effect of any order made in such proceedings;
- (*f*) in the case of an application by the surviving party, the applicant's means;
- (*g*) in the case of an application by the personal representatives of the deceased, the surviving party's means, so far as they are known to the applicants, and the information mentioned in sub-paragraphs (*a*), (*b*) and (*c*) of rule 3.4(4);
- (*h*) the facts alleged by the applicant as justifying an alteration in the agreement and the nature of the alteration sought;
- (*i*) if the application is made after the end of the period of six months from the date on which representation in regard to the deceased's estate was first taken out, the grounds on which the court's permission to entertain the application is sought.

(3) CCR Order 48, rules 3(1), 7 and 9 shall apply to an originating application under the said section 36 as they apply to an application under section 1 of the Inheritance (Provision for Family and Dependants) Act 1975.

(4) In this rule and the next following rule "the deceased" means the deceased party to the agreement to which the application relates.

Defined terms—"child", "child of the family": Matrimonial Causes Act 1973, s 52(1); "maintenance agreement": MCA 1973, s 34(2).

Scope of provision—This rule regulates, in conjunction with rr 3.4 and 3.5, an application to alter a maintenance agreement after one party's death.

"CCR Order 48, rules 3(1), 7 and 9"—CCR Ord 48, r 3(1) requires the application to be filed in the court for the district in which the deceased resided at the date of his death; r 7 provides that the application should be heard by the district judge and may be dealt with in chambers; r 9 empowers a transfer to the High Court.

3.4 Further proceedings on application under rule 3.3

(1) Without prejudice to his powers under RSC Order 15 (which deals with parties and other matters), the district judge may at any stage of the proceedings direct that any person be added as a respondent to an application under rule 3.3.

(2) RSC Order 15, rule 13 (which enables the court to make representation orders in certain cases), shall apply to the proceedings as if they were mentioned in paragraph (1) of the said rule 13.

(3) Where the application is in a county court, the references in paragraphs (1) and (2) to RSC Order 15 and Order 15, rule 13 shall be construed as references to CCR Order 5 and Order 5, rule 6 respectively.

(4) A respondent who is a personal representative of the deceased shall, within 14 days after the time limited for giving notice of intention to defend, file an affidavit in answer to the application stating –

- (*a*) full particulars of the value of the deceased's estate for probate, after providing for the discharge of the funeral, testamentary and administration expenses, debts and liabilities payable thereout, including the amount of the inheritance tax or any other tax replaced by that tax and interest thereon;
- (*b*) the persons or classes of persons beneficially interested in the estate (giving the names and addresses of all living beneficiaries) and the value of their interests so far as ascertained, and
- (*c*) if such be the case, that any living beneficiary (naming him) is a minor or a patient within the meaning of rule 9.1.

(5) If a respondent who is a personal representative of the deceased does not file an affidavit stating the matters mentioned in paragraph (4) the district judge may order him to do so.

(6) A respondent who is not a personal representative of the deceased may, within 14 days after the time limited for giving notice of intention to defend, file an affidavit in answer to the application.

(7) Every respondent who files an affidavit in answer to the application shall at the same time lodge a copy, which the proper officer shall serve on the applicant.

Amendments—SI 1991/2113.

Defined terms—"district judge", "proper officer": r 1.2(1).

"time limited for giving notice of intention to defend" (r 3.4(4), (6))—The period allowed for giving such notice is 14 days after service of the application, or such other time as may be fixed (r 10.8(2)).

3.5 Application of other rules to proceedings under section 35 or 36 of Act of 1973

(1) The following rules shall apply, with the necessary modifications, to an application under section 35 or 36 of the Act of 1973, as if it were an application for ancillary relief –

(*a*) in the case of an application under either section, rules 2.60, 2.62(4) to (6), 2.63, 2.64, 2.65 and 10.10;
(*b*) in the case of an application under section 35, rule 2.66; and
(*c*) in the case of an application under section 36, rule 2.66(1) and (2).

(2) Subject to paragraph (1) and to the provisions of rules 3.2 to 3.4, these rules shall, so far as applicable, apply with the necessary modifications to an application under section 35 or section 36 (as the case may be) of the Act of 1973, as if the application were a cause, the originating application or summons a petition, and the applicant the petitioner.

Defined terms—"ancillary relief": r 1.2(1).

General Note—The Family Proceedings (Amendment No 2) Rules 1999 have amended FPR 1991, rr 2.52–2.77 in respect of claims for ancillary relief started on or after 5 June 2000. The amended version of the rules is printed in this edition. A claim to vary a maintenance agreement is not a claim for ancillary relief. Family Proceedings (Amendment No 2) Rules 1999, r 20 provides that the unamended version of those rules applies to a claim to vary a maintenance agreement. The unamended version is printed in earlier editions of *The Family Court Practice*. See **non-ancillary relief** under r 2.51A.

Scope of provision—This rule applies to an application to vary a maintenance agreement certain rules which are applicable to pre-5 June 2000 claims for ancillary relief, the text of the rules being as printed in earlier editions, namely: r 2.60 (service of an affidavit on named person alleged to have committed adultery or improperly associated); r 2.62(4) (taking of oral evidence, ordering the attendance of any person to give evidence, and ordering a party to the application to give discovery, produce documents or provide a further affidavit); r 2.62(5) (directions); r 2.63 (request by letter to give information or produce documents); rr 2.64 and 2.65 (interim orders and referring to judge); r 10.10 (transfer between courts). Rule 2.66 (arrangements for hearing by judge) is applied to applications under s 35 but, in the case of an application under s 36, only r 2.66(1), (2) applies.

3.6 Married Women's Property Act 1882

(1) Subject to paragraph (2) below, an application under section 17 of the Married Women's Property Act 1882 (in this and the next following rule referred to as "section 17") shall be made –

(*a*) in the High Court, by originating summons, which may be issued out of the principal registry or any district registry, or
(*b*) in a county court, by originating application,

in Form M23 and shall be supported by affidavit.

(2) An order under section 17 may be made in any ancillary relief proceedings upon the application of any party thereto in Form M11 by notice of application or summons.

(3) An application under section 17 to a county court shall be filed –

(*a*) subject to sub-paragraph (*b*), in the court for the district in which the applicant or respondent resides, or
(*b*) in the divorce county court in which any pending matrimonial cause has been commenced by or on behalf of either the applicant or the respondent,

or in which any matrimonial cause is intended to be commenced by the applicant.

(4) Where the application concerns the title to or possession of land, the originating summons or application shall –

(*a*) state whether the title to the land is registered or unregistered and, if registered, the Land Registry title number; and

(*b*) give particulars, so far as known to the applicant, of any mortgage of the land or any interest therein.

(5) The application shall be served on the respondent, together with a copy of the affidavit in support and an acknowledgement of service in Form M6.

(6) Where particulars of a mortgage are given pursuant to paragraph (4), the applicant shall file a copy of the originating summons or application, which shall be served on the mortgagee; and any person so served may apply to the court in writing, within 14 days after service, for a copy of the affidavit in support; and within 14 days of receiving such affidavit may file an affidavit in answer and shall be entitled to be heard on the application.

(7) If the respondent intends to contest the application, he shall, within 14 days after the time allowed for sending the acknowledgement of service, file an affidavit in answer to the application setting out the grounds on which he relies, and lodge in the court office a copy of the affidavit for service on the applicant.

(8) If the respondent fails to comply with paragraph (7), the applicant may apply for directions; and the district judge may give such directions as he thinks fit, including a direction that the respondent shall be debarred from defending the application unless an affidavit is filed within such time as the district judge may specify.

(9) A district judge may grant an injunction in proceedings under section 17 if, but only so far as, the injunction is ancillary or incidental to any relief sought in those proceedings.

(10) Rules 2.62(4) to (6) and 2.63 to 2.66 shall apply, with the necessary modifications, to an application under section 17 as they apply to an application for ancillary relief.

(11) Subject to the provisions of this rule, these rules shall apply, with the necessary modifications, to an application under section 17 as if the application were a cause, the originating summons or application a petition, and the applicant a petitioner.

Defined terms—"ancillary relief", "district judge": r 1.2(1); "matrimonial cause": Matrimonial and Family Proceedings Act 1984, s 32.

General Note—The Family Proceedings (Amendment No 2) Rules 1999 have amended FPR 1991, rr 2.52–2.77 in respect of claims for ancillary relief started on or after 5 June 2000. The amended version of the rules is printed in this edition. A claim under the Married Women's Property Act 1882 is not a claim for ancillary relief. Family Proceedings (Amendment No 2) Rules 1999, r 20 provides that the unamended version of those rules applies to a claim under MWPA 1882. The unamended version is printed in earlier editions of *The Family Court Practice*. See **non-ancillary relief** under r 2.51A.

Form of application and supporting affidavit—Application may be made either in existing proceedings for ancillary relief using Form 11 or by originating summons or application in Form M23. In all cases the application must identify whether any land is registered or unregistered, give particulars of any mortgage or third party interest and must be supported by an affidavit setting out the applicant's case.

Service—In addition to the respondent being served, any mortgagee must be served with a copy of the application (but not the supporting affidavit) so that the mortgagee may intervene if he wishes.

Respondent's affidavit—Within 28 days of service the respondent must file an answering affidavit and if he does not do so, the district judge may direct him to do so and ultimately may debar him from defending.

Injunctions—The district judge may grant an injunction if the injunction is ancillary or incidental to the claim for relief.

Application treated as if application for ancillary relief—The following of the rules regulating the conduct of a pre-5 June 2000 claim for ancillary relief apply:
(*a*) r 2.63 (request for and order to provide information and documents);
(*b*) r 2.62(4), (5) (district judge to hear case, power to take oral evidence, to order the parties to give discovery, produce documents or swear further affidavit, to order the attendance of any person (including a non-party) to give evidence and to give directions);
(*c*) r 2.64 (interim orders); and
(*d*) rr 2.65, 2.66 (power to refer case to judge).

3.7 Exercise in principal registry of county court jurisdiction under section 17 of Married Women's Property Act 1882

(1) Where any proceedings for divorce, nullity or judicial separation which are either pending in the principal registry, or are intended to be commenced there by the applicant are or will be treated as pending in a divorce county court, an application under section 17 by one of the parties to the marriage may be made to the principal registry as if it were a county court.

(2) In relation to proceedings commenced or intended to be commenced in the principal registry under paragraph (1) of this rule or transferred from the High Court to the principal registry by an order made under section 38 of the Act of 1984 –

(*a*) section 42 of the Act of 1984 and the rules made thereunder shall have effect, with the necessary modifications, as they have effect in relation to proceedings commenced in or transferred to the principal registry under that section; and
(*b*) CCR Order 4, rule 8 and rule 3.6(3) (which relate to venue) shall not apply.

(3) Rule 1.4(1) shall apply, with the necessary modifications, to proceedings in, or intended to be commenced in, the principal registry under paragraph (1) of this rule as it applies to matrimonial proceedings.

Defined terms—"divorce county court", "principal registry", r 1.2(1).

Scope of provision—This rule is relevant only to applications under s 17 which are made in the principal registry. It provides the option, at the choice of the applicant, to make the application to the principal registry as though it were a county court, but this option is available only where the applicant is a party to a suit for divorce, nullity or judicial separation which is either pending in the principal registry or is intended to be commenced there and which is being treated as pending in a divorce county court. Thus, in the absence of such proceedings, an application under s 17 in the principal registry has to be in the High Court.

Procedure—See *Secretary's Circular of 14 August 1972*.

Lodging office copy of the register—Where title to real or leasehold property is registered, the applicant should as soon as possible (and in any event by the time of the first hearing) lodge an up-to-date office copy of the register with the court. Land Registration Act 1925, s 112 (as amended) permits inspection and copying of entries on the register.

3.8 Applications under Part IV of the Family Law Act 1996 (Family Homes and Domestic Violence)

(1) An application for an occupation order or a non-molestation order under Part IV of the Family Law Act 1996 shall be made in Form FL401.

(2) An application for an occupation order or a non-molestation order made by a child under the age of sixteen shall be made in Form FLA401 but shall be treated, in the first instance, as an application to the High Court for leave.

(3) An application for an occupation order or a non-molestation order which is made in other proceedings which are pending shall be made in Form FL401.

(4) An application in Form FL401 shall be supported by a statement which is signed by the applicant and is sworn to be true.

(5) Where an application is made without giving notice, the sworn statement shall state the reasons why notice was not given.

(6) An application made on notice (together with the sworn statement and a notice in Form FL402) shall be served by the applicant on the respondent personally not less than 2 days before the date on which the application will be heard.

(7) The court may abridge the period specified in paragraph (6).

(8) Where the applicant is acting in person, service of the application shall be effected by the court if the applicant so requests.

This does not affect the court's power to order substituted service.

(9) Where an application for an occupation order or a non-molestation order is pending, the court shall consider (on the application of either party or of its own motion) whether to exercise its powers to transfer the hearing of that application to another court and shall make an order for transfer in Form FL417 if it seems necessary or expedient to do so.

(10) Rule 9.2A shall not apply to an application for an occupation order or a non-molestation order under Part IV of the Family Law Act 1996.

(11) A copy of an application for an occupation order under section 33, 35 or 36 of the Family Law Act 1996 shall be served by the applicant by first-class post on the mortgagee or, as the case may be, the landlord of the dwelling-house in question, with a notice in Form FL416 informing him of his right to make representations in writing or at any hearing.

(12) Where the application is for the transfer of a tenancy, notice of the application shall be served by the applicant on the other cohabitant or spouse and on the landlord (as those terms are defined by paragraph 1 of Schedule 7 to the Family Law Act 1996) and any person so served shall be entitled to be heard on the application.

(13) Rules 2.62(4) to (6) and 2.63 (investigation, requests for further information) shall apply, with the necessary modifications, to –

- (*a*) an application for an occupation order under section 33, 35 or 36 of the Family Law Act 1996, and
- (*b*) an application for the transfer of a tenancy,

as they apply to an application for ancillary relief.

(14) Rule 3.6(7) to (9) (Married Women's Property Act 1882) shall apply, with the necessary modifications, to an application for the transfer of a tenancy, as they apply to an application under rule 3.6.

PART III

(15) The applicant shall file a statement in Form FL415 after he has served the application.

Amendments—Substituted by SI 1997/1893.

Defined terms—"court": r 1.2(1); "cohabitant": FLA 1996, s 62(1); "dwelling-house": FLA 1996, s 63(1), (4); "non-molestation order", "occupation order": FLA 1996, ss 39, 42.

Scope of provision—This rule regulates the procedure for applications under Family Law Act 1996, Pt IV, ie applications for occupation or non-molestation orders under ss 33–42, and transfers of contractual or statutory tenancies (for spouses, former spouses who have not remarried and cohabitants) under s 53 and Sch 7.

Code for applying for occupation and non-molestation orders—The application is made in Form FL401 (r 3.8(3)), supported by a sworn statement (r 3.8(4)). If made ex parte, the sworn statement should state why notice was not given, having regard to the criteria set out in FLA 1996, s 45 (r 3.8(5)). The application should be served personally on the respondent not less than two days before the hearing, although the court may abridge time (r 3.8(6), (7)). The two days must be business days, excluding Saturdays, Sundays, Christmas Day, Good Friday and bank holidays (r 1.5(4), (6)). If the applicant is acting in person, the court can effect service. In any event, the court can order substituted service (r 3.8(8)). Where the application is made by a child aged under 16 it is treated as an application to the High Court for leave (r 3.8(2)) and the provisions of r 9.2A (whereby certain minors can sue or defend without a next friend or guardian ad litem) do not apply (r 3.8(10)). An application for an occupation order under FLA 1996, s 33, 35 or 36 must be served on the mortgagee or landlord with notice in Form FL416 (r 3.8(11)). Orders for the discovery of documents, the attendance of any witnesses and "r 2.63 enquiries" are made in the same way as an application for ancillary relief (r 3.8(13)). If an applicant (perhaps from an ethnic minority and with little or no knowledge of English) does not know the identity of the mortgagee or landlord, there is no reason in principle why an order binding the applicant and respondent cannot be made. It is suggested that such an order can be conditional upon the applicant using his best endeavours to serve the mortgagee or landlord who would have the right to be heard on being so served, subsequent to the order made between the parties.

Transfer of tenancy application—Notice of the application is served on both the other party and the landlord. After service, the applicant should file Form FL415 (r 3.8(15)). If the tenancy is either in the other party's name or in joint names, the other party can frustrate the application by surrendering the tenancy (for the ability of one joint tenant to give an effective notice to quit without any consultation with the other see *Hammersmith and Fulham London Borough Council v Monk* [1992] 1 FLR 465). At the outset of proceedings, consideration should be given to applying (initially ex parte) for an injunction to restrain the other party from ending the tenancy by notice to quit or surrender (*Bater v Greenwich London Borough Council* [1999] 2 FLR 993). The application for an injunction can be made to the district judge (r 3.8(14) applying r 3.6(9)). If the application is contested, the respondent should file an affidavit in answer within 14 days of the time for sending acknowledgement of service (r 3.8(14) applying r 3.6(7)). If he does not, the applicant can apply to debar the respondent from defending (r 3.6(8)). Discovery of documents, orders for the attendance of witnesses and "r 2.63 enquiries" are made in the same way as a pre-5 June 2000 application for ancillary relief (r 3.8(13) applying rr 2.62(4)–(6), 2.63). Interim orders can be made under r 2.64.

3.9 Hearing of applications under Part IV of the Family Law Act 1996

(1) An application for an occupation order or a non-molestation order under Part IV of the Family Law Act 1996 shall be dealt with in chambers unless the court otherwise directs.

(2) Where an order is made on an application made ex parte, a copy of the order together with a copy of the application and of the sworn statement in support shall be served by the applicant on the respondent personally.

(3) Where the application is for an occupation order under section 33, 35 or 36 of the Family Law Act 1996, a copy of any order made on the application shall be

served by the applicant by first-class post on the mortgagee or, as the case may be, the landlord of the dwelling-house in question.

(4) A copy of an order made on an application heard inter partes shall be served by the applicant on the respondent personally.

(5) Where the applicant is acting in person, service of a copy of any order made on the hearing of the application shall be effected by the court if the applicant so requests.

(6) The following forms shall be used in connection with hearings of applications under Part IV of the Family Law Act 1996 –

(*a*) a record of the hearing shall be made on Form FL405, and

(*b*) any order made on the hearing shall be issued in Form FL404.

(7) The court may direct that a further hearing be held in order to consider any representations made by a mortgagee or a landlord.

(8) An application to vary, extend or discharge an order made under Part IV of the Family Law Act 1996 shall be made in Form FL403 and this rule shall apply to the hearing of such an application.

Amendments—Substituted by SI 1997/1893.

Scope of provision—This rule governs the procedure for an application for an order under FLA 1996, Pt IV, irrespective of whether the application is an originating process or is made in pending family proceedings. The court also has power to make non-molestation orders of its own motion (FLA 1996, s 42(2)(*b*)).

"in chambers" (r 3.9(1))—These words refer to the fact that the hearing should be in private, as opposed to open court, rather than the room in which the hearing is held.

Service on respondent—Personal service on the respondent in r 3.9(2) (ex parte orders) and in r 3.9(4) (inter partes orders) is required. In the former case, the respondent must also be served with a copy of the sworn statement used as evidence to obtain the ex parte order. Ex parte orders always have to be reconsidered at a full hearing (FLA 1996, s 45(3)) and either the date, time and place of the full hearing must be clear on the face of the ex parte order itself or the respondent must also be served with notice of the full hearing in Form FL402.

Landlords and mortgagees—Rule 3.9(3) requires service by post on the landlord or mortgagee of any occupation order made under s 33, 35 or 36. Rule 3.9(7) enables the court to direct a further hearing to consider representations from landlords or mortgagees. The court's additional powers in FLA 1996, s 40 include the power to impose an obligation to discharge rent, mortgage payments etc.

"non-molestation order"—See FLA 1996, s 42 and notes thereon.

"occupation order"—See FLA 1996, ss 33–41 and notes thereon.

Prescribed forms—FL401 (Application for a non-molestation/occupation order); FL402 (Notice of Proceedings); FL403 (Application to vary, extend or discharge an order); FL404 (Order); FL405 (Record of hearing); FL406 (Power of Arrest).

Form of order—Form FL404. The specimen clauses (set out in FPR 1991, App 1) are intended to assist in the drafting of orders.

3.9A Enforcement of orders made on applications under Part IV of the Family Law Act 1996

(1) Where a power of arrest is attached to one or more of the provisions ("the relevant provisions") of an order made under Part IV of the Family Law Act 1996 –

(*a*) the relevant provisions shall be set out in Form FL406 and the form shall not include any provisions of the order to which the power of arrest was not attached; and
(*b*) a copy of the form shall be delivered to the officer for the time being in charge of any police station for the applicant's address or of such other police station as the court may specify.

The copy of the form delivered under sub-paragraph (*b*) shall be accompanied by a statement showing that the respondent has been served with the order or informed of its terms (whether by being present when the order was made or by telephone or otherwise).

(2) Where an order is made varying or discharging the relevant provisions, the proper officer shall –

(*a*) immediately inform the officer who received a copy of the form under paragraph (1) and, if the applicant's address has changed, the officer for the time being in charge of the police station for the new address; and
(*b*) deliver a copy of the order to any officer so informed.

(3) An application for the issue of a warrant for the arrest of the respondent shall be made in Form FL407 and the warrant shall be issued in Form FL408.

(4) The court before whom a person is brought following his arrest may –

(*a*) determine whether the facts, and the circumstances which led to the arrest, amounted to disobedience of the order, or
(*b*) adjourn the proceedings and, where such an order is made, the arrested person may be released and –
 (i) be dealt with within 14 days of the day on which he was arrested; and
 (ii) be given not less than 2 days' notice of the adjourned hearing.

Nothing in this paragraph shall prevent the issue of a notice under CCR Order 29, rule 1(4) if the arrested person is not dealt with within the period mentioned in sub-paragraph (*b*)(i) above.

(5) The following provisions shall apply, with the necessary modifications, to the enforcement of orders made on applications under Part IV of the Family Law Act 1996 –

(*a*) RSC Order 52, rule 7 (power to suspend execution of committal order);
(*b*) (in a case where an application for an order of committal is made to the High Court) RSC Order 52, rule 2 (application for leave);
(*c*) CCR Order 29, rule 1 (committal for breach of order);
(*d*) CCR Order 29, rule 1A (undertakings);
(*e*) CCR Order 29, rule 3 (discharge of person in custody);

and CCR Order 29, rule 1 shall have effect, as if for paragraph (3), there were substituted the following –

"(3) At the time when the order is drawn up, the proper officer shall –

(*a*) where the order made is (or includes) a non-molestation order and (*b*) where the order made is an occupation order and the court so directs, issue a copy of the order, indorsed with or incorporating a notice as to the consequences of disobedience, for service in accordance with paragraph (2)."

(6) The court may adjourn consideration of the penalty to be imposed for contempts found provided and such consideration may be restored if the respondent does not comply with any conditions specified by the court.

(7) Where the court makes a hospital order in Form FL413 or a guardianship order in Form FL414 under the Mental Health Act 1983, the proper officer shall –

(*a*) send to the hospital any information which will be of assistance in dealing with the patient;
(*b*) inform the applicant when the respondent is being transferred to hospital.

(8) Where a transfer direction given by the Secretary of State under section 48 of the Mental Health Act 1983 is in force in respect of a person remanded in custody by the court under Schedule 5 to the Family Law Act 1996, the proper officer shall notify –

(*a*) the governor of the prison to which that person was remanded; and
(*b*) the hospital where he is detained,

of any committal hearing which that person is required to attend and the proper officer shall give notice in writing to the hospital where that person is detained of any further remand under paragraph 3 of Schedule 5 to the Family Law Act 1996.

(9) An order for the remand of the respondent shall be in Form FL409.

(10) In paragraph (4) "arrest" means arrest under a power of arrest attached to an order or under a warrant of arrest.

Amendments—Inserted by SI 1997/1893.

"power of arrest"—See FLA 1996, s 47 and notes thereon. Most, if not all, non-molestation orders have a power of arrest attached to some of their provisions.

"relevant provisions" (r 3.9A(1))—The order will be on Form FL404, drafted from the specimen clauses in FPR 1991, App 1. Invariably the order contains several provisions and the court must decide to which of these a power of arrest is to be attached: these are the "relevant provisions". Form FL406 is then drafted containing only the relevant provisions.

Delivery to the police (r 3.9A(1)(*b*))—Form FL406 is delivered, after the respondent has been told of the order, to the police. Unless a different police station is specified, Form FL406 is delivered to the officer in charge of the police station for the applicant's address. Where the police force in question has a Domestic Violence Unit based at a particular police station it may be preferable to specify that police station. It is important that the police are not told of the power of arrest before the respondent knows of the order, otherwise there is a risk that the police may exceed their powers. Hence the requirement in r 3.9A(1) for the statement of service to accompany Form FL406 when it is delivered to the police. If the "relevant provisions" are subsequently varied the onus is on the court to notify the police (r 3.9A(2)).

Arrest without warrant—See FLA 1996, s 47(6). A constable may arrest without warrant a person whom he has reasonable cause for suspecting to be in breach of a relevant provision.

"warrant for the arrest of the respondent" (r 3.9A(3))—See FLA 1996, s 47(8) and notes thereon. A warrant for the arrest of the respondent can be sought either where the injunction does not contain a power of arrest at all, or where the respondent is alleged to be in breach of one of the provisions which is not a "relevant provision". The application for a warrant must be "substantiated on oath" (FLA 1996, s 47(9)) and the better practice is for the application in Form FL407 to be supported by affidavit, rather than expect the court to receive oral evidence. The affidavit provides a record of the alleged breaches.

Warrant of arrest—The warrant is in Form FL408. It can be "backed for bail" with or without conditions, including a recognizance and/or surety. It is submitted that conditions will be rare (see commentary on FLA 1996, s 47 and Sch 5).

"committal for breach of order" (r 3.9A(5))—The warrant of arrest procedure is an additional method of bringing the respondent before the court for an alleged breach. The procedure of applying for a warrant of committal under CCR Ord 29 continues (see CCR Ord 29 and notes thereon). Where the injunction does contain a power of arrest and the respondent is alleged to be in breach of a relevant provision but the police have not in fact arrested the respondent, it is not possible to apply for a warrant of arrest (see wording of FLA 1996, s 47(8)) and the applicant must proceed under CCR Ord 29.

Contempt of court—The court's powers to punish for breach of an injunction are contained in the Contempt of Court Act 1981.

FLA 1996, s 58 provides that the court's powers to punish for contempt of court, arising out of breach of an order under FLA 1996, Pt IV, may be exercised by the "relevant judicial authority". That term is defined in FLA 1996, s 63(1). It means:

(*a*) where the order was made by the High Court, a judge of that court.

(*b*) where the order was made by a county court, a judge or district judge of that or any other county court (but not a deputy district judge).

(c) where the order was made by a magistrates' court, any magistrates' court.

Sentencing—The guideline case on sentencing is *Hale v Tanner* [2000] 2 FLR 879. On a committal application the court has to direct itself whether committal to prison is appropriate. The full range of sentencing options available to the criminal courts is not available but there is still a range of options. If prison is appropriate, the length of sentence and whether it should be suspended are separate questions. The length of sentence depends on the court's objectives: one objective is to mark disapproval of disobedience of its order; another is to secure future compliance. The length needs to bear some reasonable relationship to the two years' maximum. Suspension is wider than in criminal cases and its length requires separate consideration. The context of the breach may be aggravating or mitigating. The court should bear in mind any parallel proceedings and may have to take the outcome into account. The court should explain the choices it has made in a particular case. On the facts of *Hale v Tanner*, a sentence of six months for abusive and threatening telephone calls was reduced to 28 days. See also *Wilson v Webster* [1998] 1 FLR 1097 (fourteen days increased on appeal to three months) and *Neil v Ryan* [1998] 2 FLR 1069 (suspended sentence replaced by one of immediate committal).

Adjournments—Rule 3.9A(4) gives the court power to adjourn proceedings against a person arrested under either a power of arrest, or a warrant of arrest (r 3.9A(10)). However, if that person is released, the rule makes it clear that he must be dealt with within 14 days of the day of his arrest and, if he is not, the court would have no power to deal with him pursuant to that arrest (but the power to proceed under CCR Ord 29 is expressly preserved). Rule 3.9A(6) enables the court to adjourn consideration of the penalty for a proven contempt. Although it is not mentioned in the rule, the court does have power to vary or extend the injunction or to issue a new injunction altogether (perhaps including provisions in more defined terms). This course of action may be preferable to adjourning. Further, the court could impose a suspended sentence of imprisonment.

RSC Ord 52 (Committals)—See notes thereon.

CCR Ord 29 (Committal for breach of order or undertaking)—See notes thereon.

Remand—The High Court and county courts have been brought into line with magistrates' court procedure and now have power to remand (see FLA 1996, s 47 and Sch 5 and notes thereon). Remand can be in custody for up to 8 days (3 days if in police cells) or on bail.

"hospital order", "guardianship order" (r 3.9A(7))—FLA 1996, s 48 gives the court power to remand for medical reports. The "relevant judicial authority"(see **Contempt of court** above) is given the same powers as the Crown Court under Mental Health Act 1983, s 35.

Prescribed forms—FL404 (Order); FL406 (Power of Arrest); FL407 (Application for a Warrant of Arrest); FL408 (Warrant of Arrest); FL409 (Remand Order); FL410 (Recognizance of respondent); FL411 (Recognizance of respondent's surety); FL412 (Bail Notice); FL413 (Hospital Order/Interim Hospital Order); FL414 (Guardianship Order).

3.10 Applications under Part IV of the Family Law Act 1996: bail

(1) An application for bail made by a person arrested under a power of arrest or a warrant of arrest may be made either orally or in writing.

(2) Where an application is made in writing, it shall contain the following particulars –

(*a*) the full name of the person making the application;

(*b*) the address of the place where the person making the application is detained at the time when the application is made;

(*c*) the address where the person making the application would reside if he were to be granted bail;

(*d*) the amount of the recognizance in which he would agree to be bound; and

(*e*) the grounds on which the application is made and, where a previous application has been refused, full particulars of any change in circumstances which has occurred since that refusal.

(3) An application made in writing shall be signed by the person making the application or by a person duly authorised by him in that behalf or, where the person making the application is a minor or is for any reason incapable of acting, by a guardian ad litem acting on his behalf and a copy shall be served by the person making the application on the applicant for the Part IV order.

(4) The persons prescribed for the purposes of paragraph 4 of Schedule 5 to the Family Law Act 1996 (postponement of taking of recognizance) are –

(*a*) a district judge

(*b*) a justice of the peace

(*c*) a justices' clerk

(*d*) a police officer of the rank of inspector or above or in charge of a police station, and

(*e*) (where the person making the application is in his custody) the governor or keeper of a prison.

(5) The person having custody of the person making the application shall –

(*a*) on receipt of a certificate signed by or on behalf of the district judge stating that the recognizance of any sureties required have been taken, or on being otherwise satisfied that all such recognizances have been taken; and

(*b*) on being satisfied that the person making the application has entered into his recognizance,

release the person making the application.

(6) The following forms shall be used –

(*a*) the recognizance of the person making the application shall be in Form FL410 and that of a surety in Form FL411;

(*b*) a bail notice in Form FL412 shall be given to the respondent where he is remanded on bail.

Amendments—SI 1997/1893.

Remand—FLA 1996, s 47(7) gives the court power to remand a person arrested pursuant to a power of arrest, and s 47(10) gives a like power in the case of persons arrested pursuant to a warrant of arrest. Remand can be either in custody or on bail.

Remand in custody or on bail—Magistrates' courts have power to remand under Magistrates' Courts Act 1980, ss 128 and 129. FLA 1996, s 47(11) and Sch 5 have introduced a similar scheme into the High Court and county courts (see **Scope of provision** under FLA 1996, Sch 5).

Contempt proceedings—FLA 1996, s 58 enables the "relevant judicial authority" to deal with a contempt of court arising out of a failure to comply with an order under FLA 1996, Pt IV (see notes on r 3.9A above). Wherever possible, the court will deal with the contempt at the first hearing. Where this is not possible (eg because there is a factual dispute but the applicant is not present to give evidence) the court will have to adjourn and will then decide whether the respondent should be remanded. Only if the court remands in custody will the question of an application for bail under r 3.10 arise.

Bail applications—Rule 3.10 prescribes a procedure for an application for bail by a person arrested under a power of arrest or warrant of arrest.

Recognizance—A recognizance is an obligation or bond acknowledged before a court. The person acknowledging it, that is the person bound by it, is called the conusor or cognisor. The object of a recognizance is to secure the performance of an act by the conusor, such as to appear at court on a particular day. If the obligation is not performed the recognizance can be estreated.

Conditional bail—It is submitted that conditional bail will be rare in applications under FLA 1996, Pt IV. Bail in a criminal case is to ensure that the defendant attends his trial. However, in a civil case, provided that the court is satisfied that the defendant has notice of the hearing, the court can proceed in the absence of the defendant. Unconditional bail is just as likely to secure the defendant's attendance as conditional bail.

Prescribed forms—FL409 (Remand Order); FL410 (Recognizance of respondent); FL411 (Recognizance of respondent's surety); FL412 (Bail Notice).

"bail notice in Form FL412"—It is submitted that Form FL412 is seriously flawed. It contains the words "The court is satisfied that you disobeyed the order made on [*date*] at the [ ] Court by [*specify breaches proven*]". If the court is so satisfied it will surely punish the contempt at the hearing. What would be the purpose of a remand on bail? Fortunately, a remand on bail (cf a remand in custody) is likely to be rare. Where the court does remand on bail these words invariably have to be deleted. See further **Scope of provision** under FLA 1996, Sch 5.

3.11 Proceedings in respect of polygamous marriage

(1) The provisions of this rule shall have effect where a petition, originating application or originating summons asks for matrimonial relief within the meaning of section 47(2) of the Act of 1973 in respect of a marriage where either party to the marriage is, or has during the subsistence of the marriage been, married to more than one person (in this rule referred to as a polygamous marriage).

(2) The petition, originating application or originating summons –

(*a*) shall state that the marriage in question is polygamous;
(*b*) shall state whether or not there is, to the knowledge of the petitioner or applicant, any living spouse of his or hers additional to the respondent or, as the case may be, any living spouse of the respondent additional to the petitioner or applicant (in this rule referred to as an additional spouse); and
(*c*) if there is any additional spouse, shall give his or her full name and address and the date and place of his or her marriage to the petitioner or applicant or, as the case may be, to the respondent, or state, so far as may be applicable, that such information is unknown to the petitioner or applicant.

(3) Without prejudice to its powers under RSC Order 15 (which deals with parties) or CCR Order 15 (which deals with amendment) the court may order that any additional spouse –

(*a*) be added as a party to the proceedings; or
(*b*) be given notice of –
(i) the proceedings; or
(ii) of any application in the proceedings for any such order as is mentioned in section 47(2)(*d*) of the Act of 1973.

(4) Any order under paragraph (3) may be made at any stage of the proceedings and either on the application of any party or by the court of its own motion and, where an additional spouse is mentioned in a petition or an acknowledgement of service of a petition, the petitioner shall, on making any application in the proceedings or, if no previous application has been made in the proceedings, on making a request for directions for trial, ask for directions as to whether an order should be made under paragraph (3).

(5) Any person to whom notice is given pursuant to an order under paragraph (3) shall be entitled, without filing an answer or affidavit, to be heard in the proceedings or on the application to which the notice relates.

Amendments—SI 1996/816.

Defined terms—"court": r 1.2(1); "matrimonial relief": Matrimonial Causes Act 1973, s 47(2).

Proceedings in relation to a polygamous marriage (r 3.11(1))—The fact that a marriage is polygamous does not prevent a party to it seeking matrimonial relief or a declaration of validity in respect of it (MCA 1973, s 47). Rule 3.11 deals with matrimonial relief and r 3.12 (inter alia) with declarations as to validity of marriages. "Matrimonial relief" includes decrees under MCA 1973, Pt I (eg for divorce or nullity), applications for financial relief under MCA 1973 (including an order in cases of neglect to maintain: MCA 1973, s 27) and applications for financial relief following foreign matrimonial proceedings (Matrimonial and Family Proceedings Act 1984, Pt III).

Additional spouse (r 3.11(2))—The pleading by which the cause is begun must state whether or not the marriage is polygamous; if it is polygamous, the name and other particulars (if known) of any other spouse of the petitioner or applicant or of the respondent must be given.

Joinder of, or notice to, additional spouse (r 3.11(3))—Once an additional spouse is identified in the petition or application, the court has a discretion as to whether to order that the additional spouse be (*a*) joined as a party or (*b*) given notice of the proceedings. RSC Ord 15, r 4 and CCR Ord 15, r 1(1)(*b*) provide for joinder of parties with leave of the court and, in the case of the county court, by the court on its own motion (CCR Ord 15, r 1(3)). Rule 3.11(3) gives the court an absolute discretion as to joinder of parties or the giving of notice and at any stage in the proceedings (r 3.11(4)), but such discretion is likely to be exercised on principles similar to those applicable in civil actions. Joinder is generally relevant where some common question of law or fact is involved and any rights to relief claimed arise out of the same transaction or transactions – in this case, the marriage or marriages (see RSC Ord 15, r 4(1)). One of the purposes of these rules is to avoid multiplicity of proceedings. In considering whether to give notice, the court will wish to consider, as far as possible, the prejudice to a party of not being given notice. It is submitted that, in the first instance, the appropriate course of action is generally for an additional spouse to be given notice; only rarely should they be joined as a party in the first instance.

Application to join as a party—Where an additional spouse is given notice, she does not automatically achieve party status (*Re T (Divorce: Interim Maintenance: Discovery)* [1990] 1 FLR 1), although certain particular rights are conferred on her by r 3.11(5). Thus, on being given notice and if she wishes to be joined, the additional spouse must make application to intervene (RSC Ord 15, r 4; CCR Ord 15, r 1(1)(*b*), (3)). Such application is made on notice (by summons in the High Court) to the district judge (r 10.9) supported by affidavit. That affidavit should set out the nature of the additional spouse's interest in the proceedings and of any claim in the proceedings she may want to make; in presenting the application, the additional spouse should have in mind the factors considered in **Joinder of, or notice to, additional spouse** above. In view of the tenor of r 3.11(3)–(5), refusal of an application to be joined must be rare.

PART III

Consideration of order under r 3.11(3) on directions or application (r 3.11(4))—This rule places a duty on the petitioner (or applicant, presumably) – but not on any respondent who applies or seeks directions for trial in the proceedings – to draw to the court's attention the question of whether or not an order should be made under r 3.11(3) on making any application in the proceedings or seeking directions for trial. Further, there is a duty on the district judge, when considering directions in such cases, to check whether directions as to any additional spouse have been given and, if given, that they have been complied with (*Practice Direction of 14 May 1973*, para 4). If directions have not been given, or not complied with, the district judge should withhold directions for trial until he is satisfied as to compliance with the rule.

"Any person to whom notice is given ... shall be entitled ... to be heard" (r 3.11(5))—This widely drawn provision gives to an additional spouse served only with notice something akin to party status whilst enabling her to evade the necessity of filing evidence or of being subject to, for example, orders for discovery (*Re T (Divorce: Interim Maintenance: Discovery)* [1990] 1 FLR 1). Despite this rule, if justice is to be done to an additional spouse's position, it would seem prudent for her to apply to be joined, thus allowing her evidence to be considered properly at the hearing of any application or the trial of the cause. Further, if she wishes to make any application of her own, she should apply to be joined as a party in her own right.

3.12 Application under section 55 of Act of 1986 for declaration as to marital status

(1) Unless otherwise directed, a petition by which proceedings are begun under section 55 of the Act of 1986 for a declaration as to marital status shall state –

(*a*) the names of the parties to the marriage to which the application relates and the residential address of each of them at the date of the presentation of the petition;

(*b*) the place and date of any ceremony of marriage to which the application relates;

(*c*) the grounds on which the application is made and all other material facts alleged by the petitioner to justify the making of the declaration;

(*d*) whether there have been or are continuing any proceedings in any court, tribunal or authority in England and Wales or elsewhere between the parties which relate to, or are capable of affecting, the validity or subsistence of the marriage, divorce, annulment or legal separation to which the application relates, or which relate to the matrimonial status of either of the parties, and, if so –

(i) the nature, and either the outcome or present state of those proceedings,
(ii) the court, tribunal or authority before which they were begun,
(iii) the date when they were begun,
(iv) the names of the parties to them,
(v) the date or expected date of the trial,
(vi) any other facts relevant to the question whether the petition should be stayed under Schedule 1 to the Domicile and Matrimonial Proceedings Act of 1973;

and any such proceedings shall include any which are instituted otherwise than in a court of law in any country outside England and Wales, if they are instituted before a tribunal or other authority having power under the law having effect there to determine questions of status, and shall be treated as continuing if they have begun and have not been finally disposed of;

(*e*) where it is alleged that the court has jurisdiction based on domicile, which of the parties to the marriage to which the application relates is domiciled in England and Wales on the date of the presentation of the petition, or died before that date and was at death domiciled in England and Wales.

(*f*) where it is alleged that the court has jurisdiction based on habitual residence, which of the parties to the marriage to which the application relates has been habitually resident in England and Wales, or died before that date and had been habitually resident in England and Wales throughout the period of one year ending with the date of death;

(*g*) where the petitioner was not a party to the marriage to which the application relates, particulars of his interest in the determination of the application.

(2) Where the proceedings are for a declaration that the validity of a divorce, annulment or legal separation obtained in any country outside England or Wales in respect of the marriage either is or is not entitled to recognition in England and Wales, the petition shall in addition state the date and place of the divorce, annulment or legal separation.

(3) There shall be annexed to the petition a copy of the certificate of any marriage to which the application relates, or, as the case may be, a certified copy of any decree of divorce, annulment or order for legal separation to which the application relates.

(4) Where a document produced by virtue of paragraph (3) is not in English it shall, unless otherwise directed, be accompanied by a translation certified by a notary public or authenticated by affidavit.

(5) The parties to the marriage in respect of which a declaration is sought shall be petitioner and respondent respectively to the application, unless a third party is applying for a declaration, in which case he shall be the petitioner and the parties to the marriage shall be respondents to the application.

Defined terms—"the Act of 1986": r 1.2(1).

Declarations as to marital status—Family Law Act 1986, s 55(1) permits any person to apply to the High Court or a county court for one or more of the following declarations in relation to a marriage specified in the application:

(*a*) a declaration that the marriage was at its inception a valid marriage;
(*b*) a declaration that the marriage subsisted on a date specified in the application;
(*c*) a declaration that the marriage did not subsist on a date so specified;
(*d*) a declaration that the validity of a divorce, annulment or legal separation obtained in any country outside England and Wales in respect of the marriage is entitled to recognition in England and Wales;
(*e*) a declaration that the validity of a divorce, annulment or legal separation so obtained in respect of the marriage is not entitled to recognition in England and Wales.

Section 55(2) restricts jurisdiction to entertain such applications to cases where either of the parties to the relevant marriage is domiciled in England and Wales on the date of the application, has been habitually resident in England and Wales throughout the period of one year ending with that date or died before that date and either (i) was at death domiciled in England and Wales, or (ii) had been habitually resident in England and Wales throughout the period of one year ending with the date of death.

Section 55(3) provides that, where the application is made by any person other than a party to the marriage to which the application relates, the court shall refuse to hear the application if it considers that the applicant does not have a sufficient interest in the determination of that application.

Procedure generally in proceedings for a declaration as to marital status—See r 3.16 and Procedural Guide 14.

"under Schedule 1 to the Domicile and Matrimonial Proceedings Act 1973" (r 3.12(1)(*d*)(vi))—Domicile and Matrimonial Proceedings Act 1973, Sch 1, para 9 gives the court a discretion to stay proceedings, including those for a declaration as to the validity of a marriage of the petitioner or a declaration as to the subsistence of such a marriage where there are

PART III

concurrent proceedings elsewhere in respect of the same marriage and certain conditions are satisfied.

3.13 Application under section 55A of Act of 1986 for declaration of parentage

(1) Unless otherwise directed, a petition by which proceedings are begun under section 55A of the Act of 1986 for a declaration of parentage shall state –

(*a*) the full name and the sex, date and place of birth and residential address of the petitioner (except where the petitioner is the Secretary of State);

(*b*) where the case is not an excepted case within section 55(A)(4) of the Act of 1986; either the petitioner's interest in the determination of the application, or that section 27(2) of the Act of 1991 applies;

(*c*) if they are known, the full name and the sex, date and place of birth and residential address of each of the following persons (unless that person is the petitioner) –

(i) the person whose parentage is in issue;

(ii) the person whose parenthood is in issue; and

(iii) any person who is acknowledged to be the father or mother of the person whose parentage is in issue;

(*d*) if the petitioner, the person whose parentage is in issue or the person whose parenthood is in issue, is known by a name other than that which appears in the certificate of his birth, that other name shall also be stated in the petition and in any decree made thereon;

(*e*) if it is known, the full name of the mother, or alleged mother of the person whose parentage is in issue, at the date of –

(i) her birth;

(ii) her first marriage;

(iii) the birth of the person whose parentage is in issue; and

(iv) her most recent marriage;

if it was at any of those times different from her full name at the date of the presentation of the petition;

(*f*) the grounds on which the petitioner relies and all other material facts alleged by him to justify the making of the declaration;

(*g*) whether there are or have been any other proceedings in any court, tribunal or authority in England and Wales or elsewhere relating to the parentage of the person whose parentage is in issue or to the parenthood of the person whose parenthood is in issue, and, if so –

(i) particulars of the proceedings, including the court, tribunal or authority before which they were begun, and their nature, outcome or present state,

(ii) the date they were begun,

(iii) the names of the parties, and

(iv) the date or expected date of any trial in the proceedings;

(*h*) that either the person whose parentage is in issue or the person whose parenthood is in issue –

(i) is domiciled in England and Wales on the date of the presentation of the petition;

(ii) has been habitually resident in England and Wales throughout the period of one year ending with that date; or

(iii) died before that date and either was at death domiciled in England and Wales or had been habitually resident in England and Wales throughout the period of one year ending with the date of death; and (*i*) the nationality, citizenship or immigration status of the person whose parentage is in issue and of the person whose parenthood is in issue, and the effect which the granting of a declaration of parentage would have upon the status of each of them as regards his nationality, citizenship or right to be in the United Kingdom.

(2) Unless otherwise directed, there shall be annexed to the petition a copy of the birth certificate of the person whose parentage is in issue.

(3) The respondents to the application shall be –

(i) the person whose parentage is in issue; and

(ii) any person who is, or who is alleged to be, the mother or father of the person whose parentage is in issue;

excluding the petitioner.

(4) The prescribed officer for the purposes of section 55A(7) of the Act of 1986 shall be the proper officer within the meaning of rule 1.2(1).

(5) Within 21 days after a declaration of parentage has been made, the prescribed officer shall send to the Registrar General a copy of the declaration in Form M30 and the petition.

Amendments—Substituted by SI 2001/821; amended by SI 2003/184.

Declaration of parentage—Family Law Act 1986, s 55A(1) permits any person to apply to the High Court, a county court or a magistrates' court for a declaration that a person named in the application is or was the parent of another person so named. Section 56(3) restricts the court's jurisdiction to cases where the applicant is domiciled in England and Wales on the date of the application or has been habitually resident in England and Wales throughout the period of one year ending with that date.

Procedure generally in proceedings for a declaration of parentage—See r 3.16 and Procedural Guide 42.

"Within 21 days" (r 3.13(5))—As to the computation of time, see r 1.5.

3.14 Application under section 56(1)(b) and (2) of Act of 1986 for declaration of legitimacy or legitimation

(1) Unless otherwise directed, a petition by which proceedings are begun under section 56(1)(*b*) and (2) of the Act of 1986 for a declaration of legitimacy or legitimation shall state –

(*a*) the name of the petitioner, and if the petitioner is known by a name other than that which appears in the certificate of his birth, that other name shall be stated in the petition and in any decree made thereon;

(*b*) the date and place of birth of the petitioner;

(*c*) if it is known, the name of the petitioner's father and the maiden name of the petitioner's mother and, if it is different, her current name, and the residential address of each of them at the time of the presentation of the petition;

(*d*) the grounds on which the petitioner relies and all other material facts alleged by him to justify the making of the declaration; and

(*e*) either that the petitioner is domiciled in England and Wales on the date of the presentation of the petition or that he has been habitually resident in England and Wales throughout the period of one year ending with that date.

(2) Unless otherwise directed, there shall be annexed to the petition a copy of the petitioner's birth certificate.

(3) The petitioner's father and mother, or the survivor of them, shall be respondents to the application.

Defined terms—"the Act of 1986": r 1.2(1).

Declaration of legitimacy or legitimation—Family Law Act 1986, s 56 provides for these declarations. Section 56(1)(*b*) permits any person to apply to a county court or the High Court for a declaration that he is the legitimate child of his parents. Section 56(2) permits any person to apply to a county court or the High Court for one (or for one, or, in the alternative, the other) of the following declarations, that is to say:
(*a*) a declaration that he has become a legitimated person;
(*b*) a declaration that he has not become a legitimated person.

Section 56(3) restricts the court's jurisdiction to cases where the applicant is domiciled in England and Wales on the date of the application; or has been habitually resident in England and Wales throughout the period of one year ending with that date.

Procedure generally in proceedings for a declaration of legitimacy or legitimation—See r 3.16 and Procedural Guide 41.

3.15 Application under section 57 of Act of 1986 for declaration as to adoption effected overseas

(1) Unless otherwise directed, a petition by which proceedings are begun under section 57 of the Act of 1986 for a declaration as to an adoption effected overseas shall state –

(*a*) the names of those persons who are to be respondents pursuant to paragraph (4) and the residential address of each of them at the date of the presentation of the petition;
(*b*) the date and place of the petitioner's birth;
(*c*) the date and place of the adoption order and the court or other tribunal or authority which made it;
(*d*) all other material facts alleged by the petitioner to justify the making of the declaration and the grounds on which the application is made;
(*e*) either that the petitioner is domiciled in England and Wales on the date of the presentation of the petition or that he has been habitually resident in England and Wales throughout the period of one year ending with that date.

(2) There shall be annexed to the petition a copy of the petitioner's birth certificate (if it is available this certificate should be the one made after the adoption referred to in the petition) and, unless otherwise directed, a certified copy of the adoption order effected under the law of any country outside the British Islands.

(3) Where a document produced by virtue of paragraph (2) is not in English, it shall, unless otherwise directed, be accompanied by a translation certified by a notary public or authenticated by affidavit.

(4) The following shall, if alive, be respondents to the application, either –

(*a*) those whom the petitioner claims are his adoptive parents for the purposes of section 39 of the Adoption Act 1976; or
(*b*) those whom the petitioner claims are not his adoptive parents for the purposes of that section.

Defined terms—"Act of 1986": r 1.2(1); "British Islands": Interpretation Act 1978, Sch 1.

Scope of provision—This rule makes provision for the procedure applicable to an application under Family Law Act 1986, s 57 for a declaration concerning an adoption that has been effected overseas. Section 57 is concerned with two types of foreign adoption: (*a*) an "overseas adoption", as defined by Adoption Act 1976, s 72(2), which is an adoption which ranks automatically as an adoption order under the law of England and Wales; and (*b*) an adoption recognised by the law of England and Wales and effected under the law of any country outside the British Islands. The Adoption (Designation of Overseas Adoptions) Order 1973 specifies those countries whose statute law adoptions rank as "overseas adoptions" under s 57. For further discussion, see under AA 1976, s 38.

Petition (r 3.15(1))—The petition must include those matters set out in r 3.15(1). The conclusion of the petition must accord with FPR 1991, App 2, para 4.

"adoption effected overseas"—See FLA 1986, s 57(1).

Petitioner (r 3.15(1))—In every case the petitioner will be the person whose status as an adopted child is the subject of the application (FLA 1986, s 57(1)). A child who is still a minor may begin the application by acting through a next friend (r 9.2(1)).

3.16 General provisions as to proceedings under rules 3.12, 3.13, 3.14 and 3.15

(1) A petition under rule 3.12, 3.13, 3.14 or 3.15 shall be supported by an affidavit by the petitioner verifying the petition and giving particulars of every person whose interest may be affected by the proceedings and his relationship to the petitioner.

Provided that if the petitioner is under the age of 18, the affidavit shall, unless otherwise directed, be made by his next friend.

(2) Where the jurisdiction of the court to entertain a petition is based on habitual residence the petition shall include a statement of the addresses of the places of residence of the person so resident and the length of residence at each place either during the period of one year ending with the date of the presentation of the petition or, if that person is dead, throughout the period of one year ending with the date of death.

(3) An affidavit for the purposes of paragraph (1) may contain statements of information or belief with the sources and grounds thereof.

(4) Except in the case of a petition under rule 3.13, a copy of the petition and every document accompanying it shall be sent by the petitioner to the Attorney General at least one month before the petition is filed and it shall not be necessary thereafter to serve these documents upon him.

(5) If the Attorney General has notified the court that he wishes to intervene in the proceedings, the proper officer shall send to him a copy of any answer and, in the case of a petition under rule 3.13, of the petition and every document accompanying it.

(6) When all answers to the petition have been filed the petitioner shall issue and serve on all respondents to the application a request for directions as to any other persons who should be made respondents to the petition or given notice of the proceedings.

(7) When giving directions in accordance with paragraph (6) the court shall consider whether it is desirable that the Attorney General should argue before it any question relating to the proceedings, and if it does so consider and the Attorney General agrees to argue that question, the Attorney General need not file an answer and the court shall give directions requiring him to serve on all parties to the proceedings a summary of his argument.

(8) Persons given notice of proceedings pursuant to directions given in accordance with paragraph (6) shall within 21 days after service of the notice upon them be entitled to apply to the court to be joined as parties.

(9) The Attorney General may file an answer to the petition within 21 days after directions have been given under paragraph (7) and no directions for trial shall be given until that period and the period referred to in paragraph (8) have expired.

(10) The Attorney General, in deciding whether it is necessary or expedient to intervene in the proceedings, may have a search made for, and may inspect and bespeak a copy of, any document filed or lodged in the court offices which relates to any other family proceedings referred to in proceedings.

(11) Declarations made in accordance with section 55, section 56(1)(*a*), section 56(1)(*b*) and (2) and section 57 of the Act of 1986 shall be in the forms prescribed respectively in Forms M29, M30, M31 and M32.

(12) Subject to rules 3.12, 3.13, 3.14 and 3.15 and this rule, these rules shall, so far as applicable and with the exception of rule 2.6(1), apply with the necessary modifications to the proceedings as if they were a cause.

Amendments—SI 2001/821.

Defined terms—"cause": r 1.2(1).

Procedures that apply—The basic framework of proceedings to which this rule applies is similar to that of matrimonial causes. Rule 3.16(12) has the effect that, subject to the more specific provision made in this part, the rules apply to proceedings under rr 3.12–3.15 as if they were causes. Thus, the proceedings are required to be begun by petition (r 2.2(1)) and many other provisions of Pt II apply with appropriate modifications; of course this rule prevails over anything inconsistent which Pt II may say about causes and is supplemented in respect of each particular type of declaration proceedings by the even more specific provision made by the rule dealing with the type in question: r 3.12 in relation to declarations as to marital status, r 3.13 in respect of declarations of parentage, r 3.14 in respect of declarations of legitimacy or legitimation, and r 3.15 in relation to declarations as to adoptions affected overseas. Rules 3.12 to 3.15 deal with the contents of the petition and party status slightly differently for each type of declaration and contain any provision peculiar to the declaration concerned.

Proceedings covered by this rule are also affected by procedural provisions made by the Family Law Act 1986 itself. These are noted against the rule relating to each type of declaration where they are specific to that type but s 58(3)–(5) makes the following general provision:

> "(3) A court, on the dismissal of an application for a declaration under this Part, shall not have power to make any declaration for which an application has not been made.
>
> (4) No declaration which may be applied for under this Part may be made otherwise than under this Part by any court.
>
> (5) No declaration may be made by any court, whether under this Part or otherwise –
>
> (*a*) that a marriage was at its inception void;
> (*b*) (*repealed*)".

Proceedings may be heard in camera—FLA 1986, s 60(4) provides: "The court hearing an application under this Part may direct that the whole or any part of the proceedings shall be heard in camera, and an application for a direction under this subsection shall be heard in camera unless the court otherwise directs".

Attorney General's role—FLA 1986, s 59(1)–(3) provides as follows:

> "(1) On an application to a court for a declaration under this Part [ie any covered by r 3.16] the court may at any stage of the proceedings, of its own motion or on the application of any party to the proceedings, direct that all necessary papers in the matter be sent to the Attorney-General.
>
> (2) The Attorney-General, whether or not he is sent papers in relation to an application to a court for a declaration under this Part, may –

(*a*) intervene in the proceedings on that application in such manner as he thinks necessary or expedient, and

(*b*) argue before the court any question in relation to the application which the court considers it necessary to have fully argued.

(3) Where any costs are incurred by the Attorney-General in connection with any application to a court for a declaration under this Part, the court may make such order as it considers just as to the payment of those costs by parties to the proceedings."

There are two main reasons for these provisions. First, to minimise the risk of success of unopposed, or collusive, proceedings brought fraudulently to obtain a declaration. Section 58(2) provides that "Any declaration made under this Part shall be binding on Her Majesty and all other persons"; this creates scope for collusive proceedings to be brought for the purpose of obtaining some collateral result in relation to the state or other third parties, such as British citizenship. The role of the Attorney General is therefore not dissimilar to that which the Queen's Proctor may play in undefended divorce proceedings. Secondly, quite apart from this aspect, s 58(1) provides that "Where on an application to a court for a declaration under this Part the truth of the proposition to be declared is proved to the satisfaction of the court, the court shall make that declaration unless to do so would manifestly be contrary to public policy". The Attorney General may wish to express a view on the requirements of public policy in a particular case.

"shall be sent by the petitioner to the Attorney General" (r 3.16(4))—The chambers of the Attorney General are at 9, Buckingham Gate, London SW1E 6JP.

"within 21 days" (r 3.16(8), (9))—As to computation of time, see r 1.5.

PART III

3.17 Application for leave under section 13 of Act of 1984

(1) An application for leave to apply for an order for financial relief under Part III of the Act of 1984 shall be made ex parte by originating summons issued in Form M25 out of the principal registry and shall be supported by an affidavit by the applicant stating the facts relied on in support of the application with particular reference to the matters set out in section 16(2) of that Act.

(2) The affidavit in support shall give particulars of the judicial or other proceedings by means of which the marriage to which the application relates were dissolved or annulled or by which the parties to the marriage were legally separated and shall state, so far as is known to the applicant –

(*a*) the names of the parties to the marriage and the date and place of the marriage;

(*b*) the occupation and residence of each of the parties to the marriage;

(*c*) whether there are any living children of the family and, if so, the number of such children and the full names (including surname) of each and his date of birth or, if it be the case, that he is over 18;

(*d*) whether either party to the marriage has remarried;

(*e*) an estimate in summary form of the appropriate amount or value of the capital resources and net income of each party and of any minor child of the family;

(*f*) the grounds on which it is alleged that the court has jurisdiction to entertain an application for an order for financial relief under Part III of the Act of 1984.

(3) The proper officer shall fix a date, time and place for the hearing of the application by a judge in chambers and give notice thereof to the applicant.

Defined terms—"the Act of 1984", "principal registry", "proper officer": r 1.2(1).

Manner of application—The application is made ex parte, out of the principal registry only, in Form M25 supported by affidavit and it is heard by a judge and not a district judge.

"order for financial relief"—The orders for financial relief which may be made under MFPA 1984, Pt III comprise broadly the orders that may be made under Matrimonial Causes Act 1973, ss 23, 24 and 24B.

3.18 Application for order for financial relief or avoidance of transaction order under Part III of the Act of 1984

(1) An application for an order for financial relief under Part III of the Act of 1984 shall be made by originating summons issued in Form M26 out of the principal registry and at the same time the applicant, unless otherwise directed, shall file an affidavit in support of the summons giving full particulars of his property and income.

(2) The applicant shall serve a sealed copy of the originating summons on the respondent and shall annex thereto a copy of the affidavit in support, if one has been filed, and a notice of proceedings and acknowledgement of service in Form M28, and rule 10.8 shall apply to such an acknowledgement of service as if the references in paragraph (1) of that rule to Form M6 and in paragraph (2) of that rule to seven days were, respectively, references to Form M28 and 31 days.

(3) Rules 2.57, 2.59, 2.61, 2.62(5) and (6), 2.63 and 2.66(1) and (2) shall apply, with the necessary modifications, to an application for an order for financial relief under this rule as they apply to an application for ancillary relief made by notice in Form M11 and the court may order the attendance of any person for the purpose of being examined or cross-examined and the discovery and production of any document.

(4) An application for an interim order for maintenance under section 14 or an avoidance of transaction order under section 23 of the Act of 1984 may be made, unless the court otherwise directs, in the originating summons under paragraph (1) or by summons in accordance with rule 10.9(1) and an application for an order under section 23 shall be supported by an affidavit, which may be the affidavit filed under paragraph (1), stating the facts relied on.

(5) If the respondent intends to contest the application he shall, within 28 days after the time limited for giving notice to defend, file an affidavit in answer to the application setting out the grounds on which he relies and shall serve a copy on the applicant.

(6) In respect of any application for an avoidance of transaction order the court may give such a direction or make such appointment as it is empowered to give or make by paragraph (3) and rule 2.59 shall apply, with the necessary modifications, to an application for an avoidance of transaction order as it applies to an application for an avoidance of disposition order.

(7) Where the originating summons contains an application for an order under section 22 of the Act of 1984 the applicant shall serve a copy on the landlord of the dwelling house and he shall be entitled to be heard on the application.

(8) An application for an order for financial relief under Part III of the Act of 1984 or for an avoidance of transaction order shall be determined by a judge.

Defined terms—"the Act of 1984", "ancillary relief", "principal registry": r 1.2(1).

Manner of application (r 3.18(1), (2), (7))—Application must be made by originating summons in Form M26 issued out of the principal registry and supported by an affidavit disclosing means. As r 2.59 is applied to such applications, the affidavit must state whether the land is registered or unregistered, give its title number, and give details of any mortgagee or third party interest in the same way as for an application for ancillary relief after divorce proceedings in this country. If the application is to transfer a tenancy, the landlord must be served so that he can be heard. If the application is to set aside a transaction made with the intention of defeating the claim, the person to whom the property has been transferred must be identified and served.

General Note—The Family Proceedings (Amendment No 2) Rules 1999 have amended FPR 1991, rr 2.52–2.77 in respect of claims for ancillary relief started on or after 5 June 2000. The amended version of the rules is printed in this edition. A claim for financial relief after overseas proceedings is not a claim for ancillary relief. Family Proceedings (Amendment No 2) Rules 1999, r 20 provides that the unamended version of those rules applies to a claim for financial relief after overseas proceedings. The unamended version is printed in earlier editions of *The Family Court Practice*. See **non-ancillary relief** under r 2.51A.

Ancillary relief (r 3.18(3))—The following provisions (the text of which are printed in *The Family Court Practice 1999*) concerning ancillary relief apply:

(*a*) r 2.57 (separate representation for children; mandatory if a proposed variation of settlement is sought which will adversely affect their rights, otherwise discretionary);
(*b*) r 2.59 (service on mortgagees, the person in whose favour a disposition has been made etc);
(*c*) r 2.61 (consent applications);
(*d*) r 2.62(5) (district judge's power to give directions); and
(*e*) r 2.63 (request for information).

Although the judge or district judge may order the attendance of any person, including a third party to give evidence, there is no power to make a production order against any third party. Thus, where it is desired to obtain a document from a third party, a subpoena duces tecum with leave (if in the High Court) or a witness summons duces tecum without leave (if in the county court) must be issued (*Roker International Properties v Couvaras* [2000] 2 FLR 976).

Interim orders (r 3.18(4))—An application for an interim order is made either in the originating summons or by ordinary summons in the High Court or, in the county court, by notice of application in accordance with CCR Ord 13, r 1.

Respondent's affidavit (r 3.18(5))—The respondent must file an affidavit 28 days after the end of the period of 31 days which is allowed for the return of the acknowledgement of service under r 3.18(2).

"avoidance of transaction order" (r 3.18(6))—This is a reference to an order under MFPA 1984, s 23 to restrain or set aside a disposal made with the intention of defeating a claim where the applicant has obtained leave to make a claim for financial relief under Pt III of that Act.

"an application for an order under section 22 of the Act of 1984" (r 3.18(7))—This is an application under MFPA 1984, s 22 for an order transferring a tenancy (equivalent to an order under Matrimonial Homes Act 1983, Sch 1).

"determined by a judge" (r 3.18(8))—All hearings under MFPA 1984, Pt III are before a judge, but the effect of r 3.18(3), which applies inter alia r 2.62(5) to applications under Pt III, is that a district judge may give directions.

3.19 Application for order under section 24 of Act of 1984 preventing transaction

(1) An application under section 24 of the Act of 1984 for an order preventing a transaction shall be made by originating summons issued in Form M27 out of the principal registry and shall be supported by an affidavit by the applicant stating the facts relied on in support of the application.

(2) The applicant shall serve a sealed copy of the originating summons on the respondent and shall annex thereto a copy of the affidavit in support and a notice of proceedings and acknowledgement of service in Form M28 and rule 10.8 shall apply to such an acknowledgement of service as if the references in paragraph (1) of that rule to Form M6 and in paragraph (2) of that rule to seven days were, respectively, references to Form M28 and 31 days.

(3) If the respondent intends to contest the application he shall, within 28 days after the time limited for giving notice of intention to defend, file an affidavit in

answer to the application setting out the grounds on which he relies and shall serve a copy on the applicant.

(4) The application shall be determined by a judge.

(5) Rule 2.66 (except paragraph (3)) shall apply, with the necessary modifications, to the application as if it were an application for ancillary relief.

Defined terms—"the Act of 1984", "ancillary relief", "principal registry": r 1.2(1).

3.20 Consent to marriage of minor

(1) An application under section 3 of the Marriage Act 1949 (in this rule referred to as "section 3") for the consent of the court to the marriage of a minor shall be dealt with in chambers unless the court otherwise directs.

(2) The application may be heard and determined by a district judge.

(3) An application under section 3 may be brought without the intervention of the applicant's next friend, unless the court otherwise directs.

(4) Where an application under section 3 follows a refusal to give consent to the marriage every person who has refused consent shall be made a defendant to the summons or a respondent to the application, as appropriate.

(5) The application shall, unless the court orders otherwise, be served not less than seven days before the date upon which the application is to be heard.

Jurisdiction—Marriage Act 1949, s 3(1) sets out a general rule that children (ie those under the age of 18) who are not widows or widowers may not marry under a superintendent registrar's certificate, or a common licence (see s 3(3)), without the consent of the persons mentioned in s 3(1A). However, this is subject to two provisos. First, where consent cannot be obtained by reason of the absence, inaccessibility or disability of the only person whose consent is required, s 3(1)(*a*) allows the court, on application, to consent to the marriage. Secondly, s 3(1)(*b*) provides as follows: "if any person whose consent is required refuses his consent, the court may, on application being made, consent to the marriage, and the consent of the court so given shall have the same effect as if it had been given by the person whose consent is refused". Section 1(5) provides that, for the purposes of s 3, "the court" means the High Court, the county court of the district in which any applicant or respondent resides or a court of summary jurisdiction appointed for the commission area in which any applicant or respondent resides. For the procedure on such an application in a magistrates' court see the Magistrates' Courts (Guardianship of Minors) Rules 1974. Section 3(6) provides that "Nothing in this section shall dispense with the necessity of obtaining the consent of the High Court to the marriage of a ward of court". The practical effect of this is to require an application which relates to a ward of court to be made to the High Court or to any county court to which the wardship proceedings have been transferred under Matrimonial and Family Proceedings Act 1984, s 38(2)(*b*). Strictly, the consent under Marriage Act 1949, s 3(1)(*b*) is in addition to the common law requirement of the court's consent to the marriage of its ward and a problem may therefore arise if for some reason the county court in which the wardship proceedings are pending is not in a county court district in which the applicant or respondent resides. In those circumstances it would seem that, technically at any rate, two applications must be made to different county courts: one for wardship consent and one for the statutory consent.

Procedure generally—In the High Court, the application is required by RSC Ord 5, r 3 to be made by originating summons and those provisions of the RSC relating to proceedings begun by that method will apply subject to the specific provision of r 3.20 and the rest of these rules (eg FPR 1991, Pt X). In a county court, the application is required by CCR Ord 3, r 4 to be made by originating application (it is not an action to be commenced by plaint under Ord 3, r 1 because it does not seek relief against the respondents nor does it seek to compel them to consent); the provisions of the CCR relating to proceedings on an originating application will apply subject to these rules.

"unless the court otherwise directs" (r 3.20(1))—An application for such a direction may be made at the start of the hearing; if a party wishes the question to be determined in advance, the procedure directed by r 10.9 should be followed.

"without the intervention of the applicant's next friend" (r 3.20(3))—This is an exception to the general rule that children must bring proceedings through a next friend (see r 9.2(1)) and is no doubt made because those who would, in general civil proceedings, be most likely to undertake the role of next friend are likely to be those who are withholding their consent. The court retains a discretion to require a next friend to be used.

"every person who has refused consent" (r 3.20(4))—This refers to those whose consent is required under Marriage Act 1949, s 3(1A). The description of the relevant persons varies according to the circumstances (eg the existence of various types of order under CA 1989), and the requirements are set out in MA 1949, s 3(1A).

"defendant to the summons or a respondent to the application" (r 3.20(4))—The former is appropriate in the High Court, the latter in a county court (see **Procedure generally** above).

"application" (r 3.20(5))—In r 3.20(5), "application" means originating summons or originating application as the case may be.

"served not less than seven days before" (r 3.20(5))—Service is governed by rr 10.2 and 10.3. As to computation of time, see r 1.5.

3.21 Application under section 27 of the Act of 1991 for declaration of parentage

(1) Rule 4.6 shall apply to an application under section 55A of the Act of 1986 (declarations of parentage) as it applies to an application under the Act of 1989.

(2) Where an application under section 55A of the Act of 1986 has been transferred to the High Court or a county court the court shall, as soon as practicable after a transfer has occurred, consider what directions to give for the conduct of the proceedings.

(3) Without prejudice to the generality of paragraph (2), the court may, in particular, direct that –

(*a*) the proceedings shall proceed as if they had been commenced by originating summons or originating application;

(*b*) any document served or other thing done while the proceedings were pending in another court, including a magistrates' court, shall be treated for such purposes as may be specified in the direction as if it had been such document or other thing, being a document or other thing provided for by the rules of court applicable in the court to which the proceedings have been transferred, as may be specified in the direction and had been served or done pursuant to any such rule;

(*c*) a pre-trial hearing shall be held to determine what further directions, if any, should be given.

(4) The application may be heard and determined by a district judge.

Amendments—Inserted by SI 1993/295; amended by SI 2001/821.

Defined terms—"the Act of 1989", "court", "district judge": r 1.2(1).

Allocation of proceedings under CSA 1991, s 27—Children (Allocation of Proceedings) Order 1991, art 3 provides for applications for declaration of parentage to be issued in the magistrates' court (art 3(1)(*s*)); see also Family Proceedings Courts (Child Support Act 1991) Rules 1993. C(AP)O 1991, art 7(1) provides for the transfer of any proceedings in art 3(1) to a county court in the circumstances there described.

"Rule 4.6 shall apply" (r 3.21)—FPR 1991, r 4.6 deals with procedure where proceedings are transferred to a county court by the magistrates' court, or transferred back to the magistrates' court by a county court.

"consider what directions to give" (r 3.21(2))—A duty is placed on the court to give directions. There is no duty to fix a date for a directions appointment (cf r 4.4(2)(*a*) on commencement of a CA 1989 application), as r 3.21(3)(*a*) specifically leaves the fixing of a pre-trial review to the court's discretion.

"commenced by originating summons or originating application" (r 3.21(3)(*a*))—The application is started in the magistrates' court by application under Family Proceedings Courts (Child Support Act 1991) Rules 1993, r 3 (in accordance with procedures under Family Proceedings Courts (Matrimonial Proceedings etc) Rules 1991, rr 2–16), and is thus framed in terms appropriate to the magistrates' court. The effect of directing that the application proceed as an originating summons in the High Court or originating application in the county courts will ensure that the transferred application proceeds in accordance with a set of rules appropriate to the court to which it is transferred, ie RSC Ord 7 in the High Court and CCR Ord 3, r 4 in the county courts.

Directions for scientific tests—Probably the most common direction to be sought under this rule will be for scientific tests, provided for under Family Law Reform Act 1969, s 20. Either party may apply for such a direction.

Appeals from district judge's decisions—The assignment of all proceedings under the Child Support Act 1991 to the Family Division by High Court (Distribution of Business) Order 1993, art 2 makes applications for declaration of parentage under CSA 1991, s 27 "family proceedings" within the terms of FPR 1991, and thus appeals from the district judge are governed by RSC Ord 58 in the High Court and FPR 1991, r 8.1 in the county court.

3.22 Appeal under section 20 of Act of 1991

(1) Rule 4.6 shall apply to an appeal under section 20 of the Act of 1991 (appeals to appeal tribunals) as it applies to an application under the Act of 1989.

(2) Where an appeal under section 20 of the Act of 1991 is transferred to the High Court or a county court, Rule 3.21(2) and (3) shall apply to the appeal as it applies to an application under section 55A of the Act of 1986.

Amendments—Inserted by SI 1993/295; amended by SI 2001/821.

Defined terms—"the Act of 1991", "the Act of 1989": r 1.2(1).

Scope of provision—This rule, with rr 3.21 and 3.23, was added following the coming into operation of the Child Support Act 1991 to set up a procedure for appeals which relate to issues of parentage following assessment by the child support officer and where these appeals are transferred to the High Court or a county court. The rule adopts the provisions of r 3.21, but is silent as to whether a district judge may hear the application (cf r 3.21(4)).

"an appeal under s 20 of the Act of 1991"—CSA 1991, s 20 provides for appeals under the Act to go to the child support appeal tribunal, except for appeals on the issue of parentage which, by virtue of Child Support Appeals (Jurisdiction of Courts) Order 2002, must go to a civil court which, in the first instance, will be the magistrates' court (Children (Allocation of Proceedings) Order 1991, art 3(1)(*t*)).

Extent of use of the provision—Child Support Act 1991, s 26 provides that, where a parent denies parentage in his response to an application under the Act, the calculation is prevented from proceeding unless there has already been what amounts to a finding of paternity or the child has been adopted. In the absence of such a finding, there must be an application under s 27 for a declaration of parentage and, until that is resolved, the calculation cannot proceed. An appeal under s 20 on the issue of parentage can only arise where this issue is contested following the calculation. Consequently, given the provisions of s 26, it is difficult to envisage circumstances in which there could ever be an appeal under s 20 which relates to parentage.

Allocation of, and procedure on, appeal—In the event that an appeal under this section should proceed through the courts, allocation of the application and procedure on its transfer is identical to that set out in FPR 1991, r 3.21, except that the appeal cannot apparently be heard by a district judge.

"Rule 4.6 shall apply" (r 3.22(1))—FPR 1991, r 4.6 deals with procedure where proceedings are transferred to a county court by the magistrates' court, or transferred back to the magistrates' court by a county court.

3.23 Appeal from Child Support Commissioner

(1) This rule shall apply to any appeal to the Court of Appeal under section 25 of the Act of 1991 (appeal from Child Support Commissioner on question of law).

(2) Where leave to appeal is granted by the Commissioner, the notice of appeal must be served within 6 weeks from the date on which notice of the grant was given in writing to the appellant.

(3) Where leave to appeal is granted by the Court of Appeal upon an application made within 6 weeks of the date on which notice of the Commissioner's refusal of leave to appeal was given in writing to the appellant, the notice of appeal must be served –

(*a*) before the end of the said period of 6 weeks; or
(*b*) within 7 days after the date on which leave is granted,

whichever is the later, or within such other period as the Court of Appeal may direct.

Amendments—Inserted by SI 1993/295.

Defined terms—"the Act of 1991": r 1.2(1).

"section 25 of the Act of 1991" (r 3.23(1))—CSA 1991, s 25 provides for appeals from the Child Support Commissioner with leave and on a point of law. In the first instance, the application for leave is to the Child Support Commissioner (s 25(2)(*a*)) or, failing that, to the Court of Appeal (s 25(2)(*b*), (4)). The Child Support Commissioners (Procedure) Regulations 1992, reg 25 sets out the procedure for obtaining leave from the Child Support Commissioner.

Procedure on appeal—Procedure on appeal to the Court of Appeal is governed by CPR 1998, Pt 52.

PART IV
PROCEEDINGS UNDER THE CHILDREN ACT 1989

4.1 Interpretation and application

(1) In this Part of these rules, unless a contrary intention appears –

a section or schedule referred to means the section or schedule so numbered in the Act of 1989;
"a section 8 order" has the meaning assigned to it by section 8(2);
"application" means an application made under or by virtue of the Act of 1989 or under these rules, and "applicant" shall be construed accordingly;
"child", in relation to proceedings to which this Part applies –

(*a*) means, subject to sub-paragraph (*b*), a person under the age of 18 with respect to whom the proceedings are brought, and
(*b*) where the proceedings are under Schedule 1, also includes a person who has reached the age of 18;

"children and family reporter" means an officer of the service who has been asked to prepare a welfare report under section 7(1)(*a*);

"children's guardian" –

(*a*) means an officer of the service appointed under section 41 for the child with respect to whom the proceedings are brought; but

(*b*) does not include such an officer appointed in relation to proceedings specified by Part IVA;

"directions appointment" means a hearing for directions under rule 4.14(2);

"emergency protection order" means an order under section 44;

"leave" includes permission and approval;

"note" includes a record made by mechanical means;

"parental responsibility" has the meaning assigned to it by section 3;

"recovery order" means an order under section 50;

"specified proceedings" has the meaning assigned to it by section 41(6) and rule 4.2(2); and

"welfare officer" means a person who has been asked to prepare a welfare report under section 7(1)(*b*).

(2) Except where the contrary intention appears, the provisions of this Part apply to proceedings in the High Court and the county courts –

(*a*) on an application for a section 8 order;

(*b*) on an application for a care order or a supervision order;

(*c*) on an application under section 4(1)(*a*), 4(3), 5(1), 6(7), 13(1), 16(6), 33(7), 34(2), 34(3), 34(4), 34(9), 36(1), 38(8)(*b*), 39(1), 39(2), 39(3), 39(4), 43(1), 43(12), 44, 45, 46(7), 48(9), 50(1) or 102(1);

(*d*) under Schedule 1, except where financial relief is also sought by or on behalf of an adult;

(*e*) on an application under paragraph 19(1) of Schedule 2;

(*f*) on an application under paragraph 6(3), 15(2) or 17(1) of Schedule 3;

(*g*) on an application under paragraph 11(3) or 16(5) of Schedule 14; or

(*h*) under section 25.

Amendments—SI 1991/2113; SI 2001/821.

4.2 Matters prescribed for the purposes of the Act of 1989

(1) The parties to proceedings in which directions are given under section 38(6), and any person named in such a direction, form the prescribed class for the purposes of section 38(8) (application to vary directions made with interim care or interim supervision order).

(2) The following proceedings are specified for the purposes of section 41 in accordance with subsection (6)(i) thereof –

(*a*) proceedings under section 25;

(*b*) applications under section 33(7);

(*c*) proceedings under paragraph 19(1) of Schedule 2;

(*d*) applications under paragraph 6(3) of Schedule 3;

(*e*) appeals against the determination of proceedings of a kind set out in sub-paragraphs (*a*) to (*d*).

(3) The applicant for an order that has been made under section 43(1) and the persons referred to in section 43(11) may, in any circumstances, apply under section 43(12) for a child assessment order to be varied or discharged.

(4) The following persons form the prescribed class for the purposes of section 44(9) (application to vary directions) –

(*a*) the parties to the application for the order in respect of which it is sought to vary the directions;
(*b*) the children's guardian;
(*c*) the local authority in whose area the child concerned is ordinarily resident;
(*d*) any person who is named in the directions.

Amendments—SI 1991/2113; SI 2001/821.

Defined terms—"applicant", "application", "children's guardian": r 4.1(1).

Parties to proceedings in which s 38(6) directions are given (r 4.2(1))—The parties are the applicant and the respondents as listed in App 3, subject to any directions as to parties made by the court under r 4.7.

"section 38(6)" (r 4.2(1))—CA 1989, s 38(6) empowers the court to make directions regarding medical or psychiatric examination or other assessment of a child where it makes an interim care or supervision order.

"section 38(8)" (r 4.2(1))—CA 1989, s 38(8) empowers the court to vary a direction made under s 38(6) on the application of a person within any class prescribed by rules of court. Rule 4.2(1) is the only such rule of court which applies in county courts and the High Court.

"section 41" (r 4.2(2))—CA 1989, s 41 imposes a duty on the court in any "specified proceedings" to appoint a children's guardian for the child concerned, unless it is satisfied that it is not necessary to do so to safeguard his interests. Section 41(6) specifies many of the proceedings in which this duty arises and s 41(6)(*i*) provides for rules of court to specify further proceedings. Rule 4.2(2) is the only rule of court which so specifies for the purposes of proceedings in county courts and the High Court.

"proceedings under section 25" (r 4.2(2)(*a*))—These are proceedings concerning the use of secure accommodation to restrict the liberty of a child.

"applications under section 33(7)" (r 4.2(2)(*b*))—Application may be made under CA 1989, s 33(7) for leave to change the surname of a child in respect of whom a care order is in force (see eg *Re J (A Minor) (Change of Name)* [1993] 1 FLR 699), as may an application for leave to remove a child in care from the jurisdiction.

"proceedings under paragraph 19(1) of Schedule 2" (r 4.2(2)(*c*))—These are proceedings by a local authority for the court's approval of arrangements for a child in its care to live outside England and Wales.

"applications under paragraph 6(3) of Schedule 3" (r 4.2(2)(*d*))—Application may be made under CA 1989, Sch 3, para 6(3) by a supervisor who seeks to have the period of a supervision order extended.

"section 43(1)" (r 4.2(3))—Under CA 1989, s 43(1), an application may be made for a child assessment order.

"the persons referred to in section 43(11)" (r 4.2(3))—CA 1989, s 43(11) sets out certain people who must normally be given notice of an application for a child assessment order (including the child's parents and anyone else with parental responsibility). The same group of people (and the original applicant for the order) are allowed, by virtue of r 4.2(3) to apply for the order to be varied or discharged.

"the prescribed class for the purposes of section 44(9)" (r 4.2(4))—CA 1989, s 44 enables the court to make emergency protection orders and, where it does so, it may, under s 44(6), give directions as to the medical, psychiatric or other assessment of the child or contact with him. Section 44(9) provides that such directions can be varied at any time on the application of a person falling within any class of person prescribed by rules of court; r 4.2(4) is the only rule which prescribes such a class for the purposes of county courts and the High Court.

"the parties to the application" (r 4.2(4)(*a*))—All that the rather convoluted form of words in r 4.2(4)(*a*) means is that, where there has been an emergency protection order and ancillary directions for medical, psychiatric or other assessment, the parties to the emergency protection application may apply to vary the ancillary directions.

"children's guardian" (r 4.2(4)(*b*))—Proceedings under CA 1989, s 44 are specified proceedings for the purposes of s 41, with the result that a children's guardian will normally have been appointed for the child.

"ordinarily resident" (r 4.2(4)(*c*))—This term is not defined in the rules, but the concept appears a number of times in CA 1989, and reference should be made to the annotations under s 31 of that Act, and to s 105(6).

"any person who is named in the directions" (r 4.2(4)(*d*))—The directions referred to are the assessment directions made under s 44(6) (see **"the prescribed class for the purposes of section 44(9)"** above).

4.3 Application for leave to commence proceedings

(1) Where the leave of the court is required to bring any proceedings to which this Part applies, the person seeking leave shall file –

(*a*) a written request for leave in Form C2 setting out the reasons for the application; and

(*b*) a draft of the application (being the documents referred to in rule 4.4(1A)) for the making of which leave is sought together with sufficient copies for one to be served on each respondent.

(2) On considering a request for leave filed under paragraph (1), the court shall –

(*a*) grant the request, whereupon the proper officer shall inform the person making the request of the decision, or

(*b*) direct that a date be fixed for the hearing of the request, whereupon the proper officer shall fix such a date and give such notice as the court directs to the person making the request and such other persons as the court requires to be notified, of the date so fixed.

(3) Where leave is granted to bring proceedings to which this Part applies the application shall proceed in accordance with rule 4.4; but paragraph (1)(*a*) of that rule shall not apply.

(4) In the case of a request for leave to bring proceedings under Schedule 1, the draft application under paragraph (1) shall be accompanied by a statement setting out the financial details which the person seeking leave believes to be relevant to the request and containing a declaration that it is true to the maker's best knowledge and belief, together with sufficient copies for one to be served on each respondent.

Amendments—SI 1994/3155.

Defined terms—"application": r 4.1(1); "court": r 1.2(1); "leave": r 4.1(1); "proper officer": r 1.2(1).

Court to which the leave request should be made—Generally, the leave request is made to the court that will entertain the proceedings if leave is granted. An application by a child for leave to apply for s 8 orders (contact, prohibited steps, residence and specific issue orders) where he is to be the subject of the proposed application raises issues that are more appropriate for determination in the High Court and should be transferred there for hearing (*Practice Direction of 22 February 1993*; *Re AD (A Minor)* [1993] 1 FCR 573). As to the appropriate court for leave applications by natural parents of adopted children, see *Re T (Adopted Children: Contact)* [1995] 2 FLR 792, CA, under **Procedure on application for leave being filed**.

"proceedings to which this Part applies" (r 4.3(1))—Part IV applies to the proceedings listed in r 4.1(2).

"written request for leave" (r 4.3(1)(*a*))—The written request for leave should be made in Form C2 (see App 1 to these rules), which requires the full names of the child concerned. The applicant must provide detailed information identifying himself and his relationship to the child; the nature of the orders for which he is applying in relation to each child; the full names and addresses of all respondents to be served with the application; a brief outline of his reasons for applying for leave; and a brief description of any plans he has for the child. Care should be taken to cover any factors which are especially relevant to the instant case (for example, in the case of an application under CA 1989, s 4(3), the child's understanding). If the applicant is applying for an order under CA 1989, s 8, he must not, without leave of the court, make a full statement at this point in the proceedings, although he may be required to do so at a later stage (see prohibition contained in r 4.17(4)).

Where no written request is filed—In *Re O (Minors) (Leave to Seek Residence Order)* [1994] 1 FLR 172, leave to apply for a residence order was granted ex parte by the family proceedings court, despite the fact that the applicant for leave had not filed a written request for leave. Ewbank J was of the view that the absence of a written request did not automatically invalidate the interim residence order which the magistrates went on to make and, in a matter of emergency, it was wrong to think that a court must be constrained by rules demanding that bits of paper must be issued. However, he did reduce the period of the interim order from one month to 11 days.

"draft of the application (being the documents referred to in rule 4.4(1A))" (r 4.3(1)(*b*))—Rule 4.4 deals with the procedure for making substantive applications. The documents referred to in r 4.4(1A) are (i) whichever is appropriate of Forms C1 to C4 or C51, and (ii) such of the supplemental Forms C10 and C11 to C20 as may be appropriate. Where there is no appropriate form, the application should be made in writing (r 4.4(1A)(*b*)). Where the application is made in respect of more than one child of the family, all the children should be included on one application (r 4.4(1A)).

"respondents" (r 4.3(1)(*b*))—The reference to respondents is, of course, a reference to those who will be respondents to the proceedings if leave is given; there are no prescribed respondents to the request for leave.

Procedure on application for leave being filed (r 4.3(2), (3))—There is no power to *refuse* leave on the papers; if the court is not convinced of the merits of the written request, it has no choice but to direct a hearing. There is power to *grant* leave on the papers or on an ex parte application, but it is clear that this will rarely be appropriate. The discretion whether or not to direct a hearing must be exercised judicially and, except in cases of emergency, the interests of justice require that notice be given to parties likely to be affected (*Re M (Prohibited Steps Order: Application for Leave)* [1993] 1 FLR 275; *Re SC (A Minor) (Leave to Seek Residence Order)* [1994] 1 FLR 96; *Re W (Minor) (Contact Application: Procedure)* [1999] Fam Law 853; see also *Nottinghamshire County Council v P* [1993] 2 FLR 134 to the effect that it is inappropriate for a local authority to apply ex parte for leave to issue an application for a prohibited steps order). Often, potential respondents to the main application will be obvious candidates to receive such notice. However, the following particular situations may arise:

(*a*) *Application for leave by a child* – generally desirable for everyone with parental responsibility to be given notice (*Re SC (A Minor) (Leave to Seek Residence Order)* (above))

(*b*) *Application for leave by a natural parent or sibling of an adopted child* – the procedure should be designed to ensure that adoptive parents are not unnecessarily disturbed by such applications for contact and that the judge hearing the application has as much relevant information as possible. It will normally be appropriate for the court to direct that the adoption agency (often a local authority) should in the first instance be given notice of the application for leave. The application for leave should not be treated as if it were the substantive application, and thus the local authority should not be given the opportunity of becoming a party to the application so as to have the same right of appeal as the applicant. Nor should the Official Solicitor necessarily be brought in as a respondent to the application for leave; in some cases, it may be necessary to transfer the application to the High Court and bring in the Official Solicitor, but that should not be the general rule (*Re T (Adopted Children: Contact)* [1995] 2 FLR 792, CA, disagreeing with *Re C (A Minor) (Adopted Child: Contact)* [1993] Fam 210, [1993] 2 FLR 431, FD). In *Re S (Contact: Application by Sibling)* [1998] 2 FLR 897, FD Charles J contemplates (p 913) that there may be two stages to the leave application where an adopted child is concerned. At the first stage, the applicant for leave would have to establish that there was a good arguable case for court intervention. The adopters would then normally be given an opportunity to respond to the evidence the applicant had adduced on the leave application before the court resolved whether or not to grant leave. This is in line with the directions actually given by the Court of Appeal in *Re T* (above) (case remitted to the county court with the adopters having a fixed period to provide their reasons for failing to give the progress report they had promised; if reasons were given, the leave application was to be considered in the light of them, if not, leave was to be granted).

Where notice is to be given to persons other than the applicant, due regard should be had, in fixing the hearing date, to the fact that they may well need to seek legal advice.

Sometimes, argument may be all that is required at the hearing (*Re W (Contact: Application by Grandparent)* [1997] 1 FLR 793, FD suggests that applications for leave are almost always applications on the papers and without the benefit of a court welfare report) but there may be occasions when it is appropriate to seek a court welfare report under s 7 and sometimes there may be factual issues that require determination (eg the level of understanding of the child on an application under CA 1989, s 4(3)) and oral evidence may have to be called, which may include cross-examination as in *Re A (A Minor) (Residence Order: Leave to Apply)* [1993] 1 FLR 425. If interpreted literally, the rules themselves may give little guidance as to the procedure at the leave hearing because it appears that the bulk of them may not apply at all to a request for leave. A clear distinction is made in r 4.3 between the *request* for leave and the *application* for which leave is sought, and it would seem to follow that, strictly speaking, rules dealing with applications (for example rr 4.4 and 4.5) cannot therefore apply to the request for leave. Rules referring to *proceedings* (such as rr 4.14, 4.17 and 4.21(2)) are equally inapplicable given that no proceedings can be brought in a leave case until after leave has been granted, as are rules making reference to *parties* as there can be no parties until proceedings have been launched. However, it appears from Form C2 (which refers throughout to a r 4.3 request as an "application") that the distinction between the request and the application may, in fact, be a distinction without a difference, and that a r 4.3 request is appropriately classed as an application. In default of other guidance, the court can, of course, regulate its own procedure (see, for example, *Re W (Secure Accommodation Order: Attendance at Court)* [1994] 2 FLR 1092).

If the court grants leave, the draft application will stand as the application, and the applicant may proceed to service in accordance with r 4.4(1)(*b*), as r 4.3(3) provides.

Request for leave to bring proceedings under Schedule 1 (r 4.3(4))—CA 1989, Sch 1 contains provisions with regard to financial provision for children. Rule 4.3(4) applies to applications for permission under para 7(2) and leave under para 11(3) (which deal with certain applications after the death of a parent).

Representation of the child on application for leave—A request for leave does not fall within the meaning of "specified proceedings" for the purposes of CA 1989, s 41(6) so there is no presumption that a children's guardian will be appointed.

Appeal against grant of leave—In relation to the possibility of an appeal by a person or body who was not a party to the original leave application, see *Re M (Prohibited Steps Order) (Application for Leave)* [1993] 1 FLR 275.

4.4 Application

(1) Subject to paragraph (4), an applicant shall –

(*a*) file the documents referred to in paragraph (1A) below (which documents shall together be called the "application") together with sufficient copies for one to be served on each respondent, and

(*b*) serve a copy of the application together with Form C6 and such (if any) of Forms C7 and C10A as are given to him by the proper officer under paragraph (2)(*b*) on each respondent such number of days prior to the date fixed under paragraph (2)(*a*) as is specified for that application in column (ii) of Appendix 3 to these rules.

(1A) The documents to be filed under paragraph (1)(*a*) above are –

(*a*) (i) whichever is appropriate of Forms C1 to C4 or C51, and

(ii) such of the supplemental Forms C10 or C11 to C20 as may be appropriate, or

(*b*) where there is no appropriate form a statement in writing of the order sought,

and where the application is made in respect of more than one child, all the children shall be included in one application.

(2) On receipt of the documents filed under paragraph (1)(*a*) the proper officer shall –

(*a*) fix the date for a hearing or a directions appointment, allowing sufficient time for the applicant to comply with paragraph (1)(*b*),

(*b*) endorse the date so fixed upon Form C6 and, where appropriate, Form C6A, and

(*c*) return forthwith to the applicant the copies of the application and Form C10A if filed with it, together with Form C6 and such of Forms C6A and C7 as are appropriate.

(3) The applicant shall, at the same time as complying with paragraph (1)(*b*), serve Form C6A on the persons set out for the relevant class of proceedings in column (iv) of Appendix 3 to these rules.

(4) An application for –

(*a*) a section 8 order,

(*b*) an emergency protection order,

(*c*) a warrant under section 48(9),

(*d*) a recovery order, or

(*e*) a warrant under section 102(1)

may be made ex parte in which case the applicant shall –

(i) file the application in the appropriate form in Appendix 1 to these rules –

(*a*) where the application is made by telephone, within 24 hours after the making of the application, or

(*b*) in any other case, at the time when the application is made, and

(ii) in the case of an application for a section 8 order or an emergency protection order, serve a copy of the application on each respondent within 48 hours after the making of the order.

(5) Where the court refuses to make an order on an ex parte application it may direct that the application be made inter partes.

(6) In the case of proceedings under Schedule 1, the application under paragraph (1) shall be accompanied by a statement in Form C10A setting out the financial details which the applicant believes to be relevant to the application, together with sufficient copies for one to be served on each respondent.

Amendments—SI 1991/2113; SI 1992/2067; SI 1994/3155.

Defined terms—"applicant", "application": r 4.1(1); "child", "court": r 1.2(1); "directions appointment", "emergency protection order": r 4.1(1); "prohibited steps order": CA 1989, s 8(1); "proper officer": r 1.2(1); "section 8 order": CA 1989, s 8(2); "specific issue order": CA 1989, s 8(1).

Procedure where a matrimonial cause or an application under Matrimonial Causes Act 1973, s 19 is pending—Rule 2.40(1) provides that, where a matrimonial cause or an application under MCA 1973, s 19 is pending, an application by a party to the cause or by any other person for an order under CA 1989, Pt I or II in relation to a child of the family has to be made in the cause. By virtue of r 2.40(3), a cause is treated as pending for the purposes of r 2.40 for one year after the last hearing or judicial intervention in the cause and r 1.2(2) (which provides that unless the context otherwise requires, a cause begun by petition is treated as pending for the purposes of the rules notwithstanding that a final decree or order has been made on the petition) does not apply. By virtue of r 2.40(2), if, while a cause is pending, proceedings are begun otherwise than in the pending cause (as, for example, where care proceedings are brought with regard to a child of the family), a concise statement of the nature of the proceedings must be filed forthwith by the person beginning the proceedings or, if he is not a party to the cause, by the petitioner.

"the application" (r 4.4(1), (1A))—Rule 4.4(1A) sets out the prescribed forms to be used in relation to substantive applications. Forms C1 to C5 and C51 are the main application forms. Form C1 is simply headed "Application for an order" and should generally be used if none of the more specific forms (ie C2 to C5 and C51) is appropriate. Form C2 is to be used for an application for leave to commence proceedings, an application for an order or directions in existing family proceedings and an application to be joined as, or cease to be, a party in existing family proceedings. Form C3 is for an application for an order authorising search for, taking charge of, and delivery of a child. Form C4 is for an application for an order for disclosure of a child's whereabouts. Form C5 is for an application concerning the registration of a child-minder or provider of day care. Form C51 is for an application for a parental order. If all the forms are inappropriate, the application simply has to be in writing (r 4.4(1A)(*b*), and FPC(CA 1989)R 1991, r 4(1A)(*b*)), but care must be taken to include all the relevant information.

The main application form has to be accompanied by a supplemental form in accordance with r 4.4(1A)(*a*)(ii) (and FPC(CA 1989)R 1991, r 4(1A)(*a*)(ii)) if any of the supplemental forms is appropriate to the case. In certain situations, notably applications for private law orders under CA 1989, s 8, no supplemental form exists. Forms C10 and C11 to C20 cater for applications for; financial provision for a child (C10); emergency protection orders (C11); warrants to assist a person authorised by an emergency protection order (C12); a care or supervision order (C13); authority to refuse contact to a child in care (C14); contact with a child in care (C15); a child assessment order (C16); an education supervision order (C17); an extension of an education supervision order (C17A); a recovery order (C18); a warrant of assistance (C19); an order to hold a child in secure accommodation (C20).

Copies of the prescribed forms may be purchased from HMSO, Jordans etc.

When drafting the application, as much relevant material as possible should be included in response to the prompts on the form, subject always to the particular restrictions on giving a full statement where the application is for a s 8 order (see r 4.17(4), and FPC(CA 1989)R 1991, r 17(4)). Where the applicant is not in possession of all the information required, this fact should be stated rather than leaving part of the form blank.

Where there is more than one child (r 4.4(1A))—Where the application is made in respect of more than one child of the family, all the children should be included in one application.

Withdrawal of application—Once the application has been filed, it cannot be withdrawn without leave of the court (r 4.5).

Written statements of evidence—Normally, no written evidence is filed with the application form; it will be filed at a later stage in accordance with the directions of the court or, in the absence of directions, before the hearing or appointment (r 4.17). However, Form C5 and a number of the supplemental forms specifically request that, if the applicant is relying on a report or other documentary evidence, a copy should be enclosed with the form.

Addresses—Certain addresses are generally required on the application form (including the applicant's and the child's). Where an applicant is unwilling to give an address (for example because of fear of violence from one of the respondents), r 10.21 provides that the address can be given to the court separately on the prescribed form.

Sufficient time for the applicant to comply with r 4.4(1)(b)—The date of the hearing or directions appointment should be fixed by reference to the minimum notice periods set out in App 3. If unusual difficulty is anticipated in serving the respondent(s), this should be drawn to the attention of the proper officer when the court documents are filed so that extra time can be allowed.

Service (r 4.4(1)(*b*))—The applicant, and not the court, is responsible for service of the application. As to service generally, see rr 4.8, 10.2, 10.3 and 10.6.

Application forms (r 4.4(1A)(*a*)(i), (ii))—See under **"the application"** above.

Forms C6, C6A, C7 and C10A (r 4.4(2)(*b*), (*c*))—Form C6 gives notice of the proceedings to persons who are parties to them, and a copy of the application will accompany the notice. The notice itself contains information to assist the recipient to take the next step in the proceedings. If Form C7 (acknowledgement) is enclosed with Form C6, the recipient must fill it in and return it to the court, and serve a copy on the other parties. If the applicant has asked the court to order the recipient of Form C6 to make a payment for a child, the recipient must also fill in a statement of his financial means (Form C10A). Form C6A gives notice of the proceedings to persons who are non-parties.

"serve Form C6A on the persons ... in column (iv) of Appendix 3" (r 4.4(3))—Column (iv) of App 3 to these rules sets out those persons who must be served with notice of the proceedings, but who are not parties. Form C6A gives notice to persons who are non-parties of the existence of the proceedings; it sets out the date and venue of the first hearing or appointment, but does not usually contain a copy of the application. There are cases in which it is inappropriate to divulge by way of notice any more than the bare minimum information required. If the recipient of the notice wishes to become a party to the proceedings, he must first apply to the court for leave in Form C2 and follow the procedure in r 4.7(2). Only if his request is granted will he be entitled to the full documentation. As to the method of giving notice, see r 10.7. As to the filing in Form C9 of a statement of service of the notice, see r 4.8(7)(*b*). Where a party wishes to seek a direction that a person should not be served with the proceedings (where otherwise there is a duty to serve him according to App 3), the party concerned should apply to the court under r 4.8(8) (*Re X (Care: Notice of Proceedings)* [1996] 1 FLR 186).

Power to make ex parte orders (r 4.4(4))—This provision has been amended to add s 8 orders to the list of orders that can be made ex parte. It is interesting that it was felt necessary to make this amendment as it had been held in *Re B (A Minor) (Residence Order: Ex Parte)* [1992] 2 FLR 1, CA that an ex parte residence order could be granted notwithstanding that it was not, at that time, within the list in r 4.4(4). Despite the express wording of r 4.4(4), a question has been raised in *Re O (A Minor) (Medical Treatment)* [1993] 2 FLR 149 as to whether a specific issue order may be made ex parte. In that case, the judge accepted the joint submission of counsel that an "issue" cannot effectively be "determined" ex parte, but the matter cannot be regarded as finally decided and, in *Re R (A Minor) (Blood Transfusion)* [1993] 2 FLR 757, Booth J said that she would be very surprised if the words of the statute had to be interpreted so narrowly as to deny the court power to give such relief where it was otherwise justified and the circumstances compelled an ex parte hearing.

The signs are that the courts are not construing the r 4.4(4) list as exhaustive (see *Re J (A Minor) (Change of Name)* [1993] 1 FLR 699 in which an ex parte application for leave to change the name of a child in care was granted). However, it is clear that ex parte orders will not be granted readily, see eg *Re G (Minors) (Ex Parte Interim Residence Order)* [1993] 1 FLR 910; *Re P (A Minor) (Ex Parte Interim Residence Order)* [1993] 1 FLR 915; *M v C (Children Orders: Reasons)* [1993] 2 FLR 584 (all with regard to the limited circumstances in which an interim residence order should be made ex parte); *R v St Albans Magistrates' Court ex parte J* [1993] Fam Law 518 (CA 1989, s 75 application to cancel registration as childminder not normally to be dealt with ex parte); *Re R (A Minor) (Blood Transfusion)* [1993] 2 FLR 757 (on application for authority to give a blood transfusion, strenuous efforts should be made to arrange an inter partes hearing). In *Re B (Minors) (Care: Procedure)* [1994] Fam Law 72, Bracewell J held that a court should only allow ex parte applications for adjournment of proceedings for reduction of contact in exceptional circumstances; if a hearing was to take place without the parents being present, their legal representatives should be permitted access, subject to undertakings or directions not to pass the information to their clients. Except in exceptional circumstances, it is highly undesirable that an ex parte order should be allowed to stand for more than 7 days; a 12-week ex parte residence order in favour of a grandmother was plainly wrong (*Re Y (A Minor) (Ex Parte Interim Orders)* [1994] Fam Law 127). In *Note: Re J (Children: Ex Parte Orders)* [1997] 1 FLR 606, Hale J made certain observations about ex parte orders following consultation with the President of the Family Division. She stressed that the courts have a special responsibility to ensure that ex parte orders which could harm the interests of an adult or child are not made without a good reason. Orders requiring the handing over of a very young child to a parent with whom he has not lived for some time should only be made in exceptional circumstances. Applicants for ex parte orders and their legal advisers must be scrupulously careful in relation to the application itself and to the implementation of any order which might be made. It is incumbent on the applicant's legal advisers to understand any order and to represent it accurately to others. If there is some doubt about their interpretation, urgent clarification should be sought from the court on an inter partes basis. The police should always have a clear understanding of their role in relation to the order. Counsel should never advise on the effect of an order made in their absence without being satisfied of the exact terms of the order, which will generally involve reading it.

"warrant under section 48(9)" (r 4.4(4)(*c*))—This refers to a warrant authorising a constable to assist a person who is having difficulty enforcing an emergency protection order.

"recovery order" (r 4.4(4)(*d*))—A recovery order is an order under CA 1989, s 50 for the recovery of a child who has been abducted, has run away etc.

"warrant under section 102(1)" (r 4.4(4)(*e*))—This refers to a warrant authorising a constable to assist a person who is having difficulty enforcing various powers under CA 1989 (for example, the power to inspect children who are in children's homes or who are accommodated by voluntary organisations).

Telephone ex parte applications—In exceptional cases, where the application is particularly urgent, it can be made by telephone. It is suggested that the first approach is made to the court office where it is intended that the application will ultimately be filed. If the office is closed or cannot arrange for a judge to consider the matter, contact can always be made through the Royal Courts of Justice in London (Tel: 020 7947 6000).

Procedure for ex parte orders—Where ex parte orders are sought, Munby J has set out in *Re S (Ex Parte Orders)* [2001] 1 FLR 308 guidelines which state that:

(1) It is appropriate, generally, in the Family Division for the court to require the applicant (and, where appropriate, the applicant's solicitors) to give the following undertakings:
  (*a*) where proceedings have not yet been issued, to issue and serve on the respondent, either by some specified time or as soon as practicable, proceedings either in the form of the draft produced to the court or otherwise as may be appropriate;
  (*b*) where the application has been made otherwise than on sworn evidence, to cause to be sworn, filed and served on the respondent as soon as practicable an affidavit substantially in the terms of that produced to the court or, as the case may be, confirming the substance of what was said to the court by the applicant's counsel or solicitors; and
  (*c*) subject to (*a*) and (*b*), to serve on the respondent as soon as practicable: (i) the proceedings; (ii) a sealed copy of the order; (iii) copies of the affidavit(s) and exhibit(s) containing the evidence relied on by the applicant; and (iv) notice of the return date and details of the application to be made on that date.

(2) Whether or not express undertakings have been given, and subject to any order to the contrary, an applicant who obtains ex parte injunctive relief is under an obligation to the court, and his solicitor is under an obligation both to the court and his client, to carry out the steps referred to above.

(3) A person who finds himself unable to comply timeously with his undertaking should apply for an extension of time before the time for compliance has expired, or pass the task to someone who has available the time in which to do it.

(4) Persons injuncted are entitled to be given, if they ask, proper information as to what happened at the hearing and told what documents etc were lodged with the court and what legal authorities were cited to the judge. The applicant's lawyers should respond forthwith to any reasonable request from the respondent or his lawyers, for copies of the materials read by the judge or for information about what took place at the hearing. It would, therefore, be prudent for those acting for the applicant to keep a proper note of the proceedings.

Re S (above) concerned a without notice application by the father to forestall the removal by the mother of the children of the family from the jurisdiction. Munby J also gave guidance in the earlier case of *Re W (Ex Parte Orders)* [2000] 2 FLR 927 as to the procedure to be followed in seeking an ex parte injunction in the Family Division in relation to ancillary relief proceedings where a writ of sequestration was sought.

Ex parte application on notice—Although no provision is made for it in the Rules, a procedure has evolved, as a matter of practice and fairness, whereby an ex parte application can be made on informal notice (see eg *Croydon LBC v A (No 3)* [1992] 2 FLR 350). This procedure must not be used, however, as a way of getting what should be a proper inter partes hearing more quickly than would otherwise be the case.

Application on short notice as alternative to ex parte application—Where possible, it is preferable for an application to be served and for notice to be abridged (see r 4.8) than for an ex parte application to be made (see eg *Re B (A Minor) (Residence Order: Ex Parte)* [1992] 2 FLR 1, CA).

Service of the ex parte orders (r 4.4(4)(ii))—Service of an order of the kind specified in r 4.4(4)(iii) within the period of 48 hours there prescribed is mandatory. Failure to serve within the period might generate argument as to enforceability of the order and therefore, in order to avoid problems, an applicant who knows that there is likely to be difficulty in complying with the time-limit for service should seek directions at the same time as the initial ex parte application is made. Rule 4.8 gives the court power to direct that a requirement as to service shall not apply or that service shall be effected in an alternative manner and r 4.14 gives a general power to vary time-limits. As to the computation of time, see r 1.5; as to the extension of time-limits, see rr 4.15(1) and 4.14(2).

Refusal of an application for an ex parte order (r 4.4(5))—Where it is directed that the application is to be heard inter partes, before there can be a hearing the applicant will have to file the application, if this has not already been done, serve copies in accordance with r 4.4(1) and give notice in Form C6A in accordance with r 4.4(3). Where an ex parte application has been refused by the court the former jurisdiction of the Court of Appeal to hear a renewed application for an ex parte order as provided by CPR 1998, Sch 1, RSC Ord 59, r 14(3) no longer applies. There appear to be no similar provisions in CPR 1998, Pt 52 (as supplemented by PD52) which now governs appeals relating to orders made after 2 May 2000.

Application to set aside ex parte order—Where an ex parte order has been made and the absent party wishes to challenge it, the appropriate course is to apply to the judge who made it to vary or rescind the order. There is no purpose, in anything other than a wholly exceptional case, in making such an application ex parte. Notice (albeit short notice if justified by the urgency of the situation) should be given to the other parties (*Re P (A Minor) (Ex Parte Interim Residence Order)* [1993] 1 FLR 915; see also *Re H (Wardship: Ex Parte Orders)* [1994] 2 FLR 981, CA.

"proceedings under Schedule 1"—CA 1989, Sch 1 contains provisions with regard to financial provision for children. In a case in which leave has been granted to bring an application under Sch 1, the draft application filed on the request for leave will have been accompanied by a financial statement by virtue of r 4.3(4) and no further action need be taken to satisfy r 4.4(6).

Fees—See the Family Proceedings Fees Order 1999.

4.5 Withdrawal of application

(1) An application may be withdrawn only with leave of the court.

(2) Subject to paragraph (3), a person seeking leave to withdraw an application shall file and serve on the parties a written request for leave setting out the reasons for the request.

(3) The request under paragraph (2) may be made orally to the court if the parties and either the children's guardian or the welfare officer or children and family reporter are present.

(4) Upon receipt of a written request under paragraph (2) the court shall –

(*a*) if –

(i) the parties consent in writing,

(ii) the children's guardian has had an opportunity to make representations,

and

(iii) the court thinks fit,

grant the request, in which case the proper officer shall notify the parties, the children's guardian and the welfare officer or children and family reporter of the granting of the request, or

(*b*) direct that a date be fixed for the hearing of the request in which case the proper officer shall give at least 7 days' notice to the parties, the children's

PART III

guardian and the welfare officer or children and family reporter, of the date fixed.

Amendments—SI 2001/821.

Defined terms—"application": r 4.1(1); "court": r 1.2(1); "children's guardian", "leave": r 4.1(1); "proper officer": r 1.2(1); "children and family reporter": r 4.1(1).

Court's approach to application—In *Re F (A Minor) (Care Order: Withdrawal of Application)* [1993] 2 FLR 9, Hollings J held that withdrawal of an application is a matter which must be considered by the court as carefully as any other application in respect of a child in proceedings under CA 1989. The court must hear evidence from the children's guardian before deciding to allow the proceedings to be withdrawn. In *London Borough of Southwark v B* [1993] 2 FLR 559, the Court of Appeal held that, since an application for leave to withdraw does not involve the court in considering directly whether any existing order should be varied or discharged, the welfare checklist in CA 1989, s 1(3) does not specifically apply. However, the checklist is available to the court as an aide-memoire to assist it in reaching a decision. An application under r 4.5(1) (and FPC(CA 1989)R 1991, r 5(1)) involves the determination of a "question with respect to the upbringing of a child", and so the paramountcy principle in CA 1989, s 1(1) applies. The paramount consideration for the court is whether the withdrawal of the proceedings would promote or conflict with the welfare of the child concerned. The court must look at each case on its facts to see if there is some "solid advantage to the child to be derived from continuing the proceedings". For a recent application of the test see *Re N (Leave to Withdraw Care Proceedings)* [2000] 1 FLR 134 where the court refused the application of the local authority for leave to withdraw care proceedings.

Withdrawal of proceedings – European Convention for the Protection of Human Rights and Fundamental Freedoms 1950—Where an application is made to withdraw public law child care proceedings on the basis that to continue them would amount to an interference with the right of the parents of the child concerned under Article 8(1) of the Convention to respect for their private and family life, the court must assess whether such interference is necessary to protect one of the interests set out in Art 8(2) *(Re N (Leave to Withdraw Care Proceedings)* [2000] 1 FLR 134). Where there is a serious conflict between the interests of the child and one of its parents which can only be resolved to the disadvantage of one of them, the interests of the child must prevail under Art 8(2) (*Hendriks v The Netherlands* (1982) 5 EHRR 223).

"written request for leave" (r 4.5(2))—The written request for leave to withdraw proceedings should be made in Form C2. The form requires the names and date of birth of the child concerned, and details as to the identity of the person making the request and as to his relationship with the child. The reasons for seeking leave to withdraw the proceedings must be clearly set out, and particular attention should be paid to the effect that withdrawal will have on the child.

Service—See r 4.8, and also rr 10.2, 10.3 and 10.6.

Parties—In the usual case where the request is made by the applicant, the parties are the respondents stipulated in App 3, column (iii) (unless they have ceased to be a party by order of the court under r 4.7) and any other person whom the court has permitted to be joined as a party under r 4.7.

Oral application in the presence of the parties (r 4.5(3))—The court is permitted by r 4.16 to proceed with a hearing or directions appointment in the absence of one or more respondents, but it appears from the wording of r 4.5(3) that this would not be an acceptable course in respect of an oral request for leave to withdraw proceedings. The court must not entertain an oral request for leave to withdraw proceedings in the absence of the children's guardian either, even if his legal representative is present (*Re F (A Minor) (Care Order: Withdrawal of Application)* [1993] 2 FLR 9). It is possible that the applicant may change his mind almost immediately after filing the application and wish to raise the question of withdrawing the proceedings orally at the first directions hearing. At this stage, it may be that neither the children's guardian nor the children and family reporter will have been appointed, so neither could be present. This ought not to debar the making of an oral request. FPC(CA 1989)R 1991, r 5(3), the equivalent provision for magistrates' courts, is much clearer on this point than r 4.5(3). It is not impossible (although it is very unusual) to have both a children's guardian and a children and family reporter in the same case. Where this occurs, the wording of the rule suggests that it will suffice if the oral application is made in the presence of one or the other though it is doubted whether, in practice, it would normally be prudent to proceed to determine the application without notification to both the children's guardian and a children and family reporter.

Hearing of an oral request under r 4.5(3)—Although r 4.5(3) does not specifically provide for an oral request to be adjourned for hearing, there will be cases in which, for one reason or another, it will be impossible to resolve the question immediately, and the court must therefore have power (possibly under r 4.14(2)) to direct that a date be fixed for the hearing just as it would under r 4.5(4)(*b*) had a written request been made.

Consent of the parties in writing (r 4.5(4)(*a*)(i))—A party may be unwilling to consent for reasons connected with the substantive application itself (for example because he feels that the child requires the protection of the particular order being sought and therefore does not feel that it would be in the child's best interests for the proceedings to be abandoned) or alternatively may withhold his written consent in order to force a hearing at which he will seek to raise the issue of costs; for a case in which the possibility of a wasted costs order was canvassed in conjunction with the withdrawal of proceedings, see *Re O (A Minor) (Wasted Costs Application)* [1994] 2 FLR 842.

"7 days' notice" (r 4.5(4)(*b*))—As to the computation of time, see r 1.5. As to the method of giving notice (by post, fax etc) see r 10.7.

Granting a written request—Where the request is made orally under r 4.5(3) or where a hearing is directed under r 4.5(4)(*b*), the children and family reporter may have an opportunity to make known to the court his views as to whether it should be granted whereas, in the case of a written request made with consent in writing, he is not consulted in advance, merely told if the request is granted. In contrast, the children's guardian is guaranteed the opportunity to make representations in response to a written request by virtue of r 4.5(4)(*a*)(ii).

Procedure prior to and at the hearing—In contrast to the request for leave to bring proceedings (see r 4.3), a request to withdraw proceedings is undoubtedly made in the course of those proceedings and any of the Pt IV procedural rules which are appropriate will apply (see r 4.1(2)). In particular, directions may be given under r 4.14; r 4.16 applies as to attendance; r 4.17 as to documentary evidence; and r 4.21 as to the hearing.

4.6 Transfer

(1) Where an application is made, in accordance with the provisions of the Allocation Order, to a county court for an order transferring proceedings from a magistrates' court following the refusal of the magistrates' court to order such a transfer, the applicant shall –

(*a*) file the application in Form C2, together with a copy of the certificate issued by the magistrates' court, and

(*b*) serve a copy of the documents mentioned in sub-paragraph (*a*) personally on all parties to the proceedings which it is sought to have transferred,

within 2 days after receipt by the applicant of the certificate.

(2) Within 2 days after receipt of the documents served under paragraph (1)(*b*), any party other than the applicant may file written representations.

(3) The court shall, not before the fourth day after the filing of the application under paragraph (1), unless the parties consent to earlier consideration, consider the application and either –

(*a*) grant the application, whereupon the proper officer shall inform the parties of that decision, or

(*b*) direct that a date be fixed for the hearing of the application, whereupon the proper officer shall fix such a date and give not less than 1 day's notice to the parties of the date so fixed.

(4) Where proceedings are transferred from a magistrates' court to a county court in accordance with the provisions of the Allocation Order, the county court shall consider whether to transfer those proceedings to the High Court in accordance with that Order and either –

(*a*) determine that such an order need not be made,
(*b*) make such an order,
(*c*) order that a date be fixed for the hearing of the question whether such an order should be made, whereupon the proper officer shall give such notice to the parties as the court directs of the date so fixed, or
(*d*) invite the parties to make written representations, within a specified period, as to whether such an order should be made; and upon receipt of the representations the court shall act in accordance with sub-paragraph (*a*), (*b*) or (*c*).

(5) The proper officer shall notify the parties of an order transferring the proceedings from a county court or from the High Court made in accordance with the provisions of the Allocation Order.

(6) Before ordering the transfer of proceedings from a county court to a magistrates' court in accordance with the Allocation Order, the county court shall notify the magistrates' court of its intention to make such an order and invite the views of the clerk to the justices on whether such an order should be made.

(7) An order transferring proceedings from a county court to a magistrates' court in accordance with the Allocation Order shall –

(*a*) be in Form C49, and
(*b*) be served by the court on the parties.

(8) In this rule "the Allocation Order" means the Children (Allocation of Proceedings) Order 1991 or any Order replacing that Order.

Amendments—SI 1991/2113; SI 1994/3155.

Defined terms—"court", "parties", "proper officer": r 1.2(1).

Application to county court to transfer proceedings from magistrates' court (r 4.6(1))—Children (Allocation of Proceedings) Order 1991, art 9 enables such transfers to be ordered and sets out the criterion.

"county court"—In this context, the meaning of "county court" is extended to include the principal registry in its role as a divorce county court (Children (Allocation of Proceedings) Order 1991, art 19).

"file" (r 4.6(1), (2))—Defined in relation to county courts by CCR Ord 2, r 4 and extended to cover use of the post (CCR Ord 2, r 5). Not specifically defined for High Court purposes.

Forms C2 and C50 (r 4.6(1)(*a*))—Form C2 is the prescribed form to be used for an order or directions in existing family proceedings. The applicant is required to give the names and date of birth of the child concerned, and to give details identifying himself and his relationship to the child. He must also set out clearly in Form C2 his reasons for applying for a transfer of the proceedings from a magistrates' court, paying particular attention to the criteria set out in Children (Allocation of Proceedings) Order 1991, art 9. Where the magistrates' court (or the justices' clerk) has been requested (under the Allocation Order) to transfer a case and has refused to do so, Family Proceedings Courts (Children Act 1989) Rules 1991, r 6(1) requires it to set out, in a certificate in Form C50, the reasons for the refusal.

Service—Service is governed by r 4.8, but the provisions of r 4.8(1) are expressed to be subject to the requirement of personal service in r 4.6(1)(*b*). Therefore, the options of postal service and service on a solicitor are not available. Rule 4.8(4) applies so as to allow service on a child to be effected on someone other than the child himself, although this must, as in the case of other parties, be done personally rather than by post.

"written representations" (r 4.6(2), (4)(*d*))—No form is prescribed for written representations. The case number should appear clearly at the top with other particulars sufficient to identify the application concerned.

"parties consent to earlier consideration" (r 4.6(3))—This rule leaves open how the court is to satisfy itself that the parties consent. In view of the urgency, a letter by post may be impractical, and the court may be reluctant to accept a telephone call in case consent is subsequently disputed.

Notice (r 4.6(3)(*b*), (4)(*c*))—The mode of giving notice is governed by r 10.7.

Transfer from magistrates' court to county court (r 4.6(4))— Articles 7 to 9 of the Allocation Order make provision for such transfers.

Transfer from county court or High Court (r 4.6(5))— Articles 10 to 13 of the Allocation Order make provision for such transfers.

"notify" (r 4.6(5), (6))—This word may attract r 10.7, which governs the mode of giving "notice".

Transfer from county court to magistrates' court (r 4.6(6))— Article 11 of the Allocation Order makes provision for such transfers. It is not clear how the justices' clerk's views are to be invited or given, or how much time he is to be allowed to give them. It is submitted that the method and timing must be reasonable in all the circumstances, including the urgency with which a conclusion needs to be reached.

"served by the court" (r 4.6(7)(*b*))—Service generally is governed by r 4.8. In this context "the court" has a wider meaning than that provided by r 1.2(1) (the judge or district judge). Service may be effected by the proper officer or on his behalf.

Own motion procedure—Rule 4.6(1), (2) and (3) applies only where a party applies for a transfer order. Children (Allocation of Proceedings) Order 1991, arts 10, 11, 12 and 13 expressly enable the court to order a transfer to a magistrates' court, a county court or the High court of its own motion. Where the court wishes to make such a transfer, it is likely to act by way of a direction under r 4.14(2)(*h*).

Forms—The prescribed forms for applications made in proceedings under CA 1989 are set out in Appendix 1 to these rules.

4.7 Parties

(1) The respondents to proceedings to which this Part applies shall be those persons set out in the relevant entry in column (iii) of Appendix 3 to these rules.

(2) In proceedings to which this Part applies, a person may file a request in Form C2 that he or another person –

- (*a*) be joined as a party, or
- (*b*) cease to be a party.

(3) On considering a request under paragraph (2) the court shall, subject to paragraph (4) –

- (*a*) grant it without a hearing or representations, save that this shall be done only in the case of a request under paragraph (2)(*a*), whereupon the proper officer shall inform the parties and the person making the request of that decision, or
- (*b*) order that a date be fixed for the consideration of the request, whereupon the proper officer shall give notice of the date so fixed, together with a copy of the request –
  - (i) in the case of a request under paragraph (2)(*a*), to the applicant, and

(ii) in the case of a request under paragraph (2)(*b*), to the parties, or

(*c*) invite the parties or any of them to make written representations, within a specified period, as to whether the request should be granted; and upon the expiry of the period the court shall act in accordance with sub-paragraph (*a*) or (*b*).

(4) Where a person with parental responsibility requests that he be joined under paragraph (2)(*a*), the court shall grant his request.

(5) In proceedings to which this Part applies the court may direct –

(*a*) that a person who would not otherwise be a respondent under these rules be joined as a party to the proceedings, or

(*b*) that a party to the proceedings cease to be a party.

Amendments—SI 1992/2067; SI 1994/3155.

Defined terms—"applicant": r 4.1(1); "court": r 1.2(1); "parental responsibility": r 4.1(1), CA 1989, s 3; "proper officer": r 1.2(1).

Factors in decision whether to join or discharge a party—There is no guidance in the rules or CA 1989 as to the factors that the court should take into account in making decisions about parties. The following propositions can be extracted from the authorities.

(*a*) It appears that CA 1989, s 1(1) does not apply in this context. Where the request is for joinder, see *North Yorkshire County Council v G* [1993] 2 FLR 732; *G v Kirklees MBC* [1993] 1 FLR 805; *Re A and W (Minors) (Residence Order: Leave to Apply)* [1992] 2 FLR 154, CA. As to discharge, in *Re W (Discharge of Party to Proceedings)* [1997] 1 FLR 128, Hogg J held that, in considering an application by a mother that the father cease to be a party to her proceedings for the discharge of a care order, the welfare of the children was important but not paramount. In this extreme case, the father was discharged from the proceedings, and his views would be stated by the guardian ad litem ("children's guardian").

(*b*) Where an applicant seeks to become a party in existing proceedings in order to apply for a s 8 order, the guidelines in s 10(9) are applicable even though he does not expressly seek leave to apply for a s 8 order (*G v Kirklees MBC* (above); see also *North Yorkshire County Council v G* (above) – where a child sought to become a party to care proceedings relating to his younger brother the court should apply the criteria in s 10(9) together with those in s 1(3). See also *W v Wakefield City Council* [1995] 1 FLR 170 – s 10(9) applied where an aunt sought a residence order in respect of her niece and applied to become a party to separate care proceedings relating to her nephew.

(*c*) Where the natural father of a child who does not have parental responsibility for him applies for leave to be joined as a party to care proceedings concerning the child, albeit at a late stage, there is a presumption that his application should be granted unless there is some justifiable reason for refusing it. There is no requirement for the court to consider the CA 1989, s 10(9) factors for granting leave to seek a s 8 order in this context (*Re B (Care Proceedings: Notification of Father Without Parental Responsibility)* [1999] 2 FLR 408; *Re F (Care: Party Status: Directions)* [1999] Fam Law 294 – unmarried father was granted party status where serious allegations were made against him and were likely to form the basis of threshold criteria; *Re P (Care Proceedings: Father's Application to be Joined as Party)* [2001] 1 FLR 781 – father's application refused as he had had every opportunity to participate in the care proceedings at an early stage and had chosen not to. This was not a breach of the European Convention for the Protection of Human Rights and Fundamental Freedoms 1950, Art 6 (right to fair trial), because it was the father's fault he had not applied earlier. Furthermore, there was no breach of Art 8 (right to respect for private and family life) as the father's rights had to be balanced against those of the children and the children needed a speedy conclusion to the proceedings).

(*d*) The court is not precluded from considering all the circumstances and these include the overall merits of the case for a s 8 order for, if the applicant does not have a reasonable prospect of success, there is no purpose in joining him as a party (*G v Kirklees MBC* (above)). However, *Re M (Care: Contact: Grandmother's Application for Leave)* [1995] 2 FLR 86, CA, criticises *G v Kirklees MBC* as setting the test as to the prospects of success of the application too high, and it appears, by analogy with *Re M*, and from comments in *Re G (Child Case: Parental Involvement)* [1996] 1 FLR 857, CA, at 865H, that a good arguable case may suffice.

(*e*) Another material consideration is whether the person who seeks to be joined has an independent separate point of view to put forward. Where he does not, he may not be allowed to be joined (*North Yorkshire County Council v G* (above), and see **Separate representation of parties** below). Clearly, the court will seek to control wasted time and costs in making its decision on joinder (*Re B and H (Minors) (Costs: Legal Aid)* [1994] 1 FLR 327).

(*f*) By analogy with the decision of Hollings J in *Re A (A Minor) (Residence Order: Leave to Apply)* [1993] 1 FLR 425 (determining an application for leave to apply for a residence order), no doubt the wishes of the child can also be part of the relevant circumstances.

(*g*) There may be situations in which current foster-parents are joined as respondents to care proceedings but, in ordinary circumstances, the court would not regard it as appropriate because, in most cases, it would run counter to the policy of CA 1989, ss 9(3) and 10(3) (*Re G (Minors) (Interim Care Order)* [1993] 2 FLR 839; see further **Separate representation of parties** below).

(*h*) It is not correct, given the restrictions on applications by local authorities for private law orders, to join as a party to s 8 proceedings by a father for contact a local authority which has carried out a s 37 investigation but decided not to apply for a care or supervision order (*F v Cambridgeshire County Council* [1995] 1 FLR 516, FD).

(*i*) It is not always necessary to add an individual to proceedings as a party simply in order to make a prohibited steps order against him, nor is it necessary for him even to be present in court, although no doubt a person against whom an injunctive order was made would be given leave to make a s 8 application to vary or discharge it or given liberty to apply on notice to vary the order under s 11(7)(*d*) (*Re H (Prohibited Steps Order)* [1995] 1 FLR 638, CA (prohibited steps order against former cohabitee of mother to prevent him having contact with the children).

(*j*) As to the appropriate parties to an application for sanction for the sterilisation of a minor, see *Practice Note of 2 April 2001 (Official Solicitor: Appointment in Family Proceedings)*, to be read in conjunction with *Practice Note of March 2001 (Officers of CAFCASS Legal Services and Special Casework: Appointment in Family Proceedings)* (both are set out in Part IV of this work).

(*k*) It may be appropriate to give leave to intervene for a specific purpose rather than joining a person as a party as *Re S (Care: Residence: Intervener)* [1997] 1 FLR 497, CA illustrates. Care and residence proceedings were pending. Inter alia, allegations of sexual abuse in the past had been made against the mother's husband by his now adult niece. He was given leave to intervene but not to be made a party, taking part in the proceedings to the limited extent of his involvement in the case. The local authority would have to notify him and serve him with the relevant documents if they wished to pursue the allegations against him. He and his counsel would be present at a convenient time and he would have the opportunity to give evidence and counsel could cross-examine witnesses relevant to the allegations. However, there is no right for satellite parties against whom allegations are being made in care proceedings to intervene and each case must be looked at on its own merits (*Re H (Care Proceedings: Intervener)* [2000] 1 FLR 775). In *Re H* the parents argued that their 17-year-old daughter (D) had made false allegations of sexual abuse by her father and had persuaded her 9-year-old sister (C) to do the same. It was held that there was no need for D to have leave to intervene in the care proceedings relating to C so as to enable D to protect herself in those proceedings. D would have no protection when giving evidence in the parallel criminal proceedings being brought against her father and it would not assist her to have protection in one set of proceedings when she would not receive it for the other. However, in *Re H (Children) (Care Proceedings: Sexual Abuse)* [2000] 2 FCR 499 the court held that where, in the course of care proceedings specific allegations of child sexual abuse are made against a non-party and brought for preliminary issue trial, it is vital that that person's evidence is before the court at that stage, even if he is unlikely to have party status at the substantive hearing. See also *Re L (Police Investigation: Privilege)* [1996] 1 FLR 731, HL in which an application by the police for disclosure of medical reports was determined without the police being joined as a party to the care proceedings.

Joinder of child as respondent—Where a child seeks to make an application concerning himself, he must seek leave under CA 1989, s 10. In certain situations, the child is automatically a respondent to proceedings begun by others, notably where the proceedings are specified (see CA 1989, s 41) as for example proceedings for a care order or an emergency protection order (see FPR 1991, App 3). Where this is not the case, a child who seeks to become a respondent must apply under r 4.7 as did a 9-year-old girl in *Re N (A Minor)* (unreported) 25 September 1997, CA in relation to her father's application for contact with her. Where the application to be joined as a respondent succeeds, rr 9.2 and 9.2A will dictate whether the child can instruct his solicitor independently or whether he must do so through a children's guardian.

By analogy with the situation where a child seeks leave under CA 1989, s 10 to commence proceedings, it may be that applications by children to be joined as respondents should be transferred to the High Court (see **Court to which the leave request should be made** under r 4.3).

Separate representation of parties—Guidance as to the representation of parties is given in *Re M (Minors) (Sexual Abuse: Evidence)* [1993] 1 FLR 822, where the Court of Appeal held that grandparents should not intervene in CA 1989 proceedings unless they have a separate point of view to put forward. Here, where their interests were identical to those of the mother, the court could have been told by the mother and the children's guardian of their offer to care for the children, and they could simply have been called as witnesses in support of her case. In *North Yorkshire County Council v G* [1993] 2 FLR 732, magistrates were wrong to permit the brother of a child subject to care proceedings to be joined as a party in the proceedings when he had no independent point of view to present. He could carry out a supportive role to his mother (who was a party) simply by being present (there being no objection to that course from the parties) or by being a witness. In *Re BJ (Care: Third Party Intervention)* [1999] Fam Law 613 the court refused to join a 12-year-old boy as intervener to protect his own interests where allegations had been made that he had sexually abused one of the two children who were the subjects of the care proceedings in question. The current care proceedings did not directly involve the boy, his situation was being considered in another local authority area and his interests were being properly safeguarded by his mother. Furthermore, the court observed that intervener status brings with it onerous responsibilities which it would be inappropriate to impose on a child of his age. In *Re G (Minors) (Interim Care Order)* [1993] 2 FLR 839, the Court of Appeal said that it would not normally be appropriate for foster-parents to be joined as respondents in proceedings in which the future upbringing of children in their care is in issue although, in that case, there were exceptional circumstances to justify such a course. Where a number of parties are putting forward essentially the same case, serious consideration should be given to the degree of separate representation of those parties that is strictly necessary (*Birmingham City Council v H (No 3)* [1994] 1 FLR 224, HL). For a case in which there should have been separate representation, see *Re P (Representation)* [1996] 1 FLR 486, CA (of seven children represented by one solicitor, the eldest rejected the local authority's care plan and the six younger children, through the children's guardian, accepted it; eldest child should be represented by a separate solicitor, as it was impossible for a single advocate both to support the care plan and to attack it on behalf of the dissenting child). As to the de-merits of local authorities using employed solicitors rather than specialist local counsel as representatives in contested child care cases, see *Re B (Local Authorities: Representation) (Note)* [1996] 1 FLR 56. Reference should also be made to *Re B and H (Minors) (Costs: Legal Aid)* [1994] 1 FLR 327 as to the legal aid implications of duplicating representation. As to representation on appeal, it should be borne in mind that it may be justifiable for a party to play an active role at first instance but not on appeal and, in those circumstances, costs might be ordered against him in relation to the appeal (*Re O (Costs: Liability of Legal Aid Board)* [1997] 1 FLR 465, CA).

Children as parties where separately represented—As to whether there is jurisdiction to order separate representation for children who are the subject of proceedings without adding them as parties, see *L v L (Minors) (Separate Representation)* [1994] 1 FLR 156.

"proceedings to which this Part applies" (r 4.7(1))—See r 4.1(2).

"request in Form C2" (r 4.7(2))—The request should be made in prescribed Form C2. The reasons for the request to be joined as a party, or to cease to be a party, should be set out in as much detail as possible and, where the person making a request to be joined as a party has parental responsibility, this should be clearly stated as it will entitle him to have his request granted as of right (r 4.7(4)). The rule is wide enough to entitle a person to request that someone else be joined or cease to be a party. So, for example, where a respondent's interest in the proceedings has come to an end, perhaps because the child ceased to live with him some time ago, the applicant may apply for him to be removed as a party. Where the request is by one person that another be joined as a party, r 4.7 makes no provision for him to be consulted in advance as to his views with the result that a person might find himself a party to proceedings without knowing of the possibility in advance. Bearing in mind that participation in proceedings can have serious financial and other implications, the court should be alive to this danger and make what enquiries it can as to the willingness of the person concerned to be a party.

Granting request without a hearing (r 4.7(3)(*a*))—Only a request to be joined as a party may be granted without a hearing and without consultation with the other parties. Where an existing party requests that he should cease to be a party, the other parties must either be invited to make written representations on the subject under r 4.7(3)(*c*) or have the opportunity to make representations on or prior to the date fixed for consideration of the request under r 4.7(3)(*b*).

Fixing a date for consideration of the request (r 4.7(3)(*b*))—It is clear that decisions as to the joinder or withdrawal of parties are the province of the court itself rather than of the proper officer of the court, but r 4.7(3)(*b*) does not stipulate what form the consideration of the request to be joined as or cease to be a party should take. A hearing is not expressly mentioned in r 4.7(3)(*b*) itself but it is implicit in the requirement that notice of the date fixed be given to the parties and in the general terms of r 4.7(3) that some form of hearing is envisaged. However any party who did not wish to attend could presumably send his representations to the court in writing instead.

"within a specified period" (r 4.7(3)(*c*))—For provisions as to time, see rr 1.5 and 4.15. If the period specified by the court for the making of representations is inadequate, an extension should be sought under r 4.14(2).

Own motion procedure (r 4.7(5))—This provision empowers the court to make an order joining a new party or discharging an existing party of its own motion.

4.8 Service

(1) Subject to the requirement in rule 4.6(1)(*b*) of personal service, where service of a document is required under this Part (and not by a provision to which section 105(8) (Service of notice or other document under the Act) applies) it may be effected –

(*a*) if the person to be served is not known by the person serving to be acting by solicitor –
  (i) by delivering it to him personally, or
  (ii) by delivering it at, or by sending it by first-class post to, his residence or his last known residence, or

(*b*) if the person to be served is known by the person serving to be acting by solicitor –
  (i) by delivering the document at, or sending it by first-class post to, the solicitor's address for service,
  (ii) where the solicitor's address for service includes a numbered box at a document exchange, by leaving the document at that document exchange or at a document exchange which transmits documents on every business day to that document exchange, or
  (iii) by sending a legible copy of the document by facsimile transmission to the solicitor's office.

(2) In this rule "first-class post" means first-class post which has been pre-paid or in respect of which pre-payment is not required.

(3) Where a child who is a party to proceedings to which this Part applies is not prosecuting or defending them without a next friend or guardian ad litem under rule 9.2A and is required by these rules or other rules of court to serve a document, service shall be effected by –

(*a*) the solicitor acting for the child, or

(*b*) where there is no such solicitor, the children's guardian or the guardian ad litem, or

(*c*) where there is neither such a solicitor nor a children's guardian nor a guardian ad litem, the court.

(4) Service of any document on a child who is not prosecuting or defending the proceedings concerned without a next friend or guardian ad litem under rule 9.2A shall, subject to any direction of the court, be effected by service on –

(*a*) the solicitor acting for the child, or
(*b*) where there is no such solicitor, the children's guardian or the guardian ad litem, or
(*c*) where there is neither such a solicitor nor a children's guardian nor a guardian ad litem, with leave of the court, the child.

(5) Where the court refuses leave under paragraph (4)(*c*) it shall give a direction under paragraph (8).

(6) A document shall, unless the contrary is proved, be deemed to have been served –

(*a*) in the case of service by first-class post, on the second business day after posting, and
(*b*) in the case of service in accordance with paragraph (1)(*b*)(ii), on the second business day after the day on which it is left at the document exchange.

(7) At or before the first directions appointment in, or hearing of, proceedings to which this Part applies the applicant shall file a statement in Form C9 that service of –

(*a*) a copy of the application and other documents referred to in rule 4.4(1)(*b*) has been effected on each respondent, and
(*b*) notice of the proceedings has been effected under rule 4.4(3);

and the statement shall indicate –

(i) the manner, date, time and place of service, or
(ii) where service was effected by post, the date, time and place of posting.

(8) In proceedings to which this Part applies, where these rules or other rules of court require a document to be served, the court may, without prejudice to any power under rule 4.14, direct that –

(*a*) the requirement shall not apply;
(*b*) the time specified by the rules for complying with the requirement shall be abridged to such extent as may be specified in the direction;
(*c*) service shall be effected in such manner as may be specified in the direction.

Amendments—SI 1992/456; SI 1992/2067; SI 1994/3155; SI 2001/821.

Defined terms—"business day": r 1.5(6); "child": r 4.1(1); "court": r 1.2(1); "directions appointment", "children's guardian", "leave": r 4.1(1).

The relationship with the provisions of FPR 1991, Part X—Part X contains provisions as to service which apply to all family proceedings but subject to the provisions of any other part of the rules. The provisions of this rule therefore prevail over those in Pt X. Only where a particular matter is not covered by this rule (for example, service out of England and Wales, which is covered by r 10.6) is Pt X relevant.

"Subject to ... r 4.6(1)(b)" (r 4.8(1))—Rule 4.6(1)(*b*) requires personal service of an application to a county court under the Children (Allocation of Proceedings) Order 1991 for an order for the transfer of proceedings from a magistrates' court to a county court or the High Court after the refusal of the magistrates' court to order a transfer.

Documents—The term "document" is not defined in the rules. In this rule it is clearly used in a wide sense to include such documents as a copy of the application itself, any written statement of evidence under r 4.17(1)(*a*) and experts' reports under r 4.17(1)(*b*). In contrast, the term has a rather narrower ambit in r 4.17(1)(*b*).

"section 105(8)" (r 4.8(1))—Certain service requirements derive from CA 1989 itself rather than from the rules (for example service of a copy of a residence order before enforcement under CA 1989, s 14). Where this is so, s 105(8) (which is more restrictive than r 4.8) governs service. In the more usual case where the requirement for service derives from the rules, this rule applies.

"If the person to be served is not known ... to be acting by solicitor" (r 4.8(1)(*a*))—This covers both the situation where it is known that the person to be served has no solicitor and the situation where there is uncertainty as to whether he has or not. Presumably it also applies where it is known that the person to be served has a solicitor but not which firm is acting so that service in accordance with r 4.8(1)(*b*) is impossible.

Service by fax—Although r 4.8(6) provides for presumptions as to when a posted document or one left at a document exchange is taken to have been served, it does not make any provision with regard to a faxed document. It appears that RSC Ord 65, r 5(2B) therefore applies (see r 1.3), with the result that, unless the contrary is shown, the date of service of a document faxed before 4 pm on a business day is deemed to be the day of transmission and, in any other case, the business day next following.

"proceedings to which this Part applies" (r 4.8(7))—Part IV applies to the proceedings listed in r 4.1(2).

FPR 1991, r 9.2A—Rule 9.2A enables a child who has obtained leave or who has instructed a solicitor who considers him able to give instructions in relation to the proceedings, to begin, prosecute or defend proceedings without a next friend or guardian. Where r 4.8(3) or (4) refers to a guardian ad litem in the context of r 9.2A, the definition of the term in r 4.1(1) is overridden, since the office of a guardian ad litem for the purposes of r 9.2A is completely different to that of a s 41 children's guardian whose much wider functions are set out in r 4.11.

Service by a child (r 4.8(3))—As to the duty of the child's solicitor, children's guardian or guardian ad litem to carry out service on behalf of the child, see r 4.12(2).

Service on a child (r 4.8(4), (5))—As to the duty of the child's solicitor, children's guardian or guardian ad litem to accept service on behalf of the child and to advise him, if he has sufficient understanding, of the contents of the documents, see r 4.12(2). Where there is an application for leave to serve the child, r 4.3 does not apply, since that rule is confined to applications for leave to commence proceedings. No doubt leave to serve on a child may most conveniently be sought by means of a directions application under r 4.14, which expressly empowers the court to give directions as to service (r 4.14(2)(*e*)). If leave is refused, the court will give a direction under r 4.8(8) (r 4.8(5)). For a case in which the court deemed it inappropriate for the child to be served, see *Re J (A Minor) (Change of Name)* [1993] 1 FLR 699.

"unless the contrary is proved" (r 4.8(6))—As, for example, where the document is returned undelivered see *R v London County Quarter Sessions Appeal Committee ex parte Rossi* [1956] 1 QB 682, [1956] 2 WLR 800. If a document is proved to have been received before the date specified in r 4.8(6), the date of service is the actual date of receipt (*Hodgson v Hart District Council* [1986] 1 WLR 317, [1986] 1 All ER 400).

"statement in Form C9" (r 4.8(7))—Form C9 requires the applicant to give details of service of the application on each of the other parties, and to give details of service on persons to whom notice has to be given in accordance with column (iv) of App 3 to these rules. The details must include the manner, date, time and place of service; where service was effected by post, the date, time and place of posting must be given.

"each respondent" (r 4.8(7)(*a*))—As to who the respondents are, see r 4.7.

Notice under rule 4.4(3) (r 4.8(7)(*b*))—Rule 4.4(3) obliges the applicant to serve notice in Form C6A of the proceedings and of the date and place of the first hearing or appointment on the persons set out in column (iv) of App 3 to these rules.

Directions under r 4.8(8)—Such a direction would no doubt be sought in accordance with the procedure set out in r 4.14. Rule 4.8(8) permits the court to dispense with service or to dictate an alternative means of service. Where a party seeks a direction for leave not to serve a person with proceedings (where service is otherwise required by App 3), r 4.8(8) confers on the court a general discretion to direct that the rule as to service should be disapplied. In exercising that discretion, the welfare of the child is not the paramount consideration, although it is an important consideration (*Re X (Care: Notice of Proceedings)* [1996] 1 FLR 186 – where the court was entitled to consider, quite independently of the welfare of the child, the effect on the child's family which would be likely if notice of the public law proceedings were to be served on the putative father. The court considered per curiam that, in a case where service of proceedings would give rise to a very real danger of serious violence, the court would have a discretion to direct that notice of proceedings need not be served on a particular individual, notwithstanding that service would otherwise be required under the rules).

4.9 Answer to application

(1) Within 14 days of service of an application for a section 8 order or an application under Schedule 1, each respondent shall file, and serve on the parties, an acknowledgement of the application in Form C7.

(2) (*deleted*)

(3) Following service of an application to which this Part applies, other than an application under rule 4.3 or for a section 8 order, a respondent may, subject to paragraph (4), file a written answer, which shall be served on the other parties.

(4) An answer under paragraph (3) shall, except in the case of an application under section 25, 31, 34, 38, 43, 44, 45, 46, 48 or 50, be filed, and served, not less than 2 days before the date fixed for the hearing of the application.

Amendments—SI 1994/3155.

Defined terms—"application": r 4.1(1); "section 8 order": CA 1989, s 8(2).

Scope of provision—This rule deals with the obligation of respondents to file and serve an answer.

"within 14 days of service" (r 4.9(1))—As to the computation of time, see r 1.5; as to the extension of time, see rr 4.15(1) and 4.14(2).

Service—See r 4.8.

Parties—See r 4.7.

Form C7—Each respondent to an application for a s 8 order or an order under CA 1989, Sch 1 must serve on the other parties to the proceedings an acknowledgement in Form C7. Form C7 requires the respondent to give details identifying himself and his solicitor (if he has one) and to give an address to which correspondence may be sent. The respondent must state when he received the application, whether he opposes it, and whether he intends to apply to the court for an order. If the respondent indicates that he does wish to apply for an order himself, that indication is not tantamount to making the application, which must be launched using an application form in the normal way (see r 4.4). Form C7 allows only a small space for the respondent to say whether or not he opposes the application. He is not invited to give his side of the picture at this early stage. This is deliberate, since in s 8 cases the filing of evidence and giving of information is strictly controlled (see r 4.17(4), (5)). The acknowledgement should, therefore, restrict itself to the fact of opposition. If the applicant has asked the court to order the respondent to make a payment for a child under CA 1989, Sch 1, the respondent must also fill in a statement of his financial means in Form C10A.

"Schedule 1" (r 4.9(1))—CA 1989, Sch 1 contains provisions with regard to financial provision for children.

"application to which this Part applies" (r 4.9(3))—For the applications to which Pt IV applies, see r 4.1(2).

"application under rule 4.3" (r 4.9(3))—This is an application for leave to commence proceedings.

Written answer under r 4.9(3)—Where the prescribed forms are not applicable, the respondent's written answer must be drafted from scratch. It is suggested that a similar format to that used in the prescribed form is adopted and the same sort of matters covered. Rule 4.9(3) provides that the respondent *may* file a written answer; he is not obliged to do so as he is under r 4.9(1). However, should he choose to file an answer (and obviously, from a practical point of view, it is imperative that he does if he seriously wishes to contest the application), he must abide by the time limits set out in r 4.9(4). Rule 4.9(1) makes it quite plain it is the respondent who must serve an acknowledgement in the prescribed form. Rule 4.9(3) is a little ambiguous but the obligation must still be that of the respondent; service through the court does not fit into the scheme of Pt IV.

"not less than 2 days before the date fixed for the hearing of the application" (r 4.9(4))—There is a distinction between the hearing of the application (by reference to which the deadline for the answer is fixed) and the directions appointments which are likely to take place in the run up to the hearing. Under r 4.14(2), the court has power to curtail (or extend) the time allowed for filing an acknowledgement or answer, and will no doubt consider at one of the directions appointments whether the time for filing should be brought forward in order to ensure that all parties have knowledge of the respondent's case sufficiently far in advance of the hearing.

Exceptions to r 4.9(4)—Where the application is made under one of the provisions listed in r 4.9(4), there is no time fixed by the rules for the filing and service of the respondent's written answer, although the court could fix a time using its power under r 4.14(2) to dictate a timetable for the proceedings.

"section 25, 31, 34, 38, 43, 44, 45, 46, 48 or 50" (r 4.9(4))—These provisions of CA 1989 are concerned with the following: s 25 (application for authority to keep a child in secure accommodation); s 31 (application for care or supervision order); s 34 (application with regard to contact with a child in care); s 38 (interim orders in care or supervision proceedings or where the court gives a direction to a local authority to investigate a child's circumstances); s 43 (child assessment orders); s 44 (emergency protection orders); s 45 (supplementary provisions with regard to emergency protection orders, including applications for their extension and discharge); s 46 (application for emergency protection order by police who have a child in their protection); s 48 (applications for additional powers to assist in finding children who are or may be in need of emergency protection); and s 50 (recovery orders to assist where a child has run away, been abducted etc).

4.10 Appointment of children's guardian

(1) As soon as practicable after the commencement of specified proceedings, or the transfer of such proceedings to the court, the court shall appoint a children's guardian, unless –

- (*a*) such an appointment has already been made by the court which made the transfer and is subsisting, or
- (*b*) the court considers that such an appointment is not necessary to safeguard the interests of the child.

(2) At any stage in specified proceedings a party may apply, without notice to the other parties unless the court directs otherwise, for the appointment of a children's guardian.

(3) The court shall grant an application under paragraph (2) unless it considers such an appointment not to be necessary to safeguard the interests of the child, in which case it shall give its reasons; and a note of such reasons shall be taken by the proper officer.

(4) At any stage in specified proceedings the court may, of its own motion, appoint a children's guardian.

(4A) The court may, in specified proceedings, appoint more than one children's guardian in respect of the same child.

(5) The proper officer shall, as soon as practicable, notify the parties and any welfare officer or children and family reporter of an appointment under this rule or, as the case may be, of a decision not to make such an appointment.

(6) Upon the appointment of a children's guardian the proper officer shall, as soon as practicable, notify him of the appointment and serve on him copies of the application and of documents filed under rule 4.17(1).

(7) A children's guardian appointed by the court under this rule shall not –

(*a*) be a member, officer or servant of a local authority which, or an authorised person (within the meaning of section 31(9)) who, is a party to the proceedings;

(*b*) be, or have been, a member, officer or servant of a local authority or voluntary organisation (within the meaning of section 105(1)) who has been directly concerned in that capacity in arrangements relating to the care, accommodation or welfare of the child during the five years prior to the commencement of the proceedings; or

(*c*) be a serving probation officer who has, in that capacity, been previously concerned with the child or his family.

(8) When appointing a children's guardian the court shall consider the appointment of anyone who has previously acted as children's guardian of the same child.

(9) The appointment of a children's guardian under this rule shall continue for such time as is specified in the appointment or until terminated by the court.

(10) When terminating an appointment in accordance with paragraph (9), the court shall give its reasons in writing for so doing.

(11) Where the court appoints a children's guardian in accordance with this rule or refuses to make such an appointment, the court or the proper officer shall record the appointment or refusal in Form C47.

Amendments—SI 1994/3155; SI 2001/821.

Defined terms—"application", "child": r 4.1(1); "court": r 1.2(1); "children's guardian": r 4.1(1); "proper officer": r 1.2(1); "specified proceedings": CA 1989, s 41(6) and r 4.2(2); "voluntary organisation": CA 1989, s 105(1); "welfare officer or children and family reporter": r 4.1(1).

Appointment—The obligation to appoint a children's guardian in specified proceedings unless the circumstances are as described in r 4.10(1)(*b*) is imposed by CA 1989, s 41(1). The purpose of r 4.10(1) is to require the appointment to be made as soon as practicable after the commencement of the proceedings, or the arrival of transferred proceedings if the transferring court has not already made an appointment. The appointment is likely to be made by way of a direction under r 4.14(2)(*d*) (which can be done quickly and without a hearing as long as the parties are given the opportunity to make written representations; this would have the advantage of enabling the guardian to be in place in time to attend the first actual directions appointment). Where proceedings in which a guardian has already been appointed are transferred, the appointment continues to subsist unless terminated in accordance with r 4.10. Curiously, r 4.10(1)(*a*) refers only to the court which made the transfer, which seems to produce the strange result that where proceedings are transferred to a third court it is apparently required to appoint a guardian if the existing one had been appointed by the first court rather than by the second one (for example, where a justices' clerk had appointed a guardian before transferring the proceedings to a county court under Children (Allocation of Proceedings) Order 1991, art 7, and the county court had immediately transferred the proceedings on to the High Court under art 12, see r 4.6(4)). In such circumstances, the third court may wish, as a purely formal step, to issue a new Form C47 re-appointing the existing guardian to avoid any doubt about whether the rule has been breached.

The focus on "commencement" and "transfer" in r 4.10(1)(*a*) seems inappropriate for some types of specified proceedings. Any non-specified family proceedings will become "specified" at any time while they are pending if a direction under CA 1989, s 37(1) (investigation of the child's circumstances) is given, or if the court begins to consider making a s 8 order in respect of a child who is in care (see CA 1989, s 41(6)(*b*), (*e*)). In those circumstances, the requirement really means as soon as practicable after the proceedings become specified. In view of the requirement of r 4.10(1), the application procedure and own motion power provided by r 4.10(2)–(4) will need to be invoked only where the court or a party thinks that the initial decision that a children's guardian was unnecessary has proved to be too optimistic in the light of the development of the proceedings during their interlocutory stages, or where the first guardian has died or been removed under this rule.

Appointment of guardian as a result of a s 37 direction—See **"direction under section 37(1)"** under CA 1989, s 41.

Appointment not necessary (r 4.10(1)(*b*))—See eg *Re J (A Minor) (Change of Name)* [1993] 1 FLR 699.

Who may be appointed—Rule 4.10(7)(*a*), (*b*) makes provision which may make individuals ineligible for selection to act as children's guardian in particular proceedings if they have a close connection with the local authority concerned in the case or with any local authority if they have actually been involved with the arrangements for the child in that capacity within the previous five years. Rule 4.10(7)(*c*) also excludes probation officers unless they have not been involved with the child or his family in that capacity (see *Devon CC and Others v S and Others* [1993] 1 FLR 842, where a welfare officer (children and family reporter) from previous proceedings was ineligible on account of being a probation officer). Rule 4.10(8) requires the court to consider re-appointing anyone who has acted as the children's guardian in previous proceedings; the requirement is to do no more than consider re-appointing such a person, but the court will usually lean in favour of such a re-appointment as the previous knowledge of the child and the earlier proceedings will tend to enable the guardian better to safeguard the child's interests in the new proceedings. This approach was followed in *Re J (Adoption: Appointment of GAL)* [1999] 2 FLR 86 where, although the guardian's appointment had technically ceased on the making of a care order, she had continued to be involved in later residence proceedings, had attended a strategy meeting when adoption was discussed and had apparently agreed at the meeting that adoption was best for the child. The mother's application to disqualify the guardian from acting in the adoption proceedings was refused on the basis that the fact that in the course of lengthy proceedings the guardian had had to express adverse views of the mother did not amount to bias against her and the advantages of appointing a guardian with such a high degree of familiarity with the case and the child were overwhelming.

Duration of appointment—When appointing a guardian, the court may specify the length of the appointment; otherwise the appointment will last until terminated by the court (r 4.10(9)). The latter will be the more usual course. Where a guardian has been appointed as a result of a direction under CA 1989, s 37 (investigation of the child's circumstances), it is good practice for the order making his appointment to contain a direction that the guardian's continuing involvement be reviewed on completion of the s 37 report (*Re CE (Section 37 Direction)* [1995] 1 FLR 26). Rule 4.10 does not specify what procedure is to be followed to terminate an appointment except to require the reasons to be given once the decision has been taken (r 4.10(10)); this is in contrast with the provision of r 4.12(3) and (4) in relation to the child's solicitor. Rule 4.14(2)(*d*) specifically mentions the appointment of a guardian as something that can be dealt with under the direction-making procedure and it is submitted that this embraces the termination of such an appointment. Rule 4.14(3)(*a*) would therefore require the parties to be consulted first. Usually, this would enable the children's guardian to make his own views known, but, where the child's solicitor is taking his instructions directly from the child (see r 4.12(1)(*a*)), it is suggested that the court should allow the guardian to make representations before removing him altogether. This procedure was followed in *Re M (Terminating Appointment of Guardian ad Litem)* [1999] 2 FLR 717 where it was said that a court which terminated a guardian's appointment of its own motion should follow the procedure set out in r 4.14(3)(*a*) giving the guardian notice of the course proposed by the court and the opportunity to attend and be heard or to make written representations. If a guardian does act manifestly contrary to the child's best interests, the court will remove him even though neither his good faith nor his diligence is in issue. In reaching a responsible and considered decision, on which another mind might possibly take a different view, a guardian does not act manifestly contrary to the child's best interests (*Re A (Conjoined Twins: Medical Treatment) (No 2)* [2001] 1 FLR 267). Derivative applications, such as those to discharge a care order or to regulate contact with a child in care, are separate proceedings and not a continuation of the original care proceedings for this purpose (see the structure of s 41(6)); therefore the original guardian's appointment will not automatically carry over into the new proceedings. Indeed, once a care order has been made, the children's guardian has no function in relation to the actions of the local authority under the order, and the court has no power to add a direction to a care order that the guardian ad litem (children's guardian) continue his involvement with the child (*Kent County Council v C* [1993] 1 FLR 308). See also **"Starred" care plans** under CA 1989, s 31. When a supervision order is made the proceedings are not to be treated as concluded until the order has ceased; and, unless terminated by the court, the guardian's role continues. In such cases the court, the local authority and the guardian should consider, as part of the care plan, the role (if any) the guardian is to play in the implementation of the order; in the absence of agreement the role of the guardian should be the subject of court directions (*Re MH (A Child) and Re SB and MB (Children)* [2001] 2 FLR 1334). However, in *Oxfordshire County Council v L and F* [1997] 1 FLR 235 applications in respect of disclosure of documents in care proceedings to the police and the removal of injunctions restricting publication of material within care proceedings were made the day after care proceedings were concluded and the guardian ad litem (children's guardian) was allowed to continue to represent the child, despite the fact that her locus standi was far from clear. Where a guardian ad litem (children's guardian) has been appointed for the purposes of an emergency protection order, she is no longer the guardian ad litem (children's guardian) when the emergency protection order has expired and there are no pending proceedings (*Re M (Prohibited Steps Order: Application for Leave)* [1993] 1 FLR 275). A literal reading of r 4.10(9) would seem to suggest that the court cannot remove a guardian who had been appointed by a magistrates' court (ie before transferring the proceedings up), because the appointment would not have been made "under this rule" (it would have been made under Family Proceedings Courts (Children Act 1989) Rules 1991, r 10); however, it is submitted that there is scope for construing the provision to include such cases.

Where interests of children conflict—There is usually no reason why a guardian ad litem (children's guardian) should not properly represent children whose interests conflict (*Re T and E (Proceedings: Conflicting Interests)* [1995] 1 FLR 581, FD).

Appointment of second guardian—FPR 1991, r 4.10(4A) allows the appointment of a second children's guardian in specified proceedings where the particular circumstances of the case require it, for example where additional enquiries need to be undertaken in an area that is a considerable distance from the court hearing area, they may be carried out by a local children's guardian.

"notify" (r 4.10(5), (6))—The manner of notification does not seem to be regulated, since r 4.8 (service of documents) does not seem to apply.

"authorised person" (r 4.10(7)(*a*))—CA 1989, s 31(9) provides that "authorised person" means the NSPCC and any of its officers and any person (or the officers of any body) authorised by the Secretary of State to bring proceedings under s 31 (ie for a care or supervision order).

Refusal to make an appointment (r 4.10(11))—The concept of a refusal imports a request to act in the way refused, but it is submitted that it is appropriate for the prescribed form to be completed not only where the court refuses an application under r 4.10(2) but also where the court initially decides not to make an appointment under r 4.10(1). The court may then comply with r 4.10(5) by despatching a copy of the form.

4.11 Powers and duties of officers of the service

(1) In carrying out his duty under section 7(1)(*a*) or section 41(2), the officer of the service shall have regard to the principle set out in section 1(2) and the matters set out in section 1(3)(*a*) to (*f*) as if for the word "court" in that section there were substituted the words "officer of the service".

(2) The officer of the service shall make such investigations as may be necessary for him to carry out his duties and shall, in particular –

(*a*) contact or seek to interview such persons as he thinks appropriate or as the court directs;

(*b*) obtain such professional assistance as is available to him which he thinks appropriate or which the court directs him to obtain.

(3) In addition to his duties, under other paragraphs of this rule, or rules 4.11A and 4.11B, the officer of the service shall provide to the court such other assistance as it may require.

(4) A party may question the officer of the service about oral or written advice tendered by him to the court.

Amendments—SI 1991/2113; SI 2001/821.

Defined terms—"application", "child": r 4.1(1); "court": r 1.2(1); "directions appointment", "children's guardian"; "note": r 4.1(1); "officer of the service": CJCSA 2000, s 11(3); "proper officer": r 1.2(1).

"the principle set out in section 1(2)" (r 4.11(1))—As modified by r 4.11(1) for this purpose, CA 1989, s 1(2) provides that "In any proceedings in which any question with respect to the upbringing of a child arises, the officer of the service shall have regard to the general principle that any delay in determining the question is likely to prejudice the welfare of the child".

"the matters set out in section 1(3)(a) to (f)" (r 4.11(1))—This rule makes it clear that officers must have regard to the welfare checklist when carrying out all aspects of their duties under s 41(2); see CA 1989, s 1(3)(*a*)–(*f*).

"professional assistance" (r 4.11(2)(*b*))—This term is not defined but includes the services of all types of expert witness.

Questioning the officer of the service (r 4.11(4))—In the case of written advice, this right would crystallise at the hearing at which the issue addressed by the advice (be it interim or final) is to be considered but, if a pre-trial directions appointment is held after the report becomes available, it may assist the clarification of the issues to be dealt with at the full hearing if the parties question the guardian at the appointment.

Comparison of roles of children's guardian and children and family reporter—In *Re S (A Minor) (Guardian ad Litem/Welfare Officer)* [1993] 1 FLR 110, it was held that, although the power exists both at first instance (CA 1989, s 7) and on appeal (ss 7, 94(5)) to appoint a welfare officer or children and family reporter in public law proceedings, such an appointment should not be made when (as will normally be the case) a children's guardian has already been appointed, save in exceptional circumstances. Rule 4.11 sets out powers and duties shared by all officers of the service. Rule 4.11A gives the children's guardian additional powers which reflect the guardian's extra duty to represent the child in court and to instruct legal representation for the child if necessary. Rule 4.11B sets out additional powers and duties of a children and family reporter who is to provide a report under CA 1989, s 7(1)(*a*) and enables the reporter to consider whether the child should be a party to the proceedings and to notify the court should he feel that is necessary. In *L v L (Minors) (Separate Representation)* [1994] 1 FLR 156, however, whilst not dissenting from the general principle in *Re S (A Minor) (Guardian ad Litem/Welfare Officer)* (above), the Court of Appeal hoped that the court welfare officer (children and family reporter), who had already begun investigations in a difficult case, would report despite the appointment of a children's guardian to represent the children.

4.11A Additional powers and duties of children's guardian

(1) The children's guardian shall –

(*a*) appoint a solicitor to represent the child unless such a solicitor has already been appointed; and

(*b*) give such advice to the child as is appropriate having regard to his understanding and, subject to rule 4.12(1)(*a*), instruct the solicitor representing the child on all matters relevant to the interests of the child including possibilities for appeal, arising in the course of the proceedings.

(2) Where the children's guardian is an officer of the service authorised by the Service in the terms mentioned by and in accordance with section 15(1) of the Criminal Justice and Court Services Act 2000, paragraph 1(*a*) shall not require him

to appoint a solicitor for the child if he intends to have conduct of the proceedings on behalf of the child unless –

(*a*) the child wishes to instruct a solicitor direct; and
(*b*) the children's guardian or the court considers that he is of sufficient understanding to do so.

(3) Where it appears to the children's guardian that the child –

(*a*) is instructing his solicitor direct, or
(*b*) intends to conduct and is capable of conducting the proceedings on his own behalf,

he shall inform the court and from then he –

(i) shall perform all of his duties set out in rule 4.11 and this rule, other than duties under paragraph (1)(*a*) of this rule, and such other duties as the court may direct;
(ii) shall take such part in the proceedings as the court may direct; and
(iii) may, with leave of the court, have legal representation in the conduct of those duties.

(4) Unless excused by the court, the children's guardian shall attend all directions appointments in and hearings of the proceedings and shall advise the court on the following matters –

(*a*) whether the child is of sufficient understanding for any purpose including the child's refusal to submit to a medical or psychiatric examination or other assessment that the court has power to require, direct or order;
(*b*) the wishes of the child in respect of any matter relevant to the proceedings, including his attendance at court;
(*c*) the appropriate forum for the proceedings;
(*d*) the appropriate timing of the proceedings or any part of them;
(*e*) the options available to it in respect of the child and the suitability of each such option including what order should be made in determining the application; and
(*f*) any other matter concerning which the court seeks his advice or concerning which he considers that the court should be informed.

(5) The advice given under paragraph (4) may, subject to any order of the court, be given orally or in writing; and if the advice be given orally, a note of it shall be taken by the court or the proper officer.

(6) The children's guardian shall, where practicable, notify any person whose joinder as a party to those proceedings would be likely, in the opinion of the children's guardian, to safeguard the interests of the child of that person's right to apply to be joined under rule 4.7(2) and shall inform the court –

(*a*) of any such notification given;
(*b*) of anyone whom he attempted to notify under this paragraph but was unable to contact; and
(*c*) of anyone whom he believes may wish to be joined to the proceedings.

(7) The children's guardian shall, unless the court otherwise directs, not less than 14 days before the date fixed for the final hearing of the proceedings –

(*a*) file a written report advising on the interests of the child; and
(*b*) serve a copy of the filed report on the other parties.

(8) The children's guardian shall serve and accept service of documents on behalf of the child in accordance with rule 4.8(3)(*b*) and (4)(*b*) and, where the child has

not himself been served, and has sufficient understanding, advise the child of the contents of any document so served.

(9) If the children's guardian inspects records of the kinds referred to in section 42, he shall bring to the attention of –

(*a*) the court; and

(*b*) unless the court otherwise directs, the other parties to the proceedings,

all records and documents which may, in his opinion, assist in the proper determination of the proceedings.

(10) The children's guardian shall ensure that, in relation to a decision made by the court in the proceedings –

(*a*) if he considers it appropriate to the age and understanding of the child, the child is notified of that decision; and

(*b*) if the child is notified of the decision, it is explained to the child in a manner appropriate to his age and understanding.

Amendments—Inserted by SI 2001/821.

Duties of children's guardian—CA 1989, s 41(2)(*b*) places the children's guardian under a duty to safeguard the interests of the child in the manner prescribed by rules of court. This rule prescribes how this general duty is to be performed and lays far more specific duties on the children's guardian than those which are upon guardians ad litem under Pt IX or in general civil proceedings. In *R v Cornwall County Council ex parte G* [1992] 1 FLR 270, it was emphasised that guardians ad litem (children's guardians) are independent in the performance of their duties; and it was accordingly held that a local authority had acted unlawfully in seeking to restrict the number of hours spent by guardians on each individual case. A children and family reporter (CFR) also acts independently and exercises an independent discretion as to the nature of his investigations and enquiries. The relationship between the judge and the CFR is a collaborative one. The CFR executes that part of the judge's function which is inquisitorial. The judge should give due weight to the outcome of the CFR's investigations (*Re M (Disclosure: Children and Family Reporter)* [2002] EWCA Civ 1199, [2002] 2 FLR 893).

If a care order is made, the guardian ad litem (children's guardian) has no role in relation to the way in which the local authority performs its duties under the order, and the court has no power to direct the continuing involvement of the guardian ad litem (children's guardian) (*Kent County Council v C* [1993] 1 FLR 308). The guardian may find himself requested to act as a collator of expert reports and to produce for the court a schedule of the areas of agreement and dispute (*Re C (Expert Evidence: Disclosure: Practice)* [1995] 1 FLR 204). In *Re L (Care Proceedings: Disclosure to Third Party)* [2000] 1 FLR 913 the guardian was asked, as an officer of the court, to disclose information concerning the psychiatric condition of a mother to the UK Central Council for Nursing, Midwifery and Health Visiting.

Duties of children's guardian where local authority documents appear to be protected by public interest immunity—See **Documents which appear to be protected from disclosure by public interest immunity** under CA 1989, s 42 and FPR 1991, r 4.23.

"subject to r 4.12(1)(a)" (r 4.11A(1)(*b*))—Rule 4.12(1)(*a*) allows the solicitor to take instructions direct from the child where the child is capable, having regard to his understanding, to give them.

Child's understanding—Rule 4.11A refers a number of times to the understanding of a child. The courts have considered the question of a child's understanding in the following cases which, although not all arising in relation to this particular rule, should assist in this context: *Re S (A Minor) (Independent Representation)* [1993] 2 FLR 437, CA; *Re H (A Minor) (Role of Official Solicitor)* [1993] 2 FLR 552, FD; *Re K, W and H (Minors) (Medical Treatment)* [1993] 1 FLR 854; *Re CT (A Minor) (Wardship: Representation)* [1993] 2 FLR 278. See **"able ... to give such instructions on his own behalf"** under r 4.12.

"he shall inform the court" (r 4.11A(3))—Where it appears to the guardian ad litem (children's guardian) that the child is instructing his solicitor direct or intends to, and is capable of, conducting the proceedings on his own behalf, he should inform the court of the relevant

PART III

circumstances on a directions appointment (*Re M (Minors) (Care Proceedings: Child's Wishes)* [1994] 1 FLR 749). This means that he should either report the matter to the court at the next directions appointment or, if there is no such appointment fixed, immediately take out an appointment for directions so that the question of representation can be considered and decided by the court because: (1) there may be an issue about the capacity of the child to give coherent and consistent instructions, and expert evidence may be required to resolve the issue; (2) the court has a duty to ensure that the proceedings are disposed of promptly and in the most effective manner; (3) the other parties, particularly the child's parents, have a right to know at an early stage how their child is to be represented in the proceedings and what view their child is expressing; and (4) it is important for the court to know in advance whether or not the child and the children's guardian are to be separately represented so that the judge, when reading the papers in advance, can be alert to all issues.

Hybrid proceedings—In hybrid proceedings, or in any straightforward adoption proceedings, where the wishes and feelings of the child are in conflict with the guardian's assessment of welfare and disposal, it may be necessary to give the child an independent voice through his own legal representation (*Re O (Transracial Adoption: Contact)* [1995] 2 FLR 597 – where the court considered an application for adoption of a child in the care of the local authority together with applications by the mother for discharge of the care order and the making of a residence order in her favour).

Guardian detached from child (r 4.11A(3))—Where the child's solicitor is taking instructions from the child himself (see r 4.12(1)), the role of the children's guardian remains wholly in the discretion of the court. The court may feel that it would be beneficial, particularly if the detachment occurred at a late stage in the course of the proceedings, for the guardian to have full liberty to present a case as if he were a party to the proceedings (by calling evidence, cross-examining other parties' witnesses, addressing argument etc, for which purposes he would probably wish his own legal representation to be authorised under r 4.11A(3)(*b*)(iii)) and by making a report in the usual way. This ensures that a neutral view of the best interests of the child is advanced since, where the guardian does retain a role, CA 1989, s 41(1)(*b*) continues to require him to perform it for the purpose of safeguarding the interests of the child. However, the court may think it right to permit only a smaller role or even to terminate the guardian's appointment altogether under r 4.10(9).

In the ordinary case where conflict arises, the solicitor first appointed continues in the case putting the views, wishes and feelings of the child, and the guardian finds a fresh advocate to assist him in his continuing role as defined by the court; however, in *Re P (Representation)* [1996] 1 FLR 486, the reverse was ordered where there were seven children involved, one of whom wished to instruct her own lawyer late in the proceedings; it was decided to appoint a fresh solicitor for the one, and the original solicitor would continue to represent the remaining six.

"the children's guardian ... shall advise the court" (r 4.11A(4))—It is not part of the children's guardian function to adopt a judicial role or to seek to assess material which he does not have the expertise to assess (*B v B (Child Abuse: Contact)* [1994] 2 FLR 713 – the guardian sought to analyse interviews with children about sexual abuse, and Wall J held that this was a specialised skill which should only be undertaken by an expert in the field). However, it is proper for the guardian to offer his opinion on child care and related matters to the court where he has the experience in his background to justify offering such an opinion (*G v A Borough Council* [2000] Fam Law 11). See also *Re N (Child Abuse: Evidence)* [1996] 2 FLR 214 – a guardian may state that his belief in what the child says is the reason for his conclusion in his report and for the advice that he gives to the court, but it is best for his report and evidence to acknowledge expressly that it is the court's decision as to whether the child should be believed. In *Re M and R (Child Abuse: Evidence)* [1996] 2 FLR 195 the evidence of an expert's opinion dealing with issues such as whether a child should be believed was admissible; however, the final decision is that of the judge alone. Presumably the guardian can rely on such admissible expert evidence in forming his conclusions and recommendations, while acknowledging that the final decision is that of the court.

In *Re K (Supervision Orders)* [1999] 2 FLR 303 Wall J held that a guardian's opinions about threshold criteria could not be ruled inadmissible, even if they were at odds with all the other parties. However, the guardian must be careful not to usurp the function of the court and would be wise to predicate any recommendations on the premise that the court will make certain findings of fact. The guardian had a duty to represent the child and put all matters relevant to the child's welfare before the court. The guardian is the child's protection against poor social work practice, procedural delay and collusive agreements. However, where the local authority and the mother had reached a sensible agreement which clearly protected the child and was in no sense collusive, the guardian should think long and hard before seeking to upset that agreement or before putting forward contentious alternative proposals.

Child's capacity to refuse to be examined etc (r 4.11A(4)(*a*))—CA 1989, s 38(6) provides that a child of sufficient understanding may refuse to submit to an examination or assessment directed by a court making an interim care or supervision order; s 43(8) allows a child who is of sufficient understanding to make an informed decision to refuse to submit to a medical or psychiatric examination or other assessment which would otherwise have been authorised by a child assessment order. In *Re H (A Minor) (Care Proceedings: Child's Wishes)* [1993] 1 FLR 440 at 449A, Thorpe J said, in relation to the child's capacity under CA 1989, s 38(6) to make an informed decision whether to refuse to submit to a psychiatric examination, that "the level of understanding that enables a child to make an informed decision whether to refuse to submit to a psychiatric examination is in all practical senses a much higher level of understanding than is required to enable him to give instructions to a solicitor on his own behalf". It is useful to compare this with the power of the court, in exercising the inherent jurisdiction of the High Court, to override the child's wishes in respect of medical treatment (see *Re W (A Minor) (Consent to Medical Treatment)* [1993] 1 FLR 1).

Confidentiality—The report of the guardian is confidential and should not be disclosed to anyone other than the parties to the proceedings and their legal advisers without leave of the court. The same rule appears to extend to the information collected by the guardian in the course of his investigation for the report. In *Oxfordshire County Council v P* [1995] 1 FLR 552, FD, Ward J (as he then was) placed a wide interpretation on FPR 1991, r 4.23 and the duties of confidentiality in children cases, and held that the guardian had fallen into the error (potentially amounting to contempt of court) of making a witness statement to the police without leave of the court about an admission made to her by the mother of a baby who was the subject of care proceedings that she had caused the child's injuries. The guardian had also informed social services of the admission, but was not criticised for this because the cloak of confidentiality is not lifted when information is exchanged in relation to proceedings between parties to the proceedings if the information remains confidential to the proceedings. In *Cleveland County Council v F* [1995] 1 FLR 797, Hale J followed the decision in *Oxfordshire County Council v P* (above) and held that any incriminating statements which the mother might make to the guardian or social worker were adequately protected from disclosure by CA 1989, s 98 and FPR 1991, r 4.23. However, in *Re G (Social Worker: Disclosure)* [1996] 1 FLR 276, Butler-Sloss LJ gave a restrictive interpretation of r 4.23 and held that the guidelines set out in *Oxfordshire County Council v P* (above) and in *Cleveland County Council v F* (above) were possibly misleading insofar as Ward and Hale JJ appeared to equate the position of the social worker with that of the guardian in holding that any incriminating statements which the mother might make to the guardian or social worker were adequately protected from disclosure by CA 1989, s 98 and FPR 1991, r 4.23. It appears that the confidentiality of information obtained as a result of pending family proceedings, but not yet reduced to writing and filed, may differ according to the status of the person who receives the information and, in particular, the position of a children's guardian may differ from that of the social worker. In *Re G*, Butler-Sloss LJ held that the guardian was appointed by CA 1989, s 41 and his powers and duties were laid down by s 42 of that Act which gave him a right of access to local authority records. He had no function outside the proceedings to which he had been appointed. When those proceedings were completed, his function was ended. It might be that disclosure of all documents emanating from, or information given to, the guardian would be subject to the leave of the court. This role contrasted with that of the social worker. All information garnered by social workers is confidential, covered by public interest immunity and not to be disclosed to those not engaged (as may be, for example, the police, paediatricians, the child protection case conference) in the investigation and protection process. Some of the information (but only some) will be in the custody and control of the court, and will require court leave before it is disclosed even to those involved in the investigation and protection process; this does not include an oral statement made by a parent to a social worker, even if recorded on the social work file, provided it has not been filed with the court so as to bring it within r 4.23. However, Butler-Sloss LJ did not wish to express a view, in the absence of argument, as to the scope of the guardian's duty to the court and whether it excluded the duty to inform the police of admissions of criminal offences, without obtaining leave of the civil court. Her Ladyship acknowledged that the different positions of social worker and guardian might create a certain anomaly, in that the same statement given to different people might be subject to different rules of confidentiality, but held that that might be a necessary consequence of their different statutory roles. See also *Re R (Care Proceedings: Disclosure)* [2000] 2 FLR 751. However, leave of the court was not required for a CAFCASS officer to disclose information obtained in private law proceedings to the local authority (*Re M (Disclosure: Children and Family Reporter)* [2002] EWCA Civ 1199, [2002] 2 FLR 893).

The principle of confidentiality is strictly confined so that, once proceedings are at an end, the further distribution of the guardian's report is a matter to be controlled by the court (*Re C (Guardian ad Litem: Disclosure of Report)* [1996] 1 FLR 61 – where, at the conclusion of care proceedings, leave was given to disclose the guardian's report to a family centre which offered therapeutic treatment to the children concerned, it was held that the court should be told for whom the distribution of the report was particularly required, and some investigation should be made into who should properly see the report). As to confidentiality generally, see r 4.23.

Where a children's guardian becomes aware of information that the child does not wish to be revealed to another party in the proceedings, it can never be proper for the guardian to promise the child that the information will be withheld from the court. In an unusually sensitive case involving an older child, a guardian could properly tell the child that the judge would be told that the child did not wish the information to be disclosed to a particular party, and why. In such a case, the court was required to balance the right of a properly concerned party to disclosure of information submitted to the court on which the judge's conclusion might in some measure be based, against the paramount interest of the child (*Re C (Disclosure)* [1996] 1 FLR 797, which applied the principles in *Re D (Adoption Reports: Confidentiality)* [1996] AC 593, [1995] 2 FLR 687 to proceedings under CA 1989). Such cases should be transferred to the High Court (*Re C (Disclosure)* above).

For the position with regard to showing the children's guardian's report to an expert, see **Written report by children's guardian** below.

Where interests of children conflict—See under r 4.10.

Written report by children's guardian—It is a matter for the discretion of the court whether a report of a children's guardian in public law proceedings can be made available to a court hearing related private law proceedings and to the parties thereto. If two courts are dealing with different sets of proceedings concerning siblings (an exceptional situation, as it is normally right for one court to deal with all proceedings where siblings are concerned), the report should normally be made available to both (*W v Wakefield City Council* [1995] 1 FLR 170).

Re T and E (Proceedings: Conflicting Interests) [1995] 1 FLR 581 stresses the importance of the guardian's report being read by any expert witness whose evidence goes either to the disposal of the case or to issues canvassed in the report. Any leave to show papers to an expert should be drawn widely enough to cover this step.

Attendance of child at court—Whilst the court can allow the child who is the subject of an application to attend court, it must always bear in mind that attendance is likely to be harmful to the child and should only permit it if satisfied that it is in the interests of the child (*Re W (Secure Accommodation Order: Attendance at Court)* [1994] 2 FLR 1092 and see, further, **Use of the power to exclude** under r 4.16). The fact that the child would need to be physically restrained during the hearing in order to control him (as in *Re W (Secure Accommodation Order: Attendance at Court)*, above) would, in itself, be sufficient ground for refusing to allow the child to be in court. Further examples given in *Re W* of situations in which the court would not allow a child to be present are where there is a prospect of disturbance or unruliness in court or the possibility of the child being educationally subnormal or where the child is much younger than the 10-year-old boy in that case. Young children should be discouraged from attending appeals from the justices in family proceedings. Where a guardian is proposing to arrange for a young child to be present, he should give the question very careful thought beforehand and be prepared to explain his reasons to the judge (*Re C (A Minor) (Care: Child's Wishes)* [1993] 1 FLR 832, which concerned a girl of 13).

"notify" and "notification" (r 4.11A(6))—It is submitted that these words do not attract r 10.7 (mode of giving notice) because, although it might have been argued that "notify" was cognate with "notice", the use of "notification" rather than "notice" in conjunction with it indicates the contrary.

"not less than 14 days" (r 4.11A(7))—The requirement as to the time for filing a report may be extended only by direction of the court under r 4.14 (r 4.15(1)). See r 1.5 for how to compute the fourteen-day period.

Service—Service of documents under r 4.11A(7) is governed by r 4.8.

Inspection of records (r 4.11A(9))—CA 1989, s 42 allows a children's guardian, at all reasonable times, to examine and copy local authority records which were compiled in connection with the making, or proposed making, of any application under CA 1989 in relation to the child concerned or in connection with the authority's social services functions in relation to the child and gives him a similar right in relation to authorised person's records. Section 41(2) and (3) makes any copies taken admissible in evidence of certain matters. A guardian ad litem (children's guardian) is entitled to see case records prepared by the local authority giving detailed information concerning prospective adopters and to include the relevant information derived from it in his report to the court (*Re T (A Minor) (Guardian ad Litem: Case Record)* [1994] 1 FLR 632). As to the limitations on what the guardian may inspect under s 42 and on disclosure of what he has seen, see under CA 1989, s 42.

Where court differs from children's guardian's advice—The court is not bound to follow the recommendation of the children's guardian but, just as with a welfare officer or children and family reporter, must give careful consideration to any argument advanced by him and, where it differs, must explain its reasons carefully (*S v Oxfordshire County Council* [1993] 1 FLR 452; *Re W (A Minor) (Secure Accommodation Order)* [1993] 1 FLR 692; *Knowsley Metropolitan Borough Council v U* [1993] Fam Law 545).

Duties of children's guardian and local authority to consult one another—Guardians should think long and hard before opposing an agreement between the local authority and the parents of a child subject to care proceedings if it appears to be sensible and appears to protect the child. However, where the guardian has considered the matter carefully and has reached the conclusion that the course proposed by the local authority does not protect the child, the guardian's duty is to safeguard the interests of the child and to put before the court her view as to how best the child's welfare is to be promoted (*Re N (Leave to Withdraw Care Proceedings)* [2000] 1 FLR 134 – where the local authority sought leave to withdraw care proceedings but the guardian successfully opposed the application). In *Re N* (above) Bracewell J criticised the local authority for its failure to consult the guardian and consider her views before taking the decision to apply to withdraw (at 136H). Conversely, in *Re K (Supervision Orders)* [1999] 2 FLR 303, Wall J stressed the independent role of the guardian in representing the child and putting matters relevant to the child's welfare before the court; in addition he stressed the need for the guardian to consider carefully before seeking to upset a sensible agreement between the authority and the parents.

4.11B Additional powers and duties of a children and family reporter

(1) The children and family reporter shall –

(*a*) notify the child of such contents of his report (if any) as he considers appropriate to the age and understanding of the child, including any reference to the child's own views on the application and the recommendation of the children and family reporter; and

(*b*) if he does notify the child of any contents of his report, explain them to the child in a manner appropriate to his age and understanding.

(2) Where the court has –

(*a*) directed that a written report be made by a children and family reporter; and

(*b*) notified the children and family reporter that his report is to be considered at a hearing,

the children and family reporter shall –

(i) file the report; and

(ii) serve a copy on the other parties and on the children's guardian (if any),

by such time as the court may direct and if no direction is given, not less than 14 days before that hearing.

(3) The court may direct that the children and family reporter attend any hearing at which his report is to be considered.

(4) The children and family reporter shall advise the court if he considers that the joinder of a person as a party to the proceedings would be likely to safeguard the interests of the child.

(5) The children and family reporter shall consider whether it is in the best interests of the child for the child to be made a party to the proceedings.

(6) If the children and family reporter considers the child should be made a party to the proceedings he shall notify the court of his opinion together with the reasons for that opinion.

Amendments—Inserted by SI 2001/821.

Filing and service of written reports (r 4.11B(2))—The parties and their legal representatives and the children's guardian will need to digest the written report prior to the hearing; they may also wish to follow up certain matters covered in it (for example, by calling the child's teacher to amplify favourable statements made to the children and family reporter or by calling evidence to rebut assertions contained in the report). It is therefore most important that the report should be available to them in good time and this means that any filing date set by the court should be sufficiently far in advance of the hearing. A failure by the children and family reporter or the court to observe this requirement may be reason to seek an adjournment.

Attendance of children and family reporter (r 4.11B(3))—A children and family reporter is obliged to attend a hearing only if required to do so by a direction under r 4.11B(3). A party who wishes to question the children and family reporter should therefore seek a direction from the court that his attendance is required. For an example of the circumstances in which the court might be right to decline to accede to a request for such a direction, see *Re H (Contact: Principles)* [1994] 2 FLR 969 (contact case in which court welfare officer could not have added anything by attendance, especially as she had been unable to see the father and child together). See also the cases set out in **Court differing with recommendation in welfare report** under CA 1989, s 7. Only in exceptional circumstances will the children and family reporter be asked to see the judge in the absence of the parties (*Official Solicitor v K* [1965] AC 201, (1963) FLR Rep 520, applied in *Re C (A Minor: Irregularity of Practice)* [1991] 2 FLR 438).

Withholding children and family reporter's report from the parties—In exceptional cases, the report may contain sensitive material which ought not to be shown to the parties. Rule 4.11B allows the children and family reporter no discretion to withhold the report or any part of it. However, the court does have power under r 4.14 to give directions with regard to the service of documents and the preparation of reports under CA 1989, s 7. It is therefore suggested that where the children and family reporter feels that part or all of his report should not be shown to a party or certain parties, he should draw this to the court's attention when filing it (which he should do earlier than normal, if possible, so as to allow time for the problem to be sorted out) and apply for directions. The principles applicable on such an application are set out in **Submission of evidence** under r 4.14. Because it is for the judge to decide whether or not evidence must be disclosed to the parties, a children and family reporter/court welfare officer, who is normally a compellable witness, cannot guarantee confidentiality to a person who makes allegations to him whilst he is investigating the circumstances of the case (*Re G (Minors) (Welfare Report: Disclosure)* [1993] 2 FLR 293). In *Re M (Minors) (Disclosure of Evidence)* [1994] 1 FLR 760, the Court of Appeal held that it was inappropriate for the judge to have made an order which prevented the welfare report containing the children's wishes being revealed because those wishes were already in the public domain.

4.12 Solicitor for child

(1) A solicitor appointed under section 41(3) or in accordance with rule 4.11A(1)(*a*) shall represent the child –

(*a*) in accordance with instructions received from the children's guardian (unless the solicitor considers, having taken into account the views of the children's guardian and any direction of the court under rule 4.11A(3), that the child wishes to give instructions which conflict with those of the children's guardian and that he is able, having regard to his understanding, to give such instructions on his own behalf in which case he shall conduct the proceedings in accordance with instructions received from the child), or

(*b*) where no children's guardian has been appointed for the child and the condition in section 41(4)(*b*) is satisfied, in accordance with instructions received from the child, or

(*c*) in default of instructions under (*a*) or (*b*), in furtherance of the best interests of the child.

(2) A solicitor appointed under section 41(3) or in accordance with rule 4.11A(1)(*a*) shall serve and accept service of documents on behalf of the child in accordance with rule 4.8(3)(*a*) and (4)(*a*) and, where the child has not himself been served and has sufficient understanding, advise the child of the contents of any document so served.

(3) Where the child wishes an appointment of a solicitor under section 41(3) or in accordance with rule 4.11A(1)(*a*) to be terminated, he may apply to the court for an order terminating the appointment; and the solicitor and the children's guardian shall be given an opportunity to make representations.

(4) Where the children's guardian wishes an appointment of a solicitor under section 41(3) to be terminated, he may apply to the court for an order terminating the appointment; and the solicitor and, if he is of sufficient understanding, the child, shall be given an opportunity to make representations.

(5) When terminating an appointment in accordance with paragraph (3) or (4), the court shall give its reasons for so doing, a note of which shall be taken by the court or the proper officer.

(6) Where the court appoints a solicitor under section 41(3) or refuses to make such an appointment, the court or the proper officer shall record the appointment or refusal in Form C48.

Amendments—SI 1994/3155; SI 2001/821.

Defined terms—"child": r 4.1(1); "court": r 1.2(1); "note": r 4.1(1); "proper officer": r 1.2(1).

Solicitors to whom the rule applies—This rule applies to two types of solicitor:

(*a*) those appointed under CA 1989, s 41(3) which, in combination with s 41(4), enables the court to appoint a solicitor for a child who does not already have one if:
   (i) no children's guardian has yet been appointed;
   (ii) the child has sufficient understanding to instruct a solicitor and wishes to do so; and
   (iii) it appears to the court that it would be in the child's best interests for him to be represented by a solicitor.

(*b*) those appointed by the child's guardian in accordance with r 4.11A (except that r 4.12(4) does not apply, presumably because there is nothing to stop the children's guardian dismissing the solicitor in the usual way where the solicitor had been appointed in the first place not by the court but by the children's guardian).

As the appointment of a solicitor under s 41 can only be made in specified proceedings (see *Re W (A Minor) (Contact)* [1994] 1 FLR 843, FD, and also the tenor of the judgment of Sir Thomas Bingham MR in *Re S (A Minor) (Independent Representation)* [1993] Fam 263, [1993] 2 FLR 437, CA), and there is only a children's guardian to act under r 4.11A if there are specified proceedings, it therefore seems to be the case that r 4.12 can only be relevant in specified proceedings as defined in CA 1989, s 41(6).

"able ... to give such instructions on his own behalf" (r 4.12(1)(*a*))—Guidance on the application of the test in r 4.12(1)(*a*) was given by Thorpe J in *Re H (A Minor) (Care Proceedings: Child's Wishes)* [1993] 1 FLR 440. He said that a child of 15 would not necessarily have sufficient understanding to instruct, but the test was a lower one than that under CA 1989, s 38(6) (which allows a child to refuse to submit to a medical or psychiatric examination or assessment if he is of sufficient understanding to make an informed decision). Thorpe J rejected the argument that emotional disturbance could not, on its own, negative ability to instruct. A child had to have sufficient rationality within the understanding to instruct a solicitor, and it might be that the level of emotional disturbance would be such as to remove the necessary degree of rationality that leads to coherent and consistent instruction. In cases involving an able, intelligent but emotionally disturbed child, the court should apply rr 4.11 and 4.12 realistically to ensure that not only was the professional voice of the children's guardian heard (with separate representation under r 4.11) but also the wishes and feelings of the child, however limited the horizon, were similarly presented. Assistance may also be obtained from authorities dealing with the understanding of a child in other contexts under CA 1989 and the associated rules:

(*a*) In *Re S (A Minor) (Independent Representation)* [1993] Fam 263, [1993] 2 FLR 437, CA (unsuccessful application by 11-year-old boy under r 9.2A(4) to be allowed to dispense with the services of the Official Solicitor as his children's guardian in residence proceedings) the Court of Appeal stressed that the tests in r 9.2A are framed with regard to the child's understanding and not his age (as is also the case with r 4.12(1)(*a*)). They held that "what has become known as 'Gillick competence' is the appropriate test in relation to the sufficiency of a child's understanding" under CA 1989 and the rules. Different children have different levels of understanding at the same age, and understanding "has to be assessed relatively to the issues in the proceedings. Where any sound judgment on these issues calls for insight and imagination which only maturity and experience can bring, both the court and the solicitor will be slow to conclude that the child's understanding is sufficient". The court also commented that the difference between a child being able, having regard to his understanding, to give instructions to a solicitor (as required by r 9.2A(1)(*b*) and, of course, by r 4.12(1)(*a*)) and being of sufficient understanding to participate in proceedings as a party without a next friend or children's guardian (see r 9.2A(6)) was more apparent than real, in that the court would not generally allow a child to participate as a party without legal representation, so the real issue in both situations would be whether the child had sufficient understanding to give coherent instructions.

(*b*) In *Re H (A Minor) (Role of Official Solicitor)* [1993] 2 FLR 552, FD (successful application by 15-year-old boy under FPR 1991, r 9.2A(4) to be allowed to dispense with the services of the Official Solicitor as his children's guardian in wardship proceedings) Booth J pointed out that participating as a party goes beyond instructing a solicitor in that it includes, for example, the opportunity to give evidence and be cross-examined. Determining that the boy did have sufficient understanding to participate as a party in proceedings without a children's guardian, the judge endorsed the test in *Re S (A Minor) (Independent Representation)* (above), and said that it had to be considered in the light of all the circumstances of the case and in the light of what had already happened as well as what is likely to happen in the course of the proceedings in the future. It was not for the court, in applying the test, to take into account what the court may or may not consider to be in the best interests of the child. Note, however, that the court retained the assistance of the Official Solicitor as amicus curiae.

(*c*) In *Re K, W and H (Minors) (Medical Treatment)* [1993] 1 FLR 854, FD, Thorpe J refused an application under FPR 1991, r 9.2A(4) having found that three adolescent children did not have sufficient understanding to participate without the Official Solicitor in proceedings by a special hospital unit in relation to their treatment.

(*d*) In *Re C (Residence: Child's Application for Leave)* [1995] 1 FLR 927, FD (application by 14-year-old girl under CA 1989, s 10 for leave to make a s 8 application that she be permitted to live with her mother), the girl was found to have sufficient understanding to make the proposed application.

(*e*) *Re A (Care: Discharge Application by Child)* [1995] 1 FLR 599, FD looks at the question of understanding from the point of view of the right of a child to make representations under r 4.16(2).

Under r 4.12(1)(*a*), it is apparently the solicitor's consideration of the child's understanding that is material. There does not seem to be any express provision for the court to override this such as there is under r 9.2A(10) (see *Re CT (A Minor) (Wardship: Representation)* [1993] 2 FLR 278). However, one of the issues on which Thorpe J adjudicated on the appeal in *Re H (A Minor) (Care Proceedings: Child's Wishes)* (above) was whether the solicitor instructed for the child should have taken his instructions from the child or from the children's guardian. Thorpe J suggested that, if there was any real question as to whether the child's emotional disturbance was so intense that he could not give instructions, that question should be the subject of specific expert opinion from experts already involved in the case. No doubt, failing any other more appropriate provision, r 4.14 will entitle the court to become involved in this issue. See further *Re M (Minors) (Care Proceedings: Child's Wishes)* [1994] 1 FLR 749 and **"he shall so inform the court"** under r 4.11A(3). Guidance may also be available to a solicitor who is unsure whether or not it is appropriate to take instructions direct from a child from one or more of the following sources: the helpline operated by the Law Society Family Law Committee; the Solicitors Family Law Association Code of Practice; a children and family reporter; an expert already involved in the case; a nominated care district judge; and the Official Solicitor.

"the condition in section 41(4)(b)" (r 4.12(1)(*b*))—The condition is that the child has sufficient understanding to instruct a solicitor and wishes to do so. For the meaning of "sufficient understanding to instruct a solicitor", see **"able ... to give such instructions on his own behalf"** above.

Removal of solicitor (r 4.12(3)–(5))—Curiously, it seems that the child may apply for the removal of a solicitor under r 4.12(3) even where he is not of sufficient understanding to do so (cf r 4.12(4) where, if the children's guardian applies for the removal of such a solicitor, the child may make representations only if he is of sufficient understanding). A literal reading of r 4.12(3) and (4) would seem to suggest that the court cannot remove a solicitor who had been appointed by a children's guardian when the proceedings had been pending in a magistrates' court before being transferred up because the appointment would not have been made "in accordance with rule 4.11A(1)(*a*)" (it would have been made in accordance with Family Proceedings Courts (Children Act 1989) Rules 1991, r 11A(1)(*a*)); however, it is submitted that there is scope for construing the provision to include such cases.

Opportunity to make representations (r 4.12(3), (4))—The "opportunity to make representations" is a flexible concept that leaves the question of whether they should be oral or written, and the time within which they should be made, to be determined by the court according to the context in which the question arises.

Reasons for terminating appointment of solicitor or children's guardian to be given by the court (r 4.12(5))—Where the court terminates the appointment of a solicitor or children's guardian, this rule now requires the court to give its reasons for doing so, and requires that a note of the reasons be taken by the court or by the proper officer. The simple fact that the court has ordered a termination of the solicitor's appointment is to be formally recorded in Form C48. No doubt the court's written reasons will therefore form an appendix to the duly completed Form C48.

4.13 Welfare officer

(1) Where the court has directed that a written report be made by a welfare officer in accordance with section 7(1)(*b*), the report shall be filed at or by such time as the court directs or, in the absence of such a direction, at least 14 days before a relevant hearing; and the proper officer shall, as soon as practicable, serve a copy of the report on the parties and any children's guardian.

(2) In paragraph (1), a hearing is relevant if the proper officer has given the welfare officer notice that his report is to be considered at it.

(3) After the filing of a report by a welfare officer, the court may direct that the welfare officer attend any hearing at which the report is to be considered; and

(*a*) except where such a direction is given at a hearing attended by the welfare officer the proper officer shall inform the welfare officer of the direction; and

(*b*) at the hearing at which the report is considered any party may question the welfare officer about his report.

(3A) The welfare officer shall consider whether it is in the best interests of the child for the child to be made a party to the proceedings.

(3B) If the welfare officer considers the child should be made a party to the proceedings he shall notify the court of his opinion together with the reasons for that opinion.

(4) This rule is without prejudice to any power to give directions under rule 4.14.

Amendments—SI 1992/2067; SI 2001/821.

Defined terms—"court": r 1.2(1); "children's guardian": r 4.1(1); "proper officer": r 1.2(1); "welfare officer": r 4.1(1).

Related provision—CA 1989, s 7 makes provision for the request for a welfare report.

Further annotations—Detailed guidance on all aspects of welfare reports can be found in the annotations to CA 1989, s 7 and rr 4.11 and 4.11B. See also *Best Practice Guidance on Section 37(1) Directions* under CA 1989, s 37.

Meaning of "welfare officer" (r 4.13(1))—The CJCSA 2000 introduced the Children and Family Court Advisory and Support Service (CAFCASS). The term "officer of the service" is defined in CJCSA, s 11(3), and is used to denote the various categories of people appointed to undertake investigations and prepare reports for the court in children and family cases. Where a court directs, pursuant to s 7(1)(*b*), a local authority to report upon matters relating to the welfare of the child, the author of the report is described as a "welfare officer". The term "welfare officer" is retained only for the purpose of describing that local authority officer in those specified circumstances. Where the court appoints an officer of the service to report to it under CA 1989, s 7(1)(*a*) he is now called a "children and family reporter".

Filing and service of written reports (r 4.13(1))—The principles relating to the filing and service of written reports by the welfare officer are similar to those concerning the filing and service of reports by a children and family reporter under r 4.11B(2); see **Filing and service of written reports** under r 4.11B.

Attendance of welfare officer (r 4.13(3))—The principles relating to the attendance of the welfare officer are similar to those concerning the attendance of a children and family reporter under r 4.11B(3); see **Attendance of children and family reporter** under r 4.11B.

"any party may question the welfare officer" (r 4.13(3)(*b*))—Although the wording of r 4.13(3)(*b*) differs slightly from that in r 4.11(4), which permits the questioning of an "officer of the service" about oral or written advice tendered by him to the court, since a welfare officer is an "officer of the service" (see definition in CJCSA 2000, s 11) reference should be made to **Questioning an officer of the service** under r 4.11 for guidance. As to the way in which a welfare officer/children and family reporter gives his evidence to the court, see further under CJCSA 2000, s 16 and **Withholding children and family reporter's report from the parties** under r 4.11B. For an explanation of the difference between a welfare officer and a children and family reporter, see **Meaning of "welfare officer"** (above).

Withholding welfare officer's report from the parties—Similar principles apply to a report prepared by a welfare officer in accordance with CA 1989, s 7(1)(*b*), to those which apply to a report prepared by a children and family reporter pursuant to r 4.11B; see **Withholding children and family reporter's report from the parties** under r 4.11B.

4.14 Directions

(1) In this rule, "party" includes the children's guardian and, where a request or a direction concerns a report under section 7, the welfare officer or children and family reporter.

(2) In proceedings to which this Part applies the court may, subject to paragraph (3), give, vary or revoke directions for the conduct of the proceedings, including –

- (*a*) the timetable for the proceedings;
- (*b*) varying the time within which or by which an act is required, by these rules or by other rules of court, to be done;
- (*c*) the attendance of the child;
- (*d*) the appointment of a children's guardian, a guardian ad litem, or of a solicitor under section 41(3);
- (*e*) the service of documents;
- (*f*) the submission of evidence including experts' reports;

(*g*) the preparation of welfare reports under section 7;
(*h*) the transfer of the proceedings to another court;
(*i*) consolidation with other proceedings.

(3) Directions under paragraph (2) may be given, varied or revoked either –

(*a*) of the court's own motion having given the parties notice of its intention to do so, and an opportunity to attend and be heard or to make written representations,
(*b*) on the written request in Form C2 of a party specifying the direction which is sought, filed and served on the other parties, or
(*c*) on the written request in Form C2 of a party specifying the direction which is sought, to which the other parties consent and which they or their representatives have signed.

(4) In an urgent case the request under paragraph (3)(*b*) may, with the leave of the court, be made –

(*a*) orally, or
(*b*) without notice to the parties, or
(*c*) both as in sub-paragraph (*a*) and as in sub-paragraph (*b*).

(5) On receipt of a written request under paragraph (3)(*b*) the proper officer shall fix a date for the hearing of the request and give not less than 2 days' notice in Form C6 to the parties of the date so fixed.

(6) On considering a request under paragraph (3)(*c*) the court shall either –

(*a*) grant the request, whereupon the proper officer shall inform the parties of the decision, or
(*b*) direct that a date be fixed for the hearing of the request, whereupon the proper officer shall fix such a date and give not less than 2 days' notice to the parties of the date so fixed.

(7) A party may apply for an order to be made under section 11(3) or, if he is entitled to apply for such an order, under section 38(1) in accordance with paragraph (3)(*b*) or (*c*).

(8) Where a court is considering making, of its own motion, a section 8 order, or an order under section 31, 34 or 38, the power to give directions under paragraph (2) shall apply.

(9) Directions of a court which are still in force immediately prior to the transfer of proceedings to which this Part applies to another court shall continue to apply following the transfer, subject to any changes of terminology which are required to apply those directions to the court to which the proceedings are transferred, unless varied or discharged by directions under paragraph (2).

(10) The court or the proper officer shall take a note of the giving, variation or revocation of a direction under this rule and serve, as soon as practicable, a copy of the note on any party who was not present at the giving, variation or revocation.

Amendments—SI 1994/3155; SI 2001/821.

Defined terms—"child": r 4.1(1); "court": r 1.2(1); "directions appointment", "children's guardian", "leave": r 4.1(1); "proper officer": r 1.2(1); "section 8 order": CA 1989, s 8(2); "children and family reporter": r 4.1(1).

Case management—*Practice Direction of 31 January 1995* deals with a number of important aspects of preparation for and conduct of hearings. Reference must be made to it at the earliest possible stage in every case, since it imposes considerable obligations on legal representatives and is likely to have a bearing on many aspects of the conduct of a matter. Great assistance is also to be derived from the *Handbook of Best Practice in Children Act cases* produced by the Children Act Advisory Committee (set out in Part IV of this work as *Best Practice Guidance of June 1997*). See also the practical guidance given by Charles J in *Re R (Care: Disclosure: Nature of Proceedings)* [2002] 1 FLR 755 (a public law case) as to the proper preparation of cases brought under CA 1989 (dealt with more fully in **Preparation of public law cases** under CA 1989, s 31). See also **Disclosure – impact of the European Convention for Human Rights and Fundamental Freedoms 1950** under FPR 1991, r 4.23, and in particular the judgment of Munby J in *Re L (Care: Assessment: Fair Trial)* [2002] EWHC 1379 (Fam), [2002] 2 FLR 730.

Deciding whether case should be heard in the Administrative Court or Family Division—In *A (A Patient) v A Health Authority; Re J; The Queen on the Application of S v Secretary of State for the Home Department* [2002] EWHC 18 (Fam/Admin), [2002] 1 FLR 845, two cases raised the issue of whether disputes between family members and a public authority should be regarded as issues of private or public law and whether they should be heard in the Family Division or the Administrative Court. The court held that where cases plainly involve only issues of public law, although they concern the welfare of either children or incompetent adults, then the proper course is to apply to the Administrative Court for judicial review. But if cases may, in part, involve some issues of public law but are also private law cases about the best interests of a child or an incompetent adult then the proper course is to apply to the Family Division. If the task for the judge is to come to a decision for, and on behalf of, a child or incompetent adult, then the welfare of that person must be the paramount consideration. On the other hand, if the task for the judge is to review the decision of a public authority taken in exercise of its statutory power, then the governing principles are those of public law.

Extended meaning of party (r 4.14(1))—The normal meaning of "party" is extended by this rule so that a children's guardian, as well as the child whose interests he represents (who would normally be the party), may request and be consulted about directions. The involvement of the children and family reporter with regard to directions is more limited and arises only where a request for directions or a direction concerns a welfare report under CA 1989, s 7 (eg where the children and family reporter has encountered difficulty in preparing his report within the time specified by the court and wishes to seek an extension).

"report under section 7" (r 4.14(1))—A court considering any question with respect to a child under CA 1989 is entitled by s 7 to request a welfare report.

"proceedings to which this Part applies" (r 4.14(2))—Part IV applies to the proceedings listed in r 4.1(2).

"directions for the conduct of the proceedings" (r 4.14(2))—The court has a very wide discretion to grant directions. The matters listed in r 4.14(2) are only examples of the types of issue that might arise. A directions hearing will almost inevitably be required in a case of any substance and a date for it is fixed by the court office in accordance with r 4.4(2) when the application is commenced or when it is received from the transmitting court. Being an interlocutory matter, directions can be given by a district judge (see Family Proceedings (Allocation to Judiciary) Directions 1999 (as amended by the Family Proceedings (Allocation to Judiciary) (Amendment) Directions 2002)), although a judge can, and may well have occasion to, give directions as well. Care proceedings are non-adversarial in character (see *Re L (Police Investigation: Privilege)* [1996] 1 FLR 731, HL) and, in practice, judges dealing with directions hearings in such cases adopt an interventionist style. Directions hearings should not be treated as a formality; they enable the court to come firmly to grips with the case and ensure that it is tightly timetabled and prepared for its final hearing at the earliest opportunity. Where a party feels that the case is not making satisfactory progress, he should take out a summons for directions to ensure that progress is made (*B v B (Child Abuse: Contact)* [1994] 2 FLR 713; see also *Re A and B (Minors) (No 2)* [1995] 1 FLR 351, FD, and **Timetable for the proceedings** below). Reference to *Practice Direction of 31 January 1995* is essential in considering what directions are necessary. In public law proceedings it should now be routine for the court to direct the local authority to set out a clear schedule of facts upon which it seeks a finding by the court and upon the basis of which it is alleged that the threshold is crossed (see **Schedule of facts** under CA 1989, s 31).

Directions hearings normally take place in chambers (see r 4.16(7)), and parties who receive notice of the appointment are normally required to attend (see r 4.16(1)). Proforma directions and best practice notes to be adopted nationally and in all tiers of court for directions hearings in family cases have been issued by the Children Act Advisory Committee and are set out as *Best Practice Note of January 1995* in Part IV of this work. As to directions for the conduct of cases involving expert witnesses, see **Practice on leave applications and in instructing and calling experts** under r 4.18. For specific guidance as to what should happen at a pre-hearing review see **Pre-hearing reviews** (below).

Pre-hearing reviews—The purpose of a pre-hearing review is to enable the advocates concerned to ascertain that everything has been done which needs to be done to ensure that the case is ready for hearing. In *Re G, S and M (Wasted Costs)* [2000] 1 FLR 52 Wall J laid down guidelines as to what should happen at a pre-hearing review. At 71C he observed that: "Counsel and solicitors should go to such reviews with a complete mental or documentary 'checklist'. This should, of course, include a list of witnesses who are to be called at the final hearing, the length of time their evidence is likely to take; and, where expert witnesses in particular are concerned, the issues which they are to address; and when, in the context of the case, they are going to be called. It is for this purpose that the witness 'template' referred to in *Re EC (Disclosure of Material)* [1996] 2 FLR 123, 128G was devised. In my view such a template should be standard practice for a case of any complexity … That is so not least because it concentrates the minds of the advocates on the length of time a witness will need and, by direct inference, the issues which that witness will address." Wall J went on to say (at 72B) "that when advocates attend a pre-hearing review it is their *collective* responsibility to ensure:

(1) that the issues in the case to be addressed at the final hearing are clearly identified;

(2) that the evidence to address those issues is either already available or that directions are sought from the court to ensure that it is available in good time for the hearing;

(3) that all the expert witnesses in the case have been sent – or will prior to giving evidence be sent – all relevant material which has emerged since their reports were written; or where the material required by an expert witness had not been seen by that witness, that the material would be sent and a further report, if necessary, commissioned;

(4) that the witnesses required to give evidence at the hearing have been identified;

(5) that the length of time required for the evidence of each witness has been appropriately estimated;

(6) that the witnesses have been timetabled;

(7) that expert witnesses, in particular, have been allotted specific dates and times for their evidence; and that the length of time allotted for their evidence has been carefully assessed to ensure that it can be given without the witnesses being inconvenienced by having to return to court on a second occasion to complete their evidence;

(8) that the documents required for the cases are in good order and bundled appropriately; that there is a chronology and, where required, a short statement of case from each party;

(9) that the guardian's ("children's guardian's") report will be available in proper time for the hearing;

(10) that appropriate reading time and time for an extempore judgment has been allowed to the judge.".

Finally, Wall J also made it clear that "the court has a duty at the pre-hearing review to adopt a proactive and rigorous approach to the issues in the case with a view to ensuring that all the issues have been appropriately defined and addressed (at 72G)".

In *Re R (Care: Disclosure: Nature of Proceedings)* [2002] 1 FLR 755, Charles J emphasised that all parties have a duty throughout the period of preparation of a case for hearing to keep all pre-trial matters under review, including the preparation of evidence, disclosure and the instruction of experts; in a public law case these matters are not purely the responsibility of the local authority and the guardian. The case contains useful guidance on the proper preparation of public law cases. For further useful guidance see **Preparation of public law cases** under CA 1989, s 31 and **Disclosure – impact of the European Convention for Human Rights and Fundamental Freedoms 1950** under FPR 1991, r 4.23, and in particular the judgment of Munby J in *Re L (Care: Assessment: Fair Trial)* [2002] EWHC 1379 (Fam), [2002] 2 FLR 730.

Continuity of judge and legal representatives—Judicial continuity is important (*Re M (Minors) (Judicial Continuity)* [1993] 1 FLR 903, CA). For cases proceeding in the Family Division of the High Court at the Royal Courts of Justice in London, see *President's Direction of 22 March 2002* (set out in Part IV of this work), which details the procedure to be followed to avoid delay and achieve the highest possible degree of judicial continuity. The Lord Chancellor's Advisory Committee, jointly chaired by Coleridge J and Munby J, has drafted a protocol which sets out a national model for judicial case management in public law cases. The protocol aims to reduce delay and improve the efficient administration of such cases by establishing best practice guidelines and setting target times for each stage of the care process. It is envisaged that each Care Centre will develop a local protocol for distributing the pre-hearing steps between the judges available. Circuit judges will continue to conduct final hearings, but where appropriate the expertise of district judges may be utilised for the Case Management Conference, the Child Dispute Resolution Appointment and the Pre-Hearing Review. It is expected that the protocol will be launched by the Lord Chancellor and the President of the Family Division in April/May 2003 and thereafter be embodied in a President's Practice Direction to be issued in May 2003. It is hoped that full implementation of the protocol will be achieved in October 2003.

Recent cases have stressed the benefits of judicial continuity in the management of a case, including in the interlocutory stages (*Re CB and JB (Care Proceedings: Guidelines)* [1998] 2 FLR 211, FD; *Re F (Contact: Enforcement: Representation of Child)* [1998] 1 FLR 691, CA). The pre-trial review must always be before the trial judge as should any hearing as to evidential or timetabling issues (*Re CB and JB*). Where there is a split hearing, it is very important that the same judge should hear both limbs (*Re G (Care Proceedings: Split Trials)* [2001] 1 FLR 872). Where there has been a hearing under CA 1989 before a Family Division judge, after the conclusion of which further questions arise as to whether papers and records used in the hearing may be disclosed to third parties for other purposes, then wherever possible the Family Division judge who conducted the hearing should hear the subsequent application for disclosure as he has full knowledge of the background and issues involved (*A Health Authority v X and Others* [2002] EWCA Civ 2014, [2002] 1 FLR 1045, CA). There is also a need for continuity of counsel and solicitors advising the various parties (*Re CB and JB*).

Split hearings—*Re S (Care Proceedings: Split Hearing)* [1996] 2 FLR 773, FD, gives guidance as to split hearings. Consideration should be given to whether questions of fact, such as an allegation of physical or sexual abuse, might need to be determined at a preliminary stage, so that the substantive hearing can proceed more speedily and focus on the child's welfare with greater clarity. Local authorities and children's guardians, in particular, should give assistance to the court in identifying cases which are suited to such a split hearing. Where this is appropriate, the court can give early directions for the filing of medical evidence and statements and a hearing as to factual issues, which hearing will sometimes be possible within weeks of the care application being filed. It was held by the Court of Appeal in *Re O and N (Care: Preliminary Hearing)* [2002] EWCA Civ 1271, [2002] 2 FLR 1167 that in preparing for a preliminary hearing it is the responsibility of solicitors and counsel for all parties to agree the issues to be resolved, or failing agreement to invite the court to rule on them at an early directions appointment. Such an appointment should be attended by those who will conduct the hearing. The issues should be formulated and drawn up in an order directing a preliminary hearing of those issues, or of the questions of fact to be resolved. The questions should be formulated so as to permit the court on the preliminary hearing to answer "yes or no" wherever possible, or otherwise with the minimum narrative. At the preliminary hearing, an order should be drawn up recording those answers. If questions are properly formulated at the earliest opportunity, proper directions can be given as to the evidence to be filed to answer them; and no more than is relevant to those issues should be admitted. Once findings of fact are made, any further assessments that are necessary can be timetabled. Where there is a split hearing, it is very important that the same judge should hear both limbs of the case if possible. The judge hearing the first part should be requested to ensure that the order at the end of the first part indicates that the second part should be reserved to him or her, if available (*Re G (Care Proceedings: Split Trials)* [2001] 1 FLR 872). *Re CB and JB (Care Proceedings: Guidelines)* [1998] 2 FLR 211, FD demonstrates how a failure to hold a split hearing (in that case, to resolve who was responsible for the severe shaking of one of the children) can cause obfuscation, delay and the waste of resources and gives valuable guidance as to the procedure to be followed with regard to evidence, assessments etc where a split hearing is scheduled. Similarly in *Re CD and MD (Care Proceedings: Practice)* [1998] 1 FLR 825 (another case of head injuries to a child) there should have been a split hearing. Even where the parents make limited concessions which mean that the threshold criteria are proved, the court still has a discretion, as part of the proper management of the proceedings in the child's best interests, to order that there be a trial in relation to the threshold criteria where this is necessary to resolve a core factual issue without the determination of which the experts involved in the case are unable to advise on child protection (*Re D (Child: Threshold Criteria)* [2001] 1 FLR 274 – where in proceedings relating to her second child the mother accepted that she had failed to supervise her first child, resulting in his admission to hospital for ingestion of substances, but where the issue as to whether such ingestion was due to deliberate abuse or carelessness by the mother remained unresolved. The experts said that they were unable to advise on issues of child protection and care without a determination of this issue). Where an expert is asked to express an opinion, he must have all the relevant information, including a copy of any judgment given earlier in the case; the summary of a judgment is not sufficient (*Re G (Care Proceedings: Split Trials)* (above). *Re T (A Minor) (Procedure: Alleged Sexual Abuse) (No 1)* [1996] 2 FCR 370, however, sounds a cautionary note about splitting the evidence on the primary facts as to sexual abuse from the evidence as to what risk there will be in the future if it is established. The Court of Appeal has jurisdiction to hear an appeal against findings of fact on preliminary issues made at the first part of a split hearing in care proceedings where those findings are of crucial importance to the final care decision to be made (*Re B (Split Hearing: Jurisdiction)* [2000] 1 FLR 334 – where the judge had made findings in relation to non-accidental injury suffered by a child subject to an interim care order and the local authority, supported by the children's guardian, appealed the findings on the basis that the judge had preferred the lay evidence of the child's grandmother to that of two medical experts. The Court of Appeal treated the matter as a preliminary hearing of causation in which the issues were so crucial to the final decision that those findings could be treated as determinative; the findings therefore fell within County Courts Act 1984, s 77, so that the court had jurisdiction to hear the appeal).

Repeated applications—As to the possibility of renewing an application previously refused by the court, see *Re F (A Minor) (Care Proceedings: Directions)* [1995] 3 FCR 601, FD (children's guardian whose first application for psychological assessment of child was refused by magistrates was entitled, by virtue of FPC(CA 1989)R 1991, r 14(2), to renew the application a fortnight later).

Dismissal of proceedings at directions stage—In *Re B (Contact: Stepfather's Opposition)* [1997] 2 FLR 579, CA the judge summarily dismissed a father's application for contact at a directions hearing without hearing any evidence and ordered that he should not make further applications without leave of the court. The father was not present and had not been warned that his application might be dismissed in that way. He appealed. It was properly conceded that, in an appropriate case, a contact application can be dismissed on a directions hearing. The Court of Appeal pointed out that, in the exercise of that power, the court must bear in mind that the more Draconian the order and the more unique the situation, the greater the need for the court to be satisfied that grave harm is virtually certain to befall the child if the court follows its usual procedure and investigates the matter on its merits. In that case, there was a real risk that if the contact proceedings continued, the child's family unit would be damaged by the stepfather rejecting both the child and her mother with resulting harm to the child. The Court of Appeal dismissed the father's appeal, considering that (although it appears that individual members of the Court of Appeal might have taken different action in the crisis faced by the judge) the judge had not erred in principle. It is worth noting, however, that the Official Solicitor was to remain involved and the court clearly contemplated that contact may be arranged. In *Re A (Application for Leave)* [1998] 1 FLR 1, the Court of Appeal reaffirmed the view that, in appropriate cases, an application may be determined at a directions appointment if the content of the statements and the children and family reporter's report indicate that it should go no further. This principle is clearly demonstrated in *Re W (Minors)* (unreported) 15 December 1998, CA, where the judge at first instance had already heard and determined in favour of the father one bitterly fought residence dispute between the parties relating to their two children. The mother made a further application for residence and when the parties appeared before the same judge for the pre-hearing review he took the unusual steps of: (i) dismissing the application at that stage on the basis that even if everything the mother said was accepted it would be unlikely to affect the existing order for residence; and (ii) making an order under CA 1989, s 91(14) preventing the mother from making any further applications for residence in respect of the children without leave of the court. The Court of Appeal upheld the first instance decision, observing:

> "Of course, it is normally the case that children's cases are heard on oral evidence … which is tested under cross-examination. But it is quite clear from a number of decisions of this court and decisions at first instance that a judge does have a discretion as to whether or not there should be a full hearing permitted with oral evidence. This is particularly the case when there has already been one full investigation by the court which has produced a particular result, as here. The judge in so acting would obviously have to look carefully at the case and weigh a number of important considerations: Was the material available before the court sufficient to enable him to take that particular course? Was the outcome likely to be affected by fresh evidence or cross-examination? Would the denial of the opportunity for the mother to cross-examine witnesses or produce evidence of her own be likely to produce a skewed result and be unfair to her? Was the expert evidence available before the court sufficient? Would it be likely to be changed in the light of cross-examination or further evidence? and, above all, the welfare of the children and the likely effect on them of continuing litigation. If

that was likely to be detrimental to the welfare of the children that would be a factor which would weigh very heavily in the scales. Finally, of course, the ultimate question for the judge: Would the full hearing be likely realistically to produce any different result to that which had already been reached?".

For further examples of situations in which an application may be brought to a premature end, see **Full hearing not always appropriate** under r 4.21.

Timetable for the proceedings and time estimates (r 4.14(2)(*a*))—The court is put firmly in control of the timetable for proceedings under CA 1989 in an effort to avoid delay which CA 1989, s 1(2) stresses is likely to be prejudicial to the welfare of a child. Section 11(1) obliges the court, when dealing with proceedings in which any question of making a s 8 order arises, to draw up a timetable with a view to determining the question at issue without delay and to give such directions as it considers appropriate to ensure adherence to the timetable; s 32(1) is a similar provision relating to proceedings under CA 1989, Pt IV. Rule 4.15(2) obliges the court dealing with any proceedings to which Pt IV of these rules applies to fix a date for the next hearing upon the transfer of such proceedings, or adjourning or concluding an interlocutory hearing or appointment. Subject to these positive duties, however, the court has a wide discretion as to how the timetable for a case is set. In reaching decisions about timetabling, the time-limits set by the rules for various steps will have to be taken into account (although the court does have power under r 4.14 to abridge or extend these where necessary, see **Variation of time-limits** below). The general undesirability of delay will have to be balanced against the need to give sufficient time for all parties to prepare their cases properly, for the children's guardian or children and family reporter to investigate, for reports to be obtained etc. It must also be borne in mind that there are cases in which the child's welfare can be better secured by postponing a final resolution of the application for a short time, for example where a parent suffers from psychiatric illness and is receiving treatment which it is anticipated will be successful. What is required is a timetable that prevents the case from drifting without hustling it along at a pace which sacrifices the interests of the parties and the welfare of the child. For comments on the benefits of planned and purposeful delay, see *C v Solihull MBC* [1993] 1 FLR 290 and *Hounslow LBC v A* [1993] 1 FLR 702. See also **Interim care order or full care order?** under CA 1989, s 38.

Where a case is transferred to the High Court with a time estimate of five days or more, an early directions hearing should be sought before a High Court judge, whether or not a date is also fixed for the substantive hearing of the application (*Practice Direction of 5 March 1993*). For cases proceeding in the Family Division of the High Court at the Royal Courts of Justice in London, see *President's Direction of 22 March 2002* (set out in Part IV of this work), which details the procedure to be followed to avoid delay and achieve the highest possible degree of judicial continuity. In any case estimated to last 5 days or more and in which no pre-trial review has been ordered, application should be made for a pre-trial review which should, when practicable, be listed at least 3 weeks before the hearing and be conducted by the judge or district judge who is going to hear the case and be attended by the advocates who are going to represent the parties at the hearing (*Practice Direction of 31 January 1995*). See **Pre-hearing reviews** (above). As *B v B (Child Abuse: Contact)* [1994] 2 FLR 713 stresses, directions hearings are not a formality. They are there so that the court can come firmly to grips with the case and ensure that it is tightly timetabled and prepared for its final hearing at the earliest opportunity. It is the duty of the court to be precise in the directions it gives. If there is a risk of drift or delay, the court should not give leave to the parties to apply for further directions but should fix a date at which further directions will be given. Where there is a children's guardian, he should regularly review the file and, if the case is not making satisfactory progress, he should take out a summons for directions. *B v B (Minors) (Interviews and Listing Arrangements)* [1994] 2 FLR 489 points out that open-ended orders which do not focus the minds of the parties and their advisers on a specific hearing date should not be made.

Practice Direction of 22 November 1993 sets out the obligations of the parties with regard to the giving of time estimates in High Court cases, and proper time estimates are, of course, vital in all cases. Guidance as to the giving of accurate time estimates is contained in *Re MD and TD (Minors) (Time Estimates)* [1994] 2 FLR 336 (set out in Part IV of this work as *Practice Note of 2 February 1994*). It is pointed out that directions appointments at which time estimates are discussed are very important, and every effort should be made to ensure that, when counsel is briefed to attend a directions appointment, he or she is either the barrister who will have conduct of the substantive hearing and has addressed his or her mind to the estimated length of the hearing or, where a substitute has to take the brief, that he or she is fully instructed on the point. In *Re EC (Disclosure of Material)* [1996] 2 FLR 123 (subsequently appealed to the Court of Appeal at [1996] 2 FLR 725 but not on this point), Wall J praised the use of a timetable template identifying all the witnesses who were to be called to give oral evidence and assigning a specified time to each, with detailed estimates of the time to be spent in examination-in-chief, cross-examination and re-examination. This is dealt with more fully in **Pre-hearing reviews** (above).

In determining any application to adjourn a case involving children, as well as in fixing the timetable for the proceedings, the court has to consider delay, and the interests of the other parties have to be assessed in the light of the principle that delay in determining a question concerning a child's upbringing is likely to prejudice his welfare (*Re SW (A Minor) (Care Proceedings)* [1993] 2 FLR 609, noted more fully in **Hearing or directions appointment in the absence of applicant** under r 4.16). An application for an adjournment can be granted ex parte, but such application should only be made in exceptional circumstances and where it would be in the best interests of the children to justify such a course. Even then, those representing the parties should be in attendance, either having given undertakings or subject to a direction of the court not to pass on the information to their clients (*Re B (Minors) (Care: Procedure)* [1994] Fam Law 72, in which a local authority applied ex parte to adjourn an application relating to contact with a child in care so that it would carry out investigations into allegations of sexual abuse against a parent without the parents learning of the allegations).

Urgent hearings on Circuit before Family Division judges—The President has issued guidance to courts regarding arrangements for providing additional High Court judges on circuit in cases of special need, other than appeals from magistrates under CA 1989, s 94 (see *President's Guidance of 17 December 1993*).

Variation of time-limits (r 4.14(2)(*b*))—Time-limits set by the rules or other rules of court for proceedings to which Pt IV applies may be extended only by direction of the court under r 4.14; the parties cannot agree an extension between themselves. (see r 4.15(1)). This rule also gives the court power to abridge time-limits (for example the minimum number of days specified in App 3 for service) in an appropriate case. It is worth noting that there is no express prohibition on the abridgement of a time-limit by agreement between the parties and it would therefore seem that it is possible to do so, although it may be unlikely to arise in practice.

Attendance of the child (r 4.14(2)(*c*))—As to the attendance of the child at directions appointments and hearings, see r 4.16(1) and (2).

Appointment of a children's guardian (r 4.14(2)(*d*))—CA 1989, s 41 obliges the court to appoint a children's guardian for a child concerned in specified proceedings (such as care and supervision order proceedings) unless satisfied that it is not necessary to do so in order to safeguard his interest; r 4.10 sets out the normal procedure for the appointment of such a guardian. There is no provision in CA 1989 for the appointment of a children's guardian for a child involved in non-specified proceedings. As far as the rules are concerned, a children's guardian can be appointed in non-specified proceedings under r 9.5 (see eg *L v L (Minors) (Separate Representation)* [1994] 1 FLR 156). It appears that it is to such an appointment that the words "or otherwise" in r 4.14(2)(*d*) refer (*Essex CC v B* [1993] 1 FLR 866 – see further under FPC(CA 1989)R 1991, r 14; see also *Re S (A Minor) (Independent Representation)* [1993] 2 FLR 437 at 445C per Sir Thomas Bingham MR, where he suggests that, where the court has dismissed a children's guardian earlier in the relevant proceedings in order to enable the child to participate as a party in his own right but then later decides that the child lacks the necessary understanding so as to participate, it can use its "general power to appoint under r 4.14(2)(*d*) and r 9.5"). Whether r 4.14(2)(*d*) might ever have a wider application, however, remains somewhat uncertain. A children's guardian appointed in non-specified proceedings will not receive funding from the Legal Services Commission, and probably not from his own panel. Where a guardian has been appointed in the course of an investigation under CA 1989, s 37 at the conclusion of which the local authority decides not to apply for a care or supervision order, it would be possible for the High Court or a county court to direct that the guardian should continue to be involved under FPR 1991, r 9.5. However, this should only be done where the guardian consents, where funding is available and where the guardian has a continuing role to play despite the changed status of the proceedings (*Re CE (Section 37 Direction)* [1995] 1 FLR 26).

Appointment of a solicitor under s 41(3) (r 4.14(2)(*d*))—CA 1989, s 41(3) enables the court to appoint a solicitor to represent a child concerned in specified proceedings where he has no children's guardian, where he is of sufficient understanding to instruct a solicitor and wants to do so or where it appears that it would be in his best interests for him to be represented by a solicitor (see *Re H (A Minor) (Care Proceedings: Child's Wishes)* [1993] 1 FLR 440). In contrast to the position with regard to the appointment of a children's guardian, there is no rule dealing specifically with the procedure for the appointment of such a solicitor so this must be carried out under this rule, although r 4.12(6) imposes a duty on the court to record the appointment. Where there is a children's guardian, he generally has a duty to appoint a solicitor for the child under r 4.11(2). An appointment by the children's guardian is not made under s 41(3) and the court cannot therefore give directions with regard to it. However it is presumed that should the court's assistance be required at a later stage (for example, if a question arises as to how the solicitor should carry out his duties under r 4.12), directions under this rule could be sought on the basis that the matter arises in connection with the conduct of the proceedings. An application by the child for termination of the solicitor's appointment would, however, have to be made under r 4.12(3).

There is no power to appoint a solicitor for a child under s 41(3) in non-specified proceedings (*Re W (A Minor) (Contact)* [1994] 1 FLR 843).

Service of documents (r 4.14(2)(*e*))—As to service generally, see rr 4.8, 10.2, 10.3 and 10.6. The power to give directions about service under this rule is supplementary to the power of the court to give directions under r 4.8(8).

Submission of evidence (r 4.14(2)(*f*))—Rule 4.14 gives the court a very broad power to deal with questions concerning the submission of evidence. For example, such directions may be given as are necessary for the purposes of r 4.17, which lays down the rules about the filing and service of written and oral evidence (see *R v Nottinghamshire County Council* [1993] Fam Law 625, discussed in **Non-compliance with r 4.17** under r 4.17). Presumably directions may be given as to the use of evidence arising out of an unauthorised examination of a child (see r 4.18(3)), and it may be possible for questions of admissibility of evidence to be resolved. Questions of relevance/admissibility should normally be referred to the judge who will be conducting the final hearing (*Re CB and JB (Care Proceedings: Guidelines)* [1998] 2 FLR 211, FD).

Where disclosure of material to a party may be damaging to the child concerned in the proceedings, the court has power, in an appropriate case, to direct that the information should be withheld. Such a direction will only be given in exceptional circumstances. The principles have been set out in a number of cases including *Official Solicitor v K* [1965] AC 201, (1963) FLR Rep 520, *Re B (A Minor) (Disclosure of Evidence)* [1993] 1 FLR 191, CA, *Re G (Minors) (Welfare Report: Disclosure)* [1993] 2 FLR 293, CA, and *Re M (Minors) (Disclosure of Evidence)* [1994] 1 FLR 760, CA. In *Re D (Adoption Reports: Confidentiality)* [1995] 2 FLR 687, the House of Lords gave very full consideration to the whole question of disclosure. Although this was in the context of an adoption application, Lord Mustill's formulation of the test for non-disclosure is the test in Children Act proceedings as well, and was applied in care proceedings in *Re C (Disclosure)* [1996] 1 FLR 797, FD and endorsed in *Re M (Disclosure)* [1998] 2 FLR 1028, CA. Accordingly, the position is as follows:

(*a*) It is a fundamental principle of fairness that a party is entitled to disclosure of all materials which might be taken into account by a court when reaching a decision adverse to that party – non-disclosure is the exception, and not the rule.

(*b*) When faced with a non-disclosure application, the court should first consider whether disclosure would involve a *real possibility of significant harm* to the child.

(*c*) If so, the court should next consider whether the overall interests of the child would benefit from non-disclosure, weighing the interest of the child in having the material properly tested against the magnitude of risk that harm would occur and the gravity of that harm.

(*d*) If the court is satisfied that the interests of the child point towards non-disclosure, it should finally weigh that consideration against the interest of the parent or other party in having an opportunity to see and respond to the material, taking into account the importance of the material to the issues in the case.

(*e*) The court should be rigorous in its examination of the risk and gravity of the feared harm to the child, and should order non-disclosure only where the case for it is compelling. To say that harm must be certain is to pitch the test too high, but "a powerful combination of likelihood and seriousness of harm will be required before the requirements for a fair trial can be overridden" (*Re D* at 694H).

As *Re M* stresses, welfare of the child is not the paramount consideration. A proper balance has to be struck between the welfare consideration and the requirements of the administration of fair justice. See *Re B, R and C (Children)* (unreported), CA, LTL 12 November 2002 – Doc No C9900426, where the Court of Appeal reinstated an order requiring disclosure of medical reports by the mother in family proceedings, emphasising that the court will only withhold evidence from disclosure to another party if such disclosure would be so detrimental to the children's welfare as to outweigh the normal requirements of a fair trial.

Re C (Disclosure) (above) considered the procedure to be followed where an application for non-disclosure is made. Johnson J declined to lay down rigid rules, taking the view that the procedure in each case will be determined by the court in the light of the particular circumstances and demands of the case, so as to enable the court to carry out the appropriate balancing exercise.

This approach was endorsed by the Court of Appeal in *Re M (Disclosure)* [1998] 2 FLR 1028 and should be the norm, subject to any necessary variations in individual cases. Accordingly:

(1) The application should be transferred to the High Court.

(2) Notice of the application should be given to the party from whom the material is intended to be withheld.

(3) It is essential that any party to whom the information was not to be revealed should have the opportunity of making representations to the court.

(4) In many cases it will be appropriate to follow the practice endorsed in *Official Solicitor v K* [1965] AC 201, (1963) FLR 520; namely disclosure in the first instance to counsel only and thereafter counsel would have the opportunity to apply for onward transmission to the client.

The possibility of hearings or part of hearings being held ex parte is not excluded but should arise only rarely. For example, where there is material in a document upon which the judge is asked to make a decision whether to disclose but the judge needs assistance from a party in some way in order to ascertain the meaning of the document, he could properly ask for such help before making his decision whether the document should be disclosed (*Re M* at p1033F).

Where certain information is to have limited distribution, special arrangements will have to be made with regard to filing it in court (in *Re C*, the children's guardian was to provide the restricted information to the judge in a confidential supplementary report dealing only with that information), and the court will have to take administrative steps to ensure that it is not disclosed inadvertently. Some assistance as to the way in which the matter might be dealt with in the court office can be gained from the *Secretary's Circular of 10 February 1981*, which applied before CA 1989 came into force. See also *Re K (Adoption: Disclosure of Information)* [1997] 2 FLR 74, FD in which the procedure in adoption cases was distinguished from that contemplated by *Re C* for care cases and it was also pointed out that, where the party from whom it is sought to conceal information is not represented, giving notice of the application about the evidence may defeat the object of the exercise.

As *Re C* contemplates, circumstances can change, and the importance of maintaining confidentiality decline. *Re B (A Minor) (Disclosure of Evidence)* (above) stresses the importance of any order for non-disclosure being only for the shortest period possible consonant with preserving the child's welfare. The question of disclosure generally is further discussed in r 4.23 and, in particular, **Disclosure – impact of the European Convention for Human Rights and Fundamental Freedoms 1950**.

Where there is material that is kept confidential, the judge should say clearly in his judgment whether he is taking it into account or not (*Re M (Minors) (Disclosure of Evidence)* (above)).

In CA 1989 proceedings, statements by parties in conciliation meetings are not admissible, except in the very unusual case where the statement clearly indicates that the maker has in the past caused, or is likely in future to cause, serious harm to the well-being of a child. Even in such a case, there is a discretion whether or not to admit the evidence, and it should be admitted only if the public interest in protecting the interests of the child outweighs the public interest in preserving the confidentiality of attempted conciliation (*Re D (Minors) (Conciliation: Privilege)* [1993] 1 FLR 932, CA). As to the confidentiality of conciliation appointments at the principal registry, see *Practice Direction of 18 October 1991*.

Bundles and other particular matters—*Practice Direction of 10 March 2000* (set out in Part IV of this work) came into force on 2 May 2000. It applies to the preparation of court bundles in: (i) all High Court hearings throughout the country; (ii) all hearings in the Royal Courts of Justice whether High Court or not; (iii) all hearings with a time estimate of half a day or more in all care centres, family hearing centres and divorce county courts whether before a judge or a district judge. "Hearing" means all hearings, including directions hearings and pre-hearing reviews (*Re CH (Family Proceedings: Court Bundles)* [2000] 2 FCR 193). The only exceptions are where: (i) the hearing is too urgent to allow time for the bundle; or (ii) the court directed otherwise. In essence, the applicant is primarily responsible for the preparation of the court bundle unless another party agrees to do it (para 2.1). It must contain copies of all documents relevant to the hearing in chronological order, paginated and indexed and divided into separate sections as follows:

(*a*) applications and orders;

(*b*) statements and affidavits;

(*c*) experts' reports and other reports including those of a children's guardian; and

(*d*) other documents, divided into further sections as may be appropriate.

Paragraph 2.2 of the *Practice Direction* states that when the nature of a hearing is such that a complete bundle is not necessary then it may comprise simply the relevant documents, but the summary at the start of the bundle must state that the bundle is limited or incomplete. In these circumstances, the summary should set out only those matters which the court needs to know for the purpose of the hearing and the management of the case. At the start of the bundle there must be (para 3.1):

(*a*) a summary of the background limited if possible to one A4 page;
(*b*) a statement of the issue(s) to be determined;
(*c*) a summary of the order or directions sought by each party;
(*d*) a chronology if it is a final hearing or if the summary is insufficient;
(*e*) skeleton arguments as may be appropriate, with copies of all authorities relied on.

If possible, the bundle must be agreed. The party preparing the bundle must paginate it and provide an index to all other parties prior to the hearing (para 3.2). The bundle should normally be contained in a ring binder or lever arch file limited to 350 pages in each file. Where there is more than one bundle each should be clearly distinguishable. Bundles must be lodged, if practicable, 2 clear days prior to the hearing. For hearings in the Royal Courts of Justice bundles must be lodged with the Clerk of the Rules. All bundles must have clearly marked on the outside, the title and number of the case, the hearing date and time and, if known, the name of the judge hearing it (para 3.3). After each hearing which is not a final hearing, the party responsible for the bundle must retrieve it from the court. The bundle, with any additional documents, must be re-lodged for further hearings (para 4). In *Re CH* (above) Wall J gave further guidance as to the interpretation and applicability of the *Practice Direction.* The shorter the hearing, the more important it is that the documents should be in good order. It is wholly unacceptable to expect the judge to attempt to find out what any application is about by reference to the court file, since the court file is not a working tool for the judge, but is simply a complete record of the proceedings. It is also good practice for the parties to agree an essential reading list for the judge prior to the start of a case and to lodge it at the start of the bundle. Failure to comply with the *Practice Direction* will often lead to costs penalties for those found to be at fault.

Video conferencing facilities at the Royal Courts of Justice—Video conferencing facilities are available in the Royal Courts of Justice and the procedure to be adopted where it is desired to use these facilities is specified in *Practice Direction of 14 January 2002* (set out in Part IV of this work).

Citation of authorities—See *Practice Note of 9 April 2001 (Citation of Authorities)* which includes the following points:

(*a*) it will remain the duty of advocates to draw the attention of the court to any authority not cited by an opponent which is adverse to the case being advanced;
(*b*) a judgment falling into one of the specified categories cannot in future be cited before any court unless it clearly indicates that it purports to establish a new principle or to extend the present law. In respect of judgments delivered after the date of the direction that indication must be present in or clearly deducible from the language used in the judgment;
(*c*) the direction applies to the following categories of judgment: applications attended by one party only; applications for permission to appeal; decisions on applications that only decided that the application was arguable; and county court cases, unless cited in a county court in order to demonstrate current authority at that level on an issue in respect of which no decision at a higher level of authority is available;
(*d*) an advocate will be required to justify the decision to cite authority which merely seeks to apply decided law to the facts and does not otherwise extend the existing law;
(*e*) advocates will in future be required to state, in respect of each authority that they wish to cite, the proposition of law that the authority demonstrates, and the parts of the judgment that support that proposition. If it is desired to cite more than one authority in support of a given proposition, advocates must state the reason for taking that course (in the skeleton argument or similar document);
(*f*) any bundle or list of authorities prepared for the use of any court must in future bear a certification by the advocate responsible for arguing the case that the requirements of this paragraph have been complied with in respect of each authority included.

Note also that *Practice Note of 11 January 2001 (Judgments: Neutral Citation)* provides for a new method of numbering approved judgments in a neutral way. With effect from 11 January 2001, Court of Appeal family cases come within the Court of Appeal (Civil Division) and will have the following form of citation: eg *Smith v Jones* [2001] EWCA Civ 123. The judgment will be given in numbered paragraphs and if it is desired to cite more than one paragraph then square brackets should be used: eg *Smith v Jones* [2001] EWCA Civ 123 at [12]–[14].

Discovery by party—Representatives must address their minds in advance of the hearing to the need for pre-trial discovery. For example, it is not uncommon for a party to public law proceedings to require sight of social work notes. It is not to be thought that in every case there should be carte blanche discovery of social work notes and records. In each instance, a proper case for discovery must be made out. But applications for discovery should precede the trial and be part of the preparatory process rather than taking place during the trial. This means that the lawyers should consider, as an essential part of the process of preparation, the issues in the case and the material which will be required for the presentation of those issues. If documents are material, the proper course is to request them from social services first and, if disclosure is resisted, to apply well before the trial for disclosure (*Re JC (Care Proceedings: Procedure)* [1995] 2 FLR 77, FD). If a problem as to public interest immunity arises, the procedure to be followed is set out under r 4.17. For useful guidance as to the conduct and recording of meetings and the provision of documents in care proceedings see the judgment of Munby J in *Re L (Care: Assessment: Fair Trial)* [2002] EWHC 1379 (Fam), [2002] 2 FLR 730 which is referred to in more detail in **Disclosure – impact of the European Convention for Human Rights and Fundamental Freedoms 1950** under r 4.23.

Discovery by non-party—In *D v D (County Court Jurisdiction: Injunctions)* [1993] 2 FLR 802, the Court of Appeal held that the court had no jurisdiction to make orders for discovery by a non-party in family proceedings. The correct procedure by which a party could adduce in evidence documents in the possession of a non-party was by subpoena duces tecum (in the High Court) or by witness summons (in a county court). Even in children cases, the court has no general power to garner documentary evidence of its own motion. The judge at first instance had been wrong to order all documents, concerning investigations into the family, in the possession of the police and social services to be disclosed to the court and to the parties' solicitors.

There have been a number of recent cases concerning the gathering of evidence from non-parties, including *Re A and B (Minors) (No 2)* [1995] 1 FLR 351 (police and local authority investigation material needed for private law proceedings), *Nottinghamshire CC v H* [1995] 1 FLR 115 (CPS documents), *Re R (Child Abuse: Video Evidence)* [1995] 1 FLR 451 (police and hospital video tapes), *Re M (Child Abuse: Video Evidence)* [1995] 2 FLR 571 (police video tapes of interviews), *Cleveland County Council v F* [1995] 1 FLR 797 (police file relating to death of sibling including Home Office pathologist's report), *Cheshire County Council v C* [1995] 2 FLR 862 (documents and tapes held by Scottish prosecution authorities), *Re A Solicitor (Disclosure of Confidential Records)* [1997] 1 FLR 101 (hospital records relating to family interviews ordered to be disclosed to legal and medical advisers only; mother's solicitors fined for breaching order by sending copies to mother), *Re S (Contact: Evidence)* [1998] 1 FLR 798, CA (leave to father to issue subpoena against police to produce video and audio recordings of child's sexual abuse allegations and details of findings of police surgeon who examined the child).

Disclosure – impact of the European Convention for Human Rights and Fundamental Freedoms 1950—It is essential that a parent be placed in a position where he may obtain access to information which is relied on by the authorities in taking measures of protective care (*TP and KM v United Kingdom* [2001] 2 FLR 549). See further under r 4.23.

Preparation of welfare reports (r 4.14(2)(*g*))—As to welfare reports generally, see CA 1989, s 7 and rr 4.11B and 4.13. Directions may be sought under this rule where, for example, there are problems in complying with the request for a welfare report, either because of time constraints or for other reasons, or where the children and family reporter or welfare officer considers that part of his report contains sensitive·material which ought not to be shown to the parties in the normal way.

Transfer of proceedings (r 4.14(2)(*h*))—The transfer of proceedings between courts is governed by the Children (Allocation of Proceedings) Order 1991, which was made under CA 1989, Sch 11. Rule 4.6 deals specifically with:

(*a*) the procedure for transfer where the county court is asked to reverse the decision of a magistrates' court not to send proceedings up to the county court;
(*b*) the procedure whereby the county court sends proceedings down to a magistrates' court; and
(*c*) the procedure whereby the county court considers whether to transfer on to the High Court a case that it receives from a magistrates' court.

Any directions as to transfer that are not covered by r 4.6 may be given under this rule. The provisions of r 4.15(2), which deal with the obligation to fix a date for the receiving court next to consider the case and to notify the parties of the date, are also important in this context.

Consolidation with other proceedings (r 4.14(2)(*i*))—Clearly it is desirable wherever possible for directions to be given as to transfer between courts, consolidation etc. so that all linked proceedings can be heard and determined together; this will be the case, for example, where there are separate applications with regard to several children of the same family (see eg *W v Wakefield*

PART III

City Council [1995] 1 FLR 170) or more than one set of proceedings concerning an individual child which ought logically to be heard together. If the family proceedings court refuses to transfer upwards, for example, an application under CA 1989, s 8 for consolidation with "linked" county court proceedings, no "appeal" to the district judge is permissible. In those circumstances, one possible solution may be to seek leave to withdraw the s 8 application so that it could be started afresh in the county court. However, the Legal Services Commission may well resist the granting of public funding for "re-starting" such proceedings in the county court, when the family proceedings court was prepared to hear them originally. Another solution, in suitable circumstances, might be to seek judicial review of the magistrates' court's decision to refuse to transfer the proceedings (*R v South East Hampshire Family Proceedings Court ex parte D* [1994] 2 FLR 190 – a magistrates' court fell into error in limiting itself to the question of delay and thus precluded itself from considering the interests of the child on an application for an upwards transfer).

Notice of court's intention to give directions of its own motion (r 4.14(3)(*a*))—By virtue of r 10.7, unless otherwise directed, notice must generally be given in writing and by one of the methods set out in RSC Ord 65, r 5; the parties can therefore normally expect to receive written notice of the court's intention to give directions of its own motion. However, there will be situations in which oral notice is all that is feasible (for example, where there is special urgency or where the court becomes aware of the need for a particular direction only during the course of a hearing and proposes to make it there and then). In such a case, the court may give a direction dispensing with the need for written notice but must ensure that the parties have an opportunity to be heard (written representations are unlikely to be practical in such circumstances) in order to comply with r 4.14(3)(*a*).

"written representations" (r 4.14(3)(*a*))—There is no prescribed form, and no particular format is specified.

Written directions in difficult child care cases—In *Re A and B (Minors) (No 2)* [1995] 1 FLR 351, the view was expressed that, as a general rule, it is bad practice for directions in difficult child care cases to be sought and given in writing without the attendance of the parties.

"representatives" (r 4.14(3)(*c*))—Although it does not say so, r 4.14(3)(*c*) presumably means legal representatives.

Service—See rr 4.8, 10.2, 10.3 and 10.6.

Procedure in urgent cases (r 4.14(4))—Where the court gives leave in an urgent case, r 4.14(4) permits a party to apply orally on notice or orally without notice or in writing without notice.

Notice of request (r 4.14(5))—It appears, curiously enough, that, where an urgent request for directions is made in accordance with r 4.14(4) and happens to be in writing, r 4.14(5) applies so as to require the proper officer to fix a date for the hearing of the request and give notice to the parties. This could, in some cases, prevent the court from dealing with the matter with the urgency required thus defeating the object of r 4.14(4). However, because r 4.14(5) refers only to written requests, it does not apply where the request is made orally and the direction sought can be made immediately notwithstanding that the other parties may know nothing of the application (but see *Re B (Minors) (Care: Procedure)* [1994] Fam Law 72 discussed in **Timetable for the proceedings** above). It is only in an urgent case that, exceptionally, the application may be made orally or without notice (*Re W (A Minor) (Interim Care Order)* [1994] 2 FLR 892). As to the computation of time, see r 1.5; as to varying time-limits, see r 4.14(2).

Application of FPR 1991 to the directions hearing—Those of the Pt IV rules which are relevant will apply to the directions hearing; see particularly r 4.16 as to attendance, r 4.17 as to the filing of documentary evidence and r 4.21 as to procedure at the hearing.

"section 11(3)" (r 4.14(7))—CA 1989, s 11(3) gives the court power to grant a s 8 order at any time in the course of the proceedings even though it is not in a position to dispose finally of those proceedings.

"section 38(1)" (r 4.14(7))—CA 1989, s 38(1) concerns the making of interim care or supervision orders. Only local authorities and authorised persons are entitled to apply for such orders.

"in accordance with paragraph 3(b) or (c)" (r 4.14(7))—The provisions of r 4.14(4) relax the requirements of r 4.14(3)(*b*) to the extent that an oral ex parte application may suffice in certain cases. This relaxation may not have been meant to apply to applications under ss 11(3) and 38(1) but, as r 4.14(7) is currently drafted, it does and permits, for example, an oral ex parte application for an interim care order by a local authority provided leave is given. It is suggested that it ought perhaps to be read subject to r 4.4(4), which expressly lists those applications which may be made ex parte, and does not include applications under ss 11(3) and 38(1); however, the court in *Re B (Minors) (Residence Order)* [1992] Fam 162, CA did not feel constrained by that rule in relation to an ex parte interim residence order, which was not at that time within the ambit of r 4.4(4). Reference should be made to *Re C (A Minor) (Interim Care)* [1994] 1 FCR 447 (where an ex parte interim care order was in fact made) and to *Re W (A Minor) (Interim Care Order)* [1994] 2 FLR 892 (local authority accepted an interim supervision order would be appropriate and then, at a hearing at which the mother was not present, applied without notice to her for an interim care order).

"order under section 31, 34 or 38" (r 4.14(8))—CA 1989, s 31 is concerned with care and supervision orders; s 34 provides for orders regulating contact with a child in care; and s 38 is concerned with interim care and supervision orders.

"unless varied or discharged by directions under paragraph (2)" (r 4.14(9))—Presumably, in the case of a transfer from a county court to a magistrates' court, the proviso will also apply to any variation or discharge by the receiving court under the equivalent provision (Family Proceedings Courts (Children Act 1989) Rules 1991, r 14(2)).

Note of the giving, variation or revocation of a direction (r 4.14(10))—The prescribed form for general directions is contained in App 1.

Public interest immunity—Where an issue arises as to whether, because of public interest immunity, certain material (often material in the possession of the local authority) should or should not be disclosed, guidance as to the procedure to be followed can be derived from *Re C (Expert Evidence: Disclosure: Practice)* [1995] 1 FLR 204; *Re R (Care: Disclosure: Nature of Proceedings)* [2002] 1 FLR 755 and *Re C* [2002] LTL, 9 April 2002 – Doc No C0102987, noted further under r 4.17.

4.15 Timing of proceedings

(1) Where these rules or other rules of court provide a period of time within which or by which a certain act is to be performed in the course of proceedings to which this Part applies, that period may not be extended otherwise than by direction of the court under rule 4.14.

(2) At the –

(*a*) transfer to a court of proceedings to which this Part applies,
(*b*) postponement or adjournment of any hearing or directions appointment in the course of proceedings to which this Part applies, or
(*c*) conclusion of any such hearing or directions appointment other than one at which the proceedings are determined, or so soon thereafter as is practicable,

the court or the proper officer shall –

(i) fix a date upon which the proceedings shall come before the court again for such purposes as the court directs, which date shall, where paragraph (*a*) applies, be as soon as possible after the transfer, and
(ii) give notice to the parties, the children's guardian or the welfare officer or children and family reporter of the date so fixed.

Amendments—SI 2001/821.

Defined terms—"court": r 1.2(1); "directions appointment", "children's guardian": r 4.1(1); "proper officer": r 1.2(1); "children and family reporter": r 4.1(1).

PART III

Related provisions—Other provisions affecting the timing of proceedings include CA 1989, ss 1(2) (general principle that delay is likely to be prejudicial to the welfare of a child), 11(1) (obligation of the court in s 8 proceedings to draw up a timetable) and 32(1) (obligation of the court in proceedings under Part IV of the Act to draw up a timetable) and r 4.14 (power of the court to give directions as to time-limits, timetabling etc).

"proceedings to which this Part applies" (r 4.15(1))—Part IV applies to the proceedings listed in r 4.1(2).

Computation of time—See r 1.5.

Variation of time-limits (r 4.15(1))—Time-limits may not be extended except by direction of the court. However, there is nothing in the rules to prevent the parties from shortening time-limits by agreement.

Failure to observe time-limits—Where a local authority failed to submit written evidence as directed by the court and to comply with a direction to serve documents, the family proceedings court was correct in giving leave for statements to be filed out of time because it was vital in the interests of the children that the court should have the best information available. The sanction for failure to comply with directions was a costs order, where appropriate (*R v Nottinghamshire County Council* [1993] Fam Law 625).

Fixing a new date on transfer (r 4.15(2)(*a*))—The provisions of r 4.15(2) as to the responsibilities of the transferring or receiving court for fixing the next date and notifying the parties are ambiguous. On balance, it seems more likely that the obligation rests on the receiving court; however, it is clearly good practice for the transferring court to consult the proposed receiving court about dates in any event, so that any acceleration or delay that may result from the transfer can be taken into account in deciding whether transfer is an appropriate course of action (as required by Children (Allocation of Proceedings) Order 1991). The *CAAC Handbook of Best Practice in Children Act cases* (set out in Part IV of this work as *Best Practice Guidance of June 1997*) which also contains further helpful advice as to the procedure on transfer (see "Section 3 – First appointments in public law cases in the county courts: the role of the court"), suggests that the receiving court should fix a directions appointment when consulted about the transfer; the parties, if they are present in the transferring court, can then be informed of the new date immediately thus avoiding any postal delays or misunderstandings.

Where a case is proceeding in, or is transferred to, the High Court and an urgent hearing on Circuit is required before a High Court judge of the Family Division, enquiries should first be made as to the availability of such a judge in the area. It may be possible for the President of the Family Division to arrange for an additional High Court judge to go out to the Circuit specifically to hear the case (see *President's Guidance of 17 December 1993*). Where a case is transferred to the High Court with a time estimate of 5 days or more, an early directions hearing should be sought before a High Court judge, whether or not a date is also fixed for the substantive hearing of the application (*Practice Direction of 5 March 1993*). See also the observations made by Wall J in *Re MD and TD (Minors) (Time Estimates)* [1994] 2 FLR 336 (set out in Part IV of this work as *Practice Note of 2 February 1994*) and *Re A and B (Minors) (No 2)* [1995] 1 FLR 351 as to the desirability of fixing directions hearings in cases which are likely to be complex and/or lengthy.

Fixing a new date (r 4.15(2)(*c*))—The court must keep a tight rein on the proceedings ensuring that a new date is fixed, either at the end of the interim hearing or directions appointment while the parties are still at court or as soon as practicable thereafter.

Fixing a new date is not only a case of finding an appropriate court slot for the matter to be heard. CA 1989, s 1(2) must always be kept in mind, and other provisions of the Act may also impose constraints (see, for example, s 38(4), which limits the duration of interim care orders). Parties and their legal representatives must be in a position to inform the court of their availability for future hearings and that of their witnesses.

Notice—As to the giving of notice, see r 10.7.

4.16 Attendance at directions appointment and hearing

(1) Subject to paragraph (2), a party shall attend a directions appointment of which he has been given notice in accordance with rule 4.14(5) unless the court otherwise directs.

(2) Proceedings or any part of them shall take place in the absence of any party, including the child, if –

(*a*) the court considers it in the interests of the child, having regard to the matters to be discussed or the evidence likely to be given, and

(*b*) the party is represented by a children's guardian or solicitor;

and when considering the interests of the child under sub-paragraph (*a*) the court shall give the children's guardian, the solicitor for the child and, if he is of sufficient understanding, the child an opportunity to make representations.

(3) Subject to paragraph (4), where at the time and place appointed for a hearing or directions appointment the applicant appears but one or more of the respondents do not, the court may proceed with the hearing or appointment.

(4) The court shall not begin to hear an application in the absence of a respondent unless –

(*a*) it is proved to the satisfaction of the court that he received reasonable notice of the date of the hearing; or

(*b*) the court is satisfied that the circumstances of the case justify proceeding with the hearing.

(5) Where, at the time and place appointed for a hearing or directions appointment one or more of the respondents appear but the applicant does not, the court may refuse the application or, if sufficient evidence has previously been received, proceed in the absence of the applicant.

(6) Where at the time and place appointed for a hearing or directions appointment neither the applicant nor any respondent appears, the court may refuse the application.

(7) Unless the court otherwise directs, a hearing of, or directions appointment in, proceedings to which this Part applies shall be in chambers.

Amendments—SI 2001/821.

Defined terms—"applicant", "application", "child": r 4.1(1); "court": r 1.2(1); "directions appointment", "children's guardian": r 4.1(1).

Related provisions—Other provisions relating to attendance include r 4.11(4), which imposes a duty on the children's guardian to attend directions appointments and hearings and requires him to advise the court as to whether the child is of sufficient understanding to make representations under r 4.16(2) and as to the wishes of the child in respect of any relevant matter, including his attendance at court; r 4.14(2)(*c*), which is a general power enabling the court to give directions as to the attendance of the child, and CA 1989, s 95, which empowers a court hearing proceedings under Pt IV or V of the Act (or considering whether to make an order under those Parts) to require the attendance of the child and to make supplementary orders to secure that attendance.

"a party shall attend a directions appointment" (r 4.16(1))—By virtue of the fact that r 4.16(1) is dealing with directions appointments under r 4.14, "party" carries the extended meaning in that rule and includes the children's guardian and, where a request or direction concerns a report under s 7, the children and family reporter or welfare officer (see r 4.14(1)). The children's guardian is, in any event, obliged by r 4.11(4) to attend all directions appointments unless excused by the court. As to the children and family reporter, there appears to be a conflict between r 4.11B (the effect of which is that a children and family reporter is only obliged to attend a hearing if required to do so by a specific direction) and r 4.16(1) (which requires attendance at all directions hearings unless otherwise directed); the same conflict arises in relation to a welfare officer who prepares a report under s 7(1)(*b*), whose attendance is only required if there is a specific direction to that effect pursuant to r 4.13(3). In practice, r 4.11B prevails in relation to the children and family reporter and r 4.13 prevails in relation to the welfare officer, so that they will not be in attendance unless this has been specifically required.

"notice in accordance with r 4.14(5)" (r 4.16(1))—Notice, of not less than two days, is given under r 4.14(5) for a directions appointment which has been arranged in response to a written request of a party where the other parties have not signified their consent. It is curious that, in contrast, r 4.16(1) does not appear to make attendance obligatory where notice of an appointment is given under r 4.14(6)(*b*), ie where a written request has been made by a party for directions to which the other parties do consent but which the court is not prepared to grant. Nor, it would seem, is attendance necessary under r 4.16(1) where the court simply fixes a directions hearing of its own motion, as it is entitled to do under r 4.4 and will often do as a matter of course when an application is first filed. It is suggested that this is an oversight in the rules.

"unless the court otherwise directs" (r 4.16(1))—The court is given a complete discretion as to the circumstances in which to dispense with the attendance of a party at a directions hearing and can do so either of its own motion (for example when sending out notice of the appointment) or on the request of a party. It is suggested that the power to give the necessary direction derives from r 4.16(1) itself rather than from r 4.14. If this were not so, the provisions of r 4.14 as to notice and as to the fixing of a hearing of a request for directions would apply, with the result that the court might well end up having to hold a *preliminary* directions hearing (which the parties might all have to attend) about whether to require attendance at the directions hearing.

Seeking a direction dispensing with attendance at a directions appointment—On the assumption that the power to give directions about attendance derives from r 4.16(1) itself (see **"unless the court otherwise directs"** above), there is no set procedure for seeking a direction excusing a party from attendance at a directions appointment. An advance request in writing may be made if there is time (for guidance as to the manner of making such a request, see **Written request for directions in Form C2** under r 4.14), but there does not appear to be any reason why an oral request should not be made in appropriate circumstances. For example, where a court is fixing the next appointment at the conclusion of giving directions, it might be asked, in special circumstances, to dispense with the attendance of one of the parties on the next occasion.

Use of the power to exclude (r 4.16(2))—Generally, all parties (including the child himself if he is a party) are entitled to be present throughout the proceedings. Rule 4.16(2) empowers the court to exclude a party where the criteria laid down are satisfied; it is in mandatory terms and contrasts with r 4.16(3), (5) and (6), which confers on the court a discretion as to whether to proceed with a hearing or appointment where a party fails to attend. Rule 4.16(2) will no doubt normally come into play where it is the child who should be excluded for his own good. For the attitude of the courts towards the attendance of children at hearings, see **Child at court** below. Rule 4.16(2) may also be used where, for some reason, another party's presence would impede a proper hearing, for example in the very rare case where an older child is to give evidence and would find it distressing to do so in the presence of a parent who is alleged to be guilty of a serious sexual assault on him or her. However, in such a situation, the giving of the child's evidence by video link or behind a screen may be a better course. Exceptionally, an application for an adjournment can be granted ex parte, but only where the best interests of the children justify such a course of action. Even then, those representing the parties should be in attendance, either having given undertakings or being subject to a direction of the court not to pass on the information to their clients (*Re B (Minors) (Care: Procedure)* [1994] Fam Law 72 – local authority applied ex parte to adjourn application relating to contact with child in care so that it could carry out investigations into allegations of sexual abuse against a parent without the parents learning of the allegations). As to the procedure to be followed where an application is made to withhold material from a party to proceedings, see *Re C (Disclosure)* [1996] 1 FLR 797, FD, which is considered fully in **Submission of evidence** under r 4.14.

Child at court—The effect of r 4.16(1) is to require the child, if he is a party, to be present at directions appointments unless the court otherwise directs. As it is not generally considered that it is wise for children to attend court (see below), it might be appropriate to seek, at an early stage in proceedings, a direction excusing the child from attendance at directions hearings. There is no obligation on the child to attend hearings other than directions hearings but, if he is a party, he is entitled to do so unless excluded under r 4.16(2) or otherwise by order of the court.

The attitude of the court towards the attendance of children has consistently been a cautious one. In *Re C (A Minor) (Care: Child's Wishes)* [1993] 1 FLR 832 (appeal from a magistrates' court to the High Court), the subject of a care order application, a 13-year-old girl who was young for her years, had been present throughout the majority of the hearing before the judge and throughout the appeal hearing. The judge commented that it would be a pity if the presence of children as young as this at the hearing of High Court appeals from magistrates in family proceedings were to be allowed to develop unquestioningly into a settled practice, and that listening to lawyers debating one's future was not an experience that should in normal circumstances be wished upon any young child. Where children's guardians were proposing to arrange for a young child to be present at an appeal, they should give that question very careful thought beforehand and be prepared, if necessary, to explain their reasons to the court. In *Re W (Secure Accommodation Order: Attendance at Court)* [1994] 2 FLR 1092, Ewbank J said that attending court is likely to be harmful for a child and should only be permitted if the court is satisfied it is in the child's interests. The judge held that r 4.16(2) (which is in similar terms to FPC(CA 1989)R 1991, r 16(2)) applies only to one set of circumstances. In other circumstances, the child's interests will prevail. In addition to the consideration of the interests of the child, the court has an inherent power to control its own proceedings which entitles it to decide to proceed in the child's absence. The fact that the child would need to be physically restrained during the hearing in order to control him (as in *Re W*) would, in itself, be sufficient ground for refusing to allow the child to be in court. Further examples given in *Re W* of situations in which the court would not allow a child to be present are where there is a prospect of disturbance or unruliness in court or the possibility of the child being educationally subnormal or where the child is much younger than the 10-year-old boy in that case. *Re C (Residence: Child's Application for Leave)* [1995] 1 FLR 927, FD, contains further reference to the disadvantages of a child being present during a hearing. See also *Re HB (Abduction: Children's Objections) (No 2)* [1998] 1 FLR 564, FD as to concerns that may arise where a youngish child participates in litigation.

In *Re A (Care: Discharge Application by Child)* [1995] 1 FLR 599, Thorpe J touched on the question of whether or not a child applicant (in that case a 14-year-old boy seeking the discharge of a care order) should give evidence in proceedings, stating that the balance between recognising and upholding the rights of children who are parties to Children Act litigation to participate and be heard, and the need to protect children from exposure to material that might be damaging, is a delicate one, and the question of participation of the child has to be addressed by the trial judge at a relatively early stage in the proceedings, with a full perspective of the issues and the statements and reports and due regard to r 4.16(2). *Re M (Family Proceedings: Affidavits)* [1995] 2 FLR 100, CA, stresses that it is quite wrong in the normal case for a child (in that case, a child of 12/13) who is the subject of a dispute between parents in family proceedings to be "dragged into the arena" and asked to swear an affidavit, and that it is not the practice in family proceedings for children to give evidence.

Care proceedings: more than one local authority involved—Where the applicant local authority will not be the authority responsible for operating the arrangements for the child once an order is made, the need for the second local authority to attend court to deal with issues arising must be borne in mind (*L v London Borough of Bexley* [1996] 2 FLR 595). See also *Re C (Care Order: Appropriate Local Authority)* [1997] 1 FLR 544, FD.

"the party is represented by a children's guardian or solicitor" (r 4.16(2)(*b*))—It is not clear whether a party is represented by a solicitor simply by virtue of the fact that he has instructed a solicitor or whether he is so represented only if the solicitor is actually in attendance at the relevant hearing. The latter interpretation would seem more in keeping with the spirit of the rule. Similarly, although the rule is silent as to whether, following a decision that proceedings shall take place in the absence of a party, that party's solicitor or children's guardian is entitled to remain in court, he must, as a general rule, be entitled to continue to participate in the hearing in order to safeguard the excluded party's interests (see, for example, *Re B (Minors) (Care: Procedure)* [1994] Fam Law 72 – justices should not have excluded representatives of respondents from ex parte application for adjournment of hearing relating to contact with children in care). In *Re AS (Secure Accommodation Order)* [1999] 1 FLR 103, FD, considering the requirement for legal representation of the child concerned in secure accommodation proceedings (CA 1989, s 25(6)), the court held that to be effective, legal representation must involve the taking of instructions. It was not sufficient for the child to be represented at the hearing by a solicitor and counsel who had not been able to take any instructions because the child had not been informed of the hearing.

Child of sufficient understanding to make representations (r 4.16(2))—There are a number of situations in which the rules or the Act oblige the court to evaluate the understanding of the child (see, for example, s 4(4) with regard to parental responsibility agreements, s 10(8) with regard to leave to apply for a s 8 order, and s 43(8) with regard to medical and other examinations). No criteria are laid down as to what constitutes sufficient understanding and what is sufficient for one purpose may not, of course, be sufficient for another; the court will have to take a decision on the particular facts of each case. The authorities on the understanding of a child are collected together under **"able ... to give such instructions on his own behalf"** under FPR 1991, r 4.12. Where there is a children's guardian he will advise the court as to the level of the child's understanding and the child's wishes in accordance with r 4.11(4) and where there is a children and family

PART III

reporter, he can be asked to assist. Alternatively, the assessment will have to be based upon how the child appears and what he (or his legal representative on his behalf) says in court or the judge or district judge could, presumably, exercise his discretion to see him privately if appropriate (see further **Judge seeing child** under r 4.21). In certain cases, it may be necessary for evidence to be heard on the question from the expert or experts already involved in the case.

"opportunity to make representations" (r 4.16(2))—The rules do not require that there should be an opportunity for *oral* representations so, although oral representations will be usual, presumably an opportunity to make written representations will suffice.

Hearing or directions appointment in the absence of a respondent (r 4.16(3), (4))—Rule 4.16(3) and (4) give the court a wide discretion to entertain proceedings in the absence of a respondent and even go so far as to permit the court, in an appropriate case, to proceed to hear an application where the respondent is absent because he has not had reasonable notice of the hearing date. The court is not likely to go to this extreme very often but, where it is prepared to do so, it may be inclined to safeguard the position of the respondent by providing, for example, that he shall be entitled to apply within a certain number of days of service of the order upon him to have it varied or discharged (for a similar sort of order, see *Re D (A Minor) (Child: Removal from Jurisdiction)* [1992] 1 FLR 637). Where an application is made at the hearing itself for an order which is different in kind from that previously applied for, the respondent must be given the opportunity to be present at the hearing, and should be given the chance to cross-examine witnesses called by the applicant (*Re W (A Minor) (Interim Care Order)* [1994] 2 FLR 892, CA). In *Re M (Judge's Discretion)* [2001] EWCA Civ 1428, [2002] 1 FLR 730 the parties had agreed directions to be put before the court at an interim hearing in care proceedings and had assumed that it would be uncontested. Consequently, the mother, local authority and children's guardian were not present save by counsel. The judge refused to renew the interim care order and instead made a wholly different order, granting residence to the grandparents, without giving the parties an opportunity to make representations or to call evidence. The Court of Appeal held that the judge was wholly wrong and set aside the order, replacing it with the proposal agreed between the parties.

Re SW (A Minor) (Care Proceedings) [1993] 2 FLR 609, a care order application, is an example of the type of situation in which the court may decide to proceed in the absence of a respondent. The mother had changed her accommodation and failed to keep the local authority, her solicitor or the court informed of her whereabouts or to make proper arrangements for her mail to be collected or forwarded. When she failed to attend for the final hearing, her solicitor sought an adjournment, arguing that she was keen to oppose the application and may have become confused as to the date. She had, however, been in touch with the local authority, had full knowledge of the hearing date and had expressed to the social worker that day by telephone that she was not certain that she should come to court as she could not face a room full of people or the possible consequences. The justices concluded that she had had adequate notice of the hearing and that it would not be in the child's best interests to adjourn, and made a care order and an order terminating contact, both of which orders were upheld on appeal. Booth J pointed out that delay was a matter which had to be considered on any application to adjourn cases involving children, and the interests of the other parties had to be assessed in the light of the principle that delay in determining a question concerning a child's upbringing was likely to prejudice his welfare. She also stressed the responsibility of an adult party to keep his legal advisers or the court fully informed as to where and how he might be contacted. It is noteworthy that, whilst the mother in *Re SW* (above) knew that the court would be asked to make a care order, she did not know that it would also be asked to make an order that she should have no contact with the child. Legal advisers should therefore, as Booth J said, ensure that their clients are made well aware of the court's power in family proceedings to make a wide range of orders under CA 1989 of its own motion. Contrast, however, *Re W (A Minor) (Interim Care Order)* (above).

Dismissal of proceedings at directions stage—In *Re B (Contact: Stepfather's Opposition)* [1997] 2 FLR 579, CA the judge summarily dismissed a father's application for contact at a directions hearing without hearing any evidence and ordered that he should not make further applications without leave of the court. The father was not present and had not been warned that his application might be dismissed in that way. He appealed. It was properly conceded that, in an appropriate case, a contact application can be dismissed on a directions hearing. The Court of Appeal pointed out that, in the exercise of that power, the court must bear in mind that the more Draconian the order and the more unique the situation, the greater the need for the court to be satisfied that grave harm is virtually certain to befall the child if the court follows its usual procedure and investigates the matter on its merits. In that case, there was a real risk that if the contact proceedings continued, the child's family unit would be damaged by the stepfather rejecting both the child and her mother with resulting harm to the child. The Court of Appeal dismissed the father's appeal, considering that (although it appears that individual members of the Court of Appeal might have taken different action in the crisis faced by the judge) the judge had not erred in principle. It is worth noting, however, that the Official Solicitor was to remain involved and the court clearly contemplated that contact may be arranged. In *Re A (Application for Leave)* [1998] 1 FLR 1, the Court of Appeal reaffirmed the view that, in appropriate cases, an application may be determined at a directions appointment if the content of the statements and the children and family reporter's report indicate that it should go no further. For further examples of situations in which an application may be brought to a premature end, see **Full hearing not always appropriate** under r 4.21 (and under FPC(CA 1989)R 1991, r 21).

"reasonable notice of the date of the hearing" (r 4.16(4)(*a*))—Where it is the court's obligation to give notice to the respondents of a hearing date, proof will be found in the court file. Where it is the applicant's responsibility, he will have to prove that the respondent has had reasonable notice. Rule 10.7 makes provision as to the appropriate method of giving notice and r 4.8 with regard to service and the filing of a statement as to service in Form C9. However, it is possible that the respondent may have had reasonable notice of the hearing date even if it has not been given (or cannot be proved) in accordance with these rules. Rule 4.16(4) does not specify that the notice has to be in writing to be reasonable, and oral notice may suffice where, for example, the respondent was present at the last hearing when the new date was fixed. Alternatively, he may have shown in some way that he knows of the date of the hearing, for example by writing to the court about it or by telling one of the parties that he has no intention of coming to court on such and such a day. For a further example, see *Re SW (A Minor) (Care Proceedings)* [1993] 2 FLR 609. Where there has been an interim care or supervision order and no change in this is sought, a notification in the antecedent order that the renewal hearing will take place on a certain day is sufficient; there is no need to go through the formality of serving another piece of paper. However, if a change is intended in the nature of the order which is being sought on the subsequent occasion, then normally specific notice of at least 2 clear days should be given by the party which seeks the new form of order *Re W (A Minor) (Interim Care Order)* [1994] 2 FLR 892, and see further **"in accordance with paragraph 3(b) or (c)"** under r 4.14).

For certain applications, minimum notice periods are laid down in the rules themselves or in App 2, and it may be difficult in such cases to satisfy the court that a lesser period of notice is "reasonable".

Hearing or directions appointment in the absence of applicant (r 4.16(5))—The court has a discretion whether or not to refuse the application in the absence of the applicant. Rule 16(5) refers only to the court proceeding with the application or refusing it, but there will be many cases (for example where there is doubt as to whether the applicant has had reasonable notice of the time and place of a hearing) where the appropriate course is to adjourn the application, fixing another date for it to be heard. If the applicant fails to turn up for no good reason on more than one occasion or has indicated that he no longer wishes to proceed with his case, the court will no doubt give very serious consideration to refusing the application. However, it must be borne in mind that such a course of action would be tantamount to permitting the withdrawal of an application, and such leave is not granted as a matter of course (see under r 4.5).

"sufficient evidence has previously been received" (r 4.16(5))—Rule 4.16(5) specifically refers to evidence and not to statements, information etc. For example, where the applicant does not appear at the resumed hearing of a part-heard matter, the court may already have heard from witnesses whose evidence is sufficient to justify proceeding in the applicant's absence. Where, however, the applicant is absent at an earlier stage, the court may be in possession, at best, of written statements of the substance of the oral evidence that the parties intend to adduce at the hearing filed under r 4.17. Although the statements will be dated and signed and contain a declaration in accordance with r 4.17(1)(*a*)(iii), they are not equivalent to affidavits, and they are certainly not "oral evidence" although, according to Ward J (as he then was) in *S v Merton London Borough* [1994] 1 FCR 186, [1994] Fam Law 321, they are capable of standing as a form of documentary evidence. It is, therefore, a moot point whether they, or indeed any other documents filed in accordance with r 4.17 (such as experts' reports), constitute evidence on the basis of which the court could decide to proceed in the absence of the applicant.

There is no requirement that the evidence should have come from the applicant himself or from his witnesses; evidence adduced by any party may suffice.

Where neither applicant nor respondent attends (r 4.16(6))—Although r 4.16(6) refers only to the court's discretion to refuse the application, it must also have power in an appropriate case either to adjourn it or to grant it.

PART III

Hearings in chambers (r 4.16(7))—Robes are not worn for chambers hearings. Only the officers of the court, the parties and their legal representatives, the children's guardian, the children and family reporter and the witnesses will normally be allowed into the court and, if appropriate, even witnesses may be excluded save during the period when they are actually giving evidence. As to the publication of information relating to children's proceedings heard in private, see Administration of Justice Act 1960, s 12. The court has a discretion to sit in open court. It may do so where, for example, the case decides a point of law that is of general importance or where issues of public interest arise and it considers it appropriate to give judgment in open court, providing, where desirable in the interests of the child, appropriate directions to avoid identification. However, as *Re PB (Hearings in Open Court)* [1996] 2 FLR 765, CA, comments, the evidence relating to the welfare of a child will rarely be heard in public. In *Re B (Hearings in Open Court)* [1997] Fam Law 508, FD, the court refused an application by the Crown Prosecution Service for family proceedings to be heard in open court so that they could consider more fully the parallel criminal case against the father and also refused the alternative application that a CPS representative be present in chambers to hear the medical evidence. Appeals from the magistrates under CA 1989, s 94 are not within r 4.16 and are normally held in open court, not in chambers (*London Borough of Croydon v R* [1997] 2 FLR 675).

Court of Appeal standing instructions against identification of child—Whilst it is highly desirable that appellate proceedings, wherever possible, should be in open court, in the great majority of cases involving children this could have adverse consequences for the children. It has been accepted, therefore, by the Court of Appeal that in general the identity of the child should be protected by means of an order restricting publication of information which could lead to his identity. Under standing instructions of the Court of Appeal, orders in such terms have almost invariably been made in cases involving children. Without standing instructions, there would always be a risk that the court might fail, through oversight, to give the direction that the restriction should be included. If there were unusual circumstances which made publicity desirable then the court could decide to depart from standing instructions (*Re R (Court of Appeal: Order Against Identification)* [1999] 2 FLR 145).

Children's hearings in private do not breach European Convention for the Protection of Human Rights and Fundamental Freedoms 1950, Art 6—Hearing children cases in England and Wales in private, without public pronouncement of judgment, does not breach the European Convention for the Protection of Human Rights and Fundamental Freedoms, Art 6 (*B v UK and P v UK* [2001] 2 FLR 261). It was held in *B v UK and P v UK* (above) that if judgment were pronounced publicly that would to a large extent frustrate the aims of holding the proceedings in chambers.

"proceedings to which this Part applies" (r 4.16(7))—Part IV applies to the proceedings listed in r 4.1(2).

4.17 Documentary evidence

(1) Subject to paragraphs (4) and (5), in proceedings to which this Part applies a party shall file and serve on the parties, any welfare officer or children and family reporter and any children's guardian of whose appointment he has been given notice under rule 4.10(5) –

- (*a*) written statements of the substance of the oral evidence which the party intends to adduce at a hearing of, or a directions appointment in, those proceedings, which shall –
  - (i) be dated,
  - (ii) be signed by the person making the statement,
  - (iii) contain a declaration that the maker of the statement believes it to be true and understands that it may be placed before the court; and
  - (iv) show in the top right hand corner of the first page –
    - (*a*) the initials and surname of the person making the statement,
    - (*b*) the number of the statement in relation to the maker,
    - (*c*) the date on which the statement was made, and
    - (*d*) the party on whose behalf it is filed; and

(*b*) copies of any documents, including experts' reports, upon which the party intends to rely at a hearing of, or a directions appointment in, those proceedings,

at or by such time as the court directs or, in the absence of a direction, before the hearing or appointment.

(2) A party may, subject to any direction of the court about the timing of statements under this rule, file and serve on the parties a statement which is supplementary to a statement served under paragraph (1).

(3) At a hearing or a directions appointment a party may not, without the leave of the court –

(*a*) adduce evidence, or
(*b*) seek to rely on a document,

in respect of which he has failed to comply with the requirements of paragraph (1).

(4) In proceedings for a section 8 order a party shall –

(*a*) neither file nor serve any document other than as required or authorised by these rules, and
(*b*) in completing a form prescribed by these rules, neither give information, nor make a statement, which is not required or authorised by that form,

without the leave of the court.

(5) In proceedings for a section 8 order no statement or copy may be filed under paragraph (1) until such time as the court directs.

Amendments—SI 1992/2067; SI 2001/821.

Defined terms—"court": r 1.2(1); "directions appointment", "children's guardian", "leave": r 4.1(1); "section 8 order": CA 1989, s 8(2); "children and family reporter": r 4.1(1).

Case management—*Practice Direction of 31 January 1995* deals with a number of important aspects of the preparation for and the conduct of hearings, and reference should be made to it when dealing with documentary evidence. See also the *CAAC Handbook of Best Practice in Children Act cases* (set out in Part IV of this work as *Best Practice Guidance of June 1997*) and the useful guidance given in relation to public law cases by Charles J in *Re R (Care: Disclosure: Nature of Proceedings)* [2002] 1 FLR 755 (dealt with more fully in **Preparation of public law cases** under CA 1989, s 31). For useful guidance as to the conduct and recording of meetings and the provision of documents in care proceedings see the judgment of Munby J in *Re L (Care: Assessment: Fair Trial)* [2002] EWHC 1379 (Fam), [2002] 2 FLR 730 which is referred to in more detail in **Disclosure – impact of the European Convention for Human Rights and Fundamental Freedoms 1950** under r 4.23. See also **Bundles and other particular matters** under r 4.14.

"Subject to paragraphs (4) and (5)" (r 4.17(1))—It is most important to note that the automatic requirement to file and serve written statements of evidence and copies of documents does not apply in proceedings for a s 8 order; in such proceedings, the documentation to be filed and served is strictly limited in order to provide the parties with an opportunity to resolve issues amicably before inflammatory statements are exchanged. See further **Forms and documentary evidence in s 8 cases** below.

"proceedings to which this Part applies" (r 4.17(1))—Part IV applies to the proceedings listed in r 4.1(2).

"a party shall file and serve" (r 4.17(1))—The obligation to serve is that of the party himself, not of the court.

Parties—Broadly speaking, the parties to proceedings are the applicant and the respondents set out in the relevant entry in App 3, column (iii). As to the power of the court to order that a person be joined as or cease to be a party, see r 4.7.

Written statements of intended oral evidence (r 4.17(1)(*a*))—Providing the statement is dated, signed and contains the requisite declaration and r 4.17(1)(*a*)(iv)/FPC(CA 1989)R 1991, r 17(1)(*a*)(iv) information, its format is a matter for the individual practitioner. The title of the case and the case number should be clearly marked on the document as should the name of the maker of the statement. As for the body of the statement, it is suggested that it is sensible to use numbered paragraphs such as those used in affidavits as this makes reference to the document in court much easier; at the very least, the pages of the statement should be numbered. Headings may be used to identify the different topics covered by the maker of the statement. It is also helpful if, wherever possible, events are described in chronological order. Archaic language such as "I verily believe" should be avoided. The inclusion of a substantial amount of hearsay should also be avoided (see *Re P (Minors) (Child Abuse: Medical Evidence)* [1988] 1 FLR 328) and, where it is included, the source of information should be declared or good reason for not doing so should be given (*Practice Direction of 31 January 1995*). A common mistake that leads to the introduction of unnecessary amounts of hearsay, particularly in local authority statements in care cases, is to assume that each individual statement must tell the *whole* story. Generally, the correct approach is for each witness to deal only with that part of the evidence in relation to which he has direct knowledge. The court will then be able to assemble the complete picture from all the statements and other documents, no doubt assisted by a written chronology and an opening which includes a chronological résumé of events. All parties have a duty in family proceedings not to be tendentious in the presentation of their evidence, and that duty is particularly acute in relation to local authority evidence; the duty of local authorities to be objective, fair and balanced cannot be over-emphasised (*Re JC (Care Proceedings: Procedure)* [1995] 2 FLR 77, FD; *TP and KM v United Kingdom* [2001] 2 FLR 549). The duty of disclosure is considered further under r 4.18/FPC(CA 1989)R 1991, r 18 and in **Disclosure – impact of the European Convention for Human Rights and Fundamental Freedoms 1950** under r 4.23.

Where a witness, including the children's guardian, has compiled contemporaneous notes of events and incidents which are relevant to his evidence, then these should be fully disclosed and exhibited to his statement or report (*Re R (Care: Disclosure: Nature of Proceedings)* [2002] 1 FLR 755 – where the failure of the foster-parent, the children's guardian and further witnesses to disclose their contemporaneous notes until called for by the judge during the hearing, led to the local authority having to abandon allegations of serious sexual abuse and to rely on other allegations to support its case for care orders). *Re R* is considered in more detail in **Preparation of public law cases** under CA 1989, s 31. See also the useful guidance as to the conduct and recording of meetings and the provision of documents in care proceedings in the judgment of Munby J in *Re L (Care: Assessment: Fair Trial)* [2002] EWHC 1379 (Fam), [2002] 2 FLR 730 which is referred to in more detail in **Disclosure – impact of the European Convention for Human Rights and Fundamental Freedoms 1950** under r 4.23.

It is the substance of the oral evidence that has to be included in the statement. Whilst a witness will not, therefore, be allowed without leave to raise fresh matters which have not been covered in his statement (r 4.17(3)/FPC(CA 1989)R 1991, r 17(3)), he ought not to be prevented from elaborating (within reason) on relevant matters which were included, although the intention of the *Practice Direction of 31 January 1995* appears to be largely to prevent this. The rule is not clear as to whether the written statement is itself evidence. It is certainly not "oral evidence", and it needs to be identified by the witness when he attends to give evidence and its truth attested to or affirmed (*S v Merton London Borough* [1994] 1 FCR 186, [1994] Fam Law 321). Ward J (as he then was) did indicate, however, that a written statement was capable of standing as a form of documentary evidence.

Where the attendance of the witness is not necessary because the other parties are prepared to accept the contents of the statement without cross-examination, there appears to be no reason why the same approach should not be taken as with an unchallenged affidavit or expert report. The court will already be in possession of the relevant document, and the advocates should simply indicate that it has been agreed that it should stand as evidence without the attendance of the maker. It should be indicated whether the contents of the statement are agreed (ie there is no challenge to them and it is agreed that they are accurate) or whether, as can happen exceptionally, it has been decided that, although the contents are not agreed, areas of dispute will be indicated to the court in submissions only, rather than being explored in cross-examination as well.

Cases decided on documentary evidence and argument—See **Full hearing not always appropriate** under r 4.21.

Filing of copies of documents (r 4.17(1)(*b*))—The obligation under r 4.17(1)(*b*)/FPC(CA 1989)R 1991, r 17(1)(*b*) to file copies of documents extends only to documents on which a party intends to rely. Although a party is likely to be obliged to *disclose* experts' reports which are adverse to his case and on which he does not therefore intend to rely (*Re L (Police Investigation: Privilege)* [1996] 1 FLR 731, HL, and see further under r 4.18/FPC(CA 1989)R 1991, r 18), r 4.17(1)(*b*)/r 17(1)(*b*) does not oblige him to *file* copies. However, in practice, the leave to place the papers before the expert or to have the child examined for the purposes of the report is likely to have been expressly conditional on the report being both filed and served.

Note particularly the restrictions on filing and serving any document in proceedings for a s 8 order other than as required or authorised by the rules – see further **Forms and documentary evidence in s 8 cases** below.

Public interest immunity—The rules on public interest immunity qualify the general principle that parties to an application for a care order must file and serve copies of any documents on which they intend to rely in the proceedings. The limits of immunity are not clear: the categories of public interest are not closed and may alter over time (see *D v National Society for the Prevention of Cruelty to Children* [1978] AC 171, (1977) FLR Rep 181). Social work records are covered by public interest immunity, and *Re M (A Minor) (Disclosure of Material)* [1990] 2 FLR 36, CA, sets out the balancing exercise that must be done where application is made for disclosure. In exercising its discretion, the court has to weigh up whether the public interest in protecting the social work records overrides the public interest that the party to proceedings should obtain the information sought in order to obtain legal redress. It is for the party seeking discovery to establish the need for the production of the documents and, whilst it may be necessary for the court to inspect the documents in some cases in order to decide whether production should be ordered, a court can only inspect documents where it has definite grounds for expecting to find material of real importance to the party seeking disclosure.

However, in *Re R (Care: Disclosure: Nature of Proceedings)* [2002] 1 FLR 755 Charles J held that *Re M* (above) should be treated with caution and be carefully reconsidered in the light of developments in the law and practice relating to public interest immunity, in particular since *R v Chief Constable of West Midlands Police ex parte Wiley* [1995] 1 AC 274, which resulted in the "class claim" to public interest immunity becoming a matter of history. He held that:

"(*a*) any case on public interest immunity that precedes *In re Wiley* or post-dates it but does not include a careful consideration of that case and the developments in the law and practice relating to public interest immunity that followed should be regarded with caution and carefully reconsidered. For example, in my judgment, that applies to the decision of the Court of Appeal in *Re M (A Minor: Disclosure of Material)* [1990] 2 FLR 36;

(*b*) general statements that one sees in textbooks and hears that social work records are covered by public interest immunity, which is a widely stated class claim, should now be consigned to history;

(*c*) anyone advancing a claim to public interest immunity in respect of material held by a local authority should take advice and set out with particularity the harm that it is alleged will be caused to the public interest, for example the proper conduct of the duties of a local authority in respect of the protection of children, if material which passes the threshold test for disclosure is disclosed with or without appropriate redaction in the relevant proceedings; and

(*d*) before embarking on a claim of public interest immunity (or another argument for opposing disclosure) consideration should be given to the question whether the material passes the threshold test for disclosure and if so why."

Charles J emphasised the point that Munby J made in *Re B (Disclosure to Other Parties)* [2001] 2 FLR 1017 (discussed in more detail under r 4.23 – see **Disclosure – impact of the European Convention for Human Rights and Fundamental Freedoms 1950**), in respect of claims for non-disclosure based on Art 8 of the ECHRFF, that a compelling case for non-disclosure based on public interest immunity needs to be made out and any non-disclosure must go no further than is strictly necessary, having regard to the competing public interests. Furthermore, he expressed the view that "both local authorities and guardians ad litem should be more willing than they seem to be at present to exhibit their notes of relevant conversations and incidents that are relied on as evidence for findings at the threshold or welfare stage of proceedings, rather than to embark on what is a time-consuming and difficult exercise of preparing summaries of those notes." Charles J commended the Official Solicitor's practice of exhibiting attendance records to his report and said that it would have been beneficial if this practice had been adopted by both the local authority and the guardian in this case and, indeed, it would be likely to be beneficial in many other cases. In *Re R* (above) the failure of the foster-parent, the children's guardian and further witnesses to disclose their contemporaneous notes until called for by the judge during the hearing led to the local authority having to abandon allegations of serious sexual abuse and to rely on other allegations to support its case for care orders.

Further guidance by Charles J was given in *Re C* [2002] LTL, 9 April – Doc No C0102987, a case in which the local authority received information that the father was involved in serious criminal activity and likely to harm and abduct the child and so sought directions on disclosure from the police of information about the father. The police agreed to disclose information about the father's convictions and arrests but not otherwise, contending that to disclose further material about the father's possible criminal activity was likely to seriously harm the proper functioning of the police and the strong public interest in proper investigation and persecution of crime. Charles J held, inter alia, that:

(1) The parties to the care proceedings would not be prejudiced by not being given further detail from the police, while the public interest could have been harmed by it.
(2) *Nottinghamshire County Council v H* [1995] 1 FLR 115 had to be reconsidered in the light of *R v Chief Constable of West Midlands Police, ex parte Wiley* [1995] 1 AC 274.
(3) A person was entitled to disclosure of all material taken into account by a decision-maker when reaching a decision adverse to that person. Non-disclosure of relevant material to one party was exceptional.
(4) The general position was that confidentiality was not a valid reason for non-disclosure of material that passed the relevant threshold test.
(5) The stages of any issue relating to disclosure were:
 (*a*) Whether the relevant threshold test was satisfied; and
 (*b*) If so, whether there were nevertheless grounds for refusing disclosure.

In *Re W (Disclosure to Police)* [1998] 2 FLR 135, the Court of Appeal considered the status of local authority working papers, such as information and notes used to prepare an assessment report for court. The assessment report had been filed at court but the notes had not. Unless there is an order of the court to the contrary, such confidential information has to be dealt with by the local authority in accordance with the guide 'Working Together'. It is protected by public interest immunity from general publication but should be shared with the police without prior reference to the court where necessary for the protection of children. This decision is expressly confined, however, to documents held by and information known to social workers and has no application to the position of a children's guardian or children and family reporter appointed for court proceedings. It should also be noted that leave must be sought in the normal way to show documents that have been filed with the court (such as the assessment report here) to the police.

As to the immunity of adoption files, see *Re H (Criminal Proceedings: Disclosure of Adoption Records)* [1995] 1 FLR 964, FD, and, for a case concerning disclosure of Crown Prosecution Service documents, see *Nottinghamshire County Council v H* [1995] 1 FLR 115. In the latter case, attention was drawn to the children's guardian's power under CA 1989, s 42 to examine the local authority's social work records. The court's discretion in Children Act proceedings will be exercised in the light of this power.

Re C (Expert Evidence: Disclosure: Practice) [1995] 1 FLR 204 provides guidance as to the procedure to be followed where an issue arises, because of public interest immunity, as to whether certain material should or should not be disclosed. If documents held by the local authority are apparently relevant but appear to be protected from disclosure by public interest immunity, a letter should be written by the local authority to the parties' legal advisers and to the children's guardian drawing general attention to the existence of the documents and inviting an application to the court if disclosure of the relevant documents is required. The appropriate procedure would be to seek directions as to the service of documents pursuant to r 4.14(2)(*e*)/FPC(CA 1989)R 1991, r 14(2)(*e*), or directions as to the submission of evidence pursuant to r 4.14(2)(*f*)/FPC(CA 1989)R 1991, r 14(2)(*f*). The local authority should identify and flag the documents which they believe are, or may be, relevant and, if possible, a short précis of the information should be prepared in order to assist the court which is to make the decision. If the court orders disclosure of the documents and if the nature of the précis satisfies the party affected that the material identified and disclosed is sufficient, the directions hearing can proceed on a short basis. If the précis does not achieve agreement and the other party wishes to see more of the files, some further guide to the file should be provided so that the court can carry out the balancing exercise envisaged in *Re M (A Minor) (Disclosure of Material)* (above), taking into account the comments of Charles J in *Re R* (above) and Munby J in *Re B (Dislosure to Other Parties)* (above). It is for the court to make the decision as to disclosure of documents covered by public interest immunity. It is important for the local authority to draw the children's guardian's attention to any matters of concern within the documents, since his full knowledge of the material may enable him to assist the court as to its relevance.

As to the difficult issue of the extent to which the local authority is free to waive public immunity without leave of the court, see inter alia, *D v NSPCC* above, *Air Canada v Secretary of*

State for Trade [1983] 2 AC 394, at p 446, *Re M (A Minor) (Disclosure of Material)* (above), *Makanjuola v Commissioner of Police for the Metropolis* [1992] 3 All ER 617, CA, at p 623, *R v Chief Constable of the West Midland Police ex p Wiley* [1995] 1 AC 274, HL, *Re C (Expert Evidence: Disclosure: Practice)* (above).

Time for filing statements and documents (r 4.17(1))—Directions will normally be given under r 4.14 for all but the very early stages of the proceedings. It is suggested that directions should be specific. Solicitors should identify the deponents of proposed statements and the relevance of their evidence, and a timetable for the filing of statements should be drawn up. This has the additional advantage that the court is in a far better position to assess the reasonableness of any estimate of the length of the final hearing.

Where there is no direction as to filing and service, all that is required is that the statements should be filed and served before the hearing or appointment but as much notice as feasible should, of course, be given to other parties in an effort to reduce the possibility of an adjournment being granted so that allegations contained in the statements may be properly met. Rule 4.17 is mandatory and, accordingly, even with an interim hearing, the parties' statements should be filed before the interim hearing in the absence of any other direction (*S v Merton London Borough* [1994] 1 FCR 186, [1994] Fam Law 321 dealing with the corresponding provision, FPC(CA 1989)R 1991, r 17). Clearly, in this context, r 4.17 requires the filing at this early stage only of those statements which deal with the issues arising at the interim hearing. It would not be realistic to suppose that all (or, in some cases, any) of the statements for the final hearing will be ready. In proceedings for a s 8 order, special restrictions apply to the filing and serving of statements and documents – see **Forms and documentary evidence in s 8 cases** below.

Confidentiality of filed documents—Once filed, documents are confidential and can only be disclosed to the persons specified in r 4.23 or with leave.

Supplementary statements (r 4.17(2))—There is no restriction on what may be included in a supplementary statement. It may therefore deal with fresh matters arising since the making of the original statement or fill in gaps in the material contained in the original statement. Directions may have been given specifically about the timing of filing of supplementary statements but a general direction that "all statements" must be filed by a particular date would also cover supplementary statements, even though not expressly mentioned. If there are no relevant directions, the supplementary statement must be filed before the hearing or appointment in accordance with r 4.17(1). As to amendment of documents, see r 4.19.

Non-compliance with r 4.17(1) (r 4.17(3))—Rule 4.17(3) not only prevents a witness who has not filed a statement at all from giving evidence without leave, it also requires an application for leave before a witness who has filed a statement can give evidence on matters outside its scope. If the court feels that any party has been prejudiced by not receiving advance notice in accordance with r 4.17(1), it may refuse leave. However, as a matter of practice, most courts are reluctant to refuse to entertain evidence which has a bearing on the welfare of a child purely because of a breach of procedural rules. The alternative is to adjourn the proceedings for an appropriate period so that proper instructions can be taken etc. In such circumstances, an application for a costs order against the party who is in breach or for a wasted costs order may be appropriate. In *R v Nottinghamshire CC* [1993] Fam Law 625, for example, a local authority failed to submit written evidence as directed by the court and to comply with a direction to serve documents, but leave was given for statements to be filed out of time because it was vital in the interests of the children that the court should have the best information available. As to the form of the application for leave, it is clear that r 4.3 does not apply as the leave required is not leave to bring proceedings, and it is suggested that the granting of leave to adduce evidence is, in fact, a direction as to the conduct of the proceedings which should be sought in accordance with r 4.14.

Forms and documentary evidence in s 8 cases (r 4.17(4), (5))—The documentation to be filed and served in s 8 cases is strictly controlled in order to prevent matters becoming inflamed by comments and allegations in forms, statements and reports before the parties have had an opportunity to resolve matters amicably by negotiation. Broadly summarised, the position is as follows:

(*a*) In a normal case, certain documents are required by the rules to be filed and served and do not require leave. These include the application form (r 4.4(1)), a statement of service in Form C9 (r 4.8(7)) and the acknowledgement of the application (r 4.9(1)). Care must be taken in each case to include only such information as is required by the form.

(*b*) An answer is not required or authorised by the rules (see r 4.9) and should not be filed or served without leave.

PART III

(*c*) Statements or copies of other documents (including experts' reports) on which a party intends to rely should not be filed or served until the court so directs. The term "statement" in r 4.17(5) refers back to r 4.17(1)(*a*) and "copy" must refer back to r 4.17(1)(*b*). The court will normally address questions as to the filing of statements and documents at an early directions hearing to ensure that all relevant evidence is exchanged and filed with the court in advance of the hearing to which it relates, but not so early in proceedings that it jeopardises the possibility of an amicable resolution of the issues between the parties. Where advance planning of this kind is not possible, eg where a party wishes to rely on a statement for which leave has not yet been granted in order to support an urgent interim application, the statement should be prepared in accordance with r 4.17(1) and taken to the hearing, and the court should be invited to give leave for it to be filed forthwith.

An application for leave under r 4.17(4) is not covered by r 4.3, not being an application for leave to bring proceedings. The procedure set out in r 4.14 is recommended.

Service—See r 4.8 and Pt X.

Withholding disclosure—See **Submission of evidence** under r 4.14.

Discovery by non-party—See under r 4.14.

Bundles—See **Bundles and other particular matters** under r 4.14.

Need to file care plan—In public law cases, the local authority has a duty to file a care plan (see *Manchester City Council v F (Note)* [1993] 1 FLR 419 and under CA 1989, s 31). Note that the Adoption and Children Act 2002, s 124 inserts a new s 31A into CA 1989. Once it comes into force it will place a statutory duty on the local authority to prepare a care plan (to be known as a "s 31A care plan") in every case in which it seeks a care order; see further under s 31.

4.18 Expert evidence – examination of child

(1) No person may, without the leave of the court, cause the child to be medically or psychiatrically examined, or otherwise assessed, for the purpose of the preparation of expert evidence for use in the proceedings.

(2) An application for leave under paragraph (1) shall, unless the court otherwise directs, be served on all parties to the proceedings and on the children's guardian.

(3) Where the leave of the court has not been given under paragraph (1), no evidence arising out of an examination or assessment to which that paragraph applies may be adduced without the leave of the court.

Amendments—SI 2001/821.

Defined terms—"application", "child": r 4.1(1); "court": r 1.2(1); " children's guardian", "leave": r 4.1(1).

CAAC Handbook of Best Practice in Children Act cases—Much assistance as to all aspects of the instruction of experts can be found in this Handbook at "Section 5 – Experts and the courts" (set out in Part IV of this work as *Best Practice Guidance of June 1997*).

"No person" (r 4.18(1))—The prohibition is a blanket one, applying not just to parties to the proceedings and parents of the child but also, for example, to children's guardians, social workers and general practitioners requested to refer a child so that an expert report can be prepared for court.

"or otherwise assessed" (r 4.18(1))—For example, assessment by a clinical or educational psychologist, an independent social worker or a trained counsellor.

"for the purpose of the preparation of expert evidence for use in the proceedings" (r 4.18(1))—The rule is perhaps more loosely drafted than intended and might allow, for example, for a preliminary examination or assessment of the child without leave (for instance by the child's general practitioner) for the purpose of obtaining advice as to whether it would be worth arranging for a comprehensive examination or assessment by an expert whose evidence would then be used in the proceedings. However, given the reluctance of the courts to allow children to be subjected to examinations, and in particular to multiple examinations, it is anticipated that the rule will be interpreted widely so that such preliminary investigations will also require leave.

Putting the documents before an expert—Where a court has named an expert to be instructed in a case, it is not necessary to seek further leave to disclose documents to him (r 4.23(1)(*f*)). In cases where the court may be unlikely to grant leave for an examination or assessment of the child, one option may be to seek leave from the court to place the documentary evidence before an expert for an opinion on the papers only. Where appropriate, an application for leave for an examination or assessment may then be reinforced by a letter or short report from the expert confirming that he considers an examination or assessment necessary. There are strict restrictions on disclosing documents held by the court (see r 4.23).

Procedure on application for leave: FPR 1991 provisions—Whereas the courts have provided much guidance as to the correct way to make a leave application (see below), the rules are virtually silent as to the procedure, save for the provisions as to service contained in r 4.18(2). Rule 4.3 does not apply (it is limited to applications for leave to bring proceedings), and r 4.4 is not designed to cover applications in the course of proceedings. It is therefore suggested that the r 4.14 directions procedure should be used, suitably modified to accommodate the service requirements of r 4.18(2). It is suggested that Form C2 is appropriate for an application for leave since it amounts to an application for an order or directions in existing family proceedings. Form C2 requires the name and date of birth of the child concerned and details as to the identity of the applicant and his relationship with the child. The order or directions sought should be described clearly, together with brief reasons why the application has been made. See also the proforma directions and best practice notes to be adopted nationally and in all tiers of courts as approved by the Children Act Advisory Committee for directions hearings in family cases, as set out as *Best Practice Note of January 1995* in Part IV of this work. In accordance with the general scheme of Pt IV of the rules, service is the obligation of the person applying for leave. As to service generally, see r 4.8 and Pt X.

Principles governing grant of leave—Whether leave will be granted will depend upon the circumstances of the case. Although it may be that the court will take the view that CA 1989, s 1(1) does not strictly apply to the decision (*Re A and W (Minors) (Residence Order: Leave to Apply)* [1992] 2 FLR 154, CA; *Re A (A Minor) (Residence Order: Leave to Apply)* [1993] 1 FLR 425; *G v Kirklees MBC* [1993] 1 FLR 805), the court will pay great attention to the welfare of the child in any event. It will also consider the interests of the parties, and the need for a fair hearing at which the issues can be properly determined (as to which, see, for example, *R v Hampshire County Council ex parte K* [1990] 1 FLR 330; *Re A (A Minor) (Residence Order: Leave to Apply)* (above); *G v Kirklees MBC* (above); and *Re D (Adoption Reports: Confidentiality)* [1995] 2 FLR 687, HL) and the delay principle (*H v Cambridgeshire County Council* [1996] 2 FLR 566, FD). In considering whether to grant leave, the court should seek to identify the issue which forms the basis of the local authority's application, and consider whether it would be usefully addressed by the proposed evidence; leave to obtain expert evidence can be refused on the ground that the evidence does not bear sufficiently on the issue that falls for determination (*H v Cambridgeshire County Council* (above)).

For guidance on medical evidence about children, including guidance as to the duties of a medical expert, see *Re C (Minors) (Wardship: Medical Evidence)* [1987] 1 FLR 418; *Re R (A Minor) (Experts' Evidence) (Note)* [1991] 1 FLR 291 (set out in Part IV of this work as *Practice Note of 27 July 1990*); *Re M (Minors) (Sexual Abuse: Evidence)* [1993] 1 FLR 822; *B v B (Child Abuse: Contact)* [1994] 2 FLR 713; *Re AB (Child Abuse: Expert Witnesses)* [1995] 1 FLR 181; *Manchester City Council v B* [1996] 1 FLR 324 (as to the limits on the value of medical research and the need for experts to have relevant expertise); *Note: Vernon v Bosley (Expert Evidence)* [1998] 1 FLR 297 and *Vernon v Bosley (No 2)* [1998] 1 FLR 304.

In deciding whether to seek leave for an expert, it must be borne in mind that, whilst expert evidence dealing with issues, including the expert's opinion about the ultimate issue, is admissible by virtue of Civil Evidence Act 1972, this is subject to the overriding requirement of relevance which, together with questions of weight, is a matter for the judge; the final decision is the judge's and his alone (*Re M and R (Child Abuse: Evidence)* [1996] 2 FLR 195, CA). Questions of relevance/admissibility should be referred to the judge who will be conducting the final hearing (*Re CB and JB (Care Proceedings: Guidelines)* [1998] 2 FLR 211, FD).

Where leave for an examination is given, the court will usually try to limit the number of examinations to which the child is subjected. Wherever possible the examination should be conducted by one expert agreed upon by all parties (or, in default of agreement, the Official Solicitor holds a list of experts and could nominate an appropriate person) or there should be a single examination which the parties' experts are all invited to attend. Alternatively, the court may grant leave solely to the children's guardian to arrange an examination or assessment. The dangers of the court granting a general leave, rather than leave for the instruction of a particular expert or experts, can be seen from *Note: Re B (Child Sexual Abuse: Standard of Proof)* (above) in which, following the grant of leave in general terms without limitations, eleven psychiatrists/psychologists became involved in the proceedings.

Psychiatric and psychological reports—If consideration is being given to obtaining a psychiatric or psychological report, the purpose of the report must be clearly identified. On what issue will it assist the court? It is not uncommon for a child psychiatrist or psychologist to be instructed to assess and advise upon the appropriate course to be taken with regard to a child, dealing with questions such as whether rehabilitation to a parent should be attempted or whether adoption is the right course, what the risks of a placement in the family are etc. An example of a case in which such a report was needed is *Re CH (Care or Interim Care Order)* [1998] 1 FLR 402, CA. An adult psychiatric or psychological report on a party can also be helpful in the right case. However *Re CB and JB (Care Proceedings: Guidelines)* [1998] 2 FLR 211 reveals the dangers of obtaining such evidence to address the wrong issue or at the wrong stage of the proceedings. Wall J held that it was not an appropriate application of the principles laid down in *Re M and R (Child Abuse: Evidence)* [1996] 2 FLR 195, CA for expert psychiatric or psychological evidence to be routinely adduced as to the propensity of a parent to injure a child or as to the likelihood of the parent having done so, particularly where the court is dealing with an issue of fact in a split hearing. A psychiatric or psychological assessment of the parties should not be permitted at the first stage of a split trial unless the particular facts of the case demonstrate that such evidence is or is likely to be directly relevant to the factual issue to be tried. Expert evidence of the assessment of risk once the threshold criteria have been established is, however, another matter. The essence of such an assessment is that it should be based on the facts found by the court and parental reaction to them. Furthermore, where an expert is asked to express an opinion, he must have all the relevant information, including a copy of any judgment already given in the case; the summary of a judgment is not sufficient (*Re G (Care Proceedings: Split Trials)* [2001] 1 FLR 872). When timetabling a split hearing, it may be appropriate to put in place a timetable for the second stage of the hearing and to give leave prior to the first stage of the hearing for a party to show the papers to a psychiatrist or psychologist if and when the threshold criteria are established, thus enabling the party to pencil in appointments and establish a timetable for the assessment. The purpose of the leave, however, is simply to ensure time is not wasted and the second stage of the hearing is not held up.

Practice on leave applications and in instructing and calling experts—Wall J has issued guidelines in *Re G (Minors) (Expert Witnesses)* [1994] 2 FLR 291 which govern the grant of leave and consequential directions for expert evidence in children's cases. Further valuable assistance is also to be gained from other cases such as *Re C (Expert Evidence: Disclosure: Practice)* [1995] 1 FLR 204, FD (which contains detailed specimen directions which should normally be given), *Re R (Child Abuse: Video Evidence)* [1995] 1 FLR 451, FD, *Re A and B (Minors) (No 2)* [1995] 1 FLR 351, *Re T and E (Proceedings: Conflicting Interests)* [1995] 1 FLR 581, *Re CS (Expert Witnesses)* [1996] 2 FLR 115, FD, *Re CB and JB (Care Proceedings: Guidelines)* [1998] 2 FLR 211, FD and *Re R (Care: Disclosure: Nature of Proceedings)* [2002] 1 FLR 755. What follows here is largely derived from *Re G* but with additions from the other authorities. Propositions for which no authority is given are from *Re G*, the sources of other propositions are identified specifically:

(*a*) generalised orders giving leave for the papers to be shown to "an expert" or "experts" should never be made. In each case, the expert or area of expertise should be identified;

(*b*) as part of the process of granting or refusing leave, either for the child to be examined or for papers in the case to be shown to an expert, the advocates have a positive duty to place all relevant information before the court, and the court has a positive duty to inquire into that information and in particular into the following matters:

  (i) the category of expert evidence which the party in question seeks to adduce;

  (ii) the relevance of the expert evidence sought to be adduced to the issues arising for decision in the case;

  (iii) whether or not the expert evidence can properly be obtained by the joint instruction of one expert by two or more of the parties;

  (iv) whether or not expert evidence in any given category may properly be adduced by only one party (eg by the children's guardian) or whether it is necessary for experts in the same discipline to be instructed by more than one party;

(*c*) a party proposing to apply for leave should supply to all the other parties and file with the court at least 10 days before the application date a written explanation of the area of expertise of the proposed expert with reasons why the court should grant leave (*Re C (Expert Evidence: Disclosure: Practice)*);

(*d*) where the court exercises its discretion to grant leave for the papers to be shown to a particular expert, the court should, where possible, give directions as to:

(i) the availability for each expert and each party of copies of all the letters of instruction to experts and lists of documents supplied to those experts (*Re C (Expert Evidence: Disclosure: Practice)*)

(ii) the time-scale in which the evidence should be produced;

(iii) the disclosure of any expert report both to the parties and to the other experts in the case;

(iv) discussions between experts following mutual disclosure of reports;

(v) the filing of further evidence by the experts or parties stating the areas of agreement and/or disagreement between the experts;

(*e*) where it is impractical to give such directions at the time leave to disclose the papers is granted, the court should set a date for a further directions appointment at which the appropriate directions can be given;

(*f*) where local authorities wish to carry out an assessment, the court should carefully set out the time-scale within which it is to be completed and fix an early directions appointment following the date set for completion to consider the further conduct of the case, including the necessity for expert evidence. If possible, a date should be set for final hearing prior to completion of the assessment, but it is probable that this cannot be done until the assessment is complete and the issues in the case emerge. The fact that the timetable set may need to be revised will not necessarily be a reason not to timetable (*E v Humberside County Council and S* [1996] Fam Law 444, FD).

It follows that advocates who seek the leave of the court to disclose papers to an expert must apply their minds at an early stage of the proceedings to the issues in the case to which medical evidence will be relevant. Applications for leave to instruct experts should be made at as early a stage in the proceedings as is possible, commensurate with the state of the evidence. Advocates must come to the directions appointment at which the application is to be decided prepared to satisfy the tribunal as to the need for expert evidence of the specified type sought. Given the pressures of work on expert witnesses, particular experts should be identified and instructed at the earliest possible moment and, whenever possible, an inquiry should be made of the expert concerned to ensure that he or she can meet the likely timetable of the case.

In *Re M (Minors) (Care Proceedings: Child's Wishes)* [1994] 1 FLR 749 (and see also *Re MD and TD (Minors) (Time Estimates)*, above), Wall J pointed out that:

(*a*) It is important that medical experts who are asked to give reports or opinions in child cases are fully instructed. The letter of instruction should always set out the context in which the expert's opinion is sought and define carefully the specific questions the expert is being asked to address.

(*b*) Careful thought should be given to the selection of the papers to be sent to the expert; they should be relevant and sufficient for the expert to venture a sound opinion. The letter of instruction should always list the documents sent. *Re CS (Expert Witnesses)* [1996] 2 FLR 115, FD, points out that the expert should never be provided with an unsorted pile of papers and, to assist him, should have an agreed chronology and background history.

(*c*) The letter of instruction should always be disclosed to the other parties and included in the bundle of documents to be used in court. Where the expert is to be jointly instructed, the letter of instruction should, as *Re CB and JB* (above) says, be agreed by all those instructing the expert and the order giving leave needs to have built in provisions to ensure that the despatch of the letter is not delayed by difficulties in agreeing its terms. This is usually achieved by a direction that the letter be agreed by a given date and in default of agreement as to its terms, the matter be relisted urgently for a short appointment before the judge or district judge who made the direction. However where one party is given leave to instruct an expert, there is no particular reason, according to *Re CB and JB*, why that party should be required to agree the terms of the letter with the other parties.

(*d*) Doctors and other experts should not hesitate to request further information and ask for additional documentation.

(*e*) Doctors who have had other clinical experience of the child outside the litigation (for example, if they have treated him before) should ensure that all their clinical material is available for inspection by the court and by other experts, including all medical notes, hospital records, photographs, correspondence and X-rays.

(*f*) Experts who are going to give evidence at the trial should be kept up to date on relevant developments (see *Re G, S and M (Wasted Costs)* [2000] 1 FLR 52 – where the failure to keep experts up to date resulted in a wasted costs order against counsel for the local authority; *Re G (Care Proceedings: Split Trials)* [2001] 1 FLR 872 – the information to be provided to the expert includes a copy of any judgment already given in the case, the summary of a judgment

PART III

is not sufficient). Any expert whose evidence goes to the disposal of the case or to the issues raised in the children's guardian's report should read the children's guardian's report before giving evidence (*Re T and E (Proceedings: Conflicting Interests)* [1995] 1 FLR 581).

(*g*) Experts should always be invited to confer with each other before the trial in an attempt to reach agreement or limit the issues. *Re C (Expert Evidence: Disclosure: Practice)* [1995] 1 FLR 204, FD, suggests a direction that their letters of instruction should point out as a condition of instructing the expert the requirement to prepare, after discussion with the other experts, a joint document setting out the areas of agreement and dispute. *Re R (Child Abuse: Video Evidence)* [1995] 1 FLR 451, FD, suggests that it would be good practice for the solicitor for one of the parties, usually for the guardian, to be responsible for convening the meeting between the experts. A co-ordinator, normally the children's guardian or the local authority, should collate the experts' reports and produce a schedule for the court (*Re C (Expert Evidence: Disclosure: Practice)*). *Re CB and JB* gives considerable further assistance as to experts' meetings. Where there is agreement on paper between the experts, there is no need to hold a meeting; when they disagree, serious consideration should be given to a telephone conference provided that it has a proper agenda, is called to answer specific questions and is properly chaired and minuted. Experts' meetings must be properly constituted to meet their particular objective and care must be taken to ensure that separate meetings of different disciplines are complementary and have the same objective. Meetings must be clearly focussed. The most appropriate chair is the solicitor instructed by the children's guardian. There is need for co-operation in the preparation for and conduct of the meetings. Questions must be carefully formulated. A proper record must always be kept and the results of the meeting distilled into a statement jointly signed. Quite apart from the experts' meeting, the experts are free to have such discussions, informal or otherwise, as may assist in informing their opinion of the case but it is essential that a record of discussions (however brief they may be) is kept and the experts, in their reports or otherwise, inform those instructing them that such discussions have taken place and state how (if at all) the discussions have influenced their thinking about the case.

(*h*) Careful (and early) co-operative planning between lawyers for the different parties should be undertaken to ensure the experts' availability and that they can be called to give evidence in a logical sequence. Consideration should be given to collecting expert evidence of a particular type together, irrespective of the fact that the witnesses are called for different parties, for example, having a paediatricians' day so that each can listen to the others' evidence and comment on it. In *Re T and E (Proceedings: Conflicting Interests)*, Wall J said that the time has come to be much more stringent about timetabling expert evidence. Experts should not be kept waiting and the time required for their evidence should be carefully scheduled so as to avoid the need for an expert to return on another occasion to complete his evidence.

(*i*) Where an expert's opinion is uncontentious and he is not required for cross-examination, that fact should be established as early as possible in the preparations for trial and the expert notified accordingly.

Further guidance is given in *Re R (Care: Disclosure: Nature of Proceedings)* [2002] 1 FLR 755, where the failure of the experts and those instructing them to discuss and make clear what the parties wanted the experts to do caused severe problems. Charles J held that:

(1) letters of instruction must be carefully prepared and precedents should be used only as a basis and a check to see that all matters are covered and should not simply be reproduced;
(2) the expert must consider carefully the terms of the instructions and whether he or she can fulfil them by applying his or her general approach or an adaptation thereof; it would be sensible to invite the expert to confirm this expressly before he or she embarks upon the assessment;
(3) all parties must consider with care the terms of the instructions and the information coming from the expert as to his or her approach;
(4) all involved should consider and review the report of an expert when it is received and, where relevant, raise points with the expert and other parties relating to the performance of the expert's instructions, his or her reasoning, the factual basis of his or her views and the relevance of his or her views to the proceedings;
(5) all involved in giving joint instruction should take a full part at all stages and thus attend meetings with the relevant experts, or at least comment in respect of them;
(6) if an expert is not jointly instructed, those who do not join in the instructions should nonetheless: (*a*) consider how that expert should be instructed; and (*b*) his or her report, and raise points on both as soon as is practicable;
(7) if, as here, an expert has videoed interviews, that fact should be disclosed and consideration should be given to the desirability of the expert reviewing the video before completing his or her report and of the parties, if they wish to do so, viewing the videos at an early stage.

See also the useful guidance given by Munby J in *Re L (Care: Assessment: Fair Trial)* [2002] EWHC 1379 (Fam), [2002] 2 FLR 730 as to the conduct and recording of meetings between professionals and the provision of documents in care proceedings; this case is referred to in more detail in **Disclosure – impact of the European Convention for Human Rights and Fundamental Freedoms 1950** under r 4.23.

In a publicly funded case, where the parents' expert is first to report and eliminates the possibility of rehabilitation and all the other experts reach the same conclusion, the matter should be referred back to the Legal Services Commission (*Re N (Contested Care Application)* [1994] 2 FLR 992). It is very important that influential reports should be available before any pre-trial review, and there is an obligation on the advocates to draw the judge's attention at the pre-trial review to the reality that, for all experts, there is only one possible forensic conclusion. The judge can then make a realistic survey of the necessity for a full trial in the light of the reports and endeavour to see that the parents' need to put their case before the court through the witness box is not precluded but is kept within bounds that reflect the impact on the trial and its duration of exchanged reports which all advise the same conclusion (*Re N*, above). When the medical experts are unanimous as to causation and timing of injuries, with one possible exception they need not attend to give oral evidence. The possible exception is where the medical evidence is not in dispute between the doctors but the parents have not instructed an expert and have given instructions to their legal representatives that do not permit agreement with the medical evidence. In these circumstances, and depending on the issue involved, it may be appropriate for leave to be given to adduce oral evidence from one of the medical witnesses as spokesperson for the rest because there must be a fair hearing and parents who stand at risk of losing their children should not feel they are being wrongly limited in the way they put their case. However where the evidence commissioned by the parents confirms the consensus, Wall J could see no justification for oral evidence being called in the ordinary case (*Re CB and JB* above). In *H v West Sussex County Council* [1998] 1 FLR 862, Johnson J held that a mother who had been permitted in s 34 proceedings to obtain evidence from a clinical psychologist should not have been prevented from calling that evidence on the basis that it was irrelevant. Evidence in such cases, he said, should be regulated by weight not by admissibility, particularly in a case where a parent was at risk of being separated permanently from his child. Such a parent ought to be allowed to present his case in the way he chose, subject to the evidence being tendered in a responsible and professional manner. In *Re M (Contact: Restrictive Order: Supervision)* [1998] 1 FLR 721, CA, the court hearing a private law application heard from the children and family reporter that he felt that the father might require a psychiatric assessment. The father's GP gave evidence that he did not. The judge erred in not accepting the evidence of the GP which, in the absence of any other expert evidence, was said to be a conclusive contribution. Without a referral from the GP, the father would have no entrée to psychiatric services in any event.

Procedural checklist for instructing experts—In order to assist the practitioner to instruct an expert smoothly, the following checklist has been devised, drawing heavily on the recent authorities which are listed in the previous annotation. It will not, of course, cover all cases and it is not, in any event, complete on its own; reference should be made back to the authorities themselves or at least to the more detailed summary of the principles which appears above.

1 Consider the question of experts as early as possible in the proceedings, and always keep in mind any funding implications, whether your client is in receipt of public funding or paying privately.

2 Identify the issues which the expert is to address.

3 Consider whether a joint instruction of one expert between two or more parties might suffice, and pursue this line if feasible.

4 Identify the expert to be instructed (whether jointly or by your client alone), checking, in principle only (no documents at this stage), that he:

   (*a*) has the correct expertise
   (*b*) is willing to act
   (*c*) is available to report in time
   (*d*) is available to appear as required (get his availability dates if the dates for court hearings are not yet fixed).

   Preferably obtain a letter from him setting all this out.

5 Make sure your client understands the duties with regard to the disclosure of any report you obtain, even if adverse.

6 If so instructed, file the application for leave in accordance with the rules; this should be done as early as possible in the proceedings.

7 File and supply to the other parties at least 10 days before the leave hearing an explanation of the area of expertise of the expert and the reasons why the court should grant leave; it may be helpful also to draft a proposed letter of instruction and list of documents to be sent to the expert at this early stage.

8 Consider in detail what directions the court should be granting on the leave application and canvass the views of the other parties in advance (reference to the specimen directions in *Re C (Expert Evidence: Disclosure: Practice)* [1995] 1 FLR 204 should help); if sufficient is agreed, prepare a first draft of a proposed order and have copies available for the court and other parties to work with.

9 Ensure attendance at the leave hearing by a legal representative who is fully informed about the case.

10 If leave is granted, abide by any specific directions that may have been given. They are likely to be fairly detailed and all further steps listed below will be subject to them.

11 Sort out and copy the documents that the expert needs to see, being careful that your selection is relevant and sufficient. Even if a court bundle is not yet in existence, tether the documents and number the "bundle" right through so that the expert can refer to passages conveniently in his report. If your numbering system can be agreed with the other parties and translated in due course into the numbering in the court bundle, so much the better.

12 Send a letter of instruction (including a list of documents supplied to the expert) to the expert, together with copies of the documents. Draw the expert's attention in the letter to any particular directions that affect him and, in any event:

(*a*) set out precisely the issues which you want him to address
(*b*) summarise the context in which his opinion is sought
(*c*) invite him to seek any further information/documentation he needs from you
(*d*) make sure he appreciates he will be required to meet with other experts before the hearing to establish areas of agreement/disagreement and to embody these in a statement
(*e*) be clear about deadlines for the meeting with other experts, reporting to the court etc.
(*f*) depending on how experienced the expert is as a witness, consider forwarding to him (or offering to forward) a selection of the authorities setting out guidance as to how an expert should approach his task in a children's case.

The draft letter of joint instruction of an expert, which is annexed to the *Children Act Advisory Committee Annual Report 1994/95* and is set out as *Best Practice Note of January 1996* in Part IV of this work, may prove a helpful starting point. However account needs to be taken of the reservations expressed by Wall J about it in *Re CB and JB* (above).

13 Send a copy of your letter of instruction and list to other parties.

14 Include the letter and list in the court bundle.

15 On receipt of the other side's letter of instruction and list, send them to your expert. Also send, from time to time, any new papers that may be relevant to the expert's view, including the other side's expert's report and, in most cases, the children's guardian's report. Update your expert scrupulously on other relevant developments as well.

16 Serve and file your expert's report on receipt and ensure that you receive a copy of the other parties' reports as scheduled.

17 Upon receipt of the expert's report, all parties and legal advisers to check whether they wish to put any further points to the expert, including points as to his reasoning and points as to what facts or matters the expert has considered and whether he agrees that other facts or matters are relevant and would make a difference.

18 Ensure that, where there is more than one expert on a particular issue and their views are different, they meet before the hearing to attempt to reach agreement or to limit the issues between them, thereafter identifying areas of agreement and dispute and encapsulating them in a further statement(s) for the court. Depending on the form of the statement(s), it may be necessary to arrange for a separate schedule to be drawn up isolating what is agreed and what is not. This can be the responsibility of the children's guardian or local authority or of one of the other parties. Ensure that the schedule etc is served on all parties and filed with the court.

19 (*a*) All involved in giving joint instructions should take a full part at all stages and thus attend meetings with the relevant experts, or at least comment in respect of them.
(*b*) If an expert is not jointly instructed, those who do not join in the instructions should nonetheless consider: (i) how that expert should be instructed; and (ii) his report, and raise points on both as soon as is practicable.

20 If your expert should change his advice, communicate this to the other parties and have him record it in a form that is appropriate for the court.

21 Consider with the other parties how best to arrange the timing of the oral evidence of the experts at the hearing – do they wish to sit in on each other's evidence, can evidence of a similar sort be grouped together on a particular day etc? Calculate carefully the time set aside for the experts' evidence so that arrangements can be made for them to attend without being kept waiting and so that they do not run the risk of having to return on another unscheduled occasion to conclude. Inform your expert of when he is to attend and make sure that the other parties are also aware.

22 Where an expert's view appears to be uncontentious, check with the other parties that he will not be required to attend to give oral evidence (ensuring that there is a clear understanding as to whether or not the expert's report will still form part of the bundle for the court's attention or not) and notify him as soon as possible.

23 If all the experts are of one view which points to only one tenable conclusion for the proceedings, draw this to the attention of the court at the pre-trial directions hearing so that the substantive hearing can be planned accordingly.

24 If an expert has videoed interviews that fact should be disclosed and it is desirable that the expert reviews the video before completing his report. Early consideration should also be given to whether the parties wish to view the videos.

25 At all times, keep in mind any public funding implications that the experts' opinions may have.

26 If difficulties of any kind are encountered, seek further directions.

Pre-hearing reviews—It is of vital importance that where expert witnesses are to be called at the final hearing the advocates who attend the pre-hearing review ensure that they identify clearly the issues which the respective experts are to address and when, in the context of the case, they are to be called. For specific guidelines as to what should happen at a pre-hearing review see **Pre-hearing review** under r 4.14.

Duty to disclose report obtained pursuant to examination or assessment—The House of Lords has considered the question of disclosure of reports in *Re L (Police Investigation: Privilege)* [1996] 1 FLR 731, and the position appears to be as follows:

(*a*) Litigation privilege is a creature of adversarial procedure, whereas CA 1989, Pt IV proceedings are essentially non-adversarial, the primary consideration of the court in such cases being the welfare of the child. Litigation privilege does not therefore arise in relation to reports obtained in public law proceedings, where the reports could not have been prepared without the leave of the court to disclose court papers to the expert or for the child to be examined (at 739A inter alia). It follows that such reports must be disclosed to all parties subject only to the possibility (at 740F et seq) that the party who commissioned the report could claim to be excused from disclosing it by virtue of the privilege against self-incrimination.

(*b*) Where in public law proceedings a party omits, in breach of r 4.18 or r 4.23 (or in breach of FPC(CA 1989)R 1991, r 18 or r 23), to seek leave of the court before commissioning a report, it is suggested that that report cannot be privileged either and must also be disclosed. Reference should be made, on this point, to *Vernon v Bosley (No 2)* [1998] 1 FLR 304, CA in which, looking at the position of expert reports in private law proceedings concerning children, Thorpe LJ dismissed as absurd the argument that litigation privilege arose with regard to the reports because, by an oversight, the order granting leave to serve and file reports from the experts did not also grant leave to disclose court papers to them.

(*c*) *Re L* deals with proceedings under CA 1989, Pt IV. It is not therefore express authority with regard to duties of disclosure of reports in private law proceedings. However, the reasoning adopted in *Re L* applies equally to private law proceedings, and it seems very likely that reports in such proceedings will also be held to be unprotected by privilege. Such is the view expressed by the Court of Appeal in *Vernon v Bosley (No 2)* (above).

(*d*) Local authorities must not withhold from the court or the other parties any reports and information which are material to the case (see *R v Hampshire CC ex parte K* [1990] 1 FLR 330; *Oxfordshire CC v M* [1994] 1 FLR 175; *TP and KM v United Kingdom* [2001] 2 FLR 549). Their duty is to give first consideration to the welfare of the child and, as *R v Hampshire CC ex parte K* demonstrates, the child's welfare requires that the other parties be provided with all relevant information, whether it assists the local authority's case or not, so that a fair hearing can be ensured. The local authority must therefore volunteer to the other parties copies of all reports that come into its possession, and social workers must ensure that, in giving evidence, they do not withhold anything that is material (*L v L (Child Abuse: Access)* [1989] 2 FLR 16; see also *Re A and Others (Minors) (Child Abuse: Guidelines)* [1992] 1 FLR 439, [1991] 1 WLR 1026; *Manchester CC v S* [1991] 2 FLR 370; *Re C (Expert Evidence: Disclosure: Practice)* [1995] 1 FLR 204, FD; *Re B (Minors) (Care Proceedings)* [1994] 1 FCR 471; *Re JC (Care Proceedings: Procedure)* [1995] 2 FLR 77, FD).

(*e*) Whether a party other than a local authority simply has to disclose an unprivileged report *if ordered to do so*, or must *volunteer* disclosure, has been expressly left open (at 740E). In favour of a duty to volunteer disclosure are *Essex County Council v R* [1993] 2 FLR 826 (Thorpe J), *Re DH (A Minor) (Child Abuse)* [1994] 1 FLR 679 (Wall J – the principle that there is a duty to volunteer disclosure should be followed unless and until the Court of Appeal rules otherwise), *Oxfordshire County Council v P* [1995] 1 FLR 552 and *Practice Direction of 31 January 1995* (para 4). *Vernon v Bosley (No 2)* (above) contains instructive discussion, in the context of civil proceedings for negligence, as to the duty of disclosure of a party and the importance of the duty not to mislead the court or the other parties to the proceedings. To limit the scope for argument arising in family proceedings, it is suggested that the order granting leave to commission a report ought always to include an express requirement that the report be filed and served on all other parties.

(*f*) The position with regard to reports which a party is able to commission without first seeking leave under r 4.18 or r 4.23 (or under FPC(CA 1989) R 1991, r 18 or r 23) – for example, a medical report dealing only with a parent's psychiatric history and present mental state – remains unclear, as does the position in relation to reports which do not come into existence in the Children Act proceedings (for example, a report commissioned for parallel criminal proceedings or in support of a civil claim for damages). Reference should be made to *Vernon v Bosley (No 2)* (above) in which the existence of evidence given in family proceedings and the judgment of that court should have been disclosed to the defendant's advisers in the parallel civil proceedings.

(*g*) Nothing in *Re L* affects the privilege which attaches to communications between a solicitor and his client, which remains absolute (see also, in this regard, *R v Derby Magistrates' Court ex parte B* [1996] 1 FLR 513, HL; *S CC v B* [2000] 2 FLR 161 and see **Leave under r 4.23(1)** in the annotations to r 4.23). It is clear that the instructions of a party to his legal adviser are therefore privileged. The position as to witness statements obtained from lay witnesses (as opposed to medical and other experts) is not clear. As Lord Nicholls points out in his dissenting speech in *Re L* (at 746E), it is difficult to discern a sound distinction between experts and witnesses of fact whose statements may be just as relevant and important to the issue before the court.

(*h*) Whereas, normally, all parties will be entitled to see all the documentation filed in a case, the court does have power in exceptional circumstances to withhold disclosure from a particular party (see further **Submission of evidence** under r 4.14 or under FPC(CA 1989)R 1991, r 14).

It is inevitable, given the uncertainty that continues despite *Re L*, that there will be occasions when the practitioner has grave doubts as to what the proper course would be concerning disclosure. It is suggested that in certain cases it may be appropriate to seek the court's directions by means of a r 4.14 (or FPC(CA 1989)R 1991, r 14) directions appointment. Where such a situation arises in the family proceedings court, it may be advisable to consider transfer to the county court. Care will have to be taken to ensure that the process of seeking directions does not, of itself, reveal the information which may turn out to be privileged. Once the other parties are aware of the name of an expert who may provide useful information, there is nothing to prevent them from requiring him to come to court to give evidence at their behest, even though they may turn out not to be entitled to a copy of his report, and, if the other parties learn something of the contents of the report, even if not the name of the expert, that too may cause unfair prejudice. Furthermore, an application to the trial judge may reveal information to him which it would be impossible for him to ignore in dealing with the substantive application. In view of these factors, it may be necessary to arrange for the directions hearing to be listed before a judge other than the trial judge (though the comments of Wall J in *Re CB and JB (Care Proceedings: Guidelines)* [1998] 2 FLR 211 in a rather different context should be considered), and consideration may exceptionally have to be given to making the application ex parte in the first instance. A further option, in a case in which it is clear that problems are likely to arise about disclosure even though no specific reports have yet come into existence, is to seek directions in advance as to what the duty of disclosure would be in particular circumstances, for example with regard to reports which it is anticipated will be sought by those representing the client in his criminal defence. The courts are not unfamiliar with "advisory" directions of this sort (see, for example, *Cleveland County Council v F* [1995] 1 FLR 797, FD; *Re G (Social Worker: Disclosure)* [1996] 1 FLR 276).

As to the duty of a solicitor who might be able to protect a child at risk if he passed on confidential material in his possession to the court, social services or the police, see the guidelines issued by The Law Society which are summarised at [1991] Fam Law 461. See also The Law Society's guidance on disclosure of reports in children cases, set out at [1994] Fam Law 540. For an example of an order overriding professional privilege between a solicitor and his client, see *Re B (Abduction: Disclosure)* [1995] 1 FLR 774, CA, (solicitor ordered to disclose any information or communication from his client which might assist in ascertaining the whereabouts of the client, who had abducted his two small children and disappeared).

Where the party who commissioned the expert report does not intend to rely on it, he will not call the witness to give evidence; if he did, he would not be able to cross-examine. Other parties must therefore consider whether they wish to call the expert. In the event that no-one wishes to call the maker of a report, Wall J said in *Re DH (A Minor) (Child Abuse)* [1994] 1 FLR 679 that the court could properly treat that person as a court witness and allow all the parties to cross-examine. Naturally, this course would only be adopted if the report contained information which was material to the court's decision. The possibility of the court calling a witness so that he can be cross-examined is also raised in *Re P (Witness Summons)* [1997] 2 FLR 447, CA.

Conflict of forensic medical evidence—Where there is a stark conflict of forensic medical evidence a judge should not decline to choose between the medical opinions; instead he should invite the parties to agree a tertiary referral. To leave the evidence unresolved makes the disposal stage problematic (*Re W and P (Children)* LTL, 30 April 2002 – Doc No C9500819).

Cases concerning subdural haematomas, brain injury or retinal haemorrhages—In *Re A and D (Non-accidental Injury: Subdural Haematomas)* [2002] 1 FLR 337, Butler-Sloss P laid down (at para 41) general guidelines for the conduct of cases involving issues of brain injury, subdural haematomas or retinal haemorrhages. In light of the fact that experts now consider that the degree of force required to cause subdural haematomas need not be as great as previously believed, the President said, per curiam, that the court must be careful not to jump to conclusions, nor accept too readily the diagnosis of non-accidental injury in "brain injury" cases; equally, there is no research that entitles judges to dismiss out-of-hand the clinical experience of paediatricians and other medical experts derived from examining these children. The courts must continue to deal with medical evidence on the basis of generally recognized medical opinion, giving due weight in the individual case to any advances in medical knowledge. Since this is a difficult area, in any case where contested issues on brain injury, subdural haematomas or retinal haemorrhages are raised in the immediate future, it would be wise for courts to consider where the case would best be tried, depending on the facts of the case and a realistic approach to the likely medical evidence to be called.

Disclosure – impact of the European Convention for Human Rights and Fundamental Freedoms 1950—See under r 4.23.

Distinction between therapeutic experts and forensic experts—The role of the expert who is engaged to treat the person concerned is not to be muddled with the role of an expert whose task is to compile a forensic report on the person concerned for the purpose of the proceedings (*Re B (Sexual Abuse: Expert's Report)* [2000] 1 FLR 871 – a child psychiatrist who was treating a girl in relation to whom there were allegations of sexual abuse by the father could not make a proper forensic contribution to the father's proceedings for enforcement of his contact order).

Evidence obtained in disregard of r 4.18(1)—There is no absolute bar on the use of material obtained pursuant to an unauthorised examination or assessment, and there may be circumstances in which it is in the interests of the child that such evidence be admitted despite the breach of the rules; for an example of a local authority being given leave to adduce evidence despite having breached directions as to filing etc, see *R v Nottinghamshire CC* [1993] Fam Law 625. However, breach of r 4.18(1) is likely to be treated as a very serious matter and the court will obviously require a full explanation as to how it came about before being prepared to grant leave for the evidence to be adduced. It is suggested that the application for leave should normally be made in accordance with r 4.14 and that Form C2 be used (see **Procedure on application for leave** above). It is contrary to good practice to provide an expert with information about the case in an anonymous form in an attempt to avoid the need for court permission, and bad practice for expert witnesses who understand that their opinion is required for court proceedings to accept anonymous instructions; such breaches may lead to costs penalties (*Re A (Family Proceedings: Expert Witnesses)* [2001] 1 FLR 723).

Sterilisation applications—The *Practice Note of 2 April 2001 (Official Solicitor: Appointment in Family Proceedings)*, to be read in conjunction with *Practice Note of March 2001 (Officers of CAFCASS Legal Services and Special Casework: Appointment in Family Proceedings)* sets out important considerations with regard to expert evidence in sterilisation cases.

4.19 Amendment

(1) Subject to rule 4.17(2), a document which has been filed or served in proceedings to which this Part applies, may not be amended without the leave of the court which shall, unless the court otherwise directs, be requested in writing.

(2) On considering a request for leave to amend a document the court shall either –

PART III

(*a*) grant the request, whereupon the proper officer shall inform the person making the request of that decision, or

(*b*) invite the parties or any of them to make representations, within a specified period, as to whether such an order should be made.

(3) A person amending a document shall file it and serve it on those persons on whom it was served prior to amendment; and the amendments shall be identified.

Defined terms—"court": r 1.2(1); "leave": r 4.1(1); "proper officer": r 1.2(1).

"subject to rule 4.17(2)" (r 4.19(1))—Rule 4.17 provides for the filing of written statements of the substance of the oral evidence which a party intends to adduce. Although the written statement itself cannot be amended without leave once it is filed or served, r 4.17(2) does permit additions and alterations to be made by supplementary statement.

"proceedings to which this Part applies" (r 4.19(1))—Part IV applies to the proceedings listed in r 4.1(2).

"document which has been filed or served" (r 4.19(1))—The term "document" is not defined in the rules and seems to have different meanings depending on the context. For example, it has a much wider meaning in r 4.8 (which deals with service) than in r 4.17(1)(*b*), where it is used in contrast to "written statements" in r 4.17(1)(*a*). It is suggested that the term is used in a wide sense in r 4.19 to encompass all documents filed or served – application forms, written requests for directions, statements of evidence etc. Amendment is prohibited if the document has been either filed or served. An unsigned draft, if served in an effort to avoid delay, is probably not caught by this rule nor, presumably, covered by the confidentiality safeguards of r 4.23.

Leave to be requested in writing (r 4.19(1))—It is suggested that a request for leave to amend should be made by way of application for an order or directions in existing family proceedings using Form C2. The request ought to explain clearly why amendment is necessary and it is suggested that a copy of the document in relation to which leave is sought should be attached to the request with the draft amendments clearly identified. It would be sensible, where time permits, to seek the written consent of the other parties to the amendment and to attach such consents as are forthcoming to the request as well.

Treatment of request to amend (r 4.19(2))—The court is given only two options under r 4.19(2). Either it grants the request (in which case, nobody at all needs to be consulted) or it invites representations (in which case the court chooses which party or parties to consult). Rather strangely, it therefore appears that the court is not entitled to refuse the request without some sort of consultation with at least some of the parties, but that this consultation process need not necessarily involve the one party (the applicant for leave) who would be likely to produce arguments to dissuade the court from refusing the request.

Representations under r 4.19(2)(b)—Rule 4.19(2)(*b*) appears to envisage that representations will be made in writing, but there is no express prohibition on oral representations and these may well be more appropriate where, for example, the court permits the request for leave to amend to be made orally at a hearing attended by the other parties.

Identifying the amendments (r 4.19(3))—Traditionally, first amendments of a writ or originating summons are marked in red and second amendments in green, but this rule does not require this and word processors offer much more convenient methods of identification (bold type, underlining, italics and so on). A key should be provided so that it is clear how amendments have been marked.

Service—As to service generally, see rr 4.8, 10.2, 10.3 and 10.6.

4.20 Oral evidence

The court or the proper officer shall keep a note of the substance of the oral evidence given at a hearing of, or directions appointment in, proceedings to which this Part applies.

Defined terms—"court": r 1.2(1); "directions appointment", "note": r 4.1(1); "proper officer": r 1.2(1).

Scope of provision—This rule provides for a record to be kept of the oral evidence adduced at a hearing or directions appointment in proceedings under CA 1989.

"proceedings to which this Part applies"—Part IV applies to the proceedings listed in r 4.1(2).

"The court or the proper officer"—In courts where recording equipment is used, there will be a record of the oral evidence on tape (r 4.1(1) provides that "note" includes a record made by mechanical means). Alternatively, a shorthand writer may take a verbatim note (see r 10.15 as to official shorthand notes). If neither of these methods is available, the judge or district judge will make a full note of the substance of the evidence in his notebook.

"the substance of the oral evidence"—It is the substance of the oral evidence that r 4.20 requires to be recorded. There is no express duty under the rule to keep a note of opening and closing submissions and argument, although, curiously, where the hearing or directions appointment takes place outside normal court office hours, r 4.21(8) may oblige the court or the proper officer to take a note of the substance of these too. However, in *Hampshire County Council v S* [1993] 1 FLR 559, it was held in relation to the family proceedings courts that, where competing submissions are made in the absence of oral evidence, the justices' clerk should make a note of the submissions of the parties and, if the children's guardian gives oral evidence to the court, the clerk's note should refer to that fact and to the nature of the advice (as there is a duty to do under FPC(CA 1989)R 1991, r 11(5) and under FPR 1991, r 4.11(5) in any event). The order of the court must be recorded in accordance with other provisions of the rules.

4.21 Hearing

(1) The court may give directions as to the order of speeches and evidence at a hearing or directions appointment, in the course of proceedings to which this Part applies.

(2) Subject to directions under paragraph (1), at a hearing of, or directions appointment in, proceedings to which this Part applies, the parties and the children's guardian shall adduce their evidence in the following order –

- (*a*) the applicant,
- (*b*) any party with parental responsibility for the child,
- (*c*) other respondents,
- (*d*) the children's guardian,
- (*e*) the child, if he is a party to the proceedings and there is no children's guardian.

(3) After the final hearing of proceedings to which this Part applies, the court shall deliver its judgment as soon as is practicable.

(4) When making an order or when refusing an application, the court shall –

- (*a*) where it makes a finding of fact state such finding and complete Form C22; and
- (*b*) state the reasons for the court's decision.

(5) An order made in proceedings to which this Part applies shall be recorded, by the court or the proper officer, either in the appropriate form in Appendix 1 to these rules or, where there is no such form, in writing.

(6) Subject to paragraph (7), a copy of an order made in accordance with paragraph (5) shall, as soon as practicable after it has been made, be served by the proper officer on the parties to the proceedings in which it was made and on any person with whom the child is living.

(7) Within 48 hours after the making ex parte of –

(*a*) a section 8 order, or
(*b*) an order under section 44, 48(4), 48(9) or 50,

the applicant shall serve a copy of the order in the appropriate form in Appendix 1 to these Rules on –

(i) each party,
(ii) any person who has actual care of the child or who had such care immediately prior to the making of the order, and
(iii) in the case of an order referred to in sub-paragraph (*b*), the local authority in whose area the child lives or is found.

(8) At a hearing of, or directions appointment in, an application which takes place outside the hours during which the court office is normally open, the court or the proper officer shall take a note of the substance of the proceedings.

Amendments—SI 1992/456; SI 1992/2067; SI 1994/3155; SI 2001/821.

Defined terms—"applicant", "child": r 4.1(1); "court": r 1.2(1); "directions appointment", "children's guardian": r 4.1(1); "parental responsibility": CA 1989, s 3; "proper officer": r 1.2(1).

Scope of provision—This rule contains various provisions regulating the conduct of hearings and directions appointments, including provisions as to the giving of judgments and the recording and service of orders.

Case management—*Practice Direction of 31 January 1995* deals with a number of important aspects of hearings in the High Court and county courts. Great assistance is also to be derived from the *Handbook of Best Practice in Children Act cases* produced by the Children Act Advisory Committee (set out in Part IV of this work as *Best Practice Guidance of June 1997*). See also **Bundles and other particular matters** under FPR 1991, r 4.14. See the practical guidance given as to the proper preparation of cases brought under CA 1989 in *Re R (Care: Disclosure: Nature of Proceedings)* [2002] 1 FLR 755. For further useful guidance as to the conduct and recording of meetings and the provision of documents in care proceedings see *Re L (Care: Assessment: Fair Trial)* [2002] EWHC 1379 (Fam), [2002] 2 FLR 730 which is referred to in more detail in **Disclosure – impact of the European Convention for Human Rights and Fundamental Freedoms 1950** under r 4.23.

"proceedings to which this Part applies" (r 4.21(1))—Part IV applies to the proceedings listed in r 4.1(2).

Interim hearings—*Hampshire County Council v S* [1993] 1 FLR 559, albeit decided in relation to the family proceedings court, offers valuable guidance on the conduct of interim hearings; for a full note of this case and of other matters arising in relation to interim hearings, see under FPC(CA 1989)R 1991, r 21.

Agreed orders—Although the court has an overriding judicial duty to investigate proposals which are put before it by consent, the depth of that investigation must reflect the consensus between the parties. For the position where either the parties are agreed that there should be a care order, or the parents are prepared to concede that there should be a care order, see **Agreed orders** under CA 1989, s 31. With the exception of this one area, such problems as there have been over agreed orders appear to have arisen largely in the magistrates' courts; reference to the authorities can be found under FPC(CA 1989)R 1991, r 21.

It should be standard practice for the parties to prepare a draft consent order setting out the agreed terms. This will serve to concentrate their minds on what precisely they are agreeing, thus reducing the possibility of mistakes and misunderstandings, and also make it easier for the court to identify the points at which it might depart from the agreed package and to invite submissions about them.

Children's hearings in private do not breach European Convention for the Protection of Human Rights and Fundamental Freedoms 1950, Art 6—See under r 4.16.

Full hearing not always appropriate—There can be situations in which the application before the court has so remote a prospect of a positive outcome that it is wrong to allow it to go any further, and the appropriate course is to dismiss it without hearing oral evidence or further investigation (*Cheshire County Council v M* [1993] 1 FLR 463, in which a father applied for contact under CA 1989 some years after wardship proceedings in which his children had been placed in care with a view to adoption and his contact with them had been severed following allegations of sexual abuse). The *Cheshire* case was upheld by the Court of Appeal in the similar case of *W v Ealing London Borough Council* [1993] 2 FLR 788, but was said to be applicable only in the limited class of cases in which the Children Act provided an opportunity to an applicant to seek to undermine an order made in wardship which had not been challenged on appeal.

In cases which do not fall within the limited *Cheshire County Council v M* category, the court nonetheless has a broad discretion to conduct the case as is most appropriate for the issues involved and the evidence available. It will not necessarily hold a full hearing with the parties permitted to call oral evidence and cross-examine any witnesses they may choose. Applications for residence orders or care orders or for the revocation of a care order are likely to be decided on full oral evidence, though not invariably; contact applications may be and are heard sometimes with, and sometimes without, oral evidence or with a limited amount of oral evidence. Relevant considerations in the exercise of the court's discretion include (per *Re B (Minors) (Contact)* [1994] 2 FLR 1, CA):

(*a*) whether there is sufficient evidence on which to make the decision;
(*b*) whether the proposed evidence which the applicant for a full trial wishes to adduce and whether the opportunity to cross-examine the witnesses is likely to affect the outcome of the proceedings;
(*c*) the welfare of the child and the effect of further litigation;
(*d*) whether the delay will be so detrimental to the child's well-being that exceptionally there should not be a full hearing;
(*e*) the prospects of success of the applicant for a full trial;
(*f*) whether the justice of the case requires a full investigation with oral evidence.

For a further example of a curtailed hearing, see *Re W (Care: Leave to Place outside Jurisdiction)* [1994] 2 FLR 1087) and see also *Re B (Contact: Stepfather's Opposition)* [1997] 2 FLR 579, CA noted under **Dismissal of proceedings at directions stage** under r 4.14 and the further comments of the Court of Appeal in *Re A (Application for Leave)* [1998] 1 FLR 1 at p 4F.

It is not always wrong to consider proportionality between, on the one hand, the benefits to the welfare of the child and, on the other hand, the resources (in the widest sense of the term) to be expended on the inquiry (*Re S (Contact: Evidence)* [1998] 1 FLR 798, CA). However, the court has to be careful not to deal with the matter in too peremptory a way. In *Re I and H (Contact: Right to Give Evidence)* [1998] 1 FLR 876, CA, it was said that an applicant under CA 1989 has a fundamental right to be heard. Whatever may have been the first instance judge's view in that case of the applicant's prospects of success, he should have allowed him to ask some (though not endless) questions of the children and family reporter and to give evidence himself as to his views about contact with his children. Similarly, in *H v West Sussex CC* [1998] 1 FLR 862, FD, the magistrates were held to have erred in not allowing the mother to call a psychologist whom she had instructed pursuant to leave. Johnson J said that evidence in such cases ought to be regulated by weight rather than admissibility, particularly in a case where a parent was at risk of being separated permanently from his child. He expressed a view that such a parent ought, surely, to be allowed to present his case in the way he chose, subject to the evidence being tendered in a responsible and professional manner. In *Re W (Minor) (Contact Application: Procedure)* [1999] Fam Law 853, Wilson J roundly criticised a procedure which had been generally adopted in a family proceedings court in respect of applications for leave to apply for contact where the matter was dealt with summarily, neither party was invited to attend, no order was drawn up granting leave and no reasons were given in writing or orally. This procedure was held to be unacceptable and the judge said that it must be changed.

It is clear that, where the court hears oral evidence from one side, it is wholly inappropriate not to hear from the other side (*Re F (A Minor) (Care Order: Procedure)* [1994] 1 FLR 240). In *Re F*, the justices erred in the way in which they controlled the conduct of the case. Hearing an application for an interim care order, they permitted oral evidence from the local authority but not from the father. Having heard oral evidence from one side, it was wholly inappropriate not to hear the other. The proper procedure if they had this course in mind would have been to invite submissions from all parties on the point before deciding to exclude oral evidence; the advocates had a duty not to take an adversarial view of the proceedings and, if the justices were in the process of making, or appeared likely to make, a decision which was procedurally wrong, to advise them that they were about to make a fundamental error. Reasons for a decision to refuse to hear oral evidence from a party should be given by the justices. In contrast to *Re F*, however, it was permissible for the magistrates to stop proceedings for the discharge of a care order/defined contact in *Re S and P (Discharge of Care Order)* [1995] 2 FLR 782, FD, after hearing only the mother's evidence, there being no reasonable prospect of her application succeeding. In *Re M (A Minor) (Contact)* [1994] 2 FCR 968, justices were wrong to refuse a father's application for an adjournment and to dismiss his contact application on the basis of written evidence only, even though they were concerned about extreme delay for which he had been largely responsible. Similarly, in *Re M (Contact)* [1995] 1 FLR 1029, FD, whilst it was acknowledged that there were cases in which an application was so hopeless that the court would be entitled to dismiss it effectively out of hand, the magistrates had been wrong to dismiss this application by a father for staying contact on the papers only and without hearing oral evidence. It is difficult to envisage circumstances in which an interim contact order could properly be made where the principle of contact was genuinely in dispute and where there were substantial factual issues relating to the child which were unresolved without the court hearing oral evidence or having the advice of an expert such as the children and family reporter (*Re D (Contact: Interim Order)* [1995] 1 FLR 495), though see *Re B (Contact: Stepfather's Opposition)* (above) for a case in which the judge took the exceptional course of dismissing a contact application at the directions stage without hearing evidence.

As to the possibility of estoppel, see *K v P (Children Act Proceedings: Estoppel)* [1995] 1 FLR 248, FD; *Re S, S and A (Care Proceedings: Issue Estoppel)* [1995] 2 FLR 244, FD; *Re S (Discharge of Care Order)* [1995] 2 FLR 639, CA, and *Re B (Children Act Proceedings: Issue Estoppel)* [1997] 1 FLR 285, FD.

For the proper course in cases which are hopeless because of adverse experts' reports, see under r 4.18.

Organising the evidence—Logistical problems with witnesses arise, in particular, in relation to experts. For suggestions as to how to tackle this, see under r 4.18.

Facilitated communication—It is dangerous for a court in family proceedings to rely on evidence provided by facilitated communication, a process in which a helper supports the hand or arm of the person with communication difficulties while using a keyboard or typing device, in support of allegations of abuse made by the individual (*Re D (Evidence: Facilitated Communication)* [2001] 1 FLR 148).

Order of speeches (r 4.21(1))—Whereas r 4.21(2) establishes a normal order in which the parties and children's guardian will adduce their evidence, this rule is silent as to the normal order for speeches. The court may give directions under r 4.21(1) if necessary, but tradition generally dictates that all the respondents have their say first, the applicant goes next and the children's guardian last. Where one legal representative has made oral representations, the others in the case should not be confined to written representations (*Re E (Minors)* [1991] TLR 300).

Continuing duty of advocates—Where an advocate's submissions on the primary issue fail, it is very important that he continue to present the views of his client during the ensuing debate as to the implementation and drawing of the order (*Buckinghamshire County Council v M* [1994] 2 FLR 506).

Legal representation at hearing – the right to a fair trial under Art 6, European Convention for the Protection of Human Rights and Fundamental Freedoms 1950—Generally, it is important for parents in cases where the outcome could be the permanent loss of their children, for the parents to have equality of representation and to have a sense that a full and sympathetic hearing has taken place (*Re G (Adoption Proceedings: Representation of Children)* [2001] 1 FCR 353). The loss by parents of legal representation on the first day of care proceedings (leaving them to conduct their own case) will not necessarily amount to a breach of Art 6 (the right to a fair trial) (*Re B and T (Care Proceedings: Legal Representation)* [2001] 1 FLR 485 – where the parents had had skilled legal advice in the preparation of the case and had changed lawyers on four previous occasions, the judge had supported the parents at the final hearing and had a duty not only to the parents but also to the children who were entitled to an early determination of their future). However, in care proceedings the complexity of the case, the importance of what is at stake and the highly emotive nature of the subject matter mean that the principles of litigants having effective access to the court and of fairness require that they should receive the assistance of a lawyer (*P, C and S v UK* [2002] 2 FLR 631, ECHR – where the procedures adopted gave the appearance of unfairness and prevented the parents from properly putting forward their case, in breach of ECHRFF 1950, Arts 6 and 8).

McKenzie friend—In relation to proceedings in public (ie in open court), a litigant in person should be allowed to have a *McKenzie* friend to assist by prompting, taking notes and quietly giving advice unless the judge is satisfied that fairness and the interests of justice do not require a litigant to have such assistance. However, that right belongs to the litigant, not to the friend. The only right a *McKenzie* friend has is the right, as a member of the public, to be present in open court. That right does not apply to chambers proceedings, as these are, by definition, not open to the public. Where the proceedings are in chambers the litigant in person should be allowed to have a *McKenzie* friend unless the proceedings are in private. Where the proceedings are in private, the confidential nature of the proceedings which make it appropriate for them to be held in private may make it undesirable in the interests of justice for a *McKenzie* friend to assist. Where the proceedings are in chambers, the judge has a discretion whether to permit the presence of a *McKenzie* friend, and the exercise of that discretion can be challenged only by the litigant in person. When a judge refuses to allow a litigant in person the assistance of a *McKenzie* friend he should give his reasons. The assistance of a *McKenzie* friend is available for the benefit of the litigant in person and whether or not a *McKenzie* friend is paid or unpaid for his services he has no right to provide those services; the court is solely concerned with the interests of the litigant in person (see *R v Bow County Court ex parte Pelling* [1999] 2 FLR 1126, CA; *Re G (Chambers Proceedings: McKenzie Friend)* [1999] 2 FLR 59; *Re M (Contact: Family Assistance: McKenzie Friend)* [1999] 1 FLR 75, CA; *Re H (Chambers Proceedings: McKenzie Friend)* [1997] 2 FLR 423, CA). There is a strong presumption in family proceedings in favour of permitting a *McKenzie* friend to be present unless the judge is satisfied that fairness and the interests of justice do not require it (*Re H McKenzie Friend: Pre-Trial Determination)* [2002] EWCA Civ 1444, [2002] 1 FLR 39). However, the court can prevent a *McKenzie* friend from continuing to act as such where the assistance given is inimical to the efficient administration of justice, for example, where the friend is indirectly running the case or using the litigant as a puppet (*Noueiri v Paragon Finance plc* [2001] EWCA Civ 1402, [2002] Fam Law 16).

Advocate to the court (amicus curiae)—The Attorney-General, Lord Goldsmith QC, in conjunction with Lord Woolf CJ, has issued a *Memorandum of 19 December 2001 – Requests for the Appointment of an Advocate to the Court* (set out in Part IV of this work) which details the replacement provisions for the appointment of an advocate to the court (*amicus curiae*) in appropriate cases. In most cases an advocate to the court is appointed by the Attorney-General following a request by the court. However, in some cases, an advocate to the court will be appointed by the Official Solicitor or CAFCASS where the issue is one in which their experience of representing children and adults under a disability gives them special experience. The division of function between them is outlined in *Practice Notes of March 2001* and *2 April 2001* (both are set out in Part IV of this work). The procedure and circumstances for requesting an advocate to the court to be appointed by the Official Solicitor or CAFCASS are the same as those applying to requests to the Attorney-General. In cases of extreme urgency, telephone requests may be made (NB the *Memorandum* contains all relevant contact telephone numbers, addresses etc). In some cases, the Official Solicitor himself will be appointed as advocate to the court. He may be given directions by the court authorising him to obtain documents, conduct investigations and enquiries and to advise the court. He may appear by counsel or an in-house advocate (see para 12 of the *Memorandum*).

"parties" (r 4.21(2))—Broadly speaking, the parties to proceedings are the applicant and the respondents set out in the relevant entry in App 3, column (iv). As to the power of the court to order that a person be joined as or cease to be a party, see r 4.7. The children's guardian is not personally a party (although the child whose interests he represents may be) but, to an extent, he participates in the proceedings as if he were and the rules are drafted to facilitate this (as in r 4.21(2) and also, for example, r 4.14).

"child, if he is a party to the proceedings" (r 4.21(2))—If the child is bringing the application, no doubt his status as applicant (within r 4.21(2)(*a*)) will prevail over his status as child (within r 4.21(2)(*e*)) and he will adduce his evidence first. A child who is responding to an application and has a Part IX children's guardian but no s 41 children's guardian will fall within r 4.21(2)(*e*) as a Part IX children's guardian is not the same as a children's guardian for the purposes of Pt IV (see the definition in r 4.1(1)).

Where the child and his children's guardian part company (r 4.21(2))—Rule 4.21(2) does not expressly cover the situation where the child and the children's guardian part company because the child is instructing his solicitor direct (see r 4.12(1)) or intends and is able to conduct the proceedings on his own behalf. In this case, r 4.11(3) dictates that the children's guardian takes such part in the proceedings as the court may direct and may, with the leave of the court, have his own legal representation. When it comes to the order of adducing evidence, the guardian falls within r 4.21(2)(*d*) but the child does not fall within r 4.21(2)(*e*) so the court will have to give directions.

Questioning the children's guardian (r 4.21(2)(*d*))—The children's guardian cannot simply put in his written report; he must submit to questioning on this and on any other oral or written advice that he tenders to the court under r 4.11 if any party so requires (r 4.11(11); see also *Hampshire County Council v S* [1993] 1 FLR 559).

Court calling witness—As the semi-inquisitorial nature of Children Act proceedings has increasingly become accepted, the practice has developed of the court itself occasionally calling a witness where fairness dictates that an advocate should be able to cross-examine the witness and normal procedure would confine him to examination-in-chief (*Re P (Witness Summons)* [1997] 2 FLR 447, CA).

Witness anonymity—A court will give anonymity to a professional social worker witness in care proceedings only in highly exceptional cases (*Re W (Care Proceedings: Witness Anonymity)* [2002] EWCA Civ 1626, [2003] Fam Law 65 – where it was held that the guidance as to witness anonymity given in the criminal jurisdiction has parallels for public law cases such as care proceedings; in this case the threat of violence from adults who faced permanent separation from their children was held to be a professional hazard of social work, and not exceptional).

Judge seeing child—The judge's decision whether or not personally to interview a child is, above all, a question for the exercise of judicial discretion. Certainly, the judge is under no obligation to see a child in private before he decides what order to make (*Re R (A Minor) (Residence: Religion)* [1993] 2 FLR 163). The judge will decide who should be present during an interview with children, but he cannot promise the children absolute confidentiality, and he must tell the parties what the child has said to him so that they may deal with it (*H v H (Child: Judicial Interview)* [1974] 1 WLR 595, [1974] 1 All ER 1145; *Elder v Elder* [1986] 1 FLR 610; *Dickinson v Dickinson* (1983) Fam Law 174). *B v B (Minors) (Interviews and Listing Arrangements)* [1994] 2 FLR 489, CA, contains much valuable guidance on the subject of seeing children, including the following:

(*a*) The discretion to see children in private must be exercised cautiously; it should in no sense be automatic or routine.

(*b*) It should also be exercised only after hearing submissions from the parties; there must be a good reason for the judge to see a child, and it must be perceived by the judge that it is in the interests of the child to see him. The ascertainment of the child's wishes and feelings is, where relevant, normally the province of the children and family reporter or the children's guardian, who can be cross-examined in the normal way.

(*c*) If a judge does see a child, it is preferable for the interview to take place once the evidence in the case has been completed but before speeches. Then, if necessary, there can be further evidence, or counsel can take instructions and address the court on any issues arising from it.

(*d*) It is of the utmost importance, when the judge does see a child, for him to make it clear to the child that the responsibility for the ultimate decision is the court's, not the child's. The judge should also make it clear to the child that he may not be able to do what the child wants because he has to take an overall view of the child's welfare. The judge in *B v B* was said to have "directed himself impeccably in accordance with the decision of this court in *B v S (Formerly B)* (1973) 118 SJ 219, by making it clear to the children when he saw them that he could not promise them that he would not disclose to their parents what they said to him; indeed, he went further and told the children that there could be no secrets relating to what they talked about and that he would have to tell both parents what had been said".

Any interview between the judge and the child should take place at the court (*L v L (Access: Contempt)* [1991] FCR 547, (1991) 135 Sol Jo 152).

Judge seeing advocates—Thorpe LJ observed in *Re CH (Care or Interim Care Order)* [1998] 1 FLR 402, CA that it seemed to him undesirable that judges should encourage or permit significant exchanges between the advocates unrecorded in the privacy of the judge's room. If it is thought desirable by the advocates or by the judge that exchanges should take place without the clients and other persons being present, those exchanges can be in the court room in chambers where they will be fully recorded.

Delivery of judgment and the reasons for it (r 4.21(3), (4))—This rule allows for judgment to be reserved in an appropriate case providing that it is delivered as soon as practicable. The judgment, whether reserved or not, must state any findings of fact and the reasons for the court's decision. These must be set out with sufficient detail and clarity to make clear the facts upon which reliance is placed and the matters taken into account in exercising discretion and reaching a decision, though a judgment is not to be approached as a summing-up and is not an assault course. The Court of Appeal recognises that judges work under enormous time and other pressures and will not interfere simply because an ex tempore judgment given at the end of a long day is not as polished or thorough as it might otherwise be. Although it is not always necessary or appropriate for the judge to go through the s 1(3) "checklist" item by item, the checklist is an extremely useful and important discipline in ensuring that all relevant factors are considered and balanced. The fact that neither party is making any complaints about the other is not a good reason for not going through the checklist *(B v B (Residence Order: Reasons for Decision)* [1997] 2 FLR 602, CA). For the arrangements for delivery of written judgments in the High Court and Court of Appeal and also as to the availability of approved versions of ex tempore judgments in these courts, see *Practice Statement of 22 April 1998* and *Practice Statement of 25 November 1998*.

Departing from an expert's opinion—The court is entitled to depart from the opinion of an expert although, if it does so, it must explain its reasons (*Re B (Care: Expert Witnesses)* [1996] 1 FLR 667). Where there is a conflict between experts, the court must address and resolve that conflict insofar as it is relevant to the issues before the court and it is entitled to give greater weight to the opinion of one expert as against that of another, provided that proper reasons are given (*Re J (Expert Evidence: Hearsay)* [1999] 2 FLR 661; *Re W and P (Children)* LTL, 30 April 2002 – Doc No C9500819). Where there is a stark conflict of forensic medical evidence, a judge should not decline to choose between the medical opinions; instead he should invite the parties to agree a tertiary referral. To leave the evidence unresolved makes the disposal stage problematic (*Re W and P* (above)). Where experts are unanimous in their opinion as to a person's core personality and emotional state, it is not open to the judge to reject that expert evidence purely on the basis of his own appraisal of the person when giving oral evidence (*Re M (Residence)* [2002] EWCA Civ 1052, [2002] 2 FLR 1059).

"when making an order or when refusing an application" (r 4.21(4))—When the court makes an order or refuses an application it must, where it makes a finding of fact, state such finding and complete Form C22. Form C22 requires the court to: identify the child concerned in the proceedings; indicate whether the hearing was on notice or ex parte; list the reports and statements which it has read; identify those persons whose oral evidence it has heard in reaching its decision; list those in attendance at court during the hearing; and identify their representatives (if any). The court must also go on to state the reasons for its decision (as to which, see the preceding annotation). Any findings of fact, and the reasons for the court's decision, must be stated when an order is made or an application is refused in the interlocutory stages of the proceedings, not just after the final hearing.

Form of order—The prescribed forms are set out in App 1 to these rules. Where the order is by consent, it should say so (see *Chandless-Chandless v Nicholson* [1942] 2 KB 321, [1942] 2 All ER 315). Where the court makes no order, there should still be a written order to that effect (*S v R (Parental Responsibility)* [1993] 1 FCR 331). If appropriate, it is possible for the order to recite the intention of the parties at the time of the order, as a preliminary to stating that the court considered an order unnecessary (*Re T (Adoption: Contact)* [1995] 2 FLR 251, CA and see also *M v M (Defined Contact Application)* [1998] 2 FLR 244, FD in which there was an order of "no order as to defined contact" but with the parents' joint wishes and expectations set out in the preamble). See also *Re B (Supervision Order: Parental Undertaking)* [1996] 1 FLR 676 for the possibility of recording the agreement of a parent to seek treatment as a preamble to a supervision order. Where a court has directed the determination of specific issues, the judgment of the court performing the task should first address those issues in turn, and specifically, so that it is evident that there has been a complete and thorough performance of the operation (*Re M and MC (Care: Issues of Fact: Drawing of Orders)* [2002] EWCA Civ 499, [2003] Fam Law 64). Those findings should then be set out in the order drawn to record the outcome of the proceedings. The order can then go on to make such further directions as are appropriate.

"order under section 44, 48(4), 48(9) or 50" (r 4.21(7)(*b*))—CA 1989, s 44 provides for the making of emergency protection orders. Section 48 contains various powers to assist in the execution of emergency protection orders and in finding children who may be in need of emergency protection. Under s 48(4), where an emergency protection order authorises the applicant to enter specified premises in relation to one child and the court is satisfied that there is reasonable cause to believe that there may be another child in relation to whom an emergency protection order ought to be made on the premises as well, it may authorise a search for that other child. Under s 48(9), the court may issue a warrant authorising a constable to assist in the exercise of powers under an emergency protection order. Section 50 provides for recovery orders, ie orders in relation to a child who is in care, subject to an emergency protection order or in police protection and who has run away, been taken away, gone missing etc.

Proceedings under CA 1989—FPR 1991, r 4.16(7) provides that, unless the court otherwise directs, a hearing of, or directions appointment in, proceedings to which this Part applies must be heard in chambers.

Hearings in care proceedings—*Oxfordshire CC v M* [1994] 1 FLR 175 highlights the fact that care proceedings do not have an essentially adversarial character (as do *Re L (Police Investigation: Privilege)* [1996] 1 FLR 731 and *Re S (Contact: Evidence)* [1998] 1 FLR 798, CA) and that judges in the Family Division (and, in practice, the county courts as well) dealing with directions hearings in such cases adopt an interventionist style and, at the substantive hearing, have substantially greater control over the deployment of evidence and argument than a judge hearing other civil proceedings. *Practice Direction of 31 January 1995* dictates increased court control in all family proceedings. The following are examples of the practical consequences, in private and public children proceedings, of the non-adversarial approach: *B v B (Minors) (Interviews and Listing Arrangements)* [1994] 2 FLR 489 – parties not to countenance delay for tactical advantage; *Re MD and TD (Minors) (Time Estimates)* [1994] 2 FLR 336 (set out in Part IV of this work as *Practice Note of 2 February 1994*) – co-operative time estimating; *Re M (Minors) (Care Proceedings: Child's Wishes)* [1994] 1 FLR 749 – co-operative planning for trial; *Re F (A Minor) (Care Order: Procedure)* [1994] 1 FLR 240, *Re K and Others (Minors) (Disclosure)* [1994] 1 FLR 377 – disclosure application. Proceedings by a child-minder challenging the refusal of a local authority to register her are, however, adversarial (*London Borough of Sutton v Davis (Costs) (No 2)* [1994] 2 FLR 569).

Split hearings—See the annotations to CA 1989, s 31.

Official Solicitor's guidance on sterilisation—The *Practice Note of 2 April 2001 (Official Solicitor: Appointment in Family Proceedings)*, to be read in conjunction with *Practice Note of March 2001 (Officers of CAFCASS Legal Services and Special Casework: Appointment in Family Proceedings)* sets out the procedure on sterilisation applications. Normally, the preferred course is to raise questions of sterilisation of a minor or mentally incompetent adult by an application within the inherent jurisdiction but, with a minor, it is possible for a specific issue order to be sought instead.

4.21A Attachment of penal notice to section 8 order

CCR Order 29, rule 1 (committal for breach of order or undertaking) shall apply to section 8 orders as if for paragraph (3) of that rule there were substituted the following –

"(3) In the case of a section 8 order (within the meaning of section 8(2) of the Children Act 1989) enforceable by committal order under paragraph (1), the judge or the district judge may, on the application of the person entitled to enforce the order, direct that the proper officer issue a copy of the order, indorsed with or incorporating a notice as to the consequences of disobedience, for service in accordance with paragraph (2), and no copy of the order shall be issued with any such notice indorsed or incorporated save in accordance with such a direction".

Amendments—Inserted by SI 1992/2067.

"enforceable by committal order under paragraph (1)"—CCR Ord 29, r 1(1) provides for orders to be enforceable by committal where they require a person to do, within a specified time, or to abstain from doing, an act. However, orders that are purely declaratory cannot be enforced by committal. An order made in the High Court or a county court under CA 1989, s 8 for residence or contact will usually be declaratory and not injunctive. A declaratory order which provides for reasonable contact cannot have a penal notice incorporated in, or endorsed on, it (*D v D (Access: Contempt: Committal)* [1991] 2 FLR 34). Before a penal notice can be added, a contact order should contain clearly defined terms – see *Re H (Contact: Enforcement)* [1996] 1 FLR 614 (this case concerned enforcement of a contact order under Magistrates' Courts Act 1980, s 63, but the principles seem equally applicable to FPR 1991, r 4.21A and subsequent committal proceedings). In *Re N (A Minor) (Access: Penal Notice)* [1992] 1 FLR 134, the Court of Appeal upheld the refusal of a county court judge to make a specific access order (now "contact order") incorporating a penal notice; the judge had found that the child no longer wished to see the father and would suffer serious emotional upset if he was forced against his will to do so. Accordingly, it will rarely be appropriate to meet breach of a s 8 order with committal (see *Re L (Minors) (Access Order: Enforcement)* [1989] 2 FLR 359; *Re M (Minors) (Access: Contempt: Committal)* [1991] 1 FLR 355). However, in *A v N (Committal: Refusal of Contact)* [1997] 1 FLR 533 the Court of Appeal upheld the committal to prison of a mother who persistently flouted contact orders made by the courts, and said that, when considering whether to commit such a mother, the welfare of the child was a relevant consideration but not paramount. See also *Z v Z (Refusal of Contact: Committal)* [1996] 1 FCR 538, where a penal notice was attached to a defined contact order, the mother subsequently refused to comply with the contact order and was committed to prison for a period of six weeks, she purged her contempt after two nights and agreed to co-operate with the order, and the judge then altered the sentence to one of three weeks but suspended the sentence for a period of four months, after which time he indicated that the issue of contact would be reviewed. If a committal is sought following the attachment of a penal notice to a s 8 order, the procedure under CCR Ord 29, r 1(1) must be followed carefully, as for any other committal. As the nature of specific issue and prohibited steps orders will vary infinitely, the test must be applied in relation to the contents of the order in each case.

4.22 Appeals

(1) Where an appeal lies –

(*a*) to the High Court under section 94, or
(*b*) from any decision of a district judge to the judge of the court in which the decision was made,

it shall be made in accordance with the following provisions; and references to "the court below" are references to the court from which, or person from whom, the appeal lies.

(2) The appellant shall file and serve on the parties to the proceedings in the court below, and on any children's guardian –

(*a*) notice of the appeal in writing, setting out the grounds upon which he relies;
(*b*) a certified copy of the summons or application and of the order appealed against, and of any order staying its execution;
(*c*) a copy of any notes of the evidence;
(*d*) a copy of any reasons given for the decision.

(2A) In relation to an appeal to the High Court under section 94, the documents required to be filed by paragraph (2) shall, –

(*a*) where the care centre listed in column (ii) of Schedule 2 to the Children (Allocation of Proceedings) Order 1991 against the entry in column (i) relating to the petty sessions area or London commission area in which the court below is situated –
   (i) is the principal registry, or
   (ii) has a district registry in the same place,
   be filed in that registry, and
(*b*) in any other case, be filed in the district registry, being in the same place as a care centre within the meaning of article 2(*c*) of the said Order, which is nearest to the court below.

(3) The notice of appeal shall be filed and served in accordance with paragraph (2)(*a*) –

(*a*) within 14 days after the determination against which the appeal is brought, or
(*b*) in the case of an appeal against an order under section 38(1), within 7 days after the making of the order, or

(*c*) with the leave of the court to which, or judge to whom, the appeal is to be brought, within such other time as that court or judge may direct.

(4) The documents mentioned in paragraph (2)(*b*) to (*d*) shall, subject to any direction of the court to which, or judge to whom, the appeal is to be brought, be filed and served as soon as practicable after the filing and service of the notice of appeal under paragraph (2)(*a*).

(5) Subject to paragraph (6), a respondent who wishes –

(*a*) to contend on the appeal that the decision of the court below should be varied, either in any event or in the event of the appeal being allowed in whole or in part, or

(*b*) to contend that the decision of the court below should be affirmed on grounds other than those relied upon by that court, or

(*c*) to contend by way of cross-appeal that the decision of the court below was wrong in whole or in part,

shall, within 14 days of receipt of notice of the appeal, file and serve on all other parties to the appeal a notice in writing, setting out the grounds upon which he relies.

(6) No notice under paragraph (5) may be filed or served in an appeal against an order under section 38.

(7) In the case of an appeal mentioned in paragraph (1)(*a*) an application to –

(*a*) withdraw the appeal,

(*b*) have the appeal dismissed with the consent of all the parties, or

(*c*) amend the grounds of appeal,

may be heard by a district judge.

(8) An appeal of the kind mentioned in paragraph (1)(*a*) shall, unless the President otherwise directs, be heard and determined by a single judge.

Amendments—SI 1992/2067.

Defined terms—"district judge", "district registry", "principal registry": r 1.2(1).

Scope of provision—This rule sets out the procedure for appeals under CA 1989 from the family proceedings court and from a district judge. It does not apply to appeals in other family proceedings, which are governed in the High Court by RSC Ord 58 and in the county court by r 8.1.

Notice of appeal—An appeal must be made, by filing and serving the notice of appeal within 14 days of the decision to be appealed, unless the appeal is against an interim care or supervision order, in which case it must be served within seven days. The period for service may be altered by the High Court, on application, to provide a longer or shorter period (r 4.22(3)(*c*)).

Appeals under s 94—CA 1989, s 94 provides that all appeals under the Act from family proceedings courts must be to the High Court. Such appeals must be made in accordance with this rule (and RSC Ord 55, subject to this rule). The appeal should be commenced by filing the documents referred to in r 4.22(2) in the nearest registry which is a care centre to the court in which the order appealed from was made (r 4.22(2A)). In *Re U(T) (A Minor) (Care Order: Contact)* [1993] 2 FCR 565, Douglas Brown J held that r 4.22(2), which sets out the documents to be filed on appeal, does not include reports and witness statements filed in the proceedings; however, it should do, and the rule should be read as if it does. Therefore, in addition to the documents listed in r 4.22(2), an appellant should file a bundle of the evidence filed in the proceedings to which the appeal relates. It would seem good practice, and in accordance with practice before the Court of Appeal, that a paginated bundle containing all documents for the appeal hearing be filed with the court. Only the findings of fact and reasons announced by the justices under FPC(CA 1989)R 1991, r 21 may be considered on the appeal; the justices may not supplement these by later, additional reasons or findings (*Hillingdon LBC v H* [1992] 2 FLR 372). The notes of evidence of the hearing before the justices should be legible and clear to read on appeal (*Re W and S (Minors) (Contact)* [1992] 2 FCR 665). The appeal will be heard and determined by a High Court judge who will normally sit in open court (see *Practice Direction of 31 January 1992*). The hearing of the appeal will take the same form as an appeal heard by the Court of Appeal, namely a consideration of whether the court below exercised its discretion properly in reaching its decision in accordance with the principles of *G v G* [1985] FLR 894, [1985] 1 WLR 647 (see *Croydon LBC v A* [1992] 2 FLR 341; *Re CB (Parental Responsibility Order)* [1993] 1 FLR 920 at 924C; *Re W, Re A, Re B (Change of Name)* [1999] 2 FLR 930 at 937). Where it is unlikely that the case can be listed without delay on circuit, arrangements will be made for the appeal to be heard in London (see *Oxfordshire County Council v R* [1992] 1 FLR 648). Any application for a stay pending appeal must be made to the High Court; the family proceedings court has no power to grant a stay (*Re O* [1992] 2 FLR 7).

Appeals from the district judge—This rule relates only to appeals involving proceedings described in r 4.1(2), ie CA 1989 proceedings. An appeal from the decision of a district judge in other family proceedings must be in accordance with RSC Ord 58 (High Court) or r 8.1 (county court). An appeal from a district judge sitting in the Principal Registry of the Family Division (who has an enlarged jurisdiction by virtue of C(AP)O 1991, art 19 to make care orders, akin to that of a county court judge) is in accordance with the principles of *G v G* (above) (*Re S (Appeal from Principal Registry: Procedure)* [1997] 2 FLR 856).

Hopeless appeals—See notes to FPR 1991, r 8.1.

4.23 Confidentiality of documents

(1) Notwithstanding any rule of court to the contrary, no document, other than a record of an order, held by the court and relating to proceedings to which this Part applies shall be disclosed, other than to –

(*a*) a party,
(*b*) the legal representative of a party,
(*c*) the children's guardian,
(*d*) the Legal Aid Board, or
(*e*) a welfare officer or children and family reporter,
(*f*) an expert whose instruction by a party has been authorised by the court,

without leave of the judge or district judge.

(2) Nothing in this rule shall prevent the notification by the court or the proper officer of a direction under section 37(1) to the authority concerned.

(3) Nothing in this rule shall prevent the disclosure of a document prepared by an officer of the service for the purpose of –

(*a*) enabling a person to perform functions required by regulations under section 62(3A) of the Justices of the Peace Act 1997;
(*b*) assisting an officer of the service who is appointed by the court under any enactment to perform his functions.

(4) Nothing in this rule shall prevent the disclosure of any document relating to proceedings by an officer of the service to any other officer of the service unless that other officer is involved in the same proceedings but on behalf of a different party.

Amendments—SI 1997/1056; SI 2001/821.

Defined terms—"court": r 1.2(1); "children's guardian", "leave": r 4.1(1); "officer of the service": r 1.2(1); "proper officer": r 1.2(1); "children and family reporter": r 4.1(1).

Related provisions—See also Administration of Justice Act 1960, s 12, which prohibits the publication of information regarding wardship and other children proceedings held in private without leave and makes unauthorised publication contempt of court.

"no document ... held by the court" (r 4.23(1))—This rule is wide enough to cover not only documents filed by the parties before the hearing but also reports by the children's guardian and welfare officer, notes of evidence taken by the judge, documentary exhibits handed in during the hearing, any transcript or written note of the judgment etc. Once the written statement of a party's intended evidence has been filed, it too is covered by the rule. The only document which is exempt is a record of an order.

"proceedings to which this Part applies" (r 4.23(1))—See r 4.1(2).

"**except as is necessary in the course of the preparation of the case**" (r 4.23(1))—These words have been added by the Family Proceedings (Amendment) Rules 2001 so as to amend the provisions relating to the disclosure of documents. The purpose of the amendment is to permit disclosure without the leave of the court where this is necessary for the preparation of a case. In particular, it is intended to assist litigants in person and to facilitate discussions with experts advising in the case.

No leave necessary for CAFCASS officer to disclose material to local authority—Leave of the court is not required for the CAFCASS officer to disclose material to the local authority as a matter of law (*Re M (Disclosure: Children and Family Reporter)* [2002] EWCA Civ 1199, [2002] 2 FLR 893). Rule 4.23 expressly protects the confidentiality of documents and it cannot be argued that the CAFCASS officer is prevented from reporting to the local authority concerns resulting from investigations simply because at a later date they will be recorded in the report to the judge (*Re M* (above) para [19]). Communication between two professionals exchanging information in the course of their respective functions, each acting in furtherance of the protection of children, does not constitute publication breaching the privacy of the contemporaneous CA 1989 proceedings (paras [21], [66], [67]). The Children and Family Reporter (CFR) acts independently and exercises a discretion as to the nature and extent of his investigations and inquiries. He executes that part of the judge's function which is inquisitorial and the judge should give due weight to the outcome of his investigations (paras [26], [85]). In exercising his discretion the CFR should be mindful of the judge's power within private law proceedings to order a s 37 investigation and also the availability of emergency protection orders under CA 1989, s 44. He should always consider taking his concerns to the judge rather than to the local authority. Much will depend on the state of the proceedings – the later the proceedings the more likely it is that the judge will have knowledge of the parties and insight built up over the course of previous hearings (para [27]). Where the CFR's suspicions are raised by an interview with the child alone or by a home visit he must exercise an independent professional judgment. There may be circumstances in which the decision will be to go immediately to the judge. Alternatively, his instinct may be to go to the social services without delay. As a matter of practice the exercise of his discretion cannot be fettered by any rule requiring prior referral to the court. Any such referral to the local authority should be reported to the judge at the earliest convenient opportunity to enable the judge, who controls the proceedings, to consider the impact of the development and the need for consequential directions. Any decision to suspend an inquiry must be that of the judge and not the CFR (paras [38], [43]).

Extent of prohibition on disclosure—Unless he is listed in r 4.23(1), covered by r 4.23(3) or specific leave is given, a person can neither be given a copy of any document held by the court nor be allowed to see it. Note that the extent of prohibition on disclosure has been altered by the new words added to the end of r 4.23(1) and annotated above under "**except as is necessary in the course of the preparation of the case**". Clearly the provision governs how the court staff handle documents in their possession; it also restricts how legal advisers and others deal with copies that they have. For example, it is not permitted, without leave of the judge or district judge, to disclose copies of any documents held by the court to a medical expert for his use in preparing a report. In order to ensure the confidentiality of welfare reports, the practice is for each report to be endorsed with a warning that it must not be shown nor its contents revealed to any person other than a party or a legal adviser to a party (see *Practice Direction of 24 February 1984*, which applies in the High Court and which has been followed in the lower courts).

In *Re W (Disclosure to Police)* [1998] 2 FLR 135, CA, the ambit of r 4.23 was considered. The mother had made an admission to social workers which was written down by them in their notes and also in an assessment report which was filed with the court in the care proceedings. The Court of Appeal held that the only document protected by r 4.23 was the assessment report; the working papers were not within the ambit of the rule nor were they protected from disclosure by Administration of Justice Act 1960, s 12. However, they were protected by the principles of confidentiality and public interest immunity. In so far as disclosure by the local authority to the police and other agencies involved in child protection was concerned, the local authority must comply with the procedures in "Working Together" which sets out a policy of free exchange of information between agencies where it is necessary for the protection of children.

The restricted approach to r 4.23 taken in *Re W* is in line with *Re G (Social Worker: Disclosure)* [1996] 1 FLR 276, CA. There the local authority wished to disclose to the police any information they may obtain from the parents about injuries to their child. It was held that they did not need leave of the court to disclose information imparted to a social worker and recorded in case notes or a report which for one reason or another never reached the court. Ward J in *Oxfordshire CC v P (a Minor)* [1995] 1 FLR 552, FD and Hale J in *Cleveland CC v F* [1995] 1 FLR 797 were in error in considering that r 4.23 extended to oral statements made by a parent to a social worker.

It is difficult to say, given the relatively short resume of facts given in the case, whether *Re M (Disclosure)* [1998] 1 FLR 734 represents a slightly different point of view from the Court of Appeal from that expressed in *Re W* and *Re G*. In *Re M*, experts were instructed in care proceedings to investigate the circumstances surrounding the deaths of earlier children in the family. In relation to the child who was the subject of the proceedings, the mother made admissions as to her responsibility for bizarre things that had happened to the child. Thorpe LJ appears to have accepted that before disclosing the mother's statement of responsibility and the developing expertise to the child protection conference, the local authority needed leave under AJA 1960, s 12(1)(*a*) and r 4.23. He found the judge to have erred in giving leave for disclosure to the police alone and not to the relevant National Health Trust because it might alert them to a possible negligence action against them. He stressed the importance of the fullest co-operation between the family justice system and the child protection conference and substituted leave without restrictions involving the Health Trust.

The position of a children's guardian or a children and family reporter appears to be different from the position of a social worker. *Re W* is concerned solely with documents held by and information known to social workers and the court expressly said that its decision has no application to the wholly different position of a children's guardian or a children and family reporter. The guardian's position was also distinguished from that of the local authority in *Re G* and the court commented that it may be more restricted and it might be, though no concluded view was expressed, that leave is required for the disclosure of all documents emanating from or information given to the guardian. In *Oxfordshire CC v P* (above), Ward J held that information collected by a children's guardian in the course of investigations for her report was confidential; she should not, without leave, have given a statement to the police concerning the mother's admission to her that she had caused injuries to her baby. This will not, however, prevent disclosure by the guardian for the purposes specifically set out in r 4.23(3).

In *Vernon v Bosley (No 2)* [1998] 1 FLR 304, CA, r 4.23 was said not to prevent the disclosure of the existence of documents in family proceedings but to prevent "the disclosure of their contents without leave".

A local authority (whose ambit will always embrace various different departments and operations) should be particularly careful in deciding to whom within its establishment it may show copies of court documents without leave; in *Re C (Minors) (Guardian ad Litem: Disclosure of Report)* [1996] 1 FLR 61, FD, the local authority (which had been a party to care proceedings) was held to be wrong in its contention that it did not need leave to show the report of the children's guardian, after the conclusion of the proceedings, to a family centre which formed part of its social services department and was going to treat the children. The principle of confidentiality must be strictly preserved. As the family centre embraced a number of people, the court would need to investigate, in considering a leave application, to whom in particular it was desired that the report should be shown.

Although an application by a solicitor to reveal knowledge acquired in the course of care proceedings in criminal proceedings in which he was also acting did not fall strictly within r 4.23, leave was required and an application in accordance with the rule might be the best way to seek it (*Re A (Criminal Proceedings: Disclosure)* [1996] 1 FLR 221, CA). An alternative would be an application under Administration of Justice Act 1960, s 12 or the inherent jurisdiction.

"**Disclosure of documents prepared by an officer of the service**" (r 4.23(3))—This sub-rule is amended by the Family Proceedings (Amendment) Rules 2001. An "officer of the service" has the same meaning as in the Criminal Justice and Court Services Act 2000 which established the Children and Family Court Advisory and Support Service ("CAFCASS"). The new names for the different professional duties undertaken by officers are set out in the annotation under CJCSA 2000, s 11. The sub-rule applies to documents prepared by an officer of the service (as defined in r 1.2(1)) when disclosure is to be for one of the two purposes set out therein. The purpose of the new provisions is to allow disclosure of documents to the Magistrates' Courts Service Inspectorate in the course of their Children and Family Court Advisory and Support Service (CAFCASS) duties under CJCSA 2000, s 17. It also allows disclosure of documents where this would assist an officer of the service to perform any of his functions.

Leave under r 4.23(1)—When determining whether to grant an application for leave under r 4.23, the court has to carry out a balancing exercise. In *Re L (Police Investigation: Privilege)* [1996] 1 FLR 731, the House of Lords endorsed (at 741G) the "careful review", carried out by the Master of the Rolls in the Court of Appeal (see [1995] 1 FLR 999 at 1016D et seq), of a number of cases concerning disclosure of documents. The discretion to order or refuse disclosure must be exercised judicially. Many factors are potentially relevant, depending on the facts. Where material has come into existence in the course of proceedings to determine, whether in wardship or under the Children Act, how the welfare of the child will be best served, it is plain that consideration of the welfare of the child will be a major factor in the exercise of the discretion:

> "if disclosure will promote the welfare of the child, it will readily be ordered; if disclosure will not affect the welfare of the child, other considerations are likely to carry the day one way or the other; if disclosure will prejudice the welfare of the child, [it] may nevertheless be ordered if there are potent reasons for [it], but the court will be much more reluctant to make the order. It is plain that the public interest in the fair administration of justice, and the right of a criminal defendant to defend himself, are accepted as potent reasons for disclosure. If, on the other hand, it could be shown that disclosure would for some reason be unfair or oppressive to a party to the wardship or Children Act proceedings, that would weigh against an order for disclosure." (*Re L* (CA) at 1019C).

In *S CC v B* [2000] 2 FLR 161, Charles J considered a case in which there were care proceedings and also criminal charges arising out of an injury to the child concerned. The father proposed to instruct different experts in each set of proceedings. The children's guardian and the local authority sought disclosure of the identity of the experts in the criminal proceedings and their reports and notes in order to ensure that the court had all the relevant material and to gain access to any more detailed or inconsistent accounts they might contain of the circumstances of the injury. The father claimed privilege relying on *R v Derby Magistrates' Court ex parte B* [1996] AC 487. The guardian relied on *Re L* (above) and the duty in family cases to disclose all relevant material concerning the welfare of the child and contested the existence of privilege. Charles J held that the father's claim to privilege prevailed for a number of detailed reasons, including:

(1) the *Derby* case (above) establishes that where legal professional privilege attaches to material, it is absolute;
(2) although the decision in the *Derby* case (above) relates only to communications between solicitors and clients, the effect of the decision is not so confined. Legal professional privilege applies to both communications between the father and his solicitor for receiving advice as to and preparing his defence in the criminal proceedings and direct or indirect communications between the father and the medical experts instructed for the same purposes;
(3) nothing in *Re L* (above) prevents the father from asserting legal professional privilege in the Children Act proceedings in respect of his communications (direct or indirect) with the medical experts instructed in the criminal proceedings or in respect of their reports, nor does it mean he has only a qualified right to assert that the material should not be disclosed in the Children Act proceedings;
(4) although there is a high duty of full and frank disclosure in proceedings in the Family Division concerning the welfare of children, the existence of that duty does not override the right of a party to the proceedings to claim legal professional privilege which arises in, or in connection with, other proceedings;
(5) as a witness or potential witness should not volunteer material covered by legal professional privilege and should not be compelled by the court to provide it unless he has the consent of the person who has the benefit of the privilege, the father could refuse to disclose the names of his criminal case experts and should not be ordered to do so.

Applications for leave under r 4.23 can arise in many different circumstances. Applications for leave for disclosure to an expert and for disclosure to a general practitioner are dealt with in separate notes below. The following are further examples:

(*a*) **Disclosure for criminal proceedings/investigation** *Re EC (Disclosure of Material)* [1996] 2 FLR 725, CA, lists matters that will be amongst those relevant on an application for disclosure to the police:
 (i) the welfare and interest of the child concerned and of other children generally;
 (ii) the maintenance of confidentiality in children cases and the importance of encouraging frankness;

(iii) the public interest in the administration of justice and the prosecution of serious crime;
(iv) the gravity of the alleged offence and the relevance of the evidence to it;
(v) the desirability of co-operation between the various agencies concerned with the welfare of children;
(vi) in cases where s 98(2) applies, the terms of the section itself, namely that the witness was not excused from answering incriminating questions and that any statement of admission would not be admissible against him in criminal proceedings; fairness to the person who had incriminated himself and any others affected by the incriminating statement would also be relevant considerations; and
(vii) any other material disclosure which has already taken place.

In *Re EC*, disclosure to the police was permitted of the medical evidence and transcripts of oral evidence given by medical witnesses at the care hearing, parts of the judgment, parts of statements made in the proceedings by the parents, and transcripts of parts of the oral evidence of the parents and other family members, even where the material was covered by CA 1989, s 98(2).

In *Re W (Disclosure to Police)* [1998] 2 FLR 135, CA, the court stressed that judges ought not to frustrate the investigation of potential crimes (which includes the dissipation of unfounded suspicions against the innocent) without good reason, even more so when the police are working alongside the social workers. There will be cases where the evidence is peripheral and the harm of giving leave will outweigh the value of the information. But the police investigations require them to put together a jigsaw of information in order to carry out their public duty. There, leave was granted in care proceedings for the police to see an assessment report setting out the mother's admission that she had harmed her child.

See also: *Re L (Police Investigation: Privilege)* [1996] 1 FLR 731, HL (disclosure to police of a medical report commissioned for the purposes of care proceedings by the mother); *Re D (Minors) (Wardship: Disclosure)* [1994] 1 FLR 346, CA (father and grandfather permitted to use wardship documents in order to establish their defence on charges of indecency); *Re A (Criminal Proceedings: Disclosure)* [1996] 1 FLR 221, CA (solicitor permitted to make limited disclosure of information which he had learned in care proceedings to defence counsel for use in criminal proceedings); *Oxfordshire County Council v L and F* [1997] 1 FLR 235, FD (disclosure of material from care proceedings to the police, children's guardian taking part in disclosure application although her locus was not clear as the care proceedings had ended); *A Chief Constable v A County Council, AB (A Child) (By His Children's Guardian SM, DH and RW)* [2002] EWHC 2198 (Fam), (unreported) LTL, 5 November 2002 Doc No C014008, Wall J (where medical evidence filed in care proceedings was disclosed to the police for use in potential criminal investigations into the deaths of two young children). In *A Chief Constable* (above) the judgment of Wall J contains an important summary of the principles to be applied in disclosure applications and gives guidance as to the appropriate legal advice to be given by lawyers to parents who are subject to investigation into allegations of child abuse.

In determining whether incriminating material should be disclosed to the police, fairness to the person incriminating himself and others, and the dangers of oppression, are material considerations for the court in family proceedings (*Re M (Care Proceedings: Disclosure: Human Rights)* [2001] 2 FLR 1316 – where the court refused an application by the police for a written admission by the mother in care proceedings of her responsibility for injuries to the child concerned; bearing in mind the mother's admission was crucial to the court's determination of what happened, and also the element of compulsion in her giving oral evidence, it was held to be unfair to the mother to disclose it; there was a danger of oppression in the use that would be made of it).

(*b*) **Disclosure for civil proceedings** *Re Manda (Wardship: Disclosure of Evidence)* [1993] 1 FLR 205 (former ward permitted to disclose wardship papers to experts for purpose of a potential negligence claim against local authority and others) and see *Vernon v Bosley No 2* [1998] 1 FLR 304 in which the whole question of disclosure of family documents in civil proceedings was considered at length.

(*c*) **Disclosure for immigration proceedings** *Re F (A Minor) (Disclosure: Immigration)* [1994] 2 FLR 958 (Children Act statements released for immigration proceedings).

(*d*) **Disclosure for allied children proceedings** *W v Wakefield City Council* [1995] 1 FLR 170, FD (children's guardian's report in public law proceedings made available to court hearing allied private law proceedings and parties in those proceedings).

(*e*) **Disclosure for future therapy** *Re C (Guardian ad Litem: Disclosure of Report)* [1996] 1 FLR 61 (disclosure of children's guardian's report to local authority family centre which was going to treat the children).

(*f*) **Disclosure to the General Medical Council** *A County Council v W and Others* [1997] 1 FLR 574 (doctor found to have sexually abused his daughter; documents from care proceedings disclosed to GMC so they could decide whether to take action); *Re A (Disclosure* *of Medical Records to the GMC)* [1998] 2 FLR 641, FD (GMC investigating following criticism by judge of medical evidence in a case involving a child and wanting disclosure of documents from the court file; procedure on disclosure application considered).

(*g*) **Disclosure to probation service** *Re R (Disclosure)* [1998] 1 FLR 433 (Official Solicitor's report and psychiatrist's report on probation officer involved as a party in private law proceedings disclosed to the father's chief probation officer).

(*h*) **Disclosure to child protection case conference** See *Re W (Disclosure to Police)* [1998] 2 FLR 135, CA and *Re M (Disclosure)* [1998] 1 FLR 734 noted under **Extent of prohibition on disclosure**.

(*i*) **Disclosure by local authorities and/or police to alert others to risk to children in general** *Re V (Sexual Abuse: Disclosure)*; *Re L (Sexual Abuse: Disclosure)* [1999] 1 FLR 267, CA (not appropriate to allow local authorities to be given leave to disclose findings of sexual impropriety made in care proceedings to, in one case, another local authority and, in the other, the area Youth Football League, though the court recognised that there may be occasions when a local authority has a duty to pass on information about abuse and abusers to other local authorities, for example when children who are at risk move to another local authority area or when the local authority is responding to enquiries from another authority who are conducting enquiries into a possible abuser). In *Re C (Disclosure: Sexual Abuse Findings)* [2002] EWHC 234 (Fam), [2002] 2 FLR 375 the local authority and the police were given leave to disclose a copy of the judge's findings in care proceedings, that C had sexually abused children and was a paedophile who posed a considerable risk to any child, to C's current landlord (but not to future landlords at that stage). In *R (J and P) v West Sussex County Council and Wiltshire County Council* [2002] EWHC 1143 (Admin), [2002] 2 FLR 1192, QBD, Sullivan J, the local authority's decision to disclose to the mother of four children the fact that the maternal grandmother's partner was a Schedule 1 offender (having been convicted of indecent assault on his stepdaughter) was upheld on an application for judicial review.

(*j*) **Disclosure to victims** In *Re X (Disclosure of Information)* [2001] 2 FLR 440, X was found to have sexually abused the two children who were the subject of the proceedings and also four other people. Leave was given to disclose the findings to the four non-parties, their mothers, social workers, legal advisers and the CICB. The main purpose was to show the victims that their evidence had been accepted, to support therapy and to support compensation claims.

(*k*) **Disclosure for possible disciplinary proceedings** In *A Health Authority v X and Others* [2001] EWCA Civ 2014, [2002] 1 FLR 1045, CA, a health authority sought an order for the production of specified case papers and the GP records of two named individuals who had been involved in public law care proceedings, with a view to possible disciplinary proceedings; the application was allowed subject to express conditions.

(*l*) **Disclosure by the children's guardian to police and local authorities** In *Re D & M (Disclosure: Private Law)* (unreported), LTL 20/12/2002, Doc No AC0104335, Hedley J held that where a father had been granted contact with his daughters and it had subsequently emerged that he had been engaged in an unlawful sexual relationship with his half-sister, that information could only be disclosed by the guardian to the police and social services with the court's permission. Confidentiality attaching to the information of the criminality belongs to the court and not to the guardian so that the guardian's report and other documents are covered by r 4.23; this includes any information obtained in preparing the report. In this case the disclosure of the evidence to the police was not authorised by the court, although the guardian was permitted to reveal the information to the local authorities in the areas in which the children and the father resided, on terms that neither local authority made any further disclosure.

Leave for disclosure to expert—Applications for leave may frequently be motivated by the desire of a party to obtain an expert's report on a particular aspect of the case, for example a report from a child psychiatrist on the merits of continuing contact with a child or a report from a paediatrician on allegations of sexual abuse. If it is intended that the child himself should be examined as part of the expert's investigation, an application for leave under r 4.23(1) will have to be coupled with an application for leave under r 4.18. An application for leave under this rule alone may however be appropriate where the party seeks an expert's preliminary assessment, which may include his opinion that an examination of the child is appropriate or necessary; such an assessment may then be used to support an application under r 4.18. Alternatively, where a party acknowledges that it would be inappropriate for the child to be subjected to medical examination, an application under this rule could stand alone with a view to a report being obtained based solely on the papers in the case. For further guidance as to instructing experts and leave applications related thereto, see under r 4.18.

Leave for disclosure to general practitioner—Consideration needs to be given to obtaining leave for medical reports prepared for children proceedings to be released to the child's GP to assist in treatment of the child and to provide important information to be included in the child's medical records. The primary responsibility rests with those who have parental responsibility for the child, but the question also needs to be addressed by the children's guardian or children and family reporter or by the court itself. See further the *Children Act Advisory Committee Annual Report 1994/95*, p 33 et seq.

Principles governing applications for disclosure—The general principles governing applications for disclosure in family proceedings are discussed in detail in **Submission of evidence** under r 4.14.

Disclosure – impact of the European Convention for Human Rights and Fundamental Freedoms 1950—It is essential that a parent be placed in a position where he may obtain access to information which is relied on by the authorities in taking measures of protective care (*TP and KM v United Kingdom* [2001] 2 FLR 549). *TP and KM v UK* (above) established that a parent may claim an interest in being informed of the nature and extent of abuse sustained by his child, although there can be no absolute right to view, for example, videos of interviews. Nevertheless, the potential importance of such interviews renders it necessary for careful consideration to be given to whether they should be disclosed to the parents. The local authority may reasonably not be regarded by a parent as being able to approach the issue with objectivity. The ECHR held that the question of whether crucial material should be disclosed should, therefore, not be decided by the local authority or the medical authority responsible for the medical professional who conducted it. It should not be the sole responsibility of the parent, or lie at his initiative, to obtain the evidence on which a decision to remove his child is based. The positive obligation on the contracting state to protect the interests of the family requires that this material be made available to the parent concerned, even in the absence of any request by the parent. If there are doubts as to whether this poses a risk to the welfare of the child, the matter should be submitted to the court at the earliest stage possible in the proceedings for it to resolve the issues involved. A failure by the authority to submit such an issue to the court for determination may deprive a party of an adequate involvement in the decision-making process concerning the care of the child and thereby the requisite protection of their interests and may thus amount to a breach of Art 8 (the right to respect for private and family life) (as was the case in *TP and KM v United Kingdom* (above)).

The entitlement to a fair trial under Art 6 is absolute, but that does not mean an absolute and unqualified right on the part of the parents to see all the documents in care proceedings concerning their children (*Re B (Disclosure to Other Parties)* [2001] 2 FLR 1017). Since the HRA 1998, it is no longer the case that the only interests capable of denying a litigant access to documents are the interests of the children concerned. The interests of anyone else who is involved, whether as victim, party or witness, and who can demonstrate that his Art 8 rights are sufficiently engaged, are also relevant (*Re B* (above)). It was held in *Re B* (above) that although the litigant is prima facie entitled, under Art 6, to disclosure of all materials that might be taken into account by the court, the Art 8 rights of the parents, as well as of the children, must be afforded due respect. Consequently, a limited qualification of the right to see the documents may be appropriate if directed towards that clear and proper objective. Non-disclosure must be limited to what the situation demands, and is justified only when the case is compelling or strictly necessary, with the court being rigorous in its examination of the feared harm and any difficulty caused to the litigant, counter-balanced by procedures designed to ensure a fair trial (see *Re B* (above) – where the harm that would be suffered by disclosure would be wholly disproportionate to any legitimate forensic purpose served). See also *Re R (Care: Disclosure: Nature of Proceedings)* [2002] 1 FLR 755 which reinforces the approach of Munby J to disclosure and *Re C* [2002] LTL, 9 April 2002 – Doc No C0102987 (discussed in more detail at **Public interest immunity** under r 4.17).

The local authority when seeking to take a child into care, is under a heavy obligation to ensure that the procedure at all stages is transparent and fair, both in and out of court. In particular, it is vital that a litigant has a proper opportunity in care proceedings to examine and comment on experts' reports and other documents being considered by the court and to cross-examine witnesses interviewed and relied on therein (*Re L (Care: Assessment: Fair Trial)* [2002] EWHC 1379 (Fam), [2002] 2 FLR 730). See also *Re B (Disclosure to other parties)* [2001] 2 FLR 1017 (referred to in the paragraph above) and *Re R (Care: Disclosure: Nature of Proceedings)* [2002] 1 FLR 755 and *Re C* [2002] LTL, 9 April 2002 – Doc No C0102987 which are discussed further in **Public interest immunity** under r 4.17. In *Re L* (above), Munby J set out guidelines in relation to the conduct and recording of meetings and the provision of documents in care proceedings:

1 Social workers should, as soon as ever practicable:

(*a*) Notify parents of material criticisms of and deficits in their parenting or behaviour and of the expectations of them; and

(*b*) Advise them how they may remedy or improve their parenting or behaviour.

2 All the professionals involved (social workers, social work assistants, children's guardians, expert witnesses and others) should at all times keep clear, accurate, full and balanced notes of all relevant conversations and meetings between themselves and/or with parents, other family members and others involved with the family.

3 The local authority should at an early stage of the proceedings make full and frank disclosure to the other parties of all key documents in its possession or available to it, including, in particular, contact recordings, attendance notes of meetings and conversations and minutes of case conferences, core group meetings and similar meetings. Early provision should then be afforded for inspection of any of these documents. Any objection to the disclosure or inspection of any document should be notified to the parties at the earliest possible stage in the proceedings and raised with the court by the local authority without delay.

4 Social workers and guardians should routinely exhibit to their reports and statements notes of relevant meetings, conversations and incidents.

5 Where it is proposed that the social workers and/or guardian should meet with a jointly appointed or other sole expert witness instructed in the case (ie a "professionals meeting", as opposed to a meeting of experts chaired by one of the legal representatives in the case – usually the children's guardian's solicitor):

(*a*) There should be a written agenda circulated in advance to all concerned;

(*b*) Clear written notice of the meeting should be given in advance to the parents and/or their legal representative, accompanied by copies of the agenda and of all documents to be given or shown to the expert and notice of all issues relating to or criticisms of a parent, or a non-attending party, which it is intended to raise with the expert;

(*c*) The parent, or non-attending party, should have a clear opportunity to make representations to the expert prior to and/or at the meeting on the documents, issues and/or criticisms of which he or she has been given notice;

(*d*) A parent or other party, who wishes to, should have the right to attend and/or be represented at the professionals' meeting;

(*e*) Clear, accurate, full and balanced minutes of the professionals' meeting (identifying in particular what information has been given to the expert and by whom) should be taken by someone nominated for that task before the meeting begins;

(*f*) As soon as possible after the professionals' meeting the minutes should be agreed by those present as being an accurate record of the meeting and then be immediately disclosed to all parties.

However, there may be cases in which the disclosure of court papers to people directly involved in care proceedings, plus a limited class of people in close and confidential relationship with them, may be in the best interests of the children (*Re X (Disclosure of Information)* [2001] 2 FLR 440). See under sub-para (*j*) **Disclosure to victims** (above).

Procedure on leave applications—Rule 4.3 does not apply to the leave application (it is limited to applications for leave to bring proceedings). It is suggested that the directions procedure in r 4.14 should be used, and that the application for leave might be formulated in Form C2, which is appropriate for the making of an application for an order or directions in existing family proceedings.

Unopposed applications to discharge or modify orders for limited disclosure—Where there is an unopposed application to discharge or modify an order for limited disclosure, it may not be necessary for the applicant to make a formal application, with all the trouble and expense of instructing solicitors and counsel. In *A Health Authority v X (Discovery: Medical Conduct) (No 2)* [2002] EWHC 26 (Fam), [2002] 1 FLR 383, Munby J said that, whilst he was not setting out general practice guidelines on this topic, he would suggest that if the application is straightforward and unopposed then it might appropriately be made in the first instance by post or fax to the judge, and be dealt with as a paper application without the need for attendance by the parties, unless the judge otherwise directs. It would be a matter for the applicant to decide what papers he should lodge with the judge, but if the matter was to be dealt with as a paper application, at a minimum the judge would expect to receive: (i) a draft of the precise order which the court is being invited to make; (ii) a short witness statement explaining why the application is being made; and (iii) letters showing that the application is not opposed.

Direction that statements remain confidential—In *Cleveland County Council v F* [1995] 1 FLR 797, FD (which must now be read subject to subsequent authorities such as *Re G (Social*

Worker: Disclosure) [1996] 1 FLR 276, CA and *Re W (Disclosure to Police)* [1998] 2 FLR 135, CA), it was held that the court had power to direct that statements that might be made by the mother in care proceedings to a party to the case or their representative or to the children's guardian should remain confidential and should not be disclosed to anyone other than a party or the court. Any such direction could not bind (although it may influence) future judges in the exercise of their discretion in any subsequent application for the disclosure of the evidence. In this case, however, the court declined to give such a direction.

Departing from an expert's opinion—See under r 4.21.

"direction under section 37(1) to the authority concerned" (r 4.23(2))—Under CA 1989, s 37(1), the court may require a local authority to investigate the circumstances of a child where a question as to his welfare arises in family proceedings and it appears that it may be appropriate for there to be a care or supervision order. Local authorities do not feature in the list of those entitled to disclosure of documents as of right but may receive notification of a s 37(1) direction under r 23(2). Rule 4.26 deals further with s 37 directions and provides, inter alia, for service on the authority of copies of such documentary evidence as the court directs.

4.24 Notification of consent

(1) Consent for the purposes of –

(*a*) section 16(3), or
(*b*) section 38A(2)(*b*)(ii) or 44A(2)(*b*)(ii), or
(*c*) paragraph 19(3)(*c*) or (*d*) of Schedule 2,

shall be given either –

(i) orally in court, or
(ii) in writing to the court signed by the person giving his consent.

(2) Any written consent given for the purposes of subsection (2) of section 38A or section 44A, shall include a statement that the person giving consent –

(*a*) is able and willing to give to the child the care which it would be reasonable to expect a parent to give him; and
(*b*) understands that the giving of consent could lead to the exclusion of the relevant person from the dwelling-house in which the child lives.

Amendments—SI 1997/1893.

Defined terms—"court": r 1.2(1).

Scope of provision—This rule sets out the procedure for signifying consent in certain cases under CA 1989. It does not apply to all consents that are required under the Act, only to those specified.

"section 16(3)" (r 4.24(*a*))—CA 1989, s 16(3) requires that every person to be named in a family assistance order, other than the child, must consent to the making of that order.

"section 38A(2)(*b*)(ii) or 44A(2)(*b*)(ii)" (r 4.24(1)(*b*))—CA 1989, s 38A(2)(*b*)(ii) requires that a person (whether a parent or some other person) who is willing and able to care for a child at home, where the child is subject to an interim care order, must consent to the inclusion of an exclusion order in the interim care order in respect of the person who is putting the child at risk. Similarly CA 1989, s 44A(2)(*b*)(ii) requires that a person (whether a parent or some other person) who is willing and able to care for a child at home, where the child is the subject of an emergency protection order, must consent to the inclusion in that order of an exclusion order in respect of the person who is putting the child at risk.

"paragraph 19(3)(c) or (d) of Schedule 2" (r 4.24(*b*))—CA 1989, Sch 2, para 19(3)(*c*) requires the consent of a child in care to living in a country outside England and Wales. Paragraph 19(3)(*d*) requires the consent of every person who has parental responsibility for a child in care to the child living in a country outside England and Wales.

"orally in court" (r 4.24(i))—Bearing in mind the definition of "court" in r 1.2(1), oral consent must be given before a judge or district judge. There is no requirement that the consent should be given in evidence, so it appears that the person giving consent need not be sworn. Indeed, where the person who is consenting orally is represented by a lawyer, it is likely to be the general practice that the legal representative will tell the court of the consent rather than the person himself who will simply confirm what has been said. Strictly speaking, r 4.20, which requires the noting of oral evidence, does not therefore apply, nor are there any other provisions of the rules which require a note to be made of the giving of consent, but it is quite plain that such a note will have to be taken by the court.

Written consent (r 4.24(ii))—There is no prescribed form of written consent; the only guidance in the rules is that the consent should be signed by the person consenting. Clearly, as well as identifying the consenting party and including the signed (and dated) consent, the document must identify the child and the provision under which the consent is given and must refer to any order or proceedings that are relevant (such as the family proceedings where the consent is given under CA 1989, s 16, or the care order where the consent is given under Sch 2, para 19), giving the number thereof. However, r 4.24(2) does stipulate certain matters that must be included in the written consent to be given under CA 1989, ss 38A(2) and 44A(2).

Where the making of a court order depends on the giving of consent—The giving of consent is a condition precedent to the making of a family assistance order under CA 1989, s 16(3) and also the inclusion of an exclusion requirement in an interim care order or emergency protection order (CA 1989, ss 38A(1) and 44A(1)). Although the prescribed form of family assistance order does not require it, it is therefore suggested that, for the avoidance of doubt, the order should recite the requisite consents and state whether they were given orally or in writing. The same should also be done where the court gives approval under Sch 2, para 19(1). Form C23 and Form C33 provide for the recital of the requisite consents for the inclusion of an exclusion requirement in an emergency protection order and an interim care order.

4.24A Exclusion requirements: interim care orders and emergency protection orders

(1) This rule applies where the court includes an exclusion requirement in an interim care order or an emergency protection order.

(2) The applicant for an interim care order or emergency protection order shall –

(*a*) prepare a separate statement of the evidence in support of the application for an exclusion requirement;

(*b*) serve the statement personally on the relevant person with a copy of the order containing the exclusion requirement (and of any power of arrest which is attached to it);

(*c*) inform the relevant person of his right to apply to vary or discharge the exclusion requirement.

(3) Where a power of arrest is attached to an exclusion requirement in an interim care order or an emergency protection order, a copy of the order shall be delivered to the officer for the time being in charge of the police station for the area in which the dwelling-house in which the child lives is situated (or of such other station as the court may specify) together with a statement showing that the relevant person has been served with the order or informed of its terms (whether by being present when the order was made or by telephone or otherwise).

(4) Rules 3.9(5), 3.9A (except paragraphs (1) and (3)) and 3.10 shall apply, with the necessary modifications, for the service, variation, discharge and enforcement of any exclusion requirement to which a power of arrest is attached as they apply to an order made on an application under Part IV of the Family Law Act 1996.

(5) The relevant person shall serve the parties to the proceedings with any application which he makes for the variation or discharge of the exclusion requirement.

(6) Where an exclusion requirement ceases to have effect whether –

(*a*) as a result of the removal of a child under section 38A(10) or 44A(10),

(*b*) because of the discharge of the interim care order or emergency protection order, or

(*c*) otherwise,

the applicant shall inform –

(i) the relevant person,

(ii) the parties to the proceedings

(iii) any officer to whom a copy of the order was delivered under paragraph (3), and

(iv) (where necessary) the court.

(7) Where the court includes an exclusion requirement in an interim care order or an emergency protection order of its own motion, paragraph (2) shall apply with the omission of any reference to the statement of the evidence.

Amendments—Inserted by SI 1997/1893.

Defined terms—"applicant/application": r 4.1(1); "care order": CA 1989, ss 31(11), 105(1); "child": r 4.1(1); "court": r 1.2(1); "emergency protection order": r 4.1(1); "exclusion requirement": CA 1989, s 38A(3); "relevant person": CA 1989, s 38A(2)(*a*).

Applicant for interim care order or emergency protection order (r 4.24A(2))—The applicant in the case of an interim care order will generally be the local authority (or other authorised person) who has made the original application under CA 1989, s 31(1). Section 38 gives the court power to make an interim care order where the care/supervision proceedings are adjourned. Section 38 also gives the court power to make an interim care order where it gives a direction under s 37(1) for the local authority to investigate the child's circumstances. It is not clear who is the applicant for the purpose of r 4.24A(2) in such a situation or, indeed, whether there is one at all. It may be that this is unlikely to cause a problem given that it is difficult to foresee the court being in a position to incorporate an exclusion requirement anyway at such an early stage. If the court did consider such a course appropriate, it could act of its own motion in including the requirement, in which case r 4.24A(7) would dispense with the need for a statement of the evidence.

The applicant in the case of an emergency protection order can be any person (s 44(1)) though it is most likely to be a local authority.

Separate statement of evidence (r 4.24A(2))—The applicant will already have completed forms with regard to the application for an interim care order/emergency protection order. The statement of evidence in support of the exclusion requirement must be separate. There is no prescribed form. Reference must be made to the provisions of CA 1989, s 38A or 44A and in particular to the conditions for the inclusion of an exclusion requirement which are set out in ss 38A(2) and 44A(2). The question of the ability of another person living in the home to care for the child and the consent of that person to the exclusion requirement (ss 38A(2)(*b*) and 44A(2)(*b*)) will no doubt be covered in the statement but it should be noted that it is also the subject of a separate procedural rule, r 4.24. Best practice in respect of the separate statement of evidence to be served in support of an application for an exclusion requirement demands that the statement should:

(1) be separate and self-standing;

(2) set out in a concise form the factual material upon which the applicant relies;

(3) state the statutory requirements for obtaining an exclusion order, under CA 1989, s 38A(2) (for interim care orders) or s 44A(2) (for emergency protection orders), in particular the relevant subsections, with a summary of the evidence in support; and

(4) make it clear that the exclusion requirement sought is a requirement that a particular person should leave the dwelling-house in which the child is living, and/or prohibit the person from entering the dwelling house in which the child is living, and/or exclude the person from a defined area surrounding the dwelling-house in which the child is living (*Re W (Exclusion: Statement of Evidence)* [2000] 2 FLR 666).

If the court orders an exclusion requirement of its own motion, in the absence of the relevant person, it will usually be appropriate for the court to direct that a concise statement be prepared of the evidence led at the hearing, with the other matters set out above, to be served personally on the relevant person. If the hearing was before justices then it will be desirable also to serve their findings and reasons on the relevant person. This will ensure that he receives the appropriate information to allow him to make an application to vary or discharge the order. If the person was present in court and heard the evidence led against him, the court might, in appropriate circumstances, disapply any requirements as to service of the relevant statement. It is not necessary to make a specific application for an exclusion requirement under the Rules and therefore no separate application form is necessary; the question of exclusion is simply ancillary to the application for an interim care order or emergency protection order. The consent of the other person living in the dwelling-house can be given either orally in court or in writing, signed by that person; written consent should provide the necessary details of the person able and willing to give the child the care which it would be reasonable to expect a parent to give, and it should state that that person understood that the giving of consent could lead to the exclusion of the relevant person from the dwelling-house in which the child was living. Once the appropriate statement has been served, it will not be necessary at subsequent renewals of the order to serve the separate statement again, unless there has been a further hearing, and the grounds have changed (*Re W* (above)).

Serve on relevant person (r 4.24A(2))—The "relevant person" is the person who is excluded. It is interesting to note that service on this person of the supporting statement is only required once an order has been made; there is no specific requirement that he be given advance notice that there is a question of such a provision being included and there has not been an amendment of App 3 to cater for exclusion requirements. The "relevant person" may be a party to the proceedings in any event. Even if not, he is likely to know of the possibility of an exclusion requirement being imposed because an approach will have been made to another person living in the home in order to ensure that the requisite consent etc will be forthcoming for CA 1989, s 38A(2)(*b*) or 44A(2)(*b*). It remains to be seen to what extent the courts consider it appropriate to join as a party a relevant person, who is not a party, for the purpose of arguing the issue of an exclusion requirement or perhaps to allow him or her to intervene for this limited purpose without becoming a party. It may be that the relevant person will be excluded from the home almost summarily and then left to rely upon his or her right to seek a variation or discharge of the order under s 39(3A) and (3B) or s 45(8A) and (8B).

"inform the relevant person of his right to apply to vary or discharge" (r 4.24A(2)(*c*))—The rules do not say whether the "relevant person" should be informed orally or in writing. Given that personal service of the statement and order is required, it would seem sensible for the information to be given orally at the time of service but for the documents also to be accompanied by a written notice of the right to apply to vary or discharge. Where the exclusion requirement is included in an interim care order, the right to seek variation/discharge is contained in CA 1989, s 39(3A) (with regard to the exclusion requirement itself) and s 39(3B) (with regard to any attendant power of arrest). For an emergency protection order, the relevant provisions are s 45(8A) and (8B).

Power of arrest (r 4.24A(3))—If a power of arrest is attached to an order, the *President's Direction of 17 December 1997 (Children Act 1989: Exclusion Requirement)* requires that, unless the person to whom the exclusion requirement refers was given notice of the hearing and attended it, the name of that person and the fact that an order has been made including an exclusion requirement to which a power of arrest has been attached shall be announced in open court at the earliest opportunity. Note that, by virtue of r 4.24A(3), a copy of an order including a power of arrest is only to be delivered to the police station once the relevant person is aware of its terms. This may be because he was present when it was made or because he has subsequently been told about it or service has been effected.

Rules 3.9(5) etc (r 4.24A(4))—Rule 3.9(5) dictates service of a copy of any order by the court where the applicant is acting in person and requests this. Rule 3.9A deals with enforcement of orders which have powers of arrest attached, including also the duty to inform the police where an order with a power of arrest is subsequently varied or discharged. Rule 3.10 deals with bail after arrest. Family Law Act 1996, Pt IV contains the provisions dealing with family homes and domestic violence.

Application for variation/discharge (r 4.24A(5))—Rule 4.4 would seem to apply given that the relevant person is making "an application". There does not appear to be a notice period for the variation/discharge application. The periods set out in App 3 for discharge applications under ss 39 and 45 do not apply as they refer specifically to certain subsections of ss 39 and 45 but do not mention s 39(3A) or 45(8A). Presumably, in the absence of any specific form, Form C2 should be used for the relevant person's application. The parties to the proceedings who have to be served will be the parties to the care proceedings or to the emergency protection order application as appropriate. This may not include the person who is caring for the child in the absence of the relevant person but common sense dictates that he or she is likely to be affected by any discharge or variation and ought to be notified of the application. Indeed, it may be that the court will consider it desirable that when an exclusion requirement is included in reliance upon care to be delivered by someone who is not presently a party to the proceedings, that person should be joined so that he or she is entitled to be kept aware of developments and to make representations. Alternatively, he or she may be eligible for notice under App 3, column (iv) *All applications* as a person "who [is] caring for the child at the time when the proceedings are commenced".

Parties to the proceedings (r 4.24A(6)(*c*)(ii))—This phrase refers to the parties to the care proceedings or emergency protection proceedings, depending on the type of order to which the exclusion requirement was attached. This may not include the person caring for the child in the absence of the excluded person but it would seem necessary to inform him or her as well.

"(where necessary) the court" (r 4.24A(6)(*c*)(iv))—It is suggested that it would be sensible to inform the court as a matter of course.

4.25 Secure accommodation – evidence

In proceedings under section 25, the court shall, if practicable, arrange for copies of all written reports before it to be made available before the hearing to –

(*a*) the applicant;
(*b*) the parent or guardian of the child;
(*c*) any legal representative of the child;
(*d*) the children's guardian; and
(*e*) the child, unless the court otherwise directs;

and copies of such reports may, if the court considers it desirable, be shown to any person who is entitled to notice of the proceedings in accordance with these rules.

Amendments—SI 2001/821.

Defined terms—"applicant", "child": r 4.1(1); "court": r 1.2(1); "guardian": CA 1989, s 103; "children's guardian": r 4.1(1).

"proceedings under section 25"—CA 1989, s 25 concerns the use of secure accommodation and must be read in conjunction with the Children (Secure Accommodation) Regulations 1991 and the Children (Secure Accommodation) (No 2) Regulations 1991. The regulations provide that a local authority wishing to keep a child in secure accommodation for more than 72 hours in any 28-day period must seek authority from the court (Children (Secure Accommodation) Regulations 1991, reg 10(1)).

"parent" (r 4.25(*b*))—This term is not defined in the rules or CA 1989 (see **Meaning of "parent"** under CA 1989, s 10).

"any person entitled to notice in accordance with these rules"—See r 4.4 and App 3 for the persons so entitled.

Copies of reports—There appears to be a distinction between those persons listed in r 4.25(*a*)–(*e*) and persons who are simply entitled to notice in accordance with the rules. The former must have copies of reports made available to them if practicable, whereas the latter are allowed only sight of the reports, and then only if the court considers it desirable.

Form of application—Part IV applies to secure accommodation proceedings, which must therefore be started in accordance with r 4.4. The prescribed forms are Form C1 and supplementary Form C20. Form C1 requires the applicant to give the name and date of birth of the child concerned, to identify himself and to give details of his relationship to the child. The form requires details of: any other proceedings which concern the child; the respondents to the application; other persons to whom notice is to be given; the present arrangements for the care of the child; any involvement with the child by Social Services; the arrangements for the health and education of the child; the identity of the child's parents; the family of the child, ie siblings etc;

and other adults who live at the child's address. The applicant must then fill in the supplementary Form C20 in which he is required to set out the grounds for the application, the reasons for applying and the length of order applied for. Copies of reports or other documentary evidence on which the applicant relies should be enclosed with the prescribed forms, together with details as to the dates and authors of the documents. The respondents and the persons who are to receive notice of the proceedings are set out in App 3 in the normal way and all the usual provisions as to evidence, the hearing and so on apply.

An application for remand in secure accommodation may also be made in criminal proceedings under Children and Young Persons Act 1969, s 25.

Hearsay—Proceedings under CA 1989, s 25 are "family proceedings", and hearsay evidence contained in reports and statements is admissible, although its weight will be a matter for judicial discretion (see *Oxfordshire County Council v R* [1992] 1 FLR 648).

Delay—It is essential that there should be no delay whatsoever in the hearing of a case which concerns the liberty of the subject, such as an appeal in a secure accommodation case. In any appeal from the justices in a matter of urgency, the procedure set out in *Oxfordshire County Council v R* [1992] 1 FLR 648 at 651H–652A should be followed. Thus if, when the appeal is entered in the district registry of the appropriate care centre, no High Court judge is available to hear it, it is the duty of the appellant's solicitor to make the district registry aware of the need for urgency and to invite the district registry or the district judge to list the matter at the nearest court where an early hearing can take place before a High Court judge. Where any difficulty is encountered, an application for directions can always be made to a High Court judge sitting either at the appropriate care centre or in London (*Re W (A Minor) (Secure Accommodation Order)* [1993] 1 FLR 692).

Other procedural matters—See CA 1989, s 25 and the notes to that section; see also Children (Secure Accommodation) Regulations 1991 and Children (Secure Accommodation) (No 2) Regulations 1991.

4.26 Investigation under section 37

(1) This rule applies where a direction is given to an appropriate authority by the High Court or a county court under section 37(1).

(2) On giving a direction the court shall adjourn the proceedings and the court or the proper officer shall record the direction in Form C40.

(3) A copy of the direction recorded under paragraph (2) shall, as soon as practicable after the direction is given, be served by the proper officer on the parties to the proceedings in which the direction is given and, where the appropriate authority is not a party, on that authority.

(4) When serving the copy of the direction on the appropriate authority the proper officer shall also serve copies of such of the documentary evidence which has been, or is to be, adduced in the proceedings as the court may direct.

(5) Where a local authority informs the court of any of the matters set out in section 37(3)(*a*) to (*c*) it shall do so in writing.

Amendments—SI 1994/3155.

Defined terms—"court", "proper officer": r 1.2(1).

Guidance on use of CA 1989, s 37—See *Best Practice Guidance on Section 37(1) Directions* under CA 1989, s 37, which stresses the importance of the local authority being informed as quickly as possible of a s 37 direction, and advises that an immediate telephone notification should be made, then confirmed in writing in compliance with r 4.26(3). See also *CAAC Handbook of Best Practice in Children Act cases,* App A, item IV on local authority assessments (set out in Part IV of this work as *Best Practice Guidance of June 1997*).

"appropriate authority" (r 4.26(1))—This phrase refers back to s 37; s 37(5) sets out which authority should be named in any given case.

"record the direction in Form C40" (r 4.26(2))—Form C40 constitutes a direction to a specified local authority to undertake an investigation under s 37(1) and it sets out the full name and date of birth of the child concerned. The court specifies in the order those documents which must be served on the local authority and sets down the date by which the local authority must report in writing to the court.

"parties" (r 4.26(3))—As r 4.26 does not widen the normal meaning of "parties" to the proceedings so as to include the welfare officer as a party (as does r 4.14(1) for example), it appears that the parties are simply the applicant and the respondents.

Documentary evidence which may accompany copy of direction (r 4.26(4))—Rule 4.26(4) is important because it enables the court to ensure that the local authority carrying out the investigation receives the documentary evidence that it will need to do its job properly. However, the authority does not simply have access to the whole court file; the court has a discretion as to precisely which documents should be provided and must give a direction about this when making the s 37(1) direction. The making of such a direction will count as leave, thus overriding the confidentiality provisions of r 4.23.

Service—As to service, see rr 4.8, 10.2 and 10.3.

"matters set out in section 37(3)(a) to (c)" (r 4.26(5))—Where a local authority undertakes a s 37 investigation and decides not to apply for a care or supervision order in relation to the child concerned, by virtue of s 37(3) it must inform the court of the reasons for its decision, how it has helped or intends to help the child and his family and any other action it has taken or is intending to take with respect to the child. Rule 4.26(5) ensures that this information is passed to the court in writing. There is no prescribed form and a letter or report should suffice.

Disclosure of s 37 reports—It is good practice for s 37 reports to be disclosed to the parties and for a direction to this effect to be given whenever a s 37 report is ordered (*Re CE (Section 37 Direction)* [1995] 1 FLR 26 at 48).

Other procedural matters—In *Re CE (Section 37 Direction)* [1995] 1 FLR 26, FD, Wall J recommended that the court should fix a date by which the local authority's report is to be provided and a directions appointment shortly thereafter at which the report will be considered (and the position of the children's guardian reviewed, see **"direction under section 37(1)"** under CA 1989, s 41). There is no provision in the rules for the attendance of a representative of the local authority at such a directions appointment and, in the normal run of cases, a letter accompanying the report and setting out any particular points which the local authority wishes to bring to the court's attention will suffice, although the court might see fit to invite the local authority to attend in a particular case and it would be highly unlikely that the request would be refused (*Re CE (Section 37 Direction)*, above).

4.27 Direction to local education authority to apply for education supervision order

(1) For the purposes of section 40(3) and (4) of the Education Act 1944 a direction by the High Court or a county court to a local education authority to apply for an education supervision order shall be given in writing.

(2) Where, following such a direction, a local education authority informs the court that they have decided not to apply for an education supervision order, they shall do so in writing.

Amendments—SI 1994/3155; SI 1997/1893.

Defined terms—"court": r 1.2(1); "education supervision order": CA 1989, s 36(2).

Repeal of Education Act 1944, ss 37, 39 and 40—Education Act 1944, ss 37, 39 and 40 were repealed by Education Act 1993, Sch 19, para 11, Sch 21, Pt I; those provisions of the Education Act 1993 were brought into force with effect from 1 October 1993 by SI 1993/1975. Therefore, the text of the rule above and the annotations below should be read in the light of that repeal.

Scope of provision—This rule contains procedural provisions ancillary to the power of the court under Education Act 1944, s 40 to direct a local education authority to apply for an education supervision order in relation to a child.

Direction under Education Act 1944, s 40(3) and (4)—By virtue of Education Act 1944, s 40(3), where a person is convicted of an offence under s 37 of that Act (failure to comply with a school attendance order) or is charged with an offence under s 39 (duty of parents to secure regular attendance of registered pupils), the court by which he is convicted or before which he is charged may direct the local education authority to apply for an education supervision order. Section 40(4) deals with the duty of the court, where the local education authority has applied for an education supervision order, to direct in certain circumstances that an existing school attendance order shall cease to be in force.

"education supervision order" (r 4.27(1))—Application for an education supervision order is made under CA 1989, s 36.

Direction by court to a local education authority to be in writing (r 4.27(1))—There is no prescribed form to be used by the court when directing a local education authority to apply for an education supervision order. It is suggested that Form C21 (the general form of order for directions) be used.

Notification by local education authority of intention not to apply (r 4.27(2))—There is no prescribed form to be used by the local education authority when notifying the court of its intention not to apply for an order, and none of the general forms in App 1 is appropriate. It is presumed that an explanatory letter would therefore suffice or, alternatively, that the education authority could draw up a formal document more in the nature of a pleading. The important thing is to ensure that the court can identify the case to which the written notification applies; accordingly, the document used must:

(*a*) quote the case name and number,

(*b*) give the full name and date of birth of the child, and

(*c*) refer to the court's direction to the education authority to apply for an education supervision order and give the date of it.

The decision not to apply must be clearly communicated to the court together with the reasons for it (Education Act 1944, s 40(3A)). The education authority has a duty under s 40(3B) to communicate the reasons before the end of a period of eight weeks beginning with the date on which the direction was given.

4.28 Transitional provision

Nothing in any provision of this Part of these rules shall affect any proceedings which are pending (within the meaning of paragraph 1 of Schedule 14 to the Act of 1989) immediately before these rules come into force.

PART IVA
PROCEEDINGS UNDER SECTION 30 OF THE HUMAN FERTILISATION AND EMBRYOLOGY ACT 1990

4A.1 Interpretation

(1) In this Part of these Rules –

"the 1990 Act" means the Human Fertilisation and Embryology Act 1990;

"the birth father" means the father of the child, including a person who is treated as being the father of the child by section 28 of the 1990 Act where he is not the husband within the meaning of section 30 of the 1990 Act;

"the birth mother" means the woman who carried the child;

"the birth parents" means the birth mother and the birth father;

"the husband and wife" means the persons who may apply for a parental order where the conditions set out in section 30(1) of the 1990 Act are met;

"parental order" means an order under section 30 of the 1990 Act (parental orders in favour of gamete donors) providing for a child to be treated in law as a child of the parties to a marriage.

"parental order reporter" means an officer of the service appointed under section 41 of the Children Act 1989 in relation to proceedings specified by paragraph (2).

(2) Applications under section 30 of the 1990 Act are specified proceedings for the purposes of section 41 of the Children Act 1989 in accordance with section 41(6)(i) of that Act.

Amendments—Inserted by SI 1994/2165; amended by SI 2001/821.

Defined terms—"who carried the child": HFEA 1990, s 2(3).

Scope of provision—The rules in this Part have been introduced as a result of the coming into force of HFEA 1990, s 30, which concerns the making of parental orders. They amend these rules by prescribing the procedure to be followed in relation to applications made in the High Court and the county court for a parental order and other related interlocutory applications, ie for the removal of a child from the home of a person with whom he lives; for the return of a child who has been removed, and an injunction prohibiting the removal of a child referred to in the Parental Orders (Human Fertilisation and Embryology) Regulations 1994. Separate but similar rules apply in relation to applications made in the family proceedings court.

"specified proceedings" (r 4A.1(2))—By classifying applications for a parental order as "specified proceedings", such applications are included within the categories of case in which the court must appoint a parental order reporter for the child.

PART III

4A.2 Application of Part IV

Subject to the provisions of this Part, the provisions of Part IV of these Rules shall apply as appropriate with any necessary modifications to proceedings under this Part except that rules 4.7(1), 4.9, 4.10(1)(*b*), 4.10(11), 4.11A(1), 4.11A(3) and 4.12 shall not apply.

Amendments—Inserted by SI 1994/2165; amended by SI 2001/821.

Scope of provision—The procedure laid down for public law applications concerning children is made applicable to applications under s 30, save for certain exceptions. These exceptions relate to rules regarding: (i) who should be made parties, and the form and time-limits within which the applications must be served and an answer filed, for which provision is made in the rules; (ii) the exclusion of all the provisions which provide for a solicitor to be appointed to represent the child; and (iii) the discretionary power of the court to appoint a parental order reporter. In applications under s 30, the appointment of a parental order reporter by the court is mandatory.

4A.3 Parties

The applicants shall be the husband and wife and the respondents shall be the persons set out in the relevant entry in column (iii) of Appendix 3.

Amendments—Inserted by SI 1994/2165.

4A.4 Acknowledgement

Within 14 days of the service of an application for a parental order, each respondent shall file and serve on all the other parties an acknowledgement in Form C52.

Amendments—Inserted by SI 1994/2165; amended by SI 1994/3155.

Defined terms—"application": r 4.1(1); "parental order": HFEA 1990, s 30.

"within 14 days"—For computation of time, see r 1.5. As regards an application for an extension of time, rr 4.14(2) and 4.15(1) will apply.

4A.5 Appointment and duties of the parental order reporter

(1) As soon as practicable after the application has been filed the court shall consider the appointment of a parental order reporter in accordance with section 41(1) of the Children Act 1989.

(2), (3) (*revoked*)

(4) In addition to such of the matters set out in rules 4.11 and 4.11A as are appropriate to the proceedings, the parental order reporter shall –

(i) investigate the matters set out in section 30(1) to (7) of the 1990 Act;
(ii) so far as he considers necessary, investigate any matter contained in the application form or other matter which appears relevant to the making of a parental order;
(iii) advise the court on whether there is any reason under section 6 of the Adoption Act 1976, as applied with modifications by the Parental Orders (Human Fertilisation and Embryology) Regulations 1994, to refuse the parental order.

Amendments—Inserted by SI 1994/2165; amended by SI 2001/821.

Defined terms—"application": r 4.1(1).

Appointment—Practitioners should note that, unlike public law proceedings where the court has a discretion under r 4.10(*b*) not to appoint a parental order reporter if it considers that such an appointment is not necessary to safeguard the interest of the child, r 4A.2 specifically excludes that right in applications under HFEA 1990, s 30 – the appointment of a parental order reporter is mandatory in s 30 applications. Although the remaining provisions of r 4.10 are not excluded by r 4A.2, it is submitted that, because the appointment of a parental order reporter is mandatory, the provisions of r 4.10(2)–(4) are inapplicable.

Duties of parental order reporter—This rule lays down the specific duties, in addition to those prescribed by r 4.11(4), that a parental order reporter must carry out; in particular, he must advise the court, as in cases of adoption, whether, having regard to all the circumstances and the need to safeguard and promote the welfare of the child, there is any reason for refusing the parental order.

4A.6 Personal attendance of applicants

The court shall not make a parental order except upon the personal attendance before it of the applicants.

Amendments—Inserted by SI 1994/2165.

Defined terms—"parental order": HFEA 1990, s 30.

4A.7 Copies of orders

(1) Where a parental order is made by a court sitting in Wales in respect of a child who was born in Wales and the applicants so request before the order is drawn up, the proper officer shall obtain a translation into Welsh of the particulars set out in the order.

(2) Within 7 days after the making of a parental order, the proper officer shall send a copy of the order to the Registrar General.

(3) A copy of any parental order may be supplied to the Registrar General at his request.

Amendments—Inserted by SI 1994/2165.

Defined terms—"applicants": r 4A.3; "parental order": HFEA 1990, s 30; "proper officer": r 1.2(1).

4A.8 Amendment and revocation of orders

(1) An application under paragraph 4 of Schedule 1 to the Adoption Act 1976 as modified by the Parental Orders (Human Fertilisation and Embryology) Regulations 1994 for the amendment of a parental order or the revocation of a direction to the Registrar General may be made ex parte in the first instance but the court may require notice of the application to be served on such persons as it thinks fit.

(2) Where the application is granted, the proper officer shall send to the Registrar General a notice specifying the amendments or informing him of the revocation and shall give sufficient particulars of the order to enable the Registrar General to identify the case.

Amendments—Inserted by SI 1994/2165.

Defined terms—"parental order": HFEA 1990, s 30; "proper officer": r 1.2(1).

4A.9 Custody, inspection and disclosure of documents and information

(1) All documents relating to proceedings for a parental order shall, while they are in the custody of the court, be kept in a place of special security.

(2) Any person who obtains any information in the course of, or relating to proceedings for a parental order shall treat that information as confidential and shall only disclose it if –

(*a*) the disclosure is necessary for the proper exercise of his duties, or

(*b*) the information is requested –

(i) by a court or public authority (whether in Great Britain or not) having power to determine proceedings for a parental order and related matters, for the purpose of discharge of its duties in that behalf, or

(ii) by a person who is authorised in writing by the Secretary of State to obtain the information for the purposes of research.

Amendments—Inserted by SI 1994/2165.

Defined terms—"parental order": HFEA 1990, s 30.

4A.10 Application for removal, return etc of child

(1) An application under sections 27(1), 29(1) or 29(2) of the Adoption Act 1976 as applied with modifications by the Parental Orders (Human Fertilisation and Embryology) Regulations 1994 shall be made on notice in proceedings under section 30 of the 1990 Act.

(2) The proper officer shall serve a copy of the application and a notice of the date of the hearing on all the parties to the proceedings under section 30, on the

guardian ad litem and on any other person or body, not being the child, as the court thinks fit.

(3) The court may at any time give directions as to the conduct of the application under this rule.

Amendments—Inserted by SI 1994/2165.

Scope of provision—The Parental Orders (Human Fertilisation and Embryology) Regulations 1994 extend certain provisions of the Adoption Act 1976, with modifications, to applications under HFEA 1990, s 30. This rule lays down the procedure to be followed in interlocutory applications made in s 30 proceedings for: (i) leave to remove a child from the home of a person with whom he lives (s 27(1)); (ii) an order for the return of a child who has been removed from the home of a person with whom he lives (s 29(1)); and (iii) an order directing a person not to remove the child from the home of a person with whom he lives (s 29(2)). Although the rule does not specifically refer to it, the court also has power on an application made to it to make a search and recovery order under AA 1976, s 29(3) (see Parental Orders (Human Fertilisation and Embryology) Regulations 1994, Sch 1). The Family Proceedings Courts (Children Act 1989) Rules 1991 make reference to the form of order to be used, but the FPR 1991 do not prescribe a form. It is submitted that, where such an order is made, it should be drawn on Form C28 or C31 with the necessary modification.

It will be observed that, whereas the application for a parental order is made on the prescribed form, the aforesaid applications are to be made on notice within the substantive application, as in other applications in civil proceedings in the High Court or a county court. It is to be noted, however, that Adoption Rules 1984, r 47 provides that such applications are to be made, if the proceedings are pending, by notice in those proceedings or, if no such application is pending, by originating process. In the family proceedings court, the matter is dealt with by way of a complaint. It is submitted that, in order to provide uniformity and consistency, where an application is made for a search and recovery warrant, the application should be in like form as an application in Form C19 (an application for a warrant of assistance under CA 1989, s 102), as the provision of FPC(CA 1989)R 1991 makes specific reference to that section or, alternatively, Form C3 with the necessary modifications.

Respondents—Rule 4A.10(2) makes provision for the persons who should be served with notice of the applications. Generally, the respondents to the applications will be all the persons who were parties to the proceedings under HFEA 1990, s 30 and any person or body as the court may direct.

Service—This rule does not set the time-limit for such application, and so the rules applicable in other family applications will apply; accordingly, notice of the application must be at least 2 business days after the day of service (r 1.5(4) – see also r 3.9(5), unless time has been abridged under CCR Ord 13, r 4(1)).

Documents—The rules do not prescribe the documents to be filed in support of any application to which they relate. Since the adoption provisions have been incorporated in the regulations with modification, the procedure followed in adoption proceedings should apply, ie the application should be supported by an affidavit or, preferably, a statement in accordance with r 4.17 so as to provide conformity and consistency in all family proceedings.

PART V
WARDSHIP

5.1 Application to make a minor a ward of court

(1) An application to make a minor a ward of court shall be made by originating summons and, unless the court otherwise directs, the plaintiff shall file an affidavit in support of the application when the originating summons is issued.

(2) Rule 4.3 shall, so far as applicable, apply to an application by a local authority for the leave of the court under section 100(3) of the Act of 1989.

(3) Where there is no person other than the minor who is a suitable defendant, an application may be made ex parte to a district judge for leave to issue either an ex parte originating summons or an originating summons with the minor as defendant thereto; and, except where such leave is granted, the minor shall not be made a defendant to an originating summons under this rule in the first instance.

(4) Particulars of any summons issued under this rule in a district registry shall be sent by the proper officer to the principal registry for recording in the register of wards.

(5) The date of the minor's birth shall, unless otherwise directed, be stated in the summons, and the plaintiff shall –

(*a*) on issuing the summons or before or at the first hearing thereof lodge in the registry out of which the summons issued a certified copy of the entry in the Register of Births or, as the case may be, in the Adopted Children Register relating to the minor, or

(*b*) at the first hearing of the summons apply for directions as to proof of birth of the minor in some other manner.

(6) The name of each party to the proceedings shall be qualified by a brief description, in the body of the summons, of his interest in, or relation to, the minor.

(7) Unless the court otherwise directs, the summons shall state the whereabouts of the minor or, as the case may be, that the plaintiff is unaware of his whereabouts.

(8) Upon being served with the summons, every defendant other than the minor shall forthwith lodge in the registry out of which the summons issued a notice stating the address of the defendant and the whereabouts of the minor or, as the case may be, that the defendant is unaware of his whereabouts and, unless the court otherwise directs, serve a copy of the same upon the plaintiff.

(9) Where any party other than the minor changes his address or becomes aware of any change in the whereabouts of the minor after the issue, or, as the case may be, service of the summons, he shall, unless the court otherwise directs, forthwith lodge notice of the change in the registry out of which the summons issued and serve a copy of the notice on every other party.

(10) The summons shall contain a notice to the defendant informing him of the requirements of paragraphs (8) and (9).

(11) In this rule any reference to the whereabouts of a minor is a reference to the address at which and the person with whom he is living and any other information relevant to the question where he may be found.

Defined terms—"district judge": r 1.2(1); "local authority": CA 1989, s 105(1); "minor": Family Law Reform Act 1969, s 1; "proper officer": r 1.2(1).

Scope of provision—It is now mandatory to file an affidavit in support of the application when the originating summons is issued unless the court otherwise directs. This rule also provides for the procedure set out in r 4.3 to apply to an application by a local authority for leave of the court to issue proceedings and places on the chief clerk (instead of the district judge) the duty of sending to the principal registry the particulars of any summons issued in the district registry.

Commencement of application—An application to ward a child may only be made after its birth; an unborn child cannot be warded (*Re F (In Utero) (Wardship)* [1988] Fam 122, [1988] 2 FLR 307).

Venue—All causes and matters relating to wardship are assigned to the Family Division by Supreme Court Act 1981, Sch 1. SCA 1981, s 41 provides that no minor shall be made a ward of court except by virtue of an order to that effect made by the High Court.

Transfer of proceedings—Wardship proceedings, other than those under CA 1989, may be transferred for hearing to the county court pursuant to Matrimonial and Family Proceedings Act 1984, s 38(2), which makes provision for the transfer of wardship proceedings, except applications for an order that a minor be made or cease to be a ward of court either of the court's own motion or on the application of any party to the proceedings. *Practice Direction of 5 June 1992* provides, inter alia, for proceedings to be dealt with in the High Court where it appears to the court that by reason of the complexity, difficulty or gravity of the issues they ought to be tried in the High Court. The following proceedings must be dealt with in the High Court unless the issues of fact or law make them more suitable for trial in a county court:
(*a*) proceedings in which the Official Solicitor is or becomes the guardian ad litem of the ward or of a party to the proceedings;
(*b*) proceedings in which a local authority is or becomes a party;
(*c*) proceedings in which an application for blood tests is made;
(*d*) proceedings where an application is opposed on the ground of want of jurisdiction;
(*e*) proceedings where there is a substantial foreign element involved;
(*f*) proceedings where there is an opposed application for leave to take the child permanently out of the jurisdiction or where there is an application for a temporary removal and it is opposed on the ground that the child may not be returned.

Unless the parties consent before a transfer is made, they must be given an opportunity of being heard on the question (r 10.10(4)).

Practice on determining venue—Since county courts do not have jurisdiction to make a child a ward or make an order that a child should cease to be a ward of court, *Registrar's Direction of 23 July 1987* provides for the practice to be adopted when the tier of court is being considered. The current standard practice is that, on the first appointment following the issue of the originating summons, the High Court, if it considers that wardship should continue, confirms wardship and directs that the child remains a ward of court during his minority or until further order. If such a direction is given there is no need to repeat it in subsequent orders, including any order on the substantive hearing of the originating summons. Where such a direction is given, and provided that the matter is not one which under *President's Direction of 5 June 1992* must be dealt with in the High Court, consideration should be given to transferring the case, in whole or in part, to the county court. In any case which is so transferred where the county court concludes that it is not appropriate to deal with the matter because it is of the opinion that the minor should not remain a ward, it should transfer the case back to the High Court.

Jurisdiction—The jurisdiction of the High Court in wardship derives from the inherent jurisdiction of the court (for applications under this general and wider jurisdiction see RSC Ord 7) based on the principle that all subjects owe allegiance to the Crown and in return the Crown and protects its subjects. In relation to children, the Crown as parens patriae has the right and duty to take care of those who are not able to take care of themselves (see *Re P (GE) (An Infant)* [1965] Ch 568, [1965] 2 WLR 1; *Re N (Infants) (No 2)* [1967] Ch 512, [1967] 2 WLR 691; *Re L (An Infant)* [1968] P 119, [1968] 3 WLR 1645; *S v S* [1972] AC 24, [1970] 3 WLR 366). The court under its inherent jurisdiction has power to make any order or determine any issue in respect of a child or an adult unless restricted by legislation or case law; eg by the Family Law Act 1986 and the Child Abduction and Custody Act 1985. In the exercise of its wardship jurisdiction the High Court has jurisdiction if and only if the child is habitually resident in England and Wales, or is present in England and Wales and is not habitually resident in any other part of the UK, provided that jurisdiction is not excluded by Family Law Act 1986, s 3(2) or, where it is so excluded, the ward is present in England and Wales on the relevant date (within the meaning of s 3(6)) and the court considers that the immediate exercise of its powers is necessary for the ward's protection. Where the dispute relates to matters of public law, before commencing proceedings consideration should be given to the nature of the issues upon which a determination is sought. If the court is required to review the decision of a public authority taken in the exercise of its statutory power, the governing principles that will apply will be those of public law and not those governed by reference to the inherent jurisdiction of the court. In such cases the application should be made in the Administrative Court for judicial review and not in the Family Division (*A (A Patient) v A Health Authority; Re J: The Queen on the Application of S v Secretary of State for the Home Department* [2002] EWHC 18 (Fam/Admin), [2002] 1 FLR 845).

Jurisdiction based on habitual residence—For meaning of habitual residence, see under CACA 1985, Sch 1, Art 4. It is for the applicant to establish that the court has jurisdiction. Once this burden has been discharged and it is shown that the child was habitually resident in England when the proceedings were commenced, the court will exercise its jurisdiction even if the child is and was born outside the jurisdiction when the application is heard (*B v H (Habitual Residence:*

Wardship) [2002] 1 FLR 388; *Re B-M (Wardship: Jurisdiction)* [1993] 1 FLR 979; *Re S (Custody: Habitual Residence)* [1998] 1 FLR 122; see also *F v S (Wardship: Jurisdiction)* [1993] 2 FLR 686, CA). The "relevant date", where an application is made for an order, is the date of the application or first application if two or more are determined together or, where no such application is made, the date of the order (FLA 1986, s 3(6)). On the basis of the decision in *Ikimi v Ikimi* [2001] 2 FLR 1288, quaere whether a child, like his parent, can be habitually resident in two countries.

Restrictions under CA 1989—CA 1989, ss 91 and 100 have imposed further restrictions on the powers of the High Court under its inherent jurisdiction by restricting the use of the wardship jurisdiction and curtailing applications by local authorities in relation to the care, supervision and accommodation of children (see **Local authority as plaintiff** below). Where a care order is made with respect to a child who is a ward of court, the making of the care order discharges the wardship (CA 1989, s 91(4)). CA 1989, s 100(2) prohibits the exercise of the inherent jurisdiction so as to require a child to be placed in care, put under supervision or accommodated by or on behalf of a local authority, so as to make a child who is a subject of a care order or a deemed care order a ward of court or so as to confer on any local authority power to determine any question connected with any aspect of parental responsibility for a child.

The wardship jurisdiction of the court should not be invoked until it is clear that the issues concerning the child cannot effectively be resolved under CA 1989 (*Re CT (A Minor) (Wardship: Representation)* [1993] 2 FLR 278). See also *Re R (A Minor) (Blood Transfusion)* [1993] 2 FLR 757 and *Re O (A Minor) (Medical Treatment)* [1993] 2 FLR 149 under **Medical treatment** below. However, the court has power to grant injunctions ancillary to care orders under Supreme Court Act 1981, s 37. This power is not part of the High Court's inherent jurisdiction with respect to children referred to in CA 1989, s 100 (see further annotation thereunder).

Exercise of court's discretion to use powers—The court's power to exercise its inherent jurisdiction is discretionary, and it may refuse to exercise its power if it considers it inappropriate to do so. There are numerous examples of cases where the court has declined to exercise its jurisdiction (see *Re Dunhill (An Infant)* (1967) 111 Sol Jo 113, where the sole object of the proceedings was to gain publicity; *Re O (A Minor) (Wardship: Adopted Child)* [1978] Fam 196, [1977] 3 WLR 725, proceedings issued by the natural parents after an adoption order; *Re F (A Minor) (Wardship: Immigration)* [1990] Fam 125, [1989] 1 FLR 233, proceedings issued to frustrate immigration laws (cf *Re K and S (Minors) (Wardship: Immigration)* [1992] 1 FLR 432; *Re K (Minors) (Non-patrials: Wardship)* [1992] FCR 385); *Re JS (A Minor) (Wardship: Boy Soldier)* [1990] Fam 182, [1991] 1 FLR 7, where the exercise of the court's powers to prevent a boy soldier being arrested under military law, was considered both inappropriate and contrary to public policy; *Re K (Wards: Leave to Call as Witnesses)* [1988] 1 FLR 435, refusal to intervene on the question of whether a child should give evidence in criminal proceedings once he has made a statement to the police: see also *Re X (A Minor) (Wardship: Jurisdiction)* [1975] Fam 47, [1975] 2 WLR 335; *Re W (Wardship: Publication of Information)* [1992] 1 FLR 99). In *C v C (Access Order: Enforcement)* [1990] 1 FLR 462, it was held that wardship proceedings are unnecessary where appropriate steps may be taken within the divorce jurisdiction; on the basis of this decision, the court may decline to exercise jurisdiction in wardship where relief is available under CA 1989. In *Re C (A Minor) (Wardship: Jurisdiction)* [1991] 2 FLR 168, where the court was asked to direct or order a school to educate a ward against its wishes, it was held that it was beyond the practical boundary of the court's wardship jurisdiction to grant a mandatory injunction against the school. The court has exercised its powers under the inherent jurisdiction in child abduction cases to order the return of a child to the country of its habitual residence (*Re O (Child Abduction: Custody Rights)* [1997] 2 FLR 702) and to order the delivery up of a foreign passport (*Re A-K (Foreign Passport: Jurisdiction)* [1997] 2 FLR 569).

Examples of powers of the court—Since proceedings under the inherent jurisdiction of the High Court are classed as "family proceedings" (CA 1989, s 8(3)(*a*)), the court may make all the orders which can be made in family proceedings. In addition, the court has power to make a wide range of injunctions for a child's protection. Such orders include orders to prevent an undesirable association; to restrain publicity (see *Thompson and Venables v News Group Newspapers, Associated Newspapers Ltd and MGN Ltd* [2001] 1 FLR 791; *Re AB (Wardship: Jurisdiction)* [1985] FLR 470, [1984] 1 WLR 1422) but, because of the need to balance the freedom of the press against the protection of a ward, any such order must be drawn in clear and precise terms (*Re L (A Ward) (Publication of Information)* [1988] 1 FLR 255, [1988] 1 All ER 418; *Re W (Wardship: Publication of Information)* [1992] 1 FLR 99, in which the principles to be applied in publication cases were referred to; see also *Re C (A Minor) (No 2) (Wardship: Publication of Information)* [1990] 1 FLR 263, CA).

Medical treatment—The court has given its consent to medical treatment where the parents have refused to do so (*Re B (A Minor) (Wardship: Medical Treatment)* (1982) FLR 117); where the patient, whether a child or an adult, has refused to consent (*Re E (A Minor) (Wardship: Medical Treatment)* [1992] 2 FCR 197; *Re R (A Minor) (Wardship: Consent to Treatment)* [1992] Fam 11, [1992] 1 FLR 190; *Re J (A Minor) (Medical Treatment)* [1992] 2 FLR 165; *Re H (Mental Patient: Diagnosis)* [1993] 1 FLR 28; *Re T (An Adult) (Consent to Medical Treatment)* [1992] 2 FLR 458); to the termination of a pregnancy (*Re G-U (A Minor) (Wardship)* [1984] FLR 811; *Re P (A Minor)* [1986] 1 FLR 272) – in the case of possible termination of a psychiatric patient's pregnancy, hospitals should have a protocol to deal with any application in good time, so that the termination can be carried out at the earliest opportunity and the patient should be referred to independent legal advice at an early stage (*Re SS (Medical Treatment: Late Termination)* [2002] 1 FLR 445); to sterilisation (*Re B (A Minor) (Wardship: Sterilisation)* [1988] AC 199, [1987] 2 FLR 314; *Re P (A Minor) (Wardship: Sterilisation)* [1989] 1 FLR 182 – for the approach adopted in respect of male sterilisation see *Re A (Male Sterilisation)* [2000] 1 FLR 549); to making a choice between two alternative surgical interventions (*Re S (Sterilisation: Patient's Best Interests)* [2000] 2 FLR 389; *Re ZM and OS (Sterilisation: Patient's Best Interests)* [2000] 1 FLR 523); see also *Re F (Adult: Court's Jurisdiction)* [2000] 2 FLR 512, CA. However, where a patient is an adult and of sound mind and, in anticipation of entering into a condition such as PVS, has given clear instructions that in such an event he is not to be given medical care designed to keep him alive, the court will respect his wishes and decline to intervene (*Re AK (Medical Treatment: Consent)* [2001] 1 FLR 129). See also *Practice Note of June 1996*; *Re W (Mental Patient: Sterilisation)* [1993] 1 FLR 381. In determining whether a person has sufficient capacity to refuse treatment, the court will apply the three-stage test laid down in *Re C (Refusal of Medical Treatment)* [1994] 1 FLR 31: namely (i) whether it has been established that his capacity has been so reduced by his illness that he does not understand the nature, purpose and effect of the proposed medical treatment; (ii) whether he has comprehended and retained information regarding the treatment offered; (iii) whether he has believed it and weighed it in the balance when making a choice (see the application of this test in cases of caesarean section: *Re MB (Medical Treatment)* [1997] 2 FLR 426; *Re S (Adult: Surgical Treatment)* [1993] 1 FLR 26; *Norfolk and Norwich Healthcare (NHS) Trust v W* [1996] 2 FLR 613; *Rochdale Healthcare (NHS) Trust v C* [1997] 1 FCR 274). See also *Re JT (Adult: Refusal of Medical Treatment)* [1998] 1 FLR 48. With regard to the patient's right to choose, in *B v An NHS Hospital Trust* [2002] EWHC 429, [2002] 1 FLR 1090, the President of the Family Division set out the following guidelines:

(*a*) there was a presumption that a patient had the mental capacity to make decisions whether to consent to or refuse medical or surgical treatment offered to him or her;

(*b*) if mental capacity was not in issue and the patient, having been given the relevant information and offered the available options, chose to refuse the treatment that decision had to be respected by the doctors. Considerations that the best interest of the patient would indicate that the decision should be to consent to treatment were irrelevant;

(*c*) If there was concern or doubt about the mental capacity of the patient, that doubt should be resolved as soon as possible, by the doctors within the hospital or NHS Trust or by other normal medical procedures;

(*d*) meanwhile, while the question of capacity was being resolved, the patient, had to be cared for in accordance with the judgment of the doctors as to the patient's best interests;

(*e*) If there were difficulties in deciding whether the patient had sufficient mental capacity, particularly if the refusal might have grave consequences for the patient, it was important that those considering the issue should not confuse the question of mental capacity with the nature of the decision made by the patient, however grave the consequences. The view of the patient might reflect a difference in values rather than an absence of competence and the assessment of capacity should be approached with that firmly in mind. The doctors cannot allow their emotional reaction to, or strong disagreement with, the decision of the patient to cloud their judgment in answering the primary question whether the patient had mental capacity to make the decision;

(*f*) in the rare case where disagreement still existed about competence, it was of the utmost importance that the patient was fully informed of the steps being taken and made a part of the process. If the option of enlisting independent outside expertise was being considered the doctor should discuss that with the patient so that any referral to a doctor outside the hospital would be, if possible, on a joint basis with the aim of helping both sides to resolve the disagreement. It might be crucial to the prospects of a good outcome that the patient was involved before the referral was made and felt equally engaged in the process;

(*g*) if the hospital was faced with the dilemma which the doctors did not know how to resolve, it had to be recognised and further steps taken as a matter of priority. Those in charge could not allow a situation of deadlock or drift to occur;

(*h*) if there was no disagreement about competence but the doctors were for any reason unable to carry out the wishes of the patient, their duty was to find other doctors who would do so;

(*i*) if all appropriate steps to seek independent assistance from medical experts outside the hospital had failed, the NHS Trust should not hesitate to make an application to the High Court or seek the advice of the Official Solicitor;

(*j*) the treating clinicians and the hospital should always have in mind that a seriously physically disabled patient who was mentally competent had the same right to personal autonomy and the make decisions as any other person with mental capacity.

As to when it is appropriate to invoke the court's inherent jurisdiction as opposed to an application for a specific issue order under CA 1989, see *Devon County Council v S* [1993] 1 FLR 842 and *Re O (A Minor) (Medical Treatment)* [1993] 2 FLR 149; cf *Re R (A Minor) (Blood Transfusion)* [1993] 2 FLR 757. Such an application should be heard inter partes where possible in the High Court. For procedure concerning withdrawal of medical treatment see *Practice Note of 1 May 2001* and *President's Direction of 14 December 2001* (set out in Part IV of this work) and in relation to issues governing the right to life see *An NHS Trust v M; An NHS Trust v H* [2001] 2 FLR 367.

Application must be in respect of minor—The subject of the proceedings must be under 18. An unborn child cannot be made a ward of court (*Re F (In Utero)* [1988] Fam 122, [1988] 2 FLR 307; see also *Paton v British Pregnancy Advisory Service Trustees* [1978] QB 276, [1978] 3 WLR 687).

Application to be by originating summons (r 5.1(1))—This rule does not specify the form of the originating summons. The form to be used must therefore be that required by RSC Ord 7, r 2 (ie Form 8 in Appendix A), but adapted to contain the information required by this rule. An originating summons must contain a statement of the question on which the plaintiff seeks the determination or direction of the court, or a statement of the relief or remedy claimed (RSC Ord 7, r 3). Where a concurrent summons is necessary RSC Ord 6, r 6 will apply. This form of process is unusual in wardship proceedings but may be necessary where the proceedings have an international element and the summons is required to be served both within the jurisdiction and out of the jurisdiction.

Supporting documents (r 5.1(1), (5))—The affidavit in support of the application is filed with the originating summons unless the court otherwise directs. The plaintiff must lodge a certified copy of the birth certificate or, as the case may be, a copy of the entry in the Adopted Children Register relating to the minor either when the originating summons is issued or at any time before or at the first hearing before the court. If the birth certificate is not available for some reason, a direction should be sought from the court at the first appointment as to the manner of proving the birth of the minor.

Plaintiff (r 5.1(1), (6))—The applicant is the plaintiff. Any person may issue wardship proceedings with respect to a child but he must show that he has some genuine interest in, or relation to, the minor and particulars of this are required to be given in the body of the originating summons. If there is any doubt about the interest of the plaintiff the recording officer of the court will refer the matter to a district judge, who may dismiss the originating summons or refer it to a judge for consideration (see *Re Dunhill (An Infant)* (1967) 111 Sol Jo 113, where the applicant was a nightclub owner whose motive for the application was to obtain publicity). In the case of an application by a natural parent after an adoption order a strong prima facie case must be shown (*Re O (A Minor) (Wardship: Adopted Child)* [1978] Fam 196, [1977] 3 WLR 725). A guardian ad litem (children's guardian) appointed under CA 1989 is unlikely to have locus standi as plaintiff (*A v Berkshire CC* [1989] 1 FLR 273).

Ward as plaintiff/defendant—The minor himself may apply for an order making him a ward, but he must do so by his next friend (r 9.2) – see *L v L (Minors) (Separate Representation)* [1994] 1 FLR 156; *Practice Note of 2 April 2001*; *Re CT (A Minor) (Wardship: Representation)* [1993] 2 FLR 278. FPR 1991, r 9.2A applies to wardship as it applies to proceedings under CA 1989. See also Thorpe J, 'Independent Representation for Minors' [1994] Fam Law 20.

Local authority as plaintiff (r 5.1(2))—A local authority must obtain the leave of the court before it can commence proceedings under the inherent jurisdiction of the court in respect of children (CA 1989, s 100(3)). The application for leave must be made in accordance with the provisions of r 4.3. The local authority must prepare a written request for leave setting out the reasons for the application together with a draft of the originating summons (see **Application to**

be by originating summons above). In the written request the local authority must show that the remedy or relief it wishes to obtain cannot be achieved other than through the making of an order within the court's inherent jurisdiction, that it is entitled to apply for the order under that jurisdiction and that there is reasonable cause to believe that if the court's inherent jurisdiction is not exercised with respect to the child he is likely to suffer significant harm (CA 1989, s 100(4), (5)). The local authority may, however, apply for injunctive relief ancillary to care orders by virtue of the court's statutory powers under Supreme Court Act 1981, s 37, without the need for leave to make such an application (*Re P (Care Orders: Injunctive Relief)* [2000] 2 FLR 385 and *C v K (Inherent Jurisdiction: Exclusion Order)* [1996] 2 FLR 506).

Whilst it has been observed that the local authority should not be prevented or discouraged from invoking the court's inherent jurisdiction where its powers under CA 1989 are found to be insufficient (see *London Borough of Southwark v B* [1993] 2 FLR 559), reference should be made to the cases cited under **Medical treatment** above when considering the legal framework under which the application should be made.

Defendant (r 5.1(3), (6))—Usually the parent of the minor is a defendant, but any person who has an interest, in or relation to, the minor may be named as a defendant. The minor may be made a defendant only with the leave of the court and may defend only by a guardian ad litem. When a minor is made a party, the Official Solicitor is no longer the first person to be invited to act as guardian ad litem. The Official Solicitor's responsibilities have been taken over by CAFCASS. For appointment of a CAFCASS officer as children's guardian and when the Official Solicitor will continue to play a role see respectively *Practice Note of March 2001 (Officers of CAFCASS Legal Services and Special Casework: Appointment in Family Proceedings)* and *Practice Note of 2 April 2001 (Official Solicitor: Appointment in Family Proceedings)* (both are set out in Part IV of this work). The Official Solicitor will not be appointed to act for the child where he is or has already acted for another party in the proceedings (*A v B and Hereford and Worcester County Council* [1986] 1 FLR 289). The decision of a court appointing the Official Solicitor is not open to appeal (*Taylor v Taylor* [1975] Fam Law 151).

Undesirable association—*Practice Direction of 16 June 1983* directs that, in cases in which the ward has formed or is seeking to form an association with another person which is considered to be undesirable, that other person should not be made a party to the originating summons.

Whereabouts of the child (r 5.1(7)–(11))—The originating summons must state the child's whereabouts or as the case may be that the plaintiff is unaware of his whereabouts. There is a duty on the defendant likewise to disclose the child's whereabouts. A solicitor is under a duty to disclose information which may assist in locating a ward even if such information has been conveyed to him in confidence by his client (*Ramsbotham v Senior* (1869) LR 8 Eq 575, (1869) FLR Rep 591). Information about the child's whereabouts may also be obtained through Government departments by applying in accordance with *Practice Direction of 13 February 1989*. In such cases the request to the appropriate department is made through the court and must certify that the child cannot be traced and is believed to be with the person whose address is sought. The applicant must provide the court with the information set out in the direction. An undertaking will also be required from the applicant or his solicitor that the information given in response to the inquiry will be used solely for the purpose of assisting in tracing the person concerned or the child. A collection and/or location order (formerly known as find and return and seek and locate orders respectively) may be sought in the prescribed form (for the forms see *Emergency Remedies in the Family Courts* (Family Law, Issue 12)) directing the tipstaff to ascertain the child's whereabouts and to search for, find and recover the child and, if necessary, arrest any person who fails to comply with the order. Where such an order is obtained, the tipstaff must be provided with all available information as to the child's whereabouts. The court also has power to order disclosure of the whereabouts of a child and recovery of a child under Family Law Act 1986, ss 33 and 34. Where an order is sought for the return of a child about to arrive by air and the plaintiff requires information to enable him to meet the aeroplane, the judge should be asked to include in his order a direction that the airline and, if he has the information, the immigration officer at the appropriate airport should supply the necessary information to the plaintiff. A person who already has an order for the return of a child should apply to a judge ex parte for such a direction (*Practice Direction of 18 January 1980*). In cases where the child has been abducted, the court may consider that press publicity may assist in tracing the child. In such cases the judge should adjourn for a period of about 10 minutes to enable representatives of the press to attend so that the widest possible publicity may be given (*Practice Direction of 22 July 1979*).

Service (r 5.1(8))—As to service generally, see rr 10.2–10.6. Service outside the jurisdiction may be effected without leave in accordance with these rules or, where proceedings are pending in the High Court, in accordance with RSC Ord 11, rr 5 and 6, or, where proceedings are pending in a divorce county court, in accordance with CCR Ord 8, rr 8–10.

Change of address (r 5.1(9))—There is a duty on the defendant to notify any change of his or her address, or that of the minor, after service of the summons, but in the case of the plaintiff a similar duty applies from the commencement of the proceedings.

Removal of the ward from the jurisdiction—Subject to Family Law Act 1986, s 38, a ward may not be removed from England and Wales without the leave of the court. This injunction applies as soon as the originating summons is issued and the summons will be endorsed with such a notice. The exception in s 38 provides that where the ward's parents are involved in proceedings for divorce, nullity or judicial separation in respect of their marriage in another part of the UK or the ward is habitually resident in another part of the UK (except where that other part is Scotland and the ward has attained the age of 16), the court will not prevent the removal of the ward to that other part of the UK without the court's consent or to any other place without the consent of either the appropriate court in that part of the UK or the court where the matrimonial proceedings are pending.

By virtue of CA 1989, s 13(2), a person in whose favour a residence order has been made does not require leave to remove a child who is the subject of that order for a period of less than a month. It is suggested that a removal pursuant to the provisions of CA 1989, s 13(2) without a specific direction from the court would be contrary to the parental role of the court as parens patriae and the immediate injunction that is imposed as soon as a child is made a ward of court. If, within the wardship proceedings, the court is minded to make a residence order whilst continuing the wardship, then it should also give directions regarding the right to remove the child from the jurisdiction, as it did prior to CA 1989, by way of a general leave with conditions attached.

Practice Direction of 15 May 1987 makes provision as to the issue of passports for wards of court. As to the procedure on an application for leave to take a ward out of the jurisdiction, see *Practice Direction of 14 May 1984*.

Ward as witness in criminal proceedings—*Registrar's Direction of 11 November 1987* and *Registrar's Direction of 18 July 1988* make provision as to the procedure to be followed where a ward is required as a witness in criminal proceedings or is the subject of a criminal investigation.

Publicity and disclosure of evidence—Administration of Justice Act 1960, s 12(1) provides that the publication of information relating to wardship proceedings before any court sitting in private is a contempt of court (see also Contempt of Court Act 1981, s 12; Children Act 1989, ss 2, 97(2) and *Harris v Harris; Attorney-General v Harris* [2001] 2 FLR 895). In all other respects, the ward enjoys no greater protection against unwelcome publicity than other children. If the information relates to the ward but not to the proceedings, there is no contempt (*Re F (A Minor) (Publication of Information)* [1977] Fam 58, [1977] 1 All ER 114). No contempt is committed by the media in interviewing a ward or publishing or broadcasting such an interview. The issue in each case will be whether an injunction is necessary to protect the child from a clear and identifiable harm and whether the injunction sought is proportionate to that aim. In the absence of an injunction, it is not a contempt of court to publish information about the ward; if a wider protection is required, application should be made for an order specifically providing for the wider protection. In such cases, the court will balance the rights of the media to publish information against the need to protect the welfare of the child to uphold the effective functioning of the court's wardship jurisdiction (*Re W (Wardship: Discharge: Publicity)* [1995] 2 FLR 466; *Re H (Minors) (Injunction: Public Interest)* [1994] 1 FLR 519 and *Re R (Wardship: Restrictions on Publication)* [1994] Fam 254, [1994] 2 FLR 637; see also *R v Central Independent Television plc* [1994] Fam 192, [1994] 2 FLR 151). For the principles which the court will apply, see *Re W (Wardship: Publication of Information)* [1992] 1 FLR 99. These guidelines were followed in *A v M (Family Proceedings: Publicity)* [2000] 1 FLR 562.

Where an injunction is sought, the effect of which would be to impose a restraint on the freedom of the press and the media generally, the application should be transferred to the High Court, and the Official Solicitor should be invited to represent the child (*Re H (Minors) (Injunction: Public Interest)* [1994] 1 FLR 519). When considering such an application, the court will balance the right of a person and of the media to publish information and matters of public interest against the need to protect the welfare of the child and the risk of harm to the child. The welfare of the child, however, is not the paramount consideration but, when public interest turns into public curiosity, public interest in the protection of the child becomes the greater public interest, and the interest of the child becomes "the more important factor" (*Re Manda (Wardship:*

Disclosure of Evidence) [1993] 1 FLR 205; see also *A v M (Family Proceedings: Publicity)* [2000] 1 FLR 562 and *G (Celebrities: Publicity)* [1999] 1 FLR 409). The court's jurisdiction, however, can only be invoked where the child concerned is the subject of the proceedings before the court and the court is concerned with the care and upbringing of the child (*R v Central Independent Television plc* [1994] Fam 192). See also under Administration of Justice Act 1960, s 12. For standard forms on Press/Publicity orders see *Emergency Remedies in the Family Courts* (Family Law), Appendix 8.

5.2 Enforcement of order by tipstaff

The power of the High Court to secure, through an officer attending upon the court, compliance with any direction relating to a ward of court may be exercised by an order addressed to the tipstaff.

Scope of provision—For the purposes of the Family Law Act 1986, s 34, the tipstaff is the "officer of the court" to whom orders are directed.

5.3 Where minor ceases to be a ward of court

(1) A minor who, by virtue of section 41(2) of the Supreme Court Act 1981, becomes a ward of court on the issue of a summons under rule 5.1 shall cease to be a ward of court –

(*a*) if an application for an appointment for the hearing of the summons is not made within the period of 21 days after the issue of the summons, at the expiration of that period;

(*b*) if an application for such an appointment is made within that period, on the determination of the application made by the summons unless the court hearing it orders that the minor be made a ward of court.

(2) Nothing in paragraph (1) shall be taken as affecting the power of the court under section 41(3) of the said Act to order that any minor who is for the time being a ward of court shall cease to be a ward of court.

(3) If no application for an appointment for the hearing of a summons under rule 5.1 is made within the period of 21 days after the issue of the summons, a notice stating whether the applicant intends to proceed with the application made by the summons must be left at the registry in which the matter is proceeding immediately after the expiration of that period.

Defined terms—"minor": Family Law Reform Act 1969, s 1.

Scope of provision—This rule replaces RSC Ord 90, r 4. Its purpose is to ensure that the immediate protection afforded on the issue of proceedings is not abused but that the matter is brought before the court for consideration without delay. If application is not made as required the wardship lapses and the automatic protection of the court is lost. The originating summons continues to remain effective and there are three steps which may be taken to restore the wardship. These are:

(*a*) to issue an ordinary summons within the proceedings and seek an order to revive the wardship;

(*b*) to continue the proceedings and obtain a final order on the substantive hearing; or

(*c*) to issue a fresh originating summons.

Supreme Court Act 1981, s 41 (r 5.3(1), (2))—Section 41 is concerned with wards of court; s 41(2) provides that a minor becomes a ward on the making of the application, but it does not apply in respect of a child who is subject to a care order (s 41(2A)); s 41(3) merely recites the High Court's power to order that a wardship shall cease.

First appointment (r 5.3(1))—If a request for the date for a first appointment is not made within the 21 days of the issue of the originating summons, the wardship lapses. Provided the date has been obtained, the wardship continues notwithstanding the fact that the date for the hearing of the first appointment is later than 21 days after the commencement of the proceedings. In the principal registry, the applicant is given a form of application for the first appointment on the issue of the originating summons and it is advisable to complete the form then and apply for the date for the first appointment at once.

The first "appointment for the hearing of the summons" is, in effect, a hearing for directions to be given, for timetables to be set and for the court to deal with any other interlocutory matter such as the evidence, examination by experts, disclosure of evidence, attendance of witnesses etc. Unless the wardship has already been confirmed at a hearing before a judge, it is important to obtain an order at this hearing that the child remain a ward until further order or for such other period as may be deemed fit. The court may also make interim orders relating, for example, to residence and contact.

The directions which may be made by the court at a first appointment may include all those relevant to proceedings under CA 1989 (see r 4.14). Particular provision is made in *Practice Direction of 1 November 1985* (as to the obtaining of psychiatric reports), in FPR 1991, r 4.18 (as to medical and psychiatric examination of a child) and in *Practice Direction of 18 October 1991* (as to the district judge's power to refer a summons for conciliation where orders under CA 1989, s 8 are sought).

Delay—The general principle in CA 1989, s 1(2) (delay prejudicial to the welfare of child) applies in wardship proceedings, although *Practice Direction of 16 July 1981* also makes special provision to combat delay in such proceedings.

5.4 Adoption of minor who is a ward of court

(1) An application for leave –

(*a*) to commence proceedings to adopt a minor who is a ward, or
(*b*) to commence proceedings to free such a minor for adoption,

may be ex parte to a district judge.

(2) Where a local authority has been granted leave to place a minor who is a ward with foster parents with a view to adoption it shall not be necessary for an application to be made for leave under paragraph (1)(*a*) or (*b*) unless the court otherwise directs.

(3) If the applicant for leave under paragraph (1)(*a*) or (*b*), or a local authority which has applied for leave as referred to in paragraph (2), or a foster parent so requests, the district judge may direct that any subsequent proceedings shall be conducted with a view to securing that the proposed adopter is not seen by or made known to any respondent or prospective respondent who is not already aware of his identity except with his consent.

(4) In paragraphs (1) and (3) "proceedings" means proceedings in the High Court or in a county court.

Defined terms—"local authority": CA 1989, s 105(1); "minor": Family Law Reform Act 1969, s 1.

Scope of provision—An application for leave must be made if it is desired to commence proceedings for adoption in respect of a ward. This application may be made ex parte. On an application for leave, the duty of the court is to consider whether, on the proposed adoption application, the applicant might reasonably succeed, and not whether adoption is in the best interests of the child (*F v S (Adoption: Ward)* [1973] Fam 203, [1973] 2 WLR 178). The requirement for leave is a procedural one and may be dispensed with (*Re H (A Minor)* (1981) Fam Law 146).

Application by local authority (r 5.4(2))—In view of the restrictions under CA 1989, s 100(3) on local authority applications for wardship, it is difficult to envisage any circumstance when r 5.4(2) will be necessary.

Procedure—Application is by summons before a district judge. The rules provide that the application may be made ex parte, but the district judge may direct that notice be given to all interested parties. The summons should be supported by an affidavit sworn by the applicant.

5.5 Orders for use of secure accommodation

No order shall be made with the effect of placing or keeping a minor in secure accommodation, within the meaning of section 25(1) of the Act of 1989 unless the minor has been made a party to the summons.

Amendments—Inserted by SI 1991/2113; amended by SI 1992/456.

5.6 Notice to provider of refuge

Where a child is staying in a refuge which is certified under section 51(1) or 51(2) of the Act of 1989, the person who is providing that refuge shall be given notice of any application under this Part of these rules in respect of that child.

Amendments—Inserted by SI 1991/2113.

PART VI
CHILD ABDUCTION AND CUSTODY

6.1 Interpretation

In this Part, unless the context otherwise requires –

(*a*) "the Act" means the Child Abduction and Custody Act 1985 and words or expressions bear the same meaning as in that Act;

(*b*) "the Hague Convention" means the convention defined in section 1(1) of the Act and "the European Convention" means the convention defined in section 12(1) of the Act.

Amendments—Part title amended by SI 1994/3155.

"the Hague Convention"—The Hague Convention is the Convention on the Civil Aspects of International Child Abduction signed at The Hague on 25 October 1980 and is set out in Sch 1 to the 1985 Act. It seeks to protect rights of custody and access, and seeks to provide through legal process for the expeditious return to the country of a child's habitual residence any child who is under the age of 16 and who has been wrongfully removed to, or retained in, another Contracting State.

"the European Convention"—The European Convention is the European Convention on Recognition and Enforcement of Decisions Concerning Custody of Children and on the Restoration of Custody of Children signed in Luxembourg on 20 May 1980 and is set out in CACA 1985, Sch 2. It provides for (i) the recognition and enforcement of decisions relating to custody where there has been an improper removal of a child in breach of such a decision, (ii) the recognition and enforcement of an access order for organising or securing rights of access, (iii) the recognition of a custody or access order, and (iv) the registration of custody orders against abduction.

6.2 Mode of application

(1) Except as otherwise provided by this Part, every application under the Hague Convention and the European Convention shall be made by originating summons, which shall be in Form No 10 in Appendix A to the Rules of the Supreme Court 1965 and issued out of the principal registry.

(2) An application in custody proceedings for a declaration under section 23(2) of the Act shall be made by summons in those proceedings.

Amendments—SI 1997/1893.

Defined terms—"custody proceedings": Child Abduction and Custody Act 1985, s 27(1); "European Convention": CACA 1985, s 12(1); "Hague Convention": CACA 1985, s 1(1); "originating summons": RSC Ord 1, r 4.

Application (r 6.2(1))—The application by originating summons in Form 10 must be intituled "In the matter of the Child Abduction and Custody Act 1985 and in the matter of [the child in respect of whom the application is made]". The applicant will be the plaintiff, and the abductor will be the defendant.

"declaration under section 23(2)" (r 6.2(2))—CACA 1985, s 23(2) provides that a court which makes a decision about a child who has been removed from the UK may also declare the removal to be unlawful for the purposes of the European Convention.

6.3 Contents of originating summons: general provisions

(1) The originating summons by which any application is made under the Hague Convention or the European Convention shall state –

- (*a*) the name and date of birth of the child in respect of whom the application is made;
- (*b*) the names of the child's parents or guardians;
- (*c*) the whereabouts or suspected whereabouts of the child;
- (*d*) the interest of the plaintiff in the matter and the grounds of the application; and
- (*e*) particulars of any proceedings (including proceedings out of the jurisdiction and concluded proceedings) relating to the child,

and shall be accompanied by all relevant documents including but not limited to the documents specified in Article 8 of the Hague Convention or, as the case may be, Article 13 of the European Convention.

Defined terms—"child": Child Abduction and Custody Act 1985, Sch 1, Art 4, Sch 2, Art 1(*a*); "European Convention": CACA 1985, s 12(1); "Hague Convention": CACA 1985, s 1(1); "originating summons": RSC Ord 1, r 4.

Originating summons—Since the originating summons is in Form 10, before the matters set out in this rule are set out, a concise statement of the relief or remedy claimed must be included.

"the interest of the plaintiff" (r 6.3(1)(*d*))—In relation to an application under the Hague Convention, the applicant may be any person, institution or other body, who claims that a child has been removed or retained in breach of custody rights (CACA 1985, Sch 1, Art 8). In the case of an application under the European Convention, the applicant may be any person who has obtained in a Contracting State a decision relating to the custody of a child and who wishes to have that decision recognised or enforced (CACA 1985, Sch 2, Art 4). In *Re J (A Minor) (Abduction: Ward of Court)* [1989] Fam 85, [1990] 1 FLR 276, it was held that the applicant did not himself have to have custody rights in order to be able to apply under Sch 1, Art 8; he had to show that the removal was in breach of custody rights attributed to a person, an institution or any other body so that it was wrongful within the meaning of Art 3. Article 5 provides that custody rights include rights relating to the care of the person of the child and, in particular, the right to determine the child's place of residence. Therefore, since the wardship court has parental jurisdiction with regard to its wards including the right to determine place of residence, removal without leave of the court was wrongful within the meaning of Art 3 (see also *Re C (A Minor) (Abduction)* [1989] 1 FLR 403).

"grounds of the application" (r 6.3(1)(*d*))—Where the Hague Convention applies, the essential ground of application is that there has been a wrongful removal or retention (see **Wrongful**

removal or retention under CACA 1985, Sch 1, Art 3). In the case of an application under the European Convention, the essential ground to secure enforcement by an order for the return of the child to the person in whose favour the custody order was made is that there has been an improper removal.

The essential principle of the Hague Convention is the enforcement of rights of custody rather than rights under court orders. Thus there is no necessity for there to be a court order before the Convention operates. A court order will be an advantage, however, because under CACA 1985, Sch 1, Art 15 the judicial or administrative authorities (the High Court in England and Wales or the Court of Session in Scotland (s 4)) of a Contracting State may, prior to the making of an order for the return of the child, request that the applicant obtain from the authorities of the state of the habitual residence of the child (see **Habitual residence** under CACA 1985, Sch 1, Art 4) a decision or other determination that the removal or retention was wrongful within the meaning of Art 3 of the Convention, where such a decision or determination may be obtained in that State.

The applicant's active participation in family proceedings commenced in England by the defendant does not prevent the applicant from making an application under the Hague Convention for the return of the child to the country of his habitual residence ((*Re B (Minors) (Abduction) (Nos 1 and 2)* [1993] 1 FLR 988 and 993).

"particulars of any proceedings" (r 6.3(1)(*e*))—The applicant must identify the court in which and the date when the order was made and give particulars of the order which was made.

"accompanied by all relevant documents" (r 6.3(1))—In the case of applications under the Hague Convention, CACA 1985, Sch 1, Art 8 requires that the application be accompanied or supplemented by an authenticated copy of any relevant decision or agreement; a certificate or affidavit emanating from the Central Authority, or other competent authority, of the State of the child's habitual residence, or from a qualified person, concerning the relevant law of that State; and any other relevant document. In the case of applications under the European Convention, the documents which must accompany a request for recognition or enforcement are those set out in Sch 2, Art 13, namely:

"(*a*) a document authorising the central authority of the State addressed to act on behalf of the applicant or to designate another representative for that purpose;

(*b*) a copy of the decision which satisfies the necessary conditions of authenticity;

(*c*) in the case of a decision given in the absence of the defendant or his legal representative, a document which establishes that the defendant was duly served with the document which instituted the proceedings or an equivalent document;

(*d*) if applicable, any document which establishes that, in accordance with the law of the State of origin, the decision is enforceable;

(*e*) if possible, a statement indicating the whereabouts or likely whereabouts of the child in the State addressed;

(*f*) proposals as to how the custody of the child should be restored."

Translation of documents—In the case of applications under the Hague Convention, CACA 1985, Sch 1, Art 24 provides that "any application, communication or other document sent to the Central Authority of the requested State shall be in the original language, and shall be accompanied by a translation into the official language or one of the official languages of the requested State or, where that is not feasible, a translation into French or English".

Proof of documents and evidence—In applications under the Hague Convention, for the purposes of Art 14 (which allows the judicial or administrative authorities of the requested state to take notice of decisions in the state of the child's habitual residence), a decision or determination of a judicial or administrative authority outside the UK may be proved by a duly authenticated copy of the decision or determination; and any document purporting to be such a copy shall be deemed to be a true copy unless the contrary is shown (CACA 1985, s 7(1)). A copy is duly authenticated if it bears the seal, or is signed by a judge or officer, of the authority in question (s 7(2)). For the purposes of Arts 14 and 30 of the Hague Convention any such document as is mentioned in Art 8 (see **"accompanied by all relevant documents"** above) or a certified copy of any such document, is sufficient evidence of anything stated in it (s 7(3)). Similar provisions apply under s 22 in respect of applications under the European Convention.

6.4 Contents of originating summons: particular provisions

(1) In applications under the Hague Convention, in addition to the matters specified in rule 6.3 –

(*a*) the originating summons under which an application is made for the purposes of Article 8 for the return of a child shall state the identity of the person alleged to have removed or retained the child and, if different, the identity of the person with whom the child is presumed to be;

(*b*) the originating summons under which an application is made for the purposes of Article 15 for a declaration shall identify the proceedings in which the request that such a declaration be obtained was made.

(2) In applications under the European Convention, in addition to the matters specified in rule 6.3, the originating summons shall identify the decision relating to custody or rights of access which is sought to be registered or enforced or in relation to which a declaration that it is not to be recognised is sought.

Defined terms—"child": Child Abduction and Custody Act 1985, Sch 1, Art 4; "decision relating to custody": CACA 1985, Sch 2, Art 1(*c*); "decision relating to rights of access": CACA 1985, s 27(4); "originating summons": RSC Ord 1, r 4.

"for the purposes of Article 15" (r 6.4(1)(*b*))—Article 15 provides that an application may be made by any person appearing to have an interest in the matter for a declaration that a removal of any child from, or his retention outside, the state of his habitual residence was wrongful. CACA 1985, s 8 provides that the High Court (or the Court of Session) may make such declarations as respects wrongful removal from or retention outside the UK. This provision requires the application to identify the proceedings outside the UK for which such a declaration is required.

PART III

6.5 Defendants

The defendants to an application under the Act shall be –

(*a*) the person alleged to have brought into the United Kingdom the child in respect of whom an application under the Hague Convention is made;

(*b*) the person with whom the child is alleged to be;

(*c*) any parent or guardian of the child who is within the United Kingdom and is not otherwise a party;

(*d*) the person in whose favour a decision relating to custody has been made if he is not otherwise a party; and

(*e*) any other person who appears to the court to have a sufficient interest in the welfare of the child.

Defined terms—"child": Child Abduction and Custody Act 1985, Sch 1, Art 4, Sch 2, Art 1(*a*). "decision relating to custody": CACA 1985, Sch 2, Art 1(*c*); "Hague Convention": CACA 1985, s 1(1).

Defendants—The effect of this rule is that the following persons will be defendants: the child's abductor; any harbourer of the child; the parent or guardian of the child (if not the applicant); any person in whose favour an order listed in CACA 1985, Sch 3 has been made (if not the applicant); and any other person who has an interest in the welfare of the child.

6.6 Acknowledgement of service

The time limit for acknowledging service of an originating summons by which an application is made under the Hague Convention or the European Convention shall be seven days after service of the originating summons (including the day of service) or, in the case of a defendant referred to in rule 6.5(*d*) or (*e*), such further time as the Court may direct.

Defined terms—"European Convention": Child Abduction and Custody Act 1985, s 12(1); "Hague Convention": CACA 1985, s 1(1); "originating summons": RSC Ord 1, r 4.

Time-limits—In the case of a defendant in whose favour a decision relating to custody has been made (and who is not a party by virtue of falling within r 6.5(*a*)–(*c*)), or any other person who has an interest in the welfare of the child, the court has a discretion to extend the time-limit. Similarly, the court has power to abridge the period of time in order to give such interim directions as it thinks fit for the purpose of securing the welfare of the child concerned or for preventing changes in the circumstances relevant to the determination of the application (CACA 1985, s 5). The court may also dispense with service (r 6.9). The seven days or such other time begins to run after service. As to the computation of time, see r 1.5.

Service—As to service generally, see rr 10.2–10.6.

6.7 Evidence

(1) The plaintiff, on issuing an originating summons under the Hague Convention or the European Convention, may lodge affidavit evidence in the principal registry in support of his application and serve a copy of the same on the defendant with the originating summons.

(2) A defendant to an application under the Hague Convention or the European Convention may lodge affidavit evidence in the principal registry and serve a copy of the same on the plaintiff within seven days after service of the originating summons on him.

(3) The plaintiff in an application under the Hague Convention or the European Convention may within seven days thereafter lodge in the principal registry a statement in reply and serve a copy thereof on the defendant.

Defined terms—"European Convention": Child Abduction and Custody Act 1985, s 12(1); "Hague Convention": CACA 1985, s 1(1); "originating summons": RSC Ord 1, r 4.

Plaintiff's affidavit (r 6.7(1))—The filing of an affidavit in support of the plaintiff's application is not mandatory. The information required to be placed before the court under the provisions of CACA 1985, Sch 1, Art 8 or Sch 2, Art 13 and the rules will be set out in the originating summons or the accompanying documents. It is customary to file an affidavit confirming the truth of the matters there set out. A copy of the affidavit should be served on the defendant with the originating summons.

Defendant's affidavit (r 6.7(2))—If a defendant wishes to exercise his right to file an affidavit in answer, it must be filed and served within 7 days after service of the originating summons on him.

If the application is under the Hague Convention and is opposed, the defendant's affidavit/statement should set out simply and concisely the nature of the defence under the Convention and the Article or Articles relied upon, eg to show that Sch 1, Art 3 does not apply (ie that the removal or retention was not wrongful) or that Art 13 applies (eg by alleging that the removal was consented to or that there is a grave risk that return would expose the child to psychological harm). If a specific defence is to be raised, it must be mentioned in the affidavit, or notice of intention should be given (*Re W (Abduction: Procedure)* [1995] 1 FLR 878).

In cases under the European Convention, the defendant's affidavit would seek to show that the ground set out in CACA 1985, Sch 2, Arts 9 and 10 apply. Article 9 provides for the court to refuse to enforce any decision on procedural grounds; Art 10 provides for such refusal where enforcement is clearly contrary to the child's interests or where the child is habitually resident in the state concerned.

Preparation—Care should be taken to ensure that the written statements are succinct and confined to the issues, which must be identified. "The parties' legal advisers have a duty to the court to see that this is the case and should not permit the inevitable emotions which underlie such cases to provoke irrelevance, prejudice and prolixity" (per Connell J in *Re S (Abduction: Intolerable Situation: Beth Din)* [2000] 1 FLR 454). *President's Direction of 10 March 2000* (set out in Pt IV of this work) should be followed in all hearings irrespective of the duration of the case. The only exception is where by reason of the urgency of the application it is not reasonably practicable to prepare a bundle (*Re CH (Family Proceedings: Court Bundles)* [2000] 2 FCR 193). It is the duty of solicitors and counsel to ensure that such bundles are produced. Where poor presentation of a case in the absence of bundles has an adverse effect on the timing of a case, that part of the costs of those responsible will be disallowed on taxation. Skeleton arguments setting out all relevant issues should also be lodged (*Re W (Abduction: Procedure)* [1995] 1 FLR 878).

Oral evidence—Once a child has been found and surrendered, there is no power to order a person to give evidence. The desirability of introducing such a power by way of amendment was considered in *Re D (A Minor) (Child Abduction)* [1989] 1 FLR 97 and in *Re E (A Minor) (Abduction)* [1989] 1 FLR 135. It was held that the evidence in proceedings under CACA 1985 was by way of affidavit and that the parties had no right to give oral evidence in support of their affidavit, although the court had a discretion to admit it.

In *Re F (A Minor) (Child Abduction)* [1992] 1 FLR 548, Butler-Sloss LJ said that proceedings under the Convention were summary in nature and designed to provide a speedy resolution of disputes over children and secure the prompt return of children wrongfully removed from the country of habitual residence. There was no right to give oral evidence, although the court had a discretion to admit it. There was a real danger that, if oral evidence were to be generally admitted in such cases, it would become impossible for them to be dealt with expeditiously, and the purpose of the Convention might be frustrated. See also *V v B (A Minor) (Abduction)* [1991] 1 FLR 266. The admission of oral evidence was refused in *Re K (Abduction: Child's Objections)* [1995] 1 FLR 977, where the mother sought to adduce such evidence in order for the court to make findings of fact which would substantiate the basis for the exercise of the discretion under Art 13. The court held that it was not necessary for there to be specific findings of fact in order for the defence under Art 13(*b*) to succeed. However, in *Re G (Abduction: Psychological Harm)* [1995] 1 FLR 64 and *N v N (Abduction: Article 13 Defence)* [1995] 1 FLR 107, on the particular facts of the case, the oral evidence of experts was received.

As to the introduction on appeal of additional evidence (particularly evidence which was available at the trial), see *Re S (Minors) (Abduction)* [1993] 1 FCR 789; the principles laid down in *Ladd v Marshall* (1954) FLR Rep 422 were relaxed because the mother and her legal advisers had had only three days to prepare the evidence and the case was one which was difficult by reason of the fact that it dealt with children of dual nationality. The court held that, in appropriate cases, the *Ladd v Marshall* rules should be relaxed where the welfare of children required the court to see additional evidence.

6.8 Hearing

Any application under the Act (other than an application (*a*) to join a defendant, (*b*) to dispense with service or extend the time for acknowledging service, or (*c*) for the transfer of proceedings) shall be heard and determined by a judge and shall be dealt with in chambers unless the court otherwise directs.

Defined terms—"judge": r 1.2(1).

6.9 Dispensing with service

The court may dispense with service of any summons (whether originating or ordinary) in any proceedings under the Act.

"court may"—Since "court" is defined in r 1.2(1) to include a district judge, and an application to dispense with service is not expressly reserved to a judge by r 6.8, it would appear that such an application may be heard by a district judge.

6.10 Adjournment of summons

The hearing of the originating summons under which an application under the Hague Convention or the European Convention is made may be adjourned for a period not exceeding 21 days at any one time.

Defined terms—"European Convention": Child Abduction and Custody Act 1985, s 12(1); "Hague Convention": CACA 1985, s 1(1); "originating summons": RSC Ord 1, r 4.

Delay—When dealing with any application for an adjournment of an application under the Hague Convention, the court will be mindful that it may be required to give reasons for any delay beyond six weeks in reaching a decision under CACA 1985, Sch 1, Art 11.

"not exceeding 21 days"—As to computation of time, see r 1.5.

6.11 Stay of proceedings

(1) A party to proceedings under the Hague Convention shall, where he knows that an application relating to the merits of rights of custody is pending in or before a relevant authority, file in the principal registry a concise statement of the nature of the application which is pending, including the authority before which it is pending.

(2) A party –

- (*a*) to pending proceedings under section 16 of the Act, or
- (*b*) to proceedings as a result of which a decision relating to custody has been registered under section 16 of the Act,

shall, where he knows that such an application as is specified in section 20(2) of the Act or section 42(2) of the Child Custody Act 1987 (an Act of Tynwald) is pending in or before a relevant authority, file a concise statement of the nature of the application which is pending.

(3) The proper officer shall on receipt of such a statement as is mentioned in paragraph (1) or (2) notify the relevant authority in which or before whom the application is pending and shall subsequently notify it or him of the result of the proceedings.

(4) On the court receiving notification under paragraph (3) above or equivalent notification from the Court of Session, the High Court in Northern Ireland or the High Court of Justice of the Isle of Man –

- (*a*) where the application relates to the merits of rights of custody, all further proceedings in the action shall be stayed unless and until the proceedings under the Hague Convention in the High Court, Court of Session, the High Court in Northern Ireland or the High Court of Justice of the Isle of Man, as the case may be, are dismissed, and the parties to the action shall be notified by the proper officer of the stay and of any such dismissal accordingly, and
- (*b*) where the application is such a one as is specified in section 20(2) of the Act, the proper officer shall notify the parties to the action.

(5) In this rule "relevant authority" includes the High Court, a county court, a magistrates' court, the Court of Session, a sheriff court, a children's hearing within the meaning of Part III of the Social Work (Scotland) Act 1968, the High Court in Northern Ireland, a county court in Northern Ireland, a court of summary jurisdiction in Northern Ireland, the High Court of Justice of the Isle of Man, a court of summary jurisdiction in the Isle of Man or the Secretary of State.

Amendments—SI 1994/2890.

Defined terms—"Hague Convention": Child Abduction and Custody Act 1985, s 1(1); "proper officer": r 1.2(1); "relevant authority": r 6.11(5); "rights of custody": CACA 1985, Sch 1, Art 5.

"section 16 of the Act" (r 6.11(2))—CACA 1985, s 16 provides for the registration of decisions relating to custody in accordance with the European Convention.

6.12 Transfer of proceedings

(1) At any stage in the proceedings under the Act the court may, of its own motion or on the application by summons of any party to the proceedings issued on two days' notice, order that the proceedings be transferred to the Court of Session, the High Court in Northern Ireland or the High Court of Justice of the Isle of Man.

(2) Where an order is made under paragraph (1) the proper officer shall send a copy of the order, which shall state the grounds therefor, together with the originating summons, the documents accompanying it and any evidence, to the Court of Session, the High Court in Northern Ireland or the High Court of Justice of the Isle of Man, as the case may be.

(3) Where proceedings are transferred to the Court of Session, the High Court in Northern Ireland or the High Court of Justice of the Isle of Man the costs of the whole proceedings both before and after the transfer shall be at the discretion of the Court to which the proceedings are transferred.

(4) Where proceedings are transferred to the High Court from the Court of Session, the High Court in Northern Ireland or the High Court of Justice of the Isle of Man the proper officer shall notify the parties of the transfer and the proceedings shall continue as if they had begun by originating summons under rule 6.2.

Amendments—SI 1994/2890.

Defined terms—"originating summons": RSC Ord 1, r 4; "proper officer": r 1.2(1).

"two days' notice" (r 6.12(1))—The court has power to dispense with service of a summons under r 6.9 and would no doubt have power to dispense with the requirement of notice under this rule. As to the computation of time, see r 1.5.

6.13 Interim directions

An application for interim directions under section 5 or section 19 of the Act may where the case is one of urgency be made ex parte on affidavit but shall otherwise be made by summons.

Powers of the court on interim directions—By virtue of CACA 1985, ss 5 and 19, where an application has been made to a court in the UK under either convention, the court may at any time before the application is determined give such interim directions as it thinks fit for the purpose of securing the welfare of the child concerned or of preventing changes in the circumstances relevant to the determination of the application. The court has the power to deal with all interlocutory matters. In addition the provisions of CACA 1985, Sch 1, Arts 7 and 10 and Sch 2, Art 5 require all appropriate steps to be taken to ascertain the whereabouts of the child and to ensure his return. Thus the court will have power to deal with all matters as it would under its inherent jurisdiction; this includes the power to make a collection and location order; to order the defendant to deliver the child; and to order the disclosure of the child's whereabouts. This order may be directed to the solicitors who are acting for the offending party. In such cases, the order should require the solicitors to disclose information which is within their knowledge or control as to the whereabouts of the offending party and the child and information which is capable of assisting in tracing their whereabouts. The order should also include an injunction forbidding the individual to disclose the existence of the order until it has been served and complied with, or until the tipstaff has had an opportunity to follow up the information and retrieve the child (*Re H (Abduction: Whereabouts Order to Solicitors)* [2000] 1 FLR 766). In addition to the court's powers to order disclosure the court has additional powers under the CACA 1985, s 24A, where adequate information as to the child's whereabouts is not available, to order any person whom it has reason to believe may have relevant information to disclose it to the court (see also r 6.16).

The court also has powers to grant injunctions; to order a children and family reporter's report to be prepared (ss 6, 21); to give specific directions for trial; to order publicity (*Re D (A Minor)*

PART III

(Child Abduction) [1989] 1 FLR 97); to dispense with service (r 6.9); to adjourn the hearing for up to 21 days (r 6.10); and to stay the proceedings (r 6.11).

On a directions hearing the court should consider including in the direction a provision that the parties should identify: (i) any undertakings that they seek; and (ii) any undertakings that they are prepared to give (*Re M (Child Abduction: Existence of Undertaking)* [2000] 3 FCR 693).

6.14 (*revoked*)

6.15 Revocation and variation of registered decisions

(1) This rule applies to decisions which have been registered under section 16 of the Act and are subsequently varied or revoked by an authority in the Contracting State in which they were made.

(2) The court shall, on cancelling the registration of a decision which has been revoked, notify –

(*a*) the person appearing to the court to have care of the child,
(*b*) the person on whose behalf the application for registration of the decision was made, and
(*c*) any other party to that application,

of the cancellation.

(3) The court shall, on being notified of the variation of a decision, notify –

(*a*) the person appearing to the court to have care of the child, and
(*b*) any party to the application for registration of the decision

of the variation and any such person may apply by summons in the proceedings for the registration of the decision, for the purpose of making representations to the court before the registration is varied.

(4) Any person appearing to the court to have an interest in the matter may apply by summons in the proceedings for the registration of a decision for the cancellation or variation of the registration.

Defined terms—"child": Child Abduction and Custody Act 1985, Sch 2, Art 1(*a*); "Contracting State": CACA 1985, s 13(1).

Scope of provision—This rule makes provision as to the cancellation or variation of a registered decision where that decision has been varied or cancelled by a judicial or administrative authority in the country where the decision was originally given. It should be read together with CACA 1985, s 17, which places a duty on the person on whose behalf the application for registration was made to notify the court in which the decision of the variation or revocation is registered. Where the decision is revoked the court will cancel the registration and will give notice to the parties of the cancellation. There is no provision for the parties to make representations before the cancellation takes place. In a case where the decision has been varied, the court will notify the parties and any such person will have the right to make representations before the registration is varied. In addition, r 6.15(4) gives any person who has an interest in the matter the right to apply by summons for the registration of a variation or cancellation of a decision. There is no further provision in respect of such an application, such as for the filing of evidence, the time for service and for filing any affidavit in support or reply, but, before the court deals with such an application, applying the provisions of r 6.15(3), the court should give the other party the opportunity to make representations.

6.16 Orders for disclosure of information

At any stage in proceedings under the European Convention the court may, if it has reason to believe that any person may have relevant information about the child who is the subject of those proceedings, order that person to disclose such information and may for that purpose order that the person attend before it or file affidavit evidence.

Defined terms—"child": Child Abduction and Custody Act 1985, Sch 2, Art 1(*a*); "European Convention": CACA 1985, s 12(1).

Scope of provision—This rule reinforces the provisions of CACA 1985, s 24A, which enables the court, where adequate information as to the child's whereabouts is not available, to order any person who it has reason to believe may have relevant information to disclose it. A person is not excused from complying with an order under s 24A by reason that to do so may incriminate him or his spouse of an offence (s 24A(2)). A statement or admission made in compliance with such an order will not be admissible in evidence against the person or his spouse in proceedings for any offence other than perjury. The court has power to order the attendance of a witness and to give information about the whereabouts of the child (see *Re D (A Minor) (Child Abduction) Note* [1989] 1 FLR 97). Where an order for disclosure is made, the form of order should provide for the disclosure of "all information possessed by [the named person/s] as to the past movements and present whereabouts of the child or of the defendant" (*Re D (A Minor) (Child Abduction) (Note)* [1989] 1 FLR 97 at 100).

"in proceedings under the European Convention"—This rule applies to proceedings under the European Convention only, although CACA 1985, s 24A applies to proceedings under either convention.

6.17 Applications and orders under sections 33 and 34 of the Family Law Act 1986

(1) In this rule "the 1986 Act" means the Family Law Act 1986.

(2) An application under section 33 of the 1986 Act shall be in Form C4 and an order made under that section shall be in Form C30.

(3) An application under section 34 of the 1986 Act shall be in Form C3 and an order made under that section shall be in Form C31.

(4) An application under section 33 or section 34 of the 1986 Act may be made ex parte in which case the applicant shall file the application –

(*a*) where the application is made by telephone, within 24 hours after the making of the application, or

(*b*) in any other case at the time when the application is made,

and shall serve a copy of the application on each respondent 48 hours after the making of the order.

(5) Where the court refuses to make an order on an ex parte application it may direct that the application be made inter partes.

Amendments—Inserted by SI 1994/3155.

Powers and practice—See Procedural Guides 54 and 56 and the notes under FLA 1986, ss 33, 34.

PART VII
ENFORCEMENT OF ORDERS

Chapter 1. General

7.1 Enforcement of order for payment of money etc

(1) Before any process is issued for the enforcement of an order made in family proceedings for the payment of money to any person, an affidavit shall be filed

verifying the amount due under the order and showing how that amount is arrived at.

In a case to which CCR Order 25 rule 11 (which deals with the enforcement of a High Court judgment in the county court) applies, the information required to be given in an affidavit under this paragraph may be given in the affidavit filed pursuant to that rule.

(2) Except with the leave of the district judge, no writ of fieri facias or warrant of execution shall be issued to enforce payment of any sum due under an order for ancillary relief or an order made under the provisions of section 27 of the Act of 1973 where an application for a variation order is pending.

(3) Where a warrant of execution has been issued to enforce an order made in family proceedings pending in the principal registry which are treated as pending in a divorce county court, the goods and chattels against which the warrant has been issued shall wherever they are situate, be treated for the purposes of section 103 of the County Courts Act 1984 as being out of the jurisdiction of the principal registry.

(4) The Attachment of Earnings Act 1971 and CCR Order 27 (which deals with attachment of earnings) shall apply to the enforcement of an order made in family proceedings in the principal registry which are treated as pending in a divorce county court as if the order were an order made by such a court.

(5) Where an application under CCR Order 25, rule 3 (which deals with the oral examination of a judgment debtor) relates to an order made by a divorce county court –

(*a*) the application shall be made to such divorce county court as in the opinion of the applicant is nearest to the place where the debtor resides or carries on business, and

(*b*) there shall be filed with the application the affidavit required by paragraph (1) of this rule and, except where the application is made to the court in which the order sought to be enforced was made, a copy of the order shall be exhibited to the affidavit;

and accordingly paragraph (2) of the said rule 3 shall not apply.

Defined terms—"ancillary relief": r 1.2(1); "debtor": CCR Ord 25, r 1; "district judge", "divorce county court", "family proceedings", "principal registry", "variation order": r 1.2(1).

"enforcement of an order made in family proceedings" (r 7.1(1))—Rules 7.1–7.6 modify for family proceedings the rules relating to enforcement contained in RSC and CCR as they were before 26 April 1999.

Affidavit verifying amount due (r 7.1(1))—An affidavit is always required before issuing process to enforce a money judgment. This contrasts with the requirement for a certificate of amount due on the issue of a warrant of execution (CCR Ord 26, r 1(1)) and the absence of any similar general requirement on issue of a writ of fieri facias. The information called for by this rule may be incorporated in the affidavit required in the case of enforcement of a High Court judgment in the county court; and in other cases where an affidavit would in any event be required the same practice is in fact generally accepted.

If the amount is due under a High Court order, or under a county court order for at least £5,000 upon which interest is recoverable, then the calculation of the interest claimed should be set out in the affidavit or exhibited to it and (in the county court) a second copy provided.

"where an application for a variation order is pending" (r 7.1(2))—In such a case leave is needed to issue execution against goods (other methods of enforcement require an application, which would be subject to similar considerations to the application for leave). The affidavit filed should state whether a variation application is pending and, if so, recite or exhibit a copy of the order giving leave. Alternatively, the solicitor's certificate will be accepted (*Registrar's Direction of 5 March 1957* [1957] 1 All ER 860).

Principal registry (r 7.1(3))—The principal registry has no "district" for the purpose of execution against goods.

Oral examination (r 7.1(5))—In the case of a county court application for an order for oral examination, the application must be made to the divorce county court nearest the debtor's home or place of business. This replaces the requirement in CCR Ord 25, r 3(2) that it be made to the debtor's home county court. It is not the practice first to seek transfer of the cause, notwithstanding CCR Ord 25, r 2. A copy of the order must be exhibited to the affidavit if the application is not made to the court which made the order. (In the case of a cause which has since been transferred this should be taken to mean the court in which the cause is currently proceeding.) The county court's power to order an oral examination is limited to the case of a judgment obtained in the county court (see CCR Ord 25, r 3(1)).

7.2 Committal and injunction

(1) Subject to RSC Order 52, rule 6 (which, except in certain cases, requires an application for an order of committal to be heard in open court) an application for an order of committal in family proceedings pending in the High Court shall be made by summons.

(2) Where no judge is conveniently available to hear the application, then, without prejudice to CCR Order 29, rule 3(2) (which in certain circumstances gives jurisdiction to a district judge) an application for –

(*a*) the discharge of any person committed, or
(*b*) the discharge by consent of an injunction granted by a judge,

may be made to the district judge who may, if satisfied of the urgency of the matter and that it is expedient to do so, make any order on the application which a judge could have made.

(3) Where an order or warrant for the committal of any person to prison has been made or issued in family proceedings pending in the principal registry which are treated as pending in a divorce county court or a county court, that person shall, wherever he may be, be treated for the purposes of section 122 of the County Courts Act 1984 as being out of the jurisdiction of the principal registry; but if the committal is for failure to comply with the terms of an injunction, the order or warrant may, if the court so directs, be executed by the tipstaff within any county court district.

(3A) Where an order or warrant for the arrest or committal of any person has been made or issued in proceedings under Part IV of the Family Law Act 1996 pending in the principal registry which are treated as pending in a county court, the order or warrant may, if the court so directs, be executed by the tipstaff within any county court district.

(4) For the purposes of section 118 of the County Courts Act 1984 in its application to the hearing of family proceedings at the Royal Courts of Justice or the principal registry, the tipstaff shall be deemed to be an officer of the court.

Amendments—SI 1997/1893.

Defined terms—"district judge", "divorce county court", "family proceedings", "principal registry": r 1.2(1).

Application to commit (r 7.2(1))—Somewhat unusually, High Court committal applications are to be made by summons (rather than by motion) even though, subject to exceptions, they must be heard in open court. The exceptions are set out in RSC Ord 52, r 6, but the one most commonly encountered in family matters will be that the order breached was made in proceedings concerning children.

Discharge (r 7.2(2))—As regards the county court at least, the extension of the district judge's power to discharge is more apparent than real as he has that power generally under CCR Ord 29, r 3(2) unless the committal order otherwise directs. If the order does so direct, the district judge is unlikely to be satisfied that it is "expedient" to rely on this rule.

7.3 Transfer of county court order to High Court

(1) Any person who desires the transfer to the High Court of any order made by a divorce county court in family proceedings except an order for periodical payments or for the recovery of arrears of periodical payments shall apply to the court ex parte by affidavit stating the amount which remains due under the order, and on the filing of the application the transfer shall have effect.

(2) Where an order is so transferred, it shall have the same force and effect and the same proceedings may be taken on it as if it were an order of the High Court.

Defined terms—"divorce county court", "family proceedings": r 1.2(1); "periodical payments": Matrimonial Causes Act 1973, s 21, CA 1989, Sch 1, para 1.

Scope of provision—This rule authorises the transfer of certain orders from the county court to the High Court as distinct from the transfer of the proceedings under Matrimonial and Family Proceedings Act 1984, s 39.

Periodical payments (r 7.3(1))—The procedure provided by this rule is not available to enforce periodical payments orders or arrears under them.

"effect" (r 7.3(2))—An order transferred under this rule becomes a High Court order for all purposes. (This contrasts with the qualification set out in County Courts Act 1984, s 42(6), which does not apply to family proceedings).

Chapter 2. Judgment summonses

7.4 General provisions

(1) In this chapter, unless the context otherwise requires –

"order" means an order made in family proceedings for the payment of money;

"judgment creditor" means a person entitled to enforce an order under section 5 of the Debtors Act 1869;

"debtor" means a person liable under an order;

"judgment summons" means a summons under the said section 5 requiring a debtor to attend court.

(2) An application for the issue of a judgment summons may be made –

(*a*) in the case of an order of the High Court, to the principal registry, a district registry or a divorce county court, whichever in the opinion of the judgment creditor is most convenient,

(*b*) in the case of an order of a divorce county court, to whichever divorce county court is in the opinion of the judgment creditor most convenient,

having regard (in either case) to the place where the debtor resides or carries on business and irrespective of the court or registry in which the order was made.

(3) The application shall be made by filing a request in Form M16 together with the affidavit required by rule 7.1(1) and, except where the application is made to the registry or divorce county court in which the order was made, a copy of the order shall be exhibited to the affidavit.

(3A) The judgment creditor must file with the request copies of all written evidence on which he intends to rely.

(4) A judgment summons shall not be issued without the leave of a judge if the debtor is in default under an order of commitment made on a previous judgment summons in respect of the same order.

(5) Every judgment summons shall be in Form M17 and shall be served on the debtor personally together with copies of the written evidence referred to in paragraph (3A) not less than 14 days before the hearing and at the time of service there shall be paid or tendered to the debtor a sum reasonably sufficient to cover his expenses in travelling to and from the court at which he is summoned to appear.

(6) CCR Order 28, rule 3 (which deals among other things with the issue of successive judgment summonses) shall apply to a judgment summons, whether issued in the High Court or a divorce county court, but as if the said rule 3 did not apply CCR Order 7, rule 19(2).

(7) Successive judgment summonses may be issued notwithstanding that the judgment debtor has ceased to reside or carry on business at the address stated in Form M16 since the issue of the original judgment summons.

(7A) The following documents must be served personally on the debtor –

(*a*) where the proceedings are in the High Court and the court has summonsed the debtor to attend and he has failed to do so, the notice of the day and time fixed for the adjourned hearing;
(*b*) where the proceedings are in the county court, an order made under section 110(1) of the County Courts Act 1984;
(*c*) in either case, copies of the judgment summons, the affidavit required by rule 7.1(1) and all written evidence referred to in paragraph (3A).

(7B) No person may be committed on an application for a judgment summons unless –

(*a*) where the proceedings are in the High Court, the court has summonsed the debtor to attend, he has failed to do so, and he has also failed to attend the adjourned hearing;
(*b*) where the proceedings are in the county court, an order is made under section 110(2) of the County Courts Act 1984; or
(*c*) the judgment creditor proves that the debtor –
   (i) has or has had since the date of the order the means to pay the sum in respect of which he has made default; and
   (ii) has refused or neglected or refuses or neglects to pay that sum.

(7C) The debtor may not be compelled to give evidence.

(8) Where an applicant has obtained one or more orders in the same application but for the benefit of different persons –

(*a*) he shall be entitled to issue a judgment summons in respect of those orders on behalf of any judgment creditor without (where the judgment creditor is a child) seeking leave to act as his next friend; and
(*b*) only one judgment summons need be issued in respect of those orders.

(9) On the hearing of the judgment summons the judge may –

(*a*) where the order is for lump sum provision or costs, or

PART III

(*b*) where the order is for maintenance pending suit or other periodical payments and it appears to him that the order would have been varied or suspended if the debtor had made an application for that purpose,

make a new order for payment of the amount due under the original order, together with the costs of the judgment summons, either at a specified time or by instalments.

(10) If the judge makes an order of committal, he may direct its execution to be suspended on terms that the debtor pays to the judgment creditor the amount due, together with the costs of the judgment summons, either at a specified time or by instalments, in addition to any sums accruing due under the original order.

(11) All payments under a new order or an order of committal shall be made to the judgment creditor unless the judge otherwise directs.

(12) Where an order of committal is suspended on such terms as are mentioned in paragraph (10) –

(*a*) all payments thereafter made under the said order shall be deemed to be made, first, in or towards the discharge of any sums from time to time accruing due under the original order and, secondly, in or towards the discharge of a debt in respect of which the judgment summons was issued and the costs of the summons;

(*b*) CCR Order 28, rule 7(4) and (5) (which deal with an application for a further suspension) shall apply to the said order, whether it was made in the High Court or a divorce county court; and

(*c*) the said order shall not be issued until the judgment creditor has filed an affidavit of default on the part of the debtor.

Amendments—SI 2003/184.

Defined terms—"divorce county court", "family proceedings": r 1.2(1); "lump sum": Matrimonial Causes Act 1973, s 21, CA 1989, Sch 1, para 1; "maintenance pending suit": MCA 1973, s 22; "periodical payments": MCA 1973, s 21, CA 1989, Sch 1, para 1; "principal registry": r 1.2(1).

"section 5 of the Debtors Act 1869" (r 7.4(1))—The section provides:

"Subject to the provisions hereinafter mentioned, and to the prescribed rules, any court may commit to prison for a term not exceeding six weeks, or until payment of the sum due, any person who makes default in payment of any debt or instalment of any debt due from him in pursuance of any order or judgment of that or any other competent court. Provided –

(1) That the jurisdiction by this section given of committing a person to prison shall, in the case of any court other than the superior courts of law and equity, be exercised only subject to the following restrictions; that is to say

(*a*) be exercised only by a judge or his deputy, and by an order made in open court and showing on its face the ground on which it is issued;

(*b*) (*repealed*)

(*c*) be exercised only as respects a judgment of a county court by a county court judge or his deputy.

(2) That such jurisdiction shall only be exercised where it is proved to the satisfaction of the court that the person making default either has or has had since the date of the order or judgment the means to pay the sum in respect of which he has made default, and has refused or neglected, or refuses or neglects, to pay the same.

Proof of the means of the person making default may be given in such manner as the court thinks just.

For the purpose of considering whether to commit a debtor to prison under this section, the debtor may be summoned in accordance with the prescribed rules.

For the purposes of this section any court may direct any debt due from any person in pursuance of any order or judgment of that or any other competent court to be paid by instalments, and may from time to time rescind or vary such order.

No imprisonment under this section shall operate as a satisfaction or extinguishment of any debt or demand or cause of action, or deprive any person of any right to take out execution against the lands, goods or chattels of the person imprisoned, in the same manner as if such imprisonment had not taken place.

Any person imprisoned under this section shall be discharged out of custody upon a certificate signed in the prescribed manner to the effect that he has satisfied a debt or instalment of a debt in respect of which he was imprisoned, together with the prescribed costs (if any)."

The provision that proof of the debtor's means may be given by summoning him to be examined on oath has been removed by the amendment made to the section by the Civil Procedure (Modification of Enactments) Order 2002. The amendment is a consequence of the finding in *Mubarak v Mubarak and others* [2001] 1 FLR 698, CA that the provision was incompatible with the Human Rights Act 1998, the proceedings being of a penal character and the requirement amounting to compulsory self-incrimination. It is for the creditor to prove the necessary facts (see **"the judgment creditor proves"** below) by such other evidence as he can muster. Amendments have also been made to the CPR and, latterly, these Rules in consequence of the same decision.

The jurisdiction which the section confers may now be exercised by the High Court only in respect of a High Court maintenance order (ie a maintenance order enforceable by the High Court (Administration of Justice Act 1970, s 28(1)), which includes an order registered in or transferred to the High Court) and by the county court in respect of a High Court or a county court maintenance order, as well as in respect of certain orders for payment of taxes etc (Administration of Justice Act 1970, s 11). The term "maintenance order" is defined by Administration of Justice Act 1970, s 28 and Sch 8; in addition to periodical payments the definitions in Sch 8 include "other payments made or having effect as if made under" the provisions there referred to, including, for example, MCA 1973, Pt II, which provides for lump sum and other orders for payment of money which would not normally be thought of as maintenance orders. An obligation to pay pursuant to an undertaking may be enforced by this procedure (*Symmons v Symmons* [1993] 1 FLR 317).

Venue (r 7.4(2))—Which venue is "convenient" depends inter alia on the *debtor's* residence or place of business. The summons cannot be issued in a county court which is not a divorce county court.

Issue (r 7.4(3))—Even in the High Court, a request (Form M16) is filed and the summons (Form M17) is made up by the court.

Evidence (r 7.4(3A))—The requirement, inserted by Family Proceedings (Amendment) Rules 2003, is to file all the written evidence on which the creditor intends to rely. Copies will be served on the debtor (r 7.4(5)). The object is to secure compliance with HRA 1998 as applied in *Mubarak v Mubarak* (above). Thus, the written statements of witnesses on whose oral evidence it is intended to rely should be included. No doubt, if additional evidence came to light before the hearing, it would be admitted provided it had been copied to the debtor promptly and in sufficient time before the hearing to enable him to deal with it.

"the adjourned hearing" (r 7.4(7A)(*a*))—The rule assumes that the hearing originally fixed by the judgment summons will have been adjourned – possibly on the debtor's failure to attend. However, see **"the judgment creditor proves"** below.

"order made under section 110(1)" (r 7.4(7A)(*b*))—This is an order to attend the adjourned hearing. The section enables, but does not require, the judge so to order if the debtor fails to attend. See **"the judgment creditor proves"** below.

"No person may be committed … unless" (r 7.4(7B))—It is necessary to distinguish the "offences" for which committal can be imposed. Failure to attend in response to a judgment summons itself does not carry a penalty (save, perhaps, in costs). Failure to comply with an order of the High Court to attend an adjourned hearing is punishable as contempt of court (covered by r 4.7(7B)(*a*)). Failure to comply with such an order made, under CCA 1984, s 110(1), by a county court may be met by imprisonment of up to 14 days (s 110(2), covered by r 7.4(7B)(*b*)). Refusal

PART III

or neglect to pay the judgment debt carries imprisonment of up to 6 weeks (Debtors Act 1869, s 5, covered by r 7.4(7B)(*c*)).

"the judgment creditor proves" (r 7.4(7B)(*c*))—It is not a requirement that the debtor be in attendance. Where the judge is satisfied that the judgment summons has been duly served, with evidence which proves that the debtor has or has had the means to pay and neglects or refuses (or has neglected or refused) to pay, he is not obliged to exercise his power to order the debtor to attend an adjourned hearing. See further **Order for attendance** under CCR Ord 28, r 4. Particularly in a case where the evidence demonstrates that the debtor is aware of the hearing, chooses to absent himself, is able to pay and is defying the court's order, the judge may find that an adjournment and order to attend, with consequent costs, would serve no purpose; and exercise his power to commit under s 5 without first making such an order. (The debtor would, of course, still be able to apply to set aside the order made in his absence.) An order made in these circumstances might well be suspended for a short period to enable the debtor to pay.

The evidence must show that the debtor has or had the means to pay (*Buckley v Crawford* [1893] 1 QB 105; *R v Birmingham County Court Judge* [1902] 2 KB 283). His conduct must be in the nature of a contempt (*Re Edgcome, ex parte Edgcome* [1902] 2 KB 403), although it is his means and not his general conduct which are the relevant consideration (*Abecasis v Brandon* [1947] LJR 325). The standard of proof of the debtor's means is the criminal standard, that is beyond reasonable doubt (*Woodley v Woodley* [1992] 2 FLR 417, CA). After the making of a bankruptcy order, the debtor will usually no longer have the means to pay and, in those circumstances, a committal order will not be made unless his failure to pay before the bankruptcy was such as to merit punishment (*Woodley v Woodley (No 2)* [1993] 2 FLR 477, CA). The debtor's means include gifts received (*Re Park, ex parte Koster* (1885) 14 QBD 597), but not future sums which may be received such as a husband's allowance to his wife (*Barefoot v Clarke* [1949] 2 KB 97, [1949] 1 All ER 1039). Child benefit and certain social security benefits paid in respect of children must be ignored.

Gaps in the evidence as to the debtor's means can no longer be made good by requiring him to submit to questioning (r 7.4(7C)). It seems unlikely that any evidence he gave, under compulsion, on oral examination under CCR Ord 26, r 3 will be admitted.

As an alternative to a committal order the court may make an attachment of earnings order (Attachment of Earnings Act 1971, s 3(4)). For this purpose, proof of the debtor's means to the civil standard only would be needed. A further alternative is to make a new order under r 7.4(9). If the proceedings concern a "qualifying periodical maintenance order" within the meaning of Maintenance Enforcement Act 1991, s 1 then, under s 1(4)(*a*), the court may of its own motion make a "means of payment order", whether as an alternative to or in aid of a suspended committal order or a new order.

New order (r 7.4(9))—This alternative to a committal order effectively gives the periodical payments debtor further time to pay the arrears. It is available only if the judge believes that an application to vary or suspend would have succeeded. It allows time for such an application to be made and for the question then to be considered whether some or all of the arrears should be remitted. The judge hearing a judgment summons does not himself have power to remit. Accordingly, this rule does not contemplate that the judge will make a new order for, or a suspended committal order on, payment of anything other than "the amount due, together with the costs of the judgment summons". A new order may of course also be made in respect of a lump sum order.

Default where committal order suspended (r 7.4(12)(*c*))—The judgment creditor must file an affidavit of default by the debtor so that the order may issue; in the county court, a request under CCR Ord 28, r 11(1) for the issue of a committal warrant must also be filed. No opportunity is given to the debtor to dispute the assertion that the terms of the suspension have been breached. He would be able to apply, after his arrest, for the warrant to be set aside. Nevertheless, it may be that this provision will not survive a challenge under HRA 1998.

Continued default after committal—Only one term of imprisonment can be imposed in respect of an unpaid amount (*Evans v Wills* (1876) 1 CPD 229). This would not prevent a second judgment summons in respect of fresh arrears under the same periodical payments order.

Forms—Request to issue: M16; judgment summons: M17.

7.5 Special provisions as to judgment summonses in the High Court

(1) (*revoked*)

(2) Witnesses may be summoned to prove the means of the debtor in the same manner as witnesses are summoned to give evidence on the hearing of a cause, and writs of subpoena may for that purpose be issued out of the registry in which the judgment summons is issued.

(3) Where the debtor appears at the hearing, the travelling expenses paid to him may, if the judge so directs, be allowed as expenses of a witness, but if the debtor appears at the hearing and no order of committal is made, the judge may allow to the debtor, by way of set-off or otherwise, his proper costs, including compensation for loss of time, as upon an attendance by a defendant at a trial in court.

(4) Where a new order or an order of committal is made, the proper officer of the registry in which the judgment summons was issued shall send notice of the order to the debtor and, if the original order was made in another registry, to the proper officer of that registry.

(5) An order of committal shall be directed to the tipstaff, for execution by him, or to the proper officer of the county court within the district of which the debtor is to be found, for execution by a deputy tipstaff.

(6), (7) (*revoked*)

Amendments—SI 2003/184.

Defined terms—"debtor", "judgment creditor", "judgment summons": r 7.4(1); "new order": r 7.4(9); "proper officer": r 1.2(1).

"the High Court" (r 7.5)—RSC as they were before 26 April 1999 do not themselves make provision for judgment summons proceedings in the High Court.

Creditor's evidence—The provision which permitted the judgment creditor to give evidence by affidavit (r 7.5(1)) has been removed.

Costs—If costs are to be determined by detailed assessment, any committal order will omit reference to costs, which will be dealt with by a separately drawn order (*Registrar's Direction of 14 January 1959*).

7.6 Special provisions as to judgment summonses in divorce county courts

(1) CCR Order 25, rules 3, 4 and 11 (which deal with the oral examination of debtors and the execution of High Court orders in county courts) and Order 28, rules 1, 2, 3(2), 5, 7(3), 9(2) and 10(3) (which deal with the issue of a judgment summons in a county court and the subsequent procedure) shall not apply to a judgment summons issued in a divorce county court.

(2) CCR Order 28, rule 9(1) (which relates to a judgment summons heard in a county court on a judgment or order of the High Court) shall apply to such a summons as if for the words "the High Court" there were substituted the words "any other court" where they first appear and "that other court" where they next appear.

(3) CCR Order 28, rule 7(1) and (2) (which relates to the suspension of a committal order) shall apply to such a summons subject to rule 7.4(10) and (11) of these Rules.

Amendments—SI 2003/184.

Defined terms—"judgment summons": r 7.4(1).

Oral examination (r 7.6(1))—The disapplication of CCR Ord 25, rr 3 and 4 from judgment summonses is not understood as they do not appear to have any relevance to the procedures created by CCR Ord 28 or to r 7.4 or 7.5.

Creditor's evidence—The provision which permitted the judgment creditor to give evidence by affidavit (CCR Ord 28, r 5) has been removed.

Chapter 3. Registration and enforcement of custody orders

7.7 Registration under Family Law Act 1986

(1) In this Chapter, unless the context otherwise requires –

"the appropriate court" means, in relation to Scotland, the Court of Session and, in relation to Northern Ireland, the High Court and, in relation to a specified dependent territory, the corresponding court in that territory;

"the appropriate officer" means, in relation to the Court of Session, the Deputy Principal Clerk of Session, in relation to the High Court in Northern Ireland, the Master (Care and Protection) of that court and, in relation to the appropriate court in a specified dependent territory, the corresponding officer of that court;

"Part I order" means an order under Part I of the Act of 1986;

"registration" means registration under Part I of the Act of 1986, and "register" and "registered" shall be construed accordingly;

"specified dependent territory" means a dependent territory specified in column 1 of Schedule 1 to the Family Law Act 1986 (Specified Dependent Territories) Order 1991.

(2) The prescribed officer for the purposes of sections 27(4) and 28(1) of the Act shall be the family proceedings department manager of the principal registry and the functions of the court under sections 27(3) and 28(1) of the Act of 1986 shall be performed by the proper officer.

Amendments—SI 1994/2890; SI 1997/1056.

Scope of provision—This rule provides for the interpretation of rr 7.8 to 7.15, which replace RSC Ord 90, rr 48 to 56 and set out the procedure for the registration and enforcement of orders under Family Law Act 1986, ss 25 to 31. As amended, it includes references, where appropriate, to the Isle of Man pursuant to the Family Law Act 1986 (Dependent Territories) Order 1991, which brought orders made in the Isle of Man in relation to children within the reciprocal recognition and enforcement provisions of FLA 1986.

"Part I order" (r 7.7(1))—"Part I orders" are the orders set out in Family Law Act 1986, s 1. The orders to which Part I of the 1986 Act applies now include the following:

(*a*) a section 8 order made by a court in England and Wales under CA 1989 other than an order varying or discharging such an order;

(*b*) an order made by civil court in Scotland with respect to the custody, care or control of a child, access to a child or the education or upbringing of a child but excluding orders made under certain enactments set out under FLA 1986, s 1(1)(*b*);

(*c*) an order made by a court in Northern Ireland under Guardianship of Infants Act 1886, s 5 or Matrimonial Causes (Northern Ireland) Order 1978, art 45(1) or (2);

(*d*) an order made by the High Court in England and Wales or Northern Ireland in the exercise of its inherent jurisdiction relating to wardship, so far as it gives care and control of a child to any person or provides for the education of, or for access to, a child; but excluding any order varying or discharging such an order and any orders relating to a child in favour of the Northern Ireland Department of Health and Social Services;

(*e*) any order which would have been a custody order by virtue of FLA 1986, s 1 in any form in which it was in force at any time before its amendment by CA 1989, otherwise than as excluded by that section;

(*f*) an order made by a court in a specified dependent territory corresponding to any order within paragraphs (*a*) to (*e*) above.

Since the Family Law Act 1986 is not retrospective, it does not affect any orders made before the Act came into force, and orders which vary or revoke previous orders are excluded.

7.8 Application to register English Part I order

(1) An application under section 27 of the Act of 1986 for the registration of a Part I order made by the High Court shall be made by lodging in the principal registry or the district registry, as the case may be, a certified copy of the order, together with a copy of any order which has varied any of the terms of the original order and an affidavit by the applicant in support of his application, with a copy thereof.

(2) An application under section 27 of the Act of 1986 for the registration of a Part I order made by a county court shall be made by filing in that court a certified copy of the order, together with a certified copy of any order which has varied any of the terms of the original order and an affidavit in support of the application, with a copy thereof.

(3) The affidavit in support under paragraphs (1) and (2) above shall state –

(*a*) the name and address of the applicant and his interest under the order;

(*b*) the name and date of birth of the child in respect of whom the order was made, his whereabouts or suspected whereabouts and the name of any person with whom he is alleged to be;

(*c*) the name and address of any other person who has an interest under the order and whether it has been served on him;

(*d*) in which of the jurisdictions of Scotland, Northern Ireland or a specified dependent territory the order is to be registered;

(*e*) that, to the best of the applicant's information and belief, the order is in force;

(*f*) whether, and if so where, the order is already registered; and

(*g*) details of any order known to the applicant which affects the child and is in force in the jurisdiction in which the Part I order is to be registered;

and there shall be exhibited to the affidavit any document relevant to the application.

(4) Where the documents referred to in paragraphs (1) and (3), or (2) and (3), as the case may be are to be sent to the appropriate court, the proper officer shall –

(*a*) retain the original affidavit and send the other documents to the appropriate officer;

(*b*) record the fact of transmission in the records of the court; and

(*c*) file a copy of the documents.

(5) On receipt of notice of the registration of a Part I order in the appropriate court the proper officer shall record the fact of registration in the records of the court.

(6) If it appears to the proper officer that the Part I order is no longer in force or that the child has attained the age of 16, he shall refuse to send the documents to the appropriate court and shall within 14 days of such refusal give notice of it, and the reason for it, to the applicant.

PART III

(7) If the proper officer refuses to send the documents to the appropriate court, the applicant may apply to the judge in chambers for an order that the documents (or any of them) be sent to the appropriate court.

Amendments—SI 1994/2890.

Defined terms—"appropriate court": r 7.7(1); "district registry", "principal registry", "proper officer": r 1.2(1); "registration": r 7.7(1).

"certified copy"—Family Law Act 1986, s 42(1) provides that "certified copy" in relation to an order of any court means a copy certified by the prescribed officer of the court to be a true copy of the order or of the official record of the order.

Documents—A certified copy and a copy of the original order, any order which has varied any of the terms of the original order and any further orders obtained (eg an additional order under Family Law Act 1986, s 33 or s 34), together with an affidavit in support and a copy must be filed.

Contents of affidavit (r 7.8(3))—Any information which might assist in locating the whereabouts or suspected whereabouts of the child should be set out. The affidavit must give the name of any person, with whom the child is alleged to be, not simply that of the person who abducted the child. The affidavit must state whether the order has been served. In order to avoid any difficulties arising, it is best to give full particulars of service and, in the case of personal service, a separate affidavit of service should be exhibited to the affidavit or included with the accompanying documents. The information under r 7.8(3)(*g*) relates to any orders which may have been obtained in Scotland or Northern Ireland. Where the order refers to more than one child the affidavit should identify the child or children in respect of whom registration is sought.

Jurisdiction in which order is to be registered—An order may be registered in Scotland or Northern Ireland or in both jurisdictions. In most cases registration in one jurisdiction will suffice but there will be cases where it is desirable to have the order registered in both jurisdictions, particularly where there is a fear that the child may be moved about in order to avoid being traced.

Sending documents to the appropriate court (r 7.8(4))—No particular method is prescribed. The transmission may take the form of sending the documents to the appropriate court by post, by document exchange or by fax, which is a mode of service approved of under RSC Ord 65, r 5 and FPR 1991, r 10.2 (see also *Hastie & Jenkerson v McMahon* [1990] 1 WLR 1575).

Registration by the appropriate court (r 7.8(5))—Family Law Act 1986, s 27(4) imposes a duty on the prescribed officer of the receiving court to cause the order to be registered forthwith, ie as soon as practicable having regard to the circumstances and nature of the act to be done (see *Re Southam ex parte Lamb* (1881) 19 Ch D 169, [1881] 5 All ER 391; and *Re Muscovitch ex parte M* [1939] Ch 694, [1939] 1 All ER 135).

Appeal from refusal to send the documents (r 7.8(7))—The appeal must be to a judge not a district judge. The rules do not set out any prescribed form for the notice of appeal. The form used for notice of appeal from a district judge's decision is appropriate, suitably modified. Neither the Family Law Act 1986 nor the rules set any time-limits for appealing. The notice of appeal should nevertheless be filed as soon as is practicable because the whole purpose of registration is enforcement without delay. Since there is no other party to be served, there is no reason why the appeal procedure should not be put into action forthwith.

7.9 Registration of orders made in Scotland, Northern Ireland or a specified dependent territory

On receipt of a certified copy of an order made in Scotland, Northern Ireland or a specified dependent territory for registration, the prescribed officer shall –

(*a*) record the order in the register by entering particulars of –

(i) the name and address of the applicant and his interest under the order;

(ii) the name and whereabouts or suspected whereabouts of the child, his date of birth, and the date on which he will attain the age of 16; and

(iii) the terms of the order, its date and the court which made it;

(*b*) file the certified copy and accompanying documents; and

(*c*) give notice to the court which sent the certified copy and to the applicant for registration that the order has been registered.

Amendments—SI 1994/2890.

Defined terms—"specified dependent territory": r 7.1(1).

7.10 Revocation and variation of English order

(1) Where a Part I order which is registered in the appropriate court is revoked or varied, the proper officer of the court making the subsequent order shall –

(*a*) send a certified copy of that order to the appropriate officer, and to the court which made the Part I order, if that court is different from the court making the subsequent order, for filing by that court;

(*b*) record the fact of transmission in the records of the court; and

(*c*) file a copy of the order.

(2) On receipt of notice from the appropriate court of the amendment of its register, the proper officer in the court which made the Part I order and in the court which made the subsequent order shall each record the fact of amendment.

Amendments—SI 1994/2890.

Defined terms—"appropriate court", "Part I order": r 7.7(1); "proper officer": rr 1.2(1), 7.7(1); "register", "registered": r 7.7(1).

Scope of provision—This rule should be read together with Family Law Act 1986, s 28, which makes provision for the cancellation and variation of registered orders. Similar provision is made for the registration of Scottish and Northern Ireland orders and orders made in the Isle of Man in r 7.11 but, unlike r 7.11, there is no provision for the court of its own motion to cancel an order which has ceased to have effect, otherwise than by revocation or variation.

"certified copy"—See r 7.8.

7.11 Registration of revoked, recalled or varied orders made in Scotland, Northern Ireland or a specified dependent territory

(1) On receipt of a certified copy of an order made in Scotland, Northern Ireland or a specified dependent territory which revokes, recalls or varies a registered Part I order, the proper officer shall enter particulars of the revocation, recall or variation, as the case may be, in the register, and give notice of the entry to –

(*a*) the court which sent the certified copy,

(*b*) if different, the court which made the Part I order,

(*c*) the applicant for registration, and

(*d*) if different, the applicant for the revocation, recall or variation of the order.

(2) An application under section 28(2) of the Act of 1986 shall be made by summons and may be heard and determined by a district judge.

(3) If the applicant for the Part I order is not the applicant under section 28(2) of the Act of 1986 he shall be made a defendant to the application.

(4) Where the court cancels a registration of its own motion or on an application under paragraph (2), the proper officer shall amend the register accordingly and shall give notice of the amendment to the court which made the Part I order.

Amendments—SI 1994/2890.

Defined terms—"district judge": r 1.2(1); "Part I order": r 7.7(1); "proper officer": rr 1.2(1), 7.7(1); "register", "registered", "specified dependent territory": r 7.7(1).

Cancellation on application (r 7.11(2))—An application under Family Law Act 1986, s 28(2) is made by summons and is heard by a district judge. The rules do not set any time limits for service of the application nor do they prescribe any other procedure for the filing of evidence or the hearing. The application should be supported by an affidavit setting out the basis upon which the order is sought. The defendant should have a right to reply. Since there is no specific provision regarding the mode of service, the provisions of rr 10.2 to 10.6 will apply.

Cancellation of the court's own motion (r 7.11(4))—No provision is made for the court to give notice to any party. In such cases the court should give the parties an opportunity to be heard or have the consent of both parties to the cancellation of the registration. Where the parties or either of them intimate that they wish to be heard, the court should fix a date, time and place for the hearing and give notice of the same to the parties.

7.12 Interim directions

(1) An application for interim directions under section 29 of the Act of 1986 may be heard and determined by a district judge.

(2) The parties to the proceedings for enforcement and, if he is not a party thereto, the applicant for the Part I order, shall be made parties to the application.

Defined terms—"Part I order": r 7.7(1).

7.13 Staying and dismissal of enforcement proceedings

(1) An application under section 30(1) or 31(1) of the Act of 1986 may be heard and determined by a district judge.

(2) The parties to the proceedings for enforcement which are sought to be stayed and, if he is not a party thereto, the applicant for the Part I order shall be made parties to an application under either of the said sections.

(3) Where the court makes an order under section 30(2) or (3) or section 31(3) of the Act of 1986, the proper officer shall amend the register accordingly, and shall give notice of the amendment to the court which made the Part I order and to the applicants for registration, for enforcement and for the stay or dismissal of the proceedings for enforcement.

Defined terms—"Part I order": r 7.7(1); "proper officer": r 1.2(1); "registration": r 7.7(1).

Filing of evidence and hearing—There are no specific provisions in the rules but, since the application will be dealt with as a matter of urgency, the court may exercise its powers to give interim directions under Family Law Act 1986, s 29, and will set a timetable to suit the emergency and secure the welfare of the child.

7.14 Particulars of other proceedings

A party to proceedings for or relating to a Part I order who knows of other proceedings (including proceedings out of the jurisdiction and concluded proceedings) which relate to the child concerned shall file an affidavit stating –

(*a*) in which jurisdiction and court the other proceedings were instituted;
(*b*) the nature and current state of such proceedings and the relief claimed or granted;
(*c*) the names of the parties to such proceedings and their relationship to the child; and
(*d*) if applicable, and if known, the reasons why the relief claimed in the proceedings for or relating to the Part I order was not claimed in the other proceedings.

Defined terms—"Part I order": r 7.7(1).

7.15 Inspection of register

The following persons, namely –

(*a*) the applicant for registration of a registered Part I order,
(*b*) any person who satisfies a district judge that he has an interest under the Part I order, and
(*c*) any person who obtains the leave of a district judge,

may inspect any entry in the register relating to the order and may bespeak copies of the order and of any document relating thereto.

Defined terms—"Part I order", "register": r 7.7(1).

"any person who obtains ... leave" (r 7.15(*c*))—Rule 7.15(*c*) should be read with r 10.20 which is wider and sets out other categories of persons who may be permitted to inspect and bespeak copies of any document filed in the court.

Chapter 4. Enforcement of maintenance orders

7.16 Interpretation

In this chapter –

"the Act of 1920" means the Maintenance Orders (Facilities for Enforcement) Act 1920;
"the Act of 1950" means the Maintenance Orders Act 1950;
"the Act of 1958" means the Maintenance Orders Act 1958;
"the Act of 1965" means the Matrimonial Causes Act 1965;
"the Act of 1971" means the Attachment of Earnings Act 1971;
"the Act of 1972" means the Maintenance Orders (Reciprocal Enforcement) Act 1972;
"English maintenance order" means a maintenance order made in the High Court.

7.17 Registration etc of orders under Act of 1920

(1) The prescribed officer for the purposes of section 1(1) of the Act of 1920 shall be the senior district judge, and on receiving from the Secretary of State a copy of a maintenance order made by a court in any part of Her Majesty's dominions outside the United Kingdom to which the Act of 1920 extends he shall cause the order to be registered in the register kept for the purpose of that Act (in this rule referred to as "the register").

The copy of the order received from the Secretary of State shall be filed in the principal registry.

(2) An application for the transmission of an English maintenance order under section 2 of the Act of 1920 shall be made to the district judge by lodging in the principal registry a certified copy of the order and an affidavit stating the applicant's reasons for believing that the person liable to make payments under the order is resident in some part of Her Majesty's dominions outside the United Kingdom to which the Act of 1920 extends, together with full particulars, so far as known to the applicant, of that person's address and occupation and any other information which may be required by the law of that part of Her Majesty's dominions for the purpose of the enforcement of the order.

(3) If it appears to the district judge mentioned in paragraph (2) that the person liable to make payments under the English maintenance order is resident in some part of Her Majesty's dominions outside the United Kingdom to which the Act of 1920 extends, he shall send the certified copy of the order to the Secretary of State for transmission to the Governor of that part of Her Majesty's dominions.

Particulars of any English maintenance order sent to the Secretary of State under the said section 2 shall be entered in the register and the fact that this has been done shall be noted in the records of the court.

(4) Where an English maintenance order has been made in a cause or matter proceeding in a district registry, an application for the transmission of the order under the said section 2 may be made to the district judge of that registry and paragraphs (2) and (3) of this rule shall have effect as if for reference to the principal registry there were substituted references to the district registry.

The proper officer shall send to the principal registry for entry in the register particulars of any order sent by him to the Secretary of State.

(5) Any person who satisfies a district judge that he is entitled to or liable to make payments under an English maintenance order or a maintenance order made by a court in any part of Her Majesty's dominions outside the United Kingdom to which the Act of 1920 extends or a solicitor acting on behalf of any such person or, with the leave of a district judge, any other person may inspect the register and bespeak copies of any order which has been registered and of any document filed therewith.

Proceedings under Part II of Act of 1950

7.18 Interpretation of rules 7.18 to 7.21

In this rule and rules 7.19 to 7.21 –

"the clerk of the Court of Session" means the deputy principal clerk in charge of the petition department of the Court of Session;

"maintenance order" means a maintenance order to which section 16 of the Act of 1950 applies;

"Northern Irish order" means a maintenance order made by the Supreme Court of Northern Ireland;

"register" means the register kept for the purposes of the Act of 1950;

"the registrar in Northern Ireland" means the chief registrar of the Queen's Bench Division (Matrimonial) of the High Court of Justice in Northern Ireland;

"registration" means registration under Part II of the Act of 1950 and "registered" shall be construed accordingly;

"Scottish order" means a maintenance order made by the Court of Session.

7.19 Registration etc of English order

(1) An application for the registration of an English maintenance order may be made by lodging with the proper officer a certified copy of the order, together with an affidavit by the applicant (and a copy thereof) stating –

(*a*) the address in the United Kingdom, and the occupation, of the person liable to make payments under the order;
(*b*) the date of service of the order on the person liable to make payments thereunder or, if the order has not been served, the reason why service has not been effected;
(*c*) the reason why it is convenient that the order should be enforceable in Scotland or Northern Ireland, as the case may be;
(*d*) the amount of any arrears due to the applicant under the order; and
(*e*) that the order is not already registered.

(2) If it appears to the district judge that the person liable to make payments under the order resides in Scotland or Northern Ireland and that it is convenient that the order should be enforceable there, the proper officer shall (subject to paragraph (6) below) send a certified copy of the order and the applicant's affidavit to the clerk of the Court of Session or to the registrar in Northern Ireland, as the case may be.

(3) On receipt of notice of the registration of an English maintenance order in the Court of Session or the Supreme Court of Northern Ireland, the proper officer shall –

(*a*) cause particulars of the notice to be entered in the register;
(*b*) note the fact of registration in the records of the court; and
(*c*) send particulars of the notice to the principal registry.

(4) Where an English order registered in the Court of Session or the Supreme Court of Northern Ireland is discharged or varied the proper officer of the court ordering the discharge or variation shall give notice thereof to the clerk of the Court of Session or to the registrar in Northern Ireland, as the case may be, by sending him a certified copy of the order discharging or varying the maintenance order.

(5) Where the registration of an English maintenance order registered in the Court of Session or the Supreme Court of Northern Ireland is cancelled under section 24(1) of the Act of 1950, notice of the cancellation shall be sent (as required by section 24(3)(*a*) of that Act) to the proper officer, and on receipt of such notice he shall cause particulars of it to be entered in Part I of the register.

(6) Where the order sought to be registered was made in a county court, this rule shall apply as though references to the Court of Session, the clerk of the Court of Session, the Supreme Court of Northern Ireland and the registrar of Northern Ireland were references to the sheriff court, the sheriff-clerk of the sheriff court, the court of summary jurisdiction and the clerk of the court of summary jurisdiction respectively.

7.20 Registration etc of Scottish and Northern Irish orders

(1) In relation to a Scottish or Northern Irish order the prescribed officer for the purposes of section 17(2) of the Act of 1950 shall be the proper officer of the principal registry.

(2) On receipt of a certified copy of a Scottish or Northern Irish order for registration, the proper officer shall –

(*a*) cause the order to be registered in Part II of the register and notify the clerk of the Court of Session or the registrar in Northern Ireland, as the case may be, that this has been done; and

(*b*) file the certified copy and any statutory declaration or affidavit as to the amount of any arrears due under the order.

(3) An application under section 21(2) of the Act of 1950 by a person liable to make payments under a Scottish order registered in the High Court to adduce before that court such evidence as is mentioned in that section shall be made by lodging a request for an appointment before a district judge of the principal registry; and notice of the date, time and place fixed for the hearing shall be sent by post to the applicant and to the person entitled to payments under the order.

(4) The prescribed officer to whom notice of the discharge or variation of a Scottish or Northern Irish order registered in the High Court is to be given under section 23(1)(*a*) of the Act of 1950 shall be the proper officer, and on receipt of the notice he shall cause particulars of it to be registered in Part II of the register.

(5) An application under section 24(1) of the Act of 1950 for the cancellation of the registration of a Scottish or Northern Irish order shall be made ex parte by affidavit to a district judge of the principal registry who, if he cancels the registration, shall note the cancellation in Part II of the register, whereupon the proper officer shall send notice of the cancellation to the clerk of the Court of Session or the registrar in Northern Ireland, as the case may be, and also to the clerk of any magistrates' court in which the order has been registered in accordance with section 2(5) of the Act of 1958.

(6) A person entitled to payments under a Scottish or Northern Irish order registered in the High Court who wishes to take proceedings for or with respect to the enforcement of the order in a district registry may apply by letter to the senior district judge of the principal registry who may, if satisfied that the order ought to be enforceable in the district registry, make an order accordingly on such terms, if any, as may be just.

Amendments—SI 1997/1893.

7.21 Inspection of register

Any person who satisfies a district judge of the principal registry that he is entitled to or liable to make payments under a maintenance order of a superior court or a solicitor acting on behalf of any such person or, with the leave of the district judge, any other person may inspect the register and bespeak copies of any such order which is registered in the High Court under Part II of the Act of 1950 and of any statutory declaration or affidavit filed therewith.

Registration etc of certain orders under the Act of 1958

7.22 Application and interpretation of rules 7.22 to 7.29

Section 21 of the Act of 1958 shall apply to the interpretation of this rule and rules 7.23 to 7.29 as it applies to the interpretation of that Act; and in those rules –

"cause book" includes cause card; and
"the register" means any register kept for the purposes of the Act of 1958.

7.23 Application for registration

(1) An application under section 2(1) of the Act of 1958 for the registration in a magistrates' court of a maintenance order shall be made by lodging with the proper officer –

(i) a certified copy of the maintenance order, and
(ii) two copies of the application in Form M33.

(2) The period required to be prescribed by rules of court for the purpose of section 2(2) of the Act of 1958 shall be 14 days.

(3) The proper officer shall cause the certified copy of an order required by the said section 2(2) to be sent to the justices' chief executive for a magistrates' court to be endorsed with a note that the application for registration of the order has been granted and to be accompanied by a copy of the application lodged under paragraph (1).

(4) On receipt of notice that a maintenance order has been registered in a magistrates' court in accordance with section 2(5) of the Act of 1958, the proper officer shall enter particulars of the registration in the records of the court.

Amendments—SI 1992/2067; SI 2001/821.

Defined terms—"maintenance order": Administration of Justice Act 1970, Sch 8; "proper officer": r 1.2(1).

"maintenance order" (r 7.23(1))—As to the extended meaning of this expression, see **"section 5 of the Debtors Act 1869"** under r 7.4. A nominal order for a spouse only will not be registered, and a maintenance pending suit or interim order will only be registered in special circumstances, eg where a final order at the same rate is expected to follow shortly (*Practice Direction of 10 March 1980*). If an order in favour of a child is expected to be registered, it should not be expressed to be direct to the child unless there is some positive benefit (*Practice Direction of 10 March 1980*).

Method of and grounds supporting application (r 7.23(1))—The court may grant the application if it thinks fit (MOA 1958, s 2(1)); there is no absolute right to registration. Form M33 requires grounds to be given. The application is made by lodging the prescribed documents rather than under r 10.9 (ie it is made ex parte) but as always in the case of such an application the district judge may give the respondent the opportunity to make representations. If the order granting the application is made ex parte then as in the case of all such orders the respondent may apply for it to be reconsidered.

"certified copy" (r 7.23(1)(ii))—This means a copy certified by the proper officer to be a true copy of the original (MOA 1958, s 2(7)).

"period required to be prescribed" (r 7.23(2))—The period runs from when the application is granted but ends when registration is effected if that is within the 14 days. MOA 1958, s 2(2) prohibits enforcement during this period, and requires that within it the court to which the application is made be satisfied by the applicant that no earlier enforcement remains outstanding. On being so satisfied that court sends the certified copy order to the justices' chief executive of the magistrates' court for the area where the payer appears to be (MOA 1958, s 2(2)(*b*)). If the court is not so satisfied within the prescribed period the grant of the application becomes void.

"sent to the justices' chief executive" (r 7.23(3))—On receipt of the certified copy order, the justices' chief executive causes the maintenance order to be registered in the magistrates' court (MOA 1958, s 2(5)).

Effect of registration—Any existing attachment of earnings order ceases to have effect on registration (Attachment of Earnings Act 1971, s 11(1)(*a*)). Any existing means of payment order under Maintenance Enforcement Act 1991, s 1(7) continues to have effect (MOA 1958, s 2(6ZA)(*a*)), but, if there is no such order in force, the magistrates' court must order the payments to be made to the justices' chief executive for that or another magistrates' court (s 2(6ZA)(*b*)); in either case, the order may subsequently be varied or revoked (s 2(6ZB)(*b*)). The order is enforceable by the same procedures as if it had been made in the magistrates' court (MOA 1958, s 3(1), (2)), subject to minor modifications. No other proceedings (eg in the original court) may be taken for its enforcement (s 3(4)).

7.24 Registration in a magistrates' court of an order registered in the High Court

On receipt of notice that a maintenance order registered in the High Court in accordance with section 17(4) of the Act of 1950 has been registered in a magistrates' court in accordance with section 2(5) of the Act of 1958, the proper officer shall cause particulars of the registration to be entered in Part II of the register.

Defined terms—"proper officer": r 1.2(1); "the register": r 7.22.

"maintenance order"—As to the extended meaning of this expression, see **"section 5 of the Debtors Act 1869"** under r 7.4.

7.25 Registration of magistrates' court order

On receipt of a certified copy of a magistrates' court order sent to him pursuant to section 2(4)(*c*) of the Act of 1958, the proper officer shall cause the order to be registered in the High Court by filing the copy and making an entry in the register or, where the copy order is received in a district registry, in the cause book and shall send notice to the justices' chief executive for the magistrates' court that the order has been duly registered.

Amendments—SI 2001/821.

Defined terms—"district registry", "proper officer": r 1.2(1).

Effect of registration—Any existing attachment of earnings order ceases to have effect (Attachment of Earnings Act 1971, s 11(1)(*a*)). Any order as to the method of payment within Magistrates' Courts Act 1980, s 59(6) (payment otherwise than to the clerk) continues to have effect but any order to pay to the clerk ceases to have effect (Maintenance Orders Act 1958, s 2(6)). The court may vary the order as to method of payment or make a means of payment order under Maintenance Enforcement Act 1991, s 1(7) (MOA 1958, s 4A). The order is enforceable as a High Court order and not otherwise (MOA 1958, s 3(1), (4)).

7.26 Registration in the High Court of an order registered in a magistrates' court

(1) This rule applies where a sheriff court in Scotland or a magistrates' court in Northern Ireland has made an order for the registration in the High Court of an order previously registered in a magistrates' court in England and Wales in accordance with section 17(4) of the Act of 1950, and has sent a certified copy of the maintenance order to the proper officer of the High Court, pursuant to section 2(4)(*c*) of the Act of 1958.

(2) On receipt of the certified copy, the proper officer shall cause the order to be registered in the High Court by filing the copy and making an entry in the register, and shall send notice of the registration to the justices' chief executive for the original court and also to the justices' chief executive for the magistrates' court in which the order was registered in accordance with section 17(4) of the Act of 1950.

Amendments—SI 2001/821.

Defined terms—"maintenance order": Administration of Justice Act 1970, Sch 8; "proper officer": r 1.2(1); "the register": r 7.22.

"maintenance order"—As to the extended meaning of this expression, see **"section 5 of the Debtors Act 1869"** under r 7.4.

7.27 Variation or discharge of registered order

(1) Where the court makes an order varying or discharging an order registered in a magistrates' court under Part I of the Act of 1958, the proper officer shall send a certified copy of the first-mentioned order to the justices' chief executive for the magistrates' court.

(2) Where a certified copy of an order varying an order registered in a magistrates' court under Part I of the Act of 1958 is received from the justices' chief executive for the magistrates' court, the proper officer shall file the copy and enter particulars of the variation on the same documents or in the same records as particulars of registration are required by rule 7.23(4) to be entered.

(3) Where a certified copy of an order varying or discharging an order made by a magistrates' court and registered in the High Court under Part I of the Act of 1958 is received from the justices' chief executive for the magistrates' court, the proper officer shall –

(*a*) file the copy,
(*b*) enter particulars of the variation or discharge in the register or, where the copy order is received in a district registry, in the cause book, and
(*c*) send notice of the variation or discharge to any proper officer of a county court –
  (i) who has given notice to the proper officer of proceedings taken in that court for the enforcement of the registered order, or
  (ii) to whom any payment is to be made under an attachment of earnings order made by the High Court for the enforcement of the registered order.

Amendments—SI 2001/821.

Defined terms—"cause book": r 7.22; "proper officer": r 1.2(1); "the register": r 7.22.

Variation of order—Applications to vary the rate of payment must be made to the magistrates' court (Maintenance Orders Act 1958, s 4(2)), unless made in proceedings to vary some other provision in the order (s 4(5)(*a*)) or unless either party is not present in England or Wales (s 4(5)(*b*)). If variation proceedings are pending in one court, no variation application may be made to the other (s 4(6)). The magistrates' court may remit a variation application to be heard by the original court (s 4(4)).

Discharge of order—MOA 1958 does not give magistrates' courts power to discharge a registered order made by the High Court or county court; nor is it thought that the High Court has power to discharge a registered order made by a magistrates' court. An application for discharge must be made to the original court.

7.28 Appeal from variation etc of order by magistrates' court

An appeal to the High Court under section 4(7) of the Act of 1958 shall be heard and determined by a Divisional Court of the Family Division, and rule 8.2 shall apply as it applies in relation to an appeal from a magistrates' court under the Domestic Proceedings and Magistrates' Courts Act 1978.

Scope of provision—Maintenance Orders Act 1958, s 4(2) requires that variation of the rate of payment under an order which has been registered in a magistrates' court be dealt with by the court of registration, and s 4(7) provides a right of appeal to the High Court against any such variation or refusal to vary in similar terms to DPMCA 1978, s 29(1) in the case of variation of an order to which that Act applies. This rule applies r 8.2 to the former kind of appeal as it applies to the latter.

7.29 Cancellation of registration

(1) A notice under section 5 of the Act of 1958 by a person entitled to receive payments under an order registered in the High Court must be given to the proper officer.

(2) Where the High Court gives notice under the said section 5, the proper officer shall endorse the notice on the certified copy mentioned in rule 7.27(1).

(3) Where notice under the said section 5 is given in respect of an order registered in the High Court, the proper officer on being satisfied by an affidavit by the person entitled to receive payments under the order that no process for the enforcement of the order issued before the giving of the notice remains in force, shall –

- (*a*) cancel the registration by entering particulars of the notice in the register or cause book, as the case may be, and
- (*b*) send notice of the cancellation to the justices' chief executive for the court by which the order was made and, where applicable, to the justices' chief executive for the magistrates' court in which the order was registered in accordance with section 17(4) of the Act of 1950 stating, if such be the case, that the cancellation is in consequence of a notice given under subsection (1) of the said section 5.

(4) On receipt of notice from the justices' chief executive for a magistrates' court that the registration in that court under the Act of 1958 of an order made by the High Court or a county court has been cancelled, the proper officer shall enter particulars of the cancellation on the same documents or in the same records as particulars of registration are required by rule 7.23(4) to be entered.

(5) On receipt of notice from the justices' chief executive for a magistrates' court that the registration in that court under the Act of 1958 of an order registered in the High Court in accordance with section 17(4) of the Act of 1950 has been cancelled, the proper officer shall note the cancellation in Part II of the register.

Amendments—SI 2001/821.

Defined terms—"cause book": r 7.22; "proper officer": r 1.2(1); "the register": r 7.22.

"notice under section 5" (r 7.29(1))—Cancellation of the registration of a maintenance order is achieved by service of notice upon the court in which it is registered. This rule deals with the High Court and county court procedures on giving and receiving such notice.

"person entitled to receive payments" (r 7.29(1))—Such a person is entitled as of right to give notice to cancel the registration (MOA 1958, s 5(1)).

"High Court gives notice" (r 7.29(2))—Either the High Court or a county court may, on varying or discharging the maintenance order, give notice of cancellation (MOA 1958, s 5(2)). It is only on such an occasion that the court has power (and therefore that the payer may apply) to discharge the registration. (Oddly, it appears that only the High Court must endorse its notice on the certified copy of the variation or discharge order required to be sent under r 7.27(1).)

"on being satisfied" (r 7.29(3))—No enforcement step may be taken once the notice has been served (MOA 1958, s 5(4)(*a*)). The registration is not actually cancelled upon receipt of the notice but only when no outstanding enforcement process remains in force (s 5(4)(*c*)(i)).

Notice of cancellation given to the magistrates' court—The notice is not effective to cancel the registration while variation proceedings are pending there: MOA 1958, s 5(4)(*c*)(ii).

Effect of cancellation—If the court of registration was the magistrates' court, any order requiring the payments to be made to the clerk ceases to have effect but any other order as to method of payment, including a "means of payment" order under Maintenance Enforcement Act 1991, s 1 continues in force (MOA 1958, s 5(5)). If the maintenance order is a magistrates' court order, any order as to method of payment, including such a "means of payment" order continues in force; otherwise, the payments are made to the clerk (s 5(6)).

Proceedings under Act of 1972

7.30 Interpretation of rules 7.31 to 7.39

(1) Expressions used in rules 7.31 to 7.39 which are used in the Act of 1972 have the same meanings as in that Act.

(2) The references in the Act of 1972 to the prescribed officer shall be construed as references to the proper officer within the meaning of rule 1.2(1).

(3) The reference in section 21 of the Act of 1972 to the proper officer shall be the proper officer within the meaning of rule 1.2(1).

Amendments—SI 1996/816.

7.31 Application for transmission of maintenance order to reciprocating country

An application for a maintenance order to be sent to a reciprocating country under section 2 of the Act of 1972 shall be made by lodging with the court –

(*a*) an affidavit by the applicant stating –

- (i) the applicant's reason for believing that the payer under the maintenance order is residing in that country, and
- (ii) the amount of any arrears due to the applicant under the order, the date to which those arrears have been calculated and the date on which the next payment under the order falls due;

(*b*) a certified copy of the maintenance order,

(*c*) a statement giving such information as the applicant possesses as to the whereabouts of the payer,

(*d*) a statement giving such information as the applicant possesses for facilitating the identification of the payer (including, if known to the applicant, the name and address of any employer of the payer, his occupation and the date and place of issue of any passport of the payer) and

(*e*) if available to the applicant, a photograph of the payer.

7.32 Certification of evidence given on provisional order

Where the court makes a provisional order under section 5 of the Act of 1972 the document required by subsection (4) of that section to set out or summarise the evidence given in the proceedings shall be authenticated by a certificate signed by the district judge.

7.33 Confirmation of provisional order

(1) On receipt of a certified copy of a provisional order made in a reciprocating country, together with the document mentioned in section 5(5) of the Act of 1972, the proper officer shall fix a date, time and place for the court to consider whether or not the provisional order should be confirmed, and shall send to the payee under the maintenance order notice of the date, time and place so fixed together with a copy of the provisional order and that document.

(2) The proper officer shall send to the court which made the provisional order a certified copy of any order confirming or refusing to confirm that order.

7.34 Taking of evidence for court in reciprocating country

(1) The High Court shall be the prescribed court for the purposes of taking evidence pursuant to a request by a court in a reciprocating country under section 14 of the Act of 1972 where –

- (*a*) the request for evidence relates to a maintenance order made by a superior court in the United Kingdom, and
- (*b*) the witness resides in England and Wales.

(2) The evidence may be taken before a judge or officer of the High Court as the court thinks fit, and the provisions of RSC Order 39 shall apply with the necessary modifications as if the evidence were required to be taken pursuant to an order made under rule 1 of that Order.

(3) The county court shall be the prescribed court for the purposes of taking evidence pursuant to a request by a court in a reciprocating country pursuant to section 14 of the Act of 1972 where the request for evidence relates to a maintenance order made by a county court which has not been registered in a magistrates' court under the Act of 1958.

(4) Paragraph (2) shall apply to the taking of such evidence as though references therein to the High Court and RSC Order 39 were to the county court and CCR Order 20, rule 13 respectively.

7.35 Notification of variation or revocation

Where the court makes an order (other than a provisional order) varying or revoking a maintenance order a copy of which has been sent to a reciprocating country in pursuance of section 2 of the Act of 1972, the proper officer shall send a certified copy of the order to the court in the reciprocating country.

7.36 Transmission of documents

Any document required to be sent to a court in a reciprocating country under section 5(4) or section 14(1) of the Act of 1972 or by rule 7.33(2) or 7.36 shall be sent to the Lord Chancellor for transmission to that court unless the district judge is satisfied that, in accordance with the law of that country, the document may properly be sent by him direct to that court.

7.37 Application of rules 7.30 to 7.36 to Republic of Ireland

(1) In relation to the Republic of Ireland rules 7.30 to 7.36 shall have effect subject to the provisions of this rule.

(1A) A reference to the Act of 1972 in this rule, and in any rule which has effect in relation to the Republic of Ireland by virtue of this rule, shall be a reference to the said Act as modified by Schedule 2 to the Reciprocal Enforcement of Maintenance Orders (Republic of Ireland) Order 1993.

(2) The following paragraphs shall be added to rule 7.31 –

"(*f*) a statement as to whether or not the payer appeared in the proceedings in which the maintenance order was made and, if he did not, the original or a copy certified by the applicant or his solicitor to be a true copy of a document which establishes that notice of the institution of the proceedings was served on the payer;

(*g*) a document which establishes that notice of the order was sent to the payer, and

(*h*) if the payer received legal aid in the proceedings in which the order was made, a copy certified by the applicant or his solicitor to be a true copy of the legal aid certificate.".

(3) For rule 7.32 there shall be substituted the following rule –

"7.32 Certification of evidence given on application for variation or revocation

(1) Where an application is made to the court for the variation or revocation of an order to which section 5 of the Act of 1972 applies, the certified copy of the application and the documents required by subsection (3) of that section to set out or summarise the evidence in support of the application shall be authenticated by a certificate signed by the district judge.".

(4) Rule 7.33 shall not apply.

(5) For rule 7.35 there shall be substituted the following rule –

"7.35 Notification of variation or revocation

Where the High Court makes an order varying or revoking a maintenance order to which section 5 of the Act of 1972 applies, the proper officer shall send a certified copy of the order and a statement as to the service on the payer of the documents mentioned in subsection (3) of that section to the court in the Republic of Ireland by which the maintenance order is being enforced.".

(6) Rule 7.36 shall not apply.

Amendments—SI 1996/816.

7.38 Application of rules 7.30 to 7.36 to the Hague Convention countries

(1) In relation to the Hague Convention countries, rules 7.30, 7.31, 7.34, 7.35 and 7.36 shall have effect subject to the provisions of this rule, but rules 7.32 and 7.33 shall not apply.

(1A) A reference to the Act of 1972 in this rule, and in any rule which has effect in relation to the Hague Convention countries by virtue of this rule, shall be a reference to the said Act as modified by Schedule 3 to the Reciprocal Enforcement of Maintenance Orders (Hague Convention Countries) Order 1993.

(2) A reference in rules 7.31 and 7.34 to a reciprocating country shall be construed as a reference to a Hague Convention country.

(3) The following words shall be inserted after paragraph (*a*)(ii) of rule 7.31 –

"and

(iii) whether the time for appealing against the order has expired and whether an appeal is pending;".

(4) The following paragraphs shall be inserted after paragraph (*e*) of rule 7.31 –

"(*f*) a statement as to whether or not the payer appeared in the proceedings in which the maintenance order was made, and, if he did not, the original or a copy certified by the applicant or his solicitor to be a true copy of a document which establishes that notice of the institution of proceedings, including notice of the substance of the claim, was served on the payer;

(*g*) a document which establishes that notice of the order was sent to the payer;

(*h*) a written statement as to whether or not the payee received legal aid in the proceedings in which the order was made, or in connection with the application under section 2 of the Act of 1972 and, if he did, a copy certified by the applicant or his solicitor to be a true copy of the legal aid certificate.".

(5) In relation to the Hague Convention countries the following rules shall apply in place of rules 7.35 and 7.36 –

"7.35 Notification of variation or revocation

(1) Where the court makes an order varying or revoking a maintenance order to which section 5 of the Act of 1972, as modified, applies, and the time for appealing has expired without an appeal having been entered, the proper officer shall send to the Lord Chancellor such documents as are required by subsection (8) of that section, as it applies to Hague Convention countries, including a certificate signed by the district judge that the order of variation or revocation is enforceable and that it is no longer subject to the ordinary forms of review.

(2) Where either party enters an appeal against the order of variation or revocation he shall, at the same time, inform the proper officer thereof by a notice in writing.

7.36 Transmission of documents

Any document required to be sent to a court in a Hague Convention country shall be sent to the Lord Chancellor for transmission to the court.".

Amendments—SI 1996/816.

7.39 Application of rules 7.30 to 7.36 to a specified State of the United States of America

(1) In this rule unless the context otherwise requires –

"specified State" means a State of the United States of America specified in Schedule 1 to the Reciprocal Enforcement of Maintenance Orders (United States of America) Order 1995.

(2) In relation to a specified State, rules 7.30, 7.31, 7.34, 7.35 and 7.36 shall have effect subject to the provisions of this rule, but rules 7.32 and 7.33 shall not apply.

(3) A reference to the Act of 1972 in this rule, and in any rule which has effect in relation to a specified State by virtue of this rule, shall be a reference to the said Act as modified by Schedule 3 to the Reciprocal Enforcement of Maintenance Orders (United States of America) Order 1995.

(4) A reference in rules 7.31 and 7.34 to a reciprocating country shall be construed as a reference to a specified State.

(5) Paragraph (*c*) of rule 7.31 shall not apply to a specified State.

(6) The following paragraphs shall be inserted after paragraph (*a*)(ii) of rule 7.31 –

"(iii) the address of the payee;

(iv) such information as is known as to the whereabouts of the payer; and

(v) a description, so far as is known, of the nature and location of any assets of the payer available for execution.".

(7) A reference in paragraph (*b*) of rule 7.31 to a certified copy shall be construed as a reference to 3 certified copies.

(8) In relation to a specified State the following rules shall apply in place of rules 7.35 and 7.36 –

"7.35 Notification of variation of revocation

Where the court makes an order varying or revoking a maintenance order to which section 5 of the Act of 1972, as modified, applies, the proper officer shall send to the Secretary of State such documents as are required by subsection (7) of that section, as it applies to specified States.

7.36 Transmission of documents

Any document required to be sent to a court in a specified State shall be sent to the Secretary of State for transmission to the court."

Amendments—Inserted by SI 1996/816.

Chapter 5. Registration and enforcement under the Council Regulation

7.40 Interpretation

In this chapter "judgment" is to be construed in accordance with the definition in Article 13 of the Council Regulation.

Amendments—Inserted by SI 2001/821.

7.41 Filing of applications

Every application to the High Court under the Council Regulation, other than an application under rule 7.49 for a certified copy of a judgment, shall be filled with the principal registry.

Amendments—Inserted by SI 2001/821.

7.42 Application for registration

An application for registration of a judgment under Article 21(2) of the Council Regulation shall be made without notice being served on any other party.

Amendments—Inserted by SI 2001/821.

7.43 Evidence in support of application

(1) An application for registration under Article 21(2) of the Council Regulation must be supported by a statement that is sworn to be true or an affidavit –

(*a*) exhibiting –

(i) the judgment or a verified or certified or otherwise duly authenticated copy thereof together with such other document or documents as may be requisite to show that, according to the law of the Contracting State in which it has been given, the judgment is enforceable and has been served;

(ii) in the case of a judgment given in default, the original or a certified true copy of the document which establishes that the party in default was served with the document instituting the proceedings or with an equivalent document;

(iii) where it is the case, a document showing that the party making the application is in receipt of legal aid in the Contracting State in which the judgment was given;

(iv) where the judgment or document is not in the English language, a translation thereof into English certified by a notary public or a person qualified for the purpose in one of the Contracting States or authenticated by witness statement or affidavit;

(v) the certificate, in the form set out in Annex IV or Annex V of the Council Regulation, issued by the Contracting State in which judgment was given;

(*b*) stating –

(i) whether the judgment provides for the payment of a sum or sums of money;

(ii) whether interest is recoverable on the judgment or part thereof in accordance with the law of the State in which the judgment was given, and if such be the case, the rate of interest, the date from which interest is recoverable, and the date on which interest ceases to accrue;

(*c*) giving an address within the jurisdiction of the court for service of process on the party making the application and stating, so far as is known to the witness, the name and the usual or last known address or place of business of the person against whom judgment was given; and

(*d*) stating to the best of the information or belief of the witness –

(i) the grounds on which the right to enforce the judgment is vested in the party making the application;

(ii) as the case may require, either that at that date of the application the judgment has not been satisfied, or the part or amount in respect of which it remains unsatisfied.

(2) Where the party making the application does not produce the documents referred to in paragraphs (1)(*a*)(ii) and (iii) of this rule, the court may –

(*a*) fix a time within which the documents are to be produced;

(*b*) accept equivalent documents; or

(*c*) dispense with production of the documents.

Amendments—Inserted by SI 2001/821.

7.44 Order for registration

(1) An order giving permission to register a judgment under Article 21(2) of the Council Regulation must be drawn up by the court.

(2) Every such order shall state the period within which an appeal may be made against the order for registration and shall contain a notification that the court will not enforce the judgment until after the expiration of that period.

(3) The notification referred to in paragraph (2) shall not prevent any application for protective measures under Article 12 of the Council Regulation pending final determination of any issue relating to enforcement of the judgment.

Amendments—Inserted by SI 2001/821.

7.45 Register of judgments

There shall be kept in the principal registry by the proper officer a register of the judgments ordered to be registered under Article 21(2) of the Council Regulation.

Amendments—Inserted by SI 2001/821.

7.46 Notice of registration

(1) Notice of the registration of a judgment under Article 21(2) of the Council Regulation must be served on the person against whom judgment was given by delivering it to him personally or by sending it to him at his usual or last known address or place of business or in such other manner as the court may direct.

(2) Permission is not required to serve such a notice out of the jurisdiction and rule 10.6 shall apply in relation to such a notice.

(3) The notice of the registration must state –

(*a*) full particulars of the judgment registered and the order for registration;
(*b*) the name of the party making the application and his address for service within the jurisdiction;
(*c*) the right of the person against whom judgment was given to appeal against the order for registration; and
(*d*) the period within which an appeal against the order for registration may be made.

Amendments—Inserted by SI 2001/821.

7.47 Enforcement of judgment

(1) A judgment registered under Article 21(2) of the Council Regulation shall not be enforced until after the expiration of the period specified in accordance with rule 7.44(2) or, if that period has been extended by the Court, until after the expiration of the period so extended.

(2) Any party wishing to apply for the enforcement of a judgment registered under Article 21(2) of the Council Regulation must produce to the proper officer a witness statement or affidavit of service of the notice of registration of the judgment and of any order made by the court in relation to the judgment.

(3) Nothing in this rule shall prevent the court from granting protective measures under Article 12 of the Council Regulation pending final determination of any issue relating to enforcement of the judgment.

Amendments—Inserted by SI 2001/821.

7.48 Application for recognition

(1) Registration of the judgment under these rules shall serve for the purposes of Article 14(3) of the Council Regulation as a decision that the judgment is recognised.

PART III

(2) Where it is sought to apply for recognition of a judgment, the rules of this chapter shall apply to such application as they apply to an application for registration under Article 21(2) of the Council Regulation, with the exception that the applicant shall not be required to produce –

(*a*) a document or documents which establish that according to the law of the Contracting State in which it has been given the judgment is enforceable and has been served, or

(*b*) the document referred to in rule 7.43(1)(*a*)(iii).

Amendments—Inserted by SI 2001/821.

7.49 Enforcement of judgments in other Contracting States

(1) Subject to rules 10.16(2) and 10.20, an application for a certified copy of a judgment referred to in Article 32(1) of the Council Regulation must be made to the court which made the order on a witness statement or affidavit without notice being served on any other party.

(2) A witness statement or affidavit by which such an application is made must –

(*a*) give particulars of the proceedings in which the judgment was obtained;

(*b*) have annexed to it a copy of the petition or application by which the proceedings were begun, the evidence of service thereof on the respondent, copies of the pleadings and particulars, if any, and a statement of the grounds on which the judgment was based together, where appropriate, with any document showing that the applicant is entitled to legal aid or assistance by way of representation for the purposes of the proceedings;

(*c*) state whether the respondent did or did not object to the jurisdiction, and, if so, on what grounds;

(*d*) show that the judgment has been served in accordance with rules 4.8, 10.2, 10.3, 10.4, 10.5, 10.6, 10.16 or 10.17 and is not subject to any order for the stay of proceedings;

(*e*) state that the time for appealing has expired, or, as the case may be, the date on which it will expire and in either case whether notice of appeal against the judgment has been given; and

(*f*) state –

(i) whether the judgment provides for the payment of a sum of money;

(ii) whether interest is recoverable on the judgment or part thereof and if so, the rate of interest, the date from which interest is recoverable, and the date on which interest ceases to accrue.

(3) The certified copy of the judgment shall be an office copy sealed with the seal of the court and signed by the district judge and there shall be issued with the copy of the judgment a certified copy of any order which has varied any of the terms of the original order.

Amendments—Inserted by SI 2001/821.

7.50 Authentic instruments and court settlements

Rules 7.40 to 7.49 (except rule 7.43(1)(*a*)(ii)) shall apply to an authentic instrument and a settlement to which Article 13(3) of the Council Regulation applies, as they apply to a judgment subject to any necessary modifications.

Amendments—Inserted by SI 2001/821.

PART VIII
APPEALS

8.1 Appeals from district judges

(1) Except where paragraph (2) applies, any party may appeal from an order or decision made or given by the district judge in family proceedings in a county court to a judge on notice; and in such a case –

(*a*) CCR Order 13 rule 1(10) (which enables the judge to vary or rescind an order made by the district judge in the course of proceedings), and

(*b*) CCR Order 37 rule 6 (which gives a right of appeal to the judge from a judgment or final decision of the district judge),

shall not apply to the order or decision.

(2) Any order or decision granting or varying an order (or refusing to do so) –

(*a*) on an application for ancillary relief, or

(*b*) in proceedings to which rules 3.1, 3.2, 3.3 or 3.6 apply,

shall be treated as a final order for the purposes of CCR Order 37, rule 6.

(3) On any appeal to which paragraph (2) applies –

(*a*) the appeal shall be limited to a review of the decision or order of the district judge unless the judge considers that in the circumstances of the case it would be in the interests of justice to hold a rehearing;

(*b*) oral evidence or evidence which was not before the district judge may be admitted if in all the circumstances of the case it would be in the interests of justice to do so, irrespective of whether the appeal be by way of review or rehearing.

(4) Unless the court otherwise orders, any notice under this rule must be issued within 14 days of the order or decision appealed against and served not less than 14 days before the day fixed for the hearing of the appeal.

(5) Appeals under this rule shall be heard in chambers unless the judge otherwise directs.

(6) Unless the court otherwise orders, an appeal under this rule shall not operate as a stay of proceedings on the order or decision appealed against.

(7) This rule does not apply to any appeal by a party to proceedings for the assessment of costs against a decision in those proceedings.

Amendments—SI 1997/1893; SI 2003/184.

Defined terms—"ancillary relief", "district judge": r 1.2(1); "family proceedings": r 1.2(1), Matrimonial and Family Proceedings Act 1984, s 32.

Scope of provision—This rule, together with r 4.22, provides for appeals from the district judge in the county court in family proceedings. In relation to decisions or judgments of the district judge in the county court which do not fall within the definition of family proceedings, appeals are governed by CCR Ord 37, r 6 alone. Rule 4.22 governs all appeals from the district judge in relation to decisions or judgments in proceedings under CA 1989 (including Sch 1 to that Act, except where financial relief is sought for an adult), as specified under r 4.1(2)).

Rule 8.1(1) includes orders made by a district judge exercising a jurisdiction which previously could only be exercised by a judge, ie pronouncing decrees nisi (*Marya v Marya* [1995] 2 FLR 911). Rule 8.1(3), as substituted by the Family Proceedings (Amendment) Rules 2003, provides that the appeal is *not* a rehearing unless it is in the interests of justice that there should be. Further, irrespective of the nature of the hearing, fresh evidence may be admitted if it is in the interests of justice to do so. It would seem to be good practice that the nature of the hearing and evidence to be given at the appeal should be considered in advance at a preliminary or directions hearing .

Relationship with CCR Ord 37, r 6—Any appeal in relation to an order granting or varying ancillary relief, or in proceedings to which r 3.1 (application in case of failure to provide reasonable maintenance), 3.2, 3.3 (applications for alterations of maintenance agreement), 3.6 (Married Women's Property Act 1882) apply, is treated as an appeal against a final order for the purposes of CCR Ord 37, r 6 (which gives a party to the proceedings a right of appeal to the judge, unless he consented to the order). No permission to appeal is necessary (*Bright v Bright* [2002] EWCA Civ 1412, 10 September 2002, CA). CCR Ord 37, r 6 empowers the judge to set aside the order and make any other order or remit the matter for rehearing or direct a new trial. Appeals not referred to above, which include orders or decisions to which r 3.11 (proceedings in respect of a polygamous marriage) or 3.12 (declaration as to marital status) apply, are specifically excluded from CCR Ord 37, r 6 and from CCR Ord 13, r 1(10), which provides a judge with power to hear an appeal from the district judge. Nevertheless, r 8.1(1) provides the power of appeal, apparently envisaging an appeal to the judge in the same way as CCR Ord 37, r 6, but without giving the judge the powers therein provided.

Relationship with FPR 1991, r 4.22—FPR 1991, r 4.22 is concerned with appeals (from district judges of the High Court and county court) in relation to proceedings specified in r 4.1(2). It seems that if the decision is one to which r 4.1(2) applies the appeal should be in accordance with r 4.22. Otherwise, if the appeal relates to an order or decision made in family proceedings in the county court, this rule governs the procedure for the appeal. In any event the time for appealing under both rules is 14 days, and the procedure on such appeals is the same. Where the appeal relates to a decision or order not made within family proceedings the appeal must be made in accordance with CCR Ord 37, r 6.

Preliminary considerations—Before pursuing an appeal, it is important to establish that this is the correct course. A district judge can correct an error on the face of the order (under the "slip rule": CCR Ord 15, r 5) and has power to vary his own interim or ex parte order (*Re A (A Minor) (Challenging Ex Parte Order)* [1993] Fam Law 661) or to order a rehearing of a final order where "no error of the court is alleged" (see CCR Ord 37, r 1). In *B-T v B-T (Divorce: Procedure)* [1990] 2 FLR 1, Ward J held that the power of the county court to order a rehearing is limited to cases where there has been non-disclosure of material information which a party had a duty to place before the court. If information becomes available later, this should be a matter for appeal.

In *Benson v Benson (Deceased)* [1996] 1 FLR 692, it was held that an application can be made under CCR Ord 37, r 1 to the district judge to set aside an order made by consent, an order made as a result of fraud, mistake or material non-disclosure, or where there has been a new event to invalidate the basis of the order (see also *Re C (Financial Provision: Leave to Appeal)* [1993] 2 FLR 799). An application to set aside is as appropriate as an appeal.

Procedure—A notice of appeal must be issued within 14 days of the decision which is the subject of the appeal. The appellant should lodge the bundle of documentation that was before the district judge, together with a note of judgment. Unless the district judge has provided a written judgment, the note should be prepared by the advocate and agreed by the other parties and approved by the district judge.

On an appeal from the decision of a district judge in the county court in relation to proceedings where periodical payments, a lump sum or property are in issue, or a difficult or important question, whether of law or otherwise, is raised, the appeal should be transferred to the High Court for hearing, whether on application by a party or otherwise (*Practice Direction of 5 June 1992*).

Permission to appeal—To appeal an order after the time for appealing has expired, permission to appeal is required. In order to obtain leave to appeal, the following requirements must be satisfied: (i) it is necessary to show that new events have occurred since the making of the order which invalidate the basis or fundamental assumption on which the order was made; (ii) those events must have occurred within a relatively short time of the order having been made (in most cases, not more than a few months); (iii) the application for leave to appeal out of time should be made reasonably promptly; and (iv) the grant of leave should not prejudice third parties who have acquired interests in property in good faith and for valuable consideration (*Barder v Barder* [1988] AC 20, [1987] 2 FLR 480; *Jenkins v Livesey (formerly Jenkins)* [1985] AC 424, [1985] FLR 813; see also *B v B (Financial Provision : Leave to Appeal)* [1994] 1 FLR 219).

Hopeless appeals—The High Court has jurisdiction under RSC Ord 18, r 19 and its inherent jurisdiction to dismiss a hopeless appeal and order that no such appeal be brought without leave (see *Grepe v Loam* (1887) 37 Ch 168, followed in *B v B (Unmeritorious Applications)* [1999] 1 FLR 505, Bracewell J).

Adoption appeals—Where an appeal is made against an adoption order, the appellant should make an immediate application for a stay pending the appeal (to prevent the child meeting the judge) coupled with an application for an expedited hearing (*Re PJ (Adoption: Practice on Appeal)* [1998] 2 FLR 252).

8.1A Appeals from orders made under Part IV of the Family Law Act 1996

(1) This rule applies to all appeals from orders made under Part IV of the Family Law Act 1996 and on such an appeal –

- (*a*) paragraphs (2), (3), (4), (5), (7) and (8) of rule 4.22,
- (*b*) paragraphs (5) and (6) of rule 8.1, and
- (*c*) paragraphs (4)(*e*) and (6) of rule 8.2,

shall apply subject to the following provisions of this rule and with the necessary modifications.

(2) The justices' chief executive for the magistrates' court from which an appeal is brought shall be served with the documents mentioned in rule 4.22(2).

(3) Where an appeal lies to the High Court, the documents required to be filed by rule 4.22(2) shall be filed in the registry of the High Court which is nearest to the magistrates' court from which the appeal is brought.

(4) Where the appeal is brought against the making of a hospital order or a guardianship order under the Mental Health Act 1983, a copy of any written evidence considered by the magistrates' court under section 37(1)(*a*) of the 1983 Act shall be sent by the justices' chief executive to the registry of the High Court in which the documents relating to the appeal are filed in accordance with paragraph (3).

(5) A district judge may dismiss an appeal to which this rule applies for want of prosecution and may deal with any question of costs arising out of the dismissal or withdrawal of an appeal.

(6) Any order or decision granting or varying an order (or refusing to do so) in proceedings in which an application is made in accordance with rule 3.8 for –

- (*a*) an occupation order as described in section 33(4) of the Family Law Act 1996,
- (*b*) an occupation order containing any of the provisions specified in section 33(3) where the applicant or the respondent has matrimonial home rights, or
- (*c*) a transfer of tenancy,

shall be treated as a final order for the purposes of CCR Order 37, rule 6 and, on an appeal from such an order, the judge may exercise his own discretion in substitution for that of the district judge and the provisions of CCR Order 37, rule 6 shall apply.

Amendments—Inserted by SI 1997/1893; amended by SI 2001/821.

Procedure—The appeal is by way of notice served and filed, setting out the grounds of appeal within 14 days of the determination (r 4.22(2), (3), as applied by r 8.1A(1)(*a*)). The appellant must file and serve a copy of the notes of evidence and reasons as soon as practicable after the notice of appeal (r 4.22(2), (4), as applied by r 8.1A(1)(*a*)). Service must also be effected upon the justices' chief executive (r 8.1A(2)). If an application is to be made to extend the time in which the appeal may be brought a certificate setting out the reasons for the delay must be provided (r 8.2(4)(*e*), as applied by r 8.1A(1)(*c*)). A respondent may file and serve a respondent's notice which must be within 14 days of receipt of the notice of appeal, if grounds as specified in r 4.22(5) apply. The appeal is heard by a single judge (r 4.22(8), as applied by r 8.1A(1)(*a*)) in chambers (r 8.1(5), as applied by r 8.1A(1)(*b*)).

Relationship with CCR Ord 37, r 6—Ord 37, r 6 provides a right of appeal from a district judge to a county court judge. See further the notes to FPR 1991, r 8.1. Under r 8.1A(6) the orders listed are treated as final, so as to provide a right of appeal, and it is also established that the judge may exercise discretion afresh on consideration of such an appeal.

Stay pending appeal—The issue of the notice of appeal does not operate as a stay of the order which is the subject of the appeal (r 8.1A(6), as applied by r 8.1A(1)(*b*)). The magistrates' court has no power to grant a stay (*Re O (A Minor) (Care Order: Education: Procedure)* [1992] 2 FLR 7), hence a separate application for a stay must be made (under RSC Ord 55, r 6A).

8.2 Appeals under Domestic Proceedings and Magistrates' Courts Act 1978

(1) Subject to paragraph (9) below, every appeal to the High Court under the Domestic Proceedings and Magistrates' Courts Act 1978 shall be heard by a Divisional Court of the Family Division and shall be entered by lodging three copies of the notice of motion in the principal registry.

(2) The notice must be served, and the appeal entered, within 6 weeks after the date of the order appealed against.

(3) Notice of the motion may be served in accordance with RSC Order 65, rule 5.

(4) On entering the appeal, or as soon as practicable thereafter, the appellant shall, unless otherwise directed, lodge in the principal registry –

- (*a*) three certified copies of the summons and of the order appealed against, and of any order staying its execution,
- (*b*) three copies of the clerk's notes of the evidence,
- (*c*) three copies of the justices' reasons for their decision,
- (*d*) a certificate that notice of the motion has been duly served on the clerk and on every party affected by the appeal, and
- (*e*) where the notice of the motion includes an application to extend the time for bringing the appeal, a certificate (and a copy thereof) by the appellant's solicitor, or the appellant if he is acting in person, setting out the reasons for the delay and the relevant dates.

(5) If the clerk's notes of the evidence are not produced, the court may hear and determine the appeal on any other evidence or statement of what occurred in the proceedings before the magistrates' court as appears to the court to be sufficient.

(6) The court shall not be bound to allow the appeal on the ground merely of misdirection or improper reception or rejection of evidence unless, in the opinion of the court, substantial wrong or miscarriage of justice has been thereby occasioned.

(7) A district judge may dismiss an appeal to which this rule applies for want of prosecution or, with the consent of the parties, may dismiss the appeal or give leave for it to be withdrawn, and may deal with any question of costs arising out of the dismissal or withdrawal.

(8) Any interlocutory application in connection with or for the purpose of any appeal to which this rule applies may be heard and disposed of before a single judge.

(9) Where an appeal to which this rule applies relates only to the amount of any periodical or lump sum payment ordered to be made, it shall, unless the President otherwise directs, be heard and determined by a single judge, and in that case –

(*a*) for the references in paragraphs (1) and (4)(*a*), (*b*) and (*c*) to three copies of the documents therein mentioned there shall be substituted references to one copy;

(*b*) the parties may agree in writing or the President may direct that the appeal be heard and determined at a divorce town.

Scope of provision—The procedure for appeals under the Domestic Proceedings and Magistrates' Courts Act 1978 are set out in this rule. This rule therefore takes precedence over RSC Ord 55 which describes the general procedure for appeals to the High Court; RSC Ord 55, r 1(4) provides that RSC Ord 55 is subject to any other provision.

Notice of motion (r 8.2(1))—The notice of motion should be in the form set out in the Schedule to *Practice Direction of 11 May 1977*, which must include the grounds of appeal and must state that the whole of the order, or part or parts of the order, is appealed against. The notice must be served on all the parties and on the justices' clerk.

8.3 Appeals under section 13 of the Administration of Justice Act 1960

Proceedings within paragraph 3(*d*) of Schedule 1 to the Supreme Court Act 1981 shall be heard and determined by a Divisional Court of the Family Division and rule 8.2(4) shall apply, with the necessary modifications, to such proceedings.

Amendments—Inserted by SI 1991/2113.

Scope of provision—Appeals from an order of punishment for contempt made by an inferior court lie to a Divisional Court of the High Court (Administration of Justice Act 1960, s 13(2)). "Proceedings on appeal under section 13 of the Administration of Justice Act 1960 from an order or decision made under section 63(3) of the Magistrates' Courts Act 1980 to enforce an order of a magistrates' court made in matrimonial proceedings or with respect to the guardianship of a minor" are assigned to the Family Division of the High Court (Supreme Court Act 1981, Sch 1, para 3(*d*). Thus, an appeal from a committal order made under MCA 1980, s 63(3) for disobedience of a protection order made under Domestic Proceedings and Magistrates' Courts Act 1978, s 16 lies to a Divisional Court of the Family Division, and the requirements of r 8.2(4) as to documentation apply. It is submitted that an appeal against committal for disobedience of an order under CA 1989, s 8 or s 11(7) also lies to the Family Division, even though SCA 1981, Sch 1, para 3(*d*) still refers to a decision to enforce an order "with respect to the guardianship of a minor".

Procedure for appeal against enforcement penalty—An appeal against a penalty imposed under Magistrates' Courts Act 1980, s 63(3), to which Supreme Court Act 1981, Sch 1, para 3(*d*) applies, is governed by RSC Ords 55 and 57 and FPR 1991, rr 8.2(4), 8.3. It is brought by originating motion in the Family Division of the High Court.

PART IX
DISABILITY

9.1 Interpretation and application of Part IX

(1) In this Part –

"patient" means a person who, by reason of mental disorder within the meaning of the Mental Health Act 1983, is incapable of managing and administering his property and affairs;

"person under disability" means a person who is a minor or a patient;

"Part VII" means Part VII of the Mental Health Act 1983.

(2) So far as they relate to minors who are the subject of applications, the provisions of this Part of these rules shall not apply to proceedings which are specified proceedings within the meaning of section 41(6) of the Children Act 1989 and, with respect to proceedings which are dealt with together with specified proceedings, this Part shall have effect subject to the said section 41 and Part IV of these rules.

(3) Rule 9.2A shall apply only to proceedings under the Act of 1989 or the inherent jurisdiction of the High Court with respect to minors.

Amendments—SI 1991/2113; SI 1992/456.

Defined terms—"minor": Family Law Reform Act 1969, ss 1(2), 12.

Scope of provision—This rule defines persons under a disability with whom Pt IX is concerned and sets out the scope of Part IX in relation to children. The remainder of Pt IX regulates the conduct of proceedings by and against a person under disability, and (subject to certain exceptions in relation to minors) ensures that a patient is represented by a next friend or guardian ad litem (as appropriate). However, it does not deal with all relevant matters, and r 1.3 ensures that the RSC and CCR (as appropriate) fill any procedural gaps left by the FPR (see, in particular, RSC Ord 80 and CCR Ord 10). These references are to RSC/CCR in their final form as at 26 April 1999, prior to the Civil Procedure Rules 1998 coming into force. For non-family proceedings, reference should now be made to CPR 1998, Pt 21 (reproduced in this volume).

Persons under disability—There are two distinct categories of person under disability:

(*a*) "minors", who are by reason of age deemed incapable of acting personally in all except specified proceedings; and

(*b*) "patients", who are treated as incapable of conducting the proceedings.

It is possible for a minor also to be a patient, and this may be relevant if that condition will continue to subsist on ceasing to be a minor (eg in regard to the disposal of money awarded to the minor). Thus a minor who has severe learning disabilities will continue to be under disability even after attaining majority.

"minors" (r 9.1(2), (3))—A minor is defined by Family Law Reform Act 1969, ss 1 and 12 as a person who is under the age of 18. The term is used in Pt IX rather than "child" which is used elsewhere in the rules and is more generally used in matters of family law (see, for example, the definition of "child" in CA 1989, s 105(1)). The differing usage within the rules reflects the differing pre-consolidation sources of the various provisions; the term "minor" is used in Pt IX to harmonise with the terminology of CCR Ord 10 (which deals with persons under a disability). The two words mean exactly the same thing and no significance attaches to the choice of one in any context rather than the other. RSC Ord 80 (which also deals with disability) uses the term "infant", which may be said to be interchangeable with "minor" (FLRA 1969, s 1(2)).

"mental disorder" (r 9.1(1))—Mental Health Act 1983, s 1(2) defines "mental disorder" as "mental illness, arrested or incomplete development of mind, psychopathic disorder and any other disorder or disability of mind"; s 1(3) provides that nothing in the definition is to be construed as implying that a person may be dealt with as suffering from mental disorder by reason only of promiscuity, immoral conduct, sexual deviancy or dependence on alcohol or drugs. This definition is extremely wide and makes no reference to the degree of impairment, but it provides a useful screening process because merely being eccentric is not a basis for being deprived of one's right to conduct litigation. Medical evidence is required to confirm the diagnosis of a specific mental disorder. There are basically three categories of person who come within the definition of mental disorder, namely those with:

(*a*) *mental illness* The largest group comprises elderly people who become mentally impaired (eg by senile dementia or Alzheimer's disease);

(*b*) *learning disabilities* The expression "learning difficulties" is sometimes used and the previous term was "mental handicap"; and

(*c*) *brain damage* If the damage was caused during the developmental years (eg in childbirth), this will be classed as learning disabilities.

"patients" (r 9.1(1))—For the purpose of FPR 1991, "patient" means a person who, by reason of mental disorder, is incapable of managing and administering his property and affairs. The same definition is used to establish the jurisdiction of the Court of Protection to administer the property and affairs of patients under Part VII (ss 93–113) of the Mental Health Act 1983. It is also used in RSC Ord 80 and CCR Ord 10, although in the latter the term used is "mental patient" (there is no significance in this). There are two distinct components in this definition, namely (i) being mentally disordered, and (ii) being incapable. Whilst mental incapacity per se may result in a transaction being invalid or unenforceable, it is only when the individual is incapable "by reason of mental disorder" that the law takes away personal rights or powers and enables these to be delegated. Incapacity due to other causes, such as being under the influence of drink or drugs, is not sufficient.

Similarly, being mentally disordered (ie within one of the above categories) does not necessarily result in being a patient; an assessment must still be made of capacity. Thus an individual may be sectioned under the provisions of the Mental Health Act, yet not a patient as regards court proceedings because the criteria are different. An individual with learning disabilities may still have the capacity to manage his affairs, especially if they are very basic, although the need to participate in proceedings may tip the balance.

Presumptions as to capacity—There is a legal presumption that adults are competent until the contrary is proved. This presumption is relevant to the burden of proof. In general, the person who alleges that an individual lacks capacity must prove this, but the standard of proof is the civil standard, namely on the balance of probabilities rather than beyond reasonable doubt. Capacity must be assessed at the time that the decision is to be taken because it can vary. If an individual has previously been found to lack capacity there is no presumption of continuance, but if there is clear evidence of incapacity for a considerable period then the burden of proof may be more easily discharged even though it remains on whoever asserts incapacity.

Doubts about capacity may arise for several reasons, but these should not be confused with tests of capacity. Thus the status of the individual (being elderly and living in a nursing home), the outcome of a decision (one that no person in his right mind would be expected to reach) or appearance, behaviour or conversation may cause capacity to be questioned, but these factors do not determine capacity. It is not unusual for outward appearances to create a false impression of lack of capacity and, in all these situations, a proper assessment should be made. Physical disabilities may obstruct the power of speech or movement even where mental capacity is not affected, and other methods of communication must then be attempted.

Communication difficulties and physical disabilities—Lack of competence to deal with financial and personal affairs may arise through mental incapacity, an inability to communicate, or a combination of the two. A procedure is then needed for the affairs to be handled by some other person or body on behalf of that individual. The present court rules do not recognise this distinction and only enable proceedings to be conducted by a representative (the next friend or guardian ad litem) in the case of incapacity due to mental disorder.

Where the ability of an individual to conduct or participate in proceedings is impaired due to physical disabilities, steps can be taken by the court to overcome these. Thus the loop system may be provided for those who are hard of hearing, an interpreter may be provided for those with communication difficulties, and enlarged print may be used on all documents for those whose sight is impaired. If necessary, hearings should be conducted in a courtroom or chambers with disabled access.

Tests of capacity—There is no universal test of capacity. Legal capacity depends on understanding rather than wisdom; the quality of the decision is irrelevant as long as the person understands what he is deciding. Legal tests vary according to the particular transaction or act involved but are generally issue specific; ie they relate to the matters which the individual is required to understand. As capacity depends on time and context a decision as to capacity in one context does not bind a court which has to consider the same issue in a different context. A person who is incapable of managing his affairs may nevertheless be capable of getting married, signing an enduring power of attorney or making a will, because the matters to be taken into account are different. For a full explanation of the various tests that apply for different purposes, reference should be made to the joint Law Society and BMA publication *Assessment of Mental Capacity* (1995).

Ability to rely upon advice—The extent to which an individual with impaired capacity may rely upon the advice of others was considered by Boreham J in *White v Fell* (1987), unreported but quoted by Wright J in *Masterman-Lister v Brutton & Co and Jewell & Home Counties Dairies* [2002] EWHC 417 (QB), [2002] All ER (D) 247 (Mar):

> "Few people have the capacity to manage all their affairs unaided. In matters of law, particularly litigation, medicine, and given sufficient resources, finance professional advice is almost universally needed and sought. For instance, if the plaintiff succeeds in her claim for compensation … then she will need to take, consider and act upon appropriate advice. … It may be that she would have chosen, and would choose now, not to take advice, but that is not the question. The question is: is she capable of doing so? To have that capacity she requires first the insight and understanding of the fact that she has a problem in respect of which she needs advice. …
>
> Secondly, having identified the problem, it will be necessary for her to seek an appropriate adviser and to instruct him with sufficient clarity to enable him to understand the problem and to advise her appropriately.
>
> Finally, she needs sufficient mental capacity to understand and to make decisions based upon, or otherwise give effect to such advice as she may receive. … she may not understand all the intricacies of litigation, or of a settlement, or of a wise investment policy. … But if that were the appropriate test then quite a substantial proportion of the adult population might be regarded as under disability."

Assessment of capacity—There have been relatively few reported cases on the assessment of capacity, and until recently none relating to capacity to manage and administer property and affairs, despite the extent to which this test is applied. Mental capacity is a question of fact, so any issue of capacity can only be determined by a judge in legal proceedings, acting not as a medical expert but as a lay person influenced by personal observation and on the basis of evidence not only from doctors but also from those who know the individual. For comprehensive guidance as to the manner in which capacity should be assessed, reference should be made to *Assessment of Mental Capacity* (above).

"Property and affairs"—It becomes necessary to consider what property and affairs should be taken into account when applying the test of a "patient" in different contexts. It has been held that "affairs" does not extend to physical care and/or treatment but includes "only business matters, legal transactions or other dealings of a similar kind" (*Re F (Mental Patient: Sterilisation)* [1990] 2 AC 1).

Despite the wording of the definition of "patient", the Court of Appeal has now concentrated on the issue-specific nature of tests of capacity and decided that the test relates to the individual and his immediate problems. Unlike for the Court of Protection jurisdiction, it is not necessary to consider the totality of the property and affairs of the alleged patient when contemplating litigation. Thus:

> "the test to be applied … is whether the party to legal proceedings is capable of understanding, with the assistance of such proper explanation from legal advisers and experts in other disciplines as the case may require, the issues on which his consent or decision is likely to be necessary in the course of those proceedings. If he has capacity to understand that which he needs to understand in order to pursue or defend a claim, I can see no reason why the law – whether substantive or procedural – should require the interposition of a next friend or guardian ad litem (or, as such a person is now described in the Civil Procedure Rules, a litigation friend)."

The mental abilities required include the ability to recognise a problem, obtain and receive, understand and retain relevant information, including advice; the ability to weigh the information (including that derived from advice) in the balance in reaching a decision, and the ability to communicate that decision (*Masterman-Lister v Brutton & Co and Jewell & Home Counties Dairies* [2002] EWCA Civ 1889, [2002] All ER (D) 297 (Dec)).

Medical evidence—The evidence of a medically qualified person is required as to a diagnosis of mental disorder, and a psychologist is not qualified in this respect. In regard to the separate issue of mental capacity, a medical practitioner is regarded by the courts as an expert (even though he may not be) and entitled to express an opinion. Such opinion is merely part of the evidence, and the evidence of a psychologist, carer or social worker may be relevant. The court must decide whether the opinion of a medical witness has been formed on sufficient grounds and on the basis of the correct legal test. The typical medical practitioner has little knowledge of the various legal tests of capacity, so the appropriate test should be spelt out, and it should be explained that different tests apply to different types of decision.

Any medical witness asked to assist in relation to capacity needs to know the area of the alleged patient's activities in relation to which his advice is sought (*Masterman-Lister v Brutton & Co and Jewell & Home Counties Dairies* [2002] EWCA Civ 1889, [2002] All ER (D) 297 (Dec)). All relevant information should be provided, so when the test is whether the individual is incapable of managing his affairs the doctor must, if the jurisdiction of the Court of Protection is being considered, be given some idea of the nature and complexity of those affairs. But if this question arises in the context of litigation, the doctor will need to know what decisions the individual will be called upon to make for the conduct of that litigation. Only if the doctor has this information can he express an opinion as to whether the individual is capable of managing those affairs.

Issues as to capacity—There is unlikely to be any issue as to whether a party is a minor, but issues can arise as to whether a party is a patient. Such issue may be raised by the court or one of the parties, or by a next friend or guardian ad litem if there is doubt about whether a party has recovered capacity. It will then be necessary for the proceedings to be stayed while the issue is determined.

The child as party (r 9.1(2))—Certain applications under CA 1989 may be brought by the child himself (for example, an application as to contact under CA 1989, s 34 where the child is in care or, with leave, an application under s 4 for an order terminating a parental responsibility agreement or order) and, in other cases, the child will be joined as a respondent (for example, in care proceedings). A child is a person under a disability in legal proceedings and Pt IX applies except in relation to children who are the subject of applications in specified proceedings within the meaning of s 41(6). The position may be summarised as follows:

(*a*) Every child who brings proceedings which are non-specified or of which he is not the subject falls within Pt IX and must act by a next friend (r 9.2(1)) unless he either obtains the leave of the court (r 9.2A(1)(*a*)) or has instructed a solicitor who considers that he is able, having regard to his understanding, to give instructions in relation to the proceedings (r 9.2A(1)(*b*)).

(*b*) A child who responds to proceedings which are not specified proceedings must act by the guardian ad litem appointed for him under Pt IX (r 9.2(1)) unless he falls within r 9.2A(1)(*a*) or (*b*) (see under (*a*) above).

(*c*) A child who is the subject of specified proceedings (which will be the case, in broad terms, in public law matters) will generally be a party to those proceedings but will require no Part IX guardian ad litem as Pt IX does not apply (r 9.1(2)). However, he will normally have a s 41 guardian whose wider role, as set out in r 4.11, will include the Part IX functions.

(*d*) In exceptional cases, the child may be a party but have neither a Part IX guardian ad litem nor a s 41 guardian even though he does not fall within r 9.2A(1). This will occur when the child is the subject of an application in specified proceedings (so that Pt IX does not apply) but the court decides that it is not necessary to appoint a s 41 guardian in order to safeguard his interests (s 41(1)); or where, in Pt IX proceedings, no guardian is appointed under r 9.2(5) or otherwise.

Representation of children in specified proceedings (r 9.1(2))—Rules 9.2, 9.3 and 9.5 apply to children in relation to all family proceedings except for specified proceedings of which they are the subject. This exception is made because a special regime for the participation and representation of children in specified proceedings is provided by CA 1989, s 41 and rr 4.10 to 4.12. That special regime applies only to children who are the subject of the application, that is the child in respect of whom the order is sought. Children may be parties to proceedings in other capacities and their participation in those circumstances will be governed by Pt IX. In practice, the most common example is where the mother of the child who is the subject of the proceedings is herself under the age of 18. The mother must always be a respondent (because she will always have parental responsibility for the child by virtue of CA 1989, s 2 and App 3 to the rules requires those with parental responsibility to be made a respondent to all specified proceedings). The father may also be a minor but he is required to be a respondent only where he has acquired parental responsibility for the child under CA 1989, s 4. Appendix 3 will also require a child to be made a respondent if his contact with a child in care is sought to be regulated under CA 1989, s 34(2). It is unlikely that other categories of person who are required to be made respondents by App 3 will be children. However, the court has a general discretion to permit others to become parties (see r 4.7) and Pt IX will apply to any who are aged under 18.

Mixed proceedings—The reference to "proceedings which are dealt with together with the specified proceedings" in the closing words of r 9.1(2) is obscure. It seems to focus only on the concept of specified and unspecified proceedings being "dealt with together" rather than the situation where what would otherwise have been separate proceedings of each type have lost their separate identity by reason of the more fundamental process of consolidation or never acquired separate identities because the application of the one type had been made in the course of pre-existing proceedings of the other type. However, specific provision would seem to be otiose to deal with the former situation because the fact that separate proceedings are merely being heard together clearly does not affect the applicability of the relevant participation regime (ie CA 1989, s 41 and rr 4.10 to 4.12 or Part IX – see **Representation of children in specified proceedings** above) to each individual set of proceedings. By contrast, the result where there has been a consolidation would seem to be obscure in the absence of specific provision which the rule does not provide. On general principles, where an application of one type is made in the course of pre-existing proceedings of another type, the new application becomes part of those proceedings and is governed by their character. It would be anomalous for the question to be determined in this way because it will be fortuitous which application happened to be made first. It is submitted that, despite the deficiencies of the drafting of the rule, it makes it clear that the regime of CA 1989, s 41 is to prevail. The court may therefore feel justified in applying the s 41 regime to at least the "specified" part of a single set of umbrella proceedings (whether they assumed that character by consolidation or by application within pre-existing unspecified proceedings) and possibly to the whole of the proceedings.

Scope of r 9.2A (r 9.1(3))—Rule 9.2A applies only to proceedings under CA 1989 or the inherent jurisdiction of the High Court with respect to children. Because this restriction is in addition to the restriction of the scope of Pt IX contained in r 9.1(2), r 9.2A will apply only in such proceedings if they are not specified proceedings, or if they are specified proceedings but the child is not the subject of them.

"inherent jurisdiction of the High Court with respect to minors" (r 9.1(3))—This jurisdiction embraces wardship proceedings (see Pt V) and any proceedings which seek an exercise of the High Court's inherent jurisdiction with respect to children outside the procedural framework of wardship.

Inherent jurisdiction of the High Court with respect to adults—In relation to adults, the inherent jurisdiction of the High Court derived from the Royal Prerogative (sometimes referred to as the power of the Crown as parens patriae) has been taken away and replaced by the Mental Health Act powers. Unfortunately, these are largely restricted to financial management and the detention and treatment of mental patients. Other areas of decision-making are not dealt with, including personal affairs and medical treatment, hence the High Court only has power to make declarations (*Re F (Sterilisation: Mental Patient)* [1989] 2 FLR 376), supported where necessary by injunctions (*Re S (Hospital Patient: Jurisdiction)* [1995] Fam 26, [1995] 1 FLR 302). Problems of this nature are likely to be encountered during family proceedings involving a patient. For further consideration of this topic, reference may be made to Law Commission Report No 231 *Mental Incapacity* (1995), the Green Paper *Who Decides? Making Decisions on behalf of Mentally Incapacitated Adults* (December 1997) and the LCD Report *Making Decisions* (October 1999).

Reference should be made to *Practice Note of 1 May 2001* (Official Solicitor: Declaratory Proceedings: Medical and Welfare Decisions for Adults who Lack Capacity) and *President's Direction of 14 December 2001* (Declaratory Proceedings Concerning Incapacitated Adults: Medical and Welfare Decisions) – both are set out in Part IV of this work.

Need for Court of Protection involvement—See the note under CPR 1998, r 21.11.

Human rights—When a person is treated as a patient, whether or not as a result of an order of the court, he is thereby deprived of important rights, long cherished by English law and now safeguarded by the European Convention on Human Rights. Although the Rules do not contain any requirement for a judicial determination of the question of whether or not capacity exists courts should always, as a matter of practice, at the first convenient opportunity, investigate the question of capacity whenever there is any reason to suspect that it may be absent other than in cases where the Court of Protection is already involved – see *Masterman-Lister v Brutton & Co and Jewell & Home Counties Dairies* [2002] EWCA Civ 1889, [2002] All ER (D) 297 (Dec).

9.2 Person under disability must sue by next friend etc

(1) Except where rule 9.2A or any other rule otherwise provides, a person under disability may begin and prosecute any family proceedings only by his next friend and may defend any such proceedings only by his guardian ad litem and, except as otherwise provided by this rule, it shall not be necessary for a guardian ad litem to be appointed by the court.

(2) No person's name shall be used in any proceedings as next friend of a person under disability unless he is the Official Solicitor or the documents mentioned in paragraph (7) have been filed.

(3) Where a person is authorised under Part VII to conduct legal proceedings in the name of a patient or on his behalf, that person shall, subject to paragraph (2) be entitled to be next friend or guardian ad litem of the patient in any family proceedings to which his authority extends.

(4) Where a person entitled to defend any family proceedings is a patient and there is no person authorised under Part VII to defend the proceedings in his name or on his behalf, then –

(*a*) the Official Solicitor shall, if he consents, be the patient's guardian ad litem, but at any stage of the proceedings an application may be made on not less than four days' notice to the Official Solicitor, for the appointment of some other person as guardian;

(*b*) in any other case, an application may be made on behalf of the patient for the appointment of a guardian ad litem;

and there shall be filed in support of any application under this paragraph the documents mentioned in paragraph (7).

(5) Where a petition, answer, originating application or originating summons has been served on a person whom there is reasonable ground for believing to be a person under disability and no notice of intention to defend has been given, or answer or affidavit in answer filed, on his behalf, the party at whose instance the document was served shall, before taking any further steps in the proceedings, apply to a district judge for directions as to whether a guardian ad litem should be appointed to act for that person in the cause, and on any such application the district judge may, if he considers it necessary in order to protect the interests of the person served, order that some proper person be appointed his guardian ad litem.

(6) Except where a minor is prosecuting or defending proceedings under rule 9.2A, no notice of intention to defend shall be given, or answer or affidavit in answer filed, by or on behalf of a person under disability unless the person giving the notice or filing the answer or affidavit –

(*a*) is the Official Solicitor or, in a case to which paragraph (4) applies, is the Official Solicitor or has been appointed by the court to be guardian ad litem; or

(*b*) in any other case, has filed the documents mentioned in paragraph (7).

(7) The documents referred to in paragraphs (2), (4) and (6) are –

(*a*) a written consent to act by the proposed next friend or guardian ad litem;

(*b*) where the person under disability is a patient and the proposed next friend or guardian ad litem is authorised under Part VII to conduct the proceedings in his name or on his behalf, an office copy, sealed with the seal of the Court of Protection, of the order or other authorisation made or given under Part VII; and

(*c*) except where the proposed next friend or guardian ad litem is authorised as mentioned in sub-paragraph (*b*), a certificate by the solicitor acting for the person under disability –

(i) that he knows or believes that the person to whom the certificate relates is a minor or patient, stating (in the case of a patient) the grounds of his knowledge or belief and, where the person under disability is a patient, that there is no person authorised as aforesaid, and

(ii) that the person named in the certificate as next friend or guardian ad litem has no interest in the cause or matter in question adverse to that of the person under disability and that he is a proper person to be next friend or guardian.

Amendments—SI 1991/2113; SI 1992/456.

Defined terms—"court", "district judge", "family proceedings": r 1.2(1); "minor": Family Law Reform Act 1969, ss 1(2), 12; "notice of intention to defend": rr 1.2(1), 10.8; "Part VII", "patient", "person under disability": r 9.1(1).

Scope of provision—Rule 9.2(1) sets out the general rule that persons under disability may only begin and prosecute proceedings by a next friend and may only defend them by a guardian ad litem, subject to specific exceptions in other rules. These exceptions relate to minors and there are no exceptions in the case of patients. Rule 9.2(2)–(7) sets out the procedures for acquiring a next friend or guardian ad litem in various circumstances.

Exceptions to general rule—A minor need not act by a next friend or guardian ad litem where r 9.2A or any other rule so provides. Rule 3.20(3) (application for consent to marry) does so provide, and r 7.4(8)(*a*) enables someone to issue a judgment summons on behalf of a minor in certain circumstances without seeking leave to act as his next friend.

"next friend" and "guardian ad litem"—These terms are not defined for the purposes of this Part. It must be emphasised that a guardian ad litem under Pt IX is conceptually different from its homonym under Pt IV and that the definition in r 4.1(1) applies only to the phrase when used in Pt IV. The next friends and guardians ad litem referred to in Pt IX are conceptually identical to those in general civil proceedings; "section 41 guardians" by contrast have a different role (see r 4.11). In specified proceedings, there may be guardians of each type, because the minor who is the subject of the proceedings may have a "section 41 guardian" and other minor parties may have a Pt IX guardian. The universal term used by the Civil Procedure Rules 1998 (Pt 21) is "litigation friend".

Who is appointed—Any person authorised under Part VII of the Mental Health Act 1983 (ie as a receiver appointed by the Court of Protection – see generally s 96(1)) to conduct legal proceedings in the name or on behalf of a patient may, subject to filing the relevant document, become the next friend or guardian ad litem in accordance with such authority (r 9.2(3), (2)). There is no provision in these rules comparable to CCR Ord 10, r 1(3) empowering the court to appoint someone else, so if problems arise (eg the authorised person does not wish to act), reference should be made to the Court of Protection. A registered attorney of the patient under an enduring power is not specifically mentioned in the rules, but would be an obvious person to appoint as next friend or guardian ad litem because he will control his financial affairs. The Official Solicitor is to be the guardian ad litem if he consents (r 9.2(4)(*a*)) but in practice he will only consent if there is no-one else suitable and willing to act. It is not necessary to approach him in all cases, and the court will not be concerned to ascertain whether he has declined to consent before appointing someone else.

Apart from the above, there is no restriction on who may be a next friend or guardian ad litem, except that the person appointed must be within the jurisdiction and not under disability. Furthermore, there is no provision to prevent an unsuitable person (eg someone with a conflict of interest) from initially being appointed or thereafter continuing to act, apart from the need for the solicitor acting to file a limited certificate as to suitability (r 9.2(7)(*c*)(ii)). If the court becomes aware of the person's unsuitability, it may remove him under RSC Ord 80, r 3(4) and substitute another person as next friend or guardian ad litem, but there is no express duty to monitor the situation.

Powers of the next friend and guardian ad litem—The specific powers and duties of a next friend and guardian ad litem are not generally set out in Pt IX. RSC Ord 80 and CCR Ord 10 apply where they are compatible with the specific provisions of these rules (see r 1.3) and the principles that have developed in case-law in the context of general civil proceedings will similarly apply. It follows that a next friend or guardian ad litem may do anything required or authorised to be done by a party (RSC Ord 80, r 2(2); CCR Ord 10, r 12). But the next friend or guardian ad litem has no powers or status outside the conduct of the particular proceedings in which he is appointed; so, if money is awarded to a patient, the next friend or guardian ad litem has no authority to receive or expend that money. The money may only be dealt with pursuant to the directions of the court and, in this respect, reference must be made to RSC Ord 80, r 12 or CCR Ord 10, r 11, as appropriate. Similarly, any settlement or compromise will have to be approved by the court under RSC Ord 80, r 11 or CCR Ord 10, r 10; there are no equivalent provisions in FPR 1991.

Need for a solicitor—A next friend or guardian ad litem must act by a solicitor in the High Court (RSC Ord 80, r 2(3)); there is no similar requirement in the county court. Whether a next friend or guardian ad litem must act by a solicitor in family proceedings in the county court is far from clear. There is no express provision to this effect in FPR 1991, but r 9.2(7) requires a certificate by "the solicitor acting for the patient" to be filed before a person's name is used as next friend or guardian ad litem. The problem is likely to arise if that solicitor wishes to be withdrawn from the record, or the next friend or guardian ad litem seeks to serve notice of acting in person. The requirement for a solicitor to act on appointment of a next friend or guardian ad litem points to the need for a solicitor throughout the proceedings, but it may be a matter for the discretion of the court, depending on the complexity of the proceedings and the capacity of the next friend or guardian ad litem to continue to conduct them alone.

Replacement or removal of next friend or guardian ad litem—Except where the guardian ad litem is the Official Solicitor (r 9.2(4)(*a*)), there is no procedure in these rules (or CCR) for a next friend or guardian ad litem to be replaced or removed by order of the court. If problems arise, reference may be made (r 1.3) to the procedure in the High Court (RSC Ord 80, r 3(4)), which may also be adopted in a county court pursuant to County Courts Act 1984, s 76. For a case in which problems arose see *Re A (Conjoined Twins: Medical Treatment) (No 2)* [2001] 1 FLR 267, CA and the notes to CPR 1998, r 21.7.

No need for court appointment of next friend—A next friend may be appointed simply by filing the relevant documents (r 9.2(2), (7)). It is strange that there is no requirement for the person under disability to be notified that proceedings are being brought in his name, since he may wish to dispute that he is under disability.

Appointment of guardian ad litem—No notice of intention to defend may be given, or answer or affidavit in answer filed, by or on behalf of a minor or patient unless the person giving the notice or filing the answer or affidavit is the Official Solicitor or has been appointed by the court to be guardian ad litem (r 9.2(6)(*a*)) or, in any other case, has filed the relevant documents (r 9.2(6)(*b*)). In the case of a minor, there is no further formality. It seems that, for a patient, an application must then be made for appointment of the guardian ad litem (r 9.2(4)(*b*)), unless the Official Solicitor is to act and has already consented (r 9.2(4)(*a*)) or a person has been authorised by the Court of Protection to conduct the proceedings (r 9.2(4), (3)).

Documents to be filed (r 9.2(7))—A written consent to act must be filed by the proposed next friend or guardian ad litem in all cases (r 9.2(7)(*a*)). Unlike other civil proceedings in the county court, there is no requirement for a next friend to file an undertaking to be responsible for costs. In addition, unless the person to be appointed is the Official Solicitor (r 9.2(2)) or a person has been authorised by the Court of Protection to conduct the proceedings (r 9.2(7)(*b*)), the solicitor acting for the patient must file a certificate containing the statements set out in r 9.2(7)(*c*). This certificate goes beyond the requirements of CCR or RSC. It may presumably be signed by a member or other responsible employee of the firm duly authorised in that behalf by the solicitor in question.

Where the proposed next friend or guardian ad litem is authorised under Part VII of the Mental Health Act 1983 (ie as a receiver appointed by the Court of Protection) to conduct legal proceedings in the name or on behalf of a patient, an office copy of the order or other authorisation sealed with the official seal of the Court of Protection is filed (r 9.2(4)(*b*)) and a solicitor's certificate is not required.

Official Solicitor (r 9.2(2), (4)(*a*), (6)(*a*))—The expression is not defined for the purposes of these rules, but it is obvious from the context that it means the Official Solicitor to the Supreme Court provided for by Supreme Court Act 1981, s 90. The Official Solicitor may be contacted at 81 Chancery Lane, London WC2A 1DD Tel 0171 911 7127, Fax 0171 911 7105.

If r 9.2(4) is interpreted literally, it would require an approach to be made to the Official Solicitor to see if he consents to act before anyone else could be appointed as a guardian ad litem, but this is not the way the Official Solicitor interprets the rule. He should only be approached if there is no-one else suitable to act, and any order making such appointment should be expressed as being subject to his consent. He will usually consent to act, subject to appropriate medical evidence being produced, provided that his costs of so acting will be met. Where there are practical difficulties in obtaining such medical evidence, the Official Solicitor may be consulted. Save in the most urgent of cases, it is unlikely that the Official Solicitor will be able to complete his enquiries in less than three months. Accordingly, a lengthy adjournment of the proceedings might be necessary, and a substantive hearing should not be fixed within such period of his initial appointment without consulting him. Where the circumstances of the case justify the involvement of the Official Solicitor, a completed questionnaire, and a copy of the order appointing him (subject to his consent) and the court file, should be sent to his office.

Appointment by court (r 9.2(5))—Rule 9.2(5) provides a mechanism for the district judge to become aware of the fact that a party may be under disability and has not acquired a next friend or guardian ad litem by the usual means, as evidenced by the party's failure to respond in the appropriate manner to the first process to be served on him in the proceedings. An application must then be made to the district judge for directions as to whether a guardian ad litem should be appointed for that party. The district judge is empowered "if he considers it necessary in order to protect the interests of the person served" to order that some proper person be appointed his guardian ad litem. It is not clear whether this enables a guardian ad litem to be appointed in respect of a party who is not a patient, but this is unlikely (although this appears to be authorised by the wording of the rule). At most, this provision ensures that there is an enquiry as to whether the respondent is under disability, in which event his interests may need to be protected by the appointment of a guardian.

Another puzzling feature of r 9.2(5) is the reference to "answer", which can envisage only two situations. The first is that the person under disability is the petitioner, but in that case the paragraph can have no application because it allows only a guardian ad litem to be appointed while r 9.2(1) clearly provides that the person prosecuting proceedings may do so only by a next friend (unless one concludes that r 9.2(5) is a rule which "otherwise provides" within the meaning of r 9.2(1), in which case the curious result is that a guardian ad litem can be appointed under r 9.2(5)). The alternative explanation would be that r 9.2(5) refers to an answer served on another respondent, but in that case the provision would seem to be otiose because that respondent would already have failed to respond to service of the petition which would already have triggered the paragraph.

Appointment by court for minors—Although it is not expressly provided, the district judge should clearly not make an appointment under r 9.2(5) if it is clear that r 9.2A applies and the minor wishes to avail himself of his right to prosecute or defend the proceedings without a next friend or guardian ad litem. Such an appointment would be futile because the child could require the removal of any such appointee under the terms of r 9.2A(5)–(6).

Court appointments are also possible under r 9.2A(10) and the court may make a substitution under RSC Ord 80, r 3(4). It is not clear how the court should go about finding someone to appoint. The panel established under CA 1989, s 41(7) is not available for this type of guardian ad litem and, in many of the types of proceedings covered by Pt IX, the child's natural next friend or guardian ad litem will be a party to the proceedings and have a conflict of interest. If a panel guardian ad litem is appointed in non-specified proceedings, he will not receive funding from the Legal Services Commission, and probably not from his own panel.

Written consent to act (r 9.2(7)(*a*))—Practice Form No PF 169 may conveniently be used.

9.2A Certain minors may sue without next friend etc

(1) Where a person entitled to begin, prosecute or defend any proceedings to which this rule applies, is a minor to whom this Part applies, he may subject to paragraph (4), begin, prosecute or defend, as the case may be, such proceedings without a next friend or guardian ad litem –

(*a*) where he has obtained the leave of the court for that purpose; or
(*b*) where a solicitor –
  (i) considers that the minor is able, having regard to his understanding, to give instructions in relation to the proceedings; and
  (ii) has accepted instructions from the minor to act for him in the proceedings and, where the proceedings have begun, is so acting.

(2) A minor shall be entitled to apply for the leave of the court under paragraph (1)(*a*) without a next friend or guardian ad litem either –

(*a*) by filing a written request for leave setting out the reasons for the application, or
(*b*) by making an oral request for leave at any hearing in the proceedings.

(3) On considering a request for leave filed under paragraph (2)(*a*), the court shall either –

(*a*) grant the request, whereupon the proper officer shall communicate the decision to the minor and, where the leave relates to the prosecution or defence of existing proceedings, to the other parties to those proceedings, or
(*b*) direct that the request be heard ex parte, whereupon the proper officer shall fix a date for such a hearing and give to the minor making the request such notice of the date so fixed as the court may direct.

(4) Where a minor has a next friend or guardian ad litem in proceedings and the minor wishes to prosecute or defend the remaining stages of the proceedings without a next friend or guardian ad litem, the minor may apply to the court for leave for that purpose and for the removal of the next friend or guardian ad litem; and paragraph (2) shall apply to the application as if it were an application under paragraph (1)(*a*).

(5) On considering a request filed under paragraph (2) by virtue of paragraph (4), the court shall either –

(*a*) grant the request, whereupon the proper officer shall communicate the decision to the minor and next friend or guardian ad litem concerned and to all other parties to the proceedings, or
(*b*) direct that the request be heard, whereupon the proper officer shall fix a date for such a hearing and give to the minor and next friend or guardian ad litem concerned such notice of the date so fixed as the court may direct;

provided that the court may act under sub-paragraph (*a*) only if it is satisfied that the next friend or guardian ad litem does not oppose the request.

(6) Where the court is considering whether to –

(*a*) grant leave under paragraph (1)(*a*), or
(*b*) grant leave under paragraph (4) and remove a next friend or guardian ad litem,

it shall grant the leave sought and, as the case may be, remove the next friend or guardian ad litem if it considers that the minor concerned has sufficient understanding to participate as a party in the proceedings concerned or proposed without a next friend or guardian ad litem.

(6A) In exercising its powers under paragraph (6) the court may order the next friend or guardian ad litem to take such part in the proceedings as the court may direct.

(7) Where a request for leave is granted at a hearing fixed under paragraph (3)(*b*) (in relation to the prosecution or defence of proceedings already begun) or (5)(*b*), the proper officer shall forthwith communicate the decision to the other parties to the proceedings.

(8) The court may revoke any leave granted under paragraph (1)(*a*) where it considers that the child does not have sufficient understanding to participate as a party in the proceedings concerned without a next friend or guardian ad litem.

(9) Without prejudice to any requirement of CCR Order 50, rule 5 or RSC Order 67, where a solicitor is acting for a minor in proceedings which the minor is prosecuting or defending without a next friend or guardian ad litem by virtue of paragraph (1)(*b*) and either of the conditions specified in the paragraph (1)(*b*)(i) and (ii) cease to be fulfilled, he shall forthwith so inform the court.

(10) Where –

(*a*) the court revokes any leave under paragraph (8), or

(*b*) either of the conditions specified in paragraph (1)(*b*)(i) and (ii) is no longer fulfilled,

the court may, if it considers it necessary in order to protect the interests of the minor concerned, order that some proper person be appointed his next friend or guardian ad litem.

(11) Where a minor is of sufficient understanding to begin, prosecute or defend proceedings without a next friend or guardian ad litem –

(*a*) he may nevertheless begin, prosecute or defend them by his next friend or guardian ad litem; and

(*b*) where he is prosecuting or defending proceedings by his next friend or guardian ad litem, the respective powers and duties of the minor and next friend or guardian ad litem, except those conferred or imposed by this rule shall not be affected by the minor's ability to dispense with a next friend or guardian ad litem under the provisions of this rule.

Amendments—Inserted by SI 1992/456; amended by SI 1997/1893.

Defined terms—"court": r 1.2(1); "minor": Family Law Reform Act 1969, ss 1(2), 12; "proper officer": r 1.2(1).

"entitled to begin, prosecute or defend any proceedings" (r 9.2A(1))—Rule 9.2A(1) makes it clear that this rule does not confer any rights to party status which minors would not otherwise enjoy but merely affects whether a next friend or guardian ad litem is required when minors are parties. Unlike "begin", "prosecute or defend" refers to a continuing course of action; therefore, if in the course of proceedings which a child had been prosecuting or defending without a next friend or guardian ad litem in reliance on one (or both) of the grounds in r 9.2A(1), the ground (or both of them) ceases to apply, the child is unable to continue prosecuting or defending the remaining stages of the proceedings unless and until he acquires a next friend or guardian ad litem. Rule 9.2A(1)(*a*) ceases to apply only if the leave is revoked by the court under r 9.2A(8), in which case the court would be able to appoint a next friend or guardian ad litem under rule 9.2A(10). Where r 9.2A(1)(*b*) ceases to apply, the solicitor concerned must so inform the court under r 9.2A(9) and the court is similarly able to make an appointment under r 9.2A(10). Before, or in default of, such an appointment, a next friend may begin to act under r 9.2(2) simply by filing the documents referred to in r 9.2(7). In the case of guardians ad litem, the more specific wording of r 9.2(6) may mean it does not apply, depending on the stage already reached in the proceedings, but in that case the similar provision of RSC Ord 80, r 3(6) would seem to fill the gap.

"next friend" and "guardian ad litem"—See under r 9.2.

Leave of the court (r 9.2A(1)(*a*))—The criterion for granting leave is set out in r 9.2A(6). Where a child wishes to act as a litigant in person, the court's leave must be obtained, since r 9.2A(1)(*b*) is obviously inapplicable. Even where a child has retained a solicitor, the solicitor may still wish leave to be sought if he is unsure of whether r 9.2A(1)(*b*)(i) is satisfied, or he is unwilling to shoulder the responsibility of deciding that it is satisfied. The court, rather than the solicitor, always has the ultimate right to decide whether a child who comes before it as a party without a next friend or guardian ad litem has the necessary ability, having regard to his understanding, to instruct his solicitor (*Re CT (A Minor) (Wardship: Representation)* [1993] 2 FLR 278).

Solicitor's acceptance of instructions (r 9.2A(1)(*b*))—The test which applies under r 9.2A(1)(*b*)(i) is, in substance, the same as that which governs whether a solicitor should accept instructions from a child who is the subject of specified proceedings (see r 4.12(1)(*a*)). See also *Re CT (A Minor) (Wardship: Representation)* [1993] 2 FLR 278 (above) and **"sufficient understanding"** below.

"filing" (r 9.2A(2)(*a*))—Defined in relation to county courts by CCR Ord 2, r 4 and extended to cover use of the post (CCR Ord 2, r 5). Not specifically defined for High Court purposes.

"written request for leave" (r 9.2A(2)(*a*))—No particular form of request is required, but full details in support of the request should be included as this may obviate the need for a hearing to be directed (see r 9.2A(3)).

Ex parte nature of request (r 9.2A(3)(*b*), (5)(*b*))—Whether a minor should be allowed to dispense with a next friend or guardian ad litem is a matter between the minor and the court (and the next friend or guardian ad litem if one is already acting). It is implicit that the other parties to the proceedings (or proposed parties to proceedings which the minor wishes to begin) have no standing in relation to questions under this rule, even though they may have their own reasons for wishing a particular outcome. The rules do not expressly or implicitly confer any right on the parents of the child or anyone else to be heard on the child's application. However, the judge always has a discretion (not conferred by the rules), in the course of hearing such an application, to hear the representations of the child's parents or others in the interests of justice (*Re S (A Minor) (Independent Representation)* [1993] 2 FLR 437).

Removal of next friend or guardian ad litem (r 9.2A(4))—It is implicit in r 9.2A(4) that where a next friend or guardian ad litem is already acting he must be removed before a child may avail himself of r 9.2A(1). In *Re H (A Minor) (Role of Official Solicitor)* [1993] 2 FLR 552, FD, the Official Solicitor was removed as guardian ad litem for a 15-year-old boy in wardship proceedings. However, the Official Solicitor was asked to continue to participate in the proceedings as amicus curiae (see **Role of Official Solicitor as amicus curiae (advocate to the court)** below). For obvious reasons r 9.2A(4), by applying r 9.2A(2), enables the child to make an application for his next friend or guardian ad litem to be dismissed without going through (and thus requiring the consent of) the next friend or guardian ad litem.

"sufficient understanding" (r 9.2A(6))—See **"able ... to give such instructions on his own behalf"** under r 4.12.

Revocation of leave (r 9.2A(8))—The court may wish to revoke leave in two main types of case. First, the complexity of the proceedings may materially increase during the course of the interlocutory process by the making of new applications in the course of them, the joinder of new parties or the raising of new and complicated factual or evidential issues that were not originally foreseen. Without altering its assessment of the child's level of understanding, the court may conclude that it is insufficient in the changed circumstances (see **"sufficient understanding"** above). Secondly, through experiencing how the child conducts the interlocutory stages of the proceedings, the court may simply conclude that it was wrong to grant the leave in the first place. Where this occurs, the court can use its general power in r 4.14(2)(*d*) to direct that a guardian ad litem be appointed (*Re S (A Minor) (Independent Representation)* [1993] 2 FLR 437 at 444G).

"any requirement of CCR Order 50, rule 5 or RSC Order 67" (r 9.2A(9))—These provisions require notice to be given of a change of solicitor or where a solicitor ceases to act without being replaced.

Minor's right to use next friend or guardian ad litem where he qualifies to act without one (r 9.2A(11))—The effect of r 9.2A(11)(*b*) is to make it clear that, if such a child chooses to have a next friend or guardian ad litem, their relationship is to be unaffected by this rule. The exception to this is that the child may change his mind and obtain the next friend's or guardian ad litem's removal under r 9.2A(4)–(6). A next friend or guardian ad litem must conduct the proceedings in what he considers to be the child's best interests and, if they disagree about what these are, the child must either accept the decision of his next friend or guardian ad litem or dispense with him. The child cannot overrule him, and the next friend or guardian ad litem should not allow a threat of removal to influence his judgment.

Role of Official Solicitor as amicus curiae (advocate to the court)—Where the Official Solicitor is removed as guardian ad litem as a result of a successful application by the child under r 9.2A, the court is very likely to consider inviting him to continue to assist the court during the proceedings in the role of amicus curiae (advocate to the court). See *Re H (A Minor) (Role of Official Solicitor)* [1993] 2 FLR 552, FD and *Re H (A Minor) (Care Proceedings: Child's Wishes)* [1993] 1 FLR 440.

9.3 Service on person under disability

(1) Where a document to which rule 2.9 applies is required to be served on a person under disability, it shall be served –

(*a*) in the case of a minor who is not also a patient, on his father or guardian or, if he has no father or guardian, on the person with whom he resides or in whose care he is;

(*b*) in the case of a patient –

(i) on the person (if any) who is authorised under Part VII to conduct in the name of the patient or on his behalf the proceedings in connection with which the document is to be served, or

(ii) if there is no person so authorised, on the Official Solicitor if he has consented under rule 9.2(4) to be the guardian ad litem of the patient, or

(iii) in any other case, on the person with whom the patient resides or in whose care he is:

Provided that the court may order that a document which has been, or is to be served on the person under disability or on a person other than one mentioned in sub-paragraph (*a*) or (*b*) shall be deemed to be duly served on the person under disability.

(2) Where a document is served in accordance with paragraph (1) it shall be indorsed with a notice in Form M24; and after service has been effected the person at whose instance the document was served shall, unless the Official Solicitor is the guardian ad litem of the person under disability or the court otherwise directs, file an affidavit by the person on whom the document was served stating whether the contents of the document were, or its purport was, communicated to the person under disability and, if not, the reasons for not doing so.

Amendments—SI 1992/2067.

Defined terms—"minor": Family Law Reform Act 1969, ss 1(2), 12; "patient": r 9.1(1).

Scope of provision—This rule prescribes the manner in which a "document to which rule 2.9 applies" is to be served on a person under disability. The rule applies to petitions used to commence proceedings of any kind mentioned in r 2.1 or, presumably, under Family Law Act 1986, s 55, 56(1), (2) or 57 (by virtue of r 3.16(12)). Petitions include an answer served on a party cited (r 2.16). Supplemental or amended petitions are also included (r 2.11(8)) but, in such cases, a guardian ad litem would already have been appointed and so service on the person under disability is not required.

This rule thus applies only to service of a narrow range of documents, basically petitions in matrimonial causes for divorce, nullity of marriage, judicial separation and presumption of death and dissolution. In the absence of other provisions in these rules, service of documents commencing other family proceedings must be governed in the High Court by RSC Ord 80 and in the county court by CCR Ord 10 (by virtue of r 1.3).

"document to which rule 2.9 applies" (r 9.3(1))—See **Scope of provision** above.

"Official Solicitor"—See under r 9.2.

"filing"—See under r 9.2A.

"guardian ad litem"—See **"next friend" and "guardian ad litem"** under r 9.2.

Person to be served—The rule requires the petition to be served on the person authorised by the Court of Protection to conduct the proceedings on behalf of the person under disability or, if none, the Official Solicitor if he has agreed to act. This assumes that steps have been taken in advance to enable the proceedings to be dealt with. If that is not the case, the petition must be served on the person with whom the patient resides or in whose care he is, on the assumption that such person will then take appropriate steps to arrange a representative ("guardian ad litem"). Service on a proper officer of the local social services authority or other guardian when the patient is under a guardianship order, or the district health authority when the patient has been compulsorily admitted to hospital under the Mental Health Act 1983, may be sufficient.

Communication to person under disability—There is no requirement for service on the person under disability personally, but the court will, unless there is good reason to the contrary, wish to be satisfied that the proceedings have been brought to the attention of that person in case he wishes to dispute being under disability or alert some person to take steps on his behalf (eg seek appointment as guardian ad litem). Hence the petitioner or other party initiating the proceedings is required to file an affidavit by the person on whom the petition is served.

Mode of service—Service on a person under disability is to be effected through the petitioner (r 2.9(2)(*a*)), and the normal procedure of postal service by the court does not apply. A solicitor may still accept service on behalf of one of the nominated persons (r 10.2), and the general rules as to service apply (see rr 10.2–10.6).

Deemed service—The court may in any case order that a petition which has been, or is to be, served on a person under disability, or a person other than one mentioned in this rule, is deemed to be duly served on the person under disability (proviso to r 9.3(1)). This provision enables the court to proceed with the appointment of a guardian ad litem when service is not otherwise possible.

9.4 Petition for nullity on ground of mental disorder

(1) Where a petition for nullity has been presented on the ground that at the time of the marriage the respondent was suffering from mental disorder within the meaning of the Mental Health Act 1983 of such a kind or to such an extent as to be unfitted for marriage, then, whether or not the respondent gives notice of intention to defend, the petitioner shall not proceed with the cause without the leave of the district judge.

(2) The district judge by whom an application for leave is heard may make it a condition of granting leave that some proper person be appointed to act as guardian ad litem of the respondent.

Defined terms—"cause", "district judge": r 1.2(1); "notice of intention to defend": r 10.8(1).

Scope of provision—This rule makes special provision for respondents to nullity petitions under Matrimonial Causes Act 1973, s 12(*e*).

"mental disorder" (r 9.4(1))—See under r 9.1.

Leave to proceed—A petition under MCA 1973, s 12(*d*) cannot proceed without leave of the court; before granting leave, the district judge will want to consider whether a guardian ad litem for the respondent should be appointed in accordance with r 9.2. If the district judge thinks it appropriate, he may make leave to proceed conditional on the appointment of a guardian ad litem. It is not clear whether this provision authorises the appointment of a guardian ad litem for a respondent who is not a patient, but this is unlikely. At most, this provision ensures that there is an enquiry as to whether the respondent is under disability, in which event his interests may need to be protected by the appointment of a guardian.

9.5 Separate representation of children

(1) Without prejudice to rules 2.57 and 9.2A, if in any family proceedings it appears to the court that it is in the best interests of any child to be made a party to the proceedings, the court may appoint –

(*a*) an officer of the service;
(*b*) (if he consents) the Official Solicitor; or
(*c*) (if he consents) some other proper person,

to be the guardian ad litem of the child with authority to take part in the proceedings on the child's behalf.

(2) An order under paragraph (1) may be made by the court of its own motion or on the application of a party to the proceedings or of the proposed guardian ad litem.

(3) The court may at any time direct that an application be made by a party for an order under paragraph (1) and may stay the proceedings until the application has been made.

(4) (*revoked*)

(5) Unless otherwise directed, a person appointed under this rule or rule 2.57 to be the guardian ad litem of a child in any family proceedings shall be treated as a party for the purpose of any provision of these rules requiring a document to be served on or notice to be given to a party to the proceedings.

(6) Where the guardian ad litem appointed under this rule is an officer of the service, rules 4.11 and 4.11A shall apply to him as they apply to a children's guardian appointed under section 41 of the Children Act 1989.

Amendments—SI 1992/456; SI 2001/821.

Defined terms—"child", "court", "family proceedings": r 1.2(1).

"rule 2.57" (r 9.5(1), (5))—Rule 2.57 makes similar provision in relation to proceedings for a variation of settlement and other types of ancillary relief. The duplication seems attributable only to the different derivation of Pts II and IX.

"rule 9.2A" (r 9.5(1))—This rule allows minors to participate in proceedings without a guardian ad litem. Therefore, a guardian ad litem should not be appointed under r 9.5 if the child wishes to act without one and the condition in r 9.2A as to his capacity is satisfied.

"in any family proceedings" (r 9.5(1))—The exclusion of specified proceedings within the meaning of CA 1989, s 41(6) (see **Representation of children in specified proceedings** under r 9.1) restricts the effect of this rule.

"child" (r 9.5(1))—"child" means the same as "minor", which is used in the other rules in this Part. No significance attaches to the choice of word (see **"minors"** under r 9.1).

"child to be made a party to the proceedings" (r 9.5(1))—In *L v L (Minors) (Separate Representation)* [1994] 1 FLR 156, the Court of Appeal indicated that children should generally be made parties for practical reasons and that the appointment of a guardian ad litem (children's guardian) for a child in private law proceedings presupposed that the child would be made a party to those proceedings unless, in any particular case (as in Adoption Rules 1984, r 15(3)), there was an express provision to the contrary.

CAFCASS Legal/Official Solicitor—It is unusual to appoint a guardian and separate representation for a child in private law cases (*Re D (A Child)* (unreported), 8 November 2001, CA). In a difficult case, where it is felt that a child needs separate representation, CAFCASS Legal should be invited to provide a guardian to represent the child and take over the child's case. If CAFCASS Legal decline to deal with the case, consideration should be given to appointing a local guardian and solicitor to represent the child (*Re W (A Child)* (unreported), 22 November 2001, CA). See *Practice Note of March 2001 (Officers of CAFCASS Legal Services and Special Casework: Appointment in Family Proceedings)* and *Practice Note of 2 April 2001 (Official Solicitor: Appointment in Family Proceedings)* (both are set out in Part IV of this work).

"some other proper person" (r 9.5(1)(*c*))—This sub-rule permits a solicitor to act as solicitor and guardian (*Re N (Residence: Appointment of Solicitor: Placement with Extended Family)* [2001] 1 FLR 1028). In *Re K (Replacement of Guardian ad Litem)* [2001] 1 FLR 663 it was held that such a course is generally undesirable. Similarly, there was no objection in principle to a well-known and respected charitable organisation representing a child (*Re A (Contact: Separate Representation)* [2001] 1 FLR 715).

Continuing role of children's guardian when "specified proceedings" cease to be "specified"—It is possible for the High Court or a county court to direct that a guardian ad litem continue to be involved under r 9.5 even though proceedings which had been "specified proceedings", within the meaning of CA 1989, s 41(6)(*b*), have ceased to be "specified" (for example, where a local authority, as a result of a s 37 direction by the court, investigates the circumstances of a child but decides to make no application for a public law order in respect of him). However, this course can only be taken if: (i) the children's guardian consents to it; (ii) there is funding available; and (iii) the children's guardian has a continuing role to play in the matter despite the changed status of the proceedings (*Re CE (Section 37 Direction)* [1995] 1 FLR 26).

"guardian ad litem"—See **"next friend" and "guardian ad litem"** under r 9.2.

Manner of application—Application should be made in accordance with r 10.9.

PART X
PROCEDURE (GENERAL)

10.1 Application

The provisions of this Part apply to all family proceedings, but have effect subject to the provisions of any other Part of these rules.

Defined terms—"family proceedings": r 1.2(1).

10.2 Service on solicitors

(1) Where a document is required by these rules to be sent to any person who is acting by a solicitor, service shall, subject to any other direction or order, be effected –

(*a*) by sending the document by first class post to the solicitor's address for service; or

(*b*) where that address includes a numbered box at a document exchange, at that document exchange or at a document exchange which transmits documents every business day to that document exchange; or

(*c*) by fax (as defined by RSC Order 1, rule 4(1)) in accordance with the provisions of RSC Order 65, rule 5(2B).

(2) Any document which is left at a document exchange in accordance with paragraph (1)(*b*) shall, unless the contrary is proved, be deemed to have been served on the second day after the day on which it is left.

(3) Where no other mode of service is prescribed, directed or ordered, service may additionally be effected by leaving the document at the solicitor's address.

Defined terms—"business day": r 1.5(6); "document exchange": r 1.2(1).

"subject to any other direction or order" (r 10.2(1))—This reservation does not seem to give the court *carte blanche* to dispense with the requirements of the rule; it is a cross-reference to any power conferred elsewhere to give orders or directions about service, such as that conferred by r 4.14(2)(*e*) or the power to authorise substituted service under RSC Ord 65, r 4 or CCR Ord 7, r 8 (both of which are attracted by FPR 1991, r 1.3).

Fax (r 10.2(1)(*c*))—RSC Ord 1, r 4(1) defines "fax" to mean "the making of a facsimile copy of a document by the transmission of electronic signals". Order 65, r 5(2B) provides that:

"Service by fax may be effected where –

(*a*) the party serving the document acts by a solicitor,
(*b*) the party on whom the document is served acts by a solicitor and service is effected by transmission to the business address of such a solicitor,
(*c*) the solicitor acting for the party on whom the document is served has indicated in writing to the solicitor serving the document that he is willing to accept service by fax at a specified fax number and the document is transmitted to that number, and for this purpose the inscription of a fax number on the writing paper of a solicitor shall be deemed to indicate that such a solicitor is willing to accept service by fax at that number in accordance with this paragraph unless he states otherwise in writing, and
(*d*) as soon as practicable after service by fax the solicitor acting for the party serving the document dispatches a copy of it to the solicitor acting for the other party by any of the other methods prescribed for service by paragraph (1), and if he fails to do so the document shall be deemed never to have been served by fax.

Where the fax is transmitted on a business day it shall, unless the contrary is shown, be deemed to be served on that day, and, in any other case, on the business day next following."

It would seem from the wording by which r 10.2(1)(*c*) applies RSC Ord 65, r 5(2B) that the reference to "paragraph (1)" in r 5(2B)(*d*) means Ord 65, r 5(1) and is not to be construed for this purpose as meaning the corresponding provision in FPR 1991 (ie the other provisions of r 10.2). Therefore the confirmatory "hard copy" need only be served in compliance with Ord 65 r 5(1), which differs from r 10.2 in that it permits second-class post to be used and provides a residual alternative method of service of "such other manner as the court may direct". "Business day" is defined for the purposes of Ord 65, r 5 by r 5(4)(*b*) in terms similar to those in the definition in FPR 1991, r 1.5(6).

Where service is effected by fax, the transmission confirmation slips which most types of machine emit should be retained and, where it may prove important to show that service was effected before 4 pm, the accuracy of the machine's clock should be checked lest the confirmation slip erroneously records that the message was transmitted after 4 pm.

"second day after the day on which it is left" (r 10.2(2))—This phrase is to be construed literally as r 1.5 does not apply to exclude non-business days etc.

10.3 Service on person acting in person

(1) Subject to paragraph (3) and to any other direction or order, where a document is required by these rules to be sent to any person who is acting in person, service shall be effected by sending the document by first class post to the address given by him or, if he has not given an address for service, to his last known address.

(2) Subject to paragraph (3), where no other mode of service is prescribed, directed or ordered, service may additionally be effected by delivering the document to him or by leaving it at the address specified in paragraph (1).

(3) Where it appears to the district judge that it is impracticable to deliver the document to the person to be served and that, if the document were left at or sent by post to, the address specified in paragraph (1) it would be unlikely to reach him, the district judge may dispense with service of the document.

Defined terms—"district judge": r 1.2(1).

"Subject to ... any other direction or order" (r 10.3(1))—See **"subject to any other direction or order"** under r 10.2. The interpretation there advanced is reinforced in the context of r 10.3 because r 10.3(3) would otherwise be otiose and the preconditions for dispensation laid down there would be futile.

"address given by him" (r 10.3(1))—Usually this means the address given on the relevant process or pleading or to any new address notified by the person concerned, but it is sensibly vague to allow for an address to be given in any manner.

Application to dispense with service (r 10.3(3))—An application to dispense with service may be made in accordance with r 10.9, subject to any procedure expressly provided for in the Part relating to the proceedings in question.

10.4 Service by bailiff in proceedings in principal registry

Where, in any proceedings pending in the principal registry which are treated as pending in a divorce county court, a document is to be served by bailiff, it shall be sent for service to the proper officer of the county court within the district of which the document is to be served.

Defined terms—"divorce county court", "principal registry", "proper officer": r 1.2(1).

Scope of provision—This rule sets out how bailiff service is to be effected in county court divorce proceedings pending in the principal registry.

10.5 Proof of service by officer of court etc

(1) Where a petition is sent to any person by an officer of the court, he shall note the date of posting in the records of the court.

(2) Without prejudice to section 133 of the County Court Act 1984 (proof of service of summonses etc) a record made pursuant to paragraph (1) shall be evidence of the facts stated therein.

(3) Where the court has authorised notice by advertisement to be substituted for service and the advertisement has been inserted by some person other than the proper officer, that person shall file copies of the newspapers containing the advertisement.

Defined terms—"proper officer": r 1.2(1).

"court"—The reference to "court" in r 10.5(3) seems to attract the definition in r 1.2(1) (a judge or the district judge), but in both places where the word is used in r 10.5(1) it seems to mean the High Court or county court to which the petition is sent.

County Courts Act 1984, s 133 (r 10.5(2))— Section 133(1) enables the service of any summons or other process issued from a county court which is served by an officer of a court to be proved by a certificate in prescribed form under the hand of that officer showing the fact and mode of the service.

Substituted service (r 10.5(3))—Substituted service may be authorised under RSC Ord 65, r 4 or CCR Ord 7, r 8 (as applied by FPR 1991, r 1.3).

10.6 Service out of England and Wales

(1) Any document in family proceedings may be served out of England and Wales without leave either in the manner prescribed by these rules or –

(*a*) where the proceedings are pending in the High Court, in accordance with RSC Order 11, rules 5 and 6 (which relates to the service of a writ abroad); or

(*b*) where the proceedings are pending in a divorce county court, in accordance with CCR Order 8, rules 8 to 10 (which relate to the service of process abroad).

(2) Where the document is served in accordance with RSC Order 11, rules 5 and 6, those rules and rule 8 of the said Order 11 (which deals with expenses incurred by the Secretary of State) shall have effect in relation to service of the document as they have effect in relation to service of notice of a writ, except that the official

certificate of service referred to in paragraph (5) of the said rule 5 shall, if the document was served personally, show the server's means of knowledge of the identity of the person served.

(3) Where the document is served in accordance with CCR Order 8, rules 8 to 10, those rules shall have effect subject to the following modifications –

(*a*) the document need not be served personally on the person required to be served so long as it is served in accordance with the law of the country in which service is effected;

(*b*) the official certificate or declaration with regard to service referred to in paragraph (6) of the said rule 10 shall, if the document was served personally, show the server's means of knowledge of the identity of the person served; and

(*c*) in paragraph (7) of the said rule 10 the words "or in the manner in which default summonses are required to be served" shall be omitted.

(4) Where a petition is to be served on a person out of England and Wales, then –

(*a*) the time within which that person must give notice of intention to defend shall be determined having regard to the practice adopted under RSC Order 11, rule 4(4) (which requires an order for leave to serve a writ out of the jurisdiction to limit the time for appearance) and the notice in Form M5 shall be amended accordingly;

(*b*) if the petition is to be served otherwise than in accordance with RSC Order 11, rules 5 and 6, or CCR Order 8, rules 8 to 10, and there is reasonable ground for believing that the person to be served does not understand English, the petition shall be accompanied by a translation, approved by the district judge, of the notice in Form M5, in the official language of the country in which service is to be effected or, if there is more than one official language of that country, in any one of those languages which is appropriate to the place where service is to be effected; but this sub-paragraph shall not apply in relation to a document which is to be served in a country in which the official language, or one of the official languages, is English.

(5) Where a document specifying the date of hearing of any proceedings is to be served out of England and Wales, the date shall be fixed having regard to the time which would be limited under paragraph (4)(*a*) for giving notice of intention to defend if the document were a petition.

Defined terms—"district judge", "divorce county court", "family proceedings": r 1.2(1); "notice of intention to defend": r 10.8(1).

RSC Ord 11, rr 4(4), 5, 6, 8 and CCR Ord 8, rr 8–10—See *Civil Court Service* (Jordan Publishing Ltd) and *The County Court Practice* respectively for the text of these provisions, bearing in mind the way in which they are modified in family proceedings by this rule.

10.7 Mode of giving notice

Unless otherwise directed, any notice which is required by these rules to be given to any person shall be in writing and, may be given in any manner in which service may be effected under RSC Order 65, rule 5.

RSC Order 65, r 5—Order 65, r 5 permits service to be effected by leaving the document at the proper address, by post, through a document exchange, by fax, or in such other manner as the court may direct.

10.8 Notice of intention to defend

(1) In these rules any reference to a notice of intention to defend is a reference to an acknowledgement of service in Form M6 containing a statement to the effect that the person by whom or on whose behalf it is signed intends to defend the proceedings to which the acknowledgement relates, and any reference to giving notice of intention to defend is a reference to returning such a notice to the court office.

(2) In relation to any person on whom there is served a document requiring or authorising an acknowledgement of service to be returned to the court office, references in these rules to the time limited for giving notice of intention to defend are references –

(*a*) to seven days after service of the document, in the case of notice of intention to defend a petition under Part II of these rules, and
(*b*) in any other case, to 14 days or such other time as may be fixed.

(3) Subject to paragraph (2) a person may give notice of intention to defend notwithstanding that he has already returned to the court office an acknowledgement of service not constituting such a notice.

Computation of time—The computation of time under this rule is governed by r 1.5.

10.9 Mode of making applications

Except where these rules, or any rules applied by these rules, otherwise provide, every application in family proceedings –

(*a*) shall be made to a district judge;
(*b*) shall, if the proceedings are pending in the High Court, be made by summons or, if the proceedings are pending in a divorce county court, be made in accordance with CCR Order 13, rule 1 (which deals with applications in the course of proceedings).

Defined terms—"district judge", "divorce county court", "family proceedings": r 1.2(1).

Summons—This is normally in chambers and RSC Ord 32 applies to regulate the procedure to be followed.

CCR Ord 13, r 1—This makes general provision for applications and orders in the course of proceedings.

10.10 Orders for transfer of family proceedings

(1) Where a cause is pending in the High Court, the district judge of the registry in which the cause is pending or a judge may order that the cause be transferred to another registry.

(2) Where a cause is pending in a divorce county court, the court may order that the cause be transferred to another divorce county court.

(3) Paragraphs (1) and (2) shall apply to applications in causes as they apply to causes; but before making an order for transfer of an application the court shall consider whether it would be more convenient to transfer the cause under paragraph (1) or (2), as the case may be.

(4) The court shall not, either of its own motion or on the application of any party, make an order under paragraph (1), (2) or (3) unless the parties have either –

(*a*) had an opportunity of being heard on the question, or
(*b*) consented to such an order.

(5) Where the parties, or any of them, desire to be heard on the question of a transfer, the court shall give the parties notice of a date, time and place at which the question will be considered.

(6) Paragraphs (4) and (5) shall apply with the necessary modifications to an order for the transfer of family proceedings under section 38 or 39 of the Act of 1984 as they apply to an order under paragraph (1) or (2) of this rule.

(7) Paragraphs (4) and (5) shall not apply where the court makes an order for transfer under paragraphs (1), (2) or (3) in compliance with the provisions of any Order made under Part I of Schedule 11 to the Children Act 1989.

Defined terms—"the Act of 1984", "cause", "court", "divorce county court": r 1.2(1); "family proceedings": Matrimonial and Family Proceedings Act 1984, s 32; "judge": r 1.2(1); "pending": r 1.2(2).

Notice (r 10.10(5))—The giving of notice is regulated by r 10.7.

Matrimonial and Family Proceedings Act 1984, ss 38 and 39 (r 10.10(6))—Section 38 provides for the transfer of family proceedings from the High Court to county courts and s 39 provides for transfer in the other direction. Neither section applies to proceedings under CA 1989 or the Adoption Act 1976 (see Children (Allocation of Proceedings) Order 1991, art 5). The only modification to paragraphs (4) or (5) that is necessary is to construe the reference in (4) to "an order under paragraph (1), (2) or (3)" as being a reference to s 38 or 39.

Orders under CA 1989, Sch 11, Pt I (r 10.10(7))—Children (Allocation of Proceedings) Order 1991, art 5 disapplies Matrimonial and Family Proceedings Act 1984, ss 38 and 39 to proceedings under CA 1989 or the Adoption Act 1976 and does not require the transfer of any proceedings other than under CA 1989 or AA 1976; therefore, r 10.10(7) is in fact superfluous because there is no overlap between the order and either r 10.10(1) or (2) or s 38 or 39.

10.11 Procedure on transfer of cause or application

(1) Where any cause or application is ordered to be transferred from one court or registry to another, the proper officer of the first-mentioned court or registry shall, unless otherwise directed, give notice of the transfer to the parties.

(2) Any provision in these rules, or in any order made or notice given pursuant to these rules, for the transfer of proceedings between a divorce county court and the High Court shall, in relation to proceedings which, after the transfer, are to continue in the principal registry, be construed –

(*a*) in the case of a transfer from the High Court to a divorce county court, as a provision for the proceedings to be treated as pending in a divorce county court, and
(*b*) in the case of a transfer from a divorce county court to the High Court, as a provision for the proceedings no longer to be treated as pending in a divorce county court.

(3) Proceedings transferred from a divorce county court to the High Court pursuant to any provision in these rules shall, unless the order of transfer otherwise directs, proceed in the registry nearest to the divorce county court from which they are transferred, but nothing in this paragraph shall prejudice any power under these rules to order the transfer of the proceedings to a different registry.

Defined terms—"cause", "divorce county court", "proper officer": r 1.2(1).

Notice (r 10.11(1), (2))—The giving of notice is regulated by r 10.7.

Principal registry (r 10.11(2))—Rule 10.11(2) is necessary because the principal registry may be treated as a part of the High Court or as a county court (see **Principal registry** under r 1.4), and so proceedings may, instead of being transferred elsewhere, merely be dealt with by the principal registry in a different role.

10.12 Evidence by affidavit

On any application made –

(*a*) in a county court, by originating application or in accordance with CCR Order 13, rule 1 (which deals with applications in the course of proceedings), or

(*b*) in the High Court, by originating summons, notice or motion,

evidence may be given by affidavit unless these rules otherwise provide or the court otherwise directs, but the court may, on the application of any party, order the attendance for cross-examination of the person making any such affidavit; and where, after such an order has been made, that person does not attend, his affidavit shall not be used as evidence without the leave of the court.

Defined terms—"court": r 1.2(1).

"application of any party"—Application should be made in accordance with r 10.9.

Filing of affidavits in principal registry—See *Registrar's Direction of 20 February 1987*.

10.13 Taking of affidavit in county court proceedings

In relation to family proceedings pending or treated as pending in a divorce county court, section 58(1) of the County Courts Act 1984 shall have effect as if after paragraph (*c*) there were inserted the following words –

"or

(*d*) a district judge of the principal registry; or

(*e*) any officer of the principal registry authorised by the President under section 2 of the Commissioners for Oaths Act 1889; or

(*f*) any clerk in the Central Office of the Royal Courts of Justice authorised to take affidavits for the purposes of proceedings in the Supreme Court.".

Defined terms—"divorce county court", "family proceedings": r 1.2(1); "pending": r 1.2(2); "the President": r 1.2(1).

Scope of provision—This rule extends the categories of people before whom affidavits may be sworn for use in county court proceedings.

"treated as pending in a divorce county court"—Certain proceedings in the principal registry are included within r 10.13 by this phrase (see r 1.4(1)).

County Courts Act 1984, s 58(1)—Section 58(1) provides that:

"An affidavit to be used in a county court may be sworn before –

(*a*) a judge or district judge of any court; or

(*b*) any justice of the peace; or

(*c*) an officer of any court appointed by the judge of that court for the purpose;

as well as before a commissioner for oaths or any other person authorised to take affidavits under the Commissioners for Oaths Acts 1889 and 1891.".

10.14 Evidence of marriage outside England and Wales

(1) The celebration of a marriage outside England and Wales and its validity under the law of the country where it was celebrated may, in any family proceedings in which the existence and validity of the marriage is not disputed, be proved by the evidence of one of the parties to the marriage and the production of a document purporting to be –

(*a*) a marriage certificate or similar document issued under the law in force in that country; or

(*b*) a certified copy of an entry in a register of marriages kept under the law in force in that country.

(2) Where a document produced by virtue of paragraph (1) is not in English it shall, unless otherwise directed, be accompanied by a translation certified by a notary public or authenticated by affidavit.

(3) This rule shall not be construed as precluding the proof of marriage in accordance with the Evidence (Foreign, Dominion and Colonial Documents) Act 1933 or in any other manner authorised apart from this rule.

Defined terms—"family proceedings": r 1.2(1).

Evidence (Foreign, Dominion and Colonial Documents) Act 1933 (r 10.14(3))—This Act, and various Orders in Council made under it, provides that certain public records in specified Commonwealth countries are admissible evidence for certain purposes.

10.14A Power of court to limit cross-examination

The court may limit the issues on which an officer of the service may be cross-examined.

Amendments—Inserted by SI 2001/821.

Scope of provision—Criminal Justice and Court Services Act 2000, s 16 provides for an officer of the service to be cross-examined, subject to rules of court. This rule allows the court to limit any such cross-examination to issues relevant to the proceedings.

10.15 Official shorthand note etc of proceedings

(1) Unless the judge otherwise directs, an official shorthand note shall be taken of the proceedings at the trial in open court of every cause pending in the High Court.

(2) An official shorthand note may be taken of any other proceedings before a judge or district judge if directions for the taking of such a note are given by the Lord Chancellor.

(3) The shorthand writer shall sign the note and certify it to be a correct shorthand note of the proceedings and shall retain the note unless he is directed by the district judge to forward it to the court.

(4) On being so directed the shorthand writer shall furnish the court with a transcript of the whole or such part as may be directed of the shorthand note.

(5) Any party, any person who has intervened in a cause, the Queen's Proctor or, where a declaration of parentage has been made under section 55A of the Act of 1986, the Registrar General shall be entitled to require from the shorthand writer a transcript of the shorthand note, and the shorthand writer shall, at the request of any person so entitled, supply that person with a transcript of the whole or any part

of the note on payment of the shorthand writer's charges authorised by any scheme in force providing for the taking of official shorthand notes of legal proceedings.

(6) Except as aforesaid, the shorthand writer shall not, without the permission of the court, furnish the shorthand note or a transcript of the whole or any part thereof to anyone.

(7) In these Rules references to a shorthand note include references to a record of the proceedings made by mechanical means and in relation to such a record references to the shorthand writer shall have effect as if they were references to the person responsible for transcribing the record.

Amendments—SI 2001/821.

Defined terms—"cause", "court", "district judge", "judge": r 1.2(1); "Registrar General": Registration Service Act 1953, s 1.

Shorthand note in relation to proceedings other than in open court in the High Court—*Practice Direction of 17 July 1973* refers to the continuation of the mechanical recording of county court matrimonial causes heard at the Royal Courts of Justice but indicates that no shorthand note will normally be taken of county court matrimonial causes tried elsewhere. It provides that in any such cause where, for some special reason, it is considered that the taking of a shorthand note would be advisable, early notice (whenever possible no later than when applying for directions for trial) must be given by the petitioner's solicitor to the district judge of the court in which the case is proceeding. Such notice must similarly be given if it is thought advisable that a shorthand note should be taken of ancillary proceedings before a judge (whether in the High Court or a divorce county court) for hearing elsewhere than at the Royal Courts of Justice.

CCR Ord 50, r 9B provides for an official shorthand note to be taken of trials in the county court, if the judge so directs. As a result of this, provision has been made for the installation and use of mechanical recording equipment at trial centres (defined by CCR Ord 1, r 3 as county courts designated by the Lord Chancellor as centres for the hearing of trials). Thus, in practice, in most care centres facilities are available for a full note to be taken of proceedings before a circuit judge. All district judges now have recording equipment in their chambers. However, the quality of the equipment varies, and recording is not automatic. Given the increased jurisdiction of district judges under Family Proceedings (Allocation to Judiciary) Directions 1999, more proceedings should be recorded and legal representatives would be wise to check that the equipment is on and functioning.

Disclosure of transcripts (r 10.15(6))—The court has a discretion as to whether transcripts of court proceedings should be disclosed. In *S v S (Inland Revenue: Tax Evasion)* [1997] 2 FLR 774 the individual circumstances of the case had to be weighed against a background of two competing public interests; namely the Inland Revenue's interest in preventing tax evasion and the public interest that in ancillary relief proceedings the parties should be candid with the court and give full and frank disclosure.

10.16 Copies of decrees and orders

(1) A copy of every decree shall be sent by the proper officer to every party to the cause.

(2) A sealed or other copy of a decree or order made in open court shall be issued to any person requiring it on payment of the prescribed fee.

Defined terms—"cause", "proper officer": r 1.2(1).

"sent" (r 10.16(1))—The method by which copies are to be sent is governed by r 10.2 or 10.3 according to whether a solicitor is acting for the recipient.

PART III

10.17 Service of order

(1) Where an order made in family proceedings has been drawn up, the proper officer of the court where the order is made shall, unless otherwise directed, send a copy of the order to every party affected by it.

(2) Where a party against whom the order is made is acting by a solicitor, a copy may, if the district judge thinks fit, be sent to that party as if he were acting in person, as well as to his solicitor.

(3) It shall not be necessary for the person in whose favour the order was made to prove that a copy of the order has reached any other party to whom it is required to be sent.

(4) This rule is without prejudice to RSC Order 45, rule 7 (which deals with the service of an order to do or abstain from doing an act), CCR Order 29, rule 1 (which deals with orders enforceable by committal) and any other rule or enactment for the purposes of which an order is required to be served in a particular way.

Defined terms—"district judge", "family proceedings", "proper officer": r 1.2(1).

Sending—The method of sending is governed by r 10.2 or 10.3 according to whether a solicitor is acting for the recipient.

10.18 No notice of intention to proceed after year's delay

RSC Order 3, rule 6 (which requires a party to give notice of intention to proceed after a year's delay) shall not apply to any proceedings pending in the High Court.

Defined terms—"pending": r 1.2(2).

10.19 Filing of documents at place of hearing etc

Where the file of any family proceedings has been sent from one divorce county court or registry to another for the purpose of a hearing or for some other purpose, any document needed for that purpose and required to be filed shall be filed in the other court or registry.

Defined terms—"divorce county court", "family proceedings": r 1.2(1).

10.20 Inspection etc of documents retained in court

(1) Subject to rule 10.21, a party to any family proceedings or his solicitor or the Queen's Proctor or a person appointed under rule 2.57 or 9.5 to be the guardian ad litem of a child in any family proceedings may have a search made for, and may inspect and bespeak a copy of, any document filed or lodged in the court office in those proceedings.

(2) Any person not entitled to a copy of a document under paragraph (1) above who intends to make an application under the Hague Convention (as defined in section 1(1) of the Child Abduction and Custody Act 1985) in a Contracting State (as defined in section 2 of that Act) other than the United Kingdom shall, if he satisfies the court that he intends to make such an application, be entitled to obtain a copy bearing the seal of the court of any order relating to the custody of the child in respect of whom the application is to be made.

(3) Except as provided by rules 2.36(4) and 3.16(10) and paragraphs (1) and (2) of this rule, no document filed or lodged in the court office other than a decree or

order made in open court shall be open to inspection by any person without the leave of the district judge, and no copy of any such document, or of an extract from any such document, shall be taken by, or issued to, any person without such leave.

Amendments—SI 1992/2067.

Defined terms—"court", "family proceedings": r 1.2(1).

Hague Convention cases (r 10.20(2))—The overlap which formerly existed between this rule and s 6.14 has been removed by the revocation of the latter.

"rules 2.36(4) and 3.16(10)"—Rule 2.36(4) relates to special procedure certificates and evidence in matrimonial causes. Rule 3.16(10) relates to inspection of documents by the Attorney General in Declaratory proceedings under the Family Law Act 1986.

Inspection of court documents (r 10.20(3))—The court has a discretion as to whether affidavits and documents produced during court proceedings should be inspected and the disclosure of part of a judgment delivered in chambers, if it is not preceded by the grant of leave, is irregular. In *S v S (Inland Revenue: Tax Evasion)* [1997] 2 FLR 774 (where disclosure to the Inland Revenue was disallowed) the individual circumstances of the case had to be weighed against a background of two competing public interests; namely the Inland Revenue's interest in preventing tax evasion and the public interest that in ancillary relief proceedings the parties should be candid with the court and give full and frank disclosure. In *R v R (Disclosure to Revenue)* [1998] 1 FLR 922 Wilson J held that the public interest in ensuring taxes are paid justified disclosure where the evidence in the court's possession is clear and relevant. In *A v A; B v B* [2000] 1 FLR 701 Charles J went further and asserted that the public interest in the administration of justice, which underpins the principle of encouraging candour in proceedings, will almost always be outweighed by the competing public interest in revenue collection. Where a husband was also party to partnership proceedings, the preferable forum for determining whether information from ancillary relief proceedings should be disclosed in the partnership proceedings was the matrimonial court. The interests of the other spouse would be given due weight. Identical principles applied whether the application was made under r 10.20(3) or CPR 1998, r 31.12(1) (*Nayler and Boyle v Beard* [2001] 2 FLR 1346).

For guidance as to the correct procedure in cases where the General Medical Council seeks disclosure of court documents relating to family proceedings in order to investigate allegations of professional misconduct see *Re A (Disclosure of Medical Records to the GMC)* [1998] 2 FLR 641 and see also FPR 1991, r 4.23.

10.21 Disclosure of addresses

(1) Subject to rule 2.3 nothing in these rules shall be construed as requiring any party to reveal the address of their private residence (or that of any child) save by order of the court.

(2) Where a party declines to reveal an address in reliance upon paragraph (1) above, he shall give notice of that address to the court in Form C8 and that address shall not be revealed to any person save by order of the court.

Amendments—SI 1991/2113; SI 1994/3155.

Defined terms—"child", "court": r 1.2(1).

"Subject to rule 2.3" (r 10.21(1))—FPR 1991, r 2.3 requires every petition in proceedings to which Pt II applies (see r 2.1) to contain the information required by App 2 to the rules, which requires certain addresses to be given.

Notice (r 10.21(2))—The giving of notice is regulated by r 10.7.

PART III

10.21A Disclosure of information under the Act of 1991

Where the Secretary of State requires a person mentioned in regulation 2(2) or (3)(*a*) of the Child Support (Information, Evidence and Disclosure) Regulations 1992 to furnish information or evidence for a purpose mentioned in regulation 3(1) of those Regulations, nothing in rules 4.23 (confidentiality of documents), 10.20 (inspection etc of documents in court) or 10.21 (disclosure of addresses) shall prevent that person from furnishing the information or evidence sought or require him to seek leave of the court before doing so.

Amendments—Inserted by SI 1993/295.

10.22 Practice to be observed in district registries and divorce county courts

(1) The President and the senior district judge may, with the concurrence of the Lord Chancellor, issue directions for the purpose of securing in the district registries and the divorce county courts due observance of statutory requirements and uniformity of practice in family proceedings.

(2) RSC Order 63, rule 11 (which requires the practice of the Central Office to be followed in the district registries) shall not apply to family proceedings.

Defined terms—"divorce county court", "the President", "senior district judge": r 1.2(1).

10.23 Transitional provisions

(1) Subject to paragraph (2) below, these rules shall apply, so far as practicable, to any proceedings pending on the day on which they come into force.

(2) Rule 8.1 shall not apply to an appeal from an order or decision made or given by a district judge in matrimonial proceedings in a divorce county court where notice of appeal has been filed before the day on which these rules come into force.

(3) Where, by reason of paragraph (1) above, these rules do not apply to particular proceedings pending on the day on which they come into force, the rules in force immediately before that day shall continue to apply to those proceedings.

(4) Nothing in this rule shall be taken as prejudicing the operation of the provisions of the Interpretation Act 1978 as regards the effect of repeals.

(5) Without prejudice to the generality of paragraph (1) above (and for the avoidance of doubt) rule 2.39 shall not apply to any proceedings which are pending within the meaning of paragraph 1(1) of Schedule 14 to the Children Act 1989.

10.24 Applications for relief which is precluded by the Act of 1991

(1) Where an application is made for an order which, in the opinion of the district judge, the court would be prevented from making by section 8 or 9 of the Act of 1991, the proper officer may send a notice in Form M34 to the applicant.

(2) In the first instance, the district judge shall consider the matter under paragraph (1) himself, without holding a hearing.

(3) Where a notice is sent under paragraph (1), no requirement of these rules, except for those of this rule, as to the service of the application by the proper officer or as to any other procedural step to follow the making of an application of the type in question, shall apply unless and until the court directs that they shall

apply or that they shall apply to such extent and subject to such modifications as may be specified in the direction.

(4) Where an applicant who has been sent a notice under paragraph (1) informs the proper officer in writing, within 14 days of the date of the notice, that he wishes to persist with his application, the proper officer shall refer the matter to the district judge for action in accordance with paragraph (5).

(5) Where the district judge acts in accordance with this paragraph, he shall give such directions as he considers appropriate for the matter to be heard and determined by the court and, without prejudice to the generality of the foregoing, such directions may provide for the hearing to be ex parte.

(6) Where directions are given under paragraph (5), the proper officer, shall inform the applicant of the directions and, in relation to the other parties, –

- (*a*) send them a copy of the application;
- (*b*) where the hearing is to be ex parte, inform them briefly –
  - (i) of the nature and effect of the notice under this rule,
  - (ii) that the matter is being resolved ex parte, and
  - (iii) that they will be informed of the result in due course; and
- (*c*) where the hearing is to be inter partes, inform them of –
  - (i) the circumstances which led to the directions being given, and
  - (ii) the directions.

(7) Where a notice has been sent under paragraph (1) and the proper officer is not informed under paragraph (4), the application shall be treated as having been withdrawn.

(8) Where the matter is heard pursuant to directions under paragraph (5) and the court determines that it would be prevented by section 8 or 9 of the Act of 1991 from making the order sought by the application, it shall dismiss the application.

(9) Where the court dismisses an application under this rule it shall give its reasons in writing, copies of which shall be sent to the parties by the proper officer.

(10) In this rule, "the matter" means the question whether the making of an order in the terms sought by the application would be prevented by section 8 or 9 of the Act of 1991.

Amendments—Inserted by SI 1993/295.

Defined terms—"the Act of 1991", "court", "district judge", "proper officer": r 1.2(1).

Scope of provision—This rule, which should be read in conjunction with r 10.25, was added following the coming into operation of the Child Support Act 1991. It provides for the district judge to give notice to a party, who appears to have made an application precluded by the Child Support Act 1991, to justify why he considers that the application should proceed.

"section 8 or 9 of the Act of 1991" (r 10.24(1))—Child Support Act 1991, ss 8(3) and 9(5) prevent any court from making, varying or reviving any orders for periodical payments for children and from varying any agreement for child maintenance.

Requirements as to service etc (r 10.24(3))—FPR 1991, rr 2.59, 2.60 deal with the procedural steps, including service, which follow the filing of an application for financial relief.

Ex parte hearing (r 10.24(5), (6))—Although all parties to the proceedings are given notice of the application and of the ex parte hearing, there seems to be no mechanism whereby one of them can be heard if they wish to make representations to the district judge at this stage. This may be desirable, since they will have an opportunity to make representation later when the full application is heard, but there will be cases where a full airing of what amounts to a preliminary issue, eg on jurisdiction and habitual residence (see CSA 1991, s 44), could save time and costs.

Withdrawal or dismissal of application (r 10.24(7), (8))—In view of the terms of r 10.25, these references to withdrawal and dismissal can be taken to apply only to that part of the application which relates to periodical payments for children where other matters are dealt with in the same application (eg property adjustment, lump sum etc).

10.25 Modification of rule 10.24 in relation to non-free-standing applications

Where a notice is sent under rule 10.24(1) in respect of an application which is contained in a petition or other document ("the document") which contains material extrinsic to the application –

(*a*) the document shall, until the contrary is directed under sub-paragraph (*c*) of this rule, be treated as if it did not contain the application in respect of which the notice was served;

(*b*) the proper officer shall, when he sends copies of the document to the respondents under any provision of these rules, attach a copy of the notice under rule 10.24(1) and a notice informing the respondents of the effect of sub-paragraph (*a*) of this paragraph; and

(*c*) if it is determined, under rule 10.24, that the court would not be prevented, by section 8 or 9 of the Act of 1991, from making the order sought by the application, the court shall direct that the document shall be treated as if it contained the application, and it may give such directions as it considers appropriate for the conduct of the proceedings in consequence of that direction.

Amendments—Inserted by SI 1993/295.

Defined terms—"court", "proper officer": r 1.2(1).

Scope of provision—This rule was introduced with the coming into operation of the Child Support Act 1991 and is the counter-balance to r 10.24. It enables the court to proceed with the remainder of an application where this includes a claim for periodical payments for children which has been delayed by a notice being issued under r 10.24(1).

"the document shall ... be treated as if it did not contain the application" (r 10.25(*a*))—The effect of this provision, which must be drawn to the attention of the respondent to the application (r 10.25(*b*)), is to enable the remainder of the application to proceed, to a final hearing if required, whether or not there is an adjudication under r 10.24. If the court holds that it is prevented by Child Support Act 1991, s 8(3) or 9(5) from hearing the application for child periodical payments, that application is dismissed (r 10.24(8)). It must be assumed that r 10.25(*a*) enables the remainder of the application still to proceed so that, in those circumstances, r 10.24(8) has the effect only of causing dismissal of that part of the application which deals with child periodical payments.

10.26 Human Rights Act 1998

(1) In this rule –

"originating document" means a petition, application, originating application, originating summons or other originating process;

"answer" means an answer or other document filed or served by a party in reply to an originating document (but not an acknowledgement of service);

"Convention right" has the same meaning as in the Human Rights Act 1998;

"declaration of incompatibility" means a declaration of incompatibility under section 4 of the Human Rights Act 1998.

(2) A party who seeks to rely on any provision of or right arising under the Human Rights Act 1998 or seeks a remedy available under that Act –

documentation. If the issue arises after the commencement of the proceedings, the application or originating documentation should be amended to include the human rights point.

Declaration of incompatibility—An application may be made under HRA 1998, s 4 to declare primary or secondary legislation incompatible with the provisions of the ECHR (as defined under HRA 1998, s 1). If such an issue is raised the application must be dealt with in the High Court (HRA 1998, s 4(5)). This means the application must be made to the High Court or transferred there. Where such an application is made, notice must also be given to the Crown to consider joinder as a party to the application (CPR 1998, r 19.4A and r 10.26(6)).

Judicial Acts—An application may be made claiming that there has been a failure to act in a way which is compatible with the provisions of the ECHR (as defined under HRA 1998, s 1). Such a claim may only be made by way of appeal, or judicial review where an appeal may not be made (HRA 1998, s 9). On such an application, where damages are sought, notice must be given to the Crown with a view to joinder (CPR 1998, r 19.4A).

10.27 Costs

(1) Order 38 of the County Court Rules 1981 and Order 62 of the Rules of the Supreme Court 1965 shall not apply to costs in family proceedings, and CPR Parts 43, 44 (except rules 44.9 to 44.12), 47 and 48 shall apply to costs in those proceedings, with the following modifications –

(*a*) in CPR rule 43.2(1)(*c*)(ii), "district judge" includes a district judge of the Principal Registry of the Family Division;

(*b*) CPR rule 44.3(2) (costs follow the event) shall not apply.

(2) Except in the case of an appeal against a decision of an authorised court officer (to which CPR rules 47.20 to 47.23 apply), an appeal against a decision in assessment proceedings relating to costs in family proceedings shall be dealt with in accordance with the following paragraphs of this rule.

(3) An appeal within paragraph (2) above shall lie as follows –

(*a*) where the decision appealed against was made by a district judge of the High Court or a costs judge (as defined by CPR rule 43.2(1)(*b*)), to a judge of the High Court;

(*b*) where the decision appealed against was made by a district judge of a county court, to a judge of that court.

(4) CPR Part 52 applies to every appeal within paragraph (2) above, and any reference in CPR Part 52 to a judge or a district judge shall be taken to include a district judge of the Principal Registry of the Family Division.

(5) The Civil Procedure Rules 1998 shall apply to an appeal to which CPR Part 52 or CPR rules 47.20 to 47.23 apply in accordance with paragraph (2) above in the same way as they apply to any other appeal within CPR Part 52 or CPR rules 47.20 to 47.23 as the case may be; accordingly the Rules of the Supreme Court 1965 and the County Court Rules 1981 shall not apply to any such appeal.

Amendments—Inserted by SI 2003/184.

APPENDIX 1

FORMS

M1	Statement of Information for a Consent Order
M2	General Heading of Proceedings

M3	Certificate with Regard to Reconciliation	
M4	Statement of Arrangements for Children	
M5	Notice of Proceedings	
M6	Acknowledgement of Service	
M7	Affidavit by Petitioner in Support of Petition	
M8	Notice of Application for Decree Nisi to be made Absolute	
M9	Certificate of Making Decree Nisi Absolute (Divorce)	
M10	Certificate of Making Decree Nisi Absolute (Nullity)	
M16	Request for Issue of Judgment Summons	
M17	Judgment Summons	
M19	Originating Application on Ground of Failure to Provide Reasonable Maintenance	
M20	Notice of Application Under Rule 3.1 or 3.2	
M21	Originating Application for Alteration of Maintenance Agreement during Parties' Lifetime	
M22	Originating Application for Alteration of Maintenance Agreement after Death of One of the Parties	
M23	Originating Summons Under Section 17 of the Married Women's Property Act 1882 or Section 1 of the Matrimonial Homes Act 1967	
M24	Notice to be indorsed on Document Served in Accordance with Rule 9.3	
M25	Ex Parte Originating Summons Under Section 13 of the Matrimonial and Family Proceedings Act 1984	
M26	Originating Summons Under Section 12 of the Matrimonial and Family Proceedings Act 1984	
M27	Originating Summons Under Section 24 of the Matrimonial and Family Proceedings Act 1984	
M28	Notice of Proceedings and Acknowledgement of Service	
M29	Declaration as to Marital Status Under Section 56(1)(*a*) of the Family Law Act 1986	
M30	Declaration as to Parentage Under Section 55A of the Family Law Act 1986	
M31	Declaration as to Legitimacy or Legitimation Under Section 56(1)(*b*) and (2) of the Family Law Act 1986	
M32	Declaration as to an Adoption Effected Overseas under Section 57 of the Family Law Act 1986	
M33	Application for registration of Maintenance Order in a Magistrates' Court	
M34	Notice under rule 10.24(1)	
C1	Application	for an order
C2	Application	for an order or directions in existing family proceedings
	Application	to be joined as, or cease to be, a party in existing family proceedings
	Application	for leave to commence proceedings
C3	Application	for an order authorising search for, taking charge of, and delivery of a child
C4	Application	for an order for disclosure of a child's whereabouts
C6	Notice	of proceedings [Hearing] [Directions Appointment] (*Notice to parties*)
C6A	Notice	of proceedings [Hearing] [Directions Appointment] (*Notice to non-parties*)
C7		Acknowledgement
C8		Confidential Address

C9	Statement	of Service
C10	Supplement	for an application for financial provision for a child or for variation of financial provision for a child
C10A	Statement	of Means
C11	Supplement	for an application for an Emergency Protection Order
C12	Supplement	For an application for a Warrant to assist a person authorised by an Emergency Protection Order
C13	Supplement	for an application for a Care or Supervision Order
C14	Supplement	for an application for authority to refuse contact with a child in care
C15	Supplement	for an application for contact with a child in care
C16	Supplement	for an application for a Child Assessment Order
C17	Supplement	for an application for an Education Supervision Order
C17A	Supplement	for an application for an extension of an Education Supervision Order
C18	Supplement	for an application for a Recovery Order
C19	Supplement	for a Warrant of Assistance
C20	Supplement	for an application for an order to hold a child in Secure Accommodation
C21	Order or direction	Blank
C22	Record	of hearing
C23	Order	Emergency Protection Order
C24	Order	Variation of an Emergency Protection Order Extension of an Emergency Protection Order Discharge of an Emergency Protection Order
C25	Warrant	To assist a person authorised by an Emergency Protection Order
C26	Order	Authority to keep a child in Secure Accommodation
C27	Order	Authority to search for another child
C28	Warrant	To assist a person to gain access to a child or entry to premises
C29	Order	Recovery of a child
C30	Order	To disclose information about the whereabouts of a missing child
C31	Order	Authorising search for, taking charge of, and delivery of a child
C32	Order	Care Order Discharge of a Care Order
C33	Order	Interim Care Order
C34	Order	Contact with a child in care Authority to refuse contact with a child in care
C35	Order	Supervision Order Interim Supervision Order
C36	Order	Substitution of a Supervision Order for a Care Order Discharge of a Supervision Order Variation of a Supervision Order Extension of a Supervision Order
C37	Order	Education Supervision Order
C38	Order	Discharge of an Education Supervision Order Extension of an Education Supervision Order
C39	Order	Child Assessment Order
C40	Direction	To undertake an investigation
C42	Order	Family Assistance Order

C43	Order	Residence Order Contact Order Specific Issue Order Prohibited Steps Order
C44	Order	Leave to change the surname by which a child is known Leave to remove a child from the United Kingdom
C45	Order	Parental Responsibility Order Termination of a Parental Responsibility Order
C46	Order	Appointment of a guardian Termination of the appointment of a guardian
C47	Order	Making or refusing the appointment of a children's guardian Termination of the appointment of a children's guardian
C48	Order	Appointment of a solicitor for a child Refusal of the appointment of a solicitor for a child Termination of the appointment of a solicitor for a child
C49	Order	Transfer of Proceedings to [the High Court] [a county court] [a family proceedings court]
C51		Application for a Parental Order
C52		Acknowledgement of an application for a Parental Order
C53	Order	Parental Order
C54	Notice	of Refusal of a Parental Order

FL401	Application for a non-molestation order/an occupation order
FL402	Notice of Proceedings [Hearing] [Directions Appointment]
FL403	Application to vary, extend or discharge an order in existing proceedings
FL404	Order or Direction
FL405	Record of Hearing
FL406	Power of Arrest
FL407	Application for a Warrant of Arrest
FL408	Warrant of Arrest
FL409	Remand Order
FL410	Recognizance of respondent
FL411	Recognizance of respondent's surety
FL412	Bail Notice
FL413	Hospital Order/Interim Hospital Order
FL414	Guardianship Order
FL415	Statement of Service
FL416	Notice to Mortgagees and Landlords
FL417	Transfer of proceedings to [the High Court] [a county court] [a family proceedings court]

****

Amendments—SI 1991/2113; SI 1992/456; SI 1992/2067; SI 1993/295; SI 1994/3155; SI 1997/1893; SI 1999/3491; SI 2001/821.

Specimen clauses in Form FL404

Note to specimen clauses—To assist practitioners, judges and court staff, and to ensure uniformity of practice, Form FL404 contains 41 specimen clauses. The court must make an order appropriate to the facts of the case and, as with any precedent, the specimen clauses should not be slavishly copied but should be adapted to the facts of the case. However, the clauses should be adhered to as far as is appropriate, and are therefore reproduced below.

There are also two specimen forms of penal notice, A and B. It is submitted that Notice A is virtually always preferable to Notice B.

ORDERS UNDER FAMILY LAW ACT 1996 PART IV

(*General heading followed by Notice A* **or** *Notice B and numbered options as appropriate*)

Notice A — order includes non-molestation order — penal notice mandatory

Important Notice to the Respondent [name]

This order gives you instructions which you must follow. You should read it all carefully. If you do not understand anything in this order you should go to a solicitor, Legal Advice Centre or Citizens Advice Bureau. You have a right to ask the court to change or cancel the order but you must obey it unless the court does change or cancel it.

You must obey the instructions contained in this order. If you do not, you will be guilty of contempt of court, and you may be sent to prison.

*Notice B — order does not include non-molestation order — *penal notice discretionary*

Important Notice to the Respondent [name]

This order gives you instructions which you must follow. You should read it all carefully. If you do not understand anything in this order you should go to a solicitor, Legal Advice Centre or Citizens Advice Bureau. You have a right to ask the court to change or cancel the order but you must obey it unless the court does change or cancel it.

You must obey the instructions contained in this order. *[If you do not, you will be guilty of contempt of court, and you may be sent to prison.]

OCCUPATION ORDERS UNDER S 33 OF THE FAMILY LAW ACT 1996

1. The court declares that the applicant [*name*] is entitled to occupy [*address of home or intended home*] as [*his/her*] home. **OR**

2. The court declares that the applicant [*name*] has matrimonial home rights in [*address of home or intended home*]. **AND/OR**

3. The court declares that the applicant [*name*]'s matrimonial home rights shall not end when the respondent [*name*] dies or their marriage is dissolved and shall continue until ... or further order.

It is ordered that:

4. The respondent [*name*] shall allow the applicant [*name*] to occupy [*address of home or intended home*]. **OR**

5. The respondent [*name*] shall allow the applicant [*name*] to occupy part of [*address of home or intended home*] namely: [*specify part*].

6. The respondent [*name*] shall not obstruct, harass or interfere with the applicant [*name*]'s peaceful occupation of [*address of home or intended home*].

PART III

7. The respondent [*name*] shall not occupy [*address of home or intended home*]. **OR**

8. The respondent [*name*] shall not occupy [*address of home or intended home*] from [*specify date*] until [*specify date*]. **OR**

9. The respondent [*name*] shall not occupy [*specify part of address of home or intended home*]. **AND/OR**

10. The respondent [*name*] shall not occupy [*address or part of address*] between [*specify dates or times*].

11. The respondent [*name*] shall leave [*address or part of address*] [forthwith] [within _ [*hours/days*] of service on [*him/her*] of this order.] **AND/OR**

12. Having left [*address or part of address*], the respondent [*name*] shall not return to, enter or attempt to enter [or go within [*specify distance*] of] it.

OCCUPATION ORDERS UNDER SS 35 AND 36 OF THE FAMILY LAW ACT 1996

It is ordered that:

13. The applicant [*name*] has the right to occupy [*address of home or intended home*] and the respondent [*name*] shall allow the applicant [*name*] to do so. **OR**

14. The respondent [*name*] shall not evict or exclude the applicant [*name*] from [*address of home or intended home*] or any part of it namely [*specify part*]. **AND/OR**

15. The respondent [*name*] shall not occupy [*address of home or intended home*]. **OR**

16. The respondent [*name*] shall not occupy [*address of home or intended home*] from [*specify date*] until [*specify date*]. **OR**

17. The respondent [*name*] shall not occupy [*specify part of address of home or intended home*]. **OR**

18. The respondent [*name*] shall leave [*address or part of address*] [forthwith] [within _ [*hours/days*] of service on [*him/her*] of this order.] **AND/OR**

19. Having left [*address of part of address*], the respondent [*name*] shall not return to, enter or attempt to enter [or go within [*specify distance*] of] it.

OCCUPATION ORDERS UNDER SS 37 AND 38 OF THE FAMILY LAW ACT 1996

It is ordered that:

20. The respondent [*name*] shall allow the applicant [*name*] to occupy [*address of home or intended home*] or part of it namely: [*specify*]. **AND/OR**

21. [One or both of the provisions in paragraphs 6 and 10 above may be inserted]. **AND/OR**

22. The respondent [*name*] shall leave [*address or part of address*] [forthwith] [within _ [*hours/days*] of service on [*him/her*] of this order.] **AND/OR**

23. Having left [*address or part of address*], the respondent [*name*] may not return to, enter or attempt to enter [or go within [*specify distance*] of] it.

ADDITIONAL PROVISIONS WHICH MAY BE INCLUDED IN OCCUPATION ORDERS MADE UNDER SS 33, 35 OR 36 FAMILY LAW ACT 1996

It is ordered that:

24. The [*applicant [name]*] [*respondent [name]*] shall maintain and repair [*address of home or intended home*]. **AND/OR**

25. The [*applicant [name]*] [*respondent [name]*] shall pay the rent for [*address of home or intended home*]. **OR**

26. The [*applicant [name]*] [*respondent [name]*] shall pay the mortgage payments on [*address of home or intended home*]. **OR**

27. The [*applicant [name]*] [*respondent [name]*] shall pay the following for [*address of home or intended home*]: [specify outgoings as bullet points].

28. The [*party in occupation*] shall pay to the [*other party*] £ each [*week, month, etc*] for [*address of home etc*].

29. The [*party in occupation*] shall keep and use the [*furniture*] [*contents*] [*specify if necessary*] of [*address of home or intended home*] and the [*applicant [name]*] [*respondent [name]*] shall return to the [*party in occupation*] the [*furniture*] [*contents*] [*specify if necessary*] [*no later than [date/time]*].

30. The [*party in occupation*] shall take reasonable care of the [*furniture*] [*contents*] [*specify if necessary*] of [*address of home or intended home*].

31. The [*party in occupation*] shall take all reasonable steps to keep secure [*address of home or intended home*] and the furniture or other contents [*specify if necessary*].

DURATION

Occupation orders under s 33 of the Family Law Act 1996

32. This order shall last until [*specify event or date*]. **OR**

33. This order shall last until a further order is made.

Occupation orders under ss 35 and 37 of the Family Law Act 1996

34. This order shall last until [*state date which must not be more than 6 months from the date of this order*].

35. The occupation order made on [*state date*] is extended until [*state date which must not be more than 6 months from the date of this extension*].

Occupation orders under ss 36 and 38 of the Family Law Act 1996

36. This order shall last until [*state date which must not be more than 6 months from the date of this order*].

37. The occupation order made on [*state date*] is extended until [*state date which must not be more than 6 months from the date of this extension*] and must end on that date.

NON-MOLESTATION ORDERS

It is ordered that:

38. The respondent [*name*] is forbidden to use or threaten violence against the applicant [*name*] [and must not instruct, encourage or in any way suggest that any other person should do so]. **AND/OR**

39. The respondent [*name*] is forbidden to intimidate, harass or pester [*or [specify]*] the applicant [*name*] [and must not instruct, encourage or in any way suggest that any other person should do so]. **AND/OR**

40. The respondent [*name*] is forbidden to use or threaten violence against the relevant child(ren) [*name(s) and date(s) of birth*] [and must not instruct, encourage or in any way suggest that any other person should do so]. **AND/OR**

41. The respondent [*name*] is forbidden to intimidate, harass or pester [*or [specify]*] [the relevant child(ren) [*name(s) and date(s) of birth*] [and must not instruct, encourage or in any way suggest that any other person should do so].

APPENDIX 1A

Form A	Notice of [Intention to Proceed with] an Application for Ancillary Relief
Form B	Notice of an Application under Rule 2.45
Form C	Notice of a First Appointment
Form D	Notice of a Financial Dispute Resolution Appointment
Form E	Financial Statement
Form F	Notice of Allegation in Proceedings for Ancillary Relief
Form G	Notice of Response to First Appointment
Form H	Costs Estimate
Form I	Notice of Request for Periodical Payments Order at same rate as Order for Maintenance Pending Suit

****

Amendments—Substituted by SI 1999/3491; amended by SI 2000/2267.

APPENDIX 2

CONTENTS OF PETITION

(unless otherwise directed under rule 2.3)

1 Every petition other than a petition under rules 3.12, 3.13, 3.14 or 3.15 shall state –

(*a*) the names of the parties to the marriage and the date and place of the marriage;

(*b*) the last address at which the parties to the marriage have lived together as husband and wife;

(*bb*) where it is alleged that the court has jurisdiction under the Council Regulation, state the grounds of jurisdiction under Article 2(1) of the Council Regulation.

(*c*) where it is alleged that the court has jurisdiction, other than under the Council Regulation, based on domicile –
   (i) the country in which the petitioner is domiciled, and
   (ii) if that country is not England and Wales, the country in which the respondent is domiciled;

(*d*) where it is alleged that the court has jurisdiction, other than under the Council Regulation, based on habitual residence –
   (i) the country in which the petitioner has been habitually resident throughout the period of one year ending with the date of the presentation of the petition, or
   (ii) if the petitioner has not been habitually resident in England and Wales, the country in which the respondent has been habitually resident during that period, with details in either case, including the addresses of the places of residence and the length of residence at each place;

(*e*) the occupation and residence of the petitioner and the respondent;

(*f*) whether there are any living children of the family and, if so –
   (i) the number of such children and the full names (including surname) of each and his date of birth or (if it be the case) that he is over 18, and
   (ii) in the case of each minor child over the age of 16, whether he is receiving instruction at an educational establishment or undergoing training for a trade, profession or vocation;

(*g*) whether (to the knowledge of the petitioner in the case of a husband's petition), any other child now living has been born to the wife during the marriage and, if so, the full names (including surname) of the child and his date of birth or, if it be the case, that he is over 18;

(*h*) if it be the case, that there is a dispute whether a living child is a child of the family;

(*i*) whether or not there are or have been any other proceedings in any court in England and Wales or elsewhere with reference to the marriage or to any child of the family or between the petitioner and the respondent with reference to any property of either or both of them and, if so –
   (i) the nature of the proceedings,
   (ii) the date and effect of any decree or order, and
   (iii) in the case of proceedings with reference to the marriage, whether there has been any resumption of cohabitation since the making of the decree or order;

(*ia*) whether or not there have been any applications under the Act of 1991 for a maintenance calculation in respect of any child of the family and if so –
   (i) the date of any such application, and
   (ii) details of the calculation made;

(*j*) whether there are any proceedings continuing in any country outside England and Wales which relate to the marriage or are capable of affecting its validity or subsistence and, if so –
   (i) particulars of the proceedings, including the court in or tribunal or authority before which they were begun,
   (ii) the date when they were begun,
   (iii) the names of the parties,
   (iv) the date or expected date of any trial in the proceedings, and

(v) such other facts as may be relevant to the question whether the proceedings on the petition should be stayed under Schedule 1 to the Domicile and Matrimonial Proceedings Act 1973;

and such proceedings shall include any which are not instituted in a court of law in that country, if they are instituted before a tribunal or other authority having power under the law having effect there to determine questions of status, and shall be treated as continuing if they have been begun and have not been finally disposed of;

(*k*) where the fact on which the petition is based is five years' separation, whether any, and if so what, agreement or arrangement has been made or is proposed to be made between the parties for the support of the respondent or, as the case may be, the petitioner or any child of the family;

(*l*) in the case of a petition for divorce, that the marriage has broken down irretrievably;

(*m*) the fact alleged by the petitioner for the purposes of section 1(2) of the Act of 1973 or, where the petition is not for divorce or judicial separation, the ground on which relief is sought, together in any case with brief particulars of the individual facts relied on but not the evidence by which they are to be proved;

(*n*) any further or other information required by such of the following paragraphs and by rule 3.11 as may be applicable.

2 A petition for a decree of nullity under section 12(*e*) or (*f*) of the Act 1973 shall state whether the petitioner was at the time of the marriage ignorant of the facts alleged.

3 A petition for a decree of presumption of death and dissolution of marriage shall state –

(*a*) the last place at which the parties to the marriage cohabited;

(*b*) the circumstances in which the parties ceased to cohabit;

(*c*) the date when and the place where the respondent was last seen or heard of; and

(*d*) the steps which have been taken to trace the respondent.

4 Every petition shall conclude with –

(*a*) a prayer setting out particulars of the relief claimed, including any claim for costs and any application for ancillary relief which it is intended to claim;

(*b*) the names and addresses of the persons who are to be served with the petition, indicating if any of them is a person under disability;

(*c*) the petitioner's address for service, which, where the petitioner sues by a solicitor, shall be the solicitor's name or firm and address. Where the petitioner, although suing in person, is receiving legal advice from a solicitor, the solicitor's name or firm and address may be given as the address for service if he agrees. In any other case, the petitioner's address for service shall be the address of any place in England and Wales to which documents for the petitioner may be delivered or sent.

Amendments—SI 1992/2067; SI 1993/295; SI 2001/821.

APPENDIX 3
NOTICES AND RESPONDENTS

(i) *Provision under which proceedings brought*	(ii) *Minimum number of days prior to hearing or directions appointment for service under rule 4.4(1)(b)*	(iii) *Respondents*	(iv) *Persons to whom notice is to be given*
All applications.	See separate entries below	Subject to separate entries below: every person whom the applicant believes to have parental responsibility for the child; where the child is the subject of a care order, every person whom the applicant believes to have had parental responsibility immediately prior to the making of the care order; in the case of an application to extend, vary or discharge an order, the parties to the proceedings leading to the order which it is sought to have extended, varied or discharged; in the case of specified proceedings, the child.	Subject to separate entries below: local authority providing accommodation for the child; persons who are caring for the child at the time when the proceedings are commenced; in the case of proceedings brought in respect of a child who is alleged to be staying in a refuge which is certificated under section 51(1) or (2), the person who is providing the refuge.

(i) *Provision under which proceedings brought*	(ii) *Minimum number of days prior to hearing or directions appointment for service under rule 4.4(1)(b)*	(iii) *Respondents*	(iv) *Persons to whom notice is to be given*
Section 4(1)(*a*), 4(3), 5(1), 6(7), 8, 13(1), 16(6), 33(7), Schedule 1, paragraph 19(1) of Schedule 2, or paragraph 11(3) or 16(5) of Schedule 14.	14 days.	As for "all applications" above, and: in the case of proceedings under Schedule 1, those persons whom the applicant believes to be interested in or affected by the proceedings; in the case of an application under paragraph 11(3)(*b*) or 16(5) of Schedule 14, any person, other than the child, named in the order or directions which it is sought to discharge or vary.	As for "all applications" above, and: in the case of an application for a section 8 order, every person whom the applicant believes – (i) to be named in a court order with respect to the same child, which has not ceased to have effect, (ii) to be a party to pending proceedings in respect of the same child, or (iii) to be a person with whom the child has lived for at least 3 years prior to the application, unless, in a case to which (i) or (ii) applies, the applicant believes that the court order or pending proceedings are not relevant to the application;

(i) *Provision under which proceedings brought*	(ii) *Minimum number of days prior to hearing or directions appointment for service under rule 4.4(1)(b)*	(iii) *Respondents*	(iv) *Persons to whom notice is to be given*
			in the case of an application under paragraph 19(1) of Schedule 2, the parties to the proceedings leading to the care order; in the case of an application under section 5(1), the father of the child if he does not have parental responsibility.
Section 36(1), 39(1), 39(2), 39(3), 39(4), 43(1), or paragraph 6(3), 15(2) or 17(1) of Schedule 3.	7 days.	As for "all applications" above, and: in the case of an application under section 39(2) or (3), the supervisor; in the case of proceedings under paragraph 17(1) of Schedule 3, the local education authority concerned; in the case of proceedings under section 36 or paragraph 15(2) or 17(1) of Schedule 3, the child.	As for "all applications" above, and: in the case of an application for an order under section 43(1) – (i) every person whom the applicant believes to be a parent of the child, (ii) every person whom the applicant believes to be caring for the child, (iii) every person in whose favour a contact order is in force

(i) *Provision under which proceedings brought*	(ii) *Minimum number of days prior to hearing or directions appointment for service under rule 4.4(1)(b)*	(iii) *Respondents*	(iv) *Persons to whom notice is to be given*
			with respect to the child, and (iv) every person who is allowed to have contact with the child by virtue of an order under section 34.
Section 31, 34(2), 34(3), 34(4), 34(9) or 38(8)(*b*).	3 days.	As for "all applications" above, and: in the case of an application under section 34, the person whose contact with the child is the subject of the application.	As for "all applications" above, and: in the case of an application under section 31 – (i) every person whom the applicant believes to be a party to pending relevant proceedings in respect of the same child, and (ii) every person whom the applicant believes to be a parent without parental responsibility for the child.

(i) *Provision under which proceedings brought*	(ii) *Minimum number of days prior to hearing or directions appointment for service under rule 4.4(1)(b)*	(iii) *Respondents*	(iv) *Persons to whom notice is to be given*
Section 43(12).	2 days.	As for "all applications" above.	Those of the persons referred to in section 43(11)(*a*) to (*e*) who were not party to the application for the order which it is sought to have varied or discharged.
Section 25, 44(1), 44(9)(*b*), 45(4), 45(8), 46(7), 48(9), 50(1), or 102(1).	1 day.	As for 'all applications' above, and: in the case of an application under section 44(9)(*b*) – (i) the parties to the application for the order in respect of which it is sought to vary the directions;	Except for applications under section 102(1), as for 'all applications' above, and: in the case of an application under section 44(1), every person whom the applicant believes to be a parent of the child; in the case of an application under section 44(9)(*b*) –

(i) *Provision under which proceedings brought*	(ii) *Minimum number of days prior to hearing or directions appointment for service under rule 4.4(1)(b)*	(iii) *Respondents*	(iv) *Persons to whom notice is to be given*
		(ii) any person who was caring for the child prior to the making of the order, and (iii) any person whose contact with the child is affected by the direction which it is sought to have varied; in the case of an application under section 50, the person whom the applicant alleges to have effected or to have been or to be responsible for the taking or keeping of the child.	(i) the local authority in whose area the child is living, and (ii) any person whom the applicant believes to be affected by the direction which it is sought to have varied; in the case of an application under section 102(1), the person referred to in section 102(1) and any person preventing or likely to prevent such a person from exercising powers under enactments mentioned in subsection (6) of that section.

(i) *Provision under which proceedings brought*	(ii) *Minimum number of days prior to hearing or directions appointment for service under rule 4.4(1)(b)*	(iii) *Respondents*	(iv) *Persons to whom notice is to be given*
Section 30 of the Human Fertilisation and Embryology Act 1990	14 days.	The birth parents (except where the applicants seek to dispense with their agreement under section 30(6) of the Human Fertilisation and Embryology Act 1990) and any other persons or body with parental responsibility for the child at the date of the application.	Any local authority or voluntary organisation that has at any time provided accommodation for the child.

Amendments—SI 1992/2067; SI 1994/2165.

Defined terms—"applicant", "application": r 4.1(1); "care order": CA 1989, ss 31(11), 105(1); "child": r 4.1(1); "local authority": CA 1989, s 105(1); "parental responsibility": CA 1989, s 3; "specified proceedings": CA 1989, s 41(6) and r 4.2(2).

"father"—In relation to an application under CA 1989, s 5(1), "father" includes an unmarried father by virtue of Family Law Reform Act 1987, s 1.

"parent"—In determining who is a parent of a child, no regard is paid to whether his mother and father were married at the time of his birth or not (Family Law Reform Act 1987, s 1), and so an unmarried father is included. See also **Meaning of "parent"** under CA 1989, s 10.

"every person whom the applicant believes to be a parent without parental responsibility"—In relation to an application under CA 1989, s 31, the standard of "belief" for the purposes of issuing a notice should not be set too high, particularly where both the mother of the child concerned and the man in question are asserting that the man is the father (*Re B (Care Proceedings: Notification of Father Without Parental Responsibility)* [1999] 2 FLR 408).

Family Proceedings (Allocation to Judiciary) Directions 1999, [1999] 2 FLR 799

The Lord Chancellor, in exercise of the powers conferred on him by section 9 of the Courts and Legal Services Act 1990 and with the concurrence of the President of the Family Division, hereby gives the following Directions:

Commencement and transitional arrangements—The amendments made to these Directions by the Family Proceedings (Allocation to Judiciary) (Amendment) Directions 2002 came into force on 30 August 2002 and apply to all proceedings commenced from that date onwards. The original/unamended Schedule to the 1999 Directions (as set out in *The Family Court Practice 2002*) will apply to any proceedings commenced before that date.

"section 9 of the Courts and Legal Services Act 1990"— Section 9(2) provides that these Directions have effect "regardless of any rules of court", and they therefore prevail over any inconsistent rule or provision. However, it would seem that the existence of jurisdiction is a precondition for the allocation of a type of proceedings to a particular type of judge: in other words, the Directions cannot confer jurisdiction; they may only narrow the class of judge who would otherwise have been capable of hearing the proceedings in question. Although the Directions are, of course, to be obeyed, disobedience does not vitiate jurisdiction in the legal sense, since CLSA 1990, s 9(3) provides that "Where any directions have been given under this section allocating any proceedings to specified judges, the validity of anything done by a judge in, or in relation to, the proceedings shall not be called into question by reason only of the fact that he was not a specified judge".

1 (1) These Directions shall come into force on 1 May 1999.

(2), (3) ...

2 In these Directions, in the absence of a contrary implication –

"family proceedings" and "judge" bear the meanings assigned to them in section 9 of the Courts and Legal Services Act 1990;
"nominated" in relation to a judge means a judge who has been approved as one to whom family proceedings may be allocated by the President of the Family Division;
"opposed hearing" includes an application made ex parte; and
"Schedule" means the Schedule to these Directions.

Amendments—Family Proceedings (Allocation to Judiciary) (Amendment) Directions 2002.

"family proceedings"—Courts and Legal Services Act 1990, s 9(5) provides that "family proceedings" has the same meaning as in Matrimonial and Family Proceedings Act 1984, s 32, and also includes any other proceedings which are family proceedings for the purposes of CA 1989. For the 1984 Act definition, see "family proceedings" under FPR 1991, r 1.2(1). The meaning of "family proceedings" for the purposes of CA 1989 is contained in s 8(3), (4).

"judge"—Courts and Legal Services Act 1990, s 9(5) defines "judge" to mean any person who –
(*a*) is capable of sitting as a judge for a county court district;
(*b*) is a district judge, an assistant district judge or a deputy district judge; or
(*c*) is a district judge of the principal registry of the Family Division of the High Court.

County Courts Act 1984, s 5 states that the following may sit as a judge for a county court district: every Circuit judge, every judge of the Court of Appeal, every judge of the High Court and every recorder.

"nominated"—Copies of the lists of judges who are "nominated" to sit in various classes of family proceedings may be obtained from: Family Business Branch, 6th Floor, Southside, 105 Victoria Street, London SW1E 6QT Tel: 0171 210 1673.

"Schedule"—The Schedule to these Directions (as substituted by Family Proceedings (Allocation to Judiciary) (Amendment) Directions 2002) allocates specified classes of proceedings to specified classes of judge in specified circumstances.

3 These Directions shall apply where proceedings of a class specified in column (i) of the Schedule are pending in a county court or, by virtue of section 42 of the Matrimonial and Family Proceedings Act 1984, a provision of the Children (Allocation of Proceedings) Order 1991 or of the Family Law Act 1996 (Part IV) (Allocation of Proceedings) Order 1997, treated as pending in a county court in the Principal Registry of the Family Division of the High Court.

"section 42 of the Matrimonial and Family Proceedings Act 1984"—MFPA 1984, s 42 enables matrimonial proceedings to be dealt with in the principal registry broadly as if it were a divorce county court.

Children (Allocation of Proceedings) Order 1991—C(AP)O 1991, art 19 enables certain proceedings to be dealt with by the principal registry as if that court were a county court.

Family Law Act 1996 (Part IV) (Allocation of Proceedings) Order 1997—FLA(Pt IV)(AP)O 1997, art 16 enables the principal registry to be treated as if it were a divorce county court, a family hearing centre and a care centre for the purposes of that Order.

4 Subject to the following paragraphs of these Directions, the proceedings in column (i) of the Schedule may be allocated to a judge of the description specified in the corresponding entry in column (ii), in the circumstances specified in the corresponding entry in column (iii).

"Schedule"—The Schedule to these Directions (as substituted by Family Proceedings (Allocation to Judiciary) (Amendment) Directions 2002) allocates specified classes of proceedings to specified classes of judge in specified circumstances.

5 Without prejudice to the provisions of the Schedule, any of the proceedings in column (i) of the Schedule may be allocated to –

(*a*) a judge of the Family Division of the High Court;

(*b*) a person acting as a judge of the Family Division of the High Court in pursuance of a request made under section 9(1) of the Supreme Court Act 1981 other than a former judge of the Court of Appeal or a former puisne judge of the High Court; but public family law proceedings shall be allocated only to a judge who has been nominated for them;

(*c*) a person sitting as a recorder who has been authorised to act as a judge of the Family Division of the High Court under section 9(4) of the Supreme Court Act 1981.

(*d*) a person sitting as a recorder who is a district judge (Magistrates' Courts) and who is nominated for public family law proceedings in the county court.

(*e*) a person sitting as a recorder who is a district judge of the Principal Registry of the Family Division.

Amendments—Family Proceedings (Allocation to Judiciary) (Amendment) Directions 2002.

High Court judges in county courts (para 5(*a*))—Every judge of the High Court is capable of sitting as a judge for any county court district under County Courts Act 1984, s 5(3). This paragraph enables those High Court judges assigned to the Family Division to take any category of work covered by these Directions when they are county court business.

Deputy High Court judges (para 5(*b*))—These Directions now specifically allow a person acting as a judge of the Family Division of the High Court, pursuant to a request made under Supreme Court Act 1981, s 9(1) (other than a former judge of the Court of Appeal, or a former puisne judge of the High Court), to take any category of work covered by these Directions when they are county court business. The only proviso is that "*public family law proceedings*" must only be allocated to a judge or recorder who has been "*nominated*" for them.

"public family law proceedings"—Only a judge or recorder who has been "nominated" for public family law proceedings may hear that class of proceedings.

"person sitting as a recorder" (para 5(*c*))—Queen's Counsel authorised to sit in the High Court on family matters under Supreme Court Act 1981, s 9(4) will be able to exercise the same jurisdiction when sitting as a recorder in the county court.

5A When a person sitting as a recorder is also a district judge nominated for public family law proceedings, any proceedings may be allocated to him which, under these Directions, may be allocated to a district judge nominated for public family law proceedings.

Amendments—Family Proceedings (Allocation to Judiciary) (Amendment) Directions 2002.

6 Where any family proceedings include proceedings of more than one class specified in column (i) of the Schedule, the Schedule shall apply to those classes as if they did not form part of the same proceedings.

Mixed proceedings—CA 1989 has increased the scope for applications of one type to be made in the course of other proceedings. This paragraph allows individual applications to be listed, separately from other elements of the umbrella proceedings, before a class of judge who would not have been able to hear other elements of the global proceedings. Whether such separate listing is appropriate depends of course, on the circumstances of each individual case.

7 For the purposes of paragraphs (*f*), (*g*), (*h*) and (*i*) of the Schedule, where –

(*a*) unopposed proceedings become opposed during the course of the hearing; and

(*b*) the judge before whom the hearing takes place does not fall within a description of judge to whom the proceedings would have been allocated if the proceedings had been opposed at the commencement of the trial,

he shall adjourn the hearing to a judge to whom such a hearing would be allocated by these Directions.

Defined terms—"judge": para 2.

"unopposed proceedings become opposed during the course of the trial"—Where unopposed proceedings within the classes of proceedings listed in the Schedule at paragraphs (*f*), (*g*), (*h*) and (*i*) become opposed during the course of the trial, and the judge hearing them does not fall within the category of judge to whom the proceedings would have been allocated if they had been opposed from the outset, the judge must adjourn the trial for hearing by an appropriate judge. An example of this might occur where a district judge, who is not nominated for public family law proceedings, starts the "final" hearing of a contact case where originally only the quantum of, rather than the principle of, contact was at stake (see Sch, para (*g*)), but during the trial the party with whom the children are living becomes wholly opposed to any contact taking place at all. In those circumstances, the district judge would have to adjourn the trial to a circuit judge, a district judge who is nominated for public family law proceedings or a district judge of the Principal Registry of the Family Division (para (*g*), column (iii), item (3)(*b*)(ii)) who could then hear the issue of whether or not there should be contact; the district judge could also make a temporary contact order provided that the order is (or is one of a series of orders which is) to be limited in time to the next hearing or order (para (*g*), column (iii), item 3(*b*)).

Jurisdiction of district judges—The scope of the jurisdiction is as follows:

(*a*) *Proceedings under any of the provisions of Family Law Act 1996, Pt IV* (Sch, para (*c*)) A district judge may deal with Pt IV proceedings, including ex parte applications, save that a deputy district judge may not deal with proceedings to enforce an order under Pt IV (ie by means of committal, warrant of arrest, or remand).

(*b*) *Applications for appointment or removal of a guardian under CA 1989, ss 5(1) and 6(7)* (Sch, para (*f*)) A district judge nominated for public law proceedings may appoint a guardian for a child to take over parental responsibility where a parent has died, and also may terminate such an appointment. This must be distinguished from a guardian ad litem appointed for the purposes of legal proceedings. A district judge who is not nominated, or a deputy district judge, may only deal with applications that are unopposed or interlocutory matters.

(*c*) *Orders under CA 1989, s 8* (Sch, para (*g*)) A district judge nominated for public law proceedings and a district judge of the principal registry have full jurisdiction to hear any s 8 application, including those made ex parte. However, a district judge in a county court who is not so nominated, in an application for a s 8 order, can hear:

(i) interlocutory matters;

(ii) unopposed hearings;

(iii) opposed hearings where: the application is for a contact order and the principle of contact with the applicant is unopposed (ie the issue is quantum of contact) *or* the order is (or is one of a series of orders which is) to be limited in time until the next hearing or order *and* the substantive application is returnable before a circuit judge nominated for family proceedings, or a district judge of the principal registry or a district judge nominated for public family law proceedings who has full jurisdiction in all the circumstances.

It is not clear whether an ex parte order counts as an order limited in time until the next hearing. If it does not, the district judge would have to transfer the matter to a nominated circuit judge or district judge of the principal registry or nominated district judge, for hearing.

Deputy district judges may hear (i) interlocutory matters and (ii) unopposed trials in applications under CA 1989, s 10 for a s 8 order.

(*d*) *Care and supervision orders* (Sch, para (*h*)) A district judge nominated for public law family proceedings may make a care or supervision order under CA 1989, s 31, provided that either:

(i) the proceedings are unopposed; or

(ii) where the proceedings are opposed, the only matter to be determined is the issue of contact where the principle of contact is unopposed.

(*e*) *Interim care or supervision orders* (Sch, para (*i*)) A district judge nominated for public law proceedings may now make interim care or supervision orders, even if the matter is opposed.

(*f*) *Orders under Human Fertilisation and Embryology Act 1990, s 30* (Sch, para (*m*)) In an application made under HFEA 1990, s 30, a district judge may hear interlocutory matters.

(*g*) *Powers to order disclosure of child's whereabouts, recovery of child and surrender of passports under Family Law Act 1986, ss 33, 34 and 37*) (Sch, para (*n*)) A district judge nominated for private or public law family proceedings may hear applications in respect of all these matters in all circumstances.

Public family law proceedings—Queen's Counsel authorised to sit in the High Court on family matters under Supreme Court Act 1981, s 9(4) will be able to exercise the same jurisdiction when sitting as a recorder in the county courts.

"Own motion" powers to grant a s 8 order in family proceedings—Under CA 1989, s 10(1)(*b*), "In any family proceedings in which a question arises with respect to the welfare of any child", the court can, of its own motion, grant a s 8 order where "the court considers that the order should be made even though no ... application [for a s 8 order] has been made". The 1999 Directions do not restrict to any specified judge the power of the court, of its own motion, to grant a s 8 order. Therefore, any judge, including a district judge, a deputy district judge, or any recorder can exercise this power under CA 1989, s 10 to grant a s 8 order. However, this is a power which should be exercised with extreme caution and should not be used to evade the policy of the Directions that these orders should be made by nominated judges.

SCHEDULE
ALLOCATION OF PROCEEDINGS

(i) DESCRIPTION OF PROCEEDINGS	(ii) DESCRIPTION OF JUDGE	(iii) CIRCUMSTANCES IN WHICH ALLOCATION APPLIES
(*a*) Family proceedings for which no express provision is made in this Schedule.	A circuit judge, deputy circuit judge or recorder nominated for private or public family law proceedings; a district judge of the Principal Registry of the Family Division of the High Court; or a district judge or deputy district judge.	All circumstances.
(*b*) Non-contentious or common form probate business within the meaning of section 128 of the Supreme Court Act 1981 (c 54).	A judge.	All circumstances.
(*c*) Proceedings under any of the provisions in Part IV of the Family Law Act 1996 (c.27).	A circuit judge or deputy circuit judge nominated for private or public family law proceedings;	All circumstances.
	a recorder nominated for public family law proceedings; or	All circumstances.
	a district judge of the Principal Registry of the Family Division of the High Court; or	All circumstances.
	a district judge,	All circumstances.
	a recorder nominated for private family law proceedings, a recorder or a deputy district judge.	All circumstances except proceedings to enforce an order made under Part IV.

(i) DESCRIPTION OF PROCEEDINGS	(ii) DESCRIPTION OF JUDGE	(iii) CIRCUMSTANCES IN WHICH ALLOCATION APPLIES
(*d*) Hearing of contested petition for a decree of divorce, nullity or judicial separation.	A circuit judge, deputy circuit judge or a recorder nominated for private or public family law proceedings.	All circumstances.
(*e*) Proceedings under any of the following provisions of the Adoption Act 1976 (c 36):	A circuit judge nominated for adoption proceedings; or	All circumstances.
section 14 (adoption by married couple);	a deputy circuit judge or recorder nominated for adoptionproceedings;	All circumstances.
section 15 (adoption by one person);	a district judge of the Principal Registry of the Family Division of the High Court; or	Interlocutory matters.
section 18 (freeing child for adoption);		
section 20 (revocation of order under section 18);	a district judge nominated for adoption proceedings; or	Interlocutory matters.
section 27, 28 or 29 (restrictions on removal of child);	a deputy district judge nominated for adoption proceedings	Interlocutory matters.
section 55 (adoption of children abroad).		

(i) DESCRIPTION OF PROCEEDINGS	(ii) DESCRIPTION OF JUDGE	(iii) CIRCUMSTANCES IN WHICH ALLOCATION APPLIES

(*f*)
Proceedings under any of the following provisions of the Children Act 1989 (c 41):
section 4(1)(*a*) (applications for parental responsibility by father);
section 4(3) (termination of parental responsibility);
section 5(1) (appointment of guardian);
section 6(7) (termination of guardianship);
paragraph 11(3) of Schedule 14 (discharge of existing custody etc orders).
	A circuit judge nominated for private or public family law proceedings; or	All circumstances.

	a deputy circuit judge or recorder nominated for private or public family law proceedings; or	All circumstances.
	a district judge of the Principal Registry of the Family Division of the High Court; or	All circumstances.
	a district judge nominated for private or public family law proceedings;	All circumstances.
	a district judge or deputy district judge.	(1) Interlocutory matters; or (2) unopposed hearings.
(*g*) Proceedings under any of the following provisions of the Children Act 1989 (c 41): section 13(1) (change of child's name or removal from jurisdiction); section 16(6) (reference of question of variation or discharge of section 8 order); applications under section 10 of the Children Act 1989 (c 41) for an order under section 8.	A circuit judge nominated for private or public family law proceedings; or	All circumstances.
	a deputy circuit judge or recorder nominated for private or public family law proceedings; or	All circumstances.
	a district judge of the Principal Registry of the Family Division of the High Court; or	All circumstances.
	a district judge nominated for private or public family law proceedings;	All circumstances.
	a district judge;	(1) Interlocutory matters; (2) unopposed hearings; or (3) opposed hearings where

(i) DESCRIPTION OF PROCEEDINGS	(ii) DESCRIPTION OF JUDGE	(iii) CIRCUMSTANCES IN WHICH ALLOCATION APPLIES
		(*a*) the application is for a contact order and the principle of contact with the applicant is unopposed; or (*b*) the order (i) is (or is one of a series of orders which is) to be limited in time until the next hearing or order, and (ii) the substantive application is returnable before a judge within column (ii) of this paragraph who has full jurisdiction in all circumstances.
	a deputy district judge.	(1) Interlocutory matters; or (2) unopposed hearings.
(*h*) Proceedings under any of the following provisions of the Children Act 1989 (c 41):	A circuit judge nominated for public family law proceedings; or	All circumstances.
section 25 (secure accommodation); section 31 (care and supervision orders);	a district judge of the Principal Registry of the Family Division of the High Court;	All circumstances.
section 33(7) (change of child's name or removal from jurisdiction); section 39(1), (2) or (4) (discharge and variation of care and supervision orders); paragraph 6 of Schedule 3 (supervision order); section 34 (parental contact etc with child in care);	a district judge nominated for public family law proceedings.	(1) Interlocutory matters; or (2) unopposed hearings; or (3) opposed hearings where the application is for an order under section 34 (a contact order) and the principle of contact is unopposed.

(i) DESCRIPTION OF PROCEEDINGS	(ii) DESCRIPTION OF JUDGE	(iii) CIRCUMSTANCES IN WHICH ALLOCATION APPLIES
paragraph 19(1) of Schedule 2 (arrangements to assist children to live abroad).		
(*i*) Proceedings under section 38 of the Children Act 1989 (c 41) (interim care or supervision orders).	A circuit judge nominated for public family law proceedings;	All circumstances.
	a district judge of the Principal Registry of the Family Division of the High Court; or	All circumstances.
	a district judge nominated for public family law proceedings.	All circumstances.
(*j*) Proceedings under any of the following provisions of the Children Act 1989 (c 41):	A circuit judge nominated for public family law proceedings;	All circumstances.
section 39(3) (variation of supervision order);	a district judge of the Principal Registry of the Family Division of the High Court; or	All circumstances.
section 36(1) (education supervision order);	a district judge nominated for public family law proceedings.	All circumstances.
paragraph 15(2), or 17(1) of Schedule 3 (extension and discharge of education supervision order);		
section 43 (child assessment order);		
sections 44, 45(4), 45(8), 46(7), 48(9) (order for emergency protection of child);		
section 50 (recovery order);		
applications for leave under section 91(14), (15) or (17) (further applications);		

(i) DESCRIPTION OF PROCEEDINGS	(ii) DESCRIPTION OF JUDGE	(iii) CIRCUMSTANCES IN WHICH ALLOCATION APPLIES
applications under section 21 of the Adoption Act 1976 (c 36) (substitution of adoption agencies).		
(*k*) Proceedings under any of the following provisions of the Child Support Act 1991 (c 48):	A circuit judge nominated for private family law proceedings; or	All circumstances.
section 20 (appeals)	a district judge of the Principal Registry of the Family Division of the High Court.	All circumstances.
(*l*) The hearing of an appeal under: (i) rule 8.1 of the Family Proceedings Rules 1991; (ii) Order 37, rule 6 of the County Court Rules 1981 as applied by the said rule 8.1; or (iii) the Children (Allocation of Proceedings) (Appeals) Order 1991 ("the 1991 Order").	A person capable of sitting as a judge of a county court district and nominated for private or public family law proceedings.	Where, under these directions, such person would have been able to hear the matter at first instance but subject to the exception contained in article 2(*b*) of the 1991 Order.
(*m*) Proceedings under s 30 of the Human Fertilisation and Embryology Act 1990 (c 37).	A circuit judge nominated for private or public family law proceedings; or	All circumstances.
	a district judge of the Principal Registry of the Family Division of the High Court; or	Interlocutory matters.
	a district judge	Interlocutory matters.

PART III

(i) DESCRIPTION OF PROCEEDINGS	(ii) DESCRIPTION OF JUDGE	(iii) CIRCUMSTANCES IN WHICH ALLOCATION APPLIES
(*n*) Proceedings under any of the following provisions of the Family Law Act 1986 (c 55) in respect of proceedings or orders made under section 8 of the Children Act 1989 (c 41): section 33 (power to order child's whereabouts); section 34 (power to order recovery of child); section 37 (surrender of passports).	A circuit judge nominated for private or public family proceedings; or	All circumstances.
	a district judge of the Principal Registry of the Family Division of the High Court; or	All circumstances.
	a district judge nominated for private orpublic family law proceedings.	All circumstances.
(*o*) Proceedings under any of the following provisions of the Family Law Act 1986 (c 55): section 55 (declaration as to marital status); section 55A (declarations of parentage); section 56 (declarations of legitimacy or legitimation); section 57 (declarations as to adoptions effected overseas).	A circuit judge nominated for private or public family law proceedings; or	All circumstances.
	a district judge of the Principal Registry of the Family Division of the High Court; or	Interlocutory matters.
	a district judge.	Interlocutory matters.

Amendments—Schedule substituted by Family Proceedings (Allocation to Judiciary) (Amendment) Directions 2002.

Family Proceedings Courts (Child Support Act 1991) Rules 1993, SI 1993/627

Citation, commencement, interpretation and transitional provision

1 These Rules may be cited as the Family Proceedings Courts (Child Support Act 1991) Rules 1993 and shall come into force on 5 April 1993.

2 In these rules –

"the Act of 1991" means the Child Support Act 1991,

"court" means a family proceedings court constituted in accordance with section 66 and 67 of the Magistrates' Courts Act 1980 or a single justice who is a member of a family panel.

Scope of provision—This rule provides a brief definition of two terms within the rules. The definition of "court" is almost identical to that contained in the Family Proceedings Courts (Children Act 1989) Rules 1991 and the Family Proceedings Courts (Matrimonial Proceedings etc) Rules 1991, and it is to these two sets of rules that reference should, in the first instance, be made where terms in these Rules are not defined.

3 Rules 6 to 8 shall apply only to applications filed on or after 5 April 1993.

Scope of provision—This rule provides that applications can only be delayed, by reason of apparently being precluded by Child Support Act 1991, s 8(3) or 9(5), where such applications were made after the coming into operation of the Act.

4 (1) Rules 2 to 16 of the Family Proceedings Courts (Matrimonial Proceedings etc) Rules 1991 shall apply as appropriate to an appeal under section 20 (appeal against decision of child support officer), where the proceedings are to be dealt with in accordance with the Child Support Appeals (Jurisdiction of Courts) Order 1993.

(2) The respondent to an appeal under section 20 of the Act of 1991 shall be the Secretary of State.

(3) (*revoked*)

(4) Where the justices' clerk or the court is considering whether or not to transfer proceedings under section 20 of the Act of 1991 to another court, rules 6, 14(2)(*h*), (4) and (11) and rule 32 of the Family Proceedings Courts (Children Act 1989) Rules 1991 shall also apply as appropriate.

Amendments—SI 2001/778.

Defined terms—"the Act of 1991", "court": r 2, "justices' clerk": FPC(CA 1989)R 1991, r 1(2).

Scope of provision—This rule applies to parentage appeals (CSA 1991, s 20). In respect of such proceedings, it applies the Family Proceedings Courts (Matrimonial Proceedings etc) Rules 1991, defines who may be respondents, and applies certain provisions of the Family Proceedings Courts (Children Act 1989) Rules 1991 to a consideration of their transfer. Although this rule appears in a section headed, amongst other things, "transitional provisions", the arrangements which the rule sets out are not transitional.

"Rules 2 to 16 of the Family Proceedings Courts (Matrimonial Proceedings etc) Rules 1991" (r 4(1))—These rules deal predominantly with procedural matters in the family proceedings courts when the magistrates are dealing with questions of financial relief as between spouses.

PART III

"an appeal under section 20" (r 4(1))—It is difficult to envisage circumstances in which a parentage appeal under CSA 1991, s 20 might arise (see **Extent of use of the provision** under FPR 1991, r 3.22). The Child Support Appeals (Jurisdiction of Courts) Order 2002 provides that parentage appeals go to a "court" and not to the child support appeal tribunal. In this case, the court is the family proceedings court (Children (Allocation of Proceedings) Order 1991, art 3(1)(*t*)).

"the Secretary of State" (r 4(2))—The Secretary of State in this context is the Secretary of State for Social Security.

Application of FPC(CA 1989)R 1991 (r 4(4))—The rules which apply here refer to the following: r 6 deals with the procedure for transferring proceedings from one family proceedings court to another, or from such a court to a county court; r 14 deals with directions, those sub-rules referring specifically to a transfer of proceedings; and r 32 deals with delegation by the justices' clerk to other staff of the court.

Proceedings transferred to a county court—If proceedings under CSA 1991, s 20 are transferred to a county court or up to the High Court, FPR 1991, rr 3.21 and 3.22 apply to the appeal or application.

5 Disclosure of information under the Act of 1991

Where the Secretary of State requires a person mentioned in regulation 2(2) or (3)(*a*) of the Child Support (Information, Evidence and Disclosure) Regulations 1992 to furnish information or evidence for a purpose mentioned in regulation 3(1) of those Regulations, nothing in rule 23 of the Family Proceedings Courts (Children Act 1989) Rules 1991 or rule 14 of the Family Proceedings Courts (Matrimonial Proceedings etc) Rules 1991 (confidentiality of documents) shall prevent that person from furnishing the information or evidence sought or shall require him to seek leave of the court before doing so.

Scope of provision—This rule, in almost identical terms to FPR 1991, r 10.21A, enables the Secretary of State to seek information from parties to proceedings and disapplies other rules which might otherwise have required that party to seek leave of the court to disclose or have enabled him to claim confidentiality for those documents.

"the Secretary of State"—The Secretary of State in this context is the Secretary of State for Social Security.

Application of the rule—This rule applies not only to proceedings under CSA 1991, s 20 but also to any proceedings in the family proceedings courts where there may be information or evidence sought by the Secretary of State.

"regulation 2(2) or (3)(a) of the Child Support (Information, Evidence and Disclosure) Regulations 1992"—CS(IED)R 1992, reg 2 places various individuals and institutions under a duty to provide information or evidence to the Secretary of State where an assessment of child support maintenance is being undertaken. Amongst those who might be required to provide information are parents of the child (reg 2(2)(*a*)), a person alleged to be a parent (reg 2(2)(*b*)) or courts which have certain relevant information (reg 2(2)(*e*), (3)(*a*)).

"for a purpose mentioned in regulation 3(1)"—CS(IED)R 1992, reg 3(1) places a limitation on the reasons for which the Secretary of State is entitled to seek information; however, this limit is widely drawn and includes identification and tracing of absent parents, information to enable a variety of decisions to be made and identification of related court proceedings. It seems likely that any documents or pleadings relating to existing or previous proceedings relevant to a child could be required by the Secretary of State.

6 Applications for relief which is precluded by the Act of 1991

(1) Where an application is made for an order which, in the opinion of the justices' clerk, the court would be prevented from making by section 8 or 9 of the

Act of 1991, the justices' chief executive may send a notice in the appropriate form to the applicant and the provisions of rule 4(1) to (3) of the Family Proceedings Courts (Matrimonial Proceedings etc) Rules 1991 (service) shall apply as appropriate.

(2) Where a notice is sent under paragraph (1), no requirement of any rules, except for those of this rule, as to the service of the application or as to any other procedural step applicable to the making of an application of the type in question, shall apply unless and until the court directs that such rules shall apply or that they shall apply to such extent and subject to such modifications as may be specified in the direction.

(3) Where an applicant who has been sent a notice under paragraph (1) informs the justices' chief executive in writing, within 14 days of the date of the notice, that he wishes to persist with his application, the justices' clerk shall give such directions as he considers appropriate for the matter to be heard and determined by the court and, without prejudice to the generality of the foregoing, such directions may provide for the hearing to be ex parte.

(4) Where directions are given under paragraph (3), the justices' chief executive shall inform the applicant of the directions and, in relation to the other parties, –

(*a*) where the hearing is to be ex parte, inform them briefly –
- (i) of the nature and effect of the notice under this rule,
- (ii) that the matter is being resolved ex parte, and
- (iii) that they will be informed of the result in due course; and

(*b*) where the hearing is to be inter partes, inform them of –
- (i) the circumstances which led to the directions being given, and
- (ii) the directions.

(5) Where a notice has been sent under paragraph (1) and the justices' chief executive is not informed under paragraph (3) the application shall be treated as having been withdrawn.

(6) Where the matter is heard pursuant to directions under paragraph (3) and the court determines that it would be prevented by section 8 or 9 of the Act of 1991 from making the order sought by the application, it shall dismiss the application.

(7) Where the court dismisses an application under this rule it shall give its reasons in writing, copies of which shall be sent to the parties by the justices' chief executive.

(8) In this rule, "the matter" means the question whether the making of an order in the terms sought by the application would be prevented by section 8 or 9 of the Act of 1991.

(9) Rule 15 of the Family Proceedings Courts (Matrimonial Proceedings etc) Rules 1991 (delegation by justices' clerk) shall apply as appropriate to anything authorised to be done by or to a justices' clerk under this rule or rule 7.

Amendments—SI 2001/615.

Defined terms—"the Act of 1991", "court": r 2; "justices' clerk", "justices' chief executive": FPC(CA 1989)R 1991, r 1(2).

Scope of provision—This rule has a similar effect, for family proceedings courts, to FPR 1991, r 10.24.

"section 8 or 9 of the Act of 1991" (r 6(1))—Child Support Act 1991, ss 8(3) and 9(5) prevent any court from making, varying or reviving any orders for periodical payments for children and from varying any agreement for child maintenance.

"in the appropriate form" (r 6(1))—This form is not defined in the main part of the Rules, although the form CSA 1, in Appendix 1, is stated to "have effect" (r 8). This form is the family proceedings courts equivalent of M34 (applicable in the High Court and county courts).

"rule 4(1) to (3) of the Family Proceedings Courts (Matrimonial Proceedings etc) Rules 1991" (r 6(1))—FPC(MP etc)R 1991, r 4 deals with service of documents. Rule 4(1)–(3) is to be read in the context of the court sending documents to the applicant, either by personal service, by first-class post or to the applicant's solicitor.

Requirements as to service etc (r 6(3))—FPC(MP etc)R 1991, rr 4–8 deal with the procedural steps, including service, which follow the filing of an application for financial relief in the family proceedings courts.

Ex parte hearing (r 6(3), (4))—Although all parties to the proceedings are given notice of the application and of the ex parte hearing, there seems to be no mechanism whereby a respondent can insist on being heard if he wishes to make representations to the court at this stage. This may be desirable, since he will have an opportunity to make representation later when the full application is heard, but there will be cases where a full airing of what amounts to a preliminary issue, eg on jurisdiction and habitual residence (see CSA 1991, s 44), could save time and costs.

Withdrawal or dismissal of application (r 6(5), (6))—In view of the terms of r 7, these references to withdrawal and dismissal can be taken to apply only to that part of the application which relates to periodical payments for children where other matters are dealt with in the same application (eg lump sum, spousal periodical payments etc).

Determination or dismissal by the court (r 6(6), (7))—Although it is the justices' clerk who carries out the administrative functions, it is the magistrates themselves who take the decisions as to whether or not the application should proceed.

"Rule 15 of the Family Proceedings Courts (Matrimonial Proceedings etc) Rules 1991" (r 6(9))—FPC(MP etc)R 1991, r 15 enables the justices' clerk to delegate his decisions to appropriate members of his staff.

7 Modification of rule 6 in relation to non-free-standing applications

Where a notice is sent under rule 6(1) in respect of an application which is contained in an application, answer or other document ("the document") which contains material extrinsic to the application –

(*a*) the document shall, until the contrary is directed under sub-paragraph (*c*) of this rule, be treated as if it did not contain the application in respect of which the notice was served;

(*b*) the justices' chief executive shall send to the respondents a copy of the notice under rule 6(1) and a notice informing the respondents of the effect of sub-paragraph (*a*) of this paragraph; and

(*c*) if it is determined, under rule 6, that the court would not be prevented, by section 8 or 9 of the Act of 1991 from making the order sought by the application, the court shall direct that the document shall be treated as if it contained the application, and it may give such directions as it considers appropriate for the conduct of the proceedings in consequence of that direction.

Amendments—SI 2001/615.

Defined terms—"the Act of 1991", "court": r 2; "justices' clerk": FPC(CA 1989)R 1991, r 1(2).

Scope of provision—This rule has a similar effect, for family proceedings courts, to FPR 1991, r 10.25. It enables the court to proceed with the remainder of an application where this includes a claim for periodical payments for children which has been delayed by a notice being issued under r 6(1).

"the document shall ... be treated as if it did not contain the application" (r 7(*a*))—The effect of this provision, which must be drawn to the attention of the respondent to the application (r 7(*b*)), is to enable the remainder of the application to proceed – to a final hearing if required – whether or not there is an adjudication under r 6. If the court holds that it is prevented by Child Support Act 1991, s 8(3) or 9(5) from hearing the application for child periodical payments, that application is dismissed (r 6(6)). It must be assumed that r 7(*a*) enables the remainder of the application still to proceed so that, in those circumstances, r 6(6) has the effect only of causing dismissal of that part of the application which deals with child periodical payments.

****

Family Proceedings Courts (Children Act 1989) Rules 1991, SI 1991/1395

ARRANGEMENT OF RULES

PART I
INTRODUCTORY

PART II
GENERAL

PART IIA
PROCEEDINGS UNDER SECTION 30 OF THE HUMAN FERTILISATION AND EMBRYOLOGY ACT 1990

PART III
MISCELLANEOUS

PART I
INTRODUCTORY

1 Citation, commencement and interpretation

(1) These Rules may be cited as the Family Proceedings Courts (Children Act 1989) Rules 1991 and shall come into force on 14 October 1991.

(2) Unless a contrary intention appears –

a section or schedule referred to means the section or schedule in the Act of 1989,

"application" means an application made under or by virtue of the Act of 1989 or under these Rules, and "applicant" shall be construed accordingly, "business day" means any day other than –

(*a*) a Saturday, Sunday, Christmas Day or Good Friday; or
(*b*) a bank holiday, that is to say, a day which is, or is to be observed as, a bank holiday, or a holiday, under the Banking and Financial Dealings Act 1971, in England and Wales,

"child" –

(*a*) means, in relation to any relevant proceedings, subject to sub-paragraph (*b*), a person under the age of 18 with respect to whom the proceedings are brought, and
(*b*) where paragraph 16(1) of Schedule 1 applies, also includes a person who has reached the age of 18,

"children and family reporter" means an officer of the service who has been asked to prepare a welfare report under section 7(1)(*a*);

"children's guardian" –

(*a*) means an officer of the service appointed under section 41 for the child with respect to whom the proceedings are brought; but
(*b*) does not include such an officer appointed in relation to proceedings specified by rule 21A;

"contribution order" has the meaning assigned to it by paragraph 23(2) of Schedule 2,

"court" means a family proceedings court constituted in accordance with sections 66 and 67 of the Magistrates' Courts Act 1980 or, in respect of those proceedings prescribed in rule 2(5), a single justice who is a member of a family panel,

"directions appointment" means a hearing for directions under rule 14(2),

"emergency protection order" means an order under section 44,

"file" means deposit with the justices' chief executive,

"form" means a form in Schedule 1 to these Rules with such variation as the circumstances of the particular case may require,

"justices' chief executive" means a justices' chief executive appointed under section 40 of the Justices of the Peace Act 1997;

"justices' clerk" has the meaning assigned to it by section 70 of the Justices of the Peace Act 1979 and includes any person who performs a justices' clerk's functions by virtue of rule 32,

"leave" includes approval,

"officer of the service" has the same meaning as in the Criminal Justice and Court Services Act 2000;

"note" includes a record made by mechanical means,

"parental responsibility" has the meaning assigned to it by section 3,

"parties" in relation to any relevant proceedings means the respondents specified for those proceedings in the third column of Schedule 2 to these Rules, and the applicant,

"recovery order" means an order under section 50,

"relevant proceedings" has the meaning assigned to it by section 93(3),

"section 8 order" has the meaning assigned to it by section 8(2),

"specified proceedings" has the meaning assigned to it by section 41(6) and rule 2(2),

"the 1981 rules" means the Magistrates' Courts Rules 1981,

"the Act of 1989" means the Children Act 1989,

"welfare officer" means a person who has been asked to prepare a welfare report under section 7(1)(*b*).

Amendments—SI 2001/615; SI 2001/818.

"paragraph 16 of Schedule 1" (r 1(2))—CA 1989, Sch 1 relates to financial provision for children.

2 Matters prescribed for the purposes of the Act of 1989

(1) The parties to proceedings in which directions are given under section 38(6), and any person named in such a direction, form the prescribed class for the purposes of section 38(8)(*b*) (application to vary directions made with interim care or interim supervision order).

(2) The following proceedings are specified for the purposes of section 41 in accordance with subsection (6)(i) thereof –

(*a*) proceedings (in a family proceedings court) under section 25;
(*b*) applications under section 33(7);
(*c*) proceedings under paragraph 19(1) of Schedule 2;
(*d*) applications under paragraph 6(3) of Schedule 3.

(3) The applicant for an order that has been made under section 43(1) and the persons referred to in section 43(11) may, in any circumstances, apply under section 43(12) for a child assessment order to be varied or discharged.

(4) The following persons form the prescribed class for the purposes of section 44(9)(*b*) (application to vary directions) –

(*a*) the parties to the application for the order in respect of which it is sought to vary the directions;
(*b*) the children's guardian;
(*c*) the local authority in whose area the child concerned is ordinarily resident;
(*d*) any person who is named in the directions.

(5) The following proceedings are prescribed for the purposes of section 93(2)(*i*) as being proceedings with respect to which a single justice may discharge the functions of a family proceedings court, that is to say, proceedings –

(*a*) where an ex parte application is made, under sections 10, 44(1), 48(9), 50(1), 75(1) or 102(1),
(*b*) subject to rule 28, under sections 11(3) or 38(1),
(*c*) under sections 4(3)(*b*), 7, 14, 34(3)(*b*), 37, 41, 44(9)(*b*) and (11)(*b*)(iii), 48(4), 91(15) or (17), or paragraph 11(4) of Schedule 14,
(*d*) in accordance with any Order made by the Lord Chancellor under Part I of Schedule 11, and
(*e*) in accordance with rules 3 to 8, 10 to 19, 21, 22, or 27.

Amendments—SI 1991/1991; SI 2001/818.

Defined terms—"applicant", "application", "children's guardian", "parties": r 1(2).

"section 38(6)" (r 2(1))—CA 1989, s 38(6) empowers the court to make directions regarding medical or psychiatric examination or other assessment of a child where it makes an interim care or supervision order.

"section 38(8)(b)" (r 2(1))—CA 1989, s 38(8)(*b*) empowers the court to vary a direction made under s 38(6) on the application of a person within any class prescribed by rules of court; r 2(1) is the only such rule of court which applies in magistrates' courts.

"section 41" (r 2(2))—CA 1989, s 41 imposes a duty on the court in any "specified proceedings" to appoint a children's guardian for the child concerned, unless it is satisfied that it is not necessary to do so to safeguard his interests. Section 41(6) specifies many of the proceedings in which this duty arises and s 41(6)(*i*) provides for rules of court to specify further proceedings. Rule 2(2) is the only rule of court which so specifies for the purposes of magistrates' courts.

"proceedings ... under section 25" (r 2(2)(*a*))—These are proceedings concerning the use of secure accommodation to restrict the liberty of a child.

"applications under section 33(7)" (r 2(2)(*b*))—Application may be made under CA 1989, s 33(7) for leave to change the surname of a child in respect of whom a care order is in force (see eg *Re J (A Minor) (Change of Name)* [1993] 1 FLR 699), as may an application for leave to remove a child in care from the jurisdiction.

"proceedings under paragraph 19(1) of Schedule 2" (r 2(2)(*c*))—These are proceedings by a local authority for the court's approval of arrangements for a child in its care to live outside England and Wales.

"applications under paragraph 6(3) of Schedule 3" (r 2(2)(*d*))—Application may be made under CA 1989, Sch 3, para 6(3) by a supervisor who seeks to have the period of a supervision order extended.

"section 43(1)" (r 2(3))—Under CA 1989, s 43(1), an application may be made for a child assessment order.

"the persons referred to in section 43(11)" (r 2(3))—CA 1989, s 43(11) sets out certain people who must normally be given notice of an application for a child assessment order (including the child's parents and anyone else with parental responsibility). The same group of people (and the original applicant for the order) are allowed, by virtue of r 2(3), to apply for the order to be varied or discharged.

"the prescribed class for the purposes of section 44(9)(b)" (r 2(4))—CA 1989, s 44 enables the court to make emergency protection orders and, where it does so, it may, under s 44(6), give directions as to the medical, psychiatric or other assessment of the child or contact with him. Section 44(9)(*b*) provides that such directions may be varied at any time on the application of a person falling within any class of person prescribed by rules of court; r 2(4) is the only rule which prescribes such a class for the purposes of magistrates' courts.

"the parties to the application" (r 2(4)(*a*))—All that the rather convoluted form of words in r 2(4)(*a*) means is that, where there has been an emergency protection order and ancillary directions for medical, psychiatric or other assessment, the parties to the emergency protection application may apply to vary the ancillary directions.

"children's guardian" (r 2(4)(*b*))—Proceedings under CA 1989, s 44 are specified proceedings for the purposes of s 41, with the result that a children's guardian will normally have been appointed for the child.

"ordinarily resident" (r 2(4)(*c*))—This term is not defined in the rules, but the concept appears a number of times in CA 1989, and reference should be made to the annotations under s 31 of that Act, and to s 105(6).

"any person who is named in the directions" (r 2(4)(*d*))—The directions referred to are the assessment directions made under s 44(6) (see **"the prescribed class for the purposes of section 44(9)(b)"** above).

"section 93(2)(i)" (r 2(5))—CA 1989, s 93(2)(*i*) empowers the making of rules authorising a single justice to discharge the functions of a magistrates' court with respect to such relevant proceedings as may be prescribed; r 2(5) is such a rule.

"ex parte application" (r 2(5)(*a*))—Any application which is made without notice (or without proper notice) having been given is an ex parte application. Only certain orders may be sought ex parte. Most of these are listed in r 4(4) which also sets out the procedure to be followed on an ex parte application, including the requirement that the leave of the justices' clerk to make the application must be obtained.

"sections 10, 44(1), 48(9), 50(1), 75(1) or 102(1)" (r 2(5)(*a*))—These sections of CA 1989 deal with the following matters – s 10: power of court to make s 8 orders; s 44(1): application for an emergency protection order; s 48(9): application for a warrant authorising a constable to assist in the enforcement of an emergency protection order; s 50(1): application for a recovery order in relation to a child who has been abducted, run away etc; s 75 has been repealed and replaced by

PART III

s 79K (see Care Standards Act 2000, s 79(1)); s 102(1): application for a warrant authorising a constable to assist in the exercise of certain powers to search for children and inspect premises.

"subject to rule 28" (r 2(5)(*b*))—Rule 28 limits the power of a single justice to make an order under ss 11(3) and 38(1).

"sections 11(3) or 38(1)" (r 2(5)(*b*))—CA 1989, s 11(3) empowers the court to make a s 8 order before it is in a position to dispose finally of the proceedings in question; for example, where the proceedings have to be adjourned for a period and the court feels it necessary to regulate where the child is going to live by making an interim residence order pending the resumed hearing. Section 38(1) empowers the court to make an interim care or supervision order where an application for a full care or supervision order is adjourned, or where the court gives a direction under s 37(1) that the local authority should investigate the child's circumstances with a view to it possibly making a care or supervision order.

Provisions specified in r 2(5)(c)—A number of the provisions of CA 1989 which are specified in r 2(5)(*c*) are provisions requiring leave of the court before certain proceedings may be commenced or certain steps may be taken. Rule 2(5)(*c*) has not been particularly happily drafted in that, in relation to certain of the specified statutory provisions, it is open to argument as to whether it is the *leave* application with which the single justice is empowered to deal (as, it is suggested, was almost certainly intended) or the *substantive* application which will follow should leave be given.

As to the individual provisions specified, CA 1989, s 4(3)(*b*) authorises a child to seek an order terminating a parental responsibility order or agreement in respect of him provided that he has the leave of the court. As drafted, it is arguable that a single justice has power to determine the application itself (rather than just the leave application) where it is made by a child, but it is suggested that this cannot have been the intention of the draftsman. CA 1989, s 7 empowers the court (which, by virtue of r 2(5)(*c*), may consist of a single justice) to require a welfare report. Section 14 proceedings relate to the enforcement of residence orders. Section 34 allows certain people to apply for orders with regard to contact with a child in care; under s 34(3)(*b*) certain applicants must first seek leave to apply. Again the intention of r 2(5)(*c*) is almost certainly to empower a single justice to deal with the application for leave but the wording is ambiguous and leaves room for the argument that, in addition, a single justice may determine a contact application made by someone who has obtained leave in accordance with s 34(3)(*b*).

Section 37 gives the court in any family proceedings in which a question arises with respect to the welfare of any child power to direct the local authority to investigate the child's circumstances with a view to a care or supervision order possibly being made. Section 41 provides for the appointment by the court of a children's guardian or a solicitor for a child concerned in specified proceedings such as care proceedings etc.

For the effect of s 44(9)(*b*) see **"the prescribed class for the purposes of section 44(9)(b)"** above.

Section 44(11) applies where, after the making of an emergency protection order, it is proposed to return a child or allow his removal from the place where he has been detained. It specifies the rules of precedence by reference to which the applicant is to determine to whom he must deliver the child. The first choice is the person from whom the child has been removed, but, if that is not reasonably practicable, one of the other possibilities is, in accordance with s 44(11)(*b*)(iii), such other person as the applicant (with the agreement of the court) considers appropriate. Rule 2(5)(*c*) empowers a single justice to signify the requisite agreement.

Section 48 includes miscellaneous provisions to assist in finding children who may be in need of emergency protection. Under s 48(4), the court may authorise a search of premises for a child with respect to whom there is reasonable cause to believe an emergency protection order ought to be made. Both s 91(15) and (17) prohibit the making of repeat applications within six months in certain cases without leave (for example, no application for the discharge of a care or supervision order may be made within six months of the last such application). A single justice is empowered by r 2(5)(*c*) to give such leave. Finally, CA 1989, Sch 14, para 11(4) prohibits a child from applying for the discharge of an existing order except with the leave of the court. Rule 2(5)(*c*) permits a single justice to give such leave.

"Order made by the Lord Chancellor under Part I of Schedule 11" (r 2(5)(*d*))—Under CA 1989, Sch 11, para 3, the Lord Chancellor is empowered to specify the circumstances in which a single justice may exercise the jurisdiction of a magistrates' court to make an emergency protection order or deal with specified questions with respect to the transfer of proceedings to another court. A single justice is already empowered, by r 2(5)(*a*), to deal with an ex parte application for an emergency protection order and, by r 2(5)(*c*), to vary directions attached to an emergency protection order and to approve the return of a child on such an order to a proposed person.

"in accordance with ... [rule] 27" (r 2(5)(*e*))—Rule 2(5)(*e*) poses interpretation problems. Read logically, it means that any proceedings "in accordance with" the rules specified in r 2(5)(*e*) are prescribed proceedings and may be dealt with by a single justice. However, all applications under CA 1989 *must* be made as prescribed under r 4 and thus "in accordance with" that rule; it ought to follow that a single justice can deal with every single application under CA 1989, but plainly this is not what was intended and not what has occurred in practice. Rule 2(5)(*e*) must therefore have another meaning. One possibility is that it entitles a single justice to exercise any of the powers given to the court under the rules listed so that, for example, when refusing an ex parte application he could, under r 4(5), direct that the application be made inter partes. Is he, however, limited to exercising these powers in proceedings with which he has been specifically empowered to deal or can he exercise them in any proceedings whatsoever? Can he, for instance, grant leave under r 3 to a person who has previously been barred by the court under s 91(14) from seeking a particular type of order without leave? If a single justice can grant leave to such a person, even though s 91(14) is not one of the statutory provisions expressly assigned to his province by r 2(5)(*a*) to (*d*), it is not clear why the draftsman has listed specifically other leave applications that can be made to a single justice.

Stipendiary magistrates—Not all stipendiary magistrates are empowered to hear CA 1989 matters (see Family Proceedings Courts (Constitution) Rules 1991, Family Proceedings Courts (Constitution) (Metropolitan Areas) Rules 1991 and *Leeds City Council v C* [1993] 1 FLR 269).

Power of justices' clerks—There is no equivalent rule to r 2(5) which, instead of gathering together the powers of a single justice, gathers together those of a justices' clerk. Reference must be made to the terms of each individual rule and to the Justices' Clerks Rules 1999. In summary, a justices' clerk may:

(*a*) give leave for the making of ex parte applications under r 4(4);
(*b*) transfer proceedings to another family proceedings court or to the county court under r 6(1);
(*c*) give directions as to service under r 8(4) and (8);
(*d*) appoint a children's guardian in specified proceedings under r 10(1);
(*e*) give various directions under r 11 as to how the children's guardian should carry out his duties;
(*f*) appoint a solicitor in accordance with s 41(3) to represent the child (r 12(6));
(*g*) give, vary and revoke directions for the conduct of the proceedings under r 14, and under various other rules as well (for example, under r 13 with regard to the children and family reporter and under r 17 with regard to the filing of statements and documents etc);
(*h*) give leave under r 18 for a child to be medically or psychiatrically examined or otherwise assessed;
(*i*) give leave under r 19 to amend a document which has been filed or served;
(*j*) give leave under r 23 for documents to be disclosed;
(*k*) grant an interim s 8 order or an interim care or supervision order providing the conditions set out in r 28 are satisfied;
(*l*) issue a witness summons under Magistrates' Courts Act 1980, s 97 as applied by r 33.

In addition, he has numerous functions of a more administrative nature, such as fixing dates for hearings, and directions appointments, giving notice of certain forthcoming hearings, notifying parties of decisions of the court and serving copies of reports.

PART II
GENERAL

3 Application for leave to commence proceedings

(1) Where the leave of the court is required to bring any relevant proceedings, the person seeking leave shall file –

(*a*) a written request for leave in Form C2 setting out the reasons for the application, and (*b*) a draft of the application (being the documents referred to in rule 4(1A)) for the making of which leave is sought together with sufficient copies for one to be served on each respondent.

(2) On considering a request for leave filed under paragraph (1), the court shall –

(*a*) grant the request, whereupon the justices' chief executive shall inform the person making the request of the decision, or

(*b*) direct that a date be fixed for a hearing of the request, whereupon the justices' clerk shall fix such a date and the justices' chief executive shall give such notice as the court directs to the person making the request and to such other persons as the court requires to be notified, of the date so fixed.

(3) Where leave is granted to bring any relevant proceedings, the application shall proceed in accordance with rule 4; but paragraph (1)(*a*) of that rule shall not apply.

Amendments—SI 1994/3156; SI 2001/615.

Defined terms—"application", "the court", "file", "form", "justices' chief executive", "justices' clerk", "leave": r 1(2); "relevant proceedings": r 1(2), CA 1989, s 93(3).

Relevant proceedings—Relevant proceedings are those listed in s 93(1)(*a*)–(*c*), ie proceedings brought under CA 1989, under the provisions of any statutory instrument made under it or under any amendment made by that Act to any other enactment.

Court to which the leave request should be made—An application by a child for leave to apply for s 8 orders (contact, prohibited steps, residence and specific issue orders) where he is to be the subject of the proposed application raises issues that are more appropriate for determination in the High Court and should be transferred there for hearing (*Practice Direction of 22 February 1993*; *Re AD (A Minor) (Child's Wishes)* [1993] 1 FCR 573, [1993] Fam Law 405). As to the appropriate court for leave applications by natural parents of adopted children, see *Re T (Adopted Children: Contact)* [1995] 2 FLR 792, CA (noted in **Procedure on application for leave being filed** under FPR 1991, r 4.3). Although *Re T* disagrees with some of the advice contained in *Re C (A Minor) (Adopted Child: Contact)* [1993] 2 FLR 431, it is suggested that the net result of the two cases is still that such applications should be transferred by the magistrates courts for hearing by the higher courts; whether the application will be transferred on to the High Court will be determined by the county court. An application by a local authority for leave to issue an application for a prohibited steps order should be transferred to the county court (*Nottinghamshire County Council v P* [1993] 2 FLR 134, CA).

"written request for leave" (r 3(1)(*a*))—The written request for leave should be made in Form C2 (see Sch 1 to these rules), which requires the full names of the child concerned. The applicant must provide detailed information identifying himself and his relationship to the child; the nature of the orders for which he is applying in relation to each child; the full names and addresses of all respondents to be served with the application; a brief outline of his reasons for applying for leave; and a brief description of any plans he has for the child. Care should be taken to cover any factors which are especially relevant to the instant case (for example, in the case of an application under CA 1989, s 4(3), the child's understanding). If the applicant is applying for an order under CA 1989, s 8, he must not, without leave of the justices' clerk or the court, make a full statement at this point in the proceedings, although he may be required to do so at a later stage (see prohibition contained in r 17(4)).

Where no written request is filed—In *Re O (Minors) (Leave to Seek Residence Order)* [1994] 1 FLR 172, leave to apply for a residence order was granted ex parte by the family proceedings court despite the fact that the applicant for leave had not filed a written request for leave. Ewbank J was of the view that the absence of a written request did not automatically invalidate the interim residence order which the magistrates went on to make and, in a matter of emergency, it was wrong to think that a court must be constrained by rules demanding that bits of paper must be issued. However, he did reduce the period of the interim order from one month to 11 days.

"draft of the application (being the documents referred to in rule 4(1A))" (r 3(1)(*b*))—Rule 4 deals with the procedure for making substantive applications. The documents referred to in r 4(1A) are (i) whichever is appropriate of Forms C1 to C5 or C51, and (ii) such of the supplemental Forms C10 and C11 to C20 as may be appropriate. Where there is no appropriate form, the application should be made in writing (r 4(1A)(*b*)). Where the application is made in respect of more than one child of the family, all the children should be included on one application (r 4(1A)).

"respondent" (r 3(1)(*b*))—The reference to respondents is, of course, a reference to those who will be respondents to the proceedings if leave is given; there are no prescribed respondents to the request for leave.

Procedure on application for leave being filed (r 3(2), (3))—There is no power to *refuse* leave on the papers; if the court is not convinced of the merits of the written request, it has no choice but to direct a hearing. There is power to *grant* leave on the papers or on an ex parte application, but it is clear that this will rarely be appropriate. The discretion whether or not to direct a hearing must be exercised judicially and, except in cases of emergency, the interests of justice require that notice be given to parties likely to be affected (*Re M (Prohibited Steps Order: Application for Leave)* [1993] 1 FLR 275; *Re SC (A Minor) (Leave to Seek Residence Order)* [1994] 1 FLR 96; *Re W (Minor) (Contact Application: Procedure)* [1999] Fam Law 853; see also *Nottinghamshire County Council v P* [1994] Fam 18, [1993] 2 FLR 134 to the effect that it is inappropriate for a local authority to apply ex parte for leave to issue an application for a prohibited steps order before a single justice of the family proceedings court, and such applications should be transferred to the county court and should not be dealt with ex parte). Where the justices decide to proceed ex parte, their reasons for this decision and any findings of fact must be recorded and stated in accordance with r 21 (*Re M (Prohibited Steps Order: Application for Leave)* [1993] 1 FLR 275). Where a hearing with regard to leave is directed, potential respondents to the main application would be the obvious candidates to receive notice of it. Where notice is being given to persons other than the applicant, due regard should be had, in fixing the hearing date, to the fact that they may well need to seek legal advice.

Sometimes argument may be all that is required at the hearing (*Re W (Contact: Application by Grandparent)* [1997] 1 FLR 793, FD suggests that applications for leave are almost always applications on the papers and without the benefit of a court welfare report) but there may be occasions when it is appropriate to seek a court welfare report under CA 1989, s 7 and sometimes there may be factual issues that require determination (the level of understanding of the child on an application under CA 1989, s 4(3) for example) and oral evidence may have to be called, which may include cross-examination as in *Re A (A Minor) (Residence Order: Leave to Apply)* [1993] 1 FLR 425. Although the magistrates should not, on an application for leave, hold a full and detailed investigation of the case, where there were two competing factual accounts as to whether leave to make a s 8 contact application should be granted, they should have heard evidence, not in extensive form but from the main parties, rather than refusing the leave application after reading a letter in support and a statement in opposition and hearing oral submissions (*Re F and R (Section 8 Order: Grandparents' Application)* [1995] 1 FLR 524, FD).

If interpreted literally, the rules give little guidance as to the procedure at the leave hearing. A distinction is made in r 3 between the *request* for leave and the *application* for which leave is sought, and, strictly speaking, rules dealing with applications (for example rr 4 and 5) should not therefore apply to the request for leave. Rules relating to *proceedings* (such as rr 14, 17 and 21(3)) are equally inapplicable given that no proceedings can be brought in a leave case until after leave has been granted, as are rules making reference to *parties* as there can be no parties until proceedings have been launched. However, it appears from Form C2 (which refers throughout to a r 3 request as an "application") that the distinction between the request and the application may, in fact, be a distinction without a difference and that a r 3 request is appropriately classed as an application. In default of other guidance, the court can, of course, regulate its own procedure in any event (see, for example, *Re W (Secure Accommodation Order: Attendance at Court)* [1994] 2 FLR 1092).

The justices' reasons for their decision as to leave and any findings of fact should be recorded and stated in accordance with r 21, whether or not the leave application has been heard ex parte (*Re M (Prohibited Steps Order: Application for Leave)* [1993] 1 FLR 275, *T v W (Contact: Reasons for Refusing Leave)* [1996] 2 FLR 473, FD). If the court grants leave, the draft application will stand as the application, and the applicant may proceed to service in accordance with r 4(1)(*b*), as r 3(3) provides.

Representation of the child on application for leave—A request for leave does not fall within the meaning of "specified proceedings" for the purpose of CA 1989, s 41(6), and so there is no presumption that a children's guardian will be appointed.

PART III

Appeal against grant of leave—An order granting leave (and presumably an order refusing leave) can be appealed under CA 1989, s 94 and the appeal can be brought by a person or body (such as a local authority) who was not a party to the original leave application (*Re M (Prohibited Steps Order: Application for Leave)* [1993] 1 FLR 275).

4 Application

(1) Subject to paragraph (4), an applicant shall –

(*a*) file the documents referred to in paragraph (1A) below (which documents shall together be called the "application") together with sufficient copies for one to be served on each respondent, and

(*b*) serve a copy of the application together with Form C6 and such (if any) of Forms C7 and C10A as are given to him by the justices' chief executive under paragraph 2(*b*) on each respondent such minimum number of days prior to the date fixed under paragraph (2)(*a*) as is specified in relation to that application in column (ii) of Schedule 2 to these Rules.

(1A) The documents to be filed under paragraph (1)(*a*) above are –

(*a*) (i) whichever is appropriate of Forms C1 to C5 or C51, and

(ii) such of the supplemental Forms C10 or C11 to C20 as may be appropriate, or

(*b*) where there is no appropriate form a statement in writing of the order sought,

and where the application is made in respect of more than one child, all the children shall be included in one application.

(2) On receipt by the justices' chief executive of the documents filed under paragraph (1)(*a*) –

(*a*) the justices' clerk shall fix the date, time and place for a hearing or a directions appointment, allowing sufficient time for the applicant to comply with paragraph (1)(*b*), and

(*b*) the justices' chief executive shall –

(i) endorse the date, time and place so fixed upon Form C6, and where appropriate, Form C6A, and

(ii) return forthwith to the applicant the copies of the application and Form C10A if filed with it, together with Form C6, and such of Forms C6A and C7 as are appropriate.

(3) The applicant shall, at the same time as complying with paragraph (1)(*b*), serve Form C6A on the persons set out in relation to the relevant class of proceedings in column (iv) of Schedule 2 to these Rules.

(4) An application for –

(*a*) a section 8 order,

(*b*) an emergency protection order,

(*c*) a warrant under section 48(9),

(*d*) a recovery order, or

(*e*) a warrant under section 102(1),

may, with leave of the justices' clerk, be made ex parte in which case the applicant shall –

(i) file with the justices' chief executive or the court the application in the appropriate form in Schedule 1 to these Rules at the time when the application is made or as directed by the justices' clerk, and

(ii) in the case of an application for a prohibited steps order, or a specific issue order, under section 8 or an emergency protection order, and also in the case of an application for an order under section 75(1) where the application is ex parte, serve a copy of the application on each respondent within 48 hours after the making of the order.

(5) Where the court refuses to make an order on an ex parte application it may direct that the application be made inter partes.

(6) In the case of proceedings under Schedule 1, the application under paragraph (1) shall be accompanied by a statement in Form C10A setting out the financial details which the applicant believes to be relevant to the application, together with sufficient copies for one to be served on each respondent.

Amendments—SI 1992/2068; SI 1994/3156; SI 2001/615.

Defined terms—"applicant", "application", "child", "court", "directions appointment", "emergency protection order", "file", "form", "justices' chief executive", "justices' clerk", "leave": r 1(2); "prohibited steps order": CA 1989, s 8(1); "section 8 order": CA 1989, s 8(2); "specific issue order": CA 1989, s 8(1).

Procedure where a matrimonial cause or an application under Matrimonial Causes Act 1973, s 19 is pending—Where any such cause is pending and the child who is to be the subject of an application under CA 1989 to a magistrates' court is a child of the family in relation to that cause, reference should be made to FPR 1991, r 2.40. See also under FPR 1991, r 4.4.

"the application" (r 4(1), (1A))—Rule 4(1A) sets out the prescribed forms to be used in relation to substantive applications (see Sch 1 to these rules for the complete list of prescribed forms). For further details see under FPR 1991, r 4.4.

Where there is more than one child (r 4(1A))—Where the application is made in respect of more than one child of the family, all the children should be included on one application. This is a significant change from the former procedure, which required separate application forms to be filed in respect of each child of the family.

Written statements of evidence—Normally, no written evidence is filed with the application form; it will be filed at a later stage in accordance with the directions of the justices' clerk or the court or, in the absence of directions, before the hearing or appointment (r 17). However, Form C5 and a number of the supplemental forms specifically request that, if the applicant is relying on a report or other documentary evidence, a copy should be enclosed with the form.

Addresses—Certain addresses are generally required to be included on the application form, including those of the applicant and sometimes the child. Where an applicant is unwilling to give an address (for example, because of fear of violence from one of the respondents), r 33A provides that the address may be given to the court separately on Form C8.

Service (r 4(1)(*b*), (3))—It is the applicant who is responsible for service of the application, not the court. Form C9 is a statement of service of the application/notice of proceedings, and reference should be made to r 8(7) for the applicant's duty to file it. Rule 8 also deals with service generally.

Sufficient time for the applicant to comply with r 4(1)(b)—The date of the hearing or directions appointment should obviously be fixed by reference to the minimum notice periods set out in Sch 2. If unusual difficulty is anticipated in serving the respondent(s), this should be drawn to the attention of the justices' clerk when the court documents are filed so that extra time is allowed.

Forms C6, C6A, C7 and C10A (r 4(1)(*b*), (2)(*b*), (*c*))—Form C6 gives notice of the proceedings to persons who are parties to them and contains information to assist the recipient to take the next step in the proceedings. Form C6A is a similar notice to non-parties. If Form C7 (acknowledgement) is enclosed with Form C6, the recipient must fill it in and return it to the court, and serve a copy on the other parties. If the applicant has asked the court to order the recipient of Form C6 to make a payment for a child, the recipient must also fill in a statement of his financial means (Form C10A).

"serve Form C6A on the persons ... in column (iv) of Schedule 2" (r 4(3))—Column (iv) of Schedule 2 to these rules sets out those persons who must be served with notice of the proceedings but who are not parties, and Form C6A is used for this purpose. It sets out the date and venue of the first hearing or appointment but includes very few details of the application and is not accompanied by a copy of it. If the recipient of the notice wishes to become a party to the proceedings, he must apply to the court in Form C2, following the procedure in r 7(2). Only if his request is granted will he be entitled to the full documentation. As to the filing in Form C9 of a statement of service of Form C6A notice, see r 8(7)(*b*). Where a party wishes to seek a direction that a person should not be served with the proceedings (where otherwise there is a duty to serve him according to Sch 2), the party concerned should apply to the court under r 8(8) *(Re X (Care: Notice of Proceedings)* [1996] 1 FLR 186).

Withdrawal of applications—Once the application has been filed, it cannot be withdrawn without leave of the court (r 5).

Power to make ex parte orders (r 4(4))—This provision has been amended to add s 8 orders to the list of orders that can be made ex parte. For detailed discussion of this topic see under FPR 1991, r 4.4.

"warrant under section 48(9)" (r 4(4)(*c*))—This refers to a warrant authorising a constable to assist a person who is having difficulty enforcing an emergency protection order.

"recovery order" (r 4(4)(*d*))—A recovery order is an order under CA 1989, s 50 for the recovery of a child who has been abducted, run away, etc.

"warrant under section 102(1)" (r 4(4)(*e*))—This refers to a warrant authorising a constable to assist a person who is having difficulty enforcing various powers under the CA 1989 (for example, the power to inspect children who are in children's homes or who are accommodated by voluntary organisations).

"leave of the justices' clerk" (r 4(4))—The requirement to obtain leave from the justices' clerk before an application is made ex parte is in contrast to the position in the High Court and county courts where an ex parte application may be launched without preliminaries. Given the urgency that usually attends ex parte applications, there may not be time for much formality in seeking leave and a telephone call to the justices' clerk may be all that is possible.

Ex parte applications by telephone—Although r 4(4) does not expressly mention telephone applications in the way that FPR 1991, r 4.4(4) does, there is nothing that dictates that a face to face hearing with a magistrate is required. In an appropriate case, therefore, the justices' clerk could give leave by telephone, dispense with the need to file the application form at the time of the application and give directions as to filing at a later time and put the applicant in telephone contact with a magistrate who could grant the ex parte order.

Ex parte application on notice—Although no provision is made for it in the Rules, a procedure has evolved, as a matter of practice and fairness, whereby an ex parte application can be made on informal notice (see eg *Croydon LBC v A (No 3)* [1992] 2 FLR 350). This procedure must not be used, however, as a way of getting what should be a proper inter partes hearing more quickly than would otherwise be the case.

Application on short notice as alternative to ex parte application—Where possible, it is preferable for an application to be served and for notice to be abridged (see r 8) than for an ex parte application to be made (see eg *Re B (A Minor) (Residence Order: Ex Parte)* [1992] 2 FLR 1, CA).

"application for an order under s 75(1)" (r 4(4)(ii))—Note that s 75(1) has been repealed and replaced by s 79K (see Care Standards Act 2000, s 79(1)). The new provision in s 79K provides for the emergency cancellation or variation of a childminder's registration in order to protect a child or children from significant harm; this can be done without notice to the childminder concerned. However, it is suggested that such an application should normally be determined with appropriate notice to the childminder in accordance with s 79L (see *R v St Albans Magistrates' Court ex parte J* [1993] Fam Law 518 for the principles applied under the pre-existing law).

6 Transfer of proceedings

(1) Where, in any relevant proceedings, the justices' chief executive or the court receives a request in writing from a party that the proceedings be transferred to another family proceedings court or to a county court, the justices' chief executive or court shall issue an order or certificate in the appropriate form in Schedule 1 to these Rules, granting or refusing the request in accordance with any Order made by the Lord Chancellor under Part I of Schedule 11.

(2) Where a request is granted under paragraph (1), the justices' chief executive shall send a copy of the order –

(*a*) to the parties,
(*b*) to any children's guardian, and
(*c*) to the family proceedings court or to the county court to which the proceedings are to be transferred.

(3) Any consent given or refused by a justices' clerk in accordance with any Order made by the Lord Chancellor under Part I of Schedule 11 shall be recorded in writing by the justices' clerk at the time it is given or refused or as soon as practicable thereafter.

(4) Where a request to transfer proceedings to a county court is refused under paragraph (1), the person who made the request may apply in accordance with rule 4.6 of the Family Proceedings Rules 1991 for an order under any Order made by the Lord Chancellor under Part I of Schedule 11.

Amendments—SI 1994/3156; SI 2001/615; SI 2001/818.

Defined terms—"court", "children's guardian", "justices clerk", "parties": r 1(2); "relevant proceedings": r 1(2), CA 1989, s 93(3).

"an order or certificate" (r 6(1))—Where the request for transfer is refused, the justices' clerk or the court must issue a certificate in Form C50 giving the reasons for the refusal. If appropriate, an application to a county court for transfer can then follow in accordance with FPR 1991, r 4.6. Where the request for transfer is granted, it is not a certificate but an order that the court or justices' clerk issues and this must be in Form C49, setting out the reasons for the transfer.

"any order under Part I of Schedule 11" (r 6(1), (4))—Children (Allocation of Proceedings) Order 1991, arts 6 (transfer between magistrates' courts), 7 and 8 (transfer to a county court by order of the magistrates' court) are relevant to the reference in r 6(1); art 9 is relevant to the reference in r 6(4).

"send" (r 6(2))—This term is not defined and does not seem to attract r 8 (service of documents).

FPR 1991, r 4.6 (r 6(4))—This rule sets out the procedure by which an application can be made to a county court to pluck proceedings from the magistrates' court under Children (Allocation of Proceedings) Order 1991, art 9. Article 9 and FPR 1991, r 4.6 enables any party to make the application to the county court. It is therefore submitted that r 6(4) does not restrict the ability to make such an application to "the person who made the request".

Own motion procedure—Rule 6(1) and (2) applies only where a party applies for a transfer order. Children (Allocation of Proceedings) Order 1991, art 7(1) expressly enables the court to order a transfer to a county court of its own motion and this is implicit in arts 6 and 8. Where the court or a clerk wishes to make such a transfer they are likely to act by way of a direction under r 14(2)(*h*).

7 Parties

(1) The respondents to relevant proceedings shall be those persons set out in the relevant entry in column (iii) of Schedule 2 to these Rules.

(2) In any relevant proceedings a person may file a request in Form C2 that he or another person –

(*a*) be joined as a party, or
(*b*) cease to be a party.

(3) On considering a request under paragraph (2) the court shall, subject to paragraph (4) –

(*a*) grant it without a hearing or representations, save that this shall be done only in the case of a request under paragraph (2)(*a*), whereupon the justices' chief executive shall inform the parties and the person making the request of that decision, or
(*b*) order that a date be fixed for the consideration of the request, whereupon the justices' chief executive shall give notice of the date so fixed, together with a copy of the request –
   (i) in the case of a request under paragraph (2)(*a*), to the applicant, and
   (ii) in the case of a request under paragraph (2)(*b*), to the parties, or
(*c*) invite the parties or any of them to make written representations, within a specified period, as to whether the request should be granted; and upon the expiry of the period the court shall act in accordance with sub-paragraph (*a*) or (*b*).

(4) Where a person with parental responsibility requests that he be joined under paragraph (2)(*a*), the court shall grant his request.

(5) In any relevant proceedings the court may direct –

(*a*) that a person who would not otherwise be a respondent under these Rules be joined as a party to the proceedings, or
(*b*) that a party to the proceedings cease to be a party.

Amendments—SI 1994/3156; SI 2001/615.

Defined terms—"applicant", "court", "file", "justices' chief executive", "justices' clerk": r 1(2); "parental responsibility": r 1(2), CA 1989, s 3; "parties": r 1(2); "relevant proceedings": r 1(2), CA 1989, s 93(3).

Factors in decision whether to join or discharge a party—There is no guidance in the rules or CA 1989 as to the factors that the court should take into account in making decisions about parties. For detailed discussion of the factors to be considered see under FPR 1991, r 4.7.

Joinder of child as respondent—Where a child seeks to make an application concerning himself, he must seek leave under CA 1989, s 10. In certain situations, the child is automatically a respondent to proceedings begun by others, notably where the proceedings are specified (see CA 1989, s 41) as for example proceedings for a care order or an emergency protection order (see FPC(CA 1989)R 1991, Sch 2). Where this is not the case, a child who seeks to become a respondent must apply to be joined as a party as would any adult party. This was the course adopted by a 9-year-old girl in *Re N (A Minor)* (unreported) 25 September 1997, CA, in relation to her father's application for contact with her. By analogy with the situation where a child seeks leave under CA 1989, s 10 to commence proceedings, it seems likely that applications by children to be joined as respondents should be transferred to the higher courts (see **Court to which the leave request should be made** under r 3).

Separate representation of parties—For a discussion of the relevant case-law see under FPR 1991, r 4.7.

Children as parties where separately represented—As to whether there is jurisdiction to order separate representation for children who are the subject of proceedings without adding them as parties, see *L v L (Minors) (Separate Representation)* [1994] 1 FLR 156.

"request in Form C2" (r 7(2))—The request should be made in prescribed Form C2. The reasons for the request should be set out as cogently as possible and, where the person making a request to be joined as a party has parental responsibility, this should be clearly stated as it will entitle him to have his request granted as of right (r 7(4)). The rule is wide enough to entitle a person to request that someone else be joined or cease to be a party. So, for example, where a respondent's interest in the proceedings has come to an end, perhaps because the child ceased to live with him some time ago, the applicant may apply for him to be removed as a party. Where the request is by one person that another be joined as a party, r 7 makes no provision for him to be consulted in advance as to his views, with the result that a person might find himself a party to proceedings without knowing of the possibility in advance. Bearing in mind that participation in proceedings can have serious financial and other implications, the court should be alive to this danger and make what enquiries it can as to the willingness of the person concerned to be a party.

Granting request without a hearing (r 7(3)(*a*))—Only a request to be joined as a party may be granted without a hearing and without consultation with the other parties. Where an existing party requests that he should cease to be a party, the other parties must either be invited to make written representations on the subject under r 7(3)(*c*) or have the opportunity to make representations on or prior to the date fixed for consideration of the request under r 7(3)(*b*).

Fixing a date for consideration of the request (r 7(3)(*b*))—It is clear that decisions as to the joinder or withdrawal of parties are the province of the court itself rather than of the justices' clerk, but r 7(3)(*b*) does not stipulate what form the consideration of the request to be joined as or cease to be a party should take. A hearing is not expressly mentioned in r 7(3)(*b*) itself but it is implicit in the requirement that notice of the date fixed be given to the parties and in the general terms of r 7(3) that some form of hearing is envisaged. However any party who did not wish to attend could presumably send his representations to the court in writing instead.

"within a specified period" (r 7(3)(*c*))—For provisions as to time, see r 15. If the period specified by the court for the making of representations is inadequate, an extension should be sought under r 14(2).

Obligations under r 21—Rule 21(5), (6) applies to a decision whether or not to grant a request under r 7; the magistrates must set out the principal matters that exercise them in coming to their decision, even on an application where no evidence is called (*North Yorkshire County Council v G* [1993] 2 FLR 732).

Own motion procedure (r 7(5))—Rule 7(5) empowers the court to make an order joining a new party or discharging an existing party of its own motion.

8 Service

(1) Where service of a document is required by these Rules (and not by a provision to which section 105(8) (service of notice or other document under the Act) applies) it may be effected –

- (*a*) if the person to be served is not known by the person serving to be acting by solicitor –
  - (i) by delivering it to him personally, or
  - (ii) by delivering it at, or by sending it by first-class post to, his residence or his last known residence, or
- (*b*) if the person to be served is known by the person serving to be acting by solicitor –
  - (i) by delivering the document at, or sending it by first-class post to, the solicitor's address for service,
  - (ii) where the solicitor's address for service includes a numbered box at a document exchange, by leaving the document at that document exchange or at a document exchange which transmits documents on every business day to that document exchange, or
  - (iii) by sending a legible copy of the document by facsimile transmission to the solicitor's office.

(2) In this rule, "first-class post" means first-class post which has been pre-paid or in respect of which pre-payment is not required.

(3) Where a child who is a party to any relevant proceedings is required by these Rules to serve a document, service shall be effected by –

(*a*) the solicitor acting for the child,
(*b*) where there is no such solicitor, the children's guardian, or
(*c*) where there is neither such a solicitor nor a children's guardian, the justices' chief executive.

(4) Service of any document on a child shall, subject to any direction of the justices' clerk or the court, be effected by service on –

(*a*) the solicitor acting for the child,
(*b*) where there is no such solicitor, the children's guardian, or
(*c*) where there is neither such a solicitor nor a children's guardian, with leave of the justices' clerk or the court, the child.

(5) Where the justices' clerk or the court refuses leave under paragraph (4)(*c*), a direction shall be given under paragraph (8).

(6) A document shall, unless the contrary is proved, be deemed to have been served –

(*a*) in the case of service by first-class post, on the second business day after posting, and
(*b*) in the case of service in accordance with paragraph (1)(*b*)(ii), on the second business day after the day on which it is left at the document exchange.

(7) At or before the first directions appointment in, or hearing of, relevant proceedings, whichever occurs first, the applicant shall file a statement in Form C9 that service of –

(*a*) a copy of the application and other documents referred to in rule 4(1)(*b*) has been effected on each respondent, and
(*b*) notice of the proceedings has been effected under rule 4(3);

and the statement shall indicate –

(i) the manner, date, time and place of service, or
(ii) where service was effected by post, the date, time and place of posting.

(8) In any relevant proceedings, where these rules require a document to be served, the court or the justices' clerk may, without prejudice to any power under rule 14, direct that –

(*a*) the requirement shall not apply;
(*b*) the time specified by the rules for complying with the requirement shall be abridged to such extent as may be specified in the direction;
(*c*) service shall be effected in such manner as may be specified in the direction.

Amendments—SI 1992/2068; SI 1994/3156; SI 2001/615; SI 2001/818.

Defined terms—"business day", "child", "court", "directions appointment", "children's guardian", "justices' clerk", "leave", "parties": r 1(2); "relevant proceedings": r 1(2), CA 1989, s 93(3).

Documents—"document" is not defined in the rules. In this rule it is clearly used in a wide sense to include such documents as a copy of the application itself, any written statement of evidence under r 17(1)(*a*) and experts' reports under r 17(1)(*b*). In contrast the term has a rather narrower ambit in r 17(1)(*b*).

"section 105(8)" (r 8(1))—Certain service requirements derive from CA 1989 itself rather from these rules (for example service of a copy of a residence order before enforcement under CA 1989, s 14). Where this is so, s 105(8) (which is more restrictive than r 8) governs service. In the more usual case where the requirement for service derives from these rules, this rule applies.

"if the person to be served is not known ... to be acting by solicitor" (r 8(1)(*a*))—This covers both the situation where it is known that the person to be served has no solicitor and the situation where there is uncertainty as to whether he has or not. Presumably it also applies where it is known that the person to be served has a solicitor but not which firm is acting so that service in accordance with r 8(1)(*b*) is impossible.

Service by fax—Although r 8(6) provides for presumptions as to when a posted document or one left at a document exchange will be taken to have been served, it does not make any provision with regard to a faxed document. In the higher courts, RSC Ord 65, r 5(2B) applies to the effect that, unless the contrary is shown, the date of service of a document faxed before 4 pm on a business day will be deemed to be the day of transmission and in any other case the business day next following. There being no equivalent provision for magistrates' courts, it is suggested that a similar principle should apply.

Service by a child (r 8(3))—As to the duty of the child's solicitor and children's guardian to carry out service on behalf of the child, see rr 12(2) and 11(8).

Service on a child (r 8(4))—As to the duty of the child's solicitor and children's guardian to accept service on behalf of the child and to advise him, if he has sufficient understanding, of the contents of the documents, see rr 12(2) and 11(8). Where there is an application for leave to serve the child, r 3 does not apply as it is confined to applications for leave to commence proceedings. No doubt leave to serve on a child may most conveniently be sought by means of a directions application under r 14, which expressly empowers the justices' clerk or court to give directions as to service (r 14(2)(*e*)). If leave is refused, the justices' clerk or court will give a direction under r 8(8) (r 8(5)). For a case in which the court deemed it inappropriate for the child to be served, see *Re J (A Minor) (Change of Name)* [1993] 1 FLR 699.

"Unless the contrary is proved" (r 8(6))—As, for example, where the document is returned undelivered (see *R v London County Quarter Sessions Appeals Committee ex parte Rossi* [1956] 1 QB 682, [1956] 2 WLR 800). If a document is proved to have been received before the date specified in r 8(6), the date of service is the actual date of receipt (*Hodgson v Hart District Council* [1986] 1 WLR 317, [1986] 1 All ER 400).

"statement in Form C9" (r 8(7))—Form C9 requires the applicant to give details of service of the application on each of the other parties, and to give details of service on persons to whom notice has to be given in accordance with column (iv) of Sch 2 to these rules. The details must include the manner, date, time and place of service; where service was effected by post, the date, time and place of posting must be given.

"each respondent" (r 8(7)(*a*))—As to who the respondents are, see r 7.

Notice under r 4(3) (r 8(7)(*b*))—Rule 4(3) obliges the applicant to serve notice in Form C6A of the proceedings and of the date and place of the first hearing or appointment on the persons set out in column (iv) of Sch 2 to these rules.

Directions under r 8(8)—Such a direction would no doubt be sought in accordance with the procedure set out in r 14; r 8(8) permits the justices' clerk or the court to dispense with service or to dictate an alternative means of service. Where a party seeks a direction for leave not to serve a person with proceedings (where service is otherwise required by Sch 2), r 8(8) confers on the court a general discretion to direct that the rule as to service should be disapplied. In exercising that discretion, the welfare of the child is not the paramount consideration, although it is an important consideration (*Re X (Care: Notice of Proceedings)* [1996] 1 FLR 186 – where the court was entitled to consider, quite independently of the welfare of the child, the effect on the child's family which would be likely if notice of the public law proceedings were to be served on the putative father. The court considered per curiam that, in a case where service of proceedings would give rise to a very real danger of serious violence, the court would have a discretion to direct that notice of proceedings need not be served on a particular individual, notwithstanding that service would otherwise be required under the rules). Where a child instructed a solicitor separately from the guardian and that solicitor only became aware of the applications before the court on the day of the hearing, the court could dispense with service upon that solicitor where the child herself had been properly informed and consulted about the proceedings the previous day (*Re C (Secure Accommodation Order: Representation)* [2001] 2 FLR 169).

9 Acknowledgement of application

Within 14 days of service of an application for a section 8 order or an application under Schedule 1, each respondent shall file and serve on the parties an acknowledgement of the application in Form C7.

Amendments—SI 1994/3156.

Defined terms—"application", "form", "parties": r 1(2); "section 8 order": CA 1989, s 8(2).

"section 8 order"—Section 8 orders are contact orders, prohibited steps orders, residence orders, specific issue orders and orders varying or discharging any such order (CA 1989, s 8(2)).

"Within 14 days of service"—As to the computation and extension of time, see r 15.

Service—See r 8.

Parties—See r 7.

Form C7—Each respondent to an application for a s 8 order or an order under CA 1989, Sch 1 must serve on the other parties to the proceedings an acknowledgement in Form C7. Form C7 requires the respondent to give details identifying himself and his solicitor (if he has one) and to give an address to which correspondence may be sent. The respondent must state when he received the application, whether he opposes it, and whether he intends to apply to the court for an order. If the respondent indicates that he does wish to apply for an order himself, that indication is not tantamount to making the application, which must be launched using an application form in the normal way (see r 4). Form C7 allows only a small space in which the respondent says whether he opposes the application. He is not invited to give his side of the picture at this early stage. This is deliberate, since in s 8 cases the filing of evidence and giving of information is strictly controlled (see r 17(4), (5)). However, if the applicant has asked the court to order the respondent to make a payment for a child under CA 1989, Sch 1, the respondent must also fill in a statement of his financial means in Form C10A.

"Schedule 1"—CA 1989, Sch 1 contains provisions with regard to financial provision for children.

Acknowledgements in other cases and answers—This rule does not contain any provision for a respondent who does not fall within the rule to file an acknowledgement, nor does it expressly permit (as r 4.9, the equivalent provision in FPR 1991, does) the filing of an answer in cases other than an application for leave to commence proceedings or for a s 8 order. In s 8 cases, the combination of r 9 and r 17(4) effectively prevents the filing of an answer without leave. However, with this one exception, the rules do not contain anything that prohibits the filing of an acknowledgement or answer and it appears that a respondent, even if not obliged to do so by r 9, could take this course where appropriate, also serving the document on the other parties.

10 Appointment of children's guardian

(1) As soon as practicable after the commencement of specified proceedings or the transfer of such proceedings to the court, the justices' clerk or the court shall appoint a children's guardian unless –

(*a*) such an appointment has already been made by the court which made the transfer and is subsisting, or (*b*) the justices' clerk or the court considers that such an appointment is not necessary to safeguard the interests of the child.

(2) At any stage in specified proceedings a party may apply, without notice to the other parties unless the justices' clerk or the court otherwise directs, for the appointment of a children's guardian.

(3) The justices' clerk or the court shall grant an application under paragraph (2) unless it is considered that such an appointment is not necessary to safeguard the interests of the child, in which case reasons shall be given; and a note of such reasons shall be taken by the justices' clerk.

(4) At any stage in specified proceedings the justices' clerk or the court may appoint a children's guardian even though no application is made for such an appointment.

(4A) The justices' chief executive or the court may, in specified proceedings, appoint more than one children's guardian in respect of the same child.

(5) The justices' chief executive shall, as soon as practicable, notify the parties and any welfare officer or children and family reporter of an appointment under this rule or, as the case may be, of a decision not to make such an appointment.

(6) Upon the appointment of a children's guardian the justices' chief executive shall, as soon as practicable, notify him of the appointment and serve on him copies of the application and of documents filed under rule 17(1).

(7) A children's guardian appointed by the justices' chief executive or by the court under this rule shall not –

(*a*) be a member, officer or servant of a local authority which, or an authorised person (within the meaning of section 31(9)) who, is a party to the proceedings;

(*b*) be, or have been, a member, officer or servant of a local authority or voluntary organisation (within the meaning of section 105(1)) who has been directly concerned in that capacity in arrangements relating to the care, accommodation or welfare of the child during the five years prior to the commencement of the proceedings; or

(*c*) be a serving probation officer who has, in that capacity, been previously concerned with the child or his family.

(8) When appointing a children's guardian, the justices' clerk or the court shall consider the appointment of anyone who has previously acted as children's guardian of the same child.

(9) The appointment of a children's guardian under this rule shall continue for such time as is specified in the appointment or until terminated by the court.

(10) When terminating an appointment in accordance with paragraph (9), the court shall give reasons in writing for so doing, a note of which shall be taken by the justices' clerk.

(11) Where the justices' clerk or the court appoints a children's guardian in accordance with this rule or refuses to make such an appointment, the justices' clerk shall record the appointment or refusal in the appropriate form in Schedule 1 to these Rules.

Amendments—SI 2001/615; SI 2001/818.

Defined terms—"application", "child", "court", "children's guardian", "justices' clerk": CA 1989, s 41(6) and r 2(2); "note", "parties": r 1(2); "specified proceedings", "voluntary organisation": CA 1989, s 105(1); "welfare officer or children and family reporter": r 1(2).

Appointment—The obligation to appoint a children's guardian in specified proceedings unless the circumstances are as described in r 10(1)(*b*) is imposed by CA 1989, s 41(1). The purpose of r 10(1) is to require the appointment to be made as soon as practicable after the commencement of the proceedings, or the arrival of transferred proceedings if the transferring court or clerk has not already made an appointment. The appointment is likely to be made by way of a direction under r 14(2)(*d*) (which can be done quickly and without a hearing as long as the parties are given the opportunity to make written representations; this would have the advantage of enabling the guardian to be in place in time to attend the first actual directions appointment). Where proceedings in which a guardian has already been appointed are transferred, the appointment will continue to subsist unless terminated in accordance with this rule (r 10(1)(*a*)). Curiously, r 10(1)(*a*) refers only to the court which made the transfer, which seems to produce the strange result that where proceedings are transferred to a third court it is apparently required to appoint a guardian if the existing one had been appointed by the first court rather than by the second one (for example, where a justices' clerk had appointed a guardian before transferring the proceedings to a county court under Children (Allocation of Proceedings) Order 1991, art 7, and the county court had later transferred the proceedings down to a different magistrates' court under art 11). In such circumstances, the third court may wish, as a purely formal step, to issue a new Form C47 appointing the existing guardian to avoid any doubt about whether the rule has been breached.

The focus on "commencement" and "transfer" in r 10(1)(*a*) seems inappropriate for some types of specified proceedings. Any non-specified family proceedings will become "specified" at any time while they are pending if a direction under s 37(1) (investigation of the child's circumstances) is given or if the court begins to consider making a s 8 order in respect of a child who is in care (see CA 1989, s 41(6)(*b*), (*e*)). In those circumstances the requirement really means as soon as practicable after the proceedings become specified. In view of the requirement of r 10(1), the application procedure and own motion power provided by r 10(2)–(4) will need to be invoked only where the court or a party thinks that the initial decision that a children's guardian was unnecessary has proved to be too optimistic in the light of the development of the proceedings during their interlocutory stages, or where the first guardian has died or been removed under this rule.

Appointment not necessary (r 10(1)(*b*))—See eg *Re J (A Minor) (Change of Name)* [1993] 1 FLR 699 and see further **"direction under s 37(1)"** under CA 1989, s 41.

Who may be appointed—Rule 10(7)(*a*) and (*b*) makes provision which may make individuals ineligible for selection to act as children's guardian in particular proceedings if they have a close connection with the local authority concerned in the case or with any local authority if they have actually been involved with arrangements for the child in that capacity within the previous five years. Rule 10(7)(*c*) excludes probation officers unless they have not been involved with the child or his family in that capacity (see *Devon CC and Others v S and Others* [1993] 1 FLR 842, where a welfare officer (children and family reporter) from previous proceedings was ineligible on account of being a probation officer). Rule 10(8) requires the court or the clerk to consider re-appointing anyone who has acted as the children's guardian in previous proceedings; the requirement is to do no more than consider re-appointing such a person but the clerk or court will usually lean in favour of such a re-appointment as previous knowledge of the child and the earlier proceedings will tend to increase the guardian's competence and safeguard the child's interests in the new proceedings. In *Re M (Minors) (Judicial Continuity)* [1993] 1 FLR 903, the Court of Appeal emphasised the desirability of judicial continuity in family cases. The fact that a judge had had to express firm views about one of the parties in an earlier hearing did not disqualify him from considering subsequent applications between the same parties. In view of the wording in r 10(8), it would seem likely that the courts will adopt a similar approach to the appointment, as children's guardian in care proceedings, of a person who had previously acted as children's guardian.

Duration of appointment—When appointing a guardian, the clerk or the court may specify the length of the appointment; otherwise the appointment will last until terminated by the court (r 10(9), and see *Re CE (Section 37 Direction)* [1995] 1 FLR 26, FD). The latter will be the more usual course. No procedure is specified to terminate an appointment, except to require that the reasons be given and noted once the decision has been taken (r 10(10)); this is in contrast with the provision made by r 12(3) and (4) in relation to the child's solicitor. Rule 14(2)(*d*) specifically mentions the appointment of a guardian as something that may be dealt with under the direction-making procedure and it is submitted that this embraces the termination of such an appointment. The matter is complicated in these rules because the justices' clerk and those authorised under r 32 may exercise the direction-giving power under r 14 and, although the justices' clerk or substitute under r 32 may appoint a children's guardian and exercise most of the functions of the court under this rule, only the court may remove a children's guardian under r 10(9). It is submitted that the termination may be dealt with as a direction subject to that restriction. On that basis, r 14(3)(*a*) would require the parties to be consulted first. Usually, this would enable the children's guardian to make his own views known, but, where the child's solicitor is taking his instructions directly from the child (see r 12(1)(*a*)), it is suggested that the court should allow the guardian to make representations before removing him altogether. This procedure was followed in *Re M (Terminating Appointment of Guardian ad Litem)* [1999] 2 FLR 717. Wall J was quite clear in *Re CE (Section 37 Directions)*, above, that the termination of a guardian's appointment where the appointment originally depended on s 41(6)(*b*) and the proceedings had since ceased to be specified should be carried out by the court only after the court has given the matter due consideration and heard representations from the guardian and the other parties. He suggested that it should accordingly be the practice, where an appointment was made by virtue of s 41(6)(*b*), for the order making the appointment to contain a direction that the question of the guardian's continuing involvement be reviewed on completion of the s 37 report and for a directions appointment to be fixed for a date shortly after the date on which the s 37 report was due to be received by the court.

Derivative applications, such as those to discharge a care order or to regulate contact with a child in care, are separate proceedings and not a continuation of the original care proceedings for this purpose (see the structure of s 41(6)); therefore the original guardian's appointment will not automatically carry over into the new proceedings. Indeed, once a care order is made, the guardian ad litem (children's guardian) has no function in relation to the way in which the local authority acts under the order, and the court has no power to add a direction to a care order that the guardian ad litem (children's guardian) should continue his involvement with the child (*Kent County Council v C* [1993] 1 FLR 308). Similarly, it seems that, where a guardian ad litem (children's guardian) has been appointed for the purposes of an emergency protection order, she is no longer the guardian ad litem (children's guardian) when the emergency protection order has expired and there are no pending proceedings (*Re M (Prohibited Steps Order: Application for Leave)* [1993] 1 FLR 275). A literal reading of r 10(9) would seem to suggest that a magistrates' court cannot remove a guardian who was appointed by a county court or the High Court before the proceedings were transferred to it because the appointment would not have been made "under this rule" but under FPR 1991, r 4.10; however, it is submitted that there is scope for construing the provision to include such cases.

Where interests of children conflict—There is usually no reason why a guardian ad litem (children's guardian) should not properly represent children whose interests conflict (*Re T and E (Proceedings: Conflicting Interests)* [1995] 1 FLR 581, FD).

Appointment of second guardian—Rule 10(4) allows the appointment of a second children's guardian in specified proceedings where the particular circumstances of the case require it, for example where additional enquiries need to be undertaken in an area that is a considerable distance from the court hearing area they may be carried out by a local children's guardian.

"notify" (r 10(5), (6))—The manner of notification does not seem to be regulated; r 8 (service of documents) does not seem to apply.

"authorised person" (r 10(7)(*a*))—CA 1989, s 31(9) provides that "authorised person" means the NSPCC and any of its officers and any person (or the officers of any body) authorised by the Secretary of State to bring proceedings under s 31 (ie for a care or supervision order).

Refusal to make an appointment (r 10(11))—The concept of a refusal imports a request to act in the way refused, but it is submitted that it is appropriate for the prescribed form to be completed not only where the clerk or the court refuses an application under r 10(2) but also where the court initially decides not to make an appointment under r 10(1). The court may then comply with r 10(5) by despatching a copy of the form.

"the appropriate form in Schedule 1" (r 10(11))—The appropriate form is C47.

PART III

11 Powers and duties of officers of the service

(1) In carrying out his duty under section 7(1)(*a*) or section 41(2), the officer of the service shall have regard to the principle set out in section 1(2) and the matters set out in section 1(3)(*a*) to (*f*) as if for the word "court" in that section there were substituted the words "officer of the service".

(2) The officer of the service shall make such investigations as may be necessary for him to carry out his duties and shall, in particular –

(*a*) contact or seek to interview such persons as he thinks appropriate or as the court directs;

(*b*) obtain such professional assistance as is available to him which he thinks appropriate or which the justices' clerk or the court directs him to obtain.

(3) In addition to his duties, under other paragraphs of this rule, or rules 11A or 11B, the officer of the service shall provide to the justices' chief executive, the justices' clerk and the court such other assistance as he or it may require.

(4) A party may question the officer of the service about oral or written advice tendered by him to the justices' chief executive, the justices' clerk or the court under this rule.

Amendments—SI 2001/818.

Defined terms—"application", "child", "court", "directions appointment", "children's guardian", "justices' clerk", "note", "parties": r 1(2); "officer of the service": CJCSA 2000, s 11(3).

"the principle set out in section 1(2)" (r 11(1))—As modified by r 11(1) for this purpose, CA 1989, s 1(2) provides that "In any proceedings in which any question with respect to the upbringing of a child arises, the officer of the service shall have regard to the general principle that any delay in determining the question is likely to prejudice the welfare of the child.".

"the matters set out in section 1(3)(a) to (f)" (r 11(1))—This rule makes it clear that officers of the service must have regard to the welfare checklist when carrying out all aspects of their duties under s 41(2); see CA 1989, s 1(3)(*a*)–(*f*).

"professional assistance" (r 11(2)(*b*))—This term is not defined but includes the services of all types of expert witness.

Questioning the officer of the service (r 11(4))—In the case of written advice, this right would crystallise at the hearing at which the issue addressed by the advice (be it interim or final) is to be considered; however, if a pre-trial directions appointment is held after the report becomes available, it may assist the clarification of the issues to be dealt with at the full hearing if the parties question the guardian at the appointment.

Comparison of roles of children's guardian and children and family reporter—In *Re S (A Minor) (Guardian ad Litem/Welfare Officer)* [1993] 1 FLR 110, it was held that, although the power exists both at first instance (CA 1989, s 7) and on appeal (ss 7, 94(5)) to appoint a welfare officer or children and family reporter in public law proceedings, such an appointment should not be made when (as will normally be the case) a children's guardian has already been appointed, save in exceptional circumstances. Rule 11 sets out powers and duties shared by all officers of the service. Rule 11A gives the children's guardian additional powers which reflect the guardian's extra duty to represent the child in court and to instruct legal representation for the child if necessary. Rule 11B sets out additional powers and duties of a children and family reporter who is to provide a report under CA 1989, s 7(1)(*a*) and enables the reporter to consider whether the child should be a party to the proceedings and to notify the court should he feel that is necessary. In *L v L (Minors) (Separate Representation)* [1994] 1 FLR 156, however, whilst not dissenting from the general principle in *Re S (A Minor) (Guardian ad Litem/Welfare Officer)* (above), the Court of Appeal hoped that the court welfare officer (children and family reporter), who had already begun investigations in a difficult case, would report despite the appointment of a children's guardian to represent the children.

11A Additional powers and duties of children's guardian

(1) The children's guardian shall –

(*a*) appoint a solicitor to represent the child unless such a solicitor has already been appointed; and

(*b*) give such advice to the child as is appropriate having regard to his understanding and, subject to rule 12(1)(*a*), instruct the solicitor representing the child on all matters relevant to the interests of the child including possibilities for appeal, arising in the course of the proceedings.

(2) Where it appears to the children's guardian that the child –

(*a*) is instructing his solicitor direct, or

(*b*) intends to conduct and is capable of conducting the proceedings on his own behalf,

he shall inform the court through the justices' chief executive and from then he –

(i) shall perform all of his duties set out in rule 11 and this rule, other than duties under paragraph (1)(*a*) of this rule, and such other duties as the justices' clerk or the court may direct;

(ii) shall take such part in the proceedings as the justices' clerk or the court may direct; and

(iii) may, with leave of the justices' clerk or the court, have legal representation in the conduct of those duties.

(3) Unless excused by the justices' clerk or the court, the children's guardian shall attend all directions appointments in and hearings of the proceedings and shall advise the court on the following matters –

(*a*) whether the child is of sufficient understanding for any purpose including the child's refusal to submit to a medical or psychiatric examination or other assessment that the court has the power to require, direct or order;

(*b*) the wishes of the child in respect of any matter relevant to the proceedings including his attendance at court;

(*c*) the appropriate forum for the proceedings;

(*d*) the appropriate timing of the proceedings or any part of them;

(*e*) the options available to it in respect of the child and the suitability of each such option including what order should be made in determining the application; and

(*f*) any other matter concerning which the justices' chief executive, the justices' clerk or the court seeks his advice or concerning which he considers that the justices' chief executive, the justices' clerk or the court should be informed.

(4) The advice given under paragraph (3) may, subject to any order of the court, be given orally or in writing; and if the advice be given orally, a note of it shall be taken by the justices' clerk or the court.

(5) The children's guardian shall, where practicable, notify any person whose joinder as a party to those proceedings would be likely, in the opinion of the officer of the service, to safeguard the interests of the child of that person's right to apply to be joined under rule 7(2) and shall inform the justices' chief executive or the court –

(*a*) of any such notification given;

(*b*) of anyone whom he attempted to notify under this paragraph but was unable to contact; and

(*c*) of anyone whom he believes may wish to be joined to the proceedings.

(6) The children's guardian shall, unless the justices' clerk or the court otherwise directs, not less than 14 days before the date fixed for the final hearing of the proceedings –

(*a*) file a written report advising on the interests of the child;
(*b*) serve a copy of the filed report on the other parties.

(7) The children's guardian shall serve and accept service of documents on behalf of the child in accordance with rule 8(3)(*b*) and (4)(*b*) and, where the child has not himself been served, and has sufficient understanding, advise the child of the contents of any document so served.

(8) If the children's guardian inspects records of the kinds referred to in section 42, he shall bring to the attention of –

(*a*) the court, through the justices' chief executive; and
(*b*) unless the court or the justices' clerk otherwise directs, the other parties to the proceedings,

all records and documents which may, in his opinion, assist in the proper determination of the proceedings.

(9) The children's guardian shall ensure that, in relation to a decision made by the justices' clerk or the court in the proceedings –

(*a*) if he considers it appropriate to the age and understanding of the child, the child is notified of that decision; and
(*b*) if the child is notified of the decision, it is explained to the child in a manner appropriate to his age and understanding.

Amendments—Inserted by SI 2001/818.

Duties of children's guardian—CA 1989, s 41(2)(*b*) places the children's guardian under a duty to safeguard the interests of the child in the manner prescribed by rules of court. This rule prescribes how this general duty is to be performed. In *R v Cornwall County Council ex parte Cornwall and Isles of Scilly Guardians ad Litem and Reporting Officers Panel* [1992] 1 WLR 427, it was emphasised that guardians ad litem are independent in the performance of their duties; and it was accordingly held that a local authority had acted unlawfully in seeking to restrict the number of hours spent by guardians on each individual case. If a care order is made, the guardian ad litem (children's guardian) has no function in relation to the way in which the local authority acts under the order, and the court cannot direct any continuing involvement by the guardian ad litem (children's guardian) (*Kent County Council v C* [1993] 1 FLR 308).

The guardian may find himself requested to act as a collator of expert reports and to produce a schedule for the court of the areas of agreement and dispute (*Re C (Expert Evidence: Disclosure: Practice)* [1995] 1 FLR 204).

Public interest immunity—Where an issue arises as to whether, because of public interest immunity, certain material (often material in the possession of the local authority) should or should not be disclosed, guidance as to the procedure to be followed can be derived from *Re C (Expert Evidence: Disclosure: Practice)* [1995] 1 FLR 204, noted further in **Public interest immunity** under r 17.

"subject to r 12(1)(a)" (r 11A(1)(*b*))—Rule 12(1)(*a*) allows the solicitor to take instructions direct from the child where the child is capable, having regard to his understanding, to give them.

Child's understanding—See annotation under FPR 1991, r 4.12.

"he shall inform the court" (r 11A(2))—Where it appears to the guardian ad litem (children's guardian) that the child is instructing his solicitor direct or intends to, and is capable of, conducting the proceedings on his own behalf, he should inform the court of the relevant circumstances on a directions appointment (*Re M (Minors) (Care Proceedings: Child's Wishes)* [1994] 1 FLR 749). This means that he should either report the matter to the court at the next directions appointment or, if there is no such appointment fixed, immediately take out an appointment for directions so that the question of representation can be considered and decided by the court. Wall J set out in *Re M (Minors) (Care Proceedings: Child's Wishes)* (above) the reasons why the involvement of the court and the other parties is so important: (1) there may be an issue about the capacity of the child to give coherent and consistent instructions, and expert evidence may be required to resolve the issue; (2) the court has a duty to ensure that the proceedings are disposed of promptly and in the most effective manner; (3) the other parties, particularly the child's parents, have a right to know at an early stage how their child is to be represented in the proceedings and what view their child is expressing; and (4) it is important for the court to know in advance whether or not the child and the children's guardian are to be separately represented so that the court, when reading the papers in advance, can be alert to all issues.

Guardian detached from child (r 11A(2))—Where the child's solicitor is taking instructions from the child himself (see r 12(1)), the role of the children's guardian is wholly in the discretion of the clerk or the court. The clerk or the court may feel that it would be beneficial, particularly if the detachment occurred at a late stage in the course of the proceedings, for the guardian to have full liberty to present a case as if he were a party to the proceedings (by calling evidence, cross-examining other parties' witnesses, addressing argument etc, for which purposes he would probably wish his own legal representation to be authorised under r 11A(2)(iii)) and by making a report in the usual way. This ensures that a neutral view of the best interests of the child is advanced since, where the guardian does retain a role, CA 1989, s 41(1)(*b*) continues to require him to perform it for the purpose of safeguarding the interests of the child. However, it may be thought right to permit only a smaller role, or even to terminate the guardian's appointment altogether under r 10(9) (the latter may be done by "the court").

In the ordinary case where conflict arises, the solicitor first appointed continues in the case putting the views, wishes and feelings of the child, and the guardian finds a fresh advocate to assist him in his continuing role as defined by the court; however, in *Re P (Representation)* [1996] 1 FLR 486, the reverse was ordered where there were seven children involved, one of whom wished to instruct her own lawyer late in the proceedings; it was decided to appoint a fresh solicitor for the one, and the original solicitor would continue to represent the remaining six.

"the children's guardian ... shall advise the court" (r 11A(3))—It is not part of the children's guardian's function to adopt a judicial role or to seek to assess material which is not within his own expertise. See further under FPR 1991, r 4.11A.

Child's capacity to refuse to be examined etc (r 11A(3)(*a*))—CA 1989, s 38(6) provides that a child of sufficient understanding may refuse to submit to an examination or assessment directed by a court making an interim care or supervision order; s 43(8) allows a child who is of sufficient understanding to make an informed decision to refuse to submit to a medical or psychiatric examination or other assessment which would otherwise have been authorised by a child assessment order. In *Re H (A Minor) (Care Proceedings: Child's Wishes)* [1993] 1 FLR 440 at 449A, Thorpe J said, in relation to the child's capacity under CA 1989, s 38(6) to make an informed decision whether to refuse to submit to a psychiatric examination, that "the level of understanding that enables a child to make an informed decision whether to refuse to submit to a psychiatric examination is in all practical senses a much higher level of understanding than is required to enable him to give instructions to a solicitor on his own behalf". It is useful to compare this with the power of the court, in exercising the inherent jurisdiction of the High Court, to override the child's wishes in respect of medical treatment (see *Re W (A Minor) (Consent to Medical Treatment)* [1993] 1 FLR 1).

Confidentiality—The report of the guardian is confidential and should not be disclosed to anyone other than the parties to the proceedings and their legal advisers without leave of the court. See also under FPR 1991, r 4.11A. As to confidentiality generally see r 23.

Where interests of children conflict—There is usually no reason why a guardian ad litem (children's guardian) should not properly represent children whose interests conflict (*Re T and E (Proceedings: Conflicting Interests)* [1995] 1 FLR 581, FD).

Written report by children's guardian—It is a matter for the discretion of the court whether a report of a children's guardian in public law proceedings can be made available to a court hearing related private law proceedings and to the parties thereto. If two courts are dealing with different sets of proceedings concerning siblings (an exceptional situation, as it is normally right for one court to deal with all proceedings where siblings are concerned), the report should normally be made available to both (*W v Wakefield City Council* [1995] 1 FLR 170).

PART III

Re T and E (Proceedings: Conflicting Interests) [1995] 1 FLR 581 stresses the importance of the guardian's report being read by any expert witness whose evidence goes either to the disposal of the case or to issues canvassed in the report. Any leave to show papers to an expert should be drawn widely enough to cover this step.

Attendance of child at court—Whilst the court can allow the child who is the subject of an application to attend court, it must always bear in mind that attendance is likely to be harmful to the child and should only permit it if satisfied that it is in the interests of the child (*Re W (Secure Accommodation Order: Attendance at Court)* [1994] 2 FLR 1092 and see, further, **Use of the power to exclude** under r 16). The fact that the child would need to be physically restrained during the hearing in order to control him (as in *Re W (Secure Accommodation Order: Attendance at Court)*, above) would, in itself, be sufficient ground for refusing to allow the child to be in court. Further examples given in *Re W* of situations in which the court would not allow a child to be present are where there is a prospect of disturbance or unruliness in court or the possibility of the child being educationally subnormal or where the child is much younger than the 10-year-old boy in that case. Young children should be discouraged from attending appeals from the justices in family proceedings. Where a guardian is proposing to arrange for a young child to be present, he should give the question very careful thought beforehand and be prepared to explain his reasons to the court (*Re C (A Minor) (Care: Child's Wishes)* [1993] 1 FLR 832, which concerned a girl of 13).

Note of guardian's oral advice (r 11A(4))—The clerk's note should refer to the fact that advice was given to the court and indicate the nature of the advice (*Hampshire CC v S* [1993] 1 FLR 559).

"notify" (r 11A(5))—The manner of notification is not regulated; r 8 (service of documents) does not seem to apply.

"not less than 14 days" (r 11A(6))—This requirement as to the time for filing a report may be extended only by direction of the clerk or the court under r 14 (r 15(4)). See r 15 for how to compute the fourteen-day period.

Service—Service of documents under r 11A(6) is governed by r 8.

Inspection of records (r 11A(8))—CA 1989, s 42 allows a children's guardian, at all reasonable times, to examine and copy local authority records which were compiled in connection with the making, or proposed making, of any application under CA 1989 in relation to the child concerned, or in connection with the authority's social services functions in relation to the child and gives him a similar right in relation to an authorised person's records. Section 41(2) and (3) makes any copies taken admissible in evidence of certain matters. A guardian ad litem (children's guardian) is entitled to see a case record prepared by the local authority giving detailed information concerning prospective adopters and to include the relevant information derived from it in his report to the court (*Re T (A Minor) (Guardian ad Litem: Case Record)* [1994] 1 FLR 632). As to the limitations on what the guardian may inspect under s 42 and on disclosure of what he has seen, see under CA 1989, s 42.

Where court differs from children's guardian's advice—The court is not bound to follow the recommendation of the children's guardian but, just as with a children and family reporter, must give careful consideration to any argument advanced by him and, where it differs, must explain its reasons carefully (*S v Oxfordshire County Council* [1993] 1 FLR 452; *Re W (A Minor) (Secure Accommodation Order)* [1993] 1 FLR 692; *Knowsley Metropolitan Borough Council v U* [1993] Fam Law 545).

Duties of children's guardian and local authority to consult each other—See under FPR 1991, r 4.11A.

11B Additional powers and duties of a children and family reporter

(1) In addition to his duties under rule 11, the children and family reporter shall –

(*a*) notify the child of such contents of his report (if any) as he considers appropriate to the age and understanding of the child, including any reference to the child's own views on the application and the recommendation of the children and family reporter; and

(*b*) if he does notify the child of any contents of his report, explain them to the child in a manner appropriate to his age and understanding.

(2) Where the court has –

(*a*) directed that a written report be made by a children and family reporter; and

(*b*) notified the children and family reporter that his report is to be considered at a hearing,

the children and family reporter shall –

(i) file his report; and

(ii) serve a copy on the other parties and on the children's guardian (if any),

by such time as the court may direct and if no direction is given, not less than 14 days before that hearing.

(3) The court may direct that the children and family reporter attend any hearing at which his report is to be considered.

(4) The children and family reporter shall advise the court if he considers that the joinder of a person as a party to the proceedings would be likely to safeguard the interests of the child.

(5) The children and family reporter shall consider whether it is in the best interests of the child for the child to be made a party to the proceedings.

(6) If the children and family reporter considers the child should be made a party to the proceedings he shall notify the court of his opinion together with the reasons for that opinion.

Amendments—Inserted by SI 2001/818.

Filing and service of written reports—See under FPR 1991, r 4.11B.

Attendance of children and family reporter—See under FPR 1991, r 4.11B.

Withholding children and family reporter's report from the parties—See under FPR 1991, r 4.11B.

12 Solicitor for child

(1) A solicitor appointed under section 41(3) or in accordance with rule 11A(1)(*a*) shall represent the child –

(*a*) in accordance with instructions received from the children's guardian (unless the solicitor considers, having taken into account the views of the children's guardian and any direction of the court under rule 11A(2), that the child wishes to give instructions which conflict with those of the children's guardian and that he is able, having regard to his understanding, to give such instructions on his own behalf in which case he shall conduct the proceedings in accordance with instructions received from the child), or

(*b*) where no children's guardian has been appointed for the child and the condition in section 41(4)(*b*) is satisfied, in accordance with instructions received from the child, or (*c*) in default of instructions under (*a*) or (*b*), in furtherance of the best interests of the child.

(2) A solicitor appointed under section 41(3) or in accordance with rule 11A(1)(*a*) shall serve and accept service of documents on behalf of the child in accordance with rule 8(3)(*a*) and (4)(*a*) and, where the child has not himself been served and has sufficient understanding, advise the child of the contents of any document so served.

(3) Where the child wishes an appointment of a solicitor under section 41(3) or in accordance with rule 11A(1)(*a*) to be terminated, he may apply to the court for an order terminating the appointment; and the solicitor and the children's guardian shall be given an opportunity to make representations.

(4) Where the children's guardian wishes an appointment of a solicitor under section 41(3) to be terminated, he may apply to the court for an order terminating the appointment; and the solicitor and, if he is of sufficient understanding, the child, shall be given an opportunity to make representations.

(5) When terminating an appointment in accordance with paragraph (3) or (4), the court shall give reasons for so doing, a note of which shall be taken by the justices' clerk.

(6) Where the justices' clerk or the court appoints a solicitor under section 41(3) or refuses to make such an appointment, the justices' clerk shall record the appointment or refusal in the appropriate form in Schedule 1 to these Rules and the justices' chief executive shall serve a copy on the parties and, where he is appointed, on the solicitor.

Amendments—SI 2001/615; SI 2001/818.

Defined terms—"child", "court", "children's guardian", "justices' clerk", "note", "parties": r 1(2).

Solicitors to whom the rule applies—This rule applies to two types of solicitor:

(*a*) those appointed under CA 1989, s 41(3), which, in combination with s 41(4), enables the court to appoint a solicitor for a child who does not already have one if:

- (i) no children's guardian has yet been appointed;
- (ii) the child has sufficient understanding to instruct a solicitor and wishes to do so; and
- (iii) it appears to the court that it would be in the child's best interests for him to be represented by a solicitor.

(*b*) those appointed by the children's guardian in accordance with r 11A (except that r 12(4) does not apply, presumably because there is nothing to stop the children's guardian dismissing the solicitor in the usual way where the solicitor had been appointed in the first place not by the clerk or court but by the children's guardian).

As the appointment of a solicitor under s 41 can only be made in specified proceedings (see *Re W (A Minor) (Contact)* [1994] 1 FLR 843, FD, and also the tenor of the judgment of Sir Thomas Bingham MR in *Re S (A Minor) (Independent Representation)* [1993] Fam 263, [1993] 2 FLR 437, CA), and there is only a children's guardian to act under r 11A if there are specified proceedings, it therefore seems to be the case that r 12 can only be relevant in specified proceedings as defined by CA 1989, s 41(6).

"able ... to give such instructions on his own behalf" (r 12(1)(*a*))—See under FPR 1991, r 4.12.

"the condition in section 41(4)(b)" (r 12(1)(*b*))—The condition is that the child has sufficient understanding to instruct a solicitor and wishes to do so. For the meaning of "sufficient understanding to instruct a solicitor" see **"able ... to give such instructions on his own behalf"** under FPR 1991, r 4.12.

Removal of solicitor (r 12(3)–(5))—Curiously, it seems that the child may apply for the removal of a solicitor under r 12(3) even where he is not of sufficient understanding to do so (cf r 12(4) where, if the children's guardian applies for the removal of such a solicitor, the child may make representations only if he is of sufficient understanding). A literal reading of r 12(3) and (4) would seem to suggest that the court cannot remove a solicitor who was appointed by a children's guardian when the proceedings were pending in a county court or in the High Court before being transferred down because the appointment would not have been made "in accordance with rule 11A(1)(*a*)" (ie it would have been made in accordance with FPR 1991, r 4.11A(1)(*a*)); however, it is submitted that there is scope for construing the provision to include such cases.

Opportunity to make representations (r 12(3), (4))—See under FPR 1991, r 4.12.

Reasons for terminating appointment of solicitor or children's guardian to be given by the court (r 12(5))—See under FPR 1991, r 4.12.

13 Welfare officer

(1) Where the court or a justices' clerk has directed that a written report be made by a welfare officer in accordance with section 7(1)(*b*), the report shall be filed at or by such time as the court or justices' clerk directs or, in the absence of such a direction, at least 14 days before a relevant hearing; and the justices' chief executive shall, as soon as practicable, serve a copy of the report on the parties and any children's guardian.

(2) In paragraph (1), a hearing is relevant if the justices' chief executive has given the welfare officer notice that his report is to be considered at it.

(3) After the filing of a written report by a welfare officer, the court or the justices' clerk may direct that the welfare officer attend any hearing at which the report is to be considered; and

(*a*) except where such a direction is given at a hearing attended by the welfare officer, the justices' chief executive shall inform the welfare officer of the direction; and

(*b*) at the hearing at which the report is considered any party may question the welfare officer about his report.

(3A) The welfare officer shall consider whether it is in the best interests of the child for the child to be made a party to the proceedings.

(3B) If the welfare officer considers the child should be made a party to the proceedings he shall notify the court of his opinion together with the reasons for that opinion.

(4) This rule is without prejudice to the court's power to give directions under rule 14.

Amendments—SI 1992/2068; SI 2001/615; SI 2001/818.

Defined terms—"court", "justices' chief executive", "justices' clerk", "file", "parties", "children's guardian", "welfare officer": r 1(2).

Related provision—CA 1989, s 7 makes provision for the request for a welfare report.

Further annotations—Detailed guidance on all aspects of welfare reports can be found in the annotations to CA 1989, s 7. See also *Best Practice Guidance on Section 37(1) Directions* under CA 1989, s 37.

"welfare officer in accordance with section 7(1)(b)" (r 13(1))—This refers to cases in which a court considers any question with respect to a child under CA 1989 and decides to use its powers under s 7(1)(*b*) to ask a local authority officer to report to the court on matters relating to the welfare of the child concerned. For this purpose only the term "welfare officer" is retained. CJCSA 2000 has now introduced the Children and Family Court Advisory and Support Service (CAFCASS) and in most other contexts the reference to "welfare officer" has now been replaced by other types of officer: see annotation under CJCSA 2000, s 11. For further information about the role and duties of an officer of the service see under rr 11 and 11B and under FPR 1991, rr 4.11 and 4.11B.

Filing and service of written reports (r 13(1))—The principles relating to the filing and service of written reports by the welfare officer are similar to those concerning the filing and service of reports by a children and family reporter under r 11B(2); see **Filing and service of written reports** under r 11B and FPR 1991, r 4.11B.

Attendance of welfare officer (r 13(3))—The principles relating to the attendance of the welfare officer are similar to those concerning the attendance of a children and family reporter under r 11B(3); see **Attendance of children and family reporter** under r 11B and FPR 1991, r 4.11B.

"any party may question the welfare officer" (r 13(3)(*b*))—See under FPR 1991, r 4.13.

Withholding welfare officer's report from the parties—Similar principles apply to a report prepared by a welfare officer in accordance with CA 1989, s 7(1)(*b*), to those which apply to a report prepared by a children and family reporter pursuant to r 11B; see **Withholding children and family reporter's report from the parties** under r 11B and FPR 1991, r 4.11B.

14 Directions

(1) In this rule, "party" includes the children's guardian and, where a request or direction concerns a report under section 7, the welfare officer or children and family reporter.

(2) In any relevant proceedings the justices' clerk or the court may, subject to paragraph (5), give, vary or revoke directions for the conduct of the proceedings, including –

- (*a*) the timetable for the proceedings;
- (*b*) varying the time within which or by which an act is required, by these Rules, to be done;
- (*c*) the attendance of the child;
- (*d*) the appointment of a children's guardian, or of a solicitor under section 41(3);
- (*e*) the service of documents;
- (*f*) the submission of evidence including experts' reports;
- (*g*) the preparation of welfare reports under section 7;
- (*h*) the transfer of the proceedings to another court in accordance with any Order made by the Lord Chancellor under Part I of Schedule 11;
- (*i*) consolidation with other proceedings;

and the justices' clerk shall, on receipt of an application by the justices' chief executive, or where proceedings have been transferred to his court, consider whether such directions need to be given.

(3) Where the justices' clerk or a single justice who is holding a directions appointment considers, for whatever reason, that it is inappropriate to give a direction on a particular matter, he shall refer the matter to the court which may give any appropriate direction.

(4) Where a direction is given under paragraph (2)(*h*), an order shall be issued in the appropriate form in Schedule 1 to these Rules and the justices' chief executive shall follow the procedure set out in rule 6(2).

(5) Directions under paragraph (2) may be given, varied or revoked either –

- (*a*) of the justices' clerk's or the court's own motion, the justices' chief executive having given the parties notice of the intention to do so and an opportunity to attend and be heard or to make written representations, (*b*) on the written request in Form C2 of a party specifying the direction which is sought, filed and served on the other parties, or

(*c*) on the written request in Form C2 of a party specifying the direction which is sought, to which the other parties consent and which they or their representatives have signed.

(6) In an urgent case, the request under paragraph (5)(*b*) may, with the leave of the justices' clerk or the court, be made –

(*a*) orally,

(*b*) without notice to the parties, or

(*c*) both as in sub-paragraph (*a*) and as in sub-paragraph (*b*).

(7) On receipt of a request by the justices' chief executive under paragraph (5)(*b*) the justices' clerk shall fix a date for the hearing of the request and the justices' chief executive shall give not less than 2 days' notice in Form C6 to the parties of the date so fixed.

(8) On considering a request under paragraph (5)(*c*) the justices' clerk or the court shall either –

(*a*) grant the request, whereupon the justices' chief executive shall inform the parties of the decision, or

(*b*) direct that a date be fixed for the hearing of the request, whereupon the justices' clerk shall fix such a date and the justices' chief executive shall give not less than 2 days' notice to the parties of the date so fixed.

(9) Subject to rule 28, a party may request, in accordance with paragraph 5(*b*) or (*c*), that an order be made under section 11(3) or, if he is entitled to apply for such an order, under section 38(1), and paragraphs (6), (7) and (8) shall apply accordingly.

(10) Where, in any relevant proceedings, the court has power to make an order of its own motion, the power to give directions under paragraph (2) shall apply.

(11) Directions of the justices' clerk or a court which are still in force immediately prior to the transfer of relevant proceedings to another court shall continue to apply following the transfer, subject to any changes of terminology which are required to apply those directions to the court to which the proceedings are transferred, unless varied or discharged by directions under paragraph (2).

(12) The justices' clerk or the court shall record the giving, variation or revocation of direction under this rule in the appropriate form in Schedule 1 to these Rules and the justices' chief executive shall serve, as soon as practicable, a copy of the form on any party who was not present at the giving, variation or revocation.

Amendments—SI 1991/1991; SI 1994/3156; SI 2001/615; SI 2001/818.

Defined terms—"child", "court", "directions appointment", "children's guardian", "justices' chief executive", "justices' clerk", "leave", "parties": r 1(2); "relevant proceedings": r 1(2), CA 1989, s 93(3); "children and family reporter": r 1(2).

Case management—*Practice Direction of 31 January 1995* deals with a number of important aspects of hearings in the High Court and county courts. It is not applicable to the family proceedings courts, but reference should nevertheless be made to it for the valuable guidance that it gives on the conduct of cases. The President of the Family Division has indicated to the Justices' Clerks' Society that the guidance should be followed by the family proceedings courts (see the *Children Act Advisory Committee Annual Report 1994/95*, p 55). As to the use of the Practice Direction in the magistrates' courts, see also *Re S and P (Discharge of Care Order)* [1995] 2 FLR 782, FD. Great assistance is also to be derived from the *Handbook of Best Practice in Children Act cases* produced by the Children Act Advisory Committee (set out in Part IV of this work as *Best Practice Guidance of June 1997*). See also **Bundles and other particular matters** under FPR 1991, r 4.14 for guidance on the preparation of documentary evidence. See also the practical guidance given by Charles J in *Re R (Care: Disclosure: Nature of Proceedings)* [2002] 1 FLR 755 (a public law case) as to the proper preparation of cases brought under CA 1989 (dealt with more fully in **Preparation of public law cases** under CA 1989, s 31). Further useful information is contained in **Disclosure – impact of the European Convention for Human Rights and Fundamental Freedoms 1950** under FPR 1991, r 4.23, and in particular the judgment of Munby J in *Re L (Care: Assessment: Fair Trial)* [2002] EWHC 1379 (Fam), [2002] 2 FLR 730.

Extended meaning of "party" (r 14(1))—The normal meaning of "party" is extended by this rule so that a children's guardian, as well as the child whose interests he represents (who would normally be the party), may request and be consulted about directions. The involvement of the children and family reporter with regard to directions is more limited and arises only where a request for directions or a direction concerns a welfare report under CA 1989, s 7, for example where the children and family reporter has encountered difficulty in preparing his report within the time-limit specified by the court and wishes to seek an extension.

"report under section 7" (r 14(1))—A court considering any question with respect to a child under CA 1989 is entitled by s 7 to request a welfare report.

"directions for the conduct of the proceedings" (r 14(2))—The justices' clerk and the court have a very wide discretion to grant directions. The matters listed in r 14(2) are only examples of the types of issue that might arise. A directions hearing will almost inevitably be required in a case of any substance and a date for it is fixed by the justices' clerk in accordance with r 4(2) when the application is commenced or when it is received from the transmitting court. The intention of r 16(1) appears to be that parties who receive notice of the appointment should normally be required to attend, but that rule is poorly drafted (see **"notice in accordance with rule 14(5)"** under r 16). Proforma directions and best practice notes to be adopted nationally and in all tiers of court for directions hearings in family cases have been issued by the Children Act Advisory Committee and are set out as *Best Practice Note of January 1995* in Part IV of this work. Directions hearings are not a formality in any case but enable the court to come firmly to grips with the case (*B v B (Child Abuse: Contact)* [1994] 2 FLR 713, and see *Re A and B (Minors) (No 2)* [1995] 1 FLR 351, FD, and under **Timetable for the proceedings** below). As to directions for the conduct of cases involving expert witnesses, see **Practice on leave applications and in instructing and calling experts** under r 18. For specific guidance as to what should happen at a pre-hearing review see **Pre-hearing review** under FPR 1991, r 4.14. In public law proceedings it should now be routine for the court to direct the local authority to set out a clear schedule of facts upon which it seeks a finding by the court and upon the basis of which it is alleged that the threshold is crossed (see **Schedule of facts** under CA 1989, s 31).

Pre-hearing review—See under FPR 1991, r 4.14.

Continuity of judge and legal representatives—See under FPR 1991, r 4.14.

Split hearings—See under FPR 1991, r 4.14.

Repeated applications—As to the possibility of renewing an application previously refused by the court, see *Re F (A Minor) (Care Proceedings: Directions)* [1995] 3 FCR 601, FD (children's guardian whose first application for psychological assessment of child was refused by magistrates was entitled, by virtue of r 14(2), to renew the application a fortnight later).

Dismissal of proceedings at directions stage—See under FPR 1991, r 4.14.

Timetable for the proceedings and time estimates (r 14(2)(*a*))—The court is put firmly in control of the timetable for proceedings under CA 1989 in an effort to avoid delay, which CA 1989, s 1(2) stresses is likely to be prejudicial to the welfare of a child. Section 11(1) obliges the court, when dealing with proceedings in which any question of making a s 8 order arises, to draw up a timetable with a view to determining the question at issue without delay and to give such directions as it considers appropriate to ensure adherence to the timetable; s 32(1) is a similar provision relating to proceedings under CA 1989, Pt IV; and r 15(5) obliges a court dealing with any relevant proceedings to fix a date for the next hearing on the transfer of such proceedings, or adjourning or concluding an interlocutory hearing or appointment. Subject to these positive duties, however, the court has a wide discretion as to how the timetable for a case is set. In reaching decisions about timetabling, the time-limits set by the rules for various steps will have to be taken into account (although the court does have power under r 14 to abridge or extend these where necessary, see **Variation of time-limits** below). The general undesirability of delay will have to be balanced against the need to give sufficient time for all parties to prepare their cases properly, for the children's guardian or children and family reporter to investigate, for reports to be obtained etc. It will also need to be borne in mind that there are cases in which the child's welfare can be better secured by postponing a final resolution of the application for a short time, for example where a parent suffers from psychiatric illness and is receiving treatment which it is anticipated will be successful. What is required is a timetable that prevents the case from drifting without hustling it along at a pace which sacrifices the interests of the parties and the welfare of the child. For comments on the benefits of planned and purposeful delay, see *C v Solihull MBC* [1993] 1 FLR 290 and *Hounslow LBC v A* [1993] 1 FLR 702. See also **Interim care order or full care order?** under CA 1989, s 38.

As *B v B (Child Abuse: Contact)* [1994] 2 FLR 713 stresses, directions hearings are not a formality. They are there so that the court can come firmly to grips with the case and ensure that it is tightly timetabled and prepared for its final hearing at the earliest opportunity. It is the duty of the court to be precise in the directions it gives. If there is a risk of drift or delay, the court should not give leave to the parties to apply for further directions but should fix a date at which further directions will be given. Where there is a children's guardian, he should regularly review the file and, if the case is not making satisfactory progress, should take out a summons for directions. *B v B (Minors) (Interviews and Listing Arrangements)* [1994] 2 FLR 489 points out that open-ended orders which do not focus the minds of the parties and their advisers on a specific hearing date should not be made.

Guidance as to the giving of accurate time estimates is contained in *Re MD and TD (Minors) (Time Estimates)* [1994] 2 FLR 336 (set out in Part IV of this work as *Practice Note of 2 February 1994*) and, although principally concerned with the higher courts, should also be helpful in magistrates' court proceedings. It is pointed out that directions appointments at which time estimates are discussed are very important and every effort should be made to ensure that, when counsel is briefed to attend a directions appointment, he or she is either the barrister who will have conduct of the substantive hearing and has addressed his or her mind to the estimated length of the hearing or, where a substitute has to take the brief, that he or she is fully instructed on the point. By the same token, where a solicitor appears on a directions appointment in the magistrates' courts, he will need to be fully in the picture in order to assist the court properly. In *Re EC (Disclosure of Material)* [1996] 2 FLR 123 (subsequently appealed to the Court of Appeal at [1996] 2 FLR 725 but not on this point), Wall J praised the use of a timetable template identifying all the witnesses who were to be called to give oral evidence and assigning a specified time to each, with detailed estimates of the time to be spent in examination-in-chief, cross-examination and re-examination.

In determining any application to adjourn a case involving children, as well as in fixing the timetable for the proceedings, the court has to consider delay, and the interests of the other parties have to be assessed in the light of the principle that delay in determining a question concerning a child's upbringing is likely to prejudice his welfare (*Re SW (A Minor) (Care Proceedings)* [1993] 2 FLR 609, noted more fully in **Hearing or directions appointment in the absence of applicant** under r 16). An application for an adjournment can be granted ex parte, but such application should only be made in exceptional circumstances and where it would be in the best interests of the children to justify such a course. Even then, those representing the parties should be in attendance, either having given undertakings or subject to a direction of the court not to pass on the information to their clients (*Re B (Minors) (Care: Procedure)* [1994] Fam Law 72, in which a local authority applied ex parte to adjourn an application relating to contact with a child in care so that it would carry out investigations into allegations of sexual abuse against a parent without the parents learning of the allegations).

Variation of time-limits (r 14(2)(*b*))—Time-limits set by the rules for relevant proceedings may be extended only by direction of the justices' clerk or the court under r 14 (r 15(4)); the parties cannot agree an extension between themselves (see r 15(4)). This rule also gives the court power to abridge time-limits (for example, the minimum number of days specified in Sch 2 for service) in an appropriate case. It is worth noting that there is no express prohibition on the abridgement of a time-limit by agreement between the parties and it would therefore seem that it is possible to do so, although it may be unlikely to arise in practice.

Attendance of the child (r 14(2)(*c*))—As to the attendance of the child at directions appointments and hearings, see r 16(1) and (2).

Appointment of a children's guardian (r 14(2)(*d*))—CA 1989, s 41 obliges the court to appoint a children's guardian for a child concerned in specified proceedings (such as care and supervision order proceedings) unless satisfied that it is not necessary to do so in order to safeguard his interests; r 10 sets out the normal procedure for the appointment of such a guardian. There is no provision in CA 1989 for the appointment of a children's guardian for a child involved in non-specified proceedings. In such proceedings in a county court and the High Court (for example in a straightforward application for a residence order), a children's guardian may be appointed for the child under FPR 1991, r 9.5, but there is no equivalent rule in the magistrates' courts. In *Essex CC v B* [1993] 1 FLR 866, Douglas Brown J held that, accordingly, there is no power or authority in the family proceedings court to appoint a children's guardian in cases not covered by CA 1989, s 41 and suspected that the words "or otherwise" in r 14(2)(*d*) had been left in in error. The possibility that Wall J was expressing a different view in *Re W (A Minor) (Contact)* [1994] 1 FLR 843 now looks unlikely, given his acceptance of the *Essex CC v B* principle in *Re CE (Section 37 Direction)* [1995] 1 FLR 26.

Appointment of a solicitor under s 41(3) (r 14(2)(*e*))—CA 1989, s 41(3) enables the court to appoint a solicitor to represent a child concerned in specified proceedings where he has no children's guardian, where he is of sufficient understanding to instruct a solicitor and wants to do so or where it appears that it would be in his best interests for him to be represented by a solicitor. In contrast to the position with regard to the appointment of a children's guardian under s 41, there is no rule dealing specifically with the procedure for the appointment of such a solicitor so this must be carried out under this rule (although r 12(6) imposes a duty on the court to record the appointment). Where there is a children's guardian, he generally has a duty to appoint a solicitor for the child under r 11(2). An appointment by the children's guardian is not made under s 41(3) and the court cannot therefore give directions with regard to it. However it is presumed that should the court's assistance be required at a later stage (for example if a question arises as to how the solicitor should carry out his duties under r 12), directions under this rule could be sought on the basis that the matter arises in connection with the conduct of the proceedings. An application by the child for termination of the solicitor's appointment would, however, have to be made under r 12(3).

There is no power to appoint a solicitor for a child under s 41(3) in non-specified proceedings (*Re W (A Minor) (Contact)* [1994] 1 FLR 843).

Service of documents (r 14(2)(*e*))—As to service generally, see r 8 and Magistrates' Courts Rules 1981, r 67 (applied by virtue of r 34(2)). The power to give directions about service under this rule is supplementary to the power of the justices' clerk or the court to give directions under r 8(8).

Submission of evidence (r 14(2)(*f*))—Rule 14 gives the justices' clerk or the court a very broad power to deal with questions concerning the submission of evidence. For example, such directions may be given as are necessary for the purposes of r 17, which lays down the rules about the filing and service of written and oral evidence (see *R v Nottinghamshire CC* [1993] Fam Law 625, discussed in **Non-compliance with r 17** under r 17). Presumably, directions may be given as to the use of evidence arising out of an unauthorised examination of a child (see r 18(3)), and it may be possible for questions of admissibility of evidence to be resolved.

Where disclosure of material to a party may be damaging to the child concerned in the proceedings, the court has power, in an appropriate case, to direct that the information should be withheld. Such a direction will only be given in exceptional circumstances. The principles are set out in **Submission of evidence** under FPR 1991, r 4.14. *Re C (Disclosure)* [1996] 1 FLR 797, FD (endorsed by *Re M (Disclosure)* [1998] 2 FLR 1028, CA), suggests that, where a question of withholding disclosure arises, the case should normally be dealt with by the High Court. There is also support for the view that such matters should not be heard in the magistrates' court in *Re B (Minors) (Care: Procedure)* [1994] Fam Law 72 (once arguments are advanced that an adjournment application should be heard ex parte because of allegations about which the parents should not be made aware, the case should be transferred immediately to a care centre to be heard by a judge).

In CA 1989 proceedings, statements by parties in conciliation meetings are not admissible, except in the very unusual case where the statement clearly indicates that the maker has in the past caused, or is likely in future to cause, serious harm to the well-being of a child. Even in such a case, there is a discretion whether or not to admit the evidence, and it should be admitted only if the public interest in protecting the interests of the child outweighs the public interest in preserving the confidentiality of attempted conciliation (*Re D (Minors) (Conciliation: Privilege)* [1993] 1 FLR 932, CA).

Assistance on the assembly of evidence into a convenient form for the court can be found in *B v B (Court Bundles: Video Evidence) (Note)* [1994] 1 FLR 323 (set out in Part IV of this work as *Practice Note of 11 November 1993)*, and also *Practice Direction of 31 January 1995*.

Bundles and other particular matters—The court may wish to consider giving directions about bundles of evidence for the final hearing. There is no reason why the practice of the higher courts in this regard should not be adopted in the magistrates' courts. For further guidance see under FPR 1991, r 4.14.

Citation of authorities—See under FPR 1991, r 4.14.

Discovery by party—Representatives must address their minds in advance of the hearing to the need for pre-trial discovery. For further guidance see under FPR 1991, r 4.14. If a problem as to public interest immunity arises, the procedure to be followed is set out under r 17.

Discovery by non-party—In *D v D (County Court Jurisdiction: Injunctions)* [1993] 2 FLR 802, the Court of Appeal held that the court had no jurisdiction to make orders for discovery by a non-party in family proceedings. The correct procedure by which a party could adduce in evidence documents in the possession of a non-party was by subpoena duces tecum (in the High Court) or by witness summons (in a county court). Even in children cases, the court has no general power to garner documentary evidence of its own motion. The judge at first instance had been wrong to order all documents concerning investigations into the family, in the possession of the police and social services to be disclosed to the court and to the parties' solicitors.

By analogy with *D v D*, the proper course in the magistrates' court is no doubt to seek a witness summons against the non-party under Magistrates' Courts Act 1980, s 97, as applied by r 33 of these Rules.

For further discussion of the recent case-law on this topic see under FPR 1991, r 4.14.

Disclosure – impact of the European Convention for Human Rights and Fundamental Freedoms 1950—See under FPR 1991, r 4.23.

Preparation of welfare reports (r 14(2)(*g*))—As to welfare reports generally, see CA 1989, s 7 and rr 11B and 13. Directions may be sought under this rule where, for example, there are problems in complying with the request for a welfare report, either because of time constraints or for other reasons, or where the children and family reporter or welfare officer considers that part of his report contains sensitive material which ought not to be shown to the parties in the normal way.

Transfer of proceedings (r 14(2)(*h*))—The transfer of proceedings between courts is governed by the Children (Allocation of Proceedings) Order 1991, which was made under CA 1989, Sch 11. Rule 6 deals specifically with the position where the justices' clerk or the court receives a written request from a party for a transfer to another family proceedings court or to a county court. Any directions as to transfer that are not covered by r 6 may be given under this rule (for example, where the decision to transfer is made of the justices' clerk's or the court's own motion).

Consolidation with other proceedings (r 14(2)(*i*))—Clearly it is desirable, wherever possible, for directions to be given as to transfer between courts, consolidation etc, so that all linked proceedings can be heard and determined together. For further guidance see under FPR 1991, r.4.14.

Justices' clerk's duty to consider need for directions (r 14(2))—The duty to consider the need for directions arises on receipt of the application or on transfer. See also the duty of the justices' clerk under r 4(2) to fix a hearing or directions appointment and under r 15(5) to fix a date for the proceedings to come before the court as soon as possible after the transfer of proceedings.

Order of transfer (r 14(4))—The appropriate form is C49.

"opportunity to attend and be heard or to make written representations" (r 14(5)(*a*))—It appears that it will suffice if the parties are either given the opportunity to attend an oral hearing or the opportunity to make written representations, as the justices' clerk or the court thinks fit, although the rule could be read so as to require that the parties be given the choice whether to make their representations orally or in writing. There is no prescribed form for written representations and no particular format is specified.

Written directions in difficult child care cases—*Re A and B (Minors) (No 2)* [1995] 1 FLR 351 expresses the view that, as a general rule, it is bad practice for directions in difficult child care cases to be sought and given in writing without the attendance of the parties.

"representatives" (r 14(5)(*c*))—Although it does not say so, r 14(5)(*c*) presumably means legal representatives.

Service—As to service generally, see r 8.

Procedure in urgent cases (r 14(6))—Where the justices' clerk or the court gives leave in an urgent case, r 14(6) permits a party to apply orally on notice or orally without notice or in writing without notice.

Notice of request (r 14(7))—It is debatable whether r 14(7) applies when the request is made in accordance with r 14(6) rather than in the conventional way in writing on notice under r 14(5)(*b*). It would appear that, technically, a request in accordance with r 14(6) is still made under r 14(5)(*b*), thus imposing a duty on the clerk to fix a hearing date and give the requisite notice to the parties but, in some cases, this would prevent the court from dealing with the matter with the urgency required, so defeating the object of r 14(6). However, the alternative interpretation is not without its problems either (see **"and paragraphs (6), (7) and (8) shall apply accordingly"** below). As to the computation of time for notice, see r 15 as to varying time-limits, see r 14(2).

"Subject to rule 28" (r 14(9))—Rule 28 limits the power of a justices' clerk or single justice to make orders under CA 1989, ss 11(3) and 38(1) (see below) to cases in which the order is sought by consent and is in identical terms to the last such order made in the proceedings.

"section 11(3)" (r 14(9))—CA 1989, s 11(3) gives the court power to grant a s 8 order at any time in the course of the proceedings even though it is not in a position to dispose finally of those proceedings.

"section 38(1)" (r 14(9))—CA 1989, s 38(1) concerns the making of interim care or supervision orders. Only local authorities and authorised persons are entitled to apply for such orders.

"and paragraphs (6), (7) and (8) shall apply accordingly" (r 14(9))—The application of r 14(6) means that, in an urgent case, a written or oral application for an order under CA 1989, s 11(3) or 38(1) can be made without notice if the justices' clerk or the court gives leave. Whether this means that interim orders under ss 11(3) and 38(1) may be granted ex parte, so that, for example, a local authority could obtain an ex parte interim care order, is unclear. If r 14(7) applies (see **Notice of request** above), the strict answer ought to be that they cannot as the clerk will have to respond to the application by fixing a date for the hearing of the request and giving notice to the parties. If r 14(7) does not apply, there is room for argument. Reference should be made to *Re C (A Minor) (Interim Care)* [1994] 1 FCR 447 (where an ex parte interim care order was in fact made) and to *Re B (A Minor) (Residence Order: Ex Parte)* [1992] 2 FLR 1, CA, in which an ex parte interim residence order was granted despite the provisions of FPR 1991, r 4.4(4) (the county court and High Court equivalent of r 4(4) of these rules) which lists those applications which may be made ex parte and which, at the time that the case was decided, did not mention residence orders. FPR 1991, r 4.4(4) and r 4(4), even as amended in the light of *Re B* (above), do not include applications for orders under either s 11(3) or s 38(1). See also *Re W (A Minor) (Interim Care Order)* [1994] 2 FLR 892 (local authority accepted an interim supervision order would be appropriate and then, at a hearing at which the mother was not present, applied without notice to her for an interim care order).

"unless varied or discharged by directions under paragraph (2)" (r 14(11))—Presumably, in the case of a transfer from a magistrates' court to a county court, the proviso will also apply to any variation or discharge by the receiving court under the equivalent provision (FPR 1991, r 4.14(2)).

Record of the giving, variation or revocation of a direction (r 14(12))—For the general directions form, see the prescribed form in Sch 1.

Application of the rules to the directions hearing—Those of the rules which are relevant will apply to the directions hearing. See particularly r 16 as to attendance, r 17 as to the filing of documentary evidence and r 21 as to procedure at the hearing.

Public interest immunity—Where an issue arises as to whether, because of public interest immunity, certain material (often material in the possession of the local authority) should or should not be disclosed, guidance as to the procedure to be followed can be derived from *Re C (Expert Evidence: Disclosure: Practice)* [1995] 1 FLR 204; *Re R (Care: Disclosure: Nature of Proceedings)* [2002] 1 FLR 755 and *Re C* [2002] LTL, 9 April 2002 – Doc No C0102987, noted further under r 17 and FPR 1991, r 4.17.

15 Timing of proceedings

(1) Any period of time fixed by these Rules, or by any order or direction, for doing any act shall be reckoned in accordance with this rule.

(2) Where the period, being a period of 7 days or less, would include a day which is not a business day, that day shall be excluded.

(3) Where the time fixed for filing a document with the justices' chief executive expires on a day on which the office of the justices' chief executive is closed, and for that reason the document cannot be filed on that day, the document shall be filed in time if it is filed on the next day on which the office of the justices' chief executive is open.

(4) Where these Rules provide a period of time within which or by which a certain act is to be performed in the course of relevant proceedings, that period may not be extended otherwise than by a direction of the justices' clerk or the court under rule 14.

(5) At the –

(*a*) transfer to a court of relevant proceedings,

(*b*) postponement or adjournment of any hearing or directions appointment in the course of relevant proceedings, or

(*c*) conclusion of any such hearing or directions appointment other than one at which the proceedings are determined, or so soon thereafter as is practicable,

(i) the justices' clerk shall fix a date upon which the proceedings shall come before him or the court again for such purposes as he or the court directs, which date shall, where paragraph (*a*) applies, be as soon as possible after the transfer, and

(ii) the justices' chief executive shall give notice to the parties and to the children's guardian or the welfare officer or children and family reporter of the date so fixed.

Amendments—SI 2001/615; SI 2001/818.

Defined terms—"business day", "court", "directions appointment", "children's guardian", "justices' chief executive", "justices' clerk": r 1(2); "relevant proceedings": r 1(2), CA 1989, s 93(3); "children and family reporter": r 1(2).

Related provisions—Other provisions affecting the timing of proceedings include CA 1989, ss 1(2) (general principle that delay is likely to be prejudicial to the welfare of a child), 11(1) (obligation of court in s 8 proceedings to draw up a timetable) and 32(1) (obligation of the court in proceedings under Part IV of the Act to draw up a timetable), and r 14 (power of the court to give directions as to time-limits, timetabling etc).

Variation of time-limits (r 15(4))—Time-limits may not be extended except by direction of the justices' clerk or the court; however, there is nothing in the rules to prevent the parties from shortening time-limits by agreement.

Failure to observe time-limits—Where a local authority failed to submit written evidence as directed by the court and to comply with a direction to serve documents, the family proceedings court was correct in giving leave for statements to be filed out of time because it was vital in the interests of the children that the court should have the best information available. The sanction for failure to comply with directions was a costs order, where appropriate (*R v Nottinghamshire CC* [1993] Fam Law 625).

Fixing a new date on transfer (r 15(5))—The provisions of r 15(5)(*a*) are ambiguous, suggesting that the justices' clerk must fix a date and sent out the requisite notices either when receiving a case by transfer or when transferring a case to another magistrates' court or to a county court. On balance, it seems likely that the rule is intended to apply where a magistrates' court receives a case from another court but not when it transfers a case elsewhere. However, in the latter situation, it is clearly good practice for the transferring court to consult the proposed receiving court about dates in any event, so that any acceleration or delay that may result from the transfer can be taken into account in deciding whether transfer is an appropriate course of action (as required by Children (Allocation of Proceedings) Order 1991, arts 6 and 7). Furthermore, contact between transferring and receiving courts will be inevitable where the transfer is from one magistrates' court to another, as C(AP)O 1991, art 6 requires the consent of the receiving court to be given before transfer. A sensible approach would be for the receiving court, if possible, to fix a directions appointment when consulted about the transfer; the parties, if they are present in the transferring court, can then be informed of the new date immediately, thus avoiding any postal delays or misunderstandings. This is the course advised by the *CAAC Handbook of Best Practice in Children Act cases* (set out in Part IV of this work as *Best Practice Guidance of June 1997*) which also contains further helpful advice as to the procedure on transfer (see "Section 3 – First appointments in public law cases in the county courts: the role of the court").

Fixing a new date at hearing (r 15(5))—The justices' clerk must keep a tight rein on the proceedings, ensuring that a new date is fixed either at the end of the interim hearing or directions appointment whilst the parties are still at court or as soon as practicable thereafter.

Fixing a new date is not only a case of finding an appropriate court slot for the matter to be heard. CA 1989 s 1(2) (the delay principle) must always be kept in mind and other provisions of the Act may also impose constraints (see, for example, s 38(4), which limits the duration of interim care orders). Parties and their legal representatives must be in a position to inform the court of their availability for future hearings and that of their witnesses.

16 Attendance at directions appointment and hearing

(1) Subject to paragraph (2), a party shall attend a directions appointment of which he has been given notice in accordance with rule 14(5) unless the justices' clerk or the court otherwise directs.

(2) Relevant proceedings shall take place in the absence of any party including the child if –

- (*a*) the court considers it in the interests of the child, having regard to the matters to be discussed or the evidence likely to be given, and
- (*b*) the party is represented by a children's guardian or solicitor;

and when considering the interests of the child under sub-paragraph (*a*) the court shall give the children's guardian, solicitor for the child and, if he is of sufficient understanding, the child, an opportunity to make representations.

(3) Subject to paragraph (4) below, where at the time and place appointed for a hearing or directions appointment the applicant appears but one or more of the respondents do not, the justices' clerk or the court may proceed with the hearing or appointment.

(4) The court shall not begin to hear an application in the absence of a respondent unless –

- (*a*) it is proved to the satisfaction of the court that he received reasonable notice of the date of the hearing; or
- (*b*) the court is satisfied that the circumstances of the case justify proceeding with the hearing.

(5) Where, at the time and place appointed for a hearing or directions appointment, one or more respondents appear but the applicant does not, the court may refuse the application or, if sufficient evidence has previously been received, proceed in the absence of the applicant.

(6) Where at the time and place appointed for a hearing or directions appointment neither the applicant nor any respondent appears, the court may refuse the application.

(7) If the court considers it expedient in the interests of the child, it shall hear any relevant proceedings in private when only the officers of the court, the parties, their legal representatives and such other persons as specified by the court may attend.

Amendments—SI 2001/818.

Defined terms—"applicant", "application", "child", "court", "directions appointment", "children's guardian", "justices' clerk", "parties": r 1(2); "relevant proceedings": r 1(2), CA 1989, s 93(3).

Related provisions—Other provisions relating to attendance include r 11(4), which imposes a duty on the children's guardian to attend directions appointments and hearings and requires him to advise the court as to the wishes of the child in respect of any relevant matter, including his attendance at court; r 14(2)(*c*), which is a general power enabling the court to give directions as to the attendance of the child, and CA 1989, s 95, which empowers a court hearing proceedings under Pt IV or V of the Act, or considering whether to make an order under those parts, to require the attendance of the child and to make supplementary orders to secure that attendance.

"a party shall attend a directions appointment" (r 16(1))—By virtue of the fact that r 16(1) is dealing with directions appointments under r 14, "party" carries the extended meaning in that rule and includes the children's guardian and, where a request or direction concerns a report under s 7, the children and family reporter or welfare officer (see r 14(1)). The children's guardian is, in any event, obliged by r 11(4) to attend all directions appointments unless excused by the court or the justices' clerk. As to the children and family reporter, there appears to be a conflict between r 11B(3) (the effect of which is that a children and family reporter is only obliged to attend a hearing if required to do so by a specific direction) and r 16(1) (which requires attendance at all directions hearings unless otherwise directed); the same conflict arises in relation to a welfare officer who prepares a report under s 7(1)(*b*), whose attendance is only required if there is a specific direction to that effect pursuant to r 13(3). In practice, r 11B prevails in relation to the children and family reporter and r 13 prevails in relation to the welfare officer, so that they will not be in attendance unless this has been specifically required. For an explanation of the difference between a children and family reporter and a welfare officer see annotation under FPR 1991, r 4.13.

"notice in accordance with rule 14(5)" (r 16(1))—Rule 16(1) appears to be poorly drafted. The only notice that is specifically required to be given in accordance with r 14(5) is the notice that has to be given to the parties under r 14(5)(*a*), where the court or the justices' clerk intends, of its/his own motion, to give, vary or revoke directions under r 14(2). There will not necessarily be any directions hearing to go with the r 14(5)(*a*) notice (or at least not a hearing which the parties can be obliged to attend) as all that is required by r 14(5)(*a*) is that the parties be given an opportunity to attend and be heard or to make written representations. Where a party makes a written request for directions under r 14(5)(*b*) or (*c*), a notice of a directions hearing may follow but it is not, strictly speaking, given in accordance with r 14(5) but rather in accordance with r 14(7) or (8)(*b*). It is suggested that, despite the loose drafting, r 16(1) is meant to require attendance in response to such notices. The equivalent provision for county courts and the High Court (FPR 1991, r 4.16(1)) is not much more happily drafted but clearly does require attendance at a directions hearing arranged in pursuance of a written request of a party under the FPR equivalent of r 14(5)(*b*) (r 4.14(3)(*b*)), though not, perhaps, under the FPR equivalent of r 14(5)(*c*) (r 4.14(3)(*c*)).

"unless the justices' clerk or the court otherwise directs" (r 16(1))—The justices' clerk and the court are given a complete discretion as to the circumstances in which to dispense with the attendance of a party at a directions hearing and can do so either of his/its own motion (for example when sending out notice of the appointment) or on the request of a party. It is suggested that the power to give the necessary direction derives from r 16(1) itself rather than from r 14. If this were not so, the provisions of r 14 as to notice and as to the fixing of a hearing of a request for directions would apply, with the result that the clerk or the court might well end up having to hold a *preliminary* directions hearing (which the parties might all have to attend) about whether to require attendance at the directions hearing.

Attendance of parties at hearing for grant of leave to make an application—The grant of leave to apply for a s 8 order is a substantial judicial decision which falls to be determined by reference to CA 1989, s 10(9) and by consideration of the prima facie merits of the application, undertaken in the ordinary case, in the presence in court of both parties (*Re W (Contact Application: Procedure)* [2000] 1 FLR 263 – where the justices erred in dealing with an application for leave without arranging for a hearing in the presence of both parties).

Seeking a direction dispensing with attendance at a directions appointment—On the assumption that the power to give directions about attendance derives from r 16(1) itself (see **"unless the justices' clerk or the court otherwise directs"** above), there is no set procedure for seeking a direction excusing a party from attendance at a directions appointment. An advance request in writing may be made if there is time (for guidance as to the manner of making such a request, see **Written request for directions in Form C2** under r 14), but there does not appear to be any reason why an oral request should not be made in appropriate circumstances. For example, where a clerk is fixing the next appointment at the conclusion of giving directions, he might be asked, in special circumstances, to dispense with the attendance of one of the parties on the next occasion.

Use of the power to exclude (r 16(2))—Generally, all parties (including the child himself if he is a party) are entitled to be present throughout the proceedings. Rule 16(2) empowers the court (not, in this case, the justices' clerk) to exclude a party where the criteria laid down are satisfied; it is in mandatory terms and contrasts with r 16(3), (5) and (6) which confers on the court or the justices' clerk a discretion as to whether to proceed with a hearing or appointment where a party fails to attend. Rule 16(2) will no doubt normally come into play where it is the child who should be excluded for his own good. For the attitude of the courts towards the attendance of children at hearings, see **Child at court** below. Rule 16(2) may also be used where, for some reason, another party's presence would impede a proper hearing, for example in the very rare case where an older child is to give evidence and would find it distressing to do so in the presence of a parent who is alleged to be guilty of a serious sexual assault on him or her. However, in such a situation, the giving of the child's evidence by video link or behind a screen may be a better course. Exceptionally, an application for an adjournment can be granted ex parte, but only where the best interests of the children justify such a course of action. Even then, those representing the parties should be in attendance, either having given undertakings or being subject to a direction of the court not to pass on the information to their clients (*Re B (Minors) (Care: Procedure)* [1994] Fam Law 72 – local authority applied ex parte to adjourn application relating to contact with child in care so that it could carry out investigations into allegations of sexual abuse against a parent without the parents learning of the allegations).

Child at court—The effect of r 16(1) is to require the child, if he is a party, to be present at directions appointments unless the court otherwise directs. As it is not generally considered that it is wise for children to attend court (see below), it might be appropriate to seek, at an early stage in proceedings, a direction excusing the child from attendance at directions hearings. There is no obligation on the child to attend hearings other than directions hearings but, if he is a party, he is entitled to do so unless excluded under r 16(2) or otherwise by order of the court. See under FPR 1991, r 4.16 for further discussion of the attitude of the courts towards the attendance of children at court.

Care proceedings: more than one local authority involved—Where the applicant local authority will not be the authority responsible for operating the arrangements for the child once an order is made, the need for the second local authority to attend court to deal with issues arising must be borne in mind (*L v London Borough of Bexley* [1996] 2 FLR 595). See also *Re C (Care Order: Appropriate Local Authority)* [1997] 1 FLR 544, FD.

"Relevant proceedings" (r 16(2))—The term "relevant proceedings" has the meaning assigned to it by CA 1989, s 93(3), ie any application made or proceedings brought under any of the provisions listed in s 93(1) and any part of such proceedings. Therefore, although r 16(2) does not specifically say that the court can exclude a party from a part of proceedings, it can do so. Similarly it has power under r 16(7) to hear part of the proceedings in private.

"The party is represented by a children's guardian or solicitor" (r 16(2)(*b*))—It is not clear whether a party is represented by a solicitor simply by virtue of the fact that he has instructed a solicitor or whether he is so represented only if the solicitor is actually in attendance at the relevant hearing. For further guidance as to how this is to be interpreted see under FPR 1991, r 4.16.

Child of sufficient understanding to make representations (r 16(2))—There are a number of situations in which the rules or the Act oblige the court to evaluate the understanding of the child (see, for example, s 4(4) with regard to parental responsibility agreements, s 10(8) with regard to leave to apply for a s 8 order, and s 43(8) with regard to medical and other examinations). No criteria are laid down as to what constitutes sufficient understanding and what is sufficient for one purpose may not, of course, be sufficient for another; the court will have to take a decision on the particular facts of each case. The authorities on the understanding of a child are collected together under **"able ... to give such instructions on his own behalf"** under FPR 1991, r 4.12. Where there is a children's guardian, he will advise the court as to the level of the child's understanding and the child's wishes in accordance with r 11(4) and where there is a children and family reporter, he can be asked to assist. Alternatively, the assessment will have to be based upon how the child appears and what he (or his legal representative on his behalf) says in court. In county courts and the High Court, the judge or district judge may decide to see a child privately if appropriate, but it is rarely right for magistrates to do so (see further **Magistrates seeing the child privately** under r 21). In certain cases, it may be necessary for evidence to be heard on the question from the expert or experts already involved in the case.

"opportunity to make representations" (r 16(2))—The rules do not require that there should be an opportunity for *oral* representations so, although oral representations will be usual, presumably an opportunity to make written representations will suffice.

Hearing or directions appointment in the absence of a respondent (r 16(3), (4))—Rule 16(3) and (4) gives the clerk or the court a wide discretion to entertain proceedings in the absence of a respondent and even go so far as to permit an application to proceed to a hearing, despite the fact that the respondent is absent because he has not had reasonable notice of the hearing date. The court is not likely to go to this extreme very often but, where it is prepared to do so, it may be inclined to safeguard the position of the respondent by providing, for example, that he shall be entitled to apply within a certain number of days of service of the order upon him to have it varied or discharged (for a similar sort of order, see *Re D (A Minor) (Child: Removal from Jurisdiction)* [1992] 1 FLR 637). Where an application is made at the hearing itself for an order different in kind from that previously applied for, the respondent must be given the opportunity to be present at the hearing, and should be given the chance to cross-examine witnesses called by the applicant (*Re W (A Minor) (Interim Care Order)* [1994] 2 FLR 892, CA). For further discussion of the case-law relating to this topic see under FPR 1991, r 4.16.

Although r 16(4) refers only to the *court* being unable to proceed in the absence of a respondent unless one of the conditions set out is satisfied, it cannot be intended that the *justices' clerk* should be free to proceed in disregard of the rule, and it is assumed that he is equally bound to pay attention to the limitations it imposes.

Dismissal of proceedings at directions stage—For further guidance as to when the court may or may not summarily dismiss an application at a directions hearing without hearing any evidence see under FPR 1991, r 4.16.

"reasonable notice of the date of the hearing" (r 16(4)(*a*))—Where it is the court's obligation to give notice to the respondents of a hearing date, proof will be found in the court file. Where it is the applicant's responsibility, he will have to prove that the respondent has had reasonable notice. Rule 8 makes provision with regard to service and the filing of a statement as to service in Form C9. However, it is possible that the respondent may have had reasonable notice of the hearing date even if it has not been given (or cannot be proved) in accordance with these rules. Rule 16(4) does not specify that the notice has to be in writing to be reasonable, and oral notice may suffice where, for example, the respondent was present at the last hearing when the new date was fixed. Alternatively, he may have shown in some way that he knows of the date of the hearing, for example by writing to the court about it or by telling one of the parties that he has no intention of coming to court on such and such a day. For a further example, see *Re SW (A Minor) (Care Proceedings)* [1993] 2 FLR 609. Where there has been an interim care or supervision order and no change in this is sought, a notification in the antecedent order that the renewal hearing will take place on a certain day is sufficient; there is no need to go through the formality of serving another piece of paper. However, if a change is intended in the nature of the order which is being sought on the subsequent occasion, then normally specific notice of at least 2 clear days should be given by the party which seeks the new form of order (*Re W (A Minor) (Interim Care Order)* [1994] 2 FLR 892, and see further **"and paragraphs (6), (7) and (8) shall apply accordingly"** under r 14).

For certain applications, minimum notice periods are laid down in the rules themselves or in Sch 2, and it may be difficult in such cases to satisfy the court that a lesser period of notice is "reasonable".

Hearing or directions appointment in the absence of applicant (r 16(5))—The court has a discretion whether or not to refuse the application in the absence of the applicant. Rule 16(5) refers only to the court proceeding with the application or refusing it, but there will be many cases (for example, where there is doubt as to whether the applicant has had reasonable notice of the time and place of a hearing) where the appropriate course is to adjourn the application, fixing another date for it to be heard. If the applicant fails to turn up for no good reason on more than one occasion or has indicated that he no longer wishes to proceed with his case, the court will no doubt give very serious consideration to refusing the application. However, it must be borne in mind that such a course of action would be tantamount to permitting the withdrawal of an application, and such leave is not granted as a matter of course (see under r 5).

"sufficient evidence has previously been received" (r 16(5))—The rule specifically refers to evidence and not to statements, information etc. For example, where the applicant does not appear at the resumed hearing of a part-heard matter, the court may already have heard from witnesses whose evidence is sufficient to justify proceeding in the applicant's absence. Where, however, the applicant is absent at an earlier stage, the court may be in possession, at best, of written statements of the substance of the oral evidence that the parties intend to adduce at the hearing filed under r 17. Although the statements will be dated and signed and contain a declaration in accordance with r 17(1)(*a*)(iii), they are not equivalent to affidavits and they are certainly not "oral evidence"; nevertheless, per Ward J in *S v Merton London Borough* [1994] 1 FCR 186, [1994] Fam Law 321, they are capable of standing as a form of documentary evidence. It is therefore a moot point whether they, or any other documents filed in accordance with r 17 (such as experts' reports), constitute evidence on the basis of which the court could decide to proceed in the absence of the applicant.

There is no requirement that "sufficient evidence" should have come from the applicant himself or from his witnesses; evidence adduced by any party may suffice.

Where neither applicant nor respondent attends (r 16(6))—Although r 16(6) refers only to the court's discretion to refuse the application, it must also have power in an appropriate case either to adjourn it or to grant it.

Presence of legal representative (r 16(4), (5), (6))—Magistrates' Courts Act 1980, s 122 provides that an absent party who is represented by a legal representative is deemed not to be absent, except that appearance by a legal representative will not satisfy any provision of any enactment expressly requiring the presence of the party.

Hearings in private (r 16(7))—As *Re PB (Hearings in Open Court)* [1996] 2 FLR 765, CA, shows, children cases are rarely heard in public. A direction under r 16(7) will therefore normally be appropriate (although note the comment of Butler-Sloss LJ at 768H that, whilst in general the public is not admitted to family proceedings in the magistrates' court, the press often are). In *Re B (Hearings in Open Court)* [1997] Fam Law 508, FD, Hale J refused an application by the Crown Prosecution Service for family proceedings to be heard in open court so that they could consider more fully the parallel criminal case against the father and also refused the alternative application that a CPS representative be present in chambers to hear the medical evidence. Even if the court does not consider it necessary to sit in private, there are limitations imposed by Magistrates' Courts Act 1980, s 69 (as applied by CA 1989, s 97(8)) on the persons who may be present during family proceedings. On the whole, the categories of those who may be present under s 69 are wider than those permitted where a direction is made under r 16(7): for example, s 69 allows the press to be present as a general rule, whereas r 16(7) does not.

Publication of information about a child involved in proceedings before a magistrates' court in which any power under CA 1989 may be exercised by the court with respect to that or any other child is restricted by CA 1989, s 97 and Magistrates' Courts Act 1980, s 71 (as applied by CA 1989, s 97(8)) which restricts the information that may be included in newspaper reports and broadcasts.

Children's hearings in private do not breach European Convention for the Protection of Human Rights and Fundamental Freedoms 1950, Art 6—See under FPR 1991, r 4.16.

17 Documentary evidence

(1) Subject to paragraphs (4) and (5), in any relevant proceedings a party shall file and serve on the parties, any welfare officer or children and family reporter and any children's guardian of whose appointment he has been given notice under rule 10(5) –

(*a*) written statements of the substance of the oral evidence which the party intends to adduce at a hearing of, or a directions appointment in, those proceedings, which shall –
- (i) be dated,
- (ii) be signed by the person making the statement,
- (iii) contain a declaration that the maker of the statement believes it to be true and understands that it may be placed before the court, and
- (iv) show in the top right hand corner of the first page –
  - (*a*) the initials and surname of the person making the statement,
  - (*b*) the number of the statement in relation to the maker,
  - (*c*) the date on which the statement was made, and
  - (*d*) the party on whose behalf it is filed; and

(*b*) copies of any documents, including, subject to rule 18(3), experts' reports, upon which the party intends to rely, at a hearing of, or a directions appointment in, those proceedings,

at or by such time as the justices' clerk or the court directs or, in the absence of a direction, before the hearing or appointment.

(2) A party may, subject to any direction of the justices' clerk or the court about the timing of statements under this rule, file and serve on the parties a statement which is supplementary to a statement served under paragraph (1).

(3) At a hearing or directions appointment a party may not, without the leave of the justices' clerk, in the case of a directions appointment, or the court –

(*a*) adduce evidence, or
(*b*) seek to rely on a document,

in respect of which he has failed to comply with the requirements of paragraph (1).

(4) In proceedings for a section 8 order a party shall –

(*a*) neither file nor serve any document other than as required or authorised by these Rules, and
(*b*) in completing a form prescribed by these Rules, neither give information, nor make a statement, which is not required or authorised by that form,

without the leave of the justices' clerk or the court.

(5) In proceedings for a section 8 order, no statement or copy may be filed under paragraph (1) until such time as the justices' clerk or the court directs.

Amendments—SI 1992/2068; SI 2001/818.

Defined terms—"court", "directions appointment", "file", "children's guardian", "justices' clerk", "leave", "parties": r 1(2); "relevant proceedings": r 1(2), CA 1989, s 93(3); "section 8 order": CA 1989, s 8(2); "children and family reporter": r 1(2).

Case management—*Practice Direction of 31 January 1995* deals with a number of important aspects of hearings in the High Court and county courts. It is not applicable to the family proceedings courts, but reference should nevertheless be made to it for the valuable guidance that it gives on the conduct of cases (see *Re S and P (Discharge of Care Order)* [1995] 2 FLR 782). See also the *CAAC Handbook of Best Practice in Children Act cases* (set out in Part IV of this work as *Best Practice Guidance of June 1997*). See also **Bundles and other particular matters** under FPR 1991, r 4.14 for guidance on the preparation of documentary evidence. See also the practical guidance given by Charles J in *Re R (Care: Disclosure: Nature of Proceedings)* [2002] 1 FLR 755 (a public law case) as to the proper preparation of cases brought under CA 1989 (dealt with more fully in **Preparation of public law cases** under CA 1989, s 31). For useful guidance as to the conduct and recording of meetings and the provision of documents in care proceedings see the judgment of Munby J in *Re L (Care: Assessment: Fair Trial)* [2002] EWHC 1379 (Fam), [2002] 2 FLR 730 which is referred to in more detail in **Disclosure – impact of the European Convention for Human Rights and Fundamental Freedoms 1950** under r 4.23.

"Subject to paragraphs (4) and (5)" (r 17(1))—It is most important to note that the automatic requirement to file and serve written statements of evidence and copies of documents does not apply in proceedings for a s 8 order; in such proceedings the documentation to be filed and served is strictly limited in order to provide the parties with an opportunity to resolve issues amicably before inflammatory statements are exchanged. See further **Forms and documentary evidence in s 8 cases** below.

"a party shall file and serve" (r 17(1))—The obligation to serve is that of the party himself, not of the court.

Parties—Broadly speaking, the parties to proceedings are the applicant and the respondents set out in the relevant entry in Sch 2, column (iii). As to the power of the court to order that a person be joined as or cease to be a party, see r 7.

Written statements of intended oral evidence (r 17(1)(*a*))—See under FPR 1991, r 4.17.

Cases decided on documentary evidence and argument—See **Full hearing not always appropriate** under r 21.

Filing of copies of documents (r 17(1)(*b*))—See under FPR 1991, r 4.17.

"subject to rule 18(3)" (r 17(1)(*b*))—Rule 18 requires that leave should be sought before a child can be medically or psychiatrically examined or otherwise assessed for the purposes of preparing expert evidence for use in the proceedings. Where prior leave has not been obtained, r 18(3) makes the evidence arising out of the examination or assessment inadmissible unless the court gives leave for it to be adduced. The effect of r 17(1)(*b*) is, therefore, to require the filing only of copies of experts' reports which have been properly obtained or in respect of which special leave has been given under r 18(3).

Time for filing statements and documents (r 17(1))—Directions will normally be given under r 14 for all but the very early stages of the proceedings. It is suggested that directions should be specific. Solicitors should identify the deponents of proposed statements and the relevance of their evidence, and a timetable for the filing of statements should be drawn up. This has the additional advantage that the court is in a far better position to assess the reasonableness of any estimate of the length of the final hearing.

Where there is no such direction, all that is required is that the statements should be filed and served before the hearing or appointment, but as much notice as feasible should, of course, be given to other parties in an effort to reduce the possibility of an adjournment being granted so that allegations contained in the statements may be properly met. Rule 17 is mandatory and, accordingly, even with an interim hearing, the parties' statements should be filed before the interim hearing, in the absence of any other direction (*S v Merton London Borough* [1994] 1 FCR 186, [1994] Fam Law 321). Clearly, in this context, r 17 requires the filing at this early stage only of those statements which deal with the issues arising at the interim hearing. It would not be realistic to suppose that all (or, in some cases, any) of the statements for the final hearing will be ready. In proceedings for a s 8 order, special restrictions apply to the filing and service of statements and documents – see **Forms and documentary evidence in s 8 cases** below.

Confidentiality of filed documents—Once filed, documents are confidential and can only be disclosed to the persons specified in r 23 or with leave.

Supplementary statements (r 17(2))—There is no restriction on what may be included in a supplementary statement. It may therefore deal with fresh matters arising since the making of the original statement or fill in gaps in the material contained in the original statement. Directions may have been given specifically about the timing of filing of supplementary statements but a general direction that "all statements" must be filed by a particular date would also cover supplementary statements even though not expressly mentioned. If there are no relevant directions, the supplementary statement must be filed before the hearing or appointment in accordance with r 17(1). As to amendment of documents, see r 19.

Non-compliance with r 17(1) (r 17(3))—Rule 17(3) not only prevents a witness who has not filed a statement from giving evidence without leave, it also requires an application for leave before a witness who has filed a statement can give evidence on matters outside its scope. If the justices' clerk or the court feels that any party has been prejudiced by not receiving advance notice in accordance with r 17(1), leave may be refused. However, as a matter of practice, most courts are reluctant to refuse to entertain evidence which has a bearing on the welfare of a child purely because of a breach of procedural rules. The alternative is to adjourn the proceedings for an appropriate period so that proper instructions can be taken etc. In such circumstances, an application for a costs order against the party who is in breach or for a wasted costs order may be appropriate. In *R v Nottinghamshire CC* [1993] 1 FCR 576, [1993] Fam Law 625, for example, a local authority failed to submit written evidence as directed by the court and to comply with a direction to serve documents, but leave was given for statements to be filed out of time because it was vital in the interests of the children that the court should have the best information available. As to the form of the application for leave, it is clear that r 3 does not apply, as the leave required is not leave to bring proceedings, and it is suggested that the granting of leave to adduce evidence is, in fact, a direction for the conduct of the proceedings which should be sought in accordance with r 14.

Forms and documentary evidence in s 8 cases (r 17(4), (5))—The documentation to be filed and served in s 8 cases is strictly controlled in order to prevent matters becoming inflamed by comments and allegations in forms, statements and reports before the parties have had an opportunity to resolve matters amicably by negotiation. Broadly summarised, the position is as follows:

(*a*) In a normal case, certain documents are required by the rules to be filed and served and do not require leave. These include the application form (r 4(1)), a statement of service in Form C9 (r 8(7)) and the acknowledgement of the application (r 9(1)). Care must be taken in each case to include only such information as is required by the form.

(*b*) An answer is not required or authorised by the rules (see r 9) and should not be filed or served without leave.

(*c*) Statements or copies of other documents (including experts' reports) on which a party intends to rely should not be filed or served until the justices' clerk or court so directs. The term "statement" in r 17(5) refers back to r 17(1)(*a*) and "copy" must refer back to r 17(1)(*b*). The justices' clerk or court will normally address questions as to the filing of statements and documents at an early directions hearing to ensure that all relevant evidence is exchanged and filed with the court in advance of the hearing to which it relates but not so early in proceedings that it jeopardises the possibility of an amicable resolution of the issues between the parties. Where advance planning of this kind is not possible, e.g. where a party wishes to rely on a statement for which leave has not yet been granted in order to support an urgent interim application, the statement should be prepared in accordance with r 17(1) and taken to the hearing and the clerk/court should be invited to give leave for it to be filed forthwith.

An application for leave under r 17(4) is not covered by r 3, not being an application for leave to bring proceedings. The procedure set out in r 14 is recommended.

Service—See r 8.

Withholding disclosure—See **Submission of evidence** under r 14 above and under FPR 1991, r 4.14.

Discovery by non-party—See under r 14.

Bundles—See **Bundles and other particular matters** under FPR 1991, r 4.14.

Need to file care plan—In public law cases, the local authority has a duty to file a care plan (see *Manchester City Council v F (Note)* [1993] 1 FLR 419 and under CA 1989, s 31).

Public interest immunity—See under FPR 1991, r 4.17. Where an issue arises as to public interest immunity, it will no doubt normally be appropriate to consider whether the case should be transferred to the county court for determination.

18 Expert evidence – examination of child

(1) No person may, without the leave of the justices' clerk or the court, cause the child to be medically or psychiatrically examined, or otherwise assessed, for the purpose of the preparation of expert evidence for use in the proceedings.

(2) An application for leave under paragraph (1) shall, unless the justices' clerk or the court otherwise directs, be served on all the parties to the proceedings and on the children's guardian.

(3) Where the leave of the justices' clerk or the court has not been given under paragraph (1), no evidence arising out of an examination or assessment to which that paragraph applies may be adduced without the leave of the court.

Amendments—SI 2001/818.

Defined terms—"application", "child", "court", "children's guardian", "justices' clerk", "leave": r 1(2).

CAAC Handbook of Best Practice in Children Act cases—Much assistance as to all aspects of the instruction of experts can be found in this Handbook, at "Section 5 – Experts and the courts" (set out in Part IV of this work as *Best Practice Guidance of June 1997*).

"No person" (r 18(1))—The prohibition is a blanket one, applying not just to parties to the proceedings and parents of the child but also, for example, to children's guardians, social workers and general practitioners requested to refer a child so that an expert report can be prepared for court.

"or otherwise assessed" (r 18(1))—For example, assessment by a clinical or educational psychologist, an independent social worker or a trained counsellor.

"for the purpose of the preparation of expert evidence for use in the proceedings" (r 18(1))—See under FPR 1991, r 4.18.

Putting the documents before an expert—See under FPR 1991, r 4.18.

Procedure on application for leave: FPC(CA 1989)R 1991 provisions—Whereas the courts have provided much guidance as to the correct way to make a leave application (see below), the rules are virtually silent as to the procedure, save for the provisions as to service contained in r 18(2). Rule 3 does not apply (it is limited to applications for leave to bring proceedings) nor is r 4 designed to cover applications such as this in the course of proceedings. It is therefore suggested that the r 14 directions procedure should be used, duly modified to accommodate the service requirements of r 18(2). It is suggested that Form C2 is appropriate for an application for leave since it amounts to an application for an order or directions in existing family proceedings. Form C2 requires the name and date of birth of the child concerned and details as to the identity of the applicant and his relationship with the child. The order or directions sought should be described clearly, together with brief reasons why the application has been made. In accordance with the general scheme of the rules, service is the obligation of the person applying for leave. As to service generally, see r 8.

Principles governing grant of leave—See under FPR 1991, r 4.18.

Practice on leave applications and in instructing and calling experts—See under FPR 1991, r 4.18.

Pre-hearing reviews—It is of vital importance that where expert witnesses are to be called at the final hearing the advocates who attend the pre-hearing review ensure that they identify clearly the issues which the respective experts are to address and when, in the context of the case, they are to be called. For specific guidelines as to what should happen at a pre-hearing review see **Pre-hearing review** under FPR 1991, r 4.14.

Duty to disclose report obtained pursuant to examination or assessment—For guidance as to the question of disclosure of reports in family proceedings see under FPR 1991, r 4.18.

Conflict of forensic medical evidence—See under FPR 1991, r 4.18.

Cases concerning subdural haematomas, brain injury or retinal haemorrhages—See under FPR 1991, r 4.18.

Distinction between therapeutic experts and forensic experts—See under FPR 1991, r 4.18.

Evidence obtained in disregard of r 18(1)—There is no absolute bar on the use of material obtained pursuant to an unauthorised examination or assessment, and there may be circumstances in which it is in the interests of the child that such evidence be admitted despite the breach of the rules; for an example of a local authority being given leave to adduce evidence despite having breached directions as to filing etc, see *R v Nottinghamshire CC* [1993] Fam Law 625. However, breach of r 18(1) is likely to be treated as a very serious matter and the court will obviously require a full explanation as to how it came about before being prepared to grant leave for the evidence to be adduced. It is suggested that the application for leave should normally be made using the procedure laid down by r 14 for directions appointments and that Form C2 be used. Whereas the initial leave for the examination/assessment can be given by the justices' clerk or the court, the court itself must consider an application for leave to adduce evidence following a breach of r 18(1).

It is contrary to good practice to provide an expert with information about the case in an anonymous form in an attempt to avoid the need for court permission, and bad practice for expert witnesses who understand that their opinion is required for court proceedings to accept anonymous instructions; such breaches may lead to costs penalties (*Re A (Family Proceedings: Expert Witnesses)* [2001] 1 FLR 723).

Departing from an expert's opinion—See under r 21.

19 Amendment

(1) Subject to rule 17(2), a document which has been filed or served in any relevant proceedings may not be amended without the leave of the justices' clerk or the court which shall, unless the justices' clerk or the court otherwise directs, be requested in writing.

(2) On considering a request for leave to amend a document the justices' clerk or the court shall either –

- (*a*) grant the request, whereupon the justices' chief executive shall inform the person making the request of that decision, or
- (*b*) invite the parties or any of them to make representations, within a specified period, as to whether such an order should be made.

(3) A person amending a document shall file it with the justices' chief executive and serve it on those persons on whom it was served prior to amendment; and the amendments shall be identified.

Amendments—SI 2001/615.

Defined terms—"court", "file", "justices' clerk", "leave", "parties": r 1(2); "relevant proceedings": r 1(2), CA 1989, s 93(3).

"Subject to rule 17(2)" (r 19(1))—Rule 17 provides for the filing of written statements of the substance of the oral evidence which a party intends to adduce. Although a written statement cannot be amended once it is filed or served, r 17(2) does permit additions and alterations to be made by supplementary statement.

"a document which has been filed or served" (r 19(1))—The term "document" is not defined in the rules and seems to have different meanings depending on the context. For example, it has a much wider meaning in r 8 (which deals with service) than in r 17(1)(*b*), where it is used in contrast to "written statement" in r 17(1)(*a*). It is suggested that the term is used in a wide sense in r 19 to encompass all documents filed or served – application forms, written requests for directions, statements of evidence etc. Amendment is prohibited if the document has been either filed or served. An unsigned draft, if served in an effort to avoid delay, is probably not caught by this rule nor, presumably, covered by the confidentiality safeguards of r 23.

Leave to be requested in writing (r 19(1))—It is suggested that a request for leave to amend should be made by way of application for an order or directions in existing family proceedings using Form C2. The request ought to explain clearly why amendment is necessary, and it is suggested that a copy of the document in relation to which leave is sought should be attached to the request with the draft amendments clearly identified. It would be sensible, where time permits, to seek the written consent of the other parties to the amendment and to attach such consents as are forthcoming to the request as well.

Treatment of request to amend (r 19(2))—The justices' clerk or court is given only two options under r 19(2). Either the request is granted (in which case nobody at all needs to be consulted) or representations are invited (in which case the justices' clerk or the court chooses which party or parties to consult). Rather strangely, it therefore appears that there is no power to refuse the request without some consultation with at least some of the parties, but that this consultation process need not necessarily involve the one party (the applicant for leave) who would be likely to produce arguments against the refusal of the request.

Representations under r 19(2)(b)—Rule 19(2) appears to envisage that representations will be made in writing, but there is no express prohibition on oral representations and these may well be more appropriate where, for example, the justices' clerk or the court permits the request for leave to amend to be made orally at a hearing attended by the other parties.

Identifying the amendments (r 19(3))—Traditionally, in the higher courts, first amendments of a writ or originating summons are marked in red and second amendments in green, but this rule does not require this and word processors offer much more convenient methods of identification (bold type, underlining, italics and so on). A key should be provided so that it is clear how amendments have been marked.

Service—As to service of the amended document, see r 8.

20 Oral evidence

The justices' clerk or the court shall keep a note of the substance of the oral evidence given at a hearing of, or directions appointment in, relevant proceedings.

Defined terms—"court", "directions appointment", "justices' clerk", "note": r 1(2); "relevant proceedings": r 1(2), CA 1989, s 93(3).

Scope of provision—This rule provides for a record to be kept of the oral evidence adduced at a hearing or directions appointment in proceedings under CA 1989.

"The justices' clerk or the court"—A record made by mechanical means such as a tape recording does qualify as a note for the purposes of the rule (see the definition of "note" in r 1(2)), but until magistrates' courts are equipped with recording equipment, the justices' clerk will normally take the formal notes of the oral evidence in longhand.

"the substance of the oral evidence"—It is not feasible for verbatim notes of oral evidence to be taken in most courts. Questions and answers will rarely be noted separately but will be run together so that a witness's evidence reads as an unbroken narrative. Care must be taken to ensure that a note is made of the substance of all the witness's statements in the witness box, unless it is plain to everyone that they are wholly irrelevant. If the notetaker is selective, difficulties may arise later in the hearing or on appeal due to the incompleteness of the record. There is no express duty under the rule to keep a note of opening and closing addresses, argument etc; however, in *Hampshire County Council v S* [1993] 1 FLR 559, the court held that, where competing submissions are made in the absence of oral evidence, the justices' clerk should make a note of the submissions of the parties and, if the children's guardian gives oral evidence to the court, the clerk's note should refer to that fact and to the nature of the advice (as there is a duty to do under r 11(5) in any event). In *Re W and S (Minors) (Contact)* [1993] Fam Law 360, Bracewell J commented that it is essential that, where there is an appeal from the magistrates under CA 1989, s 94, all documentation, including the notes of evidence, should be provided to the appeal court in typescript. It would also be helpful for an appeal court if the clerk's notes included a list identifying any written statements which were before the justices and considered by them and information as to which parties were present and whether they were legally represented (*Leicestershire CC v G* [1994] 2 FLR 329); the need to complete Form C22 does now in any event oblige the court to provide this information in certain cases (see r 21(6)). The order of the magistrates' court must be recorded in accordance with other provisions of the rules. The justices' clerk must also record the reasons for the court's decision and any findings of fact in writing (r 21(5)).

21 Hearing

(1) Before the hearing, the justice or justices who will be dealing with the case shall read any documents which have been filed under rule 17 in respect of the hearing.

(2) The justices' clerk at a directions appointment, or the court at a hearing or directions appointment, may give directions as to the order of speeches and evidence.

(3) Subject to directions under paragraph (2) at a hearing of, or directions appointment in, relevant proceedings, the parties and the children's guardian shall adduce their evidence in the following order –

(*a*) the applicant,
(*b*) any party with parental responsibility for the child,
(*c*) other respondents,
(*d*) the children's guardian,
(*e*) the child if he is a party to the proceedings and there is no children's guardian.

(4) After the final hearing of relevant proceedings, the court shall make its decision as soon as is practicable.

(5) Before the court makes an order or refuses an application or request, the justices' clerk shall record in writing –

(*a*) the names of the justice or justices constituting the court by which the decision is made, and
(*b*) in consultation with the justice or justices, the reasons for the court's decision and any findings of fact.

(6) When making an order or when refusing an application, the court, or one of the justices constituting the court by which the decision is made shall –

(*a*) where it makes a finding of fact state such finding and complete Form C22; and
(*b*) state the reasons for the court's decision.

(7) As soon as practicable after the court announces its decision –

(*a*) the justices' clerk shall make a record of any order made in the appropriate form in Schedule 1 to these Rules or, where there is no such form, in writing; and
(*b*) subject to paragraph (8), the justices' chief executive shall serve a copy of any order made on the parties to the proceedings and on any person with whom the child is living.

(8) Within 48 hours after the making of an order under section 48(4) or the making, ex parte, of –

(*a*) a section 8 order, or
(*b*) an order under section 44, 48(9), 50 or 75(1),

the applicant shall serve a copy of the order in the appropriate form in Schedule 1 to these Rules on –

(i) each party,
(ii) any person who has actual care of the child, or who had such care immediately prior to the making of the order, and
(iii) in the case of an order referred to in sub-paragraph (*b*), the local authority in whose area the child lives or is found.

Amendments—SI 1992/2068; SI 1994/3156; SI 2001/615; SI 2001/818.

Defined terms—"applicant", "child", "court", "directions appointment", "children's guardian", "justices' chief executive", "justices' clerk": r 1(2); "parental responsibility": CA 1989, s 3; "parties": r 1(2); "relevant proceedings": r 1(2), CA 1989, s 93(3).

Case management—*Practice Direction of 31 January 1995* deals with a number of important aspects of hearings in the High Court and county courts. It is not applicable to the family proceedings courts, but reference should nevertheless be made to it for the valuable guidance that it gives on the conduct of cases (see *Re S and P (Discharge of Care Order)* [1995] 2 FLR 782). Great assistance is also to be derived from the *Handbook of Best Practice in Children Act cases* produced by the Children Act Advisory Committee (set out in Part IV of this work as *Best Practice Guidance of June 1997*). See also **Bundles and other particular matters** under FPR 1991, r 4.14. See also the practical guidance given by Charles J in *Re R (Care: Disclosure: Nature of Proceedings)* [2002] 1 FLR 755 (a public law case) as to the proper preparation of cases brought under CA 1989 (dealt with more fully in **Preparation of public law cases** under CA 1989, s 31). For useful guidance as to the conduct and recording of meetings and the provision of documents in care proceedings see the judgment of Munby J in *Re L (Care: Assessment: Fair Trial)* [2002] EWHC 1379 (Fam), [2002] 2 FLR 730 which is referred to in more detail in **Disclosure – impact of the European Convention for Human Rights and Fundamental Freedoms 1950** under r 4.23.

"documents ... filed under rule 17" (r 21(1))—Rule 17 obliges the parties (except in proceedings for a s 8 order) to file written statements of the substance of the oral evidence which they intend to adduce at a hearing or directions appointment and copies of any documents including experts' reports upon which they intend to rely at a hearing or directions appointment. There may also be written statements and documents filed in s 8 cases, but only if the court or the justices' clerk has given leave and directions as to filing.

The justices must comply with their duty to read the papers even where the application is an interim one and should not entertain argument about whether it might be unfair for them to read statements because not all parties have yet filed them (*Hampshire County Council v S* [1993] 1 FLR 559, as to which see **Interim hearings** below; see also *S v Merton London Borough* [1994] 1 FCR 186, [1994] Fam Law 321, referred to further under **Need for evidence** below). The reading should be done in advance of the hearing to avoid delay (*M v C (Children Orders: Reasons)* [1993] 2 FLR 584).

Interim hearings—*Hampshire County Council v S* [1993] Fam 158, [1993] 1 FLR 559 provides valuable guidance as to the conduct of interim hearings. The justices in that case had, on submissions only and without reading the statements filed or the children's guardian's report, made an interim order reducing the contact that the parents had to a child in care. On appeal, it was held that they had made a number of serious errors, and Cazalet J also gave some general guidance with the approval of the President. The following points were made:

(*a*) The discretion that justices have under r 21(2) to give directions as to the order of speeches and evidence must always be exercised judicially. Not having read the statements, these justices were not in a position properly to exercise the discretion and were in error in directing that the application would be dealt with on the basis of submissions only. If they had read the statements and decided, because of shortage of time, that they would hear submissions only, they should, bearing in mind the substantial change that the interim order would occasion in arrangements, have taken steps to ensure an early final hearing. However, if justices find that they are unable to provide the appropriate hearing time, they must, when an urgent interim order may have to be made, consider taking steps pursuant to r 14(2)(*h*) by transferring the proceedings laterally to an adjacent family proceedings court.

(*b*) The justices had an obligation to read the statements filed and the children's guardian's report. They had not done so because the parents had not filed any statements yet, but this problem should have been addressed by directions requiring the parents to file before the interim hearing short written statements dealing only with the immediate issues, thus enabling the justices to have before them the substance of each party's case in writing.

(*c*) When an interim order may be made which will lead to a substantial change in a child's position, justices should consider permitting limited oral evidence to be led and challenged by way of cross-examination restricted to the issues essential at the interim stage. If necessary, the court will have to intervene to ensure that there is not a "dress rehearsal" of the full hearing.

(*d*) Justices should always ensure that they have before them, if possible, a written advice from the children's guardian. When there are substantial issues between the parties, the guardian should, if possible, be at court to give oral advice. A party who is opposed to a recommendation made by the guardian should normally be given an opportunity to put questions to him or her in regard to advice given to the court.

(*e*) Justices are not required to make a final conclusion at an interim hearing which will usually be required so as to establish a holding position pending a final hearing which they must always ensure takes place at the earliest possible date.

(*f*) As circumstances will almost certainly not permit full evidence to be heard on an interim application, justices should rarely make findings as to disputed facts. These will have to be left over for the final hearing.

(*g*) Justices must always comply with the mandatory requirements of the rules. As well as reading documents in accordance with r 21(1) before the hearing, these include r 21(5) (written record of reasons and findings) and r 21(6) (findings of fact and reasons to be stated when giving decision). As to the possibility of deferring the announcement of the court's decision, see **The decision and the reasons for it** below.

Guidance as to interim hearings can also be derived from *Re W (A Minor) (Interim Care Order)* [1994] 2 FLR 892, CA, which endorses the *Hampshire* case. As to the making of interim contact orders on the basis of the papers only, without hearing oral evidence and/or having the advice of a children and family reporter or other experts, see *Re D (Contact: Interim Order)* [1995] 1 FLR 495, further noted under **Full hearing not always appropriate** below.

For information as to interim orders in care proceedings, see under CA 1989, s 38.

Agreed orders—Although the court has an overriding judicial duty to investigate proposals which are put before it by consent, the depth of that investigation must reflect the consensus between the parties. In *Devon CC v S and Others* [1992] Fam 176, [1992] 2 FLR 244, the justices insisted on hearing oral evidence at some length on an agreed interim care order application, and then later conducted a day's hearing of an agreed application to convert the interim order to a full order. On appeal, this was held to have been inappropriate. It was also held that, where the court intends to depart from the agreed terms, it must first tell the parties the nature of the proposed departure and allow submissions. The practice adopted in the higher courts, whereby the parties submit a draft consent order setting out the agreed terms, was commended. Such a draft order cannot, of course, bind the court but it does serve to concentrate the minds of the parties on the terms they are agreeing, thus reducing the possibility of mistakes and misunderstandings, and makes it easier for the justices to define the points at which they might tentatively depart from the agreed package. In *M v Warwickshire County Council* [1994] 2 FLR 593, where the justices had made a 12-month supervision order when all the parties sought a 6-month supervision order, they should first have put the longer duration specifically to the expert witnesses and to the advocates and, in their reasons, should specifically have explained the justification for rejecting the consensus of the parties. *S v E (Access to Child)* [1993] 1 FCR 729 (decided under the pre-CA 1989 law but still relevant) stressed that, whilst magistrates are not bound to rubber stamp what the parties agree, there must be truly exceptional circumstances for justices to discard arrangements sensitively negotiated between the parties with the assistance of legal advice (here intended as provisional during a period when the natural father was being reintroduced to his child after an extensive break in contact).

As to the extent of the court's duty to investigate where either the parties are agreed that there should be a care order or the parents are prepared to concede that there should be a care order, see **Agreed orders** under CA 1989, s 31.

Need for evidence—Rule 21(3) clearly contemplates that evidence will be adduced, even on an application for an interim order. Unless and until the maker of a statement filed under r 17 attests to or affirms the truth of the contents of the statement, although capable of standing on its own as a form of documentary evidence, the statement is not oral evidence at all. Representations of the solicitor for one of the parties do not constitute evidence on which the court can act, particularly where the application is contested (*S v Merton London Borough* [1994] 1 FCR 186, [1994] Fam Law 321).

Full hearing not always appropriate—There can be situations in which the application before the court has so remote a prospect of a positive outcome that it is wrong to allow it to go any further (*Cheshire County Council v M* [1993] 1 FLR 463). For guidance as to the circumstances in which it is appropriate for this to happen see under FPR 1991, r 4.21.

Organising the evidence—Logistical problems with witnesses arise, in particular, in relation to experts. For suggestions as to how to tackle this, see under r 18.

Order of speeches (r 21(2), (3))—Whereas r 21(3) establishes a normal order in which the parties and children's guardian will adduce their evidence, this rule is silent as to the normal order for speeches. The court can give directions under r 21(2) if necessary, but it may be convenient to follow the practice dictated by tradition in the higher courts whereby all the respondents have their say first, the applicant goes next and the children's guardian goes last. Where one legal representative has made oral representations, the others in the case should not be confined to written representations (*Re E (Minors)* [1991] TLR 300, CA).

Opportunity to address the court—Attention has been drawn to the following particular circumstances in which advocates are entitled to expect an opportunity to address the court before it makes its decision:

(*a*) Where the justices' clerk refers the justices to case-law that has not been canvassed already in court, the advocates should be given an opportunity to address the court on the authorities (*Re S (Minors) (Contact)* [1993] 2 FCR 325; *Re U(T) (A Minor) (Care Order: Contact)* [1993] 2 FCR 565, [1994] Fam Law 316).

(*b*) Where the justices intend to make an order which is additional to or differs from that sought by the parties, the advocates should be given the opportunity to address the court on the proposed order (*M v Warwickshire County Council* [1994] 2 FLR 593; *Re S (Contact: Prohibition of Applications)* [1994] 2 FLR 1057).

(*c*) Where the justices are proposing to refuse to hear oral evidence from a party (*Re F (A Minor) (Care Order: Procedure)* [1994] 1 FLR 240).

Continuing duty of advocates—Where an advocate's submissions on the primary issue fail, it is very important that he continue to present the views of his client during the ensuing debate as to the implementation and drawing of the order (*Buckinghamshire County Council v M* [1994] 2 FLR 506).

Legal representation at hearing – the right to a fair trial under Art 6, European Convention for the Protection of Human Rights and Fundamental Freedoms 1950—See under FPR 1991, r 4.21.

McKenzie friend—See under FPR 1991, r 4.21.

Advocate to the court (amicus curiae)—See under FPR 1991, r 4.21.

"parties" (r 21(3))—The parties are, according to r 1(2), the respondents specified in the third column of Sch 1 and the applicant. As to the power of the court to order that a person be joined as or cease to be a party, see r 7. The children's guardian is not personally a party (although the child whose interests he represents may be) but, to an extent, he participates in the proceedings as if he were and the rules are drafted to facilitate this (as in r 21(3) and also, for example, r 14).

Child as party (r 21(3))—If the child is bringing the application, no doubt his status as applicant (within r 21(3)(*a*)) will prevail over his status as child (within r 21(3)(*e*)) and he will adduce his evidence first.

Where the child and his children's guardian part company (r 21(3))—Rule 21(3) does not expressly cover the situation where the child and the children's guardian part company because the child is instructing his solicitor direct (see r 12(1)) or intends and is able to conduct the proceedings on his own behalf. In such a case, r 11(3) dictates that the children's guardian takes such part in the proceedings as the justices' clerk or the court may direct and may, with the leave of the justices' clerk or the court, have his own legal representation. When it comes to the order of adducing evidence, the guardian falls within r 21(2)(*d*) but the child does not fall within r 21(2)(*e*) so the justices' clerk or the court will have to give directions.

Questioning the children's guardian (r 21(3)(*d*))—The children's guardian cannot simply put in his written report; he must submit to questioning on this and on any other oral or written advice that he tenders to the court under r 11 if any party so requires (r 11(11); see also *Hampshire County Council v S* [1993] 1 FLR 559).

Court calling witness—See under FPR 1991, r 4.21.

Magistrates seeing the child privately—Whilst a judge has the discretion to see a child privately (see under FPR 1991, r 4.21), magistrates should only do so in rare and exceptional cases where a children's guardian or children and family reporter is involved. If justices do see a child in private, it is crucial that they make known to the parties any matter that the child has told them which may affect their own views or which may influence the decision that they are likely to reach (*Re M (A Minor) (Justices' Discretion)* [1993] 2 FLR 706). For a case in which the magistrates wrongly saw a child in their room, see *Re W (A Minor) (Contact)* [1994] 1 FLR 843. Where a judge interviews a child, it is normally preferable for this to be after evidence and before speeches (*B v B (Minors) (Interviews and Listing Arrangements)* [1994] 2 FLR 489, fully noted under FPR 1991, r 4.21).

The decision and the reasons for it (r 21(4)–(6))—Reasons must be given whenever an order is made or an application refused including, for example, interim orders (*W v Hertfordshire County Council* [1993] 1 FLR 118; *Hampshire County Council v S* [1993] 1 FLR 559), a refusal to shorten a prescribed notice period or to make an ex parte order (*Essex CC v F* [1993] 1 FLR 847), the determination of the length of a secure accommodation order (*Re W (A Minor) (Secure Accommodation Order)* [1993] 1 FLR 692), a decision to proceed to determine an application for leave under CA 1989, s 10 ex parte and the decision whether to grant such leave (*Re M (Prohibited Steps Order: Application for Leave)* [1993] 1 FLR 275), a refusal to give leave for a child psychiatrist to become involved in the case and to transfer the matter to the High Court (*London Borough of Croydon v R* [1997] 2 FLR 675, FD where there was particular need to give reasons as the application for directions had been referred to the court by the justices' clerk under r 14(7)). For consideration of whether there may be a class of quite exceptional cases in which reasons need not be given, see *T v W (Contact: Reasons for Refusing Leave)* [1996] 2 FLR 473 and see *London Borough of Croydon v R* (above) in which Wall J, not wishing to place an intolerable burden on justices, expressed his view that not every order for directions requires reasons to be given but that where the issue is contentious and requires a ruling from the court after full argument, it is good practice as well as obedience to the rules for succinct reasons to be given for the course taken.

Although the rules require the decision to be made as soon as practicable (r 21(4), and see *Devon CC v S and Others* [1992] Fam 176, [1992] 2 FLR 244), it can be better in certain circumstances (eg where the hearing lasts beyond normal hours) to adjourn the making of the order or the giving of the decision until the following court day or the earliest possible other date, on which subsequent occasion only one justice need return to court to state the decision, findings of fact and reasons (see *Oxfordshire County Council v R* [1992] 1 FLR 648; *Hampshire CC v S* [1993] 1 FLR 559; *Hillingdon LBC v H* [1992] 2 FLR 372). What is not permissible, however, is for the justices to announce their order before they have finished writing down their reasons and then to give reasons and announce their findings on the following day (*Re K (Minors) (Justices' Reasons)* [1993] Fam Law 615; *W v Hertfordshire CC* [1993] 1 FLR 118; *Re W (A Minor) (Contact)* [1994] 1 FLR 843). Furthermore, the findings of fact and reasons stated in court must tally with those recorded in writing (*W v L (Family Proceedings: Reasons)* [1993] 1 FCR 591; *S v S (Children: Periodical Payments)* [1993] 1 FLR 606).

Failure to observe the requirements of r 21(5) and (6) can vitiate the decision of the justices and lead to their orders being set aside on appeal (see, amongst many other examples, *W v Hertfordshire CC* [1993] 1 FLR 118, *Re W (A Minor) (Contact)* [1994] 1 FLR 843). There continue to be cases in which justices have run into problems in providing the reasons for their decision and in which the higher courts have given guidance as to how it should be done. For example, the Court of Appeal in *Re B (Procedure: Family Proceedings Court)* [1993] Fam Law 209 stated that it was helpful if the justices first set out the relevant facts in chronological order or under convenient headings, making it clear what was in dispute and what was not, and then make findings on any disputed matters. It was also said to be helpful if, in giving reasons for their decision, the justices mentioned the factors which they had brought into the balancing exercise,

PART III

even if obvious. This was not to say that every point, however trivial, had to be dealt with, but an appellate court would need to know the basis for the decision. On the format of reasons, see also *Re O (A Minor) (Care Order: Education: Procedure)* [1992] 2 FLR 7 and *Essex CC v B* [1993] 1 FLR 866 and *Re D (Contact: Interim Order)* [1995] 1 FLR 495 as to the need to deal with matters set out in CA 1989. If, in the case of an interim application, the justices decide that they cannot make findings of fact and deliberately refrain from detailed investigation as part of the overall strategy of reaching a final conclusion only on the final hearing, this is a reasoning process that should be explained in their reasons (*F v R (Contact: Justices' Reasons)* [1995] 1 FLR 227). Where the justices give inadequate reasons for their decision, they cannot retrieve the situation by sending extended reasons to the appeal court on receiving notice of appeal (see *Hillingdon LBC v H* [1992] 2 FLR 372), or by corresponding with the appellate court (*Re F (A Minor) (Care Order: Withdrawal of Application)* [1993] 2 FLR 9). It is also inappropriate for the justices to solicit general guidance from, or to communicate with, the appellate court, particularly in the submission of considerations which they believed justified their determination; anything which supported the justices' order must be contained within their stated reasons, and it was not open to them further to reason their conclusion in response to the knowledge that there was an appeal (*Re WB (Residence Orders)* [1995] 2 FLR 1023, FD). The Court of Appeal commented in *Re M (Section 94 Appeals)* [1995] 1 FLR 546 that an appellate court might be less ready to assume that magistrates have taken relevant factors into account if they have not referred to them in their reasons than it might in the case of an experienced judge, but that the justices' reasons are not intended to be a judgment and that an appellate court should be slow to interfere with magistrates' decisions as it would be to interfere with any other tribunal charged with the duty to make decisions in the exercise of discretion. See also *Re C (Care or Supervision Order)* [1999] 2 FLR 621, where Sir Stephen Brown P upheld the decision of the magistrates to follow the recommendation of the children's guardian to make a care order instead of the supervision order sought by the local authority, saying that the case revolved around the exercise of discretion by the magistrates and (at 624H) that "... the justices in giving reasons do not write a reasoned judgment, as one would expect from a judge, but in this case they have set out very clearly their reasons in a form of which they could justly be proud. I do not believe it can be argued that in this case they erred in a way which could be said to be 'plainly wrong'". In *Re P (Contact: Discretion)* [1998] 2 FLR 696, FD it was recognised that the requirement that a decision to make or refuse an order could only be announced in court after the findings and reasons in support had been recorded in writing was an onerous one and it was said to be important that the appellate court did not take too pedantic an approach to a document produced in such circumstances. The key issues for the appellate court were whether the legal principles had been correctly identified, whether the material factors, particularly any under s 1(3), had been afforded sufficient weight in the balancing exercise and whether the decision was plainly wrong. For a case in which the court, dealing with an appeal in which the magistrates had failed to give adequate reasons, filled in the gaps and upheld the magistrates' decision, see *Oxfordshire County Council v R* [1997] Fam Law 828, FD.

The *CAAC Handbook of Best Practice in Children Act cases*, App A, item X contains detailed guidance compiled by Mr Justice Cazalet as to the preparation of justices' written findings and reasons (set out in Part IV of this work as *Best Practice Guidance of June 1997*).

Departing from an expert's opinion—The court is entitled to depart from the opinion of an expert although, if it does so, it must explain its reasons (*Re B (Care: Expert Witnesses)* [1996] 1 FLR 667). Where there is a conflict between experts, the court must address and resolve that conflict insofar as it is relevant to the issues before the court and it is entitled to give greater weight to the opinion of one expert as against that of another, provided that proper reasons are given (*Re J (Expert Evidence: Hearsay)* [1999] 2 FLR 661. It is unusual for a magistrates' court to hear a case involving a conflict of expert evidence. In the event that the case is not transferred to a county court, see annotation under FPR 1991, r 4.21(4).

Form C22 and formal order (r 21(6), (7))—When the court makes an order or refuses an application, the court (or one of the justices who constituted the court) must, where it makes a finding of fact, state such finding and complete Form C22. Form C22 requires the court to: identify the child concerned in the proceedings; indicate whether the hearing was on notice or ex parte; list the reports and statements which it has read; identify those persons whose oral evidence it has heard in reaching its decision; list those in attendance at court during the hearing; and identify their representatives (if any). Form C22 is not a record of the order as required in r 21(7). That order has to be made on whichever of the other prescribed forms is appropriate to the case or, in default of an appropriate form, in writing. Where the order is by consent, it should say so (see *Chandless-Chandless v Nicholson* [1942] 2 KB 321, [1942] 2 All ER 315). Where the justices make no order, there should still be a written order to that effect (*S v R (Parental Responsibility)* [1993] 1 FCR 331). If appropriate, it is possible for the order to recite the intention of the parties at the time of the order, as a preliminary to stating that the court considered an order unnecessary (*Re T (Adoption: Contact)* [1995] 2 FLR 251, CA and see also *M v M (Defined Contact Application)* [1998] 2 FLR 244, FD in which there was an order of "no order as to defined contact" but with the parents' joint wishes and expectations set out in the preamble). The justices should give careful consideration to the practical effect of making no order (*D v D (Application for Contact)* [1994] 1 FCR 694, FD). As to the possibility of recording the agreement of a parent to seek treatment as a preamble to a supervision order, see *Re B (Supervision Order: Parental Undertaking)* [1996] 1 FLR 676.

"order under section 48(4)" (r 21(8))—CA 1989, s 48 contains various powers to assist in the execution of emergency protection orders and in finding children who may be in need of emergency protection. Under s 48(4), where an emergency protection order authorises the applicant to enter specified premises in relation to one child and the court is satisfied that there is reasonable cause to believe that there may be another child in relation to whom an emergency protection order ought to be made on the premises as well, it may authorise a search for that other child.

"order under section 44, 48(9), 50 or 75(1)" (r 21(8)(*b*))—CA 1989, s 44 provides for the making of emergency protection orders. Under s 48(9), the court may issue a warrant authorising a constable to assist in the exercise of powers under an emergency protection order. An order under s 50 is a recovery order in relation to a child who is in care or subject to an emergency protection order or in police protection and who has run away, been taken away, gone missing etc. Section 75 has been repealed and replaced by s 79K (see Care Standards Act 2000, s 79(1)). The new provision in s 79K provides for the emergency cancellation or variation of a childminder's registration in order to protect a child or children from significant harm; this can be done without notice to the childminder concerned. However, it is suggested that such an application should normally be determined with appropriate notice to the childminder in accordance with s 79L (see *R v St Albans Magistrates' Court ex parte J* [1993] Fam Law 518 for the principles applied under the pre-existing law).

Power to hear proceedings in private—See **Hearings in private** under r 16.

Children's hearings in private do not breach European Convention for the Protection of Human Rights and Fundamental Freedoms 1950, Art 6—See under FPR 1991, r 4.16.

Hearings in care proceedings—See under FPR 1991, r 4.21.

Split hearings—See the annotations to CA 1989, s 31 and FPR 1991, r 4.14.

PART IIA
PROCEEDINGS UNDER SECTION 30 OF THE HUMAN FERTILISATION AND EMBRYOLOGY ACT 1990

21A Interpretation

(1) In this Part of these Rules –

"the 1990 Act" means the Human Fertilisation and Embryology Act 1990;

"the birth father" means the father of the child, including a person who is treated as being the father of the child by section 28 of the 1990 Act where he is not the husband within the meaning of section 30 of the 1990 Act;

"the birth mother" means the woman who carried the child;

"the birth parents" means the birth mother and the birth father;

"the husband and wife" means the persons who may apply for a parental order where the conditions set out in section 30(1) of the 1990 Act are met;

"parental order" means an order under section 30 of the 1990 Act (parental orders in favour of gamete donors) providing for a child to be treated in law as a child of the parties to a marriage.

PART III

"parental order reporter" means an officer of the service appointed under section 41 of the Children Act 1989 in relation to proceedings specified by paragraph (2).

(2) Applications under section 30 of the 1990 Act are specified proceedings for the purposes of section 41 of the Children Act 1989 in accordance with section 41(6)(i) of that Act.

Amendments—Inserted by SI 1994/2166; amended by SI 2001/818.

Defined terms—"who carried the child": HFEA 1990, s 2(3).

Scope of provision—The rules in this Part have been introduced as a result of the coming into force of HFEA 1990, s 30, which concerns the making of parental orders. They amend these rules by prescribing the procedure to be followed in relation to applications made in the family proceedings court for a parental order and other related interlocutory applications, ie for the removal of a child from the home of a person with whom he lives; for the return of a child who has been removed, and an injunction prohibiting the removal of a child referred to in the Parental Orders (Human Fertilisation and Embryology) Regulations 1994.

"specified proceedings" (r 21A(2))—By classifying applications for a parental order as "specified proceedings", such applications are included within the categories of case in which the court must appoint a parental order reporter for the child.

21B Application of the remaining provisions of these Rules

Subject to the provisions of this Part, the remaining provisions of these Rules shall apply as appropriate with any necessary modifications to proceedings under this Part except that rules 7(1), 9, 10(1)(*b*), 10(11), 11A(1), 11A(2) and 12 shall not apply.

Amendments—Inserted by SI 1994/2166; amended by SI 2001/818.

Scope of provision—The procedure laid down for public law applications concerning children is made applicable to applications under s 30, save for certain exceptions. These exceptions relate to rules regarding: (i) who should be made parties, and the form and time-limits within which the applications must be served and an answer filed, for which provision is made in the rules; (ii) the exclusion of all the provisions which provide for a solicitor to be appointed to represent the child; and (iii) the discretionary power of the court to appoint a parental order reporter. In applications under s 30, the appointment of a parental order reporter by the court is mandatory.

21C Parties

The applicants shall be the husband and wife and the respondents shall be the persons set out in the relevant entry in column (iii) of Schedule 2.

Amendments—Inserted by SI 1994/2166.

21D Acknowledgement

Within 14 days of the service of an application for a parental order, each respondent shall file and serve on all the other parties an acknowledgement in Form C52.

Amendments—Inserted by SI 1994/2166; amended by SI 1994/3156.

Defined terms—"application": r 1(2); "parental order": HFEA 1990, s 30.

"within 14 days"—For computation of time, see r 15. As regards an application for an extension of time, see r 15(4) (cf FPR 1991, rr 4.14(2) and 4.15(1)).

21E Appointment and duties of the parental order reporter

(1) As soon as practicable after the application has been filed, the justices' clerk shall consider the appointment of a parental order reporter in accordance with section 41(1) of the Children Act 1989.

(2) (*revoked*)

(3) In addition to such of the matters set out in rules 11 and 11A as are appropriate, the parental order reporter shall –

(i) investigate the matters set out in section 30(1) to (7) of the 1990 Act;

(ii) so far as he considers necessary, investigate any matter contained in the application form or other matter which appears relevant to the making of a parental order;

(iii) advise the court on whether there is any reason under section 6 of the Adoption Act 1976, as applied with modifications by the Parental Orders (Human Fertilisation and Embryology) Regulations 1994, to refuse the parental order.

Amendments—Inserted by SI 1994/2166; amended by SI 2001/818.

Defined terms—"application": r 4.1(1).

Appointment—Practitioners should note that, unlike public law proceedings where the court has a discretion under r 10(*b*) not to appoint a parental order reporter if it considers that such an appointment is not necessary to safeguard the interest of the child, r 21B specifically excludes that right in applications under HFEA 1990, s 30 – the appointment of a parental order reporter is mandatory in s 30 applications. Although the remaining provisions of r 10 are not excluded by r 21B, it is submitted that, because the appointment of a parental order reporter is mandatory, the provisions of r 10(2)–(4) are inapplicable.

Duties of parental order reporter—This rule lays down the specific duties, in addition to those prescribed by r 11(9), that a parental order reporter must carry out; in particular, he must advise the court, as in cases of adoption, whether, having regard to all the circumstances and the need to safeguard and promote the welfare of the child, there is any reason for refusing the parental order.

21F Personal attendance of applicants

The court shall not make a parental order except upon the personal attendance before it of the applicants.

Amendments—Inserted by SI 1994/2166.

Defined terms—"parental order": HFEA 1990, s 30.

21G Copies of orders

(1) Where a parental order is made by a court sitting in Wales in respect of a child who was born in Wales and the applicants so request before the order is drawn up, the justices' chief executive shall obtain a translation into Welsh of the particulars set out in the order.

(2) Within 7 days after the making of a parental order, the justices' chief executive shall send a copy of the order to the Registrar General.

(3) A copy of any parental order may be supplied to the Registrar General at his request.

Amendments—Inserted by SI 1994/2166; amended by SI 2001/615.

Defined terms—"applicants": r 21C; "parental order": HFEA 1990, s 30.

Scope of provision—This rule regulates the service of orders on the Registrar General, who is required by Parental Orders (Human Fertilisation and Embryology) Regulations 1994, Sch 2, para 5 to maintain a Parental Order Register at the General Office similar to the Adopted Children Register.

21H Amendment and revocation of orders

(1) Any application made under paragraph 4 of Schedule 1 to the Adoption Act 1976 as modified by the Parental Orders (Human Fertilisation and Embryology) Regulations 1994 for the amendment of a parental order or for the revocation of a direction to the Registrar General shall be made to a family proceedings court for the same petty sessions area as the family proceedings court which made the parental order, by delivering it or sending it by post to the justices' chief executive.

(2) Notice of the application shall be given by the justices' chief executive to such persons (if any) as the court thinks fit.

(3) Where the application is granted, the justices' chief executive shall send to the Registrar General a notice specifying the amendments or informing him of the revocation and shall give sufficient particulars of the order to enable the Registrar General to identify the case.

Amendments—Inserted by SI 1994/2166; amended by SI 2001/615.

Defined terms—"parental order": HFEA 1990, s 30.

21I Keeping of registers, custody, inspection and disclosure of documents and information

(1) Such part of the register kept in pursuance of rules made under the Magistrates' Courts Act 1980 as relates to proceedings for parental orders shall be kept in a separate book and the book shall not contain particulars of any other proceedings.

(2) The book kept in pursuance of paragraph (1) and all other documents relating to the proceedings for a parental order shall, while they are in the custody of the court, be kept in a place of special security.

(3) Any person who obtains information in the course of, or relating to proceedings for a parental order, shall treat that information as confidential and shall only disclose it if –

(*a*) the disclosure is necessary for the proper exercise of his duties, or

(*b*) the information is requested –

(i) by a court or public authority (whether in Great Britain or not) having the power to determine proceedings for a parental order and related matters, for the purpose of the discharge of its duties in that behalf, or

(ii) by a person who is authorised in writing by the Secretary of State to obtain the information for the purposes of research.

Amendments—Inserted by SI 1994/2166.

Defined terms—"parental order": HFEA 1990, s 30.

21J Application for removal, return etc of child

(1) An application under sections 27(1), 29(1) or 29(2) of the Adoption Act 1976 as applied with modifications by the Parental Orders (Human Fertilisation and Embryology) Regulations 1994 shall be made by complaint to the family proceedings court in which the application under section 30 of the 1990 Act is pending.

(2) The respondents shall be all the parties to the proceedings under section 30 and such other person or body, not being the child, as the court thinks fit.

(3) The justices' chief executive shall serve notice of the time fixed for the hearing, together with a copy of the complaint on the guardian ad litem who may attend on the hearing of the application and be heard on the question of whether the application should be granted.

(4) The court may at any time give directions as to the conduct of the application under this rule.

(5) Where an application under this rule is determined, the justices' chief executive shall serve notice of the determination on all the parties.

(6) A search warrant issued by a justice of the peace under section 29(4) of the Adoption Act 1976 (applied as above) (which relates to premises specified in an information to which an order made under the said section 29(1) relates, authorising a constable to search the said premises and if he finds the child to return the child to the person on whose application the said order was made) shall be in a warrant form as if issued under section 102 of the Children Act 1989 (warrant to search for or remove a child) or a form to the like effect.

Amendments—Inserted by SI 1994/2166; amended by SI 2001/615.

Scope of provision—The Parental Orders (Human Fertilisation and Embryology) Regulations 1994 extend certain provisions of the Adoption Act 1976, with modifications, to applications under HFEA 1990, s 30. This rule lays down the procedure to be followed in interlocutory applications made in s 30 proceedings for: (i) leave to remove a child from the home of a person with whom he lives (s 27(1)); (ii) an order for the return of a child who has been removed from the home of a person with whom he lives (s 29(1)); and (iii) an order directing a person not to remove the child from the home of a person with whom he lives (s 29(2)). The court also has power on an application made to it to make a search and recovery order under AA 1976, s 29(4) (see Parental Orders (Human Fertilisation and Embryology) Regulations 1994, Sch 1). The FPC(CA 1989)R 1991 make reference to the form for the search warrant to be issued in warrant form, if issued under CA 1989, s 102, or a form to the like effect. It is submitted that, where such an order is made, it should be drawn on Form C28 or C31 with the necessary modification.

It will be observed that, whereas the application for a parental order is made on the prescribed form, the aforesaid applications are to be made by complaint in the court in which the substantive application is pending. The rules do not make any other reference to the procedure applicable to these applications. Since the reference is to a remedy provided by the Adoption Act 1976, Magistrates' Courts (Adoption) Rules 1984, rr 27 and 29 should be consulted for the procedure to be followed. However, it is submitted that, where an application is made for a search and recovery warrant, the application should be in like form as an application in Form C19 (an application for a warrant of assistance under CA 1989, s 102), as the provision of FPC(CA 1989)R 1991 makes specific reference to that section or, alternatively, Form C3.

Respondents—This rule makes provision for the persons who should be served with notice of the applications. Generally, the respondents to the applications will be all the persons who were parties to the proceedings under HFEA 1990, s 30 and any person or body as the court may direct.

Service—This rule does not set the time-limit for such application, and so the rules applicable in other family applications will apply; accordingly, notice of the application must be at least 7 business days after the day of service (r 15(2)).

PART III

Documents—The rules do not prescribe the documents to be filed in support of any application to which they relate. It is submitted that, as in all other family proceedings under CA 1989, the application for any of the related orders should be supported by statements as prescribed for applications under CA 1989. In adoption applications, the information is given on oath or affirmation where the application is for a search warrant under AA 1976, s 29(4).

PART III
MISCELLANEOUS

22 Costs

(1) In any relevant proceedings, the court may, at any time during the proceedings in that court, make an order that a party pay the whole or any part of the costs of any other party.

(2) A party against whom the court is considering making a costs order shall have an opportunity to make representations as to why the order should not be made.

Defined terms—"court", "party": r 1(2); "relevant proceedings": r 1(2), CA 1989, s 93(3).

"opportunity to make representations" (r 22(2))—It is anticipated that the opportunity afforded will normally be to make oral representations, but there appears to be nothing to prevent written representations being invited or made in an appropriate case.

Court's approach to orders for costs—It is not usual for costs orders to be made in children's cases (*Gojkovic v Gojkovic (No 2)* [1992] Fam 40, [1991] 2 FLR 233). This is so in proceedings between parents and other relations, but also applies to proceedings in which a local authority is a party when it is unusual for the authority to be ordered to pay the costs of the other parties (save perhaps for making a contribution to the Official Solicitor's costs in the higher courts); see *Re M (Local Authority's Costs)* [1995] 1 FLR 533. However, courts are certainly willing to consider the issue of costs, particularly in the case of persistent or aggressively pursued applications which either harass the respondent or are mounted without the least prospect of success. In all cases the issue of costs remains within the discretion of the court. The general rule is succinctly stated by Butler Sloss LJ in *Re G (Costs: Child Case)* [1999] 2 FLR 250: "It is unusual to order costs, although it will be appropriate to order costs when a parent, even a litigant in person, goes beyond the limit of what is reasonable to pursue the application before the court ... because it is an unusual order, it ought to be clear on the face of the transcript, either in the judgment or preferably in the order for costs, as to why it is that the normal situation is not being followed." For examples of costs being awarded against a party who had been unreasonable in the conduct of the litigation see *R v R (Costs: Child Case)* [1997] 2 FLR 95 and *Re B (A Minor)* [1999] 2 FLR 221. One of the factors that the court should consider in an application for costs is the impact of the expense of contesting the proceedings on the welfare of the child and the ability of a parent to support the child (*R v R (Costs: Child Case)* (above)). Where the proceedings are adversarial it is more usual to order costs as in *London Borough of Sutton v Davis (Costs) (No 2)* [1994] 2 FLR 569 where a child-minder had appealed to the magistrates' court against a local authority's refusal to register her.

London Borough of Sutton v Davis (Costs) (No 2) (above) also dealt with the quantification of costs under r 22. In the magistrates' courts in civil proceedings, there is no system for the taxation of costs. Where the successful party is legally aided, the justices have jurisdiction to make any of three forms of order:

(*a*) to order an adjournment of the hearing pending an assessment by the area director of the Legal Services Commission;

(*b*) to order payment of costs in such an amount as the director might in the future assess (or a proportion of that future assessment); or

(*c*) to proceed at once to make an order in a specified sum (as was done in the *Davis* case).

Course (*c*) can be particularly unsatisfactory and normally, pending reform of the civil costs system in the magistrates' courts, where the successful party is legally aided and the costs are large, the court should consider courses (*a*) and (*b*) first. However, the justices in the *Davis* case were held not to have been wrong in proceeding at once to specify the amount of costs nor in the figure they carefully arrived at.

In *Davis*, the justices had the benefit of a detailed bill of costs prepared by the solicitors to Mrs Davis and served on the local authority. Clearly, it is essential that such documentation is available to the court and, well in advance of the hearing, to the other parties, if a claim for costs is contemplated.

For a further example of a costs order under r 22, see *Hillingdon London Borough Council v H* [1993] Fam 43, [1992] 2 FLR 372.

22A Power of court to limit cross-examination

The court may limit the issues on which an officer of the service may be cross-examined.

Amendments—Inserted by SI 2001/818.

Scope of provision—Criminal Justice and Court Services Act 2000, s 16 provides for an officer of the service to be cross-examined, subject to rules of court. This rule allows the court to limit any such cross-examination to issues relevant to the proceedings.

23 Confidentiality of documents

(1) No document, other than a record of an order, held by the court and relating to relevant proceedings shall be disclosed, other than to –

(*a*) a party,
(*b*) the legal representative of a party,
(*c*) the children's guardian,
(*d*) the Legal Aid Board, or
(*e*) a welfare officer or children and family reporter, or
(*f*) an expert whose instruction by a party has been authorised by the court,

without leave of the justices' clerk or the court.

(2) Nothing in this rule shall prevent the notification by the court or the justices' chief executive of a direction under section 37(1) to the authority concerned.

(3) Nothing in this rule shall prevent the disclosure of a document prepared by an officer of the service for the purpose of –

(*a*) enabling a person to perform functions required under section 62(3A) of the Justices of the Peace Act 1997;
(*b*) assisting an officer of the service who is appointed by the court under any enactment to perform his functions.

(4) Nothing in this rule shall prevent the disclosure of any document relating to proceedings by an officer of the service to any other officer of the service unless that other officer is involved in the same proceedings but on behalf of a different party.

Amendments—SI 1997/1895; SI 2001/615; SI 2001/818.

Defined terms—"court", "children's guardian", "justices' chief executive", "justices' clerk", "leave", "parties": r 1(2); "relevant proceedings": r 1(2), CA 1989, s 93(3); "children and family reporter": r 1(2).

Related provisions—See also CA 1989, s 97, which provides for rules to be made authorising magistrates' courts to sit in private in cases under the Act and makes it an offence to publish material identifying the child involved, Magistrates' Courts Act 1980, s 71, which relates to publication of particulars of family proceedings, and Administration of Justice Act 1960, s 12, which prohibits the publication of information regarding wardship and other children proceedings held in private without leave and may make unauthorised publication contempt of court.

"No document ... held by the court" (r 23(1))—This rule is wide enough to cover not only documents filed by the parties before the hearing but also reports by the children's guardian and

PART III

children and family reporter, notes of evidence taken by the justices' clerk, documentary exhibits handed in during the hearing and the record of the justices' reasons. Once the written statement of a party's intended evidence has been filed, it too is covered by the rule. The only document which is exempt is a record of an order.

"except as is necessary in the course of the preparation of the case" (r 23(1))—These words have been added by the Family Proceedings Courts (Children Act 1989) (Amendment) Rules 2001 so as to amend the provisions relating to disclosure of documents. The purpose of the amendment is to permit disclosure without the leave of the court where this is necessary for the preparation of a case. In particular, it is intended to assist litigants in person and to facilitate discussions with experts advising in the case.

Extent of prohibition on disclosure—Unless he is listed in r 23(1), covered by r 23(3) or specific leave is given, a person can neither be given a copy of any document held by the court nor be allowed to see it. Clearly the provision governs how the court staff handle documents in their possession; it also restricts how legal advisers and others deal with copies that they have. For example, it is not permitted, without leave of the justices' clerk or the court, to disclose copies of any documents held by the court to a medical expert for his use in preparing a report. In order to ensure the confidentiality of welfare reports, the practice is for each report to be endorsed with a warning that it must not be shown nor its contents revealed to any person other than a party or a legal adviser to a party (see *Practice Direction of 24 February 1984*, which applies in the High Court and which has been followed in the lower courts).

For further annotation, see under FPR 1991, r 4.23.

"disclosure of a document prepared by an officer of the service" (r 23(3))—This sub-rule is amended by the Family Proceedings Courts (Children Act 1989) (Amendment) Rules 2001. An "officer of the service" has the same meaning as in CJCSA 2000 which established the Children and Family Court Advisory and Support Service ("CAFCASS"). The new names for the different professional duties undertaken by officers are set out in the annotation under CJCSA 2000, s 11. The sub-rule applies to documents prepared by an officer of the service (as defined in r 1.2(1)) when disclosure is to be for one of the two purposes set out therein. The purpose of the new provisions is to allow disclosure of documents to the Magistrates' Courts Service Inspectorate in the course of their Children and Family Court Advisory and Support Service (CAFCASS) duties under CJCSA 2000, s 17. It also allows disclosure of documents where this would assist an officer of the service to perform any of his functions.

Leave under r 23(1)—See under FPR 1991, r 4.23.

Leave for disclosure to expert—Applications for leave may frequently be motivated by the desire of a party to obtain an expert's report on a particular aspect of the case, for example a report from a child psychiatrist on the merits of continuing contact with a child or a report from a paediatrician on allegations of sexual abuse. If it is intended that the child himself should be examined as part of the expert's investigation, an application for leave under r 23(1) will have to be coupled with an application for leave under r 18. An application for leave under r 23(1) alone may however be appropriate where the party seeks an expert's preliminary assessment, which may include his opinion that an examination of the child is appropriate or necessary; such an assessment may then be used to support an application under r 18. Alternatively, where a party acknowledges that it would be inappropriate for the child to be subjected to medical examination, the application under r 23(1) could stand alone with a view to a report being obtained based solely on the papers in the case. For further guidance as to instructing experts and leave applications related thereto, see under r 18 and FPR 1991, r 4.18.

Leave for disclosure to general practitioner—Consideration needs to be given to obtaining leave for medical reports prepared for children proceedings to be released to the child's GP to assist in treatment of the child and to provide important information to be included in the child's medical records. The primary responsibility rests with those who have parental responsibility for the child, but the question also needs to be addressed by the children's guardian or children and family reporter or by the court itself. See further the *Children Act Advisory Committee Annual Report 1994/95*, p 33 et seq.

Disclosure – impact of the European Convention for Human Rights and Fundamental Freedoms 1950—See under FPR 1991, r 4.23.

Procedure on leave applications—Rule 3 does not apply to the leave application (it is limited to applications for leave to bring proceedings), and it is suggested that the directions procedure in r 14 should therefore be used. Form C2 might be an appropriate form.

Direction that statements remain confidential—See under FPR 1991, r 4.23.

"direction under section 37(1) to the authority concerned" (r 23(2))—Under CA 1989, s 37(1), the court may require a local authority to investigate the circumstances of a child where a question as to his welfare arises in family proceedings and it appears that it may be appropriate for there to be a care or supervision order. Local authorities do not feature in the list of those entitled to disclosure of documents as of right but may receive notification of a s 37(1) direction under r 23(2). Rule 27 deals further with s 37 directions and provides, inter alia, for service on the authority of copies of such documentary evidence as the court directs.

24 Enforcement of residence order

Where a person in whose favour a residence order is in force wishes to enforce it he shall file a written statement describing the alleged breach of the arrangements settled by the order, whereupon the justices' clerk shall fix a date, time and place for a hearing of the proceedings and the justices' chief executive shall give notice, as soon as practicable, to the person wishing to enforce the residence order and to any person whom it is alleged is in breach of the arrangements settled by that order, of the date fixed.

Amendments—SI 2001/615.

"wishes to enforce"—Under CA 1989, s 14(1) a residence order may be enforced under MCA 1980, s 63(3), in addition to any other available procedures for enforcement, eg under FLA 1986, s 34(3).

25 Notification of consent

(1) Consent for the purposes of –

(*a*) section 16(3), or
(*b*) section 38A(2)(*b*)(ii) or 44A(2)(*b*)(ii), or
(*c*) paragraph 19(1) of Schedule 2,

shall be given either –

(i) orally in court, or
(ii) in writing to the justices' chief executive or the court and signed by the person giving his consent.

(2) Any written consent given for the purposes of subsection (2) of section 38A or section 44A, shall include a statement that the person giving consent –

(*a*) is able and willing to give to the child the care which it would be reasonable to expect a parent to give him; and
(*b*) understands that the giving of consent could lead to the exclusion of the relevant person from the dwelling-house in which the child lives.

Amendments—SI 1997/1895; SI 2001/615.

Defined terms—"court", "justices' clerk": r 1(2).

"section 16(3)" (r 25(*a*))—CA 1989, s 16(3) requires that every person to be named in a family assistance order, other than the child, must consent to the making of such an order.

"section 38A(2)(*b*)(ii) or 44A(2)(*b*)(ii)" (r 25(2))—CA 1989, s 38A(2)(*b*)(ii) requires that a person (whether a parent or some other person) who is willing and able to care for a child at home, where the child is subject to an interim care order, must consent to the inclusion of an exclusion order in the interim care order in respect of the person who is putting the child at risk. Similarly CA 1989, s 44A(2)(*b*)(ii) requires that a person (whether a parent or some other person) who is willing and able to care for a child at home, where the child is the subject of an emergency protection order, must consent to the inclusion in that order of an exclusion order in respect of the person who is putting the child at risk.

"paragraph 19(1) of Schedule 2" (r 25(*c*))—CA 1989, Sch 2, para 19(1) provides that a local authority may not arrange for, or assist in arranging for, any child in its care to live outside England and Wales unless it has the approval of the court. Paragraph 19(3) provides that the court shall give such approval only if *inter alia* it is satisfied that the child concerned has consented to live in the country in question and every person with parental responsibility has consented to the move; it is to these consents that r 25(*c*) relates.

"orally in court" (r 25(i))—Bearing in mind the definition of "court" in r 1(2), it seems that, in contrast to written consent, oral consent cannot simply be given to a justices' clerk but must be given before a family proceedings court. However there is no requirement that the consent should be given in evidence so it appears that the person giving consent need not be sworn. Indeed, where the person who is consenting orally is represented by a lawyer, it is likely to be the general practice that the legal representative will tell the court of the consent rather than the person himself who will simply confirm what has been said. Strictly speaking, r 20, which requires the noting of oral evidence, does not therefore apply, nor are there any other provisions of the rules which require a note to be made of the giving of consent but it is quite plain that such a note will have to be taken by the court.

Written consent—There is no prescribed form for the written consent and the only guidance in the rules is that it should be signed by the person consenting. Clearly, as well as identifying the consenting party and including the signed (and dated) consent, the document must identify the child and the provision under which the consent is given and must refer to any order or proceedings that are relevant (such as the family proceedings where the consent is given under CA 1989, s 16, or the care order where the consent is given under Sch 2, para 19), giving the number thereof. However, r 25(2) does stipulate certain matters that must be included in the written consent to be given under CA 1989, ss 38A(2) and 44A(2).

Where a court order is dependent on the giving of consent—The giving of consent is a condition precedent to the making of a family assistance order under CA 1989, s 16(3) and also the inclusion of an exclusion requirement in a interim care order or emergency protection order (CA 1989, ss 38A(1) and 44A(1)). Although the prescribed form of family assistance order does not require it, it is therefore suggested that, for the avoidance of doubt, the order should recite the requisite consents and state whether they were given orally or in writing. The same should also be done where the court gives approval under Sch 2, para 19(1). Form C23 and Form C33 provide for the recital of the requisite consents for the inclusion of an exclusion requirement in an emergency protection order and an interim care order.

25A Exclusion requirements: interim care orders and emergency protection orders

(1) This rule applies where the court includes an exclusion requirement in an interim care order or an emergency protection order.

(2) The applicant for an interim care order or emergency protection order shall

(*a*) prepare a separate statement of the evidence in support of the application for an exclusion requirement;
(*b*) serve the statement personally on the relevant person with a copy of the order containing the exclusion requirement (and of any power of arrest which is attached to it);
(*c*) inform the relevant person of his right to apply to vary or discharge the exclusion requirement.

(3) Where a power of arrest is attached to an exclusion requirement in an interim care order or an emergency protection order, a copy of the order shall be delivered

to the officer for the time being in charge of the police station for the area in which the dwelling-house in which the child lives is situated (or of such other station as the court may specify) together with a statement that the relevant person has been served with the order or informed of its terms (whether by being present when the order was made or by telephone or otherwise).

(4) Rules 12A(3), 20 (except paragraphs (1) and (3)) and 21 of the Family Proceedings Courts (Matrimonial Proceedings etc) Rules 1991 shall apply, with the necessary modifications, for the service, variation, discharge and enforcement of any exclusion requirement to which a power of arrest is attached as they apply to an order made on an application under Part IV of the Family Law Act 1996.

(5) The relevant person shall serve the parties to the proceedings with any application which he makes for the variation or discharge of the exclusion requirement.

(6) Where an exclusion requirement ceases to have effect whether –

- (*a*) as a result of the removal of a child under section 38A(10) or 44A(10),
- (*b*) because of the discharge of the interim care order or emergency protection order, or
- (*c*) otherwise,

the applicant shall inform –

- (i) the relevant person,
- (ii) the parties to the proceedings,
- (iii) any officer to whom a copy of the order was delivered under paragraph (3), and
- (iv) (where necessary) the court.

(7) Where the court includes an exclusion requirement in an interim care order or an emergency protection order of its own motion, paragraph (2) shall apply with the omission of any reference to the statement of the evidence.

Amendments—Inserted by SI 1997/1895.

Defined terms—"applicant/application": r 1(2); "care order": CA 1989, ss 31(11), 105(1); "child", "court", "emergency protection order": r 1(2); "exclusion requirement": CA 1989, s 38A(3); "parties": r 1(2); "relevant person": CA 1989, s 38A(2)(*a*).

Inclusion of exclusion requirement—CA 1989, s 38A contains the court's power to include an exclusion requirement in an interim care order and to attach a power of arrest thereto. Section 44A is the corresponding provision with regard to an emergency protection order.

Applicant for interim care order or emergency protection order (r 25A(2))—The applicant, in the case of an interim care order, will generally be the local authority (or other authorised person) who has made the original application under CA 1989, s 31(1). Section 38 gives the court power to make an interim care order where the care/supervision proceedings are adjourned. Section 38 also gives the court power to make an interim care order where it gives a direction under s 37(1) for the local authority to investigate the child's circumstances. It is not clear who is the applicant for the purpose of r 25A(2) in such a situation or, indeed, whether there is one at all. It may be that this is unlikely to cause a problem, given that it is difficult to foresee the court being in a position to incorporate an exclusion requirement anyway at such an early stage. If the court did consider such a course appropriate, it could act of its own motion in including the requirement, in which case r 25A(7) would dispense with the need for a statement of the evidence.

The applicant in the case of an emergency protection order can be any person (s 44(1)), though it is most likely to be a local authority.

Separate statement of evidence (r 25A(2))—The applicant will already have completed forms with regard to the application for an interim care order/emergency protection order. The statement of evidence in support of the exclusion requirement must be separate. There is no prescribed form.

PART III

Reference must be made to the provisions of CA 1989, s 38A or 44A and in particular to the conditions for the inclusion of an exclusion requirement which are set out in ss 38A(2) and 44A(2). The question of the ability of another person living in the home to care for the child and the consent of that person to the exclusion requirement (ss 38A(2)(*b*) and 44A(2)(*b*)) will no doubt be covered in the statement but it should be noted that it is also the subject of a separate procedural rule, r 25. For best practice guidance in relation to the procedure to be adopted in relation to the separate statement of evidence see under FPR 1991, r 4.24A.

Serve on relevant person (r 25A(2))—The "relevant person" is the person who is excluded. It is interesting to note that service on this person of the supporting statement is only required once an order has been made; there is no specific requirement that he be given advance notice that there is a question of such a provision being included and there has not been an amendment of Sch 2 to cater for exclusion requirements. The "relevant person" may be a party to the proceedings in any event. Even if not, he is likely to know of the possibility of an exclusion requirement being imposed because an approach will have been made to another person living in the home in order to ensure that the requisite consent, etc will be forthcoming for CA 1989, s 38A(2)(*b*) or 44A(2)(*b*). It remains to be seen to what extent the courts consider it appropriate to join as a party a "relevant person" who is not a party, for the purpose of arguing the issue of an exclusion requirement, or perhaps to allow him or her to intervene for this limited purpose without becoming a party. It may be that the relevant person will be excluded from the home almost summarily and then left to rely upon his or her right to seek a variation or discharge of the order under s 39(3A) and (3B) or s 45(8A) and (8B).

"inform the relevant person of his right to apply to vary or discharge"(r 25A(2)(*c*))—The rules do not say whether the "relevant person" should be informed orally or in writing. Given that personal service of the statement and order is required, it would seem sensible for the information to be given orally at the time of service but for the documents also to be accompanied by a written notice of the right to apply to vary or discharge. Where the exclusion requirement is included in an interim care order, the right to seek variation/discharge is contained in CA 1989, s 39(3A) (with regard to the exclusion requirement itself) and s 39(3B) (with regard to any attendant power of arrest). For an emergency protection order, the relevant provisions are s 45(8A) and (8B).

Power of arrest (r 25A(3))—If a power of arrest is attached to an order, the *President's Direction of 17 December 1997 (Children Act 1989: Exclusion Requirement)* requires that, unless the person to whom the exclusion requirement refers was given notice of the hearing and attended it, the name of that person and the fact that an order has been made including an exclusion requirement to which a power of arrest has been attached shall be announced in open court at the earliest opportunity. Note that, by virtue of r 25A(3), a copy of an order including a power of arrest is only to be delivered to the police station once the relevant person is aware of its terms. This may be because he was present when it was made, or because he has subsequently been told about it, or service has been effected.

Rules 12A(3), 20 ... and 21 of the Family Proceedings Courts (Matrimonial Proceedings etc) Rules 1991 (r 25A(4))—See the notes under each rule. Family Law Act 1996, Pt IV contains the provisions dealing with family homes and domestic violence.

Application for variation/discharge (r 25A(5))—Rule 4 would seem to apply given that the relevant person is making "an application". There does not appear to be a notice period for the variation/discharge application. The periods set out in Sch 2 for discharge applications under ss 39 and 45 do not apply as they refer specifically to certain subsections of ss 39 and 45 but do not mention s 39(3A) or 45(8A). Presumably, in the absence of any specific form, Form C2 should be used for the relevant person's application. The parties to the proceedings who have to be served will be the parties to the care proceedings or to the emergency protection order application, as appropriate. This may not include the person who is caring for the child in the absence of the relevant person but common sense dictates that he or she is likely to be affected by any discharge or variation and ought to be notified of the application. Indeed, it may be that the court will consider it desirable that when an exclusion requirement is included in reliance upon care to be delivered by someone who is not presently a party to the proceedings, that person should be joined so that he or she is entitled to be kept aware of developments and to make representations. Alternatively, he or she may be eligible for notice under Sch 2, column (iv) *All applications* as a person "who [is] caring for the child at the time when the proceedings are commenced".

Parties to the proceedings (r 25A(6)(*c*)(ii))—This phrase refers to the parties to the care proceedings or emergency protection proceedings, depending on the type of order to which the exclusion requirement was attached. This may not include the person caring for the child in the absence of the excluded person but it would seem necessary to inform him or her as well.

"(where necessary) the court" (r 25A(6)(*c*)(iv))—It is suggested that it would be sensible to inform the court as a matter of course.

26 Secure accommodation

In proceedings under section 25, the justices' chief executive shall, if practicable, arrange for copies of all written reports before the court to be made available before the hearing to –

(*a*) the applicant,
(*b*) the parent or guardian of the child,
(*c*) any legal representative of the child,
(*d*) the children's guardian, and
(*e*) the child, unless the justices' clerk or the court otherwise directs;

and copies of such reports may, if the court considers it desirable, be shown to any person who is entitled to notice of the proceedings in accordance with these Rules.

Amendments—SI 2001/615; SI 2001/818.

Defined terms—"applicant", "child", "court": r 1(2); "guardian": CA 1989, s 105; "children's guardian", "justices' clerk": r 1(2).

"proceedings under section 25"—CA 1989, s 25 concerns the use of secure accommodation and must be read with the Children (Secure Accommodation) Regulations 1991 and the Children (Secure Accommodation) (No 2) Regulations 1991. The regulations provide that a local authority wishing to keep a child in secure accommodation for more than 72 hours in any 28-day period must seek authority from the court (Children (Secure Accommodation) Regulations 1991, reg 10(1)).

"parent" (r 26(*b*))—This term is not defined in the rules or CA 1989 (see **Meaning of "parent"** under CA 1989, s 10).

"any person entitled to notice in accordance with these rules"—See r 4 and Sch 2.

Copies of reports—There appears to be a distinction between those persons listed in r 26(*a*)–(*e*) and persons who are simply entitled to notice in accordance with the rules. The former must have copies of reports made available to them if practicable, whereas the latter are allowed only sight of the reports, and then only if the court considers it desirable.

Form of application—As secure accommodation proceedings arise under CA 1989, s 25 and the regulations made under that section, they are relevant proceedings (see CA 1989, s 93(3)) and the procedural provisions of the rules as to method of application, notice, evidence, hearing and so on apply. The prescribed forms are Form C1 and supplementary Form C20. Form C1 requires the applicant to give the name and date of birth of the child concerned, to identify himself and to give details of his relationship to the child. The form requires details of: any other proceedings which concern the child; the respondents to the application; other persons to whom notice is to be given; the present arrangements for the care of the child; any involvement with the child by Social Services; the arrangements for the health and education of the child; the identity of the child's parents; the family of the child, ie siblings etc; and other adults who live at the child's address. The applicant must then fill in the supplementary Form C20 in which he is required to set out the grounds for the application, the reasons for applying and the length of order applied for. Copies of reports or other documentary evidence on which the applicant relies should be enclosed with the prescribed forms, together with details as to the dates and authors of the documents.

An application for remand in secure accommodation may also be made in criminal proceedings under Children and Young Persons Act 1969, s 23.

Hearsay—Proceedings under s 25 are "family proceedings" and hearsay evidence contained in reports and statements is admissible, although its weight will be a matter for judicial discretion (see *Oxfordshire County Council v R* [1992] 1 FLR 648).

Delay—It is essential that there should be no delay whatsoever in the hearing of a case which concerns the liberty of the subject, such as an appeal in a secure accommodation case. In any appeal from the justices in a matter of urgency, the procedure set out in *Oxfordshire County Council v R* [1992] 1 FLR 648 at 651H–652A should be followed. Where any difficulty is encountered, an application for directions can always be made to a High Court judge sitting either at the appropriate care centre or in London (*Re W (A Minor) (Secure Accommodation Order)* [1993] 1 FLR 692).

Other procedural matters—See CA 1989, s 25 and annotation thereto; see also Children (Secure Accommodation) Regulations 1991 and Children (Secure Accommodation) (No 2) Regulations 1991.

27 Investigation under section 37

(1) This rules applies where a direction is given to an appropriate authority by a family proceedings court under section 37(1).

(2) On giving a direction the court shall adjourn the proceedings and the justices' clerk or the court shall record the direction in Form C40.

(3) A copy of the direction recorded under paragraph (2) shall, as soon as practicable after the direction is given, be served by the justices' chief executive on the parties to the proceedings in which the direction is given and, where the appropriate authority is not a party, on that authority.

(4) When serving the copy of the direction on the appropriate authority the justices' chief executive shall also serve copies of such of the documentary evidence which has been, or is to be, adduced in the proceedings as the court may direct.

(5) Where a local authority informs the court of any of the matters set out in section 37(3)(*a*) to (*c*) it shall do so in writing.

Amendments—SI 1991/1991; SI 1994/3156; SI 2001/615.

Defined terms—"court", "form", "justices' chief executive", "justices' clerk", "parties": r 1(2).

Guidance on use of CA 1989, s 37—See *Best Practice Guidance on Section 37(1) Directions* under CA 1989, s 37, which stresses the importance of the local authority being informed as quickly as possible of a s 37 direction, and advises that an immediate telephone notification should be made, then confirmed in writing in compliance with r 27(3). See also *CAAC Handbook of Best Practice in Children Act cases,* App A, item IV on local authority assessments (set out in Part IV of this work as *Best Practice Guidance of June 1997*).

"appropriate authority" (r 27(1))—This phrase refers back to CA 1989, s 37; s 37(5) sets out which authority should be named in any given case.

"record the direction in Form C40" (r 27(2))—Form C40 constitutes a direction to a specified local authority to undertake an investigation under s 37(1) and it sets out the full name and date of birth of the child concerned. The court specifies in the order those documents which must be served on the local authority (pursuant to r 27(4)) and sets down the date by which the local authority must report in writing to the court.

"parties" (r 27(3))—As r 27 does not widen the normal meaning of "parties" to the proceedings so as to include the children and family reporter as a party (as does r 14(1), for example), it appears that the parties are simply the applicant and the respondents.

Documentary evidence which may accompany copy of direction (r 27(4))—Rule 27(4) is important because it enables the court to ensure that the local authority carrying out the investigation receives the documentary evidence that it will need to do its job properly. However, the authority does not simply have access to the whole court file; the court has a discretion as to precisely which documents should be provided and must give a direction about this when making the s 37(1) direction. The making of such a direction will count as leave thus overriding the confidentiality provisions of r 23.

Service—As to service, see r 8.

"matters set out in section 37(3)(a) to (c)" (r 27(5))—Where a local authority undertakes a s 37 investigation and decides not to apply for a care or supervision order in relation to the child concerned, by virtue of s 37(3) it must inform the court of the reasons for its decision, how it has helped or intends to help the child and his family and any other action it has taken or is intending to take with respect to the child. Rule 27(5) ensures that this information is passed to the court in writing. There is no prescribed form and a letter or report should suffice.

Disclosure of s 37 reports—It is good practice for s 37 reports to be disclosed to the parties and for a direction to this effect to be given whenever a s 37 report is ordered (*Re CE (Section 37 Direction)* [1995] 1 FLR 26, FD, at 48).

Other procedural matters—In *Re CE (Section 37 Direction)* [1995] 1 FLR 26, FD, Wall J recommended that the court should fix a date by which the local authority's report is to be provided and a directions appointment shortly thereafter at which the report will be considered (and the position of the children's guardian reviewed, see **"direction under section 37(1)"** under CA 1989, s 41). There is no provision in the rules for the attendance of a representative of the local authority at such a directions appointment and, in the normal run of cases, a letter accompanying the report and setting out any particular points which the local authority wishes to bring to the court's attention will suffice, although the court might see fit to invite the local authority to attend in a particular case and it would be highly unlikely that the request would be refused (*Re CE (Section 37 Direction)*, above).

28 Limits on the power of justices' clerk or a single justice to make an order under section 11(3) or section 38(1)

A justices' clerk or single justice shall not make an order under section 11(3) or section 38(1) unless –

(*a*) a written request for such an order has been made to which the other parties and any children's guardian consent and which they or their representatives have signed,

(*b*) a previous such order has been made in the same proceedings, and

(*c*) the terms of the order sought are the same as those of the last such order made.

Amendments—SI 2001/818.

Defined terms—"children's guardian", "justices' clerk", "parties": r 1(2).

"order under section 11(3)"—An order under s 11(3) is, effectively, an interim s 8 order.

"order under section 38(1)"—An order under s 38(1) is an interim care or supervision order.

"representatives" (r 28(*a*))—It is assumed that this term means legal representatives.

Satisfying the conditions—All three conditions must be satisfied before the order can be made. It follows that a single justice or justices' clerk can never grant the first interim order in a case but only a second or subsequent interim order, and then only if it is by consent and in identical terms to the last such order and there is a written, signed request.

In *C v Solihull MBC* [1993] 1 FLR 290, Ward J reminded magistrates that, by virtue of r 28, the extension of an interim arrangement can be made administratively with the co-operation and consent of all concerned whilst a programme of assessment is completed, and then the matter restored for a full and final hearing once the inquiry is complete. In *Re J (Minors) (Care: Care Plan)* [1994] 1 FLR 253, however, Wall J expressed unhappiness, in view of the possible implications in terms of delay, about the uncritical use of CA 1989, s 38(4) and of this rule to extend interim orders. As to the duties of local authorities and courts in relation to the making of interim care orders, see also *Re G (Minors) (Interim Care Order)* [1993] 2 FLR 839, *Re W (A Minor) (Interim Care Order)* [1994] 2 FLR 892, and **Nature of interim orders** under CA 1989, s 38. Reference should also be made to *CAAC Handbook of Best Practice in Children Act cases* (set out in Part IV of this work as *Best Practice Guidance of June 1997*), at "Section 2 – Renewal of interim care orders".

Written and signed request—It is suggested that the written request may be made in Form C2, signed by all concerned, even though this is not particularly well suited to the situation under r 28. Alternatively, the *Handbook of Best Practice* (see above) contains a draft application form which is tailored to this particular situation. It will not always be practical for all parties to endorse their consent on the written request itself and, in these circumstances, it ought to suffice if copies are signed and filed with the original.

Section 11(3) or s 38(1) order made by justices' clerk—The justices' clerk's power to make orders under ss 11(3) and 38(1) derives from Justices' Clerks Rules 1999, Sch, para 41. As to the scope of the justices' clerk's powers generally, see **Powers of justices' clerks** under r 2.

****

30 Contribution orders

(1) An application for a contribution order under paragraph 23(1) of Schedule 2 shall be accompanied by a copy of the contribution notice served in accordance with paragraph 22(1) of that Schedule and a copy of any notice served by the contributor under paragraph 22(8) of that Schedule.

(2) Where a local authority notifies the court of an agreement reached under paragraph 23(6) of Schedule 2, it shall do so in writing through the justices' chief executive.

(3) An application for the variation or revocation of a contribution order under paragraph 23(8) of Schedule 2 shall be accompanied by a copy of the contribution order which it is sought to vary or revoke.

Amendments—SI 2001/615.

Defined terms—"application": r 1(2); "contribution order": CA 1989, Sch 2, para 23(2); "court", "justices' clerk": r 1(2).

General Note—CA 1989, Sch 2, paras 21 to 25 set up a scheme whereby local authorities can obtain, either by agreement or by order of the court, a contribution towards the maintenance of children they are looking after.

"paragraph 23(1) of Schedule 2" (r 30(1))—CA 1989, Sch 2, para 23(1) enables a local authority to apply for a contribution order where it has served a contribution notice and the proposed contributor has either failed to reach an agreement about contributions within a month of service of the notice or has withdrawn his agreement to contribute.

Contribution notice (r 30(1))—A contribution notice under CA 1989, Sch 2, para 22(1) is a notice specifying the weekly sum that the local authority considers that the proposed contributor should contribute and the arrangements for payment.

Contributor's notice—Under CA 1989, Sch 2, para 22(8), a contributor who has agreed his liability to contribute can withdraw that agreement by serving a written notice on the local authority.

Agreement under para 23(6) (r 30(2))—Where a contribution order is in force and the local authority serve a fresh contribution notice (specifying a different rate of payment, for example), the local authority and the contributor may make a new agreement about contributions under CA 1989, Sch 2, para 22(6). This agreement has the effect of discharging the contribution order and the local authority must, under para 23(7), notify the court of the agreement and the date on which it took effect. Rule 30(2) provides that this notification should be in writing through the justices' clerk.

Variation or revocation under para 23(8) (r 30(3))—CA 1989, Sch 2, para 23(8) provides that a contribution order may be varied or revoked on the application of the contributor or the local authority.

31 Direction to local education authority to apply for education supervision order

(1) For the purposes of section 40(3) and (4) of the Education Act 1944, a direction by a magistrates' court to a local education authority to apply for an education supervision order shall be given in writing.

(2) Where, following such a direction, a local education authority informs the court that they have decided not to apply for an education supervision order, they shall do so in writing.

Amendments—SI 1994/3156; SI 1997/1895.

Defined terms—"court": r 1(2); "education supervision order": CA 1989, s 36(2).

Repeal of Education Act 1944, ss 37, 39 and 40—Education Act 1944, ss 37, 39 and 40 were repealed by Education Act 1993, Sch 19, para 11, Sch 21, Pt I; those provisions of the Education Act 1993 were brought into force with effect from 1 October 1993 by SI 1993/1975. Therefore, the text of the rule above and the annotations below should be read in the light of that repeal.

Direction under Education Act 1944, s 40(3) and (4)—By virtue of Education Act 1944, s 40(3), where a person is convicted of an offence under s 37 of that Act (failure to comply with a school attendance order) or is charged with an offence under s 39 (duty of parents to secure regular attendance of registered pupils), the court by which he is convicted or before which he is charged may direct the local education authority to apply for an education supervision order. Section 40(4) deals with the duty of the court, where the local education authority has applied for an education supervision order, to direct in certain circumstances that an existing school attendance order shall cease to be in force.

"education supervision order" (r 31(1))—Application for an education supervision order is made under CA 1989, s 36.

Direction by court to a local education authority to be in writing (r 31(1))—There is no prescribed form to be used by the court when directing a local education authority to apply for an education supervision order. It is suggested that Form C21 (the general form of order for directions) be used.

Notification by local education authority of intention not to apply (r 31(2))—There is no prescribed form to be used by the local education authority when notifying the court of its intention not to apply for an order nor are any of the general forms in Sch 1 appropriate. It is presumed that an explanatory letter would therefore suffice or, alternatively, the education authority could draw up a formal document more in the nature of a pleading. The important thing is to ensure that the court can identify the case to which the written notification applies so whatever document is used must:

(*a*) quote the case name and number;

(*b*) give the full name and date of birth of the child;

(*c*) refer to the court's direction to the education authority to apply for an education supervision order and give the date of it.

The decision not to apply must be clearly communicated to the court together with the reasons for it (Education Act 1944, s 40(3A)). The education authority has a duty under s 40(3B) to communicate the reasons before the end of a period of eight weeks beginning with the date on which the direction was given.

31A Applications and orders under sections 33 and 34 of the Family Law Act 1986

(1) In this rule "the 1986 Act" means the Family Law Act 1986.

(2) An application under section 33 of the 1986 Act shall be in Form C4 and an order made under that section shall be in Form C30.

(3) An application under section 34 of the 1986 Act shall be in Form C3 and an order made under that section shall be in Form C31.

(4) An application under section 33 or section 34 of the 1986 Act may be made ex parte in which case the applicant shall file the application –

(*a*) where the application is made by telephone, within 24 hours after the making of the application, or

(*b*) in any other case at the time when the application is made,

and shall serve a copy of the application on each respondent 48 hours after the making of the order.

(5) Where the court refuses to make an order on an ex parte application it may direct that the application be made inter partes.

Amendments—Inserted by SI 1994/3156.

Powers and practice—See Procedural Guides 54 and 55 and the notes under FLA 1986, ss 33, 34.

32 Delegation by justices' clerk

(1) In this rule, "employed as a clerk in court" has the same meaning as in rule 2(1) of the Justices' Clerks (Qualifications of Assistants) Rules 1979.

(2) Anything authorised to be done by, to or before a justices' clerk under these Rules, or under paragraphs 13 to 15C of the Schedule to the Justices' Clerks Rules 1970 as amended by Schedule 3 to these Rules, may be done instead by, to or before a person employed as a clerk in court where that person is appointed by the magistrates' courts committee to assist him and where that person has been specifically authorised by the justices' clerk for that purpose.

(3) Any authorisation by the justices' clerk under paragraph (2) shall be recorded in writing at the time the authority is given or as soon as practicable thereafter.

Defined terms—"justices clerk": r 1(2).

Scope of provision—This rule permits a justices' clerk to delegate his functions to a person employed as a clerk in court who has been appointed by the magistrates' courts committee to assist the justices' clerk.

Powers of justices' clerk—See under r 2.

33 Application of section 97 of the Magistrates' Courts Act 1980

Section 97 of the Magistrates' Courts Act 1980 shall apply to relevant proceedings in a family proceedings court as it applies to a hearing of a complaint under that section.

Defined terms—"family proceedings court": Magistrates' Courts Act 1980, s 67(1); "relevant proceedings": r 1(2), CA 1989, s 93(3).

Scope of provision—As to the power of a justices' clerk to issue a witness summons under s 97, see Justices' Clerks Rules 1999, Sch, para 42.

Use of MCA 1980, s 97 to compel attendance of children as witnesses—See **Children as witnesses in family proceedings** under CA 1989, s 96.

33A Disclosure of addresses

(1) Nothing in these Rules shall be construed as requiring any party to reveal the address of their private residence (or that of any child) except by order of the court.

(2) Where a party declines to reveal an address in reliance upon paragraph (1) he shall give notice of that address to the court in Form C8 and that address shall not be revealed to any person except by order of the court.

Amendments—Inserted by SI 1994/3156.

Defined terms—"child", "court", "party": r 1(2).

Scope of provision—This rule is the magistrates' court equivalent of FPR 1991, r 10.21 and lays down the procedure to be followed where a party declines to reveal his (or a child's) private address.

33B Setting aside on failure of service

Where an application has been sent to a respondent in accordance with rule 8(1) and, after an order has been made on the application, it appears to the court that the application did not come to the knowledge of the respondent in due time, the court may of its own motion set aside the order and may give such directions as it thinks fit for the rehearing of the application.

Amendments—Inserted by SI 1997/1895.

Scope of provision—This rule allows the court to set aside an order and give directions for a rehearing of a matter where an order has been made on an application, if it appears to the court that, despite service in accordance with r 8(1), the respondent did not know in due time of the application. Presumably the respondent will have to adduce evidence of this lack of knowledge.

34 Consequential and minor amendments, savings and transitionals

(1) Subject to paragraph (3) the consequential and minor amendments in Schedule 3 to these Rules shall have effect.

(2) Subject to paragraph (3), the provisions of the 1981 rules shall have effect subject to these Rules.

(3) Nothing in these Rules shall affect any proceedings which are pending (within the meaning of paragraph 1 of Schedule 14 to the Act of 1989) immediately before these Rules come into force.

Schedule 3—Schedule 3 amends the Justices' Clerks Rules 1999.

"the 1981 Rules shall have effect subject to these Rules" (r 34(2))—The Magistrates' Courts Rules 1981 are applicable to proceedings under CA 1989 but, where a matter is covered by both these rules and MCR 1981, these rules will prevail, as this rule and MCR 1981, r 3 make clear.

PART III

"immediately before these Rules come into force" (r 34(3))—These rules came into force on 14 October 1991.

SCHEDULE 1
FORMS

C1	Application	for an order
C2	Application	for an order or directions in existing family proceedings
	Application	to be joined as, or cease to be, a party in existing family proceedings
	Application	for leave to commence proceedings
C3	Application	for an order authorising search for, taking charge of, and delivery of a child
C4	Application	for an order for disclosure of a child's whereabouts
C5	Application	concerning the registration of a child-minder or a provider of day care
C6	Notice	of proceedings [Hearing] [Directions Appointment] (*Notice to parties*)
C6A	Notice	of proceedings [Hearing] [Directions Appointment] (*Notice to non-parties*)
C7		Acknowledgement
C8		Confidential Address
C9	Statement	of Service
C10	Supplement	for an application for financial provision for a child or for variation of financial provision for a child
C10A	Statement	of Means
C11	Supplement	for an application for an Emergency Protection Order
C12	Supplement	For an application for a Warrant to assist a person authorised by an Emergency Protection Order
C13	Supplement	for an application for a Care or Supervision Order
C14	Supplement	for an application for authority to refuse contact with a child in care
C15	Supplement	for an application for contact with a child in care
C16	Supplement	for an application for a Child Assessment Order
C17	Supplement	for an application for an Education Supervision Order
C17A	Supplement	for an application for an extension of an Education Supervision Order
C18	Supplement	for an application for a Recovery Order
C19	Supplement	for a Warrant of Assistance
C20	Supplement	for an application for an order to hold a child in Secure Accommodation
C21	Order or direction	Blank
C22	Record	of hearing
C23	Order	Emergency Protection Order
C24	Order	Variation of an Emergency Protection Order Extension of an Emergency Protection Order Discharge of an Emergency Protection Order
C25	Warrant	To assist a person authorised by an Emergency Protection Order
C26	Order	Authority to keep a child in Secure Accommodation
C27	Order	Authority to search for another child

C28	Warrant	To assist a person to gain access to a child or entry to premises
C29	Order	Recovery of a child
C30	Order	To disclose information about the whereabouts of a missing child
C31	Order	Authorising search for, taking charge of, and delivery of a child
C32	Order	Care Order
		Discharge of a Care Order
C33	Order	Interim Care Order
C34	Order	Contact with a child in care
		Authority to refuse contact with a child in care
C35	Order	Supervision Order
		Interim Supervision Order
C36	Order	Substitution of a Supervision Order for a Care Order
		Discharge of a Supervision Order
		Variation of a Supervision Order
		Extension of a Supervision Order
C37	Order	Education Supervision Order
C38	Order	Discharge of an Education Supervision Order
		Extension of an Education Supervision Order
C39	Order	Child Assessment Order
C40	Direction	To undertake an investigation
C41	Order	Cancellation of the registration of a child-minder or a provider of day care
		Removal, Variation or Imposition of a requirement on a child-minder or a provider of day care
C42	Order	Family Assistance Order
C43	Order	Residence Order
		Contact Order
		Specific Issue Order
		Prohibited Steps Order
C44	Order	Leave to change the surname by which a child is known
		Leave to remove a child from the United Kingdom
C45	Order	Parental Responsibility Order
		Termination of a Parental Responsibility Order
C46	Order	Appointment of a guardian
		Termination of the appointment of a guardian
C47	Order	Making or refusing the appointment of a children's guardian
		Termination of the appointment of a children's guardian
C48	Order	Appointment of a solicitor for a child
		Refusal of the appointment of a solicitor for a child
		Termination of the appointment of a solicitor for a child
C49	Order	Transfer of Proceedings to [the High Court] [a county court] [a family proceedings court]
C50	Certificate	Refusal to transfer proceedings
C51		Application for a Parental Order
C52		Acknowledgement of an application for a Parental Order
C53	Order	Parental Order
C54	Notice	of Refusal of a Parental Order

Amendments—SI 2001/818.

SCHEDULE 2

RESPONDENTS AND NOTICE

(i) *Provision under which proceedings brought*	(ii) *Minimum number of days prior to hearing or directions appointment for service under rule 4(1)(b)*	(iii) *Respondents*	(iv) *Persons to whom notice is to be given*
All applications.	See separate entries below	Subject to separate entries below, every person whom the applicant believes to have parental responsibility for the child; where the child is the subject of a care order, every person whom the applicant believes to have had parental responsibility immediately prior to the making of the care order; in the case of an application to extend, vary or discharge an order, the parties to the proceedings leading to the order which it is sought to have extended, varied or discharged; in the case of specified proceedings, the child.	Subject to separate entries below: the local authority providing accommodation for the child; persons who are caring for the child at the time when the proceedings are commenced; in the case of proceedings brought in respect of a child who is alleged to be staying in a refuge which is certificated under section 51(1) or (2), the person who is providing the refuge.

(i) *Provision under which proceedings brought*	(ii) *Minimum number of days prior to hearing or directions appointment for service under rule 4(1)(b)*	(iii) *Respondents*	(iv) *Persons to whom notice is to be given*
Section 4(1)(*a*), 4(3), 5(1), 6(7), 8, 13(1), 16(6), 33(7), 77(6), Schedule 1, paragraph 19(1), 23(1) or 23(8) of Schedule 2, or paragraph 8(1) of Schedule 8, or paragraph 11(3) or 16(5) of Schedule 14.	14 days.	Except for proceedings under section 77(6), Schedule 2, or paragraph 8(1) of Schedule 8, as for "all applications" above, and – in the case of an application under paragraph 11(3)(*b*) or 16(5) of Schedule 14, any person, other than the child, named in the order or directions which it is sought to discharge or vary; in the case of proceedings under section 77(6), the local authority against whose decision the appeal is made; in the case of proceedings under Schedule 1, those persons whom the applicant believes to be interested in or affected by the proceedings;	As for "all applications" above, and – in the case of an application under paragraph 19(1) of Schedule 2, the parties to the proceedings leading to the care order; in the case of an application under section 5(1), the father of the child if he does not have parental responsibility.

PART III

(i) *Provision under which proceedings brought*	(ii) *Minimum number of days prior to hearing or directions appointment for service under rule 4(1)(b)*	(iii) *Respondents*	(iv) *Persons to whom notice is to be given*
		in the case of an application under paragraph 23(1) of Schedule 2, the contributor; in the case of an application under paragraph 23(8) of Schedule 2 – (i) if the applicant is the local authority, the contributor, and (ii) if the applicant is the contributor, the local authority In the case of an application under paragraph 8(1) of Schedule 8, the local authority against whose decision the appeal is made; in the case of an application for a section 8 order, every person whom the applicant believes – (i) to be named in a court order with respect to the same child, which has not ceased to have effect,	

(i) *Provision under which proceedings brought*	(ii) *Minimum number of days prior to hearing or directions appointment for service under rule 4(1)(b)*	(iii) *Respondents*	(iv) *Persons to whom notice is to be given*
		(ii) to be a party to pending proceedings in respect of the same child, or (iii) to be a person with whom the child has lived for at least three years prior to the application, unless, in a case to which (i) or (ii) applies, the applicant believes that the court order or pending proceedings are not relevant to the application.	
Section 36(1), 39(1), 39(2), 39(3), 39(4), 43(1), or paragraph 6(3), 15(2) or 17(1) of Schedule 3.	7 days.	As for "all applications" above, and – in the case of an application under section 39(2) or (3), the supervisor; in the case of proceedings under paragraph 17(1) of Schedule 3, the local education authority concerned;	As for "all applications" above, and – in the case of an application for an order under section 43(1) – (i) every person whom the applicant believes to be a parent of the child, (ii) every person whom the applicant

(i) *Provision under which proceedings brought*	(ii) *Minimum number of days prior to hearing or directions appointment for service under rule 4(1)(b)*	(iii) *Respondents*	(iv) *Persons to whom notice is to be given*
		in the case of proceedings under section 36 or paragraph 15(2) or 17(1) of Schedule 3, the child.	believes to be caring for the child, (iii) every person in whose favour a contact order is in force with respect to the child, and (iv)every person who is allowed to have contact with the child by virtue of an order under section 34.
Section 31, 34(2), 34(3), 34(4), 34(9) or 38(8)(*b*).	3 days.	As for "all applications" above, and – in the case of an application under section 34, the person whose contact with the child is the subject of the application.	As for "all applications" above, and – in the case of an application under section 31 – (i) every person whom the applicant believes to be a party to pending relevant proceedings in respect of the same child, and (ii) every person whom the applicant believes to be a parent without parental responsibility for the child.

(i) *Provision under which proceedings brought*	(ii) *Minimum number of days prior to hearing or directions appointment for service under rule 4(1)(b)*	(iii) *Respondents*	(iv) *Persons to whom notice is to be given*
Section 43(12).	2 days.	As for "all applications" above.	Those of the persons referred to in section 43(11)(*a*) to (*e*) who were not party to the application for the order which it is sought to have varied or discharged.
Section 25, 44(1), 44(9)(*b*), 45(4), 45(8), 46(7), 48(9), 50(1), 75(1) or 102(1).	1 day.	Except for applications under section 75(1) or 102(1), as for "all applications" above, and – in the case of an application under section 44(9)(*b*) – (i) the parties to the application for the order in respect of which it is sought to vary the directions; (ii) any person who was caring for the child prior to the making of the order, and (iii) any person whose contact with the child is affected by the direction which it is sought to have varied;	As for "all applications" above, and – in the case of an application under section 44(1), every person whom the applicant believes to be a parent of the child; in the case of an application under section 44(9)(*b*) – (i) the local authority in whose area the child is living, and (ii) any person whom the applicant believes to be affected by the direction which it is sought to have varied.

(i) *Provision under which proceedings brought*	(ii) *Minimum number of days prior to hearing or directions appointment for service under rule 4(1)(b)*	(iii) *Respondents*	(iv) *Persons to whom notice is to be given*
		in the case of an application under section 50, the person whom the applicant alleges to have effected or to have been or to be responsible for the taking or keeping of the child;	
		in the case of an application under section 75(1), the registered person; in the case of an application under section 102(1), the person referred to in section 102(1) and any person preventing or likely to prevent such a person from exercising powers under enactments mentioned in subsection (6) of that section.	
Section 30 of the Human Fertilisation and Embryology Act 1990.	14 days.	The birth parents (except where the applicants seek to dispense with their agreement under section 30(6) of the Human Fertilisation and Embryology Act 1990) and any	Any local authority or voluntary organisation that has at any time provided accommodation for the child.

(i) *Provision under which proceedings brought*	(ii) *Minimum number of days prior to hearing or directions appointment for service under rule 4(1)(b)*	(iii) *Respondents*	(iv) *Persons to whom notice is to be given*
		other persons or body with parental responsibility for the child at the date of the application.	

Amendments—SI 1992/2068; SI 1994/2166.

Defined terms—"applicant", "application": r 1(2); "care order": CA 1989, ss 31(11), 105(1); "child": r 1(2); "local authority": CA 1989, s 105(1); "relevant proceedings": r 1(2), CA 1989, s 93(3); "specified proceedings": rr 1(2), 2(2), CA 1989, s 41(6).

"father"—In relation to an application under CA 1989, s 5(1), "father" includes an unmarried father by virtue of Family Law Reform Act 1987, s 1.

"parent"—In determining who is a parent of a child, no account is taken of whether his mother and father were married at the time of his birth (Family Law Reform Act 1987, s 1), with the result that an unmarried father is included. See also **Meaning of "parent"** under CA 1989, s 10.

"every person whom the applicant believes to be a parent without parental responsibility"—In relation to an application under CA 1989, s 31, the standard of "belief" for the purposes of issuing a notice should not be set too high, particularly where both the mother of the child concerned and the man in question are asserting that the man is the father (*Re B (Care Proceedings: Notification of Father Without Parental Responsibility)* [1999] 2 FLR 408).

****

Family Proceedings Courts (Matrimonial Proceedings etc) Rules 1991, SI 1991/1991

ARRANGEMENT OF RULES

PART I
INTRODUCTORY

PART II
MATRIMONIAL PROCEEDINGS UNDER THE DOMESTIC PROCEEDINGS AND MAGISTRATES' COURTS ACT 1978, PROCEEDINGS UNDER SECTION 55A OF THE FAMILY LAW ACT 1986 AND PROCEEDINGS UNDER PART IV OF THE FAMILY LAW ACT 1996

PART I
INTRODUCTORY

1 Citation, commencement and transitional

(1) These Rules may be cited as the Family Proceedings Courts (Matrimonial Proceedings etc) Rules 1991 and shall come into force on 14 October 1991 except that paragraph 3(7) of Schedule 2 to these Rules shall come into force on 7 October 1991.

(2) Nothing in these Rules shall affect any proceedings which are pending (within the meaning of paragraph 1 of Schedule 14 to the Children Act 1989) immediately before these Rules come into force.

PART II
MATRIMONIAL PROCEEDINGS UNDER THE DOMESTIC PROCEEDINGS AND MAGISTRATES' COURTS ACT 1978, PROCEEDINGS UNDER SECTION 55A OF THE FAMILY LAW ACT 1986 AND PROCEEDINGS UNDER PART IV OF THE FAMILY LAW ACT 1996

Amendments—SI 1997/1894; SI 2001/778.

2 Interpretation, application and savings

(1) In this Part of these Rules, unless a contrary intention appears –

any reference to a rule shall be construed as a reference to a rule contained in these Rules; and any reference in a rule to a paragraph shall be construed as a reference to a paragraph of that rule,

"application" means an application for an order made under or by virtue of the Act, the Family Law Act 1986 or the Family Law Act 1996, as the case may be and "application" shall be construed accordingly,

"business day" means any day other than –

(*a*) a Saturday, Sunday, Christmas Day or Good Friday; or

(*b*) a bank holiday, that is to say, a day which is, or is to be observed as, a bank holiday or a holiday under the Banking and Financial Dealings Act 1971 in England and Wales,

"court" means a family proceedings court constituted in accordance with sections 66 and 67 of the Magistrates' Courts Act 1980 or, in respect of those proceedings prescribed in rule 25, a single justice who is a member of a family panel,

"directions appointment" means a hearing for directions under rule 6(1),

"file" means deposit with the justices' chief executive,

"form" means a form in Schedule 1 to these Rules and, where a form is referred to by number, means the form so numbered in that Schedule, with such variation as the circumstances of the particular case may require;

"note" includes a record made by mechanical means,

"respondent" includes, as the case may be, more than one respondent,

"the Act" means the Domestic Proceedings and Magistrates' Courts Act 1978.

(2) Expressions used in this Part of these Rules have the meaning which they bear in the Act, the Family Law Act 1986 or the Family Law Act 1996, as the case may be.

(3) This Part of these Rules shall not apply in relation to any such application or order as is referred to in paragraph 1 or 2 of Schedule 1 to the Domestic Proceedings and Magistrates' Courts Act 1978 (transitional provisions); and, accordingly, the Magistrates' Courts (Matrimonial Proceedings) Rules 1960 shall continue to apply in relation to any such application or order but with the following modification, that is to say, on any complaint made by virtue of paragraph 2(*d*) of the said Schedule 1 for the variation or revocation of a provision requiring access to a child to be given to a grandparent, rule 7 of the said Rules of 1960 shall be construed as applying to the complaint as it applies to a complaint made by virtue of section 8 of the Matrimonial Proceedings (Magistrates' Courts) Act 1960 and as if paragraph (5) of that rule included a reference to that grandparent.

(4) Subject to rule 1(2), the provisions of the Magistrates' Courts Rules 1981 shall have effect subject to this Part of these Rules.

Amendments—SI 1997/1894; SI 2001/615; SI 2001/778.

3 Applications

(1) Subject to paragraph (3) and rule 3A an applicant shall –

(*a*) file the application in the appropriate form in Schedule 1 to these Rules or, where there is no such form, in writing, together with sufficient copies for one to be served on the respondent, and

(*b*) serve a copy of the application, endorsed in accordance with paragraph (2)(*b*), together with any notice attached under paragraph (2)(*c*), on the respondent at least 21 days prior to the date fixed under paragraph (2)(*a*).

(2) On receipt by the justices' chief executive of the documents filed under paragraph (1)(*a*) –

(*a*) the justices' clerk shall fix the date, time and place for a hearing or a directions appointment, allowing sufficient time for the applicant to comply with paragraph (1)(*b*), and

(*b*) the justices' chief executive shall –

(i) endorse the date, time and place so fixed upon the copies of the application filed by the applicant, and

(ii) return the copies to the applicant forthwith.

(3) A court may proceed on an application made orally where it is made by virtue of section 6(4) of the Act and where an application is so made paragraph (1) shall not apply.

(4) (*repealed*)

Amendments—SI 1992/2068; SI 1997/1894; SI 2001/615.

Defined terms—"application", "court", "directions appointment", "file", "form", "respondent", "the Act": r 2(1).

"application" (r 3(1))—Application in the appropriate form, rather than a complaint, is required.

"sufficient copies" (r 3(1))—There may be more than one respondent and sufficient copies of the application must be filed to allow one copy for each respondent.

3A Applications under Part IV of the Family Law Act 1996

(1) An application for an occupation order or a non-molestation order under Part IV of the Family Law Act 1996 (Family Homes and Domestic Violence) shall be made in Form FL401.

(2) An application for an occupation order or a non-molestation order which is made in other proceedings which are pending shall be made in Form FL401.

(3) An application in Form FL401 shall be supported –

(*a*) by a statement which is signed and is declared to be true; or

(*b*) with the leave of the court, by oral evidence.

(4) An application in Form FL401 may, with the leave of the justices' clerk or of the court, be made ex parte, in which case

(*a*) the applicant shall file with the justices' chief executive or the court the application at the time when the application is made or as directed by the justices' clerk; and

(*b*) the evidence in support of the application shall state the reasons why the application is made ex parte.

(5) An application made on notice (together with any statement supporting it and a notice in Form FL402) shall be served by the applicant on the respondent personally not less than 2 business days prior to the date on which the application will be heard.

(6) The court or the justices' clerk may abridge the period specified in paragraph (5).

(7) Where the applicant is acting in person, service of the application may, with the leave of the justices' clerk, be effected in accordance with rule 4.

(8) Where an application for an occupation order or a non-molestation order is pending, the court shall consider (on the application of either party or of its own motion) whether to exercise its powers to transfer the hearing of that application to another court and the justices' clerk or the court shall make an order for transfer in Form FL417 if it seems necessary or expedient to do so.

(9) Where an order for transfer is made, the justices' chief executive shall send a copy of the order –

(*a*) to the parties and

(*b*) to the family proceedings court or to the county court to which the proceedings are to be transferred.

(10) A copy of an application for an occupation order under section 33, 35 or 36 of the Family Law Act 1996 shall be served by the applicant by first-class post on the mortgagee or, as the case may be, the landlord of the dwelling-house in question, with a notice in Form FL416 informing him of his right to make representations in writing or at any hearing.

(11) The applicant shall file a statement in Form FL415 after he has served the application.

(12) Rule 33A of the Family Proceedings Courts (Children Act 1989) Rules 1991 (disclosure of addresses) shall apply for the purpose of preventing the disclosure of addresses where an application is made in Form FL401 as it applies for that purpose in proceedings under the Children Act 1989.

Amendments—Inserted by SI 1997/1894; amended by SI 2001/615.

Defined terms—"application", "court", "file": r 2(1).

"non-molestation order"—See FLA 1996, s 42 and notes thereon.

"occupation order"—See FLA 1996, ss 33–41 and notes thereon.

"application for an occupation order" (r 3A(1), (2))—An application for an occupation order which involves any disputed question as to a party's entitlement to occupy any property by virtue of a beneficial estate or interest or contract, or by virtue of any statutory right to remain in occupation, may not be entertained in a magistrates' court unless the determination of the question is unnecessary in order to deal with the application or to make the order (FLA 1996, s 59(1)).

"may abridge the period" (r 3A(6))—The court or justices' clerk may abridge notice in applications made on notice but it does not appear that notice can be dispensed with. Note the different wording of r 4(5).

PART III

Prescribed forms—FL401 (Application for a non-molestation/occupation order); FL402 (Notice of Proceedings); FL403 (Application to vary, extend or discharge an order); FL404 (Order); FL405 (Record of hearing); FL406 (Power of Arrest); FL415 (Statement of service); FL416 (Notice to landlord); FL417 (Order for transfer).

3B Applications under section 55A of the Family Law Act 1986

(1) An application for a declaration of parentage under section 55A of the Family Law Act 1986 shall be made in Form FL423.

(2) An application in Form FL423 shall be supported by a statement which is signed and is declared to be true. Provided that if the applicant is under the age of 18, the statement shall, unless otherwise directed, be made by his next friend.

(3) A statement under paragraph (2) may contain statements of information or belief with the sources and grounds thereof.

(4) Within 14 days of service of the application the respondent shall file and serve on the parties an answer to the application in Form FL423.

(5) Where the respondent or one of the respondents is a child, the justices' clerk or the court may at any stage in the proceedings appoint a guardian ad litem, but only if it considers that such an appointment is necessary to safeguard the interests of the child.

(6) The justices' chief executive shall send a copy of the application and every document accompanying it and of any answer to the Attorney General if he has notified the court that he wishes to intervene in the proceedings.

(7) When all answers to the application have been filed the applicant shall issue and serve on all respondents to the application a request for directions for the conduct of the proceedings, including directions as to any other persons who should be made respondents to the application or given notice of the proceedings.

(8) When giving directions in accordance with paragraph (7) the court shall consider whether it is desirable that the Attorney General should argue before it any question relating to the proceedings, and if it does so consider and the Attorney General agrees to argue that question –

- (i) the justices' chief executive shall send a copy of the application and every document accompanying it and of any answer to the Attorney General;
- (ii) the Attorney General need not file an answer; and
- (iii) the court shall give him directions requiring him to serve on all parties to the proceedings a summary of his argument.

(9) Persons giving notice of proceedings pursuant to directions given in accordance with paragraph (7) shall within 21 days after service of the notice upon them be entitled to apply to the court to be joined as parties.

(10) The Attorney General may file an answer to the application within 21 days after directions have been given in accordance with paragraph (7) and no directions for the hearing shall be given until that period and the period referred to in paragraph (9) have expired.

(11) The Attorney General, in deciding whether it is necessary or expedient to intervene in the proceedings, may have a search made for, and may inspect and obtain a copy of, any document filed in the court offices which relates to any other family proceedings referred to in proceedings.

(12) Where the justices' clerk or the court is considering whether or not to transfer proceedings under section 55A of the Family Law Act 1986 to another court, rules

6, 14(2)(*h*), (4) and (11) and 32 of the Family Proceedings Courts (Children Act 1989) Rules 1991 shall apply as appropriate.

(13) A declaration made in accordance with section 55A of the Family Law Act 1986 shall be in Form FL424.

(14) The prescribed officer for the purposes of section 55A(7) of the Family Law Act 1986 shall be the justices' chief executive, who shall, within 21 days after a declaration of parentage has been made, send to the Registrar General a copy of the declaration and of the application.

Amendments—Inserted by SI 2001/778.

4 Service

(1) Where service of a document is required by these Rules it may be effected, unless the contrary is indicated –

(*a*) if the person to be served is not known by the person serving to be acting by solicitor –

(i) by delivering it to him personally, or

(ii) by delivering at, or by sending it by first-class post to, his residence or his last known residence, or

(*b*) if the person to be served is known by the person serving to be acting by solicitor –

(i) by delivering the document at, or sending it by first-class post to, the solicitor's address for service,

(ii) where the solicitor's address for service includes a numbered box at a document exchange, by leaving the document at that document exchange or at a document exchange which transmits documents on every business day to that document exchange, or

(iii) by sending a legible copy of the documents by facsimile transmission to the solicitor's office.

(2) In this rule, "first-class post" means first-class post which has been pre-paid or in respect of which pre-payment is not required.

(3) A document shall, unless the contrary is proved, be deemed to have been served –

(*a*) in the case of service by first-class post, on the second business day after posting, and

(*b*) in the case of service in accordance with paragraph (1)(*b*)(ii), on the second business day after the day on which it is left at the document exchange.

(4) At or before the first directions appointment in, or hearing of, the proceedings, whichever occurs first, the applicant shall file a statement that service of a copy of the application has been effected on the respondent and the statement shall indicate –

(*a*) the manner, date, time and place of service, or

(*b*) where service was effected by post, the date, time and place of posting.

(5) In any proceedings under the Act, the justices' clerk or the court may direct that a requirement in this Part of these Rules to serve a document shall not apply or shall be effected in such manner as the justices' clerk or the court directs.

PART III

Amendments—SI 1997/1894.

Defined terms—"business day", "directions appointment", "file", "the Act": r 2(1).

5 Answer to application

Within 14 days of service of an application for an order under section 2, 6, 7 or 20 of the Act, the respondent shall file and serve on the parties an answer to the application in the appropriate form in Schedule 1 to these Rules.

Defined terms—"application", "file", "form", "respondent", "the Act": r 2(1).

"shall file and serve"—For the power of the justices' clerk or court to vary the requirements as to service, see r 4(5).

6 Directions

(1) In any proceedings under the Act, the justices' clerk or the court may, subject to paragraph (3), give, vary or revoke directions for the conduct of the proceedings, including –

(*a*) the timetable for the proceedings;
(*b*) varying the time within which or by which an act is required, by this Part of these Rules, to be done;
(*c*) the service of documents; and
(*d*) the submission of evidence;

and the justices' clerk shall, on receipt of an application by the justices' chief executive, consider whether such directions need to be given.

(2) Where the justices' clerk or a single justice who is holding a directions appointment considers, for whatever reason, that it is inappropriate to give a direction on a particular matter, he shall refer the matter to the court which may give an appropriate direction.

(3) Directions under paragraph (1) may be given, varied or revoked either –

(*a*) of the justices' clerk's or the court's own motion, the justices' chief executive having given the parties notice of the intention to do so and an opportunity to attend and be heard or to make written representations,
(*b*) on the written request of a party specifying the direction which is sought, which request has been filed and served on the other parties, or
(*c*) on the written request of a party specifying the direction which is sought, to which the other parties consent and which they or their representatives have signed.

(4) In an urgent case, the request under paragraph (3)(*b*) may, with the leave of the justices' clerk or the court, be made –

(*a*) orally,
(*b*) without notice to the other parties, or
(*c*) both as in sub-paragraph (*a*) and as in sub-paragraph (*b*).

(5) On receipt of a request by the justices' chief executive under paragraph (3)(*b*) the justices' clerk shall fix a date for the hearing of the request and the justices' chief executive shall give not less than 2 days' notice to the parties of the date so fixed.

(6) On considering a request under paragraph (3)(*c*) the justices' clerk or the court shall either –

(*a*) grant the request, whereupon the justices' chief executive shall inform the parties of the decision, or

(*b*) direct that a date be fixed for the hearing of the request, whereupon the justices' chief executive shall fix such a date and the justices' chief executive shall give not less than 2 days' notice to the parties of the date so fixed.

(7) The justices' clerk or the court shall take a note of the giving, variation or revocation of a direction under this rule and the justices' chief executive shall serve, as soon as practicable, a copy of the note on any party who was not present at the giving, variation or revocation.

Amendments—SI 2001/615.

Defined terms—"note", "the Act": r 2(1).

Matters in respect of which directions may be given (r 6(1))—Any directions for the conduct of the proceedings appear to be permissible even though they may be outside the range of matters referred to in r 6(1)(*a*)–(*d*).

Duty to refer to court for directions (r 6(2))—The duty to refer arises only where a particular directions issue is raised by the clerk, single justice or one of the parties. It is submitted that where all are agreed (explicitly or implicitly) that no direction is necessary, no duty of referral is imposed.

"own motion" (r 6(3)(*a*))—A direction under r 6(3)(*a*) may be given only after notice to the parties.

"2 days' notice" (r 6(5))—The two-day period does not include a day which is not a business day (see r 7(2)).

Service of copy of notice of directions (r 6(7))—Although there is a clear duty to serve a copy of the note of the direction or its variation or revocation, it is submitted that the serving of a written note of any direction is good practice regardless of whether a party was present or not.

7 Timing of proceedings

(1) Any period of time fixed by this Part of these Rules, or by any order or direction, for the doing of any act shall be reckoned in accordance with this rule.

(2) Where the period, being a period of 7 days or less, would include a day which is not a business day, that day shall be excluded.

(3) Where the time fixed for filing a document with the justices' chief executive expires on a day on which the office of the justices' chief executive is closed, and for that reason the document cannot be filed on that day, the document shall be filed in time if it is filed on the next day on which the office of the justices' chief executive is open.

(4) Where these Rules provide a period of time within which or by which a certain act is to be performed in the course of proceedings, that period may not be extended otherwise than by a direction of the justices' clerk or the court under rule 6(1).

(5) At the –

(*a*) postponement or adjournment of any hearing or directions appointment in the course of proceedings, or

(*b*) conclusion of any such hearing or directions appointment other than one at which the proceedings are determined, or as soon thereafter as is practicable,

(i) the justices' clerk shall fix a date upon which the proceedings shall come before him or the court again for such purposes as he or the court directs, and

(ii) the justices' chief executive shall serve, in accordance with these Rules, a copy of the order made on the parties to the proceedings.

Amendments—SI 1997/1894; SI 2001/615.

Defined terms—"business day", "directions appointment", "the Act": r 2(1).

8 Attendance at directions appointment and hearing

(1) Subject to paragraph (2), a party shall attend a directions appointment of which he has been given notice in accordance with rule 6(3) unless the justices' clerk or the court otherwise directs.

(2) Subject to rules 18(2) and 22(2), the court shall not begin to hear an application in the absence of the respondent unless –

(*a*) it is proved to the satisfaction of the court that he received reasonable notice of the date of the hearing; or

(*b*) the court is satisfied that the circumstances of the case justify proceeding with the hearing.

(3) Where, at the time and place appointed for a hearing, the respondent appears but the applicant does not, the court may refuse the application or, if sufficient evidence has previously been received, proceed in the absence of the applicant.

(4) Where at the time and place appointed for a hearing neither the applicant nor the respondent appears, the court may refuse the application.

Amendments—SI 1997/1894.

Defined terms—"applicant", "application", "directions appointment", "respondent", "the Act": r 2(1).

9 Documentary evidence

(1) In any proceedings the parties shall file and serve on the other parties –

(*a*) written statements of the substance of the oral evidence which the party intends to adduce at a hearing of, or a directions appointment in, those proceedings, which shall –

(i) be dated,

(ii) be signed by the person making the statement, and

(iii) contain a declaration that the maker of the statement believes it to be true and understandings that it may be placed before the court, and

(*b*) copies of any documents upon which the party intends to rely at a hearing of, or a directions appointment in, those proceedings,

at or by such time as the justices' clerk or the court directs or, in the absence of a direction, before the hearing or appointment.

(2) A party may, subject to any direction of the justices' clerk or the court about the timing of statements under this rule, file and serve on the parties a statement which is supplementary to a statement served under paragraph (1).

(3) At a hearing or directions appointment a party may not, without the leave of the justices' clerk in the case of a directions appointment, or the court –

(*a*) adduce evidence, or
(*b*) seek to reply on a document,

in respect of which he has failed to comply with the requirements of paragraph (1).

Amendments—SI 1992/2068; SI 1997/1894..

Defined terms—"directions appointment", "file", "the Act": r 2(1).

10 Amendment

(1) Subject to rule 9(2), a copy of a document which has been filed or served in any proceedings may not be amended without the leave of the justices' clerk or the court which shall, unless the justices' clerk or the court otherwise directs, be requested in writing.

(2) On considering a request for leave to amend a document the justices' clerk or the court shall either –

(*a*) grant the request, whereupon the justices' chief executive shall inform the person making the request of that decision, or
(*b*) invite the parties or any of them to make representations, within a specified period, as to whether such an order should be made.

(3) A person amending a document shall file it with the justices' chief executive and serve it on those persons on whom it was served prior to amendment; and the amendments shall be identified.

Amendments—SI 1997/1894; SI 2001/615.

Defined terms—"file", "the Act": r 2(1).

11 Oral evidence

The justices' clerk or the court shall keep a note of the substance of the oral evidence given at a hearing of, or directions appointment in, any proceedings.

Amendments—SI 1997/1894.

Defined terms—"directions appointment", "note", "the Act": r 2(1).

12 Hearing

(1) Before the hearing, the justice or justices who will be dealing with the case shall read any documents which have been filed under rule 9 in respect of the hearing.

(2) The justices' clerk at a directions appointment or the court at a hearing or directions appointment, may give directions as to the order of speeches and evidence.

(3) Subject to directions under paragraph (2), at a hearing of, or directions appointment in, proceedings, the parties shall adduce their evidence in the following order –

(*a*) the applicant,
(*b*) the respondent other than the child, and
(*c*) the child if he is a respondent.

(4) After the final hearing of proceedings, the court shall make its decision as soon as is practicable.

(5) Before the court makes an order or refuses an application, the justices' clerk shall record in writing –

(*a*) the names of the justice or justices constituting the court by which the decision is made, and
(*b*) in consultation with the justice or justices, the reasons for the court's decision and any findings of fact.

(6) When making an order or when refusing an application, the court, or one of the justices constituting the court by which the decision is made, shall state any findings of fact and the reasons for the court's decision.

(7) After the court announces its decision –

(*a*) the justices' clerk shall, as soon as practicable, make a record of the order made in the appropriate form, in writing, and
(*b*) the justices' chief executive shall serve, in accordance with these Rules, a copy of the order made on the parties to the proceedings.

(8) The justices' chief executive shall supply a copy of the record of the reasons for a decision made in pursuance of paragraph (5)(*b*) to any person on request, if satisfied that it is required in connection with an appeal or possible appeal.

Amendments—SI 1997/1894; SI 2001/615.

Defined terms—"applicant", "directions appointment", "respondent": r 2(1).

Order of speeches and evidence—The normal order of speeches and evidence is set out in r 12(3) but r 12(2) enables the justices' clerk at a directions hearing or the court at a hearing to vary the order. This power is of particular value in reducing the amount of time a professional witness is required to spend at a hearing.

"state" (r 12(6))—Rule 12(6) appears to require an oral statement of the findings of fact and the reasons for the court's decision.

Record of reasons—The duty to supply a copy of the record of the reasons arises only where the justices' clerk is satisfied that it is required in connection with an appeal or possible appeal. In other cases, the parties must be satisfied with the oral statement of the hearing given under r 12(6), unless the justices' clerk is prepared to supply the written record ex gratia.

12A Hearing of applications under Part IV of the Family Law Act 1996

(1) This rule applies to the hearing of applications under the Part IV of the Family Law Act 1996 and the following forms shall be used in connection with such hearings –

(*a*) a record of the hearing shall be made on Form FL405, and
(*b*) any order made on the hearing shall be issued in Form FL404.

(2) Where an order is made on an application made ex parte, a copy of the order together with a copy of the application and of any statement supporting it shall be served by the applicant on the respondent personally.

(3) Where the applicant is acting in person, service of a copy of an order made on an application made ex parte shall be effected by the justices' chief executive if the applicant so requests.

(4) Where the application is for an occupation order under section 33, 35 or 36 of the Family Law Act 1996, a copy of any order made on the application shall be served by the applicant by first-class post on the mortgagee or, as the case may be, the landlord of the dwelling-house in question.

(5) A copy of an order made on an application heard inter partes shall be served by the applicant on the respondent personally.

(6) Where the applicant is acting in person, service of a copy of the order made on an application heard inter partes may, with the leave of the justices' clerk, be effected in accordance with rule 4.

(7) The court may direct that a further hearing be held in order to consider any representations made by a mortgagee or a landlord.

Amendments—Inserted by SI 1997/1894; amended by SI 2001/615.

Defined terms—"application", "respondent": r 2(1).

Scope of provision—Although this rule is expressed to apply to hearings of applications under FLA 1996, Pt IV, procedural requirements are also contained in r 12 above. Rule 12A imposes additional requirements as to the record of the hearing, the issue and service of any order, rights to a copy of the order and a further hearing of any mortgagee or landlord.

Service on respondent—Personal service on the respondent in r 12A(2) (ex parte orders) and in r 12A(6) (inter partes orders) is required. In the former case, the respondent must also be served with a copy of the application and any statement supporting it. Where the applicant is acting in person, the justices' chief executive, if so requested shall effect service of an ex parte order or may give leave for the less onerous service provisions of r 4 to be employed. Ex parte orders always have to be reconsidered at a full hearing (FLA 1996, s 45(3)) and either the date, time and place of the full hearing must be clear on the face of the ex parte order itself or the respondent must also be served with notice of the full hearing in Form FL402.

Landlords and mortgagees—Rule 12A(4) requires service by post on the landlord or mortgagee of any occupation order made under s 33, 35 or 36. Rule 12A(7) enables the court to direct a further hearing to consider representations from landlords or mortgagees. The court's additional powers in FLA 1996, s 40 include a power to impose an obligation to discharge rent, mortgage payments etc.

"non-molestation order"—See FLA 1996, s 42 and notes thereon.

"occupation order"—See FLA 1996, ss 33–41 and notes thereon.

12B Applications to vary etc orders made under Part IV of the Family Law Act 1996

An application to vary, extend or discharge an order made under Part IV of the Family Law Act 1996 shall be made in Form FL403 and rules 12 and 12A shall apply to the hearing of such an application.

Amendments—Inserted by SI 1997/1894.

Defined terms—"application", "form": r 2(1).

13 Costs

(1) In any proceedings, the court may, at any time during the proceedings, make an order that a party pay the whole or any part of the costs of any other party.

(2) A party against whom the court is considering making a costs order shall have an opportunity to make representations as to why the order should not be made.

Amendments—SI 1997/1894.

Defined terms—"the Act": r 2(1).

Scope of provision—This rule provides a wide discretion to the court to make orders for costs at any time during the proceedings. Costs do not necessarily follow the event, and the only restriction imposed is that the party against whom an order is contemplated must be given an opportunity to make representations. Where such party has failed to attend the hearing, there should be an adjournment to allow the party to attend or make written representations. In the event of a failure to respond, the court may proceed to make an order against the party in his absence.

14 Confidentiality of documents

No document, other than a record of an order, held by the court and relating to proceedings shall be disclosed other than to –

(*a*) a party,
(*b*) the legal representative of a party, or
(*c*) the Legal Aid Board,

without leave of the justices' clerk or the court.

Amendments—SI 1997/1894.

Defined terms—"the Act": r 2(1).

Scope of provision—Disobedience of this rule would amount to a contempt of court.

15 Delegation by justices' clerk

(1) In this rule, "employed as a clerk in court" has the same meaning as in rule 2(1) of the Justices' Clerks (Qualifications of Assistants) Rules 1979.

(2) Anything authorised to be done by, to or before a justices' clerk under this Part of these Rules, or under paragraph 15 or 15D of the Schedule to the Justices' Clerks Rules 1970 as amended by Schedule 2 to these Rules, may be done instead by, to or before a person employed as a clerk in court where that person is appointed by the Magistrates' Courts Committee to assist him and where that person has been specifically authorised by the justices' clerk for that purpose.

(3) Any authorisation by the justices' clerk under paragraph (2) shall be recorded in writing by the justices' chief executive at the time the authority is given or as soon as practicable thereafter.

Amendments—SI 2001/615.

"employed"—It would seem that the powers may be delegated only to a person employed as a clerk. A person acting in a self-employed capacity as an "agency clerk" cannot be so authorised.

16 Application of enactments governing procedure in proceedings brought on complaint

(1) Section 53(3) of the Magistrates' Courts Act 1980 (orders with the consent of the defendant without hearing evidence) shall apply to applications under section 20 of the Act for the variation of orders for periodical payments, as it applies to complaints for the variation of the rate of any periodical payments ordered by a magistrates' court to be made.

(2) Section 97 of the Magistrates' Courts Act 1980 (issue of a witness summons) shall apply to proceedings as it applies to a hearing of a complaint under that section.

Amendments—SI 1997/1894.

Defined terms—"the Act": r 2(1).

17 Orders made under section 6 in the absence of the respondent

For the purposes of subsection (9)(*a*), (*b*) and (*c*) of section 6 of the Act, evidence of the consent of the respondent to the making of the order, of the financial resources of the respondent and of the financial resources of the child shall be by way of a written statement in the appropriate form in Schedule 1 to these Rules signed by the respondent or, where the application is in respect of financial provision for a child and the child has completed the appropriate form, the child.

Defined terms—"respondent", "the Act": r 2(1).

18 Application under section 7

(1) Where, under subsection (4) of section 7 of the Act, a court decides to treat an application under section 7 as if it were an application for an order under section 2 of the Act, the court shall indicate orally which of grounds (*a*) and (*b*) in that subsection it considers applicable and a memorandum of the decision and the grounds therefor shall be entered in the court's register.

(2) Where a court decides as aforesaid and the respondent is not then present or represented in court, or the respondent or his representative does not then agree to the continuance of the hearing, the court shall adjourn the hearing and the justices' chief executive shall serve notice of the decision and the grounds therefor on the respondent in the appropriate form in Schedule 1 to these Rules.

Amendments—SI 2001/615.

Defined terms—"application", "respondent", "the Act": r 2(1).

19 Respondent on application under section 20 or section 20A

(1) The respondent on an application for the variation or revocation of an order under section 20 of the Act shall be the party to the marriage in question other than the applicant and, where the order requires payments to be made to or in respect of a child who is 16 years of age or over, that child.

(2) The respondents on an application for the revival of an order under section 20A of the Act shall be the parties to the proceedings leading to the order which it is sought to have revived.

Defined terms—"respondent", "the Act": r 2(1).

20 Enforcement of orders made on applications under Part IV of the Family Law Act 1996

(1) Where a power of arrest is attached to one or more of the provisions ("the relevant provisions") of an order made under Part IV of the Family Law Act 1996 –

(*a*) the relevant provisions shall be set out in Form FL406 and the form shall not include any provisions of the order to which the power of arrest was not attached; and

(*b*) a copy of the form shall be delivered to the officer for the time being in charge of any police station for the applicant's address or of such other police station as the court may specify.

The copy of the form delivered under sub-paragraph (*b*) shall be accompanied by a statement showing that the respondent has been served with the order or informed of its terms (whether by being present when the order was made or by telephone or otherwise).

(2) Where an order is made varying or discharging the relevant provisions, the justices' chief executive shall –

(*a*) immediately inform the officer who received a copy of the form under paragraph (1) and, if the applicant's address has changed, the officer for the time being in charge of the police station for the new address; and

(*b*) deliver a copy of the order to any officer so informed.

(3) An application for the issue of a warrant for the arrest of the respondent shall be made in Form FL407 and the warrant shall be issued in Form FL408 and delivered by the justices' chief executive to the officer for the time being in charge of any police station for the respondent's address or of such other police station as the court may specify.

(4) The court before whom a person is brought following his arrest may –

(*a*) determine whether the facts, and the circumstances which led to the arrest, amounted to disobedience of the order, or

(*b*) adjourn the proceedings and, where such an order is made, the arrested person may be released and

(i) be dealt with within 14 days of the day on which he was arrested; and

(ii) be given not less than 2 business days' notice of the adjourned hearing.

Nothing in this paragraph shall prevent the issue of a notice under paragraph (8) if the arrested person is not dealt with within the period mentioned in sub-paragraph (*b*)(i) above.

(5) Paragraphs (6) to (13) shall apply for the enforcement of orders made on applications under Part IV of the Family Law Act 1996 by committal order.

(6) Subject to paragraphs (11) and (12), an order shall not be enforced by committal order unless –

(*a*) a copy of the order in Form FL404 has been served personally on the respondent; and

(*b*) where the order requires the respondent to do an act, the copy has been so served before the expiration of the time within which he was required to do the act and was accompanied by a copy of any order, made between the date of the order and the date of service, fixing that time.

(7) At the time when the order is drawn up, the justices' chief executive shall –

(*a*) where the order made is (or includes) a non-molestation order, and

(*b*) where the order made is an occupation order and the court so directs,

issue a copy of the order, indorsed with or incorporating a notice as to the consequences of disobedience, for service in accordance with paragraph (6).

(8) If the respondent fails to obey the order, the justices' chief executive shall, at the request of the applicant, issue a notice in Form FL418 warning the respondent that an application will be made for him to be committed and, subject to paragraph (12), the notice shall be served on him personally.

(9) The request for issue of the notice under paragraph (8) shall be treated as a complaint and shall –

(*a*) identify the provisions of the order or undertaking which it is alleged have been disobeyed or broken;

(*b*) list the ways in which it is alleged that the order or undertaking has been disobeyed or broken;

(*c*) be supported by a statement which is signed and is declared to be true and which states the grounds on which the application is made,

and, unless service is dispensed with under paragraph (12), a copy of the statement shall be served with the notice.

(10) If an order in Form FL419 (a committal order) is made, it shall include provision for the issue of a warrant of committal in Form FL420 and, unless the court otherwise orders –

(*a*) a copy of the order shall be served personally on the person to be committed either before or at the time of the execution of the warrant; or

(*b*) the order for the issue of the warrant may be served on the person to be committed at any time within 36 hours after the execution of the warrant.

(11) An order requiring a person to abstain from doing an act may be enforced by committal order notwithstanding that a copy of the order has not been served personally if the court is satisfied that, pending such service, the respondent had notice thereof either –

(*a*) by being present when the order was made;

(*b*) by being notified of the terms of the order whether by telephone or otherwise.

(12) The court may dispense with service of a copy of the order under paragraph (6) or a notice under paragraph (8) if the court thinks it just to do so.

(13) Where service of a notice to show cause is dispensed with under paragraph (12) and a committal order is made, the court may of its own motion fix a date and time when the person to be committed is to be brought before the court.

(14) Paragraphs (6) to (10), (12) and (13) shall apply to the enforcement of undertakings with the necessary modifications and as if

(*a*) for paragraph (6) there were substituted the following –

"(6) A copy of Form FL422 recording the undertaking shall be delivered by the justices' chief executive to the party giving the undertaking

(*a*) by handing a copy of the document to him before he leaves the court building; or

(*b*) where his place of residence is known, by posting a copy to him at his place of residence; or

(*c*) through his solicitor,

and, where delivery cannot be effected in this way, the justices' chief executive shall deliver a copy of the document to the party for whose benefit the undertaking is given and that party shall cause it to be served personally as soon as is practicable."

(*b*) in paragraph (12), the words from "a copy" to "paragraph (6) or" were omitted.

(15) Where a person in custody under a warrant or order, desires to apply to the court for his discharge, he shall make his application in writing attested by the governor of the prison showing that he has purged or is desirous of purging his contempt and the justices' chief executive shall, not less than one day before the application is heard, serve notice of it on the party (if any) at whose instance the warrant or order was issued.

(16) The court by whom an order of committal is made may by order direct that the execution of the order of committal shall be suspended for such period or on such terms or conditions as it may specify.

(17) Where execution of an order of committal is suspended by an order under paragraph (16), the applicant for the order of committal must, unless the court otherwise directs, serve on the person against whom it was made a notice informing him of the making and terms of the order under that paragraph.

(18) The court may adjourn consideration of the penalty to be imposed for contempts found proved and such consideration may be restored if the respondent does not comply with any conditions specified by the court.

(19) Where the court makes a hospital order in Form FL413 or a guardianship order in Form FL414 under the Mental Health Act 1983, the justices' chief executive shall –

(*a*) send to the hospital any information which will be of assistance in dealing with the patient;
(*b*) inform the applicant when the respondent is being transferred to hospital.

(20) Where a transfer direction given by the Secretary of State under section 48 of the Mental Health Act 1983 is in force in respect of a person remanded in custody by the court, the justices' chief executive shall notify –

(*a*) the governor of the prison to which that person was remanded; and
(*b*) the hospital where he is detained,

of any committal hearing which that person is required to attend and the justices' chief executive shall give notice in writing to the hospital where that person is detained of any further remand.

(21) An order for the remand of the respondent shall be in Form FL409 and an order discharging the respondent from custody shall be in Form FL421.

(22) In paragraph (4) "arrest" means arrest under a power of arrest attached to an order or under a warrant of arrest.

Amendments—Substituted by SI 1997/1894; amended by SI 2001/615.

Defined terms—"application", "respondent", "form": r 2(1).

"power of arrest"—See FLA 1996, s 47 and notes thereon. Under FLA 1996, Pt IV it is now more common to attach a power of arrest than was previously the practice under the Domestic Proceedings and Magistrates' Courts Act 1978.

"relevant provisions" (r 20(1))—The order will be on Form FL404, drafted from the specimen clauses in Sch 1 (set out in this work at FPR 1991, App 1). Invariably the order contains several provisions and the court must decide to which of these a power of arrest is to be attached: these are the "relevant provisions". Form FL406 is then drafted containing only the relevant provisions.

Delivery to the police (r 20(1)(*b*))—Form FL406 is delivered, after the respondent has been told of the order, to the police. Unless a different police station is specified, Form FL406 is delivered to the officer in charge of the police station for the applicant's address. Where the police force in question has a Domestic Violence Unit based at a particular police station it may be preferable to specify that police station. It is important that the police are not told of the power of arrest before the respondent knows of the order, otherwise there is a risk that the police may exceed their powers. Hence the requirement in r 20(1) for the statement of service to accompany Form FL406 when it is delivered to the police. If the "relevant provisions" are subsequently varied the onus is on the court to notify the police (r 20(2)).

Arrest without warrant—See FLA 1996, s 47(6). A constable may arrest without warrant a person whom he has reasonable cause for suspecting to be in breach of a relevant provision.

"warrant for the arrest of the respondent" (r 20(3))—See FLA 1996, s 47(8) and notes thereon. A warrant for the arrest of the respondent can be sought either where the order does not contain a power of arrest at all, or where the respondent is alleged to be in breach of one of the provisions which is not a "relevant provision". The application for a warrant must be "substantiated on oath" (FLA 1996, s 47(9)).

Warrant of arrest—The warrant is in Form FL408. It can be "backed for bail" with or without conditions, including a recognizance and/or surety. It is submitted that conditions will be rare (see commentary on FLA 1996, s 47 and Sch 5).

"committal for breach of order" (r 20(5))—The warrant of arrest procedure is an additional method of bringing the respondent before the court for an alleged breach. Where the order does contain a power of arrest and the respondent is alleged to be in breach of a relevant provision but the police have not in fact arrested the respondent, it is not possible to apply for a warrant of arrest (see wording of FLA 1996, s 47(8)) and the procedure under r 20(8) must be followed.

Contempt of court (r 20(18))—The court's primary concern is to secure future compliance with its order, rather than to punish a past breach.

FLA 1996, s 58 provides that the court's powers to punish for contempt of court, arising out of breach of an order under FLA 1996, Pt IV, may be exercised by the "relevant judicial authority". That term is defined in FLA 1996, s 63(1). It means:

(*a*) where the order was made by the High Court, a judge of that court.

(*b*) where the order was made by a county court, a judge or district judge of that or any other county court (but not a deputy district judge).

(c) where the order was made by a magistrates' court, any magistrates' court.

Adjournments—Rule 20(4) gives the court power to adjourn proceedings against a person arrested under either a power of arrest, or a warrant of arrest (r 20(22)). However, the rule makes it clear that a person must be dealt with within 14 days of his arrest and, if he is not, the court would have no power to deal with him pursuant to that arrest (but the power to proceed under r 20(8) is expressly preserved by r 20(4)). Rule 20(18) enables the court to adjourn consideration of the penalty for a proven contempt.

Remand—Remand can be in custody for up to 8 days (3 days if in police cells) or on bail.

"hospital order", "guardianship order" (r 20(19))—FLA 1996, s 48 gives the court power to remand for medical reports. The "relevant judicial authority"(see **Contempt of court** above) is given the same powers as the Crown Court under Mental Health Act 1983, s 35.

Prescribed forms—FL404 (Order); FL406 (Power of Arrest); FL407 (Application for a Warrant of Arrest); FL408 (Warrant of Arrest); FL409 (Remand Order); FL410 (Recognizance of respondent); FL411 (Recognizance of respondent's surety); FL412 (Bail Notice); FL413 (Hospital Order/Interim Hospital Order); FL414 (Guardianship Order).

21 Applications under Part IV of the Family Law Act 1996: bail

(1) An application for bail made by a person arrested under a power of arrest or a warrant of arrest may be made either orally or in writing.

(2) Where an application is made in writing, it shall contain the following particulars –

(*a*) the full name of the person making the application;

(*b*) the address of the place where the person making the application is detained at the time when the application is made;

(*c*) the address where the person making the application would reside if he were to be granted bail;

(*d*) the amount of the recognizance in which he would agree to be bound; and

(*e*) the grounds on which the application is made and, where a previous application has been refused, full particulars of any change in circumstances which has occurred since that refusal.

(3) An application made in writing shall be signed by the person making the application or by a person duly authorised by him in that behalf or, where the person making the application is a minor or is for any reason incapable of acting, by a guardian ad litem acting on his behalf and a copy shall be served by the person making the application on the applicant for the Part IV order.

(4) The following forms shall be used:

(*a*) the recognizance of the person making the application shall be in Form FL410 and that of a surety in Form FL411;

(*b*) a bail notice in Form FL412 shall be given to the respondent where he is remanded on bail.

Amendments—Substituted by SI 1997/1894.

Defined terms—"application", "form": r 2(1).

Remand—FLA 1996, s 47(7) gives the court power to remand a person arrested pursuant to a power of arrest, and s 47(10) gives a like power in the case of persons arrested pursuant to a warrant of arrest. Remand can be either in custody or on bail.

Remand in custody or on bail—Magistrates' courts have power to remand under Magistrates' Courts Act 1980, ss 128 and 129. FLA 1996, s 47(11) and Sch 5 have introduced a similar scheme into the High Court and county courts (see **Scope of provision** under FLA 1996, Sch 5).

Contempt proceedings—FLA 1996, s 58 enables the "relevant judicial authority" to deal with a contempt of court arising out of a failure to comply with an order under FLA 1996, Pt IV. Wherever possible, the court will deal with the contempt at the first hearing. Where this is not possible (eg because facts are disputed but neither the applicant nor the arresting officer is present to give evidence) the court will have to adjourn and will then decide whether the respondent should be remanded. Only if the court remands in custody will the question of an application for bail under r 21 arise.

Recognizance—A recognizance is an obligation or bond acknowledged before a court. The person acknowledging it, that is the person bound by it, is called the conusor or cognisor. The object of a recognizance is to secure the performance of an act by the conusor, such as to appear at court on a particular day. If the obligation is not performed the recognizance can be estreated.

Prescribed forms—FL409 (Remand Order); FL410 (Recognizance of respondent); FL411 (Recognizance of respondent's surety); FL412 (Bail Notice).

"bail notice in Form FL412"—It is submitted that Form FL412 is seriously flawed. It contains the words "The court is satisfied that you disobeyed the order made on [*date*] at the [ ] Court by [*specify breaches proven*]". If the court proposes to remand the arrested person on bail during an adjournment it should delete this erroneous finding. However, it is likely that bail conditions would be less effective in providing interim protection to the complainant than, for example, a variation to or an expansion of the existing injunction (see further **Scope of provision** under FLA 1996, Sch 5).

22 Proceedings by or against a person outside England and Wales for variation or revocation of orders under section 20

(1) The jurisdiction conferred on a court by virtue of section 20 of the Act shall, subject to the provisions of this rule, be exercisable even though the proceedings are brought by or against a person residing outside England and Wales.

(2) Subject to paragraph (3), where a court is satisfied that the respondent has been outside England and Wales for the whole of the period beginning one month before the making of the application and ending with the date of the hearing, it may proceed with an application made under section 20 of the Act provided that –

(*a*) the applicant has taken steps to notify the respondent of the making of the application and of the time and place appointed for the hearing by –

(i) causing a notice in writing to that effect to be delivered to the respondent;

(ii) causing a notice in writing to that effect to be sent by post addressed to the respondent at his last known or usual place of abode or at his place of business or at such other address at which there is ground for believing that it will reach the respondent, in accordance with directions given for the purpose by a justice acting for the same petty sessions area as that of the court; or

(iii) causing a notice to that effect to be inserted in one or more newspapers, in accordance with directions given as aforesaid; and

(*b*) it is reasonable in all the circumstances to proceed in the absence of the respondent.

(3) The court shall not make the order for which the application is made unless it is satisfied that during the period of 6 months immediately preceding the making of the application the respondent was continuously outside England and Wales or was not in England and Wales on more than 30 days and that, having regard to any communication to the court in writing purporting to be from the respondent, it is reasonable in all the circumstances to do so.

(4) A court shall not exercise its powers under section 20 of the Act so as to increase the amount of any periodical payments required to be made by any person under the Act unless the order under that section is made at a hearing at which that person appears or a statement has been filed under rule 4(4) that service of a copy of the application has been effected on the respondent.

(5) Paragraph (1) of rule 67 of the Magistrates' Courts Rules 1981 shall apply for the purpose of proving the delivery of a written notice in pursuance of paragraph (2)(*a*)(i) as it applies for the purpose of proving the service of a summons. In relation to a solemn declaration made outside the United Kingdom, paragraph (1) of the said rule 67, as applied by this paragraph, shall have effect as if for the reference to the authorities mentioned in the said paragraph (1) there were substituted a reference to a consular officer of Her Majesty's Government in the United Kingdom or any person for the time being authorised by law, in the place where the declarant is, to administer an oath for any judicial or other legal purpose.

(6) Paragraph (2) of the said rule 67 shall apply for the purpose of proving the sending of a written notice in pursuance of paragraph (2)(*a*)(ii) or the insertion of a notice in a newspaper in pursuance of paragraph (2)(*a*)(iii) as it applies for the purpose of proving the service of any process, provided, as respects the insertion of a notice in a newspaper, that a copy of the newspaper containing the notice is annexed to the certificate.

Defined terms—"applicant", "application", "directions", "respondent", "the Act": r 2(1).

Scope of provision—The powers are strictly limited by r 22(2) (notification of application), r 22(3) (residence requirements) and r 22(4) (no increase in the amount of the order unless the payer is present or a statement of service has been filed).

23 Entries in court's registers

(1) Where the justices' chief executive receives notice of any direction made by the High Court or a county court under section 28 of the Act by virtue of which an order made by the court under the Act ceases to have effect, particulars thereof shall be entered in the court's register.

(2) Where the hearing of an application under section 2 of the Act is adjourned after the court has decided that it is satisfied of any ground mentioned in section 1 and the parties to the proceedings agree to the resumption of the hearing in accordance with section 31 by a court which includes justices who were not sitting when the hearing began, particulars of the agreement shall be entered in the court's register.

Amendments—SI 2001/615.

Defined terms—"application", "the Act": r 2(1).

24 Setting aside on failure of service

Where an application has been sent to a respondent in accordance with rule 4(1) and, after an order has been made on the application, it appears to the court that the application did not come to the knowledge of the respondent in due time, the court may of its own motion set aside the order and may give such directions as it thinks fit for the rehearing of the application.

Amendments—Substituted by SI 1997/1894.

Defined terms—"the Act": r 2(1).

25 Proceedings with respect to which a single justice may discharge the functions of a court

The following proceedings are prescribed as proceedings with respect to which a single justice may discharge the functions of a court, that is to say, proceedings –

(*a*) in which an application is made ex parte for an occupation order or a non-molestation order under Part IV of the Family Law Act 1996;
(*b*) in accordance with rules 3, 3A(2), (6) and (8), 4, 6 (except paragraph (2)), 7 to 14 and 20(4).

Amendments—Substituted by SI 1997/1894.

Defined terms—"the Act": r 2(1).

Specified functions under the rules—The functions which may be discharged by a single justice under the rules include: the hearing of an oral application for an agreed order under Domestic Proceedings and Magistrates' Courts Act 1978, s 6(4) (r 3(3)); variation of service requirements (r 4(5)); giving, variation or revocation of directions (r 6(1)); directing extensions of time, fixing dates etc (r 7(4), (5)); functions relating to attendance at proceedings or proceeding in absence (r 8); timing of submission and service of documentary evidence, and giving leave not covered by filed statements (r 9(1), (3)); granting leave to amend documents (r 10); keeping notes of oral evidence (r 11); giving directions on the order of speeches and evidence and stating findings of fact and reasons (r 12(2), (5)(*b*)); making orders for costs (r 13); granting leave to disclose documents (r 14).

SCHEDULE 1
FORMS

****

FL401	Application for a non-molestation order/an occupation order
FL402	Notice of Proceedings [Hearing] [Directions Appointment]
FL403	Application to vary, extend or discharge an order in existing proceedings
FL404	Order or Direction
FL405	Record of Hearing
FL406	Power of Arrest
FL407	Application for a Warrant of Arrest
FL408	Warrant of Arrest
FL409	Remand Order
FL410	Recognizance of respondent
FL411	Recognizance of respondent's surety
FL412	Bail Notice
FL413	Hospital Order/Interim Hospital Order
FL414	Guardianship Order
FL415	Statement of Service
FL416	Notice to Mortgagees and Landlords
FL417	Transfer of proceedings to [the High Court] [a county court] [a family proceedings court]
FL418	Notice to show good reason why an order for your committal to prison should not be made
FL419	Order of Committal or other order upon proof of disobedience of a court order or breach of an undertaking
FL420	Warrant of Committal to prison
FL421	Notice of Discharge from Custody under Warrant of Committal
FL422	General Form of Undertaking
FL423	Application for a declaration of parentage under section 55A of the Family Law Act 1986 and respondent's notice
FL424	Declaration of parentage under section 55A of the Family Law Act 1986

Amendments—SI 1997/1894; SI 2001/778.

Specimen clauses in Form FL404—The specimen clauses in Form FL404 are set out in FPR 1991, App 1.

****

Family Proceedings Fees Order 1999, SI 1999/690

1 Citation and commencement

This Order may be cited as the Family Proceedings Fees Order 1999 and shall come into force on 26 April 1999.

2 Interpretation

In this Order, unless the context otherwise requires –

(*a*) a fee referred to by number means the fee so numbered in Schedule 1 to this Order;

(*b*) a rule or form referred to by number alone means the rule or form so numbered in the Family Proceedings Rules 1991; and

(*c*) expressions also used in the Family Proceedings Rules 1991 have the same meaning as in those Rules;

(*d*) "LSC" means the Legal Services Commission established under section 1 of the Access to Justice Act 1999;

(*e*) "Funding Code" means the code approved under section 9 of the Access to Justice Act 1999.

Amendments—SI 2000/640.

"This Order"—This Order replaces the Family Proceedings Fees Order 1991 (as amended). The object of the Order is to prescribe court fees payable in family proceedings. Unless a contrary intention appears art 2 confirms that rules or forms referred to in the Order are taken from FPR 1991 and terminology has the same meaning as in FPR 1991. Schedule 1 contains the fees payable in respect of the various forms of process or other provision set out.

3 Fees to be taken

The fees set out in column 2 of Schedule 1 to this Order shall be taken in family proceedings in the High Court or in a county court in respect of the items described in column 1 in accordance with and subject to the directions specified in column 1.

Defined terms—"family proceedings": FPR 1991, r 1.2(1).

Scope of provision—This article provides for the fees payable in family proceedings as specified in Schedule 1. The Order is concerned only with the High Court and the county courts.

"family proceedings"—By virtue of art 2, it is clear that the definition adopted by FPR 1991, r 1.2 applies.

4 Exemptions, reductions and remissions

(1) No fee shall be payable under this Order by a party who, at the time when a fee would otherwise become payable –

(*a*) is in receipt of –

(i) legal advice and assistance under Part II or Part III of the Legal Aid Act 1988 in connection with the matter to which the proceedings relate; or

(ii) Legal Help as defined in, and provided in accordance with, the Funding Code in connection with the matter to which the proceedings relate, or

(*b*) is in receipt of any qualifying benefit and is not in receipt of either –

(i) representation under Part IV of the Legal Aid Act 1988 for the purposes of the proceedings; or

(ii) funding provided by the LSC for the purposes of the proceedings and for which a certificate has been issued under the Funding Code certifying a decision to fund services for that party, or

(*c*) is not a beneficiary of a trust fund in court of a value of more than £50,000 and is –

(i) under the age of eighteen, or

(ii) a person for whose financial relief an order under paragraph 2 of Schedule 1 to the Children Act 1989 is in force or is being applied for.

(2) The following are qualifying benefits for the purposes of paragraph (1)(*b*) above –

(*a*) income support;

(*b*) working families' tax credit, provided that the amount (if any) to be deducted under section 128(2)(*b*) of the Social Security Contributions and Benefits Act 1992 has been determined at not more than £70 a week;

(*bb*) disabled person's tax credit, provided that the amount (if any) to be deducted under section 129(5)(*b*) of the Social Security Contributions and Benefits Act 1992 has been determined at not more than £70 a week; and

(*c*) income-based jobseeker's allowance under the Jobseekers Act 1995.

PART III

Amendments—SI 1999/2549; SI 2000/640.

"Part III of the Legal Aid Act 1988" (art 4(1)(*a*))—Legal Aid Act 1988, Pt III defines the basis on which a person receives advice under the "green form" scheme, namely if he is receiving income support, working families' tax credit, jobseeker's allowance or disabled person's tax credit, or if his disposable income and capital are below the level prescribed by rules made under the Act.

"paragraph 2 of Schedule 1 to the Children Act 1989" (art 4(1)(*c*))—This paragraph enables persons aged over 18 to seek financial relief against their parents in certain circumstances.

"Fee exempt" form—On filing process or when claiming the benefit of art 4, the litigant files a form with the court; the front of the court file may then be marked accordingly.

5 Where it appears to the Lord Chancellor that the payment of any fee prescribed by this Order would, owing to the exceptional circumstances of the particular case, involve undue hardship, he may reduce or remit the fee in that case.

Application for reduction or remission—Applications to remit fees are dealt with by individual courts to whom fees will be paid. Application is made at the time of filing process upon the form provided at court. A decision will be made by court staff and, in due course, communicated to the applicant when either a request for the fee will be sent out; or the application will issue and proceedings will be under way on a fee remitted basis.

Criteria for remitting fees—Remission is entirely a matter for the Lord Chancellor's discretion; and it is by no means clear how this discretion is to be exercised. It is reasonable to expect that the level of disposable income and capital is around the level of income support (see similar provisions in Supreme Court Fees Order 1999, art 6 and County Court Fees Order 1999, art 6).

5A (1) Subject to paragraph (2), where a fee has been paid at a time –

(*a*) when, under article 4, it was not payable, the fee shall be refunded;

(b) where the Lord Chancellor, if he had been aware of all the circumstances, would have reduced the fee under article 5, the amount by which the fee would have been reduced shall be refunded; and

(c) where the Lord Chancellor, if he had been aware of all the circumstances, would have remitted the fee under article 5, the fee shall be refunded.

(2) No refund shall be made under paragraph (1) unless the party who paid the fee applies within 6 months of paying the fee.

(3) The Lord Chancellor may extend the period of 6 months referred to in paragraph (2) if he considers that there is good reason for an application being made after the end of the period of 6 months.

Amendments—Inserted by SI 2000/640.

****

SCHEDULE 1
FEES TO BE TAKEN

Column 1 *Number and description of fee*	*Column 2* *Amount of fee*
Section 1—Fees to be taken in the High Court and in the county courts	
Commencement of proceedings	
1.1 On filing originating proceedings where no other fee is specified	£120
1.2 On presenting any petition, other than a second petition with leave granted under rule 2.6(4)	£150
1.3 On applying for either a non-molestation order or an occupation order under Part IV of the Family Law Act 1996, or on applying simultaneously for both a non-molestation order and an occupation order	£40
1.4 On amending a petition or presenting a second or subsequent petition with leave granted under rule 2.6(4)	£50
1.5 On filing an answer to a petition or a cross-petition	£100
1.6 On an application for an order under Part III of the Solicitors Act 1974 for the assessment of costs payable to a solicitor by his client; or on the commencement of costs-only proceedings	£30

Column 1 *Number and description of fee*	*Column 2* *Amount of fee*
2 *Proceedings under the Children Act 1989*	
On filing an application or requesting leave under the following provisions of the Children Act 1989 –	
2.1 *Parental responsibility, guardians, section 8 orders etc*	
(*a*) section 4(1)(*a*), or (3), 5(1), 10(1) or (2)	£80
(*b*) section 6(7), or 13(1)	£80
2.2 *Financial provision for children*	
(*a*) paragraph 1(1), 2(1), 6(5) or 14(1) of Schedule 1	£80
(*b*) paragraph 1(4), 2(5), 5(6), 6(7), 6(8), 8(2), 10(2), or 11 of Schedule 1	£80
2.3 *Secure accommodation*	
(*a*) section 25	£80
2.4 *Care, supervision, etc*	
(*a*) section 31	£80
For the purposes of fee 2.4(*a*) a care order does not include an interim care order, and a supervision order does not include an interim supervision order.	
(*b*) section 33(7), 38(8)(*b*), 39(1), (2), (3) or (4), paragraph 6 of Schedule 3 or paragraph 11(3) of Schedule 14	£80
2.5 *Contact with child in care*	
(*a*) section 34(2), (3), (4) or (9)	£80
2.6 *Placement abroad*	
(*a*) paragraph 19(1) of Schedule 2	£80
2.7 *Education supervision*	
(*a*) section 36(1)	£80
(*b*) paragraph 15(2) or 17(1) of Schedule 3	£80
2.8 *Child assessment order*	
(*a*) section 43(1)	£80
2.9 *Emergency protection*	
(*a*) section 43(12)	£80
(*b*) section 44, 45, 46 or 48	£80
2.10 *Recovery of children*	
(*a*) section 50	£80
2.11 *Miscellaneous*	
(*a*) section 102	£80
2.12 *Appeals*	
(*a*) On commencing an appeal under section 94 of, or paragraph 23(11) of Schedule 2 to, the Children Act 1989	£80

Column 1 *Number and description of fee*	*Column 2* *Amount of fee*
2.13 *Interim care/supervision orders*	
(*a*) On an application for an interim care order or an interim supervision order to be made under section 38(1) of the Children Act 1989 where an application for a care order or an application for a supervision order has already been made, and at least one interim care order or at least one interim supervision order has been made in the proceedings	£30
Fee 2	
In the notes to fee 2 "numbered fee" means each of the following fees: 2.1(*a*); 2.1(*b*); 2.2(*a*); 2.2(*b*); 2.3(*a*); 2.4(*a*); 2.4(*b*); 2.5(*a*); 2.6(*a*); 2.7(*a*); 2.7(*b*); 2.8(*a*); 2.9(*a*); 2.9(*b*); 2.10(*a*); 2.11(*a*); 2.12(*a*); 2.13(*a*).	
Where an application is made or filed, or (as the case may be) leave is sought or an appeal commenced, under or relating to provisions of the Children Act 1989 which are listed in two or more different numbered fees, each of those fees shall be payable.	
Where an application is made or filed, or (as the case may be) leave is sought or an appeal commenced under or relating to two or more provisions of the Children Act 1989 which are listed in the same numbered fee, that fee shall be payable only once.	
Where the same application is made or filed, or (as the case may be) leave is sought or an appeal commenced, in respect of two or more children at the same time, only one fee shall be payable in respect of each numbered fee.	
3 *Adoption and wardship applications*	
3.1 On commencing proceedings under the Adoption Act 1976 other than under section 21 of that Act	£120
3.2 On commencing proceedings under section 21 of the Adoption Act 1976	£120
3.3 On applying for the exercise by the High Court of its inherent jurisdiction with respect to children	£120

Column 1 *Number and description of fee*	*Column 2* *Amount of fee*
4 *Applications in proceedings*	
4.1 On an application for an order without notice or by consent (including an application to make a decree nisi absolute) except where separately listed in this schedule	£30
4.2 On a request for directions for trial (other than in uncontested divorce proceedings, in which no fee is chargeable) except where separately listed in this schedule	£30
4.3 On an application on notice except where separately listed in this schedule	£60
4.4 On an application on notice for ancillary relief, or on filing a notice of intention to proceed with an application for ancillary relief other than an application for an order by consent	£80
5 *Appeal from a district judge*	
5.1 On filing a notice of appeal from a district judge to a judge	£80
6 *Searches*	
6.1 On making a search in the central index of decrees absolute kept at the Principal Registry of the Family Division for any specified period of ten calendar years or, if no such period is specified, for the ten most recent years, and, if appropriate, providing a certificate of decree absolute	£20
6.2 On making a search in the central index of parental responsibility agreements kept at the Principal Registry of the Family Division in accordance with regulations made under section 4(2) of the Children Act 1989 and, if appropriate, providing a copy of an agreement	£20
6.3 On making a search in the index of decrees absolute kept at any divorce county court or district registry for any specified period of ten calendar years or, if no such period is specified, for the ten most recent years, and if appropriate, providing a certificate of decree absolute	£5
7 *Copy documents*	
7.1 On a request for a copy of a document (other than where fee 7.2 applies):	
(*a*) for the first page (except the first page of a subsequent copy of the same document supplied at the same time)	£1
(*b*) per page in any other case	20p

PART III

Column 1 *Number and description of fee*	*Column 2* *Amount of fee*
Fee 7.1 shall be payable for a faxed copy or for examining a plain copy and marking it as an examined copy.	
Fee 7.1 shall be payable whether or not the copy is issued as an office copy.	
7.2 On a request for a copy of a document required in connection with proceedings and supplied by the party making the request at the time of copying, for each page	20p
7.3 On a request for a copy of a document on a computer disk or in other electronic form, for each such copy	£3
8 *Determination of costs*	
Transitional Provision Where a bill of costs (or a request for detailed assessment or a request for a detailed assessment hearing as the case may be) is filed pursuant to an order made by the court before the coming into operation of this Order the fees payable shall be those which applied immediately before the coming into force of this Order.	
8.1 On the filing of a request for detailed assessment where the party filing the request is legally aided or is funded by the LSC and no other party is ordered to pay the costs of the proceedings	£80
8.2 On the filing of a request for a detailed assessment hearing in any case where fee 8.1 does not apply; or on the filing of a request for a hearing date for the assessment of costs payable to a solicitor by his client pursuant to an order under Part III of the Solicitors Act 1974	£130
Where there is a combined party and party and legal aid, or a combined party and party and LSC, or a combined party and party, legal aid and LSC determination of costs, fee 8.2 shall be attributed proportionately to the party and party, legal aid, or LSC (as the case may be) portions of the bill on the basis of the amount allowed.	
8.3 On a request for the issue of a default costs certificate	£40
8.4 On an appeal against a decision made in detailed assessment proceedings or on a request or an application to set aside a default costs certificate	£50

Column 1 *Number and description of fee*	*Column 2* *Amount of fee*
8.5 On applying for the court's approval of a certificate of costs payable from the Community Legal Service Fund	£20
Fee 8.5 is payable at the time of applying for approval and is recoverable only against the Community Legal Service Fund	
9 *Registration of maintenance orders*	
On an application for a maintenance order to be –	
9.1 registered under the Maintenance Orders Act 1950 or the Maintenance Orders Act 1958	£30
9.2 sent abroad for enforcement under the Maintenance Orders (Reciprocal Enforcement) Act 1972	£30
10 (*repealed*)	
Section 2—Fees to be taken in the county courts only	
11 *Service*	
11.1 On a request for service by bailiff, of any document except: (*a*) an order for a debtor to attend the adjourned hearing of a judgment summons; (*b*) an interpleader summons under an execution; (*c*) an order made under section 23 of the Attachment of Earnings Act 1971 (enforcement provisions); or (*d*) an order for a debtor to attend an adjourned oral examination of his means	£10
12 *Enforcement in the county courts*	
12.1 On an application for or in relation to enforcement of a judgment or order of a county court or through a county court, by the issue of a warrant of execution against goods except a warrant to enforce payment of a fine	(*a*) Where the amount for which the warrant issues does not exceed £125………£25 (*b*) Where the amount for which the warrant issues exceeds £125………£45

Column 1 *Number and description of fee*	*Column 2* *Amount of fee*
12.2 On a request for a further attempt at execution of a warrant at a new address following a notice of the reason for non-execution (except a further attempt following suspension)	£20
12.3 On an application to question a judgment debtor or other person on oath in connection with enforcement of a judgment	£40
12.4 On an application for a garnishee order nisi or a charging order nisi, or the appointment of a receiver by way of equitable execution	£50
Fee 12.4 shall be payable in respect of each party against whom the order is sought.	
12.5 On an application for a judgment summons	£80
12.6 On the issue of a warrant of possession or a warrant of delivery	£80
Where the recovery of a sum of money is sought in addition, no further fee is payable.	
12.7 On an application for an attachment of earnings order (other than a consolidated attachment of earnings order) to secure money due under an order made in family proceedings	£50
Fee 12.7 is payable for each defendant against whom an order is sought.	
Fee 12.7 is not payable where the attachment of earnings order is made on the hearing of a judgment summons.	
13 *Sale*	
13.1 For removing or taking steps to remove goods to a place of deposit	The reasonable expenses incurred
Fee 13.1 is to include the reasonable expenses of feeding and caring for animals.	
13.2 For advertising a sale by public auction pursuant to section 97 of the County Courts Act 1984	The reasonable expenses incurred
13.3 For the appraisement of goods	5p in the £1 or part of a £1 of the appraised value
13.4 For the sale of goods (including advertisements, catalogues, sale and commission and delivery of goods)	15p in the £1 or part of a £1 on the amount realised by the sale or such other sum as the district judge may consider to be justified in the circumstances

Column 1 *Number and description of fee*	*Column 2* *Amount of fee*
13.5 Where no sale takes place by reason of an execution being withdrawn, satisfied or stopped	(*a*) 10p in the £1 or part of a £1 on the value of the goods seized, the value to be the appraised value where the goods have been appraised or such other sum as the district judge may consider to be justified in the circumstances; and in addition (*b*) any sum payable under fee 13.1, 13.2 or 13.3
Section 3—Fees to be taken in the High Court only	
14 *Enforcement in the High Court*	
14.1 On sealing a writ of execution/possession/delivery	£20
Where the recovery of a sum of money is sought in addition to a writ of possession and delivery, no further fee is payable.	
14.2 On an application to question a judgment debtor or other person on oath in connection with enforcement of a judgment	£40
14.3 On an application for a garnishee order nisi or a charging order nisi, or the appointment of a receiver by way of equitable execution	£50
Fee 14.3 shall be payable in respect of each party against whom the order is sought.	
14.4 On an application for a judgment summons	£80
14.5 On a request or application to register a judgment or order; or for leave to enforce an arbitration award; or for a certified copy of a judgment or order for use abroad	£30
15 *Affidavits*	
15.1 On taking an affidavit or an affirmation or attestation upon honour in lieu of an affidavit or a declaration; and	£5
15.2 for each exhibit referred to and required to be marked	£2

Amendments—SI 2000/640; SI 2000/938; SI 2000/1545.

****

High Court (Distribution of Business) Order 1993, SI 1993/622

1 This order may be cited as the High Court (Distribution of Business) Order 1993 and shall come into force on 5 April 1993.

2 There shall be assigned to the Family Division all proceedings in the High Court under the Child Support Act 1991.

****

"all proceedings"—Such proceedings will be rare (eg declarations of parentage under CSA 1991, s 27 and transferred upwards), and may include judicial review applications brought as a result of the Act.

Intercountry Adoption (Hague Convention) Regulations 2003, SI 2003/118

ARRANGEMENT OF REGULATIONS

PART 1
GENERAL

Commencement—These Regulations come into force on 1 June 2003.

PART 1
GENERAL

1 Citation, commencement and application

(1) These Regulations may be cited as the Intercountry Adoption (Hague Convention) Regulations 2003 and shall come into force on 1 June 2003.

(2) These Regulations apply to England and Wales only.

2 Interpretation

In these Regulations –

"the 1976 Act" means the Adoption Act 1976;

"the 1999 Act" means the Adoption (Intercountry Aspects) Act 1999;

"the Adoption Agencies Regulations" means the Adoption Agencies Regulations 1983 subject to the modifications set out in Schedule 4;

"adoption agency" means a local authority or an appropriate voluntary organisation which is an accredited body for the purposes of the Convention;

"adoption panel" has the same meaning as in the Adoption Agencies Regulations;

"CA of the receiving State" means, in relation to a Convention country other than the United Kingdom, the Central Authority of the receiving State;

"CA of the State of origin" means, in relation to a Convention country other than the United Kingdom, the Central Authority of the State of origin;

"contact order" has the meaning given in section 8(1) of the Children Act 1989;

"eligible to adopt", except in regulation 8(4)(*a*), has the meaning given in regulation 4;

"prospective adopter" means a married couple or a person who makes an application under regulation 3;

"receiving State" has the same meaning as in Article 2 of the Convention;

"relevant Central Authority" means –

(*a*) in Part 2 –
  (i) in relation to a prospective adopter who is habitually resident in England, the Secretary of State; and
  (ii) in relation to a prospective adopter who is habitually resident in Wales, the National Assembly for Wales; and

(*b*) in Part 3 –
  (i) in relation to a local authority in England, the Secretary of State; and
  (ii) in relation to a local authority in Wales, the National Assembly for Wales;

"relevant local authority" in Part 2 has the meaning given in regulation 15;

"State of origin" has the same meaning as in article 2 of the Convention.

PART 2
REQUIREMENTS, PROCEDURE, RECOGNITION AND EFFECT OF ADOPTION IN ENGLAND AND WALES WHERE THE UNITED KINGDOM IS THE RECEIVING STATE

3 Application for determination of eligibility, and assessment of suitability, to adopt

(1) A married couple or a person habitually resident in the British Islands who wishes to adopt a child habitually resident in a Convention country outside the British Islands shall apply to an adoption agency for a determination of eligibility, and an assessment of his suitability, to adopt.

(2) An application under this regulation shall be made in writing and include such information as the agency may require.

4 Eligibility requirements

An adoption agency may not consider any person eligible to adopt unless the application under regulation 3 is made by a married couple or one person and –

(*a*) in the case of an application by a married couple they have both –
  (i) attained the age of 21 years; and
  (ii) been habitually resident in any part of the British Islands for a period of not less than 1 year ending with the date of the application; or

(*b*) in the case of an application by one person, he –

(i) has attained the age of 21 years; and

(ii) has been habitually resident in any part of the British Islands for a period of not less than 1 year ending with the date of the application.

5 Requirement to provide counselling and information

(1) Where an application is made in accordance with regulation 3, the adoption agency must –

(*a*) provide a counselling service for the prospective adopter;

(*b*) explain to him the legal implications of adoption and the procedure in relation to adopting a child under the Convention; and

(*c*) provide him with written information about the matters referred to in sub-paragraph (*b*).

(2) Paragraph (1) does not apply if the adoption agency is satisfied that the requirements set out in that paragraph have been carried out in respect of the prospective adopter by another adoption agency.

6 Requirement to carry out police checks

(1) An adoption agency must take steps to obtain –

(*a*) in respect of the prospective adopter, an enhanced criminal record certificate within the meaning of section 115 of the Police Act 1997 including the matters specified in subsection (6A) of that section; and

(*b*) in respect of any other member of his household aged 18 or over, an enhanced criminal record certificate under section 115 of that Act.

(2) An adoption agency may not consider a person to be suitable to be an adoptive parent if he or any member of his household aged 18 or over –

(*a*) has been convicted of an offence specified in Schedule 2 to the Adoption Agencies Regulations committed at the age of 18 or over; or

(*b*) has been cautioned by a constable in respect of such an offence which, at the time the caution was given, he admitted.

7 Requirement to notify

(1) The adoption agency must notify a prospective adopter in writing as soon as possible after becoming aware that –

(*a*) he is not eligible to adopt because he does not meet the requirements of regulation 4; or

(*b*) he is not suitable to be an adoptive parent by virtue of regulation 6.

(2) In a case to which paragraph (1)(*b*) applies the notification must specify the conviction, or as the case may be, the caution in question.

8 Procedure in respect of carrying out an assessment

(1) Where the adoption agency –

(*a*) is satisfied that the prospective adopter is eligible to adopt in accordance with the provisions in regulation 4; and (*b*) considers he may be suitable to be an adoptive parent following any information provided or made available as a consequence of the carrying out of the requirements imposed by regulation 5 or otherwise,

it must set up a case record in respect of him and place on it any information obtained under that regulation or otherwise.

(2) The adoption agency must obtain such particulars as are referred to in Part VI of Schedule 1 to the Adoption Agencies Regulations together with, so far as is reasonably practicable, any other relevant information which may be required by the adoption panel.

(3) The adoption agency must obtain a written report –

(*a*) from a registered medical practitioner about the health of the prospective adopter which must deal with matters specified in Part VII of Schedule 1 to the Adoption Agencies Regulations;

(*b*) about the premises where the prospective adopter intends to live with any child who might be adopted by him; and

(*c*) of each of the interviews with the persons nominated by the prospective adopter to provide personal references for him,

and in a case where the agency is not the local authority in whose area the prospective adopter has his home, it must also obtain a written report about him from that authority.

(4) The adoption agency must prepare a written report which must –

(*a*) state the Convention country from which the prospective adopter wishes to adopt a child, confirm that he is eligible to adopt a child under the law of that Convention country and provide any other information which that Convention country usually requires;

(*b*) include the agency's assessment of the prospective adopter's suitability to be an adoptive parent;

(*c*) include any other observations of the agency on the matters referred to in regulations 3 to 6 and this regulation; and

(*d*) include information and observations regarding the prospective adopter's identity, background, family and medical history, social environment, reasons for adoption, ability to undertake an intercountry adoption as well as the characteristics of the children for whom he would be qualified to care for and any other information which may be relevant.

(5) The adoption agency must notify the prospective adopter that his application is to be referred to the adoption panel and at the same time send him a copy of the agency's report referred to in paragraph (4), inviting him to send any observations in writing to the agency on the report within 28 days, beginning with the date on which the notification was sent.

(6) At the end of the period of 28 days referred to in paragraph (5) (or earlier if any observations made by the prospective adopter are received before the 28 days has expired) the adoption agency must pass the report referred to in paragraph (4) together with all relevant information obtained by it under this regulation (including the prospective adopter's observations on the report), to the adoption panel.

9 Function of adoption panel

(1) Subject to paragraph (2), the function of an adoption panel is to consider the case of the prospective adopter referred to it by the adoption agency and make a

recommendation to that agency as to whether the prospective adopter is suitable to be an adoptive parent.

(2) In considering what recommendation to make, the adoption panel –

(*a*) must consider and take into account all information and reports passed to it in accordance with regulation 8(6);

(*b*) may request the adoption agency to obtain any other relevant information which the panel considers necessary; and

(*c*) may obtain legal advice as it considers necessary in relation to the case.

10 Adoption agency decision and notification

(1) The adoption agency must take into account the recommendation of the adoption panel in coming to a decision about whether the prospective adopter is suitable to be an adoptive parent.

(2) No member of an adoption panel shall take part in any decision made by the adoption agency under paragraph (1).

(3) If the adoption agency decide to approve the prospective adopter as suitable to be an adoptive parent, it must notify him in writing of its decision.

(4) If the adoption agency consider that the prospective adopter is not suitable to be an adoptive parent, it must –

(*a*) notify the prospective adopter in writing that it proposes not to approve him as suitable to be an adoptive parent;

(*b*) send with that notification its reasons together with a copy of the recommendations of the adoption panel, if different; and

(*c*) invite the prospective adopter to submit any representations he wishes to make within 28 days.

(5) If within the period of 28 days referred to in paragraph (4), the prospective adopter has not made any representations, the adoption agency may proceed to make its decision and shall notify the prospective adopter in writing of its decision together with the reasons for that decision.

(6) If within the period of 28 days referred to in paragraph (4), the adoption agency receive further representations from the prospective adopter, it may refer the case together with all the relevant information to the adoption panel for further consideration.

(7) The adoption panel must reconsider any case referred to it under paragraph (6) and make a fresh recommendation to the adoption agency as to whether the prospective adopter is suitable to be an adoptive parent.

(8) The adoption agency must make a decision on the case but if the case has been referred to the adoption panel under paragraph (6) it must make the decision only after taking into account any recommendation of the adoption panel made under paragraph (7).

(9) As soon as possible after making the decision under paragraph (8), the adoption agency must notify the prospective adopter in writing of its decision, stating its reasons for that decision if they do not consider the prospective adopter to be suitable to be an adoptive parent, and of the adoption panel's recommendations, if this is different from the adoption agency's decision.

PART III

11 Procedure following approval by adoption agency

(1) Where the adoption agency is satisfied that the prospective adopter is eligible to adopt and has approved him as suitable to be an adoptive parent ("the decision") it must send to the relevant Central Authority –

(*a*) written confirmation of the decision; and
(*b*) the report prepared for the purpose of regulation 8(4).

(2) The relevant Central Authority may seek further information from the adoption agency, if that Authority considers it is appropriate to do so.

(3) If the relevant Central Authority is satisfied that the adoption agency has complied with these Regulations and that all the relevant information has been supplied by that agency, the Authority must send to the CA of the State of origin –

(*a*) a certificate in the form set out in Schedule 1 confirming that the –
  (i) prospective adopter is eligible to adopt;
  (ii) prospective adopter has been assessed in accordance with these Regulations;
  (iii) prospective adopter has been approved as suitable to be an adoptive parent;
  (iv) child will be authorised to enter and reside permanently in the United Kingdom if entry clearance, and leave to enter or remain as may be necessary, is granted and not revoked or curtailed and a Convention adoption order or Convention adoption is made;
(*b*) a copy of the decision; and
(*c*) a copy of the report prepared for the purpose of regulation 8(4).

(4) The relevant Central Authority must notify the adoption agency and the prospective adopter in writing that the certificate and the documents referred to in paragraph (3) have been sent to the CA of the State of origin.

12 Procedure following receipt of the Article 16 Information from the CA of the State of origin

(1) Where the relevant Central Authority receive from the CA of the State of origin, the Article 16 Information relating to the child whom the CA of the State of origin considers should be placed for adoption with the prospective adopter, the relevant Central Authority must send that Information to the adoption agency.

(2) The adoption agency must consider the Article 16 Information and –

(*a*) send that Information to the prospective adopter;
(*b*) meet with him to discuss the Article 16 Information and the proposed placement; and
(*c*) if appropriate, offer a counselling service and further information as required.

(3) Where –

(*a*) the procedure in paragraph (2) has been followed;
(*b*) the prospective adopter (and where the prospective adopters are a married couple each of them) has visited the child in the State of origin; and
(*c*) after that visit to the child, the prospective adopter confirmed in writing that he –
  (i) has visited that child; and
  (ii) wishes to proceed to adopt the child,

the adoption agency must notify the relevant Central Authority that the requirements specified in sub-paragraph (*a*), (*b*) and (*c*) have been satisfied and at the same time it must confirm that it is content that the adoption should proceed.

(4) Where the relevant Central Authority has received notification from the adoption agency under paragraph (3), the relevant Central Authority shall –

(*a*) notify the CA of the State of origin that –
  (i) the prospective adopter wishes to proceed to adopt the child;
  (ii) it is prepared to agree with the CA of the State of origin that the adoption may proceed; and
(*b*) confirm to the CA of the State of origin that –
  (i) in the case where the requirements specified in section 1(5A) of the British Nationality Act 1981 are met that, the child will be authorised to enter and reside permanently in the United Kingdom; and
  (ii) in any other case, if entry clearance and leave to enter and remain, as may be necessary, is granted and not revoked or curtailed and a Convention adoption order or a Convention adoption is made, the child will be authorised to enter and reside permanently in the United Kingdom.

(5) The relevant Central Authority must inform the adoption agency and the prospective adopter when the agreement under Article 17(*c*) of the Convention has been made.

(6) If, at any stage before the agreement under Article 17(*c*) of the Convention is made, the CA of the State of origin notifies the relevant Central Authority that it has decided the proposed placement should not proceed, the relevant Central Authority must inform the adoption agency of the CA of the State of origin's decision and the agency must then inform the prospective adopter and return the documents referred to in paragraph (2) to that Authority who must then return them to the CA of the State of origin.

(7) If, at any stage before the child is placed with him, the prospective adopter notifies the adoption agency that he does not wish to proceed with the adoption of the child, that agency must inform the relevant Central Authority and return the documents to that Authority who must in turn notify the CA of the State of origin of the prospective adopter's decision and return the documents to the CA of the State of origin.

(8) Following any agreement under Article 17(*c*) of the Convention and the placement of the child by the adoption agency with the prospective adopter, the prospective adopter must accompany the child on entering the United Kingdom unless, in the case of a married couple, the agency and the CA of the State of origin have agreed that it is necessary for only one of them to do so.

(9) For the purposes of this regulation "the Article 16 Information" means –

(*a*) the report referred to in Article 16(1) of the Convention including information about the child's identity, adoptability, background, social environment, family history, medical history including that of the child's family, and any special needs of the child;
(*b*) proof of confirmation that the consents of the persons, institutions and authorities whose consents are necessary for adoption have been obtained in accordance with Article 4 of the Convention; and
(*c*) the reasons for the CA of the State of origin's determination on the placement.

13 Duty of adoption agency before the arrival of the child in England or Wales

Where the adoption agency is informed by the relevant Central Authority that the agreement under Article 17(*c*) of the Convention has been made and the adoption may proceed, that agency must –

(*a*) send a written report of the child's health history and current state of health, so far as it is known, to the prospective adopter's registered medical practitioner, if any, together with particulars of the placement;
(*b*) in a case where the adoption agency is not the local authority within whose area the prospective adopter has his home, notify that authority of the particulars of the placement; and
(*c*) notify the local education authority within whose area the prospective adopter has his home in writing of the particulars of the placement if the child is of compulsory school age within the meaning of section 8 of the Education Act 1996 or the adoption agency's medical adviser considers the child to have special needs or to be disabled.

14 Requirements following arrival of the child in the United Kingdom but no Convention adoption is made in the State of origin

Regulations 15 to 19 apply where, following agreement between the relevant Central Authority and the CA of the State of origin under Article 17(*c*) of the Convention that the adoption may proceed, no Convention adoption is made, or applied for, in the State of origin but the child is placed with the prospective adopter in the State of origin and he then returns to England or Wales with the child.

15 Duty of prospective adopter to notify local authority

A prospective adopter with whom the child is placed must within the period of fourteen days beginning with the date on which he brings the child into the United Kingdom give notice to the local authority within whose area he has his home ("the relevant local authority") of –

(*a*) his intention to apply for an adoption order to be made as a Convention adoption order in accordance with section 22 of the 1976 Act (notification to local authority of adoption application); or
(*b*) his intention not to give the child a home.

16 Duty of prospective adopter where the child is placed with them

(1) The prospective adopter with whom the child is placed is not required to allow the child to visit or stay with any person, or otherwise to allow contact between the child and any person, except under a contact order.

(2) Subject to paragraphs (3) and (4), the prospective adopter may not cause or permit –

(*a*) the child to be known by a new surname; or
(*b*) the child to be removed from the United Kingdom,

unless the court gives leave or the relevant local authority agree.

(3) Paragraph (2)(*a*) does not apply if the competent authority of the State of origin has agreed the child may be known by a new surname.

(4) Paragraph (2)(*b*) does not apply if the removal of the child is for a period of less than one month by the prospective adopter.

17 Prospective adopter unable to proceed with application to adopt

Where the child is placed with the prospective adopter or regulation 20 applies and the prospective adopter gives notice to the relevant local authority that he does not wish to proceed with the adoption and no longer wishes to give the child a home, that authority must –

(*a*) receive the child from him before the end of the period of 7 days beginning with the giving notice; and

(*b*) notify the relevant Central Authority of his decision not to proceed with the adoption.

18 Removal of the child by the relevant authority

(1) Subject to paragraph (4), where the child is placed with the prospective adopter or regulation 20 applies and the relevant local authority are of the opinion that –

(*a*) the continued placement of the child with the prospective adopter is not in the child's best interests; and

(*b*) the child should not remain with the prospective adopter,

that authority must give notice to the prospective adopter of their opinion.

(2) The prospective adopter must, not later than the end of the period of 7 days beginning with the giving of notice, return the child to the authority.

(3) Where the relevant local authority give notice under paragraph (1), they must also give notice to the relevant Central Authority that they have requested the return of the child.

(4) Where a notice under paragraph (1) is given, but –

(*a*) before the notice was given an application for a Convention adoption order was made; and

(*b*) the application has not been disposed of,

the prospective adopter is not required by virtue of the notice to return the child to the authority unless the court so orders.

(5) This regulation does not affect the exercise by any local authority or other person of any power conferred by any enactment or the exercise of any power of arrest.

19 Breakdown of placement

(1) This regulation applies where –

(*a*) the prospective adopter notifies the relevant local authority under regulation 17 that he does not wish to proceed with the adoption;

(*b*) the relevant local authority have removed the child from the home of the prospective adopter in accordance with regulation 18; or

(*c*) an application for a Convention adoption order is refused, or a Convention adoption or a Convention adoption order is annulled pursuant to section 53(1) of the 1976 Act.

PART III

(2) Where the relevant local authority are satisfied that it would be in the child's best interests to be placed for adoption with another prospective adopter habitually resident in the United Kingdom they must seek to identify a suitable adoptive parent for the child.

(3) Where the relevant local authority have identified another prospective adopter who is eligible to adopt and has been assessed in accordance with these Regulations and approved as suitable to be an adoptive parent in accordance with regulations 3 to 10 –

- (*a*) that authority must notify the relevant Central Authority in writing that –
  - (i) another prospective adopter has been identified; and
  - (ii) the requirements, procedures and notifications as provided for in regulations 3 and 10 have been complied with; and
- (*b*) the requirements specified in regulation 11(1) shall apply in respect of that prospective adopter.

(4) Where the relevant Central Authority has been notified in accordance with paragraph (3) –

- (*a*) regulation 11(2) to (4) shall apply in respect of that other prospective adopter;
- (*b*) it shall inform the CA of the State of origin of the proposed placement; and
- (*c*) it shall agree that placement with the CA of the State of origin in accordance with the provisions in this Part of these Regulations.

(5) Where the relevant local authority are not satisfied it would be in the child's best interests to be placed for adoption with another prospective adopter in England or Wales, it must liaise with the relevant Central Authority to arrange for the return of the child to his State of origin.

(6) Before coming to any decision under this regulation, the relevant local authority must have regard to the wishes and feelings of the child, having regard to his age and understanding, and, where appropriate, obtain his consent in relation to measures to be taken under this regulation.

20 Convention adoptions subject to a probationary period

(1) This regulation applies where –

- (*a*) the child has been placed with the prospective adopters by the competent authority of the State of origin and a Convention adoption has been applied for by the prospective adopter in the State of origin but the child's placement with the prospective adopter is subject to a probationary period before the Convention adoption is made; and
- (*b*) the prospective adopter returns to England or Wales with the child before that probationary period is completed and the Convention adoption is made in the State of origin.

(2) The relevant local authority must, if requested by the competent authority of the State of origin, submit a report about the placement to that authority and such a report must be prepared within such timescale and contain such information as the competent authority may reasonably require.

21 Prescribed requirements for the purposes of making a Convention adoption order

(1) For the purposes of section 17 of the 1976 Act (requirements in respect of adoption order made as a Convention adoption order), where the United Kingdom is the receiving State the prescribed requirements are –

(*a*) both spouses (in the case of an application by a married couple) or the applicant (in the case of an application by one person) have been habitually resident in any part of the British Islands for a period of not less than 1 year ending with the date of the application;

(*b*) the child to be adopted has not attained the age of 18 years on the date of the application;

(*c*) the child to be adopted was, on the date on which the agreement under Article 17(*c*) was made, habitually resident in a Convention country outside the British Islands; and

(*d*) in a case where the applicant (in the case of an application by one person) or one of the spouses (in the case of an application by a married couple) is not a British citizen by virtue of the British Nationality Act 1981, the Home Office has confirmed that the child is authorised to enter and reside permanently in the United Kingdom.

PART III

22 Procedural requirements following a Convention adoption order or Convention adoption

(1) Where a Convention adoption order is made by a court in England or Wales, the court must send a copy of that order to the relevant Central Authority.

(2) On receipt of an order under paragraph (1), the relevant Central Authority must issue a certificate in the form set out in Schedule 2 certifying that the adoption has been made in accordance with the Convention.

(3) A copy of the certificate issued under paragraph (2) must be sent to –

(*a*) the CA of the State of origin;

(*b*) the adoptive parents; and

(*c*) the adoption agency and, if different, the relevant local authority.

(4) Where the relevant Central Authority receive a certificate under Article 23 of the Convention in respect of a Convention adoption made in that Convention country, the relevant Central Authority must send a copy of that certificate to –

(*a*) the adoptive parents; and

(*b*) the adoption agency.

23 Refusal of a court in England or Wales to make a Convention adoption order

Where an application for a Convention adoption order is refused by the court or is withdrawn, the prospective adopter must return the child to the relevant local authority within the period determined by the court.

24 Annulment of a Convention adoption order or a Convention adoption

Where a Convention adoption order or a Convention adoption is annulled under section 53(1) of the 1976 Act the court must send a copy of the order to –

(*a*) the relevant Central Authority for onward transmission to the CA of the State of origin;

(*b*) the adoptive parents; and

(*c*) the adoption agency and, if different, the relevant local authority.

PART 3
REQUIREMENTS AND PROCEDURE IN ENGLAND AND WALES WHERE THE UNITED KINGDOM IS THE STATE OF ORIGIN

25 Duty of adoption agency in respect of assessment of a child

(1) This regulation applies where –

(*a*) a local authority (referred to in this Part as "the LA") –

(i) has decided that adoption is in the best interests of a child under regulation 11(1) of the Adoption Agencies Regulations ("the first decision");

(ii) has considered the possibilities for placement of that child within the British Islands; and

(iii) considers that adoption by a person habitually resident in a Convention country outside the British Islands may be in the child's best interests; and

(*b*) the child is free for adoption by virtue of an order made under section 18 of the 1976 Act, section 18 of the Adoption (Scotland) Act 1978 or Article 17(1) or 18(1) of the Adoption (Northern Ireland) Order 1987.

(2) The LA must refer the case of the child to the adoption panel together with –

(*a*) the documents referred to in regulation 7(2)(*e*) of the Adoption Agencies Regulations originally sent to the adoption panel; and

(*b*) a report from the child's social worker –

(i) as to why he considers that adoption by a person habitually resident in a Convention country outside the British Islands may be in the child's best interests, and

(ii) if appropriate, having regard to the child's age and understanding, on the child's views and wishes in relation to adoption.

26 Function of adoption panel

(1) The adoption panel must consider the case of the child and make a recommendation to the LA as to whether adoption by a person habitually resident in a Convention country outside the British Islands is in the best interests of the child.

(2) In considering what recommendation to make, the adoption panel must have regard to the duties imposed upon the LA by sections 6 and 7 of the 1976 Act (duty to promote the welfare of the child and religious upbringing of adopted child) and must –

(*a*) consider and take into account all the information and reports passed to it under regulation 25(2);

(*b*) request the LA to obtain any other relevant information which the adoption panel considers necessary; and

(*c*) obtain legal advice in relation to the case as may be necessary.

27 Decision and notification

(1) The LA must make a decision on the case referred to the adoption panel only after taking into account the recommendation of the adoption panel.

(2) No member of an adoption panel shall take part in any decision made by the LA under paragraph (1).

(3) The LA must notify the relevant Central Authority –

(*a*) of the name and age of the child;
(*b*) of the reasons why they consider that the child may be suitable for adoption by a person habitually resident in a Convention country outside the British Islands;
(*c*) of the date the freeing order under section 18 of the 1976 Act, section 18 of the Adoption (Scotland) Act 1978 or Article 17(1) or 18(1) of the Adoption (Northern Ireland) Order 1987 was made; and
(*d*) of any other information that Authority may require.

(4) The relevant Central Authority is to maintain a list of children who are notified to that Authority under paragraph (3) and shall make the contents of that list available for consultation by other Central Authorities within the British Islands.

(5) Where a LA –

(*a*) places for adoption a child whose details have been notified to the relevant Central Authority under paragraph (3); or
(*b*) determines that adoption by a person habitually resident in a Convention country outside the British Islands is no longer in the best interests of such a child,

they must notify the relevant Central Authority accordingly and that Authority must remove the details relating to that child from the Convention list.

(6) In this regulation and regulation 28 "Convention list" means –

(*a*) in relation to a relevant Central Authority, a list of children notified to that Authority in accordance with paragraph (3); or
(*b*) in relation to any other Central Authority within the British Islands, a list of children notified to that Authority in accordance with provisions which correspond to paragraph (3).

28 Receipt of the Article 15 Report from the CA of the receiving State

(1) This regulation applies where –

(*a*) the relevant Central Authority receives a report from the CA of the receiving State which has been prepared for the purposes of Article 15 of the Convention ("the Article 15 Report");
(*b*) the Article 15 Report relates to a prospective adopter who is habitually resident in that receiving State ("a Convention prospective adopter"); and
(*c*) the Convention prospective adopter wishes to adopt a child who is habitually resident in England or Wales.

(2) If the relevant Central Authority is satisfied the Convention prospective adopter meets the following requirements –

(*a*) in respect of age and marital status as provided for in sections 14 and 15 of the 1976 Act; and (*b*) in the case of a married couple, both Convention prospective adopters are, or in the case of a single Convention prospective adopter, that prospective adopter is habitually resident in a Convention country outside the British Islands,

the Authority must consult the Convention list and may, if the Authority considers it appropriate, consult any Convention list maintained by another Central Authority within the British Islands.

(3) The relevant Central Authority may pass a copy of the Article 15 Report to any other Central Authority within the British Islands for the purpose of enabling that Authority to consult its Convention list.

(4) Where the relevant Central Authority identifies a child on the Convention list who may be suitable to be adopted by the Convention prospective adopter, that Authority must send the Article 15 Report to the LA which referred the child's details to the Authority.

(5) The LA must consider the Article 15 Report and where it considers that it may be appropriate to place the child for adoption with the Convention prospective adopter it must refer the proposed placement for adoption to the adoption panel together with –

(*a*) the Article 15 Report;
(*b*) the documents and report referred to in regulation 25(2);
(*c*) its observations on the proposed placement; and
(*d*) any other relevant information about the child.

29 Duty of adoption panel in respect of proposed placement

(1) The adoption panel must consider the proposed placement referred to it by the LA under regulation 25 and make a recommendation to the LA, as to whether –

(*a*) the Convention prospective adopter is a suitable adoptive parent for the child; and
(*b*) the proposed placement is in the best interests of the child.

(2) In considering what recommendation to make under paragraph (1), the adoption panel –

(*a*) must have regard to the child's upbringing and his ethnic, religious and cultural background;
(*b*) must have regard to the duties imposed upon the LA by sections 6 and 7 of the 1976 Act (duty to promote welfare of child and religious upbringing of adopted child);
(*c*) must have regard to the documents and the Article 15 Report referred to it under regulation 28(4);
(*d*) may request the LA to obtain any other relevant information which the adoption panel considers necessary; and
(*e*) may obtain legal advice as it considers necessary in relation to the case.

30 LA decision in respect of placement

(1) The LA must make a decision about the proposed placement only after having taken into account the recommendations of the adoption panel.

(2) No member of an adoption panel shall take part in any decision made by the LA under paragraph (1).

31 Preparation of the Article 16 information for the CA of the receiving State

(1) Where the LA decides under regulation 30 that the proposed placement is in the best interests of the child and the adoption may proceed, it must prepare a report for the purposes of Article 16(1) of the Convention which must include –

(*a*) information about the child's identity, suitability for adoption, background, social environment, family history, medical history including that of the child's family, and any special needs of the child; and
(*b*) the reasons for their decision.

(2) The LA must send the report referred to in paragraph (1) to the relevant Central Authority together with –

(*a*) evidence that a freeing order has been made in respect of the child;
(*b*) written observations relating to the child's upbringing and to his or her ethnic, religious and cultural background; and
(*c*) the report, if any, referred to in regulation 25(2)(*b*)(ii).

(3) The relevant Central Authority must send the report and information referred to it under paragraph (2) to the CA of the receiving State.

(4) The relevant Central Authority may notify the CA of the receiving State that it is prepared to agree that the adoption may proceed provided that CA has confirmed that –

(*a*) the Convention prospective adopter has agreed to adopt the child and has received such counselling as may be necessary;
(*b*) the Convention prospective adopter has confirmed that he will accompany the child to the receiving State, unless where the Convention prospective adopter is a married couple, the LA and the CA of the receiving State have agreed that it is necessary for only one of them to do so;
(*c*) it is content for the adoption to proceed; and
(*d*) the child is or will be authorised to enter and reside permanently in the Convention country if a Convention adoption is made in that Convention country or a Convention adoption order is made in the United Kingdom.

(5) Subject to paragraph (7), the relevant Central Authority may not make an agreement under Article 17(*c*) of the Convention with the CA of the receiving State unless the LA have confirmed to that Authority that –

(*a*) it has met the Convention prospective adopter;
(*b*) the Convention prospective adopter has visited the child; and
(*c*) the Convention prospective adopter is content for the adoption to proceed.

(6) A LA may not place a child for adoption with a Convention prospective adopter unless the agreement under Article 17(*c*) of the Convention has been made and the relevant Central Authority must advise the LA when that agreement has been made.

(7) In paragraph (5), the reference to "Convention prospective adopter" means in the case where the Convention prospective adopters are a married couple, both of them.

PART III

32 Prescribed requirements for the purposes of making a Convention adoption order

For the purposes of section 17 of the 1976 Act (requirements in respect of an adoption order made as a Convention adoption order) the prescribed requirements are in the case where the United Kingdom is the State of origin –

(*a*) both spouses (in the case of an application by a married couple) are, or the applicant (in the case of an application by one person) is, habitually resident in a Convention country outside the British Islands on the date of the application;

(*b*) the child to be adopted is free for adoption by virtue of an order made under section 18 of the 1976 Act, section 18 of the Adoption (Scotland) Act 1978, or Article 17(1) or 18(1) of the Adoption (Northern Ireland) Order 1987;

(*c*) the child to be adopted is habitually resident in any part of the British Islands on the date of the application; and

(*d*) the child to be adopted has not attained the age of 18 years on the date of the application.

33 Procedural requirements following a Convention adoption order or Convention adoption

(1) Where a Convention adoption order is made by a court in England or Wales, the court must send a copy of that order to the relevant Central Authority.

(2) On receipt of an order under paragraph (1), the relevant Central Authority must issue a certificate in the form set out in Schedule 2 certifying that the Convention adoption order has been made in accordance with the Convention.

(3) A copy of the certificate must be sent to the –

(*a*) CA of the receiving State; and

(*b*) LA.

(4) Where the relevant Central Authority receives a certification of the adoption having been made in accordance with the Convention from the competent authority of the receiving State, the relevant Central Authority must send a copy of that certification to the LA.

PART 4
MISCELLANEOUS

****

36 Offences

Any person who contravenes or fails to comply with –

(*a*) regulation 15 (notification to local authority);

(*b*) regulation 18(2) (return of child to relevant local authority);

(*c*) regulation 18(4) (return of child to relevant authority as ordered by the court); or

(*d*) regulation 23 (return of child to relevant authority within period prescribed by court), without reasonable excuse is guilty of an offence and liable on summary conviction to imprisonment for a term not exceeding three months, or a fine not exceeding level 5 on the standard scale, or both.

37 Transitional and consequential provisions

(1) These Regulations shall not apply in relation to the case of any prospective adopter who wishes to adopt a child from a Convention country outside the British Islands which has been referred by the adoption agency (dealing with the case) to the adoption panel before the date on which these Regulations come into force.

(2) No application may be made for a Convention adoption order under section 17 of the 1976 Act unless the arrangements for the adoption of the child have been made in accordance with these Regulations.

****

Justices' Clerks Rules 1999, SI 1999/2784

****

2 The things specified in the Schedule to these Rules, being authorised to be done by, to or before a single justice of the peace for a petty sessions area, may be done by, to or before the justices' clerk for that area.

SCHEDULE

****

Family etc

37 The determination that a complaint for the revocation, discharge, revival, alteration, variation or enforcement of an affiliation order be dealt with by a magistrates' court acting for another petty sessions area in accordance with the provisions of rule 41 or 59 of the Magistrates' Courts Rules 1981.

38 The transfer of proceedings in accordance with any order made by the Lord Chancellor under Part I of Schedule 11 to the Children Act 1989.

39 The appointment of a children's guardian or solicitor for a child under section 41 of the Children Act 1989.

40 The giving, variation or revocation of directions in accordance with rule 6 of the Family Courts (Matrimonial Proceedings etc.) Rules 1991 or rule 14 of the Family Proceedings Courts (Children Act 1989) Rules 1991.

41 The making of an order, in accordance with rule 28 of the Family Proceedings Courts (Children Act 1989) Rules 1991, under sections 11(3) or 38(1) of the Children Act 1989.

42 By virtue of rule 33 of the Family Proceedings Courts (Children Act 1989) Rules 1991, the issuing of a witness summons under section 97 of the Magistrates' Courts Act 1980 in relevant proceedings within the meaning of section 93(3) of the Children Act 1989.

43 The request of a welfare report under section 7 of the Children Act 1989.

44 By virtue of rule 16(2) of the Family Proceedings Courts (Matrimonial Proceedings etc) Rules 1991, the issuing of a witness summons under section 97 of the Magistrates' Courts Act 1980 in proceedings under the Domestic Proceedings and Magistrates' Courts Act 1978.

Amendments—SI 2002/3220.

Legal Aid in Civil Proceedings (Remuneration) Regulations 1994, SI 1994/228

1 Citation, commencement and transitional provisions

(1) These Regulations may be cited as the Legal Aid in Civil Proceedings (Remuneration) Regulations 1994 and shall come into force on 25 February 1994.

(2) Subject to paragraph (3) below, these Regulations apply to proceedings in respect of which a certificate is granted on or after 25 February 1994.

(3) Where a certificate was granted before 25 February 1994 to an assisted person whose solicitor represents any other assisted person in the same proceedings under a certificate granted on or after 25 February 1994, the provisions of these Regulations shall not apply as regards the costs payable under the later certificate.

(4) Proceedings in respect of which a certificate was granted before 25 February 1994 shall be treated as if these Regulations had not been made notwithstanding any amendment issued under Part VII of the General Regulations on or after that date.

2 Interpretation

(1) In these Regulations –

"CPR" means the Civil Procedure Rules 1998, and a reference to a rule or a Part, prefixed by "CPR", means the rule or (as the case may be) Part so numbered in the CPR;
"General Regulations" means the Civil Legal Aid (General) Regulations 1989;
"legal aid area" means an area specified by the Board under regulation 4(1) of the General Regulations and "legal aid area 1" means the area so numbered by the Board;
"prescribed rate" means the fee or hourly rate specified in the Schedules to these Regulations corresponding to the relevant item or class of work, the level of court and the location of the solicitor's office;
"relevant authority" means the Area Director in the case of an assessment and the taxing officer in the case of a taxation;

(2) Unless the context otherwise requires, expressions used in CPR Parts 43 to 48 or in the General Regulations shall have the same meanings as in those Rules or Regulations.

Amendments—SI 1996/645; SI 1999/3098.

3 Scope

These regulations apply to proceedings to which Part IV of the Legal Aid Act 1988 applies except –

(*a*) proceedings in the House of Lords;
(*b*) proceedings in the Court of Appeal;
(*c*) proceedings in magistrates' courts;
(*d*) proceedings to which regulation 3(2)(*a*) or 3(2)(*b*) of the Legal Aid in Family Proceedings (Remuneration) Regulations 1991 applies;
(*e*) proceedings to which section 29 of the Legal Aid Act 1988 applies;
(*f*) proceedings to which Part XV of the General Regulations (Particular Courts and Tribunals) applies.

4 Remuneration

(1) Subject to paragraphs (3A) to (3D), the amounts to be allowed to solicitors on a determination of the costs of an assisted person under regulation 107A of the General Regulations shall be –

(*a*) in accordance with Schedule 1 to these Regulations or, where the work done was done by a person or body (other than the Board) acting under the terms of a franchising contract which was entered into by the Board pursuant to its powers under section 4 of the Legal Aid Act 1988, in accordance with Schedule 2;
(*b*) in accordance with CPR rule 44.4(6) where the costs incurred relate to the kind of work to which that paragraph applies;
(*c*) in accordance with CPR rules 44.3 to 44.5 where no provision is made in the Schedules to these Regulations for the kind of work to which the costs relate.

(2) The relevant authority, in determining costs referred to at 3 in the Schedules to these Regulations, shall allow costs at the higher rate specified where the office of the solicitor for the assisted person where the work was done is situated within legal aid area 1.

(3) Subject to paragraphs (3A) to (3D), the relevant authority shall determine disbursements (including counsel's fees) in accordance with CPR Parts 43 to 48.

(3A)–(3D) ...

(4) Subject to these Regulations, the sums to be allowed to legal representatives in connection with the representation of an assisted person in proceedings to which these Regulations apply, shall be determined in accordance with Part XII of the General Regulations and CPR Parts 43 to 48.

Amendments—SI 1996/645; SI 1999/3098.

5 Enhancement

(1) Upon a determination the relevant authority may allow fees at more than the prescribed rate subject to the provisions of this regulation where it appears to the relevant authority, taking into account all the relevant circumstances, that –

(*a*) the work was done with exceptional competence, skill or expertise;
(*b*) the work was done with exceptional dispatch; or
(*c*) the case involved exceptional circumstances or complexity.

(2) Where the relevant authority considers that any item or class of work should be allowed at more than the prescribed rate, it shall apply to that item or class of work a percentage enhancement in accordance with the following provisions of this regulation.

(3) In determining the percentage by which fees should be enhanced above the prescribed rate the relevant authority shall have regard to –

(*a*) the degree of responsibility accepted by the solicitor;
(*b*) the care, speed and economy with which the case was prepared;
(*c*) the novelty, weight and complexity of the case.

(4) Except in proceedings to which paragraph (5) applies, the percentage above the prescribed rate by which fees for work may be enhanced shall not exceed 100%.

(5) In proceedings in the High Court, the relevant authority may allow an enhancement exceeding 100% where it considers that, in comparison with work in other High Court proceedings which would merit 100% enhancement, the item or class of work relates to exceptionally complex matters which have been handled with exceptional competence or dispatch.

(6) In proceedings to which paragraph (5) applies, the percentage above the prescribed rate by which fees for work may be enhanced may exceed 100% but shall not exceed 200%.

(7) The relevant authority may have regard to the generality of proceedings to which these Regulations apply in determining what is exceptional within the meaning of this regulation.

6 Reduction of costs

(1) Upon a determination the relevant authority may allow costs in respect of any item or class of work at less than the prescribed rate where it appears reasonable to do so having regard to the competence or dispatch with which the item or class of work was done.

(2) Paragraph (1) is without prejudice to regulation 109 of the General Regulations.

SCHEDULE 1

Column 1	Column 2 *High Court*	Column 3 *County Court or Magistrates' Court*
WORK		
1 Routine letters out	£7.40 per item	£6.50 per item
2 Routine telephone calls	£4.10 per item	£3.60 per item
3 All other preparation work including any work which was reasonably done arising out of or incidental to the proceedings, interviews with client, witnesses, and other parties; obtaining evidence; preparation and consideration of, and dealing with, documents, negotiations and notices; dealing with letters written	£74.00 per hour (£78.50 per hour	£65.00 per hour £69.00 per hour
and received and telephone calls which are not routine	where solicitor's office situated within legal aid area 1)	
4 Attending counsel in conference or at the trial or hearing of any summons or application at court, or other appointment	£36.40 per hour	£32.00 per hour
5 Attending without counsel at the trial or hearing of any cause or the hearing of any summons or other application at court, or other appointment	£74.00 per hour	£65.00 per hour
6 Travelling and waiting in connection with the above matters	£32.70 per hour	£28.75 per hour

Amendments—Substituted by SI 1996/645.

Note as to figures—The figures shown in this Schedule are those set by SI 1996/645 with effect from 1 April 1996. The previous figures specified the same sums but did not apply to the magistrates' court.

SCHEDULE 2

Column 1	Column 2 *High Court*	Column 3 *County Court or Magistrates' Court*
WORK		

Column 1	Column 2 *High Court*	Column 3 *County Court or Magistrates' Court*
1 Routine letters out	£7.50 per item	£6.60 per item
2 Routine telephone calls	£4.15 per item	£3.65 per item
3 All other preparation work including any work which was reasonably done arising out of or incidental to the proceedings, interviews with client, witnesses, and other parties; obtaining evidence; preparation and consideration of, and dealing with, documents, negotiations and notices; dealing with letters written and received and telephone calls which are not routine	£75.00 per hour (£79.50 per hour where solicitor's office situated within legal aid area 1)	£66.00 per hour £70.00 per hour
4 Attending counsel in conference or at the trial or hearing of any summons or application at court, or other appointment	£37.00 per hour	£32.50 per hour
5 Attending without counsel at the trial or hearing of any cause or the hearing of any summons or other application at court, or other appointment	£75.00 per hour	£66.00 per hour
6 Travelling and waiting in connection with the above matters	£33.25 per hour	£29.20 per hour

Amendments—Inserted by SI 1996/645.

General Note—The procedure for detailed assessment of CLS public funding (legal aid) bills is still governed by Civil Legal Aid (General) Regulations 1989 (as amended by Civil Legal Aid (General) (Amendment) Regulations 2000). Primarily, they update the old regulations to harmonise them with terminology used under CPR 1998. CLA(G)R 1989, Pt XII remains the current basis for detailed assessment of legal aid bills and to that extent CPR 1998, Pts 44 and 47 do not apply to such detailed assessments (CPR 1998, r 44.17). The Remuneration Regulations define the rates of remuneration payable.

Note as to figures—The figures shown in this Schedule are those set by SI 1996/645 with effect from 1 April 1996.

Bases for detailed assessment—There are three regimes under which costs in family proceedings may be considered for detailed assessment:
(i) Civil Procedure Rules 1998, Pt 47;
(ii) Legal Aid in Family Proceedings (Remuneration) Regulations 1991;
(iii) Legal Aid in Civil Proceedings (Remuneration) Regulations 1994.

All three apply to proceedings in county courts and in the Supreme Court. Only (ii) applies to family proceedings in the magistrates' (family proceedings) courts. The separate regime for private and between parties bills under Family Proceedings (Costs) Rules 1991 was replaced by the introduction of CPR 1998.

Terminology—Attempts by the Lord Chancellor to exclude the term "legal aid" from his new scheme have been patchy, and often illogical. The regulations under consideration make no attempt to comply with the general bowdlerisation.

Which regime applies?—The applicable regime is as follows:
(i) Only family proceedings covered by LAFP(R)R 1991, reg 3(2)(*a*)–(*bb*) are assessed under those regulations. Other family proceedings (such as adoption, child abduction) are covered by LACP(R)R 1994.
(ii) All other family proceedings are covered by LACP(R)R 1994 where public funding (legal aid) detailed assessment applies.
(iii) Where (*a*) legal aid does not apply or (*b*) where a legally aided party has his bill assessed on a between parties basis as a receiving party, CPR 1998 apply.

Indemnity rules—It should be recalled that a between parties detailed assessment for a legally aided client is the exception to the indemnity rule (that a legal representative cannot charge a paying party more than he would have charged his clients). On such a detailed assessment, the solicitor can charge such rate as may be available to him (CLA(G)R 1989, reg 107B(4)), regardless of the amounts set out in the Schedules to the remuneration regulations.

"family proceedings"—For the present, in the context of legal aid detailed assessment and remuneration the term "family proceedings" refers back to a variety of otherwise defunct legislation, including old costs rules and the long repealed MCA 1973, s 50 (set out below). Detailed assessments to which the term "family proceedings" applies can therefore be summarised as follows:
(1) *Care proceedings* – all proceedings under CA 1989, Pts IV and V plus secure accommodation applications (s 25).
(2) *Prescribed family proceedings* – consist of the following:
(*a*) proceedings to which rules made under MCA 1973 would have applied;
(*b*) all proceedings under CA 1989 (other than care proceedings); and
(*c*) other forms of family proceedings such as under CSA 1991, s 27 etc
(3) *Proceedings under Family Law Act 1996 Part IV* (occupation orders and domestic violence).

Matrimonial Causes Act 1973, s 50—The relevant part of MCA 1973, s 50 (now repealed) is s 50(1)(*a*)–(*d*), which reads as follows:

"(*a*) this Act, the Matrimonial Causes Act 1967 (which confers jurisdiction on county courts in certain matrimonial proceedings) or section 45 of the Courts Act 1971 (transfer of matrimonial proceedings between High Court and county court etc);
(*b*) proceedings in the High Court or a divorce county court for an order under Schedule 1 to the Matrimonial Homes Act 1983 (transfer of certain tenancies on divorce etc);
(*c*) certain other proceedings in the High Court, that is to say –
(i) proceedings in the High Court under section 17 of the Married Women's Property Act 1882, not being proceedings in the divorce registry treated by virtue of rules made under this section for the purposes of section 45 of the Courts Act 1971 as pending in a county court;
(ii) proceedings in the High Court under section 1 of the Matrimonial Homes Act 1983 (rights of occupation of matrimonial home for spouse not otherwise entitled);
(iii) proceedings in which the only substantive relief sought is a declaration with respect to a person's matrimonial status;
(*d*) any enactment passed after this Act which relates to any matter dealt with in this Act or the Matrimonial Causes Act 1967;".

Table: forms of detailed assessment—In the table below the form of detailed assessment in each type of family proceedings is shown by columns as follows:
(i) Between parties (*inter partes*) detailed assessment;
(ii) CLS public funding in all courts save family proceedings courts;
(iii) CLS public funding in family proceedings courts.

In rows alongside each type of process indicated is the delegated legislation under which detailed assessment is undertaken as follows:
1 CPR 1998, Pt 43
2 LACP(R)R 1994
3 LAFP(R)R 1991, Sch 1 (care proceedings)

PART III

4 LAFP(R)R 1991, Sch 2(*a*) (prescribed family proceedings, other than care proceedings and proceedings under FLA 1996, Pt IV)

5 LAFP(R)R 1991, Sch 2(*b*) (proceedings in the family proceedings courts other than care proceedings)

6 LAFP(R)R 1991, Sch 2(*a*), col 3 (proceedings under FLA 1996, Pt IV in High Court, county courts or family proceedings courts)

Form of family process	(i)	(ii)	(iii)
Adoption Act 1976	1	2	5
Child Abduction and Custody Act 1985	1	2	–
Child Support Acts – appeals	1	4	5
Children Act 1989 (other than Pts IV and V)	1	4	5
Children Act 1989, Pts IV and V	1	3	3
Domestic Proceedings and Magistrates' Courts Act 1978	–	–	5
Family Law Act 1986	1	2	–
Family Law Act 1996, Pt IV	1	6	6
Human Fertilisation and Embryology Act 1990, s 30	1	4	–
Inheritance (Provision for Family and Dependants) Act 1975	1	2	–
Injunctions in inherent jurisdiction (free-standing)	1	2	–
Judicial review in family proceedings	1	2	–
Married Women's Property Act 1882	1	4	–
Matrimonial and Family Proceedings Act 1984, Pt III	1	4	–
Matrimonial Causes Act 1973	1	4	–
Protection from Harassment Act 1997 (tort)	1	2	–
Trusts of Land and Appointment of Trustees Act 1996, s 14	1	2	–
Wardship and the inherent jurisdiction	1	2	–

Graduated fees—The effect of the Community Legal Service (Funding) (Counsel in Family Proceedings) Order 2001 is to remove references to counsel's fees in respect of funding certificates granted after 1 May 2001, save for the following (CLS(F)(CFP)O 2001, art 4):

(i) proceedings where the main hearing lasts for more than 10 days (art 4(3));

(ii) appeals to the Divisional Court, the Court of Appeal and the House of Lords (art 4(4));

(iii) where another party to the proceedings is to pay the costs of the funded client (art 4(6)).

Legal Aid in Family Proceedings (Remuneration) Regulations 1991, SI 1991/2038

1 Citation, commencement and transitional provisions

(1) These Regulations may be cited as the Legal Aid in Family Proceedings (Remuneration) Regulations 1991 and shall come into force on 14 October 1991.

(2) Subject to paragraph (3), these Regulations shall apply to remuneration payable in respect of work done on or after 14 October 1991 and remuneration payable in respect of work done in proceedings commenced before that date shall

be determined as if these Regulations and the Legal Aid in Criminal and Care Proceedings (Costs) (Amendment) (No 3) Regulations 1991 had not been made:

Provided that regulation 3 of, and Schedule 1 to, these Regulations shall apply to remuneration payable in respect of work done or on after 14 October 1991 in relation to care proceedings (within the meaning of section 27 of the Legal Aid Act 1988) as if those proceedings were care proceedings within the meaning of these Regulations.

(3) For the purposes of determining remuneration payable in respect of work done before 14 October 1991 in relation to proceedings of a kind described in paragraph (*a*) of the definition of "prescribed family proceedings", Schedule 2 to the Rules shall have effect as if that Schedule were substituted for Schedule 2(*a*) to these Regulations and Schedule 2 (as so substituted) shall have effect as it had effect during the year in which the work in question was done.

Amendments—SI 1991/2112.

"these Regulations shall apply"(reg 1(2))—These regulations provide for remuneration for legal representatives in family proceedings in respect of legally aided clients. They bring care proceedings within the ambit of family proceedings costs rather than, as before, allied to criminal costs.

Schedules—The schedules contain fixed scales of costs for use in care proceedings (Sch 1) and in prescribed family proceedings (Sch 2).

2 Interpretation

(1) In these Regulations, unless the context otherwise requires –

"the relevant authority" means the Area Director in the case of an assessment and the costs officer in the case of a detailed assessment, and "determination" shall mean an assessment or detailed assessment as the case may be;

"care proceedings" means proceedings for an order under Part IV or V of the Children Act 1989 and includes proceedings under section 25 of that Act (secure accommodation orders);

"fee-earner" means a solicitor, a legal executive or any clerk who regularly does work for which it is appropriate to make a direct charge to a client;

"the General Regulations" means the Civil Legal Aid (General) Regulations 1989;

"prescribed family proceedings" means –

(*a*) proceedings commenced before 14 October 1991 with respect to which rules made under section 50 of the Matrimonial Causes Act 1973 applied immediately before the date of the coming into force of these Regulations;

(*b*) proceedings commenced on or after 14 October 1991 to which those rules would have applied if they had continued in force on and after that date, other than proceedings under Part IV of the Family Law Act 1996;

(*c*) proceedings under the Children Act 1989, excluding care proceedings;

(*d*) proceedings under sections 20 or 27 of the Child Support Act 1991 in the High Court, a county court or a magistrates' court;

(*e*) proceedings under section 30 of the Human Fertilisation and Embryology Act 1990 in the High Court, a county court or a magistrates' court;

"the Rules" means the Matrimonial Causes (Costs) Rules 1988.

(2) Unless the context otherwise requires –

(*a*) expressions used in the Rules, the Family Proceedings Rules 1991 and in the General Regulations shall have the same meanings as in those Rules or Regulations;

(*aa*) the expressions "detailed assessment", "costs judge" and "costs officer" shall have the meanings given to them in Part 43 of the Civil Procedure Rules 1998; and

(*b*) any reference in these Regulations to a regulation, Part or Schedule by number means the regulation, Part or Schedule so numbered in these Regulations.

Amendments—SI 1991/2112; SI 1993/1117; SI 1994/230; SI 1996/650; SI 1997/2394; SI 2001/830.

Defined terms—"Area Director": Civil Legal Aid (General) Regulations 1989, reg 3(1).

3 Remuneration

(1) The sums to be allowed to legal representatives in connection with family proceedings shall be determined in accordance with these Regulations, Part XII of the General Regulations, the Family Proceedings (Costs) Rules 1991 and paragraphs 1(3), (4)(*a*) and (5) and paragraph 2(2)(*a*) of Part I of Schedule 1 to the Rules.

(1A) The following paragraphs of this regulation shall apply solely on a determination under regulation 107A of the General Regulations.

(2) Subject to the following paragraphs, the amounts to be allowed on determination under this regulation shall be –

(*a*) in accordance with Schedule 1 where the certificate was issued in relation to care proceedings;

(*b*) in accordance with Schedule 2 where the certificate was issued in relation to prescribed family proceedings, or, in relation to proceedings in a magistrates' court, any family proceedings other than care proceedings, or proceedings under Part IV of the Family Law Act 1996;

(*bb*) in accordance with the county court rate in column 3 of Schedule 2(*a*) where the certificate was issued in relation to proceedings in the High Court, a county court or a magistrates' court under Part IV of the Family Law Act 1996;

(*c*) in accordance with the Legal Aid in Civil Proceedings (Remuneration) Regulations 1994 where the certificate was issued in relation to family proceedings not falling within sub-paragraph (*a*), (*b*) or (*bb*);

(*d*) in accordance with paragraph (2) of rule 8 of the Rules where the costs incurred relate to the kind of work to which that paragraph applies;

(*e*) in accordance with paragraph 1(1) of Part I of Schedule 1 to the Rules where no provision is made in the Schedules to these Regulations for the kind of work to which the costs relate.

(3) Where a certificate relating to proceedings under paragraph 2(*c*) is extended to cover proceedings falling within sub-paragraphs (*a*) or (*b*), the amounts to be allowed on determination shall be in accordance with Schedule 1 or 2 as the case may be, or, if it is extended to cover proceedings falling within both sub-paragraphs, in accordance with Schedule 2.

(3A) Where a certificate relating to proceedings under paragraph 2(*c*) is extended to cover proceedings falling within sub-paragraph (*bb*), the amounts to be allowed on determination shall be in accordance with that sub-paragraph.

(4) On determination the relevant authority –

(*a*) in allowing costs under item 4 of Part I of Schedule 1, shall allow costs at the higher rate where the work was done by a fee-earner whose office is situated within legal aid area 1;

(*b*) in allowing costs under item 4 of Part I of Schedule 2(*a*), shall allow costs at the higher rate where at the time when the relevant work was done the proceedings were conducted in the principal registry or in another court on the South-Eastern Circuit;

(*bb*) in allowing costs under Parts I to III and V of Schedule 1 and Parts I to III and V of Schedule 2, shall allow the rates specified in Schedules 1A and 2A where the work done was done by a person or body who is authorised to carry out work in family proceedings by a contract with the Legal Services Commission and references in these Regulations to Schedule 1 or 2 shall, subject to paragraph (4A), in relation to such work, be construed as references to Schedule 1A or, as the case may be, 2A;

(*c*) may allow a larger amount than that specified in column 2 or column 3, as the case may be, of Parts I, II, III and V of Schedules 1 and 2(*a*) where it appears to him reasonable to do so having regard to –

(i) the exceptional competence with which the work was done, or

(ii) the exceptional expedition with which the work was done, or

(iii) any other exceptional circumstances of the case,

but, without prejudice to regulation 109 of the General Regulations or rules 15 or 16 of the Rules, the relevant authority may in respect of any item in Part I, II, III or V of Schedule 1 or 2(*a*) allow a lower amount than that specified in column 2 or column 3 of that Part, as the case may be, where it appears to him reasonable to do so having regard to any failure on the part of the solicitor to provide timely preparation or advice, or for any similar reason.

(4A) Except in relation to prescribed family proceedings in a magistrates' court, where paragraph (4)(*bb*) applies and the relevant work is done by a member of a relevant panel the relevant authority shall, subject to paragraph (4B), allow whichever is the higher of –

(*a*) an amount 15% higher than the amount in Schedule 1A or (as the case may be) 2A(*a*) which he would have allowed but for this paragraph and paragraph (4)(*c*); and

(*b*) if he decides to award such an amount, a larger amount than that specified in column 2 or column 3, as the case may be, of Parts I, II, III and V of Schedule 1A or (as the case may be) 2A(*a*), awarded in accordance with paragraph (4)(*c*).

(4B) Paragraph (4A) shall not apply in relation to any item if, but for that paragraph, the relevant authority would, in accordance with regulation 3(4)(*c*), have allowed a lower amount for that item than the one in Part I, II, III or V of Schedule 1A or 2A(*a*).

(5) Without prejudice to regulation 109 of the Legal Aid General Regulations or rules 14 or 15 of the Rules, where a standard fee is specified in Part IV of Schedules 1 or 2(*a*) for work done by junior counsel that fee shall be allowed unless the relevant authority considers that it would be unreasonable to do so, in which case he shall allow such lesser or greater fee as may be reasonable:

Provided that the fee allowed shall not exceed any maximum fee which is specified unless the relevant authority considers that, owing to the time and labour expended by counsel or to any other special circumstance of the case, the maximum fee specified would not provide reasonable remuneration for some or all of the work done, in which case the fee to be allowed shall be in the discretion of the relevant authority.

(6) For the purpose of determining which of the brief fees provided by item 12 of Schedule 1 and item 13 of Schedule 2(a) should be allowed –

(*a*) a one hour fee shall be allowed where the hearing lasts for one hour or less than one hour;

(*b*) a half day fee shall be allowed where the hearing lasts for more than one hour and –

(i) begins and ends before the luncheon adjournment; or

(ii) begins after the luncheon adjournment and ends before 5.30 pm;

(*c*) a full day fee shall be allowed where the hearing lasts for more than one hour and –

(i) begins before and ends after the luncheon adjournment but before 5.30 pm; or

(ii) begins after the luncheon adjournment and ends after 5.30 pm; and

(*d*) a more than a full day fee shall be allowed where the hearing –

(i) begins before the luncheon adjournment and ends after 5.30 pm on the same day; or

(ii) begins on one day and continues into a subsequent day.

(7) In exercising his discretion under this regulation or in relation to any provision of the Schedules where the amount of costs to be allowed is in his discretion, the relevant authority shall exercise his discretion in accordance with paragraph 1(2) of Part I of Schedule 1 to the Rules.

(8) Disbursements (other than counsel's fees) for which no allowance is made in Schedules 1 or 2(*a*) shall be determined and allowed, or disallowed, according to the general principles applicable to the taxation of costs in Parts 43 to 48 of the Civil Procedure Rules 1998.

(9) In this regulation –

(*a*) "relevant panel" means –

(i) the Solicitors' Family Law Association Accredited Specialist Panel; or

(ii) in relation to work done under a certificate which includes proceedings relating to children, the Law Society's Children Act Panel;

(iii) the Law Society Family Law Panel Advanced; and

(*b*) "proceedings relating to children" means proceedings in which the welfare of children is determined, including, without limitation, proceedings under the Children Act 1989 or under the inherent jurisdiction of the High Court in relation to children.

Amendments—SI 1994/230; SI 1996/650; SI 1997/2394; SI 2001/830; SI 2002/710.

Defined terms—"care proceedings": reg 2(1); "certificate": Civil Legal Aid (General) Regulations 1989, reg 3(1); "determination", "the General Regulations", "prescribed family proceedings": reg 2(1); "principal registry": FPR 1991, r 1.2(1); "relevant authority", "the Rules": reg 2(1).

"legal representatives"—These regulations cover remuneration for "legal representatives", the term used in Supreme Court Act 1981, s 51(13) (elaborated by Courts and Legal Services Act 1990, s 119(1)). "Legal representative" is there defined to mean a person entitled to a right of audience and to conduct litigation. In Legal Aid Act 1988, s 43 "legal representative" is defined by reference to authorised advocates (which includes solicitors and barristers) or authorised litigators, being those entitled to conduct litigation, which is potentially a wider definition than that used in Supreme Court Act 1981, s 51(13). It is not clear which definition covers these regulations.

"the amounts to be allowed" (reg 3(2))—This regulation introduces five regimes for remuneration in various forms of family proceedings. It distinguishes between (*a*) proceedings under CA 1989, Pts IV and V; (*b*) prescribed family proceedings and family proceedings (other than care proceedings) in magistrates' courts; (*c*) family proceedings other than those covered by reg 3(2)(*a*) and (*b*); (*d*) non-contentious costs in family proceedings; and (*e*) proceedings not otherwise covered in reg 3(2). The amounts available for remuneration are set out in the various schedules and rules to which reference is made in the regulation. Where the amount to be allowed is a reasonable amount, all factors known to the taxing officer are to be taken into account (*L v L (Legal Aid Taxation)* [1996] 1 FLR 873, CA).

"Where a certificate ... is extended" (reg 3(3))—By virtue of Civil Legal Aid (General) Regulations 1989, regs 46(3) and 51(*b*)(iii), a certificate in family proceedings (as defined by Civil Legal Aid (General) Regulations 1989, reg 3(1)) may be extended to cover more than one action, cause or matter. Thus, for example, a certificate for adoption proceedings could be amended to cover an application for a residence order if the adoption application failed.

Higher rates (reg 3(4))—This regulation provides for higher rates to be allowed on taxation or assessment. In particular it grants an element of discretion to the Area Director or taxing officer where exceptional competence or expedition are demonstrated by solicitors (but not counsel – see **"lesser or greater fee" for junior counsel** below). Members of the Law Society's Children, SFLA accredited specialist and Family Law Panels may wish to seek the uplift available to them.

"exceptional circumstances" (reg 3(4)(*c*)(iii))—The significance of the term "exceptional circumstances" for the purposes of taxation was considered by Cazalet J and two assessors in *Re Children Act 1989 (Taxation of Costs)* [1994] 2 FLR 934, although they refused to define it. The solicitor concerned in the case appeared as advocate, while the local authority was represented by leading counsel in proceedings involving allegations of violence to a child and resulting in a six-day hearing. The following were held to be amongst the principal factors in assessing "exceptional circumstances":

(*a*) *Children Panel membership* Membership of The Law Society's Children Panel was an exceptional circumstance justifying the taxing officer in considering the exercise of his discretion to allow a higher amount; and this was so even though the solicitor was not representing a child.
(*b*) *Solicitor advocacy* This is not of itself an exceptional circumstance, but advocacy by a panel member is an exceptional circumstance which may justify an enhancement.
(*c*) *Length of hearing* A long hearing is not necessarily an exceptional circumstance, but a hearing of more than two days might be expected to justify an enhancement.
(*d*) *Transfer upwards* This is not an exceptional circumstance, but may provide an indication of complexity and weight.
(*e*) *Conflicts of expert evidence* Conflict of detailed medical evidence or a proliferation of expert witnesses (as distinct from merely contested expert evidence) is likely to constitute exceptional circumstances.
(*f*) *Sexual or other serious abuse* Detailed contested allegations of serious sexual or other abuse may – but will not necessarily – constitute exceptional circumstances.
(*g*) *Conflict between guardian ad litem and child* This may result in an enhancement.
(*h*) *Children with different needs* Representation of children with differing needs may lead to an enhancement.

Specific identification of items for enhancement—Specific items to which an enhancement is claimed must be identified: a generalised mark-up is not sufficient (*Re Children Act 1989 (Taxation of Costs)* [1994] 2 FLR 934). An explanation of any enhancement sought should be provided and should be applied separately to specific areas of work.

Lower amounts (reg 3(4))—A lower amount may be awarded where a solicitor (but not counsel – see **"lesser or greater fee" for junior counsel** below) has acted inefficiently or given bad advice. This does not affect any power in the taxing officer or Area Director to disallow or reduce wasted costs (Civil Legal Aid (General) Regulations 1989, reg 109) or the court's or district judge's power to order a legal representative to pay costs or to disallow wasted costs (Civil Procedure

Rules 1998, r 48.7). However the criteria under reg 3(4) are less stringent than those relating to "wasted costs" and reduction may therefore be more easily justified under this regulation on legal aid taxation or assessment.

"lesser or greater fee" for junior counsel (reg 3(5))—The facility to increase counsel's fees relates to the time spent in preparation, where the set fees in Pt IV of Sch 1 or 2 are inadequate, or to the case where there are exceptional circumstances. In such circumstances the taxing officer or Area Director has a limited discretion to allow a higher fee. In *F v F (Costs: Ancillary Relief)* [1995] 2 FLR 702, Cazalet J held that "special" in reg 3(5) had a different meaning from "exceptional" in reg 3(4)(*c*), thus entitling counsel to breach the discretionary barrier more easily than solicitors (and see *Re H (Costs: Care Proceedings)* [1995] 2 FLR 733, Cazalet J with assessors, where it was held that the degree to which a case was exceptional was tempered where an advocate for the child with a guardian ad litem performed a role supportive of the local authority).

Lower fees for counsel—It is also possible for the taxing officer or Area Director to reduce counsel's fees. No basis for considering this is suggested save that it would be unreasonable to allow the full fee. Perhaps the basis for reduction of solicitors costs (failure to provide timely preparation or advice or similar reasons – see **Lower amounts** above) might be used in appropriate cases. This regulation does not affect any power in the taxing officer or Area Director to disallow or reduce wasted costs (Civil Legal Aid (General) Regulations 1989, reg 109) or the court's or district judge's power to order a legal representative to pay costs or to disallow wasted costs (Civil Procedure Rules 1998, r 48.7).

Excessive representation—Parties should consider joint representation, especially by counsel, where there were no significant differences in the case which they intended to put before the court (*Birmingham City Council v H (No 3)* [1994] 1 FLR 224, HL).

Disbursements allowed (reg 3(8))—These provisions must be read subject to the fact that if prior authority to incur an expense or take a step in proceedings has been obtained under Civil Legal Aid (General) Regulations 1989, Pt VII then no question as to the propriety of that expense or step can be raised on taxation (Civil Legal Aid (General) Regulations 1989, reg 63(1)); unless (*a*) the solicitor or assisted person knew or ought to have known at the time of incurring it that the need for the expenditure had passed (reg 63(2)); or (*b*) the High Court exercises its inherent jurisdiction over the extent to which costs are to be allowed under Supreme Court Act 1981, s 51(3) (see eg *Re Solicitors, Re Taxation of Costs* [1982] 1 WLR 745, [1982] 2 All ER 683, where costs were disallowed even though a solicitor had authority under Pt VII (as it now is) because he failed also to obtain the client's instructions to incur the expenditure).

Costs draftsman's fees—The prescribed rate for "preparing the bill" allowed at item 18 in the Schedules below is the amount to be allowed for this item, rather than the timed amount, in accordance with *Practice Direction about Costs*, para 4.18 (*Re C (Legal Aid: Preparation of Bill of Costs)* [2001] 1 FLR 602, CA). A discretionary amount is allowed for "Preparing for and attending detailed assessment" whenever a legal representative does any work on a bill which has been provisionally assessed, even though no appointment is ultimately taken out.

SCHEDULE 1

CARE PROCEEDINGS

Part I—Preparation

Column 1	Column 2 *High Court*	Column 3 *County Court or Magistrates' Court*
ITEM		

1 Writing routine letters	£4.25 per item *(£4.15)*	£3.65 per item *(£3.60)*
2 Receiving routine letters	£2.10 per item *(£2.05)*	£1.85 per item *(£1.80)*
3 Routine telephone calls	£4.25 per item *(£4.15)*	£3.65 per item *(£3.60)*
4 All other preparation work including any work which was reasonably done arising out of or incidental to the proceedings, interviews with client, witnesses, and other parties; obtaining evidence; preparation and consideration of, and dealing with, documents, negotiations and notices; dealing with letters written and received and telephone calls which are not routine	£65.50 per hour *(£64.50)* (£69.75 per hour *(£68.75)* for a fee-earner whose office is situated within legal aid area 1)	£58.00 per hour *(£57.25)* £61.25 per hour *(£60.25)*
5 Travelling and waiting time in connection with the above matters	£32.00 per hour *(£31.50)*	£29.25 per hour *(£28.75)*

Part II—Conferences with counsel

6 Attending counsel in conference	£37.00 per hour *(£36.50)*	£32.50 per hour *(£32.00)*
7 Travelling and waiting	£32.00 per hour *(£31.50)*	£29.25 per hour *(£28.75)*

Part III—Attendances

8 Attending with counsel at the trial or hearing of any cause or the hearing of any summons or other application at court, or other appointment	£37.00 per hour *(£36.50)*	£32.50 per hour *(£32.00)*
9 Attending without counsel at the trial or hearing of any cause or the hearing of any summons or other application at court, or other appointment	£64.00 per hour *(£63.00)*	£64.00 per hour *(£63.00)*
10 Travelling and waiting	£32.00 per hour *(£31.50)*	£29.25 per hour *(£28.75)*

Part IV—Fees for Junior Counsel

11 With a brief on an unopposed application for an injunction, or procedural issue	Standard £88.25 *(£87.00)* Maximum £146.25 *(£144.00)*	£76.25 *(£75.00)* £127.00 *(£125.00)*
12 With a brief on the trial of a cause or matter or on the hearing of an application where the hearing lasts for		
(*a*) one hour	Standard £133.50 *(£131.50)* Maximum £268.00 *(£264.00)*	£114.25 *(£112.50)* £228.50 *(£225.00)*
(*b*) a half day	Standard £184.75 *(£182.00)* Maximum £304.50 *(£300.00)*	£159.25 *(£157.00)* £268.00 *(£264.00)*
(*c*) a full day	Standard £368.50 *(£363.00)* Maximum £584.75 *(£576.00)*	£317.75 *(£313.00)* £508.50 *(£501.00)*
(*d*) more than a full day	Discretionary *(Discretionary)*	Discretionary *(Discretionary)*
13 For each day or part of a day on which the trial of a cause or matter, or the hearing of an ancillary application, or a children appointment, is continued after the first day	Discretionary *(Discretionary)*	Discretionary *(Discretionary)*
14 Conference (including time reasonably spent in preparation and conference, but not otherwise remunerated)	Standard £20.25 per half hour *(£20.00)*	Standard £17.75 per half hour *(£17.50)*
15 (*a*) Complex items of written work (such as advices on evidence, opinions and affidavits of a substantial nature, requests for particulars or answers)	Standard £96.25 per item *(£94.75)*	Standard £82.75 per item *(£81.50)*
(*b*) All other written work	Standard £57.00 per item *(£56.25)*	Standard £50.25 per item *(£49.50)*
16 Except where the court is within 40 kilometres of Charing Cross or where there is no local Bar in the court town, or within 40 kilometres thereof, for travelling time	Standard £18.50 per hour plus expenses *(£18.25)*	Standard £15.85 per hour plus expenses *(£15.65)*

Part V—Detailed assessment and appeal in relation to detailed assessment (High Court and County Court only)

17 Preparing the bill (where allowable) and completing the detailed assessment (excluding preparing for and attending the detailed assessment)	£32.00–£89.25 *(£31.50–£88.00)*	£32.00–£51.00 *(£31.50–£50.25)*
18 Preparing for and attending the detailed assessment (including travelling and waiting)	Discretionary *(Discretionary)*	Discretionary *(Discretionary)*
19 Appeal to costs judge, district judge or judge (including preparation)	Discretionary *(Discretionary)*	Discretionary *(Discretionary)*

Amendments—Substituted by SI 1996/650; amended by SI 1996/1555; SI 2001/830.

Note as to figures—The principal figures set out in this Schedule are applicable from 1 April 1996, except the sums shown in Item 2 (Receiving routine letters) which are effective from 8 July 1996. The previous figures, specified by SI 1992/596 with effect from 1 April 1992, are shown italicised within brackets below each of the corresponding current figures.

SCHEDULE 1A
CARE PROCEEDINGS

Part I—Preparation

Column 1	Column 2 *High Court*	Column 3 *County Court or Magistrates' Court*
ITEM		
1 Writing routine letters	£4.70 per item	£4.10 per item
2 Receiving routine letters	£2.35 per item	£2.05 per item
3 Routine telephone calls	£4.70 per item	£4.10 per item
4 All other preparation work including any work which was reasonably done arising out of or incidental to the proceedings, interviews with client, witnesses, and other parties; obtaining evidence; preparation and consideration of, and dealing with, documents, negotiations and notices; dealing with letters written and received and telephone calls which are not routine	£73.15 per hour (£77.85 per hour	£64.90 per hour £68.20 per hour
	for a fee-earner whose office is situated in the Legal Services Commission's London Region)	

5 Travelling and waiting	£35.75 per hour	£32.45 per hour

Part II—Conferences with counsel

6 Attending with counsel in conference	£41.25 per hour	£36.30 per hour
7 Travelling and waiting	£35.75 per hour	£32.45 per hour

Part III—Attendances

8 Attending with counsel at the trial or hearing of any cause or the hearing of any summons or other application at court, or other appointment	£41.25 per hour	£36.30 per hour
9 Attending without counsel at the trial or hearing of any cause or the hearing of any summons or other application at court, or other appointment	£73.15 per hour (£77.85 per hour for a fee-earner whose office is situated in the Legal Services Commission's London Region)	£71.50 per hour
10 Travelling and waiting	£35.75 per hour	£32.45 per hour

Part V—Detailed assessment and appeal in relation to detailed assessment (High Court and County Court only)

	High Court	*County Court*
17 Preparing the bill (where allowable) and completing the detailed assessment (excluding preparing for and attending the hearing of the detailed assessment)	£35.75–£99.85	£35.75–£56.95
18 Preparing for and attending the detailed assessment (including travelling and waiting)	Discretionary	Discretionary
19 Appeal to costs judge, district judge or judge (including preparation)	Discretionary	Discretionary

Amendments—Inserted by SI 1996/650; amended by SI 1996/1555; SI 2001/830; SI 2001/1255; SI 2001/2417.

Note as to figures—The figures set out in this Schedule are applicable from 2 April 2001, except the sums shown in Item 17 (Preparing the bill and completing the detailed assessment) which are effective from 26 July 2001.

SCHEDULE 2
PRESCRIBED FAMILY PROCEEDINGS

(a) High Court and county court proceedings

Part I—Preparation

Column 1	Column 2 *High Court*	Column 3 *County Court*
ITEM		
1 Writing routine letters	£4.25 per item *(£4.15)*	£3.65 per item *(£3.60)*
2 Receiving routine letters	note 1	note 2
3 Routine telephone calls	£4.25 per item *(£4.15)*	£3.65 per item *(£3.60)*
4 All other preparation work including any work which was reasonably done arising out of or incidental to the proceedings, interviews with client, witnesses, and other parties; obtaining evidence; preparation and consideration of, and dealing with, documents, negotiations and notices; dealing with letters written and received and telephone calls which are not routine	Where the proceedings were conducted in the divorce registry or in another court on the South Eastern Circuit at the time when the relevant work was done: £46.75 per hour *(£46.00)* All other circuits: £43.75 per hour *(£43.00)*	 £41.00 per hour *(£40.25)* £38.75 per hour *(£38.20)*
5 In addition to items 1–4 above, to cover the general care and conduct of the proceedings	plus 50% *(plus 50%)*	plus 50% *(plus 50%)*
6 Travelling and waiting time in connection with the above matters	£32.00 per hour *(£31.50)*	£29.25 per hour *(£28.75)*

Part II—Conferences with counsel

7 Attending counsel in conference	£37.00 per hour *(£36.50)*	£32.50 per hour *(£32.00)*
8 Travelling and waiting	£32.00 per hour *(£31.50)*	£29.25 per hour *(£28.75)*

Part III—Attendances

9 Attending with counsel at the trial or hearing of any cause or the hearing of any summons or other application at court, or other appointment	£37.00 per hour *(£36.50)*	£32.50 per hour *(£32.00)*
10 Attending without counsel at the trial or hearing of any cause or the hearing of any summons or other application at court, or other appointment	£55.75 per hour *(£55.00)*	note 3
11 Travelling and waiting	£32.00 per hour *(£31.50)*	£29.25 per hour *(£28.75)*

Part IV—Fees for Junior Counsel

12 With a brief on an unopposed application for an injunction, or procedural issue	Standard £88.25 *(£87.00)* Maximum £146.25 *(£144.00)*	£76.25 *(£75.00)* £127.00 *(£125.00)*
13 With a brief on the trial of a cause or matter or on the hearing of an ancillary application or on a children appointment where the hearing lasts for		
(*a*) one hour	Standard £133.50 *(£131.50)* Maximum £268.00 *(£264.00)*	£114.25 *(£112.50)* £228.50 *(£225.00)*
(*b*) a half day	Standard £184.75 *(£182.00)* Maximum £304.50 *(£300.00)*	£159.25 *(£157.00)* £268.00 *(£264.00)*
(*c*) a full day	Standard £368.50 *(£363.00)* Maximum £584.75 *(£576.00)*	£317.75 *(£313.00)* £508.50 *(£501.00)*
(*d*) more than a full day	Discretionary *(Discretionary)*	Discretionary *(Discretionary)*
14 For each day or part of a day on which the trial of a cause or matter, or the hearing of an ancillary application, or a children appointment, is continued after the first day	Discretionary *(Discretionary)*	Discretionary *(Discretionary)*

15 Conference (including time reasonably spent in preparation and conference, but not otherwise remunerated)	Standard £20.25 per half hour *(£20.00)*	Standard £17.75 per half hour *(£17.50)*
16 (*a*) Complex items of written work (such as advices on evidence, opinions and affidavits of a substantial nature, requests for particulars or answers)	Standard £96.25 per item *(£94.75)*	Standard £82.75 per item *(£81.50)*
(*b*) All other written work	Standard £57.00 per item *(£56.25)*	Standard £50.25 per item *(£49.50)*
17 Except where the court is within 40 kilometres of Charing Cross or where there is no local Bar in the court town, or within 40 kilometres thereof, for travelling time	Standard £18.50 per hour plus expenses *(£18.25)*	Standard £15.85 per hour plus expenses *(£15.65)*

Part V—Detailed assessment and appeal in relation to detailed assessment

18 Preparing the bill (where allowable) and completing the detailed assessment (excluding preparing for and attending the detailed assessment)	£32.00–£89.25 *(£31.50–£88.00)*	note 4
19 Preparing for and attending the detailed assessment (including travelling and waiting)	Discretionary *(Discretionary)*	Discretionary *(Discretionary)*
20 Appeal to costs judge, district judge or judge (including preparation)	Discretionary *(Discretionary)*	Discretionary *(Discretionary)*

(b) Magistrates' court proceedings

Class of work	*Rate*	
Preparation	£44.00 per hour *(£43.25)*	(£46.75 per hour for a fee-earner whose office is situated within legal aid area 1) *(£46.00)*
Advocacy	£55.25 per hour *(£54.50)*	
Attendance at court where counsel assigned	£30.00 per hour *(£29.50)*	

Travelling and waiting	£24.60 per hour *(£24.25)*	
Routine letters written and routine telephone	£3.40 per item *(£3.35)*	(£3.55 per item for a fee-earner whose office is situated within legal aid area 1) *(£3.50)*

Amendments—Substituted by SI 1996/650; amended by SI 1996/1555; SI 1997/2394; SI 2001/830.

Note as to figures—The principal figures set out in this Schedule are applicable from 1 April 1996. The previous figures, specified by SI 1992/596 with effect from 1 April 1992, are shown italicised within brackets below each of the corresponding current figures.

See the following notes concerning exceptions to the above:

1 1 April 1992 to 31 March 1996: **£2.05 per item**; 1 April 1996 to 7 July 1996: **£2.05**; from 8 July 1996: **£2.10**.

2 1 April 1992 to 31 March 1996: **£1.80 per item**; 1 April 1996 to 7 July 1996: **£1.80**; from 8 July 1996: **£1.85**.

3 1 April 1992 to 31 March 1996: **£52.00 per hour**; 1 April 1996 to 31 October 1997: **£52.75**; from 1 November 1997: **£55.25**.

4 1 April 1992 to 31 March 1996: **£31.50–50.25**; 1 April 1996 to 7 July 1996 : **£32.00–51.75**; from 8 July 1996: **£32.00–51.00**.

SCHEDULE 2A
PRESCRIBED FAMILY PROCEEDINGS

(a) High Court and county court proceedings

Part I—Preparation

Column 1	Column 2 *High Court*	Column 3 *County Court*
ITEM		
1 Writing routine letters	£7.05 per item	£6.15 per item
2 Receiving routine letters	£3.50 per item	£3.10 per item
3 Routine telephone calls	£7.05 per item	£6.15 per item
4 All other preparation work including any work which was reasonably done arising out of or incidental to the proceedings, interviews with client, witnesses, and other parties; obtaining evidence; preparation and consideration of, and dealing with, documents, negotiations and notices; dealing with letters	Where proceedings were conducted in the divorce registry or in another court on the South Eastern Circuit at the time when the relevant work was done:	
written and received and	£78.40 per hour	£68.50 per hour

telephone calls which are not routine	All other circuits: £73.05 per hour	£64.80 per hour
6 Travelling and waiting time in connection with the above matters	£35.75 per hour	£32.45 per hour

Part II—Conferences with counsel

7 Attending counsel in conference	£41.25 per hour	£36.30 per hour
8 Travelling and waiting	£35.75 per hour	£32.45 per hour

Part III—Attendances

9 Attending with counsel at the trial or hearing of any cause or the hearing of any summons or other application at court, or other appointment	£41.25 per hour	£36.30 per hour
10 Attending without counsel at the trial or hearing of any cause or the hearing of any summons or other application at court, or other appointment	Where proceedings were conducted in the divorce registry or in another court on the South Eastern Circuit at the time when the relevant work was done: £78.40 per hour All other circuits: £73.05 per hour	£68.50 per hour £64.80 per hour
11 Travelling and waiting	£35.75 per hour	£32.45 per hour

Part V—Detailed assessment and appeal in relation to detailed assessment

18 Preparing the bill (where allowable) and completing the detailed assessment (excluding preparing for and attending the hearing of the detailed assessment)	£35.70–£99.85	£35.70–£56.95
19 Preparing for and attending the hearing of the detailed assessment (including travelling and waiting)	Discretionary	Discretionary
20 Appeal to costs judge, district judge or judge (including preparation)	Discretionary	Discretionary

(b) Magistrates' court proceedings

Class of work	*Rate*	
Preparation	£48.95 per hour	(£52.25 per hour for a fee-earner whose office is situated in the Legal Services Commission's London Region)
Advocacy	£61.90 per hour	
Attendance at court where counsel assigned	£33.30 per hour	
Travelling and waiting	£27.50 per hour	
Routine letters written and telephone calls	£3.80 per item	(£4.00 per item for a fee-earner whose office is situated in the Legal Services Commission's London Region)

Amendments—Inserted by SI 1996/650; amended by SI 1996/1555; SI 1997/2394; SI 2001/830; SI 2001/2417.

Note as to figures—The figures set out in this Schedule are applicable from 2 April 2001, except the sums shown in Item 18 (Preparing the bill and completing the detailed assessment) which are effective from 26 July 2001.

Magistrates' Courts Rules 1981, SI 1981/552

ARRANGEMENT OF RULES

General

Remand

Domestic proceedings

Orders for periodical payments

Satisfaction, enforcement and application of payments

Register

Evidence – General

Recognizances and bail

Warrant

Summons

Miscellaneous

General

1 Citation, operation and revocations

(1) These Rules may be cited as the Magistrates' Courts Rules 1981 and shall come into operation on 6th July 1981.

(2) The Rules mentioned in the Schedule to these Rules are hereby revoked; but where proceedings were commenced before 6th July 1981 and the old enactments within the meaning of paragraphs 1 and 2(2) of Schedule 8 to the Magistrates' Courts Act 1980 continue to apply by virtue of paragraph 2(1) of the said Schedule 8, the provisions of the Rules so mentioned continue to apply and nothing in these Rules affects those provisions.

"These Rules ..."—These rules were made under Magistrates' Courts Act 1980, ss 144 and 145, and are principally designed to provide rules of practice for the implementation of those provisions. These rules have effect subject to the Family Proceedings Courts (Children Act 1989) Rules 1991 and the Family Proceedings Courts (Matrimonial Proceedings etc) Rules 1991 (see r 3).

2 Interpretation

(1) In these Rules –

"the Act of 1978" means the Domestic Proceedings and Magistrates' Courts Act 1978;
"the Act of 1980" means the Magistrates' Courts Act 1980;
"the Act of 1989" means the Children Act 1989;
"the Act of 1998" means the Crime and Disorder Act 1998;
"child" means a person who has not attained the age of 18;
"contribution order" has the meaning assigned to it in paragraph 23(2) of Sch 2 to the Act of 1989;
"judgment summons" has the meaning assigned to it by rule 58.

(2) In these Rules "legal aid order" and "statement of means" have the meanings assigned to them by regulation 31(1) of the Legal Aid in Criminal Proceedings (General) Regulations 1968.

(3) In these Rules a reference to the person with whom a child has his home shall be construed in accordance with the Act of 1989, except that, in the case of any child in the care of a local authority, the local authority shall be treated for the purposes of these Rules as the person with whom the child has his home.

(4) In these Rules a reference to "the authorised persons for the area in which they are employed" is a reference to the persons employed by an authority which performs its functions within that area who are authorised to execute warrants within that area in pursuance of rule 3 of the Magistrates' Courts (Civilian Fine Enforcement Officers) (No 2) Rules 1990.

(5) Any requirement in these Rules that a document shall be in the prescribed form shall be construed as a requirement that the document shall be in the form prescribed in that behalf by rules made under section 144 of the Act of 1980, or a form to like effect.

(6) In these Rules any reference to a rule shall be construed as a reference to a rule contained in these Rules; and any reference in a rule to a paragraph shall be construed as a reference to a paragraph of that rule.

Amendments—SI 1990/1190; SI 1990/2260; SI 1991/1991; SI 2000/3361.

"prescribed in that behalf by rules" (r 2(5))—Forms have been so prescribed by the Magistrates' Courts (Forms) Rules 1981.

3 Saving for the Family Proceedings Courts (Children Act 1989) Rules 1991 and the Family Proceedings Courts (Matrimonial Proceedings etc) Rules 1991

The provisions of these Rules shall have effect subject to the provisions of the Family Proceedings Courts (Children Act 1989) Rules 1991 and the Family Proceedings Courts (Matrimonial Proceedings etc) Rules 1991.

Amendments—SI 1991/1991.

Information and complaint

4 Information and complaint

(1) An information may be laid or complaint made by the prosecutor or complainant in person or by his counsel or solicitor or other person authorised in that behalf.

(2) Subject to any provision of the Act of 1980 and any other enactment, an information or complaint need not be in writing or on oath.

(3) It shall not be necessary in an information or complaint to specify or negative an exception, exemption, proviso, excuse or qualification, whether or not it accompanies the description of the offence or matter of complaint contained in the enactment creating the offence or on which the complaint is founded.

Scope of provision—This rule specifies who may make a complaint and provides for the general proposition that it is not necessary to prove the positive of a negative by providing that an exception, exemption etc need not be specified or negatived in a complaint.

****

Summary trial of information and hearing of complaint

****

14 Order of evidence and speeches: complaint

(1) On the hearing of a complaint, except where the court determines under section 53(3) of the Act of 1980 to make the order with the consent of the defendant without hearing evidence, the complainant shall call his evidence, and before doing so may address the court.

(2) At the conclusion of the evidence for the complainant the defendant may address the court, whether or not he afterwards calls evidence.

(3) At the conclusion of the evidence, if any, for the defence, the complainant may call evidence to rebut that evidence.

(4) At the conclusion of the evidence for the defence and the evidence, if any, in rebuttal, the defendant may address the court if he has not already done so.

(5) Either party may, with the leave of the court, address the court a second time, but where the court grants leave to one party it shall not refuse leave to the other.

(6) Where the defendant obtains leave to address the court for a second time his second address shall be made before the second address, if any, of the complainant.

Scope of provision—It should be noted that separate procedures are specified for the hearing of applications; see, for example, Family Proceedings Courts (Matrimonial Proceedings etc) Rules 1991, r 12.

"the defendant may address the court", (r 14(2))—The right to address the court is retained even after a submission of no case to answer (*Disher v Disher* [1965] P 31, [1963] 2 WLR 21). Dismissal on the grounds of no case to answer may be of the court's own motion or on the defendant's submission. The complainant is entitled to address the court before dismissal (*Mayes v Mayes* [1971] 1 WLR 679, [1971] 2 All ER 397).

"the complainant may call evidence to rebut" (r 14(3))—Although r 14(3) does not restrict the right to call evidence in rebuttal, the cases show that the right is restricted to matters which have arisen unexpectedly in the course of the defence case. If the matters could have been foreseen the right to call evidence in rebuttal does not exist (see, for example, *Price v Humphries* [1958] 2 QB 353, [1958] 3 WLR 304).

Evidence—There is no general power to receive unsworn statements in civil proceedings except by agreement (*Aggas v Aggas* [1971] 1 WLR 1409, [1971] 2 All ER 1497).

Addressing the court—The defendant may restrict the right of the complainant to have the last word by reserving his address to the conclusion of the evidence for the defence.

****

16 Form of conviction or order

(1) A form of summary conviction or order made on complaint shall be drawn up if required for an appeal or other legal purpose, and if drawn up shall be in such one of the prescribed forms as is appropriate to the case.

(2) ...

****

Remand

23 Remand on bail for more than 8 days where sureties have not entered into recognizances

Where the court, with a view to a person's being remanded on bail under paragraph (*a*) of section 128(6) of the Act of 1980 for a period exceeding 8 days, has fixed the amount of the recognizances to be taken for that purpose but commits that person to custody because the recognizances of the sureties have not yet been taken, the warrant of commitment shall direct the governor or keeper of the prison or place to which he is committed to bring him before the court at the end of 8 clear days or at such earlier time as may be specified in the warrant, unless in the meantime the sureties have entered into their recognizances.

****

Domestic proceedings

****

38 Certification of records

For the purposes of section 84(2) of the Act of 1978 (which provides that a copy of any record made by virtue of section 84 of the reasons for a decision of a magistrates' court shall, if certified by such officer of the court as may be prescribed, be admissible as evidence of those reasons) the certifying officer shall be the justices' chief executive for the magistrates' court concerned.

Amendments—SI 2001/610.

"certified"—No form of certification is prescribed; the words "certified true copy", signed by the justices' chief executive, would appear to be sufficient.

Orders for periodical payments

39 Method of making periodical payments

(1) Where a magistrates' court makes a means of payment order, the clerk of the court shall record on the order for periodical payments to which the means of payment order relates, the means of payment which the court has ordered and the justices' chief executive shall notify in writing, as soon as practicable, the person liable to make payments under the order of how payments are to be made.

(2) Where the court orders that payments by the debtor to the creditor are to be made to the justices' chief executive for the court or to the justices' chief executive for any other magistrates' court under section 59(3)(*b*) of the Act of 1980, the

justices' chief executive to whom the payments are ordered to be made shall notify the person liable to make the payments of the hours during which, and the place at which, payments are to be made.

(3) The clerk to the court to whom any periodical payments are made shall send them by post to –

(*a*) the person entitled to them; or
(*b*) if the person entitled to them is a child, to the child or to the person with whom the child has his home:

Provided that the justices' chief executive may –

(*a*) at the request of the person entitled to the payments; or
(*b*) if the person entitled to them is a child, at the request of the child or the person with whom the child has his home,

make other arrangements for making the payments.

(4) If a person makes any periodical payments to the justices' chief executive for a magistrates' court otherwise than in person at the office of the justices' chief executive, he shall do so at his own risk and expense.

(5) Where the court orders the payments by the debtor to the creditor be made by a method of payment falling within section 59(6) of the Act of 1980 (standing order, etc), the justices' chief executive for the court shall notify the person liable to make payments under the order of the number and location of the account into which the payments should be made.

(6) Where the justices' chief executive for a magistrates' court receives an application from an interested party under section 20ZA(2) of the Act of 1978, section 60(4) of the Act of 1980 or paragraph 6A(2) of Schedule 1 to the Children Act 1989 for the method of payment to be varied, the justices' chief executive shall notify in writing, as soon as practicable, that party and, where practicable, any other interested party, of the result of the application, including any decision to refer the matter to the court; where the clerk of the court grants the application, he shall record the variation on the order for periodical payments to which the variation relates.

(7) In this rule "means of payment order" means an order of a magistrates' court under paragraphs (*a*) to (*d*) of section 59(3) of the Act of 1980.

Amendments—SI 1992/457; SI 2001/610.

Sending periodical payments by post (r 39(3))—The cost of sending payments by post should be borne by the court and not the creditor (see Home Office Circular 214/1971).

Rule 39(5)–(7) has been added as a result of the Maintenance Enforcement Act 1991 to give effect to the making of an order for payment by standing order and to prescribe the procedure for dealing with an application to vary a method of payment.

40 Duty of justices' chief executive to notify arrears of periodical payments

Where an order under section 59(1) of the Act requires periodical payments to be made to the justices' chief executive for a magistrates' court and the payments are at any time in arrears to an amount equal –

(*a*) in the case of payments to be made monthly or less frequently, to twice the sum payable periodically; or
(*b*) in any other case, to four times the sum payable periodically,

the justices' chief executive shall, unless it appears to him that it is unnecessary or inexpedient to do so, give to the person entitled to the payments or, if that person is a child, to the child or the person with whom the child has his home notice in writing stating the particulars of the arrears.

Amendments—SI 2001/610.

"unnecessary or inexpedient"—The justices' chief executive has a wide discretion. Notice is given to allow the payee to provide authority to enforce the order. In many courts, continuing authority to enforce is obtained and notification of arrears is of little significance.

41 Revocation, variation etc of orders for periodical payments

(1) This rule shall apply to a complaint for the revocation, discharge, revival, alteration or variation of a magistrates' court maintenance order or order enforceable as a magistrates' court maintenance order, but shall not apply –

(*a*) where jurisdiction is confined by paragraph (*a*) of subsection (2) of section 88 of the Children and Young Persons Act 1933 to courts appointed for the commission area where the person liable is residing;

(*b*) where an order has been made under the proviso to subsection (4) of that section;

(*c*) to a contribution order;

(*d*) to a complaint for an order under section 26(4) of the Children Act 1948;

(*e*) to a complaint for an order under section 22(1) of the Maintenance Orders Act 1950.

(2) A complaint to which this rule applies may be made to a justice of the peace acting for the same petty sessions area as the responsible court or to a justice of the peace acting for the petty sessions area where the complainant is for the time being.

(3) A justice of the peace shall not take action on a complaint to which this rule applies unless either the complainant has furnished him with written particulars –

(*a*) of the nature of the evidence that the complainant proposes to adduce at the hearing of the complaint and the names and addresses and, if known to him, the occupations of his witnesses; and

(*b*) of the occupations of the complainant and defendant and the address of the complainant and last address of the defendant known to the complainant

or the justice is acting for the same petty sessions area as the responsible court and it appears to him that the last address of the defendant known to the complainant is within that area.

(4) Where a complaint to which this rule applies is made to a justice of the peace acting for the same petty sessions area as the responsible court, and it appears to him that either of the places stated in the said particulars as being the addresses of the complainant and defendant is within another petty sessions area, then, if the justice determines that the complaint could more conveniently be dealt with by a magistrates' court acting for that other petty sessions area, he shall cause the justices' chief executive for the responsible court to send by post to the justices' chief executive for that other court the complaint, the said particulars and a copy of any relevant record of reasons for a decision kept in pursuance of rule 36.

(5) Where the places stated in the said particulars as being the addresses of the complainant and the defendant appear to the justice to be outside the petty sessions area for which the justice is acting and in other and different petty sessions areas,

the reference in the last preceding paragraph to another petty sessions area shall be construed as a reference to such one of those other areas aforesaid as appears to the justice convenient.

(6) On receipt by the justices' chief executive for a magistrates' court of a complaint, the particulars and a copy of any relevant record of reasons under paragraph (4), he shall bring the complaint before the court, and the court shall issue a summons requiring the defendant to appear before it, and shall hear and determine the complaint.

(7) Where a complaint to which this rule applies is made to a justice of the peace acting for a petty sessions area other than that for which the responsible court acts, the justice shall cause the justices' chief executive for the magistrates' court acting for that other petty sessions area to send the complaint, the said particulars and the said copy of any relevant record of reasons by post to the justices' chief executive for the responsible court; and the justices' chief executive for the responsible court shall bring the complaint before the court; and thereupon paragraphs (4) to (6) shall have effect as if the complaint had been made and the particulars and the copy of any relevant record of reasons furnished to a justice of the peace acting for the same petty sessions area as the responsible court.

(8) Notwithstanding the foregoing provisions of this rule, a justice to whom a complaint is made may refer the complaint to the responsible court which may, in such case or when the complaint is brought before the court in accordance with paragraph (6), cause the complaint, the particulars and the copy of any relevant record of reasons to be sent by post to the justices' chief executive for the court which made the original order and that chief executive and that court shall proceed in accordance with the provisions of paragraph (6).

(9) Where a magistrates' court makes an order on a complaint to which this rule applies affecting an order made by another magistrates' court or affecting an order under which payments are made to the justices' chief executive for another magistrates' court, the justices' chief executive for the first-mentioned court shall cause a copy of the order to be sent to the justices' chief executive for that other court.

(10) In this rule "responsible court" means –

(*a*) where payments under the order are made to the justices' chief executive for a magistrates' court, that court;

(*b*) where payments are not so made, the court which made the order.

Amendments—SI 2001/610.

Defined terms—"responsible court": r 41(10).

"section 22(1) of the Maintenance Orders Act 1950" (r 41(1)(*e*))—Section 22(1) relates to discharge and variation of maintenance orders between England, Scotland and Northern Ireland.

"if the justice determines that the complaint could more conveniently be dealt with" (r 41(4))—If the complaint is not made on oath, the complaint and determination as to venue may also be made by the justices' clerk (Justices' Clerks Rules 1999). In determining convenience, representations should be allowed where necessary in the interests of fairness (*R v Wareham Magistrates' Court ex parte Seldon* [1988] 2 FLR 269, [1988] 1 WLR 825).

"send by post ... the complaint, the said particulars and a copy of any relevant record of reasons" (r 41(4))—For information to be sent with the complaint see Home Office Circular 278/1947 and *John v John (Practice Note)* [1959] 1 WLR 60, 1 All ER 389. The justices' chief executive should send any information which would be helpful to the other court in dealing with the complaint, eg on enforcement of the order, details of the payment history; on variation, details of the defendant's circumstances when the order was made.

****

43 Service of copy of order

Where a magistrates' court makes, revokes, discharges, suspends, revives, alters or varies a magistrates' court maintenance order or order enforceable as a magistrates' court maintenance order or allows time or further time for payment of a lump sum under any such order or orders payment of a lump sum under any such order to be paid by instalments or various any such order for payment by instalments the court shall cause a copy of its order to be served on the defendant by delivering it to him or by sending it by post in a letter addressed to him at his last known or usual place of abode.

Amendments—SI 1989/384.

"sending it by post"—Service is deemed to be effected by properly addressing, prepaying and posting a letter containing the document. Unless the contrary is proved, it is deemed to have been effected, in the case of first class mail, on the second working day after posting and, in the case of second class mail, on the fourth working day after posting. Working days are Mondays to Fridays, excluding bank holidays (Interpretation Act 1978, s 7).

44 Remission of sums due under order

(1) Before remitting the whole or any part of a sum due under a magistrates' court maintenance order or an order enforceable as a magistrates' court maintenance order under section 95 of the Act of 1980, the court shall, except save where it appears to it to be unnecessary or impracticable to do so, cause the person in whose favour the order is made or, if that person is a child, the child or the person with whom the child has his home to be notified of its intention and shall afford to such person a reasonable opportunity to make representations to the court, either orally at an adjourned hearing of the complaint for enforcement or in writing and such representations shall be considered by the court.

(2) Any written representations may be considered by the court if they purport to be signed by or on behalf of the person in whose favour the order is made or, if that person is a child, by or on behalf of the child or the person with whom the child has his home.

Amendments—SI 1989/384.

Requirement to notify person in whose favour the order is made (r 44(1))—Rule 44(1) is mandatory, and the normal remedy where such notice is not given is by way of case stated under MCA 1980, s 111. Judicial review will only be granted in exceptional circumstances (*R v Bristol Magistrates' Court ex parte Hodge* [1997] 1 FLR 88).

45 Duty of justices' chief executive to notify remarriage of person entitled to payments under a maintenance order

(1) Where the justices' chief executive for a magistrates' court to whom any payments under an order to which this rule applies are required to be made is notified in writing by or on behalf of the person entitled to payments under such an order, the person liable to make payments under such an order or the personal representatives of either of those persons that the person so entitled has remarried, the justices' chief executive shall forthwith in writing so notify the justices' chief

PART III

executive for or other appropriate officer of each of the courts mentioned in paragraph (2) for which he is not the justices' chief executive.

(2) The courts referred to in paragraph (1) are –

(*a*) any court which has made a relevant order or, in the case of a provisional order made under section 3 of the Maintenance Orders (Facilities for Enforcement) Act 1920 or section 3 of the Maintenance Orders (Reciprocal Enforcement) Act 1972, the court which confirmed the order;

(*b*) if a relevant order has been transmitted abroad for registration under section 2 of the said Act of 1920 or section 2 of the said Act of 1972, the court in which the order is registered; and

(*c*) if a complaint for the enforcement of a relevant order has been sent to a court under rule 59(2), that court.

(3) This rule applies to an order in relation to which section 4(2) of the Act of 1978 applies, an order to which section 38 of the Matrimonial Causes act 1973 applies and an attachment of earnings order made to secure payments under either of the above-mentioned orders and in paragraph (2) "relevant order" means any such order to which the payments referred to in paragraph (1) relate.

Amendments—SI 2001/610.

Satisfaction, enforcement and application of payments

****

48 To whom payments are to be made

(1) A person adjudged by the conviction of a magistrates' court to pay any sum shall, unless the court otherwise directs, pay that sum, or any instalment of that sum, to the justices' chief executive for the court.

(2) Where payment of any sum or instalment of any sum adjudged to be paid by the conviction or order of a magistrates court is made to any person other than the justices' chief executive for the court, that person, unless he is the person to whom the court has directed payment to be made or, in the case of a child, is the person with whom the child has his home, shall, as soon as may be, account for and, if the justices' chief executive so requires, pay over the sum or instalment to the justices' chief executive for the court.

(3) Where payment of any sum adjudged to be paid by the conviction or order of a magistrates' court, or any instalment of such a sum, if directed to be made to the justices' chief executive for some other magistrates' court, the justices' chief executive for the court that adjudged the sum to be paid shall pay over any sums received by him on account of the said sum or instalment to the justices' chief executive for that other court.

Amendments—SI 1992/457; SI 2001/610.

49 Duty of justices' chief executive to give receipt

The justices' chief executive for a magistrates' court shall give or send a receipt to any person who makes a payment to him in pursuance of a conviction or order of a magistrates' court and who asks for a receipt.

Amendments—SI 2001/610.

50 (*revoked*)

51 Application for further time

An application under section 75(2) of the Act of 1980, or section 22 of the Act of 1978, may, unless the court requires the applicant to attend, be made in writing.

Amendments—SI 1989/384; SI 1991/1991.

52 Notice of date of hearing of means inquiry etc

Where a magistrates' court, under subsection (1) of section 86 of the Act of 1980 (power of magistrates' court to fix day for appearance of offender at means inquiry etc), has fixed a day on which an offender must appear in person before the court and, under subsection (3) of that section, fixes a later day in substitution for the day previously fixed, service of the notice of the substituted day may be effected in any manner in which service of a summons may be effected under rule 99(1).

52A Review of terms of postponement of warrant of commitment

An application under section 77(5) of the Magistrates' Courts Act 1980 may be made in writing or in person and where under that subsection a justice of the peace refers such an application to the court, notice of the time and place fixed under section 77(6) for the hearing of the application may be deemed to have been given if it is sent by registered post or the recorded delivery service addressed to the applicant at his last known address, notwithstanding that the notice is returned as undelivered or is for any other reason not received by the applicant.

"application under section 77(5) of the Magistrates' Courts Act 1980"—This is an application to vary the time or conditions of postponement of a warrant of commitment for non-payment.

53 Notice to defendant before enforcing order

(1) A warrant of distress shall not be issued for failure to pay a sum enforceable as a civil debt unless the defendant has been previously served with a copy of the minute of the order, or the order was made in his presence and the warrant is issued on that occasion.

(2) A warrant of commitment shall not be issued for disobedience to an order of a magistrates' court unless the defendant has been previously served with a copy of the minute of the order, or the order was made in his presence and the warrant is issued on that occasion:

Provided that this paragraph shall not apply to –

(*a*) an order to pay money; or
(*b*) an expedited order under section 16(2) and (6) of the Act of 1978.

(3) A copy of the minute of the order shall be served under this rule by delivering it to the defendant or by sending it to him by post in a letter addressed to him at his last known or usual place of abode.

(4) In relation to an order under section 16 of the Act of 1978 (other than an expedited order under subsections (2) and (6) of that section) paragraphs (2) and

PART III

(3) shall have effect as if for the references to a copy of a minute of the order there were substituted references to a copy of the order.

Scope of provision—This rule limits the circumstances in which a warrant of distress or committal may be issued for enforcement of a civil debt. It does not apply to the enforcement of a magistrates' court maintenance order.

"order of a magistrates' court" (r 53(2))—See Magistrates' Courts Act 1980, s 63.

"sending it to him by post" (r 53(3))—See Interpretation Act 1978, s 7 for the presumption of due delivery.

54 Execution of distress warrant

(1) A warrant of distress issued for the purpose of levying a sum adjudged to be paid by a summary conviction or order –

(*a*) shall name or otherwise describe the person against whom the distress is to be levied;

(*b*) shall be directed to the constables of the police area in which the warrant is issued or to the civilian enforcement officers for the area in which they are employed, or to a person named in the warrant and shall, subject to, and in accordance with, the provisions of this rule, require them to levy the said sum by distress and sale of the goods belonging to the said person;

(*c*) may where it is directed to the constables of a police area, instead of being executed by any of those constables, be executed by any person under the direction of a constable.

(2) The warrant shall authorise the person charged with the execution of it to take as well any money as any goods of the person against whom the distress is levied; and any money so taken shall be treated as if it were the proceeds of the sale of goods taken under the warrant.

(3) The warrant shall require the person charged with the execution to pay the sum to be levied to the justices' chief executive for the court that issued the warrant.

(3A) A warrant to which this rule applies may be executed by the persons to whom it was directed or by any of the following persons, whether or not the warrant was directed to them –

(*a*) a constable for any police area in England and Wales, acting in his own police area;

(*b*) where the warrant is one to which section 125A of the Act of 1980 applies, a civilian enforcement officer within the meaning of section 125A of the Act of 1980;

(*c*) where the warrant is one to which section 125A of the Act of 1980 applies, any of the individuals described in section 125B(1) of the Act of 1980;

and in this rule any reference to the person charged with the execution of a warrant includes any of the above persons who is for the time being authorised to execute the warrant, whether or not they have the warrant in their possession at the time.

(3B) A person executing a warrant of distress shall –

(*a*) either –

(i) if he has the warrant with him, show it to the person against whom the distress is levied, or

(ii) otherwise, state where the warrant is and what arrangements may be made to allow the person against whom distress is levied to inspect it;

(*b*) explain, in ordinary language, the sum for which distress is levied and the reason for the distress;

(*c*) where the person executing the warrant is one of the persons referred to in paragraph (3A)(*b*) or (*c*) above, show the person against whom distress is levied a written statement under section 125A(4) or 125B(4) as appropriate; and

(*d*) in any case, show documentary proof of his identity.

(4) There shall not be taken under the warrant the clothing or bedding of any person or his family or the tools, books, vehicles or other equipment which he personally needs to use in his employment, business or vocation, provided that in this paragraph the word "person" shall not include a corporation.

(5) The distress levied under any such warrant as aforesaid shall be sold within such period beginning not earlier than the 6th day after the making of the distress as may be specified in the warrant, or if no period is specified in the warrant, within a period beginning on the 6th day and ending on the 14th day after the making of the distress: Provided that with the consent in writing of the person against whom the distress is levied the distress may be sold before the beginning of the said period.

(5A) The clerk of the court which issued the warrant may, on the application of the person charged with the execution of it, extend the period within which the distress must be sold by any number of days not exceeding 60; but following the grant of such an application there shall be no further variation or extension of that period.

(6) The said distress shall be sold by public auction or in such other manner as the person against whom the distress is levied may in writing allow.

(7) Notwithstanding anything in the preceding provisions of this rule, the said distress shall not be sold if the sum for which the warrant was issued and the charges of taking and keeping the distress have been paid.

(8) Subject to any direction to the contrary in the warrant, where the distress is levied on household goods, the goods shall not, without the consent in writing of the person against whom the distress is levied, be removed from the house until the day of sale; and so much of the goods shall be impounded as is in the opinion of the person executing the warrant sufficient to satisfy the distress, by affixing to the articles impounded a conspicuous mark.

(9) The person charged with the execution of any such warrant as aforesaid shall cause the distress to be sold, and may deduct out of the amount realised by the sale all costs and charges incurred in effecting the sale; and he shall return to the owner the balance, if any, after retaining the amount of the sum for which the warrant was issued and the proper costs and charges of the execution of the warrant.

(10) The person charged with the execution of any such warrant as aforesaid shall as soon as practicable send to the justices' chief executive for the court that issued it a written account of the costs and charges incurred in executing it; and the justices' chief executive shall allow the person against whom the distress was levied to inspect the account within one month after the levy of the distress at any reasonable time to be appointed by the court.

(11) If any person pays or tenders to the person charged with the execution of any such warrant as aforesaid the sum mentioned in the warrant, or produces a receipt

for that sum given by the justices' chief executive for the court that issued the warrant, and also pays the amount of the costs and charges of the distress up to the time of the payment or tender or the production of the receipt, the person as aforesaid shall not execute the warrant, or shall cease to execute it, as the case may be.

Amendments—SI 1983/523; SI 1990/1190; SI 1992/729; SI 1999/2765; SI 2001/167; SI 2001/610.

"sale of the goods" (r 54(1)(*b*))—A landlord may not distrain or claim upon goods seized under a distress warrant. The Landlord and Tenant Act 1709, s 1 (which provides for payment by a sheriff to a landlord in respect of any arrears of rent before goods are removed under an execution) does not apply to goods seized under a justices' distress warrant (*Potts v Hickman* [1941] AC 2112, [1940] 4 All ER 491).

"conspicuous mark" (r 54(8))—It is an offence under Magistrates' Courts Act 1980, s 78(4) to remove marked goods or to deface or remove the mark.

"costs and charges" (r 54(10))—It is an offence to exact excessive costs and charges (Magistrates' Courts Act 1980, s 78(5)).

55 Payment after imprisonment imposed

(1) The persons authorised for the purposes of section 79(2) of the Act of 1980 to receive a part payment are –

(*a*) unless there has been issued a warrant of distress or commitment, the justices' chief executive for the court enforcing payment of the sum, or any person appointed under section 88 of that Act to supervise the offender;

(*b*) where the issue of a warrant of commitment has been suspended on conditions which provide for payment to be made to the justices' chief executive for some other magistrates' court, that chief executive;

(*c*) any constable holding a warrant of distress or commitment or, where the warrant is directed to some other person, that person;

(*d*) the governor or keeper of the prison or place in which the defaulter is detained, or other person having lawful custody of the defaulter:

Provided that –

(i) the said governor or keeper shall not be required to accept any sum tendered in part payment under the said subsection (2) except on a week-day between 9 o'clock in the morning and 5 o'clock in the afternoon; and

(ii) no person shall be required to receive in part payment under the said subsection (2) an amount which, or so much of an amount as, will not procure a reduction of the period for which the defaulter is committed or ordered to be detained.

(2) Where a person having custody of a defaulter received payment of any sum he shall note receipt of the sum on the warrant of commitment.

(3) Where the justices' chief executive for a court other than the court enforcing payment of the sums receives payment of any sum he shall inform the justices' chief executive for the other court.

(4) Where a person appointed under section 88 of the Act of 1980 to supervise an offender receives payment of any sum, he shall send it forthwith to the justices' chief executive for the court which appointed him.

(5) (*ceased to have effect*)

Amendments—SI 2001/610.

"unless there has been issued a warrant of distress or commitment" (r 55(1)(*a*))—A warrant of commitment has not been issued where the issue of the warrant has been suspended on conditions.

****

58 Civil debt: judgment summons

(1) A summons issued on a complaint made for the purposes of section 96 of the Act of 1980 (in these rules referred to as a "judgment summons") shall be served on the judgment debtor personally:

Provided that if a justice of the peace is satisfied by evidence on oath that prompt personal service of the summons is impracticable, he may allow the summons to be served in such a way as he may think just.

(2) Unless the judgment debtor appears and consents to an immediate hearing, the court shall not hear the complaint unless the summons was served at least 3 clear days before the hearing.

(3) Service of a judgment summons outside the commission area for which the justice issuing the summons acted may, without prejudice to any other provision of these rules enabling service of a summons to be proved, be proved by affidavit.

Scope of provision—This rule makes provision for the service or substituted service of a judgment summons. It should be noted that, although there is some overlap of terminology, a judgment summons in the magistrates' court is substantially different from that in the county court.

"section 96 of the Act of 1980" (r 58(1))—The obligations under this rule are imposed in respect of civil debt enforcement under Magistrates' Courts Act 1980, s 96. The rule is not applicable to enforcement of a magistrates' court maintenance order as a separate procedure is defined under Magistrates' Courts Act 1980, s 93.

"if a justice of the peace is satisfied ... he may allow the summons to be served in such a way as he may think just" (r 58(1))—The summons should be endorsed by the justice with the points under the rule with which he is satisfied. If alternative service is authorised ("substituted service"), the method of service should also be endorsed on the summons. The method of substituted service is entirely within the justices' discretion.

"3 clear days" (r 58(2))—A longer period of notice may be appropriate where substituted service is allowed.

"without prejudice to any other provision" (r 58(3))—For example under r 67.

59 Enforcement of magistrates' court maintenance orders etc

(1) Subject to the following provisions of this rule, a complaint for the enforcement of a magistrates' court maintenance order, or an order enforceable as a magistrates' court maintenance order, shall be heard by the court that made the order:

Provided that –

(*a*) where –

PART III

(i) the complainant is the person in whose favour the order was made or, if that person is a child, is the child or the person with whom the child has his home; and

(ii) the complainant resides in a petty sessions area other than that for which the court acts; and

(iii) payment is directed to be made either to the complainant or the justices' chief executive for a magistrates' court acting for the petty sessions area,

the complaint may be heard by the last-mentioned court;

(*b*) where the complainant is the justices' chief executive for a magistrates' court, the complaint may be heard by that court.

(2) Where a complaint is made to a justice of the peace for the enforcement of such an order as aforesaid and it appears to him that the defendant is for the time being in some petty sessions area other than for which the justice is acting and that the order may be more conveniently enforced by a magistrates' court acting for that area, the justice shall cause the justices' chief executive for the court to send the complaint by post to the justices' chief executive for a magistrates' court acting for that other petty sessions area, and for that purpose shall write down the complaint if this has not already been done.

(3) On receipt by the justices' chief executive for a magistrates' court of a complaint sent under the last preceding paragraph, he shall bring it before the court; and the court shall issue a summons or warrant for procuring the appearance of the defendant before it, and shall hear and determine the complaint.

(4) If, after a complaint has been sent to the justices' chief executive for a magistrates' court under this rule, the justices' chief executive for the court to which the complaint was made receives any payment under the order, he shall forthwith send by post to the justices' chief executive to whom the complaint was sent a certificate of the amount of the payments and of the date when it was made.

(5) If, after a complaint has been sent as aforesaid, payment under the order is made, not to the justices' chief executive for the court to which the complaint was originally made, but to the person specified in the order or, in the case of a child, to the person with whom the child has his home, that person shall forthwith inform the justices' chief executive for the amount and date as aforesaid and the justices' chief executive shall forthwith send a certificate of the amount and date as required by the last preceding paragraph.

(6) A certificate under this rule purporting to be signed by the justices' chief executive for the court to which the complaint was originally made shall be admissible as evidence on the hearing of the complaint that the amount specified in the certificate was paid on the date so specified.

(7) This rule shall not apply –

(*a*) where jurisdiction is confined by section 88(2)(*a*) of the Children and Young Persons Act 1933, to courts having jurisdiction in the place where the person liable is residing;

(*b*) to a contribution order.

Amendments—SI 1989/384; SI 2001/610.

"magistrates' court maintenance order" (r 59(1))—This term is defined in MCA 1980, s 150(1), and includes orders made under the following provisions: Domestic Proceedings and Magistrates' Courts Act 1978, Pt I; National Assistance Act 1948, s 43; Supplementary Benefits Act 1976, s 18; Social Security Act 1986, s 24; Maintenance Orders Act 1958; Maintenance Orders Act 1950, Pt II; Maintenance Orders (Facilities for Enforcement) Act 1920; Maintenance

Orders (Reciprocal Enforcement) Act 1972; Matrimonial Proceedings (Magistrates' Courts) Act 1960 and CA 1989, Sch 1.

"Where a complaint is made to a justice of the peace" (r 59(2))—Where the complaint is not made on oath, this function may be exercised by the justices' clerk (Justices' Clerks Rules 1999).

"shall write down the complaint" (r 59(2))—By virtue of r 4(2), a complaint need not be in writing. An oral complaint must be written down if it is to be sent to another magistrates' court.

Warrants (r 59(3))—Before a warrant is issued, the court must be sure that the complaint was made on oath.

"forthwith send ... a certificate of the amount of the payment" (r 59(4))—It is of vital importance that this requirement is complied with. A failure to send details of payments may result in the receiving court issuing process wrongly, or delays in the enforcement of remaining arrears while proceedings are adjourned for the investigation of the defendant's claim that payments have been made (see Home Office Circular 278/1947).

60 Enforcement where periodical payments made under more than one order

(1) Where periodical payments are required to be made to any person by another person under more than one periodical payments order, proceedings for the recovery of the payments may be brought by way of one complaint. Any such complaint shall indicate the payments due under each order referred to in the complaint.

(2) Any sum paid to the justices' chief executive for a magistrates' court on any date by a person liable to make payments under 2 or more periodical payments orders which is less than the total sum required to be paid on that date to that chief executive by that person in respect of those orders (being orders one of which requires payments to be made for the benefit of a child to the person with whom the child has his home and one or more of which requires payments to be made to that person either for his own benefit or for the benefits of another child who has his home with him) shall be apportioned between the orders in proportion to the amounts respectively due under each order over a period of one year and if, as a result of the apportionment, the payments under any such order are no longer in arrears the residue shall be applied to the amount due under the other order or (if there is more than one other order) shall be apportioned as aforesaid between the other orders.

(3) For the purposes of calculating the apportionment of any sum under paragraph (2) –

(*a*) a month shall be treated as consisting of 4 weeks; and
(*b*) a year shall be treated as consisting of 52 weeks.

Amendments—SI 1983/523; SI 2001/610.

61 Notice of adjudication on complaint for enforcement of a magistrates' court maintenance order etc

A magistrates' court shall give notice in writing to the complainant of its adjudication on a complaint for the enforcement of a magistrates' court maintenance order, or order enforceable as a magistrates' court maintenance order, unless the complainant is present or is the justices' chief executive for the court.

Amendments—SI 1989/384; SI 2001/610.

62 Particulars relating to payment of lump sum under a magistrates' court maintenance order etc to be entered in register

Where a magistrates' court allows time for payment of a lump sum required to be paid under a magistrates' court maintenance order, or order enforceable as a magistrates' court maintenance order, or orders that any such lump sum shall be paid by instalments or varies the number of instalments payable, the amount of any instalment payable or the date on which any instalment becomes payable, particulars thereof shall be entered in the register or in any separate record kept for the purpose of recording particulars of lump sum payments.

Amendments—SI 1989/384.

63 Notice of date of reception in custody and discharge

(1) Where in proceedings to enforce a magistrates' court maintenance order, or an order enforceable as a magistrates' court maintenance order, the defendant is committed to custody, then on his discharge the governor or keeper of the prison or place of detention shall send to the justices' chief executive for the court that committed the defendant a certificate showing the dates of the defendant's reception and discharge; and that chief executive shall, if the payments under the order are required to be made to the justices' chief executive for any other court, send the certificate to the last-mentioned justices' chief executive.

(2) ...

Amendments—SI 1989/384; SI 2001/610.

"magistrates' court maintenance order"—See the list of orders under Magistrates' Courts Act 1980, s 92.

64 Direction that money found on defaulter shall not be applied in satisfaction of debt

Where the defaulter is committed to, or ordered to be detained in, a prison or other place of detention, any direction given under section 80(2) of the Act of 1980 shall be endorsed on the warrant of commitment.

Scope of provision—This rule requires any direction under Magistrates' Courts Act 1980, s 80(2) to be endorsed on the warrant of commitment. If no direction is given or no endorsement made, any monies found will be applied to the debt.

"section 80(2) of the Act of 1980"—This subsection makes provision for the application of any money found on a person committed to prison for non-payment of a magistrates' court maintenance order.

****

Register

66 Register of convictions etc

(1) The justices' chief executive for every magistrates' court shall keep a register in which there shall be entered –

(*a*) a minute or memorandum of every adjudication of the court;

(*b*) a minute or memorandum of every other proceeding or thing required by these rules or any other enactment to be so entered.

(2) The register shall be in the prescribed form, and entries in the register shall include, where relevant, such particulars as are provided for in the said form.

(3) Particulars of any entry relating to a decision about bail or the reasons for any such decisions or the particulars of any certificate granted under section 5(6A) of the Bail Act 1976 may be made in a book separate from that in which the entry recording the decision itself is made, but any such separate book shall be regarded as forming part of the register.

(3A)–(10B) ...

(11) The entries shall be signed or their accuracy certified by one of the justices, or the justice, before whom the proceedings to which they relate took place, or by the clerk who was present when those proceedings took place or, in the case of an entry required by paragraphs (3A) and (3B), where the consent or withdrawal of consent was not given or made (as the case may be) when the accused was present before the court, by the justices' chief executive or justice who received the notification:

Provided that, where the proceedings took place before a justice or justices sitting elsewhere than in a petty sessional court-house, the justices or, as the case may be, one of the justices may instead of signing an entry in the register, send to the justices' chief executive whose duty it is to keep the register a signed return of the proceedings containing the particulars required to be entered in the register; and the justices' chief executive shall enter the return in the register.

(11A) Any certificates made by virtue of paragraph (11) shall be kept with and as part of the register.

(12) Every register shall be open to inspection during reasonable hours by any justice of the peace, or any person authorised in that behalf by a justice of the peace or the Lord Chancellor.

Amendments—SI 1992/709; SI 1993/1183; SI 2001/610.

Adoption register—See Magistrates' Courts (Adoption) Rules 1984, r 32 for special provisions relating to the adoption register.

"minute or memorandum" (r 66(1))—A certified extract from the register is admissible evidence under r 68.

"adjudication" (r 66(1))—This includes the dismissal of a complaint (*Baker v Baker (Practice Note)* [1961] 1 WLR 1016, [1961] 2 All ER 746). The register is an official record of the justices' decision but the decision exists independently of the record. The justices' clerk is acting within the scope of his duty if he corrects a verbal error in an entry in the register (*R v Manchester Justices ex parte Lever* [1937] 2 KB 96, [1937] 3 All ER 4 and *R v Huntingdon Justices ex parte Simpkin and Coombes* (1959) 123 JP 166).

"the clerk who was present" (r 66(11))—This means the court clerk who was actually present, and not necessarily the justices' clerk.

****

Evidence – General

67 Proof of service, handwriting etc

(1) The service on any person of a summons, process, notice or document required or authorised to be served in any proceedings before a magistrates' court, and the handwriting or seal of a justice of the peace or other person on any warrant,

summons, notice, process or documents issued or made in any such proceedings, may be proved in any legal proceedings by a document purporting to be a solemn declaration in the prescribed form made before a justice of the peace, commissioner for oaths, clerk of a magistrates' court or registrar of a county court or a sheriff or sheriff clerk (in Scotland) or a clerk of petty sessions (in Northern Ireland).

(2) The service of any process or other document required or authorised to be served, the proper addressing, pre-paying and posting or registration for the purposes of service of a letter containing such a document, and the place, date and time of posting or registration of any such letter, may be proved in any proceedings before a magistrates' court by a document purporting to be a certificate signed by the person by whom the service was effected or the letter posted or registered.

(3) References in paragraph (2) to the service of any process shall, in their application to a witness summons, be construed as including references to the payment or tender to the witness of his costs and expenses.

"The service of any process ... may be proved" (r 67(2))—A certificate of service is not conclusive proof of service (see *Maher v Gower (formerly Kubilius)* (1982) FLR 287).

68 Proof of proceedings

The register of a magistrates' court, or any document purporting to be an extract from the register and to be certified by the justices' chief executive as a true extract, shall be admissible in any legal proceedings as evidence of the proceedings of the court entered in the register.

Amendments—SI 2001/610.

69 Proof that magistrates' court maintenance orders, maintenance orders etc have not been revoked etc

A certificate purporting to be signed by the justices' chief executive for a magistrates' court, and stating that no minute or memorandum of an order revoking, discharging, suspending, reviving, altering or varying a magistrates' court maintenance order, or order enforceable as a magistrates' court maintenance order or an order made under Part I of the Act of 1978 enforceable otherwise than as a magistrates' court maintenance order made by the court is entered in the register of the court shall, in any proceedings relating to the enforcement of the order or the revocation, discharge, suspension, revival, alteration or variation of the order, be evidence that the order has not been revoked, discharged, suspended, revived, altered or varied.

Amendments—SI 1989/384; SI 2001/610.

****

Recognizances and bail

****

83 Application to vary order for sureties or dispense with them

Where a person has been committed to custody in default of finding sureties and the order to find sureties was made at the instance of another person, an application under section 118 of the Act of 1980 shall be made by complaint against that other person.

84 Notice of enlargement of recognizances

(1) If a magistrates' court before which any person is bound by a recognizance to appear enlarges the recognizance to a later time under section 129 of the Act in his absence, it shall give him and his sureties, if any, notice thereof.

(2) If a magistrates' court, under section 129(4) of the Act of 1980, enlarges the recognizance of a surety for a person committed for trial on bail, it shall give the surety notice thereof.

****

86 Requirements to be complied with before release

(1) Where a magistrates' court has fixed the amount in which a person (including any surety) is to be bound by a recognizance, the recognizance may be entered into –

- (*a*) in the case of a surety in connection with bail in criminal proceedings where the accused is in a prison or other place of detention, before the governor or keeper of the prison or place as well as before the persons mentioned in section 8(4)(*a*) of the Bail Act 1976;
- (*b*) in any other case, before a justice of the peace, a justices' clerk, a justices' chief executive, a police officer who either is of the rank of inspector or above or is in charge of a police station or, if the person to be bound is in a prison or other place of detention, before the governor or keeper of the prison or place; or
- (*c*) where a person other than a police officer is authorised under section 125A or 125B of the Act of 1980 to execute a warrant of arrest providing for a recognizance to be entered into by the person arrested (but not by any other person), before the person executing the warrant.

(2) The justices' chief executive for a magistrates' court which has fixed the amount in which a person (including any surety) is to be bound by a recognizance or, under section 3(5), (6) or (6A) of the Bail Act 1976, imposed any requirement to be complied with before a person's release on bail or any condition of bail shall issue a certificate in the prescribed form showing the amount and conditions, if any, of the recognizance or, as the case may be, containing a statement of the requirement or condition of bail; and a person authorised to take the recognizance or do anything in relation to the compliance with such requirement or condition of bail shall not be required to take or do it without production of the certificate as aforesaid.

(3) If any person proposed as a surety for a person committed to custody by a magistrates' court produces to the governor or keeper of the prison or other place of detention in which the person so committed is detained a certificate in the prescribed form to the effect that he is acceptable as a surety, signed by any of the justices composing the court or the clerk of the court and signed in the margin by

PART III

the person proposed as surety, the governor or keeper shall take the recognizance of the person so proposed.

(4) Where the recognizance of any person committed to custody by a magistrates' court or of any surety of such a person is taken by any person other than the court which committed the first-mentioned person to custody, the person taking the recognizance shall send it to the justices' chief executive for that court:

Provided that, in the case of a surety, if the person committed has been committed to the Crown Court for trial or under any of the enactments mentioned in rule 17(1), the person taking the recognizance shall send it to the appropriate officer of the Crown Court.

Amendments—SI 2001/167; SI 2001/610.

Scope of provision—This rule makes provision for the taking of recognizances at a time after the amount is fixed under Magistrates' Courts Act 1980, s 119.

87 Notice to governor of prison etc where release from custody is ordered

Where a magistrates' court has, with a view to the release on bail of a person in custody, fixed the amount in which he or any surety of such a person shall be bound or, under section 3(5), (6) or (6A) of the Bail Act 1976, imposed any requirement to be complied with before his release or any condition of bail –

(*a*) the justices' chief executive for the court shall give notice thereof to the governor or keeper of the prison or place where that person is detained by sending him such a certificate as is mentioned in rule 86(2);

(*b*) any person authorised to take the recognizance of a surety or do anything in relation to the compliance with such requirement shall, on taking or doing it, send notice thereof by post to the said governor or keeper in the prescribed form and, in the case of a recognizance of a surety, shall give a copy of the notice to the surety.

Amendments—SI 2001/610.

88 Release when recognizances have been taken or requirements complied with

Where a magistrates' court has, with a view to the release on bail of a person in custody, fixed the amount in which he or any surety of such a person shall be bound or, under section 3(5) or (6) of the Bail Act 1976, imposed any requirement to be complied with before his release and given notice thereof in accordance with these Rules to the governor or keeper of the prison or place where that person is detained, the governor or keeper shall, when satisfied that the recognizances of all sureties required have been taken and that all such requirements have been complied with –

(*a*) in the case of bail in criminal proceedings, unless he is in custody for some other cause, release him;

(*b*) in the case of bail otherwise than in criminal proceedings, take the recognizances of that person if this has not already been done and, unless he is in custody for some other cause, release him.

****

Warrant

94 Committal to custody to be by warrant

A justice of the peace shall not commit any person to a prison, young offender institution or a remand centre, or to a police station under section 128(7) of the Act of 1980, or to customs detention under section 152 of the Criminal Justice Act 1988 except by a warrant of commitment.

Amendments—Substituted by SI 1988/2132.

95 Warrant to be signed

Except where signature by the clerk of a magistrates' court is permitted by rule 109 or by the Magistrates' Courts (Forms) Rules 1981, every warrant under the Act of 1980 shall be signed by the justice issuing it.

95A Warrant issued out of hours

Where a warrant is issued by a justice of the peace for any petty sessions area at a time when the office of the justices' chief executive for that area is closed, the applicant for the warrant shall within 72 hours serve upon the justices' chief executive any information on which the warrant was issued.

Amendments—Inserted by SI 1993/1183; amended by SI 2001/610.

96 Warrant of arrest

(1) A warrant issued by a justice of the peace for the arrest of any person shall require the persons to whom it is directed, that is to say, the constables of the police area in which the warrant is issued, or the civilian enforcement officers for the police area specified in the warrant, or any persons named in that behalf in the warrant, to arrest the person against whom the warrant is issued.

(2) The warrant shall name or otherwise describe the person for whose arrest it is issued, and shall contain a statement of the offence charged in the information or, as the case may be, the ground on which the warrant is issued.

(3) A warrant to which this rule applies may be executed by the persons to whom it was directed or by any of the following persons, whether or not the warrant was directed to them –

(*a*) a constable for any police area in England and Wales, acting in his own police area;

(*b*) where the warrant is one to which section 125A of the Act of 1980 applies, a civilian enforcement officer within the meaning of section 125A of the Act of 1980;

(*c*) where the warrant is one to which section 125A of the Act of 1980 applies, any of the individuals described in section 125B(1) of the Act of 1980;

and in this rule any reference to the person charged with the execution of a warrant includes any of the above persons who is for the time being authorised to execute the warrant, whether or not they have the warrant in their possession at the time.

(4) A person executing a warrant of arrest shall, upon arresting the person against whom the warrant is issued –

(*a*) either

PART III

(i) if he has the warrant with him, show it to the person against whom the warrant is issued, or

(ii) otherwise, state where the warrant is and what arrangements may be made to allow the person arrested to inspect it;

(*b*) explain, in ordinary language, the offence or default with which the person is charged and the reason for the arrest;

(*c*) where the person executing the warrant is one of the persons referred to in paragraph (3)(*b*) or (*c*) above, show the person arrested a written statement under section 125A(4) or 125B(4) as appropriate; and

(*d*) in any case, show documentary proof of his identity.

(5) A warrant of arrest issued under any of the provisions in paragraph (6) shall cease to have effect when –

(*a*) the sum in respect of which the warrant is issued is paid to the person charged with the execution of the warrant;

(*b*) that sum is tendered to and refused by the person charged with the execution of the warrant; or

(*c*) a receipt for that sum given by –

(i) the justices' chief executive for the court which issued the warrant; or

(ii) the charging or billing authority,

is produced to the person charged with the execution of the warrant.

(6) Those provisions are –

(*a*) sections 83(1), 83(2), 86(4) and 93(5) of the Act of 1980;

(*b*) regulation 42(5)(*b*) of the Community Charges (Administration and Enforcement) Regulations 1989;

(*c*) regulation 17(5)(*b*) of the Non-Domestic Rating (Collection and Enforcement) (Local Lists) Regulations 1989; and

(*d*) regulation 48(5)(*b*) of the Council Tax (Administration and Enforcement) Regulations 1992.

Amendments—SI 2001/167.

Defined terms—"the authorised persons for the police area": r 2(4).

97 Warrant of commitment

(1) A warrant of commitment or detention, other than a warrant committing a person to customs detention under section 152 of the Criminal Justice Act 1988, issued by a justice of the peace –

(*a*) shall name or otherwise describe the person committed or detained;

(*b*) shall contain a statement of the offence with which the person committed or detained is charged, or of which he has been convicted, or of any other ground on which he is committed;

(*c*) shall be directed to a person named in the warrant or to the constables of the police area in which the warrant is issued or to the civilian enforcement officers for the area in which they are employed and to the governor or keeper of the prison or place of detention specified in the warrant, and shall require –

(i) the named person or the constables or civilian enforcement officers to arrest the person committed or detained, if he is at large, and convey him to that prison or place and deliver him with the warrant to the governor or keeper;

(ii) the governor or keeper to keep in his custody the person committed or detained until that person be delivered in due course of law, or until the happening of an event specified in the warrant, or for the period specified in the warrant, as the case may be.

(1A) A warrant issued by a justice of the peace committing a person to customs detention under section 152 of the Criminal Justice Act 1988 –

(*a*) shall name or otherwise describe the person committed;
(*b*) shall contain a statement of the offence with which the person committed is charged;
(*c*) shall be directed to the officers of Her Majesty's Customs and Excise and shall require those officers to keep the person committed in their custody, unless in the meantime he be otherwise delivered in due course of law, for a period (not exceeding 192 hours) specified in the warrant.

(1B) A warrant of commitment or detention other than a warrant committing a person to customs detention under section 152 of the Criminal Justice Act 1988 may be executed by the persons to whom it was directed or by any of the following persons, whether or not the warrant was directed to them –

(*a*) a constable for any police area in England and Wales, acting in his own police area;
(*b*) where the warrant is one to which section 125A of the Act of 1980 applies, a civilian enforcement officer within the meaning of section 125A of the Act of 1980;
(*c*) where the warrant is one to which section 125A of the Act of 1980 applies, any of the individuals described in section 125B(1) of the Act of 1980;

and in this rule any reference to the person charged with the execution of a warrant includes any of the above persons who is for the time being authorised to execute the warrant, whether or not they have the warrant in their possession at the time.

(1C) A person executing a warrant of commitment or detention shall, upon arresting the person against whom the warrant is issued –

(*a*) either
 (i) if he has the warrant with him, show it to the person against whom the warrant is issued, or
 (ii) otherwise, state where the warrant is and what arrangements may be made to allow the person against whom the warrant was issued to inspect it;
(*b*) explain, in ordinary language, the offence or default with which the person is charged and the reason for the commitment or detention;
(*c*) where the person executing the warrant is one of the persons referred to in paragraph (1B)(*b*) or (*c*) above, show the person against whom the warrant was issued a written statement under section 125A(4) or 125B(4) as appropriate; and
(*d*) in any case, show documentary proof of his identity.

(2) A warrant of commitment or detention, other than a warrant committing a person to customs detention under section 152 of the Criminal Justice Act 1988, may be executed by conveying the person committed or detained to any prison or place of detention in which he may lawfully be detained and delivering him there together with the warrant; and, so long as any person is detained in any such prison or place other than that specified in the warrant, the warrant shall have effect as if the other prison or place were the prison or place specified in it.

(3) Notwithstanding the preceding provisions of this rule, a warrant of commitment or detention issued in pursuance of a valid conviction, or of a valid order requiring the person committed or detained to do or abstain from doing anything, shall not, if it alleges that the person committed or detained has been convicted, or ordered to do or abstain from doing that thing, be held void by reason of any defect in the warrant.

(4) The governor or keeper of the prison or place of detention at which any person is delivered in pursuance of a warrant of commitment or detention shall give to the constable or other person making the delivery a receipt for that person.

(5) Notwithstanding the preceding provisions of this rule, a warrant of a justice of the peace to commit to custody any person who to the justice's knowledge is already detained in a prison or other place of detention shall be delivered to the governor or keeper of the prison or place of detention in which that person is detained.

(6) A warrant of commitment or detention issued under any of the provisions in paragraph (7) shall cease to have effect if, at any time before the person for whose commitment or detention the warrant was issued is placed in custody –

(*a*) the sum in respect of which the warrant is issued, together with the costs and charges, if any, of the commitment, is paid to the person charged with the execution of the warrant;
(*b*) that sum is tendered to and refused by the person charged with the execution of the warrant; or
(*c*) a receipt for that sum given by –
  (i) the justices' chief executive for the court which issued the warrant; or
  (ii) the charging or billing authority,

is produced to the person charged with the execution of the warrant.

(7) Those provisions are –

(*a*) sections 76 and 136 of the Act of 1980;
(*b*) section 40 of the Child Support Act 1991;
(*c*) regulation 41(1) of the Community Charges (Administration and Enforcement) Regulations 1989;
(*d*) regulation 16(3)(*a*) of the Non-Domestic Rating (Collection and Enforcement) (Local Lists) Regulations 1989; and
(*e*) regulation 47(3)(*a*) of the Council Tax (Administration and Enforcement) Regulations 1992.

(8) A warrant of commitment issued for the enforcement of a maintenance order to which Part I of the Maintenance Orders Act 1958 applies shall cease to have effect if, at any time when the defendant is not already detained in pursuance of the warrant, the person charged with the execution of the warrant is informed –

(*a*) that an application for registration of the order has been granted under section 2 of the Maintenance Orders Act 1958; or
(*b*) that notice seeking the cancellation of such registration has been given under section 5 of that Act.

Amendments—SI 1988/2132; SI 1990/1190; SI 2001/167.

Defined terms—"the authorised persons for the police area": r 2(4).

Procedure—For the form of a warrant of commitment see Magistrates' Courts (Maintenance Orders Act 1958) Rules 1959.

Circumstances in which warrant may be held void (r 97(3))—Despite the general rule that a warrant "shall not ... be held void by virtue of a defect", it may be avoided in the case of a fundamental error. In *R v Doherty ex parte Isaacs* (1910) 74 JP 304, a warrant was issued in error on the grounds of non-payment of an order although payment had been made; the warrant was quashed by certiorari.

Summons

98 Form of summons

(1) A summons shall be signed by the justice issuing it or state his name and be authenticated by the signature of the clerk of a magistrates' court.

(2) A summons requiring a person to appear before a magistrates' court to answer to an information or complaint shall state shortly the matter of the information or complaint and shall state the time and place at which the defendant is required by the summons to appear.

(3) A single summons may be issued against a person in respect of several informations or complaints; but the summons shall state the matter of each information or complaint separately and shall have effect as several summonses, each issued in respect of one information or complaint.

"signed by the justice" (r 98(1))—The signature may be in the form of a rubber stamp and may be applied by the justice or a person acting with his general or specific authority (*R v Brentford Justices ex parte Catlin*) [1975] QB 455, [1975] 2 WLR 506). For power to authorise the signature of summonses in batches, see *R v Gateshead Justices ex parte Tesco Stores* [1981] QB 470, [1981] 2 WLR 419. Summonses may be signed by a justices' clerk (r 109 and Justices' Clerks Rules 1999).

99 Service of summons etc

(1) Service of a summons issued by a justice of the peace on a person other than a corporation may be effected –

(*a*) by delivering it to the person to whom it is directed; or

(*b*) by leaving it for him with some person at his last known or usual place of abode; or

(*c*) by sending it by post in a letter addressed to him at his last known or usual place of abode.

(2) (*revoked*)

(3) Service for the purposes of the Act of 1980 of a summons issued by a justice of the peace on a corporation may be effected by delivering it at, or sending it by post to, the registered office of the corporation, if that office is the United Kingdom, or, if there is no registered office in the United Kingdom, any place in the United Kingdom where the corporation trades or conducts its business.

(4) Paragraph (3) shall have effect in relation to a document (other than a summons) issued by a justice of the peace as it has effect in relation to a summons so issued, but with the substitution of references to England and Wales for the references to the United Kingdom.

(5) Any summons or other document served in manner authorised by the preceding provisions of this rule shall, for the purposes of any enactment other than the Act of 1980 or these Rules requiring a summons or other document to be served in any particular manner, be deemed to have been as effectively served as if it had been served in that manner; and nothing in this rule shall render invalid the service of a summons or other document in that manner.

(6) Sub-paragraph (*c*) of paragraph (1) shall not authorise the service by post of –

(*a*) a summons requiring the attendance of any person to give evidence or produce a document or thing; or

(*b*) a summons issued under any enactment relating to the liability of members of the naval, military or air forces of the Crown for the maintenance of their wives and children, whether legitimate or illegitimate.

(7) In the case of a summons issued on an application for an order under section 16 or 17(1) of the Act of 1978 (powers of court to make orders for the protection of a party to a marriage or a child of the family) service of the summons shall not be effected in manner authorised by sub-paragraph (*b*) or (*c*) of paragraph (1) unless a justice of the peace is satisfied by evidence on oath that prompt personal service of the summons is impracticable and allows service to be effected in such manner.

(8) Where this rule or any other of these Rules provides that a summons or other document may be sent by post to a person's last known or usual place of abode that rule shall have effect as if it provided also for the summons or other document to be sent in the manner specified in the rule to an address given by that person for that purpose.

(9) This rule shall not apply to a judgment summons.

Amendments—SI 1983/523; SI 1993/1183.

Service of summons—Service may be proved in accordance with r 67.

Service in Scotland and Northern Ireland—See also Summary Jurisdiction (Process) Act 1881, s 4 and Maintenance Orders Act 1950, s 15 for service in Scotland and Northern Ireland.

"place of abode" (r 99(1))—Service under r 99(1)(*b*) or (*c*) is not permitted other than at the person's place of abode, although postal service at a person's business premises is permissible if that address has been nominated under r 99(8).

Proof of service (r 99(1))—The same degree of proof of service is required in the case of an adjournment notice in family proceedings (*Unitt v Unitt* (1981) FLR 89).

Service by post—Although postal service is normally effective, a witness summons may not be served by post (r 99(6)).

Judgment summons (r 99(9))—For service of a judgment summons see r 58.

****

Miscellaneous

****

105 Application for alteration of maintenance agreement under s 35 of Matrimonial Causes Act 1973 or under s 15 of the Family Law Reform Act 1987

An application to a magistrates' court under section 35 of the Matrimonial Causes Act 1973 for the alteration of a maintenance agreement shall be by complaint.

Amendments—SI 1989/384; SI 1991/1991.

106 Proceedings against person outside the United Kingdom on application for variation etc of certain maintenance orders

(1) The period referred to in section 41(2A) of the Maintenance Orders (Reciprocal Enforcement) Act 1972 (which provide that, subject to certain conditions, a magistrates' court may, if it is satisfied that the respondent has been outside the United Kingdom during such period as may be prescribed by rules, proceed on an application made under sections 11B or 11C of the Guardianship of Minors Act 1971 notwithstanding that the respondent has not been served with the summons) shall be the whole of the period beginning one month before the making of the application and ending with the date of the hearing.

(2) Before proceeding in any such case as is referred to in the said section 41(2A), the court shall be satisfied that, in addition to the matter referred to in those subsections, the applicant has taken steps to notify the respondent of the making of the application and of the time and place appointed for the hearing by –

- (*a*) causing a notice in writing to that effect to be delivered to the respondent; or
- (*b*) causing a notice in writing to that effect to be sent by post addressed to the respondent at his last known or usual place of abode or at his place of business or at such other address at which there is ground for believing that it will reach the respondent, in accordance with directions given for the purpose by a justice of the peace acting for the same petty sessions area as that of the court; or
- (*c*) causing a notice to that effect to be inserted in one or more newspapers, in accordance with directions given as aforesaid;

and that it is reasonable in all the circumstances to proceed in the absence of the respondent.

(3) In any such case as is referred to in the said section 41(2A), the court shall not make the order for which the application is made unless it is satisfied that during the period of 6 months immediately preceding the making of the application the respondent was continuously outside the United Kingdom or was not in the United Kingdom on more than 30 days and that, having regard to any communication to the court in writing purporting to be from the respondent, it is reasonable in all the circumstances so to do.

(4) Paragraph (1) of rule 67 of these Rules shall apply for the purpose of proving the delivery of a written notice in pursuance of paragraph (2)(*a*) as it applies for the purpose of proving the service of a summons.

In relation to a solemn declaration made outside the United Kingdom, paragraph (1) of the said rule 67 as applied by this paragraph, shall have effect as if for the reference to the authorities mentioned in the said paragraph (1) there were substituted a reference to a consular officer of Her Majesty's Government in the United Kingdom or any person for the time being authorised by law, in the place where the declarant is, to administer an oath for any judicial or other legal purpose.

(5) Paragraph (2) of the said rule 67 shall apply for the purpose of proving the sending of a written notice in pursuance of paragraph (2)(*b*) or the insertion of a notice in a newspaper in pursuance of paragraph (2)(*c*) as it applies for the purpose of proving the service of any process, provided, as respects the insertion of a notice in a newspaper, that a copy of the newspaper containing the notice is annexed to the certificate.

Amendments—SI 1989/384.

107 Application for summons to witness or warrant for his arrest

(1) An application for the issue of a summons or warrant under section 97 or 97A of the Act of 1980 or paragraph 4 of Schedule 3 to the Act of 1998 may be made by the applicant in person or by his counsel or solicitor.

(2) An application for the issue of such a summons may be made by delivering or sending the application in writing to the justices' chief executive for the magistrates' court.

Amendments—SI 1983/523; SI 1997/706; SI 2000/3361; SI 2001/610.

****

109 Signature of forms prescribed by rules made under the Act of 1980

(1) Subject to paragraph (2), where any form prescribed by Rules made or having effect as if made under section 144 of the Act of 1980 contains provision for signature by a justice of the peace only, the form shall have effect as if it contained provision in the alternative for signature by the clerk of a magistrates' court.

(2) This rule shall not apply to any form of warrant, other than a warrant of commitment or of distress, or to any form prescribed in the Magistrates' Courts (Forms) Rules 1981.

Magistrates' Courts (Adoption) Rules 1984, SI 1984/611

ARRANGEMENT OF RULES

PART I
INTRODUCTORY

PART II
FREEING FOR ADOPTION

PART I
INTRODUCTORY

1 Citation, operation and revocations

(1) These Rules may be cited as the Magistrates' Courts (Adoption) Rules 1984 and shall come into operation on 27 May 1984.

(2) The Magistrates' Courts (Adoption) Rules 1976, the Magistrates' Courts (Adoption) (Amendment) Rules 1979 and the Magistrates' Courts (Adoption) (Amendment) Rules 1981 are hereby revoked; but where an application for an adoption order has been made before 27 May 1984 and has not been determined by that date, the provisions of the said Rules continue to apply in connection with that application and nothing in these Rules affects those provisions.

"These Rules ..."—The rules were made under Magistrates' Courts Act 1980, s 144 and Adoption Act 1976, s 66(2). They govern the procedure for adoption or freeing for adoption proceedings in magistrates' courts. Procedure in the High Court and county courts is governed by the Adoption Rules 1984.

Consolidation of earlier rules (r 1(2))—The rules consolidate, with amendments, the Magistrates' Courts (Adoption) Rules 1976 and the Magistrates' Courts (Adoption) (Amendment) Rules 1979. The earlier rules are revoked.

2 Interpretation

(1) In these Rules, the following expressions shall, unless the context otherwise requires, have the meaning hereby respectively assigned to them, that is to say –

"the 1976 Act" means the Adoption Act 1976;
"the 1989 Act" means the Children Act 1989;
"adoption agency" means a local authority or approved adoption society;
"the child" means the person whom the applicant for an adoption order proposes to adopt or, as the case may be, the person the adoption agency proposes should be freed for adoption;
"children's guardian" means an officer of the service appointed to act on behalf of the child in accordance with section 65(1)(*a*) of the 1976 Act;
"interim order" means an order under section 25 of the 1976 Act;
"regular armed forces of the Crown" means the Royal Navy, the regular forces as defined by section 225 of the Army Act 1955, the regular air force as defined by section 223 of the Air Force Act 1955, the Queen Alexandra's Royal Naval Nursing Service and the Women's Royal Naval Service;
"reporting officer" means an officer of the service appointed in accordance with section 65(1)(*b*) of the Act.

(2) Expressions which are used in these Rules which are used in the 1976 Act and the 1989 Act have the same meaning as in those Acts.

(3) In these Rules, unless the context otherwise requires, any reference to a rule or to a Schedule shall be construed as a reference to a rule contained in these Rules or to a Schedule hereto, and any reference in a rule to a paragraph shall be construed as a reference to a paragraph of that rule.

(4) In these Rules, any reference to a form shall be construed as a reference to the form so numbered in Schedule 1 to these Rules or to a form substantially to the like effect, with such variations as the circumstances may require.

Amendments—SI 1991/1991; SI 2001/820.

Defined terms—"adoption agency": r 2(1) (see also Adoption Act 1976, s 1(4)); "approved adoption society", "child": AA 1976, s 72(1); "Convention adoption order": AA 1976, ss 17, 72(1); "local authority": CA 1989, s 105(1).

Expressions used in AA 1976 and CA 1989 (r 2(2))—Adoption Rules 1984, r 2(2) makes provision for a meaning within the CA 1989 to have priority over any conflicting meaning attributed to it under AA 1976. This rule makes no such priority but provides that expressions used in AA 1976 and CA 1989 will have the same meaning within these rules. One problem created by conflicting meanings is that under CA 1989 the meaning of "parent" includes the unmarried father, whereas under AA 1976 the unmarried father is not included within that term (see **Parent** under r 4).

3 Extent

These Rules shall apply only to proceedings under the 1976 Act.

Amendments—SI 1991/1991.

Scope of provision—Proceedings in a magistrates' court under the Adoption Act 1976 are governed by these rules and not by the Family Proceedings Courts (Children Act 1989) Rules 1991 or the Family Proceedings Courts (Matrimonial Proceedings etc) Rules 1991.

PART II
FREEING FOR ADOPTION

4 The application

(1) An application to free a child for adoption shall be in Form 1 and shall be made to a family proceedings court acting for the area within which either the child or a parent or guardian of the child is at the date of the application by delivering it, or sending it by post to that court, together with all documents referred to in the application.

(2) The applicant shall be the adoption agency and the respondents shall be –

(*a*) each parent or guardian of the child;
(*b*) any local authority or voluntary organisation which has parental responsibility for, is looking after, or which is caring for, the child; and
(*f*) any person liable by virtue of any order or agreement to contribute to the maintenance of the child.

(3) The court may at any time direct that any other person or body, except the child, be made a respondent to the application.

(4) The applicant shall supply to the justices' chief executive three copies of –

(*a*) Form 1, together with any other documents required to be supplied, and
(*b*) a report in writing covering all the relevant matters specified in Schedule 2.

Amendments—SI 1991/1991; SI 2001/615.

Defined terms—"adoption agency": r 2(1) (see also Adoption Act 1976, s 1(4)); "caring for", "child": CA 1989, s 105(1); "free a child for adoption": AA 1976, s 18; "guardian": CA 1989, s 105(1); "local authority": AA 1976, s 72(1); "looking after": CA 1989, s 22(1); "parental responsibility": CA 1989, s 3; "voluntary organisation": CA 1989, s 105(1).

Substantive law—The relevant substantive law is AA 1976, ss 18–21.

Commencement of an application to free for adoption—An application to magistrates must be made to a family proceedings court by delivery in person or by post (r 4(1)). See also under Adoption Rules 1984, r 4.

Transfer between courts—The Children (Allocation of Proceedings) Order 1991 applies to adoption proceedings.

Application to dispense with parental consent—Where the applicant intends to request the court to dispense with parental consent under AA 1976, s 16(2), the request must, unless otherwise directed, be made in the application, or, if made subsequently, by notice to the justices' clerk (r 7(1)).

Parties (r 4(2), (3))—The applicant will be the adoption agency. The application must be made in the name of an officer of the agency who has been authorised to do so (Sch 1, Form 1). The respondents will be those listed in r 4(2). The court may at any time direct that any other person or body be made a respondent, with the exception that the child may not be directed to be a respondent.

Parent (r 4(2)(*a*))—See under AR 1984, r 4.

The child and the children's guardian as parties (r 4(2), (3))—The child may not be joined as a party in the magistrates' court (r 4(3)). A children's guardian may be joined as a respondent in an appropriate case (see **Legal representation of the children's guardian** under AR 1984, r 6).

Documents to be filed (r 4(4)(*a*))—In any proceedings to free a child for adoption in the magistrates' court, the applicant must file three copies of the following documents with the court:
(*a*) the application in Form 1;
(*b*) a written report prepared in accordance with Sch 2;
(*c*) the birth certificate, or certificate of previous adoption, which should be attached to the application (see notes to Form 1);
(*d*) if a parent or guardian has agreed to the making of an adoption order, any document signifying that agreement (which may be, but need not necessarily be, in Form 2: see r 8). If that agreement has been signified in a document executed outside England and Wales, the document must be filed with the application (r 8);
(*e*) where the application requests the court to dispense with the agreement of a parent or guardian, a statement of facts must be filed in support of that request (r 7).

Schedule 2 report (r 4(4)(*b*))—See under AR 1984, r 4.

5 Appointment and duties of reporting officer

(1) As soon as practicable after the application has been made or at any stage thereafter, if it appears that a parent or guardian of the child is willing to agree to the making of an adoption order and is in England or Wales, the court shall appoint a reporting officer in respect of that parent or guardian, and shall send to him a copy of the application and any documents attached thereto and of the report supplied by the applicant.

(2) The same person may be appointed as reporting officer in respect of two or more parents or guardians of the child.

(3) The reporting officer shall not be a member or employee of the applicant or any respondent body nor have been involved in the making of any arrangements for the adoption of the child.

(4) The reporting officer shall –

(*a*) ensure so far as is reasonably practicable that any agreement to the making of an adoption order is given freely and unconditionally and with full understanding of what is involved;
(*b*) confirm that the parent or guardian has been given an opportunity of making a declaration under section 18(6) of the 1976 Act that he prefers not to be involved in future questions concerning the adoption of the child;
(*c*) witness the signature by the parent or guardian of the written agreement to the making of an adoption order;
(*d*) investigate all the circumstances relevant to that agreement and any such declaration;
(*e*) where it is proposed to free a child whose mother and father were not married at the time of his birth for adoption and his father is not his guardian, interview any person claiming to be the father in order to be able to advise the court on the matters listed in section 18(7) of the 1976 Act; but if more than one reporting officer has been appointed, the court shall nominate one of them to conduct the interview; and
(*f*) on completing his investigations make a report in writing to the court, drawing attention to any matters which, in his opinion, may be of assistance to the court in considering the application.

(5) With a view to obtaining the directions of the court on any matter, the reporting officer may at any time make such interim report to the court as appears to him to be necessary; and in particular, the reporting officer shall make a report if a parent or guardian of the child is unwilling to agree to the making of an adoption order, and in such a case the justices' chief executive shall notify the applicant.

(6) The court may, at any time before the final determination of the application, require the reporting officer to perform such further duties as the court considers necessary.

(7) The reporting officer shall attend any hearing of the application if so required by the court.

(8) Any report made to the court under this rule shall be confidential.

(9) The powers of the court to appoint a reporting officer under paragraph (1), to nominate one reporting officer to conduct an interview under paragraph (4)(*e*), to give directions following the making of an interim report in accordance with paragraph (5) and to require the reporting officer to perform further duties under paragraph (6) shall also be exercisable, before the hearing of the application, by a single justice or by the justices' clerk.

Amendments—SI 1989/384; SI 1991/1880; SI 2001/615; SI 2001/820.

Defined terms—"person whose father and mother were not married to each other at the time of his birth": Family Law Reform Act 1987, s 1.

Scope of provision—This rule is made under Adoption Act 1976, s 65. A reporting officer is appointed in every application for a freeing order where a parent or guardian, who is in England and Wales, appears willing to consent to the making of an adoption order. It is consent to an adoption order, rather than the freeing order, that is relevant. The focus of the reporting officer's work is the parent or guardian in respect of whom the appointment is made.

Appointment of reporting officer (r 5(1))—The appointment may be made by a single justice or by the justices' clerk (r 5(9)). The same person may be appointed as reporting officer in respect of two or more parents or guardians (r 5(2)), and the same officer may also be acting as children's guardian in respect of the child concerned.

Parent—See under Adoption Rules 1984, r 4.

Written agreement (r 5(4)(*a*), (*c*))—See under AR 1984, r 5.

Declaration under AA 1976, s 18(6)—See under AR 1984, r 5.

Parent or guardian unwilling to agree to adoption (r 5(5))—See under AR 1984, r 5.

Confidential reports (r 5(8))—See under AR 1984, r 5.

Justices' clerk (r 5(9))—Family Proceedings Courts (Children Act 1989) Rules 1991, r 32 does not apply to proceedings under AA 1976; consequently, the justices' clerk does not have the power to delegate his powers under these rules to a subordinate.

6 Appointment and duties of children's guardian

(1) As soon as practicable after the application has been made, or after receipt of the statement of facts supplied under rule 7, if it appears that a parent or guardian of the child is unwilling to agree to the making of an adoption order, the court shall appoint a children's guardian of the child and shall send to him a copy of the application, together with any documents attached thereto, the statement of facts and the report supplied by the applicant.

(2) Where there are special circumstances and it appears to the court that the welfare of the child requires it, the court may at any time appoint a children's guardian of the child, and where such an appointment is made the court shall indicate any particular matters which it requires the children's guardian to investigate, and the court shall send the children's guardian a copy of the

application, together with any documents attached thereto, and the report supplied by the applicant.

(3) The same person may be appointed as reporting officer under rule 5(1) in respect of a parent or guardian who appears to be willing to agree to the making of an adoption order, and as children's guardian of the child under this rule; and, whether or not so appointed as reporting officer, the children's guardian may be appointed as reporting officer in respect of a parent or guardian of the child who originally was unwilling to agree to the making of an adoption order but who later signifies his or her agreement.

(4) The children's guardian shall not be a member or employee of the applicant or any respondent body nor have been involved in the making of any arrangements for the adoption of the child.

(5) With a view to safeguarding the interests of the child before the court, the children's guardian shall, so far as is reasonably practicable –

- (*a*) investigate –
  - (i) so far as he considers necessary, the matters alleged in the application, the report supplied by the applicant and, where appropriate, the statement of facts supplied under rule 7, and
  - (ii) any other matters which appear to him to be relevant to the making of an order freeing the child for adoption;
- (*b*) advise whether, in his opinion, the child should be present at the hearing of the application; and
- (*c*) perform such other duties as appear to him to be necessary or as the court may direct.

(6) On completing his investigations the children's guardian shall make a report in writing to the court, drawing attention to any matters which, in his opinion, may be of assistance to the court in considering the application.

(7) With a view to obtaining the directions of the court on any matter, the children's guardian may at any time make such interim report to the court as appears to him to be necessary.

(8) The court may, at any time before the final determination of the application, require the children's guardian to perform such further duties as the court considers necessary.

(9) The children's guardian shall attend any hearing of the application unless the court otherwise orders.

(10) Any report made to the court under this rule shall be confidential.

(11) The power of the court to appoint a children's guardian under paragraph (1) or (2), to require the performance by the children's guardian of particular duties in accordance with paragraph (2), (5)(*c*) or (8), and to give directions following the making of an interim report in accordance with paragraph (7) shall also be exercisable, before the hearing of the application, by a single justice or by the justices' clerk.

Amendments—SI 1991/1991; SI 2001/820.

Defined terms—"statement of facts": r 7.

Scope of provision—This rule is made under Adoption Act 1976, s 65. Where a parent or guardian is unwilling to give his consent to adoption, the court must appoint a children's guardian of the child. The children's guardian's duties in adoption proceedings are governed by these rules and not by Family Proceedings Courts (Children Act 1989) Rules 1991, r 11.

"report supplied by the applicant" (r 6(1))—The report referred to is the Schedule 2 report supplied under r 4(4).

Parent—See under Adoption Rules 1984, r 4.

Appointment of children's guardian (r 6(2))—See under AR 1984, r 6.

Legal representation of the children's guardian—In the magistrates' court the child cannot be made a party to the proceedings, but the court may join the children's guardian as a respondent (r 4(3)). See **Legal representation of the children's guardian: county court** under AR 1984, r 6.

Confidential report (r 6(10))—See under AR 1984, r 5.

Justices' clerk (r 6(11))—See under r 5.

7 Statement of facts in dispensation cases

(1) Where the adoption agency applying for an order freeing a child for adoption intends to request the court to dispense with the agreement of a parent or guardian of the child on any of the grounds specified in section 16(2) of the 1976 Act, the request shall, unless otherwise directed, be made in the application, or, if made subsequently, by notice to the justices' chief executive, and there shall be attached to the application or notice three copies of the statement of facts on which the applicant intends to rely.

(2) Where the applicant has been informed by a person with whom the child has been placed for adoption that he wishes his identity to remain confidential, the statement of facts supplied under paragraph (1) shall be framed in such a way as not to disclose the identity of that person.

(3) Where a statement of facts has been supplied under paragraph (1), the justices' chief executive shall, where and as soon as practicable, inform the parent or guardian of the request to dispense with his agreement and shall send to him a copy of the statement supplied under paragraph (1).

(4) The justices' chief executive shall also send a copy of the statement supplied under paragraph (1) to the children's guardian and to the reporting officer if a different person.

Amendments—SI 1991/1991; SI 2001/615; SI 2001/820.

Defined terms—"adoption agency": r 2(1) (see also Adoption Act 1976, s 1(4)).

Scope of provision—Where the court is to determine whether the consent to adoption of a parent or guardian should be dispensed with under AA 1976, s 16, the applicant agency must file a statement of facts on which it intends to rely in support of its contention that consent should be dispensed with.

Statement of facts—See under Adoption Rules 1984, r 7.

Parent—See under AR 1984, r 4.

Confidentiality (r 7(2))—See under AR 1984, r 7.

Children's guardian—For the appointment and duties of the children's guardian, see r 6.

Reporting officer—For the appointment and duties of the reporting officer, see r 5.

8 Agreement

(1) Any document signifying the agreement of a person to the making of an adoption order may be in Form 2, and if executed by a person outside England and Wales before the commencement of the proceedings, shall be filed with the application.

(2) If the document is executed in Scotland it shall be witnessed by a Justice of the Peace or a Sheriff.

(3) If the document is executed in Northern Ireland it shall be witnessed by a Justice of the Peace.

(4) If the document is executed outside the United Kingdom it shall be witnessed by one of the following persons –

(*a*) any person for the time being authorised by law in the place where the document is executed to administer an oath for any judicial or other legal purpose;
(*b*) a British consular officer;
(*c*) a notary public; or
(*d*) if the person executing the document is serving in any of the regular armed forces of the Crown, an officer holding a commission in any of those forces.

Defined terms—"United Kingdom": Interpretation Act 1978, Sch 1.

Scope of provision—The agreement to adoption of a parent or guardian may be given in writing or orally to the court. This rule sets out the formal requirements for the form of agreement, witnessing of the signature and filing of the resulting document. A written agreement which does not comply with this provision may nevertheless be accepted by the court. Where a document purports to be witnessed in accordance with this rule, there is a rebuttable presumption that it is validly witnessed (Adoption Act 1976, s 61(2)).

Effect of giving agreement—See under Adoption Rules 1984, r 8.

Parent—See under AR 1984, r 4.

9 Notice of hearing

(1) As soon as practicable after the application has been made, the justices' clerk shall fix a time for the hearing of the application and the justices' chief executive shall serve notice of the hearing on all the parties, the reporting officer and the children's guardian (if appointed) in Form 3.

(2) The reporting officer and the children's guardian (if appointed), but no other person, shall be served with a copy of the application and the report supplied by the applicant, and that report shall be confidential.

Amendments—SI 2001/615; SI 2001/820.

Scope of provision—This rule provides for the listing of the application for hearing.

Service (r 9(1))—See under Adoption Rules 1984, r 9.

Reporting officer—For the appointment and duties of the reporting officer, see r 5.

Children's guardian—For the appointment and duties of the children's guardian, see r 6.

Confidential reports—See under AR 1984, r 5.

Directions—Unlike the corresponding rule in the Adoption Rules 1984, and unlike the Family Proceedings Courts (Children Act 1989) Rules 1991, there is no provision in this rule requiring the magistrates' court to give directions. In practice, however, the court may consider giving directions within a short time after the filing of the application and after the filing of any report from the reporting officer or the children's guardian.

10 The hearing

(1) On the hearing of the application any person upon whom notice is required to be served under rule 9 may attend and be heard on the question whether an order freeing the child for adoption should be made.

(2) Any member or employee of a party which is a local authority, adoption agency or other body may address the court if he is duly authorised in that behalf.

(3) Where the court has been informed by the applicant that the child has been placed with a person (whether alone or jointly with another) for adoption and that person wishes his identity to remain confidential, the proceedings shall be conducted with a view to securing that any such person is not seen by or made known to any respondent who is not already aware of his identity except with his consent.

(4) Subject to paragraph (5), the court shall not make an order freeing the child for adoption except after the personal attendance before the court of a representative of the applicant duly authorised in that behalf and of the child.

(5) If there are special circumstances which, having regard to the report of the children's guardian (if any), appear to the court to make the attendance of the child unnecessary, the court may direct that the child need not attend.

(6) If there are special circumstances which appear to the court to make the attendance of any other party necessary, the court may direct that that party shall attend.

Amendments—SI 2001/820.

Defined terms—"adoption agency": r 2(1) (see also Adoption Act 1976, s 1(4)).

Hearing in private—No person may be present during the hearing, other than the officers of the court, the parties and their representatives and witnesses and other persons directly connected with the case (Magistrates' Courts Act 1980, s 69(3)).

Procedure in contested case—See under Adoption Rules 1984, r 10.

Evidence—See under AR 1984, r 10.

"attend and be heard" (r 10(1))—The parties, the reporting officer and the children's guardian may attend and be heard on the question of whether a freeing order should be made. The children's guardian must attend the hearing unless the court directs otherwise (r 6(9)).

Member or employee of adoption agency (r 10(2))—The applicant agency may be represented by a non-lawyer member or employee who is duly authorised to address the court.

Attendance of the child (r 10(5))—See under AR 1984, r 10.

11 Proof of identity of child etc

(1) Where proof of the identity of the child is required for any purpose, any fact tending to establish his identity with a child to whom a document relates may be proved by affidavit.

PART III

(2) Where any such fact is proved by affidavit, the attendance of a witness at the hearing to prove that fact shall not be compelled unless the fact is disputed or for some special reason his attendance is required by the court.

(3) Where the precise date of the child's birth is not proved to the satisfaction of the court, the court shall determine the probable date of his birth and the date so determined may be specified in the order freeing the child for adoption as the date of his birth.

(4) Where the place of birth of the child cannot be proved to the satisfaction of the court but it appears probable that the child was born in the United Kingdom, the Channel Islands or the Isle of Man, he may be treated as having been born in the registration district and sub-district in which the court sits, and in any other case (where the country of birth is not proved) the particulars of the country of birth may be omitted from the order freeing the child for adoption.

Defined terms—"Adopted Children Register": Adoption Act 1976, s 50; "United Kingdom": Interpretation Act 1978, Sch 1.

Proof of date and place of birth—Where a child is freed for adoption, identifying the probable date and place of birth of the child in those proceedings is sufficient proof of the date and place of birth in any subsequent adoption proceedings (r 24(5)).

12 Application for revocation of order freeing a child for adoption

(1) An application by a former parent for an order revoking an order freeing the child for adoption shall be made in Form 4 to the court which made the order to which the application relates by delivering it, or sending it by post to that court, together with all documents referred to in the application.

(2) Notice of the application shall be served on all persons who were parties to the proceedings in which the order freeing the child for adoption was made and on any adoption agency which has parental responsibility for the child by virtue of section 21 of the 1976 Act, save that notice shall not be served on a party to the earlier proceedings who was joined as a party by virtue of rule 4(2)(*b*).

(3) As soon as practicable after the application has been made, the justices' clerk shall fix a time for the hearing of the application and the court (or a single justice or the justices' clerk) shall appoint a children's guardian of the child in accordance with rule 6(4) and the justices' chief executive shall send to him a copy of the application and any documents attached thereto.

(4) The children's guardian shall have the same duties as if he had been appointed under rule 6 but as if in that rule –

(*a*) the reference to an order freeing the child for adoption was a reference to the revocation of an order freeing the child for adoption; and

(*b*) each reference to the report supplied by the applicant was omitted.

Amendments—SI 1991/1991; SI 2001/615; SI 2001/820.

Defined terms—"adoption agency": r 2(1) (see also Adoption Act 1976, s 1(4)); "former parent": AA 1976, s 19(1); "parental responsibility": CA 1989, s 3.

Scope of provision—A former parent who has not made a declaration under AA 1976, s 18(6) (that he prefers not to be involved in future questions concerning the adoption of the child – see **Declaration under AA 1976, s 18(6)** under Adoption Rules 1984, r 5) may, in certain limited circumstances, apply for the freeing order to be revoked under AA 1976, s 20. This rule sets out the procedure applicable to such an application.

Application to be made to the court which made the original freeing order (r 12(1))—This rule and the text of Form 4 make it plain that the application for revocation must be made to the court that made the original freeing order.

Parties (r 12(2))—See under AR 1984, r 12.

Justices' clerk (r 12(3))—See under r 5.

Children's guardian (r 12(3), (4))—For the appointment and duties of the children's guardian, see under r 6.

Schedule 2 report (r 12(4)(*b*))—See under AR 1984, r 12.

13 Joint application for parental responsibility by adoption agencies

(1) An application by two adoption agencies under section 21(1) of the 1976 Act shall be made in the appropriate form prescribed in Schedule 1 to these Rules to a court acting for the area within which the child is at the date of the application by delivering it, or sending it by post, to that court, together with all documents referred to in the application.

(2) Notice of any order made under section 21 of the 1976 Act shall be sent by the court to the court which made the order under section 18 of the 1976 Act (if a different court) and to any former parent (as defined in section 19(1) of the 1976 Act) of the child.

Amendments—SI 1991/1991.

Defined terms—"adoption agency": r 2(1) (see also Adoption Act 1976, s 1(4)).

Scope of provision—Under AA 1976, s 21, the court may vary the original freeing order under s 18 by giving parental responsibility for the child to another adoption agency ("the substitute agency") in place of the agency for the time being having parental responsibility for the child under the s 18 order ("the existing agency"). The amended title to this rule differs from the corresponding provision in Adoption Rules 1984, r 13 ("Substitution of one adoption agency for another").

Joint application—An application for substitution under AA 1976, s 21 must be made jointly by the existing agency and the would-be substitute agency (AA 1976, s 21(2)). The application should be made to the court for the area in which the child is at the date of the application.

"appropriate form"—The application must be in accordance with Form 5 (Sch 1). The application must state the reasons why the transfer would be in the best interest of the child, together with the reasons that make the transfer administratively desirable.

Notice—There is no requirement to serve the application on the parties to the original proceedings (contrast r 12(2)). The only requirement is that any "former parent" (see AA 1976, s 19(1)) must be informed of the making of the application (Form 5, para 4).

PART III
ADOPTION ORDERS

14 Application for a serial number

If any person proposing to apply to a domestic court for an adoption order wishes his identity to be kept confidential, he may, before making his application, apply to the justices' chief executive for a serial number to be assigned to him for the

PART III

purposes of identifying him in connection with the proposed application, and a number shall be assigned to him accordingly.

Amendments—SI 2001/615.

Defined terms—"adoption order": Adoption Act 1976, s 12(1).

Scope of provision—If an applicant for an adoption order wishes his identity to be kept confidential, he may apply for a serial number to be assigned to him. If a serial number has been assigned, the proceedings must be conducted with a view to ensuring that the applicant is neither seen by, nor made known to, any respondent who is not already aware of his identity (r 23(3)). Ultimately the court retains the power to order disclosure of the identity of the adopters; that power should be exercised in the manner applicable to disclosure of other confidential material (*Re X (Adoption: Confidentiality Procedure)* [2002] EWCA Civ 828, [2002] 2 FLR 476) (see **Confidential reports** under r 5).

"domestic court"—This phrase was missed by the amending legislation; the reference is to "family proceedings court".

15 The application

(1) An application for an adoption order shall be in Form 6 and shall be made to a family proceedings court acting for the area within which the child is at the date of the application by delivering it, or sending it by post to that court, together with all documents referred to in the application.

(2) The applicant shall be the proposed adopter and the respondents shall be –

(*a*) each parent or guardian (not being an applicant) of the child, unless the child is free for adoption;

(*b*) any adoption agency having parental responsibility for the child by virtue of section 18 or 21 of the 1976 Act;

(*c*) any adoption agency named in the application or in any form of agreement to the making of the adoption order as having taken part in the arrangements for the adoption of the child;

(*d*) any local authority to whom the applicant has given notice under section 18 of the 1975 Act of his intention to apply for an adoption order;

(*e*) any local authority or voluntary organisation which has parental responsibility for, is looking after, or is caring for, the child; and

(*f*)–(*i*) (*revoked*)

(*j*) where the applicant proposes to rely on section 15(1)(*b*)(ii) of the 1976 Act, the spouse of the applicant.

(3) The court may at any time direct that any other person or body, except the child, be made a respondent to the application.

(4) The applicant shall supply to the justices' chief executive three copies of –

(*a*) Form 6, together with any other documents required to be supplied, and

(*b*) where the child was not placed for adoption with the applicant by an adoption agency, save where the applicant or one of the applicants is a parent of the child, reports by a registered medical practitioner made not more than three months earlier on the health of the child and of each applicant, covering the matters specified in Schedule 3.

Amendments—SI 1991/1991; SI 2001/615.

Defined terms—"adoption agency": r 2(1) (see also Adoption Act 1976, s 1(4)); "caring for", "child", "guardian", "local authority": CA 1989, s 105(1); "looking after": CA 1989, s 22(1); "parental responsibility": CA 1989, s 3; "voluntary organisation": CA 1989, s 105(1).

Substantive law—The relevant substantive law is AA 1976, ss 12–16.

Transfer between courts—The Children (Allocation of Proceedings) Order 1991 applies to adoption proceedings.

Application to dispense with parental consent—Where the applicant intends to request the court to dispense with parental consent under AA 1976, s 16(2), the request must, unless otherwise directed, be made in the application, or, if made subsequently, by notice to the justices' clerk (r 19(1)).

"applicant" (r 15(2))—See under Adoption Rules 1984, r 15.

Respondents—(r 15(2), (3))—Each of those referred to in r 15(2)(*a*)–(*j*) must be made respondents to the application. Any other person or body may be joined as a respondent by the court, save for the child. See also under AR 1984, r 15.

Parent (r 15(2)(*a*))—See under AR 1984, r 4.

"notice under section 18 of the 1975 Act" (r 15(2)(*d*))—The reference to Children Act 1975, s 18 is no longer appropriate but has yet to be corrected by amendment. The reference should be to AA 1976, s 22, which replaced s 18.

Person liable to maintain the child—Following the amendment of these rules by the Family Proceedings Courts (Matrimonial Proceedings etc) Rules 1991, r 15(2)(*h*) (which provided for any person liable by virtue of an order or agreement to contribute to the maintenance of the child to be a respondent) has been deleted, whereas the corresponding provision of AR 1984, as amended, has remained in force. There is no obvious explanation for this anomaly.

The child and the children's guardian as parties (r 15(2), (3))—See under r 4.

Documents to be filed with application (r 15(4))—At the commencement of the proceedings, the applicant must supply the justices' clerk with three copies of the following documents:
(*a*) the application (Form 6);
(*b*) if there are two applicants who are married to each other, their marriage certificate;
(*c*) in any other case, documentary evidence of marital status should be supplied; if a married applicant is applying alone, the applicant should attach any documentary evidence in support of the application being granted without the non-applicant spouse (AA 1976, s 15(1)(*b*));
(*d*) a medical report on the health of each applicant and on the child made during the three months prior to the application (in accordance with Sch 3), but no medical report is required if the child was placed for adoption by an adoption agency or is the child of one of the applicants;
(*e*) either the child's birth certificate or, if appropriate, a copy of the entry in the Adopted Children Register relating to his previous adoption;
(*f*) if the child has been freed for adoption, a copy of the freeing order and any order transferring parental responsibility to another adoption agency under AA 1976, s 21;
(*g*) if the parent or guardian has given his agreement to the making of an adoption order, and that agreement has been signified in a document executed outside England and Wales before the commencement of the proceedings, it should be filed with the originating process;
(*h*) where the application requests the court to dispense with the agreement of a parent, the statement of facts relied on in support of that request.

16 Preliminary examination of application

If it appears to the justices' clerk on receipt by the justices' chief executive of the application for an adoption order that the court –

(*a*) may be precluded, by virtue of section 22(4) of the 1975 Act, from proceeding to hear the application, or
(*b*) may, for any other reason appearing in the application, have no jurisdiction to make an adoption order,

he shall bring the relevant matter to the attention of the court and the application shall not be proceeded with unless the court gives directions as to the further conduct of the application.

Amendments—SI 2001/615.

Scope of provision—The court must conduct a preliminary examination of the application to determine whether there are any potential issues as to jurisdiction.

Justices' clerk—See under r 5.

"section 22(4) of the 1975 Act" (r 16(*a*))—The court must not proceed to hear an application for an adoption order in relation to a child where a previous application for a British adoption order, made in relation to the child by the same person or persons, was refused by any court, unless when refusing the application the court ordered that Adoption Act 1976, s 24(1) would not apply, or it appears to the court that because of a change of circumstances or some other reason it is proper to proceed. The reference to Children Act 1975, s 22(4) has escaped amendment. The reference should be read as a reference to AA 1976, s 24(1), which replaced CA 1975, s 22(4).

17 Appointment and duties of reporting officer

(1) As soon as practicable after the application has been made or at any stage thereafter, if the child is not free for adoption and if it appears that a parent or guardian of the child is willing to agree to the making of an adoption order and is in England and Wales, the court shall appoint a reporting officer in respect of that parent or guardian, and shall send to him a copy of the application and any documents attached thereto.

(2) The same person may be appointed as reporting officer in respect of two or more parents or guardians of the child.

(3) The reporting officer shall not be a member or employee of the applicant or any respondent body (except where a local authority is made a respondent only under rule 15(2)(*d*)) nor have been involved in the making of any arrangements for the adoption of the child.

(4) The reporting officer shall –

(*a*) ensure so far as is reasonably practicable that any agreement to the making of the adoption order is given freely and unconditionally and with full understanding of what is involved;
(*b*) witness the signature by the parent or guardian of the written agreement to the making of the adoption order;
(*c*) investigate all the circumstances relevant to that agreement; and
(*d*) on completing his investigations make a report in writing to the court, drawing attention to any matters which, in his opinion, may be of assistance to the court in considering the application.

(5) Paragraphs (5) to (8) of rule 5 shall apply to a reporting officer appointed under this rule as they apply to a reporting officer appointed under that rule; and paragraph (9) of rule 5 shall apply in relation to the appointment of a reporting officer under this rule as it applies in relation to such an appointment made under that rule.

Amendments—SI 1991/1991; SI 2001/820.

Defined terms—"free for adoption": Adoption Act 1976, s 18.

Scope of provision—This rule is made under AA 1976, s 65. A reporting officer is appointed in every application for an adoption order where a parent or guardian who is in England and Wales appears willing to consent to the making of an adoption order. The focus of the reporting officer's work is the parent or guardian in respect of whom he is appointed.

Appointment of a reporting officer (r 17(1))—See under r 5.

Parent—See under r 4.

Written agreement (r 17(4)(*a*), (*b*))—See under AR 1984, r 5.

Parent or guardian unwilling to agree to adoption (r 17(5))—See under AR 1984, r 5.

Confidential reports (r 17(5))—See under AR 1984, r 5.

18 Appointment and duties of children's guardian

(1) As soon as practicable after the application has been made, or after receipt of the statement of facts supplied under rule 19, if the child is not free for adoption and if it appears that a parent or guardian of the child is unwilling to agree to the making of the adoption order, the court shall appoint a children's guardian of the child and shall send him a copy of the application together with any documents attached thereto.

(2) Where there are special circumstances and it appears to the court that the welfare of the child requires it, the court may at any time appoint a children's guardian of the child and where such a appointment is made the court shall indicate any particular matters which it requires the children's guardian to investigate and the court shall send the children's guardian a copy of the application together with any documents attached thereto.

(3) The same person may be appointed as reporting officer under rule 17(1) in respect of a parent or guardian who appears to be willing to agree to the making of the adoption order, and as children's guardian of the child under this rule; and, whether or not so appointed as reporting officer, the children's guardian may be appointed as reporting officer in respect of a parent or guardian of the child who originally was unwilling to agree to the making of an adoption order but who later signifies his or her agreement.

(4) The children's guardian shall not be a member or employee of the applicant or any respondent body (except where a local authority is made a respondent only under rule 15(2)(*d*)) nor have been involved in the making of any arrangements for the adoption of the child.

(5) With a view to safeguarding the interests of the child before the court the children's guardian shall so far as is reasonably practicable –

- (*a*) investigate –
  - (i) so far as he considers necessary, the matters alleged in the application, any report supplied under rule 22(1) or (2) and, where appropriate, the statement of facts supplied under rule 19;
  - (ii) any other matters which appear to him to be relevant to the making of an adoption order;
- (*b*) advise whether, in his opinion, the child should be present at the hearing of the application; and
- (*c*) perform such other duties as appear to him to be necessary or as the court may direct.

(6) Paragraphs (6) to (10) of rule 6 shall apply to a children's guardian appointed under this rule as they apply to a children's guardian appointed under that rule; and paragraph (11) of rule 6 shall apply in relation to the appointment of a children's

guardian under this rule as it applies in relation to such an appointment made under that rule.

Amendments—SI 1991/1991; SI 2001/820.

Defined terms—"statement of facts": r 19.

Scope of provision—This rule is made under Adoption Act 1976, s 65. Where a parent or guardian is unwilling to give his consent to adoption, the court must appoint a children's guardian of the child. The children's guardian's duties in adoption proceedings are governed by these rules and not by Family Proceedings Courts (Children Act 1989) Rules 1991, r 11.

Parent—See under r 4.

Appointment of children's guardian (r 18(2))—See under Adoption Rules 1984, r 6.

Legal representation of children's guardian—See under AR 1984, r 6.

Confidential reports (r 18(6))—See under AR 1984, r 5.

19 Statement of facts in dispensation cases

(1) Where the child is not free for adoption and the applicant for the adoption order intends to request the court to dispense with the agreement of a parent or guardian of the child on any of the grounds specified in section 16(2) of the 1976 Act, the request shall, unless otherwise directed, be made in the application or, if made subsequently, by notice to the justices' chief executive and there shall be attached to the application or notice three copies of the statement of facts on which the applicant intends to rely.

(2) Where a serial number has been assigned to the applicant under rule 14, the statement of facts supplied under paragraph (1) shall be framed in such a way as not to disclose the identity of the applicant.

(3) Where a statement of facts has been supplied under paragraph (1), the justices' chief executive shall, where and as soon as practicable, inform the parent or guardian of the request to dispense with his agreement and shall send to him a copy of the statement supplied under paragraph (1).

(4) The justices' chief executive shall also send a copy of the statement supplied under paragraph (1) to the children's guardian and to the reporting officer if a different person.

Amendments—SI 1991/1880; SI 2001/615; SI 2001/820.

Defined terms—"free for adoption": Adoption Act 1976, s 18.

Scope of provision—Where the court is to determine whether the consent of a parent or guardian should be dispensed with under AA 1976, s 16, the applicant must file a statement of the facts on which he intends to rely in support of his contention that consent should be dispensed with.

Statement of facts—See under Adoption Rules 1984, r 7.

Children's guardian—For the appointment and duties of the children's guardian, see r 18.

Reporting officer—For the appointment and duties of the reporting officer, see r 17.

20 Agreement

(1) Any document signifying the agreement of a person to the making of the adoption order may be in Form 7, and, if executed by a person outside England and Wales before the commencement of the proceedings, shall be filed with the application.

(2) If the document is executed outside England and Wales it shall be witnessed by one of the persons specified in rule 8(2), (3) or (4), according to the country in which it is executed.

Scope of provision—The agreement to adoption of a parent or guardian may be given in writing or orally to the court. This rule sets out the formal requirements for the form of agreement, witnessing of the signature and filing of the resulting document. A written agreement which does not comply with this provision may nevertheless be accepted by the court. Where a document purports to be witnessed in accordance with this rule, there is a rebuttable presumption that it is validly witnessed (Adoption Act 1976, s 61(2)).

Effect of giving agreement—See under Adoption Rules 1984, r 8.

21 Notice of hearing

(1) Subject to paragraph (4), as soon as practicable after the application has been made the justices' clerk shall fix a time for the hearing of the application and the justices' chief executive shall serve notice of the hearing on all the parties, the reporting officer and the children's guardian (if appointed) in Form 8.

(2) In a case where section 22 of the 1976 Act applies, the justices' chief executive shall send a copy of the application and, where appropriate, of the report supplied under rule 15(4), to the local authority to whom notice under that section was given.

(3) No person other than the reporting officer, the children's guardian (if appointed) and, in cases where section 22 of the 1976 Act applies, the local authority to whom notice under that section was given, shall be served with a copy of the application.

(4) Where section 22 of the 1976 Act applies, the justices' clerk shall fix a time for the hearing so that the hearing takes place on a date not less than three months from the date of the notice given to the local authority under that section.

Amendments—SI 1991/1991; SI 2001/615; SI 2001/820.

Scope of provision—This rule provides for the listing of the application for hearing.

Adoption Act 1976, s 22—See under Adoption Rules 1984, r 21.

Application not to be served on parents (r 21(3))—See under AR 1984, r 21.

Service (r 21(1))—See under AR 1984, r 9.

Reporting officer—For the appointment and duties of the reporting officer, see r 17.

Children's guardian—For the appointment and duties of the children's guardian, see r 18.

Directions—See under r 9.

PART III

22 Reports by adoption agency or local authority

(1) Where the child was placed for adoption with the applicant by an adoption agency, that agency shall supply, within six weeks of receipt of the notice of hearing under rule 21, three copies of a report in writing covering the matters specified in Schedule 2.

(2) Where the child was not placed for adoption with the applicant by an adoption agency, the local authority to whom the notice under section 22 of the 1976 Act was given shall supply, within six weeks of receipt of the notice of hearing under rule 21, three copies of a report in writing covering the matters specified in Schedule 2.

(3) The court may request a further report under paragraph (1) or (2) and may indicate any particular matters it requires such a further report to cover.

(4) The justices' chief executive shall send a copy of any report supplied under paragraph (1) or (2) to the reporting officer and to the children's guardian (if appointed).

(5) No other person shall be supplied with a copy of any report supplied under paragraph (1) or (2) and any such report shall be confidential.

Amendments—SI 1991/1991; SI 2001/615; SI 2001/820.

Defined terms—"adoption agency": r 2(1) (see also Adoption Act 1976, s 1(4)).

Scope of provision—In every adoption case, whether the child's parents are in agreement or not, the relevant local authority or adoption agency must compile a written report covering all the relevant matters set out in Sch 2 to these rules (see **Schedule 2 report** under r 4).

Timing and authorship of report (r 22(1), (2))—See under Adoption Rules 1984, r 22.

Reporting officer—For the appointment and duties of the reporting officer, see r 17.

Children's guardian—For the appointment and duties of the children's guardian, see r 18.

23 The hearing

(1) On the hearing of the application any person upon whom notice is required to be served under rule 21 may attend and be heard on the question whether an adoption order should be made.

(2) Any member or employee of a party which is a local authority, adoption agency or other body may address the court if he is duly authorised in that behalf.

(3) If a serial number has been assigned to the applicant under rule 14, the proceedings shall be conducted with a view to securing that he is not seen by or made known to any respondent who is not already aware of the applicant's identity except with his consent.

(4) Subject to paragraphs (5) and (7), the court shall not make an adoption order or an interim order except after the personal attendance before the court of the applicant and the child.

(5) If there are special circumstances which, having regard to the report of the children's guardian (if any), appear to the court to make the attendance of the child unnecessary, the court may direct that the child need not attend.

(6) If there are special circumstances which appear to the court to make the attendance of any other party necessary, the court may direct that that party shall attend.

(7) In the case of an application under section 14(1A) or (1B) of the 1976 Act, the court may in special circumstances make an adoption order or an interim order after the personal attendance of one only of the applicants, if the application is verified by a declaration made by the applicant who does not attend and witnessed by a justice of the peace, a justices' clerk within the meaning of section 70 of the Justices of the Peace Act 1979, or, if made outside the United Kingdom, by any of the persons specified in rule 8(4).

Amendments—SI 1991/1991; SI 2001/820.

Defined terms—"adoption agency": r 2(1) (see also Adoption Act 1976, s 1(4)).

Scope of provision—This rule makes a number of specific provisions with regard to the hearing of an adoption application. In the absence of specific provision, the hearing will be conducted, at the discretion of the court, in accordance with the general rules of evidence and procedure.

Hearing in private—See under r 10.

Procedure in contested case—See under Adoption Rules 1984, r 10.

Evidence—See under AR 1984, r 10.

"attend and be heard" (r 23(1))—The parties, the reporting officer and the children's guardian may attend and be heard on the question of whether a freeing order should be made. The children's guardian must attend the hearing unless the court directs otherwise (rr 6(9), 18(6)).

Member or employee of adoption agency (r 23(2))—The applicant agency may be represented by a non-lawyer member or employee who is duly authorised to address the court.

Serial number case (r 23(3))—The operation of this rule will inevitably mean that the applicant and those who do not know the applicant's identity may not be in the courtroom at the same time. The normal approach of courts is to conduct most of the hearing in the absence of the applicant. If the applicant is called to give evidence, the roles are reversed and those who do not know the applicant's identity must leave the courtroom.

Personal attendance of the applicant and the child (r 23(4)–(7))—See under AR 1984, r 23.

24 Proof of identity of child etc

(1) Where proof of the identity of the child is required for any purpose, any fact tending to establish his identity with a child to whom a document relates may be proved by affidavit.

(2) Where any such fact is proved by affidavit, the attendance of a witness at the hearing to prove that fact shall not be compelled unless the fact is disputed or for some special reason his attendance is required by the court.

(3) Subject to paragraph (5), where the precise date of the child's birth is not proved to the satisfaction of the court, the court shall determine the probable date of his birth and the date so determined may be specified in the adoption order as the date of his birth.

(4) Subject to paragraph (5), where the place of birth of the child cannot be proved to the satisfaction of the court but it appears probable that the child was born in the United Kingdom, the Channel Islands or the Isle of Man, he may be treated as having been born in the registration district and sub-district in which the court sits,

and in any other case (where the country of birth is not proved) the particulars of the country of birth may be omitted from the adoption order.

(5) Where the child is free for adoption, any order made identifying the probable date and place of birth of the child in the proceedings under section 18 of the 1976 Act shall be sufficient proof of the date and place of birth of the child in proceedings to which this rule applies.

Amendments—SI 1991/1991.

Defined terms—"Adopted Children Register": Adoption Act 1976, s 50; "United Kingdom": Interpretation Act 1978, Sch 1.

Scope of provision—This rule allows the identity of the child to be presumed proved where the birth certificate relied on in the application relates to the certificate filed with a written form of agreement. The rule also allows the court to determine the child's date or place of birth where there is no precise evidence available.

25 Further proceedings after interim order

Where the court has made an interim order, the justices' clerk shall fix a time for the further hearing of the application, such hearing to be on a date before the order expires, and shall send notice in Form 8 of the date of the hearing to all the parties and to the children's guardian (if appointed) not less than one month before that date.

Amendments—SI 2001/820.

Defined terms—"interim order": Adoption Act 1976, s 25.

Scope of provision—An interim order is an order, made on an application for an adoption order, whereby the court postpones the determination of the application and makes an order giving parental responsibility for the child to the applicant for a probationary period not exceeding two years (AA 1976, s 25). This rule provides for the relisting of the case prior to the expiry of the probationary period.

Children's guardian—For the appointment and duties of the children's guardian, see r 18.

****

PART IV
MISCELLANEOUS

27 Application for removal, return etc of child

(1) An application –

(*a*) for leave under section 27 or 28 of the 1976 Act to remove a child from the home of a person with whom the child lives,

(*b*) under section 29(1) of the 1976 Act for an order for the return of a child who has been removed from the home of a person with whom the child lives,

(*c*) under section 29(2) of the 1976 Act for an order directing a person not to remove a child from the home of a person with whom the child lives,

(*d*) under section 30(2) of the 1976 Act, for leave to give notice of an intention not to allow a child to remain in a person's home, or

(*e*) under section 20(2) of the 1976 Act, for leave to place a child for adoption, shall be made in accordance with paragraph (2).

(2) The application under paragraph (1) above shall be made by complaint –

(*a*) if an application for an adoption order or an order under section 18 or 20 of the 1976 Act is pending, to the family proceedings court in which the application is pending; or

(*b*) if no such application is pending, to the family proceedings court in whose area the applicant lives or, in the case of an application made under section 28 of the 1976 Act, the court in whose area the child is:

Provided that if an application is pending under paragraph (1) above, any further application concerning the home of the child shall be made to the family proceedings court in which that original application is pending.

(3) The respondents shall be –

(*a*) in a case where proceedings for an adoption order or an order under sections 18 or 20 of the 1976 Act are pending (or where such proceedings have subsequently been commenced), all the parties to those proceedings;

(*b*) in any other case, any person against whom an order is sought in the application and the local authority to whom the prospective adopter has given notice under section 22 of the 1976 Act; and

(*c*) in any case, such other person or body, not being the child, as the court thinks fit.

(4) If in any application under this rule a serial number has been assigned to a person who has applied or who proposes to apply for an adoption order, or such a person applies to the justices' chief executive in that behalf before making that application and a serial number is assigned accordingly –

(*a*) the justices' chief executive shall ensure that a summons directed to any of the respondents does not disclose the identity of that person to any respondent to the application under this rule who is not already aware of that person's identity, and

(*b*) the proceedings on the application under this rule shall be conducted with a view to securing that he is not seen by or made known to any party who is not already aware of his identity except with his consent.

(5) The justices' chief executive shall serve notice of the time fixed for the hearing on the reporting officer and children's guardian (if any), together with a copy of the complaint: and on the hearing of the application the reporting officer and children's guardian may attend and be heard on the question of whether the application made should be granted.

(6) Unless otherwise directed, any prospective adopter who is a respondent under this rule and who wishes to oppose the application shall make his application for an adoption order within 14 days of the service upon him of the summons or before or at the time of the hearing of the application under this rule, whichever is the sooner.

(7) The court may at any time give directions, and if giving directions under paragraph (6) shall give directions, as to the conduct of any application under this rule and in particular as to the appointment of a children's guardian of the child.

(8) Any member or employee of a party which is a local authority, adoption agency or other body may address the court at the hearing of an application under this rule if he is duly authorised in that behalf.

PART III

(9) Where an application under paragraph (1)(*a*) or (*d*) is granted or an application under paragraph (1)(*b*) or (*c*) is refused, the court may thereupon, if application for an adoption order has been made, treat the hearing of the application as the hearing of the application for an adoption order and refuse an adoption order accordingly.

(10) Where an application under this rule is determined the justices' chief executive shall serve notice of the effect of the determination on all the parties.

(11) A search warrant issued by a justice of the peace under section 29(4) of the 1976 Act (which relates to premises specified in an information to which an order made under the said section 29(1) relates, authorising a constable to search the said premises and if he finds the child to return the child to the person on whose application the said order was made) shall be in a warrant form as per section 102 of the 1989 Act (warrant to search for or remove a child) or a form to the like effect.

Amendments—SI 1991/1991; SI 2001/615; SI 2001/820.

Application (r 27(2))—If there are adoption, freeing or revocation applications pending, the ancillary application must be made to the court where those proceedings are pending. Where there is no main application pending, the ancillary application must be made to the family proceedings court in whose area the applicant lives (or for an application under AA 1976, s 28, in whose area the child lives). There is no standard form for such an application, which should be made by complaint. If there is already an ancillary application pending, a further application concerning the home of the child must be made to the family proceedings court which is seised of the first application.

Respondents (r 27(3))—It is the responsibility of the applicant to ensure that the correct respondents are served with a copy of the complaint (see *Re L (A Minor) (Adoption: Procedure)* [1991] 1 FLR 171).

Serial number (r 27(4))—See generally under r 14. If there is no adoption application pending, a prospective adopter may apply for a serial number under this rule to preserve anonymity.

Reporting officer—For the appointment and duties of the reporting officer, see r 17.

Children's guardian—For the appointment and duties of the children's guardian, see r 18.

Issue of adoption application (r 27(6))—See under Adoption Rules 1984, r 47(7).

Justices' clerk (r 27(10))—A justices' clerk has jurisdiction to determine an application under this rule (see further under r 5).

"warrant form as per section 102 of the 1989 Act" (r 27(11))—The form of warrant under CA 1989, s 102 is prescribed by Family Proceedings Courts (Children Act 1989) Rules 1991, Sch 1, Form CHA63.

28 Amendment and revocation of orders

(1) Any application made under paragraph 4 of Schedule 1 to the 1976 Act for the amendment of an adoption order or the revocation of a direction to the Registrar General, or under section 52 of, and Schedule 2 to, the 1976 Act (or section 1(1) of the Adoption Act 1960), for the revocation of an adoption order, shall be in Form 9, and shall be made to a family proceedings court acting for the same petty sessions area as the family proceedings court which made the adoption order, by delivering it or sending it by post to the justices' chief executive.

(2) Notice of the application shall be given by the justices' chief executive to such persons (if any) as the court thinks fit.

(3) Where the application is granted, the justices' chief executive shall send to the Registrar General a notice specifying the amendments or informing him of the revocation and shall give sufficient particulars of the order to enable the Registrar General to identify the case.

Amendments—SI 1991/1991; SI 2001/615.

Scope of provision—Under Adoption Act 1976, Sch 1, para 4, the court which made an adoption order may, on the application of the adopter or the adopted person, amend the order by the correction of any error in the particulars contained within it. The adopted child's name may be changed within one year of the making of the adoption order. This rule makes provision for the procedure for the amendment of orders and the rectification of the Registers. The procedure also applies to applications for the revocation of adoptions on a subsequent legitimation under AA 1976, s 52.

Notice (r 28(2))—Unlike the rules applicable to the High Court or county courts, applications for amendment and revocation may not be dealt with ex parte in a magistrates' court.

28A Power of court to limit cross examination

The court may limit the issues on which a children's guardian or a reporting officer may be cross-examined.

Amendments—Inserted by SI 2001/820.

29 Service of documents

(1) Unless otherwise directed, any document under these rules may be served –

(*a*) on a corporation or body of persons, by delivering it at, or sending it by post to, the registered or principal office of the corporation or body;

(*b*) on any other person, by delivering it to him, or by sending it by post to him at his usual or last known address.

(2) A note of service or non-service shall be endorsed on a copy of Form 3 or Form 8.

(3) In the case of a document sent by post to a person's usual or last known address in accordance with paragraph (1)(*b*), the court may treat service as having been effected notwithstanding that the document has been returned undelivered.

Defined terms—"body of persons": Adoption Act 1976, s 72(1).

Scope of provision—This rule governs the service of documents in all magistrates' court proceedings under AA 1976; however, it lacks the detail and refinement of the corresponding provision within Family Proceedings Courts (Children Act 1989) Rules 1991, r 8.

Post (r 29(1))—The class of post is not specified. If first-class post is used, service may be deemed to have been achieved on the second business day after posting (by analogy with FPC(CA 1989)R 1991, r 8(6)(*a*)). This rule does not provide for service via facsimile transmission or via the document exchange.

30 Costs

(1) On the determination of an application or on the making of an interim order, the court may make such order as to the costs as it thinks just and, in particular, may order the applicant to pay –

(*a*) the expenses incurred by the reporting officer and the children's guardian (if appointed), and (*b*) the expenses incurred by any respondent in attending the hearing,

or such part of those expenses as the court thinks proper.

(2) Determination of an application in this rule includes a refusal to proceed with the application or withdrawal of the application.

Amendments—SI 2001/820.

Scope of provision—This order gives the court power to order the payment of costs and expenses. Although the power to order costs is available, it is rarely exercised in adoption proceedings. Note that the power is exercisable even where there has been a refusal to proceed with the application, or the application has been withdrawn (r 30(2)).

31 Notice and copies of orders etc

(1) In applications to which these rules apply orders shall be made in the form indicated in this paragraph –

Description of order	*Form*
(*a*) Order under section 18 of the 1976 Act	10
(*b*) Order under section 20 of the 1976 Act	11
(*c*) Interim order	12
(*d*) Adoption order	13

(2) Where an adoption order is made by a court sitting in Wales in respect of a child who was born in Wales (or is treated under rule 24(4) as having been born in the registration district and sub-district in which that court sits) and the adopter so requests before the order is drawn up, the justices' chief executive shall supply a translation into Welsh of the particulars set out in the order.

(3) Within 7 days of the making of an order in an application to which these rules apply, the justices' chief executive shall send a copy of the order (and of any translation into Welsh required to be supplied under paragraph (2)) to the applicant.

(4) Within 7 days of the making of an adoption order, the justices' chief executive shall send a copy of the order (and of any translation into Welsh supplied under paragraph (2)) to the Registrar General; where a translation into Welsh under paragraph (2) has been supplied, the English text shall prevail.

(5) Where an order to which paragraph 1(*a*), (*b*) or (*d*) applies is made or refused or an order to which paragraph 1(*c*) applies is made, the justices' chief executive shall serve notice to that effect on every respondent.

(6) (*revoked*)

(7) The justices' chief executive shall serve notice of the making of an order to which paragraph 1(*a*), (*b*) or (*d*) applies on any court in Great Britain which appears to him to have made any such order as is referred to in section 12(3) of the 1976 Act (orders relating to the parental responsibility for, and the maintenance of, the child).

(8) A copy of any order may be supplied to the Registrar General at his request.

(9) A copy of any order may be supplied to the applicant.

(10) A copy of any order may be supplied to any other person with the leave of the court.

Amendments—SI 1991/1991; SI 2001/615.

Scope of provision—This rule makes provision for the drafting of orders in proceedings under the Adoption Act 1976. Orders must be drawn in accordance with the appropriate form in Sch 1.

32 Keeping of registers, custody, inspection and disclosure of documents and information

(1) Such part of the register kept in pursuance of rules made under the Magistrates' Courts Act 1980, as relates to proceedings under Part II of the 1976 Act shall be kept in a separate book and shall contain the particulars shown in Form 14 and the book shall not contain particulars of any other proceedings except proceedings under the 1976 Act (or under any previous enactment relating to adoption).

(2) Any declaration by a parent or guardian or a former parent of a child that he prefers not to be involved in future questions concerning the adoption of the child which is required to be recorded by the court in accordance with sections 18(6) or 19(4) of the 1976 Act shall be recorded in the book kept in pursuance of paragraph (1).

(3) The book kept in pursuance of paragraph (1) and all other documents relating to proceedings mentioned in that paragraph shall, while they are in the custody of the court, be kept in a place of special security.

(4) A party who is an individual and is referred to in a confidential report supplied to the court by an adoption agency, a local authority, a reporting officer or a children's guardian may, for the purposes of the hearing, be supplied with a copy of that part of any such report which refers to him, subject to any direction given by the court that –

(*a*) no part of one or any of the reports shall be revealed to that party, or
(*b*) the part of one or any of the reports referring to that party shall be revealed only to that party's legal advisers, or
(*c*) the whole or any other part of one or any of the reports be revealed to that party.

(5) Any person who obtains any information in the course of, or relating to, any proceedings mentioned in paragraph (1), shall treat that information as confidential and shall only disclose it if –

(*a*) the disclosure is necessary for the proper exercise of his duties, or
(*b*) the information is requested –
  (i) by a court or public authority (whether in Great Britain or not) having power to determine adoptions and related matters, for the purpose of the discharge of its duties in that behalf, or
  (ii) by the Registrar General, or a person authorised in writing by him, where the information requested relates only to the identity of any adoption agency which made the arrangements for placing the child for adoption in the actual custody of the applicants, and of any local authority which was notified of the applicant's intention to apply for an adoption order in respect of the child, or
  (iii) by a person who is authorised in writing by the Lord Chancellor to obtain the information for the purposes of research.

(5A) Nothing in this rule shall prevent the disclosure of a document prepared by an officer of the service for the purpose of –

(*a*) enabling a person to perform functions required under section 62(3A) of the Justices of the Peace Act 1997; and

PART III

(*b*) assisting an officer of the service who is appointed by the court under any enactment to perform his functions.

(5B) Nothing in this rule shall prevent the disclosure of any document relating to proceedings by an officer of the service to any other officer of the service unless that other officer is involved in the same proceedings but on behalf of a different party.

(6) Save as required or authorised by a provision of any enactment or of these Rules or with the leave of the court, no document or order held by or lodged with the court in proceedings under the 1976 Act (or under any previous enactment relating to adoption) shall be open to inspection by any person, and no copy of any such document or order, or of an extract from any such document or order, shall be taken by or issued to any person.

Amendments—SI 1991/1991; SI 1992/709; SI 2001/820.

Defined terms—"adoption agency": r 2(1) (see also Adoption Act 1976, s 1(4)).

Scope of provision—This rule requires a magistrates' court to discharge its duty (under the Magistrates' Courts Act 1980) of maintaining a record of proceedings under AA 1976 by recording the information in a separate book from other court proceedings (r 32(1)–(3)).

Inspection by an individual (r 32(4))—See **Confidential reports** under Adoption Rules 1984, r 5.

Reporting officer—For the appointment and duties of the reporting officer, see rr 5 and 17.

Children's guardian—For the appointment and duties of the children's guardian, see rr 6 and 18.

Confidential information (r 32(5))—See under AR 1984, r 53.

"disclosure is necessary" (r 32(5)(*a*))—See under AR 1984, r 53.

33 Proceedings to be by way of complaint etc

Save in so far as special provision is made by these Rules, proceedings on an application shall be regulated in the same manner as proceedings on complaint, and accordingly for the purposes of this rule the application shall be deemed to be a complaint, the applicant to be a complainant, the respondents to be defendants and any notice served under these rules to be a summons; but nothing in this rule shall be construed as enabling a warrant of arrest to be issued for failure to appear in answer to any such notice.

Defined terms—"complaint": Magistrates' Courts Rules 1981, r 4.

Scope of provision—Unlike proceedings under CA 1989, which are commenced by application, proceedings before magistrates under the Adoption Act 1976 are deemed to be by complaint and therefore subject to the general provisions of the Magistrates' Courts Rules 1981, in particular r 4.

****

SCHEDULE 2

MATTERS TO BE COVERED IN REPORTS SUPPLIED UNDER RULES 4(4), 22(1) OR 22(2)

So far as is practicable, the report supplied by the adoption agency or, in the case of a report supplied under rule 22(2), the local authority shall include all the following particulars –

1 The Child

(*a*) Name, sex, date and place of birth and address;
(*b*) whether the child's father and mother were married to each other at the time of his birth;
(*c*) nationality;
(*d*) physical description;
(*e*) personality and social development;
(*f*) religion, including details of baptism, confirmation or equivalent ceremonies;
(*g*) details of any wardship proceedings and of any court orders relating to parental responsibility for the child or to maintenance and residence;
(*h*) details of any brothers and sisters, including dates of birth, arrangements concerning with whom they are to live and whether any brother or sister is the subject of a parallel application;
(*i*) extent of contract with members of the child's natural family and, if the father and mother of the child were not married to each other at the time of his birth, his father, and in each case the nature of the relationship enjoyed;
(*j*) if the child has been looked after by or is in the care of a local authority or has been cared for by a voluntary organisation, details (including dates) of any placements with foster parents, or other arrangements in respect of the care of the child, including particulars of the persons with whom the child has had his home and observations on the care provided;
(*k*) date and circumstances of placement with prospective adopter;
(*l*) names, addresses and types of schools attended with dates, and educational attainments;
(*m*) special needs in relation to the child's health (whether physical or mental) and his emotional and behavioural development and whether he is subject to a statement under the Education Act 1981;
(*n*) what, if any, rights to or interests in property or any claim to damages, under the Fatal Accidents Act 1976 or otherwise, the child stands to retain or lose if adopted;
(*o*) wishes and feelings in relation to adoption and the application, including any wishes in respect of religious and cultural upbringing; and
(*p*) any other relevant information which might assist the court.

2 Each Natural Parent, including where appropriate the father who was not married to the child's mother at the time of his birth

(*a*) Name, date and place of birth and address;
(*b*) marital status and date and place of marriage (if any);
(*c*) past and present relationship (if any) with the other natural parent, including comments on its stability;
(*d*) physical description;

(*e*) personality;
(*f*) religion;
(*g*) educational attainments;
(*h*) past and present occupations and interests;
(*i*) so far as available, names and brief details of the personal circumstances of the parents and any brothers and sisters of the natural parent, with their ages or ages at death;
(*j*) wishes and feelings in relation to adoption and the application, including any wishes in respect of the child's religious and cultural upbringing;
(*k*) reasons why any of the above information is unavailable; and
(*l*) any other relevant information which might assist the court.

3 Guardian

Give the details required under paragraph 2(*a*), (*f*), (*j*), and (*l*).

4 Prospective Adopter

(*a*) Name, date and place of birth and address;
(*b*) relationship (if any) to the child;
(*c*) marital status, date and place of marriage (if any) and comments on stability of relationship;
(*d*) details of any previous marriage;
(*e*) if a parent and step-parent are applying, the reason why they prefer adoption to a residence order;
(*f*) if a natural parent is applying alone, the reasons for the exclusion of the other parent;
(*g*) if a married person is applying alone, the reasons for this;
(*h*) physical description;
(*i*) personality;
(*j*) religion, and whether willing to follow any wishes of the child or his parents or guardian in respect of the child's religious and cultural upbringing;
(*k*) educational attainments;
(*l*) past and present occupations and interests;
(*m*) particulars of the home and living conditions (and particulars of any home where the prospective adopter proposes to live with the child, if different);
(*n*) details of income and comments on the living standards of the household;
(*o*) details of other members of the household (including any children of the prospective adopter even if not resident in the household);
(*p*) details of the parents and any brothers or sisters of the prospective adopter, with their ages or ages at death;
(*q*) attitudes to the proposed adoption of such other members of the prospective adopter's household and family as the adoption agency or, as the case may be, the local authority considers appropriate;
(*r*) previous experience of caring for children as step-parent, foster parent, childminder or prospective adopter and assessment of ability in this respect, together where appropriate with assessment of ability in bringing up the prospective adopter's own children;
(*s*) reasons for wishing to adopt the child and extent of understanding of the nature and effect of adoption;
(*t*) any hopes and expectations for the child's future;
(*u*) assessment of ability to bring up the child throughout his childhood;
(*v*) details of any adoption allowance payable;

(*w*) confirmation that any referees have been interviewed, with a report of their views and opinion of the weight to be placed thereon; and

(*x*) any other relevant information which might assist the court.

5 Actions of the adoption agency or local authority supplying the report

(*a*) Reports under rules 4(4) or 22(1) –

(i) brief account of the agency's actions in the case, with particulars and dates of all written information and notices given to the child, his natural parents and the prospective adopter;

(ii) details of alternatives to adoption considered;

(iii) reasons for considering that adoption would be in the child's best interests (with date of relevant decision); and

(iv) reasons for considering that the prospective adopter would be suitable to be an adoptive parent and that he would be suitable for this child (with dates of relevant decisions) or, if the child has not yet been placed for adoption, reasons for considering that he is likely to be so placed;

OR

(*b*) Reports under rule 22(2) –

(i) confirmation that notice was given under section 18 of the 1975 Act, with the date of that notice;

(ii) brief account of the local authority's actions in the case; and

(iii) account of investigations whether child was placed in contravention of section 11 of the 1976 Act.

6 Generally

(*a*) Whether any respondent appears to be under the age of majority or under a mental disability; and

(*b*) whether, in the opinion of the body supplying the report, any other person should be made a respondent (for example, a person who was not married to the mother of the child at the time of his birth and who claims to be the father of the child, a spouse or ex-spouse of a natural parent, a relative of a deceased parent, or a person with parental responsibility).

7 Conclusions

(This part of the report should contain more than a simple synopsis of the information above. As far as possible, the court should be given a fuller picture of the child, his natural parents and, where appropriate, the prospective adopter.)

(*a*) Except where the applicant or one of them is a parent of the child, a summary by the medical adviser to the body supplying the report, of the health history and state of health of the child, his natural parents and, if appropriate, the prospective adopter, with comments on the implications for the order sought and on how any special health needs of the child might be met;

(*b*) opinion on whether making the order sought would be in the child's best long-term interests, and on how any special emotional, behavioural and educational needs of the child might be met;

(*c*) opinion on the effect on the child's natural parents of making the order sought;

(*d*) if the child has been placed for adoption, opinion on the likelihood of full integration of the child into the household, family and community of the prospective adopter, and on whether the proposed adoption would be in the best long-term interests of the prospective adopter;

(*e*) opinion if appropriate, on the relative merits of adoption and a residence order; and

(*f*) final conclusions and recommendations whether the order sought should be made (and, if not, alternative proposals).

Amendments—SI 1989/384; SI 1991/1991.

SCHEDULE 3

REPORTS ON THE HEALTH OF THE CHILD AND OF THE APPLICANT(S)

This information is required for reports on the health of a child and of his prospective adopter(s). Its purpose is to build up a full picture of their health history and current state of health, including strengths and weaknesses. This will enable the local authority's medical adviser to base his advice to the court on the fullest possible information, when commenting on the health implications of the proposed adoption. The reports made by the examining doctor should cover, as far as practicable, the following matters.

1 The Child

Name, date of birth, sex, weight and height.

(*a*) A health history of each natural parent, so far as is possible, including –

(i) name, date of birth, sex, weight and height;

(ii) a family health history, covering the parents, the brothers and sisters and the other children of the natural parent, with details of any serious physical or mental illness and inherited and congenital disease;

(iii) past health history, including details of any serious physical or mental illness, disability, accident, hospital admission or attendance at an out-patient department, and in each case any treatment given;

(iv) a full obstetric history of the mother, including any problems in the ante-natal, labour and post-natal periods, with the results of any tests carried out during or immediately after pregnancy;

(v) details of any present illness including treatment and prognosis;

(vi) any other relevant information which might assist the medical adviser; and

(vii) the name and address of any doctor(s) who might be able to provide further information about any of the above matters.

(*b*) A neo-natal report on the child, including –

(i) details of the birth, and any complications;

(ii) results of a physical examination and screening tests;

(iii) details of any treatment given;

(iv) details of any problems in management and feeding;

(v) any other relevant information which might assist the medical adviser; and

(vi) the name and address of any doctor(s) who might be able to provide further information about any of the above matters.

(*c*) A full health history and examination of the child, including –
   (i) details of any serious illness, disability, accident, hospital admission or attendance at an out-patient department, and in each case any treatment given;
   (ii) details and dates of immunisations;
   (iii) a physical and developmental assessment according to age, including an assessment of vision and hearing and of neurological, speech and language development and any evidence of emotional disorder;
   (iv) for a child over five years of age, the school health history (if available);
   (v) any other relevant information which might assist the medical adviser; and
   (vi) the name and address of any doctor(s) who might be able to provide further information about any of the above matters.

(*d*) The signature, name, address and qualifications of the registered medical practitioner who prepared the report, and the date of the report and of the examinations carried out.

2 The Applicant

(If there is more than one applicant, a report on each applicant should be supplied covering all the matters listed below.)

(*a*) (i) name, date of birth, sex, weight and height;
   (ii) a family health history, covering the parents, the brothers and sisters and the children of the applicant, with details of any serious physical or mental illness and inherited and congenital disease;
   (iii) marital history, including (if applicable) reasons for inability to have children;
   (iv) past health history, including details of any serious physical or mental illness, disability, accident, hospital admission or attendance at an out-patient department, and in each case any treatment given.
   (v) obstetric history (if applicable);
   (vi) details of any present illness, including treatment and prognosis;
   (vii) a full medical examination;
   (viii) details of any daily consumption of alcohol, tobacco and habit-forming drugs;
   (ix) any other relevant information which might assist the medical adviser; and
   (x) the name and address of any doctor(s) who might be able to provide further information about any of the above matters.

(*b*) The signature, name, address and qualifications of the registered medical practitioner who prepared the report, and the date of the report and of the examinations carried out.

Magistrates' Courts (Attachment of Earnings) Rules 1971, SI 1971/809

ARRANGEMENT OF RULES

****

2 Interpretation

(1) Sections 2 and 25(1) of the Act shall apply to the interpretation of these Rules as they apply to the interpretation of the Act.

(2) The Interpretation Act 1978 shall apply to the interpretation of these Rules as it applies to the interpretation of an Act of Parliament.

(3) Any reference in these rules to "the Act" is a reference to the Attachment of Earnings Act 1971.

(4) Any reference in these Rules to any enactment or rule is a reference to that enactment or rule as amended by any enactment or rule.

(5) Any reference in these Rules to a form in the Schedule to these Rules shall include a reference to a form to the like effect with such variations as the circumstances may require.

(6) Any reference in these Rules to an attachment of earnings order shall be construed subject to the provisions of Rule 23.

****

4 Jurisdiction as respects complaints for an attachment of earnings order

A magistrates' court shall have the jurisdiction to hear a complaint for an attachment of earnings order if it would have jurisdiction to enforce payment of any arrears under the related maintenance order.

Defined terms—"maintenance order": r 2(1), Attachment of Earnings Act 1971, s 2(*a*), Sch 1.

Scope of provision—Jurisdiction is no longer dependent on the power to enforce a periodical payments order as a result of the amendment of Attachment of Earnings Act 1971, s 3(3) by Maintenance Enforcement Act 1991, Sch 2, paras 3, 4. An attachment of earnings order may now be made on the making, variation, registration or confirmation of a range of orders; these additional powers are noted against the relevant statutory provisions.

5 Attachment of earnings order

An attachment of earnings order shall be in the form numbered 1 in the Schedule to these Rules.

6 Service of orders and notices

(1) Where a magistrates' court makes an attachment of earnings order or an order varying or discharging such an order, the justices' chief executive for the court shall cause a copy of the order to be served on the employer and shall send a copy of the order to the debtor.

(2) Where an attachment of earnings order made by a magistrates' court ceases to have effect as provided in section 8 or 11 of the Act, notice of cessation shall be given to the employer.

(3) The notice required by the preceding paragraph shall be given by the justices' chief executive for the magistrates' court –

(*a*) which made or confirmed the maintenance order (in a case to which section 11(1)(*c*) of the Act applies);
(*b*) in which the maintenance order is registered under any enactment (in a case to which section 11(1)(*a*), (*b*) or (*d*) of the Act applies); or
(*c*) which issued the warrant of commitment or exercised the power conferred by section 77(2) of the Magistrates' Courts Act 1980 (in a case to which section 8 of the Act applies).

Amendments—SI 2001/615.

Defined terms—"the employer": Attachment of Earnings Act 1971, s 25(1); "maintenance order": r 2(1), AEA 1971, s 2(*a*), Sch 1.

7 Particulars of debtor

The particulars of the debtor for the purpose of enabling him to be identified which, so far as they are known, are to be included in an attachment of earnings order under section 6(3) of the Act shall be –

(*a*) full name and address;
(*b*) place of work;
(*c*) nature of work and works number, if any.

8 Notice of application for appropriate variation order

The justices' chief executive for a magistrates' court, by which an application under section 10 of the Act for the appropriate variation of an attachment of earnings order is to be heard, shall give notice in writing of the time and place appointed for the hearing of the application to the person entitled to receive payment under the related maintenance order (whether directly or through the officer of any court).

Amendments—SI 2001/615.

Defined terms—"maintenance order": r 2(1), Attachment of Earnings Act 1971, s 2(*a*). Sch 1.

9 Jurisdiction as respects complaints for the discharge and variation of attachment of earnings order

(1) This Rule shall apply to a complaint for the discharge or variation of an attachment of earnings order except where the related maintenance order –

(*a*) is an affiliation order to which section 88(2)(*a*) of the Children and Young Persons Act 1933 applies;
(*b*) is an order made under section 87 of that Act;
(*c*) is an order made under section 43 of the National Assistance Act 1948;
(*d*) is an order made under section 30 of the Children and Young Persons Act 1963.

(2) Where a complaint is made to a justice of the peace acting for the same petty sessions area as the court which made the attachment of earnings order and it appears to him that –

(*a*) the person in whose favour the attachment of earnings order was made, or
(*b*) the debtor,

is for the time being in some petty sessions area other than that for which the justice is acting, or that the complainant is the justices' chief executive for a magistrates' court acting for such other area, then, if it appears to the justice that the complaint may be more conveniently dealt with by a magistrates' court acting for that other area, he may cause the justices' chief executive for the court to send the complaint by post to the justices' chief executive for the other court and for that purpose shall write down the complaint, if this has not already been done.

(3) On receipt by the justices' chief executive for a magistrates' court of a complaint under the preceding paragraph, he shall bring the complaint before the court and the court shall issue a summons requiring the person appropriate under section 19(4) of the Act to appear before it, and shall hear and determine the complaint.

Amendments—SI 2001/615.

Defined terms—"maintenance order": r 2(1), Attachment of Earnings Act 1971, s 2(*a*), Sch 1.

Scope of provision—This rule has been substantially reduced in impact by amendments made by the Maintenance Enforcement Act 1991 (see r 4).

"justice of the peace" (r 9(2))—The same power applies where complaint is made to a justices' clerk (see r 22(2)(*b*)).

10 Complaints for variation or discharge of attachment of earnings orders against persons outside the United Kingdom

(1) Where a complaint for the variation or discharge of an attachment of earnings order is made against a person who resides outside the United Kingdom and that person does not appear at the time and place appointed for the hearing of the complaint, then, subject to paragraph (2) of this Rule, the court may, if it thinks it reasonable in all the circumstances to do so, proceed to hear and determine the complaint in accordance with section 20(3) of the Act if it is proved to the satisfaction of the court that the complainant has taken any of the following steps to give the person against whom the complaint is made notice of the complaint and of the time and place appointed for the hearing thereof, that is to say–

(*a*) has caused written notice of the matters aforesaid to be delivered to the said person;

(*b*) has caused written notice of the matters aforesaid to be sent by post addressed to the said person at his last known or usual place of abode or at his place of business or at some other address at which there is ground for believing that it will reach him; or

(*c*) has caused notice of the matters aforesaid to be inserted in one or more newspapers on one or more occasions.

(2) Where it is proposed to take any such steps as are mentioned in subparagraph (*b*) or (*c*) of the preceding paragraph, the complainant shall apply for directions to a justice of the peace acting for the same petty sessions area as the court by which the complaint is to be heard, and the taking of such steps shall be effective for the purposes of this Rule only if they were taken in accordance with the directions given by the said justice.

(3) Paragraph (1) of Rule 67 of the Magistrates' Courts Rules 1981 shall apply for the purposes of proving the delivery of a written notice in pursuance of sub-paragraph (*a*) of paragraph (1) of this Rule as it applies for the purpose of proving the service of a summons.

In relation to a solemn declaration made outside the United Kingdom, paragraph (1) of the said Rule 67, as applied by this paragraph, shall have effect as if for the reference to the authorities mentioned in the said paragraph (1) there were substituted a reference to a consular officer of Her Majesty's Government in the United Kingdom or any person for the time being authorised by law, in the place where the declarant is, to administer an oath for any judicial or other legal purpose.

(4) Paragraph (2) of the said Rule 67 shall apply for the purpose of proving the sending of a written notice in pursuance of sub-paragraph (*b*) of paragraph (1) of this Rule, or the insertion of a notice in a newspaper in pursuance of sub-paragraph (*c*) thereof, as it applies for the purpose of proving the service of any process, provided, as respects the insertion of a notice in a newspaper, that a copy of the newspaper containing the notice is annexed to the certificate.

"justice of the peace" (r 10(2))—Directions may also be given by a justices' clerk see (r 22(2)(*c*)).

11 Complaints by debtors for variation or discharge of attachment of earnings orders against persons who cannot be found

(1) Where a complaint by the debtor for the variation or discharge of an attachment of earnings order is made against a person and that person does not appear at the time or place appointed for the hearing of the complaint, then, subject to paragraph (2) of this Rule, the court may, if it thinks it reasonable in all the

circumstances to do so, proceed to hear and determine the complaint, notwithstanding the absence of proof that that person had knowledge of the summons as required by Rule 99 of the Magistrates' Court Rules 1981, if it is proved to the satisfaction of the court that the summons in respect of the complaint was served in accordance with the provisions of Rule 99 of those Rules and the complainant has caused notice of the complaint and of the time and place appointed for the hearing thereof to be inserted in one or more newspapers on one or more occasions.

(2) Where it is proposed to rely upon the provisions of the preceding paragraph of this Rule, the complainant shall apply for directions to a justice of the peace acting for the same petty sessions area as the court by which the complaint is to be heard, and the giving of notice in a newspaper shall be effective for the purposes of this Rule only if the notice was given in accordance with the directions given by the said justice.

(3) Paragraph (2) of Rule 67 of the Magistrates' Courts Rules 1981 shall apply for the purpose of proving the insertion of a notice in a newspaper in pursuance of paragraph (1) of this rule as it applies for the purpose of proving the service of any process, provided that a copy of the newspaper containing the notice is annexed to the certificate.

"justice of the peace" (r 11(2))—Directions may also be given by a justices' clerk (r 22(2)(*c*)).

12 Variation of attachment of earnings order on change of employment

Where an attachment of earnings order has lapsed under section 9(4) of the Act on the debtor's ceasing to be in the employment of the person to whom the order was directed and it appears to a magistrates' court, acting for the same petty sessions area as the court which made the order, that the debtor has subsequently entered the employment of a person (whether the same as before or another), the court may, of its own motion, vary the order by directing it to that person and may make any consequential amendment to the order made necessary by this variation.

"magistrates' court"—These powers may also be exercised by a justices' clerk (r 22(2)(*d*)).

13 Discharge of attachment of earnings order by court of its own motion

(1) Where it appears to a magistrates' court acting for the same petty sessions area as the magistrates' court which made the attachment of earnings order that the debtor is not in the employment of the person to whom the order is directed and that the likelihood of the debtor's entering the employment of any person is not such as to justify preserving the order, the court may, of its own motion, discharge the order.

(2) Where a magistrates' court has made an attachment of earnings order and, by virtue of section 7, 21 or 30 of the Matrimonial Proceedings and Property Act 1970, the related maintenance order ceases to have effect because of the remarriage of the person entitled to receive payments under it, a magistrates' court acting for the same petty sessions area as that court may, of its own motion, discharge the attachment of earnings order, if there are no arrears to be recovered.

"magistrates' court" (r 13(1))—This power of discharge may also be exercised by a justices' clerk (r 22(2)(*d*)).

14 Temporary variation of protected earnings rate

(1) A justice of the peace acting for the same petty sessions area as the magistrates' court which made the attachment of earnings order may, on a written application made by the debtor on the ground of a material change in the debtor's resources and needs since the order was made or last varied, by order (hereinafter referred to as a temporary variation order) vary the attachment of earnings order for a period of not more than four weeks by an increase of the protected earnings rate.

(2) A temporary variation order shall be in the form numbered 3 in the Schedule to these Rules.

(3) The justices' chief executive for the magistrates' court which made the attachment of earnings order shall cause a copy of any temporary order to be served on the employer and shall give him notice if the temporary variation order is discharged and the justices' chief executive shall also send a copy to the person entitled to receive payments under the related maintenance order (whether directly or through an officer of any court).

(4) Where an application for the variation or discharge of an attachment of earnings order is made to a magistrates' court and there is in existence a temporary variation order in respect of the attachment of earnings order, the court may, of its own motion, discharge the temporary variation order.

Amendments—SI 2001/615.

"justice of the peace" (r 14(1))—This power to vary may also be exercised by a justices' clerk (r 22(2)(*e*)).

****

18 Method of making payment under attachment of earnings order

(1) A justices' chief executive for a magistrates' court to whom any payment under an attachment of earnings order is to be made shall notify the employer and the person entitled to receive payments under the related maintenance order of the hours during which, and the place at which, payments are, subject to the provisions of this Rule, to be made and received.

(2) If an employer sends by post any payments under an attachment of earnings order to a justices' chief executive for a magistrates' court, he shall do so at his own risk and expense.

(3) A justices' chief executive for a magistrates' court may send by post any payment under an attachment of earnings order to the person entitled to receive payments under the related maintenance order at the request and at the risk of that person.

Amendments—SI 2001/615.

Defined terms—"the employer": Attachment of Earnings Act 1971, s 25(1).

19 Payments under attachment of earnings order after imprisonment imposed

(1) Where imprisonment or other detention has been imposed for the purpose of enforcing a maintenance order, the justices' chief executive for a magistrates' court to whom any payment under a related attachment of earnings order is to be made –

PART III

(*a*) in relation to such a payment shall be a person authorised to receive the said payment for the purposes of section 79(2) of the Magistrates' Courts Act 1980 (which relates to release from custody and reduction of detention on payment);

(*b*) on receiving such a payment shall notify the person authorised for the said purposes by Rule 55 of the Magistrates' Courts Rules 1981 of the sum received.

(2) Where a person receives notice of the receipt of a sum under the preceding paragraph of this Rule, he shall note the receipt of that sum on the warrant of commitment, if any, held by him.

Amendments—SI 2001/615.

20 Service of orders and notices

Where under section 14 of the Act (which relates to statements of earnings etc) an order is directed to the debtor or to a person appearing to be an employer of the debtor or where under these Rules a copy of an order is to be served or a notice is to given to any person –

(*a*) service may be effected on, or notice may be given to a person, other than a corporation, by delivering it to the person to whom it is directed or by sending it by post in a letter addressed to him at his last known or usual place of abode, or, in the case of an employer or a person appearing to be an employer of the debtor, at his place of business;

(*b*) service may be effected on, or notice given to, a corporation by delivering the document at, or sending it to –

(i) such office or place as the corporation may, for the purpose of this Rule, have specified in writing to the court in relation to the debtor or to a class or description of person to which he belongs, or

(ii) the registered office of the corporation if that office is in England and Wales or, if there is no registered office in England and Wales, any place therein where the corporation trades or conducts its business.

Defined terms—"the debtor": Attachment of Earnings Act 1971, s 2(*e*); "the employer": AEA 1971, s 25(1).

21 County court records

(1) Where a justices' chief executive for a magistrates' court causes a copy of an order or notice to be given to any person under Rule 6 of these Rules, he shall cause a copy of the order or notice to be given also to the proper officer of the county court for the district in which the debtor resides.

(2) Where the justices' chief executive for a magistrates' court which has made an attachment of earnings order is informed of a debtor's change of address, he shall notify the new address to the proper officer of the county court for the district in which the debtor resided before the change of address.

Amendments—SI 2001/615.

22 Justices' clerks

(1) The things specified in paragraph (2) of this Rule, being things authorised to be done by, to or before a single justice of the peace for a petty sessions area, may be done by, to or before the justices' clerk for that area.

(2) The things referred to in paragraph (1) above are –

(*a*) the power to make an order under section 14(1) or (2) of the Act (power of court to obtain statements of earnings, etc) before the hearing of an application to a magistrates' court for an attachment of earnings order, or for the variation or discharge of such an order;

(*b*) the determination that a complaint for the discharge or variation of an attachment of earnings order dealt with by a magistrates' court acting for another petty sessions area in accordance with Rule 9 of these Rules;

(*c*) the giving of directions under Rule 10 or 11 of these Rules;

(*d*) the discharge or variation by the court of its own motion of an attachment of earnings order in accordance with Rule 12 or 13 of these Rules;

(*e*) the temporary variation of an attachment of earnings order by an increase of the protected earnings rate in accordance with Rule 14 of these Rules;

(*f*) the making of an order under Rule 16 of these Rules (transfer of fines etc with view to making consolidated attachment order).

Defined terms—"single justice": Attachment of Earnings Act 1971, s 25(1).

****

Magistrates' Courts (Civil Jurisdiction and Judgments Act 1982) Rules 1986, SI 1986/1962

ARRANGEMENT OF RULES

PART I

CITATION, COMMENCEMENT AND INTERPRETATION

PART II

REGISTRATION OF MAINTENANCE ORDERS

PART I
CITATION, COMMENCEMENT AND INTERPRETATION

1 Citation and commencement

These Rules may be cited as the Magistrates' Courts (Civil Jurisdiction and Judgments Act 1982) Rules 1986 and shall come into operation on 1 January 1987.

"These Rules"—These rules contain detailed provisions for the application of the Civil Jurisdiction and Judgments Act 1982.

2 Interpretation

In these Rules –

"the 1982 Act" means the Civil Jurisdiction and Judgments Act 1982;
"the court's register", in relation to a justices' chief executive, means the register kept by the justices' chief executive in pursuance of Rule 66 of the Magistrates' Courts Rules 1981.

Amendments—SI 2001/615.

PART II
REGISTRATION OF MAINTENANCE ORDERS

3 The prescribed officer

The prescribed officer of a magistrates' court for the purposes of the 1982 Act and the Civil Jurisdiction and Judgments Order 2001 shall be the justices' clerk.

Amendments—SI 2002/194.

Defined terms—"the 1982 Act": r 2.

4 Registration of maintenance orders

(1) Where a justices' chief executive receives an application under Article 31 of the 1968 Convention for enforcement of a maintenance order made in a Contracting State other than the United Kingdom he shall, subject to Articles 27 and 28 of that Convention and to paragraph (3) and (4) of this Rule, cause the order to be registered in his court by means of a minute or memorandum entered and signed by him in the court's register.

(1A) Where a justices' chief executive receives an application under Article 38 of the Regulation for enforcement of a maintenance order made in a Regulation State other than the United Kingdom he shall, subject to Articles 34 and 35 of the Regulation and to paragraphs (3) and (4) of this Rule, cause the order to be registered in his court by means of a minute or memorandum entered and signed by him in the court's register.

(2) Before registering an order under paragraph (1) or (1A) of this Rule the justices' chief executive shall take such steps as he thinks fit for the purpose of ascertaining whether the payer under the order to which the application relates is residing within the jurisdiction of the court, and shall consider any information he possesses (whether provided by the applicant or otherwise) as to the nature and location of the payer's assets.

(3) If, after taking such steps and considering such information as are mentioned in paragraph (2) above, the justices' chief executive is satisfied that the payer under the order is not residing within the jurisdiction of the court he shall, subject to paragraph (4) of this Rule, refuse the application and return the documents relating thereto to the Lord Chancellor of State with a statement giving such information as he possesses as to the whereabouts of the payer and the nature and location of his assets.

(4) If, after taking such steps and considering such information as are mentioned in paragraph (2) above, the justices' chief executive is satisfied that the payer is not residing within the jurisdiction of the court but that there are assets against which, after registration in the High Court under Part I of the Maintenance Orders Act 1958, the order could be enforced, he shall cause the order to be registered in accordance with paragraph (1) or (1A) of this Rule.

Provided that where the justices' chief executive is of the opinion that the payer is residing within the jurisdiction of another magistrates court in England and Wales he may, if he thinks fit, and notwithstanding the provisions of this paragraph, refuse the application and return the documents relating thereto to the Lord Chancellor in accordance with paragraph (3) above.

(5) If the justices' chief executive refuses an application made under Article 31 of the 1968 Convention or under Article 38 of the Regulation, he shall cause notice of his decision to be sent to the applicant, at the address provided by the applicant.

(6) Where an order has been registered under paragraph (1) or (1A) of this Rule the justices' chief executive who was responsible for its registration shall cause a written notice stating that it has been duly registered in his court to be sent to –

(*a*) the Lord Chancellor;
(*b*) the payer under the order to which the registration relates;
(*c*) the applicant, at the address provided by the applicant.

(7) Where an order has been registered under paragraph (1) or (1A) of this Rule and the justices' chief executive who was responsible for its registration is of the opinion that the order, or a part thereof, is one which would be appropriate for enforcement in the High Court he shall notify the applicant accordingly and shall notify the applicant also of the possibility of an application by the applicant for registration of the whole or part of the order in the High Court under Part I of the Maintenance Orders Act 1958.

Amendments—SI 1992/709; SI 2001/615; SI 2002/194.

Defined terms—"Contracting State": CJJA 1982, s 1(3); "his register": r 2; "maintenance order": CJJA 1982, s 15(1); "the 1968 Convention": CJJA 1982, s 1(1).

PART III

5 Appeals from decision as to registration

An appeal under Article 36 or under Article 40 of the 1968 Convention or under Article 43 of the Regulation shall be by way of complaint to the magistrates' court in which the order is registered, or in which the application for its registration has been refused, as the case may be.

Amendments—SI 2002/194.

Defined terms—"the 1968 Convention": CJJA 1982, s 1(1).

6 Payment of sums due under a registered order

(1) When an order is registered under section 5(3) of the 1982 Act or under Article 38 of the Regulation, the court shall order that payment of sums due thereunder shall be made to the justices' chief executive for the registering court during such hours and at such place as that justices' chief executive may direct.

(1A) The justices' chief executive to whom payments are ordered to be made (whether by virtue of an order under paragraph (1) above or by virtue of an order of the court under the 1982 Act), shall send those payments by post to the court which made the order or to such other person or authority as that court or the Lord Chancellor may from time to time direct.

(2) Where it appears to a justices' chief executive to whom payments by way of periodical payments under any maintenance order are made that any sums payable under the order are in arrear he may and, if such sums are in arrear to an amount equal to four times the sum payable weekly, he shall, whether the person for whose benefit the payment should have been made requests him to do so or not, proceed in his own name for the recovery of those sums, unless it appears to him that it is unreasonable in the circumstances to do so.

(3) Without prejudice to the foregoing provisions of this Rule, the justices' chief executive of the registering court shall take reasonable steps to notify the person to whom payments are due under a registered order of the means of enforcement available in respect of it, including, in an appropriate case, the possibility of registration of the whole or part of the order in the High Court under Part I of the Maintenance Orders Act 1958.

Amendments—SI 1992/457; SI 1992/709; SI 2001/615; SI 2002/194.

Defined terms—"the 1982 Act": r 2.

6A (1) Where, in the exercise of the duty imposed under rule 6(1) above, or in the exercise of the powers conferred by virtue of section 5(5B) of the Act of 1982, the court orders that payments under the order are to be made by a particular means, the clerk of the court shall record on the order the means of payment which the court has ordered and the justices' chief executive shall notify in writing, as soon as practicable, the person liable to make payments under the order of how payments are to be made.

(2) Where, in the exercise of the aforesaid powers, the court orders payment to the justices' chief executive for the court, or to the justices' chief executive for any other magistrates' court, by a method of payment falling within section 59(6) of the Magistrates' Courts Act 1980 (standing order, etc), the justices' chief executive for the court to whom payments are to be made shall notify the person liable to make the payments under the order of the number and location of the account into which the payments are to be made.

Amendments—Inserted by SI 1992/457; amended by SI 2001/615; SI 2002/194.

Scope of provision—Rule 6A was added as a consequence of the Maintenance Enforcement Act 1991. Rule 6A(1) requires the clerk to record the method of payment and notify the payer accordingly (and the reference to "rule 9(1) above" should, presumably, read "rule 6(1) above"); r 6A(2) requires the justices' chief executive to notify the payer of the details of the account into which payments are to be made where an order for payment by standing order has been made.

7 Variation and revocation of registered orders

Where a maintenance order which has been registered for enforcement in a magistrates' court has been varied or revoked by an order made by a competent court in a Contracting State or a Regulation State the justices' chief executive for the court in which the order is registered shall, on receiving notice of the variation or revocation, register the order of variation or revocation by means of a minute or memorandum entered and signed by him in his register, and shall cause notice of the same to be given in writing by post to the payee and to the payer under the order to which the variation or revocation relates.

Amendments—SI 2001/615; SI 2002/194.

Defined terms—"Contracting State": CJJA 1982, s 1(3); "maintenance order": CJJA 1982, s 15(1).

8 Transfer of registered orders

(1) Where the justices' chief executive for the court where an order is registered is of the opinion that the payer under the registered order is residing within the jurisdiction of another magistrates' court in England and Wales he shall transfer the order to that other court by sending the information and documents relating to the registration of the order (that is, the information and documents required under Articles 46 and 47 of the Convention or under Article 53 of the Regulation, as appropriate) to the justices' chief executive for that other court, and shall cause notice of the same to be given to the payee under the order to which the transfer relates, and to the Lord Chancellor.

Provided that where an application is pending in the registering court for the registration of the whole or part of the order in the High Court under Part I of the Maintenance Orders Act 1958, the justices' chief executive shall not transfer the order, or such part of it to which the application relates, under this paragraph.

(2) On the transfer of an order under paragraph (1) above the justices' chief executive for the court to which it is transferred shall register the order in the like manner as if an application for registration had been received under Rule 4 of these Rules.

(3) The justices' chief executive who is required by the foregoing provisions of this Rule to send to the justices' chief executive for another court information and documents relating to the registration of an order shall send with that information and those documents –

- (*a*) a certificate of arrears, if applicable, signed by him;
- (*b*) a statement giving such information as he possesses as to the whereabouts of the payer and the nature and location of his assets; and
- (*c*) any other relevant documents in his possession relating to the case.

Amendments—SI 1992/709; SI 2001/615; SI 2002/194.

PART III

9 Cancellation of registered orders

Subject to Rule 8 of these Rules, where the justices' chief executive for the court where an order is registered is of the opinion that the payer under the registered order is not residing within the jurisdiction of that court and has no assets against which, after registration in the High Court under Part I of the Maintenance Orders Act 1958, the order could be enforced he shall cancel the registration of the order and shall cause notice of the same to be given to the payee under the order to which the cancellation relates and shall send the information and documents relating to the registration of the order (that is, the information and documents required under Articles 46 and 47 of the Convention or under Article 53 of the Regulation, as appropriate) to the Lord Chancellor, together with such information and documents as are referred to in Rule 8(3)(*a*), (*b*) and (*c*) of these Rules.

Amendments—SI 1992/709; SI 2001/615; SI 2002/194.

PART III
APPLICATIONS FOR MAINTENANCE UNDER ARTICLE 5(2) OF THE 1968 CONVENTION OR UNDER ARTICLE 5(2) OF THE REGULATION

10 Complaint against a person residing outside the United Kingdom

(1) This Rule applies where a complaint is made to a magistrates' court by a person who is domiciled or habitually resident in England and Wales against a person residing in a Contracting State or a Regulation State other than the United Kingdom, and the complaint is one in respect of which the court has jurisdiction to make a maintenance order by virtue of Article 5(2) of the 1968 Convention or Article 5(2) of the Regulation.

(2) On the making of a complaint to which paragraph (1) of this Rule applies, the following documents, that is to say –

(*a*) notice of the institution of the proceedings, including a statement of the grounds of the complaint;
(*b*) a statement signed by the justices' chief executive, giving such information as he possesses as to the whereabouts of the defendant;
(*c*) a statement giving such information as the justices' chief executive possesses for facilitating the identification of the defendant, and
(*d*) where available, a photograph of the defendant;

shall be sent by that clerk to the Lord Chancellor.

(3) The justices' chief executive shall give the defendant notice in writing of the date fixed for the hearing by sending the notice by post addressed to his last known or usual place of abode.

(4) Where the defendant makes any written representations or adduces any documentary evidence in advance of the hearing, a copy of the representations or evidence shall be served on the complainant by the justices' chief executive before the hearing.

(5) In considering whether or not to make a maintenance order pursuant to a complaint to which paragraph (1) of this Rule applies, where the defendant does not appear and is not represented at the hearing the court shall take into account any representations made and any evidence adduced by him or on his behalf under paragraph (4) above and, where the defendant does appear or is represented at the

hearing, the court may take any such representations or evidence into account in addition to any oral representations made or evidence adduced at the hearing.

(6) Where a maintenance order has been made under this Rule in respect of a complaint in relation to which the court has jurisdiction by virtue of Article 5(2) of the 1968 Convention, the justices' chief executive shall cause notice thereof to be given to the defendant by sending a copy of the order by post addressed to his last known or usual place of abode and, on application by the complainant, shall give to the complainant the following documents, that is to say –

(*a*) a certified copy of the order;

(*b*) a written statement signed by the justices' clerk as to whether or not the defendant appeared in the proceedings in which the order was made, and, if he did not appear, the original or a certified copy of a document which establishes that the document mentioned in paragraph (2)(*a*) of this Rule had been served on the defendant;

(*c*) a document which establishes that notice of the order was sent to the defendant; and

(*d*) a written statement signed by the justices' clerk as to whether or not the complainant received legal aid in the proceedings;

with a view to an application being made by the complainant for registration and enforcement under Articles 31 and 32 of the 1968 Convention.

(7) Where a maintenance order has been made under this Rule in respect of a complaint in relation to which the court has jurisdiction by virtue of Article 5(2) of the Regulation, the justices' chief executive shall cause notice thereof to be given to the defendant by sending a copy of the order by post addressed to his last known or usual place of abode and, on application by the complainant, shall give to the complainant the following documents –

(*a*) a certified copy of the order; and

(*b*) a completed certificate in the form of Annex V to the Regulation;

with a view to an application being made by the complainant for registration and enforcement under Articles 38 and 39 of the Regulation.

Amendments—SI 1992/709; SI 2001/615; SI 2002/194.

Defined terms—"Contracting State": CJJA 1982, s 1(3); "maintenance order": CJJA 1982, s 15(1); "the 1968 Convention": CJJA 1982, s 1(1).

11 Application for variation and revocation of a maintenance order

(1) This Rule applies where an application is made to a magistrates' court for the variation or revocation of a maintenance order where the payer under the order is residing in a Contracting State or a Regulation State other than the United Kingdom.

(2) Where an application to which this Rule applies is made by the payee, the following documents, that is to say –

(*a*) notice of the institution of the proceedings, including a statement of the grounds of the application;

(*b*) a statement signed by the justices' chief executive, giving such information as he possesses as to the whereabouts of the respondent;

(*c*) a statement giving such information as the clerk possesses for facilitating the identification of the respondent; and

(*d*) where available, a photograph of the respondent;

shall be sent by that justices' chief executive to the Lord Chancellor.

(3) Where an application to which this Rule applies is made by the payee –

(*a*) The justices' chief executive shall give the respondent notice in writing of the date fixed for the hearing by sending the notice by post addressed to his last known or usual place of abode;

(*b*) where the respondent makes any written representations or adduces any documentary evidence in advance of the hearing, a copy of the representations or evidence shall be served on the applicant by the justices' chief executive before the hearing;

(*c*) the court, in considering whether to vary or revoke the order, shall, where the payer does not appear and is not represented at the hearing, take into account any representations made and any evidence adduced by or on his behalf under sub-paragraph (*b*) above and, where the payer does appear or is represented at the hearing, the court may take any such representations or evidence into account, in addition to any oral representations or evidence adduced at the hearing.

(4) Where an application to which this Rule applies is made by the payer, the justices' chief executive shall arrange for the service of the document mentioned in paragraph (2)(*a*) of this Rule on the payee.

(5) Where upon an application to vary or revoke a maintenance order where the payer under the order is residing in a Contracting State the court varies or revokes the order, the justices' chief executive shall cause notice thereof to be given to the respondent by sending a copy of the order of variation or revocation by post addressed to his last known or usual place of abode and, on application by the applicant, shall give to the applicant the following documents, that is to say –

(*a*) a certified copy of the order of variation or revocation;

(*b*) a written statement, signed by the justices' clerk as to whether or not the respondent appeared in the proceedings for the variation or revocation of the order and if he did not appear the original or a certified copy of a document which establishes that the notice of the institution of the proceedings had been served on the respondent;

(*c*) a document which establishes that notice of the order of variation or revocation was sent to the respondent; and

(*d*) a written statement signed by the justices' clerk as to whether or not the applicant or the respondent received legal aid in the proceedings;

with a view to an application being made by the applicant for registration and enforcement of the order of variation or revocation under Articles 31 and 32 of the 1968 Convention.

(6) Where upon an application to vary or revoke a maintenance order where the payer under the order is residing in a Regulation State the court varies or revokes the order, the justices' chief executive shall cause notice thereof to be given to the respondent by sending a copy of the order of variation or revocation by post addressed to his last known or usual place of abode and, on application by the applicant, shall give to the applicant the following documents –

(*a*) a certified copy of the order of variation or revocation; and

(*b*) a completed certificate in the form of Annex V to the Regulation;

with a view to an application being made by the applicant for registration and enforcement of the order of variation or revocation under Articles 38 and 39 of the Regulation.

Amendments—SI 1992/709; SI 1993/617; SI 2001/615; SI 2002/194.

Defined terms—"Contracting State": CJJA 1982, s 1(3); "maintenance order", "payer": CJJA 1982, s 15(1); "the 1968 Convention": CJJA 1982, s 1(1).

12 Copies of, and certificates in connection with, maintenance orders

(1) Without prejudice to the provisions of Rules 10(6), 10(7), 11(5) and 11(6) of these Rules, a person wishing to obtain for the purposes of an application for recognition or enforcement in a Contracting State or a Regulation State a copy of a maintenance order made by a magistrates' court in England and Wales, and a certificate giving particulars relating to the order and the proceedings in which it was made, may apply in writing to the justices' chief executive for that court.

(2) An application under paragraph (1) above shall specify –

(*a*) the names of the parties to the proceedings in the magistrates' court;

(*b*) the date or approximate date of the proceedings in which the maintenance order was made, and the nature of those proceedings;

(*c*) the Contracting State or the Regulation State in which the application for recognition or enforcement has been made or is to be made;

(*d*) the postal address of the applicant.

(3) A justices' chief executive who receives an application under paragraph (1) of this Rule shall send by post to the applicant at the address indicated in the application for the purpose an authenticated copy of the order concerned.

(4) For the purposes of paragraph (3) of this Rule a copy of an order shall be deemed to be authenticated if it is accompanied by a statement signed by the justices' chief executive that it is a true copy of the order concerned and giving particulars of the proceedings in which it was made.

(5) A person wishing to obtain for the purposes of an application made or to be made in another Contracting State or in another Regulation State or in another part of the United Kingdom in connection with a maintenance order which is registered in a magistrates' court in England and Wales a certificate giving particulars of any payments made and any arrears which have accrued under the order while so registered may apply in writing to the justices' chief executive for the registering court, and a justices' chief executive who receives such an application shall send by post to the applicant at the address indicated in the application for the purposes a certificate giving the information so requested.

Amendments—SI 2001/615; SI 2002/194.

Defined terms—"Contracting State": CJJA 1982, s 1(3); "maintenance order": CJJA 1982, s 15(1).

PART IV
EVIDENCE IN MAINTENANCE PROCEEDINGS

13 Admissibility of documents

(1) Subject to paragraph (2) of this Rule, a statement contained in –

(*a*) a document which purports to set out or summarise evidence given in proceedings in a court in another part of the United Kingdom or another Contracting State or another Regulation State;

(*b*) a document which purports to have been received in evidence in proceedings in a court in another part of the United Kingdom or another Contracting State or another Regulation State;

(*c*) a document which purports to set out or summarise evidence taken in another part of the United Kingdom or in another Contracting State or another Regulation State for the purpose of proceedings in a court in England and Wales under the 1982 Act, whether in response to a request made by such a court or otherwise; or

(*d*) a document which purports to record information relating to the payments made under an order of a court in another part of the United Kingdom or another Contracting State or another Regulation State;

shall, in any proceedings in a magistrates' court in England and Wales relating to a maintenance order to which the 1982 Act applies, be admissible as evidence of any fact stated therein to the same extent as oral evidence of that fact is admissible in those proceedings.

(2) Paragraph (1) of this Rule shall not apply unless the document concerned has been made or authenticated by the court in the other part of the United Kingdom or the other Contracting State or the other Regulation State, as the case may be, or by a judge or official of that court, in accordance with paragraph (3), (4) or (5) of this Rule.

(3) A document purporting to set out or summarise evidence given as mentioned in paragraph (1)(*a*) above, or taken as mentioned in paragraph (1)(*c*) above, shall be deemed to be authenticated for the purposes of that paragraph if the document purports to be certified by the judge or official before whom the evidence was given or by whom it was taken, or to be the original document containing or recording or, as the case may be, summarising, the evidence or a true copy of that document.

(4) A document purporting to have been received in evidence as mentioned in paragraph (1)(*b*) above, or to be a copy of a document so received, shall be deemed to be authenticated for the purposes of that paragraph if the document purports to be certified by a judge or official of the court in question to be, or to be a true copy of, a document which has been so received.

(5) A document purporting to record information as mentioned in paragraph (1)(*d*) above shall be deemed to be authenticated for the purposes of that paragraph if the document purports to be certified by a judge or official of the court in question to be a true record of the payments made under the order concerned.

(6) It shall not be necessary in any proceedings in which evidence is to be received under this Rule to prove the signature or official position of the person appearing to have given such a certificate.

(7) Nothing in this Rule shall prejudice the admission in evidence of any document which is admissible in evidence apart from this Rule.

(8) Any request by a magistrates' court in England and Wales for the taking or providing of evidence by a court in another part of the United Kingdom or another Contracting State or another Regulation State for the purpose of proceedings under the 1982 Act or the Regulation shall be communicated in writing to the court in question.

Amendments—SI 2002/194.

Defined terms—"Contracting State": CJJA 1982, s 1(3); "maintenance order": CJJA 1982, s 15(1); "the 1982 Act": r 2.

14 Evidence for the purposes of proceedings outside England and Wales

(1) Subject to paragraph (2) below, where for the purposes of any proceedings in a court in another part of the United Kingdom or in a Contracting State or in a Regulation State other than the United Kingdom relating to a maintenance order a request is made by or on behalf of that court for the taking in England and Wales of evidence of a person residing therein relating to matters specified in the request, the following magistrates' courts shall have power to take that evidence, that is to say –

(*a*) where the maintenance order to which the proceedings in the court in the other part of the United Kingdom or Contracting State or Regulation State relate was made by a magistrates' court, the court which made the order;

(*b*) where the maintenance order to which those proceedings relate is registered in a magistrates' court, the court in which the order is registered;

(*c*) a magistrates' court which has received such a request from the Lord Chancellor.

(2) The power conferred by paragraph (1) above may, with the agreement of a court having that power, be exercised by any other magistrates' court which, because the person whose evidence is to be taken resides within its jurisdiction or for any other reason, the first mentioned court considers could more conveniently take the evidence; but nothing in this paragraph shall derogate from the power of any court specified in paragraph (1) above.

(3) Before taking the evidence of a person under paragraph (1) or (2) above, a magistrates' court shall give notice of the time and place at which the evidence is to be taken to such persons and in such manner as it thinks fit.

(4) Subject to paragraph (5) below, where the evidence of a person is to be taken by a magistrates' court under the foregoing provisions of this Rule –

(*a*) the evidence shall be taken in the same manner as if that person were a witness in proceedings on a complaint;

(*b*) any oral evidence so taken shall be put into writing and read to the person who gave it, who shall be required to sign the document; and

(*c*) the justices by whom the evidence of any person is so taken shall certify at the foot of any document setting out the evidence of, or produced in evidence by, that person that such evidence was taken, or a document received in evidence, as the case may be, by them.

(5) Where such a request as is mentioned in paragraph (1) above includes a request that the evidence be taken in a particular manner, the magistrates' court by which the evidence was taken shall, so far as circumstances permit, comply with that request.

(6) Any document such as is mentioned in paragraph (4)(*c*) above shall be sent to the court in the Contracting State or the Regulation State by or on behalf of which the request was made.

Amendments—SI 1992/709; SI 2002/194.

Defined terms—"Contracting State": CJJA 1982, s 1(3); "maintenance order": CJJA 1982, s 15(1).

Magistrates' Courts (Costs Against Legal Representatives in Civil Proceedings) Rules 1991, SI 1991/2096

1 Citation, commencement and interpretation

(1) These Rules may be cited as the Magistrates' Courts (Costs Against Legal Representatives in Civil Proceedings) Rules 1991 and shall come into force on 14 October 1991.

(2) In these Rules –

"interested party" means the party benefiting from the wasted costs order and, where he is a legally assisted person, within the meaning of section 2(11) of the 1988 Act, the Legal Aid Board;

"the 1988 Act" means the Legal Aid Act 1988;

"wasted costs order" means any action taken by a court under section 145A of the Magistrates' Courts Act 1980.

Scope of provision—These Rules make provision for costs to be disallowed, or a costs order to be made, against a legal or other representative, for the whole or any part of wasted costs incurred by a party in civil proceedings in magistrates' courts. Orders may be made by the court of its own motion or upon application, at any time within 6 months of the date upon which the relevant proceedings are disposed of by the court and only after giving the representative concerned a reasonable opportunity to make representations. Provision is also made for an appeal to the Crown Court against the making of a wasted costs order.

2 General

(1) A wasted costs order may provide that the whole or any part of the wasted costs incurred by a party shall be disallowed or (as the case may be) met by the legal or other representative concerned and the court shall specify the amount of such costs.

(2) Subject to paragraph (7) below, a court may make a wasted costs order either on the application of a party to the proceedings or on its own motion and when doing so the justices' clerk shall make a record of the order in writing, and the reasons for the decision of the court.

(3) Before making a wasted costs order, the court shall allow the legal or other representative a reasonable opportunity to appear before it and show cause why the order should not be made.

(4) Subject to paragraphs (5) and (6) below, any payments which are required to be made by a legal or other representative under a wasted costs order shall be made to the party who has incurred the wasted costs.

(5) Where the party who has incurred wasted costs is receiving assistance by way of representation under Part III of the 1988 Act and which has been approved under regulation 22 of the Legal Advice and Assistance Regulations 1989, any payments which are required to be made by a legal or other representative under a wasted costs order shall be paid to the justices' chief executive in accordance with regulation 31 of those Regulations.

(6) Where the party who has incurred wasted costs is being granted representation under Part IV of the 1988 Act, any payments which are required to be made by a legal or other representative under a wasted costs order shall be paid to the

justices' chief executive in accordance with regulation 89(*a*) of the Civil Legal Aid (General) Regulations 1989.

(7) A court shall not make a wasted costs order after the end of the period of six months beginning with the date on which the proceedings are disposed of by the court.

(8) Where a wasted costs order has been made, the justices' chief executive shall, as soon as practicable, serve a copy of the order on any interested party and on the legal or other representative concerned.

Amendments—SI 2001/615.

"Wasted costs"—Wasted costs includes costs incurred by a party as a result of any improper, unreasonable or negligent act or omission on the part of any legal or other representative (Magistrates' Courts Act 1980, s 145A(2)). For the meaning of "improper, unreasonable or negligent" and the procedure to be adopted see annotation to Civil Procedure Rules 1998, r 48.7.

"Legal or other representative"—Magistrates' Courts Act 1980, s 145A(3) defines "legal or other representative" as any person who is exercising a right of audience or a right to conduct litigation on behalf of any party to proceedings.

3 Appeals

(1) A legal or other representative against whom a wasted costs order is made may appeal to the Crown Court.

(2) Subject to paragraph (4) below, an appeal shall be instituted within 21 days of the wasted costs order being made by the appellant giving notice in writing to the justices' chief executive for the court which made the order, stating the grounds of appeal.

(3) The appellant shall, as soon as practicable after instituting the appeal, serve a copy of the notice and grounds of appeal, including any application for an extension of the time in which to appeal granted under paragraph (4) below, on any interested party.

(4) The time limit within which an appeal may be instituted may, for good reason, be extended before or after it expires by a judge of the Crown Court and, where it is so extended, the court to which the appeal is made shall give notice of the extension to the appellant, the justices' chief executive for the court which made the wasted costs order and any interested party.

(5) The court to which the appeal is made shall give notice of the hearing date to the appellant, the justices' chief executive for the court which made the wasted costs order and any interested party and shall allow the interested party to make representations either orally or in writing.

(6) The court hearing the appeal may affirm, vary or revoke the order as it thinks fit and shall notify its decision to the appellant, any interested party and the justices' chief executive for the court which made the order.

Amendments—SI 2001/615.

Magistrates' Courts (Family Law Act 1986) Rules 1988, SI 1988/329

****

6 Duty to give statement of other proceedings

(1) A party to proceedings for or relating to a Part I order in a magistrates' court in England and Wales who knows of other proceedings (including proceedings out of the jurisdiction and concluded proceedings) which relate to the child concerned shall provide to the court a statement giving the information set out in Form 2 in the Schedule to these Rules, and, for this purpose, the justices' chief executive for a magistrates' court in which proceedings for or relating to a Part I order are pending shall, as soon in those proceedings as may be practicable, notify the parties of the provisions of this rule by sending to each party a notice in the said Form 2 or in a similar form.

(2) Paragraph (1) above shall not apply in relation to proceedings commenced in a magistrates' court before 4 April 1988.

Amendments—SI 1991/1991; SI 2001/615.

"Part I order"—This term is defined by r 2(1) as meaning a Part I order within the meaning of any of ss 1, 32, 40 and 42(5) and (6) of the Family Law Act 1986. In relation to magistrates' courts in England and Wales, it means a s 8 order under CA 1989 other than an order varying or discharging such an order (Family Law Act 1986, s 1(1)(*a*), (2)(*a*)).

****

Magistrates' Courts (Guardianship of Minors) Rules 1974, SI 1974/706

1 Citation and commencement

These Rules may be cited as the Magistrates' Courts (Guardianship of Minors) Rules 1974 and shall come into operation on 8 May 1974.

2 Interpretation

(1) In these Rules, the following expressions have the meanings hereby respectively assigned to them, that is to say –

"the Act of 1949" means the Marriage Act 1949;
"court" means a magistrates' court except as provided by rule 9(9);
"the Rules of 1968" means the Magistrates' Courts Rules 1968, as amended.

(2) In these Rules, unless the context otherwise requires, any reference to a rule shall be construed as a reference to a rule contained in these Rules and any

reference in a rule to a paragraph shall be construed as a reference to a paragraph of that rule.

(3) (*repealed*)

(4) In these Rules, unless the context otherwise requires, any reference to any enactment shall be construed as a reference to that enactment as amended, extended or applied by any subsequent enactment.

(5) The Interpretation Act 1889 shall apply for the interpretation of these Rules as it applies for the interpretation of an Act of Parliament.

Amendments—SI 1989/384; SI 1991/1991.

"Magistrates' Courts Rules 1968" (r 2(1))—These rules have been revoked and replaced by the Magistrates' Courts Rules 1981; the reference to the 1968 Rules must now be read as a reference to the 1981 Rules (see Interpretation Act 1978, ss 17(2)(*a*), 23(1)).

"Interpretation Act 1889" (r 2(5))—This reference should be construed as a reference to the Interpretation Act 1978 (see s 25(2)).

****

5 Procedure for application for consent to marriage

(1) An application for the consent of the court to the marriage of a child under section 3 of the Act of 1949 (marriages of persons under 18) may be made, either orally or in writing, to a justice of the peace for the commission area in which the applicant or any respondent resides.

(2) Upon receiving such an application as is referred to in paragraph (1) the justice shall, where the application was in consequence of a refusal to give consent to the marriage, give to any person whose consent is required and who has refused consent a notice of the application and of the date, time and place appointed for the hearing thereof.

(3) Rule 82 of the Rules of 1968 (service of summons, etc) shall apply in relation to the service of a notice given in accordance with paragraph (2) as it applies in relation to the service of the summons issued on a person other than a corporation.

(4) The provisions of Part II of the Magistrates' Courts Act 1952 relating to the hearing of a complaint and of rule 14 of the Rules of 1968 (order of evidence and speeches) shall apply to the hearing of such an application as is referred to in paragraph (1) as if it were made by way of complaint but as if for any reference therein to the complainant, the complaint, the defendant and his defence there were substituted references, respectively, to the applicant, the application, the respondent and his case.

Amendments—SI 1980/1585; SI 1989/384.

Defined terms—"the Act of 1949", "court", "the Rules of 1968": r 2(1).

Jurisdiction—Marriage Act 1949, s 3(1) sets out a general rule that children (ie those under the age of 18) who are not widows or widowers may not marry under a superintendent registrar's certificate (or a common licence, see s 3(3)) without the consent of the persons mentioned in s 3(1A). However, this is subject to two provisos: first, where someone's consent cannot be obtained by reason of absence or disability and he is the only person whose consent is required, s 3(1)(*a*) allows the court, on application, to consent to the marriage; secondly, s 3(1)(*b*) provides as follows: "if any person whose consent is required refuses his consent, the court may, on application being made, consent to the marriage, and the consent of the court so given shall have the same effect as if it had been given by the person whose consent is refused". Section 1(5) provides that for the purposes of s 3, "the court" means the High Court, the county court of the district in which any applicant or respondent resides or a court of summary jurisdiction appointed for the commission area (within the meaning of the Justices of the Peace Act 1979) in which any applicant or respondent resides (for procedure on such an application in a county court or the High Court, see FPR 1991, r 3.20). Section 3(6) provides that "Nothing in this section shall dispense with the necessity of obtaining the consent of the High Court to the marriage of a ward of court". The practical effect of this is to exclude the jurisdiction of the magistrates' court by requiring an application to be made to the High Court or to any county court to which the wardship proceedings had been transferred under Matrimonial and Family Proceedings Act 1984, s 38(2)(*b*)). Technically, the consent under MA 1949, s 3(1)(*b*) is in addition to the common law requirement of the court's consent to the marriage of its ward; the former may still be sought from a magistrates' court in addition to seeking, separately, the leave of the wardship court, but it will be sensible to make a single application for both purposes to the wardship court.

"any person ... who has refused consent" (r 5(2))—This refers to those whose consent is required under MA 1949, s 3(1A). The description of those who consent is required varies according to the circumstances (eg where a care order is in force the consent of the local authority is required in addition to the consent of a parent or guardian) The requirements are set out in s 3(1A) as follows:

"(*a*) subject to paragraphs (*b*) to (*d*) of this subsection, the consent of:
(i) each parent (if any) of the child who has parental responsibility for him; and
(ii) each guardian (if any) of the child;

(*b*) where a residence order is in force with respect to the child, the consent of the person or persons with whom he lives, or is to live, as a result of the order (in substitution for the consents mentioned in paragraph (*a*) of this subsection);

(*c*) where a care order is in force with respect to the child, the consent of the local authority designated in the order (in addition to the consents mentioned in paragraph (*a*) of this subsection);

(*d*) where neither paragraph (*b*) nor (*c*) of this subsection applies but a residence order was in force with respect to the child immediately before he reached the age of sixteen, the consent of the person or persons with whom he lived, or was to live, as a result of the order (in substitution for the consents mentioned in paragraph (*a*) of this subsection)."

"Rule 82 of the Rules of 1968" (r 5(3))—This rule has been revoked and replaced by r 99 of the 1981 Rules.

"Part II of the Magistrates' Courts Act 1952" (r 5(4))—This has been repealed and replaced by Part II of the Magistrates' Courts Act 1980. In *R v Uxbridge Justices ex parte Commissioner of Police for the Metropolis* [1981] QB 829, [1981] 3 WLR 410, Sir George Baker P said that there is no power for a magistrates' court to make an order as to costs in applications under Marriage Act 1949, s 3, because the proceedings are by application and not by complaint. This was *obiter* in proceedings relating to police property, and the court does not seem to have had its attention drawn to the significance of the fact that Magistrates' Courts Act 1980, s 64 (empowering costs to be awarded in proceedings on complaint) is in Part II of the Act and thus, apparently, applied to applications by this rule. The dictum was repeated with approval in *R v Salisbury and Tisbury and Mere Combined Juvenile Court ex parte Ball* [1986] 1 FLR 1 (per Kennedy J at 4), but this was again *obiter* in other proceedings and the validity of the analogy with applications under MA 1949, s 3 was not evaluated.

"rule 14 of the Rules of 1968" (r 5(4))—This rule has been revoked and replaced by r 14 of the 1981 Rules.

****

Magistrates' Courts (Maintenance Orders Act 1958) Rules 1959, SI 1959/3

ARRANGEMENT OF RULES

PART I
PROCEDURE UNDER PART I OF THE ACT

PART III
MISCELLANEOUS AND SUPPLEMENTAL

PART I
PROCEDURE UNDER PART I OF THE ACT

1 Applications for registration under section 2(3) of the Act

An application for the registration in the High Court of a magistrates' court order need not be in writing or on oath.

Defined terms—"magistrates' court order": Maintenance Orders Act 1958, s 1(3).

2 Manner in which magistrates' court is to be satisfied as to various matters

(1) An applicant wishing to show, in accordance with section 2A(1) of the Act, that the order to which the application relates, though deemed to have been made by a magistrates' court in England, was in fact made in another part of the United Kingdom or a country or territory outside the United Kingdom and that by the law

of that part or of that country or territory interest is recoverable under the order may do so by producing the original court order or an authenticated copy thereof showing the date or time from which and the rate at which interest is so recoverable.

(2) For the purposes of paragraph (1) of this Rule, a copy shall be deemed to be authenticated if it purports to be certified by a judge or official of the court which made the original order to be a true copy of the original order, but it shall not be necessary to prove the signature or official position of the person appearing to have given such a certificate.

(3) Where an application for the registration in the High Court of a magistrates' court order is granted, the court shall be satisfied in the manner provided by paragraph (5) of this Rule that no process for the enforcement of the order issued before the grant of the application remains in force.

(4) Where the court receives notice given under section 5 of the Act (which relates to the cancellation of registration), the court shall be satisfied in the manner provided by paragraph (5) of this Rule that no process for the enforcement of the order issued before the giving of the notice remains in force and that no proceedings for the variation of the order are pending in a magistrates' court.

(5) For the purpose of satisfying the court as to the matters referred to in paragraphs (3) and (4) of this Rule –

(*a*) if the person through or to whom payments are ordered to be made is the justices' chief executive for a magistrates' court, there shall be produced a certificate in that behalf purporting to be signed by the justices' chief executive in the form numbered 1, 2 or 3, as the case may be, in the Schedule to these Rules;

(*b*) in any other case, there shall be produced a document purporting to be a statutory declaration in that behalf in the form numbered 5 or 6, as the case may be, in the Schedule to these Rules.

Amendments—SI 1986/1962; SI 2001/615.

Defined terms—"magistrates' court": Maintenance Orders Act 1958, s 21(1); "magistrates' court order": MOA 1958, s 1(3).

2A Receipt by magistrates' court of notice of registration in the High Court of order previously registered in magistrates' court

Where a magistrates' court receives from the High Court notice of the registration in the High Court of an order made by a sheriff court in Scotland or a court of summary jurisdiction in Northern Ireland and previously registered in that magistrates' court in accordance with s 17(4) of the Act of 1950, the justices' chief executive for the court shall cause the particulars of such notice to be entered in the register.

Amendments—Inserted by SI 1980/1896; amended by SI 2001/615.

Defined terms—"magistrates' court": Maintenance Orders Act 1958, s 21(1); "register": r 25(6); "registered": MOA 1958, s 1(3).

"Act of 1950"—Maintenance Orders Act 1950.

3 Copy of magistrates' court order sent to the High Court for registration

(1) Where an application for the registration of a magistrates' court order is granted and the court is satisfied that no process issued for the enforcement of the order before the grant of the application remains in force, the court shall, in accordance with paragraph (*c*) of subsection (4) of section two of the Act, cause the justices' chief executive to send a copy of the order, certified to be a true copy thereof in the form numbered 7 in the Schedule to these Rules to the appropriate officer of the High Court.

(2) Where the court is satisfied in accordance with Rule 1A above that interest is recoverable under the order in respect of which the application has been granted the court shall, in accordance with section 2A(1) of the Act, cause the justices' chief executive to send, together with the certified copy of the order mentioned in paragraph (1) of this rule, a certificate in respect of the interest so recoverable in the form numbered 4 in the Schedule to these Rules to the appropriate officer of the High Court.

Amendments—SI 1980/1896; SI 1986/1962; SI 2001/615.

Defined terms—"magistrates' court order": Maintenance Orders Act 1958, s 1(3).

PART III

4 Registration of High Court or county court order in a magistrates' court

Where a justices' chief executive for a magistrates' court in accordance with paragraph (*b*) of subsection (2) of section two of the Act receives from an officer of the High Court or the district judge of a county court a certified copy of a High Court or county court order, he shall cause the order to be registered in his court by means of a memorandum entered and signed by him in the register and shall send written notice to that officer of the High Court or the district judge of the county court, as the case may be, that it has been duly registered.

Amendments—SI 2001/615.

Defined terms—"certified copy": Maintenance Orders Act 1958, s 2(7); "magistrates' court": MOA 1958, s 21(1); "register": r 25(6); "registered": MOA 1958, s 1(3).

4A Registration in magistrates' court of order made in Court of Session or High Court in Northern Ireland

Where a justices' chief executive for a magistrates' court, in pursuance of section 2(2)(*b*) of the Act, receives from the appropriate officer of the original court in Scotland or Northern Ireland a certified copy of an order made by the Court of Session or the High Court in Northern Ireland, he shall cause the order to be registered in his court by means of a memorandum entered and signed by him in the register and shall send written notice to the appropriate officer of the High Court and to the appropriate officer of the original court that the order has been duly registered.

Amendments—Inserted by SI 1980/1896; amended by SI 2001/615.

Defined terms—"appropriate officer of the High Court", "appropriate officer of the original court": r 25(4); "certified copy": Maintenance Orders Act 1958, s 2(7); "magistrates' court": MOA 1958, s 21(1); "original court", "registered": MOA 1958, s 1(3).

5 Notices as respects payments through a justices' chief executive for a magistrates' court

(1) A notice under subsection (6ZC) of section 2 of the Act that the payments under a High Court or county court order or an order made by the Court of Session or the High Court in Northern Ireland have, on its registration in a magistrates' court, become payable through the justices' chief executive for a magistrates' court shall be given by the justices' chief executive for the court of registration in the form numbered 8 in the Schedule to these Rules.

(2) A notice under subsection (6ZC) of section 2 of the Act that the payments under a magistrates' court order or an order made by a sheriff court in Scotland or a court of summary jurisdiction in Northern Ireland and registered in a magistrates' court under Part II of the Act of 1950 have, on its registration in the High Court, ceased to be payable to a justices' chief executive for a magistrates' court shall be given by the justices' chief executive for the administering court and shall be in the form numbered 9 in the Schedule to these Rules and, where payments have been payable through a justices' chief executive other than the justices' chief executive for the administering court, he shall send a copy of the said notice to that other justices' chief executive.

(3) A notice under subsection (5)(*b*) of section 5 of the Act that the registration in a magistrates court of a High Court or county court order or an order made by the Court of Session or the High Court in Northern Ireland has been cancelled and that payments thereunder have ceased to be payable through a justices' chief executive for a magistrates' court shall be given by the justices' chief executive for the court of registration and shall be in the form numbered 10 in the Schedule to these Rules and, where payments have been payable through a justices' chief executive other than the justices' chief executive for the court of registration, he shall send a copy of the said notice to that other justices' chief executive.

(4) A notice given in accordance with the preceding provisions of this Rule shall be delivered to the person liable to make payments under the order to which the notice relates or sent by post to that person at his last known address.

Amendments—SI 1980/1896; SI 1992/457; SI 2001/615.

Defined terms—"administering court": r 25(5); "county court order", "High Court order": Maintenance Orders Act 1958, s 1(3); "magistrates' court": MOA 1958, s 21(1); "registered": MOA 1958, s 1(3).

5A (1) Where, in the exercise of the duty imposed by section 2(6ZA)(*b*) of the Act, or in the exercise of the powers conferred by section 3(2A) or (2B) or section 4(2A), (5A) or (5B) of the Act, a magistrates' court orders that payments under a registered order are to be made by a particular means, the clerk of the court shall record on the copy of the order the means of payment which the court has ordered and the justices' chief executive shall notify in writing, as soon as practicable, the person liable to make payments under the order of how payments are to be made.

(2) Where, in the exercise of any of the aforesaid powers, the court orders that payments be made by the debtor to the creditor or by the debtor to the justices' chief executive for the court or to the justices' chief executive for any other magistrates' court by a method of payment falling within section 59(6) of the Magistrates' Courts Act 1980 (standing order, etc), the justices' chief executive for the court which makes the order to whom payments are to be made shall notify the person liable to make the payments under the order of the number and location of the account into which the payments should be made.

(3) Where, under section 60(4) of the Magistrates' Courts Act 1980, as applied by section 4(5A) of the Act or as modified by section 4(5B) of the Act, the justices' chief executive for the court receives an application from an interested party for the method of payment to be varied, the justices' chief executive shall notify in writing, as soon as practicable, that party and, where practicable, any other interested party, of the result of the application, including any decision to refer the matter to the court; where the clerk of the court grants the application he shall record the variation on the copy of the order.

Amendments—Inserted by SI 1992/457; amended by SI 2001/615.

6 Remission to the original court of application for variation of registered maintenance order

An order under subsection (4) of section four of the Act remitting an application for the variation of a High Court or county court order registered in a magistrates' court to the original court shall be in the form numbered 11 in the Schedule to these Rules.

Defined terms—"county court order", "High Court order": Maintenance Orders Act 1958, s 1(3); "magistrates' court": MOA 1958, s 21(1); "original court", "registered": MOA 1958, s 1(3).

7 Notice of variation, remission, discharge or cancellation of registration by a magistrates' court of a registered order

(1) Where a High Court or county court order registered in a magistrates' court is, under subsection (2) of section four of the Act, varied by a magistrates' court, the justices' chief executive for the last-mentioned court shall give notice of the variation to the High Court or county court, as the case may be.

(2) Where an application for the variation of a High Court or county court order registered in a magistrates' court is, under subsection (4) of section four of the Act, remitted to the original court by a magistrates' court, the justices' chief executive for the last-mentioned court shall give notice of the remission to the High Court or county court, as the case may be.

(3) Where the registration of a High Court or county court order in a magistrates' court is, under subsection (4) of section five of the Act, cancelled by the court of registration, the justices' chief executive for the last-mentioned court shall give notice of cancellation to the High Court or county court, as the case may be, stating, if such be the case, that the cancellation is in consequence of a notice given under subsection (1) of the said section five.

(3A) Where the registration in a magistrates' court of an order made in the Court of Session or the High Court in Northern Ireland is cancelled under section 5(4) of the Act by that magistrates' court, the justices' chief executive for that magistrates' court shall give notice of the cancellation to the appropriate officer of the original court and to the appropriate officer of the High Court (where the order is registered by virtue of Part II of the Act of 1950).

(3B) Where the registration in a magistrates' court of an order under Part II of the Act of 1950 is cancelled by that magistrates' court by virtue of section 5(4) of the Act the justices' chief executive for the court shall give notice of the cancellation to the appropriate officer of the original court and to the appropriate officer of the High Court (where the order is registered under Part I of the Act).

(4) Where a magistrates' court order registered in the High Court is varied or discharged by a magistrates' court, the justices' chief executive for the

last-mentioned court shall give notice of the variation or discharge, as the case may be, to the High Court.

(5) Notice under the preceding provisions of this Rule shall be given by sending to the appropriate officer of the High Court or the registrar of the county court, as the case may be, a copy of the order of variation, remission, cancellation or discharge, as the case may be, certified to be a true copy thereof by the justices' chief executive for the magistrates' court and marked, in the case of a High Court maintenance order, with the title and cause number, if any, and in the case of a county court maintenance order, with the plaint or application number.

(6) For the purposes of the preceding paragraph the appropriate officer of the High Court shall be –

- (*a*) in relation to a High Court order registered in a magistrates' court, the officer to whom notice of registration was given under Rule 4 of these Rules;
- (*b*) in relation to a magistrates' court order registered in the High Court, the officer to whom a copy of the order was sent under Rule 3 of these Rules.

(7) Where a magistrates' court order registered in the High Court is discharged by a magistrates' court and it appears to the last-mentioned court that no arrears remain to be recovered, notice under subsection (3) of section five of the Act shall be given by an endorsement in the form numbered 12 in the Schedule to these Rules on the certified copy of the order of discharge referred to in paragraph (5) of this Rule.

Amendments—SI 1980/1896; SI 2001/615.

Defined terms—"appropriate officer of the High Court", "appropriate officer of the original court": r 25(4); "county court order", "High Court order": Maintenance Orders Act 1958, s 1(3); "magistrates' court": MOA 1958, s 21(1); "original court", "registered": MOA 1958, s 1(3).

8 Notices received from the High Court or a county court or from a person entitled to payments

Subject to rule 8A below where any notice is received –

- (*a*) of the registration in the High Court of a magistrates' court order;
- (*b*) of the discharge or variation by the High Court or a county court of a High Court or county court order registered in a magistrates' court;
- (*bb*) of the discharge or variation by the Court of Session or High Court in Northern Ireland of an order made by such court and registered in a magistrates' court;
- (*c*) under subsection (1) or (2) of section five of the Act (which relates to the cancellation of registration);

the justices' chief executive for the magistrates' court shall cause particulars of the notice to be registered in his court by means of a memorandum entered and signed by him in the register and, in the case of a notice under subsection (1) or (2) of section five of the Act, shall cause the person in possession of any warrant of commitment, issued but not executed, for the enforcement of the order to be informed of the giving of the notice.

Amendments—SI 1980/1896; SI 2001/615.

Defined terms—"county court order", "High Court order": Maintenance Orders Act 1958, s 1(3); "magistrates' court": MOA 1958, s 21(1); "magistrates' court order": MOA 1958, s 1(3); "register": r 25(6); "registered": MOA 1958, s 1(3).

8A Notice of cancellation of registration in High Court under Part I of the Act

Where any notice is received by a court that the registration of an order in the High Court has been cancelled under section 5(4) of the Act, the justices' chief executive for the court shall cause the particulars of the notice to be entered in the register.

Amendments—Inserted by SI 1980/1896; amended by SI 2001/615.

9 Jurisdiction as respects complaints for variation of High Court maintenance orders

Rule 34 of the Magistrates' Courts Rules 1952 (which relates to jurisdiction to hear certain complaints), shall apply to a complaint for the variation of a High Court or county court order registered in a magistrates' court as if the order were a magistrates' court maintenance order made by the court of registration and as if in paragraph (4) of the said Rule for the words "shall cause" there were substituted the words "may cause".

Amendments—SI 1977/1890; SI 1989/384.

Defined terms—"county court order", "High Court order": Maintenance Orders Act 1958, s 1(3); "magistrates' court": MOA 1958, s 21(1); "registered": MOA 1958, s 1(3).

"Rule 34 of the Magistrates' Courts Rules 1952"—See now Magistrates' Courts Rules 1981, r 41(4).

****

PART III
MISCELLANEOUS AND SUPPLEMENTAL

21 Administering court to be informed of proceedings in foreign court

Where any decision is reached, or warrant of distress or commitment is issued, in pursuance of a complaint or application relating to a maintenance order or the enforcement of a maintenance order (including an application under section twelve of the Act, which relates to the determination whether payments are earnings), being a complaint or application heard by a magistrates' court other than the administering court –

(*a*) the justices' chief executive for the first-mentioned court shall forthwith send by post to the justices' chief executive for the administering court an extract from the register containing a minute or memorandum of the decision or of the issue of the warrant as the case may be;

(*b*) on receipt of the extract the last-mentioned justices' chief executive shall enter the minute or memorandum in his register.

Amendments—SI 2001/615.

Defined terms—"administering court", r 25(5); "magistrates' court": Maintenance Orders Act 1958, s 21(1); "register": r 25(6).

PART III

22 Review of committals

(1) Where for the purpose of enforcing a maintenance order a magistrates' court has exercised its power under subsection (2) of section sixty-five of the Magistrates' Courts Act 1952, or subsection (3) or (5) of section eighteen of the Act to postpone the issue of a warrant of commitment and under the terms of the postponement the warrant falls to be issued, the justices' chief executive for the court shall give notice to the defendant in the form numbered 15 in the Schedule to these Rules and shall attach to the said notice a copy of the form numbered 16 in the said Schedule.

(2) An application under subsection (1) of the said section eighteen requesting that the warrant shall not be issued shall be in the form numbered 16 in the Schedule to these Rules and shall be delivered to the justices' chief executive for the court or sent to him by post.

(3) For the purposes of subsection (2) of the said section eighteen the period for the receipt by the justices' chief executive of an application under subsection (1) of the said section shall be the period of eight days beginning with the day on which the justices' chief executive sends to the defendant the notice referred to in paragraph (1) of this Rule.

(4) An application under subsection (4) of the said section eighteen requesting that a warrant of commitment which has been executed shall be cancelled shall be in the form numbered 17 in the Schedule to these Rules.

(5) Where an application by a defendant under subsection (1) or (4) of the said section eighteen is considered by the court the justices' chief executive for the court shall give notice of the decision of the court, if the person in question is not present –

- (*a*) to the person in whose favour the maintenance order in question was made; and
- (*b*) except where an application under subsection (1) of the said section eighteen is dismissed, to the defendant.

(6) Where on considering an application by a defendant under subsection (4) of the said section eighteen the court –

- (*a*) makes an order under paragraph (*b*) of subsection (5) of the said section for the cancellation of the warrant of commitment; or
- (*b*) remits under subsection (6) of the said section the whole or any part of the sum in respect of which the warrant was issued;

the justices' chief executive for the court shall forthwith give written notice of the decision to the person in charge of the prison or other place in which the defendant is detained.

Amendments—SI 2001/615.

Defined terms—"defendant", "magistrates' court": Maintenance Orders Act 1958, s 21(1).

"subsection (2) of section sixty-five of the Magistrates' Courts Act 1952" (r 22(1))—See now Magistrates' Courts Act 1980, s 77(2).

23 Warrants of commitment

(1) A warrant of commitment for the enforcement of a maintenance order, being an affiliation order or an order enforceable as an affiliation order, issued in pursuance of a complaint under section seventy-four of the Magistrates' Courts Act

1952, as amended by section sixteen of the Act, shall be in the form numbered 18 in the Schedule to these Rules:

Provided that where the issue of the warrant has been postponed under section sixty-five of the Magistrates' Courts Act 1952, or under section eighteen of the Act the warrant shall be in the form numbered 19 in the Schedule to these Rules.

(2) (*revoked*)

Amendments—SI 1971/809.

"section seventy-four of the Magistrates' Courts Act 1952" (r 23(1))—See now Magistrates' Courts Act 1980, s 93.

"section sixty-five of the Magistrates' Courts Act 1952" (r 23(1))—See now MCA 1980, s 77(2).

****

25 Interpretation

(1) Subsection (3) of section one of the Act shall apply to the interpretation of Part I of these Rules as it applies to the interpretation of Part I of the Act.

(2) Section twenty-one of the Act shall apply to the interpretation of these Rules as it applies to the interpretation of the Act.

(3) The Interpretation Act 1889 shall apply to the interpretation of these Rules as it applies to the interpretation of an Act of Parliament.

(4) In these Rules –

"the Act" means the Maintenance Orders Act 1958;

"the Act of 1950" means the Maintenance Orders Act 1950;

"appropriate officer of the High Court" means the Senior Registrar of the Principal Registry of the Family Division of the High Court or such district registrar as may be specified by the applicant;

"appropriate officer of the original court" means –

(i) the Sheriff-clerk, in the case of a sheriff court in Scotland;

(ii) the clerk of petty sessions, in the case of a magistrates' court in Northern Ireland;

(iii) the Deputy Principal Clerk of Session, in the case of the Court of Session;

(iv) the Chief Registrar of the Queen's Bench Division (Matrimonial), in the case of the High Court of Justice in Northern Ireland.

(5) Any reference in these Rules to the administering court in relation to a maintenance order or a related attachment of earnings order is a reference to the magistrates' court –

(*a*) which made the maintenance order;

(*b*) in which the maintenance order is registered under the Act, under Part II of the Maintenance Orders Act 1950, or under the Maintenance Orders (Facilities for Enforcement) Act 1920; or

(*c*) by which the maintenance order was confirmed under the Maintenance Orders (Facilities for Enforcement) Act 1920.

(6) Any reference in these Rules to the register is a reference to the register kept in accordance with Rule 54 of the Magistrates' Courts Rules 1968.

PART III

(7) Any reference in these Rules to a form in the Schedule to these Rules shall include a reference to a form to the like effect with such variations as the circumstances may require.

Amendments—SI 1980/1896.

"Interpretation Act 1889" (r 25(3))—This Act was consolidated in the Interpretation Act 1978; the reference to the 1889 Act must be construed as a reference to the 1978 Act.

"Rule 54 of the Magistrates' Courts Rules 1968" (r 25(6))—See now Magistrates' Courts Rules 1981, r 66.

****

Magistrates' Courts (Reciprocal Enforcement of Maintenance Orders) Rules 1974, SI 1974/668

1 These Rules may be cited as the Magistrates' Courts (Reciprocal Enforcement of Maintenance Orders) Rules 1974 and shall come into operation on 8 May 1974.

2 (1) In these Rules, unless the context otherwise requires –

"the Act" means the Maintenance Orders (Reciprocal Enforcement) Act 1972; and

"the court's register", in relation to a justices' chief executive, means the register kept by the justices' chief executive in pursuance of rule 54 of the Magistrates' Courts Rules 1968.

(2) The Interpretation Act 1889 shall apply for the interpretation of these Rules as it applies for the interpretation of an Act of Parliament.

Amendments—SI 2001/615.

"rule 54 of the Magistrates' Courts Rules 1968" (r 2(1))—See now Magistrates' Courts Rules 1981, r 66.

"Interpretation Act 1889" (r 2(2))—This reference should be construed as a reference to the Interpretation Act 1978.

3 The officer of any court, by or in relation to whom anything is to be done in pursuance of any provision of Part I of the Act shall, where that court is a magistrates' court, be the justices' clerk.

4 (1) An application under section 2 of the Act (transmission of maintenance order made in the United Kingdom for enforcement in reciprocating country) may, where the court which made the maintenance order to which the application relates is a magistrates' court, be made in writing by or on behalf of the payee under the order.

(2) Any application made in pursuance of paragraph (1) above shall –

(*a*) specify the date on which the order was made;

(*b*) contain such particulars as are known to the applicant of the whereabouts of the payer and the nature and location of his assets;

(*c*) specify any matters likely to assist in the identification of the payer;

(*d*) where possible, be accompanied by a recent photograph of the payer.

(3) In this rule, "the payer" means the payer under the order to which the application relates.

Amendments—SI 1986/1962.

4A (1) In this rule "an application" means –

(*a*) an application under section 3 of the Act for a provisional maintenance order against a person residing in a reciprocating country,

(*b*) an application under section 5 of the Act for the variation or revocation of a maintenance order made in the United Kingdom, or

(*c*) an application under section 9 of the Act for the variation or revocation of a maintenance order registered by a court in the United Kingdom.

(2) An application shall be filed in an appropriate form.

(3) Where the justices' chief executive receives such an application –

(*a*) the justices' clerk shall fix the date, time and place for a hearing or a directions appointment, and

(*b*) the justices' chief executive shall notify the applicant of the date, time and place so fixed.

Amendments—Inserted by SI 1993/617; amended by SI 2001/615.

4B (1) This rule applies to proceedings under section 5(5), 7 or 9(6) of the Act for the confirmation of a provisional order made in a reciprocating country.

(2) On receipt of the order and accompanying documents referred to in section 5(5), 7 or 9(6) of the Act –

(*a*) the justices' clerk shall fix the date, time and place for a hearing or a directions appointment allowing sufficient time for service under this rule to be effected at least 21 days before the date so fixed; and

(*b*) the justices' chief executive shall serve a copy of the order and documents on the resident party together with a notice stating the date, time and place so fixed.

(3) Within 14 days of service under this rule the resident party shall file an answer to the provisional order in an appropriate form.

Amendments—Inserted by SI 1993/617; amended by SI 2001/615..

4C (1) Schedule A1 to these Rules shall apply to proceedings pursuant to rules 4A and 4B above.

(2) In Schedule A1 as it applies to rule 4A, "the resident party" and "the non-resident party" shall be taken to mean –

(*a*) in the case of an application under sub-paragraph (*a*) of rule 4A(1), the applicant and the respondent respectively;

(*b*) in the case of an application under sub-paragraph (*b*) of rule 4A(1), the payee and the payer respectively under the order in question; and (*c*) in the case of an application under sub-paragraph (*c*) of rule 4A(1), the payer and payee respectively under the order in question.

(3) In rule 4B and in Schedule A1 as it applies to that rule, "the resident party" and "the non-resident party" shall be taken to mean the payer and the payee respectively under the order in question.

Amendments—Inserted by SI 1993/617.

5 A document setting out or summarising any evidence, required by section 3(5)(*b*), 5(4), or 9(5) of the Act (provisional orders) to be authenticated shall be authenticated by a certificate, signed by one of the justices before whom that evidence was given, that the document is the original document containing or recording or, as the case may be, summarising that evidence or a true copy of that document.

6 (1) Subject to paragraph (2) below, any documents required by section 5(4) or 9(5) of the Act to be sent to a court in a reciprocating country shall be sent to that court by post.

(2) Where the court to which the documents are to be sent is in a country specified in Schedule 1 to these Rules, such documents shall be sent to the Secretary of State for transmission to that court.

7 (1) For the purposes of compliance with section 5(9) of the Act (revocation by United Kingdom court of provisional order) there shall be served on the person on whose application the maintenance order was made a notice which shall –

(*a*) set out the evidence received or taken, as the case may be, in pursuance of that subsection;
(*b*) inform that person that it appears to the court that the maintenance order ought not to have been made; and
(*c*) inform that person that if he wishes to make representations with respect to the evidence set out in the notice he may do so orally or in writing and that if he wishes to adduce further evidence he should notify the justices' chief executive for the magistrates' court which made the maintenance order.

(2) Where a justices' chief executive receives notification that the person on whose application the maintenance order was made wishes to adduce further evidence –

(*a*) the justices' clerk shall fix a date for the hearing of such evidence; and
(*b*) the justices' chief executive shall send that person written notice of the date fixed.

Amendments—SI 2001/615.

8 (1) Where a certified copy of an order, not being a provisional order, is received by a justices' chief executive who is required under any provision of Part I of the Act to register the order, he shall cause the order to be registered in his court by means of a minute or memorandum entered and signed by him in the court's register.

(2) Where any magistrates' court makes or confirms an order which is required under section 7(5) or 9(10) of the Act to be registered, the justices' chief executive shall enter and sign a minute or memorandum thereof in the court's register.

(3) Every minute or memorandum entered in pursuance of paragraph (1) or (2) above shall specify the section of the Act under which the order in question is registered.

Amendments—SI 2001/615.

9 (1) When an order is registered under section 6(3) of the Act, the court shall order that payment of sums due thereunder shall be made to the justices' chief executive for the registering court during such hours and at such place as that justices' chief executive may direct.

(1A) A justices' chief executive to whom payments are ordered to be made (whether by virtue of an order under paragraph (1) above or by virtue of an order of the court under the Act) shall send those payments by post to the court which made the order or to such other person or authority as that court or the Secretary of State may from time to time direct:

Provided that if the court which made the order is in one of the countries or territories specified in Schedule 2 to these Rules, the justices' chief executive shall, unless the Secretary of State otherwise directs, send any such sums to the Crown Agents for Overseas Governments and Administrations for transmission to the person to whom they are due.

(2) Where it appears to a justices' chief executive to whom payments by way of periodical payments under any maintenance order are made that any sums payable under the order are in arrear he may and, if such sums are in arrear to an amount equal to four times the sum payable weekly under the order, he shall, whether the person for whose benefit the payment should have been made requests him to do so or not, proceed in his own name for the recovery of those sums, unless it appears to him that it is unreasonable in the circumstances to do so.

Amendments—SI 1992/457; SI 2001/615.

9A Without prejudice to Rule 9 above, the justices' chief executive of the registering court shall take reasonable steps to notify the person to whom payments are due under a registered order of the means of enforcement available in respect of it, including, in an appropriate case, the possibility of registration of the whole or a part of the order in the High Court under Part I of the Maintenance Orders Act 1958.

Amendments—Inserted by SI 1986/1962; amended by SI 2001/615.

9B (1) Where, in the exercise of the duty imposed under rule 9(1) above, or in the exercise of the powers conferred by virtue of section 7(5A), section 8(4A) or section 9(1ZA) of the Act, the court orders that payments under the order are to be made by a particular means, the clerk of the court shall record on the copy of the order the means of payment which the court has ordered and the justices' chief executive shall notify in writing, as soon as practicable, the person liable to make payments under the order of how payments are to be made.

(2) Where, in the exercise of the aforesaid powers, the court orders payment to the justices' chief executive for the court, or to the justices' chief executive for any

other magistrates' court, by a method of payment falling within section 59(6) of the Magistrates' Courts Act 1980 (standing order, etc), the justices' chief executive for the court to whom payments are to be made shall notify the person liable to make the payments under the order of the number and location of the account into which the payments are to be made.

(3) Where, under section 60(4) of the Magistrates' Courts Act 1980, as modified by section 9(1ZA) of the Act, the justices' chief executive for the court receives an application from an interested party for the method of payment to be varied, the justices' chief executive shall notify in writing, as soon as practicable, that party and, where practicable, any other interested party, of the result of the application, including any decision to refer the matter to the court; where the clerk of the court grants the application, he shall record the variation on the copy of the order.

Amendments—Inserted by SI 1992/457; amended by SI 2001/615.

10 (1) Subject to paragraph (2) below, where a request is made by or on behalf of a court in a reciprocating country for the taking in England and Wales of the evidence of a person residing therein, the following magistrates' courts shall have power under section 14(1) of the Act (obtaining of evidence needed for purpose of certain proceedings) to take that evidence, that is to say –

(*a*) where the maintenance order to which the proceedings in the court in the reciprocating country relate was made by a magistrates' court, the court which made the order;

(*b*) where the maintenance order to which those proceedings relate is registered in a magistrates' court, the court in which the order is registered;

(*c*) a magistrates' court which has received such a request from the Secretary of State.

(2) The power conferred by paragraph (1) above may, with the agreement of a court having that power, be exercised by any other magistrates' court which, because the person whose evidence is to be taken resides within its jurisdiction or for any other reason, the first-mentioned court considers could more conveniently take the evidence; but nothing in this paragraph shall derogate from the power of any court specified in paragraph (1) above.

(3) Subject to paragraph (4) below, where the evidence of any person is to be taken by a magistrates' court under the foregoing provisions of this rule –

(*a*) the evidence shall be taken in the same manner as if that person were a witness in proceedings on a complaint;

(*b*) any oral evidence so taken shall be put into writing and read to the person who gave it, who shall be required to sign the document, and

(*c*) the justices by whom the evidence of any person is so taken shall certify at the foot of any document setting out the evidence of, or produced in evidence by, that person that such evidence was taken, or document received in evidence, as the case may be, by them.

(4) Where such a request as is mentioned in paragraph (1) above includes a request that the evidence be taken in a particular manner, the magistrates' court by which the evidence is taken shall, so far as circumstances permit, comply with that request.

(5) Any document such as is mentioned in paragraph (3)(*c*) above shall be sent –

(*a*) where the request for the taking of the evidence was made by or on behalf of a court in a country specified in Schedule 1 to these Rules, to the Secretary of State for transmission to that court;

(*b*) in any other case, to the court in the reciprocating country by or on behalf of which the request was made.

11 Any request under section 14(5) of the Act for the taking or providing of evidence by a court in a reciprocating country shall, where made by a magistrates' court, be communicated in writing to the court in question.

12 (1) Where a magistrates' court makes an order, not being a provisional order, varying a maintenance order to which section 5 of the Act (variation and revocation of maintenance order made in the United Kingdom) applies, the justices' chief executive shall send written notice of the making of the order to the Secretary of State; and where the order is made by virtue of paragraph (*a*) or (*b*) of subsection (3) of that section, he shall send such written notice to the court in a reciprocating country which would, if the order had been a provisional order, have had power to confirm the order.

(2) Where a magistrates' court revokes a maintenance order to which section 5 of the Act applies, the justices' chief executive shall send written notice of the revocation to the Secretary of State and to the court in a reciprocating country which has power to confirm that maintenance order, or by which the order has been confirmed, or in which the order is registered for enforcement, as the case may be.

(3) Where under section 9 of the Act (variation and revocation of maintenance order registered in United Kingdom court) a magistrates' court makes an order, not being a provisional order, varying or revoking a registered order, the justices' chief executive shall send written notice of the making of the order to the court in a reciprocating country which made the registered order.

(4) Where under section 7(2) of the Act (confirmation by United Kingdom court of provisional maintenance order made in reciprocating country) a magistrates' court confirms an order to which section 7 of the Act applies, the justices' chief executive shall send written notice of the confirmation to the court in a reciprocating country which made the order.

Amendments—SI 2001/615.

13 (1) Where a justices' chief executive –

(*a*) registers under section 6(3) of the Act (registration in United Kingdom court of maintenance order made in reciprocating country) an order to which section 6 of the Act applies; or

(*b*) registers under section 7(5) of the Act an order which has been confirmed in pursuance of section 7(2) of the Act,

he shall send written notice to the Secretary of State that the order has been duly registered.

(2) (*revoked*)

(3) Where a justices' chief executive registers a maintenance order under section 10(4) of the Act, he shall send written notice to the Secretary of State that the order has been duly registered.

PART III

Amendments—SI 1975/2236; SI 1979/170; SI 2001/615.

14 (1) Where a justices' chief executive cancels the registration of a maintenance order under section 10(1) of the Act (cancellation of registration and transfer of order), he shall send written notice of the cancellation to the payer under the order.

(2) Where a justices' chief executive registers a maintenance order under section 6(3), 7(5), 9(10), 10(4), 10(5) or 23(3) of the Act, he shall send to the payer under the order written notice stating –

(*a*) that the order has been duly registered;
(*b*) that sums due under the order should be paid to the justices' clerk; and
(*c*) the hours during which and the place at which such payments should be made.

Amendments—SI 1975/2236; SI 2001/615.

SCHEDULE A1

RULES OF PROCEDURE

1 In this Schedule, and in any rule where this Schedule applies to proceedings pursuant to that rule, unless the context otherwise requires –

"business day" means any day other than –

(*a*) a Saturday, Sunday, Christmas or Good Friday; or
(*b*) a bank holiday, that is to say, a day which is, or is to be observed as, a bank holiday, or a holiday, under the Banking and Financial Dealings Act 1971, in England and Wales,

"directions appointment" means a hearing for directions under paragraph 4 below,
"file" means deposit with the justices' chief executive,
"justices' chief executive" means a justices' chief executive appointed under section 40 of the Justices of the Peace Act 1997;
"leave" includes approval,
"note" includes a record made by mechanical or electronic means, and
"proceedings" means proceedings to which this Schedule applies.

"any rule where this Schedule applies"—The Schedule prescribes the procedure to be followed in proceedings under Maintenance Orders (Reciprocal Enforcement) Act 1972, ss 3, 5, 7 and 9.

2 Transfer of proceedings

(1) Where –

(*a*) any proceedings are relevant proceedings within the meaning of section 93 of the Children Act 1989, and
(*b*) the justices' chief executive or the court receives a request in writing from the resident party that the proceedings be transferred to another magistrates' court,

the justices' clerk or court shall issue a certificate in the appropriate form, granting or refusing the request in accordance with any Order made by the Lord Chancellor under Part I of Schedule 11 to the Children Act 1989.

(2) Where a request is granted under paragraph (1) the justices' chief executive shall send a copy of the certificate –

- (*a*) to the resident party,
- (*b*) to the Lord Chancellor's Department, and
- (*c*) to the magistrates' court to which the proceedings are to be transferred.

(3) Any consent given or refused by a justices' clerk in accordance with any Order made by the Lord Chancellor under Part I of Schedule 11 shall be recorded in writing by the justices' clerk at the time it is given or refused or as soon as practicable thereafter.

3 Service

(1) Where service of a document is required by this Schedule or by a rule where this Schedule applies to proceedings pursuant to that rule it may be effected, unless the contrary is indicated –

- (*a*) if the person to be served is not known by the person serving to be acting by solicitor –
  - (i) by delivering it to him personally, or
  - (ii) by delivering it at, or by sending it by first-class post to, his residence or last known residence, or
- (*b*) if the person to be served is known by the person serving to be acting by solicitor –
  - (i) by delivering the document at, or sending it by first-class post to, the solicitor's address for service,
  - (ii) where the solicitor's address for service includes a numbered box at a document exchange, by leaving the document at that document exchange or at a document exchange which transmits documents on every business day to that document exchange, or
  - (iii) by sending a legible copy of the document by facsimile transmission to the solicitor's office.

(2) In this paragraph, "first-class post" means first-class post which has been pre-paid or in respect of which pre-payment is not required.

(3) A document shall, unless the contrary is proved, be deemed to have been served –

- (*a*) in the case of service by first-class post, on the second business day after posting, and
- (*b*) in the case of service in accordance with sub-paragraph (1)(*b*)(ii), on the second business day after the day on which it is left at the document exchange.

(4) In any proceedings where this Schedule, or a rule where this Schedule applies, requires a document to be served, the court or the justices' clerk may, without prejudice to any power under paragraph 4 below, direct that –

- (*a*) the requirement shall not apply;
- (*b*) the time specified by the rules for complying with the requirement shall be abridged to such extent as may be specified in the direction;
- (*c*) service shall be effected in such manner as may be specified in the direction.

PART III

4 Directions

(1) The justices' clerk or the court may give, vary or revoke directions for the conduct of the proceedings, including –

(*a*) the timetable for the proceedings,
(*b*) varying the time within which or by which an act is required by this Schedule or by a rule where this Schedule applies to proceedings pursuant to that rule to be done,
(*c*) the service of documents, and
(*d*) the submission of evidence

and, where the justices' chief executive receives such an application or any other document by which proceedings are commenced, the justices' chief executive shall consider whether such directions need to be given.

(2) Where the justices' clerk or a single justice who is holding a directions appointment considers, for whatever reason, that it is inappropriate to give a direction on a particular matter, he shall refer the matter to the court which may give any appropriate direction.

(3) Directions under sub-paragraph (1) may be given, varied or revoked either –

(*a*) of the justices' clerk's or the court's own motion having given the resident party an opportunity to attend and be heard or to make written representations, or
(*b*) on the written request of either party specifying the direction which is sought.

(4) Where the justices' chief executive receives a request under sub-paragraph (3)(*b*) the justices' clerk shall –

(*a*) make the direction sought, or
(*b*) fix a date for a hearing to consider the request.

"justices' clerk" (para 4(1)–(4))—For the power of delegation available to the justices' clerk in respect of these duties, see para 12 below.

5 Timing of proceedings

(1) Any period of time fixed by this Schedule or by a rule where this Schedule applies to proceedings pursuant to that rule, or by any order or direction, for doing any act shall be reckoned in accordance with this rule.

(2) Where the period, being a period of 7 days or less, would include a day which is not a business day, that day shall be excluded.

(3) Where the time fixed for filing a document with the justices' chief executive expires on a day on which the office of the justices' chief executive is closed, and for that reason the document cannot be filed on that day, the document shall be filed in time if it is filed on the next day on which the office of the justices' chief executive is open.

(4) Where this Schedule or a rule where this Schedule applies to proceedings pursuant to that rule provides a period of time within which or by which a certain act is to be performed in the course of relevant proceedings, that period may not be extended otherwise than by a direction of the justices' clerk or the court under paragraph 4(1) above.

(5) At the –

(*a*) transfer to a court of proceedings,
(*b*) postponement or adjournment of any hearing or directions appointment in the course of relevant proceedings, or
(*c*) conclusion of any such hearing or directions appointment other than one at which the proceedings are determined, or so soon thereafter as is practicable,
   (i) the justices' clerk shall fix a date upon which the proceedings shall come before him or the court again for such purposes as he or the court directs, which date shall, where paragraph (*a*) applies, be as soon as possible after the transfer, and
   (ii) the justices' chief executive shall give notice to the resident party of the date so fixed.

6 Attendance at directions appointment and hearing

(1) The resident party shall attend a directions appointment of which he has been given notice in accordance with paragraph 4 above unless the justices' clerk or the court otherwise directs.

(2) Where at the time and place appointed for a hearing or directions appointment the resident party does not appear the justices' clerk or the court shall not proceed with the hearing or appointment unless –

(*a*) the proceedings relate to an application filed by the resident party, or
(*b*) the court is satisfied that the resident party has received reasonable notice of the hearing or appointment.

(3) Where at the time and place appointed for a hearing or directions appointment the non-resident party does not appear the court may proceed with the hearing or appointment where the proceedings relate to an order or application sent by the Lord Chancellor to the court under the Act.

(4) Nothing in this Schedule shall be taken as preventing either party from appearing at any hearing or directions appointment.

7 Documentary evidence

(1) A party shall file, at or by such time as the justices' clerk or the court directs or, in the absence of a direction, before the hearing or appointment –

(*a*) written statements of the substance of the oral evidence which he intends to adduce at a hearing or a directions appointment, which shall –
   (i) be dated,
   (ii) be signed by the person making the statement,
   (iii) contain a declaration that the maker of the statement believes it to be true and understands that it may be placed before the court, and
   (iv) show in the top right-hand corner of the first page –
      (*a*) the initials and surname of the person making the statement,
      (*b*) the number of the statement in relation to the maker,
      (*c*) the date on which the statement was made, and
      (*d*) the party on whose behalf it is filed, and
(*b*) copies of any documents upon which he intends to rely at a hearing or a directions appointment.

(2) A party may, subject to any direction of the justices' clerk or the court about the timing or statements under this rule, file a statement which is supplementary to a statement served under sub-paragraph (1).

PART III

(3) Where a non-resident party files a statement or document under this rule, he shall also file a copy of it for service on the resident party; and the justices' chief executive shall on receipt of that copy serve it on the resident party.

(4) At a hearing or directions appointment a party may not without the leave of the justices' clerk, in the case of a directions appointment, or the court –

(*a*) adduce evidence, or
(*b*) seek to rely on a document,

in respect of which he has failed to comply with the requirements of sub-paragraphs (1) and, where applicable, (3).

8 Amendment

(1) A party amending a document shall file the amended document with the justices' chief executive; and the amendments shall be identified.

(2) Paragraph 7(3) above applies to an amended document filed under this paragraph.

9 Oral evidence

The justices' clerk or the court shall keep a note of the substance or any oral evidence given at a hearing or directions appointment.

10 Hearing

(1) Before the hearing, the justice or justices who will be dealing with the case shall read any documents which have been filed under paragraph 7 above in respect of the hearing.

(2) The justices' clerk at a directions appointment, or the court at a hearing or directions appointment, may give directions as to the order of speeches and evidence.

(3) After the final hearing, the court shall make its decision as soon as is practicable.

(4) Before the court makes an order or refuses an application, the justices' clerk shall record in writing –

(*a*) the names of the justice or justices constituting the court by which the decision is made, and
(*b*) in consultation with the justice or justices, the reasons for the court's decision and any findings of fact.

(5) After the court announces its decision, the justices' clerk shall as soon as practicable make a record in writing of any order.

(6) Where, under subsection (4) of section 7 of the Domestic Proceedings and Magistrates' Courts Act 1978, a court decides to treat an application under section 7 as if it were an application for an order under section 2 of that Act, the court shall indicate orally which of grounds (*a*) and (*b*) in that subsection it considers applicable and a memorandum of that decision and the grounds therefor shall be entered in the court's register.

11 Confidentiality of documents

(1) No document, other than a record of an order, held by the court and relating to any proceedings shall be disclosed, other than to –

(*a*) a party,
(*b*) the legal representative of a party,
(*c*) the Lord Chancellor's Department, or
(*d*) the Legal Aid Board,

without leave of the justices' clerk or the court.

12 Delegation by justices' clerk

(1) In this paragraph, "employed as a clerk in court" has the same meaning as in rule 2(1) of the Justices' Clerks (Qualifications of Assistants) Rules 1979.

(2) Anything authorised to be done by, to or before a justices' clerk under this Schedule or under a rule to which this Schedule applies may be done instead by, to or before a person employed as a clerk in court where that person is appointed by the magistrates' courts committee to assist him and where that person has been specifically authorised by the justices' clerk for that purpose.

(3) Any authorisation by the justices' clerk under sub-paragraph (2) shall be recorded in writing at the time the authority is given or as soon as practicable thereafter.

"appointed by the magistrates' courts committee" (para 12(2))—This appears to exclude "agency clerks", since the delegated powers may only be exercised by a person appointed by the relevant committee.

13 Application of section 97 of the Magistrates' Courts Act 1980

(1) Subject to sub-paragraph (2) below, section 97 of the Magistrates' Courts Act 1980 shall apply to proceedings to which this Schedule applies as it applies to a hearing of a complaint under that section.

(2) The power of a justice under section 97 of that Act to issue a witness summons may be exercised by a justices' clerk.

Amendments—Schedule inserted by SI 1993/617; amended by SI 2001/615.

SCHEDULE 1
RECIPROCATING COUNTRIES TO WHICH DOCUMENTS ARE TRANSMITTED VIA THE SECRETARY OF STATE

British Columbia
New Zealand
Nova Scotia
Ontario
Ghana
India
Kenya
New Brunswick
Northwest Territories of Canada
The Republic of South Africa

PART III

Alberta
Saskatchewan
Turks and Caicos Islands
United Republic of Tanzania (except Zanzibar)
Papua New Guinea
Zimbabwe
Nunavut

Amendments—SI 1979/170; SI 1983/1148; SI 2002/1734.

SCHEDULE 2
COUNTRIES AND TERRITORIES IN WHICH SUMS ARE PAYABLE THROUGH CROWN AGENTS FOR OVERSEAS GOVERNMENTS AND ADMINISTRATIONS

Gibraltar
Barbados
Bermuda
Ghana
Kenya
Fiji
Hong Kong
Singapore
Turks and Caicos Islands
United Republic of Tanzania (except Zanzibar)
Anguilla
Falkland Islands and Dependencies
St Helena

Amendments—SI 1979/170; SI 1983/1148.

Magistrates' Courts (Reciprocal Enforcement of Maintenance Orders) (Hague Convention Countries) Rules 1980, SI 1980/108

1 These rules may be cited as the Magistrates' Courts (Reciprocal Enforcement of Maintenance Orders) (Hague Convention Countries) Rules 1980 and shall come into operation on 1 March 1980.

"These rules"—These rules contain detailed provisions for the application of the Maintenance Orders (Reciprocal Enforcement) Act 1972 to the countries listed in Reciprocal Enforcement of Maintenance Orders (Hague Convention Countries) Order 1993, Sch 1 (ie "the Hague Convention countries"). These rules also apply (with modifications) to applications under Part I of the 1972 Act involving the States listed in Schedule 1 to the Reciprocal Enforcement of Maintenance Orders (United States of America) Order 1995.

2 In these Rules, unless the context otherwise requires –

"the Act" means the Maintenance Orders (Reciprocal Enforcement) Act 1972 as applied with such exceptions, adaptations and modifications as are specified in the Reciprocal Enforcement of Maintenance Orders (Hague Convention Countries) Order 1979; and

"the court's register", in relation to a justices' chief executive means the register kept by the justices' chief executive in pursuance of Rule 54 of the Magistrates' Courts Rules 1968.

Amendments—SI 2001/615.

"Rule 54 of the Magistrates' Courts Rules 1968"—See now Magistrates' Courts Rules 1981, r 66.

3 The officer of any court, by or in relation to whom anything is to be done in pursuance of any provision of Part I of the Act shall, where that court is a magistrates' court, be the justices' clerk.

4 (1) An application under section 2 of the Act (transmission of maintenance order made in the United Kingdom for recognition and enforcement in Hague Convention country) shall where the court which made the maintenance order to which the application relates is a magistrates' court, be made in writing by or on behalf of the payee under the order.

(2) Any application made in pursuance of paragraph (1) above shall –

(*a*) specify the date on which the order was made;
(*b*) contain such particulars as are known to the applicant of the whereabouts of the payer and the nature and location of his assets;
(*c*) specify any matters likely to assist in the identification of the payer;
(*d*) where possible, be accompanied by a recent photograph of the payer.

(3) In this rule "the payer" means the payer under the order to which the application relates.

Amendments—SI 1986/1962.

4A (1) In this rule, "an application" means –

(*a*) an application under section 3 of the Act for a maintenance order against a person residing in a Hague Convention country,
(*b*) an application under section 5 of the Act for the variation or revocation of a maintenance order made in the United Kingdom, or
(*c*) an application under section 9 of the Act for the variation of a maintenance order registered by a court in the United Kingdom.

(2) An application shall be filed in an appropriate form.

(3) Where the justices' chief executive receives such an application –

(*a*) the justices' clerk shall fix the date, time and place for a hearing or a directions appointment; and
(*b*) the justices' chief executive shall notify the applicant of the date, time and place so fixed.

Amendments—Inserted by SI 1993/617; amended by SI 1999/2002; SI 2001/615.

4B (1) Schedule 1A to these Rules shall apply to proceedings pursuant to rule 4A above.

(2) In Schedule 1A as it applies to rule 4A, "the resident party" and "the non-resident party" shall be taken to mean –

(*a*) in the case of an application under sub-paragraph (*a*) of rule 4A(1), the applicant and the respondent respectively,
(*b*) in the case of an application under sub-paragraph (*b*) of rule 4A(1), the payee and payer respectively under the order in question, and
(*c*) in the case of an application under sub-paragraph (*c*) of rule 4A(1), the payer and payee respectively under the order in question.

Amendments—Inserted by SI 1993/617.

5 (1) Where a justices' chief executive is required under any provision of Part I of the Act to register a maintenance order, he shall cause the order to be registered in his court by means of a minute or memorandum entered and signed by him in the court's register.

(2) Every minute or memorandum entered in pursuance of paragraph (1) above shall specify the section of the Act under which the order in question is registered.

(3) Where a maintenance order is under any provision of Part I of the Act registered in a magistrates' court, the justices' chief executive shall send written notice of the registration to the Secretary of State.

Amendments—SI 2001/615.

6 Where under section 5(4)(*b*) of the Act a copy of any representations made or evidence adduced by or on behalf of the payer in an application by the payee for the variation or revocation of a maintenance order to which section 5 of the Act applies, is required to be served on the payee before the hearing, the justices' chief executive for the magistrates' court to which the application is made shall arrange for a copy of such representations or evidence to be sent to the payee by post.

Amendments—SI 2001/615.

7 (1) Any notice required under section 6(8) of the Act (notice of registration in United Kingdom court of maintenance order made in Hague Convention country) to be served on the payer under a maintenance order shall, where the order is registered in a magistrates' court, be in the form in Part I of Schedule 2 to these Rules, or in a form to the like effect.

(2) Where a magistrates' court to which an appeal is made under section 6(9) of the Act sets aside the registration of a maintenance order, the justices' chief executive shall send written notice of the court's decision to the Secretary of State.

(3) Any notice required under section 6(11) of the Act (notice that maintenance order made in Hague Convention country has not been registered in United Kingdom court) to be given to the payee under a maintenance order shall, where the appropriate court is a magistrates' court, be in the form in Part I of Schedule 2 to these Rules or in a form to the like effect.

Amendments—SI 2001/615.

8 (1) When an order is registered under section 6(3) of the Act, the court shall order that payment of sums due thereunder shall be made to the justices' chief executive for the registering court during such hours and at such place as that justices' chief executive may direct.

(1A) A justices' chief executive to whom payments are ordered to be made (whether by virtue of an order under paragraph (1) above or by virtue of an order of the court under the Act) shall send those payments by post to the payee under the order.

(2) Where it appears to a justices' chief executive to whom payments by way of periodical payments under any maintenance order are to be made that any sums payable under the order are in arrear he may and, if such sums are in arrear to an amount equal to four times the sum payable weekly under the order, he shall, whether the person for whose benefit the payment should have been made requests him to do so or not, proceed in his own name for the recovery of those sums, unless it appears to him that it is unreasonable in the circumstances to do so.

Amendments—SI 1986/1962; SI 1992/457; SI 2001/615.

8A Without prejudice to Rule 8 above, the justices' chief executive of the registering court shall take reasonable steps to notify the person to whom payments are due under a registered order of the means of enforcement available in respect of it, including, in an appropriate case, the possibility of registration of the whole or part of the order in the High Court under Part I of the Maintenance Orders Act 1958.

Amendments—Inserted by SI 1986/1962; amended by SI 2001/615.

8B (1) Where, in the exercise of the duty imposed under rule 8(1) above, or in the exercise of the powers conferred by virtue of section 8(4A) or section 9(1ZA) of the Act, the court orders that payments under the order are to be made by a particular means, the clerk of the court shall record on the copy of the order the means of payment which the court has ordered and the justices' chief executive shall notify in writing, as soon as practicable, the person liable to make payments under the order of how payments are to be made.

(2) Where, in the exercise of any of the aforesaid powers, the court orders payment to the justices' chief executive for the court, or to the justices' chief executive for any other magistrates' court, by a method of payment falling within section 59(6) of the Magistrates' Courts Act 1980 (standing order, etc), the justices' chief executive for the court to whom payments are to be made shall notify the person liable to make the payments under the order of the number and location of the account into which the payments are to be made.

(3) Where, under section 60(4) of the Magistrates' Courts Act 1980, as modified by section 9(1ZA) of the Act, the justices' chief executive for the court receives an application from an interested party for the method of payment to be varied, the justices' chief executive shall notify in writing, as soon as practicable, that party and, where practicable, any other interested party, of the result of the application, including any decision to refer the matter to the court; where the clerk of the court then grants the application, he shall record the variation on the copy of the order.

Amendments—Inserted by SI 1992/457; amended by SI 2001/615.

PART III

9 (1) Subject to paragraph (2) below, where a request is made by or on behalf of a court in a Hague Convention country for the taking in England and Wales of the evidence of a person residing therein, the following magistrates' courts shall have power under section 14(1) of the Act (obtaining of evidence needed for purpose of certain proceedings) to take that evidence, that is to say –

(*a*) where the maintenance order to which the proceedings in the court in the Hague Convention country relate was made by a magistrates' court, the court which made the order;

(*b*) where the maintenance order to which those proceedings in the court in the Hague Convention country relate was made by a court in a Hague Convention country, the court in which the order is registered;

(*c*) a magistrates' court which has received such a request from the Secretary of State.

(2) The power conferred by paragraph (1) above may, with the agreement of a court having that power, be exercised by any other magistrates' court which, because the person whose evidence is to be taken resides within its jurisdiction or for any other reason, the first-mentioned court considers could more conveniently take the evidence; but nothing in this paragraph shall derogate from the power of any court specified in paragraph (1) above.

(3) Subject to paragraph (4) below, where the evidence of any person is to be taken by a magistrates' court under the foregoing provisions of this Rule –

(*a*) the evidence shall be taken in the same manner as if that person were a witness in proceedings on a complaint;

(*b*) any oral evidence so taken shall be put into writing and read to the person who gave it who shall be required to sign the document; and

(*c*) the justices by whom the evidence of any person is so taken shall certify at the foot of any document setting out the evidence of, or produced in evidence by, that person that such evidence was taken, or document received in evidence, as the case may be, by them.

(4) Where such a request as is mentioned in paragraph (1) above includes a request that the evidence be taken in a particular manner, the magistrates' court by which the evidence is taken shall, so far as circumstances permit, comply with that request.

10 (1) Where a justices' chief executive cancels the registration of a maintenance order under section 10(1) of the Act (cancellation of registration and transfer of order) he shall send written notice of the cancellation to the payer under the order.

(2) Where a justices' chief executive registers a maintenance order under section 10(4) of the Act, he shall send written notice to the Secretary of State and to the payer under the order that the order has been duly registered.

Amendments—SI 2001/615.

11 Where a justices' chief executive serves a notice on a payer under a maintenance order who resides in a Hague Convention country under any provision of Part I of the Act, he shall send a document which establishes that the notice was so served to the Secretary of State.

Amendments—SI 2001/615.

12 (1) Where the justices' chief executive for a magistrates' court receives from the Secretary of State notice of the institution of proceedings, including notice of the substance of the claim, in a Hague Convention country in relation to the making, variation or revocation of a maintenance order and it appears to the justices' chief executive that the person against whom those proceedings have been instituted is residing within the petty sessions area for which the court acts, the justices' chief executive shall serve the notice on that person by sending it by post in a registered letter addressed to him at his last known or usual place of abode.

(2) Where it appears to a justices' chief executive who has received such a notice from the Secretary of State that the person against whom the proceedings have been instituted is not so residing, the justices' chief executive shall return the notice to the Secretary of State with an intimation to that effect.

Amendments—SI 2001/615.

SCHEDULE 1

ENABLING POWERS

Section 15 of the Justices of the Peace Act 1949, as extended by section 122 of the Magistrates' Courts Act 1952;

The following provisions of the Maintenance Orders (Reciprocal Enforcement) Act 1972, as extended by Article 3 of the Reciprocal Enforcement of Maintenance Orders (Hague Convention Countries) Order 1979, namely,

section 2(3) and (4) (see Rules 3 and 4);
section 3(5)(*b*), (6A) and (6D) (see Rule 3);
section 5(3), (4)(*c*), (6), (7) and (10) (see Rules 3 and 5);
section 5(4)(*b*) (see Rule 6);
section 6(2), (3), (5), (6), (7), (8), (10), (11) and (12) (see Rules 3, 5, 7 and Schedule 2);
section 8(5) (see Rule 8);
section 8(6) (see Rule 3);
section 9(3), (4)(*b*) and (*c*), (6), (7) and (8) (see Rules 3 and 5);
section 10(1), (2), (3), (4), (5) and (7) (see Rules 3, 5 and 10);
section 11(1)(*b*) (see Rule 3);
section 14(1) (see Rule 9);
section 16(1) (see Rule 8);
section 18(1) (see Rule 9).

(Note: the references to Rules are to the Rules in this SI which give effect to the enabling powers to which the rules relate.)

SCHEDULE 1A

RULES OF PROCEDURE

1 In this Schedule, and in any rule where this Schedule applies to proceedings pursuant to that rule, unless the context otherwise requires –

"business day" means any day other than –

(*a*) a Saturday, Sunday, Christmas or Good Friday; or

PART III

(*b*) a bank holiday, that is to say, a day which is, or is to be observed as, a bank holiday, or a holiday, under the Banking and Financial Dealings Act 1971, in England and Wales,

"directions appointment" means a hearing for directions under paragraph 4 below,

"file" means deposit with the justices' chief executive,

"justices' chief executive" means a justices' chief executive appointed under section 40 of the Justices of the Peace Act 1997;

"leave" includes approval,

"note" includes a record made by mechanical or electronic means, and

"proceedings" means proceedings to which this Schedule applies.

"any rule where this Schedule applies"—The Schedule prescribes the procedure to be followed in proceedings under Maintenance Orders (Reciprocal Enforcement) Act 1972, ss 3, 5, and 9.

2 Transfer of proceedings

(1) Where –

(*a*) any proceedings are relevant proceedings within the meaning of section 93 of the Children Act 1989, and

(*b*) the justices' chief executive or the court receives a request in writing from the resident party that the proceedings be transferred to another magistrates' court,

the justices' clerk or court shall issue a certificate in the appropriate form, granting or refusing the request in accordance with any Order made by the Lord Chancellor under Part I of Schedule 11 to the Children Act 1989.

(2) Where a request is granted under paragraph (1) the justices' chief executive shall send a copy of the certificate –

(*a*) to the resident party,

(*b*) to the Lord Chancellor's Department, and

(*c*) to the magistrates' court to which the proceedings are to be transferred.

(3) Any consent given or refused by a justices' clerk in accordance with any Order made by the Lord Chancellor under Part I of Schedule 11 shall be recorded in writing by the justices' clerk at the time it is given or refused or as soon as practicable thereafter.

Scope of provision—This paragraph provides for the transfer of relevant proceedings between magistrates' courts.

3 Service

(1) Where service of a document is required by this Schedule or by a rule where this Schedule applies to proceedings pursuant to that rule it may be effected, unless the contrary is indicated –

(*a*) if the person to be served is not known by the person serving to be acting by solicitor –

(i) by delivering it to him personally, or

(ii) by delivering it at, or by sending it by first-class post to, his residence or last known residence, or

(*b*) if the person to be served is known by the person serving to be acting by solicitor –

(i) by delivering the document at, or sending it by first-class post to, the solicitor's address for service,

(ii) where the solicitor's address for service includes a numbered box at a document exchange, by leaving the document at that document exchange or at a document exchange which transmits documents on every business day to that document exchange, or

(iii) by sending a legible copy of the document by facsimile transmission to the solicitor's office.

(2) In this paragraph, "first-class post" means first-class post which has been pre-paid or in respect of which pre-payment is not required.

(3) A document shall, unless the contrary is proved, be deemed to have been served –

(*a*) in the case of service by first-class post, on the second business day after posting, and

(*b*) in the case of service in accordance with sub-paragraph (1)(*b*)(ii), on the second business day after the day on which it is left at the document exchange.

(4) In any proceedings where this Schedule, or a rule where this Schedule applies, requires a document to be served, the court or the justices' clerk may, without prejudice to any power under paragraph 4 below, direct that –

(*a*) the requirement shall not apply;

(*b*) the time specified by the rules for complying with the requirement shall be abridged to such extent as may be specified in the direction;

(*c*) service shall be effected in such manner as may be specified in the direction.

4 Directions

(1) The justices' clerk or the court may give, vary or revoke directions for the conduct of the proceedings, including –

(*a*) the timetable for the proceedings,

(*b*) varying the time within which or by which an act is required by this Schedule or by a rule where this Schedule applies to proceedings pursuant to that rule to be done,

(*c*) the service of documents, and

(*d*) the submission of evidence

and, where the justices' chief executive receives such an application or any other document by which proceedings are commenced, the justices' chief executive shall consider whether such directions need to be given.

(2) Where the justices' clerk or a single justice who is holding a directions appointment considers, for whatever reason, that it is inappropriate to give a direction on a particular matter, he shall refer the matter to the court which may give any appropriate direction.

(3) Directions under sub-paragraph (1) may be given, varied or revoked either –

(*a*) of the justices' clerk's or the court's own motion having given the resident party an opportunity to attend and be heard or to make written representations, or

(*b*) on the written request of either party specifying the direction which is sought.

(4) Where the justices' chief executive receives a request under sub-paragraph (3)(*b*) the justices' clerk shall –

(*a*) make the direction sought, or
(*b*) fix a date for a hearing to consider the request.

"justices' clerk" (para 4(1)–(4))—For the power of delegation available to the justices' clerk in respect of these duties, see para 12 below.

5 Timing of proceedings

(1) Any period of time fixed by this Schedule or by a rule where this Schedule applies to proceedings pursuant to that rule, or by any order or direction, for doing any act shall be reckoned in accordance with this rule.

(2) Where the period, being a period of 7 days or less, would include a day which is not a business day, that day shall be excluded.

(3) Where the time fixed for filing a document with the justices' chief executive expires on a day on which the office of the justices' chief executive is closed, and for that reason the document cannot be filed on that day, the document shall be filed in time if it is filed on the next day on which the office of the justices' chief executive is open.

(4) Where this Schedule or a rule where this Schedule applies to proceedings pursuant to that rule provides a period of time within which or by which a certain act is to be performed in the course of relevant proceedings, that period may not be extended otherwise than by a direction of the justices' clerk or the court under paragraph 4(1) above.

(5) At the –

(*a*) transfer to a court of proceedings,
(*b*) postponement or adjournment of any hearing or directions appointment in the course of relevant proceedings, or
(*c*) conclusion of any such hearing or directions appointment other than one at which the proceedings are determined, or so soon thereafter as is practicable,
 (i) the justices' clerk shall fix a date upon which the proceedings shall come before him or the court again for such purposes as he or the court directs, which date shall, where paragraph (*a*) applies, be as soon as possible after the transfer, and
 (ii) the justices' chief executive shall give notice to the resident party of the date so fixed.

6 Attendance at directions appointment and hearing

(1) The resident party shall attend a directions appointment of which he has been given notice in accordance with paragraph 4 above unless the justices' clerk or the court otherwise directs.

(2) Where at the time and place appointed for a hearing or directions appointment the resident party does not appear the justices' clerk or the court shall not proceed with the hearing or appointment unless –

(*a*) the proceedings relate to an application filed by the resident party, or
(*b*) the court is satisfied that the resident party has received reasonable notice of the hearing or appointment.

(3) Where at the time and place appointed for a hearing or directions appointment the non-resident party does not appear the court may proceed with the hearing or appointment where the proceedings relate to an order or application sent by the Lord Chancellor to the court under the Act.

(4) Nothing in this Schedule shall be taken as preventing either party from appearing at any hearing or directions appointment.

7 Documentary evidence

(1) A party shall file, at or by such time as the justices' clerk or the court directs or, in the absence of a direction, before the hearing or appointment –

(*a*) written statements of the substance of the oral evidence which he intends to adduce at a hearing or a directions appointment, which shall –
- (i) be dated,
- (ii) be signed by the person making the statement,
- (iii) contain a declaration that the maker of the statement believes it to be true and understands that it may be placed before the court, and
- (iv) show in the top right-hand corner of the first page –
  - (*a*) the initials and surname of the person making the statement,
  - (*b*) the number of the statement in relation to the maker,
  - (*c*) the date on which the statement was made, and
  - (*d*) the party on whose behalf it is filed, and

(*b*) copies of any documents upon which he intends to rely at a hearing or a directions appointment.

(2) A party may, subject to any direction of the justices' clerk or the court about the timing or statements under this rule, file a statement which is supplementary to a statement served under sub-paragraph (1).

(3) Where a non-resident party files a statement or document under this rule, he shall also file a copy of it for service on the resident party; and the justices' chief executive shall on receipt of that copy serve it on the resident party.

(4) At a hearing or directions appointment a party may not without the leave of the justices' clerk, in the case of a directions appointment, or the court –

(*a*) adduce evidence, or
(*b*) seek to rely on a document,

in respect of which he has failed to comply with the requirements of sub-paragraphs (1) and, where applicable, (3).

8 Amendment

(1) A party amending a document shall file the amended document with the justices' chief executive; and the amendments shall be identified.

(2) Paragraph 7(3) above applies to an amended document filed under this paragraph.

9 Oral evidence

The justices' clerk or the court shall keep a note of the substance or any oral evidence given at a hearing or directions appointment.

PART III

10 Hearing

(1) Before the hearing, the justice or justices who will be dealing with the case shall read any documents which have been filed under paragraph 7 above in respect of the hearing.

(2) The justices' clerk at a directions appointment, or the court at a hearing or directions appointment, may give directions as to the order of speeches and evidence.

(3) After the final hearing, the court shall make its decision as soon as is practicable.

(4) Before the court makes an order or refuses an application, the justices' clerk shall record in writing –

(*a*) the names of the justice or justices constituting the court by which the decision is made, and
(*b*) in consultation with the justice or justices, the reasons for the court's decision and any findings of fact.

(5) After the court announces its decision, the justices' clerk shall as soon as practicable make a record in writing of any order.

(6) Where, under subsection (4) of section 7 of the Domestic Proceedings and Magistrates' Courts Act 1978, a court decides to treat an application under section 7 as if it were an application for an order under section 2 of that Act, the court shall indicate orally which of grounds (*a*) and (*b*) in that subsection it considers applicable and a memorandum of that decision and the grounds therefor shall be entered in the court's register.

11 Confidentiality of documents

(1) No document, other than a record of an order, held by the court and relating to any proceedings shall be disclosed, other than to –

(*a*) a party,
(*b*) the legal representative of a party,
(*c*) the Lord Chancellor's Department, or
(*d*) the Legal Aid Board,

without leave of the justices' clerk or the court.

12 Delegation by justices' clerk

(1) In this paragraph, "employed as a clerk in court" has the same meaning as in rule 2(1) of the Justices' Clerks (Qualifications of Assistants) Rules 1979.

(2) Anything authorised to be done by, to or before a justices' clerk under this Schedule or under a rule to which this Schedule applies may be done instead by, to or before a person employed as a clerk in court where that person is appointed by the magistrates' courts committee to assist him and where that person has been specifically authorised by the justices' clerk for that purpose.

(3) Any authorisation by the justices' clerk under sub-paragraph (2) shall be recorded in writing at the time the authority is given or as soon as practicable thereafter.

"appointed by the magistrates' courts committee" (para 12(2))—This appears to exclude "agency clerks", since the delegated powers may only be exercised by a person appointed by the relevant committee.

13 Application of section 97 of the Magistrates' Courts Act 1980

(1) Subject to sub-paragraph (2) below, section 97 of the Magistrates' Courts Act 1980 shall apply to proceedings to which this Schedule applies as it applies to a hearing of a complaint under that section.

(2) The power of a justice under section 97 of that Act to issue a witness summons may be exercised by a justices' clerk.

Amendments—Schedule inserted by SI 1993/617; amended by SI 2001/615.

****

Magistrates' Courts (Reciprocal Enforcement of Maintenance Orders) (Republic of Ireland) Rules 1975, SI 1975/286

1 These Rules may be cited as the Magistrates' Courts (Reciprocal Enforcement of Maintenance Orders) (Republic of Ireland) Rules 1975 and shall come into operation on 1 April 1975.

"These Rules"—These rules modify the Maintenance Orders (Reciprocal Enforcement) Act 1972 to provide a separate code for the making and receiving of maintenance claims to and from the Republic of Ireland.

2 (1) In these Rules, unless the context otherwise requires –

"the Act" means the Maintenance Orders (Reciprocal Enforcement) Act 1972 as applied with such exceptions, adaptations and modifications as are specified in the Reciprocal Enforcement of Maintenance Orders (Republic of Ireland) Order 1974; and

"the court's register", in relation to a justices' chief executive, means the register kept by the justices' chief executive in pursuance of rule 54 of the Magistrates' Courts Rules 1968.

(2) The Interpretation Act 1889 shall apply to the interpretation of these Rules as it applies to the interpretation of an Act of Parliament.

Amendments—SI 2001/615.

"rule 54 of the Magistrates' Courts Rules 1968" (r 2(1))—See now Magistrates' Courts Rules 1981, r 66.

"Interpretation Act 1889" (r 2(2))—This reference should be construed as a reference to the Interpretation Act 1978.

3 The officer of any court, by or in relation to whom anything is to be done in pursuance of any provision of Part I of the Act shall, where the court is a magistrates' court, be the justices' clerk.

4 (1) An application under section 2 of the Act (transmission of maintenance order made in United Kingdom for enforcement in Republic of Ireland) may, where the court which made the maintenance order to which the application relates is a magistrates' court, be made in writing by or on behalf of the payee under the order.

(2) Any application made in pursuance of paragraph (1) above shall –

(*a*) specify the date on which the order was made;
(*b*) contain such particulars as are known to the applicant of the whereabouts of the payer;
(*c*) specify any matters likely to assist in the identification of the payer;
(*d*) where possible, be accompanied by a recent photograph of the payer.

(3) In this rule, "the payer" means the payer under the order to which the application relates.

4A (1) An application under section 3 of the Act for a provisional order or under section 5 of the Act for the variation or revocation of a maintenance order or a provisional order made in the United Kingdom shall be filed in an appropriate form.

(2) Where the justices' chief executive receives such an application –

(*a*) the justices' clerk shall fix the date, time and place for a hearing or a directions appointment; and
(*b*) the justices' chief executive shall notify the applicant of the date, time and place so fixed.

Amendments—Inserted by SI 1993/617; amended by SI 2001/615.

4B (1) Schedule A1 to these Rules shall apply to proceedings pursuant to rule 4A above.

(2) In Schedule A1 as it applies to rule 4A, "the resident party" and "the non-resident party" shall be taken to mean –

(*a*) in the case of an application for a provisional order, the applicant and the respondent respectively, and
(*b*) in the case of an application for the variation or revocation of a maintenance order or a provisional order, the payee and the payer respectively under the order in question.

Amendments—Inserted by SI 1993/617.

5 A document setting out or summarising any evidence, required by section 3(5)(*b*) or 5(2) of the Act to be authenticated, shall be authenticated by a certificate, signed by one of the justices before whom that evidence was given, that the document is the original document setting out or, as the case may be, summarising that evidence or a true copy of that document.

6 Where under section 3(6A) of the Act a person is required to be notified of the date fixed for the hearing at which confirmation of a provisional order is to be considered, the justices' chief executive for the magistrates' court which made the provisional order shall send that person written notice of the date fixed.

Amendments—SI 2001/615.

7 Any documents required by section 5(4) of the Act to be sent to a court in the Republic of Ireland shall be sent to that court by post.

8 (1) Where a justices' chief executive is required under any provision of Part I of the Act to register an order, he shall cause the order to be registered in his court by means of a minute or memorandum entered and signed by him in the court's register.

(2) Every minute or memorandum entered in pursuance of paragraph (1) above shall specify the section of the Act under which the order in question is registered.

Amendments—SI 2001/615.

9 (1) Any notice required under section 6(6) of the Act (notice of registration in United Kingdom court of maintenance order made in Republic of Ireland) to be served on the payer under a maintenance order shall, where the order is registered in a magistrates' court, be in the form in Part I of the Schedule to these Rules, or in a form to the like effect.

(2) Where a magistrates' court to which an appeal is made under section 6(7) of the Act sets aside the registration of a maintenance order, the justices' chief executive shall send written notice of the court's decision to the payee under the order.

(3) Any notice required under section 6(10) of the Act (notice that maintenance order made in Republic of Ireland has not been registered in United Kingdom court) to be given to the payee under a maintenance order shall, where the appropriate court is a magistrates' court, be in the form in Part II of the Schedule to these Rules or in a form to the like effect.

Amendments—SI 2001/615.

10 (1) When an order is registered under section 6(3) of the Act, the court shall order that payment of sums due thereunder shall be made to the justices' chief executive for the registering court during such hours and at such place as that justices' chief executive may direct.

(1A) A justices' chief executive to whom payments are ordered to be made (whether by virtue of an order under paragraph (1) above or by virtue of an order of the court under the Act) shall send those payments by post to the payee under the order, or where a public authority has been authorised by the payee to receive the payments, to that public authority.

(2) Where it appears to a justices' chief executive to whom payments under any maintenance order are made that any sums payable under the order are in arrear he shall, if the person for whose benefit the payment should have been made so requests in writing, proceed in his own name for the recovery of those sums, unless it appears to him that it is unreasonable in the circumstances to do so.

(3) Where it appears to such a justices' chief executive that any sums payable under the order are in arrear to an amount equal to four times the sum payable weekly under the order he shall give to the person for whose benefit the payment should have been made notice in writing stating the particulars of the arrears.

Amendments—SI 1992/457; SI 2001/615.

10A (1) Where, in the exercise of the duty imposed under rule 10(1) above, or in the exercise of the powers conferred by virtue of section 8(4A) of the Act, the court orders that payments under the order are to be made by a particular means, the clerk of the court shall record on the copy of the order the means of payment which the court has ordered and notify in writing, as soon as practicable, the person liable to make payments under the order of how payments are to be made.

(2) Where, in the exercise of the aforesaid powers, the court orders payment to the justices' chief executive for the court, or to the justices' chief executive for any other magistrates' court, by a method of payment falling within section 59(6) of the Magistrates' Courts Act 1980 (standing order, etc), the justices' chief executive for the court to whom payments are to be made shall notify the person liable to make the payments under the order of the number and location of the account into which the payments are to be made.

Amendments—Inserted by SI 1992/457; amended by SI 2001/615.

11 (1) Subject to paragraph (2) below, where a request is made by or on behalf of a court in the Republic of Ireland for the taking in England and Wales of the evidence of a person residing therein, the following magistrates' courts shall have power under section 14(1) of the Act (obtaining of evidence needed for purpose of certain proceedings) to take that evidence, that is to say –

(*a*) where the maintenance order to which the proceedings in the court in the Republic of Ireland relate was made by a magistrates' court, the court which made the order;
(*b*) where the maintenance order to which those proceedings relate is registered in a magistrates' court which has received such a request from the Secretary of State.

(2) The power conferred by paragraph (1) above may, with the agreement of a court having that power, be exercised by any other magistrates' court which, because the person whose evidence is to be taken resides within its jurisdiction or for any other reason, the first-mentioned court considers could more conveniently take the evidence; but nothing in this paragraph shall derogate from the power of any court specified in paragraph (1) above.

(3) Subject to paragraph (4) below, where the evidence of any person is to be taken by a magistrates' court under the foregoing provisions of this rule –

(*a*) the evidence shall be taken in the same manner as if that person were a witness in proceedings on a complaint;
(*b*) any oral evidence so taken shall be put into writing and read to the person who gave it, who shall be required to sign the document; and
(*c*) the justices by whom the evidence of any person is so taken shall certify at the foot of any document setting out the evidence of, or produced in evidence by, that person that such evidence was taken, or document received in evidence, as the case may be, by them.

(4) Where such a request as is mentioned in paragraph (1) above includes a request that the evidence be taken in a particular manner, the magistrates' court by which the evidence is taken shall, so far as circumstances permit, comply with that request.

12 Where a magistrates' court makes an order varying or revoking a maintenance order to which section 5 of the Act (variation and revocation of maintenance order made in United Kingdom) applies, the justices' chief executive shall send written notice of the making of the order to the Secretary of State.

Amendments—SI 2001/615.

13 (1) Where a justices' chief executive registers under section 6(3) of the Act (registration in United Kingdom court of maintenance order made in Republic of Ireland an order to which section 6 of the Act applies), he shall send written notice to the Secretary of State that the order has been duly registered.

(2) Where a justices' chief executive cancels the registration of a maintenance order under section 10(1) of the Act (cancellation of registration and transfer of order), he shall send written notice of the cancellation to the payer under the order.

(3) Where a justices' chief executive registers a maintenance order under section 10(4) of the Act, he shall send written notice to the Secretary of State and to the payer under the order that the order has been duly registered.

Amendments—SI 2001/615.

14 (1) Where the justices' chief executive for a magistrates' court receives from the Secretary of State a notice of the issue of the summons or other originating document in proceedings in the Republic of Ireland in relation to the making, variation or revocation of a maintenance order and it appears to that justices' chief executive that the person against whom those proceedings have been instituted is residing within the petty sessions area for which the court acts, the justices' chief executive shall serve the notice on that person by sending it by post in a registered letter addressed to him at his last known or usual place of abode.

(2) Where it appears to a justices' chief executive who has received such a notice from the Secretary of State that the person against whom the proceedings have been instituted is not so residing, the justices' chief executive shall send the notice to the Secretary of State.

(3) Where a justices' chief executive serves a notice in pursuance of paragraph (1) above he shall send a document which establishes that the notice was so served to the Secretary of State for transmission to the responsible authority in the Republic of Ireland.

Amendments—SI 2001/615.

SCHEDULE A1

RULES OF PROCEDURE

1 In this Schedule, and in any rule where this Schedule applies to proceedings pursuant to that rule, unless the context otherwise requires –

"business day" means any day other than –

(*a*) a Saturday, Sunday, Christmas or Good Friday; or

(*b*) a bank holiday, that is to say, a day which is, or is to be observed as, a bank holiday, or a holiday, under the Banking and Financial Dealings Act 1971, in England and Wales,

"directions appointment" means a hearing for directions under paragraph 4 below,

"file" means deposit with the justices' chief executive,

"justices' chief executive" means a justices' chief executive appointed under section 40 of the Justices of the Peace Act 1997,

"leave" includes approval,

"note" includes a record made by mechanical or electronic means, and

"proceedings" means proceedings to which this Schedule applies.

"any rule where this Schedule applies"—The Schedule prescribes the procedure to be followed in proceedings under Maintenance Orders (Reciprocal Enforcement) Act 1972, ss 3 and 5.

2 Transfer of proceedings

(1) Where –

(*a*) any proceedings are relevant proceedings within the meaning of section 93 of the Children Act 1989, and

(*b*) the justices' chief executive or the court receives a request in writing from the resident party that the proceedings be transferred to another magistrates' court,

the justices' clerk or court shall issue a certificate in the appropriate form, granting or refusing the request in accordance with any Order made by the Lord Chancellor under Part I of Schedule 11 to the Children Act 1989.

(2) Where a request is granted under paragraph (1) the justices' chief executive shall send a copy of the certificate –

(*a*) to the resident party,

(*b*) to the Lord Chancellor's Department, and

(*c*) to the magistrates' court to which the proceedings are to be transferred.

(3) Any consent given or refused by a justices' clerk in accordance with any Order made by the Lord Chancellor under Part I of Schedule 11 shall be recorded in writing by the justices' clerk at the time it is given or refused or as soon as practicable thereafter.

3 Service

(1) Where service of a document is required by this Schedule or by a rule where this Schedule applies to proceedings pursuant to that rule it may be effected, unless the contrary is indicated –

(*a*) if the person to be served is not known by the person serving to be acting by solicitor –

(i) by delivering it to him personally, or

(ii) by delivering it at, or by sending it by first-class post to, his residence or last known residence, or

(*b*) If the person to be served is known by the person serving to be acting by solicitor –

(i) by delivering the document at, or sending it by first-class post to, the solicitor's address for service,

(ii) where the solicitor's address for service includes a numbered box at a document exchange, by leaving the document at that document exchange or at a document exchange which transmits documents on every business day to that document exchange, or

(iii) by sending a legible copy of the document by facsimile transmission to the solicitor's office.

(2) In this paragraph, "first-class post" means first-class post which has been pre-paid or in respect of which pre-payment is not required.

(3) A document shall, unless the contrary is proved, be deemed to have been served –

(*a*) in the case of service by first-class post, on the second business day after posting, and

(*b*) in the case of service in accordance with sub-paragraph (1)(*b*)(ii), on the second business day after the day on which it is left at the document exchange.

(4) In any proceedings where this Schedule, or a rule where this Schedule applies, requires a document to be served, the court or the justices' clerk may, without prejudice to any power under paragraph 4 below, direct that –

(*a*) the requirement shall not apply;

(*b*) the time specified by the rules for complying with the requirement shall be abridged to such extent as may be specified in the direction;

(*c*) service shall be effected in such manner as may be specified in the direction.

4 Directions

(1) The justices' clerk or the court may give, vary or revoke directions for the conduct of the proceedings, including –

(*a*) the timetable for the proceedings,

(*b*) varying the time within which or by which an act is required by this Schedule or by a rule where this Schedule applies to proceedings pursuant to that rule to be done,

(*c*) the service of documents, and

(*d*) the submission of evidence

and, where the justices' chief executive receives such an application or any other document by which proceedings are commenced, the justices' chief executive shall consider whether such directions need to be given.

(2) Where the justices' clerk or a single justice who is holding a directions appointment considers, for whatever reason, that it is inappropriate to give a direction on a particular matter, he shall refer the matter to the court which may give any appropriate direction.

(3) Directions under sub-paragraph (1) may be given, varied or revoked either –

(*a*) of the justices' clerk's or the court's own motion having given the resident party an opportunity to attend and be heard or to make written representations, or

(*b*) on the written request of either party specifying the direction which is sought.

(4) Where the justices' chief executive receives a request under sub-paragraph (3)(*b*) the justices' clerk shall –

(*a*) make the direction sought, or
(*b*) fix a date for a hearing to consider the request.

"justices' clerk" (para 4(1)–(4))—**For the power of delegation available to the justices' clerk in respect of these duties, see para 12 below.**

5 Timing of proceedings

(1) Any period of time fixed by this Schedule or by a rule where this Schedule applies to proceedings pursuant to that rule, or by any order or direction, for doing any act shall be reckoned in accordance with this rule.

(2) Where the period, being a period of 7 days or less, would include a day which is not a business day, that day shall be excluded.

(3) Where the time fixed for filing a document with the justices' chief executive expires on a day on which the office of the justices' chief executive is closed, and for that reason the document cannot be filed on that day, the document shall be filed in time if it is filed on the next day on which the office of the justices' chief executive is open.

(4) Where this Schedule or a rule where this Schedule applies to proceedings pursuant to that rule provides a period of time within which or by which a certain act is to be performed in the course of relevant proceedings, that period may not be extended otherwise than by a direction of the justices' clerk or the court under paragraph 4(1) above.

(5) At the –

(*a*) transfer to a court of proceedings,
(*b*) postponement or adjournment of any hearing or directions appointment in the course of relevant proceedings, or
(*c*) conclusion of any such hearing or directions appointment other than one at which the proceedings are determined, or so soon thereafter as is practicable,

(i) the justices' clerk shall fix a date upon which the proceedings shall come before him or the court again for such purposes as he or the court directs, which date shall, where paragraph (*a*) applies, be as soon as possible after the transfer, and
(ii) the justices' chief executive shall give notice to the resident party of the date so fixed.

6 Attendance at directions appointment and hearing

(1) The resident party shall attend a directions appointment of which he has been given notice in accordance with paragraph 4 above unless the justices' clerk or the court otherwise directs.

(2) Where at the time and place appointed for a hearing or directions appointment the resident party does not appear the justices' clerk or the court shall not proceed with the hearing or appointment unless –

(*a*) the proceedings relate to an application filed by the resident party, or
(*b*) the court is satisfied that the resident party has received reasonable notice of the hearing or appointment.

(3) Where at the time and place appointed for a hearing or directions appointment the non-resident party does not appear the court may proceed with the hearing or appointment where the proceedings relate to an order or application sent by the Lord Chancellor to the court under the Act.

(4) Nothing in this Schedule shall be taken as preventing either party from appearing at any hearing or directions appointment.

7 Documentary evidence

(1) A party shall file, at or by such time as the justices' clerk or the court directs or, in the absence of a direction, before the hearing or appointment –

- (*a*) written statements of the substance of the oral evidence which he intends to adduce at a hearing or a directions appointment, which shall –
  - (i) be dated,
  - (ii) be signed by the person making the statement,
  - (iii) contain a declaration that the maker of the statement believes it to be true and understands that it may be placed before the court, and
  - (iv) show in the top right-hand corner of the first page –
    - (*a*) the initials and surname of the person making the statement,
    - (*b*) the number of the statement in relation to the maker,
    - (*c*) the date on which the statement was made, and
    - (*d*) the party on whose behalf it is filed, and
- (*b*) copies of any documents upon which he intends to rely at a hearing or a directions appointment.

(2) A party may, subject to any direction of the justices' clerk or the court about the timing or statements under this rule, file a statement which is supplementary to a statement served under sub-paragraph (1).

(3) Where a non-resident party files a statement or document under this rule, he shall also file a copy of it for service on the resident party; and the justices' chief executive shall on receipt of that copy serve it on the resident party.

(4) At a hearing or directions appointment a party may not without the leave of the justices' clerk, in the case of a directions appointment, or the court –

- (*a*) adduce evidence, or
- (*b*) seek to rely on a document,

in respect of which he has failed to comply with the requirements of sub-paragraphs (1) and, where applicable, (3).

8 Amendment

(1) A party amending a document shall file the amended document with the justices' chief executive; and the amendments shall be identified.

(2) Paragraph 7(3) above applies to an amended document filed under this paragraph.

9 Oral evidence

The justices' clerk or the court shall keep a note of the substance or any oral evidence given at a hearing or directions appointment.

PART III

10 Hearing

(1) Before the hearing, the justice or justices who will be dealing with the case shall read any documents which have been filed under paragraph 7 above in respect of the hearing.

(2) The justices' clerk at a directions appointment, or the court at a hearing or directions appointment, may give directions as to the order of speeches and evidence.

(3) After the final hearing, the court shall make its decision as soon as is practicable.

(4) Before the court makes an order or refuses an application, the justices' clerk shall record in writing –

(*a*) the names of the justice or justices constituting the court by which the decision is made, and
(*b*) in consultation with the justice or justices, the reasons for the court's decision and any findings of fact.

(5) After the court announces its decision, the justices' clerk shall as soon as practicable make a record in writing of any order.

(6) Where, under subsection (4) of section 7 of the Domestic Proceedings and Magistrates' Courts Act 1978, a court decides to treat an application under section 7 as if it were an application for an order under section 2 of that Act, the court shall indicate orally which of grounds (*a*) and (*b*) in that subsection it considers applicable and a memorandum of that decision and the grounds therefor shall be entered in the court's register.

11 Confidentiality of documents

(1) No document, other than a record of an order, held by the court and relating to any proceedings shall be disclosed, other than to –

(*a*) a party,
(*b*) the legal representative of a party,
(*c*) the Lord Chancellor's Department, or
(*d*) the Legal Aid Board,

without leave of the justices' clerk or the court.

12 Delegation by justices' clerk

(1) In this paragraph, "employed as a clerk in court" has the same meaning as in rule 2(1) of the Justices' Clerks (Qualifications of Assistants) Rules 1979.

(2) Anything authorised to be done by, to or before a justices' clerk under this Schedule or under a rule to which this Schedule applies may be done instead by, to or before a person employed as a clerk in court where that person is appointed by the magistrates' courts committee to assist him and where that person has been specifically authorised by the justices' clerk for that purpose.

(3) Any authorisation by the justices' clerk under sub-paragraph (2) shall be recorded in writing at the time the authority is given or as soon as practicable thereafter.

"appointed by the magistrates' courts committee" (para 12(2))—This appears to exclude "agency clerks", since the delegated powers may only be exercised by a person appointed by the relevant committee.

13 Application of section 97 of the Magistrates' Courts Act 1980

(1) Subject to sub-paragraph (2) below, section 97 of the Magistrates' Courts Act 1980 shall apply to proceedings to which this Schedule applies as it applies to a hearing of a complaint under that section.

(2) The power of a justice under section 97 of that Act to issue a witness summons may be exercised by a justices' clerk.

Amendments—Schedule inserted by SI 1993/617; amended by SI 2001/615.

****

Magistrates' Courts (Reciprocal Enforcement of Maintenance Orders) (United States of America) Rules 1995, SI 1995/2802

1 Citation and commencement

These Rules may be cited as the Magistrates' Courts (Reciprocal Enforcement of Maintenance Orders) (United States of America) Rules 1995 and shall come into force on 1 December 1995.

"These Rules"—These rules apply the provisions of the Magistrates' Courts (Reciprocal Enforcement of Maintenance Orders) (Hague Convention Countries) Rules 1980, with modifications, to applications under Part I of the Maintenance Orders (Reciprocal Enforcement) Act 1972 as amended by the Reciprocal Enforcement of Maintenance Orders (United States of America) Order 1995.

2 Interpretation

In these Rules "the 1980 Rules" means the Magistrates' Courts (Reciprocal Enforcement of Maintenance Orders) (Hague Convention Countries) Rules 1980 and any reference to a rule by number alone shall be construed as a reference to the rule so numbered in the 1980 Rules.

3 Application of the 1980 Rules

Rules 2 to 12 of and Schedule 1A to the 1980 Rules shall apply in respect of the matters which are to be prescribed under Part I of the Maintenance Orders (Reciprocal Enforcement) Act 1972 as set out in Schedule 3 to the Reciprocal Enforcement of Maintenance Orders (United States of America) Order 1995 as if –

(*a*) for the reference in rule 2 to the Magistrates' Courts (Reciprocal Enforcement of Maintenance Orders) (Hague Convention Countries) Order 1979 there were substituted a reference to the Magistrates' Courts

(Reciprocal Enforcement of Maintenance Orders) (United States of America) Order 1995;

(*b*) for rule 4(2)(*b*) there were substituted the following –

"(*b*) contain a sworn statement signed by the payee giving the following information –

(i) the address of the payee;

(ii) such information as is known as to the whereabouts of the payer; and

(iii) a description, so far as is known, of the nature and location of any assets of the payer available for execution;";

(*c*) rules 4A(1)(*a*) and 4B(2)(*a*) were omitted;

(*d*) for the reference to section 5(4)(*b*) of the Act in rule 6 there were substituted a reference to rule 5(5)(*c*);

(*e*) rule 7 were omitted;

(*f*) for references in rules 4, 9, 11 and 12 to "Hague Convention country", wherever they appear, there were substituted references to "specified State".

Magistrates' Courts (Recovery Abroad of Maintenance) Rules 1975, SI 1975/488

1 These Rules may be cited as the Magistrates' Courts (Recovery Abroad of Maintenance) Rules 1975 and shall come into operation on 12 April 1975.

"These Rules"—These rules provide for the application of Pt II of the Maintenance Orders (Reciprocal Enforcement) Act 1972.

2 (1) In these Rules, unless the context otherwise requires –

"the Act" means the Maintenance Orders (Reciprocal Enforcement) Act 1972; and

"the court's register", in relation to a justices' chief executive, means the register kept by the justices' chief executive in pursuance of rule 54 of the Magistrates' Courts Rules 1968.

(2) The Interpretation Act 1889 shall apply to the interpretation of these Rules as it applies to the interpretation of an Act of Parliament.

Amendments—SI 2001/615.

"rule 54 of the Magistrates' Courts Rules 1968" (r 2(1))—See now Magistrates' Courts Rules 1981, r 66.

"Interpretation Act 1889" (r 2(2))—This reference should be construed as a reference to the Interpretation Act 1978.

3 The officer of any court, by or in relation to whom anything is to be done in pursuance of any provision of Part II of the Act, shall, where that court is a magistrates' court, be the justices' clerk.

3A (1) Where the justices' chief executive receives an application for the recovery of maintenance in England and Wales sent from the Lord Chancellor to a magistrates' court under section 27B of the Act –

(*a*) the justices' clerk shall fix the date, time and place for a hearing or a directions appointment, allowing sufficient time for service under this rule to be effected at least 21 days before the date so fixed; and

(*b*) the justices' chief executive shall serve copies of the application and any accompanying documents, together with a notice stating the date, time and place so fixed, on the respondent.

(2) Within 14 days of service under this rule, the respondent shall file an answer to the application in the appropriate form.

Amendments—Inserted by SI 1993/617; amended by SI 2001/615.

4 Where a magistrates' court dismisses an application under section 27A of the Act (application for recovery of maintenance), or an application by a person in a convention country for the variation of a registered order, the justices' chief executive shall send written notice of the court's decision to the Secretary of State and any such notice shall include a statement of the justices' reasons for their decision.

Amendments—SI 1993/617; SI 2001/615.

5 (1) Where a magistrates' court makes an order which is required under section 27C(7) of the Act to be registered, the justices' clerk shall enter and sign a minute or memorandum of the order in the court's register.

(2) Where a justices' chief executive in pursuance of section 32(2) or (3) of the Act (transfer of orders), receives a certified copy of an order, he shall cause the order to be registered in his court by means of a minute or memorandum entered and signed by him in the court's register.

(3) Every minute or memorandum entered in pursuance of paragraph (1) or (2) above shall specify the section and subsection of the Act under which the order in question is registered.

Amendments—SI 1993/617; SI 2001/615.

5A Where an application under section 26(1) or (2) of the Act or a certificate under section 26(3A) of the Act is required to be registered in a magistrates' court in pursuance of the Recovery of Maintenance (United States of America) Order 1979, the justices' chief executive shall enter and sign a minute or memorandum of the application or certificate in his register.

Amendments—Inserted by SI 1979/1561; amended by SI 2001/615.

6 (1) Where a justices' chief executive registers an order in pursuance of section 27C(7) or 32(2) or (3) of the Act, he shall send written notice to the Secretary of State that the order has been duly registered.

(2) Where a justices' chief executive is required by section 32(6) of the Act to give notice of the registration of an order he shall do so by sending written notice to the officer specified in that subsection that the order has been duly registered.

Amendments—SI 1993/617; SI 2001/615.

7 (1) A justices' chief executive to whom payments are made by virtue of section 27C, section 33(3A) or section 34A of the Act shall send those payments by post to such person or authority as the Lord Chancellor may from time to time direct.

(2) Where it appears to the justices' chief executive to whom payments under a registered order are made that any sums payable under the order are in arrear he may and, if such sums are in arrear to an amount equal –

(*a*) in the case of payments to be made monthly or less frequently, to twice the sum payable periodically; or
(*b*) in any other case, to four times the sum payable periodically,

he shall, whether the person for whose benefit the payment should have been made requests him to do so or not, proceed in his own name for the recovery of those sums, unless it appears to him that it is unreasonable in the circumstances to do so.

Amendments—SI 1980/1584; SI 1993/617; SI 2001/615.

7A (1) Where, in the exercise of the duty imposed under section 27C of the Act, or in the exercise of the powers conferred by virtue of section 33(3A) or section 34A of the Act, the court orders that payments under the order are to be made by a particular means, the clerk of the court shall record on the copy of the order the means of payment which the court has ordered and the justices' chief executive shall notify in writing, as soon as practicable, the person liable to make payments under the order of how the payments are to be made.

(2) Where, in the exercise of any of the aforesaid powers, the court orders payment to the clerk of the court, or to the justices' chief executive for any other magistrates' court, by a method of payment falling within section 59(6) of the Magistrates' Courts Act 1980 (standing order, etc) the justices' chief executive for the court to whom payments are to be made shall notify the person liable to make the payments under the order of the number and location of the account into which the payments are to be made.

(3) Where, under section 34A(4) of the Act, the justices' chief executive for the court receives an application from an interested party for the method of payment to be varied, the justices' chief executive shall notify in writing, as soon as practicable, that party and, where practicable, any other interested party, of the result of the application, including any decision to refer the matter to the court; where the clerk of the court grants the application he shall record the variation on the copy of the order.

Amendments—Inserted by SI 1993/617; amended by SI 2001/615.

7B (1) In this rule "an application" means an application under section 34 of the Act for the variation or revocation of a registered order.

(2) An application which is made directly to the registering court shall be filed in an appropriate form.

(3) Where the justices' chief executive receives an application, either filed in accordance with paragraph (2) or sent from the Lord Chancellor under section 34(3) of the Act –

(*a*) the justices' clerk shall fix the date, time and place for a hearing or a directions appointment; and (*b*) the justices' chief executive shall notify the applicant of the date, time and place so fixed.

Amendments—Inserted by SI 1993/617; amended by SI 2001/615.

8 (1) Notice under section 35(4) of the Act (variation of orders by magistrates' courts) of the making of an application for the variation or revocation of a registered order and of the time and place appointed for the hearing of the application shall be in the form specified in the Schedule to these Rules and shall be sent by post by the justices' chief executive to the Secretary of State for onward transmission to the appropriate authority in the convention country in which the respondent is residing.

(2) The time appointed for the hearing of the said complaint shall be not less than six weeks later than the date on which the said notice is sent to the Secretary of State.

Amendments—SI 1993/617; SI 2001/615.

9 (1) Where a magistrates' court receives from the Secretary of State a request under section 38(1) of the Act (taking evidence at request of court in convention country) to take the evidence of any person, that evidence shall be taken in accordance with the provisions of this rule.

(2) Subject to paragraph (3) below –

(*a*) the evidence shall be taken in the same manner as if the person concerned were a witness in proceedings on a complaint;

(*b*) any oral evidence so taken shall be put into writing and read to the person who gave it, who shall be required to sign the document; and

(*c*) the justices by whom the evidence of any person is so taken shall certify at the foot of any document setting out the evidence of, or produced in evidence by, that person that such evidence was taken, or document received in evidence, as the case may be, by them.

(3) Where the request referred to in section 38(1) of the Act includes a request that the evidence be taken in a particular manner, the court by which the evidence is taken shall, so far as circumstances permit, comply with that request.

10 (1) Where a justices' chief executive receives from the Secretary of State a request under section 38(1) of the Act to take the evidence of any person, that evidence shall be taken in accordance with the provisions of this rule.

(2) Subject to paragraph (3) below –

(*a*) the person whose evidence is to be taken shall be examined on oath by or before the justices' clerk;

(*b*) any oral evidence shall be put into writing and read to that person who shall be required to sign the document; and

(*c*) the justices' clerk shall certify at the foot of any document setting out the evidence of, or produced in evidence by, that person that such evidence was taken, or document received in evidence, as the case may be, by him.

(3) Where the request referred to in section 38(1) of the Act includes a request that the evidence be taken in a particular manner the justices' clerk by whom the evidence is taken shall, so far as circumstances permit, comply with that request.

(4) For the purposes of this rule a justices' clerk shall have the like power to administer oaths as has a single justice of the peace.

Amendments—SI 2001/615.

11 Any document such as is mentioned in paragraph (2)(*c*) of rule 9 or 10 of these Rules shall be sent to the Secretary of State for onward transmission to the appropriate authority in the convention country in which the request referred to in section 38(1) of the Act originated.

12 (1) Schedule 2 shall apply to proceedings pursuant to rules 3A and 7B above.

(2) In Schedule 2 as it applies to rule 3A, "the resident party" and "the non-resident party" shall be taken to mean the respondent and the applicant respectively.

(3) In Schedule 2 as it applies to rule 7B, "the resident party" and "the non-resident party" shall be taken to mean the payer and the payee under the order in question respectively.

Amendments—Inserted by SI 1993/617.

****

SCHEDULE 2

RULES OF PROCEDURE

1 In this Schedule, and in any rule where this Schedule applies to proceedings pursuant to that rule, unless the context otherwise requires –

"business day" means any day other than –

(*a*) a Saturday, Sunday, Christmas or Good Friday; or

(*b*) a bank holiday, that is to say, a day which is, or is to be observed as, a bank holiday, or a holiday, under the Banking and Financial Dealings Act 1971, in England and Wales,

"directions appointment" means a hearing for directions under paragraph 4 below,

"file" means deposit with the justices' chief executive,

"justices' chief executive" means a justices' chief executive appointed under section 40 of the Justices of the Peace Act 1997;

"leave" includes approval,

"note" includes a record made by mechanical or electronic means, and

"proceedings" means proceedings to which this Schedule applies.

"any rule where this Schedule applies"—The Schedule prescribes the procedure to be followed in proceedings under Maintenance Orders (Reciprocal Enforcement) Act 1972, ss 27B and 34.

2 Transfer of proceedings

(1) Where –

(*a*) any proceedings are relevant proceedings within the meaning of section 93 of the Children Act 1989, and (*b*) the justices' chief executive or the court receives a request in writing from the resident party that the proceedings be transferred to another magistrates' court,

the justices' clerk or court shall issue a certificate in the appropriate form, granting or refusing the request in accordance with any Order made by the Lord Chancellor under Part I of Schedule 11 to the Children Act 1989.

(2) Where a request is granted under paragraph (1) the justices' chief executive shall send a copy of the certificate –

(*a*) to the resident party,
(*b*) to the Lord Chancellor's Department, and
(*c*) to the magistrates' court to which the proceedings are to be transferred.

(3) Any consent given or refused by a justices' clerk in accordance with any Order made by the Lord Chancellor under Part I of Schedule 11 shall be recorded in writing by the justices' clerk at the time it is given or refused or as soon as practicable thereafter.

Scope of provision—This paragraph provides for the transfer of relevant proceedings between magistrates' courts.

3 Service

(1) Where service of a document is required by this Schedule or by a rule where this Schedule applies to proceedings pursuant to that rule it may be effected, unless the contrary is indicated –

(*a*) if the person to be served is not known by the person serving to be acting by solicitor –
  (i) by delivering it to him personally, or
  (ii) by delivering it at, or by sending it by first-class post to, his residence or last known residence, or
(*b*) if the person to be served is known by the person serving to be acting by solicitor –
  (i) by delivering the document at, or sending it by first-class post to, the solicitor's address for service,
  (ii) where the solicitor's address for service includes a numbered box at a document exchange, by leaving the document at that document exchange or at a document exchange which transmits documents on every business day to that document exchange, or
  (iii) by sending a legible copy of the document by facsimile transmission to the solicitor's office.

(2) In this paragraph, "first-class post" means first-class post which has been pre-paid or in respect of which pre-payment is not required.

(3) A document shall, unless the contrary is proved, be deemed to have been served –

(*a*) in the case of service by first-class post, on the second business day after posting, and
(*b*) in the case of service in accordance with sub-paragraph (1)(*b*)(ii), on the second business day after the day on which it is left at the document exchange.

(4) In any proceedings where this Schedule, or a rule where this Schedule applies, requires a document to be served, the court or the justices' clerk may, without prejudice to any power under paragraph 4 below, direct that –

(*a*) the requirement shall not apply;
(*b*) the time specified by the rules for complying with the requirement shall be abridged to such extent as may be specified in the direction;
(*c*) service shall be effected in such manner as may be specified in the direction.

4 Directions

(1) The justices' clerk or the court may give, vary or revoke directions for the conduct of the proceedings, including –

(*a*) the timetable for the proceedings,
(*b*) varying the time within which or by which an act is required by this Schedule or by a rule where this Schedule applies to proceedings pursuant to that rule to be done,
(*c*) the service of documents, and
(*d*) the submission of evidence

and, where the justices' chief executive receives such an application or any other document by which proceedings are commenced, the justices' chief executive shall consider whether such directions need to be given.

(2) Where the justices' clerk or a single justice who is holding a directions appointment considers, for whatever reason, that it is inappropriate to give a direction on a particular matter, he shall refer the matter to the court which may give any appropriate direction.

(3) Directions under sub-paragraph (1) may be given, varied or revoked either –

(*a*) of the justices' clerk's or the court's own motion having given the resident party an opportunity to attend and be heard or to make written representations, or
(*b*) on the written request of either party specifying the direction which is sought.

(4) Where the justices' chief executive receives a request under sub-paragraph (3)(*b*) the justices' clerk shall –

(*a*) make the direction sought, or
(*b*) fix a date for a hearing to consider the request.

"justices' clerk" (para 4(1), (4))—For the power of delegation available to the justices' clerk in respect of these duties, see para 12 below.

5 Timing of proceedings

(1) Any period of time fixed by this Schedule or by a rule where this Schedule applies to proceedings pursuant to that rule, or by any order or direction, for doing any act shall be reckoned in accordance with this rule.

(2) Where the period, being a period of 7 days or less, would include a day which is not a business day, that day shall be excluded.

(3) Where the time fixed for filing a document with the justices' chief executive expires on a day on which the office of the justices' chief executive is closed, and for that reason the document cannot be filed on that day, the document shall be

filed in time if it is filed on the next day on which the office of the justices' chief executive is open.

(4) Where this Schedule or a rule where this Schedule applies to proceedings pursuant to that rule provides a period of time within which or by which a certain act is to be performed in the course of relevant proceedings, that period may not be extended otherwise than by a direction of the justices' clerk or the court under paragraph 4(1) above.

(5) At the –

(*a*) transfer to a court of proceedings,
(*b*) postponement or adjournment of any hearing or directions appointment in the course of relevant proceedings, or
(*c*) conclusion of any such hearing or directions appointment other than one at which the proceedings are determined, or so soon thereafter as is practicable,
  (i) the justices' clerk shall fix a date upon which the proceedings shall come before him or the court again for such purposes as he or the court directs, which date shall, where paragraph (*a*) applies, be as soon as possible after the transfer, and
  (ii) the justices' chief executive shall give notice to the resident party of the date so fixed.

6 Attendance at directions appointment and hearing

(1) The resident party shall attend a directions appointment of which he has been given notice in accordance with paragraph 4 above unless the justices' clerk or the court otherwise directs.

(2) Where at the time and place appointed for a hearing or directions appointment the resident party does not appear the justices' clerk or the court shall not proceed with the hearing or appointment unless –

(*a*) the proceedings relate to an application filed by the resident party, or
(*b*) the court is satisfied that the resident party has received reasonable notice of the hearing or appointment.

(3) Where at the time and place appointed for a hearing or directions appointment the non-resident party does not appear the court may proceed with the hearing or appointment where the proceedings relate to an order or application sent by the Lord Chancellor to the court under the Act.

(4) Nothing in this Schedule shall be taken as preventing either party from appearing at any hearing or directions appointment.

7 Documentary evidence

(1) A party shall file, at or by such time as the justices' clerk or the court directs or, in the absence of a direction, before the hearing or appointment –

(*a*) written statements of the substance of the oral evidence which he intends to adduce at a hearing or a directions appointment, which shall –
  (i) be dated,
  (ii) be signed by the person making the statement,
  (iii) contain a declaration that the maker of the statement believes it to be true and understands that it may be placed before the court, and
  (iv) show in the top right-hand corner of the first page –

(*a*) the initials and surname of the person making the statement,
(*b*) the number of the statement in relation to the maker,
(*c*) the date on which the statement was made, and
(*d*) the party on whose behalf it is filed, and

(*b*) copies of any documents upon which he intends to rely at a hearing or a directions appointment.

(2) A party may, subject to any direction of the justices' clerk or the court about the timing or statements under this rule, file a statement which is supplementary to a statement served under sub-paragraph (1).

(3) Where a non-resident party files a statement or document under this rule, he shall also file a copy of it for service on the resident party; and the justices' chief executive shall on receipt of that copy serve it on the resident party.

(4) At a hearing or directions appointment a party may not without the leave of the justices' clerk, in the case of a directions appointment, or the court –

(*a*) adduce evidence, or
(*b*) seek to rely on a document,

in respect of which he has failed to comply with the requirements of sub-paragraphs (1) and, where applicable, (3).

8 Amendment

(1) A party amending a document shall file the amended document with the justices' chief executive; and the amendments shall be identified.

(2) Paragraph 7(3) above applies to an amended document filed under this paragraph.

9 Oral evidence

The justices' clerk or the court shall keep a note of the substance or any oral evidence given at a hearing or directions appointment.

10 Hearing

(1) Before the hearing, the justice or justices who will be dealing with the case shall read any documents which have been filed under paragraph 7 above in respect of the hearing.

(2) The justices' clerk at a directions appointment, or the court at a hearing or directions appointment, may give directions as to the order of speeches and evidence.

(3) After the final hearing, the court shall make its decision as soon as is practicable.

(4) Before the court makes an order or refuses an application, the justices' clerk shall record in writing –

(*a*) the names of the justice or justices constituting the court by which the decision is made, and
(*b*) in consultation with the justice or justices, the reasons for the court's decision and any findings of fact.

(5) After the court announces its decision, the justices' clerk shall as soon as practicable make a record in writing of any order.

(6) Where, under subsection (4) of section 7 of the Domestic Proceedings and Magistrates' Courts Act 1978, a court decides to treat an application under section 7 as if it were an application for an order under section 2 of that Act, the court shall indicate orally which of grounds (*a*) and (*b*) in that subsection it considers applicable and a memorandum of that decision and the grounds therefor shall be entered in the court's register.

11 Confidentiality of documents

(1) No document, other than a record of an order, held by the court and relating to any proceedings shall be disclosed, other than to –

(*a*) a party,
(*b*) the legal representative of a party,
(*c*) the Lord Chancellor's Department, or
(*d*) the Legal Aid Board,

without leave of the justices' clerk or the court.

12 Delegation by justices' clerk

(1) In this paragraph, "employed as a clerk in court" has the same meaning as in rule 2(1) of the Justices' Clerks (Qualifications of Assistants) Rules 1979.

(2) Anything authorised to be done by, to or before a justices' clerk under this Schedule or under a rule to which this Schedule applies may be done instead by, to or before a person employed as a clerk in court where that person is appointed by the magistrates' courts committee to assist him and where that person has been specifically authorised by the justices' clerk for that purpose.

(3) Any authorisation by the justices' clerk under sub-paragraph (2) shall be recorded in writing at the time the authority is given or as soon as practicable thereafter.

"appointed by the magistrates' courts committee" (para 12(2))—This appears to exclude "agency clerks", since the delegated powers may only be exercised by a person appointed by the relevant committee.

13 Application of section 97 of the Magistrates' Courts Act 1980

(1) Subject to sub-paragraph (2) below, section 97 of the Magistrates' Courts Act 1980 shall apply to proceedings to which this Schedule applies as it applies to a hearing of a complaint under that section.

(2) The power of a justice under section 97 of that Act to issue a witness summons may be exercised by a justices' clerk.

Amendments—Schedule inserted by SI 1993/617; amended by SI 2001/615.

Maintenance Orders Act 1950 (Summary Jurisdiction) Rules 1950, SI 1950/2035

PART I
TRANSFER OF WIFE MAINTENANCE PROCEEDINGS

1 (1) Where proceedings under section 1 of the Domestic Proceedings and Magistrates' Courts Act 1978 are begun against a defendant residing in Scotland or Northern Ireland in a court having jurisdiction by virtue of subsection (3) of section 1 of the said Act, then, upon an application in that behalf made by the defendant in accordance with paragraph (2) of this Rule, a justice acting for the same place as that court may, if it appears that the case could be more conveniently heard in a court of summary jurisdiction have jurisdiction in the place where the parties last ordinarily resided together as man and wife, determine that the proceedings shall be removed into the last-mentioned court.

(2) An application under the foregoing paragraph may be made orally or in writing by or on behalf of the defendant and, unless the defendant applies in person, there shall be lodged with the justices' chief executive for the court in which the proceedings under the said section 1 have been begun a statutory declaration by the defendant which shall state the grounds upon which the application is made and the address of the defendant to which notices may be sent.

(3) The justice adjudicating on an application made under paragraph (1) of this Rule shall, unless he determines that the application shall be refused forthwith, afford to the complainant an opportunity of making representations, either orally or in writing, thereon.

(4) Where a justice determines under paragraph (1) of this Rule that the proceedings under the said section 1 shall be removed into another court of summary jurisdiction, he shall cause the justices' chief executive for the court in which the said proceedings have been begun to send to the clerk of that other court the complaint, a copy of the summons and any other relevant documents; and, on receipt thereof in that other court, the complaint shall be deemed to have been made in, and the summons to have been issued by, that other court, and any justice acting for the same place as that other court may appoint a time and place for the hearing of the proceedings which, upon notice thereof being sent by registered post to the complainant and defendant, shall be deemed to have been the time and place appointed in the summons.

Amendments—SI 2001/615.

PART II
PROCEDURE UNDER PART II OF THE ACT IN RELATION TO MAINTENANCE ORDERS MADE BY COURTS OF SUMMARY JURISDICTION IN ENGLAND

2 (1) An application for the registration in a court in Scotland or Northern Ireland under Part II of the Act of a maintenance order made by a court of summary jurisdiction in England may be made, either orally or in writing by or on behalf of the person entitled to the payments thereunder, to a justice acting for the same place as the court which made the order; and, unless the applicant appears in person, there shall be lodged with the justices' chief executive for the court which made the order a statutory declaration by the applicant which shall contain the particulars specified in paragraph (2) of this Rule.

(2) A statutory declaration lodged under the foregoing paragraph shall state –

(*a*) the address of the person liable to make the payments under the order;
(*b*) the reason why it is convenient that the order should be enforced in Scotland or Northern Ireland, as the case may be;
(*c*) unless a certificate of arrears is lodged under section 20 of the Act, the amount of any arrears due under the order;
(*d*) that the order is not already registered under Part II of the Act.

(3) If it appears to the justice dealing with an application made as aforesaid that the person liable to make the payments under the order resides in Scotland or Northern Ireland, and that it is convenient that the order should be enforceable there, he shall cause the justices' chief executive for the court which made the order to send to the sheriff-clerk of the sheriff court in Scotland, or, as the case may be, to the clerk of the court of summary jurisdiction in Northern Ireland, having jurisdiction in the place in which the person liable to make the payments under the order appears to be –

(*a*) a certified copy of the order;
(*b*) the certificate of arrears or statutory declaration (if any);
(*c*) if no statutory declaration has been lodged, written notice of the address of the person liable to make the payments under the order.

(4) A memorandum of any proceedings taken under the foregoing provisions of this Rule for the registration of a maintenance order in a court in Scotland or Northern Ireland shall be entered in the register; and on the receipt by the justices' chief executive for the court which made the order (who shall be the prescribed officer of that court for the purposes of subsection (4) of section 17 of the Act) of notice under the said subsection (4) of the registration of the order he shall cause particulars of the notice to be registered in his court by means of a memorandum entered and signed by him in the register.

Amendments—SI 2001/615.

"sheriff-clerk" (r 2(3))—See Home Office Circular 241/1950 for addresses of sheriff-clerks.

3 (1) An application to a court of summary jurisdiction in England under sub-section (5) of section 22 of the Act to adduce evidence in connection with a maintenance order made by that court and registered in a court in Scotland or Northern Ireland may be made orally by or on behalf of the applicant and the proceedings may be ex parte.

(2) The court in which application is made under the last foregoing paragraph shall cause a transcript or summary of any evidence taken therein to be sent to the clerk of the court in which the order is registered.

(3) The justices' chief executive for the court of summary jurisdiction in England by which a maintenance order registered in a court in Scotland or Northern Ireland was made shall be the prescribed officer to whom any transcript or summary of evidence adduced in the court in Scotland or Northern Ireland under the said subsection (5) shall be sent.

Amendments—SI 2001/615.

PART III

4 (1) Where a maintenance order made by a court of summary jurisdiction in England and registered in a court in Scotland or Northern Ireland is varied under subsection (1) of section 22 of the Act by the court in which it is registered, the justices' chief executive for the court which made the order shall be the prescribed officer to whom, under subsection (1) of section 23 of the Act, notice of the variation shall be given; and on receipt of such notice he shall cause particulars of the same to be registered in his court by means of a memorandum entered and signed by him in the register.

(2) Where a maintenance order made by a court of summary jurisdiction in England and registered in a court in Scotland or Northern Ireland is discharged or varied by the court which made it, the justices' chief executive for that court shall give notice of the discharge or variation to the clerk of the court in which the order is registered by sending to him a certified copy of the order discharging or varying the maintenance order.

Amendments—SI 2001/615.

5 (1) An application under subsection (2) of section 24 of the Act for the cancellation of the registration of a maintenance order made by a court of summary jurisdiction in England and registered in a court in Scotland or Northern Ireland may be made, either orally or in writing by or on behalf of the person liable to make the payments thereunder, to a justice acting for the same place as the court which made the order; and, unless the applicant appears in person, there shall be lodged with the justices' chief executive for the court which made the order a statutory declaration by the applicant stating the facts upon which he relies in support of the application.

(2) If it appears to the justice dealing with an application made as aforesaid that the person liable to make the payments under the order has ceased to reside in Scotland or Northern Ireland, as the case may be, he shall cause the justices' chief executive for the court which made the order to send notice to that effect to the clerk of the court in which the order is registered.

Amendments—SI 2001/615.

6 On the cancellation under section 24 of the Act of the registration in a court in Scotland or Northern Ireland of a maintenance order made by a court of summary jurisdiction in England, the justices' chief executive for the last-mentioned court shall be the prescribed officer to whom, under subsection (3) of the said section 24, notice of the cancellation shall be given; and on receipt of such notice he shall cause particulars of the same to be registered in his court by means of a memorandum entered and signed by him in the register.

Amendments—SI 2001/615.

PART III
PROCEDURE IN COURTS OF SUMMARY JURISDICTION IN ENGLAND UNDER PART II OF THE ACT IN RELATION TO MAINTENANCE ORDERS MADE BY COURTS IN SCOTLAND OR NORTHERN IRELAND

7 The justices' chief executive for the court of summary jurisdiction in England specified in paragraph (*b*) of subsection (3) of section 17 of the Act shall be the prescribed officer for the purpose of subsection (2) of the said section 17, and on receiving, in pursuance of that section, a certified copy of a maintenance order made by a court in Scotland or Northern Ireland he shall cause the order to be registered in his court by means of a memorandum entered and signed by him in the register, and shall send written notice to the clerk of the court by which the order was made that it has been duly registered.

Amendments—SI 2001/615.

8 An application for the variation under subsection (1) of section 22 of the Act of the rate of the payments under a maintenance order registered under Part II of the Act in a court of summary jurisdiction in England shall be made by way of complaint in accordance with the Magistrates' Courts Act 1980, and thereupon a summons may be issued directed to any person whom the justice to whom the complaint is made may consider proper to answer the same.

9 (1) An application to a court of summary jurisdiction in England under sub-section (5) of section 22 of the Act to adduce evidence in connection with a maintenance order registered therein under Part II of the Act may be made orally by or on behalf of the applicant and the proceedings may be ex parte.

(2) The court in which application is made under the last foregoing paragraph shall cause a transcript or summary of any evidence taken therein to be sent to the clerk of the court in Scotland or Northern Ireland by which the order was made.

(3) The justices' chief executive for the court of summary jurisdiction in England in which a maintenance order is registered under Part II of the Act shall be the prescribed officer to whom any transcript or summary of evidence adduced under the said subsection (5) in the court in Scotland or Northern Ireland by which the order was made shall be sent.

Amendments—SI 2001/615.

9A (1) An application to a magistrates' court under section 21(2) of the Act to adduce evidence in connection with a maintenance order made by the Court of Session and registered in the magistrates' court under Part I of the Act of 1958 by virtue of section 1(2) of the Act of 1958 may be made orally by or on behalf of the applicant and the proceedings may be ex parte.

(2) The court in which application is made under paragraph (1) above shall cause a transcript or summary of any evidence taken therein to be sent to the Deputy Principal Clerk of Session.

Amendments—Inserted by SI 1980/1895.

9B (1) Where, in the exercise of the duty imposed by section 19(2) of the Act or in the exercise of the powers conferred by virtue of section 18(2ZA) or section 22(1A) or (1E) of the Act, a court of summary jurisdiction orders that payments under a registered order are to be made by a particular means, the clerk of the court shall record on the copy of the order the means of payment which the court has ordered and the justices' chief executive shall notify in writing, as soon as practicable, the person liable to make payments under the order of how payments are to be made.

(2) Where, in the exercise of any of the aforesaid powers, the court orders payment to the justices' chief executive for the court, or to the justices' chief executive for any other magistrates' court, by a method of payment falling within section 59(6) of the Magistrates' Courts Act 1980 (standing order, etc), the justices' chief executive for the court to whom payments are to be made shall notify the person liable to make the payments under the order of the number and location of the account into which the payments should be made.

(3) Where, under section 60(4) of the Magistrates' Courts Act 1980, as modified by section 22(1E) of the Act, the justices' chief executive for the court receives an application from an interested party for the method of payment to be varied, the justices' chief executive shall notify in writing, as soon as practicable, that party and, where practicable, any other interested party, of the result of the application, including any decision to refer the matter to the court; where the clerk of the court grants the application, he shall record the variation on the copy of the order.

Amendments—Inserted by SI 1992/457; amended by SI 2001/615.

10 (1) Where a maintenance order registered under Part II of the Act in a court of summary jurisdiction in England is varied under subsection (1) of section 22 of the Act by that court, the justices' chief executive for the court shall –

(*a*) give notice of the variation to the clerk of the court in Scotland or Northern Ireland by which the order was made; and

(*b*) if the order is registered in the High Court under Part I of the Act of 1958 by virtue of section 1(2) of the Act of 1958, give notice of the variation to the appropriate officer of the High Court,

by sending to the clerk of the court and, where necessary, the appropriate officer of the High Court, a certified copy of the order of variation.

(2) Where a maintenance order registered under Part II of the Act in a court of summary jurisdiction in England is discharged or varied by any other court, the justices' chief executive for the court in which it is registered shall be the prescribed officer to whom under section 23(2) of the Act notice of the discharge or variation shall be given; and on receipt of a certified copy of an order discharging or varying the registered order, he shall cause particulars of the same to be registered in his court by means of a memorandum entered and signed by him in the register.

Amendments—SI 2001/615.

11 (1) An application under subsection (1) of section 24 of the Act for the cancellation of the registration of a maintenance order registered under Part II of the Act in a court of summary jurisdiction in England shall be made to the justices' chief executive for that court by lodging with him a written application in that behalf (which shall state the date of the registration of the order) together with a copy of the order the registration of which it is sought to cancel.

(2) Where, in pursuance of an application made as aforesaid, the justices' chief executive cancels the registration of the maintenance order he shall send written notice of the cancellation to the clerk of the court by which the order was made and, where the order is registered in the High Court under Part I of the Act of 1958 by virtue of section 1(2) of the Act of 1958, to the appropriate officer of the High Court.

Amendments—SI 2001/615.

12 Where a maintenance order is registered under Part II of the Act in a court of summary jurisdiction in England, the justices' chief executive for that court shall be the prescribed officer to whom notice shall be sent under subsection (2) of section 24 of the Act that the person liable to make the payments under the order has ceased to reside in England; and on receipt of such notice the justices' chief executive shall cancel the registration of the order and shall send written notice of the cancellation to the clerk of the court by which the order was made and, where the order is registered in the High Court under Part I of the Act of 1958 by virtue of section 1(2) of the Act of 1958, to the appropriate officer of the High Court.

Amendments—SI 2001/615.

12A Where the justices' chief executive for a magistrates' court in which a maintenance order is registered under Part I of the Act of 1958 receives a notice of cancellation under section 24(3) of the Act from the appropriate officer of the High Court, he shall –

(*a*) cause the particulars of such notice to be entered in the register; and
(*b*) cancel the registration under the said Part I; and
(*c*) give notice of the cancellation to the appropriate officer of the court in Scotland or Northern Ireland, as the case may be, which made the order, that is to say either –
  (i) the Deputy Principal Clerk of Session, in the case of the Court of Session; or
  (ii) the Chief Registrar of the Queen's Bench Division (Matrimonial), in the case of the High Court of Justice in Northern Ireland.

Amendments—Inserted by SI 1980/1895; amended by SI 2001/615.

PART IV
FORMS

13 (1) A notice under subsection (4) of section 19 of the Act that the payments under a maintenance order made by a sheriff court in Scotland or a court of summary jurisdiction in Northern Ireland have become payable through or to any officer or person shall be in the form number 1 in the Schedule to these Rules, or any form to the like effect, and shall be sent by registered post by the justices' chief executive for the court to the person liable to make the payments under the order at his last known address.

(2) A notice under the said subsection (4) that the payments under a maintenance order made by a court of summary jurisdiction in England have, on its registration under Part II of the Act in a court of Scotland or Northern Ireland, ceased to be payable through or to any officer or person shall be in the form number 2 in the Schedule to these Rules, or any form to the like effect, and shall be sent by registered post by the justices' chief executive for the first-mentioned court to the person liable to make the payments under the order at his last known address.

Amendments—SI 2001/615.

"sent by registered post" (r 13(2))—The notice may be sent by recorded delivery (Recorded Delivery Act 1962).

14 A certificate lodged under subsection (1) of section 20 of the Act as to the amount of any arrears due under a maintenance order made by a court of summary

PART III

jurisdiction in England shall be in the form number 3 in the Schedule to these Rules, or any form to the like effect.

15 A notice under subsection (5) or subsection (5A) of section 24 of the Act of the cancellation of the registration under Part II of the Act of a maintenance order in a court of summary jurisdiction in England shall be in the form number 4 in the Schedule to these Rules, or any form to the like effect, and shall be sent by registered post by the justices' chief executive for that court to the person liable to make the payments under the order at his last known address.

Amendments—SI 1992/457; SI 2001/615.

"sent by registered post"—The notice may be sent by recorded delivery (Recorded Delivery Act 1962).

PART V
INTERPRETATION AND COMMENCEMENT

16 (1) In Parts II to V of these Rules, unless the context otherwise requires, the following expressions have the meanings hereby respectively assigned to them –

"maintenance order" has the same meaning as in Part II of the Act;
"the Act" means the Maintenance Orders Act 1950;
"the Act of 1958" means the Maintenance Orders Act 1958;
"appropriate officer of the High Court" means the Senior Registrar of the Principal Registry of the Family Division of the High Court or the district registrar of the relevant district registry;
"register" means the register kept in accordance with rule 54 of the Magistrates' Courts Rules 1968;

and other expressions used in these Rules have the meanings assigned to them in section 28 of the Act.

(2) References in Part III of these Rules to the clerk of the court by which the order was made shall be construed, in relation to a maintenance order made by a county court in Northern Ireland, as references to the Clerk of the Crown and Peace for the appropriate county in Northern Ireland.

(3) The Interpretation Act 1889, shall apply to the interpretation of these Rules as it applies to the interpretation of an Act of Parliament.

"rule 54 of the Magistrates' Courts Rules 1968" (r 16(1))—See now Magistrates' Courts Rules 1981, r 66.

"Interpretation Act 1889" (r 16(3))—This reference should be construed as a reference to the Interpretation Act 1978.

Maintenance Orders (Facilities for Enforcement) Rules 1922, SR & O 1922/1355

1 The copy of an Order made by a court outside the United Kingdom and received by the Lord Chancellor under section 1 of the Maintenance Orders (Facilities for Enforcement) Act 1920, shall, unless the Order was made by a Court of Superior Jurisdiction, be sent to the justices' chief executive for the petty sessions area in which the defendant is alleged to be living.

Amendments—SI 1992/709; SI 2000/1875; SI 2001/615.

2 The copy of a Provisional Order made by a court outside the United Kingdom and received by the Lord Chancellor under section 4 of the Act shall be sent to a Court of Summary Jurisdiction in the manner provided by the foregoing Rule, with the accompanying documents and a requisition for the issue of a notice of hearing.

Amendments—SI 1992/709; SI 1993/617.

2A On receipt of an order in accordance with rule 2 above the justices' chief executive to whom it is sent shall serve upon the person against whom the order is made certified copies of the order and of the accompanying documents, together with the notice required to be served under section 4 of the Act.

Amendments—Inserted by SI 1993/617; amended by SI 2001/615.

3 The justices' chief executive to whom any Order is sent in accordance with the above Rules shall enter it in his register on the date on which he receives it in the same manner as though the Order had been made at his court, distinguishing it from the other entries in such manner as he may find most convenient, so as to show that it is entered in pursuance of the Act.

Amendments—SI 2001/615.

4 When an Order provisionally made outside the United Kingdom has been confirmed, with or without modification, under section 4 of the Act, by a Court of Summary Jurisdiction, or the court has decided not to confirm it, the justices' chief executive shall send notice thereof to the court from which it issued, and also to the Lord Chancellor.

Amendments—SI 1992/709; SI 2001/615.

5 When an order is registered in a Court of Summary Jurisdiction under section 1 of the Act, the court shall order that payments due thereunder shall be made to the justices' chief executive.

Amendments—SI 1992/457; SI 2001/615.

5A (1) This rule applies in respect of an order which is being or has been registered by a Court of Summary Jurisdiction under section 1 of the Act or in respect of a Provisional Order which is being or has been confirmed by a Court of Summary Jurisdiction under section 4 of the Act.

PART III

(2) Where, in the exercise of the duty imposed under rule 5 above, or in the exercise of the powers conferred by virtue of section 4(5A) or (6A) of the Act, a Court of Summary Jurisdiction orders that payments under the order are to be made by a particular means, the clerk of the court shall record on the copy of the order the means of payment which the court has ordered and the justices' chief executive shall notify in writing, as soon as practicable, the person liable to make payments under the order of how payments are to be made.

(3) Where, in the exercise of any of the aforesaid powers, the court orders payment to the justices' chief executive for the court, or to the justices' chief executive for any other magistrates' court, by a method of payment falling within section 59(6) of the Magistrates' Courts Act 1980 (standing order, etc), the justices' chief executive for the court to whom payments are to be made shall notify the person liable to make the payments under the order of the number and location of the account into which the payments should be made.

(4) Where, under section 60(4) of the Magistrates' Courts Act 1980, as modified by section 4(6A) of the Act, the justices' chief executive receives an application from an interested party for the method of payment to be varied, he shall notify in writing, as soon as practicable, that party and, where practicable, any other interested party, of the result of the application, including any decision to refer the matter to the court; where the clerk of the court grants the application, the justices' chief executive shall record the variation on the copy of the order.

Amendments—Inserted by SI 1992/457; amended by SI 2001/615.

6 Where an Order has been registered in a Court of Summary Jurisdiction under section 1 of the Act, or a Provisional Order has been confirmed by a Court of Summary Jurisdiction under section 4 of the Act, the justices' chief executive to whom the payments are ordered to be made shall collect the moneys due under the Order in the same manner as though it were a magistrates' court maintenance order and may take proceedings in his own name for enforcing payment, and shall send the moneys, when so collected, to the court from which the Order originally issued or to such other person or authority as that court or the Lord Chancellor may from time to time direct. Provided that if the court from which the Order originally issued is in Malta or in a Colony not possessing responsible Government or in a British Protectorate other than Northern or Southern Rhodesia, the moneys so collected shall be paid to the Crown Agents for the Colonies for transmission to the person to whom they are due.

Amendments—SI 1989/384; SI 1992/457; SI 1992/709; SI 2001/615.

"Lord Chancellor may from time to time direct"—In Home Office Circular 139/1970, it is directed that payments under a New Zealand court order are to be made to the New Zealand Department of Social Security. The relevant addresses are listed in the appendix to the Circular.

"Crown Agents for the Colonies"—The responsibilities of the Crown Agents for the colonies are undertaken by the Crown Agents for Overseas Governments and Administrations, 4 Millbank, London SW1.

6A (1) In this rule "an application" means –

(*a*) an application under section 3 of the Act for a provisional order,
(*b*) an application under section 4A of the Act for variation or revocation of a maintenance order made in the United Kingdom, or
(*c*) an application under section 4A of the Act for variation or revocation of a maintenance order confirmed in the United Kingdom.

(2) An application shall be filed in an appropriate form.

(3) On receipt of such an application by the justices' chief executive –

(*a*) the justices' clerk shall fix the date, time and place for a hearing or a directions appointment; and

(*b*) the justices' chief executive shall notify the applicant of the date, time and place so fixed.

Amendments—Inserted by SI 1993/617; amended by SI 2001/615.

6B (1) The Schedule to these Rules shall apply to proceedings pursuant to rules 2A and 6A above.

(2) In the Schedule as it applies to rule 2A, "the resident party" and "the non-resident party" shall be taken to mean the payer and the payee respectively under the order in question.

(3) In the Schedule as it applies to rule 6A, "the resident party" and "the non-resident party" shall be taken to mean –

(*a*) in the case of an application under sub-paragraph (*a*) of rule 6A(1), the applicant and respondent respectively,

(*b*) in the case of an application under sub-paragraph (*b*) of rule 6A(1), the payee and payer respectively under the order in question, and

(*c*) in the case of an application under sub-paragraph (*c*) of rule 6A(1), the payer and payee respectively under the order in question.

Amendments—Inserted by SI 1993/617.

7 When a Provisional Order made under section 3 of the Act has been remitted under subsection (4) of that section to a Court of Summary Jurisdiction for the purpose of taking further evidence, notice specifying the further evidence required and the time and place fixed for taking it shall be sent by the justices' chief executive to the person on whose application the Provisional Order was made.

Amendments—SI 2001/615.

****

SCHEDULE 2
RULES OF PROCEDURE

1 In this Schedule, and in any rule where this Schedule applies to proceedings pursuant to that rule, unless the context otherwise requires –

"business day" means any day other than –

(*a*) a Saturday, Sunday, Christmas or Good Friday; or

(*b*) a bank holiday, that is to say, a day which is, or is to be observed as, a bank holiday, or a holiday, under the Banking and Financial Dealings Act 1971, in England and Wales,

"directions appointment" means a hearing for directions under paragraph 4 below,

"file" means deposit with the justices' chief executive,

"justices' chief executive" means a justices' chief executive appointed under section 40 of the Justices of the Peace Act 1997,

"justices' clerk" has the meaning assigned to it by section 70 of the Justices of the Peace Act 1979 and includes any person who performs a justices' clerk's functions by virtue of paragraph 12 below,

"leave" includes approval,

"note" includes a record made by mechanical or electronic means, and

"proceedings" means proceedings to which this Schedule applies.

"any rule where this Schedule applies"—The Schedule prescribes the procedure to be followed in proceedings under Maintenance Orders (Reciprocal Enforcement) Act 1972, ss 2A, 3 and 4A.

2 Transfer of proceedings

(1) Where –

(*a*) any proceedings are relevant proceedings within the meaning of section 93 of the Children Act 1989, and

(*b*) the justices' chief executive or the court receives a request in writing from the resident party that the proceedings be transferred to another magistrates' court,

the justices' clerk or court shall issue a certificate in the appropriate form, granting or refusing the request in accordance with any Order made by the Lord Chancellor under Part I of Schedule 11 to the Children Act 1989.

(2) Where a request is granted under paragraph (1) the justices' chief executive shall send a copy of the certificate –

(*a*) to the resident party,

(*b*) to the Lord Chancellor's Department, and

(*c*) to the magistrates' court to which the proceedings are to be transferred.

(3) Any consent given or refused by a justices' clerk in accordance with any Order made by the Lord Chancellor under Part I of Schedule 11 shall be recorded in writing by the justices' clerk at the time it is given or refused or as soon as practicable thereafter.

Scope of provision—This paragraph provides for the transfer of relevant proceedings between magistrates' courts.

3 Service

(1) Where service of a document is required by this Schedule or by a rule where this Schedule applies to proceedings pursuant to that rule it may be effected, unless the contrary is indicated –

(*a*) if the person to be served is not known by the person serving to be acting by solicitor –

(i) by delivering it to him personally, or

(ii) by delivering it at, or by sending it by first-class post to, his residence or last known residence, or

(*b*) if the person to be served is known by the person serving to be acting by solicitor –

(i) by delivering the document at, or sending it by first-class post to, the solicitor's address for service,

(ii) where the solicitor's address for service includes a numbered box at a document exchange, by leaving the document at that document exchange or at a document exchange which transmits documents on every business day to that document exchange, or

(iii) by sending a legible copy of the document by facsimile transmission to the solicitor's office.

(2) In this paragraph, "first-class post" means first-class post which has been pre-paid or in respect of which pre-payment is not required.

(3) A document shall, unless the contrary is proved, be deemed to have been served –

(*a*) in the case of service by first-class post, on the second business day after posting, and

(*b*) in the case of service in accordance with sub-paragraph (1)(*b*)(ii), on the second business day after the day on which it is left at the document exchange.

(4) In any proceedings where this Schedule, or a rule where this Schedule applies, requires a document to be served, the court or the justices' clerk may, without prejudice to any power under paragraph 4 below, direct that –

(*a*) the requirement shall not apply;

(*b*) the time specified by the rules for complying with the requirement shall be abridged to such extent as may be specified in the direction;

(*c*) service shall be effected in such manner as may be specified in the direction.

PART III

4 Directions

(1) The justices' clerk or the court may give, vary or revoke directions for the conduct of the proceedings, including –

(*a*) the timetable for the proceedings,

(*b*) varying the time within which or by which an act is required by this Schedule or by a rule where this Schedule applies to proceedings pursuant to that rule to be done,

(*c*) the service of documents, and

(*d*) the submission of evidence

and, where the justices' chief executive receives such an application or any other document by which proceedings are commenced, the justices' chief executive shall consider whether such directions need to be given.

(2) Where the justices' clerk or a single justice who is holding a directions appointment considers, for whatever reason, that it is inappropriate to give a direction on a particular matter, he shall refer the matter to the court which may give any appropriate direction.

(3) Directions under sub-paragraph (1) may be given, varied or revoked either –

(*a*) of the justices' clerk's or the court's own motion having given the resident party an opportunity to attend and be heard or to make written representations, or

(*b*) on the written request of either party specifying the direction which is sought.

(4) Where the justices' chief executive receives a request under sub-paragraph (3)(*b*) the justices' clerk shall –

(*a*) make the direction sought, or

(*b*) fix a date for a hearing to consider the request.

"justices' clerk" (para 4(1)–(4))—For the power of delegation available to the justices' clerk in respect of these duties, see para 12 below.

5 Timing of proceedings

(1) Any period of time fixed by this Schedule or by a rule where this Schedule applies to proceedings pursuant to that rule, or by any order or direction, for doing any act shall be reckoned in accordance with this rule.

(2) Where the period, being a period of 7 days or less, would include a day which is not a business day, that day shall be excluded.

(3) Where the time fixed for filing a document with the justices' chief executive expires on a day on which the office of the justices' chief executive is closed, and for that reason the document cannot be filed on that day, the document shall be filed in time if it is filed on the next day on which the office of the justices' chief executive is open.

(4) Where this Schedule or a rule where this Schedule applies to proceedings pursuant to that rule provides a period of time within which or by which a certain act is to be performed in the course of relevant proceedings, that period may not be extended otherwise than by a direction of the justices' clerk or the court under paragraph 4(1) above.

(5) At the –

(*a*) transfer to a court of proceedings,
(*b*) postponement or adjournment of any hearing or directions appointment in the course of relevant proceedings, or
(*c*) conclusion of any such hearing or directions appointment other than one at which the proceedings are determined, or so soon thereafter as is practicable,
  (i) the justices' clerk shall fix a date upon which the proceedings shall come before him or the court again for such purposes as he or the court directs, which date shall, where paragraph (*a*) applies, be as soon as possible after the transfer, and
  (ii) the justices' chief executive shall give notice to the resident party of the date so fixed.

6 Attendance at directions appointment and hearing

(1) The resident party shall attend a directions appointment of which he has been given notice in accordance with paragraph 4 above unless the justices' clerk or the court otherwise directs.

(2) Where at the time and place appointed for a hearing or directions appointment the resident party does not appear the justices' clerk or the court shall not proceed with the hearing or appointment unless –

(*a*) the proceedings relate to an application filed by the resident party, or
(*b*) the court is satisfied that the resident party has received reasonable notice of the hearing or appointment.

(3) Where at the time and place appointed for a hearing or directions appointment the non-resident party does not appear the court may proceed with the hearing or appointment where the proceedings relate to an order or application sent by the Lord Chancellor to the court under the Act.

(4) Nothing in this Schedule shall be taken as preventing either party from appearing at any hearing or directions appointment.

7 Documentary evidence

(1) A party shall file, at or by such time as the justices' clerk or the court directs or, in the absence of a direction, before the hearing or appointment –

(*a*) written statements of the substance of the oral evidence which he intends to adduce at a hearing or a directions appointment, which shall –
(i) be dated,
(ii) be signed by the person making the statement,
(iii) contain a declaration that the maker of the statement believes it to be true and understands that it may be placed before the court, and
(iv) show in the top right-hand corner of the first page –
(*a*) the initials and surname of the person making the statement,
(*b*) the number of the statement in relation to the maker,
(*c*) the date on which the statement was made, and
(*d*) the party on whose behalf it is filed, and

(*b*) copies of any documents upon which he intends to rely at a hearing or a directions appointment.

(2) A party may, subject to any direction of the justices' clerk or the court about the timing or statements under this rule, file a statement which is supplementary to a statement served under sub-paragraph (1).

(3) Where a non-resident party files a statement or document under this rule, he shall also file a copy of it for service on the resident party; and the justices' chief executive shall on receipt of that copy serve it on the resident party.

(4) At a hearing or directions appointment a party may not without the leave of the justices' clerk, in the case of a directions appointment, or the court –

(*a*) adduce evidence, or
(*b*) seek to rely on a document,

in respect of which he has failed to comply with the requirements of sub-paragraphs (1) and, where applicable, (3).

8 Amendment

(1) A party amending a document shall file the amended document with the justices' chief executive; and the amendments shall be identified.

(2) Paragraph 7(3) above applies to an amended document filed under this paragraph.

9 Oral evidence

The justices' clerk or the court shall keep a note of the substance or any oral evidence given at a hearing or directions appointment.

10 Hearing

(1) Before the hearing, the justice or justices who will be dealing with the case shall read any documents which have been filed under paragraph 7 above in respect of the hearing.

PART III

(2) The justices' clerk at a directions appointment, or the court at a hearing or directions appointment, may give directions as to the order of speeches and evidence.

(3) After the final hearing, the court shall make its decision as soon as is practicable.

(4) Before the court makes an order or refuses an application, the justices' clerk shall record in writing –

- (*a*) the names of the justice or justices constituting the court by which the decision is made, and
- (*b*) in consultation with the justice or justices, the reasons for the court's decision and any findings of fact.

(5) After the court announces its decision, the justices' clerk shall as soon as practicable make a record in writing of any order.

(6) Where, under subsection (4) of section 7 of the Domestic Proceedings and Magistrates' Courts Act 1978, a court decides to treat an application under section 7 as if it were an application for an order under section 2 of that Act, the court shall indicate orally which of grounds (*a*) and (*b*) in that subsection it considers applicable and a memorandum of that decision and the grounds therefor shall be entered in the court's register.

11 Confidentiality of documents

(1) No document, other than a record of an order, held by the court and relating to any proceedings shall be disclosed, other than to –

- (*a*) a party,
- (*b*) the legal representative of a party,
- (*c*) the Lord Chancellor's Department, or
- (*d*) the Legal Aid Board,

without leave of the justices' clerk or the court.

12 Delegation by justices' clerk

(1) In this paragraph, "employed as a clerk in court" has the same meaning as in rule 2(1) of the Justices' Clerks (Qualifications of Assistants) Rules 1979.

(2) Anything authorised to be done by, to or before a justices' clerk under this Schedule or under a rule to which this Schedule applies may be done instead by, to or before a person employed as a clerk in court where that person is appointed by the magistrates' courts committee to assist him and where that person has been specifically authorised by the justices' clerk for that purpose.

(3) Any authorisation by the justices' clerk under sub-paragraph (2) shall be recorded in writing at the time the authority is given or as soon as practicable thereafter.

"appointed by the magistrates' courts committee" (para 12(2))—This appears to exclude "agency clerks", since the delegated powers may only be exercised by a person appointed by the relevant committee.

13 Application of section 97 of the Magistrates' Courts Act 1980

(1) Subject to sub-paragraph (2) below, section 97 of the Magistrates' Courts Act 1980 shall apply to proceedings to which this Schedule applies as it applies to a hearing of a complaint under that section.

(2) The power of a justice under section 97 of that Act to issue a witness summons may be exercised by a justices' clerk.

Amendments—Schedule inserted by SI 1993/617; amended by SI 2001/615.

Parental Responsibility Agreement Regulations 1991, SI 1991/1478

1 Citation, commencement and interpretation

(1) These regulations may be cited as the Parental Responsibility Agreement Regulations 1991 and shall come into force on 14 October 1991.

(2) In these Regulations, "the Principal Registry" means the principal registry of the Family Division of the High Court.

2 Form of parental responsibility agreement

A parental responsibility agreement shall be made in the form set out in the Schedule to these Regulations.

Form of agreement—The prescribed form is C(PRA) (inserted by SI 1994/3157) and comes with explanatory notes. As to evidence of identity, see further *Court Business* (June 1995), referred to at [1995] Fam Law 385, which also points out that, whilst the person who witnesses the signatures on Form C(PRA) (who must be a justice of the peace, a justices' clerk or a court official who is authorised by the judge to administer oaths) need not be attached to a court *with family jurisdiction*, solicitors cannot witness the signatures because they are not officers of either the magistrates' courts or the county courts.

3 Recording of parental responsibility agreement

(1) A parental responsibility agreement shall be recorded by the filing of the agreement, together with two copies, in the Principal Registry.

(2) Upon the filing of documents under paragraph (1), an officer of the Principal Registry shall seal the copies and send one to the child's mother and one to the child's father.

(3) The record of an agreement under paragraph (1) shall be made available, during office hours, for inspection by any person upon –

(*a*) written request to an officer of the Principal Registry, and
(*b*) payment of such fee as may be prescribed in an Order under section 41 of the Matrimonial and Family Proceedings Act 1984 (fees in family proceedings).

Defined terms—"parental responsibility agreement": CA 1989, s 4(1)(*b*).

Scope of provision—This regulation prescribes the method by which a parental responsibility agreement must be recorded. CA 1989, s 4(2) provides that, unless the regulations are complied with, the agreement is not valid for the purposes of CA 1989.

"payment of such fee as may be prescribed" (reg 3(3)(*b*))—The fee is prescribed by Family Proceedings Fees Order 1999, Sch 1, fee 6.2 and includes the cost of providing a copy of the agreement, if appropriate.

****

Pensions on Divorce etc (Provision of Information) Regulations 2000, SI 2000/1048

ARRANGEMENT OF REGULATIONS

General Note—These regulations provide for the information that the pension provider must disclose (reg 2), specify the formula for the valuation of pension benefits (reg 3), specify the information that the pension provider must provide once given notice that a pension sharing or attachment order may be made (reg 4), specify the information that both parties must give after an order has been made before the four month implementation period can begin (reg 5) and the information that the pension provider must give after notice of a pension sharing or earmarking order and after it has implemented the order (regs 7, 8 and 10).

Calculation of the cash equivalent transfer value—By a combination of reg 3 of these regulations and Divorce (Pensions) Regulations 2000, SI 2000/1123, reg 3 (the text of which is annotated in the notes under Matrimonial Causes Act 1973, s 24B) the method of calculating the CETV is prescribed in all cases (except for pension schemes administered overseas) in the highly technical formulae of these regulations. All these technical formulae have in common the fact that they are founded on taking the value of the pension rights on the basis that the member left service at the time of the valuation.

The CETV valuation will not therefore contain any element for past service reserve, ie schemes where funds have already been put aside for any future pay rises for the member or for any discretionary benefits. Further, informed opinion suggests (see "Black and White in Pensions" [2001] Fam Law 462) that the CETV of a member in the uniformed services can significantly understate the real value of the pension rights and that of a man on the point of retirement can overestimate the value of such rights.

The satellite regulations to pension sharing are silent as to whether other evidence can be led as to the true value of the CETV in such cases. It is suggested that even if it is held that the only evidence as to the CETV is on the basis prescribed by reg 3, it is nevertheless permissible (subject to proportionality) to lead expert evidence on the issue of what any given sharing or attachment would provide each of the parties.

The CETV is a calculation of the transfer value, at the current time of the total of the following elements in a pension scheme:

(i) the member's pension at retirement;
(ii) the lump sum benefit payable on death after leaving active membership of the scheme but before retirement;
(iii) the lump sum payable on retirement;
(iv) the lump sum payable on death after retirement; and
(v) the spouse's pension payable either on the member's death after leaving active membership of the scheme but before retirement or after the member's retirement.

The CETV therefore does *not* include the value of any lump sum death in service benefit nor the value of the spouse's pension if the member died in service. A valuation of the CETV alone therefore ignores the value of the death in service package which in many public service and company pension schemes is substantial.

1 Citation, commencement and interpretation

(1) These Regulations may be cited as the Pensions on Divorce etc (Provision of Information) Regulations 2000 and shall come into force on 1 December 2000.

(2) In these Regulations –

"the 1993 Act" means the Pension Schemes Act 1993;
"the 1995 Act" means the Pensions Act 1995;
"the 1999 Act" means the Welfare Reform and Pensions Act 1999;
"the Charging Regulations" means the Pensions on Divorce etc (Charging) Regulations 2000;
"the Implementation and Discharge of Liability Regulations" means the Pension Sharing (Implementation and Discharge of Liability) Regulations 2000;
"the Valuation Regulations" means the Pension Sharing (Valuation) Regulations 2000;
"active member" has the meaning given by section 124(1) of the 1995 Act;
"day" means any day other than –

(*a*) Christmas Day or Good Friday; or
(*b*) a bank holiday, that is to say, a day which is, or is to be observed as, a bank holiday or a holiday under Schedule 1 to the Banking and Financial Dealings Act 1971;

"deferred member" has the meaning given by section 124(1) of the 1995 Act;
"implementation period" has the meaning given by section 34(1) of the 1999 Act;
"member" means a person who has rights to future benefits, or has rights to benefits payable, under a pension arrangement;
"money purchase benefits" has the meaning given by section 181(1) of the 1993 Act;
"normal benefit age" has the meaning given by section 101B of the 1993 Act;
"notice of discharge of liability" means a notice issued to the member and his former spouse by the person responsible for a pension arrangement when that person has discharged his liability in respect of a pension credit in accordance with Schedule 5 to the 1999 Act;
"notice of implementation" means a notice issued by the person responsible for a pension arrangement to the member and his former spouse at the

beginning of the implementation period notifying them of the day on which the implementation period for the pension credit begins;

"occupational pension scheme" has the meaning given by section 1 of the 1993 Act;

"the party with pension rights" and "the other party" have the meanings given by section 25D(3) of the Matrimonial Causes Act 1997;

"pension arrangement" has the meaning given in section 46(1) of the 1999 Act;

"pension credit" means a credit under section 29(1)(*b*) of the 1999 Act;

"pension credit benefit" means the benefits payable under a pension arrangement or a qualifying arrangement to or in respect of a person by virtue of rights under the arrangement in question which are attributable (directly or indirectly) to a pension credit;

"pension credit rights" means rights to future benefits under a pension arrangement or a qualifying arrangement which are attributable (directly or indirectly) to a pension credit;

"pension sharing order or provision" means an order or provision which is mentioned in section 28(1) of the 1999 Act;

"pensionable service" has the meaning given by section 124(1) of the 1995 Act;

"person responsible for a pension arrangement" has the meaning given by section 46(2) of the 1999 Act;

"personal pension scheme" has the meaning given by section 1 of the 1993 Act;

"qualifying arrangement" has the meaning given by paragraph 6 of Schedule 5 to the 1999 Act;

"retirement annuity contract" means a contract or scheme approved under Chapter III of Part XIV of the Income and Corporation Taxes Act 1988;

"salary related occupational pension scheme" has the meaning given by regulation 1A of the Occupational Pension Schemes (Transfer Values) Regulations 1996;

"the Regulatory Authority" means the Occupational Pensions Regulatory Authority;

"transfer day" has the meaning given by section 29(8) of the 1999 Act;

"transferee" has the meaning given by section 29(8) of the 1999 Act;

"transferor" has the meaning given by section 29(8) of the 1999 Act.

"trustees or managers" has the meaning given by section 46(1) of the 1999 Act.

Amendments—SI 2000/2691.

2 Basic information about pensions and divorce

(1) The requirements imposed on a person responsible for a pension arrangement for the purposes of section 23(1)(*a*) of the 1999 Act (supply of pension information in connection with divorce etc) are that he shall furnish –

(*a*) on request from a member, the information referred to in paragraphs (2) and (3)(*b*) to (*f*);

(*b*) on request from the spouse of a member, the information referred to in paragraph (3); or

(*c*) pursuant to an order of the court, the information referred to in paragraph (2), (3) or (4),

to the member, the spouse of the member, or, as the case may be, to the court.

(2) The information in this paragraph is a valuation of pension rights or benefits accrued under that member's pension arrangement.

(3) The information in this paragraph is –

(*a*) a statement that on request from the member, or pursuant to an order of the court, a valuation of pension rights or benefits accrued under that member's pension arrangement, will be provided to the member, or, as the case may be, to the court;

(*b*) a statement summarising the way in which the valuation referred to in paragraph (2) and sub-paragraph (*a*) is calculated;

(*c*) the pension benefits which are included in a valuation referred to in paragraph (2) and sub-paragraph (*a*);

(*d*) whether the person responsible for the pension arrangement offers membership to a person entitled to a pension credit, and if so, the types of benefits available to pension credit members under that arrangement;

(*e*) whether the person responsible for the pension arrangements intends to discharge his liability for a pension credit other than by offering membership to a person entitled to a pension credit; and

(*f*) the schedule of charges which the person responsible for the pension arrangement will levy in accordance with regulation 2(2) of the Charging Regulations (general requirements as to charges).

(4) The information in this paragraph is any other information relevant to any power with respect to the matters specified in section 23(1)(*a*) of the 1999 Act and which is not specified in Schedule 1 or 2 to the Occupational Pension Schemes (Disclosure of Information) Regulations 1996 (basic information about the scheme and information to be made available to individuals), or in Schedule 1 or 2 to the Personal Pension Schemes (Disclosure of Information) Regulations 1987 (basic information about the scheme and information to be made available to individuals), in a case where either of those Regulations applies.

(5) Where the member's request for, or the court order for the provision of, information includes a request for, or an order for the provision of, a valuation under paragraph (2), the person responsible for the pension arrangement shall furnish all the information requested, or ordered, to the member –

(*a*) within 3 months beginning with the date the person responsible for the pension arrangement receives that request or order for the provision of the information;

(*b*) within 6 weeks beginning with the date the person responsible for the pension arrangement receives the request, or order, for the provision of the information, if the member has notified that person on the date of the request or order that the information is needed in connection with proceedings commenced under any of the provisions referred to in section 23(1)(*a*) of the 1999 Act; or

(*c*) within such shorter period specified by the court in an order requiring the person responsible for the pension arrangement to provide a valuation in accordance with paragraph (2).

(6) Where –

(*a*) the member's request for, or the court order for the provision of, information does not include a request or an order for a valuation under paragraph (2); or

(*b*) the member's spouse requests the information specified in paragraph (3), the person responsible for the pension arrangement shall furnish that information to the member, his spouse, or the court, as the case may be, within one month beginning with the date that person responsible for the pension arrangement receives the request for, or the court order for the provision of, the information.

(7) At the same time as furnishing the information referred to in paragraph (1), the person responsible for a pension arrangement may furnish the information specified in regulation 4(2) (provision of information in response to a notification that a pension sharing order or provision may be made).

3 Information about pensions and divorce: valuation of pension benefits

(1) Where an application for financial relief under any of the provisions referred to in section 23(1)(*a*)(i) or (iii) of the 1999 Act (supply of pension information in connection with domestic and overseas divorce etc in England and Wales and corresponding Northern Ireland powers) has been made or is in contemplation, the valuation of benefits under a pension arrangement shall be calculated and verified for the purposes of regulation 2 of these Regulations in accordance with –

(*a*) paragraph (3), if the person with pension rights is a deferred member of an occupational pension scheme;

(*b*) paragraph (4), if the person with pension rights is an active member of an occupational pension scheme;

(*c*) paragraphs (5) and (6), if –

(i) the person with pension rights is a member of a personal pension scheme; or

(ii) those pension rights are contained in a retirement annuity contract; or

(*d*) paragraphs (7) to (9), if –

(i) the pension of the person with pension rights is in payment;

(ii) the rights of the person with pension rights are contained in an annuity contract other than a retirement annuity contract; or

(iii) the rights of the person with pension rights are contained in a deferred annuity contract other than a retirement annuity contract.

(2) Where an application for financial provision under any of the provisions referred to in section 23(1)(*a*)(ii) of the 1999 Act (corresponding Scottish powers) has been made, or is in contemplation, the valuation of benefits under a pension arrangement shall be calculated and verified for the purposes of regulation 2 of these Regulations in accordance with regulation 3 of the Divorce etc (Pensions) (Scotland) Regulations 2000 (valuation).

(3) Where the person with pension rights is a deferred member of an occupational pension scheme, the value of the benefits which he has under that scheme shall be taken to be –

(*a*) in the case of an occupational pension scheme other than a salary related scheme, the cash equivalent to which he acquired a right under section 94(1)(*a*) of the 1993 Act (right to cash equivalent) on the termination of his pensionable service, calculated on the assumption that he has made an application under section 95 of that Act (ways of taking right to cash equivalent) on the date on which the request for the valuation was received; or

(*b*) in the case of a salary related occupational pension scheme, the guaranteed cash equivalent to which he would have acquired a right under section 94(1)(*aa*) of the 1993 Act if he had made an application under section

95(1) of that Act, calculated on the assumption that he has made such an application on the date on which the request for the valuation was received.

(4) Where the person with pension rights is an active member of an occupational pension scheme, the valuation of the benefits which he has accrued under that scheme shall be calculated and verified –

(*a*) on the assumption that the member had made a request for an estimate of the cash equivalent that would be available to him were his pensionable service to terminate on the date on which the request for the valuation was received; and

(*b*) in accordance with regulation 11 of and Schedule 1 to the Occupational Pension Schemes (Transfer Values) Regulations 1996 (disclosure).

(5) Where the person with pension rights is a member of a personal pension scheme, or those rights are contained in a retirement annuity contract, the value of the benefits which he has under that scheme or contract shall be taken to be the cash equivalent to which he would have acquired a right under section 94(1)(*b*) of the 1993 Act, if he had made an application under section 95(1) of that Act on the date on which the request for the valuation was received.

(6) In relation to a personal pension scheme which is comprised in a retirement annuity contract made before 4th January 1988, paragraph (5) shall apply as if such a scheme were not excluded from the scope of Chapter IV of Part IV of the 1993 Act by section 93(1)(*b*) of that Act (scope of Chapter IV).

(7) Except in a case to which, or to the extent to which, paragraph (9) applies, the cash equivalent of benefits in respect of a person referred to in paragraph (1)(*d*) shall be calculated and verified in such manner as may be approved in a particular case by –

(*a*) a Fellow of the Institute of Actuaries;

(*b*) a Fellow of the Faculty of Actuaries; or

(*c*) a person with other actuarial qualifications who is approved by the Secretary of State, at the request of the person responsible for the pension arrangement in question, as being a proper person to act for the purposes of this regulation in connection with that arrangement.

(8) Except in a case to which paragraph (9) applies, cash equivalents are to be calculated and verified by adopting methods and making assumptions which –

(*a*) if not determined by the person responsible for the pension arrangement in question, are notified to him by an actuary referred to in paragraph (7); and

(*b*) are certified by the actuary to the person responsible for the pension arrangement in question as being consistent with "Retirement Benefit Schemes – Transfer Values (GN11)" published by the Institute of Actuaries and the Faculty of Actuaries and current at the date on which the request for the valuation is received.

(9) Where the cash equivalent, or any portion of it represents rights to money purchase benefits under the pension arrangement in question of the person with pension rights, and those rights do not fall, either wholly or in part, to be valued in a manner which involves making estimates of the value of benefits, then that cash equivalent, or that portion of it, shall be calculated and verified in such manner as may be approved in a particular case by the person responsible for the pension arrangement in question, and by adopting methods consistent with the requirements of Chapter IV of Part IV of the 1993 Act (protection for early leavers – transfer values).

(10) Where paragraph (3), (4) or (9) has effect by reference to provisions of Chapter IV of Part IV of the 1993 Act, section 93(1)(*a*)(i) of that Act (scope of Chapter IV) shall apply to those provisions as if the words "at least one year" had been omitted from section 93(1)(*a*)(i).

4 Provision of information in response to a notification that a pension sharing order or provision may be made

(1) A person responsible for a pension arrangement shall furnish the information specified in paragraph (2) to the member or to the court, as the case may be –

(*a*) within 21 days beginning with the date that the person responsible for the pension arrangement received the notification that a pension sharing order or provision may be made; or

(*b*) if the court has specified a date which is outside the 21 days referred to in sub-paragraph (*a*), by that date.

(2) The information referred to in paragraph (1) is –

(*a*) the full name of the pension arrangement and address to which any order or provision referred to in section 28(1) of the 1999 Act (activation of pension sharing) should be sent;

(*b*) in the case of an occupational pension scheme, whether the scheme is winding up, and, if so, –

(i) the date on which the winding up commenced; and

(ii) the name and address of the trustees who are dealing with the winding up;

(*c*) in the case of an occupational pension scheme, whether a cash equivalent of the member's pension rights, if calculated on the date the notification referred to in paragraph (1)(*a*) was received by the trustees or managers of that scheme, would be reduced in accordance with the provisions of regulation 8(4), (6) or (12) of the Occupational Pension Schemes (Transfer Values) Regulations 1996 (further provisions as to reductions of cash equivalents);

(*d*) whether the person responsible for the pension arrangement is aware that the member's rights under the pension arrangement are subject to any, and if so, to specify which, of the following –

(i) any order or provision specified in section 28(1) of the 1999 Act;

(ii) an order under section 23 of the Matrimonial Causes Act 1973 (financial provision orders in connection with divorce etc.), so far as it includes provision made by virtue of section 25B or 25C of that Act (powers to include provisions about pensions);

(iii) an order under section 12A(2) or (3) of the Family Law (Scotland) Act 1985 (powers in relation to pensions lump sums when making a capital sum order) which relates to benefits or future benefits to which the member is entitled under the pension arrangement;

(iv) an order under Article 25 of the Matrimonial Causes (Northern Ireland) Order 1978, so far as it includes provision made by virtue of Article 27B or 27C of that Order (Northern Ireland powers corresponding to those mentioned in paragraph (2)(*d*)(ii));

(v) a forfeiture order;

(vi) a bankruptcy order;

(vii) an award of sequestration on a member's estate or the making of the appointment on his estate of a judicial factor under section 41 of the Solicitors (Scotland) Act 1980 (appointment of judicial factor);

(*e*) whether the member's rights under the pension arrangement include rights specified in regulation 2 of the Valuation Regulations (rights under a pension arrangement which are not shareable);

(*f*) if the person responsible for the pension arrangement has not at an earlier stage provided the following information, whether that person requires the charges specified in regulation 3 (charges recoverable in respect of the provision of basic information), 5 (charges in respect of pension sharing activity), or 6 (additional amounts recoverable in respect of pension sharing activity) of the Charging Regulations to be paid before the commencement of the implementation period, and if so –

(i) whether that person requires those charges to be paid in full; or

(ii) the proportion of those charges which he requires to be paid;

(*g*) whether the person responsible for the pension arrangement may levy additional charges specified in regulation 6 of the Charging Regulations, and if so, the scale of the additional charges which are likely to be made;

(*h*) whether the member is a trustee of the pension arrangement;

(*i*) whether the person responsible for the pension arrangement may request information about the member's state of health from the member if a pension sharing order or provision were to be made;

(*k*) whether the person responsible for the pension arrangement requires information additional to that specified in regulation 5 (information required by the person responsible for the pension arrangement before the implementation period may begin) in order to implement the pension sharing order or provision.

Amendments—SI 2000/2691.

5 Information required by the person responsible for the pension arrangement before the implementation period may begin

The information prescribed for the purposes of section 34(1)(*b*) of the 1999 Act (information relating to the transferor and the transferee which the person responsible for the pension arrangement must receive) is –

(*a*) in relation to the transferor –

(i) all names by which the transferor has been known;

(ii) date of birth;

(iii) address;

(iv) National Insurance number;

(v) the name of the pension arrangement to which the pension sharing order or provision relates; and

(vi) the transferor's membership or policy number in that pension arrangement;

(*b*) in relation to the transferee –

(i) all names by which the transferee has been known;

(ii) date of birth;

(iii) address;

(iv) National Insurance number; and

(v) if the transferee is a member of the pension arrangement from which the pension credit is derived, his membership or policy number in that pension arrangement;

(*c*) where the transferee has given his consent in accordance with paragraph 1(3)(*c*), 3(3)(*c*) or 4(2)(*c*) of Schedule 5 to the 1999 Act (mode of discharge of liability for a pension credit) to the payment of the pension credit to the person responsible for a qualifying arrangement –

PART III

(i) the full name of that qualifying arrangement;
(ii) its address;
(iii) if known, the transferee's membership number or policy number in that arrangement; and
(iv) the name or title, business address, business telephone number, and, where available, the business facsimile number and electronic mail address of a person who may be contacted in respect of the discharge of liability for the pension credit;

(*d*) where the rights from which the pension credit is derived are held in an occupational pension scheme which is being wound up, whether the transferee has given an indication whether he wishes to transfer his pension credit rights which may have been reduced in accordance with the provisions of regulation 16(1) of the Implementation and Discharge of Liability Regulations (adjustments to the amount of the pension credit – occupational pension schemes which are underfunded on the valuation day) to a qualifying arrangement; and

(*e*) any information requested by the person responsible for the pension arrangement in accordance with regulation 4(2)(i) or (*k*).

6 Provision of information after the death of the person entitled to the pension credit before liability in respect of the pension credit has been discharged

(1) Where the person entitled to the pension credit dies before the person responsible for the pension arrangement has discharged his liability in respect of the pension credit, the person responsible for the pension arrangement shall, within 21 days of the date of receipt of the notification of the death of the person entitled to the pension credit, notify in writing any person whom the person responsible for the pension arrangement considers should be notified of the matters specified in paragraph (2).

(*a*) the person whom the person entitled to the pension credit nominated pursuant to regulation 4(2)(*j*) to receive pension credit benefit; and

(*b*) any other person whom the person responsible for the pension arrangement considers should be notified,

of the matters specified in paragraph (2).

(2) The matters specified in this paragraph are –

(*a*) how the person responsible for the pension arrangement intends to discharge his liability in respect of the pension credit;

(*b*) whether the person responsible for the pension arrangement intends to recover charges from the person nominated to receive pension credit benefits, in accordance with regulations 2 to 9 of the Charging Regulations, and if so, a copy of the schedule of charges issued to the parties to pension sharing in accordance with regulation 2(2)(*b*) of the Charging Regulations (general requirements as to charges); and

(*c*) a list of any further information which the person responsible for the pension arrangement requires in order to discharge his liability in respect of the pension credit.

Amendments—SI 2000/2691.

7 Provision of information after receiving a pension sharing order or provision

(1) A person responsible for a pension arrangement who is in receipt of a pension sharing order or provision relating to that arrangement shall provide in writing to the transferor and transferee, or, where regulation 6(1) applies, to the person other than the person entitled to the pension credit referred to in regulation 6 of the Implementation and Discharge of Liability Regulations (discharge of liability in respect of a pension credit following the death of the person entitled to the pension credit), as the case may be –

(*a*) a notice in accordance with the provisions of regulation 7(1) of the Charging Regulations (charges in respect of pension sharing activity – postponement of implementation period);

(*b*) a list of information relating to the transferor or the transferee, or, where regulation 6(1) applies, the person other than the person entitled to the pension credit referred to in regulation 6 of the Implementation and Discharge of Liability Regulations, as the case may be, which –

(i) has been requested in accordance with regulation 4(2)(i) and (*k*), or, where appropriate, 6(2)(*c*), or should have been provided in accordance with regulation 5;

(ii) the person responsible for the pension arrangement considers he needs in order to begin to implement the pension sharing order or provision; and

(iii) remains outstanding;

(*c*) a notice of implementation; or

(*d*) a statement by the person responsible for the pension arrangement explaining why he is unable to implement the pension sharing order or agreement.

(2) The information specified in paragraph (1) shall be furnished in accordance with that paragraph within 21 days beginning with –

(*a*) in the case of sub-paragraph (*a*), (*b*) or (*d*) of that paragraph, the day on which the person responsible for the pension arrangement receives the pension sharing order or provision; or

(*b*) in the case of sub-paragraph (*c*) of that paragraph, the later of the days specified in section 34(1)(*a*) and (*b*) of the 1999 Act (implementation period).

8 Provision of information after the implementation of a pension sharing order or provision

(1) The person responsible for the pension arrangement shall issue a notice of discharge of liability to the transferor and the transferee, or, as the case may be, the person entitled to the pension credit by virtue of regulation 6 of the Implementation and Discharge of Liability Regulations no later than the end of the period of 21 days beginning with the day on which the discharge of liability in respect of the pension credit is completed.

(2) In the case of a transferor whose pension is not in payment, the notice of discharge of liability shall include the following details –

(*a*) the value of the transferor's accrued rights as determined by reference to the cash equivalent value of those rights calculated and verified in accordance with regulation 3 of the Valuation Regulations (calculation and verification of cash equivalents for the purposes of the creation of pension debits and credits);

(*b*) the value of the pension debit;

(*c*) any amount deducted from the value of the pension rights in accordance with regulation 9(2)(*c*) of the Charging Regulations (charges in respect of pension sharing activity – method of recovery);

(*d*) the value of the transferor's rights after the amounts referred to in sub-paragraphs (*b*) and (*c*) have been deducted; and

(*e*) the transfer day.

(3) In the case of a transferor whose pension is in payment, the notice of discharge of liability shall include the following details –

(*a*) the value of the transferor's benefits under the pension arrangement as determined by reference to the cash equivalent value of those rights calculated and verified in accordance with regulation 3 of the Valuation Regulations;

(*b*) the value of the pension debit;

(*c*) the amount of the pension which was in payment before liability in respect of the pension credit was discharged;

(*d*) the amount of pension which is payable following the deduction of the pension debit from the transferor's pension benefits;

(*e*) the transfer day;

(*f*) if the person responsible for the pension arrangement intends to recover charges, the amount of any unpaid charges –

(i) not prohibited by regulation 2 of the Charging Regulations (general requirements as to charges); and

(ii) specified in regulations 3 and 6 of those Regulations;

(*g*) how the person responsible for the pension arrangement will recover the charges referred to in sub-paragraph (*f*), including –

(i) whether the method of recovery specified in regulation 9(2)(*d*) of the Charging Regulations will be used;

(ii) the date when payment of those charges in whole or in part is required; and

(iii) the sum which will be payable by the transferor, or which will be deducted from his pension benefits, on that date.

(4) In the case of a transferee –

(*a*) whose pension is not in payment; and

(*b*) who will become a member of the pension arrangement from which the pension credit rights were derived,

the notice of discharge of liability to the transferee shall include the following details –

(i) the value of the pension credit;

(ii) any amount deducted from the value of the pension credit in accordance with regulation 9(2)(*b*) of the Charging Regulations;

(iii) the value of the pension credit after the amount referred to in sub-paragraph (*b*)(ii) has been deducted;

(iv) the transfer day;

(v) any periodical charges the person responsible for the pension arrangement intends to make, including how and when those charges will be recovered from the transferee; and

(vi) information concerning membership of the pension arrangement which is relevant to the transferee as a pension credit member.

(5) In the case of a transferee who is transferring his pension credit rights out of the pension arrangement from which those rights were derived, the notice of discharge of liability to the transferee shall include the following details –

(*a*) the value of the pension credit;
(*b*) any amount deducted from the value of the pension credit in accordance with regulation 9(2)(*b*) of the Charging Regulations;
(*c*) the value of the pension credit after the amount referred to in sub-paragraph (*b*) has been deducted;
(*d*) the transfer day; and
(*e*) details of the pension arrangement, including its name, address, reference number, telephone number, and, where available, the business facsimile number and electronic mail address, to which the pension credit has been transferred.

(6) In the case of a transferee, who has reached normal benefit age on the transfer day, and in respect of whose pension credit liability has been discharged in accordance with paragraph 1(2), 2(2), 3(2) or 4(4) of Schedule 5 to the 1999 Act (pension credits: mode of discharge – funded pension schemes, unfunded public service pension schemes, other unfunded pension schemes, or other pension arrangements), the notice of discharge of liability to the transferee shall include the following details –

(*a*) the amount of pension credit benefit which is to be paid to the transferee;
(*b*) the date when the pension credit benefit is to be paid to the transferee;
(*c*) the transfer day;
(*d*) if the person responsible for the pension arrangement intends to recover charges, the amount of any unpaid charges –
  (i) not prohibited by regulation 2 of the Charging Regulations; and
  (ii) specified in regulations 3 and 6 of those Regulations; and
(*e*) how the person responsible for the pension arrangement will recover the charges referred to in sub-paragraph (*d*), including –
  (i) whether the method of recovery specified in regulation 9(2)(*e*) of the Charging Regulations will be used;
  (ii) the date when payment of those charges in whole or in part is required; and
  (iii) the sum which will be payable by the transferee, or which will be deducted from his pension credit benefits, on that date.

(7) In the case of a person entitled to the pension credit by virtue of regulation 6 of the Implementation and Discharge of Liability Regulations, the notice of discharge of liability shall include the following details –

(*a*) the value of the pension credit rights as determined in accordance with regulation 10 of the Implementation and Discharge of Liability Regulations (calculation of the value of appropriate rights);
(*b*) any amount deducted from the value of the pension credit in accordance with regulation 9(2)(*b*) of the Charging Regulations;
(*c*) the value of the pension credit;
(*d*) the transfer day; and
(*e*) any periodical charges the person responsible for the pension arrangement intends to make, including how and when those charges will be recovered from the payments made to the person entitled to the pension credit by virtue of regulation 6 of the Implementation and Discharge of Liability Regulations.

PART III

9 Penalties

Where any trustee or manager of an occupational pension scheme fails, without reasonable excuse, to comply with any requirement imposed under regulation 6, 7 or 8, the Regulatory Authority may require that trustee or manager to pay within 28 days from the date of its imposition, a penalty which shall not exceed –

(*a*) £200 in the case of an individual, and
(*b*) £1,000 in any other case.

10 Provision of information after receipt of an earmarking order

(1) The person responsible for the pension arrangement shall, within 21 days beginning with the day that he receives –

(*a*) an order under section 23 of the Matrimonial Causes Act 1973, so far as it includes provision made by virtue of section 25B or 25C of that Act (powers to include provision about pensions);
(*b*) an order under section 12A(2) or (3) of the Family Law (Scotland) Act 1985; or
(*c*) an order under Article 25 of the Matrimonial Causes (Northern Ireland) Order 1978, so far as it includes provision made by virtue of Article 27B or 27C of that Order (Northern Ireland powers corresponding to those mentioned in sub-paragraph (*a*)),

issue to the party with pension rights and the other party a notice which includes the information specified in paragraphs (2) and (5), or (3), (4) and (5), as the case may be.

(2) Where an order referred to in paragraph (1)(*a*), (*b*) or (*c*) is made in respect of the pension rights or benefits of a party with pension rights whose pension is not in payment, the notice issued by the person responsible for a pension arrangement to the party with pension rights and the other party shall include a list of the circumstances in respect of any changes of which the party with pension rights or the other party must notify the person responsible for the pension arrangement.

(3) Where an order referred to in paragraph (1)(*a*) or (*c*) is made in respect of the pension rights or benefits of a party with pension rights whose pension is in payment, the notice issued by the person responsible for a pension arrangement to the party with pension rights and the other party shall include –

(*a*) the value of the pension rights or benefits of the party with pension rights;
(*b*) the amount of the pension of the party with pension rights after the order has been implemented;
(*c*) the first date when a payment pursuant to the order is to be made; and
(*d*) a list of the circumstances, in respect of any changes of which the party with pension rights or the other party must notify the person responsible for the pension arrangement.

(4) Where an order referred to in paragraph (1)(*a*) or (*c*) is made in respect of the pension rights of a party with pension rights whose pension is in payment, the notice issued by the person responsible for a pension arrangement to the party with pension rights shall, in addition to the items specified in paragraph (3), include –

(*a*) the amount of the pension of the party with pension rights which is currently in payment; and
(*b*) the amount of pension which will be payable to the party with pension rights after the order has been implemented.

(5) Where an order referred to in paragraph (1)(*a*), (*b*) or (*c*) is made the notice issued by the person responsible for a pension arrangement to the party with pension rights and the other party shall include –

(*a*) the amount of any charges which remain unpaid by –

(i) the party with pension rights; or

(ii) the other party,

in respect of the provision by the person responsible for the pension arrangement of information about pensions and divorce pursuant to regulation 3 of the Charging Regulations, and in respect of complying with an order referred to in paragraph (1)(*a*), (*b*) or (*c*); and

(*b*) information as to the manner in which the person responsible for the pension arrangement will recover the charges referred to in sub-paragraph (*a*), including –

(i) the date when payment of those charges in whole or in part is required;

(ii) the sum which will be payable by the party with pension rights or the other party, as the case may be; and

(iii) whether the sum will be deducted from payments of pension to the party with pension rights, or, as the case may be, from payments to be made to the other party pursuant to an order referred to in paragraph (1)(*a*), (*b*) or (*c*).

Reciprocal Enforcement of Maintenance Orders (Designation of Reciprocating Countries) Order 1974, SI 1974/556

1 This Order may be cited as the Reciprocal Enforcement of Maintenance Orders (Designation of Reciprocating Countries) Order 1974 and shall come into operation on 8 May 1974.

2 (1) In this Order –

"the Act of 1972" means the Maintenance Orders (Reciprocal Enforcement) Act 1972;

"the Act of 1920" means the Maintenance Orders (Facilities for Enforcement) Act 1920;

"column (1)" and "column (2)" mean respectively columns (1) and (2) of the Schedule to this Order.

(2) The Interpretation Act 1889 shall apply for the interpretation of this Order as it applies for the interpretation of an Act of Parliament.

"Interpretation Act 1889" (art 2(2))—This reference should be construed as a reference to the Interpretation Act 1978.

3 Each of the countries and territories specified in column (1) is hereby designated as a reciprocating country for the purposes of Part I of the Act of 1972 as regards maintenance orders of the description specified in respect of that country or territory in column (2).

"designated as a reciprocating country"—This order designates countries as reciprocating countries for the purposes of Maintenance Orders (Reciprocal Enforcement) Act 1972, s 1(1).

4 (1) Sections 5, 12 to 15, 17, 18 and 21 of the Act of 1972 shall apply in relation to a maintenance order transmitted under section 2 or 3 of the Act of 1920 to one of the countries and territories specified in column (1), being an order of the description specified in respect of that country or territory in column (2) to which immediately before the coming into operation of this Order the Act of 1920 applied, as they apply in relation to a maintenance order sent to that country or territory in pursuance of section 2 of the Act of 1972 or made by virtue of section 3 or 4 of the Act of 1972 and confirmed by a competent court in that country or territory.

(2) Sections 8 to 21 of the Act of 1972 shall apply in relation to a maintenance order made in one of the countries and territories specified in column (1), being an order of the description specified in respect of that country or territory in column (2) to which immediately before the coming into operation of this Order the Act of 1920 applied and not being an order which immediately before that date is registered in the High Court or the High Court of Justice in Northern Ireland under section 1 of the Act of 1920, as they apply in relation to a registered order.

(3) A maintenance order made by a court in one of the countries and territories specified in column (1) being an order of the description specified in respect of that country or territory in column (2) which has been confirmed by a court in England, Wales or Northern Ireland under section 4 of the Act of 1920 and is in force immediately before the coming into operation of this Order, shall be registered under section 7(5) of the Act of 1972 in like manner as if it has been confirmed by that court in England, Wales or Northern Ireland under subsection (2) of that section.

(4) Any proceedings brought under or by virtue of any provision of the Act of 1920 in a court in England, Wales or Northern Ireland which are pending immediately before the coming into operation of this Order, being proceedings affecting a person resident in one of the countries and territories specified in column (1), shall be continued as if they had been brought under or by virtue of the corresponding provision of the Act of 1972.

Transitional provision—This order applies the relevant parts of the 1972 Act to maintenance orders registered under the Maintenance Orders (Facilities for Enforcement) Act 1920 prior to the designation of a country under the 1972 Act.

SCHEDULE

COUNTRIES AND TERRITORIES DESIGNATED AS RECIPROCATING COUNTRIES

(1) Country or territory	(2) Description of maintenance orders to which designation extends
Alberta	Maintenance orders other than – (*a*) provisional affiliation orders; (*b*) maintenance orders of the description contained in paragraph (*b*) of the definition of "maintenance order" in the said section 21(1) of the Act of 1972; (*c*) orders obtained by or in favour of a public authority.
Anguilla	Maintenance orders generally.
Australian Capital Territory	Maintenance orders other than – (*a*) (*revoked*) (*b*) orders obtained by or in favour of a public authority.
Barbados	Maintenance orders generally.
Bermuda	Maintenance orders generally.
British Columbia	Maintenance orders generally.
Brunei Darussalam	Maintenance orders other than lump sum orders.
Falklands Islands and Dependencies	Maintenance orders generally.
Fiji	Maintenance orders generally.
Ghana	Maintenance orders other than – (*a*) affiliation orders; (*b*) maintenance orders of the description contained in paragraph (*b*) of the definition of "maintenance order" in the said section 21(1).
Gibraltar	Maintenance orders generally.
Hong Kong	Maintenance orders generally.
India	Maintenance orders other than – (*a*) affiliation orders; (*b*) maintenance orders of the description contained in paragraph (*b*) of the definition of "maintenance order" in the said section 21(1); (*c*) orders obtained by or in favour of a public authority.
Isle of Man	Maintenance orders generally.
Kenya	Maintenance orders other than – (*a*) affiliation orders; (*b*) maintenance orders of the description contained in paragraph (*b*) of the definition of "maintenance order" in the said section 21(1).
Malta	Maintenance orders generally.
Manitoba	Maintenance orders generally.
Nauru	Maintenance orders generally.

PART III

(1) Country or territory	(2) Description of maintenance orders to which designation extends
New Brunswick	Maintenance orders other than – (*a*) affiliation orders; (*b*) maintenance orders of the description contained in paragraph (*b*) of the definition of "maintenance order" in the said section 21(1); (*c*) orders obtained by or in favour of a public authority.
New South Wales	Maintenance orders other than – (*a*) (*revoked*) (*b*) orders obtained by or in favour of a public authority.
New Zealand	Maintenance orders generally.
Newfoundland and Labrador (formerly known as Newfoundland)	Maintenance orders generally.
Norfolk Island	Maintenance orders other than orders obtained by or in favour of a public authority.
Northern Territory of Australia	Maintenance orders other than – (*a*) (*revoked*) (*b*) orders obtained by or in favour of a public authority.
Northwest Territories of Canada	Maintenance orders other than – (*a*) affiliation orders; (*b*) maintenance orders of the description contained in paragraph (*b*) of the definition of "maintenance order" in the said section 21(1); (*c*) orders obtained by or in favour of a public authority.
Nova Scotia	Maintenance orders other than – (*a*) maintenance orders of the description contained in paragraph (*b*) of the definition of "maintenance order" in the said section 21(1) of the Act of 1972 (orders for the payment of birth and funeral expenses of child). (*b*) orders obtained by or in favour of a public authority.
Nunavut	Maintenance orders other than – (*a*) affiliation orders; (*b*) maintenance orders of the description contained in paragraph (*b*) of the definition of "maintenance order" in the said section 21(1) of the Act; (*c*) orders obtained by or in favour of a public authority.
Ontario	Maintenance orders other than – (*a*) (*revoked*) (*b*) maintenance orders of the description contained in the said paragraph (*b*), and (*c*) (*revoked*)

(1) Country or territory	(2) Description of maintenance orders to which designation extends
Papua New Guinea	Maintenance orders other than provisional affiliation orders
Queensland	Maintenance orders other than – (*a*) (*revoked*) (*b*) orders obtained by or in favour of a public authority.
The Republic of South Africa	Maintenance orders other than – (*a*) affiliation orders; (*b*) maintenance orders of the description contained in paragraph (*b*) of the definition of "maintenance order" in the said section 21(1).
St Helena	Maintenance orders generally.
Saskatchewan	Maintenance orders other than – (*a*) provisional affiliation orders; and (*b*) maintenance orders of the description contained in the said paragraph (*b*).
Singapore	Maintenance orders generally.
South Australia	Maintenance orders other than – (*a*) (*revoked*) (*b*) orders obtained by or in favour of a public authority.
Tasmania	Maintenance orders other than – (*a*) (*revoked*) (*b*) orders obtained by or in favour of a public authority.
Turks and Caicos Islands	Maintenance orders other than – (*a*) affiliation orders; (*b*) maintenance orders of the description contained in the said paragraph (*b*); (*c*) orders obtained by or in favour of a public authority.
United Republic of Tanzania (except Zanzibar)	Maintenance orders other than – (*a*) affiliation orders; (*b*) maintenance orders of the description contained in the said paragraph (*b*); (*c*) orders obtained by or in favour of a public authority.
Victoria	Maintenance orders other than – (*a*) (*revoked*) (*b*) orders obtained by or in favour of a public authority.
Western Australia	Maintenance orders other than orders obtained by or in favour of a public authority.
Zimbabwe	Maintenance orders other than – (*a*) affiliation orders; and (*b*) maintenance orders of the description contained in paragraph (*b*) of the definition of "maintenance order" in section 21(1) of the Act of 1972 (orders for the payment of birth and funeral expenses of child).

Amendments—SI 1975/2187, SI 1979/115; SI 1983/1125; SI 2001/3501; SI 2002/788.

Reciprocal Enforcement of Maintenance Orders (Hague Convention Countries) Order 1993, SI 1993/593

1 (1) This Order may be cited as the Reciprocal Enforcement of Maintenance Orders (Hague Convention Countries) Order 1993 and shall come into force on 5 April 1993.

"This Order"—This order applies the provisions of the Maintenance Orders (Reciprocal Enforcement) Act 1972, subject to specified modifications, to the countries listed in Sch 1 (ie "the Hague Convention countries"). Guidance on the application of the order can be found in Home Office Circular 15/1980.

2 In this Order, unless the context otherwise requires –

"Act" means the Maintenance Orders (Reciprocal Enforcement) Act 1972;

"court in a Hague Convention country" includes any judicial or administrative authority in a Hague Convention country;

"Hague Convention" means the Convention on the Recognition and Enforcement of Decisions Relating to Maintenance Obligations concluded at The Hague on 2 October 1973; and

"Hague Convention country" means a country or territory specified in Schedule 1 to this Order, being a country or territory (other than the United Kingdom) in which the Hague Convention is in force.

3 (1) The provisions of Part I of the Act shall apply in relation to a Hague Convention country as they apply in relation to a reciprocating country, subject to the exceptions, adaptations and modifications set out in Schedule 2 to this Order.

(2) Accordingly, Part I of the Act shall, in relation to –

(*a*) maintenance orders made by courts in the United Kingdom against persons in a Hague Convention country, and

(*b*) maintenance orders made by courts in a Hague Convention country against persons in the United Kingdom,

have effect as set out in Schedule 3 to this Order.

****

SCHEDULE 1

HAGUE CONVENTION COUNTRIES

Australia
Denmark
Federal Republic of Germany
Finland
France
Italy
Luxembourg
Netherlands (Kingdom in Europe and Netherlands Antilles)

Norway
Portugal
Republic of Estonia
Republic of Poland
Slovakia
Spain
Sweden
Switzerland
The Czech Republic
Turkey

Amendments—SI 1994/1902; SI 1999/1318; SI 2001/2567; SI 2002/2838.

****

SCHEDULE 3

PART I OF THE ACT AS MODIFIED BY SCHEDULE 2

ORDERS MADE BY COURTS IN THE UNITED KINGDOM

2 Transmission of maintenance order made in United Kingdom for recognition and enforcement in Hague Convention country

(1) Subject to subsection (2) below, where the payer under a maintenance order made, whether before, on or after 5 April 1993, by a court in the United Kingdom is residing in a Hague Convention country, the payee under the order may apply for the order to be sent to that country for recognition and enforcement.

(2) Subsection (1) above shall not have effect in relation to a maintenance order made under section 3 of this Act or to an order made by virtue of a provision of Part II of this Act.

(3) Every application under this section shall be made in the prescribed manner to the prescribed officer of the court which made the maintenance order to which the application relates.

(4) If, on an application duly made under this section to the prescribed officer of a court in the United Kingdom, that officer is satisfied that the payer under the maintenance order to which the application relates is residing in a Hague Convention country, the following documents, that is to say –

- (*a*) a certified copy of the maintenance order;
- (*b*) a certificate signed by that officer certifying that the order is enforceable and that it is no longer subject to the ordinary forms of review;
- (*c*) a certificate of arrears so signed;
- (*d*) a statement giving such information as the officer possesses as to the whereabouts of the payer;
- (*e*) a statement giving such information as the officer possesses for facilitating the identification of the payer;
- (*f*) where available, a photograph of the payer;
- (*g*) a written statement signed by that officer as to whether or not the payer appeared in the proceedings in which the maintenance order was made, and, if he did not appear, the original or a certified copy of a document which establishes that notice of the institution of the proceedings, including notice of the substance of the claim, was served on the payer;

PART III

(*h*) a document which establishes that notice of the order was sent to the payer; and
(*i*) a written statement signed by that officer as to whether or not the payee received legal aid either in the said proceedings or in connection with the said application;

shall be sent by that officer, in the case of a court in England and Wales or Northern Ireland, to the Lord Chancellor, or, in the case of a court in Scotland, to the Secretary of State, with a view to their being transmitted by the Lord Chancellor, or, as the case may be, the Secretary of State, to the appropriate authority in the Hague Convention country if he is satisfied that the statement relating to the whereabouts of the payer gives sufficient information to justify that being done.

(5) Nothing in this section shall be taken as affecting any jurisdiction of a court in the United Kingdom with respect to a maintenance order to which this section applies, and subject to section 5 any such order may be enforced, varied or revoked accordingly.

"prescribed manner"—See FPR 1991, rr 7.31, 7.38.

"prescribed officer"—In the High Court and county court, no particular officer is prescribed.

3 Power of magistrates' court to make maintenance order against person residing in Hague Convention country

(1) Where an application is made to a magistrates' court for a maintenance order by a person who is habitually resident in England and Wales against a person residing in a Hague Convention country and the court would have jurisdiction to determine the application under the Domestic Proceedings and Magistrates' Courts Act 1978 or the Children Act 1989 if at any time when the proceedings were instituted that person –

(*a*) were residing in England and Wales; and
(*b*) received reasonable notice of the date of the hearing of the application,

the court shall subject to the following provisions of this section have jurisdiction to determine the application.

(4) No enactment (or provision made under an enactment) requiring or enabling –

(*a*) a court to transfer proceedings from a magistrates' court to a county court or the High Court, or
(*b*) a magistrates' court to refuse to make an order on an application on the ground that any matter in question is one that would be more conveniently dealt with by the High Court,

shall apply in relation to an application to which subsection (1) above applies.

(5) On the making of an application to which subsection (1) above applies, the following documents, that is to say –

(*a*) notice of the institution of the proceedings, including notice of the substance of the application;
(*b*) a statement signed by the prescribed officer of the court, giving such information as he possesses as to the whereabouts of the respondent;
(*c*) a statement giving such information as the officer possesses for facilitating the identification of the respondent; and
(*d*) where available, a photograph of the respondent;

shall be sent by that officer to the Lord Chancellor with a view to their being transmitted by the Lord Chancellor to the appropriate authority in the Hague Convention country in which the respondent is residing for service on him of the document mentioned in paragraph (*a*) above if he is satisfied that the statement relating to the whereabouts of the respondent gives sufficient information to justify that being done.

(6) In considering whether or not to make a maintenance order pursuant to an application to which subsection (1) above applies the court shall take into account any representations made and any evidence adduced by or on behalf of the respondent.

(6A) Where the respondent makes any representations or adduces any evidence, a copy of the representations or evidence shall be served on the applicant by the prescribed officer of the court before the hearing.

(6B) The prescribed officer of the court shall give the respondent notice in writing of the date fixed for the hearing by sending the notice by post addressed to his last known or usual place of abode.

(6C) A maintenance order pursuant to an application in which subsection (1) above applies shall not be made unless the document mentioned in paragraph (*a*) of subsection (5) above has been served on the respondent in accordance with the law for the service of such documents in the Hague Convention country in which he is residing or in such other manner as may be authorised by the Lord Chancellor not less than six weeks previously.

(6D) Where a maintenance order has been made under this section, the prescribed officer of the court shall send the following documents, that is to say –

(*a*) a certified copy of the order;
(*b*) a certificate signed by that officer certifying that the order is enforceable and that it is no longer subject to the ordinary forms of review;
(*c*) a written statement signed by that officer as to whether or not the respondent appeared in the proceedings in which the order was made, and, if he did not appear, the original or a certified copy of a document which establishes that the document mentioned in paragraph (*a*) of subsection (5) above has been served on the payer in accordance with subsection (6C) above;
(*d*) a document which establishes that notice of the order was sent to the respondent; and
(*e*) a written statement signed by that officer as to whether or not the applicant received legal aid in the proceedings;

to the Lord Chancellor with a view to their being transmitted by him to the appropriate authority in the Hague Convention country in which the respondent resides for recognition and enforcement of the order.

(6E) A maintenance order made under this section may, subject to section 5 of this Act, be enforced, varied or revoked in like manner as any other maintenance order made by a magistrates' court.

(7) In the application of this section to Northern Ireland –

(*a*) for subsection (1) there shall be substituted –

"(1) Where a complaint is made to a magistrates' court by a person who is habitually resident in Northern Ireland against a person residing in a Hague Convention country and the complaint is one on which the court would have jurisdiction by virtue of any enactment to make a maintenance order if –

(*a*) that person were residing in Northern Ireland, and
(*b*) a summons to appear before the court to answer the complaint had been duly served on him,

the court shall have jurisdiction to hear the complaint and may make a maintenance order on the complaint.", and

(*b*) for subsection (4) there shall be substituted –

"(4) No enactment empowering a magistrates' court to refuse to make an order on a complaint on the ground that any matter in question is one which would be more conveniently dealt with by the High Court of Justice in Northern Ireland shall apply in relation to a complaint to which subsection (1) above applies.".

****

5 Variation and revocation of maintenance order made in United Kingdom

(1) This section applies to a maintenance order a certified copy of which has been sent to a Hague Convention country for recognition and enforcement of the order.

(2) The jurisdiction of a magistrates' court to revoke or vary a maintenance order shall be exercisable notwithstanding that the proceedings for the revocation or variation, as the case may be, of the order are brought by or against a person residing in a Hague Convention country.

(3) Where subsection (1) of section 60 of the Magistrates' Courts Act 1980 (revocation, variation etc of orders for periodical payment) applies in relation to a maintenance order to which this section applies, that subsection shall have effect as if for the words "by order on complaint," there were substituted "on an application being made, by order".

(4) Where an application is made by the payee to a court in England and Wales or Northern Ireland for the variation or revocation of an order to which this section applies, and the payer is residing in a Hague Convention country, the prescribed officer of the court shall send to the Lord Chancellor notice of the institution of the proceedings, including notice of the substance of the application, with a view to it being transmitted to the appropriate authority in the Hague Convention country for service on the payer.

(5) Where an application is made by the payee to a court in England and Wales or Northern Ireland for the variation or revocation of an order to which this section applies, and the payer is residing in a Hague Convention country –

(*a*) the court, in considering whether or not to vary or revoke the order, shall take into account any representations made and any evidence adduced by or on behalf of the payer;
(*b*) a copy of any such representations or evidence shall be served on the payee in the prescribed manner before the hearing;
(*c*) the prescribed officer of the court shall give the payer notice in writing of the date fixed for the hearing by sending the notice by post addressed to his last known or usual place of abode.

(6) Where an application is made by the payee to a court in England and Wales or Northern Ireland for the variation or revocation of an order to which this section applies, and the payer is residing in a Hague Convention country, the order shall

not be varied or revoked unless the document mentioned in subsection (3) above has been served on the payer in accordance with the law for the service of such a document in the Hague Convention country not less than six weeks previously.

(7) Where an application is made by the payer to a court in England and Wales or Northern Ireland for the variation or revocation of an order to which this section applies, the prescribed officer of the court shall arrange for the service of the document mentioned in subsection (4) above on the payee.

(8) Where an order to which this section applies has been varied or revoked by a court in the United Kingdom the prescribed officer of the court shall send the following documents, that is to say –

(*a*) a certified copy of the order of variation or revocation;
(*b*) a certificate signed by that officer certifying that the order of variation or revocation is enforceable and that it is no longer subject to the ordinary forms of review;
(*c*) a written statement, signed by that officer as to whether or not the respondent or, in Scotland the defender, appeared in the proceedings for the variation or revocation of the order, and, if he did not appear, the original or a certified copy of a document which establishes that notice of the institution of the proceedings has been served on the respondent, or, as the case may be, the defender; and
(*d*) a document which establishes that notice of the order of variation or revocation was sent to the respondent; and
(*e*) a written statement signed by that officer as to whether or not the payer or the payee received legal aid in the proceedings,

in the case of a court in England and Wales or Northern Ireland, to the Lord Chancellor, or, in the case of a court in Scotland, to the Secretary of State, with a view to their being transmitted by him to the appropriate authority in the Hague Convention country for recognition and enforcement of the order of variation or revocation.

(9) Where a maintenance order to which this section applies has been varied by an order made by a court in the United Kingdom the maintenance order shall, as from the date on which the order of variation took effect, have effect as varied by that order.

(10) Where a maintenance order to which this section applies has been revoked by an order made by a court in the United Kingdom the maintenance order shall, as from the date on which the order of revocation took effect, be deemed to have ceased to have effect except as respects any arrears due under the maintenance order at that date.

(11) (*revoked*)

(12) In the application of this section to Northern Ireland, in subsection (8), for the word "respondent" in each place where it occurs, there shall be substituted "defendant".

Amendments—SI 1999/1318.

ORDERS MADE BY COURTS IN HAGUE CONVENTION COUNTRIES

6 Registration in United Kingdom court of maintenance order made in Hague Convention country

(1) This section applies to a maintenance order made whether before, on or after 5 April 1993 by a competent court in a Hague Convention country.

(2) Where a certified copy of an order to which this section applies is received by the Lord Chancellor or the Secretary of State from a Hague Convention country, and it appears to him that the payer under the order is residing in the United Kingdom, he shall send the copy of the order and the accompanying documents to the prescribed officer of the appropriate court.

(3) Where the prescribed officer of the appropriate court receives from the Lord Chancellor or the Secretary of State a certified copy of an order to which this section applies, he shall, subject to the following subsections, register the order in the prescribed manner in that court.

(4) Before registering an order under this section an officer of the court shall take such steps as he thinks fit for the purpose of ascertaining whether the payer under the order is residing within the jurisdiction of the court, and if after taking those steps he is satisfied that the payer is not so residing he shall return the certified copy of the order and the accompanying documents to the Lord Chancellor or the Secretary of State, as the case may be, with a statement giving such information as he possesses as to the whereabouts of the payer.

(5) (*a*) The prescribed officer of the appropriate court may refuse to authorise the registration of the order if the court in the Hague Convention country by or before which the order was made did not have jurisdiction to make the order; and for these purposes a court in a Hague Convention country shall be considered to have jurisdiction if –

(i) either the payer or the payee had his habitual residence in the Hague Convention country at the time when the proceedings were instituted; or

(ii) the payer and the payee were nationals of that country at that time; or

(iii) the respondent in those proceedings had submitted to the jurisdiction of the court, either expressly or by defending on the merits of the case without objecting to the jurisdiction; or

(iv) in the case of an order made by reason of a divorce or a legal separation or a declaration that a marriage is void or annulled, the court is recognised by the law of the part of the United Kingdom in which enforcement is sought as having jurisdiction to make the order.

(*b*) In deciding whether a court in a Hague Convention country had jurisdiction to make an order the prescribed officer shall be bound by any finding of fact on which the court based its jurisdiction.

(6) The prescribed officer of the appropriate court may refuse to authorise the registration of the order –

(*a*) if such registration is manifestly contrary to public policy;
(*b*) if the order was obtained by fraud in connection with a matter of procedure;
(*c*) if proceedings between the same parties and having the same purpose are pending before a court in the same part of the United Kingdom and those proceedings were the first to be instituted; or

(*d*) if the order is incompatible with an order made in proceedings between the same parties and having the same purpose, either in the United Kingdom or in another country, provided that the latter order itself fulfils the conditions necessary for its registration and enforcement under this Part of this Act.

(7) Without prejudice to subsection (6) above, if the payer did not appear in the proceedings in the Hague Convention country in which the order was made, the prescribed officer of the appropriate court shall refuse to authorise the registration of the order unless notice of the institution of the proceedings, including notice of the substance of the claim, was served on the payer in accordance with the law of that Hague Convention country and if, having regard to the circumstances, the payer had sufficient time to enable him to defend the proceedings.

(8) If the order is registered under subsection (3) above, the prescribed officer of the appropriate court shall serve notice in a prescribed form on the payer and give notice to the payee that the order has been registered.

(9) The payer may, before the end of the period of one calendar month beginning with the date of service of the said notice, appeal to the court in which the order is registered to set aside the registration of the order on one of the grounds set out in paragraphs (5), (6) and (7) above.

(10) If the payer appeals to the court in which the order is registered to set aside the registration of the order, the prescribed officer of the court shall give notice to the payee of the appeal and of the date of the hearing of the appeal.

(11) If the prescribed officer refuses to register the order, he shall give notice to the payee in a prescribed form that registration has been refused.

(12) A payee to whom notice has been given by the prescribed officer of any court under subsection (11) above may, before the end of the period of two calendar months beginning with the date when the notice was given, appeal to that court against the refusal to register the order.

(13) If the payee appeals to the court against the refusal to register the order, the prescribed officer of the court shall give notice to the payer of the appeal and of the date of the hearing of the appeal.

(14) In the application of this section to Scotland –

(*a*) in subsection (8) for the words "serve notice in a prescribed form on" there shall be substituted the words "intimate to in the prescribed manner";

(*b*) in subsection (9) for the words "service of the said notice" there shall be substituted the words "the said intimation";

(*c*) in subsection (9), (10), (12) and (13), for any reference to an appeal there shall be substituted a reference to an application and cognate expressions shall be construed accordingly; and

(*d*) in subsection (11) for the words "in a prescribed form" there shall be substituted the words "in the prescribed manner".

(15) In the application of this section to Northern Ireland, in subsection (5), for the word "respondent" there shall be substituted "defendant".

Amendments—SI 1999/1318.

"public policy" (s 6(6))—The question of public policy was examined in *Armitage v Nanchen* (1983) FLR 293.

PART III

8 Enforcement of maintenance order registered in United Kingdom court

(1) Subject to subsections (2), (2A) and (2B) below, a registered order may be enforced in the United Kingdom as if it had been made by the registering court and as if that court had had jurisdiction to make it; and proceedings for or with respect to the enforcement of any such order may be taken accordingly.

(2) Subsection (1) above does not apply to an order which is for the time being registered in the High Court under Part I of the Maintenance Orders Act 1958 or to an order which is for the time being registered in the High Court of Justice in Northern Ireland under Part II of the Maintenance and Affiliation Orders Act (Northern Ireland) 1966.

(2A) Where in a maintenance order made in a Hague Convention country there are provisions which are not enforceable under this Part of this Act, this section shall apply only to the remaining provisions of the order.

(2B) The payee under a registered order may request the partial enforcement of that order.

(3) Any person for the time being under an obligation to make payments in pursuance of a registered order shall give notice of any change of address to the appropriate officer of the registering court, and any person failing without reasonable excuse to give such a notice shall be liable on summary conviction to a fine not exceeding level 2 on the standard scale.

(3A) In subsection (3) above "appropriate officer" means –

(*a*) in relation to a magistrates' court in England and Wales, the justices' chief executive for the court; and

(*b*) in relation to a court elsewhere, the clerk of the court.

(4) An order which by virtue of this section is enforceable by a magistrates' court in England and Wales shall, subject to the modifications of sections 76 and 93 of the Magistrates' Courts Act 1980 specified in subsections (4A) and (4B) below, be enforceable as if it were a magistrates' court maintenance order made by that court.

In this subsection, "magistrates' court maintenance order" has the same meaning as in section 150(1) of the Magistrates' Courts Act 1980.

(4A) Section 76 (enforcement of sums adjudged to be paid) shall have effect as if for subsections (4) to (6) there were substituted the following subsections –

"(4) Where proceedings are brought for the enforcement of a magistrates' court maintenance order under this section, the court may vary the order by exercising one of its powers under subsection (5) below.

(5) The powers of the court are –

(*a*) the power to order that payments under the order be made directly to a justices' chief executive;

(*b*) the power to order that payments under the order be made to a justices' chief executive, by such method of payment falling within section 59(6) above (standing order, etc) as may be specified;

(*c*) the power to make an attachment of earnings order under the Attachment of Earnings Act 1971 to secure payments under the order.

(6) In deciding which of the powers under subsection (5) above it is to exercise, the court shall have regard to any representations made by the debtor (within the meaning of section 59 above).

(7) Subsection (4) of section 59 above (power of court to require debtor to open account) shall apply for the purposes of subsection (5) above as it applies for the purposes of that section but as if for paragraph (*a*) there were substituted –

'(*a*) the court proposes to exercise its power under paragraph (*b*) of section 76(5) below, and'.".

(4B) In section 93 (complaint for arrears), subsection (6) (court not to impose imprisonment in certain circumstances) shall have effect as if for paragraph (*b*) there were substituted –

"(*b*) if the court is of the opinion that it is appropriate –
(i) to make an attachment of earnings order; or
(ii) to exercise its power under paragraph (*b*) of section 76(5) above.".

(5) The magistrates' court by which an order is enforceable by virtue of this section, and the officers thereof, shall take all such steps for enforcing the order as may be prescribed.

(6) In any proceedings for or with respect to the enforcement of an order which is for the time being registered in any court under this Part of this Act a certificate of arrears sent to the prescribed officer of the court shall be evidence of the facts stated therein.

(7) Subject to subsection (8) below, sums of money payable under a registered order shall be payable in accordance with the order, or such part thereof as the payee may have requested should be enforced, as from the date on which the order took effect.

(8) Where a registered order was made by a court in a Hague Convention country prior to the date of the entry into force of the Hague Convention between the United Kingdom and that country, no sums of money falling due before that date shall be payable in accordance with the order.

(9) (*applies to Scotland only*)

Amendments—SI 2001/410.

9 Variation of maintenance order registered in United Kingdom court

(1) Subject to the provisions of this section –

(*a*) the registering court shall have the like power, on an application made by the payer or payee under a registered order, to vary the method of payment of the order as if it had been made by the registering court and as if that court had had jurisdiction to make it;

(*b*) the jurisdiction of a magistrates' court to vary the method of payment of a registered order shall be exercisable notwithstanding that the proceedings for the variation of the order are brought by or against a person residing in a Hague Convention country.

(1ZA) Where the registering court is a magistrates' court in England and Wales, section 60 of the Magistrates' Courts Act 1980 (revocation, variation etc of orders for periodical payment) shall have effect in relation to the registered order –

(*za*) as if in subsection (1) for the words "by order on complaint" there were substituted "on an application being made, by order" and for the words "revoke, revive or vary the order", there were substituted "vary the order in accordance with subsection (3)";

(*zab*) as if subsection (2) were omitted;

(*a*) as if in subsection (3) –

(i) for the words "shall include", there were substituted "means the";

(ii) for the words "paragraphs (*a*) to (*d*) of section 59(3) above" there were substituted "subsection (3A) below"; and

(iii) after that subsection there were inserted –

"(3A) The powers of the court are –

(*a*) the power to order that payments under the order be made directly to a justices' chief executive;

(*b*) the power to order that payments under the order be made to a justices' chief executive by such method of payment falling within section 59(6) above (standing order, etc) as may be specified;

(*c*) the power to make an attachment of earnings order under the Attachment of Earnings Act 1971 to secure payments under the order.";

(*b*) as if in subsection (4) for paragraph (*b*) there were substituted –

"(*b*) payments under the order are required to be made to a justices' chief executive, by any method of payment falling within section 59(6) above (standing order, etc)",

and as if after the words "the court" there were inserted "which made the order";

(*c*) as if in subsection (5) for the words "to the clerk" there were substituted "in accordance with paragraph (*a*) of subsection (3A) above";

(*d*) as if in subsection (7), paragraph (*c*) and the word "and" immediately preceding it were omitted;

(*e*) as if in subsection (8) for the words "paragraphs (*a*) to (*d*) of section 59(3) above" there were substituted "subsection (3A) above";

(*f*) as if for subsections (9) and (10) there were substituted the following subsections –

"(9) In deciding, for the purposes of subsections (3) and (8) above, which of the powers under subsection (3A) above it is to exercise, the court shall have regard to any representations made by the debtor.

(10) Subsection (4) of section 59 above (power of court to require debtor to open account) shall apply for the purposes of subsection (3A) above as it applies for the purposes of that section but as if for paragraph (*a*) there were substituted –

'(*a*) the court proposes to exercise its power under paragraph (*b*) of section 60(3A) below, and'.".

(1ZB) Where the registering court is a court of summary jurisdiction in Northern Ireland, Article 86 of the Magistrates' Court (Northern Ireland) Order 1981 (revocation, variation etc, of orders for periodical payment) shall have effect in relation to the registered order –

(*za*) as if in paragraph (1) for the words "by order on complaint" there were substituted "on an application being made, by order" and for the words "revoke, revive or vary the order", there were substituted "vary the order in accordance with paragraph (3)";

(*zab*) as if paragraph (2) were omitted;

(*a*) as if in paragraph (3) –

(i) for the words "shall include", there were substituted "means the";

11 Steps to be taken by Lord Chancellor or Secretary of State where payer under certain orders is not residing in the United Kingdom

(1) If it appears to the Lord Chancellor that the payer under a maintenance order, a certified copy of which has been received by him from a Hague Convention country, is not residing in the United Kingdom or, in the case of an order which subsequently became a registered order, has ceased to reside therein, he shall send to the appropriate authority in that country –

(*a*) the certified copy of the order in question and a certified copy of any order varying that order;

(*b*) if the order has at any time been a registered order, a certificate of arrears signed by the prescribed officer;

(*c*) a statement giving such information as the Lord Chancellor or the Secretary of State possesses as to the whereabouts of the payer; and

(*d*) any other relevant documents in his possession relating to the case.

APPEALS

12 Appeals

Where in pursuance of section 9 above a registering court makes or refuses to make an order varying a registered order, the payer or the payee under the registered order shall have the like right of appeal (if any) from the order of variation or from the refusal to make it as he would have if the registered order had been made by the registering court.

EVIDENCE

13 Admissibility of evidence given in Hague Convention country

(1) A statement contained in –

(*a*) a document, duly authenticated, which purports to set out or summarise evidence given in proceedings in a court in a Hague Convention country; or

(*b*) a document, duly authenticated, which purports to set out or summarise evidence taken in that country for the purpose of proceedings in a court in the United Kingdom under this Part of this Act, whether in response to a request made by such a court or otherwise; or

(*c*) a document, duly authenticated, which purports to have been received in evidence in proceedings in a court in that country or to be a copy of a document so received; or

(*d*) a document purporting to be signed by a judicial officer, official or other competent person in a Hague Convention country which establishes that certain documents were served on a person,

shall in any proceedings in a court in the United Kingdom relating to a maintenance order to which this Part of this Act applies be admissible as evidence of any fact stated therein to the same extent as oral evidence of that fact is admissible in those proceedings.

(2) A document purporting to set out or summarise evidence given as mentioned in subsection (1)(*a*) above, or taken as mentioned in subsection (1)(*b*) above, shall be deemed to be duly authenticated for the purposes of that subsection if the document purports to be certified by the judicial officer or other person before whom the evidence was given, or, as the case may be, by whom it was taken, to be

PART III

the original document containing or recording, or, as the case may be, summarising, that evidence or a true copy of that document.

(3) A document purporting to have been received in evidence as mentioned in subsection (1)(*c*) above, or to be a copy of a document so received, shall be deemed to be duly authenticated for the purposes of that subsection if the document purports to be certified by a judge or officer of the court in question to have been, or to be a true copy of a document which has been so received.

(4) It shall not be necessary in any such proceedings to prove the signature or official position of the person appearing to have given such a certificate.

(5) Nothing in this section shall prejudice the admission in evidence of any document which is admissible in evidence apart from this section.

14 Obtaining of evidence needed for the purpose of certain proceedings

(1) Where for the purpose of any proceedings in a court in a Hague Convention country relating to a maintenance order to which this Part of this Act applies a request is made by or on behalf of that court for the taking in the United Kingdom of the evidence of a person residing therein relating to matters specified in the request, such court in the United Kingdom as may be prescribed shall have power to take that evidence and, after giving notice of the time and place at which the evidence is to be taken to such persons and in such manner as it thinks fit, shall take the evidence in such manner as may be prescribed.

Evidence taken in compliance with such a request shall be sent by the prescribed officer of the court –

(*a*) in England and Wales or Northern Ireland, to the Lord Chancellor, or
(*b*) in Scotland, to the Secretary of State,

for transmission to the appropriate authority in the Hague Convention country.

(2) Where any person, not being the payer or the payee under the maintenance order to which the proceedings in question relate, is required by virtue of this section to give evidence before a court in the United Kingdom, the court may order that there shall be paid out of moneys provided by Parliament such sums as appear to the court reasonably sufficient to compensate that person for the expense, trouble or loss of time properly incurred in or incidental to his attendance.

(3) Section 97(1), (3) and (4) of the Magistrates' Courts Act 1980 (which provide for compelling the attendance of witnesses, etc) shall apply in relation to a magistrates' court having power under subsection (1) above to take the evidence of any person as if the proceedings in the court in a Hague Convention country for the purpose of which a request for the taking of the evidence has been made were proceedings in the magistrates' court and had been begun by complaint.

(4) (*applies to Scotland only*)

(5) A court in –

(*a*) England and Wales or Northern Ireland may for the purpose of any proceedings in that court under this Part of this Act relating to a maintenance order to which this Part of this Act applies send to the Lord Chancellor, or
(*b*) Scotland may for the purpose of such proceedings in that court relating to such an action, send to the Secretary of State,

for transmission to the appropriate authority in a Hague Convention country a request for a court in a Hague Convention country to take or provide evidence relating to such matters as may be specified in the request.

(6) (*applies to Northern Ireland only*)

"court" (s 14(1))—This term is defined by FPR 1991, r 7.34.

"officer" (s 14(1))—This term is defined by FPR 1991, r 7.34.

15 Order etc made in Hague Convention country need not be proved

For the purposes of this Part of this Act, unless the contrary is shown –

(*a*) any order made by a court in a Hague Convention country purporting to bear the seal of that court or to be signed by any person in his capacity as a judge or officer of the court, shall be deemed without further proof to have been duly sealed or, as the case may be, to have been signed by that person;

(*b*) the person by whom the order was signed shall be deemed without further proof to have been a judge or officer, as the case may be, of that court when he signed it and, in the case of an officer, to have been authorised to sign it; and

(*c*) a document purporting to be a certified copy of an order made by a court in a Hague Convention country shall be deemed without further proof to be such a copy.

SUPPLEMENTAL

16 Payment of sums under orders made in Hague Convention countries: conversion of currency

(1) Payment of sums due under a registered order shall, while the order is registered in a court in England, Wales or Northern Ireland, be made in such manner and to such person as may be prescribed.

(2) Where the sums required to be paid under a registered order are expressed in a currency other than the currency of the United Kingdom, then, as from the relevant date, the order shall be treated as if it were an order requiring the payment of such sums in the currency of the United Kingdom as, on the basis of the rate of exchange prevailing at that date, are equivalent to the sums so required to be paid.

(3) Where the sum specified in any statement, being a statement of the amount of arrears due under a maintenance order made by a court in a Hague Convention country, is expressed in a currency other than the currency of the United Kingdom, that sum shall be deemed to be such sum in the currency of the United Kingdom as, on the basis of the rate of exchange prevailing at the relevant date, is equivalent to the sum so specified.

(4) For the purposes of this section a written certificate purporting to be signed by an officer of any bank in the United Kingdom certifying that a specified rate of exchange prevailed between currencies at a specified date and that at such rate a specified sum in the currency of the United Kingdom is equivalent to a specified sum in another specified currency shall be evidence of the rate of exchange so prevailing on that date and of the equivalent sums in terms of the respective currencies.

(5) In this section "the relevant date" means –

(*a*) in relation to a registered order or to a statement of arrears due under a maintenance order made by a court in a Hague Convention country, the date on which the order first becomes a registered order;

(*b*) in relation to a registered order which has been varied, the date on which the last order varying that order is registered in the registering court.

(6) (*applies to Scotland only*)

17 Proceedings in magistrates' courts

(4) Anything authorised or required by this Part of this Act to be done by, to or before the magistrates' court by, to or before which any other thing was done may be done by, to or before any magistrates' court acting for the same petty sessions area (or, in Northern Ireland, petty sessions district) as that court.

(5) Any application which by virtue of a provision of this Part of this Act is made to a magistrates' court shall be made by complaint.

(5A) Where the respondent to an application for the variation or revocation of –

(*a*) a maintenance order made by a magistrates' court in England and Wales, being an order to which section 5 of this Act applies; or

(*b*) a registered order which is registered in such a court,

is residing in a Hague Convention country, a magistrates' court in England and Wales shall have jurisdiction to hear the application (where it would not have such jurisdiction apart from this subsection) if it would have had jurisdiction to hear it had the respondent been residing in England and Wales.

(6) A magistrates' court in Northern Ireland shall have jurisdiction to hear a complaint for the variation or revocation –

(*a*) of a maintenance order made by such a court, and to which section 5 of this Act applies; or

(*b*) to hear a complaint for the variation of a registered order which is registered in that court,

if the defendant to the complaint is residing in a Hague Convention country and if the court would have had jurisdiction to hear the complaint had the defendant been residing in Northern Ireland and been served with a summons to appear before the court to answer the complaint.

(7) Where the respondent to an application –

(*a*) for the variation or revocation of a maintenance order made by a magistrates' court, being an order to which section 5 of this Act applies; or

(*b*) for the variation of a registered order registered in a magistrates' court,

does not appear at the time and place appointed for the hearing of the application, but the court is satisfied that the respondent is residing in a Hague Convention country and that the requirements of section 5(4), (6) or (7) or section 9(3), as the case may be, have been complied with, the court may proceed to hear and determine the application at the time and place appointed for the hearing or for any adjourned hearing in like manner as if the respondent had appeared at that time and place.

(7A) (*applies to Northern Ireland only*)

18 Magistrates' courts rules

(1) Without prejudice to the generality of the power to make rules under section 144 of the Magistrates' Courts Act 1980 (magistrates' courts rules), provision may be made by such rules with respect to any of the following matters, namely –

(*a*) the circumstances in which anything authorised or required by this Part of this Act to be done by, to or before a magistrates' court acting for a particular petty sessions area by, to or before an officer of that court may be done by, to or before a magistrates' court acting for such other petty sessions area as the rules may provide or by, to or before an officer of that court;

(*b*) the orders made, or other things done, by a magistrates' court, or an officer of such a court, under this Part of this Act, or by a court in a Hague Convention country, notice of which is to be given to such persons as the rules may provide and the manner in which such notice shall be given;

(*c*) the cases and manner in which courts in Hague Convention countries are to be informed of orders made, or other things done, by a magistrates' court under this Part of this Act;

(*d*) the cases and manner in which a justices' clerk may take evidence needed for the purpose of proceedings in a court in a Hague Convention country relating to a maintenance order to which this Part of this Act applies;

(*f*) the circumstances and manner in which magistrates' courts may for the purposes of this Part of this Act communicate with courts in Hague Convention countries.

(1A) For the purpose of giving effect to this Part of this Act, rules made under section 144 of the Magistrates' Courts Act 1980 may make, in relation to any proceedings brought under or by virtue of this Part of this Act, any provision not covered by subsection (1) above which –

(*a*) falls within subsection (2) of section 93 of the Children Act 1989, and

(*b*) may be made in relation to relevant proceedings under that section.

(2) (*applies to Northern Ireland only*)

****

21 Interpretation of Part I

(1) In this Part of this Act, unless the context otherwise requires –

"affiliation order" means an order (however described) adjudging, finding or declaring a person to be the father of a child, whether or not it also provides for the maintenance of the child;

"the appropriate court", in relation to a person residing in England and Wales or in Northern Ireland means a magistrates' court, and in relation to a person residing in Scotland means the sheriff court, within the jurisdiction of which that person is residing;

"certificate of arrears", in relation to a maintenance order, means a certificate certifying that the sum specified in the certificate is to the best of the information or belief of the officer giving the certificate the amount of the arrears due under the order at the date of the certificate except any arrears that accrued prior to the date of the entry into force of the Hague Convention between the United Kingdom and the Hague Convention country in which the payer is residing, or, as the case may be, that to the best of his information or belief there are no arrears due thereunder at the date of the certificate;

"certified copy", in relation to an order of a court, means a copy of the order certified by the proper officer of the court to be a true copy;

"court" includes any tribunal or person having power to make, confirm, enforce, vary or revoke a maintenance order and "competent court in a Hague Convention country" means a court having jurisdiction on one of the grounds specified in section 6(5)(*a*) above;

"maintenance order" means an order (however described), including a settlement made by or before a competent court in a Hague Convention country, of any of the following descriptions, and, in the case of an order which is not limited to the following descriptions, the part of the order which is so limited, that is to say –

(*a*) an order (including an affiliation order or order consequent upon an affiliation order) which provides for the periodical payment of sums of money towards the maintenance of any person, being a person whom the person liable to make payments under the order is, according to the law applied in the place where the order was made, liable to maintain;

(*aa*) an order which has been made in Scotland, on or after the granting of a decree of divorce, for the payment of a periodical allowance by one party to the marriage to the other party;

(*b*) an affiliation order or order consequent upon an affiliation order, being an order which provides for the payment by a person adjudged, found or declared to be a child's father of expenses incidental to the child's birth or, where the child has died, of his funeral expenses; and

(*c*) an order within the foregoing provisions of this definition made against a payer on the application of a public body which claims reimbursement of sums of money payable under the order with respect to the payee if reimbursement can be obtained by the public body under the law to which it is subject,

and, in the case of a maintenance order which has been varied (including a maintenance order which has been varied either by a court in the United Kingdom or by a competent court in a Hague Convention country whether or not the original order was made by such a court), means that order as varied:

Provided that the expression "maintenance order" shall not include an order made in a Hague Convention country of a description which that country or the United Kingdom has reserved the right under Article 26 of the Hague Convention not to recognise or enforce;

"order" means an order however described giving effect to a decision rendered by a court and, as respects Scotland, includes any interlocutor, and any decree or provision contained in an interlocutor;

"payee", in relation to a maintenance order, means the person entitled to the payments for which the order provides and includes a public body which has provided benefits for the payee and which is entitled ipso jure under the law to which it is subject to claim enforcement of the said order to the extent of the benefits so provided in place of the said person;

"payer", in relation to a maintenance order, means the person liable to make payments under the order;

"prescribed", in relation to a magistrates' court in England and Wales or in Northern Ireland, means prescribed by rules made under section 144 of the Magistrates' Courts Act 1980 or by rules made in accordance with Article 13 of the Magistrates' Courts (Northern Ireland) Order 1981, as the case may be, and in relation to any other court means prescribed by rules of court;

"registered order" means a maintenance order which is for the time being registered in a court in the United Kingdom under this Part of this Act and "registered" and "registration" shall be construed accordingly;

"registering court", in relation to a registered order, means the court in which that order is for the time being registered under this Part of this Act.

"revoke" and "revocation" include discharge.

(3) Any reference in this Part of this Act to the payment of money for the maintenance of a child shall be construed as including a reference to the payment of money for the child's education.

****

Reciprocal Enforcement of Maintenance Orders (Republic of Ireland) Order 1993, SI 1993/594

1 This Order may be cited as the Reciprocal Enforcement of Maintenance Orders (Republic of Ireland) Order 1993 and shall come into force on 5 April 1993.

2 (1) The provisions of Part I of the Maintenance Orders (Reciprocal Enforcement) Act 1972 (in this Order referred to as "the Act") shall apply in relation to the Republic of Ireland as they apply in relation to a reciprocating country, subject to the exceptions, adaptations and modifications set out in Schedule 1 to this Order.

(2) Accordingly, Part I of the Act shall, in relation to –

(*a*) maintenance orders made by courts in the United Kingdom against persons in the Republic of Ireland, and

(*b*) maintenance orders made by courts in the Republic of Ireland against persons in the United Kingdom,

have effect as set out in Schedule 2 to this Order.

SCHEDULE 2

PART I OF THE ACT AS MODIFIED BY SCHEDULE 1

ORDERS MADE BY COURTS IN THE UNITED KINGDOM

2 Transmission of maintenance order made in United Kingdom for enforcement in the Republic of Ireland

(1) Subject to subsection (2) below, where the payer under a maintenance order made, whether before, on or after 5 April 1993, by a court in the United Kingdom

is residing in the Republic of Ireland, the payee under the order may apply for the order to be sent to that country for enforcement.

(2) Subsection (1) above shall not have effect in relation to a provisional order or to an order made by virtue of a provision of Part II of this Act.

(3) Every application under this section shall be made in the prescribed manner to the prescribed officer of the court which made the maintenance order to which the application relates.

(4) If, on an application duly made under this section to the prescribed officer of a court in the United Kingdom, that officer is satisfied that the payer under the maintenance order to which the application relates is residing in the Republic of Ireland the following documents, that is to say –

(*a*) a certified copy of the maintenance order;
(*b*) a certificate signed by that officer certifying that the order is enforceable in the United Kingdom;
(*c*) a certificate of arrears so signed;
(*d*) a statement giving such information as the officer possesses as to the whereabouts of the payer;
(*e*) a statement giving such information as the officer possesses for facilitating the identification of the payer;
(*f*) where available, a photograph of the payer;
(*g*) if the payer did not appear in the proceedings in which the maintenance order was made, the original or a certified copy of a document which establishes that notice of the institution of the proceedings was served on the payer;
(*h*) a document which establishes that notice of the order was sent to the payer; and
(*i*) if the payee received legal aid in the proceedings, a written statement to that effect signed by that officer,

shall be sent by that officer, in the case of a court in England and Wales or Northern Ireland, to the Lord Chancellor, or, in the case of a court in Scotland, to the Secretary of State, with a view to their being transmitted by the Lord Chancellor, or, as the case may be, the Secretary of State, to the responsible authority in the Republic of Ireland if he is satisfied that the statement relating to the whereabouts of the payer gives sufficient information to justify that being done.

(5) Nothing in this section shall be taken as affecting any jurisdiction of a court in the United Kingdom with respect to a maintenance order to which this section applies and any such order may be enforced, varied or revoked accordingly.

Defined terms—"certificate of arrears", "certified copy", "court", "maintenance order", "payee", "payer", "provisional order": s 21(1).

"prescribed manner" (s 2(3))—See FPR 1991, rr 7.31, 7.37 and Magistrates' Courts (Reciprocal Enforcement of Maintenance Orders) (Republic of Ireland) Rules 1975, r 4.

"prescribed officer" (s 2(3), (4))—See FPR 1991, rr 7.31, 7.37 and MC(REMO)(RI)R 1975, r 3. In the High Court and county court, no particular officer is prescribed.

3 Power of magistrates' court to make and confirm provisional maintenance order against person residing in the Republic of Ireland

(1) Where an application is made to a magistrates' court for a maintenance order against a person residing in the Republic of Ireland and the court would have jurisdiction to determine the application under the Domestic Proceedings and Magistrates' Courts Act 1978 or the Children Act 1989 if that person –

(*a*) were residing in England and Wales; and

(*b*) received reasonable notice of the date of the hearing of the application,

the court shall (subject to subsection (2) below) have jurisdiction to determine the application.

(2) A maintenance order made by virtue of this section shall be a provisional order.

(4) No enactment (or provision made under an enactment) requiring or enabling –

(*a*) a court to transfer proceedings from a magistrates' court to a county court or the High Court, or

(*b*) a magistrates' court to refuse to make an order on an application on the ground that any matter in question is one that would be more conveniently dealt with by the High Court,

shall apply in relation to an application to which subsection (1) above applies.

(5) Where a court makes a maintenance order which is by virtue of this section a provisional order, the following documents, that is to say –

(*a*) a certified copy of the maintenance order;

(*b*) a document, authenticated in the prescribed manner, setting out or summarising the evidence given in the proceedings;

(*c*) a certificate signed by the prescribed officer of the court certifying that the grounds stated in the certificate are the grounds on which the making of the order might have been opposed by the payer under the order;

(*ca*) a notice addressed to the payer stating that a provisional order has been made, that it has no effect unless and until confirmed with or without alteration by the court making the order, and that in considering whether or not to confirm the provisional order the court will take into account any representations made or any evidence adduced by or on behalf of the payer within three weeks from the date of service of the notice;

(*d*) a statement giving such information as was available to the court as to the whereabouts of the payer;

(*e*) a statement giving such information as the officer possesses for facilitating the identification of the payer; and

(*f*) where available, a photograph of the payer,

shall be sent by that officer to the Lord Chancellor with a view to their being transmitted by the Lord Chancellor to the responsible authority in the Republic of Ireland if he is satisfied that the statement relating to the whereabouts of the payer gives sufficient information to justify that being done.

(6) The court which made a provisional order by virtue of this section shall not earlier than three weeks after the date of service of the notice referred to in paragraph (*ca*) of subsection (5) above consider whether or not to confirm the order and with or without alteration and shall take into account any representations made and any evidence adduced by or on behalf of the payer.

(6A) Where the payer makes any representations or adduces any evidence a copy of the representations or evidence shall be served on the person on whose application the provisional order was made before the date of the hearing at which confirmation of the provisional order will be considered and that person shall be notified in the prescribed manner of the date fixed for the hearing.

(6B) The court shall not confirm such an order unless the documents mentioned in paragraphs (*a*), (*b*), (*c*) and (*ca*) of subsection (5) above have been served on the payer in accordance with the law for the service of such documents in the Republic of Ireland and in sufficient time to enable him to arrange for his defence.

(6C) Where an order has been confirmed under this section, the prescribed officer of the court shall –

(*a*) send to the payer by registered post notice of the confirmation of the order; and

(*b*) send the following documents, that is to say –

(i) a certified copy of the maintenance order as confirmed;

(ii) a certificate signed by that officer certifying that the order is enforceable in the United Kingdom;

(iii) if the payer did not appear in the proceedings in which the order was confirmed the original or a certified copy of a document which establishes that the documents mentioned in paragraphs (*a*), (*b*), (*c*) and (*ca*) of subsection (5) above have been served on the payer;

(iv) a document which establishes that notice of the confirmation of the order has been sent to the payer by registered post;

(v) if the payee received legal aid in the proceedings, a written statement to that effect signed by that officer;

to the Lord Chancellor with a view to their being transmitted by the Lord Chancellor to the responsible authority in the Republic of Ireland.

(6D) Where the court decides not to confirm a provisional order, it shall revoke the order.

(7) (*applies to Northern Ireland only*)

Defined terms—"certified copy", "court", "maintenance order", "payer", "provisional order", "responsible authority": s 21(1).

"prescribed manner" (s 3(5)(*b*))—See Magistrates' Courts (Reciprocal Enforcement of Maintenance Orders) (Republic of Ireland) Rules 1975, r 5.

"prescribed officer" (s 3(5))—See MC(REMO)(RI)R 1975, r 3.

Notice of hearing (s 3(6A))—The notice is to be given in accordance with MC(REMO)(RI)R 1975, r 6 (see also Sch A1).

****

5 Variation and revocation of maintenance order made in United Kingdom

(1) This section applies to a maintenance order a certified copy of which has been sent to the Republic of Ireland in pursuance of section 2 of this Act and to a provisional order made in pursuance of section 3 of this Act which has been confirmed by a court in England and Wales or Northern Ireland under that section.

(2) Where subsection (1) of section 60 of the Magistrates' Courts Act 1980 (revocation, variation etc of orders for periodical payment) applies in relation to a maintenance order to which this section applies, that subsection shall have effect as if for the words "by order on complaint," there were substituted "on an application being made, by order".

(3) Where an application is made to a court in England and Wales or Northern Ireland by the payee for the variation or revocation of an order to which this section applies, and the payer is residing in the Republic of Ireland, the prescribed officer of the court shall send to the Lord Chancellor a certified copy of the application, together with a document, authenticated in the prescribed manner, setting out or summarising the evidence in support of the application, with a view to their being transmitted by him to the responsible authority in the Republic of Ireland for service on the payer.

(4) A court in England and Wales or Northern Ireland shall not vary or revoke such an order before the expiry of three weeks from the date of service of the documents mentioned in subsection (3) above and before varying or revoking the order shall take into account any representations made and any evidence adduced by or on behalf of the payer.

(5) Where such an order is varied or revoked by a court in England and Wales or Northern Ireland a certified copy of the order of the court and a statement as to the service of the documents mentioned in subsection (3) above on the payer shall be sent to the court in the Republic of Ireland by which the order is being enforced.

(6) Where a maintenance order to which this section applies has been varied by an order made by a court in the United Kingdom the maintenance order shall, as from the date on which the order of variation was made, have effect as varied by that order.

(7) Where a maintenance order to which this section applies has been revoked by an order made by a court in the United Kingdom the maintenance order shall, as from the date on which the order of revocation was made, be deemed to have ceased to have effect except as respects any arrears due under the maintenance order at that date.

Defined terms—"certified copy", "court", "maintenance order", "payee", "payer", "provisional order": s 21(1).

"prescribed officer" (s 5(3))—See FPR 1991, r 7.32 (as substituted by r 7.37) and Magistrates' Courts (Reciprocal Enforcement of Maintenance Orders) (Republic of Ireland) Rules 1975, r 3.

"prescribed manner" (s 5(3))—See FPR 1991, r 7.32 (as substituted by r 7.37) and MC(REMO)(RI)R 1975, r 5.

ORDERS MADE BY COURTS IN THE REPUBLIC OF IRELAND

6 Registration in United Kingdom court of maintenance order made in the Republic of Ireland

(1) This section applies to a maintenance order made whether before, on or after 5 April 1993 by a court in the Republic of Ireland.

(2) Where a certified copy of an order to which this section applies is received by the Lord Chancellor or the Secretary of State from the responsible authority in the Republic of Ireland, and it appears to him that the payer under the order is residing in the United Kingdom, he shall send the copy of the order and the accompanying documents to the prescribed officer of the appropriate court.

(3) Where the prescribed officer of the appropriate court receives from the Lord Chancellor or the Secretary of State a certified copy of an order to which this section applies, he shall, subject to the following subsections, register the order in the prescribed manner in that court.

(4) Before registering an order under this section an officer of a court shall take such steps as he thinks fit for the purpose of ascertaining whether the payer under the order is residing within the jurisdiction of the court, and if after taking those steps he is satisfied that the payer is not so residing he shall return the certified copy of the order and the accompanying documents to the Lord Chancellor, or, as the case may be, the Secretary of State with a statement giving such information as he possesses as to the whereabouts of the payer.

(5) The order shall not be registered –

(*a*) if such registration is contrary to public policy;
(*b*) if the payer did not appear in the proceedings in the Republic of Ireland and he was not served in accordance with the law of the place where he was residing with the summons or other notice of the institution of the proceedings in sufficient time to enable him to arrange for his defence;
(*c*) if the order is irreconcilable with a judgment given in the United Kingdom in proceedings between the same parties.

(6) If the order is registered under this section, the prescribed officer of the appropriate court shall serve notice in a prescribed form on the payer and give notice to the payee that the order has been registered.

(7) The payer may within one calendar month from the date of service of the said notice appeal to the court in which the order is registered to set aside the registration of the order on one of the grounds set out in subsection (5) above.

(8) If the payer appeals to the appropriate court to set aside the registration of the order, the prescribed officer of the court shall give notice to the payee of the appeal and of the date of the hearing of the appeal.

(9) If the payer appeals to the appropriate court to set aside the registration of the order, the court may, on the application of the payer, stay, or in Scotland sist, the proceedings if either –

(*a*) enforcement of the maintenance order has been suspended in the Republic of Ireland pending the determination of any form of appeal; or
(*b*) the time for an appeal has not yet expired and enforcement has been suspended pending the making of an appeal,

and in the latter case the court may lay down the time within which the proceedings will be stayed or sisted.

(10) If the order is not registered by virtue of subsection (5) above, the prescribed officer shall give notice to the payee in a prescribed form that the order has not been registered.

(11) A payee to whom notice has been given by the officer of any court under subsection (10) above may within one calendar month of the date of the notice appeal to that court to set aside the decision not to register the order.

(12) (*applies to Scotland only*)

Defined terms—"appropriate court", "certified copy", "court", "maintenance order", "payer", "responsible authority": s 21(1).

"prescribed officer" (s 6(2))—See FPR 1991, rr 7.32, 7.35, 7.37 and Magistrates' Courts (Reciprocal Enforcement of Maintenance Orders) (Republic of Ireland) Rules 1975, r 3.

"prescribed manner" (s 6(3))—See FPR 1991, rr 7.32, 7.35, 7.37 and MC(REMO)(RI)R 1975, r 8.

8 Enforcement of maintenance order registered in United Kingdom court

(1) Subject to subsections (1A), (2), (2A) and (2B) below, a registered order may be enforced in the United Kingdom as if it had been made by the registering court and as if that court had had jurisdiction to make it; and proceedings for or with respect to the enforcement of any such order may be taken accordingly.

(1A) During the period within which an appeal to set aside the registration of a registered order may be made under section 6(7) and until any such appeal has been determined, no measures of enforcement may be taken against the property of the payer other than those designed to protect the interests of the payee:

Provided that nothing in this subsection shall be construed as preventing a registered order from being registered as mentioned in subsection (2) below.

(2) Subsection (1) above does not apply to an order which is for the time being registered in the High Court under Part I of the Maintenance Orders Act 1958 or to an order which is for the time being registered in the High Court of Justice in Northern Ireland under Part II of the Maintenance and Affiliation Orders Act (Northern Ireland) 1966.

(2A) Where in a maintenance order made in the Republic of Ireland there are provisions which are not enforceable, this section shall apply only to the remaining provisions of the order.

(2B) The payee under a registered order may request the partial enforcement of that order.

(3) Any person for the time being under an obligation to make payment in pursuance of a registered order shall give notice of any change of address to the appropriate officer of the registering court, and any person failing without reasonable excuse to give such a notice shall be liable on summary conviction to a fine not exceeding level 2 on the standard scale.

(3A) In subsection (3) above "appropriate officer" means –

- (*a*) in relation to a magistrates' court in England and Wales, the justices' chief executive for the court; and
- (*b*) in relation to a magistrates' court elsewhere, the clerk of the court.

(4) An order which by virtue of this section is enforceable by a magistrates' court shall subject to the modifications of sections 76 and 93 of the Magistrates' Courts Act 1980 specified in subsections (4A) and (4B) below be enforceable as if it were a magistrates' court maintenance order made by that court.

In this subsection, "magistrates' court maintenance order" has the same meaning as in section 150(1) of the Magistrates' Courts Act 1980.

(4A) Section 76 (enforcement of sums adjudged to be paid) shall have effect as if for subsections (4) to (6) there were substituted the following subsections –

"(4) Where proceedings are brought for the enforcement of a magistrates' court maintenance order under this section, the court may vary the order by exercising one of its powers under subsection (5) below.

(5) The powers of the court are –

(*a*) the power to order that payments under the order be made directly to a justices' chief executive;

(*b*) the power to order that payments under the order be made to a justices' chief executive by such method of payment falling within section 59(6) above (standing order, etc) as may be specified;

(*c*) the power to make an attachment of earnings order under the Attachment of Earnings Act 1971 to secure payments under the order.

(6) In deciding which of the powers under subsection (5) above it is to exercise, the court shall have regard to any representations made by the debtor (within the meaning of section 59 above).

(7) Subsection (4) of section 59 above (power of court to require debtor to open account) shall apply for the purposes of subsection (5) above as it applies for the purposes of that section but as if for paragraph (*a*) there were substituted –

'(*a*) the court proposes to exercise its power under paragraph (*b*) of section 76(5) below, and'."

(4B) In section 93 (complaint for arrears), subsection (6) (court not to impose imprisonment in certain circumstances) shall have effect as if for paragraph (*b*) there were substituted –

"(*b*) if the court is of the opinion that it is appropriate –

(i) to make an attachment of earnings order; or

(ii) to exercise its power under paragraph (*b*) of section 76(5) above."

(5) The magistrates' court by which an order is enforceable by virtue of this section, and the officers thereof, shall take all such steps for enforcing the order as may be prescribed.

(6) In any proceedings for or with respect to the enforcement of an order which is for the time being registered in any court under this Part of this Act a certificate of arrears sent to the prescribed officer of the court shall be evidence of the facts stated therein.

(7) Subject to subsection (8) below, sums of money payable under a registered order shall be payable in accordance with the order, or such part thereof as the payee may have requested should be enforced, as from the date on which the order took effect.

(8) No sums of money accruing before 1 April 1975 under a registered order shall be payable in accordance with the order.

(9) (*applies to Scotland only*)

Amendments—Maintenance Enforcement Act 1991, Sch 1, para 13; SI 2001/410.

Defined terms—"certificate of arrears", "maintenance order", "payee", "registered order", "registering court": s 21(1).

"standing order, etc" (s 8(4A))—The methods of payment available do not include power to order payment by direct debit.

"such steps ... as may be prescribed" (s 8(5))—See Magistrates' Courts (Reciprocal Enforcement of Maintenance Orders) (Republic of Ireland) Rules 1975, r 10.

"prescribed officer" (s 8(6))—See MC(REMO)(RI)R 1975, r 3.

9 Variation and revocation of maintenance order registered in United Kingdom court

(1) Where a registered order has been varied by a court in the Republic of Ireland, the registered order shall, as from the date on which the order of variation took effect or 1 April 1975, whichever is the later, have effect as varied by that order.

(2) Where a registered order has been revoked by a court in the Republic of Ireland, the registered order shall, as from the date on which the order of revocation took effect or 1 April 1975, whichever is the later, be deemed to have ceased to have effect except as respects any arrears due under the registered order at that date.

(3) The prescribed officer of the registering court shall register in the prescribed manner any order varying a registered order.

Defined terms—"registered order", "registering court": s 21(1).

"prescribed officer" (s 9(3))—See Magistrates' Courts (Reciprocal Enforcement of Maintenance Orders) (Republic of Ireland) Rules 1975, r 3.

"prescribed manner" (s 9(3))—See Magistrates' Courts (Reciprocal Enforcement of Maintenance Orders) (Republic of Ireland) Rules 1975, r 8.

10 Cancellation of registration and transfer of order

(1) Where a registered order is revoked by an order made by a court in the Republic of Ireland and notice of the revocation is received by the registering court, the prescribed officer of the registering court shall cancel the registration; but any arrears due under the registered order at the date on which the order of revocation took effect or 1 April 1975, whichever is the later, shall continue to be recoverable as if the registration had not been cancelled.

(2) Where the prescribed officer of the registering court is of opinion that the payer under a registered order has ceased to reside within the jurisdiction of that court, he shall cancel the registration of the order and, subject to subsection (3) below, shall send the certified copy of the order to the Lord Chancellor.

(3) Where the prescribed officer of the registering court, being a magistrates' court, is of opinion that the payer is residing within the jurisdiction of another magistrates' court in that part of the United Kingdom in which the registering court is, he shall transfer the order to that other court by sending the certified copy of the order to the prescribed officer of that other court.

(4) On the transfer of an order under subsection (3) above the prescribed officer of the court to which it is transferred shall, subject to subsection (6) below, register the order in the prescribed manner in that court.

(5) Where the certified copy of an order is received by the Lord Chancellor under this section and it appears to him that the payer under the order is still residing in the United Kingdom, he shall transfer the order to the appropriate court by sending the certified copy of the order together with the related documents to the prescribed officer of the appropriate court and, subject to subsection (6) below, that officer shall register the order in the prescribed manner in that court.

(6) Before registering an order in pursuance of subsection (4) or (5) above an officer of a court shall take steps as he thinks fit for the purpose of ascertaining whether the payer is so residing, and if after taking those steps he is satisfied that the payer is not residing within the jurisdiction of the court he shall send the certified copy of the order to the Lord Chancellor.

PART III

(7) The officer of a court who is required by any of the foregoing provisions of this section to send to the Lord Chancellor or to the prescribed officer of another court the certified copy of an order shall send with that copy –

(*a*) a certificate of arrears signed by him;
(*b*) a statement giving such information as he possesses as to the whereabouts of the payer; and
(*c*) any relevant documents in his possession relating to the case.

(8) (*applies to Scotland only*)

Defined terms—"certified copy", "court", "registered order", "registering court": s 21(1).

"prescribed officer"—See Magistrates' Courts (Reciprocal Enforcement of Maintenance Orders) (Republic of Ireland) Rules 1975, r 3.

"prescribed manner" (s 10(4), (5))—See MC(REMO)(RI)R 1975, r 8.

11 Steps to be taken by Lord Chancellor or Secretary of State where payer under certain orders is not residing in the United Kingdom

(1) If it appears to the Lord Chancellor or the Secretary of State that the payer under a maintenance order, a certified copy of which has been received by him from the Republic of Ireland, is not residing in the United Kingdom, he shall send to the responsible authority in that country –

(*a*) the certified copy of the order in question;
(*b*) if the order has at any time been a registered order, a certificate of arrears signed by the prescribed officer;
(*c*) a statement giving such information as the Lord Chancellor or the Secretary of State possesses as to the whereabouts of the payer; and
(*d*) any other relevant documents in his possession relating to the case.

Defined terms—"certified copy", "maintenance order", "payer", "registered order", "responsible authority": s 21(1).

"prescribed officer" (s 11(1))—See Magistrates' Courts (Reciprocal Enforcement of Maintenance Orders) (Republic of Ireland) Rules 1975, r 3.

APPEALS

12 Appeals

(1) No appeal shall lie from a provisional order made in pursuance of section 3 of this Act by a court in England and Wales or Northern Ireland.

(2) Where in pursuance of that section any such court confirms or refuses to confirm such a provisional order, the payer or payee under the order shall have the like right of appeal (if any) from the confirmation of, or refusal to confirm, the provisional order as he would have if that order were not a provisional order and the court had made or, as the case may be, refused to make the order on the occasion on which it confirmed or, as the case may be, refused to confirm the order.

(3) Nothing in subsection (2) above shall be construed as affecting any right of appeal conferred by any other enactment.

Defined terms—"payee", "payer", "provisional order": s 21(1).

EVIDENCE

13 Admissibility of evidence given in the Republic of Ireland

(1) A statement contained in –

(*a*) a document, duly authenticated, which purports to set out or summarise evidence given in proceedings in a court in the Republic of Ireland; or

(*b*) a document, duly authenticated, which purports to set out or summarise evidence taken in that country for the purpose of proceedings in a court in the United Kingdom under this Part of this Act, whether in response to a request made by such a court or otherwise; or

(*c*) a document, duly authenticated, which purports to have been received in evidence in proceedings in a court in that country or to be a copy of a document so received; or

(*d*) a document purporting to be signed by a judge or officer of a court in the Republic of Ireland which establishes that certain documents were served on a person,

shall in any proceedings in a court in the United Kingdom relating to a maintenance order to which this Part of this Act applies be admissible as evidence of any fact stated therein to the same extent as oral evidence of that fact is admissible in those proceedings.

(2) A document purporting to set out or summarise evidence given as mentioned in subsection (1)(*a*) above, or taken as mentioned in subsection (1)(*b*) above, shall be deemed to be duly authenticated for the purposes of that subsection if the document purports to be certified by the judge or other person before whom the evidence was given, or, as the case may be, by whom it was taken, to be the original document containing or recording, or, as the case may be, summarising, that evidence or a true copy of that document.

(3) A document purporting to have been received in evidence as mentioned in subsection (1)(*c*) above, or to be a copy of a document so received, shall be deemed to be duly authenticated for the purposes of that subsection if the document purports to be certified by a judge or officer of the court in question to have been, or to be a true copy of a document which has been, so received.

(4) It shall not be necessary in any such proceedings to prove the signature or official position of the person appearing to have given such a certificate.

(5) Nothing in this section shall prejudice the admission in evidence of any document which is admissible in evidence apart from this section.

Defined terms—"court": s 21(1).

Scope of provision—This section makes provision for the admission of evidence given in the Republic of Ireland.

14 Obtaining of evidence needed for purpose of certain proceedings

(1) Where for the purpose of any proceedings in a court in the Republic of Ireland relating to a maintenance order to which this Part of this Act applies a request is made by or on behalf of that court for the taking in the United Kingdom of the evidence of a person residing therein relating to matters specified in the request, such court in the United Kingdom as may be prescribed shall have power to take that evidence and, after giving notice of the time and place at which the evidence is

to be taken to such persons and in such manner as it thinks fit, shall take the evidence in such manner as may be prescribed.

Evidence taken in compliance with such a request shall be sent by the prescribed officer of the court –

(*a*) in England and Wales or Northern Ireland, to the Lord Chancellor, or
(*b*) in Scotland, to the Secretary of State,

for transmission to the responsible authority in the Republic of Ireland.

(2) Where any person, not being the payer or the payee under the maintenance order to which the proceedings in question relate, is required by virtue of this section to give evidence before a court in the United Kingdom, the court may order that there shall be paid –

(*a*) if the court is a court in England, Wales or Scotland out of moneys provided by Parliament; and
(*b*) if the court is a court in Northern Ireland, out of moneys provided by Parliament,

such sums as appear to the court reasonably sufficient to compensate that person for the expense, trouble or loss of time properly incurred in or incidental to his attendance.

(3) Section 97(1), (3) and (4) of the Magistrates' Courts Act 1980 (which provide for compelling the attendance of witnesses, etc) shall apply in relation to a magistrates' court having power under subsection (1) above to take the evidence of any person as if the proceedings in the court in the Republic of Ireland for the purpose of which a request for the taking of the evidence has been made were proceedings in the magistrates' court and had been begun by complaint.

(4) (*applies to Scotland only*)

(5) A court in –

(*a*) England and Wales or Northern Ireland may for the purpose of any proceedings in that court under this Part of this Act relating to a maintenance order to which this Part of this Act applies, send to the Lord Chancellor, or
(*b*) Scotland may for the purpose of such proceedings in that court relating to such an action, send to the Secretary of State,

for transmission to the responsible authority in the Republic of Ireland a request for a court in the Republic of Ireland to take or provide evidence relating to such matters as may be specified in the request.

(6) (*applies to Northern Ireland only*)

Defined terms—"court", "maintenance order", "payee", "payer": s 21(1).

"such court ... as may be prescribed" (s 14(1))—See FPR 1991, r 7.34 and Magistrates' Courts (Reciprocal Enforcement of Maintenance Orders) (Republic of Ireland) Rules 1975.

"prescribed officer" (s 14(1))—See FPR 1991, r 7.34 and MC(REMO)(RI)R 1975, r 3.

15 Order etc made in the Republic of Ireland need not be proved

For the purposes of this Part of this Act, unless the contrary is shown –

(*a*) any order made by a court in the Republic of Ireland purporting to bear the seal of that court or to be signed by any person in his capacity as a judge or officer of the court, shall be deemed without further proof to have been duly sealed or, as the case may be, to have been signed by that person;

(*b*) the person by whom the order was signed shall be deemed without further proof to have been a judge or officer, as the case may be, of that court when he signed it and, in the case of an officer, to have been authorised to sign it; and

(*c*) a document purporting to be a certified copy of an order made by a court in the Republic of Ireland shall be deemed without further proof to be such a copy.

Defined terms—"certified copy", "court": s 21(1).

Scope of provision—This section provides for the proof of orders and documents made in a court in the Republic of Ireland.

SUPPLEMENTAL

16 Payment of sums under orders made in the Republic of Ireland)

Payment of sums due under a registered order shall, while the order is registered in a court in England, Wales or Northern Ireland, be made in such manner and to such person as may be prescribed.

Defined terms—"registered order": s 21(1).

"prescribed"—See Magistrates' Courts (Reciprocal Enforcement of Maintenance Orders) (Republic of Ireland) Rules 1975, r 10.

17 Proceedings in magistrates' courts

(4) Anything authorised or required by this Part of this Act to be done by, to or before the magistrates' court by, to or before which any other thing was done may be done by, to or before any magistrates' court acting for the same petty sessions area (or, in Northern Ireland, petty sessions district) as that court.

(5) Any application which by virtue of a provision of this Part of this Act is made to a magistrates' court shall be made by complaint.

(5A) Where the respondent to an application for the variation or revocation of –

(*a*) a maintenance order made by a magistrates' court in England and Wales, being an order to which section 5 of this Act applies; or

(*b*) a registered order which is registered in such a court,

is residing in the Republic of Ireland, a magistrates' court in England and Wales shall have jurisdiction to hear the application (where it would not have such jurisdiction apart from this subsection) if it would have had jurisdiction to hear it had the respondent been residing in England and Wales.

(6) A magistrates' court in Northern Ireland shall have jurisdiction to hear a complaint for the variation or revocation of a maintenance order made by such a court, being an order to which section 5 of this Act applies, if the defendant to the complaint is residing in the Republic of Ireland and the court would have jurisdiction to hear the complaint had the defendant been residing in Northern Ireland.

(7) Where the respondent to an application for the variation or revocation of a maintenance order made by a magistrates' court, being an order to which section 5 of this Act applies, does not appear at the time and place appointed for the hearing

of the application, but the court is satisfied that the respondent is residing in the Republic of Ireland, the court may proceed to hear and determine the application at the time and place appointed for the hearing or for any adjourned hearing in like manner as if the respondent had appeared at that time and place.

(7A) (*applies to Northern Ireland only*)

Defined terms—"maintenance order": s 21(1).

Commencement by complaint (s 17(5), (7))—See under s 3.

18 Magistrates' courts rules

(1) Without prejudice to the generality of the power to make rules under section 144 of the Magistrates' Courts Act 1980 (magistrates' courts rules), provision may be made by such rules with respect to any of the following matters, namely –

(*a*) the circumstances in which anything authorised or required by this Part of this Act to be done by, to or before a magistrates' court acting for a particular petty sessions area by, to or before an officer of that court may be done by, to or before a magistrates' court acting for such other petty sessions area as the rules may provide or by, to or before an officer of that court;

(*b*) the orders made, or other things done, by a magistrates' court, or an officer of such a court, under this Part of this Act, or by a court in the Republic of Ireland, notice of which is to be given to such persons as the rules may provide and the manner in which such notice shall be given;

(*c*) the cases and manner in which courts in the Republic of Ireland are to be informed of orders made, or other things done, by a magistrates' court under this Part of this Act;

(*d*) the cases and manner in which a justices' clerk may take evidence needed for the purpose of proceedings in a court in the Republic of Ireland relating to a maintenance order to which this Part of this Act applies;

(*e*) the circumstances and manner in which cases may be remitted by the magistrates' courts to courts in the Republic of Ireland;

(*f*) the circumstances and manner in which magistrates' courts may for the purposes of this Part of this Act communicate with courts in the Republic of Ireland.

(1A) For the purpose of giving effect to this Part of this Act, rules made under section 144 of the Magistrates' Courts Act 1980 may make, in relation to any proceedings brought under or by virtue of this Part of this Act, any provision not covered by subsection (1) above which –

(*a*) falls within subsection (2) of section 93 of the Children Act 1989, and

(*b*) may be made in relation to relevant proceedings under that section.

(2) (*applies to Northern Ireland only*)

Defined terms—"maintenance order": s 21(1).

Scope of provision—This section provides for the making of Rules for the application of Pt I. The Magistrates' Courts (Reciprocal Enforcement of Maintenance Orders) (Republic of Ireland) Rules 1975 have been made for this purpose.

****

21 Interpretation of Part I

(1) In this Part of this Act –

"affiliation order" means an order (however described) adjudging, finding or declaring a person to be the father of a child, whether or not it also provides for the maintenance of the child;

"the appropriate court", in relation to a person residing in England and Wales or in Northern Ireland means a magistrates' court, and in relation to a person residing in Scotland means the sheriff court, within the jurisdiction of which that person is residing;

"certificate of arrears", in relation to a maintenance order, means a certificate certifying that the sum specified in the certificate is to the best of the information or belief of the officer giving the certificate the amount of the arrears due under the order at the date of the certificate except any arrears due under the order in respect of a period ending before 1 April 1975 or, as the case may be, that to the best of his information or belief there are no arrears due thereunder at the date of the certificate;

"certified copy", in relation to an order of a court, means a copy of the order certified by the proper officer of the court to be a true copy;

"court" includes any tribunal or person having power to make, confirm, enforce, vary or revoke a maintenance order;

"maintenance order" means an order (however described) of any of the following descriptions, that is to say –

(*a*) an order (including an affiliation order or order consequent upon an affiliation order) which provides for the periodical payment of sums of money towards the maintenance of any person, being a person whom the person liable to make payments under the order is, according to the law applied in the place where the order was made, liable to maintain;

(*aa*) an order which has been made in Scotland, on or after the granting of a decree of divorce, for the payment of a periodical allowance by one party to the marriage to the other party; and

(*b*) an affiliation order or order consequent upon an affiliation order, being an order which provides for the payment by a person adjudged, found or declared to be a child's father of expenses incidental to the child's birth or, where the child has died, of his funeral expenses,

and, in the case of a maintenance order which has been varied, means that order as varied;

"order", as respects Scotland, includes any interlocutor, and any decree or provision contained in an interlocutor;

"payee", in relation to a maintenance order, means the person entitled to the payments for which the order provides;

"payer", in relation to a maintenance order, means the person liable to make payments under the order;

"prescribed", in relation to a magistrates' court in England and Wales or in Northern Ireland, means prescribed by rules made under section 144 of the Magistrates' Courts Act 1980 or by rules made in accordance with Article 13 of the Magistrates' Courts (Northern Ireland) Order 1981, as the case may be, and in relation to any other court means prescribed by rules of court;

"provisional order" means an order made by a court in England and Wales or Northern Ireland which is provisional only and has no effect unless and until confirmed, with or without alteration, by that court;

"registered order" means a maintenance order which is for the time being registered in a court in the United Kingdom under this Part of this Act;

PART III

"registering court", in relation to a registered order, means the court in which that order is for the time being registered under this Part of this Act;

"the responsible authority", in relation to the Republic of Ireland, means any person who in that country has functions similar to those of the Lord Chancellor or Secretary of State under this Part of this Act; and

"revoke" and "revocation" include discharge.

(2) For the purposes of this Part of this Act an order shall be taken to be a maintenance order so far (but only so far) as it relates to the periodical payment of sums of money as mentioned in paragraph (*a*) of the definition of "maintenance order" in subsection (1) above, to the payment of a periodical allowance as mentioned in paragraph (*aa*) of that definition, or to the payment by a person adjudged, found or declared to be a child's father of any such expenses as are mentioned in paragraph (*b*) of that definition.

(3) Any reference in this Part of this Act to the payment of money for the maintenance of a child shall be construed as including a reference to the payment of money for the child's education.

Reciprocal Enforcement of Maintenance Orders (United States of America) Order 1995, SI 1995/2709

1 This Order may be cited as the Reciprocal Enforcement of Maintenance Orders (United States of America) Order 1995 and shall come into force on 1 December 1995.

"This Order"—This order applies the provisions of the Maintenance Orders (Reciprocal Enforcement) Act 1972, subject to specified modifications, to the States listed in Sch 1. Guidance on the application of the order can be found in Lord Chancellor's Department Circular dated 22 November 1995.

2 In this Order, unless the context otherwise requires –

"the Act" means the Maintenance Orders (Reciprocal Enforcement) Act 1972; and

"specified State" means a State specified in Schedule 1 to this Order.

3 The provisions of Part I of the Act shall apply, with the exceptions, adaptations, and modifications specified in Schedule 2 to this Order, to maintenance orders made by courts in the United Kingdom and to maintenance orders made by courts in a specified State, and accordingly Part I of the Act shall, in relation to such orders, have effect as set out in Schedule 3 to this Order.

SCHEDULE 1

SPECIFIED STATES

Alaska
Arizona
Arkansas
California
Connecticut
Delaware
Florida
Indiana
Iowa
Kansas
Kentucky
Louisiana
Maine
Maryland
Massachusetts
Minnesota
Missouri
Montana
Nebraska
Nevada
New Jersey
New York
North Carolina
North Dakota
Oklahoma
Oregon
Pennsylvania
South Dakota
Texas
Utah
Vermont
Virginia
Washington
West Virginia
Wisconsin
Wyoming

****

SCHEDULE 3

PART I OF THE ACT AS MODIFIED BY SCHEDULE 2

ORDERS MADE BY COURTS IN THE UNITED KINGDOM

2 Transmission of maintenance order made in United Kingdom for enforcement in specified State

(1) Subject to subsection (2) below, where the payer under a maintenance order made, whether before, on or after 1 December 1995, by a court in the United Kingdom is residing or has assets in a specified State, the payee under the order may apply for the order to be sent to that State for enforcement.

(2) Subsection (1) above shall not have effect in relation to an order made by virtue of a provision of Part II of this Act as applied to a specified State by the Recovery of Maintenance (United States of America) Order 1993.

(3) Every application under this section shall be made in the prescribed manner to the prescribed officer of the court which made the maintenance order to which the application relates.

(4) If, on an application duly made under this section to the prescribed officer of a court in the United Kingdom, that officer is satisfied that the payer under the maintenance order to which the application relates is residing or has assets in a specified State, the following documents, that is to say –

- (*a*) three certified copies of the maintenance order;
- (*b*) a certificate signed by that officer certifying that the order is enforceable in the United Kingdom;

(*c*) a certificate of arrears so signed or, in Scotland, signed by the applicant or his solicitor;

(*d*) a sworn statement signed by the payee giving the following information –

(i) the address of the payee;

(ii) such information as is known as to the whereabouts of the payer; and

(iii) a description, so far as is known, of the nature and location of any assets of the payer available for execution;

(*e*) a statement giving such information as the officer possesses for facilitating the identification of the payer; and

(*f*) where available, a photograph of the payer;

shall be sent by that officer, in the case of a court in England and Wales or Northern Ireland, to the Lord Chancellor, or, in the case of a court in Scotland, to the Secretary of State, with a view to their being transmitted by him to the appropriate authority in the specified State if he is satisfied that the statement relating to the whereabouts of the payer and the nature and location of his assets gives sufficient information to justify that being done.

(5) Nothing in this section shall be taken as affecting any jurisdiction of a court in the United Kingdom with respect to a maintenance order to which this section applies, and, subject to section 5 below, any such order may be enforced, varied or revoked accordingly.

"prescribed manner"—See FPR 1991, rr 7.31, 7.38.

"prescribed officer"—In the High Court and county court, no particular officer is prescribed.

****

5 Variation and revocation of maintenance order made in United Kingdom

(1) This section applies to a maintenance order certified copies of which have been sent in pursuance of section 2 to a specified State for enforcement.

(2) The jurisdiction of a court in the United Kingdom to revoke, revive or vary a maintenance order shall be exercisable notwithstanding that the proceedings for the revocation, revival or variation, as the case may be, of the order are brought by or against a person residing in a specified State.

(3) Where subsection (1) of section 60 of the Magistrates' Courts Act 1980 (revocation, variation etc of orders for periodical payment) applies in relation to a maintenance order to which this section applies, that subsection shall have effect as if for the words "by order on complaint" there were substituted "on an application being made, by order".

(4) Where an application is made by the payee to a court in the United Kingdom for the variation or revocation of an order to which this section applies, and the payer is residing in a specified State, the prescribed officer of the court shall –

(*a*) in the case of a court in England and Wales or Northern Ireland, send to the Lord Chancellor, or, in the case of a court in Scotland, send to the Secretary of State, notice of the institution of the proceedings, including notice of the substance of the application, with a view to its being transmitted to the appropriate authority in the specified State for service on the payer; and (*b*) give the payer notice in writing of the date fixed for the hearing by sending the notice by post addressed to his last known or usual place of abode.

(5) Where such an application is made –

(*a*) the order shall not be varied or revoked unless the document mentioned in subsection (4)(*a*) above has been served on the payer in accordance with the law for the service of such a document in the specified State;

(*b*) the court, in considering whether or not to vary or revoke the order, shall take into account any representations made and any evidence adduced by or on behalf of the payer; and

(*c*) a copy of any such representations or evidence shall be served on the payee in the prescribed manner before the hearing.

(6) Where an application is made by the payer to a court in the United Kingdom for the variation or revocation of an order to which this section applies, the prescribed officer of the court shall arrange for the service of notice of institution of the proceedings, including notice of the substance of the application, on the payee.

(7) Where an order to which this section applies is varied or revoked by a court in the United Kingdom the prescribed officer of the court shall send the following documents, that is to say –

(*a*) three certified copies of the order of variation or revocation; and

(*b*) a written statement, signed by that officer as to whether both the payer and the payee under the order appeared in the proceedings, and, if only the applicant appeared, the original or a certified copy of a document which establishes that notice of the institution of the proceedings had been served on the other party;

in the case of a court in England and Wales or Northern Ireland, to the Lord Chancellor, or, in the case of a court in Scotland, to the Secretary of State, with a view to their being transmitted by him to the appropriate authority in the specified State for registration and enforcement of the order of variation or revocation.

(8) Where a maintenance order to which this section applies has been varied by an order made by a court in the United Kingdom or by a court in a specified State, the maintenance order shall, as from the date on which the order of variation took effect, have effect as varied by that order.

(9) Where a maintenance order to which this section applies has been revoked by an order made by a court in the United Kingdom or by a court in a specified State, the maintenance order shall, as from the date on which the order of revocation took effect, be deemed to have ceased to have effect except in respect of any arrears due under the maintenance order at that date.

(10) Where a maintenance order to which this section applies has been varied or revoked by an order made by a court in a specified State, the prescribed officer of the court shall register the order of variation or revocation in the prescribed manner.

ORDERS MADE BY COURTS IN SPECIFIED STATES

6 Registration in United Kingdom court of maintenance order made in a specified State

(1) This section applies to a maintenance order made, whether before, on or after 1 December 1995 by a court in a specified State.

PART III

(2) Where a certified copy of an order to which this section applies is received by the Lord Chancellor or the Secretary of State from the appropriate authority in a specified State, and it appears to him that the payer under the order is residing or has assets in the United Kingdom, he shall send the copy of the order to the prescribed officer of the appropriate court.

(3) Where the prescribed officer of the appropriate court receives from the Lord Chancellor or the Secretary of State a certified copy of an order to which this section applies, he shall, subject to subsection (4) below, register the order in the prescribed manner in that court.

(4) Before registering an order under this section an officer of the court shall take such steps as he thinks fit for the purpose of ascertaining whether the payer under the order is residing or has assets within the jurisdiction of the court, and if after taking those steps he is satisfied that the payer is not residing and has no assets within the jurisdiction of the court he shall return the certified copy of the order to the Lord Chancellor or the Secretary of State, as the case may be, with a statement giving such information as he possesses as to the whereabouts of the payer and the nature and location of his assets.

8 Enforcement of maintenance order registered in United Kingdom court

(1) Subject to subsection (2) below, a registered order may be enforced in the United Kingdom as if it had been made by the registering court and as if that court had had jurisdiction to make it; and proceedings for or with respect to the enforcement of any such order may be taken accordingly.

(2) Subsection (1) above does not apply to an order which is for the time being registered in the High Court under Part I of the Maintenance Orders Act 1958 or to an order which is for the time being registered in the High Court of Justice in Northern Ireland under Part II of the Maintenance and Affiliation Orders Act (Northern Ireland) 1966.

(3) Any person for the time being under an obligation to make payments in pursuance of a registered order shall give notice of any change of address to the appropriate officer of the registering court, and any person failing without reasonable excuse to give such a notice shall be liable on summary conviction to a fine not exceeding level 2 on the standard scale.

(3A) In subsection (3) above "appropriate officer" means –

(*a*) in relation to a magistrates' court in England and Wales, the justices' chief executive for the court; and

(*b*) in relation to a court elsewhere, the clerk of the court.

(4) An order which by virtue of this section is enforceable by a magistrates' court shall, subject to the modifications of sections 76 and 93 of the Magistrates' Courts Act 1980 specified in subsections (4A) and (4B) below, and subject to the modifications of Article 98 of the Magistrates' Courts (Northern Ireland) Order 1981 specified in subsection (4C) below, be enforceable as if it were a magistrates' court maintenance order made by that court.

In this subsection "magistrates' court maintenance order" has the same meaning as in section 150(1) of the Magistrates' Courts Act 1980.

(4A) Section 76 (enforcement of sums adjudged to be paid) shall have effect as if for subsections (4) to (6) there were substituted the following subsections –

"(4) Where proceedings are brought for the enforcement of a magistrates' court maintenance order under this section, the court may vary the order by exercising one of its powers under subsection (5) below.

(5) The powers of the court are –

(*a*) the power to order that payments under the order be made directly to a justices' chief executive;

(*b*) the power to order that payments under the order be made to a justices' chief executive by such method of payment falling within section 59(6) above (standing order, etc) as may be specified;

(*c*) the power to make an attachment of earnings order under the Attachment of Earnings Act 1971 to secure payments under the order.

(6) In deciding which of the powers under subsection (5) above it is to exercise, the court shall have regard to any representations made by the debtor (within the meaning of section 59 above).

(7) Subsection (4) of section 59 above (power of court to require debtor to open account) shall apply for the purposes of subsection (5) above as it applies for the purposes of that section but as if for paragraph (*a*) there were substituted –

'(*a*) the court proposes to exercise its power under paragraph (*b*) of section 76(5) below, and'."

(4B) In section 93 (complaint for arrears), subsection (6) (court not to impose imprisonment in certain circumstances) shall have effect as if for paragraph (*b*) there were substituted –

"(*b*) if the court is of the opinion that it is appropriate –

(i) to make an attachment of earnings order; or

(ii) to exercise its power under paragraph (*b*) of section 76(5) above."

(4C) Article 98 of the Magistrates' Courts (Northern Ireland) Order 1981 (enforcement of sums adjudged to be paid) shall have effect –

(*a*) as if for paragraph (7)(*a*) there were substituted the following paragraph –

"(*a*) if the court is of the opinion that it is appropriate –

(i) to make an attachment of earnings order; or

(ii) to exercise its power under paragraph (8C)(*b*)";

(*b*) as if for paragraphs (8B) to (8D) there were substituted the following paragraphs –

"(8B) Upon the appearance of a person or proof of service of the summons on him as mentioned in paragraph (4) for the enforcement of an order to which this Article applies, the court or resident magistrate may vary the order, by exercising one of the powers under paragraph (8C).

(8C) The powers mentioned in paragraph (8B) are –

(*a*) the power to order that payments under the order be made directly to the collecting officer;

(*b*) the power to order that payments under the order be made to the collecting officer, by such method of payment falling within Article 85(7) (standing order, etc) as may be specified;

(*c*) the power to make an attachment of earnings order under Part IX to secure payments under the order.

PART III

(8D) In deciding which of the powers under paragraph (8C) is to be exercised, the court or, as the case may be, a resident magistrate shall have regard to any representations made by the debtor (within the meaning of Article 85).

(8E) Paragraph (5) of Article 85 (power of court to require debtor to open account) shall apply for the purposes of paragraph (8C) above as it applies for the purposes of that Article but as if for sub-paragraph (*a*) there were substituted –

'(*a*) the court proposes to exercise its power under sub-paragraph (*b*) of Article 98(8C), and'."

(5) The magistrates' court by which an order is enforceable by virtue of this section, and the officers thereof, shall take all such steps for enforcing or facilitating the enforcement of the order as may be prescribed.

(6) In any proceedings for or with respect to the enforcement of an order which is for the time being registered in any court under this Part of this Act a certificate of arrears sent to the prescribed officer of the court shall be evidence of the facts stated therein.

(7) Sums of money payable under a registered order shall be payable in accordance with the order as from the date on which the order was made.

(9) (*applies to Scotland only*)

Amendments—SI 2001/410.

9 Variation of maintenance order registered in United Kingdom court

(1) Subject to the provisions of this section –

(*a*) the registering court shall have the like power, on an application made by the payer or payee under a registered order, to vary the order as if it had been made by the registering court and as if that court had had jurisdiction to make it;

(*b*) the jurisdiction of a magistrates' court to vary a registered order shall be exercisable notwithstanding that proceedings for the variation of the order are brought by or against a person residing in a specified State.

(1ZA) Where the registering court is a magistrates' court in England and Wales, section 60 of the Magistrates' Courts Act 1980 (revocation, variation etc of orders for periodical payment) shall have effect in relation to the registered order –

(*za*) as if in subsection (1) for the words "by order on complaint" there were substituted "on an application being made, by order";

(*a*) as if in subsection (3) for the words "paragraphs (*a*) to (*d*) of section 59(3) above" there were substituted "subsection (3A) below" and after that subsection there were inserted –

"(3A) The powers of the court are –

(*a*) the power to order that payments under the order be made directly to a justices' chief executive;

(*b*) the power to order that payments under the order be made to a justices' chief executive by such method of payment falling within section 59(6) above (standing order, etc) as may be specified;

(*c*) the power to make an attachment of earnings order under the Attachment of Earnings Act 1971 to secure payments under the order.";

(*b*) as if in subsection (4) for paragraph (*b*) there were substituted –

"(*b*) payments under the order are required to be made to a justices' chief executive by any method of payment falling within section 59(6) above (standing order, etc)",

and as if after the words "the court" there were inserted "which made the order";

(*c*) as if in subsection (5) for the words "to the clerk" there were substituted "in accordance with paragraph (*a*) of subsection (3A) above";

(*d*) as if in subsection (7), paragraph (*c*) and the word "and" immediately preceding it were omitted;

(*e*) as if in subsection (8) for the words "paragraphs (*a*) to (*d*) of section 59(3) above" there were substituted "subsection (3A) above";

(*f*) as if for subsections (9) and (10) there were substituted the following subsections –

"(9) In deciding, for the purposes of subsections (3) and (8) above, which of the powers under subsection (3A) above it is to exercise, the court shall have regard to any representations made by the debtor.

(10) Subsection (4) of section 59 above (power of court to require debtor to open account) shall apply for the purposes of subsection (3A) above as it applies for the purposes of that section but as if for paragraph (*a*) there were substituted –

'(*a*) the court proposes to exercise its power under paragraph (*b*) of section 60(3A) below, and'."

(1ZB) Where the registering court is a court of summary jurisdiction in Northern Ireland, Article 86 of the Magistrates' Courts (Northern Ireland) Order 1981 (revocation, variation etc of orders for periodical payment) shall have effect in relation to the registered order –

(*a*) as if in paragraph (3) for the words "sub-paragraphs (*a*) to (*d*) of Article 85(3)" there were substituted "paragraph (3A)" and after that paragraph there were inserted –

"(3A) The powers of the court are –

(*a*) the power to order that payments under the order be made directly to the collecting officer;

(*b*) the power to order that payments under the order be made to the collecting officer by such method of payment falling within Article 85(7) (standing order, etc) as may be specified;

(*c*) the power to make an attachment of earnings order under Part IX to secure payments under the order.";

(*b*) as if in subsection (4) for paragraph (*b*) there were substituted –

"(*b*) payments under the order are required to be made to the collecting officer by any method of payment falling within Article 85(7) (standing order, etc)",

and as if after the words "petty sessions" there were inserted "for the petty sessions district for which the court which made the order acts";

(*c*) as if in paragraph (5) for the words "to the collecting officer" there were substituted "in accordance with sub-paragraph (*a*) of paragraph (3A)";

(*d*) as if in paragraph (7), sub-paragraph (*c*) and the word "and" immediately preceding it were omitted;

(*e*) as if in paragraph (8) for the words "sub-paragraphs (*a*) to (*d*) of Article 85(3)" there were substituted "paragraph (3A)";

PART III

(*f*) as if for paragraphs (9) and (10) there were substituted the following paragraphs –

"(9) In deciding, for the purposes of paragraphs (3) and (8) above, which of the powers under paragraph (3A) above it is to exercise, the court shall have regard to any representations made by the debtor.

(10) Paragraph (5) of Article 85 (power of court to require debtor to open account) shall apply for the purposes of paragraph (3A) as it applies for the purposes of that Article but as if for sub-paragraph (*a*) there were substituted –

'(*a*) the court proposes to exercise its power under sub-paragraph (*b*) of Article 86(3A), and'."

(1A) The powers conferred by subsection (1) above are not exercisable in relation to so much of a registered order as provides for the payment of a lump sum.

(1B) The registering court shall not vary a registered order if neither the payer nor the payee under the order is resident in the United Kingdom.

(2) Where an application is made by the payer to a registering court in the United Kingdom for the variation of a registered order, and the payee is residing in a specified State, the prescribed officer of the court shall –

(*a*) in the case of a court in England and Wales or Northern Ireland, send to the Lord Chancellor, or, in the case of a court in Scotland, send to the Secretary of State, notice of the institution of the proceedings with a view to its being transmitted by him to the appropriate authority in the specified State for service on the payee; and
(*b*) give the payee notice in writing of the date fixed for the hearing by sending the notice by post addressed to his last known or usual place of abode.

(3) Where such an application is made –

(*a*) the order shall not be varied unless the document mentioned in paragraph (*a*) of subsection (2) above has been served on the payee in accordance with the law for the service of such a document in the specified State;
(*b*) the court, in considering whether or not to make or vary the order, shall take into account any representations made and any evidence adduced by or on behalf of the payee; and
(*b*) a copy of any such representations and evidence shall be served on the payer by the prescribed officer of the court before the hearing.

(4) Where an application is made by the payee to a registering court in the United Kingdom for the variation of a registered order, and the payer is residing in the United Kingdom, the prescribed officer of the court shall serve the document mentioned in paragraph (*a*) of subsection (2) above on the payer.

(5) Where a registered order is varied by a registering court in the United Kingdom the prescribed officer of the court shall send the following documents, that is to say –

(*a*) three certified copies of the order of variation;
(*b*) a written statement signed by that officer as to whether both the payer and the payee under the order appeared in the proceedings for the variation of the order, and, if only the applicant appeared, the original or a certified copy of a document which establishes that notice of the institution of the proceedings had been served on the other party,

in the case of a court in England and Wales or Northern Ireland, to the Lord Chancellor, or, in the case of a court in Scotland, to the Secretary of State, with a view to their being transmitted by him to the appropriate authority in the specified State.

(6) Where a registered order has been varied by the registering court or by a court in a specified State, the prescribed officer of the registering court shall register the variation order in the prescribed manner.

(7) Where a registered order has been varied by the registering court or by a court in a specified State, the registered order shall, as from the date on which the variation order took effect, have effect as so varied.

Amendments—SI 2001/410.

10 Cancellation of registration and transfer of order

(1) Where a registered order is revoked by an order made by a court in a specified State and notice of the revocation is received by the registering court, the prescribed officer of the registering court shall cancel the registration; but any arrears due under the registered order at the date on which the order of revocation took effect, shall continue to be recoverable as if the registration had not been cancelled.

(2) Where the prescribed officer of the registering court is of opinion that the payer under a registered order is not residing within the jurisdiction of that court and has no assets within that jurisdiction against which the order can be effectively enforced, he shall cancel the registration of the order and, subject to subsection (3) below, shall send the certified copy of the order to the Lord Chancellor.

(3) Where the prescribed officer of the registering court, being a magistrates' court, is of opinion that the payer is residing or has assets within the jurisdiction of another magistrates' court in that part of the United Kingdom in which the registering court is, he shall transfer the order to that other court by sending the certified copy of the order to the prescribed officer of that other court.

(4) On the transfer of an order under subsection (3) above the prescribed officer of the court to which it is transferred shall, subject to subsection (6) below, register the order in the prescribed manner in that court.

(5) Where the certified copy of an order is received by the Lord Chancellor under this section and it appears to him that the payer under the order is residing or has assets in the United Kingdom, he shall transfer the order to the appropriate court by sending the certified copy of the order together with the related documents to the prescribed officer of the appropriate court and, subject to subsection (6) below, that officer shall register the order in the prescribed manner in that court.

(6) Before registering an order in pursuance of subsection (4) or (5) above an officer of a court shall take such steps as he thinks fit for the purpose of ascertaining whether the payer is residing or has assets within the jurisdiction of the court, and if after taking those steps he is satisfied that the payer is not residing and has no assets within the jurisdiction of the court he shall send the certified copy of the order to the Lord Chancellor.

(7) The officer of a court who is required by any of the foregoing provisions of this section to send to the Lord Chancellor or to the prescribed officer of another court the certified copy of an order shall send with that copy –

(*a*) a certificate of arrears signed by him or, in Scotland, by the applicant or his solicitor;
(*b*) a statement giving such information as he possesses as to the whereabouts of the payer and the nature and location of his assets; and
(*c*) any relevant documents in his possession relating to the case.

(8) (*applies to Scotland only*)

11 Steps to be taken by Lord Chancellor or Secretary of State where payer under certain orders is not residing in United Kingdom

(1) If at any time it appears to the Lord Chancellor or the Secretary of State that the payer under a maintenance order, a certified copy of which has been received by him from a specified State, is not residing and has no assets in the United Kingdom, he shall send to the appropriate authority in that State or, if having regard to all the circumstances he thinks it proper to do so, to the appropriate authority in another specified State –

(*a*) the certified copy of the order in question and a certified copy of any order varying that order;
(*b*) if the order has at any time been a registered order, a certificate of arrears signed by the prescribed officer or, in Scotland, by the applicant or his solicitor;
(*c*) a statement giving such information as the Lord Chancellor or the Secretary of State possesses as to the whereabouts of the payer and the nature and location of his assets; and
(*d*) any other relevant documents in his possession relating to the case.

(2) Where the documents mentioned in subsection (1) are sent to the appropriate authority in a specified State other than that in which the order in question was made, the Lord Chancellor or the Secretary of State shall inform the appropriate authority in the specified State in which that order was made of what he has done.

APPEALS

12 Appeals

Where in pursuance of section 9 above a registering court makes, or refuses to make, an order varying a registered order, the payer or the payee under the registered order shall have the like right of appeal (if any) from the order of variation or from the refusal to make it as he would have if the registered order had been made by the registering court.

EVIDENCE

13 Admissibility of evidence given in specified State

(1) A statement contained in –

(*a*) a document, duly authenticated, which purports to set out or summarise evidence given in proceedings in a court in a specified State; or
(*b*) a document, duly authenticated, which purports to set out or summarise evidence taken in such a State for the purpose of proceedings in a court in the United Kingdom under this Part of this Act, whether in response to a request made by such a court or otherwise; or

(*c*) a document, duly authenticated, which purports to have been received in evidence in proceedings in a court in such a State or to be a copy of a document so received,

shall in any proceedings in a court in the United Kingdom relating to a maintenance order to which this Part of this Act applies be admissible as evidence of any fact stated therein to the same extent as oral evidence of that fact is admissible in those proceedings.

(2) A document purporting to set out or summarise evidence given as mentioned in subsection (1)(*a*) above, or taken as mentioned in subsection (1)(*b*) above, shall be deemed to be duly authenticated for the purposes of that subsection if the document purports to be certified by the judge, magistrate or other person before whom the evidence was given, or, as the case may be, by whom it was taken, to be the original document containing or recording, or, as the case may be, summarising, that evidence or a true copy of that document.

(3) A document purporting to have been received in evidence as mentioned in subsection (1)(*c*) above, or to be a copy of a document so received, shall be deemed to be duly authenticated for the purposes of that subsection if the document purports to be certified by a judge, magistrate or other person before whom the evidence was given to have been, or to be a true copy of a document which has been, so received.

(4) It shall not be necessary in any such proceedings to prove the signature or official position of the person appearing to have given such a certificate.

(5) Nothing in this section shall prejudice the admission in evidence of any document which is admissible in evidence apart from this section.

14 Obtaining of evidence needed for purpose of certain proceedings

(1) Where for the purpose of any proceedings in a court in a specified State relating to a maintenance order to which this Part of this Act applies a request is made by or on behalf of that court for the taking in the United Kingdom of the evidence of a person residing therein relating to matters specified in the request, such court in the United Kingdom as may be prescribed shall have power to take that evidence and, after giving notice of the time and place at which the evidence is to be taken to such persons and in such manner as it thinks fit, shall take the evidence in such manner as may be prescribed.

Evidence taken in compliance with such a request shall be sent by the prescribed officer of the court –

(*a*) in England and Wales or Northern Ireland, to the Lord Chancellor, or
(*b*) in Scotland, to the Secretary of State,

for transmission to the appropriate authority in the specified State.

(2) Where any person, not being the payer or the payee under the maintenance order to which the proceedings in question relate, is required by virtue of this section to give evidence before a court in the United Kingdom, the court may order that there shall be paid out of moneys provided by Parliament such sums as appear to the court reasonably sufficient to compensate that person for the expense, trouble or loss of time properly incurred in or incidental to his attendance.

(3) Section 97(1), (3) and (4) of the Magistrates' Courts Act 1980 (which provide for compelling the attendance of witnesses, etc) shall apply in relation to a

PART III

magistrates' court having power under subsection (1) above to take the evidence of any person as if the proceedings in the court in a specified State for the purpose of which a request for the taking of the evidence has been made were proceedings in the magistrates' court and had been begun by complaint.

(4) (*applies to Scotland only*)

(5) A court in –

(*a*) England and Wales or Northern Ireland may, for the purpose of any proceedings in that court under this Part of this Act relating to a maintenance order to which this Part of this Act applies, send to the Lord Chancellor, or

(*b*) Scotland may, for the purpose of such proceedings in that court relating to such an action, send to the Secretary of State,

for transmission to the appropriate authority in a specified State a request for a court in that State to take or provide evidence relating to such matters as may be specified in the request.

(6) (*applies to Northern Ireland only*)

"court" (s 14(1))—This term is defined by FPR 1991, r 7.34.

"officer" (s 14(1))—This term is defined by FPR 1991, r 7.34.

15 Order etc made in specified State need not be proved

For the purposes of this Part of this Act, unless the contrary is shown –

(*a*) any order made by a court in a specified State purporting to bear the seal of that court or to be signed by any person in his capacity as a judge, magistrate or officer of the court, shall be deemed without further proof to have been duly sealed or, as the case may be, to have been signed by that person;

(*b*) the person by whom the order was signed shall be deemed without further proof to have been a judge, magistrate or officer, as the case may be, of that court when he signed it and, in the case of an officer, to have been authorised to sign it; and

(*c*) a document purporting to be a certified copy of an order made by a court in a specified State shall be deemed without further proof to be such a copy.

SUPPLEMENTAL

16 Payment of sums due under orders made in specified State; conversion of currency

(1) Payment of sums due under a registered order shall, while the order is registered in a court in England, Wales or Northern Ireland, be made in such manner and to such person as may be prescribed.

(2) Where the sums required to be paid under a registered order are expressed in a currency other than the currency of the United Kingdom, then, as from the relevant date, the order shall be treated as if it were an order requiring the payment of such sums in the currency of the United Kingdom as, on the basis of the rate of exchange prevailing at that date, are equivalent to the sums so required to be paid.

(3) Where the sum specified in any statement, being a statement of the amount of any arrears due under a maintenance order made by a court in a specified State, is expressed in a currency other than the currency of the United Kingdom, that sum shall be deemed to be such sum in the currency of the United Kingdom as, on the basis of the rate of exchange prevailing at the relevant date, is equivalent to the sum so specified.

(4) For the purposes of this section a written certificate purporting to be signed by an officer of any bank in the United Kingdom certifying that a specified rate of exchange prevailed between currencies at a specified date and that at such rate a specified sum in the currency of the United Kingdom is equivalent to a specified sum in another specified currency shall be evidence of the rate of exchange so prevailing on that date and of the equivalent sums in terms of the respective currencies.

(5) In this section "the relevant date" means –

(*a*) in relation to a registered order or to a statement of arrears due under a maintenance order made by a court in a specified State, the date on which the order first becomes a registered order;
(*b*) in relation to a registered order which has been varied, the date on which the last order varying that order is registered in the registering court.

(6) (*applies to Scotland only*)

17 Proceedings in magistrates' courts

(4) Anything authorised or required by this Part of this Act to be done by, to or before the magistrates' court by, to or before which any other thing was done may be done by, to or before any magistrates' court acting for the same petty sessions area (or, in Northern Ireland, petty sessions district) as that court.

(5) Any application which by virtue of a provision of this Part of this Act is made to a magistrates' court shall be made by complaint.

(5A) Where the respondent to an application for the variation or revocation of –

(*a*) a maintenance order made by a magistrates' court in England and Wales, being an order to which section 5 of this Act applies; or
(*b*) a registered order which is registered in such a court,

is residing in a specified State, a magistrates' court in England and Wales shall have jurisdiction to hear the application (where it would not have such jurisdiction apart from this subsection) if it would have had jurisdiction to hear it had the respondent been residing in England and Wales.

(6) A magistrates' court in Northern Ireland shall have jurisdiction –

(*a*) to hear a complaint for the variation or revocation of a maintenance order made by such a court, and to which section 5 of this Act applies; or
(*b*) to hear a complaint for the variation of a registered order which is registered in that court,

if the defendant to the complaint is residing in a specified State and if the court would have had jurisdiction to hear the complaint had the defendant been residing in Northern Ireland and been served with a summons to appear before the court to answer the complaint.

(7) Where the respondent to an application –

(*a*) for the variation or revocation of a maintenance order made by a magistrates' court, being an order to which section 5 of this Act applies; or
(*b*) for the variation of a registered order registered in a magistrates' court,

does not appear at the time and place appointed for the hearing of the application, but the court is satisfied that the respondent is residing in a specified State, and that the requirements of section 5(4) or (6) or section 9(2) and (4), as the case may be, have been complied with, the court may proceed to hear and determine the application at the time and place appointed for the hearing or for any adjourned hearing as if the respondent had appeared at that time and place.

(7A) (*applies to Northern Ireland only*)

18 Magistrates' courts rules

(1) Without prejudice to the generality of the power to make rules under section 144 of the Magistrates' Courts Act 1980 (magistrates' courts rules), provision may be made by such rules with respect to any of the following matters, namely –

(*a*) the circumstances in which anything authorised or required by this Part of this Act to be done by, to or before a magistrates' court acting for a particular petty sessions area by, to or before an officer of that court may be done by, to or before a magistrates' court acting for such other petty sessions area as the rules may provide or by, to or before an officer of that court;
(*b*) the orders made, or other things done, by a magistrates' court, or an officer of such a court, under this Part of this Act, or by a court in a specified State, notice of which is to be given to such persons as the rules may provide and the manner in which such notice shall be given;
(*c*) the cases and manner in which courts in specified States are to be informed of orders made, or other things done, by a magistrates' court under this Part of this Act;
(*d*) the cases and manner in which a justices' clerk may take evidence needed for the purpose of proceedings in a court in a specified State relating to a maintenance order to which this Part of this Act applies;
(*f*) the circumstances and manner in which magistrates' courts may for the purposes of this Part of this Act communicate with courts in specified States.

(1A) For the purpose of giving effect to this Part of this Act, rules made under section 144 of the Magistrates' Courts Act 1980 may make, in relation to any proceedings brought under or by virtue of this Part of this Act, any provision not covered by subsection (1) above which –

(*a*) falls within subsection (2) of section 93 of the Children Act 1989, and
(*b*) may be made in relation to relevant proceedings under that section.

(2) (*applies to Northern Ireland only*)

****

21 Interpretation of Part I

(1) In this Part of this Act, unless the context otherwise requires –

"affiliation order" means an order (however described) adjudging, finding or declaring a person to be the father of a child, whether or not it also provides for the maintenance of the child;

"the appropriate court", in relation to a person residing or having assets in England and Wales or in Northern Ireland means a magistrates' court, and in relation to a person residing or having assets in Scotland means a sheriff court, within the jurisdiction of which that person is residing or has assets;

"certificate of arrears", in relation to a maintenance order, means a certificate certifying that the sum specified in the certificate is to the best of the information or belief of the officer or, in Scotland, the applicant or his solicitor giving the certificate the amount of the arrears due under the order at the date of the certificate or, as the case may be, that to the best of his information or belief there are no arrears due thereunder at that date;

"certified copy", in relation to an order of a court, means a copy of the order certified by the proper officer of the court to be a true copy;

"court" includes any tribunal or person having power to make, confirm, enforce, vary or revoke a maintenance order;

"maintenance order" means an order (however described) of any of the following descriptions, that is to say –

(*a*) an order (including an affiliation order or order consequent upon an affiliation order) which provides for the payment of a lump sum or the making of periodical payments towards the maintenance of any person, being a person whom the person liable to make payments under the order is, according to the law applied in the place where the order was made, liable to maintain;

(*aa*) an order which has been made in Scotland, on or after the granting of a decree of divorce, for the payment of a periodical allowance by one party to the marriage to the other party;

(*b*) an affiliation order or order consequent upon an affiliation order, being an order which provides for the payment by a person adjudged, found or declared to be a child's father of expenses incidental to the child's birth or, where the child has died, of his funeral expenses;

(*c*) an order within the foregoing provisions of this definition made against a payer on the application of a public body which claims reimbursement of sums of money payable under the order with respect to the payee if reimbursement can be obtained by the public body under the law to which it is subject,

and, in the case of a maintenance order which has been varied, means that order as varied:

"order", as respects Scotland, includes any interlocutor, and any decree or provision contained in an interlocutor;

"payee", in relation to a maintenance order, means the person entitled to the payments for which the order provides;

"payer", in relation to a maintenance order, means the person liable to make payments under the order;

"prescribed", in relation to a magistrates' court in England and Wales or in Northern Ireland, means prescribed by rules made under section 144 of the Magistrates' Courts Act 1980 or by rules made in accordance with Article 13 of the Magistrates' Courts (Northern Ireland) Order 1981, as the case may be, and in relation to any other court means prescribed by rules of court;

"registered order" means a maintenance order which is for the time being registered in a court in the United Kingdom under this Part of this Act and "registered" and "registration" shall be construed accordingly;
"registering court", in relation to a registered order, means the court in which that order is for the time being registered under this Part of this Act.
"revoke" and "revocation" include discharge;
"specified State" means a State specified in Schedule 1 to the Reciprocal Enforcement of Maintenance Orders (United States of America) Order 1995.

(3) Any reference in this Part of this Act to the payment of money for the maintenance of a child shall be construed as including a reference to the payment of money for the child's education.

Recovery Abroad of Maintenance (Convention Countries) Order 1975, SI 1975/423

****

2 The countries and territories specified in the Schedule to this Order, being countries and territories outside the United Kingdom to which the United Nations Convention on the Recovery Abroad of Maintenance done at New York on 20 June 1956 extends, are hereby declared to be convention countries for the purposes of Part II of the Maintenance Orders (Reciprocal Enforcement) Act 1972.

SCHEDULE
CONVENTION COUNTRIES

Algeria
Australia
Austria
Barbados
Belgium
Bosnia and Herzegovina
Brazil
Burkina Faso
Cape Verde
Central African Republic
Chile
Croatia
Cyprus
Czech Republic
Denmark
Ecuador
Finland

France (including the overseas departments of Guadeloupe, Guiana, Martinique and Réunion)
Comoro Archipelago
French Polynesia
New Caledonia and Dependencies
St Pierre and Miquelon
Germany
Greece
Guatemala
Haiti
Holy See
Hungary
Ireland
Israel
Italy
Luxembourg
Mexico
Monaco
Morocco
Netherlands (Kingdom in Europe, Netherlands Antilles and Aruba)
New Zealand
Niger
Norway
Pakistan
Philippines
Poland
Portugal
Romania
Slovakia
Slovenia
Spain
Sri Lanka
Suriname
Sweden
Switzerland
The Former Yugoslav Republic of Macedonia
Tunisia
Turkey
Uruguay
Yugoslavia

Amendments—SI 1996/1925; SI 2002/2839.

Recovery of Maintenance (United States of America) Order 1993, SI 1993/591

1 (1) This Order may be cited as the Recovery of Maintenance (United States of America) Order 1993.

(2) This Order shall come into force on 5 April 1993.

"This Order"—This Order applies the provisions of Pt II of the Maintenance Orders (Reciprocal Enforcement) Act 1972 to the States of the United States of America specified in the Schedule, subject to the insertion into the Act of s 26(3A). Guidance on the application of the Order can be found in Home Office Circular 172/1979.

Part I of the 1972 Act has been applied to all of the States shown in this Schedule and, additionally, to West Virginia, but with the exception of Colorado, Georgia, Hawaii, Idaho, Illinois, Michigan, New Hampshire, New Mexico, Ohio, Rhode Island and Tennessee, by the Reciprocal Enforcement of Maintenance Orders (United States of America) Order 1995. The effect is that, where there is no existing maintenance order, where an existing maintenance claim is already being enforced or where the State is included only in the Schedule to the 1993 Order, the Part II procedure continues to apply. In other cases, existing maintenance orders may be registered for enforcement under the Part I procedure.

2 In this Order, unless the context otherwise requires –

"the Act" means the Maintenance Orders (Reciprocal Enforcement) Act 1972;
"specified State" means a State specified in the Schedule to this Order.

3 (1) The provisions of Part II of the Act shall apply in relation to a specified State as they apply in relation to a convention country, subject to the modification set out in paragraph (2) below.

(2) After section 26(3) of the Act there shall be inserted –

"(3A) An application under subsection (1) or (2) above, for the purpose of recovering maintenance from a person in a specified State within the meaning of the Recovery of Maintenance (United States of America) Order 1993, and a certificate signed by a justice of the peace or, where the applicant is residing in Scotland, the sheriff, to the effect that the application sets forth facts from which it may be determined that the respondent owes a duty to maintain the applicant and any other person named in the application and that a court in the specified State may obtain jurisdiction of the respondent or his property, shall be registered in the court in the prescribed manner by the appropriate officer or, in Scotland, by the sheriff clerk in the Maintenance Orders (Reciprocal Enforcement) Act 1972 register."

****

SCHEDULE
SPECIFIED STATES

Alaska
Arizona
Arkansas
California
Colorado
Connecticut
Delaware
Florida
Georgia
Hawaii
Idaho
Illinois
Indiana
Iowa
Kansas
Kentucky
Louisiana
Maine
Maryland
Massachusetts
Michigan
Minnesota

Missouri	Montana
Nebraska	Nevada
New Hampshire	New Jersey
New Mexico	New York
North Carolina	North Dakota
Ohio	Oklahoma
Oregon	Pennsylvania
Rhode Island	South Dakota
Tennessee	Texas
Utah	Vermont
Virginia	Washington
Wisconsin	Wyoming

Rules of the Supreme Court 1965, SI 1965/1776

ARRANGEMENT OF RULES

ORDER 7
ORIGINATING SUMMONSES: GENERAL PROVISIONS

ORDER 8
ORIGINATING AND OTHER MOTIONS: GENERAL PROVISIONS

ORDER 24
DISCOVERY AND INSPECTION OF DOCUMENTS

ORDER 29
INTERLOCUTORY INJUNCTIONS, INTERIM PRESERVATION OF PROPERTY, INTERIM PAYMENTS ETC

I Interlocutory injunctions. Interim preservation of property etc

ORDER 32
APPLICATIONS AND PROCEEDINGS IN CHAMBERS

ORDER 38
EVIDENCE

I General rules

II Writs of subpoena

IV Expert evidence

ORDER 45
ENFORCEMENT OF JUDGMENTS AND ORDERS: GENERAL

ORDER 46
WRIT OF EXECUTION: GENERAL

ORDER 47
WRITS OF FIERI FACIAS

ORDER 48
EXAMINATION OF JUDGMENT DEBTOR ETC

ORDER 49
GARNISHEE PROCEEDINGS

ORDER 50
CHARGING ORDERS

PART III

ORDER 51
RECEIVERS: EQUITABLE EXECUTION

ORDER 52
COMMITTAL

ORDER 55
APPEALS TO HIGH COURT FROM COURT, TRIBUNAL OR PERSON: GENERAL

ORDER 58
APPEALS FROM MASTERS, REGISTRARS, REFEREES AND JUDGES

ORDER 65
SERVICE OF DOCUMENTS

ORDER 71
RECIPROCAL ENFORCEMENT OF JUDGMENTS AND ENFORCEMENT OF EUROPEAN COMMUNITY JUDGMENTS AND RECOMMENDATIONS ETC UNDER THE MERCHANT SHIPPING (LINER CONFERENCES) ACT 1982

ORDER 80
DISABILITY

ORDER 112
APPLICATIONS FOR USE OF BLOOD TESTS IN DETERMINING PATERNITY

****

ORDER 7
ORIGINATING SUMMONSES: GENERAL PROVISIONS

PART III

1 Application (Ord 7, r 1)

The provisions of this Order apply to all originating summonses subject, in the case of originating summonses of any particular class, to any special provisions relating to originating summonses of that class made by these Rules or by or under any Act.

Defined terms—"originating summons": Ord 1, r 4.

Scope of provision—FPR 1991 make provision for application under CA 1989 and specifically deal with applications in wardship, but they make no provision for application under the residual inherent jurisdiction of the court. Since proceedings under the residual inherent jurisdiction are assigned to the High Court by virtue of Supreme Court Act 1981, Sch 1, para 3(*b*)(i), the provisions of Ord 7 apply to such applications.

Procedure on application—In *Re F (Sterilisation: Mental Patient)* [1989] 2 FLR 376 the question of the appropriate procedure to be followed was considered by the Court of Appeal. Lord Donaldson MR (at p 392) set out directions, which were effectively amended by Lord Brandon when the case went to the House of Lords. The amended directions are as follows:

(*a*) Applications for a declaration that a proposed operation on or medical treatment of a patient can lawfully be carried out despite the inability of such patient to consent thereto should be by way or originating summons issuing out of the Family Division of the High Court.

(*b*) The applicant should normally be those responsible for the care of the patient or those intending to carry out the proposed operation or other treatment, if it is declared to be lawful.

(*c*) The patient should always be a party and should normally be a respondent. In cases in which the patient is a respondent the patient's guardian ad litem should normally be the Official Solicitor. In any cases in which the Official Solicitor is not either the next friend or the guardian ad litem of the patient or an applicant he shall be a respondent.

(*d*) With a view to protecting the patient's privacy, but subject always to the judge's discretion, the hearing will be in chambers, but the decision and the reasons for that decision will be given in open court.

Lord Brandon also commented that "there will, in cases of this kind, have to be a summons for directions heard by a judge, and it should be left for him to decide on the hearing of such summons, whether any, and, if so what, further and detailed directions should be given in the particular case before him."

The question of the appropriate procedure to be followed was considered again in *Re C (Sterilisation: Procedure)* [1990] 2 FLR 527 by Thorpe J who gave the following guidelines:

(*a*) An originating summons seeking a declaration is issued pursuant to RSC Ord 28.

(*b*) The defendant has 14 days thereafter to file an acknowledgement of service.

(*c*) The plaintiff has 14 days thereafter to file his evidence pursuant to RSC Ord 28, r 1(*a*)(i).

(*d*) The defendant has to file his evidence within 28 days thereafter pursuant to RSC Ord 28, r 1(*a*)(iv).

(*e*) The registry, on issuing the originating summons, should fix a date for directions before a judge of the Division on the first open date after eight weeks.

(*f*) On the hearing for directions, if the case appears complex and uncertain in its outcome, the judge may give further directions including directions for trial. If the case appears straightforward and without contention, he may dispose of it at that stage.
(*g*) In cases of emergency, the originating summons may be preceded by an initial application ex parte when the court, on an undertaking to issue the originating summons forthwith, may consider abridging time limits or dispensing with certain procedures.
(*h*) All evidence, including expert evidence, should be made on affidavit. Hearsay or exhibited reports from other sources should not ordinarily be regarded as admissible.
(*i*) The Official Solicitor, on receipt of a notice of any application for the sterilisation of a patient, despatches a copy of *Practice Note of 19 September 1989* and questionnaire to the plaintiff's solicitors. The *Practice Note* is issued for the guidance of practitioners and is not intended to be a mandatory code.
(*j*) The Official Solicitor normally acts as the patient's guardian ad litem but, in some cases, he will also appear as *ex officio* defendant.
(*k*) An answer to the questionnaire is not obligatory. It may be settled by the solicitor with or without the assistance of counsel and should reflect the evidence to be obtained both from the family and the expert.

Subsequent to the hearing of *Re C*, *Practice Note of 19 September 1989* has been replaced by *Practice Note of 1 May 2001*.

2 Form of summons etc (Ord 7, r 2)

(1) Every originating summons (other than an ex parte summons) shall be in Form No 8 or, if so authorised or required, in Form No 10 in Appendix A, and every ex parte originating summons shall be in Form No 11 in Appendix A.

(2) The party taking out an originating summons (other than an ex parte summons) shall be described as a plaintiff, and the other parties shall be described as defendants.

Amendments—SI 1979/1716.

Defined terms—"originating summons": Ord 1, r 4.

Forms—Form 8 is generally used where no other form is prescribed for applications for relief under the inherent jurisdiction of the court. An acknowledgement of service is required for this form. It does not give a fixed hearing date so a notice of appointment will have to be issued. Form 10 may be used only where it is prescribed or authorised. Form 11 is used when making an ex parte application.

The title of the originating summons—The originating summons must be intituled in the matter in which the application is made and if it is made under the provisions of a statute or statutes, the relevant Act or Acts must also be set out.

Parties—The applicant is the plaintiff and the responding party is the defendant and not a respondent.

3 Contents of summons (Ord 7, r 3)

(1) Every originating summons must include a statement of the questions on which the plaintiff seeks the determination or direction of the High Court or, as the case may be, a concise statement of the relief or remedy claimed in the proceedings begun by the originating summons with sufficient particulars to identify the cause or causes of action in respect of which the plaintiff claims that relief or remedy.

(2) Order 6, Rules 3 and 5, shall apply in relation to an originating summons as they apply in relation to a writ.

Defined terms—"originating summons": Ord 1, r 4.

"statement of relief or remedy" (r 3(1))—The statement must be set out with sufficient clarity. In cases relating to mental patients and sterilisation see **Procedure on application** under r 1.

"Order 6, rules 3 and 5" (r 3(2))—RSC Ord 6, rr 3 and 5 provide that the originating summons must be indorsed as to capacity and give the address of the plaintiff and/or his solicitor's name and address. Where the plaintiff is suing in person, the summons should state this and give the address of his residence. If he does not have his home within the jurisdiction then this fact must be stated on the summons and an address within the jurisdiction must be given where he can be served.

Striking out of a summons—RSC Ord 18, r 19(3) specifically provides that the provisions set out in Ord 18, r 19(1) and (2) apply to an originating summons. The court may strike out or amend it on the grounds that *(a)* it does not disclose a reasonable cause of action or defence as the case may be; or *(b)* it is scandalous, frivolous or vexatious; or *(c)* it may prejudice, embarrass or delay the fair trial of the action; or *(d)* it is otherwise an abuse of the process of the court.

****

6 Duration and renewal of summons (Ord 7, r 6)

Order 6, Rule 8, shall apply in relation to an originating summons as it applies in relation to a writ.

Defined terms—"originating summons": Ord 1, r 4.

Duration—If an originating summons is to be served out of the jurisdiction it is valid for six months; in all other cases for four months.

Renewal—The court may renew the validity of the summons from time to time for periods not exceeding four months if an application for an extension is made before the expiry of its validity or such other date as the court may allow. Where the court is satisfied that, despite all reasonable efforts, it may not be possible to serve the application within the four months, it may extend the validity of the summons for such period not exceeding 12 months. The court's power to extend the period is a discretionary one. Good reasons must be shown for the failure to serve within the time-limits and for the extension of time.

Service—See Ords 10 and 65.

****

ORDER 8
ORIGINATING AND OTHER MOTIONS: GENERAL PROVISIONS

****

2 Notice of motion (Ord 8, r 2)

(1) Except where an application by motion may properly be made ex parte, no motion shall be made without previous notice to the parties affected thereby, but the Court, if satisfied that the delay caused by proceeding in this ordinary way would or might entail irreparable or serious mischief may make an order ex parte on such terms as to costs or otherwise, and subject to such undertaking, if any, as it thinks just; and any party affected by such order may apply to the Court to set it aside.

PART III

(2) Unless the Court gives leave to the contrary, there must be at least 2 clear days between the service of notice of a motion and the day named in the notice for hearing the motion.

****

ORDER 24
DISCOVERY AND INSPECTION OF DOCUMENTS

1 Mutual discovery of documents (Ord 24, r 1)

(1) After the close of pleadings in an action begun by writ there shall, subject to and in accordance with the provisions of this Order, be discovery by the parties to the action of the documents which are or have been in their possession, custody or power relating to matters in question in the action.

(2) Nothing in this Order shall be taken as preventing the parties to an action agreeing to dispense with or limit the discovery of documents which they would otherwise be required to make to each other.

Scope of provision—This rule imposes on parties to an action – in this case commenced by writ, but the duty is to be regarded as general (see r 3 below) – the obligation to give mutual discovery of documents which are in their possession and which are relevant to the matters in issue in the proceedings. However, parties may themselves agree to dispense with, or limit the extent of, discovery.

Discovery defined—Discovery, within the terms of this Order, applies to documents and to the right of a party to any application to the court to have sight of all documents relevant to that application; accordingly, "a party to a suit must disclose all the documents in his possession, custody or power which are relevant to the matters in issue. The court has a discretion whether or not to order him to make disclosure [ie discovery] ... . The discretion is a judicial discretion, and in exercising it the court will have regard to all the circumstances" (*B v B (Matrimonial Proceedings: Discovery)* [1978] Fam 181, [1979] 1 All ER 801 per Dunn LJ at 193, 811 respectively).

Order for discovery—Where not given voluntarily, discovery can be ordered by the court, but only where discovery is "necessary for disposing fairly of the issues between the parties" (*B v B (Matrimonial Proceedings: Discovery)* (above), and see r 8 below). It will not be ordered where to do so would cause undue hardship when balanced against the need to do justice. Nor will discovery be ordered where a document is privileged from discovery, including being protected on public interest grounds – public interest immunity and "without prejudice" correspondence (r 5(2)).

Disclosure—Discovery is the means whereby disclosure (generally of documents) is compelled. In family proceedings, there is a duty to disclose all relevant documents and other information or material facts to all parties, save where that information is privileged: "full and frank disclosure" (see eg *Practice Direction of 31 January 1995*, para 4); "full relevant disclosure" (*Livesey (formerly Jenkins) v Jenkins* [1985] AC 424, [1985] FLR 813, HL, per Lord Hailsham). It has been held that local authorities in children proceedings have a particularly high duty of disclosure (*R v Hampshire County Council ex parte K* [1990] 2 QB 71, [1990] 1 FLR 330, and *Rochdale Borough Council v A* [1991] 2 FLR 192, Douglas Brown J).

Compelling discovery as between parties to an application—Where disclosure is not provided voluntarily by one party, another party to the proceedings can obtain relevant documents or information as follows:

(*a*) *Discovery of documents by order* By seeking discovery of documents under Ord 24, rr 3 and 7;

(*b*) *Evidence by interrogatories* A party may seek disclosure of facts (as distinct from documents) by interrogatories;

(*c*) *Ancillary relief proceedings* At the first appointment a district judge will give directions as to the extent to which any questions seeking information under FPR 1991, r 2.61B must be answered and what documents requested under that rule should be produced (FPR 1991, r 2.61D(2)).

Evidence from third parties—Discovery applies only as between parties to an application. The following means of securing evidence from third parties are available:

(*a*) *Subpoena or witness summons* Leave is required for issue of a subpoena (ie in the High Court) for any proceedings in chambers (Ord 32, r 7), which leave is likely to be refused where a requirement to give evidence might be oppressive for the witness (*Morgan v Morgan* [1977] Fam 122, (1976) FLR Rep 473).

(*b*) *Appointment for production of documents by third party* A party to proceedings can seek discovery from a third party prior to trial, either at a pre-trial hearing (Ord 38, r 13), or by issue of a subpoena duces tecum (witness summons in the county court) for attendance of the witness at a pre-trial hearing (*Khanna v Lovell White Durrant (a firm)* [1994] 4 All ER 267, Sir Donald Nicholls V-C). For ancillary relief applications, a procedure (similar to Ord 38, r 13; and see *Frary v Frary and anor* [1993] 2 FLR 696, CA) is provided for under FPR 1991, r 2.62(7).

(*c*) *Specific discovery by third parties* In children cases, hospitals and police have been urged to release video evidence to solicitors, on undertakings not to make copies other than for expert witnesses (*Re R (Child Abuse: Video Evidence)* [1995] 1 FLR 451, Johnson J).

Disclosure only to limited parties—Where only the court and a limited number of parties are to be informed of the contents of documents or to receive information, the court balances the need of all parties to have disclosure of all information submitted to the judge as against the needs of the child concerned in the proceedings (*Official Solicitor v K* [1965] AC 201, (1963) FLR Rep 520, HL). The procedure for such cases is set out in *Re C (Disclosure)* [1996] 1 FLR 797, Johnson J at 800G–801E – the application is dealt with on the basis that only advocates see the material initially and make submissions, but where a party (as with the mother in *Re C*) refuses to instruct her advocate to receive the material, there is no purpose in the court hearing submissions from that party.

"in an action begun by writ" (r 1(1))—Discovery is regarded as appropriate in family proceedings (*B v B (Matrimonial Proceedings: Discovery)* (above); *Re JC (Care Proceedings: Procedure)* [1995] 2 FLR 77, Wall J), and it is, in any event, an inevitable concomitant of disclosure. These words in r 1(1) can therefore be ignored.

"the close of pleadings" (r 1(1))—Properly so called, there are rarely pleadings in family cases save in the case of petitions for divorce (see FPR 1991, r 2.20(2)). Beyond this, it is impossible to be specific as to when discovery applies in the majority of family proceedings. For example:

(*a*) a rule similar to r 1(1) might be thought to apply in CA 1989, s 8 children proceedings where an application for an order under that section must be acknowledged within 14 days of the application being served (FPR 1991, r 4.9(1); FPC(CA 1989)R 1991, r 9(1)), although it is unlikely that, by that stage, the issues in the case will be clear;

(*b*) in children applications (other than for a s 8 order), the only compunction on a respondent to file an answer before the hearing is to do so two days before the hearing in public law applications (FPR 1991, r 4.9(4); FPC(CA 1989)R 1991, r 9(4)), and so a provision equivalent to r 1(1) cannot be said to be applicable in these proceedings;

(*c*) in matrimonial ancillary relief proceedings, there is a timetable for the filing of Form E etc (FPR 1991, r 2.61B).

Continuing duty of discovery—The duty of disclosure and of discovery continues until trial of the application, and thus applies to documents or information which come into existence during the course of proceedings. The classic example is a spouse's intention to remarry (see eg *Livesey (formerly Jenkins) v Jenkins* (above)) or permanently to cohabit; and, in the case of documents, it extends to documentary evidence of means: accounts, surrender values of insurance policies, pension valuations and so on. This is part of the general principle that a party may not at the hearing of an application take his opponent by surprise by producing evidence available to him prior to the hearing.

Use of documents obtained on discovery—Documents obtained on discovery can be used only for the purposes of the case, and there is an implied undertaking to this effect (*Home Office v Harman* [1983] AC 280, [1983] 1 All ER 532, HL). Documents arising in confidential proceedings (as with most family proceedings) remain confidential (see eg *D v D (Production*

Appointment) [1995] 2 FLR 497, Thorpe J). In children proceedings, documents may only be disclosed with leave of the court (FPR 1991, r 4.23; FPC(CA 1989)R 1991, r 23) save to the persons set out in the rule (even for the purposes of the case).

"discovery by the parties to the action" (r 1(1))—The scheme under Order 24 requires discovery by exchange of lists of documents (r 2 et seq). Save where ordered by the court, this requirement will rarely apply in family proceedings. However, the principle of mutuality of disclosure is as important in family proceedings as in any other.

"documents ... in their possession, custody or power" (r 1(1))—See under r 3 below.

Discovery in a discretionary jurisdiction—In a discretionary jurisdiction, as is the case with many forms of family proceedings (eg CA 1989, s 1(3), I(PFD)A 1975, s 3(1), MCA 1973, s 25(1)), the court is directed by statute to consider certain factors. Thus the words "Nothing ... shall be taken as preventing the parties to an action agreeing to dispense with or limit the discovery of documents" in r 1(2) cannot prevent the court, of its own motion, from directing the parties (despite their previous agreement) to produce documents which the court requires to see; equally, no agreement in the matrimonial ancillary relief jurisdiction can oust the jurisdiction of the court (*Hyman v Hyman* [1929] AC 601, (1929) FLR Rep 342, HL), and any agreement incorporated into a court order derives its authority, because of the discretionary nature of the jurisdiction, from the order and not from the agreement (*de Lasala v de Lasala* [1980] AC 546, (1979) FLR Rep 223, [1979] 3 WLR 390, HL).

****

3 Order for discovery (Ord 24, r 3)

(1) Subject to the provisions of this rule and of rules 4 and 8, the Court may order any party to a cause or matter (whether begun by writ, originating summons or otherwise) to make and serve on any other party a list of the documents which are or have been in his possession, custody or power relating to any matter in question in the cause or matter, and may at the same time or subsequently also order him to make and file an affidavit verifying such a list and to serve a copy thereof on the other party.

(2) Where a party who is required by rule 2 to make discovery of documents fails to comply with any provision of that rule, the Court, on the application of any party to whom the discovery was required to be made, may make an order against the first-mentioned party under paragraph (1) of this rule or, as the case may be, may order him to make and file an affidavit verifying the list of documents he is required to make under rule 2, and to serve a copy thereof on the applicant.

(3) An order under this rule may be limited to such documents or classes of document only, or to such only of the matters in question in the cause or matter, as may be specified in the order.

Stage of proceedings at which order for discovery is appropriate—Whilst the court has a discretion as to when to order on the application of a party, discovery will not normally be appropriate until issues have been defined so far as possible by statements or affidavits or other documents already exchanged (*RHM Foods Ltd v Bovril Ltd* [1982] 1 WLR 661, [1982] 1 All ER 673, CA).

"any party to a cause or matter (whether begun by writ, originating summons or otherwise)" (r 3(1))—Whilst r 2 applies only to particular forms of process, r 3 applies to any form of proceedings.

"any other party" (r 3(1))—Discovery may only be sought against a party to the proceedings, and the court should not join someone as a party to proceedings solely for the purpose of obtaining discovery against him if he otherwise has no involvement in the matter in issue (*Re T (Divorce: Interim Maintenance: Discovery)* [1990] 1 FLR 1, Ward J).

"to make and serve ... a list of ... documents" (r 3(1))—Rule 3 deals with lists of documents, since theoretically discovery relates to documents which are (or are not, if privileged) available for inspection. In practice, in family proceedings, a statement of what is available and copies of the documents themselves are more likely to be appropriate to discovery.

"documents" (r 3(1)–(3))—The term "document" includes not only information on paper or copies of such documents, but also information stored on computer (*Derby & Co Ltd v Weldon (No 9)* [1991] 1 WLR 652, [1991] 2 All ER 901) and information on video (see eg *B v B (Court Bundles: Video Evidence)* [1994] 1 FLR 323, Wall J (set out in Part IV of this work as *Practice Note of 11 November 1993)*, at para 15; *Re R (Child Abuse: Video Evidence)* [1995] 1 FLR 451, Johnson J).

"documents which are or have been in his possession, custody or power" (r 3(1))—This expression extends not only to documents which are still held by a party, but also those relevant to the case which have been held by him and those which others – eg his solicitor or a member of his staff – hold for him. There is also a continuing duty to disclose documents which come into his possession during the course of the proceedings (see **Continuing duty of discovery** under r 1).

"relating to any matter in question" (r 3(1))—Whilst apparently broad in ambit, this expression must be seen in the context of the following:

(*a*) *Relevance of evidence* The general rule of evidence that only material and evidence relevant to the issues before the court will be admissible.

(*b*) *Case management* The preference of courts generally to limit rather than encourage unlimited discovery.

(*c*) *Discovery only if necessary* See r 8 below.

****

5 Form of list and affidavit (Ord 24, r 5)

(1) A list of documents made in compliance with rule 2 or with an order under rule 3 must be in Form No 26 in Appendix A, and must enumerate the documents in a convenient order and as shortly as possible but describing each of them or, in the case of bundles of documents of the same nature, each bundle, sufficiently to enable it to be identified.

(2) If it is desired to claim that any documents are privileged from production, the claim must be made in the list of documents with a sufficient statement of the grounds of the privilege.

(3) An affidavit made as aforesaid verifying a list of documents must be in Form No 27 in Appendix A.

"documents privileged from production" (r 5(2))—In certain limited circumstances, documents and information are exempted (ie privileged) from discovery or disclosure, namely in the following four areas:

(1) Legal professional privilege Documents are exempt from discovery on grounds of legal professional privilege in the following circumstances:

(*a*) *Communications between solicitor and client* Communications between a solicitor and client (whether or not litigation is pending) are absolutely privileged (*R v Derby Magistrates' Court ex parte B* [1996] 1 FLR 513, [1995] 3 WLR 681, HL: "No exception should be allowed to the absolute nature of legal professional privilege, once established" (per Lord Taylor of Gosforth CJ at FLR 528F).

(*b*) *Communications between a solicitor and third parties (litigation pending)* In most instances, a solicitor's communications with third parties where litigation is pending are privileged. This is subject to the important exception of communications and reports which come into existence following the grant of leave by the court in children proceedings for release of confidential court documents (under FPR 1991, r 4.23 and FPC(CA 1989)R 1991, r 23). Normal "litigation privilege" (per Lord Jauncey of Tullichettle in *Re L (Police Investigation: Privilege)* [1996] 1 FLR 731, [1996] 2 WLR 395, HL) does not apply to such reports.

(2) Disclosure injurious to public interest Documents are privileged from disclosure on grounds that disclosure would injure the public interest as follows:

(*a*) *"Without prejudice" correspondence* It is public policy to encourage litigants to settle cases rather than litigate to a conclusion (*Cutts v Head* [1984] Ch 290, [1984] 1 All ER 597, CA); and therefore it is public policy to exempt from disclosure any letter or other document – whether or not marked "without prejudice" (*Chocoladefabriken Lindt & Springli AG v Nestle Co Ltd* [1978] RPC 287) - which is an attempt to settle a case (eg *Calderbank* correspondence). This principle applies to discussions with a CAFCASS officer or mediator in mediation of issues before the court (*Re D (Minors) (Conciliation: Privilege)* [1993] 1 FLR 932, CA), with the qualification that confidentiality will be overridden for the mediator/CAFCASS officer where, to withhold information (eg from the police or social services department), might effect the welfare of a child.

(*b*) *Public interest immunity* Is the public interest in the withholding of confidential documents from a party greater than the public interest that the open administration of justice on the basis of full relevant discovery as between parties (*Official Solicitor v K* [1965] AC 201, (1963) FLR Rep 520, HL). The types of material covered by public interest immunity are not closed (*D v National Society for the Prevention of Cruelty to Children* [1978] AC 171, (1977) FLR Rep 181, HL). In all cases it is a matter for the judge's discretion as to whether a document is held to be privileged from disclosure (see eg *Re C (Disclosure)* [1996] 1 FLR 797, Johnson J (child not wanting information released to a parent); and see **Public interest immunity** and **Withholding disclosure** under FPR 1991, r 4.17).

(3) Documents tending to incriminate Discovery need not be given of any document which will tend to expose the party to criminal proceedings (Civil Evidence Act 1968, s 14). This principle has been overridden in children proceedings (CA 1989, s 98(2)) where a party is immune from prosecution as a result of giving evidence about a crime. Documents arising as a result, and which tend to incriminate, can be ordered to be disclosed to the police (*Re EC (Disclosure of Material)* [1996] 2 FLR 725, CA) on the basis of balancing the need for maintaining confidentiality in family cases against the public interest in making possible a criminal trial of a serious offence.

The existence of privileged documents—The existence of privileged documents should be made known to other parties. If production of such documents is sought by a party, application should be made to the court. The procedure for a local authority to invoke public interest immunity is governed by *Re C (Expert Evidence: Disclosure: Practice)* [1995] 1 FLR 204, Cazalet J.

"a sufficient statement of the grounds of the privilege" (r 5(2))—Where privilege is sought, the document must be identified and the reason set out for privilege being claimed (based on the above categorisation).

****

7 Order for discovery of particular documents (Ord 24, r 7)

(1) Subject to rule 8, the Court may at any time, on the application of any party to a cause or matter, make an order requiring any other party to make an affidavit stating whether any document specified or described in the application or any class of document so specified or described is, or has at any time been, in his possession, custody or power, and if not then in his possession, custody or power when he parted with it and what has become of it.

(2) An order may be made against a party under this rule notwithstanding that he may already have made or been required to make a list of documents or affidavit under rule 2 or rule 3.

(3) An application for an order under this rule must be supported by an affidavit stating the belief of the deponent that the party from whom discovery is sought under this rule has, or at some time had, in his possession, custody or power the

document, or class of document, specified or described in the application and that it relates to one or more of the matters in question in the cause or matter.

****

8 Discovery to be ordered only if necessary (Ord 24, r 8)

On the hearing of an application for an order under rule 3, 7 or 7A the Court, if satisfied that discovery is not necessary, or not necessary at that stage of the cause or matter, may dismiss or, as the case may be, adjourn the application and shall in any case refuse to make such an order if and so far as it is of opinion that discovery is not necessary either for disposing fairly of the cause or matter or for saving costs.

Amendments—SI 1971/1269.

****

10 Inspection of documents referred to in pleadings, affidavits and witness statements (Ord 24, r 10)

(1) Any party to a cause or matter shall be entitled at any time to serve a notice on any other party in whose pleadings, affidavits or witness statements reference is made to any document requiring him to produce that document for the inspection of the party giving the notice and to permit him to take copies thereof.
(2) The party on whom a notice is served under paragraph (1) must, within four days after service of the notice, serve on the party giving the notice a notice stating a time within seven days after the service thereof at which the documents, or such of them as he does not object to produce, may be inspected at a place specified in the notice, and stating which (if any) of the documents he objects to produce and on what grounds.

Amendments—SI 1992/1907.

****

12 Order for production to Court (Ord 24, r 12)

At any stage of the proceedings in any cause or matter the Court may, subject to rule 13(1), order any party to produce to the Court any document in his possession, custody or power relating to any matter in question in the cause or matter and the Court may deal with the document when produced in such manner as it thinks fit.

Discretionary jurisdiction—Much in the family jurisdiction vests in the courts wide discretion to dispose of matters as the judge sees fit (see eg CA 1989, s 1(3), I(PFD)A 1975, s 3(1), MCA 1973, s 25(1). In such a jurisdiction, it becomes important for the court to demand evidence from parties of its own motion. Insofar as the power is not already implied by statute, r 13 gives the court power to seek documents from parties where these have not already been disclosed and to the extent that any such document is relevant to an issue before the court.

13 Production to be ordered only if necessary, etc (Ord 24, r 13)

(1) No order for the production of any documents for inspection or to the Court, or for the supply of a copy of any document, shall be made under any of the foregoing

rules unless the Court is of opinion that the order is necessary either for disposing fairly of the cause or matter or for saving costs.

(2) Where on an application under this Order for production of any document for inspection or to the Court, or for the supply of a copy of any document, privilege from such production or supply is claimed or objection is made to such production or supply on any other ground, the Court may inspect the document for the purpose of deciding whether the claim or objection is valid.

Amendments—SI 1987/1423.

"the order is necessary either for disposing fairly of the cause or matter or for saving costs" (r 13(1))—By contrast with r 8, this rule puts the onus on the party seeking production to show that production is necessary for the fair disposal of the case or to save costs.

****

15 Document disclosure of which would be injurious to public interest: saving (Ord 24, r 15)

The foregoing provisions of this Order shall be without prejudice to any rule of law which authorises or requires the withholding of any document on the ground that the disclosure of it would be injurious to the public interest.

Disclosure injurious to public interest—Documents which are privileged from disclosure on grounds that disclosure would injure the public interest consist of: correspondence between parties which consists of an attempt to settle a case ("without prejudice" correspondence); and confidential documents covered by public interest immunity (see **Disclosure injurious to public interest** under r 5).

Public interest immunity—Where a local authority seeks to rely on public interest immunity in relation to a confidential document, the procedure is governed by *Re C (Expert Evidence: Disclosure: Practice)* [1995] 1 FLR 204, Cazalet J.

****

ORDER 29
INTERLOCUTORY INJUNCTIONS, INTERIM PRESERVATION OF PROPERTY, INTERIM PAYMENTS ETC

I Interlocutory injunctions. Interim preservation of property etc

****

1A Cross-examination on assets disclosure affidavit (Ord 29, r 1A)

(1) Where –

(*a*) the Court has made an order restraining any party from removing from the jurisdiction of the High Court, or otherwise dealing with, any assets,
(*b*) that party has in compliance with the order, or any order made in connection with it, filed affidavit evidence as to his or any other assets, and
(*c*) the Court has ordered that that party shall be cross-examined on his affidavit,

the Court may order that the cross-examination shall be conducted otherwise than before a judge, in which case the cross-examination shall take place before a master or, if a master so orders, before an examiner of the Court.

(2) The following provisions of Order 68 shall apply to a cross-examination of a kind referred to in paragraph (1)(*c*) as if it were a trial with witnesses in the Queen's Bench or Chancery Division and as if the person presiding were the judge –

(*a*) rule 1(1) (except the words "unless the judge otherwise directs"); and
(*b*) rules 2(2) and (3) and 8.

(3) A cross-examination of a kind referred to in paragraph (1)(*c*) shall take place in chambers and no transcript or other record of it may be used by any person other than the party being cross-examined for any purpose other than the purpose of the proceedings in which the order for the cross-examination was made, unless and to the extent that that party consents or the Court gives leave.

Amendments—Inserted by SI 1992/638.

Proceedings (r 1A(3))—The proceedings referred to are the interlocutory injunction proceedings, not the main action. Cross-examination under this rule is an exceptional measure and there is no question of it becoming routine (*Yu Kong Line of Korea v Rendsburg Investment Corporation of Liberia* (1996) *The Times*, 22 October). In ancillary relief proceedings there will often be a better way of discovering assets than an application under RSC Ord 29, r 1A, such as an inspection appointment under FPR 1991, r 2.62.

2 Detention, preservation etc of subject-matter of cause or matter (Ord 29, r 2)

(1) On the application of any party to a cause or matter the Court may make an order for the detention, custody or preservation of any property which is the subject-matter of the cause or matter, or as to which any question may arise therein, or for the inspection of any such property in the possession of a party to the cause or matter.

(2) For the purpose of enabling any order under paragraph (1) to be carried out the Court may by the order authorise any person to enter upon any land or building in the possession of any party to the cause or matter.

(3) Where the right of any party to a specific fund is in dispute in a cause or matter, the Court may, on the application of a party to the cause or matter, order the fund to be paid into court or otherwise secured.

(4) An order under this rule may be made on such terms, if any, as the Court thinks just.

(5) An application for an order under this rule must be made by summons or by notice under Order 25, rule 7.

(6) Unless the Court otherwise directs, an application by a defendant for such an order may not be made before he acknowledges service of the writ or originating summons by which the cause or matter was begun.

Amendments—SI 1979/1716.

Scope of provision—This rule provides for the detention and preservation of the subject matter of a cause or matter. The rule is also directly incorporated into the CCR (CCR Ord 13, r 7(1)(*b*)), which continue to apply to family proceedings by virtue of FPR 1991, r 1.3. To some extent it overlaps with MCA 1973, s 37 but an application could be made under this rule, for example, for an order for the detention, custody or presentation of specific property such as an heirloom, dowry or engagement ring.

****

ORDER 32
APPLICATIONS AND PROCEEDINGS IN CHAMBERS

****

7 Subpoena for attendance of witness (Ord 32, r 7)

(1) A writ of subpoena ad testificandum or a writ of subpoena duces tecum to compel the attendance of a witness for the purpose of proceedings in chambers may be issued out of the Central Office, Chancery Chambers, the principal registry of the Family Division, the Admiralty and Commercial Registry or a district registry, as the case may be, if the party who desires the attendance of the witness produces a note from a judge or from a master or district judge, as the case may be, authorising the issue of the writ.

(2) In the Chancery Division and the Queen's Bench Division any master or district judge, and in the Family Division any district judge, may give such a note or may direct that the application for it be made to the judge before whom the proceedings are to be heard.

Amendments—SI 1971/1269; SI 1987/1423; SI 1994/1975.

Use of subpoena in family proceedings—Since there is no power to order an inspection appointment (FPR 1991, r 2.62(4)) in proceedings following a foreign divorce, a subpoena under this rule (perhaps with a *Khanna* appointment (see under Ord 38, r 13)) would be appropriate where documentary evidence of third parties is sought by a party (*Roker International Properties Inc and anor v Couveras and Wolf* [2000] 2 FLR 976, Wilson J).

****

10 Application to make order of House of Lords order of High Court (Ord 32, r 10)

An application to make an order of the House of Lords an order of the High Court may be made ex parte by affidavit to a master or to the Admiralty Registrar or to a district judge of the Family Division or, if the cause or matter in which the order was made proceeded in the High Court in a district registry, to the district judge of that registry.

Amendments—SI 1971/1269.

Scope of provision—Where the House of Lords reverses or varies an order on appeal, the order must be made an order of the High Court; otherwise, there would be no record in the court below of the order having been varied or reversed (see *L alias H v H* (1866) LR 1 P & M 293). Therefore, where the order of the House of Lords merely affirms the order of the court below, an application under this rule is not necessary. Where an order for costs is made, the order may be made an order of the High Court for the purposes of enforcement.

****

12 Reference of matter to judge (Ord 32, r 12)

Any master of the Queen's Bench Division or district judge of the Family Division may refer to a judge any matter which he thinks should properly be decided by a judge, and the judge may either dispose of the matter or refer it back to the master or district judge, as the case may be, with such directions as he thinks fit.

Amendments—SI 1971/1269.

13 Power to direct hearing in court (Ord 32, r 13)

(1) The judge in chambers may direct that any summons, application or appeal shall be heard in court or shall be adjourned into court to be so heard if he considers that by reason of its importance or for any other reason it should be so heard.

(2) Any matter heard in court by virtue of a direction under paragraph (1) may be adjourned from court into chambers.

Scope of provision—A judge in chambers in the High Court has power to adjourn a matter to open court and then back to chambers under this rule. This power is usually exercised when, having heard a matter in chambers, the judge considers that the whole or part of the judgment is of sufficient public interest to warrant it being given in open court.

****

ORDER 38
EVIDENCE

I General rules

1 General rule: witnesses to be examined orally (Ord 38, r 1)

Subject to the provisions of these rules and of the Civil Evidence Act 1968 and the Civil Evidence Act 1972, and any other enactment relating to evidence, any fact required to be proved at the trial of any action begun by writ by the evidence of witnesses shall be proved by the examination of the witnesses orally and in open Court.

Amendments—SI 1969/1105; SI 1979/1542.

Scope of provision—This rule states the general principle that, where a fact is to be proved in proceedings, evidence as to that fact is to be given orally and in open court, subject to certain exceptions.

Application of Order 38 in the county courts and in family proceedings—Many of the provisions of Order 38 are reproduced in Order 20 of the County Court Rules 1981. Where they are not, Order 38 will apply in the county courts pursuant to County Courts Act 1984, s 76 (application in county courts of High Court practice). RSC 1965 and CCR 1981 apply, with any necessary modifications, to family proceedings in the High Court and county courts (FPR 1991, r 1.3(1)).

"Subject to the provisions of these rules, [the Civil Evidence Acts] and any other enactment"—Categories of evidence specifically excluded from this rule include the following:

(*a*) examples from "these rules" (ie RSC 1965) where evidence may be given by other means include: affidavits (r 2); evidence adduced in such a way as the court, in its discretion, orders (r 3); and hearsay (rr 20–33); interrogatories (Ord 26); evidence taken by deposition (Ord 39) (NB Ords 26, 38 (rr 20–33) and 39 can be regarded as outside the scope of this treatment);

(*b*) Civil Evidence Act 1972, concerning admissibility of opinion evidence, which is dealt with in rr 34–41;

(*c*) Civil Evidence Act 1995, which came into force on 31 January 1997 (except ss 10 and 16(5)) and makes hearsay evidence admissible in civil proceedings (s 1), provided that notice to adduce such evidence has been given (s 2); this Act is dealt with in rr 20–24; and

(*d*) "any other enactment relating to evidence": in the family and child law field, this would include CA 1989, ss 41(11) and 42(2) (statements, evidence and copy documents obtained from the local authority treated as evidence from the children's guardian), and Children (Admissibility of Hearsay Evidence) Order 1993 (admissibility of hearsay in certain children proceedings).

"any fact required to be proved"—This rule only refers to facts (as distinct from, for example, opinion evidence) to be proved.

Evidence in the Family Division and in family courts—Most hearings in family cases are in chambers; but the rules as to the adducing of evidence are as in this Order, subject to the exceptions referred to above. For example, evidence in ancillary relief claims are dealt with in part on affidavit evidence and, in many children cases (though there is no rule on the subject), statements will often be treated as a witness's evidence-in-chief (and see *Practice Direction of 31 January 1995*, para 3: "... every witness statement or affidavit shall stand as the evidence in chief of the witness concerned" – a direction regarded more in ignorance than in observance).

Judicial immunity—A judge is not compellable as a witness where he is performing his judicial functions (*Warren v Warren* [1996] 2 FLR 777, [1996] 3 WLR 1129, CA).

2 Evidence by affidavit (Ord 38, r 2)

(1), (2) ...

(3) In any cause or matter begun by originating summons, originating motion or petition, and on any application made by summons or motion, evidence may be given by affidavit unless in the case of any such cause, matter or application any provision of these rules otherwise provides or the Court otherwise directs, but the Court may, on the application of any party, order the attendance for cross-examination of the person making any such affidavit, and where, after such an order has been made, the person in question does not attend, his affidavit shall not be used as evidence without the leave of the Court.

Defined terms—"originating summons": Ord 1, r 4(1).

"originating summons"—The form and content of an originating summons is defined by Ord 7, and the procedure applicable to them is dealt with in Ord 28.

"originating motion", "petition"—These terms are referred to (though not specifically defined), and the procedure connected with them is set out respectively in Ords 8 and 9.

3 Evidence of particular facts (Ord 38, r 3)

(1) Without prejudice to rule 2, the Court may, at or before the trial of any action, order that evidence of any particular fact shall be given at the trial in such manner as may be specified by the order.

(2) The power conferred by paragraph (1) extends in particular to ordering that evidence of any particular fact may be given at the trial –

(*a*) by statement on oath of information or belief, or
(*b*) by the production of documents or entries in books, or
(*c*) by copies of documents or entries in books, or

(*d*) in the case of a fact which is or was a matter of common knowledge either generally or in a particular district, by the production of a specified newspaper which contains a statement of that fact.

Video evidence—Evidence adduced by video can be ordered under this rule (see also Civil Evidence Act 1968, ss 2, 10; *Note: B v B (Court Bundles: Video Evidence)* [1994] 1 FLR 323, Wall J (set out in Part IV of this work as *Practice Note of 11 November 1993*). The court has jurisdiction to order that evidence from witnesses living abroad be given by video-link (*R v Horseferry Road Magistrates' Court ex parte Bennett (No 3)* (1994) *The Times*, 14 January).

Cogency of evidence—Even if leave is given under this rule, it will still be necessary for the court to consider the cogency of that evidence; see also Civil Evidence Act 1995, s 4(1) which requires the court to assess "the reliability or otherwise" of hearsay evidence and sets out (s 4(2)) a number of the factors to be taken into account by the court in this assessment.

4 Limitation of expert evidence (Ord 38, r 4)

The Court may, at or before the trial of any action, order that the number of medical or other expert witnesses who may be called at the trial shall be limited as specified by the order.

Expert evidence—This rule should be read in conjunction with Ord 38, Pt IV (expert evidence).

"number of medical or other witnesses"—This order, where made, neither compels a party to call the number of witnesses for which leave is given, nor to call any at all. Conventionally, the order is that expert evidence be agreed, failing which expert evidence be limited to one (or more) witnesses for either side. Power to limit the number of witnesses does not enable the court to disallow expert evidence altogether (*Sullivan v West Yorkshire Passenger Transport Executive* [1985] 2 All ER 134, CA), save in the case of children and family reporters (see below).

Expert evidence in children cases—Parties must address their minds as early as possible to the expert evidence needed in a children case, and thus to the number of experts to be called (*Re G (Minors) (Expert Witnesses)* [1994] 2 FLR 291, Wall J; *Re A and B (Minors) (No 2)* [1995] 1 FLR 351, Wall J). The extent to which children may be examined may – and should – be limited; and leave of the court is needed for this and for release of documents in the case to expert witnesses (FPR 1991, rr 4.18, 4.23).

Welfare reports—Where the court has ordered a children and family reporters's welfare report, it will often be wary of admitting evidence from independent welfare officers; see also **Independent welfare reports** under CA 1989, s 7 and the cases cited there.

****

12 Evidence at trial may be used in subsequent proceedings (Ord 38, r 12)

Any evidence taken at the trial of any cause or matter may be used in any subsequent proceedings in that cause or matter.

Issue estoppel distinguished—This rule is quite distinct from that of estoppel per rem judicatem; that is to say, broadly, that a person cannot deny a matter on which the court has already adjudicated, subject to certain restrictions (see eg *Re S, S and A (Care Proceedings: Issue Estoppel)* [1995] 2 FLR 244, Wilson J).

Applications to vary orders—The application of this rule will be particularly important in family proceedings in connection with applications to vary orders made earlier in the same proceedings (eg Matrimonial Causes Act 1973, s 31 (variation and discharge of certain financial relief orders), and CA 1989, s 39 (variation or discharge of care order – see also *Re S and P (Discharge of Care Order)* [1995] 2 FLR 782, Singer J). Care may be needed to distinguish between evidence which led to the making of a consent order (which might, subject to any question of estoppel, be

PART III

susceptible to challenge) and evidence used at a contested hearing, which would come within the terms of this rule.

"may be used"—It will be noted that the rule is expressed in discretionary terms. Thus, there is no obligation on the court to admit evidence from previous contested proceedings, although it is submitted that not to do so would need very strong grounds.

13 Order to produce document at proceeding other than trial (Ord 38, r 13)

(1) At any stage in a cause or matter the Court may order any person to attend any proceeding in the cause or matter and produce any document, to be specified or described in the order, the production of which appears to the Court to be necessary for the purpose of that proceeding.

(2) No person shall be compelled by an order under paragraph (1) to produce any document at a proceeding in a cause or matter which he could not be compelled to produce at the trial of that cause or matter.

"At any stage" (r 13(1))—Rule 13 may be described as the "forgotten rule" when FPR 1991, r 2.62(7) (production appointments) was incorporated into the rules which replaced the Matrimonial Causes Rules 1977 (cf *B v B (Production Appointment: Procedure)* [1995] 1 FLR 913, Thorpe J). It enables the court to require production of "any document" at an interlocutory stage of proceedings so that the documents can be evaluated in advance of a final hearing.

"compelled to produce at the trial of the matter" (r 13(2))—This is a reference to witnesses being compelled, as by subpoena duces tecum, to produce documents at the final hearing; and the case-law on this rule can be regarded as deriving from leave being sought to have discovery from third parties of documents in advance of the final hearing (*Khanna v Lovell White Durrant (a Firm)* [1995] 1 WLR 121, Sir Donald Nicholls V-C; and see Burrows [1995] Fam Law 199).

Compelling production of documents—The party who seeks documents from a third party prior to the final hearing has two courses available to him:

(*a*) the *Khanna* hearing (see further **Production and the Khanna hearing** under Ord 38, r 14) which is the simpler process and avoids seeking leave of the court for production (as distinct from leave for issue of the subpoena);

(*b*) application pursuant to r 13.

Application—Application is made on summons ex parte to the district judge for an order for production and by a process which, it is suggested, will be analogous to that commended by Thorpe J in *B v B (Production Appointment: Procedure)* [1995] 1 FLR 913 (see further **Inspection appointment** under FPR 1991, r 2.62).

Bankers' Book Evidence Act 1879—This (or the *Khanna* hearing) is the appropriate procedure to adopt for production of entries in bankers' books. Privilege may be claimed by a third party (*Waterhouse v Barker* [1924] 2 KB 759); but a bank does not breach confidentiality to its customer if it produces his bank statements when ordered so to do (*Robertson v Canadian Bank of Commerce* [1994] 1 WLR 1493, PC).

Confidentiality—The court has power to override professional privilege and confidentiality, where this is necessary to ensure full relevant disclosure (*D v D (Production Appointment)* [1995] 2 FLR 497, Thorpe J; see also *Robertson v Canadian Bank of Commerce* (above)).

II Writs of subpoena

14 Form and issue of writ of subpoena (Ord 38, r 14)

(1) A writ of subpoena must be in Form No. 28, 29, or 30 in Appendix A, whichever is appropriate.

(2) Issue of a writ of subpoena takes place upon its being sealed by an officer of the office out of which it is issued.

(3) Where a writ of subpoena is to be issued in a cause or matter which is not proceeding in a District Registry, the appropriate office for the issue of the writ is the Central Office or, if the cause or matter has been set down for trial outside the Royal Courts of Justice, either the Central Office or the registry for the district comprising the city or town at which the cause or matter has been set down for trial.

(4) Where a writ of subpoena is to be issued in a cause or matter which is proceeding in a District Registry, the appropriate office for the issue of the writ is –

(*a*) that registry, or
(*b*) if the cause or matter has been set down for trial at a city or town not comprised in the district of that registry, either that registry or the registry for the district comprising that city or town, or
(*c*) if the cause or matter has been set down for trial at the Royal Courts of Justice, either the Central Office or the registry in which the cause or matter is proceeding.

(5) Before a writ of subpoena is issued a praecipe for the issue of the writ must be filed in the office out of which the writ is to issue; and the praecipe must contain the name and address of the party issuing the writ, if he is acting in person, or the name or firm and business address of that party's solicitor and also (if the solicitor is the agent of another) the name or firm and business address of his principal.

Amendments—Inserted by SI 1969/1105; amended by SI 1971/1955.

Scope of provision—Rule 14, together with rr 17 and 18, contains the basis for issue, service and duration of writs of subpoena, and r 17 deals specifically with procedure on issue. They cover both writs of subpoena ad testificandum and subpoena duces tecum.

Proceedings in chambers—Leave for issue of a subpoena is required for any proceedings in the High Court in chambers (Ord 32, r 7). Application is to the district judge for a "note" to be produced at the time of issue of the subpoena (Ord 32, r 7(1)).

Subpoena duces tecum—As an alternative to the production appointment (see Ord 38, r 13), the court may fix a pre-hearing hearing ("*Khanna* hearing") at which a witness can be required to produce documents.

Production and the Khanna hearing—This procedure requires the issue and service of a subpoena duces tecum. This is followed by a request from the party seeking the documents that a date for consideration of the documents be fixed prior to the final hearing (a *Khanna* hearing, so-called after *Khanna v Lovell White Durrant (a Firm)* [1995] 1 WLR 121, Sir Donald Nicholls V-C). This course avoids the need for the hearing of an ex parte application which is necessary before the production appointment itself can be dealt with (as is necessary with Ord 38, r 13 and FPR 1991, r 2.62(7)), and it puts the onus on the party required to produce the documents to oppose production.

Order to produce is discretionary—The court has discretion to refuse to order production (whether under r 13 or on a subpoena duces tecum), for example where to order production would be oppressive (eg *Morgan v Morgan* [1977] Fam 122, (1976) FLR Rep 473, Watkins J) or where the evidence is not relevant to the issues before the court (eg *Frary v Frary and Another* [1993] 2 FLR 696, CA). Confidentiality may be overridden (see **Confidentiality** under r 13).

15 More than one name may be included in one writ of subpoena (Ord 38, r 15)

The names of two or more persons may be included in one writ of subpoena ad testificandum.

16 Amendment of writ of subpoena (Ord 38, r 16)

Where there is a mistake in any person's name or address in a writ of subpoena, then, if the writ has not been served, the party by whom the writ was issued may have the writ re-sealed in correct form by filing a second praecipe under rule 14(5) indorsed with the words "Amended and re-sealed".

17 Service of writ of subpoena (Ord 38, r 17)

A writ of subpoena must be served personally and, subject to rule 19, the service shall not be valid unless effected within 12 weeks after the date of issue of the writ and not less than four days or such other period as the Court may fix, before the day on which attendance before the Court is required.

Amendments—Inserted by SI 1969/1105; amended by SI 1980/1010.

Scope of provision—See notes under r 14.

18 Duration of writ of subpoena (Ord 38, r 18)

Subject to rule 19, a writ of subpoena continues to have effect until the conclusion of the trial at which the attendance of the witness is required.

Amendments—Inserted by SI 1969/1105.

Scope of provision—See notes under r 14.

19 Writ of subpoena in aid of inferior court or tribunal (Ord 38, r 19)

(1) The office of the Supreme Court out of which a writ of subpoena ad testificandum or a writ of subpoena duces tecum in aid of an inferior court or tribunal may be issued is the Crown Office, and no order of the court for the issue of such a writ is necessary.

(2) A writ of subpoena in aid of an inferior court or tribunal continues to have effect until the disposal of the proceedings before that court or tribunal at which the attendance of the witness is required.

(3) A writ of subpoena issued in aid of an inferior court or tribunal is duly served on the person to whom it is directed not less than 4 days, or such other period as the court may fix, before the day on which the attendance of that person before the court or tribunal is required by the writ that person shall not be liable to any penalty or process for failing to obey the writ.

(4) An application to set aside a writ of subpoena issued in aid of an inferior court or tribunal may be heard by a Master of the Queen's Bench Division.

****

IV Expert evidence

35 Interpretation (Ord 38, r 35)

In this part of this Order a reference to a summons for directions includes a reference to any summons or application to which, under any of these Rules, Order 25, rules 2 to 7, apply and expressions used in this Part of this Order which are used in the Civil Evidence Act 1972 have the same meanings in this Part of this Order as in that Act.

36 Restrictions on adducing expert evidence (Ord 38, r 36)

(1) Except with the leave of the Court or where all parties agree, no expert evidence may be adduced at the trial or hearing of any cause or matter unless the party seeking to adduce the evidence –

(*a*) has applied to the Court to determine whether a direction should be given under rule 37 or 41 (whichever is appropriate) and has complied with any direction given on the application, or
(*b*) has complied with automatic directions taking effect under Order 25, rule 8(1)(*b*).

(2) Nothing in paragraph (1) shall apply to evidence which is permitted to be given by affidavit or shall affect the enforcement under any other provision of these Rules (except Order 45, rule 5) of a direction given under this part of this Order.

Amendments—SI 1980/1010; SI 1987/1423.

Scope of provision—The effect of r 36 is to prevent the adducing of expert evidence at the hearing of any application, cause or matter, save as follows:
(*a*) with the leave of the court;
(*b*) where all parties have agreed the evidence;
(*c*) where the evidence is permitted to be given by affidavit; or
(*d*) where the court has directed that the evidence be disclosed in accordance with standard directions (Ord 25, r 8) or under r 37 or 41.

Application to adduce expert evidence—In the absence of agreement as to the adducing of expert evidence, a party must always apply for leave or rely on court direction (as where local court directions in financial relief cases direct agreement of valuation evidence or the limiting of evidence to one valuer to each party). Application is made on summons (or notice of application in the county courts); or application may be made at a directions appointment (eg under FPR 1991, r 4.14, provided that notice of the specific application is given to all parties: r 4.14(3)(*b*)).

Failure to seek leave—Rule 36 is based on the principle of English justice which specifies a need for mutuality and fairness between parties; thus, the consequence of failure to obtain leave is to risk exclusion of opinion evidence (subject always to the discretion of the court to admit such evidence).

Characteristics of expert evidence—In *Note: Re R (A Minor) (Experts' Evidence)* [1991] 1 FLR 291, Cazalet J (set out in Part IV of this work as *Practice Note of 27 July 1990*) summarises the characteristics of expert evidence as follows:
(*a*) opinion evidence must not be biased in favour of one party or the other, whichever party may have commissioned the report;
(*b*) opinions must be expressed objectively and clearly, and must be properly researched; and
(*c*) reports which promote a particular – or controversial – point of view must make this clear (see also *Re AB (Child Abuse: Expert Witnesses)* [1995] 1 FLR 181, Wall J).

In *Rochdale Borough Council v A and Others* [1991] 2 FLR 192, Douglas Brown J considered further and in some detail the characteristics to which expert evidence should seek to aspire.

Expert's opinion—The judge is entitled to depart from the opinion of the expert although, if he does so, he must explain his reasons (*Re B (Care: Expert Witnesses)* [1996] 1 FLR 667, CA). An expert is entitled to give evidence and make recommendations on the ultimate issue before the court (Civil Evidence Act 1972, s 5(3); *Re M and R (Child Abuse: Evidence)* [1996] 2 FLR 195, CA). Where there is a conflict between experts, the judge must address and resolve that conflict insofar as it is relevant to the issues before the court (*Sewell v Electrolux Ltd* (1997) *The Times*, 7 November, CA).

37 Direction that expert report be disclosed (Ord 38, r 37)

(1) Subject to paragraph (2), where in any cause or matter an application is made under rule 36(1) in respect of oral expert evidence, then, unless the Court considers that there are special reasons for not doing so, it shall direct that the substance of the evidence be disclosed in the form of a written report or reports to such other parties and within such period as the Court may specify.

(2) ...

Amendments—Substituted by SI 1989/2427.

"the substance of the evidence"—It should now be the practice, since *Practice Direction of 31 January 1995*, para 3, that a witness's statement will stand as his evidence-in-chief. It is, therefore, likely that the "substance" of the expert's evidence will be treated as his evidence on which he will then be cross-examined, in default of agreement of that evidence.

38 Meeting of experts (Ord 38, r 38)

In any cause or matter the Court may, if it thinks fit, direct that there be a meeting "without prejudice" of such experts within such periods before or after the disclosure of their reports as the Court may specify, for the purpose of identifying those parts of their evidence which are in issue. Where such a meeting takes place the experts may prepare a joint statement indicating those parts of their evidence on which they are, and those on which they are not, in agreement.

Amendments—Substituted by SI 1987/1423.

"the court may, if it thinks fit, direct"—The court may impose a r 38 meeting on parties, or a party may apply, by summons (on notice in the county courts), for a direction that there be such a meeting. Family judges have urged the usefulness of such meetings specifically, or impliedly, by reference to this rule (see eg *Evans v Evans* [1990] 1 FLR 319, Booth J (valuers in financial relief); *Re C (Expert Evidence: Disclosure: Practice)* [1995] 1 FLR 204, Cazalet J (medical and other witnesses in children cases)).

Condition of appointment of expert—It should be a condition of the appointment of experts in the same field of expertise that they be required to meet to identify areas of agreement (*Re S (Care Proceedings: Split Hearing)* [1996] 2 FLR 773, Bracewell J; and see *Children Act Advisory Committee Annual Report 1994/5*).

Arrangement of meetings: children proceedings—In cases under CA 1989, s 31(2) (care and supervision), the children's guardian or the local authority should co-ordinate (and, where appropriate, chair) the meetings.

Agency of experts and "without prejudice"—Whilst an expert cannot bind the party instructing him by any agreement reached at a meeting, once that agreement is ratified by the parties (eg as to valuation of matrimonial property) then privilege attaching to the information goes. Rules as to privileged information may not be so strongly upheld in children proceedings (*Oxfordshire CC v M* [1994] Fam 151, [1994] 1 FLR 175, CA).

39 Disclosure of part of expert evidence (Ord 38, r 39)

Where the Court considers that any circumstances rendering it undesirable to give a direction under rule 37 relate to part only of the evidence sought to be adduced, the Court may, if it thinks fit, direct disclosure of the remainder.

Amendments—SI 1987/1423.

"may, if it thinks fit, direct disclosure"—The rule gives the court a discretion as to whether to inhibit the disclosure of part of an expert's oral evidence, and a party may apply for an order preventing disclosure of part. Application is on summons, or on notice of application in the county courts, supported by an affidavit saying why it is "undesirable" that part of the report should be given in evidence (eg because it is irrelevant to the issues before the court, or because it contains confidential or otherwise privileged information). The court will need to be specific as to what is to be excised.

"undesirable to give a direction under rule 37"—Rule 37 applies to evidence which is to be given in court. Rule 39 thus prevents the adducing of part of that evidence before the court. It is to be distinguished from those cases where a party is prevented from seeing part of the evidence (eg of a welfare report) which the court and other parties see.

****

ORDER 45
ENFORCEMENT OF JUDGMENTS AND ORDERS: GENERAL

CPR 1998—Where the order to be enforced was obtained in proceedings which are not "family proceedings", Ords 45–51 will apply in the modified form in which they are set out in CPR 1998, Sch 1. See the annotations to FPR 1991, r 1.3.

1 Enforcement of judgment etc for payment of money (Ord 45, r 1)

(1) Subject to the provisions of these rules, a judgment or order for the payment of money, not being a judgment or order for the payment of money into the Court, may be enforced by one or more of the following means, that is to say –

- (*a*) writ of fieri facias;
- (*b*) garnishee proceedings;
- (*c*) a charging order;
- (*d*) the appointment of a receiver;
- (*e*) in the case in which rule 5 applies, an order of committal;
- (*f*) in such a case, writ of sequestration.

(2) Subject to the provisions of these rules, a judgment or order for the payment of money into Court may be enforced by one or more of the following means, that is to say –

- (*a*) the appointment of a receiver;
- (*b*) in a case in which rule 5 applies, an order of committal;
- (*c*) in such a case, writ of sequestration.

(3) Paragraphs (1) and (2) are without prejudice to any other remedy available to enforce such a judgment or order as is therein mentioned or to the power of a Court under the Debtors Acts 1869 and 1878, to commit to prison a person who makes default in paying money adjudged or ordered to be paid by him, or to the right of a person prosecuting a judgment or order for the payment of money to a person to apply under section 105(1) of the County Courts Act 1984, to have the judgment or order enforced in a county court, or to the enactments relating to bankruptcy or the winding up of companies.

(4) In this Order references to any writ shall be construed as including references to any further writ in aid of the first-mentioned writ.

Amendments—SI 1970/1208; SI 1976/337; SI 1985/69.

Scope of provision—This rule describes the ways in which a money judgment may be enforced. If the proceedings concern a "qualifying periodical maintenance order" within the meaning of Maintenance Enforcement Act 1991, s 1, the court may of its own motion make a "means of payment order" (s 1(4)(*a*)) or an attachment of earnings order (s 1(4)(*b*)).

"fieri facias" (r 1(1)(*a*))—See Ords 46 and 47.

"garnishee proceedings" (r 1(1)(*b*))—See Ord 49.

"charging order" (r 1(1)(*c*))—See Ord 50.

"appointment of a receiver" (r 1(1)(*d*), (2)(*a*))—See Ord 51.

"order of committal" (r 1(1)(*e*), (2)(*b*))—See rr 5–8 and Ord 52.

"writ of sequestration" (r 1(1)(*f*)), (2)(*c*)—See rr 5–8 and Ord 46, r 5.

Payment of money into court (r 1(2))—Execution against goods, garnishee proceedings and charging order proceedings are not available to enforce an order in this form.

"section 105(1) of the County Courts Act 1984" (r 1(3))—County Courts Act 1984, s 105(1), which enabled a judgment creditor to enforce a High Court judgment in the county court, was repealed by the Courts and Legal Services Act 1990; as regards family proceedings, it has not been replaced.

2 Notice of seizure (Ord 45, r 2)

When first executing a warrant of fieri facias, the sheriff or his officer shall deliver to the debtor or leave at each place where execution is levied a notice in Form No 55 in Appendix A informing the debtor of the execution.

Amendments—SI 1996/2892.

3 Enforcement of judgment for possession of land (Ord 45, r 3)

(1) Subject to the provisions of these rules, a judgment or order for the giving of possession of land may be enforced by one or more of the following means, that is to say –

(*a*) writ of possession;
(*b*) in a case in which rule 5 applies, an order of committal;
(*c*) in such a case, writ of sequestration.

(2) A writ of possession to enforce a judgment or order for the giving of possession of any land shall not be issued without the leave of the Court except where the judgment or order was given or made in a mortgage action to which Order 88 applies.

(3) Such leave shall not be granted unless it is shown –

(*a*) that every person in actual possession of the whole or any part of the land has received such notice of the proceedings as appears to the Court sufficient to enable him to apply to the Court for any relief to which he may be entitled, and
(*b*) if the operation of the judgment or order is suspended by subsection (2) of section 16 of the Landlord and Tenant Act 1954, that the applicant has not received notice in writing from the tenant that he desires that the provisions of paragraphs (*a*) and (*b*) of that subsection shall have effect.

A writ of possession may include provision for enforcing the payment of any money adjudged or ordered to be paid by the judgment or order which is to be enforced by the writ.

"writ of possession" (r 3(1)(*a*))—See **"leave of the Court"** below and Ord 46.

"order of committal" (r 3(1)(*b*))—See rr 5–8 and Ord 52.

"writ of sequestration" (r 3(1)(*c*))—See rr 5–8 and Ord 46, r 5.

"leave of the Court" (r 3(2))—In the High Court (unlike in the county court), leave will normally be required to issue a writ of possession. The application may generally be made ex parte by filing an affidavit (see Ord 46, r 4). The court will expect notice of the judgment or order to have been given to the defendant and (if different) the occupier, and possession to have been demanded; the affidavit must deal with these matters and give details of the tenancy of any other occupier than the person against whom the order was made (*Secretary's Circular of 19 January 1972*). Where the order was suspended subject to a condition which is said to have been broken, notice must be given to the defendant (*Fleet Mortgage and Investment Co Ltd v Lower Maisonette, 46 Eaton Place Ltd* [1972] 1 WLR 765, [1972] 2 All ER 737); in such a case the application must be made by summons.

Restitution—If, after a writ of possession has been executed, possession is unlawfully regained, the plaintiff may obtain a writ of restitution to have the occupants again evicted. Such a writ is in the nature of a writ of execution in aid of the original writ (see Ord 46, r 3 and **Warrant of restitution** under CCR Ord 26, r 17).

Forms—Affidavit seeking leave: PF No91; writ of possession: No 66.

4 Enforcement of judgment for delivery of goods (Ord 45, r 4)

(1) Subject to the provisions of these rules, a judgment or order for the delivery of any goods which does not give a person against whom the judgment is given or order made the alternative of paying the assessed value of the goods may be enforced by one or more of the following means, that is to say –

- (*a*) writ of delivery to recover the goods without alternative provision for recovery of the assessed value thereof (hereafter in this rule referred to as a "writ of specific delivery");
- (*b*) in a case in which rule 5 applies, an order of committal;
- (*c*) in a such case, writ of sequestration.

(2) Subject to the provisions of these rules, a judgment or order for the delivery of any goods or payment of their assessed value may be enforced by one or more of the following means, that is to say –

- (*a*) writ of delivery to recover the goods or their assessed value;
- (*b*) by order of the Court, writ of specific delivery;
- (*c*) in a case in which rule 5 applies, writ of sequestration.

An application for an order under sub-paragraph (*b*) shall be made by summons, which must, notwithstanding Order 65, rule 9, be served on the defendant against whom the judgment or order sought to be enforced was given or made.

(3) A writ of specific delivery, and a writ of delivery to recover any goods or their assessed value, may include provision for enforcing the payment of any money adjudged or ordered to be paid by the judgment or order which is to be enforced by the writ.

(4) A judgment or order for the payment of the assessed value of any goods may be enforced by the same means as any other judgment or order for the payment of money.

Amendments—SI 1978/579.

"alternative of paying the assessed value" (r 4(1))—The alternative forms of judgment give rise to rather different regimes for enforcement. In particular, if the judgment gives the defendant the option of paying the assessed value of the goods, the writ of delivery cannot issue until the value

PART III

has been assessed by the court and the order cannot be enforced by committal. If under such a judgment it is desired to issue a writ of specific delivery, an application may be made by summons served on the defendant, and the court may so order. If that order includes an order under r 5(3), requiring the defendant to deliver up the goods (ie without the option), that order would be enforceable by committal even though the original judgment was not. However, r 4(2)(*b*) itself requires no more than an order that the judgment may be enforced by a writ of specific delivery.

"writ of delivery" (r 4(1)(*a*), (2)(*a*))—See **"alternative of paying the assessed value"** above and Ord 46.

"order of committal" (r 4(1)(*b*))—See rr 5–8 and Ord 52.

"writ of sequestration" (r 4(1)(*c*), (2)(*c*))—See rr 5–8 and Ord 46, r 5.

Forms—Writ of specific delivery: No 64; writ of delivery of goods or assessed value: No 65.

* For rr 5–7, see Civil Procedure Rules 1998, Sch 1.

8 Court may order act to be done at expense of disobedient party (Ord 45, r 8)

If an order of mandamus, a mandatory order, an injunction or a judgment or order for the specific performance of a contract is not complied with, then, without prejudice to its powers under section 39 of the Act and its powers to punish the disobedient party for contempt, the Court may direct that the act required to be done may, so far as practicable, be done by the party by whom the order or judgment was obtained or some other person appointed by the Court, at the cost of the disobedient party, and upon the act being done the expenses incurred may be ascertained in such a manner as the Court may direct and execution may issue against the disobedient party for the amount to be ascertained and for costs.

Amendments—SI 1982/1111.

Scope of provision—Rather than coerce the person ordered to do an act into doing it himself, the court may, if it is practicable to do so, authorise it to be done by the party who obtained the order (or someone else) at the contemnor's expense. If the act is not one which requires his personal attention and a fund is available from which the expense can be met, it will be preferable to proceed under this rule. Although the rule gives powers additional to, not in substitution for, those of committal and sequestration, if the object of the order can be achieved under this rule the court will be reluctant also to commit, save in the case of blatant, contumelious contempt. In cases where large sums are at stake, the rule may be used as an adjunct to sequestration.

Undertakings—This rule does not apply in the case of a breach of an undertaking, but the court may be prepared to exercise its inherent powers to similar effect (*Mortimer v Wilson* (1885) 33 WR 927). It may be prudent to apply in the alternative for an order in the terms of the undertaking, which order could be enforced subsequently under this rule if it is not complied with.

Execution of documents—A similar but specific remedy is available, where a person has been ordered to execute a document but neglects or refuses to do so or cannot be found, under Supreme Court Act 1981, s 39.

9 Execution by or against person not being a party (Ord 45, r 9)

(1) Any person, not being a party to a cause or matter, who obtains any order or in whose favour any order is made, shall be entitled to enforce obedience to the order by the same process as if he were a party.

(2) Any person, not being a party to a cause or matter, against whom obedience to any judgment or order may be enforced, shall be liable to the same process for enforcing obedience to the judgment or order as if he were a party.

10 Conditional judgment: waiver (Ord 45, r 10)

A party entitled under any judgment or order to any relief subject to the fulfilment of any condition who fails to fulfil that condition is deemed to have abandoned the benefit of the judgment or order, and, unless the Court otherwise directs, any other person interested may take any proceedings which either are warranted by the judgment or order or might have been taken if the judgment or order had not been given or made.

11 Matters occurring after judgment: stay of execution etc (Ord 45, r 11)

Without prejudice to Order 47, rule 1, a party against whom a judgment has been given or an order made may apply to the Court for a stay of execution of the judgment or order or other relief on the ground of matters which have occurred since the date of the judgment or order, and the Court may by order grant such relief, and on such terms, as it thinks just.

Scope of provision—This rule gives the court extremely wide powers to control the execution of a judgment or order if some occurrence *since* it was given or made makes that appropriate. The rule is not confined to cases of inability to pay, nor indeed to money judgments.

"Order 47, rule 1"—Ord 47, r 1 enables the court to stay execution of a money judgment against the debtor's goods by reason of inability to pay (whenever arising) or in other special circumstances.

12 Forms of writs (Ord 45, r 12)

(1) A writ of fieri facias must be in such of the Forms Nos 53 to 63 in Appendix A as is appropriate in the particular case.

(2) A writ of delivery must be in Form No 64 or 65 in Appendix A, whichever is appropriate.

(3) A writ of possession must be in Form No 66 or 66A in Appendix A, whichever is appropriate.

(4) A writ of sequestration must be in Form No 67 in Appendix A.

Amendments—SI 1970/944.

****

ORDER 46
WRIT OF EXECUTION: GENERAL

1 Definition (Ord 46, r 1)

In this Order, unless the context otherwise requires, "writ of execution" includes a writ of fieri facias, a writ of possession, a writ of delivery, a writ of sequestration and any further writ in aid of any of the aforementioned writs.

"writ in aid"—The only writ in aid likely to be encountered in family proceedings is the writ of restitution (see **Restitution** under Ord 45, r 3).

2 When leave to issue any writ of execution is necessary (Ord 46, r 2)

(1) A writ of execution to enforce a judgment or order may not issue without the leave of the Court in the following cases, that is to say –

(*a*) where six years or more have elapsed since the date of the judgment or order;

(*b*) where any change has taken place, whether by death or otherwise, in the parties entitled or liable to execution under the judgment or order;

(*c*) where the judgment or order is against the assets of a deceased person coming to the hands of his executors or administrators after the date of the judgment or order, and it is sought to issue execution against such assets;

(*d*) where under the judgment or order any person is entitled to relief subject to the fulfilment of any condition which it is alleged has been fulfilled;

(*e*) where any goods sought to be seized under a writ of execution are in the hands of a receiver appointed by the Court or a sequestrator.

(2) Paragraph (1) is without prejudice to section 2 of the Reserve and Auxiliary Forces (Protection of Civil Interests) Act 1951, or any other enactment or rule by virtue of which a person is required to obtain the leave of the Court for the issue of a writ of execution or to proceed to execution on or otherwise to the enforcement of a judgment or order.

(3) Where the Court grants leave, whether under this rule or otherwise, for the issue of a writ of execution and the writ is not issued within one year after the date of the order granting such leave, the order shall cease to have effect, without prejudice, however, to the making of a fresh order.

Defined terms—"writ of execution": r 1.

Insolvency of debtor—In family proceedings, leave is not needed merely because a bankruptcy order has been made against the debtor.

"six years or more have elapsed" (r 2(1)(*a*))—The delay should be explained in the affidavit. The court may be reluctant to allow a stale judgment or order to be enforced and will not do so if the debtor is prejudiced by the delay.

"any change ... in the parties" (r 2(1)(*b*))—The alternative is to apply to change the party under Ord 15, r 7. It is not thought that following an order under that rule leave would also be required under this rule. An order under Ord 15, r 7 would still be needed before other enforcement proceedings were taken following a (presumably abortive) writ of execution issued with leave under this rule.

"assets of a deceased person" (r 2(1)(*c*))—Where r 2(1)(*c*) applies, a summons to the personal representatives will always be required (*Re Shephard* (1890) 43 Ch D 131).

Other cases where leave is required (r 2(2))—See the note under CCR Ord 26, r 5.

"within one year" (r 2(3))—The limitation on the time within which the writ of execution must be issued does not apply only to cases where leave is required by virtue of this rule but to all cases where leave is required.

3 Leave required for issue of writ in aid of other writ (Ord 46, r 3)

A writ of execution in aid of any other writ of execution shall not issue without the leave of the Court.

Defined terms—"writ of execution": r 1.

Writ in aid—In family proceedings it is unlikely that any writ in aid will be encountered other than the writ of restitution (see **Restitution** under Ord 45, r 3 and **Warrant of Restitution** under CCR Ord 26, r 17).

4 Application for leave to issue writ (Ord 46, r 4)

(1) An application for leave to issue a writ of execution may be made ex parte unless the Court directs it to be made by summons.

(2) Such an application must be supported by an affidavit –

(*a*) identifying the judgment or order to which the application relates and, if the judgment or order is for the payment of money, stating the amount originally due thereunder and the amount due thereunder at the date of application;

(*b*) stating, where the case falls within rule 2(1)(*a*), the reasons for the delay in enforcing the judgment or order;

(*c*) stating, where the case falls within rule 2(1)(*b*), the change which has taken place in the parties entitled or liable to execution since the date of the judgment order;

(*d*) stating, where the case falls within rule 2(1)(*c*) or (*d*), that a demand to satisfy the judgment or order was made on the person liable to satisfy it and that he refused or failed to do so;

(*e*) giving such other information as necessary to satisfy the Court that the applicant is entitled to proceed to execution on the judgment or order in question and that the person against whom it is sought to issue execution is liable to execution on it.

(3) The Court hearing such application may grant leave in accordance with the application or may order that any issue or question, a decision on which is necessary to determine the rights of the parties, be tried in any manner in which any question of fact or law arising in an action may be tried and, in either case, may impose such terms as to costs or otherwise as it thinks just.

Defined terms—"writ of execution": r 1.

Scope of provision—This rule gives the procedure for the application for leave. The application may be made ex parte on affidavit (and so may be contained in the affidavit required by FPR 1991, r 7.1(1)), but the district judge may require a summons to issue. In a case where a summons will obviously be required, time will be saved by making the application by summons (supported by the affidavit) in the first instance. The procedure specified by this rule applies to all cases where leave is needed to issue a writ of execution, not only those specified by Ord 46, except that the writ of sequestration is dealt with by r 5.

"a demand to satisfy" (r 4(2)(*d*))—Where it is sought to enforce against the assets of a deceased debtor or where the creditor has to satisfy some condition before enforcing, demand must be made of the personal representatives or the debtor, as the case may be, before application is made under this rule.

5 Application for leave to issue writ of sequestration (Ord 46, r 5)

(1) Notwithstanding anything in rules 2 and 4, an application for leave to issue a writ of sequestration must be made to a Judge by motion.

(2) Subject to paragraph (3) the notice of motion, stating the grounds of the application and accompanied by a copy of the affidavit in support of the

PART III

application, must be served personally on the person against whose property it is sought to issue the writ.

(3) Without prejudice to its powers under Order 65, rule 4, the Court may dispense with service of the notice of motion under this rule if it thinks it just to do so.

(4) The Judge hearing an application for leave to issue a writ of sequestration may sit in private in any case in which, if the application were for an order of committal, he would be entitled to do so by virtue of Order 52, rule 6 but, except in such a case, the applicant shall be heard in open court.

Sequestration—Sequestration is a process responding to contempt of court. In general terms, all the considerations which apply to committal apply to sequestration (see Ord 45, rr 5–7 and below), save that the restrictions imposed on the court's power to commit for non-compliance with a money judgment by the Debtors Acts 1869 and 1878 do not apply. It is an expensive process and, in family proceedings, leave is unlikely to be given unless the contemnor's assets are considerable; leave is also unlikely to be given if the contempt can appropriately be met by a fine, or if the judgment or order can readily be enforced by execution against goods, garnishee proceedings or the like.

Sequestration is available to enforce a restraining order or an order requiring an act to be done ("a positive order"), provided, in the latter case, that the time for doing the act is stated and has passed (see Ord 45, r 5(1)). An order to pay money (including a periodical payments order) is a positive order and, in family proceedings, will often state the time for payment. If it does not, a further order may be sought under Ord 45, r 6; however, an application for such a further order may be refused if its sole object is to found an application under this rule, unless it is shown that the debtor is wilfully neglecting or refusing to pay.

Subject to the court's power to dispense with service, which is rarely exercised, particularly in the case of a positive order, the order (bearing an appropriate "penal" notice) must have been personally served on the contemnor before the date specified so that he has had the opportunity to comply with it (see Ord 45, r 7).

Dispensing with service (r 5(3))—In view of the draconian nature of the remedy, the court exercises this power only in cases of extreme urgency (ie where it appears that the assets to be sequestrated are about to be removed from the reach of the proposed sequestrators or are being dissipated). If personal service is impracticable, the court prefers to order substituted service under Ord 65, r 4. If service is dispensed with, ie if the order giving leave is made ex parte, the order may be made subject to terms which provide some protection for the defendant (eg an undertaking as to damages), and the contemnor is entitled to have the matter reconsidered.

"sit in private ... by virtue of Order 52, rule 6" (r 5(4))—The type of case to which Ord 52, r 6 applies which is most likely to be encountered in family proceedings is the case where the order which it is sought to enforce was made in proceedings relating to children.

Effect of writ of sequestration—The writ requires the four sequestrators named to take possession of the contemnor's land and collect in his other property and hold them until further order. It does not itself automatically vest the property in them but gives them authority to demand and receive it (*Bucknell v Bucknell* [1969] 1 WLR 1204, [1969] 2 All ER 998). A mortgagee under a mortgage given after issue of the writ is not affected by it unless he had notice of the sequestration when the mortgage was given (*Ward v Booth* (1872) LR 14 Eq 195). The writ should be registered as a land charge (Land Charges Act 1972, s 6).

Application of property—The court may authorise the sale of sequestered property and payment out of the proceeds of sale (as well as out of any ready money received) of the costs and expenses of the sequestration and the judgment debt and costs due to the plaintiff. In *Mir v Mir* [1992] 1 All ER 765, a father had, in breach of an order, removed the child abroad. Sequestrators were appointed who were to use the former matrimonial home to raise funds to finance the mother's application in the foreign country for the return of the child.

Discharge—The contemnor may, on purging his contempt, apply for the sequestration to be discharged. The order, if made, will require the sequestrators to pass their final accounts, authorise payment of their outstanding costs and expenses and discharge them from liability on their paying the balance in their hands to the contemnor.

Form—Writ of sequestration: No 67.

6 Issue of writ of execution (Ord 46, r 6)

(1) Issue of a writ of execution takes place on its being sealed by an officer of the appropriate office.

(2) Before such a writ is issued a praecipe for its issue must be filed.

(3) The praecipe must be signed by or on behalf of the solicitor of the person entitled to execution or, if that person is acting in person, by him.

(4) No such writ shall be sealed unless at the time of the tender thereof for sealing –

(*a*) the person tendering it produces –

(i) the judgment or order on which the writ is to issue, or an office copy thereof,

(ii) where the writ may not issue without the leave of the Court, the order granting such leave or evidence of the granting of it,

(iii) where judgment on failure to acknowledge service has been entered against a State, as defined in section 14 of the State Immunity Act 1978, evidence that the State has been served in accordance with Order 42, rule 3A and that the judgment has taken effect; and

(*b*) the officer authorised to seal it is satisfied that the period, if any, specified in the judgment or order for the payment of any money or the doing of any other act thereunder has expired.

(5) Every writ of execution shall bear the date of the day on which it is issued.

(6) In this rule "the appropriate office" means –

(*a*) where the cause or matter in which execution is to issue is proceeding in a District Registry, that Registry;

(*b*) where the cause or matter is proceeding in the Principal Registry of the Family Division, that Registry;

(*c*) where the cause or matter is an Admiralty cause or matter or a commercial action which is not proceeding in a District Registry, the Admiralty Land Commercial Registry;

(*ca*) where the cause or matter is proceeding in the Chancery Division, Chancery Chambers;

(*d*) in any other case, the Central Office.

Amendments—SI 1971/1269; SI 1980/629; SI 1987/1423; SI 1991/1329.

Defined terms—"writ of execution": r 1.

Forms—Writ of fieri facias: Nos 53–63, praecipe: PF No 86; writ of specific delivery: No 64, praecipe: PF No 90; writ of delivery of goods or value: No 65, praecipe: PF No 90; writ of possession: No 66, praecipe: PF No 88 or 89; writ of restitution: No 68; writ of sequestration: No 67, praecipe: PF No 87.

7 (*revoked*)

8 Duration and renewal of writ of execution (Ord 46, r 8)

(1) For the purpose of execution, a writ of execution is valid in the first instance for 12 months beginning with the date of its issue.

(2) Where a writ has not been wholly executed the Court may by order extend the validity of the writ from time to time for a period of 12 months at any time beginning with the day on which the order is made, if an application for extension is made to the Court before the day next following that on which the writ would otherwise expire or such later day, if any, as the Court may allow.

(3) Before a writ the validity of which has been extended under paragraph (2) is executed either the writ must be sealed with the seal of the office out of which it was issued showing the date on which the order extending its validity was made or the applicant for the order must serve a notice (in Form No 71 in Appendix A) sealed as aforesaid, on the sheriff to whom the writ is directed informing him of the making of the order and the date thereof.

(4) The priority of a writ, the validity of which has been extended under this rule, shall be determined by reference to the date on which it was originally delivered to the sheriff.

(5) The production of a writ of execution, or of such a notice as is mentioned in paragraph (3) purporting in either case can be sealed as mentioned in that paragraph, shall be evidence that the validity of that writ, or, as the case may be, of the writ referred to in that notice, has been extended under paragraph (2).

(6) If, during the validity of a writ of execution, an interpleader summons is issued in relation to an execution under that writ, the validity of the writ shall be extended until the expiry of 12 months from the conclusion of the interpleader proceedings.

Amendments—SI 1980/629; SI 1989/1307.

Defined terms—"writ of execution": r 1.

Order to extend validity (r 8(2))—The extension is for a period of 12 months. It commences with the date of the order (unlike in the county court) so that, strangely, there may be a gap in the writ's validity if the order is made after the original date of expiry.

Priority—If extended, and whenever extended, the writ retains its original priority date. Any other execution creditors will be prejudiced (or, conversely, would be advantaged if the applicant's writ were allowed to expire). Accordingly, the applicant must afford any such creditor the opportunity of making representations. If necessary, the district judge will direct that a summons be issued. Preservation of priority will be important if there are protracted interpleader proceedings (*Practice Direction of 1 December 1981*).

Procedure on application for extension—The application is made ex parte by affidavit, which should specify the reason for preferring not to proceed by issuing a fresh writ, give the reason why (if applicable) the application is made beyond the writ's expiry and indicate the steps taken to ascertain the views of any other execution creditors, exhibiting their responses.

9 Return of writ of execution (Ord 46, r 9)

(1) Any party at whose instance or against whom a writ of execution was issued may serve a notice on the sheriff to whom the writ was directed requiring him,

within such time as may be specified in the notice, to indorse on the writ a statement of the manner in which he has executed it and to send to that party a copy of the statement.

(2) If a sheriff on whom such notice is served fails to comply with it the party by whom it was served may apply to the Court for an order directing the sheriff to comply with the notice.

Amendments—SI 1988/1340.

Defined terms—"writ of execution": r 1.

ORDER 47
WRITS OF FIERI FACIAS

1 Power to stay execution by writ of fieri facias (Ord 47, r 1)

(1) Where a judgment is given or an order made for the payment by any person of money, and the Court is satisfied, on an application made at the time of the judgment or order, or at any time thereafter, by the judgment debtor or other party liable to execution –

(*a*) that there are special circumstances which render it inexpedient to enforce the judgment or order, or

(*b*) that the applicant is unable from any cause to pay the money,

then notwithstanding anything in rule 2 or 3, the Court may by order stay the execution of the judgment or order by writ of fieri facias either absolutely or for such period and subject to such conditions as the Court thinks fit.

(2) An application under this rule, if not made at the time the judgment is given or order made, must be made by summons and may be so made notwithstanding that the party liable to execution did not acknowledge service of the writ originating summons in the action or did not state in his acknowledgment of service that he intended to apply for a stay of execution under this rule pursuant to Order 13, rule 8.

(3) An application made by summons must be supported by an affidavit made by or on behalf of the applicant stating the grounds of the application and the evidence necessary to substantiate them and, in particular, where such application is made on the grounds of the applicant's inability to pay, disclosing his income, the nature and value of any property of his and the amount of any other liabilities of his.

(4) The summons and a copy of the supporting affidavit must, not less than 4 clear days before the return day, be served on the party entitled to enforce the judgment or order.

(5) An order staying execution under this rule may be varied or revoked by a subsequent order.

Amendments—SI 1979/1716.

Scope of provision—This rule enables the court to stay execution of a judgment or order against the debtor's goods; it refers (as does the whole of this Order) to execution against goods only.

Procedure on application for stay—The application may be made at any hearing at which the judgment or order is given or made. It may also be made subsequently by summons, which must be supported by an affidavit containing the information described in r 1(3).

"special circumstances" (r 1(1)(*a*))—Special circumstances do not include the fact of a pending appeal, as an application for a stay in those circumstances would be made under the rule governing the appeal (see FPR 1991, r 8.1(6) and CPR 1998, r 52.7). It may include a pending application to set aside the judgment or order or, in the case of arrears under a periodical payments order, an application to vary the order which was lodged after the issue of the execution.

"unable from any cause to pay" (r 1(1)(*b*))—In family proceedings, except in the case of an order for costs, the court takes the debtor's ability to pay into account in making the order and, therefore, an application on this ground seems unlikely to succeed in the absence of an unexpected change in circumstances. However, if there has been such a change and if the proceedings concern a "qualifying periodical maintenance order" within the meaning of Maintenance Enforcement Act 1991, s 1, the court may, as well as suspending the execution, make a "means of payment order" (s 1(4)(*a*)) or an attachment of earnings order (s 1(4)(*b*)).

Effect of order—The order stays execution against goods only. The High Court does not usually, except on a judgment summons under Debtors Act 1869, s 5 (see FPR 1991, r 7.4(9)) or where an order has been made for a lump sum payable by instalments (see Matrimonial Causes Act 1973, s 31(2)(*d*)), make an order staying the judgment or order generally on terms of instalment payments. However, other enforcement remedies are available only in the court's discretion, and it seems likely that that discretion would be influenced by the same factors which justify stay of execution under this rule.

2 Two or more writs of fieri facias (Ord 47, r 2)

(1) A party entitled to enforce a judgment or order by writ of fieri facias may issue two or more such writs, directed to the sheriffs of different counties, at either the same time or different times, to enforce that judgment or order, but no more shall be levied under all those writs together than is authorised to be levied under one of them.

(2) Where a party issues two or more writs of fieri facias directed to the sheriffs of different counties to enforce the same judgment or order he must inform each sheriff of the issue of the other writ or writs.

3 Separate writs to enforce payment of costs etc (Ord 47, r 3)

(1) Where only the payment of money, together with costs to be taxed, is adjudged or ordered, then, if when the money becomes payable under the judgment or order the costs have not been taxed, the party entitled to enforce that judgment or order may issue a fieri facias to enforce payment of the sum (other than for costs) adjudged or ordered and, not less than 8 days after the issue of that writ, he may issue a second writ to enforce payment of the taxed costs.

(2) A party entitled to enforce a judgment or order for the delivery of possession of any property (other than money) may, if he so elects, issue a separate writ of fieri facias to enforce payment of any damages or costs awarded to him by that judgment or order.

4 No expenses of execution in certain cases (Ord 47, r 4)

Where a judgment or order is for less than £600 and does not entitle the plaintiff to costs against the person against whom the writ of fieri facias to enforce the judgment or order is issued, the writ may not authorise the sheriff to whom it is directed to levy any fees, poundage or other costs of execution.

Amendments—SI 1970/671; SI 1974/1360; SI 1977/960; SI 1981/1734.

Scope of provision—This rule prevents the recovery of costs of execution where the judgment or order is for less than £600 and does not carry with it the costs of obtaining it. This rule is intended to encourage the creditor to use county court execution in small cases. There is a potential injustice to the creditor in family proceedings, to whom this facility has not been available since County Courts Act 1984, s 105 was repealed on 1 July 1991. There will, however, be few cases where an order for so small an amount, without costs, is made in High Court family proceedings.

5 Writ of fieri facias de bonis ecclesiasticis etc (Ord 47, r 5)

(1) Where it appears upon the return of any writ of fieri facias that the person against whom the writ was issued has no goods or chattels in the county of the sheriffs to whom the writ was directed but that he is the incumbent of a benefice named in the return, then, after the writ and return have been filed, the party by whom the writ of fieri facias was issued may issue a writ of fieri facias de bonis ecclesiasticis or a writ of sequestrari de bonis ecclesiasticis directed to the bishop of the diocese within which that benefice is.

(2) Any such writ must be delivered to the bishop to be executed by him.

(3) Only such fees for the execution of any such writ shall be taken by or allowed to the bishop or any diocesan officer as are for the time being authorised by or under any enactment, including any measure of the General Synod.

Amendments—SI 1982/1111.

6 Order for sale otherwise than by auction (Ord 47, r 6)

(1) An order of the Court under section 145 of the Bankruptcy Act 1883, that a sale under an execution may be made otherwise than by public auction may be made on the application of the person at whose instance the writ of execution under which the sale is to be made was issued or the person against whom that writ was issued (in this rule referred to as "the judgment debtor") or the sheriff to whom it was issued.

(2) Such an application must be made by summons and the summons must contain a short statement of the grounds of the application.

(3) Where the applicant for an order under this rule is not the sheriff, the sheriff must, on the demand of the applicant, send to the applicant a list containing the name and address of every person at whose instance any other writ of execution against the goods of the judgment debtor was issued and delivered to the sheriff (in this rule referred to as "the sheriff's list"); and where the sheriff is the applicant, he must prepare such a list.

(4) Not less than 4 clear days before the return day the applicant must serve the summons on each of the other persons by whom the application might have been made and on every person named in the sheriff's list.

(5) Service of the summons on a person named in the sheriff's list is notice to him for the purpose of section 12 of the Bankruptcy Act 1890 (which provides that the Court shall not consider an application for leave to sell privately goods taken in execution until notice directed by rules of Court has been given to any other execution creditor).

(6) The applicant must produce the sheriff's list to the Court on the hearing of the application.

(7) Every person on whom the summons was served may attend and be heard on the hearing of the application.

"section 145 of the Bankruptcy Act 1883" (r 6(1))—The sale of goods seized in an execution for more than £20 must be by public auction, unless the court orders otherwise.

Applicant (r 6(1))—The application may be made by either party or by the sheriff.

Procedure on application—The application is by summons which must be served on any party who is not the applicant, on the sheriff if he is not the applicant and on any other known execution creditor.

Private sale—See the note under CCR Ord 26, r 15.

ORDER 48
EXAMINATION OF JUDGMENT DEBTOR ETC

1 Order for examination of judgment debtor (Ord 48, r 1)

(1) Where a person has obtained a judgment or order for the payment by some other person hereinafter referred to as "the judgment debtor" of money, the Court may, on an application made ex parte by the person entitled to enforce the judgment or order, order the judgment debtor or, if the judgment debtor is a body corporate, an officer thereof, to attend before such Master, district judge or nominated officer as the Court may appoint and be orally examined on the questions –

(*a*) whether any and, if so, what debts are owing to the judgment debtor, and
(*b*) whether the judgment debtor has any and, if so, what other property or means of satisfying the judgment or order;

and the Court may also order the judgment debtor or officer to produce any books or documents in the possession of the judgment debtor relevant to the questions aforesaid at the time and place appointed for the examination.

In this paragraph "district judge" includes the district judge of a district registry or county court, and where the Court appoints such a district judge without specifying him personally, the examination may, if he thinks fit, be conducted on his behalf by a nominated officer of that registry or county court.

(2) An order under this rule must be served personally on the judgment debtor and on any officer of a body corporate ordered to attend for examination.

(3) Any difficulty arising in the course of an examination under this rule before a nominated officer, including any dispute with respect to the obligation of the person being examined to answer any question put to him, may be referred to the senior Master or Practice Master (or, in the case of an examination at the principal registry of the Family Division, a district registry or county court, a district judge of that registry, district registry or county court respectively) and he may determine it or give such directions for determining it as he thinks fit.

(4) In this rule "nominated officer" in relation to an examination which is to take place at the Central Office, the principal registry of the Family Division, a district registry or a county court means such of the officers of that Office, registry or county court as may be nominated for the purposes of this rule by the senior Master, the senior district judge of the Family Division or the district judge of that district registry or county court respectively.

Amendments—SI 1967/829; SI 1973/1384; SI 1998/1898.

Procedure on application—The application is made ex parte by affidavit. The order must be personally served on the judgment debtor. The debtor need not be in the jurisdiction (*United Bank of Finland v Lelakis* (1996) 13 May, CA). Conduct money must be tendered or the order will not be enforced by committal (*Protector Endowment Co v Whitlam* (1877) 36 LT 467). A solicitor's undertaking to meet his reasonable costs is sufficient (*United Bank of Finland v Lelakis* (1996) 11

June, Langley J). An order adjourning the examination to a new date must also be personally served (*Beeston Shipping Ltd v Babanaft International SA, The Eastern Venture* [1985] 1 All ER 923). If the order is made, it will provide where and by whom the examination is to be conducted – no doubt the examination will, by analogy with FPR, r 7.1(5)(*a*), normally take place at the divorce county court nearest to the debtor's residence or place of business.

Procedure on examination—The examination is intended to be a rigorous cross-examination. The debtor must answer all questions fairly pertinent and properly asked and give all necessary particulars to enable the judgment creditor to recover (*Republic of Costa Rica v Strousberg* (1880) 16 Ch D 8). Any doubt whether a question should be answered will be determined by the direction of the district judge. Refusal to answer is punishable as contempt.

Other powers—If the proceedings concern a "qualifying periodical maintenance order" within the meaning of Maintenance Enforcement Act 1991, s 1, the court may of its own motion make a "means of payment order" (s 1(4)(*a*)) or an attachment of earnings order (s 1(4)(*b*)). These powers may not be exercised by a "nominated officer".

Costs—The order for the examination usually provides that the costs of obtaining the order and of the examination itself be in the discretion of the district judge at the court where the examination is conducted. If costs are allowed they are usually assessed summarily. No costs will be allowed if the examination does not yield any useful information.

Forms—Affidavit: PF No 98; order: PF No 99.

2 Examination of party liable to satisfy other judgment (Ord 48, r 2)

Where any difficulty arises in or in connection with the enforcement of any judgment or order, other than such a judgment or order as is mentioned in rule 1, the Court may make an order under that rule for the attendance of the party liable to satisfy the judgment or order and for his examination on such questions as may be specified in the order, and that rule shall apply accordingly with the necessary modifications.

3 Examiner to make record of debtor's statement (Ord 48, r 3)

The officer conducting the examination shall take down, or cause to be taken down, in writing the statement made by the judgment debtor or other person at the examination, read it to him and ask him to sign it; and if he refuses the officer shall sign the statement.

ORDER 49
GARNISHEE PROCEEDINGS

1 Attachment of debt due to judgment debtor (Ord 49, r 1)

(1) Where a person (in this Order referred to as "the judgment creditor") has obtained a judgment or order for the payment by some other person (in this Order referred to as "the judgment debtor") of a sum of money amounting in value to at least £50, not being a judgment or order for the payment of money into court, and any other person within the jurisdiction (in this Order referred to as "the garnishee") is indebted to the judgment debtor, the Court may, subject to the provisions of this Order and of any enactment, order the garnishee to pay the judgment creditor the amount of any debt due or accruing due to the judgment debtor from the garnishee, or as much thereof as is sufficient to satisfy that judgment or order and the costs of the garnishee proceedings.

(2) An order under this rule shall in the first instance be an order to show cause, specifying the time and place for further consideration of the matter, and in the meantime attaching such debt as is mentioned in paragraph (1) or so much thereof as may be specified in the order, to answer the judgment or order mentioned in that paragraph and the costs of the garnishee proceedings.

(3) Among the conditions mentioned in section 40 of the Supreme Court Act 1981 (which enables any sum standing to the credit of a person in certain types of account to be attached notwithstanding that certain conditions applicable to the account in question have not been satisfied) there shall be included any condition that a receipt for money deposited in the account must be produced before any money is withdrawn.

(4) An order under this rule shall not require a payment which would reduce below £1 the amount standing in the name of the judgment debtor in an account with a building society or a credit union.

Amendments—SI 1981/1734.

"is indebted" (r 1(1))—See the note under CCR Ord 30, r 1.

"the court may ... order" (r 1(1))—The court has a discretion whether to make the order nisi, and may decline to do so where, for example, the judgment debt is so small that the costs would be disproportionately burdensome (see **Court's discretion to make order** under CCR Ord 30, r 7.).

"in the first instance" (r 1(2))—See the note under CCR Ord 30, r 1.

Indebtedness which is subject to conditions (r 1(3))—If a liability is conditional, there may be no debt if the condition is not satisfied. In the case of balances held for the debtor by banks, building societies and the like, this difficulty is removed by Supreme Court Act 1981, s 40, which provides that requirements for notice, personal application and production of a passbook are to be disregarded and, when read with r 1(3), that any condition requiring production of a receipt must also be disregarded.

The Crown—This procedure is not available against the Crown as garnishee. An equivalent procedure is provided by Crown Proceedings Act 1947, s 27 and Ord 77, r 16. This restriction includes the National Savings Bank and, although Supreme Court Act 1981, s 139(2) enables the Lord Chancellor to make an order removing the restriction, no such order has been made.

2 Application for order (Ord 49, r 2)

An application for an order under rule 1 must be made ex parte supported by an affidavit –

(*a*) stating the name and last known address of the judgment debtor,

(*b*) identifying the judgment or order to be enforced and stating the amount of such judgment or order and the amount remaining unpaid under it at the time of the application,

(*c*) stating that to the best of the information or belief of the deponent the garnishee (naming him) is within the jurisdiction and is indebted to the judgment debtor and stating the sources of the deponent's information or the grounds for his belief, and,

(*d*) stating, where the garnishee is a deposit-taking institution having more than one place of business, the name and address of the branch at which the judgment debtor's account is believed to be held and the number of that account or, if it be the case, that all or part of this information is not known to the deponent.

Amendments—SI 1976/337; SI 1981/1734.

Defined terms—"deposit-taking institution": Supreme Court Act 1981, s 40(6); "garnishee", "judgment debtor": r 1.

"amount of such judgment ... remaining unpaid" (r 2(*b*))—If the order requires payment by a stated date then the garnishee order will not be made before that date. A garnishee order is analogous to execution against goods and will not be made where such execution would not issue (*White, Son & Pill v Stennings* [1911] 2 KB 418).

Form—Application: PF No100 (this practice form will need minor adaptation if the order to be enforced is a periodical payments order).

3 Service and effect of order to show cause (Ord 49, r 3)

(1) Unless the Court otherwise directs, an order under rule 1 to show cause must be served –

(*a*) on the garnishee personally, at least 15 days before the day appointed thereby for the further consideration of the matter, and

(*b*) on the judgment debtor, at least 7 days after the order has been served on the garnishee and at least 7 days before the day appointed for the further consideration of the matter.

(2) Such an order shall bind in the hands of the garnishee as from the service of the order on him any debt specified in the order or so much thereof as may be so specified.

Amendments—SI 1981/1734.

Defined terms—"garnishee", "judgment creditor", "judgment debtor": r 1.

Personal service on the garnishee (r 3(1)(*a*))—In the case of a corporate body, service must be effected at the registered office, but in the case of a deposit-taking institution it will be helpful (and will reduce the risk of the bank inadvertently making a payment to the debtor) also to send a copy to the branch identified in the affidavit.

Effect of order nisi—See the note under CCR Ord 30, r 4. See also r 6.

Form—Order nisi: No 72.

4 No appearance or dispute of liability by garnishee (Ord 49, r 4)

(1) Where on the further consideration of the matter the garnishee does not attend or does not dispute the debt due or claimed to be due from him to the judgment debtor, the Court may make an order absolute under rule 1 against the garnishee.

(2) An order absolute under rule 1 against the garnishee may be enforced in the same manner as any other order for the payment of money.

Amendments—SI 1981/1734.

Defined terms—"garnishee", "judgment debtor": r 1.

Court's discretion to make order (r 4(1))—See the note under CCR Ord 30, r 7.

Garnishee's expenses—Supreme Court Act 1981, s 40A authorises a deposit-taking institution to deduct from the account a sum (currently £55) in respect of its expenses, even if the amount recovered under the order is thereby reduced.

Form—Order absolute: No 73 or 74 (depending on whether the garnishee owes the judgment debtor more or less than the judgment debt).

PART III

5 Dispute of liability by garnishee (Ord 49, r 5)

Where on the further consideration of the matter the garnishee disputes liability to pay the debt due or claimed to be due from him to the judgment debtor, the Court may summarily determine the question at issue or order that any question necessary for determining the liability of the garnishee be tried in any manner in which any question or issue in an action may be tried, without, if it orders trial before a Master, the need for any consent by the parties.

Defined terms—"garnishee", "judgment debtor": r 1.

"question at issue"—See the note under CCR Ord 30, r 9. See also r 6.

6 Claims of third persons (Ord 49, r 6)

(1) If in garnishee proceedings it is brought to the notice of the Court that some other person than the judgment debtor is or claims to be entitled to the debt sought to be attached or has or claims to have a charge or lien upon it, the Court may order that person to attend before the Court and state the nature of his claim with particulars thereof.

(2) After hearing any person who attends before the Court in compliance with an order under paragraph (1) the Court may summarily determine the question at issue between the claimants or make such other order as it thinks just, including an order that any question or issue necessary for determining the validity of the claim of such other person as is mentioned in paragraph (1) be tried in such manner as is mentioned in rule 5.

Defined terms—"judgment debtor": r 1.

Scope of provision—This rule makes it clear that the power to decide issues arising in garnishee proceedings includes the power to determine third party rights. A claim to have a charge or lien over the garnished debt comes within the rule, as does a claim that the debtor is not entitled to the debt personally but as a trustee (*Roberts v Death* (1881) 8 QBD 319).

7 (*revoked*)

8 Discharge of garnishee (Ord 49, r 8)

Any payment made by a garnishee in compliance with an order absolute under this Order, and any execution levied against him in pursuance of such an order, shall be a valid discharge of his liability to the judgment debtor to the extent of the amount paid or levied notwithstanding that the garnishee proceedings are subsequently set aside or the judgment or order from which they arose reversed.

Defined terms—"garnishee", "judgment debtor": r 1.

Scope of provision—This rule provides that, to the extent that the garnishee has made payment under the order absolute (not the order nisi), he is discharged from his former liability to the judgment debtor.

9 Money in Court (Ord 49, r 9)

(1) Where money is standing to the credit of the judgment debtor in Court, the judgment creditor shall not be entitled to take garnishee proceedings in respect of that money but may apply to the Court by summons for an order that the money or

so much thereof as is sufficient to satisfy the judgment or order sought to be enforced and the costs of the application be paid to the judgment creditor.

(2) On issuing a summons under this rule the applicant must produce the summons at the office of the Accountant General and leave a copy at that office, and the money to which the application relates shall not be paid out of Court until after the determination of the application.

If the application is dismissed, the applicant must give notice of that fact to the Accountant General.

(3) Unless the Court otherwise directs, the summons must be served on the judgment debtor at least 7 days before the day named therein for the hearing of it.

(4) Subject to Order 75, rule 24, the Court hearing an application under this rule may make such order with respect to the money in Court as it thinks just.

Defined terms—"judgment creditor", "judgment debtor": r 1.

Scope of provision—The court cannot itself be the subject of garnishee proceedings. Accordingly, this rule provides a procedure which applies where the court is holding money to which the judgment debtor is entitled.

10 Costs (Ord 49, r 10)

The costs of any application for an order under rule 1 or 9, and of any proceedings arising therefrom or incidental thereto, shall, unless the Court otherwise directs, be retained by the judgment creditor out of the money recovered by him under the order and in priority to the judgment debt.

Defined terms—"judgment creditor": r 1.

Scope of provision—The judgment debt is reduced by the net amount received under the garnishee proceedings after deducting the costs of those proceedings, unless the court otherwise directs. Such a direction may be given, for example, following the trial of an issue.

Amount of costs—Ord 62, App 3, Pt III (as it was immediately before 26 April 1999) fixes the costs at *either* £148.50 including the court fee *or*, if the amount recovered is less than £150, half of the amount recovered together with the court fee. In either case, £16.25 is added if an affidavit is required to prove service. However, the court may direct otherwise, ie by assessing summarily or directing detailed assessment.

ORDER 50
CHARGING ORDERS

1 Order imposing a charge on a beneficial interest (Ord 50, r 1)

(1) The power to make a charging order under section 1 of the Charging Orders Act 1979 (referred to in this Order as "the Act") shall be exercisable by the Court.

(2) An application by a judgment creditor for a charging order in respect of a judgment debtor's beneficial interest may be made ex parte, and any order made on such an application shall in the first instance be an order, made in Form No 75 in Appendix A, to show cause, specifying the time and place for further consideration of the matter and imposing the charge in any event until that time.

(3) The application shall be supported by an affidavit –

(*a*) identifying the judgment or order to be enforced and stating the amount unpaid at the date of the application:

(*b*) stating the name of the judgment debtor and of any creditor of his whom the applicant can identify;

(*c*) giving full particulars of the subject matter of the intended charge, including, in the case of securities other than securities in Court, the full title of the securities, their amount and the name in which they stand and, in the case of funds in Court, the number of the account; and

(*d*) verifying that the interest to be charged is owned beneficially by the judgment debtor.

(4) Unless the Court otherwise directs, an affidavit for the purposes of this rule may contain statements of information or belief with the sources and grounds thereof.

(5) An application may be made for a single charging order in respect of more than one judgment or order against the debtor.

Amendments—SI 1980/629.

Defined terms—"charging order": Charging Orders Act 1979, s 1(3); "creditor", "debtor": COA 1979, s 1(1).

"debtor's beneficial interest" (r 1(2))—See **"debtor's beneficial ownership"** under CCR Ord 31, r 1.

"any order made" (r 1(2))—See **"a sufficient case"** under CCR Ord 31, r 1.

"an order ... to show cause" (r 1(2))—See **Charging order nisi** under CCR Ord 31, r 1.

Form—Charging order nisi: No 75.

2 Service of notice of order to show cause (Ord 50, r 2)

(1) On the making of an order to show cause, notice of the order shall, unless the Court otherwise directs, be served as follows –

(*a*) a copy of the order, together with a copy of the affidavit in support, shall be served on the judgment debtor;

(*b*) where the order relates to securities other than securities in Court, copies of the order shall also be served

(i) in the case of government stock for which the Bank of England keeps the Register, on the Bank of England;

(ii) in the case of government stock to which (i) does not apply, on the keeper of the register;

(iii) in the case of government stock of any body incorporated within England and Wales, on that body, or, where the register is kept by the Bank of England, on the Bank of England;

(iv) in the case of stock of any body incorporated outside England and Wales or of any state or territory outside the United Kingdom, being stock registered in a register kept in England and Wales, on the keeper of the register;

(v) in the case of units of any unit trust in respect of which a register of the unit holders is kept in England and Wales, on the keeper of the register;

(*c*) where the order relates to a fund in Court, a copy of the order shall be served on the Accountant General at the Court Funds Office; and

(*d*) where the order relates to an interest under a trust, copies of the order shall be served on such of the trustees as the Court may direct.

(2) Without prejudice to the provisions of paragraph (1), the Court may, on making the order to show cause, direct the service of copies of the order, and of the affidavit in support, on any other creditor of the judgment debtor or on any other interested person as may be appropriate in the circumstances.

(3) Documents to be served under this rule must be served at least seven days before the time appointed for the further consideration of the matter.

Amendments—SI 1980/629.

Defined terms—"debtor": Charging Orders Act 1979, s 1(1); "government stock", "stock", "unit trust": COA 1979, s 6(1).

Other creditors (r 2(2))—The district judge will usually direct service on all known creditors (see Charging Orders Act 1979, s 1(5)(*b*)), although service on prior chargees appears not to be necessary for their protection on the basis that they cannot be prejudiced by the making of the order.

"interested person" (r 2(2))—Even though it does not appear on the title, the debtor's spouse may have some beneficial interest in the matrimonial home and/or a right to occupy it. Where the debtor's home is the property to be charged, his or her spouse should therefore be identified. Similarly, if the debtor is known to have a cohabitee, he or she may have an interest and should be identified. A direction will be given under this rule that any such person identified be served (see *Harman v Glencross* [1986] Fam 81, [1986] 2 FLR 241).

3 Order made on further considerations (Ord 50, r 3)

(1) On the further consideration of the matter the Court shall either make the order absolute, with or without modifications, or discharge it.

(2) Where the order is made absolute, it shall be made in Form No 76 in Appendix A, and where it is discharged, the provisions of rule 7, regarding the service of copies of the order of discharge, shall apply.

Amendments—SI 1980/629.

Order absolute (r 3(1))—The charge is effective from the day the order nisi was made (*Haley v Barry* (1868) 3 Ch App 452).

"with or without modifications" (r 3(1))—As there is but one charging order, it cannot when made absolute be modified to extend to property which it did not charge as an order nisi.

Discharge of order (r 3(1))—See the note under CCR Ord 31, r 2.

Adjournment—Any adjournment should be to a fixed date as a general adjournment will leave the charge, in the order nisi form, in place indefinitely. It is usual when adjourning to direct that the order nisi continue in force.

Conditions—Charging Orders Act 1979, s 3(1) enables the order to be made subject to conditions.

Other powers—See the note under CCR Ord 31, r 2.

Costs—Ord 62, App 3, Pt III (as it was immediately before 26 April 1999) fixes the costs at £159 including the court fee. £16.25 is added if an affidavit is required to prove service and the court may also allow search and registration fees. However, the court may direct otherwise, ie by assessing summarily or directing detailed assessment.

Form—Charging order absolute: No 76.

4 Order imposing a charge on an interest held by a trustee (Ord 50, r 4)

(1) Save as provided by this rule, the provisions of rules 1, 2 and 3 shall apply to an order charging an interest held by a trustee as they apply to an order charging the judgment debtor's beneficial interest.

(2) Instead of verifying the judgment debtor's beneficial ownership of the interest to be charged, the affidavit required by rule 1(3) shall state the ground on which the application is based and shall verify the material facts.

(3) On making the order to show cause, the Court shall give directions for copies of the order, and of the affidavit in support, to be served on such of the trustees and beneficiaries, if any, as may be appropriate.

(4) Rules 5, 6 and 7 shall apply to an order charging an interest held by a trustee as they apply to an order charging the judgment debtor's beneficial interest, except that, where the order is made under sub-section (ii) or (iii) of section 2 (1)(*b*) of the Act references in those rules to "the judgment debtor" shall be references to the trustee.

(5) Forms No 75 and 76 in Appendix A shall be modified so as to indicate that the interest to be charged is held by the debtor as trustee or, as the case may be, that it is held by a trustee (to be named in the order) on trust for the debtor beneficially.

Amendments—SI 1980/629.

Defined terms—"debtor": Charging Orders Act 1979, s 1(1).

Trustee's interest—The three cases when this rule may apply are those set out in Charging Orders Act 1979, s 2(1)(*b*). Section 2(1)(*b*)(i) is most unlikely to apply in family proceedings; s 2(1)(*b*)(ii) and (iii) apply where the debtor is (or the debtors are) the sole beneficiary (or beneficiaries) under the trust, and enable the legal interest in the hands of the trustee as well as the beneficial interest in the hands of the debtor(s) to be charged.

5 Effect of order in relation to securities out of Court (Ord 50, r 5)

(1) No disposition by the judgment debtor of his interest in any securities to which an order to show cause relates made after the making of that order shall, so long as that order remains in force, be valid as against the judgment creditor.

(2) Until such order is discharged or made absolute, the Bank of England (or other person or body served in accordance with rule 2(1)(*b*), shall not permit any transfer of any of the securities specified in the order, or pay any dividend, interest or redemption payment in relation thereto, except with the authority of the Court, and, if it does so, shall be liable to pay the judgment creditor the value of the securities transferred or, as the case may be, the amount of the payment made or, if that value or amount is more than sufficient to satisfy the judgment or order to which such order relates, so much thereof as is sufficient to satisfy it.

(3) If the Court makes the order absolute, a copy of the order, including a stop notice as provided in Form No 76 in Appendix A, shall be served on the Bank of England, or on such other person or body specified in rule 2(1)(*b*) as may be appropriate and, save as provided in rule 7(5), rules 11 to 14 shall apply to such a notice as they apply to a stop notice made and served under rule 11.

(4) This rule does not apply to orders in respect of securities in Court.

Amendments—SI 1980/629.

Defined terms—"creditor", "debtor": Charging Orders Act 1979, s 1(1); "stop notice": COA 1979, s 5(1).

6 Effect of order in relation to funds in Court (Ord 50, r 6)

(1) Where an order to show cause has been made in relation to funds in Court (including securities in Court) and a copy thereof has been served on the Accountant General in accordance with rule 2, no disposition by the judgment debtor of any interest to which the order relates, made after the making of that order, shall, so long as the order remains in force, be valid as against the judgment creditor.

(2) If the Court makes the order absolute, a copy of the order shall be served on the Accountant General at the Court Funds Office.

Amendments—SI 1980/629.

Defined terms—"creditor", "debtor": Charging Orders Act 1979, s 1(1).

7 Discharge etc of charging order (Ord 50, r 7)

(1) Subject to paragraph (2), on the application of the judgment debtor or any other person interested in the subject matter of the charge, the Court may, at any time, whether before or after the order is made absolute, discharge or vary the order on such terms (if any) as to costs or otherwise as it thinks just.

(2) Where an application is made for the discharge of a charging order in respect of the judgment debtor's land on the ground that the judgment debt has been satisfied, the applicant shall state in his application, and the Court shall specify in its order, the title number of the land in the case of registered land, and the entry number of any relevant land charge in the case of unregistered land.

(3) Notice of an application for the discharge or variation of the order shall be served on such interested parties as the Court may direct.

(4) Where an order is made for the discharge or variation of a charging order in respect of funds in Court, a copy thereof shall be served on the Accountant General at the Court Funds Office.

(5) Where an order is made for the discharge or variation of a charging order in respect of securities other than securities in Court, a copy thereof shall be served on the Bank of England or on such other person or body specified in rule 2(1)(*b*) as may be appropriate, and the service thereof shall discharge, or, as the case may be, vary, any stop notice in respect of such securities which may be in force pursuant to the original order.

Amendments—SI 1980/629.

Defined terms—"charging order": Charging Orders Act 1979, s 1(3); "debtor": COA 1979, s 1(1).

Discharge—If the judgment debt has been paid, an order discharging the charging order is not essential since the charging order takes effect as an equitable charge and so may be discharged by a receipt in discharge; however, an application under this rule may provide a convenient way to proceed if there is difficulty in agreeing a redemption figure or if the judgment creditor is unco-operative. The order may direct the removal of any relevant entries at the Land Charges Registry or Land Registry (Charging Orders Act 1979, s 3(6)).

"on such terms ... as it thinks just" (r 7(1))—It is not only in the case of payment that discharge may be ordered. If, for example, the debtor wishes to move house, transferring the charge or part of it to the new property, the power to discharge on terms that alternative security be provided would enable such a move to take place.

8 (*revoked*)

9 Jurisdiction of Master etc to grant injunction (Ord 50, r 9)

A Master and the Admiralty Registrar and a district judge of the Family Division shall have power to grant an injunction if, and only so far as, it is ancillary or incidental to an order under rule 1, 3 or 4 and an application for an injunction under this rule may be joined with the application for the order under rule 1, 3 or 4 to which it relates.

Amendments—SI 1980/629; SI 1982/1111.

Injunction—An injunction may be sought when it is feared that the debtor is about to effect a disposal which would defeat the intended charge. Cogent evidence of the risk should be provided. An undertaking as to damages will usually be required.

Application—The application may be included in the application for the charging order nisi or may be made subsequently. A similar procedure to that on applications under Matrimonial Causes Act 1973, s 37 may be employed.

9A Enforcement of charging order by sale (Ord 50, r 9A)

General Note—This rule requires separate proceedings to be taken to seek an order for sale. Such a claim will be governed by CPR 1998. See those rules, Sch 1, RSC Ord 50, r 9A and the annotations thereto.

10 Funds in court: stop order (Ord 50, r 10)

(1) The Court, on the application of any person –

(*a*) who has a mortgage or charge on the interest of any person in funds in Court, or

(*b*) to whom that interest has been assigned, or

(*c*) who is a judgment creditor of the person entitled to that interest,

may make an order prohibiting the transfer, sale, delivery out, payment or other dealing with such funds, or any part thereof, or the income thereon, without notice to the applicant.

(2) An application for an order under this rule must be made by summons in the cause or matter relating to the funds in Court, or, if there is no such cause or matter, by originating summons.

(3) The summons must be served on every person whose interest may be affected by the order applied for and on the Accountant-General but shall not be served on any other person.

(4) Without prejudice to the Court's powers and discretion as to costs, the Court may order the applicant for an order under this rule to pay the costs of any party to the cause or matter relating to the funds in question, or of any person interested in those funds, occasioned by the application.

Defined terms—"creditor": Charging Orders Act 1979, s 1(1).

Scope of provision—This rule makes provision in relation to stop orders (within the meaning of Charging Orders Act 1979, s 5(1)) affecting funds in court.

Stop orders: general—Stop orders have the effect of preventing dealings in funds in court and the various securities over which charging orders may be obtained until further order. The purpose is to give the applicant the opportunity to make whatever application he considers necessary to protect his interests (whether under a charging order or otherwise).

Form—Stop order: No 79.

11 Securities not in court: stop notice (Ord 50, r 11)

(1) Any person claiming to be beneficially entitled to an interest in any securities of the kinds set out in section 2(2)(*b*) of the Act, other than securities in Court, who wishes to be notified of any proposed transfer or payment of those securities may avail himself of the provisions of this rule.

(2) A person claiming to be so entitled must file in the Chancery Chambers or in a District Registry –

(*a*) an affidavit identifying the securities in question and describing his interest therein by reference to the document under which it arises, and

(*b*) a notice in Form No 80 in Appendix A (a stop notice) signed by the deponent to the affidavit; and annexed to it, addressed to the Bank of England or, as the case may be, the body, state, territory or unit trust concerned,

and must serve an office copy of the affidavit, and a copy of the notice sealed with the seal of Chancery Chambers or the District Registry, on the Bank or other person or body, as provided in rule 2(1)(*b*).

(3) There must be indorsed on the affidavit filed under this rule a note stating the address to which any such notice as is referred to in rule 12 is to be sent and, subject to paragraph (4), that address shall for the purposes of that rule be the address for service of the person on whose behalf the affidavit is filed.

(4) A person on whose behalf an affidavit under this rule is filed may change his address for service for the purpose of rule 12 by serving on the Bank of England, or other person or body, a notice to that effect, and, as from the date of service of such a notice the address stated therein shall for the purpose of that rule be the address for service of that person.

Amendments—SI 1980/629; SI 1982/1111.

Defined terms—"stop notice": Charging Orders Act 1979, s 5(1).

Scope of provision—This rule specifies the procedure to issue a stop notice, which has a broadly similar effect and purpose as a stop order (see **Stop orders: general** under r 10), but in relation to securities *not* in court.

Forms—Affidavit and stop notice: No 80.

12 Effect of stop notice (Ord 50, r 12)

Where a stop notice has been served in accordance with rule 11, then, so long as the stop notice is in force, the Bank of England or other person or body on which it is served shall not register a transfer of the securities or take any other steps restrained by the stop notice until 14 days after sending notice thereof, by ordinary first class post, to the person on whose behalf the stop notice was filed, but shall not by reason only of that notice refuse to register a transfer, or to take any other step, after the expiry of that period.

Amendments—SI 1980/629.

13 Amendment of stop notice (Ord 50, r 13)

If any securities are incorrectly described in a stop notice which has been filed and of which a sealed copy has been served in accordance with rule 11, an amended stop notice may be filed and served in accordance with the same procedure and shall take effect as a stop notice on the day on which the sealed copy of the amended notice is served.

Amendments—SI 1980/629.

Defined terms—"stop notice": Charging Orders Act 1979, s 5(1).

14 Withdrawal etc of stop notice (Ord 50, r 14)

(1) The person on whose behalf a stop notice was filed may withdraw it by serving a request for its withdrawal on the Bank of England or other person or body on whom the notice was served.

(2) Such request must be signed by the person on whose behalf the notice was filed and his signature must be witnessed by a practising solicitor.

(3) The Court, on the application of any person claiming to be beneficially entitled to an interest in the securities to which a stop notice relates, may by order discharge the notice.

(4) An application for an order under paragraph (3) must be made in the Chancery Division by originating summons, and the summons must be served on the person on whose behalf a stop notice was filed.

The summons shall be in Form No 10 in Appendix A.

Amendments—SI 1979/1716; SI 1980/629.

Defined terms—"stop notice": Charging Orders Act 1979, s 5(1).

15 Order prohibiting transfer etc of securities (Ord 50, r 15)

(1) The Court, on the application of any person claiming to be beneficially entitled to an interest in any securities of the kinds set out in section 2(2)(*b*) of the Act may by order prohibit the Bank of England or other person or body concerned from registering any transfer of the securities or taking any other step to which section 5(5) of the Act applies.

The order shall specify the securities to which the prohibition relates, the name in which they stand and the steps which may not be taken, and shall state whether the prohibition applies to the securities only or to the dividends or interest as well.

(2) An application for an order under this rule must be made by motion or summons in the Chancery Division.

An originating summons under this rule shall be in Form No 10 in Appendix A.

(3) The Court, on the application of any person claiming to be entitled to an interest in any securities to which an order under this rule relates may vary or discharge the order on such terms (if any) as to costs or otherwise as it thinks fit.

Amendments—SI 1979/1716; SI 1980/629.

Forms—Stop notice: No 81.

ORDER 51
RECEIVERS: EQUITABLE EXECUTION

1 Appointment of receiver by way of equitable execution (Ord 51, r 1)

Where an application is made for the appointment of a receiver by way of equitable execution, the Court in determining whether it is just or convenient that the appointment should be made shall have regard to the amount claimed by the judgment creditor, to the amount likely to be obtained by the receiver and to the probable costs of his appointment and may direct an inquiry on any of these matters or any other matter before making the appointment.

Amendments—SI 1980/629.

"probable costs of his appointment"—In most cases, the receiver will have to provide security and, in all but the simplest, he will require ongoing remuneration. The cost is borne by the debtor in the event of successful execution, but is of course underwritten by the creditor.

2 Masters and district judges may appoint receiver etc (Ord 51, r 2)

A Master and the Admiralty Registrar and a district judge of the Family Division shall have power to make an order for the appointment of a receiver by way of equitable execution and to grant an injunction if, and only so far as, the injunction is ancillary or incidental to such an order.

Amendments—SI 1971/1269.

3 Application of rules as to appointment of receiver etc (Ord 51, r 3)

An application for the appointment of a receiver by way of equitable execution may be made in accordance with Order 30, rule 1, and rules 2 to 6 of that Order shall apply in relation to a receiver appointed by way of equitable execution as they apply in relation to a receiver appointed for any other purpose.

Scope of provision—This rule applies the provisions of RSC Ord 30 in the form in which they were immediately before 26 April 1999 as they applied to all receiverships.

"receiver by way of equitable execution"—A receiver by way of equitable execution is appointed to enable a judgment creditor to reach interests of the debtor which cannot be taken in execution by other process (*Levermore v Levermore* (1980) FLR 375, [1979] 1 WLR 1277). Often an injunction is made at the time the appointment is made in order to restrain the debtor from dealing with the assets in question. The appointment of a receiver is equitable relief granted because execution strictly so-called cannot be had. It will not be "just and convenient" to grant it (see Supreme Court Act 1981, s 37) when such execution is in fact available (*Re Shephard* (1890) Ch D 131).

There must be an asset to which the receivership is directed. Thus, a receiver cannot be appointed of the debtor's future salary (*Holmes v Millage* [1893] 1 QB 551), a disputed insurance claim (*Pearce v Johns* (1897) 41 Sol Jo 661), or his property generally (*Hamilton v Brogden* (1891) 35 Sol Jo 206); otherwise, the discretion is wide. For example, receivers may be appointed not only of the rents and profits of land vested in the debtor but of his undivided share under a trust for sale, his entitlement out of the estate of a deceased person, his interest under a trust (including a life interest), his entitlement under an annuity and the profits of his business.

Partnership share—Partnership Act 1890, s 23(2) enables the court to make a charging order in respect of the debtor's interest in a partnership and to appoint a receiver of profits and other money payable in respect of it.

Procedure on application—The application may be made by motion but will usually be made by summons to the district judge supported by the affidavit required by FPR 1991, r 7.1(1). It is usual to file a separate affidavit as to the fitness of the proposed receiver to act, sworn by some independent person who has at least five years' acquaintance of him. Any application for an injunction may be joined with the application for the appointment. An urgent application for an injunction may be made ex parte but it will be made only in temporary form, pending further consideration on the hearing of the summons—the usual undertaking as to damages may be required.

Security—Security is usually required for the receiver's due performance of his duties and, unless otherwise directed, it is provided in the form of a guarantee given by a bank or insurance company. The cost is initially borne by the creditor but, as part of the costs of the proceedings, will generally be recoverable together with the judgment debt under the receivership. Where the amounts involved are not large and the duration of the receivership will be short, a solicitor's undertaking may be offered. In a small case, the judgment creditor himself (or, presumably therefore, his solicitor) may be appointed receiver, and security may be dispensed with (*Fuggle v Bland* (1883) 11 QBD 711).

Remuneration—The receiver's remuneration, if any, is authorised by the court and is generally deducted from the proceeds of the receivership. If the proceeds are insufficient, the creditor may remain liable for the receiver's charges.

Service—The order is served on the receiver as well as all other parties.

Accounts—The receiver renders accounts to the parties from time to time in accordance with the order appointing him. If any objection is taken to the accounts, they must be lodged in court and the Master or district judge determines the issue.

Proceeds—The amounts received are paid into court and dealt with in accordance with the order.

Default of receiver—The court retains disciplinary powers over the receiver and may discharge and replace him.

Directions—The court may from time to time give directions at the receiver's request without formal application; it may, however, require a summons to be issued in appropriate circumstances.

Forms—Summons to appoint: No 82; summons combined with temporary injunction: No 83; order appointing receiver: No 84; receiver's security: Chancery Masters' PF 30.

ORDER 52
COMMITTAL

* Set out in Civil Procedure Rules 1998, Sch 1.

****

ORDER 55
APPEALS TO HIGH COURT FROM COURT, TRIBUNAL OR PERSON: GENERAL

1 Application (Ord 55, r 1)

(1) Subject to paragraphs (2), (3) and (4), this Order shall apply to every appeal which by or under any enactment lies to the High Court from any court, tribunal or person.

(2) This Order shall not apply to an appeal by case stated or to any appeal to which Order 73 applies.

(3) The following rules of this Order shall not apply to an appeal from a county court to a single judge under section 375 of the Insolvency Act 1986, but subject to the Insolvency Rules 1986, as amended, Order 59 shall, with the necessary modifications, apply to such an appeal as it applies to an appeal from a county court to the Court of Appeal.

(4) The following rules of this Order shall, in relation to an appeal to which this Order applies, have effect subject to any provision made in relation to that appeal by any other provision of these rules or by or under any enactment.

(5) In this Order references to a tribunal shall be construed as references to any tribunal constituted by or under any enactment other than any of the ordinary courts of law.

Amendments—SI 1968/1244; SI 1986/2001; SI 1989/1307.

Scope of provision—This order applies to any appeal to the High Court, but subject to any other provision in relation to such an appeal. Appeals to the High Court from family proceedings courts must be made in accordance with CA 1989, s 94 and FPR 1991, r 4.22. Therefore, where r 4.22 provides for a particular procedure to be followed, that procedure must be followed. Where there is provision within Ord 55, but not within r 4.22, then Ord 55 will apply. Rule 4.22 also governs appeals to a High Court judge from a district judge in relation to family proceedings. For other appeals to a High Court judge from a district judge see Ord 58. To determine whether an appeal from a district judge should be in accordance with FPR 1991, r 4.22 or Ord 58, see FPR 1991, r 4.1(2) and notes to FPR 1991, rr 4.22, 8.1. An appeal from an order (or the variation of an order) made under the (repealed) Guardianship of Minors Act 1971 should be by way of notice of motion under RSC Ord 55 and not pursuant to the provisions of CA 1989, s 94 or FPR 1991, r 4.22 (*B v B (Periodical Payments: Transitional Provisions)* [1995] 1 FLR 459).

2 Court to hear appeal (Ord 55, r 2)

Except where it is otherwise provided by these rules or by or under any enactment, an appeal to which this Order applies shall be assigned to the Queen's Bench Division and shall be heard and determined –

(*a*) where the decision of the High Court on the appeal is final, by a Divisional Court, and

(*b*) in any other case, by a single judge.

Amendments—SI 1977/1955.

Scope of provision—An appeal under the Domestic Proceedings and Magistrates' Courts Act 1978 or the Administration of Justice Act 1960 must be heard by a Divisional Court of the Family Division of the High Court (FPR 1991, rr 8.1, 8.2). An appeal made under CA 1989, s 94 is heard and determined by a single judge (FPR 1991, r 4.22(8)).

PART III

3 Bringing of appeal (Ord 55, r 3)

(1) An appeal to which this Order applies shall be by way of rehearing and must be brought by originating motion.

(2) Every notice of motion by which such an appeal is brought must state the grounds of the appeal and, if the appeal is against a judgment, order or other decision of a court, must state whether the appeal is against the whole or a part of that decision and, if against a part only, must specify the part.

(3) The bringing of such an appeal shall not operate as a stay of proceedings on the judgment, determination or other decision against which the appeal is brought unless the Court by which the appeal is to be heard or the court, tribunal or person by which or by whom the decision was given so orders.

Scope of provision—All appeals to which this order applies are by way of a rehearing unless any provision states otherwise. This does not mean that on an appeal to the High Court all the evidence will be recalled. The procedure is akin to an appeal to the Court of Appeal, that is to say an examination of the whole of the evidence and the course of the hearing (but see Ord 55, r 7 for the power of the court to receive further evidence). The appeal is in effect a rehearing on the documents.

Notice of appeal—Unless there is provision which states otherwise, every appeal brought in accordance with Ord 55 must be by way of a notice of motion. This rule does not apply to appeals to the High Court under CA 1989, s 94, which must be brought by a notice of appeal (FPR 1991, r 4.22(2)(*a*)). Appeals under the Domestic Proceedings and Magistrates' Courts Act 1978 and under Administration of Justice Act 1960, s 13 must be by notice of motion (FPR 1991, rr 8.2, 8.3).

Stay pending appeal—Under r 3(3) the bringing of an appeal does not operate as a stay of the proceedings or order unless the High Court orders a stay. Where the effect of the order which is the subject of the appeal is to move a child, a stay should be sought forthwith. The power of the court to make orders pending appeal under CA 1989, s 40 should be noted, but this does not give a magistrates' court power to stay the operation of an order pending appeal (*Re O (A Minor) (Care Order: Education: Procedure)* [1992] 2 FLR 7). A magistrates' court, unlike the High Court or a county court, has no power to stay the operation of its order pending appeal.

4 Service of notice of motion and entry of appeal (Ord 55, r 4)

(1) The persons to be served with notice of the motion by which an appeal to which this Order applies is brought are the following –

(*a*) if the appeal is against a judgment, order or other decision of a court, the registrar or clerk of the court and any party to the proceedings in which the decision was given who is directly affected by the appeal;

(*b*) if the appeal is against an order, determination, award or other decision of a tribunal, Minister of the Crown, government department or other person, the chairman of the tribunal, Minister, government department or person, as the case may be, and every party to the proceedings (other than the appellant) in which the decision appealed against was given.

(2) The notice must be served, and the appeal entered, within 28 days after the date of the judgment, order, determination or other decision against which the appeal is brought.

(3) In the case of an appeal against a judgment, order or decision of a court, the period specified in paragraph (2) shall be calculated from the date of the judgment or order or the date on which the decision was given.

(4) In the case of an appeal against an order, determination, award or other decision of a tribunal, Minister, government department or other person, the period

specified in paragraph (2) shall be calculated from the date on which notice of the decision, or, in a case where a statement of the reasons for a decision was given later than such notice, on which such a statement was given to the appellant by the person who made the decision or by a person authorised in that behalf to do so.

Amendments—SI 1982/1111.

Scope of provision—This rule applies only to appeals which are not made under CA 1989, as the procedure is determined by FPR 1991, r 4.22. The procedure for appeals under the Domestic Proceedings and Magistrates' Courts Act 1978 and under Administration of Justice Act 1960, s 13 must be in accordance with FPR 1991, rr 8.2, 8.3. Rule 4(2) does not apply to appeals under Administration of Justice Act 1960, s 13 (Ord 109, r 2(3)).

5 Date of hearing of appeal (Ord 55, r 5)

Unless the Court having jurisdiction to determine the appeal otherwise directs, an appeal to which this Order applies shall not be heard sooner than 21 days after service of notice of the motion by which the appeal is brought.

Uncontested appeals—An application to withdraw an appeal made pursuant to CA 1989, s 94, or to have such an appeal dismissed with consent, is subject to FPR 1991, r 4.22(7), which permits the application to be made to a district judge. This rule does not apply to appeals under Administration of Justice Act 1960, s 13 (Ord 109, r 2(3)).

6 Amendment of grounds of appeal, etc (Ord 55, r 6)

(1) The notice of the motion by which an appeal to which this Order applies is brought may be amended by the appellant, without leave, by supplementary notice served not less than 7 days before the day appointed for the hearing of the appeal, on each of the persons on whom the notice to be amended was served.

(2) Within 2 days after service of a supplementary notice under paragraph (1) the appellant must lodge two copies of the notice in the office in which the appeal is entered.

(3) Except with the leave of the Court hearing any such appeal, no grounds other than those stated in the notice of the motion by which the appeal is brought or any supplementary notice under paragraph (1) may be relied upon by the appellant at the hearing; but that Court may amend the grounds so stated or make any other order, on such terms as it thinks just, to ensure the determination on the merits of the real question in controversy between the parties.

(4) The foregoing provisions of this rule are without prejudice to the powers of the Court under Order 20.

Scope of provision—This rule permits an amendment to a notice of motion without leave. FPR 1991, r 4.22(7) provides that where in an appeal under CA 1989, s 94 the appellant seeks to amend his grounds of appeal he may apply to the district judge. This suggests that leave is required in s 94 appeals. There is no provision in r 4.22 for a supplementary notice.

"powers of the Court under Order 20" (r 6(4))—The powers, in particular that conferred by Ord 20, r 8, allow amendments for the purpose of determining the real controversy between the parties.

6A Interlocutory applications (Ord 55, r 6A)

(1) Unless the Court otherwise directs, any interlocutory application in proceedings to which this Order applies may be made to any Judge or a Master of the Queen's Bench Division or, as the case may be, any Judge or a district judge of

the Family Division, notwithstanding that the appeal has been brought by motion and is to be heard by a Divisional Court.

In this paragraph "interlocutory application" includes an application for the extension of time for the service of the notice of motion or the entry of the appeal or for the amendment of the notice of motion.

(2) In relation to an order made by a Master or district judge pursuant to paragraph (1), Order 58, rule 1 shall, where the appeal is to be heard by a Divisional Court, have effect as if a reference to that Court were substituted for the reference to a Judge in chambers.

(3) This rule is without prejudice to any statutory provision or rule of law restricting the making of an order against the Crown.

Amendments—Inserted by SI 1987/1423.

Scope of provision—The power to deal with interlocutory matters on an appeal to the High Court is also provided for in relation to appeals under CA 1989, s 94 by FPR 1991, r 4.22(7).

7 Powers of court hearing appeal (Ord 55, r 7)

(1) In addition to the power conferred by rule 6(3), the Court hearing an appeal to which this Order applies shall have the powers conferred by the following provisions of this rule.

(2) The Court shall have power to receive further evidence on questions of fact, and the evidence may be given in such manner as the Court may direct either by oral examination in court, by affidavit, by deposition taken before an examiner or in some other manner.

(3) The Court shall have power to draw any inferences of fact which might have been drawn in the proceedings out of which the appeal arose.

(4) It shall be the duty of the appellant to apply to the judge or other person presiding at the proceedings in which the decision appealed against was given for a signed copy of any note made by him of the proceedings and to furnish that copy for the use of the Court; and in default of production of such a note, or; if such note is incomplete, in addition to such note, the Court may hear and determine the appeal on any other evidence or statement of what occurred in those proceedings as appears to the Court to be sufficient.

Except where the Court otherwise directs, an affidavit or note by a person present at the proceedings shall not be used in evidence under this paragraph unless it was previously submitted to the person presiding at the proceedings for his comments.

(5) The Court may give any judgment or decision or make any order which ought to have been given or made by the court, tribunal or person and make such further or other order as the case may require or may remit the matter with the opinion of the Court for rehearing and determination by it or him.

(6) The Court may, in special circumstances, order that such security shall be given for the costs of the appeal as may be just.

(7) The Court shall not be bound to allow the appeal on the ground merely of misdirection, or of the improper admission or rejection of evidence, unless in the opinion of the Court substantial wrong or miscarriage has been thereby occasioned.

Amendments—SI 1968/1244.

Fresh evidence (r 7(2))—The court has power to receive fresh evidence on the hearing of an appeal. This provision is wider than the power of the Court of Appeal to admit fresh evidence (under CPR 1998, r 52.11(2)), but nevertheless is likely to apply only in two cases: firstly where the evidence was not available before the court below and is likely to have materially affected the court's decision, in other words evidence which might have made a difference to the decision which for some reason was not known of or not available (the magistrates' court has no power to review its own decision); secondly on a successful appeal the court may receive further evidence in order to determine the appropriate order (but see *Re W, Re A, Re B (Change of Name)* [1999] 2 FLR 930).

Notes of evidence (r 7(4))—The appellant must apply to the court from which the decision is being appealed for a copy of the notes of evidence. In the case of an appeal under CA 1989, s 94, the appellant must file and serve a copy of the notes of evidence on the parties to the appeal (FPR 1991, r 4.22(2)(*c*)). Where no notes are provided, the court may hear and determine the appeal on other evidence, but the case is liable to be remitted back for a rehearing if the High Court is unable to determine the matter without a proper record (see *Gray v Gray* [1987] 1 FLR 16). As it is common practice for district judges to have access to recording equipment, it may be prudent to ask if such equipment is being used.

Reasons for judgment—The rules for recording reasons in the magistrates' court are contained in Magistrates' Courts Rules 1981, rr 36–38. The clerk must provide a copy of a record of the reasons when asked, if satisfied that this is required for an appeal or possible appeal (r 37). The reasons should set out the matters which were in dispute and give an account of the reasoning (*Hutchinson v Hutchinson* (1981) FLR 167). The reasons should not be formulated to answer the appeal (*Faulkner v Faulkner* (1981) FLR 115). The reasons must be sufficient to enable the High Court to examine the decision (*Re M (A Minor)* (1981) Fam Law 58). See also **Notes of evidence and reasons** under CA 1989, s 94 for the duty of the justices' clerk to record the evidence and reasons.

Hopeless appeals—See notes to FPR 1991, r 8.1.

****

ORDER 58
APPEALS FROM MASTERS, REGISTRARS, REFEREES AND JUDGES

1 Appeals from certain decisions of masters etc to judge in chambers (Ord 58, r 1)

(1) Except as provided by rule 2, an appeal shall lie to a judge in chambers from any judgment, order or decision of a master, the Admiralty Registrar or a district judge of the Family Division.

(2) The appeal shall be brought by serving on every other party to the proceedings in which the judgment, order or decision was given or made a notice to attend before the judge on a day specified in the notice or on such other day as may be directed.

(3) Unless the Court otherwise orders, the notice must be issued within five days after the judgment, order or decision appealed against was given or made and must be served within five days after issue and an appeal to which this rule applies shall not be heard sooner than two clear days after such service.

(4) Except so far as the Court may otherwise direct, an appeal under this rule shall not operate as a stay of the proceedings in which the appeal is brought.

Amendments—SI 1971/1269; SI 1982/1111; SI 1987/1423.

Scope of provision—This rule applies to all decisions of a master, a district judge of the Family Division and, by virtue of r 3, any district judge in the High Court. It provides that an appeal shall be to a judge in chambers. In relation to appeals to which FPR 1991, r 4.22 applies (for which see r 4.1(2) and notes to r 4.22), the provisions of Ord 58 are modified. To determine the procedure on an appeal from the decision of a district judge of the High Court, the appellant must first determine whether the appeal is one to which FPR 1991, r 4.22 applies. If not, Ord 58 will apply without modification. If FPR 1991, r 4.22 does apply, the procedure set out there is applicable; Ord 58 will also apply, but subject to r 4.22. The time for an appeal is different under the two rules: 14 days under r 4.22; 5 days under Ord 58, r 1 (or 7 days under Ord 58, r 3). *Practice Direction of 10 March 2000* prescribes details for the filing of court bundles for such appeals.

Nature of appeal—An appeal is an actual rehearing, with the judge treating the matter as if it came to him for the first time, save that the appellant will open the appeal. The judge is entitled to give "weight it deserves to the previous decision" (*Evans v Bartlam* [1937] AC 473 at 478). An appeal from a district judge of the Principal Registry of the Family Division (who has an enlarged jurisdiction by virtue of C(AP)O 1991, art 19 to make care orders, akin to that of a county court judge) is in accordance with the principles of *G v G* [1985] FLR 894, [1985] 1 WLR 647; namely a consideration of whether the court below exercised its discretion properly in reaching its decision (*Re S (Appeal from Principal Registry: Procedure)* [1997] 2 FLR 856 and *Re W, Re A, Re B* [1999] 2 FLR 930).

****

3 Appeals from district judges (Ord 58, r 3)

(1) An appeal shall lie from any judgment, order or decision of a district judge in any cause or matter in any Division in the same circumstances and, except as provided by paragraph (2), subject to the same conditions as if the judgment, order or decision were given or made by a master or district judge in that cause or matter in that Division, and the provisions of these rules with respect to appeals shall apply accordingly.

(2) In relation to an appeal from a judgment, order or decision of a district judge, rule 1 shall have effect subject to the modification that for the reference therein to 5 days and the reference therein to 2 clear days there shall be substituted references to 7 days and 3 clear days respectively.

Amendments—SI 1987/1423.

Scope of provision—This rule equates all appeals from a district judge to those specifically dealt with in r 1, save that it provides a different time period in which the appeal must be made and served (but see **Scope of provision** under r 1).

****

6 Appeal from judge in chambers (Ord 58, r 6)

(1) Subject to section 18 of the Act and section 15(2) of the Administration of Justice Act 1960 (which restrict appeals) and to Order 53, rule 13, and without prejudice to section 13 of the said Act of 1960 (which provides for an appeal in cases of contempt of court), an appeal shall lie to the Court of Appeal from any judgment, order or decision of a judge in chambers.

Amendments—SI 1988/298.

"section 18 of the Act"—This refers to Supreme Court Act 1981, s 18.

****

ORDER 65
SERVICE OF DOCUMENTS

****

4 Substituted service (Ord 65, r 4)

(1) If, in the case of any document which by virtue of any provision of these rules is required to be served personally or is a document to which Order 10, rule 1, applies, it appears to the Court that it is impracticable for any reason to serve that document in the manner prescribed, the Court may make an order for substituted service of that document.

(2) An application for an order for substituted service may be made by an affidavit stating the facts on which the application is founded.

(3) Substituted service of a document, in relation to which an order is made under this rule, is effected by taking such steps as the Court may direct to bring the document to the notice of the person to be served.

Amendments—SI 1979/402.

****

ORDER 71
RECIPROCAL ENFORCEMENT OF JUDGMENTS AND ENFORCEMENT OF EUROPEAN COMMUNITY JUDGMENTS AND RECOMMENDATIONS ETC UNDER THE MERCHANT SHIPPING (LINER CONFERENCES) ACT 1982

****

13 Certified copy of High Court judgment (Ord 71, r 13)

(1) An application under section 10 of the Act of 1920 or section 10 of the Act of 1933 for a certified copy of a judgment entered in the High Court must be made ex parte on affidavit to a master or, in the case of a judgment given in the cause or matter proceeding in the Family Division, to a district judge of that Division.

(2) An affidavit by which an application under section 10 of the Act of 1920 is made must give particulars of the judgment, show that the judgment creditor wishes to secure the enforcement of the judgment in a part (stating which) of Her Majesty's dominions outside the United Kingdom to which Part II of that Act extends and state the name, trade or business and the usual or last known place of abode of the judgment creditor and the judgment debtor respectively, so far as known to the deponent.

(3) An affidavit by which an application under section 10 of the Act of 1933 is made must –

- (*a*) give particulars of the proceedings in which the judgment was obtained;
- (*b*) have annexed to it a copy of the writ originating summons or other process by which the proceedings were begun, the evidence of service thereof on the defendant, copies of the pleadings, if any, and a statement of the grounds on which the judgment was based;

(*c*) state whether the defendant did or did not object to the jurisdiction, and, if so, on what grounds;
(*d*) show that the judgment is not subject to any stay of execution;
(*e*) state the time for appealing has expired or, as the case may be, the date on which it will expire and in either case whether notice of appeal against the judgment has been entered; and
(*f*) state the rate at which the judgment carried interest.

(4) The certified copy of the judgment shall be an office copy sealed with the seal of the Supreme Court and indorsed with a certificate signed by a master or, where appropriate, a district judge certifying that the copy is a true copy of a judgment obtained in the High Court of England and that it is issued in accordance with section 10 of the Act of 1920 or section 10 of the Act of 1933, and the case may be.

(5) Where the application is made under section 10 of the Act of 1933 there shall also be issued a certificate (signed by a master or, where appropriate, a district judge and sealed with the seal of the Supreme Court) having annexed to it a copy of the writ originating summons or other process by which the proceedings were begun, and stating –

(*a*) the manner in which the writ, or such summons or other process was served on the defendant or that the defendant acknowledged service thereof;
(*b*) what objections, if any, were made to the jurisdiction,
(*c*) what pleadings, if any, were served,
(*d*) the grounds on which the judgment was based,
(*e*) that the time for appealing has expired or, as the case may be, the date on which it will expire,
(*f*) whether notice of appeal against the judgment has been entered, and
(*g*) such other particulars as it may be necessary to give to the court in the foreign country in which it is sought to obtain execution of the judgment,

and a certificate (signed and sealed as aforesaid) stating the rate at which the judgment carries interest.

Amendments—SI 1977/1955; SI 1979/1716; SI 1989/1307.

Scope of provision—This rule sets out the requirements to obtain a certified copy of a money judgment (other than a maintenance order) for the purpose of its enforcement in one of the countries to which the Administration of Justice Act 1920 or the Foreign Judgments (Reciprocal Enforcement) Act 1933 has been applied (see Procedural Guide 25, letters 'J' and 'K' in the Table).

****

25 Interpretation (Ord 71, r 25)

(1) In this Part of this Order –

"the Act of 1982" means the Civil Jurisdiction and Judgments Act 1982;
"Convention territory" means the territory or territories of any Contracting State, as defined by s 1(3) of the Act of 1982, to which the Brussels Conventions or the Lugano Convention as defined in s 1(1) of the Act of 1982 apply;
"judgment" is to be construed in accordance with the definition of "judgment" in s 50 of the Act of 1982;

"money provision" means a provision for the payment of one or more sums of money;

"non-money provision" means a provision for any relief or remedy not requiring payment of a sum of money;

"protective measures" means the protective measures referred to in Art 39 of Schedule 1 or of Schedule 3C to the Act of 1982.

(2) For the purposes of this Part of this Order domicile is to be determined in accordance with the provisions of ss 41 to 46 of the Act of 1982.

Amendments—Inserted by SI 1983/1181; amended by SI 1992/1907.

****

36 Enforcement of High Court judgments in other Contracting States (Ord 71, r 36)

(1) An application under section 12 of the Act of 1982 for a certified copy of a judgment entered in the High Court must be made ex parte on affidavit to the Court.

(2) An affidavit by which an application under section 12 of the Act of 1982 is made must –

(*a*) give particulars of the proceedings in which the judgment was obtained;

(*b*) have annexed to it a copy of the writ, originating summons or other process by which the proceedings were begun, the evidence of service thereof on the defendant, copies of the pleadings, if any, and a statement of the grounds on which the judgment was based together, where appropriate, with any document under which the applicant is entitled to legal aid or assistance by way of representation for the purposes of the proceedings;

(*c*) state whether the defendant did or did not object to the jurisdiction, and, if so, on what grounds;

(*d*) show that the judgment has been served in accordance with Ord 65, r 5 and is not subject to any stay of execution;

(*e*) state that the time for appealing has expired, or, as the case may be, the date on which it will expire and in either case whether notice of appeal against the judgment has been given; and

(*f*) state –

(i) whether the judgment provides for the payment of a sum or sums of money;

(ii) whether interest is recoverable on the judgment or part thereof and if such be the case, the rate of interest, the date from which interest is recoverable, and the date on which interest ceases to accrue.

(3) The certified copy of the judgment shall be an office copy sealed with the seal of the Supreme Court and there shall be issued with the copy of the judgment a certificate in Form 110, signed by one of the persons referred to in Order 1, rule 4(2) and sealed with the seal of the Supreme Court, having annexed to it a copy of the writ, originating summons or other process by which the proceedings were begun.

Amendments—Inserted by SI 1983/1181.

Scope of provision—This rule sets out the requirements to obtain a certified copy of a money judgment or other order (but not a maintenance order) for the purpose of its enforcement in one of

PART III

the European Union or European Free Trade Area countries (see Procedural Guide 25, letter 'M' in the Table).

37 Enforcement of United Kingdom judgments in other parts of the United Kingdom: money provisions (Ord 71, r 37)

(1) An application for registration in the High Court of a certificate in respect of any money provisions contained in a judgment given in another part of the United Kingdom to which section 18 of the Act of 1982 applies may be made by producing at the Central Office, within six months from the date of its issue, a certificate in the appropriate form prescribed under that Act together with a copy thereof certified by the applicant's solicitor to be a true copy.

(2) A certificate under paragraph (1) must be filed in the Central Office and the certified copy thereof, sealed by an officer of the office in which the certificate is filed, shall be returned to the applicant's solicitor.

(3) A certificate in respect of any money provisions contained in a judgment of the High Court to which section 18 of the Act of 1982 applies may be obtained by producing the form of certificate prescribed in Form 111 at the office in which the judgment is entered, together with an affidavit made by the party entitled to enforce the judgment –

(*a*) giving particulars of the judgment, stating the sum or aggregate of the sums (including any costs or expenses) payable and unsatisfied under the money provisions contained in the judgment, the rate of interest, if any, payable thereon and the date or time from which any such interest began to accrue;

(*b*) verifying that the time for appealing against the judgment has expired, or that any appeal brought has been finally disposed of and that enforcement of the judgment is not stayed or suspended; and

(*c*) stating to the best of the information or belief of the deponent the usual or last known address of the party entitled to enforce the judgment and of the party liable to execution on it.

Amendments—Inserted by SI 1983/1181.

Scope of provision—This rule sets out the requirements to obtain a certificate of a money provision in a judgment or other order (but not a maintenance order) for the purpose of its enforcement in Scotland or Northern Ireland.

38 Enforcement of United Kingdom judgments in other parts of the United Kingdom: non-money provisions (Ord 71, r 38)

(1) An application for registration in the High Court of a judgment which contains non-money provisions, being a judgment given in another part of the United Kingdom to which section 18 of the Act of 1982 applies, may be made ex parte, but the Court hearing the application may direct the issue of a summons to which paragraphs (2) and (3) of rule 2 shall apply.

(2) An application under paragraph (1) must be accompanied by a certified copy of the judgment issued under Schedule 7 to the Act of 1982 and the appropriate form prescribed for the purposes of paragraph 4(1)(*b*) of that Schedule.

(3) Rules 30 and 32 of this Order shall apply to judgments registered under Schedule 7 to the Act of 1982 as they apply to judgments registered under section 4 of that Act.

(4) Paragraphs (1) and (2) of rule 9 shall apply to applications to set aside registration of a judgment under Schedule 7 to the Act of 1982 as they apply to judgments registered under the Administration of Justice Act 1920 and the Foreign Judgments (Reciprocal Enforcements) Act 1933.

(5) A certified copy of a judgment of the High Court to which section 18 of the Act of 1982 applies and which contains any non-money provision may be obtained by an ex parte application on affidavit to the Court.

(6) The requirements in paragraph (3) of rule 37 shall apply with the necessary modifications to an affidavit made in an application under paragraph (5) of this rule.

(7) A certified copy of the judgment shall be an office copy sealed with the seal of the Supreme Court to which shall be annexed a certificate in Form 112.

Amendments—Inserted by SI 1983/1181; amended by SI 1984/1051.

Scope of provision—This rule sets out the requirements to obtain a certified copy of a judgment or other order containing a non-money provision for the purpose of enforcement of that provision in Scotland or Northern Ireland.

PART III

39 Register of United Kingdom judgments (Ord 71, r 39)

There shall be kept in the Central Office under the direction of the senior master a register of certificates in respect of judgments and of the judgments ordered to be registered in the Central Office under Schedule 6, or, as the case may be, Schedule 7 to the Act.

Amendments—Inserted by SI 1983/1181.

39A Authentic instruments and court settlements (Ord 71, r 39A)

Rules 27 to 35 inclusive (except rule 28(1)(*a*)(ii)) shall apply to:

(1) an authentic instrument to which either article 50 of Schedule 1 to the Act of 1982 or article 50 of Schedule 3C to that Act applies; and

(2) a settlement to which either article 51 of Schedule 1 to the Act of 1982 or article 51 of Schedule 3C to that Act applies,

as they apply to a judgment, subject to any necessary modifications.

Amendments—Inserted by SI 1993/2133.

Scope of provision—Authentic instruments and court settlements may be enforceable in EU and EFTA countries as judgments and orders are enforceable there. This rule applies, to such instruments and settlements, the same procedures for enforcement in the UK that apply to judgments and orders.

****

ORDER 80
DISABILITY

1 Interpretation (Ord 80, r 1)

In this Order –

"the Act" means the Mental Health Act 1983;

"patient" means a person who, by reason of mental disorder within the meaning of the Act, is incapable of managing and administering his property and affairs;

"person under disability" means a person who is an infant or a patient.

Amendments—SI 1983/1181.

Defined terms—"infant": Family Law Reform Act 1969, ss 1(2) and 12 (see below).

Scope of provision—Until 26 April 1999 this Order regulated the conduct of proceedings by and against a "person under disability" in the High Court. From that date it has been replaced by Civil Procedure Rules 1998, Pt 21 in regard to *civil proceedings* but continues to apply subject to the provisions of FPR 1991 and with the necessary modifications, to *family proceedings* in the High Court by virtue of FPR 1991, r 1.3. Most of its provisions are replaced by FPR 1991, Pt IX but there are circumstances in which reference must still be made to this Order; in the county courts, reference should be made to CCR Ord 10. Only the provisions that appear to apply in respect of family proceedings are reproduced below.

"infant"—An infant is defined by the Family Law Reform Act 1969 ss 1 and 12 as a person who is under the age of 18 – see generally note to FPR 1991, r 9.1. The term "minor" is adopted by RSC and "child" by CPR 1998, but there is no distinction.

"patient"—For a further explanation, see **"patients"** (and generally) under FPR 1991, r 9.1.

"mental disorder"—Defined by Mental Health Act 1983, s 1(3) as "mental illness, arrested or incomplete development of mind, psychopathic disorder and any other disorder or disability of mind"; see further under FPR 1991, r 9.1.

"person under disability"—Defined as an infant or a patient. It is possible for an infant also to be a patient, and this may be relevant if that condition will continue to subsist on ceasing to be an infant (eg in regard to the disposal of money awarded to the infant). Thus an infant who has severe learning disabilities will continue to be under disability even after attaining majority.

2 Person under disability must sue etc by next friend or guardian ad litem (Ord 80, r 2)

(1) …

(2) Subject to the provisions of these rules, anything which in the ordinary conduct of any proceedings is required or authorised by a provision of these rules to be done by a party to the proceedings shall or may, if the party is a person under disability, be done by his next friend or guardian ad litem.

(3) A next friend or guardian ad litem of a person under disability must act by a solicitor.

Defined terms—"person under disability": r 1.

"next friend", "guardian ad litem"—These terms are also used by FPR 1991 and relate respectively to the person bringing the proceedings and the person responding, but the term used in CPR 1998, in both cases, is litigation friend.

Powers of the next friend or guardian ad litem—The next friend or guardian ad litem may take any step in the proceedings that the party under disability could have taken (r 2(2)). There is no provision in FPR 1991 defining the authority of the next friend or guardian ad litem, but this rule (which corresponds to CCR Ord 10, r 12) may be relied on pursuant to FPR 1991, r 1.3. The next friend or guardian has no authority beyond the conduct of the proceedings.

Need for a solicitor—In the High Court, a person under disability must be represented by a solicitor (r 2(3)) in family proceedings; there is no similar requirement in the county court.

Personal liability of solicitor for costs—A solicitor who acts in any proceedings for or on behalf of a person under disability without a next friend or guardian ad litem will be held personally liable to pay any wasted costs of the proceedings incurred by the other party, assessed on the indemnity basis, even though he himself may not have been aware that the person for whom he has been acting is in fact an infant or a patient (*Yonge v Toynbee* [1910] 1 KB 215, CA). However, provided everyone has acted in good faith and there has been no manifest disadvantage to the party subsequently found to have been a patient at the relevant time it is likely that the court will regularise the position retrospectively (*Masterman-Lister v Brutton & Co and Jewell & Home Counties Dairies* [2002] EWCA Civ 1889, [2002] All ER (D) 297 (Dec)).

3 Appointment of next friend or guardian ad litem (Ord 80, r 3)

(1)–(3) …

(4) Where a person has been or is next friend or guardian ad litem of a person under disability in any proceedings, no other person shall be entitled to act as such friend or guardian, as the case may be, of the person under disability in those proceedings unless the Court makes an order appointing him such friend or guardian in substitution for the person previously acting in that capacity.

(5) Where, after any proceedings have been begun, a party to the proceedings becomes a patient, an application must be made to the Court for the appointment of a person to be next friend or guardian ad litem, as the case may be, of that party.

(6)–(8) …

Amendments—SI 1971/1269; SI 1979/1716; SI 1982/1111.

Defined terms—"person under disability": r 1.

Removal—If the court becomes aware of the person's unsuitability, it may remove him under RSC Ord 80, r 3(4) and substitute another person as next friend or guardian ad litem, but there is no express duty to monitor the situation.

Substitution—A substituted next friend or guardian ad litem, whether in the place of one who has died or who wishes to retire or who is removed for misconduct or for neglect or refusal to proceed or otherwise, must be appointed by court order. A next friend or guardian cannot retire without a court order appointing someone in his place. There are no equivalent provisions in FPR 1991 or the CCR, so reference must be made to this rule.

Supervening incapacity—This is a situation where the court may (and should) appoint a next friend or guardian ad litem. There is no provision in FPR 1991 or CCR, so RSC Ord 80, r 3(5) must be relied upon.

****

10 Compromise etc by person under disability (Ord 80, r 10)

(1) Where in any proceedings money is claimed by or on behalf of a person under disability, no settlement, compromise or payment and no acceptance of money paid into court, whenever entered into or made, shall so far as it relates to that person's claim be valid without the approval of the Court.

(2) (*revoked*)

Amendments—SI 1987/1423; SI 1988/298.

Defined terms—"person under disability": r 1.

Scope of provision—This provision ensures that compromises and settlements negotiated in any proceedings on behalf of a person under disability are approved by the court. It extends to any agreement as to costs where the recipient is under disability. Without this approval, the settlement, compromise or payment of any claim is wholly invalid and unenforceable, and is made entirely at the risk of the parties and their solicitors. It would be an abuse of the process of the court for the parties and their solicitors in any subsisting proceedings to make or act on any such settlement, compromise or payment without the court's approval. There is no similar provision in FPR 1991, Pt IX in regard to family proceedings, so reference must be made to this provision when in the High Court (or CCR Ord 10, r 10 in the county court), pursuant to FPR 1991, r 1.3.

Costs—Unless the court otherwise orders, the costs payable to a solicitor acting for a party under disability who has claimed or recovered money must be assessed and only those costs allowed on a detailed assessment should be paid (CPR 1998, r 48.5). This ensures that the plaintiff is not over-charged and that any settlement is not influenced by an attractive offer of costs.

Role of the Court of Protection—These provisions apply even where the proceedings are being conducted by the patient's receiver as next friend or guardian ad litem under the authority of the Court of Protection, but in that event the approval of the Court of Protection should also be obtained as a pre-requisite to the application to the court for approval.

11 Approval of settlement (Ord 80, r 11)

(1) Where, before proceedings in which a claim for money is made by or on behalf of a person under disability (whether alone or in conjunction with any other person) are begun, an agreement is reached for the settlement of the claim, and it is desired to obtain the Court's approval to the settlement, then, notwithstanding anything in Order 5, rule 2, the claim may be made in proceedings begun by originating summons and in the summons an application may also be made for –

(*a*) the approval of the Court to the settlement and such orders or directions as may be necessary to give effect to it or as may be necessary or expedient under rule 12, or

(*b*) alternatively, directions as to the further prosecution of the claim.

(2) ...

(3) Without prejudice to Order 7, rule 5, and Order 75, rule 36(1) an originating summons under this rule may be issued out of any district registry notwithstanding that the proceedings are assigned to the Chancery Division.

(4) An originating summons under this rule shall be in Form No 10 in Appendix A.

(5) In this rule "settlement" includes a compromise.

Amendments—SI 1979/1542; SI 1979/1716; SI 1986/632.

Defined terms—"person under disability": r 1.

Scope of provision—This provision enables a compromise or settlement reached before commencement of proceedings on behalf of a person under disability to be approved by the court. There is no equivalent provision in FPR 1991, Pt IX in regard to family proceedings, so reference must be made to this provision when in the High Court (or CCR Ord 10, r 10 in the county court), pursuant to FPR 1991, r 1.3. An ancillary relief settlement would in any event require approval of the court – see FPR 1991, r 2.61.

Costs—Any agreement as to costs should also be approved by the court, but formal assessment may be dispensed with thereby encouraging agreement by avoiding the need to pay a fee.

12 Control of money recovered by person under disability (Ord 80, r 12)

(1) Where in any proceedings –

(*a*) money is recovered by or on behalf of, or adjudged or ordered or agreed to be paid to, or for the benefit of, a person under disability, or

(*b*) money paid into court is accepted by or on behalf of a plaintiff who is a person under disability,

the money shall be dealt with in accordance with directions given by the Court under this rule and not otherwise.

(2) Directions given under this rule may provide that the money shall, as to the whole or any part thereof, be paid into the High Court and invested or otherwise dealt with there.

(3) Without prejudice to the foregoing provisions of this rule, directions given under this rule may include any general or special directions that the Court thinks fit to give and, in particular, directions as to how the money is to be applied or dealt with and as to any payment to be made, either directly or out of the amount paid into court to the plaintiff, or to the next friend in respect of moneys paid or expenses incurred for or on behalf or for the benefit of the person under disability or for his maintenance or otherwise for his benefit or to the plaintiff's solicitor in respect of costs.

(4) Where in pursuance of directions given under this rule money is paid into the High Court to be invested or otherwise dealt with there, the money (including any interest thereon) shall not be paid out, nor shall any securities in which the money is invested, or the dividends thereon, be sold, transferred or paid out of court, except in accordance with an order of the Court.

(5) …

Amendments—SI 1986/632.

Defined terms—"person under disability": r 1.

Scope of provision—This rule ensures that there is supervision of money awarded to or recovered by a person under disability. There is no similar provision in FPR 1991 so reliance must be placed on this rule pursuant to FPR 1991, r 1.3, unless the court exercises its additional powers (see notes below).

Control of money—This subject generally is beyond the scope of this volume, but the procedures adopted in regard to the award of damages may apply and would be initiated by this rule (or CCR Ord 10, r 11 in the county court). The court will control funds held on behalf of a minor but in the case of a patient reference must usually be made to the Court of Protection pursuant to Mental Health Act 1983, Pt VII. If there is a registered attorney under an enduring power it may be appropriate to release the fund to such attorney. The powers of the next friend or guardian ad litem are restricted to the conduct of the proceedings and do not extend to dealing with the financial affairs of the infant or patient (*Leather v Kirby* [1965] 3 All ER 927).

Additional powers: infant—The court will control funds held on behalf of an infant but under Ord 80, r 13 (see below) may appoint the Official Solicitor as guardian of that child's estate.

Additional powers: patient—Where a party in whose favour an order is made for financial provision is incapable by reason of mental disorder of managing and administering his property and affairs, the court has power under Matrimonial Causes Act 1973, s 40 to direct that any maintenance or lump sum be paid (or property be transferred) to a person "having charge of that party". This leaves considerable discretion to the court as to the future management of the financial provision. The person who was the next friend or guardian ad litem may of course have a sufficient continuing interest (eg as a parent) for the court to involve that person in the application of the funds in court on behalf of the minor or patient under r 11 (see above). If the incapacitated party in whose favour an order is made already has income or assets which need to be administered, or if substantial provision is to be made, it is best that the Court of Protection be left to administer the entire affairs. Where, however, there is a registered enduring power of attorney it would normally be appropriate for the attorney who is managing the affairs to receive all payments or property pursuant to the financial provision order.

Need for Court of Protection involvement—See the note under CPR 1998, r 21.11.

13 Appointment of guardian of child's estate (Ord 80, r 13)

(1) In any of the circumstances described in paragraph (2)(*a*) to (*e*) the Court may appoint the Official Solicitor to be a guardian of the estate of a child provided that –

(*a*) the appointment is to subsist only until the child reaches the age of eighteen, and

(*b*) the consent of the persons with parental responsibility for the child (within the meaning of section 3 of the Children Act 1989) –

(i) has been signified to the Court, or

(ii) in the opinion of the Court, cannot be obtained or may be dispensed with.

(2) The circumstances referred to in paragraph (1) are –

(*a*) where money is paid into court on behalf of the child in accordance with directions given under rule 12(2) (control of money recovered by person under disability);

(*b*)–(*d*) ...

(*e*) where such an appointment seems desirable to the Court.

Amendments—Inserted by SI 1991/2671.

Official Solicitor—The expression means the Official Solicitor to the Supreme Court provided for by Supreme Court Act 1981, s 90. The Official Solicitor may be contacted at 81 Chancery Lane, London WC2A 1DD Tel: 0171 911 7127, Fax 0171 911 7105.

****

16 Service of certain documents on person under disability (Ord 80, r 16)

(1) Where in any proceedings a document is required to be served personally or in accordance with Order 10, rule 1(2) on any person and that person is a person under disability this rule shall apply.

(2) Subject to the following provisions of this rule and to Order 24, rule 16(3) and Order 26, rule 6(3) the document must be served –

(*a*) in the case of an infant who is not also a patient, on his father or guardian or, if he has no father or guardian, on the person with whom he resides or in whose care he is;

(*b*) in the case of a patient, on the person (if any) who is authorised under Part VII of the Act to conduct in the name of the patient or on his behalf the proceedings in connection with which the document is to be served or, if there is no person so authorised, on the person with whom he resides or in whose care he is;

and must be served in the manner required by these rules with respect to the document in question.

(3) Notwithstanding anything in paragraph (2) the Court may order that a document which has been, or is to be, served on the person under disability or on a person other than a person mentioned in that paragraph shall be deemed to be duly served on the person under disability.

(4) A judgment or order requiring a person to do, or refrain from doing, any act, a notice of motion or summons for the committal of any person, and a writ of subpoena against any person, must, if that person is a person under disability, be served personally on him unless the Court otherwise orders.

This paragraph shall not apply to an order for interrogatories or for discovery or inspection of documents.

Amendments—SI 1979/402.

Defined terms—"infant": Family Law Reform Act 1969, ss 1(2), 12; "patient", "person under disability": r 1.

Scope of provision—The general principle is that a document in proceedings cannot be served on a patient as if he were not a patient, and if it is so served the proceedings based on it are invalid (*Cutbush v Cutbush* (1893) 37 Sol Jo 685). This principle is likely to apply also to an infant. However, certain documents must be served personally on a person under disability – see r 16(4).

This rule makes special provision for service on a person under disability. Service is effected in the normal way on the category of person specified or, in default, on "the person with whom he resides or in whose care he is". Once a next friend or guardian ad litem has been appointed, service of documents will be on that person, or the solicitor on the record instructed by that person (if any), in the usual way.

Application to family proceedings—The provision for service upon a person under disability in FPR 1991 (r 9.3) only relates to the service of a petition in matrimonial proceedings. Accordingly, the above rule must be relied upon in regard to the service of other family proceedings in the High Court upon a person under disability. It relates to the document initiating the proceedings; once a next friend or guardian ad litem has been appointed service of documents will be on that person, or the solicitor on the record instructed by that person (if any), in the usual way.

"the person ... in whose care he is"—See under CCR Ord 10, r 4.

Communication to person under disability—See under CCR Ord 10, r 4.

Deemed or substituted service—By virtue of r 16(3), deemed or substituted service on a party under a disability is permitted, thereby enabling the court to proceed with the appointment of a guardian ad litem when service is not otherwise possible.

****

ORDER 112
APPLICATIONS FOR USE OF BLOOD TESTS IN DETERMINING PATERNITY

* Set out in Civil Procedure Rules 1998, Sch 1.

****

PART III

Sharing of State Scheme Rights (Provision of Information and Valuation) (No 2) Regulations 2000, SI 2000/2914

General Note—These regulations set out the information that must be given and the method of valuation of the SERPS element of the state pension which can be subject to a pension sharing or attachment order.

1 Citation, commencement and interpretation

(1) These Regulations may be cited as the Sharing of State Scheme Rights (Provision of Information and Valuation) (No 2) Regulations 2000 and shall come into force on 1 December 2000.

(2) In these Regulations –

"the 1992 Act" means the Social Security Contributions and Benefits Act 1992;

"the 1999 Act" means the Welfare Reform and Pensions Act 1999;

"shareable state scheme rights" has the meaning given by section 47(2) of the 1999 Act.

2 Basic information about the sharing of state scheme rights and divorce

(1) The requirements imposed on the Secretary of State for the purposes of section 23(1)(*a*) of the 1999 Act (supply of pension information in connection with divorce etc) are that he shall furnish –

(*a*) the information specified in paragraphs (2) and (3) –

(i) to a person who has shareable state scheme rights on request from that person; or

(ii) to the court, pursuant to an order of the court; or

(*b*) the information specified in paragraph (3) to the spouse of a person who has shareable state scheme rights, on request from that spouse.

(2) The information specified in this paragraph is a valuation of the person's shareable state scheme rights.

(3) The information in this paragraph is an explanation of –

(*a*) the state scheme rights which are shareable;

(*b*) how a pension sharing order or provision will affect a person's shareable state scheme rights; and

(*c*) how a pension sharing order or provision in respect of a person's shareable state scheme rights will result in the spouse of the person who has shareable state scheme rights becoming entitled to a shared additional pension.

(4) The Secretary of State shall furnish the information specified in paragraphs (2) and (3) to the court or, as the case may be, to the person who has shareable state scheme rights within –

(*a*) 3 months beginning with the date the Secretary of State receives the request or, as the case may be, the order for the provision of that information;

(*b*) 6 weeks beginning with the date the Secretary of State receives the request or, as the case may be, the order for the provision of the information, if the person who has shareable state scheme rights has notified the Secretary of State on the date of the request or order that the information is needed in connection with proceedings commenced under any of the provisions referred to in section 23(1)(*a*) of the 1999 Act; or

(*c*) such shorter period specified by the court in an order requiring the Secretary of State to provide a valuation in accordance with paragraph (2).

(5) Where –

(*a*) the request made by the person with shareable state scheme rights for, or the court order requiring, the provision of information does not include a request or, as the case may be, an order for a valuation under paragraph (2); or

(*b*) the spouse of the person with shareable state scheme rights requests the information specified in paragraph (3),

the Secretary of State shall furnish that information to the person who has shareable state scheme rights, his spouse, or the court, as the case may be, within one month beginning with the date the Secretary of State receives the request or the court order for the provision of that information.

3 Information about the sharing of state scheme rights and divorce: valuation of shareable state scheme rights

Where an application for financial relief or financial provision under any of the provisions referred to in section 23(1)(*a*) of the 1999 Act has been made or is in contemplation, the valuation of shareable state scheme rights shall be calculated and verified for the purposes of regulation 2(2) of these Regulations in such manner as may be approved by or on behalf of the Government Actuary.

4 Calculation and verification of cash equivalents for the purposes of the creation of state scheme pension debits and credits

For the purposes of –

(*a*) section 49 of the 1999 Act (creation of state scheme pension debits and credits);

(*b*) section 45B of the 1992 Act (reduction of additional pension in Category A retirement pension: pension sharing);

(*c*) section 55A of the 1992 Act (shared additional pension); and

(*d*) section 55B of the 1992 Act (reduction of shared additional pension: pension sharing),

cash equivalents shall be calculated and verified in such manner as may be approved by or on behalf of the Government Actuary.

5 Revocation

The Sharing of State Scheme Rights (Provision of Information and Valuation) Regulations 2000 are revoked.

PART IV

Practice Directions

PART IV: Practice Directions

Contents

The Practice Directions in Part IV are arranged in chronological order (for a complete listing, see the Contents pages at the front of the work). The list below shows the Practice Directions arranged under the following general headings:

Adoption, Ancillary Relief, Appeals, Children, Enforcement, Inheritance, Injunctions etc, Petitions etc, Wardship and Court Work – General.

PART IV

PART IV

Practice Note
15 January 1954

Citations: [1954] 1 WLR 213; [1954] 1 All ER 230

Justices' Clerks

In a statement made in the Divisional Court of the Queen's Bench Division on 16 November 1953, about clerks to justices being present when the justices have retired to consider their decision, Lord Goddard CJ said that the ruling of that court did not apply to justices when exercising jurisdiction in matrimonial cases, as they were then subject to the directions and control of this Division. Before making any pronouncement in response to several requests for a ruling by this court on the subject, I wished to consult the judges of this Division. I now have their authority to say that they agree with the statement I am about to make. I am also authorised by the Lord Chancellor to say that he approves of it. Vaisey J also asks me to say that he agrees with it.

I wish to say at the outset that it rarely happens that an allegation of undue interference by the clerk in the decision of a complaint under the Summary Jurisdiction (Married Women) Acts is made a ground of appeal to this Divisional Court. Nevertheless, it is at least as important in cases of this class as in other cases dealt with by magistrates' courts that the decision should be that of the justices themselves, and not that of the justices and their clerk; and that not only should this be so in fact, but that nothing should be done to give the parties or the public the impression that the clerk is influencing the decision. I am, therefore, in complete agreement with the Lord Chief Justice that it should not be regarded as a matter of course that, if justices retire to consider their decision, the clerk should retire with them; moreover, whether the justices invite the clerk to retire with them, or send for him in the course of their deliberations, I agree that the clerk should always return to his place in court as soon as the justices release him, leaving them to complete their deliberations alone.

Bearing in mind that domestic proceedings are often lengthy and may involve points of law in relation to the complaint itself or to the amount of maintenance, and that this court insists that a proper note of the evidence must be kept, and that, in the event of an appeal, justices must be prepared to state the reasons for their decision, I recognise that more often than not magistrates may properly wish to refresh their recollection of the evidence by recourse to the clerk's note, or to seek his advice about the law, before coming to their decision. Having regard to the high standard of care which is generally shown by magistrates' courts in dealing with these domestic proceedings, I do not think it is necessary for me to say more than that I am confident that justices taking part in them may be trusted to act, and to ensure that they appear to act, on the fundamental principle that they alone are the judges.

Lord Merriman P

Registrar's Direction 14 January 1959

Costs of Judgment Summons

If the judge orders that the debtor should pay the full taxed costs of a judgment summons (which are considerably more than the usual fixed costs) a formal direction to that effect should be included in the order of commitment.

As the commitment order should be drawn up promptly, to enable notice to be given to the debtor, it will not usually be possible for such costs to be taxed in time for the amount to be included in the schedule to the order. All reference in the schedule to costs, counsel and conduct money, and the words "together with the prescribed costs hereinafter mentioned" in the body of the order, should therefore be deleted. A separate order for payment of the amount of the taxed costs should then be drawn up after taxation.

B. Long
Senior Registrar

Practice Note 15 December 1960

Citations: [1961] 1 All ER 129

Charge of Adultery against Girl under 16 Years

The President has approved [in its original form] the following Practice Note:

Where a petition or answer alleges adultery by a husband with a girl under sixteen years of age, application should be made to a [district judge] under Rule [2.7(1)(*b*)] or, in the case of an allegation in an answer, under that Rule as applied by Rule [2.16(1)] for directions whether the minor should be served with the petition or answer.

B. Long
Senior Registrar

Note—It is the present practice to ask for a direction under FPR 1991, r 2.7(1) as to whether the minor should be made a co-respondent.

Practice Direction 19 February 1963

Citations: [1963] 1 WLR 310; [1963] 1 All ER 611

Nullity: Appointment of Medical Inspector

1 The President has directed that Registrars and District Registrars should be guided by the principles set out below when determining under Matrimonial

Causes Rules 1957, r 24, the question whether medical inspectors of the court should be appointed to examine the parties in nullity proceedings on the ground of impotence or incapacity:

A *Undefended cases* (including cases proceeding undefended on the answer). Medical inspectors should not be appointed:

(*a*) Where the husband is the petitioner (or, in a case proceeding undefended on the answer, the respondent);

(*b*) Where the wife is the petitioner (or, in a case proceeding undefended on the answer, the respondent):

(i) if it appears from the petition that she was either a widow or divorced at the time of the marriage in question;

(ii) if it appears from the petition or otherwise that she has borne a child;

(iii) if a statement by the wife that she is not a virgin is produced to the registrar.

B *Defended cases.* Medical inspectors should be appointed to examine both parties:

(*a*) if either party requests a medical inspection of himself or herself or the other party;

(*b*) in all other cases unless in the case of a wife it appears from the pleadings or otherwise that the wife has been previously married or has borne a child, or the registrar in respect of either or both is satisfied that for other reasons medical inspection would be of no assistance to the court at the hearing.

C *Cases where the petitioner is alleging his or her own incapacity.* Medical inspectors should always be appointed.

2 *Women doctors.* A wife may request that a woman doctor or women doctors be appointed to examine her, if she prefers not to be examined by a male inspector. The solicitor for the wife should inform his client of her right to request the appointment of a woman doctor, and should satisfy the registrar at the hearing of the summons that she has been so informed.

A woman doctor is not to be appointed to examine the husband. If examination of the husband is necessary there must be a separate appointment of a male inspector or inspectors.

3 The Registrar's Direction of 21 January 1952 is hereby cancelled.

B. Long
Senior Registrar

Practice Direction
19 November 1964

Citations: [1964] 1 WLR 1473; [1964] 3 All ER 775

Divorce: Application to Expedite Decree Absolute

Wherever it is possible, there should be an application to expedite a hearing of the suit in preference to an application at or after the trial to expedite the decree absolute.

Where nevertheless an application to expedite a decree absolute is necessary, it should normally be made to the trial judge at the hearing of the suit. The petitioner (or respondent, as the case may be) should then have available all such evidence (including, where appropriate, a medical certificate as to the expected date of birth of a child) as is necessary to enable the judge to rule whether the decree absolute should be expedited. If some matter arises after decree nisi making it desirable that the decree absolute should be expedited, a party may apply to a judge in chambers for an order to that effect or for directions. The practice of referring cases to the Queen's Proctor will not in future be followed, unless the judge specifically so directs.

The following Practice Note and Direction are hereby withdrawn:

President's Direction 24 January 1944.
Practice Note 12 July 1962.

Compton Miller
Senior Registrar

Practice Direction
11 April 1968

Citations: [1968] 1 WLR 782; [1968] 2 All ER 88

Petition: Contents

Where it is desired to omit from a petition any information required to be contained therein by Appendix 2 of the [Family Proceedings Rules 1991], the petition should be filed without such information, but before service is effected an ex parte application must be made to a [district judge] for leave for the petition to stand. If leave is refused, the [district judge] will make an order requiring the petition to be amended.

Issued [in its original form] by the Senior [District Judge] with the concurrence of the Lord Chancellor.

Compton Miller
Senior Registrar

Practice Direction 18 November 1968

Citations: [1969] 1 WLR 369; [1968] 3 All ER 828

Nullity: Report by Medical Inspector

The procedure set out below should be followed in connexion with nullity suits where there has been an examination and report by an inspector appointed by the court.

The solicitor for the party having conduct of the suit at the date of trial and who wishes not to call a medical inspector to give oral evidence must so inform him at least three days before the trial. Failing this the costs of attendance of the medical inspector will have to be paid by that party in any event.

In a defended cause either party giving notice to the inspector that his attendance to give evidence is not required must also notify the other side. Unless a medical inspector has been told by both parties that he is not required to give evidence he will be entitled to assume that he must be present in court.

Fees due to a medical inspector are payable by the party at whose instigation he was appointed. In a defended case, unless both parties give notice that the medical inspector is not required, the liability for fees remains where it originated. Exceptionally, in a case listed as undefended on a respondent's answer, the liability for the inspector's fees for attending the hearing will fall on the respondent who can avoid the liability only by having given the appropriate notice to the medical inspector.

In London the clerk of the rules will continue to fix nullity suits for hearing as before, and will inform the medical inspectors on the London Panel of the dates fixed for hearing and send them a copy of the list of all cases likely to be heard on those dates.

Issued with the concurrence of the Lord Chancellor.

Compton Miller
Senior Registrar

PART IV

Practice Direction 5 July 1971

Citations: [1971] 1 WLR 1193; [1971] 2 All ER 1310

Medical Inspection in Defended Cases

In defended cases it is considered sufficient to appoint only one inspector to examine the parties.

However, where a wife objects to being examined by a man, she may request that a female doctor be appointed to examine her. The solicitor for the wife should inform his client of her right to request such an appointment and should satisfy the [district judge] at the hearing of the summons or application that she has been so informed.

A woman doctor is not to be appointed to examine the husband if either he or the inspector objects.

Issued [in its original form] by the President with the concurrence of the Lord Chancellor.

Compton Miller
Senior Registrar

Secretary's Circular 19 January 1972

Writ of Possession

An order made in proceedings under s 17 of the Married Women's Property Act 1882 may include a provision that one party is to give to the other possession of premises which were the subject matter of the application. Where such an order, made in the High Court, has not been complied with the leave of the court is necessary before a writ of possession may be issued (RSC Ord 45, r 3(2)). Application for such leave may be made ex parte but should be supported by an affidavit stating, inter alia, whether the property is solely occupied by the person ordered to give possession. If the property or part thereof is sub-let, details of the notice given to the tenants must be set out. The question whether the person(s) to give possession are protected by the Rent Acts must be considered: if the Acts apply to the property the affidavit should set out the rateable value, whether the premises are let furnished or unfurnished and other relevant matters.

Leave to issue a writ of possession must not be granted unless it is shown that every person in actual possession of the whole or part of the premises has received such notice of the proceedings as appears to the court sufficient to enable him to apply for any relief to which he may be entitled (RSC Ord 45, r 3(3)).

W. J. Pickering
Secretary

Practice Direction 17 February 1972

Citations: [1972] 1 WLR 353; [1972] 1 All ER 640

Blood Tests

When a direction is given pursuant to Part III of the Family Law Reform Act 1969 for the use of blood tests in proceedings in the Family Division and divorce county courts the arrangements for the taking and testing of blood samples will be made by the solicitor for the party on whose application the direction was given.

Where the application is proceeding at the [Principal] Registry, on receipt of a copy of the court's direction the solicitor should apply to the Registry for the necessary number of copies of the direction form prescribed by the Blood Tests (Evidence of Paternity) Regulations 1971; a form is required in respect of each person to be tested. He should, in consultation with the solicitors for the other parties, get in touch with a tester (a list of the authorised testers is available) and a sampler and make arrangements for the taking and testing of the samples. The solicitor should then complete Parts I and II of a direction form in respect of each person to be tested and attend with the forms before the [district judge] by whom the direction was given, or if it was not given by a [district judge] before the [district judge] for the day. If the [district judge] is satisfied with the arrangements he will sign the forms and return them to the solicitor with a copy of the Notes for the Guidance of Samplers.

The subsequent procedure is set out in the Regulations and in RSC Ord 112 in the case of High Court proceedings, and Order 47, rule 5 of the County Court Rules in the case of proceedings in the county courts.

Issued [in its original form] with the concurrence of the Lord Chancellor.

Compton Miller
Senior Registrar

Secretary's Circular 14 August 1972

Married Women's Property Act 1882, s 17: County Court Jurisdiction of [Principal] Registry

Under [r 3.7(1) of the Family Proceedings Rules 1991] where any proceedings for divorce, nullity of marriage or judicial separation pending in the [Principal] Registry, or are intended to be commenced there by or on behalf of the applicant, are or will be treated as pending in a divorce county court, an application by one of the parties to the marriage under s 17 of the Married Women's Property Act 1882 may be made to the [Principal] Registry as if it were a county court. (A cause may be "pending" notwithstanding that a final decree has been made.)

This rule provides an alternative to the High Court procedure, but is only permissive: High Court proceedings under s 17 may still be brought in the [Principal] Registry whether or not there are or have been matrimonial proceedings between the parties. On the other hand, the only circumstance in which county court proceedings under s 17 may be brought in the [Principal] Registry is where proceedings for divorce, nullity or judicial separation are pending in the Registry or are intended to be commenced there as if in a divorce county court.

2 *County court procedure*

The procedure in applications in the county court under s 17, which differs in many respects from that in High Court applications, is governed by [Rule 3.6 Family Proceedings Rules 1991].

3 *Issue of application*

An applicant wishing to issue a county court application under s 17 should be asked to complete Form D629, which includes a certificate as to the other proceedings the existence of which is necessary to found an application in the [Principal] Registry at county court level, and a statement of the mode of service desired. An additional fee is payable if service is to be by county court bailiff.

The originating application, in Form N393 in the County Court Practice, which is not supplied officially, must set out the order applied for and give sufficient particulars to show the grounds on which the applicant claims to be entitled to the order (Ord 3, r 4(2)(*a*)). Two copies are required.

Appointments for the first hearing will be returnable before the [district judge] for the day and fixed in the same way as in the case of High Court applications. The first hearing will be for directions and notice will be given to the applicant on Form D632.

4 *Service*

After issue of the application the Section will prepare the appropriate number of copies of Form D633 (notice to respondent) and arrange for service of the documents in the manner requested by the applicant.

5 *Answer*

The respondent should file an answer to the application, with a copy for service, within 14 days after service of the originating application. The Section will make the requisite entry in the court minutes, send the copy of the answer to the applicant's solicitor and record this on the record of service sheet.

It should be noted that the filing of an answer does not result in transfer of the application to the High Court.

The procedure at and subsequent to the first hearing will correspond to that on a High Court application.

6 *Appeal*

It should be noted that an appeal from a [district judge] in a county court application lies to a county court judge under Ord 37, r 6. [See r 8.1(1)(*b*) Family Proceedings Rules 1991.]

W. J. Pickering
Secretary

Note—FPR 1991, r 3.6(2) provides that an order under s 17 of the Married Women's Property Act 1882 may be made in ancillary relief proceedings upon the application of any party thereto in Form M11 by notice of application or summons.

Practice Direction 11 May 1973

Citations: [1973] 1 WLR 690; [1973] 2 All ER 512

Leave for Ward to Go out of the Jurisdiction

Where in wardship proceedings in the Family Division the court is satisfied that the ward should be able to leave England and Wales for temporary visits abroad without the necessity for special leave, an order may be made giving general leave for such visits, subject to compliance with the condition that the party obtaining the order (who will normally be the party having care and control of the ward) must lodge at the Registry at which the matter is proceeding at least seven days before each proposed departure:

(*a*) a written consent in unqualified terms by the other party or parties to the ward's leaving England and Wales for the period proposed;

(*b*) a statement in writing giving the date on which it is proposed that the ward shall leave England and Wales, the period of absence and the whereabouts of the minor during such absence;

and, unless otherwise directed, a written undertaking by the applicant to return the ward to England and Wales at the end of the proposed period of absence.

On compliance with these requirements a certificate, for production to the immigration authorities, stating that the conditions of the order have been complied with, may be obtained from the Registry.

Issued [in its original form] by the President of the Family Division.

D. Newton
Senior Registrar

Registrar's Direction 14 May 1973

Polygamous Marriages

1 The Matrimonial Causes Act 1973 enables the Court to grant matrimonial relief (as defined in that Act) and make declarations concerning the validity of a marriage notwithstanding that the marriage in question was entered into under a law which permits polygamy. References in this Direction to polygamous marriages include references to marriages which are only potentially polygamous.

2 [Rule 3.11(2) of the Family Proceedings Rules 1991] requires the petition, originating application or originating summons to state that the marriage is polygamous and to give details of the name and address of any additional living spouse and the date and place of the marriage to such spouse, or to state that such information is unknown to the petitioner or applicant.

3 *Commencement of Proceedings*

It will be the responsibility of the officers in the Divorce Section to peruse the petition, originating summons or originating application and boldly mark the outside of the document in every case in which the marriage is stated to be polygamous (whether or not there is any additional spouse) with the words "Polygamous Marriage".

The new case writers will be responsible for [marking] the outside of the Court Minutes prominently in red ink in the same way.

4 *Directions regarding additional spouse*

Rule [3.11(3)] provides that the Court may order that an additional spouse may either be added as a party to the proceedings or be given notice of them or of any application in the proceedings for any such order as mentioned in s 47(2)(*d*) of the Act. Rule [3.11(4)] provides that such an order may be made at any stage in the proceedings on application by any party or by the Court of its own motion, where an additional spouse is disclosed in the petition or in the acknowledgement of service the petitioner shall, on applying for directions for trial, ask for directions as to whether an order should be made under Rule [3.11(3)].

It will be the responsibility of the officer dealing with directions for trial in such cases:

(*a*) to ascertain whether directions regarding any additional spouse have been given, and if so whether they have been satisfactorily complied with; and

(*b*) if no such directions have been given, or any such directions have not been satisfactorily complied with, to withhold directions for trial until such time as the requirements of the Rule have been observed.

5 *Wording of decrees*

It will be necessary to amend the decree nisi and any subsequent certificate of decree absolute in all cases where a decree is granted in respect of an actually or potentially polygamous marriage by inserting the words "by virtue of section 47 of the Matrimonial Causes Act 1973". In decrees nisi, they should be inserted after the word "decreed" and in certificates of decree absolute immediately after the phrase "Referring to the decree made in this cause" and before the date of that decree.

D. Newton
Senior Registrar

Practice Direction 17 July 1973

Citations: [1973] 1 WLR 1015; [1973] 3 All ER 224

Matrimonial Causes: Shorthand Note

Under rule 53 of the Matrimonial Causes Rules 1971 (as amended with effect from August 1, 1973), unless the judge otherwise directs, a shorthand note will be taken of the proceedings at the trial in open court of every matrimonial cause pending in the High Court. A shorthand note may be taken of any other proceedings before a judge if directions to this effect are given by or on behalf of the Lord Chancellor.

The system of mechanical recording of the county court matrimonial causes heard at the Royal Courts of Justice will continue until further notice, but no shorthand note will normally be taken of county court matrimonial causes tried elsewhere.

In any such cause in which for some special reason it is considered that the taking of a shorthand note would be advisable early notice (whenever possible no later than when applying for directions for trial) must be given by the petitioner's solicitor to the registrar of the court in which the cause is proceeding.

Early notice must similarly be given if, for some special reason, it is thought advisable that a shorthand note should be taken of ancillary proceedings before a judge (whether in the High Court or a divorce county court) for hearing elsewhere than at the Royal Courts of Justice.

Issued with the concurrence of the Lord Chancellor.

D. Newton
Senior Registrar

Registrar's Direction 7 November 1973

Financial Protection of Respondent: Divorce on Proof of Separation

1 *Introductory*

By virtue of s 10(2) of the Matrimonial Causes Act 1973 a respondent to a petition for divorce in which the petitioner alleges two years' separation coupled with the respondent's consent to a decree being granted, or five years' separation, may apply to the court for it to consider the financial position of the respondent as it will be after the divorce.

Under the [Family Proceedings Rules 1991], the powers of the court on the hearing of such an application may be exercised by a [district judge].

2 *Filing of notice*

When a notice in Form [M]12 is tendered or sent to the Registry the officer should immediately obtain the file and ascertain whether the application can properly be made, by checking:

(*a*) if a decree nisi has not yet been pronounced, that the petitioner alleges two years' or five years' separation, coupled in the former case with the consent of the respondent to the grant of a decree; or

(*b*) if a decree has been pronounced:

  (i) that it shows that the court found that the petitioner was entitled to rely on the fact of two years' or five years' separation and has made no such findings as to any other fact mentioned in s 1(2) of the Act of 1973. (Form [M]12 may be accepted whether or not the decree states specifically that the fact of two years' or five years' separation was the only fact on which the petitioner was entitled to rely.)

  (ii) that the decree has not been made absolute.

If the application cannot properly be made it should not be accepted for filing. If the application is acceptable under (*a*) or (*b*) above, as the case may be, the officer must note the space provided on the front of the court minutes with the date of filing the notice. If the file is at Court the notice should be sent to the Clerk of the Rules, who will arrange to have it placed on the file and the court minutes marked as above. If the file has been sent to a divorce county court for hearing of the cause, an officer nominated by the [Chief] Clerk will immediately telephone the county court and check that the application is competent as above. If so, that court should be asked to note the front of the minutes as aforesaid. If the cause has not been heard the notice will be sent to the county court to be placed on the file: otherwise it will be retained in the Registry to be placed on the file when this is returned.

3 *Action when Form [M]12 is filed prior to hearing of cause*

Where a notice in Form [M]12 is filed prior to the hearing of the cause the form must show that the application will be heard on a date to be fixed. The respondent to the cause must serve a copy of Form [M]12 on the petitioner's solicitor (or the petitioner if acting in person).

In any case in which Form [M]12 has been filed prior to the hearing of the cause, if the court, on pronouncing a decree nisi, finds that the petitioner was entitled to rely on the fact of two years' or five years' separation and makes no such finding as to any other fact mentioned in s 1(2) of the Act, unless the judge deals with the

PART IV

application at the hearing it will be the duty of the associate to send a notice in Form D668 (request for appointment) to the Clerk to the Senior [District Judge] before he parts with the file, and to record on the front of the file the date on which this was done. The file itself will not be sent to the Clerk to the Senior [District Judge].

Where the cause is heard at a divorce county court the officer will, when checking the decree similarly send Form D668 to the Clerk to the Senior [District Judge] and record this on the front of the file.

If on the hearing of the cause the court finds that the petitioner was entitled to rely also on some other fact mentioned in s 1(2) of the Act, any application under s 10(2) of the Act ceases to be competent. The judge's [or district judge's] attention should be called to the fact that the application has been filed, and he should be asked by the associate [or court clerk] formally to dismiss the application. If he does so, an order dismissing the application should be drawn up as an order on decree nisi, and the associate [or court clerk] must also delete the entry on the front of the court minutes noting alongside the reason for so doing.

If, exceptionally, the judge [or district judge] deals with an application under s 10(2) at the hearing of the cause the associate [or court clerk] should carry out the appropriate part of the procedure set out in para 6.

4 *Action when Form [M]12 filed after decree nisi pronounced*

Where notice in Form [M]12 is filed after a decree nisi has been pronounced, the form must show that the application will be heard on a date to be fixed. The person filing the application should be asked to complete a form of request for an appointment (Form D668) for the hearing of the application. If the application is received through the post this form will be completed by the officer accepting the application.

The respondent to the cause must serve a copy of Form [M]12 on the petitioner's solicitor (or the petitioner if acting in person). The forms of request for appointments should be passed each day (without the relevant files) to the Clerk to the Senior [District Judge] with the request for appointments in respect of ancillary relief: the s 10(2) applications should be kept together at the front of the bundle.

5 *Arrangements for hearing of application*

The Clerk to the Senior [District Judge] will allocate the Forms D668 received from the [Divorce Branch] and from associates to the clerks to the [district judges] in rotation, ensuring that when there are delays in fixing appointments such priority as is appropriate is given to applications under s 10(2). When fixing the appointments, unless affidavits of means have already been filed, [district judges'] clerks should have regard to the time allowed by [Rule 2.45(2) and (3)] for the filing of such affidavits. Notice of the appointment must be given by the [district judges'] clerk to both parties by sending Form D285 (see [Rule 2.62(3)], applied by [Rule 2.45(5)]).

6 *Hearing of the application*

The provisions of [Rules 2.62(3) to (7) and Rule 10.10] apply to applications under s 10(2) as they do to applications for ancillary relief.

If, having heard the application, the [district judge] is satisfied under either s 10(3)(*a*) or (*b*) of the Act, or gives leave to proceed under s 10(4), his clerk must complete, sign and insert in the minutes a statement in Form D556. If the [district judge] is not so satisfied, and does not give leave to proceed, the result of the hearing of the application should be noted on the file copy of Form [M]12. Any subsequent application for an expression of satisfaction or for leave to proceed under s [10](4) should be made by restoring the application before the [district judge] by whom it was previously heard. On the further hearing the same procedure as to completion of Form D556 or noting the refusal to express satisfaction or give leave to proceed, as the case may be, should again be followed.

7 *Withdrawal of application*

Where a respondent after filing a notice in Form [M]12 elects not to proceed with the application a notice of withdrawal of the application signed by the respondent's solicitor, or by the respondent if acting in person, may be filed and served on the petitioner's solicitor without leave of the court. In this event a formal order dismissing or striking out the application is unnecessary.

On the filing of notice of withdrawal the entry on the front of the court minutes should be marked with the fact and date of withdrawal of the application.

8 *Application for decree absolute*

On any application for a decree to be made absolute in a cause in which an application under s 10(2) has been filed, the officer examining the application for decree absolute must check that the application has been finally disposed of by:

- (i) the fact that the application has ceased to be competent by reason of a finding that the petitioner was entitled to rely on a fact mentioned in s 1(2) of the Act of 1973 other than the fact of two years' or five years' separation;
- (ii) an expression of satisfaction or leave to proceed under s [10](4) recorded on Form D556;
- (iii) an order dismissing the application; or
- (iv) the withdrawal of the application.

Failing any of these the application for decree absolute must be stopped.

9 *(deleted)*

D. Newton
Senior Registrar

Registrar's Direction 11 March 1974

Discharge of Magistrates' Court Order

Where in a matrimonial cause the court makes an order for periodical payments for maintenance of a party or children replacing an existing order of a magistrates' court which provides for maintenance of the same person or persons, it is important that the latter order should at once cease to have effect so as to avoid any possibility of enforcement proceedings being taken in the magistrates' court.

The High Court or divorce county court has power under s 28 of the Domestic Proceedings and Magistrates' Courts Act 1978 to direct that an order made under Part I of the Domestic Proceedings and Magistrates' Courts Act 1978 by a magistrates' court shall cease to have effect on such date as shall be specified, and this course should be taken in preference to that of accepting an undertaking on behalf of the wife to apply to the magistrates' court for the discharge of the order.

Whenever the court orders that a magistrates' court order shall cease to have effect a copy of the order must be sent by the Registry or divorce county court to the clerk of the magistrates' court. In the [Principal] Registry the copy will be sent by the [district judge's] clerk or associate who draws the order.

To avoid any possible confusion as to the reason for sending the copy order, every such copy should be accompanied by a pro forma letter signed by or on behalf of the [district judge] stating that the copy order is sent as notification of the direction, pursuant to s 25 of the Act, that the order shall cease to have effect.

Issued [in its original form] with the concurrence of the Lord Chancellor.

D. Newton
Senior Registrar

Practice Direction 26 April 1974

Citations: [1974] 1 WLR 576; [1974] 2 All ER 400

Undertakings as to Damages

The form of interim injunction in a county court case (Form [N]16) includes a reference to an undertaking by the applicant, by his counsel or solicitor, in respect of damages sustained by the respondent. While such undertakings may be required when an interlocutory injunction is granted in an action under the general jurisdiction of the county courts, they are unnecessary and inappropriate in High Court and county court matrimonial and children's matters concerning personal conduct. An undertaking as to damages will not be incorporated in an order for an injunction unless it is specifically required by the court and has been expressly given. This is likely to occur only when the injunction concerns property matters, and then only when the claim is to protect rights (as in applications under s 17 of the Married Women's Property Act 1882) rather than to invoke discretionary powers (such as applications for transfer of property). [(See President's Direction dated 7 March 1991 and Ord 13 r 6(5) CCR.)]

Issued [in its original form] by the President of the Family Division with the concurrence of the Lord Chancellor.

R. L. Bayne-Powell
Registrar

Practice Direction 8 May 1975

Citations: [1975] 1 WLR 787; [1975] 2 All ER 384

Omission of Petitioner's Address

1 Where necessary for the protection of the petitioner a [district judge] has power by virtue of [r 2.3 of the Family Proceedings Rules 1991] to direct that the petition

in a matrimonial cause do stand notwithstanding that it omits the petitioner's place of residence.

If it is desired to omit such an address the petition should, as stated in the Registrar's Direction dated 11 April 1968, be filed omitting the information, an ex parte application being made to a [district judge] before service of the petition for leave for the petition to stand.

2 The question whether an affidavit in support of such an application is necessary is one for the discretion of the [district judge]. Any such affidavit should normally state the petitioner's place of residence, but if this is omitted, or if an affidavit is dispensed with, the petitioner's solicitor should lodge with the [district judge] a written note of the address.

3 If the [district judge] gives leave for the petition to stand, an order to this effect should be drawn up, and this should provide that the affidavit (or statement of the address, as the case may be) be sealed up and not inspected without leave of a [district judge]. This procedure must be carried out as soon as the order is made. A copy of the order should be served with the petition.

In such cases the outside of the file should be marked to indicate that leave has been given for non-disclosure of the petitioner's address.

In any case so marked care must be taken that neither the envelope containing the address nor any legal aid certificate granted to the petitioner is made available to any party who seeks to inspect the file, except by leave of a [district judge] in person.

4 If leave for the petition to stand omitting the petitioner's address is refused by the [district judge], his order should provide that the petition be amended by inserting the residence of the petitioner.

5 Where application for omission of the address is to be made, and after leave for this has been granted, care should be taken by the petitioner's solicitor that the effect of the order is not nullified by information included in other documents, eg by giving the name of the school attended by a child in the statement as to arrangements for the children or including any such detail in an affidavit subsequently filed. Such affidavits should commence "I , the petitioner in this cause (having been granted leave for my address not to be disclosed in the petition) make oath etc". If necessary, leave for the affidavit in this form to be accepted may be sought on the occasion on which it is used.

Issued [in its original form] with the concurrence of the Lord Chancellor.

D. Newton
Senior Registrar

Registrar's Direction 22 May 1975

Diversion of Payments to Department of Social Security

1 It is the policy of the Department of Social Security to invite women who have maintenance orders made in, or registered in, magistrates' courts in their favour and who receive regular payments of Supplementary Benefit to take advantage of a "diversion" arrangement if the amount payable under the maintenance order is less

PART IV

than the woman's full rate of benefit, or if, although greater than this, it is not paid, or paid only irregularly. Under the diversion arrangements the woman signs an authority for the court to pay amounts received from the husband to the Department of Social Security; she then draws her full benefit from the Department irrespective of payments made by the husband.

2 This policy has the approval of the Departments concerned and is greatly to the advantage of the payee. It can, however, operate only where payments under the order are to be made into court. As High Court or county court maintenance orders (with the exceptions mentioned below) are not payable through the court, a wife can gain this advantage only by registration of the order in a magistrate's court. [District judges] making orders of a permanent nature in the situation described in paragraph 1 may wish to encourage solicitors to ask for registration.

3 (*a*) Where an attachment of earnings order to enforce payment of maintenance is in existence in the [Principal] Registry, a District Registry or a divorce county court, or there is in force any other order requiring periodical payments into court, and the situation is as set out in paragraph 1 above, the DSS may invite the payee to sign an authority for diversion of payments under the order, and will forward such an authority to the court office.

(*b*) When such an authority is received and until it is revoked by the payee or the DSS, payments received should be remitted to such office of the DSS as is indicated in the authority, and not to the payee under the order.

(*c*) In order to facilitate the smooth operation of these arrangements, courts are asked to maintain contact with the DSS office concerned and arrange for any appropriate interchange of information: for example, notification of any cessation of payment should be given to the DSS instead of the payee under the order. Notices required by the Attachment of Earnings Act 1971 or rules thereunder to be given to the payee must, however, be so given notwithstanding the diversion of payments.

Issued [in its original form] with the concurrence of the Lord Chancellor.

D. Newton
Senior Registrar

Note—Supplementary Benefits Commission abolished in 1980.

Practice Direction 11 November 1975

Citations: [1975] 1 WLR 1640; [1975] 3 All ER 959

Issues: Procedure

1 As from 1 December 1975 the following procedure will apply in relation to the trial of an issue.

2 An order for the trial of an issue should state whether the issue is to be tried in open court or in chambers.

3 A draft issue should be drawn up by the solicitor for the plaintiff and sent to each defendant who should endorse it with his approval. The agreed draft issue

should be lodged in or sent to the court in which the cause is proceeding for settling. The settled draft issue will be returned to the solicitor for the plaintiff.

4 An engrossment of the settled draft should be sent in duplicate by the plaintiff to each defendant, who should endorse one copy to the effect that he had accepted service and return it to the plaintiff.

5 In order to set the issue down, the settled draft and engrossed copy should be sent to the court office and if the issue is to be heard in open court the same procedure will apply as for a cause. If the hearing is to be in chambers a notice of the hearing date will be sent to each party by the court. In causes proceeding in the [Principal] Registry or to be heard at the Royal Courts of Justice, this will be sent by the Clerk of the Rules.

The appendix sets out precedents of the forms to be followed.

Issued [in its original form] with the concurrence of the Lord Chancellor.

D. Newton
Senior Registrar

APPENDIX

A *Form of order for directions as to the trial of an issue*

No of 19 .

IN THE [PRINCIPAL] REGISTRY
[OR IN THE COUNTY COURT]

Mr Justice [Mr District] in Chambers

Between	AB	Petitioner
and	CD	Respondent

Upon hearing
and Upon reading

IT IS ORDERED

1 That an issue [as to whether XY is a child of CD; as to whether XY has been treated as a child of the family; as to whether AB was habitually resident in England and Wales for a period of one year ending with the date of presentation of the petition, or as the case may be] be tried;

2 That AB be the plaintiff and CD be the defendant [or as the case may be] in the said issue;

3 That the issue be heard by a judge in open court [or in chambers] on oral evidence [or as the case may be];

4 That the issue be settled by a [district judge] of this court;

[5 That the cause be stayed pending the determination of the said issue];

6 That the costs of this application be costs in the issue.

DATED the day of 19 .

B *Form of issue*

No of 19 .

IN THE [PRINCIPAL] REGISTRY
[OR IN THE COUNTY COURT]

Between AB Plaintiff
and CD Defendant

WHEREAS AB, the plaintiff in the issue affirms, and CD, the defendant in the issue denies, that [XY is a child of CD; XY has been treated as a child of the family; AB has been habitually resident in England and Wales for a period of one year ending with the date of presentation of the petition; or as the case may be].

AND WHEREAS by order dated the day of 19 , it was ordered that an issue be tried herein.

Therefore let the same be tried accordingly.

Settled

[District Judge]

DATED the day of 19 .

C *Form of order on issue*

No of 19 .

IN THE [PRINCIPAL] REGISTRY
[OR IN THE COUNTY COURT]

Between AB Plaintiff
and CD Defendant

UPON READING the issue herein, upon hearing counsel for the parties and having taken the oral evidence of AB and CD.

IT IS DECLARED that [XY is a child of CD; XY has been treated as a child of the family; AB has been habitually resident in England and Wales for a period of one year ending with the date of presentation of the petition; or as the case may be].

AND IT IS ORDERED that the defendant do pay the plaintiff's costs of this issue (or as appropriate)

DATED the day of 19 .

Practice Note 10 February 1976

Tracing Payers Overseas

Difficulties can arise where a person in this country wishes to take proceedings under the Maintenance Orders (Facilities for Enforcement) Act 1920 or Part I of the Maintenance Orders (Reciprocal Enforcement) Act 1972 to obtain or enforce a maintenance order against a payer living overseas whose address is unknown to the applicant.

To mitigate these difficulties, arrangements have now been made with the appropriate authorities in Australia, Canada, New Zealand and South Africa, whereby the court may on request ask the authorities in those countries to make enquiries with a view to tracing the whereabouts of the payer. The following procedure should be followed.

On or before an application is made for a provisional maintenance order, or for transmission of an absolute maintenance order under the above Acts by an applicant who does not know the payer's actual address in either Australia, Canada, New Zealand or South Africa, there should be completed and lodged with the [district judge] a questionnaire, in duplicate, ([Principal] Registry Form D312 or county court Form D85 as appropriate) obtainable from the registry or court office, together with a written undertaking from the solicitor (or from the applicant if acting in person) that any address of the payer received in response to the enquiries will not be disclosed or used except for the purpose of the proceedings.

This Note is issued [in its original form] with the concurrence of the Lord Chancellor.

R. L. Bayne-Powell
Senior Registrar

Practice Direction 11 May 1977

Citations: [1977] 1 WLR 609; [1977] 2 All ER 543

Notice of Motion: Simplification of Procedure

1 This Practice Direction is issued [in its original form] with the approval of the President of the Family Division. It supplements [Rule 8.2 Family Proceedings Rules 1991] which governs the normal procedure for appeals of the Divisional Court of the Family Division [under the Domestic Proceedings and Magistrates' Courts Act 1978].

2 A notice of motion on appeal to the Divisional Court should be in the form set out in the appendix to this Direction, with such modifications as may be necessary in any particular case.

3 In addition to the certificate as to service and, where appropriate, the certificate as to delay (which can be in the form "I certify that the reasons for delay are as set out in the notice of motion") required by virtue of [FPR Rule 8.2(4)(*d*) and (*e*)], the appellant's solicitor should certify whether or not there are any other matrimonial proceedings pending between the same parties. Wherever possible, all relevant certificates should be contained in the same document which should be lodged with the court on filing the notice of motion.

4 In addition to the other copies required to be lodged by [FPR Rule 8.2(4)], the appellant's solicitor (or the appellant if acting in person) must lodge in the Principal Registry three typescript copies of any manuscript document and two copies of any typescript document put in as an exhibit in the magistrates' court. Original exhibits are usually obtained by the Principal Registry from the magistrates' clerk shortly after entry of the appeal and, when necessary, the copies can be bespoken in the Registry. Original exhibits cannot be handed out to solicitors for copying.

5 All documents lodged by or on behalf of the appellant must be clearly legible and preferably in double-spaced typing. Copies produced by photographic methods must be clear. Documents which do not come up to the required standard will be rejected.

This Direction will also apply with necessary modifications to the practice in relation to adoption appeals to the Divisional Court (see Practice Note dated 7 December 1972), but will not apply to an appeal from a magistrates' order in relation to contempt of court made under s 13 of the Administration of Justice Act 1960 (as to which, see RSC Ord 109, r 2).

R. L. Bayne-Powell
Senior Registrar

APPENDIX

FORM OF NOTICE OF MOTION

No of 19 .

IN THE HIGH COURT OF JUSTICE

FAMILY DIVISION (DIVISIONAL COURT)

In the matter of an appeal under (state the appropriate Act eg Domestic Proceedings and Magistrates' Courts Act 1978)

Between	AB	Appellant
and	CD	Respondent

TAKE NOTICE that the High Court of Justice, Family Division, Royal Courts of Justice, Strand, London WC2A 2LL will, on a date to be fixed and notified to the parties, consider an appeal by AB (the husband/wife of the respondent or father/mother of the child) against the order of the magistrates' court dated the day of 19 .

1 The said order (here set out details of the magistrates' order) and (if appropriate) the full names, surnames and dates of birth of the children referred to in the order are ....

2 The appellant appeals against the whole of the said order or (here set out the part or parts of the order appealed against)

3 The appellant seeks an order that (here set out the order that is sought from the Divisional Court)

4 (If appropriate) Leave to appeal out of time is required because (here set out briefly the reason, giving any dates that are relevant).

[NB Where the delay is no more than 6 weeks (ie this notice is being filed within 12 weeks of the hearing) and has been occasioned by the obtaining of documents or legal aid and the respondent has been notified of the likelihood of an appeal, it will normally suffice to say so without giving details.]

5 The grounds of the appeal are (all the grounds should be set out; it is not sufficient to state merely that the finding was against the weight of the evidence).

DATED the day of 19 .

This notice was filed by (Signed)

whose address for service is: (Solicitor for the above-named Appellant)

To of

Practice Direction 15 June 1977

Citations: [1977] 1 WLR 759; [1977] 2 All ER 714

Expedition of Decree Absolute: Special Procedure Cases

This Direction is issued [in its original form] by the President with the approval of the Lord Chancellor.

Section 1(5) of the Matrimonial Causes Act 1973, as modified by the Matrimonial Causes (Decree Absolute) General Order 1972, provides that, unless the court fixes a shorter period, no decree may be made absolute before the expiration of six weeks from decree nisi. Having regard to this and to the extension of special procedure to virtually all undefended divorce cases, it will very rarely be necessary to make a special order giving leave for the decree absolute to be applied for in less than the period of six weeks.

If, exceptionally, such an order for expedition is sought in a special procedure case, application should be made to the judge [or district judge] on summons or by way of notice of application, as appropriate, and should be supported by any necessary evidence.

Notice of the application should be served on the other parties to the cause. Wherever it is possible, the application will be listed for hearing as soon as convenient after the pronouncement of the decree nisi.

In cases proceeding otherwise than under the special procedure, the practice contained in the President's Practice Direction dated 19 November 1964 (which envisages, whenever possible, an application to expedite the hearing of the suit in preference to an application at or after the trial for expedition of the decree absolute) should continue to be followed.

R. L. Bayne-Powell
Senior Registrar

Registrar's Direction 22 August 1978

Petitioner's Address for Service: Service Personnel

Paragraph [4(*c*)] of Appendix 2 to the [Family Proceedings Rules 1991] requires a petitioner acting in person to give [as] his address for service the address of a place in England and Wales.

Arrangements have been made with the Ministry of Defence whereby, in the case of a petitioner acting in person who is a member of the Services serving at a place overseas, the requirements of paragraph [4(*c*)] of Appendix 2 to the Rules will be satisfied if the petitioner gives as his address for service a British Forces Post Office number.

It has further been agreed that this facility may also be used by petitioning civilian employees of the Ministry of Defence serving abroad.

It should be noted that, unless a [district judge's] order has been obtained directing that the petitioner's address be omitted from the petition, the petitioner's place of residence abroad must be stated in the body of the petition in accordance with paragraph 1(*e*) of Appendix 2 to the said Rules.

Issued [in its original form] with the concurrence of the Lord Chancellor.

R. L. Bayne-Powell
Senior Registrar

Practice Direction 8 November 1978

Citations: [1978] 3 All ER 1032

Consent Orders

1 In June 1953 Vaisey J directed that a consent order made in proceedings under the Inheritance (Family Provision) Act 1938, all parties being sui juris, was not an order under that Act and accordingly that no memorandum of the order should be endorsed on the probate or letters of administration, but that it was otherwise if a compromise was approved by the court on behalf of a party not sui juris. This ruling is equally applicable to consent orders in proceedings in the Chancery Division under the Inheritance (Provision for Family and Dependants) Act 1975.

2 In the Family Division memoranda of all consent orders in proceedings under the 1975 Act are endorsed on the probate or letters of administration, whether or not the parties are all sui juris.

3 To avoid any divergence of practice between two divisions having concurrent jurisdiction, the direction of Vaisey J is now withdrawn. In future, every final order embodying terms of compromise made in proceedings in the Chancery Division under the 1975 Act shall contain a direction that a memorandum thereof shall be endorsed on or permanently annexed to the probate or letters of administration and a copy thereof shall be sent to the Principal Registry of the Family Division with the relevant grant of probate or letters of administration for endorsement, notwithstanding that any particular order may not, strictly speaking, be an order under the 1975 Act.

By the direction of the Vice-Chancellor.

R. E. Ball
Chief Master

Practice Note 22 July 1979

Citations: [1980] 2 All ER 806; (1980) 130 NLJ 683

Child Abduction: Press Publicity

In cases where a child has been abducted, a judge may consider that press publicity may assist in tracing that child.

The President is of the opinion that in such cases the judge should adjourn for a period of about ten minutes to enable representatives of the press to attend, so that the widest publicity may be given.

R. L. Bayne-Powell
Senior Registrar

Practice Direction 18 January 1980

Citations: [1980] 1 WLR 73; [1980] 1 All ER 288

Arrival of Child in England by Air

Where a person seeks an order for the return to him of children about to arrive in England by air and desires to have information to enable him to meet the aeroplane, the judge should be asked to include in his order a direction that the airline operating the flight, and, if he has the information, the immigration officer at the appropriate airport, should supply such information to that person.

To obtain such information in such circumstances in a case where a person already has an order for the return to him of children, that person should apply to a judge ex parte for such a direction.

Issued [in its original form] with the concurrence of the Lord Chancellor.

Sir John Arnold P

Practice Direction 10 March 1980

Citations: [1980] 1 WLR 354; [1980] 1 All ER 1007

Payment of Maintenance Directly to Child; Nominal Orders: Registration

(*a*) *Children's orders*

Section 77 of the Domestic Proceedings and Magistrates' Courts Act 1978, which came into operation on 1 November 1979, added a new s 53A to the Magistrates'

Courts Act 1952. [Now s 62 of the Magistrates' Courts Act 1980.] This makes provision, inter alia, for a magistrates' clerk to transmit payments under a maintenance order registered in his court, which provides for payment directly to a child, either directly to that child or to the person with whom the child has his home. It also provides that that person may proceed in his own name for variation, revival or revocation of the order and may enforce non-payment either in his own name or by requesting the magistrates to do so.

It is therefore no longer necessary for the High Court or the divorce county court when granting an application for registration to place on the order the wording required by the Practice Direction of 2 November 1977 and that Direction is hereby cancelled.

The registration in a magistrates' court of an order made direct to a child entails a considerable amount of work. Accordingly, when the court is considering the form of an order where there are children, care should be taken not to make orders for payment direct where such orders would be of no benefit to the parties or where the parties would derive no immediate tax advantage.

(*b*) *Nominal orders for spouses*

Applications for leave to register orders for nominal amounts in favour of spouses only should not be allowed and, except in special circumstances, leave to register should not be granted in respect of orders for maintenance pending suit and interim orders.

Issued [in its original form] with the concurrence of the Lord Chancellor.

R. L. Bayne-Powell
Senior Registrar

Secretary's Circular 10 February 1981

Welfare Reports

The Registrar's Circular of 15 December 1977 (page 234 of the Compendium) provides that where there are special circumstances in any particular case making it desirable that a welfare report should be seen by a Registrar before its contents are disclosed to the parties, the Court Welfare Officer or the Official Solicitor, as appropriate, will bring the matter expressly to the Registrar's attention.

If the Registrar takes the view that the report contains sensitive material which ought not to be disclosed to the parties unless the judge hearing the case expressly so directs, it must be sealed up in an envelope which should be endorsed with the name and number of the case and marked "Welfare Report. Not to be opened or shown to any party without leave".

As a warning that a file contains such a report, and to assist in identification, a red label should be stuck on the front of the envelope and on the outside of the Court Minutes.

The envelope must always be removed before the file is allowed to be inspected. It would therefore be appropriate if it were to kept inside the folder used for legal aid certificates, which is always checked and removed where appropriate whenever a file is inspected.

If a judge subsequently directs that the report may be disclosed, the envelope should be discarded and the red label warning on the Court Minutes cancelled by crossing it through.

Practice Direction 16 July 1981

Citations: [1981] 1 WLR 1162; [1981] 2 All ER 1056

Divorce: Welfare Reports

In order to make the best use of welfare officers' reports and of their time the President draws attention to the following points:

1 The time of the busy Divorce Court Welfare Service will be better spent and the time of busy judges [and district judges] saved if the court specifies those matters on which the report is to be made.

2 Such specification should never prevent the reporting officer from bringing to the notice of the court any other matters which he considers that the court should have in mind.

3 If any party considers it desirable that the reporting officer should attend the hearing, the proper course is to ask the [district judge] so to direct or, if time does not permit, to inform the reporting officer that it is proposed at the hearing to ask the judge to direct that he attends.

4 Bearing in mind that contested [Section 8 applications] often take several days to hear the parties should agree a convenient date and time for the attendance of the reporting officer in cases where his attendance is required, so that his valuable time is not wasted.

Issued [in its original form] with the concurrence of the Lord Chancellor.

R. L. Bayne-Powell
Senior Registrar

Secretary's Circular 28 September 1981

Contempt of Court

Section 14(1) of the Contempt of Court Act 1981 provides that in any case where a court has power to commit a person to prison for contempt of court and no limitation applies to the period of committal (apart from that contained in that section) the committal must be for a fixed term. This is without prejudice to the power of the court to allow an earlier discharge.

The Official Solicitor is required pursuant to a direction by the Lord Chancellor to review the cases of persons committed to prison for contempt. He may make such applications and appeals as he thinks fit either at the request of the contemnor or in his official capacity.

To enable him to do so, the [Family Proceedings] Department should henceforth send him a copy of every committal order. The covering letter should state the date of the contemnor's arrest (if known), whether or not the contemnor is legally represented and if so the name and address of the solicitors.

R. Conn
Secretary

Amendments—Secretary's Circular of 23 November 1984 (not set out here).

Practice Direction 1 December 1981

Citations: [1982] 1 All ER 319

Renewal of Writ of Fieri Facias

Since the sheriff must withdraw if the judgment creditor allows his writ of fieri facias to expire, it is important where interpleader proceedings are protracted by reason of adjournments and there may be a likelihood that they will not be completed before the date of the writ's expiry that the judgment creditor should apply to have its validity extended as is required by RSC Ord 46, r 8(2) before its expiry date. It is not considered because of the precise wording of this rule that extensions applied for after expiry could be backdated.

So that this matter can be borne in mind the sheriff's representative will inform the court at the first hearing of the interpleader summons of the date of expiry of the writ of fieri facias.

John Ritchie
Senior Master of the Supreme Court

Practice Direction 8 December 1981

Citations: [1982] 1 WLR 118; [1982] 1 All ER 319

Joinder as Parties

In the recent cases of *P v P* (unreported) and *Re F (A Minor) (Adoption: Parental Consent)* [1982] 1 All ER 321, [1982] 1 WLR 102, the Court of Appeal drew attention to the increasing tendency of [district judges] in wardship and custody cases to join the children as parties and to invite the Official Solicitor to act as guardian ad litem. In many cases up to now the parties have asked the court to order the joinder by consent, without showing any special reason for it.

The Court of Appeal emphasised that in the great majority of cases such action was unnecessary and that it added considerably to the length and expense of a hearing, without any commensurate advantage in assisting the court. The Court of Appeal made it clear that only in special circumstances should the child be joined. In most cases the child's interest will be sufficiently protected by a welfare report. It is only in exceptional cases that the joinder of the child and his representation by the Official Solicitor is likely to be of assistance to the court. This is particularly the case where a child is not old enough to express a view as to his future.

It follows from these judgments of the Court of Appeal that such orders should not be made, even by consent, unless special reasons are shown for making them. The special reasons given by the judge or [district judge] should be noted by the associate or clerk together with any special directions for inquiries or investigation to be made in the case, and a copy of the note should be sent to the Official Solicitor for his guidance.

This Direction does not, of course, apply to adoption cases in the High Court where the Rules lay down that the Official Solicitor must be appointed guardian ad litem for the child concerned.

Issued [in its original form] with the concurrence of the Lord Chancellor.

R. L. Bayne-Powell
Senior Registrar

Practice Direction 24 March 1983

Citations: (1983) FLR 450; [1983] 1 WLR 416; [1983] 1 All ER 1097

Family Division: Independent Welfare Reports

The Family Division of the High Court in matrimonial [or] wardship proceedings or any divorce county court in matrimonial proceedings may entertain the evidence of an "independent" reporter but the following points should be noted:

1 No person (other than the party who instructs the "independent" reporter) is under any obligation to discuss the case with or to be interviewed by the "independent" reporter.

2 Where the child is a ward of court, the "independent" reporter should not interview the child without leave of the court.

3 The "independent" reporter may not see a report by the court welfare officer. This is confidential to the parties and the court.

4 The court welfare officer may not discuss the case with the "independent" reporter unless authorised by the court.

5 Where the court has ordered an enquiry and report from a court welfare officer the court should not depart from the usual practice of relying on that report or of ordering a further report by a different court welfare officer.

Practitioners will bear in mind that the party wishing to obtain the services of an "independent" reporter may, if legally aided, need the authority of the area committee.

Issued [in its original form] with the concurrence of the Lord Chancellor.

Sir John Arnold P

Practice Direction 29 April 1983

Citations: (1983) FLR 514; [1983] 1 WLR 558; [1983] 2 All ER 253

Children: Removal from Jurisdiction

In matrimonial, wardship and guardianship cases the court may grant an injunction restraining the removal of a child from the court's jurisdiction. In cases in which the apparent threat comes from the holder of a foreign passport this may be the only safe course. In cases in which the child holds, or the threat comes from the holder of, a British passport the court sometimes orders the surrender of any passport issued to, or which contains particulars of, that child.

Unless the Passport Office is aware that the court has ordered a British passport to be surrendered, there may be nothing to prevent a replacement passport from being issued. Accordingly, in such cases, the court will in future notify the Passport Office in every case in which the surrender of a passport has been ordered.

Issued with the concurrence of the Lord Chancellor.

Sir John Arnold P

President's Direction 16 May 1983

Removal from Jurisdiction

The Practice Direction of 29 April 1983 provided that the court would notify the Passport Office in every case in which the surrender of a British passport has been ordered. The following is a specimen form of letter to be used in such cases.

The Chief Passport Officer
[UK Passport Agency]
Special Files
Room 215
Clive House
Petty France
London SW1H 9HD

Dear Sir

.... *v* ....

Case No ....

This is to inform you that the court has today ordered ....

[date of birth (if known) ...../...../.....]

of.. (*address*)

to surrender the passport[s] issued to, or which contains particulars of the child(ren)

Name Date of birth

(and has granted an injunction restraining removal of the child(ren) from the jurisdiction).

Please add these names to your Warning List to prevent the issue of further passport facilities for the children.

Yours faithfully

for [District Judge]

It will be the responsibility of the associate concerned to ensure that such a letter is sent. Delay must be kept to an absolute minimum.

B. P. Tickle
Senior Registrar

Practice Direction 16 June 1983

Citations: (1983) FLR 640; [1983] 1 WLR 790; [1983] 2 All ER 672

Wards of Court: Parties to the Proceedings

In cases in which the ward has formed or is seeking to form an association, considered to be undesirable, with another person, that other person should not be made a party to the originating summons. He or she should be made a defendant in a summons within the wardship proceedings for injunction or committal. Such a person should not be added to the title of the proceedings or allowed to see any documents other than those relating to the summons.

The judges of the Family Division consider that any such person should be allowed time within which to obtain representation and any order for injunction should in the first instance extend over a few days only.

This Direction supersedes that dated 15 December 1961.

Issued [in its original form] with the concurrence of the Lord Chancellor.

B. P. Tickle
Senior Registrar

Practice Direction
25 July 1983

Citations: (1983) FLR 640; [1983] 1 WLR 998; [1983] 2 All ER 1066

Contempt of Court

The President has directed that on applications for the release of a contemnor from prison the contemnor should be present in court to hear the outcome of the application.

The only exception to this practice is in those cases in which the provisions of the Mental Health Act [1983] apply and it is considered by the solicitor conducting the application that in the particular circumstances it would not be desirable for the contemnor to attend.

Issued [in its original form] with the concurrence of the Lord Chancellor.

B. P. Tickle
Senior Registrar

Practice Direction
8 December 1983

Citations: [1984] FLR 76; [1984] 1 WLR 34; [1984] 1 All ER 69

Wardship: Appointment of Guardian ad Litem

Where in wardship proceedings there are or will be two parties requiring the appointment of guardians ad litem, eg where there is a child whom the court has ordered to be joined and the parent of the child is also a minor or is incapable of managing his or her affairs, consideration should be given to the appointment of the Official Solicitor as guardian ad litem of the child party. This would not normally be suitable if the Official Solicitor has acted for the parent in other proceedings and would of course be impossible if the Official Solicitor is already guardian ad litem of the other minor or incapable party. In such a case the child party's guardian ad litem should normally be a suitable near relative who is willing to act or a divorce court welfare officer from an area outside the area of the court making the order; such a guardian ad litem would also be suitable for the other minor or disabled party if the Official Solicitor is already guardian ad litem of the child party.

Where a divorce court welfare officer is to be appointed, the order should state "a divorce court welfare officer nominated by the chief probation officer for the area of (*the selected area*)". The associate should obtain the name and address of the chief probation officer from the local divorce court welfare service.

Issued with the concurrence of the Lord Chancellor.

J. L. Arnold P

Practice Direction
24 February 1984

Citations: [1984] FLR 356; [1984] 1 WLR 446; [1984] 1 All ER 827

Court Welfare Officers' Reports

The following wording must be boldly endorsed on all Court Welfare Officers' Reports filed in Family Division proceedings and on all copies which are supplied to the parties or their solicitors.

> "This report has been prepared for the court and should be treated as confidential. It must not be shown nor its contents revealed to any person other than a party or a legal adviser to such a party. Such legal adviser may make use of the report in connection with an application for legal aid."

The Registrar's Directions dated 7 June 1973 and 8 February 1982 are hereby cancelled.

Issued with the concurrence of the Lord Chancellor.

B. P. Tickle
Senior Registrar

Practice Direction
14 May 1984

Citations: [1984] FLR 502; [1984] 1 WLR 855; [1984] 2 All ER 407

Wardship and Guardianship: Removal of Children out of England and Wales

The judges of the Family Division are of the opinion, and it is accordingly hereby directed, that an application for leave to remove a child out of England and Wales in wardship cases shall be made to a judge except in the following cases when it shall be made to the [district judge], namely:

(*a*) where the application is unopposed, or
(*b*) where the application is for the temporary removal of the child unless it is opposed on the ground that the child may not be duly returned.

The [district judge] may make such order on the application as he thinks fit or may refer it or any question arising thereon to a judge.

Issued [in its original form] with the approval of the President.

[This Direction should be read in conjunction with s 13(1) of the Children Act 1989.]

B. P. Tickle
Senior Registrar

Practice Direction 21 February 1985

Citations: [1985] FLR 355; [1985] 1 WLR 361; [1985] 1 All ER 896

Appeals from [District Judges]

1 As from 11 March 1985 on entering an appeal to a judge from a judgment, order or decision of a [district judge] exercising jurisdiction in the Family Division of the High Court or in a divorce county court the following procedure will apply.

2 Where the appellant is represented, and either party wishes to bespeak a copy of the [district judge's] notes of evidence, the appellant's solicitor shall:

(*a*) within 21 days from the date upon which the appeal is lodged, certify that either the appellant or the respondent considers that notes of evidence taken before the [district judge] are necessary for the purpose of appeal and that notes of evidence will be lodged, and

(*b*) if he has so certified, unless otherwise directed, not less than 21 days prior to the hearing of the appeal lodge a copy of the notes of evidence (which can be bespoken from the [district judge]) and of judgment (being notes prepared by the appellant's solicitor, and where the respondent is represented agreed by his legal advisers, and approved by the [district judge]).

3 Where the appellant is acting in person and the respondent is represented, the respondent's solicitor shall, after service of the notice of appeal, comply with the obligations imposed by para 2(*a*) and (*b*) above (save as to the agreement as to notes of judgment) as if he were acting for the appellant, and inform the appellant of the lodging of such notes and (if so required) supply to him a copy thereof on payment of the usual charge.

4 Where either party is represented but neither party wishes to bespeak a copy of the [district judge's] notes of evidence, a copy of the notes of judgment shall be –

(*a*) prepared by the appellant's solicitor and, if the respondent is represented, agreed by his solicitor; or

(*b*) prepared by the respondent's solicitor if the appellant is not represented,

and in any case shall be approved by the [district judge], and not less than 21 days prior to the hearing a copy of the notes shall be lodged by the solicitor who prepared them.

5 Where both parties to the appeal are acting in person the appellant shall notify the [district judge] of the appeal and the [district judge] shall, where possible, make a note for the assistance of the judge hearing the appeal and shall furnish each party with a copy of that note or certify that no note can be made.

6 This Direction supersedes the Practice Direction of 26 February 1979 and is issued [in its original form] with the approval of the President and the concurrence of the Lord Chancellor.

B. P. Tickle
Senior Registrar

Practice Direction 1 November 1985

Citations: [1985] 1 WLR 1289; [1985] 3 All ER 576

Psychiatric Reports

The Registrar's Direction of 21 February 1985 (which dealt with the question of costs of psychiatric examination and reports) referred to the need to obtain leave in wardship and matrimonial causes to subject a minor to such examination.

The President and judges of the Family Division are of the opinion that:

(*a*) such an order should normally be made only if the minor is separately represented and his representative supports the application or if the application is supported by a local authority having the care or supervision of the child;

(*b*) such an order should not normally be made unless there is or is suspected to be a specific and identifiable problem or potential problem on which the court needs assistance which can only or most conveniently be provided by a qualified psychiatrist or psychologist.

B. P. Tickle
Senior Registrar

Practice Direction 24 March 1986

Citations: [1986] 1 FLR 536; [1986] 1 WLR 443; [1986] 1 All ER 1024

Application for Adoption and for Freeing for Adoption in the High Court: Notice of Hearing

In future when the court has given notice to a natural parent asking if he or she wishes to be heard in the proceedings and such natural parent has not acknowledged the receipt of such notice within 21 days the Principal Registry will inform the applicants' solicitors and thereupon it will be the duty of the applicants' solicitors to serve any such natural parent at the latest address known to the Principal Registry with a notice in the following form:

"Notice has been sent to you of the hearing of an application made to the Family Division of the High Court for an order for the (freeing for) adoption of   of whom you are believed to be a natural parent. No acknowledgement has been received from you by the court and this is to inform you that you have the right to attend court when the application is heard by a judge so that you may give your views to the judge as to whether or not an order should be made.

If you wish to give your views to the judge will you please return the attached form to the court within the next ten days and you will then be informed of the day fixed for hearing. If the court does not hear from you within the next ten days it will be assumed that you do not wish to take any part in the proceedings

PART IV

and the application for the (freeing for) adoption order will be fixed for hearing by a judge without any further notice to you."

The latest address known to the Principal Registry will be supplied to the applicants' solicitors together with a copy of the notice with the relevant form attached for service on the natural parent. It will be for the applicants' solicitors to satisfy the court at the hearing as to service of the notice and attached form. If for some reason, such as the natural parent's absence from the jurisdiction or failure to locate that person, there is a problem in effecting personal service, the applicants' solicitors should apply to a [district judge] for directions as to service.

B. P. Tickle
Senior Registrar

Registrar's Direction 14 April 1986

Citations: [1986] 2 FLR 89; [1986] 1 WLR 475; [1986] 1 All ER 983

Children: Removal from Jurisdiction

The Child Abduction Act 1984 came into force in October 1984. Section 1 of the Act which relates to England and Wales provides that in relation to a child under 16 (and subject to certain exceptions) an offence is committed by:

(*a*) a parent or guardian of the child, or
(*b*) a person [in whose favour a residence order is in force with respect to the child]
(*c*) [in the case of a child whose parents were not married to each other at the time of his birth], a person in respect of whom there are reasonable grounds for believing that he is the father [or]
[(*d*) a person who has custody of the child]

if that person takes or sends the child out of the United Kingdom without the consent of:

(i) [the child's mother]
(ii) [the child's father, if he has parental responsibility for him]
(iii) [any guardian of the child]
[(iv) any person in whose favour a residence order is in force with respect to the child]
[(v) any person who has custody of the child or, the leave of the court granted under or by virtue of any provision of Part II of the Children Act 1989, or
if any person has custody of the child, the leave of the court which awarded custody to him.]

For the purpose of the 1984 Act, the term "custody" includes "care and control".

Under s 2 of the Act, an offence is also committed in relation to a child under the age of 16 by any person who is not mentioned in (*a*) to (*d*) above if without lawful authority or reasonable excuse he takes or detains the child (*a*) so as to remove him from the lawful control of any person having such lawful control or (*b*) so as to keep him out of the lawful control of any person entitled thereto.

With effect from 2 May 1986 ports will be informed directly by the police (instead of the Home Office) when there is a real threat that a child is about to be removed unlawfully from the country. The police will provide a 24-hour service and will liaise with Immigration Officers at the ports in an attempt to identify children at risk of removal. It is not necessary first to obtain a court order in respect of a child under 16 before police assistance is sought. If an order has been obtained, however, it should be produced to them. Where the child is between the ages of 16 and 18, it will be an essential prerequisite that an order is obtained which restricts or restrains removal, or confers custody.

No ward, however, may be removed from the jurisdiction without the leave of the court. Evidence will need to be produced to the police that the child is a ward. This may either be an order confirming wardship, an injunction, or if no such order has been made, in cases of urgency, a sealed copy of the originating summons.

Any application for assistance to prevent a child's removal from the jurisdiction must be made by the applicant or his legal representative to a police station. This should normally be the applicant's local police station. However, in urgent cases, or where the wardship originating summons has just been issued or where the court has just made the order relied on, contact may be made with any police station. If it is considered appropriate by the police, they will institute the "port-alert" system to try to prevent removal from the jurisdiction.

Where the police are asked to institute a "port-alert", they will need first to be satisfied that the danger of removal is *real* and *imminent*. "Imminent" means within 24-48 hours and "real" means that the port-alert is not being sought by or on behalf of the applicant merely by way of insurance.

The request for assistance should be accompanied by as much of the following information as possible.

The child: names, sex, date of birth, description, nationality, passport number (if known)

The person likely to remove: names, age, description, nationality, passport number (if known), relationship to child and whether child is likely to assist him or her

Person applying for a port-alert: names, relationship to child, nationality, telephone number (and solicitor's name and number if appropriate)

Likely destination

Likely time of travel and port embarkation

Grounds for port-alert (as appropriate)

1. Suspected offence under s 1 of the Child Abduction Act 1984
2. Child subject to court order

Details of person to whom the child should be returned if intercepted

If the police decide that the case is one in which the port-alert system should be used, the child's name will remain on the stop list for four weeks. After that time, it will be removed automatically unless a further application for a port stop is made.

Another measure which an interested party may take is to give notice in writing to the Passport Department, Home Office, that passport facilities should not be provided in respect of the minor either without leave of the court, or in cases other than wardship, the consent of the other parent, guardian, or person to whom custody or care and control has been granted, or the consent of the mother in the

PART IV

case of a child [whose parents were not married to each other at the time of his birth].

Issued [in its original form] with the approval of the President and the concurrence of the Lord Chancellor.

B. P. Tickle
Senior Registrar

Registrar's Direction 28 July 1986

Citations: [1986] 2 FLR 171

Children: Inquiry and Report by a Welfare Officer

A judge or [district judge], before ordering an inquiry and report by a court welfare officer, should, where local conciliation facilities exist, consider whether the case is a suitable one for attempts to be made to settle any of the issues by the conciliation process, and if so, a direction to this effect should be included in the order. If conciliation fails, any report which is ordered must be made by an officer who did not act as a conciliator.

Where the court directs an enquiry and report by a welfare officer, it is the function of the welfare officer to assist the court by investigating the circumstances of the child, or children, concerned and the important figures in their lives, to report what he sees and hears, to offer the court his assessment of the situation and, where appropriate, to make a recommendation. In such circumstances, it is not the role of the welfare officer to attempt conciliation although he may encourage the parties to settle their differences if the likelihood of a settlement arises during the course of his enquiries.

Issued [in its original form] with the approval of the President and the concurrence of the Lord Chancellor.

B. P. Tickle
Senior Registrar

Registrar's Direction 20 February 1987

Citations: [1987] 1 FLR 532; [1987] 1 All ER 546

Filing Affidavits in Cases Proceeding in the Principal Registry

Difficulties are being experienced because of the late filing of affidavits in cases proceeding in the Principal Registry.

The President and judges of the Family Division require the attention of practitioners to be drawn to the practice set out in the Registrar's Direction of 7 February 1984. Failure to comply with this practice may result in costs being disallowed or being ordered to be paid by the solicitor personally. Affidavits which are lodged in the Principal Registry within 14 days before the hearing date instead of being lodged in the Clerk of the Rules' [Branch] or with the clerk to the [district judge] may not be considered at all by the judge or the [district judge] as the case may be.

B. P. Tickle
Senior Registrar

Registrar's Direction 15 May 1987

Removal from Jurisdiction: Issue of Passports

1 *Removal from jurisdiction*

The President has directed that on application for leave to remove from the jurisdiction for holiday periods a ward of court who has been placed by a local authority with foster-parents whose identity the court considers should remain confidential, for example because they are prospective adopters, it is important that such foster-parents should not be identified in the court's order. In such cases the order should be expressed as giving leave to the local authority to arrange for the child to be removed from England and Wales for the purpose of holidays.

It is also considered permissible, where care and control has been given to a local authority, or to an individual, for the court to give general leave to make such arrangements in suitable cases, thereby obviating the need to make application for leave each time it is desired to remove the child from the jurisdiction.

2 *Issue of passports*

It is the practice of the Passport Department of the Home Office to issue passports for wards in accordance with the court's direction. This frequently results in passports being restricted to the holiday period specified in the order giving leave. It is the President's opinion that it is more convenient for wards' passports to be issued without such restriction.

The Passport Department has agreed to issue passports on this basis unless the court otherwise directs. It will, of course, still be necessary for the leave of the court to be obtained for the child's removal.

Issued with the concurrence of the Lord Chancellor.

B. P. Tickle
Senior Registrar

Registrar's Direction 23 July 1987

Transfer of Wardship Proceedings to County Court

(1) . . .

(2) . . .

(3) *Transfer of wardship proceedings to county court*

County courts do not have jurisdiction to deal with applications for an order that a minor be made, or cease to be, a ward of court. Section 38(2)(*b*) of the Matrimonial and Family Proceedings Act 1984 excludes such proceedings from the category of family proceedings which are able to be transferred from the High Court.

The current standard practice is that on the first appointment following the issue of the originating summons the court, if it considers that wardship should continue, confirms wardship and directs that the child remains a ward of court during his minority or until further order. If such a direction is given, there is no need to repeat it in subsequent orders, including any order on the substantive hearing of the originating summons. Provided that such a direction has been given, and the matter is not one which under the President's Direction of 23 February 1987 must be dealt with in the High Court, consideration should be given to transferring the case, in whole or in part, to the county court. In any case which is so transferred in which the court concludes that it is not appropriate to deal with the matter because it is of the opinion that the minor should not remain a ward, it should transfer the case back to the High Court.

Issued with the concurrence of the Lord Chancellor.

B. P. Tickle
Senior Registrar

"President's Direction of 23 February 1987"—Superseded by *Practice Direction of 5 June 1992*.

Registrar's Direction 11 November 1987

Citations: [1988] 1 FLR 183; [1987] 1 WLR 1739; [1988] 1 All ER 223

Wards of Court: Witness in Criminal Proceedings

In the case of *in Re K* reported in *The Times*, 10 September 1987, the court held that where a child has been interviewed by the police in connection with contemplated criminal proceedings and the child subsequently becomes a ward of court, no leave of the wardship court is required for the child to be called as a witness in those proceedings. Where the police desire to interview a child who is already a ward of court application must be made for leave for the police to do so. Where leave is given the order should, unless there is some special reason which requires the contrary, give leave for any number of interviews which may be required by the prosecution or the police. If it is desired to conduct any interview beyond what is permitted by the order further application should be made for this purpose.

No evidence or documents in the wardship proceedings or information about wardship proceedings should be disclosed in the criminal proceedings without the prior leave of the wardship court.

The President directs that all of the above applications be made to a judge on summons on notice to all parties.

Issued with the concurrence of the Lord Chancellor.

B. P. Tickle
Senior Registrar

"Re K"—Case now reported at [1988] 1 FLR 435, FD.

Registrar's Direction 18 July 1988

Citations: [1988] 2 FLR 260; [1988] 1 WLR 989; [1988] 2 All ER 1015

Wards of Court: Witness in Criminal Proceedings

The Registrar's Direction of 11 November 1987 set out the procedure to be followed to obtain leave for the police to interview a child who is a ward of court. It provided that all applications for leave should be made to a judge on summons on notice to all parties.

That procedure is hereby modified to the extent that where a party may become the subject of a criminal investigation and it is considered necessary for the ward to be able to be interviewed without that party knowing that the police are making enquiries, the application for leave may be made ex parte to a judge without notice to that party. Notice should, however, where practicable be given to the guardian ad litem.

There will be other occasions where the police need to deal with complaints, or alleged offences, concerning wards where it is appropriate, if not essential, for action to be taken straight away without the prior leave of the wardship court. Typical examples may be:

(*a*) serious offences against the ward such as rape, where the medical examination and the collection of forensic evidence ought to be carried out promptly;
(*b*) where the ward is suspected by the police of having committed a criminal act and the police wish to interview him in respect of that matter; or
(*c*) where the police wish to interview the ward as a potential witness.

This list is not exhaustive. There will inevitably be other instances where immediate action is appropriate.

The President and judges of the Family Division are of the opinion that, where any such instances are encountered, the police should notify the parent or foster-parent with whom the ward is living or other "appropriate adult" within the *Home Office Code of Practice for the Detention, Treatment and Questioning of Persons by Police Officers*, so that that adult has the opportunity of being present when the

PART IV

police interview the child. Additionally, if practicable the guardian ad litem (if one has been appointed) should be notified and invited to attend the police interview or to nominate a third party to attend on his behalf. A record of the interview or a copy of any statement made by the ward should be supplied to the guardian ad litem. Where the ward has been interviewed without the guardian's knowledge he should be informed at the earliest opportunity and he should also be informed (if it be the case) that the police wish to conduct further interviews. The wardship court should be appraised of the situation at the earliest possible opportunity thereafter by the guardian ad litem, the parent, foster-parent (through the local authority) or other responsible adult.

Issued with the concurrence of the Lord Chancellor.

C. F. Turner
Senior Registrar

Practice Direction 13 February 1989

Citations: [1989] 1 FLR 307; [1989] 1 WLR 219; [1989] 1 All ER 765

Disclosure of Addresses by Government Departments

The arrangements set out in the Registrar's Direction of 26 April 1988 whereby the court may request the disclosure of addresses by government departments have been further extended. These arrangements will now cover:

(*a*) tracing the address of a person in proceedings against whom another person is seeking to obtain or enforce an order for financial provision either for himself or herself or for the children of the former marriage; and,

(*b*) tracing the whereabouts of a child, or the person with whom the child is said to be, in proceedings under the Child Abduction and Custody Act 1985 or in which a [Part I order] is being sought or enforced.

Requests for such information will be made officially by the [district judge]. The request, in addition to giving the information mentioned below, should certify:

1 *In financial provision applications* either

(*a*) that a financial provision order is in existence, but cannot be enforced because the person against whom the order has been made cannot be traced; or

(*b*) that the applicant has filed or issued a notice, petition or originating summons containing an application for financial provision which cannot be served because the respondent cannot be traced.

[A "financial provision order" means any of the orders mentioned in s 21 of the Matrimonial Causes Act 1973, except an order under s 27(6) of that Act].

2 *In wardship proceedings* that the child is the subject of wardship proceedings and cannot be traced, and is believed to be with the person whose address is sought.

3 (*deleted*)

The following notes set out the information required by those departments which are likely to be of the greatest assistance to an applicant.

(1) Department of Social Security

The department most likely to be able to assist is the Department of Social Security, whose records are the most comprehensive and complete. The possibility of identifying one person amongst so many will depend on the particulars given. An address will not be supplied by the department unless it is satisfied from the particulars given that the record of the person has been reliably identified.

The applicant or his solicitor should therefore be asked to supply as much as possible of the following information about the person sought:

(i) National Insurance number;
(ii) surname;
(iii) forenames in full;
(iv) date of birth (or, if not known, approximate age);
(v) last known address, with date when living there;
(vi) any other known address(es) with dates;
(vii) if the person sought is a war pensioner, his war pension and service particulars (if known);

and in applications for financial provision:

(viii) the exact date of the marriage and the wife's forenames.

Enquiries should be sent by the [district judge] to:

Contribution Agency
Special Section A, Room 101B
Longbenton
Newcastle upon Tyne
NE98 1YX

The department will be prepared to search if given full particulars of the person's name and date of birth, but the chances of accurate identification are increased by the provision of more identifying information.

Second requests for records to be searched, provided that a reasonable interval has elapsed, will be met by the Department of Social Security.

Income Support [/Supplementary Benefit]

Where, in the case of applications for financial provision, the wife is or has been in receipt of [income support/supplementary benefit], it would be advisable in the first instance to make enquiries of the manager of the local Social Security office for the area in which she resides in order to avoid possible duplication of enquiries.

(2) [Office for National Statistics]

National Health Service Central Register

[The Office for National Statistics] administers the National Health Service Central Register for the Department of Health. The records held in the Central Register include individuals' names, with dates of birth and National Health Service number, against a record of the Family Practitioner Committee area where the patient is currently registered with a National Health Service doctor. The Central Register does not hold individual patients' addresses, but can advise courts of the last Family Practitioner Committee area registration. Courts can then apply for information about addresses to the appropriate Family Practitioner Committee for independent action.

When application is made for the disclosure of Family Practitioner Committee area registrations from these records the applicant or his solicitor should supply as much as possible of the following information about the person sought:

(i) National Health Service number;
(ii) surname;
(iii) forenames in full;
(iv) date of birth (or, if not known, approximate age);
(v) last known address;
(vi) mother's maiden name.

Enquiries should be sent by the [district judge] to:

[The Office for National Statistics]
National Health Service Central Register
Smedley Hydro, Trafalgar Road
Southport
Merseyside PR8 2HH

(3) Passport Office

If all reasonable enquiries, including the aforesaid methods, have failed to reveal an address, or if there are strong grounds for believing that the person sought may have made a recent application for a passport, enquiries may be made to the Passport Office. The applicant or his solicitor should provide as much of the following information about the person as possible:

(i) surname;
(ii) forenames in full;
(iii) date of birth (or, if not known, approximate age);
(iv) place of birth;
(v) occupation;
(vi) whether known to have travelled abroad, and, if so, the destination and dates;
(vii) last known address, with date living there;
(viii) any other known address(es), with dates.

The applicant or his solicitor must also undertake in writing that information given in response to the enquiry will be used solely for the purpose for which it was requested, ie to assist in tracing the husband in connection with the making or enforcement of a financial provision order or in tracing a child in connection with a [Part 1 order] or wardship proceedings, as the case may be.

Enquiries should be sent to:

The Chief Passport Officer
[UK Passport Agency]
Home Office
Clive House, Petty France
London SW1H 9HD

(4) Ministry of Defence

In cases where the person sought is known to be serving or to have recently served in any branch of HM Forces, the solicitor representing the applicant may obtain the address for service of financial provision or [Part I] and wardship proceedings direct from the appropriate service department. In the case of army servicemen, the solicitor can obtain a list of regiments and of the various manning and record offices from the Officer in Charge, Central Manning Support Office, Higher Barracks, Exeter, EC4 4ND.

The solicitor's request should be accompanied by a written undertaking that the address will be used for the purpose of service of process in those proceedings and that so far as is possible the solicitor will disclose the address only to the court and not to the applicant or any other person, except in the normal course of the proceedings.

Alternatively, if the solicitor wishes to serve process on the person's commanding officer under the provisions contained in s 101 of the Naval Act 1957, s 153 of the Army Act 1955 and s 153 of the Air Force Act 1955 (all of which as amended by s 62 of the Armed Forces Act 1971) he may obtain that officer's address in the same way.

Where the applicant is acting in person the appropriate service department is prepared to disclose the address of the person sought, or that of his commanding officer, to a [district judge] on receipt of an assurance that the applicant has given an undertaking that the information will be used solely for the purpose of serving process in the proceedings.

In all cases, the request should include details of the person's full name, service number, rank or rating, and his ship, arm or trade, corps, regiment or unit or as much of this information as is available. The request should also include details of his date of birth, or, if not known, his age, his date of entry into the service and, if no longer serving, the date of discharge, and any other information, such as his last known address. Failure to quote the service number and the rank or rating may result in failure to identify the serviceman or at least in considerable delay.

Enquiries should be addressed as follows:

[(*a*) Officers of Royal Navy and Women's Royal Naval Service	The Naval Secretary Room 161 Victory Building HM Naval Base Portsmouth Hants PO1 3LS
Ratings in the Royal Navy WRNS Ratings QARNNS Ratings	Captain Naval Drafting Centurion Building Grange Road Gosport Hants PO13 9XA
RN Medical and Dental Officers	The Medical Director General (Naval) Room 114 Victory Building HM Naval Base Portsmouth Hants PO1 3LS

	Naval Chaplains	Director General Naval Chaplaincy Service Room 201 Victory Building HM Naval Base Portsmouth Hants PO1 3LS
(*b*)	Royal Marine Officers	The Naval Secretary Room 161 Victory Building HM Naval Base Portsmouth Hants PO1 3LS
	Royal Marine Ranks	HQRM (DRORM) West Battery Whale Island Portsmouth Hants PO2 8DX
(*c*)	Army Officers (including WRAC and QARANC)	Army Officer Documentation Office Index Department Room F7 Government Buildings Stanmore Middlesex
	Other Ranks, Army	The Manning and Record Office which is appropriate to the Regiment or Corps
(*d*)	Royal Air Force Officers and Other Ranks Women's Royal Air Force Officers and Other Ranks (including PMRA FNS)	Ministry of Defence RAF Personnel Management 2b1(a) (RAF) Building 248 RAF Innsworth Gloucester GL3 1EZ]

General Notes

Records held by other departments are less likely to be of use, either because of their limited scope or because individual records cannot readily be identified. If, however, the circumstances suggest that the address may be known to another department, application may be made to it by the [district judge], all relevant particulars available being given.

When the department is able to supply the address of the person sought to the [district judge], it will be passed on by him to the applicant's solicitor (or, in proper cases, direct to the applicant if acting in person) on an understanding to use it only for the purpose of the proceedings.

Nothing in this practice direction affects the service in matrimonial causes of petitions which do not contain any application for financial provision, etc. The existing arrangements whereby the Department of Social Security will at the request of the solicitor forward a letter by ordinary post to a party's last known address remain in force in such cases.

The Registrar's Direction of 26 April 1988 is hereby revoked.

Issued [in its original form] with the concurrence of the Lord Chancellor.

C. F. Turner
Senior Registrar

Amendments—*Practice Direction of 20 July 1995*.

Practice Note
4 January 1990

Citations: [1990] 1 FLR 414

Adoption: Disclosure: Attorney-General

Following an exchange of correspondence between the Attorney-General and the President of the Family Division, the President has agreed that it would be sensible and wholly appropriate in future for the court to have the assistance of counsel instructed by the Attorney-General in any case where it appears that an order similar to that in *Re An Adoption Application* [1990] 1 FLR 412 may prove to be appropriate and the President is to bring the matter to the attention of the judges of the Family Division. Any person contemplating making a similar approach to the court should be aware of the Attorney-General's interest and that it has been agreed between the Attorney-General and the President of the Family Division that where it appears to the court that a similar order may be appropriate the Attorney-General should first be given an opportunity to be heard through counsel.

Attorney-General's Chambers

Registrar's Direction
5 January 1990

Citations: [1990] 1 FLR 234; [1990] 1 WLR 150; [1990] 1 All ER 382

[Family Proceedings Rules 1991, Rule 2.61]: Consent Order

The Registrar's Direction of 17 February 1986 appended a suggested form of statement of information for the purposes of r 76A of the Matrimonial Causes Rules 1977. Experience has shown that frequently the statement is inadequately completed. The statement has been revised to make it clear that the details of capital and net incomes should be stated as they are at the date of the statement (and not as they will be following implementation of the orders). Additionally, the statement should give the net equity of any property concerned and the effect of its proposed distribution.

The revised form appears in the schedule hereto. Practitioners should ensure that the information required by the new form is given in all appropriate cases.

Issued [in its original form] with the concurrence of the Lord Chancellor.

C. F. Turner
Senior Registrar

Note—The form of statement is now prescribed as Form M1 in Appendix 1 to FPR 1991.

Practice Note 27 July 1990

Citations: [1991] 1 FLR 291

Re R (A Minor) (Experts' Evidence)

In *Re R (A Minor) (Experts' Evidence)*, Cazalet J gave the following guidance on the preparation of reports and the giving of evidence by expert witnesses in cases concerning the welfare of children.

Expert witnesses are in a privileged position; indeed, only experts are permitted to give an *opinion* in evidence. Outside the legal field the court itself has no expertise and for that reason frequently has to rely on the evidence of experts. Such experts must express only opinions which they genuinely hold and which are not biased in favour of one particular party. Opinions can, of course, differ and indeed, quite frequently, experts who have expressed their objective and honest opinions will differ, but such differences are usually within a legitimate area of disagreement. On occasions, and because they are acting on opposing sides, each may give his opinion from different basic facts. This, of itself, is likely to produce a divergence.

The expert should not mislead by omissions. He should consider all the material facts in reaching his conclusions and must not omit to consider the material facts which could detract from his concluded opinion.

If experts look for and report on factors which tend to support a particular proposition or case, their reports should still:

(*a*) provide a straightforward, not a misleading opinion;
(*b*) be objective and not omit factors which do not support their opinion; and
(*c*) be properly researched.

If the expert's opinion is not properly researched because he considers that insufficient data is available, then he must say so and indicate that his opinion is no more than a provisional one.

In certain circumstances, an expert may find that he has to give an opinion adverse to his client. Alternatively, if, contrary to the appropriate practice, an expert does provide a report which is other than wholly objective – that is one which seeks to "promote" a particular case – the report must make this clear. However, such an approach should be avoided because, in my view, it would: (*a*) be an abuse of the position of the expert's proper function and privilege; and (*b*) render the report an argument, and not an opinion.

It should be borne in mind that a misleading opinion from an expert may well inhibit a proper assessment of a particular case by the non-medical professional advisers and may also lead parties, and in particular parents, to false views and hopes.

Furthermore, such misleading expert opinion is likely to increase costs by requiring competing evidence to be called at the hearing on issues which should in fact be non-contentious.

In wardship cases the duty to be objective and not to mislead is as vital as in any case, because the child's welfare, which is a matter of extreme importance, is at stake, and his/her interests are paramount. An absence of objectivity may result in a child being wrongly placed and thereby unnecessarily put at risk.

In almost all cases there is likely to be a reduction in the scale of scientific issues and a consequential saving in costs if arrangements are made for the experts on each side to discuss together their reports in advance of the hearing. Parties in wardship proceedings have a responsibility to see that such arrangements are, if possible, made. RSC Ord 38, r 38 is available, if required, to assist in achieving this end.

Practice Direction 19 August 1991

Citations: [1991] 2 FLR 384; [1991] 1 WLR 955; [1991] 3 All ER 896

Statutory Charge: Form of the Order of the Court

Regulation 90(3) of the Civil Legal Aid (General) Regulations 1989, SI 1989/339, directs that where, in proceedings under the Married Women's Property Act 1882, the Matrimonial Causes Act 1973 or the Inheritance (Provision for Family and Dependants) Act 1975 [or Sch 1 to the Children Act 1989], property is recovered or preserved for an assisted person, which by order of the court is to be used as a home or a sum of money is to be used to purchase a home for the assisted person or his dependants, the assisted person's solicitor shall inform the Area Director.

In such a case, by virtue of regs 96 and 97, the Legal Aid Board may, subject to conditions, agree to defer enforcing the statutory charge on the property recovered or preserved imposed by s 16(6) of the Legal Aid Act 1988.

To avoid any doubt whether the order of the court must expressly state that the property is to be used as a home or to purchase a home, the Legal Aid Board has agreed that a certificate incorporated in the body of the order in the following form will be regarded as a sufficient compliance with the Regulations:

> "And it is certified for the purpose of the Civil Legal Aid (General) Regulations 1989 [that the lump sum of £x has been ordered to be paid to enable the petitioner/respondent to purchase a home for himself/herself (or his/her dependants)] [that the property (*address*) has been preserved/recovered for the petitioner/respondent for use as a home for himself/herself (or his/her dependants)]."

Issued [in its original form] with the concurrence of the Lord Chancellor.

G. Angel
Senior District Judge

"Regulation 90(3) of the Civil Legal Aid (General) Regulations 1989"—See now Community Legal Service (Financial) Regulations 2000, reg 52(1)(*a*).

"s 16(6) of the Legal Aid Act 1988"—See now Access to Justice Act 1999, s 10(7).

PART IV

Practice Direction
26 September 1991

Citations: [1991] 2 FLR 462; [1991] 1 WLR 1069

Grants of Representation: Children Act 1989

The Non Contentious Probate (Amendment) Rules 1991, SI 1991/1876, in force from 14 October 1991, amend r 32 of the Non Contentious Probate Rules 1987, SI 1987/2024 which relates to grants on behalf of minors. The amendments are consequential upon the coming into effect of the Children Act 1989 (herein referred to as "the Act").

The evidence required in support of an application for such a grant in specified circumstances is as follows.

1 Where the applicant is the mother of the child she must state in the oath that she is the mother of the minor.

2 Where the applicant is the father of the child having parental responsibility under s 2(1) of the Act the oath must state that the applicant is the father of the minor and has parental responsibility under that provision.

3 Where the applicant is the father of the child, and has acquired parental responsibility as provided by s 4 of the Act the oath must state that he is the father of the minor and has parental responsibility "under an order" or "under a duly recorded parental responsibility agreement".

A copy of the order or sealed copy of the agreement recorded in the Principal Registry of the Family Division under the Parental Responsibility Agreement Regulations 1991, SI 1991/1478, must be produced.

4 Where the applicant is the father of the child and was not married to the mother at the time of the child's birth, but has parental responsibility in accordance with paras 4 or 6 of Sch 14 to the Act either:

(*a*) by virtue of an order under s 4(1) of the Family Law Reform Act 1987 or;
(*b*) by virtue of an order giving him custody or care and control of the child;

in force immediately before the commencement of Parts I and II of the Act the oath must state that he is the father of the minor and a parent having parental responsibility by virtue of such an order which was in force immediately before the commencement of the Children Act 1989.

A copy of the order must be produced in each instance.

5 Where the applicant has parental responsibility by virtue of an adoption order the oath must state that he or she is the adopter or one of the adopters of the minor by an order made within the meaning of s 12 of the Adoption Act 1976.

A copy of the order must be produced.

6 Where the applicant is a guardian who has been appointed in accordance with s 5 of the Act the oath must state that he or she is a guardian of the minor having parental responsibility by virtue of:

(*a*) an order made under s 5 of the Children Act 1989; or
(*b*) an appointment made by "AB, a parent having parental responsibility for the minor by will" (or "by deed" as appropriate); or

(*c*) an appointment made by "CD, a duly appointed guardian having parental responsibility for the minor by will" (or "by deed" as appropriate).

The order, will or deed must be produced (or in the case of a proved will, an official copy), together with such further evidence as a district judge or registrar may require in the circumstances of a case. The date of death of the person making the appointment must be included in the oath as must the date of death or any other person upon whose death the appointment takes effect.

7 An applicant who is a guardian of the child having parental responsibility by virtue of an appointment under the Guardianship of Minors Act 1971, the Sexual Offences Act 1956 or the High Court's inherent jurisdiction with respect to children which is deemed to be an appointment made and having effect under s 5 of the Children Act 1989 (by paras 12 and 13 of Sch 14 to the Act) must include such information in the oath.

A copy of the order must be produced.

G. Angel
Senior District Judge

Practice Direction 18 October 1991

Citations: [1992] 1 FLR 228; [1992] 1 WLR 147; [1992] 1 All ER 421

Conciliation: Children

The conciliation scheme which has been operating in the Principal Registry of the Family Division since 1 January 1983 has been modified from 14 October 1991 to reflect the changes brought about by the Children Act 1989.

1 *Referrals*

(i) The district judge may, at any time whilst considering arrangements for children under s 41 of the Matrimonial Causes Act 1973, direct a conciliation appointment.

(ii) When an application is made for an order under s 8 of the Children Act 1989, it shall:

  (*a*) if it is an application for a residence or contact order be referred for conciliation;

  (*b*) if it is an application for a prohibited steps or specific issue order be referred only if the applicant so requests.

(iii) The district judge may refer a summons for wardship to conciliation where orders under the said s 8 are sought. This would normally be done at the first appointment.

2 *Procedure*

There will be one conciliation list on 4 days – Monday to Thursday – of each week. The district judge will be attended by a court welfare officer.

It is essential that both the parties and any legal advisers having conduct of the case attend the appointment. The nature of the application and matters in dispute will be outlined to the district judge and the welfare officer. If the dispute continues, the parties will be given the opportunity of retiring to a private room, together with the welfare officer, to attempt to reach agreement. These discussions will be privileged and will not be disclosed on any subsequent application. Anything which is said before the district judge on such appointments will also remain privileged.

The party who has living with him or her any child aged 9 years or over in respect of whom the matter concerns, should bring that child to the conciliation appointment. If only one of two or more children concerned is aged 9, the younger child or children may attend.

Any application to adjourn a conciliation appointment must be made to a district judge.

If the conciliation is successful the district judge will make such orders, if any, as may be appropriate.

If the conciliation proves unsuccessful the district judge will give directions (including timetabling) with a view to the early hearing and disposal of the application. In such cases that district judge and court welfare officer will not be further involved in that application.

Where, in a matter referred by a district judge under para 1(1), the conciliation appointment is concluded, a certificate shall be issued by the district judge dealing with the conciliation, that the court has complied with the requirements of s 41 of the Matrimonial Causes Act 1973.

Urgent applications made by summons will be referred to the district judge of the day to determine whether they are to be referred to conciliation.

The Practice Directions of 2 November 1982, 23 September 1983 and 31 October 1984 are cancelled, save insofar as they affect pending proceedings.

G. Angel
Senior District Judge

Practice Direction 31 January 1992

Citations: [1992] 1 FLR 463; [1992] 1 WLR 261; [1992] 1 All ER 864

Children Act 1989: Appeals

Appeals from magistrates' courts to the High Court under s 94 of the Children Act 1989 are made in accordance with the provisions of r 4.22 of the Family Proceedings Rules 1991, SI 1991/1247.

Such appeals should be commenced by filing the documents referred to in r 4.22(2) in the registry, which is also a care centre, nearest to the court in which the order appealed from was made. This will usually be the care centre listed against the entry in column (i) of Sch 2 to the Children (Allocation of Proceedings) Order 1991, SI 1991/1677, for the petty sessions area or London commission area in which the magistrates' court is located. The appeal will be heard and determined by a High Court Judge of the Family Division, who will normally sit in open court. The hearing will take place as directed at the nearest convenient High Court centre.

This Direction does not affect appeals under the Domestic Proceedings and Magistrates' Courts Act 1978, which will continue to be heard by a Divisional Court of the Family Division under r 8.2 of the Family Proceedings Rules 1991.

Issued with the concurrence of the Lord Chancellor.

Sir Stephen Brown P

Practice Direction 5 June 1992

Citations: [1992] 2 FLR 87; [1992] 1 WLR 586; [1992] 3 All ER 151

Family Division: Distribution of Business

Distribution and transfer between the High Court and county courts of family business and family proceedings.

1 These directions are given under s 37 of the Matrimonial and Family Proceedings Act 1984 by the President of the Family Division, with the concurrence of the Lord Chancellor, and apply to all family proceedings which are transferable between the High Court and county courts under ss 38 and 39 of that Act. They supersede the Practice Direction given on 6 April 1988, save in respect of family proceedings concerning children pending immediately before 14 October 1991. They do not apply to:

(*a*) proceedings under the Children Act 1989 or under the Adoption Act 1976, which are governed by the Children (Allocation of Proceedings) Order 1991;

(*b*) an application that a minor be made or cease to be a ward of court, or to proceedings under Part III of the Matrimonial and Family Proceedings Act 1984, which may be heard and determined in the High Court alone.

2 (1) Family proceedings to which these directions apply (including interlocutory proceedings) shall be dealt with in the High Court where it appears to the court seised of the case that by reason of the complexity, difficulty or gravity of the issues they ought to be tried in the High Court.

(2) Without prejudice to the generality of sub-para (1), the following proceedings shall be dealt with in the High Court unless the nature of the issues of fact or law raised in the case makes them more suitable for trial in a county court than in the High Court:

(*a*) petitions under s 1(2)(*e*) of the Matrimonial Causes Act 1973 which are opposed pursuant to s 5 of that Act;

(*b*) petitions for presumption of death and dissolution of marriage under s 19 of the Matrimonial Causes Act 1973;

(*c*) proceedings involving a contested issue of domicile;

(*d*) applications under s 5(6) of the Domicile and Matrimonial Proceedings Act 1973;

(*e*) applications to restrain a respondent from taking or continuing with foreign proceedings;

(*f*) suits in which the Queen's Proctor intervenes or shows cause and elects trial in the High Court;

(*g*) proceedings in relation to a ward of court –

PART IV

(i) in which the Official Solicitor is or becomes the guardian ad litem of the ward or of a party to the proceedings;
(ii) in which a local authority is or becomes a party;
(iii) in which an application for blood tests is made;
(iv) in which an application is opposed on the grounds of want of jurisdiction;
(v) in which there is a substantial foreign element;
(vi) in which there is an opposed application for leave to take the child permanently out of the jurisdiction or where there is an application for temporary removal of a child from the jurisdiction and it is opposed on the ground that the child may not be duly returned;

(*h*) interlocutory applications involving –
(i) *Mareva* injunctions;
(ii) directions as to dealing with assets out of the jurisdiction;

(*i*) petitions in respect of declarations under Part III of the Family Law Act 1986.

3 (1) Proceedings in the county court for an order within sub-para (2) shall be heard and determined in the High Court where either the county court or any party to the proceedings considers that any such orders, if made, should be recognised and enforced in Scotland or Northern Ireland under Part I of the Family Law Act 1986.

(2) The orders referred to in sub-para (1) are those made by the county court in the exercise of its jurisdiction relating to wardship so far as it determines the living arrangements of a child or provides for the education of, or contact with, a child.

4 In proceedings where periodical payments, a lump sum or property are an issue the court shall have regard in particular to the following factors when considering in accordance with para 2(1) above whether the complexity, difficulty or gravity of the issues are such that they ought to be tried in the High Court:

(*a*) the capital values of the assets involved and the extent to which they are available for, or susceptible to, distribution or adjustment;
(*b*) any substantial allegations of fraud or deception or non-disclosure;
(*c*) any substantial contested allegations of conduct.

An appeal in such proceedings from a district judge in a county court shall be transferred to the High Court where it appears to the district judge, whether on application by a party or otherwise, that the appeal raises a difficult or important question, whether of law or otherwise.

5 Subject to the foregoing, family proceedings may be dealt with in a county court.

6 Proceedings in the High Court which under the foregoing criteria fall to be dealt with in a county court or a divorce county court, as the case may be, and proceedings in a county court which likewise fall to be dealt with in the High Court shall be transferred accordingly, in accordance with rules of court, unless to do so would cause undue delay or hardship to any party or other person involved.

Sir Stephen Brown P

Queen's Proctor—The Queen's Proctor has issued guidance on the procedure to follow when (i) a court refers a case to the Queen's Proctor and (ii) the Queen's Proctor intervenes in proceedings in a county court. This guidance is available from The Queen's Proctor, Queen Anne's Chambers, 28 Broadway, London SW1H 9JS (Tel: 0171-210-3000).

Practice Direction 22 February 1993

Citations: [1993] 1 FLR 668; [1993] 1 WLR 313; [1993] 1 All ER 820

Children Act 1989: Applications by Children

Under s 10 of the Children Act 1989, the prior leave of the court is required in respect of applications by the child concerned for s 8 orders (contact, prohibited steps, residence and specific issue orders). Rule 4.3 of the Family Proceedings Rules 1991 and r 3 of the Family Proceedings Courts (Children Act 1989) Rules 1991 set out the procedure to be followed when applying for leave.

Such applications raise issues which are more appropriate for determination in the High Court and should be transferred there for hearing.

Issued with the concurrence of the Lord Chancellor.

Sir Stephen Brown P

Practice Direction 5 March 1993

Children Act 1989: High Court – Lengthy Hearings

The President has directed that in those cases which are transferred to the High Court and in which the hearing is estimated to be lengthy (5 days or more), an early directions hearing before a High Court judge is desirable. Accordingly, either upon transfer, or as soon as it is known that the hearing is likely to be lengthy, a directions appointment should be fixed before a judge, whether or not a date is also fixed for the substantive hearing of the application.

Gerald Angel
Senior District Judge

Practice Note 5 March 1993

Citations: [1993] 1 FLR 804

Child Abduction Unit: Lord Chancellor's Department

Duties of the Central Authority for England and Wales under Article 21 of the Hague Convention on the Civil Aspects of International Child Abduction

CHILD ABDUCTION AND CUSTODY ACT 1985

In the case of *Re G (A Minor) (Hague Convention: Access)* [1993] 1 FLR 669 the Court of Appeal considered the duties of the Central Authority for England and

PART IV

Wales on receiving an application in respect of rights of access under Art 21 of the Hague Convention.

The Court of Appeal took the view that Art 21 conferred no jurisdiction to determine matters relating to access, or to recognise or enforce foreign access orders. It provides, however, for executive co-operation in the enforcement of such recognition as national law allows.

Accordingly, the duty of this Central Authority is to make appropriate arrangements for the applicant by providing solicitors to act on his behalf in applying for legal aid and instituting proceedings in the High Court under s 8 of the Children Act 1989.

If, during the course of proceedings under Art 21 of the Convention, the applicant decides to seek access instead of the return of the child, but no agreement can be reached and the provisions of the European Convention on the Recognition and Enforcement of Decisions Concerning Custody of Children and on Restoration of Custody of Children are not available, a separate application under s 8 of the Children Act 1989 will have to be made.

Central Authority for England and Wales

Practice Note 11 November 1993

Citations: [1994] 1 FLR 323

B v B (Court Bundles: Video Evidence)

After consultation with the President and with his approval Wall J made the following statement about the efficient preparation of court bundles.

1 Careful thought should always be given by the solicitors carrying the burden of the litigation to the preparation of the bundles to be used in court. This should preferably be done in consultation with counsel who is to have the conduct of the case in court and should certainly be done in consultation with the solicitors for the other parties. There should always be liaison and co-operation between the parties' legal advisers in the preparation of documents for use in court. This should be done in good time before the trial: documents which arrive late or at the last minute can then be added to existing bundles or bundled separately.

2 Where the mechanical task of putting bundles together is delegated to a clerk or junior member of staff it remains the responsibility of the solicitor or managing clerk who has the conduct of the case to check the bundles before they leave the solicitors' offices to ensure that they are in order.

3 In particular, a check should be made to ensure that all the documents copied are legible and that the photocopying process has not truncated any document so that part of it is missing. Elementary as this may sound, illegible or truncated documents are frequently found in court bundles. Where a document is found to be illegible or will not copy properly (for example because it is itself a copy or because it is an original which has been highlighted over the text) a typed version of the document should be made and inserted in the bundle next to the illegible copy.

4 Documents should be presented in a logical (usually chronological) order. The preparer of the bundles should attempt to put himself or herself in the position of the judge who is coming to the papers for the first time. Nothing is more frustrating than to open a bundle of documents and to read "I make this statement further to my previous statement of such and such a date and in answer to the respondent's statement". The judge then has the choice either of reading something which answers an allegation he has yet to read or searching the bundle for the document to which it is a reply. For these reasons it is not appropriate to bundle each party's evidence separately in different bundles or in different sections of a bundle. A chronological presentation enables the judge to read a bundle through from beginning to end without the distraction of having to search for documents which are out of sequence.

5 All bundles should be properly indexed with a description of each document and the page number at which it begins and ends.

6 Bundles should be individually paginated, and the pagination should be continuous throughout each bundle. A master bundle should be prepared and copy bundles should only be made after the master bundle has been paginated, not before. By these means only can it be ensured that everyone in court has the same document with identical pagination. Equally documents should not be presented with generalised numbering – for example, document 1 is the applicant's statement, document 2 is the respondent's statement, and so on. The aim in court is to be able to refer to bundle A page x, not bundle A, document 2, and page x of that document. The latter process is very time-wasting.

7 It is common practice for solicitors to prepare bundles for their own use and for the use of the court and to provide indices only to the solicitors for the other parties. In my judgement it is preferable for the solicitors having the conduct of the litigation to prepare all the bundles and distribute them after making a charge for photocopying. Where, however, indices only are supplied, it is the duty of the recipient solicitors to ensure that the bundles which they make up from the indices have identical pagination to the master bundles. A simple telephone call should obviate any difficulty in this regard.

8 Whilst each case varies in relation to the issues which arise from it, thought should always be given to the categorisation of documents and their distribution into individual bundles. Usually it is sensible to have a bundle of statements or affidavits (chronologically arranged) another for formal court documents and interlocutory court orders (also in chronological order) another for bundles of expert or medical reports (likewise arranged in chronological sequence) and so on.

9 Where medical records are relevant and reproduced every effort should be made to ensure that the copies are legible and photocopied in the correct order and are presented the right way up. In rare cases where a bundle of solicitors' correspondence is relevant, that correspondence should likewise be presented in chronological order. Where there are documents in manuscript (such as letters between the parties) typed copies should be provided unless the manuscript is clearly legible.

10 Rigorous pruning of unnecessary material should take place and duplication should be avoided. If a document is exhibited to an affidavit or statement and should more logically appear elsewhere (for example as a medical report in a medical bundle) a page can be inserted in the bundle from which it has been removed stating where it is to be found.

11 Wherever possible the chronology prepared by the applicant should be cross-referenced to the relevant page in the relevant bundle. Such a process can

only be achieved if the person preparing the chronology has access to the bundles in their final state, but the process is of enormous assistance to the judge. Equally a dramatis personae which identifies the parties and the principal witnesses and where their evidence is to be found is extremely useful to the judge.

12 There should always be a "witness bundle" that is to say a spare bundle for use by witnesses in the witness box. When a document needs to be put to a witness it is at the very least a discourtesy to the witness if the document has to be retrieved from a solicitor's file or counsel's papers. It is also time wasting. Moreover, the witness bundles must be kept up to date during the trial. It is the duty of the advocate having the conduct of the proceedings to ensure that this is done.

13 Bundles should be presented in a way which enables them to lie flat when opened. It is very irritating when cross-referencing documentation or making a note if the bundle snaps shut as soon as the hand is taken off it. Furthermore, staples, treasury tags or other means of holding papers together should be removed once the papers are in a file or ring binder.

14 Documents frequently arrive or emerge during the course of a trial. Provided there is agreement for their inclusion in the court bundles they should be paginated, photocopied, hole punched and inserted in the relevant bundle at the relevant place and, if possible, the index to the particular bundle amended to cover their inclusion.

15 Where videos of interviews with children form part of the evidence in the case there should either be a directions appointment at which their use is discussed and directions about their use given, alternatively the parties' respective solicitors should attempt to agree about the manner in which they are to be used. Thus:

(*a*) where there is to be a challenge to the technique used or debate as to the interpretation of what the child or interviewer has said, transcripts should be obtained and placed in a separate bundle;

(*b*) if the judge is to be asked to view the videos in private before the trial begins:

- (i) the agreement of all the parties to this course should be obtained,
- (ii) the parties should endeavour to agree those parts of the interviews which the judge should look at,
- (iii) a transcript should be provided to the judge;

(*c*) where it is intended that the video should be played in court in addition or as an alternative to a private viewing made by the judge, early arrangements should be made for the provision of the relevant equipment, agreement reached on the parts of the interviews which are to be played and transcripts provided.

President's Direction 22 November 1993

Citations: [1994] 1 FLR 108; [1994] 1 WLR 16; [1994] 1 All ER 155

Children Act 1989: Hearings before High Court Judge: Time Estimates

1 As from the date of this Direction, parties to proceedings under the Children Act 1989 or under the inherent jurisdiction of the High Court relating to children,

which are pending in the High Court in London and in other centres and which are to be heard by a judge, will be required to provide an estimate of length of the hearing (a "time estimate") in accordance with the procedure set out in the following paragraphs. This procedure is intended to enable the court and the parties to be kept fully informed of any changes in time estimates so as to facilitate the listing and disposal of cases in the most effective manner.

2 When any hearing which is expected to last *one day or more* is fixed, whether upon application or at a directions hearing or on any other occasion, the party applying for the hearing ("the applicant") and such other parties as may then be before the court, shall give a time estimate. Unless otherwise directed, this shall be in writing and shall be signed by the solicitor and by counsel, if instructed. A suitable form will be available from the court.

3 If any party to the proceedings is not before the court when the hearing is fixed, the applicant shall serve that party forthwith with a copy of the time estimate.

4 Any party served with a time estimate shall acknowledge receipt and shall inform the applicant and the court forthwith whether they agree or disagree with the estimate and, in the latter case, shall also give their own time estimate.

5 If at any time after a time estimate has been given, any party considers that the time estimate should be revised, that party shall forthwith provide the court with a further time estimate and shall serve a copy on the other parties. It is the duty of solicitors to keep counsel informed of the time estimates given in the case and it is the duty of both solicitors and counsel to keep the length of the hearing under review and to inform the court promptly of any change in the time estimate.

6 In cases where a hearing has been fixed for *less than a day*, if any party considers that it is likely to last for one day or more, then a time estimate shall be given by that party to the court and served on the other parties. If an additional application or cross-application is issued returnable on the same date, a further time estimate will only be required if the latest time estimate is affected.

7 A party shall provide a time estimate if so required by the court.

8 If, in the light of the information provided, the court considers that further directions are necessary or if any of the parties fail to provide the requisite information, a directions hearing will be fixed and notice of the appointment given to all parties by the court. In the event of a party failing to provide information when requested or if default is otherwise made in the provision of time estimates, liability for any wasted costs may arise for consideration.

9 This Direction does not apply to parties in person. Where the applicant is a party in person, the other parties to the proceedings, if represented by a solicitor, must provide a time estimate to the court immediately upon being notified of the hearing.

10 This Direction is not to be read as affecting the right of any party to apply to the court for directions at any time in relation to the listing of any application or for any other purpose.

11 The Direction dated 1 March 1984 shall continue to apply to proceedings other than proceedings under the Children Act 1989 or the inherent jurisdiction of the court relating to children.

12 Issued with the concurrence of the Lord Chancellor.

Sir Stephen Brown P

Practice Direction 23 November 1993

Citations: [1994] 1 FLR 110; [1994] 1 WLR 13; [1993] 4 All ER 960

Transfer of Inter-country Adoptions between the County Court and the High Court

In proceedings in a county court under the Adoption Act 1976 concerning a child whose place of origin is outside the United Kingdom, the question of transfer of the case to the High Court may arise. In deciding whether, under the Children (Allocation of Proceedings) Order 1991, such proceedings are appropriate for determination in the High Court, guidance may continue to be derived from the decision of the Court of Appeal in *Re N and L (Minors) (Transfer of Business)* [1988] 1 FLR 48, that transfer should be limited to those cases giving rise to issues of complexity, difficulty or gravity.

Orders for transfer should not be made of the court's own motion without the parties and the guardian ad litem (if appointed) having the opportunity of making representations on the question of transfer. It will usually be possible for the necessary enquiries to be made by letter and for the matter to be determined without a hearing. In those cases where there is an issue as to transfer, a hearing for determination of the issue should be fixed, with notice of the date, time and place of hearing given to the parties and the guardian ad litem. It will usually be impracticable to obtain the views of the natural parents or for them to be given notice of any hearing.

Issued with the approval of the President and the concurrence of the Lord Chancellor.

G. Angel
Senior District Judge

President's Guidance 17 December 1993

Urgent Hearings on Circuit before Family Division Judges: Standby Procedure

(This notice does not relate to the hearing of appeals from magistrates' courts under s 94 of the Children Act 1989.)

Where a case is proceeding in, or is transferred to, the High Court and an urgent hearing on circuit is required before a High Court judge of the Family Division, inquiries should first be made as to the availability of such a judge in the area. It may be necessary to contact circuit office to ascertain the judicial itineraries. If the case cannot be accommodated locally the President of the Family Division will consider arranging for an additional High Court judge to go out to the circuit specifically to hear the case. In order to assist the President in reaching his decision the following procedures must be followed:

1 The designated or nominated family judge must certify that the case merits an urgent hearing before a High Court judge of the Family Division.

2 Contact should be made with the Family Division liaison judge for the circuit who will require a brief summary of the issues involved and the reasons for urgency, together with the estimated length of hearing. A list of Family Division liaison judges appears at the foot of this item and the circuit office will have details of their itineraries.

If for any reason the Family Division liaison judge cannot be reached contact should be made with the President's clerk, Mrs Sheila Bell, on 071-936 6576.

Family Division liaison judges

Midland and Oxford Circuit – Mr Justice [Stuart-White]
North Eastern Circuit – Mr Justice Singer
Northern Circuit – Mr Justice [Wall]
South Eastern Circuit – Mr Justice Cazalet
Wales and Chester Circuit – Mr Justice Connell
Western Circuit – Mr Justice [Holman]

Practice Note 2 February 1994

Citations: [1994] 2 FLR 336

Re MD and TD (Minors) (Time Estimates)

After a hearing estimated at 3 days which was in fact concluded in 7 days, the judge in chambers dismissed the mother's application for a discharge of care orders and then delivered in open court a further judgment seeking to address the problems caused by underestimation of the length of a hearing in a case relating to children before a judge of the Family Division. The judge stated that he had been authorised by the President to make the following points:

"1 Any time estimate must include judicial reading time and time for the delivery of an extempore judgment in the case.

2 Time estimates should be part of ... the co-operative planning process between the lawyers for the respective parties which is designed to see that a case is properly prepared for trial. Solicitors and counsel should consult each other and their opponents so that the estimate by each side can be fully informed and if possible agreed.

3 Advocates should think realistically about their cross-examination of important witnesses and include a realistic calculation of the likely length of each witness in the overall estimate of time given.

4 Where medical experts are involved there should be careful co-operative planning to ensure that sufficient time is set aside for their evidence.

5 No estimate can be accurate unless time-limits are obeyed and evidence produced on time. Late evidence distorts the timescale.

6 Directions appointments are not formalities. On the contrary, they are extremely important, and never more so than when estimates of time are discussed. Every effort should be made to ensure that when counsel is briefed to attend a directions appointment he or she is either the barrister who will have the conduct of the substantive hearing and has addressed his or her mind

PART IV

to the estimated length of the hearing or, where a substitute has to take the brief, that he or she is fully instructed on the point. Thus, not only should the question of the likely length of the trial form an essential element in counsel's instructions, but counsel should talk freely to each other on the subject, both to opponents and to substitutes. A simple conversation in chambers or a telephone call will often suffice.

7 Whenever the question of estimating the length of a trial is undertaken or discussed in court all the persons estimating should go patiently through a mental list of:

- (i) the documents which the court will have to read and the time likely to be taken in reading;
- (ii) the likely length of the opening;
- (iii) the witnesses whose viva voce evidence will be required and the length in each case of the likely examination-in-chief, cross-examination and re-examination;
- (iv) the points of law or procedure which are likely to arise in the case and the length they will take to argue;
- (v) the number and likely length of closing speeches;
- (vi) the time likely to be needed for an extempore judgment.

These items then should be added up, together with any other factor which may be relevant in a particular case. Elementary as this process may appear, I fear it is often simply not undertaken. I make it clear that I do not exclude the judge or the district judge from this process, although it must be appreciated by the profession that the judge on a directions appointment cannot be in as good a position as the advocates as he comes to the case for the first time, often in the middle of a crowded list, has only the documents and thus little opportunity to acquire a 'feel' for the case.

8 If a case seriously overruns due to negligent or incompetent estimation of time, the courts will have to think seriously about sanctions against those responsible. The profession should be under no illusions about this. If the *Practice Direction of 22 November 1993 (Children Act 1989: Hearings before High Court Judge: Time Estimates)* is disobeyed and as a consequence a case seriously overruns, the lawyers will have to answer to a judge who has power to disallow refreshers and, in extreme cases, make wasted costs orders: see para 8 of the Practice Direction."

Practice Direction 20 December 1994

Citations: [1995] 1 FLR 458; [1995] 1 WLR 365; [1995] 1 All ER 832

Child: Change of Surname

1 (*a*) Where a person has by any order of the High Court, county court or family proceedings court been given parental responsibility for a child and applies to the Central Office, Filing Department, for the enrolment of a deed poll to change the surname (family name) of such a child who is under the age of 18 years (unless in the case of a female, she is married

below that age), the application must be supported by the production of the consent in writing of every other person having parental responsibility.

(*b*) In the absence of such consent, the application will be adjourned generally unless and until leave is given to change the surname of such child in the proceedings in which the said order was made and such leave is produced to the Central Office.

2 (*a*) Where an application is made to the Central Office, Filing Department, by a person who has not been given parental responsibility of the child by any order of the High Court, county court or family proceedings court for the enrolment of a deed poll to change the surname of such child who is under the age of 18 years (unless in the case of a female, she is married below that age), leave of the court to enrol such a deed will be granted if the consent in writing of every person having parental responsibility is produced or if the person (or, if more than one, persons) having parental responsibility is dead or overseas or despite the exercise of reasonable diligence it has not been possible to find him or her for other good reason.

(*b*) In cases of doubt, the Senior Master or, in his absence, the Practice Master, will refer the matter to the Master of the Rolls.

(*c*) In the absence of any of the conditions specified above, the Senior Master or the Master of the Rolls, as the case may be, may refer the matter to the Official Solicitor for investigation and report.

3 These directions are issued with the approval of the Master of the Rolls.

4 *Practice Direction (Minor: Change of Surname)* [1977] 1 WLR 1065 is hereby revoked and *Practice Direction (Change of Deed Poll of Surname of Child)* dated 11 April 1994 is hereby revised by the addition of the words "family proceedings court" in paras (1)(*a*) and (2)(*a*).

Keith Topley
Senior Master
Queen's Bench Division

Note—Practice Direction of 11 April 1994 is in identical terms, save for the revisions made by paragraph 4 hereof.

Best Practice Note January 1995

Form of Directions; Certificate of Time Estimate; Welfare Reports

Note: the following materials are taken from the *Children Act Advisory Committee Annual Report 1993/94*, and are reproduced with the kind permission of the President of the Family Division.

(1) Form of Directions

[*see following page*]

Form of Directions

In the

Case Number

Child(ren)'s Number

Directions

The full name(s) of the child(ren)	Boy or Girl	Date of Birth

The Application

☐ The Court orders that	be joined as [a] part[y][ies] to the proceedings
☐ The Court grants leave to	, the [1st] [2nd] [3rd] applicant, to withdraw the application for in respect of the child[ren]

Statements

☐ The Court orders that	the oral evidence which the parties shall be entitled to bring to the final hearing of this matter shall be limited to those witnesses whose statements have been filed at court and served on all other parties by the following dates: Applicant's evidence .... 1st Respondent .... 2nd Respondent .... **No further statements may be lodged with the court without the leave of the court**

Reports

☐ The Court orders that	[all parties] nominate their experts in the field[s] of by
☐ The Court requires	[the experts] jointly to examine the child[ren] by
☐ The Court orders that	the parties consult for the purpose of jointly instructing [an] expert[s] in on the following matters The parties must consult by 4 pm on and the report[s] of the [expert[s]] must be lodged at the court office by
☐ The Court orders that	the expert witnesses meet to discuss the areas of dispute revealed by the report[s] of [the expert witnesses] This meeting shall be within days of the report[s] being filed at the court office and disclosure of them to Within days of that meeting, and no later than the solicitors for must file at the court office a statement agreed by the parties. The statement must state the issues which are agreed and those which are not agreed.
☐ The Court orders that	the [Guardian ad litem] [Court Welfare Officer] file a report [on the matter of]. The report must be filed by 4 pm on The [Guardian ad litem] [Court Welfare Officer] must attend the [final hearing] [next directions hearing].
☐ The Court grants leave to	to disclose to the following papers
☐ The Court orders that	any reports which result from this disclosure must be filed at the court office and disclosed to [all the parties].
☐ The Court directs that	the serve and lodge a statement according to [Family Proceedings Rules 1991 r 4.17(1)] [Family Proceedings Courts (Children Act 1989) Rules 1991 r 17(1)] [in support of] [in answer to] the application. The statement must be lodged at the court office by 4 pm on

Reports continued overleaf

	The statement must be limited to findings of the report[s] with which [he] [she] [they] do not agree relevant matters not covered by the report[s] the matter of
Further Directions	
☐ The Court directs that	this application be listed for [further discussion] [a final hearing] before at on [**Notice** The child[ren] must [not] attend [in person] [with [his] [her] [their] solicitor] The time estimate is days
☐ The Court grants	liberty to the [parties] [Guardian ad litem] [Court Welfare Officer] to apply for urgent further directions **Notice** 24 hours' notice must be given to the Court.
Documents	
☐ The Court directs that	the [applicant][respondent] prepare a precise chronology comprising a summary of the history of the case a schedule of the lodgement of the statements a summary of the issues to be resolved between the parties The chronology must be lodged with the court office and served on the parties by 4 pm on
☐ The Court directs that	a bundle of papers for the court be prepared. The bundle must contain the chronology and the issues; all exhibits, reports and authorities; the statements lodged by all parties. The bundle must be paginated and indexed. All parties must agree the contents of the bundle. The [applicant] [respondent] [local authority] must lodge the bundle with the court office by 4 pm on
Interim orders	
☐ The Court orders that	between the date of this order and the next hearing the child[ren] be [placed] [remain] [under the supervision of] [in the care of] **Notice** This interim [care] [supervision] order may be renewed ex parte for 28 days if all the parties consent in writing. An application for renewal must be lodged at least 48 hours before the date on which the interim order ends. The application must be accompanied by written confirmation that the circumstances of the child[ren] have not changed. [This interim order is subject to [a] [specific issue] [prohibited steps] order [that] [the child[ren] reside[s] with the [applicant] [respondent] [and] the child[ren] have contact with the [applicant] [respondent] [according to Schedule [ ] which is attached]]
☐ The Court orders that	between the date of this order and the next hearing the [applicant] [respondent] pay, or cause to be paid, to the [applicant] [respondent] for the child[ren] periodical payments of £ a year. This sum is to be paid to the [applicant] [respondent] at £ a [week] [month] until further order of the Court.
Costs	
☐ The Court orders that	the [applicant] [respondent] pay the costs of this directions hearing the costs of the [applicant] [respondent] [ ] be taxed on a standard basis under the Legal Aid in Family Proceedings (Remuneration) Regulations 1991.
Ordered by	[Mr] [Mrs] Justice [His] [Her] Honour Judge District Judge [of the Family Division] Justice[s] of the Peace [Clerk of the Court] [Assistant Recorder]
on	

(2) Certificate of Time Estimate

Certificate of Time Estimate **Form**

The Court	**To be completed by the court**
	Date issued
	Case Number
The full name(s) of the child(ren)	**Child(ren)'s Number(s)**

	Hours	Minutes
Judge's preliminary reading time		
Counsel opening		
[Witness as to fact] [Parties]		
Name		
Examination in chief		
Cross examination		
Name		
Examination in chief		
Cross examination		
Name		
Examination in chief		
Cross examination		
Name		
Examination in chief		
Cross examination		
Total carried over		

	Hours	Minutes
Expert Witnesses		
Name		
Examination in chief		
Cross examination		
Name		
Examination in chief		
Cross examination		
[Guardian ad litem][Court Welfare Officer]		
Evidence		
Cross examination		
Counsel's closing speeches		
Number of counsel		
Judgment		
Total carried over		
Total estimate		

We, the undersigned counsel and solicitors for all parties in this application, certify that our estimate of the time needed to dispose of this application is given above.

Signatures of counsel and solicitors

Solicitors may sign on behalf of counsel but they must certify that they do so with the authority of counsel.

Signed

Name

Counsel Solicitor
for [Applicant] [Respondent]

Signed

Name

Counsel Solicitor
for [Applicant] [Respondent]

Signed

Name

Counsel Solicitor
for [Applicant] [Respondent]

Signed

Name

Counsel Solicitor
for [Applicant] [Respondent]

(3) Welfare Reports

Best Practice Note for the Judiciary and Family Proceedings Courts when Ordering a Court Welfare Officer's Report

1 A welfare report may only be ordered pursuant to Section 7 of the Children Act 1989 ie when a court "considering any question with respect to a child under [the] Act 'requires a report' on such matters relating to the welfare of that child as are required to be dealt with in the report". A report may not be ordered for any other purpose.

2 Before a welfare report is ordered consideration should be given to the court's power to refer parties to mediation (with the consent of the parties). This may be a mediation service or the court welfare officer, depending on local arrangements. It is important that this should not be confused with a welfare report and that any court welfare officer who may have been involved in any privileged mediation proceedings should not be the officer who undertakes the preparation of a welfare report.

3 The ordering of a welfare officer's report is a judicial act requiring inquiry into the circumstances of the child. A report should never be ordered when there is no live issue under the Children Act before the court; for example, a report must not be ordered when no formal proceedings have yet been instituted. Furthermore, save in exceptional circumstances, a report should not be ordered in response to a written request by the parties.

4 Although the exact procedures in different courts vary, there will always be some kind of preliminary appointment or hearing before the district judge, justices' clerk or family proceedings court in children's cases. This is normally the occasion on which a welfare report should be ordered. The attendance of the parties and their solicitors is required at this time to enable the court properly to inquire into the issues to be covered in the report. When a court welfare officer is present, or otherwise available, the court may consider inviting the parties to have a preliminary discussion with him or her.

5 When a welfare report is ordered the judge, district judge or justices' clerk should explain briefly to the parties what will be involved and should emphasize the need to co-operate with the welfare officer and specifically to keep any appointments made. In particular, when the principle of contact is in dispute the parties should be told that the welfare officer will probably wish to see the applicant parent alone with the child. It should also be emphasised that the report, when received, is a confidential document and must not be shown to anyone who is not a named party to the application.

6 The order for the report should specify the time by which the report should be filed and, if possible, indicate the date of the substantive hearing. The solicitors for the applicant should be handed a pro forma in the form of the model attached and asked to complete details such as name, address and telephone number on the front of the form. The judge, district judge or justices' clerk should complete the rear of the pro forma which sets out the reasons for the report and the concern of the court; this should set out succinctly the issues on which the officer is being asked to report. This part of the form should specify any documents which are to be sent to the welfare officer. This form must be fully completed and attached to the court file before the court disposes of the case.

7 An addendum report may be ordered eg for the purpose of testing an agreement between the parties or where there has been a substantial change in circumstances.

However, an addendum report should not be ordered merely because of a delay or adjournment in the listing of the substantive hearing.

8 The court will not order both a welfare report and Section 37 report.

9 It should be noted that the court welfare officers do not travel outside the United Kingdom; International Social Services are available to meet this need.

10 A court welfare officer will not attend a hearing unless specifically directed to do so by the court (Family Proceedings Rules 1991 rule 4.13 and Family Proceedings Courts (Children Act 1989) Rules 1991 rule 13). When such a direction is given the court should ensure that the officer gives evidence as soon as possible after the case has opened (and in any event on the first day) and is released after that evidence has been completed.

Best Practice Note to Court Staff when Welfare Reports have been Ordered

1 Staff should ensure that the pro forma on the court file has been fully completed by the solicitors and the judge, district judge or justices' clerk on the day that a welfare report is ordered. When this has not been done the file should be immediately referred back to the judge or, when he or she is not immediately available, to another family judge or authorised clerk.

2 A copy of the order and of the pro forma should be sent by the court to the court welfare office within whose area the child lives within 48 hours of the order being made. Copies of all documents specified on the pro forma should accompany the order. The pro forma should be date stamped with the date of despatch.

3 When a welfare report is received, it should immediately be date stamped and copies should be sent by the court to the solicitors for the parties immediately (or faxed when there is less than 7 days before the hearing) usually without reference back to the judge. Where a party acts in person a letter should be sent by the court inviting that party to call to collect the report.

4 When a hearing date (or change of date) is being considered and it appears that the parties will require the court welfare officer to attend, he or she should be consulted before the date is fixed.

[*see following page for Welfare Report Referral*]

Welfare Report Referral

About this form

- The solicitor for the applicant must fill in Part 1 (below)
- A judge or a justices' clerk will fill in Part 2 (overleaf)
- The court office will then send a copy of this form and any other papers to the court welfare office within whose area the child lives. This will be done within 48 hours.

For the use of the court office

Court

Case Number

Name of judge or clerk to the justices

Date of case review

Date of final hearing

Report ordered on

This form sent on

Report to be filed by

Part 1

The Applicant

Full name (surname in BLOCK LETTERS)	
Date of birth & Relationship to the child	Date of Birth / Relationship
Address	
Daytime Telephone Number	Home / Work
The Applicant's Solicitor	
Name and Reference	Ref.
Address	
Telephone & FAX numbers	Telephone / FAX

The Respondent

Full name (surname in BLOCK LETTERS)	
Date of birth & Relationship to the child	Date of Birth / Relationship
Address	
Daytime Telephone Number	Home / Work
The Respondent's Solicitor	
Name and Reference	Ref.
Address	
Telephone & FAX numbers	Telephone / FAX

Other relevant parties

Full name (surname in BLOCK LETTERS)	
Date of birth	
Address	

Children

Name	Date of Birth	Residing with	School Attended
1			
2			
3			
4			

Part 2

The nature of the application

For example: residence, contact, parental responsibility, prohibited steps, specific issue, (or other)

The welfare report

Give, in detail

- *the reason(s) for the Court ordering the report*
- *particular areas of concern which are to be reported on.*

About the parties

Were they interviewed at court? No ☐ Yes ☐ The Family Court Welfare Officer *(name)* ______

Was a settlement or mediation attempted? No ☐ Yes ☐ The Family Court Welfare Officer *(name)* ______

Have the parties been given copies of the information leaflet? No ☐ Yes ☐

Are there any dates when the parties will **not** be available? No ☐ Yes ☐ The dates ______

Will an interpreter be needed? No ☐ Yes ☐ The language(s) *(including signing)* ______

Are there any issues of culture or religion which the Family Court Welfare Officer should be aware of? No ☐ Yes ☐ The issue(s) ______

Are other papers attached to this form? *For example: statements, directions* No ☐ Yes ☐ The papers are **the Court Order +** ______

Is there a Child Protection issue? No ☐ Yes ☐

The Court Welfare Officer is

Give the name and address

Part 2 completed by

Name: Date:

[District] Judge ☐ Justices' Clerk ☐

Practice Direction
31 January 1995

Citations: [1995] 1 FLR 456; [1995] 1 WLR 332; [1995] 1 All ER 586

Case Management

1 The importance of reducing the cost and delay of civil litigation makes it necessary for the court to assert greater control over the preparation for and conduct of hearings than has hitherto been customary. Failure by practitioners to conduct cases economically will be visited by appropriate orders for costs, including wasted costs orders.

2 The court will accordingly exercise its discretion to limit –

(*a*) discovery;
(*b*) the length of opening and closing oral submissions;
(*c*) the time allowed for the examination and cross-examination of witnesses;
(*d*) the issues on which it wishes to be addressed;
(*e*) reading aloud from documents and authorities.

3 Unless otherwise ordered, every witness statement or affidavit shall stand as the evidence in chief of the witness concerned. The substance of the evidence which a party intends to adduce at the hearing must be sufficiently detailed, but without prolixity; it must be confined to material matters of fact, not (except in the case of the evidence of professional witnesses) of opinion; and if hearsay evidence is to be adduced, the source of the information must be declared or good reason given for not doing so.

4 It is a duty owed to the court both by the parties and by their legal representatives to give full and frank disclosure in ancillary relief applications and also in all matters in respect of children. The parties and their advisers must also use their best endeavours:

(*a*) to confine the issues and the evidence called to what is reasonably considered to be essential for the proper presentation of their case;
(*b*) to reduce or eliminate issues for expert evidence;
(*c*) in advance of the hearing to agree which are the issues or the main issues.

5 (*ceased to have effect – see President's Direction of 10 March 2000*)

6 In cases estimated to last for five days or more and in which no pre-trial review has been ordered, application should be made for a pre-trial review. It should when practicable be listed at least three weeks before the hearing and be conducted by the judge or district judge before whom the case is to be heard and should be attended by the advocates who are to represent the parties at the hearing. Whenever possible, all statements of evidence and all reports should be filed before the date of the review and in good time for them to have been considered by all parties.

7 Whenever practicable and in any matter estimated to last five days or more, each party should, not less than two clear days before the hearing, lodge with the court, or the Clerk of the Rules in matters in the Royal Courts of Justice in London, and deliver to other parties, a chronology and a skeleton argument concisely summarising that party's submissions in relation to each of the issues, and citing the main authorities relied upon. It is important that skeleton arguments should be brief.

8 (*ceased to have effect – see President's Direction of 10 March 2000*)

9 The opening speech should be succinct. At its conclusion other parties may be invited briefly to amplify their skeleton arguments. In a heavy case the court may in conjunction with final speeches require written submissions, including the findings of fact for which each party contends.

10 This practice direction which follows *Practice Direction (Civil Litigation: Case Management)* [1995] 1 WLR 262 handed down by Lord Taylor of Gosforth CJ and Sir Richard Scott V-C to apply in the Queen's Bench and Chancery Divisions, shall apply to all family proceedings in the High Court and in all care centres, family hearing centres and divorce county courts.

11 Issued with the concurrence of the Lord Chancellor.

Sir Stephen Brown P

Best Practice Note January 1996

Note: the following material is taken from the *Children Act Advisory Committee Annual Report 1994/95*, and is reproduced with the kind permission of the President of the Family Division.

Joint Instruction of Expert in Children Act Cases

DRAFT LETTER FOR JOINT INSTRUCTION[1] OF EXPERT IN CHILDREN ACT CASES

Dear [expert]

In the matter of: ***[names of children with dates of birth]***

1 We write further to the telephone conversation[2] between [*you/your secretary*] and [*name of solicitor*] on [*date*] concerning the above children.

2 **The Representatives**

In this case:

i) [*Mr/Miss/Mrs/Ms name*] of [*firm*], [*address, telephone and FAX numbers*] represents [*party*] who is/are applying for [*nature of the order*]

ii) [*Mr/Miss/Mrs/Ms name*] of [*firm*], [*address, telephone and FAX numbers*] represents [*party*] who is/are [*resisting the application/applying for*].....etc [*nature of the order*]

iii) ...

SET OUT THE SIMILAR DETAILS FOR EACH PARTY

It may also be helpful to you to know that the responsible social worker is [*name*], but please do not approach or contact [*him/her*] direct, without first discussing this with the lead solicitor (see para 3 below).

3 **The Nature of the Instructions**

Pursuant to the Order of *His/Her Honour/District Judge* ... dated ..., you are being instructed jointly by all[3] the above solicitors on behalf of each of the parties named, but on the basis that you will provide an expert opinion entirely independent of all of them. While, of course, it is expected that you will have meetings with the parents, children [*where leave is given*], social workers and guardian ad litem, nevertheless it is essential both to your role as an independent expert and to the parties' perception of your independent status, that there are no informal unrecorded discussions, or correspondence with any of the professionals or the lay parties involved in the case. If you need further information, please contact the lead solicitor[4] who is [*name of lead solicitor*] and who will provide it after consultation with the other legal advisors involved. If documents are exchanged with one party, please copy them to all the others. Where possible communication is best achieved by FAX or letter.

[*4 You will see that the court has given leave*[5] *for you to see the child(ren). How you do this is within your discretion, but if you decide not to see the child(ren) in the company of a parent or foster parent (or possibly, after consultation with the lead solicitor, the social worker), the court will need to know your reason.*]

5 **The Background**

We enclose a chronology of the main events and the court hearings to date, together with a schedule of all documents filed in the case so far. We enclose photocopies of those documents[6] which it has been agreed are necessary for you to consider and these are marked with an asterisk on the schedule. If, having perused the schedule and the documents enclosed, you consider that you require any further documents, please contact the lead solicitor who will consult with the other legal advisors. The lead solicitor will also send to you copies of any relevant documents filed after the date of this letter[7].

6 In brief, the background to the current application(s) and to your instruction in this matter is as follows:

[*Here set out the family relationships, the important areas of factual dispute, the present whereabouts of the children, the level and nature of contact with the relevant parties, and any other specific relevant issues*]

7 **Your Instructions**

You are requested kindly to consider and provide your opinion on the following issues:

[*Here set out the issues as agreed or defined by the court*]

having regard always to the principle that in determining any question with respect to the child, the child's welfare is the court's paramount consideration. If, during the course of your investigation, other issues appear to you to become relevant, please immediately contact (the lead solicitor) who, after consultation with the other legal advisors, will consider whether the scope of your instructions should be amended.

8 **Factual Issues**

Unless you have been specifically asked to do so[8], you should please avoid expressing a view regarding the factual dispute(s) as this is, of course, the province of the judge at the final hearing. Where appropriate, it will be of assistance if you are able to express your opinion on the basis of alternative findings regarding the factual dispute(s).

9 **The Timetable**

Pursuant to the above Order your report should be filed and served on or before [*time and date*]. This means by that time and date copies of your report are to reach the court office at [*address*] and each of the above named solicitors at the address given. It is crucial that you comply with this time limit as the subsequent timetable for the filing of statements and reports, and the final hearing are dependent on the receipt of your report by the due date. The final hearing is listed for [*date*] with a time estimate of [ ] days. It is expected that you will attend on [*date and time*][9]. If any of these dates or times are or become inconvenient for you, please contact [one of] the above solicitor(s) as soon as possible, as an application may have to be made to vary the dates.

Yours etc

1 The letter of instruction should be included in the court bundle.
2 See *Re G (Minors) (Expert Witnesses)* [1994] 2 FLR 291 at pp 298C–299A, and *Re M (Minors) (Care Proceedings: Child as Witness)* [1994] 1 FLR 749 at pp 758G–759B, both per Wall J. Consultation with the proposed expert should be undertaken prior to the directions appointment at which the timetable for future conduct of the case is laid down. Inconvenient dates and the timescale required of and by the expert should be ascertained in advance of the directions hearing.
3 This paragraph may be amended to accommodate instruction by only some of the parties, in which case there should be included some encouragement for the experts to meet to reduce/resolve areas of dispute. Consideration should be given to this at the directions hearing.
4 The parties should agree a "lead" solicitor who can act as the conduit for such communication. This will usually be the guardian's solicitor. If such agreement is impossible, the court may direct a lead solicitor.
5 Where relevant.
6 See *Re M* (supra) at p 758B–D.
7 It is suggested that in each case a master schedule of documents should be maintained, and kept up to date. It would normally be for the lead solicitor to have the responsibility for maintaining this schedule.
8 Such a situation might arise where a psychiatrist is asked to express an opinion on the basis of interpretation of clinical interviews and findings with regard to the likely explanations for their observations, for instance as to whether sexual abuse has occurred.
9 The phraseology here reflects the fact that many judges are reluctant to specifically order the attendance of such experts. If appropriate liaison has been effected prior to the directions appointment, an order should not be necessary.

Best Practice Guidance June 1997

Note: the following materials are taken from the *Children Act Advisory Committee Handbook of Best Practice in Children Act cases*, and are reproduced with the kind permission of the President of the Family Division.

Handbook of Best Practice in Children Act cases

INTRODUCTION

When writing its final report, the Committee thought it might be helpful to gather together in a separate document the guidance available on best practice in Children

Act proceedings with a view to providing a useful tool for the conscientious but busy practitioner. Some of this material is newly written and some is a compendium of guidance from our earlier reports updated both by experience and authoritative reported decisions. It follows that some of this guidance is firmly authoritative (deriving from binding decisions or practice directions) whilst much remains advisory, but based on accumulated experience of what works best.

The basic message of this Handbook is that the earlier matters are considered and acted upon by the parties and their advisers, and the more that can be done jointly with other parties, the better the court process can serve the interests of children. Work done in preparation, and in liaison with other parties, is rarely wasted and indeed is almost always productive in terms of avoiding, or at least reducing, the trial process which is after all both the most costly and certainly the most stressful part of the whole proceedings.

We hope that all practitioners (and not just the lawyers) will find this Handbook useful as we try to translate into practice in each case the obligation to promote the welfare of the children with whom we are dealing. We have set out this Handbook with a view primarily to ease of reference in the hope that it will find widespread use in practice.

SECTION 1 – PREPARATION FOR COURT IN CARE PROCEEDINGS

Local authority solicitors

1 At the earliest stage, when first consulted, focus on:

(*a*) the issues;
(*b*) the legal framework;
(*c*) the evidence needed to support an application;
(*d*) the proposed care plan;
(*e*) the appropriate level of court; and
(*f*) the likely time scale for concluding the court case in the light of:
  (i) the complexities involved, and
  (ii) the ages and needs of the children.

2 If counsel is to be instructed, do so at an early stage. Consider together the preparation for trial and whether transfer to the care centre is appropriate.

All parties and their legal advisers

3 By the first directions hearing, consider whether the issues of fact are stark enough to justify a split hearing, with an early resolution of factual disputes to enable a definitive care plan to be formulated and to enable the guardian ad litem to make recommended actions as to outcome. For example, this is likely to arise in cases of alleged non-accidental injury where different persons are in the frame as possible perpetrators and/or accomplices, and in cases of sexual abuse.

4 Use directions hearings imaginatively. Anticipate problems and address them in advance.

(*a*) Ensure strict compliance with timetables for filing evidence and documents.
(*b*) Inform the court, as a matter of urgency, if the timetable cannot be met for any reason.
(*c*) Be prepared in advance with dates and availability of witnesses and time needed to adduce evidence.

(*d*) Liaise with other parties to ensure that all issues are addressed at an early stage, for example:
  (i) whether transfer to the care centre would be appropriate;
  (ii) which other persons are seeking party status;
  (iii) issues of disclosure and confidentiality; or
  (iv) any assessments or experts' reports sought by any party.

(*e*) Fix the final hearing, even if only provisionally.

5 All parties, and in particular the guardian ad litem, have a duty to:

(*a*) advise the court on the timetable appropriate to the issues and timescale of the child concerned;

(*b*) keep the timetable under constant review throughout the preparation for the hearing; and

(*c*) bring to the attention of the court promptly any significant developments and seek further directions.

Instruction of experts

6 See **Section 5** below.

The care plan

7 Ensure that the issues raised by the local authority are clearly set out with a fully researched care plan, to enable the parties to know what case they have to meet.

8 If permanent placement in an alternative family is the plan, prepare the ground as far as possible without pre-empting the court's decision.

9 If the plan is for an adoptive placement, the court will be handicapped in assessing the plan and the timescale, unless the child concerned has already been considered and approved by the adoption and fostering panel, and potential suitable adoptive families have been identified. It is not good practice to await the making of a care order before obtaining such information, because the court is deprived of important background information and significant delay can occur in placing the child in the event of the court approving the plan.

10 If the plan involves a specialist placement with therapy and/or further assessment, identify the placement and any professionals involved, together with the timescale and the availability of appropriate funding.

11 If the plan depends upon the finding of facts or determination of particular issues by the court, state why and set out clear alternative proposals.

12 If no firm proposal can be made, that should be made clear and explained.

Preparing the evidence

13 Check source material and ensure that the case presented is balanced and fair.

14 If research material is to be relied upon, ensure that it is relevant and cogent.

15 Prepare a chronology and statement of issues as the case proceeds, in order to assist the court at directions hearings.

Preparation for the hearing

16 In advance of the final directions hearing, or pre-hearing review before trial, discuss with all parties whether threshold criteria are admitted and if so on what basis, so as to be able to present:

(*a*) a statement of agreed facts relevant to the threshold criteria and outcome, and a statement of remaining issues;
(*b*) a chronology; and
(*c*) a paginated bundle (core bundle if appropriate).

17 In reaching the final estimate of length of hearing:

(*a*) establish what evidence is to be called on behalf of any party;
(*b*) use the attached template or similar document, in consultation with all parties, so as to timetable the attendance of witnesses at court throughout the hearing; and
(*c*) allow time for speeches and judgment in the estimate; and
(*d*) keep the time estimate under constant review and inform the court immediately of any change.

18 In preparing the bundle for the final hearing, help the judge, parties and witnesses by:

(*a*) providing separate sections for experts' reports and interlocutory orders;
(*b*) not keeping rigidly to chronological order if it would result in documents dealing with one particular issue being scattered throughout the bundle;
(*c*) ensuring photocopied material is legible and
(*d*) having relevant handwritten documents typed.

19 Consider whether a skeleton argument will be of assistance to the court and other parties.

20 Lodge skeleton arguments with the bundle of documents. (They must *not* be handed in on the day of the hearing.)

The court

21 It is essential that judges have the opportunity to read the papers in advance of all directions appointments, and in particular before the final directions hearing, so as to ensure that all relevant matters are addressed. It is desirable and saving of court time if the judge who is listed for the full hearing also determines the final directions appointment.

SECTION 2 – RENEWAL OF INTERIM CARE ORDERS

Introduction

22 When an interim care order is made, it is normally necessary for the making of a further interim care order to be considered on at least one occasion before the final hearing. It appears that there is a variety of local practices for dealing with such cases, and, while it is not intended to encourage courts to depart unnecessarily from well-established local arrangements (particularly those which approximate closely to what is recommended below), it is thought that some guidance should be given to ensure some degree of uniformity. Although the making of further interim care orders is here described as "renewal", it must be remembered that the proper form of order is that the whole application is adjourned to the next date for further consideration.

23 The issue of renewal of interim care orders should normally be addressed at the first directions hearing. An interim care order made at the first hearing will expire after 56 days. In a majority of cases, the reality is that, once an interim care order has been made, the position is unlikely to change before the final hearing. In such cases it would be wasteful of legal costs to require all parties to attend a further hearing.

24 A court may not renew an interim care order as a matter of course, and without reconsideration. At the expiration of every interim care order, the granting of any further interim care order must be considered independently on its merits. It can never be right for a court granting an interim care order at one sitting to attempt to lay down a policy which might fetter the discretion of any future sitting in regard to the grant or refusal of a further interim care order – see *Re P (Minors) (Interim Order)* [1993] 2 FLR 742, CA.

25 It is, therefore, necessary for the court to make a judgment regarding renewal on each occasion, and the court should treat each further hearing as an opportunity to monitor the progress of the application. This does not necessarily mean that all parties should be required to attend a hearing on each occasion. The court is entitled to deal with the matter on the basis of attendance by the local authority only, provided that written consents of the other parties are produced and no party objects.

26 It is therefore suggested that, provided the parents of any child concerned (or any other party with whom the child has been living) are legally represented, provision may be made in the first directions order for a further interim care order to be made without the need for the personal attendance of all parties.

27 When any party objects to the renewal:

(*a*) that party shall set out the change of circumstances relied upon, and then:
(*b*) the court must direct an inter partes hearing, allowing sufficient time for the arguments to be heard;
(*c*) the local authority must inform the court of any objection which it receives; and
(*d*) the local authority should be prepared to report as to progress and all parties' compliance with directions.

28 The procedure would therefore be as follows.

(*a*) At the first hearing the court would make the interim care order and further order that:

"The application is adjourned to [date] when the court will consider whether a further interim care order should be made. Provided consents to the making of a further interim care order have been received, and no notice of objection has been received by the [applicant local authority] by 4.00 p.m. on [48 hours before the hearing date] no party other than the applicant need attend."

(*b*) Court staff should then list the date for the judge, district judge, or justices' clerk to deal with the application. The appointment should be allowed only a short time; if there are several such appointments, they could be blocklisted.
(*c*) If any objection is received, the court and, if appropriate, the local authority, must notify all parties urgently that they must attend. In the event of there being inadequate time to hear a contested hearing, the court must urgently fix a date for hearing and make a short term interim care order to cover the interim period.

29 Where a local authority:

(*a*) produces consents from all parties;
(*b*) confirms that all directions have been complied with; and
(*c*) considers that it might be unduly onerous to require the personal attendance of its representative, then there is no reason in principle why the court should not permit the local authority to make a written application for renewal. In such a case, responsibility would rest with the local authority to ensure that a written application was acceptable to the court, and that all parties concerned were satisfied that the papers would reach the court file in time for the hearing.

30 A suggested draft certificate is set out on the following pages.

31 This procedure should not be adopted where any party is in breach of any direction.

32 Where any parent, or other person who has had or who seeks care of the child, is unrepresented, the court should make a tailor-made order, depending on that party's significance in the case, and give notice of every hearing to that person.

[*see following page for Draft application for further interim care order*]

Draft application for further interim care order

APPLICATION for further Interim Care Order

Date present order due to expire:

Date of Final Directions/PTR:

Date of Final Hearing:

Estimated length of Final Hearing:

Respondents' representatives:

1 Name:

Address:

Telephone number:

2 Name:

Address:

Telephone number:

3 Name:

Address:

Telephone number:

Child/guardian ad litem's representative:

Name:

Address:

Telephone number:

Nature of current placement:

Has placement changed since last order?	YES/NO
Is change proposed during this order?	YES/NO
Extent of contact offered:	
Has this been taken up?	FULL/PARTIAL/NONE

Timetable

has the timetable been complied with to date?	YES/NO
can all outstanding orders be met?	YES/NO
are there any on-going assessments?	YES/NO
is it expected they will affect the timetable?	YES/NO

(If there has been any actual change in placement or any is proposed, please attach a short report addressing that matter.)

As solicitors for the [local authority] we enclose copies of consents received, and certify that we have received no notice of objection to the making of a further interim care order from any party. We apply for a further interim care order to remain in force until [date]:

signed:

date:

SECTION 3 – FIRST APPOINTMENTS IN PUBLIC LAW CASES IN THE COUNTY COURTS: THE ROLE OF THE COURT

Introduction

33 Nominated care district and Circuit judges who deal with directions appointments in public law cases have a vital role in ensuring that the case is properly brought on for hearing. Such matters as renewal of interim care orders,

decisions on split hearings, joinder of parties and timetabling are of the utmost importance and may have a crucial effect on the outcome of the case. It is, therefore, essential that the judge should have been able to read and absorb the papers in the case before the hearing otherwise it will be very difficult for him to challenge anything which the parties' representatives tell him.

The role of the family proceedings court in cases to be transferred

34 It is inevitable that first appointments are listed at very short notice. The clerk of the family proceedings court should:

(*a*) notify the care centre of the transfer by telephone and ask the date of the first appointment before the judge;
(*b*) inform all parties of the directions appointment in the care centre;
(*c*) ensure that the file of papers reaches the care centre not later than midday on the day before the hearing, using a courier service if necessary; and
(*d*) alert the district judge, by telephone if necessary, to any unusual factor in the case.

The role of the care centre

35 Listing staff in the care centre *must*:

(*a*) on the telephone, give the clerk of the family proceedings court a date for a directions hearing within two working days;
(*b*) place the file before the judge on the afternoon before the hearing;
(*c*) inform the judge of the listing of the application;
(*d*) (wherever possible) make listed time available for the judge to read the papers; and
(*e*) (wherever possible) list appointments subsequent to the first appointment before the same judge to ensure continuity of approach.

SECTION 4 – PRIVATE LAW CASES

Introduction

36 The following is a brief guide to best practice in applications made under section 8 of the Children Act. This guidance may need to be tailored to deal with cases involving unrepresented litigants.

37 Specific good practice for cases involving allegations of sexual abuse is set out in the Annex to this section.

Before proceedings

38 Consider whether the dispute between the parties could be resolved in any way other than litigation. Most areas have a mediation service which would be able to attempt to deal with disputes by way of negotiation and agreement. There is rarely anything to be lost, and normally much to be gained, by mediation.

39 At the earliest stage, if it becomes clear that negotiated or mediated settlement will not be possible, focus on:

(*a*) the issues, including the question of how crucial facts are to be proved;

(*b*) the legal framework; and
(*c*) the evidence needed to support the case to be put forward.

Issue of proceedings

40 Ensure that form C1 contains all relevant information, including a brief outline of the case (but not a detailed statement by the applicant).

41 To prevent unnecessary delay at the first directions appointment, prepare at least draft statements by:

(*a*) the applicant, and
(*b*) any witnesses who it is known will have to give evidence.

The first directions appointment

The role of the court

42 The court will fix a first directions appointment when an application is issued. The task of the court at the first appointment is to:

(*a*) investigate the issues;
(*b*) inquire into the possibility of settlement; and
(*c*) give directions in any case which has to proceed.

43 When giving directions, the court will normally:

(*a*) consider the appropriate tier of court;
(*b*) order the filing of witness statements;
(*c*) consider whether there are circumstances justifying sequential rather than simultaneous exchange;
(*d*) express times for filing (for example, of witness statements or the court welfare officer's report) by fixing a date, eg "by 28 April 1997" and not "within 14 days"; and
(*e*) include in the order the date for the next appointment and, even if only provisionally, the final hearing.

44 An order should not provide for an application to be adjourned generally unless the parties consider that it will not be necessary to return to court. In that event the order should also provide for the application to stand dismissed if not restored by a certain date.

45 The order should provide that any letter of instructions to experts (to be joint instructions wherever possible) is to be filed at court.

46 A paginated bundle of documents and chronology should be normal practice except in the simplest case.

The role of the parties

47 Parties and their legal representatives must attend directions appointments unless specifically excused.

48 A party's legal representative must have both sufficient knowledge and authority to take any necessary decisions.

49 Use the first appointment imaginatively, anticipating problems and addressing them in advance, and dealing with questions of expert evidence. (See **Section 5**)

50 When it is to be suggested that there should be contact at a contact centre or supervised contact by an individual, make enquiries to ensure that the centre or individual will be available to provide the service.

Welfare reports

51 Parties should have access to a court welfare officer, or other person qualified to assist them, at or before the first appointment. Some courts achieve this by requiring a court welfare officer to attend the first appointment, others by referring the parties to the welfare officer before the date of the first appointment. Ask about the practice of the local court if you are in any doubt.

52 If a welfare officer has attempted to mediate between the parties, he should not be involved in the case in any other way.

53 When ordering a welfare report, the guidance as to best practice under "Welfare Reports" at *Best Practice Note of January 1995* should be followed. In particular:

(*a*) the request for a report should state the issue giving rise to the request;
(*b*) addendum reports should not normally be ordered, and should not be necessary for the hearing if timetabling has been effective;
(*c*) any request for the court welfare officer to attend the final hearing should be examined carefully, and not granted as a matter of course;
(*d*) when a court requires the court welfare officer to attend a hearing, enquiry should be made to ensure that he is available; and
(*e*) the court hearing the case should allow the officer to give evidence first and then to be released.

Final directions appointments or pre-trial reviews

54 The final directions appointment, or pre-trial review, should be timetabled to take place when any welfare report and all evidence has been filed.

55 The applicant's solicitor must prepare an agreed and paginated bundle of documents, containing an index and a chronology, not less than 24 hours before the hearing.

56 The court will expect the parties' advisers to have addressed the question of what evidence can be agreed and what is in dispute. An order will be made accordingly.

57 The counsel or solicitor who will attend the final hearing should attend the pre-trial review. If this is not possible, the person attending must be thoroughly conversant with the case and competent to make any necessary concessions or admissions and to advise the lay client in respect of settlement.

The final hearing

58 Except by direction of the court, children should not attend a hearing.

59 Consider how the decision of the court is to be communicated to the children. In some cases, particularly where the court's decision is contrary to the reported wishes of the child, it may be appropriate for the court welfare officer to see the child to explain what has happened.

Annex: Flawed sexual abuse investigation

Despite the guidance in *B v B (Sexual Abuse: Procedural Delay)* [1994] 1 FLR 323 and *Re A and B (Minors) (No 2)* [1995] 1 FLR 351, problems continue to occur in private law cases where allegations of sexual abuse of a child are investigated by the police and/or social services. Frequently the cases involve an application for contact with a child, where the primary carer has refused contact on the ground that the child has been sexually abused by the applicant. Such cases cause particular difficulties where the applicant denies the allegation, and alleges that the other parent has either invented the sexual abuse or has brainwashed the child into believing that sexual abuse has occurred. The parent opposing contact may be obstructive and use delaying tactics in order to prevent contact taking place, even under supervision. If such cases are not strictly timetabled, resulting delays can achieve the object of frustrating resumption of contact, even if the court finds that sexual abuse is not proved. Good practice requires as follows:

(*a*) The legal representatives have a duty, irrespective of whether or not delay might be tactically of advantage to their client, to ensure that a case does not drift and is resolved with the minimum of delay.

(*b*) The timetable must be strictly controlled by the court and must never be left to the parties. As in public law cases, the court must monitor the procedural steps ordered, building in reviews of progress and setting stringent time limits and return dates.

(*c*) When the local authority is involved with a concurrent, but independent investigation, the principal co-ordinating agency for the determination of issues is the court, using section 7 of the Children Act 1989 which enables the court to require the local authority to report to the court on the nature, progress and outcome of the child protection investigation. Section 7 should be used to keep the parties informed of progress and material available.

(*d*) The local authority should make available a social worker to give evidence on the report and to be cross examined if so required.

(*e*) Any joint child abuse interview conducted by police and social services must follow the memorandum of good practice. Otherwise not only is the resulting interview of no forensic value, but it may impede or contaminate any further assessment of the child ordered by the court.

(*f*) The court has power to compel discovery of documents held by local authorities or the police, eg videos of interview with the child. If any arguments arise as to confidentiality, or public interest immunity, they should be determined at an early stage at a directions hearing.

(*g*) Although the court cannot compel a prosecuting authority to reach decisions speedily, the court can and should bring to the attention of the authority the need for a timely decision on criminal prosecution.

(*h*) Even when there is a police investigation, there is no good legal or social work reason why the social worker should not make contact with the parent under investigation, so that information can be given and exchanged which is relevant to the welfare of the child. The social worker should make it clear that until the police investigation is complete, the specific allegation cannot be discussed. Many parents under police investigation suffer a sense of grievance when no reason is given for denial of contact, with the result that the parent perceives the local authority as pursuing investigations with a closed mind and a presumption of guilt.

(*i*) The issue whether or not a child has been sexually abused is for decision by the court and it is essential that other agencies await that decision

PART IV

before introducing management, counselling or therapy that pre-judges the issue. Therefore, the welfare of the child demands speedy resolution of issues.

(*j*) If leave is sought to instruct an expert, it is essential to define the issues, to establish the area of expertise required and the proposed timetable, to consider joint instruction and to follow the guidance in **Section 5**. In deciding whether to grant leave for a child to be assessed the court should consider carefully the issues, and whether the court is likely to be assisted in determining whether sexual abuse has been established, as opposed to outcome, by the contribution from an expert in the field of psychological medicine.

(*k*) There is often a tension between a positive clinical finding of sexual abuse, and judicial findings that abuse has not occurred. In contested cases clinical methods will inevitably be subjected to scrutiny. Any investigation which focuses attention on the statements of the child runs the risk of producing a false result if what the child says is unreliable or if the child's primary caretaker is unreliable, particularly where the allegation emerges in bitterly contested section 8 proceedings. The dangers of a false conclusion are enhanced if the alleged perpetrator is excluded from clinical investigation. It is vital to approach a child abuse investigation with an open mind.

(*l*) Where possible directions appointments should be heard by the judge who is likely to determine the substantive issues.

(*m*) In cases in which there is a stark factual issue to be determined the court will need to consider carefully whether it is appropriate to obtain a section 7 report clarifying the issues before ordering a welfare report, whether factual issues need to be determined by the court before a welfare report is ordered as to outcome, or whether a report should be ordered at an early stage in the proceedings. Each case needs to be considered on its merits, and the court welfare service should be invited to make representations.

SECTION 5 – EXPERTS AND THE COURTS

Introduction

60 The guidance in this section applies equally to public and private law cases in which experts are instructed.

61 It is of critical importance to distinguish the respective functions of expert and judge.

(*a*) The expert forms an assessment, and expresses an opinion within the area of his expertise. This may include an opinion on the issues in the case, but the judge decides particular issues in individual cases.

(*b*) It is not for the judge to become involved in medical controversy, except in the rare case where such controversy is an issue in the case.

62 The court depends on the skill, knowledge, and above all, the professional and intellectual integrity of the expert witness.

Leave to instruct experts

The role of the instructing parties

63 Applications for leave to instruct experts should be considered by each party at the earliest possible stage of the proceedings in order to avoid serial applications by different parties seeking to counter opinions from experts which do not support their case. Such applications are likely to be refused – see *H v Cambridgeshire County Council* [1997] 1 FCR 569.

64 Advocates who seek such leave have a positive duty to place all relevant information before the court at the earliest opportunity. Applications are unlikely to succeed unless they specify:

(*a*) the category of expert evidence sought to be adduced;
(*b*) the name of the expert;
(*c*) his availability for reporting, meeting with other experts and attendance at court;
(*d*) the relevance of the expert evidence to the issues in the case;
(*e*) whether evidence can properly be obtained by both parties jointly instructing one expert; and
(*f*) whether expert evidence may properly be adduced by one party only, eg the guardian ad litem.

The role of the court

65 The court has a positive duty to enquire into the information provided by the party or parties seeking leave to instruct an expert.

66 The court should never make a generalised order for leave to disclose papers to an expert. The order should specify:

(*a*) the area of expertise;
(*b*) the issues to be addressed;
(*c*) the identity of the expert;
(*d*) the date by which the letter of instruction is to be sent;
(*e*) the documents to be released to the expert;
(*f*) the date for filing the expert's report with the court;
(*g*) a provision for experts of like discipline to communicate (as discussed below) to agree facts and define issues, together with responsibility for fixing the agenda and chairing the meeting; and
(*h*) the availability of the expert to give oral evidence, if required.

67 Expert reports based solely upon leave to disclose documents in a "paper exercise" are rarely as persuasive as those reports based on interviews and assessment as well as the documentation. *Re C (Expert Evidence: Disclosure Practice)* [1995] 1 FLR 204 provides guidance on experts, in contested cases, meeting in advance of the hearing. It should be a condition of appointment of any expert that he should be required to hold discussions with other experts instructed in the same field of expertise, in advance of the hearing, in order to identify areas of agreement and dispute, which should be incorporated into a schedule for the court. Such discussion should be chaired by a co-ordinator, such as the guardian ad litem if there is consent so to act. In advance of the meeting, the co-ordinator should prepare and circulate to all experts a schedule of issues and questions to be addressed at the meeting. The schedule should be prepared in co-operation with all parties, so that all relevant matters are considered by the experts.

68 Problems may arise when an expert's conclusion is unfavourable to the instructing party's case. The court may need to give consideration as to how that expert's evidence is to be adduced.

Letters of instruction and provision of information to experts

69 The letter of instruction should:

(*a*) define the context in which the opinion is sought;
(*b*) set out specific questions for the expert to address;
(*c*) identify any relevant issues of fact to enable each expert to give an opinion on each set of competing issues;
(*d*) specify any examinations to be permitted;
(*e*) list the documents to be sent to the expert, which should be presented in a sorted bundle and include an agreed chronology and background history; and
(*f*) require, as a condition of appointment, that the expert must, in advance of the hearing, hold discussions with other experts appointed in the same field of expertise, and produce a statement of agreement and disagreement on the issues by a specified date.

70 Always disclose the letter of instruction to the other parties, and invite them to contribute to defining the appropriate issues, relevant documentation, history, and questions to be addressed. Include the resulting letter in the bundle of documents for use in court.

71 Doctors who have clinical experience of a child before the commencement of proceedings should have all clinical material made available for inspection by the court and other experts, eg medical notes, hospital records, x-rays, photographs, and correspondence.

72 It is the instructing solicitor's duty to ensure that an expert who is to give oral evidence is kept up to date with relevant developments in the case.

73 It is the duty of the advocate calling an expert to ensure that the witness, in advance of giving oral evidence, has seen all fresh relevant material, and is aware of new developments.

Duties of experts

74 The role of the expert is to provide independent assistance to the court by way of objective, unbiased opinion, in relation to matters within his expertise. Expert evidence presented to the court must be, and be seen to be, the independent product of the expert, uninfluenced by the instructing party.

75 Acceptance of instructions imposes an obligation to

(*a*) comply with the court's timetable and
(*b*) notify the instructing solicitors promptly if there is any risk that the timetable cannot be adhered to.

76 Experts should not hesitate to seek further information and documentation when this is required. Such requests should form part of the court bundle.

77 In his report, an expert should:

(*a*) state the facts or assumptions on which his opinion is based, and not omit to consider material facts which detract from his concluded opinion;

(*b*) make it clear when a particular aspect of the case is outside his expertise;
(*c*) indicate, if appropriate, that his opinion is not properly researched because of insufficient data, and is therefore provisional; and
(*d*) inform the other parties, and, when appropriate, the court if at any time he changes his opinion on a material matter.

78 If an opinion is based, wholly or in part, on research conducted by others, the expert must:

(*a*) set this out clearly in the report;
(*b*) identify the research relied on;
(*c*) state its relevance to the points at issue; and
(*d*) be prepared to justify the opinions expressed.

79 It is unacceptable for any expert in a child case, whose evidence is relevant to the outcome, to give evidence without having read, in advance, the report of the guardian ad litem.

Assisting the experts

80 Legal advisers for the parties should co-operate, at an early stage in the preparation for trial, to ensure availability of the experts to give evidence in a logical sequence.

81 It is helpful to timetable experts, in a difficult case, to give evidence one after another, so that each can listen to the evidence of other experts, and comment on that evidence.

82 Child proceedings are non-adversarial, and it is not necessary that witnesses are called in conventional order.

83 Where it becomes clear that an expert's opinion is uncontentious, and that the expert will not be required to attend court, he must be notified at the earliest opportunity. Whenever attendance at court is necessary, the court must always try to accommodate the expert by interposing the evidence at a given time.

84 In order that all relevant matters are fully considered at the appropriate time in advance of the hearing, it is essential that advocates who will appear at the hearing are involved at the earliest stage in order to consider how the case should be prepared and progressed.

The Expert Witness Group

85 The Expert Witness Group has been active in developing an "Expert Witness Pack", which it hopes to have published in the autumn of 1997. The pack, which will be available for purchase and will be cited in bibliographies, etc, will include several pro formas and:

(*a*) draft letters of instruction and acceptance;
(*b*) a checklist for both solicitor and expert;
(*c*) guidelines and a model curriculum vitae for expert witnesses; and
(*d*) a model format for experts' reports.

86 Further information about the Expert Witness Group and the Expert Witness Pack may be obtained from: Dr Eileen Vizard, Consultant Child and Adolescent Psychiatrist, Camden and Islington Community Health Services NHS Trust, Simmons House Adolescent Unit, St. Luke's-Woodside Hospital, Woodside Avenue, London N10 3HU (Telephone: 0181 219 1883).

SECTION 6 – APPEALS FROM THE FAMILY PROCEEDINGS COURTS UNDER SECTION 94 OF THE CHILDREN ACT 1989

87 Appeals lie to a single judge of the Family Division unless the President otherwise directs. The procedure on appeal is set out in Rule 4.22 of the Family Proceedings Rules 1991.

88 Despite guidance in reported cases, problems continue to arise in the preparation and determination of such appeals.

89 Compliance with the rules and good practice requires the following.

(*a*) The merits of an appeal must be carefully and expeditiously considered. Dissatisfaction with the decision of the family proceedings court will not justify an appeal, unless the court erred in the exercise of discretion within the meaning of *G v G* [1985] FLR 894. An appeal is not a rehearing.

(*b*) Time limits are strict. An appeal must be commenced by filing and serving the notice of appeal on all parties and on any guardian ad litem within 14 days of the decision, unless the appeal is against an interim care order or interim supervision order, in which event the time limit is 7 days. The period for service may be altered by the High Court on application, to a longer or shorter period, under Rule 4.22(3)(*c*). The High Court will not grant an extension of time without good reason and advocates must be prepared to justify such applications.

(*c*) The documents set out in Rule 4.22(2) must be filed in the nearest district registry which is a care centre to the court in which the order appealed from was made. Good practice requires that all reports and witness statements filed in the proceedings should be filed for the appeal in addition to the documents identified in Rule 4.22(2).

(*d*) The family proceedings court must as a matter of urgency supply to the appellant a typed copy of the notes of evidence and of the reasons for the decision. It is detrimental to the welfare of the child concerned if there is any delay in the production of these documents.

(*e*) Strict time limits are laid down for a respondent who wishes to cross appeal, or to seek a variation, or an affirmation of the decision on grounds other than those relied upon by the family proceedings court. Within 14 days of receipt of the notice of appeal the respondent must file and serve on all parties to the appeal, a notice in writing setting out the grounds relied on. No notice may be filed or served in an appeal against an order under section 38.

90 The appeal should be set down promptly. Where it is unlikely that a case can be listed without delay on Circuit, arrangements will be made for the appeal to be heard in London.

91 In advance of the hearing the appellant must file a paginated bundle with a chronology and in all save the most simple cases, each party must file a skeleton argument. There is a duty upon advocates to file in advance an accurate time estimate of the length of hearing, and to keep the court informed of any change to that estimate.

92 Any application for a stay pending appeal must be made to the High Court. The family proceedings court has no power to grant a stay.

SECTION 7 – DISCLOSURE OF LOCAL AUTHORITY DOCUMENTS

Early consideration

93 Crown Prosecution Service and defence solicitors should give early consideration whether disclosure of records held in the possession of a local authority may be required. The appropriate time for such consideration will be at the commencement of the 4 weeks period (custody cases) or 6 weeks period (bail cases) between committal or transfer and the plea and directions hearing.

94 The parties should inform the judge of the steps that have been taken so that, if necessary, directions may be given and noted on the questionnaire.

95 Requests by the Crown Prosecution Service or the defence solicitor for disclosure should:

(*a*) be made in writing to the legal services department of the local authority who will nominate a lawyer to deal with the matter;

(*b*) provide specific details of the information required and an explanation as to why it is relevant to the proceedings, identifying as precisely as possible the category and nature of the documents for which disclosure is sought and

(*c*) be accompanied by a copy of the indictment or of the schedule of charges upon committal.

96 If the defence solicitors request information, they should notify the Crown Prosecution Service of the request and vice versa.

97 Case records will be examined by legal services and the appropriate officer to identify whether they contain the information which is sought.

98 Information which is disclosed to the defence solicitors will also be disclosed to the Crown Prosecution Service and vice versa.

99 If the case records do *not* contain the requested information, the requester will be so informed by legal services which, subject to relevance and the principle of confidentiality, may be able (but is not bound) to provide a summary of the type of information which is on file.

100 If the requester is not satisfied with the response, legal services, after appropriate consultation, will provide the name of a person to be witness summonsed to attend court with the records.

101 Where the case records do contain the information requested, legal services will disclose it so long as it is not protected by public interest immunity, legal privilege or statutory confidentiality.

102 If the local authority wishes to assert protection from disclosure for the records requested or any of them, legal services, after appropriate consultation, will provide the name of a person to be witness summonsed to attend court with the records.

103 If the local authority wishes to make representations as to why the records requested should not be disclosed, it will inform:

(*a*) the requester;
(*b*) the opposing party's representative and
(*c*) the court listing officer,

and a convenient date for listing, before a judge will be set.

104 The local authority should provide a skeleton argument and serve it on the parties and the court.

105 At the hearing:

(*a*) the witness must produce the records to the judge;
(*b*) files must be flagged to identify the documents for which immunity from disclosure is sought;
(*c*) representations will be made on behalf of the parties; and
(*d*) the judge will give appropriate directions.

106 Whenever possible, the hearing will be before the judge who will be conducting the trial. If the trial judge has not been nominated, then the hearing judge may determine the issue of disclosure.

107 The judge will give his decision in court or chambers, in the presence of the parties' representatives.

108 The judge may also give direction as to the custody of the records pending trial and as to any copies to be obtained on behalf of the parties.

109 The hearing referred to above should take place not less than 4 weeks before trial.

110 Where the requester has reasonable grounds to believe that a witness or a defendant has been involved with social services, information may be obtained by writing to the relevant department stating the witness's or defendant's name, date of birth and address.

Confidentiality of records

111 The court will normally conduct the hearing at which public interest immunity is claimed in chambers, where the local authority may be represented by a solicitor.

112 When records are disclosed to the parties by order of the court, it is on the undertaking that:

(*a*) they will only be used for the purpose of the criminal proceedings before the court; and
(*b*) their contents are revealed only to the parties and their legal representatives. (Leave of the court must be obtained for wider disclosure, eg to an expert witness.)

Costs

113 An officer of the local authority who necessarily attends court for the purpose of the proceedings otherwise than as a witness may be allowed expenses (Regulation 18(2) within Costs in Criminal Cases (General) Regulations 1986).

114 The court has no power to order payment from central funds of the cost of a search or legal costs.

115 If the court rules that the application for disclosure is frivolous or by way of a fishing expedition, it may order that costs be paid by the applicant or his legal advisers.

APPENDIX A

GUIDANCE, BEST PRACTICE NOTES AND PRO FORMAS FROM THE COMMITTEE'S PREVIOUS ANNUAL REPORTS

I Best practice guidance on section 37(1) directions

Set out in the notes to CA 1989, s 37(1).

II Urgent hearings on Circuit before Family Division judges: standby procedure

Set out as *President's Guidance of 17 December 1993*.

[*see following page for Questionnaire on guardian ad litem performance*]

PART IV

III Questionnaire on guardian ad litem performance

Name of Guardian

Name of case: No:

Part one *(To be completed by the staff)*

1. Did the GAL appoint a solicitor for the first hearing? Yes/No
2. Did the GAL attend all directions and interim hearings as appropriate? Yes/No
3. Did the GAL adhere to the court timetable? Yes/No
4. Did the GAL respond to telephone calls and letters satisfactorily? Yes/No

Part two *(To be completed by the Judge/Magistrates)*

5.Did you consider the report to be *(Tick as appropriate)*

Good
Adequate
Poor

6. Did the GAL give oral evidence *(Tick as appropriate)*

Well
Adequately
Inadequately

7. Did the GAL's argument / evidence justify the recommendation made? *(Tick as appropriate)*

Well
Adequately
Inadequately

8. If you have any further comments as to any aspects of the GAL's work please state them:

Name of court:

Date:

Signed:

Name:

Please return to:

IV Local authority assessments

Special considerations arise where the local authority wish to carry out an assessment eg a Section 37 assessment or family assessment.

In such cases the court should:

(i) Identify the purpose of the assessment.
(ii) Specify the time in which the assessment is to be carried out and direct that evidence of the outcome of the assessment be filed by a given date.
(iii) Fix a directions hearing for a date immediately after the date fixed for the completion of the assessment.
(iv) At the directions hearing the court should consider what evidence is needed to bring the case speedily and fairly to final or substantive hearing.
(v) Where the court exercises its discretion to grant leave for the papers to be shown to a particular expert, the court should go on to give directions.

These should:

- State the timescale in which the evidence in question should be produced.
- Provide for the disclosure of any written expert report both to all parties and to the other experts in the case. When a report is disclosed it should include a copy of the letter of instruction.
- Provide for discussion between experts following mutual disclosure of reports and for the filing of further evidence by the experts stating the areas of agreement and disagreement between the experts. Parties should only instruct experts who are willing to meet in advance of the hearing. When granting leave, the court must make this a condition of the appointment.

Where it proves impracticable to give such directions at the time when leave to disclose the report is granted, the court must set a date for a further directions hearing at which such directions can be given.

V Bundles of documents

Set out as *Practice Note of 11 November 1993*.

VI Best practice note for the judiciary and family proceedings courts when ordering a court welfare officer's report

Set out as *Best Practice Note of January 1995*.

VII Best practice note to court staff when welfare reports have been ordered

Set out as *Best Practice Note of January 1995*.

VIII Welfare report referral form

Set out as *Best Practice Note of January 1995*.

[*see following page for Receipt and undertaking for video recordings*]

IX Receipt and undertaking for video recordings

Name of solicitor Name of firm

Address

Telephone Solicitor's reference

I, the above named solicitor, hereby confirm that I am acting for (insert name of client):

who is a party to the proceedings currently before the court concerning (insert name of child or children):

I acknowledge receipt of the recording marked "Evidence of "

I acknowledge that this recording is and will remain the property of the Chief Constable of .... Police notwithstanding the fact that I agree to pay the reasonable expenses incurred by .... Police in providing me with this recording on loan.

I undertake that whilst the recording is in my possession I shall:

(a) not make or permit any other person to make a copy of the recording;

(b) not make or permit any disclosure of the recording or its contents to any person except when in my opinion it is strictly necessary in the interests of the child and / or the interests of justice;

(c) not part with possession of the recording to anyone other than to counsel instructed by me or to an expert witness authorised by the court, and in particular

(d) NOT PART WITH POSSESSION OF THE RECORDING TO *(insert name of client)*

(e) at all times (except whilst being played) keep the recording in a locked, secure container and not leave it unattended in vehicles or otherwise unprotected;

(f) record details of the name of any person allowed access to the recording and produce such record to an officer of .... Police upon request;

(g) ensure that any person who takes possession of the recording under paragraph (c) above is supplied with a copy of this undertaking and agrees to be bound by its terms;

(h) return the recording to .... Police immediately upon the conclusion of the proceedings or when I am no longer professionally instructed in the matter whichever is sooner;

(i) give notice to .... Police of any application to the court which may result in the variation of the terms set out in this undertaking.

Signed:
Dated:

X Guidance as to preparation of the justices' written findings and reasons - The Honourable Mr Justice Cazalet

General

1 The obligations placed upon justices and their clerks are set out succinctly in Rules 21(5) and (6) of the Family Proceedings Courts (Children Act 1989) Rules 1991. Stated summarily these require that before the court makes an order or refuses an application or request, the justices' clerk shall record in writing, in consultation with the justices, the reason for the court's decision and any finding of fact. Furthermore, when justices make an order or refuse an application, the court, or one of the justices constituting the court by which the decision is made, shall state any finding of fact or reasons for the court's decision. These provisions are straightforward and are expressed in terminology which is unequivocal. They must be interpreted literally and strictly.

2 The justices and their clerks must ensure that the reasons and findings of fact are stated at the time the order is made. They cannot be added to subsequently. The written reasons and findings of fact must accord with what is stated in court. Justices cannot make an order and then reserve judgment (a luxury which the Court of Appeal is permitted). Justices must give their reasons, and any findings made, each time they make an order or decline to make an order.

3 There can be no "back door" process. That is to say that if, on appeal, a point is taken which the justices did consider in their deliberations but omitted to put in their reasons, they cannot formally make a subsequent addendum to those reasons and supply them to the appeal court.

4 Even when the parties are agreed, there is, none the less, an overriding duty in the court to investigate the proposals advanced by the parties. However, the extent of the investigation must reflect reality and so, when an agreed order is sought, the investigation of the evidence need not and should not be dealt with in full detail unless there are concerns as to the propriety of the order. Nevertheless, it is particularly important that in cases where a care order is made by consent the basis upon which the care order is made is clearly stated, for example because of a failure to protect from an abusive spouse or an agreed non-accidental injury as set out in some statement identified in the proceedings. If this step is taken it will avoid a long and perhaps inconclusive later trawl through the evidence in the earlier case in an attempt to establish what the actual finding then was and its relevance to a different child or new family situation. Also, justices must bear in mind that it will always be important for the child's wishes (given that the child is of sufficient age and maturity for those wishes to be relevant) to be taken into consideration. A consent order sought by the parents may not always properly reflect this.

5 The Children Act has brought two fundamental changes in the way that justices conduct hearings. First they must read all the papers before coming to court (that is to say they must come into court "hot"); second they must give their reasons and findings of fact in writing. It is essential that justices are fully conversant with the written documents before the case starts. This will have one advantage in particular. The justices will know when to intervene to stop evidence being led which simply repeats what has already been stated, usually in a statement of evidence in chief. This unnecessary repetition can be extremely time wasting.

6 It is vital to remember that the findings of fact and reasons will form the basis of any appeal accordingly they must be clearly stated. In order to avoid pressure of

time when reasons are being prepared it may be appropriate to release the parties for a period or to require them to come back the next day. In this event only one of the justices concerned need attend and read out the written reasons and findings.

7 Clarity in findings and reasons is important not only so that the appeal court knows the basis on which the decision has been made but also so that the losing party knows why the decision has gone against him. It is worth remembering that decisions in family cases, unlike most other decisions in the courts, concern the future. If the losing party leaves court without understanding properly why the order has been made against him because the court has not clearly explained the reason for its decision then this will not augur well for later hearings and may well give rise to a sense of grievance which impedes the working of the order.

8 Do not be afraid to raise points with advocates during their speeches. This should help to clarify difficult points.

9 When justices make an order which differs from the advice or conclusion reached in the report of the court welfare officer or guardian ad litem it is imperative for them to set out in clear terms why they have done so. This need not be stated at great length but it must be possible for the parties (and if there is an appeal, for the appellate court) to follow the process whereby the different conclusion was reached.

10 When the arguments of the losing party are being dealt with in the findings state these first before the arguments of the party in whose favour the decision is to be made.

11 When you intervene because an advocate is being too long winded, repetitious or adversarial you will carry much more authority if you have read and fully understood the papers in the case. When you do intervene be firm, courteous and controlled.

12 When you are dealing with a care case it is usually helpful to require the advocate when opening the case for the local authority to state specifically the facts upon which he relies as establishing that the threshold criteria apply. This will enable the court to direct its mind to the material evidence as it emerges and should help to clarify at an early stage the findings which will have to be made to support a care order.

More specific guidelines in setting out reasons and findings of fact

There are a number of different proformas used by different justices for the purposes of setting out their reasons and findings of fact. Once a particular system which works satisfactorily has evolved then it would be a mistake to interfere with it in any fundamental way. I accordingly set out below some guidelines which may be of assistance in formulating reasons and findings.

1 At the start state brief details about the child, parents and any other party (this includes dealing with family, siblings and where the child makes his/her home etc).

2 State, in concise form, the competing applications (ie the orders which each party is seeking).

3 State the relevant facts not in dispute, including appropriate background details (this will include stating physical injuries, emotional or educational problems from which the child may have suffered and which are not in dispute. This will *not* deal with the cause of such injuries unless that also is not in dispute). Keep this short.

4 Set out in general form the facts in dispute (for example the cause of a non-accidental injury). This will normally involve a short statement of the competing assertions by the parties concerned.

5 State your findings of fact including in particular, where appropriate, whose evidence was preferred. In general terms you should state the reasons for preferring one witness to another (for example because he or she was more convincing, because there was corroboration, or because one witness clearly had a better recollection than another and so forth). Be careful before you call a witness a liar. We are not infallible!

6 An appellate court cannot write into justices' reasons inference and findings working backwards from their conclusions. The material findings of fact must be stated so be as firm as you feel you can be when stating your findings.

7 State concisely any relevant law, and refer to the threshold criteria. Refer to any *relevant* passage of legal authority cited.

8 State your conclusions from the facts found. In particular, if you are dealing with a care case you should state why you consider the threshold criteria to apply.

9 State your decision and reasons for it, making clear that you have taken into account the welfare checklist by going through the relevant provisions.

Conclusion

The sequence stated above is the one that I usually follow. It matters not if you vary it somewhat or if your proforma follows a somewhat different sequence. The importance is that you should deal with all those particular headings.

The clerk is under a legal duty to record your findings and reasons in consultation with you. Once you have completed your deliberations you should call in the clerk and go through the record of your findings of fact and reasons. On the back of the proforma your clerk will enter the details of all the documentary evidence which was considered by the court.

Provided you follow these various heads you should cover all essential matters. The important thing is to get a system a sequence of headings under which you deal with the evidence and any submissions made by the advocates which lead on to your decision. Once you have learned to work within a particular framework, the preparation of the written findings and reasons will come much more easily.

APPENDIX B

THE OFFICIAL SOLICITOR: APPOINTMENT IN FAMILY PROCEEDINGS (PRACTICE NOTE)

Appointment as guardian ad litem of child subject of proceedings

Set out as *Practice Note of 8 September 1995*.

APPENDIX C

PRACTICE DIRECTIONS BY THE PRESIDENT OF THE FAMILY DIVISION

I Applications by children

Set out as *Practice Direction of 22 February 1993*.

II Case management

Set out as *Practice Direction of 31 January 1995*.

Practice Note 14 October 1997

Citations: [1998] 1 FLR 491; [1998] Fam Law 224

Hague Convention: Applications by Fathers without Parental Responsibility

With the approval of the Lord Chancellor, this statement has been prepared by the Lord Chancellor's Child Abduction Unit, which undertakes the duties of the Central Authority for England and Wales. Having regard to Art 27 of the Convention, this statement describes the Central Authority's current policies in respect of the acceptance of applications by fathers for the return of children for whom they do not have parental responsibility. The policies described in this statement will necessarily be modified to reflect changes in the law.

The Child Abduction Unit ("the CAU") has noticed an increasing number of applications relating to children removed or retained away from the United Kingdom whose parents are not married to each other. Such applications raise difficult questions about the position of unmarried fathers under the Hague Convention on the Civil Aspects of International Child Abduction 1980 ("the Convention").

"Wrongful removal" and "wrongful retention"

To constitute a "wrongful removal" or "wrongful retention" under the provisions of the Hague Convention, the removal or retention must be "in breach of rights of custody attributed to a person, an institution or any other body, either jointly or alone, under the law of the state in which the child was habitually resident immediately before the removal or retention …" (Art 3). A removal which is not in breach of domestic law may nevertheless be "wrongful" for the purposes of the Convention – see *Re F (A Minor) (Abduction: Custody Rights Abroad)* [1995] Fam 224, sub nom *Re F (Child Abduction: Risk if Returned)* [1995] 2 FLR 31, in which a mother who was not in breach of domestic law in removing her child from Colorado was nevertheless held to be in breach of the father's rights of custody.

"Rights of custody"

"Rights of custody" includes rights relating to the care of the person of the child and, in particular, the right to determine the child's place of residence (Art 5(*a*)).

> "The key concepts which determine the scope of the convention are not dependent for their meaning on any single legal system. Thus the expression 'rights of custody', for example, does not coincide with any particular concept

of custody in a domestic law, but draws its meaning from the definitions, structure and purposes of the convention" (*conclusion of the second meeting of the Special Commission to discuss the operation of the Convention, 1993*).[1]

1 And see *Re C (A Minor) (Abduction)* [1989] 1 FLR 403, 411F–H.

Such rights of custody may arise in particular by operation of law or by reason of a judicial or administrative decision, or by reason of an agreement having legal effect (Art 3).

The rights attributed to a person, an institution or any other body are a matter for the law of the state of the child's habitual residence, but it is for the requested state to determine whether such rights amount to "rights of custody" within the meaning of the Convention, whether at the time of removal or retention those rights were actually exercised, and whether there has been a breach of those rights.[2] A decision or other determination made pursuant to Art 15 in the state of the child's habitual residence that the removal or retention was wrongful within the meaning of Art 3 is thus not determinative, but provisional only.[3]

2 *Re F (A Minor) (Abduction: Custody Rights Abroad)* [1995] Fam 224 sub nom *Re F (Child Abduction: Risk if Returned)* [1995] 2 FLR 31.
3 *Re P (Abduction: Declaration)* [1995] 1 FLR 831.

"Rights of custody" and unmarried fathers

If an unmarried father in England and Wales has a final or interim residence order or has parental responsibility (normally acquired by way of a parental responsibility agreement or a parental responsibility order, whether or not made in consequence of a residence order)[4], he clearly has rights of custody within the meaning of the Convention. In such a case, unless the child is removed for less than one month by a person having a residence order[5], the removal or retention of the child away from the UK without the father's consent or the leave of the court is wrongful within the meaning of Art 3 of the Convention, because it breaches the father's rights of custody.[6]

4 Children Act 1989, s 12(1).
5 Children Act 1989, s 13(2).
6 Cf *Re F (A Minor) (Abduction: Custody Rights Abroad)* [1995] Fam 224, 234H–235A sub nom *Re F (Child Abduction: Risk if Returned)* [1995] 2 FLR 31, 39H–40B. Removal would also be an offence under the Child Abduction Act 1984.

Two reported English decisions appear to have expanded the concept of rights of custody to include more than strictly legal rights. It would seem from those decisions that if a father does not have parental responsibility, but immediately prior to the removal or retention was exercising parental functions over a substantial period of time, he may have "inchoate" rights of custody which constitute "rights of custody" within the meaning of the Convention. These are "the inchoate rights of those who are carrying out duties and enjoying privileges of a custodial or parental character which, though not yet formally recognised or granted by law, a court would nevertheless be likely to uphold in the interests of the child concerned" – see *Re B (A Minor) (Abduction)* [1994] 2 FLR 249, 261A–B, per Waite LJ, followed in *Re O (Child Abduction: Custody Rights)* [1997] 2 FLR 702. It is not easy to reconcile these decisions with the decision of the House of Lords in the case of *Re J (A Minor) (Abduction: Custody Rights)* [1990] 2 AC 562 sub nom *C v S (A Minor) (Abduction)* [1990] 2 FLR 442, but distinguishing features were that the persons whose rights of custody were held to have been breached were exercising their responsibilities either alone or with someone who did not have custodial rights, and also that in the one case an

PART IV

agreement relating to custody was about to be perfected and in the other custody proceedings were pending. It would seem from *Re J* that de facto joint custody is not enough.

"Rights of custody" and pending proceedings

With the exception of wardship[7], the institution and pendency of proceedings relating to a child does not of itself give rise in English law to any express or implied prohibition on the removal of the child from the jurisdiction by a mother with sole parental responsibility.[8]

7 See below.
8 As to the implied prohibition on removal during pending proceedings in other jurisdictions, see *C v C (Minors) (Child Abduction)* [1992] 1 FLR 163, in which it was held that removal of a child from New York State in breach of an *implied* prohibition on removal constituted a wrongful removal for Convention purposes.

In *Re F (A Minor) (Abduction: Custody Rights Abroad)* [1995] Fam 224, 231F–G, 238A–B, sub nom *Re F (Child Abduction: Risk if Returned)* [1995] 2 FLR 31, 36F–H, 43A–C, the view was expressed in the Court of Appeal that the existence of a court order or of pending proceedings does not automatically clothe a court with "rights of custody" within the meaning of the Convention.[9]

9 See *Re F (A Minor) (Abduction: Custody Rights Abroad)* [1995] Fam 224, 231F–G, 238A–B sub nom *Re F (Child Abduction: Risk if Returned)* [1995] 2 FLR 31, 36F–H, 43A–C.

In *B v B (Child Abduction: Custody Rights)* [1993] Fam 32, 38C, 42G, sub nom *B v B (Abduction)* [1993] 1 FLR 238, 243A, 247F, the Court of Appeal held that a foreign court seised of an application which gave it the right to determine the child's place of residence had rights of custody which were breached by the mother when she removed the child from its habitual residence. In that case, the foreign court had embarked upon the exercise of its rights of custody by adjourning the matter, giving directions as to how the matter should be dealt with, and by making an interim custody order.

In the light of these authorities, the CAU takes the view that where a mother with sole parental responsibility removes a child from the UK while proceedings relating to the child are pending, the removal may be wrongful within the meaning of Art 3 if before the date of removal the court has embarked upon the exercise of its powers and so is actively seised of the matter, but not otherwise.

The CAU does not support the view that once the court becomes actively seised of any "family proceedings" as defined by s 8(3) of the Children Act 1989, it has "rights of custody", because it can make a residence order of its own motion under the provisions of s 10(1)(*b*) of the Children Act 1989. The CAU takes the view that a court seised of "family proceedings" is simply exercising a judicial function, and cannot be said to have "rights of custody" merely because it has wide powers to make orders. An application for a residence order, by invoking the court's powers to determine the child's place of residence, would necessarily involve the exercise of the court's rights of custody within the meaning of the Convention, as would an application for an order restraining the removal of a child from the jurisdiction.[10] An application for a parental responsibility order, on the other hand, does not require the court to determine the child's place of residence, and thus would not involve an exercise by the court of rights of custody within the meaning of the Convention.

10 See *Re C (A Minor) (Abduction)* [1989] 1 FLR 403.

Note—The view expressed above that an application for a parental responsibility order does not require the court to determine the child's place of residence, and thus would not involve an exercise by the court of rights of custody within the meaning of the Convention was rejected by Hale J in *Re C (Abduction: Wrongful Removal)* [1999] 2 FLR 859, at 863D–864C. Her Ladyship observed that in making an order prohibiting removal the court was exercising rights of custody, and as the effect of a parental responsibility order was substantially equivalent to an order prohibiting removal, the court was also exercising rights of custody when making a parental responsibility order.

Restrictions on removal

If during the pendency of proceedings or when a substantive order is made a restriction is imposed on the removal of the child from the United Kingdom, any removal of the child in breach of that order will be wrongful within the meaning of the Convention. In *Re C (A Minor) (Abduction)* [1989] 1 FLR 403 it was held that an order restraining the removal of the child without the consent of the other parent created a right of custody in the non-custodial parent, in that it gave a right (by giving or withholding consent) to determine where the child should live.

Wardship proceedings; reliance on the custody rights of others

In *Re J (Abduction: Ward of Court)* [1989] Fam 85 sub nom *Re J (A Minor) (Abduction)* [1990] 1 FLR 276 it was held that the removal of a ward from the jurisdiction without the leave of the court by a mother having sole parental responsibility was wrongful, being in breach of the rights of custody attributed to the court;[11] and, further, that the father, who had no custody rights himself, could rely on the provisions of the Convention.[12]

11 Cf *Re B-M (Wardship: Jurisdiction)* [1993] 1 FLR 979 (wrongful retention of ward). The restriction on removal is modified by Family Law Act 1986, s 38.

12 At 89B. See also *Re B-M (Wardship: Jurisdiction)* [1993] 1 FLR 979, 985F–986A. In *The Ontario Court v M and M (Abduction: Children's Objections)* [1997] 1 FLR 475 Hollis J expressed the view that the Ontario court was not a legal personality, and was capable of neither suing nor being sued. It would seem, therefore, that when rights of custody are in a court, someone else must necessarily make the application for return. There are potential difficulties where, eg a parent has lost his right to rely upon a breach of his own rights of custody but seeks to rely upon a breach of the court's rights: see *Re K (Abduction: Consent: Forum Conveniens)* [1995] 2 FLR 211, 216B–E, per Waite LJ.

"Chasing orders" – orders made after removal

Occasionally a child is taken from the UK in circumstances which do not amount to a breach of rights of custody, but subsequently an order is made requiring the return of the child. The CAU takes the view that disobedience to that order can only constitute a wrongful retention within the meaning of the Convention if it can be demonstrated that the child was habitually resident in England and Wales when the order requiring the child's return was made.[13]

13 See *Re S (A Minor) (Custody: Habitual Residence)* [1997] 3 WLR 597, approving *Re B-M (Wardship: Jurisdiction)* [1993] 1 FLR 979. As to the ability of a sole holder of parental responsibility to change a child's habitual residence, see *Re M (Minors) (Residence Order: Jurisdiction)* [1993] 1 FLR 495; *Re J (A Minor) (Abduction: Custody Rights)* [1990] 2 AC 562, 578–579.

Central Authority for England and Wales

PART IV

President's Direction 17 December 1997

Citations: [1998] 1 FLR 495; [1998] Fam Law 109

Children Act 1989: Exclusion Requirement

Under s 38A(5) and s 44A(5) of the Children Act 1989 the court may attach a power of arrest to an exclusion requirement included in an interim care order or an emergency protection order. In cases where an order is made which includes an exclusion requirement, the following shall apply:

(1) If a power of arrest is attached to the order then unless the person to whom the exclusion requirement refers was given notice of the hearing and attended the hearing, the name of that person and that an order has been made including an exclusion requirement to which a power of arrest has been attached shall be announced in open court at the earliest opportunity. This may be either on the same day when the court proceeds to hear cases in open court or where there is no further business in open court on that day at the next listed sitting of the court.

(2) When a person arrested under a power of arrest cannot conveniently be brought before the relevant judicial authority sitting in a place normally used as a courtroom within 24 hours after the arrest, he may be brought before the relevant judicial authority at any convenient place but, as the liberty of the subject is involved, the press and the public should be permitted to be present, unless security needs make this impracticable.

(3) Any order of committal made otherwise than in public or in a courtroom open to the public, shall be announced in open court at the earliest opportunity. This may be either on the same day when the court proceeds to hear cases in open court or where there is no further business in open court on that day at the next listed sitting of the court. The announcement shall state (*a*) the name of the person committed, (*b*) in general terms the nature of the contempt of the court in respect of which the order of committal has been made and (*c*) the length of the period of committal.

Issued with the concurrence of the Lord Chancellor.

Sir Stephen Brown
President

President's Direction 17 December 1997

Citations: [1998] 1 FLR 496; [1998] Fam Law 109

Family Law Act 1996, Part IV

The procedure formulated in the President's Directions of 23 January 1980 and 7 March 1991, in relation to orders made under the Domestic Violence and Matrimonial Proceedings Act 1976, shall apply in respect of orders made under Part IV of the Family Law Act 1996, as follows:

(1) Where at a hearing which has been held in private, an occupation or non-molestation order is made to which a power of arrest is attached and the person to whom it is addressed was not given notice of the hearing and was not present at the hearing, the terms of the order and the name of the person to whom it is addressed shall be announced in open court at the earliest opportunity. This may be either on the same day when the court proceeds to hear cases in open court or where there is no further business in open court on that day at the next listed sitting of the court.

(2) When a person arrested under a power of arrest cannot conveniently be brought before the relevant judicial authority sitting in a place normally used as a courtroom within 24 hours after the arrest, he may be brought before the relevant judicial authority at any convenient place but, as the liberty of the subject is involved, the press and public should be permitted to be present, unless security needs make this impracticable.

(3) Any order of committal made otherwise than in public or in a courtroom open to the public, shall be announced in open court at the earliest opportunity. This may be either on the same day when the court proceeds to hear cases in open court or where there is no further business in open court on that day at the next listed sitting of the court. The announcement shall state (*a*) the name of the person committed, (*b*) in general terms the nature of the contempt of the court in respect of which the order of committal has been made and (*c*) the length of the period of committal.

Issued with the concurrence of the Lord Chancellor.

Sir Stephen Brown
President

Note—This Direction effectively replaces the President's Directions of 23 January 1980 and 7 March 1991.

PART IV

Practice Statement 22 April 1998

Citations: [1998] 1 FLR 1102; [1998] 1 WLR 825; [1998] 2 All ER 667

Supreme Court: Judgments

New arrangements for the delivery of judgments in all divisions of the High Court and in the Court of Appeal would be introduced to facilitate the availability and speedy publication of the approved text of judgments and to prevent the dissemination of unapproved texts.

The arrangements, made in agreement with Lord Woolf MR, Sir Richard Scott V-C, and Sir Stephen Brown, President of the Family Division, were to be regarded as experimental and would apply forthwith.

Lord Bingham of Cornhill CJ: Unless the court otherwise ordered, for example, if a judgment contained price-sensitive information, copies of the written judgment would be made available to the parties' legal advisers at about 4pm on the second working day before judgment was due to be pronounced on condition that the contents were not communicated to the parties themselves until one hour before the listed time for pronouncement of judgment.

Delivery to legal advisers was made primarily to enable them to consider the judgment and decide what consequential orders they should seek. The condition was imposed to prevent the outcome of the case being publicly reported before judgment was given, since the judgment was confidential until then.

Some judges might decide to allow the parties' legal advisers to communicate the contents of the judgment to their clients 2 hours before the listed time, in order that they might be able to submit minutes of the proposed order, agreed by their clients, to the judge before the judge came into court, and it would be open to judges to permit more information about the result of a case to be communicated on a confidential basis to the client at an earlier stage if good reason were shown for making such a direction.

If, for any reason, a party's legal advisers had special grounds for seeking a relaxation of the usual condition restricting disclosure to the party itself, a request for relaxation of the condition might be made informally through the judge's clerk, or through the associate, if the judge had no clerk.

A copy of the written judgment would be made available to any party who was not legally represented at the same time as to legal advisers. It had to be treated as confidential until judgment was given.

Every page of every judgment which was made available in that way would be marked "Unapproved judgment: No permission is granted to copy or use in court". These words would carry the authority of the judge and would mean what they said.

The time at which copies of the judgment were being made available to the parties' legal advisers was being brought forward 24 hours in order to enable them to submit any written suggestions to the judge about typing errors, wrong references and other minor corrections of that kind in good time, so that, if the judge thought fit, the judgment could be corrected before it was handed down formally in court.

The parties' legal advisers were therefore requested to submit a written list of corrections of that kind to the judge's clerk, or to the associate, if the judge had no clerk, by 3pm on the day before judgment was handed down.

In divisions of the court which had two or more judges, the list should be submitted in each case to the judge who was to deliver the judgment in question.

Lawyers were not being asked to carry out proofreading for the judiciary, but a significant cause of the present delays was the fact that minor corrections of that type were being mentioned to the judge for the first time in court, when there was no time to make any necessary corrections to the text.

Availability of approved versions of handed-down judgments: new arrangements

That course would make it very much easier for the judge to make any necessary corrections and to hand down the judgment formally as the approved judgment of the court without any need for the delay involved in requiring the court shorthand writer, in courts which had an official shorthand writer, to resubmit the judgment to the judge for approval.

It would always be open to the judge to direct the shorthand writer at the time of the hearing in court to include in the text of the judgment any last-minute corrections which were mentioned for the first time in court, or which it had proved impractical to incorporate in the judgments handed down.

In such an event the judge would make it clear whether the shorthand writer could publish the judgment, as corrected, as the approved judgment of the court without any further reference to the judge, or whether it should be resubmitted to the judge for approval.

It would be open to judges, if they wished, to decline to approve their judgments at the time they were delivered, in which case the existing practice of submitting the judgment for their approval would continue.

Handing down judgment in court: availability of uncorrected copies

When the court handed down its written judgment, it would pronounce judgment in open court. Copies of the written judgment would then be made available to accredited representatives of the media, and to accredited law reporters who were willing to comply with restrictions on copying, who identified themselves as such.

In cases of particular interest to the media, it would be helpful if requests for copies could be intimated to the judge's clerk, or the presiding Lord Justice's clerk, in advance of judgment, so that the likely demand for copies could be accurately estimated.

Because there would usually be insufficient time for the judge's clerk to prepare the necessary number of copies of the corrected judgment in advance, in most cases these uncorrected copies would similarly bear the warning "Unapproved Judgment: No permission is granted to copy or use in court".

The purpose of those arrangements was to place no barrier in the way of accredited representatives of the media who wished to report the judgments of the court immediately in the usual way, or to accredited law reporters who wished to prepare a summary or digest of the judgment or to read it for the purpose of deciding whether to obtain an approved version for reporting purposes.

Its purpose was to put a stop to the dissemination of unapproved, uncorrected, judgments for other purposes, while seeking to ensure that everyone who was interested in the judgment, other than the immediate parties, might be able to buy a copy of the approved judgment in most cases much more quickly than was possible at present.

If any member of the public, other than a party to the case, or any law reporter who was not willing to comply with the restrictions on copying, wished to read the written judgment of the court on the occasion when it was handed down, a copy would be made available for him or her to read and note in court on request made to the associate or to the clerk to the judge or the presiding Lord Justice.

The copy could not be removed from the court and had to be handed back after reading. The object was to ensure that such a person was in no worse a position than if the judgment had been read aloud in full.

Availability of approved judgments

In courts without an official shorthand writer, the approved judgment should contain on its frontispiece the rubric: "This is the official judgment of the court and I direct that no further note or transcript be made".

That would cover the requirements of Ord 68, r 1 of the Rules of the Supreme Court, in the cases to which that rule applied, and would provide for certainty in all other cases.

In future, all judgments delivered at the Royal Courts of Justice would be published in a common format.

For cases decided in the two divisions of the Court of Appeal and in the Crown Office List, copies of the approved judgment could be ordered from the official shorthand writers, on payment of the appropriate fee.

In the other courts in the Royal Courts of Justice, copies of the approved judgment could be ordered from the Mechanical Recording Department, on payment of the fee prescribed for copy documents. Disks containing the judgment would also be available from the official shorthand writers, and the Mechanical Recording Department, where relevant, on payment of an appropriate charge.

It was hoped that in most cases copies of the approved judgment would be available from these sources on the same day as the judgment was handed down: they should no longer be sought from judges' clerks.

Restrictions on disclosure or reporting

Anyone who was supplied with a copy of the handed-down judgment, or who read it in court, would be bound by any direction which the court might have given in a child case under s 39 of the Children and Young Persons Act 1933, or any other form of restriction on disclosure, or reporting of information in the judgment.

Availability of approved versions of ex tempore judgments

Delays had also been experienced in the publication of approved versions of ex tempore judgments, whether they were produced by the official shorthand writers or by contractors transcribing the tapes which had been mechanically recorded.

Sometimes the delay was caused in courts without an official shorthand writer because a transcript was bespoken by one of the parties a long time after the judgment was delivered. If a transcribed copy of such a judgment was to be required, in connection with an appeal, for example, it should be ordered as soon as practicable after judgment was delivered.

Delays were also sometimes caused in those cases because judgments were delivered to a judge for approval without supplying the judge with copies of the material quoted in the judgment.

In future no judge should be invited to approve any such transcript unless the transcriber had been provided by the party ordering the transcript with copies of all the material from which the judge had quoted.

If the transcript was ordered by a person who was not a party to the case, such as a law reporter, that person should make arrangements with one of the parties to ensure that the transcriber, and the judge, would have access to all the material quoted in the judgment.

From time to time delays were also caused because judges had been slow in returning approved transcripts to the transcribers. His Lordship and the other heads of division had recently asked judges, as a general rule, that they should endeavour to return approved transcripts to the transcribers within 2 weeks of their being delivered to them for approval. If anyone encountered serious delay on that account, the relevant head of division should be informed.

Citation of authorities in court

For citation of authorities in court, the practice set out in *Practice Direction (Court of Appeal: Citation of Authorities)* [1995] 1 WLR 1096, [1995] 3 All ER 256 and *Practice Statement (Court of Appeal: Authorities)* [1996] 1 WLR 854, [1996] 3 All ER 382 were to be followed in all courts to which the present Practice Statement applied.

Conclusion

The purpose of these changes, which were being made on an experimental basis after full consultation with the Court Service, was to improve the quality of service rendered by the judges to those who used the courts.

Any comments on those changes, or suggestions about further improvements in relation to the matters set out in the statement, should be addressed to Brooke LJ at the Royal Courts of Justice.

They would be taken fully into account when the time came to decide whether these arrangements should be formalised, with or without amendment, in a Practice Direction.

Bingham of Cornhill LCJ

Practice Statement 25 November 1998

Citations: [1999] 1 FLR 314; [1999] 1 WLR 1; [1999] 1 All ER 125

Supreme Court: Judgments (No 2)

I am making this further statement with the agreement of Lord Woolf MR, Sir Richard Scott V-C, and Sir Stephen Brown P. Like the earlier statement I made on 22 April 1998 *(Practice Statement (Supreme Court: Judgments)* [1998] 1 FLR 1102), this statement applies to judgments delivered in all Divisions of the High Court and the Court of Appeal.

In my earlier statement I said that the arrangements I was announcing should be regarded as experimental, and that they would be kept under review. Experience since that time has shown that in general the new arrangements are working well, but that there is scope for some fine tuning. In particular, for a number of reasons it has not proved possible for the official shorthand writers to publish the official transcripts of approved, handed down, judgments quite as quickly as we had hoped, and there has been some uncertainty as to the status of the judgment given by the court to the shorthand writers.

We have decided to retain the embargo on copying the draft judgment which is sent to the parties 2 days before a judgment is handed down. An approved judgment, when handed down in court, will now be entitled "Judgment: Approved by the court for handing down (subject to editorial corrections)", and every page of a judgment which is handed down in this form will be marked in a similar manner. There will be no embargo on copying a judgment handed down in this form, so long as its status is made clear, and at present no charge will be made for permission to copy it.

In order to make it possible for approved judgments to be handed down in this way, the parties' legal advisers will be requested to submit their written list of suggested corrections by 12 noon, not 3pm, on the day before judgment is handed down. If it is not possible to comply with this deadline, any later corrections approved by the judge will be included in the final text which the official shorthand writer (or the judge's clerk, in courts which lack an official shorthand writer) will incorporate into the approved official text of the judgment as soon as practicable.

PART IV

Where a reserved written judgment has not been reported, reference must still be made in court to the approved official transcript (if this is available) and not to the approved transcript which is handed down, since this may have been subject to late revision after the text was prepared for handing down.

We will continue to keep these experimental arrangements under review. Comments or suggestions about any aspect of the arrangements should, once again, be addressed to Brooke LJ.

Bingham of Cornhill LCJ

President's Direction 17 December 1998

Citations: [1999] 1 FLR 315

Adopted Children Register: Restriction on Disclosure

In adoption proceedings, where it is feared that the security of the placement may be put at risk if information relating to the child in the Adopted Children Register is open to inspection, the High Court may restrict disclosure. In an appropriate case, an order may be made under the court's inherent jurisdiction directing that during the minority of the child, the Registrar General of England and Wales shall not disclose the details of the adoption entered in the Adopted Children Register to any person without leave of the court.

Applications for such orders are to be made to the High Court. In county court adoption proceedings, the application for such an order should be transferred to the High Court for determination, and if prior to the making of the adoption order, the adoption proceedings should be so transferred. Pursuant to s 100(3) of the Children Act 1989, a local authority is required to obtain leave to make such an application.

Issued with the concurrence of the Lord Chancellor.

Sir Stephen Brown
President

Practice Direction 12 January 1999

Citations: [1999] 1 FLR 503

Names of Deceased: Death Certificates

In order to facilitate the operation of standing searches and caveats and to ensure the accuracy of probate records, it is directed that in all instances where the deceased died in the UK and the death has been recorded in the Register of Deaths:

(*a*) the name and dates of birth and death of the deceased as recorded in the Register shall be included in the oath lodged in support of an application made through a solicitor or probate practitioner for a grant of representation;

(*b*) the name and date of death of the deceased as recorded in the Register shall be included in the notice lodged for a standing search or caveat; and

(*c*) in any case where the name of the deceased or by which the deceased was known differs from that recorded in the Register, that name shall also be included in the oath or the notice, as the case may be.

Gerald Angel
Senior District Judge

President's Direction 22 April 1999

Citations: [1999] 1 FLR 1295; [1999] 1 WLR 1128; [1999] 3 All ER 192

Civil Procedure Rules 1998: Allocation of Cases: Costs

It is directed that upon the coming into force on 26 April 1999 of the Civil Procedure Rules 1998 ("the 1998 Rules") and the Family Proceedings (Miscellaneous Amendments) Rules 1999:

(*a*) para 3.2 of the (Civil Procedure) Practice Direction *Allocation of Cases to Levels of Judiciary* shall apply to the Family Division. District judges (including district judges of the Principal Registry) shall have jurisdiction to hear and dispose of proceedings under the Inheritance (Provision for Family and Dependants) Act 1975 and under s 14 of the Trusts of Land and Appointment of Trustees Act 1996;

(*b*) the (Civil Procedure) Practice Direction about costs, *Supplementing Parts 43 to 48 of the Civil Procedure Rules* ("the costs direction"), shall apply to family proceedings to which the Family Proceedings Rules 1991 apply and to proceedings in the Family Division. References in the costs direction to "claimant" and "defendant" are to be read as references to the equivalent terms used in family proceedings and other terms and expressions used in the costs direction shall be similarly treated. References to procedural steps and to other Parts of the 1998 Rules which have not yet been applied to family proceedings are to be read as referring to equivalent or similar procedures under the rules applicable to family proceedings, as the context may permit. The previous practice in relation to "costs reserved" will no longer be followed and such an order will have the effect specified in the costs direction. It should also be noted that the period for commencing detailed assessment proceedings will be as specified in Part 47.7 (3 months) in substitution for the period of 6 months previously applicable.

Issued with the approval and concurrence of the Lord Chancellor.

Sir Stephen Brown
President

"para 3.2 of the (Civil Procedure) Practice Direction *Allocation of Cases to Levels of Judiciary*"—Paragraph 3.2 of this Practice Direction, set out fully in Section 2 of *The Civil Court Service* (Jordan Publishing Ltd, 2000), reads as follows:

"This Practice Direction is not concerned with family proceedings. It is also not concerned with proceedings in the Family Division except to the extent that such proceedings can be

PART IV

dealt with in the Chancery Division or the Family Division eg proceedings under the Inheritance (Provision for Family and Dependants) Act 1975 or under section 14 of the Trusts of Land and Appointment of Trustees Act 1996. District Judges (including District Judges of the Principal Registry of the Family Division) have jurisdiction to hear such proceedings, subject to any Direction given by the President of the Family Division."

"(Civil Procedure) Practice Direction about costs, *Supplementing Parts 43 to 48 of the Civil Procedure Rules* ("the costs direction"), shall apply to family proceedings ..."—See further *President's Direction of 24 July 2000*.

Lord Chancellor's Direction May 1999

Citations: [1999] 2 FLR 799

See Family Proceedings (Allocation to Judiciary) Directions 1999 (as amended by Family Proceedings (Allocation to Judiciary) (Amendment) Directions 2002) set out in **Part III**.

President's Direction 9 December 1999

Citations: [2000] 1 FLR 270

Family Law Act 1996: Attendance of Arresting Officer

Under s 47(7) of the Family Law Act 1996 a person arrested under a power of arrest attached to a non-molestation order or occupation order must be brought before a judge, district judge or magistrates' court ("the relevant judicial authority") within the period of 24 hours beginning at the time of the arrest.

When the arrested person is brought before the relevant authority the attendance of the arresting officer will not be necessary, unless the arrest itself is in issue. A written statement from the arresting officer as to the circumstances of the arrest should normally be sufficient.

In those cases where the arresting officer was also a witness to the events leading to the arrest and his evidence regarding those events is required, arrangements should be made for him to attend at a subsequent hearing to give evidence.

Issued with the approval and concurrence of the Lord Chancellor.

Dame Elizabeth Butler-Sloss
President

President's Direction 10 March 2000

Citations: [2000] 1 FLR 536; [2000] 1 WLR 737; [2000] 2 All ER 287

Family Proceedings: Court Bundles

1 The following practice applies to all hearings in family proceedings in the High Court, to all hearings of family proceedings in the Royal Courts of Justice and to hearings with a time estimate of half a day or more in all care centres, family hearing centres and divorce county courts (including the Principal Registry of the Family Division when so treated), except as specified in paragraph 2.3 below, and subject to specific directions given in any particular case. "Hearing" extends to all hearings before judges and district judges and includes the hearing of any application.

2.1 A bundle for the use of the court at the hearing shall be provided by the party in the position of applicant at the hearing or by any other party who agrees to do so. It shall contain copies of all documents relevant to the hearing in chronological order, paginated and indexed and divided into separate sections, as follows:

(*a*) applications and orders;
(*b*) statements and affidavits;
(*c*) experts' reports and other reports including those of a guardian ad litem; and
(*d*) other documents, divided into further sections as may be appropriate.

2.2 Where the nature of the hearing is such that a complete bundle of all documents is unnecessary, the bundle may comprise only those documents necessary for the hearing but the summary (paragraph 3.1(*a*) below) must commence with a statement that the bundle is limited or incomplete. The summary should be limited to those matters which the court needs to know for the purpose of the hearing and for management of the case.

2.3 The requirement to provide a bundle shall not apply to the hearing of any urgent application where the circumstances are such that it is not reasonably practicable for a bundle to be provided.

3.1 At the commencement of the bundle there shall be:

(*a*) a summary of the background to the hearing limited, if practicable, to one A4 page;
(*b*) a statement of the issue or issues to be determined;
(*c*) a summary of the order or directions sought by each party;
(*d*) a chronology if it is a final hearing or if the summary under (*a*) is insufficient;
(*e*) skeleton arguments as may be appropriate, with copies of all authorities relied on.

3.2 If possible the bundle shall be agreed. In all cases, the party preparing the bundle shall paginate it and provide an index to all other parties prior to the hearing.

3.3 The bundle should normally be contained in a ring binder or lever arch file (limited to 350 pages in each file). Where there is more than one bundle, each should be clearly distinguishable. Bundles shall be lodged, if practicable, 2 clear days prior to the hearing. For hearings in the Royal Courts of Justice bundles shall be lodged with the Clerk of the Rules. All bundles shall have clearly marked on the outside, the title and number of the case, the hearing date and time and, if known, the name of the judge hearing the case.

4 After each hearing which is not a final hearing, the party responsible for the bundle shall retrieve it from the court. The bundle with any additional documents shall be re-lodged for further hearings in accordance with the above provisions.

5 This direction replaces paragraphs 5 and 8 of *Practice Direction (Case Management)* [1995] 1 FLR 456 dated 31 January 1995 and shall have effect from 2 May 2000.

6 Issued with the approval and concurrence of the Lord Chancellor.

Dame Elizabeth Butler-Sloss
President

President's Direction 25 May 2000

Citations: [2000] 1 FLR 997

Ancillary Relief Procedure

1 *Introduction*

1.1 The Family Proceedings (Amendment No 2) Rules 1999 make important amendments to the Family Proceedings Rules 1991 as from 5 June 2000. The existing "pilot scheme" rules in relation to ancillary relief which have applied since 1996 but only in specified courts will become, with significant revisions, of general application. In the same way as the pilot scheme, the new procedure is intended to reduce delay, facilitate settlements, limit costs incurred by parties and provide the court with greater and more effective control over the conduct of the proceedings.

2 *Pre-application Protocol*

2.1 The "Pre-application protocol" annexed to this Direction outlines the steps parties should take to seek and provide information from and to each other prior to the commencement of any ancillary relief application. The court will expect the parties to comply with the terms of the protocol.

3 *Financial Dispute Resolution (FDR) Appointment*

3.1 A key element in the new procedure is the Financial Dispute Resolution (FDR) appointment. Rule 2.61E provides that the FDR appointment is to be treated as a meeting held for the purposes of discussion and negotiation. Such meetings which were previously described as meetings held for the purposes of conciliation have been developed as a means of reducing the tension which inevitably arises in matrimonial and family disputes and facilitating settlement of those disputes.

3.2 In order for the FDR appointment to be effective, parties must approach the occasion openly and without reserve. Non-disclosure of the content of such meetings is accordingly vital and is an essential prerequisite for fruitful discussion directed to the settlement of the dispute between the parties. The FDR appointment is an important part of the settlement process. As a consequence of *Re D (Minors)*

(Conciliation: Disclosure of Information) [1993] Fam 231, sub nom *Re D (Minors) (Conciliation: Privilege)* [1993] 1 FLR 932, evidence of anything said or of any admission made in the course of an FDR appointment will not be admissible in evidence, except at the trial of a person for an offence committed at the appointment or in the very exceptional circumstances indicated in *Re D*.

3.3 Courts will therefore expect:

parties to make offers and proposals;
recipients of offers and proposals to give them proper consideration;
that parties, whether separately or together, will not seek to exclude from consideration at the appointment any such offer or proposal.

3.4 In order to make the most effective use of the first appointment and the FDR appointment, the legal representatives attending those appointments will be expected to have full knowledge of the case.

4 *Single joint expert*

4.1 The introduction of expert evidence in proceedings is likely to increase costs substantially and consequently the court will use its powers to restrict the unnecessary use of experts. Accordingly, where expert evidence is sought to be relied upon, parties should if possible agree upon a single expert whom they can jointly instruct. Where parties are unable to agree upon the expert to be instructed, the court will consider using its powers under Part 35 of the Civil Procedure Rules 1998 to direct that evidence be given by one expert only. In such cases parties must be in a position at the first appointment or when the matter comes to be considered by the court to provide the court with a list of suitable experts or to make submissions as to the method by which the expert is to be selected.

5 This Direction shall have effect as from 5 June 2000 and replaces *Practice Direction: Ancillary Relief Procedure: Pilot Scheme* [1997] 2 FLR 304 dated 16 June 1997.

6 Issued with the approval and concurrence of the Lord Chancellor.

Dame Elizabeth Butler-Sloss
President

"the very exceptional circumstances indicated in *Re D*"—The reference in this case was to a clear admission that one party had done harm to a child or was likely to do so in the future.

PRE-APPLICATION PROTOCOL

1 *Introduction*

1.1

1.1.1 Lord Woolf in his final *Access to Justice* Report of July 1996 recommended the development of pre-application protocols:

"to build on and increase the benefits of early but well informed settlement which genuinely satisfy both parties to dispute"

1.1.2 Subsequently, in April 2000 the Lord Chancellor's Ancillary Relief Advisory Committee agreed this Pre-application Protocol.

1.2 The aim of the pre-application protocol is to ensure that:

(*a*) pre-application disclosure and negotiation takes place in appropriate cases;
(*b*) where there is pre-application disclosure and negotiation, it is dealt with:
    (i) cost-effectively;

(ii) in line with the overriding objectives of the Family Proceedings (Amendments) Rules 1999;

(*c*) the parties are in a position to settle the case fairly and early without litigation.

1.3 The court will be able to treat the standard set in the pre-application protocol as the normal reasonable approach to pre-application conduct. If proceedings are subsequently issued, the court will be entitled to decide whether there has been non-compliance with the protocol and, if so, whether non-compliance merits consequences.

2 *Notes of guidance*

Scope of the Protocol

2.1 This protocol is intended to apply to all claims for ancillary relief as defined by FPR 1991, r 1(2). It is designed to cover all classes of case, ranging from a simple application for periodical payments to an application for a substantial lump sum and property adjustment order. The protocol is designed to facilitate the operation of what was called the pilot scheme and is from 5 June 2000 the standard procedure for ancillary relief applications.

2.2 In considering the option of pre-application disclosure and negotiation, solicitors should bear in mind the advantage of having a court timetable and court-managed process. There is sometimes an advantage in preparing disclosure before proceedings are commenced. However, solicitors should bear in mind the objective of controlling costs and in particular the costs of discovery and that the option of pre-application disclosure and negotiation has risks of excessive and uncontrolled expenditure and delay. This option should only be encouraged where both parties agree to follow this route and disclosure is not likely to be an issue or has been adequately dealt with in mediation or otherwise.

2.3 Solicitors should consider at an early stage and keep under review whether it would be appropriate to suggest mediation to the clients as an alternative to solicitor negotiation or court-based litigation.

2.4 Making an application to the court should not be regarded as a hostile step or a last resort, rather as a way of starting the court timetable, controlling disclosure and endeavouring to avoid the costly final hearing and the preparation for it.

First letter

2.5 The circumstances of parties to an application for ancillary relief are so various that it would be difficult to prepare a specimen first letter. The request for information will be different in every case. However, the tone of the initial letter is important and the guidelines in para 3.7 should be followed. It should be approved in advance by the client. Solicitors writing to an unrepresented party should always recommend that he seeks independent legal advice and enclose a second copy of the letter to be passed to any solicitor instructed. A reasonable time-limit for a response may be 14 days.

Negotiation and settlement

2.6 In the event of pre-application disclosure and negotiation, as envisaged in para 2.2 an application should not be issued when a settlement is a reasonable prospect.

Disclosure

2.7 The protocol underlines the obligation of parties to make full and frank disclosure of all material facts, documents and other information relevant to the issues. Solicitors owe their clients a duty to tell them in clear terms of this duty and of the possible consequences of breach of the duty. This duty of disclosure is an ongoing obligation and includes the duty to disclose any material changes after initial disclosure has been given. Solicitors are referred to the *Good Practice Guide for Disclosure* produced by the Solicitors Family Law Association (obtainable from the Administrative Director, 366A Crofton Road, Orpington, Kent BR2 8NN).

3 *The Protocol*

General principles

3.1 All parties must always bear in mind the overriding objective set out at FPR 1991, r 2.51B and try to ensure that all claims should be resolved and a just outcome achieved as speedily as possible without costs being unreasonably incurred. The needs of any children should be addressed and safeguarded. The procedures which it is appropriate to follow should be conducted with minimum distress to the parties and in a manner designed to promote as good a continuing relationship between the parties and any children affected as is possible in the circumstances.

3.2 The principle of proportionality must be borne in mind at all times. It is unacceptable for the costs of any case to be disproportionate to the financial value of the subject matter of the dispute.

3.3 Parties should be informed that where a court exercises a discretion as to whether costs are payable by one party to another, this discretion extends to pre-application offers to settle and conduct of disclosure (r 44.3, para 1 of the Civil Procedure Rules 1998).

Identifying the issues

3.4 Parties must seek to clarify their claims and identify the issues between them as soon as possible. So that this can be achieved they must provide full, frank and clear disclosure of facts, information and documents which are material and sufficiently accurate to enable proper negotiations to take place to settle their differences. Openness in all dealings is essential.

Disclosure

3.5 If parties carry out voluntary disclosure before the issue of proceedings the parties should exchange schedules of assets, income, liabilities and other material facts, using Form E as a guide to the format of the disclosure. Documents should only be disclosed to the extent that they are required by Form E. Excessive or disproportionate costs should not be incurred.

Correspondence

3.6 Any first letter and subsequent correspondence must focus on the clarification of claims and identification of issues and their resolution. Protracted and unnecessary correspondence and "trial by correspondence" must be avoided.

3.7 The impact of any correspondence upon the reader and in particular the parties must always be considered. Any correspondence which raises irrelevant issues or which might cause the other party to adopt an entrenched, polarised or hostile position is to be discouraged.

Experts

3.8 Expert valuation evidence is only necessary where the parties cannot agree or do not know the value of some significant asset. The cost of a valuation should be proportionate to the sums in dispute. Wherever possible, valuations of properties, shares, etc should be obtained from a single valuer instructed by both parties. To that end, a party wishing to instruct an expert (the first party) should first give the other party a list of the names of one or more experts in the relevant speciality whom he considers are suitable to instruct. Within 14 days the other party may indicate an objection to one or more of the named experts and, if so, should supply the names of one or more experts whom he considers suitable.

3.9 Where the identity of the expert is agreed, the parties should agree the terms of a joint letter of instructions.

3.10 Where no agreement is reached as to the identity of the expert, each party should think carefully before instructing his own expert because of the costs implications. Disagreements about disclosure such as the use and identity of an expert may be better managed by the court within the context of an application for ancillary relief.

3.11 Whether a joint report is commissioned or the parties have chosen to instruct separate experts, it is important that the expert is prepared to answer reasonable questions raised by either party.

3.12 When experts' reports are commissioned pre-application, it should be made clear to the expert that they may in due course be reporting to the court and that they should therefore consider themselves bound by the guidance as to expert witnesses in Part 35 of the Civil Procedure Rules 1998.

3.13 Where the parties propose to instruct a joint expert, there is a duty on both parties to disclose whether they have already consulted that expert about the assets in issue.

3.14 If the parties agree to instruct separate experts the parties should be encouraged to agree in advance that the reports will be disclosed.

Summary

3.15 The aim of all pre-application proceedings steps must be to assist the parties to resolve their differences speedily and fairly or at least narrow the issues and, should that not be possible, to assist the court to do so.

President's Direction 24 July 2000

Citations: [2000] 2 FLR 428

Costs: Civil Procedure Rules 1998

The *President's Direction: Civil Procedure Rules 1998: Allocation of Cases: Costs* [1999] 1 FLR 1295 dated 22 April 1999 applied the (Civil Procedure) Practice

Direction about costs *Supplementing Parts 43 to 48 of the Civil Procedure Rules* ("the costs direction") to family proceedings (within the Family Proceedings Rules 1991) and to proceedings in the Family Division. A further edition of the costs direction (effective from 3 July 2000) has been published and it is hereby directed that the further edition (and all subsequent editions as and when they are published and come into effect) shall extend to family proceedings and to proceedings in the Family Division in the same way as did the costs direction and to the extent applicable to such proceedings.

The further edition of the costs direction includes provisions applicable to proceedings following changes in the manner in which legal services are funded pursuant to the Access to Justice Act 1999. It should be noted that although the cost of the premium in respect of legal costs insurance (s 29) or the cost of funding by a prescribed membership organisation (s 30) may be recoverable, family proceedings (within s 58A(2) of the Courts and Legal Services Act 1990) cannot be the subject of an enforceable conditional fee agreement.

Issued with the approval of the Lord Chancellor.

Dame Elizabeth Butler-Sloss
President

President's Direction 24 July 2000

Citations: [2000] 2 FLR 429; [2000] 1 WLR 1782; [2000] 4 All ER 288

Human Rights Act 1998

1 It is directed that the following practice shall apply as from 2 October 2000 in all family proceedings:

Citation of authorities

2 When an authority referred to in s 2 of the Human Rights Act 1998 ("the Act") is to be cited at a hearing:

(*a*) the authority to be cited shall be an authoritative and complete report;
(*b*) the court must be provided with a list of authorities it is intended to cite and copies of the reports:
  (i) in cases to which *Practice Direction (Family Proceedings: Court Bundles)* (10 March 2000) [2000] 1 FLR 536 applies, as part of the bundle;
  (ii) otherwise, not less than 2 clear days before the hearing; and
(*c*) copies of the complete original texts issued by the European Court and Commission, either paper based or from the Court's judgment database (HUDOC) which is available on the internet, may be used.

Allocation to judges

3(1) The hearing and determination of the following will be confined to a High Court judge:

(*a*) a claim for a declaration of incompatibility under s 4 of the Act; or
(*b*) an issue which may lead to the court considering making such a declaration.

(2) The hearing and determination of a claim made under the Act in respect of a judicial act shall be confined in the High Court to a High Court judge and in county courts to a circuit judge.

Issued with the concurrence and approval of the Lord Chancellor.

Dame Elizabeth Butler-Sloss
President

Practice Direction 2 October 2000

Citations: [2000] 1 WLR 1886; [2000] 4 All ER 895; [2000] 1 Cr App R 147

Justices: Clerk to Court

1 A justices' clerk is responsible for:

(*a*) the legal advice tendered to the justices within the area;
(*b*) the performance of any of the functions set out below by any member of his/her staff acting as legal adviser;
(*c*) ensuring that competent advice is available to justices when the justices' clerk is not personally present in court;
(*d*) the effective delivery of case management and the reduction of unnecessary delay.

2 Where a person other than the justices' clerk, a legal adviser who is authorised to do so, performs any of the functions referred to in this direction s/he will have the same responsibilities as the justices' clerk.

The legal adviser can consult the justices' clerk or other person authorised by the justices' clerk for that purpose before tendering advice to the bench. If the justices' clerk or that person gives any advice directly to the bench, s/he shall give the parties or their advocates an opportunity of repeating any relevant submissions prior to the advice being given.

3 It will be the responsibility of the legal adviser to provide the justices with any advice they require to properly perform their functions, whether or not the justices have requested that advice, on:

(i) questions of law, including European Court of Human Rights jurisprudence and those matters set out in section 2(1) of the Human Rights Act 1998;
(ii) questions of mixed law and fact;
(iii) matters of practice and procedure;
(iv) the range of penalties available;
(v) any relevant decisions of the superior courts or other guidelines;
(vi) other issues relevant to the matter before the court;
(vii) the appropriate decision-making structure to be applied in any given case.

In addition to advising the justices it will be the legal adviser's responsibility to assist the court, where appropriate, as to the formulation of reasons and the recording of those reasons.

4 A justices' clerk or legal adviser must not play any part in making findings of fact but can assist the bench by reminding them of the evidence, using any notes of the proceedings for that purpose.

5 A justices' clerk or legal adviser can ask questions of witnesses and the parties in order to clarify the evidence and any issues in the case.

6 A legal adviser has a duty to ensure that every case is conducted fairly.

7 When advising the justices the justices' clerk or legal adviser, whether or not previously in court, shall:

(i) ensure that s/he is aware of the relevant facts;
(ii) provide the parties with the information necessary to enable the parties to make any representations they wish as to the advice before it is given.

8 At any time, justices are entitled to receive advice to assist them in discharging their responsibilities.

If they are in any doubt as to the evidence which has been given, they should seek the aid of their legal adviser, referring to his/her notes as appropriate. That should ordinarily be done in open court. Where the justices request their adviser to join them in the retiring room, that request should be made in the presence of the parties in court.

Any legal advice given to the justices other than in open court should be clearly stated to be provisional and the adviser should subsequently repeat the substance of the advice in open court and give the parties an opportunity to make any representations they wish on that provisional advice.

The legal adviser should then state in open court whether the provisional advice is confirmed or, if it is varied, the nature of the variation.

9 The performance of a legal adviser can be appraised by a person authorised by the magistrates' courts committee to do so.

For that purpose the appraiser can be present in the justices' retiring room. The content of the appraisal is confidential, but the fact that an appraisal has taken place, and the presence of the appraiser in the retiring room, should be briefly explained in open court.

10 The legal adviser is under a duty to assist unrepresented parties to present their case, but must do so without appearing to become an advocate for the party concerned.

11 The role of legal advisers in fine default proceedings or any other proceedings for the enforcement of financial orders, obligations or penalties is to assist the court. They must not act in an adversarial or partisan manner.

With the agreement of the justices a legal adviser can ask questions of the defaulter to elicit information which the justices will require to make an adjudication, for example to facilitate his or her explanation for the default.

A legal adviser can also advise the justices in the normal way as to the options open to them in dealing with the case. It will be inappropriate for the legal adviser to set out to establish wilful refusal or neglect or any other type of culpable behaviour, to offer an opinion on the facts, or to urge a particular course of action upon the justices.

The duty of impartiality is the paramount consideration for the legal adviser at all times, and that takes precedence over any role s/he may have as a collecting officer.

The appointment of other staff to "prosecute" the case for the collecting officer is not essential to ensure compliance with the law, including the Human Rights Act 1998. Whether to make such appointments is a matter for the justices' chief executive.

12 *Practice Direction (Justices: Clerk to Court)* ([1981] 1 WLR 1163) is revoked. *Practice Note (Justices' Clerks)* ([1954] 1 WLR 213) remains in force.

Lord Woolf
Lord Chief Justice

Practice Direction 11 January 2001

Citations: [2001] 1 WLR 194; [2001] 1 All ER 193; [2001] 1 Cr App R 426

Judgments: Form and Citation

Lord Woolf CJ: gave the following direction at the sitting of the court.

This practice direction is made with the concurrence of the Master of the Rolls, the Vice-Chancellor and the President of the Family Division. It represents the next stage in the process of modernising the arrangements for the preparation, distribution and citation of judgments given in every division of the High Court, whether in London or in courts outside London.

Form of judgments

1.1 With effect from 11 January 2001, all judgments in every division of the High Court and the Court of Appeal will be prepared for delivery, or issued as approved judgments, with single spacing, paragraph numbering (in the margins) but no page numbers. In courts with more than one judge, the paragraph numbering will continue sequentially through each judgment, and will not start again at the beginning of the second judgment. Indented paragraphs will not be given a number.

1.2 The main reason of these changes is to facilitate the publication of judgments on the World Wide Web and their subsequent use by the increasing numbers of those who had access to the Web. The changes should also assist those who used and wish to search judgments stored on electronic databases.

1.3 It is desirable in the interests of consistency that all judgments prepared for delivery (or issued as approved judgments) in county courts, should also contain paragraph numbering (in the margins).

Neutral citation of judgments

2.1 With effect from 11 January 2001 a form of neutral citation will be introduced in both divisions of the Court of Appeal and in the Administrative Court. A unique number will be given by the official shorthand writers to each approved judgment issued out of these courts. The judgments will be numbered in the following way:

Court of Appeal (Civil Division) [2000] EWCA Civ 1, 2, 3 etc
Court of Appeal (Criminal Division) [2000] EWCA Crim 1, 2, 3 etc
High Court (Administrative Court) [2000] EWHC Admin 1, 2, 3 etc

2.2 Under these new arrangements, paragraph 59 in *Smith v Jones*, the tenth numbered judgment of the year in the Civil Division of the Court of Appeal, would be cited: *Smith v Jones* [2001] EWCA Civ 10 at [59].

2.3 The neutral citation will be the official number attributed to the judgment by the court and must always be used on at least one occasion when the judgment was cited in a later judgment. Once the judgment is reported, the neutral citation will appear in front of the familiar citation from the law report series: thus *Smith v Jones* [2001] EWCA Civ 10 at [30], [2001] QB 124, [2001] 2 All ER 364, etc. The paragraph number must be the number allotted by the court in all future versions of the judgment.

2.4 If a judgment is cited on more than one occasion in a later judgment, it will be of the greatest assistance if only one abbreviation, if desired, is used. Thus *Smith v Jones* [2001] EWCA Civ 10 could be abbreviated on subsequent occasions to *Smith v Jones*, or *Smith's* case, but preferably not both in the same judgment.

2.5 If it is desired to cite more than one paragraph of a judgment each numbered paragraph should be enclosed with a square bracket: thus *Smith v Jones* [2001] EWCA Civ 10 at [30]–[35], or *Smith v Jones* [2001] EWCA Civ 10 at [30], [35], and [40]–[43].

2.6 The neutral citation arrangements will be extended to include other parts of the High Court as soon as the necessary administrative arrangements can be made.

2.7 The Administrative Court citation will be given to all judgments in the Administrative Court, whether they are delivered by a Divisional court or by a single judge.

Citation of judgments in court

3.1 For the avoidance of doubt, it should be emphasised that both the High Court and the Court of Appeal require that where a case has been reported in the official Law Reports published by the Incorporated Council of Law Reporting for England and Wales it must be cited from that source. Other series of reports may only be used when a case is not reported in the Law Reports.

3.2 It will in future be permissible to cite a judgment reported in a series of reports, including those of the Incorporated Council of Law Reporting, by means of a copy of a reproduction of the judgment in electronic form that has been authorised by the publisher of the relevant series, provided that: (i) the report is presented to the court in an easily legible form (a 12-point font is preferred but a 10 or 11-point font is acceptable) and (ii) the advocate presenting the report is satisfied that it has not been reproduced in a garbled form from the data source. In any case of doubt the court will rely on the printed text of the report, unless the editor of the report has certified that an electronic version is more accurate because it corrects an error contained in an earlier printed text of the report.

Concluding comments

4.1 The changes described in this practice direction follow what is becoming accepted international practice. They are intended to make it easier to distribute, store and search judgments, and less expensive and time-consuming to reproduce them for use in court. Lord Justice Brooke is still responsible for advising the Judges' Council on these matters, and any comments on these new arrangements, or suggestions about ways in which they could be improved still further, should be addressed to him at the Royal Courts of Justice, WC2A 2LL.

Lord Woolf
Lord Chief Justice

Practice Note March 2001

Citations: [2001] 2 FLR 151

Officers of CAFCASS Legal Services and Special Casework: Appointment in Family Proceedings

1 This Practice Note comes into effect on 1 April 2001 and supersedes *Practice Note (Official Solicitor: Appointment in Family Proceedings)* (4 December 1998) [1999] 1 FLR 310 issued by the Official Solicitor in relation to the representation of children in family proceedings. It is issued in conjunction with a Practice Note dealing with the appointment of the Official Solicitor in family proceedings. This Practice Note is intended to be helpful guidance, but always subject to Practice Directions, decisions of the courts and other legal guidance.

The Children and Family Court Advisory and Support Service

Appointment as children's guardian

2 The Children and Family Court Advisory and Support Service (CAFCASS) has responsibilities in relation to children in family proceedings as defined in s 12 of the Criminal Justice and Court Services Act 2000. CAFCASS has established CAFCASS Legal Services and Special Casework ("CAFCASS Legal") principally to take over the Official Solicitor's responsibilities of representing children who are the subject of family proceedings.

3 Generally it is only where it appears to the court that the child ought to have party status and be legally represented that the question of the involvement of CAFCASS Legal may arise. Normally an officer of CAFCASS in the area in which the case is proceeding will be appointed as the children's guardian, but all private law cases where it is felt necessary for the child to be joined as a party, and all High Court adoption cases, should be referred to CAFCASS Legal. CAFCASS Legal may represent children in family proceedings either in the High Court or in a county court (but not in a family proceedings court).

Private cases

4 The court will normally at the first directions appointment consider whether the child should be made a party to the proceedings. In most private law cases (non-specified proceedings), a child's interests will be sufficiently safeguarded by the commissioning of a report under s 7 of the Children Act 1989 from a children and family reporter. Children who need someone to orchestrate an investigation of the case on their behalf may need party status and legal representation: *Re A* (2001) *The Times*, February 28. Particular examples are where:

- (*a*) there is a significant foreign element such as a challenge to the English court's jurisdiction or a need for enquiries to be conducted abroad;
- (*b*) there is a need for expert medical or other evidence to be adduced on behalf of a child in circumstances where a joint instruction by the parties is impossible;
- (*c*) where a child wants to instruct a solicitor direct but has been refused leave pursuant to Family Proceedings Rules 1991, r 9.2A to instruct a solicitor;
- (*d*) an application is made for leave to seek contact with an adopted child;
- (*e*) there are exceptionally difficult, unusual or sensitive issues making it necessary for the child to be granted party status within the proceedings: such cases are likely to be High Court matters.

5 CAFCASS Legal will almost invariably accept cases where case law has pointed to the need for a child to be granted party status and to be legally represented, for instance in "special category" medical treatment cases, notably in those cases involving an application to authorise sterilisation and cases concerning disputed life sustaining treatment. Applications in such cases should be made under the inherent jurisdiction of the High Court. The Official Solicitor will have a continuing role in such cases for adult patients and for some older children who are also patients.

Public law cases

6 In most public law cases (specified proceedings) an officer of CAFCASS in the area in which the case is proceeding will be appointed as the children's guardian. It will only be appropriate for an officer of CAFCASS Legal to be appointed as children's guardian in public law cases in the High Court or the county court which are exceptionally difficult, unusual or sensitive or where either he or she, or the Official Solicitor, previously acted for the child in related public law or private law proceedings.

Adoption and surrogacy

7 Proceedings under the Adoption Act 1976 should be commenced in the High Court or transferred there and referred to CAFCASS Legal if they are exceptionally difficult, unusual or sensitive. Circumstances warranting transfer will include difficult issues about parental agreement or compliance with the law. Reference should be made to Practice Directions, decisions of the courts and other guidance. In relation to inter-country adoptions, the case of *Re R (Inter-Country Adoptions: Practice)* [1999] 1 FLR 1042 is particularly instructive. Generally only High Court adoptions will be accepted by CAFCASS Legal and not those straightforward cases where the natural parents consent (unless the Official Solicitor or an officer in CAFCASS Legal previously acted for the child in family proceedings).

8 Only exceptionally difficult, unusual or sensitive cases under s 30 of the Human Fertilisation and Embryology Act 1990 should be referred to CAFCASS Legal.

Non-subject children

9 Exceptionally, CAFCASS Legal may accept appointment on behalf of child applicants (typically seeking contact with siblings) or children who are otherwise parties to family proceedings, such as a minor mother of a child who is the subject of the proceedings. This may be appropriate to allow continuity of representation following earlier proceedings in which the child was the subject. In all cases where the child is the applicant, CAFCASS Legal will need to be satisfied that the proposed proceedings would benefit that child before proceeding.

Advising the court

10 CAFCASS Legal may be invited to act or instruct counsel as friend of the court (amicus).

Liaison with the Official Solicitor

11 In cases of doubt or difficulty, staff of CAFCASS Legal will liaise with staff of the Official Solicitor's office to avoid duplication and ensure the most suitable arrangements are made.

Appointment of an officer of CAFCASS Legal Services and Special Casework

12 Where the court considers that a child should be made a respondent to an application and represented by CAFCASS Legal it should make an order in the following terms:

(*a*) The Director of Legal Services, CAFCASS, is invited to nominate one of his officers to act as children's guardian for [name(s)]

(*b*) Upon an officer of CAFCASS Legal Services and Special Casework consenting to act as children's guardian [name(s)] will be made respondent(s) to the applications before the court.

CAFCASS Legal will normally provide a response to any invitation within 10 working days of receiving the papers referred to in para 15 below.

13 It is often helpful to discuss the question of appointment with the duty divisional manager or a lawyer at CAFCASS Legal by telephoning 020 7904 0867. It is particularly important to do so in urgent cases.

14 Save in the most urgent cases a substantive hearing date should not normally be fixed before the next directions hearing following the invitation to act.

15 The following documents should be forwarded to CAFCASS Legal without delay:

(*a*) a copy of the order and a note of the reasons for approaching CAFCASS Legal approved by the judge;

(*b*) the court file;

(*c*) whenever practicable, a bundle with summary, statement of issues and chronology (in the form required by the *President's Direction (Family Proceedings: Court Bundles)* (10 March 2000) [2000] 1 FLR 536).

The address of CAFCASS Legal Services and Special Casework is:

Newspaper House
8–16 Great New Street
London EC4 3BN
Telephone: 020 7904 0867
Fax: 020 7904 0868/9
Email: legal@cafcass.gsi.gov.uk

Charles Prest
Director of Legal Services
CAFCASS

President's Direction 16 March 2001

Citations: [2001] 1 FLR 949; [2001] Fam Law 730

Committal Applications and Proceedings in which a Committal Order may be Made

1 As from the date of this direction, the Civil Procedure Practice Direction supplemental to the Rules of the Supreme Court 1965, Ord 52 (Sch 1 to the Civil Procedure Rules 1998) and the County Court Rules 1981, Ord 29 (Sch 2 to the Civil Procedure Rules 1998) ("the CPR Direction"), shall apply to all applications in family proceedings for an order of committal in the same manner and to the same extent as it applies to proceedings governed by the Civil Procedure Rules 1998 ("the CPR") but subject to:

(*a*) the provisions of the Family Proceedings Rules 1991 ("the FPR") and the Rules applied by those Rules namely, the Rules of the Supreme Court 1965 ("RSC") and the County Court Rules 1981 ("CCR") in force immediately before 26 April 1999; and

(*b*) the appropriate modifications consequent upon the limited application of the CPR to family proceedings.

1.1 In particular, the following modification should apply:

(*a*) Where the alleged contempt is in connection with existing proceedings (other than contempt in the face of the court) or with an order made or an undertaking given in existing proceedings, the committal application shall be made in those proceedings;

(*b*) As required by FPR, r 7.2, committal applications in the High Court are to be made by summons. In county court proceedings applications are to be made in the manner prescribed by CCR, Ord 29. References in the CPR Direction to "claim form" and "application notice" are to be read accordingly;

(*c*) In instances where the CPR Direction requires more information to be provided than is required to be provided under the RSC and the CCR, the court will expect the former to be observed;

(*d*) Having regard to the periods specified in RSC, Ord 52, r 3, Ord 32, r 3(2)(*a*) and CCR, Ord 13, r 1(2), the time specified in para 4.2 of the CPR Direction shall not apply. Nevertheless, the court will ensure that adequate time is afforded to the respondent for the preparation of his defence;

(*e*) Paragraph 9 of the CPR Direction is to be read with para 3 of each of the Directions issued on 17 December 1997, entitled *Children Act 1989 – Exclusion Requirement* and *Family Law Act 1996 – Part IV*.

2 In any family proceedings (not falling within (1) above), in which a committal order may be made, including proceedings for the enforcement of an existing order by way of judgment summons or other process, full effect will be given to the Human Rights Act 1998 and to the rights afforded under that Act. In particular, Art 6 of the European Convention for the Protection of Human Rights and Fundamental Freedoms 1950 (as set out in Sch 1 to the Human Rights Act 1998) is fully applicable to such proceedings. Those involved must ensure that in the conduct of the proceedings there is due observance of the Human Rights Act 1998 in the same manner as if the proceedings fell within the CPR Direction.

3 As with all family proceedings, the CPR costs provisions apply to all committal proceedings.

4 Issued with the approval and concurrence of the Lord Chancellor.

Dame Elizabeth Butler-Sloss
President

Practice Note
2 April 2001

Citations: [2001] 2 FLR 155

Official Solicitor: Appointment in Family Proceedings

1 This Practice Note supersedes *Practice Note (Official Solicitor: Appointment in Family Proceedings)* (4 December 1998) [1999] 1 FLR 310 issued by the Official Solicitor in relation to his appointment in family proceedings. It is issued in conjunction with a Practice Note dealing with the appointment of officers of CAFCASS Legal Services and Special Casework in family proceedings. This Practice Note is intended to be helpful guidance, but always subject to Practice Directions, decisions of the court and other legal guidance.

2 The Children and Family Court Advisory and Support Service (CAFCASS) has responsibilities in relation to children in family proceedings in which their welfare is or may be in question (Criminal Justice and Court Services Act 2000, s 12). From 1 April 2001, the Official Solicitor will no longer represent children who are the subject of family proceedings (other than in very exceptional circumstances and after liaison with CAFCASS).

3 This Practice Note summarises the continuing role of the Official Solicitor in family proceedings. Since there are no provisions for parties under disability in the Family Proceedings Courts (Children Act 1989) Rules 1991, the Official Solicitor can only act in the High Court or in a county court, pursuant to Part IX of the Family Proceedings Rules 1991. The Official Solicitor will shortly issue an updated Practice Note about his role for adults under disability who are the subject of declaratory proceedings in relation to their medical treatment or welfare.

Adults under disability

4 The Official Solicitor will, in the absence of any other willing and suitable person, act as next friend or guardian ad litem of an adult party under disability, a "patient". "Patient" means someone who is incapable by reason of mental disorder of managing and administering his property and affairs (Family Proceedings Rules 1991, r 9.1). Medical evidence will usually be required before the Official Solicitor can consent to act and his staff can provide a standard form of medical certificate. Where there are practical difficulties in obtaining such medical evidence, the Official Solicitor should be consulted.

Non-subject children

5 Again in the absence of any other willing and suitable person, the Official Solicitor will act as next friend or guardian ad litem of a child party whose own welfare is not the subject of family proceedings (Family Proceedings Rules 1991, r 2.57, r 9.2 and r 9.5). The most common examples will be:

- (*a*) a child who is also the parent of a child, and who is a respondent to a Children Act 1989 or Adoption Act 1976 application. If a child respondent is already represented by a CAFCASS officer in pending proceedings of which he or she is the subject, then the Official Solicitor will liaise with CAFCASS to agree the most appropriate arrangements;
- (*b*) a child who wishes to make an application for a Children Act 1989 order naming another child (typically a contact order naming a sibling). The Official Solicitor will need to satisfy himself that the proposed proceedings would benefit the child applicant before proceeding;

(*c*) a child witness to some disputed factual issue in a children case and who may require intervener status. In such circumstances the need for party status and legal representation should be weighed in the light of *Re H (Care Proceedings: Intervener)* [2000] 1 FLR 775;

(*d*) a child party to a petition for a declaration of status under Part III of the Family Law Act 1986;

(*e*) a child intervener in divorce or ancillary relief proceedings (r 2.57 or r 9.5);

(*f*) a child applicant for, or respondent to, an application for an order under Part IV of the Family Law Act 1996. In the case of a child applicant, the Official Solicitor will need to satisfy himself that the proposed proceedings would benefit the child before pursuing them, with leave under Family Law Act 1996, s 43 if required.

6 Any children who are parties to Children Act 1989 or inherent jurisdiction proceedings may rely on the provisions of Family Proceedings Rules 1991, r 9.2A if they wish to instruct a solicitor without the intervention of a next friend or guardian ad litem. Rule 9.2A does not apply to Adoption Act 1976, Family Law Act 1986/1996 or Matrimonial Causes Act 1973 proceedings.

Older children who are also patients

7 Officers of CAFCASS will not be able to represent anyone who is over the age of 18. The Official Solicitor may therefore be the more appropriate next friend or guardian ad litem of a child who is also a patient and whose disability will persist beyond his or her eighteenth birthday, especially in non-emergency cases where the substantive hearing is unlikely to take place before the child's eighteenth birthday. The Official Solicitor may also be the more appropriate next friend or guardian ad litem in medical treatment cases such as sterilisation or vegetative state cases, in which his staff have particular expertise deriving from their continuing role for adult patients.

Advising the court

8 The Official Solicitor may be invited to act or instruct counsel as a friend of the court (amicus) if it appears to the court that such an invitation is more appropriately addressed to him rather than (or in addition to) CAFCASS Legal Services and Special Casework.

Liaison with CAFCASS

9 In cases of doubt or difficulty, staff of the Official Solicitor's office will liaise with staff of CAFCASS Legal Services and Special Casework to avoid duplication and ensure the most suitable arrangements are made.

Invitations to act in new cases

10 Solicitors who have been consulted by a child or an adult under disability (or by someone acting on their behalf, or concerned about their interests) should write to the Official Solicitor setting out the background to the proposed case and explaining why there is no other willing and suitable person to act as next friend or guardian ad litem. Where the person concerned is an adult, medical evidence in the standard form of the Official Solicitor's medical certificate should be provided.

Invitations to act in pending proceedings

11 Where a case is already before the court, an order appointing the Official Solicitor should be expressed as being made subject to his consent. The Official Solicitor aims to provide a response to any invitation within 10 working days. He will be unable to consent to act for an adult until satisfied that the party is a

"patient". A further directions appointment after 28 days may therefore be helpful. If he accepts appointment the Official Solicitor will need time to prepare the case on behalf of the child or patient and may wish to make submissions about any substantive hearing date. The following documents should be forwarded to the Official Solicitor without delay:

(*a*) a copy of the order inviting him to act (with a note of the reasons approved by the judge if appropriate);
(*b*) the court file;
(*c*) if available, a bundle with summary, statement of issues and chronology (as required by *President's Direction (Family Proceedings: Court Bundles)* (10 March 2000) [2000] 1 FLR 536).

Contacting the Official Solicitor

12 It is often helpful to discuss the question of appointment with the Official Solicitor or one of his staff by telephoning 020 7911 7127. Enquiries about family proceedings should be addressed to the Team Manager, Family Litigation.

The Official Solicitor's address is:
81 Chancery Lane
London WC2A 1DD

DX 0012 London Chancery Lane
Fax: 020 7911 7105
Email: officialsolicitor@offsol.gsi.gov.uk

Laurence Oates
Official Solicitor

Practice Direction
9 April 2001

Citations: [2001] 1 WLR 1001; [2001] 2 All ER 510; [2001] Fam Law 794

Citation of Authority

Lord Woolf CJ: gave the following direction at the sitting of the court.

Introduction

1 In recent years, there has been a substantial growth in the number of readily available reports of judgments in this and other jurisdictions, such reports being available either in published reports or in transcript form. Widespread knowledge of the work and decisions of the courts is to be welcomed. At the same time, however, the current weight of available material causes problems both for advocates and for courts in properly limiting the nature and amount of material that is used in the preparation and argument of subsequent cases.

2 The latter issue is a matter of rapidly increasing importance. Recent and continuing efforts to increase the efficiency, and thus reduce the costs, of litigation, whilst maintaining the interests of justice, will be threatened if courts are burdened with a weight of inappropriate and unnecessary authority, and if advocates are uncertain as to the extent to which it is necessary to deploy authorities in the argument of any given case.

3 With a view to limiting the citation of previous authority to cases that are relevant and useful to the court, this Practice Direction lays down a number of rules as to what material may be cited, and the manner in which that cited material should be handled by advocates. These rules are in large part such as many courts already follow in pursuit of their general discretion in the management of litigation. However, it is now desirable to promote uniformity of practice by the same rules being followed by all courts.

4 It will remain the duty of advocates to draw the attention of the court to any authority not cited by an opponent which is adverse to the case being advanced.

5 This Direction applies to all courts apart from criminal courts, including within that latter category the Court of Appeal (Criminal Division).

Categories of judgments that may only be cited if they fulfil specified requirements

6.1 A judgment falling into one of the categories referred to in paragraph 6.2 below may not in future be cited before any court unless it clearly indicates that it purports to establish a new principle or to extend the present law. In respect of judgments delivered after the date of this Direction, that indication must take the form of an express statement to that effect. In respect of judgments delivered before the date of this Direction that indication must be present in or clearly deducible from the language used in the judgment.

6.2 Paragraph 6.1 applies to the following categories of judgment:

Applications attended by one party only;
Applications for permission to appeal;
Decisions on applications that only decide that the application is arguable;
county court cases, unless:
- (*a*) cited in order to illustrate the conventional measure of damages in a personal injury case; or
- (*b*) cited in a county court in order to demonstrate current authority at that level on an issue in respect of which no decision at a higher level of authority is available.

6.3 These categories will be kept under review, such review to include consideration of adding to the categories.

Citation of other categories of judgment

7.1 Courts will in future pay particular attention, when it is sought to cite other categories of judgment, to any indication given by the court delivering the judgment that it was seen by that court as only applying decided law to the facts of the particular case; or otherwise as not extending or adding to the existing law.

7.2 Advocates who seek to cite a judgment that contains indications of the type referred to in paragraph 7.1 will be required to justify their decision to cite the case.

Methods of citation

8.1 Advocates will in future be required to state, in respect of each authority that they wish to cite, the proposition of law that the authority demonstrates, and the parts of the judgment that support that proposition. If it is sought to cite more than one authority in support of a given proposition, advocates must state the reason for taking that course.

8.2 The demonstration referred to in paragraph 8.1 will be required to be contained in any skeleton argument and in any appellant's or respondent's notice in respect of each authority referred to in that skeleton or notice.

8.3 Any bundle or list of authorities prepared for the use of any court must in future bear a certification by the advocate responsible for arguing the case that the requirements of this paragraph have been complied with in respect of each authority included.

8.4 The statements referred to in paragraph 8.1 should not materially add to the length of submissions or of skeleton arguments, but should be sufficient to demonstrate, in the context of the advocate's argument, the relevance of the authority or authorities to that argument and that the citation is necessary for a proper presentation of that argument.

Authorities decided in other jurisdictions

9.1 Cases decided in other jurisdictions can, if properly used, be a valuable source of law in this jurisdiction. At the same time, however, such authority should not be cited without proper consideration of whether it does indeed add to the existing body of law.

9.2 In future, therefore, any advocate who seeks to cite an authority from another jurisdiction must:

(i) comply in respect of that authority, with the rules set out in paragraph 8 above;
(ii) indicate in respect of each authority what that authority adds that is not to be found in authority in this jurisdiction; or, if there is said to be justification for adding to domestic authority, what that justification is; and
(iii) certify that there is no authority in this jurisdiction that precludes the acceptance by the court of the proposition that the foreign authority is said to establish.

9.3 For the avoidance of doubt, paragraphs 9.1 and 9.2 do not apply to cases decided in either the European Court of Justice or the organs of the European Convention of Human Rights. Because of the status in English law of such authority, as provided by, respectively, section 3 of the European Communities Act 1972 and section 2(1) of the Human Rights Act 1998, such cases are covered by the earlier paragraphs of this Direction.

Lord Woolf
Lord Chief Justice

Practice Note
1 May 2001

Citations: [2001] 2 FLR 158

Official Solicitor: Declaratory Proceedings: Medical and Welfare Decisions for Adults who Lack Capacity

1 This Practice Note supersedes Practice Notes dated June 1996 ((*Official Solicitor: Sterilisation)* [1996] 2 FLR 111) and 26 July 1996 ((*Official Solicitor to*

the Supreme Court: Vegetative State) [1996] 2 FLR 375). It combines the guidance given in those earlier Practice Notes, and extends it to a wider range of medical and welfare disputes leading to litigation. This Practice Note deals only with adults who lack capacity. Medical treatment or welfare disputes about children will be dealt with under the Children Act 1989 or the inherent jurisdiction in relation to children (see *Practice Note (Official Solicitor: Appointment in Family Proceedings)* (2 April 2001) [2001] 2 FLR 155 and *CAFCASS Practice Note (Officers of CAFCASS Legal Services and Special Casework: Appointment in Family Proceedings)* (March 2001) [2001] 2 FLR 151).

Jurisdiction

2 The High Court has jurisdiction to make declarations as to the best interests of an adult who lacks decision-making capacity. The jurisdiction will be exercised when there is a serious justiciable issue requiring a decision by the court. It has been exercised in relation to a range of medical treatment issues, in particular sterilisation operations and the continuance of artificial nutrition and hydration. It has also been exercised in relation to residence and contact issues. The jurisdiction is comprehensively reviewed and analysed in *Re F (Adult: Court's Jurisdiction)* [2000] 2 FLR 512.

The need for court involvement

3 Case-law has established two categories of case that will in virtually all cases require the prior sanction of a High Court judge. The first is sterilisation of a person (whether a child or an adult) who cannot consent to the operation: *Re B (A Minor) (Wardship: Sterilisation)* [1988] AC 199, [1987] 2 FLR 314 and *Re F (Mental Patient: Sterilisation)* [1990] 2 AC 1, sub nom *Re F (Sterilization: Mental Patient)* [1989] 2 FLR 376. The second is the discontinuance of artificial nutrition and hydration for a patient in a vegetative state: *Airedale NHS Trust v Bland* [1993] AC 789, 805. Further guidance about sterilisation and vegetative state cases is given below. In all other cases, doctors and carers should seek advice from their own lawyers about the need to apply to the court. In the Official Solicitor's view, applications should be made where there are disputes or difficulties as to either the patient's capacity or the patient's best interests. Guidelines were handed down by the Court of Appeal in *St George's Healthcare NHS Trust v S; R v Collins and Others ex parte S* [1999] Fam 26, 63–65, [1998] 2 FLR 728, 758–760. It was stressed in that case that a declaration made without notice would be ineffective and ought not to be made.

The application

4 Applications should be made to the Family Division of the High Court (principal or district registry). The proceedings are not, however, "family proceedings" for the purposes of the Civil Procedure Rules 1998, r 2.1(2). The Civil Procedure Rules 1998 will therefore apply.

The claim

5 In the Official Solicitor's view, the Part 8 alternative procedure is the more appropriate and a Part 8 claim form should be used. The claimant should file all evidence with the claim form. The Official Solicitor is unlikely to be in a position to file all his evidence with his acknowledgment of service. A directions hearing should therefore be fixed when the claim form is issued.

6 The relief sought should be declarations that:[1]

(1) [the patient] lacks capacity to make a decision about … [specify treatment or welfare decision at issue, eg "having a kidney transplant" or "where to live"].

(2) It is [or is not] in the existing circumstances in the best interests of [the patient] for … [specify treatment or other issue, eg "him to undergo below-knee amputation of his left leg" or "her to have contact with the claimant for at least 2 hours each week"].

1 See appendices below for suggested wording in sterilisation and PVS cases.

The evidence

7 The claimant must adduce evidence going to both capacity and best interests.

(1) *Capacity*

The court has no jurisdiction unless it is established that the patient is incapable of making a decision about the matter in issue. The test of capacity to consent to or refuse treatment is set out in *Re MB (Medical Treatment)* [1997] 2 FLR 426, 437. In the Official Solicitor's view, this test can be used for a wide range of decisions. Evidence from a psychiatrist or psychologist who has assessed the patient applying the *Re MB* test to the particular decision in question is generally required. It follows from the terms of the *Re MB* test that global psychometric test results are unlikely to be relevant. The Official Solicitor's experience is that references to the outdated and discredited concept of "mental age" are of no assistance at all. It is important for the expert assessing capacity to advise whether the patient is likely to develop capacity to make personal decisions about the matter in issue in the future.

(2) *Best interests*

In any medical case, the claimant must adduce evidence from a responsible medical practitioner not only (i) that performing the particular operation would not be negligent, but also (ii) that it is necessary in the best interests of the patient: *Re A (Male Sterilisation)* [2000] 1 FLR 549, 555. The court's jurisdiction is to declare the best interests of the patient on the application of a welfare test analogous to that applied in wardship: *Re S (Sterilisation: Patient's Best Interests)* [2000] 2 FLR 389, 403. The judicial decision will incorporate broader ethical, social, moral and welfare considerations (above, at 401). Emotional, psychological and social benefit to the patient will be considered: *Re Y (Mental Patient: Bone Marrow Transplant)* [1997] Fam 110, [1996] 2 FLR 787. The court will wish to prepare a balance sheet listing the advantages and disadvantages of the procedure for the patient. If potential advantages and disadvantages are to be relied on then the court will wish to assess in percentage terms the likelihood of them in fact occurring: *Re A (Male Sterilisation)* [2000] 1 FLR 549, 560.

The parties

8 The claimant should be the NHS Trust or other body responsible for the patient's care, although a claim may also be brought by a family member or other individual closely connected with the patient. The body with clinical or caring responsibility should in any event be made a party: *Re S (Hospital Patient: Court's Jurisdiction)* [1996] Fam 1, [1995] 1 FLR 1075.

9 The person concerned must always be a party and should normally be a defendant, with the Official Solicitor acting as litigation friend. The Official Solicitor has a standard form of medical certificate if there is any question about

whether the person concerned is a "patient" within the meaning of the Civil Procedure Rules 1998, r 21. If the Official Solicitor does not act as litigation friend, the court will wish to consider whether he should be joined as an ex officio defendant or invited to act as a friend of the court. The Official Solicitor is invariably asked to be involved in sterilisation and vegetative state cases.

The directions hearing

10 Unless the matter is urgent, the claimant should fix a directions hearing for no less than 8 weeks after the date of issue, to allow the Official Solicitor to make initial inquiries. The court should, if appropriate, be asked to hold the directions hearing in private to protect the interests of the patient: the Civil Procedure Rules 1998, r 39.2(3)(*d*). The court will use the directions hearing to:

(1) make orders where necessary to preserve the anonymity of the patient, family and other parties;
(2) set a timetable for the Official Solicitor to conduct inquiries, obtain expert evidence and file his statement or report;
(3) fix a further hearing, to serve either as a final hearing if the matter is unopposed or as a final directions hearing to fix a contested hearing.

The Official Solicitor's inquiries

11 The Official Solicitor's representative will always see the patient, review relevant medical/social work records and interview carers, family members and others close to the patient as appropriate.

12 The Official Solicitor will consider the patient's wishes and feelings, and will inquire as to any earlier views the patient may have expressed, either in writing or otherwise. The High Court may determine the effect of a purported advance statement as to future medical treatment: *Re T (Adult: Refusal of Treatment)* [1993] Fam 95, sub nom *Re T (An Adult) (Consent to Medical Treatment)* [1992] 2 FLR 458, *Re C (Refusal of Medical Treatment)* [1994] 1 FLR 31. A valid and applicable advance refusal of treatment may be determinative. Previously expressed wishes and feelings which do not amount to an effective advance decision will still be an important component in the best interests decision.

The final hearing

13 Any substantive hearing should be before a High Court judge of the Family Division. Cases proceeding unopposed may be disposed of without oral evidence. The final hearing may be in private if necessary to protect the interests of the patient: the Civil Procedure Rules 1998, r 39.2(3)(*d*). If the hearing is in public, there may be orders that the identities of parties and witnesses (other than expert witnesses) should not be disclosed: the Civil Procedure Rules 1998, r 39.2(4). An order restricting publicity will continue to have effect notwithstanding the death of the patient, unless and until an application is made to discharge it: *Re C (Adult Patient: Publicity)* [1996] 2 FLR 251. The Official Solicitor will invite the court to make an appropriate order in relation to his costs.

Consultation with the Official Solicitor

14 Members of the Official Solicitor's legal staff are prepared to discuss adult medical and welfare cases before proceedings are issued. Inquiries should be addressed to a family litigation lawyer at:

The Official Solicitor
81 Chancery Lane
London WC2A 1DD

PART IV

Telephone: 020 7911 7127
Fax: 020 7911 7105
Email: inquiries@offsol.gsi.gov.uk

Inquiries about *children* medical and welfare cases should be directed to:

CAFCASS Legal Services and Special Casework
Newspaper House
8–16 Great New Street
London EC4A 3BN

Telephone: 020 7904 0867
Fax: 020 7904 0868/9
Email: legal@cafcass.gsi.gov.uk

Staff of CAFCASS Legal will liaise with the Official Solicitor where it is unclear which office can best represent a child.

Laurence Oates
Official Solicitor

APPENDIX 1: STERILISATION CASES

1 If a sterilisation procedure is necessary for therapeutic as opposed to contraceptive purposes then there may be no need for an application to court: *Re GF (Medical Treatment)* [1992] 1 FLR 293. If, however, any case lies anywhere near the boundary line it should be referred to the court: *Re S (Sterilisation: Patient's Best Interests)* [2000] 2 FLR 389, 405.

The claim

2 The relief sought in relation to an adult should be declarations that:

(1) [The patient] lacks capacity to consent to an operation of … [specify procedure proposed, eg "tubal occlusion by Filshie clips", or "laparoscopic sub-total hysterectomy", or "vasectomy"].

(2) It is in the existing circumstances in the best interests of [the patient] for her/him to undergo an operation of … [specify procedure as above].

The evidence

3 The court must be satisfied that the patient lacks capacity and that the operation will promote the best interests of the patient, rather than the interests or convenience of the claimant, carers or public. In sterilisation cases, the best interests tests has at least three particular components.

(1) *Likelihood of pregnancy*
An operation must address a current real need. It must be shown that the patient is capable of conception and is having or is likely to have full sexual intercourse. In relation to a young woman who has no interest in human relationships with any sexual ingredient a high level of supervision is an appropriate protection: *Re LC (Medical Treatment: Sterilisation)* [1997] 2 FLR 258. Any risk of pregnancy should be identifiable rather than speculative: *Re S (Medical Treatment: Adult Sterilisation)* [1998] 1 FLR 944.

(2) *Damage deriving from conception and/or menstruation*
The physical and psychological consequences of pregnancy and childbirth for the patient should be analysed by obstetric and psychiatric experts. In the case of a male, these considerations will be different: *Re A (Male*

Sterilisation) [2000] 1 FLR 549, 557. Psychiatric evidence as to the patient's likely ability to care for and/or have a fulfilling relationship with a child should be adduced. Evidence as to any child having a disability is likely to be irrelevant: *Re X (Adult Sterilisation)* [1998] 2 FLR 1124, 1129. If the proposed procedure is intended to affect the patient's menstruation, then evidence about any detriment caused by her current menstrual cycle must also be adduced.

(3) *Medical and surgical techniques*
The court will require a detailed analysis of all available and relevant methods of addressing any problems found to be substantiated under (1) and (2) above. This analysis should be performed by a doctor or doctors with expertise in the full range of available methods. The expert should explain the nature of each relevant method and then list its advantages and disadvantages (in particular, morbidity rates, mortality rates and failure rates) for the individual patient, taking into account any relevant aspects of her physical and psychological health. The Royal College of Obstetrics and Gynaecology has published relevant evidence-based clinical guidelines (No 4: *Male and Female Sterilisation*, April 1999 and No 5: *The Management of Menorrhagia in Secondary Care*, July 1999).

APPENDIX 2: PERMANENT VEGETATIVE STATE CASES

1 It is futile to provide medical treatment, including artificial nutrition and hydration, to a patient with no awareness of self or environment and no prospect of recovery: *Airedale NHS Trust v Bland* [1993] AC 789, 869, [1993] 1 FLR 1026, 1040. The purpose of the proceedings is to establish whether the patient is in this condition. It is not appropriate to apply to court to discontinue artificial feeding and hydration until the condition is judged to be permanent. Diagnostic guidelines are not statutory provisions and a precise label may not be of importance. The court's concern is whether there is any awareness whatsoever or any possibility of change: *Re D (Medical Treatment)* [1998] 1 FLR 411, 420 and *Re H (A Patient)* [1998] 2 FLR 36. The approach of the court has been reviewed in the light of the Human Rights Act 1998 and held to be compatible with Convention rights (European Convention for the Protection of Human Rights and Fundamental Freedoms 1950): *NHS Trust A v M; NHS Trust B v H* [2001] 2 WLR 942. There has as yet been no decided case dealing with the discontinuance of artificial feeding and hydration for an adult patient with any (however minimal) awareness of self or environment.

The claim

2 All claims in these cases should be issued in the Principal Registry and will normally be heard by the President of the Family Division unless she releases the case to another Family Division judge. The relief sought should be declarations that:

(1) [The patient] lacks capacity to consent to continued life-sustaining treatment measures and is in the permanent vegetative state.
(2) It is not in the existing circumstances in the best interests of [the patient] to be given life-sustaining medical treatment measures (including ventilation, nutrition and hydration by artificial means) and such measures may lawfully be discontinued.
(3) It is in [the patient's] best interests to be given such treatment and nursing care whether at hospital or elsewhere under medical supervision as may be

appropriate to ensure he/she retains the greatest dignity until such time as his/her life comes to an end.

The medical evidence

3 The diagnosis should be made in accordance with the most up-to-date generally accepted guidelines for the medical profession. A review by a working group of the Royal College of Physicians has been endorsed by the Conference of Medical Royal Colleges (*The Permanent Vegetative State*, Royal College of Physicians Publication Unit, 1996; with addendum published in (1997) 31 J R Coll Physns 260). The review concludes that the diagnosis of permanent vegetative state should not be made until the patient has been in a continuing vegetative state following head injury for 12 months or following other causes of brain damage for 6 months. The addendum to the review emphasises that there is no urgency in making the diagnosis and the assessors should take into account descriptions given by relatives, carers and nursing staff who spend most time with the patient. The *International Working Party Report on the Vegetative State* (1996), produced by the Royal Hospital for Neuro-disability, sets out in an appendix a range of vegetative presentations.

4 The claimant should, as a minimum, adduce evidence from (i) the treating physician and (ii) a neurologist or other expert experienced in assessing disturbances of consciousness. Both should deal with the diagnosis and their professional judgment of whether continued treatment would be in the patient's best interests. The duties of doctors making the diagnosis are described in the Royal College of Physicians review.

5 The court will generally wish to see at least two reports from experts, one of whom must be independent of the treating clinical team and claimant. The Official Solicitor will usually commission the second expert report.

Other evidence

6 The claimant should also adduce evidence about the views of family members. The views of family members or others close to the patient cannot act as a veto to an application but they must be taken fully into account by the court: *Re G (Persistent Vegetative State)* [1995] 2 FCR 46, 51.

The final hearing

7 It is usual for the final hearing to be in public, with protection for the identities of parties and witnesses. Even if the matter is unopposed, it may be appropriate for at least one expert to attend to give oral evidence. Family members need not attend if this would cause distress.

President's Guidelines 1 October 2001

Adoption Proceedings: A New Approach

Aim

The overall aim of this guidance is to reduce delay and inefficiency in adoption court proceedings and to improve the service for everyone in adoption cases. The guidance applies to a wide range of adoption cases, both contested and uncontested, and should be applied flexibly.

This guidance is issued by the President of the Family Division, with the approval of the Lord Chancellor. It is freely available to all court users, including applicants who represent themselves without a lawyer. It is drafted within the framework of the Adoption Act 1976 and the Adoption Rules 1984. It will be modified in the light of experience and any new legislation.

The guidance should be applied to all adoption or freeing for adoption applications issued after 1 October 2001.

Courts and judges

The courts listed in Appendix 1 are designated as adoption centres. They have special adoption officers, and circuit judges (adoption judges) who are responsible for adoption at those courts. The adoption officer performs the duties of the "proper officer" for the purpose of the Adoption Rules 1984.

Whenever possible, an adoption application which is issued in the county court should be issued in an adoption centre. If an adoption application is issued in a county court which is not an adoption centre, it will be transferred by the court to a convenient adoption centre. This will normally be the adoption centre to which the county court of issue is linked, as shown in Appendix 1.

The adoption officer at adoption centres should arrange for all adoption hearings and directions hearings to be listed before an adoption judge. Judges should keep close oversight on the progress of adoption cases, so judicial continuity is very important. Whenever possible, a case should always be listed before the same judge unless it would cause too much delay to do so. District judges cannot make a final adoption order, but an adoption district judge may handle directions hearings under arrangements made by the local circuit judge in charge of adoption.

Active case management

Adoption cases should be actively managed by the court. As soon as an application has been issued in, or transferred to, an adoption centre, the adoption officer should, in consultation with the adoption judge and unless the adoption judge specifically otherwise directs:

(i) liaise with CAFCASS and appoint a reporting officer or children's guardian in any case in which one is required (see Adoption Rules 1984, rule 17 – reporting officer, and 18 – children's guardian);

(ii) liaise with the adoption agency (if applicable) or local authority for the area in which the applicants live, who will be required to prepare a report under Schedule 2 to the Adoption Rules 1984. The local authority should identify the Schedule 2 reporter as soon as possible;

(iii) fix a first directions hearing, to take place about four weeks later on a date convenient to the Schedule 2 reporter and the reporting officer or children's guardian (as applicable). Notice of the hearing should be given to the applicants, the birth parents and any other person with parental responsibility for the child, the adoption agency (if applicable) or the relevant local authority, and the reporting officer or children's guardian (as applicable). (Note the further important provisions, and exceptions, as to the first directions hearing under the next two paragraphs immediately below.)

The first directions hearing

It is normally extremely important that the applicants, the birth parents (if they wish), the reporting officer or children's guardian *and* the Schedule 2 reporter should all attend a first directions hearing, together with any legal representatives.

PART IV

However the adoption judge or district judge may dispense with the attendance of a particular person or with the hearing altogether if he considers it appropriate to do so; but the judge must still consider all the matters in paragraphs (i) to (xii) below and give directions as appropriate.

In a case in which the applicants have requested confidentiality and a serial number under Adoption Rules 1984, rule 14, it is vital that arrangements are made to ensure that their confidentiality is preserved and that the birth parent(s) cannot see them. In such a case, the applicants should not attend the hearing personally. If they are legally represented, arrangements should not attend the hearing personally. If they are legally represented, arrangements should be made for the applicants to be available nearby, or on the telephone, to give instructions. If they are not legally represented, arrangements should be made for the applicants to be available to speak to the judge by telephone or, if the accommodation at the court permits, in a separate secure area.

At the first directions hearing the judge should consider and give directions as to the following matters:

- (i) checking and correcting any errors or omissions in the application and supporting documents. In cases in which the applicants are applying for the agreement of the birth parent(s) to be dispensed with, the suitability of the statement of facts (required under Adoption Rules 1984, rule 7 (freeing applications) or rule 19 (adoption applications)) should be checked and further directions given as necessary:
- (ii) in cases where the child was not placed with the applicants by an adoption agency, the filing of a statement by the applicants, explaining the background to the application, their reasons for wishing to adopt, and any other relevant information. Early provision of this information may considerably help the task of the Schedule 2 reporter, children's guardian or reporting officer;
- (iii) tracing birth parents, particularly fathers, even if they do not have parental responsibility;
- (iv) specifying in conjunction with the reporters, firm and realistic timetables for the filing of any Schedule 2 report, children's guardian's report, or report by a reporting officer. It is recognised that the period of 6 weeks prescribed by Adoption Rules 1984, rule 22, for filing a Schedule 2 report is no longer realistic when the local authority are not the placing agency (eg in the case of a step-parent application). The court may set a more realistic timetable by an extension from 6 weeks to not more than 12 weeks. Once a timetable has been set, after due consultation, courts should require it to be rigorously adhered to. In setting a timetable, it is important to check whether the birth parent(s) will remain readily available to meet reporters as required;
- (v) timetabling any other evidence, including any necessary expert evidence and any evidence from the birth family;
- (vi) in inter-country adoption cases or other cases in which the child will become a British citizen if an adoption order is made, notifying the Home Office and considering whether the requirements of the Adoption (Intercountry Aspects) Act 1999 and the Adoption of Children from Overseas Regulations 2001 (SI 2001/1251) appear to have been complied with. If they have not, the case may need to be transferred to the High Court. Consideration should also be given to the guidance described in *Re R (Intercountry adoptions: Practice)* [1999] 1 FLR 1042, and the *Intercountry Adoption Guide – Practice and Procedures, April 2001*

issued by the Adoption and Permanence Team of the Department of Health;

(vii) disclosure as soon as possible of all or as much information as possible both to the applicants and to the birth families. Openness tends to reduce anxiety and encourage agreement;

(viii) consideration of mediation or other alternative dispute resolution in contested cases, subject to preserving the confidentiality of the applicants when requested;

(ix) considering whether the child should be joined as a party to the proceedings;

(x) considering whether the case needs to be heard by a High Court judge. In such a case, the judge should further consider whether the case needs to be transferred to the Principal Registry of the Family Division (which may be very inconvenient to the parties) or may be retained in the local District Registry, or in the County Court, and arrangements made for it to be heard locally by a High Court Judge;

(xi) fixing, if necessary, a second directions hearing after all written evidence is filed. This should not be necessary in an unopposed and uncomplicated case;

(xii) fixing, if possible and appropriate, the date and place for the final hearing. In certain courts in rural areas it may be appropriate (under established local arrangements) to arrange for the final hearing to take place at a more accessible court. In cases in which the applicants have requested confidentiality, it is vital that consideration is given to making arrangements to ensure that their confidentiality is preserved and that the birth parent(s) cannot see them at the hearing.

After the first directions hearing, the adoption judge, in close liaison with the adoption officer, should actively monitor the progress of the case and ensure, in particular, that the prescribed timetable is being adhered to.

Care proceedings and adoption

Many adoptions follow care cases. It is often known from the start of, or during the course of, care proceedings that the local authority propose, if a care order is made, to place the child for adoption. In such cases, the following should be borne in mind:

(i) *Simultaneous freeing proceedings*
Local authorities should keep under active consideration during care proceedings whether they should issue simultaneous proceedings to free the child for adoption. Courts should enquire whether they are doing so and, in appropriate cases, encourage them to do so. This may save much later delay, expense and unnecessary stress both to adopters and to birth parents. (See also the guidance of the Department of Health in *LAC(98)20, Adoption – achieving the right balance and LAC(99)29, Care plans and care proceedings under the Children Act 1989.*)

(ii) *Free-standing freeing proceedings*
By contrast, once a child has been placed for adoption, a free-standing application to free the child for adoption may add to delay, expense and stress and is rarely appropriate.

(iii) *Disclosure of documents from care proceedings*
So as not to delay subsequent adoption proceedings, the court hearing the care proceedings should, on making a care order, always consider and give directions and permission for disclosure to prospective adopters and/or for use in subsequent adoption proceedings of relevant documents filed in the

care proceedings. It wastes time and costs if an application has to be made later. The findings of fact made in the care proceedings are often of especial importance in later adoption proceedings. Accordingly, if the judgment or reasons are not given in writing, consideration should also be given to whether a transcript should be obtained and who will pay for it.

APPENDIX 1

Part 1 of this Appendix lists those county courts that are designated as Adoption Centres for the purpose of these guidelines.

PART 1
DESIGNATED ADOPTION CENTRES

Midland Circuit

Birmingham County Court
Coventry County Court
Derby County Court
Leicester County Court
Lincoln County Court
Northampton County Court
Nottingham County Court
Stoke-on-Trent County Court
Telford County Court
Worcester County Court
Wolverhampton County Court

Northern Circuit

Blackburn County Court
Bolton County Court
Carlisle County Court
Lancaster County Court
Liverpool County Court
Manchester County Court
Stockport County Court

North Eastern Circuit

Bradford County Court
Kingston-upon-Hull County Court
Leeds County Court
Middlesborough County Court
Newcastle County Court
Sheffield County Court
Sunderland County Court
York County Court

South Eastern Circuit

Bow County Court
Brentford County Court
Brighton County Court
Bromley County Court
Cambridge County Court
Canterbury County Court
Chelmsford County Court
Croydon County Court
Guildford County Court
Ipswich County Court
Luton County Court
Medway County Court
Milton Keynes County Court
Norwich County Court
Oxford County Court
Peterborough County Court
Principal Registry of the Family Division
Reading County Court
Romford County Court
Watford County Court

Wales and Chester Circuit

Aberystwyth County Court
Cardiff County Court
Chester County Court
Llangefni County Court
Macclesfield County Court
Newport County Court

Pontypridd County Court
Rhyl County Court
Swansea County Court
Warrington County Court

Western Circuit

Bournemouth County Court
Bristol County Court
Exeter County Court
Plymouth County Court
Portsmouth County Court
Southampton County Court
Swindon County Court
Taunton County Court
Truro County Court

Part 2 of this Appendix lists those county courts that are designated as Adoption Centres for the purpose of these guidelines and links them to those other county courts with family jurisdiction that are to transfer adoption proceedings to them.

PART 2

TRANSFER ARRANGEMENTS

(i) County court with family jurisdiction	(ii) Designated Adoption Centre
	Midland Circuit
Boston County Court	Lincoln County Court
Burton-upon-Trent County Court	Derby County Court
Chesterfield County Court	Derby County Court
Dudley County Court	Wolverhampton County Court
Hereford County Court	Worcester County Court
Mansfield County Court	Nottingham County Court
Shrewsbury County Court	Telford County Court
Stafford County Court	Stoke-on-Trent County Court
Walsall County Court	Wolverhampton County Court
	Northern Circuit
Accrington County Court	Blackburn County Court
Altrincham County Court	Manchester County Court
Barrow-in-Furness County Court	Lancaster County Court
Birkenhead County Court	Liverpool County Court
Blackpool County Court	Lancaster County Court
Burnley County Court	Blackburn County Court
Bury County Court	Bolton County Court
Chorley County Court	Blackburn County Court
Kendal County Court	Lancaster County Court
Leigh County Court	Bolton County Court
Nelson County Court	Blackburn County Court
Oldham County Court	Manchester County Court
Penrith County Court	Carlisle County Court
Preston County Court	Lancaster County Court
Rawtensall County Court	Blackburn County Court
St Helens County Court	Liverpool County Court
Salford County Court	Manchester County Court
Southport County Court	Liverpool County Court
Tameside County Court	Stockport County Court
Whitehaven County Court	Carlisle County Court

(i) County court with family jurisdiction	(ii) Designated Adoption Centre
Wigan County Court	Liverpool County Court
	North Eastern Circuit
Barnsley County Court	Sheffield County Court
Bishop Auckland County Court	Middlesbrough County Court
Consett County Court	Sunderland County Court
Darlington County Court	Middlesbrough County Court
Dewsbury County Court	Bradford County Court
Doncaster County Court	Sheffield County Court
Durham County Court	Newcastle County Court
Gateshead County Court	Newcastle County Court
Great Grimsby County Court	Kingston-upon-Hull County Court
Halifax County Court	Bradford County Court
Harrogate County Court	York County Court
Hartlepool County Court	Middlesbrough County Court
Huddersfield County Court	Bradford County Court
Keighley County Court	Bradford County Court
North Shields County Court	Newcastle County Court
Pontefract County Court	Leeds County Court
Rotherham County Court	Sheffield County Court
Scarborough County Court	York County Court
Scunthorpe County Court	Kingston-upon-Hull County Court
Skipton County Court	York County Court
South Shields County Court	Sunderland County Court
Wakefield County Court	Leeds County Court
	South Eastern Circuit
Barnet County Court	Principal Registry of the Family Division
Bedford County Court	Luton County Court
Bury St Edmunds County Court	Ipswich County Court
Chichester County Court	Brighton County Court
Colchester County Court	Chelmsford County Court
Dartford County Court	Bromley County Court
Eastbourne County Court	Brighton County Court
Edmonton County Court	Principal Registry of the Family Division
Epsom County Court	Croydon County Court
Harlow County Court	Chelmsford County Court
Hastings County Court	Brighton County Court
Hertford County Court	Watford County Court
Hitchin County Court	Luton County Court
Horsham County Court	Brighton County Court
Ilford County Court	Romford County Court
King's Lynn County Court	Norwich County Court
Kingston-upon-Thames County Court	Brentford County Court
Lambeth County Court	Principal Registry of the Family Division
Lowestoft County Court	Norwich County Court
Maidstone County Court	Medway County Court
Reigate County Court	Guildford County Court
Slough County Court	Reading County Court
Southend County Court	Chelmsford County Court
Staines County Court	Brentford County Court

(i)	(ii)
County court with family jurisdiction	Designated Adoption Centre
Thanet County Court	Canterbury County Court
Tunbridge Wells County Court	Medway County Court
Uxbridge County Court	Watford County Court
Wandsworth County Court	Principal Registry of the Family Division
Willesden County Court	Principal Registry of the Family Division
Woolwich County Court	Principal Registry of the Family Division
Worthing County Court	Brighton County Court
	Wales and Chester Circuit
Blackwood County Court	Newport County Court
Brecknock County Court	Pontypridd County Court
Bridgend County Court	Cardiff County Court
Caernarfon County Court	Llangefni County Court
Carmarthen County Court	Swansea County Court
Crewe County Court	Macclesfield County Court
Haverfordwest County Court	Swansea County Court
Llanelli County Court	Swansea County Court
Merthyr Tydfil County Court	Pontypridd County Court
Neath and Port Talbot County Court	Swansea County Court
Runcorn County Court	Warrington County Court
Welshpool and Newtown County Court	Chester County Court
Wrexham County Court	Chester County Court
	Western Circuit
Aldershot and Farnham County Court	Southampton County Court
Barnstaple County Court	Exeter County Court
Basingstoke County Court	Southampton County Court
Bath County Court	Bristol County Court
Bodmin County Court	Truro County Court
Gloucester County Court	Bristol County Court
Newport (Isle of Wight) County Court	Portsmouth County Court
Penzance County Court	Truro County Court
Salisbury County Court	Southampton County Court
Torquay and Newton Abbott County Court	Exeter County Court
Trowbridge County Court	Swindon County Court
Weston-Super-Mare County Court	Bristol County Court
Weymouth and Dorchester County Court	Bournemouth County Court
Winchester County Court	Southampton County Court
Yeovil County Court	Taunton County Court

Dame Elizabeth Butler-Sloss
President

President's Direction 14 December 2001

Citations: [2002] 1 FLR 177; [2002] 1 WLR 325; [2002] 1 All ER 794

Declaratory Proceedings Concerning Incapacitated Adults: Medical and Welfare Decisions

1 Proceedings which invoke the jurisdiction of the High Court to grant declarations as to the best interests of incapacitated adults are civil proceedings to which the Civil Procedure Rules 1998 apply. Although not assigned to any Division, having regard to their nature and the issues raised within them, such proceedings are more suitable for hearing in the Family Division.

2 Accordingly, these proceedings should be commenced, and will be determined, as follows:

(*a*) Permanent vegetative state cases should be issued in the Principal Registry of the Family Division and will be determined by the President of the Family Division or by a Judge nominated by her. Interlocutory applications will be heard by the President or by the nominated Judge.

(*b*) Other proceedings may be commenced in any registry but must be determined by a Judge of the Division. Interlocutory applications are to be heard by a Judge of the Division.

3 *Practice Note (Declaratory Proceedings: Medical and Welfare Decisions for Adults who Lack Capacity)* [2001] 2 FLR 158, dated 1 May 2001 and issued by the Official Solicitor, provides valuable guidance in relation to these proceedings and should be followed.

4 Issued with the approval of the Lord Chief Justice and the Lord Chancellor.

Dame Elizabeth Butler-Sloss
President

Attorney-General's Memorandum 19 December 2001

Citations: [2002] Fam Law 229

Requests for the Appointment of an Advocate to the Court

1 The memorandum has been agreed between the Attorney-General and the Lord Chief Justice. It gives guidance about making a request for the appointment of an advocate to the court (formerly called an amicus curiae).

2 In most cases, an advocate to the court is appointed by the Attorney-General, following a request by the court. In some cases, an advocate to the court will be appointed by the Official Solicitor or the Children and Family Court Advisory and Support Service (CAFCASS) (see paras 11 and 12 below).

The role of an advocate to the court

3 A court may properly seek the assistance of an advocate to the court when there is a danger of an important and difficult point of law being decided without the court hearing relevant argument. In those circumstances the Attorney-General may decided to appoint an advocate to the court.

4 It is important to bear in mind that an advocate to the court represents no one. His or her function is to give to the court such assistance as he or she is able on the relevant law and its application to the facts of the case. An advocate to the court will not normally be instructed to lead evidence, cross-examine witnesses, or investigate the facts. In particular, it is not appropriate for the court to seek assistance from an advocate to the court simply because a defendant in criminal proceedings refuses representation.

5 The following circumstances are to be distinguished from those where it will be appropriate for the court to seek the assistance of an advocate to the court:

(i) where a point of law which affects a government department is being argued in a case where the department is not represented and where the court believes that the department may wish to be represented;
(ii) where the Attorney believes it is necessary for him to intervene as a party in his capacity as guardian of the public interest;
(iii) where the court believes it is appropriate for a litigant in person to seek free (pro bono) assistance;
(iv) where, in a criminal trial, the defendant is unrepresented and the advocate to the court would be duplicating the prosecutor's duty as a minister of justice "to assist the court on all matters of law applicable to the case";
(v) where in a criminal case in relation to sentencing appeals there are issues of fact which are likely to arise and the prosecution ought to be represented, or it would be reasonable to ask the prosecutor to be present and address the court as to the relevant law.

6 In the first of these five cases, the court may invite the Attorney to make arrangements for the advocate to be instructed on behalf of the department. In the second, the court may grant the Attorney permission to intervene, in which case the advocate instructed represents the Attorney. In neither case is the advocate an advocate to the court.

7 In the third case the court may grant a litigant in person an adjournment to enable him or her to seek free (pro bono) assistance. In doing so, the court should bear in mind that it is likely to take longer to obtain free (pro bono) representation than funded representation. In contrast to an advocate to the court, a free (pro bono) legal representative will obtain his or her instructions from the litigant and will represent the interests of that party. His or her role before the court and duty to the court will be identical to that of any other representative of the parties. Accordingly it will not be appropriate for the court to take such a course where the type of assistance required is that provided by an advocate to the court.

8 In the fourth case the prosecutor's special duty is akin to an advocate to the court. In the fifth case, in relation to appeals against sentence where the defendant is represented, it may be preferable to request the attendance of the prosecutor, who will be able to address the court on issues of fact and law. It would not be proper for an advocate to the court to take instructions from the prosecuting authority in relation to factual matters relating to the prosecution. An advocate to the court should only be asked to address the court as to the relevant law.

Making a request to the Attorney-General

9 A request for an advocate to the court should be made by the court as soon as convenient after it is made aware of the point of law which requires the assistance of an advocate to the court. The request should set out the circumstances which have occurred, identifying the point of law upon which assistance is sought and the nature of the assistance required. The court should consider whether it would be sufficient for such assistance to be in writing in the form of submissions as to the law, or whether the assistance should include oral submissions at the hearing. The request should ordinarily be made in writing and be accompanied by the papers necessary to enable the Attorney to reach a decision on the basis of a proper understanding of the case.

10 The Attorney will decide whether it is appropriate to provide such assistance and, if so, the form such assistance should take. Before reaching a decision he may seek further information or assistance from the court. The Attorney will also ask the court to keep under review the need for such assistance. Where the circumstances which gave rise to the original request have changed, such that the court may now anticipate hearing all relevant argument on the point of law without the presence of an advocate to the court, either the court or the Attorney may ask the advocate to the court to withdraw.

Requests to the Official Solicitor or CAFCASS

11 A request for an advocate to the court may be made to the Official Solicitor or CAFCASS (Legal Services and Special Casework) where the issue is one in which their experience of representing children and adults under disability gives rise to special experience. The division of responsibility between them is outlined in Practice Notes reported at [2001] 2 FLR 151 and [2001] 2 FLR 155.

12 The procedure and circumstances for requesting an advocate to the court to be appointed by the Official Solicitor or CAFCASS are the same as those applying to requests to the Attorney-General. In cases of extreme urgency, telephone requests may be made. In some cases, the Official Solicitor himself will be appointed as advocate to the court. He may be given directions by the court authorising him to obtain documents, conduct investigations and enquiries and to advise the court. He may appear by counsel or an in-house advocate.

Lord Goldsmith QC
Attorney-General

Lord Woolf
Lord Chief Justice

Requests for an advocate to the court should be addressed as follows:

The Legal Secretary,
The Legal Secretariat to the Law Officers,
Attorney-General's Chambers,
9 Buckingham Gate,
London SW1E 6JP,
tel 020 7271 2417 (criminal), 020 7271 2413 (civil),
fax 020 7271 2434.

Official Solicitor to the Supreme Court,
81 Chancery Lane,
London WC2A 1DD,
tel 020 7911 7127, fax 020 7911 7105.

CAFCASS (Legal Services and Special Casework),
Newspaper House,
8–16 Great New Street,
London EC4A 3BN,
tel 020 7904 0867, fax 020 7904 0868/9.

For information about free (pro bono) services: Bar Pro Bono Unit, 7 Gray's Inn Square, London WC1R 5AZ, tel 020 7831 9711, fax 020 7831 9733, email enquiries@barprobonounit.f9.co.uk.

Practice Direction 14 January 2002

Citations: [2002] 1 FLR 699; [2002] 1 WLR 406; [2002] 1 All ER 1024

Video Conferencing

1 Video conferencing facilities are available in the Royal Courts of Justice ("RCJ") in Court 38. In proceedings pending in the Principal Registry of the Family Division which are to be heard in the RCJ or in First Avenue House and in which it is desired to use these facilities, the following procedure should be observed.

2

(*a*) Directions for the video conferencing hearing should be given by an order made in the proceedings. The order may be made without attendance, provided all parties consent.

(*b*) The order should specify, in general terms, the purpose of the hearing and give the date, time, place and duration of the hearing and the place or country with which the link is to be effected.

(*c*) Availability of the facilities must be ascertained prior to the order being made fixing the appointment. This can be done by communicating with those responsible for managing the video conference facility in the RCJ, ("the video managers" – Roger Little and Norman Muller, telephone 020-7947 6581; fax: 020-7947 6613). If the order is made at a hearing, the court associate or clerk will be able to make the telephone call to ascertain an available date. For orders to be made without attendance, the parties must ascertain the availability of the facilities prior to submitting the application.

(*d*) In every case, the parties must communicate with the video managers as soon as possible after the order has been made to ensure that all the necessary arrangements for the telephone link to be established are settled well in advance of the appointed date.

3 Where in any case the main hearing may be delayed because video conferencing facilities at the RCJ are not conveniently available, consideration should be given to using the video conferencing facilities at the Bar Council or the Law Society. If facilities away from the RCJ are to be used, it will be the responsibility of the party applying for the video conferencing hearing to make all the necessary arrangements with the video conferencing provider.

4 Issued with the approval of Dame Elizabeth Butler-Sloss P.

Gerald Angel
Senior District Judge

Practice Direction 14 January 2002

Citations: [2002] 1 WLR 346; [2002] 1 All ER 351; [2002] 2 Lloyd's Rep 228

Judgments: Neutral Citation

This Practice Direction is made with the concurrence of the Lord Phillips of Worth Matravers MR, Dame Elizabeth Butler-Sloss P and Sir Andrew Morritt V-C. It covers the extension of the neutral citation arrangements announced in the *Practice Direction (Judgments: Form and Citation)*, issued on 11 January 2001 ([2001] 1 WLR 194; [2001] 1 All ER 193), as foreshadowed in paragraph 2.6 of that Practice Direction.

1 With effect from 14 January 2002 the practice of neutral citation is being extended to all judgments given by judges in the High Court in London. A unique number will be furnished to every such High Court judgment from a register kept at the High Court. A unique number will also be furnished, on request (see below) to High Court judgments delivered by judges outside London.

2 The judgments will be numbered in the following way:

Chancery Division EWHC number (Ch)
Patents Court EWHC number (Pat)
Queen's Bench Division EWHC number (QB)
Administrative Court EWHC number (Admin)
Commercial Court EWHC number (Comm)
Admiralty Court EWHC number (Admlty)
Technology & Construction Court EWHC number (TCC)
Family Division EWHC number (Fam)

For example, [2002] EWHC 123 (Fam); or [2002] EWHC 124 (QB); or [2002] EWHC 125 (Ch).

3 Under these arrangements, it will be unnecessary to include the descriptive word in brackets when citing the paragraph number of a judgment. Thus paragraph 59 in *Smith v Jones* [2002] EWHC 124 (QB) would be cited: *Smith v Jones* [2002] EWHC 124 at [59].

4 There is to be no alteration to the arrangements for the neutral citation of judgments given in the two divisions of the Court of Appeal, where the official shorthand writers will continue to provide the number for the neutral citation.

As indicated above, neutral citations will not be automatically assigned to judgments delivered by judges in the High Court outside London, because they appear much less frequently in published reports. The Mechanical Recording Department, Royal Courts of Justice, Strand, London WC2A 2LL (tel no: 020-7947-7771) will supply a citation for such a judgment to anyone wishing to include it in a published report.

5 Apart from the changes set out above, the rules set out in section 2 of the earlier Practice Direction are still applicable. Brooke LJ, the judge in charge of

modernisation, is still responsible for advising the Judges' Council on these matters. Paragraph 4.1 of that Practice Direction remains unchanged.

6 Although the judges cannot dictate the form in which law publishers reproduce the judgments of the court, this form of citation contains the official number given to each judgment which they hope will be reproduced wherever the judgment is republished, in addition to the reference given in any particular series of reports.

Lord Woolf
Lord Chief Justice

President's Direction 22 March 2002

Citations: [2002] 2 FLR 367

Judicial Continuity

1 This direction applies only to cases proceeding in the Family Division of the High Court at the Royal Courts of Justice in London.

1.1 In order to achieve as much judicial continuity as possible in the hearing of cases and to avoid delay, the procedure described in this direction will apply as from 9 April 2002.

2 Applications within Part IV (Care and Supervision) of the Children Act 1989

2.1 Upon transfer to the High Court (or where applicable, commencement) the case will be allocated to a High Court judge (the Allocated judge) and a date fixed for a Case Management Conference. The Clerk of the Rules will notify the parties of the date for the Case Management Conference and the name of the Allocated judge as soon as practicable after receipt of the court file.

2.2 Within 24 hours of transfer to the High Court (or commencement), the applicant must lodge with the Clerk of the Rules, a very brief (less than one page) summary of the case. This should be delivered to the office of the Clerk of the Rules or sent by fax (020 7947 7304).

2.3 The Case Management Conference and all further hearings (including directions hearings) will be conducted by the Allocated judge, unless the case is released to another judge or when it is impracticable for the hearing to be before the Allocated judge.

2.4 As soon as practicable the Clerk of the Rules will send to the parties a copy of the Standard Directions (in the form attached to this Direction) completed by a judge (usually the Allocated judge), notifying the parties of the steps they are required to take in preparation for the Case Management Conference.

2.5 At the Case Management Conference which is to be attached by all parties, the Allocated judge will give directions, managing the case to a final hearing.

2.6 It is of the essence of this procedure that counsel retained for the final hearing should attend the Case Management Conference and any other directions hearings, except when all the directions have been agreed in advance. Counsel should therefore use their best endeavours to ensure attendance at these hearings. On occasions when one of these hearings coincides with a hearing in another case in which counsel is engaged, counsel should, whenever possible, seek release from the judge before whom they are appearing, so as to enable them to attend the directions hearing. This requirement applies equally to a solicitor who intends to appear as advocate at the final hearing.

2.7 When a case is transferred to the High Court and an urgent hearing is required prior to the Case Management Conference, the Clerk of the Rules should be requested to provide an immediate or early hearing date, if possible before the Allocated judge. This may be obtained by telephone. Accordingly, other than to appoint a children's guardian (when required), it will not usually be necessary or appropriate for the transferring court to give any directions when transferring the case to the High Court.

2.8 The final hearing will be before the Allocated judge, unless it is impracticable so to arrange.

3 Urgent Applications Court

3.1 Cases which have been allocated to a judge will not be taken by the Urgent Applications Court except to deal with an emergency. When the Allocated judge is not in London, it will nevertheless usually be possible to communicate with the judge by telephone or by fax (or email) in order to obtain directions or release of the case. A video conference may sometimes be appropriate.

4 Applications within Part II of the Children Act 1989

4.1 These cases (ie private law children cases) when commenced in or transferred to the High Court will not formally come within this direction except that judicial continuity will be observed whenever possible. The aim will be for the same judge to deal with the directions and other interlocutory hearings as well as the final hearing.

5 Ancillary Relief applications within matrimonial causes and applications for financial provision under the Children Act 1989

5.1 These applications when transferred to (or commenced in) the High Court will not formally come within this direction except that judicial continuity will be observed whenever possible, in particular in very complex cases and in cases where there are very substantial assets.

5.2 The above is subject to the requirement in rule 2.61E of the Family Proceedings Rules 1991 in relation to the judge before whom any Financial Dispute Resolution (FDR) hearing takes place.

5.3 In cases which are suitable for adjudication in the High Court by a High Court judge and in which it would be appropriate for the first appointment to be listed before a judge, for example because of the likelihood of substantial dispute about the extent of financial disclosure or the desirability of using the first appointment as an FDR, it may be appropriate for the application for transfer to be made at an early stage of the proceedings, before the date initially given for the first appointment.

6 The Standard Directions form attached to this Direction may be amended from time to time as experience requires.

Dame Elizabeth Butler-Sloss
President

IN THE HIGH COURT OF JUSTICE FD02C
FAMILY DIVISION
PRINCIPAL REGISTRY

Application of

Re

(Child(ren))

Standard directions by High Court judge (Care proceedings)

Date of this order

Upon reading the papers filed by the applicant

IT IS ORDERED by **The Honourable**

This case is to be allocated to **The Honourable**

Clerk's Tel 020 7947

The Allocated judge will be responsible for the continuous case management of this case

All future hearings in this case (including all directions and other interlocutory hearings, the pre-trial review and the final and any split hearing(s)) will be conducted by the Allocated judge and *not* by the urgent applications judge or by any other judge unless on application to the Allocated judge (if necessary in case of urgency by telephone) the Allocated judge releases the case to another judge

Case Management Conference

There will be a Case Management Conference before the Allocated judge at the Royal Courts of Justice Strand London WC2A 2LL **at**

on the

Purpose of the Case Management Conference

The purpose of the Case Management Conference is to:

- Identify and consider the issues in the case
- Consider whether there are any features requiring particular urgency
- Identify whether there is to be a contested hearing of any application for an interim care order and (if so) when such hearing should take place
- Consider what expert assessments and reports are required, when and in what disciplines
- Consider whether twin-track planning is appropriate
- Consider whether a split hearing is necessary

- Consider the time estimate(s) for the final and any split hearing(s)
- Consider whether any directions or other interlocutory hearings
  - should be before the Allocated judge
  - can be released to another judge
- Consider whether the final and any split hearing(s)
  - should be before the Allocated judge
  - can be released to another High Court judge
  - can be released to a Deputy High Court judge
- Timetable the case through to final disposal (fixing the dates of all future hearings, including all directions and other interlocutory hearings, a pre-trial review and the final and any split hearing(s) and considering the appropriate venue)
- Give directions as to
  - the format of future directions and other hearings (including where appropriate the giving of directions on paper application without the attendance of the parties or by telephone conference)
  - who is to attend future directions and other hearings
- Give directions as to the format of and the arrangements to be made for updating the Trial Bundle
- Give directions as to expert evidence (including, where appropriate, directions for the experts to meet and for the preparation of agreed schedules of agreement and disagreement)
- Give directions as to the filing by each of the Respondents of
  - evidence and
  - a response to the Local Authority's proposed Threshold Findings
- Give such further directions as are appropriate

<u>NOTE:</u> THE PARTIES and their legal representatives MUST consider each of the above matters and if appropriate liaise BEFORE the day of THE CASE MANAGEMENT CONFERENCE

<u>STANDARD DIRECTIONS</u>

to ensure that the Case Management Conference achieves these objectives

THE LOCAL AUTHORITY MUST not later than 2pm 5 working days before the date of the Case Management Conference file with the

a Bundle prepared in accordance with the *Practice Direction (Family Proceedings: Court Bundles)* [2000] 1 FLR 536. The Local Authority must at the same time serve on each of the Respondents an Index to the Bundle.

The Bundle to be prepared by the Local Authority must contain in addition to any other documents referred to in the *Practice Direction*:

- A clear and concise summary on one page of A4 paper of
  - the issues in the case and the Local Authority's plan(s) for the child(ren) and
  - any specific issues which may require to be determined at the Case Management Conference
- A Schedule of the Threshold Findings which the court is to be invited to make
- The witness statements upon which the Local Authority intend to rely
- The (Interim) Care Plan(s)

- A Listing Information Sheet indicating
  - whether the case is complex/standard/straightforward
  - whether there are any features requiring particular urgency
  - whether twin-track planning is being considered
  - whether a split hearing is necessary
  - what assessments are contemplated, when, by whom and for what purpose
  - what expert evidence it is proposed to obtain, when, from whom and for what purpose
  - the outline timetable proposed by the Local Authority
  - any other matters which may affect the length of any interlocutory or final hearing
  - A draft of the order which the Local Authority will invite the judge to make at the conclusion of the Case Management Conference

THE RESPONDENTS MUST not later than 2pm 2 working days before the date of the Case Management Conference file with the

and serve on the Local Authority copies of:

- Any response to the documents filed by the Local Authority which the judge will be invited to consider at the Case Management Conference
- A Listing Information Sheet indicating
  - whether any assessment is to be sought and (if so) when, from whom and for what purpose
  - whether any expert evidence is proposed to be obtained and (if so) when, from whom and for what purpose
  - the outline timetable proposed by the Respondent(s)
- A draft of the order which the Respondent(s) will invite the judge to make at the conclusion of the Case Management Conference

It is the DUTY OF THE PARTIES' LEGAL REPRESENTATIVES to find out so far as is possible and notify to all other parties BEFORE THE CASE

MANAGEMENT CONFERENCE the names and the availability of anybody proposed to conduct any assessment or to provide any expert evidence

THE PARTIES' LEGAL REPRESENTATIVES and all other relevant professionals who attend the Case Management Conference MUST BRING TO THE CASE MANAGEMENT CONFERENCE:

- Their professional diaries for the next 15 months and
- Details (so far as known) of the names and the availability of anybody who it is proposed should conduct any assessment or provide any expert evidence

THE PARTIES together with their legal representatives MUST ARRIVE AT COURT on the day of the Case Management Conference NO LATER THAN one hour before the time fixed for the hearing so that they can all meet together to discuss and if possible agree:

- The outline timetable to be presented to the judge holding the Case Management Conference and
- The order which the judge will be invited to make at the conclusion of the Case Management Conference

THE LOCAL AUTHORITY MUST PREPARE so that it can be handed to the judge holding the Case Management Conference at the beginning of the hearing, a schedule listing (so far as is known) the names and contact details (professional addresses and telephone/fax/DX/email numbers for)

- the lead social worker
- the Guardian ad litem
- the solicitors and counsel for each party
- any experts who have been or may be instructed

ADDITIONAL DIRECTIONS (if any)

OBSERVATIONS

Signed

A Justice of the High Court

Best Practice Guidance December 2002

Note: the following material is taken from the Best Practice Guide published by the President of the Family Division's Ancillary Relief Advisory Group.

Citations: [2003] 1 FLR 573

Instructing a Single Joint Expert

1 The *President's Practice Direction of 25 May 2000* ([2000] 1 FLR 997), encouraged the appointment of a Single Joint Expert (SJE) as follows:

> "The introduction of expert evidence in proceedings is likely to increase costs substantially and consequently the court will use its powers to restrict the unnecessary use of experts. Accordingly, where expert evidence is sought to be relied upon, parties should if possible agree upon a single joint expert whom they can jointly instruct. Where parties are unable to agree upon the expert to be instructed the court will consider using its powers under Part 35 of the Civil Procedure Rules 1998 to direct that evidence be given by one expert only. In such cases, parties must be in a position at the first appointment or when the matter comes to be considered by the court to provide the court with a list of suitable experts or make submissions as to the method by which the expert is to be selected."

2 This Best Practice Guide is intended to promote efficiency, effectiveness and economy in the management of ancillary relief cases and to assist practitioners and experts as to the procedure to be adopted when instructions are given jointly to experts in applications for ancillary relief. It is equally applicable prior to the issue of proceedings. Throughout, the principle of proportionality must be a primary consideration.

3 An expert instructed by one party separately will not usually be appointable later as an SJE. Parties should therefore consider the costs implications before appointing an expert for their own side, rather than suggesting the appointment of an SJE to the other party.

4 If parties agree to appoint an SJE, then before instructions are given, they should:

(1) obtain confirmation from the proposed expert:
- (*a*) that there is no conflict of interest;
- (*b*) that the matter is within the range of expertise of the expert;
- (*c*) that the expert is available to provide the report within a specified timescale;
- (*d*) of the expert's availability for attendance at any dates that are known to be relevant;
- (*e*) of any periods when the expert will not be available;
- (*f*) as to the expert's fee rate, basis of charging, other terms of business and best estimate of likely fee;
- (*g*) if applicable, that the expert will accept instructions on a publicly funded basis, and
- (*h*) have agreed in what proportion the SJE's fee is to be shared between them (at least in the first instance) and when it is to be paid;
- (*i*) if applicable, have obtained agreement for public funding.

5 Where parties have not agreed on the appointment of an SJE before the relevant directions appointment, they should obtain the confirmations set out in 4(1) above, in respect of all experts they intend to put to the court for the purpose of CPR 1998, r 35.7(3)(*a*).

6 Where the court directs a report by an SJE, the order should:

- (*a*) if the SJE has already been instructed, adopt the instructions already given or make such amendments to the instruction as the court thinks fit;
- (*b*) identify the SJE;
- (*c*) specify the task that the SJE is to perform;
- (*d*) provide that the instructions are to be contained in a jointly agreed letter;
- (*e*) specify the time within which the letter of instruction is to be sent;
- (*f*) specify the date by which the report must be produced;
- (*g*) provide for the date by which written questions may be put to the SJE and the date by which they must be answered;
- (*h*) make any such provision as to the SJE's fees which the court thinks appropriate.

7 The joint instructions to the SJE should reflect the proportionality principle and include:

- (*a*) basic relevant information;
- (*b*) any assumptions to be made;
- (*c*) the principal known issues;
- (*d*) the specific questions to be answered;

PART IV

(*e*) arrangements for attendance at a property, business or accountant's office or other place;
(*f*) a copy of paragraphs 1.1 to 1.6 of the *Practice Direction to CPR Part 35* (form and contents of expert's reports) and a copy of this Guide;
(*g*) a copy of the relevant parts of the court order;
(*h*) documents necessary for the expert's consideration of the case, sufficient for the purpose, clearly legible, properly sorted, paginated and indexed.

8 Upon receiving the joint letter of instruction, or subsequently should it become necessary to do so, the SJE should raise with the solicitors any issues or questions which may arise, including proportionality, lack of clarity or completeness in the instructions and the possible effect on fees of complying with the instructions.

9 Should a party wish to give supplementary instructions to the SJE, full consideration must be given to proportionality and to the possible effect on the timetable. Supplementary instructions should not be given to the SJE unless the other party has agreed or the court has sanctioned them.

10 All communications by the SJE should be addressed to both parties and the SJE should keep the parties informed of all material steps taken, by, for example, copying all correspondence to each party.

11 Any meeting or conference attended by the SJE should be proportionate to the case and should normally be with *both* parties and/or their advisers. Unless both parties have agreed otherwise in writing, the SJE should not attend any meeting or conference that is not a joint one.

12 The report of the SJE should be served simultaneously on both parties.

13 Where the SJE considers that the proportionality principle cannot be complied with in preparing the report within the terms of reference, the SJE should give notice to the parties, identifying what is perceived to be the difficulty.

14 Where the difficulty cannot be resolved by the parties and the SJE, the SJE should file a written request to the court for directions pursuant to CPR 1998, r 35.14.

15 As a last resort, the SJE may resign the joint appointment. In this event, the SJE should serve a concise statement of the reasons on both parties. Where the court has ordered his joint appointment the SJE should also serve the court with the statement.

Protocol January 2003

Child Abduction Cases Between the UK and Pakistan

The President of the Family Division and the Hon Chief Justice of Pakistan in consultation with senior members of the family judiciary of the United Kingdom ("the UK") and the Islamic Republic of Pakistan ("Pakistan"), having met on 15–17 January 2003 in the Royal Courts of Justice in London, reach the following consensus:

WHEREAS:

(*a*) Desiring to protect the children of the UK and Pakistan from the harmful effects of wrongful removal or retention from one country to the other;

(*b*) Mindful that the UK and Pakistan share a common heritage of law and a commitment to the welfare of children;

(*c*) Desirous of promoting judicial cooperation, enhanced relations and the free flow of information between the judiciaries of the UK and Pakistan; and

(*d*) Recognising the importance of negotiation, mediation and conciliation in the resolution of family disputes;

IT IS AGREED THAT:

1 In normal circumstances the welfare of a child is best determined by the courts of the country of the child's habitual/ordinary residence.

2 If a child is removed from the UK to Pakistan, or from Pakistan to the UK, without the consent of the parent with a custody/residence order or a restraint/interdict order from the court of the child's habitual/ordinary residence, the judge of the court of the country to which the child has been removed shall not ordinarily exercise jurisdiction over the child, save in so far as it is necessary for the court to order the return of the child to the country of the child's habitual/ordinary residence.

3 If a child is taken from the UK to Pakistan, or from Pakistan to the UK, by a parent with visitation/access/contact rights with the consent of the parent with a custody/residence order or a restraint/interdict order from the court of the child's habitual/ordinary residence or in consequence of an order from that court permitting the visit, and the child is retained in that country after the end of the visit without consent or in breach of the court order, the judge of the court of the country in which the child has been retained shall not ordinarily exercise jurisdiction over the child, save in so far as it is necessary for the court to order the return of the child to the country of the child's habitual/ordinary residence.

4 The above principles shall apply without regard to the nationality, culture or religion of the parents or either parent and shall apply to children of mixed marriages.

5 In cases where the habitual/ordinary residence of the child is in dispute the court to which an application is made should decide the issue of habitual/ordinary residence before making any decision on the return or on the general welfare of the child, and upon determination of the preliminary issue as to habitual/ordinary residence should then apply the general principles set out above.

6 These applications should be lodged by the applicant, listed by the court and decided expeditiously.

7 It is recommended that the respective governments of the UK and Pakistan give urgent consideration to identifying or establishing an administrative service to facilitate or oversee the resolution of child abduction cases (not covered by the 1980 Hague Convention on the Civil Aspects of International Child Abduction).

8 It is further recommended that the judiciaries, the legal practitioners and the non-governmental organisations in the UK and Pakistan use their best endeavours to advance the objects of this protocol.

9 It is agreed that the UK and Pakistan shall each nominate a judge of the superior court to work in liaison with each other to advance the objects of this protocol.

SIGNED BY: Dame Elizabeth Butler-Sloss, DBE, President of the Family Division of the High Court of England and Wales and The Hon Mr Justice Sh Riaz Ahmad, Chief Justice of the Supreme Court of Pakistan

Dame Elizabeth Butler-Sloss
President

PART V

CPR Practice Directions

PART V: CPR Practice Directions

Contents

Practice Direction – How to Start Proceedings – The Claim Form

This Practice Direction supplements CPR Part 7 (PD7)

GENERAL

1 Subject to the following provisions of this practice direction, proceedings which both the High Court and the county courts have jurisdiction to deal with may be started in the High Court or in a county court.

WHERE TO START PROCEEDINGS

2.1 Proceedings (whether for damages or for a specified sum) may not be started in the High Court unless the value of the claim is more than £15,000.

2.2 Proceedings which include a claim for damages in respect of personal injuries must not be started in the High Court unless the value of the claim is £50,000 or more (paragraph 9 of the High Court and County Courts Jurisdiction Order 1991 (SI 1991/724 as amended) describes how the value of a claim is to be determined).

2.3 A claim must be issued in the High Court or a county court if an enactment so requires.

2.4 Subject to paragraphs 2.1 and 2.2 above, a claim should be started in the High Court if by reason of:

(1) the financial value of the claim and the amount in dispute, and/or
(2) the complexity of the facts, legal issues, remedies or procedures involved, and/or
(3) the importance of the outcome of the claim to the public in general,

the claimant believes that the claim ought to be dealt with by a High Court judge.

(CPR Part 30 and the practice direction supplementing Part 30 contain provisions relating to the transfer to the county court of proceedings started in the High Court and vice-versa.)

2.5 A claim relating to Chancery business (which includes any of the matters specified in paragraph 1 of Schedule 1 to the Supreme Court Act 1981) may, subject to any enactment, rule or practice direction, be dealt with in the High Court or in a county court. The claim form should, if issued in the High Court, be marked in the top right hand corner 'Chancery Division' and, if issued in the county court, be marked 'Chancery Business'.

(For the equity jurisdiction of county courts, see section 23 of the County Courts Act 1984.)

2.6 A claim relating to any of the matters specified in subparagraphs (a) and (b) of paragraph 2 of Schedule 1 to the Supreme Court Act 1981 must be dealt with in the High Court and will be assigned to the Queen's Bench Division.

2.7 Practice directions applying to particular types of proceedings, or to proceedings in particular courts, will contain provisions relating to the commencement and conduct of those proceedings.

2.8 A claim in the High Court for which a jury trial is directed will, if not already being dealt with in the Queen's Bench Division, be transferred to that Division.

PART V

2.9 The following proceedings may not be started in a county court unless the parties have agreed otherwise in writing:

(1) a claim for damages or other remedy for libel or slander, and
(2) a claim in which the title to any toll, fair, market or franchise is in question.

2.10 (1) The normal rules apply in deciding in which court and specialist list a claim that includes issues under the Human Rights Act 1998 should be started. They also apply in deciding which procedure to use to start the claim; this Part or CPR Part 8 or CPR Part 54 (judicial review).

(2) The exception is a claim for damages in respect of a judicial act, which should be commenced in the High Court. If the claim is made in a notice of appeal then it will be dealt with according to the normal rules governing where the appeal is heard.

(A county court cannot make a declaration of incompatibility in accordance with section 4 of the Human Rights Act 1998. Legislation may direct that such a claim is to be brought before a specified tribunal.)

THE CLAIM FORM

3.1 A claimant must use Practice Form N1 or Practice Form N208 (the Part 8 claim form) to start a claim (but see paragraphs 3.2 and 3.4 below).

3.2 Rule 7.9 deals with fixed date claims and rule 7.10 deals with the Production Centre for the issue of claims; there are separate practice directions supplementing rules 7.9 and 7.10.

3.3 If a claimant wishes his claim to proceed under Part 8, or if the claim is required to proceed under Part 8, the claim form should so state. Otherwise the claim will proceed under Part 7. But note that in respect of claims in specialist proceedings (listed in CPR Part 49) and claims brought under the RSC or CCR set out in the Schedule to the CPR (see CPR Part 50) the CPR will apply only to the extent that they are not inconsistent with the rules and practice directions that expressly apply to those claims.

3.4 Other practice directions may require special practice forms to be used to commence particular types of proceedings, or proceedings in particular courts.

3.5 Where a claim which is to be served out of the jurisdiction is one which the court has power to deal with under the Civil Jurisdiction and Judgments Act 1982, the claim form and, when they are contained in a separate document, the particulars of claim should be endorsed with a statement that the court has power under that Act to deal with the claim and that no proceedings based on the same claim are pending between the parties in Scotland, Northern Ireland or another Convention territory[1].

1 'Convention territory' means the territory or territories of any Contracting State as defined by s 1(3) of the Civil Jurisdiction and Judgments Act 1982, to which the Brussels Conventions or Lugano Convention apply.

3.5A Where a claim which is to be served out of the jurisdiction is one which the court has power to deal with under Council Regulation (EC) No 44/2001 of 22 December 2000 on jurisdiction and the recognition and enforcement of judgments in civil and commercial matters, the claim form and, when they are contained in a separate document, the particulars of claim must be endorsed with a statement that the court has power under that Regulation to deal with the claim and that no proceedings based on the same claim are pending between the parties in Scotland, Northern Ireland or another Regulation State.

3.6 If a claim for damages or for an unspecified sum is started in the High Court, the claim form must:

(1) state that the claimant expects to recover more than £15,000 (or £50,000 or more if the claim is for personal injuries) or
(2) state that some enactment provides that the claim may only be commenced in the High Court and specify that enactment or
(3) state that the claim is to be in one of the specialist High Court lists (see CPR Parts 49 and 58–62) and specify that list.

3.7 If the contents of a claim form commencing specialist proceedings complies with the requirements of the specialist list in question the claim form will also satisfy paragraph 3.6 above.

3.8 If a claim for damages for personal injuries is started in the county court, the claim form must state whether or not the claimant expects to recover more than £1000 in respect of pain, suffering and loss of amenity.

3.9 If a claim for housing disrepair which includes a claim for an order requiring repairs or other work to be carried out by the landlord is started in the county court, the claim form must state:

(1) whether or not the cost of the repairs or other work is estimated to be more than £1000, and
(2) whether or not the claimant expects to recover more than £1000 in respect of any claim for damages[1].

If either of the amounts mentioned in (1) and (2) is more than £1000, the small claims track will not be the normal track for that claim.

(The Costs Practice Direction supplementing Parts 43–48 contains details of the information required to be filed with a claim form to comply with rule 44.15 (providing information about funding arrangements).)

1 See rules 16.3(4) and 26.6.

TITLE OF PROCEEDINGS

4.1 The claim form and every other statement of case, must be headed with the title of the proceedings. The title should state:

(1) the number of proceedings,
(2) the court or Division in which they are proceeding,
(3) the full name of each party,
(4) his status in the proceedings (ie claimant/defendant).

4.2 Where there is more than one claimant and/or more than one defendant, the parties should be described in the title as follows:

(1) AB
(2) CD
(3) EF Claimants
and
(1) GH
(2) IJ
(3) KL Defendants

START OF PROCEEDINGS

5.1 Proceedings are started when the court issues a claim form at the request of the claimant (see rule 7.2) but where the claim form as issued was received in the court office on a date earlier than the date on which it was issued by the court, the claim is 'brought' for the purposes of the Limitation Act 1980 and any other relevant statute on that earlier date.

5.2 The date on which the claim form was received by the court will be recorded by a date stamp either on the claim form held on the court file or on the letter that accompanied the claim form when it was received by the court.

5.3 An enquiry as to the date on which the claim form was received by the court should be directed to a court officer.

5.4 Parties proposing to start a claim which is approaching the expiry of the limitation period should recognise the potential importance of establishing the date the claim form was received by the court and should themselves make arrangements to record the date.

5.5 Where it is sought to start proceedings against the estate of a deceased defendant where probate or letters of administration have not been granted, the claimant should issue the claim against 'the personal representatives of AB deceased'. The claimant should then, before the expiry of the period for service of the claim form, apply to the court for the appointment of a person to represent the estate of the deceased.

PARTICULARS OF CLAIM

6.1 Where the claimant does not include the particulars of claim in the claim form, particulars of claim may be served separately:

(1) either at the same time as the claim form, or
(2) within 14 days after service of the claim form provided that the service of the particulars of claim is within 4 months after the date of issue of the claim form[1] (or 6 months where the claim form is to be served out of the jurisdiction[2]).

1 See rules 7.4(2) and 7.5(2).
2 See rule 7.5(3).

6.2 If the particulars of claim are not included in or have not been served with the claim form, the claim form must contain a statement that particulars of claim will follow[1].

(These paragraphs do not apply where the Part 8 procedure is being used. For information on matters to be included in the claim form or the particulars of claim, see Part 16 (statements of case) and the practice direction which supplements it.)

1 See rule 16.2(2).

STATEMENT OF TRUTH

7.1 Part 22 requires the claim form and, where they are not included in the claim form, the particulars of claim, to be verified by a statement of truth.

7.2 The form of the statement of truth is as follows:

'[I believe][the claimant believes] that the facts stated in [this claim form] [these particulars of claim] are true.'

7.3 Attention is drawn to rule 32.14 which sets out the consequences of verifying a statement of case containing a false statement without an honest belief in its truth.

(For information regarding statements of truth see Part 22 and the practice direction which supplements it.)

EXTENSION OF TIME

8.1 An application under rule 7.6 (for an extension of time for serving a claim form under rule 7.6(1)) must be made in accordance with Part 23 and supported by evidence.

8.2 The evidence should state:

(1) all the circumstances relied on,
(2) the date of issue of the claim,
(3) the expiry date of any rule 7.6 extension, and
(4) a full explanation as to why the claim has not been served.

(For information regarding (1) written evidence see Part 32 and the practice direction which supplements it and (2) service of the claim form see Part 6 and the practice direction which supplements it.)

Practice Direction – Alternative Procedure for Claims

This Practice Direction supplements CPR Part 8 (PD8)

TYPES OF CLAIM IN WHICH PART 8 PROCEDURE MAY BE USED

1.1 A claimant may use the Part 8 procedure where he seeks the court's decision on a question which is unlikely to involve a substantial dispute of fact.

1.2 A claimant may also use the Part 8 procedure if a practice direction permits or requires its use for the type of proceedings in question.

1.3 The practice directions referred to in paragraph 1.2 above may in some respects modify or disapply the Part 8 procedure and, where that is so, it is those practice directions that must be complied with.

1.4 The types of claim for which the Part 8 procedure may be used include:

(1) a claim by or against a child or patient which has been settled before the commencement of proceedings and the sole purpose of the claim is to obtain the approval of the court to the settlement,
(2) a claim for provisional damages which has been settled before the commencement of proceedings and the sole purpose of the claim is to obtain a consent judgment, and
(3) provided there is unlikely to be a substantial dispute of fact, a claim for a summary order for possession against named or unnamed defendants occupying land or premises without the licence or consent of the person claiming possession.

1.5 Where it appears to a court officer that a claimant is using the Part 8 procedure inappropriately, he may refer the claim to a judge for the judge to consider the point.

PART V

1.6 The court may at any stage order the claim to continue as if the claimant had not used the Part 8 procedure and, if it does so, the court will allocate the claim to a track and give such directions as it considers appropriate[1].

1 Rule 8.1(3).

ISSUING THE CLAIM

2.1 Part 7 and the practice direction which supplements it contain a number of rules and directions applicable to all claims, including those to which Part 8 applies. Those rules and directions should be applied where appropriate.

2.2 Where a claimant uses the Part 8 procedure, the claim form (Practice Form N208) should be used and must state the matters set out in rule 8.2 and, if paragraphs 1.2 or 1.3 apply, must comply with the requirements of the practice direction in question. In particular, the claim form must state that Part 8 applies; a Part 8 claim form means a claim form which so states.

(The Costs Practice Direction supplementing Parts 43–48 contains details of the information required to be filed with a claim form to comply with rule 44.15 (providing information about funding arrangements).)

RESPONDING TO THE CLAIM

3.1 The provisions of Part 15 (defence and reply) do not apply where the claim form is a Part 8 claim form.

3.2 Where a defendant who wishes to respond to a Part 8 claim form is required to file an acknowledgment of service, that acknowledgment of service should be in Practice Form N210[1] but can, alternatively, be given in an informal document such as a letter.

1 Rule 8.3(1)(a).

3.3 Rule 8.3 sets out provisions relating to an acknowledgment of service of a Part 8 claim form.

3.4 Rule 8.4 sets out the consequence of failing to file an acknowledgment of service.

3.5 The provisions of Part 12 (obtaining default judgment) do not apply where the claim form is a Part 8 claim form.

3.6 Where a defendant believes that the Part 8 procedure should not be used because there is a substantial dispute of fact or, as the case may be, because its use is not authorised by any rule or practice direction, he must state his reasons in writing when he files his acknowledgment of service[1]. If the statement of reasons includes matters of evidence it should be verified by a statement of truth.

1 Rule 8.8(1).

MANAGING THE CLAIM

4.1 The court may give directions immediately a Part 8 claim form is issued either on the application of a party or on its own initiative. The directions may include fixing a hearing date where:

(1) there is no dispute, such as in child and patient settlements, or

(2) where there may be a dispute, such as in claims for mortgage possession or appointment of trustees, but a hearing date could conveniently be given.

4.2 Where the court does not fix a hearing date when the claim form is issued, it will give directions for the disposal of the claim as soon as practicable after the defendant has acknowledged service of the claim form or, as the case may be, after the period for acknowledging service has expired.

4.3 Certain applications, such as a consent application under section 38 of the Landlord and Tenant Act 1954, may not require a hearing.

4.4 The court may convene a directions hearing before giving directions.

EVIDENCE

5.1 A claimant wishing to rely on written evidence should file it when his Part 8 claim form is issued[1] (unless the evidence is contained in the claim form itself).

1 Rule 8.5.

5.2 Evidence will normally be in the form of a witness statement or an affidavit but a claimant may rely on the matters set out in his claim form provided that it has been verified by a statement of truth.

(For information about (1) statements of truth see Part 22 and the practice direction that supplements it, and (2) written evidence see Part 32 and the practice direction that supplements it.)

5.3 A defendant wishing to rely on written evidence, should file it with his acknowledgment of service[1].

1 Rule 8.5(3).

5.4 Rule 8.5 sets out the times and provisions for filing and serving written evidence.

5.5 A party may apply to the court for an extension of time to serve and file evidence under Rule 8.5 or for permission to serve and file additional evidence under Rule 8.6(1).

(For information about applications see Part 23 and the practice direction that supplements it.)

5.6 (1) The parties may, subject to the following provisions, agree in writing on an extension of time for serving and filing evidence under Rule 8.5(3) or Rule 8.5(5).

(2) An agreement extending time for a defendant to file evidence under Rule 8.5(3) –

(a) must be filed by the defendant at the same time as he files his acknowledgment of service; and

(b) must not extend time by more than 14 days after the defendant files his acknowledgment of service.

(3) An agreement extending time for a claimant to file evidence in reply under Rule 8.5(5) must not extend time to more than 28 days after service of the defendant's evidence on the claimant.

Direction – Statements of Case

This Practice Direction supplements CPR Part 16 (PD16)

GENERAL

1.1 The provisions of Part 16 do not apply to claims in respect of which the Part 8 procedure is being used.

1.2 Where special provisions about statements of case are made by the rules and practice directions applying to particular types of proceedings, the provisions of Part 16 and of this practice direction apply only to the extent that they are not inconsistent with those rules and practice directions.

1.3 Examples of types of proceedings with special provisions about statements of case include –

(1) defamation claims (Part 53);
(2) possession claims (Part 55); and
(3) probate claims (Part 57).

1.4 If exceptionally a statement of case exceeds 25 pages (excluding schedules) an appropriate short summary must also be filed and served.

THE CLAIM FORM

2.1 Rule 16.2 refers to matters which the claim form must contain. Where the claim is for money, the claim form must also contain the statement of value referred to in rule 16.3.

2.2 The claim form must include an address at which the claimant resides or carries on business. This paragraph applies even though the claimant's address for service is the business address of his solicitor.

2.3 Where the defendant is an individual, the claimant should (if he is able to do so) include in the claim form an address at which the defendant resides or carries on business. This paragraph applies even though the defendant's solicitors have agreed to accept service on the defendant's behalf.

(For information about how and where a claim may be started see Part 7 and the practice direction which supplements it.)

PARTICULARS OF CLAIM

3.1 If practicable, the particulars of claim should be set out in the claim form.

3.2 Where the claimant does not include the particulars of claim in the claim form, particulars of claim may be served separately:

(1) either at the same time as the claim form, or
(2) within 14 days after service of the claim form[1] provided that the service of the particulars of claim is not later than 4 months from the date of issue of the claim form[2] (or 6 months where the claim form is to be served out of the jurisdiction[3]).

1 See rule 7.4(1)(b).
2 See rules 7.4(2) and 7.5(2).
3 See rule 7.5(3).

3.3 If the particulars of claim are not included in or have not been served with the claim form, the claim form must also contain a statement that particulars of claim will follow[1].

1 See rule 16.2(2).

3.4 Particulars of claim which are not included in the claim form must be verified by a statement of truth, the form of which is as follows:

'[I believe][the claimant believes] that the facts stated in these particulars of claim are true.'

3.5 Attention is drawn to rule 32.14 which sets out the consequences of verifying a statement of case containing a false statement without an honest belief in its truth.

3.6 The full particulars of claim must include:

(1) the matters set out in rule 16.4, and
(2) where appropriate, the matters set out in practice directions relating to specific types of claims.

3.7 Attention is drawn to the provisions of rule 16.4(2) in respect of a claim for interest.

3.8 Particulars of claim served separately from the claim form must also contain:

(1) the name of the court in which the claim is proceeding,
(2) the claim number,
(3) the title of the proceedings, and
(4) the claimant's address for service.

****

Other Matters to be Included in Particulars of Claim

7.1 Where a claim is made for an injunction or declaration in respect of or relating to any land or the possession, occupation, use or enjoyment of any land the particulars of claim must:

(1) state whether or not the injunction or declaration relates to residential premises, and
(2) identify the land (by reference to a plan where necessary).

7.2 Where a claim is brought to enforce a right to recover possession of goods the particulars of claim must contain a statement showing the value of the goods.

7.3 Where a claim is based upon a written agreement:

(1) a copy of the contract or documents constituting the agreement should be attached to or served with the particulars of claim and the original(s) should be available at the hearing, and
(2) any general conditions of sale incorporated in the contract should also be attached (but where the contract is or the documents constituting the agreement are bulky this practice direction is complied with by attaching or serving only the relevant parts of the contract or documents).

7.4 Where a claim is based upon an oral agreement, the particulars of claim should set out the contractual words used and state by whom, to whom, when and where they were spoken.

7.5 Where a claim is based upon an agreement by conduct, the particulars of claim must specify the conduct relied on and state by whom, when and where the acts constituting the conduct were done.

7.6 In a claim issued in the High Court relating to a Consumer Credit Agreement, the particulars of claim must contain a statement that the action is not one to which section 141 of the Consumer Credit Act 1974 applies.

Matters which must be Specifically set out in the Particulars of Claim if Relied on

8.1 A claimant who wishes to rely on evidence:

(1) under section 11 of the Civil Evidence Act 1968 of a conviction of an offence, or
(2) under section 12 of the above-mentioned Act of a finding or adjudication of adultery or paternity,

must include in his particulars of claim a statement to that effect and give the following details:

(1) the type of conviction, finding or adjudication and its date,
(2) the court or court-martial which made the conviction, finding or adjudication, and
(3) the issue in the claim to which it relates.

8.2 The claimant must specifically set out the following matters in his particulars of claim where he wishes to rely on them in support of his claim:

(1) any allegation of fraud,
(2) the fact of any illegality,
(3) details of any misrepresentation,
(4) details of all breaches of trust,
(5) notice or knowledge of a fact,
(6) details of unsoundness of mind or undue influence,
(7) details of wilful default, and
(8) any facts relating to mitigation of loss or damage.

General

9.1 Where a claim is for a sum of money expressed in a foreign currency it must expressly state:

(1) that the claim is for payment in a specified foreign currency,
(2) why it is for payment in that currency,
(3) the Sterling equivalent of the sum at the date of the claim, and
(4) the source of the exchange rate relied on to calculate the Sterling equivalent.

9.2 A subsequent statement of case must not contradict or be inconsistent with an earlier one; for example a reply to a defence must not bring in a new claim. Where new matters have come to light the appropriate course may be to seek the court's permission to amend the statement of case.

9.3 In clinical negligence claims, the words 'clinical negligence' should be inserted at the top of every statement of case.

The Defence

GENERAL

10.1 Rule 16.5 deals with the contents of the defence.

10.2 A defendant should deal with every allegation in accordance with rule 16.5(1) and (2).

10.3 Rule 16.5(3), (4) and (5) sets out the consequences of not dealing with an allegation.

10.4 Where the defendant is an individual, and the claim form does not contain an address at which he resides or carries on business, or contains an incorrect address, the defendant must provide such an address in the defence.

10.5 Where the defendant's address for service is not where he resides or carries on business, he must still provide the address required by paragraph 11.4.

STATEMENT OF TRUTH

11.1 Part 22 requires a defence to be verified by a statement of truth.

11.2 The form of the statement of truth is as follows:

> '[I believe][the defendant believes] that the facts stated in the defence are true.'

11.3 Attention is drawn to rule 32.14 which sets out the consequences of verifying a statement of case containing a false statement without an honest belief in its truth.

****

HUMAN RIGHTS

15.1 A party who seeks to rely on any provision of or right arising under the Human Rights Act 1998 or seeks a remedy available under that Act –

(1) must state that fact in his statement of case; and
(2) must in his statement of case –
  (a) give precise details of the Convention right which it is alleged has been infringed and details of the alleged infringement;
  (b) specify the relief sought;
  (c) state if the relief sought includes –
    (i) a declaration of incompatibility in accordance with section 4 of that Act, or
    (ii) damages in respect of a judicial act to which section 9(3) of that Act applies;
  (d) where the relief sought includes a declaration of incompatibility in accordance with section 4 of that Act, give precise details of the

PART V

legislative provision alleged to be incompatible and details of the alleged incompatibility;
(e) where the claim is founded on a finding of unlawfulness by another court or tribunal, give details of the finding; and
(f) where the claim is founded on a judicial act which is alleged to have infringed the Convention right of the party as provided by section 9 of the Human Rights Act 1998, the judicial act complained of and the court or tribunal which is alleged to have made it.

(The practice direction to Part 19 provides for notice to be given and parties joined in the circumstances referred to in (c), (d) and (f).)

15.2 A party who seeks to amend his statement of case to include the matters referred to in paragraph 16.1 must, unless the court orders otherwise, do so as soon as possible.

(Part 17 provides for the amendment of a statement of case.)

Practice Direction – Further Information

This Practice Direction supplements CPR Part 18 (PD18)

Attention is also drawn to Part 22 (Statements of Truth).

PRELIMINARY REQUEST FOR FURTHER INFORMATION OR CLARIFICATION

1.1 Before making an application to the court for an order under Part 18, the party seeking clarification or information (the first party) should first serve on the party from whom it is sought (the second party) a written request for that clarification or information (a Request) stating a date by which the response to the Request should be served. The date must allow the second party a reasonable time to respond.

1.2 A Request should be concise and strictly confined to matters which are reasonably necessary and proportionate to enable the first party to prepare his own case or to understand the case he has to meet.

1.3 Requests must be made as far as possible in a single comprehensive document and not piecemeal.

1.4 A Request may be made by letter if the text of the request is brief and the reply is likely to be brief; otherwise the Request should be made in a separate document.

1.5 If a Request is made in a letter, the letter should, in order to distinguish it from any other that might routinely be written in the course of a case,

(1) state that it contains a Request made under Part 18, and
(2) deal with no matters other than the Request.

1.6 (1) A Request (whether made by letter or in a separate document) must –
(a) be headed with the name of the court and the title and number of the claim,
(b) in its heading state that it is a Request made under Part 18, identify the first party and the second party and state the date on which it is made,

(4) where the child or patient is a claimant, undertakes to pay any costs which the child or patient may be ordered to pay in relation to the proceedings, subject to any right he may have to be repaid from the assets of the child or patient.

3.5 Where a claimant wishes to take a step in proceedings against a child or patient who does not have a litigation friend he must apply to the court for an order appointing a litigation friend.

3.6 The proposed litigation friend must satisfy the conditions in paragraph 3.4(1), (2) and (3) above and may be one of the persons referred to in paragraph 2.4 above where appropriate, or otherwise may be the Official Solicitor. Where it is sought to appoint the Official Solicitor, provision should be made for payment of his charges.

CHANGE OF LITIGATION FRIEND AND PREVENTION OF PERSON ACTING AS LITIGATION FRIEND

4.1 Rule 21.7(1) states that the court may:

(1) direct that a person may not act as a litigation friend,
(2) terminate a litigation friend's appointment,
(3) substitute a new litigation friend for an existing one.

4.2 Where an application is made for an order under rule 21.7(1), the application notice must set out the reasons for seeking it. The application must be supported by evidence.

4.3 If the order sought is the substitution of a new litigation friend for an existing one, the evidence must satisfy the court of the matters set out in paragraph 3.4 above.

4.4 The application notice must be served:

(1) on the persons referred to in paragraph 2.4 above, and
(2) on the litigation friend or person purporting to act as litigation friend.

PROCEDURE WHERE THE NEED FOR A LITIGATION FRIEND HAS COME TO AN END

5.1 Rule 21.9 deals with the situation where the need for a litigation friend comes to an end during the proceedings because either:

(1) a child who is not also a patient reaches the age of 18 (full age) during the proceedings, or
(2) a patient ceases to be a patient (recovers).

5.2 A child on reaching full age must serve on the other parties to the proceedings and file with the court a notice:

(1) stating that he has reached full age,
(2) stating that his litigation friend's appointment has ceased [1],
(3) giving an address for service[2], and
(4) stating whether or not he intends to carry on with or continue to defend the proceedings.

1 rule 21.9(4)(a).
2 See rule 6.5

5.3 If the notice states that the child intends to carry on with or continue to defend the proceedings he shall subsequently be described in the proceedings as:

'AB (formerly a child but now of full age)'

5.4 Whether or not a child having reached full age serves a notice in accordance with rule 21.9(4)(a) and paragraph 5.2(2) above, a litigation friend may at any time after the child has reached full age serve a notice on the other parties that his appointment has ceased.

5.5 The liability of a litigation friend for costs continues until a notice that his appointment to act has ceased is served on the other parties[1].

1 rule 21.9(6).

5.6 Where a patient recovers, an application under rule 21.9(3) must be made for an order under rule 21.9(2) that the litigation friend's appointment has ceased.

5.7 The application must be supported by the following evidence:

(1) a medical report indicating that the patient has recovered and that he is capable of managing and administering his property and affairs,
(2) where the patient's affairs were under the control of the Court of Protection, a copy of the order or notice discharging the receiver, and
(3) if the application is made by the patient, a statement whether or not he intends to carry on with or continue to defend the proceedings.

5.8 An order under rule 21.9(2) must be served on the other parties to the proceedings. The patient must file with the court a notice:

(1) stating that his litigation friend's appointment has ceased,
(2) giving an address for service[1], and
(3) stating whether or not he intends to carry on with or continue to defend the proceedings.

1 See rule 6.5.

SETTLEMENT OR COMPROMISE BY OR ON BEHALF OF A CHILD OR PATIENT

6.1 Where a claim by or on behalf of a child or patient has been dealt with by agreement prior to the start of proceedings and only the approval of the court to the agreement is sought, the claim:

(1) must be made using the Part 8 procedure,
(2) must include a request for approval of the settlement or compromise, and
(3) in addition to the details of the claim, must set out the terms of the settlement or compromise or have attached to it a draft consent order in Practice Form N292.

6.2 In order to approve the settlement or compromise, the information concerning the claim that the court will require will include:

(1) whether and to what extent the defendant admits liability,
(2) the age and occupation (if any) of the child or patient,
(3) the litigation friend's approval of the proposed settlement or compromise, and
(3) in a personal injury case arising from an accident –
    (a) the circumstances of the accident,
    (b) any medical reports,
    (c) where appropriate, a schedule of any past and future expenses and losses claimed and any other relevant information relating to

personal injury as set out in the practice direction which supplements Part 16 (statements of case), and

(d) where considerations of liability are raised –

(i) any evidence or police reports in any criminal proceedings or in an inquest, and

(ii) details of any prosecution brought.

6.3 (1) An opinion on the merits of the settlement or compromise given by counsel or solicitor acting for the child or patient should, except in very clear cases, be obtained.

(2) A copy of the opinion and, unless the instructions on which it was given are sufficiently set out in it, a copy of the instructions, must also be supplied to the court.

6.4 Applications for the approval of a settlement or compromise will normally be heard by a master or district judge.

(For information about structured settlements see the practice direction on structured settlements supplementing Part 40 (Judgments and Orders).)

(For information about provisional damages claims see Part 41 and the practice direction which supplements it.)

APPORTIONMENT UNDER THE FATAL ACCIDENTS ACT 1976

7.1 A judgment on or settlement in respect of a claim under the Fatal Accidents Act 1976 must be apportioned between the persons by or on whose behalf the claim has been brought.

7.2 Where a claim is brought on behalf of a dependent child or children, the money apportioned to any child must be invested on his behalf in accordance with rules 21.10 and 21.11 and paragraphs 8 and 9 below.

7.3 In order to approve an apportionment of money to a dependent child, the court will require the following information:

(1) the matters set out in paragraph 6.2(1), (2) above, and

(2) in respect of the deceased –

(a) where death was caused by an accident, the matters set out in paragraph 6.2(3)(a),(b) and (c) above, and

(b) his future loss of earnings, and

(3) the extent and nature of the dependency.

CONTROL OF MONEY RECOVERED BY OR ON BEHALF OF A CHILD OR PATIENT

8.1 Money recovered or paid into court on behalf of or for the benefit of a child or patient shall be dealt with in accordance with directions of the court under rule 21.11.

8.2 The court:

(1) may direct the money to be paid into the High Court for investment,

(2) may also direct that certain sums be paid direct to the child or patient, his litigation friend or his legal representative[1] for the immediate benefit of the child or patient or for expenses incurred on his behalf, and

(3) may direct the applications in respect of the investment of the money be transferred to a local district registry.

1 See rule 2.3 for a definition of legal representative.

8.3 The master or district judge will consider the general aims to be achieved for the money in court (the fund) by investment and will give directions as to the type of investment.

8.4 Where a child is also a patient, and likely to remain so on reaching full age, his fund should be administered as a patient's fund.

8.5 Where a child or patient is legally aided the fund will be subject to a first charge under section 16 of the Legal Aid Act 1988 (the legal aid charge) and an order for the investment of money on the child or patient's behalf must contain a direction to that effect.

GUARDIAN'S ACCOUNTS

9 Paragraph 8 of the practice direction supplementing Part 40 (Judgments and Orders) deals with the approval of the accounts of a guardian of assets of a child.

INVESTMENT ON BEHALF OF A CHILD

10.1 At the hearing of the application for the approval of the agreement the litigation friend or his legal representative should provide a CFO form 320 (request for investment) for completion by the master or district judge.

10.2 On receipt of that form in the Court Funds Office the investment managers of the Public Trust Office will make the appropriate investment.

10.3 Where an award of damages for a child is made at trial the trial judge may direct:

(1) the money to be paid into court and placed in the special investment account, and
(2) the litigation friend to make an application to a master or district judge for further investment directions.

10.4 If the money to be invested is very small the court may order it to be paid direct to the litigation friend to be put into a building society account (or similar) for the child's use.

10.5 If the money is invested in court it must be paid out to the child when he reaches full age.

INVESTMENT ON BEHALF OF A PATIENT

11.1 The Court of Protection is responsible for protecting the property of patients and is given extensive powers to do so under the Mental Health Act 1983. Fees are charged for the administration of funds by the Court of Protection and these should be provided for in any settlement.

11.2 Where the sum to be administered is:

(1) over £30,000, the order approving the settlement will contain a direction to the litigation friend to apply to the Court of Protection for the appointment of a receiver, after which the fund will be transferred to the Court of Protection,
(2) under £20,000, it may be retained in court and invested in the same way as the fund of a child, or
(3) in intermediate cases the advice of the Master of the Court of Protection should be sought.

11.3 A form of order transferring the fund to the Court of Protection is set out in Practice Form N292.

11.4 In order for the Court Funds Office to release a fund which is subject to the legal aid charge to the Court of Protection the litigation friend or his legal representative should provide the appropriate area office of the Legal Aid Board with an undertaking in respect of a sum to cover their costs, following which the area office will advise the Court Funds Office in writing of that sum, enabling them to transfer the balance to the Court of Protection on receipt of a CFO form 200 payment schedule authorised by the court.

11.5 The CFO form 200 should be completed and presented to the court where the settlement or trial took place for authorisation, subject to paragraphs 11.6 and 11.7 below.

11.6 Where the settlement took place in the Royal Courts of Justice the CFO form 200 should be completed and presented for authorisation:

(1) on behalf of a child, in the Masters' Secretary's Office, Room E214, and
(2) on behalf of a patient, in the Action Department, Room E15.

11.7 Where the trial took place in the Royal Courts of Justice the CFO form 200 is completed and authorised by the court officer.

PAYMENT OUT OF FUNDS IN COURT

12.1 Applications to a master or district judge:

(1) for payment out of money from the fund for the benefit of the child, or
(2) to vary an investment strategy,

may be dealt with without a hearing unless the court directs otherwise.

12.2 When the child reaches full age, his fund in court:

(1) where it is a sum of money will be paid out to him, and
(2) where it is in the form of investments other than money (for example shares or unit trusts), will be transferred into his name.

12.3 An application for payment out of funds being administered by the Court of Protection must be made to the Court of Protection.

(For further information on payments into and out of court see the practice directions supplementing Parts 36 and 37.)

Practice Direction – Applications

This Practice Direction supplements CPR Part 23 (PD23)

REFERENCE TO A JUDGE

1 A master or district judge may refer to a judge any matter which he thinks should properly be decided by a judge, and the judge may either dispose of the matter or refer it back to the master or district judge.

APPLICATION NOTICES

2.1 An application notice must, in addition to the matters set out in rule 23.6, be signed and include:

(1) the title of the claim,
(2) the reference number of the claim,
(3) the full name of the applicant,
(4) where the applicant is not already a party, his address for service, and
(5) either a request for a hearing or a request that the application be dealt with without a hearing.

(Practice Form N244 may be used.)

2.2 On receipt of an application notice containing a request for a hearing the court will notify the applicant of the time and date for the hearing of the application.

2.3 On receipt of an application notice containing a request that the application be dealt with without a hearing, the application notice will be sent to a master or district judge so that he may decide whether the application is suitable for consideration without a hearing.

2.4 Where the master or district judge agrees that the application is suitable for consideration without a hearing, the court will so inform the applicant and the respondent and may give directions for the filing of evidence. (Rules 23.9 and 23.10 enable a party to apply for an order made without a hearing to be set aside or varied.)

2.5 Where the master or district judge does not agree that the application is suitable for consideration without a hearing, the court will notify the applicant and the respondent of the time, date and place for the hearing of the application and may at the same time give directions as to the filing of evidence.

2.6 If the application is intended to be made to a judge, the application notice should so state. In that case, paragraphs 2.3, 2.4 and 2.5 will apply as though references to the master or district judge were references to a judge.

2.7 Every application should be made as soon as it becomes apparent that it is necessary or desirable to make it.

2.8 Applications should wherever possible be made so that they can be considered at any other hearing for which a date has already been fixed or for which a date is about to be fixed. This is particularly so in relation to case management conferences, allocation and listing hearings and pre-trial reviews fixed by the court.

2.9 The parties must anticipate that at any hearing the court may wish to review the conduct of the case as a whole and give any necessary case management directions. They should be ready to assist the court in doing so and to answer questions the court may ask for this purpose.

2.10 Where a date for a hearing has been fixed and a party wishes to make an application at that hearing but he does not have sufficient time to serve an application notice he should inform the other party and the court (if possible in writing) as soon as he can of the nature of the application and the reason for it. He should then make the application orally at the hearing.

APPLICATIONS WITHOUT SERVICE OF APPLICATION NOTICE

3 An application may be made without serving an application notice only:

(1) where there is exceptional urgency,

(2) where the overriding objective is best furthered by doing so,
(3) by consent of all parties,
(4) with the permission of the court,
(5) where paragraph 2.10 above applies, or
(6) where a court order, rule or practice direction permits.

GIVING NOTICE OF AN APPLICATION

4.1 Unless the court otherwise directs or paragraph 3 of this practice direction applies the application notice must be served as soon as practicable after it has been issued and, if there is to be a hearing, at least 3 clear days before the hearing date (rule 23.7(1)(b)).

4.2 Where an application notice should be served but there is not sufficient time to do so, informal notification of the application should be given unless the circumstances of the application require secrecy.

PRE-ACTION APPLICATIONS

5 All applications made before a claim is commenced should be made under Part 23 of the Civil Procedure Rules. Attention is drawn in particular to rule 23.2(4).

TELEPHONE HEARINGS

6.1 The court may order that an application or part of an application be dealt with by a telephone hearing.

6.1A The applicant should indicate on his application notice if he seeks a court order under paragraph 6.1. Where he has not done so but nevertheless wishes to seek an order the request should be made as early as possible.

6.2 An order under 6.1 will not normally be made unless every party entitled to be given notice of the application and to be heard at the hearing has consented to the order.

6.3 (1) Where a party entitled to be heard at the hearing of the application is acting in person, the court –
(a) may not make an order under 6.1 except on condition that arrangements will be made for the party acting in person to be attended at the telephone hearing by a responsible person to whom the party acting in person is known and who can confirm to the court the identity of the party; and
(b) may not give effect to an order under 6.1 unless the party acting in person is accompanied by a responsible person who at the commencement of the hearing confirms to the court the identity of the party.

(2) The 'responsible person' may be a barrister, solicitor, legal executive, doctor, clergyman, police officer, prison officer or other person of comparable status.

(3) If the court makes an order under 6.1 it will generally give any directions necessary for the telephone hearing.

6.4 No representative of a party to an application being heard by telephone may attend the judge in person while the application is being heard unless the other party to the application has agreed that he may do so.

6.5 If an application is to be heard by telephone the following directions will apply, subject to any direction to the contrary:

(1) The applicant's legal representative must arrange the telephone conference for precisely the time fixed by the court. The telecommunications provider must be capable of connecting the parties and the court.
(2) He must tell the operator the telephone numbers of all those participating in the conference call and the sequence in which they are to be called.
(3) It is the responsibility of the applicant's legal representative to ascertain from all the other parties whether they have instructed counsel and, if so the identity of counsel, and whether the legal representative and counsel will be on the same or different telephone numbers.
(4) The sequence in which they are to be called will be:
    (a) the applicant's legal representative and (if on a different number) his counsel,
    (b) the legal representative (and counsel) for all other parties, and
    (c) the judge.
(5) The applicant's legal representative must arrange for the conference to be recorded on tape by the telecommunications provider whose system is being used and must send the tape to the court.
(6) Each speaker is to remain on the line after being called by the operator setting up the conference call. The call may be 2 or 3 minutes before the time fixed for the application.
(7) When the judge has been connected the applicant's legal representative (or his counsel) will introduce the parties in the usual way.
(8) If the use of a 'speakerphone' by any party causes the judge or any other party any difficulty in hearing what is said the judge may require that party to use a hand held telephone.
(9) The telephone charges debited to the account of the party initiating the conference call will be treated as part of the costs of the application.

VIDEO CONFERENCING

7 Where the parties to a matter wish to use video conferencing facilities, and those facilities are available in the relevant court, they should apply to the master or district judge for directions.

NOTE OF PROCEEDINGS

8 The procedural judge should keep, either by way of a note or a tape recording, brief details of all proceedings before him, including the dates of the proceedings and a short statement of the decision taken at each hearing.

EVIDENCE

9.1 The requirement for evidence in certain types of applications is set out in some of the rules and practice directions. Where there is no specific requirement to provide evidence it should be borne in mind that, as a practical matter, the court will often need to be satisfied by evidence of the facts that are relied on in support of or for opposing the application.

9.2 The court may give directions for the filing of evidence in support of or opposing a particular application. The court may also give directions for the filing of evidence in relation to any hearing that it fixes on its own initiative. The directions may specify the form that evidence is to take and when it is to be served.

9.3 Where it is intended to rely on evidence which is not contained in the application itself, the evidence, if it has not already been served, should be served with the application.

9.4 Where a respondent to an application wishes to rely on evidence which has not yet been served he should serve it as soon as possible and in any event in accordance with any directions the court may have given.

9.5 If it is necessary for the applicant to serve any evidence in reply it should be served as soon as possible and in any event in accordance with any directions the court may have given.

9.6 Evidence must be filed with the court as well as served on the parties. Exhibits should not be filed unless the court otherwise directs.

9.7 The contents of an application notice may be used as evidence (otherwise than at trial) provided the contents have been verified by a statement of truth[1].

1 See Part 22.

CONSENT ORDERS

10.1 Rule 40.6 sets out the circumstances where an agreed judgment or order may be entered and sealed.

10.2 Where all parties affected by an order have written to the court consenting to the making of the order a draft of which has been filed with the court, the court will treat the draft as having been signed in accordance with rule 40.6(7).

10.3 Where a consent order must be made by a judge (ie rule 40.6(2) does not apply) the order must be drawn so that the judge's name and judicial title can be inserted.

10.4 The parties to an application for a consent order must ensure that they provide the court with any material it needs to be satisfied that it is appropriate to make the order. Subject to any rule or practice direction a letter will generally be acceptable for this purpose.

10.5 Where a judgment or order has been agreed in respect of an application or claim where a hearing date has been fixed, the parties must inform the court immediately. (note that parties are reminded that under rules 28.4 and 29.5 the case management timetable cannot be varied by written agreement of the parties.)

OTHER APPLICATIONS CONSIDERED WITHOUT A HEARING

11.1 Where rule 23.8(b) applies the parties should so inform the court in writing and each should confirm that all evidence and other material on which he relies has been disclosed to the other parties to the application.

11.2 Where rule 23.8(c) applies the court will treat the application as if it were proposing to make an order on its own initiative.

Applications to stay claim where related criminal proceedings

11A.1 An application for the stay of civil proceedings pending the determination of related criminal proceedings may be made by any party to the civil proceedings or by the prosecutor or any defendant in the criminal proceedings.

11A.2 Every party to the civil proceedings must, unless he is the applicant, be made a respondent to the application.

11A.3 The evidence in support of the application must contain an estimate of the expected duration of the stay and must identify the respects in which the continuance of the civil proceedings may prejudice the criminal trial.

11A.4 In order to make an application under paragraph 11A.1, it is not necessary for the prosecutor or defendant in the criminal proceedings to be joined as a party to the civil proceedings.

MISCELLANEOUS

12.1 Except in the most simple application the applicant should bring to any hearing a draft of the order sought. If the case is proceeding in the Royal Courts of Justice and the order is unusually long or complex it should also be supplied on disk for use by the court office.

12.2 Where rule 23.11 applies, the power to re-list the application in rule 23.11(2) is in addition to any other powers of the court with regard to the order(for example to set aside, vary, discharge or suspend the order).

COSTS

13.1 Attention is drawn to the costs practice direction and, in particular, to the court's power to make a summary assessment of costs.

13.2 Attention is also drawn to rule 44.13(i) which provides that if an order makes no mention of costs, none are payable in respect of the proceedings to which it relates.

Practice Direction – Interim Injunctions

This Practice Direction supplements CPR Part 25 (PD25)

JURISDICTION

1.1 High Court judges and any other judge duly authorised may grant 'search orders'[1] and 'freezing injunctions'[2].

1 Rule 25.1(1)(h).
2 Rule 25.1(1)(f).

1.2 In a case in the High Court, masters and district judges have the power to grant injunctions:

(1) by consent,
(2) in connection with charging orders and appointments of receivers,
(3) in aid of execution of judgments.

1.3 In any other case any judge who has jurisdiction to conduct the trial of the action has the power to grant an injunction in that action.

1.4 A master or district judge has the power to vary or discharge an injunction granted by any judge with the consent of all the parties.

MAKING AN APPLICATION

2.1 The application notice must state:

(1) the order sought, and
(2) the date, time and place of the hearing.

2.2 The application notice and evidence in support must be served as soon as practicable after issue and in any event not less than 3 days before the court is due to hear the application[1].

1 Rule 23.7(1) and (2) and see rule 23.7(4) (short service).

2.3 Where the court is to serve, sufficient copies of the application notice and evidence in support for the court and for each respondent should be filed for issue and service.

2.4 Whenever possible a draft of the order sought should be filed with the application notice and a disk containing the draft should also be available to the court in a format compatible with the word processing software used by the court. This will enable the court officer to arrange for any amendments to be incorporated and for the speedy preparation and sealing of the order.

EVIDENCE

3.1 Applications for search orders and freezing injunctions must be supported by affidavit evidence.

3.2 Applications for other interim injunctions must be supported by evidence set out in either:

(1) a witness statement, or
(2) a statement of case provided that it is verified by a statement of truth[1], or
(3) the application provided that it is verified by a statement of truth,

unless the court, an Act, a rule or a practice direction requires evidence by affidavit.

1 See Part 22.

3.3 The evidence must set out the facts on which the applicant relies for the claim being made against the respondent, including all material facts of which the court should be made aware.

3.4 Where an application is made without notice to the respondent, the evidence must also set out why notice was not given.

(See Part 32 and the practice direction that supplements it for information about evidence.)

URGENT APPLICATIONS AND APPLICATIONS WITHOUT NOTICE

4.1 These fall into two categories:

(1) applications where a claim form has already been issued, and
(2) applications where a claim form has not yet been issued,

and, in both cases, where notice of the application has not been given to the respondent.

4.2 These applications are normally dealt with at a court hearing but cases of extreme urgency may be dealt with by telephone.

PART V

4.3 Applications dealt with at a court hearing after issue of a claim form:

(1) the application notice, evidence in support and a draft order (as in 2.4 above) should be filed with the court 2 hours before the hearing wherever possible,
(2) if an application is made before the application notice has been issued, a draft order (as in 2.4 above) should be provided at the hearing, and the application notice and evidence in support must be filed with the court on the same or next working day or as ordered by the court, and
(3) except in cases where secrecy is essential, the applicant should take steps to notify the respondent informally of the application.

4.4 Applications made before the issue of a claim form:

(1) in addition to the provisions set out at 4.3 above, unless the court orders otherwise, either the applicant must undertake to the court to issue a claim form immediately or the court will give directions for the commencement of the claim[1],
(2) where possible the claim form should be served with the order for the injunction,
(3) an order made before the issue of a claim form should state in the title after the names of the applicant and respondent 'the Claimant and Defendant in an Intended Action'.

1 Rule 25.2(3).

4.5 Applications made by telephone:

(1) where it is not possible to arrange a hearing, application can be made between 10.00 am and 5.00 pm weekdays by telephoning the Royal Courts of Justice on 020 7947 6000 and asking to be put in contact with a High Court judge of the appropriate Division available to deal with an emergency application in a High Court matter. The appropriate district registry may also be contacted by telephone. In county court proceedings, the appropriate county court should be contacted,
(2) where an application is made outside those hours the applicant should either –
    (a) telephone the Royal Courts of Justice on 020 7947 6000 where he will be put in contact with the clerk to the appropriate Duty judge in the High Court (or the appropriate area circuit judge where known), or
    (b) the Urgent Court Business Officer of the appropriate Circuit who will contact the local Duty judge,
(3) where the facility is available it is likely that the judge will require a draft order to be faxed to him,
(4) the application notice and evidence in support must be filed with the court on the same or next working day or as ordered, together with two copies of the order for sealing,
(5) injunctions will be heard by telephone only where the applicant is acting by counsel or solicitors.

ORDERS FOR INJUNCTIONS

5.1 Any order for an injunction, unless the court orders otherwise, must contain:

(1) an undertaking by the applicant to the court to pay any damages which the respondent(s) (or any other party served with or notified of the order) sustain which the court considers the applicant should pay,

(2) if made without notice to any other party, an undertaking by the applicant to the court to serve on the respondent the application notice, evidence in support and any order made as soon as practicable,
(3) if made without notice to any other party, a return date for a further hearing at which the other party can be present,
(4) if made before filing the application notice, an undertaking to file and pay the appropriate fee on the same or next working day, and
(5) if made before issue of a claim form –
 (a) an undertaking to issue and pay the appropriate fee on the same or next working day, or
 (b) directions for the commencement of the claim.

5.2 An order for an injunction made in the presence of all parties to be bound by it or made at a hearing of which they have had notice, may state that it is effective until trial or further order.

5.3 Any order for an injunction must set out clearly what the respondent must do or not do.

Freezing Injunctions

ORDERS TO RESTRAIN DISPOSAL OF ASSETS WORLDWIDE AND WITHIN ENGLAND AND WALES

6.1 An example of a Freezing Injunction is annexed to this practice direction.

6.2 This example may be modified as appropriate in any particular case. In particular, the court may, if it considers it appropriate, require the applicant's solicitors, as well as the applicant, to give undertakings.

Search Orders

ORDERS FOR THE PRESERVATION OF EVIDENCE AND PROPERTY

7.1 The following provisions apply to search orders in addition to those listed above.

The Supervising Solicitor

7.2 The supervising solicitor must be experienced in the operation of search orders. A supervising solicitor may be contacted either through the Law Society or, for the London area, through the London Solicitors Litigation Association.

7.3 Evidence:

(1) the affidavit must state the name, firm and its address, and experience of the supervising solicitor, also the address of the premises and whether it is a private or business address, and
(2) the affidavit must disclose very fully the reason the order is sought, including the probability that relevant material would disappear if the order were not made.

7.4 Service:

(1) the order must be served personally by the supervising solicitor, unless the court otherwise orders, and must be accompanied by the evidence in support and any documents capable of being copied,

(2) confidential exhibits need not be served but they must be made available for inspection by the respondent in the presence of the applicant's solicitors while the order is carried out and afterwards be retained by the respondent's solicitors on their undertaking not to permit the respondent –

(a) to see them or copies of them except in their presence, and

(b) to make or take away any note or record of them,

(3) the supervising solicitor may be accompanied only by the persons mentioned in the order,

(4) the supervising solicitor must explain the terms and effect of the order to the respondent in every day language and advise him of his right to –

(a) legal advice, and

(b) apply to vary or discharge the order,

(5) where the supervising solicitor is a man and the respondent is likely to be an unaccompanied woman, at least one other person named in the order must be a woman and must accompany the supervising solicitor, and

(6) the order may only be served between 9.30 am and 5.30 pm Monday to Friday unless the court otherwise orders.

7.5 Search and custody of materials:

(1) no material shall be removed unless clearly covered by the terms of the order,

(2) the premises must not be searched and no items shall be removed from them except in the presence of the respondent or a person who appears to be a responsible employee of the respondent,

(3) where copies of documents are sought, the documents should be retained for no more than 2 days before return to the owner,

(4) where material in dispute is removed pending trial, the applicant's solicitors should place it in the custody of the respondent's solicitors on their undertaking to retain it in safekeeping and to produce it to the court when required,

(5) in appropriate cases the applicant should insure the material retained in the respondent's solicitors' custody,

(6) the supervising solicitor must make a list of all material removed from the premises and supply a copy of the list to the respondent,

(7) no material shall be removed from the premises until the respondent has had reasonable time to check the list,

(8) if any of the listed items exists only in computer readable form, the respondent must immediately give the applicant's solicitors effective access to the computers, with all necessary passwords, to enable them to be searched, and cause the listed items to be printed out,

(9) the applicant must take all reasonable steps to ensure that no damage is done to any computer or data,

(10) the applicant and his representatives may not themselves search the respondent's computers unless they have sufficient expertise to do so without damaging the respondent's system,

(11) the supervising solicitor shall provide a report on the carrying out of the order to the applicant's solicitors,

(12) as soon as the report is received the applicant's solicitors shall –

(a) serve a copy of it on the respondent, and

(b) file a copy of it with the court, and

(13) where the supervising solicitor is satisfied that full compliance with paragraph 7.5(7) and (8) above is impracticable, he may permit the search to proceed and items to be removed without compliance with the impracticable requirements.

GENERAL

8.1 The supervising solicitor must not be an employee or member of the applicant's firm of solicitors.

8.2 If the court orders that the order need not be served by the supervising solicitor, the reason for so ordering must be set out in the order.

8.3 The search order must not be carried out at the same time as a police search warrant.

8.4 There is no privilege against self incrimination in Intellectual Property cases (see the Supreme Court Act 1981, section 72) therefore in those cases, paragraph (4) of the respondent's entitlements and any other references to incrimination in the Search Order, should be removed.

8.5 Applications in Intellectual Property cases should be made in the Chancery Division.

8.6 An example of a Search Order is annexed to this practice direction. This example may be modified as appropriate in any particular case.

Annex

FREEZING INJUNCTION **IN THE HIGH COURT OF JUSTICE**

[ ] DIVISION

Before The Honourable Mr Justice [ ]

Claim No

Dated

Applicant

Seal

Respondent

Name, address and reference of respondent

IF YOU [ ][1] DISOBEY THIS ORDER YOU MAY BE HELD TO BE IN CONTEMPT OF COURT AND MAY BE IMPRISONED, FINED OR HAVE YOUR ASSETS SEIZED.

ANY OTHER PERSON WHO KNOWS OF THIS ORDER AND DOES ANYTHING WHICH HELPS OR PERMITS THE RESPONDENT TO BREACH THE TERMS OF THIS ORDER MAY ALSO BE HELD TO BE IN CONTEMPT OF COURT AND MAY BE IMPRISONED, FINED OR HAVE THEIR ASSETS SEIZED.

1 Insert name of Respondent.

THIS ORDER

1 This is a Freezing Injunction made against [ ] ('the Respondent') on [ ] by Mr Justice [ ] on the application of [ ] ('the Applicant'). The Judge read the Affidavits listed in Schedule A and accepted the undertakings set out in Schedule B at the end of this Order.

2 This order was made at a hearing without notice to the Respondent. The Respondent has a right to apply to the court to vary or discharge the order – see paragraph 13 below.

3 There will be a further hearing in respect of this order on [ ] ('the return date').

4 If there is more than one Respondent –

(a) unless otherwise stated, references in this order to 'the Respondent' mean both or all of them; and

(b) this order is effective against any Respondent on whom it is served or who is given notice of it.

FREEZING INJUNCTION

[*For injunction limited to assets in England and Wales*]

5 Until the return date or further order of the court, the Respondent must not remove from England and Wales or in any way dispose of, deal with or diminish the value of any of his assets which are in England and Wales up to the value of £ .

[*For worldwide injunction*]

5 Until the return date or further order of the court, the Respondent must not –

(1) remove from England and Wales any of his assets which are in England and Wales up to the value of £ ; or

(2) in any way dispose of, deal with or diminish the value of any of his assets whether they are in or outside England and Wales up to the same value.

[*For either form of injunction*]

6 Paragraph 5 applies to all the Respondent's assets whether or not they are in his own name and whether they are solely or jointly owned. For the purpose of this order the Respondent's assets include any asset which he has the power, directly or indirectly, to dispose of or deal with as if it were his own. The Respondent is to be regarded as having such power if a third party holds or controls the asset in accordance with his direct or indirect instructions.

7 This prohibition includes the following assets in particular –

(a) the property known as [*title/address*] or the net sale money after payment of any mortgages if it has been sold;

(b) the property and assets of the Respondent's business [known as [*name*]] [carried on at [*address*]] or the sale money if any of them have been sold; and

(c) any money in the account numbered [*account number*] at [*title/address*].

[*For injunction limited to assets in England and Wales*]

8 If the total value free of charges or other securities ('unencumbered value') of the Respondent's assets in England and Wales exceeds £ , the Respondent may remove any of those assets from England and Wales or may dispose of or deal with

PART V

them so long as the total unencumbered value of his assets still in England and Wales remains above £ .

[*For worldwide injunction*]

8 (1) If the total value free of charges or other securities ('unencumbered value') of the Respondent's assets in England and Wales exceeds £ , the Respondent may remove any of those assets from England and Wales or may dispose of or deal with them so long as the total unencumbered value of the Respondent's assets still in England and Wales remains above £ .

(2) If the total unencumbered value of the Respondent's assets in England and Wales does not exceed £ , the Respondent must not remove any of those assets from England and Wales and must not dispose of or deal with any of them. If the Respondent has other assets outside England and Wales, he may dispose of or deal with those assets outside England and Wales so long as the total unencumbered value of all his assets whether in or outside England and Wales remains above £ .

PROVISION OF INFORMATION

9 (1) Unless paragraph (2) applies, the Respondent must [immediately] [within hours of service of this order] and to the best of his ability inform the Applicant's solicitors of all his assets [in England and Wales] [worldwide] [exceeding £ in value] whether in his own name or not and whether solely or jointly owned, giving the value, location and details of all such assets.

(2) If the provision of any of this information is likely to incriminate the Respondent, he may be entitled to refuse to provide it, but is recommended to take legal advice before refusing to provide the information. Wrongful refusal to provide the information is contempt of court and may render the Respondent liable to be imprisoned, fined or have his assets seized.

10 Within [ ] working days after being served with this order, the Respondent must swear and serve on the Applicant's solicitors an affidavit setting out the above information.

EXCEPTIONS TO THIS ORDER

11 (1) This order does not prohibit the Respondent from spending £ a week towards his ordinary living expenses and also £ [or a reasonable sum] on legal advice and representation. [But before spending any money the Respondent must tell the Applicant's legal representatives where the money is to come from.]

[(2) This order does not prohibit the Respondent from dealing with or disposing of any of his assets in the ordinary and proper course of business.]

(3) The Respondent may agree with the Applicant's legal representatives that the above spending limits should be increased or that this order should be varied in any other respect, but any agreement must be in writing.

(4) The order will cease to have effect if the Respondent –

(a) provides security by paying the sum of £ into court, to be held to the order of the court; or

(b) makes provision for security in that sum by another method agreed with the Applicant's legal representatives.

COSTS

12 The costs of this application are reserved to the judge hearing the application on the return date.

VARIATION OR DISCHARGE OF THIS ORDER

13 Anyone served with or notified of this order may apply to the court at any time to vary or discharge this order (or so much of it as affects that person), but they must first inform the Applicant's solicitors. If any evidence is to be relied upon in support of the application, the substance of it must be communicated in writing to the Applicant's solicitors in advance.

INTERPRETATION OF THIS ORDER

14 A Respondent who is an individual who is ordered not to do something must not do it himself or in any other way. He must not do it through others acting on his behalf or on his instructions or with his encouragement.

15 A Respondent which is not an individual which is ordered not to do something must not do it itself or by its directors, officers, partners, employees or agents or in any other way.

PARTIES OTHER THAN THE APPLICANT AND RESPONDENT

16 **Effect of this order**

It is a contempt of court for any person notified of this order knowingly to assist in or permit a breach of this order. Any person doing so may be imprisoned, fined or have their assets seized.

17 **Set off by banks**

This injunction does not prevent any bank from exercising any right of set off it may have in respect of any facility which it gave to the respondent before it was notified of this order.

18 **Withdrawals by the Respondent**

No bank need enquire as to the application or proposed application of any money withdrawn by the Respondent if the withdrawal appears to be permitted by this order.

[*For worldwide injunction*]

19 **Persons outside England and Wales**

(1) Except as provided in paragraph (2) below, the terms of this order do not affect or concern anyone outside the jurisdiction of this court.

(2) The terms of this order will affect the following persons in a country or state outside the jurisdiction of this court –

(a) the Respondent or his officer or agent appointed by power of attorney;

(b) any person who –

(i) is subject to the jurisdiction of this court;

(ii) has been given written notice of this order at his residence or place of business within the jurisdiction of this court; and

(iii) is able to prevent acts or omissions outside the jurisdiction of this court which constitute or assist in a breach of the terms of this order; and

(c) any other person, only to the extent that this order is declared enforceable by or is enforced by a court in that country or state.

[*For worldwide injunction*]

20 **Assets located outside England and Wales**

Nothing in this order shall, in respect of assets located outside England and Wales, prevent any third party from complying with –

(1) what it reasonably believes to be its obligations, contractual or otherwise, under the laws and obligations of the country or state in which those assets are situated or under the proper law of any contract between itself and the Respondent; and

(2) any orders of the courts of that country or state, provided that reasonable notice of any application for such an order is given to the Applicant's solicitors.

COMMUNICATIONS WITH THE COURT

All communications to the court about this order should be sent to –

[*Insert the address and telephone number of the appropriate Court Office*]

If the order is made at the Royal Courts of Justice, communications should be addressed as follows –

Where the order is made in the Chancery Division

Room TM 505, Royal Courts of Justice, Strand, London WC2A 2LL quoting the case number. The telephone number is 0207 947 6754.

Where the order is made in the Queen's Bench Division

Room WG034, Royal Courts of Justice, Strand, London WC2A 2LL quoting the case number. The telephone number is 0207 947 6009.

Where the order is made in the Commercial Court

Room E201, Royal Courts of Justice, Strand, London WC2A 2LL quoting the case number. The telephone number is 0207 947 6826.

The offices are open between 10 am and 4.30 pm Monday to Friday.

SCHEDULE A

AFFIDAVITS

The Applicant relied on the following affidavits –

[*name*]	[*number of affidavit*]	[*date sworn*]	[*filed on behalf of*]
(1)			
(2)			

SCHEDULE B

UNDERTAKINGS GIVEN TO THE COURT BY THE APPLICANT

(1) If the court later finds that this order has caused loss to the Respondent, and decides that the Respondent should be compensated for that loss, the Applicant will comply with any order the court may make.

[(2) The Applicant will –

(a) on or before [*date*] cause a written guarantee in the sum of £ to be issued from a bank with a place of business within England or Wales, in respect of any order the court may make pursuant to paragraph (1) above; and

(b) immediately upon issue of the guarantee, cause a copy of it to be served on the Respondent.]

(3) As soon as practicable the Applicant will issue and serve a claim form [in the form of the draft produced to the court] [claiming the appropriate relief].

(4) The Applicant will [swear and file an affidavit] [cause an affidavit to be sworn and filed] [substantially in the terms of the draft affidavit produced to the court] [confirming the substance of what was said to the court by the Applicant's counsel/solicitors].

(5) The Applicant will serve upon the Respondent [together with this order] [as soon as practicable] –

(i) copies of the affidavits and exhibits containing the evidence relied upon by the Applicant, and any other documents provided to the court on the making of the application;

(ii) the claim form; and

(iii) an application notice for continuation of the order.

[(6) Anyone notified of this order will be given a copy of it by the Applicant's legal representatives.]

(7) The Applicant will pay the reasonable costs of anyone other than the Respondent which have been incurred as a result of this order including the costs of finding out whether that person holds any of the Respondent's assets and if the court later finds that this order has caused such person loss, and decides that such person should be compensated for that loss, the Applicant will comply with any order the court may make.

(8) If this order ceases to have effect (for example, if the Respondent provides security or the Applicant does not provide a bank guarantee as provided for above) the Applicant will immediately take all reasonable steps to inform in writing anyone to whom he has given notice of this order, or who he has reasonable grounds for supposing may act upon this order, that it has ceased to have effect.

[(9) The Applicant will not without the permission of the court use any information obtained as a result of this order for the purpose of any civil or criminal proceedings, either in England and Wales or in any other jurisdiction, other than this claim.]

[(10) The Applicant will not without the permission of the court seek to enforce this order in any country outside England and Wales [or seek an order of a similar nature including orders conferring a charge or other security against the Respondent or the Respondent's assets].]

NAME AND ADDRESS OF APPLICANT'S LEGAL REPRESENTATIVES

The Applicant's legal representatives are –

[*Name, address, reference, fax and telephone numbers both in and out of office hours and e-mail*]

SEARCH ORDER **IN THE HIGH COURT OF JUSTICE**

[ ] DIVISION

Before The Honourable Mr Justice [ ]

Claim No.

Dated

Applicant

Seal

Respondent

Name, address and reference of Respondent

IF YOU [ ][1] DISOBEY THIS ORDER YOU MAY BE HELD TO BE IN CONTEMPT OF COURT AND MAY BE IMPRISONED, FINED OR HAVE YOUR ASSETS SEIZED.

ANY OTHER PERSON WHO KNOWS OF THIS ORDER AND DOES ANYTHING WHICH HELPS OR PERMITS THE RESPONDENT TO BREACH THE TERMS OF THIS ORDER MAY ALSO BE HELD TO BE IN CONTEMPT OF COURT AND MAY BE IMPRISONED, FINED OR HAVE THEIR ASSETS SEIZED.

1 Insert name of Respondent.

THIS ORDER

1 This is a Search Order made against [ ] ('the Respondent') on [ ] by Mr Justice [ ] on the application of [ ] ('the Applicant'). The Judge read the Affidavits listed in Schedule F and accepted the undertakings set out in Schedules C, D and E at the end of this order.

2 This order was made at a hearing without notice to the Respondent. The Respondent has a right to apply to the court to vary or discharge the order – see paragraph 27 below.

3 There will be a further hearing in respect of this order on [ ] ('the return date').

4 If there is more than one Respondent –

(a) unless otherwise stated, references in this order to 'the Respondent' mean both or all of them; and

(b) this order is effective against any Respondent on whom it is served or who is given notice of it.

5 This order must be complied with by –

(a) the Respondent;

(b) any director, officer, partner or responsible employee of the Respondent; and

(c) if the Respondent is an individual, any other person having responsible control of the premises to be searched.

THE SEARCH

6 The Respondent must permit the following persons[1] –

(a) [ ] ('the Supervising Solicitor');

(b) [ ], a solicitor in the firm of [ ], the Applicant's solicitors; and

(c) up to [ ] other persons[2] being [*their identity or capacity*] accompanying them,

(together 'the search party'), to enter the premises mentioned in Schedule A to this order and any other premises of the Respondent disclosed under paragraph 18 below and any vehicles under the Respondent's control on or around the premises ('the premises') so that they can search for, inspect, photograph or photocopy, and deliver into the safekeeping of the Applicant's solicitors all the documents and articles which are listed in Schedule B to this order ('the listed items').

7 Having permitted the search party to enter the premises, the Respondent must allow the search party to remain on the premises until the search is complete. In the event that it becomes necessary for any of those persons to leave the premises before the search is complete, the Respondent must allow them to re-enter the premises immediately upon their seeking re-entry on the same or the following day in order to complete the search.

1 Where the premises are likely to be occupied by an unaccompanied woman and the Supervising Solicitor is a man, at least one of the persons accompanying him should be a woman.

2 None of these persons should be people who could gain personally or commercially from anything they might read or see on the premises, unless their presence is essential.

RESTRICTIONS ON SEARCH

8 This order may not be carried out at the same time as a police search warrant.

9 Before the Respondent allows anybody onto the premises to carry out this order, he is entitled to have the Supervising Solicitor explain to him what it means in everyday language.

10 The Respondent is entitled to seek legal advice and to ask the court to vary or discharge this order. Whilst doing so, he may ask the Supervising Solicitor to delay starting the search for up to 2 hours or such other longer period as the Supervising Solicitor may permit. However, the Respondent must –

- (a) comply with the terms of paragraph 27 below;
- (b) not disturb or remove any listed items; and
- (c) permit the Supervising Solicitor to enter, but not start to search.

11 Before permitting entry to the premises by any person other than the Supervising Solicitor, the Respondent may, for a short time (not to exceed two hours, unless the Supervising Solicitor agrees to a longer period), gather together any documents he believes may be [incriminating or][1] privileged and hand them to the Supervising Solicitor for him to assess whether they are [incriminating or] privileged as claimed. If the Supervising Solicitor decides that any of the documents may be [incriminating or] privileged or is in any doubt as to their status, he will exclude them from the search and retain them in his possession pending further order of the court.

12 If the Respondent wishes to take legal advice and gather documents as permitted, he must first inform the Supervising Solicitor and keep him informed of the steps being taken.

13 No item may be removed from the premises until a list of the items to be removed has been prepared, and a copy of the list has been supplied to the Respondent, and he has been given a reasonable opportunity to check the list.

14 The premises must not be searched, and items must not be removed from them, except in the presence of the Respondent.

15 If the Supervising Solicitor is satisfied that full compliance with paragraphs 13 or 14 is not practicable, he may permit the search to proceed and items to be removed without fully complying with them.

1 References to incriminating documents should be omitted from orders made in intellectual property proceedings, where the privilege against self-incrimination does not apply – see paragraph 8.4 of the practice direction.

DELIVERY UP OF ARTICLES/DOCUMENTS

16 The Respondent must immediately hand over to the Applicant's solicitors any of the listed items, which are in his possession or under his control, save for any computer or hard disk integral to any computer. Any items the subject of a dispute as to whether they are listed items must immediately be handed over to the Supervising Solicitor for safe keeping pending resolution of the dispute or further order of the court.

17 The Respondent must immediately give the search party effective access to the computers on the premises, with all necessary passwords, to enable the computers to be searched. If they contain any listed items the Respondent must cause the listed items to be displayed so that they can be read and copied.[1] The Respondent must provide the Applicant's Solicitors with copies of all listed items contained in

the computers. All reasonable steps shall be taken by the Applicant and the Applicant's solicitors to ensure that no damage is done to any computer or data. The Applicant and his representatives may not themselves search the Respondent's computers unless they have sufficient expertise to do so without damaging the Respondent's system.

1 If it is envisaged that the Respondent's computers are to be imaged (i.e. the hard drives are to be copied wholesale, thereby reproducing listed items and other items indiscriminately), special provision needs to be made and independent computer specialists need to be appointed, who should be required to give undertakings to the court.

PROVISION OF INFORMATION

18 The Respondent must immediately inform the Applicant's Solicitors (in the presence of the Supervising Solicitor) so far as he is aware –

(a) where all the listed items are;

(b) the name and address of everyone who has supplied him, or offered to supply him, with listed items;

(c) the name and address of everyone to whom he has supplied, or offered to supply, listed items; and

(d) full details of the dates and quantities of every such supply and offer.

19 Within [ ] working days after being served with this order the Respondent must swear and serve an affidavit setting out the above information[1].

1 The period should ordinarily be longer than the period in paragraph (2) of Schedule D, if any of the information is likely to be included in listed items taken away of which the Respondent does not have copies.

PROHIBITED ACTS

20 Except for the purpose of obtaining legal advice, the Respondent must not directly or indirectly inform anyone of these proceedings or of the contents of this order, or warn anyone that proceedings have been or may be brought against him by the Applicant until 4.30 p.m. on the return date or further order of the court.

21 Until 4.30 p.m. on the return date the Respondent must not destroy, tamper with, cancel or part with possession, power, custody or control of the listed items otherwise than in accordance with the terms of this order.

22 [Insert any negative injunctions.]

23 [Insert any further order]

COSTS

24 The costs of this application are reserved to the judge hearing the application on the return date.

RESTRICTIONS ON SERVICE

25 This order may only be served between [ ] am/pm and [ ] am/pm [and on a weekday][1].

26 This order must be served by the Supervising Solicitor, and paragraph 6 of the order must be carried out in his presence and under his supervision.

1 Normally, the order should be served in the morning (not before 9.30 am) and on a weekday to enable the Respondent more readily to obtain legal advice.

VARIATION AND DISCHARGE OF THIS ORDER

27 Anyone served with or notified of this order may apply to the court at any time to vary or discharge this order (or so much of it as affects that person), but they must first inform the Applicant's solicitors. If any evidence is to be relied upon in support of the application, the substance of it must be communicated in writing to the Applicant's solicitors in advance.

INTERPRETATION OF THIS ORDER

28 Any requirement that something shall be done to or in the presence of the Respondent means –

(a) if there is more than one Respondent, to or in the presence of any one of them; and
(b) if a Respondent is not an individual, to or in the presence of a director, officer, partner or responsible employee.

29 A Respondent who is an individual who is ordered not to do something must not do it himself or in any other way. He must not do it through others acting on his behalf or on his instructions or with his encouragement.

30 A Respondent which is not an individual which is ordered not to do something must not do it itself or by its directors, officers, partners, employees or agents or in any other way.

COMMUNICATIONS WITH THE COURT

All communications to the court about this order should be sent to –

[*Insert the address and telephone number of the appropriate Court Office*]

If the order is made at the Royal Courts of Justice, communications should be addressed as follows –

Where the order is made in the Chancery Division

Room TM 505, Royal Courts of Justice, Strand, London WC2A 2LL quoting the case number. The telephone number is 0207 947 6754.

Where the order is made in the Queen's Bench Division

Room WG034, Royal Courts of Justice, Strand, London WC2A 2LL quoting the case number. The telephone number is 0207 947 6009.

Where the order is made in the Commercial Court

Room E201, Royal Courts of Justice, Strand, London WC2A 2LL quoting the case number. The telephone number is 0207 947 6826.

The offices are open between 10 am and 4.30 pm Monday to Friday.

SCHEDULE A

THE PREMISES

(1) carry out a search for any documents which it is reasonable to suppose may contain information which may –
   (a) enable the party applying for disclosure either to advance his own case or to damage that of the party giving disclosure; or
   (b) lead to a train of enquiry which has either of those consequences; and

(2) disclose any documents found as a result of that search.

CLAIMS TO WITHHOLD DISCLOSURE OR INSPECTION OF A DOCUMENT

6.1 A claim to withhold inspection of a document, or part of a document, disclosed in a list of documents does not require an application to the court. Where such a claim has been made, a party who wishes to challenge it must apply to the court (see rule 31.19(5)).

6.2 Rule 31.19(1) and (6) provide a procedure enabling a party to apply for an order permitting disclosure of the existence of a document to be withheld.

INSPECTION OF DOCUMENTS MENTIONED IN EXPERT'S REPORT (RULE 31.14(2))

7.1 If a party wishes to inspect documents referred to in the expert report of another party, before issuing an application he should request inspection of the document informally, and inspection should be provided by agreement unless the request is unreasonable.

7.2 Where an expert report refers to a large number or volume of documents and it would be burdensome to copy or collate them, the court will only order inspection of such documents if it is satisfied that it is necessary for the just disposal of the proceedings and the party cannot reasonably obtain the documents from another source.

FALSE DISCLOSURE STATEMENT

8 Attention is drawn to rule 31.23 which sets out the consequences of making a false disclosure statement without an honest belief in its truth, and to the procedures set out in paragraph 27 of the practice direction supplementing Part 32.

PART V

Annex A

DISCLOSURE STATEMENT

I, the above named claimant [or defendant] [if party making disclosure is a company, firm or other organisation identify here who the person making the disclosure statement is and why he is the appropriate person to make it] state that I have carried out a reasonable and proportionate search to locate all the documents which I am required to disclose under the order made by the court on day of . I did not search:

(1) for documents predating ,
(2) for documents located elsewhere than ,
(3) for documents in categories other than .

I certify that I understand the duty of disclosure and to the best of my knowledge I have carried out that duty. I certify that the list above is a complete list of all documents which are or have been in my control and which I am obliged under the said order to disclose.

Practice Direction – Written Evidence

This Practice Direction supplements CPR Part 32 (PD32)

EVIDENCE IN GENERAL

1.1 Rule 32.2 sets out how evidence is to be given and facts are to be proved.

1.2 Evidence at a hearing other than the trial should normally be given by witness statement[1] (see paragraph 17 onwards). However a witness may give evidence by affidavit if he wishes to do so[2] (and see paragraph 1.4 below).

1 See rule 32.6(1).
2 See rule 32.15(2).

1.3 Statements of case (see paragraph 26 onwards) and application notices[1] may also be used as evidence provided that their contents have been verified by a statement of truth[2].

(For information regarding evidence by deposition see Part 34 and the practice direction which supplements it.)

1 See Part 23 for information about making an application.
2 Rule 32.6(2) and see Part 22 for information about the statement of truth.

1.4 Affidavits must be used as evidence in the following instances:

(1) where sworn evidence is required by an enactment[1], rule, order or practice direction,
(2) in any application for a search order, a freezing injunction, or an order requiring an occupier to permit another to enter his land, and
(3) in any application for an order against anyone for alleged contempt of court.

1 See, eg, s 3(5)(a) of the Protection from Harassment Act 1997.

1.5 If a party believes that sworn evidence is required by a court in another jurisdiction for any purpose connected with the proceedings, he may apply to the court for a direction that evidence shall be given only by affidavit on any pre-trial applications.

1.6 The court may give a direction under rule 32.15 that evidence shall be given by affidavit instead of or in addition to a witness statement or statement of case:

(1) on its own initiative, or
(2) after any party has applied to the court for such a direction.

1.7 An affidavit, where referred to in the Civil Procedure Rules or a practice direction, also means an affirmation unless the context requires otherwise.

AFFIDAVITS

Deponent

2 A deponent is a person who gives evidence by affidavit or affirmation.

Heading

3.1 The affidavit should be headed with the title of the proceedings (see paragraph 4 of the practice direction supplementing Part 7 and paragraph 7 of the practice direction supplementing Part 20); where the proceedings are between several parties with the same status it is sufficient too identify the parties as follows:

	Number:
AB (and others)	Claimants/Applicants
CD (and others)	Defendants/Respondents
	(as appropriate)

3.2 At the top right hand corner of the first page (and on the backsheet) there should be clearly written:

(1) the party on whose behalf it is made,
(2) the initials and surname of the deponent,
(3) the number of the affidavit in relation to that deponent,
(4) the identifying initials and number of each exhibit referred to, and
(5) the date sworn.

Body of affidavit

4.1 The affidavit must, if practicable, be in the deponent's own words, the affidavit should be expressed in the first person and the deponent should:

(1) commence 'I (*full name*) of (*address*) state on oath ',
(2) if giving evidence in his professional, business or other occupational capacity, give the address at which he works in (1) above, the position he holds and the name of his firm or employer,
(3) give his occupation or, if he has none, his description, and
(4) state if he is a party to the proceedings or employed by a party to the proceedings, if it be the case.

4.2 An affidavit must indicate:

(1) which of the statements in it are made from the deponent's own knowledge and which are matters of information or belief, and
(2) the source for any matters of information or belief.

4.3 Where a deponent:

(1) refers to an exhibit or exhibits, he should state 'there is now shown to me marked "   " the (*description of exhibit*),' and
(2) makes more than one affidavit (to which there are exhibits) in the same proceedings, the numbering of the exhibits should run consecutively throughout and not start again with each affidavit.

PART V

Jurat

5.1 The jurat of an affidavit is a statement set out at the end of the document which authenticates the affidavit.

5.2 It must:

(1) be signed by all deponents,
(2) be completed and signed by the person before whom the affidavit was sworn whose name and qualification must be printed beneath his signature,
(3) contain the full address of the person before whom the affidavit was sworn, and
(4) follow immediately on from the text and not be put on a separate page.

Format of affidavits

6.1 An affidavit should:

(1) be produced on durable quality A4 paper with a 3.5 cm margin,
(2) be fully legible and should normally be typed on one side of the paper only,
(3) where possible, be bound securely in a manner which would not hamper filing, or otherwise each page should be endorsed with the case number and should bear the initials of the deponent and of the person before whom it was sworn,
(4) have the pages numbered consecutively as a separate document (or as one of several documents contained in a file),
(5) be divided into numbered paragraphs,
(6) have all numbers, including dates, expressed in figures, and
(7) give the reference to any document or documents mentioned either in the margin or in bold text in the body of the affidavit.

6.2 It is usually convenient for an affidavit to follow the chronological sequence of events or matters dealt with; each paragraph of an affidavit should as far as possible be confined to a distinct portion of the subject.

Inability of deponent to read or sign affidavit

7.1 Where an affidavit is sworn by a person who is unable to read or sign it, the person before whom the affidavit is sworn must certify in the jurat that:

(1) he read the affidavit to the deponent,
(2) the deponent appeared to understand it, and
(3) the deponent signed or made his mark, in his presence.

7.2 If that certificate is not included in the jurat, the affidavit may not be used in evidence unless the court is satisfied that it was read to the deponent and that he appeared to understand it. Two versions of the form of jurat with the certificate are set out at Annex 1 to this practice direction.

Alterations to affidavits

8.1 Any alteration to an affidavit must be initialled by both the deponent and the person before whom the affidavit was sworn.

8.2 An affidavit which contains an alteration that has not been initialled may be filed or used in evidence only with the permission of the court.

Who may administer oaths and take affidavits

9.1 Only the following may administer oaths and take affidavits:

(1) commissioners for oaths[1],
(2) practising solicitors[2],
(3) other persons specified by Statute[3],
(4) certain officials of the Supreme Court[4],
(5) a circuit judge or district judge[5],
(6) any justice of the peace[6], and
(7) certain officials of any county court appointed by the judge of that court for the purpose[7].

1 Commissioners for Oaths Acts 1889 and 1891.
2 Section 81 of the Solicitors Act 1974.
3 Section 65 of the Administration of Justice Act 1985, s 113 of the Courts and Legal Services Act 1990 and the Commissioners for Oaths (Prescribed Bodies) Regulations 1994 and 1995.
4 Section 2 of the Commissioners for Oaths Act 1889.
5 Section 58 of the County Courts Act 1984.
6 Section 58 as above.
7 Section 58 as above.

9.2 An affidavit must be sworn before a person independent of the parties or their representatives.

Filing of affidavits

10.1 If the court directs that an affidavit is to be filed[1], it must be filed in the court or Division, or Office or Registry of the court or Division where the action in which it was or is to be used, is proceeding or will proceed.

1 Rules 32.1(3) and 32.4(3)(b).

10.2 Where an affidavit is in a foreign language:

(1) the party wishing to rely on it –
  (a) must have it translated, and
  (b) must file the foreign language affidavit with the court, and

(2) the translator must make and file with the court an affidavit verifying the translation and exhibiting both the translation and a copy of the foreign language affidavit.

EXHIBITS

Manner of exhibiting documents

11.1 A document used in conjunction with an affidavit should be:

(1) produced to and verified by the deponent, and remain separate from the affidavit, and
(2) identified by a declaration of the person before whom the affidavit was sworn.

11.2 The declaration should be headed with the name of the proceedings in the same way as the affidavit.

11.3 The first page of each exhibit should be marked:

(1) as in paragraph 3.2 above, and
(2) with the exhibit mark referred to in the affidavit.

Letters

12.1 Copies of individual letters should be collected together and exhibited in a bundle or bundles. They should be arranged in chronological order with the earliest at the top, and firmly secured.

12.2 When a bundle of correspondence is exhibited, the exhibit should have a front page attached stating that the bundle consists of original letters and copies. They should be arranged and secured as above and numbered consecutively.

Other documents

13.1 Photocopies instead of original documents may be exhibited provided the originals are made available for inspection by the other parties before the hearing and by the judge at the hearing.

13.2 Court documents must not be exhibited (official copies of such documents prove themselves).

13.3 Where an exhibit contains more than one document, a front page should be attached setting out a list of the documents contained in the exhibit; the list should contain the dates of the documents.

Exhibits other than documents

14.1 Items other than documents should be clearly marked with an exhibit number or letter in such a manner that the mark cannot become detached from the exhibit.

14.2 Small items may be placed in a container and the container appropriately marked.

General provisions

15.1 Where an exhibit contains more than one document:

(1) the bundle should not be stapled but should be securely fastened in a way that does not hinder the reading of the documents, and
(2) the pages should be numbered consecutively at bottom centre.

15.2 Every page of an exhibit should be clearly legible; typed copies of illegible documents should be included, paginated with 'a' numbers.

15.3 Where affidavits and exhibits have become numerous, they should be put into separate bundles and the pages numbered consecutively throughout.

15.4 Where on account of their bulk the service of exhibits or copies of exhibits on the other parties would be difficult or impracticable, the directions of the court should be sought as to arrangements for bringing the exhibits to the attention of the other parties and as to their custody pending trial.

Affirmations

16 All provisions in this or any other practice direction relating to affidavits apply to affirmations with the following exceptions:

(1) the deponent should commence 'I (*name*) of (*address*) do solemnly and sincerely affirm ', and
(2) in the jurat the word 'sworn' is replaced by the word 'affirmed'.

WITNESS STATEMENTS

Heading

17.1 The witness statement should be headed with the title of the proceedings (see paragraph 4 of the practice direction supplementing Part 7 and paragraph 7 of the practice direction supplementing Part 20); where the proceedings are between several parties with the same status it is sufficient to identify the parties as follows:

	Number:
AB (and others)	Claimants/Applicants
CD (and others)	Defendants/Respondents
	(as appropriate)

17.2 At the top right hand corner of the first page there should be clearly written:

(1) the party on whose behalf it is made,
(2) the initials and surname of the witness,
(3) the number of the statement in relation to that witness,
(4) the identifying initials and number of each exhibit referred to, and
(5) the date the statement was made.

Body of witness statement

18.1 The witness statement must, if practicable, be in the intended witness's own words, the statement should be expressed in the first person and should also state:

(1) the full name of the witness,
(2) his place of residence or, if he is making the statement in his professional, business or other occupational capacity, the address at which he works, the position he holds and the name of his firm or employer,
(3) his occupation, or if he has none, his description, and
(4) the fact that he is a party to the proceedings or is the employee of such a party if it be the case.

18.2 A witness statement must indicate:

(1) which of the statements in it are made from the witness's own knowledge and which are matters of information or belief, and
(2) the source for any matters of information or belief.

18.3 An exhibit used in conjunction with a witness statement should be verified and identified by the witness and remain separate from the witness statement.

18.4 Where a witness refers to an exhibit or exhibits, he should state 'I refer to the (*description of exhibit*) marked " "'

18.5 The provisions of paragraphs 11.3 to 15.4 (exhibits) apply similarly to witness statements as they do to affidavits.

18.6 Where a witness makes more than one witness statement to which there are exhibits, in the same proceedings, the numbering of the exhibits should run consecutively throughout and not start again with each witness statement.

Format of witness statement

19.1 A witness statement should:

(1) be produced on durable quality A4 paper with a 3.5 cm margin,

(2) be fully legible and should normally be typed on one side of the paper only,
(3) where possible, be bound securely in a manner which would not hamper filing, or otherwise each page should be endorsed with the case number and should bear the initials of the witness,
(4) have the pages numbered consecutively as a separate statement (or as one of several statements contained in a file),
(5) be divided into numbered paragraphs,
(6) have all numbers, including dates, expressed in figures, and
(7) give the reference to any document or documents mentioned either in the margin or in bold text in the body of the statement.

19.2 It is usually convenient for a witness statement to follow the chronological sequence of the events or matters dealt with, each paragraph of a witness statement should as far as possible be confined to a distinct portion of the subject.

Statement of truth

20.1 A witness statement is the equivalent of the oral evidence which that witness would, if called, give in evidence; it must include a statement by the intended witness that he believes the facts in it are true[1].

1 See Part 22 for information about the statement of truth.

20.2 To verify a witness statement the statement of truth is as follows:

'I believe that the facts stated in this witness statement are true'

20.3 Attention is drawn to rule 32.14 which sets out the consequences of verifying a witness statement containing a false statement without an honest belief in its truth.

Inability of witness to read or sign statement

21.1 Where a witness statement is made by a person who is unable to read or sign the witness statement, it must contain a certificate made by an authorised person.

21.2 An authorised person is a person able to administer oaths and take affidavits but need not be independent of the parties or their representatives.

21.3 The authorised person must certify:

(1) that the witness statement has been read to the witness,
(2) that the witness appeared to understand it and approved its content as accurate,
(3) that the declaration of truth has been read to the witness,
(4) that the witness appeared to understand the declaration and the consequences of making a false witness statement, and
(5) that the witness signed or made his mark in the presence of the authorised person.

21.4 The form of the certificate is set out at Annex 2 to this practice direction.

Alterations to witness statements

22.1 Any alteration to a witness statement must be initialled by the person making the statement or by the authorised person where appropriate (see paragraph 21).

22.2 A witness statement which contains an alteration that has not been initialled may be used in evidence only with the permission of the court.

Filing of witness statements

23.1 If the court directs that a witness statement is to be filed[1], it must be filed in the court or Division, or Office or Registry of the court or Division where the action in which it was or is to be used, is proceeding or will proceed.

1 Rule 32.4(3)(b).

23.2 Where the court has directed that a witness statement in a foreign language is to be filed:

(1) the party wishing to rely on it must –
 (a) have it translated, and
 (b) file the foreign language witness statement with the court, and

(2) the translator must make and file with the court an affidavit verifying the translation and exhibiting both the translation and a copy of the foreign language witness statement.

Certificate of court officer

24.1 Where the court has ordered that a witness statement is not to be open to inspection by the public[1] or that words or passages in the statement are not to be open to inspection[2] the court officer will so certify on the statement and make any deletions directed by the court under rule 32.13(4).

1 Rule 32.13(2).
2 Rule 32.13(4).

Defects in affidavits, witness statements and exhibits

25.1 Where:

(1) an affidavit,
(2) a witness statement, or
(3) an exhibit to either an affidavit or a witness statement,

does not comply with Part 32 or this practice direction in relation to its form, the court may refuse to admit it as evidence and may refuse to allow the costs arising from its preparation.

25.2 Permission to file a defective affidavit or witness statement or to use a defective exhibit may be obtained from a judge[1] in the court where the case is proceeding.

1 Rule 2.3(1); definition of judge.

STATEMENTS OF CASE

26.1 A statement of case may be used as evidence in an interim application provided it is verified by a statement of truth[1].

1 See rule 32.6(2)(a).

26.2 To verify a statement of case the statement of truth should be set out as follows:

'[I believe] [the (*party on whose behalf the statement of case is being signed*) believes] that the facts stated in the statement of case are true'.

26.3 Attention is drawn to rule 32.14 which sets out the consequences of verifying a witness statement containing a false statement without an honest belief in its truth.

(For information regarding statements of truth see Part 22 and the practice direction which supplements it.)

(Practice directions supplementing Parts 7 and 17 provide further information concerning statements of case.)

AGREED BUNDLES FOR HEARINGS

27.1 The court may give directions requiring the parties to use their best endeavours to agree a bundle or bundles of documents for use at any hearing.

27.2 All documents contained in bundles which have been agreed for use at a hearing shall be admissible at that hearing as evidence of their contents, unless –

(1) the court orders otherwise; or
(2) a party gives written notice of objection to the admissibility of particular documents.

PENALTY

28.1 (1) Where a party alleges that a statement of truth or a disclosure statement is false the party shall refer that allegation to the court dealing with the claim in which the statement of truth or disclosure statement has been made.

(2) The court may –
(a) exercise any of its powers under the rules;
(b) initiate steps to consider if there is a contempt of court and, where there is, to punish it;

(The practice direction to RSC Order 52 (Schedule 1) and CCR Order 29 (Schedule 2) makes provision where committal to prison is a possibility if contempt is proved.)

(c) direct the party making the allegation to refer the matter to the Attorney General with a request to him to consider whether he wishes to bring proceedings for contempt of court.

28.2 (1) An application to the Attorney General should be made to his chambers at 9 Buckingham Gate London SW1E 6JP in writing. The Attorney General will initially require a copy of the order recording the direction of the judge referring the matter to him and information which –
(a) identifies the statement said to be false; and
(b) explains –
(i) why it is false, and
(ii) why the maker knew it to be false at the time he made it;
and
(c) explains why contempt proceedings would be appropriate in the light of the overriding objective in Part 1 of the Civil Procedure Rules.

(2) The practice of the Attorney General is to prefer an application that comes from the court, and so has received preliminary consideration by a judge, to one made direct to him by a party to the claim in which the alleged contempt occurred without prior consideration by the court. An

application to the Attorney General is not a way of appealing against, or reviewing, the decision of the judge.

28.3 Where a party makes an application to the court for permission for that party to commence proceedings for contempt of court, it must be supported by written evidence containing the information specified in paragraph 27.2(1) and the result of the application to the Attorney General made by the applicant.

28.4 The rules do not change the law of contempt or introduce new categories of contempt. A person applying to commence such proceedings should consider whether the incident complained of does amount to contempt of court and whether such proceedings would further the overriding objective in Part 1 of the Civil Procedure Rules.

VIDEO CONFERENCING

29.1 Guidance on the use of video conferencing in the civil courts is set out at Annex 3 to this practice direction.

Annex 1

CERTIFICATE TO BE USED WHERE A DEPONENT TO AN AFFIDAVIT IS UNABLE TO READ OR SIGN IT

Sworn at this day of Before me, I having first read over the contents of this affidavit to the deponent [*if there are exhibits, add* 'and explained the nature and effect of the exhibits referred to in it'] who appeared to understand it and approved its content as accurate, and made his mark on the affidavit in my presence.

Or, (after, *Before me*) the witness to the mark of the deponent having been first sworn that he had read over etc (*as above*) and that he saw him make his mark on the affidavit. (*Witness must sign*).

CERTIFICATE TO BE USED WHERE A DEPONENT TO AN AFFIRMATION IS UNABLE TO READ OR SIGN IT

Affirmed at this day of Before me, I having first read over the contents of this affirmation to the deponent [*if there are exhibits, add* 'and explained the nature and effect of the exhibits referred to in it'] who appeared to understand it and approved its content as accurate, and made his mark on the affirmation in my presence.

Or, (after, *Before me*) the witness to the mark of the deponent having been first sworn that he had read over etc (*as above*) and that he saw him make his mark on the affirmation. (*Witness must sign*).

Annex 2

CERTIFICATE TO BE USED WHERE A WITNESS IS UNABLE TO READ OR SIGN A WITNESS STATEMENT

I certify that I [*name and address of authorised person*] have read over the contents of this witness statement and the declaration of truth to the witness [*if there are exhibits, add* 'and explained the nature and effect of the exhibits referred to in it'] who appeared to understand (a) the statement and approved its content as accurate and (b) the declaration of truth and the consequences of making a false witness statement, and made his mark in my presence.

Annex 3

VIDEO CONFERENCING GUIDANCE

This guidance is for the use of video conferencing (VCF) in civil proceedings. It is in part based, with permission, upon the protocol of the Federal Court of Australia. It is intended to provide a guide to all persons involved in the use of VCF, although it does not attempt to cover all the practical questions which might arise.

Video conferencing generally

1 The guidance covers the use of VCF equipment both (a) in a courtroom, whether via equipment which is permanently placed there or via a mobile unit, and (b) in a separate studio or conference room. In either case, the location at which the judge sits is referred to as the 'local site'. The other site or sites to and from which transmission is made are referred to as 'the remote site' and in any particular case any such site may be another courtroom. The guidance applies to cases where VCF is used for the taking of evidence and also to its use for other parts of any legal proceedings (for example, interim applications, case management conferences, pre-trial reviews).

2 VCF may be a convenient way of dealing with any part of proceedings: it can involve considerable savings in time and cost. Its use for the taking of evidence from overseas witnesses will, in particular, be likely to achieve a material saving of costs, and such savings may also be achieved by its use for taking domestic evidence. It is, however, inevitably not as ideal as having the witness physically present in court. Its convenience should not therefore be allowed to dictate its use. A judgment must be made in every case in which the use of VCF is being considered not only as to whether it will achieve an overall cost saving but as to whether its use will be likely to be beneficial to the efficient, fair and economic disposal of the litigation. In particular, it needs to be recognised that the degree of control a court can exercise over a witness at the remote site is or may be more limited than it can exercise over a witness physically before it.

3 When used for the taking of evidence, the objective should be to make the VCF session as close as possible to the usual practice in a trial court where evidence is taken in open court. To gain the maximum benefit, several differences have to be taken into account. Some matters, which are taken for granted when evidence is taken in the conventional way, take on a different dimension when it is taken by VCF: for example, the administration of the oath, ensuring that the witness understands who is at the local site and what their various roles are, the raising of any objections to the evidence and the use of documents.

4 It should not be presumed that all foreign governments are willing to allow their nationals or others within their jurisdiction to be examined before a court in England or Wales by means of VCF. If there is any doubt about this, enquiries should be directed to the Foreign and Commonwealth Office (International Legal Matters Unit, Consular Division) with a view to ensuring that the country from which the evidence is to be taken raises no objection to it at diplomatic level. The party who is directed to be responsible for arranging the VCF (see paragraph 8 below) will be required to make all necessary inquiries about this well in advance of the VCF and must be able to inform the court what those inquiries were and of their outcome.

5 Time zone differences need to be considered when a witness abroad is to be examined in England or Wales by VCF. The convenience of the witness, the parties, their representatives and the court must all be taken into account. The cost of the use of a commercial studio is usually greater outside normal business hours.

6 Those involved with VCF need to be aware that, even with the most advanced systems currently available, there are the briefest of delays between the receipt of the picture and that of the accompanying sound. If due allowance is not made for this, there will be a tendency to 'speak over' the witness, whose voice will continue to be heard for a millisecond or so after he or she appears on the screen to have finished speaking.

7 With current technology, picture quality is good, but not as good as a television picture. The quality of the picture is enhanced if those appearing on VCF monitors keep their movements to a minimum.

Preliminary arrangements

8 The court's permission is required for any part of any proceedings to be dealt with by means of VCF. Before seeking a direction, the applicant should notify the listing officer, diary manager or other appropriate court officer of the intention to seek it, and should enquire as to the availability of court VCF equipment for the day or days of the proposed VCF. The application for a direction should be made to the master, district judge or judge, as may be appropriate. If all parties consent to a direction, permission can be sought by letter, fax or e-mail, although the court may still require an oral hearing. All parties are entitled to be heard on whether or not such a direction should be given and as to its terms. If a witness at a remote site is to give evidence by an interpreter, consideration should be given at this stage as to whether the interpreter should be at the local site or the remote site. If a VCF direction is given, arrangements for the transmission will then need to be made. The court will ordinarily direct that the party seeking permission to use VCF is to be responsible for this. That party is hereafter referred to as 'the VCF arranging party'.

9 Subject to any order to the contrary, all costs of the transmission, including the costs of hiring equipment and technical personnel to operate it, will initially be the responsibility of, and must be met by, the VCF arranging party. All reasonable efforts should be made to keep the transmission to a minimum and so keep the costs down. All such costs will be considered to be part of the costs of the proceedings and the court will determine at such subsequent time as is convenient or appropriate who, as between the parties, should be responsible for them and (if appropriate) in what proportions.

10 The local site will, if practicable, be a courtroom but it may instead be an appropriate studio or conference room. The VCF arranging party must contact the listing officer, diary manager or other appropriate officer of the court which made

the VCF direction and make arrangements for the VCF transmission. Details of the remote site, and of the equipment to be used both at the local site (if not being supplied by the court) and the remote site (including the number of ISDN lines and connection speed), together with all necessary contact names and telephone numbers, will have to be provided to the listing officer, diary manager or other court officer. The court will need to be satisfied that any equipment provided by the parties for use at the local site and also that at the remote site is of sufficient quality for a satisfactory transmission. The VCF arranging party must ensure that an appropriate person will be present at the local site to supervise the operation of the VCF throughout the transmission in order to deal with any technical problems. That party must also arrange for a technical assistant to be similarly present at the remote site for like purposes.

11 It is recommended that the judge, practitioners and witness should arrive at their respective VCF sites about 20 minutes prior to the scheduled commencement of the transmission.

12 If the local site is not a courtroom, but a conference room or studio, the judge will need to determine who is to sit where. The VCF arranging party must take care to ensure that the number of microphones is adequate for the speakers and that the panning of the camera for the practitioners' table encompasses all legal representatives so that the viewer can see everyone seated there.

13 The proceedings, wherever they may take place, form part of a trial to which the public is entitled to have access (unless the court has determined that they should be heard in private). If the local site is to be a studio or conference room, the VCF arranging party must ensure that it provides sufficient accommodation to enable a reasonable number of members of the public to attend.

14 In cases where the local site is a studio or conference room, the VCF arranging party should make arrangements, if practicable, for the royal coat of arms to be placed above the judge's seat.

15 In cases in which the VCF is to be used for the taking of evidence, the VCF arranging party must arrange for recording equipment to be provided by the court which made the VCF direction so that the evidence can be recorded. An associate will normally be present to operate the recording equipment when the local site is a courtroom. The VCF arranging party should take steps to ensure that an associate is present to do likewise when it is a studio or conference room. The equipment should be set up and tested before the VCF transmission. It will often be a valuable safeguard for the VCF arranging party also to arrange for the provision of recording equipment at the remote site. This will provide a useful back-up if there is any reduction in sound quality during the transmission. A direction from the court for the making of such a back-up recording must, however, be obtained first. This is because the proceedings are court proceedings and, save as directed by the court, no other recording of them must be made. The court will direct what is to happen to the back-up recording.

16 Some countries may require that any oath or affirmation to be taken by a witness accord with local custom rather than the usual form of oath or affirmation used in England and Wales. The VCF arranging party must make all appropriate prior inquiries and put in place all arrangements necessary to enable the oath or affirmation to be taken in accordance with any local custom. That party must be in a position to inform the court what those inquiries were, what their outcome was and what arrangements have been made. If the oath or affirmation can be administered in the manner normal in England and Wales, the VCF arranging party

must arrange in advance to have the appropriate holy book at the remote site. The associate will normally administer the oath.

17 Consideration will need to be given in advance to the documents to which the witness is likely to be referred. The parties should endeavour to agree on this. It will usually be most convenient for a bundle of the copy documents to be prepared in advance, which the VCF arranging party should then send to the remote site.

18 Additional documents are sometimes quite properly introduced during the course of a witness's evidence. To cater for this, the VCF arranging party should ensure that equipment is available to enable documents to be transmitted between sites during the course of the VCF transmission. Consideration should be given to whether to use a document camera. If it is decided to use one, arrangements for its use will need to be established in advance. The panel operator will need to know the number and size of documents or objects if their images are to be sent by document camera. In many cases, a simpler and sufficient alternative will be to ensure that there are fax transmission and reception facilities at the participating sites.

The hearing

19 The procedure for conducting the transmission will be determined by the judge. He will determine who is to control the cameras. In cases where the VCF is being used for an application in the course of the proceedings, the judge will ordinarily not enter the local site until both sites are on line. Similarly, at the conclusion of the hearing, he will ordinarily leave the local site while both sites are still on line. The following paragraphs apply primarily to cases where the VCF is being used for the taking of the evidence of a witness at a remote site. In all cases, the judge will need to decide whether court dress is appropriate when using VCF facilities. It might be appropriate when transmitting from courtroom to courtroom. It might not be when a commercial facility is being used.

20 At the beginning of the transmission, the judge will probably wish to introduce himself and the advocates to the witness. He will probably want to know who is at the remote site and will invite the witness to introduce himself and anyone else who is with him. He may wish to give directions as to the seating arrangements at the remote site so that those present are visible at the local site during the taking of the evidence. He will probably wish to explain to the witness the method of taking the oath or of affirming, the manner in which the evidence will be taken, and who will be conducting the examination and cross-examination. He will probably also wish to inform the witness of the matters referred to in paragraphs 6 and 7 above (co-ordination of picture with sound, and picture quality).

21 The examination of the witness at the remote site should follow as closely as possible the practice adopted when a witness is in the courtroom. During examination, cross-examination and re-examination, the witness must be able to see the legal representative asking the question and also any other person (whether another legal representative or the judge) making any statements in regard to the witness's evidence. It will in practice be most convenient if everyone remains seated throughout the transmission.

Practice Direction – Experts and Assessors

This Practice Direction supplements CPR Part 35 (PD35)

Part 35 is intended to limit the use of oral expert evidence to that which is reasonably required. In addition, where possible, matters requiring expert evidence should be dealt with by a single expert. Permission of the court is always required either to call an expert or to put an expert's report in evidence.

EXPERT EVIDENCE – GENERAL REQUIREMENTS

1.1 It is the duty of an expert to help the court on matters within his own expertise: rule 35.3(1). This duty is paramount and overrides any obligation to the person from whom the expert has received instructions or by whom he is paid: rule 35.3(2).

1.2 Expert evidence should be the independent product of the expert uninfluenced by the pressures of litigation.

1.3 An expert should assist the court by providing objective, unbiased opinion on matters within his expertise, and should not assume the role of an advocate.

1.4 An expert should consider all material facts, including those which might detract from his opinion.

1.5 An expert should make it clear:

- (a) when a question or issue falls outside his expertise; and
- (b) when he is not able to reach a definite opinion, for example because he has insufficient information.

1.6 If, after producing a report, an expert changes his view on any material matter, such change of view should be communicated to all the parties without delay, and when appropriate to the court.

FORM AND CONTENT OF EXPERT'S REPORTS

2.1 An expert's report should be addressed to the court and not to the party from whom the expert has received his instructions.

2.2 An expert's report must:

- (1) give details of the expert's qualifications;
- (2) give details of any literature or other material which the expert has relied on in making the report;
- (3) contain a statement setting out the substance of all facts and instructions given to the expert which are material to the opinions expressed in the report or upon which those opinions are based;
- (4) make clear which of the facts stated in the report are within the expert's own knowledge;
- (5) say who carried out any examination, measurement, test or experiment which the expert has used for the report, give the qualifications of that person, and say whether or not the test or experiment has been carried out under the expert's supervision;
- (6) where there is a range of opinion on the matters dealt with in the report –
  - (a) summarise the range of opinion, and
  - (b) give reasons for his own opinion;

(7) contain a summary of the conclusions reached;
(8) if the expert is not able to give his opinion without qualification, state the qualification; and
(9) contain a statement that the expert understands his duty to the court, and has complied and will continue to comply with that duty.

2.3 An expert's report must be verified by a statement of truth as well as containing the statements required in paragraph 2.2(8) and (9) above.

2.4 The form of the statement of truth is as follows:

'I confirm that insofar as the facts stated in my report are within my own knowledge I have made clear which they are and I believe them to be true, and that the opinions I have expressed represent my true and complete professional opinion.'

2.5 Attention is drawn to rule 32.14 which sets out the consequences of verifying a document containing a false statement without an honest belief in its truth.

(For information about statements of truth see Part 22 and the practice direction which supplements it)

INFORMATION

3 Under rule 35.9 the court may direct a party with access to information which is not reasonably available to another party to serve on that other party a document which records the information. The document served must include sufficient details of all the facts, tests, experiments and assumptions which underlie any part of the information to enable the party on whom it is served to make, or to obtain, a proper interpretation of the information and an assessment of its significance.

INSTRUCTIONS

4 The instructions referred to in paragraph 2.2(3) will not be protected by privilege (see rule 35.10(4)). But cross-examination of the expert on the contents of his instructions will not be allowed unless the court permits it (or unless the party who gave the instructions consents to it). Before it gives permission the court must be satisfied that there are reasonable grounds to consider that the statement in the report of the substance of the instructions is inaccurate or incomplete. If the court is so satisfied, it will allow the cross-examination where it appears to be in the interests of justice to do so.

QUESTIONS TO EXPERTS

5.1 Questions asked for the purpose of clarifying the expert's report (see rule 35.6) should be put, in writing, to the expert not later than 28 days after receipt of the expert's report (see paragraphs 1.2 to 1.5 above as to verification).

5.2 Where a party sends a written question or questions direct to an expert, a copy of the questions should, at the same time, be sent to the other party or parties.

5.3 The party or parties instructing the expert must pay any fees charged by that expert for answering questions put under rule 35.6. This does not affect any decision of the court as to the party who is ultimately to bear the expert's costs.

SINGLE EXPERT

6 Where the court has directed that the evidence on a particular issue is to be given by one expert only (rule 35.7) but there are a number of disciplines relevant to that issue, a leading expert in the dominant discipline should be identified as the single

expert. He should prepare the general part of the report and be responsible for annexing or incorporating the contents of any reports from experts in other disciplines.

ASSESSORS

7.1 An assessor may be appointed to assist the court under rule 35.15. Not less than 21 days before making any such appointment, the court will notify each party in writing of the name of the proposed assessor, of the matter in respect of which the assistance of the assessor will be sought and of the qualifications of the assessor to give that assistance.

7.2 Where any person has been proposed for appointment as an assessor, objection to him, either personally or in respect of his qualification, may be taken by any party.

7.3 Any such objection must be made in writing and filed with the court within 7 days of receipt of the notification referred to in paragraph 6.1 and will be taken into account by the court in deciding whether or not to make the appointment (section 63(5) of the County Courts Act 1984).

7.4 Copies of any report prepared by the assessor will be sent to each of the parties but the assessor will not give oral evidence or be open to cross-examination or questioning.

Practice Direction – Judgments and Orders

This Practice Direction supplements CPR Part 40 (PD40B)

DRAWING UP AND FILING OF JUDGMENTS AND ORDERS

1.1 Rule 40.2 sets out the standard requirements for judgments and orders and rule 40.3 deals with how judgments and orders should be drawn up.

1.2 A party who has been ordered or given permission to draw up an order must file it for sealing within 7 days of being ordered or permitted to do so[1]. If he fails to do so, any other party may draw it up and file it[2].

1 Rule 40.3(3)(a).
2 Rule 40.3(3)(b).

1.3 If the court directs that a judgment or order which is being drawn up by a party must be checked by the court before it is sealed, the party responsible must file the draft within 7 days of the date the order was made with a request that the draft be checked before it is sealed.

1.4 If the court directs the parties to file an agreed statement of terms of an order which the court is to draw up[1], the parties must do so no later than 7 days from the date the order was made, unless the court directs otherwise.

1 Rule 40.3(2)(b).

1.5 If the court requires the terms of an order which is being drawn up by the court to be agreed by the parties the court may direct that a copy of the draft order is to be sent to all the parties:

(1) for their agreement to be endorsed on it and returned to the court before the order is sealed, or
(2) with notice of an appointment to attend before the court to agree the terms of the order.

PREPARATION OF DEEDS OR DOCUMENTS UNDER AN ORDER

2.1 Where a judgment or order directs any deed or document to be prepared, executed or signed, the order will state:

(1) the person who is to prepare the deed or document, and
(2) if the deed or document is to be approved, the person who is to approve it.

2.2 If the parties are unable to agree the form of the deed or document, any party may apply in accordance with Part 23 for the form of the deed or document to be settled.

2.3 In such case the judge may:

(1) settle the deed or document himself, or
(2) refer it to
  (a) a master, or
  (b) a district judge, or
  (c) a conveyancing counsel of the Supreme Court to settle.

(See also the Sale of Land practice direction supplementing CPR Part 40.)

CONSENT ORDERS

3.1 Rule 40.6(3) sets out the types of consent judgments and orders which may be entered and sealed by a court officer. The court officer may do so in those cases provided that:

(1) none of the parties is a litigant in person, and
(2) the approval of the court is not required by the Rules, a practice direction or any enactment[1].

1 Rule 40.6(2).

3.2 If a consent order filed for sealing appears to be unclear or incorrect the court officer may refer it to a judge for consideration[1].

1 Rule 3.2.

3.3 Where a consent judgment or order does not come within the provisions of rule 40.6(2):

(1) an application notice requesting a judgment or order in the agreed terms should be filed with the draft judgment or order to be entered or sealed, and
(2) the draft judgment or order must be drawn so that the judge's name and judicial title can be inserted.

3.4 A consent judgment or order must:

(1) be drawn up in the terms agreed,
(2) bear on it the words 'By Consent', and
(3) be signed by
  (a) solicitors or counsel acting for each of the parties to the order, or
  (b) where a party is a litigant in person, the litigant[1].

1 Rule 40.6(7).

3.5 Where the parties draw up a consent order in the form of a stay of proceedings on agreed terms, disposing of the proceedings[1], and where the terms are recorded in a schedule to the order, any direction for:

1 Rule 40.6(3)(b)(ii).

(1) payment of money out of court, or
(2) payment and assessment of costs

should be contained in the body of the order and not in the schedule.

CORRECTION OF ERRORS IN JUDGMENTS AND ORDERS

4.1 Where a judgment or order contains an accidental slip or omission a party may apply for it to be corrected[1].

4.2 The application notice (which may be an informal document such as a letter) should describe the error and set out the correction required. An application may be dealt with without a hearing:

(1) where the applicant so requests,
(2) with the consent of the parties, or
(3) where the court does not consider that a hearing would be appropriate.

4.3 The judge may deal with the application without notice if the slip or omission is obvious or may direct notice of the application to be given to the other party or parties.

4.4 If the application is opposed it should, if practicable, be listed for hearing before the judge who gave the judgment or made the order.

4.5 The court has an inherent power to vary its own orders to make the meaning and intention of the court clear.

1 Rule 40.10.

****

STATEMENT AS TO SERVICE OF A CLAIM FORM

7.1 Where a party to proceedings which have gone to trial requires a statement to be included in the judgment as to where, and by what means the claim form issued in those proceedings was served, application should made to the trial judge when judgment is given.

7.2 If the judge so orders, the statement will be included in a preamble to the judgment as entered.

ORDERS REQUIRING AN ACT TO BE DONE

8.1 An order which requires an act to be done (other than a judgment or order for the payment of an amount of money) must specify the time within which the act should be done.

8.2 The consequences of failure to do an act within the time specified may be set out in the order. In this case the wording of the following examples suitably adapted must be used:

(1) Unless the [claimant][defendant] serves his list of documents by 4.00 pm on Friday, January 22, 1999 his [claim][defence] will be struck out and judgment entered for the [defendant][claimant]., or
(2) Unless the [claimant][defendant] serves his list of documents within 14 days of service of this order his [claim][defence] will be struck out and judgment entered for the [defendant][claimant].

Example (1) should be used wherever possible.

NON-COMPLIANCE WITH A JUDGMENT OR ORDER

9.1 An order which restrains a party from doing an act or requires an act to be done should, if disobedience is to be dealt with by an application to bring contempt of court proceedings, have the penal notice endorsed on it as follows:

> 'If you the within-named [ ] do not comply with this order you may be held to be in contempt of court and imprisoned or fined, or [in the case of a company or corporation] your assets may be seized.'

9.2 The provisions of paragraph 8.1 above also apply to an order which contains an undertaking by a party to do or not do an act, subject to paragraph 9.3 below.

9.3 The court has the power to decline to:

(1) accept an undertaking, and
(2) deal with disobedience in respect of an undertaking by contempt of court proceedings,

unless the party giving the undertaking has made a signed statement to the effect that he understands the terms of his undertaking and the consequences of failure to comply with it.

9.4 The statement may be endorsed on the [court copy of the] order containing the undertaking or may be filed in a separate document such as a letter.

FOREIGN CURRENCY

10 Where judgment is ordered to be entered in a foreign currency, the order should be in the following form:

> 'It is ordered that the defendant pay the claimant (state the sum in the foreign currency) or the Sterling equivalent at the time of payment.'

COSTS

11.1 Attention is drawn to the costs practice direction and, in particular, to the court's power to make a summary assessment of costs and the provisions relating to interest in detailed assessment proceedings.

11.2 Attention is also drawn to costs rule 44.13(1) which provides that if an order makes no mention of costs, none are payable in respect of the proceedings to which it relates.

JUDGMENTS PAID BY INSTALMENTS

12 Where a judgment is to be paid by instalments, the judgment should set out:

(1) the total amount of the judgment,
(2) the amount of each instalment,
(3) the number of instalments and the date on which each is to be paid, and
(4) to whom the instalments should be paid.

ORDER TO MAKE AN ORDER OF THE HOUSE OF LORDS AN ORDER OF THE HIGH COURT

13.1 Application may be made in accordance with Part 23 for an order to make an order of the House of Lords an order of the High Court. The application should be made to the procedural judge of the Division, district registry or court in which the proceedings are taking place and may be made without notice unless the court directs otherwise.

13.2 The application must be supported by the following evidence:

(1) details of the order which was the subject of the appeal to the House of Lords,
(2) details of the order of the House of Lords, with a copy annexed, and
(3) a copy annexed of the certificate of the Clerk of Parliaments of the assessment of the costs of the appeal to the House of Lords in the sum of £.............

13.3 The order to make an order of the House of Lords an order of the High Court should be in form no PF68.

EXAMPLES OF FORMS OF TRIAL JUDGMENT

14.1 The following general forms may be used;

(1) judgment after trial before judge without jury – form no 45,
(2) judgment after trial before judge with jury – form no 46,
(3) judgment after trial before a master or district judge – form no 47,
(4) judgment after trial before a judge of the Technology and Construction court – form no 47 but with any necessary modifications.

14.2 A trial judgment should, in addition to the matters set out in paragraphs 5, 6 and 7 above, have the following matters set out in a preamble:

(1) the questions put to a jury and their answers to those questions,
(2) the findings of a jury and whether unanimous or by a majority,
(3) any order made during the course of the trial concerning the use of evidence,
(4) any matters that were agreed between the parties prior to or during the course of the trial in respect of
 (a) liability,
 (b) contribution,
 (c) the amount of the damages or part of the damages, and
(5) the findings of the judge in respect of each head of damage in a personal injury case.

14.3 Form no 49 should be used for a trial judgment against an Estate.

The forms referred to in this practice direction are listed in the practice direction which supplements Part 4 (Forms).

14.4 On any application or appeal concerning –

(i) a committal order;
(ii) a refusal to grant habeas corpus or
(iii) a secure accommodation order made under section 25 of the Children Act 1989,

if the court ordering the release of the person concludes that his Convention rights have been infringed by the making of the order to which the application or appeal relates, the judgment or order should so state. If the court does not do so, that failure will not prevent another court from deciding the matter.

FOR INFORMATION ABOUT

(1) Orders for provisional damages: see Part 41 and the practice direction which supplements it.
(2) Orders in respect of children and patients: see Part 22 and the practice direction which supplements it.
(3) Orders containing directions for payment of money out of court: see Parts 36 and 37 and the practice directions which supplement them.
(4) Structured settlement orders: see the separate practice direction supplementing Part 40.
(5) Taking accounts and conducting inquiries under a judgment or order: see the separate practice direction supplementing Part 40.

Practice Direction About Costs

Supplementing CPR Parts 43–48 (PDCosts)

SECTION 1 – INTRODUCTION

1.1 This practice direction supplements Parts 43 to 48 of the Civil Procedure Rules. It applies to all proceedings to which those Parts apply.

1.2 Paragraphs 57.1 to 57.9 of this practice direction deal with various transitional provisions affecting proceedings about costs.

1.3 Attention is drawn to the powers to make orders about costs conferred on the Supreme Court and any county court by section 51 of the Supreme Court Act 1981.

1.4 In these Directions –

'counsel' means a barrister or other person with a right of audience in relation to all proceedings in the High Court or in the county courts in which he is instructed to act.

'LSC' means Legal Services Commission.

'solicitor' means a solicitor of the Supreme Court or other person with a right of audience in relation to proceedings, who is conducting the claim or defence (as the case may be) on behalf of a party to the proceedings and, where the context admits, includes a patent agent.

1.5 In respect of any document which is required by these Directions to be signed by a party or his legal representative the practice direction supplementing Part 22 will apply as if the document in question was a statement of truth. (The practice direction supplementing Part 22 makes provision for cases in which a party is a child, a patient or a company or other corporation and cases in which a document is signed on behalf of a partnership).

****

PART V

SECTION 3 – MODEL FORMS FOR CLAIMS FOR COSTS

Rule 43.3 Meaning of Summary Assessment

3.1 Rule 43.3 defines summary assessment. When carrying out a summary assessment of costs where there is an additional liability the court may assess the base costs alone, or the base costs and the additional liability.

3.2 Form N260 is a model form of Statement of Costs to be used for summary assessments.

3.3 Further details about Statements of Costs are given in paragraph 13.6 below.

Rule 43.4 Meaning of Detailed Assessment

3.4 Rule 43.4 defines detailed assessment. When carrying out a detailed assessment of costs where there is an additional liability the court will assess both the base costs and the additional liability, or, if the base costs have already been assessed, the additional liability alone.

3.5 Precedents A, B, C and D in the Schedule of Costs Precedents annexed to this practice direction are model forms of bills of costs to be used for detailed assessments.

3.6 Further details about bills of costs are given in the next section of these Directions and in paragraphs 27.1 to 48.1, below.

3.7 Precedents A, B, C and D in the Schedule of Costs Precedents and the next section of this practice direction all refer to a model form of bill of costs. The use of a model form is not compulsory, but is encouraged. A party wishing to rely upon a bill which departs from the model forms should include in the background information of the bill an explanation for that departure.

3.8 In any order of the court (whether made before or after 26 April 1999) the word 'taxation' will be taken to mean 'detailed assessment' and the words 'to be taxed' will be taken to mean 'to be decided by detailed assessment' unless in either case the context otherwise requires.

SECTION 4 – FORM AND CONTENTS OF BILLS OF COSTS

4.1 A bill of costs may consist of such of the following sections as may be appropriate –

(1) title page;
(2) background information;
(3) items of costs claimed under the headings specified in paragraph 4.6;
(4) summary showing the total costs claimed on each page of the bill;
(5) schedules of time spent on non-routine attendances; and
(6) the certificates referred to in paragraph 4.15.

4.2 Where it is necessary or convenient to do so, a bill of costs may be divided into two or more parts, each part containing sections (2), (3) and (4) above. A division into parts will be necessary or convenient in the following circumstances –

(1) Where the receiving party acted in person during the course of the proceedings (whether or not he also had a legal representative at that time) the bill should be divided into different parts so as to distinguish between;
   (a) the costs claimed for work done by the legal representative; and
   (b) the costs claimed for work done by the receiving party in person.

(2) Where the receiving party was represented by different solicitors during the course of the proceedings, the bill should be divided into different parts so as to distinguish between the costs payable in respect of each solicitor.

(3) Where the receiving party obtained legal aid or LSC funding in respect of all or part of the proceedings the bill should be divided into separate parts so as to distinguish between;

(a) costs claimed before legal aid or LSC funding was granted;
(b) costs claimed after legal aid or LSC funding was granted; and
(c) any costs claimed after legal aid or LSC funding ceased.

(4) Where value added tax (VAT) is claimed and there was a change in the rate of VAT during the course of the proceedings, the bill should be divided into separate parts so as to distinguish between;

(a) costs claimed at the old rate of VAT; and
(b) costs claimed at the new rate of VAT.

(5) Where the bill covers costs payable under an order or orders under which there are different paying parties the bill should be divided into parts so as to deal separately with the costs payable by each paying party.

(6) Where the bill covers costs payable under an order or orders, in respect of which the receiving party wishes to claim interest from different dates, the bill should be divided to enable such interest to be calculated.

4.3 Where a party claims costs against another party and also claims costs against the LSC only for work done in the same period, the costs claimed against the LSC only can be claimed either in a separate part of the bill or in additional columns in the same part of the bill. Precedents C and D in the Schedule of Costs Precedents annexed to this practice direction show how bills should be drafted when costs are claimed against the LSC only.

4.4 The title page of the bill of costs must set out –

(1) the full title of the proceedings;
(2) the name of the party whose bill it is and a description of the document showing the right to assessment (as to which see paragraph 40.4, below);
(3) if VAT is included as part of the claim for costs, the VAT number of the legal representative or other person in respect of whom VAT is claimed;
(4) details of all legal aid certificates, LSC certificates and relevant amendment certificates in respect of which claims for costs are included in the bill.

4.5 The background information included in the bill of costs should set out –

(1) a brief description of the proceedings up to the date of the notice of commencement;
(2) a statement of the status of the solicitor or solicitor's employee in respect of whom costs are claimed and (if those costs are calculated on the basis of hourly rates) the hourly rates claimed for each such person.

It should be noted that 'legal executive' means a Fellow of the Institute of Legal Executives.

Other clerks, who are fee earners of equivalent experience, may be entitled to similar rates. It should be borne in mind that Fellows of the Institute of Legal Executives will have spent approximately 6 years in practice, and taken both general and specialist examinations. The Fellows have therefore acquired considerable practical and academic experience.

Clerks without the equivalent experience of legal executives will normally be treated as being the equivalent of trainee solicitors and para-legals.

(3) a brief explanation of any agreement or arrangement between the receiving party and his solicitors which affects the costs claimed in the bill.

4.6 The bill of costs may consist of items under such of the following heads as may be appropriate –

(1) attendances on the court and counsel up to the date of the notice of commencement;
(2) attendances on and communications with the receiving party;
(3) attendances on and communications with witnesses including any expert witness;
(4) attendances to inspect any property or place for the purposes of the proceedings;
(5) attendances on and communications with other persons, including offices of public records;
(6) communications with the court and with counsel;
(7) work done on documents: preparing and considering documentation, including documentation relating to pre-action protocols where appropriate, work done in connection with arithmetical calculations of compensation and/or interest and time spent collating documents;
(8) work done in connection with negotiations with a view to settlement if not already covered in the heads listed above;
(9) attendances on and communications with London and other agents and work done by them;
(10) other work done which was of or incidental to the proceedings and which is not already covered in the heads listed above.

4.7 In respect of each of the heads of costs –

(1) 'communications' means letters out and telephone calls;
(2) communications which are not routine communications must be set out in chronological order;
(3) routine communications should be set out as a single item at the end of each head.

4.8 Routine communications are letters out, e-mails out and telephone calls which because of their simplicity should not be regarded as letters or e-mails of substance or telephone calls which properly amount to an attendance.

4.9 Each item claimed in the bill of costs must be consecutively numbered.

4.10 In each part of the bill of costs which claims items under head (1) (attendances on court and counsel) a note should be made of –

(1) all relevant events, including events which do not constitute chargeable items;
(2) any orders for costs which the court made (whether or not a claim is made in respect of those costs in this bill of costs).

4.11 The numbered items of costs may be set out on paper divided into columns. Precedents A, B, C and D in the Schedule of Costs Precedents annexed to this practice direction illustrate various model forms of bills of costs.

4.12 In respect of heads (2) to (10) in paragraph 4.6 above, if the number of attendances and communications other than routine communications is twenty or more, the claim for the costs of those items in that section of the bill of costs should be for the total only and should refer to a schedule in which the full record of dates and details is set out. If the bill of costs contains more than one schedule each schedule should be numbered consecutively.

4.13 The bill of costs must not contain any claims in respect of costs or court fees which relate solely to the detailed assessment proceedings other than costs claimed for preparing and checking the bill.

4.14 The summary must show the total profit costs and disbursements claimed separately from the total VAT claimed. Where the bill of costs is divided into parts the summary must also give totals for each part. If each page of the bill gives a page total the summary must also set out the page totals for each page.

4.15 The bill of costs must contain such of the certificates, the texts of which are set out in Precedent F of the Schedule of Costs Precedents annexed to this practice direction, as are appropriate.

4.16 The following provisions relate to work done by solicitors –

(1) Routine letters out and routine telephone calls will in general be allowed on a unit basis of 6 minutes each, the charge being calculated by reference to the appropriate hourly rate. The unit charge for letters out will include perusing and considering the relevant letters in and no separate charge should be made for incoming letters.

(2) E-mails received by solicitors will not normally be allowed. The court may, in its discretion, allow an actual time charge for preparation of e-mails sent by solicitors which properly amount to attendances provided that the time taken has been recorded. The court may also, in its discretion, allow a sum in respect of routine e-mails sent to the client or others on a unit basis of 6 minutes each, the charge being calculated by reference to the appropriate hourly rate.

(3) Local travelling expenses incurred by solicitors will not be allowed. The definition of 'local' is a matter for the discretion of the court. While no absolute rule can be laid down, as a matter of guidance, 'local' will, in general, be taken to mean within a radius of 10 miles from the court dealing with the case at the relevant time. Where travelling and waiting time is claimed, this should be allowed at the rate agreed with the client unless this is more than the hourly rate on the assessment.

(4) The cost of postage, couriers, out-going telephone calls, fax and telex messages will in general not be allowed but the court may exceptionally in its discretion allow such expenses in unusual circumstances or where the cost is unusually heavy.

(5) The cost of making copies of documents will not in general be allowed but the court may exceptionally in its discretion make an allowance for copying in unusual circumstances or where the documents copied are unusually numerous in relation to the nature of the case. Where this discretion is invoked the number of copies made, their purpose and the costs claimed for them must be set out in the bill.

(6) Agency charges as between a principal solicitor and his agent will be dealt with on the principle that such charges, where appropriate, form part of the principal solicitor's charges. Where these charges relate to head (1) in paragraph 4.6 (attendances at court and on counsel) they should be included in their chronological order in that head. In other cases they should be included in head (9) (attendances on London and other agents).

4.17

(1) Where a claim is made for a percentage increase in addition to an hourly rate or base fee, the amount of the increase must be shown separately, either in the appropriate arithmetic column or in the narrative column. (For an example see Precedent A or Precedent B.)

(2) Where a claim is made against the LSC only and includes enhancement and where a claim is made in family proceedings and includes a claim for uplift or general care and conduct, the amount of enhancement, uplift and general care and conduct must be shown, in respect of each item upon which it is claimed, as a separate amount either in the appropriate arithmetic column or in the narrative column. (For an example, see Precedent C.)

'Enhancement' means the increase in prescribed rates which may be allowed by a costs officer in accordance with the Legal Aid in Civil Proceedings (Remuneration) Regulations 1994 or the Legal Aid in Family Proceedings Regulations 1991.

Costs of preparing the bill

4.18 A claim may be made for the reasonable costs of preparing and checking the bill of costs.

****

SECTION 6 – ESTIMATES OF COSTS

6.1 This section sets out certain steps which parties and their legal representatives must take in order to keep the parties informed about their potential liability in respect of costs and in order to assist the court to decide what, if any, order to make about costs and about case management.

6.2

(1) In this section an 'estimate of costs' means –

(a) an estimate of base costs (including disbursements) already incurred; and

(b) an estimate of base costs (including disbursements) to be incurred,

which a party intends to seek to recover from any other party under an order for costs if he is successful in the case. ('Base costs' are defined in paragraphs 2.2 of this practice direction.)

(2) A party who intends to seek to recover an additional liability (defined in rule 43.2) need not reveal the amount of that liability in the estimate.

6.3 The court may at any stage in a case order any party to file an estimate of base costs and to serve copies of the estimate on all other parties. The court may direct that the estimate be prepared in such a way as to demonstrate the likely effects of giving or not giving a particular case management direction which the court is considering, for example a direction for a split trial or for the trial of a preliminary issue. The court may specify a time-limit for filing and serving the estimate. However, if no time-limit is specified the estimate should be filed and served within 28 days of the date of the order.

6.4

(1) When a party to a claim which is outside the financial scope of the small claims track, files an allocation questionnaire, he must also file an estimate of base costs and serve a copy of it on every other party, unless

the court otherwise directs. The legal representative must in addition serve an estimate upon the party he represents.

(2) Where a party to a claim which is being dealt with on the fast track or the multi track, or under Part 8, files a pre-trial check list (listing questionnaire), he must also file an estimate of base costs and serve a copy of it on every other party, unless the court otherwise directs. Where a party is represented, the legal representative must in addition serve an estimate on the party he represents.

(3) This paragraph does not apply to litigants in person.

6.5 An estimate of base costs should be substantially in the form illustrated in Precedent H of the Schedule of Costs Precedents annexed to this practice direction.

6.6 On an assessment of the costs of a party the court may have regard to any estimate previously filed by that party, or by any other party in the same proceedings. Such an estimate may be taken into account as a factor among others, when assessing the reasonableness of any costs claimed.

Directions Relating to Part 44 – General Rules About Costs

SECTION 7 – SOLICITOR'S DUTY TO NOTIFY CLIENT: RULE 44.2

7.1 For the purposes of rule 44.2 'client' includes a party for whom a solicitor is acting and any other person (for example, an insurer, a trade union or the LSC) who has instructed the solicitor to act or who is liable to pay his fees.

7.2 Where a solicitor notifies a client of an order under that rule, he must also explain why the order came to be made.

7.3 Although rule 44.2 does not specify any sanction for breach of the rule the court may, either in the order for costs itself or in a subsequent order, require the solicitor to produce to the court evidence showing that he took reasonable steps to comply with the rule.

SECTION 8 – COURT'S DISCRETION AND CIRCUMSTANCES TO BE TAKEN INTO ACCOUNT WHEN EXERCISING ITS DISCRETION AS TO COSTS: RULE 44.3

8.1 Attention is drawn to the factors set out in this rule which may lead the court to depart from the general rule stated in rule 44.3(2) and to make a different order about costs.

8.2 In a probate claim where a defendant has in his defence given notice that he requires the will to be proved in solemn form (see paragraph 8.3 of the Contentious Probate practice direction supplementing Part 49), the court will not make an order for costs against the defendant unless it appears that there was no reasonable ground for opposing the will. The term 'probate claim' is defined in paragraph 1.2 of the Contentious Probate practice direction.

8.3

(1) The court may make an order about costs at any stage in a case.

(2) In particular the court may make an order about costs when it deals with any application, makes any order or holds any hearing and that order about costs may relate to the costs of that application, order or hearing.

(3) Rule 44.3A(1) provides that the court will not assess any additional liability until the conclusion of the proceedings or the part of the proceedings to which the funding arrangement relates. (Paras 2.4 and 2.5 above explain when proceedings are concluded. As to the time when detailed assessment may be carried out see para 28.1, below.)

8.4 In deciding what order to make about costs the court is required to have regard to all the circumstances including any payment into court or admissible offer to settle made by a party which is drawn to the court's attention (whether or not it is made in accordance with Part 36). Where a claimant has made a Part 36 offer and fails to obtain a judgment which is more advantageous than that offer, that circumstance alone will not lead to a reduction in the costs awarded to the claimant under this rule.

8.5 There are certain costs orders which the court will commonly make in proceedings before trial. The following table sets out the general effect of these orders. The table is not an exhaustive list of the orders which the court may make.

Term	Effect
Costs Costs in any event	The party in whose favour the order is made is entitled to the costs in respect of the part of the proceedings to which the order relates, whatever other costs orders are made in the proceedings.
Costs in the case Costs in the application	The party in whose favour the court makes an order for costs at the end of the proceedings is entitled to his costs of the part of the proceedings to which the order relates.
Costs reserved	The decision about costs is deferred to a later occasion, but if no later order is made the costs will be costs in the case.
Claimant's/ defendant's costs in the case/ application	If the party in whose favour the costs order is made is awarded costs at the end of the proceedings, that party is entitled to his costs of the part of the proceedings to which the order relates. If any other party is awarded costs at the end of the proceedings, the party in whose favour the final costs order is made is not liable to pay the costs of any other party in respect of the part of the proceedings to which the order relates.

Term	Effect
Costs thrown away	Where, for example, a judgment or order is set aside, the party in whose favour the costs order is made is entitled to the costs which have been incurred as a consequence. This includes the costs of – (a) preparing for and attending any hearing at which the judgment or order which has been set aside was made; (b) preparing for and attending any hearing to set aside the judgment or order in question; (c) preparing for and attending any hearing at which the court orders the proceedings or the part in question to be adjourned; (d) any steps taken to enforce a judgment or order which has subsequently been set aside.
Costs of and caused by	Where, for example, the court makes this order on an application to amend a statement of case, the party in whose favour the costs order is made is entitled to the costs of preparing for and attending the application and the costs of any consequential amendment to his own statement of case.
Costs here and below	The party in whose favour the costs order is made is entitled not only to his costs in respect of the proceedings in which the court makes the order but also to his costs of the proceedings in any lower court. In the case of an appeal from a Divisional Court the party is not entitled to any costs incurred in any court below the Divisional Court.
No order as to costs Each party to pay his own costs	Each party is to bear his own costs of the part of the proceedings to which the order relates whatever costs order the court makes at the end of the proceedings.

8.6 Where, under rule 44.3(8), the court orders an amount to be paid before costs are assessed –

(1) the order will state that amount, and
(2) if no other date for payment is specified in the order rule 44.8 (Time for complying with an order for costs) will apply.

Fees of counsel

8.7

(1) This paragraph applies where the court orders the detailed assessment of the costs of a hearing at which one or more counsel appeared for a party.

(2) Where an order for costs states the opinion of the court as to whether or not the hearing was fit for the attendance of one or more counsel, a costs officer conducting a detailed assessment of costs to which that order relates will have regard to the opinion stated.

(3) The court will generally express an opinion only where –

(a) the paying party asks it to do so;

(b) more than one counsel appeared for the party or,

(c) the court wishes to record its opinion that the case was not fit for the attendance of counsel.

Fees payable to conveyancing counsel appointed by the court to assist it

8.8

(1) Where the court refers any matter to the conveyancing counsel of the court the fees payable to counsel in respect of the work done or to be done will be assessed by the court in accordance with rule 44.3.

(2) An appeal from a decision of the court in respect of the fees of such counsel will be dealt with under the general rules as to appeals set out in Part 52. If the appeal is against the decision of an authorised court officer, it will be dealt with in accordance with rules 47.20 to 47.23.

****

SECTION 11 – FACTORS TO BE TAKEN INTO ACCOUNT IN DECIDING THE AMOUNT OF COSTS: RULE 44.5

11.1 In applying the test of proportionality the court will have regard to rule 1.1(2)(c). The relationship between the total of the costs incurred and the financial value of the claim may not be a reliable guide. A fixed percentage cannot be applied in all cases to the value of the claim in order to ascertain whether or not the costs are proportionate.

11.2 In any proceedings there will be costs which will inevitably be incurred and which are necessary for the successful conduct of the case. Solicitors are not required to conduct litigation at rates which are uneconomic. Thus in a modest claim the proportion of costs is likely to be higher than in a large claim, and may even equal or possibly exceed the amount in dispute.

11.3 Where a trial takes place, the time taken by the court in dealing with a particular issue may not be an accurate guide to the amount of time properly spent by the legal or other representatives in preparation for the trial of that issue.

11.4 Where a party has entered into a funding arrangement the costs claimed may, subject to rule 44.3B include an additional liability.

11.5 In deciding whether the costs claimed are reasonable and (on a standard basis assessment) proportionate, the court will consider the amount of any additional liability separately from the base costs.

11.6 In deciding whether the base costs are reasonable and (if relevant) proportionate the court will consider the factors set out in rule 44.5.

11.7 Subject to paragraph 17.8(2), when the court is considering the factors to be taken into account in assessing an additional liability, it will have regard to the facts and circumstances as they reasonably appeared to the solicitor or counsel when the funding arrangement was entered into and at the time of any variation of the arrangement.

11.8

(1) In deciding whether a percentage increase is reasonable relevant factors to be taken into account may include –
  (a) the risk that the circumstances in which the costs, fees or expenses would be payable might or might not occur;
  (b) the legal representative's liability for any disbursements;
  (c) what other methods of financing the costs were available to the receiving party.

(2) The court has the power, when considering whether a percentage increase is reasonable, to allow different percentages for different items of costs or for different periods during which costs were incurred.

11.9 A percentage increase will not be reduced simply on the ground that, when added to base costs which are reasonable and (where relevant) proportionate, the total appears disproportionate.

11.10 In deciding whether the cost of insurance cover is reasonable, relevant factors to be taken into account include:

(1) where the insurance cover is not purchased in support of a conditional fee agreement with a success fee, how its cost compares with the likely cost of funding the case with a conditional fee agreement with a success fee and supporting insurance cover;
(2) the level and extent of the cover provided;
(3) the availability of any pre-existing insurance cover;
(4) whether any part of the premium would be rebated in the event of early settlement;
(5) the amount of commission payable to the receiving party or his legal representatives or other agents.

11.11 Where the court is considering a provision made by a membership organisation, rule 44.3B(1) (b) provides that any such provision which exceeds the likely cost to the receiving party of the premium of an insurance policy against the risk of incurring a liability to pay the costs of other parties to the proceedings is not recoverable. In such circumstances the court will, when assessing the additional liability, have regard to the factors set out in paragraph 11.10 above, in addition to the factors set out in rule 44.5.

SECTION 12 – PROCEDURE FOR ASSESSING COSTS: RULE 44.7

12.1 Where the court does not order fixed costs (or no fixed costs are provided for) the amount of costs payable will be assessed by the court. This rule allows the court making an order about costs either –

  (a) to make a summary assessment of the amount of the costs, or
  (b) to order the amount to be decided in accordance with Part 47 (a detailed assessment).

12.2 An order for costs will be treated as an order for the amount of costs to be decided by a detailed assessment unless the order otherwise provides.

12.3 Whenever the court awards costs to be assessed by way of detailed assessment it should consider whether to exercise the power in rule 44.3(8) (Courts Discretion as to Costs) to order the paying party to pay such sum of money as it thinks just on account of those costs.

SECTION 13 – SUMMARY ASSESSMENT: GENERAL PROVISIONS

13.1 Whenever a court makes an order about costs which does not provide for fixed costs to be paid the court should consider whether to make a summary assessment of costs.

13.2 The general rule is that the court should make a summary assessment of the costs –

(1) at the conclusion of the trial of a case which has been dealt with on the fast track, in which case the order will deal with the costs of the whole claim, and
(2) at the conclusion of any other hearing, which has lasted not more than 1 day, in which case the order will deal with the costs of the application or matter to which the hearing related. If this hearing disposes of the claim, the order may deal with the costs of the whole claim;
(3) in hearings in the Court of Appeal to which paragraph 14 of the practice direction supplementing Part 52 (Appeals) applies

unless there is good reason not to do so, eg where the paying party shows substantial grounds for disputing the sum claimed for costs that cannot be dealt with summarily or there is insufficient time to carry out a summary assessment.

13.3 The general rule in paragraph 13.2 does not apply to a mortgagee's costs incurred in mortgage possession proceedings or other proceedings relating to a mortgage unless the mortgagee asks the court to make an order for his costs to be paid by another party. Paragraphs 50.3 and 50.4 deal in more detail with costs relating to mortgages.

13.4 Where an application has been made and the parties to the application agree an order by consent without any party attending, the parties should agree a figure for costs to be inserted in the consent order or agree that there should be no order for costs. If the parties cannot agree the costs position, attendance on the appointment will be necessary but, unless good reason can be shown for the failure to deal with costs as set out above, no costs will be allowed for that attendance.

13.5

(1) It is the duty of the parties and their legal representatives to assist the judge in making a summary assessment of costs in any case to which paragraph 13.2 above applies, in accordance with the following paragraphs.
(2) Each party who intends to claim costs must prepare a written statement of the costs he intends to claim showing separately in the form of a schedule –
    (a) the number of hours to be claimed,
    (b) the hourly rate to be claimed,
    (c) the grade of fee earner;
    (d) the amount and nature of any disbursement to be claimed, other than counsel's fee for appearing at the hearing,
    (e) the amount of solicitor's costs to be claimed for attending or appearing at the hearing,
    (f) the fees of counsel to be claimed in respect of the hearing, and
    (g) any value added tax (VAT) to be claimed on these amounts.

(3) The statement of costs should follow as closely as possible Form N260 and must be signed by the party or his legal representative. Where a litigant is an assisted person or is a LSC funded client or is represented by a solicitor in the litigant's employment the statement of costs need not include the certificate appended at the end of Form N260.

(4) The statement of costs must be filed at court and copies of it must be served on any party against whom an order for payment of those costs is intended to be sought. The statement of costs should be filed and the copies of it should be served as soon as possible and in any event not less than 24 hours before the date fixed for the hearing.

(5) Where the litigant is or may be entitled to claim an additional liability the statement filed and served need not reveal the amount of that liability.

13.6 The failure by a party, without reasonable excuse, to comply with the foregoing paragraphs will be taken into account by the court in deciding what order to make about the costs of the claim, hearing or application, and about the costs of any further hearing or detailed assessment hearing that may be necessary as a result of that failure.

13.7 If the court makes a summary assessment of costs at the conclusion of proceedings the court will specify separately –

(1) the base costs, and if appropriate, the additional liability allowed as solicitor's charges, counsel's fees, other disbursements and any VAT; and

(2) the amount which is awarded under Part 46 (Fast Track Trial Costs).

13.8 The court awarding costs cannot make an order for a summary assessment of costs by a costs officer. If a summary assessment of costs is appropriate but the court awarding costs is unable to do so on the day, the court must give directions as to a further hearing before the same judge.

13.9 The court will not make a summary assessment of the costs of a receiving party who is an assisted person or LSC funded client.

13.10 A summary assessment of costs payable by an assisted person or LSC funded client is not by itself a determination of that person's liability to pay those costs (as to which see rule 44.17 and paragraphs 21.1 to 23.17 of this practice direction).

13.11

(1) The court will not make a summary assessment of the costs of a receiving party who is a child or patient within the meaning of Part 21 unless the solicitor acting for the child or patient has waived the right to further costs (see paragraph 51.1 below).

(2) The court may make a summary assessment of costs payable by a child or patient.

13.12

(1) Attention is drawn to rule 44.3A which prevents the court from making a summary assessment of an additional liability before the conclusion of the proceedings or the part of the proceedings to which the funding arrangement relates. Where this applies, the court should nonetheless make a summary assessment of the base costs of the hearing or application unless there is a good reason not to do so.

(2) Where the court makes a summary assessment of the base costs all statements of costs and costs estimates put before the judge must be retained on the court file.

PART V

13.13 The court will not give its approval to disproportionate and unreasonable costs. Accordingly –

(a) When the amount of the costs to be paid has been agreed between the parties the order for costs must state that the order is by consent.
(b) If the judge is to make an order which is not by consent, the judge will, so far as possible, ensure that the final figure is not disproportionate and/or unreasonable having regard to Part 1 of the CPR. The judge will retain this responsibility notwithstanding the absence of challenge to individual items in the make-up of the figure sought. The fact that the paying party is not disputing the amount of costs can however be taken as some indication that the amount is proportionate and reasonable. The judge will therefore intervene only if satisfied that the costs are so disproportionate that it is right to do so.

****

SECTION 18 – COURT'S POWERS IN RELATION TO MISCONDUCT: RULE 44.14

18.1 Before making an order under rule 44.14 the court must give the party or legal representative in question a reasonable opportunity to attend a hearing to give reasons why it should not make such an order.

18.2 Conduct before or during the proceedings which gave rise to the assessment which is unreasonable or improper includes steps which are calculated to prevent or inhibit the court from furthering the overriding objective.

18.3 Although rule 44.14(3) does not specify any sanction for breach of the obligation imposed by the rule the court may, either in the order under paragraph (2) or in a subsequent order, require the solicitor to produce to the court evidence that he took reasonable steps to comply with the obligation.

****

SECTION 21 – APPLICATION OF COSTS RULES: RULE 44.17

21.1 Rule 44.17(b) excludes the costs rules to the extent that regulations under the Legal Aid Act 1988 make different provision. The primary examples of such regulations are the regulations providing prescribed rates (with or without enhancement).

21.2 Rule 44.17(a) also excludes the procedure for the detailed assessment of costs in cases to which section 11 of the Access to Justice Act 1999 applies, whether it applies in whole or in part. In these excluded cases the procedure for determination of costs is set out in Section 22 of this practice direction.

21.3 Section 11 of the Access to Justice Act 1999 provides special protection against liability for costs for litigants who receive funding by the LSC (Legal Services Commission) as part of the Community Legal Service. Any costs ordered to be paid by a LSC funded client must not exceed the amount which is reasonable to pay having regard to all the circumstances including –

(a) the financial resources of all the parties to the proceedings, and
(b) their conduct in connection with the dispute to which the proceedings relate.

21.4 In this practice direction

'cost protection' means the limit on costs awarded against a LSC funded client set out in section 11(1) of the Access to Justice Act 1999.

'partner' has the meaning given by the Community Legal Service (Costs) Regulations 2000.

21.5 Whether or not cost protection applies depends upon the 'level of service' for which funding was provided by the LSC in accordance with the Funding Code approved under section 9 of the Access to Justice Act 1999. The levels of service referred to are:

(1) Legal Help – advice and assistance about a legal problem, not including representation or advocacy in proceedings.
(2) Help at Court – advocacy at a specific hearing, where the advocate is not formally representing the client in the proceedings.
(3) Family Mediation.
(4) Legal Representation – representation in actual or contemplated proceedings. Legal Representation can take the form of Investigative Help (limited to investigating the merits of a potential claim) or Full Representation.
(5) Approved Family Help – this can take the form of Help with Mediation (legal advice in support of the family mediation process) or General Family Help (help negotiating a settlement to a family dispute without recourse to adversarial litigation).
(6) Support Funding – partial funding in expensive cases that are primarily being funded privately, under or with a view to a conditional fee agreement. Support Funding can take the form of Investigative Support (equivalent to *Investigative Help*) or Litigation Support (equivalent to *Full Representation*).

21.6 Levels of service (4) (5) and (6) are provided under a certificate (similar to a legal aid certificate). The certificate will state which level of service is covered. Where there are proceedings, a copy of the certificate will be lodged with the court.

21.7 Cost protection does not apply where –

(1) The LSC funded client receives Help at Court;
(2) the LSC funded client receives Litigation Support (but see further, paragraph 21.8);
(3) the LSC funded client receives Investigative Support (except where the proceedings for which Investigative Support was given are not pursued after the certificate is discharged). Investigative Support will not normally cover the issue of proceedings (except for disclosure), but cost protection may be relevant if the defendant seeks an assessment of pre-action costs;
(4) the LSC funded client receives Legal Help only, ie where the solicitor is advising, but not representing a litigant in person. However, where the LSC funded client receives Legal Help, eg to write a letter before action, but later receives Legal Representation or Approved Family Help in respect of the same dispute, cost protection does apply to all costs incurred by the receiving party in the funded proceedings or prospective proceedings.

21.8 Where cost protection does not apply, the court may award costs in the normal way. In the case of Litigation Support, costs that are not covered by the LSC funded client's insurance are usually payable by the LSC rather than the funded client, and the court should order accordingly (see Regulation 6 of the Community Legal Service (Cost Protection) Regulations 2000).

21.9 Where work is done before the issue of a certificate, cost protection does not apply to those costs, except where –

(1) pre-action Legal Help is given and the LSC funded client subsequently receives Legal Representation or Approved Family Help in the same dispute; or
(2) where urgent work is undertaken immediately before the grant of an emergency certificate when no emergency application could be made as the LSC's offices were closed, provided that the solicitor seeks an emergency certificate at the first available opportunity and the certificate is granted.

21.10 If a LSC funded client's certificate is revoked, cost protection does not apply to work done before or after revocation.

21.11 If a LSC funded client's certificate is discharged, cost protection only applies to costs incurred before the date on which funded services ceased to be provided under the certificate. This may be a date before the date on which the certificate is formally discharged by the LSC (*Burridge v Stafford: Khan v Ali* [2000] 1 WLR 927, [1999] 4 All ER 660, CA).

Assessing a LSC Funded Client's Resources

21.12 The first £100,000 of the value of the LSC funded client's interest in the main or only home is disregarded when assessing his or her financial resources for the purposes of S.11 and cannot be the subject of any enforcement process by the receiving party. The receiving party cannot apply for an order to sell the LSC funded client's home, but could secure the debt against any value exceeding £100,000 by way of a charging order.

21.13 The court may only take into account the value of the LSC funded client's clothes, household furniture, tools and implements of trade to the extent that it considers that having regard to the quantity or value of the items, the circumstances are exceptional.

21.14 The LSC funded client's resources include the resources of his or her partner, unless the partner has a contrary interest in the dispute in respect of which funded services are provided.

Party acting in a Representative, Fiduciary or Official Capacity

21.15

(1) Where a LSC funded client is acting in a representative, fiduciary or official capacity, the court shall not take the personal resources of the party into account for the purposes of either a Section 11 order or costs against the Commission, but shall have regard to the value of any property or estate or the amount of any fund out of which the party is entitled to be indemnified, and may also have regard to the resources of any persons who are beneficially interested in the property, estate or fund.
(2) The purpose of this provision is to ensure that any liability is determined with reference to the value of the property or fund being used to pay for the litigation, and the financial position of those who may benefit from or rely on it.

Costs against the LSC

21.16 Regulation 5 of the Community Legal Service (Cost Protection) Regulations 2000 governs when costs can be awarded against the LSC. This provision only applies where cost protection applies and the costs ordered to be paid by the LSC funded client do not fully meet the costs that would have been ordered to be paid by him or her if cost protection did not apply.

21.17 In this section and the following two sections of this practice direction 'non-funded party' means a party to proceedings who has not received LSC funded services in relation to these proceedings under a legal aid certificate or a certificate issued under the LSC Funding Code other than a certificate which has been revoked.

21.18 The following criteria set out in Regulation 5 must be satisfied before the LSC can be ordered to pay the whole or any part of the costs incurred by a non-funded party –

(1) the proceedings are finally decided in favour of a non-funded party;
(2) the non-funded party provides written notice of intention to seek an order against the LSC within 3 months of the making of the section 11(1) costs order;
(3) the court is satisfied that it is just and equitable in the circumstances that provision for the costs should be made out of public funds; and
(4) where costs are incurred in a court of first instance, the following additional criteria must also be met –
  (i) the proceedings were instituted by the LSC funded client; and
  (ii) the non-funded party will suffer severe financial hardship unless the order is made.

('Section 11(1) costs order' is defined in paragraph 22.1, below.)

21.19 In determining whether conditions (3) and (4) are satisfied, the court shall take into account the resources of the non-funded party and his partner (unless the partner has a contrary interest).

Effect of Appeals

21.20

(1) An order for costs can only be made against the LSC when the proceedings (including any appeal) are finally decided. Therefore, where a court of first instance decides in favour of a non-funded party and an appeal lies, any order made against the LSC shall not take effect until –
  (a) where permission to appeal is required, the time-limit for permission to appeal expires, without permission being granted;
  (b) where permission to appeal is granted or is not required, the time-limit for appeal expires without an appeal being brought.

(2) This means that, if the LSC funded client appeals, any earlier order against the LSC can never take effect. If the appeal is unsuccessful, the court can make a fresh order.

SECTION 22 – ORDERS FOR COSTS TO WHICH SECTION 11 OF THE ACCESS TO JUSTICE ACT 1999 APPLIES

22.1 In this practice direction:

'order for costs to be determined' means an order for costs to which section 11 of the Access to Justice Act 1999 applies under which the amount of costs payable by the LSC funded client is to be determined by a costs judge or district judge under Section 23 of this practice direction.

'order specifying the costs payable' means an order for costs to which section 11 of the Act applies and which specifies the amount which the LSC funded client is to pay.

'full costs' means, where an order to which section 11 of the Act applies is made against a LSC funded client, the amount of costs which that person would, had cost protection not applied, have been ordered to pay.

'determination proceedings' means proceedings to which paragraphs 22.1 to 22.10 apply.

'Section 11(1) costs order' means an order for costs to be determined or an order specifying the costs payable other than an order specifying the costs payable which was made in determination proceedings.

'statement of resources' means

(1) a statement, verified by a statement of truth, made by a party to proceedings setting out:
  (a) his income and capital and financial commitments during the previous year and, if applicable, those of his partner;
  (b) his estimated future financial resources and expectations and, if applicable, those of his partner ('partner' is defined in paragraph 21.4, above);
  (c) a declaration that he and, if applicable, his partner, has not deliberately foregone or deprived himself of any resources or expectations;
  (d) particulars of any application for funding made by him in connection with the proceedings; and,
  (e) any other facts relevant to the determination of his resources;

or

(2) a statement, verified by a statement of truth, made by a client receiving funded services, setting out the information provided by the client under Regulation 6 of the Community Legal Service (Financial) Regulations 2000, and stating that there has been no significant change in the client's financial circumstances since the date on which the information was provided or, as the case may be, details of any such change.

'Regional Director' means any Regional Director appointed by the LSC and any member of his staff authorised to act on his behalf.

22.2 Regulations 8 to 13 of the Community Legal Service (Costs) Regulations 2000 set out the procedure for seeking costs against a funded client and the LSC. The effect of these Regulations is set out in this section and the next section of this practice direction.

22.3 As from 5 June 2000, Regulations 9 to 13 of the Community Legal Service (Costs) Regulations 2000 also apply to certificates issued under the Legal Aid Act 1988 where costs against the assisted person fall to be assessed under Regulation 124 of the Civil Legal Aid (General) Regulations 1989. In this section and the next section of this practice direction the expression 'LSC funded client' includes an assisted person (defined in rule 43.2).

22.4 Regulation 8 of the Community Legal Service (Costs) Regulations 2000 provides that a party intending to seek an order for costs against a LSC funded client may at any time file and serve on the LSC funded client a statement of resources. If that statement is served 7 or more days before a date fixed for a hearing at which an order for costs may be made, the LSC funded client must also make a statement of resources and produce it at the hearing.

22.5 If the court decides to make an order for costs against a LSC funded client to whom cost protection applies it may either:

(1) make an order for costs to be determined, or
(2) make an order specifying the costs payable.

22.6 If the court makes an order for costs to be determined it may also:

(1) state the amount of full costs, or
(2) make findings of facts, eg, concerning the conduct of all the parties which are to be taken into account by the court in the subsequent determination proceedings.

22.7 The court will not make an order specifying the costs payable unless:

(1) it considers that it has sufficient information before it to decide what amount is a reasonable amount for the LSC funded client to pay in accordance with section 11 of the Act, and
(2) either
    (a) the order also states the amount of full costs, or
    (b) the court considers that it has sufficient information before it to decide what amount is a reasonable amount for the LSC funded client to pay in accordance with section 11 of the Act and is satisfied that, if it were to determine the full costs at that time, they would exceed the amounts specified in the order.

22.8 Where an order specifying the costs payable is made and the LSC funded client does not have cost protection in respect of all of the costs awarded in that order, the order must identify the sum payable (if any) in respect of which the LSC funded client has cost protection and the sum payable (if any) in respect of which he does not have cost protection.

22.9 The court cannot make an order under Regulations 8 to 13 of the Community Legal Service (Costs) Regulations 2000 except in proceedings to which the next section of this practice direction applies.

SECTION 23 – DETERMINATION PROCEEDINGS AND SIMILAR PROCEEDINGS UNDER THE COMMUNITY LEGAL SERVICE (COSTS) REGULATIONS 2000

23.1 This section of this practice direction deals with

(1) proceedings subsequent to the making of an order for costs to be determined,
(2) variations in the amount stated in an order specifying the amount of costs payable and
(3) the late determination of costs under an order for costs to be determined.

23.2 In this section of this practice direction 'appropriate court office' means:

(1) the district registry or county court in which the case was being dealt with when the Section 11(1) order was made, or to which it has subsequently been transferred; or
(2) in all other cases, the Supreme Court Costs Office.

23.3

(1) A receiving party seeking an order specifying costs payable by an LSC funded client and/or by the LSC may within 3 months of an order for costs to be determined, file in the appropriate court office an application in Form N244 accompanied by
    (a) the receiving party's bill of costs (unless the full costs have already been determined);
    (b) the receiving party's statement of resources; and

PART V

(c) if the receiving party intends to seek costs against the LSC, written notice to that effect.

(2) If the LSC funded client's liability has already been determined and is less than the full costs, the application will be for costs against the LSC only. If the LSC funded client's liability has not yet been determined, the receiving party must indicate if costs will be sought against the LSC if the funded client's liability is determined as less than the full costs.

(The LSC funded client's certificate will contain the addresses of the LSC funded client, his solicitor, and the relevant Regional Office of the LSC.)

23.4 The receiving party must file the above documents in the appropriate court office and (where relevant) serve copies on the LSC funded client and the Regional Director. Failure to file a request within the 3 months time-limit specified in Regulation 10(2) is an absolute bar to the making of a costs order against the LSC.

23.5 On being served with the application, the LSC funded client must respond by filing a statement of resources and serving a copy of it on the receiving party (and the Regional Director where relevant) within 21 days. The LSC funded client may also file and serve written points disputing the bill within the same time-limit. (Under rule 3.1 the court may extend or shorten this time-limit.)

23.6 If the LSC funded client fails to file a statement of resources without good reason, the court will determine his liability (and the amount of full costs if relevant) and need not hold an oral hearing for such determination.

23.7 When the LSC funded client files a statement or the 21 day period for doing so expires, the court will fix a hearing date and give the relevant parties at least 14 days notice. The court may fix a hearing without waiting for the expiry of the 21 day period if the application is made only against the LSC.

23.8 Determination proceedings will be listed for hearing before a costs judge or district judge.

23.9 Where the LSC funded client does not have cost protection in respect of all of the costs awarded, the order made by the costs judge or district judge must in addition to specifying the costs payable, identify the full costs in respect of which cost protection applies and the full costs in respect of which cost protection does not apply.

23.10 The Regional Director may appear at any hearing at which a costs order may be made against the LSC. Instead of appearing, he may file a written statement at court and serve a copy on the receiving party. The written statement should be filed and a copy served, not less than 7 days before the hearing.

Variation of an order specifying the costs payable

23.11

(1) This paragraph applies where the amount stated in an order specifying the costs payable plus the amount ordered to be paid by the LSC is less than the full costs to which cost protection applies.

(2) The receiving party may apply to the court for a variation of the amount which the LSC funded client is required to pay on the ground that there has been a significant change in the client's circumstances since the date of the order.

23.12 On an application under paragraph 23.11, where the order specifying the costs payable does not state the full costs

(1) the receiving party must file with his application the receiving party's statement of resources and bill of costs and copies of these documents should be served with the application.

(2) The LSC funded client must respond to the application by making a statement of resources which must be filed at court and served on the receiving party within 21 days thereafter. The LSC funded client may also file and serve written points disputing the bill within the same time-limit.

(3) The court will, when determining the application assess the full costs identifying any part of them to which cost protection does apply and any part of them to which cost protection does not apply.

23.13 On an application under paragraph 23.11 the order specifying the costs payable may be varied as the court thinks fit. That variation must not increase:

(1) the amount of any costs ordered to be paid by the LSC, and

(2) the amount payable by the LSC funded client,

to a sum which is greater than the amount of the full costs plus the costs of the application.

23.14

(1) Where an order for costs to be determined has been made but the receiving party has not applied, within the three month time-limit under paragraph 23.2, the receiving party may apply on any of the following grounds for a determination of the amount which the funded client is required to pay:

(a) there has been a significant change in the funded client's circumstances since the date of the order for costs to be determined; or

(b) material additional information about the funded client's financial resources is available which could not with reasonable diligence have been obtained by the receiving party at the relevant time; or

(c) there were other good reasons for the failure by the receiving party to make an application within the time-limit.

(2) An application for costs payable by the LSC cannot be made under this paragraph.

23.15

(1) Where the receiving party has received funded services in relation to the proceedings, the LSC may make an application under paragraphs 23.11 and 23.14 above.

(2) In respect of an application under paragraph 23.11 made by the LSC, the LSC must file and serve copies of the documents described in paragraph 23.12(1).

23.16 An application under paragraph 23.11, 23.14 and 23.15 must be commenced before the expiration of 6 years from the date on which the court made the order specifying the costs payable, or (as the case may be) the order for costs to be determined.

23.17 Applications under paragraphs 23.11, 23.14 and 23.15 should be made in the appropriate court office and should be made in Form N244 to be listed for a hearing before a costs judge or district judge.

****

Directions Relating to Part 47 – Procedure for Detailed Assessment of Costs and Default Provisions

SECTION 28 – TIME WHEN ASSESSMENT MAY BE CARRIED OUT: RULE 47.1

28.1

(1) For the purposes of rule 47.1, proceedings are concluded when the court has finally determined the matters in issue in the claim, whether or not there is an appeal.

(2) For the purposes of this rule, the making of an award of provisional damages under Part 41 will be treated as a final determination of the matters in issue.

(3) The court may order or the parties may agree in writing that, although the proceedings are continuing, they will nevertheless be treated as concluded.

(4) (a) A party who is served with a notice of commencement (see paragraph 32.3 below) may apply to a costs judge or a district judge to determine whether the party who served it is entitled to commence detailed assessment proceedings.

(b) On hearing such an application the orders which the court may make include: an order allowing the detailed assessment proceedings to continue, or an order setting aside the notice of commencement.

(5) A costs judge or a district judge may make an order allowing detailed assessment proceedings to be commenced where there is no realistic prospect of the claim continuing.

SECTION 29 – NO STAY OF DETAILED ASSESSMENT WHERE THERE IS AN APPEAL: RULE 47.2

29.1

(1) Rule 47.2 provides that detailed assessment is not stayed pending an appeal unless the court so orders.

(2) An application to stay the detailed assessment of costs pending an appeal may be made to the court whose order is being appealed or to the court who will hear the appeal.

SECTION 30 – POWERS OF AN AUTHORISED COURT OFFICER: RULE 47.3

30.1

(1) The court officers authorised by the Lord Chancellor to assess costs in the Supreme Court Costs Office and the Principal Registry of the Family Division are authorised to deal with claims for costs not exceeding £30,000 (excluding VAT) in the case of senior executive officers, or their equivalent, and £75,000 (excluding VAT) in the case of principal officers.

(2) In calculating whether or not a bill of costs is within the authorised amounts, the figure to be taken into account is the total claim for costs including any claim for additional liability.

(3) Where the receiving party, paying party and any other party to the detailed assessment proceedings who has served points of dispute are

agreed that the assessment should not be made by an authorised court officer, the receiving party should so inform the court when requesting a hearing date. The court will then list the hearing before a costs judge or a district judge.

(4) In any other case a party who objects to the assessment being made by an authorised court officer must make an application to the costs judge or district judge under Part 23 (General Rules about Applications for Court Orders) setting out the reasons for the objection and if sufficient reason is shown the court will direct that the bill be assessed by a costs judge or district judge.

SECTION 31 – VENUE FOR DETAILED ASSESSMENT PROCEEDINGS: RULE 47.4

31.1 For the purposes of rule 47.4(1) the 'appropriate office' means –

(1) the district registry or county court in which the case was being dealt with when the judgment or order was made or the event occurred which gave rise to the right to assessment, or to which it has subsequently been transferred; or

(2) in all other cases, including Court of Appeal cases, the Supreme Court Costs Office.

31.2

(1) A direction under rule 47.4(2) or (3) specifying a particular court, registry or office as the appropriate office may be given on application or on the court's own initiative.

(2) Before making such a direction on its own initiative the court will give the parties the opportunity to make representations.

(3) Unless the Supreme Court Costs Office is the appropriate office for the purposes of Rule 47.4(1) an order directing that an assessment is to take place at the Supreme Court Costs Office will be made only if it is appropriate to do so having regard to the size of the bill of costs, the difficulty of the issues involved, the likely length of the hearing, the cost to the parties and any other relevant matter.

SECTION 32 – COMMENCEMENT OF DETAILED ASSESSMENT PROCEEDINGS: RULE 47.6

32.1 Precedents A, B, C and D in the Schedule of Costs Precedents annexed to this practice direction are model forms of bills of costs for detailed assessment. Further information about bills of costs is set out in Section 4.

32.2 A detailed assessment may be in respect of:

(1) base costs, where a claim for additional liability has not been made or has been agreed;

(2) a claim for additional liability only, base costs having been summarily assessed or agreed;

or

(3) both base costs and additional liability.

32.3 If the detailed assessment is in respect of costs without any additional liability, the receiving party must serve on the paying party and all the other relevant persons the following documents:

(a) a notice of commencement;

(b) a copy of the bill of costs;

(c) copies of the fee notes of counsel and of any expert in respect of fees claimed in the bill;
(d) written evidence as to any other disbursement which is claimed and which exceeds £250;
(e) a statement giving the name and address for service of any person upon whom the receiving party intends to serve the notice of commencement.

32.4 If the detailed assessment is in respect of an additional liability only, the receiving party must serve on the paying party and all other relevant persons the following documents:

(a) a notice of commencement;
(b) a copy of the bill of costs;
(c) the relevant details of the additional liability;
(d) a statement giving the name and address of any person upon whom the receiving party intends to serve the notice of commencement.

32.5 The relevant details of an additional liability are as follows:
(1) In the case of a conditional fee agreement with a success fee:
(a) a statement showing the amount of costs which have been summarily assessed or agreed, and the percentage increase which has been claimed in respect of those costs;
(b) a statement of the reasons for the percentage increase goven in accordance with regulation 3(1)(a) of the Conditional Fee Agreements Regulations or regulation 5(1)(c) of the Collective Conditional Fee Agreements Regulations 2000.
(2) If the additional liability is an insurance premium: a copy of the insurance certificate showing whether the policy covers the receiving party's own costs; his opponents costs; or his own costs and his opponent's costs; and the maximum extent of that cover, and the amount of the premium paid or payable.
(3) If the receiving party claims an additional amount under section 30 of the Access of Justice Act 1999: a statement setting out the basis upon which the receiving party's liability for the additional amount is calculated.

32.6 Attention is drawn to the fact that the additional amount recoverable pursuant to section 30 of the Access to Justice Act 1999 in respect of a membership organisation must not exceed the likely cost of the premium of an insurance policy against the risk of incurring a liability to pay the costs of other parties to the proceedings as provided by the Access to Justice (Membership Organisation) Regulations 2000 Regulation 4.

32.7 If a detailed assessment is in respect of both base costs and an additional liability, the receiving party must serve on the paying party and all other relevant persons the documents listed in paragraph 32.3 and the documents giving relevant details of an additional liability listed in paragraph 32.5.

32.8
(1) The notice of commencement should be in Form N252.
(2) Before it is served, it must be completed to show as separate items:
(a) the total amount of the costs claimed in the bill;
(b) the extra sum which will be payable by way of fixed costs and court fees if a default costs certificate is obtained.

32.9
(1) This paragraph applies where the notice of commencement is to be served outside England and Wales.

(2) The date to be inserted in the notice of commencement for the paying party to send points of dispute is a date (not less than 21 days from the date of service of the notice) which must be calculated by reference to Part 6 Section III as if the notice were a claim form and as if the date to be inserted was the date for the filing of a defence.

32.10

(1) For the purposes of rule 47.6(2) a 'relevant person' means:
- (a) any person who has taken part in the proceedings which gave rise to the assessment and who is directly liable under an order for costs made against him;
- (b) any person who has given to the receiving party notice in writing that he has a financial interest in the outcome of the assessment and wishes to be a party accordingly;
- (c) any other person whom the court orders to be treated as such.

(2) Where a party is unsure whether a person is or is not a relevant person, that party may apply to the appropriate office for directions.

(3) The court will generally not make an order that the person in respect of whom the application is made will be treated as a relevant person, unless within a specified time he applies to the court to be joined as a party to the assessment proceedings in accordance with Part 19 (Parties and Group Litigation).

32.11

(1) This paragraph applies in cases in which the bill of costs is capable of being copied onto a computer disk.

(2) If, before the detailed assessment hearing, a paying party requests a disk copy of a bill to which this paragraph applies, the receiving party must supply him with a copy free of charge not more than 7 days after the date on which he received the request..

SECTION 33 – PERIOD FOR COMMENCING DETAILED ASSESSMENT PROCEEDINGS: RULE 47.7

33.1 The parties may agree under rule 2.11 (Time-limits may be varied by parties) to extend or shorten the time specified by rule 47.7 for commencing the detailed assessment proceedings.

33.2 A party may apply to the appropriate office for an order under rule 3.1(2)(a) to extend or shorten that time.

33.3 Attention is drawn to rule 47.6(1). The detailed assessment proceedings are commenced by service of the documents referred to.

33.4 Permission to commence assessment proceedings out of time is not required.

SECTION 34 – SANCTION FOR DELAY IN COMMENCING DETAILED ASSESSMENT PROCEEDINGS: RULE 47.8

34.1

(1) An application for an order under rule 47.8 must be made in writing and be issued in the appropriate office.

(2) The application notice must be served at least 7 days before the hearing.

SECTION 35 – POINTS OF DISPUTE AND CONSEQUENCES OF NOT SERVING: RULE 47.9

35.1 The parties may agree under rule 2.11 (Time-limits may be varied by parties) to extend or shorten the time specified by rule 47.9 for service of points of dispute. A party may apply to the appropriate office for an order under rule 3.1(2)(a) to extend or shorten that time.

35.2 Points of dispute should be short and to the point and should follow as closely as possible Precedent G of the Schedule of Costs Precedents annexed to this practice direction.

35.3 Points of dispute must –

(1) identify each item in the bill of costs which is disputed,
(2) in each case state concisely the nature and grounds of dispute,
(3) where practicable suggest a figure to be allowed for each item in respect of which a reduction is sought, and
(4) be signed by the party serving them or his solicitor.

35.4

(1) The normal period for serving points of dispute is 21 days after the date of service of the notice of commencement.
(2) Where a notice of commencement is served on a party outside England and Wales the period within which that party should serve points of dispute is to be calculated by reference to Part 6 Section III as if the notice of commencement was a claim form and as if the period for serving points of dispute were the period for filing a defence.

35.5 A party who serves points of dispute on the receiving party must at the same time serve a copy on every other party to the detailed assessment proceedings, whose name and address for service appears on the statement served by the receiving party in accordance with paragraph 32.3 or 32.4 above.

35.6

(1) This paragraph applies in cases in which points of dispute are capable of being copied onto a computer disk.
(2) If, within 14 days of the receipt of the points of dispute, the receiving party requests a disk copy of them, the paying party must supply him with a copy free of charge not more than 7 days after the date on which he received the request.

35.7

(1) Where the receiving party claims an additional liability, a party who serves points of dispute on the receiving party may include a request for information about other methods of financing costs which were available to the receiving party.
(2) Part 18 (further information) and the practice direction supplementing that part apply to such a request.

SECTION 36 – PROCEDURE WHERE COSTS ARE AGREED: RULE 47.10

36.1 Where the parties have agreed terms as to the issue of a costs certificate (either interim or final) they should apply under rule 40.6 (Consent judgments and orders) for an order that a certificate be issued in terms set out in the application. Such an application may be dealt with by a court officer, who may issue the certificate.

36.2 Where in the course of proceedings the receiving party claims that the paying party has agreed to pay costs but that he will neither pay those costs nor join in a consent application under paragraph 36.1, the receiving party may apply under Part 23 (General Rules about Applications for Court Orders) for a certificate either interim or final to be issued.

36.3 An application under paragraph 36.2 must be supported by evidence and will be heard by a costs judge or a district judge. The respondent to the application must file and serve any evidence he relies on at least 2 days before the hearing date.

36.4 Nothing in rule 47.10 prevents parties who seek a judgment or order by consent from including in the draft a term that a party shall pay to another party a specified sum in respect of costs.

36.5

(1) The receiving party may discontinue the detailed assessment proceedings in accordance with Part 38 (Discontinuance).
(2) Where the receiving party discontinues the detailed assessment proceedings before a detailed assessment hearing has been requested, the paying party may apply to the appropriate office for an order about the costs of the detailed assessment proceedings.
(3) Where a detailed assessment hearing has been requested the receiving party may not discontinue unless the court gives permission.
(4) A bill of costs may be withdrawn by consent whether or not a detailed assessment hearing has been requested.

SECTION 37 – DEFAULT COSTS CERTIFICATE: RULE 47.11

37.1

(1) A request for the issue of a default costs certificate must be made in Form N254 and must be signed by the receiving party or his solicitor.
(2) The request must be accompanied by a copy of the document giving the right to detailed assessment. (Section 40.4 of the Costs Practice Direction identifies the appropriate documents.)

37.2 The request must be filed at the appropriate office.

37.3 A default costs certificate will be in Form N255.

37.4 Attention is drawn to rules 40.3 (Drawing up and Filing of Judgments and Orders) and 40.4 (Service of Judgments and Orders) which apply to the preparation and service of a default costs certificate. The receiving party will be treated as having permission to draw up a default costs certificate by virtue of this practice direction.

37.5 The issue of a default costs certificate does not prohibit, govern or affect any detailed assessment of the same costs which are payable out of the Community Legal Service Fund.

37.6 An application for an order staying enforcement of a default costs certificate may be made either –

(1) to a costs judge or district judge of the court office which issued the certificate; or
(2) to the court (if different) which has general jurisdiction to enforce the certificate.

37.7 Proceedings for enforcement of default costs certificates may not be issued in the Supreme Court Costs Office.

37.8 The fixed costs payable in respect of solicitor's charges on the issue of the default costs certificate are £80.

SECTION 38 – SETTING ASIDE DEFAULT COSTS CERTIFICATE: RULE 47.12

38.1

(1) A court officer may set aside a default costs certificate at the request of the receiving party under rule 47.12(3).

(2) A costs judge or a district judge will make any other order or give any directions under this rule.

38.2

(1) An application for an order under rule 47.12(2) to set aside or vary a default costs certificate must be supported by evidence.

(2) In deciding whether to set aside or vary a certificate under rule 47.12(2) the matters to which the court must have regard include whether the party seeking the order made the application promptly.

(3) As a general rule a default costs certificate will be set aside under rule 47.12(2) only if the applicant shows a good reason for the court to do so and if he files with his application a copy of the bill and a copy of the default costs certificate, and a draft of the points of dispute he proposes to serve if his application is granted.

38.3

(1) Attention is drawn to rule 3.1(3) (which enables the court when making an order to make it subject to conditions) and to rule 44.3(8) (which enables the court to order a party whom it has ordered to pay costs to pay an amount on account before the costs are assessed).

(2) A costs judge or a district judge may exercise the power of the court to make an order under rule 44.3(8) although he did not make the order about costs which led to the issue of the default costs certificate.

38.4 If a default costs certificate is set aside the court will give directions for the management of the detailed assessment proceedings.

SECTION 39 – OPTIONAL REPLY: RULE 47.13

39.1

(1) Where the receiving party wishes to serve a reply, he must also serve a copy on every other party to the detailed assessment proceedings. The time for doing so is within 21 days after service of the points of dispute.

(2) A reply means –

(i) a separate document prepared by the receiving party; or

(ii) his written comments added to the points of dispute.

(3) A reply must be signed by the party serving it or his solicitor.

SECTION 40 – DETAILED ASSESSMENT HEARING: RULE 47.14

40.1 The time for requesting a detailed assessment hearing is within 3 months of the expiry of the period for commencing detailed assessment proceedings.

40.2 The request for a detailed assessment hearing must be in Form N258. The request must be accompanied by –

(a) a copy of the notice of commencement of detailed assessment proceedings;
(b) a copy of the bill of costs,
(c) the document giving the right to detailed assessment (see paragraph 39.4 below);
(d) a copy of the points of dispute, annotated as necessary in order to show which items have been agreed and their value and to show which items remain in dispute and their value;
(e) as many copies of the points of dispute so annotated as there are persons who have served points of dispute;
(f) a copy of any replies served;
(g) a copy of all orders made by the court relating to the costs which are to be assessed;
(h) copies of the fee notes and other written evidence as served on the paying party in accordance with paragraph 32.3 above;
(i) where there is a dispute as to the receiving party's liability to pay costs to the solicitors who acted for the receiving party, any agreement, letter or other written information provided by the solicitor to his client explaining how the solicitor's charges are to be calculated;
(j) a statement signed by the receiving party or his solicitor giving the name, address for service, reference and telephone number and fax number, if any, of –
    (i) the receiving party;
    (ii) the paying party;
    (iii) any other person who has served points of dispute or who has given notice to the receiving party under paragraph 32.10(1)(b) above;

    and giving an estimate of the length of time the detailed assessment hearing will take;
(k) where the application for a detailed assessment hearing is made by a party other than the receiving party, such of the documents set out in this paragraph as are in the possession of that party;
(l) where the court is to assess the costs of an assisted person or LSC funded client –
    (i) the legal aid certificate, LSC certificate and relevant amendment certificates, any authorities and any certificates of discharge or revocation.
    (ii) a certificate, in Precedent F(3) of the Schedule of Costs Precedents;
    (iii) if the assisted person has a financial interest in the detailed assessment hearing and wishes to attend, the postal address of that person to which the court will send notice of any hearing;
    (iv) if the rates payable out of the LSC fund are prescribed rates, a schedule to the bill of costs setting out all the items in the bill which are claimed against other parties calculated at the legal aid prescribed rates with or without any claim for enhancement: (further information as to this schedule is set out in Section 48 of this practice direction);
    (v) a copy of any default costs certificate in respect of costs claimed in the bill of costs.

40.3

(1) This paragraph applies to any document described in paragraph 40.2(i) above which the receiving party has filed in the appropriate office. The document must be the latest relevant version and in any event have been filed not more than 2 years before filing the request for a detailed assessment hearing.

(2) In respect of any documents to which this paragraph applies, the receiving party may, instead of filing a copy of it, specify in the request for a detailed assessment hearing the case number under which a copy of the document was previously filed.

40.4 'The document giving the right to detailed assessment' means such one or more of the following documents as are appropriate to the detailed assessment proceedings –

(a) a copy of the judgment or order of the court giving the right to detailed assessment;
(b) a copy of the notice served under rule 3.7 (sanctions for non-payment of certain fees) where a claim is struck out under that rule;
(c) a copy of the notice of acceptance where an offer to settle is accepted under Part 36 (Offers to settle and payments into court);
(d) a copy of the notice of discontinuance in a case which is discontinued under Part 38 (Discontinuance);
(e) a copy of the award made on an arbitration under any Act or pursuant to an agreement, where no court has made an order for the enforcement of the award;
(f) a copy of the order, award or determination of a statutorily constituted tribunal or body;
(g) in a case under the Sheriffs Act 1887, the sheriff's bill of fees and charges, unless a court order giving the right to detailed assessment has been made;
(h) a notice of revocation or discharge under Regulation 82 of the Civil Legal Aid (General) Regulations 1989.
(j) In the county courts certain Acts and Regulations provide for costs incurred in proceedings under those Acts and Regulations to be assessed in the county court if so ordered on application. Where such an application is made, a copy of the order.

40.5 On receipt of the request for a detailed assessment hearing the court will fix a date for the hearing, or, if the costs officer so decides, will give directions or fix a date for a preliminary appointment.

40.6

(1) The court will give at least 14 days notice of the time and place of the detailed assessment hearing to every person named in the statement referred to in paragraph 40.2(j) above.
(2) The court will when giving notice, give each person who has served points of dispute a copy of the points of dispute annotated by the receiving party in compliance with paragraph 40.2(d) above.
(3) Attention is drawn to rule 47.14(6) and (7): apart from the receiving party, only those who have served points of dispute may be heard on the detailed assessment unless the court gives permission, and only items specified in the points of dispute may be raised unless the court gives permission.

40.7

(1) If the receiving party does not file a request for a detailed assessment hearing within the prescribed time, the paying party may apply to the court to fix a time within which the receiving party must do so. The sanction, for failure to request a detailed assessment hearing within the time specified by the court, is that all or part of the costs may be disallowed (see rule 47.8(2)).

Suitable record of the judgment

5.12 Where the judgment to be appealed has been officially recorded by the court, an approved transcript of that record should accompany the appellant's notice. Photocopies will not be accepted for this purpose. However, where there is no officially recorded judgment, the following documents will be acceptable –

Written judgments

(1) Where the judgment was made in writing a copy of that judgment endorsed with the judge's signature.

Note of judgment

(2) When judgment was not officially recorded or made in writing a note of the judgment (agreed between the appellant's and respondent's advocates) should be submitted for approval to the judge whose decision is being appealed. If the parties cannot agree on a single note of the judgment, both versions should be provided to that judge with an explanatory letter. For the purpose of an application for permission to appeal the note need not be approved by the respondent or the lower court judge.

Advocates' notes of judgments where the appellant is unrepresented

(3) When the appellant was unrepresented in the lower court it is the duty of any advocate for the respondent to make his/her note of judgment promptly available, free of charge to the appellant where there is no officially recorded judgment or if the court so directs. Where the appellant was represented in the lower court it is the duty of his/her own former advocate to make his/her note available in these circumstances. The appellant should submit the note of judgment to the appeal court.

Reasons for Judgment in Tribunal cases

(4) A sealed copy of the tribunal's reasons for the decision.

5.13 An appellant may not be able to obtain an official transcript or other suitable record of the lower court's decision within the time within which the appellant's notice must be filed. In such cases the appellant's notice must still be completed to the best of the appellant's ability on the basis of the documentation available. However, it may be amended subsequently with the permission of the appeal court.

Advocates' notes of judgments

5.14 Advocates' brief (or, where appropriate, refresher) fee includes –

(1) remuneration for taking a note of the judgment of the court;
(2) having the note transcribed accurately;
(3) attempting to agree the note with the other side if represented;
(4) submitting the note to the judge for approval where appropriate;
(5) revising it if so requested by the judge;
(6) providing any copies required for the appeal court, instructing solicitors and lay client; and
(7) providing a copy of his note to an unrepresented appellant.

Transcripts or Notes of Evidence

5.15 When the evidence is relevant to the appeal an official transcript of the relevant evidence must be obtained. Transcripts or notes of evidence are generally not needed for the purpose of determining an application for permission to appeal.

Notes of evidence

5.16 If evidence relevant to the appeal was not officially recorded, a typed version of the judge's notes of evidence must be obtained.

Transcripts at public expense

5.17 Where the lower court or the appeal court is satisfied that an unrepresented appellant is in such poor financial circumstances that the cost of a transcript would be an excessive burden the court may certify that the cost of obtaining one official transcript should be borne at public expense.

5.18 In the case of a request for an official transcript of evidence or proceedings to be paid for at public expense, the court must also be satisfied that there are reasonable grounds for appeal. Whenever possible a request for a transcript at public expense should be made to the lower court when asking for permission to appeal.

Filing and service of appellant's notice

5.19 Rule 52.4 sets out the procedure and time-limits for filing and serving an appellant's notice. The appellant must file the appellant's notice at the appeal court within such period as may be directed by the lower court which should not normally exceed 28 days or, where the lower court directs no such period, within 14 days of the date of the decision that the appellant wishes to appeal.

5.20 Where the lower court judge announces his decision and reserves the reasons for his judgment or order until a later date, he should, in the exercise of powers under rule 52.4(2)(a), fix a period for filing the appellant's notice at the appeal court that takes this into account.

5.21 Except where the appeal court orders otherwise a sealed copy of the appellant's notice, including any skeleton arguments must be served on all respondents to the appeal in accordance with the timetable prescribed by rule 52.4(3) except where this requirement is modified by paragraph 5.9(2) in which case the skeleton argument should be served as soon as it is lodged.

5.22 Unless the court otherwise directs a respondent need not take any action when served with an appellant's notice until such time as notification is given to him that permission to appeal has been given.

5.23 The court may dispense with the requirement for service of the notice on a respondent. Any application notice seeking an order under rule 6.9 to dispense with service should set out the reasons relied on and be verified by a statement of truth.

5.24 Where the appellant is applying for permission to appeal in his appellant's notice, there is no requirement at this stage for copies of the documents referred to at paragraph 5.6 to be served on the respondents. However, if permission has been given by the lower court or permission is not required, copies of all the documents must be served on the respondents with the appellant's notice.

(Paragraph 5.6 provides for certain documents to be filed with an appellant's notice.)

Amendment of Appeal Notice

5.25 An appeal notice may be amended with permission. Such an application to amend and any application in opposition will normally be dealt with at the hearing unless that course would cause unnecessary expense or delay in which case a request should be made for the application to amend to be heard in advance.

PROCEDURE AFTER PERMISSION IS OBTAINED

6.1 This paragraph sets out the procedure where –

(1) permission to appeal is given by the appeal court; or
(2) the appellant's notice is filed in the appeal court and –
  (a) permission was given by the lower court; or
  (b) permission is not required.

6.2 If the appeal court gives permission to appeal, copies of all the documents referred to at paragraph 5.6 must be served on the respondents within 7 days of receiving the order giving permission to appeal.

(Part 6 (service of documents) provides rules on service.)

6.3 The appeal court will send the parties –

(1) notification of –
  (a) the date of the hearing or the period of time (the 'listing window') during which the appeal is likely to be heard; and
  (b) in the Court of Appeal, the date by which the appeal will be heard (the 'hear by date');
(2) where permission is granted by the appeal court a copy of the order giving permission to appeal; and
(3) any other directions given by the court.

Appeal Questionnaire in the Court of Appeal

6.4 The Court of Appeal will send an appeal questionnaire to the appellant when it notifies him of the matters referred to in paragraph 6.3.

6.5 The appellant must complete and lodge the appeal questionnaire within 14 days of the date of the letter of notification of the matters in paragraph 6.3. The appeal questionnaire must contain –

(1) if the appellant is legally represented, the advocate's time estimate for the hearing of the appeal;
(2) where a transcript of evidence is relevant to the appeal; confirmation that a transcript of evidence has been ordered where this is not already in the bundle of documents;
(3) confirmation that copies of the appeal bundle are being prepared and will be held ready for the use of the Court of Appeal and an undertaking that they will be supplied to the court on request. For the purpose of these bundles photocopies of the transcripts will be accepted;
(4) confirmation that copies of the appeal questionnaire and the appeal bundle have been served on the respondents and the date of that service.

Time estimates

6.6 The time estimate included in an appeal questionnaire must be that of the advocate who will argue the appeal. It should exclude the time required by the court to give judgment. If the respondent disagrees with the time estimate, the respondent must inform the court within 7 days of receipt of the appeal questionnaire. In the absence of such notification the respondent will be deemed to have accepted the estimate proposed on behalf of the appellant.

RESPONDENT

7.1 A respondent who wishes to ask the appeal court to vary the order of the lower court in any way must appeal and permission will be required on the same basis as for an appellant.

7.2 A respondent who wishes only to request that the appeal court upholds the judgment or order of the lower court whether for the reasons given in the lower court or otherwise does not make an appeal and does not therefore require permission to appeal in accordance with rule 52.3(1).

7.3 A respondent who wishes to appeal or who wishes to ask the appeal court to uphold the order of the lower court for reasons different from or additional to those given by the lower court must file a respondent's notice.

7.3A Paragraphs 5.1A and 5.1B of this practice direction also apply to a respondent and a respondent's notice.

Time-limits

7.4 The time-limits for filing a respondent's notice are set out in rule 52.5 (4) and (5).

7.5 Where an extension of time is required the extension must be requested in the respondent's notice and the reasons why the respondent failed to act within the specified time must be included.

Respondent's skeleton argument

7.6 Except where paragraph 7.7A applies, the respondent must provide a skeleton argument for the court where he proposes to address arguments to the court. The respondent's skeleton argument may be included within a respondent's notice. Where a skeleton argument is included within a respondent's notice it will not form part of the notice for the purposes of rule 52.8.

7.7 Where the skeleton argument is not included within a respondent's notice it should be lodged and served no later than 21 days after the respondent receives the appellant's skeleton argument.

(Rule 52.5(4) sets out the period for filing and serving a respondent's notice.)

7.7A Where the appeal relates to a claim allocated to the small claims track the respondent may provide a skeleton argument but is not required to do so.

Content of skeleton arguments

7.8 A respondent's skeleton argument must conform to the directions at paragraphs 5.10 and 5.11 above with any necessary modifications. It should, where appropriate, answer the arguments set out in the appellant's skeleton argument.

Applications within respondent's notices

7.9 A respondent may include an application within a respondent's notice in accordance with paragraph 5.5 above.

Filing respondent's notices and skeleton arguments

7.10 The respondent must lodge the following documents with his respondent's notice in every case –

(1) two additional copies of the respondent's notice for the appeal court;
(2) one copy each for the appellant and any other respondents; and

(3) two copies of any skeleton arguments.

7.11 If the respondent does not file a respondent's notice, he will not be entitled, except with the permission of the court, to rely on any ground not relied on in the lower court.

7.12 If the respondent wishes to rely on any documents in addition to those filed by the appellant he must prepare a supplemental bundle and lodge it at the appeal court with his respondent's notice. He must serve a copy of the supplemental bundle at the same time as serving the respondent's notice on the persons required to be served in accordance with rule 52.5(6).

7.13 The respondent's notice and any skeleton argument must be served in accordance with the time-limits set out in rule 52.5(6) except this requirement is modified by paragraph 7.7.

Appeals to the High Court

8.1 This paragraph applies where an appeal lies to a High Court judge from the decision of a county court or a district judge of the High Court.

8.2 The following table sets out the following venues for each circuit –

(a) Appeal centres – court centres where appeals to which this paragraph applies may be managed and heard.

(b) Hearing only centres – court centres where appeals to which this paragraph applies may be heard by order made at an appeal centre (see paragraph 8.5).

Circuit	Appeal Centres	Hearing Only Centres
Midland Circuit	Birmingham Nottingham	Lincoln Leicester Northampton Stafford
North Eastern Circuit	Leeds Newcastle Sheffield	Teesside
Northern Circuit	Manchester Liverpool Preston	Carlisle
Wales and Chester Circuit	Cardiff Swansea Chester	
Western Circuit	Bristol Winchester Exeter	Truro Plymouth

Circuit	Appeal Centres	Hearing Only Centres
South Eastern Circuit	<u>Central London</u> – Royal Courts of Justice	
	<u>Provincial</u> –	
	Lewes	Oxford
	Luton	Chelmsford
	Norwich	St Albans
	Reading	Maidstone

8.3 The appellant's notice must be filed in the district registry at an appeal centre on the circuit in which the lower court is situated. Unless the appeal court otherwise orders the appeal will be managed and heard at that appeal centre.

8.4 The appeal court may transfer an appeal to another appeal centre (whether or not on the same circuit). In deciding whether to do so the court will have regard to the criteria in rule 30.3 (criteria for a transfer order). The appeal court may do so either on application by a party or of its own initiative. Where an appeal is transferred under this paragraph, notice of transfer must be served on every person on whom the appellant's notice has been served. An appeal may not be transferred to an appeal centre on another circuit, either for management or hearing, unless the consent of a presiding judge of that circuit has been obtained.

8.5 Directions may be given for –

(a) an appeal to be heard at a hearing only centre; or
(b) an application in an appeal to be heard at any other venue,

instead of at the appeal centre managing the appeal.

8.6 Unless a direction has been made under 8.5, any application in the appeal must be made at the appeal centre where the appeal is being managed.

8.7 A respondent's notice must be filed at the appeal centre where the appellant's notice was filed unless the appeal has been transferred to another appeal centre, in which case it must be filed at that appeal centre.

8.8 The appeal court may adopt all or any part of the procedure set out in paragraphs 6.4 to 6.6.

8.9 Where the lower court is a county court:

(1) appeals and applications for permission to appeal will be heard by a High Court judge or by a person authorised under paragraphs (1), (2) or (4) of the table in section 9(1) of the Supreme Court Act 1981 to act as a judge of the High Court; and
(2) other applications in the appeal may be heard and directions in the appeal may be given either by a High Court judge or by any person authorised under section 9 of the Supreme Court Act 1981 to act as a judge of the High Court.

8.10 In the case of appeals from masters or district judges of the High Court, appeals, applications for permission and any other applications in the appeal may be heard and directions in the appeal may be given by a High Court judge or by any person authorised under section 9 of the Supreme Court Act 1981 to act as a judge of the High Court.

APPEALS TO A JUDGE OF A COUNTY COURT FROM A DISTRICT JUDGE

8A.1 The designated civil judge in consultation with his presiding judges has responsibility for allocating appeals from decisions of district judges to circuit judges.

RE-HEARINGS

9.1 The hearing of an appeal will be a re-hearing (as opposed to a review of the decision of the lower court) if the appeal is from the decision of a minister, person or other body and the minister, person or other body –

(1) did not hold a hearing to come to that decision; or
(2) held a hearing to come to that decision, but the procedure adopted did not provide for the consideration of evidence.

APPEALS TRANSFERRED TO THE COURT OF APPEAL

10.1 Where an appeal is transferred to the Court of Appeal under rule 52.14 the Court of Appeal may give such additional directions as are considered appropriate.

APPLICATIONS

11.1 Where a party to an appeal makes an application whether in an appeal notice or by Part 23 application notice, the provisions of Part 23 will apply.

11.2 The applicant must file the following documents with the notice –

(1) one additional copy of the application notice for the appeal court and one copy for each of the respondents;
(2) where applicable a sealed copy of the order which is the subject of the main appeal;
(3) A bundle of documents in support which should include –
  (a) the Part 23 application notice;
  (b) any witness statements and affidavits filed in support of the application notice;
  (c) the documents specified in paragraph 5.6(6) above in so far as they have not already been filed with the appellant's notice.

DISPOSING OF APPLICATIONS OR APPEALS BY CONSENT

Dismissal of applications or appeals by consent

12.1 These paragraphs do not apply where any party to the proceedings is a child or patient.

12.2 Where an appellant does not wish to pursue an application or an appeal, he may request the appeal court for an order that his application or appeal be dismissed. Such a request must contain a statement that the appellant is not a child or patient. If such a request is granted it will usually be on the basis that the appellant pays the costs of the application or appeal.

12.3 If the appellant wishes to have the application or appeal dismissed without costs, his request must be accompanied by a consent signed by the respondent or his legal representative stating that the respondent is not a child or patient and consents to the dismissal of the application or appeal without costs.

12.4 Where a settlement has been reached disposing of the application or appeal, the parties may make a joint request to the court stating that none of them is a child

PART V

or patient, and asking that the application or appeal be dismissed by consent. If the request is granted the application or appeal will be dismissed.

ALLOWING UNOPPOSED APPEALS OR APPLICATIONS ON PAPER

13.1 The appeal court will not normally make an order allowing an appeal unless satisfied that the decision of the lower court was wrong, but the appeal court may set aside or vary the order of the lower court with consent and without determining the merits of the appeal, if it is satisfied that there are good and sufficient reasons for doing so. Where the appeal court is requested by all parties to allow an application or an appeal the court may consider the request on the papers. The request should state that none of the parties is a child or patient and set out the relevant history of the proceedings and the matters relied on as justifying the proposed order and be accompanied by a copy of the proposed order.

Procedure for structured settlements and consent orders involving a child or patient

13.2 Settlements relating to appeals and applications where one of the parties is a child or a patient; and structured settlements which are agreed upon at the appeal stage require the court's approval.

Child

13.3 In cases involving a child a copy of the proposed order signed by the parties' solicitors should be sent to the appeal court, together with an opinion from the advocate acting on behalf of the child.

Patient

13.4 Where a party is a patient the same procedure will be adopted, but the documents filed should also include any relevant reports prepared for the Court of Protection and a document evidencing formal approval by that court where required.

Structured settlements

13.5 Where a structured settlement has been negotiated in a case which is under appeal the documents filed should include those which would be required in the case of a structured settlement dealt with at first instance. Details can be found in the practice direction which supplements CPR Part 40.

SUMMARY ASSESSMENT OF COSTS

14.1 Costs are likely to be assessed by way of summary assessment at the following hearings –

(1) contested directions hearings;
(2) applications for permission to appeal at which the respondent is present;
(3) dismissal list hearings in the Court of Appeal at which the respondent is present;
(4) appeals from case management decisions; and
(5) appeals listed for 1 day or less.

14.2 Parties attending any of the hearings referred to in paragraph 14.1 should be prepared to deal with the summary assessment.

OTHER SPECIAL PROVISIONS REGARDING THE COURT OF APPEAL

Filing of documents

15.1 (1) The documents relevant to proceedings in the Court of Appeal, Civil Division must be filed in the Civil Appeals Office Registry, Room E307, Royal Courts of Justice, Strand, London, WC2A 2LL.

(2) The Civil Appeals Office will not serve documents and where service is required by the CPR or this practice direction it must be effected by the parties.

Master in the Court of Appeal, Civil Division

15.2 When the Head of the Civil Appeals Office acts in a judicial capacity pursuant to rule 52.16, he shall be known as Master. Other eligible officers may also be designated by the Master of the Rolls to exercise judicial authority under rule 52.16 and shall then be known as deputy masters.

Judicial Review Appeals

15.3 Where the Court of Appeal gives permission to apply for judicial review under rule 52.15(3) the court may, hear the application for judicial review. This will be rare, but may be appropriate where, for example, the High Court is bound by authority or for some other reason, an appeal to the Court of Appeal will be inevitable.

15.4 Paragraphs 5.6 and 5.19 above do not apply to cases where the appeal notice seeks permission to appeal a refusal to give permission to apply for judicial review. In such cases the following documents must be filed with the appellant's notice –

(1) one additional copy of the appellant's notice for the Court of Appeal;
(2) one copy of the appellant's notice for each of the respondents to be sealed and returned;
(3) the order refusing permission to apply for judicial review;
(4) Form 86A;
(5) a copy of the original decision which is the subject of the application to the High Court;
(6) any witness statements or affidavits in support of any application included in the appellant's notice;
(7) a copy of the bundle of documents used in the High Court;
(8) the skeleton argument relied on in the High Court; and
(9) a transcript of the judgment.

15.5 The time for filing an appellant's notice in these circumstances is set out in rule 52.15(1). The arrangements for service on the respondent in paragraph 5.21 apply.

15.6 Where it is not possible to file all these documents, the appellant must indicate which documents have not yet been filed and the reasons why they are not currently available.

Listing and hear-by dates

15.7 The management of the list will be dealt with by the lis… …cer under the direction of the Master.

15.8 The Civil Appeals List of the Court of Appe… …d as follows –

- *The applications list* – applications for permission to appeal and other applications.
- *The appeals list* – appeals where permission to appeal has been given or where an appeal lies without permission being required.
- *The expedited list* – appeals or applications where the Court of Appeal has directed an expedited hearing. The current practice of the Court of Appeal is summarised in *Unilever plc v Chefaro Proprietaries Ltd (Practice Note)* [1995] 1 WLR 24.
- *The stand-out list* – appeals or application which, for good reason, are not at present ready to proceed and have been stood out by judicial direction.
- *The fixtures list* – where a hearing date for the appeal is fixed in advance.
- *The second fixtures list* – if an appeal is designated as a 'second fixture' it means that a hearing date is arranged in advance on the express basis that the list is fully booked for the period in question and therefore the case will be heard only if a suitable gap occurs in the list.
- *The short-warned list* – appeals which the court considers may be prepared for the hearing by an advocate other than the one originally instructed with a half day's notice, or, if the court so directs, 48 hours notice.

15.9 Once an appeal is listed for hearing from the short-warned list it becomes the immediate professional duty of the advocate instructed in the appeal, if he is unable to appear at the hearing, to take all practicable measures to ensure that his lay client is represented at the hearing by an advocate who is fully instructed and able to argue the appeal.

Requests for directions

15.10 To ensure that all requests for directions are centrally monitored and correctly allocated, all requests for directions or rulings (whether relating to listing or any other matters) should be made to the Civil Appeals Office. Those seeking directions or rulings must not approach the supervising Lord Justice either directly, or via his or her clerk.

Lists of authorities

15.11 Once the parties have been notified of the date fixed for hearing the appellant's advocate shall file, after consulting his opponent, for the purpose of pre-reading by the court, one bundle containing photocopies of the principal authorities upon which each side will rely at the hearing, with the relevant passages marked. There will in general be no need to include authorities for propositions not in dispute. This bundle should be made available 28 days before the hearing, unless the period of notice of the hearing is less than 28 days in which case the bundle should be filed immediately. Such bundles should not normally contain more than 10 authorities. If any party intends, during the hearing to refer to other authorities these may be included in a second agreed bundle to be filed by the parties at the hearing. Alternatively, and in place of the second bundle only, a list of authorities and text may be delivered to the office of the Head Usher of the Court no later than 5.30 pm on the last working day before the hearing is to commence.

Core bundles

15.11A Where the total number of pages to be put before the court in a full appeal exceeds 750 pages, excluding transcripts and copied authorities, the parties must file and serve a core bundle of essential documents not exceeding 150 pages.

Reserved judgments of the Court of Appeal

15.12 Unless the court orders otherwise, copies of a written judgment will be made available to the parties' legal advisers by 4 pm on the second working day before judgment is due to be pronounced on the condition that the contents are not communicated to the parties themselves until one hour before the listed time for pronouncement of judgment.

15.13 The judgment is made available to legal advisers primarily to enable them to consider the judgment and decide what consequential orders they should seek. The condition is imposed to prevent the outcome of the case being publicly reported before judgment is given, since the judgment is confidential until then. Every page of the judgment will be marked 'Unapproved judgment: No permission is given to copy or use in court'. These words carry the authority of the court.

15.14 Where a party is not legally represented a copy of the judgment will be made available to him at the same time as to legal advisers. It must be treated as confidential until pronouncement of judgment.

****

APPEALS TO THE COURT OF APPEAL

Appeal against decree nisi of divorce or nullity of marriage

21.1 (1) The appellant must file the appellant's notice at the Court of Appeal within 28 days after the date on which the decree was pronounced.

(2) The appellant must file the following documents with the appellant's notice –
- (a) the decree; and
- (b) a certificate of service of the appellant's notice.

(3) The appellant's notice must be served on the appropriate district judge (see subparagraph (6)) in addition to the persons to be served under rule 52.4(3) and in accordance with that rule.

(4) The lower court may not alter the time-limits for filing of the appeal notices.

(5) Where an appellant intends to apply to the Court of Appeal for an extension of time for serving or filing the appellant's notice he must give notice of that intention to the appropriate district judge (see subparagraph 6) before the application is made.

(6) In this paragraph 'the appropriate district judge' means, where the lower court is –
- (a) a county court, the district judge of that court;
- (b) a district registry, the district judge of that registry;
- (c) the Principal Registry of the Family Division, the senior district judge of that division.

****

Appeals in cases of contempt of court

21.4 In an appeal under section 13 of the Administration of Justice Act 1960 (appeals in cases of contempt of court), the appellant must serve the appellant's notice on the court from whose order or decision the appeal is brought in addition to the persons to be served under rule 52.4(3) and in accordance with that rule.

Appeals from Social Security or Child Support Commissioners

21.5 (1) This paragraph applies to appeals under section 25 of the Child Support Act 1991, section 24 of the Social Security Administration Act 1992 and section 15 of the Social Security Act 1998 (appeals from the decision of a Commissioner on a question of law).

(2) The appellant must file the appellant's notice within 6 weeks after the date of the Commissioner's decision on permission to appeal to the Court of Appeal was given in writing to the appellant.

(3) The appellant must serve the appellant's notice on –

(a) the Secretary of State; and

(b) any person appointed by him to proceed with a claim

in addition to the persons to be served under rule 52.4(3) and in accordance with that rule.

****

Practice Direction – Judicial Review

This Practice Direction supplements CPR Part 54 (PD54)

1.1 In addition to Part 54 and this practice direction attention is drawn to –

- section 31 of the Supreme Court Act 1981; and
- the Human Rights Act 1998.

THE COURT

2.1 Part 54 claims for judicial review are dealt with in the Administrative Court.

2.2 Where the claim is proceeding in the Administrative Court in London, documents must be filed at the Administrative Court Office, the Royal Courts of Justice, Strand, London, WC2A 2LL.

2.3 Where the claim is proceeding in the Administrative Court in Wales (see paragraph 3.1), documents must be filed at the Law Courts, Cathays Park, Cardiff, CF10 3PG.

Urgent applications

2.4 Where urgency makes it necessary for the claim for judicial review to be made outside London or Cardiff, the Administrative Court Office in London should be consulted (if necessary, by telephone) prior to filing the claim form.

JUDICIAL REVIEW CLAIMS IN WALES

3.1 A claim for judicial review may be brought in the Administrative Court in Wales where the claim or any remedy sought involves –

(1) a devolution issue arising out of the Government of Wales Act 1998; or
(2) an issue concerning the National Assembly for Wales, the Welsh executive, or any Welsh public body (including a Welsh local authority) (whether or not it involves a devolution issue).

3.2 Such claims may also be brought in the Administrative Court at the Royal Courts of Justice.

RULE 54.5 – TIME-LIMIT FOR FILING CLAIM FORM

4.1 Where the claim is for a quashing order in respect of a judgment, order or conviction, the date when the grounds to make the claim first arose, for the purposes of rule 54.5(1)(b), is the date of that judgment, order or conviction.

RULE 54.6 – CLAIM FORM

Interested parties

5.1 Where the claim for judicial review relates to proceedings in a court or tribunal, any other parties to those proceedings must be named in the claim form as interested parties under rule 54.6(1)(a) (and therefore served with the claim form under rule 54.7(b)).

5.2 For example, in a claim by a defendant in a criminal case in the Magistrates' or Crown Court for judicial review of a decision in that case, the prosecution must always be named as an interested party.

Human rights

5.3 Where the claimant is seeking to raise any issue under the Human Rights Act 1998, or seeks a remedy available under that Act, the claim form must include the information required by paragraph 16 of the practice direction supplementing Part 16.

Devolution issues

5.4 Where the claimant intends to raise a devolution issue, the claim form must –

(1) specify that the applicant wishes to raise a devolution issue and identify the relevant provisions of the Government of Wales Act 1998, the Northern Ireland Act 1998 or the Scotland Act 1998; and
(2) contain a summary of the facts, circumstances and points of law on the basis of which it is alleged that a devolution issue arises.

5.5 In this practice direction 'devolution issue' has the same meaning as in paragraph 1, schedule 8 to the Government of Wales Act 1998; paragraph 1, schedule 10 to the Northern Ireland Act 1998; and paragraph 1, schedule 6 of the Scotland Act 1998.

Claim form

5.6 The claim form must include or be accompanied by –

(1) a detailed statement of the claimant's grounds for bringing the claim for judicial review;

(2) a statement of the facts relied on;
(3) any application to extend the time-limit for filing the claim form;
(4) any application for directions; and

5.7 In addition, the claim form must be accompanied by –

(1) any written evidence in support of the claim or application to extend time;
(2) a copy of any order that the claimant seeks to have quashed;
(3) where the claim for judicial review relates to a decision of a court or tribunal, an approved copy of the reasons for reaching that decision;
(4) copies of any documents on which the claimant proposes to rely;
(5) copies of any relevant statutory material;
(6) a list of essential documents for advance reading by the court (with page references to the passages relied on); and

5.8 Where it is not possible to file all the above documents, the claimant must indicate which documents have not been filed and the reasons why they are not currently available.

Bundle of documents

5.9 The claimant must file two copies of a paginated and indexed bundle containing all the documents referred to in paragraphs 4.6 and 4.7.

5.10 Attention is drawn to rules 8.5(1) and 8.5(7).

RULE 54.7 – SERVICE OF CLAIM FORM

6.1 Except as required by rules 54.11 or 54.12(2), the Administrative Court will not serve documents and service must be effected by the parties.

RULE 54.8 – ACKNOWLEDGMENT OF SERVICE

7.1 Attention is drawn to rule 8.3(2) and the relevant practice direction and to rule 10.5.

RULE 54.10 – PERMISSION GIVEN

Directions

8.1 Case management directions under rule 54.10(1) may include directions about serving the claim form and any evidence on other persons.

8.2 Where a claim is made under the Human Rights Act 1998, a direction may be made for giving notice to the Crown or joining the Crown as a party. Attention is drawn to rule 19.4A and paragraph 6 of the Practice Direction supplementing Section I of Part 19.

8.3 A direction may be made for the hearing of the claim for judicial review to be held outside London or Cardiff. Before making any such direction the judge will consult the judge in charge of the Administrative Court as to its feasibility.

Permission without a hearing

8.4 The court will generally, in the first instance, consider the question of permission without a hearing.

Permission hearing

8.5 Neither the defendant nor any other interested party need attend a hearing on the question of permission unless the court directs otherwise.

8.6 Where the defendant or any party does attend a hearing, the court will not generally make an order for costs against the claimant.

RULE 54.11 – SERVICE OF ORDER GIVING OR REFUSING PERMISSION

9.1 An order refusing permission or giving it subject to conditions or on certain grounds only must set out or be accompanied by the court's reasons for coming to that decision.

RULE 54.14 – RESPONSE

10.1 Where the party filing the detailed grounds intends to rely on documents not already filed, he must file a paginated bundle of those documents when he files the detailed grounds.

RULE 54.15 – WHERE CLAIMANT SEEKS TO RELY ON ADDITIONAL GROUNDS

11.1 Where the claimant intends to apply to rely on additional grounds at the hearing of the claim for judicial review, he must give notice to the court and to any other person served with the claim form no later than 7 clear days before the hearing (or the warned date where appropriate).

RULE 54.16 – EVIDENCE

12.1 Disclosure is not required unless the court orders otherwise.

RULE 54.17 – COURT'S POWERS TO HEAR ANY PERSON

13.1 Where all the parties consent, the court may deal with an application under rule 54.17 without a hearing.

13.2 Where the court gives permission for a person to file evidence or make representations at the hearing of the claim for judicial review, it may do so on conditions and may give case management directions.

13.3 An application for permission should be made by letter to the Administrative Court office, identifying the claim, explaining who the applicant is and indicating why and in what form the applicant wants to participate in the hearing.

13.4 If the applicant is seeking a prospective order as to costs, the letter should say what kind of order and on what grounds.

13.5 Applications to intervene must be made at the earliest reasonable opportunity, since it will usually be essential not to delay the hearing.

RULE 54.20 – TRANSFER

14.1 Attention is drawn to rule 30.5.

14.2 In deciding whether a claim is suitable for transfer to the Administrative Court, the court will consider whether it raises issues of public law to which Part 54 should apply.

Skeleton arguments

15.1 The claimant must file and serve a skeleton argument not less than 21 working days before the date of the hearing of the judicial review (or the warned date).

15.2 The defendant and any other party wishing to make representations at the hearing of the judicial review must file and serve a skeleton argument not less than 14 working days before the date of the hearing of the judicial review (or the warned date).

15.3 Skeleton arguments must contain –

(1) a time estimate for the complete hearing, including delivery of judgment;
(2) a list of issues;
(3) a list of the legal points to be taken (together with any relevant authorities with page references to the passages relied on);
(4) a chronology of events (with page references to the bundle of documents (see paragraph 16.1);
(5) a list of essential documents for the advance reading of the court (with page references to the passages relied on) (if different from that filed with the claim form) and a time estimate for that reading; and
(6) a list of persons referred to.

Bundle of documents to be filed

16.1 The claimant must file a paginated and indexed bundle of all relevant documents required for the hearing of the judicial review when he files his skeleton argument.

16.2 The bundle must also include those documents required by the defendant and any other party who is to make representations at the hearing.

Agreed final order

17.1 If the parties agree about the final order to be made in a claim for judicial review, the claimant must file at the court a document (with 2 copies) signed by all the parties setting out the terms of the proposed agreed order together with a short statement of the matters relied on as justifying the proposed agreed order and copies of any authorities or statutory provisions relied on.

17.2 The court will consider the documents referred to in paragraph 17.1 and will make the order if satisfied that the order should be made.

17.3 If the court is not satisfied that the order should be made, a hearing date will be set.

17.4 Where the agreement relates to an order for costs only, the parties need only file a document signed by all the parties setting out the terms of the proposed order.

Practice Direction – Probate

This Practice Direction supplements CPR Part 57 (PD57)

****

IV CLAIMS UNDER THE INHERITANCE (PROVISION FOR FAMILY AND DEPENDANTS) ACT 1975

Acknowledgment of service by personal representative – rule 57.16(4)

15 Where a defendant who is a personal representative wishes to remain neutral in relation to the claim, and agrees to abide by any decision which the court may make, he should state this in Section A of the acknowledgment of service form.

Written evidence of personal representative – rule 57.16(5)

16 The written evidence filed by a defendant who is a personal representative must state to the best of that person's ability –

(1) full details of the value of the deceased's net estate, as defined in section 25(1) of the Act;

(2) the person or classes of persons beneficially interested in the estate, and –

(a) the names and (unless they are parties to the claim) addresses of all living beneficiaries; and

(b) the value of their interests in the estate so far as they are known.

(3) whether any living beneficiary (and if so, naming him) is a child or patient within the meaning of rule 21.1(2); and

(4) any facts which might affect the exercise of the court's powers under the Act.

Separate representation of claimants

17 If a claim is made jointly by two or more claimants, and it later appears that any of the claimants have a conflict of interests –

(1) any claimant may choose to be represented at any hearing by separate solicitors or counsel, or may appear in person; and

(2) if the court considers that claimants who are represented by the same solicitors or counsel ought to be separately represented, it may adjourn the application until they are.

Production of the grant

18.1 On the hearing of a claim the personal representative must produce to the court the original grant of representation to the deceased's estate.

18.2 If the court makes an order under the Act, the original grant (together with a sealed copy of the order) must be sent to the Principal Registry of the Family Division for a memorandum of the order to be endorsed on or permanently annexed to the grant in accordance with section 19(3) of the Act.

****

PART V

Practice Direction – Committal Applications

This Practice Direction is supplemental to RSC Order 52 (Schedule 1 to the CPR) and CCR Order 29 (Schedule 2 to the CPR) (PDCommittal)

GENERAL

1.1 Part I of this practice direction applies to any application for an order for committal of a person to prison for contempt of court (a 'committal application'). Part II makes additional provision where the committal application relates to a contempt in the face of the court.

1.2 Where the alleged contempt of court consists of or is based upon disobedience to an order made in a county court or breach of an undertaking given to a county court or consists of an act done in the course of proceedings in a county court, or where in any other way the alleged contempt is a contempt which the county court has power to punish, the committal application may be made in the county court in question.

1.3 In every other case (other than one within Part II of this practice direction), a committal application must be made in the High Court.

1.4 In all cases the Convention rights of those involved should particularly be borne in mind. It should be noted that the burden of proof, having regard to the possibility that a person may be sent to prison, is that the allegation be proved beyond reasonable doubt.

(Section 1 of the Human Rights Act defines 'the Convention rights'.)

PART I

COMMENCEMENT OF COMMITTAL PROCEEDINGS

2.1 A committal application must, subject to paragraph 2.2, be commenced by the issue of a Part 8 claim form (see paragraph 2.5).

2.2 (1) If the committal application is made in existing proceedings it must be commenced by the filing of an application notice in those proceedings.

(2) An application to commit for breach of an undertaking or order must be commenced by the filing of an application notice in the proceedings in which the undertaking was given or the order was made.

(3) The application notice must state that the application is made in the proceedings in question and its title and reference number must correspond with the title and reference number of those proceedings.

2.3 If the committal application is one which cannot be made without permission, the claim form or application notice, as the case may be, may not be issued or filed until the requisite permission has been granted.

2.4 If the permission of the court is needed in order to make a committal application –

(1) the permission must be applied for by filing an application notice (see CPR rule 23.2(4));

(2) the application notice need not be served on the respondent;

(3) the date on which and the name of the judge by whom the requisite permission was granted must be stated on the claim form or application notice by which the committal application is commenced;

(4) the permission may only be granted by a judge who, under paragraph 11, would have power to hear the committal application if permission were granted; and

(5) CPR rules 23.9 and 23.10 do not apply.

2.5 If the committal application is commenced by the issue of a claim form, CPR Part 8 shall, subject to the provisions of this practice direction, apply as though references to 'claimant' were references to the person making the committal application and references to 'defendant' were references to the person against whom the committal application is made (in this practice direction referred to as 'the respondent') but:

(1) the claim form together with copies of all written evidence in support must, unless the court otherwise directs, be served personally on the respondent,

(2) the claim form must set out in full the grounds on which the committal application is made and must identify, separately and numerically, each alleged act of contempt including, if known, the date of each alleged act,

(3) an amendment to the claim form can be made with the permission of the court but not otherwise,

(4) CPR rule 8.4 does not apply, and

(5) the claim form must contain a prominent notice stating the possible consequences of the court making a committal order and of the respondent not attending the hearing. A form of notice, which may be used, is annexed to this practice direction.

2.6 If a committal application is commenced by the filing of an application notice, CPR Part 23 shall, subject to the provisions of this practice direction, apply, but:

(1) the application notice together with copies of all written evidence in support must, unless the court otherwise directs, be served personally on the respondent,

(2) the application notice must set out in full the grounds on which the committal application is made and must identify, separately and numerically, each alleged act of contempt including, if known, the date of each of the alleged acts,

(3) an amendment to the application notice can be made with the permission of the court but not otherwise, and

(4) the court may not dispose of the committal application without a hearing.

(5) the application notice must contain a prominent notice stating the possible consequences of the court making a committal order and of the respondent not attending the hearing. A form of notice, which may be used, is annexed to this practice direction.

WRITTEN EVIDENCE

3.1 Written evidence in support of or in opposition to a committal application must be given by affidavit.

3.2 Written evidence served in support of or in opposition to a committal application must, unless the court otherwise directs, be filed.

3.3 A respondent may give oral evidence at the hearing, whether or not he has filed or served any written evidence. If he does so, he may be cross-examined.

3.4 A respondent may, with the permission of the court, call a witness to give oral evidence at the hearing whether or not the witness has sworn an affidavit.

CASE MANAGEMENT AND DATE OF HEARING

4.1 The applicant for the committal order must, when lodging the claim form or application notice with the court for issuing or filing, as the case may be, obtain from the court a date for the hearing of the committal application.

4.2 Unless the court otherwise directs, the hearing date of a committal application shall be not less than 14 clear days after service of the claim form or of the application notice, as the case may be, on the respondent. The hearing date must be specified in the claim form or application notice or in a Notice of Hearing or Application attached to and served with the claim form or application notice.

4.3 The court may, however, at any time give case management directions, including directions for the service of written evidence by the respondent and written evidence in reply by the applicant, or may convene and hold a directions hearing.

4.4 The court may on the hearing date –

(1) give case management directions with a view to a hearing of the committal application on a future date, or
(2) if the committal application is ready to be heard, proceed forthwith to hear it.

4.5 In dealing with any committal application, the court will have regard to the need for the respondent to have details of the alleged acts of contempt and the opportunity to respond to the committal application.

4.6 The court should also have regard to the need for the respondent to be –

(1) allowed a reasonable time for responding to the committal application including, if necessary, preparing a defence;
(2) made aware of the availability of assistance from the Community Legal Service and how to contact the Service;
(3) given the opportunity, if unrepresented, to obtain legal advice; and
(4) if unable to understand English, allowed to make arrangements, seeking the assistance of the court if necessary, for an interpreter to attend the hearing.

STRIKING OUT

5 The court may, on application by the respondent or on its own initiative, strike out a committal application if it appears to the court:

(1) that the committal application and the evidence served in support of it disclose no reasonable ground for alleging that the respondent is guilty of a contempt of court,
(2) that the committal application is an abuse of the court's process or, if made in existing proceedings, is otherwise likely to obstruct the just disposal of those proceedings, or
(3) that there has been a failure to comply with a rule, practice direction or court order.

(CPR Part 3 contains general powers for the management by the court.)

MISCELLANEOUS

6 CPR rules 35.7 (Court's power to direct that evidence is to be given by a single joint expert), 35.8 (Instructions to single joint expert) and 35.9 (Power of court to direct a party to provide information) do not apply to committal applications.

7 An order under CPR rule 18.1 (Order for a party to give additional information) may not be made against a respondent to a committal application.

8 A committal application may not be discontinued without the permission of the court.

9 A committal application should normally be heard in public (see CPR rule 39.2), but if it is heard in private and the court finds the respondent guilty of contempt of court, the judge shall, when next sitting in public, state:

(1) the name of the respondent,
(2) in general terms the nature of the contempt or contempts found proved, and,
(3) the penalty (if any) imposed.

10 The court may waive any procedural defect in the commencement or conduct of a committal application if satisfied that no injustice has been caused to the respondent by the defect.

11 Except where under an enactment a master or district judge has power to make a committal order[1], a committal order can only be made:

(1) in High Court proceedings, by a High Court judge or a person authorised to act as such[2],
(2) in county court proceedings by a circuit judge or a person authorised to act or capable by virtue of his office of acting as such[3].

1 Eg ss 14 and 118, County Courts Act 1984.
2 See s 9(1), Supreme Court Act 1981.
3 See s 5(3), County Courts Act 1984.

PART II

12 Where the committal application relates to a contempt in the face of the court the following matters should be given particular attention. Normally, it will be appropriate to defer consideration of the behaviour to allow the respondent time to reflect on what has occurred. The time needed for the following procedures should allow such a period of reflection.

13 A Part 8 claim form and an application notice are not required for Part II, but other provisions of this practice direction should be applied, as necessary, or adapted to the circumstances. In addition the judge should:

(1) tell the respondent of the possible penalty he faces;
(2) inform the respondent in detail, and preferably in writing, of the actions and behaviour of the respondent which have given rise to the committal application;
(3) if he considers that an apology would remove the need for the committal application, tell the respondent;
(4) have regard to the need for the respondent to be –
    (a) allowed a reasonable time for responding to the committal application, including, if necessary, preparing a defence;
    (b) made aware of the availability of assistance from the Community Legal Service and how to contact the Service;

(c) given the opportunity, if unrepresented, to obtain legal advice;
(d) if unable to understand English, allowed to make arrangements, seeking the court's assistance if necessary, for an interpreter to attend the hearing; and
(e) brought back before the court for the committal application to be heard within a reasonable time.

(5) allow the respondent an opportunity to –
(a) apologise to the court;
(b) explain his actions and behaviour; and,
(c) if the contempt is proved, to address the court on the penalty to be imposed on him;

(6) if there is a risk of the appearance of bias, ask another judge to hear the committal application.

(7) where appropriate, nominate a suitable person to give the respondent the information.

(It is likely to be appropriate to nominate a person where the effective communication of information by the judge to the respondent was not possible when the incident occurred.)

14 Where the committal application is to be heard by another judge, a written statement by the judge before whom the actions and behaviour of the respondent which have given rise to the committal application took place may be submitted as evidence of those actions and behaviour.

Annex

IMPORTANT NOTICE

The court has power to send you to prison and to fine you if it finds that any of the allegations made against you are true and amount to a contempt of court.

You must attend court on the date shown on the front of this form. It is in your own interest to do so. You should bring with you any witnesses and documents which you think will help you put your side of the case.

If you consider the allegations are not true you must tell the court why. If it is established that they are true, you must tell the court of any good reason why they do not amount to a contempt of court, or, if they do, why you should not be punished.

If you need advice you should show this document at once to your solicitor or go to a Citizens' Advice Bureau.

PART VI

European Regulations

PART VI: European Regulations

Contents

Council Regulation (EC) No 1347/2000

of 29 May 2000

on jurisdiction and the recognition and enforcement of judgments in matrimonial matters and in matters of parental responsibility for children of both spouses

THE COUNCIL OF THE EUROPEAN UNION

Having regard to the Treaty establishing the European Community, and in particular Article 61(*c*) and Article 67(1) thereof,

Having regard to the proposal from the Commission,

Having regard to the opinion of the European Parliament,

Having regard to the opinion of the Economic and Social Committee,

Whereas:

(1) The Member States have set themselves the objective of maintaining and developing the Union as an area of freedom, security and justice, in which the free movement of persons is assured. To establish such an area, the Community is to adopt, among others, the measures in the field of judicial co-operation in civil matters needed for the proper functioning of the internal market.

(2) The proper functioning of the internal market entails the need to improve and simplify the free movement of judgments in civil matters.

(3) This is a subject now falling within the ambit of Article 65 of the Treaty.

(4) Differences between certain national rules governing jurisdiction and enforcement hamper the free movement of persons and the sound operation of the internal market. There are accordingly grounds for enacting provisions to unify the rules of conflict of jurisdiction in matrimonial matters and in matters of parental responsibility so as to simplify the formalities for rapid and automatic recognition and enforcement of judgments.

(5) In accordance with the principles of subsidiarity and proportionality as set out in Article 5 of the Treaty, the objectives of this Regulation cannot be sufficiently achieved by the Member States and can therefore be better achieved by the Community. This Regulation does not go beyond what is necessary to achieve those objectives.

(6) The Council, by an Act dated 28 May 1998, drew up a Convention on jurisdiction and the recognition and enforcement of judgments in matrimonial matters and recommended it for adoption by the Member States in accordance with their respective constitutional rules. Continuity in the results of the negotiations for conclusion of the Convention should be ensured. The content of this Regulation is substantially taken over from the Convention, but this Regulation contains a number of new provisions not in the Convention in order to secure consistency with certain provisions of the proposed regulation on jurisdiction and the recognition and enforcement of judgments in civil and commercial matters.

(7) In order to attain the objective of free movement of judgments in matrimonial matters and in matters of parental responsibility within the Community, it is necessary and appropriate that the cross-border recognition of jurisdiction and judgments in relation to the dissolution of matrimonial ties and to parental

responsibility for the children of both spouses be governed by a mandatory, and directly applicable, Community legal instrument.

(8) The measures laid down in this Regulation should be consistent and uniform, to enable people to move as widely as possible. Accordingly, it should also apply to nationals of non-member States whose links with the territory of a Member State are sufficiently close, in keeping with the grounds of jurisdiction laid down in the Regulation.

(9) The scope of this Regulation should cover civil proceedings and non-judicial proceedings in matrimonial matters in certain States, and exclude purely religious procedures. It should therefore be provided that the reference to "courts" includes all the authorities, judicial or otherwise, with jurisdiction in matrimonial matters.

(10) This Regulation should be confined to proceedings relating to divorce, legal separation or marriage annulment. The recognition of divorce and annulment rulings affects only the dissolution of matrimonial ties; despite the fact that they may be interrelated, the Regulation does not affect issues such as the fault of the spouses, property consequences of the marriage, the maintenance obligation or any other ancillary measures.

(11) This Regulation covers parental responsibility for children of both spouses on issues that are closely linked to proceedings for divorce, legal separation or marriage annulment.

(12) The grounds of jurisdiction accepted in this Regulation are based on the rule that there must be a real link between the party concerned and the Member State exercising jurisdiction; the decision to include certain grounds corresponds to the fact that they exist in different national legal systems and are accepted by the other Member States.

(13) One of the risks to be considered in relation to the protection of the children of both spouses in a marital crisis is that one of the parents will take the child to another country. The fundamental interests of the children must therefore be protected, in accordance with, in particular, the Hague Convention of 25 October 1980 on the Civil Aspects of the International Abduction of Children. The lawful habitual residence is accordingly maintained as the grounds of jurisdiction in cases where, because the child has been moved or has not been returned without lawful reason, there has been a de facto change in the habitual residence.

(14) This Regulation does not prevent the courts of a Member State from taking provisional, including protective, measures, in urgent cases, with regard to persons or property situated in that State.

(15) The word "judgment" refers only to decisions that lead to divorce, legal separation or marriage annulment. Those documents which have been formally drawn up or registered as authentic instruments and are enforceable in one Member State are treated as equivalent to such "judgments".

(16) The recognition and enforcement of judgments given in a Member State are based on the principle of mutual trust. The grounds for non-recognition are kept to the minimum required. Those proceedings should incorporate provisions to ensure observance of public policy in the State addressed and to safeguard the rights of the defence and those of the parties, including the individual rights of any child involved, and so as to withhold recognition of irreconcilable judgments.

(17) The State addressed should review neither the jurisdiction of the State of origin nor the findings of fact.

(18) No procedures may be required for the updating of civil-status documents in one Member State on the basis of a final judgment given in another Member State.

(19) The Convention concluded by the Nordic States in 1931 should be capable of application within the limits set by this Regulation.

(20) Spain, Italy and Portugal had concluded Concordats before the matters covered by this Regulation were brought within the ambit of the Treaty: it is necessary to ensure that these States do not breach their international commitments in relation to the Holy See.

(21) The Member States should remain free to agree among themselves on practical measures for the application of the Regulation as long as no Community measures have been taken to that end.

(22) Annexes I to III relating to the courts and redress procedures should be amended by the Commission on the basis of amendments transmitted by the Member State concerned. Amendments to Annexes IV and V should be adopted in accordance with Council Decision 1999/468/EC of 28 June 1999 laying down the procedures for the exercise of implementing powers conferred on the Commission.

(23) No later than five years after the date of the entry into force of this Regulation, the Commission is to review its application and propose such amendments as may appear necessary.

(24) The United Kingdom and Ireland, in accordance with Article 3 of the Protocol on the position of the United Kingdom and Ireland annexed to the Treaty on European Union and the Treaty establishing the European Community, have given notice of their wish to take part in the adoption and application of this Regulation.

(25) Denmark, in accordance with Articles 1 and 2 of the Protocol on the position of Denmark annexed to the Treaty on European Union and the Treaty establishing the European Community, is not participating in the adoption of this Regulation, and is therefore not bound by it nor subject to its application,

HAS ADOPTED THIS REGULATION:

CHAPTER I
SCOPE

ARTICLE 1

1 This Regulation shall apply to:

(*a*) civil proceedings relating to divorce, legal separation or marriage annulment;

(*b*) civil proceedings relating to parental responsibility for the children of both spouses on the occasion of the matrimonial proceedings referred to in (*a*).

2 Other proceedings officially recognised in a Member State shall be regarded as equivalent to judicial proceedings. The term "court" shall cover all the authorities with jurisdiction in these matters in the Member States.

3 In this Regulation, the term "Member State" shall mean all Member States with the exception of Denmark.

CHAPTER II
JURISDICTION

Section 1

General Provisions

ARTICLE 2

Divorce, legal separation and marriage annulment

1 In matters relating to divorce, legal separation or marriage annulment, jurisdiction shall lie with the courts of the Member State:

(*a*) in whose territory:
- the spouses are habitually resident, or
- the spouses were last habitually resident, insofar as one of them still resides there, or
- the respondent is habitually resident, or
- in the event of a joint application, either of the spouses is habitually resident, or
- the applicant is habitually resident if he or she resided there for at least a year immediately before the application was made, or
- the applicant is habitually resident if he or she resided there for at least six months immediately before the application was made and is either a national of the Member State in question or, in the case of the United Kingdom and Ireland, has his "domicile" there:

(*b*) of the nationality of both spouses or, in the case of the United Kingdom and Ireland, of the "domicile" of both spouses.

2 For the purpose of this Regulation, "domicile" shall have the same meaning as it has under the legal systems of the United Kingdom and Ireland.

ARTICLE 3

Parental responsibility

1 The Courts of a Member State exercising jurisdiction by virtue of Article 2 on an application for divorce, legal separation or marriage annulment shall have jurisdiction in a matter relating to parental responsibility over a child of both spouses where the child is habitually resident in that Member State.

2 Where the child is not habitually resident in the Member State referred to in paragraph 1, the courts of that State shall have jurisdiction in such a matter if the child is habitually resident in one of the Member States and:

(*a*) at least one of the spouses has parental responsibility in relation to the child; and

(*b*) the jurisdiction of the courts has been accepted by the spouses and is in the best interests of the child.

3 The jurisdiction conferred by paragraphs 1 and 2 shall cease as soon as:

(*a*) the judgment allowing or refusing the application for divorce, legal separation or marriage annulment has become final; or (*b*) in those cases where proceedings in relation to parental responsibility are still pending on the date referred to in (*a*), a judgment in these proceedings has become final; or

(*c*) the proceedings referred to in (*a*) and (*b*) have come to an end for another reason.

ARTICLE 4

Child abduction

The courts with jurisdiction within the meaning of Article 3 shall exercise their jurisdiction in conformity with the Hague Convention of 25 October 1980 on the Civil Aspects of International Child Abduction, and in particular Articles 3 and 16 thereof.

ARTICLE 5

Counterclaim

The court in which proceedings are pending on the basis of Articles 2 to 4 shall also have jurisdiction to examine a counterclaim, insofar as the latter comes within the scope of this Regulation.

ARTICLE 6

Conversion of legal separation into divorce

Without prejudice to Article 2, a court of a Member State which has given a judgment on a legal separation shall also have jurisdiction for converting that judgment into a divorce, if the law of that Member State so provides.

ARTICLE 7

Exclusive nature of jurisdiction under Articles 2 to 6

A spouse who:

(*a*) is habitually resident in the territory of a Member State; or

(*b*) is a national of a Member State, or, in the case of the United Kingdom and Ireland, has his or her "domicile" in the territory of one of the latter Member States,

may be sued in another Member State only in accordance with Articles 2 to 6.

ARTICLE 8

Residual jurisdiction

1 Where no court of a Member State has jurisdiction pursuant to Articles 2 to 6, jurisdiction shall be determined, in each Member State, by the laws of that State.

2 As against a respondent who is not habitually resident and is not either a national of a Member State or, in the case of the United Kingdom and Ireland, does not have his "domicile" within the territory of one of the latter Member States, any national of a Member State who is habitually resident within the territory of

another Member State may, like the nationals of that State, avail himself of the rules of jurisdiction applicable in that State.

Section 2

Examination as to jurisdiction and admissibility

ARTICLE 9

Examination as to jurisdiction

Where a court of a Member State is seised of a case over which it has no jurisdiction under this Regulation and over which a court of another Member State has jurisdiction by virtue of this Regulation, it shall declare of its own motion that it has no jurisdiction.

ARTICLE 10

Examination as to admissibility

1 Where a respondent habitually resident in a State other than the Member State where the action was brought does not enter an appearance, the court with jurisdiction shall stay the proceedings so long as it is not shown that the respondent has been able to receive the document instituting the proceedings or an equivalent document in sufficient time to enable him to arrange for his defence, or that all necessary steps have been taken to this end.

2 Article 19 of Council Regulation (EC) No 1348/2000 of 29 May 2000 on the service in the Member States of judicial and extra-judicial documents in civil or commercial matters, shall apply instead of the provisions of paragraph 1 of this Article if the document instituting the proceedings or an equivalent document had to be transmitted from one Member State to another pursuant to that Regulation.

3 Where the provisions of Council Regulation (EC) No 1348/2000 are not applicable, Article 15 of the Hague Convention of 15 November 1965 on the service abroad of judicial and extra-judicial documents in civil or commercial matters shall apply if the document instituting the proceedings or an equivalent document had to be transmitted abroad pursuant to that Convention.

Section 3

Lis pendens and dependent actions

ARTICLE 11

1 Where proceedings involving the same cause of action and between the same parties are brought before courts of different Member States, the court second seised shall of its own motion stay its proceedings until such time as the jurisdiction of the court first seised is established.

2 Where proceedings for divorce, legal separation or marriage annulment not involving the same cause of action and between the same parties are brought before courts of different Member States, the court second seised shall of its own motion stay its proceedings until such time as the jurisdiction of the court first seised is established.

3 Where the jurisdiction of the court first seised is established, the court second seised shall decline jurisdiction in favour of that court.

In that case, the party who brought the relevant action before the court second seised may bring that action before the court first seised.

4 For the purposes of this Article, a court shall be deemed to be seised:

(*a*) at the time when the document instituting the proceedings or an equivalent document is lodged with the court, provided that the applicant has not subsequently failed to take the steps he was required to take to have service effected on the respondent; or

(*b*) if the document has to be served before being lodged with the court, at the time when it is received by the authority responsible for service, provided that the applicant has not subsequently failed to take the steps he was required to take to have the document lodged with the court.

Section 4
Provisional, including protective, measures

ARTICLE 12

In urgent cases, the provisions of this Regulation shall not prevent the courts of a Member State from taking such provisional, including protective, measures in respect of persons or assets in that State as may be available under the law of that Member State, even if, under this Regulation, the court of another Member State has jurisdiction as to the substance of the matter.

CHAPTER III
RECOGNITION AND ENFORCEMENT

ARTICLE 13

Meaning of "judgment"

1 For the purposes of this Regulation, "judgment" means a divorce, legal separation or marriage annulment pronounced by a court of a Member State, as well as a judgment relating to the parental responsibility of the spouses given on the occasion of such matrimonial proceedings, whatever the judgment may be called, including a decree, order or decision.

2 The provisions of this chapter shall also apply to the determination of the amount of costs and expenses of proceedings under this Regulation and to the enforcement of any order concerning such costs and expenses.

3 For the purposes of implementing this Regulation, documents which have been formally drawn up or registered as authentic instruments and are enforceable in one Member State and also settlements which have been approved by a court in the course of proceedings and are enforceable in the Member State in which they were concluded shall be recognised and declared enforceable under the same conditions as the judgments referred to in paragraph 1.

Section 1
Recognition

ARTICLE 14

Recognition of a judgment

1 A judgment given in a Member State shall be recognised in the other Member States without any special procedure being required.

2 In particular, and without prejudice to paragraph 3, no special procedure shall be required for up-dating the civil-status records of a Member State on the basis of a judgment relating to divorce, legal separation or marriage annulment given in another Member State, and against which no further appeal lies under the law of that Member State.

3 Any interested party may, in accordance with the procedures provided for in Sections 2 and 3 of this Chapter, apply for a decision that the judgment be or not be recognised.

4 Where the recognition of a judgment is raised as an incidental question in a court of a Member State, that court may determine that issue.

ARTICLE 15

Grounds of non-recognition

1 A judgment relating to a divorce, legal separation or marriage annulment shall not be recognised:

(*a*) if such recognition is manifestly contrary to the public policy of the Member State in which recognition is sought;
(*b*) where it was given in default of appearance, if the respondent was not served with the document which instituted the proceedings or with an equivalent document in sufficient time and in such a way as to enable the respondent to arrange for his or her defence unless it is determined that the respondent has accepted the judgment unequivocally;
(*c*) if it is irreconcilable with a judgment given in proceedings between the same parties in the Member State in which recognition is sought; or
(*d*) if it is irreconcilable with an earlier judgment given in another Member State or in a non-member State between the same parties, provided that the earlier judgment fulfils the conditions necessary for its recognition in the Member State in which recognition is sought.

2 A judgment relating to the parental responsibility of the spouses given on the occasion of matrimonial proceedings as referred to in Article 13 shall not be recognised:

(*a*) if such recognition is manifestly contrary to the public policy of the Member State in which recognition is sought taking into account the best interests of the child;
(*b*) if it was given, except in case of urgency, without the child having been given an opportunity to be heard, in violation of fundamental principles of procedure of the Member State in which recognition is sought;
(*c*) where it was given in default of appearance if the person in default was not served with the document which instituted the proceedings or with an equivalent document in sufficient time and in such a way as to enable that

person to arrange for his or her defence unless it is determined that such person has accepted the judgment unequivocally;

(*d*) on the request of any person claiming that the judgment infringes his or her parental responsibility, if it was given without such person having been given an opportunity to be heard;

(*e*) if it is irreconcilable with a later judgment relating to parental responsibility given in the Member State in which recognition is sought; or

(*f*) if it is irreconcilable with a later judgment relating to parental responsibility given in another Member State or in the non-member State of the habitual residence of the child provided that the later judgment fulfils the conditions necessary for its recognition in the Member State in which recognition is sought.

ARTICLE 16

Agreement with third States

A court of a Member State may, on the basis of an agreement on the recognition and enforcement of judgments, not recognise a judgment given in another Member State where, in cases provided for in Article 8, the judgment could only be founded on grounds of jurisdiction other than those specified in Articles 2 to 7.

ARTICLE 17

Prohibition of review of jurisdiction of court of origin

The jurisdiction of the court of the Member State of origin may not be reviewed. The test of public policy referred to in Article 15(1)(*a*) and (2)(*a*) may not be applied to the rules relating to jurisdiction set out in Articles 2 to 8.

ARTICLE 18

Differences in applicable law

The recognition of a judgment relating to a divorce, legal separation or a marriage annulment may not be refused because the law of the Member State in which such recognition is sought would not allow divorce, legal separation or marriage annulment on the same facts.

ARTICLE 19

Non-review as to substance

Under no circumstances may a judgment be reviewed as to its substance.

ARTICLE 20

Stay of proceedings

1 A court of a Member State in which recognition is sought of a judgment given in another Member State may stay the proceedings if an ordinary appeal against the judgment has been lodged.

2 A court of a Member State in which recognition is sought of a judgment given in Ireland or the United Kingdom may stay the proceedings if enforcement is suspended in the Member State of origin by reason of an appeal.

Section 2
Enforcement

ARTICLE 21

Enforceable judgments

1 A judgment on the exercise of parental responsibility in respect of a child of both parties given in a Member State which is enforceable in that Member State and has been served shall be enforced in another member State when, on the application of any interested party, it has been declared enforceable there.

2 However, in the United Kingdom, such a judgment shall be enforced in England and Wales, in Scotland or in Northern Ireland when, on the application of any interested party, it has been registered for enforcement in that part of the United Kingdom.

ARTICLE 22

Jurisdiction of local courts

1 An application for a declaration of enforceability shall be submitted to the court appearing in the list in Annex I.

2 The local jurisdiction shall be determined by reference to the place of the habitual residence of the person against whom enforcement is sought or by reference to the habitual residence of any child to whom the application relates.

Where neither of the places referred to in the first sub-paragraph can be found in the Member State where enforcement is sought, the local jurisdiction shall be determined by reference to the place of enforcement.

3 In relation to procedures referred to in Article 14(3), the local jurisdiction shall be determined by the internal law of the Member State in which proceedings for recognition or non-recognition are brought.

ARTICLE 23

Procedure for enforcement

1 The procedure for making the application shall be governed by the law of the Member State in which enforcement is sought.

2 The applicant must give an address for service within the area of jurisdiction of the court applied to. However, if the law of the Member State in which enforcement is sought does not provide for the furnishing of such an address, the applicant shall appoint a representative ad litem.

3 The documents referred to in Articles 32 and 33 shall be attached to the application.

ARTICLE 24

Decision of the court

1 The court applied to shall give its decision without delay. The person against whom enforcement is sought shall not at this stage of the proceedings be entitled to make any submissions on the application.

2 The application may be refused only for one of the reasons specified in Articles 15, 16 and 17.

3 Under no circumstances may a judgment be reviewed as to its substance.

ARTICLE 25

Notice of the decision

The appropriate officer of the court shall without delay bring to the notice of the applicant the decision given on the application in accordance with the procedure laid down by the law of the Member State in which enforcement is sought.

ARTICLE 26

Appeal against the enforcement decision

1 The decision on the application for a declaration of enforceability may be appealed against by either party.

2 The appeal shall be lodged with the court appearing in the list in Annex II.

3 The appeal shall be dealt with in accordance with the rules governing procedure in contradictory matters.

4 If the appeal is brought by the applicant for a declaration of enforceability, the party against whom enforcement is sought shall be summoned to appear before the appellate court. If such person fails to appear, the provisions of Article 10 shall apply.

5 An appeal against a declaration of enforceability must be lodged within one month of service thereof. If the party against whom enforcement is sought is habitually resident in a Member State other than that in which the declaration of enforceability was given, the time for appealing shall be two months and shall run

from the date of service, either on him or at his residence. No extension of time may be granted on account of distance.

ARTICLE 27

Courts of appeal and means of contest

The judgment given on appeal may be contested only by the proceedings referred to in Annex III.

ARTICLE 28

Stay of proceedings

1 The court with which the appeal is lodged under Articles 26 or 27 may, on the application of the party against whom enforcement is sought, stay the proceedings if an ordinary appeal has been lodged in the Member State of origin or if the time for such appeal has not yet expired. In the latter case, the court may specify the time within which an appeal is to be lodged.

2 Where the judgment was given in Ireland or the United Kingdom, any form of appeal available in the Member State of origin shall be treated as an ordinary appeal for the purposes of paragraph 1.

ARTICLE 29

Partial enforcement

1 Where a judgment has been given in respect of several matters and enforcement cannot be authorised for all of them, the court shall authorise enforcement for one or more of them.

2 An applicant may request partial enforcement of a judgment.

ARTICLE 30

Legal aid

An applicant who, in the Member State of origin, has benefited from complete or partial legal aid or exemption from costs or expenses shall be entitled, in the procedures provided for in Articles 22 to 25, to benefit from the most favourable legal aid or the most extensive exemption from costs and expenses provided for by the law of the Member State addressed.

ARTICLE 31

Security, bond or deposit

No security, bond or deposit, however described, shall be required of a party who in one Member State applies for enforcement of a judgment given in another Member State on the following grounds:

(*a*) that he or she is not habitually resident in the Member State in which enforcement is sought; or (*b*) that he or she is either a foreign national or, where enforcement is sought in either the United Kingdom or Ireland, does not have his or her "domicile" in either of those Member States.

Section 3
Common provisions

ARTICLE 32

Documents

1 A party seeking or contesting recognition or applying for a declaration of enforceability shall produce:

(*a*) a copy of the judgment which satisfies the conditions necessary to establish its authenticity; and
(*b*) a certificate referred to in Article 33.

2 In addition, in the case of a judgment given in default, the party seeking recognition or applying for a declaration of enforceability shall produce:

(*a*) the original or certified true copy of the document which establishes that the defaulting party was served with the document instituting the proceedings or with an equivalent document; or
(*b*) any document indicating that the defendant has accepted the judgment unequivocally.

ARTICLE 33

Other documents

The competent court or authority of a Member State where a judgment was given shall issue, at the request of any interested party, a certificate using the standard form in Annex IV (judgments in matrimonial matters) or Annex V (judgments on parental responsibility).

ARTICLE 34

Absence of documents

1 If the documents specified in Article 32(1)(*b*) or (2) are not produced, the court may specify a time for their production, accept equivalent documents or, if it considers that it has sufficient information before it, dispense with their production.

2 If the court so requires, a translation of such documents shall be furnished. The translation shall be certified by a person qualified to do so in one of the Member States.

ARTICLE 35

Legalisation or other similar formality

No legalisation or other similar formality shall be required in respect of the documents referred to in Articles 32, 33 or 34(2) or in respect of a document appointing a representative ad litem.

CHAPTER IV
GENERAL PROVISIONS

ARTICLE 36

Relation with other instruments

1 Subject to the provisions of Articles 38, 42 and paragraph 2 of this Article, this Regulation shall, for the Member States, supersede conventions existing at the time of entry into force of this Regulation which have been concluded between two or more Member States and relate to matters governed by this Regulation.

2

(*a*) Finland and Sweden shall have the option of declaring that the Convention of 6 February 1931 between Denmark, Finland, Iceland, Norway and Sweden comprising international private law provisions on marriage, adoption and guardianship, together with the Final Protocol thereto, will apply, in whole or in part, in their mutual relations, in place of the rules of this Regulation. Such declarations shall be annexed to this Regulation and published in the Official Journal of the European Communities. They may be withdrawn, in whole or in part, at any moment by the said Member States.

(*b*) The principle of non-discrimination on the grounds of nationality between citizens of the Union shall be respected.

(*c*) The rules of jurisdiction in any future agreement to be concluded between the Member States referred to in sub-paragraph (*a*) which relate to matters governed by this Regulation shall be in line with those laid down in this Regulation.

(*d*) Judgments handed down in any of the Nordic States which have made the declaration provided for in sub-paragraph (*a*) under a forum of jurisdiction corresponding to one of those laid down in Chapter II, shall be recognised and enforced in the other Member States under the rules laid down in Chapter III.

3 Member States shall send to the Commission:

(*a*) a copy of the agreements and uniform laws implementing these agreements referred to in paragraphs 2(*a*) and (*c*);

(*b*) any denunciations of, or amendments to, those agreements or uniform laws.

ARTICLE 37

Relations with certain multilateral conventions

In relations between Member States, this Regulation shall take precedence over the following Conventions insofar as they concern matters governed by this Regulation:

– the Hague Convention of 5 October 1961 concerning the Powers of Authorities and the Law Applicable in respect of the Protection of Minors,
– the Luxembourg Convention of 8 September 1967 on the Recognition of Decisions Relating to the Validity of Marriages,
– The Hague Convention of 1 June 1970 on the Recognition of Divorces and Legal Separations,
– The European Convention of 20 May 1980 on Recognition and Enforcement of Decisions concerning Custody of Children and on Restoration of Custody of Children,
– the Hague Convention of 19 October 1996 on Jurisdiction, Applicable law, Recognition, Enforcement and Co-operation in Respect of Parental Responsibility and Measures for the Protection of Children, provided that the child concerned is habitually resident in a Member State.

ARTICLE 38

Extent of effects

1 The agreements and conventions referred to in Articles 36(1) and 37 shall continue to have effect in relation to matters to which this Regulation does not apply.

2 They shall continue to have effect in respect of judgments given and documents formally drawn up or registered as authentic before the entry into force of this Regulation.

ARTICLE 39

Agreements between Member States

1 Two or more Member States may conclude agreements or arrangements to amplify this Regulation or to facilitate its application.

Member States shall send to the Commission:

(*a*) a copy of the draft agreements; and
(*b*) any denunciations of, or amendments to, these agreements.

2 In no circumstances may the agreements or arrangements derogate from Chapters II or III.

ARTICLE 40

Treaties with the Holy See

1 This Regulation shall apply without prejudice to the International Treaty (Concordat) between the Holy See and Portugal, signed at the Vatican City on 7 May 1940.

2 Any decision as to the invalidity of a marriage taken under the Treaty referred to in paragraph 1 shall be recognised in the Member States on the conditions laid down in Chapter III.

3 The provisions laid down in paragraphs 1 and 2 shall also apply to the following international treaties (Concordats) with the Holy See:

(*a*) Concordato lateranense of 11 February 1929 between Italy and the Holy See, modified by the agreement, with additional Protocol signed in Rome on 18 February 1984;

(*b*) Agreement between the Holy See and Spain on legal affairs of 3 January 1979.

4 Recognition of the decisions provided for in paragraph 2 may, in Italy or in Spain, be subject to the same procedures and the same checks as are applicable to decisions of the ecclesiastical courts handed down in accordance with the international treaties concluded with the Holy See referred to in paragraph 3.

5 Member States shall send to the Commission:

(*a*) a copy of the Treaties referred to in paragraphs 1 and 3;

(*b*) any denunciations of or amendments to those Treaties.

ARTICLE 41

Member States with two or more legal systems

With regard to a Member State in which two or more systems of law or sets of rules concerning matters governed by this Regulation apply in different territorial units:

(*a*) any reference to habitual residence in that Member State shall refer to habitual residence in a territorial unit;

(*b*) any reference to nationality, or in the case of the United Kingdom "domicile", shall refer to the territorial unit designated by the law of that State;

(*c*) any reference to the authority of a Member State having received an application for divorce or legal separation or for marriage annulment shall refer to the authority of a territorial unit which has received such an application;

(*d*) any reference to the rules of the requested Member State shall refer to the rules of the territorial unit in which jurisdiction, recognition or enforcement is invoked.

CHAPTER V
TRANSITIONAL PROVISIONS

ARTICLE 42

1 The provisions of this Regulation shall apply only to legal proceedings instituted, to documents formally drawn up or registered as authentic instruments and to settlements which have been approved by a court in the course of proceedings after its entry into force.

2 Judgments given after the date of entry into force of this Regulation in proceedings instituted before that date shall be recognised and enforced in accordance with the provisions of Chapter III if jurisdiction was founded on rules which accorded with those provided for either in Chapter II of this Regulation or in a convention concluded between the Member State of origin and the Member State addressed which was in force when the proceedings were instituted.

CHAPTER VI
FINAL PROVISIONS

ARTICLE 43

Review

No later than 1 March 2006, and every five years thereafter, the Commission shall present to the European Parliament, the Council and the Economic and Social Committee a report on the application of this Regulation, and in particular Articles 36, 39 and 40(2) thereof. The report shall be accompanied if need be by proposals for adaptations.

ARTICLE 44

Amendment to lists of courts and redress procedures

1 Member States shall notify the Commission of the texts amending the lists of courts and redress procedures set out in Annexes I to III. The Commission shall adapt the Annexes concerned accordingly.

2 The updating or making of technical amendments to the standard forms set out in Annexes IV and V shall be adopted in accordance with the advisory procedure set out in Article 45(2).

ARTICLE 45

1 The Commission shall be assisted by a committee.

2 Where reference is made to this paragraph, Articles 3 and 7 of Decision 1999/468 EC shall apply.

3 The committee shall adopt its rules of procedure.

ARTICLE 46

Entry into force

This Regulation shall enter into force on 1 March 2001

This Regulation shall be binding in its entirety and directly applicable in the Member States in accordance with the Treaty establishing the European Community.

Done at Brussels, 29 May 2000.

For the Council
The President
A. Costa

ANNEX I

The applications provided for by Article 22 shall be submitted to the following courts:

– in Belgium, the "tribunal de première instance"/"rechtbank van eerste aanleg"/"erstinstanzliches Gericht",

– in Germany:

  – in the district of the "Kammergericht" (Berlin). The "Familiengericht Pankow/Weissensee",
  – in the districts of the remaining "Oberlandesgerichte" to the "Familiengericht" located at the seat of the respective "Oberlandesgericht",

– in Greece, the "Μονομελές Πρωτοδικείο",

– in Spain, the "Juzgado de Primera Instancia",

– in France, the presiding Judge of the "tribunal de grande instance",

– in Ireland, the High Court,

– in Italy, the "Corte d'apello",

– in Luxembourg, the presiding Judge of the "Tribunal d'arrondissement",

– in the Netherlands, the presiding Judge of the "arrondissementsrechtbank",

– in Austria, the "Bezirksgericht",

– in Portugal, the "Tribunal de Comarca" or "Tribunal de Familia",

– in Finland, the "käräjäoikeus"/"tinsgrätt",

– in Sweden, the "Svea hovrätt",

– in the United Kingdom:

(*a*) in England and Wales, the High Court of Justice;
(*b*) in Scotland, the Court of Session;

(c) in Northern Ireland, the High Court of Justice;
(d) in Gibraltar, the Supreme Court.

ANNEX II

The appeal provided for by Article 26 shall be lodged with the courts listed below:

– in Belgium:

(a) a person applying for a declaration of enforceability may lodge an appeal with the "cour d'appel" or the "hof van beroep";
(b) the person against whom enforcement is sought may lodge opposition with the "tribunal de première instance"/"rechtbank van eerste aanleg"/"erstinstanzliches Gericht",

– in Germany, the "Oberlandesgericht",

– in Greece, the "Εφετειο",

– in Spain, the "Audiencia Provincial",

– in France, the "Cour d'appel",

– in Ireland, the High Court,

– in Italy, the "Corte d'appello",

– in Luxembourg, the "Cour d'appel",

– in the Netherlands:

(a) if the applicant or the respondent who has appeared lodges the appeal: with the "gereschtshof";
(b) if the respondent who has been granted leave not to appear lodges the appeal: with the "arrondissementsrechtbank",

– in Austria, the "Bezirksgericht",

– in Portugal, the "Tribunal da Relação",

– in Finland, the "hovioikeus"/hovrätt",

– in Sweden, the "Svea hovrätt",

– in the United Kingdom:

(a) in England and Wales, the High Court of Justice;
(b) in Scotland, the Court of Session;
(c) in Northern Ireland, the High Court of Justice;
(d) in Gibraltar, the Court of Appeal.

ANNEX III

The appeals provided for Article 27 may be brought only:

– in Belgium, Greece, Spain, France, Italy, Luxembourg and in the Netherlands, by an appeal in cassation,

– in Germany, by a "Rechtsbeschwerde",

– in Ireland, by an appeal on a point of law to the Supreme Court,

– in Austria, by a "Revisionsrekurs",

– in Portugal, by a "recurso restrito à matéria de direito",

– in Finland, by an appeal to "korkein oikeus"/högsta domstolen",

– in Sweden, by an appeal to the "Högsta domstolen",

– in the United Kingdom, by a single further appeal on a point of law.

Council Regulation (EC) No 1348/2000

of 29 May 2000

on the service in the Member States of judicial and extrajudicial documents in civil or commercial matters

THE COUNCIL OF THE EUROPEAN UNION,

Having regard to the Treaty establishing the European Community, and in particular Article 61(*c*) and Article 67(1) thereof,

Having regard to the proposal from the Commission,

Having regard to the opinion of the European Parliament,

Having regard to the opinion of the Economic and Social Committee,

Whereas:

(1) The Union has set itself the objective of maintaining and developing the Union as an area of freedom, security and justice, in which the free movement of persons is assured. To establish such an area, the Community is to adopt, among others, the measures relating to judicial cooperation in civil matters needed for the proper functioning of the internal market.

(2) The proper functioning of the internal market entails the need to improve and expedite the transmission of judicial and extrajudicial documents in civil or commercial matters for service between the Member States.

(3) This is a subject now falling within the ambit of Article 65 of the Treaty.

(4) In accordance with the principles of subsidiarity and proportionality as set out in Article 5 of the Treaty, the objectives of this Regulation cannot be sufficiently achieved by the Member States and can therefore be better achieved by the Community. This Regulation does not go beyond what is necessary to achieve those objectives.

(5) The Council, by an Act dated 26 May 1997, drew up a Convention on the service in the Member States of the European Union of judicial and extrajudicial documents in civil or commercial matters and recommended it for adoption by the Member States in accordance with their respective constitutional rules. That Convention has not entered into force. Continuity in the results of the negotiations for conclusion of the Convention should be ensured. The main content of this Regulation is substantially taken over from it.

(6) Efficiency and speed in judicial procedures in civil matters means that the transmission of judicial and extrajudicial documents is to be made direct and by rapid means between local bodies designated by the Member States. However, the Member States may indicate their intention of designating only one transmitting or receiving agency or one agency to perform both functions for a period of five years. This designation may, however, be renewed every five years.

(7) Speed in transmission warrants the use of all appropriate means, provided that certain conditions as to the legibility and reliability of the document received are observed. Security in transmission requires that the document to be transmitted be accompanied by a pre-printed form, to be completed in the language of the place where service is to be effected, or in another language accepted by the Member State in question.

(8) To secure the effectiveness of this Regulation, the possibility of refusing service of documents is confined to exceptional situations.

(9) Speed of transmission warrants documents being served within days of reception of the document. However, if service has not been effected after one month has elapsed, the receiving agency should inform the transmitting agency. The expiry of this period should not imply that the request be returned to the transmitting agency where it is clear that service is feasible within a reasonable period.

(10) For the protection of the addressee's interests, service should be effected in the official language or one of the official languages of the place where it is to be effected or in another language of the originating Member State which the addressee understands.

(11) Given the differences between the Member States as regards their rules of procedure, the material date for the purposes of service varies from one Member State to another. Having regard to such situations and the possible difficulties that may arise, this Regulation should provide for a system where it is the law of the receiving Member State which determines the date of service. However, if the relevant documents in the context of proceedings to be brought or pending in the Member State of origin are to be served within a specified period, the date to be taken into consideration with respect to the applicant shall be that determined according to the law of the Member State of origin. A Member State is, however, authorised to derogate from the aforementioned provisions for a transitional period of five years, for appropriate reasons. Such a derogation may be renewed by a Member State at five-year intervals due to reasons related to its legal system.

(12) This Regulation prevails over the provisions contained in bilateral or multilateral agreements or arrangements having the same scope, concluded by the Member States, and in particular the Protocol annexed to the Brussels Convention of 27 September 1968 and the Hague Convention of 15 November 1965 in relations between the Member States party thereto. This Regulation does not preclude Member States from maintaining or concluding agreements or arrangements to expedite or simplify the transmission of documents, provided that they are compatible with the Regulation.

(13) The information transmitted pursuant to this Regulation should enjoy suitable protection. This matter falls within the scope of Directive 95/46/EC of the European Parliament and of the Council of 24 October 1995 on the protection of individuals with regard to the processing of personal data and on the free movement of such data, and of Directive 97/66/EC of the European Parliament and of the Council of 15 December 1997 concerning the processing of personal data and the protection of privacy in the telecommunications sector.

(14) The measures necessary for the implementation of this Regulation should be adopted in accordance with Council Decision 1999/468/EC of 28 June 1999 laying down the procedures for the exercise of implementing powers conferred on the Commission.

(15) These measures also include drawing up and updating the manual using appropriate modern means.

(16) No later than three years after the date of entry into force of this Regulation, the Commission should review its application and propose such amendments as may appear necessary.

(17) The United Kingdom and Ireland, in accordance with Article 3 of the Protocol on the position of the United Kingdom and Ireland annexed to the Treaty

on European Union and the Treaty establishing the European Community, have given notice of their wish to take part in the adoption and application of this Regulation.

(18) Denmark, in accordance with Articles 1 and 2 of the Protocol on the position of Denmark annexed to the Treaty on European Union and the Treaty establishing the European Community, is not participating in the adoption of this Regulation, and is therefore not bound by it nor subject to its application,

HAS ADOPTED THIS REGULATION:

CHAPTER I
GENERAL PROVISIONS

ARTICLE 1

Scope

1 This Regulation shall apply in civil and commercial matters where a judicial or extrajudicial document has to be transmitted from one Member State to another for service there.

2 This Regulation shall not apply where the address of the person to be served with the document is not known.

ARTICLE 2

Transmitting and receiving agencies

1 Each Member State shall designate the public officers, authorities or other persons, hereinafter referred to as "transmitting agencies", competent for the transmission of judicial or extrajudicial documents to be served in another Member State.

2 Each Member State shall designate the public officers, authorities or other persons, hereinafter referred to as "receiving agencies", competent for the receipt of judicial or extrajudicial documents from another Member State.

3 A Member State may designate one transmitting agency and one receiving agency or one agency to perform both functions. A federal State, a State in which several legal systems apply or a State with autonomous territorial units shall be free to designate more than one such agency. The designation shall have effect for a period of five years and may be renewed at five-year intervals.

4 Each Member State shall provide the Commission with the following information:

(*a*) the names and addresses of the receiving agencies referred to in paragraphs 2 and 3;
(*b*) the geographical areas in which they have jurisdiction;
(*c*) the means of receipt of documents available to them; and
(*d*) the languages that may be used for the completion of the standard form in the Annex.

Member States shall notify the Commission of any subsequent modification of such information.

ARTICLE 3

Central body

Each Member State shall designate a central body responsible for:

(*a*) supplying information to the transmitting agencies;
(*b*) seeking solutions to any difficulties which may arise during transmission of documents for service;
(*c*) forwarding, in exceptional cases, at the request of a transmitting agency, a request for service to the competent receiving agency.

A federal State, a State in which several legal systems apply or a State with autonomous territorial units shall be free to designate more than one central body.

CHAPTER II
JUDICIAL DOCUMENTS

Section 1

Transmission and service of judicial documents

ARTICLE 4

Transmission of documents

1 Judicial documents shall be transmitted directly and as soon as possible between the agencies designated on the basis of Article 2.

2 The transmission of documents, requests, confirmations, receipts, certificates and any other papers between transmitting agencies and receiving agencies may be carried out by any appropriate means, provided that the content of the document received is true and faithful to that of the document forwarded and that all information in it is easily legible.

3 The document to be transmitted shall be accompanied by a request drawn up using the standard form in the Annex. The form shall be completed in the official language of the Member State addressed or, if there are several official languages in that Member State, the official language or one of the official languages of the place where service is to be effected, or in another language which that Member State has indicated it can accept. Each Member State shall indicate the official language or languages of the European Union other than its own which is or are acceptable to it for completion of the form.

4 The documents and all papers that are transmitted shall be exempted from legalisation or any equivalent formality.

5 When the transmitting agency wishes a copy of the document to be returned together with the certificate referred to in Article 10, it shall send the document in duplicate.

ARTICLE 5

Translation of documents

1 The applicant shall be advised by the transmitting agency to which he or she forwards the document for transmission that the addressee may refuse to accept it if it is not in one of the languages provided for in Article 8.

2 The applicant shall bear any costs of translation prior to the transmission of the document, without prejudice to any possible subsequent decision by the court or competent authority on liability for such costs.

ARTICLE 6

Receipt of documents by receiving agency

1 On receipt of a document, a receiving agency shall, as soon as possible and in any event within seven days of receipt, send a receipt to the transmitting agency by the swiftest possible means of transmission using the standard form in the Annex.

2 Where the request for service cannot be fulfilled on the basis of the information or documents transmitted, the receiving agency shall contact the transmitting agency by the swiftest possible means in order to secure the missing information or documents.

3 If the request for service is manifestly outside the scope of this Regulation or if non-compliance with the formal conditions required makes service impossible, the request and the documents transmitted shall be returned, on receipt, to the transmitting agency, together with the notice of return in the standard form in the Annex.

4 A receiving agency receiving a document for service but not having territorial jurisdiction to serve it shall forward it, as well as the request, to the receiving agency having territorial jurisdiction in the same Member State if the request complies with the conditions laid down in Article 4(3) and shall inform the transmitting agency accordingly, using the standard form in the Annex. That receiving agency shall inform the transmitting agency when it receives the document, in the manner provided for in paragraph 1.

ARTICLE 7

Service of documents

1 The receiving agency shall itself serve the document or have it served, either in accordance with the law of the Member State addressed or by a particular form requested by the transmitting agency, unless such a method is incompatible with the law of that Member State.

2 All steps required for service of the document shall be effected as soon as possible. In any event, if it has not been possible to effect service within one month of receipt, the receiving agency shall inform the transmitting agency by means of the certificate in the standard form in the Annex, which shall be drawn up under

the conditions referred to in Article 10(2). The period shall be calculated in accordance with the law of the Member State addressed.

ARTICLE 8

Refusal to accept a document

1 The receiving agency shall inform the addressee that he or she may refuse to accept the document to be served if it is in a language other than either of the following languages:

(*a*) the official language of the Member State addressed or, if there are several official languages in that Member State, the official language or one of the official languages of the place where service is to be effected; or

(*b*) a language of the Member State of transmission which the addressee understands.

2 Where the receiving agency is informed that the addressee refuses to accept the document in accordance with paragraph 1, it shall immediately inform the transmitting agency by means of the certificate provided for in Article 10 and return the request and the documents of which a translation is requested.

ARTICLE 9

Date of service

1 Without prejudice to Article 8, the date of service of a document pursuant to Article 7 shall be the date on which it is served in accordance with the law of the Member State addressed.

2 However, where a document shall be served within a particular period in the context of proceedings to be brought or pending in the Member State of origin, the date to be taken into account with respect to the applicant shall be that fixed by the law of that Member State.

3 A Member State shall be authorised to derogate from the provisions of paragraphs 1 and 2 for a transitional period of five years, for appropriate reasons.

This transitional period may be renewed by a Member State at five-yearly intervals due to reasons related to its legal system. That Member State shall inform the Commission of the content of such a derogation and the circumstances of the case.

ARTICLE 10

Certificate of service and copy of the document served

1 When the formalities concerning the service of the document have been completed, a certificate of completion of those formalities shall be drawn up in the standard form in the Annex and addressed to the transmitting agency, together with, where Article 4(5) applies, a copy of the document served.

2 The certificate shall be completed in the official language or one of the official languages of the Member State of origin or in another language which the Member State of origin has indicated that it can accept. Each Member State shall indicate

the official language or languages of the European Union other than its own which is or are acceptable to it for completion of the form.

ARTICLE 11

Costs of service

1 The service of judicial documents coming from a Member State shall not give rise to any payment or reimbursement of taxes or costs for services rendered by the Member State addressed.

2 The applicant shall pay or reimburse the costs occasioned by:

(*a*) the employment of a judicial officer or of a person competent under the law of the Member State addressed;

(*b*) the use of a particular method of service.

Section 2

Other means of transmission and service of judicial documents

ARTICLE 12

Transmission by consular or diplomatic channels

Each Member State shall be free, in exceptional circumstances, to use consular or diplomatic channels to forward judicial documents, for the purpose of service, to those agencies of another Member State which are designated pursuant to Article 2 or 3.

ARTICLE 13

Service by diplomatic or consular agents

1 Each Member State shall be free to effect service of judicial documents on persons residing in another Member State, without application of any compulsion, directly through its diplomatic or consular agents.

2 Any Member State may make it known, in accordance with Article 23(1), that it is opposed to such service within its territory, unless the documents are to be served on nationals of the Member State in which the documents originate.

ARTICLE 14

Service by post

1 Each Member State shall be free to effect service of judicial documents directly by post to persons residing in another Member State.

2 Any Member State may specify, in accordance with Article 23(1), the conditions under which it will accept service of judicial documents by post.

ARTICLE 15

Direct service

1 This Regulation shall not interfere with the freedom of any person interested in a judicial proceeding to effect service of judicial documents directly through the judicial officers, officials or other competent persons of the Member State addressed.

2 Any Member State may make it known, in accordance with Article 23(1), that it is opposed to the service of judicial documents in its territory pursuant to paragraph 1.

CHAPTER III
EXTRAJUDICIAL DOCUMENTS

ARTICLE 16

Transmission

Extrajudicial documents may be transmitted for service in another Member State in accordance with the provisions of this Regulation.

CHAPTER IV
FINAL PROVISIONS

ARTICLE 17

Implementing rules

The measures necessary for the implementation of this Regulation relating to the matters referred to below shall be adopted in accordance with the advisory procedure referred to in Article 18(2):

(*a*) drawing up and annually updating a manual containing the information provided by Member States in accordance with Article 2(4);
(*b*) drawing up a glossary in the official languages of the European Union of documents which may be served under this Regulation;
(*c*) updating or making technical amendments to the standard form set out in the Annex.

ARTICLE 18

Committee

1 The Commission shall be assisted by a committee.

2 Where reference is made to this paragraph, Articles 3 and 7 of Decision 1999/468/EC shall apply.

3 The Committee shall adopt its rules of procedure.

ARTICLE 19

Defendant not entering an appearance

1 Where a writ of summons or an equivalent document has had to be transmitted to another Member State for the purpose of service, under the provisions of this Regulation, and the defendant has not appeared, judgment shall not be given until it is established that:

(*a*) the document was served by a method prescribed by the internal law of the Member State addressed for the service of documents in domestic actions upon persons who are within its territory; or

(*b*) the document was actually delivered to the defendant or to his residence by another method provided for by this Regulation;

and that in either of these cases the service or the delivery was effected in sufficient time to enable the defendant to defend.

2 Each Member State shall be free to make it known, in accordance with Article 23(1), that the judge, notwithstanding the provisions of paragraph 1, may give judgment even if no certificate of service or delivery has been received, if all the following conditions are fulfilled:

(*a*) the document was transmitted by one of the methods provided for in this Regulation;

(*b*) a period of time of not less than six months, considered adequate by the judge in the particular case, has elapsed since the date of the transmission of the document;

(*c*) no certificate of any kind has been received, even though every reasonable effort has been made to obtain it through the competent authorities or bodies of the Member State addressed.

3 Notwithstanding paragraphs 1 and 2, the judge may order, in case of urgency, any provisional or protective measures.

4 When a writ of summons or an equivalent document has had to be transmitted to another Member State for the purpose of service, under the provisions of this Regulation, and a judgment has been entered against a defendant who has not appeared, the judge shall have the power to relieve the defendant from the effects of the expiration of the time for appeal from the judgment if the following conditions are fulfilled:

(*a*) the defendant, without any fault on his part, did not have knowledge of the document in sufficient time to defend, or knowledge of the judgment in sufficient time to appeal; and

(*b*) the defendant has disclosed a prima facie defence to the action on the merits.

An application for relief may be filed only within a reasonable time after the defendant has knowledge of the judgment.

Each Member State may make it known, in accordance with Article 23(1), that such application will not be entertained if it is filed after the expiration of a time to be stated by it in that communication, but which shall in no case be less than one year following the date of the judgment.

5 Paragraph 4 shall not apply to judgments concerning status or capacity of persons.

ARTICLE 20

Relationship with agreements or arrangements to which Member States are Parties

1 This Regulation shall, in relation to matters to which it applies, prevail over other provisions contained in bilateral or multilateral agreements or arrangements concluded by the Member States, and in particular Article IV of the Protocol to the Brussels Convention of 1968 and the Hague Convention of 15 November 1965.

2 This Regulation shall not preclude individual Member States from maintaining or concluding agreements or arrangements to expedite further or simplify the transmission of documents, provided that they are compatible with this Regulation.

3 Member States shall send to the Commission:

(*a*) a copy of the agreements or arrangements referred to in paragraph 2 concluded between the Member States as well as drafts of such agreements or arrangements which they intend to adopt; and
(*b*) any denunciation of, or amendments to, these agreements or arrangements.

ARTICLE 21

Legal aid

This Regulation shall not affect the application of Article 23 of the Convention on Civil Procedure of 17 July 1905, Article 24 of the Convention on Civil Procedure of 1 March 1954 or Article 13 of the Convention on International Access to Justice of 25 October 1980 between the Member States Parties to these Conventions.

ARTICLE 22

Protection of information transmitted

1 Information, including in particular personal data, transmitted under this Regulation shall be used by the receiving agency only for the purpose for which it was transmitted.

2 Receiving agencies shall ensure the confidentiality of such information, in accordance with their national law.

3 Paragraphs 1 and 2 shall not affect national laws enabling data subjects to be informed of the use made of information transmitted under this Regulation.

4 This Regulation shall be without prejudice to Directives 95/46/EC and 97/66/EC.

ARTICLE 23

Communication and publication

1 Member States shall communicate to the Commission the information referred to in Articles 2, 3, 4, 9, 10, 13, 14, 15, 17(*a*) and 19.

2 The Commission shall publish in the *Official Journal of the European Communities* the information referred to in paragraph 1.

ARTICLE 24

Review

No later than 1 June 2004, and every five years thereafter, the Commission shall present to the European Parliament, the Council and the Economic and Social Committee a report on the application of this Regulation, paying special attention to the effectiveness of the bodies designated pursuant to Article 2 and to the practical application of point (*c*) of Article 3 and Article 9. The report shall be accompanied if need be by proposals for adaptations of this Regulation in line with the evolution of notification systems.

ARTICLE 25

Entry into force

This Regulation shall enter into force on 31 May 2001.

This Regulation shall be binding in its entirety and directly applicable in the Member States in accordance with the Treaty establishing the European Community.
Done at Brussels, 29 May 2000.

For the Council
The President
A. Costa

ANNEX

REQUEST FOR SERVICE OF DOCUMENTS
(Article 4(3) of Council Regulation (EC) No 1348/2000 on the service in the Member States of judicial and extrajudicial documents in civil or commercial matters)

Reference No: …

1. TRANSMITTING AGENCY

   1.1. Identity:

   1.2. Address:

      1.2.1. Street and number/PO box:

      1.2.2. Place and code:

      1.2.3. Country:

   1.3. Tel:

   1.4. Fax (*):

1.5. E-mail (*)

2. RECEIVING AGENCY

2.1. Identity:

2.2. Address:

2.2.1. Street and number/PO box:

2.2.2. Place and code:

2.2.3. Country:

2.3. Tel:

2.4. Fax (*):

2.5. E-mail (*):

3. APPLICANT

3.1. Identity:

3.2. Address:

3.2.1. Street and number/PO box:

3.2.2. Place and code:

3.2.3. Country:

3.3. Tel (*):

3.4. Fax (*):

3.5. E-mail (*):

4. ADDRESSEE

4.1. Identity:

4.2. Address:

4.2.1. Street and number/PO box:

4.2.2. Place and code:

4.2.3. Country:

4.3. Tel (*):

4.4. Fax (*):

4.5. E-mail (*):

4.6. Identification number/social security number/organisation number/or equivalent (*):

5. METHOD OF SERVICE

5.1. In accordance with the law of the Member State addressed

5.2. By the following particular method:

5.2.1. If this method is incompatible with the law of the Member State addressed, the document(s) should be served in accordance with the law:

5.2.1.1. yes

5.2.1.2. no

6. DOCUMENT TO BE SERVED

(*a*) 6.1. Nature of the document

6.1.1. judicial

6.1.1.1. writ of summons

6.1.1.2. judgment

6.1.1.3. appeal

6.1.1.4. other

6.1.2. extrajudicial

(*b*) 6.2. Date or time-limit stated in the document (*):

(*c*) 6.3. Language of document:

6.3.1. original DE, EN, DK, EL, FI, FR, GR, IT, NL, PT, SV, others:

6.3.2. translation (*) DE, EN, DK, ES, FI, FR, EL, IT, NL, PT, SV, others:

6.4. Number of enclosures:

7. A COPY OF DOCUMENT TO BE RETURNED WITH THE CERTIFICATE OF SERVICE (Article 4(5) of the Regulation)

7.1. Yes (in this case send two copies of the document to be served)

7.2. No

1. You are required by Article 7(2) of the Regulation to effect all steps required for service of the document as soon as possible. In any event, if it is not possible for you to effect service within one month of receipt, you must inform this agency by means of the certificate provided for in point 13.
2. If you cannot fulfil this request for service on the basis of the information or documents transmitted, you are required by Article 6(2) of the Regulation to contact this agency by the swiftest possible means in order to secure the missing information or document.

Done at:

Date:

Signature and/or stamp:

(*) This item is optional.

Reference No of the receiving agency:

ACKNOWLEDGEMENT OF RECEIPT
(Article 6(1) of Council Regulation (EC) No 1348/2000)

This acknowledgement must be sent by the swiftest possible means of transmission as soon as possible after receipt of the document and in any event within seven days of receipt.

8. DATE OF RECEIPT:

Done at:

Date:

Signature and/or stamp:

NOTICE OF RETURN OF REQUEST AND DOCUMENT
(Article 6(3) of Council Regulation (EC) No 1348/2000)

The request and document must be returned on receipt.

9. REASON FOR RETURN:

9.1. The request is manifestly outside the scope of the Regulation:

9.1.1. the document is not civil or commercial

9.1.2. the service is not from one Member State to another Member State

9.2. Non-compliance with formal conditions required makes service impossible:

9.2.1. the document is not easily legible

9.2.2. the language used to complete the form is incorrect

9.2.3. the document received is not a true and faithful copy

9.2.4. other (please give details):

9.3. The method of service is incompatible with the law of that Member State (Article 7(1) of the Regulation)

Done at:

Date:

Signature and/or stamp:

NOTICE OF RETRANSMISSION OF REQUEST AND DOCUMENT TO THE APPROPRIATE RECEIVING AGENCY
(Article 6(4) of Council Regulation (EC) No 1348/2000)

The request and document were forwarded on to the following receiving agency, which has territorial jurisdiction to serve it:

10.1. Identity:

10.2. Address:

10.2.1. Street and number/PO box:

10.2.2. Place and code:

10.2.3. Country:

10.3. Tel:

10.4. Fax (*):

10.5. E-mail (*):

Done at:

Date:

Signature and/or stamp:

(*) This item is optional.

Reference No of the appropriate receiving agency:

NOTICE OF RECEIPT BY THE APPROPRIATE RECEIVING AGENCY HAVING TERRITORIAL JURISDICTION TO THE TRANSMITTING AGENCY
(Article 6(4) of Council Regulation (EC) No 1348/2000)

This notice must be sent by the swiftest possible means of transmission as soon as possible after receipt of the document and in any event within seven days of receipt.

11. DATE OF RECEIPT:

Done at:

Date:

Signature and/or stamp:

CERTIFICATE OF SERVICE OR NON-SERVICE OF DOCUMENTS
(Article 10 of Council Regulation (EC) No 1348/2000)

The service shall be effected as soon as possible. In any event, if it has not been possible to effect service within one month of receipt, the receiving agency shall inform the transmitting agency (according to Article 7(2) of the Regulation)

12. COMPLETION OF SERVICE

(*a*) 12.1. Date and address of service:

(*b*) 12.2. The document was

(A) 12.2.1. served in accordance with the law of the Member State addressed, namely

12.2.1.1. handed to

12.2.1.1.1. the addressee in person

12.2.1.1.2. another person

12.2.1.1.2.1. Name:

12.2.1.1.2.2. Address:

12.2.1.1.2.2.1. Street and number/PO box:

12.2.1.1.2.2.2. Place and code:

12.2.1.1.2.2.3. Country:

12.2.1.1.2.3. Relation to the addressee:

family employee others

12.2.1.1.3. the addressee's address

12.2.1.2. served by post

12.2.1.2.1. without acknowledgement of receipt

12.2.1.2.2. with the enclosed acknowledgement of receipt

12.2.1.2.2.1. from the addressee

12.2.1.2.2.2. another person

12.2.1.2.2.2.1. Name:

12.2.1.2.2.2.2. Address

12.2.1.2.2.2.2.1. Street and number/PO box:

12.2.1.2.2.2.2.2. Place and code:

12.2.1.2.2.2.2.3. Country:

12.2.1.2.2.2.3. Relation to the addressee:

family employee others

12.2.1.3. other method (please say how):

(B) 12.2.2. served by the following particular method (please say how):

(*c*) 12.3. The addressee of the document was informed (orally) (in writing) that he or she may refuse to accept it if it was not in an official language of the place of service or in an official language of the state of transmission which he or she understands.

13. INFORMATION IN ACCORDANCE WITH ARTICLE 7(2)

It was not possible to effect service within one month of receipt.

14. REFUSAL OF DOCUMENT

The addressee refused to accept the document on account of the language used. The documents are annexed to this certificate.

15. REASON FOR NON-SERVICE OF DOCUMENT

15.1. Address unknown

15.2. Addressee cannot be located

15.3. Document could not be served before the date or time-limit stated in point 6.2.

15.4. Others (please specify):

The documents are annexed to this certificate.

Done at:

Date:

Signature and/or stamp:

Index

References are to page numbers.